W9-AQV-834

kenrick

seminary library

Charles L. Souvay Memorial

ROBERT NORTH S.J.

ELENCHUS OF BIBLICA
1986

EDITRICE PONTIFICIO ISTITUTO BIBLICO
ROMA 1989

ROBERT NORTH S.J.

ELENCHUS OF BIBLICA

1986

kenrick

seminary library

Charles L. Souvay Memorial

WITHDRAWN

Ref
051
E39b
v.2

EDITRICE PONTIFICIO ISTITUTO BIBLICO
ROMA 1989

893306

© 1989 – E.P.I.B. – Roma

ISBN 88-7653-569-1

Editrice Pontificia Università Gregoriana
Editrice Pontificio Istituto Biblico
Piazza della Pilotta, 35 - 00187 Roma

AA	Ann Arbor
Amst	Amsterdam
B	[o/w]Berlin
Ba/Bo	Basel/Bologna
Barc	Barcelona
Bru	Brussel
C	Cambridge, Engl.
CM	Cambridge, Mass.
Ch	Chicago
Da: Wiss	Darmstadt, WissBuchg
DG	Downers Grove, IL
Dü	Düsseldorf
E	Edinburgh
ENJ	EnglewoodCliffs NJ
F	Firenze
FrB/FrS	Freiburg-Br/Schw
Fra	Frankfurt/M
GCNY	GardenCity NY
Gö	Göttingen
GR	Grand Rapids MI
Gü	Gütersloh
Ha	Hamburg
Heid	Heidelberg
Hw	Harmondsworth
J	Jerusalem
K	København
L	London
LA	Los Angeles
Lp	Leipzig
Lv(N)	Leuven (L. Neuve)
M/Mi	Madrid/Milano
Mü	München
N	Napoli
ND	NotreDame IN
Neuk	Neukirchen/Verlag
NHv	New Haven
Nv	Nashville
NY	New York
Ox	Oxford
P	Paris
Pd	Paderborn
Ph	Philadelphia
R	Roma
Rg	Regensburg
SF	San Francisco
Sto	Stockholm
Stu	Stuttgart
T/TA	Torino/Tel Aviv
Tü	Tübingen
U/W	Uppsala/Wien
Wmr	Warminster
Wsb	Wiesbaden
Wsh	Washington
Wsz	Warszawa
Wu	Wuppertal
Wü	Würzburg
Z	Zürich

In citing from this Elenchus — Nota Bene — *citando hinc*

(1) *Pretium indicatur* **$20** [*pro* **$19.95** *etc., numero rotundo*], *non sicut in fonte ibidem citato.*

Pursuing our policy of abbreviating for clarity, we have begun rounding off prices like $19.95 to $20; less often £12.90 to £13; DM 23,80 to 24. But please note that this rounding-off is **not** attributed to the **source** often cited immediately after the price: thus $13 [TDig 34,172] where the exact price is given as $12.95. This rounding-off is intended partially as a clue to inflation, since we have found that the price we cite has usually been increased during the regrettable 2-3 year lag required by editing and printing procedures of this Elenchus.

(2) *Intra titulum, utimur* **;** [**non** **:** *vel* **.** *originis*] *ad separandum subtitulum.*

We use a **semicolon** [**;**] within the title to set off a **subtitle**, which in the original is in principle given on a subsequent line without preceding punctuation , but now commonly in English with colon [**:**], in European languages with full stop [period, point **.**]. Please note that this usage **differs from that of the original title** which is being cited. We also give **English titles without capitalizing** every word, as is now done also in some English-language libraries and bibliographies. For **quotation-marks** we follow British usage: always ' [" " for quotes within quotes] even though usually the original has " " (American), « » or , ' (European). In all other respects we try to remain rigidly faithful to the original [see Elenchus 62 (1981) 6].

(3) *Cognomina americana et italiana ponuntur sub van, de, etc.; non autem alia.*

In **alphabetizing surnames** (especially in the Index) we have put American names under the prefix **van, de,** etc., since 1980, and Italian names under *della* etc. since 1984. As explained in Elenchus 65 (1984) 6, the problem is still by no means solved, and we hope that some consistent policy applicable to *all* prefix-surnames can soon be formulated on some higher international level.

Our Index in principle gives **place-names** in *italics*; otherwise only **author-surnames**; but we have begun gradually introducing titles (as was done much more amply up to 1978) where no author is available.

(4) **Elenchus of Biblica** *1985 et 1986 (vol. 1 & 2) exacte continuat formam* **Elenchi Bibliographici Biblici** *1968-84.*

As explained in Elenchus of Biblica 1 (1985) 3, that volume continues the form and content of *Elenchus bibliographicus biblicus* 49 (1968) – 65 (1984). In the present volume, renvoi (→) to the 1985 volume is given with bold-face number **1** (thus → **1**,353).

Index systematicus – Contents

Acronyms: Periodica - Series (small).
8 fig. = ISSN; *10 fig.* = ISBN *1985 (fasc. 1)*

Ⓐ: *arabice,* in Arabic.
AAR [Aids]: American Academy of Religion (➤ JAAR, not PAAR) [Aids for the Study of Religion; Chico CA].
AAS: Acta Apostolicae Sedis; Vaticano. 0001-5199.
AASOR: Annual of the American Schools of Oriental Research; CM.
Abh: Abhandlungen Gö Lp Mü etc.; ➤ DOG / DPV.
AbhChrJüDial: Abhandlungen zum christlich-jüdischen Dialog; Mü, Kaiser.
AbrNahr: Abr-Nahrain; Leiden.
AbsIran: Abstracta iranica: Téhéran, Institut français [1 (1978)] ➤ StIran.
AcAANorv: Acta ad archaeologiam et artium historiam spectantia, Inst. Norvegiae; Roma.
AcBg: Académie royale de Belgique; Bru.
Acme; Milano, Fac. Lett. Filos. 0001-494X.
AcNum: Acta Numismatica; Barc. 0211-8386 [15 (1985)].
AcSém: Actes sémiotiques; Paris [5 (1983)].
Act: Actes/Acta (Congrès, Colloque).
ActAntH: Acta Antiqua Academiae Scientiarum Hungaricae; Budapest [summarium in ActArchH].
Acta PIB: Acta Pontificii Instituti Biblici: Roma.
ActArchH/K: Acta Archaeologica; Hungarica, Budapest. 0001-5210 / København. 0065-101X.
ActClasSAfr: Acta Classica; Cape Town.
ActIran: Acta Iranica; Téhéran/Leiden.
ActOrH/K: Acta Orientalia: Budapest, Academia Scientiarum Hungarica; 0044-5975 / K (Societates Orientales Danica, Norveigica). 0001-6438.
ActPraeh: Acta Praehistorica et Archaeologica; B.
ActSum: Acta Sumerologica; Hiroshima, Univ. Linguistics. 0387-8082.
ActuBbg: Actualidad Bibliográfica (Filos. Teol.: Selecciones de Libros); Barc. 0211-4143.
ADAJ: Annual of the Department of Antiquities, Jordan; 'Amman.
ADPF: Association pour la diffusion de la pensée française; Paris ➤ RCiv.

Aeg: Aegyptus; Milano. 0001-9046.
ÄgAbh: Ägyptologische Abhandlungen; Wb.
AegHelv: Aegyptiaca Helvetica: Basel Univ. Äg. Sem. (Univ. Genève).
Aevum; Milano.
AfER: African Ecclesiastical Review; Masaka, Uganda.
AfJB: African Journal of Biblical Studies; Ibadan. [1,1 (1986)].
AfO: Archiv für Orientforschung; Graz. 3-85028-141-8.
AfTJ: Africa Theological Journal; Makumira, Tanzania. 0856-0048.
AGJU: Arbeiten zur Geschichte des Antiken Judentums und des Urchristentums; Leiden.
AIBL: Académie des Inscriptions et Belles-Lettres; P ➤ CRAI. – AIEMA ➤ BMosA.
AION [-Clas]: Annali (dell')Istituto Universitario Orientale [Classico] ➤ ArchStorAnt di Napoli.
AIPHOS: Annuaire de l'Institut de Philologie et d'Histoire Orientales et Slaves; Bru. 2-8004-0881-2.
AJA: American Journal of Archaeology; Princeton NJ. 0002-9114.
AJS: Association for Jewish Studies Review; CM 0364-0094 [6 (1981)].
Akkadica; Bruxelles/Brussel.
al.: et alii, and other(s).
ALGHJ: Arbeiten zur Literatur und Geschichte des hellenistischen Judentums; Leiden.
Al-Kibt, The Copts, die Kopten; Ha.
ALLC: Association for Literary and Linguistic Computing Bulletin; Stockport, Cheshire.
Altertum (Das); oB. 0002-6646.
AltOrF: Altorientalische Forschungen; B. 0232-8461.
AltsprU: Der altsprachliche Unterricht.
AmBapQ: American Baptist Quarterly; Valley Forge PA. 0015-8992.
AmBenR: American Benedictine Review; Richardton ND. 0002-7650.
Ambrosius, bollettino liturgico; Milano. 0392-5757.
America; NY. 0002-7049.
AmHR: American Historical Review; NY.
AmJAncH: American Journal of Ancient History; CM, Harvard [7,1 (1982)].

AmJPg: American Journal of Philology; Baltimore. 0002-9475.

AmJTPh: American Journal of Theology and Philosophy; W. Lafayette IN.

AmMessianJ: The American Messianic Jew; Ph [68 (1983)].

AmNumM: American Numismatic Society Museum Notes; NY.

AmPhTr: Transactions of the American Philosophical Society; Ph.

AmSci: American Scientist; New Haven. 0003-0996.

AmstCah: Amsterdamse cahiers voor exegese en bijbelse theologie; Kampen.

AmstMed ➤ Mededelingen.

AmStPapyr: American Studies in Papyrology; NHv.

AnAASyr: Annales Archéologiques Arabes Syriennes; Damas.

Anadolu; Ankara, Univ.

Anagénnēsis (none ©), papyrology; Athēnai [2 (1982)].

Anatolica, Annuaire pour les civilisations de l'Asie antérieure; Istanbul. 0066-1554.

AnatSt: Anatolian Studies; London.

AnAug: Analecta Augustiniana; R.

ANaut: Archaeonautica; Paris. 0154-1854 [4 (1984)].

AnBib: Analecta Biblica. Investigationes scientificae in res biblicas; R. 0066-135X.

AnBoll: Analecta Bollandiana; Bruxelles. 0003-2468.

AnBritSchAth: Annual of the British School at Athens; London.

AnCalas: Analecta Calasanctiana (religioso–cultural–histórica); Salamanca. 0569-9789.

AnCÉtRel: Annales du Centre d'Études des Religions; Bru.

AnChile: Anales de la Facultad de Teología; Santiago, Univ. Católica.

AnchorB: Anchor Bible; Garden City NY.

AnCist: Analecta Cisterciensia; Roma. 0003-2476.

AnClas: Annales Universitatis, sectio classica; Budapest.

AnClémOchr: Annuaire de l'Académie de théologie 'St. Clément d'Ochrida' [27 (1977s) paru 1982].

AnCracov: Analecta Cracoviensia (Polish Theol. Soc.); Kraków. 0209-0864.

AncSoc: Ancient Society. Katholieke Universiteit; Leuven. 0066-1619.

AncSRes: Ancient Society, resources for teachers; North Ryde NSW; Macquarie Univ. 0310-5814.

AnCTS: Annual Publication of the College Theological Society; Chico CA [not = ➤ ProcC(ath)TS].

AncW: The Ancient World; Chicago. 0160-9645.

AndrUnS: Andrews University Seminary Studies; Berrien Springs, Mich. 0003-2980.

AnEgBbg: Annual Egyptological Bibliography; Leiden.

AnÉPH: Annuaire ➤ ÉPHÉ.

AnÉth: Annales d'Éthiopie; Addis-Ababa.

AnFac: Let: Annali della facoltà di lettere, Univ. (Bari/Cagliari/Perugia).

— **Ling/T:** Annal(es) Facultat(is); linguarum, theologiae.

AnFg: Anuario de Filología; Barc.

Ang: Angelicum; Roma. 0003-3081.

AnglTR: Anglican Theological Review; Evanston IL. 0003-3286.

AnGreg: Analecta (Pont. Univ.) Gregoriana; Roma. 0066-1376.

AnHArt: Annales d'histoire de l'art et d'archéologie: Bru.

AnHConc: Annuarium Historiae Conciliorum; Paderborn.

ANilM: Archéologie du Nil Moyen; Lille. 0299-8130 [1 (1986)].

AnItNum: Annali (dell')Istituto Italiano di Numismatica; Roma.

AnJapB: Annual of the Japanese Biblical Institute; Tokyo ● ➤ Sei-Ron.

AnLetN: Annali della Facoltà di lettere e filosofia dell'Univ.; Napoli.

AnLovBOr: Analecta Lovaniensia Biblica et Orientalia; Lv.

AnOr: Analecta Orientalia: Roma, Facultas Orientalis Pont. Inst. Biblici.

AnOrdBas: Analecta Ordinis S. Basilii Magni; Roma.

AnPg: L'Année Philologique; Paris.

AnPisa: Annali della Scuola Normale Superiore; Pisa.

AnPraem: Analecta Praemonstratensia; Averbode.

AnRIM: Annual Review of the Royal Inscriptions of Mesopotamia Project; Toronto. 0822-2525.

AnRSocSR: Annual Review of the Social Sciences of Religion; The Hague. 0066-2062.

ANRW: Aufstieg und Niedergang der römischen Welt ➤ 574.

AnSacTar: Analecta Sacra Tarraconensia; Barcelona.

AnSemClas: Annali del Seminario di Studi del Mondo Classico, sezione Archeologia e Storia Antica; Napoli, Ist. Univ. Orientale [5 (1983)].

AnStoEseg: Annali di Storia dell'Esegesi; Bologna.

AntAb: Antike und Abendland; Berlin. 0003-5696.

AntAfr: Antiquités africaines; Paris. 0066-4871.

AntClas: L'Antiquité Classique; Bru.

AntClCr: Antichità classica e cristiana; Brescia.

Anthropos; 1. Fribourg/Suisse. 0003-5572. / [2. Rivista sulla famiglia; Roma 1 (1985).]

AntiqJ: Antiquaries Journal; London. 0003-5815.

Antiquity; Gloucester. 0003-5982.

Ant/ka: ⑥ Anthropologiká: Thessaloniki.

AntKu: Antike Kunst; Basel. 0003-5688.

Anton: Antonianum; Roma. 0003-6064.

AntRArch: Antiqua, Rivista d'Archeologia e d'Architettura; Roma.

AnTVal: Anales de la Cátedra de Teología en la Universidad de Valencia [1 (1984)].

AntWelt: Antike Welt; Feldmeilen.

Anvil, Anglican Ev. theol.; Bramcote, Nottingham. 0003-6226.

AnzAltW: Anzeiger für die Altertumswissenschaft; Innsbruck. 0003-6293.

AnzW: Anzeiger der österreichischen Akademie (phil./hist.); Wien. 0378-8652.

AOAT: Alter Orient und Altes Testament: Kevelaer/Neukirchen.

AOtt: Univ. München, Arbeiten zu Text und Sprache im AT; St. Ottilien.

Apollonia: Afro-Hellenic studies, under patronage of Alexandria Patriarchate; Johannesburg, Rand Afrikaans Univ. [1 (1982)].

ArBegG: Archiv für Begriffsgeschichte (Mainz, Akad.); Bonn.

ArbGTL: Arbeiten zur Geschichte und Theologie des Luthertums, Neue Folge; B.

ArbKiG: Arbeiten zur Kirchengeschichte; B.

ArbNTJud: Arbeiten zum NT und zum Judentum: Frankfurt/M. 0170-8856.

ArbNtTextf: Arbeiten zur Neutestamentlichen Textforschung; B/NY.

ArbT: Arbeiten zur Theologie (Calwer); Stu.

ARCE ➤ J [News] AmEg.

Archaeology; Boston. 0003-8113.

Archaeometry; L. 0003-813X.

Archaiognōsia ⑥; Athenai [2 (1981)].

ArchAnz: Archäologischer Anzeiger; Berlin. 0003-8105.

ArchAth: ⑥ Archaiología; Athéna [sic; 1 (1981); 2-5 (1982)].

ArchBbg: Archäologische Bibliographie zu JbDAI; Berlin.

ArchClasR: Archeologia Classica; R.

Archeo, attualità del passato; Milano [1-10 (1985)].

Archéologia; (ex-Paris) Dijon, Faton. 0570-6270 ➤ Dossiers.

ArchEph: ⑥ Archaiologikē Ephēmeris; Athēnai.

ArchInf: Archäologische Informationen; Bonn. 3-7749-2202-0.

Architectura; München. 0044-863X.

ArchMIran: Archäologische Mitteilungen aus Iran, N.F.; Berlin.

ArchNews: Archaeological News; Tallahassee FL. 0194-3413. [13 (1984)].

ArchRCamb: Archaeological Reviews from Cambridge (Eng.). 0261-4332.

ArchRep: Archaeological Reports; Wmr, British Sch. Athens. 0570-6084.

ArchStorAnt: [= a third AION] Archeologia e Storia Antica; Napoli, Univ. Ist. Or./Cl. 0393-070X.

Arctos, Acta Philologica Fennica; Helsinki. 0570-734X.

ArEspArq: Archivo Español de Arqueología; Madrid. 0066-6742.

Arethusa... wellspring of Western man; Buffalo NY. 0004-0975.

ArFrancHist: Archivum Franciscanum Historicum; Grottaferrata.

ArGlottIt: Archivio Glottologico Italiano; Firenze. 0004-0207.

ArHPont: Archivum Historiae Pontificiae; Roma.

ArKulturg: Archiv für Kulturgeschichte; Köln. 0003-9233.

ArLtgW: Archiv für Liturgiewissenschaft; Regensburg. 0066-6386.

ArOr: Archiv Orientální; Praha. 0044-8699.

ArPapF: Archiv für Papyrusforschung; Leipzig. 0066-6459.

ArRefG: Archiv für Reformationsgeschichte; Gütersloh.

ArchRep: Archaeological Reports; Wmr, British School at Athens. 0570-6084.

ArSSocRel: Archives de Sciences Sociales des Religions; Paris.

ARTANES: Aids and Research Tools in Ancient Near Eastern Studies; Malibu.

ArTGran: Archivo Teológico Granadino; Granada. 0210-1629.

ArztC: Arzt und Christ; Salzburg.

ASAE: Annales du Service des Antiquités de l'Égypte; Le Caire.

AsbTJ: The Asbury Theological Journal; Wilmore, KY.

AshlandTJ: Theological J. (Ohio).

AsMis: Assyriological Miscellanies; K, Univ. [1 (1980)].

AsnJSt: Association for Jewish Studies Newsletter; CM. 0278-4033.

ASOR: American Schools of Oriental Research; CM (**diss.**: Dissertation Series).

Asprenas... Scienze Teologiche; Napoli.

ASTI: Annual of the [Jerusalem] Swedish Theological Institute; Leiden.

At[AcBol/Tor/Tosc]: Atti [dell'Accademia... di Bologna / di Torino / Toscana].

ATANT: Abhandlungen zur Theologie des Alten & Neuen Testaments; Zürich.

ATD: Das Alte Testament Deutsch. Neues Göttinger Bibelwerk; Gö.

AteDial: Ateismo e Dialogo; Vaticano.

AtenRom: Atene e Roma; Firenze. 0004-6493.

Athenaeum: Letteratura e Storia dell'antichità; Pavia.

ˋAtiqot, English edition; J, Dept. Ant.

AtKap: Ateneum Kapłańskie; Włocławek. 0208-9041.

ATLA: American Theological Library Association; Menuchen, NJ.

AtSGlot: Atti del Sodalizio Glottologico; Milano.

Atualização, Revista de Divulgação Teológica; Belo Horizonte, MG.

AuCAfr: Au cœur de l'Afrique; Burundi [22 (1982)].

AugLv: Augustiniana; Leuven.

AugM: Augustinus; Madrid.

AugR: Augustinianum; Roma.

AugSt: Augustinian Studies; Villanova PA.

AulaO: Aula Orientalis; Barc [1 (1983)].

AusgF: Ausgrabungen und Funde; B.

AustinSB: Austin (TX) Sem. Bulletin.

AustralasCR: Australasian Catholic Record; Sydney. 0727-3215.

AustralBR: Australian Biblical Review; Melbourne.

AVA: ➤ Bei AVgA.

Axes: Paris.

BA: Biblical Archaeologist; CM. 0006-0895.

Babel, international organ of translation; Budapest, Akad.

BaBernSt: Basler und Berner Studien zur historischen und systematischen Theologie; Bern.

Babesch: Bulletin Antieke Beschaving; Haag. 0165-9367.

BaghMit: Baghdader Mitteilungen DAI; Berlin.

BAH: Bibliothèque Archéologique et Historique (IFA-Beyrouth).

BAIG: Bollettino dell'Associazione Italiana per lo studio del Giudaismo [1 (1981) = Henoch 3 (1981) 81-96].

BAngIsr: Bulletin of the Anglo-Israel Archaeological Soc.; L. 0266-2442.

BangTF: Bangalore Theological Forum. [18 (1986)].

BaptQ: Baptist [Historical Soc.] Quarterly; Oxford. 0005-576X.

BArchAfr: Bulletin archéologique des travaux historiques et scientifiques (A. Antiquités nationales) B. Afrique du Nord: P.

BArchAlg: Bulletin d'Archéologie Algérienne; Alger.

BarIlAn: Bar-Ilan Annual; Ramat-Gan. 0067-4109.

BAR-Ox: British Archaeology Reports; Oxford.

BAR-W: Biblical Archaeology Review; Washington. 0098-9444.

BArte: Bollettino d'Arte; Roma.

BAsEspOr: Boletín de la Asociación Española de Orientalistas; Madrid.

BASOR: Bulletin of the American Schools of Oriental Research; CM. 0003-097X.

BASP: Bulletin, American Society of Papyrologists; NY. 0003-1186.

BAusPrax: Biblische Auslegung für die Praxis; Stuttgart.

BayNahr: Bayn al-Nahrayn: Archevêché Chaldéen; Mossoul.

Bazmaveb (Pazmavep; Armenian); Venezia.

BBArchäom: Berliner Beiträge zur Archäometrie; Berlin. 0344-5098. [6 (1985)].

BBB: ➤ BiBasB & BoBB.

BbbOr: Bibbia e Oriente; Bornato BS.

BBudé: Bulletin de l'Association G. Budé; Paris.

BCanadB: Bulletin of the Canadian Society of Biblical Studies; Ottawa [45 (1985)].

BCanMed: Bulletin of the Canadian Mediterranean Institute [= BCIM 1 (1981)].

BCentPrei: Bollettino del Centro Camuno di Studi Preistorici; Brescia. 0057-2168.

BCentProt: Bulletin du Centre Protestant d'Études; Genève.

BCH: Bulletin de Correspondance Hellénique; Paris. 0007-4217.

BChinAc: Bulletin of the China Academy; Taipei.

BCILL: Bibliothèque des Cahiers de l'Institut de Linguistique; Lv, Peeters/P, Cerf.

BCNH-T: Bibliothèque Copte de Nag Hammadi -Textes; Québec.

Bedi Kartlisa, revue de kartvélogie; Paris. 0373-1537.

BeerSheva: ❶ Annual: Bible/ANE; J.

BEgS: Bulletin of the Egyptological Seminar; NY.

BeiATJ: Beiträge zur Erforschung des Alten Testaments und des Antiken Judentums; Bern. 0722-0790.

BeiAVgArch: Beiträge zur allgemeinen und vergleichenden Archäologie; Mü, Beck.

BeiBibExT: Beiträge zur biblischen Exegese und Theologie [ipsi: BET]; Frankfurt/M.

BeiEvT: Beiträge zur evangelischen Theologie; München.

BeiGbEx: Beiträge zur Geschichte der biblischen Exegese; Tübingen.

BeiHistT: Beiträge zur Historischen Theologie; Tübingen.

BeiNam: Beiträge zur Namenforschung N. F.; Heid. 0005-8114.

BeiÖkT: Beiträge zur ökumenischen Theologie; München, Schöningh. 0067-5172.

BeiRelT: Beiträge zur Religionstheologie; Mödling.

BeiSudan: Beiträge zur Sudanforschung; Wien, Univ.

Belleten (Türk Tarih Kurumu); Ankara.

Benedictina; Roma.

Berytus (Amer. Univ. Beirut); København.

BethM: ❶ Beth Mikra; Jerusalem. 0005-979X.

BÉtKar: Bulletin d'Études Karaïtes; Paris [1 (1983) paru 1984].

BÉtOr: Bulletin d'Études Orientales; Damas, IFAO.

BFaCLyon: Bulletin des Facultés Catholiques; Lyon. 0180-5282.

Bib ➤ Biblica. Roma. 0006-0887.

BibAfr: La Bible en Afrique [francophone]; Lomé, Togo.

BiBasB: Biblische Basis Bücher; Kevelaer/ Stuttgart.

BiBei: Biblische Beiträge, Schweizerisches Kath. Bibelwerk; Fribourg.

BibFe: Biblia y Fe; Escorial, Madrid. 0210-5209.

BibIll: The Biblical Illustrator; Nv. [12 (1986)].

BibKonf: Biblische Konfrontationen; Stu, Kohlhammer.

Bible Bhashyam, Indian Biblical Quarterly; Vedavathoor, Kottayam, Kerala. 0970-2288.

BiblEscB/EstB: Biblioteca Escuela Bíblica; M / de Estudios Bíblicos, Salamanca.

BiblETL: Bibliotheca, ETL; Leuven.

BiblHumRef: Bibliotheca Humanistica et Reformatorica; Nieuwkoop, de Graaf.

BiblHumRen: Bibliothèque d'Humanisme et Renaissance; Genève/ Paris.

Biblica: commentarii Pontificii Instituti Biblici; Roma. 0006-0887.

Biblica-Lisboa (Capuchinos: given also as Revista Bíblica).

BiblMesop: Bibliotheca Mesopotamica; Malibu CA.

Biblos 1. Coimbra; 2. Wien.

BiblScRel: Biblioteca di Scienze religiose; Roma, Salesiana.

BibNot: Biblische Notizen; Bamberg. 0178-2967.

BibOrPont: Biblica et Orientalia, Pontificio Istituto Biblico; Roma.

BibTB: Biblical Theology Bulletin; St. Bonaventure NY. 0146-1079.

BibTPaid: Biblioteca Teologica; Brescia, Paideia.

BibTSt: Biblisch-Theologische Studien; Neukirchen-Vluyn.

BibUnt: Biblische Untersuchungen; Regensburg.

BIFAO: Bulletin de l'Institut Français d'Archéologie Orientale; Le Caire. 0255-0962.

Bijd: Bijdragen, Filosofie en Theologie; Nijmegen.

BijH: Bijbels Handboek; Kampen ➤ 575; = World of the Bible; GR ➤ 576.

BiKi: Bibel und Kirche; Stuttgart.

BInfWsz: Bulletin d'Information de l'Académie de Théologie Catholique; Warszawa. 0137-7000.

BInstArch: Bulletin of the Institute of Archaeology; London. 0076-0722.

BIP[Br]: Books in Print, U.S., annual; NY, Bowker [British, L, Whitaker].

BiRes: Biblical Research; Chicago. 0067-6535.

Biserica ... Ortodoxă Română; Bucureşti.

BIstFGrec: Bollettino dell'Istituto di Filologia Greca, Univ. di Padova; Roma.

BiWelt: Die Bibel in der Welt; Stu.

BJRyL: Bulletin of the John Rylands Library; Manchester. 0301-102X.

BKAT: Biblischer Kommentar AT; Neuk.

BL: Book List, The Society for Old Testament Study. 0-905495-04-7.

BLCéramEg: Bulletin de liaison ... céramique égyptienne; Le Caire, IFAO. 0255-0903 [10 (1985)].

BLitEc [Chr]: Bulletin de Littérature Ecclésiastique [Chronique]. Toulouse. 0007-4322 [0495-9396].

BLtg: Bibel und Liturgie; Wien-Klosterneuburg.

BMB: Bulletin du Musée de Beyrouth.

BMes: Bulletin, the Society for Mesopotamian Studies; Toronto [2-4 (1982)].

BMonde ➤ CahTrB.

BMosA [ipsi AIEMA]: Bulletin d'information de l'Association internationale pour l'étude de la mosaïque antique; Paris. 0761-8808.

BO: Bibliotheca Orientalis; Leiden. 0006-1913.

BoBB: Bonner Biblische Beiträge; Königstein.

BogSmot: Bogoslovska Smotra; Zagreb. 0352-3101.

BogTrud: Ⓖ Bogoslovskiye Trudi; Moskva.

BogVest: Bogoslovni Vestnik; Ljubljana [46 (1986)].

BonnJb: Bonner Jahrbücher.

Boreas [1. Uppsala, series]; 2. Münsterische Beiträge zur Archäologie. 0344-810X.

BOriento: Biblia kaj Oriento (Esperanto) [1 (1986)].

BR: Bible Review; Wsh. 8755-6316 [1 (1985)].

BREF: Bibliographie religieuse en français; Dourgne ➤ 1042*.

BRevuo ➤ BOriento.

BritJREd: British Journal of Religious Education; London [5 (1983)].

BS: Bibliotheca Sacra; Dallas, TX. 0006-1921.

BSAA: Boletín del Seminario de Estudios de Arte y Arqueología; Valladolid.

BSAC: Bulletin de la Société d'Archéologie Copte; Le Caire.

BSeptCog: Bulletin of the International Organization for Septuagint and Cognate Studies; ND.

BSignR: Bulletin Signalétique, religions; Paris. 0180-9296.

BSLP: Bulletin de la Société de Linguistique; Paris.

BSNAm: Biblical Scholarship in North America; Atlanta, SBL.

BSNEJap ➤ Oriento.

BSOAS: Bulletin of the School of Oriental and African Studies; London. 0041-977X.

BSoc[Fr]Ég: Bulletin de la Société [Française] d'Égyptologie; Genève [Paris].

BSoGgIt: Bollettino della Società Geografica Italiana; R. 0037-8755.

BSpade: Bible and Spade; Ballston NY.

BSSulp: Bulletin [annuel] de Saint-Sulpice; Paris.

BStLat: Bollettino di Studi Latini; N.

BStor: Biblioteca di storia e storiografia dei tempi biblici; Brescia.

BSumAg: Bulletin on Sumerian Agriculture; Cambridge. 0267-0658 [2 (1985)].

BTAfr: Bulletin de Théologie Africaine; Kinshasa.

BTAM: Bulletin de Théologie Ancienne et Médiévale; Louvain. ➤ RTAM.

BThemT: Bibliothek Themen der Theologie; Stuttgart.

BToday: The Bible Today; Collegeville MN. 0006-0836.

BTrans: The Bible Translator [Technical/ Practical, each 2 annually]; Stuttgart. 0260-0943.

BtSt: Biblisch-theologische Studien (ex-Biblische Studien); Neukirchen.

BTZ: Berliner Theologische Zeitschrift; Berlin. 0724-6137.

BUBS: Bulletin of the United Bible Societies; Stu.

BudCSt: Buddhist-Christian Studies; Honolulu, Univ. 0882-0945 [4 (1984)].

Burgense; Burgos.

BurHist: Buried History; Melbourne.

BVieChr: Bible et Vie Chrétienne NS; Paris.

BViewp: Biblical Viewpoint; Greenville SC, B. Jones Univ. 0006-0925.

BWANT: Beiträge zur Wissenschaft vom Alten und Neuen Testament; Stuttgart.

BySlav: Byzantinoslavica; Praha. 0007-7712.

ByZ: Byzantinische Zeitschrift; München. 0007-7704.

Ⓖ Byzantina; Thessaloniki.

Byzantion; Bruxelles.

ByzFor: Byzantinische Forschungen; Amsterdam. 90-256-0619-9.

BZ: Biblische Zeitschrift; Paderborn. 0006-2014.

BZA[N]W: Beihefte zur ➤ ZAW[ZNW].

CAD: [Chicago] Assyrian Dictionary; Glückstadt.

CADIR: Centre pour l'Analyse du Discours Religieux; Lyon ➤ SémBib.

CAH: Cambridge Ancient History[rev]; Cambridge Univ. ➤ 577.

CahArchéol: Cahiers Archéologiques; Paris. 2-7084-0131-9.

CahCMéd: Cahiers de Civilisation Médiévale; Poitiers.

CahDAFI: Cahiers de la Délégation Archéologique Française en Iran; Paris. 0765-104-X.

CahÉv: Cahiers Évangile; Paris. 0222-8741.

CahHist: Cahiers d'Histoire; Lyon.

CahIntSymb: Cahiers Internationaux de Symbolique; Mons, Belgique.

CahLV: Cahiers voor Levensverdieping; Averbode.

CahRechScRel: Cahiers de Recherche en Sciences de la Religion; Québec.

CahRenan: Cahiers du Cercle Ernest Renan; Paris.

CahSpIgn: Cahiers de spiritualité ignatienne; Québec.

CahTrB: Cahiers de traduction biblique; Pierrefitte France. 0755-1371.

CahTun: Les Cahiers (de la Faculté des Lettres) de Tunisie; Tunis.

CalvaryB: Calvary Baptist Theological Journal; Lansdale PA. 8756-0429 [1 (1985)].

CalvinT: Calvin Theological Journal; Grand Rapids MI. 0008-1795.

CalwTMon: Calwer Theologische Monographien (A: Biblisch); Stuttgart.

CamCW: Cambridge Commentary on Writings of the Jewish and Christian World 200 BC to AD 200: C. 0-521-28554-2.

CanadCR: Canadian Catholic Review; Saskatoon.

Carmel: Tilburg.

Carmelus: Roma. 0008-6673.

CARNES: Computer-aided research in Near Eastern Studies; Malibu CA. 0742-2334.

Carthaginensia; Murcia, Inst. Teol. 0213-4381 [1 (1985)].

CathCris: Catholicism in crisis; ND.

CathHR: Catholic Historical Review; Wsh. 0008-8080.

Catholica (Moehler-Institut, Paderborn); Münster.

Catholicisme: Paris → 578.

Catholic Studies, Tokyo → Katorikku.

CathTR: Catholic Theological Review; Clayton, Australia (NTAbs 30,150: Hong Kong) [6 (1984)].

CathTSocAmPr: → PrCTSAm [AnCTS].

CATSS: Computer assisted tools for Septuagint studies: Atlanta → SBL.

CBQ: Catholic Biblical Quarterly; Washington, DC. 0008-7912.

CC: La Civiltà Cattolica; R. 0009-8167.

CCGraec/Lat/Med: Corpus Christianorum, seriés graeca / latina / continuatio mediaev.; Turnhout.

CdÉ: Chronique d'Égypte; Bruxelles.

CédCarthB: Centre d'Études et de Documentation de la Conservation de Carthage, Bulletin; Tunis.

Center Journal; Notre Dame.

CERDAC: (Atti) Centro di Ricerca e Documentazione Classica; Milano.

CETÉDOC: Centre de Traitement Électronique des Documents; Lv.

CGL: Coptic Gnostic Library → NHS.

CGMG: Christlicher Glaube in moderner Gesellschaft; FrB.

ChCu: Church and Culture; Vatican [1 (1984)].

ChH: Church History; Berne, Ind.

CHH: Center for Hermeneutical Studies in Hellenistic and Modern Culture; Berkeley CA.

Chiea; Nairobi, Catholic Higher Institute of Eastern Africa.

Chiron: Geschichte, Epigraphie; München.

CHistEI: ✪ Cathedra, History of Eretz-Israel; Jerusalem.

CHist-J: Jerusalem Cathedra.

CHJud: Cambridge History of Judaism; C → 580.

Chm: Churchman 1. (Anglican); London: 0009-661X / 2. (Humanistic); St. Petersburg FL: 0009-6628.

ChrCent: Christian Century; Chicago.

Christus; 1. Paris; 2. México.

ChrJRel: Christian Jewish Relations; L.

ChrNIsr: Christian News from Israel; J.

ChrOost: Het Christelijk Oosten; Nijmegen.

ChrSchR: Christian Scholar's Review; Houston TX.

ChrT: Christianity Today; Chicago.

ChSt: Chicago Studies; Mundelein IL.

Church: NY, Nat. Pastoral Life.

ChWoman: The Church Woman [Protestant, Roman Catholic, Orthodox, other Christian]; NY. 0009-6598.

CistSt: Cistercian Studies; ed. Getsemani KY; pub. Chimay, Belgium.

Citeaux; Achel, Belgium. 0009-7497.

Cithara: Essays in the Judaeo-Christian Tradition; St. Bonaventure (NY) Univ.

CiTom: Ciencia Tomista; Salamanca.

CiuD: Ciudad de Dios; M. 0009-7756.

CivClCr: Civiltà classica e cristiana; Genova. 0392-8632.

CiVit: Città di Vita; Firenze. [0]009-7632.

Claret: Claretianum; Roma.

ClasA: [formerly California Studies in] Classical Antiquity; Berkeley, Univ.

ClasB: Classical Bulletin; Wilmore KY.

ClasJ: Classical Journal; Greenville SC. 0009-8353.

ClasMed: Classica et Mediaevalia; København. 0106-5815.

ClasModL: Classical and Modern Literature; Terre Haute IN.

ClasOutl: The Classical Outlook; Ch [ed. Oxford OH, Miami Univ.].

ClasPg: Classical Philology; Chicago.

ClasQ: Classical Quarterly NS; Oxford. 0009-8388.

ClasR: Classical Review NS; Oxford. 0009-840X.

ClasWo: Classical World; Pittsburgh. 0009-8148.

CLehre: Die Christenlehre; Berlin.

CleR: Clergy Review; L. 0009-8736.

ClubH: Club des Hébraïsants; Boran.

CNRS: Conseil National de Recherche Scientifique; Paris.

CogF: Cogitatio Fidei; Paris.

ColcCist: Collectanea Cisterciensia; Forges, Belgique.

ColcFranc: Collectanea Franciscana; Roma. 0010-0749.

ColcT: Collectanea Theologica; Warszawa. 0137-6985.
ColcTFu: Collectanea theol. Universitatis Fujen = *Shenhsileh Lunchi*; Taipei.
CollatVl: Collationes, Vlaams... Theologie en Pastoraal; Gent.
Colloquium; Auckland, Sydney.
ColStFen: Collezione di Studi Fenici; Roma, Univ.
ComLtg: Communautés et Liturgies; Ottignies (Belgique).
Commentary; NY. 0010-2601.
CommBras: Communio Brasiliensis: Rio de Janeiro.
CommND: Communio USA; Notre Dame. 0094-2065.
CommRevue: Communio [various languages, not related to **ComSev**]: revue catholique internationale; Paris.
CommStrum: Communio, strumento internazionale per un lavoro teologico; Milano.
Communio deutsch → **IkaZ.**
ComOT: Commentaar op het Oude Testament. Kampen.
CompHum: Computers and the Humanities; Osprey FL. 0010-4817.
Compostellanum; Santiago de Compostela.
ComRatisbNT: Comentario de Ratisbona; Barc.
ComRelM: Commentarium pro Religiosis et Missionariis; Roma.
ComSev: Communio; Sevilla.
ComSpirAT/NT: Commenti spirituali dell'Antico / Nuovo Testamento; Roma.
ComTeolNT: Commentario Teologico del NT; Brescia.
ComViat: Communio Viatorum; Praha. 0010-7133.
ConBib: Coniectanea Biblica OT/NT; Malmö.
Conc: Concilium, variis linguis; P,E, etc.; deutsch = → IZT.
ConcordJ: Concordia Journal; St. Louis.
ConcordTQ: Concordia Theological Quarterly; Fort Wayne.
ConoscRel: Conoscenza religiosa; Firenze.
Consensus: Canadian Lutheran; Winnipeg.
ConsJud: Conservative Judaism; NY.

ContrIstStorAnt: Contributi dell'Istituto di Storia Antica; Milano, Univ. Sacro Cuore.
Coptologia [also for Egyptology]: Thunder Bay ONT, Lakehead Univ.
CouStR: Council for the Study of Religion Bulletin; Hanover PA.
CovQ: Covenant Quarterly; Chicago.
CRAI: Comptes rendus de l'Académie des Inscriptions et Belles-Lettres; Paris.
Creation; Oakland CA, Friends of Creation Spirituality [1,1 (1985)].
CRIPEL: Cahiers de Recherches de l'Institut de Papyrologie et d'Égyptologie de Lille [7 (1985)].
CriswT: Criswell Theological Review; Dallas [1 (1986)].
Criterio; Buenos Aires. 0011-1473.
CrkvaSv: Crkva u Svijetu; Split.
CrNSt: Cristianesimo nella Storia; Bologna. 0393-3598.
CroatC: Croatica Christiana; Zagreb.
CrossC: Cross Currents; West Nyack NJ. 0011-1953.
Crux: Vancouver. 0011-2186.
CSacSN: Corpus Sacrae Scripturae Neerlandicae Medii Aevi; Leiden.
CSCO: Corpus Scriptorum Christianorum Orientalium; Lv. 0070-0401.
CuadJer: Cuadernos Bíblicos, Institución S. Jerónimo; Valencia.
CuadFgClás: Cuadernos de Filología Clásica; M, Univ.
CuadTeol: Cuadernos de Teología; Buenos Aires [6,3 (1983)].
CuadTrad: Cuadernos de Traducción y Interpretación / Quaderns de Traducció i Interpretació; Barcelona [1 (c. 1982): BTrans 34 (1983) 148].
CuBíb: Cultura Bíblica; M: AFEBE. 0211-2493.
CurrTMiss: Currents in Theology and Mission; St. Louis. 0098-2113.
CyrMeth: Cyrillomethodianum; Thessaloniki.
D: director (in Indice etiam *auctor*) Dissertationis.
DAFI: Délégation Archéologique Française en Iran (Mém); Paris.
DAI: Deutsches Archäologisches Institut (Baghdad etc.) → Mi(tt).
DanTTs: Dansk Teologisk Tidsskrift; København.

DanVMed/Skr: Det Kongelige Danske Videnskabornes Selskap, Historisk-Filosofiske Meddelelser / Skriften; K.

DBS [= SDB], Dictionnaire de la Bible, Supplément; P ➔ 906.

Dedalo: São Paulo.

DeltChr: Deltion tes christianikēs archaiologikēs hetaireias: Athēna [4,12 (for 1984: 1986)].

DeltVM: Ⓖ Deltío vivlikôn meletôn (= Bulletin des Études Bibliques); Athēnai.

DHGE: Dictionnaire d'Histoire et de Géographie Ecclésiastiques; P ➔ 581.

Diachronica, international journal for historical linguistics; Hildesheim [1 (1984)].

Diakonia; Mainz/Wien [13 (1982)] 0341-9592; Stu [8 (1982)].

DialArch: Dialoghi di Archeologia; Milano.

DiálEcum: Diálogo Ecuménico; Salamanca. 0210-2870.

Dialog; Minneapolis. 0012-2033.

DialTP: Diálogo teológico; El Paso TX.

DictSpir: Dictionnaire de Spiritualité; P. ➔ 582.

Didaskalia; Lisboa.

DiehlBl: Diehlheimer Blätter zum Alten Testament [ipsi DBAT]; Heid.

Dionysius: Halifax, Dalhousie University. 0705-1085.

Direction; Fresno CA.

DiscEg: Discussions in Egyptology; Oxford. 0268-3083 [1 (1985)].

Disciple, the (Disciples of Christ); St. Louis. 0092-8372.

Diss [= ᴰ, etiam Director]: Dissertation.

DissA: Dissertation Abstracts International; AA/L. -A [= US]: 0419-4209 [C = Europe. 0307-6075].

DissHRel: Dissertationes ad historiam religionum (supp. Numen); Leiden.

Divinitas; Pont. Acad. Theol. Rom. (Lateranensis); Vaticano. 0012-4222.

DivThom: Divus Thomas; Piacenza. 0012-4257.

DJD: Discoveries in the Judaean Desert; Oxford.

DLZ: Deutsche Literaturzeitung; Berlin. 0012-043X.

DMA: Dictionary of the Middle Ages; NY.

DocCath: Documentation Catholique; Paris.

DoctCom: Doctor Communis; Vaticano.

DoctLife: Doctrine and Life; Dublin.

DOG: Deutsche Orient-Gesellschaft: B.

Dor: Dor le Dor; J, World Jewish.

DosA: Histoire et archéologie, les dossiers; Dijon.

DosB: Les dossiers de la Bible [suite de La Bible et son message, 1-178 (1965-83) traitant toute la Bible livre par livre]; Paris [6-10 (1985)].

DowR: Downside Review; Bath. 0012-5806.

DPA: Dizionario patristico e di antichità cristiane; Casale Monferrato ➔ 583.

DrevVost: Ⓓ Drevnij Vostok; Moskva.

DrewG: The Drew [Theological School] Gateway; Madison NJ.

DumbO: Dumbarton Oaks Papers; CM. 0070-7546.

ᴱ: editor, Herausgeber, *a cura di.*

EAfJE: East African Journal of Evangelical Theology; Machakos, Kenya.

EAsJT: East Asia Journal of Theology [combining NE & SE AJT]; Tokyo. 0217-3859.

EAPast: East Asian Pastoral Review; Manila. 0040-0564.

ÉcAnn: Écoutez et Annoncez, mensuel; Lomé, Togo [6 (1984)].

ÉchMClas: Échos du Monde Classique/Classical Views; Calgary. 0012-9356.

EcOr: Ecclesia Orans, periodica de scientiis liturgicis; R, Anselmiano [1,1 (1984)].

ÉcoutBib: Écouter la Bible; Paris.

EcuR: Ecumenical Review; Geneva.

EfMex: Efemerides Mexicana; Tlalpan.

Egb: Ergänzungsband.

ÉglRur: Église aujourd'hui en monde rural; Paris. 0223-5854.

ÉglT: Église et Théologie; Ottawa.

EgVO: Egitto e Vicino Oriente; Pisa.

ÉHRel: Études d'histoire des religions.

Einzb: Einzelband.

EkK **[Vor]:** Evangelischer-katholischer Kommentar zum NT; Z/Köln; Neukirchen-Vluyn ['Vorarbeiten'].

EkkT: Ⓖ Ekklēsía kaì Theología; L. Elenchos, ... pensiero antico; Napoli.

Elliniká; Ⓖ Thessaloniki.

Emerita: (lingüística clásica); M.

Emmanuel: St. Meinrads IN.

Enc. Biblica ➤ EnṣMiqr.

EncHebr: ❶ Encyclopaedia Hebraica; J/TA.

Enchoria, Demotistik/Koptologie; Wiesbaden. 3-447-02807-6.

EncIran: Encyclopaedia Iranica; London [I,1 (1982)] ➤ 1,732.

EncIslam: Encyclopédie de l'Islam. Nouvelle édition; Leiden/P ➤ 584.

EncKat: Encyklopedia Katolicka; Lublin ➤ 585.

Encounter (theol.); Indianapolis.

EncRel: (1) ᴱEliade M., The encyclopedia of religion; NY ➤ 585; (2) Enciclopedia delle Religioni; Firenze.

EncWSpir: World Spirituality, an encyclopedic history; NY ➤ 588.

EnṣMiqr: ❶ Enṣiqlopediya miqrā'ît, Encyclopaedia Biblica; Jerusalem.

Entschluss: Wien. 0017-4602.

EnzMär: Enzyklopädie des Märchens; B ➤ 586.

EOL: Ex Oriente Lux ➤ 1. Jb/2. Phoenix.

Eos, ... philologia; Wsz. 0012-7825.

EpAnat: Epigraphica anatolica; Bonn.

ÉPHÉ[H/R]: École Pratique des Hautes-Études, Annuaire [Hist.-Pg. / Sc. Rel.]; Paris.

EpHetVyzSpoud: ❻ Ephēmeris tēs Hetaireías tōn Vyzantinōn Spoudōn; Athēnai.

EphLtg: Ephemerides Liturgicae; R.

EphMar: Ephemerides Mariologicae; Madrid.

ÉPR: Études préliminaires aux religions orientales dans l'Empire romain; Leiden.

Eranos[/Jb]: Acta Philologica Suecana; Uppsala / Jahrbuch; Frankfurt/M (< Z).

ErbAuf: Erbe und Auftrag; Beuron.

Eretz-Israel (partly ❶), 'annual'; Jerusalem. 0071-108X.

ErfTSt/Schr: Erfurter Theologische Studien/ Schriften.

ErtFor: Ertrag der Forschung; Da, Wiss. 0174-0695.

EscrVedat: Escritos del Vedat [del Torrente]; Valencia. 0210-3133.

EsprVie: Esprit et Vie: 1. [< Ami du Clergé]; Langres; 2. (series) Chambray.

EstAgust: Estudio Agustiniano; Valladolid.

EstBíb: Estudios Bíblicos; Madrid. 0014-1437.

EstDeusto: Estudios Universidad Deusto: Madrid.

EstE: Estudios Eclesiásticos; Madrid. 0210-1610.

EstFranc: Estudios Franciscanos; Barcelona.

EsTGuat: Estudios Teológicos; Guatemala.

EstJos: Estudios Josefinos; Valladolid.

EsTLeop: Estudos Teológicos (luteran.); São Leopoldo. RS. Brasil.

EstLul: Estudios Lulianos; Mallorca.

EstMar: Estudios Marianos; Madrid.

EstMonInstJer: Estudios y Monografías, Institución S. Jerónimo (bíblica); Valencia.

EstTrin: Estudios Trinitarios; Salamanca.

EstudosB: Estudos Bíblicos; Petrópolis [no longer part of REB].

ÉtBN: Études Bibliques, Nouvelle Série; Paris. 0760-3541.

ÉtClas: Les études classiques; Namur. 0014-200X.

Eternity; Philadelphia [34 (1983)].

ÉtFranc: Études Franciscaines; Blois.

ÉtIndE: Études Indo-Européennes; Lyon.

ETL: Ephemerides Theologicae Lovanienses; Leuven. 0013-9513.

ÉtPapyr: Études [Société Égyptienne] de Papyrologie; Le Caire.

ÉtPgHist: Études de Philologie et d'Histoire; Genève, Droz.

ÉTRel: Études Théologiques et Religieuses; Montpellier. 0014-2239.

ÉtTrav: Études et Travaux; Varsovie.

Études; Paris. 0014-1941.

Euhemer (❶ hist. rel.); Warszawa. 0014-2298

EuntDoc: Euntes Docete; Roma.

EurHS: Europäische Hochschulschriften / Publ. Universitaires Européennes; Bern.

Evangel; Edinburgh. 0265-4547.

EvErz: Der evangelische Erzieher; Frankfurt/M. 0014-3413.

EvJ: Evangelical Journal; Myerstown PA [3 (1985)].

EvKL: Evangelisches Kirchenlexikon; ➤ 587.

EvKom: Evangelische Kommentare; Stuttgart. 0300-4236.

EvQ[RT]: Evangelical Quarterly [Review of Theology]; Exeter.

EvT: Evangelische Theologie, NS; München. 0014-3502.

EWest: East and West | 1. L / 2. R.

EWSp: Encyclopedia of World Spirituality; NY/L ➤ 588.

ExAud: Ex auditu, ongoing symposium annual: Princeton (sb. Pickwick) 0883-0053 [2 (1986)].

ExcSIsr: Excavations and Surveys in Israel ➤ Ḥadašot; Jerusalem. [Winona Lake: Eisenbrauns $10]. 0334-1607.

Expedition (archaeol., anthrop.); Philadelphia. 0014-4738.

Explor [sic]; Evanston. 0362-0876.

ExpTim: The Expository Times; Edinburgh. 0014-5246.

ExWNT: Exegetisches Wörterbuch zum NT; Stuttgart ➤ 894.

F&R: Faith and Reason; Front Royal VA, Christendom College. 0098-5449 [11 (1985)].

FascBíb: Fascículos bíblicos; Madrid.

Faventia: classica; Barc. 0210-7570.

fg./fil.: filologico, filosofico.

FilRTSt: Filosofia della Religione, Testi e Studi; Brescia.

Fønix [6 (1982)].

FoiTemps: La Foi et le Temps. NS; Tournai.

FoiVie: Foi et Vie; Paris. 0015-5357.

FolOr: Folia Orientalia, Polska Akademia Nauk; Kraków. 0015-5675.

Fondamenti; Brescia, Paideia [4 (1986)].

ForBib: Forschung zur Bibel; Wü/Stu.

ForBMusB: Forschungen und Berichte, Staatliche Museen zu Berlin.

ForGLehrProt: Forschungen zur Geschichte und Lehre des Protestantismus; Mü.

ForJüdChrDial: Forschungen zum jüdisch-christlichen Dialog; Neuk.

ForKiDG: Forschungen zur Kirchen- und Dogmengeschichte; Gö.

Fornvännen (Svensk Antikvarisk Forskning); Lund. 0015-7813.

ForSystÖ: Forschungen zur Systematischen & Ökumenischen Theologie; Gö.

ForTLing: Forum Theologiae Linguisticae; Bonn.

Forum; Bonner MT. 0883-4970 [1 (1985)].

ForumKT: Forum Katholische Theologie; Münster. 0178-1626 [1 (1985)].

FOTLit: Forms of OT Literature; GR, Eerdmans.

FraJudBei: Frankfurter Judaistische Beiträge: Fra.

FranBog: Franciscanum, ciencias del espíritu; Bogotá. 0120-1468.

FrancSt: Franciscan Studies; St. Bonaventure, NY. 0080-5459.

FranzSt: Franziskanische Studien; Pd.

FraTSt: Frankfurter Theologische Studien; Fra, S. Georgen.

FreibRu: Freiburger Rundbrief. ... christlich-jüdische Begegnung; FrB.

FreibTSt: Freiburger Theologische Studien; Freiburg/Br.

FreibZ: Freiburger Zeitschrift für Philosophie und Theologie; Fribourg/Suisse.

FRLANT: Forschungen zur Religion und Literatur des Alten und NTs; Gö.

FutUo: Il futuro dell'uomo; Firenze, Assoc. Teilhard. 0390-217X [12 (1985)].

GCS: Die Griechischen Christlichen Schriftsteller der ersten Jahrhunderte; oBerlin. Ⓖ *Graece*; title in Greek.

GdT: Giornale di Teologia; Brescia.

GeistL: Geist und Leben; Wü.

Genava (archéologie, hist. art); Genève. 0072-0585.

GenLing: General Linguistics; University Park PA.

Georgica: Jena/Tbilissi. 0232-4490.

GerefTTs: Gereformeerd Theologisch Tijdschrift; Kampen. 0016-8610.

Gerión, revista de Historia Antigua; Madrid, Univ. 0213-0181.

GGA: Göttingische Gelehrte Anzeigen; Göttingen. 0017-1549.

GidsBW: Gidsen bij de Bijbelwetenschap; Kampen, Kok.

GItFg: Giornale italiano di filologia; Napoli. 0017-0461.

GLÉCS: (Comptes rendus) Groupe Linguistique d'Études Chamito-Sémitiques; Paris.

GLNT: Grande Lessico del NT (< TWNT); Brescia ➤ 895.

Glotta: griech.-lat.; Göttingen. 0017-1298.

Gnomon; klass. Altertum; München. 0017-1417.

GöMiszÄg: Göttinger Miszellen ... zur ägyptologischen Diskussion; Göttingen. 0344-385X.

GöOrFor: Göttinger Orientforschungen; Würzburg.

GöTArb: Göttinger Theologische Arbeiten; Göttingen.

GraceTJ: Grace Theological Journal; Winona Lake IN. 0198-666X.

GraecChrPrim: Graecitas Christianorum Primaeva; Nijmegen, van den Vegt.

Grail, ecumenical quarterly; Waterloo ONT, St. Jerome's College [1,1 (1985)].

GrArab: Graeco-Arabica; Athenai.

GreeceR: Greece and Rome; Oxford.

Greg[LA]: Gregorianum; R, Pontificia Universitas Gregoriana [Liber Annualis].

GrenzfTP: Grenzfragen zwischen Theologie und Philosophie; Köln.

GrOrTR: Greek Orthodox Theological Review; Brookline MA. 0017-3894.

GrPT: Growing Points in Theology.

GrRByz: Greek, Roman and Byzantine Studies; CM. 0017-3916.

GrSinai: Grande Sinal, revista de espiritualidade; Petrópolis.

Gymn: Gymnasium; Heid. 0342-5231.

🔂 (Neo-)hebraiče; (modern) Hebrew.

HaBeiA: Hamburger Beiträge zur Archäologie. 0341-3152.

Ḥadašôt arkeologiyôt 🔂 [News]; J, Education ministry museum dept. ➔ ExcSIsr.

HalleB: Hallesche Beiträge zur Orientwissenschaft; Halle. 0233-2205.

Hamdard Islamicus [research]; Pakistan. 0250-7196.

Handes Amsorya [armen.]; Wien.

HarvSemMon/Ser: Harvard Semitic Monographs / (Museum) Series; CM.

HarvStClasPg: Harvard Studies in Classical Philology; CM.

HarvTR: The Harvard Theological Review; CM. 0017-8160.

HbAltW: Handbuch der Altertumswissenschaft; München.

HbAT/NT: Handbuch zum Alten/Neuen Testament; Tübingen.

HbDG: Handbuch der Dogmengeschichte; Freiburg/B.; ➔ 1,896.

HbDTG: Handbuch der Dogmen- und Theologiegeschichte; Göttingen ➔ 589.

HbOr: Handbuch der Orientalistik; Leiden.

HbRelG: Handbuch der Religionsgeschichte; Göttingen.

HDienst: Heiliger Dienst; Salzburg. 0017-9620.

HebAnR: Hebrew Annual Review; Columbus, Ohio State Univ.

HebBWJud: Hebräische Beiträge zur Wissenschaft des Judentums deutsch angezeigt: Heidelberg. [1/1s (1985)].

HebSt: Hebrew Studies; Madison WI. 0146-4094.

Helikon (Tradizione e Cultura Classica, Univ. Messina); Roma.

Hellenika; Jb. für die Freunde Griechenlands; Bochum 0018-0084; cf. ➔ Elliniká.

Helmántica (humanidades clásicas, Univ.); Salamanca.

Henceforth, journal for Advent Christian thought; Lenox MA [14 (1985s)].

Henoch (ebraismo): Torino (Univ.).

Hephaistos, Theorie / Praxis Arch.; Ha.

HerdKor: Herder-Korrespondenz; Freiburg/Br. 0018-0645.

HerdTKom, NT: Herders Theologischer Kommentar zum NT; FrB.

Heresis, revue d'hérésiologie médiévale; Villegly/Carcassonne, Centre Nat. Ét. Cathares. 0758-3737 [4s (1985)].

Hermathena; Dublin. 0018-0750.

Hermeneus, antieke cultuur; Amersfoort.

Hermeneutica; Urbino, Univ.

Hermes, Klassische Philologie; Wiesbaden. 0018-0777.

HermUnT: Hermeneutische Untersuchungen zur Theologie; Tübingen.

HervTS: Hervormde Teologiese Studies; Pretoria.

Hesperia (American School of Classical Studies at Athens); Princeton. 0018-098X.

Hethitica. Travaux édités; Lv.

HeythJ: Heythrop Journal; London. 0018-1196.

HistJ: Historical Journal; Cambridge.

HistJb: Historisches Jahrbuch; Mü. Historia; 1. Baden-Baden: 0018-2311; 2. Santiago, Univ. Católica Chile.

HistRel: History of Religions; Chicago. 0018-2710.

HLand[S]: Das Heilige Land (Deutscher Verein) Köln [(Schw. Verein); Luzern].

Hokhma; Lausanne. 0379-7465.

HolyL: Holy Land: J, OFM. 0333-4851 [5 (1985)]. ➤ **TerraS.**

Homoousios (consustancial); Buenos Aires, Ortodoxía antioquena [1 (1986)].

HomPastR: Homiletic and Pastoral Review; New York. 0018-4268.

HomRel: Homo religiosus (histoire des religions); Louvain-la-Neuve.

HorBibT: Horizons in Biblical Theology (Old & NT); Pittsburgh. 0195-9085.

Horeb: Histoire Orientation Recherche Exégèse Bible; Sèvres, ADET (Association d'Étudiants en Théologie; Fac. Prot. Paris).

Horizons (College Theology Society); Villanova PA.

Hsientai Hsüehyüan (= Universitas); Taipei.

HUC|A: Hebrew Union College [+ Jewish Institute of Religion] Annual; Cincinnati.

Humanitas; 1. Brescia; 2. Tucuman.

HumT: Humanística e Teologia; Porto [6 (1985)].

Hydra, Middle Bronze Age studies; Uppsala, Univ. [1 (1985)].

Hypom: Hypomnemata; Göttingen, VR.

HZ: Historische Zeitschrift; Mü.

IAJS: ➤ **RAMBI.**

IBMiss: International (formerly Occasional) Bulletin of Missionary Research; Minneapolis (Lutheran).

ICC: International Critical Commentary; Edinburgh.

ICI: Informations Catholiques Internationales; Paris.

IClasSt: Illinois Classical Studies; Urbana. 0363-1923 [11 (1985)].

IFA: Institut Français d'Archéologie (Orientale, Le Caire / Beyrouth).

IglV: Iglesia Viva; Valencia/Madrid.

IkaZ: Internationale Kath. Zeitschrift, Communio; Rodenkirchen. 0341-8693.

IkiZ: Internationale kirchliche Zeitschrift; Bern. 0020-9252.

ILN: Illustrated London News; London. 0019-2422.

Immanuel (ecumenical); J. 0302-8127.

Index Jewish Studies ➤ **RAMBI.**

IndIranJ: Indo-Iranian Journal; (Canberra-) Leiden. 0019-7246.

IndJT: Indian Journal of Theology; Serampore.

IndMissR: Indian Missiological Review; Shillong. [7 (1985)].

IndogF: Indogermanische Forschungen; Berlin. 0019-7262.

IndTSt: Indian Theological Studies; Bangalore, St. Peter's.

InnsBeiKultW/SpraW/TS: Innsbrucker Beiträge zur Kulturwissenschaft / Sprachwissenschaft / Theologische Studien.

IntBbg[R/Z]: Internationale Bibliographie | der Rezensionen wissenschaftlicher Literatur [10 (1980)] / der Zeitschriftenliteratur aus allen Gebieten des Wissens [16 (1980)]; Osnabrück.

IntCathRCom ➤ **CommND.**

Interp: Interpretation; Richmond VA. 0020-9643.

IntJNaut: International Journal of Nautical Archaeology L/NY. 0305-7445.

IntJPhR: International Journal for the Philosophy of Religion; The Hague.

IntRMiss: International Review of Mission; London. 0020-8582.

Iran; London, British Institute Persian Studies. 0578-6967.

IrAnt: Iranica Antiqua; Leiden.

Iraq; L, British School of Archaeology. 0021-0889.

IrBSt: Irish Biblical Studies; Belfast. 0268-6112.

Irén: Irénikon; Chevetogne. 0021-0978.

IrTQ: Irish Theological Quarterly; Maynooth. 0021-1400.

ISBEnc: International Standard Bible Encyclopedia³; GR, Eerdmans ➤ **590*.**

Islam, Der: Berlin. 0021-1818.

Islamochristiana; Roma, Pontificio Istituto di Studi Arabi. 0392-7288.

IsrEJ: Israel Exploration Journal; Jerusalem. 0021-2059.

IsrJBot/Zool: Israel Journal of Botany 0021-213X / Zoology 0021-2210: Jerusalem.

IsrLawR: Israel Law Review; Jerusalem. 0021-2237.

IsrMusJ: Israel Museum Journal; Jerusalem.

IsrNumJ[SocB]: Israel Numismatic Journal, J [Society Bulletin: TA].

IsrOrSt: Israel Oriental Studies; Tel Aviv.

Istina; Paris. 0021-2423.

IVRA (Jura); Napoli.

IZBG: Internationale Zeitschriftenschau für Bibelwissenschaft und Grenzgebiete; Pd. 0074-9745.

IZT: Internationale Zeitschrift für Theologie [= Concilium deutsch].

JAAR: Journal of the American Academy of Religion; Atlanta. 0002-7189.

J[News]AmEg: Journal [Newsletter] of the American Research Center in Egypt; Winona Lake IN (NY Columbia Univ.).

JAmScAff: Journal of the American Scientific Affiliation (evang.); Ipswich MA. 0003-0988.

JANES: Journal of the Ancient Near Eastern Society; NY, Jewish Theol. Sem. 0010-2016.

JanLing[Pract]: Janua Linguarum [Series Practica]; The Hague / Paris.

JAOS: Journal of the American Oriental Society; NHv. 0003-0279.

JapJRelSt: Japanese Journal of Religious Studies; Nagoya.

JapRel: Japanese Religions; Tokyo.

JArchSc: Journal of Archaeological Science; London/New York.

JAs: Journal Asiatique; P. 0021-762X.

JAsAf: Journal of Asian and African Studies (York Univ., Toronto); Leiden.

Javeriana → TXav.

Jb: Jahrbuch [Heid, Mainz...]; Jaarbericht.

JbAC: Jahrbuch für Antike und Christentum; Münster i. W.

JbBerlMus: Jahrbücher der Berliner Museen; wBerlin.

JbBTh: Jahrbuch für biblische Theologie; Neukirchen [1 (1986): 3-7887-1229-5]; → 236.

JbEOL: Jaarbericht van het Vooraziatisch-Egyptisch Genootschap Ex Oriente Lux; Leiden.

JBL: Journal of Biblical Literature; Atlanta. 0021-9231.

JbLtgH: Jahrbuch für Liturgik und Hymnologie; Kassel. [3-7982-0182-X: 4 (1984)].

JbNumG: Jahrbuch für Numismatik und Geldgeschichte; Regensburg.

JbÖsByz: Jahrbuch der Österreichischen Byzantinistik; W. 0378-8660.

JChrEd: Journal of Christian Education; Sydney. 0021-9657 [82s (1985)].

JCS: Journal of Cuneiform Studies; CM. 0022-0256.

JDharma: Journal of Dharma; Bangalore.

JdU: Judentum und Umwelt; Frankfurt/M.

JEA: Journal of Egyptian Archaeology; London. 0307-5133.

JEcuSt: Journal of Ecumenical Studies; Ph, Temple Univ. 0022-0558.

Jeevadhara (Christian Interpretation); Alleppey, Kerala.

JEH: Journal of Ecclesiastical History; Cambridge. 0022-0469.

JerusSt: Jerusalem studies in Jewish thought; Jerusalem [2 (1982)].

JESHO: Journal of Economic and Social History of the Orient; Leiden.

JEvTS: Journal of the Evangelical Theological Society; Wheaton IL.

JFemR: Journal of Feminist Studies in Religion; Chico CA. 8755-4178.

JField: Journal of Field Archaeology; Boston, Univ. 0093-4690.

JGlass: Journal of Glass Studies; Corning, NY. 0075-4250.

JHistId: Journal of the History of Ideas; Ph, Temple Univ. 0022-5037.

JHMR: Judaica, Hermeneutics, Mysticism, and Religion; Albany, SUNY.

JhÖsA: Jahreshefte des Österreichischen Archäologischen Institutes; Wien. 0078-3579.

JHS: Journal of Hellenic Studies; London. 0075-4269.

JIndEur: Journal of Indo-European Studies; Hattiesburg, Miss.

JIntdenom: Journal of the Interdenominational Theological Center; Atlanta GA.

JIntdis: Journal of the Society for Interdisciplinary History; CM, MIT.

JJC: Jésus et Jésus-Christ; Paris.

JJS: Journal of Jewish Studies; Oxford. 0022-2097.

JJurPap: Journal of Juristic Papyrology; Warszawa [revived 19 (1983)].

JLawA: Jewish Law Annual (Oxford); Leiden.

JLawRel: Journal of Law and Religion; St. Paul. [3 (1985)].

JMedRenSt: Journal of Medieval and Renaissance Studies; Durham NC.

JMoscPatr: [Engl.] Journal of the Moscow Patriarchate; Moscow.

JNES: Journal of Near Eastern Studies; Chicago, Univ. 0022-2968.

JNWS: Journal of Northwest Semitic Languages; Leiden.

Journal für Geschichte; Braunschweig.

JPsy&C: Journal of Psychology and Christianity; Farmington Hills MI. 0733-4273.

JPsy&Jud: Journal of Psychology and Judaism; New York.

JPsy&T: Journal of Psychology and Theology; La Mirada / Rosemead CA.

JQR: Jewish Quarterly Review (Ph, Dropsie Univ.); Winona Lake IN. 0021-6682.

JRAS: Journal of the Royal Asiatic Society; London.

JRefJud: Journal of Reform Judaism; NY. 0149-712X.

JRel: Journal of Religion; Chicago. 0022-4189.

JRelEth: Journal of Religion and Ethics; ND (ᴱRutgers). 0384-9694.

JRelHealth: The Journal of Religion and Health; New York.

JRelHist: Journal of Religious History; Sydney, Univ. 0022-4227.

JRelPsyR: Journal of Religion and Psychical Research; Bloomfield CT.

JRelSt: Journal of Religious Studies; Cleveland.

JRelTht: Journal of Religious Thought; Washington DC.

JRS: Journal of Roman Studies; London. 0075-4358.

JSArm: Journal of the Society for Armenian Studies; LA [1 (1984)].

JSav: Journal des Savants: Paris.

JScStR: Journal for the Scientific Study of Religion; NHv. 0021-8294.

JSHZ: Jüdische Schriften aus hellenistischer und römischer Zeit; Gütersloh.

JSS: Journal of Semitic Studies; Manchester. 0022-4480.

JSStEg: Journal of the Society for the Study of Egyptian Antiquities [ipsi SSEA]; Toronto. 0383-9753.

JStJud: Journal for the Study of Judaism in the Persian, Hellenistic, & Roman Periods; Leiden. 0047-2212.

JStJTht: Jerusalem Studies in Jewish Thought.

JStNT/OT: Journal for the Study of the NT/OT; Sheffield, Univ. 0142-064X / 0309-0892.

JTS: Journal of Theological Studies, N.S.: Oxford/London. 0022-5185.

JTSAfr: Journal of Theology for Southern Africa; Rondebosch.

Judaïca; Zürich.

Judaism; NY. 0022-5762.

JudTSt: Judaistische Texte und Studien; Hildesheim.

JWarb: Journal of the Warburg and Courtauld Institutes; London.

JwHist: Jewish History; Haifa [1 (1986)].

JWomen&R: Journal of Women and Religion; Berkeley [4,2 (1985)].

JyskR: Religionsvidenskabeligt Tidsskrift; Århus, Jysk [Jutland] Selskap [1 (1982)].

Kadmos; Berlin. 0022-7498.

Kairos (Religionswiss.); Salzburg.

Karawane (Die), Vierteljahresheft der Gesellschaft für Länder- und Völkerkunde; Ludwigsburg [22 (1981)].

Karthago (archéologie africaine); P.

KAT: Kommentar zum AT: Gütersloh.

KatBlät: Katechetische Blätter; Mü.

KatKenk: Katorikku Kenkyu < Shingaku; Tokyo, Sophia. 0387-3005.

KBW: Katholisches Bibelwerk; Stu [bzw. Österreich, Schweiz].

KeK: Kritisch-exegetischer Kommentar über das NT; Göttingen.

KerDo: Kerygma und Dogma; Göttingen. 0023-0707.

KerkT: Kerk en Theologie; Wageningen. 0165-2346.

Kerygma (on Indian missions); Ottawa. 0023-0693.

KingsTR: King's College Theological Review; London.

KirSef: ❶ Kiryat Sefer, Bibliographical Quarterly; J, Nat.-Univ. Libr. 0023-1851. ➤ Rambi.

KIsr: Kirche und Israel, theologische Zeitschrift; Neukirchen. 0179-7239. [1 (1986)].

KkKS: Konfessionskundliche und Kontroverstheologische Studien; Pd. Bonifacius.

KleinÄgTexte: Kleine ägyptische Texte; Wb.

Kler: ❻ Klēronomia (patristica); Thessalonikį.

Klio: oBerlin. 0075-6334.

KLK: Katholisches Leben und Kirchenreform im Zeitalter der Glaubensspaltung; Münster.

KomBeiANT: Kommentare und Beiträge zum Alten und N.T.; Düsseldorf, Patmos.

KosmosŒ: Kosmos en Œkumene: Amsterdam.

Kratylos (Sprachwissenschaft); Wsb.

KřestR [TPřil]: Křest'anská revue [Theologická Příloha]; Praha.

Ktema; Strasbourg, CEDEX.

KvinnerA: Kvinner i [women in] arkeologi i Norge; Bergen, Historisk Museum [1 (1985)].

KTB/KUB: Keilschrifttexte/urkunden aus Boghazköi; wB,Mann/oB,Akademie.

LA: ➤ Greg; SBF; [Libro Anual] México; Urug.

Labeo, diritto romano; N. 0023-6462.

Language; Baltimore.

LAPO: Littératures Anciennes du Proche-Orient; Paris, Cerf. 0459-5831.

Lateranum; R, Pont. Univ. Lateranense.

Latomus (Ét. latines); Bru. 0023-8856.

Laur: Laurentianum; R. 0023-902X.

LavalTP: Laval Théologique et Philosophique; Québec.

LDiv: Lectio Divina; Paris, Cerf.

LebSeels: Lebendige Seelsorge; Wü/FrB.

LebZeug: Lebendiges Zeugnis; Paderborn. 0023-9941.

Lěšonénu (Hebrew Language); J.

LetPastB: Lettura pastorale della Bibbia; Bologna, Dehoniane.

Levant (archeology); London.

LexÄg: Lexikon der Ägyptologie; Wb ➤ 591.

LexMA: Lexikon des Mittelalters; Mü/Z ➤ 592.

LexTQ: Lexington [KY] Theological Quarterly. 0024-1628.

LIAO: Lettre d'Information Archéologie Orientale; Valbonne, CNRS. 0750-6279.

LIGHT: Laughter in God, History, and Theology; Fort Worth [1 (1984)].

LimnOc: Limnology & Oceanography; AA.

LinceiR/Scavi/BClas: Accademia Nazionale dei Lincei. Rendiconti / Notizie degli Scavi / Bollettino Classico. 0391-8270: Roma.

LingBib: Linguistica Biblica; Bonn. 0342-0884.

Lire la Bible; P, Cerf. 0588-2257.

Listening: Oak Park IL.

LitRelFrühjud: Literatur und Religion des Frühjudentums; Wü/Gü.

LivLight: The Living Light (US Cath. Conf.); Huntington. 0024-5275.

LivWord: Living Word; Alwaye, Kerala.

LOB: Leggere oggi la Bibbia; Brescia, Queriniana.

LogosPh: Logos, philosophic issues in Christian perspective; Santa Clara, Univ. [5 (1984)].

LStClas: London studies in classical philology [8, Corolla Londiniensis 1]; Amst.

LtgJb: Liturgisches Jahrbuch; Münster/Wf.

Lucentum; prehistoria, arqueología e historia antigua; Alicante, Univ.

LumenK: Lumen; København.

LumenVr: Lumen; Vitoria.

LumièreV: Lumière et Vie; Lyon. 0024-7359.

Luther (Gesellschaft) [Jb]; Hamburg. 0340-6210 [Gö 3-525-87419-7].

LuthMonh: Lutherische Monatshefte; Hamburg. 0024-7618.

LuthTJ: Lutheran Theological Journal; North Adelaide, S. Australia.

LuthTKi: Lutherische Theologie und Kirche; Oberursel. 0170-3846.

LVitae: Lumen Vitae; Bru. 0024-7324.

LvSt: Louvain Studies.
Ⓜ magyar: *hungarice*, en hongrois.
ᴹ: *mentio, de eo*; author commented upon.
Maarav (NW Semitic; Santa Monica last 3, 1982); now Winona Lake IN.
MadMitt [B/F]: DAI Madrider Mitteilungen (Mainz: 3-8053-0831-0) [Beiträge/Forschungen].
MAGA: Mitteilungen zur Alten Geschichte und Archäologie; oB [13 (1985)].
Maia (letterature classiche); Messina. 0025-0538.
MaisD: La Maison-Dieu; P. 0025-0937.
MANE: Monographs on the Ancient Near East; 1. Leiden; 2. Malibu.
Manresa (espiritualidad ignaciana); Azpeitia-Guipúzcoa.
Manuscripta; St. Louis.
MarbTSt: Marburger Theologische Studien; Marburg.
MARI: Mari, Annales de Recherches Interdisciplinaires; Paris [2 (1983)].
Marianum; Roma.
MariolSt: Mariologische Studien; Essen.
MarSt: Marian Studies; Washington.
Masca: Museum Applied Science Center for Archaeology Journal; Ph, Univ. [3 (1984s)].
MasSt: (SBL) Masoretic Studies; Chico CA.
MatKonfInst: Materialdienst des konfessionskundlichen Instituts; Bensheim.
MatPomWykBib: Materiały pomocznicze do wykładów z biblistyki; Lublin.
Mayéutica (Agustinos Recoletos); Marcilla (Navarra).
MDOG: Mitteilungen der Deutschen Orientgesellschaft; B. 0342-118X.
Meander: Wsz Akad. 0025-6285.
Med: Mededelingen [Amst, ...]; Meddelander.
MedHum: Mediaevalia et Humanistica (Denton, N. Texas Univ.); Totowa NJ.
MeditLg: Mediterranean Language Review: Wiesbaden [1 (1983)].
MélÉcFrR: Mélanges de l'École Française de Rome. Ant. 0223-5102.
MélSR: Mélanges de Science Religieuse; Lille.
Mém: Mémoires ➤ AIBL ... AcSc, T...

MenQR: Mennonite Quarterly Review; Goshen, Ind.
Meroit: Meroitic Newsletter / Bulletin d'informations méroitiques: Paris, CNRS [24 (1985)].
MESA: Middle East Studies Association (Bulletin); Tucson, Univ. AZ.
MesopK: Mesopotamia: Copenhagen Studies in Assyriology; København.
MesopT: Mesopotamia (Archeologia, Epigrafia, Storia ... Torino); (pub. F).
MESt: Middle Eastern Studies; L.
MetB: Metropolitan Museum Bulletin; New York. 0026-1521.
MHandelsG: Münsterische Beiträge zur antiken Handelsgeschichte; Ostfildern. 0722-4532 [4 (1985)].
MHT: Materialien zu einem hethitischen Thesaurus; Heidelberg.
MiDAI-A/K/M/R: Mitteilungen des Deutschen Archäologischen Instituts: Athen / Kairo 3-8053-0885-X. / Madrid / Rom 0342-1287.
Mid-Stream, Disciples of Christ; Indianapolis. – Midstream (Jewish); NY. 0026-332X.
Mikael; Paraná, Arg. (Seminario).
MilltSt: Milltown Studies (philosophy, theology); Dublin. 0332-1428.
Minos (Filología Egea); Salamanca. 0544-3733.
MiscCom: Miscelánea Comillas, estudios históricos; M. 0210-9522.
MiscFranc: Miscellanea Francescana; Roma (OFM Conv.).
Mishkan, a theological forum on Jewish evangelism; Jerusalem, United Christian Council [1 (1984)].
Missiology; Scottdale PA.
MissHisp: Missionalia hispanica; Madrid, CSIC Inst. E. Flores [40,117 (1983)].
Mitt: Mitteilungen [Gö Septuaginta; Berliner Museen ...]; ➤ MiDAI.
Mnemosyne, Bibliotheca Classica Batava [+ Supplements]; Leiden.
ModChm: Modern Churchman; Leominster, Herf.
ModT: Modern Theology, quarterly review; Oxford, Blackwell [1,1 (1984)].
Mon: Monograph[ie], ➤ CBQ, SBL, SNTS.
MonastSt: Monastic Studies; Montreal [14 (1983)].

MondeB: Le Monde de la Bible: 1. [< Bible et Terre Sainte]; Paris. 0154-9049. – 2. Série: Genève.

Monde Copte, Le: 0399-905X.

MonStB: Monographien und Studienbücher; Wu/Giessen.

Month (Christian Thought and World Affairs); London. 0027-0172.

Moralia; Madrid [6 (1984)].

Mosaic, journal of comparative study of international literature, art, and ideas; Winnipeg [14 (1981)].

MsME: Manuscripts of the Middle East; Leiden. 0920-0401. [1 (1986)].

MüÄgSt: Münchener Ägyptologische Studien; München/Berlin.

MüBei[T]PapR: Münchener Beiträge zur [Theologie] Papyruskunde und antiken Rechtsgeschichte; Mü.

MüStSprW: Münchener Studien zur Sprachwissenschaft; Mü. ↠ AOtt.

MüTZ: Münchener Theologische Zeitschrift; St. Ottilien. 0580-1400.

Multilingua, journal of interlanguage communication; Manchester [1 (c. 1983)].

Mundus (German Research, in English); Stuttgart. 0027-3392.

Muqarnas, Islamic art and architecture; NHv, Yale [1 (1983)].

Mus: Le Muséon; LvN. 0771-6494.

MusHelv: Museum Helveticum; Basel.

MusTusc: Museum Tusculanum; København. 0107-8062.

MuzTA: ❸ Muzeon Ha-Areş NS; TA.

NachGö: Nachrichten der Akademie der Wissenschaften; Göttingen.

NarAzAfr: ❸ *Narody:* Peoples of Asia and Africa; Moskva.

NatGeog: National Geographic; Wsh.

NatGrac: Naturaleza y Gracia; Salamanca (OFM Cap.).

NBlackfr: New Blackfriars; London. 0028-4289.

NCent: The New Century Bible Commentary (reedited); Edinburgh / GR.

NChrIsr: Nouvelles Chrétiennes d'Israël: Jérusalem.

NduitseGT: Nederduitse Gereformeerde Teologiese Tydskrif; Kaapstad. 0028-2006.

NedTTs: Nederlands Theologisch Tijdschrift; Wageningen. 0028-212X.

Neotestamentica; Pretoria; NTWerk.

NEphS: Neue Ephemeris für semitische Epigraphik; Wiesbaden.

Nestor, Classical Antiquity, Indiana Univ.; Bloomington. 0028-2812.

NESTR: Near East School of Theology Review; Beirut.

New Covenant; AA.

News: Newsletter: Anat[olian Studies; NHv]; Targ[umic and Cognate Studies; Toronto]; ASOR [CM]; Ug[aritic Studies; Calgary]; ↠ JAmEg.

NHC: Nag Hammadi Codices, Egypt UAR Facsimile edition; Leiden.

NHL/S: Nag Hammadi Library in English / Studies; Leiden.

NHLW: Neues Handbuch der Literaturwissenschaft: Wb, Athenaion.

Nicolaus (teol. ecumenico-patristica); Bari.

NICOT: New International Commentary OT; Grand Rapids, Eerdmans.

NigJT: The Nigerian Journal of Theology; Owerri [1,2 (1986)].

NIGT: New International Greek Testament Commentary; Exeter/GR, Paternoster/Eerdmans.

Nikrot Zurim (*ṣûrîm*), ❸ journal of the Israel Cave Research center; Ophra.

NorJ: Nordisk Judaistik.

NorTTs: Norsk Teologisk Tidsskrift; Oslo. 0029-2176.

NotesSU: Notes on Scripture in Use; Dallas, Summer Institute of Linguistics [1 (1981)].

NotSocTLv: Notes de la Société Théologique de Louvain; Lv-N.

NOxR: New Oxford Review; Berkeley [till 1983 Oakland], American Church Union [50 (1983)].

NRT: Nouvelle Revue Théologique; Tournai. 0029-4845.

NS [NF]: Nova series, nouvelle série.

NSys: Neue Zeitschrift für systematische Theologie und Religionsphilosophie; Berlin. 0028-3517.

NT: Novum Testamentum; Leiden.

NTAbh: Neutestamentliche Abhandlungen. [N.F.]; Münster.

NTAbs: New Testament Abstracts; CM. 0028-6877.

NTDt: Das Neue Testament deutsch; Gö.

NTS: New Testament Studies; L (SNTS).
NubChr: Nubia Christiana; Warszawa, Akad. Teol. Kat. [1 (1983)].
NumC: Numismatic Chronicle; London. 0078-2696.
Numisma; Madrid. 0029-0015.
NumZ: Numismatische Zeitschrift; Wien. 0250-7838.
Numen (International Association for the History of Religions); Leiden.
NuovaUm: Nuova Umanità; Roma.
Nuovo Areopago (Il), trimestrale di cultura; Bologna, CSEO [1,1.2 (1982)].
NVFr/Z: Nova et Vetera; 1. Fribourg S. / 2. Zamora [10 (1985)].
NZMissW: Neue Zeitschrift für Missionswissenschaft; Beckenried, Schweiz. 0028-3495.
NZSysT ➤ NSys.
ObnŽiv: Obnovljeni Život (Erneuertes religiöses Leben); Zagreb.
OBO: Orbis Biblicus et Orientalis: FrS/Gö.
OEIL: Office d'édition et d'impression du livre; Paris.
ÖkRu: Ökumenische Rundschau; Stuttgart. 0029-8654.
ÖkTbKom, NT: Ökumenischer Taschenbuchkommentar; Gütersloh / Würzburg.
ÖsterrBibSt: Österreichische Biblische Studien; Klosterneuburg.
Offa, ... Frühgeschichte; Neumünster. 0078-3714.
Ohio ➤ JRelSt: Cleveland.
OIC/P/Ac: Oriental Institute Communications / Publications / Acquisitions; Ch.
OikBud: Oikumene; historia antiqua classica et orientalis; Budapest.
Olivo (El), diálogo jud.-cr.: Madrid.
OLZ: Orientalistische Literaturzeitung; Leipzig. 0030-5383.
OMRO: Oudheidkundige Mededelingen, Rijksmuseum van Oudheden; Leiden.
OneInC: One in Christ (Catholic Ecumenical); Turvey, Bedfordshire.
OnsGErf: Ons Geestelijk Erf; Antwerpen.
OnsGLev: Ons Geestelijk Leven; Tilburg.
OpAth/Rom: Opuscula Atheniensia 91-85086-80-0 / Romana 91-7042-099-8; Swedish Inst.

Opus, rivista internazionale per la storia economica e sociale dell'antichità (Siena); R.
Or: ➤ Orientalia; Roma.
OraLab: Ora et Labora; Roriz, Portugal.
OrAnt[Coll]: Oriens Antiquus [Collectio]; Roma.
OrBibLov: Orientalia et Biblica Lovaniensia; Lv.
OrChr: Oriens Christianus; Wiesbaden. 3-447-02532-8.
OrChrPer[An]: Orientalia Christiana Periodica [Analecta]; R, Pontificium Inst. Orientalium Stud. 0030-5375.
OrGand: Orientalia Gandensia; Gent.
Orientalia (Ancient Near East); Rome, Pontifical Biblical Institute. 0030-5367.
Orientierung; Zürich. 0030-5502.
Orient-Japan: Orient, Near Eastern Studies Foreign Language Annual; Tokyo. 0743-3851; cf. ❹ Oriento. 0030-5219.
Origins; Washington Catholic Conference. 0093-609X.
OrJog: Orientasi, Annual ... Philosophy and Theology; Jogjakarta.
OrLovPer[An]: Orientalia Lovaniensia Periodica [Analecta]; Lv.
OrMod: Oriente Moderno; Napoli. 0030-5472.
OrOcc: Oriente-Occidente. Buenos Aires, Univ. Salvador.
OrPast: Orientamenti Pastorali; Roma.
Orpheus; Catania.
OrSuec: Orientalia Suecana; Uppsala.
OrtBuc: Ortodoxia; Bucureşti.
OrTrad: Oral Tradition; Columbia MO, Univ. [1 (1986)].
OstkSt: Ostkirchliche Studien; Würzburg. 0030-6487.
OTAbs: Old Testament Abstracts; Washington. 0364-8591.
OTS: Oudtestamentische Studiën; Leiden. 0169-9555.
OTWerkSuidA: Die Ou Testamentiese Werkgemeenskap Suid-Afrika; Pretoria.
OudKMed: Oudheidkundige Mededelingen uit het Rijksmuseum van Oudheden; Leiden.
OvBTh: Overtures to Biblical Theology; Philadelphia.

Overview; Ch St. Thomas More Asn.
OxJArch: Oxford Journal of Archaeology; Ox. 0262-5253.
℗: *polonice,* in Polish.
p./pa./pl.: page(s)/paperback/plate(s).
PAAR: Proceedings of the American Academy for Jewish Research; Philadelphia.
Palaeohistoria; Haarlem.
PalCl: Palestra del Clero; Rovigo.
PaléOr: Paléorient; Paris.
PalSb: ℗ Palestinski Sbornik; Leningrad.
PapBritSR: Papers of the British School at Rome; London.
PAPS: Proceedings of the American Philosophical Society; Philadelphia.
PapTAbh: Papyrologische Texte und Abhandlungen; Bonn, Habelt.
PapyrolColon: Papyrologica Coloniensia; Opladen. 0078-9410.
Parabola (Myth and the Quest for Meaning); New York.
Paradigms; Louisville KY [1 (1985)].
ParOr: Parole de l'Orient; Kaslik [12 (1984s)].
ParPass: Parola del Passato; Napoli. 0031-2355.
ParSpV: Parola, Spirito e Vita, quaderni di lettura biblica; Bo, Dehoniane.
ParVi: Parole di Vita; T-Leumann.
PasT: Pastoraltheologie; Göttingen.
PatByzR: Patristic and Byzantine Review; Kingston NY [1 (1982)].
PatrStudT: Patristische Studien und Texte; B. 0553-4003.
PBSB: Petite bibliothèque des sciences bibliques; Paris, Desclée.
PenséeC: La Pensée Catholique; P.
PEQ: Palestine Exploration Quarterly; London. 0031-0328.
PerAz: Peredneaziatskij Sbornik; Moskva.
Persica: Leiden.
PerspRelSt: Perspectives in Religious Studies (Baptist); Danville VA.
PerspT: Perspectiva Teológica; Belo Horizonte [before 1981 São Leopoldo].
Pg/Ph: philolog-/philosoph-.
PgOrTb: Philologia Orientalis (Georgian Ac. Sc.); Tbilisi.
Phase; Barcelona.
PhilipSa: Philippiniana Sacra; Manila.

Philologus; oB. 0031-7985.
Phoenix; Toronto. 0031-8299.
PhoenixEOL; Leiden (not = JbEOL). 0031-8329.
Phronesis; Assen. 0031-8868.
PiTMon: Theological Monograph Series; Pittsburgh.
PJungG: Projekte und Modelle zum Dialog mit der jungen Generation; Stu.
Pneuma, Pentecostal Studies; Pasadena [7 (1985)].
PoinT: Le Point Théologique; P.
PontAcc, R/Mem: Atti della Pontificia Accademia Romana di Archeologia, Rendiconti/Memorie; Vaticano.
PracArch: Prace Archeologiczne; Kraków, Univ. 0083-4300.
PraehZ: Praehistorische Zeitschrift; Berlin. 0079-4848.
PrakT: Praktische theologie ... pastorale wetenschappen; Zwolle.
PraktArch: ℗ Praktika, Archeology Society Athens.
PrAmPhilSoc: → PAPS.
PrCambPg: Proceedings of the Cambridge Philological Society; England. 0068-6735.
PrCTSAm: Proceedings of the Catholic Theological Society of America; Villanova PA.
PredikOT/NT: De Prediking van het OT / van het NT; Nijkerk.
Presbyteri (Spiritualità pastorale); Trento.
Presbyterion; St. Louis.
PresPast: Presenza Pastorale; Roma.
PrêtreP: Prêtre et Pasteur; Montréal. 0385-8307.
Priest (The); Washington.
PrincSemB: Princeton Seminary Bulletin; Princeton NJ.
PrIrB: Proceedings of the Irish Biblical Association; Dublin, 'published annually'.
Prism; St. Paul, United Church of Christ [1 (1986)].
PrIsrAc: Proceedings of the Israel Academy of Sciences & Humanities; Jerusalem.
ProbHistChr: Problèmes de l'Histoire du Christianisme; Bruxelles, Univ.
ProcCom: Proclamation Commentaries; Philadelphia.

ProcGLM: Proceedings of the Eastern Great Lakes [+ 'and Midwest' since 5 (1985)] Bible Societies; Westerville OH.

Progetto donna, rivista bimestrale di cultura e attualità [1 (1982)].

Prooftexts, a journal of Jewish literary history; Baltimore, Johns Hopkins Univ.

PrOrChr: Proche-Orient Chrétien; Jérusalem. 0032-9622.

Prot: Protestantesimo; R. 0033-1767.

Proyección (Teología y mundo actual); Granada.

PrPrehS: Proceedings of the Prehistoric Society; Cambridge (Univ. Museum).

PrSemArab: Proceedings of the Seminar for Arabian Studies; London.

Prudentia (Hellenistic, Roman); Auckland.

PrzOr[Tom/Pow]: Przegląd Orientalistyczny, Wsz: [Tomisticzny 1 (1984) Wsz / Powszechny, Kraków].

PT: Philosophy/Theology: Milwaukee, Marquette Univ. [1 (1986)].

PubTNEsp: Publicaciones de la Facultad Teológica del Norte de España; Burgos.

PUF: Presses Universitaires de France; P.

Pulpudeva, ... culture thrace; Sofija.

Qadm: Qadmoniot ❻ Quarterly of Dept. of Antiquities; Jerusalem.

Qardom, ❻ mensuel pour la connaissance du pays; Jerusalem, Ariel.

QDisp: Quaestiones Disputatae; FrB.

Qedem: Monographs of the Institute of Archaeology: Jerusalem, Hebr. Univ.

QEtnR: Quaderni di etnologia religiosa; Milano.

QLtg: Questions Liturgiques; Lv.

QuadCatan / Chieti: Quaderni, Catania / Chieti [3 (1982)]; Univ.

QuadSemant: Quaderni di Semantica; Bologna.

QuadSemit: Quaderni di Semitistica; Firenze.

QuadUrb: Quaderni Urbinati di Cultura Classica; Urbino. 0033-4987.

Quaerendo (Low Countries: Manuscripts and Printed Books); Amst.

QuatreF: Les quatre fleuves: Paris.

QüestVidaCr: Qüestions de Vida Cristiana; Montserrat.

❻: *russice,* in Russian.

ᴿ: *recensio,* book-review(er).

RAC: Reallexikon für Antike und Christentum; Stuttgart → 594.

Radiocarbon; NHv, Yale. 0033-8222.

RAfrT: Revue Africaine de Théologie; Kinshasa/Limete.

RAg: Revista Agustiniana [de Espiritualidad hacia 18 (1977)] Calahorra.

RAMBI: Rešimat Ma'amarim bemadda'ê ha-Yahedût, Index of articles on Jewish Studies; J. 0073-5817.

RaMIsr: Rassegna mensile di Israel; Roma.

RArchéol: Revue Archéologique; Paris. 0035-0737.

RArchéom: Revue d'Archéométrie; Rennes.

RArtLv: Revue des Archéologues et Historiens d'Art; Lv. 0080-2530.

RAss: Revue d'Assyriologie et d'Archéologie Orientale; P. 2-13-039142-7.

RasT: Rassegna di Teologia; Roma [ᴱNapoli]. 0034-9644.

Raydan:

RazF: Razón y Fe; Madrid.

RB: Revue Biblique; Jérusalem / Paris. 0035-0907.

RBén: Revue Bénédictine; Maredsous. 0035-0893.

RBgNum: Revue Belge de Numismatique et Sigillographie; Bruxelles.

RBgPg: Revue Belge de Philologie et d'Histoire; Bruxelles.

RBBras: Revista Bíblica Brasileira; Fortaleza [1 (1984)].

RBíbArg: Revista Bíblica; Buenos Aires. 0034-7078.

RBkRel: The Review of Books and Religion; Durham NC, Duke Univ. [10 c. 1984].

RCatalT: Revista Catalana de Teología; Barcelona, St. Pacià.

RCiv: Éditions Recherche sur les [Grandes] Civilisations [Mém(oires) 0291-1655]. Paris → ADPF.

RClerIt: Rivista del Clero Italiano; Mi.

RCuClaMed: Rivista di Cultura Classica e Medioevale; Roma.

RÉAnc: Revue des Études Anciennes; Bordeaux. 0035-2004.

RÉArmén: Revue des Études Arméniennes. 0080-2549.

RÉAug: Revue des Études Augustiniennes; Paris. 0035-2012.

REB: Revista Eclesiástica Brasileira; Petrópolis.

RÉByz: Revue des Études Byzantines; Paris.

RECAM: Regional Epigraphic Catalogues of Asia Minor [AnSt].

RechAug: Recherches Augustiniennes; Paris. 0035-2021.

RechSR: Recherches de Science Religieuse; Paris. 0034-1258.

RecTrPO: Recueil de travaux et communications de l'association des études du Proche-Orient ancien / Collected papers of the Society for Near Eastern Studies; Montréal [2′(1984)].

RefEgy: Református Egyház; Budapest. 0324-475X.

ReferSR: Reference Services Review; Dearborn MI, Univ.

RefGStT: Reformationsgeschichtliche Studien und Texten: Münster.

RefJ: The Reformed Journal; Grand Rapids. 0486-252X.

Reformatio; Zürich.

RefR: Reformed Review; New Brunswick NJ / Holland MI.

RefTR: Reformed Theological Review; Hawthorn, Australia. 0034-3072.

RefW: The Reformed World; Geneva.

RÉG: Revue des Études Grecques; Paris. 0035-2039.

RÉgp: Revue d'Égyptologie; Paris. 2-252-02201-9.

RÉJ: Revue des Études Juives; Paris. 0035-2055.

RÉLat: Revue des Études Latines; P.

RelCult: Religión y Cultura; M.

RelEd: Religious Education (biblical; Jewish-sponsored); Chicago.

RelHum: Religious Humanism; Yellow Springs OH.

Religion [... and Religions]; Lancaster. 0048-721X.

RelIntL: Religion and Intellectual Life; New Rochelle NY, College. 0741-0549 [2 (1985)].

RelPBei: Religionspädagogische Beiträge; Kaarst. [17 (1986)].

RelSoc: Religion and Society; B/Haag.

RelSt: Religious Studies; Cambridge. 0034-4125.

RelStR: Religious Studies Review; Waterloo, Ont. 0319-485X.

RelStT: Religious Studies [Bulletin, till 1985; now] and Theology; Edmonton.

RelTAbs: Religious and Theological Abstracts; Myerstown, Pa.

RelTrad: Religious Traditions; Brisbane. 0156-1650.

RencAssInt: Rencontre Assyriologique Internationale, Compte-Rendu.

RencChrJ: Rencontre Chrétiens et Juifs; Paris. 0233-5579.

Renovatio: 1. Zeitschrift für das interdisziplinäre Gespräch; Köln [38 (1982)]: 2. (teologia); Genova.

RepCyp: Report of the Department of Antiquities of Cyprus; Nicosia.

RepertAA: Répertoire d'art et d'archéologie; Paris. 0080-0953.

REPPAL: Revue d'Études Phéniciennes-Puniques et des Antiquités Libyques; Tunis [1 (1985)].

REspir: Revista de Espiritualidad; San Sebastián.

ResPLit: Res Publica Litterarum; Kansas.

RestQ: Restoration Quarterly; Abilene TX.

RET: Revista Española de Teología; Madrid.

RevCuBíb: Revista de Cultura Bíblica; São Paulo.

RevSR: Revue des Sciences Religieuses; Strasbourg. 0035-2217.

RExp: Review and Expositor; Louisville. 0034-6373.

RFgIC: Rivista di Filologia e di Istruzione Classica; Torino.

RgStTh: Regensburger Studien zur Theologie; Fra/Bern, Lang.

RgVV: Religionsgeschichtliche Versuche und Vorarbeiten; B/NY, de Gruyter.

RHDroit: Revue historique de Droit français et étranger; Paris.

RHE: Revue d'Histoire Ecclésiastique; Louvain. 0035-2381.

RheinMus: Rheinisches Museum für Philologie; Frankfurt. 0035-449X.

Rhetorik [Jb]; Stu / Bad Cannstatt.

RHist: Revue Historique; Paris.

RHPR: Revue d'Histoire et de Philosophie Religieuses; Strasbourg. 0035-2403.

RHR: Revue de l'Histoire des Religions; Paris. 0035-1423.
RHS ➤ RUntHö; **RU** ➤ ZRUnt.
RHText: Revue d'Histoire des Textes; Paris. 2-222-03711-5.
RIC: Répertoire bibliographique des institutions chrétiennes; Strasbourg, CERDIC.
RICathP: Revue de l'Institut Catholique de Paris. 0294-4308.
RicStorSocRel: Ricerche di Storia Sociale e Religiosa; Roma.
RIDA: Revue Internationale des Droits de l'Antiquité; Bruxelles.
RINASA: Rivista dell'Istituto Nazionale di Archeologia e Storia dell'Arte; Roma.
RItNum: Rivista Italiana di Numismatica e scienze affini; Milano.
RivArCr: Rivista di Archeologia Cristiana; Città del Vaticano. 0035-6042.
RivArV: Rivista di Archeologia, Univ. Venezia; Roma.
RivAscM: [non Nuova] Rivista di Ascetica e Mistica; Roma.
RivB: Rivista Biblica Italiana; (da 1985) Bo, Dehoniane. 0393-4853.
RivLtg: Rivista di Liturgia; T-Leumann.
RivPastLtg: Rivista di Pastorale Liturgica; Brescia. 0035-6395.
RivStoLR: Rivista di Storia e Letteratura Religiosa; F. 0035-6573.
RivStorA: Rivista Storica dell'Antichità; Bologna.
RivVSp: Rivista di Vita Spirituale; Roma. 0035-6638.
RLA: Reallexikon der Assyriologie & vorderasiatischen Archäologie; B ➤ 1,905.
RLatAmT: Revista Latinoamericana de Teología; El Salvador.
RNouv: La Revue Nouvelle; Bruxelles. 0035-3809.
RNum: Revue Numismatique; Paris.
RoczOr: Rocznik Orientalistyczny; Warszawa. 0080-3545.
RoczTK: Roczniki Teologiczno-Kanoniczne; Lublin. 0035-7723.
RömQ: Römische Quartalschrift für Christliche Altertumskunde...; Freiburg/Br. 0035-7812.
RomOrth: Romanian Orthodox Church News, French Version [sic]; Bucureşti.

RPLH: Revue de Philologie, de Littérature et d'Histoire anciennes; Paris, Klincksieck. 0035-1652.
RQum: Revue de Qumrân; P. 0035-1725.
RRéf: Revue Réformée; Saint-Germain-en-Laye.
RRel: Review for Religious; St. Louis. 0034-639X.
RRelRes: Review of Religious Research; New York. 0034-673X.
RRns: The Review of Religions; Wsh. 0743-5622.
RSO: Rivista degli Studi Orientali; Roma. 0392-4869.
RSocietà; Roma [1,1 (1986)].
RSPT: Revue des Sciences Philosophiques et Théologiques; [Le Saulchoir] Paris. 0035-2209.
RStFen: Rivista di Studi Fenici: R.
RTAM: Recherches de Théologie Ancienne et Médiévale; Louvain. 0034-1266. ➤ BTAM.
RTBat: Revista Teológica (Sem. Batista); Rio de Janeiro.
RThom: Revue Thomiste; Toulouse/Bru. 0035-4295.
RTLim: Revista Teológica; Lima.
RTLv: Revue théologique de Louvain. 0080-2654.
RTPhil: Revue de Théologie et de Philosophie; CH-1066 Épalinges. 0035-1784.
RuBi: Ruch Biblijny i Liturgiczny; Kraków. 0209-0872.
RUnivOtt: Revue de l'Université d'Ottawa.
RUntHö: Religionsunterricht an höheren Schulen; Düsseldorf.
SacEr: Sacris Erudiri; Steenbrugge.
Saeculum; FrB/Mü. 0080-5319.
SAfJud: South African Judaica; Johannesburg, Witwatersrand Univ. [1 (1984)].
Sales: Salesianum; Roma. 0036-3502.
Salm: Salmanticensis; Salamanca. 0036-3537.
SalT: Sal Terrae; Santander. 0211-4569.
Sandalion (Sassari); R, Herder.
SAOC: Studies in Ancient Oriental Civilization: Ch, Univ. 0081-7554.
Sap: Sapienza; Napoli. 0036-4711.

sb.: subscription; price for members.
SBF/LA/Anal/Pub [min]: Studii Biblici Franciscani / Liber Annuus: 0081-8933 / Analecta / Publicationes series maior 0081-8971 [minor]; Jerusalem.
SBL [AramSt / CR / Mon / Diss / GRR / MasSt / NAm / SemP / TexTr]: Society of Biblical Literature: Aramaic Studies / Critical Review of Books in Religion / Monograph Series / Dissertation Series / Graeco-Roman Religion / Masoretic Studies / Biblical Scholarship in North America / Seminar Papers 0145-2711 / Texts and Translations. ➤ JBL; CATSS.
SBS [KBW]: Stuttgarter Bibelstudien; Stuttgart, Katholisches Bibelwerk.
ScandJOT: Scandinavian Journal of the Old Testament; Aarhus.
ScEsp: Science et Esprit; Montréal. 0316-5345.
SCHN: Studia ad Corpus Hellenisticum NT; Leiden.
Schönberger Hefte; Fra.
Scholars Choice; Richmond VA.
SChr: Sources Chrétiennes; P. 0750-1978.
SciTHV: Science, technology and human values; NY [8 (1983)].
ScOfRel: Science of Religion, abstracts and index of recent articles; Amst, Vrije Univ./Unesco [10 (1985)].
ScotBEv: The Scottish Bulletin of Evangelical Theology; E. 0265-4539.
ScotJT: Scottish Journal of Theology; Edinburgh. 0036-9306.
ScotR: Scottish Journal of Religious Studies; Stirling.
ScrCiv: Scrittura [scrivere] e Civiltà; T.
ScriptB: Scripture Bulletin; London. 0036-9780.
Scriptorium; Bruxelles.
ScripTPamp: Scripta theologica; Pamplona, Univ. Navarra. 0036-9764.
Scriptura; Stellenbosch.
ScriptVict: Scriptorium Victoriense; Vitoria, España.
ScrMedit: Scripta Mediterranea; Toronto, Univ. [3 (1982)].
ScuolC: La Scuola Cattolica; Venegono Inferiore, Varese. 0036-9810.
SDB [= DBS]: Supplément au Dictionnaire de la Bible; Paris ➤ 906.
SDH: Studia et documenta historiae et iuris; Roma, Pont. Univ. Later.

SDJ: Studies on the Texts of the Desert of Judah; Leiden.
Search: Dublin [5 (1982)].
SecC: The Second Century, a journal of early Christian studies; Abilene TX. 0276-7899 [5 = 1985 + 1986].
Sefarad; Madrid. 0037-0894.
SEG: Supplementum epigraphicum graecum; Withoorn.
Segmenten; Amsterdam, Vrije Univ.
SeiRon: Seisho-gaku ronshū; Tokyo, Japanese Biblical Institute.
SelT: Selecciones de Teología... artículos; Barc. - **SelL** ➤ Actu Bbg.
SémBib: Sémiotique et Bible; Lyon ➤ CADIR. 0154-6902.
Semeia (Biblical Criticism) [Supplements]; Chico CA, SBL. 0095-571X.
Seminarios ... sobre los ministerios en la Iglesia; Salamanca, Inst. Vocacional 'M. Ávila' [29 (1983)].
Seminarium; Roma.
Seminary Review; Cincinnati.
Semiotica; Amsterdam.
Semitica; Paris. 2-7200-1040-5.
Semitics; Pretoria. '84: 0-86981-312-9.
Sens; juifs et chrétiens; Paris.
SeptCogSt: ➤ B[ulletin].
Servitium, quaderni di spiritualità; Bergamo, priorato S. Egidio; publ. Casale Monferrato. 88-211-9031-5.
SEST: South-Eastern [Baptist Sem.] Studies; Wake Forest NC.
Sevārtham; Ranchi (St. Albert's College).
SGErm: ⓡ Soobščeniya gosudarstvennovo Ermitaža, Reports of the State Hermitage Museum; Leningrad. 0432-1501.
ShinKen: ⓙ *Shinyaku Kenkyū*, Studia Textus Novi Testamenti; Osaka.
ShnatM: ⓗ Shnaton la-Mikra (Annual, Biblical and ANE Studies); Tel Aviv. ➤ SMišpat.
SicArch: Sicilia archaeologica; Trapani.
SicGym: Siculorum Gymnasium; Catania.
SIMA: Studies in Mediterranean Archaeology; Göteborg.
SixtC: The Sixteenth Century Journal; St. Louis (Kirksville). 0361-0160.
SkrifK: Skrif en Kerk; Pretoria, Univ.

SMEA: Studi Micenei ed Egeo-Anatolici (Incunabula Graeca); Roma, Consiglio Naz.

SMišpat: Šnaton ha-Mišpaṭ ha-Ivri, Annual of the Institute for Research in Jewish Law [9s (1983)].

SMSR: Studi e Materiali di Storia delle religioni: Roma. [1977-82 'Studi Storico Religiosi'].

SNTS (Mon.): Studiorum Novi Testamenti Societas (Monograph Series); C.

SNTU-A/B: Studien zum NT und seiner Umwelt; Linz [Periodica / Series].

Soundings; Nashville, Vanderbilt Univ. [65 (1983)].

SovArch: ⊕ Sovyetskaja Archeologija; Moskva. 0038-5034.

Speculum (Medieval Studies); CM. 0038-7134.

SPg: Studia Philologica;

Spiritus; Paris. 0038-7665.

SpirLife: Spiritual Life; Washington. 0038-7630.

Sprache; Wien. 0038-8467.

SR: Studies in Religion / Sciences Religieuses; Waterloo, Ont. 0008-4298.

ST: (Vaticano) Studi e Testi.

ST: Studia Theologica; Oslo. 0039-338X.

Stadion, Internationale Zeitschrift fur Geschichte des Sports; Sankt Augustin [10 (1984)].

StAltägK: Studien zur altägyptischen Kultur; Hamburg. 0340-2215.

StAns: Studia Anselmiana; Roma.

StANT: Studien zum Alten und Neuen Testament; München.

StAntCr: Studi di Antichità Cristiana; Città del Vaticano.

Star: St. Thomas Academy for Research; Bangalore.

StArchWsz: Studia archeologiczne; Warszawa, Univ.

Stauròs, Bollettino trimestrale sulla teologia della Croce: Pescara [7 (1981)].

StBEC: Studies in the Bible and Early Christianity; Lewiston NY.

StBib: Dehon/Paid/Leiden: Studi Biblici; Bo, Dehoniane / Brescia, Paideia / Studia Biblica; Leiden [1 (1983)].

StBoğT: Studien zu den Boğazköy-Texten; Wiesbaden.

STBuc: Studii Teologice; Bucureşti.

StCatt: Studi cattolici; Milano. 0039-2901.

StChHist: Studies in Church History; Oxford [21 (1984)].

StChrAnt: Studies in Christian Antiquity; Wsh.

StClasBuc: Studii Clasice; Bucureşti.

StClasOr: Studi Classici e Orientali; P.

StCompRel: Studies in Comparative Religion; Bedfont, Middlesex.

StDelitzsch: Studia Delitzschiana (Institutum Judaicum Delitzschianum, Münster); Stuttgart.

StEbl: Studi Eblaiti; Roma, Univ.

StEcum: Studi Ecumenici; Verona. 0393-3687 [2 (1984)].

StEpL: Studi Epigrafici e Linguistici sul Vicino Oriente antico; Verona.

STEv: Studi di Teologia dell'Istituto Biblico Evangelico; Roma.

StFormSp: Studies in Formative Spirituality; Pittsburgh, Duquesne.

StGnes: Studia Gnesnensia; Gniezno.

StHCT: Studies in the History of Christian Thought; Leiden.

StHJewishP: Studies in the History of the Jewish People; Haifa.

StHPhRel: Studies in the History and Philosophy of Religion; CM.

StHRel [= Numen Suppl.] Studies in the History of Religions; Leiden.

StIran: Studia Iranica; Leiden.

StItFgC: Studi Italiani di Filologia Classica; Firenze.

StiZt: Stimmen der Zeit; FrB. 0039-1492.

StJudLA: Studies in Judaism in Late Antiquity; Leiden.

StLeg: Studium Legionense; León.

StLtg: Studia Liturgica; Nieuwendam.

StLuke: St. Luke's Journal of Theology; Sewanee TN.

StMiss: Studia Missionalia, Annual; Rome, Gregorian Univ.

StMor: Studia Moralia; R, Alphonsianum.

StNT [& W]: Studien zum Neuen Testament; Gütersloh; STNT ⇒ Shin-Ken. / [Studies of the NT and its World; E].

StOr: Studia Orientalia; Helsinki, Societas Orientalis Fennica. 0039-3282.

StOrRel: Studies in Oriental Religions; Wiesbaden.
StOvet: Studium Ovetense; Oviedo ('La Asunción').
StPatav: Studia Patavina; Padova. 0039-3304.
StPatrist: Studia Patristica; oBerlin.
StPostB: Studia Post-Biblica; Leiden.
StPrace: Studia i Prace = Études et Travaux, Centre d'Archéologie Méditerranéenne; Warszawa [12 (1983)].
Streven: 1. cultureel maatschappelijk maandblad; Antwerpen [50 (1982s)] 0039-2324; 2. S.J., Amst [35 (1982)].
StRicOrCr: Studi e Ricerche dell'Oriente Cristiano; Roma [5 (1982)].
StRom: Studi Romani; Roma.
Stromata (< Ciencia y Fe); San Miguel, Argentina. 0049-2353.
StRz: Studia Religioznawcze (Filozofii i Socjologii); Wsz, Univ.
StSemLgLing: Studies in Semitic Language and Linguistics; Leiden.
StTGg: Studien zur Theologie und Geistesgeschichte des 19. Jdts.; Gö, VR.
StudiaBT: Studia Biblica et Theologica; Pasadena CA. 0094-2022.
Studies; Dublin. 0039-3495.
StudiesBT: Studies in Biblical Theology; London.
Studium; 1. Madrid; 2. R. 0039-4130.
StVTPseud: Studia in Veteris Testamenti Pseudepigrapha; Leiden.
STWsz: Studia theologica Varsaviensia; Warszawa.
SubsB: Subsidia Biblica; R, Pontifical Biblical Institute.
SudanTB: Sudan Texts Bulletin; Ulster, Univ. 0143-6554. [7 (1985)].
Sumer (Archaeology-History in the Arab World); Baghdad, Dir. Ant.
SUNT: Studien zur Umwelt des NTs; Göttingen.
SUNY: State University of New York; Albany etc.
Sup.: Supplement → NT, JStOT, SDB, SEG.
Supplément, Le: autrefois 'de VSp'; P.
SvEx: Svensk Exegetisk Årsbok; U.
SVlad: St. Vladimir's Theological Quarterly; Tuckahoe NY. 0036-3227.
SvTKv: Svensk Teologisk Kvartalskrift; Lund.

SWJT: Southwestern [Baptist Seminary] Journal of Theology; Seminary Hill TX. 0038-4828.
Symbolae (graec-lat.); Oslo. 0039-7679.
Symbolon: 1. Ba/Stu; 2. Köln.
Synaxe, annuale dell'Istituto per la Documentazione e la Ricerca S. Paolo; Catania [1 (1983)].
Syria (Art Oriental, Archéologie); Paris, IFA Beyrouth.
SyrMesSt: Syro-Mesopotamian Studies (Monograph Journals); Malibu CA.
Szb: Sitzungsberichte [Univ.], phil.-hist. Klasse (Bayr./Mü. 0342-5991).
Szolgalat Ⓜ ['Dienst']; Eisenstadt, Österreich.
Ⓣ: *lingua turca,* Turkish; – ᵀtranslator.
Tablet; London. 0039-8837.
TAik: Teologinen Aikakauskirja / Teologisk Tidskrift; Helsinki.
TaiwJT: Taiwan [Presbyterian Sem.] Journal of Theology; Taipei.
TAJ: Tel Aviv [Univ.] Journal of the Institute of Archaeology. 0334-4355.
TAn: Theology Annual; Hongkong.
TanṭurYb: Ecumenical Institute for Theological Research Yearbook; J, Ṭanṭur.
TArb: Theologische Arbeiten; Stu/oB.
Tarbiẕ Ⓞ (Jewish Studies); Jerusalem, Hebr. Univ. 0334-3650.
TArg: Teología; Buenos Aires.
TAth: Ⓖ Theología; Athēnai, Synodos.
TAVO: Tübinger Atlas zum Vorderen Orient [Beih(efte)]: Wiesbaden.
TBei: Theologische Beiträge; Wuppertal.
TBer: Theologische Berichte: Z/Köln.
TBraga: Theologica; Braga.
TBud: Teologia; Budapest, Ac. Cath.
TBüch: Theologische Bücherei. (Neudrucke und Berichte 20. Jdt.); München.
TCN: Theological College of Northern Nigeria Research Bulletin; Bukuru [13 (1983)].
TDeusto: Teología-Deusto; Bilbao/M [16 (1982)].
TDienst: Theologie und Dienst; Wuppertal.
TDig: Theology Digest; St. Louis. 0040-5728.
TDNT: Theological Dictionary of the NT [< TWNT]; Grand Rapids → 907.

TDocStA: Testi e documenti per lo studio dell'Antichità; Milano, Cisalpino.

TDOT: Theological Dictionary of the Old Testament [< TWAT] GR → 596.

TEd: Theological Education; Vandalia OH [20 (1983s)].

TEFS: Theological Education [Materials for Africa, Asia, Caribbean] Fund, Study Guide; London.

Telema (réflexion et créativité chrétiennes en Afrique); Kinshasa-Gombe.

Teocomunicação; [12 (1982)].

Teresianum [ex-EphCarm]; Roma.

TerraS / TerreS: Terra Santa: 0040-3784. / La Terre Sainte; J (Custodia OFM). → **HolyL.**

TEspir: Teología Espiritual; Valencia.

TEV: Today's English Version (Good News for Modern Man); L, Collins.

TEvca: Theologia Evangelica; Pretoria, Univ. S. Africa.

TExH: Theologische Existenz heute; München.

Text; The Hague. 0165-4888.

TextEstCisn: Textos y Estudios 'Cardenal Cisneros'; Madrid, C.S.I.C.

TextPatLtg: Textus patristici et liturgici; Regensburg, Pustet.

Textus, Annual of the Hebrew Univ. Bible Project; J. 0082-3767.

TFor: Theologische Forschung; Hamburg.

TGegw: Theologie der Gegenwart in Auswahl; Münster, Regensberg-V.

TGl: Theologie und Glaube; Paderborn.

THandkNT: Theologischer Handkommentar zum NT; oB.

THAT: Theologisches Handwörterbuch zum AT; München. → **1,908.**

Themelios; L. 0307-8388.

ThemTT: Themen und Thesen der Theologie; Dü.

Theokratia, Jahrbuch des Institutum Delitzschianum; Leiden/Köln.

Ho Theológos [sic], quadrimestrale Fac. Teol. Sicilia 'S. Giovanni Ev.'; Palermo [NS 1 (1983)].

THist: Théologie Historique; P. 0563-4253.

This World; NY [3 (1982)].

Thomist, The; Wsh. 0040-6325.

Thought; Bronx NY, Fordham Univ.

TierraN: Tierra Nueva.

TimLitS: Times Literary Supplement; London.

TItSett: Teologia; Brescia (Fac. teol. Italia settentrionale).

TJb: Theologisches Jahrbuch; Leipzig.

TKontext: Theologie im Kontext; Beiträge aus Afrika, Asien, Ozeanien; Aachen. 0724-1682.

TLond: Theology; London. 0040-571X.

TLZ: Theologische Literaturzeitung; Berlin.

TolkNT: Tolkning [commentarius] av Nya Testamentet; Stockholm.

TorJT: Toronto Journal of Theology [1 (1985)].

TPast: Theologie en pastoraat; Zwolle.

TPhil: Theologie und Philosophie; Freiburg/Br. 0040-5655.

TPQ: Theologisch-praktische Quartalschrift; Linz, Österreich.

TPract: Theologia Practica; München/Hamburg. 0720-9525.

TR: Theologische Revue; Münster. 0040-568X.

TradErn: Tradition und Erneuerung (religiös-liberales Judentum); Bern.

Traditio; Bronx NY, Fordham Univ.

Tradition, a journal of orthodox Jewish thought; New York.

TRE: Theologische Realenzyklopädie; Berlin → 597.

TRef: Theologia Reformata; Woerden.

TRevNE: → **NESTR.**

TRicScR: Testi e ricerche di scienze religiose; Brescia.

TrierTZ: Trierer Theologische Zeitschrift; Trier. 0041-2945.

TrinJ: Trinity Journal; Deerfield IL.

TrinUn [St/Mon] Rel: Trinity University Studies [Monographs] in Religion, San Antonio TX.

Tripod; Hong Kong, Holy Spirit Study Centre [2 (1981)].

TRu: Theologische Rundschau; Tübingen. 0040-5698.

TS: Theological Studies; Baltimore. 0040-5639.

TSFB: Theological Students Fellowship Bulletin; Madison WI [7 (1983s)].

TsGesch: Tijdschrift voor Geschiedenis; Groningen.

TsLtg: Tijdschrift voor Liturgie; Lv.

TStAJud: Texte und Studien zum Antiken Judentum; Tübingen. 0721-8753.

TsTKi: Tidsskrift for Teologi og Kirke; Oslo. 0040-7194.

TsTNijm: Tijdschrift voor Theologie; Nijmegen (redactie). 0168-9959.

TSzem: Theologiai Szemle; Budapest. 0133-7599.

TTod: Theology Today; Princeton.

TU: Texte und Untersuchungen, Geschichte der altchristlichen Literatur; oBerlin.

Tü [ÄgBei] ThS: Tübinger [Ägyptologische Beiträge; Bonn, Habelt] Theologische Studien; Mainz, Grünewald.

[Tü]TQ: [Tübinger] Theologische Quartalschrift; Mü. 0342-1430.

TUmAT: Texte aus der Umwelt des ATs; Gütersloh ➙ 598.

TVers: Theologische Versuche; oB. 0437-3014.

TViat: Theologia Viatorum, Jb.; B; to 15 (1979s); ➙ BTZ.

TVida: Teología y Vida; Santiago, Chile. 0049-3449.

TWAT: Theologisches Wörterbuch zum Alten Testament; Stu ➙ 599.

TWiss: Theologische Wissenschaft, Sammelwerk für Studium und Beruf; Stu.

TWNT: Theologisches Wörterbuch zum NT; Stuttgart (➙ GLNT; TDNT).

TXav: Theologica Xaveriana; Bogotá.

TxK: Texte und Kontexte (Exegese); Stu.

Tyche, Beiträge zur alten Geschichte, Papyrologie und Epigraphik; Wien. [1 (1986) 3-900518-03-3].

Tychique (Chemin Neuf); Lyon.

TyndB: Tyndale Bulletin; Cambridge.

TZBas: Theologische Zeitschrift; Basel.

UF: Ugarit-Forschungen; Kevelaer/Neukirchen. 0342-2356.

Universitas; 1. Stuttgart. 0041-9079; 2. Bogotá. 0041-9060.

UnivT: Universale Teologica; Brescia.

UnSa: Una Sancta: 1. Augsburg-Meitingen; 2. Brooklyn.

UnSemQ: Union Seminary Quarterly Review; New York.

UPA: University Press of America; Wsh/ Lanham MD.

Update [new religious movements]; Aarhus [7 (1983)].

VAeg: Varia Aegyptiaca; San Antonio. 0887-4026 [1 (1985)].

VBGed: Verklaring van een Bijbelgedeelte; Kampen.

VComRel: La vie des communautés religieuses; Montréal.

VDI: ❽ Vestnik Drevnej Istorii; Moskva. 0321-0391.

Veleia, (pre-) historia, arquelogía filología clásicas; Vitoria-Gasteiz, Univ. País Vasco [1 (1984)].

Verbum; 1. SVD; R; 2. Nancy [5 (1983)].

Veritas; Porto Alegre, Univ. Católica.

VerkF: Verkündigung und Forschung; München.

VerVid: Verdad y Vida; Madrid.

VetChr: Vetera Christianorum; Bari.

Vidyajyoti (Theological Reflection); Ranchi (Delhi, Inst. Rel.St.).

VieCons: La Vie Consacrée; P/Bru.

VigChr: Vigiliae Christianae; Leiden. 0042-6032.

ViMon: Vita Monastica; Camaldoli, Arezzo.

ViPe: Vita e Pensiero: Mi, Univ. S. Cuore.

VisLang: Visible Language; Cleveland.

VisRel: Visible Religion, annual for religious iconography; Leiden [3 (1984) 90-04-07496-1].

VitaCons: Vita Consacrata; Milano.

VizVrem: ❽ Vizantijskij Vremennik; Moskva. 0136-7358.

VO: Vicino Oriente; Roma.

Vocation; Paris.

VoxEvca: Vox Evangelica; London. 0263-6786.

VoxEvi: Vox Evangelii; Buenos Aires [NS 1 (1984)].

VoxRef: Vox Reformata; Geelong, Australia.

VoxTh: Vox Theologica; Assen.

VSp: La Vie Spirituelle; Paris.

VT: Vetus Testamentum; Leiden.

WDienst: Wort und Dienst; Bielefeld. 0342-3085.

WegFor: Wege der Forschung; Da, Wiss.

WeltOr: Welt des Orients; Göttingen. 0043-2547.

WesleyTJ: Wesleyan Theological Journal; Marion IN. 0092-4245.

WestTJ: Westminster Theological Journal; Philadelphia. 0043-4388.

WEvent: Word + Event, World Catholic Federation for the Biblical Apostolate; Stuttgart; printed in Hong Kong, also in Spanish ed.

WienerSt: Wiener Studien; Wien.

Wiss: Wissenschaftliche Buchhandlung; Da.

WissPrax: Wissenschaft und Praxis in Kirche und Gesellschaft; Göttingen.

WissWeish: Wissenschaft und Weisheit; Mü-Gladbach. 0043-678X.

WMANT: Wissenschaftliche Monographien zum Alten und Neuen Testament; Neukirchen.

WoAnt: Wort und Antwort; Mainz.

Word and Spirit; Still River MA.

WorldArch: World Archaeology; Henley.

World Spirituality → EncWSp.

Worship; St. John's Abbey, Collegeville, Minn. 0043-9414.

WrocST: Wrocławskie Studia Teologiczne / Colloquium Salutis; Wrocław. 0239-7714.

WUNT: Wissenschaftliche Untersuchungen zum NT: Tübingen.

WVDOG: Wissenschaftliche Veröffentlichungen der Deutschen Orient-Gesellschaft; Berlin.

WWorld: Word and World; St. Paul.

WZ: Wissenschaftliche Zeitschrift [... Univ.].

WZKM: Wiener Zeitschrift für die Kunde des Morgenlandes; Wien. 0084-0076.

YaleClas: Yale Classical Studies; NHv.

Yermo [... monástico]; Zamora, Monte Casino.

Yuval: Studies of the Jewish Music Research Centre [incl. Psalms]; Jerusalem.

ZäSpr: Zeitschrift für die Ägyptische Sprache und Altertumskunde; Berlin. 0044-216X.

ZAss: Zeitschrift für Assyriologie & Vorderasiatische Archäologie; Berlin. 0048-5299.

ZAW: Zeitschrift für die Alttestamentliche Wissenschaft; Berlin. 0044-2526.

ZDialT: Zeitschrift für dialektische Theologie; Kampen [1 (1985)].

ZDMG: Zeitschrift der Deutschen Morgenländischen Gesellschaft; Wiesbaden.

ZDPV: Zeitschrift des Deutschen Palästina-Vereins; Stu. 0012-1169.

ZeichZt: Die Zeichen der Zeit, Evangelische Monatschrift; oBerlin.

Zeitwende (Die neue Furche); Gü.

ZeKUL: Zeszyty Naukowe Katolickiego Uniwersytetu Lubelskiego; Lublin. 0044-4405.

ZEthnol: Zeitschrift für Ethnologie; Braunschweig. 0044-2666.

ZEvEthik: Zeitschrift für Evangelische Ethik; Gütersloh. 0044-2674.

ZfArch: Zeitschrift für Archäologie: oBerlin. 0044-233X.

ZGPred: Zeitschrift für Gottesdienst und Predigt; Gü. [1 (1983)].

Zion: ●; Jerusalem. 0044-4758.

ZIT: Zeitschriften Inhaltsdienst Theologie; Tübingen. 0340-8361.

ZKG: Zeitschrift für Kirchengeschichte; Stuttgart. 0044-2985.

ZkT: Zeitschrift für katholische Theologie; Innsbruck. 0044-2895.

ZMissRW: Zeitschrift für Missionswissenschaft und Religionswissenschaft; Münster. 0044-3123.

ZNW: Zeitschrift für die Neutestamentliche Wissenschaft und die Kunde des Alten Christentums; Berlin. 0044-2615.

ZPapEp: Zeitschrift für Papyrologie und Epigraphik; Bonn. 0084-5388.

ZRGg: Zeitschrift für Religions- und Geistesgeschichte; Köln. 0044-3441.

ZRUnt: Zeitschrift für die Praxis des Religionsunterrichts; Stu.

ZSavR: Zeitschrift der Savigny-Stiftung (Romanistische) Rechtsgeschichte: Weimar. 0323-4096.

ZSprW: Zeitschrift für Sprachwissenschaft; [3 (1984)].

ZTK: Zeitschrift für Theologie und Kirche; Tübingen. 0513-9147.

ZvgSpr: Zeitschrift für vergleichende Sprachforschung; Göttingen. 0044-3646.

Zygon; Winter Park FL. 0044-5614.

I. Bibliographica

A1   *Opera collecta* 1. **Festschriften,** memorials.

1 *a)* Collected Essays (usually tit. pp., from various signed reviewers): CBQ 48 (1986) 155-163. 355-363. 577-586. 763-775; – *b) Epp* Eldon J., Collected essays: JBL 105 (1986) 173-182. 365-370. 559-9; – *c) Halleux* A. de, *al.,* ... Miscellanea: ETL 62 (1986) 9*-19*; – *d) Langlamet* F., Recueils et mélanges (tit. pp.): RB 93 (1986) 133-7. 290-5. 446-459. [609s].

2 AHLSTRÖM G., In the shelter of Elyon 1984: ➤ **1,**5: ᴿJTS 37 (1986) 467-9 (E. W. *Nicholson*).

3 ALLARD M., NWYIA P. In mem. 1984 = MUSJ 50, 1984 ➤ **1,**5*: ᴿRechSR 74 (1986) 309-314 (R. *Arnaldez*).

4 ALONSO DÍAZ José, Palabra y vida, ᴱ**Vargas-Machuca** A. 1984 ➤ 64,2 ... **1,**6: ᴿRQum 12,46 (1986) 288s (J. *Carmignac*: art. de *García Martínez* F. et de *Diez Merino* L., sur Qumran); TR 82 (1986) 283s (A. de *Oliveira*).

5 AMORE Agostino: Noscere sancta; miscellanea in memoria di ∼ OFM † 1982: Bibliotheca Pont. Athenaei Antoniani 24s, 1985 ➤ **1,**8*: ᴿNRT 108 (1986) 599 (N. *Plumat*).

6 Amsterdam, Palache Instituut, Driehonderd jaar 'Oosterse Talen', ᴱJonge H.J. de, *al.* 1986. *f*30. – ᴿPhoenixEOL 32,2 (1986) 61-63 (K. van der *Toorn*).

7 BAILLOUD Gérard: Le Néolithique de la France, ᴱ**Demoule** Jean-Paul, *Guilaine* Jean. P 1986, Picard. 463 p.; bibliog. p. 12-14. F 350. 2-7084-0303-6. 32 art.

7* BALTHASAR Hans Urs von: The analogy of beauty; essays for ∼ at eighty, ᴱ**Riches** John. E 1986, Clark. £10 [TLond 39,84 adv.].

8 BANTELMANN Albert: Offa 43 (Neumünster 1986). 389 p.; ill.; bibliog. p. 11s. 3-529-01243-2. 27 art. (Nord-Europ. Geologie).

9 BARTH Karl: Zur Theologie ∼ s, 100. Gb. = ZTK Beiheft 6. Tü 1986, Mohr. iv-271 p. 8 art.; infra.

10 BAUMGARTNER Jakob: Der Sonntag; Anspruch — Wirklichkeit — Gestalt, ∼ 60. Gb., ᴱAltermatt Alberich M., *al.* Wü/FrS 1986, Echter/Univ. 366 p.; bibliog. p. 315-338 + index 339-344. 3-429-01027-6 / FrS 3-7278-0366-5. 20 art.; 2 infra.

10* BEEDE Grace L.: Apophoreta; Latin and Greek studies in honor of, ᴱReedy J. Ch 1985, Bolchazy-Carducci. 352 p. [AnPg 56,814].

11 BERBÉRIAN Haïg, [18.IV.1887 - 3.X.1978] Armenian studies, Études arméniennes in memoriam ∼, ᴱ**Kouymjian** Dickran. Lisboa 1986, Gulbenkian. xli-883 p.; ill.; bibliog. p. xx-xli. 50 art., 1 infra.

11* BICKERMAN Elias L. [1.VII.1897 - 31.VIII.1981]: Ancient Studies in memory of ∼ = JANES 16s (1984s). v-241 p.

12 BLUMENKRANZ Bernhard: Les Juifs à l'égard [au miroir, AnPg 56,814] de l'histoire, mélanges en l'honneur de ∼ ᴱ**Dahan** Gilbert. P 1985, Picard. 416 p. – ᴿRÉJ 145 (1986) 144-150 (Danièle *Iancu-Agou*).

12* BORZSAK István septuagenario: = Acta Classica Univ. Debrecen 20 (1984).   83 p. [An Pg 56,814].

13 BOWMAN John: Abr-Nahrain 24 (1986), ᴱMuraoka T.   Leiden 1986, Brill. vii-207 p.; 6 pl. f94.   90-04-08285-9. [BL 87,17].

13* Budapest Rabbinical Seminary 1877-1977, ᴱCarmilly-Weinberger Moshe. NY 1986, Sepher-Hermon. xiv-334 + 56 p.; 13 pl.   0-87203-148-9 [BO 43,833].

14 CARATA Giuseppe: Parola e servizio; saggi ∼ XX di episcopato, ᴱSantovito Francesco; pref. Marranzini Alfredo. R 1986, Vivere In. 413 p. – ᴿCC 137 (1986,4) 403s (P. Vanzan).

15 CASSART Jean: Mélanges offerts au chanoine ∼, 75ᵉ an.: Mémoires Hist. Tournai 4.   Tournai 1984.   622 p.; ill.   20 art. sur Tournai.

15* CHASTAGNOL André, HUVELIN Hélène: Études de numismatique romaine et byzantine = Bulletin de la Société Française de Numismatique 40 (1985) 601-635 [AnPg 56,814].

16 CHETHIMATTAM J. B., Religions in dialogue; East and West meet, ᴱThundy Zacharias P., al. Lanham MD 1985, UPA.   xiv-314 p. $26.75; pa. $14.50. [Horizons 14,202, P. F. Knitter].

16* CIPROTTI Pio: Vitam impendere vero; studi in onore ∼, ᴱSchulz Winfried, Feliciani Giorgio: Utrumque ius 14.   R 1986, Pont. Univ. Lateranense.   353 p. Lit. 30.000 [TR 83,145: ecumenismo, Eucaristia, Luoghi Sacri, diaconato ..].

17 DAALEN Aleida [Liet] van, Te beginnen bij de letter Beth; opstellen over het Bijbels Hebreeuws en de Hebreeuwse Bijbel voor Dr ∼, ᴱDeurloo K. A., Hoogewoud F. J. Kampen 1985, Kok.   205 p. f36.   90-242-0923-4. [BL 87,61, J. W. Rogerson].

18 DAUMAS François (mém.):   Hommages à ∼. Montpellier 1986, Univ. I. xxv-330 p.; II. p. 331-630, 23 pl.; biobibliog. i-vii (A. Guillaumont), ix-xxv. 63 art.; 15 infra.

19 DELCOR Mathias, Mélanges bibliques et orientaux, ᴱCaquot A. al.: AOAT 215, 1985 → 1,39: ᴿÉTRel 61 (1986) 115-7 (D. Lys: immense richesse).

20 DELLER Karlheinz, Parva assyriologica, ∼, present. Saporetti C.: MesopT 21 (F 1986) 179-259; bibliog. p. 183-189.

21 DÍEZ MACHO Alejandro: Salvación en la palabra; targum-derash-berith, en memoria del profesor ∼, ᴱMuñoz León Domingo.   M 1986, Cristiandad. 848 p.; portr.; biobibliog. p. 13-22.829-848.   84-7057-390-X. [ActuBbg 24,69; BL 88, 20].   58 art.; infra.

22 DU BOULAY F. R. H.: The Church in pre-Reformation society, ᴱBarron Caroline M., Harper-Bill Christopher.   Woodbridge, Suffolk 1985, Boydell. 232 p.; bibliog. p. 228.   15 art.; 1 infra. [JEH 38,460s, G. L. Harris].

22* DIMLER Anselme: Mélanges à la mémoire I/3, Histoire cistercienne; ordres, moines; ᴱChauvin Benoît.   Arbois 1984, Chauvin.   400 p.; ill.   27 art. [RHE 81,727, J.-P. Sosson, tit. pp.].

23 DUMOULIN Heinrich; Fernöstliche Weisheit und christlicher Glaube, Festgabe für ∼ 80.Gb., ᴱWaldenfels Hans, Immoos Thomas: Dialog der Religionen.   1985 → 1,45; DM 42; 3-7867-1202-6: ᴿGregorianum 67 (1986) 589s (J. Wicki).

24 DUPONT Jacques, À cause de l'Évangile 1985 → 1,46: ᴿAntonianum 61 (1986) 180-2 (Z. I. Herman: tit. pp. anche su Testimonium).

25 EGERMANN Franz: 80 Gb., ᴱSuerbaum Werner, Maier Friedrich.   Mü 1985, Univ. Inst. Klas. Pg.   188 p.   17 art., 1 infra.

26 ELITZUR Yehuda: ❶ Studies in Bible and exegesis 2, ᴱSimon U. Ramat-Gan 1986, Bar-Ilan Univ. 282 p. $19. 965-226-062-2 [BL 87,18, no pp.].

27 ELLIS John T., Studies in Catholic history in honor of ∼ [➔ 1,47*], ᴱMinnich Nelson H., al. Wilmington 1985, Glazier. xxi-765 p. – ᴿChH 55 (1986) 136 (M. E. Marty).

28 ERVIN Howard M.: Essays on apostolic themes, ᴱElbert P. Peabody MA 1985, Hendrickson. xix-239 p. $15. 0-913573-14-0. – ᴿRefTR 45 (1986) 88 (T. L. Wilkinson); RExp 83 (1986) 644s (E. G. Hinson).

29 FEENSTRA Robert: Satura ∼ oblata. FrS 1985, Univ. xxiv-700 p.; bibliog. xv-xxiv; 693-700, ses doctorands. – ᴿRHE 81 (1986) 396 (G. Fransen: prof. d'histoire de droit à Leiden).

30 FESTUGIÈRE André-Jean, mémorial, Antiquité païenne et chrétienne, ᴱLucchesi E., Saffrey H. D. 1984 ➔ 65,47: ᴿRÉG 98 (1985) 436-9 (P. Nautin); TPhil 61 (1986) 571-6 (A. Grillmeier).

31 FISIAK Jacek: Linguistics across historical and geographical boundaries, ∼ 50th b., ᴱKastovsky Dieter: Trends in Linguistics 32. B 1986, Mouton de Gruyter. xix-777 p., biobibliog. iv-xiii; xiv + p. 779-1543. 3-11-010426-1. 125 art.; 2 infra.

32 FITZMYER Joseph A.: A wise and discerning heart; studies presented to ∼, 65th b., ᴱBrown Raymond E., Di Lella Alexander A., = CBQ 48,3 (July, 1986) 373-522; portr.; biobibliog. p. 379-386 (M. M. Bourke / J. P. Meier). 11 art., infra.

33 FLANNERY Austin: Freedom to hope, ᴱFalconer Alan, al. Dublin 1985, Columba. 103 p. – ᴿNBlackf 67 (1986) 389 (D. Byrne).

34 FUKS Alexander [1917-1978 ➔ 61,y552]: Scripta classica [.. in honorem ∼]: Yearbook of the Israel Society for the Promotion of Classical Studies, Scripta Classica Israelitica 5. J 1979s, Academic. 262 p.; portr.; bibliog. p. 1-7. $18. 0334-4509. 19 art.; 4 infra.

35 GERHARDSSON Birger: SvEx 51s (1986s), ᴱHartman Lars. 237 p.; portr.

36 GOITEIN Shelomo D.: Biblical and other studies in memory of ∼, ᴱAhroni Reuben: Hebrew Annual Review 9. Columbus 1986, Ohio State Univ. vi-381 p.; portr. [ÉTRel 62,585, tit. pp.] 24 art.; 16 infra.

37 GOÑI GAZTAMBIDE José: De la Iglesia de Navarra, estudios en honor del prof. ∼, ᴱSaranyana José I.: Teológica 40, 1984 ➔ 1,55*: ᴿEstE 61 (1986) 85s (C. Gutiérrez).

38 GRANAROLO Jean: Hommage à ∼, philologie, littératures et histoire anciennes; textes réunis par René Braun: Annales Nice, fac. lett. 50. P 1985, BLettres. 422 p.; portr.; p. 9-21, biobibliog. 36 art., 3 infra. – ᴿGitFg 35 (1986) 301s [N. Scivoletto]; Latomus 45 (1986) 226s (S. Byl).

39 GREEVEN Heinrich, Studien zum Text und zur Ethik des NTs, ∼ 80. Gb., ᴱSchrage Wolfgang: BZNW 47. ix-456 p.; bibliog. p. 450-6 (Linssen Rudolf). DM 198 [TR 83,74: tit. pp.]; infra.

40 GRIMM Harold J.: Pietas et societas; new trends in Reformation social history, essays in memory of ∼, ᴱSessions Kyle C., Bebb Phillip N. Kirkville MO 1985, SixtC. 224 p. $25 [JAAR 54,632].

41 GROSS Heinrich; Freude an der Weisung des Herrn, Beiträge zur Theologie der Psalmen, Festgabe zum 70. Gb. von ∼, ᴱHaag E., Hossfeld F.-L.: SBB 13. Stu 1986, KBW. xii-533 p.; bibliog. p. 513-8. [TR 82,425, tit. pp.] 3-460-00131-3. – Infra.

42 GÜTERBOCK Hans G., Kanišsuwar, a tribute to ∼ 75th b. (1983), ᴱHoffner Harry A., Beckman Gary M.: Assyriological Studies 23. Ch 1986, Univ. Or. Inst. vii-203 p.; p. 185-8, bibliog. supp. Beal R. H. 0-918986-44-3. 18 art.; 15 infra.

43 HAARSMA Frans: Toekomst voor de kerk? ᴱVen J.A. van der 1985
➤ 1,61: ᴿCollatVi 16 (1986) 484s (R. *Michiels*) [NedTTs 41,247, F.O. *van Gennep*].

44 HAIRE J.L.M.: Essays in honour of the late V. Rev. Prof. emeritus ~ = IrBSt 8,3 (1986) 106-160.

45 HALKIN Léon-E., Hommage au Prof. ~, 80 ans. = Bulletin de l'Institut Historique Belge de Rome 55, (1985s). 321 p. 13 art.; 2 infra.

45* HARRIS Bruce F.: = Ancient Society, Resources for Teachers [which he founded] 16,1ss (1986); appreciation p. 2-7; portr. (E.A. *Judge*).

46 HARTMAN Sven S.: Religionsvetenskapliga studier, ᴱGeels Antoon, *al.*: Religio 12. Lund 1983, Teologiska Inst. 179 p.; bibliog. p. 177. 11 art.; 1 infra.

46* HOLWERDA D.: *Schólia*; studia ad criticam interpretationemque textuum Graecorum et ad historiam iuris graeco-romani pertinentia, ᴱAerts W.J. *al.* Groningen 1985, Forsten. vii-168 p. [AnPg 56,815].

47 HOSPERS J.H.: Scripta signa vocis, studies about scripts, scriptures, scribes and languages in the Near East, ᴱVanstiphout H.L.J., *al.* Groningen 1986, Forsten. 331 p.; portr. [RelStR 13,255, J. *Sasson*; BL 88,25, P. *Wernberg-Møller*]. 90-6980-008-X. 27 art., infra.

47* HUGHES P.E.: Through Christ's word, ᴱGodfrey W. Robert, *Boyd* Jesse L. 1985 ➤ 1,68: ᴿSTEv 9 (1986) 295s (G. *Emetti*: autori e temi: *Bruce* F., *Ridderbos* H., *Kline* M.; *Dillard* R., censimento di Davide 2 Sam 24; *Spicq* C. Apc 18,17...).

48 HUNGER Herbert: Byzantios, 70 Gb., ᴱHörandner W., *al.* 1984 ➤ 1,69: ᴿRÉByz 44 (1986) 303s (J. *Darrouzès*: tit. pp.).

HUVELIN Hélène ➤ 15*.

49 JANSEN H. Ludin, The many and the one; essays on religion in the Graeco-Roman world, ᴱBorgen P.: Relieff 15. Trondheim 1985, Tapir. 265 p. NK 120. 82-519-0670-9. [BL 87,103, L.L. *Grabbe*: mostly his own articles; four by colleagues].

50 ᴱJaphet Sara: Studies in Bible, Jerusalem Hebrew University 60th Anniversary: ScrHieros 31. J 1986, Magnes. viii-437 p. $30. 0080-8369. 17 art. $22. [TR 83,250, tit. pp.].

51 KASER Max: Iuris professio, Festgabe für ~, 80. Gb., ᴱBenöhr Hans-P., *al.* W 1986, Böhlau. 437 p.; portr. [ZSav-R 105,922] 3-205-07210-3. 26 art.; 3 infra.

52 KENNER Hedwig: Pro Arte antiqua, ᴱAlzinger Wilhelm, *al.* W 1982-5, Koska. 183 p., L pl.; p. 185-373, LXXIV pl.; bibliog. p. 371-3. 3-85334-032-6; 5-0. 52 art., 4 infra.

53 KLEIN Laurentius: Dormition Abbey Jerusalem, Fs des theologischen Studienjahres .. für Abt Dr. ~. St. Ottilien 1986, Eos. 233 p.; 64 color. pl. DM 48 [TR 83,186, K. *Richter*].

54 KNOX David B.: God who is rich in mercy; essays presented to ~, ᴱO'Brien Peter T., *Peterson* David G.: Lancer Books. Homebush West NSW 1986, Anzea [GR, Baker]. xxi-422 p.; portr.; biobibliog. p. xi-xix. 0-85892-277-0. 20 art., 15 infra.

55 KRAUS Hans-Joachim: 'Wenn nicht jetzt, wann denn', ᴱGeyer H.-G. 1983 ➤ 64,64: ᴿTLZ 111 (1986) 337-340 (K. *Lüthi*).

56 KRETSCHMAR Georg: Kirchengemeinschaft — Anspruch und Wirklichkeit, Fs für ~ zum 60. Gb., ᴱHauschild Wolf-Dieter. Stu 1986, Calwer. 335 p. DM 68 [TLZ 112,89; TR 82,425].

57 LAMBTON Ann K.S.: BSOAS 49,1 (1986). 251 p.; portr.; biobibliog. p. 2-7 (J.R. *Bracken, al.*).

58 LAUFFER Siegfried: Studien zur Alten Geschichte, 70 Gb., ᴱKalcyk Hansjörg, *al.*: Historica 2. R 1986, Bretschneider. xxi-377 p.; p. 378-766, 5 pl.; p. 767-1102. Lit 1.300.000. 88-85007-70-8. 16 art., 3 infra.

59 LEBRAM Jürgen C. H.: Tradition and re-interpretation in Jewish and early Christian literature; essays in honour of ~, ᴱHenten J. W. van, *al.*: StPostB 36. Leiden 1986, Brill. viii-313 p.; portr.; bibliog., pp. 307-313 *Klaauw* J. van der. 90-04-07752-9 [NTAbs 31,96; ZAW 99,152 & JStJud 18,103: tit. pp.]. 23 art.; infra.

59* LENGELING Emil J.: Liturgie — ein vergessenes Thema der Theologie? Festgabe zum 70. Gb., ᴱRichter Klemens: QDisp 107. FrB 1986, Herder. 192 p. DM 39 [TR 83, 409-413, R. *Kaczynski*].

60 LENZENWEGER Josef: Ecclesia peregrinans, ~ zum 70. Gb. W 1986 [RHE 81,657; TPQ 135,185].

60* LEUENBERGER Robert, Erwogenes und Gewagtes, 70. Gb., ᴱGrünewald Friedhelm. Z 1986, Theol.-V. 265 p.; bibliog. p. 255-264 [TR 83,425].

61 LILLIU Giovanni: 70° compl. [➤ 1,86], ᴱSotgiu Giovanna. Cagliari 1985, Univ. 249 p.; 30 fig. 11 art.; 1 infra.

61* MCBURNEY Charles M.: Stone Age prehistory, in memory of ~, ᴱBailey G. N., *Callow* P. C 1986, Univ. xv-265 p.; 79 fig. £45. 0-521-25773-5 [AntiqJ 67,136].

62 LIPTZIN Sol: Identity and ethos; Fs for ~ 85th B., ᴱGelber Mark. Bern 1986, P.-Lang. 412 p. 23 art. on Yiddish and later literature. – ᴿDor 15 (1986s) 264-6 (L. *Shalit*).

63 MCINTYRE John, retirement: Religious imagination, ᴱMackey James P. E 1986, Univ. v-217 p. $17.50 [TDig 34,90]. 0-85224-512-2. 10 art.; 3 infra.

63* MCKANE William: A word in season, essays in honour of ~, 65th b., ᴱMartin James D., *Davies* Philip R.: JStOT Sup 42. Sheffield 1986, Univ. xi-266 p.; phot.; bibliog. p. 249-251. 1-85075-016-5; pa. 47-5. $16 [TR 83,73, tit. pp.]. 11 art.; infra.

64 MACQUARRIE John: Being and truth, essays in honour of ~, ᴱKee Alistair, L 1986, SCM. xviii-482 p.; bibliog. p. 454-462. £25 [TR 83,74]. – ᴿExpTim 98 (1986s) 216s (W. D. *Hudson*: no titles, authors, or pages).

65 MACRAE Allan A.; Interpretation and history; essays in honour of ~, ᴱHarris R. Laird, *al.* Singapore / Hatfield PA 1986, Christian Life / Biblical Theol. Sem, Library, 300 p.; bibliog. p. 31-45 (J. G. *Pakala*). $11, pa. $8 [RelStR 13,254, W. L. *Humphreys*]. 9971-991-14-4. 17 art., 15 infra.

66 MAETZKE Guglielmo: Studi di antichità in onore di ~, ᴱMarzi Costagli Maria Grazia, *Tamagno Perna* Luisa: Archaeologica 49. R 1984, Bretschneider. xvii-227 p.; p. 229-470; 471-700, IV pl. Lit. 1,000.000. ᴿArctos 19 (1985) 255s (H. *Solin*).

67 MARRANZINI Alfredo, Ecclesiae sacramentum, Studi in onore di P. ~, ᴱLorizio Giuseppe. N 1986, D'Auria. 478 p. [TR 82,237; CC 138/1,87, A. *Mastantuono*].

67* MARSILI Salvatore: Paschale mysterium, studi in memoria dell'abate Prof. ~ (1910-1983), ᴱFarnedi Giustino: StAns 91, AnalLtg 10. R 1986, Pont. Ateneo S. Anselmo. 235 p.; portr. 10 art.; 1 infra.

68 MASTON Thomas B.: Perspectives on Applied Christianity, ᴱTillman William M.ᴶ Macon GA 1986, Mercer Univ. 96 p. [= 1985 ➤ 1, 92]. $10.50. – ᴿRExp 83 (1986) 636s (Henlee *Barnette*).

68* MAYER Reinhold: 'Wie gut sind deine Zelte, Jaakow...', 60. Gb., ᴱEhrlich Ernst L., *al.* Gerlingen 1986, Bleicher. 278 p.; biobibliog. p. 253-7. 3-88350-605-2. 22 art.; 15 infra.

69 MAYS James L.:   The hermeneutical quest; essays in honor of ∼, EMiller
   D. G.: Pittsburgh Theol. Mon. 4.   Allison Park PA 1986, Pickwick. biog.
   1-10 (J. H. *Leith*); bibliog. 171-4 (J. B. *Trotti*) 0-915138-86-7. [Interp
   41,41; OTAbs 10,67]. 10 art., infra.
70 MAZZOTTI Mario: in memoria di ∼, EFarioli Campanati Raffaella = Felix
   Ravenna 127-130 (1984s). 506 p.; portr. 30 art., 1 infra.
71 MELLINK Machteld J.:   Ancient Anatolia; aspects of change and cultural
   development; essays in honor of ∼, ECanby Jeanny V.: Wisconsin Studies in Classics.   Madison 1986, Univ. Wisconsin.   xvii-120 p.; portr.;
   bibliog. p. xiii-xvii.   0-299-10620-9. [AJA 91,618, B. R. *Foster*].   11 art.;
   9 infra.
72 METZGER Bruce M.:   A South African perspective on the New Testament;
   essays presented to ∼ in S. Africa 1985, EPetzer J. H., *Hartin* P. J.
   xii-271 p.; portr.; biobibliog. 1979-84, p. 1-7.   90-04-07720-0 [NTAbs
   32,96] 20 art.; infra.
73 MEYER Robert T.,   Diakonia, Studies in honor of ∼, EHalton Thomas,
   William Joseph P. Wsh 1986, Catholic Univ. xiii-348 p.; bibliog. p. 343.
   $25.   24 art., 4 infra [< ZIT 87,354].
74 MICHALOWSKI Kazimierz: 50 lat polskich wykopalisk ... 50 years of Polish
   excavations in Egypt and the Near East; in memory of ∼, EKiss Zsolt.
   Wsz 1986, Univ., Inst. Mediterranean Archeology.
75 MIRSKY Aharon: ❶ On the path of knowledge; essays on Jewish culture,
   EMalachi Zvi.   Lod 1986, Habermann Institute [OTAbs 10,142].
76 MITXELENA Luis: Symbolae Ludovico ∼ septuagenario oblata, EMelena
   José L. Vitoria 1985, Inst. Ciencias Antigüedad.   798 p.; p. 799-1580;
   portr.; bibliog. p. 9-19. [Kratylos 32,163, H. *Schwerteck*].   84-600-4140-9.
   143 art.; 2 infra.
77 MOKHTAR Gamal Eddin: Mélanges, EPosener-Kriéger Paule. Le Caire
   1985, IFAO. xx-417 p.; ill. / 401 p.; ill. 2-7247-0019-8. 72 art.; 25 infra.
78 MOLTMANN Jürgen: Gottes Zukunft — Zukunft der Welt; Fs für ∼, 60
   Gb., EDeuser H. ...   Mü 1986, Kaiser.   581 p. DM 98. [TR 82,337].
   3-459-01632-9. – RTheologiai Szemle 29 (1986) 318-320 (S. *Szathmáry*).
78* MUND Hans-Joachim: Um die eine Kirche; evangelische Katholizität, 70.
   Gb., Mü-Gräfelfing 1984, Banaschewski. 103 p. 12 art., 3 infra [< ZIT
   1986,759].
79 NAUDÉ Beyers: Resistance and hope; South African essays in honor of ∼,
   EVilla-Vicencio Charles, *DeGruchy* John W. GR 1985, Eerdmans,
   xii-209 p. $8. – RModT 2 (1985s) 363s (K. W. *Clements*).
80 NICOLE Roger: Reformed theology in America, a history of its modern
   development, ∼ 75th b., EWells David F. GR 1985, Eerdmans. xvi-317 p.
   $17; pa. $11. [TDig 33,485].
81 NIKIPROWETZKY Valentin [15.IV.1919-19.XII.1983]: Hellenica et Judaica,
   hommage à ∼, ECaquot André, *Hadas-Lebel* Mireille, *Riaud* Jean. Lv
   1986, Peeters. 519 p.; biobibliog. p. 1-9. 511-5. Fb 2800 [NRT 109,755, tit.
   sans pp.; ZAW 99,462, tit. pp.]. 90-6831-054-2. 38 art.; 34 infra.
81* OBERHUBER Karl: Im Bannkreis des Alten Orients; Studien zur Sprach-
   und Kulturgeschichte des Alten Orients und seines Ausstrahlungsraumes,
   ∼ 70. Gb., EMeid Wolfgang, *Trenkwalder* Helga: Innsbrucker Beiträge zur
   Kulturwissenschaft 24. Innsbruck 1986, AMOE. 283 p.; ill.; bibliog.
   p. 11-15 (M. *Schretter*). [AcOrK 48,186, E. *Knudsen*]. 3-85-124-113-4. 25
   art.; 18 infra. – RZAss 76 (1986) 138 (D. O. *Edzard*).
82 OSTERHAVEN M. Eugene: Reformed Review 21,3 (Holland MI 1986)
   146-280; bibliog. 281 .. [< ZIT]. 13 art., 1 infra.

82* PENTECOST J. Dwight: Essays in honor of ~, EToussaint Stanley D.,
Dyer Charles H.   Ch 1986, Moody.   238 p. $15.90 [TR 83,337].

83 PESCE Domenico: Sapienza antica, Studi in onore di ~: Univ. Parma, Fac.
Magistero.   Mi 1985, Angeli.   406 p. Lit. 25.000 [ÉtClas 55,93].

83* PETER Rodolphe: RHPR 66,1 (1986).   130 p.; portr.; bibliog. p. 123-7.

84 PETROCCHI Massimo: L'uomo e la storia; studi storici in onore di ~,
EChiacchella Rita, Rossi Giorgio F.: Storia e Letteratura 153s.   R 1983,
Storia e Letteratura.   xix-372 p.; 448 p. – RRivStoLR 22 (1986) 392-6 (E.
Passerin d'Entrèves).

85 PFEFFER Leo: Religion and the State; essays in honor of ~, EWood James
E.   Waco 1985, Baylor.   506 p. $40. [JAAR 54,633].

86 PLOMTEUX Hugo † 15.I.1981:   Langue, dialecte, littérature; études romaines à la mémoire de ~, EAngelet C., al.: Symbolae A-12.   Lv 1983, Presses
Univ.   462 p. – RSalesianum 48 (1986) 468s (R. Bracchi: tit. sans. pp.).

87 PORADA Edith: Insight through images; studies in honor of ~, EKelly-
Buccellati Marilyn, al.: BiblMesop 21.   Malibu CA 1986, Undena.
x-269 p.; portr.; 64 pl.   0-89003-188-6; pa. 9-4.   30 art.; infra.

88 POWLES Marjorie & Cyril: Justice as mission; an agenda for the Church,
EBrown Terry, Lind Christopher.   Burlington ON 1985, Trinity.   viii-250 p.
25 art. [SR 15,123].

89 PUGLESE Salvatore M.,   Studi di Paletnologia in onore di ~. R 1985, Univ.

90 RAHNER Karl, Glaube im Prozess, EKlinger E.   1984 → 65,113; 1,114a:
RTLZ 111 (1986) 412-5 (H. Kirchner).

91 RAMBAUD M.;   Présence de César; hommage au Doyen ~, EChevallier R.
P 1985, BLettres.   546 p. – RRPLH 60 (1986) 321s (J.-C. Richard).

92 RAUBITSCHEK Antony E.:   The Greek historians; literature and history;
papers presented to ~, EJameson Michael E.   SF 1985, Stanford Univ.
xxiii-139 p.; phot.; bibliog. p. xi-xxiii [RÉG 100,514, Valerie Fromentin]
0-915838-57-5.   8 art.; 3 infra.

93 REDHARDT Jürgen: Theologische Standorte, 60. Gb., EJendorff Bernhard,
Schmalenberg Gerhard: Theol. Rel.-Päd. 4.   Giessen 1986, Univ.
Fachbereich Religionswissenschaften.   321 p. DM 15 [TR 83,242].

94 RIJKHOFF Martien: Bij de put van Jakob: exegetische opstellen aange-
boden aan ~, EWeren Wim, Poulssen Nick: TFT-Studies 5.   Tilburg 1986,
Univ. Theologische Faculteit.   ix-154 p. ƒ20.   90-361-9731-1. [TsTNijm
27,402].   7 art., infra.

95 RISCH Ernst: o-o-pe-ro-si, Fs. zum 75. Gb., EEtter Annemarie.   B 1986,
de Gruyter.   xii-770 p.; ill. DM 390.   3-11-010518-7. [Sales 49,915, tit. sans
pp.].

96 ROBINS R. H.:   Studies in the history of western linguistics in honour of ~,
EBynon Theodora, Palmer F. R.   C 1986, Univ.   x-285 p.; bibliog.
p. 279-283.   0-521-26228-3.   14 art.; 1 infra.

97 RUBÍ Basili de, O.F.M.Cap.:   EstFranc 87,386s (1987) 325-1056; ERaurell
Frederic, biog. p. 329-360; portr. (de 1944); bibliog. p. 361-377 (Anna M.
Colomer i Casanovas).   20 art.; 2 infra.

98 SAINTE CROIX G. E. M. de: Crux, essays presented to ~, 75th b.,
ECartledge P. A., Harvey F. D. [→ 1,118]: History of Political Thought
6/1s.   Exeter 1985, Academic.   xx-380 p.; bibliog. p. viii-xii.   0-90785-01-0;
pa. 2-9.   16 art., infra.

SARTORI Luigi → e118: EDianich S., Tura E. R.,   Venti anni dopo il Concilio
Vaticano II 1985; bibliog. p. 215-230.

99 SAUER Georg: 60 Gb. = Amt und Gemeinde 37 (1986) 61-76 [ZAW
99,107].

100 SCHAUENBURG Konrad: Studien zur Mythologie und Vasenmalerei, ~
zum 65. Gb., ᴱBöhr Elke, *Martini* Wolfram. Mainz 1986, von Zabern.
xii-275 p.; 48 pl. [AntiqJ 67,159, Susan *Woodford*]. 3-8053-0898-1. 47 art.
101 SCHEFFCZYK Leo: Veritati catholicae ~, ᴱZiegenaus A., *al.* 1985 ➤ 1,122:
ᴿTrierTZ 95 (1986) 54-64 (R. *Weier:* längere Analysen).
102 SCHILLER A. Arthur: Studies in Roman law in memory of ~, ᴱBagnall
Roger S., *Harris* William V. Leiden 1986, Brill. xviii-168 p.; portr.;
bibliog. p. ix-xiv (*Szladits* Charles). 90-04-07568-2 [CdÉ 62,266, J.
Bingen]. 13 art.; 2 infra.
103 SCHNEIDER Josef: Die Kraft der Hoffnung: Gemeinde und Evangelium,
Fs. für Alterzbischof ~, zum 80. Gb., ᴱHierold Alfred E. Bamberg 1986,
St. Otto. 322 p. DM 49,80 pa. [TLZ 112,252; TR 83,337; ETL 63,407, F.
Neirynck].
104 SCHWEITZER Wolfgang: Tu deinen Mund auf für die Stummen; Beiträge
zu einer solidarischen Praxis der christlichen Gemeinde, ~ 70. Gb.,
ᴱHofmann F.-M., *Mechels* E. Gü 1986, Mohn. 264 p. DM 68.
3-579-00266-X [TsTNijm 27,322, G. *Heitink*].
105 SEGOVIA Augusto: Miscelánea: Biblioteca teológica Granadina 21.
Granada 1986, Fac. Teol. 437 p. pt. 4000 [TR 82,337]. – ᴿComSev 19
(1986) 445s (M. *Sánchez*).
106 SMITH Wilfred Cantwell: The world's religions traditions; essays in
honour of ~ ᴱWhaling F. NY 1986, Crossroad. 311 p. $15 [TS 47,759].
107 SPERNA Weiland J.: Filozofische theologie; opstellen voor ~. Baarn
1985, Ambo. 215 p. ƒ 32,50. – ᴿCollatVl 16 (1986) 481 (R. *Michiels*).
108 SPULER Bertold: Freundesgabe 75. Gb., ᴱFrei Hans: IkiZ 76,4 (1986)
193-319; portr.
109 STEIGER Lothar: Theologische Brosamen, 50. Gb., ᴱFreund G.,
Stegemann E.: DiehlBl Beih 5. Heid 1985. xi-637 p. [ZAW 99,302].
110 STENDAHL Krister: Christians among Jews and Gentiles; essays in honor
of ~, 65th b., ᴱNickelsburg George W. E., *MacRae* George W. = HarvTR
79,1-3 (1986). 320 p.; biobibliog. xi-xxviii; portr.
111 STILL William: Pulpit and people; essays in honour of ~, 75th b.,
ᴱCameron M., *Ferguson* S. E 1986, Rutherford. ix-148 p.; portr.
0-946068-18-6; pa. 9-4. [CalvinT 22,163, W. *Van Dyk*]. 13 art.; 7 infra.
112 SYLVAIN Philippe: Les ultramontains canadiens-français; études d'histoire
religieuse. Montréal 1985, Boréal-Express. 349 p. ➤ d830.
113 TOAFF Elio: Annuario di Studi Ebraici 1980-1984; studi sull'Ebraismo
presentati ad ~, ᴱToaff A., Collegio Rabbinico Italiano. R 1984,
Carucci. 491 p. 12 art. – ᴿHenoch 8 (1986) 119s (G. *Miletto*).
114 Tübingen, Evangelisches Stift: In Wahrheit und Freiheit, 450 Jahre ~,
ᴱHertel Friedrich: Quellen und Forschungen zur württembergischen
Kirchengeschichte 8. Stu 1986, Calwer. 340 p. DM 38 [TLZ 112,329, W.
Sparn].
115 TUFNELL Olga [† 11.IV.1985]: Palestine in the Bronze and Iron Ages — papers in honour of ~, ᴱTubb Jonathan: Occasional Publications [0141-8505]
11. L 1985, Univ. Inst. Archaeology. £20. 0-905853-151-16. 17 art.; infra.
115* USCATESCU Jorge: Cultura y existencia humana, homenaje al prof. ~,
ᴱMerino José A. M 1985, Rens. 448 p. – ᴿVerVida 44 (1986) 127
(Consuelo *Martínez Sicluna*).
116 VALENTINI Giuseppe: Studi albanologici, balcanici, bizantini e orientali in
onore di ~ S.J.: Studi Albanesi 6. F 1986, Olschki. xl-504 p.; bibliog.
p. xi-xxxviii. Lit. 97.000. 88-222-3390-5 [CC 138/2,203, A. *Ferrua*]. 23 art.,
2 infra.

117 VAWTER Bruce: The biblical heritage in modern Catholic scholarship, 65th b., ᴱCollins John J., *Crossan* John D.   Wilmington DE 1986, Glazier. 264 p. $13 pa. [CBQ 49,365, tit. pp.; OTAbs 10,91, tit. sans pp.].

118 VEREMANS Jozef: Hommages à ∼, ᴱDecreus Freddy, *Deroux* Carl: Latomus 193.   Bru 1986.   xiii-394 p.; portr.; bibliog. p. ix-xiii.   2-87031-133-8.   37 art.; 2 infra.

119 VETTERS Hermann: [I. = JbÖsA ➤ 1,142*] II. Lebendige Altertums-wissenschaft, 70. Gb., ᴱKandler Manfred, *al.*   Wien 1985, Holzhausen. xxxi-430 pl.; LV pl.; color. phot.; bibliog. p. xv-xxv, *Bodzenta* Maria. 3-900518-01-7.   104 art., plures infra.

120 VÖGTLE Anton: Auferstehung Jesu — Auferstehung der Christen; Deu-tungen des Osterglaubens; für ∼, 75. Gb., ᴱOberlinner Lorenz: QDisp 105. FrB 1986, Herder.   200 p.   DM 29,80.   3-451-02105-6.   7 art., infra. – ᴿSNTU-A 11 (1986) 221-4 (A. *Fuchs*); TLZ 111 (1986) 896s (T. *Holtz*: tit. pp.); TR 82 (1986) 305-8 (H. *Verweyen*).

121 WIBBING Siegfried: Leben lernen im Horizont des Glaubens, 60. Gb. Landau 1986, Hochschule Rh/Pf ev. Theologie-Seminar. vii-369 p. [ZAW 99,292].

122 WILKINSON Charles K.:   Essays on Near Eastern art and archaeology in honor of ∼, ᴱHarper Prudence O.   NY 1983, Metropolitan Museum. 93 p.; bibliog. p. 9-12.   0-87099-324-0.   6 art.; infra.

123 WILLIS William H.:   Classical studies, ᴱHobson Deborah, *McNamee* Kathleen = BASP 20 (1985) 373 p.

123* WILTERDINK Garret A. — a tribute: RefR 40,1 (Holland MI 1986) 60 p. on preaching.

124 WINTER Werner: Studia linguistica diachronica et synchronica, ∼ 60. Gb.   B 1985, Mouton de Gruyter.   xxi-985 p. – ᴿSalesianum 48 (1986) 1040-2 (R. *Gottlieb*: tit. sans pp.).

125 WOLFF H. W.:   Botschaft, ᴱJeremias J. 1981 ➤ 62,185 ... 65,152:   ᴿBZ 30 (1986) 110-2 (J. *Schreiner*: tit. pp.).

125* WOLTER Allan B.:   Essays honoring ∼, ᴱFrank W. A., *Etzkorn* G. J.: Publ. Theology 10.   St. Bonaventure NY 1985, Franciscan Institute. viii-345 p. [ETL 62, p. 12*].

126 WYSS Bernhard: Catalepton, 80 Gb., ᴱ*Schäublin* C.   Ba 1985, Sem. Klass. Pg.   212 p. [AnPg 56,817].

A1.2   **Miscellanea** *unius* auctoris.

126* *Thiel* Winfried,   Alttestamentliche Forschung in Aufsatzbänden [*Fohrer* G., *Kaiser* O., *Steck* O., *Westermann* C., *Wildberger* H.]: TRu 51 (1986) 335-348.

───────

127 **Amir** Yehoshua,   Studien zum Antiken Judentum: BErfAT (0722-0790) 2. Fra 1985, Lang.   viii-123 p.   3-8204-5610-4.   6 art., infra.

128 **Bachofen** Johann J. 1815-1887, Mutterrecht und Urreligion, ⁶ʳᵉᵛ[*Marx* Rudolf], *Kippenberg* H. G.: Taschenausgabe 52.   Stu 1984. Kroner. xl-366 p. DM 25.– ᴿOLZ 81 (1986) 541-3 (C. *Onasch*).

129 **Baldwin** Barry,   Studies on Greek and Roman history and literature: London Studies in Classical Philology 15.   Amst 1985, Gieben.   xiv-588 p. 90-70265-09-5.   82 art., 2 infra.

130 **Balthasar** Hans Urs von,   Puntos centrales de la fe [< Communio-Int etc.]. M 1985, BAC.   412 p. 84-220-1186-7. – ᴿEstE 61 (1986) 458 (J. A. *Estrada*).

131 **Bammel** Ernst, Judaica: Kleine Schriften I: WUNT 37. Tü 1986, Mohr. vi-331 p. 3-16-144971-1. 40 art.; 30 infra. [BL 87,100, B. *Lindars*; 36 reprints, German and English, + 4 inedita].

132 **Ben-Chorin** Schalom, Als Gott schwieg; ein jüdisches Credo. Mainz 1986, Grünewald. 95 p. DM 14,80 pa. 3 reprints + 2 inedita [TLZ 112,431].

132* **Best** Ernest, Disciples and discipleship; studies in the Gospel according to Mark [12 reprints 1970-82]. E 1986, Clark. xi-244 p. £12. 0-567-09369-7. – RExpTim 98 (1986s) 282 (J. *Muddiman*).

133 **Bickerman** E., † 1981. Studies in Jewish and Christian history, 3: ArbGJU 9. Leiden 1986, Brill. xvi-392 p. *f* 220. 90-04-07480-5 [BL 87,102, G. I. *Davies*].

134 **Bischoff** Bernhard. Anecdota novissima [inedita]; Texte des vierten bis sechszehnten Jahrhunderts: Quellen und Untersuchungen zur lateinischen Philologie des Mittelalters 7. Stu 1984, Hiersemann. cxii-292 p.; 5 pl. – RRHE 81 (1986) 226 (H. *Silvestre* gives a 'list' of the items, but with subdivisions and comments).

135 **Bornkamm** Günther, Studien zum Neuen Testament [→ 1,156*: extraits de quatre recueils précédents, sans source]. Mü 1985, Kaiser. 334 p. – RÉTRel 61 (1986) 446 (F. *Vouga*).

136 **Bottéro** Jean, Naissance de Dieu; la Bible et l'historien: Bibliothèque des histoires. P 1986, Gallimard. 255 p.; 2 maps. F 95. 2-07-070592-7. 5 art.; infra. – RÉTRel 61 (1986) 567-9 (D. *Lys*).

137 **Bottéro** Jean, Mythes et rites de Babylone [< ÉPHÉ 1973-9], préf. *Fleury* M.: ÉPHÉH 328, 1985 → 1,a679: RZAss 76 (1986) 126s (D. O. *Edzard*: wichtig).

138 **Burgmann** Hans, Zwei lösbare Qumrânprobleme; die Person des Lügenmannes; die Interkalation im Kalender [10 art. 1971-81]. Fra 1986, Lang. 299 p. Fs 65 pa. – RJStJud 17 (1986) 240s (F. *García Martínez*).

139 **Canivet** Maria Teresa Fortuna, Scritti e memorie, ECanivet Pierre, Oliva Giorgio. Vincenza 1986, Accademia Olimpica. 396 p.; portr.; map.; p. 13-63 biog., 359-361 bibliog.; 365-391 testimonianze. Lit. 50.000. 18 art.; 5 infra.

140 **Chatillon** Jean, D'Isidore de Séville [Questiones in Vetus Testamentum, typologie origénienne] à S. Thomas d'Aquin. L 1985, Variorum Reprints. x-336 p. £30. 15 art. – RRHE 81 (1986) 331s (F. *Hockey*).

140* **Chilton** Bruce, Targumic approaches to the Gospels; essays in the mutual definition of Judaism and Christianity: Studies in Judaism. Lanham MD 1986, UPA. xii-188 p. $12.25. 0-8191-5731-7; pa. 2-5. 11 essays, 'mostly new'; infra.

141 **Cipriani** Settimio, Per una Chiesa viva [→ 1,163*; 7 ristampe]; riflessioni biblico-teologiche su temi di attualità ecclesiali. Mi 1985, Àncora. 207 p. Lit. 11.500. – RAsprenas 33 (1986) 95s (A. *Rolla*); Claretianum 26 (1986) 363s (B. *Proietti*).

142 **Collins** Raymond F., Christian morality; biblical foundations [articles 1969-1983]. ND 1986, Univ. vi-258 p. $20. [RelStR 13,158, Pheme *Perkins*].

143 ECooperman B. D., Jewish thought in the sixteenth century: Harvard Judaic Texts and Studies 2. CM 1983, Harvard Center for Jewish Studies. xix-492 p. $30; pa. $15. 0-674-47462-7. – RJAAR 54 (1986) 169 (K. P. *Bland*: dazzled); JSS 31 (1986) 111 (S. C. *Reif*).

144 **Crahay** R., D'Érasme à Campanella [3 + 2 réimprimés + 1 sur Bodin]: ProbHistChr. Bru 1985, Univ. Libre. 161 p. Fb 525. 2-8004-0893-6. – RÉTRel 61 (1986) 454s (H. *Bost*).

145 **Crüsemann** F., Wie Gott die Welt regiert; Bibelauslegungen [bzw. Vorträge]: Traktat 90. Mü 1986, Kaiser. 80 p. DM 10 [ZAW 99,137]. 4 art., infra.

146 **Culican** William, Opera selecta; from Tyre to Tartessos: SIMA pocket 40. Göteborg 1986, Åström. 720 p.; ill.; bibliog. p. 7-25 (*Sagona* A. O.). 91-86098-41-1. 36 art., 6 infra.

147 **Dagron** Gilbert, La romanité chrétienne en Orient, héritages et mutations: CS 193, 1984 ➤ 65,178: ᴿRÉByz 43 (1985) 284s (A. *Failler*).

148 **Delumeau** Jean, Ce que je crois. P 1985, Grasset. – ᴿFoiVie 85,4 (1986) 77-79 (J. *Blondel*: série d'essais, interrogation des agnostiques par un historien catholique).

149 **Dennis** George T., Byzantium and the Franks, 1350-1420: Collected Studies 150. L 1982, Variorum. 320 p. – ᴿOrChrPer 52 (1986) 453s (C. *Capizzi*).

150 **Derrett** J. Duncan M., Studies in the New Testament, 4. Midrash, the composition of Gospels, and discipline. Leiden 1986, Brill. x-244 p. ƒ112 [TR 82,162]. 90-04-07478-3. 18 art., plures infra.

151 **Dolch** Heimo, Grenzgänge zwischen Naturwissenschaft und Theologie; gesammelte Aufsätze. Pd 1986, Schöningh. 434 p. [TR 83,161].

152 **Donadoni** Sergio F., Cultura dell'Antico Egitto; scritti di ∼, 70° compleanno, ᴱ**Amadasi Guzzo** Maria G. *al.* R 1986, Univ. xii-653 p.; biog. p. vii-xii (G. *Pugliese Carratelli*); bibliog. p. 641-7 (S. *Bosticco*). 75 art.; 5 infra.

153 **Drijvers** Han J. W., East of Antioch; studies in early Syriac Christianity. L 1984, Variorum. 340 p. 0-86078-146-1. 16 art.; 7 infra.

154 **Dumézil** Georges, L'oubli de l'homme et l'honneur des dieux; esquisses de mythologie. P 1985, NRF. 335 p. – ᴿRÉLat 63 (1985) 368s (J.-C. *Richard*).

155 **Ebach** J., Ursprung und Ziel; erinnerte Zukunft und erhoffte Vergangenheit; biblische Exegesen, Reflexionen, Geschichten. Neuk 1986. 176 p. DM 34. 3-7887-1209-0 [ZAW 99,139]. 8 art., infra.

155* **Ebeling** Gerhard, Lᴜᴛʜᴇʀstudien III. Begriffsuntersuchungen — Textinterpretationen — Wirkungsgeschichtliches. Tü 1985, Mohr. xvi- 602 p.

156 **Eco** Umberto, Travels in hyper reality; essays [fringe of hermeneutical; none biblical], ᵀ*Weaver* Wm. San Diego 1986, Harcourt-BJ. xii-307 p. 0-15-191079-0.

157 **Eco** Umberto, La estrategia de la ilusión [Semiologia quotidiana]. Barc 1986, Lumen. 380 p. – ᴿRazF 214 (1986) 255s (J. L. de *Noriega*).

158 **Eisenstein** Judah D., ⊕ *Oṣar ma'amrê Tᵉnak*, collected biblical writings. J 1982, Masora. 495 p. [KirSef 59,307].

159 **Fischer** Bonifatius, Beiträge zur Geschichte der lateinischen Bibeltexte: Vetus Latina, Aus der Geschichte 12. FrB 1986, Herder. 456 p. 3-451-00496-8. 8 art.

159* **Flusser** David, Bemerkungen eines Juden zur christlichen Theologie [Aufsätze 1968-83 + 1 ineditum]. Mü 1984, Kaiser. 104 p. [RHPR 66,334].

160 **Fransen** Piet F., Hermeneutics of the Councils and other studies, ᴱ*Mertens* H. E., *Graeve* F. de 1985 ➤ 1,174: ᴿTS 47 (1986) 160-2 (R. *Kress*).

161 **Frend** W. H. C., Saints and sinners in the early Church [selection of lectures at John Carroll University, Cleveland 1981]. L 1985, Darton-LT. 183 p. £4.50. – ᴿRHE 81 (1986) 329s (F. *Hockey*).

162 **Gadamer** Hans-Georg, The relevance of the beautiful and other essays. C 1986, Univ. xxiii-191 p. 0-521-24178-2; pa. 33953-7. 10 art.

163 **Garsoian** Nina G., Armenia between Byzantium and the Sasanians. L 1985, Variorum. 340 p. 0-86078-166-6. 12 art.

164 **Gese** Hartmut, Zur biblischen Theologie; alttestamentliche Vorträge^{2rev} [^{1}1977 ➤ 60,309; Eng. 1981 ➤ 63,211]. Tü 1983, Mohr. 239 p. DM 39. [TLZ 112,24].

164* **Goldschmidt** Victor, Écrits I. Études de philosophie ancienne ... P 1984, Vrin. 280 p. [RÉG 100,517, A. *Le Boulluec*].

165 **Gómez Caffarena** J., La entraña humanista del Cristianismo [ensayos 1975-82]. Bilbao 1984, Desclée-B. 357 p. – ^{R}RazF 214 (1986) 248s (J. A. *Candela*).

165* **Grässer** Erich, Der Alte Bund im Neuen [ineditum + 10 Nachdrücke], Exegetische Studien zur Israelfrage im Neuen Testament: WUNT 35, 1985 ➤ 1,180; DM 85; pa. 49: ^{R}NRT 108 (1986) 423 (X. *Jacques*); TLZ 111 (1986) 738-740 (W. *Schmithals*).

166 **Grech** Prosper, Ermeneutica e teologia biblica. R 1986, Borla. 441 p. Lit. 32.000. 88-263-0624-9. 23 art.; 14 infra.

167 **Hahn** Ferdinand, Exegetische Beiträge zum ökumenischen Gespräch [18 art. 1970-83]: GesAufs I. Gö 1986, Vandenhoeck & R. 354 p. DM 48 [NRT 109, 423, X. *Jacques*]. 3-525-58146-7. 18 art.; plures infra.

168 **Hanson** Richard P. C., [17] Studies in Christian antiquity 1985 ➤ 1,183; £17: ^{R}ClasR 100 (1986) 359s (W. H. C. *Frend*).

169 **Harder** Günter, Kirche und Israel; Arbeiten zum christlich-jüdischen Verhältnis, ^{E}*Osten-Sacken* Peter von der, (*Scherer* Richard): Studien zu jüdischem Volk und christlicher Gemeinde 7. B 1986, Inst. Kirche und Judentum. 287 p. DM 17,80.

170 **Hengel** Martin, The Cross of the Son of God [essays 1976-81]. L 1986, SCM. 304 p. £9.50. 0-334-01963-X [ExpTim 98,190].

171 **Herrmann** Siegfried, Gesammelte Studien zur Geschichte und Theologie des Alten Testaments: TBüch 75. Mü 1986, Kaiser. 236 p. [ZAW 97,143, tit. pp.]. 3-459-01618-3. 10 reprints + 2 inedita; infra.

172 **Hick** John, Problems of religious pluralism [1 ineditum + 8 articles since 1975, preliminary to an awaited systematic volume]. NY 1985, St. Martin's. x-148 p. $20. – ^{R}RelStR 12 (1986) 264 (P. C. *Hodgson*).

173 **Höffner** Joseph, In der Kraft des Glaubens (Ansprachen, Aufsätze, Interviews, Referate, Hirtenbriefe, Predigte des Erzbischofs von Köln aus den Jahren 1969-1986): I. Glaube und Sendung; II. Kirche-Gesellschaft. FrB 1986, Herder. xviii-615 p.; ix-697 p. DM 148 [TR 83,161].

174 **Holzner** J., San Paolo e la storia delle religioni [Gesammelte Aufsätze 1947; ital. = 1956], ^{T}*Rolla* A.: Alla scoperta della Bibbia 16, 1983 ➤ 64,5508: ^{R}Henoch 8 (1986) 406 (A. *Moda*).

175 **Iserloh** Erwin, Kirche — Ereignis und Institution; Aufsätze und Vorträge, I. Kirchengeschichte als Theologie; II. Geschichte und Theologie der Reformation: RefGStT Sup. 3. Münster 1985, Aschendorff. vii-520 p., portr.; vii-510 p. DM 120 [TLZ 112,38, B. *Lohse*].

176 **Jobling** David, The sense of biblical narrative [1 Sam 13-31; Num 11; 1 Kgs 17s; 1978 ➤ 60,3607; reprinted as vol. I, 1986]; II. [Gen 2s; 1 Sam 1-12; Num 32]: JStOT Sup 39. Sheffield 1986, Univ. 153 p. 1-85075-010-6; pa. 1-4. $18.50.

176* **Kasper** Walter, Faith and the future. L 1985, Burns & O. 140 p. £8.95. 0-86012-127-5 [ExpTim 98,222].

177 **Klauck** H. J., Brot vom Himmel; biblische Texte — für heute erschlossen [41 Überlegungen]. Wü 1985, Echter. 155 p. DM 19,80. 3-429-00962-6 [NTAbs 31,113].

178 **Knoche** Ulrich, Ausgewählte Kleine Schriften, EEhlers W.: BeiKlasPg 175. Fra 1986, Hain. xvi-482 p. 3-445-02454-7.

179 **Konidaris** Gerassimos, Ökumenischer Dialog ohne 'Konsensus'; wie kann die Una Sancta wiederhergestellt werden? [Aufsätze]. Würzburg c. 1985, Königshausen-Neumann. 318 p. DM 58. – RIstina 31 (1986) 431s (B. *Dupuy*).

180 **Kraan** K. J., Charismatische zielzorg, en andere opstellen, EMees J. G.: Past. Handreiking 48. Haag 1986, Voorhoeve. 199 p. f 29,50. 90-297-0816-6 [TsTNijm 26,437].

181 **Kraft** Konrad, Gesammelte Aufsätze zur antiken Geldgeschichte und Numismatik, II, ECastritius H., *Kienast* D. Da 1985, Wiss. vii-326 p.; 14 pl.

182 KRAUS Walther, Aus allem eines; Studien zur antiken Geistesgeschichte, 80. Gb. Heid 1984, Stiehm. 485 p. DM 148. – RRPLH 60 (1986) 131s (M. *Menu*: tit. pp.).

183 KUTSCH Ernst, Kleine Schriften zum Alten Testament, zum 65. Gb., ESchmidt Ludwig, *Eberlein* Karl: BZAW 168. B 1986, de Gruyter. ix-392 p.; bibliog. p. 376-392. DM 152 [TR 83,102s, J. *Scharbert*: tit. pp. + Ursprung; ZAW 98,468s, tit. pp.]. 3-11-010316-8. 20 art., infra.

184 **Lash** Nicholas, Theology on the way to Emmaus [lectures 1982-4, not about Emmaus]. L 1986, SCM. xii-240 p. [TLond 90,138, N. *Sagovsky*]. 0-334-02352-1. – RExpTim 98 (1986s) 217 (D. F. *Ford*).

185 **Leacock** Eleanor Burke, Myths of male dominance [*Lévi-Strauss*]; collected articles on women cross-culturally. NY 1981, Monthly Review. 344 p. $17.50; pa. $10.– RRelStR 12 (1986) 263 (Sandra W. *Perpich*).

186 LOHFF Wenzel, Fundus des Glaubens; Zugänge zur Begründung elementaren Glaubenswissens [15 Art., 60. Gb.]. Gö 1986, Vandenhoeck & R. 207 p. [TR 83,312, H. *Wagner*]. DM 30.

187 **Long** Charles, Significations; signs, symbols, and images in the interpretation of religion [12 articles of a black American]. Ph 1986, Fortress. 207 p. $12.95 pa. [RelStR 13,230, J. *Evans*].

188 **Lüling** G., Sprache und archaisches Denken; Neun Aufsätze zur Geistes- und Religionsgeschichte. Erlangen 1985, H. Lüling. 239 p. DM 29,60 [ZAW 99,146].

189 **Macquarrie** John, Theology, Church and ministry. L 1986, SCM. 211 p. £6.95. 0-334-02353-X [ExpTim 98,191].

190 **Martini** Carlo M., Per una santità di popolo; lettere, discorsi e interventi 1985. Bo 1986, Dehoniane. 641 p. Lit. 25.000. 88-10-10860-4. 45 art.; 4 infra.

191 MAZAR Benjamin, (80th b.). The early biblical period [15 reprints 1945-81]. J 1986, Israel Expl. Soc. 276 p. $24. 965-221-005-6. – RBAR-W 12,6 (1986) 10.12s (P. J. *King*); PhoenixEOL 32,2 (1986) 59 (K. R. *Veenhof*).

192 **Mettinger** T. N. D., Eva och revbenet [6 art.]: Religio 16, 1984 ⮕ 65,216: RTsTKi 57 (1986) 229s (Helge S. *Kvanvig*).

193 **Michel** Otto, Dienst am Wort; gesammelte Aufsätze, EHaacker K. Neuk 1986. 288 p. DM 48 [TLZ 112,514]. 3-7887-1218-X.

194 **Muilenburg** James (1896-1974), selections EBest Thomas F., Hearing and speaking the Word. Atlanta 1985, Scholars. xv-448 p. $27.

195 **Nagel** Thomas, Über das Leben, die Seele und den Tod [Moral questions], TPrankel K.-E., *Stoecker* R. Königstein 1984, Hain. 220 p. DM 28 pa. – RZEvEth 30 (1986) 466-8 (G. *Geisthardt*).

195* **Neusner** Jacob, The public side of learning; the political consequences of scholarship in the context of Judaism: AAR Studies in Religion 40. Chico CA 1985, Scholars. xii-135 p. $18. 0-87130-860-1; pa. 1-X [NTAbs 30,253].

196 **Noth** Martin, Estudios sobre el Antiguo Testamento: BiblEstB 44, 1985
➤ 1,220*: ᴿCiuD 199 (1986) 329 (A. *Salas*); EstE 61 (1986) 479 (J. *Alonso Díaz*); SalT 74 (1986) 155.

197 **Oesterreicher** John M., The new encounter between Christians and Jews.
NY 1986, Philosophical. 470 p. $25 [TDig 33,483].

198 **Ogden** Schubert M., On theology [8 reprints 1971-82, including Revelation, Authority of Scripture]. SF 1986, Harper & R. xi-160 p. £19.95 [JBL 105, 754].

199 **Padilla** C. René, Misión integral; ensayos sobre el Reino y la Iglesia.
Buenos Aires 1986, Nueva Creación. 212 p. 0-8028-0902-2 [EstE 61,490].

200 **Panikkar** R., Myth, faith and hermeneutics, Bangalore, Asian Trading.
500 p. – ᴿAnnals Bhandarkar 1 (1985) 269-273 (V. N. *Dhavale*).

201 **Pannenberg** Wolfhart, Ética y Eclesiología, ᵀ*Martínez de Lapera* Victor
A.; Verdad e Imagen 71. Salamanca 1986, Sígueme. 261 p. 84-301-
0986-2. – ᴿActuBbg 23 (1986) 242 (F. *Manresa*: 13 art. 1962-75 más dos inéditos).

202 **Papandreou** Damaskinos, Orthodoxie und Ökumene, Gesammelte
Aufsätze, ᴱ*Schneemelcher* Wilhelm. Stu 1986, Kohlhammer. 226 p.
DM 49,80 [TLZ 112,312, H. *Krüger*].

202* **Pathrapankal** Joseph, Critical and creative; studies in Bible and theology.
Bangalore 1986, Dharmaram. xi-179 p. 14 art.; 12 infra.

203 **Patzer** Harald, Gesammelte Schriften, ᴱ*Leimbach* Rüdiger, *Seidel*
Gabriele. Stu 1985, Steiner. 515 p. 3-515-04428-0.

204 **Pfülf** Otto, Von den Herrlichkeiten der Kirchengeschichte; Gesammelte
Aufsätze 1889-1914 [< Stimmen aus Maria-Laach], ᴱ*Haacke* Rhaban.
Siegburg 1984, F. Schmitt. 1002 p.; 788 p. DM 190. – ᴿTR 82 (1986) 122s
(J. *Overath*: trotz dem Titel zeigt Kirchengeschichte als Kreuzestheologie).

205 **Plöger** Josef G., In der Nähe des Herrn; biblische Besinnungen. FrB
1986, Herder. 95 p.

206 **Prete** B., L'opera di Luca, contenuti e prospettive [ristampe, quelle già in
Storia e Teologia 1973 più altre]. T-Leumann 1986, LDC. 591 p. Lit.
35.000. – ᴿRasT 27 (1986) 384 (V. *Fusco*).

207 **Propp** Vladimir, Theory and history of folklore [essays, including *Lévi-
Strauss* attack which it answers], ᵀ*Martin* Ariadna Y. & Richard P.,
ᴱ*Liberman* Anatoly: Theory and History of Literature 5. Minneapolis
1985, Univ. Minnesota. lxxxi-252 p. $29.50; pa. $13. – ᴿRelStR 12 (1986)
134 (R. A. *Segal*).

208 **Rad** Gerhard von, Scritti sul Vecchio Testamento [1973], ᵀ*Dusini* Antonio:
Già e non ancora 74, 1984 ➤ 1,229: ᴿRivStoLR 22 (1986) 576s (P. G.
Borbone).

209 **Räisänen** Heikki, The Torah and Christ; essays in German and English on
the problem of the Law in early Christianity: Suomen Eksegeettisen Seuran
Julkaisuja, Publications of the Finnish Exegetical Soc. 45. Helsinki 1986,
Finnish Exegetical Soc., Neitsytpolku 1 b.00140. viii-377 p. 951-
9217-00-2. 13 art.; + 3 inedita, 3 infra.

210 **Rauschenbusch** Walter, Selected Writings 1984 ➤ 1,233*: ᴿPrincSemB 7
(1986) 91s (D. B. *Whitlock*).

211 **Ricoeur** Paul, Tempo e racconto [1983 ➤ 55,8451], I: Di fronte e attraverso
165. Mi 1986, Jaca. 340 p.

212 **Ricoeur** Paul, Du texte à l'action; essais d'herméneutique [I. Conflit
d'interprétations 1969]; II: Esprit. P 1986, Seuil. 414 p. 2-02-009377-4.

213 **Rosenstock-Huessy** Eugen, The origin of speech, intr. *Stahmer* Harold.
Norwich VT 1981, Argo. 142 p. [RelStR 13,238, R. R. *Williams*].

214 **Sacon** K. K., ❹ *Toki wo Ikiru* [To live through time; 40 essays, 11 on Jeremiah]. Tokyo 1986, Yorudan-sha. 246 p. Y 1800 [BL 87,54].

215 **Schieber** Alexander [d.IV.1985], Essays on Jewish folklore and comparative literature. Budapest 1985, Akadémiai. 396 p. + ❹ 56. ft 456. – ᴿJudaica 42 (1986) 106s (S. *Schreiner*).

216 SCHLICHTING Günter [TWNT-Assistent], Der Schatz im Acker der Zeit; Theologica [12 art.] et Ratisbonensia [9; zum 75. Gb.]. Fürth 1986, Flacius. 369 p. [TLZ 112,493].

217 **Schneider** Gerhard, Lukas, Theologe der Heilsgeschichte; Aufsätze zum lukanischen Doppelwerk: BoBB. Bonn 1985, Hanstein. – ᴿETL 62 (1986) 194-6 (F. *Neirynck*).

217* **Schneiders** Sandra M., New wineskins; re-imagining religious life today. Mahwah NJ 1986, Paulist. vi-309 p. $11 pa. 13 art. [TDig 33,487]. – ᴿAmerica 155 (1986) 266.268 (Colette *Mahoney*).

218 **Schoonenberg** Piet, Auf Gott hin denken; deutschsprachige Schriften zur Theologie, ᴱ*Zauner* Wilhelm. W 1986, Herder. 267 p.; bibliog. 25-28. DM 35 [TR 83,73].

219 **Schwager** Raymund, Der wunderbare Tausch; zur Geschichte und Deutung der Erlösungslehre [10 Art. < ZkT 1980-6 über Patres und *Girard* R.]. Mü 1986, Kösel. 327 p. DM 34 [TR 83, 319, J. *Werbick*]. 3-466-20279-5.

220 **Smend** Rudolf, Die Mitte des Alten Testaments, Gesammelte Studien I: BeiEvT 99. Mü 1986, Kaiser. 246 p. 3-459-01658-2 [TR 83,249]. 12 art., plures infra.

221 **Sobrino** Jon, Liberación con espíritu; apuntes para una nueva espiritualidad. Santander 1985, Sal Terrae. 219 p. – ᴿRazF 214 (1986) 364 (J. *Royo*).

222 **Stead** Christopher G., Substance and illusion in the Christian Fathers. L 1985, Variorum Reprints. xi-330 p. £30. 16 art. – ᴿRHE 81 (1986) 329 (F. *Hockey*).

223 **Steinberg** Aaron, History as experience; aspects of historical thought, universal and Jewish. NY 1983, Ktav. 486 p. – ᴿIstina 31 (1986) 226s (B. *Dupuy*).

224 **Stob** Henry, Theological reflections [29 art. 1950-80], 1981 → 62,296: ᴿThemelios 11 (1985s) 105 (B. *Demarest*).

225 **Stockmeier** Peter, Glaube und Kultur — Studien zur Begegnung von Christentum und Antike: BeiTheolRelW 1983 → 1,251: ᴿTrierTZ 95 (1986) 69s (E. *Sauser*).

226 **Stuhlmacher** Peter, Reconciliation, law and righteousness; essays in biblical theology [11 from 1960-79], ᵀᴱ*Kalin* Everett R. Ph 1986, Fortress. 200 p. 0-8006-0770-8. – ᴿExpTim 98 (1986s) 148 (D. *Hill*: ably translated).

227 **Talmon** Shamaryahu, King, cult and calendar in ancient Israel; collected studies. J 1986, Magnes. 244 p. $22. 965-223-651-9. 10 art.; infra.

228 **Torrance** Thomas F., The Christian frame of mind [four lectures 1977-84]. E 1985, Handsel. 62 p. $3.50. – ᴿRefTR 45 (1986) 29 (G. A. *Cole*: the best access to one of the great Protestant minds of this generation).

229 **Vawter** Bruce, The path of wisdom; biblical investigations: Background Books 3. Wilmington 1986, Glazier. 326 p. $12.95 pa. 0-89453-466-1 [CBQ 49,365: tit. pp. date; OTAbs 10,92, tit. without pp. or source].

230 **Vischer** Wilhelm, L'Écriture et la parole [6 inédits, 4 réimprimés]: Essais Bibliques 12, 1985 → 1,258*; Fs 25: ᴿEsprV 96 (1986) 551s (É. *Cothenet*).

231 **Whitlau** W., Niet in de hemel; verkenningen in de wereld van de Joodse traditie [32 art.]. Baarn 1985, Ten Have. 256 p. – ᴿCollatVl 16 (1986) 496s (R. *Hoet*).

232 **Wirth** Gerhard, Studien zur Alexandergeschichte [16 reprints]. Da 1985, Wiss. ix-399 p. DM 75. – ᴿClasR 100 (1986) 330 (S. *Hornblower*).

233 **Zmijewski** Josef, Das Neue Testament — Quelle christlicher Theologie und Glaubenspraxis; Aufsätze zum NT und seiner Auslegung. Stu 1986, KBW. 390 p. DM 39 [TLZ 112, 194, tit. pp.; ZkT 109,211, M. *Hasitschka*]. 3-460-32441-4. 10 art. 1973-85 + 2 inedita; infra.

A1.3 *Plurium compilationes* **biblicae.**

234 ᴱ**Armstrong** A. H., Classical Mediterranean spirituality; Egyptian, Greek, Roman: ➤ 588, Enc. World Spirituality 15. NY 1986, Crossroad. xxiv-517 p. $49.50. 0-8245-0764-9 [OTAbs 10,202].

235 ᴱ**Ashton** John (p. 1-17), The interpretation of John: IssuesRT 9. L/Ph 1986, SPCK/Fortress. x-182 p.; bibliog. p. 174-8. £7.95. 0-281-04213-6 / 0-8006-1774-6. 8 art.; infra.

235* ᴱ**Avisar** Samuel, Tremila anni di letteratura ebraica ➤ 65,1039 [antologia; commentaires bibliques 554-576; Esséniens 201-225; Qaraïtes 577-588 ...]: Cultura Ebraica, 19.22. R 1980/2, Carucci. xvi-588 p.; xvi-676 p. – ᴿRÉJ 145 (1986) 425s (J.-P. *Rothschild*).

236 *Baldermann* Ingo, al. [*Hanowski* Bernd, *Welker* Michael, Präsent. 'für die Herausgeber'], Einheit und Vielfalt biblischer Theologie: JbBT 1 (1986). 252 p. 3-7887-1229-5. 10 art.; 2 recens.; infra.

236* ᴱ**Barbero** Giorgio, *al.,* Ebraismo e cristianesimo: Storia delle idee politiche, economiche e sociali 2/1. T 1985, UTET. viii-678 p.; 21 pl. [KirSef 60,621].

237 ᴱ**Belaval** Yvon, *Bourel* Dominique, Le siècle des Lumières et la Bible: Bible de tous les temps 7. P 1986, Beauchesne. 869 p. F 480 [TLZ 112, 494 H. *Reventlow*].

238 ᴱ**Bosman** L., *Deist* F. F., Old Testament Essays 3. Pretoria 1985, Univ. 102 p. [ZAW 99,149, tit. pp.].

239 ᴱ**Burden** J. J., *Le Roux* J. H., Old Testament Essays 4 [incl. Studienreise BR-Schweiz 1984]. Pretoria 1986, Univ. 221 p. $6. [ZAW 99,295 tit. pp.].

240 ᴱ**Carson** D. A., *Woodbridge* John D., Hermeneutics, authority and canon. GR/Leicester 1986, Academie/Inter-Varsity. xii-468 p. $17 [TR 83,426]. 0-85111-572-1.

242 ᴱ**Cohen** Arthur A., *Mendes-Flohr* Paul, Contemporary Jewish religious thought; [140 specially commissioned] original essays on critical concepts, movements, and beliefs. NY 1986, Scribner's. xix-1163 p. $75. – ᴿTDig 33 (1986) 465 (W. C. *Heiser*).

243 ᴱ**Denny** Frederick M., *Taylor* Rodney L., The Holy Book in comparative perspective: Studies in Comparative Religion 1. Columbia 1985, Univ. South Carolina. viii-252 p. $20. – ᴿRelStR 12 (1986) 134 (J. *Strong*).

244 ᴱ**Elliott** John H., Social-scientific criticism of the New Testament and its social world: Semeia 35. Decatur GA 1986, Scholars (infra).

245 ᴱ**Fasching** Darrell J., The Jewish people in Christian preaching: Symposium Series, 10. NY 1985, Mellen. x-113 p. $11.95. – ᴿHorizons 13 (1986) 438 (A. *Mittleman*).

245* ᴱ**Fontaine** Jacques, *Pietri* Charles, Le monde latin antique et la Bible: Bible de tous les temps 2. P 1985, Beauchesne. 672 p. – ᴿRHE 81 (1986) 528-530 (P.-M. *Bogaert*).

246 ᴱ**Friedman** M. A., *Gil M.*, ➒ Te'uda IV; studies in Judaica. TA 1986, Univ. 275 p.; xxv p. Eng. summ. – 19 art. [ZAW 99,301 ohne pp.] – Te'uda III (1983 ➤ 65,284*) 17 art., 4 infra.

KENRICK SEMINARY LIBRARY
5200 GLENNON DRIVE
ST. LOUIS, MISSOURI 63119

247 EHahn F., Der Erzähler des Evangeliums; methodische Neuansätze in der Markusforschung: SBS 118s. Stu 1985, KBW. 200 p. DM 31,20 pa. 3-460-04181-1. 7 art., infra. – ᴿSNTU-A 11 (1986) 232-5 (A. *Fuchs*).

248 EHamenachem Ezra, ❿ *Hgwt bmqr'* ,,, biblical reflections: Israel Bible Society, in memory of Y. Roɴ, vol. 4. TA 1983, 'Am 'Obed. 206 p.

249 EHartman Geoffrey H., *Budick* Sanford, Midrash and literature [18 essays, Hebrew Univ. project 1983-5]. NHv 1986, Yale. xvii-412 p.; bibliog. p. 369-395. $37.50. 0-300-03453-9. 18 art., infra. – ᴿVT 36 (1986) 511 (S. C. *Reif*).

250 EHoffman Lawrence A., The land of Israel; Jewish perspectives. ND 1986, Univ. x-340 p. $30 [RelStR 13,171, D. R. *Blumenthal*].

251 EHoffmann R. J., The origins of Christianity; a critical introduction [excerpts from leading modern authors]. Buffalo 1985, Prometheus. 326 p. $15 pa. 0-87975-308-0 [NTAbs 30,344].

251* EHollander H. W., *Tuinstra* E. W., Bijbel vertalen; liefhebberij of wetenschap? [Bible translation, hobby or science?] Haarlem/Bru 1985, Bijbelgenootschap. 118 p. [< ETL 62, p. 13*].

252 EJeppesen K., *Cryer* F. H., Tekster og tolkninger — ti (10) studier i Det gamle testamente. Aarhus 1986, Arus. 175 p. Dk 118. 87-7457-045-5. [BL 87,66s, S. *Holm-Nielsen*: without titles or pp.].

253 EJohnston Robert K., The use of the Bible in theology; evangelical options. Atlanta 1986, Knox. $12. [0530-2 in adv Interp 40,83].

254 EJonge M. de, Outside the Old Testament: CamCW. C 1986, Univ. xv-263 p. £11.95.

255 EKraft Robert A., *Nickelsburg* George W. E., Early Judaism and its modern interpreters: SBL The Bible and its Modern Interpreters 2. Ph/Atlanta 1986, Fortress/Scholars. xviii-494 p. 0-8006-0722-8 / 0-89130-669-2; pa. 884-9. 17 art.; infra.

256 EKronholm T., *al.*, Jødedom och kristendom under de första århundradena; Nordiskt patristikprojekt 1982-1985. Oslo 1986, Univ. 308 p. Nk 240. 82-00-07688-1 [NTAbs 31,123]. 16 art.: *Jeppesen* K., New covenant; *Gerhardsson* B., Jesus and Torah; *Müller* M., intertestamental Messiah; *Olsson* B., Petrine traditions ...

257 EKvalbein H., Blant skriftlærde og fariseere; Jødedommen i oldtiden. Oslo 1984, Verbum. 274 p.; 3 maps. 82-543-0248-0. 11 art., incl. *Weyde* K. on temple; *Hvalvik* R. on Sadducees and Pharisees; *Borgen* P. on Philo [NTAbs 30,375].

258 EMcKim Donald K., A guide to contemporary hermeneutics; major trends in biblical interpretation [20 mostly reprints]. GR 1986, Eerdmans. xx-385 p. $13.95 pa. 0-8028-0094-1 [NTAbs 31,93].

260 Neusner Jacob, New humanities and academic disciplines; the case of Jewish studies. Madison 1984, Univ. Wisconsin. xxvii-187 p. $27.50. – ᴿJRel 66 (1986) 97s (M. H. *Vogel*).

261 EPalmer Bernard V., Medicine and the Bible: Christian Medical Fellowship. Exeter 1986, Paternoster. 272 p. £7.95 pa. 0-85364-423-3. 9 art.; infra. [BL 87,89, C. S. *Rodd*].

262 EPreminger Alex, *Greenstein* Edward L., The Hebrew Bible in literary criticism: Library of Literary Criticism. NY 1986, Ungar. xvi-619 p. $65. 0-8044-3266-X [OTAbs 10,195].

263 Ricoeur Paul (*Levinas* Emmanuel, *Haulotte* Edgar, *al.*) La Révélation² [¹1977 ➤ 58,250]: Publ. 7. Bru 1984, Fac. Univ. S. Louis. 238 p. 2-8028-0007-8.

264 ᴱRossano Pietro, Tradurre la Bibbia per il popolo di Dio, Morcelliana 1925-85, present. *Minelli* Stefano: Humanitas Quad. Brescia 1986, Morcelliana. 123 p. Lit. 12.000 [TR 83,161].
265 **Schelbert** G., *al.*, Methoden der Evangelien-Exegese: TBer 13. Z 1985, Benziger. 187 p. [< ETL 62, p. 17*].
266 ᴱ**Stachowiak** L., *Rubinkiewicz* R., ❷ Duch Święty — Duch Boży: Materiały pomocznicze do wykładów z biblistyki. Lublin c. 1984, KUL. 8 art.; infra [< RuBi 39,88 without date].
267 ᴱ**Stern** M., Nation and history; studies in the history of the Jewish people, I. J 1983, Shazar.
268 ᴱ**Strolz** Walter, Vom alten zum neuen Adam; Urzeitmythos und Heilsgeschichte: Oratio Dominica 13. FrB 1986, Herder. 223 p. DM 46 [TLZ 112,535].
269 ᴱ**Timberg** Thomas A., Jews in India. NY 1986, Advent. viii-374 p. $35 [RelStR 13,171, H. H. *Paper*].
270 ᴱ**Walter** Karin, Frauen entdecken die Bibel: Frauenforum. FrB 1986, Herder. 200 p. DM 19,80. – ᴿOrientierung 50 (1986) 202s, Vorabdruck [*Sturm* Vilma].
271 ᴱ**Wenham** David, *Blomberg* Craig, The miracles of Jesus: Gospel Perspectives 6. Sheffield 1986, JStOT. 457 p. $13.50 [TR 83,75: tit. pp.]. 1-85075-008-4; pa. 9-2. 13 art.; infra.

A1.4 *Plurium compilationes* **theologicae.**

274 ᴱ**Adams** James L., *al.*, The thought of Paul TILLICH. SF 1985, Harper & R. – ᴿTS 47 (1986) 723-5 (C. D. *Hardwick*: SCHARLEMANN R. on art best).
274* ᴱ**Alberigo** G., Il Vaticano II e la Chiesa: BiblCuRel 47. Brescia 1985, Paideia. 472 p. Lit. 35.000. – ᴿActuBbg 23 (1986) 54-57 (J. *Riudor*).
275 ᴱ**Ancilli** Ermanno, *Paparozzi* Maurizio, La mistica, fenomenologia e riflessione teologica [I, 115-250, esperienza di Dio nella Bibbia] 1984 → 65,315: ᴿSalesianum 48 (1986) 431-4 (A. M. *Triacca*: per la parte biblica, perché non tracciare la mistica dei seguaci di Cristo?).
275* ᴱ**Bakker** L. A. R., *Goddijn* H. P. M., Joden en christenen; een moeizaam gesprek door de eeuwen heen: Annalen van het Thijmgenootschap 73/2. Baarn 1985, Ambo. 181 p. [< ETL 62, p. 9*].
276 ᴱ**Barringer** Robert, Rome and Constantinople; essays in the dialogue of love [1982 Sts. Peter and Andrew Lectures]. Brookline MA 1984, Holy Cross Orthodox. 86 p. [73-85, *Belonick* Deborah, Feminist theology]. – ᴿOstkSt 35 (1986) 47s (Maria *Bayer*).
277 ᴱ**Basinger** David & Randall, Predestination and free will; four views of divine sovereignty and human freedom. DG 1986, InterVarsity. 180 p. $7 pa. – ᴿWestTJ 48 (1986) 391-8 (G. L. W. *Johnson*; lacks depth).
278 ᴱ**Blank** Josef, *Werbick* Jürgen, Sühne und Versöhnung: Theologie zur Zeit 1. Dü 1986, Patmos. 172 p. DM 26 [TLZ 112,460].
279 ᴱ**Braaten** Carl E., *Jenson* Robert W., Christian dogmatics in Lutheran perspective I-II. Ph 1984, Fortress. 624 p.; 640 p.; $25 each; both $46. – ᴿInterpretation 40 (1986) 191-3 (R. F. *Thiemann*).
280 ᴱ**Bruggen** C. van der, *Ladrière* J., *Morren* L., Éthique, science et foi chrétienne. Wavre 1985, Presses LvN. 410 p. [< ETL 62, p. 18*].
281 ᴱ**Brown** Neil, Christians in a pluralist society: Faith and culture 12. Sydney 1986, Catholic Inst. viii-152 p. 0-908224-11-7.
282 ᴱ**Channer** J. H., Abortion and the sanctity of human life. Exeter 1985, Paternoster. 151 p. £2.95. 0-85364-417-9. – ᴿExpTim 2d choice 97,10

(1985s) 290s (C. S. *Rodd*); TLond 39 (1986) 407s (W. M. *Jacob*: notes *Rogerson* J., Using the Bible...).

283 ᴱ**Chaunu** Pierre, L'aventure de la Reforme; le monde de Jean CALVIN: 1986, DDB/Hermé. 296 p. F 490 [Études 365, 415].

284 Chemins de la Christologie africaine: JJC 25. P 1986, Desclée. 312 p. – ᴿEsprV 96 (1986) 535s (P. *Jay*: 'livre' par décret d'éditeur).

285 ᴱ**Chinnici** Joseph P., Devotion to the Holy Spirit in [1865-1900] American Catholicism. NY 1985, Paulist. 227 p. $13. – ᴿTS 47 (1986) 561 (J. *Hennesey*).

Cikala Musharhamina M., Afrikanische Spiritualität ... Inkulturation 1986 ➤ h8.6.

287 **Communio**, revue catholique internationale 11 [= IkaZ 15 *al*.] (1986): **1.** L'Esprit saint; **2.** Les immigrés; **3.** Le Royaume; **4.** Lire l'Écriture; **5.** La pauvreté; **6.** La famille [deutsch IkaZ fasc. **2.** Reich Gottes; **3.** Die Bibel lesen; **4.** Meditation und Spiritualität].

288 **Concilium** 1986 [ital. deutsch (125) vol. 22;] **183** (franç. español 203), Christianity among world religions, ᴱ*Küng* H., *Moltmann* J.; **184** (F/E 204), Forgiveness, ᴱ*Floristán* Casiano, *Duquoc* Christian; **185** (F/E 205), Church; its law — its reality, ᴱ*Provost* James, *Wolf* Knut; — **186** (F/E 206), La religion populaire, ᴱ*Greinacher* Norbert, *Mette* Norbert; — **187** (F/E 207), Option for the poor; challenge to the rich countries, ᴱ*Boff* Leonardo, *Elizondo* Virgil; — **188** (F/E 208), Synod 1985, an evaluation, ᴱ*Alberigo* Giuseppe, *Provost* James. c. 120 p. each, F 60; Lit. 8.000; DM 15; £6/$10.

289 ᴱ**Conn** Joann W., Women's spirituality; resources for Christian development. Mahwah NJ 1986, Paulist. viii-327 p. [23 items] $12 pa. [TDig 34,96].

290 ᴱ**Coontz** Stephanie, *Henderson* Peta, Women's work, men's property; the origins of gender and class. L 1986, Verso. xi-220 p. $10 [RelStR 13,149, Kathryn A. *Rabuzzi*].

291 ᴱ**Curran** Charles E., *McCormick* Richard A., Official Catholic social teaching; readings in moral theology 5. NY 1986, Paulist. xi-459 p. $10. 25 art. – ᴿRelStR 12 (1986) 274 (T. R. *Ulshafer*: includes Catholic critique; pity no index).

292 ᴱ**Daiber** K.-F., *Luckmann* G. A., Religion in den Gegenwartsströmungen der deutschen Soziologie 1983 ➤ 1,337: ᴿZEvEth 30 (1986) 461-3 (W.-D. *Bukow*).

293 ᴱ**Deuser** Hermann, *Steinacker* Peter, Ernst BLOCHS Vermittlung zur Theologie. Mü/Mainz 1983, Kaiser/Grunewald. 222 p. DM 42. 8 art.; bibliog. – ᴿNRT 108 (1986) 598 (B. *Pottier*); RelStR 12 (1986) 271 (T. H. *West*); TR 82 (1986) 51s (H.-G. *Janssen*).

294 ᴱ**Dhavamony** M., Saints in world religions: Studia Missionalia 35. R 1986, Pont. Univ. Gregoriana.

295 ᴱ**Dijk** D. *al.*, Feministisch-theologische teksten: Sleutelteksten in godsdienst en theologie 2. Delft 1986, Meinema. 150 p. ƒ27,50. 90-211-6101-X [TsTNijm 26,438].

295* Ebraismo, ellenismo, cristianesimo = Archivio di Filosofia 53,1.2s (1985) 391 p.; 483 p. [< ETL 62, p. 11*].

296 ᴱ**Ecker** Gisela, Feminist aesthetics [11 essays], ᵀ*Anderson* Harriet. Boston 1985, Beacon. 187 p., ill. $10 [RelStR 13,62, Kathryn A. *Rabuzzi*].

297 L'Église et les hommes, 2. Révélation et traditions: Les Chemins de la Foi [manuel de collège] 2s. P 1984, Droguet & A. / Fayard. 309 p. + 291 p.; ill. F 75 chaque [NRT 109,631, A. *Toubeau*].

298 EEicher Peter, Theologie der Befreiung im Gespräch. Mü 1985, Kösel. 128 p. – RTPhil 61 (1986) 619s (M. *Sievernich*).
299 EEisenstadt S. N., The origins and diversity of axial civilizations [I. Greece; II. Israel ...]. Albany 1986, SUNY. xiii-556 p. $44.50; pa. $20 [RelStR 13,233, J. C. *Holt*].
300 EFabris Rinaldo, La spiritualità del Nuovo Testamento: Storia della Spiritualità 2. R 1985, Borla. 439 p. Lit. 25.000. 88-263-0430-0 [NTAbs 30,239]. – RTeresianum 37 (1986) 242s (V. *Pasquetto*).
301 EFaria Stella, *al.*, The emerging Christian woman; church and society perspectives. Pune 1984, Satprakashan Sanchar Kendra/Ishvant. xii-292 p. rs. 32, p. 25. – RVidyajyoti 49 (1985) 146s (Elsy *Paul*).
302 EFloristán C., *Tamayo* J.-J., El Vaticano II, veinte años después 1985 → 1,345: RNRT 108 (1986) 440s (A. *Toubeau*).
303 EFurcha E. J., *Pipkin* H. Wayne, Prophet, pastor, Protestant; the work of Huldrych ZWINGLI after five hundred years: Pittsburgh Theol. Mon. 11. Allison Park PA 1984, Pickwick. xii-192 p. $15. 11 art. – RScotJT 39 (1986) 271s (A. E. *McGrath*); SR 15 (1986) 404s (J. W. *Baker*).
304 EGeffré Claude, *Jossua* Jean-Pierre, Monotheism: Concilium 187, 1985 → 1,334: RRelStT 6 (1986) 46-48 (H. A. *Megnell*).
304* EGiltner Fern M., Women's issues in religious education. Birmingham AL 1985, Rel. Ed. viii-190 p. $13 pa. – [Horizons 14, 204-6, Maura *Campbell*].
305 EGössmann Elisabeth, Das wohlgelahrte Frauenzimmer / Eva — Gottes Meisterwerk: Archiv für philosophie- und theologiegeschichtliche Frauenforschung 1s. Mü 1985, 'iudicium'. – / 290 p. – RTR [81 (1985) *Rieger*] 82 (1986) 295s (Anne *Jensen*).
306 EGorman Margaret, Psychology and religion; a reader. NY 1985, Paulist. xi-324 p. $12. – RRelStR 12 (1986) 44 (J. F. *Byrnes*: practically equates theology/religion/spirituality).
307 EGreinacher Norbert, Konflikt um die Theologie der Befreiung: Diskussion und Dokumentation. Z 1985, Benziger. 331 p. DM 34. – RTR 82 (1986) 318-320 (R. *Nebel*).
307* EHaan W., Godsbeelden in verschillende religieuze tradities: Kahiers van het Bezinningscentrum 5. Amst 1985, Vrije Univ. 100 p. [ETL 62, p. 13*].
308 EHaddad Yvonne, *Findly* E., Women, religion, and social change. 1985 → 1,581: RHistRel 26 (1986s) 329-332 (Judith A. *Berling*).
309 EHalder Alois, *al.*, Sein und Schein der Religion 1983 → 1,353; 3-491-71036-7: REstE 61 (1986) 471 (J. J. *Alemany*).
310 EHargrove Barbara, Religion and the sociology of knowledge; modernization and pluralism in Christian thought and structure: Studies in Religion and Society 8. NY 1984, Mellen. 402 p. $50. – RRelStR 12 (1986) 136 (E. D. *McCarthy*: fine).
311 EHarries Richard, Reinhold NIEBUHR and the issues of our time. L 1986, Mowbray. 205 p. £6.95. 0-264-67051-5. – RExpTim 98 (1986s) 126 (R. J. *Elford*: rather 'Niebuhr's time', but relevant).
312 Hauschild W.-D. [9-78] *al.*, Bilanz des Lutherjubiläums: Kirchliches Jb Ev. K. Deutschland 110,1 (1983). Gü 1985, Mohn. vi-214 p. DM 48. – RTLZ 111 (1986) 569-573 (S. *Bräuer*, auch über die zwei anderen Lieferungen des Jb).
313 EHeinen K., *Bellebaum* A., Christsein zwischen Entmutigung und Hoffnung; zur Sendung der Laien in der Welt von heute. Limburg 1986, Lahn. [ZAW 99,286].
314 EHick John, *Askari* Hasan, The experience of religious diversity. Aldershot 1985, Gower. vi-236 p. 0-566-05020-X. – RExpTim 97 (1985s)

284s (J. *Ferguson*: Malachi 1,11 could only have meant that Marduk and ... Brahma are all names of the Lord); NBlackf 67 (1986) 343s (G. *D'Costa*).
314* ᴱ**Huber** W., *Tödt* I., Ethik im Ernstfall; Dietrich Bᴏɴʜᴏᴇꜰꜰᴇʀꜱ Stellung zu den Juden und ihre Aktualität: Internationales Bonhoeffer Forum, Forschung und Praxis 4. Mü 1985, Kaiser. 264 p. [ETL 62, p. 14*].
315 ᴱ**Iserloh** Erwin, *a*) Katholische Theologen der Reformationszeit [1. 1984 → 65,777]; 2 [*Fisher, More, Seripando, Nausea* ...]: KLK 45. Münster 1985, Aschendorff. 136 p.; 4 fig. DM 26 pa. – *b*) 3. KLK 46, 1986. 102 p.; 2 fig. – ᴿTLZ 111 (1986) 604s; 112,757 (S. *Bräuer*).
315* ᴱ**Jay** Elisabeth, The evangelical and Oxford movements: English Prose Texts. C 1983, Univ. 219 p. £18.50; pa. £6.95. – ᴿHeythJ 27 (1986) 200 (J. *Coulson*); RelStR 12 (1986) 171 (Lynn *Feider*: combines historico-theological and literary focus, 'Newman verbally eviscerating').
316 **Jong** L. de, inl. [*Arkel* D. van, *al*.], Veertig jaar na '45; visies op het hedendaagse antisemitisme. Amst 1985, Neulenhoff. 339 p. [ETL 62, p. 18*].
316* La pazienza di Dio e dell'uomo = **Jüngel** E., Pazienza di Dio — pazienza dell'amore. *Rahner* K., La pazienza intellettuale con sé stessi. Brescia 1985, Morcelliana. 63 p. Lit. 5.000. – ᴿAsprenas 33 (1986) 96 (B. *Belletti*).
317 ᴱ**Küng** Hans, *Tracy* David, Das neue Paradigma von Theologie; Strukturen und Dimensionen: ÖkT 13. Z/Gü 1986, Benziger/Mohn. 242 p. DM 58 [TR 82,434, tit. pp.].
318 **Lanternari** Vittorio, Festa, carisma, apocalisse [analyses of religious phenomena, including Strangelove and Jonestown; essays 1978-82; inedita by *Villa* Giorgio; *Massenzio* Marcello]; Prisma 52. Palermo 1983, Sellerio. 379 p. Lit. 20.000. – ᴿAnthropos 81 (1986) 345-7 (Gabriella *Eichinger Ferro-Luzzi*).
319 ᴱ**Lee** Philip, Communication for all; the Church and the new world information and communication order. Indore/Maryknoll/Ibadan 1986, Satprakashan/Orbis/Daystar. xiii-158 p. $12 [TR 83,135, E. *Arens*].
320 **Lepelley** Claude, présent., L'œcuménisme; unité chrétienne et identités confessionnelles: Les Quatre Fleuves 20. P 1985, Beauchesne. 123 p. F 65 [RelStR 13,247, J. F. *Puglisi*). 9 art.
321 ᴱ**Littlejohn** R., Exploring Christian theology. Lanham MD 1985, UPA. xi-530 p. [ETL 62, p. 15*].
322 ᴱ**Llewelyn** Robert, Julian [of Norwich, 'Christ our mother'], woman of our day. L 1985, Darton-LT. 144 p. £4.95. 0-232-51674-X. – ᴿCleR 71 (1986) 227-231 (sr. C. *Boulding*); ExpTim 98 (1986s) 28 (Dorothy *Bell*).
323 ᴱ**Löser** Werner, Die römisch-katholische Kirche: Die Kirchen der Welt 20. Fra 1986, Ev-V. 455 p. DM 56. – ᴿNorTTs 87 (1986) 253-5 (N. E. *Bloch-Hoell*).
323* ᴱ**Löser** W., *al*., Dogmengeschichte und katholische Theologie. Wü 1985, Echter. 538 p. [ETL 62, p. 15*].
324 ᴱ**Lorens** Eckehart, Widerstand, Recht und Frieden; ethische Kriterien legitimen Gewaltgebrauchs; eine interkonfessionelle und ideologiekritische Studie im Auftrag der Studienkommission des Lutherischen Weltbundes. Erlangen 1984, Luther -V. 173 p. DM 14 [TLZ 112, 383-6, G. *Krusche*].
325 ᴱ**Lovin** Robert W., *Reynolds* Frank E., Cosmogony and ethical order; new studies in comparative ethics [... *Knight* D., OT; *Betz* H. NT]. Ch 1985, Univ. 416 p. – ᴿSMSR 52 (1986) 324-7 (I. P. *Culianu*).
326 ᴱ**McGregor** J. F., *Reay* Barry, Radical religion in the English revolution. Ox 1984, Clarendon. ix-219 p. £19.50. 0-19-873044-6. – ᴿÉTRel 61 (1986) 604 (J. *Pons*); JTS 37 (1986) 261-4 (K. *Lindley*: influence of Christopher Hɪʟʟ).

326* ᴱMarty Martin E., *Vaux* Kenneth L., Health/Medicine and the faith
traditions. Ph 1982, Fortress. 350 p. $17. – ᴿRExp 83 (1986) 148s (B. J.
Leonard: from a Park Ridge IL Lutheran Hospital project).

327 ᴱMeadow Mary Jo, *Rayburn* Carole A., A time to weep, a time to sing;
faith journeys of women scholars of religion. Minneapolis 1985, Winston.
x-250 p. $11 pa. – ᴿJRel 66 (1986) 462s (Constance *Buchanan*).

327* ᴱMitcham Carl, *Grote* Jim, Theology and technology; essays in Christian
analysis and exegesis 1984 ⭢ 65,349: ᴿHorizons 13 (1986) 160s (D. J.
Fasching: G. BLAIR and W. FUDPUCKER crude).

328 ᴱMoss Tony, In search of Christianity [16 essays collected by the
interviewer to whom (later Bishop) David JENKINS of Durham made his
sensational statements on Virgin Birth and Resurrection]. Waterstone
1986, Firethorn [distr. Sidgwick & J.]. 244 p. £5.95. 0-947752-66-8. –
ᴿExpTim 2d choice 97,11 (1985s) 322s (C. S. *Rodd*: best, though odd
beside J. BAXTER, is Abp HABGOOD of York; we cannot live with a God
who miraculously answers our prayer for a parking-space but did not heed
the cries of Auschwitz).

328* ᴱMueller-Vollmer Kurt, The hermeneutics reader; texts of the German
tradition from the Enlightenment to the present. NY 1985, Continuum.
xi-380 p. $27.50 [Horizons 14,190, S. *Happel*].

329 ᴱO'Connell Timothy E., Vatican II and its documents; an American
reappraisal. Wilmington 1986, Glazier. 260 p. $11 pa. – ᴿRExp 83 (1986)
475s (E. G. *Hinson*: D. SENIOR candid on Revelation document).

329* Packer J. I., *al.*, Here we stand; justification by faith today. L 1986,
Hodder & S. 189 p. £5.95 pa. – ᴿThemelios 12 (1986s) 100 (T. *Baker*).

330 ᴱParkin David, The anthropology of evil [its concept in varying cultures].
NY 1985, Blackwell. iv-283 p. $35 [RelStR 13,233, J. C. *Holt*].

331 ᴱPobee J. S., *Wartenberg-Potter* D. von, New eyes for reading; biblical
and theological reflections by women from the third world. Geneva 1986,
WCC. 108 p. $6 [TS 47,759].

332 ᴱReiser Antonio, *Schoenborn* Paul G., Basisgemeinden und Befreiung
⭢ 62,8288, Lesebuch zur Theologie und christlichen Praxis in Lateinamerika. Wu 1981, Jugenddienst. 384 p. – ᴿTPhil 61 (1986) 621 (M.
Sievernich).

333 ᴱRichter Werner *al.*, The changing role of women in society, intr. *Kuhrig*
Herta: Inventories of Social Science in Europe. B 1985, Akademie.
lxx-818 p. M 68. – ᴿDLZ 107 (1986) 310-313 (Christiane *Bialas*).

334 ᴱRoffey J. W., When Jews and Christians meet. Melbourne 1985,
Victorian Council of Churches. 108 p. $7. – ᴿExpTim 98 (1986s) 154
(Julia *Neuberger*: sympathetic; superb bibliography).

335 ᴱRousseau Richard W., Christianity and Islam; the struggling dialogue; 4,
Modern theological themes; selections from literature. 1985, Ridge Row.
230 p. [JAAR 54,636].

336 ᴱRudavsky Tamar, Divine omniscience and omnipotence in medieval
philosophy; Islamic, Jewish and Christian perspectives. 1984, D. Reidel.
299 p. $54 [JAAR 54,206].

336* ᴱRussell Elizabeth, *Greenhalgh* John, 'If Christ be not risen ...'; essays in
resurrection and survival. L 1986, St. Mary's Bourne St. 110 p. $2.50.
0-95085-162-0. – ᴿExpTim 98 (1986s) 120s (M. J. *Townsend*).

337 ᴱSanter Mark, Their lord and ours. L 1982, SPCK. 160 p. £4.50. –
ᴿEvQ 58 (1986) 283 (R. *Beckwith*: most essays caution against papal
primacy; THISELTON deals with academic freedom versus church commitment).

337* ESchleip Holger, Zurück zur Natur-Religion? Wege zur Ehrfurcht vor allem Leben. Fr 1986, Bauer. 300 p. DM 28 [TR 83,144, F. *Hartl*: the ecological movement is a real religion, against which the Church should warn instead of showing sympathy].

338 ESchlick J., *Zimmermann* M., L'homosexuel(le) dans les sociétés civiles et religieuses: Recherches institutionnelles 15. Strasbourg 1985, Cerdic. 167 p. [ETL 62, p. 17*].

338* ESchweizer H., '... Bäume braucht man doch!' Das Symbol des Baumes zwischen Hoffnung und Zerstörung. Sigmaringen 1986, Thorbecke [ZAW 99,133].

339 ESenn Frank C., Protestant spiritual traditions. NY 1986, Paulist. xi-273 p. $10 [RelStR 13,333, S. *Sapp*].

339* ESiegel Seymour, *Gertel* Elliot, God in the teachings of Conservative Judaism. NY 1985, Ktav. 278 p. $20. 0-88125-066-X. – RExpTim 98 (1986s) 30 (Julia *Neuberger*: not conservative).

340 Spee H., *al.,* Diakonie; de dienst van het delen. Zwolle 1985, Waanders. 126 p. ƒ17,50 [NedTTs 41,352, A. *Noordegraaf*].

341 EStacpoole Alberic, Vatican II by those who were there. L 1986, Chapman. xv-365 p. £15. 0-225-66479-8. – RExpTim 98 (1986s) 56s (J. *Kent*: 'Mosignor' 'Tracey' ELLIS recognizes that some things at least have changed).

341* EStietencron H. von, Theologen und Theologien in verschiedenen Kulturkreisen. Dü 1986, Patmos.

342 EStone Ronald H., *Wilbanks* Dana, The peacemaking struggle [Presbyterian, biblical, ethical ...]; militarism and resistance. Lanham MD 1985, UPA. x-294 p. $9.75. – RRelStR 12 (1986) 273 (E. *Laarman*).

342* ETabb William K., Churches in struggle; liberation theologies and social change in North America. NY 1986, Monthly Review. xix-331 p. $27; pa. $11 [TDig 34,63].

343 Theologische Auseinandersetzung mit dem Denken unserer Zeit. Stu 1983s, Hänssler. 4 vol. Vol. 3, 1984, 176 p.: *Maier* G..., p. 51-62, Grundlinien eines biblischen Schriftverständnis [ZAW 99,302: luth.-pietistisch].

343* EThieberger Friedrich, (*Rabin* Else), Jüdisches Fest, jüdischer Brauch[3] [[1]1937 von Nazis beschlagnahmt]. Königstein/Ts 1985, Jüdischer Verlag Athenäum. 486 p. DM 88. – RTR 82 (1986) 154 (K. *Richter*).

344 EVerdon Timothy G., (*Dally* J.), Monasticism and the arts. Syracuse NY 1984, Univ. xii-354 p. $35; pa. $17 [RelStR 13,160, G. A. *Zinn*].

Weaver Mary Jo, NEWMAN and the Modernists: 1985 → d844.

345 Weidman Judith L., Women ministers[2] (autobiographies; adds to [1]1981 too little about ministry without ordination). SF 1985, Harper & R. 220 p. $8. – RRExp 83 (1986) 145 (Anne *Davis*).

345* EWells David F., Reformed theology in America; a history of its modern development. GR 1985, Eerdmans. 317 p. $20. – RTTod 43 (1986s) 292. 294 (D. K. *McKim*).

A1.5 *Plurium compilationes* **philologicae** *vel* **archaeologicae.**

346 EAnkersmit F. R., Knowing and telling history; the Anglo-Saxon debate: HistTheory 25,4 (= Beih 25, 1986). 100 p. 5 art.

347 EChrist Karl, Sparta: WegFor 622. Da 1986, Wiss. vi-519 p.

347* ECleere Henry, Approaches to the archaeological heritage; a comparative study of world cultural resource management systems: New Directions in Archaeology. NY 1984, Cambridge-UP. x-138 p.; 13 fig.; 8 phot.; 2 maps. – ᴿArchaeology 39,4 (1986) 66-68 (Valerie *Talmage*).

348 *Della Casa* Carlo, *al.*, Contributi di orientalistica, glottologia e dialettologia: ACME quad. 7. Mi 1986, Cisalpino. 184 p.; map. [43-52, *Mayer-Modena* M. L. su *'āmar/loquor*].

348* ᴱDouglas-Price T., Prehistoric hunter gatherers. 1985. $60. 0-12-564750-6.

349 ᴱGroll Sarah,   Papers for discussion presented by the Department of Egyptology: I (with ᴱStein H. Emily), 1981s; II (with ᴱBogot Frances) 1983ss. J 1982/5, Hebrew Univ. 302 p.; 348 p. 12 + 5 art., infra.

350 ᴱHietala Harold, Intrasite spatial analysis in archaeology. C 1985, Univ. 284 p.; 152 fig. $49.50. 0-521-25071-4. 14 art. – ᴿAJA 90 (1986) 100-102 (T. D. *Price*); JArchSc 13 (1986) 598-600 (C. *Carr*).

351 ᴱKraus O., Regulation, Manipulation und Explosion der Bevölkerungs-dichte. Gö 1986, Vandenhoeck & R. [ZAW 99,297].

352 ᴱMiller Daniel, *Tilley* Christopher, Ideology, power and prehistory 1984 ➤ 65,388: ᴿPrPrehS 52 (1986) 327-338 (S. *Shennan*).

353 ᴱOlmo Lete Gregorio del, *Aubet Semmler* María Eugenia, Los Fenicios en la península ibérica; I. Arqueología, cerámica y plástica; II. Epigrafía y lengua, glíptica y numismática, expansión y interacción cultural. Barc-Sabadell 1986, AUSA. 323 p., ill.; 391 p., ill. 84-86329-06-X. 39 art.; 27 infra.

354 ᴱRast Walter E., Preliminary reports of ASOR-sponsored excavations, 1980-4: BASOR Sup. 24. Winona Lake 1986, Eisenbrauns. 164 p. $20.

355 ᴱReynolds L. D., Texts and transmission. Ox 1983, Clarendon. xlviii-509 p. – ᴿClasR 100 (1986) 287-290 (Mirella *Ferrari*, in Italian).

355* ᴱSchiffer Michael B., Advances in archaeological theory and method 8. L 1986. ix-468 p. $75; pa. $35. [Antiquity 61,439].

356 ᴱSiebert G., Méthodologie iconographique. Strasbourg 1981 [AION 45,675].

357 Sözer Emel, Text connexity, text coherence; aspects, methods, results: Papiere zur Textlinguistik 49. Ha 1985, Burke. 3-87118-722-4.

358 ᴱStiewe Klaus, *Holzberg* Niklas, Polybios: WegFor 347. Da 1982, Wiss. xx-448 p. – ᴿGnomon 58 (1986) 4-11 (K.-E. *Petzold*).

359 ᴱVersteegh C. H. M., *al.*, The history of linguistics in the Near East [Arabic + 2 Hebrew; the expected articles on Akkadian, Coptic, Syriac were not available]: Amst. St. Ling. 3/28. Amst 1983, Benjamins. xi-265 p. – ᴿHenoch 8 (1986) 87 (B. *Chiesa*).

360 Vokotopoulou Iouha P., présent., Ⓖ *Thessalonikēn Philippou vasilissan, meletes* ... Studies on ancient Thessaloniki [reprints]. Thessaloniki 1985, Mouseio. 993 p.; ill. 71 art.; 3 infra.

361 ᴱWiseman T. P., Roman political life, 90 BC-AD 69: Studies in History. Exeter 1985, Univ. vi-81 p. £1.75 pa. 0-85989-225-5 [NTAbs 30,381].

362 ᴱZacour N. P., *Hazard* H. W., The impact of the Crusades on the Near East: [*Setton* K. M. ➤ d145] History of the Crusades 5. Madison 1985, Univ. Wisconsin. 600 + 13 p.; 4 fig.; 3 maps. – ᴿOrChrPer 52 (1986) 463-5 (V. *Poggi*).

A2 **Acta** *congressuum* .1 **biblica** [*Notitiae*, **reports** ➤ Y7.2].

363 ᴱAssaf David, Hebrew and Jewish languages; other languages: Proceedings of the Ninth World Congress of Jewish Studies, Jerusalem, August 4-12, 1985, Division D, vol. 1. J 1986, World Union of Jewish Studies. 92 p. + Ⓞ 189 p. 0333-9068. 12 art. + Ⓞ 27; 16 infra.

364 Associazione laica di cultura biblica; – *a*) 'La Bibbia e l'uomo di oggi; Atti del Convegno inaugurale, Firenze 20.X.1985. 52 p. [25-28, *Quinzio* S.; 29-34, *Ferri* E.; 35-37, *Glisenti* G.] – *b*) Atti del Seminario invernale 'In principio...', present. *Flores de Arcais* Francesco; Prato 23-26.I.1986. Settimello FI 1986, Biblia. 308 p. 11 art.; infra.

365 **Bogaert** P.-M., *al.*, Lectures bibliques; colloque du 11 novembre 1980, Bru. 1984, Institutum Iudaicum. 173 p. [ETL 62, p. 10*].

365* ᴱ**Bokser** Baruch M., History of Judaism; the next ten years [5th Max Richter Conversation, Providence 23s.VI.1980]: BrownJudSt 21, 1980 ⊁ 62,511: ᴿOLZ 81 (1986) 365-370 (A. *Goldberg*).

366 **Bori** Pier Cesare, present., 3º Seminario di ricerca su 'Storia dell'esegesi giudaica e cristiana antica', Frascati (Roma) 23-25 ott. 1985 = AnStoEseg 3 (1986). 318 p. Lit. 28.000. 88-10-20253-8. 17 art., infra.

366* ᴱ**Casciaro** José M. [p. 17-67], *al.*, Biblia y hermenéutica; VII simposio internacional de teología de la Universidad de Navarra, 10-12 abril 1985. Pamplona 1986, Univ. 742 p. 36 art.; infra.

367 ᴱ**Chmiel** Jerzy, Materiały z sympozjum biblistów — Tarnów 1985: RuBi 39,3 (1986) 177-284; p. 280-3 ❾ summary (*Matras* Tadeusz: 17-18.IX); p. 283s, addresses of the 69 participants.

368 ᴱ**Dietrich** M., *Loretz* O., Ugarit-Kolloquium zu Münster (Mai 1986) [Vorwort; Das ugaritische Alphabet]: UF 18 (1986s) 1-82 [1s.3-26].

369 ᴱ**Di Lorenzi** Lorenzo, Résurrection du Christ et des chrétiens (1 Co 15): Benedictina Bib/Œcum 8. R 1986, Abbaye S. Paul. 363 p.

370 FARRER Austin: For God and clarity; new essays in honour of ~, ᴱ**Easton** Jeffrey C., *Loades* Ann [1981 Princeton conference]: PitTMon 4. Allison Park PA/E 1983, Pickwick/Clark. xiii-205. £11.75. – ᴿHeythJ 27 (1986) 102 (B. R. *Brinkman*: every few years a group of scholars and clerics gathers to reconsider Farrer).

371 ᴱ**Galli** Giuseppe, Interpretazione e dialogo: Atti del IV Colloquio sull'Interpretazione [non biblica questa volta; intercomunicazione in diritto, istruzione, ecumenismo] (Macerata 29-30.III.1982): Univ. Fac. Lett. Fs. 16. T 1983, Marietti. 223 p. ill. 88-211-8599-0.

372 ᴱ**Galli** Giuseppe, Interpretazione e invenzione; la parabola del Figliol Prodigo [Lc 10,11-32] tra interpretazione scientifica e invenzioni artistiche; Atti dell'Ottavo Colloquio sull'Interpretazione, Macerata 17-19.III.1986: Univ. Macerata 37. Genova 1986, Marietti. 284 p. Lit. 30.000.

373 Gesù Ebreo, provocazione e mistero: IV colloquio ebraico-cristiano: Vita Monastica 158 (Camaldoli 1984) [Judaica 41,125].

374 ᴱ**Hedrick** Charles W. [introd. 1-11], *Hodgson* Robertᴶ, Nag Hammadi, Gnosticism, and early Christianity [Springfield MO seminar 1983]. Peabody MA 1986, Hendrickson. xliv-332 p. 0-913573-16-7. [BL 88,135, P. W. *Coxon*]. 13 art.; infra.

375 ᴱ**Hoffmann** R. J., *Larue* G. A., Jesus in history and myth [1985 Symposium, Michigan Univ., Ann Arbor]. Buffalo 1986, Prometheus. 217 p. $22. 0-87975-332-3 [NTAbs 31,100].

376 ᴱ**Iancu** Carol, *Lasserre* Jean-Marie, Juifs et Judaïsme en Afrique du Nord dans l'Antiquité et le Haut Moyen-Age [Colloque international sept. 1983]. Montpellier 1985, Univ. – ᴿRÉJ 145 (1986) 192s (B. *Leroy*).

377 *a*) International Organization for the Study of the Old Testament (IOSOT) Twelfth Congress .. Jerusalem, 24 August - 2 September 1986, and .. SBL [.. Septuagint, IOSCS; Masoretic, IOMS], program and 146 full-page IOSOT abstracts; 61 infra. Jerusalem 1986, Univ. xxxix-146 p. – *b*) Society of Biblical Literature, 1986 international meeting, 18-20

August, Jerusalem. 32 p. – *c*) ^E**Richards** Kent J. [➤ 392], Abstracts SBL [brief]. 15 p.; 8 infra.

378 Israël, le Judaïsme et l'Europe: XXIIIe Colloque des Intellectuels Juifs de langue française, P 24s.IV.1983: Idées. P 1984, Gallimard. 376 p. – ^RVSp 140 (1986) 748s (Annie *Perchenet*).

379 ^E**Jewett** Robert, Christology and exegesis, new approaches [SBL/AAR seminars 1981s]: Semeia 30. Atlanta 1985, Scholars. v-235 p. $10. – ^RTLZ 111 (1986) 741-4 (E. *Schweizer*).

380 ^E**Johnston** Robert K., The use of the Bible in theology/evangelical options [AAR meeting 1982]. Atlanta 1985, Knox. ix-257 p. $18; pa. $12 [Horizons 14, 146, Mary T. *Rattigan*].

381 ^E**Kertelge** Karl, Die Autorität der Schrift in der ökumenischen Gespräch [Tagung 1982, kath. orth. ev.]: ÖkRu Beih 50. Fra 1985, Lembeck. 83 p. DM 19,80. – ^RTLZ 111 (1986) 555s (H.-J. *Kühne*).

382 ^E**Kertelge** Karl, Das Gesetz im Neuen Testament [NT Arbeitstagung 1985]: QDisp 108. FrB 1986, Herder. 240 p. 3-451-02108-0. 10 art., infra.

383 [LIEBERMANN Shaul 80th b.] ❹ Researches in Talmudic literature, study conference 13-14.VI.1978. J 1983, Israel Academy. 227 p. [NTAbs 31,127].

384 ^E**Lust** J., Ezekiel and his book; textual and literary criticism and their interrelation [35^e Colloquium Biblicum Lovaniense, 27-29.VIII.1985]: BiblETL 74. Lv 1986. Univ./Peeters. 391 p. Fb 2700. 90-6186-213-2 [tit. pp. in TR 83,249; ZAW 99,289; TLZ 113,143]. 31 art., infra.

385 ^E**McConnell** Frank, The Bible and the narrative tradition [*Bloom* H., Uncanniness of the Yahwist ... 1983 conference, Santa Barbara]. Ox 1986, UP. 152 p. $17. 0-19-503698-0 [NTAbs 31,93]. – ^RTorJT 2 (1986) 281s (S. D. *Walters*); TS 47 (1986) 701-3 (R. F. *Scuka*).

386 ^E**Martins Terra** João E., A mulher na Bíblia; Liga de Estudos Bíblicos XVI Semana Bíblica Nacional [Brasília, 3-9.VI.1986] = RCuBíb 10,39s (1986). 152 p.; p. 149-152, carta do presidente, P. *Alcides*. 9 art., infra.

387 ^E**Mickelsen** A., Women, authority and the Bible [Oak Brook IL Evangelical Colloquium 1984]. DG 1986, InterVarsity. 304 p. $10. 0-87784-608-1 [NTAbs 31,93].

387* ^E**Novak** David, *Samuelson* Norbert, Creation and the end of days: Judaism and scientific cosmology: Proceedings of the 1984 meeting of the Academy for Jewish Philosophy [Ph]: Studies in Judaism. Lanham MD 1986, UPA. xx-315 p. 0-8191-55-24-1; pa. 5-X. 11 art.; 4 infra.

388 ^E**Penna** Romano (p. 419-427; Eng. 427), Paolinismo; letture di Paolo nel I e II secolo; Atti del 1º convegno di studi neotestamentari, Bocca di Magra (La Spezia), 5-7 sett. 1985 = RivB 34,4 (1986) 421-637.

389 ^E**Poswick** R. F., Bible et Informatique, le texte; Actes du premier colloque international, LvN 2-4.IX.1985: Travaux de Linguistique Quantitative 37 / Debora 3. P/Genève 1986, Champion / Slatkine. 453 p. 2-05-100769-1 [NRT 109,735, X. *Jacques*] 40 art. (many a 1 page summary); 14 infra.

390 ^E**Prato** Gian Luigi (p. 3-8; Eng. 9). Il mondo ebraico alla luce delle fonti extrabibliche, II. Il periodo postesilico; Atti del 4º convegno di studi veterotestamentari, Bocca di Magra (La Spezia), 2-4 sett. 1985 = RivB 34,1s (1986). 283 p.

391 **Prato** Gian Luigi *al.*, La storiografia della Bibbia: Atti della XXVIII Settimana Biblica 1984. Bo 1986, Dehoniane. 169 p. Lit. 18.000. 88-10-30251-6 [TR 82,161, tit. pp.]. 10 art.; infra.

391* ^E**Rendtorff** T., Charisma und Institution; Kolloquium 'Prophetie' (*Bern*-

hardt K., *Huber* W., *Locher* G., *Wolff* H. W.). Gütersloh 1985 [119-134; < JbBT 1,234].

392 **Richards** Kent H., [➔ 377*c*] Society of Biblical Literature Seminar Papers 25, 122d meeting, Nov. 22-25, 1986, Atlanta. Atlanta 1986, Scholars. 651 p. 1-55540-071-X.   49 art., infra.

393 ᴱ**Richardson** Peter (*Granskou* David),   Anti-Judaism in early Christianity I. Paul and the Gospels; II, ᴱ**Wilson** Stephen G., Separation and polemic [Canadian Society of Biblical Studies 5-year seminar]: Studies in Christianity and Judaism 2. Waterloo 1986, Laurier Univ.   xi-232 p., $18; xi-185 p., $18.50 [TDig 33,456]. 0-88920-167-6/96-X. – ᴿExpTim 98 (1986s) 118.350 (Margaret E. *Thrall*: anti-Jewish but due to specific ephemeral situations).

394 ᴱ**Rossano** Pietro,   Tradurre la Bibbia per il popolo di Dio [incontro 1985 per il 60º anniv. della Morcelliana]; pref. *Minelli* Stefano. Brescia 1986, Morcelliana.   185 p. – ᴿLaurentianum 27 (1986) 376 (G. *Veltri*); ParVi 31 (1986) 370-2 (S. *Migliasso*, dettagliato).

395 ᴱ**Smith** Robert C., *Lounibos* John,   Pagan and Christian anxiety; a response to ᴱC. R. DODDS [Pagan and Christian in an age of anxiety 1965; J. *Gager* seminar 1979]. Lanham MD 1984, UPA.   viii-239 p.   0-8191-3824-X.   10 art.; 6 infra.

396 Society for OT Study, bulletin for 1986: *a*) Winter Meeting, London 18-20 Dec. 1985: *Linders* B., Additions to the Old Greek text of Judges; *Hunter* A. G., Jer 2,31a; *Emerton* J. A., The final form of the text [... CHILDS B.]; *Cowley* R.,   Ethiopian OT commentaries; *Van Seters* J., Ex 19-24; *Collins* D., Decoding the Psalms. – *b*) Summer Meeting, Manchester 15-17 July 1986: *Anderson* A., Judicial parables in 2 Sam; *Mastin* B., Appositional order [Nebuchadnezzar / the King] in Daniel; *Stec* D., hen; *Wood* D., 1 Sam 2,1-10; *Kaiser* O., Succession narrative?; *Johnstone* W. ['holiness' redaction of Ex]; *Wansbrough* J., Arabic Bible.

397 ⊕ *Ummah* wᵉ-*tôledôtêha*, [The Jewish] People and its history, Eighth World Congress of Judaism I. Ancient and Medieval. J 1983, Shazar. 308 p. – KirSef 59 (1985) 448.

398 ᴱ**Vanhoye** Albert,   L'Apôtre Paul; personnalité, style et conception du ministère [34ᵉ Colloquium Biblicum Lovaniense, 27-29 août 1984]: BiblETL 73. Lv 1986, Univ.   xiii-474 p.   Fb2500. [TR 83,163, tit. pp.; CollatVl 17,111].   90-6186-209-4.   28 art.; infra.

399 ᴱ**Woude** A. S. van der,   Crises and perspectives; studies in Ancient Near Eastern polytheism, biblical theology, Palestinian archaeology and intertestamental literature; papers read at the joint British-Dutch OT conference held at Cambridge, U.K. 1985: OTS 24.   Leiden 1986, Brill. 149 p.   90-04-07873-8.   [BL 88,25, R. F. *Carroll*].   8 art.; infra.

399* ᴱ**Wyk** Wouter van,   Studies in the succession narrative [27th/28th OT congress of the Pretoria OT Society 1984/6]. Pretoria 1986, OT Society of S. Africa.   379 p.   0-86979-653-4 [OTAbs 10,198].

A2.3   **Acta congressuum theologica** [reports ➔ Y7.4].

400 **Abesamis** C. H. *al.*, Dieu en Asie; Chrétiens et théologiens du tiers-monde (Colloque de Wennapuwa, Sri-Lanka) [7-20.I.1979], ᵀ*Aberdam* Philippe. P 1983, Karthala.   188 p. – ᴿRAfrT 10,19 (1986) 139-143 (*Mumpele Makudi Tudiakuile*).

401 ᴱ**Agnoletto** Attilio,   Martin LUTHER e il protestantesimo in Italia; bilancio storiografico [colloquio Milano marzo 1983, Univ./Goethe Inst.]. Mi 1984, IPL.   224 p. – ᴿRHE 81 (1986) 789s (J.-F. *Gilmont*: tit. pp. +).

402 *Alberigo* G., *al.,* La chrétienté en débat; histoire, formes et problèmes actuels; colloque de Bologne, 11-15 mai 1983: Théologies, 1984 → 1,532. ^RScEspr 38 (1986) 270s (G. *Pelland*: conclusion de *Jossua* J.-P., de 'ton hautain et hargneux ... détestable'); VSp 140 (1986) 736 (Annie *Perchenet*).

403 **Appelt** Heinrich, present., Frau und spätmittelalterlicher Alltag; Internationaler Kongress Krems 2.-5.X.1984: Szb ph/h 473. Wien 1986, Österr. Akad. 615 p.; ill. 3-7001-0782-X. 20 art.; 1 infra.

404 ^E**Aranda** A., *al.,* Dios y el hombre; VI simposio internacional de teología de la Universidad de Navarra: Teológica 43. Pamplona 1985, EUNSA. 820 p. pt. 4000. - ^RNRT 108 (1986) 913s (R. *Escol*); ScriptV 33 (1986) 443-5 (F. *Ortiz de Urtaran*).

405 **[Arnaldez]**, Colloque sur le Dieu unique [millénaire de Montpellier; i. Livre et Parole de Dieu: *Abecassis* A., *Geffré, Boubekeur*]. P 1986, Buchet-Chastel. 196 p. F 100. - ^RÉTRel 61 (1986) 470 (A. *Gaillard*).

405* Athéisme et agnosticisme, Colloque de Bruxelles, Mai 1986: ProbHistChr 16 (1986). 180 + p. 12 art.; 2 infra [< ZIT].

406 ^E*Barrios V.* Marciano, Desafíos a la teología [Seminario Interdisciplinar Univ. Católica Chile, Santiago 7-10.X.1985] = TVida 27 (1986). 152 p.

406* BARTH-Symposium, Utrecht 1986: ZDialT 2,2 (Kampen 1986) 327-380 ... [< ZIT].

407 ^E**Battaglia** Vincenzo, L'incarnazione; attualità di un messaggio; studio interdisciplinare [Frati Minori del Lazio, Greccio gen. 1984]. Mi 1985, OR. 311 p. Lit. 25.000. - ^RGregorianum 67 (1986) 599s (J. *Galot*).

408 ^E**Belzen** J. A. van, *Lans* J. M. van der, Current issues in the psychology of religion; Proceedings of the third symposium [Nijmegen Aug. 1985]. Amst 1986, Rodopi. xiv-271 p. *f* 80 [TLZ 112,551 D. *Stollbert,* Katrin *Wienold*].

409 ^E**Biggar** Nigel, *al.,* Cities of gods; faith, politics and pluralism in Judaism, Christianity and Islam [Ch Divinity School conference 1982, 6 papers; + 6 others]: Contributions to the Study of Religion 16. Westport CT 1986, Greenwood. viii-244 p. $40 [TDig 34,63].

410 ^E**Blum** Paul R., Studien zur Thematik des Todes im 16. Jahrhundert [August-Bibliothek Gastseminar Apr. 1981]: W-Forschungen 22. Wolfenbüttel/Wsb 1983, /Harrassowitz. viii-198 p.; ill. DM 64 pa. → 1,544 [als 1983/5]: ^RTLZ 111 (1986) 533s (S. *Bräuer*: Schürfungen, níchts besonders biblisch; Mary *Lindemann* 125-139, 'Armen und Eselsbegräbnis ... sozialer Kontrolle').

411 ^E**Breuning** Wilhelm, Seele, Problembegriff christlicher Eschatologie [Tagung Trier 2.-5.I.1985]: QDisp 106. FrB 1986, Herder. 224 p. 3-451-02106-4. [ZAW 99,298] 6 art., 3 infra.

412 ^E**Brocke** Edna, *Bauer* Gerhard, 'Nicht im Himmel — nicht überm Meer'; Jüdisch-christliche Dialoge zur Bibel [ev. Kirchentage, 1973-83]. Neuk 1985. 206 p. - ^RFreibRu 37s (1985s) 124s (J. *Klupsch*).

413 *Brueggemann* Walter [Scripture; Mi 6,8], *al.,* To act justly, love tenderly, walk humbly; an agenda for ministers. [Portland ME meeting Nov. 1983; → b3.2] Mahwah 1986, Paulist. v-65 p. $4 pa [TDig 34,61].

414 ^E**Buck** August, Renaissance — Reformation; Gegensätze und Gemeinsamkeiten [Kongress 20.-23.XI.1983]: Wolfenbütteler Abhandlungen zur Renaissanceforschung 5. Wsb 1984, Harrassowitz. v-297 p. DM 68 [TLZ 112,518, H. *Junghans*].

415 ^E**Burke** John, A new look at preaching [Word of God institute → 64,478; also Emory Univ. conference] Good News Studies 7. Wilmington 1983, Glazier. 163 p. $7 pa. - ^RWorship 60 (1986) 278s (W. F. *Jabusch*).

416 ᴱBynum Caroline W., *Harrell* Stevan, *Richman* Paula, Gender and religion; on the complexity of symbols [University of Washington seminar]. Boston 1986, Beacon. x-326 p. $25 [RelStR 13,230, G. *Yocum*].

417 **Caprile** Giovanni, Il sinodo straordinario (24.XI.-8.XII) 1985. R 1986, Civiltà Cattolica. 627 p. [non Acta ma fedele e precisa documentazione].

418 ᴱCattaneo E., Il Concilio venti anni dopo, 2. L'ingresso della categoria 'storia' [seminario interdisciplinare Italia Meridionale 1984]: Saggi 24. R 1985, A.V.E. 221 p. Lit. 14.000. – ᴿNRT 108 (1986) 442 (A. *Toubeau*).

419 Le charisme de la vie consacrée; Actes de la Quinzième Semaine Théologique de Kinshasa (14 au 20 avril 1985). Kinshasa 1985, Fac. Théol. Catholique. 232 p. Fb 400. – ᴿETL 62 (1986) 452s (A. *Vanneste*).

420 ᴱChmiel Jerzy, Materiały z sympozjum liturgistów — Wrocław 1985 [17-18.IX.1985; summarium *Rojewski* Andrzej]: RuBi 39,4 (1986) 285-344 [344-7].

421 ᴱCirillo Luigi, (*Roselli* Amneris), Codex Manichaicus Coloniensis; Atti del Simposio Internazionale (Rende-Amantea 3-7.IX.1984): Studi e Ricerche 4. Cosenza 1986, Marra. 390 p. 88-7687-004-0. 18 art., infra.

421* Colloque de théologie missionnaire, Lyon-Francheville, 15-23 septembre 1983 = Spiritus 25,94 (P 1984). 110 p.

422 ᴱConio Caterina, Santità a confronto; Ebraismo-Taoismo-Shintoismo-Induismo-Islamismo-Cristianesimo: Quaderni 5. Mi 1985, Centro Interreligioso H. Le Saux. 189 p. – ᴿGregorianum 67 (1986) 790 (J. *Dupuis*).

423 ᴱCook James I., The Church speaks; papers of the Commission on Theology, Reformed Church in America, 1959-1984: Historical Series 15. GR 1985, Eerdmans. xviii-268 p. $15 pa. [TDig 33,356].

423* ᴱCurtis Michael, Antisemitism in the contemporary world [Rutgers conference 1983]. Boulder CO 1986, Westview. xi-333 p. $32.50. 24 art. [TDig 33,456].

424 Czwarty kongres józefologiczny [Kalisz 22-29.IX.1985] = AtKap 107,2s (1986) 191-346; p. 342-6, *Siuta* s. Dolores, ❸ XVII rencontre des Josephologues Polonais à Kalisz [9-10.IV.1986].

424* ᴱDe Jong Norman, Christian approaches to learning theory; a symposium [Trinity College, 11-12.XI.1983]. Lanham MD 1984, UPA. xvi-218 p. $12.25 pa. – ᴿCalvinT 21 (1986) 313 (R. C. *DeVries*).

425 ᴱDockrill D. W., *Tanner* R. G., The concept of spirit [Sydney conference 1984]. Auckland 1985, Prudence Sup. 231 p. $A 10. – ᴿRefTR 45 (1986) 85s (P. F. *Jensen*).

426 ᴱDurant John, Darwinism and divinity; essays on evolution and religious belief [British Society for the History of Science 1982]. Ox 1985, Blackwell. ix-210 p. $25. – ᴿTS 47 (1986) 556 (J. F. *Haught*); TTod 43 (1986s) 287s. 290 (E. E. *Daub*).

427 'Ecclesiam suam', première lettre encyclique de Paul VI (Colloque international, Rome 24-26 octobre 1980): Pubblicazioni dell'Istituto Paolo VI, 2. Brescia 1982, Studium Vita Nova. xiv-286 p. – ᴿRThom 86 (1986) 168s (N.-B. V.).

428 ᴱEdsman Carl-Martin, *al.*, Kultur, Religion och Nutrition [Institute at Uppsala 1981 to counter Gunnar *Myrdal's* view that religion is a barrier to the nutritional aid which Swedes are trying to bring to Asia]. U 1983, Univ. 361 p.; 7 fig. 16 papers in Swedish, 1 Norwegian. – ᴿAION 46 (1986) 142s (Gabriella E. *Ferro-Luzzi*).

429 L'Évêque dans l'Histoire de l'Église; Actes de la Septième Rencontre d'Histoire Religieuse tenue à Fontevraud, les 14 et 15 octobre 1983. Angers 1984, Univ. 230 p. – ᴿDivThom 88 (1985) 153-6 (B. *Ardura*).

430 EFalsini Rinaldo, La parola di Dio nella celebrazione [Atti del XXVI Convegno liturgico pastorale 22-24.II.1984]. Mi 1984, OR. 160 p. Lit. 8700. – RCC 137 (1986,3) 200 (G. *Ferraro*).

431 EFelici Sergio, Morte e immortalità nella catechesi dei Padri del III-IV secolo; convegno di studio e aggiornamento, Facoltà di Lettere cristiane e classiche, Pont. Inst. Altioris Latinitatis, Roma, 16-18 marzo 1984: BiblScRel 66. R 1985, LAS. 292 p. Lit. 35.000. 88-213-0105-2. – RCC 137 (1986,3) 548 (D. *Marafioti*); Gregorianum 67 (1986) 566s (J. *Janssens*).

432 EFelici Sergio, Spiritualità del lavoro nella catechesi dei Padri del III-IV secolo; Convegno di studio e aggiornamento, Facoltà di Lettere cristiane e classiche (Pont. Inst. Altioris Latinitatis), Roma, 15-17 marzo 1985; BiblScRel 75. R 1986, LAS(alesianum). 284 p. Lit. 35.000. 88-213-0125-7. 16 art.; 7 infra.

433 Femmes; pour quel monde? dans quelle Église?: XVe Conférence Religieuse Canadienne. Ottawa 1985. 144 p. – RNatGrac 33 (1986) 186s (D. *Castillo*).

433* EFontaine Jacques, *al.*, GRÉGOIRE le Grand; Chantilly, centre culturel Les Fontaines, 15-19 septembre 1982. P 1986, CNRS. 690 p.; front. 2-222-03914-2. 61 art.; 17 infra.

434 EFoster Durwood, *Mojzes* Paul, Society and original sin; ecumenical essays on the impact of the Fall [< (*Moon*) Unification Church seminar, Nassau 1983]. NY 1985, Paragon. v-193 p. 14 art. 6 infra → 1575. – RComSev 19 (1986) 93s (H. de *Paz Castaño*); TLZ 111 (1986) 467s (Ilse *Bertinetti*).

435 EFurcha E. J., Huldrych ZWINGLI, 1484-1531; a legacy of radical reform; Papers from the 1984 International Zwingli Symposium, McGill University. Montreal 1985, McGill. x-198 p. – RSR 15 (1986) 403s (J. W. *Baker*).

436 EGalantino Nunzio, Il Concilio venti anni dopo; il rapporto Chiesa-mondo [Seminario RasT N ...]. R 1986, AVE. 240 p. Lit. 16,500. – RCC 137 (1986,3) 197s (G. *Lorizio*).

437 EGordan P., Gott [Salzburg 29.VII-10.VIII.1985]. Graz/Kevelaer 1986, Styria/Butzon & B. 295 p. [Stromata 42,406].

438 EGregg Robert C., Arianism, historical and theological reassessments; papers from the Ninth International Conference on Patristic Studies, September 5-10, 1983, Oxford, England: PatrMon 11. CM 1985, Philadelphia Patr. Foundation. 180 p. 0-915646-10-2. – RBijdragen 47 (1986) 445s (M. *Parmentier*).

439 EGrelle Bruce, *Krueger* David A., Christianity and capitalism; perspectives on religion, liberalism and the economy [Chicago Univ. Divinity School conference Apr. 1984]: Studies in Religion and Society. Ch 1986, Center for the Scientific Study of Religion. xiii-188 p. $26; pa. $15 [TDig 33,463].

439* EGrislis Egil, The theology of Martin LUTHER; five contemporary Canadian interpretations [symposium 1983]. Winfield BC 1985, Wood Lake. 126 p. $10 pa. – RCalvinT 21 (1986) 281-4 (L. D. *Bierma*: Catholic B. MCSORLEY's contribution charitable).

440 [Groupe d'histoire religieuse de la Bussière] *a*), Pratiques de la confession; des Pères du désert à Vatican II; quinze études d'histoire: Actes 1983. P 1983, Cerf. 298 p. 2-204-02068-0. 14 art.; 1 infra. – *b*) Le diable et ses lieux: Actes 1986 [RHE 81,736, J. *Pirotte*].

441 EHarran Marilyn J., LUTHER and learning; the [Springfield OH] Wittenberg University Luther Symposium. Selinsgrove PA 1984, Susquehanna Univ. 144 p. $19.50. 6 art. – RChH 55 (1986) 230s (Maria *Grossmann*).

442 ᴱ**Haubst** Rudolf,　Der Friede unter den Religionen nach Nikolaus von KUES; Akten des Symposiums in Trier vom 13. bis 15. Oktober 1982: Mitt. Cusanus-Ges. 16 [→ 65,506]. Mainz 1984, Grünewald.　356 p. – ᴿFreibZ 33 (1986) 262-6 (R. *Imbach*).

443 ᴱ**Hinnebusch** Paul,　Contemplation and the charismatic renewal [symposium Tampa 12-14.XI.1982].　Mahwah NJ 1986, Paulist.　iii-128 p. $9 pa. – ᴿTDig 33 (1986) 465 (W. C. *Heiser*).

444 ᴱ**Hoffman** Manfred,　Martin LUTHER and the modern mind; freedom, conscience, toleration, rights [ecumenical symposium Emory/Atlanta Nov. 1983]: Toronto studies in theology 5. Lewiston NY 1985, Mellen. xii-278 p. $50 [TDig 34,85].

444* ᴱ**Ingram** Paul O., *Streng* Frederick J.,　Buddhist-Christian dialogue [Univ. Hawaii conference 1980].　Honolulu 1986, Univ.　248 p. £10. 0-8248-1050-3. – ᴿExpTim 98 (1986s) 317s (W. *Foy*).

445 ᴱ**Iserloh** Erwin, *Müller* Gerhard,　LUTHER und die politische Welt, wissenschaftliches Symposion in Worms vom 27. bis 29. Oktober 1983: HistFor 9. Wsb 1984, Steiner.　viii-256 p. DM 48. – ᴿTR 82 (1986) 43-45 (B. *Lohse*).

445* ᴱ**Jennings** Theodore W.ᴶ,　The vocation of the theologian [< Atlanta Emory Univ. consultation]. Ph 1985, Fortress.　viii-149 p. – ᴿTLond 39 (1986) 475s (D. *Nineham*).

446 ᴱ**Junghans** H.,　Martin LUTHER 1483-1983, Werk und Wirkung; Referate und Berichte des Sechsten Internationalen Kongresses für Lutherforschung, Erfurt 14.-20. Aug. 1983. = LutherJb 52 (1985) → 1,593; DM 79: ᴿTLZ 111 (1986) 11s (E. *Koch*).

447 ᴱ**Kalven** Janet [! 65,7484], *Buckley* Mary I.,　Women's spirit bonding [conference on barriers that keep feminists apart, and power of religion to overcome them]. NY 1984, Pilgrim.　x-389 p. $13. – ᴿRelStR 12 (1986) 267s (Toinette M. *Eugene*).

448 ᴱ**Keller** C.-A.,　La réincarnation; théories, raisonnnements et appréciations; un symposium [Suisse romande 1983s]. Bern 1986, Lang.　292 p. Fs 46. 3-261-03650-8. [NRT 109,769, J. *Scheuer*].

449 ᴱ**Kinnamon** Michael, *Best* Thomas F.,　Called to be one in Christ; United Churches and the ecumenical movement [supplement to Colombo acta 1981]: Faith and Order 127. Geneva 1985, WCC.　xiii-78 p. $4.75 pa. [RelStR 13,74, J. T. *Ford*; ActuBbg 25,132, J. *Boada*].

450 Das kirchliche Amt und die apostolische Sukzession; neunter bilateraler theologischer Dialog zwischen der Russischen Orthodoxen Kirche und der evangelischen Kirche in Deutschland, 12.-17.Okt.1981, Kitzingen-Schwanberg: ÖkRu Beih 49. Fra 1984, Lembeck.　143 p. DM 19,80. – ᴿTLZ 111 (1986) 299-301 (H. *Krüger*).

451 ᴱ**Klinger** Elmar, *Zerfass* Rolf,　Die Basisgemeinden — ein Schritt auf dem Weg zur Kirche des Konzils [Symposion Würzburg/Salamanca], 1984 → 1,371.598: ᴿTPhil 61 (1986) 316s (M. *Sievernich*).

452 ᴱ**Koehler** T. A.,　Proceedings of the 36th national convention of the Mariological Society of America, Dayton May 29-30, 1985: Marian Studies 36 (1985).　160 p. [TLZ 112,529 H. *Beintker*].

453 ᴱ**Kremer** Klaus,　Um die Möglichkeit oder Unmöglichkeit natürlicher Gotteserkenntnis heute [Symposium Salzburg 1982]. Leiden 1985, Brill. vii-207 p. ƒ80 [TLZ 112,217, B. *Hildebrandt*].

454 **Küng** Hans, *al.*,　Christianity and the world religions; paths of dialogue with Islam, Hinduism, and Buddhism [1984 → 1,604], ᵀ*Heinegg* Peter. GCNY 1986, Doubleday.　xx-460 p. $20 [TDig 33,464].

455 ᴱLanger H., *al.*, Met Mirjam over de Rietzee [< Hamburg Kirchentag 1981]ᵀ. Boxtel 1985, Katholieke Bijbelstichting. 86 p. Fb 300. – ᴿCollatVl (1986) 253s (J. *Bulckens*: Forum Vrouwen).

456 ᴱLawrence Fred, The Beginning and the Beyond; papers from the GADA-MER and VOEGELIN conferences: LONERGAN Workshop (Sup) 4. Atlanta 1984, Scholars. 131 p. $13.50; sb. $9. – ᴿJAAR 54 (1986) 594s (A. M. *Olson*).

457 Lectio AUGUSTINI [Settimana Agostiniana Pavese] 1-3, [commentari su] 'Le Confessioni di Agostino d'Ippona'. Palermo 1984s, Augustinus. 121 p.; 58 p.; 112 p. – ᴿTPhil 61 (1986) 578 (H. J. *Sieben*).

458 ᴱLemieux Raymond, *Richard* Réginald, Survivre ... La religion et la mort [Colloque Univ. Laval, 17-19.II.1983]: Cahiers de Recherches en Sciences de la Religion 6. Montréal 1985, Bellarmin. 285 p. – ᴿCC 137 (1986,2) 308 (J. *Joblin*); SR 15 (1986) 393s (G. *Martel*).

459 ᴱLibânio J. B., Igreja em Busca da Terra Prometida ['CEBs' VI encontro intereclesial, Trindade/Goiás, 21-25 julho 1986]: REB 46 (1986) 489-511; documento final 483-8; *al.* 512-677; ⇴ e185, *Mesters*, 6921, *Suess*.

460 ᴱLincoln Bruce, Religion, rebellion, revolution; an interdisciplinary and cross-cultural collection of essays [Minnesota Univ. symposium]. NY 1985, St. Martin's. ix-311 p. $27.50. – ᴿRelStR 12 (1986) 261s (J. *Strong*: significant on millenarian movements).

461 ᴱLindberg David C., *Numbers* Ronald L., God and nature; historical essays on the encounter between Christianity and science [Univ. Wisconsin conference, Madison 22-25.IV.1981]. Berkeley 1986, Univ. California. xi-516 p. $50; pa. $18 [TDig 34,71].

461* Llamas Enrique present., La consagración a María; teología – historia – espiritualidad [XL Semana de Estudios Marianos, Madrid 9-12.IX.1985] = EstMar 51 (1986). 351 p. [EstMar 50 (1985) = María, madre de la reconciliación].

462 *Lohfink* Gerhard [Radikalität des Ethischen im Evangelium], *al.*, Der ethische Kompromiss [Tagung Trier 1983]: Studien zur theologischen Ethik 12. FrS/FrB 1984, Univ./Herder. 148 p. Fs 29 [TR 83,418, J. *Reiter*].

463 ᴱLohse Eduard, *Wilckens* Ulrich, Gottes Friede den Völkern: Dokumentation des wissenschaftlichen Kongresses der Evang. Kirche in Deutschland und der Nordelbischen Evangelisch-Lutherischen Kirche, 17.-19.VI.1984, Kiel. Hannover 1984, Luth. V. 413 p.; 13 fig. DM 28. – [TLZ 112,469-473, G. *Krusche*].

463* ᴱMacCana P., *Meslin* M., Rencontres de religions; Actes du Colloque du Collège des Irlandais tenu sous les auspices de l'Académie Royale Irlandaise (juin 1981). P 1986, BLettres. 139 p. F 110 [NRT 109,934].

464 ᴱMcMullin Ernan, Evolution and creation [Center for Philosophy of Religion conference 1983]. ND 1986, Univ. 304 p. $25. – ᴿSWJT 29,2 (1986s) 61 (L. R. *Bush*).

464* ᴱMalamoud C., *Vernant* J.P., Corps des dieux [Colloque Rome]: Le temps de la réflexion 7. P 1986, Gallimard. 408 p. F 160 [NRT 109,935].

465 ᴱManns Peter, Martin LUTHER, 'Reformator und Vater im Glauben'; Referate aus der Vortragsreihe des Instituts für Europäische Geschichte Mainz: Abendl. Rel. G. 19. Stu 1985, Steiner. viii-412 p. DM 76 pa. [TR 83,40-43, J. *Wicks*].

466 Maria e lo Spirito Santo: Atti del 4º Simposio, R 1982/4 ⇴ 1,611*: ᴿSalmanticensis 33 (1986) 259-261 (R. *Blázquez*).

466* ᴱMarsden George, Evangelicalism and modern America [1983 Wheaton conference]. GR 1984, Eerdmans. 220 p. $9 pa. – ᴿAndrUnS 24 (1986) 195-7 (G. R. *Knight*).

467 ᴱMat Michèle, *Marx* Jacques, LUTHER, mythe et réalité [colloque...]: ProbHistChr. Bru 1984, Univ. 123 p. – ᴿScEspr 38 (1986) 278-281 (R. *Goulet*).

467* ᴱMayne Michael, Encounters; exploring Christian faith [Cambridge meeting]. L 1986, Darton-LT. vii-117 p. £3.50. 0-232-51669-3. – ᴿTLond 39 (1986) 393-5 (H. *Dawes*).

468 ᴱMeeking Basil, *Stott* John, The Evangelical-Roman Catholic dialogue on mission, 1977-84. Exeter 1986, Paternoster. 96 p. £3. 0-85364-437-3 [ExpTim 98,127].

469 ᴱMengus Raymond, L'expérience de Dieu et le Saint-Esprit; immédiateté et médiations; Actes du colloque, Strasbourg 1982: PoinT 44. P 1985, Beauchesne. 216 p. F 120. – ᴿTR 82 (1985) 367-9 (H.-J. *Jaschke*: auteurs, thèmes sans tit. pp.).

470 ᴱMetz Johann B., Die Theologie der Befreiung; Hoffnung oder Gefahr für die Kirche? [Tagung Kath. Akad. Bayern 12.-13.X.1985]: Schriften K. Ak. Bayern 122. Dü 1986, Patmos. 243 p. – ᴿTPhil 61 (1986) 620 (O. v. *Nell-Breuning*).

470* [ᴱMilčinski M. J., *Poupard* P., *al.*] Science and faith, international and interdisciplinary colloquium Ljubljana, May 10-12, 1984. Ljubljana/R 1984, Slovene Academy / Secretariat for Non Believers. 275 p. Lit. 15.000. – ᴿNRT 108 (1986) 443 (R. *Escol*].

471 ᴱMilitello Cettina, Teologia al femminile [Primo colloquio di (circa trenta) donne docenti nelle Facoltà teologiche]. Palermo 1985, Oftes. 168 p. – ᴿSalesianum 48 (1986) 1000 (M. *Midali*).

471* ᴱMiller John W., Interfaith dialogue; four approaches [meetings since 1985]. Waterloo ONT 1986, Univ. 104 p. – ᴿEcuR 38 (1986) 480s (S. *Brown*).

472 La Mission de l'Église aujourd'hui; première rencontre de théologiens Africains et Européens, Yaoundé, Kameroun, 4-11 avril 1984 = BTAf 7,13s (1985). 433 p. [TKontext 8/2,22-25]. 28 art., 6 infra [< zɪт].

472* Moingt J., *al.,* Églises, sociétés et ministères; essai d'herméneutique historique des origines du christianisme à nos jours: Conférence Centre Sèvres [1983] 7. P 1986, Centre Sèvres. 204 p. [NRT 109,790. L. *Renwart*].

473 ᴱMoltmann-Wendel E., *Schönherr* A., *Traitler* R., Seid fruchtbar und wehrt Euch; Frauentexte zum Kirchentag [1985]: Traktate 93. Mü 1986, Kaiser. 84 p. DM 10. 3-459-01643-4 [BL 87,88, A.G. *Auld*].

473* *Muller* Wilhelm K., present., Universal Church and particular church: Symposium CECC (Catholics in Europe concerned with China), Sankt Augustin, 20-23.V.1986 = VerbumSVD 27,4 (1986) 311-403.

474 ᴱ*Nesti* P., Salvezza cristiana e culture odierne, I. Salvezza e anunzio; II. Spiritualità, riconciliazione, escatologia: Atti del II Congresso Internazionale 'La Sapienza della Croce oggi', Roma, 6-9 febbraio 1984. T-Leumann 1985, LDC. 528 p. – ᴿClaretianum 26 (1986) 348-350 (B. *Proietti*).

475 ᴱNicholls Bruce J., In word and deed [GR Consultation on Evangelism and social responsibility (Lausanne Committee) 16-23.VI.1982]. Exeter 1985, Paternoster. 238 p. £6.95. ᴿRefTR 45 (1986) 55s (M. *Raiter*).

476 ᴱOelmüller Willi, Wahrheitsansprüche der Religionen heute: Kolloquium [12.-14.VI.1984] Religion und Philosophie 2. Pd 1986, Schöningh. 366 p. DM 38 [TR 82,434].

476* L'origenismo; apologie e polemiche intorno a ORIGENE; XIV incontro di studiosi dell'antichità cristiana, Roma, 9-11 maggio 1985 = AugR 26,Is (1986). 303 p.

477 ᴱOroz Reta José, San AGUSTÍN en Oxford 2º; IX Congreso Internacional de Estudios Patrísticos [5-10.IX.1983] = Augustinus 31,121s (M 1986). 292 p.

478 Ott Heinrich [Eröffnung; Schlusswort] Karl-BARTH-Symposium: TZBas 42,4 (1986) 275-362, infra.

479 ᴱPadilla C. René, Mission between the times [clarification of Lausanne 1974 Congress of World Evangelization]. GR/Exeter 1985, Eerdmans/ Paternoster. 199 p. £10.95. – ᴿRefTR 45 (1986) 56 (M. Raiter).

480 ᴱPancheri F. S., La mariologia di S. Massimiliano Kolbe; Atti del Congresso internazionale, Roma 8-12.X.1984. R 1985, Misc. Francescana. 769 p. Lit. 40.000 [NRT 109,289, L. J. Renard].

480* ᴱPanikkar R., Strolz W., Die Verantwortung des Menschen für eine bewohnbare Welt im Christentum, Hinduismus und Buddhismus [Kolloquium]: Oratio Dominica 12. FrB 1985, Herder. 191 p. DM 39,50 [Ott H., Hoffnung; Zenger E., Ps. 90: NRT 109,912, J. Scheuer].

481 ᴱPapandreou Damaskinos, al., Les dialogues œcuméniques hier et aujourd'hui [Conférence Chambésy-Genève]: Études Théologiques 5. Chambésy 1985, Centre Orthodoxe. 415 p. – ᴿFreibZ 33 (1986) 635s (G. N. Lemopoulos).

482 Papers and reports for the Disciples of Christ – Roman Catholic international commission for dialogue, 1984-5: Mid-Stream 25,4 (1986) 339-440.

483 Das Papstamt; Dienst oder Hindernis für die Ökumene? [Tagung München 1984] 1985 → 1,535*: ᴿTsTNijm 26 (1986) 97s (W. Boelens).

483* ᴱParkin David, The anthropology of evil. Ox 1985, Blackwell. iv-283 p. £22.50. – ᴿTLond 39 (1986) 154s (Edmund Leach, severe: needed the theme 'religious people classify as evil qualities which other people classify as good').

484 ᴱPearson Birger A., Goehring James E., The roots of Egyptian Christianity, Ph 1986, Fortress. 319 p. 0-8006-3100-5. – ᴿExpTim 98 (1986s) 85s (J. D. Ray).

485 a) ᴱPerkins Robert L., History and system; Hegel's philosophy of history. – b) ᴱStillman Peter G., Hegel's philosophy of spirit [Hegel Society of America meetings, 7th 1982, 8th 1984]. Albany 1984, SUNY. 256 p., $44.50, pa. $18 / xii-223 p.; $39.50, pa. $13 [RelStR 13,236, P. C. Hodgson].

486 ᴱPöltner Günther, Vetter Helmut, Naturwissenschaft und Glaube. W 1985, Herold. 152 p. DM 18. – ᴿTPQ 134 (1986) 83s (N. Pucker).

487 Portare Cristo all'uomo; Congresso del Ventennio dal Concilio Vaticano II, 18-21 febbraio 1985; I. Dialogo; II. Testimonianza; III. Solidarietà: Studia Urbaniana 22ss 1985 → 1,628*: ᴿNRT 108 (1986) 912s (J. Masson: FROSSARD plein d'humour autant que de conviction).

488 ᴱPotvin Thomas R., Richard Jean, Questions actuelles sur la foi; Actes du Congrès de la Société canadienne de théologie tenu à Montréal les 22,23 et 24 octobre 1982: Héritage et projet 27, 1984 → 1,629: ᴿSR 14 (1985) 512s (P.-E. Chabot).

489 ᴱProdi Paolo, Sartori Luigi, Cristianesimo e potere; atti del seminario Trento 21-22 giugno 1985: Trento IstScRel 10. Bo 1986, Dehoniano. 191 p. Lit. 20.000. 88-10-40360-6. 10 art.; 3 infra.

490 ᴱRacine Louis, Ferland Lucien, Dieu écrit-il dans les marges? [Congrès de la Société Canadienne de Théologie ['Le contenu de la foi est-il un préfabriqué par des spécialistes d'une autre classe ou quelque chose qui surgit du dialogue de ceux qui essaient de se parler et de s'en sortir?' (M.-M. Campbell p. 8); il s'agit d'enseigner, non pas 'la foi' mais 'ma foi'

(J. *Goulet* p. 12)]. Montréal 1984, Fides. 190 p. – ᴿScEspr 38 (1986) 282s
(R. *Morency*: fausse la vraie notion de foi).

490* ᴱ**Radmacher** Earl D., *Preus* Robert D., Hermeneutics, inerrancy and
the Bible [Chicago, Nov. 10-13, 1982]. GR 1984, Zondervan. [➤ 65,431].
921 p. $17 pa. 16 art. [32 responses]. – ᴿBS 143 (1986) 272-4 (R. B.
Zuck).

491 ᴱ**Rendtorff** Trutz, Glaube und Toleranz; das theologische Erbe der Aufklärung [Europäischer Theologenkongress, Wien 1981] ➤ 64,525; 65,533:
ᴿTPhil 61 (1986) 272-4 (A. *Schilson*).

492 ᴱ**Riccardi** Andrea, Pio XII [Congrès Bari]. Bari 1984, Laterza. viii-478 p.
18 art. – ᴿRHE 81 (1986) 216-221 (R. *Aubert*: face aux idéologies; aspects
religieux à peine indirectement).

492* **Richards** Michael, *al.* [*Frost* Francis, Œcuménisme], L'influence de la
Patristique sur la pensée religieuse anglaise [Colloque Paris XII]. P 1983,
Didier. 100 p. – ᴿBLitEc 87 (1986) 305 (H. *Crouzel*).

493 ᴱ**Ries** Julien, L'expression du sacré dans les grandes religions [Colloque
1976, I. 1978 ➤ 60,627; II. 1983 ➤ 64,526], III. Mazdéisme, cultes
isiaques, religion grecque, Manichéisme, Nouveau Testament, Vie de
l'Homo Religiosus: Homo religiosus 3. LvN 1986, Centre d.Histoire
des Religions. x-441 p.; bibliog. p. 251-6.328s; 386-397. Fb 1200. 7 art.;
infra.

494 ᴱ**Ries** Julien, Les rites d'initiation; Actes du Colloque de Liège et de
Louvain-la-Neuve, 20-21.XI.1984: Homo Religiosus 13. LvN 1986, Centre Hist. Rel. 559 p. Fb 1400.

495 ᴱ**Rose** Mary Beth, Women in the Middle Ages and the Renaissance;
literary and historical perspectives [Chicago Newberry Library conference
1983]. Syracuse NY 1986, Univ. xxviii-288 p. $30; pa. $12.50 [RelStR
13,77s, Kristine T. *Utterack*].

496 ᴱ**Rouleau** Jean-Paul, *Zylberberg* Jacques, Les mouvements religieux
aujourd'hui; théories et pratiques [colloque international Univ. Laval,
9-11.IX.1982]: Cahiers de Recherches en Sciences de la Religion 5.
Montréal 1984, Bellarmin. 392 p. – ᴿSR 15 (1986) 115-7 (R. *Chagnon*:
comprend hassidisme, féminisme, charismatiques ...).

497 ᴱ**Rouner** Leroy S., Knowing religiously [Boston Univ. lecture program]:
Boston Univ. Studies in Philosophy and Religion 7. ND 1985, Univ.
xvi-213 p. $23. 13 art. – ᴿRelStR 12 (1986) 264 (R. *Grigg*: C. Hartshorne
and A. Flew fail to focus the promised 'ragged dynamics').

498 ᴱ**Russell** Letty M., Changing contexts of our faith [NCC Faith and Order
working group]. Ph 1985, Fortress. 111 p. $5 pa. – ᴿRelStR 12 (1986) 268
(J. T. *Ford*).

498* *Schegget* G. H. ter, present., Driebergen 1986 Barth-Tagung = ZdialektT
2,1 (1986) 7-9 (– 50, al.).

499 ᴱ**Schöpsdau** Walter, Mariologie und Feminismus (29. Europäische Tagung für Konfessionskunde 1985, Bensheim); Bensheimer Hefte
64. Gö 1985, V & R. 143 p. DM 19,80. – ᴿÖkRu 35 (1986) 235s [H.
Vorster].

499* El secuestro de la verdad; los hombres secuestran la verdad con su
injusticia (Rom 1,18) [seminario Centre d'Estudis Cristians i Justícia]:
Presencia Teológica 25. Santander 1986, Sal Terrae. 191 p. 84-293-
0742-7. – ᴿActuBbg 23 (1986) 244 (I. *Salvat*).

500 ᴱ**Selge** Kurt-Victor, Internationaler Schleiermacher-Kongress Berlin
1984. B 1985, de Gruyter. xxiv-640 p.; p. 641-1319. DM 198. 3-11-
010018-5. – ᴿDLZ 107 (1986) 815-9 (J. *Rachold*).

501 ᴱSeybold Michael, Maria im Glauben der Kirche [Forum Eichstätt] 1985
➤ 1,645: ᴿForumKT 2 (1986) 155-7 (A. Ziegenaus).

502 ᴱShiels W. J., Monks, hermits and the ascetic tradition [Ecclesiastical
History society meetings of 1984 and 1985]. Ox 1985, Blackwell. xiv-460 p.
£29.50. 27 art. [RHE 81,751, F. Hockey].

503 ᴱSilbermann Alphons, Schoeps Julius H., Antisemitismus nach dem Ho-
locaust; Bestandsaufnahme und Erscheinungsformen in deutschsprachigen
Ländern: Tagung Katholische Akadamie Schwerte, April 1985. Köln
1986, Wissenschaft und Politik. 195 p. DM 26 pa. – ᴿJudaica 42 (1986)
264-6 (P. Maser).

504 Simpozij o vjerskom indiferentizmu, Zagreb 6-7. XII. 1985 = ObnŽiv
41,3s (1986) 193-269.

505 ᴱSpira Andrea, Klock Christopher, The Easter sermons of GREGORY of
Nyssa [Fourth Nyssa Colloquium, Cambridge, England 1978]: Patristic
Mon. 9. CM [!] 1981, Philadelphia Patristic. x-384 p. $10.– ᴿHeythJ 27
(1986) 88s (J. McGuckin).

506 ᴱStadelmann Helge, Glaube und Geschichte; Heilsgeschichte als Thema
der Theologie [ev. Studienkonferenz, Tübingen 1985]: Monographien und
Studienbücher. Giessen/Wu 1986, Brunnen / Brockhaus. viii-402 p.
DM 29,80 [TLZ 112,531, F. Jacob].

507 ᴱStauffer Anita, North American Academy of Liturgy, Jan. 1986 meeting,
Durham NC = Worship 60,4 (1986) 290-383; 305-311, Sloyan Gerard S.,
Response to the Berakah Award.

508 ᴱTaubes Jacob, Gnosis und Politik [Bad Homburg Kolloquium 1982; B.
Aland, D. Georgi, H. Kippenberg ...]: Religionstheorie und Politische
Theologie 2, 1984 ➤ 1,654; DM 78: ᴿRelStR 12 (1986) 297 (B. A.
Pearson).

509 Technological powers and the person; nuclear energy and reproductive
technologies: 12th Publication, 3d Workshop. St. Louis 1983, Pope John
XXIII Center. xiii-500 p. $15.95. – ᴿAngelicum 63 (1986) 161-3 (A.
Wilder: presumably not John XXII; fascinating for ecclesiologists because
the bishops' reactions are given, though anonymously).

510 ᴱTitton Gentil, Teologia feminista na América Latina [30.X-3.XI.1985,
Buenos Aires]: REB 46,181 (1986) 1-169; Documento Final 168s: 154-166,
Tamez Elsa, A força da nudez [lenda do sacerdote Topiltzin], reflexões
sobre o encontro.

511 ᴱTorrance Thomas F., Theological dialogue between Orthodox and
Reformed Churches. E 1985, Scottish Academic. xxvii-158 p. £10.50. –
ᴿRefTR 45 (1986) 26s (R. Swanton: half the volume is from Torrance
himself, with his predilection for the Greek over the Latin fathers).

511* Trapè A., al.. AGOSTINO e LUTERO; il tormento per l'uomo: Convegni di
S. Spirito 1. Palermo 1985, Augustinus. 124 p. [ETL 62, p.18*].

512 [Vallet Georges, Pietri Charles], Paul VI et la modernité dans l'Église;
Actes du colloque organisé par l'École française de Rome, 2-4 juin 1983:
CollÉcFR 72. R 1984. xxxii-875 p. – ᴿRHE 81 (1986) 623-8 (R.
Aubert).

512* Viard C., al., La présence au monde comme expérience de Dieu; sens de
la vie religieuse 'apostolique' dans l'Église [Session 7-10.II.1983]: Travaux
et Conférences 7. P 1985, Centre Sèvres. 66 p. [ETL 62, p.18*].

513 ᴱWestermann C., Träume verstehen — Verstehen durch Träume [kath.
Tagung Freiburg 1985]. Mü 1986, Schnell & S. 110 p. [ZAW 99,153].

514 ᴱWestfall W. al., Religion/culture; comparative Canadian studies, 7.
Canadian issues [congress Toronto 23-26 May 1984]. Ottawa 1985,

Association des études canadiennes.   410 p. – ᴿSR 15 (1986) 253s (P.-A. *Turcote* franç.)   & 254s (Phyllis D. *Airhart* Eng.).

A2.5   *Acta* **philologica** *et* **historica** [reports ➤ Y7.6]

515 ᴱ**Achard** Pierre, *al.*,   Histoire et linguistique [symposium Paris 1983]. P 1984, Maison des sciences de l'homme.   viii-293 p. – ᴿHistTheor 25 (1986) 115 (M.-P. *Gruenais*).

516 Actes de l'Association pour l'Encouragement des Études Grecques 1985-6: RÉG 99 (1986) IX-XLII. – Liste des membres RÉG 99 (1986) 409-419.

517 Atti del convegno internazionale 'Letterature classiche e narratologia' (Selva di Fasano, Brindisi, 6-8.X.1980): materiali e contributi per la storia narrativa greco-latina 3.   Perugia 1981, Univ. Ist. Fg. Lat.   428 p. Lit. 15.000. – ᴿArctos 19 (1985) 280s (Hannu *Riikonen*).

518 ᴱ**Amata** Biagio,   Cultura e lingue classiche; convegno di aggiornamento e di didattica, Roma 1985: Studi-Testi-Commenti patristici.   R 1986, LAS. 156 p. Lit. 20.000.   88-213-0134-6.   15 art.; ➤ d341, *Reggi* C.

519 ᴱ**Arrigoni** Giampiera,   Le donne in Grecia: Storia e Società.   R 1985, Laterza.   xxx-447 p.; 20 fig.; 24 pl.

519* ᴱ**Bianchi** Ugo,   Transition-rites, cosmic, social and individual order [Acta of Scandinavian-Italian meeting, Univ. Rome 1984].   R 1986, Bretschneider. xv-269 p. [RÉG 100,480, Y. *Vernière*].

520 ᴱ**Bremer** Dieter, *Patzer* Andreas,   Wissenschaft und Existenz, ein inter-disziplinäres Symposium [11.-12.V.1984 München, Uvo HÖLSCHER zu ehren]: WüJbAltW Bei 1.   Wü 1985, Schöningh.   111 p.   3-87717-610-0. 8 art.; 3 infra.

521 ᴱ**Brenk** Frederick E., *Gallo* Italo,   Miscellanea plutarchea; Atti del I convegno di studi su Plutarco, International Plutarch Society, sezione italiana (Roma, presso il Pont. Ist. Biblico, 23 nov. 1985): Giornale Filologico Ferrarese, Quad. 8.   Ferrara 1986.   147 p. Lit. 4000.   9 art.; 4 infra. – ᴿKoinonia 10 (N 1986) 211 (R. *Maisano*).

521* ᴱ**Colombo** Arrigo,   Religione, istituzione, liberazione; studi sul fatto religioso 1981/3 ➤ 66,488: ᴿEstE 61 (1986) 472 (J. J. *Alemany*).

522 [*David* Jean-Michel, présent.],   Rhétorique et histoire; l'exemplum et le modéle de comportement dans le discours antique et médiéval: Table Ronde 18.V.1979. Rome.   MélEcFrR-Mod 92/1.   P/Turin 1980.   179 p. [RHE 81,733, B. Van den *Abeele*].

523 **Duret** Luc,   Programme; liste des membres; compte rendu des séances de la Société des Études Latines: thèses de doctorat: RÉLat 63 (1985) i-xxxii; 1-31.

524 Eidōlopoiia; Actes du Colloque sur les problèmes de l'image dans le monde méditerranéen classique, Lourmarin 2-3.IX.1982: Archaeologica 61.   R 1985, Bretschneider.   197 p.; 4 fig.

525 (EVANGELISTI Enzo, memoriale), Giornata di Studi Camito-Semitici e Indoeuropei (Milano 11.I.1980): Atti del Sodalizio Glottologico Milanese 21 (1979s) 1-93. – ᴿOrAnt 25 (1986) 141-4 (R. *Contini*).

526 La femme dans le monde méditerranéen, I. Antiquité [Séminaire 1982s]: Travaux de la Maison de l'Orient 10.   Lyon/P 1985, Maison de l'Orient/Boccard.   190 p., incl. VI pl.   2-903264-39-2.   11 art.; 1 infra.

527 ᴱ**Flashar** Hellmut, *Gigon* Olof,   Aspects de la philosophie hellénistique: Entretiens sur l'Antiquité Classique 32, 26-31 août 1985.   Genève 1985, Hardt.   x-386 p.   9 art.; 3 infra.

528 ᴱFoxhall Lin, *Davies* John K., The Trojan war, its historicity and context;
    papers of the First Greenbank Colloquium, Liverpool 1981. Bristol 1984,
    Classical Press. x-192 p. 5 maps. £17; pa. £10. – ᴿGreeceR 33 (1986) 90
    (N.R.E. *Fisher*).

529 ᴱGiannantoni Gabriele, Diogene Laerzio storico del pensiero an-
    tico [convegno internazionale Napoli ott. 1985] = Elenchos 7 (1986).
    115 p. Lit. 25.000.

530 ᴱGiannantoni Gabriele, *Vegetti* Mario, La scienza ellenistica; Atti delle tre
    giornate di studio tenutesi a Pavia 14-16.IV.1982: Elenchos 9. N 1985,
    Bibliopolis. 509 p. 88-7088-097-4. 13 art.; 1 infra.

531 ᴱHarris W. V., The imperialism of mid-republican Rome [Colloquium
    1982]: PapMon 29, 1984 → 65,638: ᴿClasR 100 (1986) 332s (J. *Briscoe*:
    GRUEN's extra chorum paper not included).

532 ᴱHattori S., *al.,* Proceedings of the Thirteenth International Congress of
    Linguists, Aug. 29-Sept. 4, 1982, Tokyo 1983 → 1,765: ᴿIndogF 91 (1986)
    336-9 (W.*Euler*).

533 ᴱHellwig Peter, *Lehmann* Hubert, Trends in der linguistischen Daten-
    verarbeitung, Tagung 1983: Sprache und Computer 1. Hildesheim 1986,
    Olms. viii-188 p. DM 29,80. – ᴿDLZ 107 (1986) 827s (J. *Kunze*).

534 [*Kidd* I. G. al.] ᴱFlashar H., *Gigon* O., Aspects de la philosophie
    hellénistique: Entretiens Hardt 32, Genève 26-31.VIII.1985. Genève 1986,
    Hardt. 9 art.

535 ᴱKahanto I., Equality and inequality of man in ancient thought [→ 1,766];
    papers read at the Colloquium in connection with the Assemblée générale
    of the Fédération internationale des Études Classiques held in Helsinki in
    August, 1982: CommHumLit 75. Helsinki 1984, Finnish Soc. Sc. Letters.
    75 p. 951-653-120-2 [NTAbs 31,122].

536 ᴱKreissig H., *Kühnert* F., Antike Abhängigkeitsformen in den grie-
    chischen Gebieten ohne Polisstruktur und den römischen Provin-
    zen: Actes du colloque sur l'esclavage, Iéna, 29 sept. – 2 oct. 1981:
    Schriften zur Geschichte und Kultur der Antike 25. oB 1985, Akademie.
    156 p.

537 ᴱMazza Mario, *Giuffrida* Claudia, Le trasformazioni della cultura nella
    tarda antichità: Atti del Convegno Catania Univ. 27.IX.-2.X.1982. R
    1985, Jouvence. x-490 p.; p. 491-993. 40 art.; 7 infra.

538 ᴱMazzini Innocenzo, *Fusco* Franca, I testi di medicina latini antichi,
    problemi filologici e storici, Atti del convegno internazionale 26-28.IV.
    1984, Univ. Macerata: Lett. Fil. 28. R 1985, Bretschneider. 446 p.
    88-7689-003-3. 19 art.; 2 infra.

539 ᴱNagl-Docekal Herta, *Wimmer* Franz, Neue Ansätze in der
    Geschichtswissenschaft [Tagung W 1983]. W 1984, Wiss. Gesch. 167 p. –
    ᴿHistTheor 25 (1986) 319-331 (R. *Anchor*).

539* ᴱSchlerath Bernfried, (*Rittner* Veronica), Grammatische Kategorien;
    Funktion und Geschichte: Akten der VII. Fachtagung der Indoger-
    manischen Gesellschaft Berlin 20.-25. Februar 1983. Wsb 1985, Reichert.
    VIII-579 p. DM 200 [Kratylos 32,25, W. *Lehmann*].

540 ᴱSchofield Malcolm, *Striker* Gisela, The norms of nature; studies in
    Hellenistic ethics [(3d) Reimers-Stiftung conference, Bad Homburg 17-25
    August 1983. C/P 1986, Univ./Sciences de l'Homme. 287 p. 0-521-
    26623-8 / 2-7151-0147-9. 9 art.; 3 infra [Sales 49,905, G. *Abbà*].

540* [ᴱSilvestri Domenico], Atti del Convegno su 'L'analisi linguistica dei testi
    arcaici, dall'interpretazione alla traduzione' (Napoli, 11-12 novembre
    1985): AION-Clas 7 (1985) 312 p. 11 art.; 6 infra.

541 **Thomas** Y., introd., Du châtiment dans la cité; supplices corporels et peine de mort dans le monde antique; Table ronde Rome 9-11.XI. 1982: Coll. Éc. Fr. 79. R 1984, École Française. 571 p. – ᴿRHR 203 (1986) 414-7 (R. Turcan).

A2.7 Acta orientalistica.

541* ᴱ**Cohen** Amnon, *Baer* Gabriel, Egypt and Palestine; a millennium of association (868-1948) [Israel conference 1981]. J/NY 1984, Ben Zvi Inst./ St. Martin's. – ᴿJRAS (1986) 103-5 (R. G. *Irwin*).
542 ᴱ**Galter** Hannes D., Kulturkontakte und ihre Bedeutung in Geschichte und Gegenwart des Orients; Beiträge zum 1. Grazer Morgenländischen Symposion (19.3.1986): Grazer Morgenländische Studien 1. Graz 1986, Technische Univ. x-136 p. [ZAW 99,292]. 11 art.; 8 infra.
543 ᴱ**Hecker** Karl, *Sommerfeld* Walter, Keilschriftliche Literaturen; ausgewählte Vorträge der XXXII. Rencontre Assyriologique Internationale, Münster 8.-12.VII.1985: Berliner Beiträge zum Vorderen Orient 6. B 1986, Reimer. xviii-164 p.; 1 pl. 3-496-00879-2. 17 art., infra.
544 Journées des Orientalistes Belges [A. Abel; 24; date et lieu non indiqués], résumés des communications: Akkadica 49 (1986) 31-34: 3 infra.
545 ᴱ**Martin** Richard C., Approaches to Islam in religious studies [1980 symposium]. Tucson 1985, Univ. Arizona. xiii-243 p. $19 [RelStR 13,176, Issa J. *Boullata*].
545* ᴱ**Veenhof** Klaas R., Cuneiform archives and libraries; papers read at the 30ᵉ Rencontre Assyriologique Internationale, Leiden, 4-8 July 1983: Uitgaven 57. Leiden 1986, Nederlands Historisch-Archeologisch Instituut te Istanbul. x-307 p.; ill.; program p. 305-7. f 100. 90-6258-057-2. 29 art.; 20 infra.

A2.9 Acta archaeologica [reports → Y7.8].

546 [*Alberton* Bruno present.] Egitto e società antica; Atti del convegno Torino 8/9 VI - 23/24 XI 1984: Centro Toniolo / Univ. Cattolica. Mi 1985, Vita e Pensiero. xii-288 p.; 16 pl. Lit. 40.000. 88-343-3003-X. 19 art,; infra.
546* ᴱ**Ali al-Khalifa** S. H., *Rice* M., Bahrain through the ages; the archaeology [1983 meeting]. L 1986, Kegan Paul. 526 p.; 168 fig. £25. 0-7103-0112-X [BL 87,22]. 48 art.
547 ᴱ**Allchin** B., South Asian Archaeology 1981, proceedings of the Sixth International Conference of the Association of South Asian Archaeologists in Western Europe, Cambridge 5-10 July 1981. C 1984, Univ. ix-347 p.; 280 fig. £35. ᴿBO 43 (1986) 509-518 (E.C.L. *During-Caspers*).
548 Archaeological Institute of America 87th general meeting [Wsh 27-30 Dec. 1985] (Abstracts of papers with index): AJA 90 (1986) 173-226. Some 150 summaries; only 11 samples infra.
548* ᴱ**Bintliff** J.L., *Gaffney* C.F., Archaeology at the interface; studies in archaeology's relationships with history, geography, biology and physical science (Northern University Archaeologists' Research Seminar meeting at Bradford University, March 22, 1986): BAR-Int 300. Ox 1986. 132 p. £8. 0-86054-386-0. 8 art.; infra.
549 ᴱ**Bishop** M.C., Proceedings of the Roman military equipment research seminar I. 1983. Sheffield 1983, Univ. 27 p., 4 fig. – II. The production and distribution...: BAR-Int 275. Ox 1985. 377 p. £20. 0-86054-347-1. 10 art., 5 infra.

550 EBonanno Anthony, Archaeology and fertility cult in the ancient Mediterranean; papers presented at the First International Conference on
Archaeology of the Ancient Mediterranean, the University of Malta 2-5
September 1985. Amst 1986, Grüner. xii-356 p.; 21 fig.; 40 phot. 90-
6032-288-6. 28 art.; 13 infra.

551 EBonnet C., Lipiński E., Marchetti P., Religio phoenicia; Acta colloquii
Namurcensis 14-15. dec. 1984: StPhoen 4 / CollÉtClas 1. Namur 1986,
Soc. Ét. Clas. Fb 2800. 0014-200X. 23 art.; infra. – RSalesianum 48
(1986) 983s (R. Sabin: tit. sans pp.).

551* EBridel Philippe, Le site monastique copte des Kellia; sources historiques
et explorations archéologiques: Actes du Colloque de Genève 13 au 15 août
1984. Genève 1986, Univ. Mission suisse d'archéologie copte. 362 p.; 9
pl. 12 art.; 3 infra.

552 ECederlund Carl O., Postmedieval boat and ship archaeology [interna-
tional symposium Sto 1982]: BAR-Int 256/ Sto Report 20. Sto 1985,
Maritime Museum. 440 p. £33. 0-86054-327-7. – RFornvännen 81 (1986)
245 (K. Koivula).

553 Cinquième colloque du groupe de contact interuniversitaire d'études
phéniciennes et puniques [date et lieu non indiqués]; résumé des [11]
communications faites par des Belges: Akkadica 47 (1986) 79-83: 6 infra.

554 Comparative studies in the development of complex societies. Southampton 1986, World Archaeology Congress. 3 vol.

555 EFarioli Campanati R., III colloquio internazionale sul mosaico antico
[Ravenna 1980]. Ravenna 1983, Girasole. 591 p.; 32 color. pl. Lit.
150.000. – RAntClas 55 (1986) 628-630 (Janine Balty).

555* EFieller N.R.J., al., Paleobiological investigations; research design,
methods and data analysis: Symposia of the Association for Environmental
Archaeology 5B / BAR-Int 266. Ox 1985. 254 p. $20. – RAJA 90 (1986)
347 (Pam J. Crabtree).

556 EGubel E., Lipiński E., Phoenicia and its neighbours [symposium Bru
1983]: Studia Phoenicia 3. Lv 1985, Peeters. 240 p. Fb 1800. 90-6831-
029-1 [BL 87,97, J. F. Healey: tit. pp.].

557 EHaas Volkert, Das Reich Urartu, ein altorientalischer Staat im 1.
Jahrtausend v. Chr. (Konstanzer Altorientalische Symposien 1): Xenia 17.
Konstanz 1986, Univ. 138 p.; ill.

558 EHackens Tony, Schvoerer Max, Datations-caractérisation des céramiques anciennes: Bordeaux-Talence 6-18.IV. 1984, Cours intensif européen: PACT 10. P 1984, CNRS. 433 p.; ill. 2-222-03834-0. 29 art.; 2
infra.

559 EJones R.E., Catling H.W., Science in archaeology; proceedings of a
meeting held at the British School at Athens, January 1985. L 1986,
Leopard's Head. vii-56 p. 0-904887-02-2. 11 art.; 7 infra.

559* ELancel Serge, Histoire et archéologie de l'Afrique du Nord; IIe colloque
international (Grenoble, 5-9 avril, 1983). P 1985, Comité des Travaux
Historiques. 535 p.; ill. F 400. 2-7355-0084-5 [AntiqJ 67,173, C.R.
Whittaker].

560 ELangley Susan B.M., Unger Richard W., Nautical archaeology; progress
and public responsibility [1983 Victoria-Vancouver meeting]: BAR-Int 220.
Ox 1984, BAR. 219 p. $10. – RIntJNaut 15 (1986) 350s (H. Cleere).

561 ELeeuw Sander E. Van der, Pritchard Allison C., The many dimensions of
pottery; ceramics in archaeology and anthropology [meeting Lhee
14-20.III.1982]: Cingula 7. Amst 1984, Univ. xvi-797 p. 90-70319-071. 17
art.; 1 infra.

562 ᴱLouis Pierre, L'eau dans les techniques: L'homme et l'eau en Méditerranée et au Proche Orient III, Séminaire 1981s [I 1979s/81 ► 62,k468; II. 1982 ► 63,d899: ᴱMétral J.]: Travaux 11. Lyon 1986, Maison de l'orient. 128 p. 2-903264-40-6. 13 art.; 9 infra.

563 ᴱMcBryde Isabel, Who owns the past? Papers from the annual symposium of the Australian Academy of the Humanities [Canberra 1983]. Melbourne 1985, Oxford-UP. 198 p.; 13 fig. A$ 29.50. – ᴿAJA 90 (1986) 475s (Karen D. *Vitelli*); Antiquity 60 (1986) 69-71 (J. & Ruth *Megaw*).

563* ᴱMadhlum Tariq, Abdul-Razaq Muyaser S., *al.*, Researches on Ashur in the two international symposiums, 2d and 3d, held in 1979 and 1981: Sumer 42 (1986) 95-97 (-154), ❹ 31s (-88).

564 ᴱMarazzi M., *Tusa* Vincenzo, *al.*, Traffici micenei nel Mediterraneo; problemi storici e documentazione archeologica; Atti del convegno di Palermo, 11-12 maggio e 3-6 dicembre 1984: Magna Graecia 3. Taranto 1986, Ist. Stor. Arch. Magna Grecia. iv-465 p. 38 art., 20 infra.

565 Mari: À propos d'un cinquantenaire, ~ bilan et perspective: Actes du Colloque international du C.N.R.S. 620: MARI 4. P 1985, RCiv. 624 p. F 399. – ᴿZAss 76 (1986) 120-4 (M. *Stol*).

566 Mazzoleni Danilo present., Saecularia Damasiana [convegno XVI centenario, Roma 10-12.XII.1984]. R 1986, Pontificio Istituto di Archeologia Cristiana. 400 p. Lit. 60.000. 16 art.; 5 infra. – ᴿCC 137 (1986,3) 547 (A. *Ferrua*).

566* ᴱMellink Machteld J., Troy and the Trojan War; a symposium held at Bryn Mawr college October 1984. Bryn Mawr PA 1986. ix-101 p.; 20 pl.; foldout map. 7 art.; 4 infra.

567 ᴱMitchell Stephen, Armies and frontiers in Roman and Byzantine Anatolia [Swansea Colloquium Apr. 1981]: BAR-Int. 156, 1983 ► 64,724: ᴿEos 74 (1986) 155-9 (E. *Dąbrowa*, franç.).

568 ᴱMüller-Karpe Hermann, Archäologie und Geschichtsbewusstsein [Bonn DAI]: Kolloquien Allgem. Vergl. Arch. 3. Mü 1982, Beck. 124 p. 3-4060-9043-5. – ᴿBO 43 (1986) 790 (J. van *Loon*).

568* ᴱMüller-Karpe Hermann, Zur frühen Mensch-Tier-Symbiose [Bonn 1982]: Kolloquien zur Allgemeinen und Vergleichenden Archäologie 4. Mü 1983, Beck. vi-241 p. 3-406-30108-8. – ᴿBO 43 (1986) 479-482 (Louise H. van *Wijngaarden-Bakker*, with data on three earlier cognate meetings).

569 ᴱMüller-Wiener Wolfgang, Milet 1899-1980; Ergebnisse, Probleme und Perspektiven einer Ausgrabung; Kolloquium Frankfurt am Main 1980: IstMitt Beih. 31. Tü 1986, Wasmuth. 189 p.; 23 pl. 3-8030-1730-0. 16 art.; infra.

570 *North* Robert, Jordan Paleo-Ecology congress at 'Amman [April 4-11, 1983: detailed official report, containing not only summaries of all the papers (briefer than in the Acta 1985 ► 1,849) but also names and contents of all the discussion-interventions]: Orientalia 55 (1986) 205-235.

571 ᴱRaban Avner, Caesarea Maritima, 24.-28.VI.1983; Proceedings of the international workshop on ancient Mediterranean harbours 1: BAR-Int 257. Ox 1985 [► 1,869] 204 p.; ill. 0-86054-328-5. 18 art., 7 infra. – ᴿIntJNaut 15 (1986) 354-7 (D. *Blackman*).

572 Rom DAI, 150-Jahr-Feier; Ansprachen und Vorträge 4.-7. Dez. 1979; MiDAI Erg-H. 25. Mainz 1982. 209 p.; 384 fig. [non ► 61,53; 63,740] – ᴿAJA 90 (1986) 126-8 (L. *Richardson*: unequal to the occasion).

572* ᴱShelmerdine Cynthia W., *Palaima* Thomas G. [NY Symposium 1984] Pylos comes alive; industry and administration in a Mycenaean palace. NY 1984, Archaeological Institute of America. 107 p.; 13 fig. – ᴿAJA 90 (1986) 356 (J. *Rutter*).

573 ᴱStuiver Minze, *Kra* Renee S., Proceedings of the Twelfth International
Radiocarbon Conference, Trondheim, Norway [June 24-28, 1985]: Radiocarbon 28,2A (1986). xv-804 p. 81 art., 2 infra.

A3   *Opera consultationis* – **Reference works** .1 *plurium* **separately** *infra.*

574 **ANRW**: Aufstieg und Niedergang der römischen Welt, II. Prinzipat, ᴱ**Tem-
porini** H., *al.* [→ 1,880]: **12,3,** Künste, Forts. 1985; xiii-741 p.; 3-11-
009519-X; – **16,3,** ᴱ*Haase* R., Religion [römische, Allgemeines], 1986,
p. 1777-2773; 3-11-008289-6; – **18,1,** ᴱ*Haase* [die religiösen Verhältnisse in
den Provinzen], 1986; viii-871 p.; DM 580; 3-11-010050-9; – **32,4,** ᴱ*Haase,*
Sprache und Literatur (... *Plinius, Quintilian*) 1986; p.(x +) 2069-2677;
DM 380; 3-11-010840-2; – **32,5,** ᴱ*Haase,* Sprache und Literatur (flavische
Zeit, Schluss), 1986; p. 2681-3346; DM 380; 3-11-010954-0. Berlin, de
Gruyter. – ᴿAthenaeum 64 (1986) 262-4 (L. *Troiani*: 21,2); ÉtClas 54
(1986) 216 (A. *Wankenne*:13,3); Judaica 41 (1985) 51s (C. *Thoma*: 21,1s);
RÉJ 145 (1986) 137-141 (Madeleine *Petit*: 21,1); RHR 203 (1986) 107-9 (P.
Nautin: 2,21); TLZ 111 (1986) 825s (T. *Holtz*: 25,3); VigChr 40 (1986) 202-4
(J. van *Winden*: 21,2); ZSav-R 103 (1986) 621-8 (D. *Nörr*: 17,3s; 21,1s;
32,1).

575 **BijH**: Bijbels handboek, ᴱ**Woude** A.S. van der, *al.,* I, IIA, IIB 1981-3
→ 63,750 ... 65,723: ᴿTLZ 111 (1986) 806-8 (K.-D. *Schunck*: 2B).

576 **[BijH]** The world of the Bible, I., ᴱ**Woude** A. S. van der, ᵀ*Woudstra* Sierd.
GR 1986, Eerdmans. xii-400 p., (color.) ill. $35. 0-8028-2405-6. –
ᴿExpTim 98 (1986s) 196 (C. S. *Rodd*).

577 **CAH**: Cambridge Ancient History: 7/1, ᴱ**Walbank** F. W., The Hellenistic
World 1984 → 1,881 (not continuing 2/3): ᴿAJA 90 (1986) 118-120 (K. S.
Sacks); AntiqJ 66 (1986) 163s (F. *Millar*); ClasR 100 (1986) 85-89 (S.
Hornblower); Eos 74 (1986) 135-8 (A. *Świderkówna* ❸); ÉtClas 54 (1986)
424s (H.*Leclercq*).

578 Catholicisme [X,48 → 1,884] ᴱ**Mathon** G., *al.*: XI, 49, col. 1-256,
Perpignan-Pie V; 50, col. 257-511, Pie V-Plérôme. P 1986, Letouzey & A.
ᴿGregorianum 67 (1986) 372s (J. *Janssens*: 47); RHE 81 (1986) 302s (R.
Aubert: 47s); RHPR 66 (1986) 461 (P. *Maraval*: 47s); RThom 86 (1986)
169s (J. L.: 43-47); RTLv 17 (1986) 110.244 (J.-F. *Gilmont*: 46s: sujets
inattendus; 'Région apostolique parisienne' = Paris diocèse;·'Pape' mais à
part 'primauté', 'états pontificaux', 'question romaine', 'Vatican').

579 **CHIran**: The Cambridge history of Iran, II. ᴱ**Gershevitch** Ilya, The Median
and Achaemenian Periods 1985 → 1,885: ᴿAntiqJ 66 (1986) 427s (D. J.
Wiseman); GreeceR 33 (1986) 91 (N.R.E. *Fisher*).

580 **CHJud**: The Cambridge History of Judaism, ᴱ**Davies** W., *al.,* I, 1984
→ 65,728; 1,886: ᴿJBL 105 (1986) 346s (J. J. *Collins*); JJS 37 (1986) 98-100
(M. *Goodman*: an odd mixture); Midstream 32 (NY, Dec. 1986) 52-54 (J.
Strugnell); Mid-Stream 25 (Indianapolis 1986) 245s (R. *Lowery*); NedTTs
40 (1986) 240-2 (A. van der *Kooij*); Teresianum 37 (1986) 254s (F. *Foresti*);
TLZ 111 (1986) 586-8 (S. *Schreiner*: unbefriedigt).

581 **DHGE**: Dictionnaire d'histoire et de géographie ecclésiastiques [XXI,122 s,
1985 → 1,887], ᴱ**Aubert** R.; XXI, 124, – 1520, – Grégoire [+ Sup.] P 1986,
Letouzey & A. – ᴿAnBoll 104 (1986) 459 (F. *Halkin*: XX); RHE 81 (1986)
300s (H. *Silvestre*: 121).

582 **DictSpir** [XII/2, 82 → 1,888] ᴱ**Rayez** A. *al.*; XII/2, fasc. 83-85, – 2942, –
Quodvultdeus (+ Pélage). P 1986, Beauchesne. – ᴿGregorianum 67 (1986)
378s (G. *Rambaldi*: 80ss); OrChrPer 52 (1986) 222-6 (G. *Pelland*: 80ss);

RHE 81 (1986) 302, (R. *Aubert*: 80ss); RHPR 66 (1986) 460s (M. *Cheval-lier*: 80ss); ScEspr 38 (1986) 401s (P.-É. *Langevin*: 80ss); TLZ 111 (1986) 378-381 (W. *Völker* notiert unter anderem pèlerinages).

583 **DPA:** Dizionario patristico e di antichità cristiane, ᴱ**Di Berardino** Angelo: II, 1984 ➤ 1,889: ᴿRasT 27 (1986) 189s (E. *Cattaneo*: 2).

584 **EncIslam:** Encyclopédie de l'Islam² [V, 98 ➤ 1,891], VI, fasc. 99-100, Mahkama-Makhdūm, col, 1-128, ᴱ**Bosworth** C. E., *al.* Leiden/P 1986, Brill/Maisonneuve. 90-04-08313-8.

584* **EncKat:** ❷ Encyklopedia katolicka I-IV, 1973-83 ➤ 60,877 ... 1,736: ᴿSTWsz 24,1 (1986) 277-284 (A. *Zuberbier*: jako narzędzie pracy teolo-gicznej, as theological tool).

585 **EncRel:** The encyclopedia of religion; a comprehensive guide to the history, beliefs, concepts, practices, and major figures of religions past and present, ᴱ**Eliade** Mircea. NY c. 1986, Macmillan. 16 vol. 0-02-909480-1.

586 **EnzMär:** Enzyklopädie des Märchens, ᴱ**Ranke** Kurt [IV, 4s ➤ 1,892]; V, 1.2s (1986) col. 1-288, Fortuna – Freundesprobe; 289-864, – Gegenspieler. B, de Gruyter. 3-11-015 90-X; 91-8. – ᴿAnBoll 104 (1986) 246s (J. van der Straeten).

587 **EvKL:** Evangelisches Kirchenlexikon, ᴱ**Fahlbusch** E. [I,1 ➤ 1,893] – Ehe. Gö 1985, Vandenhoeck & R. – ᴿActuBbg 23 (1986) 65-67 (J. *Boada*); EvKomm 19 (1986) 353 (J. *Lell*); KerkT 37 (1986) 266s (A. J. *Bronkhorst*); TLZ 111 (1986) 257s (E. *Winkler*); TsTNijm 26 (1986) 83 (R. *Cornelissen* 1,1), 292 (B. L. de *Groot-Kopetzky* 1,2).

588 **EWSp:** Encyclopedia of World Spirituality [25 volumes foreseen ➤ 1,376*, ᴱ*McGinn* B.]: 13. ᴱ**Green** Arthur, Jewish spirituality. NY/L 1986, Cross-road/Routledge-KP. 450 p. $49.50 / £39.50. /0-7102-0926-6. – ᴿExpTim 98 (1986s) 190 (G. S. *Wakefield*).

589 **HbDTg:** Handbuch der Dogmen- und Theologiegeschichte, ᴱ**Andresen** Carl, I-II ➤ 1,897; III. ᴱ**Benrath** Gustav A., *al.*, Die Lehrentwicklung im Rahmen der Ökumenizität 1984 ➤ 65,739*; 1,g123: ᴿActuBbg 23 (1986) 57-61 (J. *Boada*: 1-3) Protestantesimo 41 (1986) 102-5 (V. *Subilia*); Sale-sianum 48 (1986) 171s (P. T. *Stella*): 1; TR 82 (1986) 59-61 (P. *Schäfer*); TsTNijm 26 (1986) 188s (T. *Schoof*); ZkT 108 (1986) 96-99 (L. *Lies*:1-3); ZRGg 38 (1986) 72-75 (R. *Heiligenthal*:1s).

590 **HbFT:** ᴱ**Kern** Walter, *al.* [1s, 1985 ➤ 1,898], 3. Traktat Kirche. FrB 1986, Herder. 288 p. DM 38. – ᴿEstE 61 (1986) 469-471 (J. J. *Alemany*: 1s); ExpTim 98 (1986s) 336 (G. *Wainwright*); TPhil 61 (1986) 601-4 (P. *Knauer*: 1s); ZkT 108 (1986) 325-328 (W. *Klausnitzer*: 1s).

590* **ISBEnc:** The international standard Bible encyclopedia³ʳᵉᵛ [¹1915, ²1929], ᴱ**Bromiley** Geoffrey W. [Vol. I, 1979 ➤ 60,884; II. 1982 ➤ 63,763] III K-P. GR/Exeter 1986, Eerdmans/Paternoster xix-1060 p. $37.50 [TDig 34,77]. 0-8028-8163-7. – ᴿExpTim 98 (1986s) 345s (R. *Coggins*: rich but defensive).

591 **LexÄg;** Lexikon der Ägyptologie, ᴱ**Helck** Wolfgang, *Westendorf* Wolfhart [VI,46 (1985) ➤ 1,900] VI,47, Verehrung – Wadi Schatt, col. 961-1119; 3-447-02602-2; – VI,48, – Witwe, – 1280; 3-447-02644-8; VI,49, – Zypress, – 1456; 3-447-02657-2: Schluss [aber noch zu erwarten: VII General-Index, Nachträge]. Wsb 1986, Harrassowitz.

592 **LexMA:** Lexikon des Mittelalters [III, 8, 1985 ➤ 1,901], ᴱ**Bautier** R.-H. *al.* Lfg. 9s. Mü 1986, Artemis. 1793-2016-2220, Elegienkomödie-Enns-Erziehung. 3-7608-9920-1; 30-5 [8903-4 vol. III]. – ᴿAnzAltW 39 (1986) 115-122 (W. *Trillitzsch*: 2); ArHPont 23 (1985) 282-4 (P. *Rabikauskas*: 2,9s; 3,1-6); RÉLat 63 (1985) 431s (J. *Fontaine*: 3,4-6); RHE 81 (1986) 223s (J. *Pycke*: 3); ZkT 108 (1986) 447-9 (H. B. *Meyer*: 3).

593 **NDNTh:** The new international dictionary of NT theology I-III, E[*Coenen*
L.] **Brown** Colin, 1975-8 → 58,4407; 60,888; [IV.] Scriptural Indexes by
Townsley D., *Bjork* R. 1985 → 1,902; 0-310-44501-9: RCalvaryB 2,1
(1986) 68 (G. H. *Lovik*); TS 47 (1986) 341s (J. A. *Fitzmyer*).
594 **RAC:** Reallexikon für Antike und Christentum [XIII,101 → 1,903], E**Dassmann** Ernst, *al.*, Sup. [1-3, 1985 → 1,904], Lfg. 4, Anredeformen-Athen I.
Stu 1986, Hiersemann. Col. 481-640. 3-772-8604-4. – RJTS 37 (1986)
612-620 (C. P. *Hammond Bammel*: 85-90: no 'God'); VigChr 40 (1986)
392-6 (J. Van *Winden*: Sup. 1ss).
595 **SDB** [X,59 → 1,906]; XI,60 Safaïtique – Saint Esprit, E**Briend** J., *Cothenet*
E. P 1986, Letouzey & A. 256 col. F 218 [BL 87,9].
595* **TDNT** 1-vol., **Bromiley** G. 1985 → 1,907: RJAAR 54 (1986) 765s (M. L.
Soards: fears misuse).
596 **TDOT:** Theological dictionary of the Old Testament, E[*Botterweck* G.J. †]
Ringgren Helmer [1. 1974 → 56,6343; 4. 1981 → 62,871], 5. *ḥrm-YHWH'*,
T*Green* David E. GR 1986, Eerdmans. xx-521 p. $27.50. 0-8028-2329-7.
– RExpTim 98 (1986s) 83 (W. *Johnstone*); SWJT 29,2 (1986) 53 (D. G.
Kent); TS 47 (1986) 740 (J. A. *Fitzmyer*).
597 **TRE:** Theologische Realenzyklopädie [XIV, 1985 → 1,909], E**Müller** Ger-
hard; 15, Heinrich II.–Ibsen. B 1986, de Gruyter. 808 p. 3-11- 008585-2. –
RCiuD 199 (1986) 334s (J. M. *Ozaeta*: 13s); ComLtg 68 (1986) 93 (J.
Dupont); DLZ 107 (1986) 437-441 (G. *Wendelkorn*: 11ss); ÉTRel 61 (1986)
157-9 (B. *Reymond*: 13); ÖkRu 35 (1986) 360 (H. *Krüger*); Protestantesimo
41 (1986) 42-44 (V. *Subilia*: 12); RHPR 66 (1986) 459s (M.-A. *Chevallier*:
13s); TLZ 111 (1986) 881-4 (E.-H. *Amberg*: 13); TPQ 134 (1986) 204s (G.
Bachl: 12s); TR 82 (1986) 274s (R. *Bäumer*: 14: *Heidegger* politisch
verharmlost); TRu 51 (1986) 224-9 (E. *Grässer*: 8ss); TZBas 42 (1986) 174s
(W. *Rordorf*: 10-12); ZkT 108 (1986) 99s (L. *Lies*: 10).
598 **TUmAT** [→ 1,910] Dietrich M. [Ugarit, Mari], *al.*, **2/1:** Religiöse Texte;
Deutungen der Zukunft in Briefen, Orakeln und Omina. Gü 1986, Mohn.
157 p. DM 116, sb. 98. 3-579-00066-7 [BL 87,95, W. G. *Lambert*: mostly
not in ANET]. – RStreven 53 (1985s) 564 (P. *Beentjes*: 1/6).
599 **TWAT:** Theologisches Wörterbuch zum Alten Testament, E[*Botterweck*
G. J. †] **Ringgren** Helmer, *Fabry* Heinz-Josef [V, 3s, 1985 → 1,911], V, 5s,
col. 513-768, *na'ar – S^edôm*; 7s, col. 769-1024, – *'ābar*; 9s, col. 1025-1207, –
'āzab [+ 605-632, deutsche Stichwörter]. Stu 1986, Kohlhammer. 3-17-
009075-5; 284-7; 465-3 (680-X Band V). – RTR 82 (1986) 369s (W. *Kornfeld*: 3-6).

A3.2   *Opera consultationis non separatim infra;* **not subindexed.**

600 **Abrams** M. H., A glossary of literary terms. NY 1981, Holt-RW. vii-220 p.
600* E**Achtemeier** Paul J. [SBL], Harper's Bible dictionary 1985 → 1,913:
RBAR-W 12,6 (1986) 58s (W. *Harrelson*); CurrTM 13 (1986) 122 (R. W.
Klein: boner 'Samaritan Pentateuch arose out of a conflict in the 5th
century'; its present shape should probably be tied to 100 B.C.E.); ExpTim
98 (1986s) 51 (C. S. *Rodd*: curiously long articles on OT/NT sociology: H.
KEE, R. WILSON); JBL 105 (1986) 699s (M. de *Jonge*: emphasis on
sociology and archeology good, but outweighs what would be expected in
more classic approaches); JStJud 17 (1986) 251s (F. *Garcia Martinez*:
high-class, but for postexilic period gives notably less on papyri than on
archeology); RExp 83 (1986) 297s (R. L. *Omanson*: best available today);
TS 47 (1986) 300s (D. J. *Harrington*).

601 [**Alexander** P. & D.] *a*) The Lion concise Bible handbook; – *b*) The Lion concise Bible encyclopedia; – *c*) The Lion concise book of Bible quotations: all abridged by [E]**Manser** Martin H. L 1986. £4.95 each. – [R]CleR 71 (1986) 347 (J. R. *Duckworth*: recommends).

601* **Alexander** David & Pat, [➤ 1,914ss] *a*) [minor revision of British 1973] Eerdmans' handbook to the Bible. GR 1987, Eerdmans. 680 p. $29.95 [RelStR 13,342, J. H. *Elliott*]. – *b*) O Mundo da Bíblia [cf. ➤ 63,775]. São Paulo 1986, Paulinas. 693 p. – [R]REB 46 (1986) 718 (L. *Garmus*).

602 **Bacharach** Jere L., A Middle East studies handbook [= [2]A Near East ... 1974]. C 1985, Univ. x-160 p. £25; pa. £9.95. – [R]BSOAS 49 (1986) 247 (D. O. *Morgan*).

602* **Barucq** A. [Égypte p. 59-105], *al.*, Écrits de l'Orient ancien et sources bibliques, AT: PBibScB 2. P 1986, Desclée. 318 p. F 135 [EsprV 97,99, L. *Monloubou*]. 2-7189-0308-2. ➤ 7546*; 7785*.

603 [E]**Boardman** John, *Griffin* Jasper, *Murray* Oswyn, The Oxford history of the classical world. Oxford 1986, Univ. x-882 p.; 300 fig.; 20 pl.; 10 maps. £25. 0-19-872112-9. – [R]Antiquity 60 (1986) 245s (F. *Stubbings*); Tablet 240 (1986) 863 (D. *Scott*: superb).

604 **Bryant** T. A., Today's dictionary of the Bible. Minneapolis 1982, Bethany. 678 p.; 14 pl. – [R]BAR-W 12,6 (1986) 60 (W. *Harrelson*).

605 [E]**Chevalier** Jean, *Cheerbrant* Alain, Diccionario de los símbolos [1969, 'symbol', not 'creed'], [T]*Silvar* Manuel, *Rodríguez* Arturo, [E]*Olives Puig* J. Barc 1986, Herder. 1107 p.; ill. pt 7500. 84-254-1514-4. – [R]ActuBbg 23 (1986) 317 (A. *Borrás*); Carthaginensia 2 (1986) 120 (F. *Oliver Alcón*).

606 [E]**Conrad** Rudi, Lexikon sprachwissenschaftlicher Termini. Lp 1985, VEB. 281 p. – [R]Salesianum 48 (1986) 769s (R. *Bracchi*).

607 **Corsten** Severin, *al.*, Lexikon des gesamten Buchwesens[2] [[1]1935-7, 3 vol., [E]*Löffler* K.; 5 vols. de 640 p. prévus; Lfg. 1, A-Ammann. Stu 1985, Hiersemann. 80 p. DM 38. – [R]RHE 81 (1986) 631 (J.-F. *Gilmont*).

608 **Cotterell** Arthur, A dictionary of world mythology[2rev] [[1]1979 ➤ 61,k718]: Oxford Paperback Reference. Ox 1986, UP. 314 p. 0-19-217747-8. – [R]Salesianum 48 (1986) 967 (R. *Della Casa*).

609 [E]**Davies** J. G., A new [U.S.: The new Westminster] dictionary of liturgy and worship [= [2]The Westminster dictionary of worship 1979]. L/Ph 1986, SCM/Westminster. xv-544 p. $30 [TDig 33,482] / £19.50. 0-334-02207-X/. – [R]ExpTim 97 (1985s) 344 (C. S. *Rodd*: some 70 new articles, many on feminism; also dance, cremation, handicapped); Themelios 12 (1986s) 69 (J. *Fenwick*); TLond 39 (1986) 493s (M. *Perham*: [1]1972 revised but not thoroughly; Handicapped replaces Gregorian Chant; Inclusive Language replaces Incense; Anglican contributors more sensitive to Roman usage than vice versa).

609* [E]**De Fiores** Stefano, *Meo* Salvatore, Nuovo dizionario di Mariologia. Cinisello Balsamo 1985, Paoline. 1560 p. Lit. 52.000. – [R]CC 137 (1986,2) 301s (V. *Caporale*); HumBr 41 (1986) 944s (A. *Biazzi*); RClerIt 67 (1986) 633-7 (S. *Meo*).

610 **de Lange** Nicholas, Atlas of the Jewish world. NY 1985, Facts on File. 240 p. 0-87196-043-5.

610* [E]**Douglas** J. D. *al.*, The [New/] illustrated Bible dictionary[2] (3 vol.; [1]1962, 1 vol.) 1980 ➤ 62,890 ... 65,765: [R]BR 2,1 (1986) 17s (H. O. *Thompson*).

611 [E]**Easterling** P. E., *Knox* B. M. W., The Cambridge history of classical literature, I. Greek literature 1985 ➤ 1,928: [R]AntClas 55 (1986) 376-380 (H. Van *Looy*); ClasR 100 (1986) 247-252 (W. G. *Arnott*).

612 [E]**Eicher** P., Neues [= *Fries* H.[2]] Handbuch theologischer Grundbegriffe [[1]1962s, 2 Bände], 1984s ➤ 1,935: [R]ComSev 19 (1986) 91s (M. de *Burgos*); Laurentianum 27 (1986) 162s (J. *Imbach*); ÖkRu 35 (1986) 122s (H. *Krüger*); SNTU-A 11 (1986) 215s (A. *Fuchs*); Universitas 41 (1986) 87 (G. *Förster*).

613 [E]**Elwell** Walter A., Evangelical dictionary of theology 1984 ➤ 65,766; 1,936: [R]BS 143 (1986) 74s (J. L. *Burns*).

614 [E]**Fabris** Rinaldo, La spiritualità del Nuovo Testamento I [sette volumi previsti]: Storia della Spiritualità 2. R 1985, Borla. 439 p. – [R]Salesianum 48 (1986) 415s (A. M. *Triacca*).

615 [R]**Fahlbusch** Erwin, Taschenlexikon Religion und Theologie [4rev] [[1]1971] 1983 ➤ 1,936*: [R]ZkT 108 (1986) 103 (L. *Lies*: aktuell, 'Narzissmus'; zweifelhaft 'theologisch').

616 **Flon** C., Le grand Atlas Universalis de l'archéologie. P 1985, Encyclopaedia Universalis. 424 p.; color. ill. – [R]RArchéol (1986) 161s (P. *Demargne*).

618 [E]**Gentz** William H., The dictionary of Bible and religion. Nv 1986, Abingdon. 1147 p.; 280 fig.; 16 pl.; 44 (color.) maps. $27. – [R]BAR-W 12,6 (1986) 57s (W. *Harrelson*).

619 **Gilliéron** Bernard, Dictionnaire biblique 1985 ➤ 1,939: [R]ÉTRel 61 (1986) 110s (J. *Pons*).

620 [E]**Goldammer** Kurt, [[1]*Bertholet* A.], Wörterbuch der Religionen [4rev]: Taschenausgabe 125. Stu 1985, Kröner. x-679 p.

621 **Grant** Michael, A guide to the ancient world; a dictionary of classical place names. NY 1986, H. W. Wilson. 728 p. $65 [RelStR 13,258, A. T. *Kraabel*].

622 **Grimal** P., The dictionary of classical mythology [1951], [T]*Maxwell-Hyslop* A. R. Ox 1985, Blackwell. ix-603 p. $35. 0-631-13209-0 [NTAbs 31,121].

622* **Grollenberg** L., *Corswant* W. [*Galbiati* Enrico present.] Dizionario enciclopedico della Bibbia e del mondo biblico. Mi 1986, Massimo. xi-850 p. Lit. 56.000. 88-7030-719-0. – [R]Antonianum 61 (1986) 489s (Z. I. *Herman*: traduzione appena ampliata di GROLLENBERG L. + CORSWANT W.; non raccomandata); ParVi 31 (1986) 320 (F. *Mosetto*: non si deve dire che bene); StCattMi 30 (1986) 793 (U. *De Martino*).

623 **Hamman** Adalbert G., Breve dizionario dei Padri della Chiesa 1983 ➤ 64,788; appendice italiana *Zani* Antonio: [R]Salesianum 48 (1986) 139 (S. *Felici*).

624 [E]**Haran** Menaḥem, ⊕ *Enṣiqlopediya 'olam ha-T[e]nak, ...* the Biblical World. Ramat-Gan 1982-4, Revivim. I (1–) 11s [KirSef 59,307].

625 *Harrelson* Walter, What is a good Bible dictionary? [survey of eight, not including Interpreter's, Encyclopedic, or MCKENZIE...]: BAR-W 12,6 (1986) 54-61.

625* **Haussig** Hans W., al., Wörterbuch der Mythologie I/4, Götter und Mythen der kaukasischen und iranischen Völker. Stu 1986, Klett-Cotta. xix-546 p.; 13 pl.; 3 maps. DM 310 [Kratylos 32,168, R. *Schmitt*].

626 **Heinz-Mohr** G., Lessico di iconografia cristiana. Mi 1984, IPL. 363 p. Lit. 30.000. – [R]Asprenas 33 (1986) 110s (A. *Rolla*).

627 [E]**Hinnells** John R., A handbook of living religions. Hmw 1985, Penguin = L 1984, Viking. 528 p. £4.95. 0-14-022342-8. – [R]ExpTim 98 (1986s) 59 (G. *Parrinder*: valuable companion to Hinnells' Penguin Dictionary of Religions 1984 ➤ 65,775).

628 **Jólesz** Károly, ⊗ Zsidó hitéleti kislexikon [Jewish faith-life]. Budapest 1985, MIOK. 253 p. ft. 190 (c. $4) – [R]Theologiai Szemle 29 (1986) 128 (J. S. *Szénási*).

628* EJones Cheslyn, *Wainwright* Geoffrey, *Yarnold* Edward [editors of The study of liturgy; here 60 authors], The study of spirituality. L 1986, SPCK. 634 p. £25; pa. £15. 0-281-04241-2; 150-4. – RExpTim 98 (1986s) 248 (R. *Howe*).

629 EKeeley Robin, Christianity in today's world [63 contributors]. GR 1985, Eerdmans. 384 p. $30 [TDig 33,356].

630 Kelly J.N.D., The Oxford dictionary of Popes. Ox 1986, UP. 347 p. 0-19-213964-9 [ExpTim 97,384].

631 EKrüger Hanfried, *al.*, Ökumene Lexikon; Kirchen, Religionen, Bewegungen: 1983 → 64,796 ... 1,949: RTrierTZ 95 (1986) 158s (E. *Sauser*).

632 Lefèvre Y., Novum glossarium mediae latinitatis ab anno DCCC usque ad annum MCC. K 1985, Munksgaard. viii-204 col. – RRHE 81 (1986) 222 (R. *Aubert*: 'Pagina 2s' = Écr. Ste).

633 LIMC: Lexicon iconographicum mythologiae classicae, EKahil Lilly, II. Z 1984, Artemis. 110 p.; vol. de 809 pl. → 65,781; 1,947: RRArchéol (1986) 159-161 (J. *Pouilloux*); RBgPg 63 (1985) 151-4 (R. *Lambrechts*).

634 ELockyer Herbert, Nelson's illustrated Bible dictionary [5500 items]. Nv 1986, Nelson. xi-1128 p.; 9 maps; 500 (color.) ill. $27. 0-8407-4955-4 [NTAbs 31,93]. – RBAR-W 12,6 (1986) 59 (W. *Harrelson*: best for color photos); SWJT 29 (1986s) 62 (A. *Fasol*).

635 Macquarrie John, ²*Childress* James F., A new dictionary of Christian Ethics. L/Ph 1986, SCM/Westminster. 678 p. £19.50. 0-334-02205-3/ 0-664-20940-8. – RExpTim 98 (1986s) 87 (C. S. *Rodd*: notable changes).

636 Maier J., *Schaefer* P., Piccola enciclopedia dell'ebraismo, TLeoni D. Casal Monferrato 1985, Marietti. 656 col. Lit. 45.000. – RAsprenas 33 (1986) 433-5 (A. *Rolla*); StPatav 33 (1986) 437s (G. *Leonardi*).

637 Maurer Helmar, Kleines Register zur Bibel; wo steht was – was steht wo? Ein Inhaltsverzeichnis zur gesamten Bibel mit Apokryphen in fortlaufender und alphabetischer Ordnung: Bibel-Kirche-Gemeinde 21. Konstanz 1986, Christl.-V. 237 p. [TLZ 112,334, V. *Hirth*].

637* EMayer Cornelius (*Chelius* K.), *al.*, Augustinus-Lexikon I/1s, Aaron-Anima. Ba 1986, Schwabe. LI-329 p. Fs 60 [TLZ 112, 730-4, H.-U. *Delius*].

638 EMehling Marianne, Knaurs Grosser Bibelführer. Mü 1985, Droemer Knaur. 684 p.; 400 color. fig.; 2700 Stichwörter. DM 49,80. – RTrierTZ 95 (1986) 230 (R. *Bohlen*: archäologische Mängel).

639 Melton J. Gordon, The encyclopedia of American religions²rev. Detroit 1986, Gale. xv-899 p. $165 [TDig 34,85].

640 Monloubou L., *Du Buit* F.M., Dictionnaire biblique universel 1985 → 65,786; 1,959: REsprV 96 (1986) 134 (A. *Marchadour*: negligences); NRT 108 (1986) 420s (X. *Jacques*).

640* Müller P.-G., Lexikon exegetischer Fachbegriffe: BBasB 1, 1985 → 1,960: RBiKi 41 (1986) 92s (J. H. *Schroedel*); SNTU-A 11 (1986) 216 (A. *Fuchs*).

641 Müller Richard A., Dictionary of Latin and Greek theological terms, drawn principally from Protestant scholastic theology. GR 1985, Baker. 340 p. $13. – RThemelios 12 (1986s) 67 (B. *Demarest*).

642 ENegev Avraham, The archaeological encyclopedia of the Holy Land ²rev [¹1972 → 54,7986]. Nv 1986, Nelson. 419 p. $25. – RSWJT 29,2 (1986s) 50s (T. *Brisco*).

643 Patrinacos Nicon D., A dictionary of Greek Orthodoxy. NY 1984, Gr. Orthodox Archdiocese. 392 p. $18. – RRelStT 6 (1986) 57s (G. C. *Papademetriou*).

644 [*Poswick*. R.-F. *al.*] Dictionnaire de la Bible et des religions du Livre 1985 ➤ 1,968: ᴿEsprV 96 (1986) 135 (L. *Monloubou*: religion du livre, l'Islam? ou de l'anti-Livre?); ÉTRel 61 (1986) 276s (D. *Lys*: beau); PrêtreP 89 (1986) 319 (J.-Y. *Garneau*).

645 ᴱ**Poupard** Paul, *al.*, Dictionnaire des religions [section 3, ᴱ*Cothenet* É., Bible et judaïsme] ²1985 ➤ 1,970: ᴿRCuBíb 10,37s (1986) 157s (J. E. *Martins Terra*); RThom 86 (1986) 164-6 (M.-V. *Leroy*: section de Cothenet sur la Bible la mieux réussie); TS 47 (1986) 341 (W. C. *Marceau*); ZMissRW 70 (1986) 87s (P. *Antes*).

646 **Richards** Laurence O., Expository dictionary of Bible words: Regency Reference Library 1985 ➤ 1,971; 0-310-39000-I: ᴿAndrUnS 24 (1986) 197-9 (W. H. *Shea*); CalvaryB 2,2 (1986) 70s (G. H. *Lovik*); ExpTim 97 (1985s) 342s (J. *Snaith*).

647 **Roty** Martine, Dictionnaire russe-français des termes en usage dans l'Église russe ²ʳᵉᵛ 1983 ➤ 63,810; 1,973: ᴿSalesianum 48 (1986) 794s (R. *Della Casa*).

648 ᴱ**Ruh** Ulrich, *al.*, Handwörterbuch religiöser Gegenwartsfragen. FrB 1986, Herder. 519 p. [TR 83,425].

648* [ᵀ*Ruiz Garrido* Constantino], Diccionario bíblico abreviado [Concise Bible encyclopedia]: Nueva Imagen 3. Estella/M 1986, VDivino/ Paulinas. 306 p.; ill. pt. 1300. 84-7151-408-7 / 84-285-1083-0 [ActuBbg 24,78].

649 ᴱ**Scholder** Klaus, **Kleinmann** Dieter, Protestantische Profile; Lebensbilder aus fünf Jarhunderten. Königstein 1983, Athenäum. 411 p. 3-7610-8257-6. – ᴿEstE 61 (1986) 252 (J. J. *Alemany*: un insólito flos sanctorum).

650 [ᴰ*Shanks* Hershel] ᴱ**Alley** James, Who's who in biblical studies and archaeology¹ 1986-7. Wsh 1986, Biblical Archaeology Society. viii-272 p. 0-9613089-3-1. 1500 names.

651 ᴱ**Shepard** Leslie, Encyclopedia of occultism and parapsychology². Detroit 1985, Gale. 3 vol.: p.xi-570; –993; –1617. 0-8103-0196-2.

652 ᴱ**Stoeckle** Bernhard, Wörterbuch der ökologischen Ethik: Bücherei 1262. FrB 1986, Herder. 159 p. DM 8,90 [TLZ 112,66, J. *Wiebering*].

653 **Stupperich** Robert, Reformatorenlexikon [300 Kurzbiographien] 1984 ➤ 1,976: ᴿTLZ 111 (1986) 673s (J. *Rogge*).

653* ᴱ**Tribout de Morembert** H., *al.*, Dictionnaire de biographie française [I, 1929] XVI: Gilbert-Guéroult; XVII,97s: – Halicka. P 1982-5, Letouzey & Â. 1528. col./511 col. [EsprV 97,431].

654 ᴱ**Urban** Hans-Jörg, *Wagner* Harald, Handbuch der Ökumenik: Möhler-Institut. ·Pd 1985s, Bonifatius. 352 p.; 272 p. DM 48; DM 36. 3-87088-454-1; 5-X. – ᴿForumKT 2 (1986) 241s (L. *Scheffczyk*); NorTTs 87 (1986) 244-8 (Ola *Tjørhom*); ÖkRu 35 (1986) 342-5. 477-9 (H. *Gaese*); TüTQ 166 (1986) 316s (R. *Reinhardt*).

655 **Weger** Karl-Heinz, La crítica religiosa en los tres últimos siglos; dicccionario de autores y escuelas [Religionskritik von der Aufklärung bis zur Gegenwart 1979 ➤ 60,1001], ᵀ*Gancho* Claudio. Barc 1986, Herder. 404 p. pt 1800. 84-254-1499-7. – ᴿActuBbg 23 (1986) 233s (J. *Boada*).

655* [➤ 1,945, **IllDConc**, dated 1985] ᴱ**Wigoder** Geoffrey, *Paul* Shalom M., *Viviano* Benedict T., *Stern* Ephraim, Illustrated Dictionary and Concordance of the Bible [...*Freedman* D., *Gilbert* M., *Murphy-O'Connor* J., *Talmon* S.]. NY/L 1986, Macmillan/Collier. 1070 p. $100 [RelStR 13,342, W. L. *Humphreys*; BL 88,26, A. G. *Auld*]. 0-02-916380-3.

656 **Young** G. Douglas, *Giancumakis* George, Young's Bible dictionary 1984
   ➤ 1,980:   ᴿBAR-W 12,6 (1986) 61 (W. *Harrelson*: numerous mis-
   spellings).

A4   Bibliographiae .1 biblicae.

657 **Allison** J. D., The Bible study resource guide². Nv 1984, Nelson. 232 p.
   $7. 0-8407-5814-6 [NTAbs 30,215].
658 **Attal** Robert, Les Juifs de Grèce; bibliographie. J 1984, BenZvi.
   215-XXIV p. – ᴿRÉJ 145 (1986) 305 (H. V. *Sephiha*).
659 **BL** [➤ 1,1002]: **Knibb** Michael A. [with this issue handing over the
   editorship to A. Graeme **Auld**], Society for Old Testament Study Book
   List 1986. 158 p. 0-905495-05-5. [£6 from Manchester Univ., M.E.J.
   Richardson].
660 **Borchert** G. L., Paul and his interpreters – an annotated bibliography:
   IBR Bibliographic Study Guides. Madison WI 1985, Theological Students
   Fellowship. vi-123 p. [1000+ items]. $3.50 pa. [NTAbs 30,360].
661 **Breslauer** S. Daniel, Modern Jewish morality; a bibliographical survey:
   Bibliographies and indexes in religious studies 8. Westport CT 1986,
   Greenwood. x-239 p. $40 [TDig 33,460].
662 *a*) *Briend* Jacques, Bulletin d'exégèse de l'Ancien Testament; – *b*) *Paul*
   André, Bulletin du Judaïsme ancien [moderne, *Bourel* D.]; – *c*) *Guillet*
   Jacques, Bulletin d'exégèse synoptique; RechSR 74 (1986) 615-629 /
   129-157 [559-574] / 221-252.
663 **Bunis** David M., Sephardic studies; a research bibliography [incorporating
   Judezmo language, literature and folklore, and historical background] 1981
   ➤ 65,802: ᴿRÉJ 145 (1986) 153-6 (H.-V. *Sephiha*).
664 **Campbell** Richard H., *Pitts* Michael R., The Bible on film: a checklist,
   1897-1980. Metuchen NJ 1981, Scarecrow. ix-214 p.; ill. [KirSef 59,286].
664* *Chilton* Bruce, Bibliographische Ergänzungen zu Die Muttersprache Jesu
   von Matthew BLACK: ➤ 140*, Targumic 1986, 153-162.
665 *a*) *Coggins* R. J., Recent continental OT literature [8 books]: ExpTim 97
   (1985s) 298-301; 98 (1986s) 362-5, (also 8 books); – *b*) *Best* Ernest, Recent
   continental NT literature [6 books; *Berger* K., *Strecker* Bergpredigt,
   Schmithals Synoptics ...]: ExpTim 97 (1985s) 328-332; 98 (1986s) 300-5
   (infra).
666 ᴱ**Dietrich** Manfred, *Loretz* O., *Delsman* W. C., *al.*, Ugarit-Bibliographie
   1967-1971, [vol. 1-4, 1973 ➤ 55,6027], Band 5, Titel, Nachträge, Register:
   AOAT 20/5. Kevelaer/Neuk 1986, Butzon & B / Neuk.-V. vii-814 p.
   3-7666-9459-6 / Neuk 3-7887-1243-0.
667 Dissertation abstracts *a*) 47 (1986s) infra; *b*) [< DissA 43,5-12 (1982s);
   44,1-6 (1983s)]: StudiaBT 13 (1983) 77-118. 226-272.
668 EHRLICH: *Stegemann* Ekkehard, *Ehrensperger* Käthy, Bibliographie Ernst
   Ludwig Ehrlich (1952-1985): Judaica 42 (1986) 113-122.
669 *García Martínez* Florentino, Bibliographie: RQum 12,46 (1986) 293-315
   [316-9, Rectification(s nombreuses) aux Tables du Numéro 44]; 12,47
   (1986) 455-480; Rollo del Templo 425-440.
670 **Gotenburg** Erwin, Bibelwissenschaften [Theologische Bibliographie]: TR
   82 (1986) 73-75 [-88]. 161-3 [-176]. 249-251 [-264]. 337-9 [-352]. 425-7 [-440].
   515-7 [-528; dazu 511-4, Dissertationen].
670* **Harrington** Daniel J., The New Testament; a bibliography: Theological
   and Biblical Resources 2, 1985 ➤ 1,997: ᴿRExp 83 (1986) 300 (R. L.
   Omanson).

671 *Hennig* John, Liturgie und das Judentum: ArLtgW 28 (1986) 163-171 [aber 165-171, 'Der Jude Jesus' und 'Judentum und Christentum in der Geschichte'; N.B. Bibliographie Hennig (1971-) 1977-86 mit Register, *Häussling* A. p. 235-246].

671* Hokhma tables 1976-85, numéros 1 à 30: Hokhma 11,31 (1986) 56-59.

672 *Hubaut* M., Bulletin du Nouveau Testament; les Évangiles synoptiques: MélSR 43 (1986) 201-215: 9 livres, infra.

673 **IZBG** [➤ 1,1006]: Internationale Zeitschriftenschau für Bibelwissenschaft und Grenzgebiete, ᴱ**Lang** Bernhard [+ 30 Mitarbeiter] 33 (1985s) 538 p. DM 158. 0074-0973 / 3-491-76033-X. 3294 items, with summaries of some 100 words, about half each in German and English; 'scholarly only' and not (according to its published norms) extending as far to the periphery as our Elenchus; categories somewhat different and in slightly different order (Text before hermeneutic; three sections Umwelt, Archäologie, Institutionen, before History and Judaism-Gnosis; only toward the end Biblical Theology, followed by 'Concepts and Symbols', then 'Bible in systematic theology', 'in the life of the community'; History of exegesis; finally 'Bible in art and literature'. The subcategories sometimes draw attention to rather few items ('African and South American translations' are mostly what we class as general translation-problems, all from BTrans except two on the proliferation of translations in Brazil). The volume, dated for 1985-6 and appearing late in 1987, contains items from 1984 and 1985, with only a couple from 1986 or 1983 [thus comparable to our 1985 volume appearing at the end of 1987]. The summaries are very informative. – ᴿTGl 76 (1986) 138.468 (J. *Gamberoni*).

674 *Janowski* Bernd, Literatur zur biblischen Theologie 1982-1985 [gegliederte nicht annotierte Bibliographie in Fortsetzung von REVENTLOW Hauptprobleme 1983]: ➤ 236, JbBT 1 (1986) 210-244. P. 243 cites an article from ThT 24 (1984), which according to p. 210 should be interpreted [from *Schwertner* S., IATG 1976 p. 320] Theologisch tijdschrift — of which the last volume was 53,1919. – 'PRS' also dubious, p. 214 + 210.

JBL index, 1942-1981. $18.45 ➤ Elenchus vol. 3 (1987).

675 JERVELL Jacob, bibliography: *Birkeflet* S.H.: NorTTs 86 (1985) 213-223.

JOSEPHUS: **Feldman** Louis H., Josephus, a supplementary bibliography 1986 ➤ 9504.

677 **Langevin** Paul-Émile, Bibliographie biblique III, 1985 ➤ 1,1007: ᴿAngelicum 63 (1986) 640 (P. *Zerafa*); BibFe 12 (1986) 251 (A. *Salas*); ETL 62 (1986) 190s (F. *Neirynck*: comble toutes les lacunes qu'il avait signalées dans le tome 2); Gregorianum 67 (1986) 533 (R. *Latourelle*); LavalTP 42 (1986) 407s (J.-C. *Filteau*); RThom 86 (1986) 502-4 (M.-V. *Leroy*); ScEspr 38 (1986) 123-5 (J.-L. *D'Aragon*); ScripTPamp 18 (1986) 962s (S. *Ausín*); TS 47 (1986) 301-3 (J.A. *Fitzmyer* notes that this Elenchus retains the advantage of indicating also book-reviews; it might be well to add here that the Elenchus covers 1200 periodicals, many admittedly quite secondary; while Langevin now covers 163).

678 *List* Harald, Thèses d'études à la Cà Foscari [Univ. Venezia, Lingua e letteratura ebrea; 19 dissertazioni; due su Giobbe (1977) e Osea (1975)]: RÉJ 145 (1986) 387s.

679 *a*) *Lys* Daniel, Bulletin d'Ancien Testament; – *b*) *Vouga* François, Bulletin de N.T., Paul et Jésus; – *c*) *Gagnebin* Laurent, Bulletin de théologie pratique; – *d*) *Dubois* Jean-Daniel, Chronique patristique III [surtout Nagʿ-Ḥammadi]; – *e*) Thèses: ÉTRel 61 (1986) 562-573, à suivre / 421-430 / 97-100 / 257-269 / 105.

680 *Martin* François, Chronique d'Ancien Testament [10 livres]: LumièreV 35,178 (1986) 89-101.
681 **Martin** Ralph P., New Testament books for pastor and teacher 1984 ➤ 65,827: ᴿInterpretation 40 (1986) 103s (J. L. *Boyce*).
682 **Mills** Watson E., A bibliography of the periodical literature on the Acts of the Apostles 1962-84: NT Sup 19. Leiden 1986, Brill. xxx-115 p. ƒ60 [TR 83,338].
683 ᴱ**Mills** Watson E., Speaking in tongues; a guide to research on glossolalia. GR 1986, Eerdmans. 536 p. $25. 0-8028-0183-8 [Bijdragen 47,466].
683* **Moir** D. L., New Testament Studies, cumulative index of volumes 1-31 (1954-1985) and of the Bulletin 1-3 (1950-1952). C 1986, Univ. 114 p.
684 MONTEFIORE: **Goldschmidt-Lehmann** Ruth P., Sir Moses Montefiore Bart., F.R.S. 1784-1885; a bibliography. J 1984, Misgav Yerushalayim. I, xviii-166 p. – ᴿRÉJ 145 (1986) 469s (Z. *Loker*).
685 RAMBI [➤ 1,1016] ❹ Index of articles on Jewish studies [scholarly items sifted from KirSef], 25 (for 1984). J 1986, National and University Library. 389 p. – 26 (1985), ᴱ**Ben-Shammai** Bitya, *al.* J 1986. 400 p. 3869 items in categories; OT p. 9-59(-83), Language 129-144; Eretz-Israel (geog. archeol.) 233-263; Index: authors, subjects, reviews (i.e. by author of books reviewed).
685* *Schade* Herwarth von, Bibliographie zur Wirkungsgeschichte der Bibel im deutschsprachigen Raum 2 (Die Veröffentlichungen 1982): Vestigia bibliae 7 (Ha 1985) 141 ... [< ZIT].
686 *Scholer* David M., Bibliographia gnostica, supplementum XV: NT 28 1986) 356-380.
687 ᴱ**Shinan** Avigdor, Bible [Eretz Israel]: KirSef 60 (1985) 12-29 [137s]. 353-401 [616-8].
688 a) *Stuhlmueller* Carroll, [*Senior Donald*] The Old [New] Testament in review: BToday 24 (1986) 56-64.199-206.270-2.333-340 [127-133.263-270]; – b) *O'Malley* Kenneth, *Hang* Fred, Audio/Visuals in review: BToday 24 (1986) 197s. 330-2.
689 *Vattioni* Francesco, Saggio di bibliografia semitica 1984-5: AION 45 (1985) 673-724; index 725-731.
690 **Wagner** Günter, The exegetical bibliography of the New Testament [1.1983 ➤ 64,865]; 2. Luke-Acts. Macon GA 1985, Mercer Univ. xii-550 p. $49.50. 0-86554-140-X. ᴿExpTim 97 (1985s) 379 (C. K. *Barrett*: not knowing all the information provided here, 'cannot complain'; but does).

A4.2 *Bibliographiae* **theologicae**.

691 *Andriessen* J., Literatuuroverzicht 1985: OnsGErf 60 (1986) 38-119.
691* *Arató* Pál, Bibliographia 1984s: ArHPont 23 (1985) 421-683.
692 ᴱ**Balter** Lucjan *al.*, Polska bibliografia nauk kościelnych za lata 1977-1979. Wsz 1986, Akad. teol. katolickiej. 306 p. 300 p. 0303-2272.
692* a) *Bataillon* Louis-J., Bulletin d'histoire des doctrines médiévales; – b) *Gy* Pierre-M., Bulletin de liturgie: RSPT 70 (1986) 255-270 / 271-280.
693 **Belle** A. van, Bibliographie: RHE 81 (1986). 525* p.
694 *Bertuletti* Angelo, *al.*, I problemi metodologici della teologia [e Scrittura] sulle Riviste di 1984/1985: TItSett 10 (1985) 339-412 [357-365] / 11 (1986) 304-378 [322-330].
695 ᴱ**Blasi** Anthony J., *Cuneo* Michael W., Issues in the sociology of religion [3852 items by theme, with author and subject index]: Garland Bib-

liographies in Sociology 8. NY 1986, Garland. xxiv-363 p. $53 [RelStR 13,51, W. *Garrett*].

696 **Bolich** Gregory C., The Christian scholar; an introduction to theological research. Lanham MD 1986, UPA. 349 p. [RelStR 13,334, J. *Moore*: totally inept].

697 Bollettino bibliografico: RivLtg 73 (1986) 715-932.

698 *Borriello* Luigi, Teologia spirituale; linee tematiche emergenti nel suo recente sviluppo bibliografico: Teresianum 36 (1985) 189-202.

699 ᴱ**Boudens** R., *al.* [*Lust* J. / *Neirynck* F., *Segbroeck* F. Van] Elenchus Bibliographicus 1986 [VT / NT]: ETL 62 (1986) 1*-531* [115*-193* / 194*-260*]: now each of the 10049 items has its own number, and these are the numbers referred in the Index p. 474*-531*.

699* **BREF** [➔ 1,1042*]. Bibliographie religieuse en français[2]. Dourgne 1985, Abbaye de St-Benoît d'En Calcat. xii-239 p. [2000 titres]. F 85. – ᴿÉTRel 61 (1986) 271 (J. *Pons*).

700 *Budweiser* F., Generalregister, Internationale Kirchliche Zeitschrift 51-75 (1961-85). Bern 1986. 49 p.

701 Bulletin bibliographique de liturgie: QLtg 66 (1985) 66-80. 167-192. 233-250; 67 (1986) 63-180. 183-202. 262-280.

702 **Buonocore** Marco, Bibliografia dei fondi manoscritti della Biblioteca Vaticana (1968-1980): ST 318s. Vaticano 1986, Biblioteca. 768 p.; p. 769-1414. 88-210-0539-9.

702* *Camps* Arnulf, Doctoral dissertations in missiology 1963-1986, Catholic University of Nijmegen: NZMissW 42 (1986) 225-8.

703 *Chopin* Claude, Bulletin bibliographique sur les ministères [*Nicolas* J. 1985; *Dupont* J. ...]: BSulp 12 (1986) 204-236.

704 **Claes** Marie-Christine, *Leroy* Suzanne, Répertoire des bibliothèques et centres de documentation en sciences religieuses de Wallonie, de Bruxelles et du Grand-Duché de Luxembourg. Namur 1986, ABTIR (= Association des Bibliothèques de Théologie et d'Information Religieuse, fondée 1983). 68 p. Fb 250. 53 bibliothèques. – ᴿRHE 81 (1986) 254 (P. *Denis* signale aussi Gids Ned/Vl 1983).

704* *Congar* Yves, Bulletin d'ecclésiologie; conciles hier et aujourd'hui: RSPT 70 (1986) 624-638 [*Sieben* H. 1984; *Stacpoole* A. 1986; *Alberigo* G., *Jossua* J.-P. 1985 ...].

705 ᴱ**Cornish** Graham, Religious periodicals directory [1763 in six geographical regions]. Santa Barbara / Oxford 1986, ABC/Clio. xi-330 p. $89. 0-87436-365-9 [NTAbs 31,90].

706 **Day** Heather F., Protestant theological education in America; a bibliography. Metuchen NJ 1985, Scarecrow. 505 p. $42.50 [JAAR 54,630].

706* *De Klerk* Peter, CALVIN bibliography 1986: CalvinT 21 (1986) 194-221.

707 Dissertations in Progress: RelStR 12 (1986) 320-326. Only a few of the more arresting titles are noted infra; but the completed dissertations [p. 189-196] relevant to this Elenchus are all infra; and also the 1986 dissertations from vol.13.

707* *Durand* G.-M. de, Bulletin de Patrologie: RSPT 70 (1986) 591-692: plusieurs infra.

708 *a*) ᴱ*Fares* D. J., *Albistur* F., Fichero de Revistas Latinoamericanas: Stromata 42 (1986) 437-490 [455-8, Sagrada Escritura]. – *b*) Pelas revistas [... Teologia - bíblica]: REB 46 (1986) 234-240.474-480.730-6.901-5 [235s.475s.731s.901s].

709 ᴱ**Garand** Monique-Cécile *al.*, Catalogue des manuscrits en écriture latine portant des indications de date, de lieu ou de copiste, VII. Ouest de la

France et Pays de Loire. P 1984, CNRS. xli-655 p.; album 215 pl. –
ᴿRHE 81 (1986) 299s (H. *Silvestre*).
710 **Gorman** G. E. & Lyn, Theological and religious reference materials, I.
[Biblical ...]; II., 1984s ➤ 1,1061: ᴿGraceTJ 7 (1986) 142s (R. *Ibach*).
710* *Granado Bellido* Carmelo, Boletín de literatura antigua cristiana
[SChr ...; *Moreschini* C.; *Crouzel* H. ...]: EstE 61 (1986) 435-445.
711 *Häussling* A., *al.*, Literaturberichte; der Gottesdienst der Kirche [in sehr
weitem Sinn] / *Severus* Emmanuel von, Spiritualität / *Limburg* Hans von,
Religionspädagogik: ArLtgW 28 (1986) 61-129 / 130-162 / 427-457 (-487).
711* *Heiser* W. Charles, Theology Digest book survey: TDig 33 (1986)
159-195. 259-296. 351-387. 455-495.
712 **Henkel** W., (*Metzler* G.), Bibliografia missionaria anno XLVIII - 1984. R
1985, Pont. Univ. Urbaniana. 375 p. – ᴿNZMissW 42 (1986) 137s (J.
Baumgartner).
713 Index international des dissertations doctorales en théologie et en droit
canonique[s!] présentées en 1985 [mais 1983 p. 490, 492, 494, 495, 496, 511,
513; 1984 p. 491, 492, 493, 494, 495, 496; 1986 p. 490, 492; sans date p. 490,
492, 493, 494]: RTLv 17 (1986) 472-536; 705 titres [N.B. 474-484 par
institutions!].
714 [ᴱ*Janssen* H. ➤ 1,1073; *Evers* Georg; nomina isto anno suppressa] Zeitschriftenschau; 1. vollständig erfasste theologische Zeitschriften aus der
Dritten Welt [5-8, list of 55 periodicals from Asia, Africa, and Latin
America]; 2. Beiträge aus sonstigen Zeitschriften; 3. Zusammenfassungen
ausgewählter Beiträge; 4. Konferenzberichte: TKontext 7,1.2 (1986) je
c.145 p.
715 ᴱ*Kalinkowski* Stanisław, Biuletyn patrystyczny: ColcT 56,1 (1986)
133-146 [C. *Mazur*, de Jan CZUJ 1886-1957]; 56,2 p. 145-155; 56, 4, p.
143-155. Each issue contains also other bibliographical bulletins
[homiletics, catechetics, sociology ...]. The first fascicle is wrongly
numbered II on title page only; the second wrongly III on index-page only.
716 Katorikku Kenkyu, 'Catholic Studies' Tokyo, General Index of volumes
XI-XXV (nrs 21-50): KatKenk 25,50 (1986) 203-242.
717 ᴱ**LaBerge** Agnes N.O., What God hath wrought [c.1919]: The higher
Christian life; sources for the study of the Holiness, Pentecostal, [feminist],
and Kestwick movements; a 48-volume facsimile series ... 24. NY 1985,
Garland. 127 p. $22 [RelStR 13,91 Kathryn A. *Rabuzzi*].
718 *Lewek* Antoni, [Doktoraty infra] magisteria 1985, c. 100 tituli thesium ❷ ...
Kroplewski T., The last will be first; *Sawicki* J., pietas in Pastoralibus;
Szamocki P., Jesus' earthly homeland ...]: STWsz 24,1 (1986) 324-7; 24,2
(1986) 297s.
719 ᴱ**Lippy** Charles H., Religious periodicals of the United States; [135]
academic and scholarly journals: Historical guides to the world's
periodicals. Westport CT 1986, Greenwood. xix-607 p. $65. – ᴿTDig 33
(1986) 477s (W. C. *Heiser*: fifty collaborators; history of each periodical).
720 **Lop** Miguel, *Ribas* Manuel, Indices 1-100 [vol. 1-25] 1962-1986: Selecciones
de Teología. Barcelona 1986. 176 p.
721 **Lucas** George R.ᴶ, The genesis of modern process thought; a historical
outline with bibliography: ATLA. Metuchen NJ 1983, Scarecrow. 231 p.
$18.50. – ᴿJAAR 54 (1986) 181 (J. *Culp*).
721* LUSCHNAT Otto, Bibliographie 75 Jahre: BTZ 3 (1986) 354-8 (U. *Jessen*).
722 LUTHER: a) ᴱ*Junghans* Helmar, *Beyer* Michael, Lutherbibliographie 1986:
LuthJb 53 (1986) 149-216 [1708 items], 216-220 Nachtrag, 221-9, Register
➤ d560. – b) **Wolf** Herbert, Germanistische Luther-Bibliographie; Martin

Luthers deutsches Sprachschaffen im Spiegel des internationalen Schrifttums der Jahre 1880-1980: Germanistische Bibliothek NF 6. Heid 1985, Winter. 403 p. DM 160; pa. 132 [TLZ 112,17, S. *Bräuer*].

722* **Margul** Tadeusz, Międzynarodowa bibliografia religioznawstwa porównawczego w układzie działowym – International bibliography of comparative religion in dictionary order. Kraków 1986, Uniw. Jagiełłon. 403 p.

723 *a) Martimort* Aimé G., Chronique de liturgie; *b) Cabié* R., ... d'histoire de la liturgie: BLitEc 87 (1986) 211-8 / 299-304.

723* [*Matagne* Charles], Tables générales 1969-1985; 101e-117e années, tomes 91-107, Nouvelle Revue Théologique. Tournai/Namur 1986, Casterman/ NRT. v-535 p. [RTLv 18,405].

724 *Mbiye* Lumbala, La théologie africaine; bibliographie sélective (1976-1980) (suite et fin): RAfrT 10,19 (1986) 109-129 (6378 items in all).

725 **Menendez** Albert J., The road to Roma; an annotated bibliography: Reference Library of Social Science 318. NY 1986, Garland. xvi-133 p. $34 [TDig 34,86].

726 [E**Nagel** Ernst J.] Bibliographie Theologie und Frieden 1,1 Monographien 1; 1,2 Thesaurus, Register. Köln 1984, Bachem. 561 p.; 245 p. DM 47,80 + 32,10 [NRT 109,131s, L.-J. *Renard*: articles de revues de parution prochaine].

727 *a) Neunheuser* Burkhard, Liturgie im Gesamtzusammenhang der Theologie; – *b) Berger* Teresa, 'Doxology' [*Wainwright* G. 1980] – 'Jubilate' [*Hardy* D., *Ford* D. 1984] – 'Liturgical theology' [*Kavanagh* A. 1985]; zum Verhältnis von Liturgie und Theologie; Publikationen aus dem englischsprachigen Raum; – *c) Häussling* Angelus A., Conférences Saint-Serge, semaines d'études liturgiques; eine bibliographische Übersicht: ArLtgW 28 (1986) 261-300 / (-356) / 247-255 / 256-9.

728 PALAU F.: **Diego Sánchez** Manuel, Bibliografía del Padre Francisco ~: Cuadernos Palautinos 3. R 1984, Carmelitas Misioneras. 98 p. – RScripTPamp 18 (1986) 978 (A. M. *Pazos*).

729 **Parker** Harold M.J, Bibliography of published articles on American Presbyterianism, 1901-1980: Bibliographies and indexes in religious studies 4. Westport CT 1985, Greenwood. xi-261 p. $37.50 [TDig 33,375].

730 **Petersen** Paul D., *Turner* David L., Index [1-6] 1980-85; GraceTJ 7 (1986) 281-315.

731 *Pié y Ninot* Salvador, Boletín bibliográfico sobre la teología del laicado hoy ante el Sínodo sobre los Laicos de 1987; perspectivas teológicas: RCatalT 11 (1986) 439-451.

732 *Pöhlmann* H.G., Zeitschriftenschau [längere Zusammenfassungen wichtigerer Artikel]: NSys 28 (1986) 101-7.238-244.330-340: RStFen 14 (1986) 257-273: Bibliografia 14.

732* RStFen 14 (1986) 257-273: Bibliografia 14.

733 Recension des revues [la plupart titre seul, avec auteur et pp.]: RSPT 70 (1986) 151-174. 289-324. 465-490. 639-670.

733* *Sabourin* Léopold, *Poggi* Vincenzo, Indices of vol. 26-50 (1960-1984): OrChrPer 52 (1986) 5-144.

734 **Schadel** Erwin, *al.*, Bibliotheca trinitariorum I, 1984 → 65,929; 1,1101: RFranzSt 67 (1985) 369 (W. *Schachten*); TPhil 61 (1986) 280s (J. *Splett*); TR 82 (1986) 299-301 (H. *Beck*); TRu 51 (1986) 431s (F. *Wagner*); ZRGg 38 (1986) 379s (W. *Kern*).

735 SCHLINK Edmund: Bibliographie II: TLZ 111 (1986) 635-9 (M. *Plathow*).

736 *Schnaubelt* J., Bibliografia storico-dottrinale [agostiniana] in Italia e Malta (1982-5): AnAug 49 (1986) 417-448.

737 Theses and dissertations at Grace Theological Seminary [Winona Lake IN], 1986: GraceTJ 7 (1986) 317-9. The fifty-some M. Div. theses are mostly on Scripture texts.

738 *Tretter* H., Bibliographie [*Röhling* H., Zeitschriftenschau]: Ostkirchliche Studien 35 (1986) 79-104. 232-280. 349-371 (-382 Autorenregister) [66-78. 217-231].

739 *Trevijano Etcheverria* R., Bibliografía patrística hispano-luso-americana IV (1983-1984): Salmanticensis 33 (1986) 87-112.

740 VDI Index 1981-1985: VDI 176 (1986,1) 219-236.

741 **Vekene** Emil van der, Bibliotheca bibliographica historiae Sanctae Inquisitionis; bibliographisches Verzeichnis des gedruckten Schrifttums zur Geschichte und Literatur der Inquisition I-II. Vaduz 1982s, Topos. lxii-601 p.; 554 p. [TR 83,207, J. *Wicks*].

742 *Visser* J., Vrucht van eigen bodem; nederlandse studies over pastorale psychologie en theologie: NedTTs 40 (1986) 322-8.

742* *Wainwright* Geoffrey, Recent continental theology, historical and systematic: ExpTim 97 (1985s) 267-271 [*Herms* E., *Subilia* V. +˙3 infra + 10]; 98 (1986s) 333-8 [35 publications].

743 *Walls* A. F., Bibliography on world mission: IntRMiss 75 (1986) 468-487.

743* *Werblowsky* R. J. Zev, Book survey [*Flasche* on WACH; *Bozóky,* Cathares; *Widengren,* Mandaeismus; and 54 other books]: Numen 33 (1986) 241-269.

744 *Zucca* Ubaldo, Indice del decennio 1977-1986: Divinitas 30 (1986) 290-330.

A4.3 *Bibliographiae* **philologicae** *et* **generales.**

745 **Baldacci** Maria Bruna, *Sprugnoli* Renzo, Informatica e biblioteche; automazione dei sistemi informativi bibliotecari. R 1983, Nuova Italia Scientifica. 239 p. Lit. 22.500. – ᴿCC 137 (1986,3) 546s (E. *Baragli*).

746 Bibliographische Beilage: Gnomon 58 (1986) 136 p. numbered separately; p. 85-96 of regular numeration: 1986 zu erwartende Neuerscheinungen des deutschsprachigen Verlagsbuchhandels.

747 Biographie Nationale, Supplément 15 (= 43). Bru 1984, Bruylant. 790 col.; vii-46 p. – ᴿRHE 81 (1986) 251-3 (J.-P. *Hendrickx*).

748 **Blum** Rudolf, Die Literaturverzeichnung im Altertum und im Mittelalter; Versuch einer Geschichte der Biobibliographie von den Anfängen bis zum Beginn der Neuzeit: Archiv für Geschichte des Buchwesens, Sonderdruck. Fra 1983, Buchhändler-Vereinigung. 256 col. DM 64. – ᴿTZBas 42 (1986) 181s (R. *Brändle*).

749 **Carnes** Pack, Fable scholarship; an annotated bibliography: Folklore Bibliog. NY 1985, Garland. xvi-382 p. $65. 0-8240-9229-3. – ᴿClasR 100 (1986) 319s (K. *Dowden*).

750 Classical and medieval philology; classical archaeology and ancient history in Sweden in the years 1984-5: Eranos 84 (1986) 171-188.

750* *Cockshaw* Pierre, *Silvestre* Hubert, *al.,* Bulletin codicologique: Scriptorium 39 (1985) 1*-191*; index 192*-220*; 46 (1986) 1*-172*; index 173*-193*.

751 **Currás** Emilia, Documentación y metodología de la investigación científica; cuaderno de trabajo. M 1985, Paraninfo. 362 p. – ᴿCiuD 199 (1986) 183 (B. *Justel*).

751* Dumbarton Oaks Papers Index 31-40 (1977-86): DumbO 40 (1986) 189-197.

752 **Escolar** Hipólito [➤ 7875], Historia de las bibliotecas: Fund. G. Sánchez Ruipérez. M 1985, Pirámide. 566 p. – [R]CiuD 199 (1986) 184 (B. *Justel*).

753 **Farina** Raffaello, Metodologia; avviamento alla tecnica del lavoro scientifico[4] [[1]1973 [2]1974 ➤ 60,1066]: BiblScRel 71, R 1986, LAS. 340 p. Lit. 20.000. 88-213-0121-4. – [R]Asprenas 33 (1986) 227s (F. *Russo*).

754 **Havlice** Patricia P., Oral history; a reference guide and annotated bibliography. Jefferson NC 1985, McFarland. iv-140 p. 0-89950-138-9.

755 *Modrzejewski* Joseph, Bibliographie de papyrologie juridique 1972-1982, II: ArPapF 32 (1986) 97-147...

756 *Packer* Margaret M., Research in classical studies for University degrees in Great Britain and Ireland, A. in progress; B. completed: BInstClas 32 (1985) 163-191 / 192-7.

757 *Pągowska* Zofia, *Szpachta* Maria, Bibliografia Meandra za lata 1946-1985: Meander 41, 11s (1986) 465-544; Indeks 545-554.

758 *Reichardt* Robert H., Humane und inhumane Aspekte einer total informatisierten Gesellschaft: Biblos 35 (1986) 1-13.

Scanlon Thomas F., Greek and Roman athletics; a bibliography 1984 ➤ a56*a*.

758* *Sempère* Sylvie, Tables, Antiquités Africaines 1-20 (1967-1984): AntAfr 21 (1985) 271-291.

759 **Sierra Bravo** R., Tesis doctorales y trabajos de investigación científica; metodología general de su elaboración y documentación. M 1986, Paraninfo, 412 p. – [R]CiuD 199 (1986) 563s (J. *Gutiérrez*).

760 **Soliday** Gerald L., History of the family and kinship; a select international bibliography. NY 1980, Kraus. $50. – [R]RBgPg 62 (1984) 874s (J.-P. *Devroey*).

761 [*Loos* Milan †] *Vavřinek* Vladimir, Bibliographie: BySlav 46 (1985) 206-308; 47 (1986) 78-168. 240-308.

A4.4 *Bibliographiae* **orientalisticae.**

761* *Caplice* Richard, *Klengel* Horst, Keilschriftbibliographie 47, 1985: Orientalia 55 (1986) 1*-126*: 1934 items in purely alphabetical order of authors, with six-page index of categories. 'With the next issue, Professor K. *Deller* of Heidelberg will resume direction of the bibliography'.

762 **Piemontese** Angelo M., Bibliografia italiana dell'Iran (1462-1982), I. Bibliografia, Geografia, Viaggi e viaggiatori, Storia, Archeologia; II. Arte, Lingua, Lettura, Letteratura, Filosofia e scienza, La Persia nella letteratura italiana e europea: Studi Asiatici min. 18/1s. N 1982, Ist. Univ. Orientale. 947 p. Lit. 100.000. – [R]AION 46 (1986) 119-134 (G. *Vercellin*).

762* *a*) *Thissen* Heinz-J., Demotistische Literaturübersicht XIV: Enchoria 14 (1986) 135-153; – *b*) Rassegna bibliografica, diritto [cuneiforme ...]: Ivra 34 (1983) 295-519 [404-429].

A4.5 *Bibliographiae* **archaeologicae.**

763 *Ambatsis* Jannis, *al.,* Register 1976-1985: Fornvännen 81 (1986) 253-287.

763* Archäologische Dissertationen: ArchAnz (1986) 139-144.

764 [E]*Balconi* Carla, *al.,* Bibliografia metodica degli studi di egittologia e di papirologia: Aegyptus 66 (1986) 299-367.

765 **Berghe** L. Vanden, Bibliographie analytique de l'archéologie de l'Irān ancien 1979 ➤ 1,1152: [R]FolOr 23 (1985s) 339-342 (Z. J. *Kapera*).

766 Bibliographie [mosaïque, I. par thèmes; II. par pays] 1982-1984 et complément des années antérieures: BMosA [= AIEMA] 11 (1986) 1-360.

767 British archaeological abstracts 19,1-2 (1986) 336 p; 2014 items, largely British, by topics subdivided chronologically.
769 Check list of recently published articles and books on glass [Ancient ...]: JGlass 28 (1986) 127-181 [136-140].
770 Hamburger Beiträge zur Archäologie, Gesamtverzeichnis der Bände 1-X und der Beihefte 1-3: HaBeiAr 11 (1984) 125-156.
771 **Hasso** M. H., A bibliometric study of the literature of archaeology: diss. City Univ. L 1978. [1649 periodicals an archaeologist should consult: Antiquity 60,5].
772 **Hermann** Werner, al., Archäologische Bibliographie 1985: DAI. B 1986, de Gruyter. xxxix-543 p.; 13069 items. 0341-8308.
773 **Herzev** R. F., Archaeology; a bibliographical guide to the basic literature. NY 1980 [Antiquity 60,5].
774 **Homès-Fredericq** Denyse, *Hennessy* J. Basil, Archaeology of Jordan, I. (of 4) Bibliography: Akkadica – Sup. 3. Bru c. 1986, Fond. Dossin.
775 *MacKay* D. Bruce, A comprehensive index to Biblical Archaeologist volumes 36-45 (1973-1982): BA. $11.95. 0-897557-008-1.
776 MONNERET: *Piemontese* Angelo M., Bibliografia delle opere di Ugo Monneret de Villard (1881-1954): RSO 58 (1984) 1-12.
777 *Nachapyetyan* V. E., Sovietskaya Archeologiya, Index 1977-1986: SovArch (1986,4) 273-304.
779 **Polenova** I. A., *Rusinova* E. S., Raboty sovetskih učenyh po assiriologii i šumerologii 1917-1983 – Arbeiten sowjetischer Gelehrter auf dem Gebiet der Assyriologie und Sumerologie. Leningrad 1984, Akad. Nauk. 83 p.
780 [EPott P. H. al.] Annual bibliography of Indian archaeology 22 (for 1967-9). Dordrecht 1982, Reidel. xvi-173 p. [2108 items]. – ROLZ 81 (1986) 68s (H. *Mode*).
782 Studii și cercetări de istorie veche și arheologie, Indice 1 (1950) - 35 (1984): IstVArh 36,1s (1985). 179 p.
783 Survey of archeology magazines: Whole Earth Review (summer 1986) [BAR-W 12,5 (1986) 12].
785 Zeitschriftenverzeichnis; Ägyptologie, Klassische Archäologie, Mittlere und Neuere Kunstgeschichte; Stand Sept. 1983: Heidelberger Bibliotheks-schriften 11. Heid 1983, Univ. 388 p.

II. Introductio

B1   *Introductio* .1 *tota vel VT* – **Whole Bible or OT.**

786 Alla scoperta della Bibbia; I. Cammino di un popolo, storia di un libro, l'Antico Testamento; II. Un solo Gesù Cristo, una moltitudine di testimoni, il Nuovo Testamento. T-Leumann 1985, LDC. 269 p.; 275 p. Lit. 14.000 ciascuno [CC 137,1986/1 dopo p. 312].
787 **Anderson** Bernhard W., Understanding the Old Testament⁴. ENJ 1986, Prentice-Hall. xv-685 p.; bibliog. p. 652-676. 0-13-936925-7. – RRelStT 6 (1986) 72s (M. *De Roche*); SWJT 29,2 (1986s) 46s (D. G. *Kent*).
788 **Armstrong** Herbert W. †, Mystery of the Ages [the Bible is in a code which has been revealed only to him]. NY 1985, Dodd Mead. xiii-383 p. $12.95. – RTDig 33 (1986) 352 (W. C. *Heiser*).
789 **Bić** M., Ze světa Starého zákona [From the OT world, first of five background–volumes]. Praha 1986, Kalich. 365 p.; 29 ill. (maps). Kčs 25.

790 **Boadt** Lawrence, Reading the Old Testament, an introduction 1984
→ 65,993; 1,1172; $6.95 pa.: RCBQ 48 (1986) 527s (X. J. Harris: a big
book for a little price); CurrTM 13 (1986) 116s (R. Gnuse); Gregorianum
67 (1986) 599 (G. L. Prato); Horizons 13 (1986) 150 (D. P. McCarthy: good
for classroom use); Interpretation 40 (1986) 305 (J. M. Bracke: needed but
premature); RB 93 (1986) 462s (J.-M. de Tarragon); RelStR 12 (1986) 64
(G. L. Mattingly).

791 **Boecker** Hans-J., al., Altes Testament 1983 → 64,1111; 65,994 [jetzt ²1986:
p. 322, Literatur-Ergänzungen]: RTeresianum 36 (1985) 233s (F. Foresti).

791* **Bruggen** J. van, Wie maakte de Bijbel; over afsluiting en gezag van het
Oude en Nieuwe Testament. Kampen 1986, Kok. 138 p. ƒ22,50
[GerefTTs 86,3 back cover; NTAbs 31,226]. 90-242-4611-3.

792 **Carmody** John & Denise L., Robbins Gregory A., Exploring the New
Testament [for use in secular universities]. ENJ 1986, Prentice-Hall.
iv-444. $27 [RelStR 13,166, R. H. Fuller].

793 **Charpentier** Étienne, a) How to read the OT / NT 1981 → 63,1086;
1,1175: RHeythJ 27 (1986) 69 (S. Greenhalgh). – b) Para ler o Antigo
Testamento. São Paulo 1986, Paulinas. 176 p. [REB 46,722].

794 **Childs** Brevard S., Introduction to the OT as Scripture 1979 → 60,1279 ...
1,1176: RVerkF 31,1 (1986) 85s (H. Seebass).

795 E**Cimosa** M., Mosetto F., Parola di vita; una introduzione alla Bibbia.
T-Leumann 1983, LDC. 398 p. Lit. 10.000.– RAsprenas 33 (1986) 348.

796 **Cortese** Enzo, Da Mosè a Esdra; i libri storici dell'antico Israele 1985
→ 1,1177: RAsprenas 32 (1985) 455-7 (S. Cipriani); CC 137 (1986,2) 403s
(G. L. Prato); RivB 34 (1986) 401s (O. Carena); TPhil 61 (1986) 250 (N.
Lohfink).

797 **Craigie** Peter C., The Old Testament; its background, growth, and
content. Nv 1986, Abingdon. 351 p.; 41 fig.; bibliog. p. 333-340. $19.
0-687-28751-0.

798 E**Deist** F. E., Vorster W. S., Words from afar: Literature of the OT 1.
Cape Town 1986, Tafelberg. x-237 p. [ZAW 99,155].

799 E**Festorazzi** Franco, Bonora A., Sisti A., Il messaggio della salvezza; gli
'Scritti' [kᵉtubîm Ps Sap ... Mcb]: Corso completo di Studi Biblici 5.
T-Leumann 1985, Elle Di Ci. 396 p. Lit. 25.000. 88-01-13829-6. – RGregorianum 67 (1986) 765 (D. Cox); RivB 34 (1986) 408-410 (Anna Passoni
dell'Acqua).

800 **Fohrer** Georg, Vom Werden und Verstehen des ATs: Siebenstern 1414.
Gü 1986, Mohn. 269 p. DM 19,80. 3-579-01414-5 [BL 87,62, C. S. Rodd:
starts with what we have and works back, e.g. P to J].

801 **Geisler** Norman L., Nix William E., A general introduction to the Bible²ʳᵉᵛ.
Ch 1986, Moody. 724 p. [TR 83,249].

802 **Gottwald** Norman K., The Hebrew Bible, a socio-literary introduction
1985 → 1,1183: RBR 2,2 (1986) 42-50 (P. K. McCarter: 'A major new
introduction'; inset p. 46s, MENDENHALL disavows); CurrTM 13 (1986)
174s (R. Gnuse); ExpTim 98 (1986s) 23 (C. S. Rodd: this book replaces
Gottwald's A light to the nations 1959 → 60,36, which Rodd preferred to
ANDERSON; and this is even better); IrBSt 8 (1986) 199s (A.D.H. Mayes);
RelStT 6 (1986) 69-72 (J. G. Taylor); TTod 43 (1986s) 580s (J.J.M.
Roberts); VT 36 (1986) 504-6 (J. A. Emerton: critical); ZAW 98 (1986) 312s
(O. Kaiser).

803 **Gutsche** Friedhardt, Schinzer Reinhard, Die Bibel kennen; Arbeitsblätter
mit Erläuterungen und Hinweisungen zur Praxis. Gö 1986, Vandenhoeck
& R. 135 p. 3-525-61255-9.

804 **Imbach** Josef, Die Bibel lesen und verstehen; eine Hinführung. Mü 1986, Kösel. 194 p. DM 24,80 [TLZ 112,495, R. *Marschner*].
805 **Kottackal** Joseph, An introduction to Bible. Kottayam, Kerala 1986, St. Thomas Sem. 204 p. rs 18.
806 **Land** B., Ein Buch wie kein anderes 1980 ➤ 61,1449 ... 64,1022: ᴿNRT 108 (1986) 620s (J.-L. *Ska*: intelligent et enthousiaste).
807 **Mannucci** Valerio, *a*) La Biblia como palabra de Dios 1985 ➤ 1,1195: ᴿCiuD 199 (1986) 120s (J. L. del *Valle*: traducción intolerable). – *b*) Bíblia, palavra de Deus. São Paulo 1985, Paulinas. 432 p.; bibliog. p. 413-421 [REB 46,227].
808 **Neusner** Jacob, The oral Torah; the sacred books of Judaism, an introduction. SF 1986, Harper & R. xvii-238 p. $20 [Judaica 42,204].
809 **Ohler** Annemarie, Studying the OT; from tradition to canon [Gattungen 1972] 1985 ➤ 1,1198: ᴿRefTR 45 (1986) 22s (J. *Woodhouse*: ignores NOTH and the debates over BARR).
810 **Ohler** Annemarie, Grundwissen Altes Testament, ein Werkbuch ... I. Pentateuch. Stu 1986, KBW. 158 p.; 53 fig.; bibliog. p. 138-144. 3-460-32431-7.
811 **Penna** Aurelio, Introduzione alla Bibbia; guida alla lettura del Vecchio e del Nuovo Testamento. Mi 1986, Mondadori. 196 p. Lit. 16.000. 88-0028456-2. – ᴿHumBr 41 (1986) 941 (M. *Orsatti*).
811* **Preuss** Horst D., Bibelkunde des Alten und Neuen Testaments I-II: Uni-Tb 887/972 [¹1980 ➤ 61,1458]³. Heid 1985s, Quelle & M. ix-237 p.; p. 239-527. 3-494-02097-3; 121-X [= ¹].
812 **Rendtorff** Rolf, *a*) Das AT, eine Einführung 1983 ➤ 64,1025 ... 1,1199: ᴿJBL 105 (1986) 304s (J. K. *Kuntz*). – *b*) The Old Testament, an introduction 1986 ➤ 1,1200 [Horizons 14,138, Alice *Laffey*, also on GOTTWALD].
813 ᴱ**Rogerson** J., Beginning OT study 1983 ➤ 64,294 ... 1,1202: ᴿHeythJ 27 (1986) 70 (S. *Greenhalgh*); RelStT 6 (1986) 77-79 (L. *Eslinger*).
814 **Schmidt** Werner H., OT introduction, ᵀO'Connell M. 1984 ➤ 65,1024; 1,1204*: ᴿCBQ 48 (1986) 316-8 (J. L. *Sullivan*); Interpretation 40 (1986) 80s (G. D. *Jordan*); Teresianum 36 (1985) 231-3 (F. *Foresti*).
815 **Soggin** Thomas, Per capire la Bibbia. T 1982, Claudiana. 165 p. Lit. 5900. – ᴿProtestantesimo 41 (1986) 248s (Maria *Fabro*).
816 **Tomić** Celestin, Pristup Bibliji; opći uvod u Sveto pismo. Zagreb 1986, Provincijalat franjevaca konventualaca. 421 p. – ᴿObnŽiv 41 (1986) 451s (J. *Šagi*).

B1.2 'Invitations' to Bible or OT.

817 ᶠALONSO SCHÖKEL Luis, El misterio de la Palabra, ᴱ**Collado** V., *Zurro* E. 1983 ➤ 64,3; 65,7: ᴿCBQ 48 (1986) 155-7 (S. *Segert*).
817* *Anderson* Bernhard W., The newness of the Old Testament: BR 2,3 (1986) 6s.
818 **Avril** A. C., *Lenhardt* P., La lettura ebraica della Scrittura (con antologia di testi rabbinici [1982 ➤ 1,1214*a*] 1984 ➤ 1,1214*b*: ᴿParVi 31 (1986) 154s (M. *Milani*).
818* *Bottéro* Jean, Le message universel de la Bible [< Vérité et poésie de la Bible 1969, 17-75]: ➤ 136, Naissance de Dieu 1986, 21-135 [p. 21: 'on December 3, 1872, the Bible lost forever its immemorial prerogative (s, of ...) "having been written or dictated by God in person", (because...) on that day G. SMITH ... declared that a Mesopotamian text on the Deluge was older than the Bible and had clearly inspired it'].

819 **Chmiel** Jerzy, ❾ Rozważania biblijne z Janem Pawłem II [biblical themes of the Pope's pronouncements during a visit in Poland 16-23.VI.1983]. Kalwaria Zebrzydowska 1985, Kalwaria. 88 p. – ᴿRuBi 39 (1986) 176 (K. *Bukowski*).

820 [*Gafni* Shlomo S.] ᴱ**Crocos** Georgette, The glory of the Old / New Testament. J 1983, Steimatsky. 256 p.each; ill.; maps [KirSef 60,360]. ➤ 65,3444.

821 **Debyser** M., La Bibbia per i miei parrochiani [1983 ➤ 64,1049],ᵀ, AT. T 1985, Gribaudi. 414 p. Lit. 22.000.

822 **Ellis** Peter F., Os homens e a mensagem do Antigo Testamento, ᵀ*Cavalca de Castro* Flávio 1985 ➤ 1,1223: ᴿRCuBíb 9,35s (1985) 156s (A. *Charbel*).

822* **Gilles** Anthony E., The people of the book 1983 ➤ 65,1054: ᴿDoctLife 35 (1985) 423s (B. *Nolan*).

823 **Goldman** Alex J., The eternal books retold. NY 1982, Pilgrim. xvi-349 p. [KirSef 59,308].

823* *Haquin* André, La Bible, mémoire vivante de la communauté qui célèbre: ComLtg 68 (1986) 101-110.

824 *Hoogen* T. van den, Schrift lezen, omtrent het selektief omgaan met de Bijbel: PrakT 13 (1986) 476-502.

825 **Kaler** Patrick, The Bible today; tough questions and straight answers. Liguori MO 1985, Publ. 64 p. $1.50. – ᴿTDig 33 (1986) 476 (W.C. *Heiser*).

826 **Kremer** Jacob, Die Bibel – ein Buch für alle; Berechtigung und Grenzen 'einfacher' Schriftlesung. Stu 1986, KBW. 85 p. DM 11,80 [TR 83,100, T. *Söding*].

828 **Lapide** Pinchas, Mit einem Juden die Bibel lesen 1982 ➤ 63,1106 ... 65,1064: ᴿJudaica 41 (1985) 56s (H.H. *Henrix*); ZRGg 38 (1986) 286s (S. *Ben-Chorin*).

829 **Lapide** P., Leggere la Bibbia con un ebreo: StBDeh 11, 1985 ➤ 1,1231: ᴿBbbOr 28 (1986) 122 (F. *Montagnini*); CC 137 (1986,3) 299s (S. *Katunarich:* affascinante). ParVi 31 (1986) 146-8 (G. *Boggio*).

830 **Levenson** Jon D., Sinai and Zion; an entry into the Jewish Bible 1985 ➤ 1,1234: ᴿBibTB 16 (1986) 34s (T.R. *Hobbs*); BL (1986) 91 (B.P. *Robinson*); ÉTRel 61 (1986) 579s (J. *Rennes*); Horizons 13 (1986) 412 (Sylvia *Maurer*); ExpTim 98 (1986s) 53 (J. *Snaith*). Interpretation 40 (1986) 302.304 (C.R. *Seitz*); JRefJud 33,2 (1986) 99-101 (G.A. *Rendsburg*); JRel 66 (1986) 68s (R.L. *Cohn*).

831* **Mackay** H.G., The story of your Bible; what every Christian should know about it. Kansas City KS 1985, Walterick. 96 p. $2.95 pa. [BS 143 (1986) 378].

832 **Marconcini** B., Cosa significa per una comunità leggere la Bibbia: Comunità e storia 4s. Arezzo 1985. – ᴿParVi 31 (1986) 157s (Maria *Grotti*).

832* **Merton** Thomas, Opening the Bible [1967 for abortive Time-Life edition]. Collegeville MN / Ph 1986, Liturgical / Fortress. 94 p. $4.95 pa. [TDig 34,86]. 0-8146-0408-0 / 0-8006-1910-2.

833 *Mielgo* C., La difícil lectura del Antiguo Testamento hecho por el Concilio Vaticano II: EstAg 21 (1986) 351-365.

833* *Monloubou* Louis, Des paroles – une parole – la Parole [... Psautier et Prophètes; dialogue d'Israël et des Nations; l'Alliance]: EsprV 96 (1986) 561-5.

834 *Murray* Robert, Do we still need the Old Testament? [SOTS survey of syllabuses gives disquieting results]: Month 248 (1986) 198-204.

835 **Olbricht** Thomas H., He loves forever; the message of the Old Testament: Journey. Austin 1980, Sweet. 174 p. [KirSef 59,316].

836 *Paul* André, La Bible ['un bien exclusivement chrétien'] et la Torah; concurrentes ou partenaires [conférence Ottawa 1986]: ScEspr 38 (1986) 285-299.

836* *Pöhlmann* Horst G., Bibel lesen ist ein Wagnis; die Schrift als Norm unseres Glaubens: EvKomm 19 (1986) 573-7.

837 **Robinson** Wayne B., The transforming power of the Bible 1984 ➤ 65,1077: RRelEd 81 (1986) 156-8 (K. *Stokes*).

838 *Rofè* A., Alle radici della nostra cultura – la Bibbia ebraica: ➤ 364, Atti del Convegno inaugurale dell'Associazione laica di cultura biblica (F 1986) 15-23 [< ZAW].

838* Gli 'Scritti' dell'AT: Messaggio della Salvezza 5. T-Leumann 1985, Elle Di Ci.

839 *Stahl* Rainer, 'Hebräische Bibel' – 'Altes Testament': ComViat 29 (1986) 79 ... [< ZIT].

839* **Stano** Franco, Letture ingenue e sovversive; storie bibliche di ieri e di oggi. R 1984, Borla. 136 p. Lit. 8000. – RCC 137 (1986,1) 306 (G. *Caprile*).

840 **Storniolo** Ivo, *Martins Balancin* Euclides, Conheça a Bíblia. São Paulo 1986, Paulinas. 246 p. [REB 46,723].

842 **Wiesel** Élie, Mensajeros de Dios; relatos y leyendas bíblicas, TMateo Fernando. Buenos Aires 1981, Seminario Rabínico Latinoamericano. 177 p. [KirSef 59,307].

843 **Wijngaards** John, Inheriting the Master's cloak [pastoral questions from the setting of the OT]. ND 1985, Ave Maria. 191 p. $4.95 pa. [BToday 24,272].

843* **Wright** Chris, Guida facile alla Bibbia [Lion]. T 1986, Elle Di Ci. 128 p. Lit. 8000. – RParVi 31 (1986) 395s (F. *Mosetto*).

B1.3 *Paedagogia biblica* – **Bible teaching techniques.**

844 *Adams* Karl-August, Bilder der Bibel – Variationen des Selbst: KatBlätt 111 (Mü 1986) 614-7 [< ZIT].

844* *Amewowo* Wynnand, Bicam; Secam's organ for biblical apostolate: AfER 28 1(96) 381-7.

845 d'*Aviau de Ternay* Henri, *Weiler* Lúcia, Um instrumental para uma leitura de conjunto da Bíblia, na perspectiva da libertação: REB 46 (1986) 760-782.

845* *Bätz* K., *Mack* R., Sachtexte / Sachbilder² (*Witzig* H., *Testa* F.) zur Bibel; Hilfen zum Verstehen und Erzählen. Lahr/Mü 1984/4, Kaufmann / Kösel. 120 p.; 31 + 24 p. DM je 22. 3-7806-0487-6; 63-9 / 3-466-36130-3; 29-X [BL 87,7, R. *Coggins*].

846 *Beaty* Earl R., A comparison of Bible College curricula among five religious groups through three eras: diss. Missouri/St. Louis 1986, DStarr R.J. 304 p. 86-09077. – DissA 47 (1986s) 487-A.

846* *Berg* H. K., Biblische Texte verfremdet [*Brecht* B.: a familiar idea needs to become unfamiliar/strange if its truth is to be fully perceived], I. Grundsätze-Methoden-Arbeitsmöglichkeiten. Stu/Mü 1986, Calwer/Kösel. 136 p. DM 19,80. 3-7668-0808-7 / Mü 3-466-36366-7 [BL 87,58s, R. E. *Clements*].

847 **Beyer** Karl, Wie bereite ich eine Bibelarbeit vor? Wu 1986 = 1976, Brockhaus. 58 p. DM 4.95 [Streven 53,953].

847* *a)* La Bibbia a fumetti I-IV. R 1985, Paoline. 155 p., Lit 15.000 ogni volume. – *b)* ᴱVanetti P., Il Vangelo. Mi 1985, Fumetti d'arte. 198 p. Lit. 19.500. – ᴿLetture 41 (1986) 282-4 (G. *Ravasi*); CC 137 (1986,1) 295s (G. *Marchesi* su Vanetti).

848 *Bissoli* Cesare, Aprire con i giovani la Bibbia: ParVi 31 (1986) 113-122.

848* **Bortfeldt** Martin B., Schüler und Bibel; eine empirische Untersuchung religiöser Orientierungen ... 13-16. Jährige. Aachen 1984. – ᴿPrakT 13 (1986) 181s (L. van der *Tuin*).

849 *Cazelles* Henri, Formation de l'esprit critique et éducation de la foi dans l'enseignement de la Bible: Bulletin de Saint-Sulpice 12 ('La formation intellectuelle des prêtres' 1986) 93-110.

850 ᴱ**Coleman** Lyman, *al.,* Serendipity New Testament for groups. NY 1986, Paulist. 504 p. $10. 0-8091-8863-8.

851 ❷ Dzieje przymierza; Biblia dla młodzieży [Youth Bible; history of the covenant = Neue Schulbibel]. Wsz 1985, Pax. 362 p. – ᴿRuBi 39 (1986) 79s (S. *Grzybek*: some books missing).

851* **Gable** C. David, National Assemblies of God youth ministry; the formation of balanced, biblical programs: diss. Fuller, ᴰ*Anderson* R. Pasadena 1986. 142 p. 86-16384. – DissA 47 (1986s) 1756-A.

852 *Grzybek* Stanisław, ❷ Formy apostolatu pismem świętym [= De usu pastorali S. Scripturae: i. interest the faithful in Scripture; ii. diffuse the Bible in the parish; iii. stimulate self and others to read it; iv. live by it each day]: RuBi 39 (1986) 55-69.

853 **Gutsche** Friedhardt, *Schinzer* Reinhard, Die Bibel kennen; 30 Arbeitsblätter mit Erläuterungen und Hinweisen zur Praxis. Gö 1986, Vandenhoeck & R. 135 p. [TLZ 112,334, V. *Hirth*].

854 **Hauer** Christian E., *Young* William A., An introduction to the Bible → 1,1188*]; a journey into three worlds. ENJ 1985, Prentice-Hall. 333 p. $27. – ᴿHorizons 13 (1986) 411s (D. J. *Grimes*: for college students); TDig 33 (1986) 473 (W. C. *Heiser*).

855 **Höffken** P., Elemente kommunikativer Didaktik in frühjüdischer und rabbinischer Literatur [Hab. Bonn]: Religionspädagogik in der Blauen Eule 1. Essen 1986, Blaue Eule. 536 p. DM 56. 3-89206-113-0 [BL 87,108, R. J. *Coggins*]. ᴿFreibRu 37s (1985s) 117s (K. *Bätz*).

856 *Korherr* Edgar J., ❷ Katecheza i diakonia (Caritas): RuBi 39 (1986) 155-172.

857 ᴱ**Lechmann** R., *Reents* C., Johann HÜBNER, Zweymal zwey und funffzig Auserlesene Biblische Historien Aus dem Alten und Neuen Testamente, Der Jugend zum Besten abgefasset [1714-1731]. Hildesheim 1986, Olms. xiv-28 + 416 p.; 85 pl. DM 118 [TLZ 112,230, G. *Adam*]. *b)* **Reents** Christine [HÜBNER Johann, Zweymal zwey und fünffzig auserlesene biblische Historien, der Jugend zum Besten abgefasst Lp 1714 (...-1902)] Die Bibel als Schul- und Hausbuch für Kinder; Werkanalyse und Wirkungsgeschichte einer frühen Schul- und Kinderbibel im evangelischen Raum: Arbeiten zur Religionspädagogik 2, 1984 → 1,1285: ᴿTLZ 111 (1986) 177s (G. *Adam*).

858 *Levenson* Jon, Hebrew Bible in colleges and universities: RelEd 81 (Ch 1986) 37-44.

858* *Mafico Temba* L. J., The Old Testament and effective evangelism in Africa: IntRMiss 75 (1986) 400-9.

859 **Marinelli** Anthony J., Yahweh and son; a teenager's guide to the Bible. NY 1986, Paulist. v-151 p. $8. 0-8091-9568-2.

860 *Martin* Gerhard M., Mehrdimensionaler Umgang mit der Bibel in Handlungsfeldern der Praktischen Theologie: VerkF 31,2 (1986) 34-46.

861 **Mesters** C., Lecturas bíblicas; guías de trabajo para un curso bíblico, ᵀ*Barrical* Nicolas. Estella 1986, VDivino. 270 p. pt. 1250. 84-7151-412-5. – ᴿBibFe 12 (1986) 367s (A. *Salas*).

862 **Mesters** Carlos, Vom Leben zur Bibel, von der Bibel zum Leben; ein Bibelkurs aus Brasilien für uns. Mü/Mainz c. 1985, Kaiser/Grünewald. 112 p.; 167 p. DM 36. – ᴿLuthMon 25 (1986) 88 (M. *Weskott*).

862* *a)* **Neuberger** Julia, The story of the Jews. – *b)* **Rye** Jennifer, The story of the Christians. C 1986, Univ. 32 p.; £3.95, pa. £1.95 each [ExpTim 98,351].

863 *Ott* Rudi, Wie mit der Bibel unterrichten? Kommentare zu bibeldidaktischen Büchern von 1980 bis 1984: RelPBei 17 (Kaarst 1986) 19-90 [< ZIT].

864 **Pikaza** X., Anunciar la libertad a los cautivos; palabra de Dios y catequesis 1985 → 1,1283: ᴿCiuD 199 (1986) 119 (A. *Salas*).

865 **Ringel** Erwin, *Kirchmayr* Alfred, Religionsverlust durch religöse Erziehung; tiefenpsychologische Ursachen und Folgerungen. W 1985, Herder. 241 p. DM 35. – ᴿTLZ 111 (1986) 696-8 (K. *Schmidt-Rost*); TPQ 134 (1986) 301s (J. *Janda*).

865* *Russell* Kenneth C., *O'Donovan* Kilian, Catholic Bible schools: CanadCathR 4 (Jan. 1986)...

866 **Schinzer** Reinhard [→ 853], Im Spiel die Bibel verstehen; Anregungen für den Umgang mit der Bibel in Gruppen. Gö 1986, Vandenhoeck & R. 156 p. 3-525-61259-1 [Apg 16,11-34; Röm 13,1-7...].

866* *Schneider* Jan H., Das Thema der Jesus-Nachfolge in einer korrelativen Didaktik: FreibZ 33 (1986) 311-325 [327-344, *Eigenmann* Urs].

867 **Shoemaker** Stephen, Retelling the biblical story. Nv 1985, Broadman. 179 p. $6.95. – ᴿRExp 83 (1986) 487s (J. A. *Smith*).

867* *Sivatte* Rafael de, Dios camina con su pueblo; catecumenado para Universitarios [Alliberament d'Israel], ᵀ*Balanzo* Sergio A. de: Pastoral 22. Santander 1984, Sal Terrae. 195 p.; maps. 84-293-0677-3 [ActuBbg 24,79].

868 *a)* *Sorger* Karlheinz, Biblische Elemente in Religionsbüchern für die Grundschule; – *b)* *Stachel* Günter, Exodus und Exodusmotiv in der Religionspädagogik; – *c)* *Florian* Helke M., Das Bild der Frau in den Religionsbüchern der Primarstufe: RelPBei 18 (Kaarst 1986) 59-75 / 99-119 / 120-130 [< ZIT].

868* **Thiselton** Anthony, Address and understanding; some goals and models of biblical interpretation as principals [sic] of vocational training: Anvil 3 (Bristol 1986) 101-118 [< ZIT].

869 **Thompson** Dorothy L., Bible study that works. GR 1984, Zondervan/ Asbury. 67 p. [ETL 62,117*].

869* **Ven** J. A. van der, Kritische Godsdienstdidactiek. Kampen 1982, Kok. 700 p. (bibliog. 700 titles) ƒ 72,50. – ᴿGerefTTs 86 (986) 54-56 (F. H. *Kuiper*).

870 **Vogt** Theophil, Bibelarbeit; Grundlegung und Praxismodelle einer biblisch orientierten Erwachsenenbildung: Praktische Wissenschaft Kirchengemeinde. Stu 1985, Kohlhammer. 173 p. DM 29,80. 3-17-009018-6. – ᴿTLZ 111 (1986) 629-631 (K. *Wegenast*).

871 *a)* *Vogt* Theophil, Bibelarbeit; *b)* *Schneider* Hans, Bibelgesellschaften; → 587, EvKL 1 (1986) 446-8 / 461-4.

872 **Wijngaards** John N. M., *a)* Communiquer la Parole; pistes et orientations pour la prédication et la catéchèse bibliques [1978 → 61,1619], ᵀ*Winandy*

Jacques: BiVChr NS (0224-8859). P 1982, Lethielleux. 270 p.; 42 fig. 2-249-61013-4. – *b*) On planning Scripture studies [➤ 1,1292]. ScrB 17 (1986s) 2-11.

873 **Wuckelt** Agnes, *a*) Tendenzkritische Auslegung alttestamentlicher Texte im schulischen Religionsunterricht: Diss. ᴱ*Görg* M. Bamberg 1986. 293 p. RTLv 18,544; TR 82,512. – *b*) Zentrale Texte des ATs, eine Praxishilfe ... Mü 1985, Kösel. 191 p. – ᴿComSev 19 (1986) 52s (M. de *Burgos*).

B2.1   **Hermeneutica** [➤ J9.1, linguistica de Deo].

874 **Alonso Schökel** Luis, Hermenéutica de la Palabra, I, Hermenéutica biblica [reprints 1959-85 + update p. 238-246: OTAbs 9,297]. Academia Christiana 37. M 1986, Cristiandad. 267 p. 84-7057- 401-5 [BL 87,127].

875 **Alonso Schökel** Luis, La Palabra Inspirada; la Biblia a la luz de la ciencia del lenguaje[3]. Academia Christiana 27. M 1986, Cristiandad. 409 p. pt. 1300. 84-7057-393-4 [BL 87,79s, R. J. *Hammer*: bibliographies updated].

876 *a*) *Basevi* Claudio, La función hermenéutica de la tradición de la Iglesia [i. insuficiencia de los métodos histórico-críticos: GADAMER; ii. Concilios]; – *b*) *Tabet* Miguel A., La perspectiva sobrenatural de la hermenéutica bíblica de santo Tomás: ScripTPamp 18 (1986) 159-174 / 175-196.

876* *a*) *Birch* Bruce C., Biblical hermeneutics in recent discussion; OT; – *b*) *Harrington* Daniel J., ... NT; – *c*) *Steinmetz* David C., Theology and exegesis; ten theses: ➤ 259, ᴱ*McKim* D., A guide to contemporary hermeneutics 1986, 3-12 / 13-20 [< RelStR 10 (1984) 1-7 / 7-10] / 27.

877 *Blank* G. Kim, Deconstruction; entering the Bible through Babel: Neotestamentica 20 (1986) 61-67. ➤ 8007-8009.

878 *a*) *Bori* Pier Cesare, Il paradigma ermeneutico antico e le sue possibili metamorfosi; – *b*) *Bettiolo* Paolo, Esegesi e purezza di cuore; la testimonianza di Dadišoʼ Qaṭraya (VII sec.), nestoriano e solitario: ➤ 365, AnStoEseg 3 (1985/6) 259-276 [277-296 discussione] / 201-213.

879 **Canévet** Mariette, GRÉGOIRE de Nysse et l'herméneutique biblique; étude des rapports entre le langage et la connaissance de Dieu 1983 ➤ 64,e73: ᴿJTS 37 (1986) 223-6 (C. *Stead*); Salesianum 48 (1986) 987 (E. *Fontana*).

880 **Cohen** E. D., The mind of the Bible believer. Buffalo 1986, Prometheus. v-423 p. $20. 0-87975-341-2 [NTAbs 31,130].

881 *Combrink* H.J.B., The changing scene of biblical interpretation: ➤ 72, ꟳMETZGER B. 1985/6, 4-17.

882 *Comstock* Gary, Truth or meaning; RICŒUR versus FREI on biblical narrative: JRel 66 (1986) 117-140.

883 *Corduan* Winfried, Humility and commitment; an approach to modern hermeneutics; Themelios 11 (1985s) 83-88.

884 **Corsani** B., Esegesi; come interpretare un testo biblico. T 1985, Claudiana. 142 p. – ᴿCiuD 199 (1986) 125 (J. *Gutiérrez*); StPatav 33 (1986) 430s (G. *Segalla*).

885 *Cotterell* Peter, Sociolinguistics and biblical interpretation: VoxEvca 16 (1986) 61-76.

885* *a*) *Cremascoli* Giuseppe, Le symbolisme des nombres dans les œuvres de Grégoire le Grand; – *b*) *Rapisarda lo Menzo* Grazia, L'Écriture sainte comme guide de la vie quotidienne dans la correspondance de Grégoire le Grand; – *c*) *Banniard* Michel, ʼIuxta uniuscuiusque qualitatemʼ; l'Écriture médiatrice chez Grégoire le Grand: ➤ 433*, GRÉGOIRE 1982/6, 445-454 / 215-225 / 477-488.

886 **Croatto** J. Severino, Hermenêutica bíblica [1984 ➤ 1,1302],[T]. São Leopoldo 1986, Sinodal. 76 p. [REB 46,724].

887 **Daschbach** Edwin, Interpreting Scripture. 1985. $6.95 pa. [TDig 33,359].

888 *David* Petre, [rum.] Neuere Verhaltensweisen im Blick auf den Wert und auf die Interpretation der Heiligen Schrift: Mitropolia Banatului 34 (1984) 128-138 [TLZ 111,479].

889 **Diel** Paul [1893-1972; [E]*Diel* Jane; franç. 1975], Symbolism in the Bible; the universality of symbolic language and its psychological significance, [T]*Marans* Nelly. SF 1986, Harper & R. x-175 p. $17.95 [TDig 34,65: the myth of the Fall, the myth of the Incarnation, and the myth of the Resurrection]. 0-86683-475-3.

889* **Dunnett** Walter M., The interpretation of Holy Scripture 1984 ➤ 1,1306: [R]BS 143 (1986) 177 (R. B. *Zuck*: p. 36s 'denies the inerrancy of the Bible'; on p. 283 this statement is retracted in light of a comment from Dunnett); RExp 83 (1986) 467s (W. *Ward*).

890 **Erickson** Richard J., James BARR and the beginnings of biblical semantics [< diss.]; Anthroscience Minigraph 1984 ➤ 65,1134: [R]JStNT 27 (1986) 117s (S. E. *Porter*).

891 **Ferguson** Duncan S., Biblical hermeneutics, an introduction. Atlanta/L 1986, Knox/SCM. 220 p. $12.95 pa. [TDig 34,68]. /o-334-01906-0.

892 **Fishbane** Michael, Biblical interpretation in ancient Israel 1985 ➤ 1,1308; bibliog. p. 545-558: [R]BL (1986) 68s (R. E. *Clements*: a major scholarly achievement, a vital prolegomenon); Interpretation 40 (1986) 418 (R. E. *Murphy*); RHR 203 (1986) 411-4 (A. *Caquot*); TLond 39 (1986) 476-8 (P. R. *Ackroyd*).

892* *a*) *Fishbane* Michael, Inner biblical exegesis; types and strategies of interpretation in ancient Israel; – *b*) *Heinemann* Joseph, The nature of the Aggadah: ➤ 249, [E]*Hartman* G., Midrash 1986, 19-37 / 41-55.

893 *Frei* Hans, The 'literal reading' of biblical narrative in the Christian tradition; does it stretch or will it break? [Scripture should be read with concern for minimal literal sense acknowledged in the community]: ➤ 385, *McConnell* F., Bible as narrative 1983/6 ... [TS 46,702, *Scuka* R.: means '*Should* be read as *has* been read'].

894 *Grech* Prosper, *a*) Il problema ermeneutico nel secondo secolo [conferenza Univ. Navarra 1985, di prossima pubblicazione]; – *b*) La nuova ermeneutica; FUCHS e EBELING [< AugR 12 (1972) 277-296]; – *c*) I principi ermeneutici di Sant'AGOSTINO; una valutazione [< Lateranum 48 (1982) 209-223]; – *d*) I 'testimonia' e la moderna ermeneutica [< NTS 19 (1976) 318-324], [T]*Camporeale* Rita: ➤ 166, Ermeneutica 1986, 108-118 / 173-194 / 119-134 / 97-107.

895 *Gribomont* J., I generi letterari nel monachesimo primitivo: Koinonia 10 (N 1986) 7-28.

896 *Grossberg* Daniel, Multiple meaning; part of a compound literary device in the Hebrew Bible: EAsJT 4,1 (1986) 77-86.

897 **Gunneweg** Antonius H. J., Comprendere l'Antico Testamento, un'ermeneutica [Vom Verstehen 1977 ➤ 58,1024], [T]*Fantoma* Giovanna: AT Sup 5. Brescia 1986, Paideia. 324 p.; bibliog. p. 297-310. Lit. 30.000.

898 *Hall* R. L., The living Word; an auditory interpretation of Scripture: Listening 21,1 (River Forest 1986) 25-42 [NTAbs 30,262].

899 *Henau* E., Schrifinterpretatie als element van kommunikatie: PrakT 13 (1986) 503-517.

900 *a*) *Illanes Maestre* José Luis, Hermenéutica bíblica y praxis de liberación; – *b*) *Pérez Fernández* Miguel, Aportación de la hermenéutica judía a la

exégesis bíblica; – c) *Mejía* Jorge, Presupuestos hermenéuticos y perspectivas de la exégesis crítica de la Biblia; – d) *Lorda Iñarra* Juan Luis, La palabra viva del Dios vivo; – e) *Chapa* Juan, Principios hermenéuticos de un filósofo neoplatónico; algunas consideraciones sobre la exegesis allegórica: ➤ 366, Hermenéutica 1985/6, 165-277 / 293-306 / 307-323 / 257-263 / 145-157.

901   **Johnson** C. B., The psychology of biblical interpretation. GR 1983, Zondervan. 119 p. $5.95. 0-310-33281-8 [BL 87,84s, R. J. *Hammer*: on American-scene fundamentalism].

901* a) *Kaiser* Walter C.ᴶ, Legitimate hermeneutics [< ᴱ*Geisler* N., Inerrancy 1979, 117-147]; – b) *Froehlich* Karlfried, Biblical hermeneutics on the move [< WWorld 1 (1981) 140-152]; – c) *Kraft* Charles H., Supracultural meanings via cultural forms [< Christianity in culture 1979, 116-146]; – d) *Padilla* C. René, The interpreted word; reflections on contextual hermeneutics [< Themelios Sept. 1981, 18-23]; – e) *Miguez Bonino* J., ... praxis [< Doing Theology 1975, 86-105]; – f) *Schüssler Fiorenza* Elisabeth, ... feminist [< Challenge of Liberation Theology 1981, 91-112]: ➤ 259, Hermeneutics 1986, 111-141 / 175-191 / 309-343 / 297-308 / 344-357 / 358-381.

902   **Kedar** Benjamin, Biblische Semantik, eine Einführung 1981 ➤ 62,1359 ... 1,1318: ᴿZRGg 38 (1986) 79-81 (B. *Mengel*).

903   **Keegan** T. J., Interpreting the Bible; a popular introduction to biblical hermeneutics 1985 ➤ 1,1319: ᴿExpTim 97 (1985s) 381 (A. T. *Lincoln*: insistently Catholic); TS 47 (1986) 741 (J. R. *Donahue*: clear, with a fine 60-term glossary).

904   **Korshin** Paul J., Typologies in England, 1650-1820. Princeton 1982, Univ. xvii-437. £26.10 – ᴿHeythJ 27 (1986) 95s (N. *Abercrombie*: shaky norms).

905   **Kugel** James L., *Greer* Rowan A., Early biblical interpretation: [ᴱ*Meeks* W.] Library of Early Christianity 3. Ph 1986, Westminster. 214 p. $19. – ᴿCCurr 36 (1986s) 232s (Pheme *Perkins*); RExp 83 (1986) 632s (E. G. *Hinson*); TTod 43 (1986s) 598.600s (B. M. *Metzger*).

906   *Kunjummen* Raju D., The single intent of Scripture – critical examination of a theological construct: GraceTJ 7 (1986) 81-110.

907   *La Potterie* Ignace de, La lettura della Sacra Scrittura 'nello Spirito'; il modo patristico di leggere la Bibbia è possibile oggi?: CC 137 (1986,3) 209-223.

908   a) *La Potterie* Ignace de, La lecture 'dans l'Esprit'; – b) *Esbroeck* Michel van, Les deux Testaments; une même vie; – c) *Boulnois* Olivier, Puis-je lire l'Écriture?; – d) *Costantini* Michel, Horizon 2001; pour une exégèse du 4ᵉ type; e) *Alves* Manuel I., Exégèse pour l'Église: Communio 11,4 ('Lire l'Écriture' 1986) 11-28 / 71-90 / 29-44 / 45-70 / 4-10; > IkaZ 15 (1986) solum 209-224, de la Potterie, 'Ist die patristische Weise der Bibellesung heute möglich?; übrigens p. 193-203, f) *König* Franz, Die Katholiken und die Bibel.

909   **Lategan** Bernard C., *Vorster* Willem S., Text and reality; aspects of reference in biblical texts 1985 ➤ 1, 1323: ᴿThemelios 12 (1986s) 60 (W. A. *Strange*); TR 82 (1986) 373s (T. *Söding*).

909* *Loubser* J. A., Die belang van die konteks in die lees van 'n teks: NduitseGT 27 (1986) 146-157.

910   **Lundin** R., *Thiselton* A. C., *Walhout* C., The responsibility of hermeneutics 1985 ➤ 1,1325: ᴿCalvinT 21 (1986) 290-6 (L. *Suidervaart*); ExpTim 97 (1985s) 381 (A. T. *Lincoln*).

911   **Mabee** Charles, Reimagining America ... biblical hermeneutics 1985 ➤ 1,1326: ᴿHorizons 13 (1986) 159 (D. J. *Fasching*).

912 *McConville* Gordon, Diversity and obscurity in Old Testament books; a hermeneutical exercise based on some later OT books: Anvil 3,1 (Bristol 1986) 33-48 [< ZIT].

912* *a) McKim* Donald K., Approaches to contemporary hermeneutics; major emphases in biblical interpretation; – *b) Timmer* David E., The Bible between Church and Synagogue; thoughts on the interpretation of the Hebrew Scriptures: RefR 39 (1985s) 86-93 / 94-106 [< ZIT].

913 *a) McKinney* Ronald H., RICŒUR's hermeneutic and the Messianic problem; – *b) Walsh* Brian J., Anthony THISELTON's contribution to biblical hermeneutics: ChrSchR 14 (1985) 211-223 / 224-235 [< ZIT],

913* *Maori* Y., The approach of classical Jewish exegetes to Peshat and Derash and its implications for the reading of the Bible today: Tradition 21,3 (1984s) 40-53 [Istina 31 (1986) 250].

914 **Martínez** José M., Hermenéutica bíblica. Barc-Terrassa 1984, Clie. 586 p. – ᴿSTEv 8,16 (1985) 284s (G. *Emetti*).

914* *Mędala* Stanisław, ❷ Formy interpretacji Biblii w Judaizmie okresu międzytestamentalnego (intertestamentario): → 367, Sympozjum 1985, RuBi 39 (1986) 212-231.

915 *Molina Palma* Mario A., La interpretación de la Escritura en el Espíritu; estudio histórico y teológico de un principio hermenéutico de la Constitución 'Dei Verbum', 12 [diss. R, PIB, ᴰ*La Potterie* I. de → 1,1336]: Burgense 27 (1986) 345-359 [350-361, bibliog.; ... antigüedad ... reposición ...].

915* *Moore* Stephen D., Negative hermeneutics, insubstantial texts; Stanley FISH and the biblical interpreter: JAAR 54 (1986) 707-719.

916 *a) Newport* J.P., Representative historical and contemporary approaches to biblical interpretation; – *b) Hull* W.E., The nature of the Bible and its message: Faith & Mission 3,2 (Wake Forest 1986) 32-48 / 3-10 [NTAbs 30,263].

916* **Oost** R., Omstreden bijbeluitleg; aspecten en achtergronden van de hermeneutische discussie rondom de exegese van het Oude Testament in Nederland; een bijdrage tot gesprek: diss ᴰ*Woude* A. van der. Groningen 1986. 121 p. – RTLv 18,540; TsTNijm 27,99.

917 *Pathrapankal* Joseph, *a)* God's Word for God's world; the task of present-day exegetes; – *b)* The living Word of God in a secular age; – *c)* Time and eternity in biblical thought: → 202*, Critical and creative 1986, 1-10 / 11-21 / 23-38.

917* **Polka** Brayton, The dialectic of biblical critique; interpretation and existence. NY / Basingstoke, Hampshire 1986, St. Martin's/Macmillan. x-191 p. $25. 0-312-19874-4 / 0-333-39257-4. [NTAbs 31,94].

918 **Prickett** Stephen, Words and The Word; language, poetic and biblical interpretation. C 1986, Univ. 305 p. £27.50. 0-521-32248-0. – ᴿExpTim 98 (1986s) 276s (M.J. *Townsend*).

918* *a) Rad* Gerhard von, Theological interpretation of the OT, ᵀ*Bright* John [< ᴱ*Mays* J., Essays 1963, 17-39]; – *b) LaSor* William S., The Sensus Plenior and biblical interpretation [< ᶠ*Harrison* E. 1978, 260-277]; – *c)* *Steinmetz* David C., The superiority of precritical exegesis [< TTod, Apr. 1980, 27-38]; – *d) Thiselton* Anthony C., The new hermeneutic [< ᴱ*Marshall* I., NT Interpretation 1977, 308-333]: → 259, ᴱ*McKim* D., Hermeneutics 1986, 28-46 / 47-64 / 65-77 / 78-107 (142-172).

919 **Richard** Ramesh P., Methodological proposals for Scripture relevance [ethics, ᴰ1982 → 64,6386]: 1. Selected issues in theoretical hermeneutics; 2. Levels of biblical meaning; 3. Application theory in relation to the New

Testament; 4. ... to the Old Testament: Bibliotheca Sacra 143 (1986) 14-25 / 122-133 / 205-217 / 302-313 [before p. 289: Bibliotheca Sacra will henceforth have new format, 24 pages more each issue; fewer and longer book-reviews].

919* *Riggs* Jack R., The 'fuller meaning' of Scripture; a hermeneutical question for Evangelicals: GraceTJ 7 (1986) 213-227.

920 *Rispoli* Gioia M., Eufonia ed ermeneutica; origine ed evoluzione di un metodo filologico e critico-letterario: Koinonia 10 (1986) 113-149.

921 **Rojtman** Betty, Feu noir sur feu blanc; essai sur l'herméneutique juive. Lagrasse 1986, Verdier. 217 p. 2-86432-047-9.

921* *Schmidt* Ludwig / *Schenk* Wolfgang, Hermeneutik AT / NT: ➤ 597, TRE 15 (1986) 137-143 / 144-150 [108-137 *Bormann* Claus von, philosophisch; 150-6 *Schröer* Henning, prak.-theol.].

922 **Schweizer** Harald, Biblische Texte verstehen; Arbeitsbuch zur Hermeneutik und Methodik der Bibelinterpretation. Stu 1986, Kohlhammer. 199 p. DM 34. 3-17-009392-4 [BL 87,77s, R. E. *Clements*: heavy].

922* *Smend* Rudolf, Nachkritische Schriftauslegung [< ᶠBARTH K. Parrhesia 1966, 215-237]: ➤ 220, Mitte des ATs 1986, 212-232.

923 *Steiger* Lothar, Humor [3. 'Biblischer Humor der Endlichkeit']: ➤ 597, TRE 15 (1986) 696-701.

923* *Steinmetz* Peter, Allegorische Deutung und allegorische Dichtung in der Alten Stoa: RheinMus 129 (1986) 18-30.

924 *Tabick* Jacqueline, The snake in the grass; the problems of interpreting a symbol in the Hebrew Bible and rabbinic writings: Religion 16 (L 1986) 155-168 [ZIT].

924* *Theissen* Gerd. Evolutionäre Religionstheorie und biblische Hermeneutik: ➤ 109, ᶠSTEIGER L., Brosamen 1985, 437-454.

925 *Thiselton* A. C., La nouvelle herméneutique [< ᴱ*Marshall* I., NT Interpretation 1977, 308-333], ᵀ*Hickel* Pascal, *al.*: Hokhma 11,33 (1986) 1-35.

925* *Thomas* Robert L., The hermeneutics of evangelical redaction criticism: JEvTS 29 (1986) 447-460 [< ZIT].

926 **Tőkés** István, ⓂA bibliai hermeneutika története [history of ...]. Kolozsvár 1985. 266 p. – ᴿTheologiai Szemle 29 (1986) 113 (L. *Gáspár Csaba*).

926* *Toker* Naphtali, ⓄQôl ha-mspr (ha-kᵉtûb) in etymological explanation: BethM 31,105 (1985s) 169-181.

927 **Vogels** W., Reading and preaching the Bible; a new semiotic approach: Background 4. Wilmington 1986, Glazier. 190 p. $9 pa. 0-89453-472-6 [NTAbs 31,96].

B2.2 Structuralismus – Analysis of narrative [➤ J9.6].

927* **Beauchamp** P., Le récit, la lettre et le corps: CogF 114, 1982 ➤ 63,1327 ... 1,1351: ᴿEsprV 96 (1986) 64 (L. *Debarge*); RechSR 74 (1986) 305-8 (J. *Calloud*: difficile mais non sans charme); ScEspr 38 (1986) 265s (G. *Novotny*: il faut relire dix fois).

928 **Berlin** Adele, Poetics and interpretation of biblical narrative: BLit 9, 1983 ➤ 64,1166 ... 1,1352: ᴿCBQ 48 (1986) 297-9 (Barbara *Green*: the book admits incompatibility with earlier biblical criticism).

929 **Greenwood** David C., Structuralism and the biblical text: Religion and Reason 32, 1985 ➤ 1,1358: ᴿÉTRel 61 (1986) 563s (D. *Lys*); TsTNijm 26 (1986) 293 (E. van *Walde*).

929* a) *Hoppe* Leslie J., A synopsis of Robert ALTER's 'The art of biblical narrative'; – b) *Cohn* Robert L., On the art of biblical narrative; – c) *Edelman* Diana, An appraisal of Robert Alter's approach: BiRes 31 (Ch 1986) 6-12 / 13-19 / 19-25.

930 *Jacobson* Richard, The structuralists and the Bible [< Interpretation 28 (1974) 146-164]: ➤ 259, ᴱ*McKim* D., Hermeneutics 1986, 280-296.

930* **Jobling** David, The sense of biblical narrative; structural analyses in the Hebrew Bible [1, 1978 ➤ 60,3607], 2 [Gn 2s; 1 Sm 1-12; Nm 32...]: JStOT Sup. 39. Sheffield 1986, Univ. 153 p. 1-85075-010-6; pa. 1-4.

931 **Leach** E., *Aycock* D. A., Structuralist interpretations of biblical myth 1983 ➤ 64, 1282 ... 1,1361: ᴿJBL 105 (1986) 126-8 (R. C. *Culley*); JTS 37 (1986) 439-442 (D. *Nineham*).

McCarthy Carmel, *Riley* William, The Old Testament short story 1986 ➤ 8022.

933 *Moberly* R. W. L., Story in the Old Testament: Themelios 11,3 (1985s) 77-83.

934 *Riley* W., Situating biblical narrative; poetics and the transmission of community values: PrIrB 9 (1985) 38-52.

935 **Sternberg** M., The poetics of biblical narrative; ideological literature and the drama of reading. Indiana Literary Biblical Series [ᴱ*Polzin* R. M.]. Bloomington 1985, Univ. xiv-580 p. $57.50. 0-253-34521-9 [BL 87,78, R. P. *Carroll*: dense, enjoyable].

935* *Vetter* Dieter, Was leistet die biblische Erzählung? Beobachtung einer Stilform als Lese- und Verstehenshilfe: BTZ 3 (1986) 190-206.

B3 *Interpretatio ecclesiastica* .1 **Bible and Church.**

936 *Alonso Schökel* Luis, diálogo, La Biblia en España, veinte años después: RazF 213 (1986) 509-522.

937 a) *Aranda Pérez* Gonzalo, Magisterio de la Iglesia y interpretación de la Escritura; – b) *Taber* Miguel A., *McGovern* Thomas, El principio hermenéutico de la inspiración del hagiógrafo en la Constitución Dogmática 'Dei Verbum'; – c) *Bandera* Armando, Lectura de la biblia 'in sinu Ecclesiae' y celebración de la Eucaristía: ➤ 366, Hermenéutica 1985/6, 529-562 / 697-713 / 715-731.

938 **Barr** James, Escaping from fundamentalism 1984 ➤ 65, 1179; 1,1373: ᴿScripB 16 (1985s) 41s (R. C. *Fuller*); TsTNijm 26 (1986) 304 (L. *Grollenberg*).

938* *Bohren* Rudolf, Gemeinde und Theologie: BTZ 3 (1986) 241-250 [251-70, *Jörns* Klaus-P., Gemeinschaft; 271-292, *Wendland* G., Ortsgemeinde; 293-306, *Langer* J., Sozialgestalt].

939 **Bolich** Gregory G., Authority and the Church 1982 ➤ 64,1430: ᴿEvQ 58 (1986) 285s (P. *Cotterell*: leaders of the house-church movements have appropriated the term 'apostle').

940 **Bradley** Robert J., *Kevane* Eugene, The Roman Catechism 1985 ➤ 1,1375: ᴱAngelicum 63 (1986) 494 (J. *Aumann*: not really as claimed 'annotated in accord with Vatican II and Post-Conciliar documents and the new Code of Canon Law').

940* **Bray** Gerald, Creeds, councils and Christ 1984 ➤ 65,1184; 1,1376*: ᴿEvQ 58 (1986) 180s (H. *Bayer*); ScotJT 39 (1986) 287s (S. G. *Hall*).

941 **Brown** Raymond E., Biblical exegesis and Church doctrine 1985 ➤ 1,159; also L 1986, Chapman; 0-225-66478-X: ᴿExpTim 97 (1985s) 342 (A. *Hanson*: his defense of Assumption without foundation in Scripture is a

counsel of despair); Furrow 57 (1986) 406s (L. *O'Reilly*); Month 248 (1986) 278s (H. *Tomnay*); TLond 39 (1986) 478-480 (E. *Franklin*); TS 47 (1986) 703s (J. P. *Galvin*); TTod 43 (1986s) 435s (R. J. *Karris*).

942 *Callahan* Sidney, Conscience reconsidered [... The Church must work toward respecting loyal dissent]: America 155 (1986) 251-3.

943 ᴱ**Carson** D. A., Biblical interpretation and the Church 1982/5 → 1,459: ᴿVidyajyoti 49 (1986) 425-7 (P. M. *Meagher*); WestTJ 48 (1986) 215s (R. R. De *Ridder*).

944 *a*) *Conway* Pierre, Scripture, tradition, Magisterium; – *b*) *Kennedy* Leonard A., The seminarian and Thomist philosophy; – *c*) *Kevane* Eugene, The synod, the catechism, and the deposit of faith; the plot to reinterpret the faith is doomed to ashes: HomPast 87,4 (1986s) 9-19 / 20-26 / 49-57.

945 *Conway* P., The 'dual magisterium'; oil and water: HomPast 86,11 (1986) 21-30 [NTAbs 31,16].

946 *Cooke* Bernard, The Vatican and the U. S. Church [... Truth cannot be legislated]: America 155 (1986) 206-8.

947 **Crocetti** Giuseppe, I Testimoni di Geova a confronto con la vera Bibbia. Mi 1985, Áncora. 184 p. Lit. 9.000. – ᴿCC 137 (1986,1) 510 (G. *Caprile*).

948 **Curran** Charles E., Faithful dissent. Kansas City c. 1986, Sheed & W. 287 p. $10. 1-55612-045-1 [America 155, 389 adv.].

949 **Davis** John J., *a*) Handbook of basic Bible texts; *b*) Foundations of evangelical theology; *c*) Theology primer. GR 1984/84/81, Baker. 158 p., $7 pa.; 282 p., $10 pa.; 111 p. $6 pa. – ᴿGraceTJ 7 (1986) 138-140 (D. S. *Dockery*).

949* **Deely** Robert P., The mandate for those who teach theology in institutes of higher studies; an interpretation of the meaning of Canon 812 of the Code of Canon Law: diss. Pont. Univ. Gregoriana, ᴰ*Urrutia* F. J., Roma 1986. 240 p. Extr. Nº 3357, xi-215 p. – RTLv 18,594.

950 *Derousseaux* L., Lire l'Écriture en Église: Ensemble 43,1 (Lille 1986) 25-32 [NTAbs 30,262].

951 *Dulles* Avery, Sensus fidelium [... is the common consent of all peoples an infallible index of truth even today?]: America 155 (1986) 240-2.263.

951* **Eblen** James E., Dei Verbum; theory and practice: diss. Claremont 1986. – RelStR 13,188.

952 *Elsbernd* Mary, Rights statements; a hermeneutical key to continuing development in magisterial teaching: ETL 62 (1986) 308-332.

953 *Floristán* Casiano, El cansament dels catòlics davant el magisteri: QVidCr 134 (1986) 34-39.

954 *Franco* Ricardo, Teología y magisterio; dos modelos de relación [< EstE 59 (1984) 3-25], ᴱ*Bernal* José M.: SelT 25 (1986) 14-26.

954* *Fuller* Reginald H., Popes, bishops and academic freedom: CCurr 36 (1986s) 404-9.

955 *Galeriu* Constantin N., Biblia in Biserica Orthodoxǎ [rum., Die Bibel in der orthodoxen Kirche]: MitropBanat 35 (1985) 592-7 [TLZ 112,782].

955* *Galli* Alberto, Teologi contro il magistero; Giuseppe COLOMBO ['e quasi tutta la scuola milanese che fa capo a TItSett']: SacDoc 31 (1986) 527-541.

956 **González Faus** J. I., La libertad de palabra en la Iglesia y en la teología 1985 → 1,1390*: ᴿRazF 212 (1985) 104s (R. de *Andrés*).

956* *Grech* Prosper, *a*) Il magistero nella Scrittura e nella tradizione [< The Magisterium in Scripture and tradition, in A positive statement (Boston 1978, St. Paul) 32-52] ᵀ*Camporeale* Rita; – *b*) Criteri di ortodossia e eresia nel NT [< AugR 25 (1985) 583-596]: → 166, Ermeneutica 1986, 50-76 / 225-241.

957 *Grisez* Germain, How to deal with theological dissent: HomPast 87,1 (1986s) 19-29; 87,3 (1986s) 49-61 [available in cassette $3.50 each, Box 34, New London CT 06320].

957* **Häring** B., *a*) Erzwingung von Verstandesgehorsam gegenüber nicht-unfehlbaren Lehren?: TGegw 29 (1986) 213-9. – *b*) The Curran case, ᵀ*Neenan* Benedict: CCurr 36 (1986s) 332-342.

958 *Hofbeck* Joseph, La télévision religieuse; tension ou polarisation entre fondamentalistes et modernistes: SR 14 (1985) 371-382.

958* **Hunter** James D., American Evangelicalism; conservative religion and the quandary of modernity [diss. Rutgers 1981, ᴰ*Berger* P.]. New Brunswick NJ 1983, Rutgers. – ᴿCalvinT 21 (1986) 247-250 (D. *Stravers*).

959 *Ibáñez Arana* Andrés, La Constitución 'Dei Verbum' y los estudios bíblicos [inaugural 1985 ➤ 1,1395]: Lumen 35 (Vitoria 1986) 58-82.

959* *Inbody* Tyron, The common ground of liberals and fundamentalists: PerspRelSt 13 (1986) 197-206 [< ᴢɪᴛ].

960 ᴱ**Johnston** Robert K., The use of the Bible in theology; evangelical options. Atlanta 1985, Knox. ix-257 p. $12 pa. [TDig 33,492]. – ᴿRExp 83 (1986) 465s (W. *Ward*).

960* *Jossua* Jean-Pierre, La condition des théologiens depuis Vatican II vue par l'un d'entre eux: ArchivScSocRel 62,1 ('Vatican II vingt ans après; une restauration catholique ?' 1986) 119-134.

961 *Kaufmann* Ludwig, *Klein* Nikolaus, Cᴜʀʀᴀɴ; um den öffentlichen Dissens in der Kirche: Orientierung 50 (1986) 185-8.

962 **Laurentin** R., *a*) Comment reconcilier l'exégèse et la foi 1984 ➤ 65,1193: ᴿScripTPamp 18 (1986) 729s (J. M. *Casciaro*). – *b*) Come riconciliare l'esegesi e la fede, ᵀ*Masini* M. Brescia 1986, Queriniana. 190 p. – ᴿRasT 27 (1986) 375-381 (V. *Fusco*: non ha impostato correttamente il problema).

962* *Losada* Joaquín, Los derechos del cristiano en la Iglesia; a propósito del 'caso Bᴏꜰꜰ': SalT 73 (1985) 491-4.

963 *McCormick* Richard A., *a*) L'affaire Cᴜʀʀᴀɴ [absolutely dissenting views, but 'if Cardinal Rᴀᴛᴢɪɴɢᴇʀ's letter were applied to theologians throughout the world, the vast majority would not qualify as Catholic theologians']: America 154 (1986) 261-7. – *b*) De affaire-Curran; mogen theologen afwijken van de officiële leer?: Streven 53 (1985s) 878-887.

964 *McCormick* Richard A., The search for truth in the Catholic context [to silence dissent is to exclude ... improvement]: America 155 (1986) 276-281.

965 **McKim** Donald K., What Christians believe about the Bible 1985 ➤ 1,1237: 0-8407-5968-1: ᴿTS 47 (1986) 740s (R. L. *Maddox*); TTod 43 (1986s) 442.444 (T. W. *Gillespie*).

965* *a*) *Marty* Martin E., Modern fundamentalism; – *b*) *Whealon* John F., Challenging fundamentalism: – *c*) *Catoir* John, Fundamentalists on the move: America 155 (1986) 133-5 / 136-8 / 142-4.

966 *a*) *Mildenberger* Friedrich, Biblische Theologie als kirchliche Schriftauslegung; – *b*) *Baldermann* Ingo, Biblische Theologie als Weg des Lernens; didaktische Strukturen in der Theologie Luthers, Bonhoeffers und dem Selbstverständnis des Kirchenbundes: ➤ 236, JbBT 1 (1986) 151-162 / 182-198.

966* *Parker* David, *a*) Fundamentalism; still fighting for the faith: Interchange 35, 33-45 [< BS 136 (1986) 69]; – *b*) The Bible Union; a case study in Australian fundamentalism; – *c*) *Rich* Joe, Hellenism and Hebraism in Australia; a case study: JRelHist 14,1 (Sydney 1986) 71 ... / 57-70 [< ᴢɪᴛ].

967 *a*) *Poulat* Émile, La querelle de l'intégrisme en France; – *b*) *Bauberot* Jean, *Willaime* Jean-Paul, Le courant évangélique français, un 'intégrisme

protestant'?; – c) *Golding* Gordon, L'évangélisme, un intégrisme protestant américain?; – d) *Alexander* Daniel, Is Fundamentalism an integrism?:
Social Compass 32 (Louvain 1985) 343-352 / 393-412 / 363-372 / 373-392
[< ZIT].
967* *Price* Robert M., Neo-Evangelicals and Scripture; a forgotten period of
ferment: ChrSchR 15 (Houghton 1986) 315-330.
968 *Raberger* Walter, Der Fundamentalismus – eine Illusion?: TPQ 134 (1986)
160-9 [... Pluralismus als Verunsicherung und Orientierungsverlust ...
Kritikimmunisierung und Irrationalismus].
969 *Rupčić* Ljudevit, Biblijska i crkveno-ljudska uvjetovanost religioznog indi-
ferentizma: ➤ 504, Simpozij = ObnŽiv 41 (1986) 213-222; 222, Biblische
und kirchen-menschliche Bedingtheiten des religiösen Indifferentismus.
970 *Schmied* Augustin, Vielfältige Autorität in der Vermittlung des Glaubens:
TGegw 29 (1986) 150-160.
970* *Schöpsdau* Walter, Die Kompetenz des Lehramts in Fragen der Moral;
zum römischen Lehrverbot für Charles CURRAN: MaterialdienstKkI 37
(Bensheim 1986) 91-95 [< ZIT].
971 ᴱ**Selvidge** Marla J., Fundamentalism today, what makes it so attractive ?
1984 ➤ 1,398: ᴿRExp 83 (1986) 303s (B. J. *Leonard*).
971* *Siefer* Gregor, Fundamentalismus und Realität; schwieriger Umgang mit
der modernen Welt; LuthMon 25 (1986) 54-7.
972 *Sloyan* Gerard S., The Bible as the book of the Church: Worship 60
(1986) 9-21.
973 **Speyer** Wolfgang, Büchervernichtung und Zensur des Geistes bei Heiden,
Juden und Christen 1981 ➤ 62,1568 ... 65,1208: ᴿTPhil 61 (1986) 582-4
(A. *Grillmeier*).
974 **Sullivan** Francis A., Magisterium 1983 ➤ 64,1353; 1,1410: ᴿLavalTP 42
(1986) 329s (R.-M. *Roberge*); RelEd 81 (1986) 148-150 (J. A. *Varacalli*);
RRel 45 (1986) 628-630 (W. J. *Bildstein*); Vidyajyoti 49 (1985) 142s (F.
Wilfred).
975 *Thiel* John E., Theological responsibility; beyond the classical paradigm
[final report of Nov. 1985 Synod cites persistence of friction between
magisterium and theologians ...]: TS 47 (1986) 573-598.
975* *Visser 't Hooft* Willem A., Teachers and the teaching authority; the
magistri and the magisterium: EcuR 38 (1986) 152-202.
976 a) *Wackenheim* Charles, Le magistère et ses connexions avec l'Écriture, la
tradition et la théologie; – b) *Duquoc* Christian, Magistère et historicité; –
c) *Faivre* Alexandre, 'Où est la vérité?'; déplacements et enjeux d'une
question; – d) *Willaime* Jean-Paul, L'autorité religieuse et sa pratique dans
la situation contemporaine; – e) *Monsarrat* Jean-Pierre, La doctrine des
Églises Réformées sur ce qu'elles refusent d'appeler magistère: LumièreV
35,180 (1986) 95-107 / 83-94 / 5-16 / 37-52 / 55-64.
977 **Walton** Marlin, Witness in biblical scholarship; a survey of recent studies
1956-80; pref. *Spindler* Marc R.: Research Pamphlet 15. Leiden 1986,
IIMO. iv-79 p. *f* 18 [TR 83,249]. 90-71387-14-3. – ᴿÉTRel 61 (1986) 579
(J. *Pons*).
978 *Weymann* Volker [al.]. Fundamentalismus; Zugänge zur Bibel, Hindernisse
und Perspektiven: Reformatio 35 (Bern 1986) 126-131 [111-147].
978* *Winck* Honoré, Les origines de la Constitution Apostolique 'Divino
afflatu', du 1ᵉʳ novembre 1911 [sur la liturgie; ne pas confondre avec
Divino Afflante Spiritu sur l'Écriture]: EphLtg 100 (1986) 340-3.
979 *Wonderly* William L., The Bible in the Church; some implications for the
translator's treatment of background information: BTrans 37 (1986) 212-6

[most of the proposals seem quite secular, e.g. 'city where David was born' instead of 'city of David' as if David possessed it].

980 **Zehr** Paul M., Biblical criticism in the life of the [Mennonite/Anabaptist] Church. Scottdale PA 1986, Herald. 109 p. $7 [RelStR 13,254, R. H. *Fuller*]. 0-8361-3404-4.

981 *Zmijewski* Josef, Schriftauslegung – ein Problem zwischen den Konfessionen [< Catholica 37 (1983) 216-257]: → 233, Das NT Quelle 1986, 19-66.

B3.2 *Homiletica* – The Bible in preaching.

981* EAycock Don M., Heralds to a new age; preaching for the twenty-first century. Elgin IL 1985, Brethren. 256 p. – RRExp 83 (1986) 144s (J. A. *Smith*).

982 EBaumann Arnulf H., *Schwemer* Ulrich, Predigen in Israels Gegenwart; Predigtmeditationen im Horizont des christlich-jüdischen Gesprächs: EKD Studienkommission 'Kirche und Judentum'. Gü 1986, Mohn. 111 p. DM 22,80 [TLZ 112,502, C. *Hinz*].

983 **Brossier** François, Dire la Bible; récits bibliques et communication de la foi [diss. 1984 → 65,1218]. P 1986, Centurion. 154 p. F 94. – RÉtudes 364 (1986) 572 (J. *Thomas*).

984 **Brueggemann** W., Hopeful imagination; prophetic voices in exile [Pastors' Conferences; on preaching; cf. → 413]: Jer 30,12-17; Ezek 36,22-32; Is 54. Ph 1986, Fortress. x-146 p. $8. 0-8006-1925-0 [BL 87,80, A. *Gelston*].

985 *Cameron* Nigel M., The pulpit bible; preaching and the logic of authority: → 111, FSTILL W. 1986, 29-37.

986 **Carl** William J.III, Preaching Christian doctrine. Ph 1984, Fortress. 167 p. $8.95 pa. – RInterpretaton 40 (1986) 104 (J. *Vannorsdall*).

986* a) *Chollet* Jean, Prédication et narration [... des textes bibliques]; – b) *Daiber* Karl-Fritz, La prédication comme institution d'intégration ecclésiale et sociale; – c) *Palard* Jacques, Prédication des laïcs et pouvoir d'interprétation dans l'Église catholique: FoiVie 85,2s (Sociologie de la prédication, 1986) 35-49 / 97-113 / 143-156.

987 a) *Cook* James I., The use of the Bible in preaching; – b) *Van Kempen* Cornelis H. J., Masters of the text; is every age the same ? : → 123*, FWILTERDINK G. = RefR 40 (1986) 6-14 / 20-25.

987* ECox James W., Biblical preaching; an expositor's treasury 1983 → 1,1422: RGraceTJ 7 (1986) 156-8 (R. L. *Overstreet*); RExp 83 (1986) 291 (J. A. *Smith*: the best); Worship 60 (1986) 186s (W. F. *Jabusch*).

988 **Dannowski** Hans W., Kompendium der Predigtlehre. Gü 1985, Mohn. 168 p. DM 19,80. – RTLZ 111 (1986) 148s (K.-P. *Hertsch*).

988* **Engemann** Wilfried, Die Verkündigung als transaktionales Ereignis zwischen Prediger und Hörer; eine Studie zur Anwendbarkeit der Transaktionsanalyse auf homiletische Fragehinsichten, Relevanzen und Probleme: Diss. Rostock 1985. vii-155 p.; 65-xix p. – TLZ 111 (1986) 478s (auct.).

989 *Gagnebin* Laurent, Trois étapes – trois distances – trois temps ['Le prédicateur confronté aux textes bibliques découvre: 1) Une distance historique et la valeur positive de l'altérité divine; 2) Le vertige du néant de l'exégèse historico-critique et la valeur positive de la pauvreté du texte; 3) L'à-venir de la prédication qui ne nous appartient pas.']: → 83*, FPETER R. = RHPR 66 (1986) 79-91; Eng. 130.

990 *Goldingay* John, The spirituality of preaching [first of a new series, 'The Pastor's Opportunities']: ExpTim 98 (1986s) 197-203.

990* **Hammar** K. G., Det som hörs – ett predikoteoretiskt perspektiv. Alvsjö 1985, Verbum. 79 p. – ᴿSvTKv 62 (1986) 133-5 (H. *Fagerberg*).

991 **Hebblethwaite** Brian, Preaching throughout the Christian year; sermons from Queen's College, Cambridge. L 1985, Mowbray. 182 p. £4.95. 0-264-67061-2. – ᴿExpTim 97 (1985s) 254 (J. M. *James*: masterly examples of the art).

992 *Hellwig* Monika K., The Church in the world; making homilies for our times: TTod 43 (1968s) 561-8.

993 **Killinger** John, Fundamentals of preaching [... importance of the Bible] 1985 → 1,1425; also Ph, SCM; $10 pa: ᴿWorship 60 (1986) 554s (A. C. *Rueter*).

994 **Leuking** F. Dean, Preaching; the art of connecting God and people. Waco 1985, Word. 128 p. $12.95. 0-8499-0480-3. – ᴿExpTim 98 (1986s) 152 (J. M. *James*: pastor of one Illinois Lutheran church ever since he was ordained there thirty years ago); RExp 83 (1986) 670s (R. *Bailey*: spells Lueking).

994* **Liefeld** Walter L., New Testament exposition; from text to sermon 1984 → 65,3716; 1,4123: ᴿBS 143 (1986) 89s (D. R. *Sunukjian*).

995 *Michel* Arlette, Éloquence et théologie de la parole chez Lacordaire: BBudé (1986) 397-407.

995* *Müller* Hans M., Homiletik: → 597, TRE 15 (1986) 526-565.

996 **Newman** Elbert B.,ᴶ A critical evaluation of the contributions of the hermeneutical approaches of representative contemporary Old Testament scholars [*Bright* J., *Achtemeier* Elizabeth, *Gowan* D.] to an appropriation of the OT for Christian preaching: diss. SW Baptist Theol. Sem. 1986. 369 p. 86-14903. – DissA 47 (1986s) 1770-A.

996* ᴱ**Nitschke** Horst, Zeichen und Wunder; Predigten [namhafter Exegeten] über Wundergeschichten des Alten und Neuen Testaments. Gü 1985, Mohn. 144 p. DM 22,80 pa. – ᴿTLZ 111 (1986) 391s (M. *Josuttis*).

997 **Pittenger** Norman, Preaching the Gospel. Wilton CT 1984, Morehouse-Barlow. 107 p. – ᴿRExp 83 (1986) 496 (L. J. *Thompson*).

997* **Preuss** Horst D., Das Alte Testament in christlicher Predigt 1984 → 65,1227; 1,1429: ᴿBTZ 3 (1986) 148-154 (H. *Grün-Rath*); Salesianum 48 (1986) 426s (M. *Cimosa*); TZBas 42 (1986) 89s (G. *Adam*).

998 **Reiterer** Friedrich V., Gottes Wort im Festkreis; Hilfen für Verkündigung und Bibelrunden: SchwerpunktAT. Graz 1983, Styria. 263 p. [KirSef 59,316].

999 **Robinson** Haddon W., a Expository preaching, principles and practice. Leicester 1986, Inter-Varsity. 229 p. £4.95. 0-85110-758-3. – ᴿExpTim 98 (1986s) 151 (J. M. *James*: good, though not modern like J. Cox 1983). – *b*) Predicare la Bibbia; svolgimento e comunicazione di messaggi espositivi. R 1984, Istituto Biblico Evangelico. 251 p. – ᴿSTEv 15 (1985) 148s (C. *Bertinelli*).

1000 *Rorem* Paul, Toward liturgical hermeneutics; some Byzantine examples: CurrTM 13 (1986) 346-353.

1001 **Rostagno** B., La fede nasce dall'ascolto; guida per la predicazione. T 1984, Claudiana. 74 p. Lit. 3800. – ᴿProtestantesimo 41 (1986) 186s (R. *Bottazzi*).

1002 **Rothermundt** Jörg, Der Heilige Geist und die Rhetorik; theologische Grundlinien einer empirischen Homiletik 1984 → 1,1431: ᴿTheologiai Szemle 28 (1985) 381s (S. *Szénási*).

1002* **Schott** Christian-Erdmann, Predigtgeschichte als Zugang zur Predigt. Stu 1986, Calwer. 135 p. DM 19,80. – ᴿBiKi 41 (1986) 188 (P.-G. *Müller*).

1003 **Scott** Bernard B., The word of God in words; reading and preaching. Ph 1985 Fortress. 94 p. $5. – RRExp 83 (1986) 633s (R. *Baily*).
1003* **Sleeth** Ronald E., God's word and our words [basic homiletics]. Atlanta 1986, Knox. 139 p. $8. 0-8042-1577-4. – RExpTim 98 (1986s) 157 (D. W. *Cleverley Ford*).
1004 *Stöger* Alois, Bibelwissenschaft und Verkündigung [II. Vat.]: TPQ 134 (1986) 330-7 [319-346].
1005 **Vogels** Walter, Reading and preaching the Bible; a new semiotic approach: Background Books 4. Wilmington 1986, Glazier. 190 p. $8.95 pa. [JBL 105,756].
1006 **Wagner** Siegfried, *Breit* Herbert, Die Menschenfreundlichkeit Gottes; alttestamentliche Predigten mit hermeneutischen Überlegungen: Beiträge zur Erforschung des ATs und des antiken Judentums 7. Fra 1986, Lang. 224 p. 3-8204-8997-5.
1007 **Wolff** H. W., Old Testament and Christian preaching, TKohl Margaret. Ph 1986, Fortress. 110 p. $8.95. 0-8006-1905-6 [BL 87,94, G. W. *Anderson*].

B3.3 **Inerrantia, inspiratio.**

1008 *Baird* J. Arthur, A living and abiding voice; the function of the Holy Word in the early Christian consensus: → 392, SBL Seminars 1986, 479-489.
1009 **Basinger** David & Randall, Inerrancy [of Scripture] and Free Will [incompatible, as response to the problem of evil]; some further thoughts: EvQ [55 (1983) 177-180; 347-353, Geisler N.] 58 (1986) 351-4.
1009* *Bauman* Michael, Why the noninerrantists are not listening; six tactical errors evangelicals commit: JEvTS 29 (1986) 317 ... [< ZIT].
1010 *Bayer* Oswald, Vernunftautorität und Bibelkritik in der Kontroverse zwischen Johann G. HAMANN und Immanuel KANT: NSys 28 (1986) 179-197; Eng. 197.
1010* *a)* **Bergèse** D., L'Église Réformée de France et l'autorité de la Bible; – *b)* *Wells* P., L'insuffisance de l'Écriture et les agents doubles: RRéf 37 (1986) 113-7 / 118-133 [< ZIT].
1011 **Bockmuehl** K., Books, God's tools in the history of salvation: Vancouver Regent College Mon 1. Colorado Springs 1986, Helmers & H. 0-88865-414-6 [BL 87,127].
1012 *Donadoni* Sergio F., *a)* L''ispirazione divina' di Sinuhe [< Acme 10 (1957) 53-55]; – *b)* Sinuhe nella correganza di Sesostri [< StClasOr 15 (1966) 275-7]: → 152, Cultura 1986, 289-291 / 105-7.
1012* *Geffré* Claude, Autorité des Écritures et autonomie de la conscience: SuppVSp 155 (1985) 65-73.
1013 *a)* *Gillespie* Thomas W., Biblical authority and interpretation; the current debate on hermeneutics; [? ineditum]; – *b)* *Provence* Thomas E., The sovereign subject matter; hermeneutics in [Barth K.] the Church Dogmatics [< diss. Fuller 1980, 136-176]: → 259, EMcKim D., Hermeneutics 1986, 192-219 / 241-262.
1014 **Gnuse** Robert, The authority of the Bible; theories of inspiration, revelation and the canon of Scripture 1985 → 1,1450: RBibTB 16 (1986) 153 (J. I. *Hunt*); Gregorianum 67 (1986) 534s (J. *Wicks*: rightly claims biblical authority is a more basic category than biblical inspiration, but underrates categories more basic still); Horizons 14 (1987) 145s (J. F. *Devine*).

1014* *Goldingay* J., Divine ideals, human stubbornness, and Scriptural inerrancy: Transformation 2,4 (Exeter 1985) 1-4 [NTAbs 30,321].

1015 *Grelot* Pierre, Dix propositions sur l'inspiration scripturaire: i. la relier à l'expérience historique d'une communauté du salut; ii. auteurs plutôt que livres inspirés; iii. ministères ANT; iv. Jésus n'écrit pas; assume les valeurs AT en dépassant les limites prévisibles; v. témoins directs et successifs; vi. préhistoire des textes, pluralité de formes revêtues par les mêmes textes inspirés; vii. valeur LXX; viii. ne pas réduire l'inspiration NT aux seuls textes finalement fixés; ix. critère hors des livres mêmes; x. imbriquée avec la théologie: EsprV 96 (1986) 97-105.

1015* **Hauck** Robert, Inspiration as apologetic; the issue of true prophecy in the Contra Celsum of ORIGEN: diss. Duke, ^D*Gregg* R. Durham NC 1985. 283 p. 86-14435. – DissA 47 (1986s) 1364-A; RelStR 13,190.

1016 *Honeycutt* Roy L., Biblical authority; a treasured heritage ! [rather than 'inerrancy']: RExp 83 (thematic issue 'The Minister' 1986) 605-622.

1016* *Ibáñez Arana* Andrés, Inspiración, inerrancia e interpretación de la S. Escritura en el Concilio Vaticano II: ScriptV 33 (1986) 5-96. 225-329.

1017 ^E**Iserloh** Erwin, *al.,* DIETENBERGER Johannes (1475-1537), Phimostomus scripturariorum [exegete-gag]. Köln 1532: Corpus Catholicorum 38. Münster 1985, Aschendorff. xciv-272 p. DM 98. 3-402-03452-2. – ^RBibHumRen 48 (1986) 542s (I. *Backus*); Gregorianum 67 (1986) 577-9 (J. *Wicks*: earliest Catholic treatise on inspiration in response to Sola Scriptura).

1017* *Johnson* Elliott E., Dual authorship and the single intended meaning of Scripture: BS 143 (1986) 218-227.

1018 *Lane* A.N.S., B. B. WARFIELD and the humanity of Scripture: VoxEvca 16 (1986) 77-94.

1019 *Moreland* J. P., The rationality of belief in inerrancy: TrinJ 7 (1986) 75-86.

1020 **Most** William G., Free from all error; authorship, inerrancy, historicity of Scripture, Church teaching, and modern Scripture scholars. Libertyville IL 1985, Franciscan. 180 p. $11.95. – ^RHomPast 87,1 (1986s) 74 (K. *Baker*: cuts through the verbiage of Scripture scholars).

1021 *Piñero-Sáenz* Antonio, Concepciones de la inspiración en FILÓN de Alejandría: ➤ 21, Mem. DÍEZ MACHO A., Salvación 1986, 223-233.

1022 **Pinnock** Clark, The Scripture principle 1984 ➤ 1,1461: ^RBS 143 (1986) 76s (N. L. *Geisler*); Horizons 13 (1986) 161s (J. *Carmody*); JBL 105 (1986) 700s (T. C. *Butler*: p. 225, inerrancy is 'a metaphor for the determination to trust God's Word completely'); RExp 83 (1986) 473 (W. L. *Hendricks*: against the term 'inerrancy'); WestTJ 48 (1986) 192-8 (K. *Wanhoozer*).

1023 *Poythress* Vern S., Divine meaning of Scripture: WestTJ 48 (1986) 241-279.

1023* **Ruokanen** Mükka, Doctrina divinitus inspirata; Martin LUTHER's position in the ecumenical problem of biblical inspiration: Luther-Agricola Publ. B 14. Helsinki 1985. 164 p. [RTLv 18,386, A de *Halleux*].

1024 **Schnabel** Eckhard, Inspiration und Offenbarung; die Lehre vom Ursprung und Wesen der Bibel. Wu 1986, Brockhaus. 264 p. DM 24,80 [TR 83,337].

1025 *Trembath* Kern R., Biblical inspiration and the believing community; a new look [< diss. Notre Dame, 'Evangelical theories...']: EvQ 58 (1986) 245-256.

1026 *Veenhof* Jan, Holy Spirit and Holy Scripture; considerations concerning the character and function of Scripture in the framework of salvation history: ScotBEvT 4 (1986) 69-84.

1027 *Vogels* Walter,   Die Inspiration in einem linguistischen Modell [< BibTB
15 (1985) 87-93]: TGegw 23 (1985) 205-214.
1028 *Vroom* H. M.,   Het schriftgezag ter diskussie in protestantse kring: PrakT
13 (1986) 427-444.

A3.4   **Traditio, canon.**

1029 **Allan** George, The importances of the past; a meditation on the authority of tradition. Albany 1986, SUNY. xiii-260 p. 0-88706-116-8;
pa. 7-6.
1030 **Barr** James, Holy Scripture, canon ... 1983 ➤ 64,1464 ... 1,1471: ᴿJRel
66 (1986) 69s (R. G. *Boling*).
1031 **Beckwith** Roger, The OT canon of the NT church 1985 ➤ 1,1472: ᴿBL
(1986) 61s (R. B. *Salters*); ExpTim 97 (1985s) 374s (R. J. *Coggins*:
demolition of traditions; less secure replacement); IrBSt 8 (1986) 207-211
(D. W. *Gooding*); RQum 12,47 (1986) 449-453 (J. *Carmignac* †); SWJT 29
(1986s) 55 (R. L. *Smith*).
1031* *Bruin* C. C.,   De Apocriefen [Catholic deuterocanonica] van het Oude
Testament in Nederlandse bijbeloverzettingen tot 1637: ➤ 59, ꜰ*Lebram* J.,
Tradition 1986, 259-267; Eng. 267s.
1032 *Christensen* Duane L.,   Joseᴘʜus and the twenty-two book canon of
Sacred Scripture: JEvTS 29 (1986) 37-46 [< ᴢɪᴛ].
1032* *Davies* W. D.,   Reflections on the Mormon 'canon': ➤ 110, ꜰSᴛᴇɴᴅᴀʜʟ
K. = HarvTR 79 (1986) 44-66.
1033 *Diebner* Bernd J.,   Zur Funktion der kanonischen Textsammlung im
Judentum der vor-christlichen Zeit–Gedanken zu einer Kanon-Her-
meneutik: DiehlB 22 (1985) 58-73.
1034 **Dittrich** Bernhard,   Das Traditionsverständnis in der Confessio Augustana und in der Confutatio: Erfurter TSt 51, 1983 ➤ 64,1472: ᴿTLZ 111
(1986) 293-5 (R. *Slenczka*); TR 82 (1986) 395s (P. *Schäfer*).
1035 **Farmer** W. R., *Farkasfalvy* D. M., ₁Formation of the NT canon 1983
➤ 64,1475 ... 1,1478: ᴿJBL 105 (1986) 168s (H. *Gamble*).
1036 **Gamble** Harry Y.,   The New Testament Canon; its making and meaning:
GuidesBS 1985 ➤ 1,1479: ᴿCBQ 48 (1986) 746s (S. B. *Marrow*: clear,
thought-provoking); Gregorianum 67 (1986) 368-370 (J. *Wicks*); RelStR 12
(1986) 163 (R. H. *Fuller*); RExp 83 (1986) 298s (R. L. *Omanson*: superb);
TR 82 (1986) 284-6 (T. *Söding*).
1036* *Hahn* Ferdinand,   a) 'Schrift und Tradition' im Urchristentum [< EvT
30 (1970) 449-468]; – b) Die heilige Schrift als älteste christliche Tradition
und als Kanon [< EvT 40 (1980) 455-466 = ÖkRu Beih 42 (1982) 46-55]:
➤ 167, Ges. Aufs. 1 (1986) 9-28 / 29-39.
1037 ᴱKaestli Daniel, *Wermelinger* Otto,   Le canon de l'AT, sa formation et
son histoire 1984 ➤ 1,477: ᴿCrNSt 7 (1986) 177-9 (A. *Tosato*); FreibZ 33
(1986) 267s (J. *Doignon*); RHE 81 (1986) 131-3 (L. *Leloir*); RivStoLR 22
(1986) 525-9 (W. *Schneemelcher*); TüTQ 166 (1986) 236s (R. *Reinhardt*);
TZBas 42 (1986) 267s (O. *Bächli*); ZkT 108 (1986) 81 (G. *Fischer*).
1038 *Kermode* Frank, The argument about canons [*Childs* B., *Barr* J.]: ➤ 385,
ꜰ*McConnell* F., Bible and narrative 1983/6 ... [TS 47,702, *Scuka* R.: does
not advance the discussion].
1038* **Koole** J. L.,   Het beslissende woord; een canonhistorisch onderzoek:
Cahiers 56. Kampen 1985, Kok. 48 p. [NedTTs 41,76].
1039 *Lemcio* Eugene E., Ephesus and the New Testament canon: BJRyL 69
(1986s) 210-234.

1039* *Loss* Nicolò M., *a*) La questione del 'canone biblico'; – *b*) La storia del testo dell'AT: ParVi 30 (1985) 147-152 . 379-384.

1040 **Meade** David G., Pseudonymity and canon; an investigation into the relationship of authorship and authority in Jewish and earliest Christian tradition: WUNT 39. Tü 1986, Mohr. 257 p.; bibliog. p. 219-229. DM 98. 3-16-145044-2.

1041 *Moloney* Francis J., 'The living voice of the Gospel' (Dei Verbum 8); some reflections on the dynamism of the Christian tradition: *a*) Salesianum 48 (1986) 225-254; – *b*) AustralasCR 63 (1986) 264-279.

1041* *Morgan* Donn F., Canon and criticism; method or madness? : AnglTR 68 (1986) 83-98.

1042 **Ohler** Annemarie, Studying the Old Testament; from tradition to canon, ᵀ*Cairns* David, 1985 ➤ 1,1198:   ᴿÉTRel 61 (1986) 566s (D. *Lys*).

1043 **Paul** André, La inspiración y el canon de las escrituras [1984 ➤ 65,1283],ᵀ. Estella 1985, VDivino. – ᴿBibFe 12 (1986) 136s (C. *Barcía*).

1044 **Sanders** James A., Canon and community; a guide to canonical criticism: GuidesBS, 1984 ➤ 65,1288; 1,1493:   ᴿBS 143 (1986) 83s (E. H. *Merrill*); Interpretation 40 (1986) 195s (K. G. *O'Connell*); JBL 105 (1986) 303s (T. W. *Overholt*).

1045 *Siegwalt* Gérard, *a*) Le canon biblique et la révélation: PosLuth 34,1 (1986) 3-21 [< ᴢɪᴛ]; – *b*) Der biblische Kanon und die Offenbarung, ᵀ*Wolff* B.: NSys 28 (1986) 51-67; Eng. 67.

1046 *Smend* Rudolf [*Merk* Otto], Bibelkanon AT [NT]: ➤ 587, EvKL 1 (1986) 468-470 [-474(-5)].

1047 **Staal** Frits, The fidelity of oral tradition and the origins of science: MedAkad Lett 49/8. Amst 1986, North-Holland. 40 p. 0-444-85669-2.

1047* *Tofană* Stelian, La sainte tradition dans la vie de l'Église selon les Écritures (roum.): STBuc 37 (1985) 633-646.

1048 *a*) *Trebolle Barrera* Julio, La dimensión textual de la catolicidad; canon, texto, midraš; – *b*) *Gribomont* Jean †, La función hermenéutica de la Tradición de la Iglesia; – *c*) *Ibáñez* Javier, *Mendoza* Fernando, Valor de los Padres en la función hermenéutica de la Tradición de la Iglesia: ➤ 366, Hermenéutica 1985/6, 343-355 / 511-527 / 601-610.

1049 *Zirker* Hans, Tradition im Islam; eine Würdigung aus christlich-theologischem Interesse: Kairos 28 (1986) 75-97.

B4   *Interpretatio humanistica* – .1   **The Bible and Man.**

1050 **Augustin** Matthias, Der schöne Mensch im AT und im hellenistischen Judentum 1983 ➤ 64,1537... 1,1495: ᴿJStJud 17 (1986) 233s (A. S. van der *Woude*: verdient Beachtung); RelStR 12 (1986) 158 (J. *Levison*: less thorough on Hellenistic texts).

1050* *a*) *Boeckler* Richard, Christus in der Krise des modernen Menschen; – *b*) *Müller-Scholl* Albrecht, Arm und Reich – und das Evangelium: Diakonie 12,1 (Stu 1986) 5-11 / 12-15 [ᴢɪᴛ].

1051 *Carmen Portela* María del, Los ancianos en la Biblia: CuBi 39,283 (1984ss) 7-20.

1053 **Claypool** John, Glad reunion; meeting ourselves in the lives of Bible men and women. Waco 1985, Word. 160 p. $8.95 [JAAR 54,203].

1054 **Crabb** Lawrence, *a*) Effective biblical counselling; – *b*) Basic principles of biblical counselling. L 1977s, Marshall. 119 p.; 192 p. £1.95; £2.50 – ᴿCleR 71 (1986) 74s (L. *Marteau*: superficial, demeaning).

1055 *Dellazari* Romano, O jovem e a bíblia: Teocomunicação 15,69 (1985) 34-46.
1055* *Fichtner* Joseph, Biblical leadership: Emmanuel 92 (1986) 520-6.577-580 [OTAbs 10,183].
1056 **Foitzik** Karl, Spiegelbilder; Begegnungen mit Gestalten des Alten Testaments: Ganz Praktisch. Mü 1980, Kaiser. 144 p. [KirSef 59,314].
1056* *Gernot* Moshe, ✪ The secular Israeli and the Bible: BethM 31,105 (1985s) 182-5 [381-3, comment of *Margalit* Othniel].
1057 a) *Giuliani* Matheus F., O trabalho — realidade bíblica; – b) *Dreher* Carlos A., O trabalhador e o trabalho sob o reino de Salomão; – c) *Pereira* Ney B., O sentido do trabalho nos livros sapienciais; – d) *Silva* Valmor da, O trabalho como festa: Estudos Bíblicos 11 [REB 46,3] (1986) 32-47 / 48-68 / 83-91 / 22-31.
1058 *Gladwin* John, W., Work, faith and freedom [Rom 4; Gn 2s; Prov 24;26] Themelios 12 (1986s) 88s.
1059 *Gremmels* Christian, Arbeit [... AT; NT]: ➤ 587, EvKL 1 (1986) 237-244.
1060 *Hertog* G. C. den, Durchbruch nach vorn; zu H. J. IWANDs Vortrag Die Bibel und die soziale Frage: ZDialT 1,2 (Kampen 1985) 149-159 ...
1061 **Katz** Robert L., Pastoral care and the Jewish tradition; empathic process and religious counseling. Ph 1985, Fortress. 120 p. $7. – ᴿTS 47 (1986) 731 (M. J. *McGinniss*).
1062 **L'Heureux** Conrad E., Life journey and the OT; an experiential approach to the Bible and personal transformation. Mahwah NJ 1986, Paulist. ix-171 p. $9. 0-8091-2828-4 [BL 87,86, A. G. *Auld*].
1062* **Reisema** G., [Geloof unterweg ➤ 63,251] Fragmenten van bijbels humanisme; waarvoor dient eigenlijk godsdienst ? Rotterdam 1981, Futile. 113 p. – ᴿGerefTTs 86 (1986) 253s (W. *Stoker*).
1063 **Tranquilli** V., Il concetto di lavoro da Aristotele a Calvino. Mi 1979, Ricciardi. viii-630 p. Lit. 35.000. – ᴿProtestantesimo 41 (1986) 179s (S. C. *Brofferio*).
1064 *Veit* Marie, Arbeit aus biblischer Perspektive: EvErz 38,1 (Fra 1986) 18-34 [NTAbs 30,325].
1065 **zur Nieden** Eckart, Mein Name ist ...; Menschen der Bibel stellen sich vor: ABC-team. Stu 1980, Christliches. 237 p. [KirSef 59,316].

B4.2 *Femina, familia*; **Woman in the Bible** [➤ H8.8s].

1065* **Adinolfi** Marco, Il femminismo della Bibbia 1981 ➤ 62,8329 ... 64,1496: ᴿParVi 30 (1985) 370-8 (C. *Marcheselli Casale*).
1066 **Bal** Mieke, Femmes imaginaires; l'Ancien Testament au risque d'une narratologie critique: Écrire les femmes. Utrecht/P 1986, H & S/Nizet. 282 p. ƒ39,50. [RechSR 74, 630].
1066* *Balkan* Kemal, Betrothal of girls during childhood in ancient Assyria and Anatolia: ➤ 42, ᶠGÜTERSLOH H., Kaniššuwar 1986, 1-8; 6 fig.
1067 **Biale** R., Women and Jewish law; an exploration of women's issues in Halakhic sources 1984 ➤ 1,1507.6630: ᴿJAAR 54 (1986) 572s (H. *Eilberg-Schwartz*); RelStR 12 (1986) 174 (Devorah *Jacobson*).
1067* **Boer** C. de, Man en vrouw in bijbels perspectief [➤ 1,1509]; een bijbels-theologische verkenning van de man-vrouw verhouding met het oog op de gemeente. Kampen 1985, Kok. 215 p. ƒ29,90. 90-242-2916-2 [NTAbs 30,364].
1068 **Brayer** Menachem M., The Jewish woman in rabbinic literature [I.] a psychosocial perspective; II. A psychohistorical perspective. Hoboken

1986, Ktav. xv-352 p.; xv-285 p. $20 each; pa. $12 [TDig 33,459]. 0-88125-071-6; 3-2; pa. 0-8; 2-4. – ᴿExpTim 98 (1986s) 222 (Julia *Neuberger*: the rabbi is banal).

1069 **Brenner** Athalya, The Israelite woman; social role and literary type in biblical narrative 1985 ➤ 1,1510: ᴿÉTRel 61 (1986) 443s (Corinne *Lanoir*); Interpretation 40 (1986) 306.308 (J. C. *McCann*: a feminist told her it is not radical enough for 'us' but dull for 'them'); VT 36 (1986) 373s (J. A. *Emerton*).

1070 **Callaway** Mary, Sing, O barren one; a study in comparative midrash: SBL diss. 91 [1978: ᴰ*Sanders* J., Columbia Univ.]. Atlanta 1986, Scholars. xii-157 p.; bibliog. p. 143-151. 0-89130-994-2; pa. 5-0.

1070* ᴱ**Cameron** A., *Kuhrt* A., Images of women in antiquity [*Ackroyd* P., in the Bible] 1983 ➤ 65,322; 1,1513: ᴿAncSRes 16 (1986) 183-6 (Suzanne *Dixon*).

1071 **Cantarella** E., Tacita muta; la donna nella città antica. R 1985, Riuniti. 63 p. Lit. 5500.

1072 *Cauvin* Jacques, La question du 'matriarcat préhistorique' et le rôle de la femme dans la préhistoire: ➤ 526, La femme dans le monde méditerranéen I (1985) 7-17.

1073 **Chalier** Catherine, Les matriarches; Sarah, Rébecca, Rachel et Léa; préf. *Lévinas* Emmanuel. P 1985, Cerf. 224 p. F 78 [TR 83,162]. – ᴿMondeB 42,1 (1986) 55 (P. I. *Fransen*); VSp 140 (1986) 726 (Annie *Perchenet*).

1073* *Crowley* Joann, Faith of our mothers; the dark night of Sara, Rebeka and Rachel: RRel 45 (1986) 531-7.

1074 *De Spirito* Angelomichele, Maschio e femmina secondo la Bibbia [*Gerstenberger* E., *Schrage* W. ital. 1984]: Studium 82 (R 1986) 265-8.

1074* *Eicher* Peter, Die Kinder der Verheissung; Partner des Bundes und Erben des Reiches: Diakonia 17 (1986) 302-9.

1075 **Evans** Mary, Woman in the Bible 1983 ➤ 64,1510... 1,1518: EvQ 58 (1986) 178-180 (P. H. *Towner*).

1076 *Exum* J. Cheryl, The mothers of Israel; the patriarchal narratives from a feminist perspective: BR 2,1 (1986) 60-67; ill.

1077 *Fantham* Elaine, Women in antiquity; a selective (and subjective) survey 1979-84: EchMClas 30 (1986) 1-24.

1078 *Goldingay* John, The Bible and sexuality?: ScotJT 39 (1986) 175-188.

1079 **Harding** Sandra, *Hintikka* Merill B., Discovering reality; feminist perspectives on epistemology, metaphysics, methodology, and philosophy of science: Synthèse 161. Dordrecht 1983, Reidel. xix-332 p. ƒ125; pa. ƒ64. 90-277-1496-7; 538-6. – ᴿBijdragen 47 (1986) 90s (A. A. *Derksen*).

1080 **Harris** Kevin, Sex, ideology and religion; the representation of women in the Bible. NJ 1984, Barnes & N. x-134 p. $22.50. – ᴿBibTB 16 (1986) 82 (Mary M. *Pazdan*).

1081 **Heister** Maria-Sybilla, Frauen in der biblischen Glaubensgeschichte 1984 ➤ 65,1316; 1,1523: BL (1986) 88 (A. G. *Auld*); ÖkRu 35 (1986) 231s (Christa *Springe*); TZBas 42 (1986) 182s (E. *Buess*).

1082 *a)* *Heschel* S., Current issues in Jewish feminist theology; – *b)* *Kellenbach* K., Jewish-Christian dialogue on feminism and religion; – *c)* *Eckardt* A. R., Christians, Jews and the women's movement: Christian Jewish Relations 19,2 (L 1986) 23-33 / 33-39 / 13-21 [< Judaica 42,271].

1083 *Horst* Pieter W. van der, The role of women in the [apocryphal, LXX-based] Testament of Job: NedTTS 40 (1986) 273-289: though the first wife is loyal but fickle and shallow, the daughters are highly gifted and take over the story: probably from a different source, in a women-dominated ecstatic-mystical group.

1083* **Huff** Margaret E., Woman in the image of God; toward a prototype for feminist pastoral counseling: diss. Boston Univ. 1986. – RelStR 13,186.

1084 *Jason* Heda, The Jewish beauty and the king; coherence in folktales; preliminary sketch of a model: ➤ 357, ᴱ*Sözer* E., Text connexity 1985, 500-525.

1085 *a) Kipper* J. Balduino, A mulher no Antigo Testamento; – *b) Minette de Tillesse* Caetano, Matrimônio e Aliança: ➤ 386, A mulher na Biblia, RCuBíb 10,39s (1986) 8-28 / 29-37.

1085* **Kirk** Martha Ann, God of our mothers; seven biblical women tell their stories. Cincinnati 1985, St. Anthony. 2 cassettes. $16.95. – ᴿRRel 45 (1986) 948s (Mary Ann *Hoope*).

1086 ᴱ**Korenhof-Scharffenorth** Mieke, *al.*, 'Aus dem Brunnen schöpfen...' Geschichten aus der hebräischen Bibel und dem Neuen Testament, von Frauen erzählt und ausgelegt. Neuk 1986. 120 p. DM 19,80 [TLZ 112, 176]. 3-7887-0790-9.

1087 *Lerner* Gerda, The creation of patriarchy [chiefly 3500-500, cuneiform and Hebrew]. NY 1986, Oxford. $22 [RelStR 13,343, Bonnie M. *Kingsley*].

1088 *Levinson* Pnina N., Die Ordination von Frauen als Rabbiner: ZRGg 38 (1986) 289-310.

1089 *Moser-Rath* Elfriede, [*al.*] Frau: ➤ 586, EnzMär 5 (1986) 100-137 [-220].

1090 **Pfister** Herta, Der an uns Gefallen findet; Frauen im Alten Testament. FrB 1986, Herder. 96 p. DM 10,80 pa. [TPQ 134,416).

1090* *Provera* Mario, La famiglia al tempo di Gesù: ParVi 31 (1986) 135-8.

1091 *Scalise* Pamela J., Women in ministry; reclaiming our Old Testament heritage: RExp 83 (1986) 7-13 (-79, *al.*).

1091* **Sheek** G. William, The Word on families; a biblical guide to family well-being. Nv 1985, Abingdon. 156 p. $7.50. – ᴿRExp 83 (1986) 671s (J. M. *Hester*).

1092 **Shenk** Barbara K., The God of Sarah, Rebekah and Rachel. Scottdale PA 1985, Herald. 132 p. $20 [BToday 24,270].

1093 **Swartley** Willard M., Slavery, sabbath, war and women 1983 ➤ 64,1658 ... 1,1572: ᴿThemelios 12 (1986s) 65 (G. R. *Palmer*).

1094 ᴱ*Swidler* A., Marriage in the world religions: JEcuST 22,1 (1985) 1-119.

1095 **Terrien** Samuel, Till the heart sings; a biblical theology of manhood and womanhood [Gn 1-3; Ct; 'Gender of God'; 'Circumcised male and polluted female'; Prov 8,22-31...] 1985 ➤ 1,1545: ᴿBibTB 16 (1986) 158s (Dianne *Bergant*); ExpTim 97 (1985s) (C. S. *Rodd*: Terrien claims 'biblical theology does not support traditional Judaism and Christianity [but] regards woman as the crown of creation'; the main thrust of the Bible 'contradicts the disbalance in favor of the male sex': special pleading?).

1096 *a) Tryon-Montalembert* Renée de, Ist das Judentum frauenfeindlich? [< Les Nouveaux Cahiers 68 (1983) 26-32], ᵀ*Hruby* Kurt; – *b) Wallach-Faller* Marianne, Veränderung im Status der jüdischen Frau; ein geschichtlicher Überblick; – *c) Posen* Jacob, Die Stellung der Frau im jüdischen Religionsgesetz (Halacha): Judaica 41 (1985) 132-141 / 152-172 / 142-151.

1096* **Vanier** Jean, Man and woman he made them. NY 1985, Paulist. 177 p. $7. – ᴿRRel 45 (1986) 942s (Mary Elizabeth *Kenel*: on the needs of handicapped persons).

1097 **Weiler** Gerda, Ich verwerfe im Lande die Kriege; das verborgene Matriarchat im AT. Mü 1984, Frauenoffensive, 424 p. DM 39,80. – ᴿBTZ 3 (1986) 144-7 (Katharina von *Kellenbach*).

1098 **Williams** James G., Women recounted 1982 ➤ 63,1579 ... 1,1547: ᴿRB 93 (1986) 154s (J. *Loza*); RechSR 74 (1986) 624s (J. *Briend*: finesse); VT 36 (1986) 124 (R. P. *Gordon*).

1099 *Zola* G., JTS, HUC and women rabbis: JRefJud 31 (1984) 39-46 [Judaica 41,64].

B4.5 *Influxus litterarius* – **The Bible as Literature**.

1100 **Bar-Efrat** Shimeon [➤ 61,1802], The art of the biblical story [= ? ◍ 1980 ➤ 64,1264]. J 1979. 239 p.

1101 *Bauman* Michael E., MILTON, subordinationism, and the two-stage Logos: WestTJ 48 (1986) 173-182.

1101* *Bierzychudek* Eduardo, Biblia y literatura en la 'Bibliografía teológica comentada del area iberoamericana': RBibArg 48 (1986) 169-174: tema preferido, Job.

1102 **Cantor** Paul A., Creature and creator; myth-making and English Romanticism [lost paradise in BLAKE, SHELLEY, BYRON....]. C 1984, Univ. xxi-223 p. £19.50. – ᴿJTS 37 (1986) 652-4 (J. *Coulson*).

1102* **Chmaitelly** Nancy A., The theme of synagogue, ecclesia, and the whore of Babylon in the visual arts and in the poetry of DANTE and CHAUCER; a background study for Chaucer's Wife of Bath: diss. Rice, ᴰ*Chance* Jane, 1986. 390 p. 86-17435. – DissA 47 (1986s) 1722s-A.

1103 **Chu-Pund** Oreida, La figura del Mesías en el teatro romántico español [11 dramas 1822-1865]: diss. Pennsylvania, ᴰ*Sebold* R. Ph 1986. 215 p. 87-03189. – DissA 47 (1986s) 4405-A.

1103* *Delgado Morales* Manuel, Lope de VEGA's 'El vaso de elección': RivStoLR 22 (1986) 56-67.

1104 *Desplanque* Christophe, Le Messie selon Gustave FLAUBERT: Hokhma 11,30 (1986) 48-55.

1104* **Fowler** David C., The Bible in Middle English literature 1985 ➤ 1,1589: ᴿHorizons 13 (1986) 166 (Marie Anne *Mayeski*); ScotJT 39 (1986) 253-5 (H. F. G. *Swanston*).

1105 *Frost* Peggy, Sight, sin, and blindness in the Samson narrative [Jg 14] and in MILTON's Samson Agonistes: Dor 15 (1986s) 150-9.

1105* **Frye** Northrop, The great code 1982 ➤ 63,1648 ... 1,1590: ᴿTheologiai Szemle 30 (1987) 190-2 (P. *Pásztor*).

1106 **Gabel** John B., *Wheeler* Charles B., The Bible as literature, an introduction. NY 1986, Oxford-UP. xiv-278 p. $20; pa. $10. 0-19-503994-7; 3-9. – ᴿOTAbs 9 (1986) 330 (L. *Greenspoon*: no documentation, 'just an impediment for most of our readers'); TDig 33 (1986) 471 (W. C. *Heiser*).

1106* **Gardner** Philip A. T., The banquet of the word; biblical authority and interpretation in SPENSER and the FLETCHERs: diss. ᴰ*Blissett* W. Toronto 1985. – DissA 47 (1986s) 909-A.

1107 **Goldsmith** Steven R., Unbuilding Jerusalem; the romantics against the apocalypse: diss. Pennsylvania. Ph 1986. 347 p. 86-23993. – DissA 47 (1986s) 2594-A.

1107* *González Caballero* Alberto, Influencia de la Biblia en El Quijote: CuBi 39,283 (1984ss) 21-67.

1108 **Gottcent** J. H., The Bible, a literary study: Masterwork Studies 2. Boston 1986, Twayne. 168 p. $18; pa. $7. 0-8057-8003-3 [NTAbs 31,92].

1109 *a)* **Harding** Anthony J., COLERIDGE and the inspired word. Toronto 1985, McGill-Queen's Univ. xiv-187 p. $27.50 [RelStR 13,159, S. *Happel*]. –

b) **Jasper** David, Coleridge as poet and religious thinker. L 1985, Macmillan. xii-195 p. £22.50. – ᴿTLond 39 (1986) 137-9 (S. *Prickett*). – *c)* *Hoffmann* Daniel, S. T. Coleridge and the attack an inerrancy: TrinJ 7,2 (1986) 55-68.

1110 ᴱ**Hirsch** David H., *Aschkenasy* Nehama, Biblical patterns in modern Hebrew literature: BrownJudSt 77, 1984 → 65,1371: ᴿJAOS 106 (1986) 581 (D. *Aberbach*: 'random, woolly, poorly edited collection' of items 'tame and dry ... far removed from the spirit and purpose of the Bible').

1111 *Jasper* D., The New Testament and literary interpretation: Religion & Literature 17,3 (ND 1985) 1-10 [NTAbs 30,263].

1111* **Johnson** Lonnell E., Portrait of the bondslave in the Bible; slavery and freedom in the work of four Afro-American poets [*Hammon* J. -1806; *Wheatley* P. -1784; *Horton* G. -1883; *Harper* F. -1911]: diss. Indiana 1986. 178 p. 86-27995. – DissA 47 (1986s) 3038s-A.

1112 **Liptzin** Sol, Biblical themes in world literature 1985 → 1,1604: ᴿBL (1986) 74s (D. J. A. *Clines*); CBQ 48 (1986) 538-540 (J. S. *Coolidge*); RÉJ 145 (1986) 183s (M. R. *Hayoun*).

1113 *Luyten* Jos, Humor in het Oude Testament: OnsGLev 63 (1986) 67-72.

1114 *a)* *Mokry* Wlodzimierz, ❷ Taras SZEWCZENKO in the sphere of biblical writings; – *b)* *Kozak* Stefan, ❷ Shevchenko's historiosophical concepts; – *c)* *Mucha* Bogusław, Biblical inspirations in Russian romantic literature. ZeKUL 25,2 (1982) 115-146; Eng. 147 / 26,2 (1983) 23-33; Eng. 34 / 3-20; Eng. 21.

1115 **Nunes Carreira** José, CAMÕES e o Antigo Testamento. Ponta Delgada 1982 [→ 64,1598]; Univ. Açores. 146 p. – ᴿCBQ 48 (1986) 159s (R. H. *McGrath*).

1115* **Perah** Pinchas, ❻ Literary form of biblical comparisons. TA 1984, 'Aqad. 94 p. – ᴿBethM 31,104 (1985s) 88-91 (Ş. *Şemiryon*).

1116 *Pineas* Rainer, Polemical use of the Scripture in the plays of John BALE: Nederlands Archief voor Kerkgeschiedenis 66 (Leiden 1986) 180-189 [< ZIT].

1116* *Polomsky* Marek, Indeks biblijny do twórczości Adama MICKIEWICZA: STWsz 24,1 (1986) 219-275.

1117 ᴱ**Preminger** Alex, *Greenstein* Edward L., The Hebrew Bible in literary criticism: A library of literary criticism. NY 1986, Ungar. xvi-619 p. $65. 0-8044-3266-X.

1118 **Robertson** D., ❹ Bungakol toshite-no Seisho [The OT and the literary critic 1977 → 58,563], ᵀ*Arai* S. Tokyo 1986, Kyobunkwan. 204 p. Y 1800 [BL 87,75, K. K. *Sacon*].

1119 ᴱ**Ryken** Leland, The New Testament in literary criticism: Library of literary criticism. NY 1985, Unger. x-349 p. $45 [TDig 33,374].

1119* **Seidel** Margot, Bibel und Christentum im dramatischen Werk Eugene O'NEILLs. Fra 1984, Lang. 339 p. Fs 71. – ᴿStreven 53 (1985s) 762s (C. *Tindemans*).

1120 **Sternberg** Meir, The poetics of biblical narrative; ideological literature and the drama of reading 1985 → 1,1617: ᴿRExp 83 (1986) 466s (J. D. W. *Watts*).

1120* **Stieg** Elizabeth J., William BLAKE and the prophetic tradition: diss. ᴰ*Wilson* M. Toronto 1985. – DissA 47 (1986s) 916-A.

1121 **Wagner** Nery A., T. S. ELIOT and the myth of Christ; an analysis of Prufrock, Tiresias and Becket: diss. George Washington Univ. 1986, ᴰ*Combs* R. 288 p. 86-08357. – DissA 47 (1986s) 526s-A.

1121* **Whallon** William, Inconsistencies; studies in the NT, the Inferno, Othello and Beowulf 1983 → 64,1608: RHeythJ 27 (1986) 474 (B. L. *Horne*: impish).

B4.6 *Interpretatio* **athea, materialistica, psychiatrica.**

1122 **Ashbrook** James B., The human mind and the mind of God; theological promise in brain research. Lanham MD 1984, UPA. xxiv-383 p. $27.25; pa. $17.50 [RelStR 13,47, A. *Siirala*].

1123 **Captain** Philip A., Eight stages of Christian growth; human development in psycho-spiritual terms [... secular psychology leads away from God's Word]. ENJ 1984, Prentice-Hall. x-218 p. $7 pa. – RRelStR 12 (1986) 134 (A. *Lester*).

1124 **Dourley** John P., The illness that we are; a Jungian critique of Christianity 1984 → 1,1620: RSR 14 (1985) 510-2 (W. P. *Zion*); TorJT 2 (1986) 142-4 (S. *Brown*).

1125 **Drewermann** Eugen, Tiefenpsychologie und Exegese 1. Die Wahrheit der Formen; Traum, Mythos, Märchen, Sage und Legende[2] [[1]1984 → 65,1396; 1,1621]. Olten 1985, Walter. 576 p.; ill. DM 78. – RTPQ 134 (1986) 201-3 (J. *Goldbrunner*, [1]); WissWeis 47 (1984) 229s (H. J. *Klauck*); ZkT 108 (1986) 197s (M. *Hasitschka*). — II. Die Wahrheit der Werke und der Worte; Wunder, Visionen, Weissagung, Apokalypse, Geschichte, Gleichnis. Olten 1985, Walter. 851 p. DM 88. – RErbAuf 62 (1986) 68s; ZAW 98 (1986) 465 (H.-C. *Schmitt*).

1126 *a)* **Nel** P., Eksegese as 'n proces van hermitologisering; 'n kritiese bespreking van die benadering van Eugen DREWERMANN: NduitseGT 27 (1986) 15-22; – *b)* **Teichert** Wolfgang, Der Psychologe als Exeget; Bibelauslegung nach Eugen Drewermann: EvKomm 19 (1986) 588. 593-5.

1127 **Ferder** Fran, Words made flesh [therapist relating psychology to Scripture]. ND 1986, Ave Maria. 183 p. $6 pa. – RTDig 33 (1986) 470 (W. C. *Heiser*).

1128 **Friedmann** Edwin H., Generation to generation; family process [also on congregation and inter-congregation level] in church and synagogue: Family therapy series. NY 1985, Guilford. x-319 p. $25. – RTDig 33 (1986) 471 (W. C. *Heiser*).

1129 **Hark** Helmut, Der Traum als Gottes vergessene Sprache; symbol-psychologische Deutung biblischer und heutiger Träume. Olten 1982, Walter. 230 p. [KirSef 59,315].

1130 **Meissner** W. W., Psychoanalysis and religious experience 1984 → 65,1402: RHorizons symposium-review 13 (1986) 389-393 (J. *McDargh*), 393-7 (Joann W. *Conn*), 397-400 (V. *Gregson*), 400-5 (S. *Moore*), Meissner response 405-410.

1131 **Stein** Dominique, Lectures psychanalytiques de la Bible. P 1985, Cerf. 144 p. F 85. 2-204-0234-6. – RÉTRel 61 (1986) 290 (J. *Ansaldi*); Études 364 (1986) 858 (J.-F. *Catalan*); RHPR 66 (1986) 251s (B. *Kaempf*).

1132 **Uleyn** A., Psychoanalytisch lezen in de Bijbel. Hilversum 1985, Gooi & S. 148 p. *f* 29. 90-304-0330-6. 8 reprints. – RTsTNijm 26 (1986) 293s (L. *Grollenberg*).

B5 **Methodus exegetica.**

1133 **Abercrombie** John A., [... how to write] Computer programs for literary analysis. Ph 1984, Univ. Pennsylvania. v-205 p. – RBTrans 37 (1986) 147s (H. P. *Scanlin*).

1134 **Armerding** Carl E., The OT and criticism 1983 → 64,1627 ... 1,1640:   ᴿBR 2,1 (1986) 19s (L. C. *Allen*).

1135 *a) Barthélemy* Dominique,   Christliche Bibelauslegung und jüdische Kommentatoren; – *b) Simon* Uriel,   Von der religiösen Bedeutung des Wortsinns der Schrift heute: Judaica 41 (1985) 207-216 / 217-237.

1136 **Barton** John, Reading the OT, method 1984 → 65,1413; 1,1642;   also 0-664-24555-2:   ᴿÉTRel 61 (1986) 564s (D. *Lys*); JBL 105 (1986) 514s (D. T. *Olson*); JTS 37 (1986) 462-5 (J. *Barr*); ScotJT 39 (1986) 128-130 (R. *Carroll*); Themelios 12 (1986s) 27s (R. L. *Alden*); Vidyajyoti 49 (1986) 427 (J. *Volckaert*).

1137 *a) Benzecri* J. P.,   Élaboration statistique de données sur ordinateur; application à l'analyse des textes; contributions attendues à l'étude de la Bible; – *b) Cochrane* Jack, Travaux de Bible et informatique en cours à Sherbrooke, Québec; – *c) Arbache* S.,   Les anciens textes bibliques; recherches appuyées par l'informatique: → 389, Bible et informatique 1985/6, 87-118 / 155-163 / 399 only.

1138 **Berger** Klaus,   Exegese und Philosophie: SBS 123s. Stu 1986, KBW. 194 p. DM 34,80 [TR 82337].

1138* *Bonora* Antonio,   Vent'anni dopo la costituzione dogmatica Dei Verbum: il metodo esegetico (critica e teologia): TItSett 10 (1985) 287-305; Eng. 306: Christological interpretation not 'added' to critical OT exegesis.

1139 **Carson** D. A.,   Exegetical fallacies 1984 → 65,1416; 1,1647: ᴿGraceTJ 7 (1986) 125s (J. *Guimont*).

1139* ᴱ**Clines** D., *al.*, Art and meaning; rhetoric in biblical literature 1982 → 64,391: ᴿVidyajyoti 49 (1986) 424s (P. M. *Meagher*).

1140 ᴱ**Coats** George W.,   Saga... narrative forms: JStOT Sup 35, 1985 → 1,274: ᴿInterpretation 40 (1986) 309s (L. *Eslinger*).

1140* *Corsani* Bruno,   Esegesi; come interpretare un testo biblico. T 1985, Claudiana. 144 p. Lit. 5500. – ᴿHumBr 41 (1986) 452s (F. *Montagnini*); Letture 41 (1984) 180s (G. *Ravasi*).

1141 **Davis** Larry J.,   Interpretation of Scripture in the evangelistic preaching of William Franklin 'Billy' GRAHAM: diss. Southern Baptist Sem. 1986, ᴰ*Drummond* L. 357 p. 87-06359. – DissA 47 (1986s) 4414-A.

1141* *Diebner* Bernd J.,   Das Ende welcher 'historisch-kritischen Methode'? Einige Überlegungen im Blick auf eine angemessene Interpretation der antik-jüdischen (hebräischen) Bibel als Religionsurkunde der Vergangenheit: DielhB 22 (1985) 9-35.

1142 *Fishbane* Michael,   The earliest biblical exegesis is in the Bible itself: BR 2,4 (1986) 42-45.

1142* ᴱ**Friedman** Richard E.,   The poet and the historian; essays in literary and historical biblical criticism: HarvSemSt 26,1983 → 64,264: ᴿJJS 37 (1986) 112s (J. *Hughes*: COOPER's life of David in Psalms seductive; CROSS 'epic' not).

1143 *Gaines* R. N.,   Philodemus on the three activities of rhetorical invention: Rhetorica 3 (Berkeley 1985) 155-163 [NTAbs 30,210].

1143* *Gross* Walter,   Sollten wir ägyptischer werden, um wirklich christlich zu sein? [*Drewermann* E., QDisp 101, 1982/4 p. 142 verwirrend, 'Wir sind als Christen zu sehr alttestamentlich und zu wenig ägyptisch, um wirklich christlich zu sein']: TüTQ 166 (1986) 234-6.

1144 *Handelman* Susan,   'Everything is in it'; rabbinic interpretation and modern literary theory: Judaism 35 (1986) 429-440.

1144* *a) Haran* Menahem,   Midrashic and literal exegesis and the critical method in biblical research; – *b) Shinan* A., *Zakovitch* Y.,   Midrash on

Scripture and midrash within Scripture: ➤ 251*, ᴱ*Japhet* S., ScrHieros 31 (1986) 19-48 / 257-277.
1145 *Hoffmann* Y., ◉ [Insufficiency of diction for dating OT texts]: ➤ 246, ᴱ*Friedman* M., Te'uda 4 (1986)...
1146 *Honko* Lauri, Gattungsprobleme: ➤ 586, EnzMär 5 (1986) 745-769.
1146* *Jucci* Elio, Il *pesher*, un ponte tra il passato e il futuro: Henoch 8 (1986) 321-7; franç. 327s.
1147 *Keller* Joseph, Biblical literary criticism; logical form and poetic function: JRelSt 13,1 (Cleveland 1985s) 15-24 [< ZIT].
1147* *Kiesow* Klaus, Der Dienst der Exegese zwischen naiver Bibellektüre und toter Gelehrsamkeit: WAntw 27 (Mainz 1986) 129-132 [< ZIT].
1148 ᴱ**Knight** D., *Tucker* G., The Hebrew Bible and its modern interpreters 1985 ➤ 1,293: ᴿETL 62 (1986) 168 (J. *Lust*); ÉTRel 61 (1986) 112s (D. *Lys*); Interpretation 40 (1986) 302 (R. E. *Murphy* stresses growth of 'biblical' as opposed to 'Syro-Palestinian' archeology); Themelios 12 (1986s) 28 (K. M. *Craig*: no sign of research after 1979).
1148* *Kourie* Celia, The historical critical method in Roman Catholic biblical scholarship: TEvca 18,3 (1985) 42-49.
1149 *a)* *Longman* Tremperᴵᴵᴵ, The literary approach to the study of the OT; promise and pitfalls; – *b)* *Dyrness* William A., Aesthetics in the OT; beauty in context; – *c)* *Osborne* Grant R., Round Four; the redaction debate continues: JEvTS 28 (1985) 385-398 / 421-432 / 399-410.
1149* *Luria* B. Z., ◉ Scripture study in our eyes: BethM 31,106 (1985s) 193-210.
1150 *Malina* B. J., Reader response theory; discovery or redundancy: Creighton Univ. Fac. Journal 5 (Omaha 1986) 55-66: reader-response criticism is suited to texts written to be read by solitary readers and its insights are already available in sociolinguistics or discourse-analysis [NTAbs 30, 263].
1150* *Myers* Edith, New directions in Catholic Bibles [against New Catholic Study Bible]: HomPast 87,2 (1986s) 52-60.
1151 *Neusner* Jacob, What do we study when we study the Bible? [i. 'the intellectual hoax of biblical studies' – vote on which sayings of Jesus are authentic; ii. philology, history, theology, not religion; iii. world-view; iv. way of life ... vii. choices of Israelite culture]: ProcIrB 10 (1986) 1-12.
1151* **Poland** Lynn M., Literary criticism and biblical hermeneutics; a critique of formalist approaches. Atlanta 1985, Scholars. 220 p. $15.25; pa. $10.25. – ᴿJRel 66 (1986) 466-8 (F. *Landy*).
1152 *Ralph* Margaret N., 'And God said what?' An introduction to biblical literary forms for Bible lovers. NY 1986, Paulist. vi-255 p. $11 [TS 47,756].
1152* *Rotenberg* Mordechai, The 'midrash' and biographic rehabilitation: JScStR 25 (1986) 41-55.
1153 *Sæbø* Magne. Om tradisjonshistorisk metode – i nye sammenhenger og perspektiver: TsTKi 57 (1986) 127-141.
1153* *Şemûdi* Joseph, Parallels and contrasts (on descriptive terms in biblical narratives): BethM 31,107 (1985s) 371-380.
1154 *Smith* P. J., Further observations on the method of discourse analysis: NduitseGT 27 (1986) 172-7.
1154* *Spencer* Aida B., An apologetic for stylistics in biblical studies: JEvTS 29 (1986) 419-428 [< ZIT].
1155 *Talmon* Shemaryahu, Emendation of biblical texts on the basis of Ugaritic parallels [= ErIsr 14 (1978) 117-124]: ➤ 251*, ScrHieros 31 (1986) 279-300.

1155* **Zehr** Paul M., Biblical criticism in the life of the Church: Scottdale 1986, Herald. 109 p. $7. 0-8361-3404-4 [ExpTim 98,319].

III. Critica Textus, Versiones

D1 **Textual Criticism**.

1156 **Barbour** Ruth, Greek literary hands, A.D. 400-1600: 1981 → 62,1874 ... 1,1672*: ᴿRBgPg 64 (1986) 104s (A. *Wouters*).

1157 ᴱ**Barthélemy** Dominique, Critique textuelle de l'AT [1.1982 → 63,720] 2. Isaïe, Jérémie, Lamentations: OBO 50/2. FrS/Gö 1986, Univ.VR. xviii-71*-1013 p. Fs 300, sb. 270. 2-8271-0322-2 / 3-525-53692-5 [BL 87,36, J. *Barr*: perverse, stifling, bizarre]. – I: ᴿJTS 37 (1986) 445-450 (J. *Barr*); KirSef 60 (1985) 366; NRT 108 (1986) 105s (J.-L. *Ska*).

1158 **Bat-Yehouda** Monique Zerdoun, Les encres noires au Moyen Âge (jusqu'à 1600); documents, études et répertoires publiés par l'Institut de recherche et d'histoire des textes. P 1983, CNRS. 437 p. – ᴿRÉJ 145 (1986) 150-3 (J.-P. *Rothschild*); Studia Islamica 64 (1986) 170s (Y. *Rāġib*).

1159 **Bischoff** Bernhard, Paléographie de l'Antiquité romaine et du Moyen Âge occidental [1979], ᵀ*Aatsma* H., *Vezin* J. P 1985, Picard. 326 p.; 23 pl. – ᴿFaventia 8,1 (1986) 151-3 (J. *Alturo i Perucho*); RÉLat 63 (1985) 265-9 (J. *Fontaine*); RHist 275 (1986) 479-481 (E. *Poulle*).

1160 **Blecua** A., Manual de crítica textual. M 1983, Castalia. 360 p. – ᴿCiuD 199 (1986) 178 (J. M. *Torrijos*).

1160* **Buzzetti** C., La Bibbia y sus transformaciones [targumim, LXX, Vulgata...]. Estella 1986, VDivino. 143 p. – ᴿBibFe 12 (1986) 356 (M. *Sáenz Galache*).

1161 *Byl* Simon, Méthode philologique (ou) et analyse codicologique: RBgPg 64 (1986) 62-67.

1162 *Cannuyer* C., Consommation et production de l'écriture à Cambron au moyen âge: Annales du Cercle royal d'histoire et d'archéologie d'Ath 49 (1982s) 119-142 [RHE 81,666].

1163 **Crown** A.D., Dated Samaritan manuscripts; some codicological implications. Sydney 1986. Unnumbered photocopies with descriptions facing each.

1164 *Crown* A.D., Studies in Samaritan scribal practices and manuscript history, IV. An index of scribes, witnesses, owners and others mentioned in Samaritan manuscripts, with a key to the principal families therein: BJRyL 68 (1985s) 317-372. – V. Samaritan binding; a chronological survey with reference to Nag Hammadi techniques: BJRyL 69 (1986s) 425-491.

1164* **De Hamel** Christopher, The history of illuminated manuscripts. Ox 1986, Phaidon. 256 p.; 250 (colour.) ill. £25. 0-7148-2361-9. [AntiqJ 67,196, Margaret *Gibson*].

1165 *Dukan* Michèle, De la difficulté à reconnaître des instruments de reglure; planche à régler (*mastara*) et cadre-patron: Scriptorium 40 (1986) 257-261.

1165* *Fornberg* Tord, Textual criticism and canon; some problems: ST 40 (1986) 45-53.

1166 *Fumagalli* Pier F., Frammenti di manoscritti ebraici medievali nelle filze e nelle legature dei volumi degli archivi e delle biblioteche di Stato italiano: Henoch 8 (1986) 49-66; franç. 66.

1167 **Gallo** Italo, Greek and Latin papyrology, ᵀ*Falivene* Maria R., *March* Jennifer R.: Classical Handbook 1. L 1986, Univ. Inst. Clas. St. 155 p.; 16 pl. 0-900587-50-4.

1168 ᴱ**Gigante** Marcello, Atti del XVII Congresso Internazionale di Papirologia (Napoli, 19-26 Maggio 1983) I-III, 1984 ➤ 65,637; 1,1680: ᴿDLZ 107 (1986) 837-9 (W. *Luppe*); Orpheus 7,1 (1986) 199-203 (M. *Capasso*).

1169 **Greenlee** J. Harold, Scribes scrolls and Scripture 1985 ➤ 1,1681: ᴿEvJ 4 (1986) 39-41 (J. D. *Yoder*); RExp 83 (1986) 295s (R. L. *Omanson*).

1170 **Hamman** A.-G., L'épopée du livre 1985 ➤ 1,1682: ᴿRÉLat 63 (1985) 264s (P. *Bourgain*).

1171 **Harrauer** H., **Sijpesteijn** P., Neue Texte aus dem antiken Unterricht. W 1985. – ᴿZPapEp 66 (1986) 71-76 (T. K. *Stephanopoulos*, Bemerkungen).

1172 *Kramer* Johannes, Sprachliche Beobachtungen an Schuldiktaten: ZPapEp 64 (1986) 246-252.

1173 **Lemaire** André, Les Écoles et la formation de la Bible dans l'ancien Israël 1981 ➤ 62,1154a... 1,1688b: ᴿJNES 45 (1986) 67-69 (B. A. *Levine*: factual but incoherent).

1174 *Metzger* Bruce M., [*Smend* Rudolf], Bibelhandschriften NT, ᵀ*Roehl* W.: ➤ 587, EvKL 1 (1986) 466-8 [AT 464-6]; col. 448-450, Ausgaben, *Köster* Beate.

1175 *Metzger* Thérèse, Ornamental micrography in medieval Hebrew manuscripts: BO 43 (1986) 377-388.

1176 **Murdoch** John E., Antiquity and the Middle Ages [book-illustration]: Album of Science 3. – ᴿSpeculum 61 (1986) 445-7 (R. B. *Thomson*).

1177 **Muzerelle** Denis, Vocabulaire codicologique; répertoire méthodique des termes français relatifs aux manuscrits: Histoire du livre 1. P 1985, Comité International de Paléographie [CEMI]. 265 p.; 60 pl. 2-903680-04-3. – ᴿRTAM 53 (1986) 192 (H. *Silvestre*).

1178 ᴱ**Nadav** Mordekhai, *Weiser* Rafael, Selected manuscripts and prints; an exhibition from the treasures of the Jewish National and University Library. J 1985. 36 p.; ➌ 92 p. 65 pl. + color. $20. – ᴿRÉJ 145 (1986) 196-8 (C. *Sirat*).

1179 [**Roberts** C. H., *Skeat* T. C., The birth of the codex 1983 ➤ 64,1705]... and the apostolic life-style: ᴿ*McCormick* M., Scriptorium 39 (1985) 150-8: RHE 81 (1986) 328: H. *Silvestre*, citant K. *Gardner*, The book in Japan, in The book through 5000 years (L 1972) 129-139: le passage du rouleau au codex s'est opéré sans qu'on puisse déceler la moindre relation avec le phénomène parallèle se produisant en Occident]; ᴿJBL 105 (1986) 359-361 (E. J. *Epp*).

1180 **Schubert** Ursula & Kurt, Jüdische Buchkunst 1983 ➤ 65,1463; 1,1702: ᴿRivStoLR 22 (1986) 579s (G. *Tamani*).

1181 **Shaheen** A. Moeiz, Scientific basis of treatment and conservation of parchment and papyrus. Cairo 1981, Antiquities Service. 278 p.; ill. – ᴿOLZ 81 (1986) 454s (M. *Fackelmann*).

1182 **Stickler** A. M., present., Le chiavi della memoria; miscellanea in occasione del I centenario della Scuola Vaticana di Paleografia, Diplomatica e Archivistica. Vaticano 1984, Assoc. Ex-Allievi. viii-612. – ᴿCC 137 (1986,1) 508s (G. *Caprile*: 15 su 19 autori donne; niente biblico notato).

1183 *Tishby* Pereș, ➌ Hebrew incunabula [... Italia]: KirSef 60 (1985) 865-922; pl. 923-962.

1183* **Zanetti** U., Les manuscrits de Dair Abû Maqâr, inventaire [... bibliques]: Cah. d'Orientalisme 11. Genève 1986, Cramer. 102 p. [VetChr 24,223].

D2.1 Biblia hebraica, Hebrew text.

1184 Barr James, The distribution of plene and defective spelling in the Masoretic text; its contribution to the study of text and language: → 377a, IOSOT summaries (1986) 13.

1185 Barthélemy Dominique, Texte, massores et facsimilé du manuscrit d'Alep: → 21, Mem. DÍEZ MACHO A., Salvation 1986, 53-63 [does not give any facsimile but comments on it].

1186 Biblia polyglotta complutensia, facsimile 1985 → 65,1469: RBiblica 67 (1986) 448s (L. Alonso Schökel); Gregorianum 67 (1986) 603 [also L. Alonso Schökel].

Borbone Pier G., Riflessioni sulla critica del testo dell'Antico Testamento ebraico 1986 → 2862.

1187 Fraser James G., A prelude to the Samaritan Pentateuch texts of the Paris polyglot Bible: → 63, FMcKANE W., A word 1986, 223-247.

1188 **Kohlenberger** J. R.III, The NIV interlinear Hebrew-English OT, 4. Isaiah-Malachi. GR 1985, Zondervan. xiii-595 p. $25. 0-310-38880-5 [BL 87,38, J. H. Eaton: splendid typography].

1188* Koller Yitshak, ❂ Signs, abbreviations, and initials in the Bible: BethM 31,104s (1985s) 10-16. 137-143.

1189 a) Lehman I. O., The biblical texts from K'ai Feng Fu and their manuscript tradition; – b) Revell E. J., Pausal phenomena and the biblical tradition in texts with Palestinian pointing: → 21, Mem. DÍEZ MACHO A., Salvación 1986, 185-191 / 235-244.

1190 Lozano Galán Marián, Jiménez Jiménez José Luis, Fragmentos [bíblicos...] de códices hebreos hallados en el archivo capitular de Tarazona: Sefarad 45 (1985) 217-236; Eng. 236. (Only a few words each except for two pages of bMo'ed Qatan.)

1191 **Lyons** David L., The vocalisation, accentuation and Masora of Codex Or. 4445 [British Museum] and their place in the development of the Tiberian Masora: diss. London 1983. 426 p. – KirSef 60 (1985) 374.

1192 **McCarter** P. KyleJ, Textual criticism; recovering the text of the Hebrew Bible. Ph 1986, Fortress. 94 p. $5. 0-8006-0471-7 [BL 87,39s, M. P. Weitzman].

1193 Moscati Sabatino, La Bibbia [?!] d'argento [rotoli di 97 mm e 39 mm contenenti (secondo Ada Yardeni) 'varie linee, nelle quali' si può riconoscere Num 6,24-27, con il nome YHWH (prima attestazione) (solo o anche il resto?) in caratteri anteriori alla forma (aramaica) del ritorno dall'esilio; trovati da Gabriel Barkay in una grotta del orlo sud del Ge-Hinnom]: Archeo 19 (Mi 1986) 4s.

1193* **Ognibeni** Bruno, È scritto 'non'; si legge 'a lui'; diciassette questioni testuali ed esegetiche nella Bibbia ebraica: diss. FrS 1985s, DSchenker A. – TR 82 (1986) 514. [= ?] Tradizioni di lettura e testo ebraico della Bibbia: diss. DBarthélemy D. FrS 1986. – RTLv 18,5443.

1194 **Shashar** Yitschak, ❂ Ketab-yad.. The Jerusalem manuscript 5702 24º [Sassoon 507] and its place in the formation of the Tiberian Textus Receptus: diss. Hebrew Univ. J 1983. 367 p. – KirSef 60 (1985) 364.

1194* **Smith** David C., An analysis of Sebirin [or Mat'en, Massoretic sigla] types for use in OT textual criticism: diss. New Orleans Baptist theol. sem. 1985, DSmith B. 155 p. 86-21468. – DissA 47 (1986) 2623s-A.

1195 *Sollamo* Raija, The source text for the translation of the Old Testament: BTrans 37 (1986) 319-322.
1196 **Weingreen** J., Introduction to the critical study of the text of the Hebrew Bible 1982 ➤ 63,1773... 65,1481: RScriptB 16 (1985s) 45s (M. *McNamara*).
1197 **Wonneberger** R., Understanding Biblia Hebraica Stuttgartensia...: SubsBPont 8, 1984 ➤ 65,1484: RVT 36 (1986) 125 (J. A. *Emerton*).
1198 *a*) *Wonneberger* R., Überlegungen zu einer maschinenlesbaren Neuausgabe der Biblia Hebraica Stuttgartensia: – *b*) *Radday* Y. T., Suggestions for standardizing biblical Hebrew text analysis for eventual computer-aided processing; – *c*) *Talstra* E., An hierarchically structured data base of biblical Hebrew texts; the relationship of grammar and encoding; – *d*) *Weil* G. E., Massorah, Massorètes et ordinateurs; les sources textuelles et les recherches automatisées: ➤ 389, Bible et informatique 1985/6, 363-379 / 287-293 (-6) / 335-349 / 351-361.

D2.2 Targum.

1199 **Chester** Andrew, Divine revelation and divine titles in the Pentateuchal Targumim: TStAntJud 14. Tü 1986, Mohr. xvi-432 p. DM 128. 3-16-145113-9 [RelStR 13,140 adv].
1200 **Churgin** Pinkhos, ESmolar Leivy, *Aberbach* Moses, Targum Jonathan to the Prophets [1927, diss. 1922] 1983 ➤ 64,1741; 1,1727: RBO 43 (1986) 769-771 (R. P. *Gordon*); CBQ 48 (1986) 319-322 (Z. *Garber*); JAOS 106 (1986) 363s (I. *Rabinowitz*); JBL 105 (1986) 164-6 (D. J. *Harrington*); JStJud 17 (1986) 272s (L. *Díez Merino*); NedTTs 40 (1986) 341-3 (A. van der *Kooij*, also on CHILTON B., Is.-Targ.).
1201 **Clarke** E. G., *al.*, Targum Pseudo-Jonathan of the Pentateuch; text and concordance. 1984 ➤ 65,1487; 1,1728: RJJS 37 (1986) 116s (R. *White*: the first concordance existing; marred by computer-traces); RB 93 (1986) 605-8 . (É. *Nodet*).
1201* **Cook** Edward M., Rewriting the Bible; the text and language of the Pseudo-Jonathan targum: diss. UCLA 1986, DSegert S. 293 p. 8606449. – DissA 47 (1986s) 164-A.
1202 **Díez Macho** A., *al.*, Targum Palaestinense in Pentateuchum I-V, 1977-80 ➤ 61,2326... 1,1729: RRÉJ 145 (186) 184s (J. *Margain*).
1203 **Díez Merino** Luis, Targum de Salmos / Job / Proverbios 1982-4 ➤ 64,2960... 1,1730: RBZ 30 (1986) 301-3 (J. *Maier*); ETL 62 (1986) 183-6 (A. *Schoors*).
1204 *a*) *Díez Merino* Luis, Grecismos y latinismos en el Targum Palestino (Neófiti 1); – *b*) *Martínez Borobio* Emiliano, Las formas D- y DY en función de pronombre relativo en el Targum Palestinense; – *c*) *Klein* Michael L., Targumic Toseftot from the Cairo Geniza; – *d*) *Tal* Abraham, Un fragment inédit du Targum Samaritain [Gn 9,6...]; – *e*) *McNamara* Martin, On Englishing the Targums: ➤ 21, Mem. DÍEZ MACHO A., Salvación 1986, 347-368 / 433-445 / 409-418 / 533-540 / 447-461.
1205 **Golomb** David M., A grammar of Targum Neofiti: HarvSemMon 34, 1985 ➤ 1,1733: RETL 62 (1986) 467s (J. *Lust*); JJS 37 (1986) 117s (S. *Brock*).
1206 *Kasher* Rimon, ⊕ Targumic conflations in the Ms Neofiti 1: HUCA 57 (1986) ⊕ 1-19.
1207 **Klein** Michael L., The fragment-targums of the Pentateuch according to their extant sources: AnBib 76, 1980 ➤ 62,1951*a*... 1,1739: RJNES 45 (1986) 157s (D. *Pardee*); KirSef 59 (1985) 294.

1208 **Klein** Michael L., Genizah manuscripts of Palestinian Targum to the Pentateuch, I-II. Cincinnati 1986, HUC. LI-363 p.; 131 p., 182 pl. Bibliog. p. xxxix-xliii. $125. 0-87820-206-4.

1209 **Le Déaut** Roger, The message of the New Testament and the Aramaic Bible (Targum) [Liturgie juive 1965 ➤ 47,677], ᵀ*Miletic* S.: Subsidia Biblica 5. R 1982, Pontifical Biblical Institute. 106 p.; bibliog. p. 93-97. 90-334-1350-7.

1209* **Le Déaut** Roger, De Bijbel van Jezus; het Nieuwe Testament en de arameese bijbelvertalingen [The message of the NT and the Aramaic Bible (Targum) 1982],ᵀ. Lv 1986, Vlaamse Bijbelstichting. 106 p.; bibliog. p. 93-97.

1210 **Levy** B. B., Targum Neophyti I., a textual study, I. Introduction, Genesis, Exodus. Lanham MD 1986, UPA. x-450 p. $36.50; pa. $21.75. 0-8191-5464-4; 5-2 [BL 87,109s, P. S. *Alexander*].

1210* *Syrén* R., Targumisterna som bibeltolkare: NorJ 5 (1984) 33-40 [< JStJud 17,143].

1211 **Tal** Abraham, ❿ The Samaritan Targum of the Pentateuch, a critical edition; III. Introduction: TStHeb 6, 1983 ➤ 64,1742 ... 1,1745: ᴿHenoch 8 (1986) 249s (S. *Noja*); Orientalia 55 (1986) 477 (S. P. *Brock*).

1212 *Weil* G. E., Targum du Pentateuque [*Le Déaut* R. I-V, 1978-81]: OLZ 81 (1986) 5-12: manuel de référence par excellence.

D3.1   *Textus graecus* – **Greek NT.**

1213 **Aland** K. & B., Der Text des NTs 1982 ➤ 63,1795 ... 1,1747: ᴿHenoch 8 (1986) 99s (B. *Chiesa*).

1213* *Aland* K., NTGraece²⁶, introd. ᵀ*Verzen* Sabin: STBuc 37 (1985) 305-347.

1214 ᴱ*Balconi* Carla, *al.*, Testi recentemente pubblicati [greci biblici e cristiani]: Aegyptus 66 (1986) 205-275 [205-7].

1214* Bericht der Hermann Kunst-Stiftung zur Förderung der neutestamentlichen Textforschung für die Jahre 1982 bis 1984. Münster 1985, H. K.-Stiftung. 128 p. [ETL 62, p. 9*].

1215 a) *Chmiel* J., *Jelonek* T., The Greek NT in the computer; a project of the Pontifical Academy of Theology at Cracow; – b) *Amphoux* C., Un nouveau répertoire des manuscrits des versions anciennes du Nouveau Testament, le 'Nouveau Gregory': ➤ 389, Bible et informatique 1985/6, 141 only/405s.

1216 ᴱ**Holeczek** Heinz, ERASMUS von Rotterdam, Novum Instrumentum, Basel, 1516 [NT gr./lat.]. Stu-Bad Cannstatt 1986, Frommann-Holzboog. xli-987 p. [facsimile] DM 340 [NRT 109,424, X. *Jacques*] 3-7728-0609-0.

1217 **Jeanne d'Arc** sr., Les Évangiles — Évangile selon Marc [➤ 3735] — Évangile selon Luc; présentation du texte grec, traduction et notes: Nouv. Coll. Budé. P 1986, BLettres/Desclée-B. xiv-117 (double) p. + fasc. 16 p.; x-201 (d.) p. + fasc. 24 p. F 225 + 330 [NRT 109, 739, X. *Jacques*].

1217* a) *Jordaan* G. J. C., Variation in word order between the Greek and Latin texts in Codex Bezae; – b) *Petzer* J. H., The papyri and New Testament textual criticism — clarity or confusion?: ➤ 72, ᶠMETZGER B., South Africa 1985/6, 99-111 / 18-31.

1218 *Metzger* Bruce M., Two manuscripts of the Greek gospels in Cape Town: Neotestamentica 20 (1986) 68s.

1218* *Muszyńska* Krystyna, ❿ The oldest NT codex in Poland (8-9 cent., from St. Maximinus monastery, acquired 1986 by National Library): RuBi 39 (1986) 492s.

1219 **Reeves** Rodney R., Methodology for determining text-types of NT manuscripts: diss. SW Baptist Sem. 1986. 329 p. 87-05906. – DissA 47 (1986s) 4116s-A.

1219* a) *Schrage* Wolfgang, Ethische Tendenzen in der Textüberlieferung des Neuen Testaments; – b) *Elliott* J. Keith, The purpose and construction of a critical apparatus to a Greek New Testament; – c) *Birdsall* J. Neville, The geographical and cultural origin of the Codex Bezae Cantabrigiensis; a survey of the status quaestionis, mainly from the palaeographical standpoint: ➤ 39, ᶠGREEVEN H., Text/Ethik 1986, 374-396 / 125-143 / 102-114.

1220 **Shields** David D., Recent attempts to defend the Byzantine text of the Greek New Testament; diss. SW Baptist Sem., ᴰ*Brooks* J., 1985. 217 p. 86-12697. – DissA 47 (1986s) 949-A.

1221 *Spottorno* Maria Victoria, El carácter expansivo del códice de Beza: ➤ 21, Mem. DÍEZ MACHO A., Salvación 1986, 689-698.

1222 **Sturz** Harry A., The Byzantine text-type and New Testament textual criticism [< diss. 1967] 1984 ➤ 65,1515; 1,1757: ᴿCBQ 48 (1986) 149s (L. W. *Hurtado*); NT 28 (1986) 282-4 (J. K. *Elliott*); WestTJ 48 (1986) 187-190 (M. *Silva*).

1223 *Thiede* C. P., Neutestamentliche Papyrologie; die ersten Handschriften, ihre Datierung und Bewertung: IBW Journal 23,10 [Pd 1985) 12-19 [NTAbs 30,135].

1224 [*Vaganay* Léon] ² **Amphoux** Christian-Bernard, Initiation à la critique textuelle du Nouveau Testament [¹ 1934]. P 1986, Cerf. 300 p. F 145. – ᴿEsprV 96 (1986) 549-551 (É. *Cothenet*: 'Vaganay genuit Duplacy, DUPLACY autem genuit Amphoux'); ETL 62 (1986) 426s (F. *Neirynck*: 'Wescott', 'Wordworth' partout, où Vaganay ¹ correctement); VSp 140 (1986) 723s (G. *Rouiller*).

1225 **Zellweger** E., Das Neue Testament im Lichte der Papyrusfunde. Bern 1985, Lang. 176 p.; 4 phot. Fs 28. 3-261-04044-0 [NTAbs 31,97].

D3.2 *Versiones graecae* – **VT, Septuaginta** etc.

1226 *Abercrombie* J., Programs for work with the Septuagint data from CATSS: ➤ 389, Bible et informatique 1985/6, 35 only.

1226* **Aly** Zaki, Three rolls of the early Septuagint; Genesis and Deuteronomy; intr. *Koenen* L. PapTAbh 27. Bonn 1980, Habelt. xiii-143 p.; 57 pl. DM 78, pa. 65. – ᴿOLZ 81 (1986) 355-7 (R. *Sollano*: this means WEVER must be checked).

1227 **Bentley** James, Secrets of Mount Sinai; the story of the world's oldest Bible – Codex Sinaiticus [➤ 1,1761] also GCNY 1986, Doubleday. 272 p. $18. – ᴿHorizons 13 (1986) 415s (Mary Rose *d'Angelo* adds: the British offered the body of Marx as part of the price; the Russians preferred sterling).

1228 ᴱ**Fernández Marcos** N., La Septuaginta en la investigación contemporánea 1983/5 ➤ 1,468: ᴿAegyptus 66 (1986) 296 (Anna *Passoni Dell'Acqua*); JJS 37 (1986) 115s (Alison *Salvesen*); JStJud 17 (1986) 101-4 (F. *García Martínez*); JTS 37 (1986) 471-4 (H. F. D. *Sparks*); Muséon 99 (1986) 181s (P.-M. *Bogaert*); Salmanticensis 33 (1986) 113s (J. M. *Sánchez Caro*).

1229 *Gruenwald* J., ⊕ [hostility of the Rabbis to LXX]: ➤ 246, ᴱ*Friedman* M., Teʿuda 4 (1986).

Harl Marguerite, La Bible d'Alexandrie... traduction du texte grec de la Septante, introduction et notes [I.] La Genèse 1986 ➤ 1384*.

1230 **Lee** J. A.,   A lexical study of the Septuagint version of the Pentateuch [diss. 1970] 1983 ➤ 64,1778... 1,1763: RJBL 105 (1986) 327s (L. *Greenspoon*); RechSR 74 (1986) 151s (A. *Paul*).

1231 *Luke* K.,   The Septuagint; an account of recent research: Bible Bhashyam 12 (1986) 131-149.

1232 *Murray* Oswyn,   Aristeasbrief, (Art.) T*Engemann* Josef: ➤ 594, RAC Sup (1986) 573-587.

1233 *Peters* Melvin K. H.,   Why study the Septuagint? BA 49 (1986) 174-181.

1234 **Schmidt** Werner,   Untersuchungen zur Fälschung historischer Dokumente bei Pseudo-Aristaios: DissKlPg 37. Bonn 1985, Habelt. x-165 p.

1235 *Stone* Richard B.,   The life and hard times of Ephraemi Rescriptus [in first person]: BToday 24 (1986) 112-8.

1235* *Talshir* Zipora,   Linguistic development and the evaluation of translation technique in the Septuagint: ➤ 251*, ScrHieros 31 (1986) 301-320.

1236 *Therath* Anthony,   A Christian Old Testament [LXX] ? : LivWord 92 (1986) 131-9 [TKontext 8/1,35].

1237 **Tov** Emanuel,   A computerized data base for Septuagint studies; the parallel aligned text of the Greek and Hebrew Bible: JNWS Sup. 1 / Computer assisted Sept., 2. Stellenbosch 1986, Univ. xviii-144 p.

1238 *Tov* Emmanuel,   Jewish Greek Scriptures [LXX; revisions]: ➤ 255, Early Judaism 1986, 221-237.

1239 *Treu* Kurt,   Christliche Papyri XII [... Gn 25s; Esther 4,4-11; Ps 90; 129; Qoh/Sir; Job 9; Is 33; – Mt 1,19s; Act 2]: ArPapF 32 (1986) 87s(-95).

1239* *Veltri* Giuseppe,   L'ispirazione della LXX tra leggenda e teologia; dal racconto di Aristea alla 'veritas hebraica' di GIROLAMO: Laurentianum 27 (1986) 3-71.

1240 FWEVERS J. W., De Septuaginta, E*Pietersma* A., *Cox* C., 1984 ➤ 1,149: RJStJud 17 (1986) 115-7 (A. *Hilhorst*).

D4   Versiones orientales.

1241 *Aland* Barbara, Bibelübersetzungen: ➤ 587, EvKL 1 (1986) 478-487.

1242 **Schmitz** Franz-Jürgen, *Mink* Gerd,   Liste der koptischen Handschriften des Neuen Testaments, I. Die sahidischen Handschriften der Evangelien, 1.: ArbNTTextF 8. B 1986, de Gruyter. xxiii-471 p. DM 148 [NRT 109, 420s, X. *Jacques*], 3-11-010256-0.

1243 *Bandrés* José L.,   The Ethiopian Anaphora of the Apostles; historical considerations: PrOrChr 36 (1986) 6-13.

1243* **Beylot** Robert,   Testamentum Domini éthiopien, édition et traduction [diss. Sorbonne]. Lv 1984, Peeters. xii-238 p. Fb 1800 [RelStR 13,353, J. F. *Puglisi*].

1244 *Luke* K.,   The Ethiopic version of the Bible: Bible Bhashyam 11 (1985) 170-188. 236-253.

1245 **Miles** John R.,   Retroversion and text criticism... [Esther] Greek to Ethiopic 1985 ➤ 1,1776: RETL 62 (1986) 170s (J. *Lust*); TLZ 111 (1986) 342-4 (Anneli *Aejmelaeus*).

1246 **Aland** Barbara,   Das Neue Testament in syrischer Überlieferung, 1. (mit *Juckel* A.) Die grossen katholischen Briefe [Jac, 1 Pt, 1 Jn]: ArbNTTextf 7. B 1986, de Gruyter. x-312 p. 3-11-010255-2. – RMuséon 99 (1986) 359-362 (A. de *Halleux*).

1247 *Baarda* T., To the roots of the Syriac Diatessaron tradition (T^A 25:1-3): NT 28 (1986) 1-25.

1248 *Petersen* William, New evidence for the question of the original language of the Diatessaron: ➤ 39, ^FGREEVEN H., Text/Ethik 1986, 325-343.

1249 *Charlesworth* James H., Semitisms in the New Testament and the need to clarify the importance of the Syriac NT: ➤ 21, Mem. DÍEZ MACHO A., Salvación 1986, 633-8.

1250 *Konigsveld* P. S. van, Peshitta institute communication 20: The monastery of Bâqûqâ in Iraq and an old owner's entry in Ms Syr. 341 of the Bibliothèque Nationale in Paris: VT 36 (1986) 235-240.

1251 *Lehmann* Henning J., The Syriac translation of the OT—as evidenced around the middle of the fourth century (in EUSEBIUS of Emesa): ScandJOT 1,1 (1986) 66-86.

1252 *McConaughy* Daniel L., Syriac manuscripts (some scriptural) in South India; the library of the St. Thomas apostolic seminary: OrChrPer 52 (1986) 432-4.

1253 *Neff* D., Recovering the erased Gospels [Sinaitic Syriac by computer-enhanced photography]: ChrTod 30,14 (1986) 17-20 [NTAbs 31,13].

1254 *Vilders* Monique, Two folios of a Syriac lectionary in Leiden (F 1965/4.7) [Mk 9,14-29; Lk 10,25-37]: OMRO 66 (1986) 77-83; 4 pl.

1255 **Cox** Claude E., Hexaplaric materials preserved in the Armenian version [1227 asterisked, 234 obeli]: SBL SepCog 21. Atlanta 1986, Scholars. xv-236 p. $13; pa. $9.75. 0-55540-028-0; 9-9. – ^RExpTim 98 (1986s) 119 (C. S. *Rodd*).

1256 **Künzle** Beda O., Das altarmenische Evangelium, I. Edition zweier altarmenischer Handschriften; II. Lexikon: EurHS 21/33. Bern 1984, Lang. 144*-293 p.; 29*-103 p. Fs 118. 3-261-03422-X. – ^RBijdragen 47 (1986) 329 (M. *Parmentier*, Eng.: transitoriness of a milestone).

1257 *a) Stone* M. E., Computer implantation of Armenian; – *b) Outtier* B., 'Vetus Iberica' un projet d'édition critique des vieilles versions géorgiennes: ➤ 389, Bible et informatique 1985/6, 323-334 / 401 only.

1258 ^EDočanašvili E., [Georgian] Mc'het'a manuscript: Pentateuch, Joshua, Judges, Ruth: SSR Georgia Academy of Sciences, Commission for the Sources of the History of Georgia. Tbilisi 1981, Mec'niereba. 544 p.

1259 ^EDočanašvili E., 1-4 Kingdoms, 1-2 Paralipomenon, 1-3 Esdras (in Georgian): Mc'het'a Manuscript. Tbilisi 1982, Mec'niereba; SSR Georgia Academy of Sciences. 472 p.

1260 ^EDočanašvili E., [in Georgian] Tobias, Judith, Esther, Job, Psalms, Proverbs: Mc'het'a Manuscript. Tbilisi 1983, Mec'niereba. 328 p.

1261 ^EDočanašvili E., Ecclesiastes, Wisdom of Solomon, Song of Solomon, Is Jer Ezek: Mc'het'a Manuscript [in Georgian]. Tbilisi 1985, Mec'niereba; SSR Georgia Academy of Sciences. 384 p. [44-49 Eces; 50-60 Wis; 61-70 Ct; ➤ Is].

1262 ^EDočanašvili E., Daniel, Minor Prophets, NT Mt-Mk-Lk: Mc'het'a Manuscript. Tbilisi 1986, Mec'niereba. 304 p. [NT p. 152-261].

1262* *Luke* K., The Georgian version of the Bible: Bible Bhashyam 12 (1986) 59-79. 249-262.

1263 *Vateishvili* J. Levanovich, Origine e vicende editoriali della prima Bibbia in lingua georgiana: Nicolaus 13,1 (1986) 85 (-130) [< ZIT].

1263* *Kutûb at-Tarîḫ* ❹ Historical books: *Al-Kitâb al-Muqaddas* p. 416-1039. Beirut 1986, Mašriq.
1264 *Higgins* A. J. B., The Arabic Diatessaron in the new Oxford edition of the Gospel according to St. Luke in Greek: JTS 37 (1986) 415-9 [3 corrections 38 (1987) 135].
1265 *Luke* K., The Arabic versions of the Bible [NT]: LivWord 91 (1985) 315-335; 92 (1986) 11-33.

1266 *Kyas* Vladimir, Zur griechischen Vorlage des altkirchenslavischen Parömienbuches [not clearly limited to Proverbs]: BySlav 46 (1985) 89-93 [94-105, *Svábová* Jana, Textvarianten].
1267 *Moszyński* Leszek, Die Tetraevangelien des Codex Zographensis und Codex Marianus als liturgische Bücher, II. Die kyrillische Etappe: BySlav 46 (1985) 78-88.
1268 *a) Nazor* Anica, The Old Testament in Croato-Glagolitic manuscript tradition; – *b) Reinhart* Johannes M., The sapiential collection in the Croatian-Glagolitic missal: ➤ 363. Congress IX-Dl, 1985/6, 69-75 / 77-84.
1269 *Sorokin* Wladimir, Der slawische Text des Neuen Testament und seine Bedeutung: Stimme der Orthodoxie 8 (1986) 40-45 [TLZ 112,176].

D5   **Versiones latinae.**

1270 *a) d'Amato* Cesario, Alcune note d'archivio sulla 'Bibbia di S. Paolo [fuori le mura]'; – *b) Gribomont* Jean †, Recherches en cours sur le Codex Paulinus: Benedictina 33 (1986) 173-7 / 337-345.
1271 **Cohen-Mushlin** Aliza, The making of a manuscript: the Worms Bible of 1148 (British Library, Harley 2803-2804) [diss. J, Hebrew Univ. 1986]: Wolfenbüttler Forschungen 25. Wsb 1983, Harrassowitz. 222 p.; 166 (color.) pl. DM 168. – ᴿSpeculum 61 (1986) 396-8 (Kristine E. *Haney*).
1272 **Fischer** Bonifatius [➤ 156], Lateinische Bibelhandschriften im frühen Mittelalter 1985 ➤ 1,173: ᴿJTS 37 (1986) 354s (G. D. *Kilpatrick*); RHE 81 (1986) 542s (P.-M. *Bogaert*); TLZ 111 (1986) 897s (G. *Haendler*: 5 reprints, analyzed).
1273 *García de la Fuente* Olegario, Sobre el uso de los adverbios en el latín bíblico: ➤ 21, Mem. DÍEZ MACHO A., Salvación 1986, 135-156.
1274 **García Moreno** Antonio, La Neovulgata; precedentes y actualidad: EUNSA teol. 47. Pamplona 1986, Univ. Navarra. 346 p. – ᴿScripTPamp 18 (1986) 919-922 (C. *Basevi*); ScriptV 33 (1986) 440s (A.*Ibáñez Arana*).
1275 **Ghiglione** Natale, L'Evangeliario purpureo di Sarezzano 1984 ➤ 1,1749: ᴿEphLtg 100 (1986) 609-611 (A. M. *Triacca*).
1275* **Harrison** Rebecca R., Jerome's revision of the Gospels: diss. Pennsylvania, ᴰO'Donnell J. Ph 1986. 355 p. 86-14809. – DissA 47 (1986s) 1311-A.
1276 **Hertz** Anselme, Le message du Christ; l'Évangéliaire d'Otton III [➤ 65,3552]. P 1984, Cerf. 48 p.; 22 color. fig.
1276* *Horst* Ulrich, Der Streit um die Autorität der Vulgata; zur Rezeption des Trienter Schriftdekrets in Spanien: Revista Univ. Coimbra 29 (1983) 152-252 [ForumKT 2 (1986) 314s (P. *Schäfer*)].

1277 **Hutz** Ferdinand,   Das Vorauer Evangeliar [Codex 346: 12 Faksim., 51 Seiten] 1983 ➤ 1,1792 [1986: 3-201-01337-4]:   ᴿTrierTZ 95 (1986) 75s (E. *Sauser*).

1278 *Jonge* H. J. de,   ERASMUS' method of translation in his version of the New Testament [in acceptably good Latin, to reform the Christian world; 250 printed editions]: BTrans 37 (1986) 135-8.

1278* **Szirmai** Julia C.,   La Bible anonyme du Ms. Paris B.N. f.fr. 763, édition critique.   Amst 1985, Rodipi.   399 p. *f*100 [GerefTTs 86,65].

1279 **Valgiglio** Ernesto,   Le antiche versioni latine del Nuovo Testamento; fedeltà e aspetti grammaticali: Koinonia 11, 1985 ➤ 1,1795:   ᴿCC 137 (1986,4) 98s (A. *Ferrua*); Maia 38 (1986) 192s (A. *Ceresa-Gastaldo*); Orpheus 7 (1986) 471s (A. V. *Nazzaro*).

D 5.5 – *Citationes apud Patres* — **the Patristic Bible**

1280 **Ehrman** Bart D.,   DIDYMUS the Blind and the text of the Gospels [cf. ᴰ1985 ➤ 1, 1797]: SBL NT in the Greek Fathers 1.   Atlanta 1986, Scholars.   xii-288 p.; bibliog. p. 276-288. $13.95.

1280* *a*) *Gribomont* Jean †,   Le texte biblique de GRÉGOIRE; – *b*) *Reinhart* Johannes M.,   Une figure stylistique dans la traduction vieux-slave des Homélies sur les Évangiles de Grégoire le Grand en comparaison avec les textes scripturaires: ➤ 433*. Grégoire 1982/6, 455-466 / 597-606.

1281 *Halleux* André de,   Glanures syro-hexaplaires dans les florilèges grégoriens: Muséon 99 (1986) 251-290.

D6 **Versiones modernae** .1 *romanicae*, **romance**.

1282 *Zsigmond* Gyula, Ⓜ The Olivetan Bible is 450 years old: Theologiai Szemle 29 (1986) 31-34.

1283 *Smeets* J. R.,   La Bible [versifiée et commentée entre 1270 et 1314] de Jehan Malkaraume (Ms. Paris, Bibl. Nat. f. fr. 903).   Assen 1978, Van Gorcum.   vii-386 p.; 351 p. *f*175. – ᴿRBgPg 62 (1984) 638-640 (P. *Verhuyck*; puts the whole Roman de Troie as a transition to Joshua; and OVID's Pyramis and Thisbe between Susanna and Ruth).

1284 **Fuentes Mendiola** A., Nuevo Testamento. M 1986, Rialp. 766 p.; maps. – ᴿStudium 26 (M 1986) 544 (L. *López de las Heras*).

1285 **Littlefield** Mark G.,   Biblia romanceada I.I.8; the 13th-century Spanish Bible contained in Escorial MS. I.I.8.   Madison WI 1983, Univ. Hispanic Seminary of Medieval Studies.   xiii-332 p.; 4 pl.; bibliog. p. 325-332; 10 microfiches.   0-942260-34-1.

1286 Sagrada Biblia [de Navarra], Santos Evangelios 1983 ➤ 1,1806:   ᴿAngelicum 63 (1986) 490s (J. *García Trapiello*: las numerosas notas, algunas de dos páginas, han procurado no sólo explicar el contenido del texto bíblico, sino también formar al lector en la doctrina cristiana en general; le auguramos el mejor resultado); Asprenas 33 (1986) 201s (C. *Marcheselli-Casale*).

1286* *Buzzetti* Carlo, Le traduzioni della Bibbia: RClerIt 67 (1986) 341-9.

1287 Parola del Signore; La Bibbia, traduzione interconfessionale in lingua corrente 1985 ➤ 1,1809;   1324 + 482 p. Lit. 20.000:   ᴿAsprenas 32 (1985) 453-5 (V. *Scippa*).

1287* **Ravasi** Gianfranco, *Saldarini* Giovanni, La Bibbia [condensata, Reader's Digest] 1985 ➤ 1,1809; Lit. 24.500: [R]Letture 41 (1986) 77-79 (G. *Ravasi*).
1288 [E]**Rossano** P., Tradurre la Bibbia per il popolo di Dio; Morcelliana 1925-1985: Humanitas Quad. 6. Brescia 1986, Morcelliana. 125 p. Lit. 12.000. – [R]RasT 27 (1986) 283s (V. *Fusco*).
1289 *Subilia* V., La traduzione confessionale della Bibbia: Protestantesimo 41 (1986) 28-33; p. 106s, *Soggin* J. A. protesta la critica della Bibbia TILC [➤ 1,1807].

D6.2   *Versiones anglicae* – **English Bible translations**.

1290 A concise history of the English Bible, with helpful notes. NY 1983, American Bible Society. 61 p.
1291 **Duthie** Alan S., [English] Bible translations and how to choose between them [best in order: Good News, New Jerusalem, New American, New English, NIV...] 1985 ➤ 1,1814: [R]BTrans 37 (1986) 342s (F. *Bruce*); RefTR 45 (1986) 86 (J. W. *Woodhouse*: his criteria are deficiencies).
1292 *Epp* Eldon J., Should 'The Book' be panned? [1984 Wheaton ed. of The Living Bible, 30 million copies sold since 1971 in 40 languages]: BR 2,2 (1986) 36-41.52: inaccurate paraphrase.
1293 *Ledyard* Gleason H., The New Life New Testament [using only some 850 different English words; circulated in West Africa but publication-data not given]: [R]BTrans 37 (1986) 436-441 (J. *Ellington*).
1294 **Levi** P., The English Bible 1534-1859. Worthing 1985 = 1974, Churchman. 222 p. £3.95 pa. 1-85093-015-5 [NTAbs 30,220].
1295 *a)* [E]**Lindsell** H., Harper study Bible [formerly with RSV text, now with] New American Standard Bible. GR 1985, Zondervan. xiii-1757 p.; 14 maps. 0-310-95065-1 [NTAbs 31,92]. – *b)* [E]**Barker** Kenneth, The NIV study Bible. GR 1985, Zondervan. 2103 p. [JAAR 54, 391]. – [R]AndrUnS 24 (1986) 286-8 (R. M. *Johnston*); BS 143 (1986) 372s (R. B. *Zuck*). – *c)* NIV [➤ 1,1823*] The New Testament, New International Version; an ecumenical Bible study edition. NY 1986, Paulist. 451 p. $7.95. 0-8091-2733-4.
1296 *Jackson* D., The theology of the NIV [subordinated to accuracy]: RestQ 27,4 (1984) 208-220 [NTAbs 30,267].
1297 *Scott* J. W., Dynamic equivalence and some theological problems in the NIV [New International Version]: WestTJ 48 (1986) 351-361.
1298 NJerB: [E]**Wansbrough** H., The New Jerusalem Bible 1985 ➤ 1,1827: [R]Furrow 57 (1986) 476s (W. *Harrington*); Gregorianum 67 (1986) 149s (J. *Dupuis*); NBlackf 67 (1986) 140-2 (I. *Robinson*); NT 28 (1986) 381 (G. D. *Kilpatrick*: still outdated in comparison with Einheitsübersetzung); TLond 39 (1986) 309s (P. *Hammond*: first choice for both private and liturgical use).
1299 *Nestle-Aland*, Greek (= [26] 7th printing 1983) + English (= RSV [2] 1971) New Testament [2]. Stu 1985, Deutsche Bibelgesellschaft. viii + 40* + 779 p. – [R]NT 28 (1986) 381s (G. D. *Kilpatrick*: dubious that this combination is 'as close as we can come to the original').
1299* **Vacca** R., La Bibbia inglese nella versione di King James; un esame storico-linguistico: diss. [D]*Binni* F. F 1985, [RivB 35,397].
1300 *Vawter* Bruce, On 'inclusive language' [W. *Michel*'s negative judgment about the Lectionary is proper; an offense against the English language]: Dialog 25,1 (St. Paul 1986) 64-67 [NTAbs 30,268].

1302 [EGinsberg H., al.] The Writings, Kethubim ... Jewish Publ. Soc. 1982
➤ 63,1877; 65,1588:   RAustralBR 34 (1986) 65s (J. J. Scullion).

6.3 Versiones germanicae – Deutsche Bibelübersetzungen.

1303 Locher Clemens,   Fragen zur 'Neuen Jerusalem Bibel' [EDeissler A.,
Vögtle A., 1985 ➤ 1,1830]: Orientierung 50 (1986) 30-34.

1304 Meid Wolfgang,   Die Auseinandersetzung germanischer mit orien-
talisch-griechischer Weltsicht am Beispiel der gotischen Bibelübersetzung:
➤ 82, FOBERHUBER K., Im Bannkreis 1986, 159-170.

1305 EMeurer Siegfried,   Die neue Lutherbibel, Beiträge zum revidierten Text
1984: Die Bibel in der Welt 21.   Stu 1985, Deutsche Bibelgesellschaft.
184 p. DM 15. – RTR 82 (1986) 115-7 (O. B. Knoch).

D6.4   Versiones nordicae et variae.

1306 Biemans J.A.A.M.,   Middelnederlandse bijbelhandschriften, beschreven:
Verzameling van middelnederlandse bijbelteksten, Catalogus.   Leiden
1984, Brill.   340 p.; ill. ƒ120.   90-04-07088-5. – RBijdragen 47 (1986) 212
(P. Nissen).

1307 Poortman Wilco C.,   Bijbel en prent, I. Boekzaal van de Nederlandse
Bijbels [IIa ... Prentbijbels; IIb. Boekzaal van de Nederlandse uitgaven van de werken van Flavius Josephus, awaited].   Haag 1983, Boekencentrum.   270 p.   ƒ165. – RNedTTs 40 (1986) 85 (C. J. Labuschagne).

1308 Outryve O. Van,   Bijbel voor de jeugd; het Nieuwe Testament.
Averbode/Boxtel 1986, Altiora/K.B.S.   284 p. – RCollatVl 16 (1986) 501s
(R. Hoet).

1309 Tromp Nico,   Pak dit boek dat openligt en eet het op; Kerk en bijbel
voor en na Vaticanum II; de Groot Nieuws Bijbel: OnsGLev 63 (1986)
20-27.

1310 Chmiel Jerzy,   ❷ Sts. Cyril and Methodius, creators of the Slavic Bible,
in the background of the Encyclical of John Paul II, 'Slavorum apostoli':
RuBi 39 (1986) 89-96.

1311 ESalminen Jorma,   Kohti uutta Kirkkoraamattua näkökulmia raamatun
kääntämiseen: Suomen eksegeettisen seuran julkaisuja 43.   Helsinki 1986,
Vammalan Kirjapaino Oy.   205 p.   951-95185-8-4.   19 art.

1312 Bottyán János,   A magyar biblia évszázadai.   Budapest 1982, Reformatus
Zsinati.   206 p., lxvii pl. [KirSef 59,314].

1313 Radó György,   The Bible in Hungarian [Bottyán J. ⓂThe centuries of the
Hungarian Bible 1982]: BTrans 37 (1986) 144s.

1314 a) Nicodemus metrop.,   ❸ The recent translation of the New Testament
(by six professors) and the Church: TAth 57 (1986) 489-502. – b) Wittig
Andreas,   Um eine umgangsgriechische Übersetzung der Heiligen Schrift:
OstkSt 35 (1986) 41-44.

1315 a) The Bible in Hindi.   Ranchi 1986.   1448 + 404 p. – b) The Bible in
Gujarate.   Anand 1981, Gujarat Sahitya Prakash. 1236-344 p.

1318 Covell R. R. [Baptist Missionary], Confucius, the Buddha, and Christ; a
history of the Gospel in Chinese: American Society of Missiology 11.
Maryknoll NY 1986, Orbis.   xviii-285 p. $14.95 [NRT 109,768, J.
Scheuer).

1319 **Rijks** Piet, A guide to Catholic Bible translations, 1. The Pacific. Stu
c. 1986, WCFBA. 147 p.; maps.

D7 *Problemata vertentis* – **Bible translation techniques.**

1320 *Achtemeier* Elizabeth, The translator's dilemma; inclusive language:
Living Light 22 (Wsh 1986) 242-5: the new Lectionary is a step in the right
direction but a bad product [NTAbs 30,267].
1321 *Albrektson* Bertil, Är översättning också tolkning? [Is translation also
interpretation?]: SvEx 51s (1986s) 13-22.
1322 **Arcaini** Enrico, Analisi linguistica e traduzione: Le Scienze del
Linguaggio 1. Bo 1986, Pàtron. 248 p. Lit. 30.000.
Bible translation, hobby or science ? [Dutch] 1985 → 251*, ᴱHollander H.
1323 **Deladrière** Valentin, Traduction en renouveau [a sort of revolt against
scholarly translations]: Libre parole 2. Bru 1986. 79 p.
1323* *Derrida* T., Théologie de la traduction: → 16*, Mem. Coppieters de
Gibson D. 1985, 165-184.
1324 *Ellingworth* Paul, *Mojola* Aloo, Translating euphemisms in the Bible:
BTrans 37 (1986) 139-143.
1324* **Firmage** Robert D., A prolegomenon to theory of translation: diss.
Utah 1986, ᴰ*Helbling* R. 361 p. 86-24441. – DissA 47 (1986s) 2612-A.
1325 ᴱGnilka Joachim, *Rüger* Hans-Peter, Die Übersetzung der Bibel —
Aufgabe der Theologie: Stuttgarter Symposion 1984/5 → 1,285: ᴿTR 82
(1986) 451s (O. B. *Knoch*); TüTQ 166 (1986) 152s (M. *Reiser*).
1326 *Grumm* Meinert, Why so many 'musts' ? [every 'must' in King James
(Crudens) is for *deî* or similar; RSV adds 35, NIV and JerB¹ less, NEB and
TEV only some 18 more; arbitrariness shown in key verses, Eph 4-6]:
CurrTM 13 (1986) 169s.
1327 *Hope* Edward R., Translating prepositions [reduces to a geometric set of
rules 'ambiguities' obvious to anyone familiar with the situation; 'he was
on the sea' means 'he was on a boat on the sea' ...]: BTrans 37 (1986)
401-412.
1328 **Lapide** Pinchas F., Hebrew in the Church; the foundations of
Jewish-Christian dialogue 1984 → 1,a86: ᴿBTrans 37 (1986) 344s (P. *Ellingworth*: contains a list of seven arguable sins of which NT translators
have been guilty).
1329 **Lapide** P., Ist die Bibel richtig übersetzt?: Siebenstern 1415. Gü 1986,
Mohn. 144 p. DM 14,80 [ZAW 99,292]. 3-579-01415-3.
1330 **Larson** Mildred L., Meaning-based translation; a guide to cross-language
equivalence. Lanham MD 1984, UPA. 537 p. – ᴿBTrans 37 (1986) 343s
(H. W. *Fehderau*).
1330* **Lee-Lim Guek Eng** Violet, Cognitive processes and linguistic forms in
Old Testament Hebrew and Chinese cultures; implications for translation:
diss. Fuller, ᴰ*Shaw* D. Pasadena 1986. 464 p. 86-16918. – DissA 47
(1986s) 1760-A.
1331 *Miller* Patrick D.ᴶ, The translation task: TTod 43 (1986s) 540-6.
1332 *Milward* Peter, Translating the Bible; has simplicity lost its merit?:
HomPast 86 (1986) 63 ...
1332* *Nichols* Anthony, Dynamic equivalence Bible translations: Colloquium
19,1 (Auckland 1986) 23-42.
1333 **Norton** Glyn P., The ideology and language of translation in Renaissance
France and their humanist antecedents: TrHumRen 201. Genève 1984,
Droz. 364 p. – ᴿBiblHumRen 48 (1986) 276-8 (M. *Jeanneret*).

1334 **Olofsson** S.,   Guds Ord och människors språk; en bok om bibelöversättning. U 1986, EFS. 91-9080-721-3 [BL 87,130].

1335 *Pence* Gary,   The inclusive language lectionary and the Church's holy 'censorship' of the Bible: CurrTM 13 (1986) 261-5 [substitution of 'Jesus' for 'he' in order to deemphasize Jesus' maleness is all right; but it is essential that the oppressions as much as the liberating words of that period be accessible to us preserved from 'improvement' of later generations]; 266-272, comment of *Graesser* Carl; 272-5 rejoinder.

1336 *Pisarska* Alicja,   On different types of translation: ➤ 31, FFISIAK J., Linguistics 1986, 1421-6.

1336* *Riebert* S.,   Die verryking van ons taalkunde-insig in klassiek Hebreeus en die vertaling van die Ou Testament: NduitseGT 27 (1986) 157-171.

1337 *Sanderfur* John,   Checking those jots and tittles [the computer can tell you there is no such word (in English) but not that in this context it is a misprint]: BTrans 37 (1986) 428-432.

1337* *Schwarz* Werner (1905-1982), Schriften zur Bibelübersetzung und mittelalterlichen Übersetzungstheorie: Vestigia Bibliae 7 (Hamburg 1985) 11-140 [< ZIT].

1338 *Shaw* Daniel,   Ethnohistory, strategy, and Bible translation; the case of WYCLIFFE and the cause of world mission: Missiology 14 (1986) 47-54.

1339 *a) Smith* Jill,   Dealing with proper nouns in translation; – *b) Loewen* Jacob A.,   Who am I translating for?: BTrans 37 (1986) 204-211 / 201-4 [for children, 239-242, *Arichea* D.; 420-428, *al.*].

1340 *Stortz* Martha E.,   Language for those who have ears to hear [inclusive is also exclusive; the new lectionary gives *one* form of conversion, but the original text must remain open to *further* conversion]: CurrTM 13 (1986) 285-291.

1341 *Throckmorton* Burton, [Inclusive] Language and the Bible: RelEd 80 (Ch 1985) 523-538 [-550 response, *Boys* Mary C. + 7 related articles].

1342 **Waard** Jan de, *Nida* Eugene A.,   From one language to another; functional equivalence in Bible translating. Nv 1986, Nelson. 224 p.; bibliog. p. 210-6. $16. 0-8407-5437-X.

1343 *Wigtil* David N.,   The independent value of ancient religious translations: ➤ 574, ANRW 2/16/3 (1984) 2052-2066.

D8   *Concordantiae, lexica specialia* – **Specialized dictionaries, synopses**.

1344 Concordance to the Peshitta version of the Aramaic New Testament 1985 ➤ **1**,1783; English dictionary supplement to the concordance. New Knoxville OH 1985, American Christian. 59 p. $2.95. – RRelStR 12 (1986) 154 (J. H. *Charlesworth*: exaggerations, chiefly in preface; English supplement of little use to learner, who needs vocalized Syriac text).

1344* **Mulder** H.,   Klein Lexicon van bibjbelse namen 1982 ➤ 65,1652: RGerefTTs 86 (1986) 42 (C. *Houtman*).

1345 **Neirynck** Frans, *Van Segbroeck* Frans,   New Testament vocabulary; a companion volume to the concordance: BiblETL 65, 1984 ➤ 65,1653; **1**,1882: REstB 44 (1986) 242s (A. *Rodriguez Carmona*).

1346 *Neirynck* F.,   New Testament Vocabulary [1984], corrections and supplement: ETL 62 (1986) 134-140.

1347 **Schierse** F. J.,   Konkordanz zur Einheitsübersetzung 1985 ➤ **1**,1887: RBiKi 41 (1986) 45s (R. *Russ*).

1348 ᴱStrothman Werner, Konkordanz zur syrischen Bibel: Die Propheten:
GöOrF 1/25, 1984 ➤ 65,1656: ᴿBiblica 67 (1986) 587s (T. *Franxman*);
WeltOr 17 (1986) 185s (R. M. *Voigt*); BO 43 (1986) 190-3 (M. J. *Mulder*).

IV. ➤ Kl	V. Exegesis generalis VT vel cum NT

D9   Commentaries on the whole Bible or OT.

1350 [Beaumont P. de ...] La Bible 'Mame' des jeunes [➤ 1,1798*]. P 1986,
Mame. 380 p. F 145. 2-7289-0230-5. – ᴿMondeB 46 (1986) 55s (F.
Brossier).
1351 ᴱBruce F. F., The international Bible commentary [one volume, based on
NIV; ¹1979 was RSV]. GR 1986, Zondervan. xv-1629 p. $24.95. 0-551-
01291-9. – ᴿSWJT 29 (1986s) 62 (A. *Fasol*).
1352 Chouraqui André, Un pacte neuf, le NT 1984 ➤ 1,1895: ᴿVSp 139 (1985)
414-6 (J. *Jordan*).
1353 ᴱFuller R. C., *Johnston* L., *Kearns* C., A new Catholic commentary on
Holy Scripture [³; ¹1953 ➤ 35,1363; ²1969 ➤ 50,1426]. Nv 1986, Nelson.
xix-1363 p. $35.
1354 ᴱGaebelein Frank E. †, Expositor's Bible Commentary [➤ 64,1910;
65,1659], 6: Isaiah, Jeremiah, Ezekiel. GR 1986, Zondervan. 996 p.
0-310-36480-9. [ExpTim 98,347].
1355 Henry M. *al.*, Bethany parallel commentary on the OT (his dated
comments at the side of two others). Minneapolis 1985. $50. – ᴿCalvaryB
2,2 (1986) 71 (G. H. *Lovik*).
1356 Kohlenberger J. R.ᴵᴵᴵ, The NIV interlinear Hebrew-English Old Testament
4. Isaiah-Malachi. xiv-591 p. $25. 0-310-38880-5 [ExpTim 98,158].
1357 Parker T. H. L., CALVIN's Old Testament commentaries. E 1986, Clark.
239 p. £15. 0-567-09365-4. [Pent. Ps. Is.]. – ᴿCalvinT 21 (1986) 241-5
(R. C. *Gamble*); ExpTim 98 (1986s) 86 (J. W. *Rogerson*); Themelios 12
(1986s) 94 (D. F. *Wright*).
1358 *Snyman* S. D., Oor die gebruik van 'n kommentaar by die eksegese van
die Ou Testament: NduitseGT 27 (1986) 51-4 [< GerefTTs 86,191].
1359 ᴱStuhlmueller Carroll, *McNamara* Martin, Old Testament message; a
biblical theological interpretation. Wilmington 1981-4, Glazier. – Data on
23 volumes in KirSef 59 (1985) 304s.
1360 ᴱWalvoord John F., *Zuck* Roy B., The Bible knowledge commentary, an
exposition of the Scriptures by Dallas Seminary faculty. Wheaton IL
1985s, Victor. I. OT, 1589 p.; II. NT, 991 p. 0-88207-813-5; NT 2-7.
1361 ᴱZodhiates Spiros, The Hebrew-Greek key study Bible, King James
version [with Strong's concordance and some notes of his own].
Chattanooga 1984, AMG. 1743 p. $39. – ᴿCalvaryB 2,1 (1986) 69 (G. H.
Lovik: not recommended).

VI. Libri historici VT

E1   Pentateuchus, Torah .1 *Textus, commentarii.*

1362 Amigo Lorenzo, El Pentatéuco de Constantinopla y la Biblia romanceada judeoespañola – criterios y fuentes de traducción. (diss.) Sa-

lamanca 1983, Univ. Pontificia. 300 p. – ᴿRÉJ 145 (1986) 156-8 (H. V. *Sephiha*).
Dočʻanasvili E., Georgian Pentateuch-Jos-Jg → 1258.
1363 **Greenbaum** Aharon, ❿ *Peruš ha-Torâh*, The biblical commentary of Rav Samuel BEN HOFNI according to Geniza manuscripts. J 1978 [→ 61,2738; 62,2152]: ᴿTarbiz 55 (1985s) 269-278 (R. *Brody*) & 279-291 (J. *Blau*); Eng. V.
1363* **Hertz** Joseph H., ⓦ Mózes öt könyve és a haftárák; héber szöveg, magyar fordítás és kommentár, ᵀ*Hevesi* Simon, *al.*². Budapest 1984, Akadémiai Kiadó. xx-544 p.; xiv-613 p.; xiv-478 p. xiv-484 p.; xiv-624 p.; maps; music. [KirSef 59,293].
1364 *Júnior* M. A., Argumentação no Comentário de FÍLON de Alexandria ao Pentateuco: Euphrosyne 13 (1985) 9-26 [< JStJud 17,137].
1364* **Levy** B. Barry, Targum Neophyti 1 [introd.; Gn, Ex], a textual study: Studies in Judaism. Lanham MD 1986, UPA. xix-450 p. 0-8191-5464-4; pa. 5-2.
1365 ᴱLohr Charles, Berndt Rainer, ANDREAS de Sancto Victore, Opera, I: Expositio super Heptateuchum: CCMed 53. Turnhout 1986, Brepols. xxi-254 p. 2-503-03531-0; pa. 2-9.
1365* **Peters** Melvin K. H., A critical edition of the Coptic (Bohairic) Pentateuch [1 Genesis; 1982 → 63,1995] 2. Exodus: SBL SeptCog 19.22. Atlanta 1985s, Scholars. xvii-137 p.; xii-111 p. $12 each, pa. $9 [JSS 32,370, K. H. *Kuhn*].
1366 ᴱSandler Pereș, ❽ Moses MENDELSOHN's commentary on the Torah, intr. *Klausner* J. J 1984, Maas. 249 p. [KirSef 59,296].

E1   *Pentateuchus*   .2 **Introductio; Fontes JEDP**

1366* *Berge* Kåre, Jahvistens tid; til dateringen av noen jahvistiske fedretekster: diss. Oslo 1985. – NorTTs 87 (1986) 40.
1367 *Bloom* Harold [→ 1,1915], From J to K, or The uncanniness of the Yahwist: → 385, ᴱ*McConnell* F., Bible and narrative 1983/6, ...
1368 *Diebner* Bernd J., 'Von der Notwendigkeit "einer umfassenden Neu-analyse des pentateuchischen Erzählungsgutes"' [G. von *Rad*, als Motto zitiert in E. *Blum* 1984]: DiehlB 22 (1985) 193-215.
1368* *Hildebrand* David R., A summary of recent findings in support of an early date for the so-called priestly material of the Pentateuch: JEvTS 29 (1986) 129-138 [< ZIT].
1369 *Labuschagne* C. L., Neue Wege und Perspektiven in der Penta-teuchforschung: VT 36 (1986) 146-162.
1370 **Noth** M., ❶ Mōse Gosho Densho-Ki [Überlieferungsgeschichte des Pentateuchs 1948], ᵀ*Yamaga* T. with bibliography update. Tokyo 1986, Nihon Kirisuto Kyōdan. 456 + 13 p. Y 5200 [BL 87,72].
1371 *Prinsloo* W. S., Response to J. A. *Loader*, 'The exilic period in Abraham KUENEN's account of Israelite religion': ZAW [96 (1984) 3-23] 98 (1986) 267-271 [Kuenen was first to use the term P; we should speak of the Graf-Kuenen-Wellhausen hypothesis].
1372 *Rose* Martin, La croissance du corpus historiographique de la Bible — une proposition [conférence Neuchâtel 1985]: RTPhil 118 (1986) 217-236.
1373 **Tengström** Sven, Die Toledotformel und die literarische Struktur der priesterlichen Erweiterungsschicht im Pentateuch: ConBibOT 17,1982 → 63,1982 ... 1,1681: ᴿJNES 45 (1986) 155s (J. D. *Levenson*).

1374 **Zaman** L., R. RENDTORFF en zijn 'Das überlieferungsgeschichtliche Problem des Pentateuch' [lic. diss. Bru ᴰ*Jagersma* H.] 1984 ➤ 1,1930: ᴿCBQ 48 (1986) 549s (C. T. *Begg*: some verve, some faults); NRT 108 (1986) 112 (J.-L. *Ska*); TLZ 111 (1986) 347-9 (K.-D. *Schunck*).

E1.3   *Pentateuchus,* **themata.**

1375 **Andrade** Barbara, Encuentro con Dios en la historia [Pentateuco; *Pannenberg* W., *Cullmann* O. ...] 1985 ➤ 1,1932: ᴿBrotéria 128 (1986) 576 (I. *Ribeiro*); CiTom 113 (1986) 398s (J. L. *Espinel*); ComSev 19 (1986) 83s (V. J. *Ansede Alonso*); NatGrac 32 (1985) 302s (D. *Montero*); VerVid 44 (1986) 143s (D. *Cervera*).

1375* *Brunner-Traut* Emma, Volkserzählungen: ➤ 591, LexÄg 6,47 (1986) 1057-1061.

1376 **Doron** P., ❿ Interpretation of difficult passages in RASHI, 1. Genesis and Exodus. Hoboken 1985, Ktav. 277 p.; Eng. 4 p. $20. 0-88125-081-3 [BL 87,104, S. C. *Reif*].

1377 **Goldberg** Oscar, L'édifice des nombres dans le Pentateuque, avec une biographie de l'auteur par Gershom *Scholem*. P 1986, Tsédek. 83 p.

1378 **Meirovich** Harvey W., Judaism on trial; an analysis of the [1929-1939 (anti-WELLHAUSEN) Joseph] HERTZ Pentateuch: diss. Jewish Theol. Sem. NY 1986. 458 p. 86-13690. – DissA 47 (1986s) 1770-A.

1379 *Menezes* Rui de, The Pentateuchal theology of land: BibleBhashyam 12 (1986) 5-28.

1380 *a*) *Van Seters* John, The Yahwist as historian: ➤ 392, SBL Seminars 1986, 37-55. – *b*) *Diebner* Bernd J., Einige Anmerkungen zu John Van Seters methodischer Skizze 'The Yahwist as Historian I-II': DiehlB 22 (1985) 36-57.

1380*· *Wright* David F., CALVIN's Pentateuchal criticism; equity, hardness of heart, and divine accommodation: CalvinT 21 (1986) 33-50.

E1.4   **Genesis;** *textus, commentarii.*

1381 **Boice** James M., Genesis, an expositional commentary [I..] II (12,1-36,43); [III. ...]: Ministry Resources Library. GR 1985, Zondervan. 382 p. $17. 0-310-21569-9. – ᴿOTAbs 9 (1986) 332 (L. *Greenspoon*: 'most people who study the Scripture have little interest in becoming bogged down in a maze of complex technical and textual issues. They turn to the Bible to find heaven-sent guidance [which Boice gives them] for today's down-to-earth problems ... Chaperone your Children; It's a Wicked, Wicked World ...').

1382 ᵀᴱ**Brunner** Fernand, *al.*, Maître ECKHART, 'Le commentaire de la Genèse' précédé des 'Prologues' 1984 ➤ 65,1694: ᴿSpeculum 61 (1986) 230 (M. L. *Führer*).

1382* **Cattiani** Luigi, RASHI di Troyes, Commento alla Genesi, pref. *De Benedetti* P.: Ascolta Israele 1, 1985 ➤ 1, 1948: ᴿAntonianum 61 (1986) 769-771 (M. *Nobile*); ParVi 31 (1986) 77-80 (M. *Perani*).

1383 **Davidson** R., ❿ Sōseiki [Cambridge Bible Genesis 1-11 (1973) and 12-50 (1979) ➤ 60,2810], ᵀ*Ohno* Y. Tokyo 1986, Shinkyō Shuppan-sha. 394 p. Y 4200 [BL 87,46].

1383* ᵀ**Fox** Everett, In the beginning 1983 ➤ 64,1954: **1,**1953: ᴿJudaism 35 (1986) 114-6 (S. A. *Geller*).

1384 **Gispen** W. H., Genesis III (25:12 - 36:43): Commentaar op het OT. Kampen 1983, Kok. 180 p. ƒ39,85. – ᴿGerefTTs 86 (1986) 44s (C. *Houtman*).

1384* **Harl** Marguerite, La Genèse: La Bible d'Alexandrie, traduction du texte grec de la Septante, introduction et notes, 1. P 1986, Cerf. 337 p. 2-204-02591-7.

1385 T**Mercier** C., EPetit F., PHILON, Quaestiones et solutiones in Genesim IV-VI e versione armeniaca 1984 ➤ 65,1703; 1,1962: RRB 93 (1986) 467 (M.-J. Pierre); RÉG 99 (1986) 214 (A. Le Boulluec).

1386 **Neri** Umberto, Genesi, versione ufficiale italiana confrontata con ebraico masoretico, greco di Settanta, siriaco della Peshitta, latino della Vulgata; Targum Onqelos, Neofiti, Pseudo-Jonathan; commenti di autori greci (ORIGENE, CIRILLO A., ...): La Bibbia interpretata dalla grande Tradizione AT 1. T 1986, Gribaudi. cxlvi-662 p. Lit. 90.000. – RAntonianum 61 (1986) 771-3 (M. Nobile: progetto promettente, realizzazione frustrante).

1387 **Neveu** Louis, Avant Abraham (Genèse I-XI) 1984 ➤ 65,1739; 1,1978: RCBQ 48 (1986) 309s (J. I. Hunt: subtitled 'researches on the processes of biblical composition', far beyond JEP, plausible but ...).

1388 E**Paramelle** Joseph, (Lucchesi Enzo), PHILON... Genèse II 1-7: 1984 ➤ 65,1704; 1,1963: RJStJud 17 (1986) 113-5 (A. Hilhorst: Vatopedi 659 brought in photocopy from Athos by Marcel RICHARD in 1963); NRT 108 (1986) 425 (X. Jacques); RB 93 (1986) 467s (M.-J. Pierre); RÉByz 44 (1986) 298s (Marie-Hélène Congourdeau); TAth 57 (1986) 926 (P. V. Paschos); VigChr 40 (1986) 204s (D. T. Runia).

1389 E**Petit** Françoise, Catenae graecae in Genesim et in Exodum, II. Collectio Coisliniana in Genesim: CCG 15. Turnhout 1986, Brepols. cxiv-308 p. bibliog. p. ix-xvi. 2-503-40151-1; pa. 2-X.

1389* Rachman Josepha, ❻ Adoption of midrashim in RASHI's commentary on the Pentateuch: ➤ 246*, Teʿuda 3 (1983) 261-8; Eng. XVIII.

1390 **Ruppert** Lothar, Das Buch Genesis 2, Kap. 25,19-50,26: Geistliche Schriftlesung 6/2, 1984 ➤ 65,1705; 1,2334* [!]: RTLZ 111 (1986) 736s (H. Seidel).

1390* **Scharbert** Josef, Genesis [1-11,1983 ➤ 1,1965] 12-50: NEchter 16. Wü 1986, Echter. P. 121-307; DM 34, sb. 29. 3-428-01035-7 [ZAW 99,297, H.-C. Schmitt].

1391 T**Stanula** E., ❻ ORYGENES, Homilie o Księgach Rodzaju, Wyjścia, Kapłańskiej [Gn Ex Lv]: Pisma Starochrześcijańskich Pisarzy 31. Wsz 1984, Akad. Teol. Katolickiej. 278 p.; 248 p. [TLZ 112, 288, J. Rohde].

1392 Ta-Shema Ysrael, ❻ An unpublished early Franco-German commentary on Bereshit and Vayikra Rabba, Mekilta and Sifre: Tarbiz 55 (1985s) 61-75; Eng. II.

1393 **Tomić** Celestin, Prapovijest spasenja Knjiga Postanka, glava 1-11. Zagreb 1986, Prov. Franjevaca Konv. 299 p.

1394 Weismann F.J., Teología y simbolismo en 'De Genesi adversus Manichaeos' de S. AGUSTÍN: Stromata 42 (1986) 217-226.

1395 E**Weitzmann** Kurt, Kessler Herbert L., The Cotton Genesis; British Library Codex Cotton Otho B.VI. Princeton 1986, Univ. xiii-250 p.; 539 fig.; portr. bibliog. p. 239-245. 0-691-04031-1.

1396 **Westermann** C., Genesis I, 1-11, TScullion J.J. 1984 ➤ 65,1711; RAndrUnS 24 (1986) 74-77 (W.H. Shea); ScotJT 39 (1986) 130-3 (J.D. Martin: why 'primeval story'? and other comments on the translation); Themelios 12 (1986s) 25 (D.W. Baker: needs supplementing with canon criticism).

1397 **Westermann** Claus, Genesis TScullion J., II, 12-36. Minneapolis 1985, Augsburg. 604 p. $30. – RParadigms 2,1 (1986) 39s (K.H. Craig); TLZ 111 (1986) 265-7 (H.-J. Zobel: deutsch Lfg. 11-23); TTod 43 (1986s) 303s (P.D. Miller).

1397* **Westermann** C., Genesis III. 37-50; ᵀ*Scullion* J. J. Minneapolis 1986, Augsburg. 269 p. [TS 47,756].

1398 **Westermann** Claus, Am Anfang; I. Mose; Die Urgeschichte, Abraham, Jacob und Esau, die Josepherzählung [Verkürzung der drei Bände ➤ 65,1710]: Kleine biblische Bibliothek 1/2. Neuk 1986. ix-259 p.; vi-235 p.; p. 262-497. DM 48. 3-7887-0759-3. – ᴿTsTNijm 26 (1986) 407 (P. *Kevers*: 'Westerman' 'Bibliotheek').

1399 **Westermann** Claus, Genesis I-II, en praktische bijbelverklaring. Kampen 1986, Kok. 220 + 185 p. Fb 672 + 590 [CollatVl 16,508].

1400 ᵀᴱ**Zucker** Moshe, SAADYA's commentary on Genesis. NY 1984, Jewish Theol. Sem.

E1.5 *Genesis*, **themata**.

1401 [*Behaghel* Otto] ⁹**Taeger** Burkhard, Heliand und Genesis: Altdeutsche Textbibliothek 4. Tü 1984, Niemeyer. xxxii-294 p. DM 82; pa. 68. – ᴿSpeculum 61 (1986) 224 (H. *Maxwell*: virtually a new book).

1402 *Coats* George W., Genesis, with an introduction to narrative literature: FOTLit 1, 1983 ➤ 64,1953 ... 1,1949: ᴿCBQ 48 (1986) 102-4 (B. O. *Long*); GraceTJ 7 (1986) 130s (G. L. *Klein*); JBL 105 (1986) 130s (W. *Brueggemann*); ScrB 16 (1985s) 46s (S. *Greenhalgh*).

1403 *Daum* Schmuel, Penînê tôra, rabbinische Weisheiten zum Pentateuch; Gedanken und Lebensweisheiten jüdischer Interpreten und Ethiker zu den Wochenabschnitten Gen/Ex. Ba 1985, Goldschmidt. 414 p. [226 Verse für Kinder.] – ᴿFreibRu 37s (1985s) 113 (C. *Thoma*).

1404 a) Midrash Rabbah, Seder Berešit, with commentary Yešuot Ya'aqob. J/Brooklyn 1985-, Dov/Fekete. I, 501 + 500 p. – b) **Neusner** Jacob, [not = ➤ 1,1960, 3 vol.] Genesis and Judaism — the perspective of Genesis Rabbah, an analytical anthology: BrownJudSt 108. Atlanta 1985, Scholars. 208 p. $29; sb. $23. 0-89130-940-3. – ᴿExpTim 98 (1986s) 153s (Julia *Neuberger*: a great service). – c) **Neusner** Jacob, Comparative midrash; the plan and program of Genesis Rabbah and Leviticus Rabbah; BrownJudSt 111. Atlanta 1986, Scholars. xiii-211 p. $28. 0-89130-958-6; pa. 9-4. [NTAbs 30,377].

1406 **Franxman** Thomas W., Genesis and the 'Jewish Antiquities' of Flavius JOSEPHUS: BibOrPont 35, 1979 ➤ 60,2508 ... 65,1713: ᴿRÉJ 145 (1986) 430s (Madeleine *Petit*: apport non négligeable).

1407 **Galbiati** Enrico, **Piazza** Alessandro, Pagine difficili della Bibbia, AT⁵ʳᵉᵛ (¹1951, ⁴1966): Sorgenti di Vita 1, 1985 ➤ 1,1976: ᴿAntonianum 61 (1986) 775-7 (Z. I. *Herman*); BL (1986) 70: (R. *Murray*; one third on early Genesis problems, creation, original sin ...); RivB 34 (1986) 405-7 (Anna *Passoni Dell'Acqua*).

1407* *Ibañez Arana* Andrés, Los valores éticos de las narraciones del Génesis: Lumen 35 (Vitoria 1986) 361-396. 473-500.

1408 **Levison** John R., 'Adam' in major authors of early Judaism: diss. Duke, ᴰ*Charlesworth* James H. Durham NC 1985. 435 p. 86-08929. – DissA 47 (1986s) 558s-A.

1409 *Neusner* J., Genesis Rabbah as polemic; an intoductory account: ➤ 36, Mem. GOITEIN S. = HebAnR 9 (Columbus 1985) 253-265 [< NTAbs 31,80].

1410 **Owens** Robert J., The Genesis and Exodus citations of APHRAHAT 1983 ➤ 64,1964 ... 1,1981: ᴿOLZ 81 (1986) 493-6 (R. *Macuch*); RB 93 (1986) 632-4 (M. J. *Pierre*).

1410* *Peters* Edward, Aenigma Salomonis; Manichaean anti-Genesis polemic and the Vitium curiositatis in Confessions III,6: AugLv 36 (1986) 48-64.

1411 **Radday** Y.T., *Shore* H., Genesis, an authorship study in computer-assisted statistical linguistics: AnBib 103, 1985 ➤ 1,1982; 88-7654-103-3: ᴿBL (1986) 79 (M.P. *Weitzman*: their special pleading should not obscure the differences they show between P and JE; their claim of Gn unity is a massive non-sequitur); RB 93 (1986) 615s (É. *Nodet*).

1412 **Rendsburg** Gary A., The redaction of Genesis. Winona Lake IN 1986, Eisenbrauns. xii-129 p. $12.50. 0-931464-25-0 [OTAbs 10,197].

1413 *Robinson* Robert B., Literary functions of the genealogies of Genesis: CBQ 48 (1986) 595-608.

1414 *a) Talstra* Eep, Genesis bit by bit [*Radday* Y., *Shore* H. 1985]; – *b) Muraoka* Takamitsu, A computer-generated 'perfect' concordance?: Biblica 67 (1986) 557-564 / 565-7 [on 66 (1985) 438, *Talshir* Z.].

1415 *Testa Bappenheim* Italo, La 'mezzaluna fertile' delle scritture genesiache, alla luce del Concilio Vaticano II: BbbOr 28 (1986) 69-78.

E1.6 **Creatio**, *Genesis 1s.*

1416 *Abir* S., Was kann die anthropologische *bāśār*-Konzeption zur Deutung der Urgeschichte beitragen?: ZAW 98 (1986) 179-198.

1416* *a) Adinolfi* Marco, Origine dell'universo; Gen 1-2,4a; – *b) De Benedetti* Paolo, Interpretazioni ebraiche del racconto della creazione; – *c) Giannarelli* Elena, Approccio alle interpretazioni cristiane antiche del racconto della creazione; – *d) Zatelli* Ida, Il lessico della creazione; – *e) Buiatti* Marcello, Modelli evolutivi e specificità dell'uomo: ➤ 364*b*, In principio 1986, 37-55 / 85-107 / 111-146 / 173-181 / 185-238; 3 fig.

1417 **Asmussen** H.-G., Biblische Urgeschichte; Gen 1-11 neu durchdacht; Adam war nicht der erste Mensch[2rev]. Heide 1985, auct. (Markt 28, D-2240). v-91 p. [ZAW 99,132].

1418 *Beauchamp* Paul, Au commencement Dieu parle, ou les sept jours de la création: Études 365 (1986) 105-116.

1419 **Blocher** Henri, *a)* In the beginning; the opening chapters of Genesis 1984 ➤ 65,1720*a*; 1,1990: also DG,$6.95: ᴿBS 143 (1986) 374s (F.R. *Howe*); EvQ 58 (1986) 258s (D. *Alexander*). – *b)* La creazione — inizio della Genesi 1984 ➤ 65,1720*b*: ᴿProtestantesimo 41 (1986) 227s (G. *Scuderi*).

1419* *Brito* E., SCHELLING et la bonté de la création: NRT 108 (1986) 499-516.

1420 **Cimosa** Mario, Genesi 1-11; alle origini dell'uomo: LoB 1/1, 1984 ➤ 1,1994: ᴿParVi 30 (1985) 461-3 (G. *Marocco*).

1420* *a) Cimosa* Mario, L'uomo e il dominio della natura in Gn 1-3; – *b) Monari* Luciano, Luci e ombre sul lavoro nell'AT; – *c) Fanuli* Antonio, Desumanizzazione e umanizzazione del lavoro nella esperienza biblica; – *d) Cirignano* Giulio, Significato e valore del lavoro nei libri sapienziali; – *e) Canfora* Giovanni, Il lavoro in Paolo: ParVi 30 (1985) 19-26 / 11-18 / 27-33 / 40-49 / 50-53.

1421 ᴱ**Dales** Richard C., *Gieben* Servus, Robert GROSSETESTE, Hexaëmeron 1982 ➤ 65,1723: ᴿHeythJ 27 (1986) 459-461 (P.O. *Lewry*).

1422 **Donders** Joseph G., Creation and human dynamism; a spirituality for life [our concern for redemption leads us to overlook the power creation left in us]. Mystic CT 1985, Twenty-Third. 100 p. $6 pa. [TDig 33,359].

1423 **Eberlein** Karl, Gott der Schöpfer — Israels Gott; eine exegetisch-hermeneutische Studie zur theologischen Funktion alttestamentlicher Schöpfungsaussagen [Diss. Erlangen, ᴰ*Kutsch* E. – RTLv 18,541 sans date]: BeiATJ 5. Fra 1986, Lang. 471 p. Fs 76.

1424 **Fohr** S. D., Adam and Eve; the spiritual symbolism of Genesis and Exodus. Lanham MD 1986, UPA. xiii-147 p. $10.25 pa. [TDig 34,69].

1425 *a) Fronzaroli* P., I racconti paralleli sulla creazione del mondo nel Vicino Oriente antico [contro *Pettinato* P. su Ebla]; – *b) Garrone* D., Genesi 2, l'origine dell'uomo; – *c) Sacchi* P., Genesi 3 e il problema del male; – *d) Rizzi* A., Ruolo del racconto biblico nello sviluppo del concetto del male: ➤ 364, Atti del Seminario invernale 'In principio ...' F 1986, Associazione laica di cultura biblica (Settimello FI 1986; 308 p.) [< ZAW 99,282 senza pp.].

1425* **Gage** Warren A., The gospel of Genesis; studies in protology and eschatology 1984 ➤ 65,1726; 1,2006: ᴿRExp 83 (1986) 294 (J. D. W. *Watts*: strains credulity but shows value of close reading).

1426 **Ganoczy** Alexander, Doctrina de la creación [1983 ➤ 65,1727], ᵀ*Bazterrica* Victor: BiblTeología 7. Barc 1986, Herder. 208 p. – ᴿCiTom 113 (1986) 630s (E. *García*); NatGrac 33 (1986) 574s (A. *Villalmonte*).

1427 **Ganoczy** Alexandre, Schöpfungstheologie heute; Skizze eines Versuchs: TLZ 111 (1986) 561-570.

1428 **Gisel** Pierre, La création... 1980 ➤ 62,2213... 1,2007: ᴿRThom 86 (1986) 297-304 (J.-M. *Maldamé*, très détaillé dans une large synthèse scientifique).

1428* **Guibert** Pierre, [Gen 1-11] Les racines de la Parole; les récits des origines 1985 ➤ 1,2007*: ᴿEsprV 96 (1986) 136 (L. *Monloubou*).

1429 **Hellenkemper** G., La création du monde; les mosaïques de Saint-Marc à Venise. P 1986, Cerf. 52 p.; ill. [NRT 109,924, A. *Wankenne*].

1429* *Herrmann* Siegfried, Die Naturlehre des Schöpfungsberichtes; Erwägungen zur Vorgeschichte von Genesis 1 [< TLZ 86 (1961) 413-424]: ➤ 171, Ges. St. 1986, 32-46.

1430 *Janssen* L. F., Weitere Beobachtungen zur creatio [lat. Gebrauch]: Mnemosyne 39 (1986) 365-382.

1431 *Jervell* Jacob, Adam: ➤ 587, EvKL 1 (1986) 40s.

1431* *Kamin* Sarah, RASHBAM's conception of the creation in light of the intellectual currents of his time: ➤ 251*, ᴱ*Japhet* S., ScrHieros 31 (1986) 91-132.

1432 *Keel* Othmar, Vernachlässigte Aspekte biblischer Schöpfungstheologie: KatBlätt 111 (Mü 1986) 168-179 [< ZIT].

1433 **Kikawada** I. M., **Quinn** A., Before Abraham was; the unity of Genesis 1-11, 1985 ➤ 1,2010: ᴿBL (1986) 73 (R. N. *Whybray*: stimulating but not solid).

1435 *Martín* Juan Pablo, La presencia de FILÓN en el Hexameron de TEÓFILO de Antioquía: Salmanticensis 33 (1986) 147-177; Eng. 177.

1436 *Mask* E. Jeffrey, Concepts from the doctrine of creation in the Kabbalah in the work of Jürgen MOLTMANN [... God our Mother]: Paradigms 2,1 (1986) 16-32.

1437 **Müller** A. M. Klaus, *Pasolini* Paul, *Braun* Dietrich, Schöpfungsglaube heute. Neuk 1985, Neuk.-V. 219 p. DM 22. – ᴿTGl 76 (1986) 357-9 (W. *Beinert*).

Nestle D., Schöpfung im Lichte des ersten Evangeliums 1985 ➤ 3331.

1438 **Niditch** Susan, Chaos to cosmos 1985 ➤ 1,2017: ᴿAustralBR 34 (1986) 66s (J. J. *Scullion*); BibTB 16 (1986) 157 (Pauline *Viviano*); ÉglT 17 (1986) 85s (W. *Vogels*: not much new); Horizons 13 (1986) 414s (R. J. *Clifford*); IrBSt 8 (1986) 46s (T. D. *Alexander*: fascinating, but).

1439 **Oneta** M., Le origini della letteratura esameronale negli autori cristiani antichi: diss. Univ. Cattolica, ᴰ*Pizzolato* P. L. Milano 1984 [RivB 35,86].

1439* **O'Shaughnessy** Thomas J., Creation and the teaching of the Qur'ān 1985: **1**,2018: ᴿExpTim 98 (1986s) 318 (W. M. *Watt*).

1440 *Pagels* Elaine H., Exegesis and exposition of the Genesis creation accounts in selected texts from Nag Hammadi: ➤ 374, ᴱ*Hedrick* C., Nag Hammadi 1983/6, 257-285 [221-238, *Perkins* Pheme ➤ d279].

1440* *a)* *Paul* André, Le récit de la Création dans les Antiquités juives de Flavius Josèphe; traduction et commentaire; – *b)* *Winston* David, Theodicy and creation of man in Philo of Alexandria; – *c)* *Radice* Roberto, Ipotesi per una interpretazione della struttura della Kosmopoiia nel De opificio mundi di Filone di Alessandria: ➤ 81, Mem. Nikiprowetzky V., Hellenica 1986, 129-137 / 105-111 / 69-78.

1441 **Ravalico** Domenica E., La creazione non è una favola. T 1986, Paoline. 184 p. Lit. 12.000. – ᴿBbbOr 28 (1986) 171s (D. *Sardini*; p. 172 correzione a p. 171 del libro recensito: Carl Sagan è astronomo, non astronautá).

1442 **Riccati** Carlo, 'Processio' et 'explicatio'; la doctrine de la création chez Jean Scot et Nicolas de Cues: Ist. Ital. St. Filosofici 6, 1983 ➤ **1**,2020: 88-7088-076-1: ᴿGregorianum 67 (1986) 153 (L. *Ladaria*).

1442* *a)* *Römer* Thomas, Genèse 1 et son milieu d'origine; – *b)* *Heintz* Jean-Georges, 'L'homme créé à l'image de Dieu'; – *c)* *Menu* Bernadette, Les récits de création en Égypte ancienne; – *d)* *Salles* Catherine, Les récits de création dans le monde grec: FoiVie 85,3 (CahBib 25, 1986) 19-29 / 53-64 / 65-77 / 79-86.

1443 *Schäfer* Peter, Adam in der jüdischen Überlieferung: ➤ 268, ᴱ*Strolz* W., Vom alten zum neuen Adam [TLZ 112,505] 69-93.

1444 *Timm* Roger E., Let's not miss the theology of the creation accounts: CurrTM 13 (1986) 97-105.

1445 *Vallin* Pierre, Les 'soirées' de Joseph de Maistre; une création théologique originale [... cosmologie; pensée des origines; marche temporelle de la Providence ...]: RechSR 74 (1986) 341-362.

1446 **Waschke** E.-J., Untersuchungen zum Menschenbild der Urgeschichte; ein Beitrag zur alttestamentlichen Theologie [Diss. Leipzig 1979, ᴰ*Wagner* S. ➤ 61,7811]: TArb 43. B 1984, EvV. 244 p. ➤ 65,1749; DM 17,50: ᴿZAW 98 (1986) 157s (H.-C. *Schmitt*).

1447 *Winston* David, Creation ex nihilo revisited; a reply to Jonathan Goldstein: JSS [35 (1984) 127-135] 37 (1986) 88-91.

1447* **Wolters** Albert M., Creation regained. Leicester 1985, Inter-Varsity. 98 p. £4. 0-85110-757-5 [ExpTim 98,254].

1448 **Zenger** Erich, Gottes Bogen in den Wolken; Untersuchungen zu Komposition und Theologie der priesterschriftlichen Urgeschichte: SBS 112, 1983 ➤ 64,6026; 65,1751: ᴿBiKi 41 (1986) 51s (F. J. *Stendebach*).

1448* **Manns** Frédéric, [Gn 1,2] Le symbole eau – Esprit: SBFAnal 19, 1983 ➤ 64,2035 ... **1**,2027: ᴿBZ 30 (1986) 303-6 (J. *Maier*).

1449 *Paradise* Bryan, Food for thought [*dešeh, 'ēśeb, 'eṣ pᵉrî*]; the Septuagint translation of Genesis 1,11-12: ➤ 63, ᶠMcKane W., A word 1986, 177-204.

1450 **Van Till** Howard J., [Gn 1,14-19] The fourth day; what the Bible and the heavens are telling us about the creation. GR/Exeter 1986, Eerdmans/Paternoster. 286 p. 0-8028-0178-1. – ᴿExpTim 98 (1986s) 382 (A. *Ford*); SWJT 29,2 (1986s) 65 (L. R. *Bush*: queries 'Calvinisticly' two-realm truth, science and religion); WestTJ 48 (1986) 410-2 (R. C. *Newman*: little is said about the fourth day).

1451 *Nascimento Washington* Roberto, [Gn 1,21; Prov. 1,4] Alguns problemas de tradução à luz da nova versão revisada 'de acordo com os melhores textos em hebraico e grego' e do Velho Testamento hebraico e da Septuaginta: RTBat 2 (1986) 72s.

1452 *a) Pérez Fernández* Miguel, Targum y midrás sobre Gn 1,25-27; 27; 3,7.21; la creación de Adán en el Targum de Pseudo-Jonatán y en Pirqé de Rabbi Eliezer; – *b) Guillén Torralba* Juan, Motivos tópicos en cuatro leyendas cósmicas de Génesis [2s; 6ss; 11; 18s]: ➤ 21, Mem. DÍEZ MACHO A., Salvación 1986, 471-487 / 157-183.

Gn 1,26, imago Dei – ➤ 1442*b*.

1453 *Ebach* J., Bild Gottes und Schrecken der Tiere; zur Anthropologie der priesterlichen Urgeschichte: ➤ 155, Ursprung 1986, 16-47 [111-125, Gen 2s].

1454 **Fantino** Jacques, L'homme image de Dieu chez saint Irénée de Lyon [diss.]: Thèses. P 1986, Cerf. viii-264 p. – [R]RThom 86 (1986) 479s (H. *Crouzel*).

1455 **Hall** Douglas J., Imaging [i.e. being the image of] God; dominion as stewardship. Exeter/GR 1986, Paternoster/Eerdmans. viii-248 p. £8. 0-8028-0244-3. [R]ExpTim 98 (1986s) 381 (J. *Mahoney* gives date as 1968, and contents as ecological).

1456 **Hoekema** Anthony A., Created in God's image. GR 1986, Eerdmans. 264 p. $20 [RelStR 13,248, T. D. *Kennedy*].

1457 *O'Donovan* Joan E., Man in the image of God; the disagreement between BARTH and BRUNNER reconsidered: ScotJT 39 (1986) 433-459.

1457* *Léna* Marguerite, L'image de Dieu; échos de Genèse 1,26 dans un cœur chrétien: FoiVie 85,6 (1986) 19-31.

1458 *Kurz* William S., Genesis [1,26s] and abortion; an exegetical text of a biblical warrant in ethics: TS 47 (1986) 668-680.

1459 *Heinen* K., 'Macht euch die Erde untertan' (Gen 1,28); Sinn und Wirkungsgeschichte eines biblischen Wortes: ➤ 313, Christsein 1986, 130-141.

1460 *Sandlin* Bryce, To have dominion over the earth: BibIll 12 (1986) 12-16 [OTAbs 10,83].

1461 *Sardini* Fausto, La terra casa dell'uomo; *kabas* e *radah*: BbbOr 28 (1986) 65-67; 68, Sardini sostituisce MONTAGNINI F. come redattore.

1462 *a) Stendebach* F. J., L'uomo creato come coppia (Gn 1,26-28); – *b) Virgulin* S., La fecondità della coppia; crescete e moltiplicatevi; – *c) Schüngel-Straumann* Helen, Il comandamento biblico sui genitori; – *d) Rochettes* Jacqueline des, Il mistero della famiglia nella tradizione ebraica; – *e) Meloni* P., La pastorale dei Padri sulla famiglia: ParSpV 14 (1986) 13-28 / 29-41 / 43-58 / 89-105 / 195-218 (-272).

1463 *a) Schenker* Adrian, Die Segnung des siebten Schöpfungstages; zum besonderen Segen in Gen 2,3; – *b) Rordorf* Willy, Die theologische Bedeutung des Sonntags bei AUGUSTIN; Tradition und Erneuerung: ➤ 10, [F]BAUMGARTNER J., Der Sonntag 1986, 19-29 / 30-43.

E1.7   *Genesis 1s*: **Bible and myth** [➤ M3.5].

1464 *Adelowo* E. Dada, A comparative study of creation stories in Yoruba religion, Islam and Judeo-Christianity: AfJT 15 (1986) 29-53.

1465 **Carre Gates** Marie-Henriette,   Casting Tiamat into another sphere;
sources for the 'Ain Samiya [NW Jericho] goblet: Levant 18 (1986) 75-81;
1 fig.; pl. XIII-XV.

1466 **Castel** François,   Commencements; les onze premiers chapitres de la Genèse; parole de Dieu et mythes de l'Orient ancien: Dossiers pour l'animation biblique 7, 1985 ➤ 1,2049:   – ᴿRechSR 74 (1986) 617 (J. *Briend*).

1467 **Day** John,   God's conflict with the dragon and the sea 1985 ➤ 1,2051:
ᴿJSS 31 (1986) 243-5 (M. C. A. *Korpel*, J. C. de *Moor*); NedTTs 40 (1986)
242 (K. A. D. *Smelik*); RB 93 (1986) 463s (J.-M. de *Tarragon*: Psalms
dated too early); VT 36 (1986) 495-9 (J. F. *Healy*); ZAW 98 (1986) 307s
(G. *Wanke*).

1467* **De Lano** Joan H.,   The 'exegesis' of Enuma Elish and Genesis 1: 1875
to 1975; a study in interpretation: diss. Marquette. Milwaukee 1985.
324 p. 86-04952. – DissA 47 (1986s) 214-A.

1468 *a) Chiozzi* Paolo, I miti dell'origine dell'uomo presso le culture primitive;
– *b) Poletto* Giannina, Cosmologia d'oggi: ➤ 364*b*, In principio 1986,
15-33 / 245-262 / 59-81.

1468* **Gibert** Pierre, Bible, mythes et récits de commencement: Parole de Dieu.
P 1986, Seuil. 287 p. F 95. 2-02-009379-0.

1469 **Graves** R., *Patai* R., Los mitos hebreos. M 1986, Alianza. 276 p. –
ᴿCiuD 199 (1986) 563 (J. L. del *Valle*); RazF 214 (1986) 249s (M. *Alcalá*).

1469* **Guilhou** Nadine, Réfléxions sur la conception du mal à travers quelques
grands mythes antiques: ➤ 18, Mém. DAUMAS F., II (1986) 361-371.

1470 *Hallbäck* Geert, Lignelse [comparison] – myte – dekonstruktion: DanTTs
49 (1986) 32-50 [< ᴢɪᴛ].

1471 **Hutter** Manfred, Altorientalische Vorstellungen von der Unterwelt;
literar- und religionsgeschichtliche Überlegungen zu 'Nergal und
Ereškigal': OBO 63, 1985 ➤ 1,2058: ᴿRB 93 (1986) 462 (M. R. *Sigrist*).

1472 *Hutter* Manfred, *ammatu*, Unterwelt in Enuma Eliš I 2: RAss 79 (1985)
187s.

1473 **Jacobsen** Thorkild, The Harab myth: SourANE 2/3, 1984 ➤ 65,1768;
0-89003-158-4: ᴿBO 43 (1986) 445.

1474 **Kaiser-Minn** Helga, Die Erschaffung des Menschen auf der spätantiken
Monumenten 1981 ➤ 62,2220... 65,1733: ᴿAnzAltW 39 (1968) 105s (R.
Pillinger).

1475 **Kunz** Bruno, Himmel, Erde, Urflut; das geheime Weltbild im Alten
Orient. Wien 1981, Böhlau. 172 p.; (color.) ill. [KirSef 59,315].

1476 *a) Lambert* W. G., Ninurta mythology in the Babylonian epic of
creation; – *b) Groneberg* Brigitte, Eine Einführungsszene in der
altbabylonischen Literatur; Bemerkungen zum persönlichen Gott: ➤ 543,
Rencontre 32, 1985/6, 55-60 / 93-108.

1477 **Lincoln** Bruce, Myth, cosmos, and society; Indo-European theme of
creation and destruction. CM 1986, Harvard Univ. viii-278 p. $22.50
[TDig 33,369].

1478 **McCurley** Foster R., Ancient myths and biblical faith; Scriptural
transformations 1983 ➤ 64,2058... 1,2060: ᴿBA 49 (1986) 61s (Z. *Zevit*).

1479 **Maclagan** David, Schöpfungsmythen, ᵀ*Schaup* Susanne. Mü 1985,
Kösel. 96 p.; 130 fig. + 19 color. – ᴿZkT 108 (1986) 89 (G. *Fischer*: aus
der amerikanischen Reihe 'Art and Imagination').

1480 *Mafico* T. J., The ancient and biblical view of the universe: JTSAf 54
(1986) 3-14.

1481 **Mann** Ulrich, Schöpfungsmythen; vom Ursprung und Sinn der Welt
1982 ➤ 63,2090; 64,2059: ᴿAnthropos 81 (1986) 738 (H.-J. *Findeis*).

1482 *Naddaf* Gérard, Hésiode, précurseur des cosmogonies grecques de type
'évolutionniste' [... compare Enuma Elish]:   RHR 203 (1986) 339-364;
Eng. 339.
1482* *Ohlig* Karl-Heinz, Ausserbiblische und biblische Schöpfungsvorstellun-
gen: Diakonia 17 (1986) 221-230.
1483 *Podbielski* Henryk, Le chaos et les confins de l'univers dans la Théogonie
d'Hésiode: ÉtClas 54 (1986) 253-263.
1484 **Ranke-Graves** Robert von, Hebräische Mythologie; über die Schöp-
fungsgeschichte und andere Mythen aus dem Alten Testament. 1986,
Reinbek [GeistL 59,308].
1484* [E]**Rosemont** Henry[J], Explorations in early Chinese cosmology. Atlanta
1984, Scholars. 171 p. $19.50; sb. $13. – [R]JAAR 54 (1986) 605-7 (C.
LeBlanc).
1485 *Smith* Morton, P Leid J 395 (PGM XIII) and its creation legend
[Abraxas: *Dieterich* A. 1891, *Reitzenstein* R. 1913]: ➤ 81, Mém.
NIKIPROWETZKY V., Hellenica 1986, 491-8.
1485* *Waschke* Ernst-Joachim, Mythos als Strukturelement und Denkka-
tegorie biblischer Urgeschichte: TVers 16 (1986) 9-22.
1486 **Westman** Heinz, The structure of biblical myths 1983 ➤ 65,1801; 1,2064:
[R]HeythJ 27 (1986) 71 (G. *Every*).
1487 **Wolkstein** Diane, *Kramer* Samuel N., Il mito sumero della vita e
dell'immortalità; i poemi della dea Inanna [1983] [T]1985 ➤ 1,2067: [R]CC
137 (1986,4) 91s (G. L. *Prato*); Salesianum 48 (1986) 785 (R. *Sabin*: prima
storia d'amore del mondo, di duemila anni più vecchia della Bibbia).

E1.8   Genesis 1s: The Bible, the Church, and Science.

1488 *Altner* Günter, Evolution, Evolutionismus: ➤ 587, EvKL 1 (1986) 1222-7.
1489 **Arcidiacono** Vincenzo, Scienza e fede. Cosenza 1984, Giordano. 246 p.
Lit. 15.000. – [R]Gregorianum 67 (1986) 187s (F. *Selvaggi*).
1490 *Baldner* Steven, Creation and science: CanadCathR 4 (May 1986)...
1491 **Bartholomew** David J., God of chance 1984 ➤ 65,1805; 1,2074: [R]JTS 37
(1986) 285 (B. *Hebblethwaite*).
1492 **Bergeron** Ernest, Le Christ universel et l'évolution selon TEILHARD de
Chardin. P 1986, Cerf. 192 p. F 65 [ÉTRel 61,623].
1492* *Blandino* Giovanni, Una dottrina contraddittoria; il darwinismo [*Mayr*
E. 1981 ...]: RasT 27 (1986) 241-253.
1493 *Bliss* Richard B., Evolution vs. Science: Christian Herald (July 1985)
40-42 [< BS 143 (1986) 71].
1493* a) *Bolognesi* Pietro, Credere nel Dio creatore; – b) *Reid* W. Stanford,
Fede cristiana e scienza, [T]*Grosso* S.; – c) *Fackerell* Edward O., Insegnare
le scienze in un'ottica cristiana, [T]*Regruto* A.: STEv 16 (1985) 153-8 /
159-189 / 190-241.
1494 **Bosshard** Stefan N., Erschafft die Welt sich selbst? Die Selbstorgani-
sation von Natur und Mensch aus naturwissenschaftlicher, philosophischer
und theologischer Sicht: QDisp 103, 1985 ➤ 1,2081*: [R]REB 46 (1986)
224s (F. *Vering*).
1494* a) *Bresch* Carsten, Evolutionslehre und Schöpfungsglaube [➤ TDig
34,139]; – b) *Bosshard* Stefan N., Gegenwart und Zukunft des Schöp-
fungsprozesses; – c) *Eder* Gernot, Thesen zur Diskussion; Naturwissenschaft – Theologie: Diakonia 17 (1986) 230-240 / 240-5 /
246-250.
1495 *Britton* Barrie, Evolution by blind chance: ScotJT 39 (1986) 341-360.

1496 a) *Carles* Jules, Du singe à l'homme; – b) *Milet* Jean, Dieu créateur; création ou évolution?: EsprV 96 (1986) 74-78 / 65-74.85-89.
1497 **Chittick** Donald E., The controversy; roots of the creation-evolution conflict. Portland OR 1984, Multnomah. 280 p. $13. – ᴿGraceTJ 7 (1986) 254s (J. C. *Whitcomb*); SWJT 29,2 (1986s) 59 (L. R. *Bush*).
1498 **Davies** Paul, a) God and the new physics ➤ 65,1821; 1,2101; Hmw 1984, Penguin; 0-671-47688-2 [= L 1983, Dent]. 229 p. + varia. – ᴿIrBSt 8 (1986) 200s (J. T. *MacCormack*). – b) Dio e la nuova fisica. Mi 1984, Mondadori. 338 p. Lit. 16.500. – ᴿStPatav 33 (1986) 627s (P. *Campogalliani*).
1498* *Dijk* P. van, Eine neue Runde im Gespräch zwischen Naturwissenschaft und Theologie: ZdialektT 2 (Kampen 1986) 149 ... [< ZIT].
1499 **Dóriga** Enrique L., El universo de NEWTON y de EINSTEIN; introducción a la filosofia de la naturaleza. Barc 1985, Herder. 277 p. – ᴿAntonianum 61 (1986) 499s (E. *Mariani*).
ᴱ**Durant** J., Darwinism and divinity 1982/5 ➤ 426.
1500 **Fischer** Klaus, Galileo GALILEI [1983 ➤ 65,1826], ᵀ*Gancho* C. Barc 1986, Herder. 184 p. – ᴿNatGrac 33 (1986) 359s (M. *González*).
1501 **Ford** Adam, Universe; God, man and science. L 1986, Hodder & S. 220 p. £6.95. 0-340-39083-2. – ᴿExpTim 98 (1986s) 33s (C. S. *Rodd*: splendid).
1502 *Freudenthal* Gad, Cosmogonie et physique chez GERSONIDE: RÉJ 145 (1986) 295-314.
1503 *Galli* Giuseppe, Questioni insolute a proposito del processo di Galileo: Angelicum 63 (1986) 276-310 [... la pena era non solo in vista di un precetto personale, eppure sproporzionata alla legge generale esistente; come spiegare il fallimento del progetto distensivo del cardinale Maculano, e l'intransigenza di Urbano VIII?...].
1504 *Gauthier* Madeleine, La 'science cosmique' est-elle une science ou une religion?: SR 15 (1986) 29-41 [3-28 al., mouvements religieux récents].
1504* **Geymonat** L., GALILEO Galilei: Nexos 13. Barc 1986, Peninsula. 236 p. – ᴿComSev 19 (1986) 481s (M. *Sánchez*).
1505 **Gilkey** Langdon, Creationism on trial; evolution and God at Little Rock. Minneapolis 1985, Winston. vii-301 p. 0-86683-780-9. – ᴿRExp 83 (1986) 640-2 (Melody *Mazuk*).
1506 **Gilson** E., From Aristotle to Darwin and back again [1971], ᵀLyon J. 1984 ➤ 1,2112: ᴿNBlackf 67 (1986) 94-96 (C. C. W. *Taylor*: translation-defects); Thomist 50 (1986) 318-323 (F. F. *Centore*).
1507 **Glässer** Alfred, Evolutive Welt und christlicher Glaube (Pierre TEILHARD de Chardin 1881-1955) 1984 ➤ 65,1829: ᴿDivThom 88 (1985) 179s (G. *Sanguineti*, sic); FranzSt 67 (1985) 374s (J. *Decorte*); TPhil 61 (1986) 476s (R. *Koltermann*).
1508 **Gowlett** John A. J., Auf Adams Spuren; die Archäologie des frühen Menschen, ᵀ*Becker* Andrea. FrB 1985, Herder. 208 p.; 110 fig., 109 phot. + 125 color.; 23 maps. – ᴿSalesianum 48 (1986) 716s (R. *Sabin*).
1509 *Hall* Norman F. & *Lucia* K. B., Is the war between science and religion over? [no]: The Humanist (May 1986) 26-28.32 [< BS 143 (1986) 367].
1510 *Haikola* Lars, Den moderna världsbilden; en ny relation naturvetenskap-religion?: SvTKv 62 (1986) 59-68.
1511 **Hedtke** Randall, The secret of the sixth edition [of The origin of species, i.e. DARWIN dropped natural selection, aimed to ungod the universe]. NY 1983, Vantage. 136 p. – ᴿRelStR 12 (1986) 265 (G. W. *Coats*).

1512 **Henderson** Charles R.,   God and Science; the death and rebirth of theism. Atlanta 1986, Knox.   186 p. $11.   0-8042-0668-6. – RExpTim 98 (1986s) 156 (D. W. D. *Shaw*).

1513 **Herrmann** E.,   Erkenntnisansprüche; eine orientierende erkenntnistheoretische Untersuchung über Fragen zum Verhältnis zwischen Religion und Wissenschaft: Studia Philosophiae Religionis 12.   Malmö 1984, Gleerup.   127 p. – RNedTTS 40 (1986) 270-2 (J. *Geurts*).

1513* **Houtman** C., *al.*,   Schepping en evolutie; het creationisme een alternatief?   Kampen 1986, Kok.   145 p. *f* 22,50 [GerefTTs 86,3 cover].

1514 **Hummel** C. E.,   The GALILEO connection; resolving conflicts between Science and the Bible.   DG 1986, InterVarsity.   293 p. $9 pa.   0-87784-500-X [NTAbs 30,257].

1515 **Hyers** Conrad,   The meaning of creation; Genesis and modern science 1984 → 1,2125:   RBL (1986) 88 (R. J. *Coggins*); BS 143 (1986) 171 (F. R. *Howe*: rests wholly on the documentary theory); CBQ 48 (1986) 718s (J. G. *Gammie*).

1516 **Jaki** Stanley L.,   Angels, apes and men 1983 → 1,2126:   RDowR 104 (1986) 35-37 (C. *Wookey*).

1516* *Kaiser* Christopher B.,   CALVIN, COPERNICUS, and CASTELLIO: CalvinT 21 (1986) 5-31.

1517 **Kamp** W. van der,   Houvast aan het hemelruim; een pleidooi voor de bijbelse opvatting dat de zon om de aarde draait [Tycho BRAHE geocentrism].   Kampen 1985, Kok.   203 p. *f* 29,90. – RGerefTTs 86 (1986) 241s (C. *Houtman*).

1517* *Klaaren* Eugene M.,   Religious origins of modern science; belief in creation in seventeenth-century thought.   Lanham MD 1985, UPA.   244 p. $12.75 [JAAR 54,400].

1518 **Köhler** Udo,   Sündenfall und Urknall; biblischer Schöpfungsbericht und moderne Kosmologie.   Stu 1983, Quell.   95 p. [KirSef 59,315].

1519 EKohn David,   The Darwinian heritage [31 essays].   Princeton 1985, Univ.   xii-1138 p. [RelStR 13,269, J. C. *Livingston*].

1520 *Koloss* Hans-Joachim,   Der ethnologische Evolutionismus im 19. Jahrhundert; Darstellung und Kritik seiner theoretischen Grundlagen: ZEthnol 111 (1986) 15-46.

1521 EKoslowski Peter, *al.*,   *a*) Evolution und Freiheit; zum Spannungsfeld von Naturgeschichte und Mensch.   Stu 1984, Hirzel.   196 p. – *b*) Evolutionstheorie und menschliches Selbstverständnis; zur philosophischen Kritik eines Paradigmas moderner Wissenschaft.   Weinheim 1984, Acta Humaniora.   104 p. – CIVITAS Resultate 5 und 6 [gegründet München 1979]. – RTPhil 61 (1986) 474-6 (J. *Splett*).

1522 **Kropf** Richard W.,   Evil and evolution; a theodicy 1984 → 1,2143: RÉglT 17 (1986) 104-6 (J. *Pambrun*).

1523 *Landucci* Pier Carlo,   *a*) Il contagio teologico del darwinismo; – *b*) Il tavolo di prova della dignità umana: Renovatio 21 (1986) 97-114 / 222-234 [537: † 28.V].

1524 *a*) *Landucci* Pier Carlo.   La contagion théologique du darwinisme; – *b*) *Lefèvre* Luc J.,   Le péché originel et les sciences humaines: PenséeC 223 (1986) 19-35 / 36-52.

1525 *Livingstone* David N.,   B. B. WARFIELD, the theory of evolution and early fundamentalism: EvQ 58 (1986) 69-83.

1526 *Lucas* E. C.,   Some scientific issues related to the understanding of Genesis 1-3:   Themelios 12 (1986s) 46-51.

1527 **McGowan** Chris,   In the beginning... a scientist shows why creationists are wrong 1984 ➤ 65,1844; **1,**2140: ᴿSWJT 29,2 (1986s) 59s (L. R. *Bush*).

1527* a) *Mackey* James B., Theology, science and the imagination; exploring the issues; – b) *Lane* Dermot A., Theology and science in dialogue; – c) *Hamill* Thomas, The Bible and the imagination; a modest sounding of the harlot's evaluation: IrTQ 52 (1986) 1-8 / 31-53 / 96-108 [19-130 *al.*].

ᴱMcMullin Ernan, Evolution and creation 1983/6 ➤ 464.

1528 **Mahin** Mark, The new scientific case for God's existence. 1985, Mindlifter. 137 p. $9 [JAAR 54,210].

1529 *Montenat* C., *al.*, Pour lire la création dans l'Évolution 1984 ➤ **1,**2148: F 47: ᴿCC 137 (1986,2) 409s (G. *Blandino*); RThom 86 (1986) 294-6 (J.-M. *Maldamé*: synthèse très soignée; un des collaborateurs est prêtre, Pascal Roux).

1530 **Montenat** C., *Planteaux* L., *Roux* P., How to read the world; creation in evolution. L 1985, SCM. 126 p. £5.50. 0-334-02053-0. – ᴿExpTim 97 (1985s) 348 (C. A. *Russell*: Teilhardian scientists, near animism if not pantheism).

1531 **Morris** Henry M., The biblical basis for modern science. GR 1984, Baker. 516 p. – ᴿSWJT 29,2 (1986s) 50 (L. R. *Bush*: Darwinism wrong; the earth less than 20,000 years old).

1532 **Morris** Henry M., Creation and the modern Christian. El Cajon CA 1985, Master. 298 p. $9. – ᴿSWJT 29,2 (1986s) 61 (L. R. *Bush*).

1532* **Murphy** George L., The trademark of God; a Christian course in creation, evolution, and salvation. Wilton CT 1986, Morehouse-Barlow. xii-138 p. 0-8192-1382-9.

1533 **Nebelsick** Harold P., Circles of God; theology and science from the Greeks to Copernicus: Theology and science at the frontiers of knowledge 2. E 1985, Scottish Academic. xxviii-284 p. $24. 0-7073-0448-2. – ᴿExpTim 98 (1986s) 125 (C. A. *Russell*).

1533* **Nicolau** Francesc, L'evolucionisme, avui. Barc 1984, Terra Nostra. 187 p. – ᴿVerVid 44 (1986) 144 (D. *Cervera*).

1534 **Olson** Raymond, Science deified and science defied; the historical significance of science in western culture from the Bronze Age to the beginnings of the modern era. Berkeley 1982, Univ. California. xv-329. $42. – ᴿHeythJ 27 (1986) 359s (S. *Talmor*).

1535 **Ortoli** Sven, *Pharabod* Jean-Pierre, Le cantique des quantiques: le monde existe-t-il?: Science et société. P 1985, La découverte. 144 p. – ᴿRThom 86 (1986) 291 (J.-M. *Maldamé*: bon malgré le titre).

1535* **Ostovich** Steven T., History, theology, and the philosophy of science [METZ J.-B., KUHN T.]: diss. Marquette. Milwaukee 1986. 324 p. 87-08732. – DissA 47 (1986s) 4423-A.

1536 **Owens** Virginia S., And the trees clap their hands; faith, perception and the New Physics 1983 ➤ **1,**2160: ᴿSpTod 38 (1986) 380-2 (K. C. *Russell*).

1537 ᴱPagano S. M., I documenti del processo di G. GALILEI: Collectanea Archivi Vaticani 21, 1984 ➤ 65,1860; **1,**2161: ᴿRHE 81 (1986) 364 (R. *Aubert*: réédition du volume déjà réédité 1877, *Gebler* K. von; 1909, *Favaro* A.).

1538 *Pannenberg* Wolfhart, The doctrine of creation and modern science: EAsJT 4,1 (Singapore 1986) 33-46.

1539 **Paul** Iaian, Science, theology and EINSTEIN 1982 ➤ 65,1861; **1,**2162: ᴿExpTim 98 (1986s) 124 (R. *Stannard*).

1540 **Peacocke** Arthur, God and the new biology. L 1986, Dent. 198 p. £11. 0-460-04699-3. – ᴿExpTim 98 (1986s) 97s (C. S. *Rodd*).

1541 **Peacocke** Arthur, Intimations of reality; critical realism in science and religion 1983/4 ➤ 1,2163: RNedTTs 40 (1986) 355s (J. van *Brakel*).

1542 *a) Pearson* Samuel C., Science and theological enterprise in early modern Europe; – *b) Grant* C. David, Science and natural theology rewed?: Encounter 47 (1986) 27-40 / 99-108.

1543 **Pitman** Michael, Adam and evolution. L 1984, Rider. 269 p. $13. – RBS 143 (1986) 370 (F. R. *Howe*: Cambridge University biology teacher; highly recommended); SWJT 29,2 (1986s) 60 (L. R. *Bush*: the Rock of Ages is more important than the ages of the rocks).

1544 **Polkinghorne** John, One world; the interaction of science and theology. L 1986, SPCK. £4.50. 0-281-04188-1. – RCleR 71 (1986) 192s (M. *Sharratt*); ExpTim 97 (1985s) 225s (C. S. *Rodd*); NBlackf 67 (1986) 344s (P. *Hodgson*); TLond 39 (1986) 386s (J. *Habgood*).

1544* EPoupard Paul card., Scienza e fede [indagine mondiale sulla fede fra scienziati ...]. Casale Monferrato 1986, Piemme. 198 p. Lit. 16.000. – RCiVit 41 (1986) 291s (Susanna *Bellizzi*).

1545 EPoupard Paul, Galileo GALILEI: Cultures et dialogue 1, 1983 ➤ 1,2170a: RRTLv 17 (1986) 107s (D. *Chavée*).

1546 **Redondi** Pietro, Galilée hérétique, TAymard M.: Bibliothèque des Idées, 1983 ➤ 64,2144: RÉtudes 365 (1986) 551s (F. *Russo*); RHPR 66 (1986) 366s (P. *Racine*).

1547 *Reid* W. Stanford, Sir J. William DAWSON on creation and evolution: RefTR 45 (1986) 13-17.

1547* **Riaza Morales** J. M., El comienzo del mundo, I. El hombre, la vida y la Tierra: BAC normal. M 1984, Católica. XXVIII-500 p. – RSalT 73 (1985) 335s (J. A. *García*).

1548 *Rosenbloom* Noah H., ⊕ Mysticism and science in MALBIM's theory of creation: HUCA 57 ⊕ 49-96; Eng. 49.

1548* **Russell** Colin A., Cross-currents; interactions between science and faith ➤ 1,2177; also GR 1985, Eerdmans. 272 p. $15. – RRExp 83 (1986) (D. R. *Stiver*).

1549 **Russo** François, Nature et méthode de l'histoire des sciences [... rapports historiques entre science et religion; Genèse; GALILÉE...]. P 1983, Blanchard. 528 p. – RRThom 86 (1986) 283-9 (J.-M. *Maldamé*).

1549* *a) Schipper* F., Over de verhouding van natuurwetenschap en theologie; – *b) Musschenga* A. W., Boedelscheiding een noodzaak ? Over de verhouding tussen theologie en natuurwetenschap: GerefTTs 86 (1986) 155-167 / 131-154.

1550 *Scotland* Nigel, DARWIN and doubt and the response of the Victorian churches: Churchman 100 (L 1986) 294-308 [< ZIT].

1550* ESpaemann Robert, al., Evolutionismus und Christentum: Civitas-Resultate 9. ix-152 p. DM 38 [TR 83,226, W. *Bröker*].

1551 **Stanesby** Derek, Science, reason and religion. L 1985, Croom Helm. xi-210 p. £20. – RModT 3 (1986s) 109s (T. E. *Burke*); TLond 39 (1986) 319s (J. *Stewart*).

1552 *Staudinger* Hugo, Die Nebenwirkung einer Reise? DARWINS Theorie und ihre Folgen: ZRGg 38 (1986) 167-185.

1553 *Stengers* Jean, Les premiers Coperniciens et la Bible: RBgPg 62 (1984) 703-719.

1554 **Strickling** James E.J, Origins; today's science, tomorrow's myth; an objective study of creationism, evolution, and catastrophism. NY 1986, Vantage. 118 p. $12. – RSWJT 29,2 (1986s) 63 (L. R. *Bush*).

1555 **Swinburne** Richard, The evolution of the soul. Ox 1986, Clarendon. 323 p. £35. – RNature 323 (1986) 679s (D. M. *MacKay*).

1556 a) *Testa Bappenheim* Italo, Sui problemi della creazione: BbbOr 28 (1986) 219-221; – b) *Testa von Bappenheim* Italo, Finalità e caso nella moderna scienza antropologica: BbbOr 28 (1986) 165-9.

1557 a) *Torrance* Thomas F., Theology and scientific inquiry; – b) *Van Dyke* Fred, Theological problems of theistic evolution; – c) *Murphy* George L., A theological argument for evolution; – d) *Thomas* Robert, The Bible as genetic code: JAmScAf 38 (1986) 2-10 / 11-18 / 19-26 / 38-40.

1558 **Torrance** Thomas F., Reality and scientific theology [1970 Dundee Harris lectures]: Theology and Science at the Frontiers of Knowledge 1. E 1985, Scottish Academic. 206 p. £10. – ᴿExpTim 97 (1985s) 217 (G. *Huelin*); JTS 37 (1986) 679-682 (J. C. *Polkinghorne*); RHPR 66 (1986) 473s (G. *Siegwalt*); RefTR 45 (1986) 57s (J. A. *Friend*); RTLv 17 (1986) 372s (D. *Chavée*); TLond 39 (1986) 323s (R. *Stannard*).

1558* **Tresmontant** Claude, L'histoire de l'univers et le sens de la création 1985 → 1,b13: ᴿRThom 86 (1986) 297 (J.-M. *Maldamé*: seul le spécialiste sera agacé par ses jugements sommaires).

1559 **Turner** David H., Life before Genesis; a conclusion; an understanding of the significance of Australian aboriginal culture. NY 1985, Lang. 185 p. [JAAR 54,632].

1559* **Van Horsen** Roger D., The contemporary search for the meaning of creation: diss. Fuller Theol. Sem., ᴰ*Brown* Colin. Pasadena 1986. 365 p. 86-19162. – DissA 47 (1986s) 2625-A.

1560 **Wallace** William A., Gᴀʟɪʟᴇᴏ and his sources... Collegio Romano 1984 → 1,2186: ᴿAngelicum 63 (1986) 140-3 (A. *Wilder*); CathHR 72 (1986) 266-8 (W. E. *Carroll*); Thomist 50 (1986) 289-292 (A. *Moreno*).

1561 **Wells** John C., Charles Hᴏᴅɢᴇ's critique of Darwinism; the argument to design: diss. Yale. NHv 1986. 265 p. 86-29517. – DissA 47 (1986s) 3460-A; RelStR 13,188.

1562 **Young** Davis A., Christianity and the age of the earth 1982 → 63,2164... 65,1889: ᴿAndrUnS 24 (1986) 288-290 (L. A. *Mitchel*: compromise).

E1.9   *Peccatum originale,* **The Sin of Eden,** *Genesis 2-3.*

1563 *Alszeghy* Zoltan, La discussione sul peccato originale [*Dubarle* A. 1983]: Gregorianum 67 (1986) 133-139.

1564 **Awn** P. J., Satan's tragedy and redemption; Iblīs in Sūfī psychology 1983 → 64,2159... 1,2198: ᴿZDMG 136 (1986) 130 (M. *Glünz*).

1565 a) *Benetollo* Ottorino, Il peccato originale nella Bibbia; – b) *Stivel* Giancarlo, Peccato originale e miti greco-romani: SacDoc 31 (1986) 472-489 / 490-506.

1566 *Bernard* Jacques, Genèse 1-3; lecture et traditions de lecture: MelSR [41 (1984) 109-128] 43 (1986) 57-77.

1567 *Bonora* Antonio, Uomo e donna in Gn 1-11: ParSpV 13 (1986) 11-26.

1568 *Borella* Jean, Méditation sur la Genèse (II); cultiver et garder; (III) L'epreuve des deux chapitres; (IV) Gen. 2; (V) La femme devant l'homme: PenséeC 221 (1986) 51-61 / 222, 53-66 / 223, 67-80 / 224, 55-62.

1569 *Cantoni* Piero, Il demonio: Renovatio 21 (1986) 379-395.

1570 *Cignelli* Lino, I due padri, Dio e Satana; una verità biblico-tradizionale: TerraS 62 (1986) 75-81.

1571 **Cini Tassinario** Agnese, Il diavolo secondo l'insegnamento recente della Chiesa: ᴰStAnt 28, 1984 → 65,1983; 1,2207: ᴿAngelicum 63 (1986) 313-8 (T. *Stancati*: utilissimo per la documentazione e lo status quaestionis; mostra non solo la complessità del problema ma anche le sue basi serie);

Asprenas 32 (1985) 462-4 (A. *Rolla*); ScripTPamp 18 (1986) 343-6 (A. *Quirós*).

1572 **Cottiaux** Jean,   La sacralisation du mariage de la Genèse aux incises matthéennes 1982 ➤ 63,7235; 65,1308:   RRBgPg 64 (1986) 162s (H. *Wattiaux*). ➤ 5979, *Dacquino* P.

1573 *De Rosa* Giuseppe,   Il diavolo; fantasie e realtà: CC 137 (1986,1) 573-7.

1574 **Dubarle** A.-M.,   Le péché originel 1983 ➤ 64,2167... 1,2210:   RTeresianum 36 (1985) 222s (G. *Blandino*).

1575 *a) Eby* Lloyd, Original sin and human value; – *b) Wells* Jonathan,   Some reflexions on the Unification [Church] account of the Fall; – *c) Kim Young Oon*,   Satan, reality or symbol?; – *d) Petersen* Sarah E.,   The fall and misogyny in JUSTIN Martyr and CLEMENT of Alexandria; – *e) Roberts* J. Deotis,   A good thing spoiled; – *f) Mojzes* Paul,   The cracked mirror: ➤ 434, Unification Seminar 1983/5, 133-148 / 62-72 / 21-36 / 37-51 / 100-105 / 106-118.

1575* *Exem* A. Van,   Genesis read by Chotanagpur tribals: Bible Bhashyam 12 (1986) 263-278.

1576 *Feilschuss-Abir* A. S.,   Erschaffung, Bestimmung und Stellung der Frau in der Urgeschichte in anthropologischer Sicht: TG1 76 (1986) 399-423.

1576* *a) Garrone* Daniele,   Genesi 2; l'origine dell'uomo; – *b) Sacchi* Paolo,   Genesi 3 e il problema del male; – *c) Rizzi* Armido,   Ruolo del racconto biblico nello sviluppo del concetto di male: ➤ 364*b*, In principio 1986, 149-169 / 265-289 / 293-308.

1577 *Greenlee* Lynn F.J,   KOHUT's self psychology and theory of narcissism; some implications regarding the fall and restoration of humanity: JPsy&T 14 (Rosemead 1986) 110-6 [< ZIT].

1577* *Holman* Jan,   Die verdraaide erfzonde: ➤ 80*, FRIJKHOFF M., Bij de put 1986, 19-45.

1578 **Holtz** Gottfried,   Die Faszination der Zwänge; Aberglaube und Okkultismus [... Wunderheilung... Der neue Satanismus]. Gö 1984, Vandenhoeck & R.   279 p. DM 42 pa. – RTLZ 111 (1986) 258-260 (H. *Obst*).

1579 *Idel* Moshe,   The origins of alchemy according to ZOSIMUS and a Hebrew parallel [... the fallen angels; *Bamberger* B. 1952; *Dimant* Devorah diss. J 1974]: RÉJ 145 (1986) 117-124.

1580 [Olu] *Igenoza* Andrew,   Christian theology and the belief in evil spirits; an African perspective: ScotBEvT 4 (1984) 39-48.

Jobling David,   The sense of [Gn 2s] 1986 ➤ 176.

1580* *Kalluveetil* Paul,   The transcending and transgressing man; the dialectical anthropology of Genesis I-XI: Bible Bhashyam 12 (1986) 85-99.

1581 **Kasujja** Augustine,   Polygenism and the theology of original sin today; Eastern African contribution to the solution of the scientific problem; the impact of polygenism in modern theology [diss. Urbaniana 3268]. Vatican 1986, Urbaniana Univ.   204 p. Lit. 18.000 [TDig 34,78].

1581* *a) Keler* Hans Von,   Gesetzt, zu bauen und zu bewahren (Gen. 2,15); – *b) Hengel* Martin,   Die Arbeit im frühen Christentum: TBei 17 (Wu 1986) 169-173 / 174-212 [< ZIT]. – *c) Kedar-Kopfstein* B.,   Eden: ➤ 599, TWAT 5,9s (1986) 1093-1103.

1582 **Kertelge** Karl, Diavolo – demoni – possessione [in prospettiva biblica p. 7-44], *al.*, Sulla realtà del male [Teufel – Dämonen – Bessessenheit]: GdT 149. Brescia 1983, Queriniana. 173 p. [p. 79-111, *Lehmann* Karl, Il diavolo – essere personale?]. – RTeresianum 37 (1986) 240s (V. *Pasquetto*).

1583 **Knapp** Markus,   'Wahr ist nur, was nicht in diese Welt passt'; die Erbsündenlehre als Ansatzpunkt eines Dialoges mit T. W. ADORNO [Diss. Wü 1983 ➤ 64,2174]. Wü 1983, Echter. x-300 p. DM 39. 3-429-00847-6. –

ᴿGregorianum 67 (1986) 371 (Z. *Alszeghy*: 'la teologia cattolica può liberarsi dal suo isolamento culturale solo in quanto si pronuncia ... [su] una concezione moderna della realtà').

1583* a) *Langer* Michael, 'In Gesellschaft der Teufel'; zur Pädagogisierung der Hölle in der katholischen Literatur der Neuzeit; – b) *Haag* Herbert, Der Teufel — Mythos und Geschichte: KatBlätter 111 (Mü 1986) 782-6 / 778-781 [< ZIT].

1584 *Marcheselli-Casale* Cesare, Satana o mistero di iniquità? personalisti e simbolisti; il confronto continua (*Cini Tassinario* A.): Asprenas 33 (1986) 373-395.

1584* **Marks** Herbert J., The language of Adam; biblical naming and poetic etymology: diss. Yale. NHv 1985. 194 p. 86-13597. – DissA 47 (1986s) 1311-A; RelStR 13,189.

1585 **Martelet** Gustave, Libre réponse à un scandale; la faute originelle, la souffrance et la mort: Théologies. P 1986, Cerf. 186 p. F 72. 2-204-02488-0. – ᴿEsprV 96 (1986) 333-5 (P. *Jay*); Études 365 (1986) 137s (R. *Marlé*); ÉTRel 61 (1986) (H. *Bost*: veut différencier le chronologiquement originel et l'humainement primordial, mais invoque la paléontologie pour préférer IRÉNÉE à AUGUSTIN); MélSR 43 (1986) 106 (M. *Huftier*); RSPT 70 (1986) 495s (J. *Bonduelle*).

1586 *Cozette* O., Le péché originel; une autre réponse à un scandale [*Martelet* G. 1986]: EsprV 96 (1986) 412-6.

1587 **Melzer** Sara E., Discourses of the Fall; a study of PASCAL's Pensées. Berkeley 1986, Univ. California. x-171 p. $23 [TDig 34,86].

1588 **Neyton** André. L'âge d'or et l'âge de fer: Confluents. P 1984, BLettres. 86 p. 2-251-33422-X.

1588* **Nothomb** P., [Gn 2s] L'homme immortel. P 1984, Albin Michel [NRT 109,901].

1589 *Ottosson* Magnus V., Eden and the land of promise [Fekheriyeh *'dn* 'enrich']: → 377a, IOSOT summaries (1986) 100.

1590 ᴱ**Perkins** Robert L., International KIERKEGAARD commentary, 8. The concept of anxiety; a simple psychological orienting deliberation on the dogmatic issue of hereditary sin. Macon GA 1986, Mercer Univ. 203 p. $19 [JAAR 54,632].

1591 *Rembaum* Joel E., Medieval Jewish criticism of the doctrine of original sin: AJS 7s (1982s) 353-382.

1592 *Rigby* P., Crítica a la interpretación de Paul RICŒUR sobre la doctrina agustiniana del pecado original, ᵀ*Anoz* J.: → 477, Congreso 1983 = AugM 31 (1986) 245-252.

1593 **Rivero** Jorge, Cantabria, cuna de la humanidad [site of Paradise and toponymy from Troy, Thebes, Jericho, Jerusalem ... are to be found in the Peña Sagra sierra]. – Ya (30 oct. 1986) (presented at London Royal Geographical society; also links Hibernia with Tiberias and Tiber ...).

1594 *Roehl* Wolfgang G., Dämonen: → 587, EvKL 1 (1986) 781-4.

1594* *Rosenzweig* Michael L., A helper equal to him: Judaism 35 (1986) 277-280.

1595 **Russell** Jeffrey B., Lucifer ... 1984 → 1,2236: ᴿSpeculum 61 (1986) 994-7 (A. E. *Bernstein*).

1596 *Schillebeeckx* Edward, Menselijke biotechniek en de 'Hand Gods': TsTNijm 26 (1986) 48-61; Eng. 61: 'In a pre-critical period, Christians equated the 'natural course of affairs' with God's will... For many Christians the Bible is the great stumbling block to speaking with an open mind; therefore [Gn 1,28; 2,5 - 3,24] are analyzed...'

1597 *Schmied* Augustin,   Stimmen zum Thema 'Erbsünde' [*Dubarle* A.; *Vanneste* A.; *Villalmonte* A. de]:   TGegw 23 (1985) 189-198.

1598 **Storms** C. Samuel,   Tragedy in Eden; original sin in the theology of Jonathán EDWARDS.   Lanham MD 1985, UPA.   xii-316 p. $25.75; pa. $12.75. – ᴿTrinJ 7 (1986) 92s (J. H. *Gerstner*); WestTJ 48 (1986) 398-404 (S. T. *Logan*).

1599 **Toorn** Karel van der,   Sin and sanction in ancient Israel and Mesopotamia: StSemNeer 22,1985 ➤ 1,2242:   ᴿBijdragen 47 (1986) 437s (P. C. *Beentjes*); ETL 62 (1986) 410s (J. *Lust*); ZAW 98 (1986) 479 (O. *Kaiser*).

1600 *Valabrega* Roberto,   L'iconografia catacombale di Adamo ed Eva: RivStLR 22 (1986) 25-55; 9 fig.

1601 *a*) *Valle* José L. del,   El matrimonio, ¿Institución creacional? [Gen 1-3]; – *b*) *Cañellas* Gabriel, ... praxis del judaísmo bíblico; – *c*) *Saenz de S. María* Miguel, ... ¿Contrato o sacramento?; – *e*) *Alonso Díaz* José. ... el problema de su indisolubilidad; – *f*) *Manrique* Andrés, ... praxis del cristianismo primitivo; – *g*) *Salas* Antonio, ... praxis pastoral hoy [bibliog.]:   Biblia y Fe 12,36 (1986) 261-271 / 272-286 / 287-301 / 302-313 / 314-324 / 325-340 / 341-359 [-362].

1602 *Villalmonte* Alejandro,   El pecado original en su historia; comentario a dos libros recientes [*Köster* H. 1982s; *Gross* J. 1960-72]:   NatGrac 33 (1986) 139-172.

1603 **Wallace** Howard N.,   The Eden narrative: HarvSemMon 32, 1985 ➤ 1,2243;   0-89-130838-5:   ᴿBiblica 67 (1986) 577-580 (J.-L. *Ska*); ÉglT 17 (1986) 233s (W. *Vogels*); ÉTRel 61 (1986) 569s (D. *Lys*); Syria 63 (1986) 444s (A. *Caquot*).

1604 *Zerwick* Max,   I problemi dei primi tre capi del Genesi [dal latino, Decima Hebdomas Biblica R 1948, < Verbum Domini 26 (1948)]: BbbOr 28 (1986) 79-94.

1605 *Komadina* A., [Postanka (Gn) 2,4-25] Pred tajnom zla i grijeha: ObnŽiv 41 (1986) 42-54; 55, Vor dem Geheimnis des Bösen und der Sünde.

1606 *Hutter* Manfred,   Adam als Gärtner und König (Gen 2,8.15): BZ 30 (1986) 258-262.

1606* **Maller** Allen S., [Gn 2,7] What about the tree of life ? [made women live longer than men]: Dor 15 (1986s) 270s.

1607 *Pathrapankal* Joseph,   'To cultivate and guard Eden' (Gen 2:15); reflections on a biblical theology of work: ➤ 202*, Critical and creative 1986, 39-48.

1607* *Beeston* A. F. L., [Gen 2,23] One flesh [= clan]: VT 36 (1986) 115-7.

1608 *Lawton* Robert B.,   Genesis 2:24, trite or tragic? [possibly 'a man *ought to* cling to his wife', hinting another shadow of fallen existence]: JBL 105 (1986) 97s.

1608* *Görg* Manfred, [Gen 2,25-3,7] Weisheit als Provokation: WissWeish 49 (1986) 8-198.

1609 *Bottéro* Jean,   *a*) Le récit du 'Péché originel' dans Genèse, II,25 - III [inédit 1949]; – *b*) Les origines de l'univers selon la Bible [< Sources orientales (1959) 187-234]: ➤ 136, Naissance de Dieu 1986, 203-221 / 155-202.

1609* **Diprose** Rinaldo,   Colonna e sostegno della Verità [... come leggere e studiare la Bibbia... esempio Gen 3 ... predicazione]. 1984, Fondi UCEB. 243 p. – ᴿSTEv 8,16 (1985) 293-9 (G. *Freri*: dice 'a cura di' Diprose, ma non indica altri autori).

1610 *Busenitz* Irvin A., Woman's desire for man; Genesis 3:16 reconsidered: GraceTJ 7 (1986) 203-212.

1611 *Vogels* Walter, Das sogenannte 'Proto-Evangelium' (Gen 3,15); verschiedene Arten, den Text zu lesen [< Sacerdos 53 (1986) 351-366]: TGegw 29 (1986) 195-203.

1611* *Alexandre* Monique, L'épée de flamme (Gen. 3,24); textes chrétiens et traditions juives: ► 81, Mém. NIKIPROWETZKY V., Hellenica 1986, 403-441.

1612 *Zipor* Moshe A., [Gen 3,25] ❾ The sword and the book; a covert midrash of the *al-tikre* type?: Tarbiz 55 (1985s) 137-9; Eng. IV. [cf. 612, *Mali* Assaf].

E2.1   Cain et Abel; *gigantes; longaevi; Genesis 4s*

1612* *Bassler* Jouette M., Cain and Abel in the Palestinian Targums; a brief note on an old controversy: JStJud 17 (1986) 56-64.

1613 *Rouillard* Hedwige, Et si Caïn voulait que l'œil le regardât? Études des transformations de Gen. 4,14 à travers la LXX et Philon d'Alexandrie: ► 81, Mém. NIKIPROWETZKY V. 1986, 79-83.

1613* *Soleh* M. Z., ❿ Cain's sin and tent-dwelling: BethM 31,106 (1985s) 287s.

1614 *Davies* Philip R., [Gen. 4,1.17] Sons of Cain: ► 63, ᶠMcKANE W., A word 1986, 35-56.

1615 **Ulrich** Anna. Kain und Abel in der Kunst. — Untersuchung zur Ikonographie und Auslegungsgeschichte [kath. Diss. Bamberg 1980]. Bamberg 1981 [Die Hegge, 3533 Willebadessen]. 301 p.; 291 fig. DM 36. – ᴿTrierTZ 95 (1986) 232s (E. *Sauser*).

1616 *Sawyer* John F. A., Cain and Hephaestus; possible relics of metal-working traditions in Genesis 4: AbrNahr 24 (1986) 155-166.

1616* *Waltke* Bruce K., Cain and his offering: WestTJ 48 (1986) 363-372.

1617 **Oduyoye** Modupe, The sons of the gods and the daughters of men; an Afro-Asiatic interpretation of Genesis 1-11: 1984 ► 65,1714: ᴿCBQ 48 (1986) 123s (J. G. *Gammie*); Vidyajyoti 49 (1985) 148s (J. *Volckaert*).

1617* *Cicchinè* C., I giganti nella Bibbia e nell'area siro-palestinese: diss. ᴰ*Fronzaroli* P. F 1979. [RivB 35,397].

1618 **Fraade** Steven D., [Gn 4,26] Enoch and his generation; pre-Israelite hero and history in postbiblical interpretation: SBL Mon 30 [diss. Pennsylvania 1980] 1984 ► 65,1944: ᴿCBQ 48 (1986) 338s (Janet *Timble*: Gn 4,26 as in Enoch and other writings); ETL 62 (1986) 177s (J. *Lust*); JBL 105 (1986) 736s (J. P. *Lewis*); JSS 31 (1986) 257-261 (G. *Brooke*).

Christensen Duane L., Job and the age of the Patriarchs in the Old Testament ► 2403.

1619 *Poulssen* N., Time and place in Genesis v: ► 399, OTS 24, 1985/6, 21-33.

E2.2   Diluvium, **The Flood,** *Atraḥasis, Gilgameš, Genesis 6 ...*

1620 *Abusch* Tzvi, Ishtar's proposal and Gilgamesh's refusal; an interpretation of the Gilgamesh epic, tablet 6, lines 1-179: HistRel 26 (1986s) 143-187.

1621 *a)* **Dijk** J. van, *Lugal ud...* Déluge 1983 ► 64,2046... **1**,2264: ᴿOLZ 81 (1986) 343-6 (M. *Krebernik*); – *b)* *Borger* R., Neue Lugal-Fragmente: Orientalia 55 (1986) 446-9.

1622 **Caduff** Gian Andrea, Antike Sintflutsagen: Hypomnemata 82. Gö 1986, Vandenhoeck & R. 308 p. 3-525-25180-7 [BL 87,94s, J. R. *Porter*].

1623 *Frot* Yves, L'interprétation ecclésiastique de l'épisode du Déluge chez les Pères des trois premiers siècles: AugR 26 (1986) 335-348.

1624 *Lambert* W. G., Niṣir or Nimuš? [Gilg. 11,140-144, Nimuš likelier as mountain where the Ark came to rest]: RAss 80 (1986) 185s.

1625 *Lange* Günter,   'Noach im Kasten'; zum Noach-Bild der Schulbibel: KatBlät 111 (Mü 1986) 21-27.
Mack B. L., Gilgamesh and the wizard of Oz [nothing about either] 1985 ➤ b899.
1626 *Silvestri* Domenico,   Il vero volto di Huwawa e la scoperta del legno: ➤ 540* Analisi 1985, AION-Clas 7 (1985) 177-190.
1627 *Saporetti* Claudio,   Gilgameš e Minosse: ➤ 20, ᶠDELLER K., MesopT 21 (F 1986) 237-247.
1627* *Tropper* Josef,   'Beschwörung' des Enkidu? Anmerkungen zur Interpretation von GEN 240-243 // Gilg. XII, 79-84:   WeltOr 17 (1986) 19-24.
1628 *Vanstiphout* H. L. J.,   Towards a reading of 'Gilgamesh and Agga', II. Construction: OrLovPer 17 (1986) 33-50.
1629 *Westhuizen* J. P. van der,   Some proposed restorations to the Atrahasīs epic: ➤ 543, Rencontre 32, 1985/6, 89-92.
1630 *Wilson* John R., The Gilgamesh epic and the Iliad: EchMClas 30 (1986) 25-42.
1631 **Poortvliet** Rien, De ark van Noach, of Ere wie ere toekomt [17 p. on Gn 6ss as occasion to portray all imaginable animals].   Kampen/Weesp 1985, Kok/van Holkema & W. 240 p. *f*99. – ᴿStreven 53 (1985s) 474s (P. *Beentjes*).

1632 *Christensen* Duane,   Janus parallelism in Genesis 6:3:   HebSt 27 (Madison 1986) 20-24 [OTAbs 10,141].
1633 *Clarke* Ernest G., [Gn 7,1] Noah; *gbr ṣdyq* or *gbr zky*: ➤ 21, Mem. DÍEZ MACHO A., Salvación 1986, 337-345.
1634 *Crüsemann* F.,   Nach der Katastrophe gesprochen (Gen 8,20-9,17): ➤ 145, Wie Gott 1986, ...
1635 *Rimbach* James A. [Gn 8,20s; Gilgameš] 'The gods like flies' — no offense intended: EAsJT 4,1 (1986) 87-97.
1636 *Oded* B.,   The Table of Nations (Genesis 10) — a socio-cultural approach: ZAW 98 (1986) 14-31.
1637 **Pilkey** John, [Gn 10] The origin of the nations.   San Diego 1984, Master. 346 p. $10 pa. – ᴿBS 143 (1986) 375s (F. R. *Howe*: reconstruction of W. JONES 1784).
1638 *Anderson* Francis I., [Gen 11] Language bridges and barriers in ancient Israelite society: ➤ 46, ᶠHARRIS B., AnSRes 16 (1986) 72-78.
1639 **Bost** Hubert,   Babel; du texte au symbole 1985 ➤ 1,2283; Fs 35; 2-8309-0035-9:   ᴿBL (1986) 64 (U. E. *Simon*); ETL 62 (1986) 171s (J. *Lust*); ÉTRel 61 (1986) 120s (D. *Lys*); MondeB 45 (1986) 53 (J.-L. *Huot*); RechSR 74 (1986) 617s (J. *Briend*: déconcerte, 'Babel devient le symbole de la mort des minorités'); RHPR 66 (1986) 218 (P. de *Robert*: p. 73 'pari' du traducteur, non parti; p. 168 'qualifier G. POSTEL de jésuite est pour le moins excessif...'); RThom 86 (1986) 341s (R. *Couffignal*); RTPhil 118 (1986) 323-5 (T. *Römer*: exégèse détaillée; ensuite 'Quel est le sens de l'entreprise humaine' ... industrialisée?); Salmanticensis 33 (1986) 371s (M. *García Cordero*); Teresianum 37 (1986) 256 (F. *Foresti*).
1639* *Miller* Patrick D., [Gn 11] Eridu, Dunnu and Babel; a study in comparative mythology: ➤ 36, Mem. GOITEIN S. = HebAnR 9 (1985) 227-251.

E2.3   **Patriarchae, Abraham;** *Gen 12...*

1640 **Abela** Anthony,   Reading the Abraham narrative in Gen 11,27-25,18 as a literary unit: diss. Pont. Ist. Biblico, ᴰ*Pisano* S. R 1986. – AcPIB 9,2 (1985s) 147s; 116; RTLv 18,540.

1640* **Bascom** Robert A., Prolegomena to the study of the itinerary genre in the Old Testament and beyond: diss. Claremont 1986, ᴰ*Sanders* J. A. 428 p. 86-06875. – DissA 47 (1986s) 206-A.

1641 a) *Baumbach* Günther, Abraham unser Vater; der Prozess der Vereinnahmung Abrahams durch das frühe Christentum: – b) *Tröger* Karl-Wolfgang, Abraham im Koran: TVers 16 (1986) 37-56 / 23-36.

1641* *Bleickert* Günter, Abraham hört auf seinen Gott; ein Gespräch mit dem Stammvater Israels: GeistL 59 (1986) 228-234.

1642 **Collin** Matthieu, Abraham: CahÉv 56. P 1986, Cerf. 68 p. F 22. 0222-9714.

1642* **DeRoche** Michael, The dynamics of promise; narrative logic in the Abraham story: diss. McMaster, ᴰ*Cooper* A. Hamilton ONT 1986. — DissA 47 (1986s) 1755-A ['Deroche']; RelStR 13,189.

1643 *Flusser* David, Abraham and the Upanishads: Immanuel 20 (J 1986) 53-66.

1643* **Gentiloni** F., Abramo contro Ulisse; un itinerario alla ricerca di Dio. T 1984, Claudiana. 123 p. – ᴿSTEv 15 (1985) 146s (P. *Bolognesi*).

1644 *Hunter* Alastair G., Father Abraham; a structural and theological study of the Yahwist's presentation of the Abraham material: JStOT 35 (1986) 3-27.

1644* *McKane* William, Abraham, ᵀ*Roehl* W.: ➤ 587, EvKL 1 (1986) 36-38.

1645 **Oberforcher** Robert, Glaube als Verheissung... Patriarchengeschichte 1981 ➤ 62,2448... 65,1975: ᴿBZ 30 (1986) 285s (O. *Wahl*).

1645* a) *Peek-Horn* Margaret, Der Gottesglaube der Vätergeschichten als Lernort für unseren Glauben; – b) *Zirker* Hans, Abraham, ein 'Muslim,' 'Freund Gottes' und 'Vorbild der Menschen': ZPraxRU 16 (Stu 1986) 3-7 / 10-17 [27-9; < zɪᴛ].

1646 *Renard* John, Images of Abraham in the writings of JALAL AD-DĪN RŪMĪ: JAOS 106 (1986) 633-640.

1647 *Sánchez Bosch* Jorge, La figura de Abrahán en Pablo y en FILÓN de Alejandría; ➤ 21, Mem. DÍEZ MACHO A., Salvación 1986, 677-688.

1648 **Schwantes** Milton, A família de Abraão e Sara; texto e contexto de Gênesis 12-25. Petrópolis / São Leopoldo 1986, Vozes / Sinodal. 91 p. – ᴿEstudos Bíblicos 12 [REB 46,4] (1985) 52 (L. *Garmus*).

1649 *Scullion* John J., 'Die Genesis ist eine Sammlung von Sagen' (Hermann GUNKEL); independent stories and redactional unity in Genesis 12-36: ➤ 377, IOSOT summaries (1986) 123.

E2.4 **Melchisedech, Sodoma:** *Genesis 14.*

1650 **Gianotto** Claudio, Melchisedek e la sua tipologia; tradizioni giudaiche, cristiane e gnostiche (sec. II a.C. - sec. III d.C) [diss. T 1978]: RivBSup 12, 1984 ➤ 65,1986: ᴿBiblica 67 (1986) 435-7 (J. *Swetnam*: a legitimizing figure); BL (1986) 120s (C. J. A. *Hickling*); CBQ 48 (1986) 747-9 (S. P. *Kealy*); CrNSt 7 (1986) 606s (B. A. *Pearson*); ÉTRel 61 (1986) 285s (J.-M. *Léonard*); ParVi 31 (1986) 389s (Clara *Burini*); RivB 34 (1986) 410-414 (Liliana *Rosso Ubigli*); RTPhil 118 (1986) 421 (Françoise *Morard*); Salesianum 48 (1986) 417s (R. *Vicent*).

1651 **Kobelski** Paul J., Melchisedek and Melchireša: CBQ Mon 10, 1981 ➤ 62,2462... 1,2303: ᴿRelStR 12 (1986) 176 (J. H. *Charlesworth*).

1652 **Mianbé Bétoudji** Denis, El, le Dieu Suprême et le Dieu des Patriarches (Genesis 14,18-20) [diss. Roma, Urbaniana, ᴰ*Spada* D.]: Religionswissenschaftliche Texte und Studien 1. Hildesheim 1986, Olms. 290 p.; bibliog. p. 245-267. 3-487-07760-4.

1653 *Myszor* W., ❷ Melchisedech (NHC IX,1) — wstęp, przekład z koptyjskiego i komentarz: STWsz 24,2 (1986) 209-226.

1654 *Willi* Thomas, Melchisedek; der alte und der neue Bund im Hebräerbrief im Lichte der rabbinischen Traditionen über Melchisedek: Judaica 42 (1986) 158-170.

E2.5   *Foedus*, **The Covenant**, *Alliance, Bund; Genesis 15 ...*

1655 **Ganne** Pierre † [cours 1964s + art. 1947/9] ᴱ*Fournier* F., 'Je suis ton Dieu et tu es mon peuple'; leçons sur l'Alliance. P 1986, Centurion. F 175. – ᴿEsprV 96 (1986) 536s (P. *Jay*).

1656 *Graetz* N. L., Sarah's three lives: JRefJud (Summer 1986) 43-48 [< Judaica 42,271].

1657 *Jensen* Hansjørgen L., Die Frauen der Patriarchen und der Raub der Sabinerinnen: ScandJOT 1,1 (1986) 104-9.

1658 *Lambrecht* Jan, 'Je serai leur Dieu et ils seront mon peuple' [Ezek 37,27; sur l'Alliance (Proche-Orient ancien, AT, NT): épilogue de son livre sur Mt 5-7]: NRT 108 (1986) 481-498.

1659 *Nicholson* E. W., Covenant in a century of study since WELLHAUSEN: ⇒ 399, OTS 24, 1985/6, 54-69.

1660 *Perlitt* Lothar [*Hübner* Hans], Bund: ⇒ 587, EvKL 1 (1986) 565-8 [-570 (-2)].

1661 *Schotsman* Paul, Het verhaal van Sara, Hanna en Elisabet omgekeerd ... Moderne voortplantingstechniek bezien vanuit de medische ethiek [i. seksualiteit, geen noodlot, maar taal en expressie van menswording; ii. ... onvervulde wens tot zwangerschap / gewenste evolutieve zwangerschap; iii. een ethisch kader omtrent vruchtbaarheidsordening]: TsTNijm 26 (1986) 28-46; Eng. 46s.

1662 *Schwarz* Joachim, Eid: ⇒ 587, EvKL 1 (1986) 987-991.

1663 *Vanel* Jean, Le livre de Sara: Lire la Bible 67, 1984 ⇒ 1,2321: ᴿVSp 140 (1986) 124s (Michèle *Morgen*).

1663* a) *Goodnick* Benjamin, Abraham's great sin [calling Sarah his sister] — a reevaluation; – b) *Katzoff* Louis, Five questions of Abraham: Dor 15 (1986s) 186-9 / 244-7.

1664 **Ha** John, Genesis 15, a theological compendium of pentateuchal history: diss. Pont. Ist. Biblico, ᴰ*Soggin* J. A. R 1986. – AcPIB 9,2 (1985s) 148s; 116; RTLv 18,541.

1665 *Johnson* Bo, [Gen 15,6] Who reckoned righteousness to whom? [*Oeming* M.]: SvEx 51s (1986s) 108-115.

1666 *Brenner* Athalya, [Gn 16; 21 ...] Female social behaviour; two descriptive patterns within the 'birth of the hero' paradigm: VT 36 (1986) 257-273.

1667 *Gitay* Zefira, Hagar's expulsion — a tale twice-told in Genesis [16,6; 21,12]: BR 2,4 (1986) 26-32; ill.

1667* *Tamez* Elsa, [Gn 16; 21; Hagar] The woman who complicated the history of salvation: CCurr 36 (1986s) 129-139.

1668 **Miller** William T., [Gn 18; 32] Mysterious encounters at Mambre and Jabbok: BrownJudSt 50, 1984 ⇒ 65,2002: ᴿÉglT 17 (1986) 234s (W. *Vogels*); JTS 37 (1986) 222s (S. P. *Brock*).

1669 *Gottlieb* I. B., Light and darkness in perpetual round; Genesis 18 and 19: ⇒ 75, ᶠMIRSKY A. 1986, 181-198.

1670 *Giguère* Paul-André, [Gn 18,12; Prov 7,18; Sg 7,2] Trois textes bibliques sur le plaisir sexuel: ÉglT 17 (1986) 311-320.

1671 **Knauf** E. A., [Gn 18,18; 21,15] Ismael; Untersuchungen zur Geschichte Palästinas und Nordarabiens im 1. Jahrtausend v. Chr. [Diss. Kiel, ᴰ*Donner* H.]: Abh DPV. Wsb 1985, Harrassowitz. IX-133 p.; map. DM 52. – ᴿWeltOr 17 (1986) 176-9 (H. M. *Niemann*); ZAW 98 (1986) 468 (H.-C. *Schmitt*).

1672 *Koener* Ulrike, Genesis 19,4/11 und 22,3/13 und der Bethlehemitische Kindermord auf dem 'Lot-Sarkophag' von S. Sebastiano in Rom: JbAC 29 (1986) 118-145; 1 fig.; pl. 16-21.

1672* *Levin* S., [Gn 19,23] The sickness of Sodom [not moral: were the babies bad? rather a universal disease ...]: Judaism 35 (1986) 281-3.

1673 *Daoust* J., [Gn 19,24] Sodome et Gomorrhe [< *Hennig* Richard, Les grandes énigmes de l'Univers: Historia 455 (nov. 1984)]: EsprV 96 (1986) 207s.

1674 *Ebach* J., [Gn 19,26] Lots Weib; der gebannte Blick auf die Katastrophe: ► 155, Ursprung 1986, 147-150.

1675 *McEvenue* Sean E., La obra del Elohista [< 'The Elohist at work', ZAW 96 (1984) 315-332; Gn 20 y 22], ᵀᴱ*Reig* Ramiro: SelT 25 (1986) 145-155.

1676 *Matthews* Victor H., The wells of Gerar [in Gen 21; 26; not archeology]: BA 49 (1986) 118-126.

E2.6   *Isaac ... The 'Aqēdâ, Genesis 22 ...*

1676* *Breitbart* Sidney, [Gn 22] The Aḳedah — a test of God: Dor 15 (1986s) 19-28.

1677 *Brock* Sebastian, [Gn 22] Two Syriac verse homilies on the binding of Isaac: Muséon 99 (1986) 61-129.

1678 *Calder* Norman. The *sa'y* and the *jabīn*; some notes on Qur'ān 37:102-3 [when Abraham's boy reached working age]: JSS 31 (1986) 17-26.

1678* *Chilton* Bruce, a) Recent discussion of the 'Aqedah [... Is 33,7 marg.]; b) Isaac and the second night, a consideration [< Biblica 61 (1980) 78-88: TargEx 12,42 not evidence that the Aqedah is pre-Christian]: ► 140*, Targumic Approaches 1986, 39-49 / 25-37 (113-135).

1679 *Harl* Marguerite, La 'ligature' d'Isaac (Gen. 22,9) dans la Septante et chez les Pères grecs: ► 81, Mém. NIKIPROWETZKY V., Hellenica 1986, 457-472; 2 fig.

1679* a) *Kreuzer* S., Das Opfer des Vaters — die Gefährdung des Sohnes — Genesis 22; – b) *Neubacher* F., Isaaks Opferung in der griechischen Alten Kirche; ᶠ*SAUER* G., Amt und Gemeinde 37 (1986) 62-70 / 72-76.

1680 a) *Maiberger* Paul, Genesis 22 und die Problematik des Menschenopfers in Israel; – b) *Drewermann* Eugen, Abrahams Opfer; Gen 22,1-19 in tiefenpsychologischer Sicht; – c) *Kilian* Rudolf, Isaaks Opferung; die Sicht der historisch-kritischen Exegese; – d) *Schroedel* Joachim H., Text, Leser und [tiefenpsychologische ...] Methode; zu Grund- und Arbeitsfragung der Schriftauslegung: BiKi 41,3 (1986) 104-112 / 113-124 / 98-103 / 125-135.

1681 *Mazor* Yair, Genesis 22; the ideological rhetoric and the psychological composition: Biblica 67 (1986) 81-88.

1681* *Mooney* E. F., Abraham and his dilemma; KIERKEGAARD's theological suspension revisited: IntJPhRel 19 (1986) 23-42.

1682 *Poulssen* Niek, Menselijk spreken over het zien van God (Gen 22,1-19): ► 80*, ᶠ*NIJKHOFF* M., Bij de put 1986, 1-18.

1683 a) *Schultz* Samuel J., [Gen 22 ...] Sacrifice in the God-Man relationship in the Pentateuch; – b) *Smick* Elmer B., Israel's struggle with the religions of Canaan: ► 65, ᶠ*MACRAE* Allan, Interpretation 1986, 109-121 / 123-133.

1684 *Pope* Marvin H., The timing of the snagging of the rain, Genesis 22:13: BA 49 (1986) 114-7.

1685 *a*) **Libera** Piotr, Le immagini dell'anima nel 'De Isaac et anima' in rapporto ad altre figure veterotestamentarie di Sant'AMBROGIO, diss. Pont. Univ. Salesiana, doct. 222, ᴰ*Riggi* C. R 1986. 92 p.; bibliog. p. 65-89. – *b*) *Nauroy* Gérard, [Gn 24; Ct 1,2] La structure du De Isaac vel anima et la cohérence de l'allégorèse d'Ambroise de Milan: RÉLat 63 (1986) 210-236.

E2.7 Jacob, *Genesis 25 ...*

1686 **Blum** Erhard, [Gn 25-31] Die Komposition der Vätergeschichte [ohne JEDP; Diss. ᴰ*Rendtorff* R.]: WMANT 57, 1984 ➤ 65,1970: ᴿETL 62 (1986) 178-181 (J. *Lust*); ÉTRel 61 (1986) 580-2 (T. *Römer*); ExpTim 97 (1985s) 298 (R. J. *Coggins*); Henoch 8 (1986) 245-9 (J. A. *Soggin*); JBL 105 (1986) 706-8 (J. *Van Seters*: approval, reservations); TLZ 111 (1986) 180-3 (R. *Albertz*).

1687 **Hendel** Ronald S., The epic of the patriarch; the Jacob cycle and the narrative traditions of Canaan and Israel: diss. Harvard 1985. 229 p. 86-62288. – DissA 47 (1986s) 208-A.

1688 *a*) *Greenfield* Jonas C., [Gn 26,31] An ancient treaty ritual and its targumic echo; – *b*) *Goshen-Gottstein* M. H., Exegetical exercises in comparative targum study (Gn 15,1) [Gn 14 ...]: ➤ 21, Mem. DÍEZ MACHO A., Salvación 1986, 391-7 / 375-389.

1689 *a*) *Friedman* Richard E., [Gn 27, Jacob] Deception for deception; who breaks the cycle?; – *b*) *Evans* Carl D., The patriarch Jacob — an 'innocent man'; moral ambiguity in the biblical portrayal; – *c*) *Mann* Thomas, Jacob takes his bride; – *d*) *Exum* J. Cheryl, The mothers of Israel; the patriarchal narrative from a feminist perspective: BR 2,1 (1986) 22-31.68 / 32-37 / 52-59 / 60-67; all color. ill. ('art').

1690 **Kuntzmann** Raymond, Le symbolisme des jumeaux au Proche-Orient ancien: Beauchesne Religions 12, 1983 ➤ 64,2325 ... 1,2333: ᴿJBL 105 (1986) 311s (A. F. *Segal*); NRT 108 (1986) 114s (J.-L. *Ska*).

1691 **Oliva** Manuel, Jacob en Betel, visión y voto (Gn 28,10-22); estudio sobre la fuente E [diss. Pont. Ist. Biblico, ᴰ*Lohfink* N., R 1973 ➤ 57,2320]. M 1975, Univ. Pont. Comillas. 148 p. – ᴿCBQ 48 (1986) 125s (E. J. *Fischer*).

1691* *Steinmetz* David C., [Gn 28] LUTHER and the ascent of Jacob's Ladder: ChH 55 (1986) 179-192.

1692 *Zucker* David J., Jacob in darkness (and light); a study in contrasts: Judaism 35 (1986) 402-413.

E2.8 *mal'ak*, Angel; *Genesis 31 ...*

1693 **Adler** G., Erinnerung an die Engel; wiederentdeckte Erfahrungen [NT]: Bücherei 1245. FrB 1986, Herder. 191 p. DM 8,90 [NRT 109, 587, A. *Toubeau*: la théologie actuelle préfère ne pas aborder l'angélologie].

1694 *Brandstetter* R., [Gn 32,24] ➌ Jacob's wrestling with God: W Drodze (1985,1) 3-20 [< RuBi 39,87].

1695 *Bühner* Jan-Adolf, Engel: ➤ 587, EvKL 1 (1986) 1030-3.

1695* *Coudert* Allison, Angels: ➤ 585, EncRel 1 (1986) 282-6.

1696 **Fossum** Jarl E., The name of God and the angel of the Lord ... Samaritan / Gnosticism: WUNT 36, 1985 ➤ 1,2344*b*: ᴿNorTTs 87 (1986) 125s (R. *Leivestad*); TLZ 111 (1986) 815s (R. *Bergmeier*).

1697 **Giudici** Maria-Pia, Qui sont les anges? [fruit de cours sur l'angélologie donné par une religieuse dans une institution romaine]. P 1985, Nouvelle Cité. 170 p. – ᴿScEspr 38 (1986) 407s (B. de *Margerie*).

1697* *Hammann* Gottfried, Le songe de Jacob et sa lutte avec l'ange (Genèse 28 et 32); repères historiques d'une lecture et de ses variations: → 83*, ꜰPᴇᴛᴇʀ R. = RHPR 66 (1986) 29-42; Eng. 130.

1698 **Klee** Vincent, Les plus beaux textes sur les Saints Anges 1985 → 1,2344*: ᴿDivinitas 30 (1986) 209s (C. *Petino*).

1699 *a)* *Pifano* Paolo, L'angelo necessario: Asprenas 33 (1986) 397-410. – *b)* *Goodman* D., Do angels eat?: JJS 37 (1986) 160-175.

1700 **Quadflieg** Josef, Das Buch von der heiligen Engeln. Donauwörth 1985, Auer. 63 p. DM 12,80. – ᴿTPQ 134 (1986) 303 (Angelika M. *Eckart*).

1701 .**Rosenberg** Alfons, Engel und Dämonen; Gestaltwandel eines Urbildes; Vorw. *Betz* Otto. Mü 1986, Kösel. 334 p.; ill. DM 48. 3-466-20278-7. – ᴿActuBbg 23 (1986) 201-3 (A. *Borràs i Feliu*).

1701* *a)* *Schmied* Wieland, Der Jakobskampf von Herbert FALKEN: Kunst und Kirche 49,1 (Linz 1986) 18-20 [< ᴢɪᴛ]. – *b)* [*Ruh* U.] Verbindlich? Päpstliche Audienzansprachen über Engel und Teufel: HerdKor 40 (1986) 454.

1702 *Smith* Morton, A note on some Jewish assimilationists; the angels [*ml'km*, 'agents', trade-union becoming family-group, with Palmyra relatives] (P. Berlin 5025b, P. Louvre 2391): → 11*, Mem. BICKERMAN E. = JANES 16s (1984s) 207-212.

1702* *Vermeylen* J., Dieu et ses représentations antinomiques dans le Livre de Jacob: → 16*, Mém. COPPIETERS de Gibson D. 1985, 591-612.

1703 *Munnich* Olivier, Note sur la Bible de PHILON; *klopophoreîn* / *klopophroneîn* en Gen. 31,26 et en Leg. All. III.20: → 81, Mém. NIKIPROWETZKY V., Hellenica 1986, 43-51.

1703* *Dotan* A., ❶ [Gen 31,35 *derek nāšîm* = pregnancy]: → 247, ᴱ*Friedman* M., Teʿuda 4 (1986)...

1704 *Jüngel* Eberhard, Festpredigt über Gen 32,23-32 im Münster zu Basel: TZBas 42 (1986) 352-360.

1705 *Lund* Jerome A., On the interpretation of the Palestinian Targumic reading *wqht* ['was benumbed'] in Gen 32:25: JBL 105 (1986) 99-103.

1706 *Caspi* Mishael M., [Gn 34] The story of the rape of Dinah; the narrator and the reader: HebSt 26 (1985) 25-45 [OTAbs 10,143].

1707 **Pitt-Rivers** Julian A., Anthropologie de l'honneur; la mésaventure de Sichem [The fate of Sichem, or, The Politics of sex (Gn 34) 1977 → 58,2950], ᵀ*Mer* Jacqueline: Les hommes et leurs signes. P 1983, Sycomore. 275 p.; 195-261: la valeur politique du sexe [KirSef 59,316].

1708 *Salkin* Jeffrey K., [Gn 34] Dinah, the Torah's forgotten woman: Judaism 35 (1986) 284-9.

E2.9   **Joseph,** *Genesis 37 ...*

1708* *a)* **Salm** Eva, [Gn 38] Juda und Tamar; eine literaturwissenschaftliche und traditionsgeschichtliche Untersuchung zu Gen 38: Diss. FrB c. 1986, ᴰ*Ruppert* L. – ZAW 98 (1986) 438. – *b)* **Golder** Mark, Genesis 38 in the context of the 'Joseph Story': diss. ᴰ*Curtis*. Manchester 1985. 297 p. – RTLv 18,541. – *c)* *Rendsburg* Gary A., David and his circle in Genesis XXXVIII: VT 36 (1986) 438-446.

1709 *Ahuvia* Abraham, ❶ Joseph's exploits: BethM 31,106 (1985s) 271-280.

1709* **Berg** M. R. van den, De Regisseur, de spelers en het grote spel; de plaats van Jozef in Gods heilsplan, een verklaring van Genesis 37-50. Kampen c. 1986, Kok. 90-242-0466-6. – ᴿNedTTs 40 (1986) 334 (M. D. *Koster*).

1710 **Goldman** Shalom L., The Joseph story in Jewish and Islamic lore: diss. NYU 1986, ᴰ*Gordon* C. H. 189 p. 87-06314. – DissA 47 (1986s) 4403-A.

1710* *Montanari* Giovanni, Giuseppe l'Ebreo della cattedra di Massimiano; prototipo del buon governo? ⇥ 70, Mem. MAZZOTTI M. = FelRav 127-130 (1984s) 305-322; 5 fig.

1711 *Renard* John, The prophet Yūsuf in the writings of JALĀL AL-DIN Rūmī: Hamdard 9,1 (1986) 11-22.

1712 **Resenhöfft** Wilhelm, *a)* Die Quellenberichte im Josef-Sinai-Komplex [Gn 37-Ex 34] 1983 ⇥ 64,2356; – *b)* Die Genesis im Wortlaut ihrer drei Quellenschriften [EurHS 23/27, 1974 ⇥ 56,1744] + Beiträge zur abschliessenden Genesis-Analyse. Fra 1984, Lang. 200+30 p. Fs 41,70. 3-261-01028-2 [BL 87,75, A. G. *Auld*: unimpressed].

1713 **Robinson** B. P., Israel's mysterious God; an analysis of some OT narratives [Joseph ...]. Newcastle 1986, Grevatt. xi-94 p. £8.45; pa. £6.50 [ZAW 99,297, I. *Kottsieper*].

1714 *Samuel* Maurice, The true character of the biblical Joseph, the brilliant failure: BR 2,1 (1986) 38-51. 68; color. ill.

1715 *Schmidt* Ludwig, Literarische Studien zur Josephsgeschichte: BZAW 167 [after *Aejmelaeus* A., Ps]. B 1986, de Gruyter. p. 121-310. 0-311-010480-6.

1716 *Westermann* C., [⇥ 1397] Der Traum im AT: ⇥ 513, Träume verstehen 1985/6, 8-23.

1717 *a)* *Brocke* Edna, Wer verkaufte Josef nach Ägypten? Gedanken zu Gen 37; – *b)* *Böhnisch* W., *al.*, Josefs Kleider; – *c)* *Perrar* Hermann-Josef, 'Brunnen lebendigen Wassers' (Gen 26,19): ZPraxRU 16 (1986) 18-20 / 21-23 / 24-26.

1718 *Longacre* Robert E., [Gen 37,28] Who sold Joseph into Egypt? ⇥ 65, ᶠMACRAE Allan, Interpretation 1986, 75-91.

1719 *Seebass* Horst, The Joseph story, Genesis 48 and the canonical process, ᵀ*Engelken* Karen: JStOT 35 (1986) 29-43.

1720 *Crocetti* Giuseppe, [Gn 49] Significato e prassi della 'benedizione' nella Bibbia: RivLtg 73 (1986) 166-187.

1721 **Drijvers** Pius, *Schilling* Peter, [Gn 49] De twaalf gezichten van de messianse mens; Jakob zegent zijn twaalf zonen. Hilversum 1986, Gooi & S. 151 p. *f* 25. – ᴿStreven 53 (1985s) 948 (P. *Bentjes*).

1721* *Heck* Joel D., Issachar; slave or freeman ? (Gen 49:14-15): JEvTS 29 (1986) 385-396 [< ZIT].

1722 **Syrén** Roger, The blessings in the Targums; a study on the targumic interpretations of Genesis 49 and Deuteronomy 33: AcÅbo [0355-578X] 64,1. Åbo 1986, Akademi. 259 p. Fm 85. 951-649-223-1 [BL 87,405, R. P. *Gordon*].

E3   **Exodus** .1 *Textus, commentarii, thema.*

1723 *Ausín* Santiago, La tradición del Éxodo en los profetas: ⇥ 366, Hermenéutica 1985/6, 423-438.

1724 *Benthem* W. van, *al.*, Verkenningen in Exodus: Bijbel en exegese, Theol. Verkenningen 2. Kampen 1986, Kok. 168 p. 90-242-4613-X [TsTNijm 26,439].

1725 **Borret** Marcel, ORIGÈNE, Homélies sur l'Exode² [¹1947]: SChr 321, 1985 ➤ 1,2378*: ᴿChH 55 (1986) 504s (R. M. *Grant*); EsprV 96 (1986) 216s (Y.-M. *Duval*); ScEspr 38 (1986) 402s (G. *Pelland*: élégant).

1726 **Burns** Rita J., Exodus, Leviticus, Numbers: OTMessage 3, 1983 ➤ 64,2365: ᴿBibTB 16 (1986) 28s (Pauline *Viviano*).

1727 *Clapham* Phillip, In search of the Exodus: Catastrophism and Ancient History 8 (LA 1986) 97-133 [71-79, *Courville* D.; OTAbs 10,133].

1728 EZECHIEL, Exagoge: *a*) **Fornaro** Pierpaolo, La voce fuori scena ... Exagogê di Ezechiele 1982 ➤ 65,2067: ᴿMnemosyne 39 (1986) 482s (P. W. van der *Horst*); RBgPg 64 (1986) 118s (J. *Schamp*). – *b*) *Gergely* T., Premier drame biblique, *exagōgē* ou 'La sortie d'Égypte' d'Ezéchiel d'Alexandrie: in ᶠDELSEMME Paul, Théâtre de toujours d'Aristôte à Kalisky, ᴱ*Debusscher* Gilbert, *Crugten* Alain Van [Bru 1983, Univ. Libre; 351 p.] 89-115 [KirSef 59,311]. – *c*) *Horbury* William, Ezekiel tragicus 106, *dōrēmata*: VT 36 (1986) 37-51. – *d*) *Arnott* W. G., Ezekiel Exagoge 208 ➤ 1,2462: (TGrF 1.128, p. 299 Snell): American Journal of Philology 106 (1985) 240s [JStJud 17 (1986) 131, *Hilhorst* A.: *énkopoi pónō* for *émponoi kópō* already suggested by *Sansone* D., Mnemosyne 4,37 (1984) 442s].

1728* *Féghali* Paul, Commentaire de l'Éxode par saint EPHREM: Parole de l'Orient 12 (Kaslik 1984s) 91-132 [< ZIT].

1729 **Fox** Everett, Now these are the names; a new English rendition of the Book of Exodus, with commentary and notes. NY 1986, Schocken. xxxvii-230 p. 0-8052-4040-9.

1730 **Goldberg** Michael, Jews and Christians; getting our stories straight 1985 ➤ 1,2381: ᴿCurrTM 13 (1986) 244 (J. C. *Rochelle*: Jews see their lives as 'trusts', Christians as 'gifts').

1731 **Hoffman** Yair, ⦿ The doctrine of the Exodus in the Bible 1983 ➤ 1,2382: ᴿBO 43 (1986) 459-461 (F. C. *Fensham*: important).

1732 **Houtman** C., Exodus I, 1:1-7:13: CommOT. Kampen 1986, Kok. 504 p. ƒ99. 90-242-0922-6 [BL 87, 50, J. W. *Rogerson*: JEPD first mentioned p. 217 in passing].

1733 **Peters** Melvin K. H., A critical edition of the Coptic (Bohairic) Pentateuch, 2. Exodus: SBL SeptCog 22. Atlanta 1986, Scholars. xi-111 p.; pa. $9, sb. $7 [ZAW 99,296]. 0-55540-030-2; pa. 1-0.

1734 **Postma** F., *al.*, Exodus, Materials in automatic text processing 1983 ➤ 64,2385 ... 1,2389: ᴿHenoch 8 (1986) 94s (P. G. *Borbone*).

1735 *Profitt* T. D., The Exodus as a revitalization movement: FolOr 23 (1985s) 237-244.

1736 **Ravasi** Gianfranco, Éxodo [1980➤ 61,3310]: Pequeno Comentário Bíblico 6. São Paulo 1985, Paulinas. 206 p. [REB 46,228].

1736* *Rodd* C. S., Which is the best commentary? VIII. Exodus: ExpTim 98 (1986s) 359-362: CHILDS.

1737 **Sanderson** Judith E., An Exodus scroll from Qumran: 4Q paleoExodᵐ and the Samaritan tradition: HarvSemSt 30. Atlanta 1986, Scholars [RQum 47,455]. xix-358 p.; bibliog. p. 347-358. $14. 1-55540-036-1.

1738 **Sarna** Nahum, *a*) Exploring Exodus; the heritage of biblical Israel. NY 1986, Schocken. xii-277 p.; bibliog. p. 247-263. $18. – ᴿBR 2,4 (1986) 46s (G. W. *Coats*: delightful). – *b*) *Sarna* Nahum M., . Exploring Exodus; the oppression: BA 49 (1986) 68-79, ill.

1739 **Schart** Aaron,   Mose und Israel im Konflikt; eine redaktionsgeschichtliche Studie zu den Wüstenerzählungen: ev. Diss. Mü 1986, ᴰ*Jeremias* J. –
RTLv 18,543.

1740 **Schmidt** Werner H.,   Exodus, Lfg. 3 [Ex 3,7...]: BK AT 2/3, 1983
➤ 1,2394:   ᴿOLZ 81 (1986) 152-4 (Eva *Osswald*); TLZ 111 (1986) 809s (J.
Conrad).

1741 *Schmidt* Werner H., Exodus: ➤ 587, EvKL 1 (1986) 1235-7.

1742 **Schuman** N. A.,   Voortvarend en vierend; stap voor stap door het boek
Exodus 1985 ➤ 1,2395:   ᴿGerefTTs 86 (1986) 243 (K. van der *Toorn*:
radio-lezingen); Streven 53 (1985s) 652 (P. *Beentjes*).

1743 **Spreafico** A.,   Esodo, memoria e promessa; interpretazioni profetiche:
RivB Sup 14, 1985➤ 1,2397:   ᴿLaurentianum 27 (1986) 374s (G. *Veltri*);
RivB 34 (1986) 403-5 (A. *Bonora*).

1743* *Stadelmann* L. I. J.,   A missão do Povo de Deus no Éxodo: PerspT 17
(1985) 343-368.

1744 **Tijn** Maartje Van,   Midrasjin I. Over de uittocht uit Egypte; van
onderdrukking en verzet. Kampen 1986, Kok. 111 p. ƒ19.90 [PrakT
13,413].

1744* *Stamatoiu* D.,   L'exode et le chéminement du peuple hébreu vers
Canaan sous la conduite de Moïse à la lumière des découvertes
archéologiques (roum.): STBuc 37 (1985) 710-724.

1745 *Strus* Andrzej,   Una liberazione dall'alto; rilettura dell'Esodo: ParVi 31
(1986) 84-93.

1746 **Walzer** Michael, Exodus and revolution 1985 ➤ 1,2401:   ᴿBAR-W 12,1
(1986) 12.14 (D. *Epstein*); JAAR 54 (1986) 805-7 (J. *Neusner*).

1747 **Wendland** Ernst H.,   Exodus: The People's Bible [NIV translation with
very conservative comment].   Milwaukee 1984, Northwestern [Publ. not
Univ.] 289 p. $7. – ᴿCurrTM 13 (1986) 376s (A. V. *Sauer*, ex-adherent of
the same trend).

1748 *Wevers* J. W.,   Translation and canonicity; a study in the narrative
portions of the Greek Exodus: ➤ 47, ꟳHOSPERS J., Scripta 1986, 295-303.

1749 **Wilson** Ian,   Exodus; the true story behind the biblical account. SF 1985,
Harper & R. 208 p. $20. 0-06-250969-1 [NTAbs 30,382].

1749* *Woudstra* Marten H.,   CALVIN interprets what 'Moses reports';
observations on Calvin's commentary on Exodus 1-19: CalvinT 21 (1986)
151-174.

E3.2   **Moyses,** *Exodus* 1 ... – Pharaoh, Goshen.

1750 *Canévet* Mariette,   Remarques sur l'utilisation du genre littéraire historique par PHILON d'Alexandrie dans la Vita Moysis, ou Moïse général en
chef - prophète: RevSR 60 (1986) 189-206.

1751 *Coats* George W.,   The failure of the hero; Moses as a model for ministry:
AsbTJ 41,2 (1986) 15-22.

1751* *a) Goedicke* Hans,   Wadi Tumilat [... Pithom; Sukkot]: ➤ 591, LexÄg
6,48 (1986) 1124-6 [on Raamses ➤ b139-b142]; – *b) Gutekunst* Wilfried,
Zauber: ➤ 591, LexÄg 6,49 (1986) 1320-1355.

1752 *Herrmann* Siegfried,   Mose [< EvT 28 (1968) 301-328]: ➤ 171, Ges. St.
1986, 47-75.

1753 **Ingersoll** R.,   Some mistakes of Moses. Buffalo 1986 = 1879, Prometheus. 270 p. $13 pa. 0-87975-361-7 [NTAbs 31,131].

1754 **Kitchen** Kenneth A.,   Pharaoh triumphant ... Ramesses II 1982
➤ 64.2377...; 1,2413:   ᴿCdÉ 61 (1986) 243-6 (Bernadette *Letellier*). – *b)*

Ramsès II, le pharaon triomphant, sa vie et son époque, [T]*Couturiati* P., *Rollinat* C. 1985 ➤ 1,2414: [R]Études 364 (1986) 560s (P. du *Bourguet*); RHist 276 (1986) 193-5 (Y. *Kœnig*).

1754* *Lange* Günter, 'Mose und der Berg in Flammen'; zum Mose-Bild der Schulbibel: KatBlätt 111 (Mü 1986) 273-281 [< ZIT].

1755 **Lehmann** J., Moses, der Religionsstifter und Befreier Israels. 1985, Heyne. 298 p. DM 9,80 [Judaica 41,256].

1756 **Martini** Carlo M., Het leven van Mozes [1980 ➤ 62,2569]: Bijbelse Spiritualiteit 3. Nijmegen 1984, Gottmer. 124 p. Fb 340. – [R]CollatVl 16 (1986) 245s (R. *Hoet*); Streven 53 (1985s) 275s (P. *Beentjes*).

1757 *Renaud* B., La figure prophétique de Moïse en Exode 3,1-4,17 [d'après W. *Schmidt*]: RB 93 (1986) 510-534; Eng. 510.

1758 a) *Renaud* Bernard, Moïse prophète et serviteur; – b) *Stehly* Ralph, Moïse pour l'Islam; – c) *Coulot* Claude, Moïse et Jésus: MondeB 44 (1986) 41s / 43s / 45s.

1758* *Rogers* Cleon, Moses; meek or miserable ? : JEvTS 29 (1986) 257-264 [< ZIT].

1759 **Schmid** H., Die Gestalt des Mose; Probleme alttestamentlicher Forschung unter Berücksichtigung der Pentateuchkrise: ErtFor 237. Da 1986, Wiss. x-144 p. DM 36; sb. 24. 3-534-09620-7 [BL 87, 77, R.J. *Coggins*: complements ErtFor 191, *Schmidt* W.H., Exodus, Sinai und Mose 1983 ➤ 64,2388].

1760 *Schmid* H., Mose im evangelischen Religionsunterricht der Grundschule und die alttestamentliche Wissenschaft: ➤ 121, [F]WIBBING S., Leben lernen 1986, 45-64.

1761 **Silver** Daniel J., Images of Moses 1982 ➤ 63,409; 65,2399: [R]RelStR 12 (1986) 174 (C. L. *Seow*).

1761* [E]**Simonetti** Manlio, GREGORIO di Nissa, La Vita di Mosè 1984 ➤ 65,2085; 1,2419: [R]BLitEc 87 (1986) 312s (H. *Crouzel*).

1762 *Stein* H. Emily, The Israel stele: ➤ 349*, [E]*Groll* S., Papers 1 (1982) 156-165.

1763 **Sweeney** Deborah, The great dedicatory inscription of Ramses II at Abydos (lines 1-79) [M. A. thesis [D]*Groll* S.]: ➤ 349*, Papers 2 (1985) 134-327.

1764 *Teeter* Emily, Observations on the presentation of the Ramesside prenomen [mostly III and XI, but including II]: VAeg 2 (1986) 175-184; 5 fig.

1765 **Wildavsky** Aaron, The nursing father; Moses as a political leader 1984 ➤ 65,2086; 1,2425: [R]BR 2,1 (1986) 12s. 17 (A. *Shinan*).

1766 **Zeligs** Dorothy F., Moses, a psychodynamic study. NY 1986, Human Sciences. 460 p. $40 [TDig 34,96].

1766* *Niccacci* Alviero, Sullo sfondo egiziano di Esodo 1-15: SBFLA 36 (1986) 7-43.

1767 *Ünal* Ahmet, [Ex 2,3] Das Motiv der Kindesaussetzung in den altanatolischen Literaturen: ➤ 543, Rencontre 32, 1985/6, 129-136.

1768 *Chiu* Andrew, [Ex 2,18; 3,1; Nm 10,29] Who is Moses' father-in-law?: EAsJT 4,1 (1986) 62-67 [Reuel 'God's friend', Hobab 'beloved', and Jethro 'His Majesty' were all appellatives for a leader whose name was forgotten].

1769 *Schmidt* Arne, Forholdet mellem det jahvistiske og elohistiske materiale i Ex. 3,1-14: DanskTTs 49 (1986) 96-109.

1770 *Couffignal* Robert, Le buisson ardent; approches nouvelles d'Exode III, 1-6: RThom 86 (1986) 644-653.

1771 *Wyatt* N., The significance of the Burning Bush: VT 36 (1986) 361-5.

1772 *Bülow-Jacobsen* Adam, *Strange* John, P. Carlsberg 49, fragment of an unknown Greek translation of the OT (Exod. 3,2-6. 12-13. 16-19); same codex as H 16 (Strasb. inv. 748): ArPapF 32 (1986) 15-21; pl. 3-6.

1773 *Levine* Etan, What is a land flowing with milk and honey? [Ex 3,8 + 14 t. Pent. + 5 t.: subsistence, not Paradise]: ➤ 21, Mem. DíEZ MACHO A., Salvación 1986, 193-204.

E3.3 **Nomen divinum, Tetragrammaton,** *Ex 3,14* ...

1773* *Doucet* Marc, Ontologie et économie dans la théologie de GRÉGOIRE le Grand; l'épisode du buisson ardent (Ex., 3,1-14]: ➤ 433*, Grégoire 1982/6, 227-234.

1774 *Görg* Manfred, Sabaoth, the 'enthroned' god: ➤ 377, IOSOT summaries (1986) 49.

1775 *Herrmann* Siegfried, Der alttestamentliche Gottesname [< EvT 26 (1966) 281-293]: ➤ 171, GesSt 1986, 76-88.

1776 **Kohata** Fujiko, Jahwist und Priesterschrift in Exodus 3-14 [Diss. Marburg, ᴰSchmidt W. H., 1985 ➤ 1,2431*]: BZAW 166. B 1986, de Gruyter. xii-372 p.; bibliog. p. 357-365. DM 94. 3-11-010649-3 [TR 83,188, J. *Scharbert*].

1777 *Kohata* Fujiko, Verzicht auf die Quellenschriften im Pentateuch? — Konsequenzen aus Textbeobachtungen in Exodus 3-14: AnJapB 12 (1986) 3-28.

1778 ᴱ**Libera** A. de, *Zum Brunn* Emilie, Celui qui est; interprétations juives et chrétiennes d'Exode 3,14: Patrimoines. P 1986, Cerf. 316 p. F 142 [NRT 109,270s, J.-L. *Ska*]. 2-204-02442-2.

1779 *Martins Terra* J. E., *a*) El, divindade dos semitas, Deus de Israel; – *b*) Noção teológica de inculturação: RCuBíb 10,39s (1986) 86-119 / 120-131.

1780 **Mettinger** Tryggve N. D., The dethronement of Sabaoth; studies in the Shem and Kabod theologies: ConBib OT 18, 1982 ➤ 63,2427 ... 1,2438: ᴿBZ 30 (1986) 116s (J. *Gamberoni*); TLZ 111 (1986) 350-2 (S. *Schreiner*). ➤ 1696, *Fossum* J.

1781 *Nebe* G. Wilhelm, Der Buchstabenname Yod als Ersatz des Tetragramms in 4 Q 511, Fragm. 10, Zeile 12 ?: RQum 12,46 (1986) 283s.

1782 **Niccacci** Alviero, *Ehyeh ašer ehyeh* (Exod. 3:14a) as 'I will be what I was' and an Egyptian parallel [Wenamun 2,27 'Is Amen-Re not now what he was?']: ➤ 377, IOSOT summaries (1986) 96.

1783 **Norin** Stig I. L., Sein Name allein ist hoch; das Jhw-haltige Suffix althebräischer Personennamen untersucht mit besonderer Berücksichtigung der alttestamentlichen Redaktionsgeschichte: ConBib OT 24. Malmö 1986, Gleerup. 227 p.; bibliog. p. 201-214. 91-40-05113-7. – ᴿNorTTs 87 (1986) 255s (H. M. *Barstad*).

1784 **Radday** Yehuda T., 'Wie ist sein Name?' (Ex 3:13): LingBib 58 (1986) 87-104; Eng. 105, 'essence' not 'personal name' is meant.

1784* *Schmidt* Anne, Forholdet mellem det jahvistiske og elohistiske materiale i Ex 3,1-14: DanTT 49 (1986) 96-109 [< ZIT].

1785 **Waaijman** Kees, De betekenis van de naam Jahwe. Kampen 1984, Kok. 189 p. *f* 31. – ᴿGerefTTs 86 (1986) 240s (C. *Houtman*); KerkT 37 (1986) 67 (B. *Maarsingh*).

1785* *Zenger* Erich, Der Gott JHWH im Spannungsfeld von Politik und Kult [*Levin* C. 1985; *Spieckermann* H. 1982...]: TR 82 (1986) 441-450.

1786 *Robinson* Bernard P., Zipporah to the rescue; a contextual study of Exodus IV 24-6: VT 36 (1986) 447-461.

1786* **Leeuwen** J.H. van, De inlijving door het bloed, of het overleveringshistorische probleem van de Pentateuch in literair perspektief, aan de hand van Exodus 4:24-26 [diss. Bru. ➤ 1,2447]. Haag 1985, Boekencentrum. 167 p. [NedTTs 41,232s, K. van der *Toorn*].

1787 *a) Glisson* Shawn D., Exodus 6:3 in Pentateuch criticism: RestQ 28 (Abilene 1985s) 135-144 [< ZIT]. – *b) Whitney* G.E., Alternative interpretations of *lō'* ['not *only*'] in Exodus 6:3 and Jeremiah 7:22: WestTJ 48 (1986) 151-9.

1788 *Wacholder* Ben Zion, A Qumranic polemic against a divergent reading of Exodus 6:20 ?: ➤ 11* Mem. BICKERMANN E. = JANES 16s (1984s) 225-8.

1788* *Van Seters* John, The plagues of Egypt; ancient tradition [no] or literary invention? [like disasters in series inflicted by the deity through Dt and prophets to Ezek, none of which know the plagues of Egypt]: ZAW 98 (1986) 31-39.

1789 *Houtman* C., On the meaning of *ûbā'ēṣîm ûbā'ăbānîm* in Exodus VII 19 ['(the sap) in the trees and (springs) in stony places' rather than merism for 'everywhere' as *Zevit*]: VT 36 (1986) 347-352.

1790 *Dorn* H.-J. *al.*, [Ex 8,3.9-11 (*Rahlfs* 7,28; 8,5-7)] Nachtrag zu dem Septuagintapapyrus VBP IV 56: ZPapEp [61 (1985) 115-121] 65 (1986) 106.

E3.4 *Pascha, sanguis, sacrificium;* **Passover, blood, sacrifice:** *Ex 11 ...*

1791 **Ben-Chorin** Schalom, Narrative Theologie des Judentums, anhand der Pessach-Haggada: Jerusalemer Vorlesungen 1985 ➤ 1,2454: ᴿArLtgW 28 (1986) 163s (J. *Hennig*); Gregorianum 67 (1986) 768s (G.L. *Prato*); JStJud 17 (1986) 82s (A. van der *Heide*: fifth instalment of a systematic treatment of Jewish theology; 1. was Jüdischer Glaube ²1979; 2. Tafeln des Bundes 1979; 3. Betendes Judentum 1980; 4. Ethik 1983); Salesianum 48 (1986) 113s (R. *Vicent*); TLZ 111 (1986) 500-2 (S. *Schreiner*); TüTQ 166 (1986) 151s (H. *Schweizer*).

1792 *a) Briend* Jacques, La pâque israélite; – *b) Grelot* Pierre, ... d'Éléphantine / intertestamentaire; – *c) Cazelles* Henri, Les fêtes de printemps; – *d) Baillet* Maurice, La pâque samaritaine en 1986; – *e) Cothenet* Édouard, La pâque dans les évangiles; – *f) Perrot* Charles, Les lectures de la synagogue / Christ notre pâque: MondeB 43 (1986) 4s / 14-21 / 6-11.15 / 27-32 (phot. coul. p. 12) / 35-39 / 24ss.33s.

1792* **Carena** Omer, Cena pasquale ebraica per comunità cristiane² 1983 (¹1980) ➤ 61,k13: ᴿParVi 30 (1985) 78 (P. *Dacquino*).

1793 *Compagnoni* Pia, La Pasqua ebraica: TerraS 62 (1986) 63-68.

1794 *Kutsch* Ernst, *a)* Erwägungen zur Geschichte der Passafeier und des Massotfestes [< ZTK 55 (1958) 1-35]; – *b)* '... am Ende des Jahres'; zur Datierung des israelitischen Herbstfestes in Ex 23,16 [(< Diss. 1955, nie veröffentlicht) < ZAW 83 (1971) 15-21]; – *c)* 'Trauerbräuche' und 'Selbstminderungsriten' im AT [< ThSt 78 (Z 1965) 23-42]: ➤ 183, KLS 1986, 29-63 / 64-70 / 78-95.

1795 *Tacik* Renate, Die Rolle des jüdischen Kindes beim Sedermahl: HLand 118,1 (1986) 2-4.

1795* *Philonenko* Marc, [Ex 12,23] PHILON d'Alexandrie et l' 'Instruction sur les Deux Esprits': ➤ 81, Mém. NIKIPROWETZKY V. 1986, 61-68.

1796 *a) Kreuzer* Siegfried, [Ex 12,40] 430 Jahre, 400 Jahre oder 4 Generationen — Zu den Zeitangaben über den Ägyptenaufenthalt der 'Israeliten': ZAW 98 (1986) 199-210. – *b) Ray* Paul J.ᴶ, The duration of the Israelite sojourn

in Egypt [430 years, as Ex 12,40H; the genealogies in Ex 6,16-27 have lacunas]: AndrUnS 24 (1986) 231-248.
1797 *Bonnet* C.,   Baal Saphon et Typhon: ⇢ 553, Cinquième: Akkadica 47 (1986) 79.
1798 *Chernus* Ira,   The rebellion at the Reed Sea; observations on the nature of midrash: HebAnR 4 (1980) 45-52 [OTAbs 10,100].
1798* *a) Thoma* Clemens,   Murrende Wüstengemeinde und ganzes Volk Gottes — Entwurf einer jüdisch-christlichen Gemeinschaftstheologie; – *b) Welten* Peter,   Zur Frage nach dem Fremden im AT: ⇢ 68*, ꟻMAYER R., Wie gut 1986, 120-9/130-8.
1799 *Chuvin* Pierre, *Yoyotte* Jean,   Documents relatifs au culte Pélusien de Zeus Casios [et ainsi à la thèse d'*Eissfeldt* du transit nord de l'Exode]: RArchéol (1986) 41-63; 9 fig.
1800 **Kratz** Reinhardt,   Rettungswunder; motiv-, traditions- und formkritische Aufarbeitung einer biblischen Gattung [Diss. ᴰ*Pesch* R.]: EurHS 23/123, 1979 ⇢ 60,3029: ᴿZkT 108 (1986) 190s (R. *Oberforcher*).
1800* *Hoffmeier* James K.,   [Ex 13,3 ...] The arm of God versus the arm of Pharaoh in the Exodus narratives: Biblica 67 (1986) 378-387.
1801 **Weimar** Peter,   Die Meerwundererzählung ... Ex 13,17-14,31: ÄgAT 9, 1985 ⇢ 1,2460: ᴿTüTQ 166 (1986) 146-8 (W. *Gross*).
1802 **Vervenne** Marc,   Het Zeeverhaal (Exodus 13,17-14,31), een literarire studie: Cath. diss. Lv 1986, ᴰ*Brekelmans* C.   352 p. – TsTNijm 26 (1986) 289; RTLv 18,544.
1803 *Graefe* Erhart,   Wunder: ⇢ 591, LexÄg 6,49 (1986) 1298s.
1803* **Ska** Jean-Louis,   Le passage de la mer; étude de la construction, du style et de la symbolique d'Ex 14,1-31 [diss. Inst. Bib. Pontifical 1984 ⇢ 65,2108]: AnBib 109. R 1986, Biblical Institute.   198 p.; bibliog. p. 181-8. $29. 88-7653-109-2. – ᴿÉTRel 61 (1986) 570s (D. *Lys*: louange, perplexités); ExpTim 98 (1986s) 376 (R. *Coggins*).
1804 *Stek* John H.,   What happened to the chariot wheels of Exodus 14:25?: JBL 105 (1986) 293s.
1805 **Howell** Maribeth,   A song of salvation, Exodus 15,1b-18: Cath. diss. Lv 1986, ᴰ*Brekelmans* C.   xlii-267 p. – TsTNijm 26 (1986) 288; RTLv 18,542.
1806 **Fanuli** Antonio, [Ex 15-34] L'uomo sulle piste di Dio; attraverso il deserto al Sinai 1984 ⇢ 65,2112; 1,2465: ᴿCC 137 (1986,2) 296s (G. *Sàvoca*).
1807 **Bienaimé** Germain,   Moïse et le don de l'eau dans la tradition juive ancienne [diss. R, Pont. Ist. Biblico 1981]: AnBib 98, 1984 ⇢ 65,2115; 1,2469: ᴿBZ 30 (1986) 303s (J. *Maier*); ETL 62 (1986) 408s (L. *Dequeker*); Istina 31 (1986) 223s (B. *Dupuy*); KirSef 59 (1985) 298; JBL 105 (1986) 737-9 (E. G. *Clarke*); NRT 108 (1986) 111s (J.-L. *Ska*).
1808 **Propp** William H.,   Water in the wilderness; the mythological background of a biblical motif: diss. Harvard 1985.   168 p. 86-02294. – DissA 47 (1986s) 212-A; HarvTR 79 (1986) 477s.
1808* **Maiberger** P., Das Manna: ÄgAT 6, 1983 ⇢ 64,2457: ᴿCrNSt 6 (1986) 601s (J. A. *Soggin*); – *b) Guglielmi* Waltraud, [Ex 16,13] Wachtel (quail, coturnix): ⇢ 591, LexÄg 6,47 (1986) 1094s.
1809 *Boyarin* Daniel,   [Ex 16,2ss] Voices in the text; midrash and the inner tension of biblical narrative: RB 93 (1986) 581-597; franç. 581s.
1809* *Van Seters* John,   Etiology in the Moses tradition; the case of Exodus 18: ⇢ 36, Mem. GOITEIN S. = HebAnR 9 (1985) 355-361.
1810 **Anati** Emmanuel,   Har Karkom montagna sacra nel deserto dell'Esodo; le scoperte archeologiche; il monte Sinai nel contesto dell'Esodo 1984 ⇢ 65,2123; 1,2477: ᴿCC 137 (1986,1) 298-300 (G. L. *Prato* won't accept

until a fragment of the tablets broken by Moses is found there); Divinitas 30 (1986) 101s (T. *Stramare*: attendiamo gli sviluppi); HumBr 41 (1986) 473s (M. *Orsatti*); Salesianum 48 (1986) 123s (B. *Amata*).

1811 **Anati** Emmanuel, The mountain of God [adv.: important new archeological evidence locates Mount Sinai]; archeological finds on the route of the Exodus. NY 1986, Rizzoli. 376 p.; 224 fig. + 152 color. $75 [Archaeology 39/5,67]. 0-8478-0723-1.

1812 *Anati* Emmanuel, Nouvelles découvertes au mont Sinaï de la Bible [sic]; la montagne de Dieu se trouve-t-elle à Har Karkom?: Archéologia 219 (1986) 30-43; (color.) ill.

1813 *a*) *Soggin* J. A., Har Karkom e le narrazioni bibliche dell'Esodo; – *b*) *Tournay* R. J., Har Karkom n'est pas le Mont Sinai; – *c*) *Gilbert* M., Har Karkom et le Mont Sinai; – *d*) *Galbiati* Enrico, Har Karkom è il monte Sinai? Identificazione possibile, cronologia impossibile; – *e*) *Luckerman* M. A., The dating of Har Karkom and Joshua; – *f*) *Cazelles* Henri, Il y a un sanctuaire mais le hiatus constitue un problème; – *g*) *Montagnini* Felice, Identificazione di Har Karkom e cronologia dell'Esodo: BCentPrei 23 (1986) (lettere) 8s / 9 / 9s / 10 / 11s / 10 / 11.

1814 **Maiberger** Paul, *a*) Topographische ... zum Sinaiproblem...: OBO 54, 1984 ⇨ 65,2128; 1,2472: RZDPV 102 (1986) 189-191 (E. A. *Knauf*). – *b*) Sinai: ⇨ 599, TWAT 5,7s (1986) 819-838 [830, *Dohmen* C.].

1814* **Ellis** Robert R., An examination of the covenant promises of Exodus 19,5-6 and their theological significance for Israel: diss. Fort Worth. – RTLv 18,541 sans date.

E3.5 **Decalogus,** *Ex 20 = Dt 5; Ex 21ss;* **Ancient Near East Law**

1815 *Beauduin* A., Les dix commandements dans la Bible et dans la catéchèse: FoiTemps 16 (1986) 205-223.

1816 **Carmichael** Calum M., Law and narrative in the Bible; the evidence of Deuteronomic laws and the Decalogue 1985 ⇨ 1,2482: RETL 62 (1986) 414s (J. *Lust*: unconvincing); JTS 37 (1986) 456-8 (A. D. H. *Mayes*: a straitjacket); TS 47 (1986) 509s (F. *Moriarty*: 'each law is based on a biblical incident rather than a life-situation' will not go unchallenged).

1817 *Crüsemann* F., Das Zehnwort vom Sinai, Magna Charta der Verantwortung von Juden und Christen: ⇨ 145, Wie Gott 1986, ...

1818 **Davidman** Joy, Smoke on the mountain; an interpretation of the Ten Commandments. Ph 1985, Westminster. 141 p. $8. 0-664-24680-X.

1818* **Douma** J., Die tien geboden, I (eerste tot derde gebod); bijdrag drs. *Lettinga* J. P.: Ethische Bezinningen 2. Kampen 1985, Van den Berg. 169 p. – RKerkT 37 (1986) 267 (B. *Maarsingh*).

1819 *a*) *Gruen* Wolfgang, O Decálogo segundo Ex 20,1-17; texto e observações; – *b*) *Carreira de Oliveira* Benjamim, O Decálogo; palavras de uma aliança; – *c*) *da Silva Airton* José, Leis de vida e leis de morte; os dez mandamentos e seu contexto social; – *d*) *Antoniazzi* Alberto, Dez mandamentos antigos e um mandamento novo: Estudos Bíblicos 9 [REB 46,1] (1986) 7-10 (24-37) / 11-23 / 38-51 / 68-76.

1820 **Hossfeld** F. L., Der Dekalog: OBO 45,1982 ⇨ 63,2471 ... 65,2136: RBbbOr 28 (1986) 64 e entrambe copertine successive (A. *Bonora*); BiKi 41 (1986) 90s (F. J. *Stendebach*).

1821 *Lefevre* Frans, De tien geboden; bijbelse en actuele betekenis [I ⇨ 1,2487] IIs: CollatVl 16 (1986) 5-36. 387-404.

1822 **Mack** Rudolf, *Volpert* Dieter, Kennen Sie die Zehn Gebote? Biblische Normen und verantwortliches Handeln: Oberstufe Religion 8. Stu 1985. – ᴿBiKi 41 (1986) 184s (N. *Hölzer*).

1823 **Metzler** E. [= *Moziani* E. (Torah of the alphabet) 1984 → 1,2492], Discovering the three-dimensional structure of the Ten Commandments: Archives for Mosaical Metrology and Mosaistics 1/2. Herborn 1986, Baalschem. 31 p. DM 18 [ZAW 99,147]. 3-924448-04-3.

1824 **Petuchowski** Jakob J., De stem van de Sinaï; een rabbijns leesboek bij de Tien geboden, praef. *Zuidema* drs. W. 1984 → 1,2494: ᴿCollatVl 16 (1986) 503 (F. *Lefevre*).

1824* *Rand* Herbert, The layout of the Decalogue on the tablets and archaeology: Dor 15 (1986s) 177-180.

1825 *Schunck* Klaus-Dietrich, LUTHER und der Dekalog: KerDo 32 (1986) 52-68; Eng. 68.

1826 *Torrell* J.-P., *a*) Les 'Collationes in decem praeceptis' de S. Thomas d'AQUIN; édition critique avec introduction et notes [à paraître dans l'édition léonine 44]: RSPT 69 (1985) 5-40.227-263; – *b*) Deux remaniements anonymes...: MedSt 40 (1978) 1-29; – *c*) La pratique pastorale d'un théologien du XIIIᵉ s.; S. Thomas d'Aquin prédicateur: RThom 82 (1982) 213-245 [RHE 81 (1986) 312 (R. *Aubert*)].

1827 **Tigay** Jeffrey H., [Ex 20,3] You shall have no other gods; Israelite religion in the light of Hebrew inscriptions: HarvSemMus 31. Atlanta 1986, Scholars. xv-114 p. 1-55540-063-9.

1828 *Croatto* J. Severino, [Ex 20,4] La exclusión de los 'otros dioses' y sus imágenes en el Decálogo: RBibArg 48 (1986) 129-139.

1829 **Dohmen** Christoph, Das Bilderverbot; seine Entstehung und Entwicklung im AT [kath. Diss. Bonn 1985]: BoBB 62, 1985 → 1,2500: ᴿETL 62 (1986) 175s (J. *Lust*: 'consequent' i.e. consistent application of editorial criticism); TZBas 42 (1986) 90s (K. *Seybold*); VerkF 31,1 (1986) 87-89 (A. *Graupner*).

1829* ᴱ**Klimkeit** H.-J., Götterbild in Kunst und Schrift [*Hoheisel* K., Judentum, 81-92; *Schützinger* H., Mesopotamien, 61-80; *Hornung* E., Ägypten, 37-60]. Bonn 1984, Grundmann. 180 p.; 49 fig. – ᴿRHPR 66 (1986) 216s (J.-G. *Heintz*).

1830 **Schroer** Silvia, In Israel gab es Bilder; Nachrichten von darstellender Kunst im Alten Testament: Diss. FrS 1985s, ᴰ*Keel* O. – TR 82 (1986) 514.

1830* *Tatum* W. Barnes, The LXX version of the Second Commandment (Ex. 20,3-6 = Deut. 5,7-10); a polemic against idols, not images: JStJud 17 (1986) 177-195.

1831 *Tsevat* Matitiahu, The prohibition of images according to the Old Testament [a) because a form of human self-veneration; *b*) because God is invisible]: → 377*a*, IOSOT summaries (1986) 137.

1832 *Alonso Díaz* José, [Ex 20,8] Valores y desvalores religiosos del sábado judaico: → 21, Mem. DíEZ MACHO A., Salvación 1986, 25-37.

1832* **Bettenzoli** G., Origine e sviluppo della tradizione sabbatica in Israele: diss. ᴰ*Fronzaroli* P. F 1978. [RivB 35,397].

1833 *Compagnoni* Pia, Il sabato ebraico: TerraS 62 (1986) 24-31.

1834 *Kutsch* Ernst, *a*) Der Sabbat — ursprünglich Vollmondtag? [ineditum]; – *b*) Menschliche Weisung — Gesetz Gottes; Beobachtungen zu einem aktuellen Thema [< ᴱ*Heine* S., Gott 1983, 77-106]: → 183, KLS 1986, 71-77 / 247-273.

1835 *Nowell* Irene, Sabbath; sign of the Covenant: BToday 24 (1986) 376-380.

1835* *Pérès* Jacques-Noël, Le quatrième commandement; de la gratitude à l'action de grâces: PosLuth 34 (1986) 200-218.

1836 a) *Schwantes* Milton, 'Seis dias trabalharás e farás toda a tua obra' — iniciação à temática do trabalho e do trabalhador na Bíblia; – b) *Erich Dobberahn* Friedrich, Trabalho e direito fundiário — observações a partir do Antigo Oriente; – c) *Burin* Aguinelo, O Sábado, descanso do trabalho: Estudos Biblicos 11 [REB 46,3] (1986) 6-21 / 69-75 / 76-82.

1836* a) *Albertz* R., Altes und Neues zum Elterngebot: Zeitschrift für Gottesdienst und Predigt 3 (1985) 22-26 [< JbBT 1, 223]; – b) *Klemm* Peter, Zum Elterngebot im Dekalog: BTZ 3 (1986) 50-60.

1837 *Ydit* M., [Ex 20,12, honor father and mother, Pe'a 1,1] A case study in Mishnaic theodicy: JRefJud 33,1 (NY 1986) 65-74 [NTAbs 30,337].

1838 **Gnuse** Robert, [Ex 20,13] You shall not steal 1985 ➤ 1,7862: ᴿCurrTM 13 (1986) 180 (W. *Henkenmeier*: proves the command protects not property but people).

1839 *Bosman* Hendrik, [Ex 20,14] Adultery, prophetic tradition and the decalogue: ➤ 377a, IOSOT summaries (1986) 19.

1840 *Boecker* Hans-J., a) [Ex 20,22 - 23,19(33)] Bundesbuch; ➤ 587, EvKL 1 (1986) 578s / 797-9.

1840* *Levi-Feldblum* Eila, ❿ [Ex 21,2; Dt 15,12] The law of the Hebrew slave; differences of style and their meaning: BetM 31,107 (1985s) 348-359.

1841 *Ellington* John, [Ex 21,22] Miscarriage or premature birth [LXX takes MT to mean that if the lost fetus is not yet recognizably formed, the punishment is a fine and not as if for a capital offense]: BTrans 37 (1986) 334-7.

1841* *Freund* R., [Ex 21,22s] The ethics of abortion in Hellenistic Judaism: Helios 10 (1983) 125-137 [< JStJud 17,137].

1842 *Herrmann* Siegfried, Das 'apodiktische Recht'; Erwägungen zur Klärung dieses Begriffs [< Mitteilungen Inst. Or.-Forsch. 15 (1969) 249-261]: ➤ 171, GesSt 1986, 89-100.

1843 *Westbrook* Raymond, Lex talionis and Exodus 21, 22-25: RB 93 (1986) 52-69.

1844 *Carmichael* Calum, [Ex 21,23 ...] a) Biblical laws of talion: ➤ 36, Mem. GOITEIN S. = HebAnR 9 (1985) 107-126; – b) Biblical laws of talion: with – c) *Daube*, David, Witnesses in Bible and Talmud. Ox 1986, Centre for Postgraduate Hebrew Studies. p. 21-39 / 1-10.

1844* *Bakon* Shimon, [Ex 22,17 ...] Witchcraft in the Bible [begins, 'When, in 1962 (!), "witches" were executed in Salem after due process, Cotton MATHER could write ...']: Dor 15 (1986s) 234-243.

1845 *Luciani* Ferdinando, Il significato di *'ad [bô' haššemeš]* in Es 22,25b: RivB 34 (1986) 391-5.

1846 *Erling* Bernhard, [Ex 22,29] First-born and firstlings in the Covenant Code: ➤ 392, SBL Seminars 1986, 470-8.

1847 **Keel** O., [Ex 23,19 ...] Das Böcklein ...: OBO 33, 1980 ➤ 61,3474 ... 65, 2184: ᴿZDPV 102 (1986) 184-9 (B. *Janowski*).

1848 *Ratner* Robert, *Zuckerman* Bruce, ['A kid in milk'? New photographs of [Ugarit] KTU 1.23, line 14: HUCA 57 (1986) 15-52; 8 pl.

1849 *Ben-Chorin* Schalom, Das althebräische Gerichtswesen: ZRGg 38 (1986) 268s.

1850 *Cole* G. A., Justice; retributive or reformative [... OT]: RefTR 45 (1986) 5-12.

1851 *de Menezes* Rui, Social justice in Israel's law: Bible Bhashyan 11 (1985) 10-46.

1851* *a) Greenberg* Moshe, More reflections on biblical criminal law; – *b) Japhet* Sara, The relationship between the legal corpora in the Pentateuch in the light of manumission laws: ➔ 251*, StHieros 31 (1986) 1-17 / 83-89.

1852 **Gropp** Douglas M., The Samaria papyri from Wâdī ed-Dâliyeh; the slave sales [... Neo-Babylonian antecedents]: diss. Harvard. CM 1986. 161 p. 86-20578. – DissA 47 (1986s) 2141-A.

1852* **Hoyles** J. A., Punishment in the Bible. L 1986, Epworth. xi-148 p. £5.95. 0-7162-0425-8 [BL 87, 84, G. *Emmerson*: more broadly on his concerns as prison-chaplain].

1853 **Jacobs** Louis, A tree of life... Jewish law 1984 ➔ 65,2166; 1,2518: ᴿJRel 66 (1986) 210-2 (D. *Novak*); RB 93 (1986) 465 (M.-J. *Pierre*).

1853* **L'Hour** J., La morale de l'Alliance, 1985 [= 1966 ➔ 48,3811], ➔ 1,2644: ᴿComLtg 68 (1986) 93s (D. *Dufrasne*).

1854 **Patrick** Dale, Old Testament Law 1985 ➔ 1,2523: also L 1986, SCM. £8.50. 0-334-02228-2: ᴿBibTB 16 (1986) 38 (R. *Gnuse*); BS 143 (1986) 178s (E. H. *Merrill*); CurrTM 13 (1986) 49s (R. W. *Nysse*); ExpTim first choice 97,10 (1985s) 289s (C. S. *Rodd*).

1855 *Sokol* Moshe Z., The autonomy of reason, revealed morality and Jewish law: RelSt 22 (1986) 423-437.

1856 **Weinfeld** M., ⊕ *Mišpat u-ṣᵉdāqâ*... righteousness in Israel and the nations; equality and freedom in ancient Israel in the light of social justice in the Ancient Near East: Perry Foundation. J 1985, Magnes. 182 p. – ᴿRB 93 (1986) 602-5 (R. *Westbrook*).

1857 *Allam* S., Réflexions sur le 'Code légal' d'Hermopolis dans l'Égypte ancienne: CdÉ 61,121 (1986) 50-75.

1858 **Cardellini** Innocenzo, Die biblischen 'Sklaven'-Gesetze im Lichte des keilschriftlichen Sklavenrechts 1981 ➔ 62,2663... 1,2514: ᴿZkT 108 (1986) 80 (G. *Fischer*).

1859 *Epsztein* Léon, La justice sociale dans le Proche-Orient ancien et le peuple de la Bible 1983 ➔ 64,2488; 65,2191: ᴿBO 43 (1986) 766s (C. van *Leeuwen*); BZ 30 (1986) 125s (H. *Niehr*).

1860 **Epsztein** Léon, Social justice in the Ancient Near East and the people of the Bible. L 1986, SCM. 178 p.; bibliog. p. 149-173. £8. 0-334-02334-3. ᴿExpTim 2d choice 97,12 (1985s) 354s (C. S. *Rodd*: 'in a Webrian manner'; author's name misspelled].

1861 *Haase* Richard, Texte zum hethitischen Recht; eine Auswahl 1984 ➔ 65,2194: ᴿWeltOr 17 (1986) 164-7 (J. *Hengstl*).

1862 **Klíma** Josef, Zakony Asyrie a Chaldeje, pokracovatele Chammurapiho. Praha 1985, Academia [ChOrInstAcq Ag87].

1863 *Klima* Josef, Le règlement du mariage dans les lois babyloniennes anciennes: ➔ 82, ᶠOBERHUBER K., Im Bannkreis 1986, 109-121.

1864 *Lorton* David, The king and the law [in ancient Egypt]: VAeg 2 (1986) 53-62; dazu 87-92, *Boochs* Wolfgang, Zur Bedeutung der *hpw*. ➔ 9335, *Kruchten* J.

1865 *Petschow* H. P. H., Beiträge zum Codex Ḫammurapi: ZAss 76 (1986) 17-75.

1866 **Ries** Gerhard, Prolog und Epilog in Gesetzen des Altertums: MüB-PapFR 76, 1983 ➔ 65,2203; 1,2542: ᴿClasR 100 (1986) 146s (T. *Honoré*);

Muséon 99 (1986) 357 (P. *Bogaert*); WeltOr 17 (1986) 167-172 (J. *Hengstl*).

1867 **Saporetti** Claudio, The Middle Assyrian Laws: 1984 ➤ 65,2205: ᴿZAss 76 (1986) 137s (D. O. *Edzard*).

1868 *Sauren* Herbert, Le mariage selon le Code d'Eshnunna: RIDA 33 (1986) 45-86.

1869 **Sick** Ulrich, Die Tötung eines Menschen und ihre Ahndung in den keilschriftlichen Rechtssammlungen unter Berücksichtigung rechtsvergleichender Aspekte: Inaug.–Diss. Tü, 1984 ➤ 65,2207; 1,2545: ᴿZAss 76 (1986) 124-6 (M. *Stol*).

1870 *a) Vandendriessche* M., Il y a 4000 ans; un homme se marie...; – *b) Sauren* H., La diandrie en Mésopotamie (résumé): Akkadica 42 (1985) 24-31 / 48 (1986) 41.

E3.6 **Cultus**, *Exodus 25-40*.

1871 **Costecalde** Claude-Bernard, Aux origines du sacré biblique. [< SDB ➤ 1,2571]. P 1986, Letouzey & A. 156 p.; bibliog. p. 143-155. 2-7350-0138-5.

1872 *Brown* John P., The Ark of the Covenant and the temple of Janus: BZ 30 (1986) 20-35.

1872* **Olyan** Saul M., Problems in the history of the cult and priesthood in ancient Israel [Am 8,14; Asherah...]: diss. Harvard 1986. 232 p. 86-02292. – DissA 47 (1986s) 211-A.

1873 **Revel-Neher** Elisabeth, L'arche d'alliance dans l'art juif et chrétien du second au dixième siècle 1984 ➤ 1,2552; F 195: ᴿJbAC 29 (1986) 218-222 (F. *Rickert*); REByz 44 (1986) 327s (C. *Walter*).

1873* **Nelson** Russell D., Studies in the development of the [Hebrew/Greek] text of the Tabernacle account: diss. Harvard, ᴰ*Cross* F. CM 1986. 392 p. 87-04482. – DissA 47 (1986s) 4075-A.

1874 **Nielsen** Kjeld, Incense in ancient Israel: VTSup 38. Leiden 1986, Brill. xi-147 p.; bibliog. p. 132-9. 90-04-07702-2.

1874* *a) Rodríguez* Ángel M., [Ex 25,8] Sanctuary theology in the Book of Exodus: AndrUnS 24 (1986) 127-145. – *b) Petit* Madeleine, [Ex 25,12 ...] Le contenu de l'Arche d'Alliance; génération et addition de thèmes [... Héb. 9,4]: ➤ 81, Mém. NIKIPROWETZKY V., Hellenica 1986, 335-346.

1875 **Dam** Cornelius van, [Ex 28,30...] The Urim and Thummim: Ref. Diss. ᴰ*Ohmann* H. Kampen 1986, Van den Berg. 344 p. (2 vol.) – TsTNijm 26 (1986) 287.

1876 **Moberly** R. W. L., At the mountain of God... Ex 32-34, 1983 ➤ 64,2532*... 1,2561: ᴿJBL 105 (1986) 132-4 (T. W. *Mann*).

1877 *Perani* Mauro, [Ex 32-34] Senso letterale e senso cabalistico nel commento di Mosheh b. NAḤMAN all'episodio del Vitello d'Oro: Henoch 8 (1986) 39-48; franç. 48.

1878 *Turiot* C., Une lecture du Veau d'Or, Exode 32: SémiotB 43 (1986) 8-22.

1878* *Agmon* Mordechai, ☯ [Ex 33,29-35] The horns of Moses' skin: BethM 31,105 (1985s) 186-8.

E3.7 **Leviticus**.

1879 ᵀᴱ**Danieli** Maria Ignazia, ORIGENE, Omelie sul Levitico: Testi Patristici 51. R 1985, Città Nuova. 349 p. Lit. 17.000. 88-311-3051-X. – ᴿCC 137 (1986,1) 503s (E. *Cattaneo*); Teresianum 37 (1986) 510 (M. *Diego Sánchez*).

1879* a) *Darling* Averill S., The levitical code; hygiene or holiness; – b) *Browne* Stanley G., Leprosy in the Bible: ➤ 261, ᴱ*Palmer* B., Medicine 1986, 85-99.258 / 101-125.259s.

1880 a) **Freedman** D. N., *Mathews* K. A., The paleo-Hebraic Leviticus scroll 1985 ➤ 1,2873*: ᴿAndrUnS 24 (1986) 272-5 (W. H. *Shea*); JStJud 17 (1986) 248-251 (F. *García Martínez*); VT 36 (1986) 501 (J. A. *Emerton*). – b) *Mathews* K. A., The Leviticus scroll (11QPaleoLev) and the text of the Hebrew bible: CBQ 48 (1986) 171-200 [200-207 Hebrew text].

1881 **Kornfeld** Walter, Leviticus; NEchter 6, 1983 ➤ 64,2535; 65,2235: ᴿJBL 105 (1986) 315s (G. J. *Wenham*: not an advance on his 1972 Lev).

1882 **Neusner** Jacob, Judaism and Scripture; the evidence of Leviticus Rabbah: ChStHistJud. Ch 1986, Univ. xxii-641 p. $50. 0-226-57614-0. – ᴿTDig 33 (1986) 481 (W. C. *Heiser*).

1882* a) *Stern* David, Midrash and the language of exegesis; a study of Vayikra Rabbah, ch. 1; – b) *Kugel* James L., Two introductions to midrash: ➤ 249, ᴱ*Hartman* G., Midrash 1986, 105-124 / 77-103.

1883 **Verhuyck** P. E. R., La Bible de Macé de la Charité, II. Levitique ... Juges. Leiden 1977, Presse Univ. lii-138 p. – ᴿRBgPg 62 (1984) 632-4 (M. *Gosman*).

1884 **Wevers** John W., a) (with *Quast* U.), Leviticus graece: Gö Septuaginta 2/2. Gö 1986, Vandenhoeck & R. 328 p. 3-525-53444-2. – b) Text history of the Greek Leviticus: AbhGö 153 / MittSeptU 19. Gö 1986, Vandenhoeck & R. 136 p. 3-525-82440-8.

1885 a) **Anderson** Gary A., [Lv 1-7 ...] Sacrifices and offerings in ancient Israel; studies in their social and political importance: diss. Harvard 1985. 212 p. 86-02281. – DissA 47 (1986s) 199-A; – b) **Marx** Alfred, Formes et fonctions du sacrifice a YHWH d'après l'Ancien Testament: diss. prot. ᴰ*Jacob* E. Strasbourg 1986. 461 p. – RTLv 18,543.

1885* **Gorman** Frank H.ᴶ, Priestly ritual and creation theology; the conceptual categories of space, time, and status in Lev. 8,14.16; Num. 19,28-39: diss. Emory, ᴰ*Hayes* J. Atlanta 1985. 439 p. 86-05733. – DissA 47 (1986s) 201s-A; RelStR 13,189.

1886 *Fernández Marcos* Natalio, [Lv 11] El 'sentido profundo' de las prescripciones dietéticas judías (Carta de Aristeas, 143-169): ➤ 21, Mem. Díez Macho A., Salvación 1986, 553-562.

1886* **Amorim** Nilton D., Desecration and defilement in the Old Testament: diss. Andrews, ᴰ*Davidson* R. Berrien Springs MI 1986. 418 p. 86-24224. – DissA 47 (1986s) 2620-A.

1887 **Seidl** Theodor, Tora für den 'Aussatz'-Fall ... Lev 13s: AOtt 1982 ➤ 63, 2581; 1,2588: ᴿCBQ 48 (1986) 127-9 (G. J. *Wenham*: not much help).

1888 Sifra, the Rabbinic commentary on Leviticus; an American translation: 1. The Leper, Lv 13:1 - 14:57, *Neusner* Jacob; 2. Support for the poor, Lv 19:5-10, *Brooks* Roger: Brown JudSt 102. Atlanta 1985, Scholars. 162 p. 0-89130-913-6; pa. 4-4.

1889 *Capelli* Piero, [Lv 14,24 ...] Alcune note al trattato Terumot della Mishna: EgVO 9 (1986) 165-173.

1890 **Azuwou Onibere** S. G., [Lv 16] Old Testament sacrifice in African tradition; a case of scape-goatism: ➤ 377a, IOSOT summaries (1986) 11.

1891 *Wright* David P., The gesture of hand placement in the Hebrew Bible [Lv 16:21 ...; one/two hands as rightly R. *Peter* 1977] and in Hittite literature: JAOS 106 (1986) 433-446.

1892 **Loretz** Oswald, [Lv 16,26] Leberschau, Sündenbock, Asasel in Ugarit und Israel [➤ 1,2591]; Leberschau und Jahwestatue in Psalm 27; Leberschau in

Psalm 74: Ug.-Bibl. Lit. 3. Altenberge 1985. 138 p.; 3 pl.; bibliog. p. 122-
135. DM 44,80. 3-88733-061-7. – ᴿZAW 98 (1986) 470s (J. van *Oorschot*).
1893 *Görg* Manfred, [Lv 17...] Fremdsein in und für Israel: MüTZ 37 (1986)
217-232.
1894 *Gewalt* Dietfried, Taube und Blinde nach Leviticus 19,14: DiehlB 22
(1985) 119-139.
1895 **Mathys** Hans-Peter, [Lv 19,18] Liebe deinen Nächsten wie dich selbst;
Untersuchungen zum alttestamentlichen Gebot der Gottesliebe Lev 19,18
[Diss. Bern]: OBO 71. FrS/Gö 1986, Univ./Vandenhoeck & R. xii-195 p.
DM 80. 3-7278-0357-6. – ᴿETL 62 (1986) 411s (J. *Lust*); ExpTim 98
(1986s) 277s (R. *Coggins*).
1895* *Schwartz* Baruch J., A literary study of the slave-girl pericope —
Leviticus 19:20-22 [< M.A. diss., Hebrew Univ. 1980]: ScrHieros 31 (1986)
241-255.
1896 *Compagnoni* Pia, [Lv 23,15-20...] La festa di Pentecoste: TerraS 62
(1986) 100-8.
1896* a) *Sierra* Sergio J., Le feste ebraiche; – b) *Boggio* Giovanni, 'Io detesto
le vostre feste'...: ParVi 31 (1986) 10-18 / 19-25.
1897 *Livingston* Dennis H., The crime of Leviticus XXIV 11: VT 36 (1986) 352-4.
1898 **Fager** Jeffrey A., Land tenure and land reform in Leviticus 25: diss. in
progress, Vanderbilt Univ. [RelStR 12,324].
1899 *Crüsemann* F., Der grössere Sabbat — oder die Weisung, sich nicht zu
Tode zu arbeiten (3. Mose 25,1-13): ⇒ 145, Wie Gott 1986, ...
1899* *Katzoff* Louis, [(Lev 25; Dt 15) Ex 23,10] Shemittah and the geography
of Israel: Dor 15 (1986s) 163-5 [this Hebrew year, 5747, is a Shemittah
year in Israel].
1900 *Di Sante* Carmine, [Lv 25,23...] La categoria della *berakah*; l'uomo biblico di fronte alla terra [< Sidic 18,2 (1985) 7-10]: HumBr 41 (1986) 377-383.
1901 *Moss* Rowland, [Lv 25,23] The land is mine ... and you are .. my tenants:
reflections on the biblical view of man and nature: ⇒ 111, ᶠSTILL W.,
Pulpit & people 1986, 103-116.

E3.8   *Numeri*, **Numbers, Balaam.**

1903 **Licht** Jacob, ❶ *Peruš al Seper Bamidbar* ... Commentary on the book of
Numbers. J 1985, Magnes. 169 p. [KirSef 60,363].
1904 *Minsuki* ❶ (Numbers): Studium Biblicum Franciscanum. Tokyo 1986,
Chūō. vi-245 p.; 2 maps. Y 2800 [BL 87,55].
1905 **Neusner** J., Sifré to Numbers; an American translation and expansion, I.
1-58; II. 59-115: BrownJudSt 118s. Atlanta 1986, Scholars. xvi-232 p.;
vi-186 p. $28 + $25. 1-55540-008-6; 10-8 [NTAbs 31,126].
1905* *Vigne* Daniel, ORIGÈNE, la XVIIᵉ homélie sur les Nombres (suite et fin)
[iv. Les tentes, ou le progrès; v. le Royaume, ou l'exaltation; vi. réflexions]:
BLitEc 87 (1986) 5-28; Eng. p. 4.

1906 **Tolila** Joëlle, Traduction et commentaires des chapitres 1 à 10 du livre
des 'Nombres' dans la 'Septante': diss. P Sorbonne 1986, ᴰ*Harl* M. – RTLv
18,543.
1906* **Olson** D. T., [Nm 1; 26] The death of the old and the birth of the new;
the framework of the Book of Numbers and the Pentateuch: BrownJudSt
71. Chico CA 1985, Scholars. viii-253 p. $30; pa. $23. 0-89130-885-7; 6-5.
[BL 87,72s, E. W. *Nicholson*].

1907 *Frymer-Kensky* Tikva, [Num 5,11-31] The trial before God of an accused adulteress: BR 2,3 (1986) 46-49.

1908 *Riesner* Rainer, [Nm 6,24-25 auf Silberplättchen] Bisher älteste Bibeltexte in Jerusalem gefunden: HLand 118,4 (1986) 13s [< Idea]. ➤ 1193, *Moscati* S.

1908* *Milgrom* Jacob, The chieftains' gifts; Numbers, chapter 7: ➤ 36, Mem. GOITEIN S. = HebAnR 9 (1985) 221-5.

1909 **Ahuis** Ferdinand, Autorität in Umbruch ... Nm 16s, 1983 ➤ 64,2566; 65,2266: ᴿTR 82 (1986) 452-4 (J. *Scharbert*).

1910 *Daoust* J. [< *Briend* J., MondeB 39 (1985) Nm 13,26...] Qadesh dans la Bible: EsprV 96 (1986) 373-5.

1911 *Stein* Hans W., Haderwasser (4. Mose 20,1-13): TBei 17 (Wu 1986) 57-62 [< ZIT].

1911* *Ferrando Lada* José L., La infidelidad de Moisés y Aarón y la protesta de los Hijos de Israel (Num 20,1-13); ensayo de lectura sincrónico-teológica: SBFLA 36 (1986) 45-61.

1912 *Smelik* K. A. D., [Num 20,14-21 ...] Dating the story of the war against Sihon and Og [600 B.C.]: ➤ 377*a*, IOSOT summaries (1986) 127.

1913 *Greiner* Albert, [Nm 21,9] Le serpent d'airain et le Crucifié: PosLuth 34,1 (1986) 22-27 [ZIT].

1913* **Davies** LeGrande, Serpent imagery in ancient Israel; the relationship between the literature and the physical remains: diss. Utah, ᴰ*Hammond* P. 286 p. 86-16076. – DissA 47 (1986s) 1786s-A.

1914 **Hackett** Jo Ann, [Nm 22-24] The Balaam text from Deir'Allā [diss. Harvard] 1984 ➤ 65,2375; 1,2628: ᴿCBQ 48 (1986) 109s (W. J. *Fulco*: splendid); JAOS 106 (1986) 364 (B. A. *Levine*); JTS 37 (1986) 476-8 (J. A. *Emerton*); OLZ 81 (1986) 473-5 (W. *Herrmann*); RelStR 12 (1986) 63 (S. D. *Sperling*); VT 36 (1986) 507s (G. I. *Davies*).

1914* **Hackett** Jo Ann, Some observations on the Balaam tradition at Deir'Allā: BA 49 (1986) 216-222; ill.

1915 *a*) *Kooij* Gerrit van der, *Puech* Émile, Tell Deir'Allā, l'inscription de Balaam; – *b*) *Brossier* François, Le combat de Jacob contre l'ange; – *c*) *Briend* Jacques, Le passage des tribus d'Israël en Transjordanie; – *d*) *Asurmendi* Jesus, Les oracles contre les nations: MondeB 46 (1986) 34s.36ss / 39 / 40ss / 43.

1915* *Luria* B. Z., ⊕ Who is Bileam ben-Beor?: BethM 31,104 (1985s) 1-5.

1916 **Rouillard** Hedwige, La péricope de Balaam (Nombres 22-24); la prose et les 'oracles' [diss. Sorbonne]: ÉtBN 4, 1985 ➤ 1, 2627: ᴿETL 62 (1986) 412-4 (J. *Lust*); ÉTRel 61 (1986) 571s (D. *Lys*: beau; brouilles); JSS 31 (1986) 245-7 (J. *Van Seters*); RechSR 74 (1986) 618s (J. *Briend*); RevSR 60 (1986) 261s (B. *Renaud*).

1917 *Safren* Jonathan D., The conclusion of the Balaam narrative (Num. 22:2-24:25): ➤ 377*a*, IOSOT summaries (1986) 119.

1918 *Klassen* William, [Nm 25,1-13] Jesus and Phineas; a rejected role model: ➤ 392, SBL Seminars 1986, 490-500.

1919 *Schiffman* Lawrence H., The law of vows and oaths (Num. 30:3-16) in the Zadokite fragments and the Temple Scroll: ➤ 377*a*, IOSOT summaries (1986) 121.

Jobling David, The sense of [Num 32] 1986 ➤ 176.

E3.9   Liber Deuteronomii.

1919* **Alghisi** A., Gli 'altri dèi' nel Deuteronomio, nell'opera storica deuteronomistica e in Geremia: diss. Milano, Univ. Cattolica 1984, ᴰ*Luciani* F. [RivB 35,86].

1920 *Bettenzoli* Giuseppe,   I Leviti e la riforma deuteronomica: RivStoLR 22 (1986) 3-23.

1921 **Bietenhard** H., (*Ljungman* H.),   Der tannaitische Midrasch Sifre Deuteronomium: Judaica et Christiana 8,   3-261-03311-8.   1985 ➤ 65,2279; 1,2633: ᴿBL (1986) 112 (C. T. R. *Hayward*); JStJud 17 (1986) 83-86 (Margarete *Schlüter*); Judaica 41 (1985) 121s (S. *Schreiner*).

1922 **Braulik** Georg,   Deuteronomium 1-16,17: NEchter AT 15.   Wü 1986, Echter.   120 p. DM 28; sb. 24.   3-429-00997-9.

1923 *Braulik* Georg,   Das Deuteronomium und die Menschenrechte: TüTQ 166 (1986) 8-24.

1924 **Ginsberg** H. L.,   The Israelian heritage of Judaism [northern Dt] 1982 ➤ 63,2622 ... 1,2640: ᴿBO 43 (1986) 183-5 (A. *Hultgård*).

1924* *Goldberg* Abraham,   ⊕ The school of Rabbi AKIBA and the school of Rabbi ISHMAEL in *Sifre* Deuteronomy, Pericopes 1-54: ➤ 246, Teʿuda 3 (1983) 7-16; Eng. vii.

1925 *Herrmann* Siegfried,   a) Die konstruktive Restauration; das Deuteronomium als Mitte biblischer Theologie [ᶠRAD G. von, Probleme 1971, 155-170]; – b) 'Bund' eine Fehlübersetzung von bᵉrīt'? [ineditum]: ➤ 171, Ges.St. 1986, 163-178 / 210-220.

1926 a) *Hoppe* Leslie J.,   Deuteronomy and the poor; – b) *Pawlikowski* John T.,   Participation in economic life [co-creation suggested in Genesis; *Vawter* B.]: BToday 24 (1986) 371-5 / 363-9.

1927 *Labuschagne* C. J.,   Some significant composition techniques in Deuteronomy: ➤ 47, ᶠHOSPERS J., Scripta 1986, 121-131.

1928 ᴱ**Lohfink** N.,   Das Deuteronomium 1983/5 ➤ 1,481: ᴿETL 62 (1986) 166-8 (R. E. *Clements*); ÉTRel 61 (1986) 584s (T. *Römer*); JTS 37 (1986) 454-6 (J. G. *McConville*: no dialogue, even of Lohfink with PERLITT; muddles along separate tracks); RechSR 74 (1986) 620 (J. *Briend*).

1929 **McConville** J. G.,   Law and theology in Deuteronomy [diss. Belfast 1980, ᴰ*Wenham* G.]: JStOT Sup 33, 1984 ➤ 65,2294: ᴿBiblica 67 (1986) 423-7 (G. *Braulik*: Hauptresultate überzeugen nicht); ScotJT 39 (1986) 257s (A. G. *Auld*); Themelios 12 (1986s) 25 (R. W. L. *Moberly*).

1930 *Marangon* Antonio,   Il Dio della liberazione e dell'Alleanza: RClerIt 67 (1986) 428-434.

1931 *Perlitt* Lothar,   Deuteronomium: ➤ 587, EvKL 1 (1986) 823-5.

1932 **Peters** Melvin K. H.,   A critical edition of the Coptic (Bohairic) Pentateuch, 5. Deuteronomy: SeptCog 15, 1983 ➤ 64,2588 ... 1, 2647: ᴿOrientalia 55 (1986) 349-354 (H. *Quecke*).

_____

1933 a) *Schedl* Claus,   Prosa und Dichtung in der Bibel; logotechnische Analyse von Dtn 1,9-18: ZAW 98 (1986) 271-5. – b) *Kaswalder* Pietro,   Lo schema geografico deuteronomista; Dt 3,8-17: SBFLA 36 (1986) 63-84; 2 maps.

1933* **Knapp** Dietrich,   Deuteronomium 4; literarische Analyse und theologische Interpretation: Diss. ᴰ*Perlitt* L.   Gö 1986. – RTLv 18,542.

1934 *Rofé* Alexander,   ⊕ Dt 4,32-40; monotheist ...: BethM 31,106 (1985s) 211-9.

1934* *Gubler* Marie-Louise,   'Der Herr wird alle Krankheit von dir nehmen' (Dtn 7,15); ein theologischer Durchblick durch das Alte Testament: Diakonia 17 (1986) 6-17.

1935 *Legrand* Lucien,   [Dt 10,18] L'étranger dans la Bible: Spiritus 27 (1986) 57-67.

1935* **Butterfield** Robert A., Deuteronomy 12-20 in cultural evolutionary perspective: diss. Lutheran School of Theology. Ch 1986. 217 p. 86-21948. – DissA 47 (1986s) 2198-A.

1936 *Palatty* Paul, The centralisation of cult in Deuteronomy (an exegetical study of Deu. 12,2-6 with a historico-critical point of view): Bible Bhashyam 12 (1986) 219-236.

1936* **Carmichael** Calum M., Women, law, and the Genesis tradition [Dt 21-24 against] 1979 → 60,3416; 62,2800: ᴿRB 93 (1986) 153s (J. *Loza*).

1937 *Davies* Eryl W., The meaning of *pî šᵉnayim* in Deuteronomy XXI 17: VT 36 (1986) 341-7.

1938 **Locher** Clemens, Die Ehre einer Frau in Israel; exegetische und rechtsvergleichende Studien zu Deuteronomium 22,13-21 [Diss. Fra St. Georgen 1984, ᴰ*Lohfink* N.]: OBO 70. FrS/Gö 1986, Univ./VR. xviii-464 p. Fs 110. 3-7278-0356-8 / VR 3-525-53697-6 [BL 87,87, A. *Mayes*].

1939 **Neudecker** Reinhard, [Dt 24,1-4] Frührabbinisches Ehescheidungsrecht: BOrPont 39, 1982 → 63,2651 ... 1,2674: ᴿOLZ 81 (1986) 158-160 (W. *Wiefel*); RB 93 (1986) 622 (É. *Nodet*).

1940 *Westbrook* Raymond, The prohibition on [sic] restoration of marriage in Deuteronomy 24:1-4: → 251*, ScrHieros 31 (1986) 387-405.

1940* *Manor* D. W., [Dt 25,5-10] A brief history of levirate marriage as it relates to the Bible: RestQ 27,3 (1984) 129-142 [NTAbs 30,206].

1941 *Shrager* Miriam Y., [Dt 25,12, cutting off woman's hand] A unique biblical law: Dor 15 (1986s) 190-194; on p. 159 editors' comment: not so unique; aspect of talion.

1941* *Lachs* Samuel T., [Dt 26,3 ...] Two related Arameans; a difficult reading in the Passover Haggadah: JStJud 17 (1986) 65-69.

1942 **Basser** Herbert W., [Dt 32, Sifre 306-341] Midrashic interpretations of the Song of Moses [diss. Toronto 1983]: AmerUnivS 7/2, 1984 → 65,2326; 1,2685: ᴿJStJud 17 (1986) 234s (H. E. *Gaylord*: severe); Judaica 41 (1985) 247s (S. *Schreiner*); RelStR 12 (1986) 81 (A. J. *Avery-Peck*).

1943 *a) Segert* Stanislav, Rendering of parallelistic structures in the Targum Neofiti; the song of Moses (Dt 32:1-43); – *b) Rodríguez Carmona* Antonio, La muerte de Moisés según el Targum Dt 34,5; – *c) Martínez Saiz* Teresa (de Jesús), La muerte de Moisés en Sifré Deuteronomio: → 21, Mem. DÍEZ MACHO A., Salvación 1986, 515-532 / 503-514 / 205-214.

1944 *Tal* Abraham, The Samaritan Targumic version of 'The Blessings of Moses' (Dt 33) according to an unpublished ancient fragment: AbrNahr 24 (1986) 178-195.

1945 *Axelsson* Lars E., [Dt 33,2 ...] God still dwells in the desert; a conception characteristic of North-Israelite Yahwism: → 377*a*, IOSOT summaries (1986) 10.

1946 *a) Robert* Philippe de, La fin de Moïse; le récit du Deutéronome; les traditions samaritaines; – *b) Maraval* Pierre, Les traditions patristiques; l'énigme de la sépulture de Moïse: MondeB 44 (1986) 21ss.24 / 27.28s.

E4.1 *Deuteronomista, XII Tribus, Amphictyonia;* **Liber Josue.**

1946* **Hoffmann** Hans-Detlef, Reform und Reformen; Untersuchungen zu einem Grundthema der deuteronomistischen Geschichtsschreibung [Diss. 1979]: ATANT 66, 1980 → 61,3579 ... 65,2331: ᴿFreibRu 37s (1985s) 102 (D. *Kinet*).

1947 **Nelson** Richard D., The double redaction of the Deuteronomistic

history: JStOT Sup 18, 1981 ➤ 62,2823 ... 65,2332: ᴿBZ 30 (1986) 112-4
(J. *Becker*); RelStT 6 (1986) 81-83 (L. *Eslinger*).
1948 *Römer* Thomas, Israël et son histoire d'après l'historiographie deutéronomiste [i. niveaux différents; ii. rôle des pères; nouvelles tendances; iii.
conception exodique ...]: ÉTRel 61 (1986) 1-19.
1949 *Smend* Rudolf, Deuteronomistisches Geschichtswerk: ➤ 587, EvKL 1
(1986) 821-3.

1950 **Anbar** [Inbar] Moshe, The Amorite tribes in Mari and the settlement of
the Israelites in Canaan 1985 ➤ 1,2688: ᴿBethM 31,105 (1985s) 189-192
(A. *Zeron*); ZAW 98 (1986) 303s (J. *Maier*); Zion 51 (1986) 361s (H. *Reviv*).
1951 *Coote* Robert B., *Whitelam* Keith W., The emergence of Israel; social
transformation and state formation following the decline in Late Bronze
Age trade: Semeia 37 (1986 ➤ b873) 107-142; bibliog. 142-7.
Freedman D., *Graf* D., Transition 1983 ➤ b876.
1952 **Halpern** Baruch, The emergence of Israel in Canaan: SBL Mon. 29, 1984
➤ 65,2337; 1,2691: ᴿBSOAS 49 (1986) 388s (J.D. *Martin*); CBQ 48
(1986) 110s (W.R. *Wifall*); JBL 105 (1986) 307-9 (D. L. *Christensen*); JRel
66 (1986) 205s (G.M. *Landes*); RechSR 74 (1986) 627 (J. *Briend*:
discernement bien informé); RelStR 12 (1986) 157 (H. *Olivier*: Halpern
maintains the biblical account is substantially historical); VT 36 (1986) 508s
(J. A. *Emerton*).
1952* **Halpern** Baruch, The constitution of the monarchy in Israel: HarvSem-
Mon 25, 1981 ➤ 62,2914 ... 65,2425: ᴿOLZ 81 (1986) 36-40 (W. *Thiel*).
1953 *a) Hauer* Chrisᴶ, From Alt to anthropology; the rise of the Israelite state;
– *b) Rogerson* J.W., Was early Israel a segmentary society ? ; – *c) Cook*
Albert, 'Fiction' and history in Samuel and Kings; JStOT 36 (1986) 3-15
/ 17-26 / 27-48.
1954 *Herrmann* Siegfried, Das Werden Israels [< TLZ 87 (1962) 561-574]:
➤ 171, GesSt 1986, 101-119 [unaltered 1962 view of Noᴛʜ's amphictyony].
1955 **Lemche** Niels P., Early Israel; [unified] anthropological and historical
studies on the Israelite society before the monarchy: VTSup 37. Leiden
1985, Brill. xv-496 p. (Dansk 1-16). *f* 168. 90-04-07853-3. – ᴿDiehlB 2
(1985) 215-222 (B.J. *Diebner*, mit zitiertem Titel, 'Es fragt sich, ob eine
Landnahmetheorie erforderlich ist' und Ausgangspunkt Loʜꜰɪɴᴋ N., 'ganz
auf Hypothesen zu verzichten ... ist auch eine, und sie ist gefährlich, weil
nicht kontrollierbar').
1956 **Mayes** A.D.H., The story of Israel between settlement and exile 1983
➤ 64,9821.2628; 1,2694: ᴿHeythJ 27 (1986) 309s (R. *Coggins*); JJS 37
(1986) 110s (J. *Hughes*).
1957 *Weinfeld* Moshe, The pattern of the Israelite settlement in Canaan [in
Joshua much as in Strabo 3,171; Thucydides 1,2,1; Plato 745b]: ➤ 377*a*,
IOSOT summaries (1986) 142.

1958 **Auld** A. Graeme, Joshua, Judges and Ruth: Daily Study Bible 1984
➤ 65,2341: ᴿEvQ 58 (1986) 358s (Joyce *Baldwin*, also on Sᴀᴡʏᴇʀ's
Isaiah); ZAW 98 (1986) 139s (O. *Kaiser*).
1958* **Benjamin** Paul, The theology of [not 'the'] land in the book of Joshua:
diss. Lutheran School of Theology, ᴰ*Klein* R. Ch 1986. 162 p. 86-21949.
– DissA 47 (1986s) 2197-A.

1959 **Butler** T. C., Joshua: Word Comm. 1983 ➤ 64,2640 ... 1,2701: [R]ScripB 16 (1985s) 49 (M. *McNamara*); TLZ 111 (1986) 14-16 (W. *Herrmann*).

1960 **Gray** John, Joshua, Judges, Ruth[3rev]. NCent [[1]1967, [2]1977]. GR/Basingstoke 1986, Eerdmans / Marshall-MS. xiii-427 p. $12.95. 0-8028-0018-1 / 0-551-01215-3. – [R]ExpTim 98 (1986s) 52 (C. S. *Rodd*: type clearer, format not; 'Deuteronomic editing' now 'Deuteronomistic redaction'); OTAbs 9 (1986) 333 (L. *Greenspoon*).

1961 **Greenspoon** Leonard J., Textual studies in the book of Joshua: HarvSemMon 28, 1983 ➤ 64,2644 ... 1,2703: [R]JBL 105 (1986) 134-6 (A. G. *Auld*); TLZ 111 (1986) 95 (W. *Hermann*: Septuagintaforschung).

1962 **Gutbrod** Karl, Das Buch vom Lande Gottes, Josua und Richter[4]: BotsAT 10, 1985 ➤ 1,2704: [R]OTAbs 9 (1986) 333 (J. J. *Collins*: homiletic).

1963 [E]**Mazal** O., Josua-Rolle (Codex Vaticanus MS. Pal. graec. 431). Graz 1983, Akad. 15 Segmente, 10,6 m Faksimile. DM 1380. – [R]TrierTZ 95 (1986) 157s (E. *Sauser*: 10. Jh. Konstantinopel, 'makedonische Renaissance').

1963* *Scognamiglio* Rosario, Giosuè nell'esegesi dei Padri: ParVi 31 (1986) 127-134, 222-9 ('Iesus'; mistero e potenza del nome), 296-302 (Es 17), 357-364, 444-452.

1964 **Stancari** Pino, La beatitudine della mitezza; lettura spirituale del libro di Giosué 1985 ➤ 1,2710: [R]CC 137 (1986,4) 511s (P. *Bovati*: stimolante).

1964* *Tov* Emanuel, The growth of the book of Joshua in the light of the evidence of the LXX translation: ➤ 251*, ScrHieros 31 (1986) 321-359.

1965 **Floss** Johannes P., Kunden oder Kundschafter? Literaturwissenschaftliche Untersuchung zu Jos 2 [I. Text, Schichtung, Überlieferung; Diss. 1982 ➤ 63,2687 ... 1,2718; [R]OLZ 81 (1986) 466-8 (R. *Stahl*)]; – II. Komposition, Redaktion, Intention: AOtt 16. St. Ottilien 1986, Eos. 187 p.

1966 *García Araya* Alfonso, [Gios 2] Rahab la convertita di Gerico, [T]De Constantiis Pio: TerraS 62 (1986) 96-98.

1966* *Coats* George W., [Jos 3,1 ...] The Ark of the Covenant in Joshua; a probe into the history of a tradition: ➤ 36, Mem. GOITEIN S. = HebAnR 9 (1985) 137-157.

1967 **Schwienhorst** Ludger, Die Eroberung Jerichos; exegetische Untersuchung zu Josua 6: SBS 122. Stu 1986, KBW. 156 p.; bibliog. p. 145-151. 3-460-04221-4. – [R]ErbAuf 62 (1986) 475s (B. *Schwank*).

1968 *Begg* Christopher T., The function of Josh 7,1-8,29 in the Deuteronomistic history: Biblica 67 (1986) 320-333; franç. 334.

1969 a) *Kempinski* Aharon, [Jos 8,30-35] Joshua's altar — an Iron Age I watchtower; – b) *Zertal* Adam, [➤ 1,2724] How can Kempinski be so wrong ! : BAR-W 12,1 (1986) 42.44-48 / 43.49-53; (color.) phot. – c) BAR-W 12,4 (1986) 64-66, Kempinski letter; p. 66 *Rainey* A. al., Zertal's 'blatant phoney'; 12/5, 16, Zertal replies to Rainey ('not an archaeologist, never saw Ebal, never read the articles ...?').

1969* *Mayes* A. D. H., [Jos 9] The Gibeonites as a historical and theological problem in the OT: ProcIrB 10 (1986) 13-25.

1970 *Gacek* Stanisław, [P] Analiza egzegetyczno-teologiczna perykopy Joz 10,12-15: STWsz 24,2 (1986) 117-143; franç. 144.

1971 **Brueggemann** Walter, [Jos 11] Revelation and violence; a study in contextualization [17th Père Marquette Lecture]. Milwaukee 1986, Marquette Univ. 72 p. $8 [TDig 34,61].

1972 *Peterson* John E.,   Priestly materials in Joshua 13-22; a return to the Hexateuch?: HebAnR 4 (1980) 131-146 [OTAbs 10,147].

1973 *Lipiński* E., Guadalhorce; une inscription du roi d'Éqron? [the king is not mentioned in Jos 13,3 nor in the preceding list of kings, nor elsewhere in the Bible, but a Padi king of Ekron is prominent in Sennacherib's inscriptions]: ➤ 353, ᴱ*Olmo Lete* G. del, Fenicios 1986, II. 85-88 [continuing OrLovPer 14 (1983) 129-165; 15 (1984) 81-132].

1974 *Mundhenk* Norm, Mount Seir [usually (to be translated) Edom, but not in Jos 15,10; and in some cases Seir is a person]: BTrans 37 (1986) 236s.

1975 *Cortese* Enzo, Josua 18,1-10 zwischen 'Tetrateuch' und 'Hexateuch': ➤ 377a, IOSOT summaries (1986) 28.

1976 *Aḥituv* Shmuel, The laws of the refuge cities [Jos 20 a late development out of Ex 21,12-14]: ➤ 377a, IOSOT summaries (1966) 2.

1976* *Rofé* Alexander, History of the cities of refuge in biblical law: *a*) ➤ 251*, ᴱ*Japhet* S., ScrHieros 31 (1986) 205-239; – *b*) ❹ BethM 31,105 (1985s) 110-133.

1977 **Mölle** Herbert, [Jos 24] Der sogenannte Landtag zu Sichem [Hab.-Diss. Essen 1979]: ForBi 42, 1980 ➤ 61,3670 ... 65,2367: ᴿEstB 44 (1986) 229-231 (J. *Trebolle*).

E4.2   *Liber Judicum:* **Richter, Judges.**

1978 **Bodine** W.R., The Greek Text of Judges: HarvSemMon 23, 1980 ➤ 61,3673 ... 1,2733: ᴿSyria 63 (1986) 452s (O. *Munnich*).

1979 **Dirksen** P.B., The transmission of the text in the Peshiṭta manuscripts of the Book of Judges 1972 ➤ 53,937; 54,1043: ᴿRuBi 39 (1987) 365s (J. *Woźniak*).

1979* *Dirksen* P.B., The relation between the ancient and the younger Peshiṭta MSS in Judges: ➤ 59, ᶠ*Lebram* J., Tradition 1986, 163-171.

1980 *Greenspahn* Frederick E., The theology of the framework of Judges: VT 36 (1986) 385-396.

1981 **Mayes** A.D.H., Judges: OTGuides 3, 1985 ➤ 1,2735: ᴿBL (1986) 76 (B. *Lindars*); ScriptB 16 (1985s) 48 (D. F. *Murray*); Themelios 12 (1986s) 26s (R.W.L. *Moberly*)

1982 *Trebolle Barrera* Julio, Historia del texto de los libros históricos e historia de la redacción deuteronomística (Jueces 2,10-3,6)* ➤ 21, Mem. Díez Macho A., Salvación 1986, 245-255.

1983 *Cavalcanti* Tereza, [Jz 4s] O profetismo das mulheres no AT – perpectivas de atualização: ➤ 510, REB 46 (1986) 38-59.

1984 *Bottéro* Jean, [Jg 5] Le plus vieux poème biblique [< Tel Quel 6 (1960) 81-91]: ➤ 136, Naissance de Dieu 1986, 139-154.

1985 **Harrington** Daniel J., [Jg 5] The prophecy of Deborah; interpretative homiletics in Targum Jonathan of Judges 5: ➤ 32, ᶠ*Fitzmyer* J., CBQ 48 (1986) 432-442.

1986 *Feldman* Louis H. [Jg 4s] Josephus' portrait of Deborah: ➤ 81, Mém. Nikiprowetzky V., Hellenica 1986, 115-128.

1987 *Stager* Lawrence E., Archaeology, ecology, and social history; background themes to the Song of Deborah: ➤ 377a, IOSOT summaries (1986) 130.

1988 *Caquot* André, Les tribus d'Israël dans le Cantique de Débora (*Juges* 5,13-17): Semitica 36 (1986) 47-70.

1989 *Kutsch* Ernst, Gideons Berufung und Altarbau, Jdc 6,11-24 [< TLZ 81 (1956) 75-84]: → 183, KIS 1986, 99-109.

1990 *MacLeod* Ian, [Jg 6,13] God with us: ExpTim 98 (1986s)19s.

1991 *Na'aman* Nadav, ❾ [Jg 9] Migdal-Shechem and the 'house of el-berith': Zion 51 (1986) 259-280; Eng. IX.

1992 *Soggin* J.A., [Jg 9,46] The Migdal temple, Migdal Šekem and the discoveries on Mt. Ebal [1982-3]: → 377a, IOSOT summaries (1986) 129 [146, Ebal cult-center related to Jos 8,30 by excavator Adam *Zertal*].

1993 **Marcus** David, [Jg 11,29-40] Jephthah and his vow. Lubbock 1986, Texas Tech. 77 p. $25; pa. $15. 0-89672-136-1; 5-3 [OTAbs 10,198].

1994 **Trible** Phyllis, [Jg 11,29-40; 19,1-30; Gn 16,1-16; 2 Sam 13,1-22] Texts of terror, literary-feminist readings of biblical narratives: OvBT 13, 1984 → 65,1331* [!] 1,2752: ᴿAbrNahr 24 (1986) 203s (Grace J. *Emmerson*); BibTB 16 (1986) 41 (Irene *Nowell*); CBQ 48 (1986) 715-7 (M.J. *Fischer*, also on ᴱGros Louis-Ackerman 1982, both as contributions to biblical theology); JAAR 54 (1986) 159-161 (Claudia V. *Camp*); JBL 105 (1986) 519-521 (B.C. *Ollenburger*); RB 93 (1986) 155s (J. *Loza*); TR 82 (1986) 110-2 (F. *Crüsemann*).

1995 *Webb* Barry G., [Jg 10,6-12,7] The theme of the Jephthah story: RefTR 45 (1986) 34-43.

1996 *Bal* M., [Jg 13-16] *a*) The rhetoric of subjectivity [Unstable Samson's quest of love is overruled by his subconscious fear of love]; *b*) Sexuality, sin and sorrow; the emergence of female character [Gen 1-3]: Poetics Today 5 (1984) 337-376 / 6 (1985) 21-42 [< ZAW].

1997 *Kegler* J., Simson – Widerstandskämpfer und Volksheld: → 109, ᶠSteiger L., Brosamen 1985, 233-255.

1998 *Margalith* Othniel, Samson's riddle and Samson's magic locks: VT 36 (1986) 225-234 (397-405, more Samson legends).

1998* *Thompson* Yakov, [Jg 14s] Samson in Timnah; Judges 14-15, form and function: Dor 15 (1986s) 249-255.

1999 *Toorn* K. van der, Judges XVI 21 in the light of the Akkadian sources: VT 36 (1986) 248-253.

E4.3   **Liber Ruth,** *'V Rotuli',* *the Five Scrolls.*

2000 *Beattie* D.R.G., Towards dating the Targum of Ruth: → 63, ᶠMcKane W., A word 1986, 205-221.

2001 **Crapon de Caprona** P., Ruth la Moabite: Essais bibliques, 1982 → 63,2728; 65,2388: ᴿRHPR 66 (1986) 224s (P. de *Robert,* entre 5 autres 'Visages de Femmes').

2002 ᴱ**Friedländer** Albert H., Bronstein Herbert, The five scrolls 1984 → 1,2767: ᴿJudaism 35 (1986) 249-251 (Adele *Berlin*).

2002* **Joüon** P. †, Ruth [1953 + corrigenda], commentaire philologique et exégétique: SubsBPont 9. R 1986, Biblical Institute. viii-100 p. $7.50. 88-7653-586-1. – ᴿNRT 109 (1987) 133 (J.-L. *Ska*).

2003 ᴱ**Kraft** Robert A., *Tov* Emanuel, Ruth: CATSS 1 [ᴱ*Abercrombie* J.R., *al.*], SBL SepCog 20. Atlanta 1986, Scholars. 325 p. $16; pa. $12. 0-89130-978-0; 9-8. – ᴿETL 62 (1986) 405s (J. *Lust*); ExpTim 98 (1986s) 119 (C.S. *Rodd*: 'Computer Assisted Tools for Septuagint Studies' project described in Introduction).

2003* **Lepre** C., Il libro di Rut, intr. comm. 1981 → 62,2885; 64,2695: ᴿParVi 31 (1986) 79 (Emanuela *Ghini*).

2004 **Mesters** Carlos, Rute, comentários. Petrópolis 1986, Vozes/ Metodista/ Sinodal. 72 p. [REB 46,895].

2005 *Milne* Pamela J.,   Folktales and fairy tales; an evaluation of two Proppian analyses of biblical narratives [*Sasson* J., Ruth; *Blenkimsopp* J., Jacob/Tobit]:   JStOT 34 (1986) 35-60.

2006 **Miskotte** K. H.,   Antwoord uit het onweer [Job]; Het gewone leven [Ruth]: Verzameld Werk 10.   Kampen 1984, Kok. – ᴿNedTTs 40 (1986) 346-350 (J. M. *Hasselaar*).

2006* *Hammer* Reuven, [Job; Ruth] Two approaches to the problem of suffering: Judaism 35 (1986) 300-5.

2007 *Moor* Johannes C. de,   The poetry of the Book of Ruth: Orientalia [53 (1984) 262-283] 55 (1986) 16-46.

2008 *Petermann* Ina J.,   Travestie in der Exegese? – Über die patriarchalische Funktionalisierung eines gynozentrischen Bibeltextes; Das Buch Ruth und seine Kommentare: DiehlB 22 (1985) 74-117.

2009 *Phillips* Anthony,   The book of Ruth – deception and shame: JJS 37 (1986) 1-17.

2010 *a) Cherok* Haim,   The book of Ruth – complexities within simplicity; – *b) Gordis* Robert,   Personal names in Ruth; a note on biblical etymologies Judaism 35 (1986) 290-7 / 298s. – *c) McCarthy* Carmel,   The Davidic genealogy in the Book of Ruth: PrIrB 9 (1985) 53-62.

2010* *Wright* G.R.H.,   The mother-maid at Bethlehem: ZAW 98 (1986) 56-72 [... Persephone; Cinderella].

E4.4 1-2 Samuel.

2011 *Abramsky* Samuel,   The attitude toward the Amorites and Jebusites in the book of Samuel [only biblical book which shows no hatred of them]: → 377*a*, IOSOT summaries (1986) 1.

2011* *a*) **Black** Jonathan,   De civitate Dei and the commentaries of GREGORY the Great, BEDE and HRABANUS Maurus on the book of Samuel: Augustinian Studies 15 (1984) 114 ... [< ZIT]; – *b*) *Vogüé* Adlabert de, Renoncement et désir; la définition du moine dans le Commentaire de GRÉGOIRE le Grand sur le premier livre des Rois: ColcCist 48 (1986) 54-70.

2012 **Campbell** Anthony F.,   Of prophets and kings; a late ninth-century document (1 Samuel 1 - 2 Kings 10): CBQ Mon 17.   Wsh 1986, Catholic Biblical Association.   vii-240 p. $7.50.   0-915170-16-7. – ᴿETL 62 (1986) 415s (E. *Eynikel*).

2013 ᴱ**Fernández Marcos** N., *Busto Saiz* J. R., THEODORETI Cyrensis Quaestiones in Reges et Par 1984 → 65,2396; 1,2778: ᴿJTS 37 (1986) 596-8 (P. M. *Parvis*); Muséon 99 (1986) 182s (J.-C. *Haelewyck*).

2014 **Garsiel** Moshe, ⊕ The first book of Samuel, a literary study of comparative structures, analogies and parallels 1983 → 64,2709 [Eng. 1,2779]: ᴿJBL 105 (1986) 137s (Y. *Gitay*).

2015 **Gordon** R. P.,   1 & 2 Samuel: OTGuides 2, 1984 → 65,2400; 1,2781: ᴿCBQ 48 (1986) 108s (G. G. *Nicol*); EvQ 58 (1986) 360s (D. F. *Payne*); VT 36 (1986) 504 (J. *Barton*).

2016 **Gordon** Robert P.,   1 & 2 Samuel, a commentary.   Exeter 1986, Paternoster.   375 p. £13.   0-85364-420-9 [ExpTim 98,347].

2017 ᴱ**Gottlieb** H., *Holm-Nielsen* S.,   Samuelsbøgerne og Kongebøgerne: Det Gamle testamente i ny oversættelse.   K 1985, Dansk. Bibelselskab.   304 p. Dk 60.   87-7523-2480 [BL 87,55].

Jobling David,   The sense of [1 Sam 1-12] 1986 → 176.

2018 *Lang* B.,   Vom Propheten zum Schriftgelehrten; charismatische Autorität im Frühjudentum: → 341*, ᴱ*Stietencorn* H. von, Theologen 1986, 89-114.

2019 **McCarter** P. K. II Samuel: AnchorB 9, 1984 ➤ 65,2402; **1**,2783:   RBA 49
(1986) 251s (F. E. *Greenspahn*); Bible Bhashyam 12 (1986) 80 (J. *Kotteckal*);
Interpretation 40 (1986) 84-86 (John R. *Spencer*); JTS 37 (1986) 139-141
(J. W. *Rogerson*); RB 93 (1986) 115-132 (F. *Langlamet*: 'Le vol. II est
supérieur au Vol. I. Qui oserait s'en plaindre?'); TLZ 111 (1986) 581-3
(H.-J. *Stoebe*).

2020 *Trebolle Barrera* Julio, El estudio textual y literario del Segundo Libro
de Samuel, a propósito del comentario de P. Kyle MCCARTER: EstB 44
(1986) 5-23.

2021 **Miscall** Peter D.,   I Samuel; a literary reading: Indiana Studies in Biblical
Literature.   Bloomington 1986, Univ.   xxv-198 p. $32.50; pa. $10. 0-253-
34247-3 [BL 87,70, J. G. *Snaith*: 'metonymic dispersion', 'specific lures'].

2022 **Nautin** Pierre & Marie-Thérèse, ORIGÈNE, Homélies sur Samuel: SChr
328. P 1986, Cerf.   239 p. F 156 [NRT 109,450 V. *Roisel*].

2023 **Newsome** J. D.J, A synoptic harmony of [RSV] Samuel, Kings, and
Chronicles, with related passages from Psalms, Isaiah, Jeremiah, and Ezra.
GR 1986, Baker.   275 p. $17.   0-8010-6744-8 [BL 87,71, A. G. *Auld*].

2024 **Pisano** Stephen,   Additions or omissions in the books of Samuel: OBO
57, 1984 ➤ 65,2409; **1**,2784:   RBiblica 67 (1986) 427-431 (H. J. *Stoebe*);
JTS 37 (1986) 458-461 (H.G.M. *Williamson*); RHPR 66 (1986) 220s (P. de
Robert); ZDMG 136 (1986) 639 (G. *Wanke*: methodisch sauber).

2025 *Kalluveettil* Paul, [1 Sam 2,4-8] The marginalizing dialectics of the Bible:
Bible Bhashyam 11 (1985) 201-214.

2025* **Schley** Donald G.J, The traditions and history of biblical Shiloh: diss.
Emory, DHayes J. Atlanta 1986. 440 p. 87-05658. – DissA 47 (1986s)
4112-A.

2026 *a) Ilan* Judith, ❹ Literary structure of 1 Sam 2,11-26:   BethM 31,106
(1985s) 268-270; – *b) Wicke* Donald W., The structure of 1 Sam 3; another
view: BZ [29 (1985) 90, *Watson* W.] 30 (1986) 256-8.

2027 **Gnuse** Robert K., [1 Sam 3,4] The dream theophany of Samuel 1984
➤ 65,2424; **1**,2790:   RBZ 30 (1986) 309s (E. S. *Gerstenberger*).

E4.5   *1 Sam 7 ... Initia potestatis regiae*, **Origins of kingship.**

2028 **Ahlström** G. W., Royal administration and national religion in ancient
Palestine 1982 ➤ 63,2778 ... **1**,2796: RJNES 45 (1986) 154s (J. *Van Seters*:
a single pattern for many states through several thousand years?); OLZ 81
(1986) 154-6 (W. *Thiel*); PEQ 118 (1986) 70s (A. R. *Millard*: intrigued,
dubious).

2028* **Arnold** Patrick M., Gibeah in Israelite history and tradition: diss.
Emory, DMiller J. M. Atlanta 1986. 325 p. 86-26507. – DissA 47 (1986s)
3024-A; RelStR 13,189.

2029 *Bettenzoli* Giuseppe, *a)* Samuel und Saul in geschichtlicher und
theologischer Auffassung: ZAW 98 (1986) 338-351; – *b)* Samuel und das
Problem des Königtums: BZ 30 (1986) 222-236.

2030 *Blidstein* Gerald J., The monarchic imperative [whether Israel was
commanded to crown a king] in rabbinic perspective: AJS 7s (1982s)
15-39.

2030* **Eron Brown** Margaret H., The one whom the Lord has chosen;
monarchy in theocracy, 1 Samuel 8:1-16:13: diss. Marquette. Milwaukee
1986. 338 p. 86-18708. – DissA 47 (1986s) 1774-A.

2031 **Camponovo** Odo, Königtum, Königsherrschaft und Reich Gottes in den frühjüdischen Schriften [Diss. FrS 1984]: OBO 58, 1984 ➤ 64,2733 ... 1,2798: ᴿCBQ 48 (1986) 328s (J. J. *Collins*); ETL 62 (1986) 188s (J. *Lust*); JStJud 17 (1986) 94-96 (A. S. van der *Woude*); JTS 37 (1986) 505s (G. I. *Davies*); NedTTs 40 (1986) 337s (M. de *Jonge*); TR 82 (1986) 193s (H. *Merklein*).

2031* **Edelman** Diana Vikander, The rise of the Israelite state under Saul: diss. Ch 1986, ᴰ*Ahlström* G. 340 p. – RTLv 18,544.

2032 *a) Frick* Frank S., Social science methods and theories of significance for the study of the Israelite monarchy; a critical review essay; – *b) Chaney* Marvin L., Systematic study of the Israelite monarchy: Semeia 37 (1986➤ b873) 9-47; bibliog. 47-52 / 53-74; bibliog. 75-77.

2033 **Gerbrandt** Gerald E., Kingship according to the Deuteronomistic History: SBL diss. 87 [Richmond 1980 ➤ 61,3740]. Atlanta 1986, Scholars. 229 p. $18; pa. $13. 0-89130-968-3; 9-1. – ᴿExpTim 98 (1986s) 119 (C. S. *Rodd*).

2034 **Gibert** Pierre, A Bíblia na origem da História [... a história como ciência surgiu precisamente quando se estabeleceu a monarquia em Israel]. São Paulo 1986, Paulinas. 390 p. [REB 46,722].

2034* *Hill* Andrew E., *Herion* Gary A., Functional Yahwism and social control in the early Israelite monarchy: JEvTS 29 (1986) 277-284 [< ᴢɪᴛ].

2035 *a) Lanoir* Corinne, La quête de la royauté; – *b) Römer* Thomas, Le mouvement deutéronomiste face à la royauté; monarchistes ou anarchistes; – *c) Gilbert* Pierre, Le prophète face au roi; Samuel et l'institution de la monarchie; – *d) Beauchamp* Paul, Le roi, fils de David et fils d'Adam; messianisme et médiation: LumièreV 35,178 (1986) 5-12 / 13-27 / 29-41 / 55-67.

2035* *Malamat* Abraham, Organs of statecraft in the Israelite monarchy: Dor 15 (1986s) 1-10. 71-78. 141-9 [listeners' comments]. 215-222 [reply].

2036 **Moftah** Ramses, Studien zum altägyptischen Königsdogma im Neuen Reich: DAI-K Sonderschrift 20. Mainz 1985, von Zabern. xiv-370 p. DM 88. – ᴿMundus 22 (1986) 201s (J. *Brinks*).

2037 *Neu* Rainer, 'Israel' vor der Entstehung des Königtums: BZ 30 (1986) 204-221.

2037* *Van Praag* Herman M., The downfall of King Saul; the neurobiological consequences of losing hope: Judaism 35 (1986) 414-428.

2038 *Talmon* Shemaryahu, *a)* Kingship and the ideology of the State [... in Biblical Israel, < ᴱ*Malamat* A., World History 1978, 3-26]; – *b)* 'In those days there was no *melek* in Israel' – Judges 18-21 [< ❶, 5th World Congress 1969/72, 135-144]; – *c)* 'The Rule of the King' – 1 Samuel 8:4-22 [< ❶ ꟳBɪʀᴀᴍ A. 1956, 45-56]: ➤ 227, King, cult 1986, 9-38 / 39-52 / 53-67.

2038* *Weber* Hans-Ruedi, Power; some biblical perspectives: EcuR 38 (1986) 265-279.

2039 **Humphreys** W. Lee, [1 Sam 9-31; Gn 2s ...] The tragic vision and the Hebrew tradition: OvBT 18. Ph 1985, Fortress. xvii-151 p. $10 pa. [TDig 33,366].

2039* **Weber-Möckl** Annette, 'Das Recht des Königs, der über euch herrschen soll'; Studien zu 1 Sam. 8,11f in der Literatur der frühen Neuzeit [Diss. Giessen]: Historische Forschungen 27. B 1986, Duncker & Humblot. 214 p. DM 88. 3-428-05963-8. – ᴿExpTim 98 (1986s) 376 (R. *Coggins*).

2040 *a) Luke* K., A verse missing from 1 Samuel 10:27-11:15: Bible Bhashyam 12 (1986) 196-212; – *b) Jung* Leo, [1 Sam 12,3-5] Samuel's conscience: HebSt 26 (1985) 47-51 (OTAbs 10,151].

2041 **Hagan** Harry,   The battle narrative of David and Saul; a literary study of
1 Sam 13 - 2 Sam 8 and its genre in the Ancient Near East: diss. Pont. Ist.
Biblico, ᴰ*Alonso Schökel* L.   R 1986. – AcPIB 9,2 (1985s) 149; 116.
2042 **Fokkelman** J. P.,   Narrative art and poetry in the books of Samuel [1.
1981 ➤ 62,2962*a*]; 2. The crossing fates [Saul's and David's 1 Sam 13 -
2 Sam 1: five acts divided into 30 scenes]: StSemNeer 23. Assen 1986, Van
Gorcum. 808 p. *f*115. 90-232-2175-3. – ᴿExpTim 98 (1986s) 182 (R.
Coggins: previous commentators dismissed as fundamentally mistaken).
2043 **Foresti** Fabrizio, [1 Sam 15] The rejection of Saul [diss. Haifa 1983] 1984
➤ 65,2434; 1,2812:   ᴿBible Bhashyam 12 (1986) 151s (J. *Kottackal*);
Henoch 8 (1986) 93s (A. *Catastini*); NRT 108 (1986) 112s (J.-L. *Ska*); RivB
34 (1986) 285-7 (P. *Tamietti*).
2044 *Edelman* Diana,   Saul's battle against Amaleq (1 Sam 15): JStOT 35
(1986) 71-84.

E4.6   *1 Sam 16...2 Sam; Accessio Davidis,*   **David's Rise.**

2045 **Brueggemann** Walter,   David's truth in Israel's imagination and memory
1985 ➤ 1,2814:   ᴿBL (1986) 65 (H.G.M. *Williamson*); Interpretation 40
(1986) 422.424 (R. S. *Dietrich*).
2045* *Cargill* Jack,   David in history; a secular approach: Judaism 35 (1986)
211-222.
2046 *Freedman* David N.,   The spelling of the name 'David' in the Hebrew
Bible, ᶠGORDIS R., ᴱ*Ahroni* R. (1983 ➤ 65,60): JAOS 106 (1986) 357-9
(Adele *Berlin*, most of her review of the Festschrift).
2047 **Friis** Heike,   Die Bedingungen für die Errichtung des Davidischen Reichs
in Israel und seiner Umwelt [1968 theol. Preisaufgabe], ᵀᴱ*Diebner* B. J.:
DiehlBl Beih. 6. Heid 1986. iv-250 p. [ZAW 99,290, G. *Wanke*].
2048 **Heym** Stefan,   The King David report. London 1984 = 1972, Sphere.
254 p. – ᴿTorJT 2 (1986) 135-139 (R.W.E. *Forrest*; novel, remarkably
suggests East German regime).
2049 ᴱ**Ishida** T.,   Studies in the period of David and Solomon and other essays
1979/82 ➤ 63,434 ... 1,2828:   ᴿHenoch 8 (1986) 88-90 (P. G. *Borbone*);
JAOS 106 (1986) 573-5 (G. W. *Ahlström*).
2050 *a) McCarter* P. Kyle,   The historical David; – *b) Petersen* David L.,
Portraits of David, canonical and otherwise; – *c) Mays* James L.,   The
David of the Psalms; – *d) Bassler* Jouette M.,   A man for all seasons;
David in rabbinic and New Testament literature: Interpretation 40 (1986)
117-129 / 130-142 / 143-155 / 156-169.
2051 **Malamat** A.,   Das davidische und salomonische Königreich: WSzb 407,
1983 ➤ 63,2788 (1982?) ... 1,2820:   ᴿJBL 105 (1986) 117s (S. E.
McEvenue); OLZ 81 (1986) 463-6 (S. *Herrmann*: aus dem ❿ lies p. 25 n. 34
Šišak nicht Schicksal).
2052 **Stryjkowski** Józef, ❿ Król David żyje (King David lives). Poznań 1984,
'W drodze'. 301 p. [RuBi 39,371].
2053 *Veijola* Timo, David: ➤ 587, EvKL 1 (1986) 794s.
2054 *Whitelam* Keith W.,   The symbols of power; aspects of royal propaganda
in the United Monarchy: BA 49 (1986) 166-173; ill.

2055 **Lingen** Anton van der,   David en Saul in I Samuel 16 - II Samuel 5;
verhalen in politiek en religie [diss.] 1983 ➤ 64,2772 ... 1,2824: ᴿCBQ 48
(1986) 120s (C. T. *Begg*); GerefTTs 86 (1986) 39s (K. van der *Toorn*); JBL
105 (1986) 136s (J. C. *VanderKam*).

2056 *Seidl* Theodor, David statt Saul; göttliche Legitimation und menschliche Kompetenz des Königs als Motive der Redaktion von I Sam 16-18: ZAW 98 (1986) 39-55.

2057 *Tov* Emanuel, [1 Sam 16-18] The David and Goliath saga; how a biblical editor combined two versions: BR 2,4 (1986) 34-41; ill.

2058 *Jongeling* B., La préposition L dans 1 Samuel 16:7 ↠ 47, ᶠHOSPERS J., Scripta 1986, 95-99.

2059 *Campbell* Antony F., From Philistine to throne (1 Samuel 16:14 - 18:16): AustralBR 34 (1986) 35-41.

2060 *Barthélemy* D. [Trois niveaux p. 47-54], *al.*, The story of David and Goliath; textual and literary criticism; papers of a joint research venture: OBO 73. FrS/Gö 1986, Univ./VR. vii-157 p. Fs 39. 3-7278-0372-X / 3-525-53702-6 [BL 87,127].

2061 *a) Lust* J. The story of David and Goliath in Hebrew and in Greek; *b) Gooding* D. W., An approach to the literary and textual problems of ... 1 Sam 16-18: ↠ 2060, OBO 73 (1986) 5-18. 87-91. 121-128. 155s / 55-86. 114-120. 121-128. 145-154.

2062 *Tov* E., The nature of the differences between MT and the LXX in 1 Sam 17-18: ↠ 2060, OBO 73 (1986) 19-46. 92-94. 129-137.

2063 *Korfmann* Manfred, Die Waffe Davids; ein Beitrag zur Geschichte der Fernwaffen und zu den Anfängen organisierten kriegerischen Verhaltens: Saeculum 37 (1986) 129-149.

2064 *Simon* Uriel, A balanced story; the stern prophet and the kind ghostwife (1 Sam 28: 3-25): ↠ 377a, IOSOT summaries (1986) 125.

2065 *Shea* William H., [2 Sam 1,19-27] Chiasmus and the structure of David's lament: JBL 105 (1986) 13-25.

2066 *Kutsch* Ernst, *a)* Wie David König wurde; Beobachtungen zu 2. Sam 2,4a und 5,3 [< ᶠWÜRTHWEIN E. 1979, 75-93]; – *b)* Die Dynastie von Gottes Gnaden; Probleme der Nathanweissagung in 2. Samuel 7 [< ZTK 58 (1961) 137-153]: ↠ 183, KLS 1986, 110-128 / 129-145.

2066* *Luria* B. Z., ⊕ [2 Sam 5,5] What happened in the *medînâ* during the years of David's rule in Hebron?: BethM 31,105 (1985s) 97-109.

2067 *a) Edelman* Diana, [2 Sm 6,3: *gib'at bet 'Abindadab* was at Gibeon, not Qiryat-Yearim] The ark's home under Saul: ↠ 377a, IOSOT summaries (1986) 35. – *b) Bakon* Shimon, [2 Sam. 6,9] How David captured Jerusalem: Dor 15 (1986s) 43s.42.

2068 **Dempster** Stephen G., [2 Sam 9,20...] Linguistic features of Hebrew narrative; a discourse analysis of narrative from the classical period: diss. ᴰ*Revell* E. Toronto 1985. – DissA 47 (1986s) 883-A.

2068* *a) McEvenue* Sean E., The basis of empire; a study of the succession narrative (2 Sam. 9-20; 1 Kings 1-2); – *b) Miller* Patrick D.ᴶ, The prophetic critique of kings; – *c) Wainwright* Geoffrey, Praying for kings; the place of human rulers in the divine plan of salvation: ExAud 2 (1986) 34-35 / 82-95 / 117-127.

2069 *Fontaine* Carole, The bearing of wisdom on the shape of 2 Samuel 11-12 and 1 Kings 3: JStOT 34 (1986) 61-77.

2069* *Stoebe* Hans J., David und Uria; Überlegungen zur Überlieferung von 2 Sam 11: Biblica 67 (1986) 388-396.

2070 *Waldman* Nahum M., [2 Sam 12,1-4; 14,5-17] Two biblical parables; irony and self-entrapment: Dor 15 (1986s) 11-18.

2070* *Coats* George W., II Samuel 12:17a: Interpretation 40 (1986) 170-5.

2071 *Crenshaw* James L., [2 Sam 12,22 + 9 postex.] The expression *mî yôdēa'* in the Hebrew Bible: VT 36 (1986) 274-288.

2072 *Vorster* Willem S.,   Readings, readers and the succession narrative; an essay on reception: ZAW 98 (1986) 351-362.

2073 *Ben-Barak* Zafrira,   Succession to the throne in Israel and in Assyria: OrLovPer 17 (1986) 85-100.

2074 *Beckman* Gary,   Inheritance and royal succession among the Hittites: ⇸ 42, ᶠGÜTERBOCK H., Kaniššuwar 1986, 13-31.

2075 *Chang* Wilson, [2 Sam 18,33] Pathos of a father; reading the Davidic court history and William FAULKNER's 'Absalom, Absalom' from a reader response perspective: ⇸ 377*a*, IOSOT Summaries (1986) 22.

2076 *Mesori-Caspi* M., [2 Sam 18,19-19,5] ❶ The running of Ahimaaz and the Cushite: BethM 31 (1985s) 59-71.

2077 *Roberts* J.J.M., [2 Sam 22:26-27; Ps 18,26-27] Does God lie? divine deceit as a theological problem in Israelite prophetic literature [God's answer must be taken in the light of the questioner's integrity]: ⇸ 377*a*, IOSOT summaries (1986) 113.

E4.7   *Libri Regum;* **Solomon, Temple: 1 Kings ...**

2078 **Auld** A. Graeme,   Kings: Daily Study Bible.   E/Ph 1986, St. Andrew/ Westminster   259 p. £4.25 [ExpTim 98,181]. 0-7152-0523-4/.

2079 **DeVries** Simon J.,   1 Kings: Word Comm. 12, 1985 ⇸ **1**,2842:   ᴿAndr-UnS 24 (1986) 186-8 (D. R. *Clark*); BA 49 (1986) 252s (B. O. *Long*); BibTB 16 (1986) 151 (D. W. *Baker*); BL (1986) 58s (G. H. *Jones*); RefTR 45 (1986) 52s (J. *Woodhouse*); TLZ 111 (1986) 583s (W. *Thiel*); VT 36 (1986) 381 (J. A. *Emerton*).

Dočّanasvili Georgian Kgs-Chr ⇸ 1259.

2080 **Hentschel** Georg,   I Könige: NEchter 10, 1984 ⇸ 65,2463:   ᴿCBQ 48 (1986) 717s (B. O. *Long*).

2081 **Jones** Gwilym,   1 and 2 Kings: I, 1 Kings 1-16:34; II. 1 Kings 17:1 - 2 Kings 25:30: NCent 1984 ⇸ **1**,2847:   ᴿAndrUnS 24 (1986) 63-69 (W. H. *Shea*: too negative on historicity); Antonianum 61 (1986) 493-5 (M. *Nobile*); ETL 62 (1986) 416s (E. *Eynikel*); Themelios 12 (1986s) 26 (D. W. *Baker*).

2082 *Lemaire* André,   Vers l'histoire de la rédaction des Livres des Rois [SBL Strasbourg 1984]: ZAW 98 (1986) 221-235; Eng. 236.

2083 **Long** Burke O., 1 Kings: FOTLit, 9, 1984 ⇸ 65,2465; **1**,2849:   ᴿJBL 105 (1986) 523s (W.M.W. *Roth*); TLZ 111 (1986) 183-5 (W. *Thiel*).

2083* *McKenzie* Steven L.,   The prophetic history and the redaction of Kings: ⇸ 36, Mem. GOITEIN S. = HebAnR 9 (1985) 203-220.

2084 **Rehm** Martin,   Das erste Buch der Könige 1979 ⇸ 60,3683 ... 65,2467: ᴿEstB 44 (1986) 227-9 (J. *Trebolle*).

2085 *Wallace* H. N.,   The oracles against the Israelite dynasties in 1 and 2 Kings: Biblica 67 (1986) 21-40; franç. 40.

2086 **Würthwein** Ernst,   Die Bücher der Könige I-II (¹1977) ²1985/1984 ⇸ **1**,2875:   ᴿAntonianum 61 (1986) 490-3 (M. *Nobile*); Gregorianum 67 (1986) 766-8 (G. L. *Prato*); JBL 105 (1986) 708s (R. D. *Nelson*).

2086* *Cohen* Shaye J. D., [1 Kgs 3,1 ...] Solomon and the daughter of Pharaoh; intermarriage, conversion, and the impurity of women: ⇸ 11*, Mem. BICKERMAN E. = JANES 16s (1984s) 23-37.

2087 *Herrmann* Siegfried, [1 Kg 3,4-15] Die Königsnovelle in Ägypten und Israel; ein Beitrag zur Gattungsgeschichte in den Geschichtsbüchern des ATs [< WZ Lp 3 (1983s) 51-62]: ⇸ 171, Ges.St. 1986, 120-144.

2088 **Kenik** Helen A., Design for kingship ... 1 Kgs 3:4-15: SBL diss. 69, 1983
   ➤ 64,2803 ... 1,2856: ᴿRechSR 74 (1986) 621s (J. *Briend*).
2089 *Gelio* Roberto, Storiografia e ideologia in 1 Re 3-10: ➤ 391, Storiografia
   1984/6, 29-52.
2090 *Cogan* Mordechai, ❷ [1 Kgs 6; 2 Chr 3,1] 'The city that 1 chose' – the
   Deuteronomistic view of Jerusalem: Tarbiz 55 (1985s) 301-9; Eng. I.
2091 **1 Reg 7, Templum:** *Zwickel* Wolfgang, [1 Kg 7,27-39] Die Kesselwagen
   im salomonischen Tempel: UF 18 (1986s) 459-461; 1 fig.
2092 *Patrich* Joseph, The *mesibbah* [stairwell] of the Temple according to the
   tractate Middot: IsrEJ 36 (1986) 215-233; 8 fig.; pl. 27A.
2093 *Christensen* Jens, Tempel – bjerg – paradis; en forestillingskreds og dens
   konstans [cluster of representations at Ugarit, Mari ...]: DanTTs 49 (1986)
   51-61 [< ZAW].
2093* *Mulder* ˙J., Die Bedeutung von Jachin und Boaz in 1 Kön. 7:21 (2 Chr.
   3:17): ➤ 59, ꜰLEBRAM J., Tradition 1986, 19-26.
2094 *Tarragon* Jean-Michel de, The physical relationship between the Ark, the
   Cherubim, the *kapporet* and the Solomonic Temple; an unsolved problem:
   ➤ 377*a*, IOSOT summaries (1986) 133.
2095 **Haran** Menahem, Temples and temple-service in ancient Israel. Winona
   Lake IN 1985 [= Ox 1978 ➤ 60,3706] Eisenbrauns. xviii-394 p.
   0-931464-18-8.
2096 **Klein** Mina C. & H. Arthur, Temple beyond time; the story of the site of
   Solomon's Temple at Jerusalem. NY 1970, Van Nostrand [Ch OrInstAc
   Ag87].

2097 *Johns* A.H., [1 Kgs 10] Solomon and the queen of Sheba; Fakhr al-Dīn
   AL-RAZI's treatment of the Qur'anic telling of the story: AbrNahr 24
   (1986) 58-81.
2098 **Vanoni** Gottfried, Literarkritik... 1 Kön 11-12: 1984 ➤ 65,2487; **1**, 2864:
   ᴿWeltOr 17 (1986) 175s (P.J. *Nel*); ZkT 108 (1986) 80s (G. *Fischer*).
2098* *Simotas* Panagiotis, Critical observations on III (I) Kings 11,19: TAth
   57 (1986) 378-385.
2099 **Barnes** William H., Studies in the chronology of the Divided Monarchy
   in Israel: diss. Harvard, ᴰ*Cross* F. CM 1986. 228 p. 86-19010. – DissA 47
   (1986s) 1846-A; HarvTR 79 (1986) 467s.
2100 *Hickman* D., The chronology of Israel and Judah I: Catastrophism and
   Ancient History 7 (1985) 57-70 [OTAbs 10,134].
2101 *Laato* Antti, New viewpoints on the chronology of the Kings of Judah
   and Israel: ZAW 98 (1986) 210-221.
2102 *Herrmann* Siegfried, Autonome Entwicklungen in den Königreichen Israel
   und Juda [< VTSup 17 (1969) 139-158]: ➤ 171, GesSt 1986, 145-162.
2102* *Smelik* K.A.D., De dynastieën van Omri en Jehu; de compositie van de
   boek Koningen (1): AmstCah 6 (1985) 43-69.
2103 *Talmon* Shemaryahu, *a*) The cult and calendar reform of Jeroboam I [=
   Divergences in calendar reckoning in Ephraim and Judah, VT 8 (1958)
   48-74]; – *b*) The Gezer Calendar and the seasonal cycle of ancient Canaan
   [< JAOS 83 (1963) 177-187]; – *c*) ... new letter [< BASOR 177 (1965)
   29-39]: ➤ 228, King, cult 1986, 113-139 / 89-112; 1 pl. / 79-88.

E4.8 *1 Regum 17-22: Elias,* **Elijah.**

2104 *Daxelmüller* C., Elias: ➤ 592, LexMA 3 (1986) 1821-3.

2105 *Kiesow* Klaus, Elija, Elischa: ➤ 587, EvKL 1 (1986) 1016s.
2106 *Payne* D. F., The Elijah cycle and its place in Kings: ➤ 44, Mem. HAIRE
    J. = IrBSt 8 (1986) 109-114.
2107 *Pick* Pinhas W., [1 Kgs 17,1] On the cognomen 'Tishbite' [< Tešub] of the
    prophet Elijah: HebSt 26 (Madison 1985) 197-202 [OTAbs 10,128].
2107* *Ukachukwu Manus* Chris: Elijah – a *nabi'* before the 'writing prophets';
    some critical reflections: AfJBSt 1,1 (1986) 25-34 [< TKontext 8/2,20].
2108 *a) Wahl* Otto, Gott behält das letzte Wort; zu den Elija- und
    Elischa-Erzählungen der Königsbücher; – *b) Zeller* Dieter, Elija und
    Elischa im Frühjudentum; – *c) Nützel* Johannes M., Elija- und
    Elischa-Traditionen im Neuen Testament: BiKi 41,4 (1986) 146-153 /
    154-159 / 160-171.
2109 **Waaijman** Kees, De profeet Elia. Nijmegen 1985, Gottmer. 160 p.
    f 20,90. – ᴿStreven 53 (1985s) 275 (P. *Beentjes*).
2110 **Carena** Omar, La comunicazione non-verbale ... 1 Re 16,29 - 2 Re 13,25:
    1981 ➤ 62,3004 ... 65,2496: ᴿBZ 30 (1986) 115s (J. *Gamberoni*).
2111 *Smend* Rudolf, Das Wort Jahwes an Elia; Erwägungen zur Komposition
    von 1 Kön 17-19 [< VT 25 (1975) 525-543]: ➤ 220, Mitte des ATs 1986,
    138-153.
2112 *Soards* Marion L.ᴶ, Elijah and the Lord's word; a study of 1 Kings 17:
    17-24: StudiaBT 13 (1983) 39-50.
2113 *Hauser* Alan J., [1 Kgs 18,1-16] Whose servant is he? Obadiah's
    indecision and the challenge posed by Death to Yahweh: ➤ 377s, IOSOT
    summaries (1986) 56.
2114 *Oeming* Manfred, Naboth, der Jesreeliter; Untersuchungen zu den
    theologischen Motiven der Überlieferungsgeschichte von 1 Reg 21: ZAW
    98 (1986) 363-382.
2114* *Dorp* J. van, Wie zal Achab verleiden? Over thema en geschiedenis van
    1 Koningen 22: 1-38: AmstCah 6 (1985) 39-52.

E4.9   *2 Reg 1 ... Elisaeus, Elisha, and down to the Exile.*

2115 *Deboys* David G., *a)* Quinta/e' in Four Reigns: TyndB 36 (1985)
    163-178; – *b)* Recensional criteria in the Greek text of II Kings [IV
    Kingdoms] JSS 31 (1986) 135-9.
2116 **Hobbs** T. R., 2 Kings: Word 13. Waco 1986, Word. xlviii-387 p. [TDig
    33,494]. – ᴿSWJT 29,2 (1986s) 47s (D. G. *Kent*); TrinJ 7,2 (1986) 115-7
    (H.G.M. *Williamson*).
2116* **LaBarbera** Robert D., Social and religious satire in the Elisha cycle:
    diss. Graduate Theological Union, ᴰ*Alter* R. Berkeley 1986. 208 p.
    86-17054. – DissA 47 (1986s) 1720-A; RelStR 13,189.

2117 *Margalit* Baruch, [2 Kgs 3,26s] Why King Mesha of Moab sacrificed his
    oldest son: BAR-W 12,6 (1986) 62s. 76.
2118 *King* Michael A., [2 Kgs 5,1-19] Naaman and the wild God of Israel:
    SpTod 38 (1986) 4-8.
2119 *Tsukimoto* Akio, 'Ein Eselkopf und 1/4 kab Taubenmist' (II Kön 6,25b):
    AnJapB 12 (1986) 77-86.
2119* *Reinhold* Gotthard G. G., The Bir-Hadad stele and the biblical kings of
    Aram: AndrUnS 24 (1986) 115-126.
2120 *Ahlström* G. W., The battle at Ramoth-Gilead in 841 B.C. [2 Kgs 8: Israel
    against Assyria, not Damascus-ally]: ➤ 377a, IOSOT summaries (1986) 3.

2120* **Barre** Lloyd M., The rhetoric of political persuasion; an examination of the literary features and political intentions of 2 Kings 9-11: diss. Vanderbilt, DKnight D. Nv 1986. 296 p. 86-16339. – DissA 47 (1986s) 1359-A; RelStR 13,189.

2121 **Trebolle-Barrera** Julio C., Jehú y Joás; texto y composición literaria de 2 Reyes 9-11, 1984 ➤ 65,2512; 1,2887*: RCBQ 48 (1986) 544s (S. Olyan); JBL 105 (1986) 521-3 (I. Mihalik); JTS 37 (1986) 141s (F. Landy: lucid); ScripTPamp 18 (1986) 963s (S. Ausín).

2122 *Foresti* Fabrizio, Il racconto della detronizzazione di Atalia (2 Reg. 11); documento di archivio o composizione deuteronomistica? [Levin C. 1982]: Teresianum 36 (1985) 203-8.

2123 *Hurowitz* Victor, Another fiscal practice in the Ancient Near East; 2 Kings 12:5-17 and a letter to Esarhaddon (LAS 277): JNES 45 (1986) 289-294.

2124 *Hart* Stephen, [2 Kgs 14,7; 2 Chr 25,11s] Selaʿ; the rock of Edom? [not Petra or Biyâra, but near Boṣra; the Amaziah story unhistorical]: PEQ 118 (1986) 91-95; 2 fig. (map).

2125 *Naʾaman* Nadav, [Pekah 2 Kgs 15,30...] Historical and chronological notes on the kingdoms of Israel and Judah in the eighth century B.C.: VT 36 (1986) 71-82.

2125* **Becking** Bob, De ondergang van Samaria; historische, exegetische en theologische opmerkingen bij II Koningen 17 [diss. Utrecht 1985]. Huis ter Heide 1985, auct. 292 p. ƒ30 [NedTTs 41,231, H. Jagersma].

2126 a) *Sanders* Michael S., Megiddo [21st dynasty Šošenq = So of 2 Kgs 17,4-6]; – b) *Sieff* Martin, Scarab in the dust; Egypt in the time of the Twenty-First Dynasty [710-565]: Catastrophism and Ancient History 8 (LA 1986) 135-140 / 7 (1985) 99-109 [OTAbs 10,135].

2127 *Zeidman* Reena, Deportations in the Neo-Assyrian empire: Catastrophism and Ancient History 7 (1985) 25-34 [OTAbs 9,271].

2127* *Roshwald* Mordecai, [2 Kgs 20,2] The wall of communication: Judaism 35 (1986) 483-6.

2128 *Begg* Christopher T., 2 Kings 20:12-19 as an element of the Deuteronomistic history: CBQ 48 (1986) 27-38.

2129 *Fewell* Danna N., Sennacherib's defeat; words at war in 2 Kings 18.13-19.37: JStOT 34 (1986) 79-90.

2130 *George* A. R., Sennacherib and the Tablet of Destinies [British Museum < Kuyunjik]: Iraq 48 (1986) 133-146.

2131 **Gonçalves** Francolino J., L'expédition de Sennachérib en Palestine dans la littérature hébraïque ancienne: ÉtBN 7. P 1986, Gabalda. 578 p. F 620. [RechSR 74,630]. 2-85021-021-8.

2132 *Herrmann* Siegfried, Hiskia: ➤ 597, TRE 15 (1986) 398-404.

2133 *Kooij* Arie van der, Das assyrische Heer vor den Mauern Jerusalems im Jahr 701 v. Chr.: ZDPV 102 (1986) 93-109.

2134 *Liwak* Rüdiger, Die Rettung Jerusalems im Jahr 701 v. Chr.; zum Verhältnis und Verständnis historischer und theologischer Aussagen [Antrittsvorlesung Bochum 1985]: ZTK 83 (1986) 137-166.

2135 *Millard* A. R., Sennacherib's attack on Hezekiah: TyndB 36 (1985) 61-77.

2135* **Vera-Chamaza** Galo W., Hiziqijjahú; reconstrucción e interpretación de las narraciones de Ezequías en base a la crítica textual, literaria, de las Formas y de la Composición: diss. Tübingen 1985s, DGross. – TR 82 (1986) 513.

2136 **Vogt** Ernst †, Der Aufstand Hiskias und die Belagerung Jerusalems 701 v. Chr.: AnBib 106. R 1986, Pont. Biblical Institute. viii-105 p.; portr. $16. 88-7653-106-X. – RExpTim 98 (1986s) 376 (R. Coggins).

2137 **Spieckermann** H.,   Juda unter Assur in der Sargonidenzeit 1982
➤ 64,2861 ... 1, 2896:   ᴿProtestantesimo 41 (1986) 108s (J. A. *Soggin*).
2138 *Begg* Christopher T.,   The reading at 2 Kings XX 13:   VT 36 (1986)
339-341.
2139 **Wiseman** D. J.,   Nebuchadrezzar and Babylon (21st Schweich Lectures
1983) 1985 ➤ 1,2908:   ᴿExpTim 98 (1986s) 53 (R. *Coggins*: 'siege' misspelt
throughout; Daniel regarded as source on Babylonian king); ZAss 76
(1986) 141-3 (M. *Dandamayev*).
2140 *Kutsch* Ernst,   Das Jahr der Katastrophe, 587 v. Chr.; kritische
Erwägungen zu neueren chronologischen Versuchen [< Biblica 55 (1974)
520-545]: ➤ 183, KLS 1986, 3-28.
2141 *Begg* Christopher T.,   [2 Kgs 25,27-30] The significance of Jehoiachin's
release; a new proposal: JStOT 36 (1986) 49-56.
2142 *Nobile* Marco,   Un contributo alla lettura sincronica della redazione
Genesi - 2 Re, sulla base del filo narrativo offerto da 2 Re 25,27-30:
Antonianum 61 (1986) 207-224; Eng. 207.

E5.1   *Chronicorum libri* – **The Chronicler.**

2143 **Becker** Joachim, 1 Chronik: NEchter 18. Wü 1986, Echter. 120 p. DM
28 [ZAW 99,284, O. *Kaiser*]. 3-429-01038-1.
2144 **Braun** Roddy,   Chronicles: Word Comm. 14 [not 13 as p. vi]. Waco
1986, Word. xlv-312 p. 0-8499-0213-4.
2145 **Im** T.-S. Das Davidbild in den Chronikbüchern [Diss. Bonn]: EurHS
23/263. Fra c. 1986, Lang. 197 p. Fs 45. 3-8204-8900-2 [BL 87,65s, R. J.
Coggins: claims messianic aspirations reflected in Chr].
2146 *Japhet* Sara,   Die Theologie der Chronikbücher und ihre Stellung
innerhalb des biblischen Denkens: HBeiWJ 1 (1985) 123 ... [< ZAW].
2147 *Johnstone* William,   Guilt and atonement, the theme of 1 and 2
Chronicles: ➤ 63, ᶠMcKANE W., A word 1986, 113-138.
2148 **Kegler** Jürgen, *Augustin* Matthias,   Synopse zum chronistischen Geschichtswerk: Beiträge zur Erforschung des ATs und des antiken
Judentums 1, 1984 ➤ 65,2539: ᴿTLZ 111 (1986) 417-9 (D. *Mathias*).
2149 **McConville** J. Gordon,   Chronicles: Daily Study Bible 1984 ➤ 65,2540;
1,2912: ᴿEvQ 58 (1986) 260-2 (D. *Schibler*).
2150 **McKenzie** Steven L.,   The Chronicler's use of the deuteronomistic history:
HarvSemMus 33, 1985 ➤ 1,2913:   ᴿÉTRel 61 (1986) 586s (F. *Smyth*:
détaillé); RechSR 74 (1986) 622s (J. *Briend*: vaut plus par ses analyses que
par sa thèse).
2151 **Micheel** Rosemarie,   Die Seher- und Prophetenüberlieferung in der Chronik 1983 ➤ 64,2872 ... 1,2914: ᴿJBL 105 (1986) 316-8 (M. P. *Graham*);
TLZ 111 (1986) 16-19 (D. *Mathias*).
2151* *Romerowski* Sylvain,   Les règnes de David et de Salomon dans les
Chroniques: Hokhma 11,31 (1986) 1-23.
2152 *Weinberg* Joel P.,   Die soziale Gruppe im Weltbild des Chronisten: ZAW
98 (1986) 72-95; Eng. 95.

2153 *Arichea* Daniel C.ᴶ,   [1 Chr 6,33] Translating biblical genealogies ['He-
man's genealogy from the bottom upwards ...']: BTrans 37 (1986) 232-4.
2154 *Hognesius* Kjell,   A note on 1 Chr 23: ScandJOT 1,1 (1986) ...
2155 *Dequeker* L.,   1 Chronicles xxiv and the royal priesthood of the
Hasmoneans: ➤ 399, OTS 24, 1985/6, 94-106.

2156 *Fleischer* Ezra, ❸ [1 Chr 25,8] Additional data concerning the 24 priestly orders: Tarbiz 47-60; Eng. II.
2157 *McConville* J. G., 1 Chronicles 28:9; Yahweh 'seeks out' Solomon: JTS 37 (1986) 105-8.
2158 *Na'aman* Nadav, [2 Chr 11,5-10] Hezechiah's fortified cities and the LMLK stamps: BASOR 261 (1986) 5-21.
2159 **Latham** James E., [2 Chr 13,5] The religious symbolism of salt 1982 ➤ 63,4449 ... 1,2921*: ᴿTR 82 (1986) 372s (J.B. *Bauer*).
2160 *Dillard* Ray, [2 Chr 17-20] The Chronicler's Josaphat: TrinJ 7 (1986) 17-22.
2160* *Kasher* Rimmon, ❸ (2 Chr 20,1-30) The saving of Jehoshaphat; extent, parallels, significance: BethM 31,106 (1985s) 242-251.
2161 *Luria* B. Z., [2 Chr 28,1-8] Oded – a prophet of God, ᵀ*Abramowitz* Chaim: Dor 15 (1986s) 256-9.
2161* *Haran* Menahem, [2 Chr 36,22] Explaining the identical lines at the end of Chronicles and the beginning of Ezra: BR 2,3 (1986) 18-20.

E5.4   *Esdrae libri,* **Ezra-Nehemiah.**

2162 *Abe* G. O., Religion and national unity; guidelines for Nigeria from the Judean exilic and post-exilic experience: AfJT 15 (1986) 63-72.
2163 *Bach* R., Esra- und Nehemiabuch: ➤ 587, EvKL 1 (1986) 1126s.
2164 *Betlyon* John W., The provincial government of Persian period Judea and the Yehud coins: JBL 105 (1986) 633-642 [*Mildenberg* L., revised to support *Cross* F. inserting another highpriest in the postexilic list].
2165 **Clines** D. J., Ezra, Nehemiah, Esther: NCent, 1984 ➤ 65,2551; 1,2930: ᴿAndrUnS 24 (1986) 53-55 (W. H. *Shea*); Antonianum 61 (1986) 773-5 (M. *Nobile*).
2165* *Cohn* Robert L., Biblical responses to catastrophe [exile 586 B.C.E.]: Judaism 35 (1986) 263-276.
2166 *Daoust* J. [< *Briend* J., MondeB 40 (1985)] Les Juifs en Babylonie: EsprV 96 (1986) 375-7.
2167 *Dumbrell* William J., The theological intention of Ezra-Nehemiah: RefTR 45 (1986) 65-72.
2168 *a*) *Eskenazi* Tamara C., In an age of prose: a literary approach to Ezra and Nehemiah: diss. Iliff, ᴰ*Richards* K. Denver 1986. 274 p. 86-16287. – DissA 47 (1986s) 1774-A. – *b*) The Chronicler and the composition of 1 Esdras: CBQ 48 (1986) 39-61.
2169 **Fensham** F. Charles, The Books of Ezra and Nehemiah: NICOT 1982 ➤ 64,2885 ... 1,2931: ᴿScripB 17 (1986s) 23 (M. *McNamara*).
2170 *a*) *Gabba* Emilio, La Palestina e gli ebrei negli storici classici fra il V e il III sec. a.C.; – *b*) *Contini* Riccardo, I documenti aramaici dell'Egitto persiano e tolemaico; – *c*) *Rossi* Adriano V., I materiali iranici; – *d*) *Cagni* Luigi, Le fonti mesopotamiche dei periodi neo-babilonese, achemenide e seleucide (VI-III sec. a.C.): ➤ 390, RivB 34 (1986) 127-141; Eng. 141 / 73-108; Eng. 109 / 55-72; Eng. 72 / 11-52; Eng. 53.
2171 **Gunneweg** Antonius H. J., Esra: KAT 19,1, 1985 ➤ 1,2931*: ᴿTLZ 111 (1986) 737s (A. *Meinhold*: theology not history; hence the commentary is fragmentary).
2172 *a*) *Hoppe* Leslie J., Biblical update; Ezra and Nehemiah; the restoration of Judah; – *b*) *Dulin* Rachel, Leaders in the restoration: BToday 24 (1986) 281-6 / 287-291.
2173 *Lang* Bernhard, Vom Propheten zum Schriftgelehrten; charismatische Autorität im Frühjudentum [... Esra, Neh, Sir]: ➤ 341*, ᴱ*Stietencron*

Heinrich von, Theologen und Theologien in verschiedenen Kulturkreisen [Dü 1986, Patmos] 89-114.
2174 *Lazarus-Yafeh* Hava, ⊕ Ezra-'Uzayr; metamorphosis of a polemical motif: Tarbiz 55 (1985s) 359-379; Eng. II.
2174* **Lo Hing Choi,** The structural relationship of the synoptic and non-synoptic passages in the book of Chronicles: diss. Southern Baptist Sem., ᴰ*Tate* M. 1986. 281 p. 86-28706. – DissA 47 (1986s) 3084-A.
2175 *McConville* J. G., Ezra-Nehemiah and the fulfilment of prophecy: VT 36 (1986) 205-224.
2176 **Williamson** H.G.M., Ezra, Nehemiah: Word Comm. 16. Waco 1985, Word. iii-517 p. $23. – ᴿCurrTM 13 (1986) 372 (R. W. *Klein*: best available); ETL 62 (1986) 417-9 (J. *Lust*); RefTR 45 (1986) 91(B.*Webb*); SWJT 29,2 (1986s) 48s (D. G. *Kent*); Themelios 12 (1986s) 93s (P. *King*); TrinJ 7 (1986) 93-96 (H. E. *Clem*).

2177 **Fahr** H., Herodot [Kyros, Kambyses] und AT: EurHS 23/266. Fra 1985, Lang. 140 p. Fs 30. 3-8204-8524-4 [BL 87,95s, F. F. *Bruce*].
2178 *Puech* Émile, [Ezra 2,43-46] The Tel el-Ful jar inscription [read Hagab, not Hananiah] and the *Nĕtînîm*: BASOR 261 (1986) 69-72; 1 fig.
2179 *Morrow* William S., *Clarke* Ernest G., The *ketib/qere* in the Aramaic portions of Ezra and Daniel: VT 36 (1986) 406-422.
2180 *Margalith* Othniel, The political role of Ezra as Persian governor: ZAW 98 (1986) 110-112.
2181 *Rubinkiewicz* Ryszard, [Ezra 9,1-10,44] The book of Noah (Hen 6-11) and Esra's reform: → 377*a*, IOSOT summaries (1986) 117.
2182 *Malul* Meir, ⊕ 'And I also shook out my garment' (Neh 5,13) – the significance of shaking out the *ḥōṣen* [designates freeing from a previous obligation, as Nuzi *ganna maṣāru*]: BethM 31,104 (1985s) 17-22 [OTAbs 9,284].
2183 *Giraudo* Cesare, [Neh 8, Lc 4] La celebrazione della Parola di Dio nella Scrittura: RivLtg 73 (1986) 593-615.
2184 *Koch* Robert, [Neh 9; Dan 9 ...] Nachexilische Bussfeiern: TGegw 23 (1985) 29-40.

E5.5   Libri Tobiae, Judith, Esther.

2185 *Bonora* Antonio, La famiglia nel libro di Tobia: ParSpV 14 1986) 59-72.
2186 *Doran* Robert, Narrative literature [... Tobit, Daniel additions, Judith]: → 255, ᴱ*Kraft* R., Early Judasim 1986, 287-310.
2187 **Drewermann** Eugen, *Neuhaus* Ingritt, Voller Erbarmen rettet er uns; Die Tobitlegende tiefenpsychologisch gedeutet 1985 → 1,2941: ᴿTPQ 134 (1986) 300s (F. *Hubmann*).
2188 ᴱ**Hanhart** Robert, Tobit: SeptGö 8/5, 1983 → 64,2899 ... 1,2942: ᴿCBQ 48 (1986) 112s (Irene *Nowell*); JBL 105 (1986) 324s (J.A.L. *Lee*, also on 1984 'Text').
2188* *Jansen* H. L., Die Hochzeitsriten im Tobitbuche [1965]: → 49, ᶠJANSEN 1985, 41-48.

2189 **Barsotti** D., Meditazione sul libro di Giuditta: Bibbia e Liturgia 29. Brescia 1985, Queriniana. 142 p.
2189* **Craven** Toni, Artistry and faith in the book of Judith: SBL diss 70, 1983 → 64,2903 ... 1,2948: ᴿJBL 105 (1986) 144s (D. E. *Gowan*).
2190 **Moore** Carey A., Judith: AnchorB 40, 1985 → 1,2948*: ᴿBibTB 16 (1986) 156s (R. *Gnuse*).

2190* *Walle* R. Vande, The book of Judith: Bible Bhashyam 12 (1986) 237-248.

2191 **Clines** David J. A., The Esther scroll: JStOT Sup 30, 1984 ➤ 65,2575; 1,2953: ᴿCBQ 48 (1986) 712-4 (B. W. *Jones*, also on Clines' NCent Ezra-Neh-Esther); Interpretation 40 (1986) 202 (W. *Brueggemann*); JSS 31 (1986) 254-6 (G. *Brooke*); JTS 37 (1986) 146-152 (H.G.M. *Williamson*: conventional methods upended).

2192 *a*) *Craghan* John F., Esther, a fully liberated woman; – *b*) *Nowell* Irene, Judith, a question of power; – *c*) *Havener* Ivan, Biblical women: BToday 24 (1986) 6-11 / 12-17 / 21-23.

2193 **Grossfeld** Bernhard, The first Targum to Esther 1983 ➤ 64,2913 ... 1,2954 [Concordance 1984 ➤ 65,2579; 1,2955]: ᴿBO 43 (1986) 466-8 (M. J. *Mulder*); EstB 44 (1986) 231-3 (L. *Diez Merino*, conc.); JBL 105 (1986) 357-9 (E. G. *Clarke*) 739s (B. B. *Levy*, concordance); OLZ 81 (1986) 571s (R. *Degen*, conc.).

2194 *Hanhart* Robert, Esterbuch: ➤ 587, EvKL 1 (1986) 1128s.

2194* *Hastoupis* Athanasios P., Ⓖ The book of Esther: TAth 57 (1986) 697-711.

2195 **Herrmann** Wolfram, Ester im Streit der Meinungen: BeiErfATJ 4. Fra 1986, Lang. 93 p. 3-8204-8947-8.

2196 *Hutter* Manfred, Iranische Elemente im Buch Esther: ➤ 542, ᴱ*Galter* H., Kulturkontakte 1986, 51-66.

2196* *Smitt* J. W., Pinksterens triumf over Purim. Kampen 1985, Van den Berg. 134 p. ƒ16,50. – ᴿKerkT 37 (1986) 66 (B. *Maarsingh*).

2197 *Waegeman* Maryse, Esther and [Aelian] Aspasia, beloved wives of Persian kings: ➤ 377*a*, IOSOT summaries (1986) 141.

2198 *Zadok* Ran, Notes on Esther [links of personal names with Persian or chiefly Imperial Aramaic]: ZAW 98 (1986) 105-110.

2199 *Margalit* M., Ⓞ 'From another place' – Esther 4,14 ['place' = God; 'other' for an obvious and well-known name]: BethM 31,104 (1985s) 6-9 [OTAbs 9,285].

2200 *Grelot* Pierre, La dispute des arbres dans le Targoum II d'Esther VII,10: ➤ 21, Mem. DÍEZ MACHO A., Salvación 1986, 399-408.

2201 *Thornton* T.C.G., [Esth 7,10] The crucifixion of Haman and the scandal of the Cross: JTS 37 (1986) 419-426.

E5.8   *Machabaeorum libri*, **1-2 Maccabees.**

2202 *Attridge* Harold W., Jewish historiography [... Maccabean; Philo, Josephus ...]: ➤ 255, Early Judaism 1986, 311-343.

2203 *Bammel* Ernst, Zum jüdischen Märtyrerkult [< TLZ 78 (1953) 119-126]: ➤ 131, Judaica 1986, 79-85.

2204 **Barsotti** Divo, Le second livre des Maccabées 1984 ➤ 65,2596; F 60: ᴿVSp 140 (1986) 126s (H. *Troadec*).

2205 **Bringmann** Klaus, Hellenistische Reform und Religionsverfolgung in Judäa: AbhGö 3/132, 1983 ➤ 64,2926 ... 1,2968: ᴿArctos 19 (1985) 301s (Heikki *Solin*); TLZ 111 (1986) 100-2 (K.-D. *Schunck*).

2206 **Dommershausen** Werner, 1 Makkabäer; 2 Makkabäer: NEchter 12. Wü 1985, Echter 188 p. 3-429-00955-3.

2207 **Doran** Robert, Temple propaganda ... 2 Mcb: CBQ Mon 12, 1981 ➤ 62,3091 ... 1,2974: ᴿBZ 30 (1986) 288s (J. *Maier*).

2208 **Fischel** H. A., The First Book of Maccabees, commentary. NY 1985, Schocken. 123 p. 0-8052-0793-7.

2209 **Fischer** T., Seleukiden und Makkabäer 1980 → 61,3960 ... 1,2969: ^RBZ 30 (1986) 284s (J. *Maier*).

2209* *Gabba* Emilio, [1-2 Mcb] The Holy Spirit, the Roman Senate, and BOSSUET: 11*, Mem. BICKERMAN E. = JANES 16s (1984s) 55-65.

2210 **Goldstein** Jonathan A., II Maccabees: AnchorB 41A, 1983 → 64,2931 ... 1,2975: ^RBible Bhashyam 11 (1985) 107s (J. *Kottackal*); Gregorianum 67 (1986) 147-9 (G. L. *Prato*); Interpretation 40 (1986) 87.90 (R. *Doran*); RQum 12,46 (1986) 285-7 (P.-M. *Bogaert*).

2210* *Hallo* William W., The concept of eras from Nabonassar to Seleucus: → 11*, Mem. BICKERMAN E. JANES 16s (1984s) 143-151.

2211 *Heard* Warren J., The Maccabean martyrs' contribution to Holy War: EvQ 58 (1986) 291-318.

2211* **Henten** Jan W. van, De joodse martelaren als grondleggers van een nieuwe orde; een studie uitgaande van 2 en 4 Makkabeeëns: diss. Leiden 1986, ^D*Lebram* J. 439 p. – RTLv 18,545; TsTNijm 27,100.

2212 *Jacobson* Howard, Visions of the past; Jews and Greeks: Judaism 35 (1986) 407-482.

2212* *Jossa* Giorgio, La storiografia giudeo-ellenistica; il secondo libro dei Maccabei e la Guerra Giudaica di GIUSEPPE Flavio: → 391, Storiografia 1984/6, 93-102.

2213 *Macina* R., L'énigme des prophéties et oracles à portée 'Macchabéenne' et leur application *ek prosópou* selon l'exégèse antiochienne: OrChr 70 (1986) 86-109.

2214 **Martola** Nils, Capture and liberation ... 1 Mcb, ^D1984 → 1,2971: ^RJBL 105 (1986) 533s (D. J. *Harrington*).

2214* *Orrieux* Claude, Les papyrus de Zénon et la préhistoire du mouvement maccabéen: → 81, Mém. NIKIPROWETZKY V., Hellenica 1986, 321-333.

2215 *Passoni dell'Acqua* Anna, Le testimonianze papiracee relative alla 'Siria e Fenicia' in età tolemaica (I papiri di Zenone e le ordinanze reali): → 390 RivB 34 (1986) 233-283; Eng. 283.

2216 *Nodet* Étienne, La dédicace, les Maccabées et le Messie: RB 93 (1986) 321-375; Eng. 321.

2217 a) *Saulnier* Christiane, L'hellénisation; l'armée séleucide; les Maccabées; – b) *Siat* Jeannine, L'art de vivre dans le monde hellénistique; – c) *Starcky* Jean, Les hasmonéens: MondeB 42 (1986) 5-12.23-29 / 12-18 / 38-46; ill.

2218 *Vanhetloo* Warren, Four hundred silent years [no revelation from Malachi until John Baptist]: CalvaryB 2,1 (1986) 33-50.

2218* *Katzoff* R., [1 Mcb 12,6-18] Jonathan and late Sparta: AmJPg 106 (1985) 485-9 [< JStJud 17,281].

2219 *Mihoc* Vasile, La péricope II Maccabées 12,39-46, fondement des prières de l'Église pour les morts [en roumain]: OrtBuc 37 (1985) 533-540.

2220 **Stern** Menahem, ⊕ The treaty between Judaea and Rome in 161 B.C.E.: Zion 51 (1986) 3-28; Eng. I.

VII. Libri didactici VT

E6.1 *Poesis .1 metrica,* **Biblical versification.**

2221 **Alter** Robert, The art of biblical poetry 1985 → 1,2978: ^RBR 2,3 (1986) 10-12 (B. *Halpern*); Horizons 14 (1987) 139s (Denise D. *Hopkins*); Religion

and Intellectual Life 3,3 (New Rochelle 1986) 120-2 (H. J. *Levine*); RExp 83 (1986) 473s (J. D. W. *Watts*).
2222 *Andersen* T. David, Problems in analysing Hebrew poetry: EAsJT 4,2 (1986) 68-94.
2223 **Berlin** Adele, The dynamics of biblical parallelism 1985 ➤ 1,2983: ᴿBL (1986) 62 (W. G. E. *Watson*); RelStR 12 (1986) 282 (S. D. *Sperling*: JAKOBSON influence); VT 36 (1986) 256 (J. A. *Emerton*).
2225 **Cohen** Mark E., Sumerian hymology; the Eršemma: HUCA Sup 2, 1981 ➤ 62,3108*; 64,2944: ᴿTLZ 111 (1986) 733-5 (J. *Oelsner*).
2226 *Freedman* David N., Acrostic poems in the Hebrew Bible, alphabetic and otherwise: ➤ 32, ᶠFITZMYER J., CBQ 48 (1986) 408-431.
2227 *a)* **Grol** Hermanus Van, De versbouw in het klassieke Hebreeuws; fundamentele verkenningen, I. Metriek: diss. Amst 1986, ᴰ*Beuken* W. 266 p. – RTLv 18,544. – *b)* **Grol** Harm W. M. van, Classical Hebrew versification; fundamental explorations; 1. Metrics: diss. Kath. Theol. Hogeschool. Amst 1986. xi-267 p. ƒ45.
2228 *a)* **Korpel** M. C. A., *Moor* J. C. de, Fundamentals of Ugaritic and Hebrew poetry; – *b)* *Segert* Stanislav, Preliminary notes on the structure of the Aramaic poems in the Papyrus Amherst 61; – *c)* *Tsumura* David T., Literary insertion, AxB pattern, in Hebrew and Ugaritic – a problem of adjacency and dependency in poetic parallelism; – *d)* *Watson* W. G. E., Antithesis in Ugaritic verse: UF 18 (1986s) 173-212 / 271-299 / 351-361 / 413-9.
2229 **Krašovec** Jože, Antithetic structure in biblical Hebrew poetry [diss. 1977]: VTS 35, 1984 ➤ 65,2604; 1, 2990: ᴿBO 43 (1986) 656-8 (P. *Höffken*); JBL 105 (1986) 704s (J. L. *Kugel*: framework too classical).
2230 *Loretz* Oswald, Kolometrie ugaritischer und hebräischer Poesie; Grundlagen, Informationstheoretische und literaturwissenschaftliche Aspekte: ZAW 98 (1986) 249-266 [... Prov 9,1-6]; Eng. 266.
2231 **Watson** Wilfred G. E., Classical Hebrew poetry; a guide to its techniques: JStOT Sup 26, 1984 ➤ 65,2607; 0-905774-57-4; reedited 1986 with 100-item bibliog.; £12.50 pa.; 1-85075-048-3: ᴿBiblica 67 (1986) 120-4 (L. *Alonso Schökel*); ExpTim 97 (1985s) 376s (J. F. A. *Sawyer*: modelled on G. LEECH, Linguistic Guide to English Poetry); JAOS 106 (1986) 579s (Adele *Berlin*); RB 93 (1986) 306 (R. J. *Tournay*); TLZ 111 (1986) 178-180 (W. *Herrmann*).

E6.2 **Psalmi, textus.**

2231* *Bäumlin* Klaus, Die Zumutung der Genfer Psalmen: Reformatio 35 (Bern 1986) 272-280.
2232 **Busto Saiz** J. B., La traducción de Símaco en el libro de los Salmos: TEstCisn 22. M 1985, Cons. Naz. Inv. Ci. xxvi-756 p. – ᴿJTS 37 (1986) 556s (S. *Brock*).
2233 *Carolus-Barré* Louis, Le psautier de Peterborough et ses enluminures profanes: Bull. Antiquaires (1984) 185-193.
2234 **Corrigan** Kathleen A., The ninth century Byzantine marginal Psalters: diss. Univ. California. LA 1984. xii-271 p.
2235 **Cutler** Anthony, The aristocratic psalters in Byzantium: BiblCahArchéol 13, 1984 ➤ 1,3005; F 400: ᴿRÉByz 43 (1985) 304s (C. *Walter*).
2236 *Dennison* Lynda, An illuminator of the Queen Mary Psalter group; the ancient 6 master [diss. London 1979]: AntiqJ 66 (1986) 287-314; pl. XL-IV.

ᴱ**Doč'anašvili** E., Psalms, Georgian Mc'het'a Manuscript 1983 ➤ 1260.

2237 **Estin** Colette, Les Psautiers de JÉRÔME 1984 ➤ 65,2614; 1,3009: ᴿJStJud 17 (1986) 245-8 (A. *Hilhorst*: courage and insight; methodological errors; overuses 'second best' reference); RB 93 (1986) 149-152 (B. *Couroyer*); RÉAug 32 (1986) 197-9 (Y.-M. *Duval*).

2238 *Gabra* Gawdat, Zur Bedeutung des koptischen Psalmenbuches im oxyrhynchitischen Dialekt: GöMiszÄg 93 (1986) 37-42.

2238* *Gier* J. de, De psalmen Davids van Jacob REVIUS: TRef 29 (Woerden 1986) 267-291 [< ZIT].

2239 *Kjærgaard* Jørgen, Renæssancehumanistisk retorik i LUTHERS salmer: DanTTs 49 (1986) 1-19 [< ZIT].

2240 **Mortari** Luciana, Il salterio della tradizione 1983 ➤ 64,2963*a* ... 1,3013: ᴿBL (1986) 56 (S. B. *Brock*: overlooks English versions of Lazarus MOORE, Madras 1966-71; and of Holy Transfiguration Monastery, Boston 1974).

2241 *Pado* Włodzimierz M., ❷ De psalmis in versione J. KOCHANOWSKI [= Czy Kochanowski laicyzował Psalmy?]: RuBi 29 (1986) 33-41.

2242 **Pidoux** Pierre, Theódore de BÈZE, Psaumes mis en vers français (1551-62), prose de Loïs Budé. Genève 1984, Droz. 277 p. – ᴿScuolC 113 (1985) 593-6 (Elisabetta *Zambruno*).

2243 **Pietersma** Albert, The Acts of Phileas ... Psalter: 1984 ➤ 65,2620; 1,3014: ᴿRivStoLR 22 (1986) 542-7 (F. *Bolgiani*).

2244 The Psalter: New Skete. NY 1984, Cambridge [-UP]. xvii-286 p. – ᴿOrChrPer 52 (1986) 472s (R. *Taft*).

2245 **Stadler** Alisa, Die Berge tanzten; Die Psalmen aus dem Urtext übertragen; Vorw. **Ben Chorin** Schalom. 1986, Herold. 304 p. DL 48. – ᴿTR 82 (1986) 424 (Oda *Hagemeyer*: frei, dichterisch).

2246 **Szenci Molnár** Albert, ᴱ*Győri* János, ❿ Psalterium Ungaricum. Budapest 1984, Szépirodalmi. 405 p.; ill. – ᴿTheologiai Szemle 29 (1986) 63s (D. *Kövendi*).

2247 **Tescaroli** Livio, I Salmi nella tradizione ebraica; nuova traduzione del testo masoretico. R 1985, Città Nuova. 328 p. Lit. 20.000. – ᴿHumBr 41 (1986) 770 (A. *Bonora*).

2248 ᴱ**Thomas** Marcel, Der Psalter Ludwig des Heiligen. Graz 1985, Akad. Druck-V. 29 p.; 78 color. pl. Sch 360 [RelStR 13,253, J. *Gutmann*].

2249 **Tomić** Celestin, Psalmi; kratki uvod i tumač². Zagreb 1986, Provincijalat franjevaca konv. 382 p.

2250 *Tornaghi* Paola, I nomi propri nelle antiche versioni inglesi (4 Salteri): Rendiconti Ist. Lombardo 120 (1986) 35-62.

2251 **Wilson** Gerald H., The editing of the Hebrew Psalter⁶ [Yale 1981, ᴰ*Wilson* R.]: SBL diss. 76, 1985 ➤ 1, 3022: ᴿAustralBR 34 (1986) 70s (R. A. *Anderson*); BL (1986) 82s (P. R. *Ackroyd*); ÉglT 17 (1986) 387s (L. *Laberge*); TLZ 111 (1986) 659-661 (D. *Vetter*).

2252 **Zuber** Beat, Die Psalmen, eine Studienübersetzung unter besonderer Berücksichtigung des hebräischen Tempus: DiehlB Beih 7. Heid 1986, Univ. Wiss.-theol. Seminar. 220 p. DM 12,50.

E6.3   **Psalmi, introductio.**

2253 **Aletti** J.-N., *Trublet* J., Approche poétique et théologique des Psaumes 1983 ➤ 64,2975 ... 1,3024: ᴿAntonianum 61 (1986) 172s (M. *Nobile*: per oggi); BLitEc 87 (1986) 78s (L. *Monloubou*: méthode qui laisse au seuil des difficultés); LumièreV 35,178 (1986) 90-92 (F. *Martin*).

2254 *Alter* Robert, The Psalms; beauty heightened through poetic structure: BR 2,3 (1986) 29-41 [< The art of biblical poetry Ch. 5, 1985].

2254* *Cimosa* Mario, I salmi; rassegna bibliografica [testi (*Sàvoca* G.); introduzioni; commenti (*Lancellotti* A., *Alonso-Schökel* L., *Ravasi* G.); lettura cristiana]: ParVi 31 (1986) 352-6.

Haïk-Ventoura Suzanne, Les 150 psaumes dans leurs mélodies antiques 1985 → a68.

2255 *Hopkins* Denise D., New directions in Psalms research – good news for theology and Church: SLuke 29 (1986) 271-283 [265-270, *Dietrich* R., on Ps 2 and 5 others: OTAbs 10,61s].

2256 **Miller** Patrick D., Interpreting the Psalms [first half general (recent) approaches; second half, applied to ten psalms: 1; 2; 14; 22s; 82 (!); 90; 127; 130; 139]. Ph 1986, Fortress. x-165 p. $11 pa. 0-8006-1896-3. – ᴿExpTim 98 (1986s) 116 (J. *Eaton*); OTAbs 9 (1986) 333s (R. E. *Murphy*).

2257 **Seybold** Klaus, Die Psalmen: Urban-Tb 382. Stu 1986, Kohlhammer. 215 p. DM 24. 3-17-009424-6. – ᴿExpTim 98 (1986s) 248s (R. *Coggins*).

E6.4 **Psalmi, commentarii.**

2258 **Allen** Leslie C., Psalms 101-150; Word Comm. 21, 1985 → 64,2976; 1,3032; $20; 0-8499-0220-7. – ᴿExpTim 98 (1986s) 52 (C. S. *Rodd*: learned but lacks sparkle); GraceTJ 7 (1986) 129s (R.D. *Patterson*).

2259 **Borgogno** C., S. AGOSTINO d'Ippona, Commento ai salmi di lode: Letture cristiane delle origini 26. T 1986, Paoline. 350 p. Lit. 16.000. 88-215-0957-5. – ᴿCiVit 41 (1986) 484 (B. *Farnetani*).

2260 **Brueggemann** Walter, The message of the Psalms, a theological commentary 1984 → 1,3035: ᴿAndrUnS 24 (1986) 184-6 (W. H. *Shea*); CurrTM 13 (1986) 48s (R. *Gnuse*); JBL 105 (1986) 710s (L. C. *Allen*).

2261 *a)* Ciccarese Maria Pia, La composizione del 'corpus' asteriano sui Salmi; – *b)* Prinzivalli Emanuela, Codici interpretativi del Commento ai Salmi di DIDIMO; – *c)* Tuccari Luciana, Il Salterio Ag 11 della Biblioteca di Grottaferrata; → 365, AnStoEseg 3 (1985/6) 7-42 / 43-56 / 65-70.

2262 **Clifford** Richard J., Psalms 1-72 / 73-150: OT 22s. Collegeville MN 1985, Liturgical. 79 p.; 87 p. $3 each [TDig 33,464].

2263 **Craigie** Peter C., Psalms 1-50: Word Comm. 19, 1983 → 64,2980 ... 1,3037: ᴿTLZ 111 (1986) 95-97 (H. *Seidel*).

2264 **Deissler** Alfons, I salmi, esegesi e spiritualità [1964 → 47,1770], ᵀ*Nobile Ventura* Ornella M.: Scritturistica. R 1986, Città Nuova. 535 p. Lit. 35.000. 88-311-3610-0. – ᴿLetture 41 (1986), 866s (G. *Ravasi*).

2265 **Girard** Marc, Les psaumes (1-50) 1984 → 65,2642; 1,3039: ᴿBiblica 67 (1986) 286s (J.-N. *Aletti*: quatre remèdes pour les volumes suivants); Divinitas 30 (1986) 100s (T. *Stramare*); JTS 37 (1986) 142-4 (P. *Wernberg-Møller*); NRT 108 (1986) 107s (J.-L. *Ska*); ScEspr 38 (1986) 125s (J. *Harvey*); VSp 140 (1986) 727s (A. *Schenker*).

2266 **Knight** G. A. F., Psalma [I, 1982 → 1,3041]; II: Daily Study Bible. Ph 1983, Westminster. xiii-368 p. $16; pa.$9: ᴿCBQ 48 (1986) 295 (J. *Endres*: his hermeneutical stance, the piety and belief of the individual Christian, seldom adjusts to the Sitz im Leben).

2267 **McNamara** Martin, Glossa in Psalmos; the Hiberno-Latin Gloss on the psalms of Codex Palatinus Latinus 68 (Psalms 39:11-151:7): ST 310. Vatican 1986, Biblioteca. 387 p.; bibliog. p. 78-86.

Orazzo Antonio, La salvezza in ILARIO.. 'Tractatus super Psalmos' 1986 → 5916.

2268 **Phillips** J., Exploring the Psalms II. Ps. 42-72. Neptune NJ 1986, Loizeaux. 285 p. $15. 0-87213-685-X [NTAbs 30,258].

2269 **Ravasi** Gianfranco, Il libro dei Salmi 3 vol. 1981-4 ➤ 62,3147 ... 1,3043: ᴿCC 137 (1986,3) 395-9 (G. L. *Prato*); ParVi 31 (1986) 374-7 (T. *Lorenzin*); TItSett 11 (1986) 182-193 (A. *Bonora*).

2270 **Ravasi** Gianfranco, I salmi [ridotto dai tre volumi Dehoniani], introduzione, traduzione, commento: BUR poesia L-601. Mi 1986, Rizzoli. 430 p. [RivB 35,385]. ➤ 2309.

2271 **Rondeau** Marie-Josèphe, Les commentaires patristiques du Psautier II: OrChrAn 220, 1985 ➤ 1,3047: ᴿNRT 108 (1986) 582s (V. *Roisel*); RÉAug 32 (1986) 265 (R. *Braun*); RevSR 60 (1986) 268-270 (Mariette *Canévet*); RSPT 70 (1986) 596-9 (G. M. de *Durand*); TLZ 111 (1986) 827s (K. *Treu*).

2272 ᵀᴱ*Ruiz* Guillermo, Avec et comme les Pères, lire les Psaumes: EsprV 96 (1986) 565-8.

2273 *Simonetti* Manlio, La tecnica esegetica di TEODORETO nel Commento ai Salmi: VetChr 23 (1986) 81-116.

2274 **Stuhlmueller** Carroll, Psalms I-II: DTMessage 21s, 1983 ➤ 64,2999 ... 1,3052: ᴿJBL 105 (1986) 318 (P. D. *Miller*).

2275 **Weiser** A., ➓ *Shihen-chū* [Psalmen[8] 1979 ➤ 60,4021] 42-89 hen, ᵀ*Shioya* Y. Tokyo 1985, ATD-NTD Seisho Chūkai Kankō-kai. 337 p. Y 3600 [BL 87,56].

2276 **Westermann** Claus, [41] Ausgewählte Psalmen [+ Lam 5] 1984 ➤ 65,2657; 1,3055: ᴿCBQ 48 (1986) 534s (J. F. *Craghan*); SvTKv 62 (1986) 123s (T. *Kronholm*).

E6.5 **Psalmi, themata.**

2277 *Barré* Michael L., The formulaic pair *ṭôb (wᵉ) ḥesed* in the Psalter: ZAW 98 (1986) 100-5.

2278 **Bazak** Jacob, ➓ [Ps 25; 34; 37; 111s; 119; 145] Structures and contents in the Psalms; geometric structural patterns in the seven alphabetical psalms 1984 ➤ 65,2661 [index !]: ᴿJBL 105 (1986) 709s (Y. *Gitay*: the author is a criminologist).

2279 **Bellinger** W. H.ᴶ, Psalmody and prophecy [diss]: JStOT Sup 27, 1984 ➤ 65,2661; 1,3058: ᴿCBQ 48 (1986) 711s (L. *Boadt*); JBL 105 (1986) 524s (J. *Blenkinsopp*); RB 93 (1986) 148s (R. J. *Tournay*).

2280 *Brueggemann* Walter, The costly loss of lament: JStOT 36 (1986) 57-71.

2281 *Brzegowy* Tadeusz, 'Miasto Boże' w Psałterzu: ColcT 56,4 (1986) 37-58; 58s, 'La cité de Dieu' dans le Psautier.

2282 **Eaton** John H., Kingship and the Psalms[2] [= ¹SCM 1976 ➤ 58,3539 + 20 p. appendix]. Sheffield 1986. JStOT. 247 p. £7. 0-905774-89-2 [ExpTim 98,191]. – ᴿZAW 98 (1986) 465 (H.-C. *Schmitt*).

2282* *a)* **Ferris** Paul W.ᴶ, The genre of communal lament in the Bible and the Ancient Near East: diss. Dropsie. Ph 1985. 321 p. 86-05512. – DissA 47 (1986s) 542-A. – *b)* **Fuchs** Guido, Die 'Feinde' in den Psalmen und ihre christliche Deutung im Psalmlied, dargestellt an den Liedern Nikolaus SELNECKERS (1530-1592): Diss. Würzburg 1985s, ᴰ*Langgärtner*. – TR 82 (1986) 513.

2283 *a)* *Gamberoni* Johann, Der einzelne in den Psalmen; – *b)* *Scharbert* Josef, Das 'wir' in den Psalmen auf dem Hintergrund altorientalischen Betens; – *c)* *Reinelt* Heinz, Gottes Herrschaftsbereich nach den Aussagen der Psalmen; – *d)* *Schmuttermayr* Georg, Vom Gott unter Göttern zum einzigen Gott; zu den Spuren der Geschichte des Jahweglaubens in den

Psalmen: ➤ 41, ^FGROSS H., Freude 1986, 107-123 / 297-324 / 265-274 / 349-374.

2283* **Haar** Murray J., The God-Israel relationship in the community lament psalms: diss. Union. Richmond 1985. 205 p. 86-1377. – DissA 47 (1986s) 1368-A.

2284 **Haglund** Erik, Historical motifs in the Psalms [diss. U 1983]: ConBibOT 23, 1984 ➤ 65,2665; 1,3061: ^RBbbOr 28 (1986) 14 (F. *Montagnini*); CBQ 48 (1986) 533s (J. F. *Craghan*); ÉTRel 61 (1986) 125s (D. *Lys*).

2285 *Hoffman* Yair, ☉ The transition from despair to hope in the individual-lament psalms: Tarbiz 55 (1985s) 161-172; Eng. I.

2286 **Kim** Ee Kon, ☉ The rapid change of mood in the lament psalms; a matrix for the establishment of a Psalm theology (diss). Seoul 1985, Theological Study Inst. 267 p. – ^RTTod 43 (1986s) 464s (J, J. M. *Roberts*).

2287 **Kraus** H. J., Teología de los Salmos 1985 ➤ 1,3063b: ^RBibFe 12 (1986) 251 (A. *Salas*); CiTom 113 (1986) 625 (J. L. *Espinel*); EstE 61 (1986) 478s (J. *Alonso Díaz*); NatGrac 33 (1986) 176 (D. *Montero*); RBibArg 48 (1986) 125s (A. J. *Levoratti*); Studium 26 (M 1986) 354 (L. *López de las Heras*); VerVid 44 (1986) 465s (V. *Casas*).

2288 **Kraus** Hans-Joachim, Theology of the Psalms [1979 ➤ 60,4042], ^TCrim Keith. Minneapolis 1986, Augsburg. 235 p. $25 [TDig 34,80].

2288* **Łach** Józef, ☉ Biblijna idea miłości ... L'idée biblique de la charité qui sauve, à la lumière du Psautier: diss. Wsz 1986, ^DMuszyński H. – RTLv 18,542.

2289 a) *McCandless* J. Bardarah, Enfleshing the Psalms; – b) *McConnell* Taylor, Oral cultures and literate research: RelEd 81 (Ch 1986) 372-391 / 341-355 [< ZIT]; – c) *McConville* J. G., Statement of assurance in psalms of lament: IrBSt 8 (1986) 64-75.

2289* **Rasmussen** Tarald, Inimici ecclesiae; das ekklesiologische Feindbild in Luthers 'Dictata super Psalterium' (1513-1515) im Horizont der theologischen Tradition: Diss. Olso 1985. – NorTTs 87 (1986) 40.
    Reed Stephen A., Food in the Psalms ^D1985 ➤ b744.

2290 *Roslon* Józef W., ☉ Zbawienie jako życie w oparciu o księgę Psalmów (De notione salutis ut vitae in psalmis): ➤ 367, Sympozjum 1985, RuBi 39 (1986) 177-197.

2291 *Scippa* Vincenzo, Il figlio e la figlia nei Salmi; ricerca di semantica e di antropologia biblica: Asprenas 33 (1986) 263-289.

2292 *Tournay* Raymond J., La dimension prophétique de la psalmique israélite à l'époque du Second Temple: ➤ 377a, IOSOT summaries (1986) 135.

2293 **Wilson** Gerald H., The use of royal psalms at the 'seams' of the Hebrew Psalter: JStOT 35 (1986) 85-94.

2294 **Witczyk** Henryk, Teofania w psalmach [diss. Kraków]. Kraków 1985, Polskie Towarzystwo Teologiczne. 200 p. – ^RColcT 56,3 (1986) 185-190 (T. *Brzegowy*); RuBi 39 (1986) 531s (A. *Tronina*).

E6.6   *Psalmi: oratio, liturgia;* **Psalms as prayer.**

2294* *Abruden* Dumitrun Le psautier dans la spiritualité orthodoxe (roum.) STBuc 37 (1985) 453-470.

2295 **Aejmelaeus** Anneli, The traditional prayer in the Psalms: BZAW 167 [with *Schmidt* L., Josephsgesch.]. B 1986, de Gruyter. p. 1-119. DM 140 [TR 83,74]. 3-11-010480-6 / NY 0-89925-279-6.

2296 **Allen** Ronald B., Lord of song; the Messiah revealed in the Psalms, foreword *Shea* George B. Portland OR 1985, Multnomah. 177 p. 0-88070-129-3.

2297 **Alonso Schökel** Luis, Pregare i Salmi [115; 137; 87; 102; Lc 1,46-55]: Settimana Biblica Casalpina 1, present. *Morero* V.; appendice *Buzzetti* C. T-Pragelato 1986. 129 p.

2298 **Alonso Schökel** Luis, Treinta Salmos; poesia y oración[2] [¹1980 ➤ 62,3193]: Inst. S. Jer. M 1986, Cristiandad. 471 p. 88-7057-292-X; pa. 1-1.

2298* **Anderson** Bernhard W., Out of the depths; the psalms speak for us today ²ʳᵉᵛ [¹1970] 1983 ➤ 64,3021; 65,2682: ᴿCBQ 48 (1986) 293-5 (J. *Endres*).

2299 **Beaucamp** Évode, Israel en prière; des Psaumes au Notre Père 1985 ➤ 1,3071: ᴿAngelicum 63 (1986) 134-6 (J. *García Trapiello*); PrOrChr 36 (1986) 183s (P. *Ternant*).

2300 **Cox** Dermot, I salmi, incontri col Dio vivente [1984 ➤ 65,2692]. Mi, Paoline. 168 p. – ᴿBbbOr 28 (1986) (E. P.).

2301 **Craghan** John, The Psalms, prayers ... 1985 ➤ 1,3076: ᴿCurrTM 13 (1986) 116 (R. *Gnuse*): RExp 83 (1986) 119s (E. G. *Hinson*: scholarly, practical).

2302 **Esquerda Bifet** Juan, Todo es mensaje; experiencia cristiana de los Salmos[2]. M 1983, Paulinas. 310 p. 84-285-0878-X.

2303 *Fischer* Balthasar, Die Psalmen als Stimme der Kirche 1982 ➤ 63,204; 64,3032: ᴿTLZ 111 (1986) 211s (W.-D. *Hauschild*).

2304 *Fischer* Balthasar, Eine Predigt Johann Henry NEWMANS aus dem Jahre 1840 zur Frage des christlichen Psalmenverständnisses: ➤ 41, ᶠGROSS H., Freude 1986, 69-79.

2305 [**Hamman** A. G. 1980] I salmi pregati da S. AGOSTINO, ᵀ*Parenzan* Annamaria. Mi 1986, Paoline. 336 p. – ᴿSalesianum 48 (1986) 988 (B. *Amata*).

2306 **Janecko** Benedict, The Psalms, heartbeat of life and worship. St. Meinrad IN 1986, Archabbey. xiii-85 p. 0-87029-203-X.

2307 **López Martín** Julián, La oración de las Horas; historia, teología y pastoral del oficio divino: Mundo y Dios 24. Salamanca 1984, Secr. Trinitario. 251 p. – ᴿRB 93 (1986) 312 (J. *Loza*).

2308 **Michelsen** Leif M., Rop til Herren; et utvalg gammeltestamentlige salmer 1984 ➤ 1, 3088: ᴿTsTKi 57 (1986) 227s (Helge S. *Kvanvig*).

2309 *a) Morard* Loyse, Psaumes et prière chrétienne: FoiTemps 16 (1986) 423-441. – *b) Singer* Susanne F., The power of the Psalms in our time [*Scharansky* A. ...]: BR 2,3 (1986) 4 only.

2309* *Ravasi* G. [➤ 2269s], I canti di Israele; preghiera e vita di un popolo: La Bibbia nella storia. Bo 1986, Dehoniane. 304 p. Lit. 18.000. – ᴿStPatav 33 (1986) 691s (M. *Milani*).

2310 *Stolz* Fritz, Psalmen im nachkultischen Raum: ThSt 129, 1983 ➤ 64,3107: ᴿJBL 105 (1986) 140s (L. G. *Perdue*: 'post-cultic piety').

2311 *Trublet* Jacques, Psaumes: ➤ 582, DictSpir XII/2 (1986) 2504-2562 [-2568, commentaires, *Solignac* Aimé].

2312 *Vesco* Jean-Luc, La lecture du Psautier selon l'Épître de Barnabé: RB 93 (1986) 5-37.

2312* *Westermann* Claus, Das Beten der Psalmen und unser Beten: ZeichZt 40 (1986) 243-6.

2313 **White** R. E. O., A Christian handbook to the Psalms 1984 ➤ 65,2713; 1,3101: ᴿSTEv 9,18 (1986) 284-6 (P. *Finch*); Vidyajyoti 49 (1985) 480s (J. *Volckaert*).

2313* *Zirnheld* Claire-Agnès, Les psaumes; antiquités ou sources vives?: VieCons 58 (1986) 146-161. 232-242.

E6.7   *Psalmi:* **verse-numbers.**

2314 *Conti* Martino, La via della beatitudine e della rovina secondo il Salmo 1: Antonianum 61 (1986) 3-39; eng. 3.

2314* *Thomas* Marlin E., Psalms 1 and 112 as a paradigm for the comparison of wisdom motifs in the Psalms: JEvTS 29 (1986) 15-24 [< ZIT].

2315 a) *Marböck* Johannes, Zur frühen Wirkungsgeschichte von Ps 1; – *b)* *Kornfeld* Walter, [Ps 1,1-6; 2,1-4] Ein unpublizierter Psalmtext aus der Kairoer Genizah; – *c)* *Zenger* Erich, 'Wozu tosen die Völker ...?'; Beobachtungen zur Entstehung und Theologie des 2. Psalms: ➤ 41, ᶠGROSS H., Freude 1986, 207-222 / 191-7 / 495-509; 2 fig.

2315* *Sasson* Victor, The language of rebellion in Psalm 2 and in the plaster texts from Deir'Alla: AndrUnS 24 (1986) 147-154.

2316 *Willis* John T., A cry of defiance – Psalm 2: ➤ 377*b*, SBL Jerusalem summaries (1986) 9.

2317 *Auffret* Pierre, 'Qui nous fera voir le bonheur?' Étude structurelle du Psaume 4 [... *Girard* M. 1984]: NRT 108 (1986) 342-355.

2318 *Wahl* Otto, Du allein, Herr, lässt mich sorglos ruhen; die frohe Botschaft von Ps 4: ➤ 41, ᶠGROSS H., Freude 1986, 457-470.

2318* a) **Allen** Ronald B., [Ps 8] The majesty of man; the dignity of being human 1984 ➤ 65,2720; $12: ᴿBS 143 (1986) 79 (F. R. *Howe*); GraceTJ 7 (1986) 135s (T. *Craigen*). – *b)* *Cimosa* Mario, Dio, uomo e cosmo nel Salmo 8: ParVi 31 (1986) 335-9.

2319 *Görg* Manfred, Alles hast du gelegt unter seine Füsse; Beobachtungen zu Ps 8,7b im Vergleich mit Gen 1,28; ➤ 41, ᶠGROSS H., Freude 1986, 125-148.

2319* *Beintker* Horst, Christologische Gedanken LUTHERS zum Sterben Jesu, bei Auslegung von Psalm 8 und Psalm 22 im Kommentar von 1519 bis 1521 und verwandten Texterklärungen: ArRefG 77 (1986) 5-30.

2320 *Schweikhart* Wilfried, [Ps 9s; 25; 34; 37; 111] Gottes Lob von A-Z; alphabetischen Psalmen in alphabetischer Übersetzung: FreibRu 37s (1985s) 49-51.

2321 **Steingrimsson** Sigurdur Ö. [Ps 15; 24; Is 33,14-16] Tor der Gerechtigkeit ... Einzugsliturgien: AOtt 1984 ➤ 65,2724; 1,3113: ᴿCBQ 48 (1986) 322s (W. *Brueggemann*); JBL 105 (1986) 525s (J. T. *Willis*: important despite 200 errors and 75 unkeyed abbreviations); RB 93 (1986) 149 (R. J. *Tournay*); TPQ 134 (1986) 75 (H. *Irsigler*); WeltOr 17 (1986) 172s (P. J. *Nel*).

2322 **Waaijman** Kees, Psalmen [15... 150] om Jeruzalem: VBGed. Kampen 1985, Kok. 152 p. ƒ22,50. – ᴿPrakT 13 (1986) 622s (J. *Kahmann*); Streven 53 (1985s) 852s (P. *Beentjes*).

2323 *Hossfeld* Frank-Lothar, Der Wandel des Beters in Ps 18; Wachstumsphasen eines Dankliedes: ➤ 41, ᶠ*Gross* H., Freude 1986, 171-190.

2324 *Couroyer* B., [Ps 18,36b] Ta droite assiste mon épée: RB 93 (1986) 38-47; 48-51, *Puech* Émile, Note paléographique.

2325 *Allen* Leslie C., David as exemplar of spirituality; the redactional function of Psalm 19: Biblica 67 (1986) 544-6.

2326 *Loretz* Oswald, Ugaritologische und kolometrische Anmerkungen zu Ps 19A: UF 18 (1986s) 223-9.

2327 *Halporn* James W., CASSIODORUS' Commentary on Psalms 20 and 21; text and context: RÉAug 32 (1986) 92-102.

2328 **Fuchs** Ottmar, Die Klage als Gebet ... Ps 22: 1982 ➤ 63,3157 ... 1,3124: ᴿArLtgW 28 (1986) 416-426 (A. R. *Müller*); TR 82 (1986) 370-2 (A. *Deissler*).

2329 *a) Weimar* Peter, Psalm 22; Beobachtungen zur Komposition und Entstehungsgeschichte; – *b) Stenger* Werner, Strukturale 'relecture' von Ps 23: ➤ 41, ᶠGʀᴏss H., Freude 1986, 471-494 / 441-455.

2330 *Lundbom* Jack R., Psalm 23, song of passage: Interpretation 40 (1986) 5-16.

2331 *Auffret* Pierre, 'Yahvé m'accueillera'; étude structurale du Psaume 27: ScEspr 38 (1986) 97-113.

2332 *Gordon* Cyrus H., Psalm 29 and the dance of Shiva: ➤ 377*b*, SBL Jerusalem summaries (1986) 9.

2333 **Kloos** Carola J. L., [Ps 29; Ex 15,1-18 ...] Yhwh's combat with the sea; a Canaanite tradition in the religion of ancient Israel: diss. Leiden 1986, ᴰ*Mulder* M. 243 p. – TsTNijm 26 (1986) 288.

2334 **Loretz** Oswald, Ps 29; Kanaanäische El- und Baaltraditionen in jüdischer Sicht 1984 ➤ 65,2315; 1,3129: ᴿRB 93 (1986) 304 (R. J. *Tournay*); TR 82 (1986) 112 (K. *Seybold*); ZAW 98 (1986) 316 (H.-C. *Schmitt*).

2335 *Tromp* Nicolas J., La louange réaliste du Psaume 30 (29), 'Ne pas séparer ce que Dieu a uni': ETL 62 (1986) 257-266.

2336 *Bellinger* W. H.ᴶ, Psalms of the falsely accused; a reassessment [Ps 31; 64; 28: malicious gossip; not courtroom-scene]: ➤ 392, SBL Seminars 1986, 463-9.

2337 *Richards* Kent H., Psalm 34: Interpretation 40 (1986) 175-180.

2337* *Hunter* J. H., Die vertaling van Psalm 36:10 in die Nuwe Afrikaanse Vertaling van die Bybel: NduitseGT 26 (1985) 404-8.

2338 *Angerstorfer* Andreas, Der Mensch nach Ps 39,6f und Targum Ps 39,6f; Vergänglichkeitsaussage und Auferstehungshoffnung: ➤ 41, ᶠGʀᴏss H., Freude 1986, 1-15.

2339 *Ishikawa* R., ❶ A literary interpretation of the Psalms, taking the case from the Psalms 42-43: Kirisutokyō Kenkyū (1986) 46-81 [OTAbs 10,63].

2340 *Whitley* C. F., Textual and exegetical observations on Ps 45,4-7: ZAW 98 (1986) 277-282: Elohim = 'the anointed one'.

2341 *Schweizer* Harald, 'Ein feste Burg ...' Der Beitrag der Prädikate zur Aussageabsicht von Ps 46: TüTQ 166 (1986) 107-119.

2341* *Barucq* André, Quelques réflexions à propos du Psaume 49 et des 'Chants du harpiste': ➤ 18, Mem. DAUMAS F. I (1986), 67-73.

2342 *Willis* John T., Four assessments of sacrifice in Psalm 50: ➤ 377*a*, IOSOT summaries (1986) 143.

2343 *Anoz* José, El salmo 50 [51] en los escritos agustinianos: AugM 31 (1986) 293-342.

2344 **Martini** Carlo M., [Ps 51] Das Gebet der Versöhnung; Betrachtungen zum Psalm 'Miserere', ᵀ*Schmittinger* H. FrB 1986, Herder. 96 p. DM 12,80 [TLZ 111,720].

2345 *Weber* Timothy, Mercy and our many selves; a meditation on Psalm 51: CurrTM 13 (1986) 42-45.

2346 *Jackson* M., Formica Dei; Augustine's enarratio in Psalmum 66.3: VigChr 40 (1986) 153-168.

2347 **Carniti** Cecilia sr., Il Salmo 68; studio letterario [diss. 1984, Pont. Ist. Biblico, ᴰ*McCarthy* D. ➤ 65,2748]: 1985 ➤ 1,3146: ᴿBL (1986) 65 (R. *Murray*: well argued with insight and literary sensitivity); Claretianum 26 (1986) 358-360 (M. *Zappella*); ParVi 31 (1986) 377s (T. *Lorenzin*).

2348 *Allen* Leslie C., The value of rhetorical criticism in Psalm 69: JBL 105 (1986) 577-598.

2348* **Pezhumkattil** Abraham, The image of the Servant of the Lord in Psalm 69,2-30 in comparison to the other 'Servant-Psalms': diss. Pont. Univ. Gregoriana, ᴰ*Simian-Yofre* H. R 1986. xiii-410 p. – RTLv 18,543.

2349 **Schelling** P., [Ps 73-83; 50] De Asafpsalmen, hun samenhang en achtergrond [Proefschrift prot. Fac. Brussel] 1985 ➤ 1,3147: ᴿNedTTs 40 (1986) 332s (N. J. *Tromp*); Streven 53 (1985s) 562s (P. *Beentjes*).

2349* *Anders* Dan, Amadeus; when good things happen to bad people; Psalm 73: RestQ 28,1 (Abilene 1985s) 11-16.

2350 **Irsigler** Hubert, Psalm 73 — Monolog eines Weisen; Text, Programm, Struktur [Hab.-D. Mü, ᴰ*Richter* W.]: AOtt 20, 1984 ➤ 65,2749; 1,3148: ᴿAION 46 (1986) 115 (J. A. *Soggin* su AOtt 11-20); JSS 31 (1986) 250-2 (J. *Gray*); RB 93 (1986) 304s (R. J. *Tournay*); TPQ 134 (1986) 299s (J. *Marböck*); WeltOr 17 (1986) 173-5 (P. J. *Nel*).

2351 *Tromp* Nico, Het heil komt uit het Noorden (Ps. 75): OnsGLev 63 (1986) 160s.

2352 *Gameleira Soares* Sebastião A., Salmos — história, poesia e oração (Uma leitura do Salmo 77): Estudos Bíblicos 10 (1986) 8-27 [58-60, *Barros Souza* Marcelo de, Os Salmos nas lutas das comunidades cristãs].

2353 *Bonner* Gerald, [Ps 81G,6] AUGUSTINE's conception of deification: JTS 37 (1986) 369-386.

2354 *Stendebach* Franz J., Glaube und Ethos; Überlegungen zu Ps 82: ➤ 41, ᶠGROSS H., Freude 1986, 425-440.

2355 *It* K., ❶ The structure and theme of Ps 84: Kōbe Jogakuin Daigaku Ronshū 33 (1986) 19-37 [OTAbs 10,64].

2356 *Tromp* Nico, Een tranendal (Psalm 84,7): OnsGLev 63 (1986) 46-50.

2357 *Booij* T., Royal words in Psalm LXXXIV: VT 36 (1986) 117-121.

2358 *Haag* Ernst, Psalm 88: ➤ 41, ᶠGROSS H., Freude 1986, 149-170.

2359 *Mosca* Paul G., Once again the heavenly witness [*ba-šaḥaq*] of Ps 89:38: JBL 105 (1986) 27-37.

2360 **Veijola** Timo, Verheissung in der Krise... Exilszeit ... Ps 89: 1982 ➤ 63,3193 ... 65,2758: ᴿJBL 105 (1986) 141s (E. S. *Gerstenberger*); JTS 37 (1986) 144s (J. G. *Snaith*); OLZ 81 (1986) 562-6 (J. *Conrad*).

2361 *Datema* C., *Allen* P., LEONTIUS, presbyter of Constantinople, the author of Ps.-Chrysostom, In Psalmum 92 (CPG 4548): VigChr 40 (1986) 169-182.

2361* **Howard** David M., The structure of Psalms 93-100: diss. Michigan, ᴰ*Freedman* D. N. AA 1986. 279 p. 86-12539. – DissA 47 (1986s) 883-A.

2362 **Braulik** Georg, Gottes Ruhe — das Land oder der Tempel? Zu Psalm 95,11: ➤ 41, ᶠGROSS H., Freude 1986, 33-44.

2363 *Auffret* Pierre, Essai de structure littéraire du Psaume 103: FolOr 23 (Kraków 1985s) 197-225.

2364 **Barker** David G., The waters of the earth; an exegetical study of Psalm 104: 1-9: GraceTJ 7 (1986) 57-80.

2365 **Auffret** Pierre, Essai sur la structure littéraire du Psaume 105: BibNot Beih. 3. Mü 1985, Görg. 137 p.

2365* *Thompson* Yaakov, [Ps 106 reflects] A missing hexateuchal narrative concerning child sacrifice: Dor 15 (1986s) 38-42.

2366 *Schnider* Franz, Rettung aus Seenot; Ps 107,23-32 und Mk 4,35-41: ➤ 41, ᶠGROSS H., Freude 1986, 375-393.

2367 *a*) *Becker* Joachim, Zur Deutung von Ps 110,7; – *b*) *Fabry* Heinz-Josef, 11Q Psᵃ und die Kanonizität des Psalters: ➤ 41, ᶠGROSS H., Freude 1986, 17-31 / 45-67.

2368 *Sacon* K. K., **O** A methodological remark on exegesis and preaching of Psalm 113: Nihon no Shingaku 25 (1986) 26-42 [OTAbs 10,64].

2369 *Tromp* Nico, Die rotsen herschiep tot sijpelend water, graniet tot borrelende wel (Ps. 114,8): OnsGLev 63 (1986) 266-272.

2370 *Lohfink* Norbert, Ps 114/115 (M und G) und die deuteronomische Sprachwelt: → 41, ᶠGROSS H., Freude 1986, 199-205.

2371 *Carpino* Fabiola, ORIGENE, EUSEBIO e ILARIO sul Salmo 118: → 365, AnStoEseg 3 (1985/6) 57-64.

2372 *Kutsch* Ernst, Deus humiliat et exaltat; zu LUTHERs Übersetzung von Psalm 118,21 und Psalm 18,36 [< ZTK 61 (1964) 193-220]: → 183, KLS 1986, 348-375.

2373 *Amir* Yehoshua, Psalm 119 als Zeugnis eines protorabbinischen Judentums [< GRINTZ Y., Te'uda 2 (1982) 57-81]: → 127, Studien 1985, 1-34.

2373* ᴱ**Bucichowski** Wacław, MATHEUS de Cracovia, Lectura super Beati immaculati: Textus et Studia 19/1s. Wsz 1984, Akademia Teologii Katolickiej. 203 p.; 247 p.

2374 *Schreiner* Josef, Leben nach der Weisung des Herrn; eine Auslegung des Ps 119: → 41, ᶠGROSS H., Freude 1986, 395-424.

2375 **Beyerlin** Walter, Weisheitliche Vergewisserung mit Bezug auf den Zionskult; Studien zum 125. Psalm: OBO 68, 1985 → 1,3171: ᴿETL 62 (1986) 187 (J. *Lust*).

2376 *Fleming* Daniel E., [Ps 127,1] 'House'/'city'; an unrecognized parallel word pair: JBL 105 (1986) 689-693.

2377 **Auffret** P., Et comment pourrait-elle chanter? La lecture du Psaume 136 dans les Lettres de Thérèse de Lisieux, suivie d'une analyse de la poésie Vivre d'Amour. Monte-Carlo 1985, Regain. F 150 [NRT 109,477].

2377* *Maertens* Grégoire, 'Nous souvenant de Sion...' (Ps 136): ComLtg 68 (1986) 111-6.

2378 *Schedl* Claus, Die alphabetisch-arithmetische Struktur von Psalm CXXXVI: VT [35 (1985) 129-138, *Bazak* J.] 36 (1986) 489-494.

2379 *Bayer* Bathja, Babylonian court music and Asaphite apologetics; a rationale for Ps. 137:1-7: → 377a, IOSOT summaries (1986) 14.

2381 *Hartmann* Benedikt, Exegetische und religionsgeschichtliche Studie zu Psalm 141:5d-7: → 59, ᶠLEBRAM J., Tradition 1986, 27-37.

2382 *a)* **Ruppert** Lothar, Aufforderung an die Schöpfung zum Lob Gottes; zur Literar-, Form- und Traditionskritik von Ps 148; – *b)* *Füglister* Notger, Ein garstig Lied — Ps 149: → 41, ᶠGROSS H., Freude 1986, 275-296 / 81-105.

2383 *Ceresko* Anthony R., Psalm 149; poetry, themes (Exodus and Conquest) and social function: Biblica 67 (1986) 177-194; franç. 194.

E7.1   **Job,** *Textus, commentarii.*

2384 **Alonso Schökel** L., *Sicre Díaz* J. L., Job, comentario teológico y literario: Nueva Biblia Española 1983 → 64,3149... 1,3184: ᴿCBQ 48 (1986) 318s (R. E. *Murphy*: original but dialogues more with Spanish classics than with modern authors); JBL 105 (1986) 138s (C. T. *Begg*); NRT 108 (108s (J.-L. *Ska*); ScEspr 38 (1986) 126-8 (G. *Novotny*).

2384* *a)* *Braga* Gabriella, Moralia in Iob — epitomi dei secoli VII-X e loro evoluzione; – *b)* *Fontaine* Jacques, AUGUSTIN, GRÉGOIRE et ISIDORE; esquisse d'une recherche sur le style des Moralia in Iob; – *c)* *Doignon* Jean, 'Blessure d'affliction' et 'blessure d'amour' (Moralia 6,25,42); une fonction de thème de la spiritualité patristique de CYPRIEN à Augustin: ➤ 433*, Grégoire 1982/6, 561-8 / 499-509 / 297-303.

2385 *Deselaers* Paul [kath.; Exegese], *al.*, Sehnsucht nach dem lebendigen Gott; das Buch Ijob: BPrax 8. Stu 1983, KBW. 160 p. DM 22,80. – ᴿCBQ 48 (1986) 305s (A. R. *Ceresko*: the series team includes also a pastoral theologian, a Protestant pastor, and three others).

2386 **Ebach** Jürgen, Hiob, Hiobbuch: ➤ 597, TRE 15 (1986) 360-373; bibliog. 373-380 !

2387 **Finateri** Serafino, *Ozawa* Paul K., ❾ Job: Franciscan Biblical Institute. Tokyo 1986, Chūō Shuppan-sha. vi-327 p. Y 3500. 4-8056-8916-1 [OTAbs 10,93].

2388 **Fronius** Hans [etchings; text by *Marböck* Johannes ➤ 61,4272], Das Buch Hiob. Klosterneuburg 1980, ÖsKBW. 103 p. – ᴿRelStR 12 (1986) 159 (J. L. *Crenshaw*: stunning).

2389 **Gross** Heinrich, Ijob: NEchter AT. Wü 1986, Echter. 152 p. DM 34; sb. 29. 3-429-00998-7.

2390 **Guinan** Michael D., Job: OT 19. Collegeville MN 1986, Liturgical. 87 p. $3 pa. [TDig 33,464].

2391 **Habel** Norman, The Book of Job 1985 ➤ 1,3195: ᴿBijdragen 47 (1986) 440 (P. C. *Beentjes*); Paradigms 2,1 (1986) 40s (D. M. *Fleming*); SvTKv 62 (1986) 41s (T. N. D. *Mettinger*); VT 36 (1986) 507 (J. A. *Emerton*).

2392 *Hagedorn* Dieter & Ursula, Zur Katenenüberlieferung des Hiobkommentar von DIDYMUS dem Blinden: ➤ 123, ᶠWILLIS W., BASP 20 (1985) 55-78.

2393 ᴱ**Hagedorn** Ursula & Dieter, OLYMPIODOR Diakon von Alexandria, Kommentar zu Hiob: PatrTSt 24, 1984 ➤ 65,2788; 1,3197: ᴿBO 43 (1986) 465s (P. *Allen*).

2394 *Hidal* Sten, Hjältedikt eller själens resa — synen på Jobs bok i fornkyrkan: SvTKv 62 (1986) 69-76.

2394* **Hussain** Haider A., Yefet BEN ALI's commentary on the Hebrew text of the Book of Job I-X.: diss. St. Andrews 1986. 500 p. – RTLv 18,544.

2395 **Janzen** J. G., Job. Atlanta 1985, Knox. 272 p. $19. ᴿTTod 43 (1986s) 578.580 (R. N. *Boyce*).

2396 *Le Déaut* Roger, Usage implicite de l' *'al tiqré* dans le Targum de Job de Qumrân ? : ➤ 21, Mem. DÍEZ MACHO A., Salvación 1986, 419-431.

2396* *Luyten* Jos, A new commentary on the book of Job [*Habel* N. ➤ 2391]: LvSt 11,1 (1986) 60.

2397 **Montgolfier** Jeannine de, Traduction et commentaire du 'De interpellatione Job et David' d'AMBROISE de Milan: diss. Sorbonne, ᴰ*Fontaine*. P 1986. – RTLv 18,551.

2397* **Pixley** Jorge, El libro de Job: Com. bíblico latinoamericano. San José CR 1982, Cebila. 233 p. – ᴿTVida 27 (1986) 336s (R. *Dell'Aquila* F.).

2398 *Rodd* C. S., Which is the best commentary? IV. Job [*Gibson* J. 1985; *Habel* N. OTLibrary 1985; but special value is found in the composite-commentaries, *Irwin* W. in Peake's 1962 and *MacKenzie* R. A. F. in Jerome (Chapman) 1970]: ExpTim 97 (1985s) 356-360.

2398* *Schreiner* Susan E., 'Through a mirror dimly'; CALVIN's sermons on Job: CalvinT 21 (1986) 175-193.

2399 **Selms** A. Van, Job, a practical commentary, ᵀ*Vriend* John: Text & Interpretation [Tekst en Toelichting 1984 ➤ 65,2797]. GR 1985, Eerdmans. vii-160 p. $9. 0-8028-0101-3. – ᴿCalvinT 21 (1986) 303-9 (A. *Wolters*); RelStT 6 (1986) 67s (L. *Eslinger*).

2400 **Simundson** Daniel J., The message of Job; a theological commentary. Minneapolis 1986, Augsburg. 159 p. $10 [TS 48, 389 D. J. *Harrington*].

2401 **Ziegler** Joseph, Beiträge zum griechischen Iob: AbhGö pg/h 147, 1985
→ 1,3205; DM 68: ᴿBijdragen 47 (1986) 440s (Tamis *Wever*); TR 82
(1986) 281-3 (H.-P. *Müller*).
2402 **Ziegler** J., Iob: Göttinger Septuaginta 11/4, 1982 → 63,3246... 65,2800:
ᴿNRT 108 (1986) (C. *Martin*).

E7.2   *Job: themata,* **Topics**... *Versiculi,* **Verse-numbers.**

2403 *Christensen* D., Job and the age of the Patriarchs in the Old Testament:
PerspRelSt 13 (1986) 225-8 [< ZAW].
2404 *a) Clines* David J. A., False naivety in the prologue to Job; – *b) Gordis*
Robert, Job and ecology (and the significance of Job 40:15): → 36, Mem.
GOITEIN S. = HebAnR 9 (1985) 127-136 / 189-202.
2405 **Eaton** J. H., Job: OTGuides. Sheffield 1985, JStOT. 68 p. £3. – ᴿCBQ
48 (1986) 708s (D. J. *Harrington*, also on ᴱ*Aufrecht*).
2406 **Fohrer** G., Studien zum Buche Hiob: BZAW 159, 1983 → 64,164; 65,2804:
ᴿBO 43 (1986) 464s (H. *Haag*); OLZ 81 (1986) 565s (H. *Seidel*).
2407 *Geyer* Carl-Friedrich, Das Hiobbuch im christlichen und nachchrist-
lichen Kontext; Anmerkungen zur Rezeptionsgeschichte: Kairos 28 (1986)
174-195.
2408 *Gorringe* Timothy J., Job and the Pharisees ['Be holy as I am holy'
underlies both]: Interpretation 40 (1986) 17-28.
2409 **Gutiérrez** Gustavo, Hablar de Dios desde el sufrimiento del inocente;
una reflexión sobre el libro de Job: Pedal 183. Lima/Salamanca 1986,
CEP/ Sígueme. 226 p. (187 p.) 84-301-1002-X. – ᴿActuBbg 23 (1986) 213
(R. de *Sivatte*); ComSev 19 (1986) 428s (V. J. *Ansede Alonso*); LumenV 35
(1986) 557 (F. *Ortiz de Urtaran*); RCatalT 11 (1986) 457s (J. I. *González
Faus*).
2410 *Hoffmann* Yair, La ironía en el libro de Job [< Immanuel 17 (1984)
7-21], ᵀᴱ*Muñoza* Antolín de la: SelT 25 (1986) 231-9.
2411 **Huber** Paul, Hiob, Dulder oder Rebell? Byzantinische Miniaturen zum
Buch Hiob in Patmos, Rom, Venedig, Sinai, Jerusalem und Athos. Dü
1986, Patmos. 264 p.; 256 (color.) fig. 3-491-77639-2.
2412 *Huberlant* François-X., Commentaire excessif du livre de Job: VSp 140
(1986) 235-241.
2413 *Klaus* Nathan, ❿ Between Job and his friends: BethM 31,105 (1985s)
152-168.
2414 **Lévêque** J., Job, el libro y el mensaje: CuadBib 53. Estella 1986,
VDivino. 62 p. pt. 250. 84-7151-496-6. – ᴿBibFe 12 (1986) 367 (M. *Sáenz
Galache*); ScripTPamp 18 (1986) 964 (F. *Varo*).
2415 **Loades** A. L., KANT and Job's comforters. 1985, Avero. 174 p. [JAAR
54,400].
2415* **Loyd** Douglas E., Patterns of interrogative rhetoric in the
[speeches/poetic sections] of the book of Job: diss. Iowa, ᴰ*Kuntz* J. K.
Iowa City 1986. 328 p. 86-22792. – DissA 47 (1986s) 2616-A 'speeches'
[RelStR 13,189 'poetic sections'].
2416 *Maia* Pedro A., Paixão de Jó e paixão de Cristo: RCuBíb 10,39s (1986)
132-148.
2416* **Perraymond** Myla, Giobbe nell'iconografia sepolcrale e nella primitiva
letteratura cristiana: diss. Ist. Arch. Cristiana, ᴰ*Recio* P. R 1986. – RTLv
18,563.
2417 *Smick* Elmer B., Semeiological interpretation of the book of Job [*Vawter*
B. 1983; *Alonso Schökel* L., *Ricœur* P. (Semeia 19,1981)...]: WestTJ 48
(1986) 135-149.

2418 **Vermeylen** J.,   Job, ses amis et son Dieu: StB 2.   Leiden 1986, Brill.
100 p. ƒ32.   90-04-07649-2. – [R]ExpTim 98 (1986s) 117 (R. *Coggins*: shows
four stages of composition, earliest in Persian period); ZAW 98 (1986) 480s
(H.-C. *Schmitt*).
2419 *Weissblüth* S. [OTAbs 9,292]. ❿ Meaning of Job's chastisements: BethM
31,104 (1985s) 72-77.
2420 **Yaeger** Yaacov, ❿ *Be'urim* ... Researches on the book of Job.   J 1983,
Zak.   174 p. [KirSef 60,363].

2421 **Day** Peggy L.,   [Job 1s; Nm 22,22-35; Zech 3,1-7; 1 Chr 21,1-22,1] *Śāṭān*
in the Hebrew Bible: diss. Harvard.   CM 1986. 207 p. – DissA 47 (1986s)
4418-A; HarvTR 79 (1986) 471.
2422 *Blois* Kees F. de, [Job 1,6 ...] How to deal with Satan? [LXX 21 t.
Diábolos, 13 in Job; meaning shifts from OT to NT; 'Satan' as proper name
often used ...; basically public prosecutor]: BTrans 37 (1986) 301-9.
2423 *Cox* Dermot,   A rational inquiry into God; chapters 4-27 of the Book of
Job: Gregorianum 67 (1986) 621-657; franç. 658.
2423* *a) Riggans* Walter,   A note on Job 6:8-10; suicide and death-wishes; – *b)*
Wolfers David, [Job 12] 'Greek' logic in the book of Job: Dor 15 (1986s)
173-6 / 166-172.
2424 *Kutsch* Ernst,   *a)* Unschuldsbekenntnis und Gottesbegegnung; der
Zusammenhang zwischen Hiob 31 und 38 ff. [ineditum]; – *b)* Hiob;
leidender Gerechter — leidender Mensch [< KerDo 19 (1973) 197-214]; –
c) Vom Grund und Sinn des Leidens nach dem AT [< [E]SCHULZE H. Das
leidende Mensch 1974, 73-84]: ➤ 183, KLS 1986, 308-335 / 290-307 /
336-347.
2424* *a) O'Connor* Daniel,   The futility of myth-making in theodicy; Job
38-41; – *b) Finan* Thomas,   The myth of the innocent sufferer; some Greek
paradigms: PrIrB 9 (1985) 81-99 / 121-135.
2425 **Oorschot** Jürgen van,   Die Gottesreden des Hiobbuches; eine literar- und
redaktionsgeschichtliche Studie zu Hiob 38,1-42,6: Diss. [D]*Kaiser* O.   Marburg 1986. – RTLv 18,543.
2425* *Rowold* Henry,   Mi hû'? Lî hû? Leviathan and Job in Job 41:2-3: JBL
105 (1986) 104-109.
2426 *Cimosa* Mario,   L'intercessione di Giobbe in LXX Gb 42,7-10:
Salesianum 48 (1986) 513-538.
2426* *Morrow* William,   Consolation, rejection, and repentance in Job 42:6:
JBL 105 (1986) 211-225.

E7.3   *Canticum canticorum*, **Song of Solomon** – *textus, commentarii.*

2427 **Arminjon** Blaise,   La cantate de l'Amour, lecture suivie du Cantique des
Cantiques; préf. *Lubac* H. de. 1983 ➤ 64,3215 ... 1,3248: [R]DivThom 88
(1985) 148-151 (P.-L. *Carle*: contraste, 'au moment où la critique
exégétique adopte fréquemment le style triumphaliste, multiplie les
affirmations péremptoires, sans appel, se décerne volontiers un brevet
d'infaillibilité ...'); ÉglT 17 (1986) 90s (L. *Laberge*); FoiTemps 16 (1986)
179-181 (Monique *Foket*).
2428 **Barsotti** Divo,   Le Cantique des Cantiques [1980 ➤ 61,4343], [T]*Solms*
Élisabeth de, 1983 ➤ 64,3217: [R]ScEspr 38 (1986) 128 (B. de *Margerie*).
2429 [E]**Bélanger** Rodrigue,   *a)* GRÉGOIRE le Grand,   Commentaire sur le
Cantique des Cantiques: SChr 314, 1984 ➤ 65,2840; 1,3249: [R]JTS 37

(1986) 600-3 (Carole *Straw*); RHR 203 (1986) 442s (J. *Doignon*). – *b)* Anthropologie et Parole de Dieu dans le commentaire de Grégoire le Grand sur le Cantique des Cantiques: → 433*, Grégoire 1982/6, 245-254.

2430 **Brésard** Luc, BERNARD et ORIGÈNE commentent le Cantique [= Colct-Cist 44 (1982)] 1983 → 64,3218 ... 1,3250: ᴿRÉAug 31 (1985) 189-192 (Solange *Sagot*).

2431 **Carr** G. Lloyd, The Song of Solomon, an introduction and comm.: Tyndale Comm. 1984 → 65,2843; 1,3251: ᴿCBQ 48 (1986) 306 (A. R. *Ceresko*: relentlessly literalist, no space for allegorical or Marian); EvQ 58 (1986) 158s (Joyce *Baldwin*).

2432 **Colombo** Dalmazio, Cantico dei Cantici 1985 → 1,3252: ᴿCC 137 (1986,3) 439 (G. *Mucci*).

2433 **Falk** Marcia, Love lyrics 1982 → 63,3292 ... 1,3253: BZ 30 (1986) 114s (J. *Gamberoni*).

2434 **Fischer** James A., Song of Songs, Ruth, Lamentations, Ecclesiastes, Esther: OT 24. Collegeville MN 1986, Liturgical. 111 p. $3 [TDig 33,464].

2435 **Garbini** G., Calchi lessicali greci nel 'Cantico dei Cantici': LinceiAt 8/39 (1984) 149-160.

2436 **Goulder** Michael, The song of fourteen songs: JStOT Sup 36. Sheffield 1986, Univ. 94 p. £12; pa. £5. 0-905774-86-8; 7-6. – ᴿExpTim 98 (1986s) 24s (J. F. *Healey*); VT 36 (1986) 506 (J. A. *Emerton*).

2437 *Kamin* Sarah, ➊ A Latin [Vat 1053, 105-114] version of RASHI's commentary on the Song of Songs (13th century?): Tarbiz 55 (1985s) 381-411; Eng. III.

2438 **Keel** Othmar, Das Hohelied: Z BK. Z 1986, Theol.-V. 268 p.; 145 fig. Fs 33,50. 3-290-14739-8. – ᴿExpTim 98 (1986s) 182 (R. *Coggins*: lively delight in sexuality).

2438* *a) Martel* G. De, Fragment inédit d'un commentaire anonyme sur le Cantique: SacEr 28 (1985) 557-561; – *b)* **Morassi** S., Il 'Commento al Cantico dei Cantici' di APONIO: diss. ᴰ*Ceresa-Gastaldo* A. Genova 1984 [RivB 35,86].

2439 **Osculati** Roberto, Cantico dei Cantici 1985 → 1,3262: ᴿCC 137 (1986,3) 439 (G. *Mucci*: per gli ignari dell'esegesi).

2440 **Patterson** Paige, Song of Solomon: Everyman's Comm. Ch 1986, Moody. 124 p. $6. – ᴿSWJT 29,2 (1986s) 51 (L. R. *Bush*).

2441 **Ravasi** Gianfranco, Cantico dei Cantici 1985 → 1,3264: ᴿCC 137 (1986,3) 439 (G. *Mucci*); HumBr 41 (1986) 451 (A. *Bonora*); StPatav 431s (M. *Milani*).

2442 ᴱ**Simonetti** Manlio, ORÍGENES, comentario al Cantar de los Cantares, ᵀ*Velasco Delgado* A.: BibliotPatr 1. M 1986, Ciudad Nueva. 287 p. – ᴿScripTPamp 18 (1986) 968 (D. *Ramos-Lissón*).

2443 **Terrinoni** Ubaldo, El Cantar de los Cantares. Buenos Aires 1985, Paulinas. 144 p. [REB 46,471].

2444 **Tournay** Raymond J., Quand Dieu parle aux hommes le langage de l'amour ...: RB Ca 21, 1982 → 63,3305 ... 1,3266: ᴿCBQ 48 (1986) 324s (J. Cheryl *Exum*: can be read messianically but *was* not).

2445 ᴱ**Vregille** B. de, **Neyrand** L., APPONIUS, In Canticum Canticorum expositio: CCLat 19. Turnhout 1986, Brepols. cxx-537 p. [CETEDOC 84 p. + 13 microfiches]. 2-503-00191-6; pa. 2-4.

E7.4   **Canticum**. *themata, versiculi.*

2446 *Alster* Bendt, Sumerian love songs: RAss 79 (1985) 127-159.

2447 ᴱAntoniono Normanno, ORIGENE, Esortazione al martirio; Omelie sul Cantico dei Cantici. Mi 1985, Rusconi. 184 p. Lit. 18.000. – ᴿCC 137 (1986,2) 615 (E. Cattaneo).

2448 Augustin Matthias, Schönheit und Liebe im Hohenlied und dessen jüdische Auslegung im 1. und 2. Jahrhundert: → 377a, IOSOT summaries (1986) 8.

2449 Billigheimer Samuel, The concept of love in Jewish religious philosophy: AbrNahr 24 (1986) 27-50.

2450 Casalis G., al., Un chant d'amour insolite; le Cantique des cantiques. 1984. – ᴿProtestantesimo 41 (1986) 45s (D. Garone).

2451 Doignon Jean, HILAIRE lecteur du commentaire d'ORIGÈNE sur le Cantique des Cantiques? À propos de l'image psalmique du filet tendu à l'âme: → 476*, L'Origenismo 1985 = AugR 26 (1986) 251-260.

2452 a) Elliott Timothea, Lo sposo e la sposa nel Cantico dei cantici; – b) Rochettes Jacqueline des, L'incontro 'sposo-sposa' nella liturgia sinagogale: ParSpV 13 (1986) 57-68 / 69-84.

2453 Esquerda Bifet Juan, Hemos conocido el amor; meditaciones sobre el Cantar de los Cantares. M 1982, BAC. xi-203 p. 84-220-1066-6.

2453* Fassetta Raffaele, Le mariage spirituel dans les Sermons de saint BERNARD sur le Cantique: ColcCist 48 (1986) 155-180. 251-265.

2454 Fox M. V., The Song of Songs and the ancient Egyptian love songs 1985 → 1,3271: ᴿJAAR 54 (1986) 775s (J. B. White); JSS 31 (1986) 252-4 (C. J. Eyre); RelStR 12 (1986) 65 (J. Crenshaw: superb); TLZ 111 (1986) 419-421 (W. Herrmann); VT 36 (1986) 499-501 (J. D. Ray +? J. A. Emerton).

2455 Goldmann Christoph, Du bist schön, meine Freundin; das Hohenlied der Liebe Salomons in Texten der Bibel und Bildern von Marc Chagall: Forum Religion 1 (Stu 1986) 2-12.

2456 Landy Francis, Paradoxes of Paradise 1983 → 64,3239... 1,3278: ᴿHeythJ 27 (1986) 184s (J. F. A. Sawyer); JAAR 54 (1986) 592s (J. Cheryl Exum); RelStR 12 (1986) 159 (J. L. Crenshaw: psychoanalysis likely to be rejected, chiefly because of convolution).

2456* Matter E. A., Eulogium sponsi de sponsa; canons, monks, and the Song of Song: Thomist 49 (1985) 551-574.

2457 Miller Patricia C., 'Pleasure of the text, text of pleasure'; eros and language in ORIGEN's Commentary on the Song of Songs: JAAR 54 (1986) 241-253.

2458 Müller Hans-Peter, Vergleich und Metapher im Hohenlied: OBO 56, 1984 → 65,2868; 1,3284: ᴿBO 43 (1986) 648s (P. Höffken); JBL 105 (1986) 712-4 (T. Polk).

2459 Murphy Roland E., History of exegesis as a hermeneutical tool; the Song of Songs: BibTB 16 (1986) 87-91.

2460 Pos[e]ner-Kriéger P., Les chants d'amour de l'ancienne Égypte: MondeB 45 (1986) 42s.

2460* Rabinowitz Z. M., ❶ On the ancient form of Midrash Shir ha-Shirim Rabba (according to Geniza fragments): Teʿuda 3 (1983) 83-90; Eng. viii.

2461 Reventlow Henning, Hoheslied: → 597, TRE 499-502 (-514, al., Auslegungsgeschichte).

2461* Shoshar Michael, ❶ Song of Songs and Bedouin love-song: BethM 31,107 (1985s) 360-370.

2462 Walter Hans-Ulrich, Das Hohelied — eine alttestamentliche Sprengung der alttestamentlichen Diskriminierung der Frauen: DiehlB 22 (1985) 140-174.

2462* *Frank* Karl S., Geordnete Liebe; Cant 2,4b in der patristischen Auslegung: WissWeis 49,1 (1986) 15-30.

E7.5   *Libri sapientiales* – **Wisdom literature.**

2463 **Auffret** Pierre, La sagesse a bâti sa maison; études de structures littéraires [Gn 2Sam Pss Lc 18]: OBO 49, 1982 ➤ 64,134; 65,2626: ᴿCBQ 48 (1986) 99-101 (J. R. *Lundbom*).

2464 *Beckman* Gary, Proverbs and proverbial allusions in Hittite: JNES 45 (1986) 19-30.

2465 **Bergant** Dianne, What are they saying about Wisdom literature? 1984 ➤ 65,2876: ᴿCBQ 48 (1986) 296 (J. A. *Gladson*: more about scholars than about text, esp. Job); Interpretation 40 (1986) 312 (Claudia V. *Camp*: 'Cliff Notes').

2466 **Blenkinsopp** Joseph, Wisdom and law in the OT 1983 ➤ 64,3250... 1,3297: ᴿHeythJ 27 (1986) 310s (R. N. *Whybray*).

2466* *a*) *Bonora* Antonio, Il metodo 'educativo' sapienziale; – *b*) *Bissoli* Cesare, Il 'giovane' nel mondo biblico; – *c*) *Monari* Luciano, Figure giovanili nella Bibbia: ParVi 31 (1986) 28-37 / 9-19 / 20-27.

2467 *Bontempi* Franco, Il problema della morale e della realtà nella tradizione sapienziale: Servitium 44 (1986) 14-28.

2468 **Brunner-Traut** E., Lebensweisheit der alten Ägypter 1985 ➤ 1,3802: ᴿMundus 22 (1986) 7s (G. *Förster*).

2469 **Crenshaw** J. L., OT wisdom 1981 ➤ 62,3420... 1,3303: ᴿRelStT 6 (1986) 73-75 (L. *Eslinger*).

2469* *Curtis* Edward M., Old Testament wisdom; a model for faith-learning integration: ChrSchR 15 (1985) 213-227.

2470 *Es* Hildo van, De kunst van het sturen; Spreuken uit Egypte en Israël. Delft 1985, Meinema. 120 p. *f* 19.50. – ᴿStreven 53 (1985s) 565 (P. *Bentjes*: delightful).

2471 *Fidalgo* José Antonio, Hermenéutica bíblica de Santo Tomás de AQUINO; interpretación de la Sabiduría del Antiguo Testamento: ➤ 366, Hermenéutica 1985/6, 477-486.

2472 *Foster* John L., Texts of the Egyptian composition 'The instruction of a man for his son' in the [Ch] Oriental Institute Museum: JNES 45 (1986) 213-202 + 8 fig.

2473 *Fox* Michael V., Egyptian onomastica and biblical wisdom: VT 36 (1986) 302-310.

2474 *Galtier* Hannes D., Probleme historisch-lehrhafter Dichtung in Mesopotamien: ➤ 543, Rencontre 32, 1985/6, 71-79.

2475 **Gilbert** M., *Aletti* J.-N., A Sabedoria e Jesus Cristo [1980 ➤ 62, 3425]: Cadernos Bíblicos 32. São Paulo 1985, Paulinas. 102 p. [REB 46, 227].

2476 **Golka** Friedemann W., Die Königs- und Hofsprüche und der Ursprung der israelitischen Weisheit: VT 36 (1986) 13-36.

2477 *González Caballero* Alberto, Influencia de la Biblia en los refranes [... maxims] españoles: EstE 61 (1986) 173-213; índice 213-7.

2478 **Helck** Wolfgang, Die Lehre des Djedefhor und die Lehre eines Vaters an seinen Sohn: KlÄgTexte 8, 1984 ➤ 65,2891; 1,3309: DM 24,80: ᴿBO 43 (1986) 398-400 (A. *Roccati*).

2479 **Lévêque** J., Sagesse de l'Égypte ancienne: CahEv Sup. 46, 1983 ➤ 1,2214: ᴿBL (1986) 106 (K. A. *Kitchen*).

2480 **Lichtheim** Miriam, Late Egyptian wisdom literature in the international context: OBO 52, 1983 ➤ 64,3267 ... 1,3315: ᴿEnchoria 14 (1986) 189-197 (H.-J. *Thissen*).

2481 *Mack* Burton L., *Murphy* Roland E., Wisdom literature: ➤ 255, ᴱ*Kraft* R., Early Judaism 1986, 371-410.

2482 **Norrick** Neal R., How proverbs mean; semantic studies in English proverbs: Trends in Linguistics 27. B 1985, Mouton. xi-213 p.; bibliog. p. 203-210. 3-11-010196-3. – ᴿSalesianum 48 (1986) 491s (R. *Della Casa*).

2483 *Pié i Ninot* Salvador, La literatura sapiencial bíblica; una actualidad bibliográfica creciente: ActuBbg [22 (1985) 202-211] 23 (1986) 163-174: *Winston* D., *Larcher* C., *Reese* J., *Bizzetti* P. ...

2484 *Pola* T., Die Frau in der Weisheit: ➤ 343, Theol. Auseinandersetzung 3 (1984) 105-122.

2485 *Posener* G., *Lévêque* Jean, Les sagesses égyptiennes ... biblique: MondeB 45 (1986) 36-39 / 39-41.

2486 *Pozzo* Vittorio, Proverbi cristiani in TS: TerraS 62 (1986) 139-142.

2487 **Rad** G. von, Sabiduria en Israel [1970], ᵀ*Minguez* D. M 1985 [➤ 1,3324*] = 1973, Cristiandad. 408 p. – ᴿCiuD 199 (1986) 122 (J. L. del *Valle*).

2488 *a) Ravasi* Gianfranco, La famiglia nella letteratura sapienziale: ParSpV 14 (1986) 73-87. – *b) Rogers* Alan D., ' Human prudence and implied divine sanctions in Malagasy proverbial wisdom: JRelAf 15 (1985) 216-226 [< ZIT].

2488* **Sandelin** Karl-Gustav, Wisdom as a nourisher [NTAbs 31,380]; a study of an Old Testament theme; its development within early Judaism and its impact on early Christianity: AcÅbo hum 64/3. Åbo 1986, Akademi. 274 p. Fm 85. 951-649-323-8.

2489 **Schimanowski** G., Weisheit und Messias ... Präexistenzchristologie: WUNT 2/17, 1985 ➤ 1,3327: ᴿTGegw 29 (1986) 253s (H. *Giesen*).

2490 *Schneider* Theo M., From wisdom sayings to wisdom texts I: BTrans 37 (1986) 128-135.

2491 **Sheppard** G., Wisdom as a hermeneutical construct: BZAW 151, 1980 ➤ 61,4411 ... 65,2907: ᴿTsTKi 57 (1986) 232-4 (M. *Sæbø*).

2491* *a) Smith* Mark J., Weisheit, demotische [demotic wisdom literature, in English]; – *b) Guglielmi* Waltraud, Vergleich: ➤ 591, LexÄg 6,47s (1986) 1192-1204 / 986-9.

2492 **Shupak** Nili [➤ 1,3328], ⊕ *Munaḥim* ... Selected terms in the biblical wisdom literature in comparison with the Egyptian wisdom literature: diss. Hebrew Univ. J 1984. 460 p. – KirSef 60 (1985) 364.

2493 *Vanel* A. † 1978, Sagesse (Courant de): ➤ 595, SDB 11,60 (1986) 4-58.

2494 *Van Es* Rowland D., The Hebrew sage as a model for theological leadership in the Philippines [diss. Toa Fong Shan]: EAsJT 4,1 (1986) 195s.

2495 **Washington** Harold C., Wealth and poverty in the wisdom literature of the Old Testament; a sociological and canon-critical study: diss. in progress, Princeton [RelStR 12,324].

E7.6   **Proverbiorum liber**, *themata, versiculi.*

2496 **Aitken** Kenneth, Proverbs: Daily Study Bible. E 1986, St. Andrew. 264 p. £4.25. 0-7152-0533-1 [ExpTim 98,181].

2497 **Alden** Robert L., Proverbs 1983 ➤ 65,2914; 1,3334: ᴿCBQ 48 (1986) 297 (J. A. *Gladson*: conservative; Egyptian scribes used Proverbs); WestTJ 48 (1986) 183s (B. *Waltke*: some weaknesses).

2498 **Alonso Schökel** L., *Vilchez Lindez* J., Proverbios 1984 ➤ 65,2915; 1,3335: RCiuD 199 (1986) 121 (J. L. del *Valle*); JBL 105 (1986) 712 (C. T. *Begg*: pleasing turns of phrase); QVidCr 131s (1986) 227 (V. *Pagès*).

2499 **Boadt** Lawrence E., Introduction to Wisdom literature; Proverbs: Collegeville Comm OT 18. Collegeville 1986, Liturgical. 103 p. $3 pa. [TDig 33,464].

2500 **Delitzsch** Franz, Salomonisches Spruchbuch. Giessen 1985 = 1873, Brunnen. 556 p. DM 78 [ZAW 98,463].

2501 **Dietrich** Werner, Das Buch der Sprüche 1985 ➤ 1,3337: RStreven 53 (1985s) 276 (P. *Bentjes*).

2501* **Díez Merino** Luis, Targum de Proverbios [Villa-Amil] 1984 ➤ 65,2919; 1,1730: RStudium 26 (M 1986) 144s (L. *López de las Heras*).

2502 *Hurvitz* Avi, ❿ Studies in the language of the Book of Proverbs — concerning the use of the construct state *ba'al*-X: Tarbiz 55 (1985s) 1-17; Eng. I.

2503 *Lévêque* Jean, Proverbes: ➤ 582, DictSpir XII/2, 2459-2464.

2504 **Michaud** Robert, La literatura sapiencial; Proverbios y Job 1985 ➤ 1,3342: RBibFe 12 (1986) 368 (M. *Sáenz Galache*).

2505 **Plöger** Otto, Sprüche Salomos (Proverbia) BKAT 17, 1984 ➤ 1,3334: RCBQ [46 (1984) 322s] 48 (1986) 312-5 (L. G. *Perdue*); JBL 105 (1986) 526 (R. E. *Murphy*).

2506 **Rothenberg** Meir, ❿ Epigrams of the Book of Proverbs. TA 1984, Reshafim. – RBethM 31,104 (1985s) 94s (R. *Levi*).

2507 **Saebø** M., Fortolkning til Salomos Ordspråk, Forkynneren, Høysangen, Klagesangene [Prov Qoh Ct Lam]: Bibelverket. Oslo 1986, Luther/Lunde. 351 p. Nk 285. 82-531-6059-3 [BL 87, 76, G. W. *Anderson*].

2508 [**Zornberg** Avivah], EWengrov Charles, The commentary of r. Meir Leibush MALBIM on the Book of Proverbs, abridged. J 1982, Feldheim. 327 p. [KirSef 60,361].

2509 **Doll** P., Menschenschöpfung... Prov 1-9. 20-29: SBS 117, 1985 ➤ 1,2001: RBL (1986) 85 (R. N. *Whybray*).

2510 **Lang** Bernhard, Wisdom and the book of Proverbs [1,20-33; 8,1-35; 9,1-6.13], an Israelite goddess re-defined [Frau Weisheit 1975 ➤ 57,2914]. NY 1986, Pilgrim. 192 p. $11. 0-8298-0568-0. – RExpTim 98 (1986s) 25s (R. N. *Whybray*: persuasive but unconvincing).

2511 *Murphy* Roland E., *a*) Wisdom's song; Proverbs 1:20-33: ➤ 32, RFITZMYER J., CBQ 48 (1986) 456-467; – *b*) Proverbs and theological exegesis: ➤ 69, FMAYS J., Hermeneutical 1986, 87-95.

2512 *Cohen* Chaim (Harold), Two misunderstood verses in the Book of Proverbs (3:9; 6:30): ➤ 377a, IOSOT summaries (1986) 26.

2513 **Cottini** Valentino, [Prov 12,28...] La vita futura nel libro dei Proverbi [diss. 1982] 1984 ➤ 65,2930: RCBQ 48 (1986) 104s (M. *Kolarcik*); ÉglT 17 (1986) 87-90 (L. *Laberge*).

2514 *Friedlander* Yehuda, ❿ 'The words of a talebearer are as wounds' (Proverbs 18:8); on Megillat Yuḥasin attributed to Rabbi Mendel LANDSBERG of Kremnitz: HUCA 57 (1986) 21-38; facsim.

2515 *Isola* Antonino, [Prov 19,5, martyr/testis], L'esegesi biblica del Sermo 286 di AGOSTINO: VetChr 23 (1986) 267-281.

2516 **Nare** Laurent, Proverbes salomoniens et proverbes mossi; étude comparative à partir d'une nouvelle analyse de Pr 25-29: EurHS 23/283. Fra 1986, Lang. xiv-461 p. Fs 76. 3-8204-8968-1.

2517 *Van Leeuwen* Raymond C., *a*) Proverbs XXV 27 once again: VT 36 (1986) 105-114; – *b*) Proverbs 30,21-33 and the biblical world upside down: JBL 105 (1986) 599-610.

2518 *Olmo Lete* Gregorio del, Nota sobre Prov 30,19: Biblica 67 (1986) 68-74.

2518* *Levin* Yael, [Prov 31,1-31] 'The valiant woman' in Jewish cult: BethM 31,107 (1985s) 339-347.

E7.7   *Ecclesiastes* – **Qohelet,** *themata, versiculi.*

2519 *Amir* Yehoshua, Doch ein griechischer Einfluss auf das Buch Kohelet? [< BethM 10 (1965) 36-42]: ➤ 127, Studien 1985, 35-50.

2520 **Beek** M.A., Prediker, Hooglied: Prediking OT, 1984 ➤ 65,2935: ᴿKerkT 37 (1986) 68-70 (G. de *Ru*); RB 93 (1986) 301 (J. *Barink,* aussi sur Esther, Josué, Nombres, Zacharie).

2521 *Bottéro* Jean, L'Ecclésiaste et le problème du Mal [< NClio 7ss (1955ss) 139-149 = RechTMore 11 (1976)]: ➤ 136, Naissance de Dieu 1986, 221-251.

2522 *Caneday* Ardel B., Qoheleth; enigmatic pessimist or godly sage?: GraceTJ 7 (1986) 21-56.

2523 **Davidson** Robert, Ecclesiastes and Song of Solomon: Daily Study Bible. E 1986, St. Andrew. 162 p. £4.25 (price same as 264 p. Proverbs). 0-7152-0537-4. – ᴿExpTim 98 (1986s) 181s (D. *Coggan* chuckles assent).

2524 **Eaton** Michael A., Ecclesiastes: Tyndale Comm. 1983 ➤ 64,3305... 1,3367: ᴿEvQ 58 (1986) 259s (G. J. *Wenham*).

2525 *Gammie* John G., Stoicism and anti-Stoicism in Qoleleth: ➤ 36, Mem. GOITEIN S. = HebAnR 9 (1985) 169-187.

2526 *Hastoupis* Athanasios P., Ⓖ The book of Ecclesiastes: TAth 57 (1986) 300-328.

2526* **Johnson** Raymond E., The rhetorical question as a literary device in Ecclesiastes: diss. Southern Baptist Sem. 1986, ᴰ*Tate* M. 333 p. 87-02213. – DissA 47 (1986s) 3787s-A.

2527 **Kobayashi** Yoichi, The concept of limits in Qoheleth: diss. Southern Baptist Sem. 1986, ᴰ*Tate* M. 235 p. 86-28704. – DissA 47 (1986s) 3083-A.

2527* *Kottsieper* Ingo, Die Bedeutung der W[ur]z[eln] ʿ ṢB und SKN in Koh 10,9; ein Beitrag zum hebr[äischen] Lexikon: UF 18 (1986s) 213-222.

2528 **Japhet** S., *Salters* R.B., The commentary of R. Samuel ben Meir RASHBAM on Qoheleth. J/Leiden 1985, Magnes/Brill. 256 p.; 17 pl. $28. 965-223-517-2. – ᴿBL (1986) 53s (C. T. R. *Hayward*).

2529 **Kronholm** T., Den verksamme Guden; ett bidrag till Predikarens verklighetsuppfattning, speciellt hans teologi: Religio 4, 1982 ➤ 65,2938; 1,3371: ᴿBL (1986) 73s (B. *Albrektson*).

2530 *Leanza* Sandro, Sulle fonti del Commentario all'Ecclesiaste di GIROLAMO: ➤ 365, AnStoEseg 3 (1985/6) 173-199.

2531 **Loader** J.A., Ecclesiastes, a practical commentary, ᵀ*Vriend* J.: GR 1986, Eerdmans. vii-136 p. $7 [Exeter, Paternoster £6.20]. 0-8028-0102-1 [BL 87,52, R. B. *Salters*].

2532 *Loewenclau* Ilse von, Kohelet und Sokrates — Versuch eines Vergleiches: ZAW 98 (1986) 327-338.

2533 ᴱ**Lucà** Santo, Anonymus in Ecclesiasten: CCG 11, 1983 ➤ 64,3314; 65,2942: ᴿHeythJ 27 (1986) 89-91 (J. A. *Munitiz*); Koinonia 10 (N 1986) 99s (A. *Garzya*).

2533* *Saracino* Francesco, Qohelet, il vino e la morte: ParVi 31 (1986) 186-190.

2534 *Schröer* Henning, Unterrichtsideen zum Prediger Salomo: EvErz 38 (Fra 1986) 188 ... [< ZIT].
2535 *Navarro Peiró* Ángeles, Variantes del texto hebreo babilónico de Proverbios del Ms. Ec 1 respecto al texto tiberiense: 21, Mem. DÍEZ MACHO A., Salvación 1986, 215-221.

2536 *Fox* Michael V., [Qoh 1,2] The meaning of *hebel* for Qohelet: JBL 105 (1986) 409-427 [absurd].
2537 *Ogden* Graham S., The interpretation of *dôr* in Ecclesiastes 1,4 [cyclic movement of nature]: JStOT 34 (1986) 91s.
2538 *Müller* Hans.Peter, Theonome Skepsis und Lebensfreude — Zu Koh 1,1-3,15: BZ 30 (1986) 1-19.
2539 *Labate* Antonio, [Eces 2,10.24] Sui due frammenti di IPPOLITO all'Ecclesiaste: VetChr 23 (1986) 177-181.
2539* *Youngblood* Ronald F., Qoheleth's 'dark house' (Eccl 12:5): JEvTS 29 (1986) 397-410 [< ZIT].

E7.8   *Liber Sapientiae*: **Wisdom of Solomon.**

2540 *Amir* Yehoshua, Die Gestalt des Thanatos in der 'Weisheit Salomos' < JJS 30 (1979) 154-178]: ➤ 127, Studies 1985, 51-82.
2541 **Bizzeti** Paolo, Il libro della Sapienza; struttura e genere leterario: RivB Sup 11,1984 ➤ 65,2954: RCBQ 48 (1986) 525-7 (D. *Winston*); CC 137 (1986,1) 610s (G. L. *Prato*); JBL 105 (1986) 718s (J. M. *Reese*); Salesianum 48 (1986) 162s (M. *Cimosa*); StPatav 33 (1986) 692s (G. *Leonardi*).
2542 *Drijvers* H. J. W., The Peshitta of Sapientia Salomonis: 47, FHOSPERS J., Scripta 1986, 15-30.
2543 *Gilbert* M., Sagesse de Salomon: ➤ 595, SDB 11,60 (1986) 58-119 [153-6, Esprit Saint dans ...].
2544 (*Ziegler* Joseph) **Hübner** Hans, Wörterbuch der [Gö] Sapientia Salomonis 1985 ➤ 1,3384: RBL (1986) 124 (J. G. *Snaith*).
2544* *Hübner* Hans, Zur Ethik der Sapientia Salomonis: ➤ 39, FGREEVEN H., Text/Ethik 1986, 166-187.
2545 **Larcher** C., Le livre de la Sagesse ou la Sagesse de Salomon: ÉtBN 1, 1983 ➤ 64,3332... 1,3385: RCBQ 48 (1986) 119s (J. M. *Reese*, 1), 721-3 (*Reese*, 2: Larcher regards words as static entities with meanings fixed, often by etymology); JBL 105 (1986) 719s (R. E. *Murphy*, 2).
2546 **Rybolt** John E., Wisdom / Sirach: OT 20s. Collegeville MN 1986, Liturgical. 63 p.; 112. $3 each [TDig 33,464].
2547 **Schmitt** Armin, Das Buch der Weisheit; ein Kommentar. Wü 1986, Echter. 140 p. DM 24 [TR 83,337].
2548 EThiele Walter, Sapientia Salomonis: VLat 11/1, 1977-85 ➤ 64,3337... 1,3387: RRÉLat 63 (1985) 290s (J. *Fontaine*); RHE 81 (1986) 133-5 (J. *Gribomont* †).
2548* *Vilchez* J., El libro de la Sabiduría y la teoría sobre la transmutación de los elementos: ➤ 105, FSegovia A., 1986 ...
2549 *Webster* Edwin C., Structural unity in the Book of Wisdom [*Reese* J., *Wright* A.] EAsJT 4,1 (1986) 98-112.

2550 *Sisti* Adalberto, L'ateismo degli empi di Sap. 2: BbbOr 28 (1986) 41-54.

2551 *Schmitt* Armin, Der frühe Tod des Gerechten nach Weish 4,7-19; ein Psalmthema in Weisheitlicher Fassung: 41, [F]GROSS H., Freude 1986, 325-349.
2552 *Rooden* Peter T. van, Die antike Elementarlehre und der Aufbau von Sapientia Salomonis 11-19: → 59, [F]LEBRAM J., Tradition 1986, 81-96.
2553 *Busto Saiz* José R., [Sab 11,2 - 19,22] La intención del midras del libro de la Sabiduria sobre el Éxodo: → 21, Mem. DÍEZ MACHO A., Salvación 1986, 65-78.
2554 *Poniży* Bogdan, The cognition of God according to the Book of Wisdom (13: 1-9): → 377a, IOSOT summaries (1986) 105.

E7.9   *Ecclesiasticus, Siracides;* **Wisdom of Jesus Sirach.**

2555 *Beentjes* Pancratius C., Some misplaced words in the Hebrew manuscript C of Ben Sira: Biblica 67 (1986) 397-401.
2556 *Boccaccini* Gabriele, Origine del male, libertà dell'uomo e retribuzione nella Sapienza di Ben Sira: Henoch 8 (1986) 1-35; franç. 35-37.
2557 **Boccaccio** Pietro, *Berardi* Guido, Ecclesiasticus; textus hebraeus secundum fragmenta reperta. R 1986, Pont. Ist. Biblico. 38 p., facsimiles.
2558 *Carmignac* Jean, L'infinitif absolu chez Ben Sira et à Qumrân: RQum 12,46 (1986) 251-260; deutsch, Eng. 261.
2559 *Gilbert* Maurice, JÉRÔME et Ben Sira [changé de vue sur sa canonicité?]: → 377a, IOSOT summaries (1986) 45.
2560 *Martin* James D., Ben Sira — a child of his time: → 93, [F]MCKANE M., A word 1986, 141-161.
   Rybolt comm. 1986 → 2546.
2561 **Sanders** J.T., Ben Sira and demotic wisdom: SBL Mon 28, 1983 → 64,3347 ... 1,3395: [R]Enchoria 14 (1986) 199-201 (H.-J. *Thissen*); JBL 105 (1986) 145-7 (J. *Gladson,* also on LICHTHEIM M.); JSS 31 (1986) 83s (K. A. *Kitchen*).
2562 **Schnabel** Eckhard J., Law and wisdom from Ben Sira to Paul; a tradition-historical enquiry into the relation of law, wisdom, and ethics [diss. Aberdeen 1983]: WUNT 2/16, 1985 → 1,3396: [R]ExpTim 98 (1986s) 54 (R. *Bauckham*); NorTTs 87 (1986) 189s (R. *Leivestad*); NRT 108 (1986) 748s (X. *Jacques*).
2563 **Trenchard** Warren C., Ben-Sira's view of women 1982 → 63,3415 ... 1,3397: [R]JAOS 106 (1986) 578s (Sarah J. *Tanzer*: fine).

2564 *Bronznick* Norman M., [Sir 14,2; 30,39; 35,12] An unrecognized denotation of the verb *ḥsr* in Ben-Sira and rabbinic Hebrew [Pi. 'to shame']: → 36, Mem. GOITEN S. = HebAnR 9 (1985) 91-105.
2565 **Lee** Thomas R., Studies in the form of Sirach 44-50: SBL diss. 75 [Berkeley Grad. Theological Union 1979 → 60,4598]. Atlanta 1986, Scholars. 275 p. $18; pa. $14. 0-89130-834-2; 5-0. – [R]ExpTim 98 (1986) 119 (C. S. *Rodd*).
2566 **Mack** Burton L., Wisdom and the Hebrew epic; Ben Sira's hymn in praise of the Fathers 1985 → 1,3403: [R]JIStJud 17 (1986) 259-261 (P. C. *Beentjes*).
2567 *Martin* J. D., Ben Sira's hymn to the fathers; a messianic perspective: → 399, OTS 24, 1985/6, 107-123.
2568 **Reiterer** Friedrich V., 'Urtext' und Übersetzungen; Sprachstudie über Sir 44,16-45,26: AOtt 12, 1980 → 61,4512 ... 1,3404: [R]JNES 45 (1986) 331s (D. *Pardee*: spells partly Sira, partly Sirah without point).

2569 *Kieweler* H. V., [Sir 44,19-21] Abraham und der Preis der Väter bei Ben
Sira: ➤ 99, ᶠSAUER G., Amt und Gemeinde 37 (1986) 70-72.
2570 *Peterca* Vladimir, Das Porträt Salomos bei Ben Sirach (45,12-22) (Ein
Beitrag zu der Midraschexegese): ➤ 372*a*, IOSOT summaries (1986) 102.
2571 *Di Lella* Alexander A., Sirach 51:1-12; poetic structure and analysis of
Ben Sira's psalm: ➤ 32, ᶠFITZMYER J., 48 (1986) 395-407.

VIII. Libri prophetici VT

E8.1.   **Prophetismus.**

2572 **Alonso Schökel** Luis, *Sicre Díaz* José Luis, Profetas 1983 / I Profeti 1984
➤ 61,4515... 1,3406:   ᴿBiblica 67 (1986) 431-5 (E. S. *Gerstenberger*); CC
137 (1986,4) 511 (G. J. *Prato*: malgrado la ricchezza, alcuni spropositi).
2573 **Amsler** S., Les actes des prophètes 1985 ➤ 1,3407:   ᴿProtestantesimo 41
(1986) 110s (M. *Grube*); RTPhil 118 (1986) 325s (H. *Mottu*); Salesianum 48
(1986) 412s (M. *Cimosa*).
2574 **Asurmendi** Jesús, Le prophétisme; des origines à l'époque moderne 1985
➤ 1,3409; 2-85313-102-5:   ᴿÉTRel 61 (1986) 121s (J. *Pons*: 'le plus vieux
métier du monde n'est pas celui que vous pensiez').
2575 [ᴱ*Auneau* J.] **Amsler** S., *al.*, Les prophètes et les livres prophétiques 1985
➤ 1,264:   ᴿEstE 61 (1986) 487s (J. M. *Ábrego*); RThom 86 (1986) 667s
(M.-V. *Leroy*: Auneau, catholique, a été le maître d'œuvre de cette colla-
boration œcuménique).
2575* **Bacchiocchi** Samuel, Hal LINDSEY's prophetic jigsaw puzzle; five predictions that failed. Berrien Springs MI 1985, Biblical Perspectives. 90 p.
$3. − ᴿGraceTJ 7 (1986) 252s (C. L. *Turner*: dispensationalism challenged).
2576 **Barack** Nathan A., God speaks naturally; an organic perspective on the
Prophets; pref. *Wagner* Stanley M.: Denver Center for Judaic Studies.
Middle Village NY 1983, J. David. xv-247 p. [KirSef 60,366].
2577 **Barton** John, Oracles of God; perception of ancient prophecy in Israel
after the Exile. L 1986, Darton-LT. 324 p.; bibliog. p. 302-310. £13.
0-232-51666-9. − ᴿExpTim 98 (1986s) 66-68 (C. S. *Rodd*: exhilarating).
2578 *Bentjes* Panc, Profeten binden heden en toekomst op het hart: OnsGLev
63 (1986) 118-123.
2579 **Blenkinsopp** Joseph, A history of prophecy in Israel 1983 ➤ 64,3364...
1,3411:   ᴿJStOT 34 (1986) 119s (R. *Carroll*); ScripTPamp 18 (1986) 966s
(G. *Aranda*).
2580 *a) Borchert* R., Zur sozialen Botschaft der Propheten des 8. Jahrhunderts: ➤ 121, ᶠWIBBING S. 1986, 2-21; − *b) Bresciani* Edda, Oracles
d'Égypte et prophéties bibliques: MondeB 45 (1986) 44s.
2581 *Bovati* Pietro, Alla ricerca del profeta, I. Una presenza singolare nel
cammino del popolo di Dio; II. Criteri per discernere i veri profeti: RClerIt
67 (1986) 110-118. 179-188.
2581* **Bresinger** Terry L., Lions, wind, and fire; a study of prophetic similes:
diss. Drew. Madison NJ 1985. − RelStR 13,189.
2582 **Brueggemann** Walter, La imaginación profética [1978 ➤ 60,4639]: Presencia Teológica 28. Santander 1986, Sal Terrae. 138 p. 84-293-0749-4
[ActuBbg 24,75, R. de *Sivatte*]. − ᴿSalT 74 (1986) 331s (J. A. *García*).
2582* **Buber** M., La fede dei Profeti 1985 ➤ 1,3614*b*:   ᴿParVi 31 (1986) 381-3
(B. *Marconcini*).

2583 *Bullock* C. Hassel, An introduction to the Old Testament prophetic books. Ch 1986, Moody. 291 p. $20 [TR 83,162]. 0-8024-4142-4.

2584 *Chalender* Pierrette & Gérard, Le discours prophétique: approche linguistique et textuelle: FoiVie 85,1 (1986) 23-31.

2584* *Clements* Ronald S., Prophecy as literature; a re-appraisal: ➤ 69, ᶠMAYS J. 1986, 59-76.

2585 **Correa** Germán, Profetas y salmistas 1981 ➤ 62,3533 ... 64,3371: ᴿPhase 26 (1986) 366s (J. *Roca*).

2586 **Crenshaw** James L., Los falsos profetas [1971 ➤ 53,2111], ᵀ*Ábrego* José M. Bilbao 1986, Desclée-B. 183 p. – ᴿEstAg 21 (1986) 641s (C. *Mielgo*); NatGrac 33 (1986) 333 (D. *Montero*).

2587 ᶠ**Fohrer** Georg, Prophecy: BZAW 150, 1980 ➤ 61,71; 63,78: ᴿBZ 30 (1986) 108-110 (J. *Schreiner*).

2588 **Graffy** Adrian, A prophet confronts his people; the disputation speech in the prophets: AnBib 104, 1984 ➤ 65,3006; 1,3420: ᴿBL (1986) 71s (R. B. *Salters*); JBL 105 (1986) 714s (T. M. *Raitt*: more interested in packaging than religious meaning).

2589 **Green** J. B., How to read prophecy. Leicester 1986, Inter-Varsity. 154 p. £4.50. 0-85110-760-5 [BL 87,64, G. I. *Emmerson*: sound and practical].

2590 **Hagemann** Ludwig, Propheten — Zeugen des Glaubens; koranische und biblische Deutungen: Islam und westliche Welt 7, 1985 ➤ 1,3421: ᴿDer Islam 63 (1986) 337s (H. *Schützinger*); Salesianum 48 (1986) 419 (M. *Cimosa*: brillante); ZkT 108 (1986) 86 (W. *Kern*).

2590* *Hardmeier* Chr., Die judäische Unheilsprophetie; Antwort auf einen Gesellschafts- und Normenwandel im Israel des 8. Jahrhunderts vor Christus: Der altsprachliche Unterricht 26 (1983) 20-44 [< JbBT 1,234].

2591 *Harris* E. Laird, Prophecy, illustration and typology: ➤ 65, ᶠMACRAE Allan, Interpretation 1986, 57-66.

2592 **Herbrechtsmeier** William E., False prophecy and canonical thinking: diss. in progress, Columbia Univ. [RelStR 12,324].

2593 **Herrmann** Siegfried, Prophetie und Wirklichkeit in der Epoche des babylonischen Exils [< ᴱSCHLATTER T., Arb. Theol. 1.32 (1967)]: ➤ 171, GesSt 1986, 179-209.

2594 *Israeli* Shlomit, The true prophet of the Old Testament, the good scribe of Anastasi I, and their similar attitude towards morality: ➤ 349, ᴱ*Groll* S., Papers 2 (1985) 97-133.

2594* **Jaramillo Rivas** Pedro, La injusticia y la opresión en el lenguaje figurado de los profetas: diss. Pont. Univ. Gregoriana, ᴰ*Conroy* C. R 1986. xxxv-528 p. – RTLv 18,542.

2595 **Koch** Klaus, The Prophets, 2. Babylonian and Persian periods 1984 ➤ 64,3387; 65,3014: ᴿComSev 19 (1986) 84s (M. de *Burgos*); JBL 105 (1986) 528s (G. W. *Ramsey*).

2596 **Kraus** Hans-Joachim, Prophetie heute! Die Aktualität biblischer Prophetie in der Verkündigung der Kirche. Neuk 1986, Neuk-V. 94 p. 3-7887-1246-5.

2597 *Kühn* Rolf, L'attitude des prophètes vis-à-vis du culte: Teresianum 37 (1986) 263-286.

2598 *Lang* Bernhard, Vom Propheten zum Schriftgelehrten; charismatische Autorität im Frühjudentum: ➤ 341*, Theologen 1986, 89-114.

2598* **La Rondelle** Hans K., The Israel of God in prophecy; principles of prophetic interpretation 1983 ➤ 64,3392: ᴿGraceTJ 7 (1986) 126-8 (D. L. *Turner*: scores several direct hits against some dispensationalists).

2599 *Légasse* Simon, Prophétisme, Écriture sainte: → 582, DictSpir XII/2 (1986) 2410-2434 [-2446, dans l'Église, *Vallin* Pierre].

2600 *Luke* K., Prophecy in Israel and Arabia: LivWord 92 (1986) 83-109 [TKontext 8/1,35].

2600* *a*) *McCaughey* J. Davis, Imagination in the understanding of the prophets; – *b*) *MacKinnon* D. M., The evangelical imagination; – *c*) *Watson* Gerard, Imagination and religion in classical thought: → 62*, ᶠMcINTYRE J., Religious imagination 1986, 161-174 / 175-185 / 29-54.

2601 *a*) *Malchow* Bruce V., The prophetic contribution to dialogue: BibTB 16 (1986) 127-131; – *b*) *Michot* J., Prophétie et divination selon AVICENNE: Revue Philosophique de Louvain 83 (1985) 507-535 [RSPT 70 (1986) 309].

2601* *Neher* André, L'essenza del profetismo [³1983; español < français 1975 → 57,3048], ᵀ*Piattelli* Elio. Casale Monferrato 1984, Marietti. 290 p. Lit. 28.000. – ᴿParVi 30 (1985) 395-7 (G. *Boggio*).

2602 *Niditch* Susan, The symbolic vision in biblical tradition [diss. ᴰCross F.] 1983 → 64,3403 ... 1,3437: ᴿBZ 30 (1986) 124s (B. *Lang*); JBL 105 (1986) 123s (R. R. *Clifford*).

2603 *Overholt* Thomas W., Prophecy in cross-cultural perspective; a sourcebook for biblical researchers [texts from various cultures]: SBL Sour 17. Atlanta 1986, Scholars. vi-386 p. $27 [TDig 34,89]. 0-89130-900-4; pa. 1-2.

2603* *Pleins* J. David, Biblical ethics and the poor; the language and structures of poverty in the writings of the Hebrew prophets: diss. Michigan, ᴰ*Mendenhall* G. AA 1986. 349 p. 86-21355. – DissA 47 (1986s) 2201s - A.

2604 *Prince* Derek, Biblische Prophetie und der Nahe Osten (Israel — Gottes Zeiger an der Weltenuhr) [The last word on the Middle East], ᵀ*Neumann* K. H. Erzhausen 1982, Leuchter. [KirSef 59,2497, Eng. 261].

2605 *Ribera* Josep, El profetismo según el Targum Jonatán y el Targum Palestinense: → 21, Mem. DÍEZ MACHO A., Salvación 1986, 489-501.

2606 *Rofé* A., ❶ The prophetical stories 1982 → 63,3496 ... 65,3029: ᴿHenoch 8 (1986) 92s (A. *Catastini*).

2606* *Ruiz* Gregorio († 29.VIII.1986), Los profetas, modelo de actitud en la iglesia hoy; SalT 74 (1986) 643-654.

2607 *Savoca* Gaetano, I profeti d'Israele, voce del Dio vivente: La Bibbia nella storia 3, 1985 → 1,3444; 220 p.; Lit. 15.000: ᴿActuBbg 23 (1986) 220 (R. de *Sivatte*); HumBr 41 (1986) 617 (M. *Orsatti*); ParVi 31 (1986) 235s (B. *Marconcini*); StPatav 33 (1986) 689-691 (M. *Milani*).

2608 *Schenker* Adrian, Gerichtsverkündigung und Verblendung bei den vorexilischen Propheten: RB 93 (1986) 563-580.

2608* *Schmidt* Georg †, Das Prophetenbild des H. G. A. EWALD [Diss.] Marburg, Univ. DM 20. – ZAW 98 (1986) 483.

2609 *Sicre* J. L., 'Con los pobres de la tierra'; la justicia social en los profetas de Israel 1984 → 65,3034; 1,3447: ᴿAngelicum 63 (1986) 131-4 (J. *García Trapiello*, detallado e muy favorable); BL (1986) 95s (J. R. *Porter*: unusual; wide and sound scholarship); CiTom 113 (1986) 593 (J. L. *Espinal*); CiuD 199 (1986) 330 (J. L. del *Valle*); Igreja e Missão 131 (1986) 91s (S. O.: inquietante); QVidCr 131s (1986) 227 (V. *Pagès*).

2610 *Sicre* José L., Los profetas de Israel y su mensaje; antología de textos. M 1986, Cristiandad. 253 p. – ᴿCiTom 113 (1986) 629 (J. A. *Marcén*); SalT 74 (1986) 335s (J. A. *García*).

2611 *Sobosan* Jeffrey G., Christian commitment and [Hebrew Bible] prophetic living. Mystic CT 1986, Twenty-Third. xv-122 p. $6 [RelStR 13,231, D. M. *Hammond*].

2611* **Streefland** J., Profetie in Israël I-II [➤ 64,3418; 65,3037] III. de Ge-
schriften uit Tenach. Nijkerk 1983, Callenbach. [224 p., ƒ37,50] 272 p.,
ƒ39,50; 184 p., ƒ37,50. – ᴿGerefTTs 86 (1986) 42 (C. *Houtman*).

2612 **Sublon** Roland, Menteur et prophète, préf. *Israël* Lucien: Connivence. P
1984, Desclée-B. 298 p. F 79. – ᴿAngelicum 63 (1986) 131 (P. *Zerafa*:
'discorso ponderato, spesso allegorico e delle volte allegorico' ! ...
come l'uomo moderno, le grandi figure bibliche non riescono ad afferrare la
verità, o non la riconoscono una volta afferrata).

2613 **Virgulin** S., Profeti e sapienti 1985 ➤ 1,3456: ᴿBL (1986) 97 (J. R.
Porter).

2613* *Vogels* Walter, The biblical prophets as diviners and magicians:
Kerygma 20,46 (1986) 3-28.

2614 **Weippert** Helga, *al.*, Beiträge zur prophetischen Bildersprache in Israel
und Assyrien: OBO 64, 1985 ➤ 1,3458: ᴿBO 43 (1986) 654-6 (P. *Höffken*);
ETL 62 (1986) 170 (J. *Lust*); NedTTs 40 (1986) 335s (K. A. D. *Smelik*:
< FrS symposium 1984); TR 82 (1986) 23 (B. *Lang*).

2615 *Westermann* D. C., Zur Erforschung und zum Verständnis der Prophetischen Heilsworte [i. nicht Gerichtsworte; ii. Gliederung, Sammlungen;... Entwicklung; iii. eschatologisch; iv. exil./nachex.]: ZAW 98
(1986) 1-13.

2616 **Wolff** Hans-W., Confrontations with the Prophets 1983 ➤ 64,240b...
1,3460: ᴿBibTB 16 (1986) 43 (E. A. *Wcela*).

2617 *Wolff* Hans W., a) Prophets and institutions in the Old Testament [<
ᴱRendtorff T., Charisma und Institution 87-101 without documentation],
ᵀTrapp Thomas: CurrTM 13 (1986) 5-12. – b) 'So sprach Jahwe zu mir, als
die Hand mich packte'; was haben die Propheten erfahren [< Zeitwende
55 (Karlsruhe 1984) 65-75]: TGegw 23 (1985) 77-86.

2618 a) *Wood* Fred M., Thus saith the Lord; the prophet's call to attention; –
b) *Travis* James, Of dreams and visions: BibIll 12 (1986) 22s / 72-76
[OTAbs 10,85].

E8.2 **Proto-Isaias**, *textus, commentarii.*

ᴱ**Dočʻanašvili** E., [Ecclesiastes...] Isaiah [p. 71-153]; Jeremiah [p. 154-254
(-282)]; Ezekiel [p. 283-372]: Mcʻḫetʻa Manuscript (in Georgian) 1985
➤ 1261.

2619 ᴱ**Dumortier** Jean, Jean CHRYSOSTOME, Commentaire sur Isaïe: SChr
304, 1983 ➤ 64,3436; 65,3053: ᴿBijdragen 47 (1986) 217s (J. *Declerck*);
RBgPg 64 (1986) 122s (J. *Schamp*).

2620 ᴱ**Goshen-Gottstein** Moshe H., ⊕ The book of Isaiah [I 1975 ➤ 57,850] II.
Chapters 22-44, 1984 ➤ 65,3055: J, Magnes; p. 81-204; $40. – ᴿCBQ 48
(1968) 532s (R. J. *Owens*).

2620* **Grogan** Geoffrey W., Isaiah: ➤ 1354, Expositor's Bible Commentary 6
(1986) ...

2621 *Gryson* Roger, Les anciennes versions latines du livre d'Isaïe; signification et voies d'une recherche: RTLv 17 (1986) 22-37; Eng. 127.

2622 ᴱ**Guinot** Jean-Noël, THÉODORET de Cyr, Commentaire sur Isaie II: SChr
295 [315] 1982 ➤ 63,3525... 1,3466: ᴿBijdragen 47 (1986) 214s (J.
Declerck); JTS 37 (1986) 598-600 (P. M. *Parvis*); RHR 203 (1986) 441s (P.
Nautin); RTAM 53 (1986) 198 (G. *Michiels*); TLZ 111 (1986) 214 (F.
Winkelmann: konstruktiv kritisch).

2623 ᴱ**Hofman** Y., *al.*, ⊕ Yᵉšaʻyâh: Enṣiqlopediya ʻOlam ha-TNK. Ramat Gan
1986, Revivim. 280 p. [ZAW 99,288, J. *Maier*].

2624 **Jay** Pierre, L'exégèse de saint JÉRÔME d'après son 'Commentaire sur Isaïe' 1985 → 1,3467: ᴿChH 55 (1986) 359s (R. B. *Eno*); ColcT 56,3 (1986) 194-6 (W. *Myszor*); FreibZ 33 (1986) 269-278 (D. *Barthélemy*); RSPT 70 (1986) 611-3 (G.-M. de *Durand*).

2625 **Jensen** Joseph, Isaiah 1-39: OTMessage 8, 1984 → 65,3058; 1,3468: ᴿInterpretation 40 (1986) 198.200 (M. A. *Throntveit*).

2626 **Kilian** Rudolf, Jesaja 1-39: ErFor 200, 1983 → 64,3441; 1,3470: ᴿCBQ 48 (1986) 719-721 (J. M. *Berridge*).

2627 **Kilian** Rudolf, Jesaia 1-12: NEchter 17. Wü 1986, Echter. 96 p. DM 24.

2627* ᵀ**Millet** J., *al.*, Isaïe expliqué par les Pères: Les Pères dans la Foi. P 1983, Desclée-B. 144 p. – ᴿBLitEc 87 (1986) 154-6 (H. *Crouzel*).

2628 **Oswalt** J. N., The Book of Isaiah, chapters 1-39: NICOT. GR/Exeter 1986, Eerdmans/Paternoster. xiii-746 p. £26.60 [ZAW 99,296, O. *Kaiser*].

2629 **Partain** Jack [ch. 1-12], *Deutsch* Richard, A guide to Isaiah 1-39: TEF Study Guide 21. L 1986, SPCK. x-262 p. £6. 0-281-04182-2. – ᴿBL (1986) 56 (R. E. *Clements*, aimed at Asia-Africa); ExpTim 97 (1985s) 383 [C. S. *Rodd*: updating of series originally intended for users of English as second language, but useful also for all].

2630 ᴱ**Pérez Castro** F., El códice de profetas de El Cairo, IV. Isaías, edición de su texto y masoras: TEstCisn 36. M 1986, Cons. Sup. Inv. Ci. 227 p. pt. 2800. 84-00-06174-8.

2630* **Porath** Renatus, Die Sozialkritik im Jesajabuch; redaktionsgeschichtliche Analyse: ev. Diss. Mü 1986s, ᴰ*Jeremias* J. – RTLv 18,543.

2631 **Ridderbos** Jan, Isaiah [Korte Verklarung 1950], ᵀ*Vriend* John: Bible Student's Commentary 1985 → 1,3473: ᴿOTAbs 9 (1986) 335s (J. I. *Hunt*).

2632 **Watts** John D. W., Isaiah 1-33: Word Comm. 24. Waco 1985, Word. lvii-449 p. $25. 0-8499-0223-1. – ᴿETL 62 (1986) 419s (J. *Lust*: no source-criticism; unity of Isaiah assumed; a challenge); ExpTim 98 (1986s) 52 (C. S. *Rodd*: a new line, 'vision genre'); GraceTJ 7 (1986) 246s (G. L. *Klein*); SWJT 29,2 (1986s) 52 (D. G. *Kent*).

2633 *Weinberg* Zvi, ❹ Notes of Jakob BARTH to the consolation passages of Isaiah, to Song of Songs and to Qohelet: BethM 31,104 (1985s) 78-87.

E8.3   [Proto-]Isaias 1-39, *themata, versiculi.*

2634 *Cañellas* Gabriel, La 'ḥokmāh' en el profeta Isaias: → 21, Mem. DíEZ MACHO A., Salvación 1986, 79-88.

2635 *Cazelles* Henri, D'Ex 22,4 à Is 6,13 par les Targums: 21, Mem. DíEZ MACHO A., Salvación 1986, 329-336.

2636 *Dumbrell* William J., The purpose of the book of Isaiah: TyndB 36 (1985) 111-128.

2636* **Guigui** A., Isaïe à la lumière du Targoum de Yonatan BEN OUZIEL: 365, *Bogaert* P.-M., Lectures 1984, 55-68.

2637 *Hardmeier* Christof, Jesajaforschung im Umbruch: VerkF 31,1 (1986) 3-31.

2637* **Hollerich** Michael J., The godly polity in the light of prophecy; a study of EUSEBIUS of Caesarea's commentary on Isaiah: diss. Chicago Divinity School 1986. – RelStR 13,189.

2638 *Jensen* Joseph, Yahweh's plan in Isaiah and in the rest of the Old Testament: → 32, ᶠFITZMYER J., CBQ 48 (1986) 443-455.

2638* **Johnston** Ann, The concept of waiting in the Isaianic corpus; a rhetorical critical study of selected texts: diss. Boston Univ. 1986, ᴰ*Richardson* H. N. 311 p. 86-16997. – DissA 47 (1986s) 1776-A; RelStR 13,190.

2639 *Kooij* Arie van der, Accident or method? On 'analogical' interpretation in the Old Greek of Isaiah and in 1QIsᵃ: BO 43 (1986) 366-376.

2640 **Nielsen** Kirsten, For et træ er der håb [Job 14,7, 'there is hope for a tree (, if cut down, it will sprout again)']; om træet som metafor i Jes 1-39: Bibel og historie 8, 1985 ➤ 1,3478: ᴿBL (1986) 77 (K. *Jeppesen*); NorTTs 87 (1986) 43s (A. S. *Kapelrud*).

2641 *Nielsen* Kirsten, Reinterpretation of metaphors; tree metaphors in Isaiah 1-39 [three (trees) 5,1-7; 27,2-6; 1,29-31]: ➤ 377*a*, IOSOT summaries (1986) 97.

2642 *Ljung* Inger, [Is 1-39; *Nielsen* K. diss. Århus 1985]: DanskTTs 49 (1986) 81-95 [OTAbs 9,239].

2643 *Otzen* B., [Is 1-39] Profetbog og billedsprog [*Nielsen* K. diss. 1985]: Religionsvidenskabeligt Tidsskrift 8 (1986) 43-54 [< ZAW].

2644 **Schmitt** John J., Isaiah and his interpreters. NY 1985, Paulist. vi-137 p. $9. 0-8091-2826-8. – Themes of doom, conversion, covenant, promise, purification associated with Isaiah have a solid foundation in the book; Isaiah is a fellow-believer who guides us in our religious striving. P. 94 finds in von RAD a basis for rejecting current views of the originality of prophetic religion; and p. 119 holds that the complete book of Isaiah 1-66 'is where one finds the words of Isaiah'. – ᴿExpTim 98 (1986s) 346s (R. *Carroll*: lively, pious).

2644* *Stein* J. W., Isaiah and statesmanship: Journal of Church and State 27 (1985) 83-97.

2645 *Watts* John D. W., The characterization of Yahweh in the vision of Isaiah [i.e. the whole book, as Is 1,1]: RExp 83 (1986) 439-450.

2645* *Wodecki* Bernard, Synonymic designation of Jerusalem in Is. I-XXXIX: ➤ 377*a*, IOSOT summaries (1986) 145.

2646 **Loretz** O., Der Prolog des Jesaja-Buches (1,1-2,5): UgBLit 1, 1984 ➤ 65,3086; 1,3482: ᴿBO 43 (1986) 185s (R. J. *Coggins*).

2647 *Doron* Pinchas, Methodology of Targum Jonathan; analysis of non-literal renderings in Isaiah 1: ➤ 21, Mem. DíEZ MACHO A., Salvación 1986, 369-374.

2648 *Hasel* Gerhard F., 'New moon and sabbath' in eighth century Israelite prophetic writings (Isa 1:13; Hos 2:13; Am 8:5): ➤ 377*a*, IOSOT summaries (1986) 55.

2649 *Kutsch* Ernst, 'Wir wollen miteinander rechnen'; zu Form und Aussage von Jes 1,18-20 [ᶠSCHREINER J. 1982, 23-33]; ➤ 183, KlS 1986, 146-156.

2650 *Willis* John T., Lament reversed — Isaiah 1,21ff: ZAW 98 (1986) 236-248.

2651 **Wiklander** Bertil, Prophecy as literature; a text-linguistic and rhetorical approach to Isaiah 2-4: ConBib OT 22, 1984 ➤ 65,3058; 1,3487: ᴿAndr-UnS 24 (1986) 77s (N.-E. *Andreasen*); ÉTRel 61 (1986) 585 (J. *Pons*); VT 36 (1986) 123 (J. A. *Emerton*); JBL 105 (1986) 527s (G. T. *Sheppard*).

2652 *Lohfink* Gerhard, 'Schwerter zu Pflugscharen ! '; die Rezeption von Jes 2,1-5 par Mi 4,1-5 in der Alten Kirche und im Neuen Testament: TüTQ 166 (1986) 184-209.

2653 *Folmer* Margaretha L., A literary analysis of the 'Song of the Vineyard' (Is. 5:1-7): JbEOL 29 (1985s) 106-123.

2654 *Luria* B. Z., ◍ What is the vineyard in Isaiah's proverb ? BethM 31,107 (1985s) 289-292.

2655 a) *Niehr* Herbert, Zur Gattung von Jes 5,1-7; – b) *Evans* Craig A., On Isaiah's use of Israel's sacred tradition: BZ 30 (1986) 99-104 / 92-99.

2656 *Reventlow* Henning, [Is 6,1-9,6; *Budde* K. 1928] Die sog. 'Denkschrift' — eine überholte Hypothese: ➤ 377a, IOSOT summaries (1986) 110.

2656* *Chilton* Bruce, The Temple in the Targum of Isaiah [rarely *heykal* as 6,1; 24 times *bêt miqdašâ'* 'sanctuary house']: ➤ 140*, Targumic 1986, 51-61.

2657 *Nielsen* Kirsten, Is 6:1 - 8:18 as dramatic writing: ST 40 (1986) 1-16.

2657* ᴱ**Dumortier** Jean, Jean CHRYSOSTOME, Homélies sur Ozias: SChr 277, 1981 ➤ 62,3640... 65,3096: ᴿRTAM 53 (1986) 196s (G. *Michiels*, aussi sur le Comm. Is. SChr 304).

2658 *Klijn* A. F. J., JÉRÔME, Isaïe 6 et l'Évangile des Nazaréens: VigChr 40 (1986) 245-250.

2658* *Evans* Craig A., Isa 6:9-13 in the context of Isaiah's theology: JEvTS 29 (1986) 139-140 [ZIT].

2659 *Ambros* Arne A., [Is 6,9 ...] 'Höre, ohne zu hören' zu Koran 4,46 (48): ZDMG 136 (1986) 15-22.

2660 *Weiss* Meir, [Is 7,3] The contribution of literary theory to biblical research illustrated by the problem of She'ar-Yashub: ➤ 251*, ScrHieros 31 (1986) 373-386.

2661 *Laato* Antti, [Is 7,14; 9,5] Immanuel; who is God with us? Hezekiah or Messiah ! ➤ 377a, IOSOT summaries (1986) 74.

2662 *Strus* Andrzej, ◍ Rozwój proroctwa o Emmanuelu jako przykład hermeneutyki w Starym Testamencie (De momento hermeneutico prophetiae de Emmanuele): ➤ 367, Sympozjum 1985, RuBi 39 (1986) 197-211.

2663 **Thompson** Michael E. W., Situation... Syro-Ephraimite war 1982 ➤ 63,2882... 1,3499: ᴿHeythJ 27 (1986) 185s (R. E. *Clements*).

2664 *Marin* Marcello, [Is 8,4: 2 Reg 21H,9] Bibbia e filologia patristica; note di lettura: VetChr 23 (1986) 73-79.

2665 *Gilead* Ḥayyim, ◍ [Is 10,27] *wᵉ-ḥubbal 'al mi-pᵉnê šāmen*: BethM 31,105 (1985s) 134-6.

2666 *Chilton* Bruce, [Is 10,32s] Sennacherib; a synoptic relationship among Targumim of Isaiah: a) ➤ 392, SBL Seminars 1986, 544-554; – b) ➤ 140*, Targumic 1986, 163-177.

2667 a) *Stachowiak* L., ◍ The gifts of the Spirit for the line of David and his coming universal kingdom of peace (Is 11,1-10); – b) *Homerski* J., ◍ The gift of the Holy Spirit in the teaching of the prophets: ➤ 266, Duch Święty 23-38 / 9-22.

2668 *Ebach* J., [Is 11,6] Ende des Feindes oder Ende der Feindschaft ? Der Tierfrieden bei Jesaja und Vergil: ➤ 155, Ursprung 1986, 75-89 [151-6, Jos 32,17].

2668* *Jeppesen* Knud, The Maśśē' Bābel in Isaiah 13-14: PrIrB 9 (1985) 63-80.

2669 *Etz* Donald V., Is Isaiah XIV 12-15 a reference to Comet Halley?: VT 36 (1986) 289-301.

2670 *Schvindt* Claudio, Análisis literario y de la relectura de las tradiciones en Isaías 19,16-25: RBigArg 48 (1986) 51-59.

2671 *Sawyer* John F. A., 'Blessed be my people Egypt' (Isaiah 19.25); the context and meaning of a remarkable passage: ➤ 63, ᶠMcKANE W., A word 1986, 57-71.

2672 *Gosse* Bernard, Le 'moi' prophétique de l'oracle contre Babylone d'Isaïe XXI, 1-10: RB 93 (1986) 70-84.
2673 *Chiera* G., Is. 23, l'elegia su Tiro: RStFen 14 (1986) 3-19.
2674 *a) Tsirkin* Ju. B., [Is 23,10...] The Hebrew Bible and the origin of Tartessian power; – *b) Fernández-Miranda* M., Helva, ciudad de los tartessios; – *c) Brunnens* G., Le rôle de Gadès dans l'implantation phénicienne en Espagne: → 353, E*Olmo Lete* G. del, Fenicios II = AulaOr 4 (1986) 179-185, T*Chistonogova* L. / 227-261; 15 fig. ['tartesios' en los títulos corrientes] / 211-225; T*Fernández Jurado* J. / 187-192.
2674* **Lewis** Dale J., A rhetorical critical analysis of Isaiah 24-27: diss. Southern Baptist Sem., D*Smothers* T., 1985. 220 p. 86-06145. – DissA 47 (1986s) 948-A.
2675 **Steck** Odil Hannes, Bereitete Heimkehr; Jesaja 35 als redaktionelle Brücke zwischen dem Ersten und dem Zweiten Jesaja: SBS 121, 1985 → 1,3513; DM 26,80: R*Bijdragen* 47 (1986) 439 (W. *Beuken*); BL (1986) 80s (R. E. *Clements*); Streven 53 (1985s) 952s (P. *Beentjes*).
2676 *Alonso Schökel* Luis, *Carniti* Cecilia, 'In testa', Is 35,10: RivB 34 (1986) 397-9.
2677 *Smelik* K. A. D., Distortion of Old Testament prophecy; the purpose of Isaiah xxxvi and xxxvii: → 399, OTS 24, 1985/6, 70-93.

E8.4 **Deutero-Isaias 40-52:** *commentarii, themata, versiculi.*

2678 *Carena* Omar, [→ 7464] L'idea del 'resto' come rivendicazione morale nei confronti del potere conquistatore: → 391, Storiografia 1984/6, 53-64.
2679 **Clifford** Richard J., Fair spoken and persuading; an interpretation of Second Isaiah 1984 → 65,3122; 1,3516: R*CBQ* 48 (1986) 299s (Elizabeth *Achtemeier*: a few overlookings).
2679* **Hausmann** Jutta, Der nachexilische Restgedanke; Studien zum Selbstverständnis der nachexilischen Gemeinde: Diss. D*Preus* H. Erlangen 1986. 325 p. – RTLv 18,542.
2680 *Hermisson* Hans-Jürgen, Deuterojesaja-Probleme: VerkF 31,1 (1986) 53-84.
2681 **Jerger** Günter, 'Evangelium des Alten Testaments'; die Grundbotschaft des Propheten Deuterojesaja in ihrer Bedeutung für den Religionsunterricht [Diss. FrB 1985s, D*Biemer*: TR 82 (1986) 512]: SBB 14. Stu 1986, KBW. vii-469 p. DM 39. 3-460-00141-0.
2682 **Knight** George A. F., Servant theology; a commentary on the Book of Isaiah 40-55[2]: 1984 [¹1965] → 65,3125; 1,3521: R*AndrUnS* 24 (1986) 194s (N.-E. *Andreasen*); HeythJ 27 (1986) 44 (G. G. *Nicol*: not really 'revised'; the series in general provides inadequate space for defense of views adopted); ScotJT 39 (1986) 259-262 (Norma D. *Stewart*); TLZ 111 (1986) 884s (D. *Mathias*).
2683 *Lindars* Barnabas, Good tidings to Zion; interpreting Deutero-Isaiah today: BJRyL 68 (1985s) 473-497.
2684 *Mettinger* Tryggve N. D., In search of the hidden structure; YHWH as king in Isaiah 40-55: SvEx 51s (1986s) 148-157.
2685 **Sawyer** J. F. A., Isaiah vol. 2: Daily Study Bible. E/Ph 1986, St. Andrew / Westminster. x-225 p. £4.25. 0-7152-0528-5 / [BL 87,55].
2686 **Scullion** John, Isaiah 40-66: OTMessage, 1982 → 63,3603; 65,3128: R*BibTB* 16 (1986) 158 (Chris *Franke*).

2687 *Whybray* R. Norman, Two recent studies on Second Isaiah [*Beuken* W. 1979/83; *Clifford* R. 1984]: JStOT 34 (1986) 109-117.

2688 **Kern** Brigitte A. A., Tröstet, tröstet mein Volk ! Zwei rabbinische Homilien zu Jesaja 40,1 (PesR 30 und PesR 29/30): FraJudSt 7. Fra 1986, Ges. Judaist. Studien. 520 p. 3-922056-04-0.

2689 *Berlin* Adele, Isaiah 40:4; etymological and poetic considerations: HebAnR 3 (1979) 1-6 [OTAbs 9,297].

2689* *McNeese* Art, The God of no respect (Isaiah 40:12-31): RestQ 28 (1985s) 79-86 < zɪᴛ].

2690 *a*) *Bizeul* Yves, *Ganzevoort* Inge, Créateur et aménagement de l'espace dans l'hymne de louange d'Ésaïe 40,12-31: – *b*) *Smyth* Françoise, Les espaces du IIᵉ Ésaïe; de la route impériale à l'avènement de la parole: FoiVie 85,5 (CahBib 25, 1986) 42-51 / 31-41.

2691 *Williamson* H. G. M., Isaiah 40,20 — a case of not seeing the wood for the trees: Biblica 67 (1986) 1-19; franç. 20.

2691* *Sicre* J. L., El cántico del nuevo Éxodo (Is. 42,14-17): ➤ 105, ᶠ*Segovia* A. 1986...

2692 **Grimm** W., Die Heimkehr der Jakobskinder (Jes. 43,1-7) 1985 ➤ 1,3528: ᴿBL (1986) 87 (R. N. *Whybray*: pushes NT relevance).

2693 *Kutsch* Ernst, 'Ich will meinen Geist ausgiessen auf deine Kinder', Jes 44,1-5 < Mem. Fʀöʀ K. 1981, 122-133]: ➤ 183, Kʟs 1986, 157-168.

2694 *Clements* Roland E., Isaiah 45:20-25: Interpretation 40 (1986) 392-7.

2695 **Steck** Odil H., Heimkehr auf der Schulter oder/und der Hüfte, Jes 49,22b/60,4b: ZAW 98 (1986) 275-7.

E8.5 *Isaiae 53ss, Carmina Servi YHWH:* **Servant-Songs.**

2696 *Begg* Christopher, Zedekiah and the Servant [not mentioned among the 15 candidates of C. *North*'s ²1956 classic, though suggested by the early *Coppens* J. 1950]: ETL 62 (1986) 393-8.

2696* **Goldingay** John, God's prophet, God's servant; a study in Jeremiah and Isaiah 1984 ➤ 65,3146; 1,3535: ᴿCBQ 48 (1986) 531s (G. A. *Yee*)

2697 *Grelot* Pierre, I canti del Servo del Signore 1983 ➤ 65,3147*b*: ᴿAsprenas 32 (1985) 457s (V. *Scippa*).

2698 *Haag* Herbert, Der 'Gottesknecht' bei Deuterojesaja im Veständnis des Judentums: Judaica 41 (1985) 27-36.

2699 *Jakovljević* Radivoj, The sense of Ebed Yahweh's suffering: ➤ 377*a*, IOSOT summaries (1986) 64.

2700 **Kleinknecht** Karl T., Der leidende Gerechtfertigte ... und Paulus: WUNT 2/13, 1984 ➤ 1,3539: ᴿActuBbg 23 (1986) 214s (X. *Alegre* S.); Gregorianum 67 (1986) 367s (R. *Penna*); NRT 108 (1986) 122s (X. *Jacques*); RThom 86 (1986) 326s (H. *Ponsot*); Salmanticensis 33 (1986) 125-7 (R. *Trevijano*); TLZ 111 (1986) 429-431 (C. *Wolff*).

2701 *Kutsch* Ernst, Sein Leiden und Tod — unser Heil; eine Auslegung von Jesaja 52,13 - 53,12 = BibSt 52 (Neuk 1967)]: 183, Kʟs 1986, 169-196.

2702 **Lindsey** F. D., The Servant Songs 1985 ➤ 1,3541: ᴿBL (1986) 55 (R. N. *Whybray*: competent dignity).

2703 **Ljung** Inger, Tradition and interpretation; a study of the use and application of formulaic language in the so-called Ebed YHWH-psalms 1978

➤ 60,4858 ... 62,3708:   ᴿCBQ 48 (1986) 121-3 (J.K. *Kunst*: too dissertational).

2704 **Mesters** Carlos, La mission du peuple qui souffre; la non-violence des pauvres dans les quatre Chants d'Isaïe [Botschaft 1982; Zending 1984 ➤ 63,3637; 65,3151]: Lire la Bible 68. P 1984, Cerf. 157p. F 57. – ᴿVSp 140 (1986) 125s (T. *Chary*).

2705 **Mettinger** Tryggve N.D., A farewell to the servant songs; a critical examination of an exegetical axiom 1983 ➤ 64,3525 ... 1,3542: ᴿCBQ 48 (1986) 116-8 (S. *Greenhalgh*: not quite); ÉTRel 61 (1986) 124s (D. *Lys*); Interpretation 40 (1986) 310.312 (F.J. *Gaiser*: to read with H.-J. HERMISSON's answer TRu 49,209).

2705* *Simian-Yofre* Horacio, *Ringgren* Helmer, [*al.*], 'Ebed YHWH: ➤ 599, TWAT 5,7s (1986) [982-]1003-1012.

2706 **Leene** H., [Is 50,1-3.4-9, The Servant's voice] De stem van de knecht als metafoor; beschouwingen over de compositie van Jesaja 50, 1980 ➤ 61,4714; 90-242-0205-1: ᴿNedTTs 40 (1986) 174 (M.D. *Koster*).

2706* *Ruppert* L., Schuld und Schuld-Lösen nach Jes 53: ➤ 64,504, ᴱ*Kaufmann* G., Schulderfahrung 1979/82, 17-34.

E8.6 [Trito-]Isaias 56-66.

2707 **Bastiaens** Jean, *al.*, Trito-Isaiah; an exhaustive concordance of Isa 56-66, especially with reference to Deutero-Isaiah; an example of computer assisted research: Applicatio, informatica-toepassingen in de theologie 4,1984 ➤ 65,3160; *f*37,50: ᴿJNWS 13 (1985s) 221 (W.T. *Claassen*).

2708 **Knight** George A.F., Isaiah 56-66: International Theological Comm. 1985 ➤ 1,3550: ᴿExpTim 97 (1985s) 278 (C.S. *Rodd*: less old-fashioned than his Is 40-55).

2709 **Polan** Gregory J., In the ways of justice toward salvation; a rhetorical analysis of Isaiah 56-59 [diss. Ottawa: TR 83,249]: AmerUnivSt 7/13. NY 1986, Lang. xiv-360p. 0-8204-0280-X.

2710 *Beuken* W.A.M., Isa. 56:9 - 57:13 — an example of the Isaianic legacy of Trito-Isaiah: ➤ 59, ꜰLEBRAM J., Tradition 1986, 48-64.

2711 **Mouw** Richard J., When the kings come marching in; Isaiah [60] and the New Jerusalem 1983 ➤ 64,3459; 1,3557: ᴿGraceTJ 7 (1986) 245s (S.R. *Schrader*).

2712 *Steck* Odil H., *a*) Der Grundtext in Jesaja 60 und sein Aufbau: ZTK 83 (1986) 261-296; – *b*) Der Rachetag in Jesaja LXI 2: ein Kapitel redaktionsgeschichtlicher Kleinarbeit: VT 36 (1986) 323-333.

2713 *Anderson* T. David, Renaming and wedding imagery in Isaiah 62: Biblica 67 (1986) 75-80.

2714 **Beuken** W.A.M., Abraham weet van ons niet (Jes. 63:16); de grond van Israëls vertrouwen tijdens de ballingschap [Inaug. Nijmegen 1986]. Nijkerk 1986, Callenbach. 32p. [PhoenixEOL 32/2,7].

2715 *Webster* Edwin C., A rhetorical study of Isaiah 66: JStOT 34 (1986) 93-108 [errata corrected 35,121].

E8.7 Jeremias.

2716 *Blanchet* R., *al.*, Jérémie, un prophète en temps de crise: Dossier pour l'animation biblique, 1985 ➤ 1,3564: ᴿBL (1986) 62s (W. *McKane*); Protestantesimo 41 (1986) 165-7 (M. *Grube*); ZAW 98 (1986) 461s (G. *Wanke*).

E8.7 Jeremiah text and commentaries 229

2716* *Boggio* Giovanni, [Geremia] Un uomo senza maschera: ParVi 31 (1986) 94-100.

2717 **Brueggemann** Walter, Hopeful imagination; prophetic voices in exile [Jer Ezek 2-Is 587 B.C.]. Ph 1986, Fortress. x-146 p. $8 pa. 0-8006-1925-1 [OTAbs 10,95].

2718 **Carroll** Robert P., Jeremiah, a commentary: OTLibrary. L/Ph 1986 SCM/Westminster. ix-874 p. £20. 0-334-02093-X/. – ᴿExpTim 98 (1986s) 24 (C. S. *Rodd*); TS 48 (1986) 343-7 (W. *Brueggemann*).

2719 *a) Carroll* Robert P., Arguments for dismantling the book of Jeremiah and deconstructing the prophet: → 377a, IOSOT summaries (1986) 21. – *b) Brueggemann* Walter, A second reading of Jeremiah after the dismantling: ExAud 1 (1985) 156-168.

2720 *Conroy* Charles, Jeremiah and sainthood: [J. *Bright*: he didn't make it]: → 294, ᴱ*Dhavamony* M., Saints = StMiss 35 (1986) 1-40.

2720* **Cruells i Viñas** Antoni, El *dabar* en Jeremías: diss. ᴰ*Raurell* F. – RTLv 18,541; ActuBbg 24,77. Barc 1986, auct. 300 p. 84-398-6898-7.

2721 **Davidson** Robert, *a)* Jeremiah I: Daily Study Bible 1983 → 64,3466; 1,3569: ᴿCBQ 48 (1986) 105s (J. *Limburg* doubts the claim 'if this book was written by a sane man with an orderly mind, he has done his best to confuse us'). – *b)* Jeremiah vol. 2 [ch. 21-52] and Lamentations: Daily Study Bible. Ph 1986, Westminster. IX-214 p. $15; pa. $8 [JBL 105,750].

2722 *Feinberg* Charles L., Jeremiah: → 1354, Expositor's Bible Commentary 6 (1986)...

2723 *Hayward* C. T. R., Jewish traditions in JEROME's commentary on Jeremiah and the Targum of Jeremiah: PrIrB 9 (1985) 100-120.

2724 **Herrmann** Siegfried, Jeremia: BK AT 12. Neuk 1986, Neuk-V.

2725 **Holladay** W. L., Jeremiah 1 (-25); Hermeneia. Ph/L 1986, Fortress/ SCM. xxii-682 p. $45/£41. 0-8006-0017-X / 0-334-00778-X [BL 87,49, R. P. *Carroll*: 'magnificent but not exegesis'].

2726 **Klages** G., *Heinemeyer* K., Prophetie im Unterricht, dargestellt an Jeremia; Modell eines fachspezifischen Kurses. Hannover 1986, Luther-haus. 190 p. [ZAW 99,292, G. *Wanke*).

2727 [*Klostermann* E.] ²**Nautin** P., ORIGENES, Jeremiahomilien, Klage-liederkommentar, Erklärung der Samuel- und Königsbücher: GCS, 1983 → 64,3557; 1,3573: ᴿTLZ 111 (1986) 212s (H. *Kraft*); TR 82 (1986) 462s (R. M. *Hübner*).

2728 **McKane** William, Jeremiah I: New ICC [first OT to appear]. E 1986, Clark. cxxii-658 p. £25. 0-567-05042-4. – ᴿExpTim 97 (1985s) 309 (C. S. *Rodd*).

2729 **Martens** Elmer A., Jeremiah: Believers' Church Bible Comm. Scottdale PA 1986, Herald. 327 p. $35.15 [JBL 105,753].

2730 *Moore* Michael S., Jeremiah's progressive paradox: RB 93 (1986) 386-414.

2732 **Paterson** Robert M. ['Patterson' OTAbs 8 (1985) 206; → 1,3574, ch. 1-24], Kitab Yeremia, fasal 25-52. Jakarta 1985, Gunung Mulia. 210 p. Rp 2750. – ᴿOTAbs 9 (1986) 336s (*ipse*).

2733 ᴱ**Perdue** Leo G., *Kovacs* Brian W., A prophet to the nations... Jeremiah [23 reprints] 1984 → 65,301; 1,3577: ᴿJAAR 54 (1986) 147-9 (W. E. *Lemke*).

2734 *Pixley* Jorge V., ¿A qué partido político perteneció Jeremías ?: RBibArg 48 (1986) 31-49.

2735 **Polk** Timothy, The prophetic persona; Jeremiah and the language of the self: JStOT Sup 32, 1984 → 65,3185; 1,3579: ᴿCBQ 48 (1986) 727-9 (J. R.

Lundbom: reserves); JTS 37 (1986) 461s (R. E. *Clements*); RB 93 (1986) 303 (R. J. *Tournay*); TLond 39 (1986) 140-2 (R. *Coggins*: 'it looks as if authority has passed from the word of God and the historical figure of the prophet and has arrived on the literary critics' desk').

2736 *a*) *Riaud* Jean, 'Le Puissant t'emportera dans ta tente'; la destinée ultime du Juste selon les Paralipomena Jeremiae Prophetae; – *b*) *Charlesworth* James H., Greek, Persian, Roman, Syrian and Egyptian influences on early Jewish theology; a study of the History of the Rechabites: ➤ 81, Mém. NIKIPROWETZKY V. 1986, 257-265 / 219-243.

2737 **Ridouard** A., Geremia; la prova della fede 1984 ➤ 65,3186*b*: ᴿParVi 31 (1986) 150s (B. *Marconcini*).

2737* *Rodd* C. S., Which is the best commentary? VI. Jeremiah [bypasses (his own, editor's) formulation of the question, fairly treats them all]: ExpTim 98 (1986s) 171-5.

2738 *Rofé* Alexander, ❻ Jeremiah and his book — summary: BethM 31,107 (1985s) 308-315.

2739 **Rosenberg** A. J., Jeremiah, a new English translation, incl. RASHI comm., II. NY 1985, Judaica. xxii, p. 210-442, maps [KirSef 60,361].

2740 **Schreiner** Josef, Jeremia [I, 1981 ➤ 62,3747], II: 25,15-52,34: NEchter 3. Wü 1984, Echter. pp. 149-282. DM 28. – ᴿCBQ 48 (1986) 729s (J. I. *Hunt*); TR 82 (1986) 275-9 (Helga *Weippert*).

2740* **Seitz** Christopher R., Theology in conflict; reactions to the Exile in the book of Jeremiah: diss. Yale. NHv 1986. 587 p. 87-01082. DissA 47 (1986s) 3450-A; RelStR 13,189.

2741 **Soderlund** Sven, The Greek text of Jeremiah; a revised hypothesis [< diss. Glasgow 1978]: JStOT Sup 47. Sheffield 1986, Univ. 304 p. £18.50; pa. £9. 1-85075-028-9; 7-9. – ᴿExpTim 97 (1985s) 343 (R. *Carroll*: salutary); JSS 31 (1986) 247-9 (B. *Lindars*); ZAW 98 (1986) 476 (G. *Wanke*).

2742 **Stulman** Louis, The prose sermons of the Book of Jeremiah; a redescription of the correspondences with the Deuteronomistic literature in the light of recent text-critical research [diss. Drew 1982 ➤ 64,3560]: SBL diss. 83. Atlanta 1986, Scholars. vii-157 p.; bibliog. p. 147-157. $13.25; sb. $8.75 [ZAW 99,300, G. *Wanke*].

2743 **Stulman** Louis, The other text of Jeremiah [➤ 1,3583]; a reconstruction of the Hebrew text underlying the Greek version of the prose sections of Jeremiah, with English translation. Lanham MD 1985, UPA. 171 p. $12.75. – ᴿJSS 31 (1986) 249s (W. *McKane*).

2744 *Thiel* Winfried, Ein Vierteljahrhundert Jeremia-Forschung: VerkF 31,1 (1986) 32-52.

2745 **Vieweger** Dieter, Die Spezifik der Berufungsgeschichte Jeremias und Ezechiels im Umfeld ähnlicher Einheiten des Alten Testaments: Diss. Lp 1985]: BErfAT 6. Fra 1986, Lang. 180 p.; bibliog. p. 145-164. 3-8204-8948-7: ᴿETL 62 (1986) 421 (J. *Lust*).

2746 *Weiss* Herold, How can Jeremiah compare the migration of birds to knowledge of God's justice?: BR 2,3 (1986) 42-45.

2747 **Wisser** Laurent, Jérémie, critique de la vie sociale 1982 ➤ 63,3682... 1,3591: ᴿProtestantesimo 41 (1986) 165 (J. A. *Soggin*).

_____

2748 [Jer 1] *a*) **Augustin** Gary C., Jeremiah's religious call as a model for adversity in ministry from a Jungian perspective: diss. Southern Baptist

Theol. Sem. 1986, ᴰ*Rowatt* G. W. 284 p. 86-19027. – DissA 47 (1986s) 2621-A. – *b*) **Vieweger** Dieter, Die Spezifik der Berufungsberichte Jeremias und Ezechiels 1986 ➤ 2745. – *c*) **Williams** David T., The call of Jeremiah: diss. Pretoria, ᴰ*Loader* J. 313 p. – RTLv 18,544 sans date.

2748* *a*) *Arenhoevel* Diego (†), Ohnmacht und Macht des prophetischen Wortes; die Berufung des Jeremia (Jer 1,1-10): WAntw 27 (Mainz 1986) 143-9 < zɪт].

2749 *Dorn* Louis, [Jer 2,4...] The unexpected as a speech device; shifts of thematic expectancy in Jeremiah: BTrans 37 (1986) 216-222.

2749* **Althann** Robert, A philological analysis of Jeremiah 4-6 in the light of NW Semitic: BibOrPont 38, 1983 ➤ 64,3571; 1,3599: ᴿJBL 105 (1986) 319s (W. L. *Holladay*: implausible); RelStR 12 (1986) 159 (D. L. *Petersen*: valuable).

2750 *Odashima* Taro, Wie entstand die Grundgestalt von Jer. V ? ; die Sprüche Jeremias und ihre Bearbeitung in der Nachexilszeit: ➤ 377*a*, IOSOT summaries (1986) 99.

2751 *a*) *Holt* Else K., Jeremiah's temple sermon and the Deuteronomists; an investigation of the redactional relationship between Jeremiah 7 and 26; – *b*) *Lundbom* J. R., Baruch, Seraiah, and expanded colophons in the Book of Jeremiah: JStOT 36 (1986) 73-87 / 89-114.

2752 *Kutsch* Ernst, *a*) Weisheitsspruch und Prophetenwort; zur Traditionsgeschichte des Spruches Jer 9,22-23 < BZ 25 (1981) 161-179]; – *b*) '... denn Jahwe vernichtet die Philister'; Erwägungen zu Jer 47,1-7 [< ᶠWOLFF H. W. 1981, 253-267]: ➤ 183, KɪS 1986, 197-215 / 216-230.

2753 *Sternberger* Jean-Pierre, Un oracle royal[e] à la source d'un ajout rédactionnel aux 'Confessions' de Jérémie; hypothèses se rapportant aux 'Confessions' de Jérémie XII et XV: VT 36 (1986) 462-473.

2754 *Seybold* Klaus, Der 'Löwe' von Jeremia XII 8; Bemerkungen zu einem prophetischen Gedicht: VT 36 (1986) 93-104.

2755 *Sisson* Jonathan P., [Jer 14,13] Jeremiah and the Jerusalem conception of peace: JBL 105 (1986) 429-442.

2756 **Lubac** Henri de, 'Du hast mich betrogen, Herr!' — Der ORIGE-NES-Kommentar über Jeremia 20,7. Einsiedeln 1984, Johannes. 120 p. DM 17. – ᴿTrierTZ 95 (1986) 162s (E. *Sauser*).

2757 *Grossberg* Daniel, Pivotal polysemy in Jeremiah XXV 10-11A: VT 36 (1986) 481-5.

2757* *Mendecki* Norbert, ℗ Czy Jr 31,7-9 jest pokrewny orędziu Deutero-izajasza?: ColcT 56,2 (1986) 43-52; 52s, Berührungen mit der Botschaft Dt-Jes?

2758 **Levin** Christoph, [Jer 31,31] Die Verheissung des Neuen Bundes in ihrem theologiegeschichtlichen Zusammenhang ausgelegt: FRLANT 137, 1985 ➤ 1,3616: ᴿBL (1986) 92 (E. W. *Nicholson*); CBQ 48 (1986) 723s (R. *Gnuse*, unconvinced); ÉTRel 61 (1986) 117-120 (T. *Römer*); TsTNijm 26 (1986) 85 (L. *Grollenberg*); ZAW 98 (1986) 149s (G. *Wanke*).

2759 **Compton** Robert B., [Jer 31 + 12 times] An examination of the New Covenant in the Old and New Testament: diss. Grace 1986, ᴰ*Kent* H. 361 p. 87-02958. – DissA 47 (1986s) 3786-A; GraceTJ 7 (1986) 319.

2760 *Lee* L. W., The new covenant in Jeremiah: BibIll 12 (Nv 1986) 24-29 [OTAbs 10,73].

2761 **Wilfong** Marsha M., [Jer 31,33... Ezek 11,19 ... Dt 30,6] God's promised action on the human heart; deliverance from faulty reasoning: diss. Union Theol. Sem. Richmond 1986. 255 p. 86-27543. – DissA 47 (1986s) 3075-A.

2762 *Wacholder* Ben Zion, The 'sealed' Torah versus the 'revealed' Torah; an exegesis of Damascus Covenant V,1-6 and Jeremiah 32,10-14: RQum 12,47 (1986) 351-367; franç. 367s; deutsch 368.

2763 **Ábrego** José M., Jeremías y el final del reino; lectura sincrónica de Jer 36-45: EstJer 3, 1983 ➤ 64,3599; 1,3619: [diss. Pont. Ist. Biblico, ᴰ*Alonso Schökel* L., R 1982]: ᴿCBQ 48 (1986) 292s (L. *Laberge*: exaggerates hidden meanings); JBL 105 (1986) 319 (C. T. *Begg*); NRT 108 (1986) 109s (J.-L. *Ska*).

2764 *Ball* Jeffrey D., [Jer 36] Towards a new understanding of the Jeremiah scroll; the problem and recent scholarship: StudiaBT 13 (1983) 51-75.

2764* **Bellis** Alice O., The structure and composition of Jeremiah 50:2-51:58: diss. Catholic Univ., ᴰ*Fitzgerald* Aloysius. Wsh 1986. 347 p. 86-11639. – DissA 47 (1986s) 883-A.

2765 *Gosse* Bernard, La malédiction contre Babylone de Jérémie 51,59-64 et les rédactions du livre de Jérémie: ZAW 98 (1986) 392-399.

E8.8   **Lamentationes**, *Threni; Baruch.*

2766 *Alexander* P. S., The textual tradition of Targum Lamentations: Abr-Nahr 24 (1986) 1-26.

2767 *Alster* Bendt, E d i n - n a   ú - s a g - g á: econstruction, history, and interpretation of a Sumerian cultic lament: ➤ 543, Rencontre 32, 1985/6, 19-31.

2768 **Boecker** H. J., Klagelieder 1985 ➤ 1,3622: ᴿExpTim 97 (1985s) 375 (R. J. *Coggins*).

2769 **Dori** Zachariya, ❻ Megillat Êkâ, targum and midrash. Petah-Tikvah 1984, auct. 138 p.; ill.; maps [KirSef 59,296].

2769* *Ellison* H. L., Lamentations: ➤ 1354, Expositor's Bible Commentary 6 (1986) ...

2770 **Gross** Heinrich, Klagelieder; *Schreiner* Josef, Baruch: NEchter 14. Wü 1986, Echter. 89 p. DM 24, sb. 19,80. 3-429-00998-7 [BL 87,48, R. A. *Mason*: Gross sets forth various views and leaves issues open; Schreiner gives his own view].

2771 *Salters* R. B., Lamentations 1.3; light from the history of exegesis: ➤ 63, ᶠMᴄKᴀɴᴇ W., A word 1986, 73-89.

_____

2772 **Murphy** Frederick J., The structure and meaning of Second Baruch [diss. Harvard 1984, ᴰ*Cross* F.]: SBL diss. 78, 1985 ➤ 1,3629: ᴿAustralBR 34 (1986) 78-80 (Anne E. *Gardner*); Biblica 67 (1986) 590-2 (P.-M. *Bogaert*); CBQ 48 (1986) 752s (J. J. *Collins*).

2773 **Sayler** Gwendolyn B., Have the promises failed? A literary analysis of 2 Baruch: SBL diss 72 [Iowa City 1982, ᴰ*Nickelsburg* G.] ➤ 65,3225; 1,3631: ᴿAustralBR 34 (1986) 77s (Anne E. *Gardner*); BL (1986) 135 (M. A. *Knibb*); CBQ 48 (1986) 315s (J. J. *Collins*); Gregorianum 67 (1986) 359 (G. L. *Prato*); JBL 105 (1986) 349s (Anitra B. *Kolenkow*).

2774 *Alonso Schökel* Luis, Jerusalén inocente intercede; Baruc 4, 9-19: ➤ 21, Mem. Dɪᴇᴢ Mᴀᴄʜᴏ A., Salvación 1986, 39-51.

E8.9   **Ezechiel**: *textus, commentarii; themata, versiculi.*

2774* *Alexander* Ralph H., Ezekiel: ➤ 1354, Expositor's Bible Commentary 6 (1986) ...

2775 **Asurmendi** J. M., O profeta Ezequiel: Cadernos Bíblicos 33. São Paulo 1985, Paulinas. 89 p. [REB 46,228].

2776 *Baltzer* Dieter, Ezechiel: ➤ 587, EvKL 1 (1986) 1248-1250.

2777 **Brownlee** William H., Ezekiel 1-19: Word Comm. 28. Waco 1986, Word. xlii-321 p. 0-8499-0227-4.

2777* ᵀᴱ**Bürke** Georg, GREGOR der Grosse, Homilien zu Ezechiel: Christliche Meister 21, 1983 ➤ 1,3637: ᴿTrierTZ 95 (1986) 155 (E. *Sauser*).

2778 **Burnier-Genton** Jean, Ézéchiel fils d'homme 1982 ➤ 63,3733... 1,3639: ᴿHenoch 8 (1986) 95s (P. G. *Borbone*).

2779 **Cody** Aelred, Ezekiel, with an excursus on OT priesthood: OTMessage 11, 1984 ➤ 65,3229; 1,3640: ᴿCBQ 48 (1986) 300s (M. *Hillmer*: well-turned phrases).

2780 **Craigie** P. C., ❹ Ezekieru-sho [1983 ➤ 65,3230], ᵀTomoeda K. Tokyo 1986, Shinkyō Shuppan-sha. 494 p. Y 2900 [BL 87,45].

2781 **Greenberg** Moshe, Ezekiel 1-20: AnchorB 22, 1983 ➤ 64,3618... 1,3643: ᴿBASOR 262 (1986) 91-93 (M. *Fishbane*); JBL 105 (1986) 142-4 (W. B. *Barrick*); NRT 108 (1986) 110s (J.-L. *Ska*).

2782 *a*) *Greenberg* Moshe, What are valid criteria for determining inauthentic matter in Ezekiel?; – *b*) *Baltzer* Dieter, Literarkritische und literarhistorische Anmerkungen zur Heilsprophetie im Ezechiel-Buch; – *c*) *Boadt* Lawrence, Rhetorical strategies in Ezekiel's oracles of judgment; – *d*) *Joyce* Paul M., Ezekiel and individual responsibility; – *e*) *Dohmen* Christoph, Das Problem der Gottesbeschreibung im Ezechielbuch; – *f*) *Begg* Christopher T., The non-mention of Ezekiel in the Deuteronomic history, the book of Jeremiah and the Chronistic history: ➤ 384, Ezekiel 1985/6, 123-135 / 166-181 / 182-200 / 317-321 / 330-4 / 340-3.

2782* **Hurvitz** Avi, A linguistic study of the relationship between... P & Ezekiel 1982 ➤ 63,1970; 64,3620: ᴿScripB 16 (1985s) 47 (M. *McNamara*).

2783 **Job** John, Watchman in Babylon; a study guide to Ezekiel 1983 ➤ 1,3643*; also Pocket 32. Exeter 1983, Paternoster. 101 p. £2.20 – ᴿCBQ 48 (1986) 116s (S. *Greenhalgh*).

2783* **Krüger** Thomas, Geschichtskonzepte im Ezechielbuch: ev. Diss. Mü 1986, ᴰBaltzer K. – RTLv 18,542.

2784 **Kutsch** Ernst, Die chronologischen Daten des Ezechielbuches: OBO 62, 1985 ➤ 1,3644; 3-7278-0327-4 / VR 3-525-53685-2. ᴿETL 62 (1986) 181s (J. *Lust*: this is the contribution referred to ZAW 1983 by B. *Lang* in Biblica 1983, 226); RB 93 (1986) 441-5 (B. *Gosse*).

2785 *a*) *Lust* Johan, The use of textual witnesses for the establishment of the text; the shorter and longer texts of Ezekiel; – *b*) *Spottorno* Victoria, Some lexical aspects of the Greek text of Ezekiel; – *c*) *Mulder* M. J., Die neue Pešitta-Ausgabe von Ezechiel; – *d*) *Verdegaal* C. M. L., The Jewish influence on the Ezekiel-translation of the English and Dutch authorized versions; – *e*) *Lemaire* André, Les formules de datation dans Ézéchiel à la lumière des données épigraphiques récentes; – *f*) *Raurell* Frederic, The polemical role of the *árchontes* and *aphēgoúmenoi* in Ez LXX: ➤ 384, ᴱLust J., Ezekiel 1985/6, (1-)7-20 / 78-84 / 101-110 / 111-9 / 359-366 / 85-89.

2785* **Lust** J., The computer and the hypothetical translators of Ezekiel: ➤ 389, Bible et informatique 1985/6, 265-274.

2786 **Maarsingh** B., Ezechiël I, 1985 ➤ 1,3646: ᴿBL (1986) 55s (P. R. *Ackroyd*: sensible); Streven 53 (1985s) 666 (P. *Beentjes*).

2787 **McGregor** Leslie J., The Greek text of Ezekiel [diss. Belfast]: SBL SeptCog 18, 1985 ➤ 1,3647: ᴿAustralBR 34 (1986) 67-70 (G. *Jenkins*);

ETL 62 (1986) 182s (J. *Lust*: computer-results); JSS 31 (1986) 84-87 (T. *Muraoka*); TLZ 111 (1986) 885-8 (Anneli *Aejmelaeus*, Eng.); TrinJ 7,2 (1986) 111-5 (L. *Perkins*).

2788 *Monloubou* L., Ézéchiel; autour du problème Religion et foi: EsprV 96 (1986) 391-7.

2789 a) **Morel** C., GRÉGOIRE le Grand, Homélies sur Ézéchiel I: SChr 327. P 1986, Cerf. 543 p. F 216 [NRT 109,451, A. *Harvengt*] 2-204-02584-4. – b) *Morel* Charles, La 'rectitudo' dans les homélies de GRÉGOIRE le Grand sur Ezéchiel (Livre I): ➤ 433*, Grégoire 1982/6, 289-295.

2790 *Mulder* Martin J., Einige Beobachtungen zum Peschittatext von Ezechiel in seinen Beziehungen zum masoretischen Text, zur Septuaginta und zum Targum: ➤ 21, Mem. DÍEZ MACHO A., Salvación 1986, 463-470.

2791 ᴱ**Nielsen** K., *Jeppesen* K., Hezekiels bog: Det Gamle testamente i ny oversættelse. K 1985, Dansk. Bibelselskab. 139 p. Dk 84 [BL 87,55]. 87-7523-203-0.

2792 *Pons* Jacques, Polémique à Tel-Aviv en 591 av. J.-C. ['Lisez Ezéchiel... avec 10% d'herméneutique et 90% d'Esprit-Saint']: ÉTRel 61 (1986) 165-175.

2793 *Tov* Emanuel, Recensional differences between the MT and LXX of Ezekiel: ETL 62 (1986) 89-101.

2794 **Zimmerli** W., Ezekiel II, 1983 ➤ 64,3628; 1,3653: ᴿJBL 105 (1986) 321s (R. M. *Hals*).

2795 a) *Clements* R. E., The chronology of redaction in Ez 1-24; – b) *Tromp* Nicholas J., The paradox of Ezekiel's prophetic mission; towards a semiotic approach of Ezekiel 3,22-27; – c) *Bogaert* P.-M., Les deux rédactions conservées (LXX et TM) d'Ézéchiel 7; – d) *Becker* Joachim, Ez 8-11 als einheitliche Komposition in einem pseudepigraphischen Ezechielbuch; – e) *Hossfeld* Frank L., Die Tempelvision Ez 8-11 im Licht unterschiedlicher methodischer Zugänge; – f) *Dijkstra* Meindert, The glosses in Ezekiel reconsidered; aspects of textual transmission in Ezekiel 10: ➤ 384, ᴱ*Lust* J., Ezekiel 1985/6, 283-294 / 201-213 / 21-47 / 136-150 / 151-165 / 55-77.

2795* *Stone* Michael E., The Armenian vision of Ezekiel [Ch. 1]: ➤ 110, ꟳSTENDAHL K. = HarvTR 79 (1986) 261-9.

2796 *Pons* J., [Ézéchiel 2] De CHOURAQUI à la Bible en Français [Courant: rend mieux justice au sens en s'éloignant parfois du texte; mais Chouraqui nous rappelle 'la traduction doit-elle être plus claire que l'original?']: ÉTRel 61 (1986) 415-9.

2797 a) *Simian-Yofre* Horacio, La métaphore d'Ézéchiel 15; – b) *Renaud* Bernard, L'alliance éternelle d'Éz. 16,59-63 et l'alliance nouvelle de Jér 31,31-34; – c) *Pons* Jacques, Le vocabulaire d'Éz 20; le prophète s'oppose à la vision deutéronomiste de l'histoire; – d) *Rendtorff* Rolf, Ez 20 und 36,16ff im Rahmen der Komposition des Buches Ezechiel; – e) *Maarsingh* B., Das Schwertlied in Ez 21,13-22 und das Erra-Gedicht; – f) *Fuhs* Hans F., Ez 24; Überlegungen zu Tradition und Redaktion des Ezechielbuches: ➤ 384, ᴱ*Lust* J., Ezekiel 1985/6, 234-247 / 335-9 / 214-233 / 260-5 / 350-8 / 266-282.

2797* **Chrostowski** Waldemar, Ᵽ Interpretacja dziejów Izraela... L'interprétation de l'histoire d'Israël chez Ezek 16,20 et 23 et leur réinterprétation dans la Septante et le Targum: diss. Wsz 1986, ᴰ*Muszyński* H. – RTLv 18,541.

2798 *Prinsloo* W.W.,   Esegiël 19; een, twee of drie treuerliedere: NduitseGT 26 (1985) 260-270.
2798* *Allen* L.C.,   A textual torso in Ezekiel 22:20:   JSS 31 (1986) 131-3.
2799 *Gosse* Bernard,   Le recueil d'oracles contre les nations d'Ézéchiel XXV-XXXII dans la rédaction du livre d'Ézéchiel: RB 93 (1986) 535-562; Eng. 535.
2800 *Schweizer* H.,   Die vorhergesehene Katastrophe; der Sturz des Welten-baumes (Ez 31): ➤ 340, Bäume 1986, 89-108 [ZAW 99,133].
2801 *a) Nobile* Marco,   Beziehung zwischen Ez 32,17-32 und der Gog-Perikope (Ez 38-39) im Lichte der Endredaktion; – *b) Willmes* Bernd,   Dif-ferenzierende Prophezeiungen in Ez 34; – *c) Lang* Bernhard, [Ezek 37] Street theater, raising the dead, and the Zoroastrian connection in Ezekiel's prophecy; – *d) Lust* Johan,   The final text and textual criticism, Ez 39,28; – *e) Goudoever* J. van, [Ezek 40-48] Ezekiel sees in exile a new temple-city at the beginning of a Jobel year; – *f) Monloubou* Louis,   La signification du culte selon Ézéchiel: ➤ 384, Ezekiel 1985/6, 255-9 / 248-254 / 297-316; 2 fig. / 48-54 / 344-9 / 322-9.
2801* *Freund* Joseph, ❶ [Ezek 33,32] Lo, you are to them as *šîr 'agabim*: BethM 31,105 (1985s) 144-151.
2802 **Willmes** Bernd,   Die sogenannte Hirtenallegorie Ez 34 [< Diss. Bochum 1983]: BeiBExT 19, 1984 ➤ 65,3255; 1,3662: ᴿBO 43 (1986) 461-4 (W. *Die-trich*); CBQ 48 (1986) 545s (W.E. *Lemke*: tedious); JBL 105 (1986) 715s (Carol *Newsom*: does not notice that *sô'n* fem. for 'people' masc. takes both masculine and feminine verbs and suffixes); ZkT 108 (1986) 85s (G. *Glassner*).
2803 *Ellul* Danielle,   *a)* Ézéchiel 37; du chaos à la vie: – *b)* Ézéchiel 40-41; le nouveau Temple; un conglomérat confus de prescriptions sacerdotales, ou l'épure prophétique d'une création sanctifiée?:   FoiVie 85,5 (CahBib 25, 1986) 3-8 / 9-17.
2804 *Scholz* Ruediger,   'Bible scholars generally agree that the prophecies recorded in Ezekiel 38 and 39 are about Russia'; zur evangelicalen Rezeption von Ez. 37-39 [USA Electronic Church Radio Bible Class ...]: DiehlB 22 (1985) 179-189.
2805 *Haynman* Irma & Victor,   The people 'Rosh' of Ezekiel 38:2,3; 39:1: ➤ 377a, IOSOT summaries (1986) 57.
2806 *Niditch* Susan,   Ezekiel 40-48 in a visionary context: CBQ 48 (1986) 208-224.
2807 *Hurvitz* Avi,   The term *liškot šarim* (Ezek 40:44) and its place in the cultic terminology of the Temple [< ❶ ErIsr 14 (1978) 100-4]: ➤ 251*, ᴱ*Japhet* S., ScrHieros 31 (1986) 49-62.

E9.1   **Apocalyptica VT.**

2808 **Collins** John J.,   The apocalyptic imagination; an introduction to the Jewish matrix of Christianity 1984 ➤ 65,3262; 1,3667: ᴿBR 2,3 (1986) 12s (L.H. *Schiffman*); CBQ 48 (1986) 332-4 (Martha *Himmelfarb*: excellent, some queries); JAAR 54 (1985) 140s (J.C. *VanderKam*); JTS 37 (1986) 484-490 (C.C. *Rowland*); RQum 12,47 (1986) 446-8 (F. *García Martínez*).
2809 *Collins* John J.,   Apocalyptic literature: ➤ 255, ᴱ*Kraft* R., Early Judaism 1986, 345-370.
2810 *Delcor* Mathias,   Le passage du temps prophétique au temps apocalyptique: ➤ 21, Mem. DÍEZ MACHO A., Salvación 1986, 97-134.

2811 *Gignoux* Philippe, Nouveaux regards sur l'Apocalyptique iranienne: CRAI (1986) 334-346.

2812 ᴱHanson Paul D., Visionaries and their apocalypses: IssuesRelT 2, 1983 ➤ 64,274 ... 1,3672: ᴿCBQ 48 (1986) 113-5 (M. B. *Dick*).

2813 ᴱHellholm David, Apocalypticism in the Mediterranean world and the Near East 1979/83 ➤ 64,403 ... 1,3675: ᴿJStJud 17 (1986) 224-232 (F. *Garcia Martinez*); TLZ 111 (1986) 591-4 (T. *Holtz*).

2814 *Kippenberg* Hans G. [*Koch* Klaus], Apokalyptik [AT-NT]: ➤ 587, EvKL 1 (1986) 190-2 [192-9].

2815 *Koenen* L., Manichaean apocalypticism at the crossroads of Iranian, Egyptian, Jewish and Christian thought: ➤ 421, Codex Manichaicus 1984/6, 285-332.

2816 *Moore* Hamilton, The problem of Apocalyptic as evidenced in recent discussion: IrBSt 8 (1986) 76-91.

2817 *Ruston* Roger, Apocalyptic and the peace movement: NBlackf 67 (1986) 204-215.

2818 *a*) *Sacchi* Paolo, Jewish Apocalyptic; – *b*) *Abecassis* Armand, The meaning and message of Jewish apocalyptic; – *c*) *Stiassny* M.J., Apocalyptic in Judaism; its eclipse: SIDIC 18,3 (1985) 4-9 / 10s / 12-17.

2819 *VanderKam* James C., The prophetic-sapiential origins of apocalyptic thought: ➤ 63, ᶠMᴄKᴀɴᴇ W., A word 1986, 163-176.

E9.2 **Daniel:** *textus, commentarii; themata, versiculi.*

2820 *Aberbach* Moshe, ➊ Role of Nebukadnezzar in the book of Daniel: BethM 31,104 (1985s) 23-30.

2821 **Anderson** Robert A., Signs and wonders ... Daniel 1984 ➤ 65,3275; 1,3685: ᴿScotJT 39 (1986) 263-5 (R.J. *Way*).

2822 **Beale** G.K., The use of Daniel in Jewish apocalyptic literature and in the Revelation of St. John [diss. Cambridge] 1984 ➤ 65,3276; 1,3688: ᴿCBQ 48 (1986) 552s (J.R. *Keating*); JBL 105 (1986) 734s (Adela Y. *Collins*); JStJud 17 (1986) 80-82 (A.S. van der *Woude*).

2823 **Bodenmann** Reinhard, Naissance d'une exégèse; Daniel dans l'Église ancienne des trois premiers siècles: BeiGBibEx 28. Tü 1986, Mohr. xviii-442 p.; bibliog. p. 400-419. DM 98. 3-16-145143-0 [RelStR 13,140 adv.].

2824 *a*) *Bonora* Antonio, La storiografia nel libro di Daniele; – *b*) *Garbini* Giovanni, Abramo fra i caldei di Nabonedo [sic]: ➤ 391, Storiografia 1984/6, 77-91 / 65-76.

2825 *Cantó* Josefa, Servio, los Scholia Danielis e Isɪᴅᴏʀᴏ (Etym. 18): ➤ 76, ᶠMɪᴛxᴇʟᴇɴᴀ L. 1985, 307-316.

2826 **Collins** John J., Daniel: FOTLit 20, 1984 ➤ 1,3691: ᴿAndrUnS 24 (1986) 56-62 (A.J. *Ferch*: his 167-4 dating throws caution to the wind); JTS 37 (1986) 478-484 (M. *Casey*: shows clearly how out-of-touch form critics are with ancient Jewish culture).

2827 *Coxon* Peter W., The 'list' genre and narrative style in the court tales of Daniel: JStOT 35 (1986) 95-121.

2828 **Davies** P.R., Daniel: OTGuides 4, 1985 ➤ 1,3692: ᴿBL (1986) 67 (P.W. *Coxon*); ScripB 16 (1985s) 44s (A. *Graffy*); Themelios 12 (1986s) 26 (R.W.L. *Moberly*).

ᴱDočʻanašvili E., Daniel, Georgian Mcʻḫetʻa Manuscript 1986 ➤ 1262.

2829 *Hanhart* Robert, Daniel: ➤ 587, EvKL 1 (1986) 790-2.

2830 **Jeske** John C., Daniel: The People's Bible. Milwaukee 1985, North-western Publ. 229 p. $6.50 pa. – ᴿCurrTM 13 (1986) 377s (A. V. *Sauer*: Jeske more than Daniel 'makes one wince').

2831 **Koch** K., Daniel: BK AT 22/1 [Dan 1,1-21] Neuk 1986. 80 p. DM 26,80 [ZAW 99,284, H.-C. *Schmitt*].

2832 **Lacocque** André, Daniel et son temps 1983 ➤ 64,3668... 1,3697: ᴿSalesianum 48 (1986) 164 (M. *Cimosa*); Teresianum 36 (1985) 228s (F. *Foresti*).

2832* **Mickelsen** A. Berkeley, Daniel and Revelation; riddles or realities ? 1984 ➤ 65,3287; 1,3699: ᴿBS 143 (1986) 84s (J. F. *Walvoord*: more confusion than clarity; not authentic prophecy).

2833 **Russell** D. S., ❶ Danieru-sho [Daniel 1981 ➤ 62,8868], ᵀ*Makino* R. Tokyo 1981, Shinkyō. 381 p. Y 2400 [BL 87,54].

2834 **Towner** W. Sibley, Daniel 1984 ➤ 1,3703: ᴿCBQ 48 (1986) 129 (G. W. *Buchanan*); JBL 105 (1986) 322s (J. J. *Collins*).

2834* *Wenham* David, The kingdom of God and Daniel: ExpTim 98 (1986s) 132-4.

2835 **Stanley** John E., The use of the symbol of four world empires to inspire resistance to or acceptance of Hellenism in Daniel 2, Daniel 7, 4 Ezra 11-12, Revelation 13, and [*Josephus*] Antiquities of the Jews; insights from the sociology of knowledge and sect analysis: diss. Iliff. Denver 1986. 306 p. 86-12008. – DissA 47 (1986s) 941-A.

2835* *Walton* John H., The four kingdoms of Daniel: JEvTS 29 (1986) 25-36 [< ZIT].

2836 *Calleja* Joseph, The use of Daniel 3 in the Eclogae Propheticae (chs. 1-9) of CLEMENT of Alexandria: AugR 26 (1986) 401-411.

2837 *Coxon* Peter W., The great tree of Daniel 4: ➤ 63, ꟳMcKANE W., A word 1986, 91-111.

2837* *Boogaart* T. A., Daniel 6; a tale of two empires: RefR 39 (1985s) 106-113 < ZIT].

2838 **Haag** Ernst, [Dan 6,22] Die Errettung Daniels aus der Löwengrube; Untersuchung zum Ursprung der biblischen Danieltradition: SBS 110, 1983 ➤ 64,3679 ... 1,3713: ᴿCBQ 48 (1986) 306s (G. W. *Buchanan*: confident Quellenscheidung).

2839 *Newsom* C. A., The past as revelation; history in apocalyptic literature [... Dan 7-12; 1 Henoch 80-90]; Quarterly Review 4 (1984) 40-53 [5 (1985) 96-108, *Gammie* J. G.].

2840 **Porter** Paul A., [Dan 7s] Metaphors and monsters, 1985 ➤ 1,3715: ᴿAustralBR 34 (1986) 71 (Mary *Reaburn*); BO 43 (1986) 658-660 (P. *Höffken*); ExpTim 97 (1985s) 342 (J. *Goldingay*: finds 'shepherd' dominant though unmentioned); RExp 83 (1986) 296s (J. D. W. *Watts*).

2841 *Mosca* Paul G., Ugarit and Daniel 7; a missing link: Biblica 67 (1986) 496-517; franç. 517.

2842 *a) Raabe* Paul R., Daniel 7; its structure and role in the book; – *b) Wilson* Gerald H., Wisdom in Daniel and the origin of apocalyptic: ➤ 36, Mem. GOITEIN S. = HebAnR 9 (1985) 267-275.

2843 *Shea* William H., The Neo-Babylonian historical setting for Daniel 7: AndrUnS 24 (1986) 31-36.

2844 **Betz** O., Jesus und das Danielbuch [I.: *Grimm* W. 1984 ➤ 65,3283] II. Die Menschensohnworte Jesu und die Zukunftserwartung des Paulus (Daniel 7,13-14): ArbNTJud 6/2. Fra 1985, Lang. 176 p. Fs 38 pa. 3-8204-5543-4 [NTAbs 30,349].

2845 *Manns* Frédéric, [Dan 8,16...] L'angelo Gabriele nella letteratura ebraica: TerraS 62 (1986) 12-14.

2846 *Walters* Stanley D., [Dan 8,17+] The end (of what?) is at hand : TorJT 2 (1986) 23-46.

2847 *Goldingay* John, [Dan 9] Nebuchadnezzar = Antiochus Epiphanes [same number value (*Cornill* C.) but only in Dan 1,1 spelling, of only *some* mss.]: ZAW 98 (1986) 439.

2848 *Spangenberg* I. J. J., Daniël 9; 'n voorspelling van die kruisigingsdatum van Jesus Christus?: NduitseGT 26 (1985) 271-281 [NTAbs 30,142].

2849 *a) Bogaert* Pierre-Maurice, La chronologie dans la dernière vision de Daniel (Dn 10,4 et 12,11-12); – *b) Hadas-Lebel* Mireille, Rome 'quatrième empire' et le symbole du porc: ➤ 81, Mém. NIKIPROWETZKY V., Hellenica 1986, 207-211 / 297-312.

2850 *Kooij* Arie van der, A case of reinterpretation in the Old Greek of Daniel 11: ➤ 59, ᶠLEBRAM J., Tradition 1986, 72-80.

2851 **Bacchini** M., L'utilizzazione e la trasformazione di un passo biblico (Dan. XIII,1-64) nel romanzo religioso 'La Susanna' di Ferrante PALLAVICINO (1615-1644): diss. Bologna 1985, ᴰ*Pesce* M. [RivB 35,85].

2852 **Engel** Helmut, [Dan 13] Die Susanna-Erzählung: OBO 61, 1985 ➤ 1,3723: ᴿBiblica 67 (1986) 580-6 (Zipora *Talshir*); ETL 62 (1986) 406s (J. *Lust*); RTLv 17 (1986) 222-4 (P.-M. *Bogaert*: précis et original); TR 82 (1986) 23-25 (H. *Seebass*); VT 36 (1986) 383s (W. *Horbury*); ZAW 98 (1986) 143 (H.-C. *Schmitt*); ZDMG 136 (1986) 638s (G. *Wanke*: wichtig).

2853 *Lange* Nicolas de, La lettre d'ORIGÈNE à Africanus sur l'histoire de Suzanne: SChr 302 [avec *Harl* M., Philocalie ➤ 64,e18] 1983 ➤ 65,d458: ᴿRHR 203 (1986) 76 (A. *Le Boulluec*).

2854 *Saporetti* Claudio, [Dan 13] Il primo racconto poliziesco; 'giallo' nell'antica Mesopotamia: Archeo 13 (1986) 36-39; ill.

2855 *Loewenthal* Elena, Tradizioni deuterocanoniche nel mondo ebraico medievale; Daniele, il dracone e Abacuc (Dan. 14,22-42): Henoch 8 (1986) 185-221; franç. 221s.

2856 *a) Woude* A. S. van der, Erwägungen zur Doppelsprachigkeit des Buches Daniel; – *b) Molenberg* C., [deuteroc. Dan 14] Habakkuk's dinner; an apocryphal story and its aftermath: ➤ 47, ᶠHOSPERS J., Scripta 1986, 306-316 / 155-162.

2857 *Rassart-Debergh* M., Les trois hébreux dans la fournaise en Égypt et en Nubie chrétiennes: RSO 58 (1984) 141-151.

E9.3 *Prophetae minores,* **Dodekapropheton ... Hosea, Joel.**

2858 **Deissler** Alfons, Zwölf Propheten II: Obadja, Jona, Micha, Nahum, Habakkuk: NEchter 8, 65,3306; 1,3726: ᴿCBQ 48 (1986) 304s (E. D. *Mallon*).

2859 **Holm-Nielsen** S., Tolvprofetbogen fortokelt. K 1985, Bibelselskab. 288 p. Dk 165. 87-7523-236-7 [BL 87,50, K. *Jeppesen*].

2860 **Keil** C. F., Die zwölf kleinen Propheten [= ³1888]. Giessen 1985, Brunnen. viii-718 p. DM 88. 3-7655-9204-8 [BL 87,51, R. N. *Whybray*].

2860* **Lee Chun-wing** Adam, The concept of kingship in the Book of the Twelve: diss. Southern Baptist Sem. 1986, ᴰ*Watts* J. 274 p. 86-28705. – DissA 47 (1986s) 3083s-A.

2861 ᵀ**Nishizu** Joseph, *Urano* Michael, ❶ Joel, Amos, Obadiah, Jonah, Micah, Nahum, and Habakkuk: Franciscan Biblical Institute. Tokyo

1986, Chuo Shuppansha. vi-342 p., map. Y 3500. 4-8056-8914-5 [OTAbs 10,94].

2861* a) *Abramowitz* Chaim, Hosea's true marriage: – b) *Katzoff* Louis, Hosea and the fertility cult; – c) *Bakon* Shimon, Hosea — his message: Dor 15 (1986s) 79-83 / 84-87 / 88-96.

2862 *Borbone* Pier Giorgio, Riflessioni sulla critica del testo dell'Antico Testamento ebraico in riferimento al libro di Osea: Henoch 8 (1986) 281-309; franç. 309.

2863 **Calvin** John, Hosea and Joel, ᵀ*Owen* John. E 1986, Banner of Truth. 529-xxx p. £7. – ᴿRefTR 45 (1986) 93 (R. *Swanton*).

2864 *Day* John, Pre-deuteronomic allusions to the Covenant in Hosea and Psalm LXXVIII: VT 36 (1986) 1-12.

2865 **Emmerson** Grace I., Hosea, an Israelite prophet in Judean perspective: JStOT Sup 28, 1984 → 65,3314: 1,3733: ᴿEvQ 58 (1986) 159-163 (C. J. H. *Wright*); Interpretation 40 (1986) 86s (R. F. *Melugin*); JBL 105 (1986) 529s (J. M. *Ward*); SvTKv 62 (1986) 125s (B. *Karlgren*); TLZ 111 (1986) 661s (G. *Wallis*).

2866 *Hastoupis* Athanasios P., ⑥ The book of Hosea: TAth 57 (1986) 503-520.

2867 *Holt* Else K., *Da'at Elohîm* und *chesed* im Buche Hosea: ScandJOT 1 (1986) 87-103.

2868 **Jeremias** Jörg, Der Prophet Hosea: ATD 24/1, 1983 → 64,3701... 1,3736: ᴿCBQ 48 (1986) 115s (M. J. *Buss*); FreibRu 37s (1985s) 103s (A. *Deissler*).

2869 *Jeremias* Jörg, Hosea, Hoseabuch: → 597, TRE 15 (1986) 586-598.

2870 *Neef* Heinz-Dieter, Der Septuaginta-Text und der Masoreten-Text des Hoseabuches im Vergleich: Biblica 67 (1986) 195-220; franç. 220.

2871 a) *Virgulin* Stefano, La sposa infedele in Osea; – b) *Ravasi* Gianfranco, Il rapporto uomo-donna, simbolo dell'alleanza, nei profeti: ParSpV 13 (1986) 27-39 / 41-56.

2871* a) *Kruger* Paul, Woord en Beeld in Hosea 2: NduitseGT 26 (1985) 386-403; – b) *Semriyon* Ş., [Hos 2,9] ⑥ 'I will go back to my former husband': BethM 31,107 (1985s) 293-7.

2872 *Lundbom* Jack R., Contentious priests and contentious people in Hosea IV 1-10: VT 36 (1986) 52-70.

2873 *Muraoka* Takamitsu, Hosea V in the Septuagint version: AbrNahr 24 (1986) 120-138.

2874 *Nissinen* Martti, Hos 6,1-3 repentance; true or false?: → 377a, IOSOT summaries (1986) 98.

2874* *Weiden* Wim van der, 'Barmherzigkeit will ich, nicht Opfer' [Hos 6,6; Mt 9,13; 12,7] (indonesisch): Orientasi 18 (1986) 9-24 [< TKontext 8/2,43].

2875 *Paul* Shalom M., *Maśśa' melek śārîm* — Hosea 8:8-10 and ancient Near Eastern royal epithets: → 251*, ScrHieros 31 (1986) 193-204.

2876 *Schüngel-Straumann* Helen, Gott als Mutter in Hosea 11: TüTQ 166 (1986) 119-124 [...Gynaikomorphismen als Gegenteil nicht zu Andromorphismen sondern zu Anthropomorphismen].

2877 *Gese* Hartmut, Jakob und Mose; Hosea 12:3-14 als einheitlicher Text: → 59, ꟻLEBRAM L., Tradition 1986, 38-47.

2878 *McKenzie* Steven L., The Jacob tradition in Hosea XII 4-5: VT 36 (1986) 311-322.
2878* **Franklyn** Paul N., Prophetic cursing of apostasy; the text, forms, and traditions of Hosea 13: Diss. Vanderbilt, ᴰ*Crenshaw* J., Nv 1986. 260 p. 86-26555. – DissA 47 (1986s) 3073s-A. – RelStR 13,189.

2879 *Garrett* Duane A., The structure of Joel: JEvTS 28 (1985) 289-297.
2880 *Kutsch* Ernst, Heuschreckenplage und Tag Jahwes in Joel 1 und 2 [< TZ 18 (1962) 81-94]: → 183, KʟS 1986, 231-244.
2881 **Prinsloo** W. S., The theology of the book of Joel: BZAW 163, 1985 → 1,3757: ᴿBL (1986) 94 (R. E. *Clements*).
2882 *Redditt* Paul L., The book of Joel and peripheral prophecy [515-445 B.C., not priestly]: CBQ 48 (1986) 225-240.
2883 *Tobias* Hugh, Joel, his life and times: BibIll 12 (1986) 56-59 [OTAbs 10,76].

E9.4 **Amos.**

2884 **Auld** A. Graeme, Amos: OT Guides. Sheffield 1986, JStOT. 89 p. £3. 1-85075-005-X. – ᴿExpTim 98 (1986s) 117 (C. S. *Rodd*: fine, taxing; the series is edited by R. N. Wʜʏʙʀᴀʏ and published by JStOT 'for the British Old Testament Society').
2885 **Bartczek** Günter, Prophetie und Vermittlung; zur literarischen Analyse und theologischen Interpretation der Visionsberichte des Amos [→ 62, 3914]: EurHS 23/120. Fra 1980, Lang. 330 p. – Kir Sef 59 (1985) 297.
2886 **Bjørndalen** Anders J., Untersuchungen zur allegorischen Rede der Propheten Amos und Jesaja: BZAW 165. B 1986, de Gruyter. xi-398 p.; bibliog. p. 355-387. DM 168. 3-11-010105-X. – ᴿExpTim 98 (1986s) 363s (R. *Coggins*); ZAW 98 (1986) 461 (H.-C. *Schmitt*).
2887 *Bohlen* Reinhold, Zur Sozialkritik des Propheten Amos: TrierTZ 95 (1986) 282-301.
2888 **Calvin** John, Amos and Obadiah, ᵀ*Owen* John. E 1986, Banner of Truth. 513-xvi p. £7 [RefTR 45,93].
2890 *a) Dines* Jennifer, Reading the Book of Amos: ScriptB 16 (1985s) 26-32; – *b) Finley* Thomas J., An evangelical response to the preaching of Amos: JEvTS 28 (1985) 411-420.
2891 *Kallikuzhuppil* John, Liberation in Amos and Micah: Bible Bhashyam 11 (1985) 214-223.
2892 **Leeuwen** C. van, Amos: PredikOT 1985 → 1,3764: ᴿGerefTTs 86 (1986) 183-6 (A. van der *Wal*); NedTTs 40 (1986) 334s (P. B. *Dirksen*); Streven 53 (1985s) 855 (P. *Beentjes*).
2893 **Martin-Achard** R., Re'emi S. Paul, God's people in crisis ... Amos/ Lam 1984 → 65,3343: 1,3768: ᴿBZ 30 (1986) 289s (R. *Bohlen*); CBQ 48 (1986) 725s (S. *Greenhalgh*: not related to contemporary issues as series claims).
2894 **Martin-Achard** R., Amos, l'homme, le message, l'influence 1984 → 65, 3342; 1,3767: ᴿSalesianum 48 (1986) 164s (M. *Cimosa*); ScotJT 39 (1986) 262s (A. W. *Morrison*).
2895 **Ruiz** Gregorio, Don Isaac ᴀʙʀᴀʙᴀɴᴇʟ... Amos 1984 → 65,3345; 1,3770: ᴿComSev 19 (1986) 85s (M. de *Burgos*); JBL 105 (1986) 590s (N. *Both*); JStJud 17 (1986) 117s (A. van der *Heide*).

2896 **Schmitt** A., Ein offenes Wort; das Prophetenbuch Amos für unsere Zeit erschlossen 1985 → 1,3771: RClaretianum 26 (1986) 394s (B. *Proietti*).
2897 *Thiel* Winfried, Amos: → 587, EvKL 1 (1986) 124-6.
2898 **Wal** Adri van der [→ 65,3348], *Talstra* Eep, Amos; concordance and lexical surveys: Applicatio, Informatica-toepassingen in de Theologie 2. Amst 1984, Vrije Univ. 136 p. *f*29,50 [JNWS 13,221, W. T. *Claassen*].
2899 **Witaszek** Gabriel, I profeti Amos e Micha nella lotta per la giustizia sociale nell'VIII secolo a.C.: diss. Pont. Univ. Gregoriana, N° 3325, DHamel E. R 1986. 302 p. bibliog. p. 183-205. – RTLv 18,544.

2900 *Geyer* John B., [Am 1s; Is 13-23; Jer 46-51; Ezek 25-32] Mythology and culture in the oracles against the nations: VT 36 (1986) 129-145.
2901 *Barré* Michael L., The meaning of *l' 'šybnw* in Amos 1:3-2:6: JBL 105 (1986) 611-631.
2902 **Barstad** Hans M., [Am 2,7s ...] The religious polemics of Amos ...: VT Sup 34, 1984 → 65,3354; 1,3775: RCBQ 48 (1986) 709-711 (J. D. *Newsome*).
2903 *Schenker* Adrian, Steht der Prophet unter dem Zwang zu weissagen, oder steht Israel vor der Evidenz der Weisung Gottes in der Weissagung des Propheten? Zur Interpretation von Amos 3, 3-8: BZ 30 (1986) 250-6.
2904 *Wicke* Donald W., Two perspectives (Amos 5:1-17): CurrTM 13 (1986) 89-96.
2905 *Schmitt* John J., The virgin of Israel; meaning and use of the phrase in Amos [5,2] and Jeremiah: → 377*a*, IOSOT summaries (1986) 122.
2906 *Jackson* Jared J., Amos 5,13 contextually understood: ZAW 98 (1986) 434s.
2906* *Cornick* David, [Amos 5,14s] Amos's legacy to us: ExpTim 98 (1986s) 342-4.
2907 *Hauan* Michael J., The background and meaning of Amos 5:17b: HarvTR 79 (1986) 337-348.
2908 *Smelik* K. A. D., The meaning of Amos V 18-20: VT 36 (1986) 246-8.
2909 *Hardmeier* C., [Am 7,10-17] Alttestamentliche Exegese und linguistische Erzählforschung: WDienst 18 (1985) 49-71 [=] Old Testament exegesis and linguistic narrative research: Poetics 15 (1986) 89-109 [< ZAW].
2910 *Smend* Rudolf, *a*) Das Nein des Amos [EvT 23 (1963) 404-423]; – *b*) 'Das Ende ist gekommen'; ein Amoswort in der Priesterschrift [Am 8,2; Gn 6,13; FWOLFF H. 1981, 67-72]: → 220, Mitte des ATs 1986, 85-103 / 154-9.

E9.5 Jonas.

2911 *a*) *Alexander* T. Desmond, Jonah and genre; – *b*) *Lawrence* Paul J. N., Assyrian nobles and the Book of Jonah: TyndB 36 (1985) 35-59 / 37 (1986) 121-132.
2912 **Almbladh** Karin, Studies in the Book of Jonah: AcU Semit. 7. U 1986, Almqvist & W. 53 p. 91-554-1535-0.
2913 *Artes* Allen, Jonah. Black Mountain NC 1984, Lorien. vi-58 p.; maps. [KirSef 59,313].
2914 *Butler* Vincent E., Seaweed on my head [Jonah 'partly humorous', NAB]: BToday 24 (1986) 249-253.
2914* *Christensen* Duane L., Andrzej PANUFNIK and the structure of the book of Jonah; icons, music and literary art: JEvTS 28 (1985) 133-140 [OTAbs 9,305s].

2915 ᴱDuval Y.-M., JÉRÔME, ... Sur Jonas: SChr 323, 1985 ➤ 1,3784: RÉLat 63 (1985) 285-7 (J. *Fontaine*); RHPR 66 (1986) 345 (D. A. *Bertrand*).
2915* **Ghini** Emanuela, Scandalo di un amore senza frontiere; il libro di Giona. T-Leumann 1982, Elle Di Ci. 116 p. Lit. 3000. – ᴿParVi 30 (1985) 463s (I. G. *Zedde*: due m p. 463; una p. 402; 420).
2916 *Golka* Friedemann W., Jonaxegese und Antijudaismus: KIsr 1 (1986) 51-61.
2917 *Guilmin* Serge, Jona: ÉTRel 61 (1986) 189-193.
2918 *Halpern* Baruch, *Friedman* Richard E., Composition and paronomasia in the book of Jonah: HebAnR 4 (1980) 79-92 [OTAbs 10,178].
2919 **Heinrich** Klaus, Parmenides und Jona; vier Studien über das Verhältnis von Philosophie und Mythologie. Ba 1982, Stroemfeld. 221 p., Jona 61-129 [KirSef 59,315].
2920 *Jacob* Edmond, Le prophète Jonas: Tychique 59 (1986) 23-27.
2920* *Lawrence* Paul J. N., Assyrian nobles and the book of Jonah: TyndB 37 (1986) 121-132.
2921 **Magonet** Jonathan, Form and meaning; studies in literary techniques in the book of Jonah 1983 ➤ 64,3749 ... 1,3792: ᴿTLZ 111 (1986) 495s (E. *Otto*: required reading).
2922 *Herrmann* Siegfried, Hans Walter WOLFFS Verständnis des Buches Jona [ineditum]: ➤ 171, Ges. St. 1986, 221-231.
2923 **Nowell** Irene, Jonah, Tobit, Judith: ᴵOT 25. Collegeville MN 1986, Liturgical. 94 p. $3 [TDig 33,464].
2924 *a*) *Robinson* Noel P. (f.), The Middle English *Patience*, the preacher-poet Jonah, and their common mission; – *b*) *Clark* Susan L., *Wassermann* Julian N., Jews, Gentiles and prophets; the sense of community in *Patience*: AmBenR 37 (1986) 130-142 / 230-255.
2925 **Steffen** Uwe, Jona und der Fisch; der Mythos von Tod und Wiedergeburt: Symbole. Stu 1982, Kreuz. 189 p. [KirSef 59,316].

E9.6   *Michaeas*, **Micah.**

2926 **Hillers** Delbert R., Micah: Hermeneia, 1984 ➤ 65,3380; 1,3802: ᴿInterpretation 40 (1986) 200 (C. *Graesser*); JAAR 54 (1986) 350-2 (J. L. *Mays*); Henoch 8 (1986) 401-4 (P. G. *Borbone*).
2926* **Luker** Lamontte M., Doom and hope in Micah; the redaction of the oracles attributed to an eighth-century prophet: diss. Vanderbilt, ᴰ*Harrelson* W. Nv 1985. 86-07519. – DissA 47 (1986s) 559-A; RelStR 13,189.
2927 **Smith** Ralph L., Micah-Malachi: Word Comm 32, 1984 ➤ 65,3383; 1,3807: ᴿCBQ 48 (1986) 730s (G. M. *Tucker*); JBL 105 (1986) 532s (L. *Boadt*); RefTR 45 (1986) 25s (J. *Woodhouse*: less independent judgment than some of the series).
2927* **Wolff** Hans Walter, Dodekapropheton 4: Micha: BK 14/4, 1982 ➤ 63,3871 ... 1,3808: ᴿFreibRu 37s (1985s) 107s (D. *Kinet*).
2928 *Woude* A. S. van der, Profeet en Establishment ... Micha 1985 ➤ 1,3809: ᴿBL (1986) 83 (P. R. *Ackroyd*); Streven 53 (1985s) 950 (P. *Beentjes*); TsTNijm 26 (1986) 177s (L. *Grollenberg*).

2929 *Álvarez Barredo* Miguel, El abuso de poder y los derechos humanos in Mi 2,1-5: Carthaginensia 2 (1986) 129-144.

2930 *Vincent* Jean M., Michas Gerichtswort gegen Zion (3,12) in seinem Kontext: ZTK 83 (1986) 167-187.

2931 *Cathcart* Kevin J., *Jeppesen* Knut, More suggestions on Mic 6,14: ScandJOT 1 (1986) 110-5.

2932 *Grelot* Pierre, Michée 7,6 dans les évangiles et dans la littérature rabbinique: Biblica 67 (1986) 363-377.

E9.7 *Abdias, Sophonias...* Obadiah, Zephaniah, Nahum.

2933 *Renaud* B., Le livre de Sophonie; le jour de YHWH thème structurant de la synthèse rédactionnelle: RevSR 60 (1986) 1-33.

2934 **Seybold** Klaus, Satirische Prophetie; Studien zum Buch Zefanja. Stu 1985, KBW. 121 p. DM 26,80. 3-460-04201-X. – ᴿStreven 53 (1985s) 951s (P. *Beentjes*).

2935 *Zalcman* Lawrence, Ambiguity and assonance at Zephaniah II 4: VT 36 (1986) 365-371.

2936 *Achtemeier* Elizabeth, Nahum — Malachi: Interpretation Comm. Atlanta 1986, Knox. x-201 p. 0-8042-3129-X.

2937 **Coggins** R., (*Réemi* S.), Israel among the nations [Nah Obad (Esth)] 1985 1,3822: ᴿComSev 19 (1986) 430 (V. J. *Ansede Alonso*); Themelios 12 (1986s) 94 (M. J. *Selman*).

2938 **Heflin** J. N. Boo, Nahum, Habakkuk, Zephaniah, and Haggai: Bible Study Commentary. GR 1985, Zondervan. 190 p. $8. – ᴿSWJT 29 (1986s) 52 (H. B. *Hunt*).

2938* **House** Paul R., Zephaniah as a prophetic drama: diss. Southern Baptist Theol. Sem. 1985, ᴰ*Watts* J. 216 p. 86-19032. – DissA 47 (1986s) 2188-A.

E9.8 *Habacuc,* Habakkuk.

2939 *Gunneweg* A. H. J., Habakuk und das Problem des leidenden Ṣaddîq: ZAW 98 (1986) 400-415.

2939* **Haak** Robert D., Habakkuk among the prophets: diss. ᴰ*Ahlström* G. Ch 1986. 463 p. – RTLv 18,541.

2940 **Lloyd-Jones** David M., From fear to faith; studies in the book of Habakkuk: Summit. GR 1982 = c. 1950, Baker. [KirSef 59,303].

2941 **Nitzan** Bilha, ⊙ Pesher Habakkuk, a scroll from the wilderness of Judaea (1Q pHab), text, introduction and commentary. J 1986, Bialik. xviii-222 p. [RQum 47,455].

2942 *Ortega Monasterio* Maria Teresa, Las Masoras de A, C y L en el libro de Habacuc: Henoch 8 (1986) 149-184; franç. 184.

2943 *Peckham* Brian, The vision of Habakkuk: CBQ 48 (1986) 617-636.

2943* *Ahuvia* Abraham, ⊙ [Hab 1,1-2,4] Why do you look on faithless men? [Hab 1,13]: BethM 31,107 (1985s) 320-7.

2944 *a) Cathcart* Kevin J., Legal terminology in Habakkuk 2: 1-4: PrIrB 10 (1986) 103-110; – *b) Zuurmond* R., De rechtvaardige zal door geloof leven; Habakkuk 2:4 bij Joden en Christenen vóór het jaar 135: AmstCah 6 (1985) 162-173.

2945 **Hiebert** Theodore, God of my victory; the ancient hymn in Habakkuk 3: HarvSemMon 38. Atlanta 1986, Scholars. xii-205 p. $17.

2947 *Tsumura* David T.,   Niphal with an internal object in Habakkuk 3:9a:
JSS 31 (1986) 11-16.

E9.9   *Aggaeus,* **Haggai** – *Zacharias,* **Zechariah** – *Malachias,* **Malachi.**

2950 **Petersen** David L.,   Haggai and Zechariah 1-8, 1984 → 65,3408; 1,3835:
ᴿBiblica 67 (1986) 119s (J. A. *Soggin*); BL (1986) 57 (R. A. *Mason*); CBQ
48 (1986) 311s (E. M. *Meyers*: praise with a couple of queries); CurrTM 13
(1986) 47s (R. W. *Klein*: first comprehensive and insightful commentary in
English); Interpretation 40 (1986) 186-8 (R. F. *Melugin*); JBL 105 (1986)
716s (Carol *Meyers*); RB 93 (1986) 147s (R. J. *Tournay*).
2952 **Sakkos** Sergios N., Ⓖ *Hypomnema...* Memoir on the prophet Haggai.
Thessaloniki 1984. 92 p. – ᴿTAth 57 (1986) 261s (P. *Simotas*).
2954 **Wolff** H. W.,   Dodekapropheton 6. Haggai: BK 14/6. Neuk 1986.
ix-100 p. DM 42, sb. 38. 3-7887-1244-9 [BL 87,57, R. N. *Whybray*].
2955 *Prinsloo* W. S.,   The cohesion of Haggai 1:4-11: → 377*a*, IOSOT
summaries (1986) 106.

2956 **Bergdall** Chaney R.,   Zechariah's program of restoration; a rhetorical
critical study of Zechariah 1-8: diss. Fuller, ᴰ*Bush* F. Pasadena 1986.
302 p. 86-19157. – DissA 47 (1986s) 2187-A.
2957 **Cataldo** Antonio,   CIRILLO d'Alessandria, Commento ai profeti minori
Zaccaria e Malachia: Testi Patristici 60. R 1986, Città Nuova. 378 p.
2958 **Ruffin** Michael L.,   Symbolism in Zechariah; a study in functional unity:
diss. Southern Baptist Theol. Sem. 1986, ᴰ*Watts* J. 249 p. 86-19034. –
DissA 47 (1986s) 2189s-A.
2959 **Schöttler** Heinz-G.,   Gottes heiliges Volk und die Heidenvölker; die
Neuordnung des Gottesvolkes nach Sach 1-6: Diss. Trier 1985s, ᴰ*Haag* E.
– TR 82 (1986) 513.
2960 **Woude** A. S. van der, Zacharia: PredikOT, 1984 → 65,3413; 1,3842: ᴿBijdragen 47 (1986) 58s (P. C. *Beentjes*).
2961 *Richter* Hans-F.,   Die Pferde in den Nachtgesichten des Sacharja: ZAW
98 (1986) 96-100.
2962 *Stuhlmueller* Carroll, [Zc 9,1-10 ...] Justice toward the poor: BToday 24
(1986) 385-390.
2963 *Garbini* Giovanni,   La luce di Zaccaria 14,6: Henoch 8 (1986) 311-8;
franç. 318s.

2964 **Kaiser** Walter C.ᴶ,   Malachi; God's unchanging love 1984 → 65,3423:
ᴿCBQ 48 (1986) 537s (B. E. *Shafer*: new genus, not approved); Themelios
12 (1986s) 27 (E. C. *Lucas*).
2965 *Klein* Ralph W.,   A valentine for those who fear Yahweh; the book of
Malachi: CurrTM 13 (1986) 143-152.
2966 *Or* Daniel, Ⓞ Malachi, last of the prophets, and his link to Moses:
BethM 31,107 (1985s) 316-9.
2967 **Paterson** Robert M.,   Kitab nabi Maleakhi. Jakarta 1985, Gunung
Mulia. 60 p. Rp 860. – ᴿOTAbs 9 (1986) 337 (*ipse*).
2968 *Snyman* S. D.,   Antitheses in the Book of Malachi: *a*) → 377*a*, IOSOT
summaries (1986) 128; – *b*) in Malachi 1, 2-5: ZAW 98 (1986) 436-8.
2969 *Woude* A. S. van der,   Malachi's struggle for a pure community;

reflections on Malachi 2: 10-16: ➤ 59, FLEBRAM J., Tradition 1986, 65-71.
2970 *Glazier-McDonald* Beth, Malachi 2:12, '*ēr we'ōneh* — another look: JBL 105 (1986) 295-8.

IX. NT Exegesis Generalis

F1.   **New Testament Introduction.**

2971 *Block* Per, Teorier om kristendomens uppkomst; utkast till en typologi: SvEx 51s (1986s) 23-31.
2972 **Brown** Schuyler. The origins of Christianity; a historical introduction to the NT 1984 ➤ 54, 3433; 1,3855*:   RSR 15 (1986) 118s (R. *Crouse*); TLZ 11 (1986) 191s (G. *Haufe*).
2972* **Charlesworth** J. H., The background and foreground of Christian origins: PrIrB 10 (1986) 40-54.
2973 **Childs** Brevard S.,   The New Testament as canon; an introduction ➤ 65,3446; 1,3858:   RAustralBR (1986) 72s (N. M. *Watson*); Interpretation 40 (1986) 407-411 (D. Moody *Smith*); JTS 37 (1986) 161-4 (M. *Davies*); TLond 39 (1986) 60-62 (J. *Drury*: does boldly what so many do covertly, subjecting the whole historical process to revealed dogma).
2974 **Chilton** Bruce, Beginning New Testament study. L 1986, SPCK. xii-196 p.; map. £6.   0-281-04210-1. – RCleR 71 (1986) 462s (J. R. *Duckworth*); ExpTim 98 (1986s) 214 (Margaret *Davies*: better than Linda FOSTER).
2975 **Collins** Raymond F.,   Introduction to the NT 1984 ➤ 64,3810 ... 1,3859: REvQ 58 (1986) 166-8 (S. *Travis*); Neotestamentica 20 (1986) 70s (Mrs C. *Kourie*).
2976 **Conzelmann** Hans, **Lindemann** Andreas,   Arbeitsbuch zum Neuen Testament[8]: Uni-TB 52.   1985.   xvi-458 p.   3-26-145007-8.
2977 **Conzelmann** Hans, **Lindemann** Andreas, Guida allo studio del NT, TE*Pesce* M.   Casale M 1986, Marietti. xvi-454 p. Lit. 46.000. – RRClerIt 67 (1986) 718s (G. *Borgonovo*).
2978 **Cullmann** Oscar,   Einführung in das NT[2] [[1]1966, Que sais-je? 1231 ➤ 48,109], T*Vogelsanger-de Roche* I: Siebenstern 1409. Gü 1984, Mohn. 158 p.   DM 9,80. – RTLZ 111 (1986) 23s (P. *Pokorný*).
2979 **Dahmus** J.,   The puzzling gospels; suggested explanations of puzzling passages in Matthew, Mark, Luke and John: Basics of Christian Thought 3. Ch 1985, More.   168 p. $11.   0-88347-182-5 [NTAbs 30,351].
2980 **Dalbesio** Anselmo.   Il vangelo; storia di un libro e di un'esperienza di fede 1979 [1981 ➤ 63,4144]: RRivLtg 73 (1986) 428s (G. *Crocetti*).
2981 **Derron** Pascale, PHOCYLIDÈS, Sentences: Coll. Budé. P 1986, BLettres. cxvi-55 (doubles) p.   2-352-00385-1.
2982 **Egger** Wilhelm,   Kleine Bibelkunde zum Neuen Testament 1984 ➤ 63,3440; auch Lp 1985, St. Benno. 152 p.
2983 **Ernst** Josef, *Backhaus* Knut, Studium Neues Testament.   Pd 1986, Bonifatius.   122 p. DM 12,80. – RTR 82 (1986) 454 (O. B. *Knoch*).
2984 **Freed** Edwin D.,   The New Testament; a critical introduction. Belmont CA 1986, Wadsworth.   xiii-449 p.; 25 phot. $27.   0-534-05388-2 [NTAbs 30,217].
2985 **Giesen** Heinz, Jesustradition, das Evangelium und die Evangelien [*Stuhlmacher* P. 1983; *Cancik* H. 1984]: TGgw 29 (1986) 47-55.

2985* a) *Guillet* Jacques, L'Évangile; du bonheur à la joie; – b) *Dumas* André, Le bonheur, sujet biblique: QuatreF 23s (1986) 21-31 / 9-19.
2986 **Hock** Ronald F., *O'Neil* Edward N., The chreia [propaedeutic anecdote] in ancient rhetoric, I. The progymnasmata: SBL TTr 27, GrRRel 9, 1985 ➤ 1,3863* : ᴿRelStR 12 (1986) 289 (R. P. *Sonkowsky*).
2987 **Hoerber** R. G., Reading the New Testament for understanding. St. Louis 1986, Concordia. 211 p.; 4 maps. $7.50 pa. 0-570-03988-6 [NTAbs 31,92].
2988 *Hommel* Hildebrecht, Sebasmata... zum frühen Christentum 1983s ➤ 65,202: ᴿCurrTM 13 (1986) 56s (E. *Krentz* praises as reminder of Hommel's seminar Antikes im NT which he attended).
2989 **Johnson** L. T., The writings of the New Testament, an interpretation. Ph 1986, Fortress. xiv-593 p. $35; pa. $19. 0-8006-0886-0; 6 [NTAbs 31,92]. – ᴿTS 47 (1986) 699s (D. J. *Harrington*).
2990 *Kantzenbach* Friedrich W., Häresie oder Methodenzwang? [*Berger* P. 1980; *Mayer* A. 1983 ...]: ZRGg 38 (1986) 49-57.
2991 *Linstrand* Jan F., Diogenes LAERTIUS and the *Chreia* tradition: ➤ 529, D. Laerzio 1985 = Elenchos 7 (1986) 217-243.
2992 **Koester** Helmut, Introduction to the NT 1982 ➤ 64,3828b... 1,3873: ᴿRÉAug 31 (1985) 144s (A. *Le Boulluec*); ScotJT 39 (1986) 133-5 (J. D. G. *Dunn*).
2992* **Lohse** E., L'ambiente del Nuovo Testamento 1980 ➤ 61,5171b... 1,3877: ᴿSTEv 15 (1985) 127-132 (M. *Clemente*).
2993 **Loi** Vincenzo, Le origini del cristianesimo 1984 ➤ 1,3878: ᴿCC 137 (1986,1) 307 (N. *Uricchio*).
2994 **Ludwig** Charles, Ludwig's handbook of New Testament rulers and cities [= ²Cities/Rulers in NT times 1976]. Denver 1983, Accent. 243 p. $7 pa. – ᴿCalvaryB 2,1 (1986) 67s (G. H. *Lovik*).
2995 **Maass** Fritz [O. EISSFELDTs Mitherausgeber], Was ist Christentum ? ³ Tü 1982. 148 p. – ᴿDiehlB 22 (1985) 222-5 (B. J. *Diebner*, unter Titel 'Die christliche Weltrevolution ist fällig').
2996 a) *Mackay* Peter W., The coming revolution; the new literary approaches to the New Testament [< Theological Educator 9 (1979) 32-46]; – b) *Keifert* Patrick R., Mind reader and maestro; models for understanding biblical interpreters [< WWorld 1 (1980) 153-168]: ➤ 259, ᴱ*McKim* D., Hermeneutics 1986, 263-279 / 200-238.
2997 **Mann** D., Mit dem Neuen Testament im Gespräch, I. Evangelien und Apostelgeschichte: Arbeitsbücherei für den Hauskreis 1. Konstanz 1985, Christliche V-A. 159 p DM 14,80. – ᴿSNTU-A 11 (1986) 217s (A. *Fuchs*).
2998 **Marxsen** Willi, Introducción al NT 1983 ➤ 64,3832... 1,3882: ᴿEstE 61 (1986) 81s (F. *Pastor Ramos*).
2999 *Marxsen* W., Orientierung am Neuen Testament?: Pastoraltheologie 74 (1985) 2-16.
3000 **Michiels** Robrecht, Evangelie en evangelies: Nikè-Didachè 1. Amersfoort 1986, Acco. 184 p. *f*29,75. 90-334-0933-X. – ᴿCollatVl 16 (1986) 499 (P. *Schmidt*).
3001 **Minette de Tillesse** C., Evangelho = Revista Bíblica Brasileira 2 (Fortaleza 1985) 109-136; 3 (1986) 5-31.37-68.77-95.101-119.125-154 [NRT 109,741, X. *Jacques*].
3002 *Moloney* Francis J., The living voice of the Gospel; the Gospels today. NY 1986, Paulist. xii-252 p. 0-8091-2887-X.
3002* **Nash** Ronald H., Christianity and the Hellenistic world 1984 ➤ 65, 3462: ᴿBS 143 (1986) 173s (J. A. *Witmer*).

3003 **Newbigin** Lesslie, Foolishness to the Greeks. GR/L 1986, Eerdmans/SPCK. 156 p. $8. 0-8028-0176-5 / 0-281-04232-2. – ᴿExpTim 98 (1986s) 65s (C. S. *Rodd*: the Christian Bible has to be read within a believing community).

3004 **Reese** James M., Experiencing the Good News; the NT as communication; Good News Studies 10, 1984 ➤ 65,3842; 1, 3889: ᴿCBQ 148 (1986) 148s (Mary C. *Boys*).

3005 **Robinson** Donald, abp. Faith's framework; the structure of the NT. Exeter c. 1985, Paternoster. 152 p. £4.20. – ᴿKerkT 37 (1986) 70 (G. de *Ru*).

3006 *Robinson* James M., The Gospels as narrative [counters *Childs* B.]: ➤ 385, ᴱ*McConnell* F., Bible and narrative 1983/6...

3007 **Roetzel** Calvin J., The world that shaped the New Testament. Atlanta 1985, Knox. ix-120 p. 0-8042-0455-1. – ᴿChH 55 (1986) 508-510 (R. M. *Grant*).

3007* **Rouet** Albert, Hombres y cosas del Nuevo Testamento 1982 ➤ 63, 3942*b*; 64,3841: ᴿBrotéria 122 (1986) 236s (F. de Sales *Baptista*).

3008 *a*) *Rougier* L., Jean-Baptiste et Jésus; deux évangiles télescopés; – *b*) *Chevalon* M., Désordre et contradictions dans les Écritures [NT]; CahRenan 33,139 (1985) 29-32 / 34,144 (1986) 31-35 [NTAbs 30,268s].

3009 **Scott** B. B., The Word of God in words; reading and preaching the Gospels: Resources for Preaching. Ph 1985, Fortress. 94 p. $5 pa. 0-8006-1142-X [NTAbs 30,357].

3010 **Segalla** Giuseppe, Panorama letterario del Nuovo Testamento [Panorama storico 1984 ➤ 9614; teologico, atteso]: LoB 3,6. Brescia 1986, Queriniana. 247 p. Lit. 20.000 [NRT 109,736s, X. *Jacques*].

3011 ᴱ**Segovia** Fernando F., Discipleship in the NT [Marquette symposium, Milwaukee 15-17.IV.1982] 1985 ➤ 1,491, not '*and* the NT': ᴿCBQ 48 (1986) 771s (J. *Kodell*; should become normative format for such collections... notes after each chapter); ExpTim 97 (1985s) 378s (B. G. *Powley*: KELBER challengingly holds Mark wrote against gnosticizing portrayal of Jesus as bearer of secret words); Themelios 12 (1986s) 62 (H. J. B. *Combrink*); TS 48 (1986) 350-2 (D. *Goldsmith*).

3012 **Stuhlmacher** Peter, Vom Verstehen des Neuen Testaments; eine Hermeneutik²ʳᵉᵛ [¹1979 ➤ 60,5334]: NTD Grundrisse 6. Gö 1986, Vandenhoeck & R. 275 p.; bibliog. p. 257-265. 3-525-51355-6.

3013 *Stuhlmacher* Peter, Evangelium: ➤ 587, EvKL 1 (1986) 1217-1221.

3014 **Tenney** Merrill C., [¹1953, ²1961] ³ʳᵉᵛ *Dunnett* Walter M. 1985 ➤ 1,3898: AndrUnS 24 (1986) 199s (R. M. *Johnston*); RExp 83 (1986) 299 (R. L. *Omanson*: presuppositions).

3015 **Thiemann** Ronald F., Revelation and theology; the Gospels as narrated promise. ND 1985, Univ. 272 p. $24 [BToday 24,268].

3016 **Thivollier** Pierre, The Gospel story [pictures, cartoons, text]ᵀ. Sydney 1985, CCD. 384 p. A$24. – ᴿAustralasCR 63 (1986) 342 (B. *Lucas*).

3017 **Walsh** Michael, The triumph of the meek; why early Christianity succeeded. L/SF 1986, Boxby/ Harper & R. 256 p. $18 [JBL 105,756].

3018 **Weaver** Mary Jo, Introduction to Christianity. Belmont CA 1984, Wadsworth. xx-268 p. – ᴿSR 15 (1986) 411 (H. *Remus*: for collegians ignorant of the diversity of Christianity).

3019 **Weder** Hans, Neutestamentliche Hermeneutik: Grundrisse zur Bibel. Z 1986, Theol.-V. 452 p.; bibliog. p. 436-8; 441-452.

3020 ᴱ**Wenham** David, The Jesus tradition outside the Gospels [1 Cor... 1 Pt...] 1985 ➤ 1,317: ᴿJTS 37 (1986) 540-3 (A. J. M. *Wedderburn*).

3021 **Wikenhauser** A. [1952], ²*Schmid* J., Introduzione al NT, ᵀᴱ*Montagnini* F. 1981 ➤ 62,4045 ... 1,3902: ᴿHenoch 8 (1986) 100s (A. *Moda*).

3022 **Wrege** Hans-Theo, Wirkungsgeschichte des Evangeliums; Erfahrungen, Perspektiven und Möglichkeiten 1981 ➤ 62,4046; 64,3850: ᴿZRGg 38 (1986) 71 (F. W. *Kantzenbach*).

3022* **Young** John, The case against Christ [suavely demolished]. L 1986, Hodder & S. 206 p. £2. 0-340-39371-8 [ExpTim 98,286].

F1.2   *Origo Evangeliorum;* the Origin of the Gospels.

3023 *Berger* Paul-Richard, Zum Aramäischen der Evangelien und der Apostelgeschichte [*Black* M. ³1967, ᵀ*Schwarz* G. 1982]: TR 82 (1986) 1-18 (17-22, *Black*, Erwiderung).

3024 *Breytenbach* Cilliers, Das Problem des Übergangs von mündlicher zu schrifticher Überlieferung: Neotestamentica 20 (1986) 46-57.

3025 **Crossan** John Dominic, Sayings parallels; a workbook for the Jesus tradition: Foundations & Facets NT. Ph 1986, Fortress. xx-233 p. $15. ➤ 8109, *Cameron* R.

3026 **Foster** Linda, Four for the Gospel makers. L 1986, SCM. 127 p. £4. 0-334-02005-0 [JStNT 27,120].

3027 **Gerhardsson** Birger, The Gospel tradition: ConBibNT 15. Lund 1986, Liber. 47 p.

3028 **Grelot** Pierre, Évangiles et tradition apostolique ... 'Christ hébreu' 1984 ➤ 65,3488; 1,3911: ᴿAngelicum 63 (1986) 129 (S. *Parsons*); Salesianum 48 (1986) 429 (M. *Cimosa*: pericolo per la Chiesa).

3029 **Grelot** Pierre, L'origine des Évangiles; controverse avec J. CARMIGNAC [†]: Apologique. P 1986, Cerf. 154 p. F 82 [NRT 109,425, X. *Jacques*]. 2-204-02608-5.

3029* **Hengel** Martin, Die Evangelienüberschriften: Szb Heid ph/h 1984/3. Heid 1984, Winter. 51 p. [NedTTS 41,315, T. *Baarda*].

3030 *Hurst* L. D., The neglected role of semantics in the search for the Aramaic words of Jesus: JStNT 28 (1986) 63-80.

3031 **Kelber** Werner H., The oral and the written Gospel 1983 ➤ 64,3877; 65,3491: ᴿInterpretation 40 (1986) 72-75 (J. D. G. *Dunn*); TorJT 2 (1986) 149-151 (J. S. *Kloppenborg*).

3032 **Kelly** Joseph, Why is there a New Testament?: Background Books 5. Wilmington/L 1986, Glazier/ Chapman. 200 p. $9 pa. [TDig 34,79]. 0-225-66483-6/.

3033 **Meagher** John C., Five gospels; an account of how the Good News came to be 1983 ➤ 64,3880 ... 1,3914: ᴿÉglT 17 (1986) 238-240 (W. *Vogels*).

3034 **Perrier** Pierre, Karozoutha; annonce orale de la bonne nouvelle en araméen et Évangiles gréco-latins. P/Montréal 1986, Médiaspaul/Paulines. 704 p. F 220 [MélSR 43,227]. P 2-7122-0248-1/ M 2-89039-344-5.

3035 **Pokorný** Petr, Zur Entstehung der Evangelien [SNTS main paper, Trondheim 1985]: NTS 32 (1986) 393-403.

3036 *Rasco* Emilio, Deformación y formación de los Evangelios; de Claude TRESMONTANT a Pierre GRELOT: Gregorianum 67 (1986) 329-339.

3037 **Riesner** Rainer, Jesus als Lehrer² [< Diss.]; WUNT 7, 1984 ➤ 62,4080 ... 1,3917: ᴿStudia Monastica 28 (Barc 1986)) 221 (A. *Iturrialde*).

3039 *De Santis* Luca, Per una riflessione criteriologica in vista della definizione del genere letterario dei vangeli canonici: Angelicum 63 (1986) 169-186.

3040 **Schenk** Wolfgang, Evangelium — Evangelien — Evangeliologie; ein

'hermeneutisches' Manifest: TExH 216. Mü c. 1985, Kaiser. 128 p. –
RRechSR 74 (1986) 233-5 (J. *Guillet*).
3041 **Schwarz** Günther, 'Und Jesus sprach'; Untersuchungen zur aramäischen
Urgestalt der Worte Jesu: BWANT 118, 1985 ➤ 1,3919:   RBL (1986) 136s
(J. A. *Emerton*); CBQ 48 (1986) 571-3 (D. J. *Harrington*: methodological
snares); TPQ 134 (1986) 77 (A. *Fuchs*).
3042 *Spadafora* Francesco,   Data di composizione degli Evangeli [*Robinson* J.,
Redating 1976; *Tresmontant* C. 1983; *Carmignac* J. 1984]:   Divinitas 30
(1986) 78-84.
3043 ᴱ**Stuhlmacher** Peter,   Das Evangelium und die Evangelien 1982/3 ➤ 64,
428: RBZ 30 (1986) 129-132 (H. *Merklein*); HeythJ 27 (1986) 73 (B. *McNeil*);
RechSR 74 (1986) 229-233 (J. *Guillet*); TLZ 111 (1986) 507-510 (J. *Roloff*).

F1.3   **Historicitas**, *chronologia* **Evangeliorum.**

3044 **Dockx** S. † 9.XI.1985,   Chronologies néotestamentaires [²; ¹1976] et Vie
de l'Église primitive; recherches exégétiques 1984 ➤ 65,3509;   1,3924:
REsprV 96 (1986) 110 (L. *Walter*: dix études séparées); ETL 62 (1986) 434s
(F. *Neirynck*); JTS 37 (1986) 200-2 (F. F. *Bruce*).
3045 *France* R. T.,   Chronological aspects of 'Gospel Harmony':   VoxEvca 16
(1986) 33-59.
3046 [*George* A. †] **Grelot** P., Évangiles et histoire / Les Paroles de Jésus-Christi
Introduction a la Bible III. NT, 6s³. P 1986, Desclée.   338 p.; 364 p.; F
168 chaque. 2-7189-0292-2; 3-9. – REsprV 96 (1986) 545-7 (É. *Cothenet*);
Études 365 (1986) 119s (P. *Gibert*); MélSR 43 (1986) 208-210 (M. *Hubaut*);
RICathP (1986) 125s (M. *Quesnel*) & 127-9 (M. *Morgen*); VSp 140 (1986)
724s (T. *Chary*).
3047 *Léon-Dufour* Xavier,   I vangeli e la storia di Gesù ⁵ [1963],   ᵀ*Rossano*
Piero: Parola di Dio 2/4. Cinisello Balsamo MI 1986, Paoline.   544 p.
88-215-0586-9.
3048 *Merkley* Paul,   The Gospels as historical testimony: EvQ 58 (1986) 319-336.
3049 **Ory** Armand.   Riscoprire la verità storica dei Vangeli; una iniziazione all'esegesi funzionale [ned. 1978; Initiation 1984 ➤ 1,3930], ᵀ*Terribile* Sergio: Sorgenti di Vita 18.   Mi 1986, Massimo.   239 p. Lit. 15.000.   88-7030- 720-4.
3050 **Robinson** J. A. T.,   Possiamo fidarsi del NT? [1977 ➤ 58s,702] 1980
➤ 62,4115: RProtestantesimo 41 (1986) 168s (P. *De Petris*).
3051 **Robinson** John A. T.,   Wann entstand das Neue Testament? [Redating
1976 ➤ 57,223; ⁴1981], ᵀ*Madey* Johannes.   Pd/Wu 1986, Bonifatius/
Brockhaus. 383 p. DM 32. – RBiKi 41 (1986) 185s (P.-G. *Müller*).
3052 *Ellis* E. Earle,   Die Datierung des Neuen Testaments [*Robinson* J. A. T.
1976; SNTS 1979], ᵀ*Betz* Isolde: TZBas 42 (1986) 409-430: even if
Robinson is not right in all details, the traditional NT dating rests on feeble
foundations.
3054 **Stott** J. R. W.,   The authentic Jesus; the certainty of Christ in a skeptical
world [against recent disturbing theological statements]. DG 1985,
Inter-Varsity.   95 p. $3 pa. 0-87784-619-7 [NTAbs 30, 357].
3055 **Wilson** Ian,   Jesus, the evidence 1985 ➤ 1,3932 but L 1984, Weidenfeld &
N. 207 p. £11: RScotJT 39 (1986) 126-8 (P. *Forster*).

F1.4   *Jesus historicus* –   **The human Jesus.**

3055* *Agouridis* Sabbas, ⑤ Investigation of the 'historical Jesus' by recent
European research [*sképsis*]: DeltioVM 15,2 (1986) 5-22.

3056 **Alfonso** Regina M., How Jesus taught; the methods and techniques of the master. Staten Island 1986, Alba. xiii-129 p. $7 pa. [TDig 34,57].

3057 **Anderson** Norman, The teaching of Jesus 1983 ➤ 64,3907; 65,3523; ᴿEvQ 58 (1986) 169 (S. *Travis*: gathers momentum as it goes).

3058 *Ardusso* Franco, Dalle 'Vite di Gesù' alla 'Storia di Gesù; 1. Da LANDOLFO a RENAN; 2. Prima e dopo BULTMANN: 3. In Francia e Italia fino a RICCIOTTI; 4. Da Bultmann a oggi: ParVi 31 (1986) 66-72 / 123-6 / 212-220 / 288-295.

3059 **Badia** Leonard F., Jesus, introducing his life and teaching 1985 ➤ 1,3934; 0-8091-2689-3: ᴿTS 47 (1986) 551 (J. H. *McKenna*: simple).

3059* **Barr** James, Exegesis as a theological discipline reconsidered and the shadow of the Jesus of history: ➤ 69, ᶠMAYS J., Hermeneutical Quest 1986, 11-45 [also published separately by Union Theological Seminary, Richmond].

·3060 **Baumotte** Manfred, Die Frage nach dem historischen Jesus; Texte aus drei Jahrhunderten: Reader Theologie 1984 ➤ 65,3525: ᴿActuBbg 23 (1986) 98 (J. *Boada*); ZKG 97 (1986) 261s (W. *Schmithals*).

3060* *Beaude* Pierre-Marie, Per leggere Gesù di Nazaret [Jésus de N. 1983 ➤ 64,3909], ᵀ*De Rosa* R. R 1985, Borla. 128 p. Lit. 12.000. – ᴿLetture 41 (1986) 684s (G. *Ravasi*); StPatav 33 (1986) 453s (G. *Segalla*).

3061 *Blank* J., Karl BARTH und die Frage nach dem irdischen Jesus: ZDialT 2 (Kampen 1986) 176-192 [< ZIT].

3061* **Blázquez** Ricardo, Jesús, el evangelio de Dios. M 1985, Marova. 309 p. – ᴿNatGrac 33 (1986) 175 (D. *Montero*).

3062 **Braun** Herbert, Jesus — der Mann aus Nazareth und seine Zeit [1969 ➤ 51,2632; um 12 Kapitel erweiterte Studienausgabe: Radikalität; Qumran]. Stu 1984, Kreuz. 3-7831-0758-X. – ᴿEstE 61 (1986) 459s [J. *García Pérez*]; ÉTRel 61 (1986) 425-7 (F. *Vouga*: passé trop inaperçu à côté de KÄSEMANN, BORNKAMM).

3063 **Bredin** Eamonn, *a)* Rediscovering Jesus; challenge of discipleship. Blackrock-Dublin/Mystic CT 1986, Columba/Twenty-Third. xiii-289 p. $10 pa. [JBL 105,750]. – *b)* Disturbing the peace; the way of disciples [... historical truth of the Gospels]. Dublin 1985, Columba. 318 p. £8 pa. – ᴿDoctLife 36 (1986) 218s (G. J. *Norton*).

3064 **Bruce** F. F., *a)* Jesus, Lord and Savior: The Jesus Library. DG 1986, Inter-Varsity. 228 p. $8 pa. 0-87784-932-3. – *b)* The Real Jesus. L 1985, Hodder & S. 232 p. £6. 0-340-38174-4 [ExpTim 98,223].

3065 **Castillo** José M., *Estrada* Juan A., El proyecto de Jesús: Verdad e imagen 94, 1983/5 ➤ 1,553: ᴿQVidCr 131s (1986) 231s (J. *Bosch*); RazF 213 (1986) 439s (R. de *Andrés*); TVida 27 (1986) 230s (M. *Arias Reyero*); VerVid 44 (1986) 468 (V. *Casas*).

3066 *Charlesworth* James H., *a)* Research on the historical Jesus: PrIrB 9 (1985) 19-37 [NTAbs 30,270]; *b)* From barren mazes to gentile rappings; the emergence of Jesus research: PrincSemB 7 (1986) 221-230 [< ZIT].

3067 **Doriga** Enrique L., Semblanza de Jesucristo. Barc 1986, Herder. 73 p. – ᴿLumenV 35 (1986) 565 (F. *Ortiz de Urtaran*).

3068 **Doyon** Jacques, L'option fondamentale de Jésus: Notre temps 28. Montréal/P 1984, Paulines/Médiaspaul. 214 p. – ᴿÉglT 17 (1986) 240s (N. *Provencher*).

3069 **Doyon** Jacques, Love before the Law; Jesus Christ's fundamental option. Slough 1986, St. Paul. 184 p. £5.25. 0-85439-250-5. – ᴿExpTim 98 (1986s) 27 (E. *Franklin*: orthodox but trivial).

3070 **Drane** John W., Jésus et les quatre évangiles [1979], TLaroche F., 1984 ► 65,3538: ᴿVSp 139 (1985) 258 (L. Dewailly).

3071 **Dunn** James D. G., The evidence for Jesus [to straighten out a 1984 BBC broadcast]. Ph 1985, Westminster. xlv-113. $9 [RelStR 13, 262, R. H. Fuller].

3071* **Eichholz** G., Das Rätsel des historischen Jesus 1984 ► 65,3542: ᴿSt-Patav 33 (1986) 438 (G. Segalla).

3072 Ellis Ieuan, Dean FARRAR and the quest for the historical Jesus: TLond 39 (1986) 108-115.

3073 **Espeja** Jesús, La experiencia de Jesús: Paradosis 1, 1984 ► 1,3954: ᴿLumenV 35 (1986) 546 (F. Ortiz de Urtaran); ScriptV 33 (1986) 441s (A. Eguiluz).

3074 **Fabris** Rinaldo, Gesù di Nazareth, storia e interpretazione[2] 1983 ► 1,3955a: ᴿCiTom 113 (1986) 400s (J. L. Espinel); Teresianum 37 (1986) 236s (V. Pasquetto).

3075 **Fabris** Rinaldo, Jesús de Nazaret, historia e interpretación 1985 ► 1,3955b: ᴿEstE 61 (1986) 459 [J. García Pérez]; RazF 213 (1986) 216s (también J. García Pérez); Studium 26 (M 1986) 543 (P. Blázquez); VerVid 44 (1986) 465s (V. Casas).

3076 Freshwater Mark E., C. S. LEWIS and the quest for the historical Jesus: diss. Florida State 1985, ᴰCunningham L. 296 p. 86-07376. – DissA 47 (1986s) 553s-A.

3077 Galot Jean, a) 'Christ as our ancestor' [Nyamiti C.] et christologie africaine, – b) Jésus de l'histoire et Christ de la foi: Telema 12,46 (1986) 37-40 / 55-66.

3078 **Goergen** Donald J., A theology of Jesus [5-vol 4-step Christology: i. Jesus research; ii. historical retrieval; iii. hermeneutical reconstruction; iv. socioethical evaluation], I. The mission and ministry of Jesus [i. Christology as an invitation to an encounter; Jesus' roots in Palestinian Judaism; Jesus and the people; ii. solidarity with God, origins of mission, prophet from Nazareth, apocalypticism; iii. solidarity with people, compassionate sage] Wilmington 1986, Glazier. 316 p. $13. 0-89453-603-6 [NTAbs 31,112].

3079 **Goffi** Tullo, Gesù di Nazareth nella sua esperienza spirituale 1983 ► 64,3927; 65,3548: ᴿProtestantesimo 41 (1986) 114s (A. Moda).

3079* **Guidetti** Armando, Conoscenza storica di Gesù di Nazareth 1981 ► 62,4104; 63,4031: ᴿParVi 30 (1985) 397s (A. Casalegno).

3080 **Habermas** Gary R., Ancient evidence for the life of Jesus. Nv 1984, Nelson. 187 p. $7 pa. – ᴿBS (1986) 169s (E. R. Howe).

3080* Jaspard J.-M., Jésus-Christ est-il modèle d'identification pour les jeunes? En quoi? Jusqu'où?: FoiTemps 16 (1986) 62-75.

3081 Kampling Rainer, Jesus von Nazaret – Lehrer und Exorzist: BZ 30 (1986) 237-248.

3082 Kissinger W., The lives of Jesus 1985 ► 1,3964: ᴿBrethren Life and Thought 31 (Oak Brook IL 1986) 61-63 (R. Mc Fadden).

3082* Kocher Michel, Jésus communicateur; essai sur la figure du communicateur chrétien, I: Hokhma 11,33 (1986) 63-80...

3083 **Kümmel** Werner G., Dreissig Jahre Jesusforschung: BoBB 60, 1985 ► 1,3965: ᴿActuBbg 23 (1986) 103s (J. Boada); ExpTim 98 (1986s) 302 (E. Best); MélSR 43 (1986) 206-8 (M. Hubaut); RTLv 17 (1986) 363s (Alice Dermience); Salesianum 48 (1986) 443 (A. Amato); SNTU-A 11 (1986) 220s (A. Fuchs); TLZ 111 (1986) 801-3 (G. Haufe); TRu 51 (1986) 426-8 (E. Grässer).

3084 **Lampen** John, Twenty questions about Jesus. L 1985, Quaker Home Service. 97 p. £3. 0-85245-186-5 [ExpTim 98,95].

3085 **Langevin** G., Gesù il Cristo nell'attuale ricerca esegetica [Jésus aujourd'hui, Radio Canada 1980], ᵀ*Rizzi* A., 1985 ➤ 1,296: ᴿTeresianum 37 (1986) 506s (V. *Pasquetto*).

3086 **Lealman** Brenda, Christ — who's that? L c. 1985, 'CEM'. 28 p. 0-905-02281-5. – ᴿExpTim 97 (1985s) 255 [C. S. *Rodd*: valuable material, for children].

3087 *McGuckin* John A., The sign of the prophet; the significance of meals in the doctrine of Jesus: ScripB 16 (1985s) 35-40.

3087* **Marcel** Pierre, Face à la critique; Jésus et les Apôtres; esquisse d'une logique chrétienne: RRéf Sup 37,3 (1986) 1-172 [< ZIT].

3088 **Martín Descalzo** José Luis, Vida y misterio de Jesús de Nazaret, I. Los comienzos: Nueva Alianza 103. Salamanca 1986, Sígueme. 347 p. 84-301-0993-5. – ᴿActuBbg 23 (1986) 241s (F. de *P. Solá*); BibFe 12 (1986) 363s (A. *Salas*); LumenV 35 (1986) 555s (F. *Ortíz de Urtaran*); NatGrac 33 (1986) 560s (D. *Montero*); RazF 214 (1986) 250s (R. de *Andrés*).

3089 **Mascall** E. L., Jesus — who he is and how we know him 1985 ➤ 1,3970; 0-232-51653-7: ᴿGregorianum 67 (1986) 803 (J. *Galot*).

3090 ᴱ**Miguez Bonino** J. Faces of Jesus (13 essays) 1984 ➤ 65,348: ᴿThemelios 12 (1986s) 63s (G. R. *Palmer*).

3091 *Murphy* Cullen, 'Who do men say that I am?'; Interpreting Jesus in the modern world [surveys of key figures since *Reimarus* in their backgrounds, interviews with *Küng* etc.]: Atlantic 258,6 (Dec. 1986) 37-58.

3092 **Neumann** Johannes, Der galiläische Messias; eine Untersuchung über Leben, Wirken und Tod des historischen Jesus und den Ursprung des Glaubens an die Auferstehung Jesu: Die Entstehung des Christentums 1. Ha 1986, Neumann. xii-82 p. DM 19,80 [TLZ 112,350].

3093 **O'Collins** Gerald, Interpreting Jesus 1983 ➤ 64,3949... 1,3973: ᴿHeythJ 27 (1986) 345-7 (J. P. *Galvin*, also on DWYER J., TATUM W.); ScripTPamp 18 (1986) 381s (L. F. *Mateo-Seco*).

3094 **O'Grady** John F., Das menschliche Antlitz Gottes, Modelle zum Verständnis des Jesus von Nazaret [Models of Jesus 1981 ➤ 62,4170], Vorw. *Zahrnt* Heinz. Olten 1983, Walter. 229 p. – ᴿZRGg 38 (1986) 49-57 (F. W. *Kantzenbach*).

3095 *O'Malley* William J., Jesus the warm fuzzy: America 154 (1986) 204-6.

3096 **Pals** Daniel L., The Victorian 'Lives' of Jesus 1982 ➤ 63,4059... 65,3571: ᴿAndrUnS 24 (1986) 70-74 (J. L. *Brunie*).

3097 **Pelikan** Jaroslav, Jesus through the centuries; his place in the history of culture 1985 ➤ 1,3975; $22.50: ᴿAmerica 154 (1986) 166 (J. M. *Powers*); CalvinT 21 (1986) 299-303 (F. C. *Roberts*); Month 248 (1986) 276s (L. *Swain*); RRel 45 (1986) 626s (J. L. *Casteel*); Speculum 61 (1986) 982-4 (Caroline W. *Bynum*); TLond 39 (1986) 302-4 (J. L. *Houlden*); TS 47 (1986) 537s (M. E. *Hussey*); TTod 43 (1986s) 102s (D. G. *Dawe*, also on *Brown* C., *Thompson* W.).

3098 **Quéré** France, Les ennemis de Jésus 1985 ➤ 1,3978; 2-02-008679-4: ᴿÉTRel 61 (1986) 131s (M. *Bouttier*); Études 365 (1986) 136s (D. *Farnham*); RTLv 17 (1986) 90s (J. *Dupont* cite 'Attardons-nous à cette idée; et si Jésus n'avait rencontré chaque jour que la faveur des hommes?').

3098* **Rajcak** J., La figura di Gesù Cristo nella recente ricerca sovietica: diss. Pont. Univ. Urbaniana, ᴰ*Virgulin* S. Roma 1984 [RivB 35,87].

3099 **Ravasi** G., Gesù una buona notizia⁵ 1983 [1982 ➤ 64,3952*]: ᴿProtestantesimo 41 (1986) 47s (G. *Scuderi*).

3100 **Richard** Cliff,   Jesus me and you.   L 1985, Hodder & S.   127 p. £5.
0-340-36932-9 [ExpTim 98,63].
3101 **Rosenberg** Roy A.,   Who was Jesus?   Lanham MD 1986, UPA.   vii-
123 p. $9.25.   0-8191-5177-7; pa. 8-5.
3102 *Schlageter* Johannes,   Das Menschsein Jesu Christi in seiner zentralen
Bedeutung für Schöpfung und Geschichte bei Johannes Duns SCOTUS und
heute: WissWeish 47 (1984) 23-36.
3102* *Schneider* Jan H.,   Das Thema der Jesus-Nachfolge in einer korrelativen
Didaktik: FreibZ 33 (1986) 311-325.
3103 **Schweitzer** Albert,   Storia della ricerca sulla vita di Gesù [1906, ³1984
➤ 65,3518], ᵀ*Coppellotti* Francesco: Biblioteca di storia e storiografia dei
tempi biblici 4.   Brescia 1986, Paideia.   776 p. Lit. 70.000.
Simonis Walter,   Jesus von Nazareth; seine Botschaft vom Reich Gottes und
der Glaube der Urgemeinde; historisch-kritische Erhellung der Ursprünge
des Christentums 1985 ➤ 5544.
3104 **Simonis** Walter,   Das Reich Gottes ist mitten unter euch; Neuorientierung
an Jesu Lahre und Leben.   Dü 1986, Patmos.   103 p.   3-491-77655-4.
3105 **Sloyan** Gerard S.,   Jesus in focus; a life in its setting 1983 ➤ 64,3955...
1,3984:   ᴿInterpretation 40 (1986) 424.426 (M. H. *Hoope*).
3106 **Sloyan** Gerard S.,   The Jesus tradition; images of Jesus in the West [some
apocrypha and Fathers, Francis Assisi/Sales, Teresa Avila/Lisieux...].
Mystic CT 1986, Twenty-Third.   vii-121 p. $6 pa. [TDig 33,488].
3106* **Stein** R. H.,   Difficult passages in the Gospels 1984 ➤ 1,3986:   ᴿWestTJ
48 (1986) 379s (J. W. *Scott*).
3107 *Stenger* Werner,   Sozialgeschichtliche Wende und historischer Jesus:
Kairos 28 (1986) 11-22.
3108 **Stock** Klemens,   Christus in der heutigen Exegese; Standortbestim-
mung und Ausblick [i. Der Graben zwischen vorösterlichem Jesus und
nachösterlichem Christus ist weniger tief; ii. Die Suche nach dem
'historischen Jesus' geht weiter; iii. Distanz zur historisch-kritischen
Exegese wächst; iv. Versuche einer Heimholung Jesu ins Judentum; v.
Neue Ansätze (Wirkungsgeschichte, Rhetorische Analyse, Methoden-
reflexion, Analogie); 4 Leitlinien; Johannes und Markus]: GeistL 59 (1986)
215-228.
3109 **Theissen** Gerd,   Der Schatten des Galiläers; historische Jesusforschung in
erzählender Form.   Mü 1986, Kaiser.   269 p. DM 32 [TLZ 112,437, W.
Trilling] 3-459-01656-6.
3110 **Thompson** William M.,   The Jesus debate; a survey and synthesis [!
➤ 1,3989*]; NY 1985, Paulist.   437 p. 0-8091-2666-4:   ᴿExpTim 97 (1985s)
281s (E. *Franklin*); Furrow 57 (1986) 266s (E. *Bredin*); Gregorianum 67
(1986) 547-9 (J. *Dupuis*); NRT 108 (1986) 908-910 (L. *Renwart*: has he
thrown out the spine with the straitjacket?); TLZ 111 (1986) 620-2 (P.
Pokorný); TS 47 (1986) 530s (Susan A. *Ross*).
3111 **Trudinger** P.,   Honest to Jesus; on NOT being a Christian [Jesus dis-
claimed being Messiah/God]. Winnipeg 1983, Frye.   vi-64 p.   0-919741-
14-2 [NTAbs 30,358].
3112 *Varga* Zsigmond J., Ⓜ Jesus the Teacher — formal aspects, theological
content: Theologiai Szemle 28 (1985) 1-6.
3113 **Veenhof** Jan,   De dubbele Jesus; [radio-]meditaties over teksten van de
evangelisten.   Baarn 1985, Ten Have.   134 p. – ᴿNedTTs 40 (1986) 88 (M.
de *Jonge*).
3114 **Wahlberg** R. C.,   Jesus according to a woman.   NY 1986 = 1975,
Paulist.   100 p. $5 [TS 47,756].

3115 **Watson** David, *Jenkins* Simón, Jesús entonces y ahora [cf. deutsch 1984
➤ 65,3699]. M 1984, PPC. 189 p. – ᴿTVida 27 (1986) 232 (J.M.
Guerrero).

3116 **Weiss** Hans-Friedrich, Kerygma und Geschichte; Erwägungen zur Frage
nach Jesus im Rahmen der Theologie des Neuen Testaments 1983
➤ 64,3962: ᴿTLZ 111 (1986) 505s (N. *Walter*).

3117 **Winstanley** Michael, Come and see [lively critical study of the Gospels
with ample footnote and Scripture reference]. L 1985, Darton-LT. 148 p.
£4. 0-232-51639-1. – ᴿExpTim 97 (1985s) 319 [C.S. *Rodd*: the author is
Rector of the Student Community of the Catholic College at Ushaw,
Durham, esteemed preacher and retreat-giver].

3118 *Wright* N.T., 'Constraints' and the Jesus of history [*Harvey* A. 1982]:
ScotJT 39 (1986) 189-210.

F1.5   *Jesus et Israel* – **Jesus the Jew.**

3119 *a) Agua Pérez* Agustín del, El papel de la 'escuela midrásica' en la
configuración del Nuevo Testamento; – *b) Fuentes Mendiola* Antonia,
Presupuestos teológicos del midrásh judaico; – *c) Díez Merino* Luis,
Exculpación-inculpación de los antepasados de Israel en la tradición
targúmica: ➤ 366, Hermenéutica 1985/6, 391-408 / 409-421 / 357-390.

3120 **Aron** Robert, Così pregava l'ebreo Gesù 1982 ➤ 64,3966: ᴿParVi 31
(1986) 313-5 (M. *Perani*).

3121 **Barnard** W.J., *Riet* P. van 't, Zonder Tora leest niemand wel;
bouwstenen voor een leeswijze van de evangeliën gebaseerd op Tenach en
joodse traditie. Kampen 1986, Kok. 188 p. *f*28,50. 90-242-4129-4
[TsTNijm 26,436].

3122 **Ben-Chorin** Schalom, Fratello Gesù; un punto di vista ebraico sul
Nazareno, ᵀ*Scandiani* G.; 1985 ➤ 1,3993: ᴿParVi 31 (1986) 74s (G. *Se-
galla*); RClerIt 67 (1986) 717s (P. *De Benedetti*); Salesianum 48 (1986) 413
(R. *Vincent*); Sapienza 39 (1986) 480s (B. *Belletti*); StPatav 33 (1986) 702-4
(Teresa *Salzano*); Teresianum 37 (1986) 256s (F. *Foresti*).

3123 **Bianchi** Enzo, Un rabbi che amava i banchetti; l'Eucaristia narrata ai
bambini. Casale Monferrato 1985, Marietti. 48 p.; ill. (Luzzati E.). Lit.
14.000. – ᴿHumBr 41 (1986) 136s (G. *Vaggi*).

3123* **Brandon** S.G.F., Gesù e gli Zeloti [1967] 1983 ➤ 1,3997: ᴿParVi 31
(1985) 441-5 (G. *Jossa*).

3124 **Callan** Terrance, Forgetting the root; the emergence of Christianity from
Judaism. Mahwah NJ 1986, Paulist. vii-131 p. $6 pa. [TDig 33,461].
0-8091-2778-4.

3125 **Cazelles** Henri, Naissance de l'Église; secte juive rejetée? 1968 ²1983
➤ 65,4629: ᴿVSp 139 (1985) 258s (T. *Chary*).

3126 **Chilton** Bruce D., *a)* A Galilean Rabbi and his Bible; Jesus' use of the
interpreted Scripture of his time: GoodNewsSt 8, 1984 ➤ 65,3597; 1,3999:
ᴿCBQ 48 (1986) 329-331 (M. *McNamara*: very fine); Interpretation 40
(1986) 92 (D.J. *Harrington*); – *b)* A Galilean Rabbi and his Bible; Jesus'
own interpretation of Isaiah [SPCK] 1984: ᴿEvQ 58 (1986) 268-270 (I.H.
Marshall); IrBSt 8 (1986) 197s (D.R.G. *Beattie*: slippery); Salesianum 48
(1986) 414 (R. *Vicent*).

3127 *Corbett* John, The Pharisaic revolution and Jesus as embodied Torah:
SR 15 (1986) 375-391.

3128 **Di Segni** R., Il Vangelo del Ghetto 1985 ➤ 1,4001; 237 p.: ᴿHenoch 8
(1986) 406-412 (Elena *Loewenthal*).

3129 *Du Buit* F. M., Pharisiens: ➤ 578, Catholicisme XI, 49 (1986) 135-9.

3130 **Falk** Harvey, Jesus the Pharisee; a new look at the Jewishness of Jesus 1985 ➤ 1,4003: ᴿCBQ 48 (1986) 558s (E. J. *Fisher*: Jewish Orthodox continuer of J. EMDEN, with little use of biblical or NEUSNER criticism); Encounter 47 (1986) 180s (C. M. *Williamson*); TLZ 111 (1986) 588s (G. *Baumbach*: könnte nicht einer historisch-kritischen Nachprüfung standhalten); TS 47 (1986) 551s (A. J. *Tambasco*: Emden or Emdem?); WestTJ 48 (1986) 375s (M. *Silva*).

3131 *Fattorini* Gino, Gesù e la festa [...si rivela durante la festa]: ParVi 31 (1986) 191-8.

3132 *Flusser* David, Thesen zur Entstehung des Christentums aus dem Judentum: KIsr 1 (1986) 62-70.

3133 *Gaston* L., Jesus the Jew in the Apostolic writings [part of a special isue assessing P. VAN BUREN, Theology of the Jewish-Christian reality]: Religion & Intellectual Life 3,4 (New Rochelle 1986) 55-59 [NTAbs 31,14].

3134 *a) Geftman* Rina, Jésus de Nazareth, fils d'Israël; – *b) Dubois* Marcel, La personne de Jésus entre les juifs et les chrétiens: Tychique 60 (1986) 7-12 / 13-15.

3135 **Genot-Bismuth** Jacqueline, Un homme nommé Salut; genèse d'une hérésie à Jérusalem. P 1986, O.E.I.L. 340 p. F 145 [Judaica 42,206].

3136 **Hagner** Donald A., The Jewish reclamation of Jesus 1984 ➤ 65,3605; 1,4010: ᴿJRefJud 33,1 (1986) 97-100 (R. A. *Rosenberg*); Themelios 12 (1986s) 104 (J. *Woodhead*).

3137 **Heyer** C. J. den, De messiaanse weg II. Jezus [TsTNijm 26,437] van Nazaret. Kampen 1986, Kok. 270 p. ƒ44,50. 90-242-4114-6.

3138 **Hooker** Morna D., Continuity and discontinuity; early Christianity in its Jewish setting. L 1986, Epworth. iv-76 p. £4. 0-7162-0429-0.

3139 *Horsley* Richard A., [➤ 9570s] Popular prophetic movements at the time of Jesus; their principal features and social origins: JStNT 26 (1986) 3-27.

3140 *Lapide* P., Er wandelte nicht auf dem Meer; ein jüdischer Theologe liest die Evangelien: Tb 1410. Gü 1984. 125 p. DM 12,80 [Judaica 41,127].

3141 **Lapide** Pinchas, Geen nieuw gebod; een joodse visie op de evangelien [Er wandelte nicht auf dem Meer 1984]. Baarn 1985, Ten Have. 116 p. ƒ-16,50. – ᴿCollatVl 16 (1986) 493s (R. *Hoet*); Streven 53 (1985s) 276 (P. *Beentjes*).

3141* **Lapide** P., *Küng* H. [➤ 57,4311] Jezus in tegenspraak; een jods-christelijke dialoog. Kampen 1986, Kok. 59 p. ƒ9,50 [PrakT 13,626].

3142 **Lapide** P., *Luz* U., Jezus de Jood; thesen van een jood, antwoorden van een Christen [1979]. Kampen/Antwerpen 1985, Kok/Patmos. 184 p. – ᴿCollatVl 16 (1986) 494s (R. *Hoet*); PrakT 13 (1986) 401s (Marien vanden *Boom*); Streven 53 (1985s) 666s (H. *Roeffaers*).

3143 **McNamara** Martin, Palestinian Judaism and the NT: Good News Studies 4, 1983 ➤ 64,3998 ... 1,4018: ᴿEstE 61 (1986) 122s (A. *Vargas-Machuca*); Henoch 8 (1986) 250-2 (G. *Boccaccini*).

3143* **Müller** Karlheinz, Das Judentum in der religionsgeschichtlichen Arbeit am NT: JudUmw 6, 1983 ➤ 64,3991 ... 1,4019: ᴿTLZ 111 (1986) 102s (W. *Wiefel*).

3144 **Neusner** Jacob, Judaism in the beginning of Christianity 1984 ➤ 65,3615; 1,4020: ᴿScotJT 39 (1986) 408-410 (R. B. *Salters*).

3145 **Neusner** Jacob, Le judaïsme à l'aube du christianisme, ᵀBagot Jean-Pierre: Lire la Bible 71. P 1986, Cerf. 169 p. F 85. 2-204-02453-8. – ᴿActuBbg 23 (1986) 217s (X. *Alegre* S.: 'profundo conocedor del judaísmo'); Brotéria 123 (1986) 106s 106s (I. *Ribeiro*); EsprV 96 (1986) 445s (L. *Mon-*

loubou); RÉJ 145 (1986) 434s (Madeleine *Petit*); TsTNijm 26 (1986) 409 (M. *Poorthuis*).

3146 *Puente Ojea* Gonzalo, L'idéologie populaire messianique; Jésus et la révolution juive de son temps: ➤ 5446, Messianisme 1983, 21-132.

3147 **Ronai** A., *Wahle* H. sr., Das Evangelium — ein jüdisches Buch? Eine Einführung in die jüdischen Wurzeln des Neuen Testaments: Bücherei 1298. FrB 1986, Herder. 190 p. DM 10. 3-451-08298-5 [NTAbs 31,115].

3148 **Rowland** Christopher, *a)* Christian origins; an account of the most important Messianic sect of Judaism. L 1985, SPCK. xx-428 p.; bibliog. p. 377-409. ➤ 1,4026: ᴿBL (1986) 134 (J. M. *Lieu*); JTS 37 (1986) 159-161 (also J. *Lieu*); NBlackf 67 (1986) 193s (R. *Morgan*); ScripB 17 (1986s) 24s (J. A. *McGuckin*); Themelios 12 (1986s) 29s (D. de *Lacey*); TLond 39 (1986) 312-4 (M. *Goulder* hopes critics will not assume Q much longer). – *b)* Christian origins; from messianic movement to Christian religion. Minneapolis 1985, Augsburg. XX-428 p. – ᴿRelStT 6 (1986) 44s (G. *Hamilton*).

3149 **Russell** D. S., From early Judaism to early Church. Ph 1986, Fortress. 150 p. $6. 0-334-00496-9 [RelStR 13,171s, J. *Neusner*: dated, uncritical].

3150 **Saldarini** Anthony J., Jesus and Passover. NY 1984, Paulist. 116 p. ➤ 65,3618; 1,4027: ᴿBibTB 16 (1986) 38 (L. F. *Badia*); ComSev 19 (1986) 89s (V. J. *Ansede Alonso*); Interpretation 40 (1986) 206s (N. *Theiss*).

3151 **Sanders** E. P., Jesus and Judaism 1985 ➤ 1,4028: ᴿCBQ 48 (1986) 569-571 (D. *Senior*); JJS 37 (1986) 103-6 (P. S. *Alexander*); JRel 66 (1986) 203s (J. J. *Collins*: lucid); JTS 37 (1986) 510-3 (J. D. G. *Dunn*: challenging and valuable); Paradigms 2,1 (1986) 41-43 (J. P. *Mason*); RelStT 6 (1986) 86-88 (M. *Desjardins*); TLond 39 (1986) 142-4 (Judith *Lieu*); WWorld 6 (1986) 239s (D. *Tiede*).

3152 **Schelkle** Karl H., Israel im Neuen Testament 1985 ➤ 1,4029: ᴿFreibRu 37s (1985s) 106s (P. *Fiedler*).

3153 **Schlichting** Günter, Ein jüdisches Leben Jesu... Tam-ū-mū'ād: WUNT 24, 1982 ➤ 63,4128... 1,4030: ᴿTPhil 61 (1986) 570s (W. *Feneberg*).

3154 *Scroggs* R., The Judaizing of the New Testament: ChThSemRegister 76,1 (1986) 36-45 [NTAbs 30,326].

3155 *Steinhauser* Michael G., The Targums and the New Testament: TorJT 2 (1986) 262-278.

3155* *Talmon* Shemaryahu, Gott und Mensch — eine zeitgenössische jüdische Ansicht: ➤ 68*, ᶠMᴀʏᴇʀ R., Wie gut 1986, 185-190.

3156 *Tomson* Peter J., The names Israel and Jew in ancient Judaism and in the New Testament: Bijdragen 47 (1986) 120-139. 266-289; Eng. 140.289.

3157 *Vermes* Geza, Jesus and the world of Judaism 1983 ➤ 65,3628; 1,4033: ᴿEstE 61 (1986) 124-6 (A. *Vargas-Machuca*); Judaism 35 (1986) 361-4 (D. *Flusser*).

3158 **Weber** Hans-Ruedi, Jesus e as crianças [... judáica, pagã]. São Leopoldo 1986, Sinodal. 96 p. [REB 46,898].

3159 **Carmignac** J., Traductions hébraïques des Évangiles 1-3, 1982 ➤ 63, 4086... 1,4038: ᴿTR 82 (1986) 113-5 (P. *Kuhn*).

3160 ᴱ**Carmignac** Jean, Die vier Evangelien ins Hebräische übersetzt von Franz *Delitzsch* (1877-1890-1902), kritischer Apparat der zwölf Auflagen von Hubert *Klein*: TrHébÉv 4, 1984 ➤ 65,3635; 1,4039: ᴿGregorianum 67 (1986) 769s (G. L. *Prato*).

3161 ᴱCarmignac J., Traductions hébraïques 5. *D'Allemand* Judah, *Fry* T. [1838 + 1864] 1985: ⇥ 1,4040: ᴿIstina 31 (1986) 229s (B. *Dupuy*).

3162 *Howard* George, The textual nature of an old Hebrew version of Matthew [1555]: JBL 105 (1986) 49-63.

F1.6   *Jesus in Ecclesia* – **The Church Jesus.**

3163 *Ardura* Bernard, Le Christ dans la spiritualité de la Réforme grégorienne [1074]: DivThom 88 (1985) 24-41; lat. 24.

3164 *Barruffo* Antonio, Nuove forme di esperienza religiosa cristiana [... Gesù, il Vivente; riscoperta dello Spirito Santo; ritorno alle radici cristiane; gusto della parola di Dio ...]: RasT 27 (1986) 535-558.

3164* *Blauvelt* Livingston ᴶ, Does the Bible teach Lordship salvation? [i.e. for salvation a person must accept Jesus as his savior from sin]: BS 143 (1986) 37-45.

3165 **Blázquez** Ricardo, Jesús sí; la Iglesia también 1983 ⇥ 64,4014 ... 1,4045*: ᴿComSev 19 (1986) 251s (V. J. *Ansede Alonso*); Teresianum 36 (1985) 235s (S. *Ros García*).

3165* **Germain** E., Jésus-Christ dans les catéchismes: JJC 27. P 1986, Desclée. 269 p. F 135. 2-7189-0307-4 [RechSR 74,630].

Gertler Thomas, Jesus Christus — die Antwort der Kirche auf die Frage nach dem Menschsein: ErfurtTSt 52, 1986 ⇥ 5611.

3166 *Guthrie* Donald, Biblical authority and New Testament scholarship [Laing lecture 1985]: VoxEvca 16 (1986) 7-23.

3167 **Herbst** Karl, Was wollte Jesus selbst? Die vorkirchlichen Jesusworte in den Evangelien² I (¹1979), II (¹1981). Dü 1986, Patmos. 275 p.; 295 p. 3-491-77372-5; 226-5.

3168 **Koestler** Martin, Stirbt Jesus am Christentum? Ein Plädoyer für die ursprüngliche Verkündigung Jesu: Siebenstern 1417. Gü 1986, Mohn. 192 p. DM 14,80 [TLZ 112,114].

3169 **Marzola** Oddone, Gesù Cristo centro vivo della fede; dall'esperienza religiosa all'annuncio cristiano: Corona Lateranensis 36. R 1986, Pont. Univ. Lateranensis. xvi-386 p.; bibliog. p. 355-372.

3170 *Muller* Richard A., Emanuel V. GERHART on the 'Christ-Idea' as fundamental principle: WestTJ 48 (1986) 97-117.

3172 **Sheehan** Thomas, The first coming; how the Kingdom of God became Christianity. NY 1986, Random. xii-287 p.; bibliog. p. 275-287. $19 [RechSR 74,631]. 0-394-51198-0.

3173 **Subilia** V., 'Solus Christus'; il messaggio cristiano nella prospettiva protestante: Sola Scriptura 10. T 1985, Claudiana. 162 p. Lit. 9500. – ᴿNRT 108 (1986) 152 (L. *Renard*); Protestantesimo 41 (1986) 121-4 (G. *Conte*).

3174 **Trisoglio** Francesco, Cristo en los Padres de la Iglesia; las primeras generaciones cristianas ante Jesús, antología de textos, ᵀ*Martínez Riu* A.: TeolFilos 161. Barc 1986, Herder. 335 p. – ᴿLumenV 35 (1986) 566 (F. *Ortiz de Urtaran*).

3176 **White** Leland J., Christ and the Christian movement; Jesus in the New Testament, the Creeds and modern theology 1985 ⇥ 1,4053; 0-8189-0484-4: ᴿBibTB 16 (1986) 161 (M. G. *Lawler*).

F1.7   *Jesus 'anormalis'*: **to atheists, psychoanalysts, romance ...**

3177 **Aubrun** Jean, Les oubliés de l'Évangile: Épiphanie. P 1986, Cerf. 155 p. F 63. – ᴿVSp 140 (1986) 726s (sr. *Marie-Pascale*: imaginaire).

3178 *Bovon* François, De Jésus de Nazareth au Christ Pantocrator [... créateur de l'univers]: FoiVie 85,5 (CahBib 25, 1986) 87-96.

3179 *Brisset* A., Les agrapha dans la tradition islamique: CahRenan 32,136 (1984) 178-187 [NTAbs 30,339].

3180 **Bynum** Caroline W., Jesus as mother 1982 ➤ 63,4167... 1,4063: ᴿHeythJ 27 (1986) 194s (Margaret *Hebblethwaite*); Worship 60 (1986) 181s (T. D. *McGonigle*).

3181 **Cipriani** Roberto, Il Cristo rosso; riti e simboli, religione e politica nella cultura popolare; intr. *Poulat* E. R 1985, Ianua. xxi-248 p. Lit. 30.000. – ᴿRasT 27 (1986) 281s (N. *Galantino*).

3182 **Cragg** Kenneth, Jesus and the Muslim; an exploration. L [➤ 1,4069 !] 1985, Allen & U. 315 p. $17.50. 0-042-97046-6. – ᴿExpTim 98 (1986s) (G. *Parrinder*: parallel to his 1984 'Muhammad and the Christian'); Islamochristiana 12 (1986) 239-242 (J. *Slomp*); TS 47 (1986) 547-9 (W. *Teasdale*).

3183 *DeJong* Mary G., 'I want to be like Jesus'; the self-defining power of evangelical hymnody ['feminization' of deity; 'masculine' Christianity]: JAAR 54 (1986) 461-484; bibliog. 484-493.

3184 **Gallup** G.ᴶ, *O'Connell* G., Who do Americans say that I am? What Christians can learn from opinion polls. Ph 1986, Westminster. 129 p. $10 [TS 47,759].

3185 *Glenn* J., Prometheus and Christ: ClasB 62,1 (Wilmore KY 1986) 1-5.

3186 **Grönbold** Günter, Jesus in Indien; das Ende einer Legende [*Kersten* H. 1983; *Obermeier* S. ²1983] 1985 ➤ 1,4080: ᴿMundus 22 (1986) 279-282 (K.-H. *Golzio*: kaum 'das Ende').

3187 **Hawkin** David J., Christ and modernity. Waterloo 1986, W. Laurier Univ. 181 p. $13 [C$10.95 !] 0-88920-193-5. – ᴿExpTim 98 (1986s) 1s (C. S. *Rodd*).

3188 *Kamykowski* Łukasz, ℗ Współczesne niechrześcijańskie studia o Jezusie: AnCracov 18 (1986) 251-271; 271, Les études contemporaines non-chrétiennes sur Jésus.

3189 **Kelsey** Morton T., Christo-Psychology 1982 ➤ 64,4058... 1,4088: ᴿDoct-Life 35 (1985) 178-180 (B. *Cosgrave* spells 'Kesley'); HeythJ 27 (1986) 349 (R. *Moloney* †); RRel 45 (1986) 311s (Elisabeth *Liebert*).

3190 **Khaouam** Mounir, Le Christ dans la pensée moderne d'Islam et dans le Christianisme [diss. Univ. S. Joseph]: Beyrouth 1983, Khalifé. 374 p. [P 1985 ➤ 1,4089]: ᴿIslamochristiana 12 (1986) 250-2 (M. *Borrmans*).

3191 *Klatt* Norbert, Der Essäerbrief [*Kissener* Hermann, Wer war Jesus? 1906 = 1968; The Crucifixion by an eye-witness 1907 = 1977]; zur geistesgeschichtlichen Einordnung einer Fälschung: ZRGg 38 (1986) 32-48.

3192 **McCarthy** Vincent A., Quest for a philosophical Jesus; Christianity and philosophy in ROUSSEAU, KANT, HEGEL, and SCHELLING. Macon GA 1986, Mercer Univ. xv-240 p. $29 [TDig 34,82].

3193 *Matsas* Nestor, Les mémoires de Jésus d'après le manuscrit [imaginé, de la main de Jésus même] de la Mer Morte [℗], ᵀ*Comberousse* P.: Confluents 15. P 1984, BLettres. 164 p. – ᴿSalesianum 48 (1986) 424 (R. *Vicent*).

3194 **Menacherry** Cheriyan, An Indian philosophical approach to the personality of Jesus Christ. R 1986, Urbaniana Univ. 89 p. – ᴿGregorianum 67 (1986) 801 (J. *Dupuis*).

3195 *Meulenberg* Leo F.J., 'Mein armer Vetter, der du die Welt erlösen gewollt'; die Gestalt Jesu im religiösen Werdegang von Heinrich HEINE: KerDo 32 (1986) 71-98; 98 'the appearance of Jesus...'.

3196 **Otero Silva** Miguel †, La piedra que era Cristo. Bogotá 1984, Oveja Negra. 162 p. – ᴿSalesianum 48 (1986) 737s (Ge. C.: novela histórica).

3197 **Panikkar** Raimundo, Der unbekannte Christus im Hinduismus, ᵀ*Risse* Heike, *al.*; Dialog der Religionen. Mainz 1986, Grünewald. 168 p. DM 39 [TGl 76,483].

3198 **Rajcak** Józef, Gesù nella ricerca sovietica contemporanea. Casale Monferrato 1985, Piemme. 176 p. Lit. 16.000. – ᴿNRT 108 (1986) 907s (L. *Renwart*).

3199 *a) Richardson* William J., Psychoanalysis and the God-question; – *b) Miller* David L., 'Attack upon Christendom'; the anti-Christianism of depth psychology; – *c) Kerrigan* William, The case-history of Christianity; a double-cross; – *d) Scott* Charles E., The pathology of the father's role; LACAN and the symbolic order: Thought 61 (1986) 68-83 / 56-67 / 23-33 / 118-130.

3199* *Sardini* Fausto, Gesù Cristo, la figura che più ha affascinato gli scrittori: BbbOr 28 (1986) 157-163.

3200 **Schonfield** Hugh J., The original New Testament; a radical translation. SF 1985, Harper & R. 168 p. $20. – ᴿRExp 83 (1986) 292 (R. L. *Omanson*: eccentric, but forces focusing Judaism content).

3201 **Slusser** Gerald H., From Jung to Jesus; myth and consciousness in the New Testament. Atlanta 1986, Knox. x-170 p. $11 pa. 0-8042-1111-6. [NTAbs 31,95]. – ᴿCCurr 36 (1986s) 485s (Carolyn M. *Craft*).

3202 *Stein* D., Lectures psychanalytiques de la Bible; l'enfant prodigue, Marie, saint Paul et les femmes 1985 ➤ 1,4103: ᴿMélSR 43 (1986) 213-5 (M. *Hubaut*: sur Marie rappelle POHIER).

3203 *Tröger* Karl-W., Jesus as prophet in Islam, Judaism and Christianity [< Kairos 24 (1982) 100-9], ᵀᴱ *Asen* B.: TDig 33 (1986) 126-8.

3204 *Urvoy* Dominique, La religion musulmane et la preuve de la divinité de Jésus selon Jacques ABBADIE (1654-1727): Islamochristiana 12 (1986) 73-91.

3205 **Wehr** Gerhard, Stichwort Damaskus-Erlebnis; der Weg zu Christus nach C. G. JUNG; Psyche und Glaube 3. Stu 1982, Kreuz. 191 p. – ᴿRHPR (1986) 250 (B. *Kæmpf*: sustained parallel to Paul).

3206 *Willers* Ulrich, 'Aut Zarathustra aut Christus'; die Jesus-Deutung NIETZSCHES im Spiegel ihrer Interpretationsgeschichte; Tendenzen und Entwicklungen von 1900-1980: TPhil 61 (1986) 236-249.

F2.1 *Exegesis creativa* – **innovative methods.**

3207 **Agua Pérez** Agustín del, El método midrásico y la exégesis del NT 1985 ➤ 1,4112: ᴿAugR 26 (1986) 581s (P. *Grech*); Salmanticensis 33 (1986) 117s (J. M. *Sánchez Caro*); ScripTPamp 18 (1986) 272-4 (J. M. *Casciaro*).

3208 *Albrektson* Ray, The feasibility of a microcomputer based New Testament research system: EAsJT 4,2 (1986) 62-67.

3209 *Benjamin* Don C., Form criticism today; mapping the OT [as itself a form of folk-art; nothing on maps or geography]: BToday 24 (1986) 315-321.

3210 **Berger** Klaus, Formgeschichte des NTs 1984 ➤ 63,3705 ... 1,4115: ᴿAntonianum 61 (1986) 495-7 (Z. I. *Herman*); BZ 30 (1986) 265-7 (W. *Radl*); CBQ 48 (1986) 734s (D. E. *Aune*); ÉTRel 61 (1986) 427 (F. *Vouga*); LingBib 58 (1986) 105s (W. *Magass*); LuthMon 25 (1986) 89 (J. *Schoon*); Protestantesimo 41 (1986) 119-121 (B. *Corsani*); RBibArg 48 (1986) 122-4 (J. *Denker*); TGegw 29 (1986) 58s (H. *Giesen*); TR 82 (1986) 195-7 (I. *Broer*).

Berger Klaus, Exegese und Philosophie: SBS 123s 1986 ➤ 1138.
3211 **Bultmann** R., NT and mythology, [R]*Ogden* S. [deutsch = 1941 ➤ 1,3922]
1985 ➤ 1,g75: [R]Vidyajyoti 49 (1985) 527s (J. *Volckaert*).
3212 **Chevallier** Max-Alain, L'exégèse du NT, initiation à la méthode 1984
➤ 65,3707; 1,4116: [R]ÉTRel 61 (1986) 432s (M. *Carrez*); ScEspr 38 (1986)
263-5 (P.-É. *Langevin*).
Chilton Bruce, Targumic approaches to the Gospels; essays in the mutual
definition of Judaism and Christianity 1986 ➤ 140*.
3214 *Donelson* L. R., The Gospel as linguistic freedom; a New Testament
critique of contemporary evangelism: Austin Sem. Bulletin 100,8 (1985)
31-39.
3215 *Fisher* Simon, Half-way demythologisation?: ModT 3 (1986s) 245-254.
3216 **Frankemölle** Hubert, Biblische Handlungsanweisungen 1983 ➤ 65,3711:
[R]ActuBbg 23 (1986) 211s (X. *Alegre* S.).
3217 *Hahn* Ferdinand, Der Beitrag der katholischen Exegese zur neutestamentlichen Forschung [< VerkFor 2 (1973s) 83-98]: ➤ 167, Ges. Aufs. 1
(1986) 336-351.
3218 [E]**Harvey** Anthony E., Alternative approaches to New Testament study
1985 ➤ 1,291: [R]ExpTim 97 (1985s) 378 (W. R. *Telford*: illuminating, not
so alternative); NorTTs 87 (1986) 121s (R. *Leivestad*); Themelios 12 (1986s)
98s (M. *Turner*); TLond 39 (1986) 226s (E. *Leach*).
3219 *Hübner* Hans, Entmythologisierung: ➤ 587, EvKL 1 (1986) 1034-6.
3220 **Jaspert** B., Sackgassen im Streit mit Rudolf BULTMANN; hermeneutische Probleme der Bultmannrezeption in Theologie und Kirche. St. Ottilien 1985, EOS. 117 p. DM 8,80. 3-88096-005-4 [NTAbs 30,344]. –
[R]EvKomm 19 (1986) 288 (O. *Merk*).
3220* *Kantzer* Kenneth K., Redaction criticism; handle with care: ChrTod
18 (1985) 111-121 [< BS 143 (1986) 168].
3221 **Kennedy** George A., NT interpretation through rhetorical criticism
1984 ➤ 65,3478; 1,4121: [R]CurrTM 13 (1986) 57s (R. H. *Smith*); Interpretation 40 (1986) 91s (J. D. *Kingsbury*); JBL 105 (1986) 328-330 (R. M.
Fowler); JTS 37 (1986) 166s (H. D. *Betz*); RExp 83 (1986) 113s (R. B. *Vin-
son*).
3222 **Kenny** Antony, A stylometric study of the New Testament. Ox 1986,
Clarendon. xiii-127 p. £20 [TR 82,427].
3223 **Lührmann** Dieter, Auslegung des NTs 1984 ➤ 65,3717; DM 21: [R]Ev-
Komm 19 (1986) 49s (W. *Schenk*).
3324 a) *Meyer* Ben F., Conversion and the hermeneutics of consent; – b)
Stanton Graham N., Interpreting the New Testament today; – c) *Nations*
Archie L., Historical criticism and the current methodological crisis
[< ScotJT 36 (1983) 59-71]: ExAud 1 (1985) 36-46 [2 (1986) 7-18] / 1
(1985) 63-73 / 125-132.
3224* **Michel** Karl-Heinz, Sehen und glauben; Schriftauslegung in der
Auseinandersetzung mit Kerygmatheologie und historisch-kritischer
Forschung: TDienst 31, 1982 ➤ 63,4233: DM 8,80: [R]TZBas 42 (1986)
268s (R. *Riesner*).
3225 *Muñoz León* Domingo, Deraš neotestamentario y deraš intertestamentario (avance de un proyecto): ➤ 21, Mem. DÍEZ MACHO A., Salvación 1986, 657-676.
3225* *Nichol* Chris, Updating Adolf von HARNACK; the tension between myth
and its embodiment; country music, the New Testament and sexuality:
Colloquium 19,1 (Auckland 1986) 33-42.
3226 **Nida** E. A. *al.*, Style and discourse, with special reference to the text of the

Greek New Testament 1983 ➤ 64,1892.3855; 1,486: ᴿGraceTJ 7 (1986) 133s (D. A. *Black*).

3226* *Pisarek* Stanisław, ❷ Historia oddziaływania tekstu (Wirkungsgeschichte) jako nowa metoda w badaniu Nowego Testamentu: RuBi 39 (1986) 96-107.

3227 **Simpson** H. Mitchell, The conflicting hermeneutics of Rudolf BULTMANN and A. T. ROBERTSON; dimensions of biblical authority in a Southern Baptist controversy: diss. Florida State 1986, ᴰ*Hill* S. 263 p. 87-08196. – DissA 47 (1986s) 4416-A.

3228 **Trilling** Wolfgang, L'annuncio di Gesù; orientamenti esegetici [Die Botschaft 1978 ➤ 58,6068a; 60,5678], ᵀ*Sacchi* Anna: StBPaid 74. Brescia 1986, Paideia. 135 p. Lit. 14.000.

·3229 *Tuszyński* Kazimierz, ❷ Bultmannowski postulat demitologizacji i egzystencjalnej interpretacji Ewangelii w ujęciu współczesnej literatury teologicznej w Polsce: STWsz 24,1 (1986) 19-38; Eng. 38s.

F2.2 *Unitas VT-NT:* The Unity of the Two Testaments.

3230 **Beauchamp** Paul, L'uno e l'altro Testamento; saggio di lettura [1976], ᵀ*Moretti* A. 1985 ➤ 1,4134: ᴿParVi 31 (1986) 388s (T. *Caruso*).

3231 *Black* Matthew, The theological appropriating of the OT by the NT: ScotJT 39 (1986) 1-17.

3232 **Bruns** Paul C., Is your word list complete? [the NT, often disseminated long before any OT is available in a given language, contains many passages which cannot be understood without familiarity with cited OT passage]: BTrans 37 (1986) 228-231 [445s, *Thomas* K. on Gal 4,24 Hagar].

3233 *Crossan* John D., From Moses to Jesus; parallel themes: BR 2,2 (1986) 18-28; color ill.

3234 **Daniel** E. Randolph, Abbot Joachim of FIORE, Liber de concordia Noui ac Veteris Testamenti [first four books]. Ph 1983, American Philosophical. 455 p. $18. – ᴿJAAR 54 (1986) 169s (B. *McGinn*).

3235 ᴱ**De Gennaro** Giuseppe, L'Antico Testamento interpretato dal Nuovo [L'Aquila 7, 1982s], 1985 ➤ 1,464; Lit. 40.000: ᴿCC 137 (1986,2) 93s (G. *Giachi*).

3236 ᴱ**Doré** Joseph, L'Ancien et le Nouveau: CogF 11, 1982 ➤ 63,289; 1,4143: ᴿEsprV 96 (1986) 95s (L. *Debarge*).

3236* *Esbroeck* M. van, La notion d'accomplissement de l'Écriture: ➤ 365, *Bogaert* F.-M., Lectures bibliques 131-141.

3237 *Evans* M. J., The Old Testament as Christian Scripture: VoxEvca 16 (1986) 25-32.

3237* **Ferguson** Duncan S., Biblical hermeneutics; an introduction. Atlanta 1986, Knox. iv-220 p. $13 [RelStR 13,334, (B. *Ollenburger*: really on the use of the Bible by Christians].

3238 **Grässer** E., Der Alte Bund im Neuen 1985 ➤ 1,180.4144: ᴿSNTU-A 11 (1986) 224-7 (A. *Fuchs*).

3239 *Grogan* G. W., The relationship between prophecy and typology: ScotBEvT 4 (1986) 5-16.

3240 **Hanson** A. T., The living utterances of God; the NT exegesis of the Old 1983 ➤ 64,4119... 1,4145: ᴿJTS 37 (1986) 194s (C. K. *Barrett*: really about how we today differ).

3241 **Hirsch** Emanuel, al., ᴱ*Müller* Hans M. Das Alte Testament und die Predigt des Evangeliums, Tü/Gosler 1986 = 1936, Katzmann/Thuhoff. 179 p. 3-7803-0435-9 / 3-823887-11-5.

3242 **Kaiser** Walter C., The uses of the Old Testament in the New 1985 ➤ 1, 4147: ᴿBS 143 (1986) 279s (D. L. *Bock*); SWJT 29 (1986s) 60 (D. G. *Kent*).
3243 *Kraus* Hans-Joachim, Das Alte Testament in der 'bekennenden Kirche': KIsr 1 (1986) 26-46.
3244 **LaRondelle** Hans K., The Israel of God in prophecy [... NT fulfilment]; principles of prophetic interpretation 1983 ➤ 65,3742; 1,4150: ᴿSWJT 29,2 (1986s) 54s (H. B. *Hunt*: excellent critique of classical dispensationalism).
3245 **Longobardo** Luigi, ILARIO di Poitiers, Trattato sui misteri; per una lettura cristiana dell'AT 1984 ➤ 1,4151: ᴿSalesianum 48 (1986) 442 (B. *Amata*).
3245* *Oeming* Manfred, Unitas Scripturae? Eine Problemskizze: ➤ 236, JbBT 1 (1986) 48-70.
3246 **Pannenberg** Wolfhart, *Kaufmann* Arthur, Gesetz und Evangelium: Szb Mü 1986/2. Mü 1986, Bayr. Akad. 48 p. 3-7696-1540-9.
3247 **Schelkle** Karl H., Israel im Neuen Testament. Da 1985, Wiss. xix-136 p. DM 39 [TLZ 112,100, W. *Stegemann*].
3248 **Van Roo** William A., Telling about God, I [Promise and fulfillment]: AnGreg 242. R 1986, Pont. Univ. Gregoriana. xii-375 p. 88-7652-548-3.
3248* *Venturi* Gianfranco, Tutta la Scrittura è annuncio del mistero di Cristo: ParVi 30 (1985) 446-451.

F2.3   *Unitas interna – NT –* **Internal unity.**

3249 *Deer* Donald S., Unity and diversity in the New Testament: ➤ 472, BTAf 7,13s (1985) 91-105 [< TKontext 8/2,23].

3249* **Hanson** Paul D., L'Écriture une et diverse; interprétation théologique [Diversity of Scripture 1982 ➤ 63,1043], ᵀ*Bagot* J.-P.: LDiv 122, 1985 ➤ 1,4159: ᴿBL (1986) 87s (B. P. *Robinson*: 'the translator does not attempt to mitigate the infelicities of Hanson's prose style'); Études 364 (1986) 714s (P. *Gibert*); RTPhil 118 (1986) 329s (H. *Mottu*); VSp 140 (1986) 727 (G. *Rouiller*: pénible; à quel public?).
3250 *Zumstein* Jean, Pluralidad y autoridad de los escritos neotestamentarios [< LumiereV 34 (1985) 19-32], ᵀᴱ*Gari* José A.: SelT 25 (1986) 49-56.

F2.5   *Commentarii –* **Commentaries on the whole NT.**

3251 ᴱ**Harrington** W., *Senior* D., New Testament Message, 22 volumes; 3-6 Mt Jn 4th printing; Mk Lk 3d. Wilmington/Dublin 1984, Glazier/Veritas. – ᴿFurrow 57 (1986) 479s (B. *McConvery*).
3251* *Mignon* Christian, BARCLAY's feet of clay [page-headings, The clay in Barclay: Daily Study Bible Gospels dangerous for our Catholic people]: Vidyajyoti 49 (1985) 456-463; 463s, rejoinder by *Meagher* P.
3252 ᴱ**Reeve** Anne, ERASMUS' Annotations on the New Testament; The Gospels, facsimile of the final Latin text (1535) with all the earlier variants (1516, 1519, 1522 and 1527). L 1986, Duckworth.

| X. Evangelia |

F2.6   **Evangelia Synoptica;** *textus, commentarii.*

3252* **Anneau** J. *al.*, Evangelhos sinóticos e Atos dos Apóstolos. São Paulo 1986, Paulinas. 306 p. [REB 46,722].

3253 **Boismard** M.-É., *Lamouille* A., Synopsis graeca quattuor Evangeliorum. Lv 1986, Peeters. lxxviii-418 p. Fb 2000 [NRT 109, 737, X. *Jacques*].

3253* **Denaux** Adelbert, *Vervenne* Marc, Synopsis van de eerste drie evangeliën. Lv/Turnhout 1986, Vlaamse Bijbelstichting / Brepols. lxv-332 p. Fb 1175. – ᴿNRT 108 (1986) 949s (X. *Jacques*); PrakT 13 (1986) 615 (M. *Menken*); Streven 53 (1985s) 847-850 (P. *Beentjes*).

ᴱ**Dočanašvili** E., Matthew, Mark, Luke, in the Georgian Mc'het'a Manuscript 1986 ➤ 1262, p. 152-261.

3254 *Elliott* J.K., An examination of the text and apparatus of three recent Greek synopses [*Orchard* in general uses a form longer than *Aland* or *Huck*; his chief merit lies in furnishing data for Griesbach proponents]: NTS 32 (1986) 557-582.

3255 ᴱ**Funk** Robert W., New Gospel parallels, I. The Synoptic Gospels [II. John] 1985 ➤ 1,4169: ᴿCBQ 48 (1986) 744-6 (M. L. *Soards*: brilliant, incomplete).

3256 **Huck** Albert, ᴮ*Greeven* Heinrich, Synopse der drei ersten Evangelien 1981 ➤ 62,4396... 65,3761: ᴿAnJapB 12 (1986) 126-130 (M. *Sato*).

3257 **Kudasiewicz** Józef, ❷ Ewangelie synopticzne dzisiaj: Więzi 53. Wsz 1986, Biblioteka Więzi. 427 p.; bibliog. p. 413-424.

3258 *a) Neirynck* F., Once more, the making of a synopsis [ALAND, VBS, Dungan D.]; – *b) Orchard* J. B., The 'neutrality' of vertical-column synopses: ETL 62 (1986) 141-154 / 155s [on Neirynck 61 (1985) 161-6].

3259 **Orchard** John B., A synopsis of the four Gospels in Greek arranged according to the Two-Gospel hypothesis 1983 ➤ 64,4155... 1,4172: ᴿRB 93 (1986) 470s (M.-É. *Boismard*).

3260 **Poppi** Angelico, Sinossi dei quattro vangeli, I. Testo 1983 ➤ 64,4156... 1,4173: ᴿRB 93 (1986) 471 (M.-É. *Boismard*).

3261 **Schmithals** Walter, Einleitung in die drei ersten Evangelien: Lehrbuch 1985 ➤ 1,4177; DM 58: ᴿCBQ 48 (1986) 758s (F. F. *Matera*); ETL 62 (1986) 192-4 (F. *Neirynck*); JTS 37 (1986) 519-521 (C. M. *Tuckett*: Mark used both pre/post-Christological Q); RB 93 (1986) 471s (B. T. *Viviano*, franç.); TGegw 29 (1986) 255s (H. *Giesen*).

3262 **Wünsch** Dietrich, Evangelienharmonien im Reformationszeitalter; ein Beitrag zur Geschichte der Leben-Jesu-Darstellungen: ArbKG 52, 1983 ➤ 64,4159... 1,4178: ᴿCrNSt 7 (1986) 640s (M. *Wriedt*); TLZ 111 (1986) 460-2 (S. *Strohm*).

F2.7 *Problema synopticum:* **The** (Two-Source / Q) **Synoptic Problem.**

3263 **Carmignac** Jean, La naissance des Évangiles Synoptiques 1984 ➤ 65, 3769; 1,4180: ᴿAngelicum 63 (1986) 130s (S. *Parsons*); BLitEc 87 (1986) 146s (S. *Légasse*); EstE 61 (1986) 97s (J. *Iturriaga*); RechSR (1986) 227-9 (J. *Guillet*: non); Protestantesimo 41 (1986) 46s (B. *Corsani*); RB 93 (1986) 624s (M.-É. *Boismard*).

3264 **Carmignac** Jean, La nascita dei vangeli sinottici: Problemi e dibattiti 2. Mi-Cinisello Balsamo 1985, Paoline. 110 p. Lit. 75.000. – ᴿParVi 31 (1986) 459-461 (M. *Làconi*: fuori il campo di competenza dell'autore); STEv 9 (1986) 291s (G. *Emetti*).

3265 ᴱ**Crossan** John D., Sayings parallels; a workbook for the Jesus tradition [in four categories: parables, aphorisms. sayings, and stories]: Foundations & Facets. Ph 1986, Fortress. 233 p. $25; pa. $15. ·0-8006-2109-3; 1909-9. – ᴿCurrTM 13 (1986) 254 (J. C. *Rochelle*: 'startling, dangerous; why? look up for yourself'); ExpTim 98 (1986s) 350 (C. S. *Rodd*).

3266 *a) Cunningham* S., The Synoptic problem; a summary of the leading theories; – *b) Onwu* N., 'Don't mention it'; Jesus' instruction to healed persons: AfJBSt 1,1 (1986) 48-58 / 35-47 [< TKontext 8/2,20].

3266* **Farmer** William R., The synoptic problem, a critical analysis 1976 = 1964 ➤ 58,4460 ... 62,4404:   ᴿEstB 44 (1986) 239s (A. *Rodríguez Carmona*).

3267 *Farmer* W. R., The Church's stake in the question of Q: Perkins Journal 39,3 (1986) 9-19 [NTAbs 31,17].

3268 *Neirynck* F., *Segbroeck* F. Van, Q bibliography, additional list 1981-1985 [to Logia 1982 ➤ 63,37, p. 561-588]: ETL 62 (1986) 157-165.

3268* *Prior* Michael P., A 'Copernican' revolution, or GRIESBACH re-buried [ORCHARD J. B.]: ScripB 17 (1986s) 14-19.

3269 *Robinson* James M., On bridging the gulf from Q to the Gospel of Thomas (or vice versa)?: ➤ 374, ᴱ*Hedrick* C., Nag Hammadi 1986, 127-175.

3270 **Rolland** Philippe, Les premiers évangiles ... problème synoptique: LDiv 116, 1984 ➤ 65,3781; 1,4194: ᴿBLitEc 87 (1986) 145s (S. *Légasse*: utile et en partie convaincant); ÉglT 17 (1986) 388-390 (M. *Dumais*); EsprV 96 (1986) 111s (L. *Walter*); MélSR 43 (1986) 203-6 (M. *Hubaut*: non); RechSR 74 (1986) 225-7 (J. *Guillet*); RTLv 17 (1986) 213-5 (T. P. *Osborne*).

3271 *a) Scholer* David M., Q bibliography: 1981-1986; – *b) Kloppenborg* John S., The function of apocalyptic language in Q: ➤ 392, SBL Seminars 1986, 27-36 / 224-235.

3271* **Scott** J. W., Luke's preface and the Synoptic Problem: diss. ᴰ*Wilson* R. St. Andrews. xlii-467 p. – RTLv 18,550 sans date.

3272 **Stoldt** Hans-Herbert, Geschichte und Kritik der Markushypothese² [¹1977 ➤ 60,5764*]. Giessen 1986, Brunnen. 269 p. DM 34. – ᴿETL 62 (1986) 427s (F. *Neirynck*); SNTU-A 11 (1986) 218-220 (A. *Fuchs*).

3273 **Tuckett** C. M., The revival of the GRIESBACH hypothesis [diss. Lancaster 1979] 1983 ➤ 64,4174 ... 1,4194: ᴿHeythJ 27 (1986) 187s (J. B. *Orchard*).

3274 ᴱ**Tuckett** C. M., Synoptic studies; the Ampleforth conferences of 1982 and 1983: 1984 ➤ 65,441: ᴿCBQ 48 (1986) 161-3 (J. S. *Kloppenborg*); ScotJT 39 (1986) 265s (D. C. *Parker*).

3275 **Wheeler** Frank E., Textual criticism and the Synoptic Problem; a textual commentary on the minor agreements of Matthew and Luke against Mark; diss. Baylor. Waco 1985. 487 p. 86-06998. – DissA 47 (1986s) 555-A; RelStR 13,190.

3276 **Zeller** Dieter, Kommentar zur Logienquelle: Stu KlKomm NT 21, 1984 ➤ 65,3786; 1,4197: ᴿCBQ 48 (1986) 353s (J. S. *Kloppenborg*).

F2.8   *Synoptica:* **themata.**

3277 **Bayer** Hans F., Jesus' predictions of vindication and resurrection; the provenance, meaning, and correlation of the Synoptic predictions: WUNT 2/20. Tü 1986, Mohr. xi-289 p. DM 78. 3-16-145014-0. – ᴿExpTim 98 (1986s) 214 (A. *Chester*); Themelios 12 (1986s) 96s (C. L. *Blomberg*).

3278 *Blomberg* Craig L., Synoptic studies; some recent methodological developments and debates [98 items]: Themelios 12 (1986s) 38-46.

3279 *Butts* James R., The chreia in the Synoptic gospels: BibTB 16 (1986) 132-8.

3280 **Dupont** Jacques, Études sur les Evangiles synoptiques 1985 ➤ 1,169: ᴿCollatVl 16 (1986) 119s (A. *Denaux*); Gregorianum 67 (1986) 542s (L. *Sabourin*).

3281 **Hendriks** W. M. A., Karakteristiek woordgebruik in de synoptische evangelies: kath. diss. Nijmegen, ᴰ*Iersel* B. van. 596 p. – TsTNijm 26 (1986) 289.

3282 **Kelber** W. H., The oral and the written Gospel; the hermeneutics of speaking and writing in the Synoptic tradition, Mark, Paul, and Q: 1983 ➤ 64,3877.4181 ... 1,4201: ᴿMélSR 43 (1986) 201-3 (M. *Hubaut*).

3283 *Kloppenborg* John S., The formation of Q and antique instructional genres: JBL 105 (1986) 443-462.

3284 *Làconi* Mauro, Vangeli sinottici; un annuncio per la Chiesa di oggi: SacDoc 31 (1986) 8-28.

3285 *Lindemann* Andreas, Erwägungen zum Problem einer 'Theologie der synoptischen Evangelien': ZNW 77 (1986) 1-33.

3286 **Melbourne** Bertram L., Slow to understand; the disciples in Synoptic perspective: diss. Andrews, ᴰ*Terian* A. Berrien Springs MI 1986. 320 p. 87-04324. – DissA 47 (1986s) 4115-A.

3287 *Neusner* Jacob, The Synoptic Problem in rabbinic literature; the cases of the Mishna, Tosepta, Sipra, and Leviticus Rabba: JBL 105 (1986) 499-507.

3288 *Palatty* Paul, Discipleship in the Synoptic Gospels: Bible Bhashyam 11 (1985) 224-235.

3289 **Pasquetto** Virgilio, Annuncio del Regno, i grandi temi dei Vangeli sinottici riproposti al cristiano d'oggi [saggi inediti o senza riferimento]. N 1985, Dehoniane. 507 p. Lit. 25.000. – ᴿRasT 27 (1986) 285-7 (C. *Marucci*); StPatav 33 (1986) 438s (G. *Segalla*); Teresianum 37 (1986) 258 (B. G. *Moriconi*).

3289* **Piper** Ronald A., Wisdom in the Sayings of Jesus, with special reference to 'Q' tradition: diss. ᴰ*Stanton*. L 1986. 300 p. – RTLv 18,549.

3290 **Polag** A., Die Christologie der Logienquelle [Diss. 1969] 1977 ➤ 58,4542 (Index !): ᴿHenoch 8 (1986) 102s (L. *Moraldi*).

3290* **Reicke** Bo, The roots of the Synoptic Gospels. Ph 1986, Fortress. x-189 p.

3291 *Sacchi* Paolo, I sinottici furono scritti in ebraico? Una valida ipotesi di lavoro [*Tresmontant* C., *Carmignac* J.]: Henoch 8 (1986) 67-78.

3292 **Sellew** Philip H., Early collections of Jesus' words; the development of dominical discourses: diss. Harvard. CM 1986. 296 p. 87-01114. – DissA 47 (1986s) 3453-A; HarvTR 79 (1986) 481.

3293 **Silvola** Kalevi, Lapset ja Jeesus; traditio- ja redaktiohistoriallinen tutkimus synoptisten Evankeliumien lapsiperikoopeista: Suomen Eksegeettisen Suran Julkaisuja 41. Helsinki 1984, Vammalan Kirjapaino Oy. 188 p. 951-95185-6-8.

3294 **Tuck** Sherrie A., The form and function of sayings-material in Hellenistic biographies of philosophers: diss. Harvard ... – HarvTR 79 (1986) 483.

3295 **Tuckett** C. M., Nag Hammadi and the Gospel tradition; synoptic tradition in the Nag Hammadi Library: StNT&W. E 1986, Clark. xi-194 p.; bibliog. p. 169-177. 0-567-09364-6.

F3.1 Matthaei evangelium: textus, commentarii.

3300 **Aranda Pérez** G., El evangelio de san Mateo en copto sahidico: TEstCisn 35, 1984 ➤ 65,3802; 1,4208: ᴿCBQ 48 (1986) 550s (D. *Johnson*); Muséon 99 (1986) 187 (Y. *Janssens*); NT 28 (1986) 284 (G. D. *Kilpatrick*: 'we lack now only John' — but QUECKE's 'announced' Sahidic John also appeared in 1984 ➤ 65,4769); ScripTPamp 18 (1986) 276s (M. *Guerra*).

3302 **Da Spinetoli** Ortensio, Matteo, il vangelo della Chiesa[4] [[1]1971] 1983
➤ 65,3820: [R]Teresianum 37 (1986) 241s (V. *Pasquetto*).

3303 *France* R.T., Matthew: Tyndale NT. Leicester/GR 1985, Inter-
Varsity/Eerdmans. 416 p. £4.25. – [R]Themelios 12 (1986s) 94s (D. A.
Hagner) & 92s (G. *Maier*).

3304 **Gnilka** Joachim, Das Matthäusevangelium I: Herders Theol. Komm. NT
1. FrB 1986, Herder. bibliog. p. xi-xvi. – [R]ExpTim 98 (1986s) 301 (E.
Best).

3306 **Limbeck** Meinrad, Matthäus-Evangelium: Kl. Komm. NT 1. Stu 1986,
KBW. 312 p. 3-460-15311-3.

3307 **Luz** Ulrich, Das Evangelium nach Matthäus (Mt 1-7): EkK 1/1, 1985
➤ 1,4213; DM 69: [R]ÉTRel 61 (1986) 429s (F. *Vouga*); Streven 53 (1985s)
380s (P. *Beentjes*); Teresianum 37 (1986) 503s (V. *Pasquetto*); TsTNijm 26
(1986) 295 (S. van *Tilborg*).

3308 *MacArthur* John F., Matthew 1-7: MacArthur NT Comm. Ch 1985,
Moody. 505 p. $15 [TR 83,250].

3309 *Maier* Gerhard, Three commentaries on Matthew; a review [*Luz* U.;
Carson A., *France* R.]: Themelios 12 (1986s) 89-93.

3310 **Melles** Cornelia H., St. Matthew in Lamut [Tungus-Altaic], the Kazan
edition of 1880 reprinted with a preface: 'Debter-DebTher-Debtelin' 5.
Budapest 1984, Akadémia. xi-139 p. – [R]AION 46 (1986) 141s (O.
Durand).

3310* **Mounce** Robert H., Matthew ➤ 1,4214: Good News Comm. SF 1985,
Harper & R, xv-292 p. $11 pa. – [R]CalvinT 21 (1986) 320 (S. *Kistemaker*).

3311 *Neidhart* Walter, Wissenschaftliche Erklärung des Matthäus und
Probleme heutiger christlicher Praxis [*Luz* U. 1985]: Reformatio 35 (1986)
2-7.

3312 [E]**Paulus** Beda, Pascasii RADBERTI Expositio in Matheo Libri XII:
CCMed 56 + AB [➤ 65,3817]. Turnhout 1984, Brepols. lxi-1599 p. Fb
16.650. 2-503-03561-2; 3-9; 5-5 [+ Instrumenta lexicologica Cetedoc,
183 p. + 38 microfiches; Fb 3750; 2-503-63562-5]. – [R]Bijdragen 47 (1986)
336 (M. *Schneiders*).

3314 **Zahn** T., Das Evangelium des Matthäus [[4]1922] ➤ 1,4223: [R]SNTU-A
11 (1986) 229s (A. *Fuchs*: eine gute Idee).

F3.2 **Themata** *de Matthaeo.*

3314* **Breukelman** F.H., De theologie van de Evangelist Mattheüs, 1. De
ouverture van het Evangelie: Bijbelse Theologie 3/1. Kampen 1984, Kok.
236 p. *f*35 pa. – [R]KerkT 37 (1986) 71 (M. H. *Bolkestein*).

3315 **Brooks** Stephenson H., The history of the Matthean community as
reflected in the M sayings traditions: diss. Columbia. NY 1986. 288 p.
86-10745. – DissA 47 (1986s) 938-A.

3315* **Doohan** Leonard, Matthew; spirituality for the 80's and 90's: 1985
➤ 1,4232; 0-839680-19-X: [R]ÉglT 17 (1986) 390s (R. P. *Hardy*: good).

3316 *Doohan* Leonard, Ecclesial sharing in Matthew's Gospel: BToday 24
(1986) 254-9.

3317 *Doyle* B.R., 'Crowds' in Matthew; texts and theology: Catholic
Theological Review 6 (Clayton, Australia 1984) 28-33 [NTAbs 30,144].

3318 **Edwards** R.A., Matthew's story of Jesus 1985 ➤ 1,4236: [R]Neo-
testamentica 20 (1986) 75 (H. J. B. *Combrink*).

3319 *Fabris* Rinaldo, Per una lettura del Vangelo di Matteo: RClerIt 67
(1986) 814-824.

3320 **Ford** W. Herschel †, Sermons you can preach on Matthew 1985
➤ 1,4239: ᴿExpTim 97 (1985s) 254 (J. M. *James*: simplistic; a century out
of date).

3320* *a) Hadiwardoyo* A. Purwa, Die Grundlage des christlichen moralischen
Lebens — im Matthäusevangelium; - *b) Kieser* Bernhard, Das Neue
Testament — formt es den sittlichen Charakter der Christen?: Orientasi 18
(indonesisch 1986) 100-113 / 79-99 [< TKontext 8/2,43].

3321 *Hamel* Eduardo, A não-violéncia em S. Mateus; reflexões bíblico-teo-
lógicas: Brotéria 123 (1986) 554-560.

3321* *Hellholm* David, En textgrammatisk konstruktion i Matteusevangeliet
[7,28; 11,1; 13,53; 19,1; 26,1]: SvEx 51s (1986s) 80-89.

3322 *Hill* David, In quest of Matthaean Christology [... *Gerhardsson* B. 1979]:
➤ 44, Mem. HAIRE J. = IrBSt 8 (1986) 135-142.

3323 *Howard* George, Was the Gospel of Matthew originally written in
Hebrew [new evidence: Shem Tob]:ᐧBR 2,4 (1986) 14-25; ill.

3323* **Jullien de Pommerol** Patrice, Il vangelo come racconto; analisi
morfologica del Vangelo di Matteo [1980] 1983 ➤ 64,4218; 65,3829:
ᴿParVi 30 (1985) 70-73 (S. *Migliasso*: errori dell'originale corretti, altri
introdotti).

3324 **Kennedy** Eugene, The choice to be human; Jesus alive in the Gospel of
Matthew. CCNY 1985, Doubleday. 263 p. $16. - ᴿRelStR 12 (1986) 293
(R. C. *Leslie*: the Kingdom is to be found not through institutionalized
ritual but in common people living out the truth in their own personal
ways).

3325 **Kingsbury** Jack D., Matthew as story. Ph 1986, Fortress. x-149 p. $10
pa. [TDig 33,368]. - ᴿTTod 43 (1986s) 438.440 (F. W. *Burnett*).

3326 **Martini** Carlo M., Ich bin bei euch; Leben im Glauben nach dem
Matthäusevangelium, ᵀ*Berz* A, 1985 ➤ 1,4252: ᴿTLZ 111 (1986) 769s (M.
Behnisch).

3327 **Massaux** Éduard [actuellement Recteur honoraire LvN; diss. Lv 1950,
ᴰ*Cerfaux* L.:] Influence de l'Évangile de saint Matthieu sur la littérature
chrétienne avant saint Irénée, réimprimé avec présentation de *Neirynck* F.,
et bibliographie 1950-85 de *Dehandschutter* B.: BiblETL 75. Lv 1986,
Univ./Peeters. xxvii-850 p. 90-6186-214-0. - ᴿETL 62 (1986) 399-403 (F.
Neirynck).

3327* *Mauser* Ulrich W., Christian community and governmental power in
the gospel of Matthew: ExAud 2 (1986) 46-54.

3328 **Mohrlang** Roger, Matthew and Paul; a comparison of ethical
perspectives: SNTS Mon 48, 1984 ➤ 65,3835; 1,4254: ᴿCiTom 113 (1986)
589s (J. L. *Espinel*); Interpretation 40 (1986) 95s (L. E. *Keck*); JRel 66
(1986) 206 (H. D. *Betz*).

3329 *Mosetto* Francesco, Rassegna bibliografica sul Vangelo di Matteo
[... commentari]: ParVi 31 (1986) 438-443.

3330 *Müller* Mogens, Mattaeusevangeliets messiasbillede; et forsøg på at
bestemmen Mattaeusevangeliets forståelse af Jesu messianitet: SvEx 51s
(1986s) 168-179.

3331 **Nestle** D., 'Wenn du im Garten wandelst, lerne den Glauben'; Schöpfung
im Lichte des ersten Evangeliums. [Mt]. FrB 1985, Herder. 158 p.
DM 8,90. 3-451-08214-4 [NTAbs 30,355].

3332 **Ogawa** Akira, L'histoire de Jésus chez Matthieu 1979 ➤ 60,5861 ...
65,3837: ᴿHenoch 8 (1986) 253-6 (L. *Moraldi*).

3333 *Pilch* John J., The health care system in Matthew, a social science
analysis: BibTB 16 (1986) 102-6.

3334 **Price** Stephen G., The accusation of hypocrisy in Matthew's Gospel: diss. Marquette, [D]*Edwards* R. Milwaukee 1985. 318 p. 86-04961. – DissA 47 (1986s) 218-A.

3335 **Przybylski** Benno, Righteousness in Matthew and his world of thought [diss. [D]*Sanders* E.]: SNTS Mon 41, 1980 ► 61,5996... 1,4259: [R]EstE 61 (1986) 120s (A. *Vargas-Machuca*).

3336 *Russell* E. A., 'Antisemitism' in the Gospel of Matthew: IrBSt 8 (1986) 183-196.

3337 **Senior** Donald, What are they saying about Matthew? 1983 ► 64,4226; 65,3842: [R]Interpretation 40 (1986) 98s (D. E. *Garland*: sure-footed).

3338 **Sigal** P., The Halakah of Jesus of Nazareth according to the Gospel of Matthew [diss. Pittsburgh Theol. Sem., [D]*Hare* D.]. Lanham MD 1986, UPA. xi-269 p. $23.75; pa. $13.25. 0-8191-5210-2; 1-0 [NTAbs 30,357; Judaism 35,506].

3339 [E]**Stanton** Graham, The interpretation of Matthew 1983 ► 64,4329... 1,4266: [R]BibTB 16 (1986) 41 (Karen A. *Barta*).

3340 **Stock** Klemens, Jesus — Künder der Seligkeit; Betrachtungen zum Matthäus-Evangelium. Innsbruck 1986, Tyrolia. 158 p. 3-7022-1597-2.

3341 **Wilkins** Michael J., The concept of disciple in Matthew's Gospel as reflected in the use of the term *mathētēs*: diss. Fuller Theol. Sem., [D]*Martin* R. Pasadena 1986. 389 p. 86-19163. – DissA 47 (1986s) 2204-A.

3341* **Zumstein** Jean, Matthieu le théologien. CahÉv 58. P 1986, Cerf. 68 p. F 22. 0222-9714.

F3.3 Mt 1s (Lc 1s) *Infantia Jesu* – Infancy Gospels.

3342 *Siotis* Markos A., ⊚ The forefathers of Jesus Christ according to the flesh: TAth 57 (1986) 127-154. 273-299.

3343 **Brown** Raymond E., Matthew's genealogy of Jesus Christ; a challenging Advent homily: Worship 60 (1986) 483-490.

3344 *Stramare* Tarcisio, Per un riesame della genealogia di Matteo [1,1-17]: BbbOr 28 (1986) 3-13.

3345 *Mussies* Gerard, Parallels to Matthew's version of the pedigree of Jesus: NT 28 (1986) 32-47.

3346 **Bell** James B., [E]*Abrams* Richard L. [co-author of Searching for your ancestors], The roots of Jesus. GCNY 1984, Doubleday. xii-195. $14. – [R]RelStR 12 (1986) 292 (R. H. *Fuller* speaks only of Abrams as author).

3347 *Brändle* Francisco, ⊕ L'histoire de Joseph et son influence sur la théologie de St. Joseph selon l'Évangile de St. Matthieu, [T]*Bardski* K.: ► 424, Kongres 1985/6, 227-238.

3348 *Bostock* Gerald, Virgin birth or human conception? [Joseph-Mary confrontation in BLAKE's Jerusalem; *Wainwright* G. the most probable, Zechariah was the father; the only important thing is 'Jesus conceived through an act of pure obedience, which was unaffected by physical desire or by psychological need']: ExpTim 97 (1985s) 260-3; 98 (1986s) [139s *Benson*] 331-3.

3349 *Benson* G. P., Virgin birth, virgin conception: ExpTim [97 (1985s) 260 *Bostock*, Zechariah the father] 98 (1986s) 139s.

3350 *Brown* Raymond E., Gospel infancy narrative research from 1976 to 1986; part I (Matthew): ► 32, [F]FITZMYER J., CBQ 48 (1986) 468-483.

3350* **Brown** Raymond E., La nascita del Messia secondo Matteo e Luca [1977] 1981 ► 63,4374*b*; 64,4239: [R]ParVi 30 (1985) 474-6 (M. *Orsatti*).

3351 *a*) *Brändle* Franciscus, San José desde el Evangelio: – *b*) *Ros García*

Salvador, 'Carpintero' e 'Hijo del carpintero' (Mc 6,3; Mt 13,55); el oficio de José y de Jesús; notas de Cristología inductiva; – c) *Verd* Gabriel M., ¿Era San José de Belén? Una hipótesis sobre Lc 2,3-5; – d) *Llamas* Enrique, San José y la Virgen María: EstJos 40,80 (1986) 153-162 / 163-177 / 179-184 / 185-203.

3352 *Dobraczynski* Jan, La sombra del Padre; historia de José de Nazaret. M 1984 ³1985, Palabra. 331 p. [EstJos 40,263].

3353 **Firpo** Giulio, Il problema cronologico della nascita di Gesù 1983 ➤ 64,4244... 1,4273: ᴿJBL 105 (1986) 149s (Casimir *Bernas*: a broader survey of critical method than the title indicates); Protestantesimo 41 (1986) 167s (E. *Stretti*); RBgPg 64 (1986) 159 (P. *Salmon*).

3354 **Hendrickx** Herman, Studies in the Synoptic Gospels; the Infancy narratives etc. [Manila 1975-9] 1984 ➤ 65,3790: ᴿIrBSt 8 (1986) 47s (B. M. *Nolan*); JStNT 26 (1986) 121-5 (D. *Hill*: all four volumes should be on every teacher's desk); NBlackf 67 (1986) 147s (H. B. *Green*).

3355 **Laurentin** René, The truth of Christmas; beyond the myths, the gospels of the infancy of Jesus [Les évangiles de l'enfance; vérité de Noël 1982 ➤ 63,4384; not Les évangiles de Noël 1985 ➤ 1,4280], ᵀ*Wrenn* Michael J., al.: Studies in Scripture. Petersham MA 1986, St. Bede's. xx-569 p. $30 pa. [NTAbs 31,102]. 0-932506-34-8.

3356 **Laurentin** René, I Vangeli dell'infanzia di Cristo; la verità del Natale al di là dei miti; esegesi e semiotica, storicità e teologia [1982]: Parola di Dio 2/1. Mi-Cinisello Balsamo 1985 (²1986). 712 p. Lit. 30.000. – ᴿParVi 31 (1986) 383-5 (M. *Làconi*); StPatav 33 (1986) 441 (G. *Segalla*).

3357 *Manns* Frédéric, La natività di Gesù nel protovangelo di Giacomo, ᵀ*de Constantiis* Pio: TerraS 62 (1986) 128-131.

3357* **Moolan** John, The period of Annunciation-Nativity in the East [Syrian] calendar; its background and place in the liturgical year. Kottayam, Kerala 1985, St. Thomas Sem. xxxiii-297 p. – ᴿBible Bhashyam 12 (1986) 150 (T. *Mannooramparampil*).

3358 ᴱMoreschini Claudio, GREGORIO Nazianzeno, Omelie sulla Natività (Discorsi 38-40): Testi Patristici 39. R 1983, Città Nuova. 165 p. 88-311-3039-0.

3358* **Paul** A., Il vangelo dell'infanzia secondo Matteo (letture bibliche) [1968 ➤ 50,2511],ᵀ. R 1986, Borla. 200 p. Lit. 12.000. – ᴿStPatav 33 (1986) 695 (G. *Segalla*).

3359 **Perrin** Joseph, Un juste nommé Joseph 1985 ➤ 1,4287: ᴿEstJos 40 (1986) 261 (J. A. *Carrasco*).

3360 **Ruedi-Weber** Hans, Immanuel; the coming of Jesus in art and the Bible. Geneva 1984, WCC. 122 p.; ill. $13. 2-8254-0793-3. – ᴿExpTim 97 (1985s) 255 [C. S. *Rodd*: very high quality].

3361 *Scotland* N. A. D., Conceived by the Holy Spirit, born of the Virgin Mary [if not by parthenogenesis, then the sperm was provided by Joseph or by another man or by the Holy Spirit]: EvTR 10,1 (Exeter 1986) 27-32.

3362 *Segalla* Giuseppe, Matteo 1-2; dalla narrazione teologica della tradizione alla teologia kerygmatica della redazione: TItSett 11 (1986) 197-225; Eng. 225.

3363 *Ercoliani* Lorenzo, [Lc 2,21] La circoncisione ebraica e la festa cristiana: BbbOr 28 (1986) 227-9.

3364 *a) Stramare* Tarcisio, La circoncisión de Jesús; significado exegético y teológico; – b) *Morán* José A., La paternidad de San José en el pueblo cristiano: EstJos 40,79 (1986) 3-13 / 15-30.

3365 *Vorster* W. S., The annunciation of the birth of Jesus in the Protevangelium of James: ➤ 72, FMETZGER B., South Africa 1985/6. 33-53.

Magi, Mt 2, 1-12:

3366 *Boldorini* Alberto, Sic itur ad astra, o della cometa di Halley: Renovatio 21 (1986) 659-681 [... *Cassini* G. e altri osservatori c. 1680].

3367 **Bussagli** Mario, *Chiappori* Maria Grazia, I Magi; realtà storica e tradizione magica. Mi 1985, Rusconi. 266 p. – RSalesianum 48 (1986) 961s (R. *Sabin*).

3368 *Daoust* J., Les Mages étaient-ils des Nabatéens? [*Charbel* A.]: EsprVie 96 (1986) 706-8.

3369 **Irwin** Kathleen M., The liturgical and theological correlations in the associations of representations of the Three Hebrews and the Magi in the Christian art of late antiquity: diss. Graduate Theological Union. Berkeley 1985. – RelStR 13,189.

3370 *Phipps* Williams E., The Magi and Halley's Comet: TTod 43 (1986s) 88-92.

3371 **Ravasi** Gianfranco, Videro il Bambino e sua Madre. Mi 1984, Àncora. 164 p. – RDivinitas 30 (1986) 194 (C. *Petino*).

3372 *Scorza Barcellona* Francesco, 'Oro e incenso e mirra' (Mt 2,11): II: ➤ 365, AnStoEseg [I. 2 (1985)137-147] 3 (1986) 227-245.

3373 **Strobel** A. [Mt 2,1-12] Der Stern von Bethlehem; ein Licht in unserer Zeit? Fürth/Bay. 1985, Flacius. 79 p. DM 13,80. 3-924022-13-5 [NTAbs 30,358].

3374 *a*) *Nodet* Étienne, L'illusion hérodienne ou la royauté introuvable; – *b*) *Cazeaux* Jacques, 'Toi, Bethléem, n'es-tu pas le parent pauvre des clans de Juda?' Le thème du 'roi' dans l'Évangile de Jean [18,37; 1,19s ...]: LumièreV 35,178 (1986) 43-54 / 69-88.

3374* *Howard* Tracy L., The use of Hosea 11:1 in Matthew 2:15; an alternative solution: Bibliotheca Sacra 143 (1986) 314-328.

3375 *Giannarelli* Elena, [Mt 2,18] Rachele e il pianto della madre nella tradizione cristiana antica: ➤ 365, AnStoEseg 3 (1985/6) 215-226.

3376 **Daniel-Ange**, Dieu à douze ans. P 1983, Sigier/Cerf. 70 p. F 70 – RVSpl 140 (1986) 265 (P. *Lambert*).

3377 **Sánchez-Silva** José M., Jesús creciente, introito imaginario a la vida oculta del Señor: Narraciones juveniles 2. M 1985, Dyrsa. 192 p. – RRThom 86 (1986) 520 [J.-M. *F(abre)* compare les Pseudépigraphes et *Rievaulx* Aelred de, Quand Jésus eut douze ans: SC(hr) 60, 1958; *Aron* Robert, Les années obscures de Jésus 1960; Ainsi priait Jésus enfant 1968].

F3.4 Mt 3... *Baptismus Jesu,* **Beginning of the Public Life.**

3378 *Bammel* Ernst, *a*) Die Versuchung Jesu nach einer jüdischen Quelle [ineditum]; – *b*) Jesus und ein anderer [ineditum]; – *c*) Seventeen apostles [< JTS 20 (1969) 434f]; – *d*) What is thy name? [< NT 12 (1970) 223-8]: ➤ 131, Judaica 1986, 253-6 / 157-174 / 209 only / 210-5.

3379 **Neugebauer** Fritz, Jesu Versuchung; Wegentscheidung am Anfang. Tü 1986, Mohr. vi-120 p. 3-16-145120-1.

3380 **Panier** Louis, [Mt 4,1-11] Récit et commentaire de la tentation de Jésus au désert; approche sémiotique du discours interprétatif: Thèses, 1984 ➤ 65,3903; 1,4318: RRB 93 (1986) 613s (É. *Nodet*); RTLv 17 (1986) 89s (C. *Focant*); ScEspr 38 (1986) 261-3 (J.-Y. *Thériault*: réussi).

3381 **Rey** Bernard, Les tentations et le choix de Jésus: Lire la Bible 72. P
1986, Cerf. 164 p. F 70. – ᴿMélSR 43 (1986) 211 (M. *Hubaut*).
3381* *a) Schegget* G. H. ter, Christologie und Jesusbild an Hand der
Versuchungsgeschichte Jesu; – *b) Heyer* C. J. den, Die Versuchungs-
erzählung in den Evangelien; – *c) Wengst* Klaus, Anmerkungen zur
Barthschen Auslegung der Versuchungsgeschichte aus heutiger exegetischer
Perspektive; – *d) Bakker* L. A. R., Jesus als Stellvertreter für unsere
Sünden und sein Verhältnis zu Israel bei Karl BARTH: ➤ 406*,
Barth-Tagung 1986, 7-9 / 10-20 / 21-38 / 39... [< ZIT].
3382 *Shea* John J., Christian faith and the temptations of Christ: ChSt 25,1
(1986) 65-78.
3383 *Odero* José M., El debate de Jesús con Satán (Mt 4,5-7; Lc 4,9-12)
(Cuestiones teológicas sobre fe y hermenéutica): ➤ 366, Hermenéutica
1985/6, 241-255.
3384 *Chevallier* Max-Alain, L'apologie du baptême d'eau à la fin du premier
siècle; introduction secondaire de l'étiologie dans les récits du baptême de
Jésus: NTS 32 (1986) 528-543.
3385 *Crawford* L., La légende de 'la vie cachée de Jésus' [in an Essene
community with John Baptist]: CahRenan 34,141 (1985) 32-39 [NTAbs
30,271].
3386 **Infante** Renzo, L'amico dello sposo; Giovanni Battista [diss. Univ.
Gregoriana] 1984 ➤ 65,3887: ᴿSalesianum 48 (1986) 420 (C. *Bissoli*).
3387 *Kieffer* René, Judiska reningar och det dop som Jesus kommer med
[Jewish purifications and the baptism Jesus brought]: SvEx 51s (1986s)
116-126.
3388 *Lupieri* Edmondo, Santi, dèi e missionari; un caso di primitivo
sincretismo religioso maya-cristiano, con particolare attenzione alla figura
del Battista: SMSR 52 (1986) 113-127.

F3.5   **Mt 5... Sermon on the Mount** [... *plain, Lk 6,17*].

3389 *Allison* Dale C., Jesus and Moses (Mt 5:1-2): ExpTim 98 (1986s) 203-5.
3390 **Alt** Franz, Vrede is mogelijk; de politiek van de Bergrede [1983
➤ 65,3907]. Baarn 1984, Ten Have. 112 p. Fb 290. – ᴿCollatVl 16 (1986)
244 (R. *Hoet*).
3391 *Baumann* Rolf, Bergpredigt und Weltfrieden III. Von der 'Frie-
densvision' zu konkreten Schritten: Orientierung 50 (1986) [5-9.20-23]
89-93.
3392 **Betz** Hans D., Studien zur Bergpredigt 1985 ➤ 1,4322: ᴿÉTRel 61 (1986)
427s (F. *Vouga*); RThom 86 (1986) 312-5 (L. *Devillers*); RTLv 17 (1986)
88s (J. *Dupont*).
3393 **Betz** Hans D., Essays on the Sermon on the Mount 1985 ➤ 1,4323:
ᴿHorizons 13 (1986) 420 (N. *McEleney* is unconvinced); JTS 37 (1986)
521-3 (G. N. *Stanton*: origin unconvincing, otherwise fine); SpTod 38
(1986) 265s (B. T. *Viviano*); TTod 43 (1986s) 132.134 (R. A. *Edwards*).
3393* **Buckley** Michael, Let peace disturb you. L 1985, Collins Fount. 159 p.
£2. 0-00-626947-8 [ExpTim 98,286].
3394 *Burchard* Christoph, Bergpredigt: ➤ 587, EvKL 1 (1986) 433-6.
3395 *Catchpole* David R., Jesus and the Community of Israel — the inaugural
discourse in Q: BJRyL 68 (1985s) 296-316.
3396 **Donaldson** Terence L., Jesus on the mountain; a study in Matthean
theology [diss. Toronto 1981, ᴰ*Longenecker* R.]: JStNT Sup 8, 1985
➤ 1,4328: ᴿBiblica 67 (1986) 402-4 (R. A. *Gundry*: relation to Zion

unproved); CBQ 48 (1986) 740s (R. A. *Edwards*); JTS 37 (1986) 524-6 (W. L. *Kynes*: Mt 4,8 and four other episodes beside the Sermon).

3397 *a) Farmer* William R., The Sermon on the Mount: a form-critical and redactional analysis of Matt 5:1-7:29; – *b) Kea* Parry V., The Sermon on the Mount; ethics and eschatological time; – *c) Fowler* Robert M., [Mt 3,17; 28,2...] Reading Matthew reading Mark; observing the first steps toward meaning-as-reference in the Synoptic Gospels: ↦ 392, SBL Seminars 1986, 56-87 / 88-98 / 1-16.

3398 **Giavini** Giovanni, Ma io vi dico; esegesi e vita attorno al Discorso della Montagna [= ²Tra la folla al discorso della Montagna 1980 ↦ 61,5686]: Aggiornamenti teologici 8. Mi 1985, Àncora. 211 p. Lit. 10.000. – ᴿClaretianum 26 (1986) 378-380 (B. *Proietti*); CC 137 (1986,1) 410 (J. *Janssens*); ParVi 31 (1986) 466-8 (G. *Alluvione*); RivAscM 1 (1986) 93 (G. *D'Urso*).

3399 ᴱ**Ginzel** Günther B., Die Bergpredigt, jüdisches und christliches Glaubensdokument; eine Synopse der Texte 1985 ↦ 1,4331: ᴿTLZ 111 (1986) 888s (P. von der *Osten-Sacken* calls him 'Herausgeber' who renders superfluous earlier works not only of FRIEDLANDER and MONTEFIORE but even of BILLERBECK); TR 82 (1986) 119s (T. *Söding*).

3400 **Kodjak** Andreij, A structural analysis of the Sermon on the Mount: Religion and Reason 34. B 1986, Mouton de Gruyter. x-234 p. DM 98 [TR 83,75].

3401 **Lambrecht** Jan, Ich aber sage euch; die Bergpredigt als programmatische Rede Jesu 1984 ↦ 65,3919; 1,4334: ᴿCBQ 48 (1986) 145s (J. D. *Kingsbury*: a bit elementary); JTS 37 (1986) 175-7 (H. B. *Green*); RB 93 (1986) 156s (B. T. *Viviano*, franç.); RThom 86 (1986) 309-12 (L. *Devillers*); StPatav 33 (1986) 439s (G. *Segalla*).

3402 **Lambrecht** Jan, 'Eh bien! Moi je vous dis'; le discours-programme de Jésus (Mt 5-7; Lc 6,30-49), ᵀ*Dermience* Alice: LDiv 25. P 1986, Cerf. 265 p. F 138. 2-20402512-7. – ᴿMélSR 43 (1986) 212 (M. *Hubaut*).

3403 **Lambrecht** J., The Sermon on the Mount 1985 ↦ 1,4335: ᴿRExp 83 (1986) 460s (M. G. *Reddish*: not successfully midpoint between scientific and popular); TS 47 (1986) 342s (C. *Bernas*).

3404 **Lapide** Pinchas, Die Bergpredigt — Utopie oder Programm? 1982 ↦ 63,4431 ... 65,3920: ᴿTZBas 42 (1986) 83s (J. *Thomas*).

3405 **Lapide** Pinchas, The sermon on the mount; utopia or program for action? Maryknoll NY 1986, Orbis. vii-148 p. – ᴿScripB 17,1 (1986s) back cover (M. *Prior*).

3406 **Lapide** Pinchas, O Sermão da Montanha; utopia o programa? Petrópolis 1986, Vozes. 136 p. [REB 46,468].

3407 *Larson* Stan, The Sermon on the Mount; what its textual transformation discloses concerning the historicity of the Book of Mormon: TrinJ 7 (1986) 23-45.

3407* *a) Marxsen* Willi, Der Streit um die Bergpredigt — ein exegetisches Problem? Anmerkungen zum Umgang mit der Sprache; – *b) Schneider* Gerhard, Die Bitte um das Kommen des Geistes im lukanischen Vaterunser (Lk 11,2 v.l.); – *c) Schroeder* Hans H., Haben Jesu Worte über Armut und Reichtum Folgen für das soziale Verhalten? : ↦ 39, ᶠGREEVEN H., Text/Ethik 1986, 315-324 / 344-373 / 397-409.

3408 *Mattill* A. J., The sermon on the mount; how not to live: American Rationalist 31,2 (St. Louis 1986) 95-98 [< NTAbs 31,19].

3409 *Németh* Tamás, Ⓦ Ethics in the Sermon on the Mount: Theologiai Szemle 28 (1985) 146-8.

3409* *Simoens* Yves, The sermon on the mount; light for the Christian conscience: LVitae 41 (1986) 127-143.
3410 *Siotes* N. A., Le sermon sur la Montagne dans la littérature du XIXᵉ s.: ⓖ Rizáreios Ekklesiastikē Paideía 3 (198-) 223-241 [RHE 81,356 donne en grec Rigáreios et n'indique pas l'an].
3411 **Strecker** G., Die Bergpredigt 1984 ➤ 65,3929; 1,4344: ᴿEvKomm 19 (1986) 182 (H.-W. *Kuhn*); Teresianum 36 (1985) 229-231 (F. *Foresti*); TLZ 111 (1986) 194-6 (R. A. *Guelich*).
3412 *Szénási* J. Sándor, ⓜ Jesus and the Law: Theologiai Szemle 29 (1986) 239-241.
3413 *White* Leland J., Grid and group in Matthew's community; the righteousness/honor code in the Sermon on the Mount: Semeia 35 (1986) 61-88; bibliog. 89s.
3414 **Schnackenburg** Rudolf, Alles kann wer glaubt; Bergpredigt und Vaterunser in der Absicht Jesu 1984 ➤ 65,3923; 1,4341: ᴿColcT 56,2 (1986) 189 (S. *Moysa*).

F3.6 **Mt 5,3-11 (Lc 6,20-22) Beatitudines.**

3414* **Blanch** Stuart, The way of blessedness. L 1985, Hodder & S. 231 p. £2 [ExpTim 98,286].
3415 **Broer** Ingo, Die Seligpreisungen der Bergpredigt; Studien zur Überlieferung und Interpretation: BoBB 61. Bonn 1986, Hanstein. 104 p. DM 38. – ᴿSNTU-A 11 (1986) 230-2 (A. *Fuchs*); TPQ 134 (1986) 402 (A. *Stöger*).
3416 *a)* **Broer** Ingo, Anmerkungen zum Gesetzesverständnis des Matthäus; – *b)* *Fiedler* Peter, Die Tora bei Jesus und in der Jesusüberlieferung; – *c)* *Dautzenberg* Gerhard, Gesetzeskritik und Gesetzesgehorsam in der Jesustradition: ➤ 382*, ᴱ*Kertelge* K., Gesetz 1985/6, 128-145 / 71-77 / 46-70.
3417 *Cabodevilla* J. M., Las formas de felicidad son ocho; comentario a las bienaventuranzas 1984 ➤ 65,3936: ᴿCiTom 113 (1986) 145 (A. *Bandera*).
3418 **Coste** René, Le grand secret des Béatitudes; une théologie [➤ 1,4352*] et une spiritualité pour aujourd'hui. P 1985, S.O.S. 300 p. F 110. 2-7185-0962-7. – ᴿÉtudes 364 (1986) 716 (J. *Thomas*); Gregorianum 67 (1986) 780s (G. *Rambaldi*); VSp 140 (1986) 745 (J. *Robert*).
3419 *Galligan* John S., The Augustinian connection; beatitudes and gifts: SpTod 38 (1986) 53-62.
3420 *Lapide* P., The Beatitudes: Emmanuel 92 (1986) 322-9.355 [< NTAbs 31,20].
3421 *Romaniuk* Kazimierz bp., ⓟ The oldest form of the beatitudes forming the introduction to the Sermon on the Mount: Przegląd Tomistyczny 1 (1984) 75-86 [< RuBi 39,86].
3421* **Sánchez** L. Manuel, Pensamientos breves sobre las Bienaventuranzas. Lima 1985, CEP. 134 p. – ᴿPerspT 18 (1986) 415s (J. *Oliveira Souza*).
3422 *a)* *Beyerhaus* Peter, [Mt 5,3] 'Blessed are the poor in spirit' — the theology of the poor in biblical perspective; – *b)* *Seccombe* David P., Take up your cross; ➤ 54, ᶠKNox D., God rich 1986, 153-163 / 139-151.
3423 *a)* *Sicari* Antonio, 'Au commencement' était la Béatitude de la pauvreté; – *b)* *Lacoste* Jean-Yves, Approches d'un scandale [il ne faut pas retirer à la béatitude des pauvres son caractère scandaleux]: Communio 11,5 (P 1986) 8-17 / 45-50 [non in IkaZ].

3424 *Helewa* Giovanni, [Mt 5,7] 'Beati i misericordiosi'; RivVSp 40 (1986) 10-29. 113-126. 220-239.

3425 *Holmes* Michael W., The text of Matthew 5.11: NTS 32 (1986) 283-6: context shows *pseudómenoi* should be included, against Nestle-Aland[26].

3426 *a) Stenger* Werner, [Mt 5,11] Die Seligpreisung der Geschmähten: – *b)* *Krieger* Klaus S, [Mt 24,23s] Das Publikum der Bergpredigt: Kairos 28 (1986) 33-60 / 98-119.

3427 *Fornberg* T., [Mt 5,21-48] Matthew and the school of Shammai; a study in the Matthean antithesis: Theology and Life 7 (Hong Kong 1984) 35-59 [NTAbs 30,146].

3428 *Levison* John R., Responsible initiative in Matthew 5:21-48: ExpTim 98 (1986s) 231-4.

3429 *Trilling* Wolfgang, [Mt 5,27...] Zum Thema Ehe und Ehescheidung im Neuen Testament: TVers 16 (1986) 73-84.

3430 **Heth** W. A., *Wenham* G. J., [Mt 5,32; 19,9] Jesus and divorce 1984 ➤ 65,3952; 1,4367: [R]EvQ 58 (1986) 361s (J. *Barclay*); TrinJ 7,2 (1986) 100-2 (S. D. *Hull*).

3432 **Stramare** Tarcisio, Matteo divorzista? Studio su Mt. 5,32 e 19,9: StBPaid 76. Brescia 1986, Paideia. 95 p. Lit. 10.000 [TR 83,338].

3433 *a) Bastiaens* Jean, 'Oog voor oog, tand voor tand'; over ver-geld-ing en verzoening (Mt 5, 38-39); – *b) Weren* Wim, Bergrede en halacha: ➤ 94, [F]RIJKHOFF M., Bij de put 1986, 72-97 / 46-71.

3434 *Sahlin* Harald, Ett svårt ställe i Bergspredikan (Mt 5:39-42) [*ponērô*]: SvEx 51s (1986s) 214-8.

3435 *Łach* Jan, ❷ Obowiązek pojednania i miłości (De obligatione reconciliationis et amoris, Mt 5,43-48): ➤ 367, Sympozjum 1985 = RuBi 39 (1986) 231-243.

F3.7 Mt 6,9-13 (Lc 11,2-4) *Oratio Jesu,* Pater Noster, **The Lord's Prayer** [➤ H1.4]

3436 *Bischoff* Bernhard, BERENGAR von Tours, eine zweite Auslegung des 'Pater Noster' (vor 1088): ➤ 134, Anecdota 1984... [< RHE 81,226].

3437 [E]**Bühring** Gernot, Vaterunser Polyglott; das Gebet des Herrn — in 42 Sprachen mit 75 Textfassungen. Ha c. 1986, Buske. 278 p. DM 19,80. – [R]LuthMon 25 (1986) 325 (J. *Jeziorowski*).

3438 *Pirlot* Sabine, Het Onze Vader in de sacramentsbediening: CollatVl 16 (1986) 37-54.

3439 *Rodríguez* Isidoro, 'Padre nuestro, que estás en los cielos' [mejor 'en el cielo']: NatGrac 33 (1986) 327-9.

3440 **Sabugal** Santos, Abbà... La oración del Señor (Historia y exégesis teológica): BAC 467. M 1985, Católica. xxiv-759 p. 84-220-1201-4. – [R]Angelicum 63 (1986) 486-8 (J. *Salguero*); AugR 26 (1986) 582-4 (P. *Grech*); BibFe 12 (1986) 131s (A. *Salas*); BZ 30 (1986) 268-270 (H. E. *Lona*; Ziel nicht erreicht); Gregorianum 67 (1986) 773 (J. *Galot*).

3441 *Sabugal* Santos, La tradición pre-redaccional del Padrenuestro: Nat-Grac 32 (1985) 233-266.

3442 **Schnurr** Klaus B., Hören und handeln; lateinische Auslegungen des Vaterunsers in der alten Kirche 1985 ➤ [D]65,3985] 1,4393; [R]Salesianum 48 (1986) 447 (B. *Amata*); SNTU-A 11 (1986) 257-9 (F. *Weissengruber*); TsTNijm 26 (1986) 298 (J. *Waldram*).

3443 *Verheul* A., Le 'Notre Père' et l'Eucharistie: QLtg 67 (1986) 159-179.

3444 *Burtness* J.H., [Mt 6,4.18] Now you see it, now you don't; ethical reflections on a textual variant in Matthew six [*en tô phanerô* out of place]: WWorld 6,2 (1986) 161-9 [NTAbs 30,278].

3445 *Hastoupis* Athanasios P., ⊚ The passages Matth. 6.6 and John 20,16-17: TAth 57 (1986) 855s.

3446 *Buetubela* Balembo, Et ne nous soumets pas à la tentation ...; la difficile actualisation de Mt 6,13: RAfrT 10,19 (1986) 5-13.

3447 *Tum* Janusz, ❷ 'Szukajcie najpierw królestwa Bożego i jego sprawiedliwości, a to wszystko będzie wam dodane'; analiza Mt 6,17-7,12: STWsz 24,1 (1986) 61-97; deutsch 97s.

3448 *Wolbert* Werner, [Mt 7,1] Die Goldene Regel und das ius talionis [Antrittsvorlesung Münster 13.XI.1985]: TrierTZ 95 (1986) 169-181.

3449 *Behnisch* M., [Mt 7,12] The golden rule as an expression of Jesus' preaching: Bangalore Theological Forum 17,1 (1985) 83-97 [NTAbs 30,147].

3450 **Wegner** Uwe, Der Hauptmann von Kafarnaum (Mt 7,28a; 8,5-10.13)...: WUNT 2/14, 1985 ➤ 1,4401: ᴿKerkT 37 (1986) 270-2 (P. W. van der *Horst*); TGegw 29 (1986) 253 (H. *Giesen*).

3451 *Lambrecht* Jan, Een nieuwe Nederlandse synopsis [*Denaux-Vervenne* 1986]; het gebruik van Mt. 8, 18-27: CollatVl 16 (1986) 405-428.

F4.1 **Mt 9-12 ...** *Miracula Jesu* – **The Gospel Miracles.**

3452 *Bauermeister* Paul, Healing; mission and ministry of the Church: CurrTM 13 (1986) 205-213.

3453 **Beck** Daniel A., Miracle and the mechanical philosophy; the theology of Robert BOYLE in its historical context: diss. Notre Dame 1986. 273 p. 87-02205. – DissA 47 (1986s) 3784s-A.

3454 **Brown** Colin, Miracles and the critical mind 1984 ➤ 65,3996; **1,4413**: ᴿEvQ 58 (1986) 271s (J. S. *Wright* †); TLZ 111 (1986) 301s (H. *Reventlow*).

3455 **Brown** Colin, That you may believe 1985 ➤ **1,4414**: ᴿGraceTJ 7 (1986) 235-244 (G. J. *Zemek*).

3456 **Burns** R. M., The great debate on miracles 1981 ➤ 65,3997; **1,4415**: ᴿHeythJ 27 (1986) 96s (J. *O'Higgins*: very readable).

3457 *Campbell* Ted A., John WESLEY and Conyers MIDDLETON on divine intervention in history: ChH 55 (1986) 39-49.

3458 *a) Craig* William L., The problem of miracles; a historical and philosophical perspective; – *b) Maier* Gerhard, Zur neutestamentlichen Wunderexegese im 19. und 20. Jahrhundert; – *c) Yamauchi* Edwin, Magic or miracle? Diseases, demons and exorcisms; – *d) Blackburn* Harry L., 'Miracle working *theîoi ándres*' in Hellenism (and Hellenistic Judaism); – *e) Harris* Murray J., 'The dead are restored to life'; miracles of revivification in the Gospels; – *f) Blomberg* Craig L., The miracles as parables: ➤ 271, Miracles 1986, 9-48 / 49-87 / 89-183 / 185-218 / 295-326 / 327-361 (443-457).

3459 **Crasta** Patrick M., Miracle and magic; style of Jesus and style of magician: diss. Pont. Univ. Gregoriana, ᴰ*Latourelle* R. R 1985. Excerpt. 104 p.; bibliog. p. 60-97.

3460 *Fueter* Paul D., The therapeutic language of the Bible: *a)* BTrans 37 (1986) 309-319; – *b)* IntRMiss 75 (Geneva 1986) 211-221.

3461 **Gardner** Rex, Healing miracles; a doctor investigates. L 1986, Darton-LT. 214 p. £5. 0-232-51640-5. – ᴿExpTim 98 (1986s) 194s (C. S. *Rodd*: includes people in Chile miraculously receiving silver fillings in their teeth during a service, each filling marked by a cross); p. 219, note also J. *Wilkinson* on S. PARSONS; Themelios 12 (1986s) 100s (R. *Cowley*).

3462 **Glöckner** Richard, Neutestamentliche Wundergeschichten und das Lob der Wundertaten Gottes in den Psalmen 1983 ➤ 64,4364... 1,4422:

ᴿRechSR 74 (1986) 239 (J. *Guillet*: contre la thèse depuis REITZENSTEIN du *theîos anēr*).

3463 **González Faus** J.I.,   Clamor del Regno 1982 ⮕ 63,4497...1,4423: ᴿTVida 27 (1986) 327s (A. *Bentué*).

3464 *Graham* David J.,   Jesus as miracle worker [...Hellenistic parallels; current views]: ScotBEvT 4 (1986) 85-96.

3465 **Guardini** Romano,   Miracoli e segni, ᵀ*Colombi* Giulio: Opera 25.   Brescia 1985, Morcelliana.   64 p. Lit. 4000. – ᴿHumBr 41 (1986) 778 (B. *Belletti*).

3466 **Harper** Michael,   The healings of Jesus: The Jesus library.   L 1986, Hodder & S.   194 p.   £6.   0-340-27235-X. – ᴿExpTim 98 (1986s) 84 (C. *Davey*: convinced rather than convincing).

3467 *Joubert* Jean-Marie,   Ce qu'est un miracle selon Ludwig WITTGENSTEIN: RThom 86 (1986) 115-126.

3468 **Kee** H.C.,   Medicine, miracle and magic in New Testament times: SNTS Mon 55.   C 1986, Univ.   170 p.   £19.50.   0-521-32309-6. – ᴿExpTim 98 (1986s) 247s (J. L. *Houlden*).

3469 **Kee** Howard C.,   Miracle in the early Christian world 1983 ⮕ 64,4368... 1,4428:   ᴿCrNSt 7 (1986) 608s (N. *Brox*); JBL 105 (1986) 150-2 (J. H. *Elliott*: Golden Bough broken, history of religions cradle fallen: but what to replace it?).

3470 *Knoch* Otto B.,   'Diese Zeichen sind aufgeschrieben, damit ihr glaubt' (Joh 20,31); Überlegungen zur Eigenart, Bedeutung und kerygmatischen Auslegung der Wundererzählungen der Evangelien: KatBlätt 111 (Mü 1986) 180-9.265-272 [< ZIT].

3471 **Latourelle** René,   Miracles de Jésus et théologie du miracle: Recherches NS 8.   Montréal/P 1986, Bellarmin/Cerf.   400 p. – ᴿGregorianum 67 (1986) 603s (*ipse*); RThom 86 (1986) 654-9 (J.-P. *Torrell*); ScEspr 38 (1986) 257-260 (A. *Charbonneau*).

3472 **Lewis** C.S.,   Les miracles; étude préliminaire, ᵀ*Blondel* Jacques.   P 1985, 'S.P.B.'   183 p. – ᴿRHPR 66 (1986) 479s (R. *Voeltzel*).

3473 *Long* Valentine,   Miracles, a test of faith: HomPast 86,6 (1986) 11-16.

3474 **Mosetto** Francesco,   I miracoli evangelici nel dibattito tra Celso e ORIGENE: BiblScRel 76.   R 1986, LAS.   172 p. Lit. 20.000. – ᴿScripTPamp 18 (1986) 968s (N. *Merino*).

3475 **Peláez del Rosal** Jesús,   Los milagros de Jesús en los evangelios sinópticos; morfología e interpretación: EstNT 3, 1984 ⮕ 1,4437; 84-398-2499-9; 1606-5:   ᴿEstE 61 (1986) 476s (J. *Iturriaga*).

3476 **Penndu** Théophile,   Les miracles de Jésus; signes du monde nouveau.   Montréal 1985, Levain.   352 p. [Études 364,424].

3476* *Samuel* David,   Making room in history for the miraculous: Churchman 100 (L 1986) 46...; 101-113 [< ZIT].

3477 *Schoedel* William R. / *Malina* Bruce J. [both on *Kee* H., *Remus* H., *Theissen* G. 1983; *Gallagher* E. 1982]: RelStR 12 (1986) 31-35 / 35-39.

3477* *Schrage* Wolfgang,   Heil und Heilung im NT: EvT 46 (1986) 197-214.

3478 **Shorter** Aylward,   Jesus and the witchdoctor; an approach to healing and wholeness 1985 ⮕ 1,4442:   ᴿCleR 71 (1986) 36 (Vera *von der Heydt*); EAPast 23 (1986) cover after p. 98 (F. *Gómez*); ModT 3 (1986s) 274-6 (S. *Pattison*); Themelios 12 (1986s) 31s (J.J. *Stamoolis*); ZMissRW 70 (1986) 48-52 (H.-J. *Becken*).

3479 *Becken* Hans-Jürgen,   Jesus und Medizinmann: ZMissR 70 (1986) 48-52.

3480 *a)* Sigal Pierre,   L'homme et le miracle dans la France médiévale, XIᵉ-XIIᵉ s. [< diss. Paris I, 1981] 1985 ⮕ 1,4443:   ᴿRHE 81 (1986) 716s (G. *Hendrix*); RThom 86 (1986) 504s (B. *Montagnes*). – *b)* **Kselman** T.A.,

Miracles and prophecies in nineteenth-century France. New Brunswick NJ 1984, Rutgers. 283 p. $27.50. - ᴿCrNSt 7 (1986) 430-3 (L. *Ferrari*).

3481 **Sims** Andrew C. P., Demon possession; medical perspective in a western culture: ➤ 261, ᴱ*Palmer* B., Medicine 1986, 165-189. 264.

3482 **Staudinger** H., *Schlüter* J., An Wunder glauben? Gottes Allmacht und moderne Welterfahrung: Bücherei 1258. FrB 1986, Herder. 127 p. DM 7,90 [NRT 109,592, A. *Toubeau*].

3483 **Ward** Benedicta, Miracles and the medieval mind 1982 ➤ 63,4516... 1,4448: ᴿMélSR 43 (1986) 99-101 (H. *Platelle*).

3484 [*Wenham* David,] Miracles then and now: Themelios 12,1 (1986s) 1-4.

3485 **Wenisch** B., Geschichten oder Geschichte? Theologie des Wunders 1981 ➤ 62,4609... 1,4450: ᴿLaurentianum 27 (1986) 383s (J. *Imbach*).

3486 **Wilkinson** John, Healing [a weasel-word] in semantics, creation and redemption: ScotBEvT 4 (1986) 17-37.

3487 **Wilms** F. E., I miracoli nell'Antico Testamento: StBDeh 12. Bo 1985, Dehoniane. 350 p. - ᴿAsprenas 33 (1986) 203s (S. *Cipriani*); ParVi 31 (1986) 378-380 (G. *Boggio*).

3487* **Wojciechowski** Tadeusz, Ⓟ Aus der Problematik der Wunder: AnCracov 18 (1986) 35-59; deutsch 59.

3488 *Rolland* Philippe, [Mt 9,4; 12,24; 22,18...]: ETL 62 (1986) 118-121.

3489 **Bartnicki** Roman, Ⓟ *a*) Uczeń Jezusa jako głosiciel Ewangelii [the disciple of Jezus as mouthpiece of the Gospel], tradycja i redakcja Mt 9,35-11,1: 1985 ➤ 1,4453: ᴿColcT 56,4 (1986) 175-8 (J. *Łach*); RuBi 39 (1986) 174s (S. *Grzybek*). - *b*) Le disciple de Jésus comme héraut de l'Évangile; tradition et rédaction de Mt 9,35-11,1: Hab. Wsz AkadCath. 1984. - BinfWsz (1986,1) 29-31.

3490 **Crockett** Bennie R.ᴶ, The missionary experience of the Matthean community; a redactional analysis of Matthew 10: diss. New Orleans Baptist Sem. 1986, ᴰ*Glaze* R. 232 p. 87-06823. - DissA 47 (1986s) 4421s-A.

3491 **Adinolfi** Marco, [Mt 10,1...] L'apostolato dei Dodici nella vita di Gesù 1985 ➤ 1,4454: ᴿAntonianum 61 (1986) 203 (*ipse*); CC 137 (1986,3) 438 (J. *Janssens*).

3492 *Horbury* W., [Mt 10,1] The twelve and the phylarchs: NTS 32 (1986) 503-527.

3492* *Rossé* Gérard, La scelta dei Dodici: NuovaUm 8,46s (1986) 11-27.

3493 **White** Vernon, [Mt 10,29] The fall of a sparrow; a concept of special divine action. Exeter 1985, Paternoster. 208 p. £7.50 pa. - ᴿTLZ 111 (1986) 913s (J. *Langer*).

3495 **Verseput** Donald, The rejection of the humble messianic king; a study of the composition of Matthew 11-12: EurHS 23/201. Fra 1986, Lang. 480 p. Fs 77 [TR 83,250]. 3-8204-9781-1.

3496 **Cameron** Peter S., Violence and the Kingdom; the interpretation of Matthew 11:12 [diss. Cambridge 1979]: ArbNTJud 5, 1984 ➤ 65,4036: ᴿCBQ 48 (1986) 133-5 (Karen A. *Barta*).

3497 *Doyle* R., Matthew 11:12 — a challenge to the evangelist's community: Colloquium 18,1 (Auckland 1985) 20-30 [NTAbs 30,148].

3498 *O'Callaghan* José, La variante 'se gritan ... diciendo', de Mt 11,16-17: EstE 61 (1986) 67-70.

3499 *Rimbach* James A., [Mt 11,25...] God-talk or baby-talk; more on 'Abba': CurrTM [12/1 (1985) 9, *Quere* R.] 13 (1986) 232-5 [what J. JEREMIAS really

says is that *abba* was used also as a respectful address to old men, but never forgetting that it derived from the language of small children].
3500 *Doyle* B. Rod, A concern of the Evangelist; Pharisees in Matthew 12: AustralBR 34 (1986) 17-34.
3500* *Chilton* Bruce, [Mt 12,24-30 < Gn 4,8] A comparative study of synoptic development; the dispute between Cain and Abel in the Palestinian Targums and the Beelzebul controversy in the Gospels [< JBL 101 (1982) 553-562]: → 140*, Targumic approaches 1986, 137-149.
3501 *Neirynck* F., Mt 12,25a/Lc 11,17a et la rédaction des Évangiles: ETL 62 (1986) 122-133.
3502 *Romaniuk* Kazimierz bp. ℗ 'Być dzieckiem' [to be a child] według Biblii: Communio ℗ (1985,3) 3-17 [< RuBi 39,86].
3502* *Flusser* David, [Mt 12,32] Die Sünde gegen den heiligen Geist: → 68*, FMAYER R., Wie gut 1986, 139-144.

F4.3   Mt 13... *Parabolae Jesu* – **The Parables.**

3503 *Baasland* Ernst, Zum Beispiel der Beispielerzählungen; zur Formenlehre der Gleichnisse und zur Methodik der Gleichnisauslegung: NT 28 (1986) 193-219.
3504 **Baudler** Georg, Jesus im Spiegel seiner Gleichnisse; das erzählerische Lebenswerk Jesu — ein Zugang zum Glauben. Stu/Mü 1986, Calwer/ Kösel. 330 p.; bibliog. p. 321-330. DM 38 pa. [TR 83,75]. Stu 3-7668-0804-4 / Mü 3-466-36263-6.
3505 *Boyarin* D., Rhetoric and interpretation; the case of the nimshal [explanation of *mašal*]; Prooftexts 5,3 (Baltimore 1985) 269-276.
3506 **Bruin** Paul, Gleichnisse, die Lieblingssprache Jesu. Luzern 1982-4, Rex. 100 p. – RFreibRu 37s (1985s) 100s (P. *Fiedler*: Beispiele antijüdischer Klischeen).
3507 *Cole* Dick T., A response to [J. D.] FOSTER and [G. T.] MORAN's 'PIAGET and parables; the convergence of secular and Scriptural views of learning': JPsy&T [13 (1985s) 97-103] 14 (1986) 49-53; rejoinder 54-58.
3508 *Crossan* J. D., In fragments, the aphorisms of Jesus 1983 → 64,4404... 1,4476: RForum 1,1 (1985) 15-21 (B. B. *Scott*) & 23-30 (W. H. *Kelber*) & 1,2 (1985) 31-64 (V. K. *Robbins*); Interpretation 40 (1986) 92.94 (D. O. *Via*).
3509 *Dömötör* Akos, Ⓜ Characteristics of the parables in Protestant preaching: Theologiai Szemle 28 (1985) 15-21.
3510 **Drury** John, The parables in the Gospels; history and allegory 1985 → 1,4478: RInterpretation 40 (1986) 426. 428 (R. W. *Lyon*); IrBSt 8 (1986) 43s (E. *Best*); JTS 37 (1936) 172-4 (M. D. *Goulder*: challenges redaction-criticism and allegory-rejection, but without quite enough accuracy); Themelios 11 (1985s) 99 (D. *Wenham*); TLond 39 (1986) 228-230 (J. *Muddiman*); TS 47 (1986) 183s (R. F. *O'Toole*).
3511 **Erlemann** Kurt, Das Gottesbild der synoptischen Gleichnisse: Diss. DBerger K. Heid 1986s. – RTLv 18,546.
3512 **Espinel** José Luis, La poesía de Jesús [... parábolas]: Glosas 10. Salamanca 1986, San Esteban. 295 p. pt. 1200. 84-85045-71-8. – RCiTom 113 (1986) 385-8 (J. *Huarte*); LumenV 35 (1986) 546s (F. *Ortiz de Urtaran*); NatGrac 33 (1986) 334 (V. *Muñiz*); RazF 214 (1986) 467 (R. de *Andrés*); ScriptV 33 (1986) 442s (A. *Eguiluz*).
3513 **Fusco** Vittorio, Oltre la parabola 1983 → 64,4412... 1,4483: RDivinitas 30 (1986) 193s (C. *Petino*); Salesianum 48 (1986) 417 (C. *Bissoli*: tesi di

JÜLICHER-DODD-JEREMIAS riaffermata contro nord-americani secolarizzanti).

3514 **Harnisch** Wolfgang, Die Gleichniserzählungen Jesu; eine hermeneutische Einführung: UTB 1343, 1985 ➤ 1,4485: ᴿExpTim 98 (1986s) 302s (E. *Best*: his own views, as distinct from his two WegFor compilations); TR 82 (1986) 26-28 (E. *Arens*).

3514* **Hendrickx** Herman, The Parables of Jesus. L/SF 1986, Chapman/Harper & R. 291 p. $15. 0-225-664860 / 0-06-254815-8. – ᴿExpTim 98 (1986s) 280 (J. M. *Court*: if less strikingly successful than his four-volume series, fault of the material).

3515 **Johannsen** Friedrich, Gleichnisse Jesu im Religionsunterricht; Anregungen und Modelle für die Grundschule: Siebenstern 757. Gü 1986, Mohn. 96 p., ill. [TLZ 112,149].

3516 **Kjärgaard** Mogens S., Metaphor and parable; a systematic analysis of the specific structure and cognitive function of the Synoptic similes and parables qua metaphors: AcTheolDanica 19. Leiden 1986, Brill. 264 p.

3517 **La Maisonnneuve** Dominique de, Parábolas rabínicas [1,4490]: ᵀ*Darrical* Nicolás: Documentos en torno a la Biblia 12. Estella 1985, VDivino. 63 p. pt. 500. 84-7151-452-4. – ᴿBibFe 12 (1986) 367 (M. *Sáenz Galache*).

3518 **Lambrecht** Jan, Once more astonished 1981 ➤ 62,4656... 65,4063: ᴿHeythJ 27 (1986) 74s (J. N. *Birdsall*).

3519 **Mussner** Franz, Il messaggio delle parabole di Gesù² [1961, ²1964], ᵀ*Masini* Mario [¹1971 ᵀ*Colavero* G. ➤ 53,3304*]. Brescia 1986, Queriniana. 108 p. Lit. 8000. – ᴿBbbOr 28 (1986) 125 (F. *Sardini*); ScuolC 114 (1986) 748 (F. *Baj*: sulle 23 delle 24 parabole che hanno un identico messaggio).

3520 *Newman* Robert C., Perspective transformation by means of parables: ➤ 65, ᶠMᴀᴄRᴀᴇ A., Interpretation 1986, 139-154.

3521 **Rossel** W., Zonder parabels sprak Hij niet; gelovig leven in het licht van de evangelische parabels 1985 ➤ 1,4493: ᴿCollatVl 16 (1986) 124 (J. *Lambrecht*).

3522 *Rossow* F. C., The Gospel-potential of our Lord's parables: ConcordJ 12,1 (1986) 3-8 [NTAbs 30,276].

3523 **Rupp** Walter, Erstaunliche Gleichnisse; das Himmelreich ist wie... Graz 1985, Styria. 148 p. 10 fig. (Graw H.); Sch 168. – ᴿZkT 108 (1986) 196s (L. *Jorissen*).

3524 *Schmidt-Leukel* Perry, Zur Funktion der Gleichnisrede bei Buddha und Jesus: MüTZ 37 (1986) 116-133.

3525 **Schramm** T., *Löwenstein* K., Unmoralische Helden; anstössige Gleichnisse Jesu. Gö 1986, Vandenhoeck & R. 204 p.

3526 **Soldati** Joseph A., Talking like gods; new voices of authority: ➤ 395, ᴱ*Smith* R., Pagan and Christian anxiety 1979/84, 169-190.

3527 **Stern** David, The rabbinic parable; from rhetoric to poetics: ➤ 392, SBL Seminars 1986, 631-643.

3528 **Thielicke** Helmut, Das Bilderbuch Gottes; Reden über die Gleichnisse Jesu. Stu 1986, Quell. 304 p.

3529 ᴱ**Thoma** Clemens, *Lauer* Simon, Die Gleichnisse der Rabbinen; I. Pešiqtā de Rav KᴀHᴀNᴀ Einleitung, Übersetzung, Parallelen, Kommentar, Texte: JudChr 10. Bern 1986, Lang. 430 p. 3-261-03596-X.

3530 *Wailes* Stephen L., Why did Jesus use parables? The medieval discussion: MedHum 13 (Totowa 1985) 43-64.

3531 **Westermann** Claus, Vergleiche und Gleichnisse im ANT 1984 ➤ 65,4071; 1,4502: ᴿActuBbg 23 (1986) 223 (X. *Alegre* S.); BO 43 (1986) 650-4 (P.

Höffken); JBL 105 (1986) 512s (J. G. *Williams*: a retired professor launching out into a new area of investigation); WissWeis 47 (1984) 228 (H.-J. *Klauck*).

3532 **Wojciechowski** Michał, ℗ Czynności symbologiczne... Des actions symboliques de Jésus sur l'arrière-plan de l'Ancien Testament: diss. ᴰ*Łach* J., Wsz 1986. – RTLv 18,551.

3533 **Battaglia** Oscar, Le parabole del Regno [sette in Mt 13] 1985 → 1,4505 [index!]: ᴿAsprenas 33 (1986) 336s (A. *Rolla*).

3533* *Schaupp* Klemens, 'Ein Sämann ging aufs Feld, um zu säen...'; zur Frage der Integration von psychologischer Hilfestellung und geistlicher Begleitung: GeistL 59 (1986) 269-275.

3534 **Gilles** Jean, [Mt 13,55] I 'fratelli e sorelle' di Gesù [normalmente tali, non parenti]; per una lettura fedele del Vangelo: Piccola Biblioteca Teologica 16, 1985 → 1,4512: ᴿBbbOr 28 (1986) 122 (F. *Montagnini*: l'autore è filologo cattolico; la serie è valdese, introduzione di *Corsano* B. p. 5-15; segue un 'commento al libro' di U. A. *Interlandi*, insegnante cattolico sorpreso che R. PESCH abbia chiesto la soppressione del suo Excursus relativo nell'edizione italiana); CC 137 (1986,3) 192-4 (V. *Fusco*: ingenuità e lacune, commenti di cattolici non esegeti); EphMar 36 (1986) 189 (S. *Blanco*: la cuestión no afecta la filiación divina); HumBr 41 (1986) 454s (A. *Orsatti*: non va per un cattolico); ParVi 31 (1986) 237-240 (M. *Galizzi*: perfino contro LUTERO); Studium 26 (M 1986) 544s (L. *López de las Heras*).

3535 *a)* *Kruse* Heinz, ❶ The brothers of Jesus [*Pesch* R.; Mk 6,3]: KatKenk 25,50 (1986) 1-36; Eng. i-iv; – *b)* *Drăguşin* Valeriu, 'Les frères' du Seigneur à la lumière de l'exégèse orthodoxe (roum.): STBuc 37 (1985) 381-9.

3536 *O'Callaghan* Josep, Sobre tres variants de Mt 14,6.15.18: RCatalT 11 (1986) 27-30.

3537 **Berg** W., [Mt 14,22...] Die Rezeption alttestamentlicher Motive im NT — dargestellt an den Seewandelerzählungen [Hab.-D. Mü 1978, ᴰ*Scharbert* J. → 60,6142; 61,4684]. Fr 1979, Hochschul-V. ix-374 p. DM 55. – ᴿBZ 30 (1986) 105s (G. *Dautzenberg*); SNTU-A 11 (1986) 227s (A. *Fuchs*).

3538 **Heil** John P., Jesus walking on the sea... Matt 14: 22-33: AnBib 87, 1981 → 62,4685... 65,4078: ᴿRB 93 (1986) 472s (M.-É. *Boismard*).

3539 *Schwartz* Daniel R. [Mt 15,1-20] Viewing the holy utensils (P. Ox. V, 840): NTS 32 (1986) 153-9.

3539* *Baumgarten* Albert I., [Mt 15,5] Korban and the Pharisaic Parádosis: → 11*, Mem. ᶠBICKERMAN E. = JANES 16s (1984) 5-17.

3540 *O'Callaghan* José, La variante 'palabra' o 'precepto' en Mt 15,6: EstE 61 (1986) 421-3.

3541 *Maier* John P., Matthew 15:21-28: Interpretation 40 (1986) 397-402.

3542 *Onwu Neenanya* [Contents: Nienanya], Jesus and the Canaanite woman (Mt. 15:21-28): Bible Bhashyam 11 (1985) 130-143.

3543 *O'Callaghan* José, *a)* Consideraciones críticas sobre Mt 15,35-36a: Biblica 67 (1986) 360-2. – *b)* [Mt 16,11] La variante neotestamentaria 'levadura de los panes': Biblica 67 (1986) 98-100.

F4.5 **Mt 16**... *Primatus promissus* – **the promise to Peter.**

3544 *Bonino* Serge-Thomas, La place du pape dans l'Église selon saint Thomas d'AQUIN: RThom 86 (1986) 392-422.

3544* *Chilton* Bruce, Shebna, Eliakim, and the promise to Peter: ➤ 140*, Targumic 1986, 63-80.

3545 **Chirico** Peter, Infallibility: the crossroads of doctrine 1983 ➤ 64,4463; 1,4529:   ᴿHeythJ 27 (1986) 222s (G. *Newlands*).

3546 **Claudel** Gérard, La confession de Pierre; trajectoire d'une période évangélique: diss. ᴰ*Schlosser* J. Strasbourg 1986. 488 p.; 331 p. – RTLv 18,546.

3547 *Crawford* L., Tu es Pierre, et sur cette pierre...: CahRenan 33,139 (1985) 13-16: a first Matthew got the text from Essenes (1QH 7,8s) and a second Matthew applied it to Peter [NTAbs 30,280].

3548 *Fabris* Rinaldo, San Pietro apostolo nella prima Chiesa: StMiss 35 (R 1986) 41-70.

3549 *Fornberg* Tord, Peter — the High Priest of the new covenant ? : EAsJT 4,1 (1986) 113-121.

3550 *Frohnhofen* Herbert, 'Forma' und 'forma Petri'; Anmerkungen zu ihrer Bedeutungsgeschichte bis zu Papst LEO dem Grossen: TrierTZ 95 (1986) 208-217.

3551 *Galvin* John P., Papal primacy in contemporary Roman Catholic theology: TS 47 (1986) 653-667.

3552 **Iannice** M., Il primato di Pietro in alcuni momenti della storia dell'esegesi: diss. Cosenza 1984, ᴰ*Leanza* S. [RivB 35,85].

3553 *Lambrecht* Jan, 'Du bist Petrus' — Mt 16,16-19 und das Papsttum: SNTU-A 11 (1986) 5-32.

3554 **Pepka** Edward P., The theology of St. Peter's presence in his successors according to St. LEO the Great, diss. Catholic Univ., ᴰ*Eno* R., Wsh 1986. 331 p. 86-13472. – DissA 47 (1986s) 1371s-A.

3555 **Smith** Terence V., Petrine controversies in early Christianity; attitudes towards Peter in Christian writings of the first two centuries [diss. London 1981]: WUNT 2/15, 1985 ➤ 1,4538:   ᴿAugR 26 (1986) 579s (E. *Peretto*); NRT 108 (1986) 758s (X. *Jacques*); RHPR (1986) 237s (C. *Grappe*).

3556 ᴱ**Tekippe** Terry J., Papal infallibility; an application of LONERGAN's theological method 1983 ➤ 64,360; 65,4096:   ᴿHeythJ 27 (1986) 354s (P. *Chirico*).

3557 **Thiede** Carsten P., Simon Peter; from Galilee to Rome. Exeter 1986, Paternoster. 272 p.; bibliog. p. 197-211. £8. 0-85364-386-5. – ᴿExpTim 98 (1986s) 281s (F. F. *Bruce*); Themelios 12 (1986s) 103 (I. H. *Marshall*).

3558 **Tillard** J.-M., *a)* L'Évêque de Rome 1982 ➤ 63,903 ... 1,4539:   ᴿRThom 86 (1986) 127-133 (M.-V. *Leroy*); Vidyajyoti 49 (1985) 50s (R. *Lewicki*).

3559 *a) Winkler* Gerhard B., Kirchenfürst oder Seelsorger? Vom Wandel des päpstlichen Selbstverständnisses [... Abstreifen der Herrschaftsstrukturen unter dem Druck der Ereignisse ...]; – *b) Zinnhobler* Rudolf, Petrusamt und Ökumene; zum gegenwärtigen Stand der Diskussion: TPQ 134 (1986) 5-12 / 13-21.

3560 **Vigen** Larry A., 'To think the things of God'; a discoursive reading of Matthew 16:13-18;35:   diss. Vanderbilt; ᴰ*Patte* D. Nv 1985. 429 p. 86-07531. – DissA 47 (1986s) 554-A; RelStR 13,190.

3561 *Wright* Benjamin G.ᴵᴵᴵ, A previously unnoticed Greek variant of Matt 16:14 — 'Some say John the Baptist ...': JBL 105 (1986) 694-7.

3562 ᴱ**Coune** Michael, [Mt 17] Joie de la Transfiguration d'après les Pères d'Orient. Bellefontaine 1985, Abbaye. 263 p. F 78. – ᴿVSp 140 (1986) 730 (D. *Cerbelaud*).

3563 McGuckin John A., The Transfiguration of Christ in Scripture and tradition: StBEC 9. Lewiston NY 1986, Mellen. xvi-333 p. 0-88946-609-2.

3564 Zmijewski Josef, Der Glaube und seine Macht, eine traditionsgeschichtliche Untersuchung zu Mt 17,20; 21,21; Mk 11,23; Lk 17,6 [< FZIMMERMANN H. 1980, 81-103]: ⇒ 233, Das NT Quelle 1986, 265-292.

3565 Bauckham Richard, [Mt 17,24-27] The coin in the fish's mouth: ⇒ 271, Miracles 1986, 219-252.

3566 Elkins Jorge, Análisis lingüístico estructural de la parábola del siervo sin entrañas (Mt 18,21-26): CuBi 39,283 (1984ss) 68-77.

3567 Mateu y Llopis Felipe, [Mt 18,24-30] Talentum argenti y talenta auri; del Evangelio d San Mateo a los diplomas hispanos anteriores a 1126: ⇒ 21, Mem. DÍEZ MACHO A., Salvación 1986, 735-748.

3568 Ganswinkel Albert van, Ehescheidung und Wiederheirat in neutestamentlicher und moraltheologischer Sicht [Mt 19,9 moicheúein; Mk 10,12 apolyménē; 1 Kor 7,10-16 ápistos; Eph 5,32 mystērion...]: TGl 76 (1986) 193-211.

Heth W., Wenham G., Jesus and divorce 1985 ⇒ 3430; Stramare T., Matteo divorzista? 1986 ⇒ 3432.

3569 Wenham Gordon J., The syntax of Matthew 19.9: JStNT 28 (1986) 17-23.

3570 Quesnell Quentin, Hacerse eunucos por el reino de los cielos [Mt 19,10-12]. M 1986, Rama Dorada. 52 p. – RBibFe 12 (1986) 368s (A. Salas).

3571 Côté Pierre-René, Les eunuques pour le Royaume (Mt 19,12): ÉglT 17 (1986) 321-334.

3571* Luck Ulrich, Die Frage nach dem Guten; zu Mt 19,16-30 und Parr.: ⇒ 39, FGREEVEN H., Text/Ethik 1986, 282-297.

3572 EPizzolato Luigi F., [Mt 19,16-22] Per foramen acus; il cristianesimo antico di fronte alla pericope evangelica del 'giovane ricco': Studia patristica mediolanensia 14. Mi 1986, Univ. Cattolica/ViPe. viii-565 p. 88-343-0171-4. 9 art. [Dal Covolo Enrico, 79-108 in CLEMENTE e ORIGENE; Scaglioni Carlo, 329-528, CRISOSTOMO, AGOSTINO].

3572* Pausch Alfons & Jutta, [Mt 19,24] Steuern in der Bibel. Köln 1986, O. Schmidt. 103 p. DM 24. – RBiKi 41 (1986) 187s (P.-G. Müller).

F4.8 Mt 20 ... Regnum eschatologicum – Kingdom eschatology.

3573 Ardizzoni Anthos, I disoccupati dell'ultima ora (Riflessioni su Matteo 20,1-20): GitFg 37 (1985) 3-14.

3574 Barré Michael L., [Mt 20,1-16] The workers in the vineyard: BToday 24 (1986) 173-180.

3575 Bonzi M., Analisi della parabola degli operai nella vigna (Mt. 20,1-16): diss. Univ. Cattolica, DGhiberti G. Milano 1985 [RivB 35,86].

3575* Lämmermann Godwin, Ist das gerecht ? Das Gleichnis von den Gärtnern im Weinberg (Mt 20,1-16) im Religionsunterricht einer 6. Klasse: EvErz 38 (1986) 482-499.

3576 Schottroff Luise, Bibelarbeit über Matthäus 20,1-16: Junge Kirche 47 (Bremen 1986) 322-5.

3576* Sorger Karlheinz, Die Parabel vom gütigen Herrn des Weinbergs (Mt 20,1-16): KatBlätt 111 (Mü 1986) 190-2 [< ZIT].

3577 Wegner Uwe, Justiça para os desempregados – reflexões sobre Mt 20,1-15: Estudos Bíblicos 11 [REB 46,3] (1986) 92-109.

3578 *Meyer* Paul W.,   Matthew 21:1-11:   Interpretation 40 (1986) 180-5.
3579 *Kingsbury* Jack D., [Mt 21,33-46] The parable of the wicked husbandmen and the secret of Jesus' divine sonship in Matthew; some literary-critical observations: JBL 105 (1986) 643-655.
3580 *Morrice* W. G., *a*) [Mt 21,33-46] The parable of the tenants and the Gospel of Thomas; – *b*) [Mt 13,44] The parable of the hidden treasure [and the Gospel of Thomas]:   ExpTim 98 (1986s) 104-7/ 112s.
3581 **Snodgrass** Klyne, [Mt 21,33-46; Mk 12,1-12] The parable of the wicked tenants: WUNT 27, 1983 ➤ 64,4506 ... 1,4562:   ᴿHeythJ 27 (1986) 448s (J.D.M. *Derrett*: a joy to read); TLZ 111 (1986) 361s (G. *Haufe*).
3582 *Aarde* A. G. van,   Plot as mediated through point of view; Mt 22:1-14 – a case study: ➤ 72, ᶠMETZGER B., South Africa 1985/6, 62-75.
3582* *a*) *Oster* Richard E., [Mt 22,19] 'Show me a denarius'; symbolism of Roman coinage and Christian beliefs: RestQ 28 (1985s) 107 ... [< ZIT]; – *b*) *Bori* Pier Cesare, 'Date a Cesare quel che è di Cesare ...' (Mt 22,21); linee di storia dell'interpretazione antica: CrNSt 7 (1986) 451-464.
3583 *Canning* R.,   AUGUSTINE on the identity of the neighbour and the meaning of true love for him 'as ourselves' (Matt. 22,39) and 'as Christ has loved as' (Jn 13,34):   AugLv 36 (1986) 161-239.
3584 *Plass* Paul, [Mt 22,39 ...] Antinomy and exegesis in KIERKEGAARD: TZBas 42 (1986) 26-39.
3585 *Schürmann* Heinz,   Die Redekomposition wider 'dieses Geschlecht' und seine Führung in der Redenquelle (vgl. Mt 23,1-39 par Lk 11,37-54); Bestand – Akoluthie – Kompositionsformen: SNTU-A 11 (1986) 33-81.
3586 *Derrett* J.D.M.,   Receptacles and tombs (Mt 23,24-30) [tirade against Pharisees]: ZNW 77 (1986) 255-266.
3587 *Winkle* Ross E., [Mt 23:29 - 24:2] The Jeremiah model for Jesus in the Temple [in NT only Mt refers to Jeremiah by name]:   AndrUnS 24 (1986) 155-172.
3588 **Kühschelm** Roman,   Jüngerverfolgung ... Mt 23,29: ÖstBSt 5, 1983 ➤ 64,4517 ... 1,4568:   ᴿTLZ 111 (1986) 105-7 (H.-T. *Wrege*).
3589 *Míguez* Néstor O.,   Continuidad y ruptura, confrontación y conflicto; elementos para una aproximación socio-política a Mateo 23-24: RBibArg 48 (1986) 153-167.
3590 **Agbanou** Victor K.,   Le discours eschatologique de Matthieu 24-25: ÉtBN 20, 1983 ➤ 65,4125; 1,4570:   ᴿRechSR 74 (1986) 242s (J. *Guillet*: clair, suggestif).
3591 **Dupont** Jacques, [Mt 24s] Les trois Apocalypses synoptiques: LDiv 121, 1985 ➤ 1,4572:   ᴿCBQ 48 (1986) 741-3 (R. D. *Witherup*: balanced, not much new); EsprV 96 (1986) 442-4 (L. *Monloubou*); ÉTRel 61 (1986) 287s (E. *Cuvillier*); FoiTemps 16 (1986) 181 (C. *Focant*); JTS 37 (1986) 532s (T. F. *Glasson*); MélSR 43 (1986) 212s (M. *Hubaut*); NRT 108 (1986) 752s (X. *Jacques*); RThom 86 (1986) 321-3 (L. *Devillers*); Salmanticensis 33 (1986) 372 (R. *Trevijano*).
3592 **Kimball** William R., [Mt 24s] What the Bible says about the great tribulation. Joplin MO 1983, College = GR 1984, Baker. x-291 p. $8 pa. – ᴿAndrUnS 24 (1986) 191-4 (H. K. *LaRondelle*).
3593 **Hart** John F.,   A chronology of Matthew 24: 1-44 ['immediately after the tribulation']: diss. Grace Theol. Sem., ᴰ'Sproule J., 1986. 287 p. 86-19649. – DissA 47 (1986s) 2188-A; GraceTJ 7 (1986) 319.
3594 **Wenham** David,   The rediscovery of Jesus' eschatological discourse [Mt 24,1-36]: Gospel Perspectives 4, 1984 ➤ 65,4126; 1,4574:   ᴿCBQ 48 (1986) 351-3 (F. W. *Burnett*); EvQ 58 (1986) 364-7 (T. J. *Geddert*: his p. 239 is too

late to let the reader know Matthew wrote with a copy of Mark in front of him); Themelios 11 (1985s) 99 (G. *Stanton*).

3595 *a) Fleddermann* Harry, [Mt 24,43s] The householder and the servant left in charge; – *b) McKnight* Scot, Jesus and the End-Time; Matthew 10:23; – *c) Borg* Marcus J., A temperate case for a noneschatological Jesus: ➤ 392, SBL Seminars 1986, 17-26 / 501-520 / 521-535.

3596 **Puig i Tarrèch** A., [Mt 25,1-13] La parabole des dix vierges: AnBib 102/ColSPacià 28, 1983 ➤ 64,4525; 1,4578: ᴿRechSR 74 (1986) 243s (J. *Guillet*).

3596* **Marin** Marcello, Ricerche sull'esegesi agostiniana della parabola delle dieci vergini (Mt 25,1-13) 1981 ➤ 62,4741 ... 65,4129: ᴿCrNSt 7 (1986) 609-611 (C. *Scaglioni*).

3597 *Lemcio* Eugene E., The parables of the great supper and the wedding feast; history, redaction and canon: HorBT 8,1 (Pittsburgh 1986) 1-26.

3597* *Marguerat* Daniel, Le jugement dans l'évangile de Matthieu [diss. Lausanne 1981]: Le monde de la Bible 1981 ➤ 62,4462 ... 1,4585: ᴿRThom 86 (1986) 315-9 (L. *Devillers*: remarquable).

3598 *Vara* J., Dos conjeturas textuales sobre Mt 25,21.23 y Mt 26,32/17,22 y par.: Salmanticensis 33 (1986) 81-86.

3599 *Donahue* John R., [Mt 25,31-46] The 'parable' of the sheep and the goats; a challenge to Christian ethics [redimensioning L. *Cope* 1969: not 'universal charity' but 'punishment for not accepting the Gospel']: TS 47 (1986) 3-31.

3599* *Frahier* Louis-Jean, La prédication de Luther sur Mt 25,31-46: RICathP 19 (1986) 101-118.

3600 **Pikaza** X., Hermanos de Jesús y servidores de los más pequeños (Mt 25,31-46) 1984 ➤ 65,4133; 1,4583: ᴿComSev 19 (1986) 248-250 (V. J. *Ansede Alonso*); RazF 212 (1985) 217 (R. de *Andrés*).

F5.1   *Redemptio; Mt 26, Ultima coena;* **The Eucharist** ➤ H7.4.

3601 **Alonso Schökel** Luis, Meditaciones bíblicas sobre la Eucaristía: Ritos y símbolos 21. Santander 1986, Sal Terrae. 151 p. 84-293-0961-3.

3602 *Alonso Schökel* Luis, Meditazioni sulla celebrazione eucaristica, 1. Il segno della croce; [2.] La liturgia penitenziale ...]: ViConsacr 22 (1986) 95-100. 193-9. 264-271. 341-7. 437-443. 525-531. 621-9. 713-720. 809-816.

3603 **Bätzing** Georg, Die Eucharistie als Opfer der Kirche nach Hans Urs von BALTHASAR: Kriterien 74. Einsiedeln 1986, Johannes. 164 p. [TR 82,259].

3604 **Baigorri** L., Eucaristía. Estella 1985, VDivino. 114 p. – ᴿBibFe 12 (1986) 250 (A. *Salas*: sin presentación científica).

3605 *Bartnik* Czesław, ⊕ Eucharystia uniwersalna: ColcT 56,2 (1986) 5-17; franç. 17.

3606 *Beer* Peter, G. B. SALA and E. SCHILLEBEECKX on the Eucharistic presence: a critique: ScEspr 38 (1986) 31-48.

3607 *Bergeron* Richard, La souffrance dans la pâque de Jésus: PrêtreP 89 (1986) 130-137.

3608 *Bieritz* K.-H., *Roloff* J. Abendmahl: ➤ 587, EvKL 1 (1986) 5-9-13 (-31 al.).

3609 *Biffi* Inos, Scrittura e liturgia nel Sacro Triduo: Ambrosius 62 (1986) 101-6.

3610 **Bishop** Jonathan, The covenant, a reading 1982 ➤ 63,4663; 65,4536: ᴿAmBenR 37 (1986) 336-348 (J. *Leinenweber*; cites J. M. *Cameron*, New York Review, 'an original work of theology').

3610* **Bode** Franz-Josef, Gemeinschaft mit dem lebendigen Gott; die Lehre der Eucharistie bei Matthias J. SCHEEBEN: PdTheolSt 16. Pd 1986, Schöningh. xiii-522 p. [TR 83,403, E. *Fastenrath*].

3611 *Bosshard* Stefan N., Zur Bedeutung der Anamneselehre für ein ökumenisches Eucharistieverständnis: ZkT 108 (1986) 155-163.

3612 **Bürgener** Karsten, Amt und Abendmahl und was die Bibel dazu sagt. Bremen 1985, St. Johannes-Sodenmatt. 123 p.

3613 **Bürki** Bruno, Cène du Seigneur – Eucharistie de l'Église; le cheminement des Églises réformées romandes et française depuis le XVIIIe siècle, d'après leurs textes liturgiques; A. Textes; B. Commentaire: Cahiers Œcuméniques 17. FrS 1985, Univ. 175 p.; 224 p. 2-8271-0298-4. – ᴿÉTRel 61 (1986) 617s (B. *Reymond*); JTS 37 (1986) 693-7 (B. D. *Spinks*); TS 47 (1986) 709-711 (E. J. *Cutrone*: valuable).

3614 *Ferraro* Giuseppe, L'eucaristia nelle encicliche 'Redemptor Hominis', 'Dives in Misericordia' e 'Dominum et Vivificantem': RasT 27 (1986) 289-301.

3615 **Gesteira Garza** Manuel, L'Eucaristia, misterio de comunión 1983 ➤ 64,4553; 1,4602: ᴿSalmanticensis 33 (1986) 254-6 (D. *Salado*: esplendido).

3615* *Gesteira Garza* Manuel, La transustanciación eucarística; ¿ un milagro o un misterio?: MiscCom 44 (1986) 339-383.

3616 **Giraudo** Cesare, La struttura letteraria della preghiera eucaristica ... *tôdâ*, *bᵉrākâ*: AnBib 92, 1981 ➤ 62,4765 ... 65,4154: ᴿÉtRel 61 (1986) 590 (F. *Smyth*: manque l'anamnèse); OrChr 70 (1986) 197-9 (G. *Winkler*: bahnbrechend, nicht überzeugend).

3617 *Hahn* Ferdinand, Thesen zur Frage einheitsstiftender Elemente in Lehre und Praxis des urchristlichen Herrenmahls [< ᶠBORNKAMM G. 1980, 415-424]: ➤ 167, Ges. Aufs. 1 (1986) 232-241 (-336, 5 verwandte Art.).

3618 **Heron** Alasdair I. C., Table and tradition 1983 ➤ 65,4163; 1,4608: ᴿChH 55 (1986) 83 (R. L. *Harrison*).

3619 *Hobbs* R. Gerald, L'exégèse des Psaumes par Martin BUCER dans le contexte de la querelle eucharistique [colloque 1984, Bucer et la Concorde de Wittenberg]: RTPhil 118 (1986) 318s (somm.).

3619* *Hollenweger* Walter J., Le dernier repas; une liturgie eucharistique narrative et théâtrale [Jüngermesse/Gomer 1983],ᵀᴱ: Hokhma 11,32 (1986) 1-11.

3620 **Huels** John M., One table, many laws; essays on Catholic eucharistic practice. Collegeville MN 1986, Liturgical, 112 p. $6 pa. [TDig 34,76].

3621 *Jilek* August, Diakonia im Herrenmahl; Sinndeutung des Opfergangs aus der Stiftung der Eucharistie: LtgJb 36 (1986) 46-57.

3622 *Kasper* Walter, Unidad y pluralidad de aspectos en la Eucaristía [< IKZ 14 (1985) 196-215], ᵀᴱ*Alemany* Alvaro: SelT 25 (1986) 338-349.

3623 **Kilpatrick** G. D., The Eucharist in Bible and liturgy 1983 ➤ 64,4562 ... 1,4614: ᴿEstB 44 (1986) 247-9 (N. *Fernández Marcos*); EvQ 58 (1986) 86-89 (J. B. *Green*); NT 28 (1986) 94s (J. K. *Elliott*).

3624 *Koch* Ernst, Johannes BUGENHAGENS Anteil am Abendmahlsstreit zwischen 1525 und 1532: TLZ 111 (1986) 705-730.

3624* **Kyndal** Erik, Nadverlære og nadverfællesskab; den lutherske nadverlære kritisk belyst ud fra Ny Testamente og den økumeniske samtale i nutiden 1984 ➤ 1,4618: ᴿTsTKi 57 (1986) 316s (O. *Tjørhom*).

3625 *Lamberts* J., Eucharistie et Esprit-Saint: QLtg 67 (1986) 33-52 [81-86, Liturgie, L. *Leijssen*].

3626 *Laurance* John D., The Eucharist as imitation of Christ: TS 47 (1986) 286-296.

3627 ᴱLehmann Karl, Schlink Edmund, Das Opfer Jesu Christi und seine Gegenwart in der Kirche; Klärungen zum Opfercharakter des Herrenmahles: Dialog der Kirchen 3, 1983 → 64,512: ᴿTPQ 134 (1986) 404s (J. B. *Bauer*: Gn 22 kultätiologisch); TR 82 (1986) 403-410 (M. M. *Garijo-Guembe*).

3628 **Léon-Dufour** X., Le partage du pain eucharistique selon le NT 1982 → 63,4689 ... 1,4621: ᴿRB 93 (1986) 473s (M.-E. *Boismard*: riche).

3629 **Lies** Lothar, ORIGENES' Eucharistielehre im Streit der Konfessionen; die Auslegungsgeschichte seit der Reformation: InnsbThSt 15, 1985 → 1,4624: ᴿETL 62 (1986) 441-3 (A. de *Halleux*); TR 82 (1986) 396-8 (H. *Feld*).

3630 *McCabe* Herbert, Holy Thursday, the mystery of unity: NBlackf 67 (1986) 56-69.

3631 **Macy** Gary, The theologies of the Eucharist in the early scholastic period; a study of the salvific function of the sacrament ... [diss. Cambridge] 1984 → 65,4170*; 1,4627: ᴿHorizons 13 (1986) 168s (Eileen *Kearney*); JRel 66 (1986) 438s (J. *van Engen*); JTS 37 (1986) 629-632 (D. *Luscombe*); NRT 108 (1986) 916s (J.-Y. *Lacoste*).

3632 *Marcel* Pierre, La communication du Christ avec les siens; la parole et la cène: RRef 37,1 (1986) 5-53 [< ZIT].

3633 **Menconi** Valeria, Verbo fatto uomo fatto pane; le pagine più belle sull'Eucaristia. R 1985, Assoc. Internaz. Mariana. 818 p. – ᴿDivinitas 30 (1986) 208 (G. *Concetti*).

3633* *Mertin* Andreas, Schmidt Heinz-Ulrich, 'Nehmet und esset ...'; das Abendmahl im Bild der Zeit: Forum Religion 3 (Stu 1986) 2-11 [< ZIT].

3634 *Moore* Gareth, Transubstantiation for beginners [... like paper money]: NBlackf 67 (1986) 530-7.

3635 *Oftestad* Bernt T., 'Historia' und 'utilitas'; methodologische Aspekte der Abendmahlstheologie bei Martin CHEMNITZ: ArRefG 77 (1986) 186-224; Eng. 225.

3636 **Reumann** John, The Supper of the Lord; the New Testament, ecumenical dialogues, and Faith and Order on Eucharist 1985 → 1,4639; $14: ᴿCBQ 48 (1986) 757s (G. S. *Sloyan*); CurrTM 13 (1986) 117s (R. W. *Roschke*: it's fun to see Benedictines anticipating Reformation debates); TLZ 112 (1987) 775-7 (H.-C. *Schmidt-Lauber*); TS 47 (1986) 344s (E. J. *Cutrone*).

3637 *Rogowski* Roman E., ❷ La transsubstantiation pascale: AtKap 106 (1986) 24-33.

3637* *Roux* Jean-Marie, Corporéité et symbole eucharistique: BLitEc 87 (1986) 29-55; Eng. p. 54: 'a real presence – a bodily one as it were – of the thing symbolised in the symboliser'.

3638 *a) Rubianes* Jesús, La Eucaristía; praxis en el judaismo bíblico; – *b)* *Gallego* Epifanio, ... perspectiva sinóptica; – *c)* *Calle* Francisco de la, ... joánica; – *d)* *Municio* Fidela, ... presencia del resucitado; – *e)* *Villar* Evaristo, ... praxis del cristianismo naciente; – *f)* *Tous* Lorenzo, ... perspectiva social; – *g)* *Galdeano Ochoa* J. Luis, ... praxis pastoral, hoy; – *h)* *Salas* Antonio, Eucaristía y comunión; reflexión teológica desde la praxis sacramentaria: BibFe 12,35 (1986) 149-157 / 158-173 / 174-184 / 185-195 / 196-209 / 210-222 / 223-232 / 233-246 [-248 bibliog.].

3639 **Sayés** J. A., El misterio eucarístico: BAC 482, Historia Salutis 16. M 1986, Católica. xix-433 p. [NRT 109,605, R. *Escol*].

3640 **Schenker** Adrian, L'Eucaristia nell'Antico Testamento: Già e non ancora 87. Mi 1982, Jaca. 184 p. Lit. 13.000. – ᴿBenedictina 33 (1986) 582s (E. *Tuccimei*).

3641 **Schmemann** A. († 1983) L'Eucharistie, sacrement du Royaume: L'Échelle de Jacob. P 1985, O.E.I.L./YMCA. 277 p. F 98. – ᴿNRT 108 (1986) 917s (A. *Toubeau*).

3641* *Scordato* Cosimo, La dimensione cosmica dell'Eucaristia nella riflessione di TEILHARD de Chardin: Asprenas 33 (1986) 123-148.

3642 *Steiger* Lothar, Die Predigt und ihr Kommentar, sum Beispiel Mt 26,1-13: BTZ 3 (1986) 172-7.

3643 *Stepelevich* Lawrence S., HEGEL and the Lutheran Eucharist: HeythJ 27 (1986) 262-274.

3644 *Suggit* J. N., The perils of Bible translation; an examination of the Latin versions of the words of institution of the Eucharist: → 72, ᶠMETZGER B., South Africa 1985/6, 54-61.

3645 **Trimp** C., Woord, Water en Wijn: Bij-tijds Geloven. Kampen 1985, Kok. 116 p. *f* 19,50 pa. – ᴿKerkT 37 (1986) 276 (M. H. *Bolkestein*).

3645* *Veerkamp* Ton, Das mystifizierte Abendmahl – der mystifizierte Messias: Forum Religion 4 (Stu 1986) 7-11 [< ZIT].

3646 *a) Volk* Ernst, Evangelische Akzente [Eng. p. 206 'Luther's accents'] im Verständnis der Eucharistie [zu PANNENBERG W., KÜHN U.]: KerDo 32 (1986) 188-205. – *b) Widmann* Peter, En lutersk besindelse på Nadveren [the Supper]: DanTTs 49 (1986) 279 ... [< ZIT].

3646* **Walker** Michael, The theology of the Lord's Supper amongst English Baptists in the nineteenth century: diss. London 1986. – RTLv 18,559.

3647 **Yousif** Pierre, L'Eucharistie [parole absente] chez saint *Ephrem* de Nisibe [diss. Strasbourg]: OrChrAn 224, 1984 → 65,4190: ᴿMuséon 99 (1986) 209-212 (A. de *Halleux*); NRT 108 (1986) 915s (V. *Roisel*); RelStR 12 (1986) 263s (E. G. *Mathews*).

F5.3 **Mt 26,30 ||... : Passio Christi; Passion-Narrative.**

3648 **Allison** D. C., The end of the ages has come; an early interpretation of the Passion and Resurrection of Jesus. Ph 1985, Fortress. xiii-194 p. $20. 0-8006-0753-8 [NTAbs 30,226].

3649 **Axmacher** Elke, 'Aus Liebe will mein Heyland sterben'; Untersuchungen zum Wandel des Passions [-libretti, -predigten; Bach-] verständnisses im frühen 18. Jahrhundert. Stu 1984, Hänssler. 257 p. DM 58. – ᴿTR 82 (1986) 209-211 (W. *Baier*); ZKG 97 (1986) 132-5 (G. A. *Krieg*).

3650 *Bammel* Ernst, *a)* Die Blutgerichtsbarkeit in der römischen Provinz Judäa vor dem ersten jüdischen Aufstand [< JJS 25 (1974) 35-49]; – *b)* Crucifixion as a punishment in Palestine [< ᶠMOULE C., Trial of Jesus 1970, 162-5]; – *c)* Die Bruderfolge im Hochpriestertum der herodianisch-römischen Zeit [< ZDPV 90 (1974) 61-68]; – *d)* Der Tod Jesu in einer 'Toledoth Jeschu'-Überlieferung [< ASTI 6 (1968) 124-131]; – *e)* Christus parricida [Altercatio Simonis; < VigChr 26 (1972) 259-262]: → 131, Judaica 1986, 59-72 / 76-78 / 21-27 / 196-204 / 216-9.

3651 **Bernard-Marie** fr., La passione secondo la Bibbia,ᵀ. N 1984, Dehoniane. – ᴿTeresianum 37 (1986) 257 (L. *Gaetani*).

3652 **Brown** R. E., A crucified Christ in Holy Week; essays on the four Gospel Passion narratives [< Worship]. Collegeville MN 1986, Liturgical. 71 p. $4. – ᴿRExp 83 (1986) 629s (M. C. *Parsons*).

3652* *Cârstoiu* Joan, La Croix et la Résurrection du Sauveur à la lumière du NT (roum.): STBuc 37 (1985) 355-364.

3653 ᵀᴱ**Ceresa-Gastaldo** Aldo, MASSIMO il Confessore, Meditazioni sull'agonia di Gesù. R 1985, Città Nuova. 112 p. Lit. 7.000. 88-311-3050-1. – ᴿCC 137 (1986,2) 195 (E. *Cattaneo*: cristologia, monotelismo).

3654 **Cousin** Hugues, Le prophète assassiné; histoire des textes évangéliques de la Passion; intr. *Duquoc* C. 1976 ➤ 57,4834...: ᴿRB 93 (1986) 625s (M.-E. *Boismard*).

3655 *Crawford* L., Non, Jésus n'est part mort sur le Golgotha ! : CahRenan 33,142 (1985) 17-29; 34,143 (1986) 20-22; 34,144 (1986) 37-43 (NTAbs 30,273].

3656 **Dawe** Donald G., The death and resurrection of God. Atlanta 1985, Knox. 205 p. $16. ... 0527-2 [Interp 40,83]. – ᴿTTod 43 (1986s) 290s (M. *Root*: aims to mediate among religions).

3657 **Edwards** Wm. D., *Gabel* Wesley J., *Hosmer* Floyd E., On the Physical Death of Jesus Christ: Journal of American Medical Association, 255,11 (March 21, 1986), 1455-1463.

3658 **Fricke** Weddig, Standrechtlich gekreuzigt; Person und Prozess des Jesus aus Galiläa. Fra-Buchschlag 1986, Mai. 304 p. DM 38 [TR 83,265] 3-87936-169-X.

3659 [*Danieli* G.] Gesù e la sua morte, XXVII Settimana Biblica 1982/4 ➤ 65,411: ᴿAngelicum 63 (1986) 489s (T. *Stancati*).

3660 *Ghiberti* Giuseppe, Il modello del 'giusto sofferente' nella passione di Gesù: ➤ 391, Storiografia 1984/6, 153-168.

3661 **Gilly** René, Passion de Jésus; les conclusions d'un médecin. P 1985, Fayard. 157 p.; F 59 pa. 2-213-01570-8. – ᴿEsprV 96 (1986) 60-62 (A. M. *Dubarle*: erreurs fâcheuses).

3661* *Girard* René, The Gospel Passion as victim's story [< The Scapegoat c. 1986], ᵀ*Freccero* Yvonne: CCurr 36 (1986s) 28-38.

3662 Har vi två kulturer? Till dateringen av Jesu död [Vad astronomerna utgick från ... astronomins bidrag ... astronomernas bidrag i Nature (1983, 743: *Humphreys* C.) ...]: SvEx 51s (1986s) 192-202.

3663 **Harvey** Nicholas P., Death's gift. L 1985, Epworth. 152 p. £4. – ᴿScotJT 39 (1986) 397-9 (J. *Dominian*).

3663* *Imbert* Jean, Le procès de Jésus: RICathP 19 (1986) 53-66(-69, réponse aux questions).

3664 **Kelly** J.N.D., Aspects of the Passion. L 1985 = 1970, Mowbray. 93 p. £3. 0-264-67035-3 [NTAbs 30,366].

3665 **Leenhardt** F. J., La mort et le testament de Jésus 1983 ➤ 64,4610 ... 1,4678: ᴿProtestantesimo 41 (1986) 228s (E. *Stretti*).

3666 **Léon-Dufour** Xavier, Life and death in the New Testament; the teachings of Jesus and Paul [Face à la mort, Jésus et Paul 1979 ➤ 60,6263], ᵀ*Prendergast* Terrence. SF 1986, Harper & R. xxxiii-316 p. 0-06-061094-9.

3667 *a*) *Lodge* John C., Matthew's passion-resurrection narrative; – *b*) [Mark] *Senior* Donald, Crucible of truth ...; – *c*) [Luke] *LaVerdiere* E.; – *d*) [John] *Fuller* Reginald H.: ChSt 25,1 (1986) 3-20 / 21-34 / 35-50 / 51-63.

3668 *McCabe* Herbert, Good Friday; the mystery of the Cross: NBlackf 67 (1986) 104-114.

3669 **Matera** Frank J., Passion narratives and Gospel theologies; interpreting the Synoptics through their Passion stories: Theological Inquiries. NY 1986, Paulist. xi-256 p.; bibliog. p. 245-253. $13. 0-8091-2775-X [NTAbs 31,102]. – ᴿExpTim 98 (1986s) 279s (E. *Franklin*).

3670 **Moo** Douglas J., The OT in the Gospel Passion narratives [diss. St. Andrew, ᴰ*Black* M.] 1983 ➤ 64,4621 ... 1,4683: ᴿBibTB 16 (1986) 37s (J. H. *Neyrey*); Interpretation 40 (1986) 94s (G. S. *Sloyan*); RB 93 (1986) 474s (M.-É. *Boismard*).

3671 **Morris** Clayton L., The Saint Matthew Passion of J. S. Bach; an examination of the composer's theological interpretation of the Pas-

sion narrative: diss. Graduate Theological Union. – RelStR 13,189 sans date.
3672 *Müller* Klaus W., Schierlingstrank und Kreuzestod: Anmerkungen zu den Prozessen gegen Sokrates und Jesus: AntAb 32 (1986) 66-87.
3673 *a) Pawlikowski* John T., The trial and death of Jesus; reflections in light of a new understanding of Judaism; – *b) O'Donovan* Leo J., The word of the Cross [*Rahner* K.]: ChSt 25,1 (1986) 79-94 / 95-110.
3674 *Perry* John M., The three days in the Synoptic Passion predictions: CBQ 48 (1986) 637-654.
3674* *Ramos* Felipe F., Los relatos de la Pasión: StLeg 26 (1985) 9-78.
3675 *Rinaldi* Bonaventura, Passione di Gesù Cristo; appunti di storia e di teologia: ScuolC 114 (1986) 716-728.
3676 **Rivkin** Ellis, What crucified Jesus? The political execution of a charismatic. L 1986, SCM. 79 p. £4. 0-334-01798-X. – ᴿEstE 61 (1986) 380s (A. *Vargas-Machuca*: serie de afirmaciones no demostradas o inexactas); ExpTim 97 (1985s) 280 (J. R. *Bartlett*: but 'under Tiberius all was quiet', BARNETT P. 1975); Interpretation 40 (1986) 313s (D. C. *Duling*); ModT 3 (1986s) 207 (Frances *Young*); TLond 39 (1986) 400-2 (S. C. *Barton*).
3677 *Ruckstuhl* Eugen, Zur Chronologie der Leidensgeschichte Jesu (2. Teil): SNTU-A 11 (1986) 97-129.
3678 ᴱ**Salas** Antonio, Jesús; entrega – muerte – resurrección: Dios te hable 4. M 1986, BibFe. 112 p. – ᴿBibFe 12 (1986) 253 (M. *Saenz Galache*).
3678* **Schürmann** Heinz, Gottesreich – Jesu Geschick; Jesu ureigener Tod im Licht seiner Basileia-Verkündigung 1983 ➤1,4690: ᴿTPQ 134 (1986) 401s (J. *Kremer*).
3679 **Schürmann** H., Gesù di fronte alla propria morte; riflessioni esegetiche e prospettive 1983 ➤ 64,4630 ... 1,4692: ᴿProtestantesimo 41 (1986) 229s (D. *Tomasetto*).
3680 **Senior** Donald, The Passion of Jesus in the Gospel of Matthew 1985 ➤ 1,4693: ᴿCBQ 48 (1986) 573s (F. W. *Burnett*); RExp 83 (1986) 457s (M. G. *Reddish*); TS 47 (1986) 552s (J. M. *Reese*).
3681 *Soards* M. L., The question of a pre-Markan Passion narrative: Bible Bhashyam 11 (1985) 144-169.
3682 Il Testamento di Gesù: trasmissione della Radio Vaticana [Quaresima-estate 1985]. R 1985, Rogate. 280 p. Lit. 13.000. – ᴿCC 137 (1986,3) 101s (E. *Sonzini*).
3683 **Topping** Frank, An impossible God [meditations on the Passion]. L 1985, Collins/Fount. 141 p. £2. 0-00-626927-3. – ᴿExpTim 98 (1986s) 63 [C. S. *Rodd*: people will need no urging to 'by'].
3684 *Pettersen* Alvyn, [Mt 26,39] Did ATHANASIUS deny Christ's fear ? : ScotJT 39 (1986) 327-340.
3685 **Post** Paulus G. J., De haanscène in de vroeg-christelijke kunst 1984 ➤ 1,4702: ᴿGregorianum 67 (1986) 793-5 (J. *Janssens*).
3685* *Flusser* David, [Mt 26,68] 'Who is it that struck you?' : Immanuel 20 (1986) 27-32.
3686 **Witherup** Ronald D., The cross of Jesus; a literary-critical study of Matthew 27: diss. Union. Richmond 1985. 409 p. 86-13771. – DissA 47 (1986s) 1363-A.
3687 *Desautels* Luc, La mort de Judas (Mt 27,3-10; Ac 1,15-26): ScEspr 38 (1986) 221-239.
3688 *Stalter-Fouilloy* Danielle, Les maudits [... Judas]: RHPR 66 (1986) 451-8; Eng. 491.

3689 ᴱWagner Harald, Judas Iskariot; menschliches oder heilsgeschichtliches Drama? Fra 1985, Knecht. 144 p. DM 22. – ᴿErbAuf 62 (1986) 475.

3690 *Haacker* Klaus, 'Sein Blut über uns'; Erwägungen zu Matthäus 27,25: KIsr 1 (1986) 47-50.

3691 **Kampling** Rainer, Das Blut Christi und die Juden; Mt 27,25 bei den lateinsprachigen christlichen Autoren bis zu LEO dem Grossen: NT Abh NF 16, 1984 ➤ 65,4237; 1,4706: ᴿRHPR 66 (1986) 352s (J. *Doignon*).

3692 **Mora** Vincent, [Mt 27,25] Le refus d'Israël: LDiv 124. P 1986, Cerf. 182 p. F 100. 2-204-02438-4. – ᴿCC 137 (1986,3) 541 (V. *Fusco*); EsprV 96 (1986) 555s (S. *Légasse*); TR 82 (1986) 457-9 (F. *Mussner*)

F5.6   **Mt 28 ‖ :   Resurrectio.**

3693 *Alsup* John, Auferstehung, ᵀ*Roloff* J.: ➤ 587, EvKL 1 (1986) 309-313 (-315 dogm.).

3694 **Andronikof** Costantin, Il senso della Pasqua nella liturgia bizantina, I. I giorni della preparazione e della passione; II. I cinquanta giorni della festa: Liturgia e Vita 6s. T-Leumann 1986, Elle Di Ci. 326 p.; 220 p. – ᴿScuolC 114 (1986) 738-741 (M. *Navoni*).

Bayer Hans F., Jesus' prediction of vindication and resurrection ... Synoptics 1986 ➤ 3277.

3695 *Blank* Josef, Sucht den Lebenden nicht bei den Toten; zum gegenwärtigen Stand der theologischen Diskussion um die Auferstehung Jesu: Orientierung 50 (1986) 62-65.

3696 La bonne nouvelle de la Résurrection / La buona novella della risurrezione, ᵀ*De Rosa* Elena. R 1986, Borla. 200 p. Lit. 12.000. – ᴿLetture 41 (1986) 682s (A. *Scurani*).

3697 *Broer* Inge, *al.,* [ᴱ**Oberlinner** Lorenz], Auferstehung Jesu – Auferstehung der Christen; Deutungen des Osterglaubens: QDisp 105. FrB 1986, Herder. 199 p. DM 28,80. – ᴿHerdKor 40 (1986) 150 (U. *Ruh*).

3698 **Caba** José, Resucitó Cristo, mi esperanza; estudio exegético: BAC 475. M 1986, Católica. xxxii-407 p.; bibliog. p. xvii-xxx. pt. 2200. 84-220-1230-8. ᴿGregorianum 67 (1986) 805s (*ipse*).

3698* **Cichal** Krzysztof, Il mistero della Resurrezione di Gesù Cristo nella 'Kirchliche Dogmatik' di Karl BARTH: diss. Angelicum, Roma. – RTLv 18,571 sans date.

3699 *Davis* Stephen, Was Jesus raised bodily? ['not advocated by any scholar or theologically sophisticated Christian' p. 141]: ChrSchR 15 (1985) ... [< CalvinT 21 (1986) 111].

3699* **Fuller** Reginald H., The formation of the Resurrection narratives 1980 = 1971 ➤ 61,6019: ᴿRB 93 (1986) 626s (M.-É. *Boismard*).

3700 *Goitia* José de, El origen de la fe pascual según Rudolf PESCH [... y *Winden* H. 1982]: EstE 61 (1986) 23-65.

3701 *Hallman* J. M., The resurrection of Jesus and the origin of Christology: Encounter 47,2 (1986) 219-231 [NTAbs 31,16].

Harris M. J., Raised immortal 1983 ➤ 7172.

3703 **Harris** Murray J., Easter in Durham; Bishop JENKINS and the Resurrection of Jesus 1985 ➤ 1,4722: ᴿVidyajyoti 49 (1985) 526 (P. M. *Meagher*).

3704 **Harrison** Ted, The Durham phenomenon [press misunderstandings of *Jenkins* on Resurrection, cognate analysis by K. *Ward*...]. L 1985, Darton-LT. 184 p. £1.85. – ᴿMonth 248 (1986) 67 (M. *Smith*).

3705 **Hempelmann** Heinzpeter,   Die Auferstehung Jesu Christi – eine historische Tatsache? Eine engagierte Analyse 1982 ➤ 63,4799; DM 14,80: [R]TZBas 42 (1986) 268 (R. *Riesner*: Antwort an Nobelpreisträger H. BÖLL).

3706 **Hendrickx** H.,   The resurrection narratives of the synoptic Gospels[2rev] 1984 ➤ 65,3790:   [R]Neotestamentica 20 (1986) 77s (W. S. *Vorster*).

3707 **Ignatius IV** (patriarch of Antioch), The Resurrection and modern man, [T]*Bigham* Stephen; pref. *Clement* Oliver.   Crestwood NY 1985, St. Vladimir. 96 p. – [R]RelStR 12 (1986) 268 (Elizabeth A. *Johnson*).

3708 **Kessler** Hans, Sucht den Lebenden nicht bei den Toten; die Auferstehung ... 1985 ➤ 1,4727: [R]BZ 30 (1986) 271-4 (R. *Schnackenburg*); TR 82 (1986) 52-54 (W. *Kirchschläger*); ZkT 108 (1986) 70-74 (H. *Verweyen*).

3709 *a*) **Kessler** Hans,   Die Auferstehung Jesu, Mitte und Kriterium christlichen Glaubens; – *b*) *Bollag* Michel,   Auferstehung im Judentum im Lichte liturgischer und rabbinischer Texte: Judaica 42 (1986) 211-230 / 231-9.

3710 *Kümmel* Werner G.,   Eine jüdische Stimme zur Auferstehung Jesu [*Lapide* P.]: TRu 51 (1986) 92-97.

3711 *a*) *Lindars* Barnabas, Jesus risen; bodily resurrection but no empty tomb; – *b*) *Jasper* David, The poetry of the Resurrection: TLond 39 (1986) 90-96 / 96-102.

3712 *McCabe* Herbert,   The Easter vigil; the mystery of new life: NBlackf 67 (1986) 157-169.

3713 **McKenzie** R. A.,   The first day of the week; the mystery and message of the empty tomb.   NY 1985, Paulist. iii-87 p. $5 pa. 0-8091-2735-0 [NTAbs 30,355].

3714 *Margerie* Bertrand de,   Le troisième jour, selon les Écritures, il est ressuscité; importance théologique d'une recherche exégétique: RevST 60 (1986) 158-188.

3715 **Nützel** Johannes M.,   Da gingen ihnen die Augen auf; Wege zu österlichen Glauben.   FrB 1986, Herder. 79 p. DM 9,80 [TLZ 111,836].

3716 *O'Collins* Gerald,   Beyond David JENKINS [bishop of Durham; fear that orthodox belief in the empty tomb and the virgin birth may lessen Christian commitment to social justice]: Tablet 240 (1986) 830s.

3717 *O'Collins* Gerald,   The resurrection of Jesus; four contemporary challenges: Catholic Theological Review 6 (Clayton, Australia 1984) 5-10 [NTAbs 30,143].

3718 **O'Donovan** Oliver,   Resurrection and moral order.   Nottingham c. 1986, Inter-Varsity. $15. 0-85111-745-7. [ScotJT 39,550 adv].

3719 **Osborne** Grant R.,   The Resurrection narratives 1984 ➤ 65,4263; 1,4732: [R]JBL 105 (1986) 726-8 (J. E. *Alsup*: some weaknesses); Themelios 11 (1985s) 99s (J. B. *Green*); WestTJ 48 (1986) 190-2 (R. T. *France*: aim good).

3720 **Perkins** Pheme, Resurrection 1984 ➤ 65,4265; 1,4733: [R]CurrTM 13 (1986) 185s (R. H. *Smith*: very fine; but does not tell us concisely what she thinks actually happened to Jesus after Good Friday); JTS 37 (1986) 164-6 (C.F.D. *Moule*: rather wooden; elementary blunders); Month 248 (1986) 67s (L. *Swain*); NBlackf 67 (1986) 146 (C. F. *Evans*); ScotJT 39 (1986) 243s (J. W. *Rogerson*).

3720* **Perret** Jacques, *a*) Ressuscité ? approche historique 1984 ➤ 65,4266; 1,4735: [R]BLitEc 87 (1986) 219s (S. *Légasse*); – *b*) Gesù è davvero risorto? Una ricerca storica: Il popolo cristiano. T 1986, SEI. 108 p. Lit. 8000. – [R]StPatav 33 (1986) 696 (G. *Segalla*).

3721 [TE]**Poque** Suzanne,   Saint AUGUSTIN, Jésus-Christ mort et ressuscité pour nous: Foi Vivante 214. P 1986, Cerf. 125 p. – [R]EsprV 96 (1986) 543s (J. *Pintard*).

3721* **Proczek** Zygmunt, Les relations bibliques concernant les christophanies; étude apologétique: diss. Acad. Cath. Wsz 1983, ᴰ*Myśków* J. – BInfWsz (1986,1) 35-37.

3722 **Richards** H.J., The first Easter; what really happened? [< British 1976 revised]. Mystic CT 1986, Twenty-third. viii-116. $6. – ᴿTS 47 (1986) 744s (P. *Perkins*: still 1976 status, and crucial 'not' fell out p.48).

3723 *Schützeichel* Heribert, Die Bedeutung der Auferstehung Christi: TrierTZ 95 (1986) 98-114.

3724 **Smith** Robert H., Easter gospels 1983 ↠ 64,4676 ... 1,4738: ᴿInterpretation 40 (1986) 100.102 (J.J. H. *Price*); JBL 105 (1986) 152-4 (W.O. *Walker*).

3724* *Ukachukwu Manus* Chris, The resurrection of Jesus; some critical and exegetical considerations in the Nigerian context: NigJT 1,2 (1986) 28-45 [< TKontext 8/2,20].

3725 *Jonge* M. de, Matthew 27:51 in early Christian exegesis: ↠ 110, ᶠSTENDAHL K. = HarvTR 79 (1986) 67-79.

3725* *a) Maisch* Ingrid, Die österliche Dimension des Todes Jesu; zur Osterverkündigung in Mt 27,51-54; – *b) Gollinger* Hildegard, 'Wenn einer stirbt, lebt er dann wieder auf?' (Ijob 14,14); zum alttestamentlich-jüdischen Hintergrund der Deutung der dem Kreuzestod nachfolgenden Erfahrung der Jünger mit dem Bekenntnis zur Auferweckung Jesu; – *c) Oberlinner* Lorenz, Zwischen Kreuz und Parusie; die eschatologische Qualität des Osterglaubens: ↠ 120, ᶠVÖGTLE A., Auferstehung 1986, 96-123 / 11-38 / 63-95.

3726 *Nauerth* Claudia, Ein Fingerring aus El-Hibe mit den Frauen am Grabe: DiehlB 22 (1985) 175-8; fig. p.174.

3727 **Soler Quintillá** Gerardo, '¡Alegraos!' (Mt 28,9); para una teología y pastoral del gozo a partir de la vigilia pascual: diss. 3255 Pont. Univ. Urbaniana. R 1984, Univ. Gregoriana. 162 p.; bibliog. p.21-30.

3728 *Horst* P.W. van der, Once more, the translation of *hoi dé* in Matthew 28.17 [not all but some of the disciples present]: JStNT 27 (1986) 27-30.

3729 *Hill* David, The conclusion of Matthew's Gospel; some literary-critical observations: IrBSt 8 (1986) 54-63.

F6.1   **Evangelium Marci** – *Textus, commentarii.*

3730 **Achtemeier** Paul J., Mark²ʳᵉᵛ [¹1975 ↠ 56,2929]: Proclamation Comm. Ph 1986, Fortress. v-138 p. $7 pa. 0-8006-1916-1 [NTAbs 31,97].

3731 **Gnilka** Joachim, El evangelio según Marcos I-II [1978s ↠ 60,6371], ᵀ*Martínez de Lapera* V.A.: BiblEstB 55s. Salamanca 1986, Sígueme. 369 p.; 428 p. – ᴿCiTom 113 (1986) 623s (J.L. *Espinel*).

3732 **Heyer** C.J. den, Marcus I-II, een praktische Bijbelverklaring. Kampen 1985, Kok. 173 p., 169 p. *f*25,50; 25,90. – ᴿKerkT 37 (1986) 74 (M.H. *Bolkestein*, I); Streven 53 (1985s) 276-8. 852s (P. *Beentjes*).

3733 **Hurtado** Larry, Mark: Good News comm. 1984 ↠ 65,4295: ᴿInterpretation 40 (1986) 316s (L. *Williamson*).

3734 **Iersel** Bas van, Marcus: Belichting van het Bijbelboek. Boxtel/Brugge 1986, Katholieke Bijbelstichting / Tabor. 270 p. *f*24,75. 90-6173-380-1 / Tabor 90-6597-492-X.

3735 **Jeanne d'Arc** sr., Évangile selon Marc; présentation du texte grec, traduction et notes: Nouvelle collection de textes et documents, Les évangiles. P 1986, BLettres / Desclée-B. xxii-136 p. + 16 p. à part (verbes et mots difficiles). – ᴿRThom 86 (1986) 668s (M-E. *Lauzière*, enthousiasme lyrique pour sa 'sobriété absolue'); Études 365 (1986) 281 (P. *Lamarche*); MondeB 45 (1986) 54s (F. *Brossier*); Salesianum 48 (1986) 978s (R. *Sabin*).

3736 **Mann** Christopher S., Mark ...: AnchorB 27. GCNY 1986, Doubleday. xxvi-714 p. $20 [TDig 34,84]. 0-385-03253-6.

3737 **Mentz** Hermann, Das Markus-Evangelium neu erzählt. Gö 1986, Vandenhoeck & R. 122 p. 3-525-60370-3.

3738 **Mourlon Beernaert** Pierre, Saint Marc: Le temps de lire 2, 1985 ➤ 1,4752*: ᴿNRT 108 (1986) 429s (X. *Jacques*: Marc au théâtre, p. 19).

3739 **Pesch** Rudolf, L'evangelo della comunità primitiva [1979] 1984 ➤ 65,4297: ᴿProtestantesimo 41 (1986) 230s (A. *Moda*).

3740 **Pohl** Adolf, Das Evangelium des Markus: Studienbibel. Wu 1986, Brockhaus. 604 p.; bibliog. p. 599-604. 3-417-25122-2; pa. 022-6.

3741 **Powell** Ivor, Mark's superb gospel. GR 1985, Kregel. 432 p. [TR 83,250].

3742 *Quesnel* Michel, Comment lire un évangile; Saint Marc 1984 ➤ 65,4300; 1,4755: ᴿNRT 108 (1986) 428s (X. *Jacques*: simple lecture, non théorie que suggère le titre).

3743 **Stébé** M.-H., *Goudet* M.-O., Marc commenté par JÉRÔME et Jean CHRYSOSTOME: Les Pères dans la Foi. P 1986, Desclée-B. 172 p. F 77. – ᴿEsprV 96 (1986) 552s (É. *Cothenet*).

3743* *Ziesler* John A., Which is the best commentary ? VII. The Gospel according to Mark [Jerome best of one-volume commentaries (by E.J. *Mally*); *Cranfield* all we have on the Greek; *Hurtado* best all-around]: ExpTim 98 (1986s) 263-7.

F6.2 *Evangelium Marci,* **Themata.**

3744 *Alegre* X., Marcos o la corrección de una ideología triunfalista; pautas para la lectura de un evangelio beligerante y comprometido: RLatAmT 2,6 (1985) 229-263 [< NTAbs 31,23].

3745 *Beavis* Mary Ann, Mark's teaching on faith: BibTB 16 (1986) 139-142.

3747 **Best** Ernest, Mark, the Gospel as story 1983 ➤ 65,4314; 1,4763: ᴿEvQ 58 (1986) 363s (T.J. *Geddert*); HeythJ 27 (1986) 75s (M. *Smith*); JBL 105 (1986) 335s (Joanna *Dewey*); Neotestamentica 20 (1986) 69 (W.S. *Vorster*); Salmanticensis 33 (1986) 119s (R. *Trevijano*); TLZ 111 (1986) 594s (W. *Vogler*).

Best Ernest, Disciples and discipleship; studies in the Gospel according to Mark 1986 ➤ 132*.

3748 **Black** Carl Clifton, An evaluation of the investigative method and exegetical results of redaction criticism of the Gospel of Mark; the role of the disciples as a test-case in current research: diss. Duke, ᴰ*Smith* D.M. Durham NC 1986. 522 p. 86-24368. – DissA 47 (1986s) 2615-A; RelStR 13,189 ['text-case'].

3749 **Blackburn** Barry L., A critique of the 'Theios Aner' concept as an interpretative background of the miracle traditions used by Mark: diss. Aberdeen. – RTLv 18,545, sans date.

3750 **Booth** Roger P., Jesus and the laws of purity; tradition history and legal history in Mark: JStNT Sup 13. Sheffield 1986, JStOT. 277 p. $13.50.

3751 **Breytenbach** Cilliers, Nachfolge und Zukunftserwartung nach Markus; eine methodenkritische Studie [Diss. München 1983, ᴰ*Hahn* F.]: ATANT 71, 1984 ➤ 65,4318; 1,4765: ᴿKerkT 37 (1986) 73s (G. *Mussies*); Salmanticensis 33 (1986) 122-4 (R. *Trevijano*); TLZ 111 (1986) 667-9 (N. *Walter*).

3752 ᴱ**Cancik** Hubert, Markus-Philologie: WUNT 33, 1984 ➤ 65,273.4321; 1,4767: ᴿJRel 66 (1986) 70s (A.J. *Droge*); TLZ 111 (1986) 357-360 (F. *Neugebauer*).

3753 **Cárdenas Pallares** José, A poor man called Jesus; reflections on the Gospel of Mark [México 1982], ᵀ*Barr* Robert R. Maryknoll NY 1986, Orbis. viii-136 p. $9 pa. 0-88344-398-8. – ᴿNorTTs 87 (1986) 251-3 (K. *Nordstokke*); TsTNijm 26 (1986) 411s (S. van *Tilborg*).

3754 **Clévenot** Michel, [mostly *Bélo*'s Mark] Materialist approaches to the Bible, ᵀ*Nottingham* William J., 1985 ➤ 1,4771: ᴿCBQ 48 (1986) 331s (S.P. *Kealy:* Marxist jargon grates).

3755 **Derrett** J.D.M., The making of Mark I-II 1985 ➤ 1,4774: ᴿCBQ 48 (1986) 557s (Q. *Quesnell:* unconvincing); TLZ 111 (1986) 360s (P. *Pokorný*).

3756 **Dschulnigg** Peter, Sprache, Redaktion und Intention des Markusevangeliums[Diss. Luzern]: SBB 11, 1984 ➤ 1,4776: ᴿBZ 30 (1986) 132-4 (M. *Reiser*); NT 28 (1986) 280s (J.K. *Elliott*); TR 82 (1986) 198 (D. *Dormeyer*).

3757 *Fackelmann* Anton †, Präsentation christlicher Urtexte aus dem ersten Jahrhundert, geschrieben auf papyrus; vermutlich Notizschriften des Evangelisten Markus?: Anagénēsis 4,1 (1986) 25-36.

3758 *Ferrario* Fulvio, La cristologia di Marco; appunti su alcune piste della ricerca recente: BbbOr 28 (1986) 15-31 [... *Kingsbury* J., funerali della teoria dell''uomo divino'].

ᴱ**Hahn** F., Der Erzähler ... in der Markusforschung 1985 ➤ 246*.

3759 *Halsema* J.H. van, ⓜ Mystery as a literary form in the Gospels according to Mark and John [< GerefTTs (1983) 1-17], ᵀ*Timár* Gabriella: Theologiai Szemle 28 (1985) 201-6.

3760 **Hengel** Martin, Studies in the Gospel of Mark 1985 ➤ 1,4779: ᴿBibTB 16 (1986) 154 (A. *Stock*); EstE 61 (1986) 243s (A. *Vargas-Machuca*); NBlackf 67 (1986) 199s (Morna D. *Hooker*); RB 93 (1986) 436-441 (P. *Grelot*); TLond 39 (1986) 311s (E. *Best*).

3761 *Hiosan* C., Theology of Eucharist in the Gospel of Mark: CathTR 6 (1984) 61-68 [NTAbs 30,150].

3762 **Hooker** Morna D., The message of Mark 1983 ➤ 65,4334: ᴿHeythJ 27 (1986) 312s (Marion *Smith*).

3763 **Kato** Zenji, Die Völkermission im Markusevangelium; eine redaktionsgeschichtliche Untersuchung [Diss. Bern]: EurHS 23/252. Bern 1986, Lang. Fs 59,40. – TR 83,75. 3-261-04040-8.

3764 *a*) **Keller** Joseph, Jesus and the critics; a logico-critical analysis of the Marcan confrontation; – *b*) *Bishop* Jonathan, *Parabole* and *parrhesia* in Mark: Interpretation 40 (1986) 29-38 / 39-52.

3765 **Kingsbury** Jack D., The Christology of Mark's Gospel 1983 ➤ 64,4730 ... 1,4782: ᴿTLZ 111 (1986) 818s (P. *Pokorný*).

3766 *Lemcio* Eugene E., The intention of the evangelist Mark: NTS 32 (1986) 187-206.

3767 *Loimaranta* L.K., Mark's inserenda, a key to the early history of the Synoptic gospel text: ➤ 389, Bible et informatique 1985/6, 235-241.

3768 **McGann** Diarmuid, The journeying self ... Mk/Jung 1985 ➤ 1,4787: ᴿHorizons 13 (1986) 193s (F. *Dorff*).

3769 **Malbon** Elizabeth S., Narrative space and mythic meaning in Mark. SF 1986, Harper. 212 p. $25 [TS 48,598]. 0-06-254540-X.

3770 *Malbon* Elizabeth S., *a*) Disciples/Crowds/Whoever; Markan characters and readers: NT 28 (1986) 104-130; – *b*) Pharisees, chief priests, scribes, and elders; a literary study of Markan characteristics: ➤ 377*b*, SBL Jerusalem summaries (1986) 2s. – ➤ 3783*b*.

3771 **Maloney** Elliott C., Semitic interference in Marcan syntax ᴰ1981 ➤ 62,4941 ... 1,4788: ᴿTheologiai Szemle 28 (1985) 125-7 (Valeria *Csonka*).

3772 **Manicardi** Ermenegildo, Il cammino di Gesù nel Vangelo di Marco [diss.R]: AnBib 96, 1981 ➤ 62,4942 ... 65,4343: ᴿRechSR 74 (1986) 240 (J. *Guillet*: netteté sans ombre).

3773 *Moore* W. Ernest, 'Outside' and 'inside' [;] a Markan motif: ExpTim 98 (1986) 39-43.

3774 **Naickaparampil** Michael, Jesus as teacher in Mark; a redaction-critical study of the didactic terminology in the second gospel: diss. Pont. Ist. Biblico, ᴰ*Vanhoye* A. R 1986. ix-137 p.; bibliog. p. 113-137. – AcPIB 9,2 (1985s) 149s; 116.

3775 *Neusner* Jacob, Death-scenes and farewell stories; an aspect of the master-disciple relationship in Mark and in some Talmudic tales: ➤ 110, ꟻStendahl K. = HarvTR 79 (1986) 187-197.

3776 *Neyrey* Jerome H., Idea of purity in Mark's Gospel: Semeia 35 (1986) 91-124; bibliog. 125-8.

3777 **Peabody** David B., Mark as composer. Macon GA 1986, Mercer Univ. 392 p. $60. 0-86554-197-3 [BR 2/2,5].

3778 **Quintanar** Gerardo, El rechazo del Judaismo en Marcos; una investigación sobre el motivo del rechazo del Judaismo en la redacción del evangelio según san Marcos: diss. ᴰ*Gourgues* M. Ottawa 1986. – RTLv 18,549.

3779 **Robbins** Vernon K., Jesus the teacher; a socio-rhetorical interpretation of Mark 1984 ➤ 65,4355: ᴿJAAR 54 (1986) 604s (P. J. *Achtemeier*); TLZ 111 (1986) 107-9 (J. *Becker*); TR 82 (1986) 28s (R. *Pesch*).

3779* *Schenke* Ludger, Der Aufbau des Markusevangeliums – ein hermeneutischer Schlüssel: BibNot 32 (1986) 54-82.

3780 *Scott* J., Story and discipleship in Mark's Gospel: Friends' Quarterly 23,11 (Ashford UK 1985) 583-594 [NTAbs 30,151].

3781 **Standaert** B., Marcus geweld en genade; de actualiteit van het Marcusevangelie: Woord en Beleving 6, 1985 ➤ 1,4804*b*: ᴿCollatVl 16 (1986) 482s (W. Van *Soom*).

3782 *Stegemann* Ekkehard W., Zur Rolle von Petrus, Jakobus und Johannes im Markusevangelium: TZBas 42 (1986) 366-374.

3783 *a) Stock* Augustine, [Mk prologue] Jesus, hypocrites and Herodians; – *b) Malbon* Elizabeth S., Mark; myth and parable: BibTB 16 (1986) 3-7; 2 fig./8-17. – ➤ 3770.

3784 **Suh Joong Suck,** Discipleship and community in the Gospel of Mark: diss. Boston Univ., ᴰ*Kee* H. 1985. 86-02779; DissA 47 (1986s) 563-A; RelStR 13,190.

Telford William, The interpretation of Mark 1985 ➤ 1,314.

3784* ᴱ**Tuckett** Christopher, The messianic secret: Issues in Religion and Theology 1, 1983 ➤ 64,303: ᴿCrNSt 7 (1986) 602s (P. F. *Beatrice*).

3785 **Via** Dan O.ᴶ, The ethics of Mark's Gospel – in the middle of time 1985 ➤ 1,4808: ᴿBibTB 16 (1986) 160s (A. *Stock*); CiTom 13 (1986) 587-9 (J. L. *Espinel*); ExpTim 97 (1985s) 279 (J. I. H. *McDonald*: hermeneutically sensitive but not without predilections); TR 82 (1986) 375s (R. *Pesch*).

3786 **Vincent** John J., Radical Jesus [Mark]. L 1986, Marshall Pickering. 130 p. £2. 0-551-01344-3. – ᴿExpTim 98 (1986s) 158 [C. S. *Rodd*: those who won't like it should read it].

3787 ᴱVincent John J., Starting all over again; hints of Jesus in the city ['The sweep of the story of Mark is that of a sick world, a weak Church, but a strong God' (*Franklin* M. p. 39)]. Geneva 1981, World Council of Churches. 66 p. Fs 8. – ᴿNedTTs 40 (1986) 91 (J. A. B. *Jongeneel*).

3787* a) *Vorster* Willem W., Markus – Sammler, Redaktor, Autor oder Erzähler? ᵀ*Huber* Brigitte; – b) *Tannehill* Robert C., Die Jünger im Markusevangelium; die Funktion einer Erzählfigur, ᵀ*Huber*; – c) *Petersen* Norman R., Die 'Perspektive' in der Erzählung des Markusev. / Die Zeitebenen im markinischen Erzählwerk; vorgestellte und dargestellte Zeit, ᵀ*Huber*; – d) *Breytenbach* Cilliers, Das Markusevangelium als episodische Erzählung; mit Überlegungen zum 'Aufbau' des zweiten Evangeliums / bibliog.; – e) *Hahn* Ferdinand, Einige Überlegungen zu gegenwärtigen Aufgaben der Markusinterpretation: ➤ 247, Erzähler 1985, 11-36 / 37-66 / 67-91.93-135 / 137-169.198-200 / 171-197.

3788 **Weiss** Wolfgang, Eine neue Lehre in Vollmacht; die Streit- und Schulgespräche im Markus-Evangelium: ev. Diss. ᴰ*Brandenburger* E. Mainz 1984. – RTLv 18,550.

3789 **Williams** J. G., Gospel against parable; Mark's language of mystery: Bible & Literature 12. Sheffield 1985, JStOT. 244 p. £17; pa. £8.50. 0-907459-44-7; 5-5 [NTAbs 30,358].

F6.3. Evangelii Marci versiculi 1,1 ...

3789* **Stock** Klemens, [Mc 1,1-13] Le pericopi iniziali del Vangelo di San Marco. R 1986, Pont. Ist. Biblico. iii-99 p.

3790 *Agua Pérez* Agustín del, El procedimiento derásico que configura el relato del bautismo de Jesús (Mc 1,9-11); estudio de crítica literaria: ➤ 21, Mem. DÍEZ MACHO A., Salvación 1986, 593-609.

3791 *Funk* R. W., Polling the pundits [Berkeley seminar as to whether Jesus spoke Mk 1,15 and 2,17]: Forum 1,1 (1985) 31-50 [NTAbs 30,139].

3792 *LaVerdiere* E. [Mk ...] Beware of the scribes: Emmanuel 92 (1986) 394-400 [< NTAbs 31,23] (316-321, The widow's mite).

3792* *Burgos Núñez* Miguel de, La acción liberadora de Jesús en la jornada de Cafarnao (Mc. 1,21-3,6): ComSev 19 (1986) 323-341.

3793 a) *Chilton* B. D., Exorcism and history; Mark 1:21-28; – b) *Twelftree* Graham H., '*Ei de ... egō ekbállō ta daimónia* [Mt 12,27] ...': ➤ 271, Miracles 1986, 253-272 / 361-400.

3794 *Evans* Craig A., Patristic Interpretation of Mark 2:26, 'When Abiathar was high priest': VigChr 40 (1986) 183-6.

3795 *Derrett* J. D. M., a) Christ and the power of choice (Mark 3,1-6); – b) Mark's techniques; the haemorrhaging woman and Jairus' daughter [< Biblica 65 (1984) 168-188 / 63 (1982) 474-505]: ➤ 150, Studies NT 4 (1986) 9-29; franç. 29 / 30-60; franç. 61.

3796 **Sánchez Román** Eloy, Proyecto y educación en Mc 3,13-19; ensayo de interpretación intercultural del proyecto de Jesús con los Doce: diss. Pont. Univ. Gregoriana, ᴰ*Lentzen-Deis* F. R 1986. 241 p. [extr. Nᵒ 3321, 200 p.; bibliog. p. 153-193]. – TR 82 (1986) 426; RTLv 18,549.

3797 *Stock* A., 'All sins will be forgiven ... but ...' [Mk 3,29 is not part of 3,28, but Mishnah-type citation of an alternative view]: Emmanuel 92,1 (1986) 18-21 [NTAbs 30,151].

3797* **Marcus** Joel, [Mk 4,1-34] The mystery of the Kingdom of God: SBL diss. 90 [NY Columbia 1985, ᴰ*Martyn* J.]. Atlanta 1986, Scholars. xiv-272 p.; bibliog. p. 235-259. $13. 0-89130-983-7; pa. 4-5.

3798 *Lohfink* Gerhard, Das Gleichnis vom Sämann (Mk 4,3-9): BZ 30 (1986) 36-69.

3799 *Parkin* Vincent, Exegesis of Mark 4:10-12: IrBSt 8 (1986) 179-182.

3800 *Hatton* Howard A., [Mk 4,24s] Unraveling the agents and events: BTrans 37 (1986) 417-420.

3801 **Hallbäck** Geert, Strukturalisme og eksegese; modellanalyser af Markus 5,21-43: Bibel og historie 4, 1983 ➤ 64,4789: ᴿSvTKv 62 (1986) 45-47 (T. *Skinstad*).

3802 *Derrett* J. D. M., *a)* Peace, sandals and shirts (Mark 6:6b-13 par.) [< HeythJ 24 (1983) 253-265]; – *b)* Crumbs in Mark [< DowR 102 (1984) 12-21]: ➤ 150, Studies NT 4 (1986) 62-74 / 82-91.

3803 *Chevalon* M., [Mk 6,17-28] Jean le Baptiste et Salomé ou l'insaisissable vérité: CahRenan 33,140 (1985) 24-26: Salome would have been a pre-adolescent [NTAbs 30,283].

3804 *Schwartz* Jacques, [Mc 6,23; Esther 5,3 ...] Récits bibliques et mœurs perses: ➤ 81, Mém. NIKIPROWETZKY V., Hellenica 1986, 267-277.

3805 *a) Barnett* P. W., The feeding of the multitude in Mark 6 / John 6; – *b)* *Wright* David F., Apologetic and apocalyptic; the miraculous in the Gospel of Peter: ➤ 271, Miracles 1986, 273-293 / 401-418.

3806 *Bassler* Jouette M., The parable [*sic,* as *Robinson* D. 1957; Mk 6,30-44; 8,1-10] of the loaves: JRel 66 (1986) 157-172.

3807 *Neugebauer* Fritz, Die wunderbare Speisung (Mk 6,30-44 parr.) und Jesu Identität: KerDo 32 (1986) 254-277; Eng. 277.

3808 *LaVerdiere* E., *a)* [Mk 6,34-44] In hundreds and fifties; – *b)* [Mk 8,1-10] The evening of the third day: Emmanuel 91 (1985) 425-9 / 502-7.

3809 **Booth** Roger P., Jesus and the laws of purity; tradition history and legal history in Mark 7: JStNT Sup 13. Sheffield 1986, JStOT. 278 p. £18.50; pa. £9. 1-850750-23-80 22-X. – ᴿExpTim 98 (1986s) 117s (J. *Muddiman*).

3809* *Slusser* Michael, [Mk 7,11] The *corban* passages in patristic exegesis: ➤ 73, ᶠMEYER R., Diakonia 1986, 101-110.

3810 *Sugirtharajah* R. S., [Mk 7:24-30] The Syrophoenician woman [account challenging us to acknowledge role of other faiths]: ExpTim 98 (1986s) 13-15.

3811 *Horton* Fred L.ᴶ, Nochmals *ephphathá* in Mk 7,34: ZNW 77 (1986) 101-8.

3812 *Gibson* Jeffrey B., The rebuke of the disciples in Mark 8.14-21: JStNT 27 (1986) 31-47.

3813 *Collange* J.-F., La déroute de l'aveugle (Mc 8,22-26); Écriture et pratique chrétienne: ➤ 83*, ᶠPETER R. = RHPR 66 (1986) 21-28; Eng. 130, 'The re-routing...'.

3814 *Miller* J. I., Was TISCHENDORF really wrong? Mark 8:26b revisited: NT 28 (1986) 97-103.

3815 **Ko Ha Fong** Maria, [Mk 8,34] Crucem tollendo Christum sequi ... in der Alten Kirche ᴰ1984 ➤ 65,4032; 1,4848: ᴿEstE 61 (1986) 444s (C. *Granado Bellido*); RSPT 70 (1986) 693s (J. M. de *Durand*); VigChr 40 (1986) 307-9 (G. Q. *Reiners*).

3816 *Russell* E. A., A plea for tolerance (Mark 9. 38-40): ➤ 44, Mem. HAIRE J. = IrBSt 8 (1986) 154-160.

3817 **Busemann** R., Die Jüngergemeinde nach Markus 10 ... BoBB 57, 1983 ➤ 64,4799 ... 1,4853: ᴿJBL 105 (1986) 154-6 (Q. *Quesnell*).

3818 *Casciaro Ramírez* José M., Un aspecto de la igualdad radical de los cónyuges en el matrimonio: Mc 10,12: ➤ 21, Mem. DÍEZ MACHO A., Salvación 1986, 623-631.

3819 *Focant* Camille, Les méthodes dans la lecture biblique; un exemple, Mc 10,13-16: FoiTemps 16 (1986) 119-139.

3820 *Maat* Paul de, 'Als een erfgenaam'? een hypothese voor de uitleg van Mc 10,13-16 ['as an heir' not 'child', though understood otherwise by Mt 19,14]: ► 94, FRIJKHOFF M., Bij de put 1986, 98-108.

3821 *Ringshausen* Gerhard, Die Kinder der Weisheit; zur Auslegung von Mk 10,13-16 par.: ZNW 77 (1986) 34-63.

3822 *Gori* Franco, La bontà di Dio nell'esegesi gnostica di Mc 10,18 (e paralleli): ► 365, AnStoEseg 3 (1985/6) 163-171.

3823 *Derrett* J. D. M., [Mk 10,25] A camel through the eye of a needle: NTS 32 (1986) 465-470.

3824 **Debergé** Pierre, Réflexion biblique et théologique sur le pouvoir à partir de Marc 10,35-45: diss. Pont. Univ. Gregoriana, ᴰ*Lentzen-Deis* F. R 1986. 454 p. – RTLv 18,546.

3825 *Brueggemann* W., [Mk 10,46-52] Theological education; healing the blind beggar: ChrCent 103 (1986) 114-6 [NTAbs 30,284].

3826 *Steinhauser* Michael G., The form of the Bartimaeus narrative (Mark 10. 46-52): NTS 32 (1986) 583-595.

3827 **Mudiso Mbâ Mundla** Jean-Gaspard, Jesus und die Führer Israels ... [Mk 11s]: NTAbh 17, 1984 ► 65,4411; 1,4860: ᴿCBQ 48 (1986) 146s (R. *Scroggs*: purpose not clear); RAfrT 10,19 (1986) 91-102 (*Atal Sa Angang*); TLZ 111 (1986) 271-4 (P. von der *Osten-Sacken*).

3828 *Hre Kio* Stephen, A prayer framework in Mark 11: BTrans 37 (1986) 323-8.

3829 *Cotter* Wendy J., [Mk 11,12-14] 'For it was not the season for figs': CBQ 48 (1986) 62-66.

3830 *Broadhead* Edwin K., Which mountain is 'this mountain'? A critical note on Mark 11:22-25: Paradigms 2,1 (1986) 33-38 [the Temple mount].

3831 **Dowd** Sharyn E., 'Whatever you ask in prayer, believe' (Mark 11:22-25); the theological function of prayer and the problem of theodicy in Mark: diss. Emory, ᴰ*Holladay* C. Atlanta 1986. 382 p. 87-05642. DissA 47 (1986s) 4113s-A.

3832 **Lee Young-Heon** Marius, Jesus und die jüdische Autorität; eine exegetische Untersuchung zu Mk 11,27 – 12,12 [diss. Innsbruck 1984]: ForBi 56. Wü 1986, Echter. vi-375 p.; bibliog. p. 245-572. 3-429-01018-7.

3833 *Marucci* Corrado, Die implizite Christologie in der sogenannten Vollmachtsfrage (Mk 11,27-33), SNTS Trondheim 1985: ZkT 108 (1986) 292-300.

3833* *Haacker* Klaus, Kaisertribut und Gottesdienst (eine Auslegung von Markus 12,13-17): TBei 17 (Wu 1986) 285-292 [< ZIT].

3834 *Rahmani* L. Y., 'Whose likeness and inscription is this?' (Mark 12:16): BA 49 (1986) 60s.

3835 **Schwankl** Otto, Die Sadduzäerfrage (Mk 12,18-27 parr.), eine exegetisch-theologische Studie zur Auferstehungserwartung: Diss. Würzburg 1985s, ᴰ*Schnackenburg* R. – TR 82 (1986) 513.

3836 *Vouga* François, Controverse sur la résurrection des morts (Marc 12,18-27): LumièreV 35,179 (1986) 49-61.

3837 **Brandenburger** Egon, Markus 13 und die Apokalyptik; FRLANT 134, 1984 ► 65,4413; 1,4869: ᴿÉTRel 61 (1986) 132-4 (M. *Bouttier*); JTS 37 (1986) 177-180 (B. *Lindars*); Salmanticensis 33 (1986) 120-2 (R. *Trevijano*); TLZ 111 (1986) 746-8 (J. *Lambrecht*); TPhil 61 (1986) 566-8 (H. *Engel*); TS 48 (1986) 348-350 (J. M. *McDermott*).

3838 **Geddert** Timothy J.,   Mark 13 in its Markan interpretative context: diss. Aberdeen. – RTLv 18,547 sans date.
3839 *Graham* Helen R.,   A Passion prediction for Mark's community; Mark 13:9-13:   BibTB 16 (1986) 18-22.
3840 *McNicol* A.,   The lesson of the fig tree in Mark 13,28-32; a comparison between two exegetical methodologies: RestQ 27 (1984) 193-207 [NTAbs 30,285].

F6.8   **Passio secundum Marcum, 14,1 ...**

3841 **Blackwell** John,   The passion as story; the plot of Mark: Resources for Preaching. Ph 1986, Fortress. 96 p. $6 pa. 0-8006-1144-6. – RCleR 71 (1986) 193 (M. *Winstanley*).
3842 **Schlier** Heinrich,   La passione secondo Marco [1974]: Già e non ancora pocket 36, 1979 ➤ 60,6281; 61,6231: RRivLtg 73 (1986) 429s (G. *Crocetti*).
3843 **Senior** Donald,   The Passion of Jesus in the Gospel of Mark 1984 ➤ 1,4879: RBibTB 16 (1986) 158 (M. *McVann*); CurrTM 13 (1986) 176s (M. I. *Wegener*) & 313 (E. *Krentz*).
3844 **Ziegler** James R.,   Holy War theology as a paradigm for understanding the Passion in the Gospel of Mark: diss. in progress, Saint Louis Univ. [RelStR 12, 325].
3845 **Feldmeier** Reinhard,   Die Krisis des Gottessohnes; die markinische Gethsemaneperikope als Schlüssel der Markuspassion: ev. Diss. DHengel M. Tübingen 1986. 271 p. – RTLv 18,546.
3846 *Kiley* Mark,   'Lord, save my life' (Ps 116:4) as generative text for Jesus' Gethsemane prayer (Mark 14:36a); CBQ 48 (1986) 655-9.
3847 *Müller* Klaus W.,   *Apéchei* (Mk 14,41) – absurda lectio?: ZNW 77 (1986) 83-100: 3 sg. impf. < *apochéō* '[God] poured out [his judgment-wrath]'.
3848 *McVann* Mark,   Conjectures about a guilty bystander; the sword slashing in Mark 12:47: Listening 21 (1986) 124-137.
3848* *Ukachukwu Manus* Chris,   The centurion's confession of faith (Mk 14:39); reflections on Mark's Christology and its significance in the life of African Christians: ➤ 472, BTAf 7,13 (1985) 261-278 [< TKontext 8/2,23].
3849 *Maartens* P. J.,   The Son of Man as compound metaphor in Mk 14:62: ➤ 72, FMetzger B., South Africa 1985/6, 76-98.
3850 *LaVerdiere* Eugene, [Mk 14,72] Peter broke down and began to cry / [Mk 16,4] It was a huge stone: Emmanuel 92 (1986,2) 70-73 / (1986,3) 125-129 [NTAbs 30,286] and other short items.
3851 **Matera** Frank J.,   The kingship of Jesus ... Mk 15:   1982 ➤ 63,4974 ... 1,4888: RJAAR 54 (1986) 182s (J. R. *Donahue*).
3852 **Schreiber** Johannes,   Der Kreuzigungsbericht des Markusevangeliums Mk 15.20b-41; eine traditionsgeschichtliche und methodenkritische Untersuchung nach William WREDE (1859-1906) [Diss. 1959, DVielhauer P.]: BZNW 48. B 1986, de Gruyter. x-517 p.; bibliog. p. 457-486. 3-11-010594-2.
3853 *Kilpatrick* G. D., Mark XV.28: ➤ 21, Mem. DíEZ MACHO A., Salvación 1986, 641-5.
3854 **Caza** Lorraine,   'Mon Dieu, mon Dieu, pourquoi m'as-tu abandonné ? ' (Marc 15,34) comme bonne nouvelle de Jésus Christ fils de Dieu, comme bonne nouvelle de Dieu pour la multitude: diss. Ottawa 1986, DTremel Y. – RTLv 18,546.
3855 **Rossé** G., [Mc 15,34 ➤ 65,4421] Il grido di Gesù in croce; una panoramica

esegetica e teologica. R 1984, Città Nuova. 166 p. Lit. 10.000 [NTAbs 31,103].

3856 *Henaut* Barry W., Empty tomb or empty argument; a failure of nerve in recent studies of Mark 16?: SR 15 (1986) 177-190 [➤ 8666, *Dawson* L.].

3857 *Backhaus* Knut, 'Dort werdet ihr Ihn sehen' (Mk 16,7); die redaktionelle Schlussnotiz des zweiten Evangeliums als dessen christologische Summe: TGl 76 (1986) 277-294.

3858 **Magness** J. Lee, [Mk 16,8] Sense and absence; structure and suspension in the ending of Mark's Gospel [diss. 1984 ➤ 1,4891]: SBL Semeia. Atlanta 1986, Scholars. 136 p. $15; pa. $11. 1-55540-006-X. – ᴿExpTim 98 (1986s) 117 (J. *Muddiman*); IrBSt 8 (1986) 206 (E. A. *Russell*).

3859 **Hug** Joseph, La finale de l'évangile de Marc (16,9-20) 1978 ➤ 60,6597 ... 63,4979: ᴿRThom 86 (1986) 319-321 (L. *Devillers*).

3860 **Mirecki** Paul A., Mark 16:9-20; composition, tradition and redaction: diss. Harvard, ᴰ*Koester* H. CM 1986. 172 p. 86-19014 – DissA 47 (1986s) 1767-A; HarvTR 79 (1986) 476s.

XII. Opus Lucanum

F7.1 *Opus Lucanum* – **Luke-Acts.**

3861 *Agua* Agustín del, El concepto Lucano de 'relato' (*diēgēsis*) como teología narrativa, la Haggada cristiana: ScriptV 33 (1986) 97-122.

3862 *Alexander* Loveday, Luke's preface in the context of Greek preface-writing: NT 28 (1986) 48-74.

3863 **Barnard** Will J., *Riet* Peter van 't, Lukas, de Jood; een Joodse inleiding op het Evangelie naar Lukas en de Handelingen der Apostelen 1984 ➤ 65,4428; 1,4895: ᴿNedTTs 40 (1986) 246s (J. T. *Nielsen*).

3864 *Bergquist* J. A., 'Good news to the poor' – why does this Lucan motif appear to run dry in the book of Acts?: Bangalore Theological Forum 18,1 (1986) 1-16 [< NTAbs 31,36].

3865 *Betori* Giuseppe, L'opera lucana nella storia dell'esegesi: ParVi 30 (1985) 385-394.

3866 *Beydon* France, Luc [-Actes] et 'ces dames de la Haute Société': ÉTRel 61 (1986) 331-341.

3867 **Carroll** John T., Eschatology and situation in Luke-Acts: diss. Princeton Theol. Sem. 1986. vi-322 p. 86-16946. – DissA 47 (1986s) 1772-A.

3868 **Casalegno** Alberto, Gesù e il tempio; studio redazionale su Luca-Atti [diss. Gregoriana, ᴰ*Mínguez* D.] 1984 ➤ 65,4431; 1,4903: ᴿBiblica 67 (1986) 282-5 (R. F. *O'Toole*); Igreja e Missão 131 (1986) 92s (R. F.); PerspT 18 (1986) 393-5 (V. *Marques*); RTLv 17 (1986) 224-6 (J. *Dupont*).

3869 ᴱ**Cassidy** R., *Scharper* P., Political issues in Luke-Acts 1983 ➤ 64,262 ... 1,4903: ᴿScripB 16 (1985s) 51s (M. *Goulder*).

3870 *Downing* F. Gerald, Freedom from the Law in Luke-Acts: JStNT 26 (1986) 49-52.

3871 **Edwards** Douglas R., Acts of the Apostles and Chariton's Chaereas and Callirhoe; a literary and sociohistorical study [Luke-Acts and the ancient romance Chaereas and Callirhoe; a comparison of their literary and social function: – RelStR 13,190, 1986], diss. Boston Univ. ᴰ*Kee* Howard C. [1987]. 223 p. 87-07080. – DissA 47 (1986s) 4414-A.

3872 **Feiler** Paul F., Jesus the prophet; the Lucan portrayal of Jesus as the prophet like Moses: diss. Princeton Theol. Sem. 1986. xiii-332 p. 86-16947. – DissA 47 (1986s) 1774s-A.

3873 a) *Fusco* Vittorio, Progetto storiografico e progetto teologico nell'opera lucana; – b) *Betori* Giuseppe, Gli Atti come opera storiografica; osservazioni di metodo: ➤ 391, Storiografia 1984/6, 123-152 / 103-122.

3874 **Ford** J.M., My enemy is my guest; Jesus and violence in Luke 1984 ➤ 65,4439; 1,4909: ᴿEvQ 58 (1986) 169-172 (W.J. *Heard*); Vidyajyoti 49 (1985) 481s (P.M. *Meagher*).

3874* *Goulder* Michael D., Did Luke know any of the Pauline letters ? : PerspRelSt 13 (1986) 97-112.

3875 *Grygliewicz* Feliks, ❷ Duch Święty [the Holy Spirit] w ujęciu św. Łukasza; ➤ 266, Duch Święty 73-80 / 89-100.

3876 *Jáuregui* José A., 'Israel' y la Iglesia en la teología de Lucas [< conferencia Jerusalén 1985]: EstE 61 (1986) 129-149.

3877 **Jervell** Jacob, The unknown Paul; essays on Luke-Acts and early Christian history 1984 ➤ 65,205; $10: ᴿBijdragen 47 (1986) 326s (B.J. *Koet*); CBQ 48 (1986) 142s (R.F. *O'Toole* dubious about the significance of Jewish Christians); EfMex 4,10 (1986) 133-6 (R. *Duarte Castillo*, también Director Responsable: 'uunknown', 'enssays', 'Luc' 'Sistory'); Interpretation 40 (1986) 428. 430 (S. *Brown*).

3878 **Juel** Donald, Luke-Acts; the promise of history 1983 ➤ 64,4842 ... **1,4913** ᴿInterpretation 40 (1986) 99s (D.E. *Garland*).

3879 *Kariamadam* Paul, India and Luke's theology of the Way: Bible Bhashyam 11 (1985) 47-60.

3880 a) *Klauck* Hans-Josef, Die Armut der Jünger in der Sicht des Lukas; – b) *Perrone* L., *Couilleu* G., La sequela di Cristo [< DizIstPerf]: Claretianum 26 (1986) 5-47 / 49-69.

3881 **Klinghardt** Matthias, Gesetz und Volk Gottes; das lukanische Verständnis des Gesetzes nach Herkunft, Funktion und seinem Ort in der Geschichte des Urchristentums: Diss. ᴰ*Berger* K. Heid. 1986s. – RTLv 18,547.

3882 **Klingsporn** Gary W., The validity of the Law in Luke-Acts: Diss. Baylor 1985. – RelStR 13,190.

3883 **Kolasny** Judette M., Pericopes of confrontation and rejection as a plot device in Luke-Acts: diss. Marquette, ᴰ*Kurz* W. Milwaukee 1985. 183 p. 86-04953. – DissA 47 (1986s) 216-A.

3883* **Kurz** William, Following Jesus; a disciple's guide to Luke and Acts. AA 1984, Servant. 140 p. $7. – ᴿBibTB 16 (1986) 34 (J. *Kodell*).

3884 **Làconi** M., Luca e la sua Chiesa. T 1986, Gribaudi. 135 p. Lit. 10.000.

3885 **Lewycky** David E., Paul's turning from the Jews to the Gentiles in Luke-Acts: diss. Marquette, ᴰ*Kurz* W. Milwaukee 1986. 267 p. 86-18712. – DissA 47 (1986s) 1777s-A.

3886 **Martin** T.W., Eschatology, history and mission in the social experience of Lucan Christians; a sociological study of the relationship between ideas and realities in Luke-Acts: diss. Oxford 1986. – RTLv 18,548.

3887 **Miller** Robert J., Prophecy and persecution in Luke-Acts: diss. Claremont 1986, ᴰ*Mack* B. 321 p. 86-06882. – DissA 47 (1986s) 211-A.

3888 *Moessner* David P., 'The Christ must suffer'; new light on the Jesus – Peter, Stephen, Paul parallels in Luke-Acts: NT 28 (1986) 220-256.

3889 *Moxnes* Halvor, Meals and the new community in Luke: SvEx 51s (1986s) 158-167.

3890 *Olsson* Birger, Mission à la Lukas, Johannes och Petrus: SvEx 51s (1986s) 180-191.

3891 **O'Toole** Robert F., The unity of Luke's theology; an analysis of Luke-Acts: GoodNewsSt 9, 1984 ➤ 65,4450; 1,4919: ᴿCBQ 48 (1986)

344-6 (D. *Hamm*: only minor queries); ComSev 19 (1986) 88s (M. de *Burgos*); Interpretation 40 (1986) 317.320.322 (W. *Pilgrim*: good but seems not to have kept up on recent studies challenging his conclusions); RRel 45 (1986) 944s (E. *Hensell*).

3892 *Pilarczyk* Krzystof, ❷ Luke-Acts bibliography, Poland 1945-1985: RuBi 39 (1986) 504-530.

Prete B., L'opera di Luca 1986 ➤ 206.

3893 *a) Ringgren* Helmer, Luke's use of the Old Testament; – *b) Kraabel* A. T., Greeks, Jews, and Lutherans in the middle half of Acts: ➤ 110, ᶠSTENDAHL K. = HarvTR 79 (1986) 227-235 / 147-157.

3894 *Russell* Walt, The anointing with the Holy Spirit in Luke-Acts: TrinJ 7 (1986) 47-63.

3895 *a) Salvador* Joaquim, A mulher em Lucas e nos Atos; – *b) Brasil Pereira* Ney, Humildade ou humilhação de Maria; – *c) Nogueira* Maria C., A mulher na vida judaica: ➤ 386, RCuBíb 10,39s (1986) 55-74 / 38-54 / 75-77.

3896 *a) Sanders* Jack T., The Jewish people in Luke-Acts; – *b) Tannehill* Robert C., Rejection by Jews and turning to Gentiles; the pattern of Paul's mission in Acts; – *c) Tiede* David L., 'Glory to thy people Israel!'; Luke-Acts and the Jews: ➤ 392, SBL Seminars 1986, 110-129 / 130-141 / 142-151.

3897 **Sanders** Jack, The Jews in Luke-Acts. L 1986, SCM. 410 p. £15. 0-334-02097-2. – ᴿExpTim 98 (1986s) 376s (D. *Mealand*).

Schneider Gerhard, Lukas, Theologe der Heilsgeschichte 1985 ➤ 217.

3898 **Seccombe** D. P., Possessions and the poor in Luke-Acts 1982 ➤ 63,5004 ... 1,4923: ᴿThemelios 12 (1986s) 95s (M. *Turner*).

3899 **Stronstad** R., The charismatic theology of St. Luke [master's diss. Vancouver 1975, ᴰ*Gasque* W.]. Peabody MA 1984, Hendrickson. viii-96 p. $5 pa. 0-913573-11-6 [NTAbs 30,358].

3900 ᴱ**Talbert** Charles H., Luke-Acts; new perspectives ... 1984 ➤ 65,440; 1,4927: ᴿCurrTM 13 (1986) 55s (R. H. *Smith*).

3901 **Tannehill** Robert C., The narrative unity of Luke-Acts, a literary interpretation; I. The Gospel according to Luke: Foundations and Facets NT. Ph 1986, Fortress. xv-334 p. 0-8006-2112-3.

3902 **Van Linden** Philip, The Gospel of Luke and Acts: Message of Biblical Spirituality. Wilmington 1986, Glazier. 193 p. $11; pa. $9. – ᴿBibTB 16 (1986) 160 (J. *Kodell*); RExp 83 (1986) 626s (J. *Polhill*).

3903 **Wagner** Günter, An exegetical bibliography of the New Testament [1. Mt-Mk 1983 ➤ 64,865], 2. Luke and Acts. Macon GA 1985, Mercer Univ. xiii-550 p. – ᴿETL 62 (1986) 428s (F. *Neirynck*: son fichier biblique de Rüschlikon-Zürich; Jean sous presse; le reste du NT, deux volumes, attendu).

3904 **Walaskay** Paul W., 'And so we came to Rome'; the political perspective of St. Luke: SNTS Mon 49, 1983 ➤ 64,4863; 1,4930: ᴿJBL 105 (1986) 338-340 (D. R. *Edwards*).

3905 **Wilson** S. G., Luke and the Law: SNTS Mon 50,1983 ➤ 65,4460; 1,4931: ᴿEvQ 58 (1986) 265-7 (S. V. *Rees*); JBL 105 (1986) 336-8 (L. T. *Johnson*).

F7.3 **Evangelium Lucae** – *Textus, commentarii*.

3906 **Bossuyt** Philippe, *Radermakers* Jean, Jesus parole de la grâce selon saint Luc 1981 ➤ 62,5068 ... 1,4936: ᴿTLZ 111 (1986) 34-36 (C. *Burchard*).

3907 **Ernst** Josef, Il vangelo di Luca [Rg 1977] 1985 ⇒ 1,4938: ᴿTeresianum 37 (1986) 507s (V. *Pasquetto*).

3908 **Fitzmyer** Joseph A., The Gospel according to Luke I-II: Anchor Bible 28, 1981/5 ⇒ 62,5051 ... **1,4939:** ᴿBibTB 16 (1986) 152 (E. *Jane Via*, 2); Bijdragen 47 (1986) 443 (J. *Lambrecht*, 2); BZ 30 (1986) 135-7 (R. *Schnackenburg*); CBQ 48 (1986) 336-8 (C. H. *Talbert*, 2: in four major areas belongs to the pre-1974 trend of Lucan studies; but he has the better of the argument); Claretianum 26 (1986) 370s (B. *Proietti*, 2); ÉTRel 61 (1986) 430 (F. *Vouga*, 2: irremplaçable, plus pour texte et bibliographie que pour la promise 'réhabilitation de Luc', mieux chez TALBERT); Furrow 57 (1986) 202s (M. *Drennan*, 2: 'Jerome A. Fitzmeyer'); Gregorianum 67 (1986) 365-7 (L. *Sabourin*: first-rate); Horizons 13 (1986) 417s (Q. *Quesnell*); JStNT 28 (1986) 124 (C. *Tuckett*, 2: a classic); JTS 37 (1986) 527-530 (J. L. *Nolland*); RQum 12,46 (1986) 289-291 (J. *Carmignac*: détails sur Qumran); TS 47 (1986) 303s (R. J. *Karris*, 2).

3909 **Fitzmyer** Joseph A., El Evangelio según Lucas, I. Introducción general. M 1986, Cristiandad. 475 p.

3910 **Galizzi** Mario, La lunga marcia di Gesù / Gesù vittima del potere: Vangelo secondo Luca 2s, 1977/9 ⇒ 58,5044; 60,6651; 61,6298: ᴿRivLtg 73 (1986) 140s (G. *Crocetti*).

3911 **Gryson** Roger, Collectio veronensis; scholia in Lucam rescripta [c. 380]: CCL 87. Turnhout 1982. Brepols. 285 p. 2-503-00871-2; pa. 2-0. – ᴿRBgPg 64 (1986) 138s (H. *Savon*).

3912 **Jeanne d'Arc** sr., Évangile selon Luc ... grec: Nouvelle Collection de Textes et Documents. P 1986, BLettres/Desclée-B. x-221 (double) p. F 330. 2-251-32020-2 / 2-220-02608-6. [⇒ 1217].

3913 **Làconi** Mauro, Commenti al Vangelo di Luca [*Schürmann* H., *Ernst* J., *Radermakers* J., *da Spinetoli* O., *Prete* B.]: SacDoc 31 (1986) 234-241.

3914 [*Legg* S. C. E. text 1935/40] The NT in Greek, the Gospel according to St. Luke, I ch. 1-12. Ox 1984, Clarendon. xvi-300. £55. 0-19-826167-5. – ᴿÉTRel 61 (1986) 448-450 (C. *Amphoux*: pas à la hauteur des signatures prestigieuses, manquait un vrai responsable; la sélection des témoins n'est pas justifiée; le seul texte établi est moyen et tardif ...); ScotJT 39 (1986) 563-6 (D. C. *Parker*).

3915 **Müller** Paul-Gerhard, Lukas-Evangelium: Kleiner Komm. NT 3. Stu 1986, KBW. 183 p. 3-460-15331-8.

3916 **Mulder** H., Lucas I [tot 9:27], een praktische bijbelberklaring: Tekst en Toelichting. Kampen 1985, Kok. 147 p. ƒ 23,50. – ᴿKerkT 37 (1986) 72s (M. H. *Bolkestein*).

3917 **Obach** Robert E., (*Kirk* Albert), A commentary on the Gospel of Luke. Mahwah NJ 1986, Paulist. iii-266 p. $9 pa. [TDig 34,88; NTAbs 30,356]. 0-8091-2763-6.

3918 **Sabourin** Léopold, L'Évangile de Luc 1985 ⇒ 1,4946: ᴿEsprV 96 (1986) 105s [É. *Cothenet*]; EstE 61 (1986) 454-6 (J. A. *Jáuregui*); RAfrT 10,19 (1986) 133s (*Buetubela Balembo*); RThom 86 (1986) 321 (L. *Devillers*: decevant; curieux mélange des genres; trop hybride pour des non-spécialistes, rien de nouveau pour les spécialistes); ScEspr 38 (1986) 260s (P.-É. *Langevin*: de grands services).

3919 **Schürmann** H., Il vangelo di Luca I, 1983 ⇒ 64,4879 ... **1,4947:** ᴿAsprenas 33 (1986) 93-95 (C. *Marcheselli-Casale*).

3920 **Schweizer** Eduard, The Good News according to Luke, ᵀ*Green* David

E. 1984 → 65,4474; 1,4949: ᴿBibTB 16 (1986) 38s (Karen A. *Barta*);
Interpretation 40 (1986) 322s (S. *Brown*).

F7.4   *Lucae themata* – **Luke's Gospel, topics.**

3921 **Dawsey** James M.,   The Lukan voice; confusion and irony in the Gospel
of Luke.   Macon GA 1986, Mercer Univ.   vi-198 p. $19.50. [TR 83,251].
0-86554-193-0.

3922 *Dawsey* James M.,   *a*) The unexpected Christ; the Lucan image: ExpTim
98 (1986s) 296-300; – *b*) What's in a name? Characterization in Luke:
BibTB 16 (1986) 143-7.

3923 **Derrett** J. D. M.,   New resolutions of old conundrums; a fresh insight
into Luke's Gospel.   Shipston-on-Stour 1986, Drinkwater.   xviii-240 p.
£15.   0-946643-17-2. – ᴿExpTim 98 (1986s) 313 (F. F. *Bruce*).

3924 **Grassi** Joseph A.,   God makes me laugh; a new approach to Luke: Good
News Studies 17.   Wilmington 1986, Glazier.   152 p. $8 pa. [TDig 34,72].
0-89453-540-4.

3925 *Hamm* Dennis,   Sight to the blind; vision as metaphor in Luke: Biblica
67 (1986) 457-477; franç. 477.

3926 *Kopas* Jane,   Jesus and women; Luke's Gospel: TTod 43 (1986s) 192-202.

3927 **Lohfink** G.,   La raccolta di Israele; una ricerca sull'ecclesiologia lucana
[Die Sammlung Israels ᴰ1975 → 55,3085].   Casale Monferrato 1983,
Marietti. – ᴿAsprenas 33 (1986) 209-211 (C. *Scanzillo*).

3927* *Makridis* Vassilios, ⑥ Why Herodians are absent in the Gospel of Luke:
DeltioVM 15,1 (1986) 45-52.

3928 **Martini** Carlos M.,   Itinerario de oración [Lucas para jóvenes < 1981
→ 64,4896],ᵀ.   Bogotá 1983, Paulinas.   95 p. – ᴿTVida 27 (1986) 233
(Lucía *Santelices*).

3929 **Martini** Carlo M.,   Was allein notwendig ist; Jesusnachfolge nach dem
Lukasevangelium 1984 → 65,4487; 1,4967:   ᴿColcT 56,4 (1986) 187s (S.
Moysa).

3930 **Martini** Carlo M.,   Hoe Lucas ons leert bidden [1981 → 64,4896]: Gebed
en leven 3.   Nijmegen 1986, Gottmer.   87 p. Fb 280. – ᴿCollatVl 16 (1986)
498 (J. *De Kesel*).

3931 *Murray* Gregory,   Did Luke use Mark? [rather Mark used Luke]: DowR
104 (1986) 268-271.

3932 **Noel** Timothy L.,   Parables in context; developing a narrative critical
approach to parables in Luke: diss. Southern Baptist sem., ᴰ*Culpepper* R.
211 p. 86-28709. – DissA 47 (1986s) 3075-A.

3933 *Ravens* D.A.S.,   St Luke and atonement: ExpTim 97 (1985s) 291-4: Luke
has, not *no* theology of the Cross, but not a sacrificial one.

3934 **Rouiller** Grégoire, *Varone* M. C.,   Il Vangelo secondo Luca; testi e telogía
[Év.S.Luc, cours de correspondance en 13 fascicules, 1980], ᵀ*Cavalieri* Ugo.
Assisi 1983, Cittadella.   463 p. Lit. 13.000. – ᴿActuBbg 23 (1986) 219 (X.
Alegre S.).

3934* *Torelli* Stefano,   Osservazioni sui pronomi e aggettivi dimostrativi nel
Vangelo di Luca (con speciale riferimento al valore testuale) e sulla loro
traduzione nella versione armena antica: Rendiconti Ist. Lombardo 119
(1985) 3-8.

3935 **Torriani** A.,   Il *deîn* riferito a Gesù nel Vangelo di Luca: diss. Univ.
Cattolica, ᴰ*Ghiberti* G.   Milano 1985. [RivB 35,86].

3936 **Yoon** Seung-Ku Victor,   Did the Evangelist Luke use the canonical
Gospel of Matthew?:   diss. Graduate Theological Union, ᴰ*Herzog* W.

Berkeley 1986.   193 p. 86-06920. – DissA 47 (1986s) 220-A; RelStR
13,190.

F7.5   *Infantia, cantica* – **Magnificat, Benedictus: Luc. 1-3.**

3937 *Baudler* Georg,   Aspekte für eine christliche Erziehung nach den
lukanischen Kindheitserzählungen: TPQ 134 (1986) 28-38.

3938 *Brown* Raymond E.,   Gospel infancy narrative research from 1976 to
1986 [I ➤ 3350]; part II (Luke): CBQ 48 (1986) 660-680.

3939 *Dawsey* J. M.,   The form and function of the nativity stories in Luke:
MeliT 36,2 (1985) 41-48 [NTAbs 31,28].

3940 **Gueuret** Agnès,   L'engendrement d'un récit: LDiv 113, ᴰ1983 ➤ 64,4912
... 1,4977: ᴿAngelicum 63 (1986) 126-8 (A. *Paretsky*: made redundant by
publication meanwhile of LAURENTIN; flawed beyond usefulness e.g. in
citing BROWN); REB 46 (1986) 222s (S. *Voigt*); RB 93 (1986) 612s (É.
Nodet).

3940* **Stock** Klemens, [Lc 1,1-38] Le prime pericopi della storia dell'Infanzia in
Lc 1-2. R 1986, Pont. Ist. Biblico. 138 p.

3941 **Muñoz Iglesias** Salvador, [Lc 1,11.26] Los Evangelios de la Infancia II.
Los anuncios angélicos previos en el Evangelio lucano de la Infancia: BAC
479. M 1986, Católica. xii-321 p.

3942 **Muñoz Iglesias** S.,   Los Cánticos del Evangelio de la Infancia 1983
➤ 64,4929 ... 1,4992: ᴿDivinitas 30 (1986) 190 (T. *Stramare*).

3943 **Farris** Stephen,   The hymns of Luke's infancy narratives: JStNT Sup 9,
1985 ➤ 1,4990: ᴿBiblica 67 (1986) 405-7 (J. *Dupont*: travail à reculons);
ExpTim 97 (1985s) 248 (Ruth B. *Edwards*); JTS 37 (1986) 530s (I. H.
Marshall); Themelios 12 (1986s) 60s (M. *Turner*).

3944 **Lemmo** Nunzio, Maria, 'figlia di Sion' a partire da Lc 1,26-38; bilancio
esegetico dal 1939 al 1982: diss. Marianum 37. R 1985. xiii-85 p. [estr.];
bibliog. p. vii-xiii.

3945 **Bemile** Paul. The Magnificat within the context and framework of Lukan
theology; an exegetical theological study of Lk 1:46-55 [diss. Rg 1983,
ᴰ*Mussner* F. ➤ 64,4924]: RgStTheol 34. Fra 1986, Lang. vii-435 p. Fs
75. 3-8204-8395-0 [NTAbs 31,98].

3946 **Gomà Civit** Isidro,   The song of salvation, the Magnificat [1982 ➤ 63,
5062], ᵀSr. *Mary of Jesus*. Slough 1986, St. Paul. 159 p. £6. 0-85439-
260-2. – ᴿExpTim 98 (1986s) 281 (F. F. *Bruce*).

3946* *Lippold* Ernst,   Die Revision der Lutherbibel von 1984, dargestellt am
Beispiel des Magnificat Lk 1,46-55: JbLtgHymn 29 (1985) 127-133.

3947 *Martini* Carlo M., *a)* Il Magnificat [conferenza episcopale brasiliana,
15.IV.1985]; – *b)* Luca, il vangelo dell'evangelizzatore [< Terra ambrosiana (nov. 1985)] ➤ 190, Per una santità di popolo 1986, 223-247 /
541-553.

3947* *a) Muñoz Iglesias* Salvador,   Génesis histórico-literaria del Magníficat; –
b) Aranda Pérez Gonzalo,   El Evangelio proclamado por María; – *c)
Molina Prieto,* Andrés,   Mensaje liberador del Magníficat y sugerencias
marginales; – *d) Schnackenburg* Rudolf,   Comentario spiritual al
Magníficat: EphMar 36 (1986) 9-27 / 29-56 / 57-88 / 133-147.

3948 *Diez Merino* L.,   [Lc 1,48] Desde ahora me felicitarán todas las
generaciones: Scripta de Maria 9 (Zaragoza 1986) 7-26.

3948* *Rousseau* François,   Les structures du Benedictus (Luc 1.68-79): NTS
32 (1986) 268-282.

3949 *Lupieri* Edmondo,   La nascita di un santo; la figura di Giovanni Battista fra l'esegesi di ORIGENE e quella di GIROLAMO: ➤ 365, AnStoEseg 3 (1985/6) 247-258.

3950 *Must* Hildegard, A diatessaric rendering in Luke 2.7: NTS 32 (1986) 136-143.

3951 *Ottey* J. L., 'In a stable born our brother' [Lk 2,7: in a cave; not as K. *Bailey*, 'like most Jewish Boys (sic), in a loving, crowded home']: ExpTim 98 (1986s) 71-73.

3952 *Prete* Benedetto, 'Oggi vi è nato ... il Salvatore che è il Cristo Signore' (Lc 2,11): RivB 34 (1986) 289-325.

3953 *LaVerdiere* E., At the table of the manger: Emmanuel 92,1 (1986) 22-27.

3954 *a*) *Muñoz Iglesias* Salvador, 'Encontraréis un niño envuelto en pañales ...' (Lc 2,12); – *b*) *Aranda Pérez* Gonzalo, Concepción virginal de Jesús y apocalíptica; a propósito de un fragmento copto sobre Henoc: ➤ 21, Mem. DÍEZ MACHO A., Salvación 1986, 647-655 / 543-552.

3955 *Pritchard* Alwyn, [Lk 2,12] The sign: ExpTim 98 (1986s) 48-50.

3955* **Plöger** Josef G., [Lk 2,25-32...] In der Nähe des Herrn; biblische Besinnungen. FrB 1986, Herder. 95 p. 3-451-20738-9.

3956 *Grelot* Pierre, Le Cantique de Siméon (Luc, II, 29-32): RB 93 (1986) 481-509; Eng. 481.

3957 *Lindemann* F.-W., [Lk 2,49] 'Wisset ihr nicht, dass ich sein muss in dem, das meines Vaters ist?': Wege zum Menschen 38 (Gö 1986) 70-76 [< ZIT].

3957* *Ruiz* Gregorio, [Lc 2,50s] Cara y cruz de la familia en el Evangelio; una tensión que no cesa: SalT 74 (1986) 379-389.

3958 **Allencherry** George, [Lc 3,21] Le baptême de Jésus dans l'oeuvre de Luc et dans la tradition baptismale de l'Église indo-chaldéenne: diss. P Inst.Cath./ Sorbonne, 1986, ᴰCothenet R. – RICathP 18 (1986) 78s; RTLv 18, 545.

3958* *Heater* Homerᴶ, A textual note on Luke 3.33: JStNT 28 (1986) 25-29.

F7.6   **Evangelium Lucae 4,1...**

3959 **Meynet** Roland, Initiation à la rhétorique biblique [Lc 4,14-30; Mt 20,29-34 ‖; Mc 10,35-52; Lc 18,31 – 19,46; Lc 22,1-53] 1982 ➤ 63,1254 ... 1,5005; ᴿEsprV 96 (1986) 109s (L. *Walter*); VSp 139 (1985) 258 (C. *Coulot*).

3960 *Álvarez Barredo* Miguel, Discurso inaugural de Jesús en Nazaret (Lc 4,16-30), clave teológica del evangelio de Lucas: Carthaginensia 2 (1986) 23-34.

3961 *Koet* B.-J., 'Today this Scripture has been fulfilled in your ears'; Jesus' explanation of Scripture in Luke 4,16-30: Bijdragen 47 (1986) 368-394; franç. 394.

3962 *Baarda* T., *Anoíxas – anaptúxas*; over de vaststelling van de tekst van Lukas 4,17 in het Diatessaron: NedTTs 40 (1986) 199-208: Eng. 208.

3963 *Nolland* J., [Lk 4,22...] Luke's use of *cháris* [a power, *Wilckens* U.; no, *Taeger* J.]: NTS 32 (1986) 614-620.

3964 **Allegro** J. M. [Lk 4,23] Physician, heal thyself [healing-movements in Essenism and Christianity and their rejection]. Buffalo 1985, Prometheus. 93 p. $14. 0-87975-305-6 [NTAbs 30,239].

3964* *Palmieri* Vincenzo, Nota a Luca, 4,25 [*hõs* consecutivo con indic.]: Sileno 12 (1986) 87-91.

3965 *Baarda* T., 'The flying Jesus'; Luke 4:29-30 in the Syriac Diatessaron: VigChr 40 (1986) 313-341.

3966 **Bouwman** Gijs, De wonderbare visvangst (Lc 5,1-11), een proeve van integrale exegese: ➤ 94, ᶠRIJKHOFF M., Bij de put 1986, 109-129.

3967 *Bammel* Ernst,   The Cambridge pericope; the addition to Luke 6.4 in Codex Bezae: NTS 32 (1986) 404-426.
3968 *a) Miller* Donald G.,   Luke 4:22-30; – *b) Cousar* Charles B.,   Luke 5:29-35; – *c) Tiede* David L.,   Luke 6:17-26; things are not as they seem: Interpretation 40 (1986) 53-58 / 58-63 / 63-68.
3969 *Brodie* Thomas L.,   Toward unravelling Luke's use of the Old Testament; Luke 7.11-17 as an imitatio of 1 Kings 17.7-24: NTS 32 (1986) 247-267.
3970 *Karris* Robert J., [Lk 7,20; 19,1-10; 12,15-21 ...] God's boundary-breaking mercy: BToday 24 (1986) 24-30.
3971 *a) Plessis* I. J. du,   Contextual aid for an identity crisis; an attempt to interpret Lk 7:35; – *b) Louw* J. P.,   Macro levels of meaning in Lk 7:36-50: ➤ 72, ᶠMETZGER B., 1985/6, 112-127 / 128-135.
3972 **Ricci** Carla,   Le donne al seguito di Gesù in Lc. 8,1-3: diss. ᴰ*Pesce* M. Bologna 1986, 256 p.; p. 257-480. [i. La questione delle 'tre Marie'; ruolo privilegiato di Maria di Magdala; ii. la condizione della donna al tempo di Gesù; iii. 'gruppo' intorno a Gesù; iv. analisi del testo].
3973 *García Pérez* José M.,   El endemoniado de Gerasa (Lc 8,26-39): EstB 44 (1986) 117-146.

F7.7   Iter hierosolymitanum *Lc 9...*

3973* *Farrell* Hobert K.,   The structure and theology of Luke's central section: TrinJ 7,2 (1986) 33-54.
3974 *Coune* Michel, [Lc 9,28-36] Saint Luc et le mystère de la Transfiguration: NRT 108 (1986) 3-12.
3975 *Hagemeyer* Oda,   Freut euch, dass eure Namen im Himmel verzeichnet sind ! (Lk 10,20): HDienst 39,4 (Salzburg 1985) 160-3.
3975* *Giblet* J.,   L'action de grâce de Jésus dans le contexte de l'Évangile de saint Luc [Lc X, 21-24]: ➤ 16*, Mém. COPPIETERS de Gibson D. 1985, 613-636.
3976 *O'Donovan* O. M. T., [Lk 10,29] Who is a person?: ➤ 282, ᴱ*Channer* J., Abortion 1985...
3977 **Brutscheck** Jutta,   Die Maria-Martha-Erzählung; eine redaktionskritische Untersuchung zu Lk 10,38-42: BoBB 64. Fra 1986, Hanstein. xiv-291 p. DM 78 [TR 82,426].
3978 *Schüssler Fiorenza* Elisabeth,   A feminist critical interpretation for liberation; Martha and Mary: Lk. 10:38-42: Religion and Intellectual Life 3,2 (New Rochelle 1986) 21-36 [NTAbs 30,289].
3979 *Erb* P. C.,   The contemplative life as the unum necessarium; in defense of a traditional reading of Luke 10:42: Mystics Quarterly 11,4 (Iowa City 1985) 161-4 [NTAbs 30,289].
3979* **Pacomio** Luciano, [Lc 11,3] Dacci ogni giorno il nostro pane; L'eucaristia secondo Luca 1983 ➤ 64,4898*b*; Lit. 6000: ParVi 30 (1985) 79 (P. *Dacquino*).
3980 *Haacker* Klaus,   Mut zum Bitten; eine Auslegung von Lukas 11,5-8: TBei 17 (Wu 1986) 1-6 [< ZIT].
3980* *Gorringe* Timothy,   A zealot option rejected ? Luke 12:13-14: ExpTim 98 (1986s) 267-270.
3981 *Jerry* S.,   'I came to cast fire upon the earth ...' (Lk 12:49); reflections on violence [in Tamil]: Marai Aruvi 10,1 (1986) 1-28 [< TKontext 8/2,35].
3981* *März* Claus-Peter,   Lk 12,54b-56 par Mt 16,2b.3 und die Akoluthie der Redequelle: SNTU-A 11 (1986) 83-96.

3982 *Derrett* J. D. M., Lk 13,10-17; 14,1-6] Positive perspectives on two Lucan miracles: DowR 104 (1986) 272-287.

3982* *Radl* Walter, Ein 'doppeltes Leiden' in Lk 13,11 ? Zu einer Notiz von Günther SCHWARZ: BibNot [20 (1983) 58 = BWANT 118 (1985)] 31 (1986) 35s.

3983 *Abel* Olivier, De l'obligation de croire; les objections de BAYLE au commentaire augustinien du 'contrains-les d'entrer' (Luc 14/16-23): ÉTRel 61 (1986) 35-49.

3984 **Welzen** Paulus H. M., Lucas, evangelist van gemeenschap; een onderzoek naar het pragmatisch effect van Lc 15,1 – 17,10: diss. ᴰIersel B. van. Nijmegen 1986. xii-265 p. – RTLv 18,550. 90-9001-292-3.

3984* *Petersen* Joan M., Greek influences upon GREGORY the Great's exegesis of Luke 15,1-11 in Homelia in Evangelium II, 34; – b) *Étaix* Raymond, Note sur la tradition manuscrite des Homélies sur l'Évangile de saint Grégoire le Grand: ➔ 433*, Grégoire 1982/6, 521-9 / 551-9.

3985 *Vanhetloo* Warren, [Lk 15,3-6; Mt 18,12s] Two ninety and nines: CalvaryB 2,2 (1986) 9-22.

3986 *Mycielski* Ludwik, ❷ [Lk 15,3-7 centum oves, 8-10 decem drachmae, 11-32 duo filii: omnes simul una] Parabola de reconciliatione; introductio biblica ad Adhortationem Apostolicam Johannis Pauli II 'Reconciliatio et paenitentia': RuBi 39 (1986) 135-155.

3986* **Hurst** Antony, [Lk 15,11-32] The prodigal son [in today's terms, drug addiction ...]: ExpTim 98 (1986s) 274s.

3987 *Lees* J. G., [Lk 15,11-32] The parable of the good father: ExpTim 97 (1985s) 246s.

3988 *Smit Sibinga* Joost, Zur Kompositionstechnik des Lukas in Lk. 15:11-32: ➔ 59, ᶠLEBRAM J., Tradition 1986, 97-113.

3988* **Poensgen** Herbert, Die Befreiung einer verlorenen Beziehung; eine biblisch-homiletische Untersuchung zu Lk 15,11-32 unter besonderer Berücksichtigung familientherapeutischer Erkenntnisse: Diss. Bamberg 1985s, ᴰ*Fuchs.* – TR 82 (1986) 512.

3989 *Zauner* Wilhelm, Busse als Fest [Lk 15,11-32]: TPQ 134 (1986) 280-2.

3990 *Baudler* Georg, Das Gleichnis vom 'betrügerischen Verwalter' (Lk 16,1-8a) als Ausdruck der 'inneren Biographie' Jesu; Beispiel einer existenz-biographischen Gleichnisinterpretation in religionspädagogischer Absicht; TGegw 23 (1985) 65-76.

3991 *Derrett* J. D. M., a) The parable of the profitable servant (Luke xvii.7-10) [< TU 126 (1982) 165-174]; – b) Luke's perspective on tribute to Caesar [< ᴱ*Cassidy* R., Political Issues 1983, 38-48]: ➔ 150, Studies NT 4 (1986) 157-166 / 196-206.

3992 *Dupont* Jacques, The master and his servant (Lk 17:7-10) [< ETL 60 (1984) 233-251 = Études Év. Syn. 2 (1985) 1098-1116]: TDig 33 (1986) 343-6.

3993 *Read* David H. C., [Lk 17,21 kingdom of God 'within you' AV, 'among you' NEB] Christ comes unexpectedly: ExpTim 98 (1986s) 21s.

3994 *Lorenzen* T., The radicality of grace; 'the pharisee and the tax collector' (Luke 18:9-14) as a parable of Jesus: Faith & Mission 3,2 [Wake Forest 1986] 66-75 [NTAbs 30,289].

3995 **Reist** Thomas, Saint BONAVENTURE as a biblical commentator; a translation and analysis of his commentary on Luke, XVIII,34-XIX,12: 1985 ➔ 1,5045*: ᴿThomist 50 (1986) 701-3 (D. V. *Monti*).

3996 **Kariamadam** Paul, The Zacchaeus story [Lk. 19,1-10], a redaction-critical investigation [< diss. R 1983, Pont. Ist. Biblico] 1985 ➔ 1,5046: ᴿBible

Bhashyam 12 (1986) 150s (G. *Mangatt*); Biblica 67 (1986) 568s (J. *Swetnam*).

3997 *Baggio* Hugo D., Zaqueu, desce da árvore. Petrópolis 1986, Vozes. 96 p. [REB 46,468: sem preocupações exegéticas].

3998 *Kerr* A. J., [Lk 19,8] Zacchaeus's decision to make fourfold restitution [*sykophantéō* really means (cheat by) false accusing; it is *Roman* law which prescribes fourfold restitution for similar cases]: ExpTim 98 (1986s) 68-71.

3999 *Kilgallen* John J., The Sadducees and resurrection from the dead; Luke 20,27-40: Biblica 67 (1986) 478-495; franç. 495.

4000 **Giblin** Charles H. [Lk 10,16s; 13,31-34; 19,41-44; 21,20-24; 23,26-32] The destruction of Jerusalem according to Luke's Gospel; a historical-typological moral: AnBib 107, 1985 ➤ 1,5052: ᴿCBQ 48 (1986) 560-2 (J. H. *Neyrey*: adds little to his sources); JTS 37 (1986) 531s (I. H. *Marshall*); TS 47 (1986) 519s (R. F. *O'Toole*).

4001 *Zmijewski* Josef, Die Eschatologiereden Lk 21 und Lk 17 [< BLeb 14 (1973) 30-40]: ➤ 233, Das NT Quelle 1986, 171-183.

F7.8 *Luc. 22 ...* **Passio.**

4002 *Brown* Raymond E., The Passion according to Luke: Worship 60 (1986) 2-9.

4003 *Derrett* J. D. M., Daniel [1-7; Lk Passion parallels] and salvation history [< DowR 100 (1982) 63-68]: ➤ 150, Studies NT 4 (1986) 132-8.

4004 *Kany* Roland, Der lukanische Bericht vom Tod und Auferstehung Jesu aus der Sicht eines hellenistischen Romanlesers: NT 28 (1986) 75-90.

4005 **Karris** Robert J., Luke, artist and theologian; Luke's Passion account as literature: Theological Inquiries 1985 ➤ 1,5053: ᴿCBQ 48 (1986) 144s (Susan M. *Praeder*); CurrTM 13 (1986) 120s (W. C. *Linss*); Interpretation 40 (1986) 207.209 (R. D. *Witherup*: broader but less thorough than SENIOR's Mt); RRel 45 (1986) 312s (R. F. *O'Toole*); TS 47 (1986) 182s (J. *Kodell*).

4006 **Neyrey** Jerome, The Passion according to Luke; a redaction study of Luke's soteriology: Theological Inquiries 1985 ➤ 1,5054: ᴿCBQ 48 (1986) 754s (W. S. *Kurz*: superb); ExpTim 97 (1985s) 279s (I. H. *Marshall*: six studies not forced into a unity; arresting ideas on every page); Furrow 57 (1986) 202s (M. *Drennan*); RelStR 12 (1986) 293s (R. H. *Fuller*: maximizes Luke's activity beyond the point of 'redaction'); TS 47 (1986) 552s (J. *Kodell*).

4007 **Tyson** J. B., The death of Jesus in Luke-Acts. Columbia 1986, Univ. S. Carolina. xi-198 p. $18. 0-87249-461-6 [NTAbs 31,104].

4008 *Lull* David J., The servant-benefactor as a model of greatness (Luke 22:24-30): NT 28 (1986) 289-305.

4008* *Kruger* H., Die twee swaarde (Luk. 22:35-53), 'n poging tot verstaan: NduitseGT 27 (1986) 191-6 [< GerefTTs 86,255].

4009 *Green* Joel B., Jesus on the Mount of Olives (Luke 22.39-46); tradition and theology: JStNT 26 (1986) 29-48.

4010 *Soards* Marion L., a) 'And the Lord turned and looked straight at Peter'; understanding Luke 22,61: Biblica 67 (1986) 518s; – b) Herod Antipas' hearing in Luke 23,8: BTrans 37 (1986) 146s.

4011 *Sylva* Dennis D., [Lk 23,45] The Temple curtain and Jesus' death in the Gospel of Luke: JBL 105 (1986) 239-250.

4012 *Karris* Robert J., Luke 23:47 and the Lucan view of Jesus' death: JBL 105 (1986) 65-74.

4013 **Guillaume** Jean-Marie, Luc interprète des anciennes traditions sur la résurrection de Jésus 1979 ➤ 60,6811 ... 62,5081: ᴿTZBas 42 (1986) 179s (A. *Moda*).

4014 *DeLeers* Stephen V., [Lk 24] The road to Emmaus: BToday 24 (1986) 100-7.

4015 *Lombardi* Roberto, ₍Emmaus; un'icona [letteraria, non archeologica] interpretativa del rapporto catechesi-liturgia nell'itinerario di fede Lateranum 52 (1986) 399-410.

4016 *Parsons* Mikael C., [Lk 24] A Christological tendency in P⁷⁵: JBL 105 (1986) 463-479.

4017 *Ross* J.M., The genuineness of Luke 24:12: ExpTim 98 (1986s) 107s.

4017* *a) Broer* Ingo, 'Der Herr ist wahrhaft auferstanden' (Lk 24,34); Auferstehung Jesu und historisch-kritische Methode; Erwägungen zur Entstehung des Osterglaubens; – *b) Fiedler* Peter, Die Gegenwart als österliche Zeit – erfahrbar im Gottesdienst; die 'Emmausgeschichte' Lk 24,13-35: ➤ 120, ᶠVöGTLE A., Auferstehung 1986, 39-62 / 124-144.

4018 *Kilpatrick* G.D., Luke 24:42-43: NT 28 (1986) 306-8.

4019 *Parsons* Mikael C., Narrative closure and openness in the plot of the third Gospel; the sense of an ending in Luke 24:50-53: ➤ 392, SBL Seminars 1986, 201-223.

XII. Actus Apostolorum

F8.1   **Acts** – *text, commentary, topics.*

4020 *Aland* Barbara, Entstehung, Charakter und Herkunft des sog. Westlichen Textes – untersucht an der Apostelgeschichte: ETL 62 (1986) 5-65 [140: analyse de *Boismard* M. annoncée par *Neirynck* F. ➤ 4025].

4021 *Banks* Robert, The Acts of the Apostles as a historical document; ➤ 46, ᶠHARRIS B., AncSRes 16 (1986) 13-18.

4022 **Baslez** Marie-Françoise, L'étranger dans la Grèce antique [➤ 65,d68; 1,f57; ... Actes]: Realia. P 1984, BLettres. 361 p.; fasc. de 40 p. fig. 2-251-33805-5. – ᴿAntClas 55 (1986) 515s (C. *Delvoye*); JHS 106 (1986) 237s (D. *Whitehead*).

4023 **Benéites** Manuel, 'Esta salvación de Dios' [Hech 28,28]; análisis narrativo estructuralista de 'Hechos': Publ. 1/35. M 1986, Univ. Pont. Comillas. xxiii-784 p. pt 3775.

4024 **Black** Robert A.ᴶ, The conversion stories in the Acts of the Apostles; a study of their forms and functions: diss. Emory, ᴰ*Holladay* C. Atlanta 1986. 263 p. 86-05727. – DissA 47 (1986s) 213s-A; RTLv 17 (1986) 492.

4025 **Boismard** M.-E., *Lamouille* A., Le texte occidental des Actes des Apôtres, reconstitution et réhabilitation, I. Introduction et texte; II. Apparat critique: Synthèse 17. P 1984 ➤ 65,4597*: RCiv. xi-232 p.; 356 p. F 320. 2-86538-120-6. – ᴿBiblica 67 (1986) 410-4 (C.-B. *Amphoux*); NRT 108 (1986) 432s (X. *Jacques*); RB 93 (1986) 598-601 (J. *Murphy-O'Connor*: total disrespect for current academic dogmas).

4026 *Bruce* F.F., *a)* Chronological questions in the Acts of the Apostles; – *b)* Paul's apologetic and the purpose of Acts: BJRyL 68 (1985s) 273-295 / 69 (1986s) 379-393.

4027 **Cappelleri** M., Le Complexiones in Acta Apostolorum di Fl. Magno Aurelio Cassiodoro, diss. ᴰ*Rallo Freni* R. Messina 1986. [RivB 35,86].

4028 **Delebecque** Édouard, Les deux Actes des Apôtres; préf. *Spicq* Ceslas: ÉtBN 6. P 1986, Gabalda. 427 p. F 496. 2-85021-018-8. – RETL 62 (1986) 431s (F. *Neirynck*).

4029 **Dupont** Jacques, Nouvelles études sur les Actes: LDiv 118, 1984 ➤ 65,184; 1,5074: RAntonianum 61 (1986) 178-180 (Z. I. *Herman*); CrNSt 7 (1986) 379-382 (R. *Fabris*).

4029* *Gignac* Francis T., Codex monacensis Graeca 147 and the text of CHRYSOSTOM's Homilies on Acts: ➤ 73, FMEYER R., Diakonia 1986, 14-21.

4030 *Hahn* Ferdinand, Der gegenwärtige Stand der Erforschung der Apostelgeschichte; Kommentare und Aufsatzbände 1980-1985 [*Schneider* G.; *Dupont* J.; *Weiser* A.; *Mussner* F. ...]: TR 82 (1986) 177-190.

4031 *Horsley* G. H. R., Speeches and dialogue in Acts [... Thuc 1,22]: NTS 32 (1986) 609-614.

4032 *Jervell* Jacob, Apostelgeschichte: ➤ 587, EvKL 1 (1986) 225-9.

4032* *Kliesch* Klaus, Apostelgeschichte: KLK NT 5. Stu 1986, KBW. 167 p. DM 19,80 [TR 83,377, D. *Dormeyer*]. 3-460-15351-2.

4033 *a) LaVerdiere* Eugene, Biblical update, Acts of the Apostles; Jesus Christ, Lord of all; – *b) Praeder* Susan M., From Jerusalem to Rome; – *c) Osiek* Carolyn, The Way, sect, Christian: BToday 24 (1986) 73-78 / 79-84 / 85s.

4034 *Lenkey* István, ⓜ Analysis of the prayers and sermons in the Acts of the Apostles with regard to their form and contents: Theologiai Szemle 28 (1985) 10-15.

Mills Watson E., A bibliography on Acts 1986 ➤ 682.

4035 **Mussner** Franz, Apostelgeschichte: EchterB 1984 ➤ 1,5087: RSNTU-A 11 (1986) 237s (J. *Ernst*).

4036 **Neudorfer** Heinz-Werner, Die Apostelgeschichte des Lukas [Kap. 1-12]: Bibel-Kommentar 8. Stu-Neuhausen 1986, Hänssler. 271 p. 3-7751-1125-5.

4037 **Pesch** Rudolf, Die Apostelgechichte [I. Kap. 1-12]: EkK NT 5. Z/Neuk 1986, Benziger/Neuk. 371 p. 3-545-23112-7 / Neuk 3-7887-0774-7.

4038 **Roloff** J., Hechos de los Apóstoles, TMínguez D. 1984 ➤ 65,4615: RCiTom 113 (1986) 146s (J. *Huarte*); CiuD 199 (1986) 333 (J. *Gutiérrez*: traducción brillante en todos los aspectos).

4039 **Saoût** Yves, Cette activité libératrice; étude des Actes des Apôtres; les disciples de Jésus devant le pouvoir, l'avoir, le savoir; préf. *Guillet* J., 1983 ➤ 1,5089*; 359 p.; F 135: RNRT 108 (1986) 929 (A. *Toubeau*: professeur d'Écriture au Nord-Cameroun).

4040 **Schneider** Gerhard, Gli Atti degli Apostoli I-II [HerdersTK 1980/2 ➤ 61,6460; 63,5154b]. CommTeol NT 5. Brescia 1985s, Paideia. I (1-8), 723 p.; II (9-28) 583 p. Lit. 70.000 + 65.000. – RAntonianum 61 (1986) 177s (M. *Nobile*); Asprenas 33 (1986) 332-6 (C. *Marcheselli-Casale*); ComSev 19 (1986) 431-3 (M. de *Burgos*); ÉtClas 54 (1986) 199 (X. *Jacques*); ParVi 31 (1986) 469-471 (M. *Làconi*).

4041 *a) Selvidge* Marla, The Acts of the Apostles; a violent aetiological legend; – *b) Kraabel* A. Thomas, Traditional Christian evidence for diaspora Judaism; the Book of Acts (page-heads 'Greeks, Jews, and Lutherans in the middle half of Acts'); – *c) Kraemer* Ross S., Hellenistic Jewish women; the epigraphical evidence; – *d) Stark* Rodney, Jewish conversion and the rise of Christianity; rethinking the received wisdom: ➤ 392, SBL Seminars 1986, 330-340 / 644-651 / 183-200 / 314-329.

4042 *Ziesler* J. A., Which is the best commentary? V. The Acts of the Apostles

[*Haenchen* for the Greek text; *Hanson* or *Marshall* for the English]: Exp-Tim 98 (1986s) 73-77.

F8.3   *Ecclesia primaeva Actuum*:   **Die Urgemeinde.**

4043 *Achtemeier* Paul J.,   An elusive unity; Paul, Acts, and the early Church [CBA presidential address, San Francisco, August 12, 1985]: CBQ 48 (1986) 1-26.

4044 **Ballast** Bruce T.,   The marks of the Church in the book of Acts; the fingerprints of God: diss. Fuller, ᴰ*Anderson* Ray S. Pasadena 1986. 166 p. 86-09170. – DissA 47 (1986s) 552-A.

4045 *Bartsch* Christian,   Frühkatholizismus: ➤ 587, EvKL 1 (1986) 1402-4.

4045* *Bieritz* Karl-Heinrich,   Rückkehr ins Haus? Sozialgeschichtliche und theologische Erwägungen zum Thema 'Hauskirche': BTZ 3 (1986) 111-126.

4046 **Bouwman** Gijs,   De Weg van het Woord; het Woord van de Weg; de wording van de jonge kerk 1985 ➤ 1,5100*:   ᴿCollatVl 16 (1986) 247s (R. *Hoet*); Streven 53 (1985s) 754 (P. *Beentjes*).

4047 *Brändle* R.,   Neues Testament und alte Kirchengeschichte: Kirchenblatt für die reformierte Schweiz: 142,3 (Ba 1986) 38s [NTAbs 30,339].

4048 **Brown** R. E., *Meier* J. P.,   Antioch and Rome 1983 ➤ 64,5048 ... 1,5102: ᴿBA 49 (1986) 63s (R. L. *Wilken*: reasonable suggestions); EvQ 58 (1986) 176s (J. *Drane*: important); HeythJ 27 (1986) 455-7 (W. *Meeks*: essentially BAUR's program; Brown's reconstruction shaky); TLZ 111 (1986) 744-6 (J. *Roloff*).

4049 **Brown** Raymond E.,   The churches the Apostles left behind 1984 ➤ 65,4626; 1,5101: ᴿAndrUnS 24 (1986) 51s (H. *Weiss*); BibTB 16 (1986) 28 (Carolyn *Osiek*); CurrTM 13 (1986) 58 (W. C. *Linss*); Interpretation 40 (1986) 90s (A. J. *Hultgren*); JBL 105 (1986) 732-4 (Carolyn *Osiek*: not 'to assure ourselves that we are right' but 'to discover where we have not been listening'); PrincSemB 7 (1986) 87-89 (B. J. *Kutcher*).

4050 **Brown** Raymond E.,   As Igrejas dos Apóstolos. São Paulo 1986, Paulinas. 196 p. [REB 46,723].

4050* *Casalegno* Alberto,   Comunhão eclesial e ministério apostólico nos Atos dos Apóstolos, ᵀ*Otacilio Leite* José: PerspT 18 (1986) 293-314.

4051 *Collins* Raymond F.,   *a*) Glimpses into some local churches of New Testament times: LavalTP 42 (1982) 291-316; – *b*) Aperçus sur quelques Églises locales à l'époque du Nouveau Testament: MaisD 165 (1986) 7-47 [-134, époques récentes]; – *c*) The local church in the New Testament: Church 2,2 (NY 1986) 23-28 [< NTAbs 31,62].

4052 **Da Spinetoli** Ortensio,   Chiesa delle origini, Chiesa del futuro: Concilio aperto. R 1986, Borla. 219 p. 88-263-0844-3.

4053 *Dupont* Jacques,   Teologia della Chiesa negli Atti degli Apostoli [corso 1983, Palermo]: StBDeh 10,1984 ➤ 65,4633: ᴿParVi 31 (1986) 471-3 (M. *Làconi*); StPatav 33 (1986) 441-3 (G. *Segalla*).

4054 **Faivre** Alexandre,   Les laïcs aux origines de l'Église 1984 ➤ 65,4635; 1,5106; 2-227-32100-8: ᴿÉglT 17 (1986) 242-4 (J. K. *Coyle*); ÉTRel 61 (1986) 470s (B. *Kaempf*); MüTZ 37 (1986) 305s (H. *Frohnhofen*); RÉAug 32 (1986) 180 (J. *Doignon*).

4055 **Faivre** Alexandre,   I laici alle origini della Chiesa [1984 ➤ 65,4635.6725] ... Paoline. 272 p. Lit 12.000. – ᴿBbbOr 28 (1986) 235s (E. P.).

4056 **Guillet** Jacques,   Entre Jésus et l'Église 1985 ➤ 1,5109; F 110; 2-02-008899-1: ᴿBrotéria 123 (1986) 476s (I. *Ribeiro*); Gregorianum 67

(1986) 554s (J. *Dupuis*); RAfrT 10,19 (1986) 131-3 (A. *Vanneste*); Salmanticensis 33 (1986) 258s (R. *Blázquez*); ScEspr 38 (1986) 266s (P.-É. *Langevin*); TS 47 (1985) 554 (C. *Bernas* does not find apparent in the title 'continuity between the words and deeds of Jesus and those of the early Church'); VSp 140 (1986) 746s (J.-M. *Poffet*).

4057 **Hahn** Ferdinand, *a*) Das Problem des Frühkatholizismus [< EvT 38 (1978) 340-357]; – *b*) Frühkatholizismus als ökumenisches Problem [< Catholica 37 (1983) 17-35]; – *c*) Das apostolische und das nachapostolische Zeitalter als ökumenisches Problem [< ÖkRu 30 (1981) 146-164]: ➤ 167, Ges. Aufs. 1 (1986) 39-56 / 57-75 / 76-94.

4058 **Harrison** Everett F., The apostolic church 1985 ➤ 1,5110; also Exeter, Paternoster, £13: ᴿChH 55 (1986) 356s (J. *Helgeland*: bad); GraceTJ 7 (1986) 263s (D. A. *Black*); RelStR 12 (1986) 294 (R. H. *Fuller*: negative on Germans except GOPPELT; will not enhance his reputation as enlightened conservative open to critical method); Themelios 12 (1986s) 61s (C. *Hemer*).

4059 **Hengel** Martin, Earliest Christianity [= Acts and the history of earliest Christianity 1979 + Property and riches in the early Church 1974]. L 1986, SCM. 244 p. £8. 0-334-00346-6 [ExpTim 98,190].

4060 **Hengel** Martin, La storiografia protocristiana; StBPaid 73. Brescia 1985, Paideia, 191 p. Lit 16.000. – ᴿComLtg 68 (1986) 318s (J. *Dupont*).

4061 *Jervell* J., Paulus in der Apostelgeschichte und die Geschichte des Urchristentums [SNTS main paper, Trondheim 1985]: NTS 32 (1986) 378-392.

4062 *Kampling* Rainer, 'Haben wir dann nicht aus der Erde ein Himmel gemacht?' Arm und Reich in der Alten Kirche: (Concilium) IZT 22 (1986) 357-363 (➤ 288; Eng. ed. 'Have we not then made a heaven of earth?' Rich and poor in the early Church, ᵀNowell R., 51-61).

4063 *Kraft* Heinrich, Dalla 'Chiesa' originaria all'episcopato monarchico: RivStoLR 22 (1986) 411-438.

4064 *Kümmel* Werner G., Das Urchristentum II/c. Taufe und Gottesdienst: TRu 51 (1986) 239-268.

4065 **Matthey** Jacques, Et pourtant la mission, perspectives actuelles selon les Actes des Apôtres [mission à longue distance fait place au rayonnement des Églises locales]. Aubonne 1985, Moulin. 100 p. – ᴿÉTRel 61 (1986) 450 (F. *Vouga*).

4066 **Meyer** B. F., The early Christians; their world mission and self-discovery: GoodNewsSt 16. Wilmington 1986, Glazier. 245 p. $13. 0-89453-542-0 [NTAbs 31,114].

4067 *Pathrapankal* Joseph, *a*) The dynamic Church in the Acts of the Apostles; – *b*) Reconciliation and the Kingdom of God [... Acts 15]: ➤ 202*, Critical and creative 1986, 85-99 / 49-69; – *c*) Die Kirche der Apostelgeschichte als Modell für unsere Zeit: ZMissRW 70 (1986) 275-287; Eng. 286s.

4068 *Ravasi* Gianfranco, Chiesa e conciliarità nel NT: Servitium 45s (1986) 11-22.

4069 *Runia* Klaas, The God-given ministry between Spirit and situation [Eph 4,11; the Apostolic Church ...]: ➤ 54, ᶠKnox D., God rich 1986, 265-286.

4070 *Russell* D. S., From early Judaism to early Church. L 1986, SCM. 149 p. £4.50. 0-334-00496-9 [ExpTim 98,159].

4071 *Sabourin* Léopold, Traits 'protocatholiques' dans le Nouveau Testament: ScEspr 38 (1986) 301-315.

4071* *Taber* Charles R., The New Testament language of quantity and growth in relation to the Church: Missiology 14 (S. Pasadena 1986) 387-400 [< ZIT].

4072 **Venetz** Hermann-Josef, C'est ainsi que l'Église a commencé [So fing es mit der Kirche an ²1981 ➤ 62,4043]: Théologies. P 1986, Cerf. 182 p.

4072* **Verbraken** P. P., Les premiers siècles chrétiens 1984 ➤ 65,4663: ᴿBLitEc 87 (1986) 232s (H. *Crouzel*).

4073 **Vouga** François, À l'aube du christianisme; une surprenante diversité. Aubonne 1986, Moulin. 96 p. – ᴿÉTRel 61 (1986) 621s (*ipse*).

4074 **Walker** Andrew, Restoring the Kingdom; the radical Christianity of the House Church movement. L 1985, Hodder & S. 303 p. £6. – ᴿThemelios 12 (1986s) 32 (J. S. *Went*).

F8.5 Acts 1 ... *Ascensio, Pentecostes; ministerium Petri*.

4075 *a) Gager* John G., Jews, Gentiles, and Synagogues in the Book of Acts; – *b) Tiede* David L., The exaltation of Jesus and the restoration of Israel in Acts 1: ➤ 110, ᶠSTENDAHL K. = HarvTR 79 (1986) 91-99 / 278-286.

4076 *Maile* John F., The Ascension in Luke-Acts: TyndB 37 (1986) 29-59.

4076* *Palatty* Paul, The Ascension of Christ in Luke-Acts: Bible Bhashyam 12 (1986) 100-117. 166-181.

4077 *Weiser* Alfons, Himmelfahrt Christi: ➤ 597, TRE 15 (1986) 330-4 (-344).

4078 *Zmijewski* Josef, *a)* Apg 1 als literarischer und theologischer Anfang der Apostelgeschichte [ineditum]; – *b)* Der Stephanusrede (Apg 7,2-53) – literarisches und theologisches [ineditum]: ➤ 233, Das NT Quelle 1986, 67-84 / 85-128.

4079 *Schwartz* Daniel R., The end of the *gê* (Acts 1:8); beginning or end of the Christian vision ? : JBL 105 (1986) 669-697.

4080 *Grogan* Geoffrey W., The significance of Pentecost in the history of salvation: ScotBEvT 4 (1986) 97-107.

4081 **Osoline** Nicolas, L'icône de la descente du Saint-Esprit; origine et évolution de ses thèmes constituants à l'époque byzantine: diss. ᴰ*Dufrenne* S. P 1985. – ÉPHÉR 94 (1985s) 657-660.

4082 *Dillon* Richard J., [Acts 2,16-21; 3,22-26] The prophecy of Christ and his witnesses according to the discourses of Acts: NTS 32 (1986) 544-556.

4083 *Pickering* S. R., P. Macquarie Inv. 360 (+ P. Mil. Vogl. Inv. 1224): Acta Apostolorum 2.30-37, 2.46-3.2: ZPapEp 65 (1986) 76-78.

4084 *Alsup* J. E., Prayer, consciousness, and the early Church; a look at Acts 2:41-47 for today: Austin Seminary Bulletin 101,4 (1985) 31-37 [NTAbs 30,298].

4085 *Hamm* Dennis, Acts 3,1-10; the healing of the Temple beggar as Lucan theology: Biblica 67 (1986) 305-319; franç. 319.

4085* *Suharyo* I., Im Namen Jesu Christi, des Nazaräers, geh umher ! (Apg 3,6, indonesisch): Orientasi 18 (1986) 69-78 [< TKontext 8/2,43].

4086 **Barbi** A., Il Cristo celeste presente nella Chiesa; tradizione e redazione in Atti 3,19-21: AnBib 64, 1979 ➤ 60,6976c ... 62,5287: ᴿTZBas 42 (1986) 180s (A. *Moda*).

4087 *Lochman* Jan M., Apokatástasis [Act 3,21]: ➤ 587, EvKL 1 (1986) 202s.

4088 *Christiansen* Ellen J., Taufe als Initiation in der Apostelgeschichte [4,4 ...]: ST 40 (1986) 55-79.

4089 *Gaventa* B. R., To speak thy word with all boldness; Acts 4:23-31: Faith & Mission 3,2 (Wake Forest 1986) 76-82 [NTAbs 30,298].

4090 *Vallauri* E., La preghiera per la parresia (Atti 4,24-31): Laurentianum 27 (1986) 185-216.

4091 *a) West* Charles.C.,   The sharing of resources [Acts 4,32-35]; a biblical reflection; – *b) Kinnamon* Michael,   The sharing of faith, the sharing of resources; – *c) Wee* Paul A.,   Biblical ethics and lending to the poor; – *d) de Lange* Harry M.,   The jubilee principle [Lv 25,10]; is it relevant for today ?:   EcuR 38 (1986) 357-369 / 370-377 / 416-430 / 437-443.

4092 **Brakemeier** Gottfried,   O socialismo da primeira Cristiandade.   São Leopoldo 1985, Sinodal.   60 p. [REB 46,230].

4093 **Mworia** Thaddeus A.,   The community of goods in Acts; a Lucan model of Christian charity: diss. Pont. Univ. Urbaniana, ᴰ*Sisti* A.   R 1986. 272 p.; bibliog. p. 251-272.

4094 *Szymik* Stefan, ❷ Actus Apost. 6,1-7 in luce investigationum recentium: RuBi 39 (1986) 477-482.

4094* **Neudorfer** H. W.,   Der Stephanuskreis in der Forschungsgeschichte seit F. C. BAUR [prot. Diss. Tübingen]: Monographien und Studienbücher 309, 1983 ➤ 64,5117; 1,5137: ᴿCrNSt 7 (1986) 428-430 (M. *Simon*).

4095 *Viviano* Benedict T.,   L'Église en perpétuelle dialectique entre Jacques et Étienne: PrOrChr 36 (1986) 3-5.

4096 *Trudinger* Paul, [Acts 7,41-49 equates Temple with golden calf] St Stephen and the 'edifice complex': DowR 104 (1986) 240-2.

4097 **Paulo** Pierre-Antoine, [Act 7,42...] Le problème ecclésial des Actes à la lumière d'Amos 1985 ➤ 1,5140: ᴿEsprV 96 (1986) 106s (É. *Cothenet*); PrOrChr 36 (1986) 190s (P. *Ternant*); RThom 86 (1986) 670 (H. *Ponsot*: clair, original, attachant).

4098 *Tosolini* Fabrizio, [Act 7,58 ... 9,1...] Paolo in *Atti* e nelle Pseudoclementine (Recognitiones I, 33-71): AugR 26 (1986) 369-400.

4099 *Bergmeier* Roland,   Die Gestalt des Simon Magus in Act 8 und in der simonianischen Gnosis – Aporien einer Gesamtdeutung: ZNW 77 (1986) 267-275.

4099* **Mead** G. R. S.,   Simon Magus; an essay on the founder of Simonianism based on the ancient sources, with a reevaluation of his philosophy and teachings.   Ch 1985, Ares.   91 p.

4100 *Gourgues* Michel,   Esprit des commencements et esprit des prolongements dans les Actes; note sur la 'Pentecôte des Samaritains' (Act., VIII, 5-25): RB 93 (1986) 376-385; Eng. 376.

4101 *Koch* Dietrich-Alex,   Geistbesitz, Geistverleihung und Wundermacht; Erwägungen zur Tradition und zur lukanischen Redaktion in Act 8,5-25: ZNW 77 (1986) 64-82.

4102 *Brodie* Thomas L.,   Towards unraveling the rhetorical imitation of sources in Acts; 2 Kgs 5 as one component of Acts 8,9-40: Biblica 67 (1986) 41-67; franç. 67.

4103 *Kleinheyer* Bruno, [Act 8,14-17] Ausgiessung des Geistes in frühchristlicher Initiationsfeier: MüTZ 37 (1986) 275-290.

4103* **Liederle** Henry I.,   Treasures old and new; interpretations of 'Spirit-baptism' in the charismatic renewal movement; an exercise in ecumenical theology: diss. ᴰ*König* A.   Pretoria 1985.   445 p. – RTLv 18,572.

4104 **Quesnel** Michel, [Act 8,16; 2,38; 10,44-48; 19,1-7] Baptisé dans l'esprit; baptême et Esprit-Saint dans les Actes des Apôtres [< diss. Institut Catholique, Paris 1984]: LDiv 120, 1985 ➤ 65,4612.4691; 1,5141; 2-204-02276-4: ᴿCBQ 48 (1986) 755s (J. C. *Turro*: Gallic logic and good sense); Gregorianum 67 (1986) 545s (J. *Galot*); RHPR 66 (1986) 230s (M.-A. *Chevallier*); RTPhil 118 (1986) 424 (*Ngayihembako Mutahinga*); TLZ 111 (1986) 431s (L. *Hartman*); VSp 139 (1985) 694s (P.-T. *Camelot*).

4105 **Martin** Clarice, The function of Acts 8:26-40 within the narrative structure of the Book of Acts; the significance of the eunuch's provenance for Acts 1:8c: diss. Duke. Durham NC 1985. – RelStR 13,190.

4106 *Calloud* J., Sur le chemin de Damas (4) Quelques lumières sur l'organisation discursive d'un texte; Actes des Apôtres 9,1-19: SémiotB 42 (1986) 1-19.

4106* *Collins* Raymond F., [Act 9,3...] Paul's Damascus experience; reflections on the Lukan account: LvSt 11 (1986) 99-118.

4107 *a)* *MacLennan* Robert S., *Kraabel* A. Thomas, [Acts 10,2 ... 13,26] The God-Fearers – a literary and theological invention; – *b)* *Tannenbaum* Robert F., Jews and God-fearers in the Holy City of Aphrodite [Aphrodisias in Turkey]; – *c)* *Feldman* Louis H., The omnipresence of the God-fearers: BAR-W 12,5 (1986) 44-53.64 / 54-57 / 58-63.64-69; ill.

4108 **Wielgat** Włodzimierz, [Act 10,41] ❾ 'Martyres prokecheirotonēmenoi hypo tou Theou'; le problème du témoignage du Peuple de Dieu: diss. ᴰ*Roslon* J..W. Wsz 1985. – RTLv 18,551; BlnfWsz (1986,4) 34-36; STWsz 24,2 (1986) 297.

4109 *Barnett* Paul W., [Act 12: Herod] Agrippa the elder and early Christianity: ➤ 54, ᶠKNOX D., God rich 1986, 123-137.

4110 *Strom* Mark R., The Old Testament background to Acts 12.20-23 [Ezck 28]: NTS 32 (1986) 289-292.

F8.7   **Act 13** ... *Itinera Pauli,*   **Paul's Journeys.**

4111 *a)* *Barbi* Augusto, Il paolinismo degli Atti; – *b)* *Moraldi* Luigi, Gli Atti apocrifi di Paolo: ➤ 388, RivB 34 (1986) 571-518; Eng. 518 / 599-612; Eng. 613.

4112 *Borse* Udo, Lukanische Kompositionen im Umfeld der ersten Missionsreise: SNTU-A 11 (1986) 169-194.

4112* *Townsend* John T., Missionary journeys in Acts and European missionary societies: AnglTR 68 (1986) 99-105.

4113 *Grech* Prosper, *a)* L'apologia di Paolo negli 'Atti degli Apostoli' [< Il pensiero di Paolo, Ist. Fg. Univ. Genova 1983, 81-94]; – *b)* Timoteo e Tito, modelli del vescovo nel periodo subapostolico [> StAns]: ➤ 166, Ermeneutica 1986, 397-410 / 411-9.

4114 **Rius-Camps** Josep, El camino de Pablo ... Hech 13-28, 1984 ➤ 65,4700; 1,5151: ᴿScripTPamp 18 (1986) 353s (C. *Basevi*).

4115 **Dumais** Marcel, Le langage de l'évangélisation; l'annonce missionnaire en milieu juif (Acts 13,16-41): Rech/Théol 16, 1975 ➤ 57,5181; 58,6677: ᴿEstB 44 (1986) 240-2 (A. *Rodríguez Carmona*).

4116 *a)* *Slingerland* Dixon, 'The Jews' in the Pauline portion of Acts [15s ...]: JAAR 54 (1986) 305-321; – *b)* *Kalu Ogbu,* Luke and the Gentile mission; a study on Acts 15: AfJBSt 1,1 (1986) 59-65 [< TKontext 8/2,20].

4116* *a)* *Bruce* Frederick F., The apostolic decree of Acts 15; – *b)* *Kilpatrick* George D., The two texts of Acts; – *c)* *Barrett* Charles L., Old Testament history according to Stephen and Paul: ➤ 39, ᶠGREEVEN H., Text/Ethik 1986, 115-124 / 188-195 / 57-69.

4117 *a)* *Radl* Walter, Das Gesetz in Apg 15; – *b)* *Weiser* Alfons, Zur Gesetzes- und Tempelkritik der 'Hellenisten': ➤ 382, ᴱ*Kertelge* K., Gesetz 1985/6, 169-174 / 146-168.

4118 *Schwartz* Daniel R., The futility of preaching Moses (Acts 15,21): Biblica 67 (1986) 276-281.

4119 *Cohen* Shaye J. D., Was Timothy Jewish (Acts 16:1-3)? Patristic exegesis, rabbinic law, and matrilineal descent: JBL 105 (1986) 251-268.

4119* *Fischer* Enno, Von der Führung Gottes; eine biblische Besinnung zu Apostelgeschichte 16,6-15: Diakonie 12 (Stu 1986) 338-340 [< ZIT].

4120 *Larsson* Edvin, [Act 16,10 ...] 'Vi'-passager och itinerarer; om traditionsunderlaget för Apg.s skildring av Paulus' missionsresor: SvEx 51s (1986s) 127-136.

4121 *Thornton* Larry R., [Acts 17,16-34] Paul's apologetic at Athens and ours: CalvaryB 2,1 (1986) 1-21.

4122 *Kilpatrick* G. D., The Acts of the Apostles, xvii.18: TZBas 42 (1986) 431s: for Greeks the real me is the soul; for Hebrews the body.

4123 *Samuel* S., [Act 17,22-31] Paul on the Areopagus; a mission perspective: Bangalore Theological Forum 18,1 (1986) 17-32 [NTAbs 31,40].

4124 **Pereira** Francis, [Acts 18,23 ...] Ephesus; climax of universalism in Luke-Acts [diss. PIB 1975, ᴰ*Martini* C.] 1983 ➤ 64,5145 ... 1,5168: ᴿJBL 105 (1986) 538-540 (E. *Richard*: convincing); JStNT 26 (1986) 119-121 (F. S. *Spencer*); RechSR 74 (1986) 247s (J. *Guillet*).

4124* *Norris* F. W., 'Christians only, but not the only Christians' (Acts 19:1-7): RestQ 28 (1985s) 97-106 [< ZIT].

4125 *Thornton* T. C. G., [Acts 19,37] The destruction of idols; sinful or meritorious: JTS 37 (1986) 121-9.

4125* *Lövestam* Evald, En gammaltestamentlig nyckel [OT clue] till Paulus-talet i Miletos (Apg 20:18-35): SvEx 51 (1986s) 137-147.

4126 *Hemer* Colin J., *a*) First person narrative in Acts 27-28; – *b*) The name of Paul: TyndB 36 (1985) 79-109 / 179-183.

4126* *Papadopoulos* K. N. ✆ [Act 27,9 ...] Earliest Christian fasting: Deltio-VM 16,1 (1987) 51-57.

4127 **Beneitez Rodríguez** Manuel, 'Esta salvación de Dios' (Hch 28,28); análisis narrativo estructuralista de Hechos: diss. Comillas, ᴰ*Vargas-Machuca* A. M 1985, – MiscCom 44 (1986) 569.

4128 **Kettenbach** Günter, Das Logbuch des Lukas: EurHS 23/276. Fra 1986, Lang. 218 p. 3-8204-8450-2.

XIV. Johannes

G1 *Corpus Johanneum*   .1 **John and his community.**

4128* *Barrett* C. K., St. John, social historian; PrIrB 10 (1986) 26-39.

4129 **Brown** R. E., La communauté du disciple bien-aimé 1983 ➤ 65,4732; 1,5177: ᴿVSp 139 (1985) 259s (T. *Chary*).

4130 *Culpepper* R. A., Synthesis and schism in the Johannine Community and the Southern Baptist Convention: PerspRelSt 13,1 (1986) 1-20 [< NTAbs 31,31].

4131 *Domeris* W. R., Christology and community; a study of the social matrix of the Fourth Gospel: ➤ 377*b*, SBL Jerusalem summaries (1986) 5.

4132 **Mbombo Kapiamba** A., Le groupe des disciples; son itinéraire de foi selon le Quatrième Évangile: diss. R 1986, Gregoriana. iv-117 p. extr.; bibliog. p. 101-114.

4133 *Locher* Clemens, La comunidad joánica y 'los judíos' [< Orientierung 48 (1984) 223-6], ᵀᴱ*Torres* María José de: SelT 25 (1986) 334-7.

4134 **Onuki** Takashi, Gemeinde und Welt im Johannesevangelium; ein Beitrag zur Frage nach der theologischen und pragmatischen Funktion des johanneischen 'Dualismus': WMANT 56, 1984 ➤ 65,4743; 1,5183: ᴿJBL 105 (1986) 728-731 (D. *Rensberger*).

4135 **Panimolle** Salvatore A., L'evangelista Giovanni; pensiero e opera letteraria del quarto evangelista 1985 ➤ 1,5184; Lit. 30.000: ᴿGregorianum 67 (1986) 543-5 (G. *Ferraro*).

4136 *Smalley* Stephen S., John's Revelation and John's community: BJRyL 69 (1986s) 549-571.

4137 **Smith** D. Moody, Johannine Christianity 1984 ➤ 65,4745: ᴿInterpretation 40 (1986) 210s (G. M. *Burge*: skilful); JAAR 54 (1986) 149s (R. *Kysar*); TLZ 111 (1986) 819s (W. *Vogler*).

4138 *Strecker* Georg, Die Anfänge der johanneischen Schule: NTS 32 (1986) 31-47.

4139 **Taeger** Jens-W., Johannesapokalypse und johanneischer Kreis; Versuch einer traditionsgeschichtlichen Ortsbestimmung am Paradigma der Lebenswasser-Thematik: Hab.-Diss. ᴰ*Klein* G. Münster 1986. – RTLv 18,550.

4140 **Witkamp** L. T., Jezus van Nazareth in de gemeente van Johannes; over de interactie van traditie en ervaring: diss. ᴰ*Baarlink* H. Kampen 1986, Van den Berg. xii-451 p. – TsTNijm 26 (1986) 287.

G1.2 **Evangelium Johannis:** *textus, commentarii.*

4140* *Aland* Kurt, Der Text des Johannes-Evangeliums im 2. Jahrhundert: ➤ 39, ᶠGREEVEN H., Text/Ethik 1986, 1-10.

4141 ᴱ**Blanc** Cécile, ORIGÈNE, Commentaire sur Saint Jean IV (livres XIX et XX): SChr 290, 1982 ➤ 63,5281 ... 1,5187: ᴿRBgPg 64 (1986) 119s (H. *Savon*).

4142 **Blank** Josef, El Evangelio según San Juan 1979-84 ➤ 65,4752; 1,5188: ᴿScripTPamp 18 (1986) 277-281 (A. *García-Moreno*).

4142* *Brearley* D., The Irish influences in the Expositio Iohannis iuxta HIERONIMUM in Angers BM 175: PrIrB 10 (1986) 72-89.

4143 **Cothenet** E., *al.,* Escritos de Juan y Carta a los Hebreos 1985 ➤ 1,5195: ᴿCiuD 199 (1986) 123s (J. *Gutiérrez*); RazF 212 (1985) 438s (R. de *Andrés*); ScripTPamp 18 (1986) 281-5 (A. *García-Moreno*).

4144 **Ellis** Peter F., The genius of John; a composition-critical commentary on the Fourth Gospel 1984 ➤ 65,4756; 1,5196: ᴿBibTB 16 (1986) 31s (U. C. von *Wahlde*); CBQ 48 (1986) 334s (J. E. *Bruns*: Procrustean bed of chiasms); Horizons 13 (1986) 153 (Sally A. *Kenel*); RelStR 12 (1986) 294 (D. M. *Smith*: unusual, following out chiastic structure of John GERHARD's unpublished 1975 Catholic University dissertation).

4145 **Giertz** B., Forkläringar till Nya Testamentet II. Johannes, Apostlagärningarna, Romarbrevet, Korintierbreven. Sto 1985, Verbum / Pro Caritate. 91-526-1253-8 / 91-85046-64-7 [NTAbs 30,342].

4146 **Gnilka** Joachim, Johannesevangelium: NEchter 1983 ➤ 64,5178; 65,4760: ᴿTR 82 (1986) 199-201 (H. *Frankemölle*).

4147 **Gruenler** Royce G., The Trinity in the Gospel of John; a thematic commentary on the fourth gospel. GR 1986, Baker. xxi-159 p. $10 pa. [CBQ 48,777].

4148 **Haenchen** Ernst, John: Hermeneia 1984 ➤ 65,4762; 1,5199: ᴿBS 143 (1986) 181s (W. H. *Harris*); CBQ 48 (1986) 140-2 (Pheme *Perkins*); Interpretation 40 (1986) 69-72 (R. *Kysar*).

4149 *Heine* Ronald E., Can the catena fragments of ORIGEN's commentary on John be trusted?: VigChr 40 (1986) 118-134.

4150 **Kysar** Robert, John: Commentaries NT. Minneapolis 1986, Augsburg. 333 p. $11. 0-8066-8860-2. – ᴿRelStR 12 (1986) 294 (D. M. *Smith*).
4150* **Cahill** Michael, LIBERMANN's commentary on John; an investigation of the rabbinical and French School influences: diss. Inst. Catholique. P 1985. xv-298 p.; 93 p. – RICathP 18 (1986) 83s (C. *Perrot*).
4151 **Lindars** Barnabas, The Gospel of John: NCent. GR 1986 = 1972, Eerdmans. 648 p. 0-8028-1864-1.
4152 **Maier** Gerhard, Johannes-Evangelium [I. 1984 ➤ 65,4763]; II [Kap.: 12-21]: Bibel-Kommentar 7. Stu-Neuhausen 1986, Hänssler. 416 p. 3-7751-1095-X.
4153 **Minear** Paul S., John, the martyr's Gospel 1984 ➤ 1,5201: ᴿCBQ 48 (1986) 341s (F. F. *Segovia*).
4154 **Morris** L., [comm. 1971 ➤ 53,2898] Reflections on the Gospel of John, I. The Word was made flesh, John 1-5. GR 1986, Baker. v-201 p.; $9 pa. 0-8010-6202-0 [NTAbs 30,355].
4155 **Pronzato** Alessandro, Un vangelo per cercare; Giovanni. T 1986, Gribaudi. 295 p. Lit. 18.000.
4156 **Quecke** Hans, Das Johannesevangelium saïdisch 1984 ➤ 65,4769: ᴿBiblica 67 (1986) 407-9 (D. *Johnson*: model scholarship); JBL 105 (1986) 341 (B. M. *Metzger*).
4157 **Serra** F., Aquí, ahora, 2000 años después I. ¿Aceptaría Jesús esta interpretación de Juan? Bilbao 1985, Desclée-B. 191 p. – ᴿCiuD 199 (1986) 554 (R. *Castellano*: comentario especial).
4157* **Salvail** Ghislaine, À la recherche de la lumière; l'Évangile selon saint Jean: De la Parole à l'Écriture 5. Montréal/P 1985, Paulines/Médiaspaul. 72 p. (ill. Villemaire Jean) [RTLv 18, 247, J. *Ponthot*].
4158 **Tresmontant** Claude, Évangile de Jean 1984 ➤ 65,4777: ᴿBenedictina 33 (1986) 227s (L. *De Lorenzi*: alquanto utile).
4158* *Wengert* Timothy J., Dating Huldrych ZWINGLI's lectures on the Gospel of John: Zwingliana 17,1 (Z 1986) 6-10.
4159 **Wijngaards** J., The Gospel of John and his letters: Message of Biblical Spirituality 11. Wilmington 1986, Glazier. 304 p. $17; pa. $13. 0-89453-561-7; 77-3 [NTAbs 30,23].
4160 **Zevini** Giorgio, Vangelo secondo Giovanni I: CommSpirNT 1984 ➤ 65,4782; 88-311-3706-9: ᴿAsprenas 32 (1985) 32 (1985) 458-460 (R. *Penna*); Gregorianum 67 (1986) 364s (G. *Ferraro*); ParVi 30 (1985) 234s (A. *Casalegno*).

G1.3 **Introductio** in Evangelium Johannis.

4161 **Barrett** C. K., Il Vangelo di Giovanni fra simbolismo e storia: Brevi Studi 4, 1983 ➤ 65,4783; 1,5212: ᴿParVi 30 (1985) 466s (S. *Migliasso*).
4162 *Becker* Jürgen, Das Johannesevangelium im Streit der Methoden (1980-1984): TRu 51 (1986) 1-78: ... ii. als literarische Einheit; iii. im Verhältnis zu den Synoptikern; iv. Schichtenanalyse, Gemeindewirklichkeit; v. Textpragmatik; ... vii. soziologisch; ... ix. religionsgeschichtlich; x. Integration, *Theobald* M. ...
4163 *Collins* Raymond F., John's Gospel; a Passion narrative?: BToday 24 (1986) 181-6.
4164 **Cope** Lamar, Faith for a new day; the new view of the Gospel of John. St. Louis 1986, 'CBP'. 127 p. $9 pa. [RelStR 13, 262, T. R. W. *Longstaff*).
4165 **Culpepper** R. A., Anatomy of the fourth Gospel, a study in literary design 1983 ➤ 64,5199 ... 1,5215: ᴿNeotestamentica 20 (1986) 73s (J. A. du *Rand*).

4166 *Foster* Donald, John come lately; the belated evangelist: ➤ 385, [E]*McConnell* F., Bible and narrative 1983/6, ...

4167 **Heekerens** Hans-Peter, Die Zeichen-Quelle der johanneischen Redaktion; ein Beitrag zur Entstehungsgeschichte des vierten Evangeliums [diss. [D]*Thyen* H., Bultmann-student]: SBS 113. Stu 1984, KBW. 145 p. 3-460-04131-5. – [R]RelStR 12 (1986) 294 (D. M. *Smith*: with Thyen holds redaction of a Gnostic Grundschrift, but rejects BULTMANN's *semeia*-source); StPatav 33 (1986) 698s (G. *Segalla*).

4168 *Iafolla* Paolo, Giovanni, figlio di Zebedeo 'il discepolo che amava' e il IV⁰ vangelo: BbbOr 28 (1986) 95-110. 143-155.

4169 *Koester* Helmut, The history-of-religions school, gnosis, and Gospel of John [Oslo Mowinckel lecture 1986]: ST 40 (1986) 115-136.

4170 **Kouam** Maurice, Structure formelle du 4e Évangile et problèmes contemporains d'une Église africaine; essai exégétique et sociologique sur la crise de foi en Jésus-Christ: diss. [D]*Le Fort* P. Bru 1986. – RTLv 18.547.

4171 **Kysar** Robert, John's story of Jesus 1984 ➤ 65,4791; 1,5223: [R]BibTB 16 (1986) 80 (U. C. von *Wahlde*); Interpretation 40 (1986) 96.98 (R. H. *Fuller*).

4172 *Marcheselli-Casale* Cesare, In cammino verso il Padre; un recente studio sul Vangelo di Giovanni [*Pasquetto* V., Da Gesù 1983]: Asprenas 33 (1986) 79-91.

4173 *a) Martyn* J. Louis, Source criticism and Religionsgeschichte in the Fourth Gospel [< Jesus and man's hope I (1970) 247-273, notes abridged]; – *b) Bornkamm* Günther, Towards the interpretation of John's gospel; a discussion of The Testament of Jesus by Ernst KÄSEMANN [< EvT 28 (1968) 8-28]: ➤ 235, [E]*Ashton* J., Interpretation of John 1986, 99-121 / 79-98.

4174 **Panimolle** S. A., L'evangelista Giovanni; pensiero e opera letteraria del quarto evangelista. R 1985, Borla. 673 p. Lit. 30.000. 88-263-0663-X [NTAbs 30,356]. – [R]StPatav 33 (1986) 447s (G. *Segalla*); Teresianum 37 (1986) 505s (V. *Pasquetto*).

4175 **Robinson** J.A.T., The priority of John 1985 ➤ 1,5234: [R]NorTTs 87 (1986) 127s (R. *Leivestad*); Themelios 12 (1986) 97s (S. S. *Smalley*); TLond 39 (1986) 398-400 (J. M. *Lieu*).

4176 *Thornecroft* John K., The redactor and the 'beloved' in John: ExpTim 98 (1986s) 135-9.

4177 **Tuñí Vancells** José O., El testimonio del evangelio de Juan 1983 ➤ 64,5217 ... 1,5240: [R]ScripTPamp 18 (1986) 679-683 (A. *García-Moreno*).

4178 *Tuñi* J.O., La vida de Jesús en el evangelio de Juan: RLatAmT 3,7 (1986) 3-43 [NTAbs 31,33].

G1.4 *Johannis themata,* topics.

4179 **Belle** Gilbert Van, Les parenthèses dans l'Évangile de Jean: SNT Auxilia 11, 1985 ➤ 1,5243: [R]CBQ 48 (1986) 761s (J. E. *Bruns*); ÉtClas 54 (1986) 198s (X. *Jacques*); JTS 37 (1986) 534-7 (J. K. *Elliott*); RHPR 66 (1986) 228 (F. *Grob*); RThom 86 (1986) 151-6 (R. *Robert*); Salesianum 48 (1986) 166s (R. *Bracchi*); VetChr 23 (1986) 91-3 (A. *Quacquarelli*).

4180 *Beutler* Johannes, Das Hauptgebot im Johannesevangelium: ➤ 382, [E]*Kertelge* K., Gesetz 1985/6, 222-236.

4181 *Bignardi* L. T., Ginōskō; la conoscenza religiosa nel quarto vangelo: diss. Univ. Cattolica, [D]*Ghiberti* G. Milano 1984. [RivB 35,86].

4182 **Bruce** F. F., The Gospel of John [from articles over thirty years; not for specialists]. Basingstoke 1983, Pickering & I. 425 p. £7. – ᴿEvQ 58 (1986) 173s (D. A. *Carson*).

4182* **Capdevila i Montaner** Vicenç-M., Liberación y divinización del hombre; teología de la gracia, I. Ev. y Cartas de san Juan 1984 ➤ 65,4804: ᴿAnVal 11 (1985) 330-2 (R. *Arnau*).

4183 *a*) *Chembakasserry* J., Johannine concept of believing and its relevance in India; – *b*) *Vellanickal* Mathew, St. John and the Advaitic experience of the Upanishads; *c*) *Nereparampil* Lucius, The spiritual vision of St. John and the Bhagavadgita: Bible Bhashyam 11 (1985) 61-67 / 68-74 / 95-106.

4184 *a*) *Collins* R. F., Proverbial sayings in St. John's Gospel: MeliT 37,1 (1986) 42-58 [< NTAbs 31,31]; – *b*) *Cârstoiu* Joan, Le sens de l''agapé' selon les écrits de l'évangéliste S. Jean (roum.): STBuc 37 (1985) 510-521.

4185 **Corsani** Bruno I miracoli di Gesù nel quarto vangelo 1984 ➤ 64,5225; 1,5248: ᴿProtestantesimo 41 (1986) 231-3 (B. *Costabel*).

4186 **Diéguez** Manuel de, Jésus [➤ 1,3950: chez Jean]. P 1985, Fayard. 492 p. F 120 [NedTTs 41, 319, H. *Heering*].

4187 **Dodd** C. H., La tradizione storica del quarto vangelo: BibTPaid 10, 1983 ➤ 64,5201 ... 1,5217; ᴿStPatav 33 (1986) 445-7 (G. *Segalla*).

4187* **Duke** Paul D., Irony in the Fourth Gospel 1985 ➤ 1,5250; $12; 0-8042-0242-7: ᴿExpTim 98 (1986s) 118 (S. S. *Smalley*).

4188 **Esquerda Bifet** Juan, Hemos visto su gloria; el camino de la contemplación según San Juan: Betania 28. M 1986, Paulinas. 235 p.

4189 **Ferraro** Giuseppe, Lo Spirito e Cristo nel vangelo di Giovanni: StBPaid 70, 1984 ➤ 65,4809; 1,5252: ᴿBLitEc 87 (1986) 219 (S. *Légasse*); CBQ 48 (1986) 743s (P. J. *Cahill*); CiuD 199 (1986) 547s (J. *Gutiérrez*); ParVi 31 (1986) 468s (D. *Cancian*); Protestantesimo 41 (1986) 48s (F. *Ferrario*: 'La Spirito' in titolo ...); RasT 27 (1986) 184-7 (D. *Marzotto*: opera di maturità, ormai decantata da questioni inutili); ScEspr 38 (1986) 131s (L. *Sabourin*: ne pose pas la question 'Qui parle dans ces discours?'); ScuolC 114 (1986) 511s (N. *Spaccapelo*).

4190 *Ferraro* Giuseppe, *a*) L'esegesi dei testi pneumatologici del Quarto Vangelo nell''In Iohannis Evangelium tractatus' e nel 'De Trinitate' di Sant'AGOSTINO: Lateranum 52 (1986) 83-214; – *b*) L'esposizione dei testi pneumatologici nel commento di TEODORO di Mopsuestia al Quarto Vangelo: Gregorianum 67 (1986) 265-295; franç. 296.

4191 *Feuillet* André, Les épousailles du Messie; la Mère de Jésus et l'Église dans le Quatrième Évangile [introd. La place de l'allégorie nuptiale dans l'ensemble de la Bible (Osée ...); 1. Les noces de Cana (Jo. II. 1-11; 2. 'L'heure' de la femme en Jo. XVI,21 / 3. Le nouvel Adam; la mère de Jésus et l'Église (nouvelle Ève) dans la Passion ... liberté souveraine, royauté et sacerdoce ... transfixion, Sacré-Cœur ... Apocalypse): RThom 86 (1986) 257-391 / 536-575.

4192 *Forkman* Göran, Människans förändring [change] – ett tema i Johannesevangeliet: SvEx 51s (1986s) 57-64.

4193 *García-Moreno* Antonio, Hermenéutica de los símbolos en San Juan: ➤ 366, Hermenéutica 1985/6, 453-475.

4194 *Giesbrecht* Herbert, The Evangelist John's conception of the Church as delineated in his Gospel: EvQ 58 (1986) 101-119.

4195 *González* Carlos I., María en el comentario de San AGUSTÍN al Evangelio de San Juan: EstE 61 (1986) 395-419.

4196 **Guillet** Jacques, Jesus Cristo no Evangelho de João: Cadernos bíblicos 31. Sâo Paulo 1985, Paulinas. 72 p. [REB 46,227].

4197 *a*) *La Potterie* Ignace de, The truth in Saint John [< RivB 11 (1963)

3-24], ᵀAshton; – b) Borgen Peder, God's agent in the Fourth Gospel [< Religions in Antiquity 1968, 137-148]; – c) Dahl Nils A., The Johannine Church and history [< Current Issues 1962, 124-142]: ➤ 235, ᴱAshton J., Interpretation of John 1986, 53-66 / 67-78 / 122-140.

4197* **La Potterie** Ignace de, Studi di cristologia giovannea²: Dabar, studi biblici e giudaistici 4... Genova 1986, Marietti. 341 p.

4198 Loader W.R.G., La estructura central de la cristología joánica [< NTS 30 (1984) 188-216], ᵀBistué Javier de, ᴱPascual Eduard: SelT 25 (1986) 323-333.

4199 a) Louw J.P., On Johannine style; – b) Geyser A.S. † 1985, Israel in the fourth gospel; – c) Nortjé ms. S., The role of women in the fourth gospel: Neotestamentica 20 (1986) 5-12 / 13-20 / 21-28.

4200 **Menken** M.J.J., Numerical literary techniques in John; the evangelist's use of numbers of words and syllables [diss. Amst]: NT Sup 55. Leiden 1985, Brill. xvi-303 p. f96. – ᴿJTS 37 (1986) 538-540 (S.S. Smalley: dubious); NorTTs 87 (1986) 183-6 (T.S. Dokka).

4201 **Moroni** A., Il nuovo Tempio nel Vangelo di Giovanni: diss. Univ. Cattolica, ᴰGhiberti G. Milano 1985. [RivB 35,86].

4202 a) Neyrey Jerome H., 'My Lord and My God'; the divinity of Jesus in John's Gospel; – b) Buchanan George W., Apostolic Christology: ➤ 392, SBL Seminars 1986, 152-171 / 172-182.

4203 **O'Day** Gail R., Revelation in the Fourth Gospel; narrative mode and theological claim [diss. Emory, ᴰBeardsley W.]. Ph 1986, Fortress. xii-143 p. 0-8006-1933-1.

4204 O'Day Gail R., Narrative mode and theological claim; a study in the Fourth Gospel: JBL 105 (1986) 657-668.

4205 **Prescott-Erickson** Robert D., The sending motif in the Gospel of John; implications for theology of mission: diss. Southern Baptist Sem. 1986, ᴰHicks W.B. 230 p. 86-28710. – DissA 47 (1986s) 3084s-A.

4206 **Rittelmeyer** Friedrich, Ich bin; Reden und Aufsätze über die sieben 'Ich bin'–Worte des Johannesevangeliums. Stu 1986, Urachhaus. 138 p. 3-87838-424-1.

4207 Salvarani Brunetto, L'Eucaristia di Didachè IX-X alla luce della teologia giovannea; un'ipotesi: RivB 34 (1986) 369-390.

4208 **Stanley** David M., 'I encountered God'; the Spiritual Exercises with the Gospel of John. St. Louis 1986, Institute of Jesuit Sources. xvi-328 p. $14; pa. $11.

4209 ᴱ**Tragan** Pius-Ramón, Fede e sacramenti negli scritti giovannei; Atti del VI convegno di teologia sacramentaria 1983/5 ➤ 1,494: ᴿSalesianum 48 (1986) 429s (A.M. Triacca).

4209* Vellanickal Mathew, [kósmos...] The world vision of John: Bible Bhashyam 12 (1986) 118-130.

4210 Weismann F.J., Cristo, Verbo creador y redentor, en la controversia antidonatista de los 'Tractatus in Johannis Evangelium' I-XVI de San AGUSTÍN: Stromata 42 (1986) 301-328.

4210* **Whitacre** R.A., Johannine polemic; the role of tradition and theology: SBL diss. 67 (Cambridge, ᴰHooker M.) 1982 ➤ 63,5372 ... 1,5273: ᴿStPatav 33 (1986) 701s (G. Segalla).

G1.5 Johannis Prologus 1,1 ...

4211 Ashton John, The transformation of wisdom; a study of the prologue of John's Gospel: NTS 32 (1986) 161-186.

4212 *Black* C. Clifton[II], St. THOMAS's commentary on the Johannine prologue; some reflections on its character and implications: CBQ 48 (1986) 681-698.

4213 *a*) *Bultmann* Rudolf, The history of religions background of the prologue to the Gospel of John [< [F]GUNKEL H. 1983, 3-26]; – *b*) *Lamarche* Paul, The prologue of John [< RechSR 52 (1964) 497-537]. [T]*Ashton*; – *c*) *Meeks* Wayne A., The man from Heaven in Johannine sectarianism [< JBL 91 (1972) 44-72]: ➤ 235, [E]*Ashton* J., Interpretation of John 1986, 18-35 / 36-52 / 141-173.

4214 *Csengödy* László, Ⓜ On the translation of the word *lógos* [1. consideration; 2. relation; 3. in law; ... 7. utterance, maxim, command; 9. expression; 10. The Word of Wisdom]: Theologiai Szemle 28 (1985) 148-155.

4215 *Duvernoy* J., [Jn 1,1-18] Le prologue de l'évangile selon saint Jean: CahRenan 33,138 (1985) 26-33: the original version was similar to Jn 17,1-26 [NTAbs 30,293].

4216 **Gwo Yun-Han,** Homiletical dialogue between The Journey to the West [China's classical novel Hsi Yu Chi] and the Johannine Logos: diss. Southern Baptist theol. sem. 1986, [D]*Chafin* K. 275 p. 86-19037. – DissA 47 (1986s) 2199-A.

4217 **Hofrichter** P., Im Anfang war der 'Johannesprolog'; das urchristliche Logosbekenntnis – die Basis neutestamentlicher und gnostischer Theologie [Hab.-Diss. Graz 1985]: BibUnt 17. Rg 1986, Pustet. iv-481 p. DM 48. 3-7917-1001-X [NTAbs 30,353]. – [R]CiuD 199 (1986) 327 (A. *Salas*); ExpTim 98 (1986s) 216 (E. *Best*); TR 82 (1986) 454-7 (R. *Schnackenburg*: kühne These).

4218 *Kermode* Frank, St. John as poet: JStNT 28 (1986) 3-16.

4219 **Pazzini** Domenico, In principio era il Logos; ORIGENE ... 1983 ➤ 64,5271 ... 1,5278: [R]TLZ 111 (1986) 127-9 (W. *Ullmann*).

4220 *Schedl* Claus, Neue Sicht der Logos-Theologie nach dem aramäischen Targum Neophyti [< [R]*Kolb* A., Theologie im Dialog (1985) 205-210]: TGegw 23 (1985) 251-4.

4221 *Schoonenberg* Piet, A sapiential reading of John's Prologue; some reflections on views of Reginald FULLER and James DUNN [30th Bellarmine Lecture (unabridged), St. Louis Univ. 29.X.1986]: TDig 33 (1986) 403-421.

4222 *Staley* Jeff, The structure of John's Prologue; its implications for the Gospel's narrative structure: CBQ 48 (1986) 241-263; chart 264.

4223 **Theobald** Michael, Im Anfang war das Wort: textlinguistische Studie zum Johannesprolog: SBS 106, 1983 ➤ 64,5273: [R]CBQ 48 (1986) 350s (K. *Brower*).

4224 **Barth** Karl, Witness to the word, a commentary on John I [Münster lectures 1925, Bonn 1933, [E]*Fürst* Walther], [T]*Bromiley* Geoffrey W. GR/Exeter 1986, Eerdmans/Paternoster xii-163 p. $6 pa. [TDig 33,458]. 0-8028-0186-2/.

4225 **Guardini** Romano, Tre interpretazioni scritturistiche [Giov 1; 1 Cor 13; Rom 8]. Brescia 1985, Morcelliana. 116 p. Lit. 8000 [HumBr 41,777].

4226 *Delebecque* Édouard, '... mais afin qu'il témoignât sur la lumière' (Jn 1,8); note sur un emploi de *hina* chez Jean: ÉtClas 54 (1986) 147-158.

4227 *Dumbrell* W.J., Law and grace; the nature of the contrast in John 1:17: EvQ 58 (1986) 25-37.

4228 *Zauner* Wilhelm, Lob der Neugierde; eine Busspredigt zu Joh 1,19-42: TPQ 134 (1986) 51s.

4229 **Stichel** Rainer, [Jn 1,45-51] Nathanael unter dem Feigenbaum ... in Literatur und Kunst 1985 → **1**,5292: ᴿMuséon 99 (1986) 203s (J. *Mossay*); RivArCr 62 (1986) 223s (V. *Saxer*).

4230 **Middleton** Thomas G., The Christology of the miraculous signs in John 2-11 and John 21: diss. New Orleans Baptist Theol. Sem. 1986, ᴰ*Simmons* B. 209 p. 86-21463. – DissA 47 (1986s) 2200s-A.

4231 **Moreira Azevedo** Carlos A., O milagre de Caná na iconografia paleocristã; catálogos dos monumentos: diss. Pont. Univ. Gregoriana, ᴰ*Martínez-Fazio* 1986, Nº 3366. 878 p. Porto 1986, Metanoia. ix-312 p.; 295 p.; bibliog. p. 275-303. – RTLv 18,562.

4232 *Bonart* Richard / *Maurer* Bernhard, Die Hochzeit zu Kana, I. Das Wunder, die Richtigkeiten und die Wahrheit / II. Das Wunder geschieht im Hören und im Vertrauen: Quatember 50,1 (Kassel 1986) 22-29 / 29 ... [< ᴢɪᴛ].

4233 *Davis* Stephen T., The miracle at Cana; a philosopher's perspective: → 271, Miracles 1986, 419-442.

4234 *Grassi* Joseph A., [Jn 2,1-12; 19,25 frames of chiastic structure] The role of Jesus' mother in John's Gospel; a reappraisal: CBQ 48 (1986) 67-80.

4235 *Trudinger* Paul, 'On the third day there was a wedding at Cana'; reflections on St John 2,1-12: DowR 104 (1986) 41-43.

4235* *Gourgues* Michel, [Jn 2,1; 19,25] Marie, la 'femme' et la 'mère' en Jean: NRT 108 (1986) 174-191.

4236 **Lausberg** Heinrich, Die Verse J. 2,7-9 des Johannes-Evangeliums; rhetorische Befunde zu Form und Sinn des Textes: NachGö 1986/5. Gö 1986, Vandenhoeck & R. 8 p. [= p. 115-125].

G1.6   Jn 3ss ... Nicodemus, Samaritana.

4237 *Mees* Michael, Das 3. Kapitel des Johannesevangeliums in früh-christlicher Sicht: Laurentianum 27 (1986) 121-137.

4238 *King* J. S., Nicodemus and the Pharisees: ExpTim [97 (1985s) 71-75, M. *Pamment* too severe] 98 (1986s) 45 only.

4239 *a) Zevini* G., Gesù lo sposo della comunità messianica (Gv 3,29); – *b) La Potterie* I, de, Le nozze messianiche e il matrimonio cristiano; – *c) Cremaschi* I., La 'donna meretrix'; il tema della chiesa-sposa nei Padri: ParSpV 13 (1986) 105-117 / 87-104 / 209-220 (-267).

4240 **Chappuis** Jean-Marc, Jésus et la Samaritaine 1982 → 64,5299: ᴿThe-ologiai Szemle 29 (1986) 119-121 (I. *Karasszon*).

4241 *Girard* Marc, Jésus en Samarie (Jean 4,1-42); analyse des structures stylistiques et du processus de symbolisation: ÉglT 17 (1986) 275-310.

4242 *Lorenzini* Ezio, [Jn 4] L'interpretazione del dialogo con la Samaritana: Orpheus 7 (1986) 134-146 [VetChr 23 (1986) 413-5, A. *Quacquarelli*].

4243 *Maggioni* Bruno, [Jn 4,7-38] Un itinerario di fede: ParVi 31 (1986) 101-4.

4244 **Poffet** Jean-Michel, La méthode exégétique d'HÉRACLÉON et d'ORI-GÈNE, commentateurs de Jn 4; Jésus, la Samaritaine et les Samaritains: Paradosis 28, 1985 → **1**,5308: ᴿAugR 26 (1986) 308-311 (E. *Peretto*); CBQ 48 (1986) 567s (G. *Rochais*: original and enlightening); JTS 37 (1986) 573s (K. J. *Torjesen*: detail-work excellent); RSPT 70 (1986) 609-611 (G.-M. *de Durand*).

4245 **Dauer** Anton, Johannes [4,46-54 ...] und Lukas ... Parallelperikopen: ForBi 50, 1984 → 65,4884; **1**,5314: ᴿBiblica 67 (1986) 124-7 (Y. *Simoens*); ColcT 56,1 (1986) 176s (S. *Mędala*).

4246 **Mees** Michael, Die Heilung des Kranken vom Bethesdateich aus Joh 5.1-18 in frühchristlicher Sicht: NTS 32 (1986) 596-608.
4247 *Tromp* Nico, Johannes 5,1-9; acht en dertig jaar gehandicapt: OnsGLev 63 (1986) 329s.
4248 *Mees* Michael, Jesu Selbstzeugnis nach Joh 5,19-30 in frühchristlicher Sicht: ETL 62 (1986) 102-117.
4249 *Möchen* Roland, [Joh 5,35; 8,56 *agalliáomai*] Johanneisches 'Jubeln': BZ 30 (1986) 248-250.

G1.7   **Jn 6... Panis Vitae.**

4250 **Beuken** Wim, *al.*, Brood uit de hemel; lijnen van Exodus 16 naar Johannes 6 tegen de achtergrond van de rabbijnse literatuur. Kampen 1985, Kok, 136 p. *f* 20. – RStreven 53 (1985s) 562 (P. *Beentjes*).
4251 *Dorman* David A., The Son of Man in John; a fresh approach through chapter 6: StudiaBT 13 (1983) 121-142.
4252 *Durkin* Kenneth, A eucharistic hymn in John 6 ? : ExpTim 98 (1986s) 168-170.
4253 *Feuillet* André, Dans le sillage de Vatican II; réflexions sur quelques versets de Jn 6 (vv. 14-15 et 67-69) et sur le réalisme historique du quatrième Évangile: Divinitas 30 (1986) 3-52.
4254 *Ben-Chorin* Schalom, [Jn 6,60] Deuteworte, Dornenkrone und Evengelienstruktur; drei exegetische Randbemerkungen: ZRGg 38 (1986) 270.
4255 *Grigsby* Bruce H., 'If any man thirsts ...'; observations on the rabbinic background of John 7, 37-39: Biblica 67 (1986) 101-8.
4256 *Robert* René, Approche littéraire de Jean, VII, 37-39: RThom 86 (1986) 257-268.
4257 *a) Krüger* Ralf-Dieter, Eine unerwartete Alternative, Jesus und die Ehebrecherin – Joh 8.1-11: Diakonie 12 (Stu 1986) 91-99; – *b) Leroy* Hubert, Jesus und die Ehebrecherin (Joh 7,53-8,11): ➤ 68*, FMAYER R., Wie gut 1986, 145-9.
4258 *Genuyt* F., Jésus, les scribes et la femme adultère: SémiotB 42 (1986) 21-31.
4259 *a) Coetzee* J.C., Jesus' revelation in the *ego eimi* sayings in John 8 and 9; – *b) Plessis* P.J. du, The Lamb of God in the Fourth Gospel; – *c) Rand* J.A. du, Plot and point of view in the Gospel of John: ➤ 72, FMETZGER B., South Africa 1985/6, 170-7 / 136-148 / 149-169.
4260 *a) Koester* Helmut, Gnostic sayings and controversy traditions in John 8:12-59; – *b) MacRae* George W. †, Gnosticism and the Church of John's Gospel: – *c) Schenke* Hans-Martin, The function and background of the Beloved Disciple in the Gospel of John: ➤ 374, EHedrick C., Nag Hammadi 1983/5, 97-110 / 89-96 / 111-125.
4261 *Delebecque* Édouard, *a)* Autour du verbe *eimi*, 'je suis', dans le quatrième évangile; note sur Jean VIII, 25: RThom 86 (1986) 83-89; – *b)* Jésus contemporain d'Abraham selon Jean 8,57: RB 93 (1986) 85-92.
4262 *a) Gillick* Laurence, [Jn 9] The man born blind; – *b) Empereur* James L., Anointing and the handicapped; – *c) Rackham* Kate, Handicapped people and ministry: Way 25 (1985) 87-95 / 122-131 / 132-9.
4263 *Painter* John, John 9 and the interpretation of the Fourth Gospel: JStNT 28 (1986) 31-61.
4264 *Manns* Frédéric, Traditions targumiques en Jean 10,1-30: RevSR 60 (1986) 135-157.
4265 *Genuyt* François, Le discours sur le bon pasteur; analyse sémiotique de Jean 10,1-21: SémiotB 41 (1986) 23-34.

4266 *Winstanley* Michael, The shepherd image in the Scriptures, a paradigm for Christian ministry: CleR 71 (1986) 197-206.

4267 *Cunningham* Mary B. [Jn 11] BASIL of Seleucia's homily on [the raising of] Lazarus, a new edition, BHG 2225: AnBoll 104 (1986) 161-184.

4268 **Kremer** Jacob L., [Jn 11,1-46] Lazarus, die Geschichte einer Auferstehung 1985 ➤ 1,5340: RErbAuf 62 (1986) 310 (B. *Schwank*); Laurentianum 27 (1986) 384s (J. *Imbach*).

4269 *Kremer* Jacob, The awakening of Lazarus [< GeistL 58 (1985) 244-258], TE*Asen* B.: TDig 33 (1986) 135-8.

4270 *Genuyt* François, Ressusciter pour apprendre à vivre et à mourir; la résurrection de Lazare selon Jean 11,1-44: LumièreV 35,179 (1986) 63-74.

4271 *Larsen* Iver, Walking in the light; a comment on John 11.9-10: BTrans 37 (1986) 432-6.

4271* *Delebecque* Édouard, 'Lazare est mort' (note sur Jean 11,14-15): Biblica 67 (1986) 89-97.

4272 *Cavallin* Hans C., Jesus gör de döda levande; Jh 11:25 jämfört med saddukéerperikopen och paulinska texter om de dödas uppståndelse som bidrag till johanneisk kristologi [Jesus makes the dead live]: SvEx 51s (1986s) 40-49.

4272* *a) Manns* Frédéric, Lecture symbolique de Jean 12,1-11: SBFLA 36 (1986) 85-110; – *b) Pathrapankal* Joseph, [Jn 12,20-26] Jesus and the Greeks; reflections on a theology of religious identity: ➤ 202*, Critical 1986, 71-84.

4273 *a) Beasley-Murray* George, John 12,31-34; the eschatological significance of the lifting up of the Son of Man; – *b) Balz* Horst, Johanneische Theologie und Ethik im Licht der 'letzten Stunde': ➤ 39, FGREEVEN H., Text/Ethik 1986, 70-81 / 35-56.

4273* *Chilton* Bruce, John XII 34 and Targum Isaiah LII 13 [< NT 22 (1980) 176-8]: ➤ 140*, Targumic 1986, 81-84.

4274 *Engelbrecht* Ben, [Jn 12,44] 'He who believes in me, believes not in me': JTSAf 54 (1986) 38-41 [< ZIT].

G1.8   **Jn 13... Sermo sacerdotalis et Passio.**

4274* **Naastepad** T. J. M., Pasen en Passie bij Johannes I, Hoofdstuk 12-17 II. 18-21. VBGed. Kampen 1986, Kok. 160 p.; 125 p. *f* 18,90 each. [GerefTTs 86,258].

4275 **Wakefield** Gordon S., The liturgy of St. John [13-21 in terms of a liturgy]. L 1985, Epworth. ix-102 p. £4. 0-7162-04134. – RExpTim 97 (1985s) 344 (J. *Lieu*).

4276 **Calloud** J., *Genuyt* F., Le discours d'adieu, Jean 13-17; analyse sémiotique. Lyon 1985, Centre pour l'analyse du discours religieux (CADIR) / Centre Thomas More. 117 p. F 60. 2-905601-00-0 / 2-905600-00-4 [NTAbs 31,98].

4277 **Hanson** R. S., Journey to Resurrection; the drama of Lent and Easter in the Gospel of John. NY 1986, Paulist. iv-81 p. $5 pa. 0-8091-2737-7 [NTAbs 31,100].

4278 **Schnackenburg** R. Ihr werdet mich sehen ... Joh 13-17, 1985 ➤ 1,5351: RColcT 56,1 (1986) 186s (S. *Mędala*).

4279 *Moloney* Francis J., The structure and message of John 13:1-38: AustralBR 34 (1986) 1-16.

4280 **Beatrice** P. F., [Gv 13,1-18] La lavanda dei piedi 1983 ➤ 64,5341; 65,4915: RRCatalT 11 (1986) 466 (M. S. *Gros i Pujol*).

4280* *Schneiders* Sandra M., The foot washing (John 13:1-20); an experiment in hermeneutics: ExAud 1 (1985) 135-146.

4281 **Beutler** J., Habt keine Angst ... Joh 14: SBS 116, 1984 ➤ 65,4921: ᴿCiuD 199 (1986) 545s (J. *Gutiérrez*); StPatav 33 (1986) 699-701 (G. *Segalla*).

4282 *Delebecque* Édouard, [Jn 14,2s; Lc 2,7] De la naissance de Jésus à la naissance d'une foi (sur un emploi 'divin' du grec *tópos* chez Luc et chez Jean): RBgPg 63 (1985) 92-98.

4282* *Vogel* Heinrich, Predigt über Joh 14,6: BTZ 3 (1986) 127-131.

4283 **Casurella** Anthony, [Jn 14,15...] The Johannine Paraclete in the Church Fathers ... [diss. ᴰ*Barrett* C., Durham 1980]: BeiGBEx 25, 1983 ➤ 64,5345 ... 1,5361: ᴿCBQ 48 (1986) 738s (R. E. *Brown*: beautifully nuanced); EvQ 58 (1986) 172 (R. *Bauckham*); HeythJ 27 (1986) 449s (A. *Meredith*).

4284 **Franck** Eskil, Revelation taught; the Paraclete in the Gospel of John: ConBib NT 14, 1985 ➤ 1,5363: ᴿNorTTs 87 (1986) 122-5 (T. S. *Dokka*); RHPR 66 (1986) 229 (F. *Grob*).

4285 *Ferraro* Giuseppe, L'esegesi dei testi del IV Vangelo sul 'paraclito' nel 'De Trinitate' di AGOSTINO: AugR 26 (1986) 437-457.

4286 a) *Szlaga* J., ❷ Salvation-history mission of the Holy Spirit according to J[ohn] 16,8-11; – b) *Grygliewicz* Feliks, ❷ John Evangelist on the Holy Spirit in the Church: ➤ 266, Duch Święty 101-114 / 89-100.

4286* *Kurichianil* John, Jesus' glorification in the Gospel of John: Bible Bhashyam 12 (1986) 42-58.

4287 **Käsemann** Ernst, [Jn 17] El testamento de Jesús 1983 ➤ 64,5354; 65,4928: ᴿDeltioVM 15,2 (1986) 94-100 (S. *Agouridis*); ScripTPamp 18 (1986) 712 (A. *Garcia-Moreno*); TVida 27 (1986) 226s (M. A. *Ferrando*).

4287* *Rossé* Gérard, Il pensiero giovanneo sull'unità nella preghiera di Gv 17: NuovaUm 8,48 (1986) 9-21.

4288 a) *Rubeaux* Francisco, [João 17] Como o Pai e Eu ... assim vós; – b) *Masi* Nicolau, Cristo, homem de conflitos; – c) *Gallazzi* Sandro, O projeto e o lugar da unidade na Igreja: Estudos Bíblicos 12 [REB 46,4] (1986, 'Unidade e conflitos na Igreja à luz do Novo Testamento') 15-23 / 38-46 / 7-14.

4289 **Claxton** David L., The distinctive emphases in the Johannine passion narrative as a key to the interpretation of John's Gospel; diss. New Orleans Baptist theol. sem. 1986, ᴰ*Glaze* R. 222 p. 86-21467. – DissA 47 (1986s) 2198-A.

4290 **La Potterie** Ignace de, La passion de Jésus selon l'évangile de Jean, texte et esprit [1983]: Lire la Bible 73. P 1986, Cerf. 212 p. F 89 [NRT 109,431, Y. *Simoens*].

4291 **Speyr** Adrienne von, Jean, naissance de l'église; méditation sur les chapitres 18-20 de l'Évangile selon saint Jean: Sycomore. P/Namur 1985, Lethielleux / Culture et Vérité. 295 + 200 p. F 105 + 70 [NRT 109,432, Y. *Simoens*: ne pouvait se tromper en choisissant – en recevant d'en haut – ce principe d'intelligibilité].

4292 **Sullivan** Roger W., The Christology of the Johannine Passion and Resurrection narratives: diss. New Orleans Baptist Sem. 1986, ᴰ*Glaze* R. 161 p. 87-06825. – DissA 47 (1986s) 4424-A.

4292* *Oliver Roman* Miguel, Jesús proclamado rey por un pagano en Juan 18.28-19.22: ComSev 19 (1986) 343-364.

4293 **Baum-Bodenbender** Rosel, Hoheit in Niedrigkeit; Johanneische Christologie im Prozess ... Joh 18,28-19,16a: ForBi 49, 1984 ➤ 65,4941; 1,5377: ᴿCBQ 48 (1986) 325-7 (R. E. *Brown*); ColcT 56,1 (1986) 173-5 (S. *Mędala*); ETL 62 (1986) 429s (F. *Neirynck*).

4294 *Charbonneau* André, 'Qu'as tu fait?' et 'D'où es-tu?'; le procès de Jésus chez Jean (18,28-19,16a): ScEspr 38 (1986) 203-219.317-329.

4295 *Giblin* Charles H., John's narration of the hearing before Pilate (John 18,28-19,16a): Biblica 67 (1986) 221-238; franç. 239.

4296 *a) Wilcox* Max, The text of the Titulus in John 19.19-20 as found in some Italian Renaissance paintings; – *b) Saunderson* Barbara, Biblical and non-biblical elements in Italian Renaissance representations of the Crucifixion: JStNT 27 (1986) 113-6 / 89-112.

4296* *a) Gillespie* Thomas W., The trial of politics and religion; John 18:28-19:16 (a sermon): ExAud 2 (1986) 69-73; – *b) Schottroff* L., 'Mein Reich ist nicht von dieser Welt'; der johanneische Messianismus: → 1,654, ᴱ*Taubes* J., Gnosis und Politik [Religionstheorie und politische Theologie 2; Mü (1984)] 97-108 [< JbBT 1,233].

4297 **Harvey** A.E., Jesus on trial, a study in the Fourth Gospel 1976 → 58,5297 ... 61,6620: ᴿDeltioVM 15,2 (1986) 91s (S. *Agouridis*).

4297* *Baarda* Tjitze, Jesus and Mary (John 20,16f) in the Second Epistle on Virginity ascribed to Clement: → 39, ᶠGREEVEN H., Text/Ethik 1986, 11-34.

4298 *Vicent Saera* Rafael, La halaka de Dt 21.22-23 y su interpretación en Qumran y en Jn 19,31-42: → 21, Mem. DÍEZ MACHO A., Salvación 1986, 699-709.

4298* **Meehan** sr. Thomas M., John 19:32-35 and 1 John 5:6-8; a study in the history of interpretation: diss. Drew. Madison NJ 1985. – RelStR 13,189; RTLv 18,548.

4299 *La Potterie* Ignace de, [Gv 19,37] 'Volgeranno lo sguardo a colui che hanno trafitto'; sangue di Cristo e oblatività: CC 137 (1986,3) 105-118.

4299* *a) Zeller* Dieter, Der Ostermorgen im 4. Evangelium (Joh 20,1-18); – *b) Nützel* Johannes M., 'Komm und sieh' - Wege zum österlichen Glauben im Johannesevangelium: → 120, ᶠVÖGTLE A. 1986, 145-161 / 162-189.

4300 *a) Carmignac* Jean, La position des linges selon Jean 20,6-7 et le linceul de Turin; – *b) Gil Vernet* J.M., Aspectos psicológicos de la agonía de Jesús [Jn 19,29]: → 21, Mem. DÍEZ MACHO A., Salvación 1986, 611-621 / 639s.

4301 *Kötzsche-Breitenbruch* Liselotte, Windel und Grablinnen: JbAC 29 (1986) 181-7; pl. 30-31.

4302 *McGehee* Michael, A less theological reading of John 20:17: JBL 105 (1986) 299-302.

4303 *Neirynck* F., Note sur Jn 20,1-18 [correction d'une citation orale de lui-même et d'une caricature en rapport à *Zeller* D. in ᴱ*Oberlinner* L., Auferstehung 1986]: ETL 62 (1986) 40s.

4304 **Faragone** Vincenzo, 'Ricevete lo Spirito Santo' (Gv 20, 22b): diss. R 1984, Pont. Univ. Gregoriana. 247 p.; bibliog. p.37-55.

4305 *Ruckstuhl* Eugen, [Jn 21] Der Jünger, den Jesus liebte: SNTU-A 11 (1986) 131-167.

4306 *a) La Potterie* Ignace de, Le témoin qui demeure; le disciple que Jésus aimait; – *b) Delebecque* Édouard, La mission de Pierre et celle de Jean; note philologique sur Jean 21: Biblica 67 (1986) 343-359 / 335-342.

G2.1　**Epistulae Johannis.**

4307 S. AUGUSTIN commente la 1ʳᵉ Lettre de saint Jean; intr. *La Potterie* I. de, *Hamman* A.-G.: Les Pères dans la Foi. P 1986, Desclée-B. 208 p. F 83. – ᴿEsprV 96 (1986) 553 (É. *Cothenet*).

4308 *Black* C. Clifton[II], The Johannine epistles and the question of Early Catholicism: NT 28 (1986) 131-158.

4309 **Bonnard** P., Les épîtres johanniques 1983 ➤ 64,5381 ... 1,5392: [R]Protestantesimo 41 (1986) 233s (B. *Costabel*).

4310 **Brown** R. E., The Epistles of John: AnchorB 30, 1982 ➤ 63,5472 ... 1,5393: [R]Biblica 67 (1986) 127-9 (P. *Bonnard*).

4311 **Brown** Raymond E., Le lettere di Giovanni, [T]*Benetazzo* Claudio: Commenti e Studi Biblici. Assisi 1986, Cittadella. 1087 p. Lit. 45.000.

4311* *Darmawijaya* S., Die Christologie des Johannes im Licht seiner Briefe (indonesisch): Orientasi 18 (1986) 45-68 [< TKontext 8/2,43].

4312 **Smalley** Stephen S., 1,2,3 John: Word Comm 51, 1984 ➤ 65,4968; **1,5397**: [R]BibTB 16 (1986) 40 (U. C. von *Wahlde*); BZ 30 (1986) 144s (H. *Klauck*); CBQ 48 (1986) 347s (P. F. *Ellis*: five underlying assumptions); Interpretation 40 (1986) 218s (P. S. *Berge*); JTS 37 (1986) 198-200 (K. *Grayston*: pastoral interest hampers judgment); PrincSemB 7 (1986) 86s (B. D. *Ehrman*); TLZ 111 (1986) 825 (T. *Holtz*); WestTJ 48 (1986)382-5 (J. W. *Scott*).

4313 *Mian* Franca, Sull'autenticità delle 'epistole giovannee' [1 Jn dall'autore dell'Ev.]: VetChr 23 (1986) 399-411.

4314 *Painter* John, The 'opponents' in 1 John: NTS 32 (1986) 48-71.

4315 **Wade** Leon R., Impeccability in 1 John; an evaluation: diss. Andrews, [D]*Blazen* I. Berrien Springs MI 1986. 336 p. 87-04322. – DissA 47 (1986s) 4117s-A.

4315* *Savon* Hervé, [1Jn 2,18...] L'Antéchrist dans l'œuvre de GRÉGOIRE le Grand: ➤ 433*, Grégoire 1982/6, 389-405.

4316 *Ferguson* Sinclair B., [1 Jn 3,1-3; Rom 9,4] The Reformed doctrine of sonship: ➤ 111, [F]STILL W., Pulpit & people 1986, 81-88.

4317 **Lieu** Judith, The second and third epistles of John, history and background: StNT&W. E 1986, Clark. x-264 p. £13. – [R]ExpTim 98 (1986s) 247 (K. *Grayston*); Themelios 12 (1986s) 98 (I. H. *Marshall*).

4318 *Malina* Bruce J., The Received View [*Malherbe* A.,] and what it cannot do ; III John and hospitality: Semeia 35 (1986) 171-189; bibliog. 191-4.

4319 *Olsson* B., [3 Jn] Structural analyses in handbooks for translators [*Malatesta* E., du *Rand* J. ...]: BTrans 37 (1986) 117-127.

G2.3   *Apocalypsis Johannis* – **Revelation**: *text, introduction.*

4320 [E]**Adams** A. W., PRIMASIUS episcopus Hadrumetinus, Commentarius in Apocalypsim: 1985 ➤ 1,5409: [R]TS 46 (1986) 348 (K. B. *Steinhauser*).

4320* *Botha* F. J., Die verklaring van die Boek Openbaring: NduitseGT 27 (1986) 29-37 [< GerefTTs 86,191].

4321 **Corsini** Eugenio, L'Apocalypse maintenant [1980], [T]*Arrighi* Renza 1984 ➤ 65,4984; 1,5413: [R]ÉTRel 61 (1986) 431s (M. *Carrez*: en 1981 avait eu lieu à la Sorbonne un débat vif et courtois, animé et informé entre Corsini et P. PRIGENT); Judaica 42 (1986) 108s (M. *Petit,* [T]*Hruby* K.); RThom 86 (1986) 675-681 (L. *Devillers*: ouvrage étrange, par un spécialiste de littérature chrétienne ancienne, étranger au monde clos des exégètes du NT; refuse l'interprétation eschatologique, apocalyptique, linéaire, anti-romaine; l'ennemi dénoncé par Jean est la Synagogue; ... très suggestif); TsTNijm 26 (1986) 87 (L. *Grollenberg*); TXav 36,78 (1986) 115s (P. *Ortiz* V.); VSp 139 (1985) 695 (J.-M. *Poffet*).

4322 **Draper** James T.[J], The unveiling. Nv 1984, Broadman. 285 p. $7.95. – [R]RExp 83 (1986) 116-9 (D. *Moody*: at last Southern Baptist 'has decided to move beyond the Protestant prejudice against Rev' by planning three books from different viewpoints; this first is Dispensational Premillenialism; to be followed by Historical Premillenial and Non-Millenial).

4323 **Durken** Daniel, a) What's this world coming to?; the Book of Revelation; 4 cassettes; – b) Understanding fundamentalism; 1 cassette. Collegeville MN 1981/3. $31; $8. [BToday 24,330s].

4324 **Esquerda Bifet** Juan, Bienvenido, Señor: Pedal 144. Salamanca 1983, Sígueme. 270 p.

4325 **Giesen** Heinz, Johannes-Apokalypse: KlKomm 18. Stu 1986, KBW. 192 p. DM 19,80. ?-460-15481-0. – ᴿTGegw 29 (1986) 258 (O. *Böcher*).

4326 **Hartingsveld** L. van, Revelation, a practical commentary [1984 ➤ 1, 5416],ᵀ. GR/Exeter 1985, Eerdmans/Paternoster. 103 p. £7. 0-8028-0100-5. – ᴿExpTim 97 (1985s) 377s (J. A. *Ziesler*: shows if you can't use Rev, at least don't misuse it).

4327 **Lops** R. L. H., La Bible de Macé de la Charité VII. Apocalypse, 1982 ➤ 1,5419: ᴿRBgPg 62 (1984) 636s (M. *Gosman*: not having any Apc. in the Aurora of Petrus RIGA as for the other books, Macé had to write this commentary himself).

4328 **Mollat** Donatien, Una lettura per oggi; l'Apocalisse [1982 ➤ 63,5531], ᵀ*Mariacher* Maria Noemi: Letture bibliche. R 1985, Borla. 197 p. Lit. 12.000. – ᴿBenedictina 33 (1986) 233s (L. *De Lorenzi*: sui generis); Letture 41 (1986) 182s (A. *Scurani*).

4329 **Müller** Ulrich B., Die Offenbarung des Johannes: ÖkTbK NT 19, 1984 ➤ 65,4996; 1,5421: ᴿRHPR 66 (1986) 240s (P. *Prigent*); ZkT 108 (1986) 192s (R. *Oberforcher*).

4330 **Prigent** Pierre, L'Apocalypse de saint Jean 1981 ➤ 62,6202 ... 1,5425: ᴿBZ 30 (1986) 145s (H. *Ritt*); RThom [84 (1984) 504s, M.-V. *Leroy*] 86 (1986) 672-5 (L. *Devillers*).

4331 **Prigent** Pierre, L'Apocalisse di S. Giovanni, traduzione e commento, [1981 ➤ 62,6202] ᵀ*Brugnoli* Piero: Commenti biblici. R 1985, Borla. 811 p. Lit 40.000. – ᴿBenedictina 33 (1986) 234-6 (L. *De Lorenzi*); CC 137 (1986,2) 609-611 (A. *Cannizzo*).

4332 **Ritt** Hubert, Offenbarung des Johannes: NEchter 21. Wü 1986, Echter. 123 p. 3-428-01042-X.

4333 **Tresmontant** Claude, Apocalypse de Jean, traduction et notes. P 1985, O. E. I. L. 511 p. F 160. – ᴿBenedictina 33 (1986) 229-232 (L. *De Lorenzi*: cerca chiarezza e semplicità, forse a troppo costo).

G2.5 *Apocalypsis,* **Revelation, topics.**

4334 **Argyriou** Astérios, Les exégèses grecques de l'Apocalypse à l'époque turque (1453-1821) 1982 ➤ 63,5493 ... 65,4978: ᴿIstina 31 (1986) 227-9 (B. *Dupuy*).

4335 **Barthélemy-Vogels** R., *Hyart* Charles, L'iconographie russe de l'Apocalypse; la 'mise à jour' des Livres Saints d'après le manuscrit no. 6 de la Collection Wittert: Liège ph/lett 241. P 1985, BLettres. x-215 p.

4336 *Beale* G. K., [➤ 2822] A reconsideration of the text of Daniel in the Apocalypse: Biblica 67 (1986) 539-543.

4337 **Bousset** W., Der Antichrist in der Überlieferung des Judentums, des Neuen Testaments und der Alten Kirche; ein Beitrag zur Auslegung der Apokalypse [1895]. Hildesheim 1983, Olms. vi-186 p. DM 38 pa. 3-487-07335-8 [NTAbs 30,360].

4337* a) *Bovon* François, Possession ou enchantement; les institutions romaines selon l'Apocalypse de Jean: CrNSt 7 (1986) 221-238; Eng. 436; – *b) Burkhardt* Helmut, Ausharren bei Jesus; Überlegungen zum theologischen Verständnis der Johannesoffenbarung: TBei 17 (Wu 1986) 234-247 [< ZIT].

4338 *Charlier* Jean-P., El Apocalipsis de San Juan ¿escritura para el fin de los tiempos o final de las Escrituras? [< LumenV 39 (1984) 419-430], ᵀᴱ*Cabié* Maïte: SelT 25 (1986) 57-63.

4339 **Collins** Adela Y., Crisis and catharsis; the power of the Apocalypse 1984 ➤ 65,5012; 1,5441: ᴿEfMex 4,11 (1986) 135-8 (R. *Duarte Castillo*); Horizons 13 (1986) 154 (W. O. *Walker*); Interpretation 40 (1986) 326-8 (R. L. *Jeske*); JBL 105 (1986) 543s (D. E. *Aune*); WWorld 6 (1986) 110s. 114 (D. *Fodness*).

4340 *a) Collins* Adela Y., Reading the Book of Revelation in the twentieth century; – *b) Barr* David L., The Apocalypse of John as oral enactment; – *c) Boring* M. Eugene, The theology of Revelation; 'the Lord our God the Almighty reigns'; – *d) Craddock* Fred B., Preaching the Book of Revelation: Interpretation 40 (1986) 229-242 / 243-256 / 257-269 / 270-282.

4341 *Collins* Adela Y., Early Christian apocalypticism; – *b) Schüssler Fiorenza* Elisabeth, The followers of the Lamb; visionary rhetoric and social-political situation: Semeia 36 (1986) 1-11 / 123-146.

4342 **Cowley** Roger W., The traditional interpretation of the Apocalypse of St. John in the Ethiopian Orthodox Church 1983 ➤ 64,5414 ... 1,5444: ᴿRasStEtiop 30 (1984ss) 186-191 (G. *Haile*).

4343 **Daalen** David van, A guide to the Revelation: TEF study guides² 20. L 1986, SPCK. 205 p. £6. 0-281-04193-8 [ExpTim 97,383].

4344 **Ellul** Jacques, Conférences sur l'Apocalypse de Jean, suivi du [1976 de lui-même] texte de l'Apocalypse. Nantes 1985, Arefppi. 182 p. – ᴿÉTRel 61 (1986) 453 (F. *Vouga*: sur tout et sur rien).

4345 *Feuillet* André, Visión de conjunto de la mística nupcial en el Apocalipsis: ScripTPamp 18 (1986) 407-430; lat. 430s; Eng. 431.

4346 *Frerichs* Wendell W., God's song of Revelation; from Easter to Pentecost in the Apocalypse: WWorld 6 (St. Paul 1986) 216-228.

4347 **Goldsworthy** Graeme, The Gospel in Revelation; Gospel and Apocalypse 1984 ➤ 65,5019 [➤ 1,5449 The lamb and the lion; the Gospel in Revelation 1985]: Vidyajyoti 49 (1985) 484.445 (sic; J. *Volckaert*).

4348 *Grassi* Joseph A., The liturgy of Revelation: BToday 24 (1986) 30-37.

4348* *a) Hahn* Ferdinand, Liturgische Elemente in den Rahmenstücken der Johannesoffenbarung; – *b) Klein* Hans, Die Gemeinschaft der Gotteskinder; zur Ekklesiologie der johanneischen Schriften: ➤ 56, ᶠKRETSCHMAR G., Anspruch 1986, 43-58 / 59-68.

4349 *Hamilton* Alastair, The Apocalypse within; some interpretations of the Book of Revelation from the sixteenth to the eighteenth century: ➤ 59, ᶠLEBRAM J., Tradition 1986, 269-283.

4350 *a) Hellholm* David, The problem of apocalyptic genre and the Apocalypse of John; – *b) Aune* David E., The apocalypse of John and the problem of genre; – *c) Thompson* Leonard, A sociological analysis of tribulation in the Apocalypse of John: Semeia 36 (1986) 13-64 / 65-96 / 147-174.

4351 **Hodder** Alan D., EMERSON's [first book] rhetoric of Revelation [of John]; 'Nature', the reader, and the apocalypse within: diss. Harvard ... – HarvTR 79 (1986) 473s.

4352 **Hofmann** H. U., LUTHER und die Johannes-Apokalypse [diss. Erlangen

1977]: BeiGBEx 24, 1982 ➤ 63,5517; 65,5021: ᴿRHPR 66 (1986) 241s (P. *Prigent*).

4353 *Jankowski* A., ❷ Syn Człowieczy [Son of Man] w Janowej Apokalipsie: Przegląd Tomistyczny 1 (1984) 39-48 [< RuBi 39,86].

4354 **Karrer** Martin, Die Johannesoffenbarung als Brief; Studien zu ihrem literarischen, historischen und theologischen Ort [diss. Erlangen-Nürnberg 1983]: FRLANT 140. Gö 1986, Vandenhoeck & R. 354 p. DM 84 [NRT 109,752, X. *Jacques*]. 3-525-53818-9.

4355 **Klein** Peter, Endzeiterwartung und Ritterideologie; die englischen Bilderapokalypsen der Frühgotik und MS Douce 180 (Ox Bodleian). Graz 1983, Akad. 241 p.; 175 fig.; 30 Faksim. DM 1160. – ᴿTrierTZ (1986) 156s (E. *Sauser*).

4356 **Kuykendall** Robert M., The literary genre of the book of Revelation; a study of the history of apocalyptic research and its relationship to John's Apocalypse: diss. SW Baptist Sem. 1986. 258 p. 86-23461. – DissA 47 (1986s) 3074-A.

4357 *Läpple* Alfred, El misterio del cordero [< ... das Christusbild: BiKi 1 (1984) 53-58], ᵀᴱ*Segarra* Montserrat: SelT 25 (1986) 64-66.

4358 ᴱ**Lambrecht** Jan, L'Apocalypse johannique et l'Apocalyptique dans le NT [Lv 30ᵉ] 1980 ➤ 61,705* ... 63,5524: ᴿRThom 86 (1986) 681-3 (L. *Devillers*).

4359 *Lempa* Henryk, ❷ Badania nad Apokalipsą św. Jana we współczesnej biblistyce polskiej (1945-1985 Polish exegetical research): ➤ 367, Sympozjum 1985 = RuBi 39 (1986) 259-274.

4360 **Lijka** Kazimierz, ❷ Motywy liturgii sakramentalnej w Apokalipsie; studium egzegetyczno-liturgiczne: diss. ᴰ*Kudasiewicz* J. Lublin 1986. 228 p. – RTLv 18,582.

4361 **Maclachlan** David, The Elect and their opponents in the Revelation of John: diss. ᴰ*Barth* M. Basel 1986. – RTLv 18,548.

4362 **Maier** Gerhard, Die Johannesoffenbarung und die Kirche: WUNT 25, 1981 ➤ 62,6191 ... 1,5454: ᴿAugR 26 (1986) 306s (P. *Grech*); BiKi 41 (1986) 49s (P.-G. *Müller*).

4363 **Maxwell** C. Mervyn, God cares [I. Daniel] II. The message of Revelation for you and your family. Boise 1985, Pacific. 573 p. $15. – ᴿAndrUnS 24 (1986) 284-6 (K. A. *Strand*: scholarly).

4364 **Mazzaferri** Frederick D., The genre of the Book of Revelation from a source-critical perspective: diss. Aberdeen. – RTLv 18,548 sans date.

4365 **Mesters** Carlos, Speranza di un popolo perseguitato; Apocalisse, una chiave di lettura, ᵀ*Demarchi* Enzo: Figure bibliche. Assisi 1985, Cittadella. 128 p. Lit. 6000. – ᴿBenedictina 33 (1986) 232s (L. *De Lorenzi*: maestria).

4366 *Newport* Kenneth, *a)* Semitic influence on the use of some prepositions in the Book of Revelation: BTrans 37 (1986) 328-334; – *b)* The use of *ek* in Revelation; evidence of Semitic influence: AndrUnS 24 (1986) 223-230.

4367 *O'Donovan* Oliver, The political thought of the Book of Revelation: TyndB 37 (1986) 61-94.

4367* **Paley** Morton D., The apocalyptic sublime [English art from 1775 to 1851 by a BLAKE scholar]. NHv 1986, Yale Univ. xii-196 p.; 85 pl. + 7 color. $35 [RelStR 13,341, K. *Lewis*].

4368 ᴱ**Patrides** C., *Wittreich* J., The Apocalypse in English renaissance thought and literature 1984 ➤ 1,301; ᴿSixtC 16 (1985) 285s (R. B. *Barnes*) & 288 (F. *Ardonilo*); TS 47 (1986) 520-2 (J. R. *Keating*).

4369 *Perini* Giovanni, Salvezza e festa in Apocalisse: ParVi 31 (1986) 199-204.

4370 **Plancke** Chantal van der,   L'Apocalypse: Le temps de lire   Bru 1984, Lumen Vitae.   112 p. – RFoiTemps 16 (1986) 283 (C. *Focant*).

4371 *Rena* John,   Women in the Gospel of John: ÉglT 17 (1986) 131-147.

4372 *Sartori* Luigi,   L'Apocalisse della fede: Hermeneutica 3 (Urbino 1983) 11-23.

4373 **Schüssler Fiorenza** Elisabeth,   The book of revelation; justice and judgment 1985 ⇥ 1,5466:   RCBQ 48 (1986) 139s (J. E. *Bruns*: a landmark); CurrTM 13 (1986) 249 (E. *Krentz*); Horizons 13 (1986) 154 (W. O. *Walker*); Interpretation 40 (1986) 430.432 (M. *Rissi*); JAAR 54 (1986) 576s (D. L. *Barr*).

4374 *a) Stanley* John E.,   The Apocalypse and contemporary sect analysis; – *b) Hills* Julian,   The Epistula Apostolorum and the genre 'Apocalypse'; –, *c) Barr* David L.,   Elephants and holograms; from metaphor to methodology in the study of John's Apocalypse: ⇥ 392, SBL Seminars 1986, 412-421 / 581-595 / 400-411.

4375 **Thompson** Steven,   The Apocalypse and Semitic syntax: SNTS Mon 52, 1985 ⇥ 1,5469:   RBL (1986) 142s (F. F. *Bruce*); StPatav 33 (1986) 449s (G. *Segalla*); TüTQ 166 (1986) 65 (M. *Reiser*: like many others, assumes we know more about what is 'Greek' than we do; thus helps neither to grasp nor to evaluate the undoubted Semitisms of Apc).

4376 *Trevès* M.,   Remarques sur l'Apocalypse: CahRenan 33,139 (1985) 33-42 [NTAbs 30,314].

4377 *Trudinger* Paul,   The Apocalypse and the Palestinian Targum: BibTB 16 (1986) 78s.

G2.6   *Apocalypsis,* **Revelation 1,1 ...**

4378 **Hemer** Colin J.,   The letters to the seven churches of Asia in their local setting [diss. DBruce F.]: JStNT Sup 11. Sheffield 1986, Univ.   xiv-338 p. $32.50; pa. $15.   0-905774-95-7. – RExpTim 98 (1986s) 55 (J. P. M. *Sweet*: archeological support for RAMSAY 1904; good index but no map); RExp 83 (1986) 630s (J. L. *Blevins*); TrinJ 7,2 (1986) 107-111 (G. *Beale*).

4379 **Hutchison** Dennis A.,   The nature of Christ's comings in Revelation 2-3: diss. Grace Theol. Sem. 1986.   309 p. 86-19650. – DissA 47 (1986s) 2199-A; GraceTJ 7 (1986) 319.

4379* *Muse* Robert L.,   Revelation 2-3; a critical analysis of seven prophetic messages: JEvTS 29 (1986) 147-162 [< ZIT].

4380 **Rinaldi** G.,   Le sette lettere dell'Apocalisse di Giovanni; problemi storici e testimonianze archeologiche 1984 ⇥ 1,5479:   RSTEv 15 (1985) 135s (G. *Emetti*).

4380* **Sharkey** Sarah A.,   The background of the imagery of the Heavenly Jerusalem in the New Testament [Gal 4,26; Heb 12,22; Rev 3,12; 21,2]: diss. Catholic Univ.,   DFitzmyer J. A. Wsh 1986.   389 p. 86-13465. – DissA 47 (1986s) 1373-A.

4381 *Dautzenberg* Gerhard,   Reich Gottes und Evangelium in der Johannesapokalypse; ein Versuch zu Apk. 4-22, 1986: Theologische Standorte ...

4381* *Hidber* Bruno,   Ostern und das Geheimnis der Weltgeschichte; das Lamm und das versiegelte Buch (Offb 5,1-6): TGegw 29 (1986) 21-28.

4382 *a) Achtemeier* Paul J.,   Revelation 5:1-14; – *b) Kelly* Balmer H., Rev. 7:9-17: – *c) Raber* Rudolph W., Rev. 21:1-8:   Interpretation 40 (1986) 283-8 / 288-295 / 296-301.

4383 *Bachmann* Michael,   [Offb 6,2] Der erste apokalyptische Reiter und die Anlage des letzten Buches der Bibel;   Biblica 67 (1986) 240-275; franç. 275.

4384 *Allison* Dale C., [Rev 9,13; 3,12] 4 Q 403 fragm. 1, col. i, 38-46 and the Revelation to John: RQum 12,47 (1986) 409-414.

4385 *Rapisarda Lo Menzo* Grazia, 'Mulier amicta sole' (Ap 12,1) fra Antico e Nuovo Testamento: ➤ 365, AnStoEseg 3 (1985/6) 139-147.

4385* *Ulrichsen* Jarl H., DYRET i Åpenbaringen; en skisse til tidhistorisk forståelse av kapitlene 13 og 17: NorTTs 87 (1986) 167-177.

4386 **Brady** David, The contribution of British writers between 1560 and 1830 to the interpretation of Revelation 13,16-18, 1983 ➤ 64,5472 ... 1,5489: ᴿHeythJ 27 (1986) 94s (A. *Hamilton*).

4387 *Oberweis* Michael, Die Bedeutung der neutestamentlichen 'Rätzelzahlen' 666 (Apk 13,18) und 153 (Joh 21,11): ZNW 77 (1986) 226-241.

4388 *Topham* Michael, [Rev 13,18 '666' number of the beast =] Hanniqola῾ītēs [2,6.15 = Balaam]: ExpTim 98 (1986s) 44s.

4389 *Altink* Willem, Theological motives for the use of 1 Chronicles 16:8-36 as background for Revelation 14:6-7: AndrUnS 24 (1986) 211-221.

4389* a) *Jensen* Joseph, [Rev 16,14s] What are they saying about Armageddon?: CurrTM 13 (1986) 292-301; – b) *Ford* J. Massyngberde, The structure and meaning of Revelation 16: ExpTim 98 (1986s) 327-331.

4390 a) *Georgi* Dieter, [Rev 18 and Horace, Carmen saeculare] Who is the true prophet?; – b) *Collins* Adela Y., Vilification and self-definition in the Book of Revelation: ᶠSTENDAHL K. = HarvTR 79 (1986) 100-126 / 308-320.

4391 *Strand* Kenneth A., Some modalities of symbolic usage in Revelation 18: AndrUnS 24 (1986) 37-46.

G2.7 **Millenniarismus**, Apc 21 ...

4392 **Cohn** Norman, Les fanatiques de l'Apocalypse; millénaristes révolutionnaires et anarchistes mystiques au Moyen Âge², ᵀ*Clémendot* Simone al.: Bibliothèque historique. P 1983, Payot. 378 p. – ᴿRHR 203 (1986) 99-101 (F. *Lestringant*: réédition justifiée d'un classique).

4393 *Creelan* Paul, [John B.] WATSON as mythmaker; the millenarian sources of Watsonian behaviorism: JScStR 24 (1985) 194-216.

4394 **Efird** James M., End-times; rapture, antichrist, millennium; what the Bible says: Contemporary Christian concerns. Nv 1986, Abingdon. 96 p. 0-687-11787-9 [NTAbs 30,364: Efrid] – ᴿRExp 83 (1986) 643s (D. *Moody*).

4395 *Haas* Mary De, Is millenarianism alive and well in white South Africa?: RelSAfr 7,1 (1986) 37-45 [< ᴢɪᴛ].

4396 *Karrer* Martin, Chiliasmus: ➤ 587, EvKL 1 (1986) 655-8.

4397 *Lightner* Robert P., Theological perspectives on Theonomy [-Post-millenialism: i.e. the Law of Moses is still God's rule of life]: 1. Theonomy and dispensationalism; 2. Nondispensational responses to theonomy; 3. A dispensational response to theonomy: Bibliotheca Sacra 143 (1986) 26-36 / 134-145 / 228-245.

4398 *Lilienfeld* Fairy von, Hesychasmus: ➤ 597, TRE 15 (1986) 282-9.

4399 a) *Mazzucco* Clementina, Il millenarismo di METODIO di Olimpo di fronte a ORIGENE; polemica o continuità?; – b) *Montserrat-Torrents* J., Origenismo y gnosis; los 'perfectos' de Metodio di Olimpo: ➤ 476*, L'origenismo 1985 = AugR 26 (1986) 73-87 / 89-101.

4400 *Seifert* Arno, Reformation und Chiliasmus; die Rolle des Martin CELLARIUS-Borrhaus: ArRefG 77 (1986) 226-263; Eng. 264.

─────────────

4401 *Mazzucco* Clementina, [Apc 20ss] Gli antichi esegeti di fronte alla

Gerusalemme celeste [< ᴱ*Gatti Perer* M., La Gerusalemme celeste 1983
➤ 64,266 ... 1,5505]: BbbOr 28 (1986) 129-141.
4402 *a) Mircea* I., Le règne du Christ de mille ans; étude exégétique de Ap
20,1-15; – *b) Galeriu* C., Le manque de fondements du millénarisme:
Ortodoxia 36,1 (1984) 29-58 / 59-72 [Istina 31 (1986) 343].
4403 **Dumbrell** William J., The end of the beginning; Revelation 21-22 and the
Old Testament [Moore College lectures 1983]. Homebush West NSW 1985,
Lancer. [16 +] 200 p. 0-85892-269-X.
4404 **Collins** Thomas, Apocalypse 22:6-21 as the focal point of moral teaching
and exhortation in the Apocalypse: diss. Pont. Univ. Gregoriana, ᴰ*Vanni*
U. R 1986. viii-366 p.; bibliog. p. 349-366. 86-25139. – DissA 47 (1986s)
2622-A; TR 82,338.
4405 *Vanni* Ugo, Lo Spirito e la sposa (Ap 22,17): ParSpV 13 (1986) 191-206.

XIII. Paulus

G3.1   **Pauli vita, stylus, chronologia.**

4406 **Barbaglio** Giuseppe. Paolo di Tarso e le origini cristiane 1985 ➤ 1,5511:
ᴿAsprenas 33 (1986) 205-7 (A. *Rolla*); Letture 41 (1986) 863-5 (G. *Ravasi*);
Protestantesimo 41 (1986) 169-171 (B. *Corsani*); RasT 27 (1986) 474s (V.
Fusco); RClerIt 67 (1986) 875s (G. *Borgonovo*).
4407 ᶠBARRETT C.K., Paul and Paulinism, ᴱ**Hooker** M., *Wilson* S. 1982
➤ 63,12 ... 1,5513: ᴿTZBas 42 (1986) 175-8 (P. *Elbert*).
4408 *Best* Ernest, Paul's apostolic authority–?: JStNT 27 (1986) 3-25.
4409 *a) Betz* H.D., Paul in the Mani biography; – *b) Rosenstiehl* J.-M.,
C.M.C. 60,13-62,9; contribution à l'étude de l'Apocalypse apocryphe de
Paul; – *c) Giuffrè Scibona* Concetta, Gnosi e salvezza nel CMC: ➤ 421,
Codex Manichaicus Coloniensis 1984/6, 215-234 / 345-353 / 355-370.
4410 **Black** David A., Paul apostle of weakness 1984 ➤ 65,5066; 1,5519:
ᴿCBQ 48 (1986) 130-2 (T.H. *Tobin*).
    Borchert G.L., Paul and his interpreters 1985 ➤ 660.
4411 **Bruce** F.F., Paul and his converts; how Paul nurtured the churches he
planted [= ²1962]. DG 1985, InterVarsity. 155 p. $6 pa. 0-87784-593-X
[NTAbs 30,360].
4412 **Bruce** F.F., The Pauline circle 1985 ➤ 1,5522: ᴿAndrUnS 24 (1986)
183s (J. *Paulien*); GraceTJ 7 (1986) 247s (D.A. *Black*); Vidyajyoti 49 (1985)
483 (P. *Meagher*).
4413 **Bruce** F.F., Mensen rondom Paulus, ᵀ*Ru* G. de. Haag 1986, Boekencentrum. 95 p. *f* 12.90. – ᴿKerkT 37 (1986) 361s (A.J. *Bronkhorst*).
4414 **Bultmann** R., Der Stil der paulinischen Predigt und die kynisch-stoische
Diatribe, ᴱ*Hübner* H.: FRLANT 13. Gö 1984 = 1910, Vandenhoeck &
R. viii-110 p. DM 34. – ᴿNRT 108 (1986) 269 (X. *Jacques*: exégète de
grande classe).
4415 *Callan* Terrance, Competition and boasting; toward a psychological
portrait of Paul: ST 40 (1986) 137-156.
4416 *Carson* David, Pauline inconsistency; Churchman 100 (L 1986) 6-45.
4417 **Cunningham** P.A., Apostle to the Gentiles; Paul as he saw himself.
Mystic CT 1986, 'Twenty-third', 100 p. $6 [TS 47,755].
4417* **Davies** W.D., Jewish and Pauline studies 1984 ➤ 65,180; 1,5523:
ᴿNorTTs 87 (1986) 4s (H. *Moxnes*).

4418 **Dietzfelbinger** Christian, Die Berufung des Paulus als Ursprung seiner Theologie [ev. Hab.-Diss. München 1982]: WMANT 58. Neuk 1985, V. xii-164 p. DM 42, sb. 37,80. 3-7887-0771-2. – ᴿBijdragen 47 (1986) 71s (J. *Delobel*); BZ 30 (1986) 277s (M. *Theobald*); NRT 108 (1986) 436 (X. *Jacques*); RThom 86 (1986) 669s (H. *Ponsot*).

4418* *Dorsey* Charles, Paul's use of *apóstolos*: RestQ 28 (Abilene 1985s) 193-200 [< ZIT].

4419 **Everts** Janet M., Testing a literary-critical hermeneutic; an exegesis of the autobiographical passages in Paul's epistles: diss. Duke, ᴰ*Price* J. Durham NC 1985. 229 p. 86-08922. – DissA 47 (1986s) 553-A; RelStR 13,190.

4420 *Forbes* Christopher, Comparison, self-praise and irony; Paul's boasting and the conventions of Hellenistic rhetoric: NTS 32 (1986) 1-30.

4421 *Frederiksen* Paula, Paul and AUGUSTINE; conversion narratives, orthodox traditions, and the retrospective self: JTS 37 (1986) 3-34.

4421* *Fung* Ronald Y. K., Révélation et tradition [couverture: traditions]; les origines de l'Évangile de Paul [< EvQ 57 (1985) 23-41],ᵀ: Hokhma 11,32 (1986) 53-70.

4422 *Giles* K., Apostles before and after Paul [... Paul's understanding of apostleship]: Churchman 99 (1985) 241-256.

4423 **Harrington** W., Jesus and Paul; signs of contradiction. Wilmington 1986, Glazier. 229 p. $13; pa. $9 [TS 48,407].

4424 *Harris* Xavier J., Paul's missionary activity: BToday 24 (1986) 241-8.

4425 **Hengel** M., Between Jesus and Paul 1983 ➤ 65,200: ᴿJTS 37 (1986) 167-171 (E. P. *Sanders* lists sheer assertions and erroneous clichés).

4426 **Hugedé** N., Saint Paul et Rome [ancienne]. P 1986, BLettres/Desclée-B. 236 p.; ill. F 95 [NRT 109,745, X. *Jacques*]. 2-251-33312-6 / Desclée 2-220-02624-8.

4427 **Hyldahl** Niels, Die paulinische Chronologie: ActTheolDan 19. Leiden 1986, Brill. vii-136 p. *f* 53 [TR 83,251]. 90-04-07908-4.

4428 **Johnson** K. L., Paul the teacher; a resource for teachers in the Church. Minneapolis 1986, Augsburg. 126 p. 0-8066-2226-1 [NTAbs 31,107].

4429 **Kaufmann** Rolf, Die Krise des Tüchtigen; Paulus und wir im Verständnis der Tiefenpsychologie 1983 ➤ 64,5514: ᴿZRGg 38 (1986) 52-54 (F. W. *Kantzenbach*).

4430 *Ker* Donald P., Missionary motivation in Paul; the Jewish environment: IrBSt 8 (1986) 162-178.

4431 **Kim** Seyoon, The origin of Paul's Gospel²: WUNT 2/4, 1984 ➤ 63,5606 ... 1,5534: ᴿNRT 108 (1986) 268s (X. *Jacques*: long postscript apprécié).

4432 **Knoch** O., 'Durch die Gnade Gottes bin ich, was ich bin'; Gestalt, Werk und Wirkung des Apostels Paulus. Ostfildern 1984, Schwaben-V. 108 p. DM 19,80. 3-7966-0594-X [NTAbs 30,361].

4433 **Lapide** P., **Stuhlmacher** P., Paul, rabbi and apostle 1984 ➤ 65,5082; 1,5536: ᴿCurrTM 13 (1986) 175s (W. C. *Linss*: two interesting monologues); Interpretation 40 (1986) 212-214 (E. *Krentz*).

4434 **Lindemann** A., Paulus im ältesten Christentum 1979 ➤ 60,7558 ... 64,5521: ᴿProtestantesimo 41 (1986) 49s (V. *Subilia*).

4435 **Luedemann** Gerd, Paul, apostle to the Gentiles ... chronology 1984 ➤ 1,5541: ᴿBibTB 16 (1986) 36 (J. L. *White*); CurrTM 13 (1986) 118s (W. C. *Linss*); Interpretation 40 (1986) 323s (J. C. *Hurd*); JTS 37 (1986) 180-2 (K. *Grayston*); NRT 108 (1986) 270s (X. *Jacques*: préface de J. KNOX remarque que l'auteur enseignait aux États-Unis 1977-82); RThom 86 (1986) 157s (H. *Ponsot*: réaffirme les positions de l'édition allemande en face des réactions); TLond 39 (1986) 58-60 (F. *Watson*: first stay in Greece ten years before inscription related to Gallio of Acts 18,12); TLZ 111 (1986) 669s (H. *Hübner*, zum Nachwort des Englischen gegen Hübners TLZ 107,741).

4435* *Lux* Rüdiger, 'Ivri anochi' – 'Ein Hebräer bin ich': ZeichZt 40 (1986) 293-300 [< ZIT].

4436 **Lyons** George, Pauline autobiography; toward a new understanding: SBL diss 73, 1985 ➤ 1,5543: ᴿCBQ 48 (1986) 750-2 (P. J. *Achtemeier*); RelStR 12 (1986) 294s (D. J. *Lull*: against apologia thesis).

4437 **Maccoby** H., The mythmaker; Paul and the invention of Christianity. SF 1986, Harper & R. xii-237 p. $18. 0-06-015582-5 [NTAbs 30,362]. – ᴿCCurr 36 (1986s) 230s (Pheme *Perkins*).

4438 *a) Malherbe* Abraham J., A physical description of Paul; – *b) Smith* Morton, Paul's arguments as evidence of the Christianity from which he diverged; – *c) Sundberg* Albert C.ᴶ, Enabling language in Paul: ➤ 110, ꟳSTENDAHL K. = HarvTR 79 (1986) 170-5 / 254-260 / 270-7.

4438* *Malherbe* Abraham J., Paul; Hellenistic philosopher or Christian pastor?: AnglTR 68 (1986) 3-15.

4439 *Norelli* Enrico, La funzione di Paolo nel pensiero di Marcione: RivB 34 (1986) 543-597; Eng. 597 [419-427, *Penna* R.].

4440 **Ollrog** Wolf-Henning, Paulus und seine Mitarbeiter: WMANT 50, 1979 ➤ 60,7566 ... 63,5617: ᴿHenoch 8 (1986) 103s (L. *Moraldi*).

4441 **Patte** Daniel, Paul's faith and the power of the Gospel; a structural introduction to the Pauline letters 1983 ➤ 64,5562; 65,5120: ᴿJBL 105 (1986) 540-3 (B. C. *Lategan*); TLZ 111 (1986) 362-4 (W. *Rebell*: the vocabulary of structuralism limits him to a few expressions which can be made clear for the general public).

4442 **Patte** Daniel, Paul, sa foi et la puissance de l'Évangile: Initiations. P 1985, Cerf. 288 p. – ᴿEsprV 96 (1986) 138 (L. *Monloubou*: réserves); FoiTemps 16 (1986) 283s (C. *Focant*); RThom 86 (1986) 323s (H. *Ponsot*: plutôt qu''Initiation', risque de désorienter même les avertis).

4443 **Patte** Daniel, Preaching Paul 1984 ➤ 65,5090; 1,5549: ᴿRPHR 66 (1986) 232 (G. *Vahanian*).

4444 ꟳ**Piédagnel** Auguste, Jean CHRYSOSTOME, Panégyriques de Saint Paul: SChr 300, 1982 ➤ 63,5623 ... 1,5550; ᴿRBgPg 64 (1986) 121s (R. *Gryson*).

4445 **Plevnik** Joseph, What are they saying about Paul? Mahwah NJ 1986, Paulist. v-114 p. $5 pa. [TDig 34,89]. 0-8091-2776-8.

4446 **Pollock** John, The Apostle; a life of Paul. Wheaton IL 1985 [= England 1971], Victor/SP. 311 p.; map. 0-88207-233-1.

4447 *Räisänen* Heikki, *a)* Paul's call experience and his later view of the Law; – *b)* The 'Hellenists' – a bridge between Jesus and Paul?; – *c)* Zionstora und biblische Theologie; zu einer Tübinger Theorie; ➤ 209, Torah 1986, 55-92 / 242-306 / 337-365.

4448 **Rebell** Walter, Gehorsam und Unabhängigkeit; eine sozial-psychologische Studie zu Paulus. Mü 1986, Kaiser. 180 p. DM 36. 3-459-01635-3. – ᴿExpTim 98 (1986s) 215s (E. *Best*).

4449 *Salzer* Elisabetta, Aspetti mistici dell'esperienza religiosa di San Paolo, III. Esperienza mistica della trasformazione esistenziale in Cristo; – IV. Esperienza mistica nella trasformazione esistenziale ad opera dello Spirito: Teresianum 36 (1985) 139-167 / 37 (1986) 393-426.

4450 **Sanders** E. P., Paulus und das palästinische Judentum: SUNT 17, 1985 ➤ 1,5552: ᴿSalesianum 48 (1986) 428 (R. *Vicent*); SNTU-A 11 (1986) 238-245 (H. *Hübner*); TLZ 111 (1986) 421-5 (C. *Wolff*); TPQ 134 (1986) 78s (A. *Fuchs*).

4451 **Sanders** E. P., Paolo e il giudaismo palestinese; studio comparativo su modelli di religione [1977 ²1984 ➤ 58,6856], ᵀ*Bori* Pier C. BiblTPaid 21. Brescia 1986, Paideia. 845 p.; bibliog. p. 761-792. Lit. 80.000. – ᴿComSev 19 (1986) 433s (M. de *Burgos*).

4452 **Schillebeeckx** Edward, [17 p.; + 100 p. phot.] Paul the Apostle 1983 ➤ 64,5539; 65,5698: ᴿBibTB 16 (1986) 38s (C. J. *Roetzel*).

4453 **Senft** Christophe, Jésus de Nazareth et Paul de Tarse: Essais Bibliques 11, 1985 ➤ 1,5555: ᴿRThom 86 (1986) 324s (H. *Ponsot*); RTPhil 118 (1986) 407-416 (J.-F. *Habermacher*: 'Paul trahit-il ou traduit-il Jésus?': identification trop rapide pourrait opérer une déhistoricisation).

4454 *Soards* Marion L. [omitted from Contents p. 125], Paul, apostle and apostolic visionary: BibTB 16 (1986) 148-150.

4454* **Stainthorpe** Fred, Tail-end gospel [the conclusions of Paul's letters (e.g. 2 Tim 4,8s) show him as a needy human being, a disappointed and lonely man, but not entirely friendless]: ExpTim 98 (1986s) 307.

4455 *Stanley* David, The apostle Paul as saint: StMiss 35 (R 1986) 71-97.

4456 *Tassin* Claude, Saint Paul et la figure du Serviteur: Spiritus 26 (P 1985) 391-9.

4457 **Thompson** William G., Paul and his message for life's journey. NY 1986, Paulist. vii-151 p. $10 pa. 0-8091-2824-1.

4458 **Trilling** Wolfgang, A conversation with Paul [Mit Paulus in Gespräch 1983 ➤ 64,5544], ᵀ*Bowden* John. L 1986, SCM. x-116 p. £4.50 0-334-01962-1.

4458* **Trilling** Wolfgang, Conversaciones con Pablo; un recorrido original por la obra del Apóstol. Barc 1986, Herder. 184 p. [Igreja e missão 132,203]. – ᴿEstAg 21 (1986) 185 (A. *Rodríguez*).

4459 *a) Vanhoye* Albert, Personnalité de Paul et exégèse paulinienne; – *b) Aletti* Jean-Noël, L'autorité apostolique de Paul; théorie et pratique; – *c) Vassiliadis* Petros, Centre of the Pauline soteriology and apostolic ministry; – *d) Radl* W., Alle Mühe umsonst? Paulus und der Gottesknecht; – *e) Baumert* Norbert, Charisma und Amt bei Paulus; – *f) Tuckett* C. M., Dt 21,33 and Paul's conversion: ➤ 398, ᴱ*Vanhoye* A., L'Apôtre Paul 1984/6, 3-15 / 229-246 / 247-253 / 144-149 / 203-228 / 345-350.

4460 *Virgulin* Stefano, Cristo al centro della missione di Paolo: RivVSp 40 (1986) 378-397.

4461 **Woods** Laurence E., St. Paul's apostolic weakness: diss. ᴰ*Lindars* B. Manchester 1985. 343 p. – RTLv 18,55.

G3.2 **Corpus paulinum;** *introductio, commentarii.*

4462 **Biser** Eugen, Paulus für Christen; eine Herausforderung; Einleitung und Textauswahl: Bücherei 1219. FrB 1985, Herder. 192 p. DM 10 [TLZ 112, 10-18, G. *Baudler*].

4463 **Bonora** A., Il libro dei Salmi nel 'corpus Paulinum'; presenza, uso, significato: diss. Pont. Univ. Gregoriana, ᴰ*Vanni* U. Roma 1986 [RivB 35,87].

4464 **Brisebois** Mireille, St. Paul: introduction to St. Paul and his letters [1984 ➤ 65,5106], ᵀ. L 1986, St. Paul. 142 p. £5.25. 0-85439-243-2. – ᴿCleR 71 (1986) 231 (J. *Green*).

4465 *Carrez* M., *al., a)* Cartas de Pablo ... 1985 ➤1,5566: ᴿScripTPamp 18 (1986) 677-9 (A. *García-Moreno*). – *b)* Lettere di Paolo, Giacomo, Pietro e Giuda: PiccEncBib 8. R 1985, Borla. 335 p. Lit. 20.000. – ᴿStPatav 33 (1986) 442s (G. *Segalla*).

4466 **Cugusi** Paolo, Evoluzione e forme dell'epistolografia latina nella tarda repubblica e nei primi secoli dell'impero con cenni sull'epistolografia preciceroniana. R 1983, Herder. 291 p. Lit. 30.000. – RArctos 19 (1985) 281s (Saara *Lilia*); Maia 37 (1985) 292s (Elisabetta *Nano*).

4467 **Davidsen** A., Paulus, inledning og kommentar til Paulus' breve og breve skrevet i Paulus' navn. K 1986, Gyldendal. 419 p. Dk 249 [TsTKi 57,239].

4468 **Exler** Francis X., The form of the ancient Greek letter of the epistolary papyri (3d c. B.C. – 3d c. A.D.); a study in Greek epistolography. Ch 1976, Ares. 140 p.

4469 *Hartman* Lars, On reading others' letters: ► 110, FSTENDAHL K. = HarvTR 79 (1986) 137-146.

4470 **Keck** Leander E., *Furnish* Victor P., The Pauline letters 1984 ► 65,5114; 1,5573: RInterpretation 40 (1986) 102s (D. W. *Kendall*); PrincSemB 7 (1986) 85s (R. E. *De Maris*).

4471 **Madsen** N., St. Paul; the Apostle and his letters. Huntington IN 1986, Our Sunday Visitor. ii-198 p. $7 pa. 0-87973-589-9 [NTAbs 31,107].

4472 **Mara** Maria Grazia, Paolo di Tarso e il suo epistolario 1983 ► 1,5575*: RParVi 30 (1985) 235-7 (F. *Mosetto*).

4473 **Marrow** Stanley B., Paul, his letters and his theology; an introduction to Paul's epistles. Mahwah NJ 1986, Paulist. iv-278 p. $10. 0-8091-2744-X. – RComLtg 68 (1986) 316 (J. *Dupont*); ExpTim 98 (1986s) 26s (R. *Lunt*: conspicuously clear English); NBlackf 67 (1986) 502 (J. A. *Ziesler*); TsTNijm 26 (1986) 412s (L. *Visschers*).

4474 **Pardee** Dennis, *al.*, Handbook of ancient Hebrew letters: SBL Sour 15, 1982 ► 63,5647 ... 1,5577: RBASOR 263 (1986) 94-96 (W. T. *Pitard*); Henoch 8 (1986) 400s (F. *Israel*); JNES 45 (1986) 152-4 (A. *Lemaire*, franç.).

4475 *a)* *Roberts* J. H., The eschatological transitions to the Pauline letter body; – *b)* *Pelser* G. M. M., Resurrection and eschatology in Paul's letters: Neotestamentica 20 (1986) 29-35 / 36-45.

4476 *a)* *Roberts* J. H., Pauline transitions to the letter body; – *b)* *Standaert* B., La rhétorique ancienne dans saint Paul; – *c)* *Neirynck* Frans, Paul and the sayings of Jesus; – *d)* *Wedderburn* A. J. M., Paul's use of the phrases 'in Christ' and 'with Christ'; – *e)* *Barrett* C. K., Boasting (*kauchâsthai* etc.) in the Pauline Epistles: ► 398, EVanhoye A., L'Apôtre Paul 1984/6, 93-99 / 78-92 / 265-321 / 362 only / 363-8.

4476* *a)* *Roberts* J. H., Transitional techniques to the letter body in the Corpus Paulinum; – *b)* *Toit* A. B. du, Hyperbolical contrasts; a neglected aspect of Paul's style: ► 72, FMETZGER B., South Africa 1985/6, 187-201 / 178-186.

4477 **Roetzel** Calvin J., The letters of Paul; conversations in context[2] [[1]1975] 1982 ► 64,5564 = L 1983, SCM. viii-149 p. £6. – RHeythJ 27 (1986) 189s (F. F. *Bruce*).

4478 **Schmithals** Walter, Die Briefe des Paulus in ihrer ursprünglichen Form 1984 ► 65,5123; 1,5581: RTLZ 111 (1986) 512s (H. M. *Schenke*: thirteen letters to Corinth, made up in part from sections of Rom and Thes).

4479 **Spadafora** Francesco, San Paolo, le lettere, I. Le due lettere ai Tessalonicesi; II. Gal – Rom; III. Cor.: Renovatio 21 (1986) 115-137 / 251-262 / 345-378.

4481 **Staab** K., Pauluskommentare aus der griechischen Kirche [1933]. [2]*Kötting* B. 1984 ► 65,5124: RNRT 108 (1986) 270 (X. *Jacques*).

4482 **Stowers** Stanley K., Letter writing in Greco-Roman antiquity: Library of Early Christianity 5. Ph 1986, Westminster. 188 p. 0-664-21909-8.
4483 **Swain** L., The people of the Resurrection, I. The apostolic letters: Good News Studies 15. Wilmington 1986, Glazier. 288 p. $13. 0-89453-290-1 [NTAbs 31,109].
4484 **Tibiletti** G., Le [34] lettere private nei papiri greci del III e IV secolo d.C., tra paganesimo e cristianesimo 1979 → 61,a664 ... 63,8330: ᴿClasR 100 (1986) 353s (P. J. *Parsons*).
4485 *Trudinger* P., Computers and the authorship of the Pauline Epistles [*Wake* W., assumes many things that are not certain: use of secretaries, fluency in Greek, stylistic development...]: Faith and Freedom 39,115 (Oxford 1986) 24-27 [< NTAbs 31,44].
4486 **White** John Lee, Light from ancient letters [Egyptian papyri 3d cent. B.C. - 3d A.D.]: Foundations and facets. Ph 1986, Fortress. xviii-238 p. $25 [TDig 34,95]. 0-8006-2110-7. – ᴿExpTim 98 (1986s) 350 (C. S. *Rodd*).

G3.3 Pauli theologia.

4486* **Beaudean** John W., Paul's theology of preaching: diss. Drew. Madison NJ 1985. – RelStR 13,187.
4487 *a) Beker* J.C., The method of recasting Pauline theology; the coherence-contingency scheme as interpretive model; – *b) Sampley* J. Paul, Overcoming traditional methods by synthesizing the theology of individual letters; – *c) Segal* Alan F., Paul and ecstasy: → 392, SBL Seminars 1986, 596-602 / 603-613 / 555-580.
4488 *a) Betz* H.D., The problem of rhetoric and theology according to the Apostle Paul; – *b) Kertelge* Karl, Der Ort des Amtes in der Ekklesiologie des Paulus; – *c) Men* Alexandre, The messianic eschatology of St Paul in connexion with the primitive preaching of the Gospel: → 398, ᴱ*Vanhoye* A., L'Apôtre Paul 1984/6, 16-48 / 184-202 / 322s.
4489 *Deidun* Thomas, Some recent attempts at explaining Paul's theology [*Käsemann* E., *Sanders* E., *Beker* J.]: Way 26 (1986) 230-242.
4490 **Friesen** Lauren D., The eagle and the dove; a three-act drama on life in the Johannine community: diss. Graduate Theological Union. Berkeley 1985. – RelStR 13,189.
4491 **Hoffmann** R. Joseph, Marcion ... radical Paulinist theology [diss. Oxford 1982] AAR 46, 1984 → 65,5131; 1,5592: ᴿJBL 105 (1986) 343-6 (J. J. *Clabeaux*: numerous strengths and weaknesses).
4492 **Huarte Osacar** Juan, Evangelio y comunidad; estudio de teología paulina 1983 → 64,5576 ... 1, 5594: ᴿTXav 36,78 (1986) 116-8 (C. *Maccise*).
4493 **Kreitzer** Larry J., Theocentricity and Christocentricity in Paul's eschatological thought; diss. ᴰ*Stanton*. London 1986. 300 p. – RTLv 18,547.
4494 *Langkammer* H., ❷ Pneumatologia świętego Pawła; → 266, Duch Święty 59-72.
4495 *Maillot* A., Les théologies de la mort du Christ chez Paul: FoiVie 85,6 (1986) 33-45.
4496 **Pobee** John S., Persecution and martyrdom in the theology of Paul: JStNT Sup 6, 1985 → 1,5604: ᴿCBQ 48 (1986) 565s (D. L. *Tiede*: dated but deep); EfMex 4,10 (1986) 130-3 (H. *Sasado*); TLZ 111 (1986) 510s (K. T. *Kleinknecht*).
4497 **Schlier** Heinrich, Linee fondamentali di una teologia paolina [1978 → 60,7674],ᵀ: BibTeolContemp 48. Brescia 1985, Queriniana. 208 p. Lit. 18.000. – ᴿParVi 31 (1986) 390-2 (G. *Segalla*).
4498 **Schnelle** Udo, Gerechtigkeit und Christusgegenwart; vorpaulinische und

paulinische Tauftheologie [ev. Diss. Göttingen] 1983 ➤ 64,5589 ... 1,5607:
ᴿSalesianum 48 (1986) 428s (C. *Bissoli*); TLZ 111 (1986) 30.

Segundo Juan Luis, The humanist Christology of Paul: Jesus of Nazareth
yersterday and today 3, 1986 ➤ 5542.

4499 **Sinclair** Scott G., The Christologies of Paul's undisputed epistles and the
Christology of Paul: diss. Graduate Theological Union, ᴰ*Leahy* T. Berkeley 1986. 185 p. 8617047. – DissA 47 (1986s) 1781-A; RelStR 13,190.

4500 **Theissen** Gerd, Psychologische Aspekte paulinischer Theologie:
FRLANT 131, 1983 ➤ 64,5591 ... 1,5609: ᴿActuBbg 23 (1986) 96 (X.
Alegre S.); Salmanticensis 33 (1986) 380-3 (R. *Trevijano*).

4501 **Thüsing** Wilhelm, Gott und Christus in der paulinischen Soteriologie, 1.
Per Christum in Deum; das Verhältnis der Christozentrik zur Theozen-
trik³ʳᵉᵛ [Hab.–Diss. 1965]: NTAbh NF 1/1. Münster 1986, Aschendorff.
xxxv-307 p. DM 48. – ᴿAntonianum 61 (1986) 498s (Z. I. *Herman*:
revisione poco felice di un libro già buono).

4501* *Tofană* Stelian, La responsabilité chrétienne selon les Épîtres de
l'Apôtre Saint Paul (en roumain): STBuc 38,5 (1986) 83-99.

4502 *Wanamaker* C. A., Christ as divine agent in Paul: ScotJT 39 (1986)
517-528.

4503 **Ziesler** John, Pauline Christianity 1983 ➤ 64,5597 ... 1,5612: ᴿHeythJ
27 (1986) 78s (T. *Deidun*).

G3.4   **Themata paulina**   [Israel et Lex ➤ G4.6].

4504 **Behrendt** Ethel L., Die verlorene Gerechtigkeit der christlichen Botschaft;
Paulus vor Jesus?: Christ im Staat 1. München 1986, auct. xxxviii-559 p.
3-922479-19-7.

4505 *Best* Thomas F., St. Paul and the decline of the miraculous: EAsJT 4,1
(1986) 68-76.

4506 **Brotherton** Dennis O., An examination of selected Pauline passages
concerning the vocational missionary; an interpretative basis for critiquing
contemporary missiological thoughts: diss. SWBaptist Sem. 1986. 239 p.
87-05898. – DissA 47 (1986s) 4107-A.

4507 **Carmack** Samuel W., Paul's affirmation of suffering in light of his
Christology: diss. SW Baptist Theol. Sem. 1985. 323 p. 86-12695. – DissA
47 (1986s) 946-A.

4508 **Cartigny** C., Le carré magique, testament de saint Paul 1984 ➤ 65,5154;
1,5621: ᴿNRT 108 (1986) 271s (X. *Jacques*; trouvé à Pompéi 1926/35 par
M. DELLA CORTE; 'sator arepo tenet opera rotas' peut être lu 'Pater
Noster' bis + a-ô).

4509 *Chamblin* Knox, Revelation and tradition in the Pauline *euangelion* [Gal
1,11s; 1 Cor 15,1s]: WestTJ 48 (1986) 1-16.

4510 *Charbel* Antônio, Questões candentes dos escritos paulinos em relação à
mulher: ➤ 386, RCuBíb 10,39s (1986) 78-85.

4511 *Corrigan* Gregory M., Paul's shame for the Gospel: BibTB 16 (1986)
23-27.

4512 *Dassmann* Ernst, Zum Paulusverständnis in der östlichen Kirche: JbAC
29 (1986) 27-39.

4513 **Dennison** W. D., Paul's two-age construction and apologetics 1985
➤ 1,5626; ᴿRefTR 45 (1986) 84 (T. L. *Wilkinson*: follower of VAN TIL;
seeks to put apologetics on a proper biblical basis).

4514 **Doohan** Helen, Leadership in Paul: Good News Studies 11, 1984
➤ 65,5073*b*; 1,5525: ᴿCBQ 48 (1986) 136s (E. *Hensell*).

4515 **Eckstein** Hans-J., Der Begriff *syneidesis* bei Paulus: WUNT 2/10, 1983

➤ 64,5622; 65,5161:   ᴿAugR 26 (1986) 305s (E. *Peretto*); BZ 30 (1986) 140-2 (R. *Schnackenburg*).

4516 **Franco** Ettore,   Comunione e partecipazione; la *koinōnia* nell'epistolario paolino [diss. S. Luigi, ᴰ*Vanni* U., N 1983: TR 82 (1986) 427]: Aloisiana 20. Brescia 1986, Morcelliana. xiii-346 p. Lit. 39.000. 88-372-1281-X. – ᴿRasT 27 (1986) 469s (V. *Fusco*).

4518 *Gómez García* X. A.,   'Evangelio' en la tradición paulina: Lumieira (1986) 161-180 [REB 46,902].

4519 **Gouvernaire** Jean,   La práctica del discernimiento bajo la guía de san Pablo.   Santander 1984, Sal Terrae.   87 p.   84-293-0682-X. – ᴿEstE 61 (1986) 87 (J. *Iturriaga*).

4520 *Güttgemanns* Erhardt,   Paulus und der désir nach dem Eschaton: LingBib 58 (1986) 7-13; Eng. 14.

4521 *Hallbäck* Geert,   Paulus og metoderne: DanTTs 49 (1986) 110-6 [< ᴢɪᴛ].

4522 **Iovino** Paolo,   Chiesa e tribolazione; il tema della 'thlipsis' nelle lettere di S. Paolo 1985 ➤ 1,5634: – ᴿRevSR 60 (1986) 266 (J. *Schlosser*).

4523 **Jaswant** Raj Joseph,   Grace in the Siddhantham and in St. Paul: diss. Salesiana, ᴰ*Amato* A.   Roma 1985.   148 p. – RTLv 18,589.

4524 **Kitzberger** Ingrid R.,   Bau der Gemeinde; das paulinische Wortfeld 'oikodome (ep)oikodomein' [Diss. ᴰ*Beilner* W.   Salzburg 1986. vi-351 p. – RTLv 18,547]: ForBi 53.   Wü 1986, Echter. ix-357 p.   3-429-01052-7.

　 Kleinknecht Karl T.,   Der leidende Gerechtfertigte ... und Paulus 1984 ➤ 2700.

4525 **Koch** Dietrich A.,   Die Schrift als Zeuge des Evangeliums; Untersuchungen zur Verwendung und zum Verständnis der Schrift bei Paulus [Hab. Mainz]: BeiHistT 69.   Tü 1986, Mohr.   406 p. DM 198 [TR 83,339].   3-16-144990-8.

4526 *Lindars* Barnabas,   The Old Testament and universalism in Paul: BJRyL 69 (1986s) 511-527.

4527 *Marcus* Joel,   The evil inclination in the letters of Paul: IrBSt 8 (1986) 8-21.

4528 **Marques** Valdir,   'Eikón' em Paulo; investigação teológica e bíblica à luz de LXX: diss. Pont. Univ. Gregoriana, ᴰ*Vanni* U.   R 1986. [RTLv 18,543]. xiv-352 p.; bibliog. p. 325-337.

4529 **Meeks** Wayne A.,   The first urban Christians; the social world of the Apostle Paul 1983 ➤ 64,5641 ... 1, also 5641; ᴿActuBbg 23 (1986) 216 (X. *Alegre* S.); HeythJ 27 (1986) 454s (T. *Deidun*); NorTTs 87 (1986) 45-47 (H. *Moxnes*); TLZ 111 (1986) 104s (W. *Rebell*); TZBas 42 (1986) 438-440 (E. L. *Miller*, Eng.); Worship 60 (1986) 178s (T. H. *Troeger*).

4530 *Newton* Michael,   The concept of purity at Qumran and in the letters of Paul: SNTS Mon 53, 1985 ➤ 1,5646: ᴿBL (1986) 132 (P. R. *Davies*: many unexamined assumptions); BSOAS 49 (1986) 568s (J. H. *Eaton*); NBlackf 67 (1986) 244s (A. R. C. *Leaney*); NRT 108 (1986) 438s (X. *Jacques*); SR 15 (1986) 401-3 (H. W. *Basser*: confused and forced interpretation of key-terms); WestTJ 48 (1986) 376-8 (F. S. *Spencer*).

4530* *Nkwoka* A. O.,   Paul's idea of the Hagioi [die Heiligen, not das Heilige as TKontext 8/2,15] and its significance for contemporary Nigerian Christianity: EAfJevT 5,1 (1986) 23-35.

4531 *Osten-Sacken* Peter von der,   The Pauline gospel and homosexuality [< BTZ 3 (1986) 28-49], ᵀᴱ*Asen* B. A.: TDig 33 (1986) 28-49 [309-312, in canon law, *Walf* K.].

4532 **Palliparambil** Jacob,   The will of God in Paul, a commitment to man; an exegetico-theological study of 'thelo-thelema' vocabulary in the writings of Paul: diss. Pont. Univ. Gregoriana, ᴰ*Vanni* U.   R 1986.   758 p. [extr. Nᵒ 3344, 236 p.] – TTLv 18,549.

4533 *Parkin* Vincent, Some comments on the Pauline prescripts: IrBSt 8 (Belfast 1986) 92-99.

4534 *Perkins* Pheme, Pauline anthropology in light of Nag Hammadi: ➤ 32, ᶠFᴛᴢᴍʏᴇʀ J., CBQ 48 (1986) 512-522.

4535 *Provera* Mario, Gerusalemme nella vita e pensiero di san Paolo: BbbOr 28 (1986) 111-120; pl. II-IV.

4536 **Puthiyidom** Mani, Confessions of faith in Pauline writings: diss. Pont. Univ. Gregoriana, ᴰ*Grech* P. R 1986. 402 p. – RTLv 18,549.

4537 **Rebell** Walter, Das Leidensverständnis bei Paulus und Iɢɴᴀᴛɪᴜs von Antiochien: NTS 32 (1986) 457-465.

4538 **Reinmuth** Eckart, Geist und Gesetz; Studien zu Voraussetzungen und Inhalt der paulinischen Paränese: Theologische Arbeiten 44. B 1986, Ev.-V. 152 p. DM 15.

4539 *Sacchi* Alessandro, [Paolo] La libertà del cristiano: ParVi 31 (1986) 105-32.

4540 **Schäfer** Klaus, Gemeinde als 'Bruderschaft'; ein Beitrag zum Kirchenverständnis des Paulus: Diss. ᴰ*Schramm* T. Hamburg 1986s. – RTLv 18,550.

4541 **Shaw** Graham, The cost of authority ... NT [Paul] 1983 ➤ 64,5658; 65,5193: ᴿHeythJ 27 (1986) 188s (B. *McNeil*).

4542 *Stegemann* E., Aspekte gegenwärtiger Paulusforschung / Zwei sozialgeschichtliche Anfragen an unser Paulusbild: EvErz 37,5 (1985) 491-502 / 480-490.

4543 *Templeton* Douglas A., Pauline investigations; peripsemata postpaulina [some 200 Wittgenstein-style assertions vaguely related to Paul and to each other: e.g. '1.4/2 And so it is'; '1.4/7 I do not wish to jump onto my horse and gallop off in all directions. I wish to have several horses at my disposal']: HeythJ 27 (1986) 26-42.

4544 *Vassiliadis* Petros, Your will be done; reflections from St. Paul: IntRMiss 75 (1986) 376-382.

4545 *Wischmeyer* Oda, a) Das Gebot der Nächstenliebe bei Paulus; eine traditionsgeschichtliche Untersuchung: BZ 30 (1986) 161-187; – b) Das Adjektiv *agapētos* in den paulinischen Briefen; eine traditionsgeschichtliche Miszelle: NTS 32 (1986) 476-480.

4546 **Zedda** Silverio, Relativo e assoluto nella morale di S. Paolo: BiblCuRel 43, 1984 ➤ 65,5204; 1,5662: ᴿAsprenas 33 (1986) 438-440 (S. *Cipriani*); ÉTRel 61 (1986) 288s (A. *Moda*: étude de maître; trop de coquilles); NRT 108 (1986) 123s (X. *Jacques*); ParVi 30 (1985) 237s (A. *Casalegno*); RTPhil 118 (1986) 423s (A. *Moda*).

4547 *Ziobro* Basil, Buddhist tradition and Paul [Rom 8,9-23; Col 1,15-20 ...]: BToday 24 (1986) 299-308.

G4   Ad Romanos   .1   *Textus, commentarii.*

4548 **Achtemeier** Paul J., Romans 1985 ➤ 1,5663: ᴿCBQ 48 (1986) 130 (R. M. *Karris* recommends); Interpretation 40 (1986) 188-190 (L. E. *Keck*: 'the triumph of God's gracious Lordship').

4549 **Barth** Karl, Der Römerbrief (Erste Fassung) 1919, ᴱ*Schmidt* H.: Gesamtausgabe 2. Z 1985, Theol.-V. xix-713 p. Fs 64 [TLZ 112,613, D. *Schellong*].

4550 **Bruce** F. F., Romans²: Tyndale NT. GR 1985 [¹1963], Eerdmans. 274 p. $6. ᴿRExp 83 (1986) 293s (R. L. *Omanson*).

4551 **Byrne** Brendan, Reckoning with Romans; a contemporary reading of Paul's Gospel: GoodNewsSt 18. Wilmington 1986, Glazier. 229 p. $13 pa. [TDig 33,461]. 0-89453-585-4.

4552 ᴱCocchini Francesca, ORIGENE, commento alla lettera ai Romani I, libri I-VII: Ascolta, Israele 2, 1985 ➤ 1,5668: ᴿParVi 31 (1986) 75-77 (Clara *Burini*); SMSR 52 (1986) 173-5 (L. *Navarra*).

4553 **Granfield** C. E. B., Romans, a shorter commentary 1985 ➤ 1,5669: ᴿNRT 108 (1986) 434 (X. *Jacques*); ScotJT 39 (1986) 268s (R. S. *Barbour*).

4554 **Dettori** Luigi, Lettera ai Romani; traduzione interlineare greco-italiana. Villanova di Guidonia 1986, Veritas. 84 p.

4555 ᴱEsnault R. H., Martin LUTHER, Commentaire de l'Épître aux Romains I. texte; gloses; scolies 1-3: Œuvres 11, 1983 ➤ 65,5207*: ᴿNRT 108 (1986) 116s (X. *Jacques*). ➤ 4561.

4556 **Hammond Bammel** Caroline P., Der Römerbrieftext des RUFIN und seine ORIGENES-Übersetzung: VLat 10, 1985 ➤ 1,5672: ᴿNRT 108 (1986) 756 (X. *Jacques*); ZkT 108 (1986) 352-4 (L. *Lies*).

4557 **Keller** C., Das Evangelium des Paulus, genannt 'Der Römerbrief'; unter Berücksichtigung des griechischen Urtextes aus dem Deutschen ins Deutsche übersetzt. B 1985, CZV. 70 p. DM 11,80. 3-7674-0239-4 [NTAbs 31,107].

4558 ᴱKooi C. van der, Teksten uit Karl BARTHS Romeinenbrief: Sleutelteksten in godsdienst en theologie 1. Delft 1986, Meinema. 103 p. f 24,50. 90-211-6100-1 [TsTNijm 26,439].

4559 **Kruijf** T. C. De, De Brief van Paulus aan de Romeinen vertaald en toegelicht: Het NT. Boxtel 1986, Katholieke Bijbelstichting. 300 p. 90-6173-349-9.

4560 **Kuhatschek** J., Romans; becoming new in Christ: Lifebuilder Bible Studies. DG 1986, Intervarsity. 94 p. $3 pa. 0-8308-1008-0 [NTAbs 31,107].

4561 **Luther** M. [➤ 4555], Commentary on the Epistle to the Romans [1515-6, published 1908], ᵀ*Mueller* J. Theodore. GR 1982 = 1954, Kregel. 223 p. – ᴿScotBEvT 4 (1986) 68s (D. F. *Wright*: translation unusably abridged).

4562 **Maillot** Alphonse, L'Épître aux Romains épître de l'œcuménisme et théologie de l'histoire 1984 ➤ 65,5210; 1,5676: ᴿBLitEc 87 (1986) 147 (S. *Légasse*); EsprV 96 (1986) 109 (L. *Walter*); NRT 108 (1986) 115s (X. *Jacques*).

4563 *Mara* Maria Grazia, Notas sobre el comentario de san AGUSTÍN a la Carta a los Romanos; exposición de algunas proposiciones de la Epist. ad Romanos, ᵀ*Santervás* M.: ➤ 477, Congreso 1983 = AugM 31 (1986) 185-194.

4564 **Parker** T. H. L., Commentaries on Romans 1532-1542 [chiefly Rom 1,18-23; 2,13-16; 3,20-28] (editor not named though introduction is in 1st person). E 1986, Clark. xii-226 p., bibliog. p. 210-222. £15. 0-567-009366-2. – ᴿExpTim 98 (1986s) 314 (J. K. *Cameron*).

4566 *Pottier* B., La 'Lettre aux Romains' de K. BARTH et les quatre sens de l'Écriture ['allégorisation assez conceptuelle et philosophique ... pour que survienne le miracle de la foi ... allergie à toute lecture ne visant pas la conversion']: NRT 108 (1986) 823-844.

4567 ᴱStrohm Stefan, BRENZ Johannes, Explicatio Epistolae Pauli ad Romanos 1 [1538]: Brenz, Werke, Schriftauslegungen 2. Tü 1986, Mohr. xvii-498 p. 3-16-144921-5.

4568 **Wilckens** U., Der Brief an die Römer I-III, 1978-82 ➤ 64,5686 ... 1,5684: ᴿHenoch 8 (1986) 256-260 (A. *Moda*).

4569 **Wrightman** Paul, Paul's later letters [Rom ...] 1984 ➤ 65,5127*b*; 1,5685: ᴿDoctLife 35 (1985) 423 (B. *Nolan*); Vidyajyoti 49 (1985) 483s (J. *Volckaert*).

4570 **Zeller** Dieter, Der Brief an die Römer: Rg NT. Rg 1985, Pustet. 304 p. DM 52. - ᴿClaretianum 26 (1986) 402s (B. *Proietti*); TGegw 29 (1986) 256s (H. *Giesen*); TGl 76 (1986) 350s (J. *Ernst*).

G4.2 *Ad Romanos: Themata*, topics.

4571 **Gaertner** Dennis C., 'The righteousness of God' in light of the theo-centric message of Romans; diss. Southern Baptist Sem. 1986, ᴰ*Polhill* J. 227 p. 87-02212. - DissA 47 (1986s) 3787-A.

4572 *González* Carlos I., La salvación por Jesuscristo en la 'Epístola a los Romanos' de K. BARTH: EfMex 4,11 (1986) 40-68.

4573 **Hultgren** Arland J., Paul's Gospel and mission; the outlook from his letter to the Romans 1985 → 1,5692: ᴿCalvinT 21 (1986) 318 (R. R. *Recker*); TDig 33 (1986) 475 (W. C. *Heiser*).

4573* *Pathrapankal* Joseph, a) The letter to the Romans and its message for our times; - b) Polarity of law and freedom in Pauline religion; - c) Pauline theology; past approaches and modern trends; - d) Pauline theology of the Church; - e) Paul and his attitude toward the Gentiles: → 202*, Critical and creative 1986, 139-151 / 153-163 / 101-113 / 115-126 / 127-138.

4574 **Peureux** Marie-Christine, Saint AUGUSTIN, lecteur de l'Épître aux Romains et de l'Épître aux Galates; de la loi de l'Esprit à l'esprit de la loi: diss. Sorbonne, ᴰ*Mandouze*. P 1986.. - RTLv 18,552.

4575 *Stuhlmacher* Peter, Der Abfassungszweck des Römerbriefes: ZNW 77 (1986) 180-193.

G4.3 *Naturalis cognitio Dei* ... **Rom 1-4.**

4575* *Raschke* Carl A., On rereading Romans 1-6 or overcoming the hermeneutics of suspicion: ExAud 1 (1985) 147-155.

4576 **Lloyd-Jones** D. Martin, Romans, an exposition of chapter 1; the Gospel of God 1985 → 1,5699: ᴿRefTR 45 (1986) 54 (W. J. *Milne*: good).

4577 *Lafontaine* René, Pour une nouvelle évangélisation; l'emprise universelle de la justice de Dieu selon l'Épître aux Romains 1,18-2,29: NRT 108 (1986) 641-665.

4578 a) *Basevì* Claudio, Exégesis cristiana de los primeros siglos a Rom 1,18-32; el hombre, Dios y la sociedad; - b) *Estrada* Bernardo, Exégesis de San Juan CRISÓSTOMO a la 'astheneia' de san Pablo: → 366, Hermenéutica 1985/6, 611-623 / 655-666.

4579 **Hugghins** Kenneth W., An investigation of the Jewish theology of sexuality influencing the references to homosexuality in Romans 1:18-32; diss. SW Baptist Sem [→ 1,5705] 1986. 291 p. 87-05904. - DissA 47 (1986s) 4114-A.

4580 *Iammarone* Luigi, [Rom 1,18-25...] L'impensabilità dell'ateismo nei riflessi della Parola di Dio [conoscibilità di Dio AT, NT; rivelazione nella storia...]: Renovatio 21 (1986) 65-95.

4581 *Keck* Leander E., Romans 1:18-23: Interpretation 40 (1986) 402-6.

4582 *Snodgrass* Klyne R., Justification by grace - to the doers; an analysis of the place of Romans 2 in the theology of Paul: NTS 32 (1986) 72-93.

4582* *Yates* J. C., The judgment of the heathen; the interpretation of Article XVIII and Romans 2:2-16: Churchman 100 (L 1986) 220-230 [< ZIT].

4583 *Lafon* Guy, La production de la loi; la pensée de la loi en Romains 2,12-27: RechSR 74 (1986) 321-340; Eng. 341.

4584 **Kottackal** J., The salvific folly of God; a biblical-theological study on the paradox of God's folly and the world's wisdom [< diss. R Pont. Univ. Gregoriana, DMollat D.]. Kottayam 1984, Oriental Institute of Religious Studies 68. 232 p. rs. 50 [NTAbs 30,366].

4585 *Cantalamessa* Raniero, 'Si è manifestata la giustizia di Dio!': la giustificazione mediante la fede (Rm 3,21-31): ViConsacr 22 (1986) 1-11 [81-94, Rom 1,18-3,20].

4586 *Piguet* J.-Claude, [Rom 3,21s vs. Jacques] La foi et les œuvres, un dialogue interdisciplinaire; RTPhil 118 (1986) 291-6.

4587 *Thompson* Richard W., Paul's double critique of Jewish boasting; a study of Rom 3,27 in its context: Biblica 67 (1986) 520-531.

4588 **Guerra** Anthony J., Romans 3:29-30 and the apologetic tradition: diss. Harvard, DKoester H. CM 1986. 130 p. 86-19012:– DissA 47 (1986s) 1766-A; HarvTR 79 (1986) 471s.

G4.4 *Peccatum originale; redemptio cosmica:* **Rom 5-8.**

4589 **McCarthy** John P., Speaking of death; toward a fundamental theological hermeneutic of death based on Romans 5 and First Corinthians 15: diss. Chicago Divinity School, 1986. – RelStR 13,188.

4590 **Reid** Marty L., An analysis of AUGUSTINE's exegesis of Romans Five; hermeneutical investigation into the contributions of Augustine's exegesis for contemporary interpretation: diss. SW Baptist Sem. 1986. 224 p. 86-23465. – DissA 47 (1986s) 2623-A; RelStR 13,190 [➤ 1,5718: 'Reid Marvin L.'].

4591 *Helewa* Giovanni, 'Fedele è Dio'; una lettura di Rom 5,1-11: Teresianum 36 (1985) 25-57.

4592 **Ferraro** C. A., Rom. 5,12-19, esempi di esegesi patristica: diss. DSfameni Gasparro G. Messina 1985. [RivB 35,86].

4593 *Herman* Zvonimir I., La novità cristiana secondo Romani 5,20-7,6; alcune osservazioni esegetiche: Antonianum 61 (1986) 225-273; Eng. 273.

4595 **Álvarez Verdes** L., El imperativo cristiano en San Pablo ... Rom 6: 1980 ➤ 61,7288b ...1,5726: REstB 44 (1986) 243-7 (R. *Koch*).

4596 **Ko Young-Min,** Der Mensch, seine Not und sein Heil; Probleme der paulinischen Anthropologie im Zusammenhang der Heilsaussagen unter besonderer Beücksichtigung von Römer 6,1-8.30: Diss. DHaacker K. Wuppertal 1986. – RTLv 18,547.

4597 *Frid* Bo, Römer 6,4-5, *Eis tòn thánaton* und *tõ homoiõmati toû thanátou autoû* als Schlüssel zu Duktus und Gedankengang in Röm 6,1-11: BZ 30 (1986) 188-203.

4598 *Segal* Alan F., Romans 7 and Jewish dietary law: SR 15 (1986) 361-374.

4599 *a) Karlberg* Mark W., Israel's history personified; Romans 7:7-13 in relation to Paul's teaching on the 'old man': TrinJ 7,1 (1986) 65-74; – *b) Snyman* A. H., Stilistiese tegnieke in Rom 7:7-13: NduitseGT 27 (1986) 23-28 [< GerefTTs 86,191].

4600 *Moo* Douglas J., Israel and Paul in Romans 7,7-12: NTS 32 (1986) 122-135.

4601 *a) Varo* Francisco, Hermenéutica paulina del Antiguo Testamento en Rom 7,7-12; – *b) d'Ors* Alvaro, 'La letra mata, el espíritu vivifica' [2 Cor 3,6]: ➤ 366, Hermenéutica 1985/6, 439-451 / 497-505.

4602 *Roquefort* Daniel, Romains 7/7s selon Jacques LACAN [conf. psychanalyse Trait-Littoral 1985]: ÉTRel 61 (1986) 343-352.

4603 *Dunn* James D.G.,   Romans 7,14-25 in the theology of Paul: ➤ 28, ᶠERVIN H., Essays on apostolic themes 1985...

4603* *Philonenko* Marc, [Rom 7,14 < Is 50,1] Sur l'expression 'vendu au péché' dans 'L'Épître aux Romains': RHR 203 (1986) 41-52; Eng. 41.

4604 *Merrill* Timothy F., ACHARD of Saint Victor and the medieval exegetical tradition; Rom 7:22-25 in a sermon on the feast of the Resurrection: WestTJ 48 (1986) 47-62.

4605 *Thompson* Richard W.,   How is the Law fulfilled in us? An interpretation of Rom 8:4:   LvSt 11,1 (1986) 31-40.

4606 *Helewa* Giovanni, 'Fedele e Dio'; una lettura di Rom 8,14-39 (I): Teresianum 37 (1986) 3-36...

4607 **Menezes** Franklin,   Life in the spirit; a life of hope; a study of Rom 8,18-30: diss. Pont. Univ. Urbaniana, ᴰ*Virgulin* S. R 1986. xix-112p. (part); bibliog. p.91-106.

4608 *Moore* Brian,   Suffering; a study on Romans 8:18-30: ➤ 111, ᶠSTILL W., Pulpit & people 1986, 141-148.

4609 **Thomas** Mary Carolyn,   Romans 8:18-30 and its relation to the current Romans debate: diss. Fordham [➤ 1,5741], ᴰ*Dillon* R.J. NY 1985. 184p. 86-12862. – DissA 47 (1986s) 949s-A.

4610 *Obeng* E.A.,   *a)* The reconciliation of Rom. 8.26f. to New Testament writings and themes: ScotJT 39 (1986) 165-174; – *b)* The origins of the Spirit intercession motif in Romans 8.26: NTS 32 (1986) 621-632.

G4.6   *Israel et Lex,* **The Law and the Jews,** *Rom 9-11.*

4611 *Aageson* James W.,   Scripture and structure in the development of the argument in Romans 9-11: CBQ 48 (1986) 265-289.

4612 *Barclay* John M.G.,   Paul and the law; observations on some recent debates: Themelios 12,1 (1986s) 5-15.

4613 **Barth** Markus,   The people of God [Das Volk Gottes; Juden und Christen in der Botschaft des Paulus < Paulus, Apostat oder Apostel 1977, 45-134],ᵀ: JStNT Sup 5, 1983 ➤ 1,5747: ᴿTLZ 111 (1986) 192-4 (M. *Rese*: sharper on Israel).

4614 *a) Beker* J.C.,   The faithfulness of God and the priority of Israel in Paul's letter to the Romans; – *b) Epp* Eldon J.,   Jewish-Gentile continuity in Paul; Torah and/or Faith (Romans 9:1-5): ➤ 110, ᶠSTENDAHL K. = HarvTR 79 (1986) 10-16 / 80-90.

4615 **Cuenca Molina** Juan F.,   *a)* Luchas antipaulinas en los dos primeros siglos de la Iglesia; el problema de la Ley: diss. Comillas, ᴰ*Pastor* F. M 1984. – MiscCom 44 (1986) 568s. – *b)* El judeo-cristianismo y la ley; a propósito del nomismo de las 'homilias clementinas': Carthaginensia 2 (1986) 35-54.

4616 *Fabris* Renzo,   La 'gelosia' nella Lettera ai Romani (9-11); per un nuovo rapporto tra ebrei e cristiani: RasT 27 (1986) 15-33.

4617 **Gorday** Peter,   Principles of patristic exegesis, Rom 9-11 ... 1983 ➤ 65, 5256; 1,5749: ᴿJBL 105 (1986) 166-8 (J.F.T. *Kelly*: favors ORIGEN over the Reformation in linking Rom 9-11 not only with Gal but also with cosmic Col).

4618 *Hofius* Otfried,   Das Evangelium und Israel; Erwägungen zu Römer 9-11: ZTK 83 (1986) 297-324.

4619 **Hübner** Hans,   Gottes Ich und Israel ... Röm 9-11: FRLANT 136, 1984 ➤ 65,5258; 1,5751: ᴿBiblica 67 (1986) 414-6 (J.-N. *Aletti*); NRT 108

(1986) 117s (X. *Jacques*); StPatav 33 (1986) 696-8 (G. *Segalla*); ZkT 108 (1986) 194 (R. *Oberforcher*).

4620 **Hübner** Hans, Law in Paul's thought, ᵀ*Greig* J., 1984 ➤ 65,5257; 1,5752: ᴿJTS 37 (1986) 183-7 (J. M. G. *Barclay*); NBlackf 67 (1986) 197s (J. A. *Ziesler*); NRT 108 (1986) 124 (X. *Jacques*).

4621 *Lambrecht* Jan, Gesetzesverständnis bei Paulus: ➤ 382, ᴱ*Kertelge* K., Gesetz 1985/6, 88-127.

4621* **Logister** W. M. E., Heilsgeschiedenis en jodendom; de Israëltheologie van PANNENBERG in discussie 1984 ➤ 1,5755: ᴿCollatVl 16 (1986) 489s (J. De *Kesel*).

4622 **Lübking** H. M., Paulus und Israel im Römerbrief: EurHS. Bern 1986, Lang. 156 p. Fs 65 [Judaica 42,269].

4623 **Mussner** Franz, Tractate on the Jews; the significance of Judaism for the Christian faith 1984 ➤ 65,5262; 1,5757: ᴿInterpretation 40 (1986) 203 (C. *Bernas*); JRel 66 (1986) 102s (M. *Wyschogrod*); TLond 39 (1986) 53-55 (U. *Simon*); WWorld 6 (1986) 105s (H. H. *Ditmanson*).

4624 **Mussner** Franz, Traité sur les juifs 1981 ➤ 62,6488*b* ... 1,5758: ᴿRÉJ 145 (1986) 489-491 (M. *Hayoun*: profonde sincérité; whitewash de Paul pure perte; ce genre de traité paraît d'un autre âge; comment peut-on écrire un 'Traité sur les juifs'? – à vrai dire, *Pour* les juifs, non contre).

4625 *Mussner* Franz, Die Psalmen im Gedankengang des Paulus in Röm 9-11: ➤ 41, ᶠGROSS H., Freude 1986, 243-263.

4626 *a*) *Penna* Romano, L'évolution de l'attitude de Paul envers les Juifs; – *b*) *Rese* Martin, Die Rettung der Juden nach Römer 11; – *c*) *Ponthot* Joseph, L'expression cultuelle du ministère paulinien selon Rom 15,16: ➤ 398, ᴱ*Vanhoye* A., L'Apôtre Paul 1984/6, 390-421 / 422-430 / 254-262.

4626* *Penna* Romano, Evoluzione dell'atteggiamento di Paolo verso gli Ebrei: Lateranum 52 (1986) 1-37.

4627 **Räisänen** H., Paul and the Law: WUNT 29, 1983 ➤ 64,5532 ... 1,5762: ᴿBZ 30 (1986) 137-140 (J. *Roloff*); HeythJ 27 (1986) 77s (F. F. *Bruce*); NorTTs 87 (1986) 47-49 (H. *Moxnes*); Salmanticensis 33 (1986) 127-9 (R. *Trevijano*); SNTU-A 11 (1986) 245-9 (N. *Walter*).

4628 *Räisänen* Heikki, *a*) Legalism and salvation by the Law [< ᴱ*Pedersen* S., Die paulinische Literatur 1980, 63-83]; – *b*) Paul's theological difficulties with the Law [< Studia Biblica 3, Oxford 1978/80, 301-320]; – *c*) Sprachliches zum Spiel des Paulus mit *nómos* [< Mem. GYLLENBERG R. 1983, 131-154]: ➤ 209, Torah 1986, 25-54 / 3-24 / 119-147.

4629 **Sanders** E. P., Paul, the Law and the Jewish people 1985 ➤ 64,5537 ... 1,5764: 0-334-01318-X [also L 1985, SCM]: ᴿEstE 61 (1986) 239-242 (F. *Pastor-Ramos*); JRel 66 (1986) 101s (L. L. *Welborn*); ModT 2 (1985s) 364s (J. L. *Houlden*); NBlackf 67 (1986) 340s (A. R. C. *Leaney*); RThom 86 (1986) 158s (H. *Ponsot*).

4630 *a*) *Deidun* Tom, [E. P. SANDERS, an assessment of two recent works, 1.] 'Having his cake and eating it'; Paul on the Law; – *b*) *Riches* John, 2. Works and words of Jesus the Jew: HeythJ 27 (1986) 43-52 / 53-62.

4631 **Schmitt** Rainer, Gottesgerechtigkeit – Heilsgeschichte – Israel in der Theologie des Paulus: EurHS 23/240, 1984 ➤ 65,5265; Fs 56: ᴿCBQ 48 (1986) 346s (J. *Plevnik*); RThom 86 (1986) 325 (H. *Ponsot*; sérieux; avec KÄSEMANN, sur l'erreur de G. KLEIN contre H. WILCKENS); TLZ 111 (1986) 890-3 (H. *Hübner*).

4632 *Schreiner* Thomas R., The Church as the new Israel and the future of ethnic Israel in Paul: StudiaBT 13 (1983) 17-38.

4633 **Schrenk** Gottlob, Die Weissagung über Israel im Neuen Testament²

[¹1951]: Theologie und Dienst 39. Giessen 1984, Brunnen. 62 p. – ᴿTR 82 (1986) 286 (R. *Kampling*: antiquiert).

4634 **Siegert** Folker, Argumentation bei Paulus, gezeigt an Röm 9-11 [Diss. Tü]: WUNT 34, 1985 ➤ 1,5766: ᴿCBQ 48 (1986) 760 (J. P. *Heil*); Gregorianum 67 (1986) 804 (R. *Penna*); Salmanticensis 33 (1986) 376-8 (R. *Trevijano*); SNTU-A 11 (1986) 249-251 (H. *Giesen*).

4634* **Watson** Francis, Paul, Judaism and the Gentiles; a sociological approach: SNTS Mon 56. C 1986, Univ. xii-246 p. £22.50. 0-521-32573-0. – ᴿExpTim 98 (1986s) 280 (B. G. *Powley*: continues STENDAHL's delutheranizing of Paul).

4635 *Welker* M., Security of expectations; reformulating the theology of law and Gospel; JRel 66 (1986) 237-260.

4635* *a) Widmann* Martin, Der Israelit Paulus und sein antijüdischer Redaktor; – *b) Mussner* Franz, Warum ich mich als Christ für die Juden interessiere: ➤ 68*, ᶠMAYER R., Wie gut 1986, 150-9 / 191-5.

4636 *a) Wiefel* Wolfgang, Paulus und das Judentum; – *b) Baumbach* Günther, Das Neue Testament – ein judenfeindliches Buch?: ZeichZt 40 (1986) 142-7 / 138-141.

4637 *Winkel* Johannes, Argumentationsanalyse von Röm 9-11: LingBib 58 (1986) 65-79; Eng. 79 'syntagmatic approach'.

4638 *a) Cocchini* Francesca, Problematiche relative a Rm 9 nel Commento di ORIGENE alla Lettera ai Romani; – *b) Pani* Giancarlo, Il De spiritu et littera nella Römerbriefvorlesung di M. LUTERO: ➤ 365, AnStoEseg 3 (1985/6) 85-97 / 109-138.

4639 **Badenas** Robert, Christ the end [*télos* 'goal'] of the Law; Romans 10,4 in Pauline perspective: JStNT Sup 10, 1985 ➤ 1,5775: ᴿExpTim 377 (Margaret *Thrall*: convincing; but did Paul change his mind since writing Galatians?).

4640 *Riggans* Walter, Romans 11:17-21: ExpTim 98 (1986s) 205s.

4641 **Refoulé** Francois, Et ainsi tout Israël sera sauvé (Romains 11,25-32): LDiv 117, 1984 ➤ 65,5281; 1,5783: ᴿBLitEc 87 (1986) 148 (S. *Légasse*); ÉglT 17 (1986) 391-5 (L. *Laberge*); EstE 61 (1986) 99s (F. *Pastor-Ramos*); NRT 108 (1986) 118s (X. *Jacques*); RHPR 66 (1986) 233s (E. *Trocmé*: écrit à Jérusalem durant les trop brèves années où R. a dirigé l'École Biblique); RHR 203 (1986) 211s (J. *Doignon*); Salmanticensis 33 (1986) 378-380 (R. *Trevijano*); VSp 139 (1985) 136s (H. *Ponsot*).

4642 *Sänger* Dieter, Rettung der Heiden und Erwählung Israels; einige vorläufige Erwägungen zu Römer 11,25-27: KerDo 32 (1986) 99-119; Eng. 119.

G4.8 Rom 12 ...

4643 *Vouga* François, L'Épître aux Romains comme document ecclésiologique (Rm 12-15) [< conférence 1986 < séminaire 1985s]: ÉTRel 61 (1986) 485-495.

4644 *Gleixner* Hans, [Röm 12,1s] Die Relevanz des christlichen Glaubens für die Ethik: TGl 76 (1986) 307-323.

4645 *Tångberg* K. Arvid, Romerbrevet 12,1-2 og parenesebegrepet i nytestamentlig forskning: TsTKi 57 (1986) 81-91.

4646 *Chłąd* Stanisław, ❷ Charismata in Rom 12,6-8: RuBi 39 (1986) 24-32.

4647 **Pohle** Lutz, Die Christen und der Staat nach Römer 13, 1984 ➤ 65,5285; 1,5790: ᴿColcT 56,1 (1986) 177-183 (S. *Mędala*); NRT 108 (1986) 119s (X. *Jacques*); TS 47 (1986) 147s (J. M. *McDermott*).

4648 **Munro** W., [Rom 13,1-9] Authority in Paul and Peter: SNTS Mon 45, 1983 ➤ 64,5743 ... 1,5786: ᴿHeythJ 27 (1986) 190s (F. F. *Bruce*).

4649 **Bielecki** S., Il cristiano nella comunità civile e matrimoniale secondo Rom. 13,1-10 ed Ef. 5,21-33: diss. Pont. Univ. Gregoriana, ᴰ*Lyonnet* S. Roma 1984. [RivB 35,87].

4650 *a) Dunn* James D. G., Romans 13:1-7; a chapter for political quietism?; – *b) Steinmetz* David C., Calvin and Melanchthon on Romans 13:1-7: ExAud 2 (1986) 55-68 / 74-81; – *c) Bakkevig* Trond, De kristnes forhold il øvrigheten i lys av Rom 13,1-7: TsTKi 57 (1986) 257-169.

4651 **Jüngel** Eberhard, [Rom 13:1-7, 'let everyone be subject to the governing authorities'], *al.*, Evangelische Christen in unserer Demokratie; Beiträge aus der Synode der evangelischen Kirche in Deutschland: Siebenstern 580. Gü 1986, Mohn. 79 p. DM 4.80. 3-579-00580-4 [NTAbs 31,113].

4651* *Potestà* Gian Luca, Rm 13,1 in OCKHAM; origine e legittimità del potere civile: CrNSt 7 (1986) 465-482.

4652 *a) Mosetto* Francesco, A chi le tasse, le tasse (Rm 13,7); – *b) Zedde* Italo G., Il denaro nell'insegnamento di Gesù; – *c) Boggio* Giovanni, Il denaro, una trappola per gli stolti [AT]; – *d) Bizzeti* Paolo, Elogio delle ricchezze: ParVi 31 (1986) 275-282 / 267-274 / 258-266 / 250-7.

4653 *Richardson* Peter, From apostles to virgins; Romans 16 and the roles of women in the early Church: TorJT 2 (1986) 232-261.

4654 *Gielen* Marlis, [Röm 16,3.5 ...] Zur Interpretation der paulinischen Formel *hē kat'oîkon ekklēsía*: ZNW 77 (1986) 109-125.

4655 *Schulz* Ray R., Romans 16:7, Junia or Junias? [or Julia P46: the Church Fathers never doubted that this was a woman among the 'apostles'; their problem was what to do about it]: ExpTim 98 (1986s) 108-110.

G5   **Epistulae ad Corinthios** *(I vel I-II)*.

4656 **Bartolomé** Juan José, 'i Ay de mí, si no evangelizara!'; una lectura de la primera carta a los Corintios para apóstoles de Cristo: Espiritualidad 8. M 1986, CCS. 182 p. 84-7043-442-X.

4657 **Ellingworth** Paul, *Hatton* Howard, A translator's handbook on Paul's First Letter to the Corinthians 1985 ➤ 1,5800: ᴿExpTim 98 (1986s) 26 (O. E. *Evans*).

4658 *Ellis* E. Earle, Traditions in 1 Corinthians: NTS 32 (1986) 481-502.

4659 *a) Frigerio* Tea, Os conflitos na Igreja de Corinto; 1ᵃ aos Corintios; – *b) Mosconi* Luis, Paulo Apóstolo; fidelidade a Jesus Cristo e ao Reino no meio dos conflitos: Estudos Bíblicos 12 [REB 46,4] (1986) 31-37 / 24-30.

4660 **Klauck** Hans-Josef, I. Korintherbrief: NEchter 7, 1984 ➤ 65,5303; 1,5804: ᴿTLZ 111 (1986) 111s sic (G. *Voigt*).

4661 **Lang** Friedrich, Die Briefe an die Korinther, übersetzt und erklärt: NTD 7¹⁶ʳᵉᵛ. Gö 1986, Vandenhoeck & R. iv-382 p. DM 48 [NRT 109,439, X. *Jacques*].

4662 **Murphy-O'Connor** Jerome, St. Paul's Corinth 1983 ➤ 64,5763 ... 1,5808: ᴿCurrTM 13 (1986) 121s (R. H. *Smith*).

4663 **Murphy-O'Connor** Jérôme, Corinthe au temps de saint Paul d'après les textes et l'archéologie [1983], ᵀ*Prignaud* Jean: BJérÉt. P 1986, Cerf. 297 p.; 11 fig. F 119. 2-204-02421-X. – ᴿBrotéria 123 (1986) 477 (I. *Ribeiro da Silva*); EsprV 96 (1986) 547-9 (É. *Cothenet*); NRT 108 (1986) 754s (X. *Jacques*).

4664 *Murphy-O'Connor* Jerome, Interpolations in 1 Corinthians: CBQ 48 (1986) 81-94.

4665 *Neyrey* Jerome H., Body [i.e. group; *Douglas* M.; and individual-body comparisons] language in 1 Corinthians; the use of anthropological models for understanding Paul and his opponents: Semeia 35 (1986) 129-164; bibliog. 165-170.

4666 **Pesch** Rudolf, Paulus ringt um die Lebensform der Kirche; vier Briefe an die Gemeinde Gottes in Korinth; Paulus – neu gesehen: Herderbücherei 1291. FrB 1986, Herder. 254 p. DM 12,90 [TR 83,25-27, H.-J. *Klauck*]. 3-451-08291-8.

4667 **Prior** David, The message in 1 Corinthians; life in the local church: The Bible Speaks Today 1985 → 1,5810: ᴿBS 143 (1986) 376s (D. L. *Bock*).

Salmon J. B., Wealthy Corinth 1984 → b335.

4669 **Schick** Eduard, Allen Alles werden; besinnliche Gedanken zum ersten Brief des Apostels Paulus an die Korinther. Stu 1984, KBW. 319 p. 3-460-32291-8.

4670 **Senft** C., La première épître de Saint Paul aux Corinthiens 1979 → 60,7921 ... 65,5312: ᴿHenoch 8 (1986) 107 (E. *Jucci*).

4671 *Walbank* Mary H., The nature of early Roman Corinth [not a refounding of Greek Corinth]: → 548, AJA 90 (1986) 220.

4672 *Xavier* Aloysius, Fuerza en la flaqueza; pastoral de Pablo en Corinto [< IndTSt (1983) 286-295], ᵀᴱ *Boix* Aureli: SelT 25 (1986) 155-9 [non p. 75; cf. p. 83].

4673 *Ziesler* John A., Which is the best commentary? III. 1 Corinthians [*Murphy-O'Connor* 1979 for the general reader; C. K. *Barrett* 1985 by far the best on the English text; on the Greek text *Conzelmann* 1969, in Hermeneia 1975]: ExpTim 97 (1985s) 263-7.

G5.3 1 Cor 1-7: *sapientia crucis ... abusus matrimonii ...*

4674 *Padgett* Alan, Feminism in First Corinthians [1-4], a dialogue with Elisabeth SCHÜSSLER FIORENZA: EvQ 58 (1986) 121-132: she has proved the existence and importance of women leaders in the early Church.

4675 *Boring* M. Eugene, [1 Cor 1,18; Rom 5,18 ...] The language of universal salvation in Paul: JBL 105 (1986) 269-292.

4676 **Davis** James A., Wisdom and Spirit ... 1 Cor 1:18-3:20: 1984 → 1,5822: ᴿAustralBR 34 (1986) 75s (J. *Painter*); Themelios 12 (1986s) 29 (A. C. *Thiselton*).

4677 **Dennison** William D., [1 Cor 1-3] Paul's two-age construction and apologetics. Lanham MD 1986, UPA. 129 p. $18.50; pa. $8.75. 0-8191-5011-8; 2-6. – ᴿExpTim 98 (1986s) 118s (Margaret E. *Thrall*).

4678 *Gooch* P. W., [1 Cor 2,9] Margaret, Bottom, Paul and the inexpressible: WWorld 6 (1986) 313-325 [< NTAbs 31,48].

4679 **Rafiński** Grzegorz, ❷ 'Duch świata – Duch z Boga' ... 'Esprit du monde – Esprit de Dieu'; le problème du contexte historico-religieux de 1 Co 2,12: diss. ᴰ*Mędala* S. Wsz 1985. – STWsz 24,1 (1986) 232s [ᴰ*Łach* J.]; RTLv 18,549.

4680 *Chłąd* Stanisław, ❷ *Theatron* (1 Kor 4,9): AnCracov 18 (1986) 185-195; 196, Theatron, la situation du chrétien dans le monde.

4681 *a) Schrage* Wolfgang, Das apostolische Amt des Paulus nach 1 Kor 4,14-17; – *b) O'Neill* J. C., 1 Corinthians 7,14 and infant baptism; – *c) Delobel* Joel, 1 Cor 11,2-16; towards a coherent interpretation; – *d) Wuellner* Wilhelm, Paul as pastor; the function of rhetorical questions in First Corinthians: → 398, ᴱ*Vanhoye* A., L'Apôtre Paul 1984/6, 103-119 / 357-361 / 369-389 / 49-77.

4681* *Derrett* J. D. M., 'Handing [not Handling as in Contents] over to Satan'; an explanation of 1 Cor. 5:1-7 [< RIDA 3/26 (1979) 11-30]: ➤ 150, Studies NT 4 (1986) 167-186.

4682 *Cole* G. A., 1 Cor 5:4 '... with my spirit': ExpTim 98 (1986s) 205.

4683 *Colella* Pasquale, Cristo nostra Pasqua? 1 Cor 5,7: BbbOr 28 (1986) 197-217.

4684 **Mitchell** Alan C., 1 Corinthians 6:1-11; group boundaries and the courts of Corinth: diss. Yale. NHv 1986. 238 p. 86-28738. – DissA 47 (1986s) 3078-A; RelStR 13,190.

4684* *a) Fuller* Reginald H., 1 Cor. 6:1-11; an exegetical paper; – *b) Taylor* Robert D., Toward a biblical theology of litigation; a law professor looks at 1 Cor. 6:1-11: ExAud 2 (1986) 96-104 / 105-116.

4685 *Shillington* G., People of God in the courts of the world; a study of 1 Corinthians 6,1-11: Direction 15,1 (Fresno 1986) 40-50 [< NTAbs 31,48].

4686 *a) Petersen* William L., Can *arsenokoîtai* be translated by 'homosexuals'? (1 Cor. 6.9; 1 Tim. 1.10): VigChr [38 (1984) 125-153, *Wright* D. against *Boswell* J.] 40 (1986) 187-191; – *b) Osten-Sacken* Peter von der, [1 Cor 6,9 ...] Paulinisches Evangelium und Homosexualität: BTZ 3 (1986) 28-49.

4687 *Claudel* G., Une lecture de 1 Co 6,12 – 7,40 [< TrierTZ 1985]: SémiotB 41 (1986) 3-19.

4688 *Byrne* Brendan, [1 Cor 6,12-20; 15,32-34] Eschatologies of resurrection and destruction; the ethical significance of Paul's dispute with the Corinthians: DowR 104 (1986) 288-298.

4689 *Radcliffe* Timothy, 'Glorify God in your bodies'; 1 Corinthians 6,12-20 as a sexual ethic: NBlackf 67 (1986) 306-314 [387s objection of G. *Loughlin*].

4690 **Baumert** Norbert, Ehe und Ehelosigkeit im Herrn ... 1 Kor 7: 1984 ➤ 65, 5327; **1**,5830: ᴿColcT 56,1 (1986) 171-3 (S. *Mędala*) & 56,4 (1986) 167-173 (D. *Tomczyk,* independenter); TAth 57 (1986) 692s (K. N. *Papadopoulos*).

4691 *a) Pesce* M., Stare in Cristo, ma continuare ad essere una carne sola; la coppia coniugale in 1 Cor 7: – *b) Barbaglio* G., L'allegoria sponsale in 2 Cor 11,2: ParSpV 13 (1986) 119-134 / 135-152.

4692 *Patronos* George P., ❻ [1 Cor 7,1-7] Marriage and celibacy according to the Apostle Paul: TAth 57 (1986) 179-243.

4693 *Zalęski* Jan, ❷ Nauka św. Pawła na temat małżeństwa [matrimonii] w 1 Kor 7,12b-13: RuBi 39 (1986) 108-111.

4694 **Bartchy** S. Scott, First-century slavery and the interpretation of 1 Corinthians 7:21: SBL diss. 11 [Harvard 1973] Atlanta 1985 = 1973, Scholars. ix-199 p.; bibliog. p. 185-199. 0-88414-022-9.

4695 *Chmiel* Jerzy, Zur Interpretation des paulinischen *hōs mē* in 1 Kor 7,29-31: AnCracov 18 (1986) 197-204.

4696 *Ramos-Lissón* Domingo, Exégesis de 1 Cor 7,32-34 en el 'De habitu virginum' de San CIPRIANO: ➤ 366, Hermenéutica 1985/6, 645-654.

4696* *Force* Paul, Une péricope 'sauvage' de Saint Paul (1 Cor. VII,34) chez les Encratites égyptiens du IV siècle?: ➤ 18, Mem. DAUMAS F. I (1986) 253-260.

4697 *Bauer* Johannes B., Was las Tertullian 1 Kor 7,39?: ZNW 77 (1986) 284-7.

G5.4 *Idolothyta ... Eucharistia:* **1 Cor 8-11.**

4698 *Kippenberg* Hans G., [1 Cor 8,10; Mcb ...] Ketmān; zur Maxime der Verstellung in der antiken und frühislamischen Religionsgeschichte: ➤ 59, ᶠLEBRAM J., Tradition 1986, 172-183.

4699 **Willis** Wendell L.,   Idol meat in Corinth ... 1 Cor 8.10 [diss. Southern Methodist 1981, ^D*Furnish* V.]: SBL Diss. 68, 1985 → 1,5833: ^RAustralBR 34 (1986) 76s (B. *Byrne*); Biblica 67 (1986) 417-9 (D. *Hamm*: good except on *koinōnia* and *syneidēsis*); CBQ 48 (1986) 575s (R. J. *Karris*: fine); Salmanticensis 33 (1986) 374-6 (R. *Trevijano*); TLZ 111 (1986) 432s (H. J. *Klauck*).

4700 *Carson* D.,   Pauline inconsistency; reflections on 1 Corinthians 9.19-23 and Galatians 2.11-14: Churchman 100,1 (1986) 6-45 [< NTAbs 31.49].

4701 *Borgen* Peder,   Nattverdtradisjonen i 1. Kor. 10 og 11 som evangelietradisjon: SvEx 51s (1986s) 32-39.

4702 *Haykin* Michael A. G.,   'In the cloud and in the sea'; BASIL of Caesarea and the exegesis of 1 Cor 10:2: VigChr 40 (1986) 135-144.

4703 *Mazza* Enrico,   L'Eucaristia di 1 Corinzi 10,16-17 in rapporto a Didachè 9,10: EphLtg 100 (1986) 193-223.

4704 *Lowery* David K.,   The head covering and the Lord's Supper in 1 Corinthians 11: 2-34: Biblïotheca Sacra 143 (1986) 155-163 [< ^E*Walvoord* J., Bible Knowledge Commentary 1985].

4705 *Padgett* A.,   'Authority over her head'; toward a feminist reading of St. Paul: Daughters of Sarah 12 (Ch 1986) 5-9 [NTAbs 30,305].

4705* *Klauck* Hans-Josef,   Eucharistie und Kirchengemeinschaft bei Paulus: WissWeis 49,1 (1986) 1-14.

4706 *Lavoie* Rosaire,   Le repas du Seigneur dans 1 Co 11,17-34; 'Vous proclamez la mort du Seigneur jusqu'à ce qu'il vienne' (1 Co 11,26): PrêtreP 89 (1986) 73-82.

4707 *Magne* J., [1 Cor 11,24s; Mk 14,25] Les paroles sur la coupe: CahRenan 32,137 (1984) 241-8 [NTAbs 30,305].

4708 *Hyldahl* Niels,   Metà tò deipnêsai, 1 Kor 11,25 (og Luk 22,20): SvEx 51s (1986s) 100-107.

G5.5   1 Cor 12 ... Glossolalia, charismata.

4709 **Aune** David E.,   Prophecy in early Christianity and the ancient Mediterranean world 1983 → 64,5808 ... 1,5845: ^RCrNSt 7 (1986) 382-9 (G. *Dautzenberg*); ÉTRel 61 (1986) 435 (M. *Carrez*); JTS 37 (1986) 542-8 (W. J. *Houston*); SWJT 29 (1986s) 55s (S. S. *Schatzmann*).

4710 *Battley* D. H.,   Charismatic renewal; a view from inside: EcuR 38 (1986) 48-56.

4711 **Baumert** Norbert,   Gaben des Geistes Jesu; Das charismatische in der Kirche. Graz 1986, Styria. 207 p. DM 24,80. – ^RGeistL 59 (1986) 238s (J. *Sudbrack*).

4712 **Bommel** J. P.,   De charismatische Opwekking als verdere Reformatie. Kampen 1985, Kok. 102 p. *f* 14,90 pa. [KerkT 37,82].

4713 **Brandt-Bessire** Daniel,   Aux sources de la spiritualité pentecôtiste. Genève 1986, Labor & F. 222 p. 2-8309-0048-0. – ^RÉTRel 61 (1986) 615s (A. *Gounelle*).

4714 *Damşa* Teodor V.,   Ist die Glossolalie oder das Zungenreden eine Bedingung für die Erlösung?: MitropBanatul 35 (1985) 23-34 [rum.; TLZ 112,782].

4714* **Fletcher** William G.,   Soviet charismatics; the Pentecostals in the USSR: AmerUnivSt 7/i. NY 1985, Lang. 200 p. Fs 57,90 [NedTTs 41,250, J. *Hebly*].

4715 *Forbes* Christopher,   Early Christian inspired speech and Hellenistic popular religion: NT 28 (1986) 257-270.

4716 **Griffiths** Michael, Serving grace [exalting 'special charismatic gifts' is wrong and divisive; *all* churches should claim *all* the Spirit's gifts]. L 1986, MARC-Europe. 127 p. £1.75. 0-947697-18-7 [ExpTim 98,255].

4717 **Grudem** Wayne A., The gift of prophecy in I Corinthians [diss. Cambridge 1978, ᴰ*Moule* C.] 1982 ➤ 63,5982... 1,5857: ᴿEvQ 58 (1986) 368-370 (M. *Turner*); Themelios 12 (1986s) 28 (J. J. *Stamoolis*).

4718 *Hoerschelmann* Werner, Vertrauen in die Kraft des Geistes; das Modell der charismatischen Gemeinde-Erneuerung; LuthMon 25 (1986) 561-3.

4718* **Karakostanoglou** Jean, Le phénomène de l'extase dans le monde grec des trois premiers siècles de notre ère: diss. Inst. Catholique, ᴰ*Wolinski* J. P 1986. ix-350 p. – RICathP 18 (1986) 71s.

4719 **Lewis** I. M., Religion in context; cults and charisms [witchcraft and cannibalism too are a manifestation of charism...]. Cambridge 1986, UP. x-139 p. $37.50; pa. $10 [TDig 34,81].

4720 **Malony** H. Newton, *Lovekin* A. Adams, Glossolalia; behavioral science perspectives on speaking in tongues. NY 1985, Oxford-UP. x-292 p. $30. – ᴿJPsy&T 14 (1986) 81 (W. P. *Wilson*).

4721 *Marcheselli Casale* Cesare, Glossolalia; estasi o profezia? [*Scippa* V. 1982]: Teresianum 37 (1986) 205-210.

4722 ᴱ**Martin** D., *Mullen* D., Strange gifts? a guide to charismatic renewal 1985 ➤ 1,378: ᴿTS 47 (1986) 178s (T. *Weinandy*: only Mullen a bit negative).

4723 *a) Merkel* Helmut, Charisma; – *b) O'Donnell* Christopher, Charismatische Bewegung, ᵀ*Mühlenberg* M.: ➤ 587, EvKL 1 (1986) 641s / 646-8.

4724 **Mills** Watson E., A theological/exegetical approach to glossolalia 1985 ➤ 1,5871: ᴿRExp 83 (1986) 298 (B. J. *Leonard*).

ᴱ**Mills** Watson E., Speaking in tongues; a guide to research on glossolalia 1986 ➤ 683.

4725 **Scanlan** Michael [T.O.R.], *Cirner* Randal J., Deliverance from evil spirits, a weapon for spiritual warfare [in the experience of charismatic communities]. – AA 1980, Servant. – ᵀ*Lowrie* Doreen, Liberazione dalle potenze delle tenebre, un'arma nel combattimento spirituale. R 1984, REM. 184 p. – ᴿBbbOr 28 (1986) 175-8 [dalla pref. di *Lippi* Adolfo C.P.].

4726 *Schnackenburg* Rudolf, Charisma und Amt in der Urkirche und heute: MüTZ 37 (1986) 233-248.

4727 *Shorter* Aylward, Christian healing and traditional medicine in Africa: Kerygma 20,46 (1986) 51-58 [deutsch TKontext 8/1,302].

4728 **Sullivan** Francis A., *a)* Die charismatische Erneuerung; Wirken und Ziele 1984 ➤ 1,5883; ᵀ*Keil* Charlotte: ᴿTPhil 61 (1986) 305s (G. L. *Müller*). – *b)* Die charismatische Erneuerung²; die biblischen und theologischen Grundlagen, ᵀ*Wörner* W., *Baumert* N.; Vorw. *Suenens* L. Graz 1986, Styria. 199 p. DM 24,80. – ᴿGeistL 59 (1986) 237s (J. *Sudbrack*).

4729 *Sullivan* Francis A., Pfingstbewegung und charismatische Gemeindeerneuerung; Geschichte — Spiritualität — Stellungnahme [< DictSp 12,1 (1984) 1036-1052]: GeistL 59 (1986) 165-184.

4730 *Tomczyk* Dominik, *a)* ✪ Die charismatische Bewegung und die Kirche, Aufgaben und Ziele; – *b)* ✪ H. MÜHLENs Theologie der charismatischen Erneuerungsbewegung: ColcT 56,4 (1986) 61-66; deutsch 67 / 56,3 (1986) 19-33; deutsch 33.

4731 *Valencourt* J. Roy, Paul's perspective on glossolalia: TCNN Bulletin 17 (N. Nigeria 1986) 3-30.

4732 *Vande Kappelle* Robert P., Prophets and mantics: ➤ 395, ᴱ*Smith* R., Pagan and Christian anxiety 1979/84, 87-111.

4733 **Vanhoye** Albert, I carismi nel Nuovo Testamento. R 1986, Pont. Ist. Biblico. 131 p.

4734 *Zevi* Maurice, The Catholic charismatic renewal: AfER 28 (1986) 293-305.

4735 **Martin** Ralph P., The spirit and the congregation ... 1 Cor 12-15, 1984 ➤ 65,5375; 1,5870: [R]RExp 83 (1986) 115 (R. L. *Omanson*: unusually relates 11-14 to 15).

4736 **Bukas-Yakabuul** Badi-Bamwimin, Pauline use of the metaphor of the body in 1 Corinthians 12-14; a paradigm study in a New Testament use of metaphor: diss. Emory, [D]*Saliers* D. Atlanta 1986. – 292 p. 86-26512. – DissA 47 (1986s) 3024s-A. – RelStR 13, 190.

4737 *Ormseth* Dennis, Showing the Body [of Christ]; reflections on 1 Corinthians 12-13 for Epiphany: WWorld 6 (1986) 97-104.

4738 *Snyman* A. H., Remarks on the stylistic parallelism in 1 Cor 13: ➤ 72, [F]METZGER B., South Africa 1985/6, 202-213.

4739 **Klein** William W., Noisy gong or acoustic vase? a note on 1 Corinthians 13,1: NTS 32 (1986) 286-9.

4740 **Richardson** William E., Liturgical order and glossolalia; 1 Corinthians 14:26c and its implications: diss. Andrews Univ., [D]*Blazen* I. Berrien Springs MI 1983. – AndrUnS 24 (1986) 47s.

4741 *Richardson* William, Liturgical order and glossolalia in 1 Corinthians 14. 26c-33a: NTS 32 (1986) 144-153.

4742 **Aworinde** Sunday O., First Corinthians 14:33b-36 in its literary and socio-historical contexts: diss. Southern Baptist Sem., [D]*Polhill* J. 246 p. 86-09082. – DissA 47 (1986s) 561-A.

4743 *Barton* Stephen C., [1 Cor 14,33-36; 11,17-34] Paul's sense of place; an anthropological approach to community formation in Corinth: NTS 32 (1986) 235-246.

4744 *Blampied* Ann B., Paul and silence for 'The Women' in 1 Corinthians 14:34-35; StudiaBT 13 (1983) 143-165.

4745 *Kroeger* C. & R., [1 Cor 14,34s] Strange tongues or plain talk?: Daughters of Sarah 12,4 (Ch 1986) 10-13 [<NTAbs 31,50].

G5.6 **Resurrectio;** *1 Cor 15* ...

4746 *a) Nickelsburg* George W. E., An *éktrōma*, though appointed from the womb; Paul's apostolic self-description in 1 Corinthians 15 and Galatians 1; – *b) Petersen* Norman R., Pauline baptism and 'secondary burial': ➤ 110, [F]STENDAHL K. = HarvTR 79 (1986) 198-205 / 217-226.

4747 *Pérez Gordo* Ángel, ¿Es 1 Cor 15 una homilía?; Burgense 27 (1986) 9-97; foldout diagram.

4748 **Biser** E., Paolo, l'ultimo testimone della Risurrezione [1981] 1984 ➤ 1,5899: [R]Asprenas 33 (1986) 435-8 (C. *Marcheselli-Casale*).

4749 [E]**De Lorenzi** L., Résurrection du Christ et des chrétiens (1 Co 15) 1983/5 ➤ 1,466: [R]BbbOr 28 (1986) 32 (M. Franca *Mottinelli*).

4750 *Meyer* Ben F. [1 Thess 4; 1 Cor 15; 2 Cor 5; Phlp 1] Did Paul's view of the resurrection of the dead undergo development?: TS 47 (1986) 363-387.

4751 **Sellin** Gerhard, Der Streit um die Auferstehung der Toten; eine religionsgeschichtliche und exegetische Untersuchung von 1 Korinther 15 [Diss. Münster]: FRLANT 138. Gö 1986, Vandenhoeck & R. 337 p. bibliog. p. 298-320. DM 86 [TR 82,251]. 3-525-53815-4. – [R]ExpTim 98 (1986s) 304s (E. *Best*).

4752 *Pastor-Ramos* Federico, 'Murió por nuestros pecados' (1 Cor 15,3; Gal 1,4); observaciones sobre el origen de esta fórmula en Is 53: EstE 61 (1986) 386-393.

4753 *Jones* Peter R., *a*) 1 Corinthians 15:8; Paul the last apostle: TyndB 36 (1985) 3-34; – *b*) Paul le dernier apôtre, 1 Corinthiens 15,8 [< TyndB 36 (1985)], ᵀ*Nzinga* Dika, *al.*: Hokhma 11,33 (1986) 36-62.

4754 *Trevijano Etcheverria* R., Los que dicen que no hay resurrección (1 Cor 15,12): Salmanticensis 23 (1986) 275-302; Eng. 302.

4755 *Zincone* Sergio, Problematiche relative alla resurrezione nell'esegesi antiochena di 1 Cor 15,20ss: → 365, AnStoEseg 3 (1985/6) 99-107.

4756 *Peters* Ted, [1 Cor 15:24s in Inclusive Language Lectionary 'Christ delivers all sovereignty to God, the Father (and Mother)'] On adding divine mothers to the Bible: CurrTM 13 (1986) 276-284 [the original revelatory symbols ought to remain accessible to us].

4757 *Mees* Michael, [1 Cor 15,38-50; 2 Cor 5,1-10...] Paulus, ORIGENES und METHODIUS über die Auferstehung der Toten: → 476*, L'origenismo 1985 = AugR 26 (1986) 103-113.

G5.9 Secunda epistola ad Corinthios.

4757* *Adloff* Kristlieb, Die missionarische Existenz des Apostels Paulus nach dem Zweiten Korintherbrief: BTZ 3 (1986) 11-27.

4758 **Bultmann** Rudolf, The second letter to the Corinthians, ᵀ*Dinkler* E. 1985 → 1,5913: ᴿCurrTM 13 (1986) 248s (W. *Wuellner*).

4759 **Carrez** Maurice, La deuxième épître de saint Paul aux Corinthiens: CommNT ² 8. Genève 1986, Labor et Fides. 260 p.

4760 **Carrez** M., La segunda carta a los corintios [1985 → 1,5914]: CuadBíb 51. Estella 1986, VDivino. 62 p. – ᴿBibFe 12 (1986) 356 (M. *Saenz Galache*).

4761 *Fóris* Éva Kalós, The understanding of the apostle's office in the Second Epistle to the Corinthians: Theologiai Szemle 29 (1986) 93-95.

4762 **Furnish** Victor P., II Corinthians: AnchorB 32A, 1984 → 65,5416; 1,5915: ᴿBiblica 67 (1986) 419-421 (R. *Penna*: fra i maggiori del secolo); Bible Bhashyam 11 (1985) 191s (M. *Vellanickal*); BZ 30 (1986) 142-4 (H.-J. *Klauck*); CBQ 48 (1986) 559s (V. P. *Branick*: one of the best of the series); Claretianum 26 (1986) 375-7 (B. *Proietti*); ÉTRel 61 (1986) 423s (F. *Vouga*); Interpretation 40 (1986) 411-3 (E. *Best*); JAAR 54 (1986) 374s (J. P. *Sampley*); JSS 31 (1986) 89s (C. K. *Barrett*); JTS 37 (1986) 189s (Margaret E. *Thrall*); NRT 108 (1986) 753s (X. *Jacques*).

4763 **Georgi** Dieter, The opponents of Paul in Second Corinthians [diss. Heid 1958: 1964],ᵀ. Ph 1986, Fortress. xv-463 p. $33 [RelStR 13,168, M. L. S-*oards*]. 0-8006-0729-5.

4763* **Klauck** Hans-Josef, 2. Korintherbrief: NEchter NT. Wü 1986, Echter. 107 p.

4764 *a*) *Lambrecht* J., The nekrōsis of Jesus; ministry and suffering in 2 Cor 4,7-15; – *b*) *Carrez* Maurice, Réalité christologique et référence apostolique de l'apôtre Paul en présence d'une église divisée; – *c*) *Dautzenberg* G., Motive der Selbstdarstellung des Paulus in 2 Kor 2,14-7,4: → 398, ᴱ*Vanhoye* A., L'Apôtre Paul 1984/6, 120-143 / 163-183 / 150-162.

4765 **Maillot** A. (*Olombel* A.), Saint Paul, Deuxième épître aux Corinthiens; l'Église sous la croix. Strasbourg 1985, Oberlin. 192 p. F 78. – ᴿMondeB 43 (1986) 55 (P. I. *Fransen*).

4766 **Madros** Peter, The pride and humility of Saint Paul in his Second Letter
to the Corinthians [Susceptibilité et humilité 1981 ➤ 62,6609; 64,5880],
T*Deuel* M. J 1986, Franciscian. 63 p. $5. [NTAbs 30,362].
4767 **Martin** R. P., 2 Corinthians: Word Comm. 40. Waco 1986, Word.
lxiii-527 p. 0-8499-0239-8 [NTAbs 30,362].
4768 *Martin* Ralph P., The setting of 2 Corinthians : TyndB 37 (1986)
3-19.
4769 **Wickham** P., Segunda epístola a los Corintios. Viladecavalls (Barc)
1984, Portavoz Evangélico. 344 p.; mapas. – ᴿStudium 26 (M 1986) 145s
(L. *López de las Heras*).

4769* *a) Hahn* Ferdinand, Ist das textkritische Problem von 2 Kor 1,7
lösbar?; – *b) Lührmann* Dieter, Freundschaft trotz Spannungen; zu
Gattung und Aufbau des Ersten Korintherbriefes; – *c) Wengst* Klaus,
'... einander durch Demut für vorzüglicher zu halten'; zum Begriff 'Demut'
bei Paulus und in paulinischer Tradition: ➤ 39, ᶠGreeven H., Text/Ethik
1986, 158-165 / 298-314 / 428-439.
4770 *Wenham* David, 2 Corinthians 1:17,18; echo of a Dominical logion; NT
28 (1986) 271-9.
4771 *Young* Frances, Note on 2 Corinthians 1: 17b: JTS 37 (1986) 404-415.
4771* **Refshauge** Ebba, [2 Cor 2,4] Tårebrevet 1984 ➤ 65,5419: ᴿJBL 105
(1986) 731s (D. E. *Aune*); JTS 37 (1986) 190s (N. *Hyldahl*).
4772 **Cherian** Kunnel K., Paul's understanding of *diakonia* as proclamation
according to 2 Corinthians 2:14-7:4: diss. Lutheran School of Theology,
ᴰ*Krentz* E. Ch 1986. 230 p. 86-21951. – DissA 47 (1986s) 2191-A.
4773 *Murphy-O'Connor* Jerome, *Pneumatikoi* and Judaizers in 2 Cor 2:14-4:6:
AustralBR 34 (1986) 42-58.
4774 **Renju Masumbulio** Peter, Semantic analysis of 2 Corinthians 2:14-3:18
[diss. ᴰ*Reiling* J., Utrecht 1986. – TsTNijm 26 (1986) 290; RTLv 18,549].
Haarlem 1986, Ned. Bijbelgenootschap. 122 p.
4775 **Hafemann** Scott J., Suffering and the Spirit; an exegetical study of II
Cor. 2:14-3:3 within the context of the Corinthian correspondence: WUNT
2/19. Tü 1986, Mohr. viii-258 p. DM 79. 3-16-144973-8. – ᴿExpTim 98
(1986s) 183s (Margaret E. *Thrall*).
4777 *a) Dumbrell* William J., Paul's use of Exodus 34 in 2 Corinthians 3; – *b)*
Morris Leon L., The Apostle Paul and his God: ➤ 54, ᶠKnox D., God
rich 1986, 179-194 / 165-178.
4778 *Stegemann* Ekkehard, Der Neue Bund im Alten; zum Schriftverständnis
des Paulus in II Kor. 3.: TZBas 42 (1986) 97-114.
4780 **Belleville** Linda L., Paul's polemic use of the Moses-Doxa tradition in 2
Corinthians 3:12-18: diss. St.Michael, ᴰ*Longenecker* R. Toronto 1986.
496 p. [microfiche National Library of Canada]. – RTLv 18,545.
4781 **Giglioli** Alberto mons., Il Signore è lo Spirito; congettura al testo di 2
Cor 3:17: RivAscM 11 (1986) 235-247.
4782 **Grech** Prosper, 2 Cor 3,17 e la dottrina paolina della conversione allo
Spirito Santo [< CBQ 17 (1955) 420-437], T*Camporeale* Rita: ➤ 166,
Ermeneutica 1986, 278-299.
4782* *Jezierska* Ewa J., ❷ 'Przemieniamy się w jego obraz' (2 Kor 3,18): Ru-
Bi 39 (1986) 112-120.
4783 *a) Best* Ernst, II Corinthians 4.7-15; life through death; – *b) Marcus* Joel,
The evil inclination in the letters of Paul: IrBSt 8 (1986) 2-7 / 9-21.

4784 *Osei-Bonsu* Joseph, Does 2 Cor. 5.1-10 teach the reception of the Resurrection body at the moment of death?: JStNT 28 (1986) 81-101.
4785 **Wonneberger** Reinhard, Syntax und Exegese ... griech. NT ... 2 Kor 5,2f; Röm 3,21-26 [diss. Heid 1974]: BeiBExT 13, 1979 → 60,8034 ... 1,5918*: ᴿCBQ 48 (1986) 152-4 (E. C. A. *Dougherty*).
4786 *Murphy-O'Connor* J., 'Being at home in the body we are in exile from the Lord' (2 Cor 5:6b): RB 93 (1986) 214-221.
4787 **Bieringer** Reimund, 'Lasst euch mit Gott versöhnen'; eine exegetische Untersuchung zu 2 Kor 5,14-21 in seinem Kontext: Diss. ᴰ*Lambrecht* J. Leuven 1986. – RTLv 18,545.
    Findeis H.-J., Versöhnung[saussagen 2 Cor 5,18 ...] 1983 → 5892.
4788 **Carson** Donald A., From triumphalism to maturity; an exposition of 2 Corinthians 10-13: 1984 Baker [1,5924]; also Leicester 1986, Inter-Varsity. – ᴿThemelios 12 (1986s) 61 (R. E. *Davies*).
4789 *Neyrey* Jerome H., Witchcraft accusations in 2 Cor 10-13; Paul in social-science perspective: Listening 21,2 (1986) 160-170 [NTAbs 31,51].
4790 **Spencer** Aida B., Paul's literary style; a stylistic and historical comparison of II Corinthians 11:16-12:13, Romans 8:9-39, and Philippians 3:2-4:13: EvTheolSoc Mon., Jackson MS, Ev. Theol. Soc. 1984 → 65,5433 [not Ada]: ᴿCBQ 48 (1986) 574s (D. M. *Sweetland*); GraceTJ 7 (1986) 251s (D. L. *Turner*); JTS 37 (1985) 300 (H. D. *Betz*); ScotJT 39 (1986) 267s (C. M. *Tuckett*).
4791 **Tabor** James D., [2 Cor 12,2] Things unutterable; Paul's ascent to Paradise in its Greco-Roman, Judaic, and early Christian contexts. Lanham MD 1986, UPA. 155 p. $23.50; pa. $11.50 [TS 48,407]. 0-8191-5643-4; pa. 4-2.
4792 *Zmijewski* Josef, Kontextbezug und Deutung von 2 Kor 12,7a; stilistische und strukturale Erwägungen zur Lösung eines alten Problems [< BZ 21 (1977) 265-272]: → 233, NT Quelle 1986, 157-167.

G6.1 Ad Galatas.

4793 *Alfsvåg* Knut, Evangeliet som autoritet; hovedtrekk i LUTHERs Galaterbrevskommentarer fra 1519: TsTKi 57 (1986) 107-126.
4794 **Barrett** C. K., Freedom and obligation; a study of the Epistle to the Galatians [Melbourne lectures 1983] 1985 → 1,5937: ᴿJTS 37 (1986) 187-9 (F. F. *Bruce*: gets to the heart of the matter); NBlackfr 67 (1986) 346s (J. A. *Ziesler*); RelStR 12 (1986) 296 (S. J. *Kraftchick*: nothing new to help one familiar with the issue); TLond 39 (1986) 224s (Judith *Lieu*); TS 47 (1986) 555 (R. J. *Karris*: outstanding).
4795 **Borse** Udo, Der Brief an die Galater: RgNT 1984 → 65,5437; 1,5938: ᴿBiKi 41 (1986) 47s (O. *Knoch*); BLitEc 87 (1986) 148s (S. *Légasse*); NRT 108 (1986) 120s (X. *Jacques*); TGegw 29 (1986) 60s (H. *Giessen*); TGl 76 (1986) 350s (J. *Ernst*); TLZ 111 (1986) 198-200 (H. *Hübner*); TPhil 61 (1986) 568s N. *Baumert*); TrierTZ 95 (1986) 145s (G. *Schmahl*).
4796 **Brinsmead** Bernard H., Galatians — dialogical response to opponents [diss. ᴰ*Cox* J.]: SBL diss. 65, 1982 → 63,5993 ... 1,5939: ᴿTLZ 111 (1986) 364s (J. *Becker*).
4797 **Bruce** F. F., The epistle to the Galatians: NIGT 1982 → 63,5994 ... 1,5940: ᴿTLZ 111 (1986) 196-8 (J. *Rohde*).
4798 *Bruce* F. F., The Spirit in the Letter to the Galatians: → 28, ᶠERVIN H., Essays on apostolic themes 1985 ...
4799 *Costa* Giuseppe, Principi ermeneutici gnostici nella lettura di Paolo

(Lettera ai GALATI) secondo lo Adv. Haer. di IRENEO: ➤ 388, RivB 34 (1986) 615-637.

4800 *Cronjé* J. V., Defamiliarization in the letter to the Galatians: ➤ 72, ᶠMETZGER B., South Africa 1985/6, 214-227.

4801 ᵀᴱ**Fatica** Luigi, AMBROSIASTER, Commento alla Lettera ai Galati: Collana di Testi Patristici 61. R 1986, Città Nuova. 138 p. 88-311-3061-7.

4802 *Hall* J., [Gal...] Paul, the Lawyer, on Law: JLawRel 3 (St. Paul 1985) 331-379 [< NTAbs 31,41].

4803 **Herman** Zvonimir I., Liberi in Cristo; saggi esegetici sulla libertà dalla Legge nella Lettera ai Galati: Spicilegium 27. R 1986, Antonianum. 234 p. Lit. 25.000 [NRT 109,750, X. *Jacques*].

4804 **Kim Chang-Nack**, Der Kampf des Paulus für das Evangelium in Galatien: ev. Diss. ᴰ*Schottroff* L. Mainz 1984. – RTLv 18,547.

4804* *a) Klein* Günter, Werkruhm und Christusruhm im Galaterbrief und die Frage nach einer Entwicklung des Paulus; ein hermeneutischer und exegetischer Zwischenruf; – *b) Lindemann* Andreas, Die biblischen Toragebote und die paulinische Ethik: ➤ 39, ᶠGREEVEN H., Text/Ethik 1986, 196-211 / 242-265.

4805 **Lategan** B. C., Die Brief aan die Galasiërs. Cape Town 1986, NG-Kerk. 117 p. R 12,50 [GerefTTs 86,258].

4805* **Mayer** Friedrich, Die Gerechtigkeit aus dem Glauben; der rechtschaffene Glaube; Betrachtungen über den Galaterbrief und den Jakobusbrief. Metzingen 1986, Franz. 170 p. 3-7722-0202-0.

4806 *Panier* L., Parcours; pour lire l'Épître aux Galates: SémiotB 42 (1986) 40-46; 43 (1986) 23-29 [1,11-2,21].

4807 **Verhoef** Eduard, Er staat geschreeven... de Oud-Testamentische Citaten in de Brief aan de Galaten [diss. Amst Vrije Univ.] 1979 ➤ 60,8071... 63,6009: ᴿTLZ 111 (1986) 109-111 (J. *Reiling*).

4808 *Gaventa* B. R., Galatians 1 and 2; autobiography as paradigm: NT 28 (1986) 309-326.

4809 *a) Kirchschläger* W., Zu Herkunft und Aussage von Gal 1,4; – *b) Berényi* Gabriella, Gal 2,20; a pre-Pauline or a Pauline text?: – *c) Walter* Nikolaus, Paulus und die Gegner des Christusevangeliums in Galatien: ➤ 398, ᴱ*Vanhoye* A., L'Apôtre Paul 1984/6, 332-9 / 340-4 / 351-6.

4809* *Hester* James D., The use and influence of rhetoric in Galatians 2:1-14: TZBas 42 (1986) 386-408.

4810 *a) Bruce* Frederick F., Conference in Jerusalem — Galatians 2:1-10; – *b) O'Brien* Peter T., The importance of the Gospel in Philippians: ➤ 54, ᶠKNOX D., God rich 1986, 195-212 / 213-233.

4810* *Mavrofidis* Sotirios, ⑨ Gal. 2,10; various aspects of scholarship between 1893-1979: DeltioVM 15,1 (1986) 20-34.

4811 *Holtz* Traugott, Der antiochenische Zwischenfall (Galater 2.11-14) [SNTS main paper, Trondheim 1985]: NTS 32 (1986) 344-361.

4812 *Winger* Michael, [Gal 2,21; 3,21] Unreal conditions in the letters of Paul: JBL 105 (1986) 110-2.

4813 *Hays* Richard B., The faith of Jesus Christ [subjective genitive in Gal 3,1-4,11] 1983 ➤ 64,5930... 1,5969: ᴿBTrans 37 (1986) 346 [P. *Ellingworth*: forces translators to render also *epangelia* varyingly as 'the promise itself' or 'the content of what God promises'); JBL 105 (1986) 156-9 (G. E. *Howard*).

4814 *Gewalt* Dietfried, Die 'fides ex auditu' und die Taubstummen; zur Auslegungsgeschichte von Gal. 3,2 und Röm. 10,14-17 [*l'Epée* C. de 1776...]: LingBib 58 (1986) 46-64; Eng. 64: not *auditus* but 'preaching', which may also be non-verbal.

4815 *Donaldson* T. L., The 'curse of the Law' and the inclusion of the Gentiles; Galatians 3,13-14: NTS 32 (1986) 94-112.

4816 *Lull* David J., 'The law was our pedagogue'; a study in Galatians 3: 19-25: JBL 105 (1986) 481-498.

4817 *Belleville* Linda L., 'Under law'; structural analysis and Pauline concept of law in Galatians 3.21-4.11: JStNT 26 (1986) 53-78.

4817* *Garland* J. M., [Gal 3,23-4,7...] Freedom [strangely embarrassing to an adolescent, who secretly yearns for childhood restrictions: thus religion today is leaning toward pre-Vatican II conservatism]: ExpTim 98 (1986s) 271-3.

4818 **MacDonald** Dennis R., [Gal 3,27s] There is no male and female; the fate of a dominical saying in Paul and Gnosticism: HarvDissRel. Ph c. 1986, Fortress. $15 [RelStR 13,87 adv].

4819 *Smit* Joop, Redactie in de brief aan de Galaten; retorische analyse van Gal. 4,12-6,18: TsTNijm 26 (1986) 113-143; Eng. 143s.

4820 *Westerholm* Stephen, On fulfilling the whole law (Gal. 5:14): SvEx 51s (1986s) 229-237.

G6.2 Ad Ephesios.

4821 **Arnold** Clinton E., The power of God and the 'Powers' of evil in Ephesians: diss. Aberdeen. – RTLv 18,545 sans date.

4822 *Dahl* Nils A., Gentiles, Christians, and Israelites in the Epistle to the Ephesians: ➤ 110, FSTENDAHL K. = HarvTR 79 (1986) 31-40.

4823 **Clark** G. H., Ephesians. Jefferson MD 1985, Trinity. xiv-230 p. $9 pa. [NTAbs 31,105].

4824 EGori Franco, Mario VITTORINO, Commentari... agli Efesini, ai Galati, ai Filippesi: Corona Patrum 8, 1981 ➤ 62,6669; 63,5939: ROrpheus 7,1 (1986) 230-2 (A. *Gallico*).

4825 **Le Peau** Andrew T. & Phyllis J., Ephesians; wholeness for a broken world. DG 1985, InterVarsity. 64 p. $3 [JAAR 54,400].

4826 *Lindemann* Andreas, Epheserbrief: ➤ 587, EvKL 1 (1986) 1049-52 (-53, Ephesus, *Wischmeyer* Wolfgang).

4827 **Russell** L. M., Imitators of God; a study book on Ephesians. NY 1984, Methodist Women's Ministries. vii-136 p. $1.50 pa. [NTAbs 30,363].

4828 *Steinmetz* Franz-Josef, Jenseits der Mauern und Zäune; somatische Verständnis der kirchlichen Einheit im Epheserbrief [*Usami* K. 1983]: GeistL 59 (1986) 202-214.

4829 **Usami** Koshi, Somatic comprehension of unity; the Church in Ephesians: AnBib 101, 1983 ➤ 64,5948... 1,5982: RRelStR 12 (1986) 164s (D. C. *Smith*: grammatical and typographical errors).

────────

4830 *Robbins* Charles J., The composition of Eph 1:3-14: JBL 105 (1986) 677-687.

4831 *Iovino* Paolo, La 'conoscenza del mistero', una inclusione decisiva nella lettera agli Efesini (1,9 e 6,19): RivB 34 (1986) 327-367.

4832 *Hartin* P. J., *Anakephalaiōsasthai tà pánta en tô Christô* (Eph 1:10): ➤ 72, FMETZGER B., South Africa 1985/6, 228-237.

4833 *Robertson* A. C., 'Hope' in Ephesians 1:18: JThSAf 14,55 (1986) 62s [< ZIT].

4834 *Allen* Thomas G., *a*) Exaltation and solidarity with Christ; Ephesians 1.20 and 2.6: JStNT 28 (1986) 103-120; – *b*) God the namer; a note on Ephesians 1,21b: NTS 32 (1986) 470-5.

4835 *a*) *Heriban* J., Da Dio ogni paternità prende nome (Ef 3,14-15); – *b*) *Ghiberti* G., 'State sottomessi'; la parenesi cristiana sulla famiglia; – *c*) *Barbaglio* G., L'uomo non separi ciò che Dio ha unito; – *d*) *Laurentin* R., La famiglia di Nazaret; il suo segreto; – *e*) *Bianchi* E., La nuova famiglia di Gesù: ParSpV 14 (1986) 143-160 / 161-177 / 121-141 / 109-120 ᵀ*Benassi* Silvestro / 179-192.

4836 *Strauss* Richard L., Like Christ; an exposition of Ephesians 4:13: Bibliotheca Sacra 143 (1986) 260-5.

4837 *a*) *Fabris* R., Il matrimonio cristiano figura dell'alleanza (Ef 5,21-33); – *b*) *Serra* A., Eva, donna dell'alleanza: ParSpV 13 (1986) 153-169 / 171-190.

4838 **Miletic** Stephen F., 'One flesh'; Eph. 5. 22-24, 5.31;. marriage and the new creation diss. Marquette. Milwaukee 1985. 155 p. 86-04957. – DissA 47 (1986s) 217-A.

4839 **Jeffrey** Peter, Stand firm [Eph 6,10-18]. Bridgend 1983, Evangelical Press of Wales. 72 p. $1.25. – ᴿEvQ 58 (1986) 287s (S. P. *Dray*: a gem).

G6.3   Ad Philippenses.

4840 **Bruce** F. F., Philippians 1983 ➤ 1,5993: ᴿInterpretation 40 (1986) 324.326 (B. *Crawford*).

4841 **Craddock** Fred B., Philippians: Interpretation comm. 1985 ➤ 1,5994: ᴿCBQ 48 (1986) 135s (Florence M. *Gillman*); Interpretation 40 (1986) 211s (R. L. *Jeske*); WWorld 6 (1986) 236-8 (Marilyn S. *Breckenridge*).

4842 **Ernst** Josef, Le Lettere ai Filippesi... Efesini. Brescia 1986, Morcelliana. 616 p. Lit. 55.000. – ᴿHumBr 41 (1986) 771 (A. *Bonora*).

4843 **Pesch** Rudolf, Paulus und seine Lieblingsgemeinde; Paulus — neu gesehen; drei Briefe an die Heiligen von Philippi 1985 ➤ 1,6007: ᴿNRT 108 (1986) 435 (X. *Jacques*); Salesianum 48 (1986) 165 (J. *Heriban*); TPhil 61 (1986) 253s (H. *Engel*: Probleme verschwiegen).

4844 **Schenk** Wolfgang, Die Philipperbriefe des Paulus 1984 ➤ 65,5504; 1,6008: ᴿTLZ 111 (1986) 436s (M. *Rese*); TPQ 134 (1986) 79 (O. B. *Knoch*: unbefriedigend).

4845 *Dąbek* Tomasz M., ❷ 'Dla mnie żyć — to Chrystus!' (Flp 1,21) — Pawłowa odpowiedź na odwieczne pytanie o sens ludzkiego życia [Paul's answer to the immemorial question of the meaning of human life]: RuBi 39 (1986) 121-126.

4846 **Heriban** Jozef, Retto phroneîn e kénōsis... Fil 2: BiblScRel 51, 1983 ➤ 64,5975 ... 1,6012: ᴿTLZ 111 (1986) 748-750 (C. *Wolff*).

4847 *Hurst* L. D., Re-enter the pre-existent Christ in Philippians 2,5-11?: NTS 32 (1986) 449-457.

4848 *Wright* N. T., *Harpagmós* and the meaning of Philippians 2:5-11: JTS 37 (1986) 321-352.

4849 **Verwilghen** Albert, [Phlp 2,5-11] Christologie et spiritualité selon saint AUGUSTIN; l'hymne aux Philippiens: THist 72, 1985 ➤ 1,6015: ᴿAnBoll 104 (1986) 249s (R. de *Fenoyl*); EsprV 96 (1986) 222 (Y.-M. *Duval*); MélSR 43 (1986) 170s (M. *Huftier*); RÉAug 31 (1985) 352s (I. *Bochet*); RÉLat 63

(1985s) 416s (aussi Y.-M. *Duval*); Salesianum 48 (1986) 179 (B. *Amata*); TS 47 (1986) 322s (W. C. *Marceau*).

4850 *Wagner* Guy, Le scandale de la Croix expliqué par le chant du Serviteur d'Ésaïe 53; réflexion sur Philippiens 2/6-11: ÉTRel 61 (1986) 177-187.

4851 **Wong Yai-Chow** Teresa, From humiliation to exaltation, a study of Phil. 2,6-11: Cath. diss. ᴰ*Lambrecht* J. Lv 1986. xlix-414 p. – TsTNijm 26 (1986) 288.

4852 *Wong Yai-Chow* Teresa, The problem of pre-existence in Philippians 2,6-11: ETL 62 (1986) 267-282; franç. 282.

4853 *Jezierska* Ewa J., Ⓞ Motyw śmierci i zmartwychwstania wiernych z Chrystusem w Flp 3,10-11 (mors et resurrectio fidelium): → 367, Sympozjum 1985 = RuBi 39 (1986) 250-9.

G6.4 Ad Colossenses.

4854 **Bruce** F. F., The epistles to the Colossians, to Philemon, and to the Ephesians: NICOT, 1984 → 65,5515: **1**,6023: ᴿCBQ 48 (1986) 132s (R. A. *Wild*); GraceTJ 7 (1986) 131-3 (H. A. *Kent*); IrBSt 8 (1986) 50s (E. *Best*); JTS 37 (1986) 191-3 (C. F. D. *Moule*); RThom 86 (1986) 671 (H. *Ponsot*: remplit les promesses de la série, non comme l'inutile réimpression de *Müller* J. † 1977, Philippians 1984); TLZ 111 (1986) 274-7 (A. *Lindemann*).

4855 **Cannon** George E., The use of traditional materials in Colossians [diss. Fuller, ᴰ*Martin* R.] 1983 → 65,5516; **1**,6024: ᴿEvQ 58 (1986) 174s (P. *O'Brien*); JBL 105 (1986) 341-3 (J. T. *Sanders*).

4856 **Gnilka** J., Der Kolosserbrief 1980 → 61,7539 ... **1**,6025: ᴿHenoch 8 (1986) 106s (E. *Jucci*).

4857 **Kiley** Mark, Colossians as pseudepigraphy: The biblical seminar 4. Sheffield 1986, JStOT. 146 p.; bibliog. p. 136-142 £8 [TR 83,75]. – ᴿExpTim 98 (1986s) 281 (Ruth B. *Edwards*).

4858 **Lindemann** Andreas, Der Kolosserbrief: Z BK NT 10, 1983 → 64,5985; 65,5520: ᴿTLZ 111 (1986) 820-2 (H.-M. *Schenke*).

4859 **Lona** Horacio E., Die Eschatologie im Kolosser- und Epheserbrief [Hab.-Diss. 1981, ᴰ*Schnackenburg* R.]: ForBi 48, 1984 → 65,5521; **1**,6027: ᴿTLZ 111 (1986) 433-6 (A. *Lindemann*).

4860 *Montagnini* Felice, La figura di Paolo nelle lettere ai colossesi e agli efesini: → 388, RivB 34 (1986) 429-449.

4861 **O'Brien** Peter T., Colossians, Philemon: WordComm 44, 1982 → 63,6076 ... **1**,6029: ᴿJTS 37 (1986) 551s (J. B. *Muddiman*).

4862 **Patzia** Arthur G., Colossians, Philemon, Ephesians: Good News Comm. 1984 → **1**,6030: ᴿRExp 83 (1986) 627s (J. *Polhill*: Baptist, and not so cramped as Lutheran TAYLOR-REUMANN).

4863 *Roth* R. P., Christ and the powers of darkness; lessons from Colossians: WWorld 6 (1986) 336-344 [< NTAbs 31,53].

4864 **Wright** N. T., The epistles of Paul to the Colossians and to Philemon; an introduction and commentary: Tyndale NT Comm. Leicester 1986, Inter-Varsity. 192 p.

4865 *Yates* Roy, Colossians and Gnosis: JStNT 27 (1986) 49-68.

4865* *Watt* J. G. van der, Colossians 1:3-12 considered as an exordium: JTSAf 57 (1986) 32-42 [< TKontext 8/2,18].

4866 *Crüsemann* F., Ein Lied über die Weise, wie Gott die Welt regiert (Kol. 1,15-23): → 145, Wie Gott 1986 ...

4866* *Rossé* Gérard, La funzione cosmica di Cristo secondo il Nuovo Testamento II: NuovaUm 8,43 (1986) 85-107; 8,45 (1986) 15-38.

4867 *Bellai* Zoltán, Ⓦ Traces of the ancient Church's liturgy of baptism in the New Testament (Col. 1:15-20): Theologiai Szemle 28 (1985) 6-9.

4867* *Botha* J., A stylistic analysis of the Christ hymn (Col 1:15-20): ➤ 72, ᶠMETZGER B., South Africa 1985/6, 238-251.

4868 **Wink** Walter, [Col 1,16] Naming the powers, 1. The language of power in the NT 1984 ➤ 65,5526: 1,6036: ᴿBibTB 16 (1986) 42 (J. M. *Reese*); BS 143 (1986) 86 (W. H. *Harris*); CBQ 48 (1986) 151s (W. S. *Kurz*: seems to repeat naively solutions the church has long found incompatible with its biblical faith); JAAR 54 (1986) 619s (J. *Koenig*); RExp 83 (1986) 120s (E. E. *Thornton*).

4869 **Wink** Walter, Unmasking the powers; the invisible forces that determine human existence: The Powers 2, Ph 1986, Fortress. 227 p. 0-8006-1902-1. – ᴿExpTim 98 (1986s) 159 [C. S. *Rodd*: trilogy completion awaited].

4870 *Messier* M., [Col 1,19 ...] Plérôme: ➤ 578, Catholicisme XI,50s (1986s) 507-515.

4872 *Hartman* Lars, 'Kroppsligen', 'personligen' eller vad? [bodily or what?] Till Kol 2:9: SvEx 51s (1986s) 72-79.

G6.5 *Ad Philemonem* – **Slavery in NT background.**

4873 *Bieżuńska-Małowist* Iza, L'esclavage dans l'Égypte gréco-romaine; quelques observations en marge de publications récentes: ➤ 123, ᶠWILLIS W., BASP 20 (1985) 7-14.

4874 **Bradley** K. R., Slaves and masters in the Roman empire 1984 ➤ 65,5534; 1,6042: ᴿClasR 100 (1986) 276 (T. *Wiedemann*); Gnomon 58 (1986) 461-3 (P. *Herz*).

4875 *Bradley* K. R., *a)* Seneca and slavery: ClasMedK 37 (1986) 171-172. – *b)* Social aspects of the slave trade in the Roman world: MünstHand 5,1 (1986) 49-58.

4876 **Corcoran** Gervase, Saint AUGUSTINE on slavery 1985 ➤ 1,6044: ᴿEstE 61 (1986) 249s (G. *Higuera*); Laurentianum 27 (1986) 385s (E. *Covi*: 'Concoran' anche nell'Indice; tesi che per Agostino la schiavitù è una conseguenza del peccato originale).

4877 *Daube* David, Onesimos: ➤ 110, ᶠSTENDAHL K. = HarvTR 79 (1986) 40-43.

4878 **Fabre** Georges, Libertus; recherches sur les rapports patron-affranchi à la fin de la République romaine ➤ 1,6045: ᴿAntClas 55 (1986) 536-8 (Marie-Thérèse *Raepsaet-Charlier*); Gnomon 58 (1986) 159-162 (H. *Chantraine*).

4879 **Garlan** Yvon, Les esclaves en Grèce ancienne 1982 ➤ 64,4006; 65,5540: ᴿGnomon 58 (1986) 71-74 (Iza *Bieżuńska-Małowist*).

4880 *a)* *Kudlien* Fridolf, Empticius servus; Bemerkungen zum antiken Sklavenmarkt; – *b)* *Wickert-Micknat* Gisela, Unfreiheit in der frühgriechischen Gesellschaft [homerisch, *Vogt* J. 1983]; Schwierigkeiten bei der Beschreibung des Phänomens: Historia 35 (1986) 240-256 / 129-146.

4881 **Laub** Franz, Die Begegnung des frühen Christentums mit der antiken Sklaverei: SBS 107, 1982 ➤ 64,6009; 65,5545: ᴿGymnasium 93 (1986) 319s (R. *Klein*); RömQ 81 (1986) 124s (auch R. *Klein*).

4882 **Lehmann** Richard, Épître à Philémon; le christianisme primitif et l'esclavage 1978 ➤ 60,8221 ... 62,6725: ᴿRHPR 66 (1986) 234s (J.-D. *Dubois*).

4883 **Lyall** Francis, Slaves, citizens, sons; legal metaphors in the Epistles 1984
➤ 65,5546; 0-310-45191-4: ᴿCalvinT 21 (1986) 270-2 (W. P. *DeBoer*);
ExpTim 98 (1986s) 55 (D. *Hill*); Interpretation 40 (1986) 214-6 (R. F.
Hock); JRS 76 (1986) 323s (A. N. *Sherwin-White*).

4884 **Patterson** Orlando, Slavery and social death; a comparative study
[< New Left Review 117 (1979) 31-67]. CM 1982, Harvard. xiii-511 p.
$30. – ᴿJNES 45 (1986) 308-311 (E. *Cruz-Uribe*, as in RIDA 29,47-71: he
did not sufficiently grasp the situation in Egypt, at least).

4885 **Peterson** Norman R., Rediscovering Paul; Philemon and the sociology of
Paul's narrative world 1985 ➤ 1,6057: ᴿTTod 43 (1986s) 139-142 (C. J.
Roetzel).

4886 *Roberts* J. H., Die brief aan Filemon; Bevryding en Christelike
verantwoordelikheid: TEv 18,3 (Pretoria 1985) 19-26 [NTAbs 30,310].

4887 *Scholl* Reinhold, Sklaverei in der Arbeitswelt der Antike im Lichte der
verschiedenen Quellenkategorien: Gymnasium 93 (1986) 476-496; pl.
V-XVI.

4888 **Vogt** Joseph, Sklaverei und Humanität [¹1965; Sup. zu ²1972, 8
Nachdrucke + 1 ineditum]: Historia Einz 44, 1983 ➤ 65,5553: ᴿRBgPg 64
(1986) 142s (J. A. *Straus*).

4889 *Yuge* Toru, Die Einstellung PLINIUS des Jüngeren zur Sklaverei: ➤ 58,
ᶠLAUFFER S. III (1986) 1089-1102.

4890 *Zmijewski* Josef, Beobachtungen zur Struktur des Philemonbriefes [BLeb
15 (1974) 273-296]: ➤ 233, Das NT Quelle 1986, 129-155.

G6.6 Ad Thessalonicenses.

4890* *Becker* Jürgen, Die Erwählung der Völker durch das Evangelium —
theologiegeschichtliche Erwägungen zum 1. Thessalonicherbrief: ➤ 39,
ᶠGREEVEN H., Text/Ethik 1986, 82-101.

4891 **Bruce** F. F., 1 & 2 Thessalonians: Word Comm. 45 ➤ 63,6099 ... 1,6063;
also Milton Keynes, 0-85009-441-0 [JStNT 27-120]. – ᴿJTS 37 (1986)
548-550 (C. J. A. *Hickling*: robust).

4892 *Collins* Raymond F., Studies on the first letter to the Thessalonians [4
inedita; 13 from 1976-83] 1984 ➤ 65,556; 1,6064: ᴿBibTB 16 (1986) 29s
(Mary Ann *Getty*); EvQ 58 (1986) 270s (I. H. *Marshall*); NRT 108 (1986)
435s (X. *Jacques*).

4892* Dans l'attente du Sauveur; les lettres de Paul aux Thessaloniciens et aux
Philippiens; Quand Dieu parle aux hommes 17. P 1986, Cerf [ActuBbg
24,81].

4893 **Demarest** Gary, 1,2 Thessalonians, 1,2 Timothy, Titus: Communicator's
Comm. 9, 1984 ➤ 65,5557: ᴿAndrUnS 24 (1986) 62s (J. *Paulien*).

4894 **Holtz** Traugott, Der erste Brief an die Thessalonicher: EkK NT 13, Z/
Neuk 1986, Benziger/Neuk. x-291 p. DM 72 [NRT 109,437, X. *Jacques*].
3-545-23110-0 / Neuk 3-7887-0752-6. – ᴿExpTim 98 (1986s) 303 (E. *Best*).

4895 **Jewett** Robert, The Thessalonian correspondence; Pauline rhetoric and
millenarian piety: Foundations and Facets. Ph 1986, Fortress. xv-240 p.;
bibliog. p. 193-213. 0-8006-2111-5.

4896 **Lecompte** C., I / II Thessalonicenzen: VBGed 1984s ➤ 65,5662: 1,6069;
ƒ19,90 each: ᴿNedTTs 40 (1986) 177s (H. W. *Hollander* cites from i p. 72
Timothy's 1 Thes 3,6:) 'H = HS ➤ S ➤ [(S ol,ol 02) ➤ (S ol *en* ol 02)];
PrakT 13 (1986) 403s (J. *Kahmann*).

4897 **Morton** A. O., *al.*, A critical concordance to I-II Thes: ComputerB 26,
1983 ➤ 64,6024: ᴿJBL 105 (1986) 159s (E. J. *Epp*).

4898 **Pesch** R., Die Entdeckung des ältesten Paulus-Briefes 1984 ➤ 65,5565; 1,6072: ᴿNRT 108 (1986) 121s (X. *Jacques*).

4898* *Roetzel* Calvin J., Theodidaktoi and handwork in Philo and 1 Thessalonians: ➤ 398, ᴱ*Vanhoye* A., L'Apôtre Paul 1984/6, 324-331.

4899 *Schnelle* Udo, Der erste Thessalonicherbrief und die Entstehung der paulinischen Anthropologie: NTS 32 (1986) 207-224.

4900 *a) Asso* Cecilia, A proposito di Paolo, 1 Thess., II 7: Maia 38 (1986) 233s (*ēpioi*, non *nēpioi* as Nestle-Aland); – *b) Janse van Rensburg* J. J., An argument for reading *nēpioi* in 1 Ts 2:7: ➤ 72, ᶠMETZGER B., South Africa 1985/6, 252-9.

4901 **Baarda** T. H., [1 Tess. 2,13-16; *Jensen* H., Gal 4,21-31; *Vos* J., Rom 9-11] Paulus en de andere Joden; exegetische bijdragen en discussie 1984 ➤ 65,266*: ᴿBijdragen 47 (1986) 327 (J. *Lambrecht*).

4901* *Günther* Hartmut, 'Das ist der Wille Gottes, eure Heiligung' (1 Th 4,3); Bindung und Freiheit im Leben der Christen: LuthTKi 10 (1986) 1-16.

4902 **Kimball** William R. [1 Thes 4,15-18; 1 Cor 15,51-53] The Rapture, a question of timing. Nv 1985, Abingdon. 208 p. $9.50 pa. – ᴿTDig 33 (1986) 476 (W. C. *Heiser*).

4903 **Aejmelaeus** Lars, Wachen vor dem Ende; die traditionsgeschichtlichen Wurzeln von 1. Thess 5:1-11 und Luk 21:34-36: Schriften 44. Helsinki 1985, Finnische Exegetische Gesellschaft. iv-157 p.; bibliog. p. 138-149 [TR 83,282, W. *Radl*]. 951-95185-9-2.

4904 **Holland** Glenn S., The tradition that you received from us; 2 Thessalonians in the Pauline tradition: diss. Chicago Divinity School 1986. – RelStR 13,190.

4905 **Müller** Peter, Anfänge der Paulusschule dargestellt am zweiten Thessalonicherbrief und am Kolosserbrief: ev. Diss. ᴰ*Hahn* F. München 1986s. – RTLv 18,548.

4906 **Moreland** Donald D., The katechon; a proposal for the translation and interpretation of 2 Thes 2,6-7 in its literary and historical context: diss. Inst. Prot. ᴰ*Carrez* M. Paris 1986. 422 p. – RTLv 18,548.

G7 Epistulae pastorales.

4907 **Clark** Gordon H., The pastoral epistles. Jefferson MD 1983, Trinity. 294 p. $10. – ᴿGraceTJ 7 (1986) 248-250 (D. A. *Black*: weak).

4908 *Dalton* William J., Pseudepigraphy in the New Testament: Catholic Theological Review 5 (Clayton, Australia 1983) 29-35 [NTAbs 30,259].

4909 *Donelson* Lewis R., Pseudepigraphy and ethical argument in the Pastoral Epistles [diss. Ch 1984 ➤ 1,6092]: Hermeneut. Unters. Theol. 22. Tü 1986, Mohr. viii-221 p. DM 78. 3-16-145009-4. – ᴿExpTim 98 (1986s) 84 (A. *Hanson*: fruitful, but 'enthymeme' and 'inductive paradigm' don't help).

4910 **Fabris** Rinaldo, Le lettere pastorali: LoB 2,11. Brescia 1986, Queriniana. 116 p. Lit. 12.000 [NRT 109,751, X. *Jacques*].

4911 *Fabris* Rinaldo, Il paolinismo nelle lettere pastorali: ➤ 388, RivB 34 (1986) 451-470; Eng. 470.

4912 **Fee** Gordon D., 1 and 2 Timothy, Titus; Good News Comm. SF 1984, Harper & R. xl-274 p. $10. 0-06-062338-1. – ᴿExpTim 98 (1986s) 84 J. A. *Ziesler*: holds they fit best Paul's own ministry; but his stress on Acts 20,30 could fit also a generation later).

4913 **Fiore** Benjamin, The function of personal example in the Socratic and Pastoral epistles: AnBib 105. R 1986, Biblical Institute Press. xviii-286 p. Lit. 50.000/$35. 88-7653-105-X.

4914 ᴱ**Günther** H., *Volk* E., D. Martin Luthers Epistel-Auslegung 5. Der erste Brief des Paulus an Timotheus; der Brief des Paulus an Titus; der erste Brief des Petrus / Johannes; der Brief an die Hebräer; der Brief an Jakobus, 1983 ➤ 65,5583; 1,6098: ᴿTLZ 111 (1986) 367s (J. *Rogge*).

4915 **Hanson** A.T., The pastoral epistles: NCent 1982 ➤ 64,6042; 65,5584: ᴿJTS 37 (1986) 193 (C.K. *Barrett*).

4915* *a) Lohse* Eduard, Das apostolische Vermächtnis — zum paulinischen Charakter der Pastoralbriefe; – *b) Kraft* Heinrich, Die Entstehung von Gemeindeverbänden: ➤ 39, ᶠGreeven H., Text/Ethik 1986, 266-281 / 217-241.

4916 **MacDonald** Dennis R., The legend and the Apostle; the battle for Paul in story and canon 1983 ➤ 64,8751 ... 1,6100: ᴿHeythJ 27 (1986) 313s (F.F. *Bruce*).

4917 *Maloney* Elliott C., Biblical authorship and the Pastoral Letters; inspired and anonymous: BToday 24 (1986) 119-123 [(Church leadership), 'the problem the Apostles left behind'].

4918 **Schwarz** Roland, Bürgerliches Christentum im NT?... Pastoralbriefen: ÖsBS 4, 1983 ➤ 64,6047 ... 1,6106: ᴿTLZ 111 (1986) 28-30 (J. *Rohde*); TPhil 61 (1986) 254s (H. *Engel*).

4919 *Towner* P.H., The present age in the eschatology of the pastoral epistles: NTS 32 (1986) 427-448.

4920 **Wolter** Michael, Die Pastoralbriefe als Paulustradition: Hab. Diss. Mainz 1984. – RTLv 18,551.

4921 *Zmijewski* Josef, *a)* Die Pastoralbriefe als pseudepigraphische Schriften — Beschreibung. Erklärung, Bewertung [< SNTU A4 (1979) 97-118]; – *b)* Apostolische Paradosis und Pseudepigraphie im NT [< BZ 23 (1979) 161-171]: ➤ 233, Das NT Quelle 1986, 197-220 / 185-196.

G7.2 1-2 ad Timotheum.

4922 **Fernando** Ajith, Leadership life style; a study of 1 Timothy. Wheaton 1985, Tyndale. – ᴿNESTR 7,1 (1986) 63 (Wanis A. *Semaan*).

4923 *Marshall* I. Howard, Church and ministry in 1 Timothy: ➤ 111, ᶠStill W., Pulpit & people 1986, 51-60.

4924 **Küchler** M., Schweigen, Schmuck und Schleier; drei neutestamentliche Vorschriften [1 Tim 2,8-15; 1 Cor 11,3-16; Gn 2-6 ...] zur Verdrängung der Frauen auf dem Hintergrund einer frauenfeindlichen Exegese des ATs im antiken Judentum: NT et Orbis Antiquus 1. FrS/Gö 1986, Univ./VR. xxii-539 p. Fs 98. 3-7278-0362-2 / 3-525-53900-2 [BL 87,109, L.L. *Grabbe*].

4925 **Gritz** Sharon M.H., A study of 1 Timothy 2,9-15 in light of the religious and cultural milieu of the first century: diss. SW Baptist Sem. 1986. 267 p. 87-05901. – DissA 47 (1986s) 4114-A.

4926 *Verner* David C., [1 Tim 3,15] The household of God; the social world of the Pastoral Epistles: SBL Diss 71, 1983 ➤ 64,6057 ... 1,6113: ᴿTLZ 111 (1986) 893-5 (B. *Holmberg*, Eng.).

4927 *Schlarb* Egbert, Miszelle zu 1 Tim 6,20: ZNW 77 (1986) 276-281.

4927* **Sârbu** Georghe, La seconde Épître de l'Apôtre St. Paul à Timothée; intr. tr. comm.; diss. en roumain: STBuc (1986) 18,2 p. 39-91; 18,3 p. 11-51; 18,4 p. 21-65; 18,5 p. 11-83; 18,6 p. 15-72; 73-83 bibliog.

4928 *Read* David H.C., [2 Tim 1,5; Eunice and Lois] Home-made religion: ExpTim 97 (1985s) 307s.

G8   Epistula ad Hebraeos.

4929 *Black* David A., The problem of the literary structure of Hebrews; an evaluation and a proposal: GraceTJ 7 (1986) 163-177.

4930 **Braun** Herbert, An die Hebräer: HNT 14, 1984 → 65,5609; 1,6117: RCBQ 48 (1986) 327s (J. *Swetnam*: not a commentary but materials gathered for one); TLZ 111 (1986) 595-8 (W.G. *Kümmel*).

4931 *a) Breneman* M., El uso del Antiguo Testamento en Hebreos; – *b) Villanueva* C., Análisis de términos que hacen a la interpretación de Hebreos; – *c) Warren* W.J., La Cristologia...: Diálogo Teológico 26 (1985) 22-35 / 10-21 / 52-64 [Stromata 42,456].

4931* *a) Bruce* F.F., The structure and argument of Hebrews; – *b) Lane* William L., Hebrews, a sermon in search of a setting; – *c) Hughes* Philip E., The Christology of Hebrews; – *d) Brown* Raymond, Pilgrimage in Faith; the Christian life in Hebrews; – *e) Clements* Ronald E., The use of the Old Testament in Hebrews: SWJT 28,1 (1985s) 6-12 / 13-19 / 19-27 / 28-35 / 36... [< ZIT].

4932 *Ellingsworth* Paul, Jesus and the Universe in Hebrews: EvQ 58 (1986) 337-350.

4933 **Esquerda Bifet** Juan, [Heb 1; 3; 5; 10; 12] La vida es un si: Pedal 179. Salamanca 1986, Sígueme. 144 p. 84-301-0995-1.

4934 **Evans** Louis H.ᴶ, Hebrews: Communicator's Comm. 10, 1985 → 1,6125: RGraceTJ (1986) 250s (H.A. *Kent*); RefTR 45 (1986) 19 (D. *Peterson*: impoverished by failure to interact with scholars).

4935 **Feld** Helmut, Der Hebräerbrief: ErtFor 228, 1985 → 1,6127: RBiKi 41 (1986) 47 (P.-G. *Müller*).

4936 *Grässer* Erich, Das wandernde Gottesvolk; zum Basismotiv des Hebräerbriefs: ZNW 77 (1986) 160-179.

4937 **Guthrie** Donald, The letter to the Hebrews 1983 [reprinted 1986]: → 64,6073; 1,6130; GR 0-8028-1427-1 / IVP 0-8511-884-4: RBibTB 16 (1986) 153 (Carol L. *Stockhausen*).

4938 **Hewitt** Thomas, L'epistola agli Ebrei, introduzione e commentario [1960], ᵀ*Bottazzi* Roberto: Commentario al NT. R 1986, 'G.B.U.' 263 p. Lit. 14.800.

4939 **Hughes** Graham, Hebrews and hermeneutics 1979 → 60,8313... 63,6152: RNedTTs 40 (1986) 86 (H.W. de *Knijff*).

4940 *Jelonek* Tomasz, ℗ Problem autorstwa listu do Hebrajczyków: AnCracov 18 (1986) 205-241; 241-3, De auctore epistolae ad Hebraeos quaestiunculae selectae.

4941 **Käsemann** Ernst, The wandering people of God... Hebrews [1939], ᵀ1984 → 65,5636; 1,6136: RCurrTM 13 (1986) 54s (R. *Gnuse*); Interpretation 40 (1986) 216.218 (R.H. *Smith*: written while in Nazi imprisonment); JTS 37 (1986) 552-4 (F.F. *Bruce*).

4942 *Loane* Marcus L., The unity of the Old and New Testaments as illustrated in the Epistle to the Hebrews: → 54, ᶠKNOX D., God rich 1986, 255-264.

4943 **Logan** Stephen P., The background of *paideia* in Hebrews: diss. Southern Baptist Sem. 1986, ᴰ*Songer* H. 248 p. 86-28707. – DissA 47 (1986s) 3084-A.

4944 **Luxton** Andrea T.J., MILTON's hermeneutics; an intertextual study of the Epistle to the Hebrews and Paradise Lost: diss. Catholic Univ.,

O'Donnell Anne. Wsh 1986. 387 p. 86-13457. – DissA 47 (1986s) 1334-A.

4945 a) *McGehee* Michael, Hebrews, the letter which is not a letter; – b) *Lauderville* Dale, Jesus, the eternal High Priest; – c) *Havener* Ivan, A concerned pastor; – d) *Hutson* Jeffrey, The author of Hebrews: BToday 24 (1986) 213-5 / 217-222 / 223-9 / 232s.

4946 **Masini** Mario, Lettera agli Ebrei; messaggio ai cristiani 1985 ➤ 1,6140: ᴿCC 137 (1986,3) 100s (A. *Vanhoye*).

4947 **Müller** Paul-Gerhard, Die Funktion der Psalmzitate im Hebräerbrief: ➤ 41, ᶠGROSS H., Freude 1986, 223-242.

4948 *Nielsen* Anders E., Sabbatsmotivet i Hebraeerbrevet: DanTTs 49 (1986) 161-176 [< ZIT].

4949 **Peterson** David, Hebrews and perfection [diss. ᴰ*Bruce* F.] 1982 ➤ 63,6156... 1,6142: ᴿJRel 66 (1986) 72s (R. *Jewett*).

4950 *Raurell* Frederic, Certes afinitats entre Ez-LXX i la carta als hebreus en el rol de la 'doxa' i dels querubins: RCatalT 11 (1986) 1-25.

4950* *Scott* J. Julius, Archēgos in the Salvation-History of the epistle to the Hebrews: JEvTS 29 (1986) 47-54 [< ZIT].

4951 *Sharp* Jeffrey R., Typology and the message of Hebrews: EAsJT 4,2 (1986) 95-103.

4952 **Steinbach** Wendelin [1516, ᴱ*Feld* Helmut], Commentarii in Epistolam ad Hebraeos I, 1984 ➤ 65,5618: ᴿTR 82 (1986) 470s (I. *Backus*).

4953 *Thurston* Robert W., PHILO and the Epistle to the Hebrews: EvQ 58 (1986) 133-143.

4954 **Übelacker** Walter, Das Rätsel des Hebräerbriefes und die Bedeutung von Hb 1,1-4 als Exordium. Lund 1986. 105 p.; bibliog. p. 95-105.

4955 *Harris* Murray J., The translation and significance of *Ho theós* in Hebrews 1:8-9: TyndB 36 (1985) 129-162.

4955* **Franco Martínez** Cesar A., El misterio de Cristo en la carta a los Hebreos; lengua y cristología de [2,9s; 4,14; 5,1-10; 9,27s]: diss. Comillas, ᴰ*Vargas-Machuca* A. M 1983. – MiscCom 44 (1986) 568.

4956 *Tait* Henry A. G., The problem of apostasy in Hebrews [3,7 - 4,13...]: ➤ 111, ᶠSTILL, W., Pulpit & people 1986, 131-9.

4957 *Kiley* Mark, [Heb 5,10; 6,20] Melchizedek's promotion to *archiereús* and the translation of *tà stoicheîa tês archês*: ➤ 392, SBL Seminars 1986, 236-245.

4958 **Hancock** Christopher, [Heb 5,14...] The priesthood of Christ in Anglican doctrine and devotion 1827-1900: diss. ᴰ*Sykes* S. Durham 1985. 461 p.; 204 p. – RTLv 18,557.

4959 *Nascimento* Luis J., El sacerdocio de Cristo en la Carta a los Hebreos: RCuBíb 10,37s (1986) 47-85.

4960 *Del Verme* Marcello, La 'prima decima' giudaica nella pericopa di Ebrei 7,1-10: Henoch 8 (1986) 339-361; franç. 361-3.

4961 *Attridge* Harold W., The uses of antithesis in Hebrews 8-10: ➤ 110, ᶠSTENDAHL K. = HarvTR 79 (1986) 1-9.

4961* *Selby* Gary S., The meaning and function of *syneídēsis* in Hebrews 9 and 10: RestQ 28 (Abilene 1985s) 145-154 [< ZIT].

4962 **Casalini** a) Nelio, L'espiazione dall'antica alla nuova alleanza secondo Ebr 9,1-14: diss. P Inst. Cath. 1986, ᴰ*Grelot* P. 287 p. – RICathP 20 (1986) 145-151; RTLv 18,546. – b) (Nello), Ebr 9,11; la tenda più grande e più perfetta: SBFLA 36 (1986) 111-170.

4963 *Camacho* Harold S.,   The altar of incense in Hebrews 9:3-4:   AndrUnS 24 (1986) 5-12.
4963* *Levoratti* Armando J.,   'Tu no has querido sacrificio ni oblación'; Salmo 40,7, Hebreos 10,5:   RBibArg 48 (1986) 1-30. 63-87. 141-152...
4964 *Miller* Merland R.,   What is the literary form of Hebrews 11?:   JEvTS 29 (1986) 411-8 [< ZIT].

G9.1   *Epistulae catholicae* (Jn ➤ G2.1) – **1 Petri.**

ᴱ**Aland** Barbara,   Die grossen katholischen Briefe 1986 ➤ 1246.
4965 **Arichea** Daniel C.,   A translator's handbook on the first letter from Peter: Helps for Translators.   NY 1980, United Bible Societies.   viii-190 p. 0-8267-0152-3.
4966 **Bénétreau** Samuel,   La première épître de Pierre: Comm. Évangélique. Vaux-sur-Seine 1984, Edifac.   287 p. F 92. – ᴿNRT 108 (1986) 757s (X. *Jacques*);_RHPR 66 (1986) 236s (L. *Miller*).
4967 **Calloud** J., *Genuyt* F.,   La première lettre de Pierre, analyse sémiotique: LDiv 109, 1982 ➤ 63,6186; 1,6170:   ᴿCrNSt 7 (1986) 179s (G. *Segalla*).
4968 **Chmiel** Jerzy, ⒫ De epistulis catholicis ut exemplar[i] praedicationis hodie: RuBi 39 (1986) 501-4.
4969 **Dijkman** Jan H. L.,   The socio-religious condition of the recipients of 1 Peter; an attempt to solve the problems of date, authority and addressees of the letter: diss. Witwatersrand 1983. – DissA 47 (1986s) 210-A.
4970 *Dijkman* J. H. L.,   *Hóti* as an introductory formula to catechetical references in 1 Peter: ➤ 72, ꜰMETZGER B., South Africa 1985/6, 260-270.
4971 **Elliott** John H.,   A home for the homeless... 1 Peter 1981 ➤ 62,6851... 1,6173:   ᴿStPatav 33 (1986) 443-5 (G. *Segalla*); SvTKv 62 (1962) 43-45 (B. *Holmberg*).
4972 **Grünewald** W. (*Junack* K.),   Das Neue Testament auf Papyrus I. Die Katholischen Briefe; Vorw. *Aland* K.: ArbNTTextf 6. B 1986, de Gruyter. xi-171 p. DM 158 3-11-010245-5. – ᴿETL 62 (1986) 433s (F. *Neirynck*).
4973 *Halas* Stanisław, ⒫ Originalność koncepcji odrodzenia według pierwszego listu św. Piotra (De novo conceptu regenerationis in Prima Petri): ➤ 367, Sympozjum 1985 = RuBi 39 (1986) 243-9.
4974 **Hurst** David,   The Commentary on the seven Catholic Epistles of BEDE the Venerable 1985 ➤ 1,6167:   ᴿAustralasCR 63 (1986) 338s (W. J. *Dalton*); TS 47 (1986) 348s (J. F. T. *Kelly*).
4975 **Lamau** Marie-Louise,   Articulation de la foi et de la pratique dans la première épître de Pierre; de l'actualisation dans l'Écriture à l'actualité de l'Écriture: diss. P, Inst. Cath. & Sorbonne 1986, ᴰ*Cothenet* E. – RICathP 19 (1986) 145-9; RTLv 18,547.
4976 *Lamau* sr. Marie-Louise,   *a*) Exhortation aux esclaves et hymne au Christ souffrant dans la 'Première épître de Pierre' [2,18-20]: MélSR 43 (1986) 121-143; – *b*) Pierre (Apôtre) — les lettres: ➤ 578, Catholicisme XI,50 (1986) 318-333 [-344, *al.*].
4977 **McDonnell** Rea,   The Catholic Epistles and Hebrews: Message of biblical spirituality 14. Wilmington 1986, Glazier. 150 p. $13; pa. $8. 0-89453-564-1; 80-3 [NTAbs 31,108].
4978 *Migliasso* Secondo,   Il paolinismo di Prima Pietro: ➤ 388, RivB 34 (1986) 519-541; Eng. 541.
4979 *Pryor* J. W.,   First Peter and the New Covenant: RefTR 45 (1986) 1-3.44-51.

4980 ᴱTalbert C. H., Perspectives on First Peter: NABPR 9. Macon GA 1986, Mercer Univ. iv-151 p. $16 pa. 0-86554-198-1 [NTAbs 31,109].
4981 Vanni Ugo, Lettere di Pietro, Giacomo e Giuda: LoB 2/13. Brescia 1986, Queriniana. 163 p. Lit. 13.000.
4982 Warden Preston D., Alienation and community in 1 Peter: diss. Duke, ᴰPrice J. Durham NC 1986. 276 p. 87-06842. – DissA 47 (1986s) 4420s-A.

4983 Kilpatrick G. D., 1 Peter 1:11 tina ē poion kairon: NT 28 (1986) 91s.
4984 Giesen Heinz, Kirche als Gottes erwähltes Volks; zum Gemeinde-verständnis von 1 Petr 2,4-10: TGegw 29 (1986) 140-9.
4985 Steuernagel V. R., An exiled community as a missionary community; a study based on 1 Peter 2:9,10: EvRT 10,1 (Exeter 1986) 8-18 [NTAbs 30,312f.
4986 Best Ernest, A first century sect [1 Pt 2,17 'honour all men; love the brotherhood' — not from Jesus; 'love the brotherhood' is on Orange Order Banners]: ➤ 44, Mem. HAIRE J. = IrBSt 8 (1986) 115-121.
4987 Peeters Robert J., Imitatio Christi: samenhang en theologie in 1 Petr 3,13 - 4,6: ➤ 94, ᶠRIJKHOFF M., Bij de put 1986, 130-153.
4988 a) Feinberg John S., 1 Peter 3; 18-20, ancient mythology, and the intermediate state: WestTJ 48 (1986) 303-336. – b) Grudem Wayne, Christ preaching through Noah?; 1 Peter 3,19-20 in the light of dominant themes in Jewish literature: TrinJ 7,2 (1986) 3-31.
4988* Johnson Dennis E., Fire in God's house; imagery from Malachi 3 in Peter's theology of suffering (1 Pet 4:12-19): JEvTS 29 (1986) 285-294 [< ZIT].
4989 Lehmann Detlef, a) 'Werdet Vorbilder der Herde' (1 Petr. 5,3); Ordnung uns Freiheit in Leben und Dienst des Pastors; – b) Distanzierte Kirchenzugehörigkeit — Problem und Herausforderung für Theologie und kirchliches Handeln: LuthTKi 10 (1986) 17-40 / 41-61.
4989* Thiede C. P., Babylon, der andere Ort; Anmerkungen zu 1 Petr 5,13 und Apg 12,17: Biblica 67 (1986) 532-8.

G9.2   2 Petri.

4990 Berger Klaus, Streit um Gottes Vorsehung; zur Position der Gegner im 2. Petrusbrief: ➤ 59, ᶠLEBRAM J., Tradition 1986, 121-135.
4991 Snyder John I., The promise of his coming; the eschatology of 2 Peter [Diss. Basel]. San Mateo CA 1986, Western. 180 p. $12.50 [TR 83,251].
4992 Thiede Carsten P., A pagan reader of 2 Peter; cosmic conflagration in 2 Peter 3 and the Octavius of Minucius Felix: JStNT 26 (1986) 79-96.
4993 Bergant Dianne, 'There are some things in them hard to understand' — 2 Peter 3:16; biblical interpretation: Listening 21 (1986) 103-114.

G9.4   Epistula Jacobi.

ᴱAland Barbara, Die grossen katholischen Briefe (Jac 1 Pt 1 Jn syr.) 1986 ➤ 1246.
4994 Barsotti Divo, Meditazione sulla lettera di Giacomo: Bibbia e Liturgia 30. Brescia 1986, Queriniana. 89 p. Lit. 8000.
4994* Bottini Giovanni C., Sentenze di Pseudo-Focilide alla luce della lettera di Giacomo: SBFLA 36 (1986) 171-181.

4995 *Cavedo* Romeo, La Chiesa primitiva e la mediazione etica; la lettera di Giacomo: Servitium 44 (1986) 29-37.

4996 *Frankemölle* Hubert, Gesetz im Jakobusbrief; zur Tradition, kontextuellen Verwendung und Rezeption eines belasteten Begriffes: ⮞ 382, ᴱ*Kertelge* G., Gesetz 1985/6, 175-221.

4996* *Kistemaker* Simon J., The theological message of James: JEvTS 29 (1986) 55-62 [< ZIT].

4997 *a) Lea* Thomas D., James, outline and introduction; – *b) Gideon* Virtus, An exposition of James 1; – *c) Cranford* Lorin L., James 2; – *d) MacGorman* J. W., James 3; – *e) Urrey* Thomas C., James 4; – *f) Munn* G. Lacoste, James 5; – *g) Palmer* Clark, Available study helps for James: SWJT 29,1 (1986s) 5-11 / 12-18 / 19-30 / 31-36 / 37-42 / 43-47 / 48s.

4998 **Moo** Douglas J., The letter of James, an introduction and commentary: Tyndale NT 16. GR / Leicester 1986, Eerdmans / Inter-Varsity 191 p. 0-8028-0079-3 / IVP 0-85111-885-2.

4999 **Popkes** Wiard, Adressaten, Situation und Form des Jakobusbriefes: SBS 125s. Stu 1986, KBW. 219 p.; bibliog. p. 211-9. [TR 83,75]. 3-460-04251-6.

5000 *a) Songer* Harold S., Introduction to James; – *b) George* Timothy, 'A right strawy epistle'; Reformation perspectives on James; – *c) Garland* David E., Severe trials, good gifts, and pure religion; James 1; – *d) Polhill* John B., Prejudice, partiality, and faith; James 2; – *e) Culpepper* R. Alan, The power of words and the tests of two wisdoms; James 3; – *f) Blevins* William L., A call to repent, love others, and remember God; James 4; – *g) Omanson* Roger L., The certainty of judgment and the power of prayer; James 5: RExp 83 (1986) 357-368 / 369-382 / 383-394 / 395-404 / 405-418 / 419-426 / 427-438.

5001 **Tamez** Elsa, Santiago, lectura latinoamericana de la epístola : Aportes. San José CR 1985, Departamento Ecuménico. 112 p. – ᴿFranBog 18 (1986) 111.

5002 **Vouga** François, L'épître de saint Jacques 1984 ⮞ 65,5700: ᴿBZ 30 (1986) 280-3 (U. *Luck*); CBQ 48 (1986) 150s (L. T. *Johnson*); JTS 37 (1986) 195-7 (C. L. *Mitton*); RHPR 66 (1986) 235s (J.-C. *Ingelaere*); St Patav 33 (1986) 448s (G. *Segalla*).

5003 *Zmijewski* Josef, Christliche 'Vollkommenheit'; Erwägungen zur Theologie des Jakobusbriefes < SNTU A5 (1980) 50-78]: ⮞ 233, Das NT Quelle 1986, 293-324.

Gideon Virtus [*al.*], An exposition of James 1 [-5] 1986 ⮞ 4997.

5004 *Rakestraw* Robert V., James 2:14-26; does James contradict the Pauline soteriology?: Criswell Theological Review 1 (Dallas 1986) 31-50 [< BS 144,220].

5004* *Schmitt* John J., You adulteresses! The image in James 4:4: NT 28 (1986) 327-337.

5005 **Bottini** G. C., La preghiera di Elia in Giacomo 5,17-18, 1981 ⮞ 63,6218 ... 65,5706: ᴿAsprenas 33 (1986) 204s (A. *Rolla*).

G9.6 **Epistula Judae.**

5006 *Dehandschutter* B., Pseudo-Cyprian, Jude and Enoch; some notes on 1 Enoch 1:9: ⮞ 59, ᶠ*Lebram* J., Tradition 1906, 114-120.

5007 *Heiligenthal* Roman, Der Judasbrief; Aspekte der Forschung in den letzten Jahrzehnten: TRu 51 (1986) 117-129.

5008 *Sellin* Gerhard, Die Häretiker des Judasbriefes [Gastvortrag Neuendettelsau 1984]: ZNW 77 (1986) 206-255.
5009 **Watson** Duane, Rhetorical criticism of Jude and 2 Peter; its contribution to interpretation and questions of literary integrity and interrelationship: diss. Duke, ᴰ*Young* F. Durham NC 1986. 299 p. 86-29332. – DissA 47 (1986s) 3454-A; RelStR 13,190.
5010 **Wickert** James R., An analysis of the use of noncanonical literature in Jude and 2 Peter: diss. SW Baptist Sem., 1985. 261 p. 86-12701. – DissA 47 (1986s) 941-A.

| XV. Theologia Biblica |

H1   **Biblical Theology** 1. [OT] **God.** [→ J9.1 *linguistica de Deo*].

5011 *a) Alston* William P., Does God have beliefs?; – *b) Legenhauser* Gary, Is God a person?: RelSt 22 (1986) 287-306 / 307-323.
5012 *Andersen* Francis I., Yahweh, the kind and sensitive God [77 OT texts]: → 54, ᶠKɴox D., God rich 1986, 41-88.
5013 **Andrade** Bárbara, Encuentro con Dios en la historia; estudio de la concepción de Dios en el Pentateuco: BiblEstB 45. Salamanca 1985, Sígueme. 250 p. 84-301-0954-4. – ᴿCiTom 113 (1986) 398s (J. L. *Espinel*); EstE 61 (1986) 458 (R. *Franco*).
5013* **Baldwin** Louis, Portraits of God; word pictures of the Deity from the earliest times through today. 1986, McFarland. 182 p. $19 [JAAR 55,193].
5014 **Balentine** Samuel S., The hidden God 1983 [diss. Ox, ᴰ*Barr* J.] → 64,6162... 1,6217: ᴿBZ 30 (1986) 292-4 (R. *Bohlen*); JAAR 54 (1986) 163s (J. K. *Kuntz*); JBL 105 (1986) 312-5 (P. D. *Miller*); TLZ 111 (1986) 264s (L. *Horák*).
5015 **Bonansea** Bernardino M., God and atheism. Wsh 1979, Catholic University of America. – ᴿAngelicum 63 (1986) 560-597 (J. M. *Quinn*: Edmund Wɪʟsoɴ wrote in 1956 'The word God is now archaic and it ought to be dropped by those who do not need it for moral support').
5015* *Breitbart* Sidney, Problem of the theodicy: Dor 15 (1986s) 223-233.
5016 *Brito* Emilio, La mort de Dieu selon Hᴇɢᴇʟ; l'interprétation d'Eberhard Jüɴɢᴇʟ [Dieu mystère du monde 1977/1983]: RTLv 17 (1986) 293-308; Eng. 391.
5017 **Burrell** David B., Knowing the unknowable God; Iʙɴ-Sɪɴᴀ, Mᴀɪ-ᴍoɴɪᴅᴇs, Aǫuɪɴᴀs. ND 1986, Univ. x-130 p. $16 [TDig 33,461].
5017* *Busto* José Ramón, La experiencia de Dios en el AT; ¿dónde y cómo sucede?: SalT 74 (1986) 763-772.
5018 *a) Castellino* Giorgio R., Il 'sorriso' di Dio nella S. Scrittura; – *b) Orfali* Moisés, Il Midraš y antropomorfismos en la polémica judeo-cristiana medieval: → 21, Mem. Díᴇz Mᴀcʜo A., Salvación 1986, 89-96 / 759-774.
5019 **Crenshaw** James L., A whirlpool of torment; Israelite traditions of God as an oppressive presence 1984 → 65,5714; 1,6224: ᴿBibTB 16 (1986) 30 (J. I. *Hunt*); CBQ 48 (1986) 528-530 (G. H. *Matties*); Horizons 13 (1986) 155s (Dolores *Greeley*); Interpretation 40 (1986) 84 (M. *Hillmer*); JBL 105 (1906) 518s (J. G. *Janzen*).
5020 **Cupitt** Don, Only human 1985 → 1,6225: ᴿTLond 39 (1986) 132-4 (K. *Surin*: neither the 'divine subject' nor the 'human subject' exists, though the 'religious subject' very much does; the only religion for today is

'anthropomonism', the belief that 'only the human community exists'); further p. 187-194 (C. *Pickstone*: Mondrian 'grin without a cat').

5021 **Delloff** Linda Marie, 'God as artist'; aesthetic theory in The Christian Century 1908-1955: diss. Chicago 1985. – RTLv 18,563.

5022 *Eaton* Jeffrey C., The miracle of atheism [cf. *Mackie* J. L., The miracle of theism 1982]: HeythJ 27 (1986) 125-136 [-177, *al.*].

Eberlein Karl, Gott der Schöpfer — Israels Gott: BeiErfATJ 5, 1986 ➤ 1423.

5023 **Evans** W. Glyn, Beloved adversary; our complex relationship with a loving God. GR 1985, Zondervan. 161 p. $6 [JAAR 54,398].

5024 **García-Murga** José R., El Dios del Antigo Testamento: El problema de Dios hoy 6. M 1985, Fund. S. María. 63 p. – ᴿMiscCom 44 (1986) 228 (J. *Gómez Caffarena*).

5025 *Görg* Manfred, Wege zu dem Einen; Perspektiven zu den Frühphasen der Religionsgeschichte Israels: MüTZ 37 (1986) 97-115.

5026 *Gootjes* N. H., The sense of divinity; a critical examination of the views of CALVIN and DEMAREST [B. A., 1982]: WestTJ 48 (1986) 337-350.

5027 **Goulder** Michael, Hick John, Why believe in God? L 1983, SCM. 117 p. £2.50. – ᴿThemelios 12 (1986s) 68 (S. *Brady*).

5027* **Graf** Gerold, Gott dennoch Recht geben; die Theodizeefrage als ein entscheidendes Problem — besonders bei LUTHER, BULTMANN und SÖLLE: EurHS 23/219. Fra 1983, Lang. 296 p. – ᴿNorTTs 87 (1986) 59-61 (J. B. *Hygen*).

5028 *Gruber* Jacques, La 'représentation' [Stellvertretung... nach dem 'Tode Gottes' 1965 ➤ 48,418] de Dorothée *Sölle*: RHPR 66 (1986) 179-210.287-318, Eng. 257.384.

5029 ᴱ**Haag** Ernst, Gott, der Einzige; zur Entstehung des Monotheismus in Israel: QDisp 104,1985 ➤ 1,288: ᴿDiehlB 22 (1985) 226-234 (B. J. *Diebner*: inquisitorisch?); RHR 203 (1986) 305-308 (A. *Caquot*: pour réfuter l'audace de B. LANG); TrierTZ 95 (1986) 143-5 (R. *Bohlen*).

5029* a) *Habachi* René, Le Dieu des philosophes et le Dieu des théologiens; – b) *Labarrière* Pierre-Jean, Le Dieu de HEGEL: LavalTP 42 (1986) 217-234 / 235-245.

5030 *Hägglund* Bengt, De providentia; zur Gotteslehre im frühen Luthertum: ZTK 83 (1986) 356-369.

5031 **Häring** Hermann, Het kwaad als vraag naar Gods macht en machteloosheid: TsTNijm 26 (1986) 351-371; Eng. 371.

5032 **Hall** Douglas J., God and human suffering. Minneapolis 1986, Augsburg. 223 p. 0-8066-2223-7 [ExpTim 98,287].

5033 **Hick** John, Gott und seine vielen Namen [God has many names 1980 ➤ 62,7253; 65,9035],ᵀ Altenberge 1985, Christlich-Islamisch. 164 p. – ᴿZMissRW 70 (1986) 325 (G. *Risse*).

5034 **Jüngel** E., God as the mystery of the world, ᵀGuder D. L. 1983 ➤ 64,6189b... 1,6240: ᴿCalvinT 21 (1986) 250-5 (J. *Bolt*); GraceTJ 7 (1986) 143-6 (J. D. *Morrison*); HeythJ 27 (1986) 79-81 (J. *O'Donnell*); Interpretation 40 (1986) 77-79 (R. P. *Scharlemann*); ScotJT 39 (1986) 551-6 (J. B. *Webster*).

5035 **Jüngel** E., Dieu mystère du monde 1983 ➤ 65,5723: ᴿScEspr 38 (1986) 5-30 (J. *Richard*: théologie évangélique/philosophique); VSp 139 (1985) 263s (R.-L. *Oechslin*).

5036 **Jüngel** E., a) Dios como misterio del mundo, ᵀVevia F. C. 1984 ➤ 65,5725, 1,6241: ᴿCiuD 199 (1986) 136s (S. *Folgado Flórez*). – b) Dio, mistero del mondo 1982 ➤ 64,6180c; 65,5724: ᴿStPatav 33 (1986) 467-9 (G. *Segalla*).

5036* *Klaiber* W., Der eine Gott — die ganze Bibel: ➤ 64,37, [F]FICK Ulrich, Mittelpunkt Bibel, [E]**Meurer** S., 1983, 167-185.

5037 *Krawczyk* Roman, ❷ La transcendance de Dieu dans l'AT: ColcT 56,3 (1986) 35-41; franç. 41.

5038 *Kyle* Richard, The divine attributes in John KNOX's concept of God: WestTJ 48 (1986) 161-172.

5039 **Lang** Bernhard, Monotheism and the prophetic minority 1983 ➤ 64,191.6188; 1,6242: [R]BO 43 (1986) 456-9 (F. *Stolz*); JBL 105 (1986) 116s (B. O. *Long*); JStOT 34 (1986) 121s (R. *Carroll*); RTLv 17 (1986) 221 (P.-M. *Bogaert*).

5040 *Lang* Bernhard, Zur Entstehung des biblischen Monotheismus: TüTQ 166 (1986) 135-142.

5041 **Lindström** Fredrik, God and the origin of evil, [T]*Cryer* F. H.: ConBibOT 21, 1983 ➤ 65,5757: [R]JBL 105 (1986) 120-2 (G. H. *Matties*).

5042 *Lyons* Andrew, *al.*, Images of God: Way 26 (1986) 267-277 (-311).

5043 **Mast** Stanley P., The wrath of God on believers: diss. Calvin Theol. Sem., [D]*Plantinga* C. GR c. 1986. vii-191 p. + bibliog. – CalvinT 21 (1986) 325.

5043* *a*) *Mauser* Ulrich, *Heìs theós* und *mónos theós* in biblischer Theologie; – *b*) *Stuhlmacher* Peter, Biblische Theologie als Weg der Erkenntnis Gottes; zum Buch von Horst SEEBASS, Der Gott der ganzen Bibel / Seebass, Antwort: ➤ 236, JbBT 1 (1986) 71-87 / 91-114.115-134.

5044 *Mayberger* Paul, Zur 'dulcedo Dei' im Alten Testament: AnCracov 18 (1986) 167-184.

5045 **Meador** Marion F., The motif of God as judge in the Old Testament: diss. SW Baptist Sem. 1986. 259 p. 86-23462. – DissA 47 (1986s) 2623-A; RelStR 13,189.

5045* *a*) *Mesle* C. Robert, The problem of genuine evil; a critique of John HICK's theodicy: JRel 66 (1986) 412-430: – *b*) *Miller* Patrick D., The sovereignty of God: ➤ 69, [F]MAYS J., Hermeneutical Quest 1986, 129-144.

5046 **Montefiore** Hugh, The probability of God 1985 ➤ 1,6253: [R]TLond 39 (1986) 134s (J. *Kent*).

5047 *Nicholson* E. W. W., Israelite religion in the pre-exilic period: a debate renewed [*Wellhausen, Weber, Albright; Mendenhall, Gottwald; Schmid* H. H., creation-theology ...]: ➤ 63, [F]McKANE W., A word 1986, 3-34.

5048 **Oberthür** Rainer, Angst vor Gott? Über die Vorstellung eines strafenden Gottes in der religiösen Entwicklung und Erziehung: RelPdSt 4. Essen 1986, Blaue Eule. 141 p. DM 24 [TR 83,416, J. *Hofmeier*].

5049 **Page** Ruth, Ambiguity and the presence of God. L 1985, SCM. viii-230. £11. 0-334-00022-X. – [R]ExpTim 97 (1985s) 283 (D. W. *Hardy*: accentuates the negative); TLond 39 (1986) 329s (K. *Surin*).

5050 [E]**Pannenberg** W., Die Erfahrung der Abwesenheit Gottes in der modernen Kultur 1978/84 ➤ 1,624: [R]ExpTim 97 (1985s) 268 (G. *Wainwright*'s 'disappointment' seems ultimately with modern iconography and privatism rather than with Pannenberg's 'habitual cool [leading into] passionate and prophetic'); TZBas 42 (1986) 270s (U. *Gerber*).

5051 *Rémy* Gérard, L'analogie selon E. JÜNGEL [trouve son modèle dans la parabole évangélique], remarques critiques; l'enjeu d'un débat: RHPR 66 (1986) 147-177; Eng. 257.

5052 **Robinson** Bernard P., Israel's mysterious God; an analysis of some Old Testament narratives. Newcastle 1986, Grevatt. xi-93 p. £7.45.

5052* *Sampson* David A., The Old Testament and God's love: RestQ 28 (1985s) 171 ... [< ZIT].

5053 *Schoonenberg* Piet,   Der Gott der Philosophen und der Gott der Bibel —
eine meta-thomistische Überlegung, ^T*Sukenik* Dietlind [zum 75. Gb.]: TPQ
134 (1986) 358-365.

5054 **Schulweis** Harold M.,   Evil and the morality of God: Jewish perspectives
3, 1984 ➤ 65,5765:   ^RJRel 66 (1986) 452-4 (C. M. *Raffel*); Judaism 35
(1986) 117-9 (K. *Seeskin*); NRT 108 (1986) 113s (J.-L. *Ska*).

5055 **Seebass** Horst,   Der Gott der ganzen Bibel 1982 ➤ 63,4263 ... 1,6261:
^RFreibRu 37s (1985s) 104s (Rita *Egger*).

5056 **Seebass** Horst,   Il Dio di tutta la Bibbia; teologia biblica per
l'orientamento alla fede, ^T*Fantoma* G.: StBPaid 72. Brescia 1985, Paideia.
293 p. Lit. 20.000 [BL 87,91].

5057 *Soviv* Aaron,   About some Scriptural divine designations [Lord of Hosts,
Glory of the Presence, the Name: shifting formulations or ever-new
meaning]: Dor 15 (1986s) 29-37.

5058 **Sponheim** Paul R.,   God — the question and the quest.   Ph 1985,
Fortress. 214 p. [Int 41, 325, G. *Guthrie*].

Stähli H. P.,   Solare Elemente im Jahweglauben des ATs: OBO 66, 1985
➤ 1,6266.

5059 **Storms** C. Samuel,   The grandeur of God; a theological and devotional
study of the divine attributes. GR 1984, Baker. 180 p. $7. – ^RBS 143
(1986) 78s (J. L. *Burns*).

5060 **Surin** Kenneth,   Theology and the problem of evil: Signposts in
Theology. Ox 1986, Blackwell. 180 p. £19.50; pa. £7. 0-631-14663-6;4-4.
– ^RExpTim 98 (1986s) 129s (C. S. *Rodd*: high praise).

5061 ^E**Thoma** Clemens, *Wyschogrod* Michael,   Das Reden von einem Gott bei
Juden und Christen [Seminar Luzern 1982s]: Judaica et Christiana 7. Bern
1984, Lang. 247 p. – ^RFreibRu 37s (1985s) 126s (G. *Klostermann*).

5062 **Unen** H. J. van,   Prodeonisme, 1. De wijsbegeerte van grond en zin; 2. de
theologie van God en zijn Rijk.   Muiderberg 1984, Pro Deo. 493 p.
f 39,50. – ^RNedTTs 40 (1986) 267s (H. *Berkhof*).

5063 **Varone** François,   Ce Dieu absent qui fait problème; religion, athéisme et
foi; trois regards sur le mystère.³ P 1984, Cerf. 230 p. 2-204-02043-5.
– ^REstE 61 (1986) 111s (J. J. *Alemany*: textos bíblicos... para la diferencia entre Dios de la religión — proyección del hombre — y Dios de
la fe).

5064 **Vázquez Moro** Ulpiano,   El discurso sobre Dios en la obra de E.
LEVINAS. Publ. Comillas 1/23. M 1982, Univ. Pontificia Comillas.
XXXI-303 p. – ^RRB 93 (1986) 307-9 (J. *Loza*).

5065 **Vorlander** Hermann,   Aspekte von Volksreligiosität im Alten Testament:
(Concilium) IZT 22 (1986) 281-5 (Eng. ed., Aspects of popular religion in
the OT, 63-70, ^T*Harrison* G.).

5066 **Walsh** James & P. G.,   Divine providence and human suffering: Message of the Fathers 17, 1985 ➤ 1,6271: ^RÉTRel 61 (1986) 144s (A.
Gounelle).

5067 **Wenham** J. M.,   The enigma of evil [= The goodness of God 1974].
Leicester 1985, Inter-Varsity. 223 p. £5. – ^RRefTR 45 (1986) 59s (D. *Kir-
kaldy*: OT; NT; good except on Hell).

5068 **Wiles** Maurice,   God's action in the world (Bampton Lectures 1986).
L 1986, SCM. 118 p. £5.95. 0-334-02028-4. – ^RExpTim 98 (1986s)
130-2 (C. S. *Rodd*: God's single act of 'continuing creation' does not
warrant calling each result of evolution a specific act of God; we say 'It's
all your fault' to a friend who had loyally urged us to make our own
choice).

5069 **Wilterdink** Garret, Tyrant or father ? A study of CALVIN's doctrine of God. Bristol IN 1985, Wyndam. 134 p.; 99 p. – RCalvinT 21 (1986) 239-241 (L. D. *Bierma*).

H1.3 *Immutabilitas* – **God's suffering; process theology.**

5069* *Boonstra* S. A., Het Godsbeeld in de procesfilosofie en procestheologie: GerefTTs 86 (1986) 168-182.

5070 **Bracken** Joseph A., The triune symbol; persons, process and community: CTS Studies in Religion 1, 1985 ➤ 1,6280: RHorizons 13 (1986) 178-180 (L. S. *Ford*: first full-scale Catholic WHITEHEAD theology).

5071 *Buri* Fritz, Das Sinn-Sein-Problem in heutiger amerikanischer Imaginations- und Prozess-Theologie: TZBas 42 (1986) 46-65.

5072 **Creel** Richard E., Divine impassibility, an essay in philosophical theology. C 1986, Univ. xiii-238 p. £25. 0-521-30317-6. – RExpTim 97 (1985s) 282 (W. D. *Hudson*: skilful); JTS 37 (1986) 682-5 (Helen *Oppenheimer*); TrinJ 7,2 (1986) 97-100 (P. D. *Feinberg*); TS 47 (1986) 707s (J. A. *Bracken*).

5073 *Dalferth* Ingolf U., The One who is worshipped; Erwägungen zu Charles HARTSHORNES Versuch, Gott zu denken: ZTK 83 (1986) 484-506.

5074 **Dodds** Michael J., The unchanging God of love; a study of the teaching of St. Thomas AQUINAS on divine immutability in view of certain contemporary criticisms of this doctrine: Studia Friburgensia NS 66. FrS 1986, Univ. xviii-489 p. – RNBlackf 67 (1986) 503s (B. *Davies*: splendid).

5075 **Egmond** Adrianus Van, De lijdende God in de Britse theologie van de negentiende eeuw; de bijdrage van NEWMAN, MCLEOD CAMPBELL en GORE aan de christelijke theopaschitische traditie: diss. DVeenhof J. Amst 1986. 292 p. – RTLv 18,573; TsTNijm 27,99.

5076 **Fretheim** Terence E., The suffering of God; an OT perspective: OvBT 14, 1984 ➤ 65,5752; 1,6285: RBibTB 16 (1986) 32 (R. *Gnuse*); Horizons 13 (1986) 151-3 (Elizabeth *Bellefontaine*); Interpretation 40 (1986) 81s (N. C. *Theiss*); JAAR 54 (1986) 578s (J. B. *White*); JBL 105 (1986) 516-8 (J. M. *Ward*: how is the divine 'presence intensified'?); SpTod 38 (1986) 91s (J. M. *Deschene*).

5077 **Frohnhofen** Herbert, Apatheia tou theou; über die Affektlosigkeit in der griechischen Antike und bei den griechisch sprechenden Kirchenvätern bis zu Gregorios Thaumaturgos: Diss. München 1985s, DStockmeier P. – TR 82 (1986) 512; RTLv 18,551.

5078 *Geisler* Norman L., *Watkins* William D., Process theology; a survey and an appraisal: Themelios 12 (1986s) 15-22.

5079 *Keller* James A., Continuity, possibility, and omniscience; a contrasting view: ProcSt 15 (1986) 1-18.

5080 *Koslowski* Peter, Der leidende Gott: TPhil 61 (1986) 562-5.

5081 **Kreuzer** Siegfried, Der lebendige Gott ...: BWANT 116, 1983 ➤ 65,5756: RBZ 30 (1986) 295s (R. *Albertz*).

5082 **McWilliams** Warren, The Passion of God; divine suffering in contemporary Protestant theology 1985 ➤ 1,6297: RJAAR 54 (1986) 380s (K. *Cauthen*).

5083 *Maldamé* Jean-Michel, Cosmologie et théologie; étude de la notion de création dans la théologie nord-américaine du 'Procès': RThom 86 (1986) 90-114.

5084 *Mascall* E. L., Das God change? Mutability and Incarnation; a review discussion [*Weinandy* T. 1985]: Thomist 50 (1986) 447-457.

5085 *Mueller* J. J.,   Process theology and the Catholic theological community: TS 47 (1986) 412-427.

5086 **O'Donnell** John,   Trinity and temporality... process theology 1983 ➤ 64,6815 ... 1,6299: ᴿTPhil 61 (1986) 288s (G. *Haeffner*).

5086* *Olson* Roger E.,   The human self-realization of God; HEGELIAN elements in PANNENBERG's Christology; PerspRelSt 13 (1986) 207-224 [< ZIT].

5087 **Pickett** Joseph R.,   God and world-loyalty; prayer from a process perspective; diss. Claremont 1986, ᴰ*Griffin* D. 280 p. 86-19082. – DissA 47 (1986s) 2195s-A; RelStR 13,188.

5088 *Rizzi* Armido,   Le sfide del pensiero debole ['impotenza di Dio', *Moltmann*; ... *Vattimo* G.]: RasT 27 (1986) 1-14.

5089 **Sia** Santiago,   God in process thought 1985 ➤ 1,6308: ᴿModT 3 (1986s) 107-9 (J. B. *Cobb*); RelSt 22 (1986) 284-6 (D. A. *Pailin*).

5090 *Staudinger* Hugo,   Gottes Allmacht und moderne Welterfahrung; Überlegungen zum Problem der Integration moderner Weltverständnisses und überkommener Offenbarungswahrheiten: ForumKT 2 (1986) 120-133.

5091 **Taylor** Mark C.,   [➤ e157s] God is love; a study in the theology of Karl RAHNER [diss. ᴰ*Ogden* S.]. Atlanta 1986, Scholars. 416 p. $25; pa. $18.25. – ᴿTTod 43 (1986s) 611 (E. O. *Springsted*: nothing wrong that process theology would not solve).

5092 **Thelekat** Paul,   God suffers evil; an attempted rapprochement of classical and neo-classical theism: diss. ᴰ*Veken* J. van der. Leuven 1986. xxxiii-395 p. – RTLv 17 (1986) 517.

5093 **Tracy** Thomas F.,   God, action, and embodiment [diss. Yale 1980] 1984 ➤ 1,6309: ᴿJTS 37 (1986) 673-6 (Grace M. *Jantzen*); Thomist 50 (1986) 706-710 (F. G. *Kirkpatrick*).

5093* *Ware* Bruce A.,   An evangelical reformulation of the doctrine of the immutability of God: JEvTS 29 (1986) 431-446 [< ZIT].

5094 **Weinandy** Thomas G.,   Does God change? The Word's becoming in the Incarnation: Studies in Historical Theology 4, 1985 ➤ 1,6993: ᴿThomist 50 (1986) 447-457 (E. L. *Mascall*); TS 47 (1986) 708s (W. L. *Porter*).

5095 *Welker* Michael,   Dogmatische Theologie und postmoderne Metaphysik; Karl BARTHs Theologie, Prozesstheologie und die Religionstheorie WHITEHEADS [< Princeton Feier, TTod 43 (1986)]: NSys 28 (1986) 311-326; Eng. 326.

5096 **Whitney** Barry L.,   Evil and the process God: TorStT 19, 1985 ➤ 1,6313: ᴿEncounter 47 (1986) 171s (L. S. *Ford*); SR 15 (1986) 108 (Pamela D. *Young*); TS 47 (1986) 187 (P. E. *Devenish*).

5097 **Williams** Trevor,   Form and vitality in the world and God; a Christian perspective. Ox 1985, Clarendon. 356 p. £22.50/$30. – ᴿInterpretation 40 (1986) 432.434 (C. M. *Wood*); TLond 39 (1986) 387-9 (Ann *Loades*); TS 47 (1986) 557s (T. W. *Tilley*); TTod 43 (1986s) 584-6 (W. *Brueggemann*).

5098 *Wilmot* Laurence F.,   God and the world; one man's search and discovery [*Whitehead* A. N.; *Lowe* V. 1982]: RelSt 22 (1986) 125-150.

H1.4   *Femininum in Deo* – **God as father and as mother.**

5098* *Achtemeier* Elizabeth,   Female language for God; should the Church adopt it?: ➤ 69, ᶠMAYS J., Hermeneutical Quest 1986, 97-114.

5099 *Arluck* Theresa E. S.,   The supreme breasted one (El shaddai): Religion and Intellectual Life 3,2 (New Rochelle 1986) 78s (poem).

5100 **Bloesch** Donald G.,   The battle for the Trinity ... inclusive God-language 1985 ➤ 1,6316: ᴿWestTJ 48 (1986) 407-9 (Susan *Fox*).

5100* **Boff** Leonardo, Das mütterliche Antlitz Gottes 1985 ⇥ 1,6316*: ᴿHerdKor 40 (1986) 102 (K. *Nientiedt*).

5101 **Bovet** René, Dieu le Père et Jésus le Christ dans la théologie féministe aux USA: cath. diss. ᴰ*Winling* R. Strasbourg 1986. 356 p. – RTLv 18,571.

5101* *Bray* Gerald, What will happen to God? (I): Churchman 100 (L 1986) 309-322 [< ZIT].

5102 **Bynum** Caroline W., Jesus as mother 1984 ⇥ 63,4167 ... 1,4063: ᴿSpeculum 61 (1986) 907-910 (R. *Boenig*).

5103 *Campos Lavall* Luciano, A afirmação de 'Deus Pai' na teologia RAHNERiana [diss. Pont. Univ. Gregoriana, R 1985]: PerspTeol 18,45 (1986) 193-213.

5104 *Camroux* Martin, The motherhood of God [Mt 23,37]: ExpTim 98 (1986s) 146s.

5105 **Carson** Anne, Feminist spirituality and the feminine divine; an annotated bibliography. Trumansburg NY 1986, Crossing. 139 p. $40 [TDig 33, 462].

5106 **Daly** Mary, Beyond God the Father; towards a philosophy of women's liberation 1985 = 1973 [⇥ 60,9862], The Women's Press £5. – ᴿTablet 240 (1986) 732 (Rosemary R. *Ruether*: Mary Daly's first book was Christian, second [this] post-Christian; third and after, anti-Christian; she is still professor of theology at Boston College).

5107 *Douglass* Jane D., CALVIN's use of metaphorical language for God; God as enemy and God as mother: ArRefG 77 (1986) 126-139, deutsch 139s.

5108 *Edwards* James R., Does God really want to be called 'Father' ? : ChrTod (Feb. 21,1986) 27-30 [< BS 143 (1986) 271].

5109 *Fatula* Mary Ann, On calling God 'Father' [Gal 4,6]: SpTod 38 (1986) 361-8.

5110 *Foss* David B., From God as mother to priest as mother; JULIAN of Norwich and the movement for the ordination of women: DowR 104 (1986) 214-226 [... no evidence for any supposed connection].

5111 *Fuster* Sebastian, ¿Hijos 'de Dios' o hijos 'del Padre'? Estudio sobre las apropiaciones: EscrVedat 16 (1986) 77-113.

5112 **Galot** Jean, Découvrir le Père; esquisse d'une théologie du Père. Lv 1985, Sintal. 208 p. Fb 610. – ᴿGregorianum 67 (1986) 201s (*ipse*).

5113 **Gelpi** Donald L., The divine mother; a trinitarian theology of the Holy Spirit 1984 ⇥ 1,6322; 0-8191-4035-X: ᴿGregorianum 67 (1986) 557s (J. *Galot*); JAAR 54 (1986) 579.581s (N. *Kollar*).

5114 **Hebblethwaite** Margaret, Motherhood and God 1984 ⇥ 65,5775; 1,6235: ᴿVidyajyoti 49 (1985) 310-312 (Marianne *Katoppo*).

5115 **Loh** Johannes, Gott der Vater; ein Beitrag zum Gespräch mit der Psychologie über den praktisch-theologischen Sinn der Vater-Symbolik: Erfahrung und Theologie 7. Fra 1984, Lang 299 p. Fs 67 pa. 3-8204-7861-2. – ᴿTLZ 111 (1986) 627 (E. R. *Kiesow*).

5116 *MacCaffrey* James, Prayer and the fatherhood of God in Matthew: CleR 71 (1986) 104-9. 135-141.

5116* *McCoy* Michael R., Our father / My father; the interpenetration of religious and familial imagery in the Puritan conception of the father: PerspRelSt 13 (1986) 45-54 [< ZIT].

5117 **Mangan** Celine, Can we still call God 'father'? 1984 ⇥ 65,5781; 1,6334: ᴿRRel 45 (1986) 467s (CarolAnn *Kenz*).

5118 **Mercadante** Linda A., The influence of gender imagery for God; a case study in theology and narrative, using the Shaker Father-Mother God

metaphor: diss. Princeton Theol. Sem. 1986. 258 p. 86-16950. – DissA 47 (1986s) 1777s-A.
5119 *Miller* John W.,   *a*) Depatriarchalizing God in biblical interpretation [*Trible* P. 1973]: CBQ 48 (1986) 609-616; – *b*) God as father in the Bible and the father image in several contemporary ancient Near Eastern myths; a comparison: SR 14 (Toronto 1985) 347-354.
5120 **Moltmann** Elizabeth & Jürgen,   Dieu homme et femme: Théologies, 1984, ➤ 65,5786. **1**,6340: ᴿScEspr 38 (1986) 406s (J.-M. *Archambault*: ᵀ[de l' 'américain'] BRUN-REYNIERS Marcelline); SR 15 (1986) 256s (G. *Durand*).
5120* *Phillips* Nancy V.,   Imaging God as mother: ➤ 123*, ᶠWILTERDINK G. = RefR 40 (1986) 41-9.
5121 *Porter* Jean,   The feminization of God; second thoughts on the ethical implications of process theology: StLuke 29 (1986) 251-260 [OTAbs 10,82].
5122 *Ramshaw-Schmidt* Gail,   Naming the Trinity; orthodoxy and inclusivity (Abba–Servant–Paraclete): Worship 60 (1986) 491-8.
5122* **Schlink** M. Basilea,   God, een Vader vol van troost.   Franeker 1986, Wever. 136 p. ƒ 10 [GerefTTs 86,259].
5123 **Schneiders** Sandra M.,   Women and the word; the gender of God in the New Testament and the spirituality of women (Madeleva lecture). Mahwah NJ 1986, Paulist. 81 p. $3 pa. [TDig 33,487].
Schüngel-Straumann Helen,   Gott als Mutter in Hosea 11: 1986 ➤ 2876.
5124 *Sölle* Dorothée,   Dios, madre de todos nosotros [< Orientierung 49 (1985) 37s], ᵀᴱ*Reig* Ramiro: SelT 25 (1986) 97-100.
5125 **Tennis** Diane,   Is God the only reliable father ? 1985 ➤ 1,6353: ᴿEncounter 47 (1986) 170s (Nadia M. *Lahutsky*).
5126 **Torwesten** Hans,   Gott ist auch Mutter. 1984, Planegg [GeistL 59,309].
5127 *Verhoeven* Alieda,   Conceito de Deus a partir da perspectiva feminina: ➤ 510, REB 46 (1986) 30-37.
5128 **Visser't Hooft** W. A.,   The fatherhood of God in an age of emancipation 1982 ➤ 63,6389... **1**,6354: ᴿRExp 83 (1986) 307s (Molly *Marshall-Green*); Protestantesimo 41 (1986) 126 (M. *Cignoni*).
5129 **Winter** Urs,   Frau und Göttin...: OBO 53, 1983 ➤ 64,1534... **1**,6356: ᴿBO 43 (1986) 493-9 (K. van der *Toorn*); BZ 30 (1986) 291s (E. S. *Gerstenberger*); JBL 105 (1986) 309-311 (Phyllis *Bird*: place of female divinity in Israelite piety and cultus); PEQ 118 (1986) 75s (D. *Collon*); VT 36 (1986) 124s (J. A. *Emerton*).

H1.7 Revelatio, theologia fundamentalis.

5130 *Albano* Peter J.,   Toward a dialectical apologetic of hope; the confrontative dimension of Paul RICŒUR's contribution to fundamental theology: SR 15 (1986) 77-88.
5131 *Alemany* José J.,   El Vaticano I, citado en 'Dei Verbum' 6: MiscCom 44 (1986) 29-44.
5132 **Alfaro** Juan,   Revelación cristiana, fe y teología 1985 ➤ 1,148: ᴿPerspT 18 (1986) 413s (A. *Casalegno*); Salmanticensis 33 (1986) 252-4 (J. L. *Ruiz de la Peña*); VerVid 44 (1986) 145 (V. *Casas*).
5133 **Allen** Diogenes,   Philosophy for understanding theology. Atlanta/L 1985, Knox/SCM. vi-287 p. $15/£9.50. 0-334-01249-X. – ᴿExpTim 98 (1986s) 21 (G. *Slater*: focusing Plato and Aristotle, not explaining why they no longer hold the field); TS 47 (1986) 555s (D. K. *McKim*: highly recommended).

5134 *Alszeghy* Zoltan, Sistema in teologia?: Gregorianum 67 (1986) 213-234.
5135 **Artola** A. M., [LESSIUS L.] De la revelación a la inspiración 1983
→ 64,1425... 1,6360: ᴿScripTPamp 18 (1986) 674-7 (J. M. *Casciaro*).
ZKG 97 (1936) 139-141 (J. M. *Sánchez Caro*).
5136 *Balthasar* Hans Urs von, Dieu est son propre exégète: Communio 11,1
(P 1986) 5-12 = Gott ist sein eigener Exeget: IkaZ 15 (1986) 8-13.
5137 **Bañares Parera** Leticia, Revelación y 'lumen propheticum' en Santo
Tomás de AQUINO: diss. Pamplona 1986, ᴰ*Illanes Maestre* J. 310 p. –
RTLv 18,539.
5138 **Barnes** Robert B.ᴶ, The concept of revelation among selected
twentieth-century theologians; James ORR, Edward J. CARNELL, and G. C.
BERKOUWER: diss. New Orleans Baptist theol. sem. 1986, ᴰ*Humphreys* F.
183 p. 86-21466. – DissA 47 (1986s) 2197-A.
5139 *a) Beardslee* William A., Scripture and philosophy; – *b) McGrath*
Brendan, Preach the Word: Listening 21 (1986) 115-123 / 171-8.
5140 **Beinert** Wolfgang, Dogmatik studieren; Einführung in dogmatisches
Denken und Arbeiten 1985 → 1,6361: ᴿSalesianum 48 (1986) 991s (D. *Valentini*).
5140* **Bentue** A., La opción creyente; introducción a la Teología
Fundamental: Lux Mundi 62. Salamanca 1986, Sígueme [= Chile 1981/3].
334 p. [Proyección 34, 240, A. *Jiménez*].
5141 **Betti** Umberto, La dottrina del Concilio Vaticano II sulla trasmissione
della Rivelazione: Spicilegium 26. R 1985, Pont. Athenaeum Antonianum.
367 p. – ᴿScripTPamp 18 (1986) 730 (A. *García-Moreno*).
5142 **Bižaca** N., Rivelazione e teologia in Gottlieb SÖHNGEN [diss. R, Pont.
Univ. Gregoriana] 1985 → 1,6363: ᴿRasT 27 (1986) 92-94 (R. *Fisichella*).
5143 *Boada* Josep, Teología fundamental [*Fries* H.; *Waldenfels* A.; *Niemann*
F., *Heinz* G.; *Latourelle* R., *Mayer* A., *Lohfink* G.; *Herms* E.]: ActuBbg 23
(1986) 7-53.
5144 *Brom* L. J. van den, Dogmatik een wetenschap; een contradictie?
[ᴱ*Sauter* G. 1971; *Pannenberg* W. 1977...]: NedTTs 40 (1986) 53-80; Eng.
81, Is dogmatics science or mere ideology?
5145 *Bucher* Theodor G., Wahrheitsgarantie der Theologie und der Beitrag
der Logik: LingBib 58 (1986) 15-43; Eng. 43; Replik, *Güttgemanns* E., 43s.
5146 **Cantalamessa** R., Ci ha parlato nel Figlio; il mistero della parola di Dio.
Mi 1984, Àncora. 136 p. – ᴿClaretianum 26 (1986) 354-7 (R. M.
Serra).
5147 *Casalis* Georges, Correct ideas don't fall from the skies; elements for an
inductive theology. Maryknoll NY 1984, Orbis. xxi-219 p. $9. – ᴿVidyajyoti 49 (1985) 145 (R. *Athickal*).
5148 **Caviglia** Giovanni, Le ragioni della speranza cristiana; teologia
fondamentale 1981 → 63,1453; 88-01-15467-4: ᴿEstE 61 (1986) 465 (J. J.
Alemany).
5149 *Chantraine* Georges, 'Dei Verbum' un enseignement et une tâche: NRT
[107 (1985) 823-837] 108 (1986) 13-26.
5150 *Charron* André, La critique de la religion, une fonction mal reconnue:
ScEspr 38 (1986) 151-179.
5150* **Christoffersen** Svein A., Identifikasjon og verifikasjon... EBELINGS
fundamentalteologi. Oslo 1984, Univ. 304 p. – ᴿNorTTs 87 (1986) 65-80
(T. *Jørgensen*, 'Teologi mellem forkyndelse og videnskabelighed', theology
straddles proclamation and scholarship).
5151 *Cipriani* Settimio, Rileggere la Dei Verbum; un documento sempre vivo e
stimolante: Asprenas 32 (1985) 361-376.

5152 **Coffey** David, Believer, Christian, Catholic; three essays in fundamental theology. Sydney 1986. 74 p.

5153 *Cook* Michael J., Revelation as metaphoric process: TS 47 (1986) 388-411.

5154 *Cooke* Vincent M., The new CALVINist epistemology [*Planting* A.; *Wolterstorff* N.]: TS 47 (1986) 273.

5155 **Craig** William L., Apologetics; an introduction. Ch 1984, Moody. 214 p. $14. – ᴿBS 143 (1986) 370s (F. R. *Howe*).

5156 **Dartigues** André, La révélation; du sens au salut [1,6370]: Le christianisme et la foi chrétienne; manuel de théologie 6 [ᴱ*Doré* Joseph; 2. *Vallin* Pierre, Les chrétiens et leur histoire; 4. *Neusch* Marcel, Les chrétiens et leur vision de l'homme; 10. *Bourgeois* Henri, L'expérience maintenant et toujours]. P 1985, Desclée. 288 p. – ᴿRSPT 70 (1986) 281-7 (B. *Rey*).

5157 *Doré* Joseph, Bulletin de théologie fondamentale; instruments de travail [*Langevin* P.; *Mondésert* C., *Fontaine-Pietri, Riché-Lobrichon, Savart-Aletti* BTT; *Niemann* F., *Fisichella* R., *Fries* R.; *Kern* W.]: RechSR 74 (1986) 441-475.

5158 *Drilling* Peter J., The pyramid or the raft; Francis Schüssler FIORENZA and Bernard LONERGAN in dialogue about foundational theology: Horizons 13 (1986) 275-290.

5159 **Dulles** Avery, Models of revelation 1983 → 64,1379... 1,6373: ᴿAfER 28 (1986) 354 (P. *Vonck*); HeythJ 27 (1986) 181-3 (G. *O'Collins*, also on SHORTER, HELM, ENGLEZAKIS); LavalTP 42 (1986) 331s (R.-M. *Roberge*).

5160 **Farley** Edward [→ d732], Ecclesial reflection; an anatomy of theological method 1982 → 63,1338... 1,6375: ᴿJTS 37 (1986) 272-4 (S. W. *Sykes*).

5161 **Fiorenza** Francis S., Foundational theology; Jesus and the Church 1985 → 65,5815; 1,6376: ᴿBibTB 16 (1986) 151s (Q. *Quesnell*: 'foundation' as of a ship which has to be repaired by part of itself); Gregorianum 67 (1986) 374-6 (J. *Wicks*); Interpretation 40 (1986) 331s (A. *Milavec*); JRel 66 (1986) 81s (Rebecca *Chopp*); LavalTP 42 (1986) 317-9 (R.-M. *Roberge*); NRT 108 (1986) 95-104 (L. *Renwart*); TPhil 61 (1986) 607-9 (J. *Beutler*).

5162 **Fisichella** Rino, La rivelazione; evento e credibilità; saggio di teologia fondamentale: Corso Teol. sist. 2. Bo 1985, Dehoniane. 391 p. – ᴿCC 137 (1986,2) 611s (R. *Latourelle*); RasT 27 (1986) 188s (G. *O'Collins*); Salesianum 48 (1986) 735-8 (G. *Groppo*).

5163 *Fisichella* Rino, Scopo e confini della teologia fondamentale [*Fries* H., *Kern* W., *Waldenfels* H.]: Gregorianum 67 (1986) 340-357.

5164 **Fries** Heinrich, Fundamentaltheologie 1985 → 1, 6379: ᴿActuBbg 23 (1986) 7-15 (J. *Boada*); EstE 61 (1986) 106 (J. *García Pérez*); MüTZ 37 (1986) 135 (G. *Wenz*); NRT 108 (1986) 93-95 (L. *Renwart*); TPhil 61 (1986) 604-6 (P. *Knauer*); TPQ 134 (1986) 69-71 (P. *Neuner*); TsTKi 57 (1986) 317s (Ola *Tjørhom*).

5165 **Ganoczy** Alexandre, Einführung in die Dogmatik: Die Theologie. Da 1983, Wiss. xvi-214 p. – ᴿSalesianum 48 (1986) 994s (F. *Meyer*).

5166 **González de Cardedal** Olegario, El lugar de la teología. M 1986, Real Academia de Ciencias Morales y Políticas. 151 p. – ᴿCarthaginensia 2 (1986) 113s (F. *Martínez Fresneda*).

5167 **Hackett** Stuart C., The reconstruction of the Christian revelation claim; a philosophical and critical apologetic 1984 → 65,5823: ᴿBS 143 (1986) 77s (N. L. *Geisler*); Themelios 12 (1986s) 65s (W. *Corduan*: a Summa contra Gentiles).

5168 *Härle* Wilfried, Widerspruchsfreiheit; Überlegungen zum Verhältnis von Glauben und Denken: NSys 28 (1986) 223-237.

5168* **Happel** Stephen, *Walter* James J., Conversion and discipleship; a Christian foundation for ethics and doctrine. Ph 1986, Fortress. 229 p. $15 pa. [Int 41,436, R. *Palmer*].

5169 **Hartmann** Michael, Ästhetik als ein Grundbegriff fundamentaler Theologie; eine Untersuchung zu Hans Urs von BALTHASAR: Diss. theol. 5. St. Ottilien 1985, EOS. viii-277 p. DM 29,60 [TR 83,311, H. *Verweyen*].

5170 **Heinrichs** Maurus, Christliche Offenbarung und religiöse Erfahrung im Dialog ➤ 1,6391 [zwischen dem Christentum und den östlichen Religionen], ᴱ*Dettloff* W. Pd 1984, Schöningh. 540 p. – ᴿLaurentianum 27 (1986) 383 (J. *Imbach*).

5171 **Heinz** Gerhard, Divinam christianae religionis originem probare; Untersuchung zur Entstehung des fundamentaltheologischen Offenbarungstraktates 1984 ➤ 65,5824; 1,6392; 3-7867-1128-3: ᴿActuBbg 23 (1986) 33-37 (J. *Boada*); EstE 61 (1986) 250s (J. J. *Alemany*); TLZ 111 (1986) 388s (B. *Hildebrandt*); TPQ 134 (1986) 81s (H. *Döring*).

5172 **Helm** Paul, Divine revelation; the basic issues: Foundations for Faith 1982 ➤ 64,1386... 1,6394: ᴿEvQ 58 (1986) 183s (R. *Olson*); Themelios 12 (1986s) 20 (N. M. *Cameron*).

5174 **Houlden** J. L., Connections; the integration of theology and faith. L 1986, SCM. v-200 p. £6. – ᴿTLond 39 (1986) 390s (P. *Selby*).

5175 *Izquierdo* César, *Odero* José Miguel, Manuales de teología fundamental [... *Boublik* W., *Cardaropoli* G., *Beni* A., *Bof* G., *Fisichella* R., *Aleu* J., *Latourelle* R., ...]: ScripTPamp 18 (1986) 625-668.

5176 **Janssens** Ben, Metaphysisches Denken und heilsgeschichtliche Offenbarung; ihre Korrespondenz im Systemversuch Hermann SCHELLS ➤ 1,6399 [Diss. Gregoriana, ᴰ*Alfaro* J.]: EurHS 23/125. Fra 1980, Lang. 413 p. – ᴿRechSR 74 (1986) 451 (J. *Doré*); TPhil 61 (1986) 278s (F. T. *Gottwald*).

5177 **Jiménez-Limón** Javier, Pagar el precio y dar razón de la esperanza cristiana hoy; dos proyectos de teología fundamental: J. B. METZ y J. L. SEGUNDO: diss. ᴰ*González Faus* J. I. Barc 1986, S. F. Borja. 809 p. – RTLv 18,587.

5178 **Jiménez Ortiz** Antonio, *a)* Los conceptos de revelación y de fe en teología fundamental de Heinrich FRIES: diss Salesiana, ᴰ*Midali* M. R 1986. Extr. 90 p. – RTLv 18,557. – *b)* La teología fundamental como teología del encuentro entre la revelación y el hombre: EstE 61 (1986) 3-21.

5179 *Jüngel* Eberhard, Tro og forståelse; om Rudolf BULTMANNS teologibegrep, ᵀ*Hjelde* Sigurd: NorTTs 87 (1986) 81-99.

5180 *Jung* Matthias, Zum Verhältnis von Philosophie und Theologie im Denken Martin HEIDEGGERS: TPhil 61 (1986) 404-413.

5181 *Kannengiesser* Charles, Begriff und Ziel historischer Theologie heute: Kairos 28 (1986) 1-10.

5182 ᴱ**Kern** Walter, *al.*, Traktat Offenbarung: HdFundT 2, 1985 ➤ 1, 898: ᴿMüTZ 37 (1986) 136 (G. *Wenz*).

5183 **Kern** Walter, *Niemann* Franz-Josef, El conocimiento teológico, ᵀ*Martínez de Lapera* Abelardo: BiblTeol 5. Barc 1986, Herder. 240 p. pt 1000. 84-354-1479-2. – ᴿActuBbg 23 (1986) 226 (F. *Manresa*); NatGrac 33 (1986) 578s (A. *Villalmonte*); QVidCr 133 (1986) 155 (J. *Bosch*); SalT 74 (1986) 335s (A. *Raffo*); ScripTPamp 18 (1986) 987 (C. *Izquierdo*).

5184 **Kessler** Michael, [FICHTE J. G. 1792] Kritik aller Offenbarung: TüTheolSt 26. Mainz 1986, Grünewald. 429 p. DM 48. [TR 83,217, H. *Verweyen*].

5185 *Knudsen* Robert D., The transcendental perspective of Westminster's apologetic: WestTJ (1986) 223-239.

5186 *Koch* Traugott, 'Denkende Aneignung des Glaubens'; zur theologischen Komponente in Erich HEINTELS 'Grundriss der Dialektik' [Da 1984]: TRu 51 (1986) 315-328.

5187 ᴱ**Latourelle** R., *O'Collins* G., *a)* Problems and perspectives of fundamental theology 1982 ➤ 64,334*a* ... 1,6404: ᴿJRel 66 (1986) 82-84 (S, *Happel*). – *b)* Problèmes et perspectives de la théologie fondamentale 1982 ➤ 65,5837: ᴿRÉAug 31 (1985) 198 (J. *Doignon*).

5188 **Laurenzi** M.C., Esperienza e rivelazione; la ricerca del giovane BARTH (1909-1921), intr. *Mancini* I. Casale Monferrato 1983, Marietti. 195 p. – ᴿProtestantesimo 41 (1986) 91-93 (S. *Rostagno*).

5189 ᴱ**Lauret** B., *Refoulé* F., Initiation à la pratique de la théologie I-V, 1982s ➤ 64,335; 1,6405: ᴿEstE 61 (1986) 104-6 (J. *García Pérez*, 2s); Thomist 50 (1986) 170-2 (W. J. *Bildstein*,1-2).

5190 ᴱ**Lauret** B., *Refoulé* F., Iniciación a la práctica de la teología, ᵀ*Urbán* A., *Godoy* R. I-II, 1984 ➤ 1,6406: ᴿSalmanticensis 3 (1986) 264-6 (A. *González Montes*).

5191 **Lauret** B., *Refoulé* F., Iniziazione... Dogmatica I-II, 1985s ➤ 1,6407: ᴿRClerIt 67 (1986) 713-7 (F. *Brambilla*).

5192 **Lavatori** R., Dio e l'uomo un incontro di salvezza; rivelazione e fede. Bo 1985, Dehoniane. 261 p. Lit. 18.000. – ᴿDivinitas 30 (1986) 197 (V. *Natalini*).

5193 **Louth** Andrew, Discerning the mystery; an essay on the nature of theology 1983 ➤ 64,1337; 65,5841: ᴿTLZ 111 (1986) 386s (G. *Wainwright*, deutsch).

5194 *McGrath* Alister E., Geschichte, Überlieferung und Erzählung; Überlegungen zur Identität und Aufgabe christlicher Theologie, ᵀ*Slenczka* R.: KerDo 32 (1986) 234-253; Eng. 253.

5195 **Mehedinţu** Viorel, Offenbarung und Überlieferung; neue Möglichkeiten eines Dialogs zwischen der Orthodoxen und der Evangelisch-Lutherischen Kirche: For SysÖkT 49. Gö 1980, Vandenhoeck & R. 352 p. DM 64 pa. – ᴿTLZ 111 (1986) 690-2 (G. *Schulz*).

5196 *Miller* John F., Disclaiming divine inspiration; a programmatic pattern [in *Propertius, Ovid, Perseus*]: WienerSt 99 (1986) 149-164.

5197 **Mondin** Battista, Introduzione alla teologia ➤ 1,6414: Problemi del nostro tempo 59. Mi 1983, Massimo. 382 p. 88-7030-459-0. – ᴿDivinitas 30 (1986) 196 (C. *Petino*); EstE 61 (1986) 377s (J. J. *Alemany*).

5198 **Newport** John P., What is Christian doctrine ? : Layman's Library of Christian Doctrine. Nv 1984, Broadman. 170 p. $6. – ᴿRExp 83 (1986) 125s (D. R. *Stiver*: identifies his Baptist view as Evangelical).

5199 **Niemann** Franz-Josef, Jesus als Glaubensgrund in der Fundamentaltheologie der Neuzeit 1983 ➤ 65,5849; 1,6420; 3-7022-1444-5. – ᴿActu-Bbg 23 (1986) 26-33 (J. *Boada*); TPhil 61 (1986) 275s (B. *Groth*); TPQ 134 (1986) 80 (P. *Neuner*); ZkT 108 (1986) 341-4 (J. *Reikerstorfer*, wie p. 497; nicht L. Kern wie p. 344).

5200 **O'Leary** Joseph S., Questioning back; the overcoming of metaphysics 1985 ➤ 1, 6423: ᴿHorizons 13 (1986) 173-5 (F. *Kerr*); RelStR 12 (1986) 269 (P. C. *Hodgson*: not 'the genuinely deconstructionist theology'; rather a radical alternative to simplistic jargonizing of HEIDEGGER and DERRIDA by C. RASCHKE and M. TAYLOR); TS 47 (1986) 526s (J. A. *Bracken*).

5200* *Pannenberg* Wolfhart, The significance of the categories 'part' and 'whole' for the epistemology of theology: JRel 66 (1986) 369-385.

5201 *Paton* Michael, On claiming less and believing more: TLond 39 (1986) 375-380.
5202 *Penelhum* Terence, Do religious beliefs need grounds? [...if religion is true, why is it not more *obviously* true?]: NedTTs 40 (1986) 227-237.
5203 ᴱ**Petuchowski** Jakob J., *Strolz* W., Offenbarung im jüdischen und christlichen Glaubensverständnis: QDisp 92, 1981 ➤ 62,553... 65,5852: ᴿZRGg 38 (1986) 282-4 (K. *Hoheisel*).
5204 **Peukert** Helmut, Science, action, and fundamental theology; toward a theology of communicative action, ᵀ*Bohman* J. [➤ 1,6425]: Studies in Contemporary German Social Thought. CM 1984, MIT. xxv-330 p. $35. 0-262-16095-1. – ᴿJPsy&T 14 (1986) 65-67 (M. K. *Mayers*).
5205 **Pfeiffer** H., Gott offenbart sich 1982 ➤ 64,1404a... 1,6426* ᴿEstE 61 (1986) 466 (J. J. *Alemany*).
5206 *Phan Tan Thanh* G., La teologia della rivelazione nell'Enchiridion Vaticanum: Angelicum 63 (1986) 419-485 [i. Vaticano II; dopo: in genere; interpretazioni globali; dimensione antropologica; rivelazione e Scrittura... e Tradizione... e Magistero... e dottrina/teologia/cultura; altre religioni].
5207 *Pöhlmann* Horst G., Apologetik: ➤ 587, EvKL 1 (1986) 213-7.
5208 **Ratzinger** Joseph, Teoría de los principios teológicos, materiales para una teología fundamental [1982 ➤ 64,250], ᵀ*Villanueva Salas* M. Barc 1985, Herder. 476 p. – ᴿLumenV 35 (1986) 583s (U. *Gil Ortega*); NatGrac 33 (1986) 164s A. *Villalmonte*); QVidCr 131s (1986) 230 (C. *Pifarré*). **Ricœur** Paul, La révélation 1984 ➤ 263.
5209 *a) Ritchie* Bruce, Theological logic: ScotBEvT 4 (1986) 109-122; – *b) Ruh* Ulrich, Auf dem Weg zu einem neuen Profil; zum gegenwärtigen Stand der Fundamentaltheologie: HerdKor 40 (1986) 287-290.
5210 *Roberge* René-Michel, Quelques ouvrages récents en théologie fondamentale; épistémologie théologique, magistère, révélation [... *Malherbe* J. sur *Ladrière*; *Paroz* P. sur *Albert* et *Ebeling*; *Virgoulay* R.] LavalTP 42 (1986) 317-332.
5210* **Rocchetta** Carlo *al.*, La teologia tra rivelazione e storia; introduzione alla teologia sistematica. Bo 1986, Dehoniane. 368 p. Lit. 20.000. – ᴿRivVSp 40 (1986) 605-7 (*ipse*); Salesianum 48 (1986) 735s (G. *Groppo*).
5211 **Ruiz Arenas** Octavio, Teología de la revelación: Colección [17 vol.] de textos básicos para seminarios latinoamericanos. Bogotá —, CELAM. – ᴿRCuBíb 10,39s (1986) 153s (J. E. *Martins Terra)*.
5212 *Rusecki* Marian, ❂ Problème de crédibilité des 'révélations privées': AtKap 106 (1986) 34-50.
5212* *Santi Cucinotta* Filippo, L'insegnamento della teologia fondamentale in Sicilia; dimensioni e prospettive: HoTheológos 3 (1985) 3-173. 271-325.
5213 *Schäfer* Rolf, Fundamentaltheologie: ➤ 587, EvKL 1 (1986) 1406-10.
5214 *Schwaiger* Georg, 'Diener des Wortes' (Lk. 1,2) oder Grösse und Grenze der Theologen: ➤ 56, ᶠKRETSCHMAR G., Anspruch 1986, 177-188.
5215 **Schwarz** Hans, Gottes Selbstoffenbarung in der jüdisch-christlichen Tradition. Gö 1984, Vandenhoeck. 99 p. DM 12,80 [Judaica 42,206 cf. ➤ 1,6435].
5216 **Shorter** Aylward, *a)* Revelation and its interpretation 1983 ➤ 64,1412... 1,6438: ᴿVidyajyoti 49 (1985) 309 (J. *Thayil*). – *b)* La revelación y su interpretación. M 1986, Paulinas. 338 p. [SalT 74 (1986) 666].
5217 **Skalicky** C., Teologia fondamentale. R 1979, Ut unum sint. 328 p. – ᴿScripTPamp 18 (1986) 632-5 (C. *Izquierdo*, J. M. *Odero*).

5218 **Sproul** Richard C. *al.*,   Classical apologetics; a rational defense of the Christian faith and a critique of presuppositional apologetics 1984 ➤ 1,6439;   0-310-44951-0:   ᴿEstE 61 (1986) 466s (J. *Alemany*); GraceTJ 7 (1986) 111-123 (G. J. *Zemek*).

5219 **Steinvorth** Alberto,   La introducción a la teología según J. S. von Drey: diss. ᴰ*Illanes* J.   Pamplona 1986. 474 p. – RTLv 18,558.

5220 *Strenski* Ivan,   Our very own 'contras'; a response to the 'St. Louis Project' report: JAAR [52 (1984) 727-757] 54 (1986) 323-335: in the 'religious studies vs. theology' controversy, favors W. May's 'Why can University philosophers philosophize, but theologians not theologize?'... with cautions.

5220* *Suda* Max Josef,   Der atheistische Hintergrund der Offenbarung... Marx: BTZ 3 (1986) 92-110.

5221 *Talmon* Shemaryahu,   Revelation in biblical times: HebSt 26 (1985) 53-70 [OTAbs 10,188].

5222 **Thiemann** Ronald E.,   Revelation and theology; the Gospel as narrated promise 1985 ➤ 1,6442:   ᴿCalvinT 21 (1986) 127-130 · (R. J. *Feenstra*); JAAR 54 (1986) 801s (J. W. *McClendon*); TS 47 (1986) 522s (T. W. *Tilley*: Harvard Divinity's new dean; clear).

5223 **Thomassen** Jürgen,   Heilswirksamkeit der Verkündigung; Kritik und Neubegründung: ThTT. Dü 1986, Patmos. 380 p. DM 48 [TR 83,132-4, E. *Arens*, holprig].

5224 *Van Den Hengel* John,   Reason and revelation in Lessing's Enlightenment: ÉglT 17 (1986) 171-194.

5225 *a)* *Vannoy* J. Robert,   Divine revelation and history in the Old Testament; – *b)* *Lewis* Gordon R.,   Three sides to every story; relating the absolutes of general and special revelation to relativists; – *c)* *Dunzweiler* Robert J., Inspiration, 'inspiredness', and the proclamation of God's word today; – *d)* *Grounds* Vernon C.,   The Bible and the modern mind: ➤ 65, ᶠMacRae Allan 1986,   67-67 / 201-210 / 185-199 / 169-183.

5226 **Velthaus** Andreas,   Hans Alberts Kritik am Offenbarungsgedanken [Diss. Mainz]: EurHS 23/284.   Fra 1986, Lang. 215 p. Fs 49. – TR 82 (1986) 435.

5227 *Verweyen* Hansjürgen,   *a)* Fundamentaltheologie; zum 'status quaestionis' [Tagung Freiburg März 1986]: TPhil 61 (1986) 321-335; – *b)* Fundamentaltheologie — eine Zwischenbilanz: TR 82 (1986) 89-102.

5228 **Vörckel** Karl,   Chancen der natürlichen Theologie.   Fernwald 1985, Litblockin. 287 p. DM 31 [TLZ 112,619, W. *Pfüller*].

5229 **Waldenfels** Hans,   Kontextuelle Fundamentaltheologie: UTB-Wiss. 1985 ➤ 1,6448: ᴿActuBbg 23 (1986) 15-21 (J. *Boada*); EstE 61 (1986) 468s (J. J. *Alemany*); Orientierung 50 (1986) 191-3 (H. *Häring*); TPhil 61 (1986) 606 (P. *Knauer*); TS 47 (1986) 704s (R. *Kress*); TSNijm 26 (1986) 303 (J. Van *Nieuwenhove*).

5230 **Walstra** J.,   Tegen beter weten in — een proeve van christelijke identiteit [diss.: some few use erudition for pastoral, but 'knowing better' is a kind of rationalism to be corrected].   Franeker 1983, Wever. – ᴿNedTTs 40 (1986) 250-2 (J. M. *Hasselaar*: read p. 206-211 of the book first).

5231 **Wilson** A. N.,   How can we know? An essay on the Christian religion. NY 1985, Athenaeum. 128 p. $11. – ᴿRExp 83 (1986) 123s (D. R. *Stiver*: sometimes those who know most know least).

5232 **Wood** Charles M.,   Vision and discernment; an orientation in theological study. Atlanta 1985, Scholars. 98 p. $16; pa. $12. – ᴿTTod 43 (1986s) 294.296.298 (N. D. *McCarter*).

5233 *Wood* Laurence W., Defining the modern concept of self-revelation ; toward a synthesis of BARTH and PANNENBERG: AsbTJ 41,2 (1986) 85-105.

H2.1 Anthropologia theologica – VT & NT.

5234 **Amata** Biagio, Problemi di antropologia arnobiana: ScRel 64, 1984 ➤ 1,6452; 172 p.; Lit. 18.000: ᴿTLZ 111 (1986) 454s (B. *Studer*).

5235 **Aruviyil** Josephus, Self-fulfilment in self-emptying in the Gita and the New Testament: diss. Angelicum. – RTLv 18,545 sans date.

5236 **Ashley** Benedict M., Theologies of the Body, humanist and Christian: Pope John XXIII Medical-Moral Research Center, 1985 ➤ 1,6454: ᴿSalesianum 48 (1986) 989-991 (G. *Abbà*: importante); TS 47 (1986) 309s (E. C. *Vacek*).

5236* **Balthasar** Hans Urs von, Man in history; a theological study. L 1982 = 1968, Sheed & W. x-341 p. £9.50 pa. 0-7220-5220-0.

5237 **Bonansea** B. M., Man and his approach to God in John Duns SCOTUS. Lanham MD 1983, UPA. 249 p. – ᴿDivThom 88 (1985) 164s (G. *Sanguineti*).

5238 *Brambilla* Franco G., Il Concilio Vaticano II e l'antropologia teologica: ScuolC 114 (1986) 663-676.

5239 **Clark** Gordon H. †, The Biblical doctrine of man ➤ 1,6467; Jefferson MD 1984, Trinity. 101 p. $6 pa.: ᴿBS 143 (1986) 170s (F. R. *Howe*: not at his best).

5239* **Comblin** J., Antropología cristiana: Teología y liberación 3/1. M 1985, Paulinas. 283 p. – ᴿSalT 74 (1986) 151 (A. *Raffo*).

5240 **Cupitt** Don, Life lines [... life's ultimate purpose]. L 1986, SCM. 232 p. £8. 0-334-00901-4 [ExpTim 98,287].

5240* *Dec* Ignacy, ℗ Antropologia encykliki 'Laborem exercens': ColcT 56,1 (1986) 5-12.

5241 **Deissler** Alfons, Wer bist du, Mensch? Die Antwort der Bibel 1985 ➤ 1,6472: ᴿColcT 56,3 (1986) 196-9 (R. *Bartnicki*); TGegw 29 (1986) 61s (F. *Rosenberg*).

5242 **Eccles** John C., Die Psyche des menschen [Gifford Lectures, The human psyche, E 1979], ᵀ*Jongejan* J., 1985 ➤ 1,6472*; ᴿMüTZ 37 (1986) 204s (A. *Kreiner*).

5243 **Elmore** Vernon O., Man as God's creation: Layman's Library of Christian Doctrine 6. Nv 1986, Broadman. 168 p. $6. – ᴿRExp 83 (1986) 462s (W. *Ward*).

5244 **Erickson** Millard T., Christian theology [I, 1983]; II [anthropology, Christology]. GR 1984, Baker. 418 p. $20. – ᴿRExp 83 (1986) 134s (C. L. *Chaney* with an awaited third volume, will surely replace STRONG and MULLINS as Baptist/Evangelical textbook).

5245 *Fernández del Riesco* Manuel, La originalidad de la condición humana desde la perspectiva etológica y sociobiológica: CiuD 199 (1986) 209-251. 435-488.

5246 *Fritzsche* Helmut, Humanisierung der Persönlichkeit in theologischer Sicht: TLZ 111 (1986) 321-336.

5247 **Galot** Jean, Perché la sofferenza? [1983 ➤ 1,6478],ᵀ. Mi 1986, Àncora. 211 p. Lit. 12.000. – ᴿParVi 31 (1986) 475s (L. *Melotti*).

5248 **González de Andía** Ysabel, Homo vivens; incorruptibilité et divinisation de l'homme selon IRÉNÉE de Lyon. P 1986, Ét. Augustiniennes. 395 p.; bibliog. p. 345-365. F 390. – ᴿTS 48 (1987) 557s (Mary Ann *Donovan*).

5249 **González de Cardedal** Olegario, La gloria del hombre; reto entre una cultura de la fe y una cultura de la increencia: BAC. M 1985, Católica. 390 p. – [R]CiuD 199 (1986) 549 (G. *Díaz*); RazFe 213 (1986) 554 (R. de *Andrés*).

5250 **Gozzelino** Giorgio, Vocazione e destino dell'uomo in Cristo; saggio di antropologia teologica fondamentale (protologia) 1985 ➤ 1,6480: [R]ParVi 30 (1985) 471-3 (L. *Melotti*).

5251 **Grossi** Vittorino. Lineamenti di antropologia patristica 1983 ➤ 65,5895: [R]Asprenas 32 (1985) 477s (L. *Longobardo*).

5252 *Guelluy* Robert, Réflexions sur l'anthropologie chrétienne; justice ou gratuité: FoiTemps 16 (1986) 163-173.

5253 **Hallensleben** Barbara, Communicatio; Anthropologie und Gnadenlehre bei Thomas de Vio CAJETAN: RefGStT 123. Münster 1985, Aschendorff. xi-640 p. DM 48 pa. [TR 83,286-9, B. *Lohse*].

5254 **Hasenfratz** Hans-Peter, Die Seele; Einführung in ein religiöses Grundphänomen (mit ausgewählten Texten). Z 1986, Theol.-V. 131 p. Fs 42 [TLZ 112,225-7, M. *Brückner*].

5255 *Hasenfratz* Hans-Peter, Seelenvorstellungen bei den Germanen und ihre Übernahme und Umformung durch die christliche Mission: ZRGg 38 (1986) 19-31.

5255* **Heiligenthal** R., Werke als Zeichen 1983 ➤ 64,6244; 65,5896: [R]TGegw 29 (1986) 58s (H. *Giesen*).

5256 **Hill** Edmund, Being human; a biblical perspective: Introducing Catholic Theology 1984 ➤ 65,5897; 1,6484: [R]DoctLife 35 (1985) 416 (G. *Daly*).

5256* **Hoekema** Anthony A., Created in God's image. GR 1986, Eerdmans. 264 p. $20 [Interpretation 41,328, D. G. *Bloesch*].

5257 **Holmes** A. F., Contours of a world view ['in God's world we can play, and whistle while we work' p. 234], I. GR/Leicester 1983, Eerdmans/ Inter-Varsity. 240 p. £6. – [R]EvQ 58 (1986) 370-2 (H. *Bayer*).

5258 *Janda* Josef, Neuer Mensch — alte Werte: TPQ 134 (1986) 375-386.

5259 **Janz** Denis R., LUTHER and late medieval Thomism; a study in theological anthropology. Waterloo 1983, W. Laurier Univ. xii-186 p. – [R]SR 15 (1986) 100s (E. *Grislis*: Luther regarded AQUINAS as Pelagian, but no indication of how much he had ever read him).

5259* *Jarpelău* Gheorghe, Fondements vétéro-testamentaires pour la colla-boration et la réconciliation des hommes (roum.): STBuc 37 (1985) 699-710.

5260 *Jonkers* Peter, Vrijheid en macht nauit christelijk perspectief; wijsgerige kanttekeningen bij RAHNERs theologische antropologie [index: anthro-pologie]: Bijdragen 47 (1986) 395-418; Eng. 419s.

5261 **Kreuter** Franz, Person und Gnade; die systematische Grundlegung des Personbegriffes in der Theo-Logie und Anthropo-Logie von J. E. von KUHN unter Berücksichtigung der Natur-Gnade-Kontroverse mit C. von SCHÄZLER [diss. Roma, Pont. Univ. Gregoriana, [D]*Alfaro* J.]. Fra 1984, Lang. 437 p. Fs 74. – [R]TR 82 (1986) 56-59 (H. *Vorgrimler*: Meisterstück).

5262 **Ladaria** Luis F., Antropologia teologica [1983 ➤ 64,6252],[T]. Ca-sale Monferrato / R 1986, Piemme / Univ. Gregoriana. 328 p. Lit. 30.000. 88-384-2210-9 [Greg 67,807]. – [R]Teresianum 37 (1986) 521s (M. *Caprioli*).

5263 **Latourelle** René, El hombre y sus problemas a la luz de Cristo, [T]*Ortiz García* Alfonso: Verdad e Imagen 84, 1984 ➤ 65,5901; 1,6491: [R]ActuBbg 23 (1986) 37-41 (J. *Boada*).

5264 **Latourelle** René, Man and his problems in the light of Jesus Christ

[L'homme 1981 ► 63,6808], ᵀ*O'Connell* Matthew. NY 1983, Alba. 395 p. $10 pa. – ᴿVidyajyoti 49 (1985) 142 (G. *Lobo*).

5265 *Laudazi* Carlo, La dimensione teologica dell'uomo: Teresianum 37 (1986) 287-317.

5266 **Lepargneur** Hubert, Antropologia do sofrimento. Aparecida 1985, Santuário. 256 p. – ᴿREB 46 (1986) 465s (E. *Ferreira Alves*).

5267 *McDermott* John M., Il senso della sofferenza: CC 137 (1986,4) 112-126.

5268 **Mondin** Battista, *a*) Il valore uomo; *b*) I valori fondamentali. R 1983/5, Dino. 253 p./210 p. Lit. 13.500 / 20.000. – ᴿCC 137 (1986,4) 612s (J. de *Finance*).

5269 **Nikonov** Kiril I., Suvremena kršćanska antropologija [... Prot.; Katol.] Moskva 1983, Univ. – ᴿObnŽiv 41 (1986) 85-96.

5270 *Nüchtern* Michael, Krankheit und Heilung; eine biblisch-theologische Besinnung: Diakonie 12 (Stu 1986) 211-5 [< ᴢɪᴛ].

5271 *O'Donnell* John, *a*) Exploring the human; theology in dialogue [*Pesch* O. 1983; *Moltmann* J. 1985; *Pannenberg* W. 1983]: Gregorianum 67 (1986) 125-132; – *b*) Der Mensch als Thema der Theologie — Theologie im Dialog [< Gregorianum 67 (1986) 125-132 über *Pesch* O., *Moltmann* J., *Pannenberg* W.], ᵀ*Gottfried* Herbert: TGegw 29 (1986) 174-180.

5272 *Orlando* Pasquale, Volere di Dio e decisione dell'uomo; un binomio dinamico: Teresianum 37 (1986) 461-482 [*Bañez-Molina*].

5273 **Pannenberg** Wolfhart, Anthropologie in theologischer Perspektive 1983 ► 64,6259 ... 1,6498: ᴿZRGg 38 (1986) 77-79 (F. W. *Kantzenbach*).

5274 **Pannenberg** W., Anthropology in theological perspective 1985 ► 1,6499: ᴿChrSchR 15 (1985) 247 ... (B. J. *Walsh*); Encounter 47 (1986) 172s (W. C. *Placher*); JAAR 54 (1986) 602s (C. *Raschke*: 'salvation equals sociality'); JPsy&T 14 (1986) 64s (G. R. *Lewis*); Paradigms 2,1 (1986) 46s (B. S. *Hildreth*); SR 15 (1986) 112s (B. *Walsh*); TLZ 111 (1986) 914-8 (E.-H. *Amberg*, also on Anthropologie 1983); TS 47 (1986) 304-6 (Elizabeth A. *Johnson*).

5275 *Papademetriou* George C., An Orthodox Christian view of man: TAth 57 (1986) 777-792.

5276 ᴱ*Pathrapankal* Joseph, 'Man' in the biblical perspective, = Jeevadhara 16,92 (1986): 89-104, prophets, *Cherian* C. M.; 105-120, psalms, *De Menezes* Rui; 121-132, wisdom, *Vande Walle* R.; 133-7, synoptics, *Crasta* Patrick; 138-148, Johannine writings, *Vellanickal* Mathew; 149-166, The man Jesus, *Rayan* Samuel.

5277 **Perrin** Michel, L'homme antique et chrétien; l'anthropologie de LACTANCE 250-325 [diss. Sorbonne 1977]: 1981 ► 64,c143 ... 1,6500: ᴿRÉAug 31 (1985) 179-181(R. *Braun*).

5278 **Pesch** Otto H., Frei sein aus Gnade 1983 ► 65,5909; 1,6501: ᴿTPQ 134 (1986) 84s (R. *Schulte*).

5279 *Peters* Jan, The function of forgiveness in social relationships, ᵀ*Nowell* R.: Concilium 184 (E 1986) 3-11 (éd. franç. ᵀ*Pardon-Genesse* M., 13-22).

5280 *a*) *Ranon* Angelo, L'AT storia di salvezza e sofferenza; – *b*) *Monari* Luciano, Le cause del dolore e del male nella predicazione profetica; – *c*) *Perrenchio* Fausto, La sofferenza dell'uomo nei Salmi; – *d*) *Cimosa* Mario, La contestazione sapienziale di Giobbe e Qoèlet; – *e*) *Bizzeti* [con una *i* anche nell'Indice] Paolo, Le cause della sofferenza e del dolore nel libro della Sapienza; – *f*) *Cavedo* Romeo, Sofferenza ed espiazione; – *g*) *Mosetto* Francesco, Fede e sofferenza secondo la prima lettera di Pietro: ParVi 30 (1985) 251-9 / 260-6 / 267-279 / 280-5 / 286-294 / 295-303 / 304-313.

5281 **Raurell** Frederic, Mots sobre l'home (Aspectes d'Antropologia Biblica): Sauri 65, 1984 ➤ 65,242.5911; 1,6508: ᴿRB 93 (1986) 152s (J. *Loza*).

5282 **Raurell** F., Lineamenti di antropologia biblica: Collana Laurentianum 1. Casale-M 1986, Piemme. 244 p. Lit. 18.000. 88-384-2301-6. – ᴿLaurentianum 27 (1986) 154-8 (G. *Veltri*: parla dell' 'antifemminismo' senza notare il peso della mariologia); ParVi 31 (1986) 380s (F. *Perrenchio*).

5283 **Ray** S. Alan, The modern soul; Michel FOUCAULT and the theological discourse of Gordon KAUFMAN and David TRACY: diss. Harvard... – HarvTR 79 (1986) 478.

5284 *Renard* Jean-Bruno, Les rites de passage; une constante anthropologique: ÉTRel 61 (1986) 227-238.

5285 **Ruiz de la Peña** Juan L., Las nuevas antropologías: Punto Limite 17, 1983 ➤ 64,6263... 1,6510: ᴿCiTom 113 (1986) 631s (E. *García*).

5286 **Rulla** Luigi M., Antropologia della vocazione cristiana, 1. Basi interdisciplinari. Casale Monferrato 1985, Piemme. 384 p. – ᴿTeresianum 37 (1986) 500 (M. *Caprioli*).

5287 **Sanna** Ignazio, L'uomo via fondamentale della Chiesa; trattato di antropologia teologica: Teologia a confronto 4, 1984 1,6511: ᴿGregorianum 67 (1986) 152s (L. *Ladaria*).

5288 *Schmidt* Werner H. [*Brendenburger* Egon], Anthropologie AT [NT]: ➤ 587, EvKL 1 (1986) 156-8 [159-164 (-6)].

5289 *Schulte* Josef, Wie sieht die Theologie den Menschen?: TGl 76 (1986) 110-118.

5289* **Sears** Elizabeth, The ages of man; medieval interpretations of the life cycle. Princeton 1986, Univ. 320 p. $55 [JAAR 55,426].

5290 **Stefani** Massimo, La antropologia di Mario VITTORINO: diss. ᴰRamos-*Lissón* D. Pamplona 1986. 320 p. – RTLv 18,552.

5291 **Thielicke** Helmut, Esencia del hombre; ensayo de antropología cristiana [Mensch sein –], ᵀ*Gancho* Claudio: TeolFilos 173. Barc 1985, Herder. 548 p. pt. 2860. 84-254-1495-4 [ActuBbg 24, 95, J. *Boada*]. – ᴿNatGrac 33 (1986) 588s A. *Villalmonte*); SalT 74 (1986) 664s (A. *Raffo*).

5292 *a)* *Tornos* Andrés, Grandeza y decepción de lo humano; – *b)* *García* José A., 'Sed perfectos...' Canto y compromiso en el acercamiento salvador de Dios; – *c)* *Fernández-Martos* José M., Psicopatología de la perfección, o la lidia del 'aguijón de la carne': SalT 74 (1986) 691-702 / 703-714 / 715-731.

Veld B. van 't, [Is 40,6s...] De klacht over de vergankelijkheid van het menselijk leven ... [diss. Utrecht] 1985 ➤ 5466.

5292* *Verweyen* Hansjürgen, Wie wird ein Existential übernatürlich? Zu einem Grundproblem der Anthropologie K. RAHNERs [Antrittsvorlesung FrB 4.VI.1985)]: TrierTZ 95 (1986) 115-131.

5293 **Viladesau** Richard, The reason for our hope; an introduction to Christian anthropology 1984 ➤ 65,5917; 1,6523: ᴿTLond 39 (1986) 48-50 (B. *Horne*: weaknesses hard to criticize since other volumes are awaited); TLZ 111 (1986) 694-6 (C. *Frey*).

5294 **Ward** Keith, The battle for the soul. L 1985, Hodder & 5. 183 p. – ᴿRelSt 22 (1986) 281s (H. P. *Owen*: the not-given subtitle shows the concern is with morality).

5294* *Westermann* Claus, *a)* The contribution of biblical thought to an understanding of our reality [lecture Munich 1984, ᵀ*Miller* Donald G.]: ➤ 69, ᶠMAYS J., Hermeneutical Quest 1986, 47-57; – *b)* Gesundheit, Leben und Tod aus der Sicht des Alten Testaments: Curare 5 (1982) 23-32 [< JbBT 1,232].

5295 **Woschitz** Karl M., De homine; Existenzweisen; Spiegelungen, Konturen, Metamorphosen des antiken Menschenbildes [Athen, Rom, Jerusalem] 1984 → 1,6525: ᴿZkT 108 (1986) 198s (M. *Hasitschka*).

5295* **Zubiri** Xavier †, El hombre y Dios. M 1984, Alianza. [ActuBbg 24,72, J. *Ordi*].

H2.8 Œcologia VT & NT   – saecularitas.

5296 **Albertz** Rainer, Verantwortung vor dem Schöpfer; die Bibel als Anleitung für einen neuen Umgang mit unserer Umwelt: Konstanzer Theol. Reden. Konstanz 1985, Christliche V. 23 p. [TLZ 112,586, S. *Wagner*].

5297 *Ángel Estrada* Luis, *al.*, Hacia una perspectiva cristiana de la ecología; su historia y su proyección actual en Colombia: FranBog 28 (1986) 85-94.

5297* **Auer** A., Umweltethik 1984 → 65,5939; 1,6528: ᴿStPatav 33 (1986) 475s (G. *Trentin*).

5298 *Baier* Klaus A., Zum Entwurf einer postmodernen Schöpfungstheologie: Deutsches Pfarrerblatt 86 (Essen 1986) 418-420 [< ZIT].

5299 *Bauckham* Richard, First steps to a theology of nature: EvQ 58 (1986) 229-244.

5300 **Bouyer** Louis, Cosmos; le monde et le gloire de Dieu 1982 → 64,6297... 1,6531: ᴿRThom 86 (1986) 304-8 (J.-M. *Maldamé*: sévère); RTLv 17 (1986) 229s (E. *Brito*).

5300* *Braun* Dietrich, Regnum hominis in naturam; Ansatz und Herkunft des naturphilosophischen Werk von Francis BACON: BTZ 3 (1986) 207-225.

5301 **Castaño-Mollor y Arranz** Manuel I., La secularidad en los escritores cristianos de los dos primeros siglos: Canónica. Pamplona 1984, Univ. Navarra. 201 p. 84-313-0869-09 [NTAbs 30,371].

5302 *Dettloff* Werner, Die christozentrische Konzeption des Johannes Duns SCOTUS als Anzatz für eine Theologie der Welt: WissWeis 48 (1985) 182-196.

5303 **Dietrich** Gerhard H., Das Verständnis von Natur und Welt bei Rudolf BULTMANN und Karl LÖWITH: eine vergleichende Studie: Diss. ᴰ*Fischer* H. Hamburg 1986. – RTLv 18,556.

5304 **Garin** George, A sacramental universe; the theology of William TEMPLE in its philosophical and theological context; Ev. diss. ᴰ*Pannenberg* W. München 1986s. – RTLv 18,557.

5305 *Gehring* Hans, *Kerstiens* Ferdinand: Macht euch die Schöpfung untertan — aber macht sie nicht kaputt ! : Diakonia 17 (1986) 270-2 (-8).

5306 *a) Giustiniani* Pasquale, Uomo e cosmo; possibili figure di un rapporto; – *b) Priotto* Michelangelo, Dal cosmo a Dio: ParVi 31 (1986) 324-7 / 328-334.

5307 *Gosling* David, Auf dem Weg zu einer glaubwürdigen ökumenischen Theologie der Natur, ᵀ*Voigt* Helga: ÖkRu 35 (1986) 129-143.

5308 *Grässer* Erich, *Kaì ēn metà tôn thēríōn* (Mk 1,13b); Ansätze einer theologischen Tierschutzethik: → 39, ꟳGREEVEN H., Text/Ethik 1986, 144-157.

5309 ᴱ**Hessel** Dieter T., For creation's sake; preaching, ecology, and justice. Ph 1985, Geneva [distr. Westminster]. 142 p. $9 pa. [TDig 33,362].

5310 *a) Hoefnagels* Harry, Christliche Verantwortung für die Schöpfung; die Haltung der Menschen gegenüber der Natur: StiZt 204 (1986) 547-558; –

b) *Immink* F. G, drs., Schepping, natuur en Openbaring: TRef 29 (Woerden 1986) 367... [< ZIT].

5310* **Houtman** Cornelis, Wereld en tegenwereld; mens en milieu in/en die Bijbel 1982 ⮕ 63,d728; 64,6245:   ᴿGerefTTs 86 (1986) 248s (M. E. *Brinkmann*).

5311 *Krawczyk* Roman, ℗ L'Ancien Testament et l'écologie: AtKap 106 (1986) 13-23.

5312 **Lamberty** Brett D., Natural cycles in ancient Israel's view of reality: diss. Claremont 1986, ᴰ*Knierim* R. 255 p.   86-19080. – DissA 47 (1986s) 1777-A; RelStR 13,189.

5312* *Lynch* Patrick J., Secularization affirms the sacred; Karl RAHNER: Thought 61 (1986) 381-393.

5313 *McPherson* James, Towards an ecological theology; ExpTim 97 (1985s) 236-240.

5313* **Martins Terra** J. E., A Bíblia e a natureza. São Paulo 1986, Loyola. 152 p.

5314 **Moltmann** Jürgen, Gott in der Schöpfung; ökologische Schöpfungslehre² 1985 ⮕ 1,6556:   ᴿMüTZ 37 (1986) 208-210 (G. *Schütz*); RHPR 66 (1966) 478s (G. *Siegwalt*).

5315 **Moltmann** Jürgen, God in creation [an ecological doctrine of creation: L, SCM]; a new theology of creation and the Spirit of God [Gifford Lectures 1984. ᵀ*Kohl* Margaret]. SF 1985, Harper & R. xvi-365 p. $26. – ᴿAmerica 155 (1986) 192-4 (B. *Ollenburger*); CCurr 36 (1986) 470-4 (G.-P. *Léonard*); CurrTM 13 (1986) 241-4 (T. *Peters*); ÉglT 17 (1986) 412-5 (J. *Pambrun*); ExpTim 97 (1985s) 285 (J. *Polkinghorne*: but modern science is not an optional extra]; Themelios 12 (1986s) 30s (L. *Osborn*); TS 47 (1986) 527-9 (T. *German*); TTod 43 (1986s) 576-8 (G. S. *Hendry*).

5316 *a*) ᴱ**Musall** Peter, Gottes Schöpfung — uns anvertraut. Offenbach/FrB 1986, Burckhardt/Christophorus. 159 p. DM 19,80. – *b*) ᴱ**Krenzer** Rolf, Habt acht auf Gottes Welt. Limburg 1986, Lahn. 208 p. DM 24,80. – ᴿTGl 76 (1986) 365s (K. *Hollmann*).

5317 **Rappaport** Roy A., Ecology, meaning, and religion.   1979, North Atlantic. 259 p. $8. – ᴿJAAR 54 (1986) 387 (R. A. *Segal*).

Ruiz de la Peña, Juan Luis, Teología de la creación 1986 ⮕ 5820.

5319 **Santmire** H. Paul, The travail of nature; the ambiguous ecological promise of Christian theology ⮕ 1,6562: Ph/L 1985, Fortress/SCM. xiii-274 p. – ᴿScotJT 39 (1986) 560s (J. B. *Taylor*); TLond 39 (1986) 392s (T. S. M. *Williams*); WWorld 6 (1986) 238s (N. *Wisnefske*).

5320 **Schmitz** P., Ist die Schöpfung noch zu retten? Umweltkrise und christliche Verantwortung. Wü 1985, Echter. 296 p. DM 29 [NRT 109,313, L. *Renwart*].

5321 ᴱ**Schottroff** Luise & Willy, Mitarbeiter der Schöpfung; Bibel und Arbeitswelt. Mü 1983, Kaiser. – ᴿTZBas 42 (1986) 441-3 (U. *Gerber*).

5322 *Schröder* Richard, Nachahmung der Natur; das aristotelische Verständnis des menschlichen Herstellens: ZEvEth 30 (1986) 373-398.

5322* *Schüssler* Werner, Paul TILLICH zum Problem der Säkularisierung: TrierTZ 95 (1986) 192-207 [lässt dem säkularen Menschen keinen Raum an dem er 'unreligiös' leben könnte].

5323 *Smend* Rudolf, Essen und trinken — ein Stück Weltlichkeit des ATs [< ᶠZIMMERLI W. 1977, 446-459]: ⮕ 220, Mitte des ATs 1986, 200-21.

5324 *a*) *Stockmeier* Peter, Die Natur im Glaubensbewusstsein der frühen Christen; Herrschaftsauftrag und Entsakralisierung; – *b*) *Irrgang* Peter,

Zur Problemgeschichte des Topos 'christliche Anthropozentrik' und seine Bedeutung für die Umweltethik: MüTZ 37 (1986) 149-161 / 185-203.

5325 *Stolz* Peter, Arbeit, Umwelt, qualitatives Wachstum — ökonomische und wirtschaftsethische Perspektiven: ZEvEth 30 (1986) 191-210.

5326 **Strachan** Gordon, Christ and the cosmos [numerology in both testaments]. L 1986, Labarum. xiv-162 p. £6.45. 0-948095-07-5 [ExpTim 98,222]. – ᴿFurrow 57 (1986) 265s (N. D. *O'Donoghue*).

5328 *Velle* Bernard, Astrotheology [inadequacy of man as sole raison d'être of the universe]: AustralasCR 63 (1986) 408-411.

H3.1   *Foedus* – **The Covenant;**   the Chosen People.

5329 **Basden** Paul A., Theologies of predestination in the Southern Baptist tradition; a critical evaluation: diss. SW Baptist Sem. 1986. – RelStR 13,187.

5329* *a) Boice* Montgomery, Cenni su la [sic] predestinazione nella storia, ᵀ*Scorza-Marzone* A.; – *b) Grottoli* Corrado, Il contesto storico della controversia arminiana-calvinista nel XVI secolo; – *c) Montanari* Roberto, Il significato dei canoni di Dordrecht sul piano pastorale [...i canoni in intero, ᵀ*Secondi* B., *Bolognesi* P.]: STEv 9,17 (1986) 3-26 / 27-43 / 44-62 [66-120].

5330 **Bühlmann** Walbert, Les peuples élus [Wenn Gott zu allen Menschen geht 1981 ➤ 63,6356], ᵀ*Leonhardon* Philippe. P/Montréal 1986, Médiaspaul/ Paulines. 446 p. F 120. 2-7122-0236-8 / M 2-89039-336-4. – ᴿEsprV 96 (1986) 556s (A.-M. *Henry*: simpliste, pessimiste).

5331 **Dumbrell** W. J., Covenant and creation 1984 ➤ 65,5966; 1,6570: ᴿRechSR 74 (1986) 624 (J. *Briend*: refuse division des sources, alliance tardive...).

5332 *Falcke* Heino, Biblical aspects of the process of mutual commitment [covenanting]: EcuR 38 (1986) 257-264.

5333 *Gherardini* Brunero, A proposito d'elezione in Karl BARTH: Lateranum 52 (1986) 289-305.

5334 *Gilchrist* Paul R., Towards a covenantal definition of tôrâ: ➤ 65, ᶠMACRAE Allan, Interpretation 1986, 93-107.

5335 **Guillén Torralba** Juan, La fuerza oculta de Dios; la elección en el Antiguo Testamento: EstJer 15, 1983 ➤ 64,6320; 1,6572: ᴿCBQ 48 (1986) 731s (C. F. *Mariottini*: sections not sufficiently interconnected); JBL 105 (1986) 122s (F. O. *Garcia-Treto*).

5336 *Hanson* Paul D., The people called; the growth of community in the Bible: Confessional perspectives. SF 1986, Harper & R. xiv-255 p. [TR 83,425].

5337 *Harbin* Michael A., The hermeneutics of covenant theology [outdated 17th century effort]: BS 143 (1986) 246-259.

5338 **Jewett** Paul K., Election and predestination; pref. *Grounds* Vernon. GR/Exeter 1985, Eerdmans/Paternoster. 147 p. $9 pa. – ᴿRHPR 66 (1986) 481 (G. *Siegwalt*); WestTJ 48 (1986) 388-391 (M. W. *Karlberg*).

5339 **McComiskey** T. E., The Covenants [➤ 1,6578] of promise; a theology of OT covenants 1985: ᴿScotBEvT 4 (1986) 66-68 (G. *McConville*).

5340 *Magonet* Jonathan, Universalism and particularism in the Hebrew Bible: Month 248 (1986) 221-5.

5341 ᴱ**Mora** Aldo, Karl BARTH, La dottrina dell'elezione divina, dalla Dogmatica ecclesiastica: Classici della Religione, 1983 ➤ 65,5958; 1,6569: ᴿProtestantesimo 41 (1986) 183s (G. *Conte*).

5342 **Nicholson** [as TDig 34,88; TR 82,426 Nicholsen] Ernest W., God and his people; covenant and theology in the Old Testament. Ox 1986, Clarendon. 244 p. £22.50. 0-19-826684-7. – ᴿExpTim first choice 97,11 (1985s) 321s (C. S. *Rodd*).

5343 **Sohn Seock-Tae**, The divine election of Israel: diss. NYU 1986, ᴰ*Levine* B. 331 p. 86-14546 . – DissA 47 (1986s) 1374-A.

5344 **Vermeylen** Jacques, Le Dieu de la promesse et le Dieu de l'Alliance; le dialogue des grandes intuitions théologiques de l'AT: LDiv 126. P 1986, Cerf. 375 p. 2-204-02594-1 [OTAbs 10,202].

5345 *Wells* Paul, Covenant, humanity, and Scripture; some theological reflections: WestTJ 48 (1986) 17-45.

5346 **Wyschogrod** Michael, The body of faith; Judaism as corporeal election 1983 ➤ 65,5979; 1,6584: ᴿJRefJud 33,1 (1986) 95-97 (E. N. *Dorff*); Judaica 41 (1985) 115-7 (G. *Klostermann*); Judaism 35 (1986) 497-500 (N. M. *Samuelson*).

H3.3   *Fides in VT* – OT Faith.

5347 **Drane** J., Old Testament faith; an illustrated documentary. SF 1986, Harper & R. 160 p. $11. 0-06-062064-1 [NTAbs 31,130].

5348 *Martin-Achard* Robert, Old Testament theologies and faith confessions [< RTPhil 117 (1985) 81-91], ᵀᴱ*Asen* B.: TDig 33 (1986) 145-8.

5349 **Mello** Alberto, Ritorna, Israele ! La conversione nella interpretazione rabbinica: Commenti ebraici antichi alla Scrittura. R 1985, Città Nuova. 207 p.; bibliog. p. 39-43. 88-311-4906-7.

5350 **Schmidt** Werner H., The faith of the OT, a history 1983 ➤ 64,6338 ... 1,6587; now paperback, Ox 1986, Blackwell; x-302 p. £8; 0-631-15305-5: ᴿHeythJ 27 (1986) 183s (R. *Coggins*).

H3.5   *Liturgia VT* – OT prayer.

5351 **Adelman** Penina V., Miriam's Well; rituals for Jewish women around the year. Fresh Meadows NY 1986, Biblio. ix-142 p.; ill. $10 [RelStR 13,174, Ruth *Langer*].

5352 *Balentine* Samuel E., Prayer in the wilderness traditions; in pursuit of divine justice: ➤ 36, Mem. GOITEIN S. = HebAnR 9 (1985) 53-74.

5353 **Ben-Chorin** Schalom, *Kaczynski* Reiter, *Knoch* Otto, Das Gebet bei Juden und Christen 1982 ➤ 65,5988: ᴿFreibRu 37s (1985s) 99s (Martina *Schlatterer*).

5354 *Brednich* Rolf W., Gebet: ➤ 586, EnzMär 5 (1986) 792-9.

5355 **Clements** R. E., The prayers of the Bible [17, none from Psalms, + 8 NT]. L/Atlanta 1986, SCM/Knox. 295 p. £8/$10. 0-334-02268-1 / 0-8042-0071-8 [= In spirit and in truth; insights from biblical prayers 1985 ➤ 1,6596]. – ᴿExpTim 98 (1986s) 24 (J. *Eaton*).

5356 **Cohen** J. M., Horizons of Jewish prayer. L 1986, United Synagogue. 368 p. £7.50 pa. 0-907104-08-8 [BL 87,103, S. C. *Reif*].

5357 *Diez Merino* L., Expresiones relativas a la consagración en la literatura bíblica y judía: ➤ 461*, XL Semana 1985, EstMar 51 (1986) 31-63.

5358 **Di Sante** C., La preghiera di Israele; alle radici della liturgia cristiana: Radici 6. Casale Monferrato 1985, Marietti. xiv-242 p. Lit. 20.000. 88-211-8334-3 [BL 87,90, A. *Gelston*]. – ᴿStPatav 33 (1986) 432-4 (Teresa *Salzano*). [EphLtg 100 (1986) 616 indica p. 191 una recensione inesistente di A. *Pistoia*].

5359 **Fabris** Rinaldo, La preghiera nella Bibbia. R 1985, Borla. 201 p. Lit. 12.000. – ᴿLetture 41 (1986) 968 (G. *Ravasi*); ParVi 31 (1986) 387s (T. *Lorenzin*).

5359* *Faur* José, Delocutive expressions in the Hebrew liturgy: ➤ 11*, Mem. BICKERMAN E. = JANES 16s (1984s) 41-54.

5360 *Fumagalli* P. F., La proclamazione della Parola di Dio nella liturgia ebraica del Sabato: EphLtg 98 (1984) 241-269.

5361 ᴱ**Green** Arthur, Jewish spirituality, from the Bible through the Middle Ages: ➤ 588, Enc. World Spirituality 13. NY 1986, Crossroad. xxv-450 p. $49.50. – ᴿTDig 33 (1986) 476 (W. C. *Heiser*).

5362 **Greenberg** Moshe, Biblical prose prayer 1983 ➤ 64,6351; 1,6605: ᴿJBL 105 (1986) 128s (J. *Corvin*).

5363 *Grelot* Pierre, Prière dans la Bible: ➤ 582, DictSpir XII,2 (1986) 2217-2247.

5364 **Heinemann** J., La preghiera ebraica [Eng. 1977 ➤ 61,b794], ᵀᴱ*Mello* Alberto. Magnano VC 1986, Qiqajon, comunità di Bose. 192 p.

5365 *Hennig* John, Das Alte Testament als Quelle der Eröffnungsverse der Messe; eine Durchsicht des Missale Romanum von 1970: ArLtgW 28 (1986) 43-60.

5366 *Homerski* Józef, ❷ Modèle de prêtre dans [les livres inspirés de] l'Ancien Testament: AtKap 106 (1986) 3-13.

5367 *Kimbrough* S. T.ᴶ, Jewish resources for Christian worship: [Methodist] Quarterly Review 6,1 (Nv 1986) 55-64.

5367* *Klappe* Jill, Sukkoth, Huttenfest, Palmzondag. Kampen 1986, Kok. 60 p. *f* 12,90 [GerefTTs 86,3 back cover].

5368 *Le Gall* Robert, La liturgie, célébration de l'Alliance: 1. Associés à l'œuvre de Dieu; 2. La liturgie dans l'Ancienne... 3. Nouvelle Alliance. Chambray-les-Tours 1981. 160 p.; 142 p.; 270 p. – ᴿRuBi 39 (1986) 83s (B. *Nadolski*).

5368* *Légasse* Simon, Pureté, purification (Écriture Sainte): ➤ 582, DictSpir XII/2 (1986) 2627-2637.

5369 *Leibovici* Sarah, Noces séfarades; quelques rites; bibliographie: RÉJ 145 (1986) 227-241.

5370 **Manns** Frédéric, La prière d'Israël à l'heure de Jésus; préf. *Flusser* D.: SBF Anal 22. J 1986, Franciscan. xii-304 p. $20 pa. [NTAbs 30,376]. – ᴿCiuD 199 (1986) 332 (J. *Gutiérrez*); EsprV 96 (1986) 554s (S. *Légasse*).

5371 *Petuchowski* Jakob, a) Jüdische Liturgie ? 'Liturgie' im christlichen und jüdischen Sprachgebrauch; – b) Wirkliche und vermeintliche messianische Elemente der Sederfeier: Judaica 41 (1985) 99-107 / 37-44.

5372 *Provera* Mario, La preghiera al tempo di Gesù: ParVi 31 (1986) 453-8.

5373 **Ravasi** Gianfranco, I Canti di Israele; preghiera e vita di un popolo: La Bibbia nella storia 5. Bo 1986, Dehoniane. 299 p. 88-10-40254-5.

5374 **Reventlow** Henning, Gebet im AT. Stu 1986, Kohlhammer. 334 p. DM 36 pa. [TR 83,338].

5375 ᴱ**Thieberger** F., Jüdisches Fest, jüdischer Brauch ³ [¹1937 confiscated]. Königstein 1985, Jüd. Athenaeum. 486 p.; ill. 3-7610-0378-1. – ᴿNedTTs 40 (1986) 338s (K. A. D. *Smelik*).

5376 **Trolin** Clifford F., Prayer and the imagination; a study of the Shemoneh Esreh, the eighteen benedictions of the daily Jewish service: diss. Graduate Theological Union, ᴰ*Matt* D. Berkeley 1986. 272 p. 86-28718. – DissA 47 (1986s) 3078s-A.

5377 *Weinfeld* Moshe, The day of the Lord; aspirations for the Kingdom of God in the Bible and Jewish liturgy: ➤ 50, ScrHieros 31 (1986) 361-372.

5378 **Wijngaards** John,   Inheriting the master's cloak; creative biblical spirituality [OT passages]. ND 1985, Ave Maria.   191 p. $5 pa. [TDig 3,494].

5379 **Wilms** Franz-E.,   Freude vor Gott; Kult und Fest in Israel 1981 ↠ 62,6995; 63,6388: ᴿBZ 30 (1986) 287s (O *Wahl*).

H3.7   VT-OT Moral Theology.

5380 *Albertz* Rainer,   Das Überleben der Familie sichern; die biblischen Aussagen über Ehe und Sexualität sind zeitbedingt: LuthMon 25 (1986) 401-5.

5381 **Ben-Chorin** Schalom,   Jüdische Ethik, anhand der patristischen Perikopen 1983 ↠ 64,6369; 65,6024: ᴿZRGg 38 (1986) 281s (Salcia *Landmann*).

5381* **Birch** Bruce C.,   What does the Lord require? ... social witness 1985 ↠ 1,6630*: ᴿInterpretation 40 (1986) 420.422 (J. M. *Bracke*).

5382 **Dan** Joseph,   Jewish mysticism and Jewish ethics [Stroum Lectures]. Seattle 1986, Univ. Washington.   xiii-133 p. $30 [CBQ 48,777].

5383 *Daube* David,   The Old Testament prohibitions of homosexuality: ZSavR 103 (1986) 447s: Lv 18,22; 20,13, like Assyrian Laws 20, envisions anal, not oral.

5384 **Cook** Ronald L.,   The neighbor concept in the Old Testament: diss. Southern Baptist Theol. Sem. 1980. ix-164 p. – KirSef 59 (1985) 298.

5384* **Hoyles** J. Arthur,   Punishment in the Bible. L 1986, Epworth.   148 p. £6.   0-7162-0425,8. – ᴿExpTim second choice 98,11 (1986s) 322s (C. S. *Rodd*: not scholarly, but on a topic too much ignored).

5385 *Hunt* Harry B.ᴶ,   Attitude toward divorce in post-exilic Judaism: BibIll 12 (1986) 62-65 [OTAbs 10,80].

5385* **Kaiser** Walter C.,   Toward Old Testament ethics 1983 ↠ 64,6380 ... 1,6635: ᴿHeythJ 27 (1986) 72 (L. *Jacobs*); STEv 15 (1985) 126s (P. *Bolognesi*).

5386 *a*) *Lubarsky* S.,   Judaism and the justification of abortion; – *b*) *Block* R., A matter of life and death; Reform Judaism and the defective child: JRefJud 31 (1984) 1-14 / 14-31 [Judaica 41,64].

5387 *a*) *Müller* Karlheinz,   Gesetz und Gesetzeserfüllung im Frühjudentum; – *b*) *Mussner* Franz,   Das Toraleben im jüdischen Verständnis: ↠ 382, ᴱKERTELGE K., Gesetz 1985/6, 11-27 / 28-45.

5388 **O'Neill** Helen C.,   Biblical truth and the morality of *ḥērem*: diss. R, Pont. Univ. S. Thomae. Providence 1984.   xvi-278 p.; bibliog. p. 261-278.

5389 *Otto* Eckart,   Kultus und Ethos in Jerusalemer Theologie; ein Beitrag zur theologischen Begründung der Ethik im Alten Testament [i. Recht und Religion im AT: ii. Ps 15 & 24; Schöpfungtheologie; iii. dialektische Entwicklung]: ZAW 98 (1986) 161-179.

5390 *Rogerson* John W.,   [on use of the Bible in the abortion debate; OT silence in comparison with Assyrian law ...]: ↠ 282, ᴱ*Channer* J., Abortion 1985 ...

5391 **Roth** Joel,   The halakhic process; a systemic analysis: Moreshet 13.   NY 1986, Jewish Theological Seminary of America.   398 p.

5392 *Seltzer* S.,   The psychological implications of mixed marriage: JRefJud 34 (1985) 21-38 [Judaica 41,255].

5393 *Tångberg* K. Arvid,   Die Bewertung des ungeborenen Lebens: ScandJOT 1,1 (1986) 51-65.

5393* *Voorwinde* S., The Temple and biblical ethics: Vox Reformata 45 (1985) 3-11.

H3.8   *Bellum et pax VT-NT* - **War and peace in the Bible.**

5394 **Atkinson** David J., Peace in our time? Some biblical groundwork. GR 1986, Eerdmans. 221 p. $5 [TDig 33,457].

5395 **Baldermann** Ingo, Der Gott des Friedens und die Götter der Macht; Biblische Alternativen: Wege des Lernens 1, 1983 ➤ 64,6400: ᴿKIsr 1 (1986) 87-89 (A. *Lohrbächer*).

5396 *Bóna* Zoltán, Ⓦ Biblical light on human aggression: Theologiai Szemle 29 (1986) 264-8.

5397 **Brown** Dale W., Biblical pacifism; a peace church perspective; pref. *Deats* Richard B. Elgin 1986, Brethren. xviii-203 p. [TR 83,249].

5398 **Brueggemann** Walter, Revelation and violence, a study in contextualization [1986 Père Marquette lecture]. Milwaukee 1986, Marquette Univ. vi-72 p. [CBQ 48,777].

5399 *De Benedetti* Paolo, La violenza e il giudaismo: Hermeneutica 4 (Urbino 1984) 51-60 [Themenheft 'Ermeneutica della violenza'; 5 (1955) 'Violenza dell'ermeneutica', i.e. forza morale non fisica].

5400 *a) Derrick* Christopher, The just war; a dilemma; - *b) Hayes* Doris K., Shalom; covenant and kingdom: CleR 71 (1986) 434-7 / 429-434.

5401 *a) Finkel* Asher, Sabbath as the way of *shalom* in the biblical tradition; - *b) Frizzell* Lawrence E., Peacemaking in the NT period; - *c) Pushparajan* A., Struggle for peace; complementary models in the context of India: JDharma 11 (1986) 115-123 / 160-171 / 172-195.

5401* **Friesen** Duane K., Christian peacemaking and international conflict; a realist pacifist perspective. Scottdale PA 1986, Herald. 304 p. $20 [RelStR 13,339, C. *Chatfield*].

5402 *Goodman* M. D., *Holladay* A. J., Religious scruples in ancient warfare: ClasQ 36 (1986) 151-171.

5403 *Grech* Prosper, 'Peace' nella Sacra Scrittura [< ᴱ*Magnani* G., Pace, disarmo e Chiesa 1984, 129-142]: 166, Ermeneutica 1986, 420-435.

5404 *Grob* Leonard M., Non-violence — a BUBERIAN perspective: JJS 37 (1986) 76-87.

5405 **Häring** Bernard, The healing power of peace and non-violence. L 1986, St. Paul. $5. 0-85439-244-0. - ᴿCleR 71 (1986) 380-5 (O. *Hardwicke*); ExpTim 98 (1986s) 150s (P. D. *Bishop*: shibboleths).

5405* **Harries** Richard, Christianity and war in a nuclear age. L 1986, Mowbray. 170 p. £5. 0-264-67053-1. - ᴿExpTim 98 (1986s) 284 (J. *Ferguson*: urbane, courteous, tolerant — but scourge of pacifism).

5406 **Hauerwas** Stanley, Against the nations; war and survival in a liberal society. Minneapolis 1985, Winston. vii-208 p. $21.35/£15. - ᴿScotJT 39 (1986) 571-4 (R. *Gill*); Thomist 50 (1986) 714-7 (Judith A. *Dwyer*); TLond 39 (1986) 316s (R. *Harries*).

5407 *Hauerwas* Stanley, A pacifist response to *In Defense of Creation* [Methodist bishops]: AsburyTJ 41,2 (1986) 5-14.

5408 **Helgeland** J. *al.*, Christian and the military 1985 ➤ 1,6677: ᴿCathCrisis 4,2 (1986) 29-31 (C. J. *Reid*).

5409 *Hoogen* Toine van den, Veiligheid en scheppingsgelooft [Security and belief in creation]; aanzetten tot een theologie van de vrede: TsTNijm 26 (1986) 372-390; 391, 'Theology of peace in the light of creation'.

5410 **Hoppe** Thomas, Friedenspolitik mit militärischen Mitteln: eine ethische

Analyse strategischer Ansätze: Theologie und Frieden 1. Köln 1986, Bachem. 318 p. [TR 83,142, R. *Weiler*].

5411 *Horsley* Richard, Ethics and exegesis; 'love your enemies' and the doctrine of non-violence: JAAR 54 (1986) 3-27; bibliog. 27-31.

5412 *Jegen* Mary Evelyn, Theology and spirituality of nonviolence: Worship 60 (1986) 119-133.

5413 **Johnson** James T., Can modern war be just? 1984 ➤ 1,6681: [R]Horizons 13 (1986) 447s (J. M. *Thompson*); TTod 43 (1986s) 104.106 (S. *Hauerwas*, L. G. *Jones*).

5414 [E]**Khoury** A., *Hünermann* P., Friede, was ist das? Die Antwort der Weltreligionen: Herderbücherei 1144, 1984 ➤ 1,6684: [R]TPQ 134 (1986) 213 (G. *Wildmann*).

5415 **Klassen** William, Love of enemies, the way to peace: OvBT 15, 1984 ➤ 65,6070; 1,6686: [R]RB 93 (1986) 298s (L. J. *Foley*); SR 14 (1985) 397s (J. *Culliton*).

5416 *Klein* Günter, Der Friede Gottes und der Friede der Welt; eine exegetische Vergewisserung am Neuen Testament: ZTK 83 (1986) 325-355.

5417 [E]**Lohfink** Norbert, Gewalt und Gewaltlosigkeit im Alten Testament: QDisp 96, 1983 ➤ 64,407*... 1,6689: [R]BZ 30 (1986) 296-8 (H. *Niehr*); TPQ 134 (1986) 400s (J. M. *Oesch*).

5418 **Lohfink** Norbert, Il Dio della Bibbia e la violenza [Gewalt und Gewaltlosigkeit 1983 ➤ 64,407*], [T]*Scandiani* Giuseppe. Brescia 1985, Morcelliana. 160 p. Lit. 16.000. – [R]Asprenas 33 (1986) 337s (B. *Belletti*); CiTom 113 (1986) 624s (M. *García Cordero*); HumBr 41 (1986) 616s (G. *Segalla*); Letture 41 (1986) 769s (A. *Carrara*); STEv 9,18 (1986) 288s (P. *Guccini*).

5419 *Lohfink* Norbert, Gewaltlosigkeit nach dem Evangelium angesichts der gesellschaftlichen Verankerung der Gewalt; Referat, Pax Christi,Bonn 28. Okt. 1984: Probleme des Friedens (Fra 1986,1) 16-27.

5420 *Miller* Richard B., Christian pacifism and just-war tenets; how do they diverge?: TS 47 (1986) 448-472.

5421 **Morey** Robert A., When is it right to fight ? Minneapolis 1985, Bethany. 143 p. 0-87123-810-1.

5422 *Murphy* Don, Can a Christian be a pacifist ?: SpTod 38 (1986) 100-110.

5423 *Nagy* Gyula, [M] The idea of nations and internationalism in Protestant theology [National Peace Council 1985]: Theologiai Szemle 29 (1986) 5-8.

5424 **Noort** Ed, Geweld in het Oude Testament; over woorden en verhalen aan de rond van de kerkelijke praktijk: TerSprake 28, 1985 ➤ 1,6700: [R]Streven 53 (1985s) 948s (P. *Beentjes*).

5425 *Oliva* Max, A scriptural approach to the ministry of justice and peace: RRel 45 (1986) 747-753.

5426 **Pawlikowski** John T., *Senior* Donald, Biblical and theological reflections on 'The challenge of peace' 1984 ➤ 65,300: [R]BibTB 16 (1986) 39s (H. *Humphrey*); Horizons 13 (1986) 206 (Anita M. *Hyslop*).

5427 *Piwowarski* Władysław, [P] La paix comme valeur fondamentale dans la doctrine sociale de l'Église: ColcT 56,3 (1986) 5-16; franç. 16s.

5428 *a) Ravasi* Gianfranco, *Shalom* e *eirene*; – *b) Mannucci* Valerio, Caino e Abele; – *c) Cimosa* Mario, La pace messianica nel Sal 72 e in Is 11,1-9; – *d) Loss* Nicolò M., Guerra e herem nell'AT uno scandalo?; – *e) Vallauri* Emiliano, Il discorso della montagna e la non violenza; – *f) De Lorenzi* Lorenzo, I conflitti e il loro superamento in 1-2 Cor: ParVi 30,2 (1985) 9-16 / 17-25 / 26-32 / 33-42 / 43-50 / 51-58.

5429 *Rendtorff* Rolf, Die Aufnahme alttestamentlicher Friedenstraditionen in die gegenwärtige Diskusssion: ➤ 109, ᶠSTEIGER L., Brosamen 1986, 331-340.

5430 **Rousseau** Félicien, Courage ou résignation et violence (Un retour aux sources de l'éthique): Recherches NS 5. Montréal 1985, Bellarmin. 311 p. 2-89007-595-8.

5431 *Sänger* Peter, Die eine Menschheit; ein Argument H.J. IWANDS gegen den Krieg: BTZ 3 (1986) 132-143.

5432 *Schmidt* Daryl, Biblical hermeneutics on peacemaking in the bishops' pastoral: BibTB 16 (1986) 47-55.

5432* *Sicre* José Luis, Valor profético y cristiano de la paz: ComSev 19 (1986) 3-18.

5433 *a) Soares-Prabhu* George, Jesus and conflict; – *b) Dalrymple* John †, Not peace but the sword; – *c) Smith* Bede, Conflict, non-violence and discipleship: Way 26 (1986) 14-23 / 4-13 / 24-32.

5434 *Sölle* Dorothee, Der Bibelgebrauch in der Friedensarbeit: Junge Kirche 47 (1986) 67-76 [< ZIT].

5435 *Stark* Axel H., Zur Friendenserziehung im Religionsunterricht: TPQ 134 (1986) 249-253.

5436 *Susin* L. C., Paz, dom e tarefa mesiânica: Teocomunicação 71 (1986) 5-19 [Stromata 42,457].

5437 *Sutor* Bernhard, Lo político en las declaraciones sobre la paz de las conferencias episcopales [< StiZt 202 (1984) 455-474], ᵀᴱ*Reig* Ramiro: SelT 25 (1986) 84-96.

5438 *Thompson* W. M., The justice and peace of the Jesus event and the gnostic temptation [to escape the 'in-between' character of the present] StFormSp 7 (1986) 393-407 [< NTAbs 31,61].

5438* *Tofană* Stelian, L'unité des chrétiens dans les efforts pour la défense de la paix et de la vie dans le monde selon le NT (roum.): STBuc 37 (1985) 365-381.

5439 ᴱ**Tröger** Karl-W., Nachfolge und Friedensdienst — — — ᴿTheologiai Szemle 29 (1986) 58-60 (T. *Ujlaki*).

5440 **Vögtle** Anton, La pace; le fonti nel NT 1984 ➤ 65,6075*b*; **1**,6717: ᴿProtestantesimo 41 (1986) 235 (F. *Ferrario*).

5441 **Wengst** Klaus, Pax romana; Anspruch und Wirklichkeit; Erfahrungen und Wahrnehmungen des Friedens bei Jesus und im Urchristentum. Mü 1986, Kaiser. 292 p. DM 39 [RelStR 13,261, J. H. *Elliott*].

5442 **Wilkinson** Alan, Dissent or conform? War, peace and the English churches 1900-1945. L 1986, SCM. 361 p. £10.50. 0-334-00416-0. – ᴿExpTim 97 (1985s) 257s (C. S. *Rodd* finds confirmed his opinion that the churches have not provided needed leadership; a leader of one of the most pacifist on August 2, 1914 turned one week later to support the war; on most social issues, churches tend to follow public opinion).

H4.1   Regnum messianicum VT.

5442* *Bacchiocchi* Samuele, Sabbatical typologies of Messianic redemption: JStJud 17 (1986) 153-176.

5443 *Boon* R., Messiaanse gemeenschap in eschatologisch perspectief: Ter Herkenning 14,1 (1986) 16-29 [< GerefTTs 86,192].

5443* **Cazelles** H., Le Messie de la Bible; christologie de l'AT 1978 ➤ 60,8696... 62,7045: ᴿProtestantesimo 41 (1986) 107s (J. A. *Soggin*).

5444 *e) Harun* Martin, Der Messias in der Apokalyptik des ersten Jahr-

hunderts (indonesisch): Orientasi 18 (1986) 25-44 [< TKontext 8/2,43].
– *b*) *Cornițescu* Em., La personne du Messie et son œuvre à la lumière
des prophéties vétérotestamentaires (en roumain): STBuc 37 (1985) 606-
614.

5444* *a*) **Khoury** Fauzy, Le messianisme dans les trois religions monothéistes:
diss. Inst. Cath. P 1986. – RICathP 19 (1986) 151s (H. *Cazelles*). – *b*)
Laperrousaz E.-M., L'attente du Messie en Palestine à la veille et au début
de l'ère chrétienne ... 1982 ⇒ 63,6433 ... 1,6732:   ᴿJSS 31 (1986) 264-6 (D.
Goodman).

5445 **Neusner** Jacob, Messiah in context 1984 ⇒ 65,6109: **1,6736**:   ᴿInterpretation 40 (1986) 203s (G. *Howard*); RÉJ 145 (1986) 406-9 (Mireille
Hadas-Lebel); TrinJ 7 (1986) 86-99 (D. A. *Hagner*).

5446 **Puente Ojea** Gonzalo, Messianisme et idéologie, ᵀ: Problèmes et
controverses. P 1983, Vrin. iv-361 p. [KirSef 59,312].

5447 ᴱ**Reem** Shmuel, ➌ *Ha-ra'yon*... The Messianic concept in Israel:
study-day for the 80th birthday of Gershom SCHOLEM, 4-5.XII.1977: 1982
⇒ 64,423:   ᴿRÉJ 145 (1986) 397-400 (M.-R. *Hayoun*).

5447* *Rizzi* A., El mesianismo en la vida cotidiana. Barc 1986, Herder.
267 p. [Proyección 34, 151, A. *Sánchez*].

5448 **Schimanowski** G., Weisheit und Messias ... Präexistenzchristologie:
WUNT 2/17, 1985 ⇒ **1,6739**:   ᴿExpTim 98 (1986s) 304 (E. *Best*).

5448* *Schunck* Klaus-Dietrich, Die Attribute des eschatologischen Messias;
Strukturlinien in der Ausprägung des alttestamentlichen Messiasbildes
[Gastvorlesung Tü Mü 1986]: TLZ 111 (1986) 641-652.

5449 **Strauss** Hans, Messianisch ohne Messias; zur Überlieferungsgeschichte
und Interpretation der sog. messianischen Texte im AT 1984 ⇒ 65,6117;
1,6741:   ᴿTLZ 111 (1986) 813-5 (K.-D. *Schunck*); TPQ 134 (1986) 74s (F.
Hubmann).

5450 *Talmon* Shemaryahu, *a*) Types of messianic expectation at the turn of the
era [< ᶠRAD G. von, Probleme 1971, given as 511-588]; – *b*) Biblical
visions of the future ideal age [no source indicated]: ⇒ 227, King, cult
1986, 202-224 / 140-164.

5451 **Tuttle** Jeffrey P., The coming *mashiah* / Messiah [1 Sam 2,10.15; Ps 2,2;
Hab 3,13; Dan 9,25s]: CalvaryB 2 (1986) 23-38.

5452 **Waschke** Ernst-Joachim, Wurzeln und Ausprägung messianischer
Vorstellungen im Alten Testament; eine traditionsgeschichtliche Untersuchung: Diss. Greifswald 1985. 244 p. – TLZ 112,78.

H4.3   **Eschatologia VT.**

5453 *Cannizzo* Antonio, L'escatologia dell'Antico Testamento: RasT 27
(1986) 385-400 [i. Esistenza di ombre nella 'Sheol', il dominio della morte,
la morte come esperienza di fede; ii. Crisi dei valori nazionali e sapienziali;
iii. L' 'eschaton' come risurrezione dei morti (periodi esilico e maccabeo) e
come comunione perenne con Dio; iv. Rivalutazione dei valori tradi-
zionali].

5454 *García Cordero* Maximiliano, La esperienza del más allá en el judaismo
contemporáneo de Jesús: CiTom 113 (1986) 209-249.

5455 *Gowan* Donald E., Eschatology in the Old Testament. Ph 1986,
Fortress. 150 p. $10. 0-8006-1906-4. – ᴿExpTim 98 (1986s) 147s
(A. H. W. *Curtis*); TDig 33 (1986) 472 (W. C. *Heiser*).

5456 *Grech* Prosper, *a*) Reinterpretazione interprofetica ed escatologia vete-
rotestamentaria [< AugR 9 (1969) 235-265]; – *b*) Saggio sul linguaggio

della scrittura e la sua interpretazione [< BibTB 6 (1976)]: ᵀ*Camporeale* Rita: ⇥ 166, Ermeneutica 1986, 5-39 / 40-58.

5457 *Haag* E., Seele und Unsterblichkeit in biblischer Sicht: ⇥ 411, ᴱ*Breuning* W., Seele 1986, 31-93.

5458 **Himmelfarb** Martha, Tours of Hell, an apocalyptic form in Jewish and Christian literature [diss. Pennsylvania] 1983: ⇥ 64,6474; 1,6745: ᴿJBL 105 (1986) 147-9 (Adela Y. *Collins*); JJS 37 (1986) 120-3 (R. *White*: broad and systematic); RHR 203 (1986) 71-73 (A. *Paul*).

5459 *Milikowsky* Chaim, ⊕ Gehenna and 'Sinners of Israel' in the light of Seder ʿOlam: Tarbiz 55 (1985s) 311-349; Eng. I.

5460 **Moraldi** L., L'aldilà dell'uomo nelle civiltà babilonese, egizia, greca, latina, ebraica, cristiana e musulmana. Mi 1985, Mondadori. 265 p. Lit. 16.500. 88-0026286-5 [BL 87, 99, F. F. *Bruce*]. – ᴿStPatav 33 (1986) 395-9 (A. *Capuzzo*).

5461 **Paull** Simcha S., Judaism's contribution to the psychology of death and dying [... Judaism on life after death]: diss. California Institute of Integral Studies, 1986. 410 p. 86-25140. – DissA 47 (1986s) 2617-A.

5462 *Preuss* Horst D. [*Karrer* Martin], Eschatologie AT [NT]: ⇥ 587, EvKL 1 (1986) 1109-1111 [-1114].

5463 **Spronk** Klaas, Beatific afterlife in Ancient Israel and the Ancient Near East [diss. Kampen 1986, ᴰ*Moor* J. de. ix-398 p. – RTLv 18,543; TsTNijm 26,286s]: AOAT 219. Kevelaer/Neuk 1986, Butzon & B. / Neuk. ix-398 p. [TR 82,338]. 3-7666-9454-5 / Neuk 3-7887-1114-0.

5464 *Stähli* Hans-Peter, Tod und Leben im Alten Testament: TGl 76 (1986) 172-193.

5465 **Talmon** Shemaryahu, Eschatology and history in biblical Judaism: Tantur Occasional Papers 2. J 1986, Ecumenical Institute. 39 p. [JBL 105, 756].

5466 **Veld** Bertus van 't, De klacht over de vergankelijkheid van het menselijk leven in het Oude Testament, tegen de achtergrond van andere Oudtestamentische en van oud-oosterse uitspraken inzake de vergankelijkheid [Die Klage über die Vergänglichkeit des menschlichen Lebens im AT], diss. Utrecht. [⇥ 1,6522]. Harderwijk 1985, Wedding. 215 p. ƒ42,50. – ᴿBijdragen 47 (1986) 438 (W. *Beuken*); NedTTs 41 (1987) 733-5 (E. *Talstra*).

5467 *Wächter* L., Tod im AT: ZeichZt 40 (1986) 35-42.

H4.5 *Totius VT theologia biblica* – **General OT biblical theology.**

5468 *Addinall* Peter, What is meant by a theology of the Old Testament? ExpTim 97 (1985s) 332-6.

5468* *Bakker* L., Het Oude Testament in de systematische Theologie: 'ThT' 24 (1984) 97-114.

5469 *Barr* James [*al.*], Biblische theologie, ᵀ*Roehl* W. ⇥ 587, EvKL 1 (1986) 488-494 [-503 im Kontext; feministisch].

5470 **Ben-Chorin** Schalom, Theologia judaica 1982 ⇥ 64,137; 65,6134: ᴿIstina 31 (1986) 224s (B. *Dupuy*).

5471 **Childs** Brevard S., Old Testament theology in a canonical context 1985 ⇥ 1,6759: ᴿBL (1986) 84 (R. E. *Clements*: fine, but not so much about canon after all); CurrTM 13 (1986) 379 (R. W. *Klein*: cryptic brevity); ÉTRel 61 (1986) 442s (D. *Lys*); ExpTim 97 (1985s) 226s (C. S. *Rodd*); JTS 37 (1986) 442-4 (Margaret *Davies*); Salesianum 48 (1986) 726s (R. *Vicent*); TTod 43 (1986s) 284.286s (W. *Brueggemann*: currently most influential OT interpreter; disappointing); VT 36 (1986) 376-8 (J. A. *Emerton*, review much longer than VT norm).

5472 *Fensham* F. C., Die verhoudingsteologie [(God-man) relationship ...] as 'n moontlike oplossing vir 'n teologie van die Ou Testament: NduitseGT 26 (1985) 246-259.

5473 **Fohrer** Georg, Storia della religione israelitica 1985 ➤ 1,6764: [R]BL (1986) 85s (R. *Murray*); ComSev 19 (1986) 241 (M. de *Burgos*); ParVi 31 (1986) 152-4 (A. *Rolla*); Salesianum 48 (1986) 416s (R. *Vicent*).

5474 *Goldsworthy* Graeme L., 'Thus says the Lord' — the dogmatic basis of biblical theology: ➤ 54, [F]KNOX D., God rich 1986, 25-40.

5475 [E]**Hayes** J. H.: *Prussner* F. C. † 1978 (diss. Ch 1952), Old Testament theology; its history and development 1985 ➤ 1,6767: [R]BibTB 16 (1986) 33s (T. A. *Hoffman*); BL (1986) 88 (J. W. *Rogerson*: usefulness not limited by failing to delimit Hayes' additions); CBQ 48 (1986) 307 (R. *Gnuse*: updating of Prussner's 1952 dissertation, Methodology in OT theology; really an excellent history of OT theology); TLond 39 (1986) 395-7 (P. *Joyce*).

5475* *McEvenue* Sean E., The Old Testament, scripture or theology?: [< Interp 35 (1981) 229-242]: ExAud 1 (1985) 115-124.

5476 **McKenzie** John L., A theology of the Old Testament. Lanham MD 1986 = 1974, UPA. 336 p. $12 [JBL 105,753].

5477 **Oeming** Manfred, Gesamtbiblische Theologien der Gegenwart 1985 ➤ 1,6777: [R]Biblica 67 (1986) 570-7 (J. A. *Soggin*); BL (1986) 93 (R. E. *Clements*); RHPR 66 (1986) 211s (E. *Jacob*: important); TüTQ 166 (1986) 227s W. *Gross*).

5478 **Patrick** D., How should the biblical theologian go about constructing a theological model? [dramatic, not metaphysical]: Encounter ˙47 (1986) 361-9 [< ZAW].

5479 **Reventlow** H., Hauptprobleme der **biblischen** Theologie: ErtFor 203, 1983 ➤ 64,6505... 1,6781: [R]BLitEc 87 (1986) 150s (S. *Légasse* déplore les parenthèses interminables, 23 lignes p. 87s); Gregorianum 67 (1986) 535-7 (G. L. *Prato*); JBL 105 (1986) 118-120 (G. F. *Hasel*).

5480 **Reventlow** H., Problems of **biblical** theology in the twentieth century. L 1986, SCM. xvii-188 p. £8. 0-334-122770-0. – [R]ExpTim 98 (1986s) 52s (A. *Hanson*: 38-line sentence p. 168s may go in German, not in English).

5481 **Reventlow** Henning, Problems of **Old Testament** theology 1985 ➤ 1,6780b: [R]ModT 2 (1985s) 278s (R. E. *Clements*); NBlackf 67 (1986) 550s (J. *Barton*).

5481* a) *Ritschl* Dietrich, 'Wahre', 'reine' oder 'neue' biblische Theologie ? Einige Anfragen zur neueren Diskussion um 'Biblische Theologie'; – b) *Bohren* Rudolf, Biblische Theologie wider latenten Deismus: – c) *Reventlow* Henning, Biblische Theologie auf historisch-kritischer Grundlage [*Oeming* M. 1985]: ➤ 236, JbBT 1 (1986) 135-150 / 163-181 / 201-9.

5482 *Rolla* Armando, La teologia cristiana dell'ebraismo; il dibattito attuale [i. Gesù; ii. Paolo; iii. Vaticano II. iv. Messia sofferente]: Asprenas 33 (1986) 235-262.

5482* **Roscam Abbing** P. J., Inleiding in de Bijbelse Theologie 1983 ➤ 64,6508: [R]GerefTTs 86 (1986) 43 (C. *Houtman*).

5483 **Schedl** Claus, Zur Theologie des Alten Testaments; der göttliche Sprachvorgang. W 1986, Herder. 248 p. Sch 275. 3-210-24828-1 [TsTN 26,438].

5484 **Schmid** Johannes H., Biblische Theologie in der Sicht heutiger Alttesta-mentler [*Gese* H.; *Westermann* C.; *Zimmerli* W.; *Gunneweg* A.]. Z/Giessen 1986, Gotthelf/Brunnen. vi-250 p. 3-85706-239-8 / 3-7655-9326-5.

5485 **Seebass** Horst, Ist biblische Theologie möglich?: Judaica 41 (1985) 194-206.

5486 *Smend* Rudolf, *a)* Die ['nicht-statische'] Mitte des Alten Testaments [<*Barth* K., Theologische Studien 101, 1970]; – *b)* Theologie im AT [< ᶠEBELING G. 1982, 11-26]: ⇥ 220, Mitte des ATs 1986, 40-84 / 104-117.

5487 **Van Buren** Paul M., A Christian theology of the people Israel: A theology of the Jewish-Christian reality 2, 1983 ⇥ 65,6165; 1,6787: ᴿWWorld 6 (1986) 106-8 (H. H. *Ditmanson*).

5487* *Ware* J. H., Rethinking the possibility of a biblical theology: PRS [? Philosophy of religion series according to ⇥ 236, JbBT 214 + 210] 10 (1983) 5-13.

5488 **Werner** Wolfgang, Studien zur alttestamentlichen Vorstellung vom Plan Jahwes: Hab.-Diss. Augsburg 1986, ᴰ*Kilian*. – TR 82 (1986) 511.

5489 **Westermann** Claus, Théologie de L'AT, ᵀ*Jeanneret* Lore 1984 ⇥ **1**,6790: ᴿETL 62 (1986) 174s (J. *Lust*: translation often clearer than the German, at other times requires validity-check); ÉTRel 61 (1986) 111s (D. *Lys*); RechSR 74 (1986) 623s (J. *Briend*); RTPhil 118 (1986) 417-9 (*Musuvaho Paluku*).

5490 **Westermann** Claus, Hoofdlijnen van een Theologie van het Oude Testament [1978] 1981 ⇥ 63,6488*b*; 64,6519: ᴿNedTTs 40 (1986) 174-7 (M. D. *Koster*: detailed analysis; weaknesses of the translation).

5490* *Westermann* Claus, Zur Frage einer biblischen Theologie [... *Ebeling* G.]: ⇥ 236, JbBT 1 (1986) 13-30.

H5.1 *Deus* – NT – **God** [as Father ⇥ 5098*-5129]

5491 *Basinger* David, The new Calvinism; a sheep in wolves' clothing [diminishes God's rigid control of human decisions]: ScotJT 39 (1986) 483-499.

5492 *Bastianon* Eugenio, Per una teologia ermeneutica [*Kasper* W., Il Dio di Gesù Cristo 1982/4]: RasT 27 (1986) 436-441.

5493 *Bauerschmidt* F. C., Doing [NT] theology in light of divine aniconicity: StLuke 29 (1986) 117-135 [NTAbs 30,270].

5494 *Dupont* Jacques, Le Dieu de Jésus: NRT 109 (1987) 321-344: i. un Dieu pour les autres; ii. qui n'admet aucun partage.

5495 **Kasper** Walter, Der Gott Jesu Christi 1982 ⇥ 64,6534 ... **1**,6795: ᴿRel-StR 12 (1986) 55 (C. J. *Peter*: remarkable erudition, worthy of highest commendation); TGegw 23 (1985) 115-123 (V. *Hahn*).

5496 **Kasper** Walter, The God of Jesus Christ 1984 ⇥ 65,6176; **1**,6796: ᴿJAAR 54 (1986) 352-4 (J. R. *Sachs*; translation poor and badly printed); JTS 37 (1986) 286-9 (J. P. *Mackey*); RelStT 6 (1986) 50s (H. A. *Meynell*); RRel 45 (1986) 625s (J. P. *Gaffney*); TLond 39 (1986) 131s (C. *Gunton*); TTod 43 (1986s) 108s (J. H. *Wright*).

5497 **Kasper** W., Il Dio di Gesu Cristo. Brescia, 1984, Queriniana. 450 p. – ᴿHumBr 41 (1986) 140 (G. *Canobbio*).

5498 **Kasper** Walter, El Dios de Jesucristo 1985 ⇥ **1**,6798: ᴿComSev 19 (1986) 440-2 (V. J. *Ansede Alonso*); EstE 61 (1986) 453s (L. *García Pérez*); NatGrac 33 (1986) 190s (B. de *Armellada*); TEspir 30 (1986) 142-4 (S. *Fuster*); VerVid 44 (1986) 465s (V. *Casas*).

5499 **Kasper** Walter, Le Dieu des chrétiens: CogF 128, 1985 ⇥ **1**,6797: ᴿEsprV 96 (1986) 91-93 (P. *Jay*); RTPhil 118 (1986) 328 (K. *Blaser*).

5500 *Mulder* D. C., 'None other gods' — 'no other name' [*Visser 't Hooft*]: EcuR 33 (1986) 209-215.

5501 **Manaranche** André, Le monothéisme chrétien 1985 ➤ 1,6800; F 110: RRHPR 66 (1986) 475-7 (P. *Lønning*).
5502 *Martin Velasco* Juan. El Dios de Jesús y la 'vuelta de lo religioso' ¿Ruido o rumor?: SalT 74 (1986) 799-809.
5503 *Pastor Félix* Alejandro, Teismo bíblico y Kerygma cristiano: Compostellanum 31 (1986) 63-98.
5504 *Simonetti* Manlio, Il problema dell'unità di Dio da Giustino a Ireneo / da Clemente a Dionigi : RivStoLR 22 (1986) 201-240 / 439-474.
5505 **Studer** B., Gott [Trinität] und unsere Erlösung im Glauben der alten Kirche. Dü 1985, Patmos. 331 p. – ROrChrPer 52 (1986) 482s (E. *Farrugia*).

H5.2 Christologia ipsius NT.

5506 **Boring** M. Eugene, Truly human / truly divine 1984 ➤ 65,6191; 1,6817: RJAAR 54 (1986) 165s (K. A. *Plank*: more coming).
5507 **Caba** José, De los evangelios al Jesús histórico; introducción a la cristología² [¹1970]: BAC 316, Historia salutis 4 [Cf. BAC 392, 1977 ➤ 58,5752]. M 1980, Católica. xl-493 p.; bibliog. p. xxix-xl. 84-220-0284-1.
5508 ECazelles H., Commission biblique pontificale, Bible et christologie 1984 ➤ 65,274; 1,6820: RRHR 203 (1986) 437s (J. *Doignon*); ScripTPamp 18 (1986) 686-9 (A. *García-Moreno*).
5509 *Charlesworth* James H., The Jewish roots of Christology; the discovery of The Hypostatic Voice: ScotJT 39 (1986) 19-41.
5510 *Chouinard* Larry, Trends in Synoptic Christology: RestQ 28 (Abilene 1985s) 201-214 [< ZIT].
5511 a) *[Delhaye* P. secr.] Commissio theologica internationalis, La conscience que Jésus avait de lui-même et de sa mission; quatre propositions avec commentaire; – b) *Galot* Jean, Le Christ terrestre et la vision [béatifique]: Gregorianum 67 (1986) 413-428 / 429-450; Eng. 450.
5512 *Delhaye* Philippe segr., Commissione Teologica Internazionale, La coscienza che Gesù aveva di sé stesso e della sua missione; quattro proposizioni commentate: CC 137 (1986,3) 53-65.
5513 [*Schönborn* Christophe von, président de sous-commission responsable] Commission théologique internationale, session d'octobre 1985, La conscience que Jésus avait de lui-même et de sa misssion ; quatre propositions avec commentaire: EsprV 96 (1986) 529-535.
5514 **Dreyfus** François, Jésus savait-il qu'il était Dieu? 1984 ➤ 65,6193; 1,6822: RCBQ 48 (1986) 137-9 (N. J. *McEleney*: will console some, but not convince many exegetes); Gregorianum 67 (1986) 162s (J. *Galot*); RHPR 66 (1986) 226s (E. *Trocmé*: attitude condescendante); RivStoLR 22 (1986) 522-5 (Donatella *Maggiorotti*); RThom 86 (1986) 476-9 (M.-J. *Nicolas*); VSp 139 (1985) 545s (J.-M. *Poffet*).
5515 **Dreyfus** François, Gesù sapeva di essere Dio? TRolfo Luigi; 1985 ➤ 1,6823; Lit. 9000: RHumBR 41 (1986) 452 (A. *Bonora*); Letture 41 (1986) 466-8 (A. *Carrara*).
5515* **Duquoc** Christian, Messianisme de Jésus et discrétion de Dieu, essai sur la limite de la christologie 1984 ➤ 65,6194; 1,6826: RGregorianum 67 (1986) 553 (J. *Dupuis*); RÉAug 32 (1986) 194s (R. *Berton*); RTPhil 118 (1986) 206 (K. *Blaser*); ScEspr 38 (1986) 267s (C.-R. *Nadeau*); ScripT-Pamp 18 (1986) 339-341 (L. F. *Mateo-Seco*); Spiritus 26 (1985) 216 (J. *Pierron*).

5516 **Duquoc** Christian, Mesianismo de Jesús y discreción de Dios; ensayo sobre los limites de la cristología, ᵀ*Godoy* Rufino: Academia Cristiana 31. M 1985, Cristiandad. 231 p. 84-7057-385-3 [ActuBbg 24, 101]. – ᴿSalT 74 (1986) 915 (J. A. *García*).

5516* **Fitzmyer** J., A Christological catechism ²1982 ⇒ 63,6563; 64,6562: ᴿRCuBíb 9,35s (1985) 151 (J. E. *Martins Terra*); Vidyajyoti 49 (1985) 312s (P. M. *Meagher*).

5517 *Fitzmyer* Joseph A., Catecismo cristológico; respuestas del NT 1984 ⇒ 65,6196; 1,6828: ᴿEstE 61 (1986) 82-84 (A. *Vargas-Machuca*); PerspT 18 (1986) 119s (C. *Palácio*).

5518 **Fitzmyer** Joseph A., Scripture and Christology; a statement of the Biblical Commission with a commentary. NY/L 1986, Paulist/Chapman. viii-110 p. $7. 0-8091-2789-X.

5519 *Fitzmyer* Joseph A., La Comisión Bíblica y la Cristología [< America dic. 1984], ᵀ*Vargas-Machuca* A.: EstE 61 (1986) 71-77.

5520 **Forte** Bruno, Jésus de Nazareth 1984 ⇒ 65,6199; 1,6831: ᴿBrotéria 122 (1986) 351s (I. *Ribeiro*); EsprV 96 (1986) 270s (P. *Jay*); VSp 139 (1985) 697s (R.-L. *Oechslin*).

5521 **Forte** Bruno, Jesús de Nazaret... cristología como historia 1983 ⇒ 65,6201: ᴿEfMex 4,11 (1986) 138-142 (V. *Girardi S.*).

5522 **Fuller** R. H., *Perkins* Pheme, Who is this Christ? Gospel Christology and contemporary faith 1983 ⇒ 64,6565; 1,6834: ᴿTsTKi 57 (1986) 215-7 (O. *Skarsaune*).

5523 **Furberg** I., Bibelkritiken och kristologin [Phlp 2,5-11; 1 Tim 3,16; Rom 1,3s; 4,25; 2 Cor 5,19]. U 1984, Stiftelsen Biblicum. 118 p. Sk 65. 91-85604-06-2 [NTAbs 30,361].

5524 **Galot** Jean, *a)* Christ, qui es-tu? Christologie I., Le témoignage de l'Écriture. Lv 1986, Sintal. 218 p. Fb 625. – ᴿNRT 108 (1986) 902s (L. *Renwart*). – *b)* ¡Cristo! ¿Tú quién eres? [1977],ᵀ: Cristología 1/Pensamiento Católico 2. M 1982, Cete. 407 p. – ᴿScripTPamp 18 (1986) 731s (J. L. *Bastero*).

5525 *Gray* William, Wisdom Christology in the New Testament; its scope and relevance: TLond 39 (1986) 448-459.

5526 *Harding* William N., An examination of passages cited by the Jehovah's Witnesses to deny Jesus is God: ⇒ 65, ꟳMᴀᴄRᴀᴇ Allan, Interpretation 1986, 273-9.

5527 **Hausherr** Irénée, The name of Christ; the names of Jesus used by the early Christians [1960]: Cistercian Studies 44, 1978 ⇒ 60,8915: ᴿHeythJ 27 (1986) 87s (J. *McGuckin*: NT part hopelessly outdated; Patristics part a classic).

5528 **Hengel** Martin, Il figlio di Dio; l'origine della cristologia e la storia della religione giudeo-ellenistica [²1977 ⇒ 58,5809], ᵀ*Cessi* V.; ᴱ*Soffritti* O. Brescia 1984, Paideia. 140 p. Lit. 12.000. – ᴿParVi 30 (1985) 467-470 (Anna *Passoni Dell'Acqua*).

5529 *Keck* Leander E., Toward the renewal of New Testament Christology [SNTS main paper, Trondheim 1985]: NTS 32 (1986) 362-377.

5530 **Lavatori** R., L'unigenito del Padre 1983 ⇒ 64,6583 ... 1,6841: ᴿDivinitas 30 (1986) 96-99 (V. *Natalini*).

5531 *a)* *Luz* Ulrich (*al.*), Christologie im NT; – *b)* *Holtz* Traugott, Christologische Hoheitstitel; ⇒ 587, EvKL 1 (1986) 704-8(-741)/741-3.

5531* *Muarquardt* Friedrich-Wilhelm, Vom gepredigten Jesus zum gelehrten Christus: EvT 46 (1986) 315-325 [Bᴀʀᴛʜ; ⇒ d945*b* *Nossol* A.].

5532 **Milet** Jean, Dieu ou le Christ? 1980 ⇒ 61,5359*... 64,6589: ᴿRTLv 17 (1986) 351-3 (A. *Vander Perre*).

5533 **Most** William G.,   The consciousness of Christ 1980 ➤ 62,7297; 63,6626:
ᴿDivinitas 30 (1986) 199s (R. M. *Schmitz* commenda); ScripTPamp 18
(1986) 702-4 (P. *O'Callaghan*).

5534 **Neyrey** Jerome H.,   Christ is community; the Christologies of the NT:
GoodNewsSt 13, 1985 ➤ 1,6845:   ᴿAustralBR 34 (1986) 74s (M. *Cole-
ridge*); CBQ 48 (1986) 743s (Susan M. *Praeder*); RExp 83 (1986) 459s (J. E.
Jones); TS 47 (1986) 553s (J. M. *Reese*: two-thirds on Gospels).

5534* *Otto* E.,   Impleta est haec Scriptura; zum Problem einer christologischen
Interpretation des Alten Testaments im Anschluss an Traugott KOCHs
Christologiekritik: ➤ 1,599, Gegenwart des Absoluten; philosophisch-
theologische Diskurse zur Christologie 1984, 156-162.

5535 *Ramos* Felipe F., Jesucristo palabra de Dios: StLeg 27 (1986) 9-52.

5535* *Richardson* H. Neil,   The Old Testament background of Jesus as
begotten of God: BR 2,3 (1986) 22-27.

5536 **Sabourin** Leopold,   Christology; basic texts in focus 1984 ➤ 65,6214;
1,6851: ᴿCBQ 48 (1986) 568s (P. *Zilonka*); Paradigms 2,1 (1986) 45s (R. W.
Coleman).

5537 *Sabourin* Léopold,   La christologie à partir de textes clés: Recherches NS
9.   Montréal/P 1986, Bellarmin/Cerf.   228 p. – ᴿEsprV 96 (1986) 553s (É.
Cothenet).

5538 *Sabourin* Léopold,   Approaches to Christology: Bible Bhashyam 12
(1986) 29-41.

5539 **Schweizer** Eduard,   Neues Testament und Christologie im Werden,
Aufsätze 1982 ➤ 63,262; 1,6853:   ᴿTZBas 42 (1986) 86-88 (W. *Wilkens*).

5540 **Segalla** Giuseppe,   La cristologia del Nuovo Testamento, un saggio[2]:
StBPaid 71, 1985 ➤ 1,6854: ᴿBiblica 67 (1987) 421-3 (J. *Swetnam*: some
omissions); CC 137 (1986,3) 194-6 (G. *Ferraro*); RCuBíb 9,35s (1985) 152s
(J. E. *Martins Terra*); TLZ 111 (1986) 895s (B. *Forte*).

5541 **Segundo** Juan Luis, [El hombre de hoy 1982 ➤ 64,6606; I. Faith and ideologies 1984 ➤ 65,6339] II. [Historia y actualidad, 1] The historical Jesus of
the Synoptics 1985 ➤ 1,6855*: ᴿCCurr 36 (1986s) 85-90 (R. *Haight*: 'a
political interpretation of Jesus'); EcuR (1986) 481s (W. *Bildstein*); ExpTim
97 (1985s) 309 (A. E. *Harvey*); Gregorianum 67 (1986) 551-3 (J. *Dupuis*);
Month 248 (1986) 106 (M. *Nevin*); ScotJT 39 (1986) 399s (N. D.
O'Donoghue); TsTNijm 26 (1986) 426s (E. *Borgman*, with all 6 ISBN).

5542 **Segundo** Juan Luis,   The humanist Christology of Paul [El hombre de hoy
ante Jesús II/1b, 1982 ➤ 64,6606]: Jesus of Nazareth yesterday and today
3.   Maryknoll NY/L 1986, Orbis/Sheed.   ix-244 p. 0-88344-221-3 / L 0-
07220-427-0.

5543 **Segundo** Juan Luis,   O homem de hoje diante de Jesus de Nazaré 2/2. São
Paulo 1985, Paulinas.   408 p. [REB 46,228].

5544 **Simonis** Walter,   Jesus von Nazareth; seine Botschaft vom Reich Gottes
und der Glaube der Urgemeinde; historisch-kritische Erhellung der
Ursprünge des Christentums.   Dü 1985, Patmos. 382 p. DM 39,80. – ᴿBZ
30 (1986) 274-6 (J. *Blank*: chaotisch); ForumKT 2 (1986) 153-5 (A. *Vögtle*).

5545 *Vellanickal* Mathew,   The filial faith of Jesus; Jesus' experience as Son of
God: Bible Bhashyam 11 (1985) 113-129.

5545* ᴱWelte B.,   La storia della cristologia primitiva; gli inizi biblici e la
formula di Nicea [Zur Frühgeschichte 1970 ➤ 52,3039: *Schlier* H., *Mussner*
F., *Ricken* F.]. StPaid 75.   Brescia 1986, Paideia.   141 p. Lit. 15.000.

H5.3   *Christologia patristica* ... **in the early Church.**

5546 **Arens** Herbert,   Die christologische Sprache LEOs des Grossen: Freib-

TSt 122, 1982 ➤ 63,6518... 1,6861: ᴿTLZ 111 (1986) 514-6 (F. *Winkelmann*).

5547 **Aubineau** Michel, Un traité inédit de christologie de SÉVÉRIEN 1983 ➤ 64,6621: 1,6862: ᴿRivStoLR 22 (1986) 160-2 (Renée H. *Dalmais*); TLZ 111 (1986) 259s (F. *Winkelman*).

5548 *Bastero de Eleizalde* Juan Luis, Hermenéutica en el símbolo de fe del Concilio de Nicea: ➤ 366, Hermenéutica 1985/6, 683-695.
Bray Gerald, Creeds, councils and Christ 1984 ➤ 940*.

5549 **Brennecke** Hanne C., Studien zur Geschichte der Homöer; der Osten bis zum Ende der homöischen Reichskirche: ev. Hab.-Diss. ᴰ*Abramowski* L. – Tübingen 1986. – RTLv 18,559.

5549* *Chang* A. B., ⊖ Christology throughout the Church's history 3: ColcFuJen 70 (1986) 441-456.

5550 *Christie* Wilhelm, Christologie und Seinsverständnis; zur Interpretation altkirchlicher Christologie bei Bernhard WELTE [Was ist Glauben? 1982; Religionsphilosophie 1978]: TGl 76 (1986) 17-37.

5551 *Cignelli* Lino, Il Cristo di San GEROLAMO: TerraS 62 (1986) 165-172.221-6.

5552 **Contri** Antonio, Gesù Cristo, Figlio di Dio e Salvatore; saggio di Cristologia patristico-storica e teologico-sistematica 1985 ➤ 1,6867; 88-01-12807-X: ᴿClaretianum 26 (1986) 364-6 (L. *Gutiérrez*); Gregorianum 67 (1986) 161s (J. *Galot*); ParVi 30 (1985) 231-4 (L. *Melotti*).

5553 **Dunn** James D. G., Christology in the making 1980 ➤ 61,8088... 1,6871: ᴿSalesianum 48 (1986) 415 (A. *Amato*: conclusione né originale né risolutiva; il problema viene semplicemente spostato).

5554 **Gahbauer** Ferdinand R., Das anthropologische Modell; ein Beitrag zur Christologie der frühen Kirche bis Chalkedon: Das östliche Christentum 35, 1984 ➤ 1,6874: ᴿRSPT 70 (1986) 600-2 (G.-M de *Durand*); Salesianum 48 (1986) 171 (B. *Amata*); TPhil 61 (1986) 261-3 (H.-J. *Höhn*); VigChr 40 (1986) 310s (H. *Frohnhofen*); ZKG 97 (1986) 275s (E. *Mühlenberg*).

5555 **Gessel** Wilhelm, Das 'homoousios' als Testfall für die Frage nach der Geltung und dem Verhältnis von Schrift und Tradition auf dem Konzil von Nizäa: AnHistConc 17 (1985) 1-8.

5556 **Grillmeier** Alois, Jesus der Christus im Glauben der Kirche I, 1979 ²1982 ➤ 60,8909... 65,6236: ᴿNatGrac 33 (1986) 576s (A. *Villalmonte*).

5557 **Grillmeier** Alois, Jesus der Christus im Glauben der Kirche 2/1, Das Konzil von Chalcedon (451) — Rezeption und Widerspruch (451-518). FrB 1986, Herder. 283 p. DM 66 [TR 83,125-9, B. *Studer*].

5558 *Guillén Preckler* Fernando, Cristo 'hombre perfecto'; anotaciones a una expresión conciliar: EfMex 4,1 (1986) 69-90.

5559 *a*) *Khalil* Samir, Une allusion au Filioque dans la 'Réfutation des Chrétiens' d' Abd al GABHAR (m. 1925); – *b*) *Schultze* Bernhard, Zur Grundlage des Filioque: ➤ 116, ᶠVALENTINI G. 1986, 361-7 / 369-411.

5560 **Löhr** Winrich A., Die Entstehung der homöischen und homöusischen Kirchenparteien; Studien zur Synodalgeschichte des 4. Jahrhunderts: Diss. ᴰ*Schäferdiek* K. Bonn 1986, Univ. 248 p. – RTLv 18,552.

5561 *Ludwig* Eugene (p. 98; ma indici *Eugene* L.), Chalcedon and its aftermath; three unresolved crises [i. Christological...]: Laurentianum 27 (1986) 98-120.

5562 *McGuckin* J. A., LACTANTIUS as theologian; an angelic Christology on the eve of Nicaea: RivStoLR 22 (1986) 492-7.

5563 **Lyons** James A., The cosmic Christ in ORIGEN and TEILHARD 1982 ➤ 63,6611... 1,6889: ᴿRHR 203 (1986) 316s (P. *Nautin*).

5564 *Mazzanti* Giorgio, Irrilevanza della cristologia di BASILIO Magno nell'opinione corrente: CrNSt 7 (1986) 565-580.

5565 *a) Moulder* James, Is a Chalcedonian Christology coherent ?; – *b) Morris* Thomas V., Reduplication and representational Christology: ModT 2 (1985s) 285-307 / 319-327.

5566 **Nijendijk** L. W., Die Christologie des Hirten des Hermas; exegetisch, religions- und dogmengeschichtlich untersucht: diss. Utrecht 1986, DReiling J. 239 p. – TsTNijm 26 (1986) 290.

5566* EOrbe Antonio, Il Cristo [antologia sec. I-IV]. Mi 1985, Mondadori. 427 p. Lit. 30.000. – RCiVit 41 (1986) 79s (C. *Toscani*); VetChr 23 (1986) 419-423 (A. *Isola*).

5567 *Pedersen* Jørgens, Ny tilgang til middelalderens kristne tænkning og dens spekulative kristologi: DanTTs 49 (1986) 177-197.

5568 **Perrone** L., La chiesa di Palestina e le controversie cristologiche 1980 ➤ 61,8197... **1**,6895: RBySlav 46 (1985) 189-191 (H. G. *Thümmel*).

5569 **Pokorný** Petr, Die Entstehung der Christologie [...post-Resurrection thought] ➤ **1**,6898: RExpTim 97 (1985s) 331s (E. *Best*: fascinating, merits translation); TLZ 111 (1986) 270-2 (G. *Haufe*).

5570 **Riestra** J. A., Cristo y la plenitud del cuerpo místico; estudio sobre la cristología de Santo Tomás de AQUINO: Teológica 44. Pamplona 1985, Univ. Navarra. 220 p. pt. 2125. – RCiTom 113 (1986) 406s (A. *Bandera*); NRT 108 (1986) 904 (L. *Renwart*).

5571 **Schönborn** Christoph von, L'icône du Christ; fondements théologiques [trinitaires et christologiques; pourquoi appelé éd. 3? traduction de [1]1976 sans tenir compte de [2]1984 sauf en ajoutant sa Postface]: Théologies. P 1986, Cerf. 254 p. F 95. – RNRT 108 (1986) 900 L. *Renwart*).

5572 **Trisoglio** Francesco, Cristo en los Padres de la Iglesia; las primeras generaciones cristianas ante Jesús; antología de textos: [1981 ➤ 63,6684], TMartínez Riu A.: Biblioteca Herder 161. Barc 1986, Herder. 336 p. pt 1800. 84-254-1446-6. – RCiuD 199 (1986) 553s (C. J. *Sánchez*); NatGrac 33 (1986) 589s (A. *Villalmonte*); ScripTPamp 18 (1986) 716s (J. L. *Bastero*).

5573 *Walter* Christopher, Christological themes in the Byzantine marginal psalters from the ninth to the eleventh century: RÉByz 44 (1986) 269-287; 11 phot.

5574 **Wéber** H., Saint BONAVENTURE, Questions disputées sur le savoir chez le Christ 1985 ➤ 1,6906; F 120: RRHE 81 (1986) 311s (P. H. *Daly*).

5575 **Welsch** Pierre J., La foi au 'Verbe fait chair' dans le De Trinitate de saint AUGUSTIN: diss. Louvain 1986, DHoussiau A. – RTLv 17 (1986) 469s, résumé.

5576 **Wesche** Kenneth W., The defense of Chalcedon in the 6th century; the doctrine of 'hypostasis' and deification in the Christology of LEONTIUS of Jerusalem: diss. Fordham, DMeyendorff J. NY 1986. 283 p. 86-15708. – DissA 47 (1986s) 1375-A.

5577 **Wright** Robert E., Art and the Incarnate Word; medieval [*Augustine*...] Christologies and the problem of literary inexpressibility: diss. Duke, DGregg R. Durham NC 1986. 313 p. 86-29334. – DissA 47 (1986s) 3423s-A.

5578 **Young** Frances M., From Nicaea to Chalcedon; a guide to the literature and its background 1983 ➤ 64,6657... **1**, 6908: RCrNSt 7 (1986) 611-4 (Marcella *Forlin Patrucco*); ScripTPamp 18 (1986) 288s (L. F. *Mateo-Seco*).

5579 **Zani** Antonio. La Cristologia di IPPOLITO 1983 ➤ 64,6658... **1**,6909: RAsprenas 33 (1986) 103 (L. *Longobardo*); RÉAug (31 (1985) 179 (J. *Doignon*); TPhil 61 (1986) 259s (H. J. *Höhn*).

5579* *Zimdars-Swartz* Sandra, A confluence of imagery; exegesis and Christology according to GREGORY the Great: ⇥ 433*, Grégoire 1982/6, 327-335.

H5.4 (*Commentationes de*) *Christologia* **moderna.**

5580 **Arias Reyero** M., Jesús el Cristo; curso fundamental de Cristologia 1982 ⇥ 63,6519; 65,6265: RScripTPamp 18 (1986) 947-950 (J. L. *Bastero*).

5581 *Aring* Paul G., La christologie dans le dialogue judéo-chrétien aujourd'hui: Istina 31 (1986) 371-387.

5582 **Auer** Johann, Jesus Christus — Gottes und Mariä 'Sohn': Kleine katholische Dogmatik 4/1. Rg 1986, Pustet. 443 p. DM 34. 3-7917-0984-4. – RDivinitas 30 (1986) 198s (R. M. *Schmitz*); Gregorianum 67 (1986) 555s (J. *Galot*: même auteur de tous les autres traités annoncés sauf Eschatologie, ce qui comporte beaucoup d'avantages); Salesianum 48 (1986) 434 (A. *Amato*: contro BROWN e FITZMYER afferma fondatamente che la concezione e la nascita verginale di Gesù appartengono al Gesù storico, come la croce e la risurrezione p. 304).

5583 *Beckwith* Francis J., Of logic and lordship; the validity of a categorical syllogism supporting Christ's deity: JEvTS 29 (1986) 429s [< ZIT].

5584 *Berg* J. van den, The idea of the pre-existence of the soul of Christ: an argument in the controversy between Arian and Orthodox in the eighteenth century: ⇥ 59, FLEBRAM J., Tradition 1986, 284-295.

5585 **Blough** N., Christologie anabaptiste: Pilgram MARPECK et l'humanité du Christ 1984 ⇥ 65,6271; 1,6916: RCrNSt 7 (1986) 636-8 (E. *Campi*); Protestantesimo 41 (1986) 177s (F. *Ferrario*); RTPhil 118 (1986) 198s (G. *Hammann*).

5586 **Boff** L., God werd mens; bezinning over Kerstmis. Averbode 1985, Altiora. 70 p. Fb 196. – RCollatVl 16 (1986) 382 (W. Van *Soom*).

5586* **Bonhoeffer** D., Cristologia [1933], EBethge E., Dudzus O. [1981], TLaurenzi Cristina [1975]: GdT 154. Brescia 1984, Queriniana. 124 p. – REphMar 36 (1986) 195 (D. *Fernández*); StPatav 33 (1986) 469 (A. *Moda*).

5587 *Bray* Gerald L., Recent trends in Christology: Themelios 12 (1986s) 52-56.

5588 **Brito** Emilio, La christologie de HEGEL 1983 ⇥ 64,6667b... 1,6921*: RTR 82 (1986) 70s (W. *Jaeschke*).

5589 *Buckley* James J., Christological inquiry; BARTH, RAHNER, and the identity of Jesus Christ: Thomist 50 (1986) 568-598.

5590 *a*) *Cajião* Silvio, La Cristología en América Latina; – *b*) *Zea* Virgilio, Jesús, su compromiso con Dios y con la historia; – *c*) *Baena* Gustavo, El sacerdocio de Cristo; – *d*) *Zapata* Guillermo, Del olvido de la Cruz a su presencia en la historia: TXav 36 (1986) 363-404 / 405-422 / 437-448 / 423-436.

5591 **Calverat** David G. A., From Christ to God 1983 ⇥ 65,6277: RHeythJ 27 (1986) 344s (J. P. *Galvin*).

5592 *Casciaro* José M., La encarnación del Verbo y la corporeidad hamana: ScripTPamp 18 (1986) 751-769; lat. 769; Eng. 769s.

5593 *Castelli* Ferdinando, François MAURIAC, II. Gesù, questo Dio in agguato: CC 137 (1986,1) [135-148] 325-336.

5594 [certosino] Il tu del Padre; Cristologia e contemplazione, T-Leumann 1985, LDC. 280 p. Lit. 10.000. TMelotti L.: La fede e la vita. – RCC 137 (1986 ?) 613s (G. *Mucci*); Claretianum 26 (1986) 361ss (B. *Proietti*).

5595 **Charlton** Terrence P., The Incarnation in the thought of Pierre TEILHARD de Chardin: diss. Boston College, 1986. 396 p. 86-16092. – DissA 47 (1986s) 1366s-A.

5596 **Chesnut** Glenn F., Images of Christ; an introduction to Christology 1984 ➤ 65,6279; **1**,6927; 0-86683-875-9:   [R]Encounter 47 (1986) 179s (C. M. *Williamson*); Gregorianum 67 (1986) 554 (J. *Dupuis*); Horizons 13 (1986) 175s (Christine M. *Bochen*).

5597 **Ciola** Nicola,   Introduzione alla Cristologia: Universale Teologica 15. Brescia 1986, Queriniana. 134 p. Lit. 10.000. – [R]CC 137 (1986,3) 536s (P. *Vanzan*); RasT 27 (1986) 579s (G. *Ferraro*; meriti e pericoli delle varie riduzioni); RClerIt 67 (1986) 639s (F. *Brambilla*).

5599 **Corrington** Gail A.,   The 'divine man'; his origin and function in Hellenistic popular religion [*Theîos anēr* was first formulated as an attempt to understand a particular Christology of the NT, that of Jesus as miracle-working Son of God. There have been strong arguments against usefulness of this paradigm. Both sides have failed to explore the milieu of popular audience addressed by the missionaries of the Greco-Roman world. Here we have that milieu, especially, and magic]: AmerUnivSt 7/17. NY 1986, P. Lang. 334 p. $35. 0-8204-0299-0.

5600 **Crawford** Robert G.,   The saga of God incarnate. Pretoria 1985, Univ. S. Africa [E: Clark]. xiii-106 p. – [R]IrBSt 8 (1986) 44s (A. E. *Lewis*: 'incarnate' seems to mean 'supremely conscious of the divine presence').

5601 *Dossi* Francesca,   Ontologia e storia in 'Gesù di Nazareth, storia di Dio, Dio della storia' di Bruno FORTE: HumBr 41 (1986) 56-71.

5602 **Doyon** Jacques,   L'option fondamentale de Jésus 1984 ➤ **1**,6937; aussi P, Médiaspaul: [R]LavalTP 42 (1986) 274s (G. *Langevin*); ScEspr 38 (1986) 269 (R. *Bergeron*: déjà vu).

5603 **Dreschner** John,   WESLEY's Christology, an interpretation [diss. Basel 1960, [D]*Barth* K.]. Dallas 1985, Southern Methodist Univ. xxi-221 p. $13 pa. – [R]TLZ 111 (1986) 615s (K. *Zehner*: reprinted with a new preface which rightly says nothing new has appeared in the meantime).

5603* **Driver** Tom F.,   Christ in a changing world; towards an ethical Christology 1981 ➤ 62,4272... 64,6674: [R]Vidyajyoti 49 (1985) 530 (R. *Athickal*).

5604 **Emeis** Dieter,   Jesus Christus — Lehrer des Lebens; katechetische Christologie 1985 ➤ **1**,6938; 3-451-20429-0:   [R]EstE 61 (1986) 460s (J. *García Pérez*); TLZ 111 (1986) 309-312 (G. *Baudler*).

5605 *Farrugia* Edward G.,   Aussage und Zusage; zur Indirektheit der Methode Karl RAHNERs veranschaulicht an seiner Christologie [diss. Tü 1981, [D]*Kasper* W.]: An Greg 233. R 1985, Pont. Univ. Gregoriana. 386 p. – [R]CC 137 (1986,4) 404s (M. van *Esbroeck*); EstE 61 (1986) 248 (L. *Ladaria*); Gregorianum 67 (1986) 775-7 (E. J. *Kilmartin*).

5606 **Fastenrath** Elmar,   Die Christologie Herman SCHELLs im Spannungsfeld des Modernismus [Inaug. Fulda 1981]: Fuldaer Theol. St. 1. St. Ottilien 1986, Eos. 32 p. DM 4,80 [TR 83,131, S. *Ernst*].

5607 **Ferrari** Pier Luigi,   Personalismo e Cristologia; meditazione cristologica di Jean MOUROUX 1984 ➤ 65,6285; **1**,6939: [R]CC 137 (1986,2) 612s (G. *Ferraro*); Divinitas 30 (1986) 200s (C. *Petino*).

5608 *Ferraro* Giuseppe,   Il mistero di Cristo nella liturgia della dedicazione dell'altare: CC 137 (1986,3) 239-251.

5608* **Flesseman-van Leer** E.,   Wie toch is Jezus van Nazareth? De christologie in discussie. Haag 1985, Boekencentrum. 167 p. 90-239-0032-4 [NedTTs 41,340, M. de *Jonge*].

5609 **Gaffney** J. Patrick,   Inexhaustible presence; the mystery of Jesus. Denville NJ 1986, Dimension. iii-197 p. $12 pa. [TDig 34,70].

5610 **Garcia** Sixto J., Christology in F. W. J. SCHELLING's Philosophie der Offenbarung; the incarnation of the second potency; diss. Notre Dame 1986. – 185 p. 98-12992. – DissA 47 (1986s) 947s-A; RelStR 13,188.

5611 **Gertler** T., Jesus Christus — die Antwort der Kirche auf die Frage nach dem Menschsein; eine Untersuchung zu Funktion und Inhalt der Christologie im ersten Teil der Pastoralkonstitution 'Gaudium et Spes' des Zweiten Vatikanischen Konzils: ErfTSt 52. Lp 1986, St. Benno. xxv-432 p. 3-7462-0036-9 [NTAbs 31,130].

5612 **Goergen** Donald J., A theology of Jesus, 1. [of 5] The mission and ministry of Jesus. Wilmington 1986, Glazier. 316 p. $13 [TS 48,584, J. P. *Galvin*].

5613 **González de Cardedal** Olegario, Jesús de Nazaret; aproximación a la cristología ² [¹1975 ➤ 57,4449... 62,7233]: BAC maior 9. M 1978, Católica. xvi-613 p. – ᴿRHPR 66 (1986) 481s (A. *Moda*: trois mérites, deux apories).

5614 *González de Cardedal* Olegario, Puntos de partida y criterios para la elaboración de una cristología sistemática [➤ 1,6945]: Salmanticensis 33 (1986) 5-52; Eng. 53s.

5615 **González Faus** J. I., La humanidad nueva; ensayo de Cristología ² ʳᵉᵛ (¹c 1974) 1984 ➤ 1,6946: ᴿRazF 212 (1985) 104s (J. *Royo*).

5616 *Grech* Prosper, *a*) Sviluppo della Cristologia nel NT [< Problemi attuali di Cristologia (R 1976, LAS) 59-74]; – *b*) L'Antico Testamento come fonte della cristologia nell'età apostolica [BibTB 5 (1975) 127-144, ᵀ*Camporeale* Rita]: – *c*) Il problema cristologico e l'ermeneutica [< Problemi e prospettive di teologia fondamentale 1980, 141-170]; – *d*) Christological motives in Pauline ethics [< ᴱ*De Lorenzi* L., Paul 1979, 541-558]: ➤ 166, Ermeneutica 1986, 318-334 / 77-96 / 135-172 / 362-381.

5617 **Hart** Thomas N., To know and follow Jesus; contemporary Christology 1984 ➤ 65,6294: ᴿGregorianum 67 (1986) 549s (J. *Dupuis*); Horizons 13 (1986) 177s (Mary T. *Rattigan*); TS 47 (1986) 185s (G. M. *Fagin*: basic thrust to change Chalcedon's 'Jesus God and man' to 'Jesus, God in man').

5618 **Havrilak** Gregory C., Eastern Christian elements in the Christology of Karl RAHNER and Jürgen MOLTMANN: contemporary trends in Catholic and Protestant thought from an Orthodox perspective: diss. Fordham, ᴰ*Meyendorff* J. NY 1985. – 317 p. 86-15720. – DissA 47 (1986s) 1369-A; RelStR 13,190.

5619 **Helminiak** Daniel A., The same Jesus; a contemporary Christology. Ch 1986, Loyola. xxiii-337 p. $16 [TDig 34,74].

5620 *Helminiak* Daniel A., Four viewpoints on the human [... humanity as graced in Christ ... *Lonergan*]; a conceptual schema for interdisciplinary studies I: HeythJ 27 (1986) 420-437.

5621 **Huovinen** Eero, Idea Christi; die idealistische Denkform und Christologie in der Theologie Hans KÜNGs [Diss. Helsinki 1978], ᵀ*Daniel* H.-C.: ArbGTLuth 6. Hannover 1985, Luth.-V. 159 p. [TLZ 112,377s, H. *Häring*].

5621* **Iammarrone** Luigi, La cristologia di E. SCHILLEBEECKX: *a*) Genova 1985, Quadrivium. 368 p. Lit. 18.000. – ᴿCiVit 41 (1986) 189 (B. *Farnetani*). – *b*) [8-9]: Renovatio [➤ 65,6299] 20 (1985) 9-55.169-218.

5622 *Krieg* Robert, Zur Aktualität der Christologie Karl ADAMS, ᵀ*Meyer* Josef: TüTQ 166 (1986) 92-107.

5623 **Lapide** Pinchas, Ieder komt tot de Vader; Karl BARTH, Barmen en een poging tot een nieuwe christologie, ᵀ*Endedijk* B. Kampen 1985, Kok. 89 p. *f* 13,90. – ᴿNedTTs 40 (1986) 244s (H. W. *Hollander*: overtuigend).

5624 **Lonergan** B., Conoscenza e interiorità; il Verbum nel pensiero di s. Tommaso [< TS 1946-9], T*Spaccapelo* Natalino, 1984 ➤ 1,6959: RAngelicum 63 (1986) 145-8 (A. *Wilder*).

5625 *McDermott* John M., The Christologies of Karl RAHNER: Gregorianum 67 (1986) 87-122.297-326; franç. 123. 327.

5626 **McGrath** Alister E., The making of modern German Christology; from the Enlightenment to Pannenberg. Ox 1986, Blackwell. viii-231 p. £19.50. 0-631-13855-2. – RExpTim 98 (1986s) 122s (B. M. G. *Reardon*: worthy successor to J. M. CREED); NRT 108 (1986) 906s (L. *Renwart*).

5627 *McGrath* Alister E., Christology and soteriology; a response to Wolfhart PANNENBERG's critique of the soteriological approach to Christology: TZBas 42 (1986) 222-236.

5628 *Martins Terra* J. E., A Cristologia de L. GOPPELT [a melhor em português, 1976-82]: RCuBíb 10,37s (1986) 148-156.

5629 *Martins Terra* J. E., *a*) Jesus sabia que era Deus?; – *c*) Cristologia de Marcos e segredo messiânico; – *c*) A consciência de Cristo / Cristocentrismo teológico de Karl RAHNER: RCuBíb 9,35s (1985) 74-83 / 93-113 / 114-150.

5630 *Martorell* J., Jon SOBRINO; un proyecto de Cristología: TEspir 30 (1986) 261-283.

5631 EMiguez **Bonino** José, Faces of Jesus; Latin American Christologies 1984 ➤ 1,6966: RNZMissW 42 (1986) 76s (S. *Herbst*).

5632 *Min* Anselm K., Christology and theology of religions; John HICK and Karl RAHNER: LvSt 11,1 (1986) 3-21.

5633 **Momose** F., To learn Jesus; a Christology from below [cf. ➤ 62,7664]: RKatKenk 25,50 (1986) 157-172 (T. *Iwashima* ❍).

5633* *Mondin* Battista, Bilancio della Cristologia contemporanea: CiVit 41 (1986) 5-18.

5634 **Morris** Thomas V., The logic of God incarnate. Ithaca NY 1986, Cornell Univ. 220 p. $20 [TDig 33,373]. – RNBlackf 67 (1986) 390s (B. *Davies*).

5635 *Muller* Richard A., Directions in the study of BARTH's Christology [*Thompson* J. 1978; *Waldrop* C. 1984]: WestTJ 48 (1986) 119-134.

5636 *Nebel* Richard, Christological aspects of the ancient Mexican-Christian popular piety in modern Mexico: VerbumSVD 27 (1986) 43-53.

5636* **Nicoletti** Michele, La dialettica dell'Incarnazione; soggettività e storia in Sören KIERKEGAARD 1983 ➤ 64,6707; 1,6967: REphMar 36 (1986) 195s (J. *Escohotado*).

5637 **Ntwite Lumu** Alexis, Les enjeux christologiques dans la crise moderniste; analyse critique de la théologie d'expression française (1900-1950): diss. DMateo-Seco L. Pamplona 1986. 347 p. – RTLv 18,558.

5638 **Ogden** Schubert, The point of Christology 1982 ➤ 63,6632... 1,6970: RThomist 50 (1986) 292-300 (T. *Weinandy*).

5639 **Ohlig** Karl-Heinz, Fundamentalchristologie; im Spannungsfeld von Christentum und Kultur. Mü 1986, Kösel. 724 p. – RExpTim 98 (1986s) 335 (G. *Wainwright*: 'Christology is a function of soteriology'); NatGrac 33 (1986) 582s (A. *Villalmonte*).

5640 *O'Meara* Thomas F., Christ in SCHELLING's Philosophy of religion: HeythJ 27 (1986) 275-289.

5641 **Orbe** A., En torno a la Encarnación: Coll. Sc. Compostellana 3. Santiago 1985. 236 p. – RCompostellanum 31 (1986) 282-5 (M. *Ferro Couselo*).

5642 *Ott* Heinrich, 'Sendung' als Grundbegriff der Christologie [< TZBas 1984]: TGegw 28 (1985) 1-6.

5643 *Peyrous* Bernard, La christologie de saint Jean EUDES: DivThom 88 (1985) 42-57; lat. 42.

5644 **Ramisch** Joseph G., The 'historical Jesus' and method in Christology; an examination of three recent Roman Catholic theologians [*Schillebeeckx* E., *Küng* H., *Kasper* W.]: diss. Catholic Univ., [D]*Loewe* W. Wsh 1986. 413 p. 86-13473. – DissA 47 (1986s) 1872-A.

5645 **Ramm** B. L., An evangelical Christology [➤ 1,6977], ecumenic and historic. Nv 1985, Nelson. 229 p. $15. 0-8407-7518-0. – [R]ExpTim 98 (1986s) 120 (M. *Casey*: no good at all).

5646 **Ratzinger** Joseph, Schauen auf den Durchbohrten; Versuche zu einer spirituellen Christologie 1984 ➤ 65,241; DM 19: [R]TLZ 111 (1986) 303s (A. *Peters*).

5647 *Renwart* Léon, Vrai Dieu, vrai homme; chronique de Christologie [*Grillmeier* A.; *Contri* A.; *Guillet* J ... *al.* (infra)]: NRT 108 (1986) 897-911.

5648 *Reymond* Robert G., The justification of theology with special application to contemporary Christology; Presbuterion 12 (Spring 1986) 1-16 [< BS 143 (1986) 368].

5650 *Ritchie* Nelly, Mulher e Cristologia: ➤ 510, REB 46 (1986) 60-72.

5651 **Rolf** Heinrich, Verheissung des Kreuzes; die Christologie Hans-J. IWANDS. Mü/Mainz 1982, Kaiser/Grünewald. 338 p. DM 48 – [R]TPQ 134 (1986) 410 (H. *Nausner*).

5652 **Rosenau** Hartmut, Die Differenz im christologischen Denken SCHELLINGS: EurHS 23/248. Fra 1985, Lang. 158 p. Fs 43. – [R]ForumKT 2 (1986) 323s (J. *Kreiml*).

5653 **Runia** Klaas, The present-day Christological debate 1984 ➤ 65,6328; **1,6978**: [R]ScotJT 39 (1986) 395s (G. *Bray*); Themelios 11 (1985s) 101s (J. F. *Colwell*).

5654 **Sayes** José Antonio, Jesucristo, ser y persona 1984 ➤ 1,6899; 84-7009-227-7: [R]Gregorianum 67 (1986) 163s (J. *Galot*).

5655 [E]**Scheffczyk** L., Problemi fondamentali della cristologia oggi [1975 ➤ 57,5740],[T]. Brescia 1983, Morcelliana. 153 p. Lit. 8000. – [R]Protestantesimo 41 (1986) 115s (D. *Tomasetto*: spiacevoli omissioni nella traduzione).

5655* **Schierse** Franz J., Cristologia: GdT 153, 1984 ➤ 1,6983: [R]EphMar 36 (1986) 194 (D. *Fernández*).

5656 **Schönborn** Christoph, Das Geheimnis der Menschwerdung. Mainz 1983, Matthias. 52 p.; 4 color. pl. DM 13,80. – [R]TrierTZ 95 (1986) 154 (E. *Sauser*).

5657 *Schwarz* Hans, Historische Kontingenz und universale Relevanz in neueren Prozess-Christologien [*Wires* J., 'The search for the Christological Jesus', StLuke 21 (1977) 19 ...]: NSys 28 (1986) 1-13; Eng. 13.

5658 *Schwoebel* Christoph, Anglo-German Christology [*McGrath* A. 1986]: TLond 39 (1986) 470-4.

5659 **Serenthà** M., Cristologia 1985 ➤ 1,6986: [R]ParVi 31 (1986) 145s (L. *Melotti*).

5660 **Serenthà** Mario, Jesus Cristo, ontem, hoje e sempre. São Paulo 1986, Salesiana. 600 p. [REB 46,725].

5661 *Serenthà* Mario, Cristologia: ScuolC 114,5 ('L'insegnamento dei trattati teologici' 1986) 538-547.

5662 **Snyder** Mary H., Contemporary Christological concerns; the contribution of Rosemary R. RUETHER: diss. St. Michael, [D]*Leonard* E. Toronto 1986. 211 p. – RTLv 18,573.

5663 **Sullivan** Maureen, Pope PAUL's Christian humanism; an inquiry into its Christological foundations: diss. Fordham. NY 1985. – RTLv 18,558.

5664 **Surin** Kenneth,   Christology, tragedy and 'ideology' [*MacKinnon* D.]:
TLond 39 (1986) 283-291.
5665 **Tadsen** Rose,   Jesus Christ in the world theology of Wilfred C. SMITH:
diss. St. Michael's (Canada), 1985. 380 p. 86-06402. – DissA 47 (1986s)
219-A.
5666 **Tilliette** X.,   La christologie idéaliste: JJC 28.   P 1986, Desclée.   238 p. F
125.   2-1789-0304-X [RechSR 74,631]. – ᴿRICathP 20 (1986) 103-5 (P.
Colin: 'voie de la théologie [à la philosophie', omis sur la couverture]).
5667 **Torre** Joseph M. de,   Divinity of Jesus Christ.   Manila 1984, Sinag-Tala.
166 p. – ᴿScripTPamp 18 (1986) 990 (C. *Izquierdo*).
5668 *Torres Queiruga* Andrés,   El Vaticano II y la cristología actual: SalT 73
(1985) 479-489.
5669 *Trembath* Kern R.,   Was the Incarnation redundant? [since all moral and
cognitive progress is possible only on the presupposition of the existence of
God? no, show E. J. CARNELL and more successfully K. *Rahner*]; a
Catholic and an Evangelical respond: Horizons 13 (1986) 43-66.
5670 **Vorgrimler** Herbert,   Jesus — Gottes und des Menschen Sohn 1984
➤ 65,6220; 1,6857:   ᴿColcT 56,2 (1986) 190s (S. *Moysa*).
5671 **Waldrop** Charles T.,   Karl BARTH's Christology 1984 ➤ 65,3549; 1,6990:
ᴿScotJT 30 (1986) 121-3 (J. *Thompson*); TS 47 (1986) 725s (J. M.
McDermott).
5672 **Webster** Eric C.,   Crosscurrents in Adventist Christology: Theology and
Religion 6, 1984 ➤ 65,6351; $26.50:   ᴿAndUnS 24 (1986) 200-3 (N.
Gulley).
5673 **Wells** David F.,   The person of Christ; a biblical and historical analysis of
the Incarnation: Foundations for Faith 1984 ➤ 1,6994:   ᴿEvJ 4 (1986)
41-45 (R. A. *Peterson*); Horizons 13 (1986) 176s (Mary T. *Rattigan*).
5674 **Wevers** Herbert E.,   Jezus Christus, van waar komt hij? Een syste-
matisch-theologisch en bijbels-theologisch onderzoek naar het oorsprongs-
denken in de christologie en de preëxistentie als facet hiervan, uitgaand van
de huidige christologie 'van beneden': diss. ᴰ*Berkhof* H.   Leiden 1986,
Meinema. 171 p. – RTLv 18,573; TsTNijm 26,287s.
5675 **Wong** Joseph H. P.,   Logos-Symbol in the Christology of Karl RAHNER
(diss. Gregoriana, R 1981, ᴰ*Neufeld* K.) 1984 ➤ 1,6997:   ᴿÉglT 17 (1986)
108-111 J. *Pambrun*); HeythJ 27 (1986) 347-9 (J. P. *Galvin*); NatGrac 33
(1986) 198s (A. *Villalmonte*).
5676 *Wong* Joseph H. P.,   *a)* Karl RAHNER's Christology of symbol and three
models of Christology: HeythJ 27 (1986) 1-25; – *b)* Karl RAHNER on the
consciousness of Jesus; implications and assessments: Salesianum 48
(1968) 255-279.
5677 *Ziegenaus* Antón,   La filiación eterna de Jesucristo como fundamento del
significado salvífico del misterio de la vida del Señor: Tierra Nueva 14,56
(Bogotá 1986) 69-84 [TKontext 8/1,72].

H5.5 *Spiritus Sanctus; pneumatologia* – **The Holy Spirit.**

5678 **Aranda** Antonio,   Estudios de pneumatología.   Pamplona 1985, Univ.
Navarra.   248 p. – ᴿComSev 19 (1986) 439s (V. J. *Ansede Alonso*); RSPT
70 (1986) 599s (G.-M. de *Durand*).
5678* *Beintker* Michael,   Zu einem unerledigten Problem der Pneumatologie:
EvT 46 (1986) 12-26.
5679 *Bentué* Antonio,   La pneumatología como tema teológico: TVida 27
(1986) 263-276.

5680 **Bilaniuk** Petro B.T., Theology and economy of the Holy Spirit, an eastern [Ukrainian] approach [Rome Pont. Inst. St. Or. Centre for Indian and Interreligious Studies, Placid Lecture 2]. Bangalore 1980, Dharmaram. xii-218. $6 [➤ 62,7400]: ᴿTR 82 (1986) 491 (M.M. *Carijo-Guembe* spells once 'Placed', once 'Placid'; 'Leider sind die griechischen Zitate voller Fehler').

5681 **Boespflug** François, Dieu dans l'art ... l'affaire Crescence 1984 ➤ 65,6357; 1,7001: ᴿEstE 61 (1986) 109s (J.Mz. *Medina*); RivStoLR 22 (1986) 178-184 (G.C. *Sciolla*); TR 82 (1986) 45-49 (W. *Messerer*).

5682 **Buchanan** J., The office and work of the Holy Spirit (1843). E 1984, Banner of Truth. 488 p. £5.50. – ᴿEvQ 58 (1986) 375s (A.T.B. *McGowan*: a welcome relief from the experience-centred).

5683 **Burns** J. Patout. *Fagin* Gerald M., The Holy Spirit: Message of the Fathers 3, 1984 ➤ 1,6359: ᴿAfER 28 (1986) 416s (Catherine *Asomugha*); CleR 71 (1986) 191s (J. *McGu[c]kin*).

5684 ᴱ**Cattaneo** Enrico, ATANASIO, lettera a Serapione, Lo Spirito Santo. R 1986, Città Nuova. 188 p. 88-311-3055-2. – ᴿRasT 27 (1986) 287s (D. *Marafioti*).

5685 **Cavalcanti** Elena, L'esperienza di Dio nei Padri Greci; il trattato 'Sullo Spirito Santo' di BASILIO de Cesarea. R 1984, Studium. 240 p. Lit. 12.000. – ᴿOrChrPer 52 (1986) 238s (T. *Špidlík*); RasT 27 (1986) 91 (E. *Cattaneo*).

5686 *Cazelles* H., Saint-Esprit AT ➤ 595, SDB 11,60 (1986) 127-153 [153-6, Sagesse, *Gilbert* M.; 156-165, Qumran, *Cothenet* É.].

5687 *Coffey* David M., A proper mission of the Holy Spirit: TS 47 (1986) 227-250.

5688 *Colombo* Giuseppe, 'Dominum et vivificantem', l'enciclica di GIOVANNI PAOLO II: TItStt 11 (1986) 109-134.

5688* **Comblin** J., Breve curso de teologia. I. Jesus Cristo e sua missão; II. O Espírito Santo e sua missão; III. A Igreja e sua missão no mundo. São Paulo 1983-5, Paulinas. 256 p.; 348 p.; 330 p. 85-05-00023-4. – ᴿPerspT 18 (1986) 120-2 (C. *Palácio*).

5689 *Dantine* Johannes, Zu Karl BARTHs Traum von einer Theologie des Heiligen Geistes: TLZ 111 (1986) 401-8.

5690 *Dreissen* Josef †, Der Heilige Geist als die Vergebung der Sünden ['ipse est remissio omnium peccatorum', sabb. ante Pentecosten super oblata; ex-Feria V Pent.]: TGl 76 (1986) 212-229.

5691 **Durrwell** F.X., El Espíritu Santo en la Iglesia [1983 ➤ 64,6750], ᵀ*Fernández Zulaica* J. Salamanca 1986, Sígueme. 199 p. – ᴿBibFe 12 (1986) 366 (A. *Salas*); NatGrac 33 (1986) 570 (A. *Villalmonte*).

5692 **Durrwell** F.X., De Heilige Geest van God [< franç.]. Tielt 1986, Lannoo. 236 p. Fb 695. – ᴿCollatVl 16 (1986) 497 (J. De *Kesel*).

5693 **Durrwell** F.X., Lo Spirito Santo alla luce del mistero pasquale 1985 ➤ 1,7013; Lit. 12.000: ᴿParVi 30 (1985) 473s (L. *Melotti*).

5694 **Durrwell** François-Xavier, Holy Spirit of God; an essay in biblical theology, ᵀ*Davies* sr. Benedict. L 1986, Chapman. viii-184 p. 0-225-66453-4.

5695 *Durrwell* F.-X., Facetten einer Theologie des Heiligen Geistes ['Der Geist des Herrn' 1986]: TGegw 29 (1986) 131-9.

5696 **Fierens** Marc, *a*) De h. Geest en de kerken; pneumatologie en oecumenisme in het werk van Y. CONGAR: CollatVl 16 (1986) 131-144; – *b*) L'Esprit Saint et la liturgie dans la pneumatologie de Y. CONGAR: QLtg 66 (1985) 221-7.

5697 **Finan** Barbara A., The mission of the Holy Spirit in the theology of Karl RAHNER: diss. Marquette, ᴰ*Masson* R. Milwaukee 1986. 285 p. 87-08740. – DissA 47 (1986s) 4422-A.

5698 *Finan* Barbara, The Holy Spirit; an issue in theology: SpTod 38 (1986) 9-18.

5699 [*Gilbert* M. *al.*] El Espíritu Santo en la Biblia: CuadBíb 52. Estella 1986, VDivino. 62 p. – ᴿBibFe 12 (1986) 370s (M. *Sáenz Galache*).

5700 *a) Guillet* J., Le Saint Esprit dans les Évangiles synoptiques [et Actes]; – *b) Lémonon* J. P., dans le corpus paulinien; – (*Vanhoye* A., Héb; al.): → 595, SDB 11,60 (1986) 172-182 [-191] / 192-256...

5701 *Hilberath* Bernd J., 'Der Herr ist und der Leben schafft'; Anstösse zur Rede vom Heiligen Geist: ZkT 108 (1986) 282-291.

5702 **Inch** Morris A., The saga of the Spirit; a biblical, systematic and historical theology of th Holy Spirit. GR 1985, Baker. 280 p. $13 pa. – ᴿTDig 33 (1986) 475 (W. C. *Heiser*).

5703 **Johannes Paulus II**, Lettera enciclica 'Dominum et vivificantem' sullo Spirito Santo nella Chiesa e nel mondo: CC 137 (1986,2) 455-487.559-589 [521-531].

5704 *Knapp* Markus, Der Begriff des Geistes in der Philosophie ADORNOS und die christliche Rede vom Heiligen Geist: TPhil 61 (1986) 507-534.

5704* *Kocher* Michel, Le Saint-Esprit, interprète des Écritures et du croyant; essai en théologie du Saint-Esprit: Hokhma 11,31 (1986) 24-47; 11,32 (1986) 12-52.

5705 **Lavatori** Renzo, Lo Spirito Santo e il suo mistero ; esperienza e teologia nel trattato 'Sullo Spirito Santo' di BASILIO: Spiritualità 4. Vaticano 1986, Libreria Editrice. 187 p. Lit. 13.000 [CiVit 41,619].

5705* El Espíritu Santo en la Biblia: Cuadernos Bíblicos 52. Estella 1986, VDivino. 62 p. pt. 250. 84-7151-480-X [ActuBbg 24,80].

5706 *Margerie* Bertrand de, Vers une relecture du concile de Florence [sur la procession et mission de l'Esprit-Saint; évitée comme 'œcuméniquement maladroite' au congrès de Rome 1982] grâce à la reconsidération de l'Écriture et des Pères grecs et latins: RThom 86 (1986) 31-81.

5706* *Mondin* Battista, Credo nello Spirito Santo: CiVit 4 (1986) 307-326.

5707 **Mowery** Robert L., The articular references to the Holy Spirit in the Synoptic Gospels and Acts: BiRes 31 (Ch 1986) 26...

5708 *Nicolas* Simonne, [JEAN-PAUL II, Dominum et vivificantem 1986] L'Esprit-Saint dans la vie de l'Église et du monde: RThom 86 (1986) 533-5.

5709 *a) Ordon* H., ❷ The Holy Spirit in the NT as power and person; – *b) Rubinkiewicz* R., ❷ 'The Spirit of God' in intertestamental messianic texts; – *c) Tronina* A., ❷ ... in pre-Christian Judaism: → 266, Duch Święty 81-88 / 39-48 / 49-58.

5710 **Packer** James I., Keep in step with the Spirit 1984 → 1,7026: ᴿEvJ 4 (1986) 37-39 (W. S. *Sailer*); GraceTJ 7 (1986) 151-3 (D. S. *Dockery*); Protestantesimo 41 (1986) 226s (M. *Cignoni*); STEv 8,16 (1985) 288-292 (P. *Finch*).

5711 *Raschini* Maria Adelaide, A proposito della Dominum et vivificantem: Renovatio 21 (1986) 639-650.

5711* *Rodríguez Fassio* Francisco J., La experiencia del Espíritu Santo en los sacramentos de iniciación: ComSev 19 (1986) 365-381.

5712 **Rosato** Philip J., The Spirit as Lord; the pneumatology of Karl BARTH 1981 → 62,7464 ... 1,7028: ᴿTTod 43 (1986s) 419s.422s (G. S. *Hendry*).

5712* *Schroer* Silvia, Der Geist, die Weisheit und die Taube; feministisch-kritische Exegese eines neutestamentlichen Symbols auf dem Hinter-

grund seiner altorientalischen und hellenistisch-frühjüdischen Traditionsgeschichte: FreibZ 33 (1986) 197-225.
5713 **Schütz** Christian, Einführung in die Pneumatologie 1985 ➤ 1,7034:
ᴿAugR 26 (1986) 598-602 (B. *Studer*); ÉTRel 61 (1986) 145 (J.-P. *Gabus*);
GeistL 59 (1986) 239s (J. *Sudbrack*); Salesianum 48 (1986) 738s (A. M.
Triacca); TLZ 111 (1986) 463-471 (J. *Dantine*).
5714 **Schweizer** Eduard, *a*) The Holy Spirit 1980 ➤ 62,7467*b* ... 1,7035: ᴿVidyajyoti 49 (1985) 313s (P. *Meagher*). – *b*) El Espíritu Santo 1984
➤ 65,6395; 1,7035: ᴿPerspT 18 (1986) 129s (F. *Taborda*).
5715 **Smail** Thomas, Au risque de ta présence [le Saint-Esprit: il n'y a *pas que*
la glossolalie]. Lausanne 1985, Ligue/Bible. 175 p. Fs 18. – ᴿÉTRel 61
(1986) 609 (A.-G. *Martin*).
5716 *Spijker* W. van 't, ⓦ The Holy Spirit in BUCER and CALVIN, ᵀ*Fükő* Dezső:
Theologiai Szemle 29 (1986) 333-342.
5717 *Suurmond* Jean-Jacques, Ethical aspects of the inner witness of the Holy
Spirit: StudiaBT 13 (1983) 3-16.
5718 *Takayanagi* Shunichi, ⓞ God's self-communication and the Holy Spirit;
an attempt to synthesize Karl RAHNER's pneumatological ideas: KatKenk
25,50 (1986) 37-84; Eng. iv-vii.
5719 *Triacca* Achille M., Pneumatologia, epicletologia o paracletologia?
Contributo alla comprensione della presenza ed azione dello Spirito Santo
da alcune visuali della teologia liturgica: Salesianum 48 (1986) 67-107.
5719* *a*) *Vanhoye* Albert, Il donarsi salvifico di Dio nello Spirito Santo:
OssRom (21.VI.1986) 1.5. – *b*) *Vauthier* E., Introduction à l'encyclique
'Dominum et vivificantem' [*Jean-Paul* II, 18.V.1986]: EsprV 96 (1986)
465-476.
5720 *Walvoord* John F., The Holy Spirit and spiritual gifts: Bibliotheca Sacra
143 (1986) 109-122 [= Oct. 1973].
5721 **Wleklik** Ireneusz, ❷ Nauka... Doctrine d'Alexandre ŻYCHLIŃSKI sur le
rôle de l'Esprit Saint dans la vie chrétienne: diss. ᴰ*Pryszmont* J. Wsz 1986.
– RTLv 18,559.
5722 *Young* R. Garland, The role of the Spirit in texts; James SANDERS, Paul
ACHTEMEIER: PerspRelSt 13 (1986) 229-240 [< ZIT].

H5.6 *Spiritus et Filius*; **'Spirit-Christology'**.

5723 *a*) *Bavel* J. van, Le rapport entre le Saint-Esprit et le Christ Jésus; – *b*)
Standaert Benoît, Le mystère de l'Esprit dans les Écritures et dans la
liturgie: QLtg 67 (1986) 94-105 / 87-93.
5724 **Congar** Yves, La parole et le souffle 1984 ➤ 65,2402; 1,7041: RBLitEc
87 (1986) 234s (A. *Dartigues*); KatKenk 25,50 (1986) 186-190 (S.
Takayanagi ❹).
5725 **Congar** Yves, La Parola e il Soffio. ᵀ 1985, Borla. 166 p. Lit. 12.000. –
ᴿParVi 31 (1986) 73s (L. *Melotti*); Salesianum 48 (1986) 435s (A. M.
Triacca).
5726 **Congar** Yves M. J., The Word and the Spirit. L/SF 1986,
Chapman/Harper & R. x-133 p. 0-225-66433-X / SF 0-86683-538-5.
5727 *Halleux* André de, Personnalisme ou essentialisme trinitaire chez les
Pères cappadociens [Filioque; ... *Régnon* T. de, *Petau* D.]: RTLv 17 (1986)
129-155.265-292; Eng. 263.
5728 **Riaud** Alexis, L'Esprit du Père et du Fils, une étude nouvelle de
l'Esprit-Saint et de la vie trinitaire 1984 ➤ 65,6392; F 48: ᴿRTLv 17
(1986) 232s (A. de *Halleux*).

5729 *a) Scheffczyk* Leo, Der Sinn des Filioque: IkaZ 15 (1986) 23-34 = Le sens du Filioque: Communio 11,1 (P 1986) 57-69, ᵀ*Fontette* Pierre de. – *b) Sicari* Antonio M., Der Heilige Geist und die 'totale' Inkarnation: IkaZ 15 (1986) 14-22 = L'Esprit du Corps: Communio 11,1 (P 1986) 13-24.

5730 *Schultze* Bernhard, Das Filioque bei EPIPHANIUS von Cypern (im Ancoratus): OstkSt 35 (1986) 105-134.

H5.7 *Ssma Trinitas* – The Holy Trinity.

5731 *Bingemer* Maria Clara L., A Trindade a partir da perspectiva da mulher: → 510, REB 46 (1986) 73-99.

5732 *Blandino* Giovanni, Questioni sull'unità e trinità di Dio: Teresianum 37 (1986) 191-204.

5733 *Blaser* Klauspeter, La remise en valeur du dogme trinitaire dans la théologie actuelle: ÉTRel 61 (1986) 395-407 [383-394 liturgie, *Vischer* W.].

5734 **Boff** Leonardo, A Trindade, a Sociedade e a libertação. Petrópolis 1986, Vozes. 206 p. – ᴿREB 46 (1986) 890-4 (E. F. *Alves*).

5735 **Bonato** Antonio, La dottrina trinitaria di CIRILLO di Gerusalemme 1983 → 64,6798; 65,6413: ᴿSalesianum 48 (1986) 434s (A. M. *Triacca*).

5736 *Bradshaw* Timothy, Karl BARTH on the Trinity; a family resemblance: ScotJT 39 (1986) 145-164.

5737 ᴱ**Breuning** Wilhelm, Trinität; aktuelle Perspectiven 1984 → 65,478*; 1,7054: ᴿZkT 108 (1986) 438-440 (L. *Lies*).

5738 *Brito* Emilio, Trinité et création; l'approche de SCHELLING: ETL 62 (1986) 66-88.

5739 **Brown** David, The divine Trinity 1985 → 1,7055: ᴿJTS 37 (1986) 669-671 (C. *Gunton*); ModT 2 (1985s) 235-256 (K. *Surin*), 257-276 response; RelSt 22 (1986) 157-161 (J. P. *Mackey*: grudgingly interested); ScotJT 39 (1986) 557-560 (A. E. *Lewis*); TLond 39 (1986) 127-9 (J. *Kent*); TS 47 (1986) 184s (T. *German*: one of the best).

5740 *Coggi* Roberto, Punti controversi di teologia trinitaria: SacDoc 31 (1986) 568-581.

5741 **Courth** F., Trinität, in der Scholastik: HbDG 2/1b, 1985 → 1,7058: ᴿTVida 27 (1986) 324s (Anneliese *Meis*); ZkT 108 (1986) 355s (L. *Lies*).

5742 **Ebied** R.Y., *Roey* A. van, *Wickham* L. R., PETER of Callinicum, Anti-Tritheist dossier: OrLovAn 10, 1981 → 62,m144; Fb1200; 90-70192-06-3: ᴿBijdragen 47 (1986) 338s (M. *Parmentier*, Eng.).

5743 *Fidalgo Herranz* José-Antonio, La SS. Trinidad en [AQUINAS] la Suma contra los gentiles; fuentes bíblicas: EstB [42 (1984) 363-389] 44 (1986) 147-194.

5744 *Forte* Bruno, Trinità come storia³: Prospettive teologiche 5, 1985 → 1, 7061: ᴿActuBbg 23 (1986) 111-5 (*J. Vives*); Claretianum 26 (1986) 371-5 (L. *Gutiérrez Vega*); Gregorianum 67 (1986) 373s (J. *O'Donnell*); ScuolC 114 (1986) 503-510 (V. *Croce*); Teresianum 37 (1986) 523s (C. *Laudazi*).

5745 *Forte* Bruno, Trinità cristiana e realtà sociale [simposio Salamanca 1986]: Asprenas 33 (1986) 355-371. .

5746 **Fortman** Edmund J., The triune God; a historical study of the doctrine of the Trinity [1972]. GR c. 1983, Baker. 408 p. $11. – ᴿEvQ (1986) 188s (J. P. *Baker*).

5747 *a) Gagnebin* Laurent, De Trinitate; questions de méthode; – *b) Groot* Art de, L'antitrinitarisme socinien: ÉTRel 61 (1986) 63-73 / 51-61.

5748 *González-Alio* José L., La Santísima Trinidad, comunión de personas: ScripTPamp 18 (1986) 11-114; lat. 114s; Eng. 115.

5748* *Guilluy* Paul, Personne: → 578, Catholicisme XI,49 (1986) 30-54.

5749 **Gunton** C. E., Enlightenment and alienation; an essay towards a trinitarian theology 1985 → 1,7065: ᴿTsTNijm 26 (1986) 307 (H. *Rikhof*).

5750 **Haddad** Rachid, La Trinité divine chez les théologiens [chrétiens] arabes (750-1050): Religions 15; 1985 → 1,7066: ᴿRSPT 70 (1986) 457s (C. *Gilliot*); RThom 86 (1986) 336s (J. *Jomier*); RTLv 17 (1986) 346-351 (A. de *Halleux*).

5751 *Haubst* Rudolf, Die 'Bibliotheca trinitariorum' und die Leitidee der 'analogia Trinitatis': TrierTZ 95 (1986) 28-37.

5752 **Heinz** Hanspeter, Trinitarische Begegnungen bei BONAVENTURA; Fruchtbarkeit einer appropriativen Trinitätstheologie: Beiträge zur Gesch. Ph. Theol. des Mittelalters NF 26. Münster 1985, Aschendorff. xv-298 p. 3-402-03921-4.

5753 **Hilberath** Bernd J., Der Personbegriff der Trinitätstheologie in Rückfrage von Karl RAHNER zu TERTULLIANs 'Adversus Praxean': InnsbTSt 17. Innsbruck 1986, Tyrolia. 365 p. DM 76 [TR 83,306-9, B. *Studer*].

5754 **Hill** Edmund, The mystery of the Trinity: Introducing Catholic Theology 4. L 1985, G. Chapman. ix-193 p. £9. 0-225-66470-4. – ᴿExpTim 98 (1986s) 30 (R. *Butterworth*: tries to reinstate AUGUSTINE and mystery).

5755 **Jansen** Reiner, Studien zu LUTHERs Trinitätslehre: BaBSt 26. Fra 1976, Lang. 232 p. Fs 54,55. – ᴿZkT 108 (1986) 440-3 (L. *Lies*: dates the volume 1976 but with no comment on why such a long review now).

5756 **Kern** Iso, Trinität — Theologische Überlegung eines Phänomenologen: FreibZ 33 (1986) 181-196.

5757 *Kiesling* Christopher, On relating to the persons of the Trinity: TS 47 (1986) 599-616.

5758 a) *La Cugna* Catherine M., Philosophers and theologians on the Trinity; – b) *Lash* Nicholas, Considering the Trinity; – c) *Williams* Roman, Trinity and Revelation; – d) *Milbank* John, The second difference; for a trinitarianism without reserve: ModT 2 (1985s) 169-181 / 183-196 / 197-212 / 213-234.

5759 ᴱ**Ladaria** L., San HILARIO de Poitiers, La Trinidad: BAC 481. M 1986, Católica. xxii-711 p. [NRT 109, 930].

5760 **Luzárraga** J., El Dios que llama; experiencia bíblica de la Trinidad en la vocación. Salamanca 1985, Secr. Trinitario. 89 p. 84-85376-55-2 [NTAbs 30,366].

5761 **Milano** Andrea, Persona in teologia; alle origini del significato di persona nel cristianesimo antico: Saggi e Ricerche 1, 1985, → 1,7079: ᴿAngelicum 63 (1986) 136-8 (G. *Grasso*); Asprenas 33 (1986) 97-101 (P. *Giustiniani*); Byzantion 56 (1986) 502s (J. *Mossay*); ÉtClas 54 (1986) 311s (X. *Jacques*); Muséon 99 (1986) 376s (J. *Mossay*); TPhil 61 (1986) 260s (H. J. *Höhn*); TR 82 (1986) 483-7 (H. R. *Drobner*).

5762 **Milet** Jean, 'Un seul Dieu en trois personnes' [... les apports de la Révélation ...]: EsprV 96 (1986) 401-412.421-440.

5763 **Miller** David L., Three faces of God; traces of the Trinity in literature and life. Ph 1986, Fortress. 164 p. $11.95 pa. [RelStR 13, 159, J. J. *Jackson*].

5764 **Min** Anselm K., The Trinity and the Incarnation; HEGEL and classical approaches: JRel 66 (1986) 173-193.

5765 **Minz** Karl-Heinz, Pleroma trinitatis; die Trinitätstheologie bei M. J. SCHEEBEN: DispTheol 10, 1982 → 64,6812; 1,7080: ᴿTPQ 134 (1986) 85 (R. *Schulte*); ZRGg 38 (1986) 380s (E. *Schadel*).

5766 **Moltmann** J., The Trinity and the Kingdom of God 1981 → 62,7453b ... 65,6527: ᴿVidyajyoti 49 (1985) 431s (T. K. *John*).

5767 **Moltmann** J., Trinité et royaume de Dieu, [T]*Kleiber* M. 1984 ➤ 65,6426; 1,7082: [R]BLitEc 87 (1986) 228-230 (A. *Dartigue*).

5768 **Moltmann** J., Trinidad y Reino de Dios 1983 ➤ 64,6813*c*,,, 1,7083: [R]TVida 27 (1986) 226 (Anneliese *Meis Wörmer*).

5768* *Moltmann* Jürgen, Trinitarier und Antitrinitarier [[E]*Schadel* E. 1984): EvT 46 (1986) 293s.

5769 **Nicolas** Jean-Hervé, Synthèse dogmatique; de la Trinité à la Trinité, préf. *Ratzinger* J., 1985 ➤ 1,7085: [R]ActuBbg 23 (1986) 175-182 (J. *Vives*); Angelicum 63 (1986) 491s (M. *Tavuzzi*: monumental); FreibZ 33 (1986) 277-9 (J.-P. *Torrell*); MélSR 43 (1986) 36-39 (B. *Rey*); NatGrac 33 (1986) 193s (A. *Villalmonte*); NRT 108 (1986) 914 (L. *Renwart*); Salesianum 48 (1986) 174 (G. *Abbà*); TS 47 (1986) 529s (J. *Farrelly*).

5770 *Patfoort* A., Missions divines et expérience des Personnes divines selon S. THOMAS: Angelicum 63 (1986) 545-559.

5771 *Plantinga* Cornelius [J], GREGORY of Nyssa and the social analogy of the Trinity: Thomist 50 (1986) 325-352.

5772 **Powell** Samuel M., The doctrine of the Trinity in nineteenth-century German Protestant [thought: RelStR 13,188], theology: Philipp MARHEINEKE, Isaak DORNER, Johann von HOFFMANN, and Alexander SCHWEITZER, diss. Claremont 1986, [D]*Verheyden* J. (1987)]. 289 p. 87-05184. – DissA 47 (1986s) 4416-A.

5773 [E]**Schadel** Erwin *al.*, Bibliotheca Trinitariorum I, 1984 ➤ 65,929*: [R]BLitEc 87 (1986) 73 (H. *Crouzel*); FreibRu 37s (1985s) 105s (K.-H. *Minz*); TüTQ 166 (1986) 73s (P. *Walter*).

5774 **Schlitt** Dale M., HEGEL's Trinitarian claim 1984 ➤ 1,7088: [R]RTLv 17 (1986) 368s (E. *Brito*); TPhil 61 (1986) 133-5 (J. *Splett*).

5775 **Schroeder** Hans-Werner, Dreieinigkeit und Dreifaltigkeit; vom Geheimnis der Trinität. Stu 1986, Urachhaus. 288 p. 3-87838-492-0.

5776 **Silberer** Michael, Die Trinitätsidee im Werk von Pavel A. FLORENSKIJ; Versuch einer systematischen Darstellung in Begegnung mit Thomas von AQUIN: Das Östliche Christentum 36. [➤ 1,7090]. Wü 1984, Augustinus. xliii-303 p. DM 43,80. – [R]TR 82 (1986) 491-5 (W. *Goerdt*).

5777 a) *Stucki* P.-A., *Vouga* F., La Trinité au musée ['une théologie risque de perdre les conditions de sa liberté non seulement quand elle traite de Dieu sans traiter en même temps de l'homme ... (mais aussi) sans le concevoir comme trinitaire ... sottises au cœur même de la modernité']; – b) *Reymond* Bernard, L'Anti-trinitarisme chez les Réformés d'expression française au début du XIXe s.: ÉTRel 61 (1986) 195-212 / 213-226.

5778 **Thurmer** John, A detection of the Trinity. Exeter 1985, Paternoster. 93 p. £3. 0-85364-395-4. – [R]ExpTim 97 (1985s) 282 (M. J. *Townsend*: enthusiasm for OT angelic trinitarianism a lost cause).

5779 *Vandervelde* George, A trinitarian framework and Reformed distinctiveness; a critical assessment of [*Bolt* J.] Christian and Reformed Today: CalvinT 21 (1986) 95-109.

5780 *Williams* Arthur H.[J], The Trinity and time [... Can it be that the phrase 'Kingdom of God/heaven' is a functional equivalent in the NT of the later term 'Trinity', first used 170 A.D. by THEOPHILUS of Antioch, referring to the first three days of creation?]: ScotJT 39 (1986) 65-81.

H5.8 *Regnum messianicum, Filius hominis* – **Messianic kingdom, Son of Man.**

5781 **Arias** Mortimer, Announcing the Reign of God; evangelization and the subversive memory of Jesus 1984 ➤ 65,6437: [R]Themelios 12 (1986s) 33 (H. M. *Conn*).

5782 **Beasley-Murray** George R., Jesus and the Kingdom of God. GR/Exeter 1986, Eerdmans/Paternoster. 446 p. $50/£20. GR 0-8028-3609-7 / Exeter 0-85364-394-6. – [R]ExpTim 97 (1985s) 376s (D. *Hill*); SWJT 29,2 (1986s) 56 (E. E. *Ellis*); TrinJ 7,2 (1986) 103-7 (C. A. *Evans*).

5783 *Bentué* Antoni, El espíritu mesiánico de Jesús: RCatalT 11 (1986) 253-381; Eng. 382.

5784 **Betz** Otto, Jesus und das Danielbuch, II. Die Menschensohnworte Jesu und die Zukunftserwartung des Paulus (Daniel 7,13-14): ArbNTJud (0170-8856) 6/2. Fra 1985, P. Lang. 196 p. 3-8204-5543-4.

5785 *Bock* Darrell L., Jesus as Lord in Acts and in the Gospel message: BS 143 (1986) 146-154.

5786 **Caragounis** Chrys C., The Son of Man; vision and interpretation: WUNT 38. Tü 1986, Mohr. ix-310 p. DM 118. 3-16-144963-0. – [R]Exp-Tim 98 (1986s) 214s (M. *Casey*: 'no problem can be illuminated by this combination of commitment and ignorance').

5787 [E]**Chilton** Bruce, The Kingdom of God in the teaching of Jesus: Issues Rel. T. 5, 1984 → 65,275; 1,7099: [R]EvQ 58 (1986) 267s (I. H. *Marshall*); Interpretation 40 (1986) 313 (R. H *Hiers*).

5787* *Chilton* Bruce, a) Jesus, the King and his Kingdom [> BR]; – b) Regnum Dei Deus est [< ScotJT 31 (1978) 261-270]; – c) Gottesherrschaft als Gotteserfahrung; Erkenntnisse der Targumforschung für den neu-testamentlichen Begriff 'Königsherrschaft Gottes' [without indication of source or translator]: → 140*, Targumic Approaches 1986, 109-112 / 99-107 / 85-97.

5788 *Coninck* Frédéric de, Le Royaume de Dieu comme critique des royaumes des hommes: FoiVie 85,6 (1986) 47-72.

5789 *Donahue* John R., Recent studies on the origin of 'Son of Man' in the Gospels: → 32, [F]FITZMYER J., CBQ 48 (1986) 484-498.

5790 **Ehler** Bernhard, Die Herrschaft des Gekreuzigten; Ernst KÄSEMANNs Frage nach der Mitte der Schrift: BZNW 46. xv-365 p. DM 146. 3-11-010397-4.

5791 **Geist** Heinz, Menschensohn und Gemeinde; eine redaktionskritische Untersuchung zur Menschensohnprädikation im Matthäusevangelium: ForBi 57. Wü 1986, Echter. xv-517 p.; bibliog. p. 444-501. 3-429-01039-X.

5791* **González-Carvajal** J., El Reino de Dios y nuestra historia: Alcance 38. Santander 1986, Sal Terrae. 158 p. [Proyección 34, 72].

5792 a) *Hartzsch* Klaus-Peter, 'Dein Reich Komme — worauf wartet die christliche Gemeinde?'; – b) *Schille* Gottfried, Ein neuer Zugang zu Jesus?: – c) *Jörns* Klaus-Peter, Das 'ordinierte Amt' als Problem des Gemeindeaufbaus: ZeichZt 40 (1986) 262-7 / 247-252 / 268-274 [< ZIT].

Heyer C. J. den, De messiaanse weg, II. Jezus van Nazareth 1986 → 3137.

5793 *Iwashima* Tadahiko, ● Salvation in Jesus; considerations about the logic of the Kingdom of God: KatKenk 25,50 (1986) 85-120; Eng. vii-x.

5794 *Jackson* Don, A survey of the 1967-1981 study of the Son of Man: RestQ 28 (Abilene 1985s) 67-78 [< ZIT].

5795 *Jüngel* Eberhard, Die Bedeutung der Reich-Gottes-Erwartung für das Zeugnis der christlichen Gemeinde: BTZ 3 (1986) 344-353.

5796 **Kearns** Rollin, Das Traditionsgefüge um den Menschensohn; ur-sprünglicher Gehalt und älteste Veränderung im Urchristentum. Tü 1986, Mohr. iv-202 p. DM 68 pa. [TR 83,251]. – [R]ExpTim 98 (1986s) 301 (E. *Best*).

5797 **Kim Seyoon**, The 'Son of Man' as the Son of God: WUNT 30, 1983 ➤ 65,6449; 1,7115: ᴿBiblica 67 (1986) 129-132 (R. *Riesner*); HeythJ 27 (1986) 76s (M. *Smith*); JAAR 54 (1986) 377s (D. R. A. *Hare*).

5797* **Kümmel** Werner G., Jesus der Menschensohn? [... 'Meinungswirrwarr']: Szb Fra 20/3, ➤ 65,6450; p. 147-188; DM 20: ᴿTR 82 (1986) 195 (R. *Pesch*).

5798 *Lange* Dietz, Zum Verhältnis von Utopie und Reich Gottes; Probleme der Begründung einer christlichen Ethik in der modernen Gesellschaft: ZTK 83 (1986) 507-542.

5799 **Lindars** Barnabas, Jesus Son of Man 1983 ➤ 64,6853... 1,7118: ᴿHeythJ 27 (1986) 31s (Marion *Smith*: courageous revision of his own views); Interpretation 40 (1986) 204.206 (W. O. *Walker*); JBL 105 (1986) 332-5 (P. L. *Achtemeier*: he and KIM SEYOON cancel each other out); JTS 37 (1986) 517-9 (G. N. *Stanton*).

5800 *Lindemann* Andreas, [*Zenger* Erich], Herrschaft Gottes, Reich Gottes NT [AT]: ➤ 597, TRE 15 (1986) 196-218 [177-189] (176s; 190-6; 218-244 *al.*).

5801 *Lindemann* Andreas Gottesherrschaft und Menschenherrschaft; Beobachtungen zum neutestamentlichen Basileia-Zeugnis und zum Problem einer theologischen Ethik des Politischen [Gastvorlesung Pd 1985]: TGl 76 (1986) 69-94.

5802 *a*) *McDermott* John, Le Royaume du NT: ➤ 287, Communio 11,3 (P 1986) 13-25 > IkaZ 15 (1986) 142-4, Gegenwärtiges und kommendes Reich Gottes; – *b*) *Balthasar* Hans Urs von, Gottes Reich und die Kirche: IkaZ 15 (1986) 124-130 > Communio 11,3 (1986) 4-12, Le Royaume de Dieu ou l'Église?

5803 *Marchesi* Giovanni, L'annuncio del Regno di Dio; novità dell'insegnamento di Gesù: CC 137 (1986,3) 460-479.

5804 *Moltmann* Jürgen, Essere cristiani, essere uomini e Regno di Dio; un dialogo con Karl RAHNER [< StiZt 203 (1985) 619-631], ᵀ*Colombi* Giulio: HumBr 41 (1986) 882-899.

5805 *Moltmann* Jürgen, Être chrétien, être homme et royaume de Dieu, dialogue avec Karl RAHNER [< StiZt Sept. 1985], ᵀ*Lang* Jean-Bernard: BCentProt 38,8 (1986) 5-22.

5806 **Müller** Mogens, Der Ausdruck 'Menschensohn' in den Evangelien [Diss. K 1984], ᵀ: AcTheolDan 17, 1984 ➤ 65,6456: *f*90: ᴿCBQ 48 (1986) 342-4 (M. E. *Boring*).

5807 **Rice** Richard, The reign of God; an introduction to Christian theology from a Seventh-Day Adventist perspective. Berrien Springs MI 1983, Andrews Univ. xx-404 p. $24. – ᴿAndrUnS 24 (1986) 80.

5808 **Schwarz** G., Jesus 'der Menschensohn'; aramaistische Untersuchungen zu den synoptischen Menschensohnworten Jesu: BWANT 119. Stu 1986, Kohlhammer. x-352 p. DM 74. 3-17-009268-5 [NTAbs 31,116].

Sheehan T., The first coming; how the Kingdom of God became Christianity 1986 ➤ 3172.

5810 **Simonis** Walter, Das Reich Gottes ist mitten unter euch; Neuorientierung an Jesu Lehre und Leben. Dü 1986, Patmos. 103 p.

5811 *Simonsen* Hejne, Dansk disputats om udtrykket 'menneskesønnen': SvEx 51s (1986s) 219-228.

5812 **Snyder** Howard A., A kingdom manifesto; calling the Church to live under God's reign [... land, justice for the poor, Jubilee Lv 25]. DG 1985, InterVarsity. 132 p. $5 pa. – ᴿCalvinT 21 (1986) 126s (R. R. *Recker*).

5813 *Sobrino* Jon, The Kingdom of God in contemporary spirituality

[Significación del Reino de Dios anunciado por Jesús, Diakonia 7,26 (Managua 1983) 94-110], ᵀᴱNichols Francis W.: TDig 33 (1986) 325-7.

H6.1   *Creatio, sabbatum NT* [➤ E3.5]; **The Creation** [➤ E1.6; H2.8].

5814 **Bacchiocchi** Samuele,   Du Sabbat au dimanche [1977 ➤ 58,8951], ᵀ*Sébire* Dominique 1984 ➤ **1**,7135:   ᴿRB 93 (1986) 314 (M.-J. *Pierre*); TR 82 (1986) 286s (R. *Staats*).

5815 *Baur* Jörg,   Theologisches Reden über die Schöpfung christlich oder vor-christlich [Konsultation Schöpfungstheologie, Elsass 1984]: NSys 28 (1986) 124-138; Eng. 138.

5816 **Bayer** O.,   Schöpfung als Anrede; zu einer Hermeneutik der Schöpfung [... against *Spinoza* and process-theology]. Tü 1986, Mohr. x-166 p. DM 39 [ZAW 99,284, O. *Kaiser*].

5816* *Hahn* Ferdinand,   Schabbat und Sonntag: EvT 46 (1986) 495-507.

5817 *Kolberg* Anfinn A.,   Søndagen som tidens sakrament: TsTKi 57 (1986) 281-295.

Moltmann Jürgen, God in creation 1985 ➤ 5315.

5818 **Müller** A. M. K.,   *Pasolini* P.,   *Braun* D.,   Schöpfungsglaube heute: Grenzgespräche 11. Neuk 1985. [< JbBT 1,236].

5819 *Richard* Lucien,   Toward a renewed theology of creation; implications for the question of human rights: ÉglT 17 (1986) 149-170.

5820 **Ruiz de la Peña** Juan,   Teología de la creación: Presencia Teológica 24. Santander 1986, Sal Terrae.   279 p.   84-293-0736-2. – ᴿBibFe 12 (1986) 369 (A. *Salas*); Burgense 27 (1986) 573-5 (J. de *Sahagún Lucas*); CiTom 113 (1986) 631s (E. *García*); ComSev 19 (1986) 443s (V. J. *Ansede Alonso*); Gregorianum 67 (1986) 777s (L. *Ladaria*); Salmanticensis 33 (1986) 251s (J.-R. *Flecha*); SalT 74 (1986) 413s (J. A. *García*).

5821 **Soelle** Dorothee, ᵀ*Cloyes* Shirley,   To work and to love; a theology of creation 1984 ➤ **1**,7148:   ᴿJAAR 54 (1986) 194s (Sharon D. *Welch*); SpTod 38 (1986) 171s (J. *Theisen*).

5822 **Sölle** Dorothee,   Lieben und arbeiten; eine Theologie der Schöpfung. Stu 1985, Kreuz.   213 p. – ᴿNatGrac 3 (1986) 587s (A. *Villalmonte*).

5822* *Zenger* E.,   Alttestamentlicher-jüdischer Sabbat und neutesta-mentlich-christlicher Sonntag: Lebendige Seelsorge 33 (1982) 249-253 [< JbBT 1,219].

H6.3   *Fides, veritas in NT* – **Faith and Truth.**

5823 **Anderführen** Jean,   À l'ombre du doute, la foi; commentaire du Symbole des Apôtres: L'Évangile et la Vie 10. Genève 1984, Labor et Fides.   268 p. 2-8309-0019-7. – ᴿÉTRel 61 (1986) 467s (J.-D. *Kraege*).

5824 **Balthasar** Hans Urs von,   Puntos centrales de la fe: BAC 464. M 1985. xiii-395 p. – ᴿBurgense 27 (1986) 317s (N. *López Martínez*); ComSev 19 (1986) 250s (V. J. *Ansede Alonso*).

5825 *Barker* K. S.,   Prancing with belief [*Chesterton* G. K. ...]: ExpTim 97 (1985s) 242-4.

5826 **Bonnet** Georges,   L'homme sauvé 1985 ➤ **1**, 7157: ᴿÉTRel 61 (1986) 466s (A. *Dupleix*); LavalTP 42 (1986) 411s (J. *Doyon*); ScEspr 38 (1986) 271s (R. *Potvin*: continuation de ses études sur la morale biblique);VSp 140 (1986) 267s (P. *Lambert*).

5826* *Brossier* Françoise,   Lire la Bible; récits bibliques et communication de la foi; préf. *Marlé* René. P 1986, Centurion.   154 p. – ᴿRICathP 19 (1986) 139s (C. *Wiener*).

5827 ᴱChenu Bruno, *Coudreau* François, *al.*, Glaube zum Leben; die christliche Botschaft [1984 → 1,7161], ᵀᴱ*Biemer* G. FrB 1986, Herder. 840 p. DM 29,80 [TLZ 112,452, A. *Rössler*].

5828 *Connolly* T. Gerard, Perichoresis and the faith that personalizes according to Jean MOUROUX [largely responsible for the now-common speaking of faith as personal encounter]: ETL 62 (1986) 356-380.

5828* *Dulles* Avery, Glaube, Glaubensbegründung und Glaubengemeinschaft [*Polanyi* M.; < TS 45 (1984) 537-550]: TGegw 23 (1985) 15-20.

5829 **Eyt** Pierre, Je crois en Dieu; commentaire du Credo. P 1985, Desclée-B. 168 p. – ᴿRICathP 18 (1986) 55-62 (H. *Cazelles*).

5829* *Gilmour* T. R., The dynamic of faith [in several Scripture verses...]: ExpTim 98 (1986s) 365-9.

5830 *Haag* Herbert, Glauben — was bedeutet mir das?: Diakonia 17 (1986) 132-4.

5831 **Hann** William, The hierarchy of truths according to Yves CONGAR o.p.: diss. Pont. Univ. Gregoriana, ᴰ*O'Collins* G. R 1986. 405 p. – RTLv 18,570.

5832 **Herrick** Jim, Against the faith; essays on deists, skeptics and atheists. NY 1985, Prometheus. 250 p. $20 [JAAR 54,204].

5833 **Holloway** Richard, The sidelong glance; conflict and commitment in Christianity today. L 1985, Darton-LT. 86 p. £3. 0-232-51652-9. – ᴿExpTim 97 (1985s) 283 (G. T. *Eddy* calls him a 'typical Angelican', whether as misprint or old-new trend is not clear).

5834 **Huddleston** Trevor, bp., I believe [Apostles' Creed]. L 1986, Collins-Fount. 88 p. £1.75. 0-00-627069-7. – ᴿExpTim 98 (1986s) 156 (W. D. *Horton*: doctrine earthed).

5835 *Indelicato* Antonino, La 'Formula nova professionis fidei' nella preparazione del Vaticano II: CrNSt 7 (1986) 305-340 [p. 335-9, il testo: 'Firmiter recipio omnia et singula ... spondeo, voveo et iuro ... sic me Deus adiuvet, et haec sancta Dei Evangelia'].

5836 *Jericó Bermejo* Ignacio, Fides ecclesiae tradita, el artículo de fe según [PEÑA, MANCIO, MEDINA: 'Escuela de Salamanca' 1559-1569]: ScriptV 33 (1986) 123-166.

5837 *Kapellari* Egon, Bischof, Das Bild des Glaubens: TPQ 134 (1986) 53-58.

5837* **Kasper** W., Einführung in den Katholischen Erwachsenenkatechismus. Dü 1985. – ᴿEvT 46 (1986) 565-571 (G. *Wenz*, 'Glaube der Kirche und kirchliche Glaubensvermittlung').

5838 **Kehl** Medard, Hinführung zum christlichen Glauben. Mainz 1984, Grünewald. 170 p. ᴿTPhil 61 (1986) 281-3 (B. *Groth*).

5839 **Kemmer** Alfons, *a)* Das Glaubensbekenntnis in den Evangelien; eine Einführung in die biblischen Ursprünge des Credo: Herderbücherei 1166. FrB 1985, Herder. 157 p. DM 9. – ᴿColcT 56,1 (1986) 184-6 (S. *Mędala*). – *b)* The creed in the Gospels, ᵀ*Schnaus* Urban. NY 1986, Paulist. v-134 p. 0-8091-2830-6.

5840 ᴱLink Hans-Georg, The roots of our common faith; faith in the Scriptures and in the early Church: Faith and Order 119, 1983/4 → 65,514*; 1,7177: Istina 31 (1986) 430s (B. *Dupuy*).

5841 ᴱLink Hans-Georg, Apostolic faith today; a handbook for study. Genève 1985, WCC. 281 p. Fs 25. 2-8254-0827-1. – ᴿÉTRel 61 (1986) 309s (A. *Gounelle*).

5842 **Lochman** Jan M., The faith we possess; an ecumenical dogmatics [... feminism → 1,7178, ᵀ*Lewis* David], Ph 1984, Fortress '... we confess'] / E 1985, Clark. 274 p. £15. 0-8006-0723-6 / 0-567-09367-0. – ᴿExpTim 97 (1985s) 281 (I. R. *Torrance*: subtle, lucid); JAAR 54 (1986) 146s (G. *Wainwright*).

5843 **Lubac** Henri de,   Christian faith; the structure of the Apostles' Creed [²1970]. L 1986, Chapman.   xv-206 p. £9.   0-225-66429-1. – ᴿExpTim 98 (1986s) 155 (G. *Slater*: claustrophobic).

5844 **McCabe** Herbert,   The teaching of the Catholic Church; a new catechism of Christian doctrine.   L 1985, Catholic Truth Society.   49 p. £0.80. – ᴿClerR 71 (1986) 344-6 (F. J. *Selman*: eschews 'person' and 'soul').

5845 *Ocvirk* Drago K.,   La foi et le Credo; essai théologique sur l'appartenance chrétienne [diss. P. Inst. Cath., ᴰ*Lafon* G.]: CogF 131.   P 1986, Cerf. 174 p. – ᴿRTLv 17 (1986) 230s (E. *Brito*).

5846 **Oury** G.-M.,   Dictionnaire de la foi catholique.   Chambray 1986, C.L.D. 269 p.; 17 fig. F 150 [NRT 109,944].

5847 **Pagé** J.-G.,   La source; au cœur de la foi en Jésus-Christ.   Montréal 1985, Bellarmin.   434 p.; 9 pl. $20.   2-89007-589-3 [NTAbs 30,366].

5847* **Paul** Geoffrey bp.,   ᴱ*Williams* Roman,   A pattern of faith.   157 p. £6. 1-85093-037-6 [ExpTim 98,319].

5848 **Perkins** Pheme,   What we believe; a biblical catechism of the Apostle's Creed.   NY 1986, Paulist.   vi-134 p. $4 pa.   0-8091-2764-4 [NTAbs 31,115].

5849 *Pöltner* Günther,   Der Glaube als Grundvollzug menschlichen Daseins: TPQ 134 (1986) 254-264.

5850 **Rahner** Karl (*Krauss* M. intervista), La fatica di credere, ᵀ*Carrozzini* A.: Esperienze Verità 2.   Cinisello Balsamo 1986, EP.   126 p. Lit. 9000. – ᴿRasT 27 (1986) 189 (E. *Cattaneo*).

5851 **Reiser** William,   An unlikely catechism; some challenges for the creedless Catholic.   Mahwah NJ 1985, Paulist.   v-173 p. $7 pa. [TDig 33,485].

5852 **Sabugal** Santos,   Credo; la fe de la Iglesia; el símbolo de la fe, historia e interpretación.   Zamora 1986, Monte Casino.   xvii-1189 p.; bibliog. p. xv-xvii.   84-8640704-4.

5853 **Schwarz** Hans,   Responsible faith; Christian theology in the light of 20th-century questions.   Minneapolis 1986; Augsburg.   448 p. $24 [TDig 34.9].

5854 **Strange** Roderick,   The Catholic Faith.   Ox 1986, UP.   186 p. $12.50; pa. £4.   0-19-826685-5; 283051-1.   – ᴿExpTim 98 (1986s) 89 (A. *Lovegrove*; high praise).

5855 **Sutherland** Stewart R.,   God, Jesus, and belief; the legacy of theism 1984 → 1,7194: ᴿJTS 37 (1986) 282-4 (D. F. *Ford*).

5856 **Theissen** Gerd,   Biblical faith, an evolutionary approach 1984 → 65,6510; 1,7198: ᴿCurrTM 13 (1986) 52s (F. *Reklau*: seminal); JTS 37 (1986) 274-6 (T. S. M. *Williams*); RExp 83 (1986) 313-5 (E. C. *Rust* writes Thiessen; 'fascinating'); Themelios 11 (1985s) 102 (L. H. *Osborn*: capitulation to evolutionary categories, ultimately a denial of Christian faith).

5857 *Urban* Hans Jörg [*Vorster* Hans / *Motel* Hans B.], Das Bekenntnis der Alten Kirche und unser Bekennen heute — aus katholischer [evangelischer / freikirchlicher] Sicht: Catholica 40 (Münster 1986) 1-15 / 16-28 / 28-38.

5858 **Velasco** Rufino,   Réplica a Ratzinger, a propósito de su libro 'Informes sobre la fe': Testimonio 8.   Bilbao 1986, Desclée-B.   94 p. – ᴿLumenV 35 (1986) 564s (F. *Ortiz de Urtaran*).

5858* **Vives** Josep,   Creer el Credo [Creure el Credo]: Alcance 37.   Santander 1986, Sal Terrae.   223 p.   84-293-0746-X [ActuBbg 24,107, I. *Salvat*].

5859 **Wood** Maurice,   This is our faith.   L 1985, Hodder & S.   160 p. £2.   0-340-38602-9.   – ᴿExpTim 97 (1985s) 283 (G. T. *Eddy*: Anglican bishop of Norwich, against York and on p. 26 Durham, who should resign: 'thought, then, is for professors of theology; bishops should stick to belief').

5860 **Zo Tchúl-Hyún**, ❸ Kern des Glaubens im Neuen Testament: Sinhak Jonmang 71 (Kwangju 1985) 4-32; 72 (1986) 2-23 [TKontext 7/2,41; 8/1,51].

H6.6 *Peccatum NT – Sin, Evil* [➤ E1.9].

5861 *Arokiasamy* S., Sinful structures in the theology of sin: Vidyajyoti 49 (1985) 486-501.

5862 **Beisser** Friedrich, *Peters* Albrecht, Sünde und Sündenvergebung; der Schlüssel zu Luthers Theologie: Bekenntnisse, Fuldaer Hefte 26. Hannover c. 1985. 83 p. – ᴿZEvEth 30 (1986) 451s (G. *Wenz*).

5863 **Brandenburger** Egon, Das Böse; eine biblisch-theologische Studie: Theologische Studien 132. Z 1986, Theol.-V. 115 p. 3-290-17132-9.

5864 *Bunn* John T., Sin, iniquity, transgression; what is the difference?: BibIll 12 (1986) 77-79 [OTAbs 10,79].

5864* *a) Casas García* Victoriano, El misterio de la iniquidad en la sagrada Escritura; – *b) Martín Velasco* Juan, ... en el mundo de las religiones: VerVid 44 (1986) 359-381 / 343-358.

5865 *Coblenz* Katharina, Sünde und Vergebung in zwischenmenschlichen Beziehungen heute; ein Beitrag zum Verständnis von Sünde und Vergebung in der Beziehung zwischen Mann und Frau: TVers 16 (1986) 187-205.

5866 **Cooke** Bernard, Reconciled sinners; healing human brokenness. Mystic CT 1986, Twenty-Third. vii-109 p. $6 pa. [TDig 34,64].

5866* *Courtes* Joseph, Sémiotique et théologie du péché [en Occident influencée par plusieurs dualismes]: AuCAf 26 (1986) 212-252 [< TKontext 8/2,21].

5867 *Gesché* Adolphe, Topiques de la question du mal [i. contra Deum; ii. pro Deo; iii. in Deo; iv. ad Deum; v. cum Deo; Conclusion]: RTLv 17 (1986) 393-418; Eng. 544.

5868 **Häring** Hermann, Das Problem des Bösen in der Theologie: Grundzüge 62. Da 1985, Wiss. vi-212 p. DM 42 [TLZ 112,459, M. J. *Suda*].

5869 *Hendry* George S., Is sin obsolescent?: PrincSemB 7 (1986) 256 ... [< ZIT].

5870 **Kelly** Henry A., The devil at baptism 1985 ➤ 1,7208: ᴿTS 47 (1986) 711s [C. W. *Gusmer*: shows with F. DÖLGER that the baptism-exorcisms preceded AUGUSTINE's view of original sin]; Worship 60 (1986) 549s (L. J. *Mitchell*).

5871 **Krötke** Wolf, Ⓜ An 'impossible possibility' for man; thoughts about the Christian interpretation of sin with reference to Karl BARTH's teaching on sin, ᵀ*Karasszon* István: Theologiai Szemle 28 (1985) 94-98.

5872 *Mestrović* Stjepan J., Anomia and sin in DURKHEIM's thought: JScStR 24 (1985) 119-136.

5873 **Munera Duque** Alberto, Pecado personal desde el pecado original; estudio en autores recientes: diss. Bogotá 1983, Pont. Univ. Javeriana. 239 p. – ᴿCiuD 199 (1986) 139 (G. *Díaz*); Divinitas 30 (1986) 205s (C. *Petino*).

5874 *a) Nocke* Frans-Josef, Einladung zur Umkehr; zum Verständnis von Sünde und Busse im NT; – *b) Berg* Horst K., Sünde, das Leben verfehlen; Beobachtungen zu Texten des ATs: [ZP]RU 16 (Stu 1986) 137-140 / 132-6 [< ZIT].

5875 **Ramm** Bernard, Offense to reason; the theology of sin. SF 1985, Harper & R. xi-187 p. $16. – ᴿTS 47 (1986) 306-8 (R. M. *Gula*).

5876 *Ricœur* Paul, Le mal, un défi à la philosophie et à la théologie [conf. Lausanne 1985]: BCentProt 38,7 (1986) 13-45.

5877 **Sabugal** Santos, Pecado y reconciliación en el mensaje de Jesús 1985
➤ 1,7217: ᴿAngelicum 63 (1986) 508 (M. F. M.); BibFe 12 (1986) 137s (A.
Salas).

5877* **Schneider-Flume** G., Die Identität des Sünders [*Erikson* E.]. Gö 1985
[NedTTs 41,242, T. *Kruijne*].

5878 **Ssempungu** David W., Punishment of sin in Baganda traditional religion
and in Christianity; an anthropological and biblico-moral study: diss.
ᴰ*Cannon* S. R 1986, Alfonsiana. 104 p. – RTLv 18,580.

5879 **Stivers** Richard, Evil in modern myth and ritual 1982 ➤ 65,6524:
ᴿJAAR 54 (1986) 196 (R. *Detweiler*: too ambitious).

5880 *Vance* Robert L., Sin and consciousness of sin in SCHLEIERMACHER:
PerspRelSt 13 (1986) 241-262 [< ZIT].

H7 Soteriologia NT.

5881 **Bayer** Oswald, Aus Glauben leben; über Rechtfertigung und Heiligung.
Stu 1984, Calwer; 80 p. DM 9.80 [RelStR 13,58, J. J. *Buckley*].

5882 *Blank* David L., The etymology of salvation in GREGORY of Nyssa's De
Virginitate [not on the root of *sōtēría*, but 'a parallel between sin and
grammatical error', 'nature can only be recovered by reversing the steps of
the decline']: JTS 37 (1986) 77-90.

5883 *Bonnard* P., Conversation biblique avec Jean DELUMEAU [Le cas Luther
1983]: FoiVie 85,5 (1985) 77-81: for LUTHER, Paul thought God neither
vindictive nor indulgent [49-56, *Senft* C.].

5884 **Boyd** Stephen B., Pilgram MARPECK [c. 1495-1556] and the justice of
Christ: diss. Harvard... – HarvTR 79 (1986) 470s.

5885 **Carlos** Otto Federico de, La salvación como curación; el concepto de
salvación en la teología y en la predicación de P. TILLICH: diss. Comillas,
ᴰ*Álvarez Bolado* A. M 1982. – MiscCom 44 (1986) 567s.

5886 ᴱ*Catarsi* Carlo, Salute/salvezza, rassegna: Religioni e Società 1,1 (R
1986) 157... [< ZIT].

5887 **Cessario** Romanus, Christian satisfaction in AQUINAS; towards a personal
understanding 1982 ➤ 65,6532: ᴿScripTPamp 18 (1986) 294-8 (P. O'Callaghan).

5888 *Corliss* Richard L., Redemption and the divine realities; a study of HICK,
and an alternative: RelSt 22 (1986) 235-248.

5889 **Criswell** W. A., Soteriology [doctrinal sermons]: Great Doctrines of the
Bible 5. GR 1985, Zondervan. 154 p. $10 pa. – ᴿAndrUnS 24 (1986) 269s
(H. K. *LaRondelle*).

5890 **Davies** D. J., Meaning and salvation in religious studies: StHistRel 46.
Leiden 1984, Brill. viii-174 p. ƒ60 [NRT 109,911, J. *Scheuer*].

5891 **Dominy** Bert, God's work of salvation: Layman's Library of Christian
Doctrine 8. Nv 1986, Broadman. 170 p. $6. – ᴿSWJT 29,2 (1986s) 45s
(D. C. *George*).

5891* **Edwards** D., What are they saying about salvation? NY 1986, Paulist.
101 p. $5 [NRT 109, 139, A. *Toubeau*].

5892 **Findeis** Hans-Jürgen, Versöhnung – Apostolat – Kirche 1983
➤ 64,6905... 1,7425: ᴿBZ 30 (1986) 279s (M. *Theobald*).

5893 *Galot* Jean, a) Le Cœur de Jésus et le mystère de l'Incarnation
rédemptrice: EsprV 96 (1986) 322-8; – b) I paradossi dell'opera di
salvezza: CC 137 (1986,1) 535-548.

5895 **Gillis** Chester, A question of final belief: an analysis and critique of the
soteriology of John HICK: diss. ᴰ*Tracy* D. Chicago 1986. – RTLv 18,572.

5896 *a)* *Goldstein* Françoise, Yom Kippur; – *b)* *Blanchet* Jean, La réconciliation selon le Nouveau Testament: Tychique 64 (1986) 19-24 / 11-18.

5897 **Gorringe** Timothy, Redeeming time; atonement through education [redefined; really about redemption and the Kingdom]. L 1986, Darton-LT. 239 p. £7. 0-232-51701-0. – [R]ExpTim 98 (1986s) 161s (C. S. *Rodd*).

5898 **Hallonsten** Gösta, Satisfactio bei TERTULLIAN; Überprüfung einer Forschungstradition: StT 39, 1984 ➤ 65,6546; 1,7252: [R]ETL 62 (1986) 449s (A.-M. *Jonckheere*); Gnomon 58 (1986) 128-133 (G. *Quispel*); JTS 37 (1986) 212-4 (S. G. *Hall*).

5899 *Hamm* Berndt, Was ist [nicht gerade lutherische sondern] reformatorische Rechtfertigungsllehre?: ZTK 83 (1986) 1-38.

5900 **Heeler** David L., A relational view of the atonement; prolegomenon to a reconstruction of the doctrine: diss. Graduate Theol. Union. Berkeley 1984. – RTLv 18,572.

5901 **Heinz** Johann, Justification and merit; LUTHER vs. Catholicism: Andrews Univ. Diss. 8. Berrien 'Springs MI 1984, Andrews Univ. xi-451 p. $15. – [R]ChH 55 (1986) 373s (M. P. *Fleischer*).

5902 *Horne* Charles M., The doctrine of salvation (1971), [2]*Nevin* Paul. Ch 1984, Moody. 112 p. $5. – [R]GraceTJ 7 (1986) 256s (D. S. *Dockery*).

5903 **Kendall** R. T., Once saved, always saved. L 1983, Hodder & S. 162 p. £4.50. – [R]EvQ 58 (1986) 184-7 (A. *Torrance*).

5904 **Kettler** Christian D., The vicarious humanity of Christ and the reality of salvation: diss. Fuller Theol. Sem. [D]*Anderson* R. Pasadena 1986. 371 p. 86-19159. – DissA 47 (1986s) 2200-A.

5905 *Kirjavainen* Haikki, Die Paradoxie des Simul-Prinzips [simul justus et peccator]: NSys 28 (1986) 29-49; Eng. 50.

5906 **McDonald** H. D., The atonement of the death of Christ [➤ 1,7263] in faith, revelation and history. GR 1985, Baker. 317 p. $20. 0-8010-6194-6. – [R]EvJ 4 (1986) 29-36 (W. S. *Sailer*); ExpTim 98 (1986s) 120 (J. *McIntyre*: no less skill than he showed in his 'Theories of Revelation' c. 1967).

5907 *McGrath* Alister E., 'The article by which the Church stands or falls' [justification]: EvQ 58 (1986) 207-228.

5908 *Maimela* Simon S., The atonement in the context of liberation theology: IntRMiss 75 (Geneva 1986) 261-9.

5909 *Manaranche* André, Pour nous, les hommes; la Rédemption: Communio 1984 ➤ 65,6561; 1,7266; 2-213-01370-5: [R]Gregorianum 67 (1986) 163 (J. *Galot*).

5910 *Marra* Bruno, Per una fenomenologia dell'espiazione [rimorso... pentimento]: RasT 27 (1986) 63-74.

5911 *Martins Terra* J. E., Os mistérios da vida de Cristo e seu valor soteriológico: RCuBíb 10,37s (1986) 6-43.

5912 *Marx* Z., Continuiteit en discontinuiteit; twee modellen van verlossing: Ter Herkenning 47,3 (1986) 154-164 [or 14,3? < GereffTs 86,256].

5913 **Morris** Leon, The atonement; its meaning and significance 1983 ➤ 64,6926... 1,7270: [R]EvQ 58 (1986) 182s (H. *Bayer*).

5914 **Naduvilekut** James, Christus der Heilsweg; soteria als theodrama im Werk Urs von BALTHASARs: Diss. [D]*Hödl* L. Bochum 1986. 395 p. – RTLv 18,572.

5914* *Nkurunziza* Deusdedit R. K., A study of St. ANSELM's 'Cur Deus homo' and a critical evaluation of his theology of satisfaction: Chiea 2,2 (Nairobi 1986) 45-58 [< TKontext 8/2,13].

5915 **Oguro** Tatsuo, Der Rettungsgedanke bei Shinran und LUTHER; eine religionsvergleichende Untersuchung. Hildesheim 1985, Olms. 159 p. [Mundus 22,313].

5916 **Orazzo** Antonio, La salvezza in ILARIO di Poitiers; Cristo salvatore dell'uomo nei 'Tractatus super Psalmos'. N 1986, D'Auria. 196 p. Lit. 19.000. – ᴿHumBr 41 (1986) 945s (L. *Amerio*).

5916* **Peterson** Robert A., CALVIN's doctrine of the Atonement 1983 ➤ 65,6567; 1,7277: ᴿSTEv 9,17 (1986) 128s (P. *Bolognesi*).

5917 *a) Plevnik* Joseph, Recent developments in the discussion concerning justification by faith; – *b) Demson* David, 'Justification by faith', the canonical principle: TorTJ 2 (1986) 47-62 / 63-78.

5918 *Riquelme Otálora* José, La justificación en el ámbito de las relaciones humanas como campo del significado de purgare: Faventia 7,1 (1985) 47-73.

5919 **Rosenkranz** Raymond R., HEGEL's soteriology; a historical perspective: diss. Guelph., ᴰ*Amstutz* J., 1985. — DissA 47 (1986s) 550s-A.

5920 *Schwager* Raymund, Der Sohn Gottes und die Weltsünde; zur Erlösungslehre von Hans Urs von BALTHASAR: ZkT 108 (1986) 5-44.

5921 *Seils* Martin, Marginalien zur lutherischen Theologie heute: NSys 28 (1986) 111-123 [< ZeichZt 37 (1983) 302-7]; [different from universalistic trend of contemporary theology and from an inclusive Christology].

5922 *Shutte* Augustinus, How Jesus saves us [Rom...]: JTSAf 55 (1986) 3-14 [TKontext 8/1,19].

5923 **Sinsin** Bayo Jean, Le salut par la mort et la résurrection de Jésus-Christ dans la pensée de Christian DUQUOC: diss. cath. ᴰ*Wackenheim* C. Strasbourg 1986. – RTLv 18,572.

5924 **Söderlund** Rune, Ex praevisa fide; zum Verständnis der Prädestinationslehre in der lutherischen Orthodoxie: ArbGTL NF 3. Hannover 1983, Lutherisches-VH. 193 p. DM 29,80. – ᴿTLZ 111 (1986) 295-8 (J. *Rogge*).

5925 **Speidell** Todd S., The Incarnation as theological imperative for human reconciliation; a Christocentric social ethic: diss. Fuller Theol. Sem., ᴰ*Anderson* R. Pasadena 1986. 281 p. 86-19161. – DissA 47 (1986s) 2203-A.

5926 **Studer** Basil, Gott und unsere Erlösung im Glauben der Alten Kirche 1985 ➤ 1,7290: ᴿAugR 26 (1986) 588-591 (M. *Simonetti*); TR 82 (1986) 467-470 (W.-D. *Hauschild*); ZkT 108 (1986) 354s (L. *Lies*: parallel zu GRILLMEIER A., ANDRESEN C.).

5927 **Studer** Basil, Dio salvatore nei Padri della Chiesa; Trinità — cristologia — soteriologia. ᵀ*Gianotti* Daniele: Cultura Cristiana Antica. R 1986, Borla. 374 p. 88-263-0638-9.

5928 *Sundén* Hjalmar, Der psychologische Aspekt in der Rechtfertigung durch den Glauben: KerDo 32 (1986) 120-131; Eng. 131.

5929 **Tuttle** George M., So rich a soil; John McLeod CAMPBELL on Christian Atonement. E 1986, Handsel. 174 p. £10.50. 0-905312-47-3. – ᴿExpTim 98 (1986s) 251s (J. *McIntyre*).

5930 *Watt* J.G. van der, Loskoping deur Christus (*lutron* en sy derivate): NduitseGT 27 (1986) 178-190 [< GerefTTs 86,255].

5931 *Webster* J.B., Atonement, history and narrative: TZBas 42 (1986) 115-131.

5932 **Wenz** Gunther, Geschichte der Versöhnungslehre in der evangelischen Theologie der Neuzeit I. II. [Hab.-Diss.]: Mon. Hist. Syst. Theol. 9.11. Mü 1984/6, Kaiser. 476 p.; 493 p., DM 130. – ᴿTLZ 111 (1986) 67-70 [112, 380] (T. *Koppehl*).

5933 **Zalar** Djuro, Der Ernst der Liebe Gottes; die Soteriologie Romano GUARDINI's: Diss. Pont. Univ. Gregoriana, ᴰ*O'Collins* G. Roma 1986. 294 p.; Extr. N⁰ 3358, 147 p. – RTLv 18,573.

5933* *Ziegenaus* Anton, La filiación eterna de Jesucristo como fundamento del significado salvador del misterio de la vida del Señor: TierraN 14,56 (1986) 69-84.

5934 **Zumkeller** Adolar, Erbsünde, Gnade, Rechtfertigung und Verdienst nach der Lehre der Erfurter Augustinertheologen des Spätmittelalters: Cassicianum 35, 1984 ➔ 1,7295: ᴿTLZ 111 (1986) 291-3 (C. *Burger*: from his imposing list of already-published researches).

H7.2 *Crux, sacrificium* – The Cross.

5935 ᴱ**Boone** Elizabeth H., Ritual human sacrifice in Mesoamerica. Wsh 1984, Dumbarton Oaks. viii-247 p.; 37 fig.; map. – ᴿArchaeology 39,1 (1986) 69 (T. H. *Charlton*; text gives name as Elizabeth H. Benson).

5936 **Carrara** Alberto, Violenza, sacro, rivelazione biblica; il pensiero di René GIRARD: Mi 1985, ViPe. 154 p. Lit. 12.000. – ᴿHumBr 41 (1986) 454 (B. *Belletti*); Sapienza 39 (1986) 370s (anche B. *Belletti*).

5937 **Cozby** James A., Gnosis and the Cross; the Passion of Christ in Gnostic soteriology as reflected in the Nag Hammadi tractates: diss. Duke, ᴰ*Wintermute* O. Durham NC 1985. 386 p. 86-10304. – DissA 47 (1986s) 939s-A; RelStR 13,190.

5938 **Deneken** Michel, Le salut par la croix dans la théologie catholique contemporaine (1930-1985): diss. cath. ᴰ*Wackenheim* C. Strasbourg 1986. 419 p. – RTLv 18,571.

5939 *Domché* Étienne, La croix et le sacrifice de sanctification: ÉTRel 61 (1986) 251-6.

5940 **Fitzgerald** Georgina, The meaning of the death of Jesus in the later Christology of Edward SCHILLEBECKX: diss. Ottawa 1985. – RTLv 18,571.

5941 *Galvin* John P., The death of Jesus in contemporary theology; systematic perspectives and historical issues: Horizons 13 (1986) 239-252.

5942 **Girard** René, La route antique des hommes pervers [... Job, victim of his people]. P 1985, Grasset. 248 p. [RCuBíb 10/39s,132].

5943 *Girard* René, Das Ende der Gewalt — Analyse des Menschheitsverhängnisses 1983 1,7304: ᴿTPhil 61 (1986) 450-3 (P. *Knauer*: no easier to read than the original in dialogue form).

5944 **Henning** Lawrence H., The Cross and pastoral care [*Hunter* R. on *Moltmann*]: CurrTM 13 (1986) 22-29.

5945 *Heusch* Luc de, Sacrifice in Africa; a structural approach, ᵀ*O'Brien* Linda, *Morton* Alice. Bloomington 1985, Indiana Univ. vii-232 p. $22.50. ᴿHistRel 26 (1986s) 214-6 (*Manabu Waida*); JRel 66 (1986) 477-9 (E. T. *Gilday*).

5946 *Leites* Nathan, Le meurtre de Jésus moyen de salut?, ᵀ*Chazelle* A. 1982 ➔ 63,6910 ... 65,6607: ᴿScripTPamp 18 (1986) 382 (L. F. *Mateo-Seco*); TR 82 (1986) 211s (J. *Schmid*).

5947 **McGrath** A. E., LUTHER's theology of the Cross 1985 ➔ 1,7323: ᴿChH 55 (1986) 99s (Maria *Grossmann*); JRel 66 (1986) 440s (K. *Hagen*); JTS 37 (1986) 250-3 (G. *Yule*); NBlackf 67 (1986) 198s (B. *Drewery*); ScotJT 39 (1986) 410s (J. *Atkinson*).

5948 **Münsterer** Hanns O., Amulettkreuze und Kreuzamulette — Studien zur religiösen Volkskunde, ᴱ*Brauneck* Manfred. Rg 1983, Pustet. 243 p.: 71 fig. DM 68. – ᴿTrierTZ 95 (1986) 157 (E. *Sauser*).

5949 **Nshue Utwanga**, Esquisse d'une réflexion théologique sur l'interprétation sacrificielle de la mort rédemptrice de Jésus; essai d'approche exégétique sur le symbolisme du sang dans la pensée chrétienne: diss. ^{D}*Le Fort* P. Bru 1986. 753 p. – RTLv 18,572.

5950 *O'Callaghan* Paul, La mediación de Cristo en su pasión: ScripTPamp 18 (1986) 771-796; lat. 796s; Eng. 797s.

5951 *Orbe* Antonio, El sacrificio de la Nueva Ley según S. IRENEO (Adv. haer. IV, 17-18): Compostellanum 31 (1986) 7-62.

5952 *Peterson* Robert A., Christ's death as an example in the New Testament: → 65, ^{F}MACRAE Allan 1986, 135-8.

5953 *Rochat* François, La mort de Jésus; une erreur tactique? [*Haley* J.]: ÉTRel 61 (1986) 325-9.

5954 a) *Rognini* Giorgio, Al di là del sacrificio [*Girard* ...]; – b) *Grassi* Piergiorgio, René GIRARD; la violenza, il sacro e il kerygma: Hermeneutica 5 (Urbino 1985) 79-114 / 65-78.

5954* *Rosa* Jean-Pierre, Per una lettura non sacrificale di René GIRARD: NuovaUm 8,44 (1986) 73-96.

5955 *Schwager* R., Der Tod Christi und die Opferkritik [< Semeia 33]: TGegw 29 (1986) 11-20.

5956 *Stetkevych* Suzanne P., Ritual and sacrificial elements in the poetry of blood-vengeance; two poems by Durayd ibn al-Simmah and Muhalhil ibn Rabīah: JNES 45 (1986) 31-43.

5957 **Stott** John, The Cross of Christ. Leicester 1986, Inter-Varsity. 383 p.; bibliog. p. 352-363. £10; pa. £6. 0-85110-638-2; 767-2 [ExpTim 98, 286].

5958 **Thachil** José, The Vedic and the Christian concept of sacrifice. Alwaye 1985, Pontifical Inst. 363 p. xxii-363 p. $12. – ^{R}JDharma 11 (1986) 307s (M. *Mundadan*).

5959 **Varone** François, Ce Dieu censé aimer la souffrance 1984 → 65,6615; 1,7336: ^{R}EstE 61 (1986) 100s (J. A. *Estrada*); ScEspr 38 (1986) 138-140 (J.-M. *Archimbault*); VSp 139 (1985) 700 (H. *Ponsot*).

5960 **Wallace** Ronald S., The atoning death of Christ: Foundations for faith → 63,6924; also L 1981, Marshall-MS. xii-147 p. £5. – ^{R}EvQ 58 (1986) 89s (R. *Bauckham*: not the usual clichés).

5961 a) *Weiser* Alfons, Der Tod Jesu und das Heil der Menschen; – b) *Merklein* Helmut, Der Tod Jesu als stellvertretender Sühnetod; – c) *Hossfeld* Frank-L., Versöhnung und Sühne; – d) *Breuning* Wilhelm, Wie kann man heute von 'Sühne' reden?: BiKi 41,2 (1986) 60-67 / 68-75 / 54-59 / 76-82.

5962 **Will** James E., Passion as tragedy; the problem of redemptive suffering in the Passion: diss. Claremont 1985. – RelStR 13,188.

H7.4 Sacramenta, Gratia.

5963 *Arnold* John, Usus sacrae Scripturae in Paenitentiali Cummeani: Periodica 75 (R 1986) 447-466.

5964 **Austin** Gerard, Anointing with the Spirit; the rite of confirmation, the use of oil and chrism. NY 1985, Pueblo. xiii-178 p. $10. – ^{R}TS 47 (1986) 558 (Prudence M. *Croke*: merits implementation).

5965 *Badham* Paul, A critique of the Lima report: ExpTim 97 (1985s) 294-8.

5966 **Barth** Gerhard, Die Taufe in frühchristlicher Zeit: BibTSt 4. Neuk 1986, Neuk.-V. 151 p. [RelStTR 13,72, R. H. *Fuller*].

5967 **Barth** Gerhard, El bautismo en el tiempo del cristianismo primitivo, T*Ruiz-Garrido* C.: BiblEstB 60. Salamanca 1986, Sígueme. 171 p. [Ci-Tom 113,622].

5968 *Békefi* Lajos, Ⓜ Reconciliation and penitence in the mission of the Church; what happened at the Sixth Synod of Bishops? [Rome 1983; Cardinal MARTINI's *vitainditó* (provocative) presentation; ... Hungarian interventions]: Theologiai Szemle 29 (1986) [... 30,49-53].

5969 *Békési* Andor, Ⓜ The benefit of the sacraments according to CALVIN: Theologiai Szemle 29 (1986) 70-77.

5970 *Bellai* Zoltán, Ⓜ Baptism in the Reformed Church in Hungary viewed in the light of the Lima Document: Theologiai Szemle 28 (1985) 85-89.

5971 *a) Biffi* Inos, Fede e comunione sacramentale (Aspetto teologico — punto di vista occidentale); – *b) Valdman* Traian, ... (orientale): Nicolaus 12 (1985) 257-266 / 267-282 [< ZIT].

5972 *Blei* Karel, De receptie van de Lima-tekst over doop, eucharistie en ambt in Nederland: NedTTs 40 (1986) 14-43; Eng. 43 [... 'whether the own tradition could fit'].

5973 **Bourgeois** Henri, On becoming Christian; Christian initiation and its sacraments. Mystic CT 1985, Twenty-Third. 153 p. $7 [JAAR 54,397].

5974 **Browning** Robert L., *Reed* Roy A., The sacraments in religious education and liturgy; an ecumenical model. Birmingham AL 1985, Religious Education. x-313 p. $15 pa. – RHorizons 13 (1986) 433s (R. A. *Duffy*); TTod 43 (1986s) 114-6 (D. *Ng*).

5975 **Burnish** Raymond, The meaning of baptism — a comparison of the teaching and practice of the fourth century with the present day. L 1986, SPCK (for Alcuin Club). xv-240 p. £10.50. 0-281-04200-4. – RExpTim 98 (1986s) 123 [from this page on in larger type] (K. W. *Clements*: significant, 'ecuminical'); TLond 39 (1986) 314s (E. *Yarnold*).

5976 **Carpin** A., Il battesimo in ISIDORO di Siviglia [diss. R, Pont. Univ. Greg.] 1984 ➤ 1,7351; 231 p.; RSalmanticensis 33 (1986) 139-141 (D. *Borobio*).

5977 *Carpin* Attilio, La confermazione in san Tommaso d'AQUINO; l'apporto della tradizione: SacDoc 31,3s (1986) 247-463.

5978 *Clerck* Paul de, La dissociation du baptême et de la confirmation au haut Moyen Âge: MaisD 168 (1986) 47-75.

5979 *Dacquino* Pietro, Storia del matrimonio cristiano alla luce della Bibbia 1984 ➤ 65,6629; 1,7355: RHumBr 41 (1986) 620 (A. *Biazzi*); Salesianum 48 (1986) 437-440 (A. M. *Triacca*: non tutto negativo). ➤ 1572.

5980 *Demmer* Klaus, Vergebung empfangen und der Versöhnung dienen; Überlegungen zur Berufung des Christen auf dem Feld des Ethos: Gregorianum 67 (1986) 235-262; ital. 263.

5981 *a) Díez* Florentino, El bautismo; praxis en las religiones primitiva [iniciación: Australia, África, América; ... Eleusis]; – *b) Cañellas* Gabriel, praxis en el judaísmo bíblico [... Qumran, Juan]; – *c) Iriarte* María Eugenia, ... experiencia mesiánica de Jesús; – *d) Manrique* Andrés, ... praxis en el cristianismo naciente; – *e) Folgado* Segundo, ... experiencia de muerte; – *f) Casas* Victoriano, ... experiencia de vida; – *g) Salas* Antonio, ... experiencia de resurrección [... Pastoral; Bibliografía]: Biblia y Fe 12,34 (1986) 5-19 / 20-31 / 32-46 / 47-59 / 60-73 / 74-92 / 93-108 [109-127 / 128-130].

5982 **Falsini** Rinaldo, L'iniziazione cristiana e i suoi sacramenti. Mi 1986, OR. 272 p. Lit. 15.000. – RCC 137 (1986,3) 196s (G. *Ferraro*).

5983 *Gervais* P., [JEAN-PAUL II], L'exhortation apostolique 'Reconciliatio et paenitentia' [2.XII.1984]: NRT 108 (1986) 192-217.

5984 *Girault* René, L'œcuménisme en marche; la 'réception' du 'BEM' en
France: Études 364 (1986) 253-266.
5984* **Guillet** Jacques, De Jésus aux sacrements: CahÉv 57. P 1986, Cerf.
68 p. F 22. 0222-9714.
5985 **Hassab Alla** Waheed, Le baptême des enfants dans la tradition de
l'Église Copte d'Alexandrie: diss. 1985 ➤ 1,7367: ᴿFreibZ 33 (1986) 276
(G. *Bavaud*); Gregorianum 67 (1986) 96 (E. *Farahian*).
5986 *Klauck* H.-J., Die Sakramente und der historische Jesus: WissWeish 47
(1984) 1-11.
5987 **Knoch** Wendelin, Die Einsetzung der Sakramente durch Christus 1983
➤ 65,6643; 1,7372; 3-402-03919-2: ᴿGregorianum 67 (1986) 155s (Z.
Alszeghy).
5988 *Lies* Lothar, Kultmysterium heute — Modell sakramentaler Begegnung;
Rückschau und Vorschau auf Odo CASEL [1888-1948]: ArLtgW 28 (1986)
2-21 [26-42, *Häussling* A., Bibliog. Casel 1967-1985]; 357-395, Häussling;
Meyer H.-B.
5989 **Limouris** G., *Vaporis* N. M., Orthodox perspectives on Baptism,
Eucharist and Ministry: Faith and Order 128. Brookline MA 1985, Holy
Cross Orthodox. 168 p. – ᴿOstSt 35 (1986) 341-4 (H. M. *Biedermann*).
5990 *Longeat* J. P., Les rites du baptême dans les homélies catéchétiques de
THÉODORE de Mopsueste: QLtg 66 (1985) 193-202 [81-95].
5991 *Louth* Andrew, Pagan theurgy and Christian sacramentalism in DENYS
the Areopagite: JTS 37 (1986) 432-8.
5992 *Lukken* Gerard, Semiotische analyse van de schuldbelijdenis aan het
begin van de Eucharistieviering: Bijdragen 47 (1986) 290-316; 317, Analyse
sémiotique de la confession des péchés au commencement de la célébration
eucharistique [possibilités: i. distance/proximité; ii. self-centered/
finality-centered; iii. for the reader to discover].
5993 *Maccarone* Michele, L'unité du baptême et de la confirmation dans la
liturgie romaine du IIIᵉ au VIIᵉ siècle, ᵀ*Delmotte* M.: Istina 31 (1986)
259-272.
5994 *MacMillan* J. Douglas, [Baptism of] The children for Christ; his covenant
seed and their covenant sign: ➤ 111, ᶠSTILL W., Pulpit & people 1986,
117-129.
5995 *Medisch* Richard, Kirchliches Amt und Eucharistie [BEM ...]: TGegw 23
(1985) 182-9.
5996 **Myers** Edward P., A study of baptism in the first three centuries: diss.
Drew. Madison NJ 1985. – RelStR 13,188.
5997 **Nardi** Carlo, Il battesimo in CLEMENTE Alessandrino 1984 ➤ 1,7381:
ᴿSalesianum 48 (1986) 445s (A. M. *Triacca*).
5998 *a)* Pannenberg Wolfhart, Christsein und Taufe: – *b)* *Butterworth* Julia K.,
Ordained to what? Ordiniert wozu?: ➤ 78*, ᶠMUND H., Um die eine
Kirche 1984, 58-65 / 44-50.
5999 **Rocchetta** Carlo, I sacramenti della fede; saggio di teologia biblica sui
sacramenti quali 'meraviglia della salvezza' nel tempo della Chiesa 1982
➤ 64,7040; 1,7385: ᴿEfMex 4,10 (1986) 136-140 (F. *González Díaz*).
6000 *Sala* Giovanni B., Von den Schwierigkeiten der Beichte heute: ForumKT
2 (1986) 281-297.
6001 *Salachas* Dimitri, Les Sacrements de l'initiation chrétienne dans la
tradition de l'Église catholique-romaine et de l'Église orthodoxe: Angelicum 63 (1986) 187-212.
6002 **Salij** Jacek [cf. ➤ 63,6977], ❷ Główne kontrowersje teologiczne wokół
komunii niemowląt (Le principali controversie teologiche a proposito

della comunione degli infanti). Wsz 1982, Akademia Teologii Katolickiej. 264 p. – RAntonianum 63 (1986) 318s (E. *Kaczyński*).

6003 **Schmitt** E., Le mariage chrétien dans l'œuvre de Saint AUGUSTIN; une théologie baptismale de la vie conjugale 1983 ➤ 65,6670: RSalmanticensis 33 (1986) 135-7 (F. R. *Aznar Gil*).

6004 **Smith** Martin L., Reconciliation; preparing for confession in the Episcopal Church. CM 1985, Cowley. 121 p. $9 pa. [TDig 34,92].

6005 *Spölgen* Johannes, 'Sollen wir unser Kind taufen lassen?' — Kirchendistanz und Taufaufschub; Anfragen und Impulse zur Kindertaufpraxis: KatBlätt 111 (Mü 1986) 204-210 [< ZIT].

6006 EThurian Max, Churches respond to BEM, I. 1986; II. 1986: Faith and Order Paper 129, 132. Geneva 1986, WCC. vi-129 p.; vii-348 p. Fs 15 + 29,50 [NRT 109,761, A. *Toubeau*].

6007 EThurian M., *Wainwright* G., Baptism and Eucharist; ecumenical convergences in celebration. Geneva/GR 1983, WCC / Eerdmans. ix-258 p. $10 / £2.25. – RNRT 108 (1986) 127s (A. *Toubeau*).

6008 **Toinet** Paul, Au commencement la famille; le sacrement de mariage: Théologie nouvelle 7. P 1985, FAC. 347 p. – RScEspr 38 (1986) 245-256 (M. *Lefebvre* offre des alternatives à cette agressivité polémique).

6008* *Vanhoye* Albert, Baptême et offrande: Prier et servir (1986) 297-313.

6009 **Vela** J. A., Reiniciación cristiana; respuesta a un bautismo 'sociológico': diss. Pont. Univ. Gregoriana. R 1984. 393 p. [Stromata 42,409].

6010 **Werbick** Jürgen, Schulderfahrung und Busssakrament. Mainz 1985, Grünewald. 172 p. DM 26,80. – RMüTZ 37 (1986) 138s (G. *Wenz*).

6011 **White** James F., Sacraments as God's self-giving. Nv 1983, Abingdon. 158 p. $9. – RHeythJ 27 (1986) 350s (Mary *Grey*).

6012 **Zerndl** Josef, Die Theologie der Firmung in der Vorbereitung und in den Akten des Zweiten Vatikanischen Konzils [diss. R, Pont. Univ. Gregoriana]: KkKSt 49. Pd 1986, Bonifatius. cxiv-454 p. DM 48 [TR 83,230, A. *Adam*).

H7.6 *Ecclesiologia, theologia missionis, laici* – The Church.

EAlberigo G. *Jossua* J., Il Vaticano II e la Chiesa 1985 ➤ 274*.

6014 **Alston** Wallace M.J, The Church: Guides to the Reformed Tradition 1984 ➤ 65,6682; 1,7401: RRExp 83 (1986) 331 (B. J. *Leonard*).

6015 *Álvarez-Suárez* Aniano, La eclesiología de la 'Redemptor Hominis' de JUAN PABLO II: Teresianum 37 (1986) 375-39.

6016 *Amaladoss* Michael, Dialogue and mission; conflict or convergence: IntRMiss 75 (Geneva 1986) 222-241.

6017 [Carlos] **Araújo Luiz**, Profecia e poder na Igreja. São Paulo 1986, Paulinas. 72 p. [REB 46,722].

6018 **Auer** Johann, Die Kirche — das allgemeine Heilssakrament: Kleine kath. Dogmatik 8, 1983 ➤ 64,7051... 1, 7404: – RFreibRu 37s (1985s) 99 (C. *Thoma*).

6019 **Auer** Johann, La Iglesia, ssacramento universal de salvación [1983 ➤ 64,7051], TGancho Claudio: Curso de Teología Dogmática 8. Barc 1986, Herder. 496 p. pt. 2650. 84-254-1467-9. – RActuBbg 23 (1986) 235 (I. *Riudor*).

6020 **Avis** Paul D. L., The Church in the theology of the Reformers 1981 ➤ 62,7737... 65,6689: REvQ 58 (1986) 91-93 (G. S. S. *Yule*).

6021 **Baier** Walter, Die Kirche als Fortsetzung des Wirkens Christi; Untersuchungen zu Leben und Werk und zur Ekklesiologie des

Münsteraner Dogmatikers Anton BERLAGE (1805-81) 1984 ➤ 1,7407: RTPQ 134 (1986) 85s (R. *Schulte*); ZkT 108 (1986) 104s (W. *Kern*).

6022 **Balthasar** Hans Urs von, The office of Peter and the structure of the Church [Der antirömische Affekt 1974 ➤ 56,4226], TEmery Andrée. SF 1986, Ignatius. 358 p. $13 [RelStR 13,333, J. *Ford*: 'the current papacy' and other allusions are outdated].

6023 **Barrett** C. K., Church, ministry and sacraments in the New Testament Exeter/GR 1985, Paternoster/Eerdmans. 110 p. £3. 0-85364-406-3. – RExpTim 97 (1985s) 309s (H. B. *Green*: controversial only on sacraments; '1 Cor 1 depreciates baptism'); TTod 43 (1986s) 135s (R. *Kress*).

6024 **Beeck** Frans J. van, Catholic identity after Vatican II; three types of faith in the one Church [Cody chair inaugural]. Ch 1985, Loyola Univ. XI-113 p. $10 [TDig 3,353].

6025 *Betti* Umberto, Chiesa di Cristo e Chiesa Cattolica; a proposito di un'espressione della 'Lumen Gentium': Antonianum 61 (1986) 726-745.

6026 *Beyer* J., Principe de subsidiarité ou 'juste autonomie' dans l'Église: NRT 108 (1986) 801-822.

6027 *Boff* Clodovis, Eine Kirche in Bewegung; biblische Grundlagen der Basisgemenden: EvKomm 19 (1986) 640-644.

6028 **Boff** Leonardo, E a Igreja se fez povo; Eclesiogênese; a Igreja que nasce da Fé do Povo. Petrópolis 1986, Vozes. 200 p. – RREB 46 (1986) 462-5 (E. *Ferreira Alves*).

6029 **Boff** Leonardo, Church, charism and power; liberation theology and the institutional Church [1981 ➤ 63,6994], TDiercksmeier J. W., 1985 ➤ 1, 7413: RHorizons 13 (1986) 180s (B. *Cooke* sees why RATZINGER is uneasy, and has his own perhaps different objections); JAAR 54 (1986) 347s (R. *Haight*); TLond 39 (1986) 307s (K. *Leech*); TS 47 (1985) 155-7 (J. P. *Hogan*).

6030 **Boff** Leonardo, Ecclesiogenesis; the base communities reinvent the Church [1977], TBarr Robert R. [➤ 1,7417] Maryknoll NY 1986, Orbis. 115 p. $10. – RThemelios 12 (1986s) 68 (W. T. *McConnell*): TierraN 14,54 (1985) 69-73 (J. *Böckmann*).

6031 *Bowe* Paul / *Regan* David, [Ireland] A church in need of conversion: DoctLife 35 (1986) 384-391 / 555-560.

6032 *Calvo Cortés* A., *Ruiz Díaz* A., Para leer una eclesiología elemental ['BUP']. Estella 1986, VDivino. 185 p. – RNatGrac 33 (1986) 567s (G. *Rodríguez*).

6033 **Canobbio** Giacomo, Si può ancora parlare di laici e di laicato?: RClerIt 67 (1986) 215-224.

6034 **Castro** Emilio, Sent free; mission and unity in the perspective of the Kingdom. GR 1985, Eerdmans. 102 p. $6 [JAAR 54,208].

6034* *Chang* Aloysius B., Ministry of the Pope and the communion of the Catholic Church [... Jin Luxian]: Tripod 36 (1986) 54-74 [Zusammenfassung, TKontext 8/2,106, G. *Evers*].

6035 **Ciola** Nicola, Il dibattito ecclesiologico in Italia; uno studio bibliografico (1963-1984). R 1986, Pont. Univ. Lateranense. 263 p. – RScripTPamp 18 (1986) 997 (J. R. *Villar*).

6036 *Citrini* Tullio, Ecclesiologia e trattato sull'ordine: ScuolC 114,5 ('L'insegnamento dei trattati teologici' 1986) 587-600.

6037 **Collet** Giancarlo, Das Missionsverständnis der Kirche in der gegenwärtigen Diskussion: TüTheolSt 24, 1984 ➤ 1,7429: RColcT 56,1 (1986) 168-170 (W. *Kowalak*); NRT 108 (1986) 927s (J. *Masson*);

NZMissW 42 (1986) 140-2 (F. *Frei*); TGegw 29 (1986) 185s (J. *Aussermair*); ZkT 108 (1986) 77-79 (K. *Piskaty*).

6038 *Colzani* Gianni,   L'ora della missione mondiale; senso e problemi di un mutamento [... la missione e una concezione 'pneumatica' della storia, e la crisi della cristologia; La missione di Gesù, spunti biblici ... Dall'egemonia alla comunione]: ScuolC 114 (1986) 677-715.

6038* **Comblin** J.,   A Igreja e sua missão no mundo.   São Paulo, Paulinas. 336 p. [REB 46,228].

6039 **Conser** Walter H.[J],   Church and confession; conservative theologians in Germany, England and America, 1815-1866.   Atlanta 1984, Mercer Univ. viii-361 p. $29. – [R]CurrTM 13 (1986) 46s (M. *Root*: biographical rather than theological sketches of leaders tinged with romanticism).

6040 *Crichton* J. D.,   Recusant writers on the priesthood of the laity [*Dymock* J. ...]: CleR 71 (1986) 455-7.

6040* **Cunningham** Lawrence S.,   The Catholic experience... NY 1985, Crossroad. 270 p. $17 [Horizons 14,387, A. *Dulles*].

6041 **Czyz** Paweł,   Il rapporto tra la dimensione cristologica e pneumatologica dell'ecclesiologia nel pensiero di Y. CONGAR: diss. Pont. Univ. Gregoriana, [D]*Békés* G.   R 1986. Extr. N⁰ 3322; v-163 p. – RTLv 18,568.

6042 *De Rosa* Giuseppe,   Istituzione e carisma nella Chiesa [CONGAR Y. 1985]: CC 137 (1986,1) 351-9.

6043 **Descy** Serge,   Introduction à l'histoire et à l'ecclésiologie de l'Église melkite.   Beyrouth 1986, St.-Paul. 126 p. – [R]ÖkRu 35 (1986) 483-5 (F. *Heyer*).

6044 **Dianich** Severino,   Chiesa in missione; per una ecclesiologia dinamica. Mi 1985, Paoline. 315 p. Lit. 15.000.

6045 **Dietrich** Wendell S.,   Christ and the Church, according to BARTH and some of his Roman Catholic critics: diss. Yale 1960! 277 p. 86-26783. – DissA 47 (1986s) 3080-A.

6046 *Dulles* Avery,   Catholic Ecclesiology since the second Vatican council: Concilium 188 (1986) [deutsch IZT 22 (1986) 412-9, [T]*Debe* Astrid; español 208 (Nov. 1986) 321-335, [T]*Valente Malla* J.].

6047 *Dulles* Avery,   Community of disciples as a model of Church: Philosophy Theology 1,2 (Milwaukee 1986) 99-120.

6048 **Dulles** A., *Granfield* P.,   The Church, a bibliography 1985 → 1,1056: [R]TS 47 (1986) 712-715 (M. A. *Fahey*: for specialists too, with lacunas).

6049 **Dyrness** William A.,   Let the earth rejoice; a biblical theology of holistic mission 1983 → 64,7074; 1,7448: [R]IntRMiss 75 (Geneva 1986) 87-89 (H. *Rowold*).

6050 **Edge** Findley B.,   The doctrine of the Laity. Nv 1985, Southern Baptist Convention. 156 p. – [R]RExp 83 (1986) 332s (W. M. *Johnson*: exciting).

6051 **Estrada** J. A.,   La Iglesia; identidad y cambio; el concepto de Iglesia del Vaticano I a nuestros días 1985 → 1,7452: [R]Burgense 27 (1986) 571-3 [N. *López Martínez*].

6051* [E]**Eyt** Pierre,   Thèmes choisis d'ecclésiologie; rapport de la Commission théologique internationale.   P 1985, Centurion.   73 p. – [R]RICathP 19 (1986) 121-4 (M. *Vidal*).

6052 **Faivre** Alexandre,   Les laïcs aux origines de l'Église 1984 → 65,6725; 1,7454; F 124: 2-227-32100-8: [R]Bijdragen 47 (1986) 74s (M. *Parmentier*, Eng.: 'lay people' are a third-century invention; including women, fourth century; silenced as in our days, fifth century).

6053 *Faivre* Alexandre,   Naissance d'un laïcat chrétien; les enjeux d'un mot: FreibZ 33 (1986) 391-429.

6054 **Figura** Michael, Das Kirchenverständnis des HILARIUS von Poitiers: FreibTSt 127. FrB 1984, Herder. 382 p. DM 98. – ᴿJbAC 29 (1986) 200-209 (M. *Durst*).

6055 **Forte** Bruno, L'Église, icone de la Trinité; brève ecclésiologie [1983]. P 1985, Médiaspaul. 107 p. – ᴿEsprV 96 (1986) 12-14 (P. *Jay*).

6056 **French** Henry F., The concept of the Church in the theology of Walter RAUSCHENBUSCH: diss. Drew. Madison NJ 1985. – RelStR 13,188.

6057 *Frost* Francis, Les laïcs dans l'Anglicanisme [conférence Paris 1986]: MélSR 43 (1986) 145-155; Eng. 155.

6058 **Galanis** Spyridon, La conception de l'Église dans la pensée théologique et les mouvements religieux en Grèce de 1830 à nos jours: diss. cath. ᴰ*Wackenheim* C. Strasbourg 1986. 440 p. – RTLv 18,568.

6059 ᴱ**Gandolfo** Giuliana, Martin LUTERO, Prediche sulla Chiesa e lo Spirito Santo: Testi della Riforma 12. T 1984, Claudiana. 182 p. – ᴿTeresianum 37 (1986) 234 (E. *Pacho*).

6060 *García Lomas* Santiago, La figura teológica y eclesiológica del laico: SalT 73,3 ('Por una desclericalización de la Iglesia' 1985) 205-217.

6061 *García Roca* Joaquín, La presencia de los cristianos en el mundo [... Aproximación al imaginario social del concilio: < Misión abierta 78 (1985) 239-249; 'extra mundum nulla salus', SCHILLEBEECKX], ᵀᴱ*Casas* Josep: SelT 25 (1986) 308-315.

6062 *Gherardini* Brunero, '... Senza macchia e senza ruga' (Ef 5,27): Divinitas 30 (1986) 111-119.

6063 a) *Giustiniani* Pasquale, Laicità come stile di Chiesa; – b) *Cavedo* Romeo, Gesù 'laico'; – c) *Dacquino* Pietro, Il sacerdozio del nuovo popolo di Dio; – d) *Mosetto* Francesco, 'Voi siete il sale della terra'...: ParVi 31 (1986) 404-8 / 409-415 / 416-425 / 426-434.

6064 *Glorieux* Achille, Les étapes préliminaires de la Constitution pastorale 'Gaudium et spes' [Vat. II sur l'Église]: NRT 108 (1986) 388-403.

6065 *González Faus* José Ignacio, Para una reforma evangélica de la Iglesia: RCatalT 11 (1986) 31-67.

6066 **González Ruiz** José M., La Iglesia a la intemperie; reflexiones postmodernas... Santander 1986, Sal Terrae. 213 p. – ᴿRazF 214 (1986) 361 (R. de *Andrés*).

6067 *Grootaers* J., Peuple de Dieu: ⇥ 578, Catholicisme XI,49 (1986) 98-121.

6068 **Grossi** Vittorino, *Di Berardino* Angelo, La Chiesa antica; ecclesiologia e istituzione 1984 ⇥ 65,6743; 1,7471: ᴿAugR 26 (1986) 585s (E. *Peretto*).

6069 **Grossi** Vittorino, Per una rilettura di S. AGOSTINO sulle relazioni Chiesa-mondo: RasT 27 (1986) 497-515.

6070 **Guder** Darell L., Be my witnesses; the Church's mission, message and messengers. GR 1985, Eerdmans. xiv-237 p. $11 pa. – ᴿTDig 33 (1986) 473 (W. C. *Heiser*).

6071 **Halton** Thomas, The Church: Message of the Fathers, 1985 ⇥ 1,7476: ᴿRelStT 6 (1986) 41s (C. C. *Hefling*); RExp 83 (1986) 331 (B. J. *Leonard*).

6072 **Hanson** P. D., The people called; the growth of community in the Bible [mostly OT: Gn 12-39; Ex 1-15.19-23 ... Dan, Mcb; Jesus Mt-Mk-Lk; the nascent Church, Mt Jn Jas Tim Lk-Acts]. SF 1986, Harper & R. xii-564 p. $32. 0-06-063700-5 [NTAbs 31,112].

6073 **Harrington** D. J., Light of all nations... Church in NT research 1982 ⇥ 63,215; 64,7089: ᴿDoctLife 36 (1986) 163s (W. G. *Jeanrond*).

6074 **Heiser** Lothar, Das Glaubenszeugnis der armenischen Kirche: Sophia 22. Trier 1983, Paulinus. 313 p.; ill. DM 48. – ᴿOstkSt 35 (1986) 346-8 (R. *Freudenberger*); TrierTZ 95 (1986) 67s (E. *Sauser*).

6075 *a*) *Hendrickx* Herman, The people of God in Holy Scripture: – *b*) *Nicolas* Adolfo, The laity in the life and mission of the Church; theological reflection; – *c*) *Coyle* Kathleen, Women in the Church; – *d*) Bibliography on laity and ministry: EAPast 23 (1986) 210-230 / 265-294 / 256-264 / 372-381.

6076 ᵀᴱ**Hinson** E.Glenn, [Patristic] Understandings of the Church. Ph 1986, Fortress. 128 p. $7 [RelStR 13,353, G. S. *Heyer*].

6077 **Höhn** Hans-Joachim, Kirche und kommunikatives Handeln ...Sozialtheorien Niklas LUHMANNs und Jürgen HABERMAS' [Diss. FrB]: FraThSt, 32. Fra 1985, Knecht. 298 p. DM 58. – ᴿTGl 76 (1986) 359s (W. *Beinert*).

6078 *Honecker* Martin, Geschichtliche Schuld [der Kirche] und kirchliches Bekenntnis; die sogenannte Stuttgarter Schulderklärung [1945; *Sauter* G. 1945 ...]: TZBas 42 (1986) 132-158.

6079 **Horst** Ulrich, Zwischen Konziliarismus ind Reformation; Studien zur Ekklesiologie im Dominikanerorden: DissHist 22. R 1985, Ist. Storico Domenicano. 189 p. – ᴿTR 82 (1986) 298s (R. *Bäumer*).

6080 **Houtepen** Anton, People of God, a plea for the Church, ᵀ*Bowden* J., 1984 ➤ 65,6750; 1,7484: ᴿRAfrT 10,19 (1986) 155s (A. *Vanneste*).

6081 **Hunter** Victor L., *Johnson* Phillip, The human Church in the presence of Christ. Macon GA 1985, Mercer Univ. 180 p. $15.50. – ᴿRExp 83 (1986) 500s (F. B. *Edge*).

6082 *Junghans* Helmar, Die Schäflein, die ihres Hirten Stimme hören; Verkündigung, Glaube und Leben in LUTHERs Beschreibung der Kirche: Luther 57 (Wu 1986) 19-34.

6083 *Kelly* Robert A., The suffering Church; a study of LUTHER's Theologia Crucis: ConcordTQ 50 (Fort Wayne 1986) 3-18.

6084 *Kern* Udo, Die durch Barmen definierte Zweireichelehre: TZBas 42 (1986) 237-254: ideales und reales Instrumentarium um Christ, Kirche, und Welt zu bestimmen.

6085 *Kolvenbach* Peter-Hans, La dimensión universal de la Iglesia [conferencia Köln 1985], ᵀ*Alcalá* M.: RazF 213 (1986) 63-73.

6086 **Kress** Robert, The Church; communion, sacrament, communication 1985 ➤ 1,7494: ᴿHorizons 13 (1986) 431s (B. *Cooke*: the power remains with management); SpTod 38 (1986) 283s (Marie S. *Reges*); TS 47 (1986) 534s (P. *Chirico*).

6087 *Laney* J. Carl, The biblical practice of Church discipline ['confrontive measures regarding a sin in the life of a believer' recently publicized by lawsuits against the pastor]: BS 143 (1986) 353-364.

6088 *Leisching* Peter, Teilhabe der Laien am dreifachen Amt Christi — ein zu realisierendes Programm: TBer 15 (1986) 39-82 [< ZIT].

6089 **Löser** W., Die RK Kirche: Kirchen der Welt. Fra 1986, Ev.-V. 455 p. – ᴿÖkRu 35 (1986) 482s (E. *Fahlbusch*).

6090 **Lohfink** Gerhard, Wie hat Jesus Gemeinde gewollt? 1982 ➤ 63,5118 ... 1,7505: TLZ 111 (1986) 24-27 (G. *Strecker*).

6091 **Lohfink** Gerhard, L'Église que voulait Jésus 1985 ➤ 1,7506; 2-204-02340-X: ᴿActuBbg 23 (1986) 43-49 (J. *Boada*); ComSev 19 (1986) 264s (M. de *Burgos*); EsprV 96 (1986) 343s (P. *Jay*); MélSR 43 (1986) 210s (M. *Hubaut*); QVidCr 131s (1986) 232 (A. *Marquès*); VSp 140 (1986) 747 (Annie *Perchenet*).

6092 **Lohfink** Gerhard, La Iglesia que Jesús quería; dimensión comunitaria de la fe cristiana [Wie hat 1982 ➤ 63,5188], ᵀ*Martínez de Lapera* Victor A.: Cristiano y sociedad 12. Bilbao 1986, Desclée-B. 202 p. pt. 1450. 84-330-0690-8 [ActuBbg 24, 97 J. I. *González Faus*].

6093 **Lohfink** G., Jesus and community, ᵀ*Galvin* John P. 1984 → 1,7507: ᴿBibTB 16 (1986) 35s (P. *Hollenbach*); CurrTM 13 (1986) 176 (H. T. *Mayer*).

6094 *Lohfink* Gerhard, Jesus und die Kirche: → 590, ᴱ**Kern** W., Traktat Kirche 1986, 49-96.

6095 **Lorenzo** Gumersindo, Una Iglesia democrática, I. Prolegómenos; II. Itinerario. Bilbao 1985, Desclée-B. 204 p.; 207 p. – ᴿCiuD 199 (1986) 339s (S. *Folgado Flórez*); RazF 214 (1986) 361s (M. *Alcalá*).

6096 *Losada* Joaquín, La Iglesia, pueblo de Dios y misterio de comunión: SalT 74 (1986) 243-256.

6097 **Mettnitzer** Arnold, Mensch und Leben der Kirche bei Ernst COMMER (1847-1928); ein Beitrag zur Geschichte der Ekklesiologie: Diss. Pont. Univ. Gregoriana, ᴰ*Antón* A. R 1986. 557 p. – RTLv 18,558.

6098 *a) Meyer* Harding, Die Thesen von FRIES und RAHNER — Versuch einer Weiterführung; eine lutherische Stellungnahme zu These II und IV; – *b) Fries* Heinrich, Die Thesen von Fries und Rahner und ihre Wirkungsgeschichte: TüTQ 166 (1986) 291-301 / 302-312.

6099 *Michiels* Robrecht, Over het zelfverstaan van de Kerk na Vaticanum II: CollatVl 16 (1986) 145-170 (-215, *Denaux* Adelbert).

6100 **Minette de Tillesse** Caetano, Nova Jerusalém, eclesiologia, I/1 Reino de Dios, estudo bíblico. Fortaleza CE 1986, Nova Jerusalém. 171 p. $40 [BL 87, 93, J. M. *Dines*: lucid].

6101 *Möller* Christian, Gemeindeaufbau jenseits der Alternative von 'Volkskirche oder Ekklesia'; zum Gespräch mit der 'Theologie des Gemeindeaufbaus' von Fritz und Christian A. SCHWARZ: TBei 17 (1986) 118-136 [< ZIT].

6102 **Mondin** B., La Chiesa primizia del Regno; trattato di ecclesiologia: Corso di Teologia Sistematica 7. Bo 1986, Dehoniane. 507 p. Lit. 28.000 [NRT 109, 592, R. *Escol*].

6103 **Mora** Abdias, Praxis and Church [DissA] / The understanding of the Church [RelStR] in the theology of liberation: diss. Baylor 1986. 416 p. 86-28281. – DissA 47 (1986s) 3080-A; RelStR 13.188.

6104 **Müller** Gerhard L., Der theologische Ort der Heiligen; Überlegungen zum ekklesiologischen Ansatz des 2. Vatikanischen Konzils: ZkT 108 (1986) 145-154.

6105 **Müller** Karl, *al.*, Missionstheologie — eine Einführung 1985 → 1,7520: ᴿZKG 97 (1986) 265s (L. *Schreiner*).

6106 **Naab** Erich, Das eine grosse Sakrament des Lebens; Studie zum Kirchentraktat des Joseph ERNST (1804-1869) mit Berücksichtigung der Lehrentwicklung in der von ihm begründeten Schule: EichSt 20, 1985 → 1,7522: ᴿTR 82 (1986) 487-491 (E. *Fastenrath*).

6107 *a) Nagy* Stanisław, La présence de l'ecclésiologie et de l'œcuménisme au IIᵉ Synode Extraordinaire [Rome sept.-déc. 1985]; – *b) Kaczyński* E., Alcuni problemi post-conciliari della Chiesa; – *c) Goldie* Rosemary, Il Sinodo e la posizione dei laici nella Chiesa e nel mondo; – *d) Accattoli* Luigi ['giornalista del Corriere della Sera'], Il Sinodo e l'opinione pubblica mondiale [coro di lode, malgrado i titoli/headlines di poca fiducia e il contrasto delle opinioni; eppure l'interesse per i mutamenti di una chiesa in ricerca è una sfida ...]: Angelicum 63 (1986) 356-367 / 368-385 / 386-395 / 396-402.

6108 *a) Navarro Ángel* M., 'Lumen Gentium' y la eclesiología del Concilio Vaticano II; – *b) Oriol* Antoni M., Sobre la relación Iglesia-Mundo en el Concilio Vaticano II; – *c) Garaygordobil* mons. Victor, La Missione en el

Concilio y repercusiones postconciliares: Lumen 35 (Victoria 1986) 83-118 / 119-146 / 301-321.

6109 a) *Nissiotis* Nikos A., † Auf dem Weg zur Gemeinschaft der Kirchen im Jahr '2000', T*Münch-Labacher* Gudrun; – b) *Klein* Laurentius, Theologische Alternative zur Konsensökumene; – c) *Dulles* Avery, Zur Überwindbarkeit von Lehrdifferenzen; Überlegungen aus Anlass zweier neuerer Lösungsvorschläge [*Fries-Rahner; Lindbeck* G.], T*Berchtold* Christoph; – d) *Ratzinger* J., Brief: TüTQ 166 (1986) 248-267 / 268-278 / 278-289 / 243-8.

6110 *Oberti* Armando, Théologie du laïcat: VieCons 58 (1986) 67-80.

6111 *O'Connell* Patrick F., 'Is the world a problem?': MERTON, RAHNER and CLARK in the Diaspora Church: AmBenR 37 (1986) 349-369.

6112 T E*O'Connor* James T., GASSER Vinzenz 1809-1879, The gift of infallibility; the official relatio on infallibility at Vatican Council I. Boston 1986, St. Paul. 126 p. $5; pa. $4 [TDig 33,363].

6113 *O'Gara* Margaret, *al.*, The nature of koinonia: ➤ 482, Mid-Stream 25 (1986) 339-350 (-374).

6114 **Pannenberg** W., The Church 1983 ➤ 64,7116... 1,7533: RHeythJ 27 (1986) 220-2 (Elizabeth A. *Johnson*).

6115 **Pannenberg** Wolfhart, Ética y eclesiología [1977], T*Martínez de Lapera* V. A. Salamanca 1986, Sígueme. 261 p. – RComSev 19 (1986) 252s (V. J. *Ansede Alonso*); NatGrac 33 (1986) 586 (A. *Villalmonte*); Studium 26 (M 1986) 356s (C. G. *Extremeño*).

6116 *Pasquetto* Virgilio, La missione di Gesù e dei suoi discepoli nell'insegnamento dei Vangeli: RivVSp 40 (1986) 355-377 [398-419, *Castellano* Jesús].

6117 *Pasztor* János, Ⓜ 'Ye shall be witnesses unto me' (thoughts on World Alliance paper 'Called to witness today'): Theologiai Szemle 28 (1985) 215-223.

6118 **Pelchat** Marc, L'ecclésiologie dans l'œuvre de Henri de LUBAC: diss. Pont. Univ. Gregoriana, D*Sullivan* F. R 1986. 508 p. Extr. Nº 3332, 120 p. – RTLv 18,569.

6119 *Peter* Carl J., The Church's treasures (*thesauri Ecclesiae*) then and now; TS 47 (1986) 251-272.

6120 *Pifano* Paolo, Per una Chiesa viva [... *Cipriani* S. 1985]: RasT 27 (1986) 458-466.

6121 *Poletti* Ugo present., Con il Sinodo dei Vescovi sulla strada del concilio [4 capitoli sulla Chiesa], a cura della Segreteria Generale della Conferenza Episcopale Italiana. R 1986, A.V.E. 78 p. Lit. 6000.

6122 **Porro** Carlo, La Chiesa; introduzione teologica. Casale Monferrato 1981, Piemme. 206 p. Lit. 16.000. – RCC 137 (1986,2) 304s (G. *Mucci*); Gregorianum 67 (1986) 803 (J. *Galot*).

6123 *Porter* D. W., 'Spreading the word'; aspects of the biblical basis of mission: Christian Brethren Review 36 (Exeter 1985) 11-20 [NTAbs 30,193].

6124 **Poulat** Émile, L'Église, c'est un monde — L'ecclésiosphère: Sciences humaines et religions. P 1986, Cerf. 282 p. F 105. 2-204-02500-3. – RÉTRel 61 (1986) 616 (B. *Reymond*).

6124* **Quiroz Magaña** Alvaro, Eclesiología en la Teología de la Liberación 1983 ➤ 64,7470; 65,7276: RComSev 19 (1986) 92s (V. J.*Ansede Alonso*).

6125 *Rausch* Thomas P., Reception past and present [used to mean acceptance of higher authority by local churches; now means also acceptance by one church (i.e. denomination) of agreements reached with another]: TS 47 (1986) 497-508.

6126 *Sartore* Domenico, La chiesa dal costato di Cristo nel pensiero di S.
Giovanni CRISOSTOMO: ➤ 67*, Mem. MARSILI S., Paschale mysterium
1986, 169-176.

6127 *Schneiders* Sandra M., Evangelical equality [... challenging the image of
the Church as a hierarchical institution]; religious consecration, mission,
and witness: SpTod 38 (1986) 293-302 ...

6128 *Schönborn* Christoph, L'Église de la terre; le royaume de Dieu et l'Église
du ciel; notes sur Lumen Gentium ch. VII: EsprVie 96 (1986) 689-697.

6129 *Schwaiger* Georg, Die konziliare Idee in der Geschichte der Kirche:
Rottenburger Jahrbuch für Kirchengeschichte 5 (Sigmaringen 1986) 11-24
[< ZIT].

6130 **Sell** Alan P. F., Saints, visible, orderly and Catholic — the Con-
gregational idea of the Church: 'WARC'. L 1986, Tavistock. 173 p.
£5.50. 92-9075-001-4. – RExpTim 98 (1986s) 186 (D. *Cornick*: varying
ideas, 'evangelical', 'denominational', 'churchly', ... American).

6131 **Senior** D., *Stuhlmueller* C., Biblia y misión; fundamentos bíblicos 1985
➤ 1,7558: RBibFe 12 (1986) 253 (A. *Salas*).

6132 **Senior** D., *Stuhlmueller* C., I fondamenti biblici della missione 1985
➤ 1,7559: RClaretianum 26 (1986) 395-7 (M. *Zappella*); ParVi 31 (1986)
317-9 (G. *Cappelletto*: leggi 'salvezza, assemblea', non 'salvazione, congregazione').

6133 **Seumois** André, Théologie missionnaire: 1. Délimitation de la fonction
missionnaire de l'Église², 1980, 179 p.; 2. Théologie de l'implantation
ecclésiale², 1980, 219 p.; 3. Salut et religions de la Gentilité², 1981, 203 p.;
4. Église missionnaire et facteurs socio-culturels², 1983, 187 p.; 5.
Dynamisme missionnaire du Peuple de Dieu, 1981, 209 p. Vaticano, Pont.
Univ. Urbaniana. – RDivinitas 30 (1986) 179-183 (C. *Petino*).

6134 **Sieben** Herman J., Traktate und Theorien zum Konzil: FraTheolSt 30.
Fra 1983, Knecht. 296 p. 3-7820-0491-4. – REstE 61 (1986) 110s (A. M.
Navas).

6135 *Sobrino* Jon, Conflict within the Church: Way 26 (1986) 33-43 [44-52,
Dunn Mary, in the family].

6136 *Staats* Reinhart, Die katholische Kirche des IGNATIUS von Antiochien
und das Problem ihrer Normativität im zweiten Jahrhundert: ZNW 77
(1986) 126-145.242-254.

6137 **Stamoolis** James J., Eastern Orthodox mission theology today.
Maryknoll NY c. 1985, Orbis. xiv-194 p. $19. – RPhilipSac 21 (1986) 486s
(L. C. *Dolor*); Themelios 12 (1986s) 33 (M. *Goldsmith*).

6138 *Stival* Giancarlo, La Chiesa 'madre' nei padri dell'Italia settentrionale
del IV-V secolo: SacDoc 31 (1986) 29-35.

6139 **Stötzel** Arnold, Kirche als 'neue Gesellschaft'; die humanisierende
Wirkung des Christentums nach Johannes CHRYSOSTOMUS [Hab.-Diss.
Mü 1980] 1984 ➤ 1,7566: RVigChr 40 (1986) 109s (H. *Frohnhofen*).

6139* *Stoevesandt* Hinrich, Gott und die [*Barth*: in der Kirche selbst falschen]
Götter: EvT 46 (1986) 457-476.

6140 *Süss* Paulo, Die schöpferische und normative Rolle der Volksreligiosität
in der Kirche: (Concilium) IZT 22 (1986) 317-324 (Eng. ed. 122-131,
T*Burns* P.).

6141 **Teissier** Henri, La mission de l'Église (L'héritage du Concile). P 1985,
Desclée. 240 p. F 84. – RÉgIT 17 (1986) 100-3 (M. *Zago*).

6142 a) *Tillard* J. M. R., Koinonia-Sacrament; – b) *Forstman* H. Jackson, The
Church as sacramental community and as community of faith: ➤ 482,
Mid-Stream 25 (1986) 375-385 (364-7) / 393-402 [-440, *al.*].

6143 **Toinet** Paul, L'être et l'Église, I [de 3], Logique de l'expérience ecclésiale 1982 ➤ 64,7144: ᴿScEspr 38 (1986) 140 (G. *Pelland*: richesse de thèmes).

6144 **Tourneux** André, Église et Eucharistie à Vatican II; étude génétique, cohérence et signification d'un thème conciliaire: diss. ᴰ*Houssiau* A. Louvain-la-Neuve 1986. iv-801 p. – RTLv 18,137.

6145 *Trudinger* Paul, The Church is dying; it had better be!: ExpTim 98 (1986s) 340s.

6146 **Valentini** Donato, Il nuovo popolo di Dio in cammino; punti nodali per una ecclesiologia attuale: BiblScRel 65 / dogm. 35, 1984 ➤ 65,6819: 1,7573: ᴿCC 137 (1986,2) 195s (G. *Mucci*); Claretianum 26 (1986) 398-400 (B. *Proietti*); ÉglT 17 (1986) 402 (A. *Peelman*); Gregorianum 67 (1986) 154 (J. *Dupuis*); TLZ 111 (1986) 237s (K. H. *Neufeld*).

6147 *Vela* Luis, *al.*, La iglesia española y la comunidad europea: EstE 61,238 (1986) 261-8 (-375).

6148 **Vermeulen** C., Cor Ecclesiae; een onderzoek naar de penumatologische consequenties van Karl BARTHs verkiezingsleer in het geheel van zijn 'Kirchliche Dogmatik': diss. Utrecht 1986, ᴰ*Hasselaar* J. 364 p. – TsTNijm 26 (1986) 280 (H. *Biezeno* summary focuses only universality of salvific plan, not mentioning either pneuma or Spirit).

6149 *Willems* Ad, Het mysterie als ideologie; de bischoppensynode over het kerkebegrip: TsTNijm 26 (1986) 157-170; Eng. 170s: the 1985 synod ideologically misused the description 'mystery' for the Church... to mask questions and problems which arise from its description as 'people of God'.

6150 **Willimon** William H., What's right with the Church? 1985 ➤ 1,7582: ᴿCurrTM 13 (1986) 60 (H. T. *Mayer*).

6151 *Winkler* Eberhard, Zur Theologie des Gemeindeaufbaus: TLZ 111 (1986) 481-492.

6152 *Wrede* Gösta, Dop och kyrkotillhörighet [Baptism and church membership]: SvTKv 62 (1986) 33-40.

6152* *Yemba* Kekumba, La mission de l'Église et son actualité théologique: ➤ 472, Yaoundé 1984 = BTAf 7,13 (1985) 333-341.

6153 *Zabala Caballero* Ignacio S., La Iglesia y su autoridad doctrinal según Domingo BAÑEZ: diss. Univ. S. Thomae (Angelicum). R 1983. 419 p. – ᴿEstE 61 (1986) 92-94 (J. *Iturriaga*).

6154 **Zizioulas** John D., Being as [not 'in' ➤ 1,7585] communion; studies in personhood and the Church. L 1985, Darton-LT. 269 p. £10. 0-232-51648-90. – ᴿExpTim 97 (1985s) 282s (B. *Horne*: breaks down the barriers we set around the Orthodox); NBlackf 67 (1986) 45-48 (J. *Saward*); ÖkRu 35 (1986) 479-481 (K. *Raiser*); TLond 39 (1986) 220-2 (J. *Macquarrie*).

H7.7 Œcumenismus – The ecumenical movement.

6155 *Abaitua* Carlos, El ecumenismo, veinte años después: Lumen 35 (Vitoria 1986) 322-341.

6156 *Amaladoss* M., Reply to objectors to his 'Faith meets faith' in Vidyajyoti 49 (1985) [109-117] 475-9.

6157 *Avis* Paul, Ecumenical theology and the elusiveness of doctrine [➤ 1,7404]. L 1986, SPCK. 140 p. £6. – ᴿIrBSt 8 (1986) 103s (R. *Boyd*: radical critique of ARCIC); Month 248 (1986) 104s (M. *Nevin*: an Anglican Ratzinger; strongly negative); RefTR 45 (1986) 83 (R. *Doyle*); TLond 39 (1986) 304s (J. *Drury*).

6158 **Avis** Paul D.L., Truth beyond word; problems and prospects for Anglican-Roman Catholic unity. CM 1985, Cowley. xv-142 p. $8 pa. [TDig 33,457].

6159 *Bartha* Tibor bp., ⑩ The history and present possibilities of the contacts between the Free Churches and other Protestant denominations in Hungary [jubilee address 1984]: Theologiai Szemle 28 (1985) 129-131.

6159* a) *Becker* Ulrich, Ökumenisches Lernen — eine Aufgabe für den Religionsunterricht? – b) *Hoppe* Joachim, Begegnung mit dem Judentum im christlichen Religionsunterricht — ein ökumenischer Lernprozess?: EvErz 38 (1986) 519-529 / 550-565.

6160 **Bermejo** Luis M., Towards Christian reunion; Vatican I, obstacles and opportunities: Jesuit Theol. Forum 2, 1984 ➤ 65,6696; 1,7411: ᴿBible Bhashyam 11 (1985) 195 (X. *Koodapuzha*); Gregorianum 67 (1986) 385-8 (F.A. *Sullivan*); Vidyajyoti 49 (1985) 51s. 15 (E.R. *Hambye*).

6161 *Bertalot* Renzo, Interpretazione e dialogo nel movimento ecumenico: ➤ 371, ᴱ*Galli* G., Interpretazione 1982/3, 47-49 (-77, discussione).

6162 **Bilsen** T.J.C. van, Kerk van alle gelovigen. Brugge 1984, Tabor. 209 p. ƒ 29,50 [TR 83,231, J. *Ambaum*].

6163 **Birmelé** André, a) 'Sola gratia'; le salut en Jésus-Christ dans les dialogues œcuméniques: prot. diss. ᴰ*Siegwalt* M. Strasbourg 1986. 570 p. – RTLv 18,569. – b) P/Genève 1986, Cerf / Labor et Fides. 472 p. F 149.

6164 a) [*Birmelé* A. présent.] Mémorandum de cinq Instituts Œcuméniques Européens [nov. 1984]. Les Églises issues de la Réforme et le Mouvement œcuménique; – b) *Lovsky*, Pour élargir l'espace de la tente œcuménique: FoiVie 85,4 (1986) 1-54 / 57-67.

6165 **Bloch-Hoell** Nils E., Katolske kristne og vi andre. Oslo 1986, Gyldendal. 271 p. Nk 136. – ᴿNorTTs 87 (1986) 178-181 (K.W. *Ruyter*).

6167 *Bouwen* Frans, Quelques dimensions importantes de la vie œcuménique en 1986, vue à partir de Jérusalem: PrOrChr 36 (1986) 63-80.

6168 *Bradshaw* Tim, Primacy and authority in the ARCIC report: TLond 39 (1986) 24-32.

6169 *Bria* Ion, The Eastern Orthodox in the ecumenical movement: EcuR 38 (1986) 216-227.

6170 a) *Brown* Wesley H., Broken walls and a whole body; – b) *Nagano* Paul M., Woven together in life and mission: AmBapQ 5,4 ('Patterns of faith' 1986) 328-335 / 336-347.

6171 a) *Bux* Nicola, Ecumenismo; riflessione su situazione ecumenica dopo 20 anni; – b) *Cardini* Franco, Lo scisma d'Oriente (III): TerraS 62 (1986) 146-8 / 32-41.

6172 **Castro** Emilio, Freedom in mission; the perspective of the Kingdom of God. an ecumenical inquiry [➤ 1,7424* = diss. Lausanne 1984, 'Sent Free' 1985 + conferences 1963-1983]. Genève 1985, WCC. 348 p. Fs 29,50. 2-8254-0824-7. – ᴿÉTRel 61 (1986) 153-5 (M. *Spindler*).

6173 **Charley** Julian, Rome, Canterbury, and the Future. Bramcote 1982, Nottingham Grove. 33 p. – ᴿIstina 31 (1986) 334 (B. *Dupuy*).

6174 *Chevallier* Max-Alain, L'unité plurielle de l'Église d'après le Nouveau Testament: ➤ 83*, ᶠPETER R. = RHPR 66 (1986) 3-20; Eng. 129.

6175 **Congar** Y., Diversity and communion 1984 ➤ 65,6706; 1,7432: ᴿCalvinT 21 (1986) 258-260 (J.H. *Kromminga*); Mid-Stream 25 (1986) 137-9 (P.J. *Mitchell*); NorTTs 87 (1986) 148 (K. *Nordstokke*); TsTKi 57 (1986) 315 (O. *Tjørhom*).

6176 *Coppola* R., Primato papale ed ecumenismo: Nicolaus 13,1 (1986) 3-28.

6177 **Cullmann** Oscar, *a*) Einheit durch Vielfalt; Grundlegung und Beitrag zur Diskussion über die Möglichkeit ihrer Verwirklichung. Tü 1986, Mohr. – *b*) L'unité par la diversité; son fondement et le problème de sa réalisation: Théologies. P 1986, Cerf [NRT 109,870, A. de *Halleux*]. 122 p. F 59.

6178 [*Damaskinos* métrop.] Les dialogues œcuméniques hier et aujourd'hui [séminaire interconfessionel, surtout Orthodoxe, 1984]: Les études théologiques de Chambésy 5. Genève-Chambésy 1985, Patriarcat œcuménique. 415 p. Fs 50 [RTLv 18,104, A. de *Halleux*].

6179 **Desseaux** Jacques. Twenty centuries of ecumenism 1984 ➤ 1,7440: RCalvinT 21 (1986) 313s (J. H. *Kromminga*).

6180 **Dobson** Edward, In search of union; an appeal to fundamentalists and evangelicals. Nv 1985, Nelson. 168 p. $5 pa. – RJPsy&Chr 5,1 (1986) 53s (B. P. *Hayton*).

6181 **Dulles** Avery, The catholicity of the Church [Oxford D'Arcy lectures 1983] 1985 ➤ 1,7443; £17.50: RExpTim 98 (1986s) 88s (B. L. *Horne*: makes valuable French contributions available); Furrow 57 (1986) 738s (J. *Caffrey*); Month 248 (1986) 246 (O. *Rafferty*); Tablet 240 (1986) 536s (F. *Kerr*).

6182 *Dulles* Avery, Catholicity and Catholicism: ConcordTQ 50 (1986) 81-94.

6183 *Dulles* Avery, Paths to doctrinal agreement; ten theses [... complete agreement is unattainable; there is a hierarchy of importance; all mainline churches share a large fund in the Apostles' Creed; others' doctrines should be admitted not repugnant to Christ's revelation even if not true; withdrawal of anathemas; hermeneutic reformulation can lead to wider acceptance ...]: TS 47 (1986) 32-47.

6184 *Dumont* Christophe-Jean, Où en est le dialogue entre l'Église catholique et l'Église orthodoxe [*Stylianos* mgr. 1985]: Istina 31 (1986) 273-292.

6185 *Dupuy* Bernard, Où en est le dialogue entre l'Orthodoxie et les Églises dites monophysites?: Istina 31 (1986) 357-370 [Rapports de rencontres, 396-412].

6186 **Duquoc** C., Des Églises provisoires 1985 ➤ 1,7446: RBijdragen 47 (1986) 58-66, franç. 66 (A. H. C. van *Eijk*) & 79 (J. *Kerkhofs*); ÉTRel 61 (1986) 156s (J. M. *Prieur*: nous ne voyons pas s'il veut le système catholique, même amélioré, ou un autre, qu'il ne décrit pas); MélSR 43 (1986) 173 (L. *Debarge*); QVidCr 131s (1986) 232s (E. *Vilanova*); RechSR 74 (1986) 308s (B. *Sesboüé*); VSp 140 (1986) 269s (J. *Robert*).

6187 **Duquoc** Christian, Kirchen unterwegs; Versuch einer ökumenischen Ekklesiologie 1985 ➤ 1,7447: RÖkRu 35 (1986) 481s [H. *Vorster*].

6188 **Duquoc** Christian, Iglesias provisionales; ensayo de eclesiología ecuménica, T*Godoy López* R.: Senda abierta 5. M 1986, Cristiandad. 172 p. 84-7057-388-8 [ActuBbg 24,96s, I. *Riudor*].

6189 **Duquoc** Christian, Provisional churches. L 1986, SCM. 116 p. £5. 0-334-01338-0. – RExpTim 98 (1986s) 169 (B. L. *Horne*; questions of an intellectual; non-answers of a Catholic); Month 248 (1986) 277 (Elizabeth *Lord*).

6190 L'Église, mystère et signe prophétique; rapport [plutôt: document conclusif] du premier colloque de l'Étude sur l'unité de l'Église et le renouveau de la communauté humaine, Chantilly (3-10 janvier 1985): Istina 31 (1986) 307-322.

6191 **Eham** Markus M., Gemeinschaft im Sakrament? Die Frage nach der Möglichkeit sakramentaler Gemeinschaft zwischen katholischen und nichtkatholischen Christen: kath. Diss. D*Finkenzeller* J. München 1986. – RTLv 18,568.

6192 *Eijk* A. H. C. van,   Ecumenical convergence on episcopal [i.e. bishops']
ministry: Bijdragen 47 (1986) 236-265.

6193 ᴱ**Fabella** Virginia, *Torres* Sergio,   Doing theology in a divided world
1983/5 ➤ 1,571*b*: ᴿGregorianum 67 (1986) 383s (J. *Dupuis*).

6194 *Fahlbusch* Erwin,   Ⓜ Ökumenismus, ein lexikographischer Umriss
[➤ Materialdienst KkI 1983/3], ᵀ*Karasszon* István: Theologiai Szemle 28
(1985) 89-94.

6195 **Fries** H., *Rahner* K.,   Einigung der Kirchen: QDisp 100, 1985
➤ 64,7081... 1,7459: ᴿForumKT 2 (1986) 244s (F. *Courth*); NorTTs 87
(1986) 53-55 (Ola *Tjørhom*).

6196 **Fries** Heinrich, *Rahner* Karl,   Unity of the Churches, an actual
posssibility 1985 ➤ 1,7460: ᴿRExp 83 (1986) 326s (E. G. *Hinson*: concede
too much from the side of Roman papacy and episcopacy).

6197 **Fries** H., *Rahner* K.,   Unione delle Chiese possibilità reale. Brescia 1986,
Morcelliana.   219 p.   Lit. 18.000. – ᴿAmbrosius 62 (1986) 473s (G.
Ferrario); HumBr 41 (1986) 948s (B. *Belletti*); ParVi (31 (1986) 74s (L.
Melotti); Sapienza 39 (1986) 489-491 (anche B. *Belletti*).

6198 *a*) **Fries** Heinrich,   Zum Stand der Ökumene aus katholischer Sicht: – *b*)
Jouanin Yves,   Simples réflexions sur la place du Judaïsme dans
l'œcuménisme: ➤ 78*, ᶠMUND H., Um die eine Kirche 1984, 86-97 / 30-43.

6199 *Fritzsche* Hellmut,   Ⓜ Christlich-marxistischer Dialog unter dem
Gesichtswinkel der DDR betrachtet, mit besonderer Rücksicht auf die
Fragen der Zusammenarbeit zwischen der christlich-theologischen und
marxistisch-philosophischen Forschungen auf den Universitäten der DDR
(Vortrag Debrecen 16.-17, Apr. 1984): Theologiai Szemle 28 (1985) 32-5.

6200 *Froehlich* Herbert,   Um ihres Auftrags willen; die katholische Kirche hat
die Pflicht, sich in den Konziliaren Prozess einzubringen: WAnt 27
(Mainz 1986) 113-7 [< ZIT].

6201 *Frost* Francis, Œcuménisme 1984 ➤ 65,6731; 1,7462: ᴿRTLv 17 (1986)
69-71 (A. de *Halleux*).

6202 *Gestrich* Christof,   Kirchliche Toleranzgewährung und kirchliches Tole-
ranzbedürfnis; Versuch theologischer Orientierung in einem schwierigen
Gelände der Neuzeit: BTZ 3 (1986) 155-167.

6203 **Girault** René, *Nicolas* Albert,   Sans tricher ni trahir; sur la grand-route
œcuménique: Rencontres 41. P 1985, Cerf.   191 p.   F 97.   2-204-02416-3. –
ᴿÉTRel 61 (1986) 311s (J.-M. *Prieur*); PrOrChr 36 (1986) 188s (P.
Ternant); RHPR 66 (1986) 244s (R. *Mehl*).

6204 *Gregson* Vernon,   LONERGAN, spirituality, and the meeting of religions.
Lanham MD 1985, UPA.   xvi-154 p. $11.75 pa. – ᴿCalvinT 21 (1986)
279-281 (A. *Vos*).

6204* **Guthrie** Shirley C.ᴶ,   Diversity in faith — unity in Christ. Ph 1986,
Westminster.   160 p. $11 [JAAR 55,431].

6205 **Hahn** Eberhard,   Wo ist die Kirche Jesu Christi? Theologische
Beurteilung kirchlicher Zertrennung anhand von Fallbeispielen: Diss.
ᴰ*Slenczka* R. Erlangen 1986.   328 p. – RTLv 18,568.

6206 *Hahn* Ferdinand, *a*) Die Einheit der Kirche und Kirchengemeinschaft in
neutestamentlicher Sicht < Einheit der Kirche, QDisp 84 (1979) 9-51]; – *b*)
Die Bedeutung des Apostelkonvents [ActAp 15] für die Einheit der
Christenheit [< ᶠFRIES H. 1982, 15-44]: ➤ 167, Ges. Aufs. 1 (1986)
116-158 / 95-115.

6207 **Heiser** Lothar,   Das Glaubenszeugnis der armenischen Kirche: Sophia 2.
Trier 1983, Paulinus.   313 p.; ill.   DM 48. – ᴿTrierTZ 95 (1986) 67s (E.
Sauser).

6208 **Herms** Eilert, Einheit der Christen ... Antwort auf den Rahner-Plan 1984 ⇒ 1,7480: ᴿActuBbg 23 (1986) 49-53 (J. *Boada*); NorTTs 87 (1986) 56s (Ola *Tjørhom*).

6209 *Hoeckmann* Remi, Ecumenism after the Extraordinary Synod [and Reagan-Gorbachev meeting in Geneva, 1985]: Angelicum 63 (1986) 598-615.

6210 **Joly** Robert, Origines et évolution de l'intolérance catholique: Laïcité. Bru 1986, Univ. 151 p. Fb 400. 2-8004-0906-1. – ᴿÉTRel 61 (1986) 617 (H. *Bost*: laïcisme militant).

6211 ᴱ**Kinnamon** M., *Best* T. F., Called to be one in Christ; United Churches and the ecumenical movement: Faith and Order 127. Geneva 1985, WCC. xiv-78 p. Fs 9.50 [RTLv 18,103, A. de *Halleux*].

6212 **Kirchengemeinschaft** in Wort und Sakrament [kath.-ev. Arbeitsgruppe]. Pd/Hannover 1984, Bonifatius / Luth. 110 p. – ᴿZkT 108 (1986) 328-332 (L. *Lies*).

6213 **Knoche** Hansjürgen, Einigung der Kirchen — mit wem? Zu den Thesen von Karl RAHNER (†) und Heinrich FRIES. Mü 1986, Behrendt. viii-177 p. DM 23 sb. [TR 83,406, A. *Klein*].

6214 **Krijnsen** C., Intercommunie; theologische discussie [since *Dockx* H.] 1969-1983: Research Pamphlet 11, 1984 ⇒ 1,7495; 90-713187-11-9: ᴿNedTTs 40 (1986) 263s (K. *Blei*).

6215 **Krüger** Hanfried, Ökumenischer Katechismus; eine kurze Einführung in Wesen, Werden und Wirken der Ökumene[8]. Fra 1985, Ev.-V. 92 p. DM 8,50 pa. [RelStR 13,152, J. T. *Ford*].

6216 *Kühn* Ulrich, Das reformatorische Proprium und die Ökumene: KerDo 32 (1986) 170-187; Eng. 187.

6217 *Küng* Hans, What is the true religion? Toward an ecumenical criteriology: JThSAf 14,56 (1986) 4-23 [< ZIT].

6218 ᵀᴱ**Legrand** H., *Meyer* H., Commission internationale catholique-lu-thérienne, Face à l'unité, ensemble de textes 1972-85. P 1986, Cerf. 396 p. F 92 [NRT 109,760, R. *Escol*].

6220 ᴱ**Lehmann** Karl, *Schlink* Edmund. Evangelium — Sakramente — Amt und die Einheit der Kirche; die ökumenische Tragweite der Confessio Augustana: Dialog der Kirchen 2, 1982 ⇒ 64,511: ᴿTPQ 134 (1986) 407s (J. B. *Bauer*).

6221 **Lemopoulos** Georges N., Le dialogue théologique entre l'Église orthodoxe et l'Église des Vieux-Catholiques: IkiZ 76 (1986) 161-190.

6222 *Loades* David M., *Aveling* J.C.H., *MacAdoo* J.R., Rome and the Anglicans; historical and doctrinal aspects of the Anglican-Roman Catholic relation [< ANRW, ᴱ*Haase* W.]. B 1982, de Gruyter. 301 p. DM 138. – ᴿEvT 38 (1986) 282 (R. *Beckwith*: RATZINGER declined); Istina 31 (1986) 334s (B. *Dupuy*).

6223 *Löser* Werner, Presencia de Cristo y apostolicidad de la Iglesia en perspectiva ecuménica [< TPhil 59 (1984) 379-392], ᵀᴱ*Alemany* Alvaro: SelT 25 (1986) 27-36.

6224 **Lowery** Mark D., Ecumenism; striving for unity amid diversity. Mystic CT 1985, Twenty-Third. 181 p. $10 pa. – ᴿCalvinT 21 (1986) 286-290 (P. G. *Schrotenboer*); RelStR 12 (1986) 270s (J. T. *Ford*).

6225 *Lubbe* Gerrie, The study of religion and inter-faith dialogue: RelSAf 7,2 (Pietermaritzburg 1986) 27-37 [Zusammenfassung, TKontext 8/2,11s, N. B. *Abeng*].

6226 **McDonnell** John J., The World Council of Churches and the Catholic

Church: Toronto Studies in Theology 21. NY 1985, Mellen. x-467 p. $40 [RelStR 13,74, J.T. *Ford*].

6227 *Maday* Johannes, Die ökumenische Relevanz der von Papst Johannes Paulus II und Patriarch Ignatius Zakka I. geschlossenen zwischenkirchlichen Vereinbarung: Catholica 40 (Münster 1986) 139-153.

6228 *Martini* Luciano, Fede implicita e cristianesimo anonimo nella teologia di Karl RAHNER: Religioni e Società 1,1 (R 1986) 68-81.

6229 *Meeking* Basil, Peace and ecumenism: Seminarium 37 (1986) 420-8.

6231 **Mikulanis** Dennis L., Authority in the Church from the perspective of recent Anglican-Roman Catholic dialogues: diss. Angelicum. R 1986. 384 p. – RTLv 18,570.

6232 **Molendijk** Arie L., Getuigen in missionair en oecumenisch verband; een studie over het begrip 'getuigen' in documenten van de Wereldraad van Kerken, de Rooms-Katholieke Kerk en de Evangelicalen, in de periode 1948-1985; praef. *Spindler* M.P. [Developments in the witness terminology and theology of the World Council of Churches and the Vatican]: IIMO Research 16. Leiden 1986, Interuniversitair Instituut voor Missiologie. iv-257- p. *f* 25. 90-71387-20-8.

6233 *Molendijk* Arie L., Carte blanche voor 'Getuigen' ['Witness' is an in-word]; ontwikkelingen in de getuigenisterminologie en -theologie binnen de Wereldraad en het Vatican: NedTTs 40 (1986) 290-304.

6234 **Montefiore** Hugh, So near and yet so far [light at the end of a long tunnel for Anglicans and Rome]. L 1986, SCM. 154 p. £6. 0-334-01517-0. – RExpTim 98 (1986s) 252 (J.K.S. *Reid*).

6235 *Moore* Alvin [J], Ecumenism, shadow and substance [*Schuon* F., 1985]: Hamdard 9,4 (1986) 89-106.

6236 **Neuner** Peter, Kleines Handbuch der Ökumene 1984 ➤ 1,962: RForumKT 2 (1986) 247-9 (M. *Seybold*); TLZ 111 (1986) 777 (H. *Kühne*).

6237 *Neuner* Peter, Unity of the churches; the ecumenical theses of Heinrich FRIES and Karl RAHNER [< Orientierung 15 (1985) 124-7 replying to attacks on the second of the eight theses], TE*Asen* B.A.: TDig 33 (1986) 103-111.

6238 *Nichols* Aidan, 'Unity of the churches'; an ecumenical controversy [< One in Christ 21,2 (1985) 139-166], TE*Asen* B.A.: TDig 33 (1986) 329-332: D. OLS' allegedly 'Vatican-line' critique hits equally Paul VI and John Paul II.

6239 *Ottlyk* Ernő, Ⓜ A joint working group of the Roman Catholic Church and the WCC: Theologiai Szemle 29 (1986) 100-103.

6240 *a*) *Pannenberg* Wolfhart, Reformation und Kirchenspaltung; – *b*) *May* Gerhard, Die Einheit der Kirche bei Irenäus; – *c*) *Stockmeier* Peter, Universalis ecclesia; Papst LEO der Grosse und der Osten: ➤ 56, FKRETSCHMAR G., Anspruch 1986, 137-148 / 69-82 / 83-92.

6241 **Pattaro** G., Corso di teologia dell'ecumenismo. Brescia 1985, Queriniana. 436 p. Lit. 25.000. – RAsprenas 33 (1986) 211-4 (Diana *Pacelli*); EphMar 36 (1986) 416s (E. *Barea*).

6242 *Peter* Carl J., Dialogo tra luterani e cattolici negli Stati Uniti; il contributo della teologia all'unità cristiana in tutto il mondo: TItSett 11 (1986) 168-180; Eng. 180.

6243 **Roux** André, Missions des Églises, mission de l'Église; histoire d'une longue marche; préf. *Mehl* Roger; *Luneau* René: Rencontres 35. P 1984, Cerf. 341 p. F 115. 2-204-02164-4. – RÉTRel 61 (1986) 152s (M. *Spindler*).

6244 **Rusch** William G., Ecumenism — a movement towards Church unity. Ph

1985, Fortress. 133 p. – ᴿNorTTs 87 (1986) 181-3 (Odo *Tjærhom*); RExp 83 (1986) 149s (E. G. *Hinson*).

6245 *a) Santovito* F., Il laicato nella chiesa missionaria; prospettiva ecumenica; – *b) Coppola* R., Primato papale ed ecumenismo: Nicolaus 13,1 (1986) 141-152 / 3-28 [< ZIT].

6246 **Sartori** L., present., Papato e istanze ecumeniche [convegno Trento 1982] 1984 ➤ 1,642: ᴿParVi 31 (1986) 74s (L. *Melotti*).

6246* *Sartori* Luigi, Ecumenismo per la Chiesa italiana [*Pataro* G., *Cereti* G.: 1985]: StPatav 33 (1986) 353-9.

6247 *Scheffczyk* Leo, Die Einheit der Kirche und die uneinige Christenheit in der 'Ökumenischen Dogmatik' von E. SCHLINK [1983]: ForumKT 2 (1986) 231-240.

6248 **Schlink** Edmund, Ökumenische Dogmatik 1983 ➤ 65,6793; 1,7552 [ed. 2, 1985]: ᴿEvT 46 (1986) 561-4 (J. *Brosseder*); Luther 57 (1986) 41-46 (H.-V. *Herntrich*: unzeitgemäss); ScotJT 39 (1986) 123s (S. W. *Sykes*); TLZ 111 (1986) 223-7 (H. *Fischer*); TZBas 42 (1986) 187-190 (A. *Jäger*); TRu 51 (1986) 98-116 (H. F. *Geisser*).

6249 **Schütte** Heinz, Ziel, Kirchengemeinschaft; zur ökumenischen Orientierung 1985 ➤ 1,7554; DM 19,80: ᴿForumKT 2 (1986) 246s (P. *Schäfer*); ÖkRu 35 (1986) 114s (A. *Rössler*); TPhil 61 (1986) 292-4 (W. *Löser*).

6250 *a) Schumacher* Joseph, Der Stand der ökumenischen Bemühungen zwischen Katholiken und Protestanten; Fakten und prinzipielle Überlegungen; – *b) Amato* Angelo, Der ökumenische Dialog zwischen Katholiken und Orthodoxen; Situation und entstandene Probleme; auf dem Weg zur Grundlagendiskussion; – *d) Brandmüller* Walter, Ökumenismus vor dem Hintergrund der Geschichte: ForumKT 2 (1986) 162-183 / 184-200 / 201-217 / 218-230.

6251 *Schwarz* Reinhard, Was gilt noch von den antirömischen Verwerfungen der Reformation?: Luther 57 (Wu 1986) 60-65 [dazu *Lohse* Bernhard 143-8].

6252 **Schwerdtfeger** Nikolaus, Gnade und Welt; zum Grundgefüge von Karl RAHNERs Theorie der 'anonymen Christen' [diss. FrB 1981, ᴰ*Lehmann* K.]: FreibThSt 123, 1982 ➤ 64,7129... 1,7555*: ᴿTPhil 61 (1986) 289s (J. *Bolewski*); ZkT 108 (1986) 68-70 (W. *Kern*).

6253 *Sesboüé* Bernard, Karl RAHNER y los 'Cristianos anónimos' [< Études 361 (1984) 521-535], ᵀᴱ*Pasqual Piqué* Antonio: SelT 25 (1986) 197-204.

6254 *a) Skowronek* Alfons, ❷ L'état de l'œcuménisme 20 ans après le Vatican II; – *b) Michalik* Józef, ❷ Les laïcs dans la communauté chrétienne; – *c) Wilkanowicz* Stefan. ❷ Le chrétien dans le Christ, dans l'Église et dans le monde: AtKap 107 (1986) 50-66 / 67-79 / 80-90.

6255 *Spuler* Bertold, Die orthodoxen Kirchen (XCIII/XCIV): IkiZ 76 (1986) 5-41 / 129-160.

6256 *Stahl* Rainer, Grunddimensionen einer ökumenischen Ekklesiologie — ein Versuch: TLZ 111 (1986) 81-90.

6257 *Stephenson* John, Wittenberg und Canterbury [lutherisch-anglikanischer Dialog [< ConcordTQ 1984, 165ss], ᵀ*Oesch* Johannes: LuthTKi 10 (1986) 129-145.

6258 *Thils* Gustave, Le ministère des successeurs de Pierre et le service de l' 'unité universelle': RTLv 17 (1986) 61-68; Eng. 128.

6259 **Tilby** Angela, Won't you join the dance? [how can Christian creeds become vital once again?] L 1985, SPCK. vii-136 p. £4. – ᴿTLond 39

(1986) 76s (S. *Platten*: her superb writing favors something livelier than a stately waltz).

6260 *a*) *Tillard* J. M. R., We are different; – *b*) *Meyer* Harding, Fundamental difference, fundamental consensus: Mid-Stream 25 (1986) 274-286 / 247-259.

6261 *Tjørhom* Ola, Den internasjonale katolsk-lutherske dialog 20 år efter Vaticanum II — et forsøk på en innføring og oppsummering: TsTKi 57 (1986) 49-63.

6262 **Tulcan** Joan, Die Einheit der Kirche und ihre dogmatischen Fundamente: Diss. ᴰ*Peters* A. Heidelberg 1986. – RTLv 18,569.

6263 **Urban** Hans J., *Wieland* Wolfgang, Zum Thema, Was ist evangelisch, was katholisch? 1984 → 1,7572: ᴿRTLv 17 (1986) 369s (E. *Brito*).

ᴱ**Urban** H. J., *Wagner* H., Handbuch der Ökumenik I, 1985 → 654.

6264 **Valentini** Donato, Dialoghi ecumenici ufficiali; bilanci e prospettive: BiblScRel 53. R 1983, LAS. 168 p.: ᴿRHE 81 (1086) 781s [R. *Aubert*].

6265 **Vattakeril** Peter, Dialogue with men of other faiths; its theological implications; a critical study of Raimundo PANIKKAR: diss. ᴰ*López-Gay* J., Pont. Univ. Gregoriana. Roma 1986. xiii-628 p.; Extr. Nᵒ. 3345, 163 p. – RTLv 18,589.

6266 *a*) *Zaphiris* Gerasimos-Chrysostomos, Ⓖ The theological dialogue between the Orthodox and Roman Catholic churches; – *b*) *Stavrides* Basil T., Ⓖ The historical presuppositions of the dialogues: TAth 57 (1986) 329-342 / 723-752.

6267 *Zekiyan* Boghos L., St. Nersēs ŠNORHALI en dialogue avec les grecs; un prophète de l'œcuménisme au XIIᵉ siècle: → 11, Mem. BERBÉRIAN H. 1986, 861-883.

H7.8   **Amt:** *Ministerium ecclesiasticum.*

6268 *Abad* José A., Los ministerios profético y sacramental del presbítero: Phase 26 (1986) 509-518.

6269 **Anderson** James D., *Jones* Ezra E., Ministry of the [Episcopal/Disciples] laity. SF 1986, Harper & Row. xxix-152 p. $15 [TDig 34,57].

6270 *Aumann* Jordan, Non-ordained ministry and lay apostolate after Vatican Council II: Angelicum 63 (1986) 403-418.

6271 **Barnett** James M., The diaconate, a full and equal order 1981 → 62,7843... 1,7590: ᴿScotJT 39 (1986) 269s (D. F. *Wright*).

6272 **Barstow** Anne L., Married priests and the reforming papacy; the eleventh-century debates: Texts and Studies in Religion 12, 1982 → 64,7155; 65,6837: ᴿHorizons 13 (1986) 423s (J. E. *Biechler*).

6273 *Bertone* Tarcisio, Il servizio del cardinalato al ministero del successore di Pietro: Salesianum 48 (1986) 109-121.

6274 *Blaisdell* Charles R., Beyond the 'profession' of ministry; the priest, the teacher, and the Christ: Encounter 47 (Indianapolis 1986) 41-60 [61-83, *Williamson* Clark M.].

6275 *Blázquez* Ricardo, El ministerio eclesial en J. A. MÖHLER: Salmanticensis 33 (1986) 303-330; Eng. 331.

6276 **Borobio** Dionisio, [Cf. 1982 → 63,7073] Ministerios laicales; manual del cristiano comprometido. M 1984, Atenas. 213 p. – ᴿRazF 214 (1986) 250s (V. *Ramallo*).

6277 **Bressolette** Claude, Le pouvoir dans la société et dans l'Église; l'ecclésiologie politique de Mgr MARET, dernier doyen de la faculté de théologie de Sorbonne au XIXᵉ siècle [→ 1,7597]; préf. *Gadille* Jacques:

Histoire des doctrines ecclésiologiques. P 1984, Cerf. 211 p. F 99. – RÉglT 17 (1986) 401s (A. *Peelman*).

6278 *Bürgener* Karsten, Amt und Abendmahl und was die Bibel dazu sagt. Bremen 1985, St. Johannes. 123 p. [JStNT 27,120].

6279 a) *Camarra Mayor* Saturnino, La identidad del presbítero en la perspectiva del Vaticano II; – b) *Aguirre* Andrés, *Fernández de Troconiz* Luis María, La formación sacerdotal; una tarea postconciliar a contracorriente: Lumen 35 (Victoria 1986) 229-256/ 257-281.

6280 *Carey* George, Reflections upon the nature of ministry and priesthood in the light of the Lima report: Anvil 3,1 (Bristol 1986) 19-32 [< ZIT].

6281 *Cheung* Alex T. M., The priest as the redeemed man; a biblical-theological study of the priesthood: JEvTS 29 (1986) 265-276 [< ZIT].

6282 a) *Clines* D., Biblical reflections on the religious professional [against]; – b) *Baigent* J. [for], Biblical practices and principles: Christian Brethren Review 37 (Exeter 1986) 57-64 / 49-55 [< NTAbs 31,62].

6283 *Coleman* John A., *al.*, A theology of ministry: Way 25 (1985) 7-18 (-53).

6284 a) *Colombi* Giulio, Il diaconato permanente; – b) *Frohnhofen* Herbert, Diaconesse nella Chiesa primitiva [< StiZt (1986) 268-278], TColombi G.: HumBr 41 (1986) 651-676 / 677-690.

6285 *Congar* Yves, Collège, primauté... conférences épiscopales ['pas d'institution divine', de LUBAC dès 1972; RATZINGER...]: EsprV 96 (1986) 385-390.

6285* *Constantin* Leonte C., Le sacerdoce dans la vie de l'Église et dans la vie des fidèles (en roumain): STBuc 38,6 (1986) 84-95.

6286 *Cornick* David, The Reformed Elder [Amt for CALVIN]: ExpTim 98 (1986s) 235-240.

6287 **Cunningham** Agnes, The bishop in the Church: Theology and Life 13, 1985 ➤ 1,7604: RTS 47 (1986) 310s (D. J. *Grimes*: prepared at CODY's request).

6288 a) *Diprose* Rinaldo, Gli anziani nella chiesa neotestamentaria; – b) *Kuen* Alfred, Istituzione e formazione degli anziani, TDel Din S. & A.; – c) *Masters* Peter, Qualità e compiti degli anziani, TFinch P.; – d) *Blandenier* Jacques, Collegialità e ministero pastorale. TCorradini G.: STEv 15 (1985) 4-17 / 18-40 / 41-67 / 68-91.

6289 **Domínguez Sánchez** Benito, El ministerio y su repercusión en la unidad. Valladolid 1984, [Agustinos]. 523 p. – REstE 61 (1986) 94-97 (J. *Iturriaga*: sin indicio de institución académica o aprobación eclesiástica; más simpatía para los documentos ecuménicos que católicos); Gregorianum 67 (1986) 384s (J. *Galot*: réagit contre les positions catholiques).

6290 *Donovan* Mary Ann, Insights on ministry; IRENAEUS: TorJT 2 (1986) 79-93.

6291 **Enrique Tarancón** card. Vicente, El sacerdote en la Iglesia y en el mundo de hoy. Salamanca 1985, Sígueme. 280 p. – RRazF 213 (1986) 661 (V. *Ramallo*).

6292 *Evans* Michael, In persona Christi — the key to priestly identity: CleR 71 (1986) 117-125.

6293 EFransen Piet T., Authority in the Church 1981/3 ➤ 64,487... 1,7009: RHeythJ 27 (1986) 353s (B. C. *Butler*).

6294 *Fusco* Vittorio, Il presbiterio [nella chiesa locale; fondazione biblico-teologica]: Asprenas 33 (1986) 5-35 [non presbiterato, ma luogo, unico nella 'chiesa locale' e intimamente legato al vescovo].

6295 **Galot** Jean, Prêtre au nom du Christ: Le Caillou Blanc 7. Cham-

bray-les-Tours 1985, C.L.D.   286 p. ➤ 1,7612; F 150;   2-85443-078-6:
ᴿGregorianum 67 (1986) 806s (ipse).

6296 **Galot** Jean, Theology of the priesthood 1984 ➤ 65,6862; 1,7613: ᴿTS 47
(1986) 159s (E. J. *Gratsch*).

6297 **Genn** Felix, Trinität und Amt nach AUGUSTINUS [Diss. ᴰ*Greshake*
➤ 1,7614]: Horizonte 23. Einsiedeln 1986, Johannes. 328 p. DM 47. –
ᴿTrierTZ 95 (1986) 231 (H. *Schützeichel*: Hinweis RATZINGERs).

6298 **Grelot** Pierre, Église et ministères... SCHILLEBEECKX 1983 ➤ 64,7178...
1,7617:   ᴿActuBbg 23 (1986) 106s (A. M. *Tortras*); ScripTPamp 18 (1986)
387s (P. *Rodríguez*); TR 82 (1986) 413s (G. *Greshake*: verdient Beachtung
auch nach den Modifizierungen in Schillebeeckx 1985).

6299 *Hahn* Ferdinand, a) Neutestamentliche Grundlagen für eine Lehre vom
kirchlichen Amt [< Dienst und Amt 1973, 7-40]; – b) Charism und Amt;
die Diskussion über das kirchliche Amt im Lichte der neutestamentlichen
Charismenlehre [< ZTK 76 (1979) 419-449]; – c) Die Petrusverheissung Mt
16,18f [< WegFor 439 (1977) 543-563]: ➤ 167, Ges. Aufs. 1 (1986) 159-184
/ 201-231 / 185-200.

6300 *Hall* Sean F., The permanent diaconate— or the divine calling to walk
on water: CleR 70 (1985) 332-6 > TDig 33 (1986) 117s [ᴱ*Asen* B.].

6301 *Hamman* Adalbert, De l'agape à la diaconie, en Afrique chrétienne:
TZBas 42 (1986) 214-221.

6302 *Harbin* Sam, The office of deacon in the local church: CalvaryB 2,1
(1986) 22-28.

6303 *Hein* Martin, *Jung* Hans-G., Bischofsamt: ➤ 587, EvKL 1 (1986)
518-522.

6304 *Hemmerle* Klaus, Diaconato ed eucaristia; il servizio ecclesiale alla luce
del paradigma liturgico [< ᴱ*Plöger* J., Der Diakon (1980) 274-281],
ᵀ*Colombi* G.: HumBr 41 (1986) 741-8.

6305 ᵀ*Hennessey* Lawrence R., *Diakonia* and *diakonoi* in the pre-Nicene
Church: ➤ 73, ꜰMEYER R., Diakonia 1986, 60-86.

6306 *Hickey* Raymond, Priesthood and the Church of the future; the case for
an auxiliary married priesthood: CleR 71 (1986) 158-164.

6307 ᴱ**Kertelge** Karl, Mission im NT: QDisp 93,1982 ➤ 63,308b... 1,7632:
ᴿNZMissW 42 (1986) 138-140 (G. *Schelbert*).

6308 *Kiesow* Ernst-R., Die Amtsfrage als aktuelle Bekenntnisfrage zwischen
Barmen und Lima: ZeichZt 40 (1986) 14-20 [2-8, *Lorenz* Wolfgang].

6309 **König** Dorothee, Amt und Askese; Priesteramt und Mönchtum bei den
lateinischen Kirchenvätern in vorbenediktinischer Zeit: Regulae Benedicti
Sup 12. St. Ottilien 1985, EOS. xi-423 p. DM 48 [TLZ 112,278, G.
Haendler].

6310 **Kruse** Colin G., New Testament models for ministry; Jesus and Paul
1984 ➤ 1,7636: ᴿCBQ 48 (1986) 339-341 (L. T. *Johnson*: illustrates the
difficulty of turning a dissertation into a pastoral theology).

6311 **Laurance** John D., 'Priest as type of Christ'... CYPRIAN 1984 ➤ 65,6881;
1,7645: ᴿSalesianum 48 (1986) 730-2 (A. M. *Triacca*: conclusioni flash o
dovute alla metodologia).

6312 *Lécuyer* Joseph, Le sacrement de l'ordination 1983 ➤ 64,7200 ...1,7646:
ᴿHeythJ 27 (1986) 451s (J. *Coventry*).

6313 **Loppa** Lorenzo, 'In persona Christi'; 'nomine Ecclesiae'; linee per una
teologia del ministero nel Concilio Ecumenico Vaticano II e nel Magistero
post-conciliare (1962-1985); Corona Lateranensis 34. R 1985, Pont. Univ.
Lateranensis. 197 p. Lit. 15.000.

6314 **McCaslin** Patrick, *Lawler* Michael G., Sacrament of service; a vision of the permanent diaconate today. Mahwah NJ 1986, Paulist. $8 pa. [TDig 34,82].

6315 *McGuckin* J. A., ORIGEN's doctrine of the priesthood [< CleR 70 (1985) 277-286; 318-325]: TDig 33 (1986) 334-6.

6316 **McKee** Elsie Anne, John CALVIN, On the diaconate and liturgical almsgiving: TravHumRen 197. Genève 1984, Droz. 309 p. – ᴿRTPhil 18 (1986) 199s (G. *Hammann*).

6317 **Manaranche** André, Le prêtre, ce prophète. P 1982, Fayard. 232 p. F 59 [RTLv 18,255, A. De *Halleux*).

6318 **Marcus** Émile [évêque de Nantes], Les prêtres. P 1984. 164 p. – ᴿAtKap 106 (1986) 185s (B. *Nadolski*).

6319 **Martelet** Gustav, Deux mille ans d'Église en question... crise de sacerdoce 1984 ➤ 65,6768... 1,7655: ᴿEstE 61 (1986) 102s (J. A. *Estrada*: engañoso; sólo cap. 5 sobre el sacerdocio); ScripTPamp 18 (1986) 563-573 (A. *Romero*).

6320 *a*) **Medina** *Estévez* Jorge, Notas sobre los ministerios de la Iglesia confiados a fieles laicos; – *b*) *Noemi Callejas* Juan, Reflexiones teológico-críticas en torno al tema del laico: TVida 27 (1986) 167-172 / 157-166.

6321 **Mondello** Vittorio, Quale Vescovo per il futuro? La dottrina dell'episcopato nella Chiesa 1984 ➤ 65,6893; 1,7657*: ᴿGregorianum 67 (1986) 560s (J. *Galot*).

6322 *Mucci* Giandomenico, Il ministero ordinato nell'ecclesiogenesi di L. BOFF: CC 137 (1986,3) 119-129 [387-394, comparando DUQUOC C.].

6323 **Nicolas** M. J., La grâce d'être prêtre. P 1986, Desclée. 203 p. F 89. – ᴿNRT 108 (1986) 938s (L. D.).

6324 *Nicolas* Marie-Joseph, Le concept intégral de sacerdoce ministériel [< La grâce d'être prêtre, à paraître]: RThom 86 (1986) 5-30.

6325 *Roberts* Richard H., Der Stellenwert des kirchlichen Amtes im ökumenischen Gespräch aus anglikanischer Sicht unter Berücksichtigung der Leuenberger Konkordie [1973] und der Lima-Erklärungen: ZTK 83 (1986) 370-403.

6326 *Röthlin* Eduard, Das Amt in der Kirche: TPQ 134 (1986) 59-62.

6327 *Ruhbach* Gerhard, Zu Kirchengemeinschaft, Abendmahl und Amt: TBei 17 (Wu 1986) [40-43, *Müller* H.-M.] 44s [< ZIT].

6328 *Russell* John L., *Rafferty* Olivier, St. James the Great [? really buried at Compostela] and Anglican Orders [invalid: Papal decrees of comparable authority]: HeythJ 27 (1986) 178-180.

6329 **Schillebeeckx** Edward, Pleidooi voor mensen in de kerk; christelijke identiteit en ambten in de kerk 1985 ➤ 1,7680; 90-244-1527-6: ᴿBijdragen 47 (1986) 340s (A. H. C. van *Eijk*).

6330 **Schillebeeckx** Edward, Christliche Identität und kirchliches Amt; Plädoyer für den Menschen in der Kirche, ᵀ*Zulauf* Hugo, 1985 ➤ 1,7681: ᴿAugR 26 (1986) 602-5 (B. *Studer*); TüTQ 166 (1986) 156-8 (W. *Kasper*); ZkT 108 (1986) 434-8 (P. *Wess*).

6331 **Schillebeeckx** Edward, The Church with a human face; a new and expanded theology of ministry 1985 ➤ 1,7682: ᴿDoctLife 36 (1986) 384 (W. *Harrington*: 'no retraction'); Furrow 57 (1986) 536-9 (W. G. *Jeanrond*: lucid and compelling); Horizons 13 (1986) 432s (M. J. *McGinniss*); JTS 37 (1986) 290-3 (A. *Hanson*); ModT 3 (1986) 114s (P. *Sedgwick*); Month 248 (1986) 103s (A. *Stacpoole*); NBlackf 67 (1986) 289-291 (M. *Richards*,

R. *Schreiter*); Tablet 240 (1986) 11s (F. A. *Sullivan*); TLond 39 (1986) 222-4 (M. *Kitchener*); TS 47 (1986) 157-9 (P. *Chirico*: too much space for the nonproductive synod of 1971).

6331* **Schillebeeckx** E., Per una Chiesa dal volto umano; identità cristiana dei ministeri nella Chiesa: BiblTeolContemp 49. Brescia 1986, Queriniana. 332 p. Lit. 30.000. – ᴿStPatav 33 (1986) 410-3 (E. R. *Tura*).

6332 **Schillebeeckx** Edward, El ministerio eclesial; responsables en la comunidad cristiana [Kerkelijk Ambt 1980 → 62,7931a], ᵀ*Díaz* J. M.: Academia Christiana 22. M 1983, Cristiandad. 237 p. pt. 800. 84-7057-339-X. – ᴿActuBbg 23 (1986) 77-82 (A. M. *Tortras*).

6333 *Schöllgen* Georg, Monepiskopat und monarchischer Episkopat [*Ignatius* Ant.]; eine Bemerkung zur Terminologie: ZNW 77 (1986) 146-151.

6334 *a*) *Segler* Franklin M., Theological foundations for ministry; – *b*) *Oates* Wayne E., The marks of a Christian leader; – *c*) *Dale* Robert D., Leadership-followership [the Apostles ...]; the Church's challenge: SWJT 29,2 (1986s) 5-18 / 19-22 / 23-28.

6335 *Škrinjar* Albin, Svećenička svetost: ObnŽiv 41 (1986) 152-6; 157, Priesterliche Heiligkeit.

6336 *Stevens* R. Paul, Liberating the laity; equipping all the saints for ministry. DG 1985, Inter-Varsity. 177 p. $6 [JAAR 54,402].

6337 *Terrien* Lawrence B., Scripture foundations of ministry; recent publications in English [*Theissen* G., *Meeks* W., *Brown* R. E. ...]: BSulp 12 (1986) 184-203.

6338 *Theodorou* Evangelos, Das Priestertum nach dem Zeugnis der byzantinischen liturgischen Texte: *a*) TAth 57 (1986) 155-172; – *b*) ÖkRu 35 (1986) 267-280.

6339 **Thurian** Max, Priesthood and ministry; ecumenical research 1983 → 64,7235... 1,6595: ᴿHeythJ 27 (1986) 351-3 (J. *Coventry*).

6340 **Trapè** Agostino, Il sacerdote uomo di Dio al servizio della Chiesa; considerazioni patristiche: Gaudium de Veritate 1. R 1985, Città Nuova. 223 p. Lit. 16.000. – ᴿBenedictina 33 (1986) 241s (S. *Spera*).

6341 **Vanhoye** Albert, Sacerdoti antichi e nuovo sacerdote secondo il NT 1985 → 1,7702: ᴿCC 137 (1986,2) 295s (G. *Ferraro*: per il lettore normale non basta citare solo numeri senza il testo biblico stesso); Claretianum 26 (1986) 400-2 (B. *Proietti*).

6342 **Vanhoye** Albert, Sacerdotes antiguos, sacerdote nuevo según el NT 1984 → 65,6926; 1,7703: ᴿCiTom 113 (1986) 147s (A. *Osuna*); PerspT 18 (1986) 401-3 (F. *Taborda*); RazF 214 (1986) 363 (V. *Ramallo*); TVida 27 (1986) 231s (J. M. *Guerrero*).

6343 **Vanhoye** Albert, Old Testament priests and the New Priest according to the New Testament, ᵀ*Orchard* J. B. Petersham MA 1986, St. Bede. xv-332 p. $25. 0-932506-38-0 [NTAbs 31,117]. – ᴿAmerica 155 (1986) 371s (D. J. *Harrington*).

6344 *Vischer* Lukas, Die Rezeption der [Vat. II] Debatte über die Kollegialität: EvT 46 (1986) 508-523.

6344* **Wess** Paul, Ihr alle seid Geschwister; Gemeinde und Priester. Mainz 1983, Grünewald. 149 p. DM 19,80. – ᴿZkT 108 (1986) 176-9 (L. *Lies*: als Stellungnahme zu GRESHAKE 'in persona Christi' und SCHILLEBEECKX 'Gemeinde-delegiert' gekünstelt und gefährlich; p. 179-185, 2 fig., *Wess*' Antwort).

6345 **Young** Frances, *Wilson* Kenneth, Focus on God [social concern is not all that matters for ministers of the Gospel]. L 1986, Epworth. 133 p. £5. 0-7162-0424-X [ExpTim 98,287].

6346 *Ziegenaus* Anton, Zum Selbstverständnis des Priesters in den Zeiten des Umbruchs: ForumKT 2 (1986) 253-267.

H8 *Liturgia, vita religiosa; oratio* – NT – **Prayer.**

6347 **Adams** H. B., What Jesus asks; meditations on questions in the Gospels. St. Louis 1986, 'CBP'. 160 p. $11 pa. 0-8272-4217-4 [NTAbs 30,381].

6347* *a) Adriani* Maurilio, Sulla santità extra-biblica: CiVit 41 (1986) 553-570 (-580, *Basetti Sani* Giulio. ... musulmana); – *b) Targonski* Francesco, Il santo e i santi nella religione ebraica: CiVit 41 (1986) 509-522.

6348 *Agouridis* Savas, **☺** The Word of God and mystical experience of the believer according to the New Testament: DeltioVM 15,1 (1986) 5-19.

6348* *Aldazábal* José, Las lecturas de la Misa: Phase 26,151 ('La Palabra de Dios en la celebración de la Misa' 1986) 9-53.

6349 **Allmen** Jean-Jacques von, Célébrer le salut; doctrine et pratique du culte chrétien: Rites et symboles 15, 1984 ➤ 1,7708: ᴿScEspr 38 (1986) 276-8 (J.-M. *Dufort*).

6350 *Alonso Schökel* Luis, Meditazioni sulla celebrazione eucaristica: Vita Consacrata 22 (1986): 1. Il segno della croce, 95-110; 2. La liturgia penitenziale, 193-199; 3s. Liturgia della Parola, 264-271. 341-347; 5s. Offertorio-Eucaristia-Beraka 437-443. 525-531; 7. Epiclesi, 621-629; 8. Anamnesi-Memoria, 713-720; 9. Consacrazione-Trasformazione, 809-816.

6351 [*Américo*] *Maia* Pedro, O Cristo de Deus para Inácio de Loyola: RCuBíb 10,37s (1986) 109-147.

6352 **Aubrun** Jean, Les oubliés de l'Évangile: Épiphanie. P 1986, Cerf. 155 p. F 63. 2-204-02443-0. – ᴿActuBbg 23 (1986) 246 (X. *Alegre* S.).

6353 **Aumann** Jordan, Christian spirituality in the Catholic tradition [... biblical, patristic briefly]. L/SF 1985, Sheed & W./ Ignatius. x-326 p. $12 [RelStR 13,74, Julia *Gatta*: dismisses Lutheran spirituality as quietistic].

6354 *a) Azevedo* Marcello, Gesù maestro di preghiera; Abba, la preghiera di Gesù; – *b) Vanhoye* Alberto, Gesù maestro di preghiera: ViConsacr 22 (1986) 26-31 [182-192] / 547-563.

6355 **Balthasar** Hans Urs von, Prayer [1955], new English ᵀ*Harrison* Graham. SF 1986, Ignatius. 31 p. $11 pa. [TDig 33,457].

6356 **Balthasar** Hans Urs von, Gli stati di vita del cristiano. Mi 1985, Jaca. 445 p. – ᴿSalesianum 48 (1986) 451s (P. *Braido*).

6357 **Barth** Karl, Prayer, [ᵀ*Terrien* Sara F.] ²*Saliers* Do E. Ph 1985, Westminster. 96 p. $8 pa. – ᴿTDig 33 (1986) 352 (W. C. *Heiser*).

6358 **Bartolomé** Juan J., Escucharás la voz del Señor, tu Dios ... 10 meditaciones bíblicas en torno a la escucha de Dios: Espiritualidad 5. M 1984, CCS. 99 p.

6359 ᴱ**Bianchi** Ugo, La tradizione dell'enkrateia, colloquio Milano 1982/5 ➤ 1,542: ᴿOrChrPer 52 (1986) 478s (G. *Pelland*).

6360 **Bilheimer** Robert S., A spirituality for the long haul; biblical risk and moral stand 1984 ➤ 65,6944: ᴿWorship 60 (1986) 86-88 (R. M. *Friday*).

6361 **Bouley** A., From freedom to formula; the evolution of the Eucharistic Prayer from oral improvisation to written texts. Wsh 1981. – ᴿVigChr 40 (1986) 192s (H. *Wegman* querics 'to improvise well is beyond the capacities of most ministers').

6362 *Bourgeon* Roger [recorded], The Gospel with Dom Helder Camara [60 meditations]. L 1986, Darton-LT. 154 p. £4. 0-232-51685-5 [ExpTim 98,23].

6363 **Bouyer** Louis, A history of Christian spirituality. Tunbridge Wells, Kent 1986, Burns & O.   I. xix-541 p., NT-Fathers; II. x-602 p., Middle Ages; III. 224 p., Orthodox-Protestant-Anglican.   0-86012-113-5; 4-3; 5-1. ᵀ*Ryan* Mary P., *al*. [1968].

6364 *Brovelli* Franco, L'arcivescovo MONTINI 'interprete' del movimento liturgico: ScuolC 114 (1986) 411-437.

6365 *Camelot* P.-T., L'évangile au désert ? : VSp 140 (1986) 362-379.

6366 *a) Comblin* José, A oração profética [... NT: Jesus]; – *b) Guerre* René, A oração das primeiras comunidades: Estudos bíblicos 10 [REB 46,2] (1986) 28-44 / 45-57.

6367 **Common** lectionary [adaptation of 1969 Roman Catholic lectionary for continued use in four or more other Christian denominations]. NY 1983, Church Hymnal. 133 p. $4.50. – ᴿCBQ 48 (1986) 524s (E. *Hensell*: chief improvement is the abandonment of post Pentecost adaptation of OT pericope to Gospel, prohibiting the OT to 'speak for itself').

6368 **Conti** Martino, La vocazione e le vocazioni nella Bibbia 1985 ➤ 1,7726: ᴿLaurentianum 27 (1986) 377-382 (F. *Raurell*: pequeños errores y 'discrepacias').

6369 **Cox** Michael, Handbook of Christian spirituality; a guide to figures and teachings from the biblical era to the twentieth century. SF 1985, Harper & R. 288 p. $15 [JAAR 54,392].

6370 *Davis* Charles, From inwardness to social action; a shift in the locus of religious experience: NBlackf 67 (1986) 114-125.

6371 *Daxelmüller* Christoph, Frömmigkeit [... Judentum, Christentum]: ➤ 586, EnzMär 5 (1986) 383-393.

6372 *Diego Sánchez* Manuel, El leccionario bíblico del 'proprium missarum OCD': Teresianum 37 (1986) 441-460.

6373 *Dion* Marie-Paul, La virginité: ÉglT 17 (1986) 5-39.

6374 **Doriga** Enrique L., Semblanza de Jesucristo [humanidad, mesianidad, divinidad]. Barc 1986, Herder. 76 p. [NatGrac 33,569].

6375 **Dorr** Donal, [... Micha 6,8] Spirituality and Justice. Dublin/Maryknoll 1984, Gill & M./ Orbis. 260 p. £6. – ᴿNorTTs 87 (1986) 115s (K. *Nordstokke*); TLond 39 (1986) 157s (C. *Elliott*: just too good for this world).

6375* *a) Dumas* André, Présence à Christ plutôt que présence du Christ [*Zundel* M.]: BICathP 20 (1986) 49-60; – *b) Durrwell* F.X., La preghiera di Gesù: NuovaUm 8,44 (1986) 7-23.

6376 *Espeja* Jesús, Jesús — creyente y contemplativo — y la contemplación cristiana: SalT 74 (1986) 843-858.

6377 **Esquerda Bifet** Juan, Te hemos seguido; espiritualidad sacerdotal. M 1986, Edica. 175 p. – ᴿNatGrac 33 (1986) 571 (G. *Rodríguez*).

6378 **Fabris** Rinaldo, La preghiera nella Bibbia: Le spighe. R 1985, Borla. 201 p. Lit. 12.000. – ᴿBenedictina 33 (1986) 573 (E. *Tuccimei*); StPatav 33 (1986) 453 (G. *Leonardi*).

6378* ᴱ**Fabris** Rinaldo, La spiritualità del NT: Storia della spiritualità 2. R 1985, Borla. 458 p. Lit. 25.000. – ᴿStPatav 33 (1986) 452s (G. *Segalla*).

6379 **Faricy** Robert, *Wicks* Robert J., Contemplating Jesus [Neumann College, Aston PA 1984]. Mahwah NJ 1986, Paulist. vi-36 p. $3 [TDig 33,361].

6380 **Felici** Sergio, Spiritualità del lavoro nella catechesi dei Padri del II-IV secolo: BiblScRel 75. R 1986, LAS(alesiano). 279 p. Lit. 35.000.

6381 **Futrell** John C., El discernimiento espiritual. Santander 1984, Sal Terrae. 101 p. 84-293-0678-1. – ᴿEstE 61 (1986) 88s (J. *Iturriaga*).

6382 *Galot* Jean, Cristo viene nel mondo? Introduzione all'Avvento: CC 137 (1986,4) 323-337.

6383 *Galot* Jean, *a*) La fonte evangelica della vita consacrata; l'impegno nella povertà [... *Légasse* S. 1966]; – *b*) Il modello evangelico della vita consacrata; Maria primo modello di verginità offerta a Dio: ViConsacr 21 (1985) 384-398 / 469-479 [22 (1986) 12-27.95-100.272-285.444-451.532-546.733-744.817-832].

6384 **García** J. A., Hogar y taller; seguimiento de Jesús y comunidad religiosa. Santander 1985, Sal Terrae. 191 p. – ᴿRazF 214 (1986) 468 (J. *Royo*).

6385 *Glotin* Édouard, Jean-Paul II à Paray-le-Monial ou pourquoi le 'cœur'? NRT 108 (1986) 685-714.

6386 **Groh** D. E., In between Advents; biblical and spiritual arrivals: The Bible for Christian Life. Ph 1986, Fortress. 63 p. $4. 0-8006-2025-9 [NTAbs 31,112].

6387 **Hamman** A. G., Orações dos primeiros cristãos: A oração dos Pobres. São Paulo 1985, Paulinas. 272 p. [REB 46,228].

6388 **Hardy** Daniel W., **Ford** David F., Praising and knowing God. Ph 1985, Westminster. 218 p. $13. – ᴿTTod 43 (1986s) 99s (W. *Brueggemann*).

6389 **Helewa** Giovanni, *Ancilli* Ermanno, La spiritualità cristiana; fondamenti biblici e sintesi storica. R/Mi 1986 [= 1984 prima parte], Teresianum / OR. 178 p. Lit. 10.000 [CC 137/4,102].

6390 *Henry* A. M., Piété: → 578, Catholicisme XI,50 (1986) 403-419.

6391 *John* br. [Taizé], The pilgrim God; a biblical journey. Wsh 1985, Pastoral. 220 p. $13. 0-912405-18-X.

6392 *Josuttis* Manfred, Gottesdienst nach SCHLEIERMACHER: VerkF 31,2 (1986) 47-79.

6393 *Kantzenbach* Friedrich W., Blinder Gehorsam; Variationen des Gehorsamsbegriffs: ZRGg 38 (1986) 208-230.

6394 *Keifert* Patrick, Modern dogma [in-words; red current, green current, yellow current (pop songs), eddies] and liturgical renewal: CurrTM 13 (1986) 214-227.

6395 *Kessel* Rob van, De krisis van de christelijke identiteit; over identiteit en spiritualiteit in de huidige krisis van geloof en kerk: TsTNijm 26 (1986) 329-349; Eng. 349s.

6396 **Łach** J., ❷ Prayer and togetherness: Communio ❷ (1985,4) 60-66 [< RuBi 39,86].

6397 *Lane* Belden C., The spirituality of the evangelical revival: TTod 43 (1986s) 169-177.

6398 ᴱ**Lang** Bernhard, Das tanzende Wort; intellektuelle Rituale im Religionsvergleich 1984 → 1,373: ᴿÉTRel 61 (1986) 107-9 (H. *Winkler*: liturgies; judéo-chrétiennes par Lang).

6399 **Leech** Kenneth, Experiencing God; theology as spirituality. SF 1985, Harper & R. vii-500 p. $21. – ᴿHorizons 13 (1986) 187s (M. *Downey*: Anglican; high level, perhaps too high, but with some errors).

6400 *Lienhard* Marc, Prier au XVIᵉ siècle; regards sur le Biblisch Bettbüchlin du strasbourgeois Othon BRUNELS [1528, année du lat. Precationes biblicae Sanctorum Patrum]: → 83*, ᶠPETER R. = RHPR 66 (1986) 43-55; Eng. 129.

6401 **Lohfink** Norbert, Das Geschmack der Hoffnung; Christsein und christliche Orden 1983 → 64,194a... 1,7772: ᴿArLtgW 28 (1986) 138 (E. von *Severus*); WissWeis 48 (1985) 233s (L. *Lehmann*).

6402 **Lohfink** N., Kirchenträume 1982 → 64,196: ᴿWissWeis 47 (1984) 234 (J. *Lang*).

6403 *Lohfink* Norbert, Die Orden als Gottes Kirchentherapie; biblische Überlegungen zur Not der Kirche und zur Not vieler Orden: Ordenskorrespondenz 27,1 (1986) 31-54.

6404 *López* Rafael, El Corazón de Cristo, obra maestra del Espíritu Santo: TierraN 15,59 (1986) 63-82.

6404* *López-Yarto* Luis, Vida religiosa y increencia; un análisis de actitudes: MiscCom 44 (1986) 385-426.

6405 *a) Luzarraga* Jesús, Espiritualidad bíblica de la Palabra de Dios; – *b) Ramos-Lissón* Domingo, El seguimiento de Cristo (en los orígenes de la espiritualidad de los primeros cristianos): TEspir 30 (1986) 181-206 / 3-27.

6406 *MacCaffrey* James, Prayer, the heart of the Gospel: CleR 71 (1986) 24-26. 68-71 (Mk).

6407 *Maccise* Camillo, Deus presente na História. São Paulo 1986, Paulinas. 110 p. [REB 46,228: Espiritualidade com fundamentos bíblicos].

6408 ᴱ*McGinn* B. *al.*, Christian spirituality; origins to the twelfth century ➤ 588, EncWSp 16, 1985 ➤ 1,376*; also 1986 Routledge-KP, £39.50: ᴿExpTim 98 (1986s) 93s (A. *Louth*: SCHNEIDERS fine; otherwise not clear for whom such an expensive book is intended); Worship 60 (1986) 551-3 (R. K. *Seasoltz*).

6409 ᴱ*Martimort* Aimé G., L'Église en prière; introduction à la liturgie ² *rev* 1983 (1s)/1984 (3) ➤ 1,7781: ᴱZkT 108 (1986) 360-2 (H. B. *Meyer*).

6410 *a) Martínez* German, Catholic liturgical reform [still needed, Christologically founded]; – *b) Anderson* Fred R., Protestant worship today; – *c) Downey* Michael, Worship between the holocausts: TTod 43 (1986s) 52-62 / 63-74 / 75-87.

6411 **Martini** Carlo M., Sulle strade del Signore; meditazioni per ogni giorno 1985 ➤ 1,7783; 88-7610-137-3: ᴿParVi 31 (1986) 146 (F. *Mosetto*).

6412 **Martini** Carlo M., Consolad a mi pueblo, ᵀ*Simó Roig* B. M 1986, Ciudad Nueva. 145 p. – ᴿNatGrac 33 (1986) 604 [C. *Compadre*].

6413 *Martini* Carlo M., *a)* Pregare la Bibbia [meditazione ai giovani, Padova 24.IX.1985]; – *b)* 'In religioso ascolto della parola di Dio' [convegno Assisi, 30.XII.1985]: ➤ 190, Per una santità di popolo 1986, 433-449 / 607-633.

6414 **Marzola** Oddone, Gesù Cristo centro vivo della fede; dall'esperienza religiosa all'annuncio cristiano: Corona Lateranensis 3. R 1986, Pont. Univ. Lateranensis. xvi-386 p. Lit. 25.000.

6415 **Moloney** F., A life of promise 1984 ➤ 65,6998; 1,7788: ᴿSpTod 38 (1986) 370-2 (R. *Wright*).

6416 **Moore** Sebastian, Let this mind be in you; the quest for identity through Oedipus to Christ. Minneapolis 1985, Winston. 174 p. $14 [JAAR 54,394].

6417 **Mulholland** M. Robert ᴶ, Shaped by the Word; the power of Scripture in spiritual formation. Nv 1985, Upper Room. 171 p. $8. – ᴿRExp 83 (1986) 655-7 (E. E. *Thornton*).

6418 *Navoni* Marco, La nuova liturgia ambrosiana delle ore; lettura storico-comparativa: ScuolC 114 (1986) 235-324.

6419 **Nicol** Martin, Meditation bei LUTHER: ForKiDG 34. Gö 1984, Vandenhoeck & R. 195 p. DM 42. – ᴿTZBas 42 (1986) 271-3 (G. *Adam*).

6420 **Orsatti** Mauro, Briciole del Vangelo — riflessioni bibliche. Mi ... Àncora. 111 p. Lit. 7000. – ᴿRivAscM 11 (1986) 334 (G. *Podio*).

6421 *Ottensmeyer* Hilary, Using the Scripture in prayer: RRel 45 (1986) 380-5.

6422 *Parlier* Jean-Luc, À l'épreuve du rite; liturgie et Bible [*Gruber* J., choix de textes pour mariage/enterrement]: ÉTRel 61 (1986) 549-553 [541-7].

6423 **Pennington** M. Basil, The manual of life; the New Testament for daily living. NY 1986, Paulist. 118 p. $5.

6423* **Pilch** John J., Wellness spirituality. NY 1985, Crossroad. 97 p. $8. – ᴿBibTB 16 (1986) 157 (Mary Ann *Getty*).

6424 *Pöhlmann* Horst G., Das Gebet bei uns Theologen und in unserer Welt: Grundsätzliches und Konkretes zum Gebet: TBei 17 (1986) 225-233.

6424* *Ponthot* Joseph, Sacré et sainteté dans le Nouveau Testament: → 493, Expression du Sacré 3 (1978/86) 289-329.

6425 *Putten* Jan W. M. van der, Der biblische Aufbau der Schriften des FRANZISKUS von Assisi: WissWeis 49,1 (1986) 74-77.

6426 **Ratzinger** Joseph, *a*) The feast of faith; approaches to a theology of the liturgy, ᵀ*Harrison* Graham. SF 1986, Ignatius. 153 p. $9 pa. [TDig 33,485]. – *b*) Journey towards Easter. Slough 1987, St. Paul. 159 p. £6. 0-85439-258-0 [ExpTim 98,319].

6427 *Renwart* Léon, Théologie de la vie religieuse; chronique bibliographique: VieCons 58 (1986) 48-61.

6428 **Ridick** Joyce, Treasures in earthen vessels; the vows, a wholistic approach [2 Cor 4,5-15]. NY 1984, Alba. xvii-166; $10 pa. – ᴿRelStR 12 (1986) 45 (Mary Margaret *Pazdan*; drawn from male authors and her own musings; no dialogue with a 'a larger world view'; exclusive language ...).

6429 *Rigo* Antonio, Le formule per la preghiera di Gesù [*to* Jesus: 'Signore Gesù Cristo, Figlio di Dio, abbi pietà di me'] nell'Esicasmo athonita: CrNSt 7 (1986) 1-18.

6430 **Rollin** Bertrand, L'appel évangélique à la pauvreté volontaire: Épiphanie. P 1985, Cerf. 152 p. F 78. – ᴿVSp 140 (1986) 730s (E. *Yon*).

6431 **Rordorf** Willy, Liturgie, foi et vie des premiers chrétiens; études patristiques: THist 75. P 1985, Beauchesne. 520 p.; bibliog. p. 15-25. F 150. 2-7010-1123-1.

6432 **Schnackenburg** Rudolf, Interpretate i segni dei tempi; meditazioni per l'Avvento. Brescia 1985, Morcelliana. 94 p. – ᴿScuolC 114 (1986) 749 (F. *Baj*).

6434 *Schneiders* Sandra M., Theology and spirituality; strangers, rivals, or partners?: Horizons 13 (1986) 253-274.

6435 *a*) *Seasoltz* R. Kevin, Lenten journey from ashes to fire; – *b*) *Walsh* Christopher J., 'And then there were Forty — — —' The origins, developments and themes of Lent: CleR 71 (1986) 40-48 / 49-52.

6436 **Sfameni Gasparro** Giulia, Enkrateia 1984 → 65,7022; 1,7814: ᴿRTLv 17 (1986) 215-8 (Kari E. *Børresen*).

6437 *Sheets* John R., La pauvreté religieuse aujourd'hui; quelques conclusions: Communio 11,5 (P 1986) 51-56 [non in IkaZ].

6438 **Simmons** Joe, The warrior; brief studies in the sources of spiritual mastery, sport, and military power [... sources of spiritual power in West and East are the same for warrior, athlete, and monk]. Lanham MD 1982, UPA. 175 p. $11.25 pa. [RelStR 13,45, W. C. *Beane*].

6439 *Sobrino* Jon, Liberación con espíritu; apuntes para una nueva espiritualidad. Santander 1985, Sal Terrae. 219 p. – ᴿEfMex 4,11 (1986) 144s (E. *Bonnín*).

6440 **Špidlík** Tomas, La spiritualità dell'Oriente cristiano; manuale sistematico. R 1985, Pont. Inst. Stud. Orientalium. 401 p. – ᴿTeresianum 37 (1986) 246 (J. *Castellano*).

6441 **Špidlík** Thomas, The spirituality of the Christian East; a systematic handbook, ᵀ*Gythiel* Anthony P.: Cistercian Studies 79. Kalamazoo 1986, Cistercian. xii-473 p. $49; pa. $18 [RelStR 13,333, J. *Wiseman*].

6442 *Stanley* David, Contemporary Gospel-Criticism and the 'Mysteries of the Life of Our Lord' in the Spiritual Exercises: in ᶠSCHNER George P., Ignatian spirituality in a secular age. (Waterloo ON 1985, Laurier; viii-128 p.) ...

6443 *Stevenson* Kenneth W., Lex orandi and lex credendi — strange bed-fellows? Some reflections on worship and doctrine: ScotJT 39 (1986) 225-241.

6444 **Taft** Robert [➤ 6924], The liturgy of the hours in East and West; the origins of the divine office and its meaning for today [= ²Liturgy of the Hours in the Christian East, ¹1984]. Collegeville 1986, Liturgical. xvii-421 p. – ᴿOrChrPer 52 (1986) 473-5 (P. F. *Bradshaw*).

6445 *Truijen* Vincent, Les lectures du Nouveau Testament dans la liturgie rénovée: QLtg 67 (1986) 235-251.

6446 **Tugwell** Simon, Ways of imperfection 1984 ➤ 1,7819: ᴿDoctLife 35 (1985) 250s (W. *Barden*); NBlackf 67 (1986) 501s (R. *Williams*); SpTod 38 (1986) 71s (Mary *Paynter*).

6446* *Tura* Ermanno R., Per una teologia che alimenti la vita ecclesiale: StPatav 33 (1986) 517-537.

6447 **Ulanov** Ann & Barry, Primary speech; a psychology of prayer. Atlanta 1982, Knox. 192 p. $10. L 1985, SCM. xi-178 p. £6. – ᴿTLond 39 (1986) 68-70 (C. *Bryant* †: aptly Jungian).

6448 **Van Kaam** Adrian, Formative spirituality, I [of 4]. NY 1983, Crossroad. xxi-330 p. $24.50. 0-8245-0544-1. – ᴿHorizons 13 (1986) 189 (F. G. *McLeod*).

6449 ᴱ**Vattioni** Francesco, Sangue e antropologia nella liturgia 1983/4 ➤ 65,549: ᴿOrChrPer52 (1986) 491s (P. *Yousif*).

6450 **Visseaux** R. N., *a)* Beten nach dem Evangelium [< Livre de vie monastique], ᵀ*Haymoz* J. Münsterschwarzach 1983, Vier Türme. 68 p. – *b)* Auf dem Weg des Evangelium; ein Buch vom geistlichen Leben — nicht nur für Mönche [= Livre de vie monastique, vollständiger Text], ᵀ*Haymoz* J. FrS 1984, Kanisius. 158 p. – ᴿArLtgW 28 (1986) 137s (E. von *Severus*).

6450* **Weismayer** Josef, Leben in Fülle; zur Geschichte und Theologie christlicher Spiritualität. Innsbruck 1983, Tyrolia. 218 p. DM 29 [TPQ 135, 193, W. *Wimmer*].

6451 *a)* *Wiéner* Claude, L'Ancien Testament dans le lectionnaire dominical; – *b)* *Trimaille* Michel, Les livres du Nouveau Testament; deuxièmes lectures; – *c)* *Duchesneau* Claude, Une liturgie qui tire son inspiration de la Sainte Écriture: MaisD 165 (1986) 47-60 / 83-105 / 119-131.

6452 *Williamson* sr. Enid, The notion of charism in the religious life: Studia Canonica 19 (Ottawa 1985) 99-114.

6453 **Zampetti** Pier Luigi, Il vangelo di mia mamma 1985 ➤ 1,7827: ᴿCC 137 (1986,2) 615s (P. *Vanzan*).

6454 **Zarri** Adriana, Il pozzo di Giacobbe; geografia della preghiera di tutte le religioni. Brescia 1985, Camunia. 376 p. Lit. 20.000. – ᴿRasT 27 (1986) 581 (A. *Cavadi*: spregiudicatezza teologico-dottrinale).

H8.2 Theologia moralis NT.

6455 *Abbà* Giuseppe, I Christian moral principles di G. GRISEZ e la Secunda pars della Summa Theologiae [... un eccellente manuale che fa problema]: Salesianum 48 (1986) 637-680.

6456 **Adams** J. E., How to help people change; the four step biblical process. GR 1986, Zondervan. xv-203 p. $8 pa. [Horizons 14,422].

6457 *Adoukonou* Barthélemy, Mariage et famille en Afrique; réflexions anthropologiques et théologiques, suggestions pastorales: Communio 11,6 ('La famille' 1986) 84-97 [non in IkaZ].

6458 **Allen** Joseph L., Love and conflict; a covenantal model of Christian ethics 1984 → 1,7829: ᴿInterpretation 40 (1986) 106 (T. *Walker*).

6459 *Anderson* J. Kerby, Artificial reproduction; a biblical appraisal [mostly limited to a few verses cited at the end]: BS 143 (1986) 61-67.

6460 **d'Aviau de Ternay** Henri, Traces bibliques dans la loi morale chez KANT: Bibliothèque des Archives de Philosophie 46. P 1986, Beauchesne. 296 p.; bibliog. p. 277-286. F 120 [TS 47, 759]. 2-7010-1130-2.

6461 **Bayer** Oswald, Nachfolge-Ethos und Haustafel-Ethos; LUTHERs seelsorgerliche Ethik: TBei 17 (Wu 1986) 24-39 [< ZIT].

6462 **Berlendis** Alfredo, La gioia sessuale, frutto proibito? La risposta della Bibbia, della Chiesa e della società. T 1985, Claudiana. 280 p. – ᴿCC 137 (1986,3) 318 (F. *Giunchedi*: al livello di certe pubblicazioni cattoliche americane condannate); NatGrac 33 (1986) 180s (E. *Rivera*); Salesianum 48 (1986) 729s (G. *Gatii*: ['faciloneria' in comparazione con il protestante serio E. *Fuchs*).

6463 *Bray* Alan, History, homosexuality and God: NBlackf 67 (1986) 538-544.

6464 **Bringas Trueba** A., El valor de la vida humana, en las Sagradas Escrituras. M 1984, Fund. S. María. 58 p. – ᴿBibFe 12 (1986) 133 (C. *Barcia*: escribe en título Bringas, en texto Brigas).

6465 *Brundage* James A., 'Allas! that evere love was synne' [CHAUCER]; sex and medieval canon law [presidential address Dec. 29, 1985: to love one's spouse was virtuous; to make love to one's spouse was shameful]: CathHR 72 (1986) 1-13.

6466 **Brunsman** Barry, ... das darf der Mensch nicht trennen? Neue Hoffnung für geschiedene Katholiken, ᵀ*Benn* Roland. Z 1986, Benziger. 223 p. DM 28 [TR 83,6064, K. *Lüdicke*: the translator seems as incompetent as the author].

6467 **Cahill** Lisa S., Between the sexes; foundations for a Christian ethics of sexuality 1985 → 1,7838: ᴿAmerica 154 (1986) 54s (J. M. *Gustafson*); CCurr 36 (1986s) 237-9 (Joan W. *Conn*); CurrTM 13 (1986) 185s (Martha E. *Stortz*); Horizons 13 (1986) 452s (J. P. *Boyle*); RelStT 6 (1986) 43s (W. *Tomm*); TLond 39 (1986) 412-4 (J. *Mathers*).

6468 *Cahill* Lisa S., Canon, authority, norms? Recent studies in biblical ethics [*Curran-McCormick*, *Daly* R.; *Verhey* A. 'amazing command of biblical materials' ...]; Interpretation 40 (1986) 414-7.

6469 *Calvo Cubillo* Quintín, Jesucristo hoy; religión y moral católicas: BUP 1. Estella 1984, VDivino. 253 p. 84-7151-368-4. – ᴿEstE 61 (1986) 90s (J. *Iturriaga*).

6470 **Cambier** Jules M., La libertà cristiana, una morale di adulti. T-Leumann 1984, Elle Di Ci. 344 p. Lit. 14.000. – ᴿParVi 30 (1985) 398-400 (A. *Sisti*: l'autore è esegeta di professione; non dice se è una traduzione).

6471 **Campbell** Alastair, The gospel of anger [it performs useful functions]. L 1986, SPCK. 118 p. £4. 0-281-04221-1. – ᴿExpTim 98 (1986s) 217 (D. *Atkinson*).

6472 *Chabassus* Henri, Jesus... Pedro, Judas e a relação de ajuda: RCuBíb 10,37s (1986) 86-108.

6473 *Cole* G. A., [Dt 21,18-21 ...] Justice; retributive or reformative?: RefTR 45 (1986) 5-12.

6474 **Collins** Raymond F., Christian morality; biblical foundations. ND 1986, Univ. vi-258 p. 0-268-00758-6.

6475 *Croteau* Jacques, Le bel amour de soi; dimension ontologique et dimension psychologique ['Aimer quelque chose ou quelqu'un, c'est toujours en quelque sort s'aimer soi-même']: ScEspr 38 (1986) 361-371.

6476 ᴱ**Daly** Robert J., Christian biblical ethics, from biblical revelation to contemporary Christian praxis; method and content 1984 ➤ 65,7049; 1,7846: ᴿBibTB 16 (1986) 30s (Carolyn *Osiek*); CBQ 48 (1986) 739s (Beverly R. *Gaventa*); JBL 106 (1985) 536-8 (J. E. *Toews*: interim report of nine-year CBA task force).

6477 **Demmer** Klaus, Deuten und handeln; Grundlagen und Grundfragen der Fundamentalmoral [Christologische Basis, zwischen Christonomismus und rein transzendentalen Elementen des Lebens Jesu ...]: Studien zur theologischen Ethik 15. FrS/FrB 1985, Univ./Herder. 240 p. DM 48 [83,140, B. *Fraling*].

6478 **Dillmann** Rainer, Das Eigentliche der Ethik Jesu; ein exegetischer Beitrag zur moraltheologischen Diskussion um das Proprium einer christlichen Ethik: TüTheolSt 23, 1984 ➤ 65,7051; 1,7847: ᴿTPhil 61 (1986) 255-7 (H.-J. *Höhn*); TR 82 (1986) 62s (W. *Wolbert*).

6479 **Drewermann** Eugen, Psychoanalyse und Moraltheogie I. Angst und Schuld. Mainz 1982, Grunewald. - ᴿZRGg 38 (1986) 82s (Ursula *Homann*).

6480 **Drewermann** Eugen, Psychoanalyse und Moraltheologie 2. Wege und Umwege der Liebe. Mainz 1983, Grünewald. 307 p. – ᴿTZBas 42 (1986) 185s. 443 (W. *Neidhart*: Grenzgänger, von beiden Seiten beschossen).

6481 **Drewermann** Eugen, Psychoanalyse und Moraltheologie 3. An den Grenzen des Lebens [cf. ➤ 1,1621ᴿ]. Mainz 1984, Grünewald. 280 p. DM 29,80. – ᴿMüTZ 37 (1986) 205s (G. *Schütz*); TGl 76 (1986) 339-349 (W. *Wolbert*); ZkT 108 (1986) 166-8 (H. *Rotter*).

6482 **Edwards** George R., Gay/Lesbian liberation; a biblical perspective [Gn 19; Jg 19 ...] 1984 ➤ 1,7848: ᴿBibTB 16 (1986) 81s (L. J. *White*).

6483 *Espinel* J. L., Biblia y moral cristiana [12 obras; *Ogletree* T.; *Daly* R.; *Lohfink* G.; *Klassen* W....]: CiTom 113 (1986) 583-595.

6484 *Faber van der Meulen* Harry, Choisir la mort? Perspectives bibliques: PosLuth 34 (1986) 147 ... [< ᴢɪᴛ].

6485 *Fabris* R., Alcuni spunti per una fondazione biblica del diritto canonico: Credere Oggi 6,5 (1985) 19-31.

6486 **Fairweather** Ian C. M., *McDonald* James I. H., The quest for Christian ethics 1984 ➤ 65,7055; 1,7851: ᴿJTS 37 (1986) 293-5 (D. *Brown*; not enough post-1975).

6487 *Frank* Isnard W., Belastendes Erbe; zur Leib- und Geschlechtsfeindlichkeit in der Kirche: Wort und Antwort 27,2 (Mainz 1986) 35-40.

6488 **Fuchs** E., *Stucki* P.-A., Au nom de l'Autre; essai sur le fondement des Droits de l'homme: Champ éthique 12. Genève 1985, Labor et Fides. 243 p. 2-8309-0022-7. – ᴿCC 137 (1986,3) 316s (J. *Joblin*); ÉTRel 61 (1986) 101-4 (J. *Ansaldi*: 'étude critique') [247-250, O. *Vallet*].

6489 **Fuchs** Eric, Sexual desire and love, ᵀ*Daigle* Marsha, 1983 ➤ 65,7057: ᴿJAAR 54 (1986) 172s (L. R. *Sachs*; not innovative, not comprehensive, not well-organized) [➤ 6462ᴿ]; JRel 66 (1986) 215s (Lisa S. *Cahill*).

6490 *Fuchs* Eric, Pour une réinterprétation éthique du dogme trinitaire: ÉTRel 61 (1986) 533-540.

6491 **Fuchs** Josef, a) Personal responsibility and Christian morality, ᵀ*Cleves* W. al.; –b) Christian ethics in a secular arena, ᵀ*Hoose* B., *McNeil* B. Wsh 1984, Georgetown Univ. v-230 p.; vii-154 p. $10 each. – ᴿHorizons 13 (1986) 450-2 (N. J. *Rigali*).

6492 *Fuchs* Josef, Christian morality; biblical orientation and human evaluation [Lecture at St. Thomas College, St. Paul, 8 April 1986]: Gregorianum 67 (1986) 745-763; deutsch 763.

6493 *Fuchs* Joseph, Marital love; Christian pluralism in the 12th century [< StiZt 110 (1985) 803-817], [TE]*Asen* B. A.: TDig 33 (1986) 313-8.

6494 **Gallagher** John, The basis for christian ethics 1985 → 1,7858: [R]CCurr 36 (1986s) 480-4 (J. R. *Pollock*); CurrTM 13 (1986) 247 (C. W. *Mangold*: rather a Catholic, philosophical ethics).

6495 **García de Haro** Ramón, *Celaya* Ignacio de, La sabiduria moral cristiana [= ²La moral 1975]: Coll. teol. 46. Pamplona 1986, EUNSA. 248 p. – [R]ScripTPamp 18 (1986) 950-4 (A. *Quirós*).

6496 **Gardner** E. Clinton, Christocentrism in Christian social ethics; a depth study of eight modern Protestants. Lanham MD 1983, UPA. 264 p. $22.50; pa. $11.75. 0-8191-2954-2; 5-0. – [R]Encounter 47 (1986) 93-95 (R. D. N. *Dickinson*).

6497 *Gerhardsson* Birger, Enhetsskapande element i Bibelns etiska mångfald: SvTKv 62 (1986) 49-58.

6498 **Gill** Robin, A textbook of Christian ethics. E 1985, Clark. xiii-571 p. £10 [TLZ 112,221-3, H. *Kress*].

6499 **Grisez** G., The way of the Lord Jesus I, 1983 → 65,7063; 1,7868: [R]AustralasCR 63 (1986) 225s (B. *Lucas*); ColcT 56,3 (1986) 199-203 (J. *Kempski*); Horizons 13 (1986) 199s (C. E. *Curran*, 'one of the authors with whom Grisez strongly disagrees'); TLond 39 (1986) 74-76 (E. J. *Bayer*: he rejects AQUINAS' doctrine that God is man's final end; rejects capital punishment but not war).

6500 *Grisez* Germain, Infallibility and contraception; a reply to Garth HALLETT: TS [43 (1982) 629] 47 (1986) 134-145.

6501 **Guindon** André, The sexual creators; an ethical proposal for concerned Christians [including how the irreversibly-homosexual and the celibate can be fecund]. Lanham MD 1986, UPA. 246 p. $28; pa. $13 [RelStR 13,249, S. G. *Post*].

6502 *Guindon* André, Homosexualités et méthodologie éthique; à propos d'un livre de Xavier *Thévenot* [bonne piste, pas assez]: ÉglT 17 (1986) 57-84.

6503 **Gustafson** James M., Ethics and theology 1984 → 65,7066; 1,7870: [R]Interpretation 40 (1986) 330s (J. P. *Gunnemann*); RelStR 12 (1986) 11-16 (G. *Meilaender*).

6503* **Hallett** Garth L., Christian moral reasoning, an analytic guide. ND 1982, Univ. 272 p. $20; pa. $9. 0-268-00740-3; 1-1. – [R]HeythJ 27 (1986) 356s (G. *Hughes*).

6504 **Hanigan** James P., As I have loved you; the challenge of Christian ethics. NY 1986, Paulist. 227 p. $10 [RelStR 13,156, M. K. *Duffey*].

6505 **Hauerwas** Stanley, The peaceable kingdom; a primer in Christian ethics 1983 → 65,7068; 1,7874: [R]Interpretation 40 (1986) 75-77 (M. *Longwood*); JRel 66 (1986) 217s (R. B. *Miller*).

6506 *Herzog* W. R., The New Testament and the question of racial justice: AmBapQ 5,1 (Valley Forge 1986) 12-32 [< NTAbs 31,65].

6507 *Houdijk* Rinus, Kerk en homoseksualiteit; veranderende opvattingen en de aard van kerkelijke reacties: TsTNijm 26 (1986) 259-281; Eng. 281 'neither Scripture nor tradition binds the modern believer to a rejection'.

6508 *Jelonek* Tomas, ❷ Posoborowa odnowa biblijna w duszpasterstwie (De renovatione biblica postconciliari in re pastorali): RuBi 39 (1986) 469-477.

6509 *Josuttis* Manfred, Kirche zwischen Angst und Macht; zur Entlassung homosexueller Pfarrer aus dem kirchlichen Dienst: Junge Kirche 47 (Bremen 1986) 412-6.

6510 ᴱKertelge Karl, Ethik im NT: QDisp 102, 1983/4 ➤ 65,422: ᴿTR 82 (1986) 117-9 (H. *Merklein*).

6511 *Klein* Ralph W., Dialog with gay and Lesbian Lutherans; a response [to 'A call for dialog', Chicago, Lutherans Concerned; iii. biblical issues, but 'our moral judgments are not limited to the Bible']: CurrTM 13 (1986) 304-6 [358-360, response (also anonymous), 'Since when has nature been set up as the arbiter of our moral decisions? (not Rom 1,26)'].

6512 **Koenig** John, New Testament hospitality; partnership with strangers as promise and mission: OvBT 17, 1985 ➤ 1,7891: ᴿTDig 33 (1986) 369 (W. C. *Heiser*).

6513 *Kroeker* P. Travis, Canada's Catholic bishops and the economy; a theological ethical analysis: TorJT 2 (1986) 3-18 (19s, 21s, responses; *Baum* Gregory; *Hutchinson* Roger).

6514 *Kuster* H. J., *Cormier* R. J., Old views and new trends; observations on the problem of homosexuality in the Middle Ages [*Boswell* J. 1980]: Studi Medievali 25 (1984) 311 (587-610).

6515 **Langkammer** Hugolin, ⊖ Etyka Nowego Testamentu; 'jeśli chcesz wejść do królestwa Bożego'. Wrocław 1985, Archidiecezja. 275 p. – ᴿRuBi 39 (1986) 367s (J. *Czerski*).

6516 **Lapide** Pinchas, Hoe heeft men zijn vijanden lief? Kampen 1984, Kok. 87 p. ƒ 12,90 [NedTTs 40,244].

6517 *Lefèvre* Luc J., Connaissance et morale dans la Bible: PenséeC 225 (1986) 42-47.

6518 **Longenecker** R., NT social ethics for today 1984 ➤ 65,7080; 1,7896: ᴿSt-Patav 33 (1986) 450s (G. *Segalla*); TLZ 111 (1986) 427s (J. H. *Friedrich*).

6519 **Lütgert** Wilhelm, Die Liebe im Neuen Testament; ein Beitrag zur Geschichte des Urchristentums. Giessen 1986 = 1905, Brunnen. xvii-275 p. 3-7655-9237-4.

6520 **Mackin** Theodore, Divorce and remarriage: Marriage in the Catholic Church, 1984 ➤ 65,7086; 1,7899: ᴿTLZ 111 (1986) 616-9 (A. *Stein*).

6521 *McCormick* Richard A., Health and medicine in the Catholic tradition [Inauguration lecture, Lv Centrum voor Bio-Medische Ethiek, Feb. 4, 1986]: ETL 62 (1986) 207-215 [207-210, Scripture].

6522 *a) McCormick* Richard A. *al.,* Notes on moral theology, 1985 [... *Ratzinger*'s 'unqualified bleakness' (*Lash*)]; – *b) Spohn* William C., The use of Scripture in moral theology: TS 47 (1986) 69-88 [102-117, *Cahill* Lisa S., sexual ethics; 117-133, *Hollenbach* D., nuclear deterrence] / 88-102.

6523 **MacIntyre** Alasdair, After virtue; a study in moral theory. ND 1981, ² ʳᵉᵛ1984, Univ. x-252 p. (² xii-292 p.), avec chapître de réponse aux critiques). – ᴿRThom 86 (1986) 137-142 (S. T. *Pinckaers*, donnant à la fin le contenu des révisions, mais en changeant 'Alasdair' en 'Alastair' et 'in moral' en 'of moral').

6524 **MacNamara** Vincent, Faith and ethics. Dublin 1985, Gill & M. 255 p. £6. 0-7171-1403-1. – ᴿExpTim 97 (1985s) 252 (R. G. *Jones*).

6525 **Malherbe** Abraham J., Moral exhortation; a Greco-Roman sourcebook: Library of Early Christianity 4. Ph 1986, Westminster. 178 p.

6526 **Maly** Karl, Handeln als Christ; eine Orientierungshilfe. Fra 1985, Knecht. 160 p. DM 21 pa. – ᴿBiKi 41 (1986) 186s (P.-G. *Müller*).

6527 *Mare* W. Harold, The work ethic of the Gospels and Acts: ➤ 65, ꟷMACRAE Allan 1986, 155-168.

6528 *a*) *Marx* Alfred, Israël et l'accueil de l'étranger selon l'Ancien Testament; – *b*) *Salles* Catherine, Le monde gréco-romain du 1er siècle; une société interculturelle?: SuppVSp 156 (1986) 5-14 / 15-28.

6529 *Mattei* P., Le divorce chez TERTULLIEN; examen de la question à la lumière des développements que le De monogamia consacre à ce sujet [... a-t-il en certains cas reconnu aux divorcés le droit (ou la simple licence) de se remarier?]: RevSR 60 (1986) 207-234.

6530 **May** William F., The physician's covenant; images of the healer in medical ethics 1983 → 64,4371: RJRel 66 (1986) 214s (E. C. *Gardner*, also on *Nelson* J. → 6538*).

6531 **Meeks** Wayne A., The moral world of the first Christians. Ph 1986, Westminster. 182 p. $19 [TS 48,541-3, L. T. *Johnson*]. 0-664-21910-1.

6532 *Meeks* Wayne A., Understanding early Christian ethics [SBL presidential address, Anaheim 23 Nov. 1985]: JBL 105 (1986) 3-11.

6533 *Merk* Otto, Neutestamentliche Ethik: → 587, EvKL 1 (1986) 1140-3.

6534 *a*) *Millar* David R., The value of human life; – *b*) *Winter* Richard, Homosexuality; – *c*) *Jackson* Douglas M., Conscience and modern medicine: → 261, Medicine and the Bible 1986, 127-143.261 / 145-163.262s / 217-236. 267s [191-216, *Hurding* Roger].

6535 **Mott** Stephen, Jesus and social ethics [three theses on NT...] 1984 → 1,7903: RRelStR 12 (1986) 57 (Pheme *Perkins*).

6536 **Naud** André, La recherche des valeurs chrétiennes; jalons pour une éducation [se réduit à: liberté, amour, prière, attitude face à l'argent]: Héritage et projet 31. Montréal 1985. 325 p. – RScEspr 38 (1986) 393-9 (G. *Plante*).

6537 *Navone* J., What is 'love'?: HomPast 86,6 (1985s) 46-50.

6538 *Neckebrouck* V., La polygynie africaine, idéal ou concession? À propos des arguments littéraires: RAfrT 10,19 (1986) 15-30.

6538* **Nelson** J. R., Human life, a biblical perspective for bioethics 1984 → 65,7094; 1,7905: RStPatav 33 (1986) 481 (G. *Trentin*).

6539 **Niebergall** A.† 1978, ERitter A. M., Ehe und Eheschliessung in der Bibel und in der Geschichte der alten Kirche; Marburger Theol. St. 18. Marburg 1985, Elwert. xxvi-267 p. DM 80. 3-7708-0806-1 [NTAbs 30,366].

6540 **O'Donovan** Oliver, Resurrection and moral order; an outline for evangelical ethics. Leicester 1986, Inter-Varsity. 284 p. £15. 0-85111-745-7. – RExpTim 98 (1986s) 188 (E. J. *Warnock*); Themelios 12 (1986s) 99s (T. *Hart*).

6541 **Ogletree** Thomas W., The use of the Bible in Christian ethics 1983 → 64,7354... 1,7909: RJRel 66 (1986) 213s (J. *Comstock*); JTS 37 (1985) 295s (K. *Ward*).

6542 **Ohrstedt** Robert J., Abortion; focus of conflict [four hidden agendas (apart from proper role of government): i. when does life begin? ii. quality of life; abortion-veto hits the poor harder; iii. family stability; iv. women's changing role]: CurrTM 13 (1986) 132-142.

6543 **Osborn** Eric, La morale dans la pensée chrétienne primitive; description des archétypes de la morale patristique [Ethical patterns 1976], TLatteur E.: THist 68, 1984 → 1,7910: RBLitEc 87 (1986) 306s (H. *Crouzel*); NRT 108 (1986) 581 (L. *Volpe*); StPatav 33 (1986) 704s (G. *Segalla*).

6544 **Payer** Pierre J., Sex and the Penitentials [really: development of a sexual code from 500 to 1150]. Toronto 1984, Univ. xii-220 p. – RSR 14 (1985) 388s (A. *Guindon*).

6545 *Peters* Ted, A book worth discussing [*MacIntyre* Alasdair, After Virtue 1981]: CurrTM 13 (1986) 113-6.

6545* **Phipps** William E., Was Jesus married? The distortion of sexuality in the Christian tradition. Lanham MD 1986, UPA. [ix-] 239 p. $11.75 pa. [CBQ 48,779].

6546 *Piegsa* Joachim, *Dobiosch* Hubert, Ist der menschliche Keim in den ersten zwei Wochen keine Person? ForumKT 2 (1986) 303-310.

6547 *Pietrantonio* Ricardo, ¿Está la justicia enraizada en el NT?: RBibArg 48 (1986) 89-119.

6548 **Pinckaers** T. Servais, Les sources de la morale chrétienne, sa méthode, son contenu, son histoire. FrS 1985, Univ. 523 p. 2-8271-0297-8. – ᴿÉT-Rel 61 (1986) 302s (J. *Ansaldi*: mépris de l'exégèse; caricature de la Réforme; surdité à l'apport des sciences humaines); Salmanticensis 33 (1986) 383s (J.-R. *Flecha*).

6549 **Piva** Pompeo, La fondazione critica della norma di moralità alla luce del Vangelo e dell'esperienza umana: diss. Antonianum, ᴰ*Perugini* L. R 1986. 93 p. extr.

6550 [*Ratzinger* Joseph prefetto] Congregazione per la dottrina della fede, Lettera ai vescovi della Chiesa Cattolica sulla cura pastorale delle persone omosessuali: OssRom 31.X. 1986,1 = CC 137 (1986,4) 367-376; 560-9, commento di *Marchesi* G.

6551 **Rey-Mermet** T., Croire 4: Pour une redécouverte de la morale 1985 ➤ 1,7920; Fb 691. – ᴿRTLv 17 (1986) 218s (M. *Dayez*).

6552 **Schmidt** Frederick W., Ethical prescription and practical justification in selected apocalyptic literature and the teaching of Jesus; advancing the debate over the relationship between ethic and eschatology: diss. ᴰ*Morgan* R. Oxford 1986. 399 p. – RTLv 18,550.

6553 **Schnackenburg** Rudolf, Die sittliche Botschaft des neuen Testament, I. Von Jesus zur Urkirche²ʳᵉᵛ [¹1954]: TheolKomm Sup 1. FrB 1986, Herder. 271 p. DM 48. 3-451-20685-4 [NTAbs 31,116]. – ᴿExpTim 98 (1986s) 303s (E. *Best*: more critically and tightly written than [Eng.] 1954).

6554 **Schuster** Josef, Ethos und kirchliches Amt; zur Kompetenz des Lehramtes in Fragen der natürlichen Sittlichkeit 1984 ➤ 1,7927: ᴿTGl (1986) 363s (W. *Wolbert*).

6555 *Segalla* Giuseppe, L'etica di Gesù da DODD a DILLMANN (1951-1984), una rassegna: TItSett 11 (1986) 24-66; Eng. 67.

6556 La sessualità nella Bibbia [Commissione Valdese-Metodista] 1984 ➤ 1,7936: ᴿSapienza 39 (1986) 213-223 (A. *Cavadi*: conforto per l'ecumenismo).

6557 **Shklar** Judith N., Ordinary vices [overlooked by the Decalogue and the Capital Sins: snobbery, hypocrisy, and in first place cruelty]. CM 1984, Harvard Univ. x-268 p. £13.20. – ᴿTLond 39 (1986) 70s (Helen *Oppenheimer*).

6558 *Soares-Prabhu* George, 'As we forgive'; interhuman forgiveness in the teaching of Jesus: Concilium 184 (E 1986) 57-65 (ed. ital. ᵀ*Gatti* E., 245-258; franç. ᵀ*Divault* A. 73-84; deutsch ᵀ*Saiber* B. 120-6).

6559 *Sobrino* Jon, Lo divino de luchar por los derechos humanos [< SalT 72 (1984) 683-697], ᴱ*Cortés i Bofill* Miquel: SelT 25 (1986) 163-8.

6560 *a) Soggin* J. Alberto, Solidarietà nel Popolo di Dio; – *b) Dacquino* Pietro, Solidarietà e mediazione nella Bibbia; – *c) Rolla* Armando, Episodi emblematici di non solidarietà nell'AT; – *e) Mosetto* Francesco, Luci paoline sulla solidarietà cristiana: ParVi 30 (1985) 170-3 / 174-182 / 183-9 / 190-200 / 201-210.

6561 **Spicq** Ceslas, Connaissance et morale dans la Bible: Études d'éthique chrétienne 13. 1985 ➤ 1,7938: ᴿGregorianum 67 (1986) 565 (É. *Hamel*);

NRT 108 (1986) 747s (X. *Jacques*); ScripTPamp 18 (1986) 683-6 (J. M. *Yanguas*).

6562 **Spohn** William C., What are they saying about Scripture and ethics? 1984 ➤ 65,7116; 1,7939: ᴿCiTom 113 (1986) 583-5 (J. *Espinel*); Horizons 13 (1986) 196s (Christine E. *Gudorf*; conceptually flawed); SWJT 29,2 (1986s) 56s (W. M. *Tillman*).

6563 **Thévenot** X., Homosexualités masculines et morale chrétienne [ch. 3/1, Écriture, surtout Gn 1-3...] 1985 ➤ 1,7944: ᴿActuBbg 23 (1986) 245 (M. *Cuyás*); FoiTemps 16 (1986) 479 (P. *Weber*); NRT 108 (1986) 291 (L. *Volpe*).

6564 *Thornton* Larry R., A biblical view of artificial insemination [only husband-sperm allowed]; CalvaryB 2,2 (1986) 56-69.

6564* **Trentin** Giuseppe, Vent'anni di teologia fondamentale in Italia (1965-1985): StPatav 33 (1986) 539-565.

6565 **Valen-Sendstad** Aksel, Innføring i kristen etikk.   Oslo 1984, Luther. 500 p. – ᴿTsTKi 57 (1986) 297-301 (I. *Asheim*).

6566 **Verhey** Allen, The great reversal; ethics & NT 1984 ➤ 65,7122; 1,7948: ᴿBibTB 16 (1986) 41s (A. D. *Jacobson*); CiTom 113 (1986) 586s (J. L. *Espinel*); JAAR 54 (1986) 161s (B. *Witherington*); JBL 105 (1986) 330-2 (W. *Willis*); JPsy&T 14 (1986) 74-76 (M. K. *Mayers*).

6567 *Vincent* D., Christian vision of marriage in the New Testament and tradition: JDharma 11 (1986) 278-286.

6568 *Walf* Knut, Homosexualität und katholisches Kirchenrecht: Orientierung 50 (1986) 54s.

6569 **Walters** John R., Perfection in New Testament theology; the relation of eschatological existence to ethical demand: diss. ᴰ*Sanders* E. Oxford 1986. 408 p. – RTLv 18,550.

6570 *Webster* John B., *a)* The imitation of Christ [... moral theology]: TyndB 37 (1986) 95-120; – *b)* Christology, imitability and ethics: ScotJT 39 (1986) 309-326.

6571 *Welker* Michael, Security of expectations; reformulating the theology of law and gospel: JRel 66 (Ch 1986) 237-260.

6572 **Wennberg** Robert N., Life in the balance; exploring the abortion controversy ['status of particular abortions may vary: some justified, some excused, many wrong, some uncertain, but all tragic... on the whole morally ojectionable']. GR 1985, Eerdmans. xi-184 p. $8. – ᴿRelStR 12 (1986) 277 (P. *Nelson*: evangelical Protestant).

6573 *Witschen* Dieter, Die streng deontologisch verstanden Idee der Gerechtigkeit, erläutert am Beispiel von KANTS absoluter Straftheorie: TPhil 61 (1986) 60-85.

6574 *Ziegler* J. G., *a)* 'Christus, der neue Adam' (GS 22); eine anthropologisch integrierte christzentrische Moraltheologie; die Vision des Vatikanum II. zum Entwurf einer Gnadenmoral: StMor 24 (R 1986) 41-70; – *b)* Vom Sein zum Leben in Christus; für eine spirituelle Moraltheologie: TR 82 (1986) 265-274.

6575 *Zmijewski* Josef, *a)* Neutestamentliche Weisungen für Ehe und Familie [< SNTU-A 9 (1984) 31-78]; – *b)* Überlegungen zum Verhältnis von Theologie und christlicher Glaubenspraxis anhand des NTs [< TGl 72 (1982) 40-78]: ➤ 233, Das NT Quelle 1986 324-378 / 223-264.

H8.4   *NT ipsum de reformatione sociali* – **Political action in Scripture.**

6576 **Antonides** Harry, Stones for bread; the Social Gospel and its contemporary legacy. Jordan Station ON 1985, Paideia. xvi-264 p. – ᴿSR 15 (1986) 407 (R. *Hutchinson*: attentive to Canadian materials, inattentive to feminism).

6577 ᴱ**Bammel** E., *Moule* C., Jesus and the politics of his day (1984 ➤ 65,267; 1,7961), paperback. NY 1985, Cambridge-UP. xi-511 p. $18. – ᴿCurrTM 13 (1986) 372 (E. *Krentz*); JBL 105 (1986) 173s (E. J. *Epp*: tit. pp.); JTS 37 (1986) 513-7 (G. N. *Stanton*: excellent).

6578 *Blackburn* J. R., The politics of Jesus: Faith & Freedom 39,115 (Oxford 1986) 37-44 [NTAbs 31,14].

6579 *a*) *Bonora* Antonio, Il potere 'politico' nell'Antico Testamento; – *b*) *Segalla* Giuseppe, Exousia nel Nuovo Testamento; il potere fra autorità di servizio e autorità di dominio; – *c*) *Pesce* Mauro, Marginalità e sottomissione; la concezione escatologica del potere politico in Paolo: ➤ 489, Cristianesimo e potere 1985/6, 21-36 / 37-42 / 43-80.

6580 **Borg** Marcus J., Conflict; holiness and politics in the teaching of Jesus [< diss. Oxford 1972, ᴰ*Caird* G.]: Studies in the Bible and Early Christianity 5, 1984 ➤ 65,7134; 1,7965: ᴿCBQ 48 (1986) 736s (J. H. *Elliott*: lacks conceptual models); JBL 105 (1986) 723s (W. R. *Farmer*: no one critical school); RelStR 12 (1986) 68 (R. H. *Fuller*).

6581 **Brown** Robert M., Unexpected news; reading the Bible with Third World eyes 1984 ➤ 65,7136: 1,7966: ᴿHorizons 13 (1986) 158s (F. X. *Meehan*); SpTod 38 (1986) 73s (J. *Alison*).

6582 **Bühler** Pierre, Kreuz und Eschatologie, eine Auseinandersetzung mit der politischen Theologie 1981 ➤ 62,7633.8170; 65,7137: ᴿLuthJb 53 (1986) 140-2 (M. *Seils*).

6583 **Burgess** John P., The problem of Scripture and political affairs as reflected in the Puritan revolution; Samuel RUTHERFORD, Thomas GOODWIN, John GOODWIN and Gerrard WINSTANLEY: diss. ᴰ*Gustafson* J. Chicago 1986. 321 p. RTLv 18,576.

6583* **Castillo** José M., *Estrada* Juan A., El proyecto de Jesús: Verdad e Imagen 94, 1985 ➤ 1,553: ᴿPerspT 18 (1986) 262s (C. *Palácio*: centenário de Lutero, Málaga 1983).

6584 **Christophe** Paul, Les pauvres et la pauvreté, des origines au XVᵉ siècle, I: Bibliothèque d'histoire du christianisme. P 1985, Desclée. 152 p. F 79. – ᴿÉtudes 364 (1986) 569s (P. *Vallin*).

6584* **Comblin** José, Introdução geral ao comentário bíblico; leitura da Biblia na perspectiva dos pobres. Petrópolis 1985, Vozes, 20 p. – ᴿPerspT 18 (1986) 395s (M. *Díaz-Mateos*).

6585 *a*) *Crampsey* James A., Jesus and power; – *b*) *Kennedy* Ted, Called to be powerless?: Way 26 (1986) 180-188 / 189-197.

6586 *Cuthbertson* Malcolm, The kingdom and the poor [OT *ebyon, dal, 'ani, rûš*; Ex 6,6; Lev 25; NT ...; the Gospel is biased to the poor]: ScotBEvT 4 (1986) 123-133.

6587 **Davis** John J., Your wealth in God's world 1984 ➤ 1,7972: ᴿBS 143 (1986) 371 (D. K. *Lowery*: for those looking for an affirmation of conservative economics).

6588 *Dijon* Xavier, Petite théologie du pouvoir [i. l'altérité juive; ii. la subversion chrétienne; iii. les deux pouvoirs; iv. la sécularisation ...]: NRT 108 (1986) 64-75.

6589 *Drescher* Hans-Georg, Demokratie, Konservatismus und Christentum; Ernst TROELTSCHs theologisches Konzept zum Umgang mit politischer Ethik auf dem Evangelisch-sozialen Kongress 1904: ZEvEthik 30 (1986) 84-98.

6590 **Eidsmoe** John, God and Caesar; Christian faith and political action. Westchester IL 1984, Crossway. xii-239 p. $8 pa. – ᴿBS 143 (1986) 82s (J. A. *Witmer*).

6591 **Elliott** Charles, Praying the Kingdom; towards a political spirituality. L 1985, Darton-LT. ix-150 p. £3.50. – ᴿMonth 248 (1986) 31 (B. B. *McClorry*).

6592 *Espinel* José Luis, Jesús y los movimientos políticos y sociales de su tiempo; estado actual de la cuestión: CiTom 113 (1986) 251-284.

6593 **Farina** Marcella, Chiesa di poveri e Chiesa dei poveri; la fondazione biblica di un tema conciliare: Il prisma 3. R 1985, LAS. 270 p.; bibliog. p. 15-44. Lit. 20.000. 88-213-0124-9. – ᴿBiblica 67 (1986) 588-590 (J. *Swetnam*); NatGrac 33 (1986) 559s (D. *Montero*); ParVi 31 (1986) 393s (B. *Marconcini*: data 1966); Salesianum 48 (1986) 810 (*ipsa*).

6594 *Flood* David, Gospel poverty and the poor: Concilium 188 (1986) 63-69 (ed. ital. La povertà evangelica e i poveri, ᵀ*Guzzetti* C. M. 739-748).

6595 *Foucachon* F., 'Jésus politicien?' [*Yoder* F. reductionist 1972]: RRéf 37 (1986) 106-112 [NTAbs 31,14].

6596 **Fraijó** M., Jesús y los marginados; utopía y esperanza cristiana. M 1985, Cristiandad. 312 p. – ᴿSalT 74 (1986) 663s (M.del *Campo Guilarte*).

6597 *a*) *Goba* Bonganjalo, The use of Scripture in the Kairos document; a biblical ethical perspective: – *b*) *Gifford* Paul, The Sola Scriptura ideal; the almost normative status of a purely contingent theological situation; – *c*) *Domeris* W. R., Biblical perspectives on the poor: JTSAf 56 (1986) 61-65 / 57 (1986) 43-56 / 57-61 [< TKontext 8/2,18].

6598 **Griffiths** Brian, The creation of wealth; a Christian's case for capitalism. DG 1985, Inter-Varsity. 160 p. $6 [JAAR 54.209].

6599 **Haley** J., The power tactics of Jesus Christ and other essays = Tacticiens de Pouvoir. P 1984, ESF [ÉTRel 61,325].

6600 **Hanson** A., Liberation theology and the New Testament [... more in OT]: Search 8,2 (Dublin 1985) 65-69.

6601 **Haughey** John C., The holy use of money; personal finances in light of Christian faith. GGNY 1986, Doubleday. xi-274 p. $17 [TS 48,595, A. J. *Tambasco*].

6602 *Heideman* Eugene P., The Bible in public life: → 82* ꜰOsterHaven M. E., RefR 39 (1985s) 222-230.

6603 *Hertog* Gerhard den, Durchbruch nach vorn; zu H. J. Iwands Vortrag Die Bibel und die soziale Frage (II): ZdialektT 2 (Kampen 1986) 89-108.

6604 *Herzog* William R.ᴵᴵ, The New Testament and the question of racial justice: AmBapQ 5 (1986) 12-32 [*al.* 2-78 < zɪᴛ].

6605 **Hexham** Irving, The Bible, justice and the culture of poverty [→ 1,7981]; emotive calls to action versus rational analysis. L 1985, Social Affairs Unit. 17 p. £2. – ᴿTLond 39 (1986) 411s (K. *Leech*, also on A. Flew and cognate pamphlets).

6606 *Higuera* Gonzalo, Aportaciones de la ética evangélica a una ética civil: SalT 73 (1985) 815-823.

6607 *Höhn* Hans-Joachim, Politischer Glaube? Massstäbe kirchlicher Stellungnahmen zu Fragen der Politik [i. Wie politisch dürfen Christen sein?; ii. Politische Vernunft und christlicher Glaube; iii. Kirche in der Politik — Politik in der Kirche; iv. Zur Einheit von Theorie und Praxis kirchlicher Sozialverkündigung]: TPhil 61 (1986) 1-23.

6607* *Hofmann* Rupert, La tentación escatológica; consideraciones sobre la teología política, y politizante después, de Ernst Bloch: TierraN 14,56 (1986) 5-21.

6608 **Hood** Robert E., Contemporary political orders and Christ; Karl BARTH's Christology and political praxis. Allison Park 1985, Pickwick. xviii-269 p. $20 [RelStR 13,245, M. *Rumscheidt*].

6609 **Hug** James E., Scripture sharing on the bishops' economic pastoral. Kansas City 1985, Leaven [BToday 24,397].

6610 *Hurst* Antony, Towards a theology of paid employment: ExpTim 98 (1986s) 260-3.

6611 **Jossa** G., Gesù e i movimenti di liberazione della Palestina: BiblCuRel 37, 1980 ➔ 61,9205... 65,7153: ᴿTZBas 42 (1986) 435s (A. *Moda*: fera date; utilement repris RasT 1982, 128-140).

6612 **Kee** Alistair, Domination or liberation; the place of religion in social conflict [Ferguson lectures]. L 1986, SCM. xii-126 p. £5.50. – ᴿExpTim 98 (1986s) 284 (J. *Ferguson*, no kin).

6613 **Kuitert** H. M., Everything is politics but politics is not everything, ᵀ*Bowden* John. L 1986, SCM. 183 p. £7. 0-3340-0418-7. – ᴿExpTim 98 (1986s) (R. G. *Jones*: not favorable to liberation theologians or any theology not academic).

6614 *Kvalbein* Hans, [Mt 5,3; Lk 16,19-31] Jesus and the poor; two texts and a tentative conclusion: Themelios 12 (1986s) 80-87.

6615 **Lane** Dermot A., Foundations for a social theology. Dublin 1984, Gill & M. – ᴿNBlackf 67 (1986) 192 (H. *Meynell*).

6616 *Lohfink* Norbert, Von der 'Anawim-Partei' zur 'Kirche der Armen'; die bibelwissenschaftliche Ahnentafel eines Hauptbegriffs der 'Theologie der Befreiung' [Psalmenkommentare *Olshausen* J. 1853; *Hupfeld* H. 1855; *Graetz* H. 1882; *Smend* R. 1882]: Biblica 67 (1986) 153-175; franç. 176.

6617 *Mangatt* George, Jesus and the poor: Bible Bhashyam 12 (1986) 157-165.

6618 *Mardones* José M., El Evangelio y los 'demonios' de la ciudad secular: SalT 74 (1986) 609-619.

6619 **Marshall** Paul, Thine is the Kingdom; a biblical perspective on the nature of government and politics today. GR 1986, Eerdmans. 160 p. $8 pa. [TDig 34,84].

6620 *Menozzi* Daniele, La Bibbia dei rivoluzionari [< Bible de tous les temps 6]: CrNSt 7 (1986) 493-513.

6621 **Miguez Bonino** José, Toward a Christian political ethics. Ph 1983, Fortress. 126 p. $6 pa. – ᴿBibTB 16 (1986) 28 (A. J. *Tambasco*); Vidyajyoti 49 (1985) 143s (S. *Arokiasamy*).

6622 **Moltmann** J., On human dignity; political theology and ethics 1984 ➔ 1,216: ᴿWestTJ 48 (1986) 212-5 (R. C. *Gamble*).

6623 *Morin* A., Biblia y política: Medellín 11 (1985) 3-16.

6624 *Nessan* Craig L., Poverty; the biblical witness and contemporary reality: CurrTM 13 (1986) 236-8.

6625 **Nissen** J., Poverty and mission; New Testament perspectives on a contemporary theme: Research Pamphlet 10. Leiden-Utrecht 1984, Interuniversitaire Institut voor Missiologie en Œcumenica. iv-308 p. – ᴿNRT 108 (1986) 311.

6626 *Nolan* Albert, The option for the poor [in the Bible...] in South Africa: NBlackf 67 (1986) 5-15.

6627 **Oakman** D. E., Jesus and the economic questions of his day. Lewiston NY 1986, Mellen. 319 p. $60 [TS 48,598].

6628 **Parente** F., Il pensiero politico ebraico [sp. maccabaico] e cristiano: Storia delle idee politiche, economiche e sociali 2/1. T 1985, UTET. 478 p. [ZAW 99,149].

6629 *Rackman* Emanuel,   The Church fathers and Hebrew political thought: HebSt 26 (1985) 241-7 [OTAbs 10,110].

6630 **Rahner** Karl,   Politische Dimensionen des Christentums; Ausgewählte Texte zu Fragen der Zeit, EVorgrimler H.   Mü 1986, Kösel.   231 p.   DM 24,80 [ActuBbg 24,94, J. *Boada*].   3-466-20277-9.

6631 *Rollin* B.,   Le radicalisme des conseils évangeliques: NRT 108 (1986) 532-554.

6632 *Rotzetter* Anton,   Plädoyer für eine prophetisch-politische Spiritualität: GeistL 59 (1986) 6-19.

6633 *Sarles* Ken L.,   A theological evaluation of the prosperity gospel ['it is God's will for every believer to be prosperous']:   BS 143 (1986) 329-352.

6634 **Schelhaas** Nimda,   De politieke theologie van Helmut GOLLWITZER, van LUTHER tot MARX [< diss. Vrije Univ.].   Kampen 1984.   162 p. – RNedTTs 40 (1986) 254-6 (G. H. *ter Schegget*).

6635 ESchirmer Dietrich [*Clévenot* M., *al.*] Die Bibel als politisches Buch; Beiträge zu einer befreienden Christologie 1980/2 ➤ 62,327; 65,7179: RTPQ 134 (1986) 80s (K. *Blumauer*).

6636 **Schottroff** Luise, *Stegemann* Wolfgang,   Jesus and the hope of the poor, TMcConnell Matthew J.   Maryknoll NY/Dublin 1986, Orbis/ Gill & M.   134 p. $10.   0-88344-255-8. – RExpTim first choice 98,11 (1986s) 321s (C. S. *Rodd*).

6637 ESchottroff Willy, *Stegemann* Wolfgang,   God of the lowly; socio-historical interpretations of the Bible, TO'Connell M. J., 1984 ➤ 65,7181; 1,8016:   RCBQ 48 (1986) 360-2 (J. H. *Neyrey*); EvQ 58 (1986) 272-4 (T. *Geddert*); Vidyajyoti 49 (1985) 422s (P. *Meagher*).

6638 *Schrey* Heinz-Horst,   Christentum und Sozialismus; ein Rückblick auf der Literatur der siebziger Jahre: TRu 51 (1986) 372-403.

6639 **Sobrino** Jon, The true Church and the poor 1984 ➤ 1,8017: RJAAR 54 (1986) 193s (R. *Haight*); NBlackf 67 (1986) 51s (A. *Kee*); TLond 39 (1986) 139s (N. *Lash*: the enemy is not atheism but idolatry, 'gods who cause death').

6640 EStumme Wayne,   Christians and the many faces of Marxism.   Minneapolis 1984, Augsburg.   159 p. $9. – RRExp 83 (1986) 136 (W. L. *Hendricks*: ten authors show all its faces covered by Lutheran Christianity; neither for nor against Marx, only how what he actually teaches merits dialogue).

6641 *Vasey* V.,   The social ideas of ASTERIUS of Amasea [...from Scripture]: AugR 26 (1986) 413-436.

6642 *Vives* Josep,   Notes sobre la 'teologia política' de l'Antic Testament: RCatalT 11 (1986) 283-310; Eng. 310.

6643 *a) Weakland* Rembert G.,   The Bible and Catholic social teaching; – *b) Senior* Donald,   The New Testament and the U.S. economy: BToday 24 (1986) 351-5 / 357-362.

6644 **Webber** Robert E.,   The Church in the world [... Church/State tension since the first century].   GR 1986, Zondervan.   331 p.   0-310-36601-1 [ExpTim 98,287].

6645 **Westland** L.,   Eredienst en maatschappij [public worship and society], een onderzoek naar de visie van A. A. van RULER, Prof. Dr. G. van der LEEUWSTICHTING en de beweging Christenen voor het Socialisme [diss. DJonker H.].   Haag 1985, Boekencentrum.   199 p. – RNedTTs 40 (1986) 258-260 (R. *Hensen*).

6646 **Wogaman** J. Philip,   Economics and ethics; a Christian enquiry.   L 1986, SCM.   145 p.   £7.   0-334-00336-0. – RExpTim 98 (1986s) 188 (R. G. *Jones*).

6647 **Yoder** John H., The priestly kingdom; social ethics as gospel 1984
➤ 1,262: ᴿJAAR 54 (1986) 622s (D. *Sturm*).

6648 **Zimbelman** Joel A., Theological ethics and politics in the thought of Juan
Luis SEGUNDO S.J. and John Howard YODER: diss. Virginia sans date. –
RelStR 13, 189.

H8.5 **Theologia liberationis latino-americana.**

6649 **Adriance** Madeleine, Opting for the poor; Brazilian Catholicism in
transition. Kansas City 1986, Sheed & W. vii-200 p. $13 pa. [TDig
33,455].

6650 *Alegre* X. *al.*, *a)* El segrest de la veritat. Barc 1986, Claret. – *b)* El
secuestro de la verdad. Santander 1986, Sal Terrae. 191 p. – ᴿComSev 19
(1986) 435 (V. J. *Ansede Alonso*); RazF 214 (1986) 453-7 (F. *Martí
Ambel*).

6651 *a) Álvarez Bolado* Alfonso, Mundialidad de las relaciones y Teología de
la Liberación; – *b) Ugalde* Luis, El futuro de la T. L.; tareas para los
próximos años; – *c) Ruiz* Gregorio, La hermenéutica de la T. L.; – *d)
Losada* Joaquin, La eclesiología de la T. L.: SalT 73 (1985) 83-98 / 99-112
/ 113-126 / 127-142.

6652 **Alves** Rubem, Protestantism and repression; a Brazilian case study
[indictment of Presbyterianism]. Maryknoll/L 1985, Orbis/SCM. xi-215 p.
$12. 0-88344-098-9 / 0-334-02278-9. – ᴿCCurr 36 (1986s) 368-370 (G. C.
Chapman); ExpTim 97 (1985s) 314s (S. *Mayor*).

6652* *Antoncich* Ricardo, *a)* Hacia una interpretación cristiana del conflicto
social; – *b)* Libertatis Nuntius et Libertatis Conscientia: Medellín 12
(1986) 64-86 / 327-348.

6653 *Ardusso* Franco, 'Libertà cristiana e liberazione' [Istruzione 1986]:
RClerIt 67 (1986) 825-833.

6653* *Azzi* Riolando, Do bom Jesus sofredor ao Cristo libertador: PerspT 18
(1986) 215-233. 343-358.

6654 *Barr* William R., Debated issues in liberation theology: TTod 43
(1986s) 510-523.

6655 *Barth* Hans-Martin, *a)* Die Theologie Leonardo BOFFs — eine
ökumenische Verheissung?: MatKonfInst 36 (1985) 107-112; – *b)* La
teologia di Leonardo BOFF; una promessa per l'ecumenismo? [Conferenza
Roma 1986, = Materialdienst Bensheim 36 (1985) 107-112], ᵀ*Rostagno* S.:
Protestantesimo 41 (1986) 193-205.

6656 **Bayer** Charles H., A guide to liberation theology for middle-class
congregations. St. Louis 1986, 'CBP'. 176 p. $13 pa. [TDig 34,59].

6657 **Bazarra** Carlos, ¿Qué es la teología de la liberación? Buenos Aires 1985,
Paulinas. 72 p. [REB 46,231].

6658 *Berbusse* Edward J., Liberation theology, an ideological invasion of the
Church; the liberation to be sought: liberation from sin: HomPast 86,6
(1986) 17-26.

6659 *Berten* Ignace, Les pauvres à l'étroit dans l'ecclésiologie romaine:
LumièreV 35,177 (1986) 75-89 [Eng. TDig 34,154].

6660 **Bloomquist** Karen, Toward the redemption of American working class
reality; a liberation theology: diss. Union Theol Sem. NY 1985. – RTLv
18,571.

6661 **Boff** Clodovis, Die Befreiung der Armen; Reflexionen zum
Grundanliegen der lateinamerikanischen Befreiungstheologie. FrS 1986,
Exodus. 164 p. Fs 19. – ᴿNorTTs 87 (1986) 166 (K. *Nordstokke*).

6662 **Boff** Clodovis, Mit den Füssen am Boden; Theologie aus dem Leben des Volkes. Dü 1986, Patmos. 256 p. DM 34. – ᴿEvKomm 19 (1986) 670s (P.-G. *Schoenborn*); NorTTs 87 (1986) 166 (K. *Nordstokke*).

6663 **Boff** Clodovis, Theologie und Praxis; die erkenntnistheoretischen Grundlagen der Theologie der Befreiung 1983 ➔ 65,7204; 1,8042: ᴿExpTim (1985s) 269 (G. *Wainwright*: 'with great sophistication'); TPhil 61 (1986) 617-9 (M. *Sievernich*).

6664 *Boff* Clodovis, *a*) Carta teológica sobre Cuba: REB 46 (1986) 348-371; – *b*) 15 tesis sobre la Teología de la Liberación: SalT 74 (1986) 311-321.

6665 **Boff** Leonardo, Aus dem Tal der Tränen ins Gelobte Land; der Weg der Kirche mit den Unterdrückten. Dü 1982 [➔ 63,7325; 64,7418]; ²1984, Patmos. 256 p. – ᴿTPhil 61 (1986) 308s (M. *Sievernich*).

6666 **Boff** Leonardo, Teología desde el lugar del pobre. Santander 1986, Sal Terrae. 148 p. – ᴿRazF 214 (1986) 473 (J. *Royo*).

6667 *Boff* Leonardo, A Igreja como misterio e la libertação integral: GrSinal 40 (1986) 85-106.

6668 **Boff** Leonardo & Clodovis, Como fazer Teologia da Libertação: Fazer 17s. Petrópolis 1986, Vozes. 141 p. – ᴿPerspT 18 (1986) 260-2 (F. *Taborda*).

6668* **Boff** L. & C., Cómo hacer teología de la liberación: Teología y Pastoral. M 1986, Paulinas. 132 p. pt 600. 84-285-1092-X. [ActuBbg 24,91, J. *Boada*]. – ᴿRazF 214 (1986) 471s (M. *Alcalá*).

6669 **Boff** Leonardo & Clodovis, Liberation theology; from confrontation to dialogue, ᵀBarr Robert R. SF 1986, Harper & R. 100 p. $9 pa. [TDig 33,459].

6670 **Boff** L. & C., Salvation and liberation 1984 ➔ 65,7208; 1,8046: ᴿVidyajyoti 49 (1985) 250s (J. *Mattam*).

6671 **Bussmann** Claus, What do you say? Jesus Christ in Latin American theology [Befreiung 1980 ➔ 62,8173], ᵀBarr R. Maryknoll NY 1985, Orbis. 185 p. $10 pa. 0-88344-711-8. – ᴿCalvinT 21 (1986) 137 (J. W. *Cooper*: nothing clear on two natures, atonement, resurrection); ExpTim 98 (1986s) 89s (A. *Kirk*: 'liberation quotes'; disappointing); Gregorianum 67 (1986) 550s (J. *Dupuis*).

6672 *a*) *Calvez* Jean-Yves, La 'théologie de la libération' critiquée et accueillie, après les deux Instructions...; – *b*) *Scannone* Juan Carlos, 'Peuple' et 'populaire'; réalité sociale, pratique pastorale et réflexion théologique en Argentine: NRT 108 (1986) 845-859 / 860-877.

6672* **Camacho** I. R., *al.*, Opción por la justicia y la libertad: Praxis Cristiana 3. M 1986, Paulinas. 614 p. – ᴿCarthaginensia 2 (1986) 325 (J. L. *Parada*).

6673 **Camara** Helder, Through the Gospel with Dom Helder. Maryknoll 1986, Orbis.

6673* *Carvalho Azevedo* Marcello de, Igreja, cultura, libertação: Brotéria 122 (1986) 483-501.

6674 **Chopp** Rebecca S., The praxis of suffering; an interpretation of liberation and political theologies. Maryknoll NY 1986, Orbis. xi-178 p. $13 pa. [TDig 34,62]. – ᴿFurrow 57 (1986) 803-5 (D. *Dorr*).

6675 **Cleary** Edward L., Crisis and change; the Church in Latin America today 1985 ➔ 1,8055: ᴿCCurr 36 (1986s) 116-8 (J. R. *Brockman*); TS 47 (1986) 752s (J. P. *Hogan*).

6676 *a*) *Cohn-Sherbok* Dan, Judaism and the theology of liberation; – *b*) *Hauerwas* Stanley, Some theological reflections on GUTIÉRREZ's use of 'liberation' as a theological concept: ModT 3 (1986s) 1-19 [> TDig 34,127] / 67-76.

6677 *Comblin* José, Teología y marxismo en América Latina [< PerspT 16 (1984) 291-311], ᵀᴱ*Suñol* Miquel: SelT 25 (1986) 183-193.

6678 **Cooper** Roy B., A critical analysis of liberation theology in the works of José MÍGUEZ-BONINO and Ronald J. SIDER: diss. SW Baptist sem. 1986. 272 p. 86-23460. – DissA 47 (1986s) 3076-A. – RelStR 13,187.

6679 *Corner* Mark, Did MARX have an ethics? [*Brenkert* G., Marx's ethics of freedom 1983, 'has little understanding of Christianity' as compared with *Miranda* J. P., Marx against the Marxists]: HeythJ 27 (1986) 437-441.

6679* *Cosgrave* William, The theology of liberation: Furrow 57 (1986) 506-516.

6680 **Costé** René, Marxist analysis and Christian faith, ᵀ*Couture* Roger A., *Cort* John C. Maryknoll NY 1985, Orbis. 232 p. – ᴿPhilipSa 20 (1985) 495-7 (M. *Marina*).

6681 *a)* *Cottier* Georges, Le christianisme et les valeurs de liberté; – *b)* *Gilbert* Paul, Métaphysique de la liberté et théologie de la libération; – *c)* *Finance* Joseph de, La liberté sous l'éclairage de la foi; – *d)* *Barriola* Miguel A., Jesús, los pobres y los otros: Seminarium 37 (1986) 522-531 / 532-547 / 548-559 / 606-624.

6682 *Croatto* J. S., La contribución de la hermenéutica bíblica a la teología de la liberación: Cuadernos de Teología 6,4 (Buenos Aires 1985) 45-69 [Stromata 42,455].

6683 *Delhaye* Philippe, Problèmes chrétiens et humains de la 'libération'; JEAN-PAUL II appelle les chrétiens à vivre l'authenticité évangélique: EsprV [1985, 7 art.] 96 (1986) 177-190.

6683* **Dussel** Enrique D., Caminos de libertação latino-americana [➤ 1,8066]: IV. Reflexões para uma Teología da Libertação, ᵀ*Cunha* Álvaro: Estudos e Debates Latino-americanos 9. São Paulo 1985, Paulinas. 294 p. 85-01-00154-0. – ᴿPerspT 18 (1986) 125s (O. *Leite*).

6684 *Dussel* E., Religiosidad popular latinoamericana, hipótesis fundamentales: Concilium 206 (M 1986) 99-113 (ed. ital. Religiosità popolare come oppressione e come liberazione; ipotesi sulla sua storia e sul presente in America Latina, ᵀ*Gatti* E., 590-606).

6685 **Dussel** Enrique, Philosophy of liberation, ᵀ*Martinez* Aquilina, *Markowsky* Christine, 1985 ➤ 1,8067: ᴿHorizons 13 (1986) 186s (R. S. *Goizueta*); RelStT 6 (1986) 64-66 (R. *Ware*).

6685* *Edwards* Anibal, Beber en su propio pozo; proyecto de seguimiento de Cristo en América Latina: StLeg 27 (1986) 101-173.

6686 *Eichinger* Werner, Politik und Mystik; Anmerkungen zur Polemik einiger Vertreter der Katholischen Soziallehre gegen die Theologie der Befreiung: Wort und Antwort 27 (Mainz 1986) 87... [< ZIT].

6687 **Ferm** Deane W., Third World liberation theologies, I. An introductory survey; II. A reader. Maryknoll NY 1986, Orbis. ix-150 p.; ix-386 p. $25 [NRT 109,297, J. *Masson*]. – ᴿFurrow 57 (1986) 542 (L. *Martin*: too limited to English works); PhilipSac 21 (1986) 165s (B. *Peña*); Themelios 12 (1986s) 64 (J. *Stamoolis*).

6688 *Ferm* Deane W., Third world liberation theology; a bibliographic survey: Choice 22 (1985) 1446-1459 [< BS 136 (1986) 70].

6689 **Fischer** Klaus P., Gotteserfahrung; Mystagogie in der Theologie Karl RAHNERs und in der Theologie der Befreiung. Mainz 1986, Grünewald. 143 p. DM 19. – ᴿNatGrac 33 (1966 571s (A. *Villalmonte*).

6690 **Frieling** Reinhard, Befreiungstheogien; Studien zur Theologie in Lateinamerika: Bensheimer Hefte 63. Gö 1984 [➤ 1,8078] ²1986, Vandenhoeck & R. 196 p. – ᴿTPhil 61 (1986) 309s M. *Sievernich*).

6691 *France* R. T., Liberation in the New Testament: EvQ 58 (1986) 3-23.
6692 *Galilea* Segundo, The spirituality of liberation: Way 25 (1985) 186-194.
6693 **Gibellini** R., Il dibattito sulla teologia della liberazione: GdT 166. Brescia 1986, Queriniana. 146 p. Lit. 12.000 [NRT 109,635, A. *Toubeau*].
6694 *Gibellini* Rosino, Temi e problemi della teologia della liberazione: RasT 27 (1986) 34-62.
6695 *Gómez Canedo* Lino. La Iglesia en Hispanoamérica y su historiografía (Realidad, nacionalismo y política): Carthaginensia 2 (1986) 303-315.
6696 *Gomez* Fausto, Paths of liberation towards freedom: PhilipSac 21 (1986) 173-211.
6697 *González* Carlos I., *a*) Il documento su 'libertà cristiana e liberazione': CC 137 (1986,2) 220-232: – *b*) La teología de la liberación a la luz del magisterio de Juan Pablo II en América Latina: Gregorianum 67 (1986) 5-46.
6698 **González** Justo L. & Catherine G., Liberation preaching; the pulpit and the oppressed. Nv 1984 [→ 1,8091], Abingdon. 127 p. – RTheologiai Szemle 29 (1986) 126s (G. *Benke*).
6699 *a*) *González Ruiz* José M., Fonaments biblics per la teologia de l'alliberament; – *b*) *Codina* Victor, ¿Perquè es conflictiva la teologia de l'alliberament?; – *c*) *Sobrino* Jon, Teología de l'alliberament i teologia europea progressista; – *d*) *López Camps* Jordi, Per a una teologia de l'alliberament a Europa: QVidCr 133 (1986) 13-24 / 39-51 / 64-85 / 86-106.
6700 *Greinacher* Norbert, Zur Situation in Lateinamerika [... Geschichte]: TüTQ 166 (1986) 61s.
6701 **Greinacher** Norbert, *Boff* Clodovis, Umkehr und Neubeginn; der Nord-Süd-Konflikt als Herausforderung an die Theologie und die Kirche Europas. FrS 1986, Exodus. 71 p. – RNorTTs 87 (1986) 204 (K. *Nordstokke*).
6702 *Guillaumin* Armand, À propos de la théologie de la libération; idéologie ou dialogue?: Spiritus 27 (1986) 12-26.
6703 **Gutiérrez** G., Beber en su propio pozo 1983 → 65,7241; 1,8100: RStromata 42 (1986) 211-6 (J. C. *Scannone*).
6704 **Gutiérrez** Gustavo, Aus der eigenen Quelle trinken; Spiritualität der Befreiung: Fundamentaltheologische Studien 12. Mü/Mainz 1986, Kaiser/Grünewald. 151 p. – RTPhil 61 (1986) 626 (M. *Sievernich*).
6705 *Gutiérrez* Gustavo, La libération par la foi — boire à son propre puits 1985 → 1,8102: RSpiritus 27 (1986) 437 (A. *Guillaumin*).
6706 **Gutiérrez** Gustavo, La force historique des pauvres [1982 → 64,7438], TGuibal Francis: CogF 137. P 1986, Cerf. 240 p. F 125. 2-204-02456-2. – RÉTRel 61 (1986) 619s (Letizia *Tomassone*); Études 365 (1986) 423s (R. *Marlé*); FoiTemps 16 (1986) 376 (G. *Harpigny*); MélSR 43 (1986) 114s (B. *Rey*).
6707 **Gutiérrez** Gustavo, Die historische Macht der Armen 1984 → 1,8104: RTPhil 61 (1986) 3113 (M. *Sievernich*).
6708 **Gutiérrez** Gustavo, *a*) Vaticano II y la Iglesia latinoamericana. Lima 1985. – *b*) Das Zweite Vatikanische Konzil und die Kirche Lateinamerikas: Adveniat Kommentare 12. Essen 1986, Bischöfliche Aktion. 47 p. – RTR 82 (1986) 508s (W. *Promper* mit Biographie; Übersetzung fehlerhaft).
6709 *Haes* René de, La liberté chrétienne et la libération, Instruction ... 22.III.1986: RAfrT 10,19 (1986) 75-89.
6710 **Haight** Roger, An alternative vision 1985 → 1,8107: RCathCris 4,1 (1986) 41-44 (Joyce A. *Little*); Horizons 13 (1986) 136-149 (G. *Baum*: 'the

creed that liberates'); RelStT 6 (1986) 62-64 (R. *Ware*); SR 15 (1986) 255s (M. *Rumscheidt*); TS 47 (1986) 308s (J.P. *Hogan*).

6711 *Haunhorst* Benno, Herr, wann hätten wir dich je leidend gesehen? Leiden und Kreuz Jesu Christi aus der Sicht der Befreiungstheologie im Unterricht: RelUnHö 29,1 (Dü 1986) 31-34 [< ZIT].

6711* a) *Hoeffner* Joseph, ¿Doctrina social de la Iglesia, o teología de la liberación?; – b) *Herr* Theodor, Teología de la liberación y doctrina social de la Iglesia; – c) *Spieker* Manfred, Revolución como sacramento; la sanctificación de la lucha de clases por la teología de la liberación: TierraN 15,57 (Bogotá 1986) 5-29 / 30-42 / 43-50.

6712 a) *Hoffmann* J.G.H., La théologie de la libération, facteur de déstabilisation de la foi?: – b) *Jones* P., La lecture matérialiste de la Bible; – c) *Foucachon* F., Jésus politicien?: RRef 37 (1986) 87-97 / 98-104 / 105... [< ZIT].

6713 *Honings* Bonifacio, La liberazione; impegno da discernere: Teresianum 37 (1986) 37-51.

6714 *Hoornaert* Eduardo, Os três fatores da nova hegemonia dentro da Igreja Católica no Brasil; fatos e perspectivas: REB 46 (1986) 371-384.

6715 *Horrell* J. Scott, Leonardo BOFF and the Latin American liberation theology movement: Creation, Social Science and Humanities Quarterly 8 (Winter 1985) 6-11 [< BS 143 (1986) 269].

6716 *Hoy* Michael, Theses for liberating the dialogue between Lutherans and Liberationists: CurrTM [12 (1985) 232-7, *Kelly* R.] 13 (1986) 38-41.

6717 *Huerga* Álvaro, La implantación de la Iglesia en el Nuevo Mundo: Angelicum 63 (1986) 227-256.

6718 **Jiménez** R., Sumario sobre la teología de la liberación. San Cristóbal, Venezuela 1984, Univ. Católica del Táchira. 130 p. [Stromata 42,278].

6718* *Jiménez* Roberto, Uno de tres conceptos claves del proyecto histórico de la teología de la liberación; la via revolucionaria hacia el socialismo: TierraN 15,59 (1986) 33-62.

6719 Carta de JOÃO PAULO II a seus Irmãos no Episcopado do Brasil, 9.IV. 1986: REB 46 (1986) 396-402.

6720 **Johnson** Wallace R., A history of Christianity in Belize, 1776-1838. Lanham MD 1986, UPA. xvii-279 p. $24.75; pa. $13.50 [TDig 33,367].

6721 *Joos* André, A criatividade na Teologia da Libertação: Igreja e Missão 133 (1986) 226-308.

6722 **Joseph** père, Les pauvres sont l'Église. P 1983, Centurion. 248 p. F 65 pa. – ᴿSpTod 38 (1986) 86-88 (Simone D. *Delery*).

6723 *Kern* Udo, Die lateinamerikanische Theologie der Befreiung in ihrem theologischen Selbstverständnis: ComViat 29 (1986) 41-66.

6724 **Kirk** J. Andrew, Theology and the Third World church. DG 1983, InterVarsity. 64 p. $3 [RelStR 13,54, J. *Dawsey*].

6725 *Kroger* Josef, Crítica profética y estrategía práctica; la Teología de la Liberación confrontada con la epistemología de HABERMAS [< TS 46 (1985) 3-20], ᵀᴱ *Vives* Josep: SelT 25 (1986) 129-139.

6726 *Lakeland* Paul, a) Liberation, the Gospel and the Church; two Vatican documents: Month 248 (1986) 185-190; – b) [Political and] Liberation theology: Way [25 (1985) 224-235] 26 (1986) 145-154.

6727 **Lane** Dermot A., Foundations for a social theory; praxis, process and salvation 1984 ➔ 1,8127; also NY 1984, Paulist. IX-192 p. $7 pa. – ᴿHorizons 13 (1986) 185s (T.J. *Tekippe* thinks that writing a book proves that theory precedes practice).

6728 *Laubier* Patrick de, Liberté chrétienne et libération [Instructions (ᴱ*Chenu* M. 1986) qui viennent d'enrichir singulièrement le trésor de l'Église ...]: RThom 86 (1986) 702-4.

6729 *Lippert* P., Libertação heisst Befreiung; einige persönliche Eindrücke zu Theologie und Kirche Brasiliens: TGegw 28 (1985) 7-14.

6730 **Lois** Julio, Teología de la liberación; opción por los pobres. M 1986, Iepala. 506 p. – ᴿRCatalT 11 (1986) 458 (J. I. *González Faus*).

6731 *Lozano* Itziar, *González* Maruja, Feminismo e movimento popular na América Latina: ↝ 510, REB 46 (1986) 122-153.

6732 *Malley* François, [Bartolomé de] Lᴀs Cᴀsᴀs y las teologías de la liberación [< VSp 139 (1985) 53-77], ᵀᴱ*Castanye* Josep: SelT 25 (1986) 254-264.

6733 *Maloney* Thomas J., The Peruvian experience as a source of liberation theology: America 154 (1986) 51s.

6734 *Márkus* Gilbert, Theologies of repression [sects fostering US-backed regimes]: NBlackf 67 (1986) 37-45.

6735 *Marlé* René, La théologie de la libération réhabilitée: Études 365 (1986) 521-536.

6736 *Marti i Ambel* Fèlix, La nostra teologia de l'alliberament; presentació del llibre 'El segrest de la veritat' [Barc 1986]: QVidCr 133 (1986) 107-111.

6737 *Mateo-Seco* Lucas F., Libertad y liberación [Instrucción 22.III.1986]: ScripTPamp 18 (1986) 873-889.

6738 *Melendez* Guillermo, Iglesia Católica y conflicto social en América Central: Cristianismo y Sociedad 89 (1986) 23-48 [Zusammenfassung, TKontext 8/2,114, M. v. *Lay*].

6739 *Min* Anselm K., Praxis and theology in recent debates: ScotJT 39 (1986) 529-549.

6740 *Mitterhöfer* Jakob, Die römischen Instruktionen zur Theologie der Befreiung: TPQ 134 (1986) 347-357.

6741 *Mondin* Battista, Il metodo dell'analisi sociale nella teologia della liberazione [↝ 1,8148]: Sapienza 39 (1986) 399-417.

6742 **Moon** C. H. S., A Korean Minjung [... 'liberation'] theology — an OT perspective. Maryknoll NY 1985, Orbis. x-83 p. $8. 0-88344-250-7 [BL 87,88, R. N. *Whybray*].

6743 **Moser** Mary Theresa, The evolution of the option for the poor in France 1880-1965. Lanham MD 1985, UPA. x-206 p. $21.50; pa. $11.50. – ᴿHorizons 13 (1986) 425s (L. J. *Weber*).

6744 *Nash* Ronald, Liberation theology; soldiers of Christ or Marx?: Eternity (July 1986) 15-22 [< BS 143 (1986) 368].

6745 **Nelson** Wilton M., Protestantism in Central America 1984 ↝ 65,7269; 1,8154: 0-8028-0024-6: ᴿÉTRel 61 (1986) 297s (J. *Pons*).

6746 **Nessan** Craig, The North American theological response to Latin American liberation theology; validity and limitations of a praxis-oriented theology: Ev. diss. ᴰ*Schwarz* H. München 1986. – RTLv 18,558.

6747 ᴱ**Nieuwenhove** J. van, Jésus et la libération en Amérique latine, ᵀ*Duboys de Lavigerie* P., *Lochmann* J.: JJC 26. P 1986, Desclée. 370 p. F 135. – ᴿÉtudes 365 (1986) 423 (R. *Marlé*).

6748 *Noceti* Emilio R., Fundamentos y líneas principales de la ética de la liberación de Enrique Dᴜssᴇʟ: Salesianum 48 (1986) 869-906.

6749 **Novak** Michael, Will it liberate? Questions about liberation theology. NT 1986, Paulist. 309 p. $15 [RelStR 331 P. *Gathie*].

6750 **Nuñes** Emilio A., Liberation theology, ᵀ*Sywulka* Paul E, 1985 ↝ 1,8155: ᴿGraceTJ 7 (1986) 257-9 (D. S. *Dockery* compares with Nᴀsʜ).

6751 *Olthuis* James H., Evolutionary dialectics and SEGUNDO's Liberation of Theology: CalvinT 21 (1986) 79-93.

6752 *Ottlyk* Ernő, Ⓜ The theology of liberation and the struggle of the oppressed: Theologiai Szemle 29 (1986) 352-8.

6753 ᴱ**Piediscalzi** Nicholas, *Theobaben* Robert G., Three worlds of Christian-Marxist encounters 1985 ➤ **1**,389: ᴿExpTim 97 (1985s) 251 (W. J. *Hollenweger*: MARX should be to theology today what Aristotle was to AQUINAS).

6754 **Planas** Ricardo, Liberation theology; the political expression of religion. Kansas City 1986, Sheed & W. vi-289 p. $13 [TS 48,596, A. T. *Hennelly*].

6755 *Post* Werner, ¿Traición a los pobres? 'Marxismo' en la Instrucción de la Congregación de la Fe [< Orientierung 48 (1984) 226-8], ᵀᴱ*Castanye* Josep: SelT 25 (1986) 289-294.

6756 *Powles* Cyril H., Cristianismo en el Tercer Mundo; ¿Cómo estudiar su historia? [< SR 13 (1984) 131-144], ᵀᴱ*Sols* Josep: SelT 25 (1986) 274-281.

6757 **Prien** Hans-Jürgen, La historia del cristianismo en América Latina [1978 ➤ **1**,8168], ᵀ*Barnadas* Josep: El peso de los días 21. Salamanca 1985, Sígueme. 1236 p. 84-301-0962-5. – ᴿNatGrac 33 (1986) 309-315 (E. *Rivera*: interpretación discutible); PerspT 18 (1986) 411 (F. *Taborda*).

6758 *Prien* Hans-Jürgen, Kirchengeschichte Lateinamerikas, ein Forschungsbericht: TLZ 111 (1986) 785-800.

6759 *Ramos Regidor* José, La spiritualità della liberazione in America Latina: Servitium 47 (1986) 10-49.

6760 *Ratzinger* Joseph, Freiheit und Befreiung; die anthropologische Vision der Instruktion 'Libertatis conscientia': IkaZ 15 (1986) 409-424; 425-439, Anmerkungen, *Santoro* Filippo [non in Communio (P 1986)].

6761 *a*) *Rayan* Samuel, Instruction on Christian freedom and liberation; some reflections on the document: Jeevadhara 16,93 ('Liberation, a red-hot issue', 1986) 228-250; 185-200, Towards an Indian theology of liberation.

6762 ᴱ**Richard** Pablo, Raíces de la Teología latinoamericana [i. colonial hasta 1808; ii. neocristiana; iii. protestante; iv. en la literatura]. San José CR 1985, DEI [Departamento Ecuménico de Investigaciones]. 432 p. [REB 46,232]. – ᴿPerspT 18 (1986) 276s (J. B. *Libânio*); ComSev 19 (1986) 255s (V. J. *Anseda Alonso*).

6763 *Richard* Pablo, *a*) Los Cristianos en la práctica política de liberación: Pasos 8 (1986) 1-8 [Zusammenfassung, TKontext 8/2,108, M. von *Lay*). – *b*) La Iglesia que nace en América Central [< Cristianismo y Sociedad 22 (1984) 71-91], ᴱ*Farràs* Josep: SelT 25 (1986) 37-48.

6764 *Richards* Glyn, Faith and praxis in liberation theology, BONHOEFFER and GANDHI: ModT 3 (1986s) 359-373.

6765 **Rodor** Amin A., The concept of the poor in the context of the ecclesiology of liberation theology: diss. Andrews, ᴰ*Dederen* R. Berrien Springs MI 1986. 485 p. 87-04323. – DissA 47 (1986s) 4117-A.

6766 ᴱ**Rottländer** Peter, Theologie der Befreiung und Marxismus. Münster 1986, Liberación. 192 p. DM 24,50. – ᴿOrientierung 50 (1986) 127-131 (I. *Ellacuría*, ᵀRottländer, al.).

6767 ᴱ**Samuel** Vinay, *Sugden* Chris, Sharing Jesus in the two thirds world 1982/4 ➤ **1**,636*: ᴿWWorld 6 (1986) 235s (D. A. *Olson*).

6768 *Sanz de Diego* Rafael M., Teología de la liberación — doctrina social de la Iglesia: RazF 214 (1986) 116-125.

6769 *a*) *Saravia* Xavier, La Bible lue dans la vie en communauté; – *b*) *Bravo* Carlos, Où le peuple joue sa vie; les communautés de base; – *c*) *Espeja* Jesús, Libération et spiritualité en Amérique Latine; – *d*) *Arroyo* Gonzalo,

Genèse et développement de la théologie de la libération; – e) Duquoc Christian, 'Une unique histoire'; réflexion autour d'un thème majeur des théologies de la libération; – f) Marlé René, Un document apaisant et bienvenu [Instruction ...]: RechSR 74 (1986) 179-184 / 49-78 / 13-48 / 185-200 / 201-215 / 216-9; French and English summaries on unnumbered pages in front of the fascicle.

6770 **Schall** James, Liberation theology 1984 ⇒ 65,7288; 1,8179: ᴿPerspRelSt 13 (1986) 65ss (E. D. Johnson).

6771 *Schwantes* Milton, Von unten gesehen; die Bibel als Buch der Befreiung gelesen: EvKomm 19 (1986) 383-7.

6772 **Segundo** Juan Luis, Theology and the Church, a response to Cardinal Ratzinger and a warning to the whole Church 1985 ⇒ 1,8184: NY 1985, Seabury. 188 p. $16. – ᴿCurrTM 13 (1986) 316.318 (R. Navarro: read first the appendix: Rome Instructio); TS 47 (1986) 531-3 (A. T. Hennelly: Council-implementation has been blocked); TTod 43 (1986s) 427s. 430 (A. Dulles does not share his perspective).

6773 **Segundo** J. L., Teología de la liberación, respuesta al card. Ratzinger [⇒ 1,8184],ᵀ. M 1985, Cristiandad. 195 p. – ᴿCiuD 199 (1986) 151s (M. A. Keller: aprueba); RazF 212 (1985) 328 (M. Alcalá).

6774 *Segundo* Juan Luis, a) Las dos teologías de la liberación en Latinoamérica [< Études 361 (1984) 149-161], ᵀᴱTortras Antoni M.: SelT 25 (1986) 283-9; – b) La opción por los pobres como clave hermenéutica para entender el Evangelio: SalT 74 (1986) 473-482.

6775 **Segundo** J. L., Teología abierta, I. Iglesia-gracia; II. Dios-sacramentos-culpa; III. Reflexiones críticas ²1984 ⇒ 1,8183: ᴿCiuD 199 (1986) 134s (S. Folgado Flóres: ¹años sesenta); SalT 74 (1986) 153 (J. Eguren).

6776 *Sievernich* Michael, a) 'Theologie der Befreiung' im interkulturellen Gespräch; ein historischer und systematischer Blick auf das Grundliegen: TPhil 61 (1986) 336-358; – b) Im Gespräch mit der Theologie der Befreiung: GeistL 59 (1986) 459-469.

6776* *Silva* António da, Liberdade cristã e doutrinação positiva: Brotéria 123 (1986) 3-15.

6777 a) *Soares-Prabhu* George M., Class in the Bible? The biblical 'poor' a social class?; – b) *Kottukapally* Joseph, Liberation theology and Marxism; – c) *D'Lima* Errol, [The] Instruction... a theological reflection: Vidyajyoti 49 (1985) 322-346 / 347-363 / 364-376.

6778 *Sobrino* Jon, a) El Vaticano II desde América Latina [< Vida Nueva 1501 (1985) 23-30], ᴱMuñoz Maxim: SelT 25 (1986) 140-4. – b) Teología de la liberación y teología europea progresista [< Misión abierta 77 (1984) 395-410], ᴱTorres María José de: SelT 25 (1986) 265-274.

6778* *Spieker* Manfred, La defensa de la doctrina social de la Iglesia ante la teología de la liberación: TierraN 14,54 (1985).

6779 *Spijkerboer* A. A., Interpellatie in naam van de vrijheid; over de ethiek van Jacques Ellul: NedTTs 40 (1986) 160-171; Eng. 171: Christians may take part in revolutionary liberation movements, but as soon as these movements make victims they must take sides with the victims.

6780 *Strohm* Theodor, Befreiungstheologie: ⇒ 587, EvKL 1 (1986) 380-3.

6781 **Tamez** Elsa, Bijbel van de onderdrukten [1979 + La hora de la vida 1978] 1985 ⇒ 1,8193: ᴿCollatVl 16 (1986) 495s (R. Hoet).

6782 **Tamez** Elsa, La Bible des opprimés [1979], ᵀBajard Migèle & Jean: BiVC NS. P 1984, Lethielleux. 139 p. 2-249-61017-7.

6783 a) *Tepe* Valfredo, Uma leitura do documento 'Libertatis conscientia'; – b) *Boff* Leonardo & Clodovis, Convocatória geral em prol da libertação

(Carta aberta ao Cardeal Ratzinger); – c) Boff Clodovis, Retrato de 15 anos da Teologia da Libertação; – d) Comblin José, O tema da reconciliação e a teologia na América Latina; – e) Suess Paulo, Revolução cultural na Sociedade e na Igreja; – f) Castelo Branco Manoel J. de F., A questão da Filosofia da Libertação: REB 46 (1986) 243-250 / 251-262 / 263-271 / 272-314 / 315-324 / 325-347.

6784 Thils Gustave, L'Instruction sur la liberté chrétienne et la libération (22 mars 1986) [comments briefly one aspect, 'Liberation Theology' as lived and proposed in Latin America]: RTLv 17 (1986) 444-452; Eng. 544.

6785 Tokos F., Teología de la liberación; más allá de los dogmas. M 1986, Cipie. 110 p. – RBibFe 12 (1986) 369s (A. Salas).

6786 Triana Servando, Liberation theology and the Bible [La interpretación de la Biblia según la 'Instrucción...': Servir 20 (Jalapa 1984) 539-559], TENichols Francis W.: TDig 33 (1986) 319-321 [-324, India].

6787 EVenetz Hermann-Josef, Vorgrimler Herbert, Das Lehramt der Kirche und der Schrei der Armen; Analysen zur Instruktion der Kongregation für die Glaubenslehre... 1985 ➤ 1,404: RTPhil 61 (1986) 629s (M. Sievernich).

6788 Vesely Ema, Teologija oslobođenia (postanak, razvoj, dvojbe): ObnŽiv 41 (1986) 18-41.

6789 Vida y reflexión; aportes de la teología de la liberación al pensamiento teológico actual. Lima 1983, CEP. 312 p. [ActuBbg 23,232].

6789* Villapadierna Carlos de, Lectura de la Biblia en el campo de la praxis [nueva estrategía... Reino de Dios en este mundo]: StLeg 27 (1986) 215-247.

6790 Vives Josep, 'La teología de la liberación es útil y necesaria'... también para el primer mundo: RazF 214 (1986) 275-288.

6791 Ward James G., The context for liberation thought: Listening 21 (1986) 43-55.

6792 Warnholtz B. Carlos, Bien común y bien público en la Iglesia: EfMex 4,10 (1986) 9-37.

6793 a) Weir J. Emmette, Liberation theology comes of age: ExpTim 98 (1986s) 3-9 [p. 5, in GUTIÉRREZ Theology of Liberation 1971 the marks of MARX are unmistakable; SOBRINO rejects Marx; exegesis-works 'in a Marxist key'; p. 8, Sobrino leaves Marx after first stage, MIRANDA after second, Gutiérrez after third]. – b) Carroll M. Daniel, ExpTim 98 (1986s) 170s: corrections, e.g. Marxism has not moved to the background but the arena of endeavour has changed; the Catholic struggle has become one of ecclesiastical power; Evangelicals underrated.

6794 Witvliet Theo, A place in the sun; liberation theology in the Third World [1984], TBowden J. 1985 ➤ 1, 8209: RÉglT 17 (1986) 404-6 (R. P. Hardy; lacks documentation); Gregorianum 67 (1986) 772s (J. Dupuis); NBlackf 67 (1986) 243s (A. Kee).

6795 Yadegari Mohammad, Liberation theology and Islamic revivalism: JRelTht 43,2 (1986s) 38-50 [< ZIT].

6796 a) Zappone Katherine E., Liberation spirituality; from suspicion to challenge; – b) Kirby Peadar, The Pope, liberation theology and the poor: DoctLife 35 (1985) 326-335 / 336-344.

H8.6 Theologiae emergentes – 'Theologies of' emergent groups.

6797 a) Abe G.O., Berith; its impact on Israel and its relevance to the Nigerian society; – b) Abogunrin S.O., Biblical research in Africa; the task ahead: AfJBSt 1,1 (1986) 66-73 / 7-24 [< TKontext 8/2,20].

6798 *Adoukonou* Barthélemy, *a*) L'anthropologie comme lieu théologique; – *b*) Pour une méthodologie du Sillon Noir: Savanes Forêts (1986,1s) 15-45 / 65-72 (-102) [< TKontext 8/2,21].

6799 **Ahrens** Theodor, Unterwegs nach der verlorenen Heimat; Studien zur Identitätsproblematik in Melanesien [und] Enthusiastisches Christentum, *Strathern* Andrew: MissionÖk 4. Erlangen 1986, Ev.-Luth. Mission. 380 p. DM 28 pa. [TLZ 112,777-780, W. *Gern*].

6800 *Amaladoss* Michael, Evangelization in Asia; a new focus?: EAPast 23,4 (1986) 440-461 [Zusammenfassung, TKontext 8/2,106, G. *Evers*].

6801 *Amaladoss* Michael, *a*) La inculturación en la India (perspectivas e interrogantes): RazF 213 (1986) 127-136. – *b*) Questions des églises d'Asie: Spiritus 27 (P 1986) 227-234.

6802 *Amaladoss* M., Faith meets faith [Hinduism – Christianity]: Vidyajyoti 49 (1985) 109-118.

6803 **Amba Oduyoye** Mercy, Hearing and knowing; theological reflections on Christianity in Africa [... how Africa can share in mission]. Maryknoll / Dublin 1986, Orbis / Gill & M. 168 p. $10 / £8.25. 0-88344-258-2 [Exp-Tim 98,286].

6804 *Ambrosio* Gianni, Cristianesimo e Cina; tra storia e cronaca [*Gernet* J. T1984]: TItSett 11 (1986) 68-78; Eng. 78.

6805 **Anijielo** Chukwuma A., Theological investigation into fear of mystical forces, with special reference to the Igbos [Diss. Innsbruck]: Stimmen der kommenden Kirche 2. Bonn 1984, Borengässer. x-195 p. DM 19,80 pa. [ZkT 108,87, W. *Kern*].

6806 **Asante** Emmanuel, The kingship of Onyame; towards an African Christian theology of the Kingdom of God; a question of continuity: diss. DSchlitt D. Ottawa 1985. ix-363 p. – RTLv 18,567.

6807 **Baer** Hans A., The black spiritual movement; a religious response to racism. Knoxville 1984, Univ. Tennessee. 231 p. $19. – RJScStR 24 (1985) 225s (S. D. *Glazier*).

6808 **Bakole wa Ilunga**, Paths of liberation; a Third World spirituality 1984 → 65,7314; 1,8217: RVidyajyoti 49 (1985) 251s (P. *Kullu*).

6809 *Berner* Ulrich, Inkulturationsprogramme in indischer und afrikanischer Theologie: Saeculum 37 (1986) 83-95.

6810 *Bevans* Stephen, Modelle kontextueller Theologie [< Missiology 13 (1985) 185-202], TGottfried Herbert: TGegw 23 (1985) 135-147.

6811 **Bleyler** Karl-Eugen, Religion und Gesellschaft in Schwarzafrika; sozialreligiöse Bewegungen und koloniale Situation. Stu 1981, Kohlhammer. 207 p. DM 49,80 [TR 83,330-2, K.J. *Tossou*].

6812 *Boff* Leonardo, A teologia [... as teologias] do Terceiro Mundo: REB 46 (1986) 847-851.

6812* *a*) *Bogaert* Michael Vanden, Social transformation of a tribal society; fall-out of evangelization in Chotanagpur; – *b*) *Kullu* Paulus, Figures of Christ in Kharia religion: Sevartham 11 (1986) 19-37 / 97-111.

6813 **Bosch** J. [cf. → 1,8246] James H. CONE, teólogo de la negritud. Valencia 1984, Ferrer. 154 p. – RComSev 19 (1986) 257 (V.J. *Ansalde Alonso*).

6814 *Brandt* Hermann, Kontextuelle Theologie als Synkretismus? Der 'neue Synkretismus' der Befreiungstheologie und der Synkretismusverdacht gegen die Ökumene: ÖkRu 35 (1986) 144-159.

6815 **Brown** Kelly D., Who is Jesus Christ for the Black community? A Black feminist critique of Black male theologians: diss. in progress, Union Theol. Sem. [RelStR 12,321].

6816 *Bujo* Benezet, Solidarity and freedom; Christian ethic in Africa [< StiZt 109 (1984) 795-804], ᵀᴱ*Hellmann* Wayne: TDig 34 (1987) 48-50.

6817 **Bukasa Kabongo** J. *al.*, Chemins de la christologie africaine [chef; ancêtre; maître d'initiation; guérisseur ...]: JJC 25. P 1986, Desclée. 317 p. F 125. – ᴿNRT 108 (1986) 910 (L. *Renwart*).

6818 *Caprile* G., La Chiesa nell'Asia sud-orientale: CC 137 (1986,1) 367-277.

6819 *Chiu* Andrew, Spirit and spirits in classical Asian religions and traditions: EAsJT 4,2 (1986) 104-120.

6820 ᴱ**Cikala Musharhamina** Mulago gwa, Afrikanische Spiritualität und christlicher Glaube; Erfahrungen der Inkulturation: Theologie der Dritten Welt 8. FrB 1986, Herder. 198 p. DM 34 [TR 83,332, K. J. *Tossou*].

6821 *Clarke* Sathianathan, Redoing Indian theology; reflections from a rural parish: Bangalore Theological Forum 18,2s (1986) 125-136 [Zusammenfassung, TKontext 8/2,100, G. *Evers*].

6822 **Coleman** Michael C., Presbyterian missionary attitudes toward American Indians, 1837-1893. Jackson 1985, Univ. Mississippi. 222 p. $25. – ᴿTTod 43 (1986s) 298-301 (D. C. *Wyckoff*).

6823 *a) Collins* Raymond, The local church in New Testament times; – *b) Uzukwu* E. E., Liturgical celebration and inculturation in Igbo Christian communities — 20 years after Vatican II: NigJT 1,2 (1986) 61-67 / 46-60 [< TKontext 8/2,20].

6823* **Comaroff** Jean, Body of power, spirit of resistance; the culture and history of a [Methodist mission: Tshidi] South African people. Ch 1985, Univ. 296 p. $32; pa. $15. [JAAR 55,384-6, I. *Hexham*].

6824 **Cone** James H., A black theology of liberation. Maryknoll NY 1986, Orbis. 154 p. – ᴿPhilipSac 21 (1986) 484-6 (B. *Peña*: about blackness or holiness rather than theology).

6825 **Cone** James H., For my people; black theology and the black church; where we have been and where we are going 1984 ⇥ 65,7320; **1**,8242: ᴿCurrTM 13 (1986) 53s (D. J. *Dallmann*: 'I felt like a voyeur').

6826 **Cone** James H., Speaking the truth [all-white education gives unbalanced view]. GR/Exeter 1986, Eerdmans/Paternoster. 167 p. £8. 0-8028-0226-5. – ᴿExpTim 98 (1986s) 283s (W. J. *Hollenweger*: our Birmingham worse).

6827 *a) Cone* James H., Black theology in American religion; – *b) Ruether* Rosemary R., Re-contextualizing theology; – *c) Hollenweger* Walter J., Intercultural theology; – *d) Taylor* Mark K., In praise of shaky ground; the liminal Christ and cultural pluralism: TTod 43 (1986s) 6-21 / 22-27 / 28-35 / 36-51.

6828 **Conn** Harvie M., Eternal Word and changing world; theology, anthropology, and missions in trialogue. GR 1984, Zondervan. 372 p. $11 pa. – ᴿWestTJ 48 (1986) 409s (J. J. *Davis*).

6829 *Crawford* R. G., Theological bombshell in South Africa ('Kairos' by 50 black ministers, addressed to both church and state): ExpTim 98 (1986s) 9-13.

6830 *a) Deer* D., Unity and diversity in the NT; – *b) Tossou Ametonu* R., L'Église du Christ en dialogue de mission dans la réalité africaine; – *c) Brookman-Amissah* J., African culture and Christian theology: ⇥ 472, Yaoundé 1984/5, 91-106 / 197-138 / 139-164.

6831 *de Gruchy* John W., The Church and the struggle for South Africa: TTod 43 (1986s) [203-] 229-243.

6832 **Deminger** Sigfrid, Evangelist på indiska vilkor; Stanley JONES och den indiska renässansen 1918-1930. Örebro 1985, Libris. 221 p. – ᴿNorTTs 87 (1986) 41s (N. E. *Bloch-Hoell*).

6833 **Diaz** Hector, A Korean theology; *Chu-gyo yo-ji*, Essentials of the Lord's teaching, by CHONG YAK-JONG Augustine (1760-1801): NZMissW Sup 35. Immensee 1986. xxi-466 p. Fs 58. 3-85824-064-8.

6834 **Dickson** Kwesi A., Theology in Africa 1984 ➤ 65,7325; **1**,8253: ᴿCalvinT 21 (1986) 260-2 (R.R. *Recker*); SpTod 38 (1986) 183s (K.B. *Maxwell*); TLond 39 (1986) 63-5 (W.J. *Hollenweger*: behind unpolemical pleasant English, lurk theological time-bombs; like Barth's Romans, would not have got by a European University board).

6835 **Donders** Joseph G., Non-bourgeois theology; an African experience of Jesus 1985 ➤ **1**,8256: ᴿNZMissW 42 (1986) 301 (W. *Bühlmann*); Spiritus 27 (1986) 217 (F. *Richard*).

6836 *D'Souza* Dinesh, The inculturation crisis ['Christianity is being tailored for the Hindus, who don't want to practice it, instead of for the Catholics, who do']: CathCris 4,3 (ND 1986) 14-16.

6837 *Dupuis* Jacques, Un decennio di riflessione nelle chiese dell'Asia; il mutato ruolo della Chiesa nei problemi socioeconomici: CC 137 (1986,2) 326-339.

6838 *a) Dussel* Enrique, Existe-t-il une théologie de la libération en Afrique et en Asie?; – *b) Kerkhofs* Jan, La 'réception' de l'instruction de 1984 en Asie et en Afrique; – *c) Marlé* René, Théologiens en procès; la théologie de la libération dans ses rapports avec l'Europe et avec les instances magistérielles: RechSR 74 (1986) 165-178 / 111-128 / 79-110; résumés français et anglais en tête de fascicule.

6839 **Eboussi Boulaga** F. [ex-SJ], Christianity without fetishes; an African critique and recapture of Christianity, ᵀ*Barr* Robert R., 1984 ➤ **1**,8260: ᴿCalvinT 21 (1986) 257 (R.R. *Recker*).

6839* *Efefe* Elonda, *Episcope* and oversight in the Church; an African perspective: Mid-Stream 25 (Indianapolis 1986) 42-48.

6840 **Elwood** Douglas J., Faith encounters ideology; Christian discernment and social change. Quezon City 1985, New Day. 320 p. $16. – ᴿTTod 43 (1986s) 593s (C.C. *West*: creative nonviolence, not only for the Philippines).

6841 *Espin* Orlando, Iroko e Ará-kolé; comentário exegético a: un mito Iorubá-Lucumí: PerspTeol 18,44 (1986) 29-61 [TKontext 8/1,114 deutsch].

6842 *Evers* Georg, *a)* Afrikanische Theologie: ➤ 587, EvKL 1 (1986) 55-57; – *b)* Indien und das Christentum; ein schweieriges, aber nicht unfruchtbares Verhältnis: HerKor 40 (1986) 291-6.

6843 *Fang* Mark, How the Chinese read the Bible: Tripod 35 (1986) 37-47 [< TKontext 8/2,84].

6844 **Filbeck** David, Social context and proclamation; a socio-cognitive study in proclaiming the Gospel cross-culturally. Pasadena 1985, Carey Library. xvi-180 p. $9 pa. [TDig 33,362].

6845 **Firinga** Michaël, Anthropologie biblique et malgache (affinités et différences): diss. cath. ᴰ*Winling* R. Strasbourg 1986. 743 p. – RTLv 18,566.

6846 *Gerber* Uwe, Kontextuelles Christentum im Neuen China — eine Herausforderung an westliche Kirchen und Theologien: TZBas 42 (1986) 159-173.

6847 **Healey** Joseph G., A fifth gospel; in search of black Christian values 1981 ➤ **1**,8272: ᴿSpiritus 27 (P 1986) 217s (F. *Richard*); Worship 60 (1986) 472s (W.D. *Murrman*).

6848 **Hiebert** Paul G., Anthropological insights for missionaries. GR 1985, Baker. 315 p. $14 [RelStR 13,54, G. *Oosterwal*].

6849 **Hiebert** Paul G.,   Cultural anthropology [... and missionaries] [2] ([1]1976). GR 1983, Baker.   476 p. $14. – [R]EvQ 58 (1986) 372s (A. F. *Walls*].

6850 *Hinkelammert* Franz,   De la doctrina social a la doctrina social [postconciliar]? : Pasos 9 (1986) 1-9 [Zusammenfassung, TKontext 8/2,115, M. v. *Lay*].

6851 *Hünermann* Peter,   Evangelisierung und Kultur; eine systematische Reflexion: TüTQ 166 (1986) 81-91.

6852 **Jesudasan** Ignatius,   A Gandhian theology of liberation 1984 ⇨ 65,7339; 1,8290:   [R]Vidyajyoti 49 (1985) (J. *Rosario*).

6853 *Jin Luxian* Aloysius,   Christian faith in the Far East — a Chinese perspective: ⇨ 473*, VerbumSVD 27 (1986) 365-375.

6854 *a*) *Joly* Raymond,   Inculturation et vie de foi; – *b*) *Uzukwu* Elochukwu, Église nigériane et inculturation; — *c*) *Tini* Osvaldo,   Fraternité et inculturation en Zambie: Spiritus 26 (P 1985) 3-32 / 33-52 / 65-92.

6855 **Kanjirathinkal** A.,   A Church in struggle [Syro-Malabar; Rome Oriental Inst. diss.].   Bangalore 1984, Dharmaram.   xviii-302 p.; rs 40. – [R]Vidyajyoti 49 (1986) 208 (E. R. *Hambye*).

6856 **Kaplan** Steven,   The Africanization of missionary Christianity; history and typology: JRelAf 16 (1986) 166-186 [< ZIT].

6857 *a*) *Kerkhofs* Jan,   Some introductory notes for a theology of the particular church; – *b*) *Amaladoss* Michael A.,   The local churches in Asia; problems and prospects; – *c*) *Waldenfels* Hans,   Universality and particularity of the Church in the case of China: ⇨ 473*, CECC = VerbumSVD 27 (1986) 313-321 / 323-343 / 345-363.

6858 **Kochumuttom** Thomas A.,   Comparative theology [⇨ 1,8298*]; Christian thinking and spirituality in Indian perspective.   Bangalore 1985, Dharmaram Coll.   x-160 p. $5 pa. – [R]TDig 33 (1986) 477 (W. C. *Heiser*).

6859 [*Kudadjie* J. N. on Ghana; *al.*,] Theology by the people.   Geneva 1986, WCC.   x-143 p. $7.50. 2-8254-0862-X. – [R]ExpTim 98 (1986s) 380 (G. T. *Eddy*).

6860 *a*) *Lee Sung-Hee*,   Women's liberation theology as the foundation for Asian theology; – *b*) *Lewis* Nantawan B.,   Asian women theology; a historical and theological analysis: EAsJT 4,2 (1986) 2-13 / 18-22.

6861 *Le Saux* H. (Swami Abhishiktananda), La contemplazione cristiana in India [Les yeux de lumière 1979].   Bo 1984, EMI.   142 p. Lit. 9000. – [R]DivThom 88 (1985) 156-8 (G. *Perigo*: insoddisfatto, con moderazione).

6862 *a*) *Lobo* Lancy,   Towards an inculturation in the non-Sanskritic tradition; – *b*) *Grant* sr. Sara,   Towards a practical Indian ecclesiology: Vidyajyoti 49 (1985) 16-28 / 29-35.

6863 *Lodewyckx* H., 'Philosophie africaine', origines et perspectives: Bijdragen 47 (1986) 141-169.

6864 **Loth** Heinrich,   Vom Schlangenkult zur Christuskirche; Religion und Messianismus in Afrika.   B 1985, Union.   270 p.; 36 fig. – [R]RAfrT 10,19 (1986) 145-7 (F. *Bontinck*).

6865 *Lubbe* Gerrie,   Christians, Muslims and liberation in South Africa: JTSAfr 56 (1986) 24-33 [Zusammenfassung, TKontext 8/2,103, N. B. *Abeng*].

6866 [F]MARAIS Ben (Barend Jacobus),   New faces of Africa; essays in honour of ~ , [E]**Hofmeyr** J. W., *Foster* W. S., 1984 ⇨ 65,98: [R]ZMissRW 70 (1986) 333s (L. A. *Mettler*).

6867 **Mayson** Cedric,   A certain sound; the struggle for liberation in South Africa.   Maryknoll NY 1985, Orbis.   145 p. $9 pa. – [R]RelStT 6 (1986) 66s (R. *Ware*).

6868 **Menacherry** Cheriyan, An Indian philosophical approach to the personality of Jesus Christ [... Radhakrishnan; Singh]. R 1986, Urbaniana Univ. viii-90 p. – RNRT 108 (1986) 905s (L. *Renwart*).

6869 *Miguez Bonino* José, Nuevas tendencias en teología: Pasos 9 (1986) 18-22 [Zusammenfassung, TKontext 8/2, 100, M. v. *Lay*].

6870 **Milingo** Emmanuel [until 1982 Catholic archbishop of Lusaka], The world in between; Christian healing and the struggle for spiritual survival 1984 ⇒ 1, 8309: RThemelios 12 (1986s) 31s (J. J. *Stamoolis*); TLond 39 (1986) 326-8 (J. S. *Robertson*, also on SHORTER).

6871 **Milner** Clyde A.II, *O'Neil* Floyd A., Churchmen and the western Indians, 1820-1920. Norman 1985, Univ. Oklahoma. 264 p. $20. – RTTod 43 (1986s) 591-3 (D. C. *Wyckoff*).

6872 **Mitchell** Henry H., *Lawler* Nicolas C., [Black 'folk'] Soul theology. SF 1986, Harper & R. 175 p. £15.25. 0-06-065764-2. [ExpTim 98,287].

6873 **Mofokeng** Takatso A., The Crucified among the crossbearers — towards a black Christology [diss.] 1983 ⇒ 65,7347; 1,8310: RIntRMiss 75 (1986) 332 (J. *Mbiti*).

6874 E**Moltmann** Jürgen, Minjung; Theologie des Volkes Gottes in Südkorea [< Minjung Theology 1979/83]. Neuk 1984. 250 p. [RelStR 13,332, R. *Maddox*].

6875 **Mondal** Asish K., The Christian minority in India, 1947-1980: diss. Graduate Theol. Union. Berkeley 1984. – RTLv 18,560.

6876 *Moon Tong Whan*, Doing theology in Korea with reference to theological education from Minjung theological viewpoint: EAsJT 4,2 (Singapore 1986) 35-45 [Zusammenfassung, TKontext 8/2, 112, G. *Evers*].

6877 *Mosala* Itumeleng J., *Tlhagale* Buti, The unquestionable right to be free; black theology from South Africa. Maryknoll NY 1986, Orbis. 206 p. $12.

6878 *Mwalunyungu* Magnus, Towards a true local indigenous Christian church: Pastoral Orientation Service 5s (Tanzania 1986) 18-26 [< TKontext 8/2, 17].

6879 *Ngindu Mushete* A., Les thèmes majeurs de la théologie africaine; ⇒ 472, BTAf 7,13 (1985) 279-292 [< TKontext 8/2,23].

6880 *Mpombo* Lokofe, L'unité de l'Église; don et appel; un exemple, le cas de l'Église du Christ au Zaïre — éléments, obstacles et perspectives: diss. DLindijer G. J. Bru 1986. 334 p. – RTLv 18,569.

6881 *Mpongo* Laurent, Pain et vin pour l'Eucharistie en Afrique noire? Le problème a-t-il été bien posé? [*Mahieu* W. de 1970]: NRT 108 (1986) 517-531.

6882 **Mundadan** A. Mathias, History of Christianity in India, 1. From the beginnning up to the middle of the sixteenth century [2. *Thekkedath* J., 1542-1700] 1984 ⇒ 1,8312: RJDharma 11 (1986) 208-211 (V. F. *Vineeth*); NZMissW 42 (1986) 154s (J. *Wicki*); ZkT 108 (1986) 216-8 (H. B. *Meyer*).

6883 **Mundadan** A. Mathias, Indian Christians search for identity and struggle for autonomy 1984 ⇒ 1,8312a: RCleR 71 (1986) 73s (J. D. *Holmes*); PrOrChr 36 (1986) 189s (F. *Gruber*); Vidyajyoti 49 (1985) 207 (E. R. *Hambye*).

6884 **Mungello** David E., Curious land; Jesuit accommodation and the origins of Sinology: Studia Leibnitiana Sup. 25. Stu 1985, Steiner. 400 p.; 20 fig. DM 96. – RRelStR 12 (1986) 317 (E. *Hsu*).

6885 *a) M veng* Engelbert, Afrikanisches Profil von Theologie und Kirche; – *b) Mutiso-Mbinda* John, Inkulturation; eine Aufgabe für die afrikanische Kirche; – *c) Tran Van Doan*, Überlegungen zu einer asiatischen Theologie: ZMissRW 70 (1986) 154-163 / 164-171 / 172-9.

6886 **Muzorewa** Gwinyai H., The origins and development of African theology 1985 ➤ **1**,8316: ᴿEncounter 47 (1986) 90-92 (R. *Burrow*); Gregorianum 67 (1986) 160s (A. *Wolanin*); NorTTs 87 (1986) 114s (K. *Nordstokke*); RExp 83 (1986) 323 (R. *Omanson*).

6887 *Neckebrouk* V., Séparatisme religieux et indigénisation en Afrique noire; pour une approche plus nuancée: Bijdragen 47 (1986) 31-57.

6888 **Neill** Stephen, A history of Christianity in India; the beginnings to A.D. 1707: 1984 ➤ 65,7353; **1**,8320: ᴿBSOAS 49 (1986) 604s (C. *Shackle*); Month 248 (1986) 178s (D. B. *Forrester*) = 308s ! ; ScotJT 39 (1986) 412 (also D. B. *Forrester*); TorJT 2 (1986) 287s (C. T. *McIntire*).

6889 **Neill** Stephen †, A history of Christianity in India, II. ➤ **1**,8320 [Protestant missions during Catholic 'frustration and decay']; C 1985, Univ. 578 p. £45. 0-521-30376-1. – ᴿExpTim 97 (1985s) 313s (G. E. *Long* hopes for a third volume from Bishop Neill's Nachlass]; ÖkRu 35 (1986) 486s (H.-W. *Gensichen*).

6890 **Newbigin** Lesslie, Foolishness to the Greeks; the gospel and Western culture [1984 Princeton Warfield lectures: inculturation is for us of the dominant culture too]. GR 1986, Eerdmans. 156 p. $8 pa. [TDig 34,87]. – ᴿNRT 108 (1986) 932s (A. H.).

6891 *Ngwey* M., Contribution des facultés de théologie catholique à la problématique du développement [colloque LvN 1985]: RTLv 17 (1986) 193-202; Eng. 264, 'it pertains to the mission of the Church to participate in this liberating transformation of all historical oppressions and to make a theological critique of mentalities, ideologies and value systems which [favor] subordinations'.

6892 *Nlenanya Onwu*, Debate on African Theology revisited: RAfrT 10,19 (1986) 31-41.

6893 **Nyamiti** C., Christ, notre ancêtre. Zimbabwe 1984 ²1985, Gweru. 151 p. – ᴿTelema 12,46 (1986) 37-40 (J. *Galot*).

6893* **O'Collins** Gerald, Jesus today; Christology in an Australian context. NY 1986, Paulist. 74 p. $5 pa. [JAAR 55,201].

6894 *O'Donohue* John, The dogmatic perversion of religion [response to the 'extreme Romanism' of C. *Derrick*'s Opus Dei position paper circulated in East Africa]: AfER 28 (1986) 312-322.

6895 **Onema Ndjate** Tharcise, De la logique de l'existence négro-africaine à l'appel du mystère chrétien pour une exploitation théologique du concept Tetela 'vie': Diss. Tübingen 1985s, ᴰKasper W. – TR 82 (1986) 513.

6896 ᴱ**Oppenheim** Frank M., The reasoning heart; toward a North American theology. Wsh 1986, Georgetown Univ. 149 p. $18; pa. $10 [TDig 33,485]. – ᴿTS 47 (1986) 745s (R. F. *Scuka*: mostly < TS 1982-4; none on Scripture).

6897 *Osborn* Eric, Variety in Australian theology: AustralBR 34 (1986) 59-64.

6898 *Paper* Jordan, The divine principle; the Bible from a Korean perspective: StRel 15 (1986) 451-460.

6899 **Park Joung Chun**, Paul TILLICH's categories for the interpretation of history; an application to the encounter of eastern and western cultures: diss. Emory 1986. – RelStR 13,188.

6900 *Pasquato* Ottorino, Evangelizzazione e cultura nei Padri (secc. IV-V): Lateranum 52 (1986) 265-288.

6901 **Pieris** Aloysius, Theologie der Befreiung in Asien; Christentum im Kontext der Armut und der Religionen: Theologie der Dritten Welt 9. FrB 1986, Herder. 270 p. [TPhil 62,320].

6902 *a) Pieris* Aloysius, Inculturation in non-Semitic Asia; – *b) Thiel* John E., Can there be a universal catechism?: Month 248 (1986) 83-87 / 88-92.

6903 **Pieris** Aloysius, A theology of liberation in Asian churches?: *a)* EAPast 23 (Manila 1986) 117-137; – *b)* [Tokyo Symposium 1985]: Month 248 (1986) 231-9.247.

6904 *Pieris* Aloysius, El Asia no semítica frente a los modelos occidentales de inculturación [< LumièreV 33 (1984) 50-62; Orientierung 49 (1985) 102-6], ᵀᴱ*Ribas* Ramón: SelT 25 (1986) 295-302.

6905 *Pirotte* Jean, Évangélisation et cultures; pour un renouveau de la missiologie historique [... missiology as the study of the historical conditions of the incarnation of Christianity]: RTLv 17 (1986) 419-443; Eng. 544.

6906 *Pittau* Giuseppe, Religioni e cristianesimo in Giappone: CC 137 (1986,4) 531-544.

6907 *Pizzuti* Domenico, Mutamento sociale e subcontinente indiano: RasT 27 (1986) 516-534.

6908 ᴱ**Pobee** J. S., *Wartenberg-Potter* B. von, New eyes for reading; biblical and theological reflections by women from the third world. Geneva 1986, World Council of Churches. viii-108 p. Fs 12 [NRT 109,121, J. *Masson*].

6909 *Ranger* Terence, Religion, development and African Christian identity: NZMissW 42 (1986) 44-67.

6910 *Roberts* J. Deotis, An Afro-American / African theological dialogue: TorJT 2 (1986) 172-187.

6911 **Rücker** Heribert, Afrikanische Theologie; Darstellung und Dialog [Rahner-Preis für theologische Forschung]: InnsbThSt 14, 1985 ➤ 1,8342: ᴿÖkRu 35 (1986) 487s (J. *Mbiti*); RAfT 10,19 (1986) 102-5 (A. *Vanneste*); TPQ 135 (1986) 205 (K. *Piskaty*).

6912 *Saldanha* Julian, Conversion without change of community: Indian Missiological Review 8,4 (Shillong 1986) 242-252 [Zusammenfassung, TKontext 8/2, 111, G. *Evers*).

6913 **Sanneh** Lamin, West African Christianity; the religious impact 1983 ➤ 1,8343: ᴿCalvinT 21 (1986) 255s (R. R. *Recker*: spicy).

6914 *Schrauf* Roberto, La Iglesia local en el proceso de decentralización y de inculturación — una eclesiología sinodal: TXav 36,78 (1986) 7-42.

6915 **Schreiter** Robert J., Constructing local theologies 1985 ➤ 1,8348; also L, SCM: ᴿAustralasCR 63 (1986) 438-441 (F. E. *George*); Salesianum 48 (1986) 1004s (D. *Valentini*); TLond 39 (1986) 129s (A. *Race*); TR 82 (1986) 137-9 (E. *Arens*).

6916 **Schreiter** R. J., Bouwen aan een eigen theologie; gelofsverstaan binnen de platselijke context, pref. *Schillebeeckx* E. 1985 ➤ 1,8348*b*: ᴿCollatVl 16 (1986) 490 (J. De *Kesel*); TsTNijm 26 (1986) 83s (J. *Heijke*: some errors of the Dutch edition, which also suppresses the index of persons and things).

6917 *Schroeder* Edward H., Lessons for Westerners from [poem of Gabriel] Sᴇᴛɪʟᴏᴀɴᴇ's Christology: CurrTM 13 (1986) 71-77 (78-80, 'I am an African').

6917* *Sin* Jaime L. Card., Human rights and poverty [UN lecture Ph 1985]; PhilipSa 20 (1985) 407-426.

6918 **Song Choan-Seng**, Tell us our names; story theology from an Asian perspective 1984 ➤ 65,8456; 1,8356: ᴿNedTTs 40 (1986) 94s (L. A. *Hoedemaker*); Vidyajyoti 49 (1986) 430s (F. *Parmar*).

6919 **Staffner** Hans, The significance of Jesus Christ in Asia: Pastoral 11, 1985 ➤ 1,8359: ᴿGregorianum 67 (1986) 382s (J. *Dupuis*); TPhil 61 (1986) 284-6 (W. *Brugger*).

6920 *Su Deci,* Three tasks in Chinese theological work today [< Nanjing Theological Review]: Ching Feng 29,4 (Hong Kong 1986) 199-206 [Zusammenfassung, TKontext 8/2,114, G. *Evers*].

6921 *Suess* Paulo, Igreja indígena — um novo jeito de ser igreja* ⇒ 459, = REB 46 (1986) 620-630.

6922 **Sundermeier** Theo, Das Kreuz als Befreiung; Kreuzes-Interpretationen in Asien und Afrika: Traktate. Mü 1985, Kaiser. 99 p. DM 13. – RÉTRel 61 (1986) 472s (J. *Rennes*).

6923 *Swetnam* James, Mexican / Philippine Catholics and the Bible: BToday: 24 (1986) 108-111 / 310-313.

6924 **Taft** Robert [⇒ 6444], Beyond East and West; problems in liturgical understanding. Wsh 1984, Pastoral. 293 p. $12 pa. – RLtgJb 36 (1986) 65s (A. *Gerhards*).

6925 *Tang* Edmond, Ostasien, Inkulturationsstrategien: Pro Mundi Vita Bulletin 104 (1986) 1-51 [Zusammenfassung TKontext 8/2,98s, G. *Evers*].

6926 *Tepe* Valfredo, Cultura e teologia [... contextual]: REB 46 (1986) 739-759.

6927 *Thangaraj* M. Thhomas [sic], Culture and Gospel; the Indian experience: NESTR 7 (1986) 107-115.

6928 *Thils* Gustave, La présence de Dieu dans un monde planétaire et pluraliste [dans toutes les cultures, diverses médiations qui peuvent relayer l'action salvifique et même sanctifiante de Dieu...]: NRT 108 (1986) 878-896.

6929 *Thunberg* Lars, Third world theologies and the appeal to history [African poem: 'God is black / Nothing is blacker than God; / all that is black receives its blackness from him'...]: ST 40 (1986) 95-113.

6930 **Vekathanam** Mathew, Christology in the Indian anthropological context Man-History-Christ, the mystery of man and of the human history: diss. Würzburg 1985s, DGanoczy A. – TR 82 (1986) 513.

6931 **Vierling** Hermann, Stammesreligion und Hermeneutik; religionswissenschaftliche Prolegomena zur Mission unter den Kenldaylan-Dayak in West Kalimantan; Diss. DGensichen W. Heid 1986. – RTLv 18,540.

6932 *Waldenfels* Hans, Universalität und Partikularität der Kirche; Fallbeispiel China: StiZt 204 (1986) 579-593.

6933 *Wang Hsien-Chih,* Some perspectives on the theological education in the light of Homeland Theology in the Taiwanese context: CTC Bulletin 6,2s (Singapore 1986) 13-21 [Zusammenfassung, TKontext 8/2,111, G. *Evers*].

6934 **Washington** Joseph R.J, Anti-blackness in English religion 1500-1800: Texts and Studies in Religion 19. NY 1985, Mellen. xix-503 p. $40. – RHorizons 13 (1986) 169s (W. D. *Lindsey*).

6935 **Wegman** Herman, Christian worship in East and West; a study guide to liturgical history, TLathrop Gordon W. NY 1985, Pueblo. xvii-390 p. $19.50 [RelStR 13,149, J. F. *Puglisi*].

6935* **Wessels** Anton, Jezus zien; hoe Jezus is overgeleverd in andere culturen. Baarn 1986, Ten Have. 174 p. ƒ25. – RStreven 53 (1985s) 854s (P. *Beentjes*).

6936 **West** Cornel, Prophesy deliverance! an Afro-American revolutionary Christianity 1982 ⇒ 65,7385; 1,8378: RRelStR 12 (1986) 118-121 (D. W. *Wills*: hard on U.S. blacks for whom 'deliverance' means 'within capitalism') & 121-4 (J. A. *Coleman*: neither major nor mature) & 124-6 (J. Deotis *Roberts*: stunning and brilliant).

6937 **Wilmore** Gayraud S., Cone James H., Teologia negra [trabalhos '60-70]. São Paulo 1986, Paulinas. 566 p. [REB 46,722].

6938 **Yamsat Pandang** [Yilji Deshi G. J.], The concept of God and spiritual beings in various Nigerian traditional religions [... the Ngas]: TCNN Bulletin 16 (N. Nigeria 1986) 27-29 [30-39] [TKontext 8/1,21].

H8.7 *Mariologia* – The Mother of Jesus in the NT.

6939 **Allchin** A. M., The joy of all creation 1984; 0-232-51611-1 ➤ 65,7395; 1,8384: [R]ExpTim 98 (1986s) 28 (G. S. *Wakefield*: credulity which sees moving statues emanates from an anti-feminist and pastorally cruel discipline); ScotJT 39 (1986) 275s (S. M. *Harris*).

6940 [E]**Beinert** W., *Petri* H., Handbuch der Marienkunde 1984 ➤ 1,919; 3-7917-0908-9: [R]Gregorianum 67 (1986) 165s (J. *Galot*); Laurentianum 27 (1986) 160s (J. *Imbach*); ÖkRu 35 (1986) 233-5 (D. *Fischinger*); TGegw 29 (1986) 246s (R. *Medisch*); TPQ 134 (1986) 197-200 (W. *Gruber*).

6941 **Beinert** W., Maria Wegleiterin der Christen: Theologie und Leben 78. Friesing 1986, Kyrios. 64 p. DM 7,20. 43-7838-0336-5 [NTAbs 31,110].

6942 [E]**Beinert** W., Il culto di Maria oggi; teologia, liturgia, pastorale [2] [Maria heute ehren, ital. [1]1978]: Parola e liturgia 12, 1985 ➤ 1,8388: [R]Claretianum 26 (1986) 342s (M. *Augé*).

6943 *Bergeon* Inger H., Maria, modelo de libertação da mulher? Reflexões de uma luterana escandinava sobre a Teologia da Libertação da América Latina, [T]*Wenzel* João I.: PerspT 18 (1986) 359-369 [Zusammenfassung, TKontext 8/2,107, M. von *Lay*].

6944 *Berger* Pamela, The goddess obscured [grain goddess transformed into saints, eventually Mary]. Boston 1985, Beacon. 213 p.; 59 ill. $20. – [R]CurrTM 13 (1986) 254 (J. C. *Rochelle*: to liberate women, men must worship the goddess unobscured, not the defeminized Virgin Mary).

6945 **Blaquière** G., L'Évangile de Marie. Nouan-le Fuzelier 1986, Lion de Juda. 198 p. F 52 [NRT 109,941].

6946 *Boff* Leonardo, Je vous salue Marie; l'Esprit et le féminin [El Ave María 1982 ➤ 63,7476], [T]*Durban* Christiane & Luc: Théologies. P 1986, Cerf. 92 p. F 64 [NRT 109,884]. 2-204-02613-1.

6947 *Bridcut* William, Our Lord's relationship with his mother: Churchman 100 (L 1986) 339 ... [< ZIT].

6948 **Brown** R. E., *al.*, Maria nel NT [1982]. Assisi 1985, Cittadella. 341 p. Lit. 30.000. – [R]Asprenas 33 (1986) 208s (A. *Rolla*).

6949 María no Novo Testamento. São Paulo 1985, Paulinas. 336 p. [REB 46,228].

6950 **Buby** Bertrand, Mary, the faithful disciple [< Sydney conferences]. NY 1985, Paulist. 139 p. $7 pa. – [R]EphMar 36 (1986) 180 (S. *Blanco*); RRel 45 (1986) 627s (Judette M. *Kolasny*); TS 47 (1986) 554s (P. *Bearsley*).

6951 *Burggraf* Jutta, Madre de la Iglesia y mujer en la Iglesia; a propósito de la 'Teología feminista': ScripTPamp 18 (1986) 575-593.

6952 **Cannone** G., La presenza del Cantico dei Cantici nella mariologia di S. Francesco di Sales: diss. Marianum, [D]*Meo* S.M. Roma 1985 [RivB 35,87].

6953 *Carroll* Michael P., The cult of the Virgin Mary; psychological origins. Princeton 1986, Univ. xv-253 p. $25 [TDig 33,462].

6954 *Composta* Dario, Una discussione ecumenica aperta; LUTERO e Maria: Divinitas 30 (1986) 85-93.

6955 **Cooper** Thomas, Worshipping Mary, I. Mary, model of Christian perfection; IIs. Loreto revisited 1-2; IV. The Queenship of Mary; [no V.] VI. The all-holy Mother of God: CleR 71 (1986) 284-9.326-8.366-9. 418-21.444-7.

6956 *Courth* Franz, *a)* Maria im aktuellen ökumenischen Gespräch: TrierTZ 95 (1986) 38-53; – *b)* Marias endgültige Verherrlichung; neue Aspekte im ökumenischen Dialog: TGegw 29 (1986) 39-46.
De Flores S., *Meo* S., Nuovo dizionario di Mariologia 1985 → 609*.

6957 *Feuillet* André, Jesus and his mother; the role of the Virgin Mary in salvation history and the place of woman in the Church [1974], ᵀ*Maluf* L., 1984 → 1,8402: ᴿScripTPamp 18 (1986) 945-7 (J. L. *Bastero*).

6958 **Galot** Jean, Maria, la donna nell'opera di salvezza 1984 → 65,7409; 1,8409: ᴿForumKT 2 (1986) 157s (F. *Courth*).

6959 *Galot* Jean, *a)* All'origine della nostra fede, la fede di Maria: CC 137 (1986,3) 359-372; – *b)* Maria, mère de l'Église: EsprVie 96 (1986) 697-703.

6960 **Gherardini** Brunero, Lutero-Maria, pro o contro? Pisa 1985, Giardini. 328 p. – ᴿCC 137 (1986,2) 511s (J. E. *Vercruysse*); Protestantesimo 41 (1986) 156-162 (E. *Campi*); ScuolC 113 (1985) 604-7 (F. *Buzzi*).

6961 *Gherardini* Brunero, L'Immacolata Concezione in Lutero: Divinitas 30 (1986) 271-283.

6962 **González-Dorado** Antonio, *a)* Mariología popular latinoamericana; de la María conquistadora a la María liberadora: CEPAG. Asunción 1985, Loyola. 122 p. – ᴿPerspT 18 (1986) 254-6 (F. *Taborda*). – *b)* De la María conquistadora a la María liberadora, ensayo sobre mariología popular latinoamericana: Medellín 12 (1986) 3-63.192-215.

6963 *Hunter* Jim E., Blessed art thou among women? Mary in the history of Christian thought: RExp 83 (1986) 35-49.

6964 *Lago Alba* Luis, María, un misterio de gracia, una historia de fe: CiTom 113 (1986) 109-117.

6965 *Laurentin* René, Bulletin sur la Vierge Marie: RSPT 69 (1985) 611-643; 70 (1986) 101-150; 121-7, Femmes et féminisme; 143-9, Œcuménisme.

6965* *Llamas Martínez* Enrique, La Mariología en el magisterio posconciliar; mariología y magisterio: EphMar 36 (1986) 221-258.

6966 **Lunari** Luigi, Maria di Nazareth. Mi 1986, Mondadori. 264 p. Lit. 20.000. – ᴿLetture 41 (1986) 823-5 (A. *Carrara*).

6967 *Maraschin* Jaci C., Mary as theologian [and priest]: EAsJT 4,1 (1986) 164s.

6968 Maria e lo Spirito Santo 1982/4 → 1,611*: ᴿGregorianum 67 (1986) 166s (J. *Galot*).

6968* **Martínez Blat** V., Dichosa tú, María; diccionario popular. Costa Rica 1986, Ludovico. 194 p. – ᴿEphMar 36 (1986) 404 (D. *Fernández*).

6969 *Martínez Sierra* Alejandro, María mediadora; un polémico tema conciliar: MiscCom 44 (1986) 3-27.

6970 *Martini* Carlo M., Lernen von Maria; Gespräche mit jungen Menschen [La donna della riconciliazione → 1,8426], ᵀ*Beyrink* Hans. Mü 1986, Neue Stadt. 80 p. DM 9,80 [TGl 76,483].

6971 **Melotti** Luigi, Maria, la madre dei viventi [= ²Maria e la sua missione 1976]; compendio di mariologia. T-Leumann 1986, LDC. 210 p. Lit. 13.000. – ᴿHumBr 41 (1986) 945 (A. *Biazzi*).

6972 **Menvielle** Louis, Marie, mère de vie, approche du mystère marial à partir d'Irénée de Lyon: Théologie 1. P 1986, Carmel. 148 p. F 110 [MélSR 43,227].

6973 **Müller** A., Reflexiones teológicas sobre María, Madre de Jesús; la mariología en perspectiva actual [1980], ᵀ*Aramayona* A. 1985 → 1,8430: ᴿCiuD 199 (1986) 136 (S. *Folgado Flórez*).

6974 **Mulack** Christa, Maria — die geheime Göttin im Christentum: Symbole, 1985 → 1,8430: ᴿLuthMon 25 (1986) 88s (J. *Jeziorowski*); NatGrac 33

(1986) 581 (A. *Villalmonte*: Maria 'en los confines de la Divinidad' ... 'cuaternidad divina').

6975 *Napiórkowski* Stanisław C. bp. ℗ Maryja w pobozności katolickiej: ColcT 56,2 (1986) 19-33.

6976 **Palazzini** card. Pietro, La Santissima Vergine; note di mariologia e riflessione mariana. Frigento (Avellino) 1984, Casa Mariana. 274 p. – ᴿDivinitas 30 (1986) 202s (F. *López-Illana*).

6977 **Pelikan** Jaroslav, *Flusser* David, *Lang* Justin, Mary; images of the mother of Jesus in Jewish and Christian perspective. Ph 1986, Fortress. 105 p.; 48 color. pl. $20 [RelStR 13,248, Elizabeth A. *Johnson*].

6978 **Ratzinger** Joseph, Daughter Zion [meditations on Marian beliefs of the Church, German conferences 1975, published 1977], ᵀ*McDermott* J. M. SF 1983, Ignatius. 92 p. – ᴿScEspr 38 (1986) 136s (B. de *Margerie*).

6979 *Salgado* Jean-Marie, La maternité spirituelle de la Sainte Vierge chez les Pères durant les quatre premiers siècles / du Vᵉ au VIIIᵉ / IXᵉ-XIᵉ: Divinitas 30 (1986) 53-77, 120-160, 240-270.

6980 **Schaffer** Christa (*Gamber* Klaus), Koimesis; der Heimgang Mariens; das Entschlafungsbild in seiner Abhängigkeit von Legende und Theologie: StPatrLtg, 15, 1985, ↠ 1,844: ᴿEphLtg 100 (1986) 613s (A. M. *Triacca*).

6981 *a*) *Schwarz* Reinhard, 'Die zarte Mutter Christi'; wie uns LUTHER über Maria lehrt; – *b*) *Schweizer* Eduard, Das Bild der Maria bei Lukas: Zeitwende 57 (Karlsruhe 1986) / 204-216 / 193-203 [< ZIT].

6982 *a*) *Senior* Donald, NT images of Mary; – *b*) *Jegen* Carol F., Mary, mother of a renewing Church; – *c*) *Stuhlmueller* Carroll, OT settings for Mary in the Liturgy; – *d*) *Havener* Ivan, The Dormition of Mary: BToday 24 (1986) 143-151 (170s) / 153-7 / 159-166 / 167-9.

6983 **Stan** Al. I., L'église orthodoxe et les religions non-chrétiennes [diss.]: Ortodoxia 36 (1984) 151-281. 323-378 [Istina 31 (1986) 343s].

6984 **Suárez** Federico, Marie de Nazareth, ᵀ*Leonardon* P. 1986 [EsprV 97,95, P. *Cousin*].

6985 **Tambasco** A. J., What are they saying about Mary? 1984 ↠ 65,7436: ᴿScripB 16 (1985) 41 (J. R. *Duckworth*).

6986 *Tanoni* Italo [Lorette, *al.*] Sociologie de la dévotion mariale: Social Compass 33 (Lv 1986) 107 (5-106) [< ZIT].

6987 **Testa** Emmanuele, Maria terra vergine, I. I rapporti della Madre di Dio con la SS. Trinità; II. Il culto mariano palestinese 1985 ↠ 1,8447: ᴿEphMar 36 (1986) 177s (D. *Fernández*); ErbAuf 62 (1986) 311s (B. *Schwank*); Salesianum 48 (1986) 449-451 (D. *Bertetto*: magistrale); TerraS 62 (1986) 54s (anche D. *Bertetto*).

6988 **T'Joen** Michel, Maria, Kerk-in-oorsprong; de Mariavisie van H. U. von BALTHASAR tegen de achtergrond van de mariologische ontwikkelingen in de twintigste eeuw: diss. Louvain 1986, ᴰ*Perre* A. Vander. lxxxvii-593 p. – RTLv 17 (1986) 470s, résumé.

6989 *Urbaniak* Katarzyna, ℗ Zaśnięcie... 'Einschlafen' der hl. Maria — die saidische Fassung; Einleitung, Übersetzung und Kommentar: StWsz 24,1 (1986) 205-218.

6990 *Vogüé* Adalbert de, Marie chez les vierges du sixième siècle [rien du genre de piété de nos jours dans la Règle de s. BENOÎT; mais proche de lui] CÉSAIRE d'Arles et GRÉGOIRE le Grand: Benedictina 33 (1986) 79-91.

6991 **Warner** Mariana, Alone of all her sex; the myth and cult of the Virgin Mary. L 1985, Picador. xx-400-xix p. £4. – ᴿScotJT 39 (1986) 282-4 (S. M. *Harris*).

6992 *Wodecki* Bernard,   ℗ Miejsce Matki Mesjasza w Piśmie Świętym; syntetyczny schemat Mariologii biblijnej: STWsz 24,1 (1986) 41-59; franç. 60.

6993 *Zervou Tognazzi* Ioanna, L'iconografia della koimisis della Santa Vergine specchio del pensiero teologico dei Padri bizantini: Studi e Ricerche sull'Oriente Cristiano 8,1s (R 1985). 52 p.

H8.8   *Feminae NT* – **Women in the NT and early Church.**

6994 *Bernhard* T., Women's ministry in the Church; a Lukan perspective: StLuke 29,4 (1986) 261-3 [< NTAbs 31,27].

6995 *a) Bottino* Adriana, Gesù e la donna; – *b) La Posta Bertalot* Mara, Il femminile nella Bibbia come espressione del mistero di Dio; – *c) Boggio* Giovanni, Donne nella Bibbia; – *d) Fanuli* Antonio, La coppia umana secondo il libro della Genesi; – *e) Rosso Ubigli* Liliana, La donna nel giudaismo antico: ParVi 30 (1985) 361-369 / 345-351 / 337-344 / 329-336 / 352-360.

6996 *a) Burrus* Virginia, Chastity as autonomy; women in the stories of the apocryphal Acts; – *b) Davies* Steven L., Women, Tertullian and the Acts of Paul; – *c) MacDonald* D., *Scrimgeour* Andrew D., Pseudo-Chrysostom's panegyric to Thecla; the heroine of the Acts of Paul in homily and art: Semeia 38 (1986 → 8123) 101-117 (-135, answering *Kaestli* J.-D.) / 139-144 (-9, *MacKay* T.) / 151-9.

6997 **Cady** Susan, *Ronan* Marian, *Taussig* Hal, Sophia, the future of feminist spirituality. SF 1986, Harper & R. 103 p. $15 [RelStR 13,333, Pamela D. *Young*: not clear whether Sophia is a name for God or a female distinct from God].

6998 *Chevalon* M., Jésus devant les femmes: CahRenan 32,132 (1984) 219-221 [NTAbs 30,271].

6999 *D'Angelo* Mary Rose, Remembering her; feminist readings of the Christian tradition: TorJT 2 (1986) 118-126.

7000 ᴱ**Dautzenberg** Gerhard, *al.*, Die Frau im Urchristentum: QDisp 95, 1983, → 64,393 ... 1,8458: ᴿTLZ 111 (1986) 589-591 (W. *Vogler*: Sachinformation, Anfragen); TPQ 134 (1986) 87 (Herlinde *Pissarek-Hudelist*).

7001 *a) Fabris* Rinaldo, Donna, Bibbia e Chiesa; – *b) Canfora* Giovanni, La donna nella Chiesa primitiva; – *c) Mara* Maria Grazia, I Padri della Chiesa e la donna; – *d) Ghini* Emanuela, Teresa d'Avila e la Sacra Scrittura: ParVi 30 (1985) 428-435 / 404-410 / 411-9 / 420-7.

7002 *Ferguson* John, Mary Magdalene [Lk 8.12]: ExpTim 97 (1985s) 275s.

7003 *Gaden* Janet & John, Women and discipleship in the NT: Way 26 (1986) 113-123.

7004 **Gramaglia** Pier Angelo, Tertulliano, De virginibus velandis (la condizione femminile nelle prime comunità cristiana) 1984 → 1,8466: ᴿAsprenas 32 (1985) 475s (L. *Longobardo*).

7005 **Grassi** Joseph A. & Carolyn, Mary Magdalene and the women in Jesus' life. Kansas City 1986, Sheed & W. vi-158 p. $8 pa. 0-934134-33-2 [NTAbs 31,100].

7006 *Harrington* Wilfrid, Paul and women [the main reason why he is regarded as a misogynist is that he was incorrectly taken to be author of the Pastorals e.g. 1 Tim 2,11s]: Religious Life Review 25 (1986) 155-163 [< NTAbs 31,41].

7007 **Heine** Susanne, Frauen der frühen Christenheit; zur historischen Kritik einer feministischen Theologie. Gö 1986, Vandenhoeck & R. 194 p. DM 22,80 [TLZ 112,751, G. *Theissen*].

7008 *Hilkert* Mary Catherine, [Mk 16,7; 1 Cor 11,5...] Women preaching the Gospel: TDig 33 (1986) 423-440.

7009 **Honoré-Lainé** Geneviève, La femme et le mystère de l'Alliance; préf. *La Potterie* Ignace de: Épiphanie. P 1985, Cerf. 140 p. F 65. 2-204-02290-X [NTAbs 31,113]. – ᴿScripTPamp 18 (1986) 711s (C.*Basevi*).

7010 **Ide** A. F., God's girls; ordination of women in the early Christian and Gnostic churches. Garland TX 1986, Tangelwüld. v-131 p. $9 pa. 0-934667-01-2 [NTAbs 30,365].

7011 *Jodl* E.-M., Frauen um Jesus — und wie es anders kam, Paulus: Kirchenblatt für die reformierte Schweiz 141 (1985) 328s.

7012 **Kirk** Martha Ann, The prophetess led them in praise; women's stories in ritual: diss. Graduate Theological Union, ᴰ*Adams* D. Berkeley 1986. 524 p. 86-17048. – DissA 47 (1986) 1759-A.

Küchler M., Schweigen, Schmuck und Schleier... einer frauenfeindlichen Exegese 1986 → 4924.

7012* **Labarge** Margaret W., A small sound of the trumpet; women in medieval life. Boston 1986, Beacon. 285 p. $22 [JAAR 55,423].

7013 *Leclercq* Jean, *a)* La femme et les femmes dans l'œuvre de saint BERNARD 1983 → 64,7657; 65,7522: ᴿLavalTP 42 (1986) 408-411 (H.-M. *Guindon*); – *b)* La donna e le donne in San Bernardo. Mi 1985, Jaca. 144 p. Lit. 15.000. – ᴿCiVit 41 (1986) 79 (C. *Tosani*).

7014 *Locher* Clemens, Frauen — im Neuen Testament unsichtbar?: Orientierung 50 (1986) 77-80.

7015 **MacHaffie** Barbara J., Her story; women in Christian tradition. Ph 1986, Fortress. viii-183 p. $10 pa [TDig 34,83]. – ᴿTTod 43 (1981s) 608 (D. W. *Kramer*: lively rewriting of Church history).

7016 **Militello** C., Donna e chiesa; la testimonianza di Giovanni CRISOSTOMO: Fac. Teol. Sicilia 3. Palermo 1985, Oftes. 254 p. Lit. 20.000. – ᴿAsprenas 33 (1986) 456.

7017 **Moloney** Francis J., Woman, first among the faithful; a NT study 1985 → 1,8477; also ND, Ave Maria: ᴿGregorianum 67 (1986) 773 (J. *Galot*); IrBSt 8 (1986) 203s (J. R. *Boyd*: also Index, not 'Maloney'); RRel 45 (1986) 938s (Judette M. *Kolasny*).

7018 *Omanson* Roger L., The role of women in the New Testament church: RExp 83 (1986) 15-25.

7019 *Osiek* Carolyn, Feminist hermeneutics: BToday 24 (1986) 18s ['the Bible contains so much that is opposed to the real God-intended freedom and dignity of all believers that it can no longer be counted upon for guidance and inspiration' (mentioned as one of various possible approaches) queried p. 193 by Claire MCHARDY, who at 73 has 'held every position in the parish open to women, and I've been content; I can't believe the Bible can't be enough for us to live "the Word incarnate and inspired" ' (DICHARRY); p. 193s, objections of B. AHERN and answer].

7020 *Ott* Elisabeth, Wer war die Frau des Pilatus? Eine Geschichte für heute: GeistL 59 (1986) 104-6.

7021 **Pirot** J., Trois amies de Jésus [Lc 7,36; Mc 14,3; Lc 8,2]: Lire la Bible 74. P 1986, Cerf. 145 p. F 66 [EsprV 97,335, L. *Walter*].

7022 **Plum** Karin F., Den tilslørede frihed; kvindehistorie [Veiled freedom; women's story] og kvindehistorier i det nye testamente [...i det gamle testamente 1983 → 65,1327]. K 1984, Reitzel. 143 p.; ill. Dk 178. 87-412-3776-5 [NTAbs 31,115].

Ricci Carla, Le donne al seguito di Gesù in Lc. 8,1-3 [1.3 Ruolo privilegiato di Maria di Magdala; ipotesi di una 'tradizione delle donne', 'teologia femminista'; 1.4, Donne e ministero], ᴰ1986 → 3972.

7023 ᴱRussell Letty M., Feminist interpretation of the Bible 1985 → 1,307: ᴿÉTRel 61 (1986) 565s (D. *Lys*: 'Ce livre peut être dangereux pour votre santé!'); JAAR 54 (1986) 608s (Carol *Meyers*); Month 248 (1986) 353s (Lavinia *Byrne*); TTod 43 (1986s) 282-4 (W. *Brueggemann*).

7024 **Schüssler Fiorenza** Elisabeth, In memory of her 1983 → 64,7405... 1,8483: ᴿBijdragen 47 (1986) 318-324 (J. *Wissink*: more help than the latest fundamental theology manuals on contextual-emancipatory versus academic theology); BSulp 12 (1986) 191-4 (L.W. *Terrien*); KIsr 1 (1986) 90-94 (Luise *Schottroff*); RExp 83 (1986) 480-2 (Molly T. *Marshall-Green*).

7025 **Schüssler Fiorenza** Elisabeth, En mémoire d'elle; essai de reconstruction des origines chrétiennes selon la théologie féministe, ᵀ*Brun* Marcelline: CogF 136. P 1986, Cerf. 482 p. F 175. – ᴿEsprV 96 (1986) 329-333 [P. *Jay*: approximations proférées sur un ton doctoral]; Études 365 (1986) 138s (R. *Marlé*); MélSR 43 (1986) 167s (M. *Huftier*); NRT 108 (1986) 759s (X. *Jacques*: parti pris, uses an eisegesis which it reproves in others); RTLv 17 (1986) 456-8 (Alice *Dermience*: stimulant, mais déforme les aspects les plus valables); SuppVSp 157 (1986) 145-9 (M. *Morgen*).

7026 **Sider** Elizabeth A., Women in the early Church. Wilmington 1983. 260 p. – ᴿDivinitas 30 (1986) 192 (T. *Stramare*).

7027 *Stebbins* C., La nature faible et souvent dangereuse de la femme dans la version en vers du XIVᵉ siècle consacrée à la Vie Saint Jehan-Baptiste: RBgPg 64 (1986) 473-495.

7028 *Sudbrack* Josef, Die Geschwister von Betanien; biblisches Zeugnis von der Menschlichkeit Jesu: GeistL 59 (1986) 83-92.

7029 **Tetlow** Elisabeth M., Women and ministry in the New Testament; called to serve: CollTheolSoc Reprints 1. Lanham MD 1985 [= 1980 → 61, 9501a], UPA. vi-164 p. $10.75 pa. – ᴿCBQ 48 (1986) 348s (Marla J. *Selvidge*: it may convince a few).

7030 **Tolbert** Mary Ann, The Bible and feminist hermeneutics [treatments of specific texts]: Semeia 28. Chico 1983, Scholars. iv-128 p. $10 [RelStR 13,254, Pamela D. *Young*].

7031 *Valerio* Adriana, Women in the 'societas christiana', 10th-12th centuries [< RasT 5 (1983) 435-446 > TGegw 28 (1985) 98-107, ᵀ*Ebermann* Bernhard], ᵀᴱ*Asen* B.: TDig 33 (1986) 155-8.

7032 *van den Doel* A., Submission in the New Testament [... wives to husbands; like Diaspora Judaism, early Christianity adapted its life-style to the environment]: Brethren Life and Thought 31,2 (Oak Brook IL 1986) 121-5 [< NTAbs 31,68].

7033 *Vanzan* Piersandro, Una donna nella Chiesa; indicazioni bibliche e interpretazioni femministe: CC 137 (1986,1) 431-444.

7034 **Witherington** Benᴵᴵᴵ, Women in the ministry of Jesus; a study of Jesus' attitudes to women and their roles as reflected in his earthly life: SNTS Mon 51, 1984 → 65,7469: 1,8489: ᴿJBL 105 (1986) 724-6 (Susan G. *De George*: too little use of apocrypha and other indications of women's greater prominence); Salesianum 48 (1986) 989 (D. *Valentini*).

H8.9 *Theologia feminae* – **Feminist theology.**

7035 ᴱ**Andolsen** Barbara, al., Women's consciousness, women's conscience. Minneapolis 1985, Winston. xxvi-310 p. $25. – ᴿTTod 43 (1986s) 594-6 (Isabel W. *Rogers*).

7035* *Andolsen* Barbara H., 'Daughters of Jefferson, daughters of boot-blacks'; racism and American feminism. Macon GA 1986, Mercer Univ. 130 p. $22; pa. $13 [JAAR 55,193].

7036 ᴱAtkinson Clarissa W., al., Immaculate and powerful; the female in sacred image and social reality 1985 ➤ 1,536: ᴿHistRel 26 (1986s) 329-331 (Judith A. Berling).

7037 a) Aubert Jean-Marie, Théologie féministe et parole d'Église; – b) Mehl Herrade, La condition des femmes-pasteurs en France: SuppVSp 157 (1986) 123-143 / 107-121.

7037* [Lucchetti] Bingemer Maria Clara, ... e a mulher rompeu o siléncio; a propósito do segundo encontro sobre a produção teológica feminina nas Igrejas cristãs: PerspT 18 (1986) 371-381.

7038 Bons-Storm Riet, De rib, de appel en de pastor; feminisme en pastoraat: PrakT 13 (1986) 346-356.

7039 Brown Earl K., Women of Mr. WESLEY's Methodism. 1984, Mellen. 261 p. $50. – ᴿJAAR 54 (1986) 167s (Carolyn D. Gifford).

7040 Carmody Denise L., The double cross; ordination, abortion, and Catholic feminism. NY 1986, Crossroad. ix-158 p. $11 pa. [TDig 33,462].

7041 a) Castelli Elizabeth, Virginity and its meaning for women's sexuality in early Christianity; – b) Cliff Michelle, I found God in myself and I loved her, I loved her fiercely; more thoughts on the work of black women artists: JFemRel 2,1 (1986) 61-88 / 7-40 [< ZIT].

7042 Clark Sandra, Hic mulier, haec vir, and the controversy over masculine women: StPg 82 (1985) 157-183.

7043 ᴱCollins Adela Y., Feminist perspectives on biblical scholarship: SBL Biblical Scholarship in North America 10, 1985 ➤ 1,276; $14; sb./pa. $9.50: ᴿAustralBR 34 (1986) 80s (J. W. Roffey); BL (1986) 13s (J..M. Lieu); ÉglT 17 (1986) 235-7 (W. Vogels); IrBSt 8 (1986) 204-6 (J. R. Boyd); VT 36 (1986) 379 (J. A. Emerton).

7044 Daly Mary, Gyn-ökologie, eine Meta-Ethik des radikalen Feminismus [1978 cf. ➤ 62,8391; 65,7490]. Mü 1981 [GeistL 59 (1986) 306].

7045 Daly Mary, Jenseits von Gottvater, Sohn & Co., Aufbruch zu einer Philosophie der Frauenbefreiung [1974 ➤ 60,9862],ᵀ. Mü 1980 [GeistL 59 (1986) 306].

7046 ᴱDayton Donald W., Holiness tracts defending the ministry of women [four, 1853-1904]. NY 1985, Garland. xii-304 p. $44 [RelStR 13,154, Pamela D. Young].

7047 Diehl Judith R., A woman's place; equal partnership in daily ministry. Ph 1985, Fortress. 107 p. – ᴿRelStR 12 (1986) 268 (Carol Doran).

7048 Dietrich G., Bible and liberation; the origins of the Bible revisited; reconstructing women's history: COELI 35 (Bru 1985) 19-23 ... [NTAbs 30,131].

7049 Dirks-Blatt Henny G., The ordination of women to the ministry in the member churches of the WARC [World Alliance of Reformed Churches]: Reformed World 39,1 (Geneva 1986) 434-443. 484-495.

7050 Dittes James E., The male predicament; being a man today ➤ 1,8532 ['manliness' is a snare meaning conformity to others' expectations; liberation can be learned from women's struggles; goal like the NT 'life-and-world-affirming God']. SF 1985, Harper. 223 p. $15 [RelStR 12,136].

7051 Dorst B., Frauenbewegung als Therapie — feministische Therapie als Frauenbewegung: Wege zum Menschen 38 (Gö 1986) 308-318 [< ZIT].

7052 Douglass Jane D., Women, freedom and CALVIN. Ph 1985, Westminster. 155 p. $12. 0-664-24663-X. – ᴿÉTRel 61 (1986) 600 (A. Gounelle); TTod 43 (1986s) 270.272s (D. Foxgrover).

7053 ᴱ**Dunayevskaya** Raya [disciple and ex-secretary of Trotsky], Women's liberation and the dialectics of revolution; reaching for the future; a 35-year collection of essays — historic, philosophic, global.   Atlanta Highlands NJ 1985, Humanities.   viii-294 p. $38.50 [RelStR 13,52, Kathryn A. *Rabuzzi*].

7054 *Echivard* Nicole,   Le rôle de la femme dans l'Église: Communio 11,1 (P 1985) 109-118 [non in IkaZ].

7055 *Edwards* Adrian,   Gender and sacrifice: NBlackf 67 (1986) 372-7 [499s, objection of Anne *Inman*].

7056 **Fraser** Elouise R.,   Karl BARTH's doctrine of humanity; a reconstructive exercise in feminist narrative theology: diss. Vanderbilt, ᴰ*Hodgson* P.   Nv 1986. 311 p. 86-16351. – DissA 47 (1986s) 1367s-A; RelStR 13,188.

7057 *Franklin* Doris,   Impact of Christianity on the status of women from the socio-cultural point of view: Religion and Society 32,2 (Bangalore 1985) 43-55 [3-70, *al.* in Hinduism, Islam, Jain].

7058 **French** Marilyn,   Jenseits der Macht; Frauen, Männer und Moral.   1985, Reinbek [Marielouise *Janssen-Jurreit* (Der Spiegel) zeigt 'naïv, harmlos': GeistL 59 (1986) 309].

7059 **Fuller y Romero** Orlando,   Women's ordination as a theological issue; a study of the controversy since 'inter insigniores': diss. Angelicum.   R 1985. 172 p. – RTLv 18,582.

7060 *a*) *Gebara* Ivone,   A mulher faz Teologia — um ensaio para reflexão; – *b*) *Prado* Consuelo de,   Eu sinto Deus de outro modo; – *c*) *Lora* Carmen, *Barnechea* Cecilia,   Reflexões sobre sexualidade e identidade da mulher: ➤ 510, REB 46 (1986) 5-14 / 15-29 / 100-121.

7061 **Giles** Kevin,   Created woman [Gn 2; Gal 3,23-8 warrant ordination; only 1 Tim 2,11-14 opposed, and may have to be struck from the canon]. Canberra 1985, Alcorn,   84 p. A$7 pa. – ᴿRefTR 45 (1986) 20 (D. *Peterson*).

7062 *a*) *Gilkes* Cheryl T.,   The role of women in the sanctified Church; – *b*) *Sanders* Cheryl J.,   The woman as preacher: JRelTht 43,1 (1986) 24-41 / 6-23 [< ZIT].

7063 **Grant** Jacquelyn,   The development and limitations of feminist Christology; towards an engagement of white women's and black women's religious experience: diss. Union. NY 1985. – RTLv 18,572.

7064 *Haight* Roger,   Women in the Church; a theological reflection: TorJT 2 (1986) 105-117.

7065 **Harrison** Beverly W.,   Making the connections; essays in feminist social ethics 1985 ➤ 1,184: ᴿJAAR 54 (1986) 584-6 (Lisa S. *Cahill*); JRel 66 (1986) 465s (Christine F. *Hinze*); TTod 43 (1986s) 454.456.458 (Jane C. *Peck*).

7066 *Hasenohr* Geneviève,   La vie quotidienne de la femme vue par l'église; l'enseignement des 'journées chrétiennes' de la fin du moyen âge: ➤ 403, Frau 1984/6, 19-101.

7067 **Hébrard** Monique, Les femmes dans l'Église 1984 ➤ 65,7509; 1,8556: ᴿÉ-TRel 61 (1986) 308 (L. *Gagnebin*: l'Église, protestante aussi, est un grand groupe essentiellement féminin dominé par un petit groupe masculin).

7068 *Heyward* Carter, *Hunt* Mary E., *Brooten* Bernadette, *al.*,   Lesbianism and feminist theology: JFemStRel 2,2 (1986) 95-108.

7069 **Hourcade** Janine,   *a*) La femme dans l'Église; les ministères féminins: diss. ᴰ*Dagens* C.   Toulouse 1986. 445 p. – RTLv 18,587. – *b*) La femme dans l'Église; étude anthropologique et théologique des ministères féminins: Croire et Savoir 7.   P 1986, Téqui.   343 p. F 160 [NRT 109,628, A. *Toubeau*].

7070 *Jennings* D. A., [letter rectifying RHYMES and making four points behind Catholic non-ordination of women]: TLond 39 (1986) 218-220.

7071 **Kaiser** Jochen-Christoph, Frauen in der Kirche; Evangelische Frauenverbände im Spannungsfeld von Kirche und Gesellschaft 1890-1945: Quellen und Materialen 27. Dü 1985, Schwann. – ᴿZKG 97 (1986) 422s (P. *Henning*).

7072 *Karant-Nunn* Susan C., The transmission of LUTHER's teaching on women and matrimony; the case of Zwickau: ArRefG 77 (1986) 31-46.

7073 *Karsay* Eszter, ⓂThe changed relationships between men and women in the economic, social, and ecclesiastical life of our days: Theologiai Szemle 29 (1986) 293-9.

7074 *a)* *King* Ursula, Feminismus; – *b)* *Siegele-Wenschkewitz* Leonore, (*Schottroff* Luise), Feministische Theologie; – *c)* *Schiersmann* Christiana, Frau (und Kirche, *Pfiffin* Ursula; -enbewegung, *Schröder* Hannelore): ➤ 587, EvKL 1 (1986) 1280-4 / 1284-1291 / 2334-7 (-2346).

7075 *Kopas* Jane, Teaching Christology in light of feminist issues: Horizons 13 (1986) 332-343.

7076 ᴱ**Lacelle** Élisabeth J., La femme, son corps, la religion 1977/83 ➤ 64,507*... 1,8577: ᴿÉglT 17 (1986) 262-6 (Micheline *Laguë*).

7077 *Langer* Heidemarie, Letting ourselves be found; stories of a feminist spirituality [from group-study of Lk 15, 8-10]: EcuR 38 (1986) 23-28.

7078 **Laurien** Hanna-Renate, Nicht Ja und nicht Amen — eine Frau in der Politik beruft sich auf das Christentum. FrB 1985, Herder. 160 p. DM 16,80. – ᴿUniversitas 41 (1986) 1213s (G. *Kleinschmidt*).

7079 **Lenz** Elinor, *Myerhoff* Barbara, The feminization of America; how women's values are changing our public and private lives. NY 1985, St. Martin's. 276 p. $16. – ᴿCCurr 36 (1986s) 239-242 (Ann-Janine *Morey*).

7079* **Lerner** Gerda, Women and history, I. The creation of patriarchy. NY 1986, Oxford-UP. 318 p. [JAAR 55,608-613, Elizabeth *Fox-Genovese*].

7080 *Lewis* Nantawan B., Asian women theology; a historical and theological analysis: EAsJT 4,2 (1986) 18-22 [Zusammenfassung, TKontext 8/2,107, G. *Evers*].

7081 *a)* *Lozano* Itziar, *González* Maruja, Feminismo y movimiento popular en América Latina; – *b)* *Gebara* Ivone, La mujer hace teología; un ensayo para la reflexión; – *c)* *Ritchie* Nelly, La mujer y cristología: Christus 51,595 (Méx 1986) 4-14 / 16-21 [REB 46 (1986) 5-14] / 29-35 [TKontext 8/1,78; deutsch 104].

7082 *McDonough* Elizabeth, Women and the new Church law: Concilium 184 (E 1986) 73-81 [deutsch IZT 22 (1986) 210-216, ᵀ*Saiber* Birgit].

7083 *Maeckelberghe* E., Vanuit de ervaring; recente ontwikkelingen in de feministische theologie van de Verenigde Staten: TsTNijm 26 (1986) 392-405.

7084 *McKelway* Alexander J., Perichoretic possibilities in BARTH's doctrine of male and female: PrincSemB 7 (1986) 231-243 [< ZIT].

7085 *Maddox* Randy L., Toward an inclusive theology; the systematic implications of the feminist critique: ChrSchR 16 (GR 1986) 7-23.

7086 *Mahowald* Mary B., A majority perspective; feminine and feminist elements in American philosophy: CCurr 36 (1986s) 410-7.

7087 *a)* *Manolache* Anca, Aus der gegenwärtigen Frauenproblematik; – *b)* *Jurca* Constantin-Eugen, Erklärung des heiligen Sakraments des Priestertums: Mitropolia Banatului 35 (1985) 342-441 / 313-322 [rum. < TLZ 112,782].

7088 *Marshall-Green* Molly, 'When keeping silent will no longer do'; a theological agenda for the contemporary Church: RExp 83 ('Women in ministry' 1986) 27-33.

7089 *Martin* John H., The ordination of women and the theologians in the Middle Ages: EscVedat 16 (1986) 115-177.

7090 **Massey** Marilyn C., Feminine soul; the fate of an ideal. Boston 1985, Beacon. xiii-219 p. $23. – ᴿJRel 66 (1986) 463s (Dawn *De Vries*).

7091 **May** Melanie A., Bonds of unity; women, theology, and the worldwide Church: diss. Harvard 1986. – HarvTR 79 (1986) 475; RelStR 13,188.

7092 **Meese** Elizabeth A., Crossing the double-cross; the practice of feminist criticism. Chapel Hill 1986, Univ. North Carolina. xii-190 p. $19; pa. $9 [RelStR 13,159, Kathryn A. *Rabuzzi*].

7093 *Meneghetti* Antonella, Donne e liturgia; 'status quaestionis' della problematica in corso: RivLtg 73 (1986) 382-391.

7094 **Moltmann-Wendel** Elisabeth, A land flowing with milk and honey [1985 ➤ 1,8595],ᵀ. L 1986, SCM. 212 p. £7. 0-334-00869-7. – ᴿExpTim 98 (1986s) 149 (Elizabeth *Moberly*); ModT 3 (1986s) 276 (Kate *Mertes*).

7095 **Morgan** John H., Women priests; an emerging ministry in the Episcopal Church (1975-1985). Bristol IN 1985, Wyndham Hall. xx-187 p. $13 pa. [TDig 33,373].

7095* **Muddiman** John & Gillian, Women, the Bible and the Priesthood. L 1984, MOW [Movement for the Ordination of Women]. 14 p. £0.50 [TLond 39,78, with similar pamphlets].

7096 *Oeyen* Christian, Priesteramt der Frau? Die altkatholische Theologie als Beispiel einer Denkentwicklung: ÖkRu 35 (1986) 254-267.

7097 ᴱ**Parvey** Constance F., L'ordinazione delle donne in una prospettiva ecumenica; uno strumento di lavoro per il futuro della chiesa [Klingenthal 1979 ➤ 62,425], ᵀ*Jacobelli* Caterina: Terzomillennio. Casale Monferrato 1983, Marietti. 133 p. – ᴿRivStoLR 22 (1986) 595s (Angela *Lostia di S. Sofia*).

7098 *Prokes* sr. M. Timothy, Woman and man; war or synergy?: Canad-CathR 4 (May 1986)...

7099 *Quigley* Michael E., Male and female symbolism in Catholic faith: HomPast 87,5 (1986s) 27-32.50-53.

7100 **Rabuzzi** Kathryn A., The sacred and the feminine; toward a theology of housework 1982 ➤ 63,7611; 64,7675: ᴿRelStR 12 (1986) 205 (June *O'Connor*: feminists need to acknowledge a richness in domestic life).

7101 **Randour** Mary Lou, Women's psyche, women's spirit; the reality of relationships. NY 1986, Columbia. 240 p. $25 [RelStR 13,327, Martha A. *Robbins*].

7102 *Robson* Jill, Women's images of God and prayer: Way 26 (1986) 91-103.

7103 *Roe* Michael D., *Warner* Carolina F., *Erickson* Shari R., A phenomenological explanation of feminism and Christian orthodoxy: JPsy&Chr. 5,1 (1986) 30-38.

7104 **Ruether** Rosemary. Sexism and God-talk; toward a feminist theology 1983 ➤ 64,7678... 1,8613: ᴿRelStR 12 (1986) 202-4 (June *O'Connor*); Salesianum 48 (1986) 1003s (D. *Valentini*).

7105 **Ruether** Rosemary R., Womanguides 1985 ➤ 1,8614: ᴿJAAR 54 (1986) 607s (Mary M. *Fulkerson*).

7106 **Ruether** Rosemary R., Woman-church; theology and practice of feminist liturgical communities. SF 1986, Harper & R. viii-306 p. $17. 0-06-066834-2 [NTAbs 31,131]. – ᴿCCurr 36 (1986s) 362-4 (R. O. *Cleary*).

7107 *Ruether* Rosemary R., *a*) Feminism and religious faith; renewal or new creation: Religion and Intellectual Life 3,2 ('Feminism and Religious Experience' 1986) 7-20: – b) Women-church; emerging feminist liturgical communities: Concilium 186 (E 1986) 52-59 (ed. franç. 71-80, ᵀ*Divault* A.).

7108 *Salamone* Frank A., Religion and repression; enforcing feminine inequality in an 'egalitarian society' [the Hune of Nigeria]: Anthropos 81 (1986) 517-528.

7109 **Schneiders** Sandra M., Women and the Word; the gender of God in the NT and the spirituality of women. NY 1986, Paulist. 81 p. $3 pa. [Horizons 14,171, Carolyn *Osiek*].

7110 **Schüssler Fiorenza** Elisabeth, Bread not stone; the challenge of feminist biblical interpretation 1985 ➤ 1,8622: ᴿJAAR 54 (1986) 141-3 (Rosemary R. *Ruether*: labored hermeneutics); RelStR 12 (1986) 197-202 (Mary *Knutsen*).

7112 **Sölle** Dorothee, The strength of the weak; toward a Christian feminist identity 1984 ➤ 65,7556; 1,8630: ᴿJPsy&T 14 (1986) 84 (Nancy S. *Duvall*); WWorld 6 (1986) 119s (Eva *Rogness*).

7113 **Soelle** D., *Schottroff* L., Mijn broeders hoedster; vrouwen lezen de Bijbel. Baarn 1986, Ten Have. 152 p. – ᴿCollarVl 16 (1986) 501 (R. *Hoet*).

7114 *Sölle* Dorothee, *a*) Frauenbewegung; Ritual und Religion: Orientierung 50 (1986) 1s; – *b*) Ritual and religion in the women's movement [< Orientierung 50 (1986) 1s]: TDig 33 (1986) 348s.

7115 **Sorge** Elga, Religion und Frau; weibliche Spiritualität im Christentum: Tb 1038, 1985 ➤ 1,8631: ᴿZAW 98 (1986) 477 (H.-C. *Schmitt*: p. 94-115, Eva).

7116 **Spencer** Aida B., Beyond the curse; women called to ministry. Nv 1985, Nelson. 223 p. $11. 0-8407-5482-5 [NTAbs 30,242]. – ᴿSWJT 29,2 (1986s) 57 (G. *Greenfield*).

7117 *Steele sr.* Elizabeth, The role of women in the Church: CurrTM 13 (1986) 13-21.

7117* **Stern** Karl, The flight from woman. 1986 [JAAR 55,436 indicates 'Paragon'; there are several publishers with that name, one in Santa Rosa CA]. 310 p. $10.

7118 *Stierle* Beate, Die Frau in Gesellschaft und Kirche: Werkstatt Gemeinde 4 (Rotenburg 1986) 112-128 [< ZIT].

7119 **Storkey** Elaine, What's right with feminism? L/GR 1985, SPCK/ Eerdmans. 186 p. £4. – ᴿCleR 71 (1986) 309s (D. *Higgins*); NBlackf 67 (1986) 49s (Kate *Mertes*).

7120 **Strachan** Elspeth & Gordon, Freeing the Feminine 1985 ➤ 1,8632: ᴿScotJT 39 (1986) 280-2 (Daphne *Hampson*).

7121 *Sudbrack* Josef, Feministische Theologie; Fragen um ein aktuelles Thema: GeistL 59 (1986) 301-316.

7122 *a*) *Thistlethwaite* Susan B., Inclusive language and linguistic blindness; – *b*) *Ringe* Sharon H., Standing toward the text: TTod 43 (1986s) 533-9 / 552-7 [540-551, *Miller* P., *Bennett* R.].

7123 *Thomas* Owen C., Feminist theology and Anglican theology: AnglTR 68 (1986) 125 ...

7124 ᴱ**Thompson** Betty, Ⓜ *Nők és férfiak az egyházban* [A chance to change; women and men in the Church, Sheffield 1981],ᵀ. Geneva 1982, WCC. – ᴿTheologiai Szemle 29 (1986) 113-116 (Eszter *Karsay*).

7125 *Tobin* Mary Luke, Women in the Church since Vatican II: America 155 (1986) 243-6.

7126 *Trapani* Giuseppe, L''Eterno Femminino' di T. de CHARDIN riletto da H. de LUBAC: Ho Theológos 3 (1985) 247-262.

Valenze Deborah M., Prophetic sons and daughters; female preaching and popular religion in industrial England 1985 ➤ d746.

7127 **Valerio** A., La questione femminile nei secoli X-XII; una rilettura storica di alcune esperienze in Campania. N 1983, D'Auria. 96 p. – ᴿPro-testantesimo 41 (1986) 116s (G. *Gonnet*).

7128 **Van Herik** Judith, FREUD on femininity and faith 1982 ➤ 64,1626.7689; 1,8640: ᴿTTod 43 (1986s) 123-6 (Diane *Jonte-Pace*).

7129 [*Vanzan* Piersandro], *Bellenzier* Maria Teresa, *Di Nicola* Giulia P., *Morra* Stella, La donna nella Chiesa e nella società. R 1986, AVE. 184 p. Lit. 16.000. – ᴿCC 137 (1986,2) 509s G. *Giachi*).

7130 *Vanzan* Piersandro, L'ordinazione sacerdotale delle donne; riflessioni in margine a un recente carteggio tra la Chiesa cattolica e la Comunione anglicana: CC 137 (1986,3) 148-154.

7131 **Walker** Barbara G., The crone; woman of age, wisdom and power. NY 1985, Harper & R. 191 p. $15 (RelStR 13,148, Ann-Janine *Morey*].

7132 *a) Walsh* Kathleen, Women's studies and the Churches; – *b) Hampson* Daphne, Feminism, its nature and implications; Month 248 (1986) 18-21 / 96-99.

7133 **Weaver** Mary Jo, New Catholic women; a contemporary challenge to traditional religious authority. SF 1986, Harper & R. 270 p. $19 [JAAR 54,633]. – ᴿCCurr 25 (1985s) 458 (Sally *Cunneen*: what do Catholic women want ?); Tablet 240 (1986) 732 (Rosemary R. *Ruether*).

7134 **Wenck** Inge, Gott ist im Mann zu kurz gekommen; eine Frau über Jesus von Nazareth. Gü 1982 [GeistL 59 (1986) 302].

7135 *Wenham* David, Men and women in the Church: Themelios 12 (1986s) 73-79.

7135* **White** Charles E., The beauty of holiness; Phoebe PALMER as theologian, revivalist, feminist and humanitarian. Asbury [JAAR 55,428: can be in Wilmore KY; but it is a name for Zondervan in GR]. 351 p. 0-310-46250-9.

7136 *Wiederanders* Gerlinne, 'Lass dich gelüsten nach der Männer Bildung, Kunst, Weisheit und Ehre'; zur Emanzipation der Frau bei SCHLEIER-MACHER: TVers 16 (1986) 119-129.

7137 *Wilson-Kastner* Patricia, Faith, feminism, and the Christ 1983 ➤ 64, 7693; 1,8646: ᴿRelStR 12 (1986) 197-202 (Mary *Knutsen*).

7138 *a) Zor-Obianga* R., Questions des femmes africaines à l'Église d'Afrique; – *b) Mayland* J. M., The community of women and men in the Church: ➤ 472, Yaoundé 1984/5, 373-382 / 383-399.

H9 **Eschatologia NT**, *spes, hope.*

7139 *Alfeche* M., The basis of hope in the resurrection of the body according to AUGUSTINE: AugLv 36 (1986) 240-296.

7140 **Allison** Dale C.ᴶ, The end of the ages has come; an early interpretation of the Passion and Resurrection of Jesus [as part of general resurrection already begun; diss. Duke 1982 ➤ 64,4598]. Ph 1985, Fortress. xiii-194 p. 0-8006-0753-8. – ᴿBS 143 (1986) 174s (J. F. *Walvoord*); ExpTim 97 (1985s) 344s (A. *Chester*: challenging, inadequate).

7141 **Baarlink** Heinrich, Die Eschatologie der synoptischen Evangelien: BWANT 120. Stu 1986, Kohlhammer. 200 p.; bibliog. p. 184-191. DM 68. 3-17-009269-3.

7142 *a*) **Barnett** Vida,   Ends — or beginnings? – *b*) **Rogers** Alan,   Suffering —
why? L c. 1985, 'CEM'. 40 p.; 42 p. 0-905022-87-2; 8-2. – ᴿExpTim 97
(1985s) 255 [C. S. *Rodd*: the most effective in this children's series: topics to
face before the full impact of adolescence].

7143 **Berentsen** J. M.,   Grave and Gospel [biblical data touching Japanese
ancestor-veneration]: ZRGg Beih. 30. Leiden 1985, Brill. x-306 p. *f* 96
[NRT 109,291, J. *Masson*].

7144 **Biffi** card. Giacomo,   Linee di escatologia cristiana 1984 → 1,8655: ᴿCC
137 (1986,2) 617 (G. *Mucci*); Protestantesimo 41 (1986) 234s (S. *Rostagno*).

7144* **Bloch** Ernst,   The principle of hope, ᵀ*Plaice* N., *al.* Ox 1986, Blackwell.
xxxiii-1420 p. £120 [JTS 38,303].

7145 *Bosch* J. P. van den,   Dood en religie; over funeraire riten, in het
bijzonder in het oude India [Voordracht Groningen 1985]: NedTTs 40
(1986) 209-226; Eng. 226.

7146 *Bougerol* Jacques-Guy,   La théologie de l'espérance aux XIIᵉ et XIIIᵉ
siècles; I. Études; 2. Textes. P 1985, Ét. Augustiniennes. 400 p.; 240 p. –
ᴿRÉAug 32 (1986) 189s (J. *Longère*); RTLv 17 (1986) 71 (P. *Delhaye*);
TsTNijm 26 (1986) 300 (J. *Waldram*).

7147 **Bourgeois** Henri,   L'espérance maintenant et toujours. P 1985, Desclée. –
ᴿBFaCLyon 79 (1986) 61 (*ipse*).

7148 *Bregman* Lucy,   The death of everyone [threatened total extinction makes
individual death meaningless]; Robert Lɪғᴛᴏɴ [The broken connection
1979], Christian theology and apocalyptic imagery: Horizons 13 (1986)
306-320.

7149 *Bria* I.,   La doctrine orthodoxe sur la vie future: Ortodoxia 36,1 (1986)
1-28 [Istina 31 (1986) 343].

7150 **Brie** J. J. de,   The soul and its immortality. Zerkegem-Jabbeke. 114 p.
[CC 137/4 dopo 208].

7151 **Bridges** James T.ᴶ,   Human destiny and resurrection in Pᴀɴɴᴇɴʙᴇʀɢ and
Rᴀʜɴᴇʀ: diss. Rice, ᴰ*Nielsen* N. = Houston 1986. 367 p. 86-17430. –
DissA 47 (1986s) 1772-A.

7152 *Brito* Emilio,   Création et eschatologie chez Sᴄʜᴇʟʟɪɴɢ: LavalTP 42
(1986) 247-267.

7153 *Buchheit* Vinzenz,   Resurrectio carnis bei Pʀᴜᴅᴇɴᴛɪᴜs: VigChr 40
(1986) 261-285.

7154 **Bühlmann** Walter,   Leben, Sterben, Leben; Fragen um Tod und Jenseits 1985 → 1,8662; 3-222-11643-1: ᴿEstE 61 (1986) 480 [J. *García
Pérez*].

7155 **Cavarnos** Constantine,   The future life according to Orthodox teaching,
ᵀ*Auxentios* & *Chrysostomos*. Etna CA 1985, Center for Traditionalist
Orthodox Studies. 88 p. $6.50 [RelStR 13,333, J. *Overbeck*].

7156 *Cherry* Christopher,   Near-Death experiences and the problem of
evidence for survival after death: RelSt 22 (1986) 397-406.

7157 *Ciccarese* M. P.,   Le più antiche rappresentazioni del purgatorio dalla
Passio Perpetuae alla fine del IX sec.: Romanobarbarica 7 (1982s) 33-76
[non chiaro perché incluso nella Bibliografia semitica di AION 45 (1985)
707].

7158 **Condrau** Gion,   Der Mensch und sein Tod; certa moriendi condicio 1984
→ 1,8668: ᴿOrientierung 50 (1986) 59s (Elisabeth *Wunderli*); TZBas 42
(1986) 186s (W. *Neidhart*: fünftes Buch des monumentalen Werkes
'Menschlich Sterben in unmenschlicher Zeit').

7159 *a*) *Cracco* Giorgio,   Gregorio e l'oltretomba; – *b*) *Duval* Yves-Marie, La
discussion entre l'apocrisiaire Grégoire et le patriarche Eutychios au sujet

de la résurrection de la chair; l'arrière-plan doctrinal oriental et occidental:
➤ 433*, Grégoire 1982/6, 255-266 / 347-366.

7160 **Daley** Brian [p. 84-248] (*Schreiner* Josef, *Lona* Horacio E.), Eschatologie in der Schrift und Patristik: HbDG 4/7a. FrB 1986, Herder. viii-248 p. 3-451-00742-8 [NTAbs 31,110]. – ᴿRCatalT 11 (1986) 454-7 (J. *Gil Ribas*).

7161 *Davis* Stephen T., Is personal identity retained in the Resurrection?: ModT 2 (1985s) 328-340.

7162 **Dewart** Joanne E. M., Death and resurrection: Message of the Fathers 22. Wilmington 1986, Glazier. 198 p. $16; pa. $10. [RelStR 13,353, F. W. *Norris*].

7263 **Fabris** R., Attualità della speranza 1984 ➤ 65,7585; 1,8676: ᴿProtestantesimo 41 (1986) 235s (G. *Plescan*).

7164 **Finger** Thomas N., Christian theology; an eschatological approach, I. Nv 1985, Nelson. 367 p. $19. – ᴿRExp 83 (1986) 482s (W. *Ward*); TDig 33 (1986) 470 (W. C. *Heiser*).

7165 **Fortman** Edmund J., Everlasting life; towards a theology of the future life. Staten Island NY 1986, Alba. xi-369 p. $10. – ᴿTDig 33 (1986) 471 (W. C. *Heiser*).

7166 **Grelot** Pierre, Dans les angoisses, l'espérance; enquête biblique 1983 ➤ 64,7718 ... 1,8683: ᴿSpiritus 25 (1984) 216s (J. *Pierron*).

7167 **Greshake** Gisbert, (*Kremer* Jacob, bibeltheologisch), Resurrectio mortuorum; zum theologischen Verständnis der leiblichen Auferstehung. Da 1986, Wiss. xii-399 p. DM 59 [TR 83,313-6, H. *Verweyen*]. 3-534-07037-2.

7168 **Gualtieri** Antonio R., The vulture and the bull; religious responses to death. Lanham MD 1984, UPA. xvi-178 p. – ᴿSR 14 (1985) 394s (W. P. *Zion*).

7169 **Guidi** Remo L., La morte nell'età umanistica: Aspetti religiosi nella letteratura del 1400. 5. Vicenza 1983, L.I.E.F. iv-712 p. Lit. 35.000. – ᴿÉglT 17 (1986) 249-251 (P. *Hurtubise*).

7170 *a)* **Haag** Ernst, Seele' und Unsterblichkeit in biblischer Sicht; – *b)* *Greshake* Gisbert, 'Seele' in der Geschichte der christlichen Eschatologie; ein Durchblick; – *c)* *Haeffner* Gerd, Vom Unzerstörbaren im Menschen; Versuch einer philosophischen Annäherung an ein problematisch gewordenes Theologoumenon: ➤ 411, *Breuning* W., Seele 1985/6, 31-93 / 107-158 / 159-191.

7171 *a)* *Harrington* Wilfrid; – *b)* *Hogan* Mary, Resurrection of the body and life everlasting: Furrow 57 (1986) 92-100 / 233-241.

7172 **Harris** Murray J., Raised immortal 1983 ➤ 64,7722 ... 1,8685: ᴿAndr-UnS 24 (1986) 188s (R. K. *McIver*); TS 47 (1986) 342s (Pheme *Perkins*: some problems); WestTJ 48 (1986) 380-2 (J. W. *Scott*).

7173 *a)* *Haufe* Günter, Individuelle Eschatologie des Neuen Testaments; – *b)* *Herms* Eilert, Die eschatologische Existenz des neuen Menschen: ZTK 83 (1986) 436-463 / 464-483.

7173* **Hawkins** Peter, Getting nowhere; Christian hope and utopian dreams [mostly analysis of various literary utopias from PLATO's Republic to B. F. SKINNER and W. PERCY]. CM 1985, Cowley. 133 p. $9 [JAAR 55,156, F. B. *Brown*].

7174 **Hebblethwaite** Brian,The Christian hope 1984 ➤ 1,8686: ᴿBS 143 (1986) 80-82 (J. F. *Walvoord*).

7175 **Heidler** Fritz, Die biblische Lehre von der Unsterblichkeit der Seele; Sterben, Tod, ewiges Leben im Aspekt lutherischer Anthropologie 1983 ➤ 64,7724 ... 1,8687: ᴿForumKT 2 (1986) 245s (A. *Ziegenaus*); LuthTKi 10 (1986) 155s (G. *Hoffmann*).

7176 **Hubbard** David A., The second coming; what will happen when Jesus returns? 1984 ➤ 1,8690: ᴿBS 143 (1986) 174 (J.F. *Walvoord*: premillennial).

7177 *Hughes* Dewi A., William W. PANTYCELYN's eschatology as seen especially in his Aurora Borealis of 1774: ScotBEvT 4 (1986) 49-63.

7178 *Kasper* Walter, Hope in Jesus' final coming [< IkaZ 14 (1985) 1-14], ᵀᴱ*Asen* B.: TDig 33 (1986) 149-154.

7179 **Kehl** Medard, Eschatologie. Mü 1986, Echter. 370 p. DM 46; pa. 34 [TLZ 112,538-40, F. *Beisser*].

7180 ᴱ**Khoury** A., *Hünermann* P., Weiterleben — nach dem Tod? Die Antwort der Weltreligionen: Herderbücherei 1202, 1985, ➤ 1,368: ᴿNZMissW 42 (1986) 294 (F. *Frei*); TPQ 134 (1986) 195-7 (F. *Reisinger*).

7181 *King* Winston L., Eschatology, Christian and Buddhist: Religion 16 (L 1986) 169-186 [< ZIT].

7182 *Kötzsche* Lieselotte, Die Seelenreinigung durch das Feuer; zu einer Jenseitsvorstellung in der römischer Katakombenmalerei: BTZ 3 (1986) 61-76; 4 fig.

7183 **Kraus** Hans-Joachim, Systematische Theologie im Kontext biblischer Geschichte und Eschatologie 1983 ➤ 65,7610; 1,8699: ᴿTLZ 111 (1986) 389-391 (J. *Langer*); TRu 51 (1986) 98-116 (H.F. *Geisser*: 'Dogmatik im Aufbruch... wohin?').

7184 **Kremer** Jacob, Gibt es keine Auferstehung der Toten?: StiZt 204 (1984) 815-828.

7185 **Küng** Hans, Eternal life? 1984 ➤ 65,7612; 1,8701: ᴿJAAR 54 (1986) 179s (N.R. *Kollar*: ignores U.S. death-awareness movement); RelStT 6 (1986) 48s (H.A. *Meynell*).

7186 **Küng** Hans, Vie éternelle? ᵀ*Rochais* Henri, 1985, 1,8702: ᴿRevSR 60 (1986) 125 (C. *Wackenheim*).

7187 *a) Lacroix* Xavier, Le corps à venir; – *b) Bühler* Pierre, Le souci de la survie et ses étranges paradoxes; – *c) Duquoc* Christian, Le jugement dernier en appel: LumièreV 35,179 (1986) 75-91 / 35-47 / 93-106.

7188 *a) Lanczkowski* Günter, Jenseitsvorstellungen in ausserchristlichen Religionen; – *b) Beinert* Wolfgang, Der Himmel ist das Ende aller Theologie [fast aus unserer Verkündigung verschwunden; nicht etwas vom Menschen Verschiedenes, sondern seine Vollendung und Erfüllung; für diesen Himmel lohnt es sich zu leben]; – *c) Woschitz* Karl M., Ersehntes und erschlossenes Leben; Skizze zum biblischen Thema 'Ewiges Leben': TPQ 134 (1886) 107-116 / 117-127 / 128-138 [-148].

7189 *Lea* Thomas D., A survey of the doctrine of the return of Christ in the Ante-Nicene Fathers: JEvTS 29 (1986) 163-178 [< ZIT].

7190 *Ledure* Y., La philosophie comme mémoire de la mort: NRT 108 (1986) 555-570.

7191 **Le Goff** Jacques, The birth of Purgatory 1984 ➤ 65,7618; 1,8709: ᴿTLond 39 (1986) 62s (G. *Rowell*).

7192 **Le Goff** Jacques, Die Geburt des Fegfeuers, ᵀ*Forkel* Ariane, 1984 ➤ 1,8710: ᴿTR 82 (1986) 38-41 (A. *Angenendt*).

7193 *Libânio* Juan B., *Bingem[ey]er* María Clara, Escatología, el nuevo cielo y la nueva tierra [Escatologia cristã], ᵀ*Ortiz García* Alfonso: Teología y liberación, 1985 ➤ 1,8711: ᴿActuBbg 23 (1986) 197-201 (I. *Riudor*); CiTom 113 (1986) 405s (J. *Díaz Murugarren*); PerspT 18 (1986) 257-260 (F. *Taborda*); RazF 213 (1986) 216s (R. de *Andrés*); SalT 74 (1986) 152 (A. *Raffo*).

7194 **McManners** John, *a)* Death and the Enlightenment; changing attitudes to death among Christians and unbelievers in eighteenth-century France

[1981]. Ox 1985 pa., UP. vii-619 p. – *b*) Morte e illuminismo; il senso della morte nella Francia del XVIII secolo. Bo 1984, Mulino. xiv-660 p. – ᴿSalesianum 48 (1986) 395s (P. *Braido*).

7195 **Martinetti** G., La vita fuori del corpo [parapsicologia... biblica]; pref. *Inardi* M. T-Leumann 1986, LDC. 326 p. Lit. 13.000. – ᴿAsprenas 33 (1986) 350.

7196 *Menken* Maarten, Reïncarnatie in het Nieuwe Testament?: OnsGLev 63 (1986) 170-7 (-185, *Logister* Wiel).

7197 *Miquel* Pierre, [*Seyssel* Chantal de], Purgatoire: → 582, DictSpir XII/2 (1986) 2652-2666 [-2676].

7198 **Morey** Robert A., Death and the afterlife 1984 → 65,7624; 1,8720: ᴿGraceTJ 7 (1986) 146-8 (G. R. *Habermas*).

7199 *Mosetto* Francesco, Nuovo cielo e nuova terra [2 Pt 3,13; Apc 21,1...]: ParVi 31 (1986) 340-351.

7200 *Müller* Gerhard L., 'Fegfeuer'; zur Hermeneutik eines umstritten Lehrstücks in der Eschatologie: TüTQ 166 (1986) 25-39.

7201 **Murphy** Marie, A critical analysis of Karl RAHNER's eschatology: diss. Fordham. NY 1985. – RTLv 18,572.

7202 ᶠNEUHÄUSLER Englebert, Eschatologie, bibeltheologisch... ᴱKilian R 1981 → 62,122: ᴿBZ 30 (1986) 107 (J. *Schreiner*).

7203 **Nocke** F.-J., Escatología 1984 → 65,7625; 1,8722: ᴿScripTPamp 18 (1986) 384s (L. F. *Mateo-Seco*).

7204 *Perrett* Roy W., Regarding immortality: RelSt 22 (1986) 219-233.

7205 *Portilla* Jorge L., *a*) El destino del hombre y del mundo; principio de esperanza; – *b*) La escatología en Leonardo BOFF: FranBog 28 (1986) 211-238 / 11-33.

7206 **Pozo** Cándido, Teología dell'aldilà. 1983 → 64,7763... 1,8729: ᴿDiv-Thom 88 (1985) 151-3 (A. *Perego*: improbabile che il Battista abbia realmente dubitato che Gesù fosse il Messia p. 405); Teresianum 36 (1985) 221s (G. *Blandino*).

7207 **Richards** Jeffrey J., The eschatology of Lewis Sperry CHAFER; his contribution to a systematization of dispensational premillennialism: diss. Drew. Madison NJ 1985. – RTLv 18,572.

7208 **Schäfer** Philipp, Eschatologie; Trient und Gegenreformation: HDG/4/7e/2, 1984 → 65,7640: ᴿTLZ 111 (1986) 534 (K. *Kändler*).

7209 *Schmied* Augustin, Rückkehr zur Übersetzung 'Auferstehung des Fleisches' [anstatt 'der Toten'; wie im Spanischen] und die Frage der 'Auferstehung im Tode': TGegw 29 (1986) 238-246.

7210 **Sonnemans** Heino, Seele — Unsterblichkeit — Auferstehung: FreibTSt 128,1984 → 1,8748: ᴿForumKT 2 (1986) 312-4 (A. *Ziegenaus*); TPhil 61 (1986) 294-6 (G. L. *Müller*).

7211 *Sonnemans* Heino, Seele, Unsterblichkeit, Auferstehung II.: Renovatio 42 (Köln 1986) 221-233.

7212 **Spronk** K., Beatific afterlife in Israel and in the Ancient Near East, ᴰ*Moor* J. C. de [diss. Calvijnstichting Kampen 1986]: AOAT 219. Neuk 1986. x-398 p. DM 129. – ᴿPhoenixEOL 32,2 (1986) 8s.

7213 **Stallaert** L., Worden wie wij zijn; argumenten voor onsterfelijkheid. Kampen 1986, Kok Agora. 167 p. ƒ19,70. 90-242-7538-5 [TsTNijm 26,438].

7214 *Ström* Åke V. / *Rasmussen* Tarald, Hölle religionsgeschichtlich / kirchengeschichtlich: → 597, TRE 15 (1986) 445-9 / 449-455 [biblisch nur Höllenfahrt Christi, 1 Pt 3,19s; Eph 4,8s: p. 455-461, *Koch* Ernst].

7215 **Stuhlmann** Rainer, Das eschatologische Mass im NT: FRLANT 132, 1983 → 64,7770... 1,8749: ᴿBZ 30 (1986) 278s (M. *Theobald*).

7216 **Toon** Peter, Heaven and hell; a biblical and theological overview. Nv 1986, Nelson. xv-223 p. $9. 0-8407-5967-3 [JStNT 27,122]. – [R]ExpTim 98 (1986s) 55s (F. F. *Bruce* is happy to learn that his own interpretation of 2 Cor 5,1-10 is not heresy, though unsatisfactory); SWJT 29 (1986s) 51 (L. R. *Bush*: queries 'all the biblical data symbolic').

7217 **Tornos Cubillo** Andrés, *a*) La esperanza en el juicio de Dios; – *b*) Esperanza come riesgo y perdición definitiva: Escatologia 6s. M 1984, Fund. S. María. 60 p.; 80 p. [MiscCom 44,227].

7218 *Trokhine* P., Espérance et salut dans le NT : Revue du Patriarcat de Moscou (1984,6) 64-71 [Istina 31 (1986) 346].

7219 *Ulrich* Hans G., Hoffnung und Verantwortung: EvT 46 (1986) 26-37.

7220 *a*) *Vogel* Winfried, The eschatological theology of Martin LUTHER, I. Luther's basic concepts: AndrUnS 24 (1986) 249-264; – *b*) *Vogler* Werner, Die 'Naherwartung' Jesu: TVers 16 (1986) 57-71.

7221 **Walle** A. R. van de, From darkness to the dawn; how belief in the afterlife affects living. [T]*Bowden* John, 1984 ➤ 65,7651; also Mystic CT 1985, Twenty-Third. 261 p. $11 pa. [TDig 33,493].

7222 *Weder* Hans, Hoffnung NT: ➤ 597, TRE 15 (1986) 484-491 (480-4; 491-8, *al.*).

7223 *Wiefel* Wolfgang, Die Herausbildung einer individuellen Eschatologie im Neuen Testament: ZeichZt 40,3 (1986) 60-64 [< NTAbs 31,68].

7224 *Woschitz* Karl M., Death and eternal life [< Ersehntes und erschlossenes Leben. TPQ 134 (1986) 128-138], [TE]*Asen* B. A.: TDig 33 (1986) 337-342.

7225 *a*) *Yeaton* Kenneth, Aspects of CALVIN's eschatology; – *b*) *Thomas* Richard, Reflections on the Resurrection frame; with what body do they come?: Churchman 100 (L 1986) 114-128. 198-209 / 210-219 [< ZIT].

H9.5 *Theologia totius NT* – **General NT Theology.**

7226 **Bultmann** R., Teología del Nuevo Testamento [1958] 1981 ➤ 62,8647*b*; 64,7788: [R]PerspT 18 (1986) 273s (J. B. *Kipper*); Teresianum 37 (1986) 502s (V. *Pasquetto*).

7226* **Davis** John J., Let the Bible teach you [collection of Bible-texts illustrating evangelical] Christian doctrine [cf. GR 1984 ➤ 1,8767]. Exeter 1985, Paternoster. 138 p. – [R]STEv 9 (1986) 294s (P. *Bolognesi*).

7227 *a*) *Fuller* Reginald H., Sir Edwyn HOSKYNS and the contemporary relevance of 'biblical theology' [< NTS 30 (1984) 321-334]; – *b*) *Hanson* Paul D., The responsibility of biblical theology to communities of faith [< TTod 37 (1980) 39-50]: ExAud 1 (1985) 25-35 / 54-62.

7228 **Goppelt** L., Teologia del Nuovo Testamento 1982s ➤ 64,7791*b*; 1,8770: [R]Teresianum 37 (1986) 239s (V. *Pasquetto*).

7229 *Kalusche* Martin, 'Das Gesetz als Thema biblischer Theologie'? Anmerkungen zu einem Entwurf Peter STUHLMACHERs [1981]: ZNW 77 (1986) 194-205.

7230 **Ladd** G.-E., Théologie du Nouveau Testament 1984 ➤ 1,8773: [R]ÉTRel 61 (1986) 446s (F. *Vouga*).

7231 **Lowry** Charles W., The first theologians [Paul; Apollos author of Heb; John]. Ch 1986, Gateway. 443 p. $8 pa. [TDig 33,372].

7232 **McCurley** Foster R., *Reumann* John, Witness of the Word; a biblical theology of the Gospel. Ph 1986, Fortress. xxv-500 p.; ill. $20 pa. 0-8006-1866-1. – [R]ExpTim 98 (1986s) 279 ([I.] H. *Marshall*).

7233 *Morgan* Robert, GABLER's bicentenary [his 1787 inugural at Altdorf was the birth of NT theology]: ExpTim 98 (1986s) 164-168.

7234 **Morris** Leon, New Testament Theology. GR 1986, Zondervan. 368 p.
$20. 0-310-45570-7. – ᴿExpTim 98 (1986s) 349s (H. *Marshall*).
7235 **Neill** S., A Gesù attraverso molti occhi; introduzione alla teologia del NT,
ᵀ*Benetazzo* C., *Suffì* N. T-Leumann 1984, LDC. 264 p. – ᴿClaretianum
26 (1986) 390s (R. M. *Serra*).
7236 *Ollenburger* Ben C., What Krister STENDAHL 'meant': — a normative
critique of 'descriptive biblical theology': HorBT 8,1 (1986) 61-[< ZIT].
7237 **Porsch** Felix, Viele Stimmen, ein Glaube 1982 ⭢ 63,7747... 1,8782:
ᴿÉglT 17 (1986) 91s (L. *Laberge*).
7238 **Robinson** Donald, Faith's framework [= 'The structure of NT theology',
1981 Moore College lectures]. Exeter/Sydney 1985, Paternoster/ Albatross.
152 p. £4.20. – ᴿETRel 61 (1986) 447 (F. *Vouga*: cinq conférences d'un
archevêque anglican australien); RefTR 45 (1986) 24s (G. *Goldsworthy*).
7239 *Schnackenburg* Rudolf, Neutestamentliche Theologie im Rahmen einer
gesamtbiblischen Theologie: ⭢ 236, JbBT 1 (1986) 31-47.
7240 **Stăniloae** Dumitru, Orthodoxe Dogmatik, ᵀ*Pitters* H., 1985 ⭢ 1,8784:
ᴿÖkRu 35 (1986) 108-112 (Dorothea *Wendebourg*); TR 82 (1986) 399-403
(A. *Siegfried*); ZKG 97 (1986) 262-5 (T. *Nikolaou*).

XVI. Philologia biblica

J1 **Hebraica** .1 *grammatica*.

7242 **Anderson** F., Forbes A., Spelling in the Hebrew Bible [Dahood Memorial
Lecture, AA Feb. 1983] pref. *Freedman* D. N.: BibOrPont 41. R 1986,
Pontifical Biblical Institute. xxii-379 p. $22. 88-7653-342-7. – ᴿAustral-
BR 34 (1986) 86-88 (A. F. *Campbell*).
7243 **Bergen** Robert D., Varieties and functions of Hebrew Waw-plus-sub-
ject-plus-perfect sentence; constructions in the narrative framework of the
Pentateuch: diss. SW Baptist Sem. 1986. 345 p. – 86-23459. – Diss A 47
(1986s) 2561-A; RelStR 13,189
7244 **Bergsträsser** Gotthelf, Introduction to the Semitic languages, ᴱ*Daniels* P.
1983 ⭢ 64,7844 ... 1,8788; ᴿRB 93 (1986) 141s (M. S. *Smith*).
7245 *Blau* Joshua, *a*) Non-phonetic conditioning of sound change and biblical
Hebrew: HebAnR 3 (1979) 7-15 [OTAbs 9,252]; – *b*) ❶ [Massoretic
Tiberian vocalization indicates only quality, not quantity]: ⭢ 246, ᴱ*Friedman* M., Teʿuda 4 (1986) ...
7246 *Booij* T., The Yavneh-Yam ostracon and Hebrew consecutive imperfect:
BO 43 (1986) 642-7.
7247 **Cohen** Daniel, ❶ Nitôaḥ taḥbîrî ... A mechanical algorithm for finding the
syntactic structure of a Hebrew sentence: diss. Hebrew Univ. 1984. 114 p. –
KirSef 60 (1985) 706.
7248 **Drummond** Samuel J., A historical critique of the problem of conditional
discourse in Hebrew; diss. Southern Baptist Sem., ᴰ*Watts* J.D.W., 1986.
297 p. 87-02211. – DissA 47 (1986s) 3787-A.
7249 **Eaton** J. H., First Studies / Readings I² / II in Biblical Hebrew. Sheffield
1980 / 1982 (¹ 1976) / 1978, JStOT. viii-143 p., $11.50; xviii-127 p., $11;
xxxi-137 p., $12.50. [RelStR 13, S. D. *Sperling*].
7250 **Garr** W. Randall, Dialect geography of Syria-Palestine 1000-586 B.C.,
1985 ⭢ 1,8791*b*. – ᴿBO (1986) 756s (G. *Janssens*); TS 47 (1986) 510-2
(J. A. *Fitzmyer*); WestTJ 48 (1986) 185s (M. *Silva*).

7250* *Greenspahn* Frederick E., Abraham IBN EZRA and the origin of some medieval grammatical terms: JQR 76 (1985s) 217-227.

7251 **Hoftijzer** J., The function and use of the imperfect forms with nun paragogicum in classical Hebrew: Studia Semitica Neerlandica 21, 1985 → 1,8794: ᴿZAW 98 (1986) 314 (H. W. *Hoffmann*).

7252 *a) Hoftijzer* J., A grammatical note on the Yavne-Yam ostracon [first '*ebdeka* is casus pendens, as NAVEH J.]; – *b) Heering* H. J., Der Mehrwert des Wortes; hermeneutische Erwägungen: → 59, ᶠLEBRAM J., Tradition 1986, 1-6 / 296-306.

7253 **Johnson** Bo, Hebräisches Perfekt und Imperfekt mit vorangehendem wᵉ 1979 → 60,a145 ... 64,7821: ᴿSvTKv 62 (1986) 177-9 (C. *Toll*).

7254 *Kesterson* John C., Cohortative and short imperfect forms in Serakim and Damascus Document: RQum 12,47 (1986) 369-382.

7255 **Körner** Jutta, Hebräische Studiengrammatik [< *Meyer* Rudolf, Hebräische Grammatik I-IV, ³1966-72] 1983 → 64,7823; 65,7688: ᴿArOr 54 (1986) 196 (O. *Klíma*); BO 43 (1986) 761-4 (C. van der *Merwe*); OLZ 81 (1986) 46-48 (W. *Thiel*); TLZ 111 (1986) 97s (E. *Jenni*).

7256 **Kutscher** E. Y., ᴱR., A history of the Hebrew language 1982 → 63,7788 ... 1,8797: ᴿOLZ 81 (1986) 151s (H. *Simon*).

7257 *Levin* Saul, The metheg according to the practice of early vocalizers: HebAnR 3 (1979) 129-139 [OTAbs 9,255].

7258 **McFall** Leslie, The enigma of the Hebrew verbal system 1982 → 62,8716 · ... 1,8801: ᴿTLZ 111 (1986) 262s (T. *Novotný*).

7259 *Müller* Hans-Peter, Aramisierende Bildungen bei verba mediae geminatae — ein Irrtum der Hebraistik?: VT 36 (1986) 423-437.

7260 **Niccacci** A., Sintassi del verbo ebraico nella prosa biblica classica: SBF Anal 127. J 1986, Franciscan. 127 p. $5 [BL 87,123, W. *Watson*].

7261 *Novetsky* Chaikie, Pseudo-verbal constructions in biblical Hebrew: diss. NYU 1986, ᴰ*Gordon* C. H. 166 p. 86-25647. – DissA 47 (1986s) 3019-A.

7262 **Qimron** Elisha, The Hebrew of the Dead Sea Scrolls: HarvSemSt 29. Atlanta 1986, Scholars. 138 p. [TR 83,338]. $14. 0-89130-889-6.

7263 *Qoller* Y., ⊕ Symbols, abbreviations, and acronyms in the Bible [Gn 15,6; Ex 10,11 ... superfluous *h* is for YHWH]: BethM 31 (1985s) 10-16 [OTAbs 9,256].

7264 *Revell* E. J., The conditioning of stress position in *Waw* consecutive perfect forms in biblical Hebrew: → 36, Mem. GOITEIN S. = HebAnR 9 (1985) 277-300.

7265 **Richter** Wolfgang, Grundlagen einer althebräischen Grammatik B-III. Der Satz: AOtt 13, 1980 → 61,a71 ... 64,7832: ᴿJNES 45 (1986) 69s (D. *Pardee*).

7266 *a) Rooy* Herculaas F. van, Conditional sentences in biblical Hebrew; – *b) Talshir* David, ⊕ Syntactical patterns in late biblical Hebrew; – *c) Chayen* Moshe J., ⊕ Suggested solutions to problems in Hebrew morphology with reference to universal phonological problems; – *d) Cohen* Daniel, ⊕ Parsing non-vocalized Hebrew texts: → 363, Congress IX-D1, 1985/6, 9-16 / ⊕ 5-8 / ⊕ 71-75 / ⊕ 117-122.

7267 **Schweizer** Harald, Metaphorische Grammatik ... in der Exegese 1981 → 62,1424 ... 1,8810: ᴿOLZ 81 (1986) 42-46 (R. *Stahl*: Bedenken über linguistische Arbeitsweise generell).

7268 **Simon** Ethelyn, *al.*, The first Hebrew primer for adults; biblical and prayerbook Hebrew². Oakland CA 1983, EKS. 316 p. $18 [BAR-W 13/6,52].

7269 **Stähli** Hans-P., Hebräische-Kurzgrammatik / Vokabular 1984 ⇥ 65, 7703; **1**,8811: ᴿTLZ 111 (1986) 98s (S. *Schreiner*).

7270 **Stähli** H.-P., ᵀ*Chiesa* B., Corso di Ebraico Biblico I. Grammatica; II. Esercizi, crestomazia e glossario. Brescia 1986, Paideia. xvi-109 p.; 191 p. Lit. 24.000 [BL 87,125s, W. *Watson*].

7271 **Thorion** Yochanan, Studien zur klassischen hebräischen Syntax 1984 ⇥ **1**,8814: ᴿBO 43 (1986) 450-5 (C. H. J. van der *Merwe*).

7272 *Thorion-Vardi* Talia, *a)* The personal pronoun as syntactical glide [sic] in the Temple Scroll and in the Masoretic Text; – *b)* 't nominativi in the Qumran literature: RQum 12,47 (1986) 421s / 423s.

7273 *Wolff* Zev, ❸ Function of 'noun' and 'verb' in biblical usage: BethM 31,104 (1985s) 39.

7274 **Zuber** Beat, Das Tempussystem des biblischen Hebräisch: BZAW 164 [1986] ⇥ **1**,8822: ᴿDiehlB 22 (1985/6) 235-7 (B. J. *Diebner*); ExpTim 98 (1986s) 213s (C. S. *Rodd*: suffix form indicative without time-value; prefix-form modal or future, as already W. H. BENNETT); GerefTTs 86 (1986) 239s (E. *Talstra*); SBFLA 36 (1986) 397-405 (A. *Niccacci*); TüTQ 166 (1986) 148-150 (W. *Gross*: absurd, nach These wie Methode); ZAW 98 (1986) 483 (H. W. *Hoffmann*).

J1.2 *Hebraica varia* **Hebrew vocabulary, inscriptions, later Hebrew.**

7275 **Armstrong** T. A. *al.*, A reader's Hebrew-English lexicon of the OT [I. II. 1980/2 ⇥ 62,8687; 63,7821], III. Isaiah-Malachi. GR 1986, Zondervan. viii-220 p. $15. 0-310-37010-8 [BL 87,122, G. J. *Emmerson*].

7276 **Avigad** N., ❸ *Bullot* ... Hebrew bullae from the time of Jeremiah. J 1986, Israel Expl. Soc. 123 p.; ill. $15. – ᴿIsrEJ 36 (1986) 119.

7277 **Avishur** Yitzhak, Stylistic studies of word-pairs in biblical and ancient Semitic literatures: AOAT 210, 1984 ⇥ 65,7711; **1**,8827: ᴿBSOAS 49 (1986) 569 (J. *Wansbrough*).

7278 *Barag* Dan, *Flusser* David, The ossuary of Yehoḥanah granddaughter of the High Priest Theophilus: IsrEJ 36 (1986) 39-42.

7279 *Bar-Ašer* Mošeh, ❸ The Hebrew base in the Šarḥ of Jewish Marocco: Lešonenu 48s (1984s) 227-252.

7280 *Bar-Magen* M., ❸ Plene and defective writings in the Torah: BethM 31,107 (1985s) 328-338.

7281 *a)* *Birnbaum* Gabriel, ❸ The noun determination in Mishnaic Hebrew; – *b)* *Nathan* Hava, ❸ Some juridical terms in Tannaitic Hebrew; – *c)* *Braverman* Natan, ❸ Concerning the language of the Mishnah and the Tosephta; – *d)* *Eldar* Ilan, ❸ Etymological word-interpretation in medieval Hebrew lexicography and biblical exegesis; – *e)* *Tobin* Yishai, ❸ Aspectual markers in modern Hebrew — a sign-oriented approach: ⇥ 363, Congress IX-D1, 1985/6, ❸ 39-43 / 23-29 / 31-38 / 49-53 / 53-60.

7282 [*Zorell* F.] **Boccaccio** Pietro, Lexicon hebraicum Veteris Testamenti: index lat.-hebr. etc. R 1984, Biblical Institute. 16* + p.913-1005. Lit. 40.000. 88-7653-557-8 [BL (1986) 144].

7283 **Bolle** Menachem E., *Pimentel* Jitschak, Woordenboek Nederlands-Hebreeuws. Naarden 1984, Strengholt. 974 p. [KirSef 60,709].

7284 *Brin* G., ❸ [expressions for time in the OT]: ⇥ 246, ᴱ*Friedman* M., Te'uda 4 (1986) ...

7285 **Brugnatelli** V., Questioni ... dei numeri cardinali semitici 1982 ⇥ 63,7828 ... **1**,8830: ᴿOrAnt 25 (1986) 144-7 (R. *Contini*).

7286 *Busi* Giulio, Materiali per una storia della filologia e dell'esegesi ebraica; Abū 'l-Walīd Marwān IBN ĠANĀḤ; AION 46 (1986) 167-195.

7287 *Cowley* Roger W., Technical terms in biblical Hebrew ? [*rîb, mabbûl, zebaḥ*...]: TyndB 37 (1986) 22-28.

7288 **Eldar** (Adler) Ilan, ❶ The Hebrew language tradition in medieval Ashkenaz (ca. 950-1350), I. Phonology and vocalization; II. Morphology: 'Edah we-lašon 4s. J 1978s. 39-XXVIII-215 p.; VI-461 p. 0-253-32600-1: ᴿEstB 44 (1986) 233-9 (L. *Díez Merino*).

7289 **Faur** Jose, Golden doves with silver dots; semiotics and textuality in rabbinic tradition: Bloomington 1985, Indiana Univ. XXIX-226 p.; bibliog. p. 202-213. $27.50 [Judaica 42,204].

7290 ᴱ**Friedman** M. *al.*, ❶ Studies in Talmudic literature, in post-biblical Hebrew, and in biblical exegesis: Teuda 3, 1983 ➤ 65,284*: ᴿBO 43 (1986) 468-470 (A. van der *Heide*).

7291 **Gordon** Amnon, The development of the participle in biblical, mishnaic, and modern Hebrew: AfrAsLing 8/3, 1982 ➤ 65,7725; 1,8839: ᴿTüTQ 166 (1986) 150s (W. *Gross*).

7292 **Grazzini** E., Studi su tre termini arcaici in ebraico biblico: diss. ᴰ*Fronzaroli* P. F 1978 [RivB 35,397, senza precisare i tre termini].

7293 **Greenspahn** Frederick E., Hapax legomena in biblical Hebrew 1984 ➤ 65,7726; 1,8840: ᴿBASOR 264 (1986) 88-90 (J. *Huehnergard*): JBL 105 (1986) 702-4 (C/H. *Cohen*); OLZ 81 (1986) 471s (W. *Herrmann*).

7294 Hebrew On-Line! [the entire vocabulary of the Hebrew Bible on a single 5¼ inch disc, IBM or compatible; 3d program, drill, words according to frequency of occurrence, without English equivalent (at first) if desired; 6th program, typed-in English word calls up the Hebrew (4th/5th, more complicated to call from the Hebrew); geared to the numbering of Strong's Concordance]. Staunton VA c. 1986, P.O.Box 96; 24401. $60. – ᴿExpTim 97 (1985s) 355s (C. S. *Rodd*: low price, high value, despite some erudite drawbacks; 'Up to ten words can be selected at one time; I did [?? not] find any particular use in this'). [JStOT 37,128 less favorable].

7295 *Höffken* Peter, Neuere Arbeiten zur Sprachgestalt alttestamentlicher Texte [5 Bücher; infra]: BO 43 (1986) 647-660.

7296 *Hookerman* Jacob, ❶ Etymological concerns in biblical Hebrew: BethM 31,106 (1985s) 220-6.298-307.

7297 *a)* *Kaddari* Menahem Z., ❶ The marked order participle — HYH as a stylistic marker of discourse in the Hebrew of the Babylonian Amora'im; – *b)* *Gluska* Isaac, ❶ The gender of *śadeh* in Mishnaic Hebrew: BarIlAn 20s (1983) 67-75, Eng. XI / 43-66, Eng. X.

7298 [**Koehler** L. †, *Baumgartner* W. †] *Stamm* J.J., Hebräisches und aramäisches Lexikon zum AT³, Lfg. 3, 1983 ➤ 64,7861; 65,7732: ᴿBZ 30 (1986) 306s (M. *Dietrich*, O. *Loretz*).

7299 *LaSor* William S., The sequence of phonemes in Semitic roots (based on evidence from Arabic): HebSt 26 (1985) 71-80 [OTAbs 10,127].

7300 *Margain* Jean, Note sur la particule *'yt* dans le Targum Samaritain: Semitica 36 (1986) 101-4.

7301 *Mishor* Mordechay, ❶ On the style of Mishnaic-Talmudic literature; the imperfect with indicative meaning: Tarbiz 55 (1985s) 345-358; Eng. II.

7302 **Mitchel** L. A., A student's vocabulary for biblical Hebrew and Aramaic ➤ 65,7736 [listing separately in purely alphabetical order the Hebrew words which occur over 500 times, over 200 etc.]: Academie. GR 1984, Zondervan. xxiv-88 p. 0-310-45461-1 [BL 86,140].

7303 *Moia* S., La traduzione di alcune semipreposizioni ebraiche nei Settanta: diss. Univ. Cattolica, ᴰ*Luciani* F. Milano 1985. [RivB 35,86].

7304 *Müller* Hans-Peter, Polysemie im semitischen und hebräischen Konjugationssystem: Orientalia 55 (1986) 365-389.

7305 **Muraoka** T., Modern Hebrew for biblical scholars; an annotated chrestomathy with an outline grammar and a glossary: JStOT Manuals 2, 1982 ➤ 63,7795; 65,7737: ᴿLešonenu 48s (1984s) 284-290 (O. R. *Schwarzwald*).

7306 **Murtonen** A., Hebrew in its West-Semitic setting; a comparative survey of non-Masoretic Hebrew dialects and traditions, A. Proper names: StSemLangL 13. Leiden 1986, Brill. xxxii-341 p. 90-04-07245-4 [RelStR 13,257, S. D. *Sperling*].

7307 ᴱ**Nir** Raphael, ❶ *Hôra'âh aqademit*... University teaching of modern Hebrew. J 1985, International Center. 171 p. [KirSef 60,707].

7308 *Puech* Émile, Les écoles dans l'Israël préexilique; données épigraphiques: ➤ 377*a*, IOSOT summaries (1986) 107.

7309 *Rabin* Chaim, L'hébreu 'mixte'; de la langue de la Mishna à la renaissance de l'hébreu [25. III. 1985]: RÉJ 145 (1986) 221-6.

7310 *Rainey* Anson F., The ancient Hebrew prefix conjugation [yaqtul(u/a); Dt 32,8-13] in the light of Amarnah Canaanite: HebSt 27 (Madison 1986) 4-19 [OTAbs 10,129].

7311 **Richter** Wolfgang, Transliteration und Transkription; Objekt- und metasprachliche Metazeichensysteme zur Wiedergabe hebräischer Texte: AOtt 19, 1983 ➤ 64,7873; 65,7739: ᴿCBQ 48 (1986) 126s (S. D. *Sperling*).

7312 **Rosen** Haiim B., La nature de l'hébreu médiéval; une grande langue de tradition à différenciation régionale: TStHeb. TA 1986, Univ. Rosenberg School. 24 p. – ᴿRÉJ 145 (1986) 441 (G. *Nahon*).

7313 **Róth** Ernst, *Striedl* Hans, Hebräische Handschriften Teil 3 ... Hamburg/Levy. Wsb 1984, Steiner. xxvi-392 p.; 3 pl. + 5 color. DM 289. 3-515-03678-4. – ᴿWeltOr 17 (1986) 184s (*P. Freimark*).

7313* **Scerbo** F., Dizionario ebraico e caldaico del Vecchio Testamento. F 1986 = 1912, LEF[lorentina]. xix-491 p. – ᴿStPatav 33 (1986) 436s (M. *Milani*).

7314 *Sáenz-Badillos* A., Los 'hapax legómena' bíblicos en Menahem BEN SARUQ: ➤ 21, Mem. DÍEZ MACHO A., Salvación 1986, 783-809.

7314* **Segal** M., *Dagut* M. B., English-Hebrew, Hebrew-English Dictionary. Jerusalem 1986, Kiryat-Sefer. 965-17-0172-2.

7315 *Shiloh* Yigal, A group of Hebrew bullae from the City of David: IsrEJ 36 (1986) 16-38; 9 fig.; pl. 4-7.

7316 **Sirat** Colette *al.*, La Ketouba de Cologne, un contrat de mariage juif à Antinoopolis [417 A.D.; partly Greek but all in Hebrew characters]: Rh/Wf Akad, Pap. Colon. 12. Opladen 1986, Westdeutscher. 72 p.; XX pl. DM 52. – ᴿCdÉ 61 (1986) 345s (J. *Bingen*).

7317 **Sirat** Colette, Les papyrus en caractères hébraïques trouvés en Égypte 1985 ➤ 1,8858: ᴿCdÉ 61 (1986) 169 (J. *Bingen*).

7318 *Slutzky* Leon, ❶ The wealth of synonyms in the Hebrew language: HebSt 26 (Madison 1985) 325-241 [OTAbs 10,129].

7319 **Smelik** K., Behouden schrift — historische documenten 1984 ➤ 1,8859: ᴿBO 43 (1986) 175 (J. A. *Soggin*: follows outdated ALBRIGHT).

7320 **Sperber** Daniel, A dictionary of Greek and Latin legal terms in rabbinic literature 1984 ➤ 65,7744: ᴿBO 43 (1986) 470s (M. J. *Mulder*); JStJud 17 (1986) 119s (G. A. *Wewers* †); Salesianum 48 (1986) 1043s (R. *Gottlieb*).

7321 **Stamm** J. J., Beiträge zur hebräischen und altorientalischen Namenkunde: OBO 30, 1980 ➤ 61,393 ... 64,7880: ᴿOLZ 81 (1986) 572-4 (J. *Oelsner*).

7322 *Terasawa* Yoshio, Hebrew loan-words in English: ➤ 31, ᶠFISIAK J. Linguistics 1986, 659-669.

7323 **Weinberg** Werner, The history of Hebrew plene spelling. Cincinnati 1985, HUC. ix-190 p. $15. 0-87820-205-6 [ZDMG 136,637, E. *Wagner*].

7324 **Werner** Fritz, Modernhebräischer Mindestwortschatz 1979 → 61,a131: ᴿRoczOr 45,1 (1986) 139-141 (R. *Marcinkowski*).

7325 **Wertheimer** Solomon A., ☉ *Be'ur šᵉmôt ha-nirdapîm* ... Torah synonyms. J 1984. XXVIII-376 p. [KirSef 59,308].

7326 *Yahalom* Yosef, *Saenz-Badillos* Ángel, ☉ Editing and emendation of the manuscript of MENAḤEM's notebook: Lešonenu 48s (1984s) 253-268.

7327 *Zakovitch* Yair, Explicit and implicit name-derivations: HebAnR 4 (1980) 167-181 [OTAbs 10,111].

J1.3 **Voces** ordine alphabetico *consonantium* **hebraicarum.**

7328 *āhab*: Zecchi A., Ricerche sul lessico di 'amicizia' e 'amore' in ebraico biblico: diss. ᴰ*Zatelli* I. F 1985 [RivB 35,397].

7329 *ûrîm*: **Van Dam** Cornelis, The Urim and Thummim; a study of an Old Testament means of revelation: diss. Kampen 1986, ᴰ*Ohmann* H. vi-344 p. – RTLv 18,543.

7330 *eḥad*: *Fassberg* Steven E., Determined forms of the cardinal number 'one' in three pentateuchal Targumim: Sefarad 45 (1985) 207-215 → 7522.

7331 *amēn*: *Chilton* Bruce, 'Amen', an approach through Syriac gospels [< ZNW 69 (1978) 203-211]: → 140*, Targumic Approaches 1986, 15-23.

7331* *ārak*: **Richter** Wolfgang, [→ 7336] Untersuchungen zur Valenz althebräischer Verben, 1. 'RK: AOtt 23, 1985 → 1, 8957 [but not initial *ayin*; *'rk* = 'lengthen' as Ex 20,12]: ᴿTüTQ 166 (1986) 229-231 (H. *Schweizer*).

7332 *ārar*: *Schottroff* Willy, Fluch: → 587, EvKL 1 (1986) 1306s.

7333 *Ašērâ*: *Day* John, Asherah in the Hebrew Bible and Northwest Semitic literature ['Ajrud gives 'extrabiblical testimony to the cult object as well as the goddess' meanings, p. 408]: JBL 105 (1986) 385-408.

7334 *bêt*: *Block* Daniel I., Israel's house; reflections on the use of *byt yśr'l* in the OT in the light of its Ancient Near Eastern environment: JEvTS 28 (1985) 257-275.

7335 *bāśār*: *Beck* Edmund, *Besrâ (sarx)* and *pagrâ (sōma)* bei EPHRÄM dem Syrer: OrChr 70 (1986) 1-22.

7336 *gābāh*: **Richter** Wolfgang, Untersuchungen zur Valenz althebräischer Verben [1. *'ārak* 1985 → 7331*]; 2. GBH, ᶜMQ, QṢR: AOtt 25. St. Ottilien 1986, EOS. xii-220 p. 3-88096-525-11.

7337 *gardali*: *Geiger* Joseph, ☉ Greek in the Talmud; an allusion to a Hellenistic epigram?: Tarbiz 55 (1985s) 606s; Eng. V.

7338 *dam*: *Babut* Jean-Marc, Que son sang soit sur sa tête [AT 40 fois]: VT 36 (1986) 474-480.

7339 *derāqôn*: **Schlüter** Margarete, 'Derāqôn' und Götzendienst 1982 → 63,7882 ... 65,7768: ᴿJQR 76 (1985s) 386s (M. *Smith*); OLZ 81 (1986) 254s (W. *Wiefel*); RÉJ 145 (1986) 435-7 (J.-P. *Rothschild*).

7340 *hāzāh*: *Gelio* Roberto, Osservazioni critiche su uno *hāzāh* 'gioire' usato per lo più in contesto liturgico (Is 28,15.18; Es 24,11; Sal 63,3; 27,4; Gb 8,17): EphLtg 100 (1986) 73-95.

7341 *hinneh*: *Kogut* Simcha, On the meaning and syntactical status of *hinneh* in biblical Hebrew: → 251*, ScrHieros 31 (1986) 133-154.

7342 *zākar*: *Boccaccini* G., 'Ricordate / dimenticate' nella tradizione giudaica e cristiana antica: diss. ᴰ*Ranchetti* M. F 1982 [RivB 35,397].

7343 *zāᶜaq*: *Raja Rao* T. J., 'Cry' [shout] in the OT: Living Word 92 (1986) 179-210.237-290.

7344 *ḥāzaq*: ⇥ 246, Te'uda 4 (1986) ... (E. *Rubinstein*).
7345 *ḥesed*: **Sakenfeld** Katharine D., Faithfulness in action; loyalty in biblical perspective 1985 ⇥ 1,8893: ᴿBibTB 16 (1986) 81 (A. E. *Zannoni*); CurrTM 13 (1986) 52 (R. *Nysse*); Horizons 13 (1986) 434-6 (Denise L. *Carmody*: passes over biblical authors' 'self-serving quality'); Interpretation 40 (1986) 308s (J. D. *Newsome*); RExp 83 (1986) 494s (Diana S. R. *Garland*).
7346 *ḥuppudum*: **Stol** Marten, Blindness and night-blindness in Akkadian: JNES 45 (1986) 295-9 [so perhaps *sanwērīm* Ps. 121:6; Dt 28:28].
7347 *Ḥerem*: **Toorn** K. van den, Ḥerem-Bethel [not a divinity parallel to (Anat-)Jahu] and Elephantine oath procedure: ZAW 98 (1986) 282-5.
7348 *tôb*: **Brin** Gershon, ➊ Some biblical uses of *tôb*: BethM 31,106 (1985s) 227-241.
7349 *tō'ēbâ*: **Pickett** Winston H., The meaning and function of *t'b / to'evah* in the Hebrew Bible: diss. HUC. Cincinnati 1985. 335 p. 86-09872. – DissA 47 (1986s) 1712-A.
7349* *yad*: **Görg** Manfred, 'Der starke Arm Pharaos' [Ex 6,1...] — Beobachtungen zum Belegspektrum einer Metapher in Pälastina und Ägypten: ⇥ 18, Mem. DAUMAS J., I (1986) 323-330.
7350 *yôm*: **Zerafa** P., The Old Testament day [did not include the night at all; only later the (preceding) eve was drawn in as a feast-vigil]: Angelicum 63 (1986) 532-544.
7351 *yônâ*: **Wissemann** Michael, *Yônāh* gleich 'Taube'? [nicht in Jer 25,38; 46,16; 50,16; Zph 3,1 wie HIERONYMUS]; zu vier Vulgataproblemen: Glotta 64 (1986) 37-48.
7352 *yāsar*: **Kennedy** James M., A structural semantic analysis of selected biblical Hebrew words for punishment/discipline: diss. Drew. Madison NJ 1986. 291 p. 86-16870. – DissA 47 (1986s) 1711-A; RelStR 13,189.
7353 *yāṣā'*: **Van Leeuwen** Raymond C., A technical metallurgical usage of *yaṣa'* [Prov 25,4]: ZAW 98 (1986) 112s.
7354 *yārā'*: **Conrad** E. W., Fear not warrior; a study of '*al tîrā*' pericopes in the Hebrew Scriptures: BrownJudSt 75, 1985 ⇥ 1,8900: ᴿBL (1986) 66s (L. L. *Grabbe*).
7355 **Shearer** Rodney H., A contextual analysis of the phrase '*al tîrā*' as it occurs in the Hebrew Bible and in selected related literature: diss. Drew. Madison NJ 1985. – RelStR 13,189.
7356 *kᵉ*: **Jongeling** K., K and variants in Punic: ⇥ 47, ꟳHOSPERS J., Scripta 1986, 101-9.
7357 *kî*: **Aejmelaeus** Anneli, Function and interpretation of *kî* in biblical Hebrew: JBL 105 (1986) 193-209.
7358 *Deller* Karlheinz, Old Assyrian *kanwarta*, Middle Assyrian *kalmarte*, and Neo-Assyrian *garmarte*: JbEOL 29 (1985s) 43-49.
7359 *lāmad*: **Ebach** Jürgen, Verstehen, Lernen und Erinnerung in der hebräischen Bibel: EvErz 38 (Fra 1986) 106-116.
7360 *malmad ha-bōqer*, Jg 3,31: BethM 31,106 (1985s) 281-6 (O. *Margalit*).
7361 *Good* Robert M., *Lāmed* [(Ug. *mdl* 'attach) guide-rope']: BASOR 262 (1986) 89s; 1 fig.
7362 *lā'ak*: **Auld** A. Graeme, Sabbath, work and creation; *mᵉla'kâh* reconsidered: Henoch 8 (1986) 273-280; franç. 280.
7363 *malē'/pímplēmi*: **Fairman** Richard G., An exegesis of 'filling' texts which refer to the doctrine of filling: diss. Grace Theol. Sem., ᴰKent H., 1986. 411 p. 86-19648. – DissA 47 (1986s) 2198-A; GraceTJ 7,319.
7364 *Powell* Marvin A., *mun-du* as an Akkadian plural loan word in Sumerian: ZAss 76 (1986) 12-17.

7365 *nābi:* *Müller* Walter W., Südsemitische Marginalien zur Etymologie von *nābī'*: BibNot 32 (1986) 31-37.

7366 *nedîriyyâ':* *Slutnik* Dov, ❸ Ascalon [*nautilía*, fugitives]: Lešonenu 48s (1984s) 299s.

7367 *nāzîr:* → 246, Te'uda 4 (1986) ... (Y. *Amit*: not a lifelong commitment).

7368 *naḥalat* Y': → 251*, ScrHieros 31 (1986) 155-192 (S. E. *Loewenstamm*, Eng.).

7369 *nāḥat* *Görg* Manfred, Marginalien zur Basis *nḥt*: BibNot 32 (1986) 20s.

7370 *nēs:* *Kasher* Rimmon, ❸ *Nēsīm* [Wunder, miracle] in the Bible: BethM 31,104 (1985s) 40-58.

7371 *nāpaḥ* 'blasen': → 599, TWAT 5,5s (1986) 519-521 (P. *Maiberger*).

7372 *nāpal* 'fallen': → 599, TWAT 5,5s (1986) 521-531 (H. *Seebass*).

7373 *næpæš* 'Seele': → 509, TWAT 5,5s (1986) 531-555 (H. *Seebass*).

7374 *niṣṣēb* / [*hit*]*yaṣṣēb* 'aufrichten': → 599, TWAT 5,5s (1986) 555-565 (J. *Reindl* †).

7375 *neṣaḥ* 'Glanz': → 599, TWAT 5,5s (1986) 565-570 (G. *Anderson*).

7376 *naṣal* [*hiṣṣîl*] 'retten': → 599, TWAT 5,5s (1986) 570-7 (F. L. *Hossfeld*, B. *Kalthoff*).

7377 *nāṣar* 'hüten' → 599, TWAT 5,5s (1986) 577-587 (-9, S. *Wagner*).

7378 *nāqab* 'durchbohren': → 599, TWAT 5,5s (1986) 589-591 (J. *Scharbert*).

7379 *nāqāh, nāqî* 'straffrei': → 599, TWAT 5,5s (1986) 591-602 (G. *Warmuth*).

7380 *nāqam* 'Rache': → 599, TWAT 5,5s (1986) 602-612 (E. *Lipiński*).

7381 *nāqap* 'umgehen': → 599, TWAT 5,5s (1986) 612-6 (F. *Reiterer*).

7382 *nēr* 'Lampe': → 599, TWAT 5,5s (1986) 616-626 (D. *Kellermann*).

7383 *nāśā'* 'heben': → 599, TWAT 5,5s (1986) 626-642 (D. *Freedman*, B. E. *Willoughby*, al.).

7384 *nāśag* 'erreichen': → 599, TWAT 5,5s (1986) 643-7 (J. *Hausmann*).

7385 *nāśî'* 'Fürst': → 599, TWAT 5,5s (1986) 647-657 (H. *Niehr*).

7386 *nāšā'* [I. 'betrügen'] II. 'leihen': → 599, TWAT 5,5s (1986) [657s, H. *Ringgren*] 658-663 (F. *Hossfeld*, E. *Reuter*).

7387 *nāšak* 'beissen, Wucher': → 599, TWAT 5,5s (1986) 665-9 (A. *Kapelrud*).

7388 *nᵉšāmāh* 'Hauch, Leben': → 599, TWAT 5,5s (1986) 669-673 (H. *Lamberty-Zielinski*).

7389 *næšæp* 'Dunkel': → 599, TWAT 5,5s (1986) 673-6 (B. *Kedar-Kopfstein*).

7390 *nāšaq* 'küssen': → 599, TWAT 5,5s (1986) 676-680 (K.-M. *Beyse*).

7391 *nātak* 'tropfen': → 599, TWAT 5,5s (1986) 689-693 (A. *Stiglmair*).

7392 *nātan* 'geben': → 599, TWAT 5,5s (1986) 693-712 (E. *Lipiński*).

7393 *nātaṣ* 'niederreissen': → 599, TWAT 5,5s (1986) 713-9 (C. *Barth* †).

7394 *nātaq* 'losreissen': → 599, TWAT 5,5s (1986) 719-723 (T. *Kronholm*).

7395 *nātar* 'springen': → 599, TWAT 5,5s (1986) 723-6 (P. *Maiberger*).

7396 *nātaš* 'herausreissen': → 599, TWAT 5,5s (1986) 727-730 (J. *Hausmann*).

7397 *sābab* 'umgeben': → 599, TWAT 5,5s (1986) 730-744 (E. *García López*).

7398 *sābal* 'tragen': → 599, TWAT 5,5s (1986) 744-8 (D. *Kellermann*).

7399 *segullāh* 'Eigentum': → 599, TWAT 5,5s (1986) 749-752 (E. *Lipiński*).

7400 *sāgar* 'schliessen': → 599, TWAT 5,5s (1986) 753-6 (H. *Ringgren*).

7401 *Sedom* 'Sodom': → 599, TWAT 5,5ss (1986) 756-769 (M. J. *Mulder*).

7402 *sûg* 'abweichen': → 599, TWAT 5,7s (1986) 769-774 (F. *Reiterer*).

7403 *sôd* 'Rat': → 599, TWAT 5,7s (1986) 775-782 (H.-J. *Fabry*).

7404 *sôp* 'Ende': → 599, TWAT 5,7s (1986) 791-4 (M. *Sæbø*); *sûp* → b706.

7405 *sûpāh* 'Sturmwind': → 599, TWAT 5,7s (1986) 800-3 (K.-M. *Beyse*).

7406 *sûr* 'abbiegen': → 599, TWAT 5,7s (1986) 803-810 (A. *Snijders*).

7407 *swt* Hif. 'verführen': → 599, TWAT 5,7s (1986) 810-814 (G. *Wallis*).

7408 *saḥar* 'durchwandeln (Händler)': ➤ 599, TWAT 5,7s (1986) 814-9 (H. *Seebass*).

7409 *sākak*, *sukkāh* 'bedecken, Hütte': ➤ 599, TWAT 5,7s (1986) 838-856 (T. *Kronholm*).

7410 *sākal* 'töricht sein': ➤ 599, TWAT 5,7s (1986) 856-9 (G. *Fleischer*).

7411 *sālaḥ* 'vergeben': ➤ 599, TWAT 5,7s (1986) 859-867 (J. *Hausmann*).

7412 *sālal*, *mesillāh* 'aufschütten, Weg': ➤ 599, TWAT 5,7s (1986) 867-872 (H.-J. *Fabry*).

7412* *samak*, *sᵉmîkāh* 'Handauflegung': ➤ 599, TWAT 5,7s (1986) 880-9 (J. *Milgrom, al.*).

7413 *sāʿad* 'stützen': ➤ 599, TWAT 5,7s (1986) 889-893 (G. *Warmuth*).

7413* *sāpad* 'trauern': ➤ 599, TWAT 5,7s (1986) 901-6 (J. *Scharbert*).

7414 *sāpah* 'wegraffen': ➤ 599, TWAT 5,7s (1986) 906-8 (H. *Ringgren*).

7415 *sāpaq* 'schlagen': ➤ 599, TWAT 5,7s (1986) 909s (H. *Ringgren*).

7416 *sāpar* 'zählen': ➤ 599, TWAT 5,7s (1986) 910-921 (J. *Conrad*), 921-9 *sôpēr* (H. *Niehr*), 921-44 *sēper* (F. *Hossfeld, al.*).

7417 *sāqal* 'Steinigung': ➤ 599, TWAT 5,7s (1986) 945-8 (A. *Kapelrud*).

7418 *sārîs* 'Hofbeamter, Kastrat': ➤ 599, TWAT 5,7s (1986) 948-954 (B. *Kedar-Kopfstein*).

7419 *seren* 'Herrscher': ➤ 599, TWAT 5,7s (1986) 955-7 (K.-D. *Schunck*).

7420 *sārar* 'störrisch sein': ➤ 599, TWAT 5,7s (1986) 957-963 (L. *Ruppert*).

7421 *sātam* 'verstopfen': ➤ 599, TWAT 5,7s (1986) 963-7 (B. *Otzen*).

7422 *sātar* 'verbergen': ➤ 599, TWAT 5,7s (1986) 967-977 (S. *Wagner*).

7423 *ʿabôṭ* 'Pfand': ➤ 599, TWAT 5,7s (1986) 1013-5 (K.-M. *Beyse*).

7424 *ʿābar* 'vorübergehen': ➤ 599, TWAT 5,7ss (1986) 1015-1033 (H. F. *Fuhs*), *ʿebrāh* 1033-9 'Zorn' (K. D. *Schunck*), *ʿibri* 1039-1056 (D. N. *Freedman*, B. E. *Willoughby*).

7425 *ʿēber*: **Loretz** Oswald, Habiru-Hebräer ...: BZAW 160, 1984 ➤ 65,7843; 1,8953: ᴿAntonianum 61 (1986) 175-7 (M. *Nobile*); Biblica 67 (1986) 287-291 (H. *Engel*), CBQ 48 (1986) 540s (A. J. *Hauser*); OLZ 81 (1986) 570s (W. *Herrmann*); RB 93 (1986) 146s (J.-M. de *Tarragon*); RechSR 74 (1986) 627s (J. *Briend*); Syria 63 (1986) 442s (A. *Caquot*).

7426 *ʿad* ['dauernd']: ➤ 599, TWAT 5,9s (1986) 1066-1074 (E. *Haag*).

7427 *ʿōz* 'Zuflucht': ➤ 599, TWAT 5,9s (1986) 1130 (H. *Ringgren*).

7428 *ʿûl* 'Kleinkind': ➤ 599, TWAT 5,9s (1986) 1131-5 (M. *Sæbø*).

7429 *ʿāwel* 'Unrecht': ➤ 599, TWAT 5,9s (1986) 1135-1144 (J. *Schreiner*).

7430 *ʿôlām* 'Dauer, Ewigkeit': ➤ 599, TWAT 5,9s (1986) 1145-1159 (H. D. *Preuss*).

7431 *ʿāwon* 'Sünde': ➤ 599, TWAT 5,9s (1986) 1160-1177 (K. *Koch*).

7432 *ʿûp* 'fliegen': ➤ 599, TWAT 5,9s (1986) 1177-1183 (A. *Stiglmair*).

7433 *ʿûr* 'erregen': ➤ 599, TWAT 5,9s (1986) 1184-1190 (J. *Schreiner*).

7434 *ʿiwwer* 'blind': ➤ 599, TWAT 5,9s (1986) 1190-3 (L. *Wächter*).

7435 *ʿāzab* 'verlassen': ➤ 599, TWAT 5,9s (1986) 1200-8 (E. *Gerstenberger*).

7436 *ʿēdāh* 'Gemeinde': ➤ 599, TWAT 5,9s (1986) 1079-1093 (J. *Milgrom, al.*).

7437 *Hurvitz* A., Beobachtungen zum priesterlichen Terminus *ʿeda* und zur Sprache der Priesterschrift: HBeiWJ 1 (1985) 39 ... [<ZAW].

7438 *ʿed* 'Zeuge': ➤ 599, TWAT 5,9s (1986) 1109-1130 (H. *Simian-Yofre, al.*).

7439 *ʿālaz*: *Vanoni* Gottfried, Das Problem der Homonymie beim althebräischen ʿLZ / ʿLṢ: BibNot 33 (1986) 29-33.

7440 *ʿam*: **Good** Robert M., The sheep of his pasture ... *ʿam*(m) 1983 ➤ 64,7981 ... 1,8956: ᴿBO 43 (1986) 181-3 (E. *Lipiński*: assumes biliterality, overlooks importance of Arabic usage); CBQ 48 (1986) 106-8 (Carol *Meyers*: weak on archeology); JBL 105 (1986) 325s (J. J. M.

Roberts: dubious); TLZ 111 (1986) 349s (Helgalinde *Staudigel*); VT 36 (1986) 503s (J. A. *Emerton*).

7441 *'ārab*: *Soden* Wolfram von, Hebräische Problemwörter [*hit'ārēb* 2 Kg 18,23; *sanwerīm* Gn 19,11, Akk. *sinnurbûm*]: UF 18 (1986s) 341-4.

7443 *pāqad*: **André** G., Determining the destiny, pqd in the OT 1980 ↠ 63,7958; 64,7988: ᴿHenoch 8 (1986) 91 (J. A. *Soggin*).

7445 *ṣedeq* / *ṣedaqah*: ↠ 377*b*, SBL Jerusalem summaries (1986) 3 (J. J. *Scullion*).

7446 **Gossai** Hemchand, *Ṣedeq, mišpat* and the social critique of the eighth century prophets: diss. ᴰ*Martin* J., St. Andrews 1986. 452 p. – RTLv 18,541.

7447 **Krasovec** Joze, La justice (ṣdq) de Dieu dans la Bible hébraïque et l'interprétation juive et chrétienne: diss. P Sorbonne/Inst. Cath. 1986, ᴰ*Levêque* J. – RICathP 20 (1986) 141-4; RTLv 18,542.

7448 *Saout* Yves, Juste et justice d'une culture à l'autre dans la Bible: Spiritus 27 (1986) 176-192.

7449 *Ṣelem*: *Dalley* Stephanie, The god Ṣalmu and the winged disk: Iraq 48 (1986) 85-101.

7450 *Ṣiqlag*: *Ray* J. D., [Gn 21,22] Two etymologies, Ziklag and Phicol: VT 36 (1986) 355-361.

7451 *qbh*: *Kaye* Alan S., The etymology of 'coffee', the Dark Brew: JAOS 106 (1986) 557s [not Abyssinian locality Kaffa, native home of the coffee plant, as Oxford Dictionary of English Etymology 1966].

7452 *qôdeš*: *Lods* Marc, Le saint et le sacré; enquête sur le vocabulaire biblique: PosLuth 34 (1986) 185-199.

7453 *Loewen* Jacob A., The translation of holy in Monkole [N. Benin]; solving a problem: BTrans 37 (1986) 222-8.

7454 *a*) *Quinzio* Sergio, Il sacro nel pensiero ebraico; – *b*) *García Bazán* Francisco, Il sacro e le religioni dell'Oriente: Fondamenti 4 (Il sacro, 1986) 125-139 / 141-172.

7455 *qḥt*: *Hoftijzer* J., Frustula epigraphica hebraica [Lachish letters *qḥt*, *m't*]: ↠ 47, ᶠHOSPERS J., Scripta 1986, 85-93.

7456 *qilléšôn* 1 Sam 13,21: BethM 31,106 (1985s) 281-6 (O. *Margalit*).

7457 *rāḥep*: *Sawyer* J. F. A., The role of Jewish studies in biblical semantics [*mᵉraḥepet* Gn 1,2; *'al-mawet* Prov 12,28; *lilit* Is 34,14; *raz* Is 24,16; *miškan*...]: ↠ 47, ᶠHOSPERS J., Scripta 1986, 201-7.

7458 *rîb*: **Bovati** Pietro, Ristabilire la giustizia: procedure, vocabolario, orientamenti [diss. 1985 ↠ **1**,8976]: AnBib 110. R 1986, Pontificio Istituto Biblico. 446 p.; bibliog. p. 368-403. 88-7653-110-6.

7459 *repā'îm*: **Barnett** R. D., Sirens and Rephaim: ↠ 71, ᶠMELLINK A., Ancient Anatolia 1986, 112-9; 8 fig.

7460 *Kutscher* Raphael, Akkadian *šadādum* / *šadādum* = 'to camp': ZAss 76 (1986) 1-3.

7460* *śādeh*: *Fry* Euan, Translating *śade* 'field' in the Old Testament: BTrans 37 (1986) 412-7.

7461 *śmḥ*: *Grossberg* Daniel, The dual glow/grow motif [Is 58,8; 9,2; Ps 97,11 ..]: Biblica 67 (1986) 547-554.

7462 *śār*: **Rüterswörden** Udo, Die Beamten der israelitischen Königszeit; eine Studie zu *śr* und vergleichbaren Begriffen [Diss. Bochum]: BZAW 117, 1985 ↠ **1**, 8983: ᴿBL (1986) 80 (G. H. *Jones*); TPQ 134 (1986) 299 (J. *Scharbert*).

7463 *še'ôl*: **Moro** V., *še'ol*; indagine sulla terminologia dell'aldilà nell'AT: diss. ᴰ*Zatelli* I. F 1979. [RivB 35,397].

7464 *še'īrît:* **Carena** O., Il resto di Israele [diss. *DLiverani* M.] 1985 → 1,8977: RParVi 31 (1986) 465s (A. *Rolla*).

7465 *šābaʿ:* Giesen Georg, Die Wurzel šbʿ 'schwören' ... Eid im AT [diss. Bonn 1981]: BoBB 56, 1981 → 63,8845; 64,8008: RKirSef 59 (1985) 299.

7466 *šāḥaz:* Millard A. R., A lexical illusion [mishnaic *mašḥezet* not a reappearance after hibernation, as *Ṭur-Sinai* claimed]: JSS 30 (1986) 1-3.

7467 *šākal:* Chiera Giovanna, Rapporti tra la base mediterranea *(a)skal* e il semitico *aškil:* AION 46 (1986) 291-3.

7468 *hiškîm:* **Janowski** Bernd, Rettungsgewissheit und Epiphanie des Heils; das Motiv der Hilfe Gottes 'am Morgen' im Alten Orient und im AT, I. Alter Orient: WMANT 59. Neuk-V. 1986. 208 p. [Mundus 22,311].

7469 *šālōm:* Klaus Nathan, ⊕ The blessing *šālôm* in the Bible: BethM 31,106 (1985s) 252-267.

7470 *Soviv* Aharon, ⊕ Meaning of *šem* in the Bible: BethM 31,104 (1985s) 31-38.

7471 *šāpaṭ:* **Niehr** Herbert, Herrschen und Richten; die Wurzel *špṭ* im Alten Orient und im AT [kath. Diss. Würzburg]: ForBi 54. Wü 1986, Echter. xii-458 p. DM 56 pa. – TR 83,74. 3-429-01012-8.

7472 *šeqel:* Mundhenk Norm, The translation of shekel [a weight, often of (precious) metal, but food in Ezek 4,10; Absalom's hair in 2 Sam 14,26]: BTrans 37 (1986) 237s.

J1.5 *Phoenicia, Ugaritica* – **North-West Semitic** [→ T5.4].

7473 *Amadasi Guzzo* M. G., L'onomastica nelle iscrizioni puniche tripolitane: RStFen 14 (1986) 21-51.

7474 *Cunchillos Ilarri* Jesús Luis, Que tout aille bien auprès de ma mère ! un quatala optatif en ugaritique?: → 21, Mem. DíEZ MACHO A., Salvación 1986, 259-266.

7475 *Dietrich* M., *Loretz* O., *a)* Baals Ablehnung niedriger Gäste (KTU 1.4 III 17-22]; – *b)* Die bipolare Position von 'l im Ugaritischen und Hebräischen; – *c)* Ug. NGŠ und NGṬ, MGṬ: UF 18 (1986s) 447s / 449s / 451s.

7476 *Dietrich* M., *Loretz* O., *a)* ṢRK im Kontext der Rede Danils in KTU 1.19 I 38-46; – *b)* Die Trauer Els und Anats (KTU 1.5 VI 11-22.31 - 1.6 I 5); – *c)* Orthographie und Inhalt im ugaritischen Brief KTU 2.16; – *d)* Ug. *bṣql 'rgz* und he. *b ṣqlnw* (2 Reg 4,42), *'gwz:* UF 18 (1986s) 97-100 / 101-110 / 111-4 / 115-120.

7477 *Dijkstra* M., *a)* An Ugaritic fable (KTU 1.93); – *b)* Another text in the shorter cuneiform alphabet (KTU 5.22): UF 18 (1986s) 125-8 / 121-3.

7478 *Faber* Alice, On the structural unity of the Eshmunazor inscription: JAOS 106 (1986) 425-432.

7479 *a) Fuentes Estañol* M. J., Corpus de las inscripciones fenicias de España; – *b) Olmo Lete* G. del, Fenicio y Ugarítico, su correlación lingüística; *c) Röllig* W., Contribución de las inscripciones fenicio-púnicas al estudio de la protohistoria de España; – *d) Hoz* J. de, Escritura fenicia y escrituras hispánicas; algunos aspectos de su relación; – *e) Sanmartín Ascaso* J., Inscripciones fenicio-púnicas del sureste hispánico I: → 353, EOlmo Lete G. del, Fenicios 1986, II. 5-30 / 31-49 / 51-58, TMartínez Teresa / 73-83 [84, útil cuadro de alfabetos fenicios] / 89-96; 13 fig.

7480 *a) Fuentes Estañol* M. J., Corpus de las inscripciones fenicias de España; – *b) Röllig* W., Contribución de las inscripciones fenicio-púnicas al estudio de la protohistoria de España, TMartínez Teresa; – *c) Sanmartín Ascaso* J., Inscripciones fenicio-púnicas del sureste hispánico I; – *d) Hoz* J. de,

Escritura fenicia y escrituras hispánicas; algunos aspectos de su relación; –
e) *Blázquez* J. M., El influjo de la cultura semitica (fenicios y cartagineses)
en la formación de la cultur ibérica: AulaOr 4 (1986) 5-30 / 51-58 / 89-96;
13 fig. / 73-84 / 163-178 [315-338, bibliog., *Pérez* C. J.].

7481 *Garr* W. Randall, On voicing and devoicing in Ugaritic: JNES 45 (1986)
45-52.

7482 *Israel* Felice, Les dialectes de Transjordanie [Ammonite, Moabite,
Édomite]: MondeB 46 (1986) 44.

7483 **Jackson** Kent P., The Ammonite language of the Iron Age 1983
➤ 64,8944 ... 1,9002: ᴿBO 43 (1986) 448-450 (E. *Lipiński*); CBQ 48 (1986)
535s (W. J. *Fulco*); Gregorianum 67 (1986) 141-3 (G. L. *Prato*); JAOS 106
(1986) 370-2 (E. G. *Clarke*).

7484 *Jongeling* K., Vowel assimilation in Punic: JbEOL 29 (1985s) 124-132.

7485 *Krahmalkov* Charles R., The qatal with future tense reference in
Phoenician: JSS 31 (1986) 5-10.

Lemaire A. [Phénicien, Araméen], *Caquot* A. [Cananéen]: ➤ 602*, [*Barucq*
A.] Écrits de l'Orient ancien et sources bibliques 1986, 213-269 (9-57);
181-212.

7486 *Malul* Meir, Some comments on, B. MARGALIT's 'Ugaritic lexicography
II': RB 93 (1986) 415-8.

7487 *Margalit* Baruch, a) Ḫ'(!)ršm in KTU 1.19.IV.60 (= CTA 19.222); a
suggested reading/emendation: VT 36 (1986) 485-9; – b) The Ugaritic
poem of AQHT; analysis and interpretation: ➤ 392, SBL Seminars 1986,
246-261.

7488 a) *Meier* Sam, Baal's fight with Yam (KTU 1.2.I.IV), a part of the Baal
myth as known in KTU 1.1.3-6 ?; – b) *Smith* Mark S., Interpreting the
Baal cycle; – c) *Tsevat* Matitiahu, Eating and drinking, hosting and
sacrificing in the epic of Aqht: UF 18 (1986s) 241-254 / 313-339 / 345-350.

7489 *Olmo Lete* G. del, Fenicio y Ugarítico; correlación lingüística: AulaOr 4
(1986) 31-49.

7490 a) *Renfroe* F., Qr-Mym's comeuppance; – b) *Moor* J. C. de, Ugaritic
lexicographical notes I [GḪT -MṬ – *pirigalu* - MŠR D]; – c) *Smith* M. S., Mt.
Ll in KTU 1.2 I 19-20: UF 18 (1986s) 455-7 / 255-261 / 458.

7491 **Segert** S., A basic grammar of the Ugaritic language 1984 ➤ 65,7912:
ᴿBL (1986) 140 (M. E. J. *Richardson*); JRAS (1986) 258-260 (E.
Ullendorff); Lešonenu 48s (1984s) 291-6 (J. *Blau*).

7492 **Siles** Jaime, Léxico de inscripciones ibéricas. M 1985, Escolar. 437 p.;
bibliog. p. 406-437. 84-505-1735-4.

7493 **Sivan** Daniel, Grammatical analysis and glossary of the Northwest
Semitic vocables in Akkadian texts of the 15th-13th c. B.C. from Canaan
and Syria: AOAT 214, 1984 ➤ 65,7914; 1, 9014: ᴿBSOAS 49 (1986) 625s
(J. *Wansbrough*).

7494 **Soldt** W. H. van, Studies in the Akkadian of Ugarit; dating and grammar, diss. Leiden 1986, ᴰ*Veenhof* K. – PhoenixEOL 32,2 (1986) 9 ['1968'].

7495 *Sznycer* Maurice, Les inscriptions néopuniques de Mididi: Semitica 36
(1986) 5-24 [25-42, *Fantar* Mhamed, stèles] pl. I-X.

7496 *Vattioni* Francesco, Lettura e interpretazione dei cuneiformi alfabetici di
Ugarit: ➤ 540*, Analisi 1985, AION-Clas 7 (1985) 131-155.

7497 a) *Verreet* Eddy, Abriss des ugaritischen Verbalsystems; – b) *Renfroe* F.,
Methodological considerations regarding the use of Arabic in Ugaritic
philology: ➤ 368, Münster colloquium, UF 18 (1986s) 75-82 / 33-74.

7498 a) *Verreet* Eddy, Beobachtungen zum ugaritischen Verbalsystem III; – b)
Huehnergard J., RS 15.86 (PRU 3,51f.) / RS 19.55 (PRU 4,293b); –

c) Sivan Daniel, Problematic lengthenings in North West Semitic spellings in the middle of the second millennium B.C.E.; – *d) Pardee* Dennis, Epigraphic notes to articles in UF 16: UF 18 (1986s) 363-386 / 169-171.453 / 301-312 / 454.

7499 *Verreet* Eddy, Der Gebrauch des Perfekts *qtl* in den ugaritischen Nebensätzen: OrLovPer 17 (1986) 71-83: JBL 105 (1986) 113s (W. H. *Shea*); JQR 76 (1985s) 258s (W. R. *Garr*).

J1.6 Aramaica.

7500 **Abbadi** Sabri, Die Personennamen der Inschriften aus Hatra: Texte und Studien zur Orientalistik 1, 1983 → 65,7997; 1,9125: ᴿArOr 54 (1986) 192s (O. *Klima*: aramäische Philologie); BSOAS 49 (1986) 625 (J. C. *Greenfield*: sometimes corrects VATTIONI F. 1981); OLZ 81 (1986) 574-6 (H. *Preissler*).

7501 **Abou-Assaf** A., *al.*, La statue de Tell Fekherye 1982 → 63,8067a ... 1,9021: ᴿBASOR 261 (1986) 91-95 (J. *Huehnergard*).

7502 **Aggoula** Basile, Inscriptions et graffites araméens d'Assour: Aion 43/2 Sup. (1985) → 1,9022: ᴿJSS 31 (1986) 240-2 (L. L. *Grabbe*).

7503 *Aggoula* Basile, Remarques sur les inscriptions hatréennes XII: Syria 63 (1986) 353-374; corrigenda p. 454.

7504 **Attardo** E., La paleografia aramaica dagli inizi al 612 a.C.: diss. Padova 1984, ᴰ*Fales* F. M. [RivB 35,86].

7505 **Beyer** Klaus, Die aramäischen Texte vom Toten Meer ... 1984 → 65,7925; 1,9027: ᴿBiblica 67 (1986) 134s (T. *Franxman*); JBL 105 (1986) 347-9 (D. J. *Harrington*); Judaica 41 (1985) 245s (S. *Schreiner*); RQum 12,46 (1986) 287s (J. *Carmignac*).

7506 **Beyer** K., The Aramaic language, its distribution and subdivisions [= Texte ch. 1], ᵀ*Healey* J. F. Gö 1986, Vandenhoeck & R. 61 p. DM 25. 3-525-53573-2 [NTAbs 31,119].

7507 *Broshi* M., *Qimron* E., A house deed sale from Kefar Baru from the time of Bar Kokhba [(long) Aramaic 'exterior'; brief Hebrew 'interior'; found among the papers of Y. *Yadin*]: IsrEJ 36 (1986) 201-214; 2 fig.; pol. 26.

7508 *Caquot* A., Hébreu et araméen: Annuaire du Collège de France (P 1983-4) 603-622 [AION 45,710].

7509 **Cook** Edward M., Word order in the Aramaic of Daniel: AfrAsLing 9/3. Malibu 1986, Undena. 16 p.

7510 *Cross* Frank M., A new Aramaic stele from Taymā' [Šahrū of Lihyan, not father of Gašmu (before Nehemiah)]: → 32, ᶠFITZMYER J., CBQ 48 (1986) 387-394; phot.; facsim.

7511 *Ellingworth* Paul, Hebrew or Aramaic? [the NT uses *hebraïsti* 7 times; only *gabbatha* and *rabboni* are clearly Aramaic, but the others probably; but the translator must face the question, 'Then why does the NT use *hebraïsti*?' and decide what *he* should use]: BTrans 37 (1986) 338-341.

7512 **Fales** Frederick M., Aramaic epigraphs on clay tablets of the Neo-Assyrian period: StSem NS 2 / Materiali per il lessico aramaico 1. R 1986, Univ. xx-287 p.; 17 pl.

7513 *a) Fassberg* Steven, ❶ Topics in the Aramaic of the Palestine Targum fragments in the light of comparative data; – *b) Beyer* Klaus, The pronunciation of Galilean Aramaic according to the Geniza fragments with Palestinian and Tiberian pointing; – *c) Solomon* Zomaya S., The state of spoken Aramaic today: → 363, Congress IX-D1, 1985/6, ❶ 17-22 / 23-30.

7514 *Fauth* Wolfgang, Lilits und Astarten in aramäischen, mandäischen und syrischen Zaubertexten: WeltOr 17 (1986) 66-94.

7515 **Fitzmyer** J. A., *Harrington* D. J., A manual of Palestinian Aramaic texts: BibOrPont 34, 1978 ⇢ 60,a432 ... 63,8084: ᴿOLZ 81 (1986) 475s (J. *Oelsner*).

7516 *Geller* M. J., Eight incantation bowls (7 Aramaic, 1 Syriac): OrLovPer 17 (1986) 101-117.

7517 **Greenfield** Jonas C., *Porten* Bezalel, The Bisitun inscription of Darius the Great, Aramaic version: CorpInscrIran 1/5/1, 1982 ⇢ 65,7931; 1,9036: ᴿCdÉ 61 (1986) 267-9 (E. *Lipiński*); Orientalia 55 (1986) 348s (A. *Lemaire*).

7518 **Krotkoff** Georg, A Neo-Aramaic dialect of Kurdistan; texts, grammar, and vocabulary: AOR 64, 1982 ⇢ 1,9045: ᴿActOrK 47 (1986) 172s (Frithiof *Rundgren*); Muséon 97 (1984) 163 (A. *Denis*).

7519 *a*) *Leemhuis* F., An early witness for a fronted /g/ in Aramaic? the case of the Tell Fekherye inscription; – *b*) *Klugkist* A., The origin of the Mandaic script: ⇢ 47, ꟳHOSPERS J., Scripta 1986, 133-142 / 111-120.

7520 **Lemaire** A., *Durand* J.-M., Les inscriptions araméennes de Sfiré ... 1984 ⇢ 65,7937; 1,9046: ᴿBASOR 264 (1986) 85s (E. *Lipiński*); BO 43 (1986) 445-7 (H. D. *Galter*); BZ 30 (1986) 308 (H. D. *Preuss*); JBL 105 (1986) 510-2 (P. E. *Dion*); OLZ 81 (1986) 351-4 (E. *Lipiński*); RAss 80 (1986) 88-93 (F. M. *Fales*).

7521 **Levias** Caspar, A grammar of Galilean Aramaic; intr. *Sokoloff* M. NY 1986, Jewish Theological Sem. xxxii p. Eng.; ◑ 343 p. 0-87334-030-2.

7522 *Lund* Jerome A., The syntax of the numeral 'one' as a noun modifier in Jewish Palestinian Aramaic of the Amoraic period: JAOS 106 (1986) 413-423.

7523 **Macuch** Rudolf, Grammatik des samaritanischen Aramäisch 1982 ⇢ 63,8095 ... 1,9049: ᴿOLZ 81 (1986) 568s (H. *Pohl*).

7523* *Margain* Jean, Notes de lexicographie araméenne; targum samaritain en Gn 1: Sefarad 44 (1984) 211-6: *ryqny* 'vide'; *y'r* 'herbe'; *qms* 'sauterelle'; *b'lpwš* 'reptile'; *tšby(t)* 'ressemblance'; *šryr* 'très'.

7524 *Martínez-Borobio* Emiliano, *Yt* and *L* before the direct object in the Aramaic of the Palestinian Targum: ⇢ 377, IOSOT summaries (1986) 87.

7525 **Mukherjee** B. N., Studies in the Aramaic edicts of Aśoka. Calcutta 1984, Indian Museum. 73 p.; X pl. r. 8. – ᴿStIran 15 (1986) 275 (G. *F-ussman*).

7526 *Muraoka* Takamitsu, A study in Palestinian Jewish Aramaic: Sefarad 45 (1985) 3-21.

7527 **Naveh** Joseph, *Shaked* Shaul, Amulets and magic bowls; Aramaic incantations of late antiquity 1985 ⇢ 1,9051: ᴿJSS 31 (1986) 96-98 (J. B. *Segal*).

7528 *Piso* I., Epigraphica (XIV), Acta Musei Napocensis 20 (1983) 103-111 [AION 45 (1985) 717].

7529 **Porten** Bezalel, *Yardeni* Ada, Textbook of Aramaic documents from ancient Egypt, newly copied, edited and translated into Hebrew and English. J 1986, Hebrew Univ. I. ix-11 p. 965-222-075-2.

7530 *Porten* Bezalel, Une autre lettre araméenne à l'Académie des Inscriptions (AI 2-4); une nouvelle reconstruction: Semitica 36 (1986) 71-86; pl. XII-XIII.

7531 *Roschinski* H. P., Eine Gefässscherbe mit aramäischen Namen aus Krefeld-Gellep: Epigraphische Studien 13 (1983) 79-86 [AION 45 (1985) 719: fig. 1 capovolta].

7531* **Sabar** Yona, ◑ Homilies in the New-Aramaic of the Kurdistani Jews. J 1985, Israel Acad. 372 p. 965-208-054-3. – ᴿKirSef 61 (1986) 42 (A. *Shinan*).

7532 **Segal** J. B. (*Smith* H. S.), Aramaic texts from North Saqqâra with some fragments in Phoenician 1983 ➤ 64,8092 ... 1,9059: ᴿCBQ 48 (1986) 541-4 (J. A. *Fitzmyer*).

7533 *Segal* J. B., Arabs at Hatra and the vicinity; marginalia on new Aramaic texts [*Ibrahim* J. K. 1981]: JSS 31 (1986) 57-80; 4 fig.

7534 ᴱ**Sokoloff** Michael, Arameans, Aramaic and the Aramaic literary tradition 1980/3 ➤ 64,8094 ... 1,9062: ᴿBO 43 (1986) 767-9 (W. R. *Garr*); OLZ 81 (1986) 265s (W. *Herrmann*).

7535 **Talmon** Zvi, ✪ Linguistic aspects of the Aramaic proverb in the Babylonian Talmud: diss. J 1984. vii-264 p.; p. 265-521 + xl; 37 fig. – KirSef 59 (1985) 523.

7536 **Vilsker** L. H., Manuel d'araméen Samaritain, ᵀ*Margain* J., 1981 ➤ 62,8895 ... 65,7949: ᴿOLZ 81 (1986) 476-8 (J. *Oelsner*).

7537 *Wesselius* J. W., The restoration of Hermopolis Letter 6 and the ransom of prisoners: ➤ 59, ᶠLᴇʙʀᴀᴍ J., Tradition 1986, 7-18.

7538 *Yassine* Khair, *Teixidor* Javier, Ammonite and Aramaic inscriptions from Tell El-Mazār in Jordan: BASOR 264 (1986) 45-50; 9 fig.

7539 *Zadok* Ron, On some Iranian names in Aramaic documents from Egypt: IndIraJ 29 (1986) 41-44.

J1.7 Syriaca.

7540 *Drijvers* H. J. W., Facts and problems in early Syriac-Speaking [...]: SecC 2 (1982) 157-175 [AION 45 (1985) 714].

7541 *Köbert* R., Heisst syr. *ḥašqbōl* 'duplex'? [vielmehr 'zusammen, gleich']: Biblica 67 (1986) 555s.

7541* *Puech* Émile, Une inscription syriaque palestinienne: SBFLA 36 (1986) 309-316; pl. 39-40.

7542 *Sixdenier* Guy, Du nouveau sur Si-Ngan-Fou ... les inscriptions syriaques: JAs 274 (1986) 469-471.

J2.1 Akkadica (sumerica).

7543 **Black** J. A., Sumerian grammar in Babylonian theory: StPohl 12, 1984 ➤ 65,7964: ᴿBO 43 (1986) 720-2 (Marie-Louise *Thomsen*); BSOAS 49 (1986) 563s, 2 fig. (M. J. *Geller* cannot accept); JRAS (1986) 95s (W. G. *Lambert*).

7543* **Civil** Miguel, *Gurney* Oliver R., *Kennedy* Douglas A., The Sag-Tablet; lexical texts in the Ashmolean Museum, Middle Babylonian grammatical texts; miscellaneous texts: Materials for the Sumerian Lexicon, Sup. 1. R 1986, Pontificium Institutum Biblicum. 103 p.; 27 pl. 88-7653-563-2.

7544 **Dandamayev** M. A., Vavilonskie Pis-tsi 1983 ➤ 64,8113 ... 1,9088: ᴿJAOS 106 (1986) 566s (B. R. *Foster*).

7545 *Dandamayev* M. A., The Late Babylonian *ambaru* [< Old Persian 'storehouse']: ➤ 11*, Mem. Bɪᴄᴋᴇʀᴍᴀɴ E. = JANES 16s (1984s) 39s.

7546 *Dunham* Sally, Sumerian words for foundation; I. Temen: RAss 80 (1986) 31-64.

Durand J., mésopotamiens; *Masson* E., hittites: ➤ 602, Écrits de l'Orient ancien 1986, 107-155 / 157-180.

7547 *Green* M. W., Archaic Uruk cuneiform: AJA 90 (1986) 464-6.

7548 a) **Greenstein** Edward I., Phonology of Akkadian syllable structure; – b) *Gai* Amikam, Predicative state and inflection of the nominal predicate in Akkadian and Syrian: AfrAsLing 9/1, 1984 ➤ 65,7977; 0-89003-156-8:

RBO 43 (1986) 723-732 (E. E. *Knudsen*); JAOS 106 (1986) 359-362 (D. O. *Edzard*: not the last word); JSS 31 (1986) 81-83 (W. von *Soden*, deutsch).

7549 *Huehnergard* John, On verbless clauses in Akkadian: ZAss 76 (1986) 218-249.

7550 *Israeli* Shlomit, A grammatical analysis of the first 23 pages of the El Amarna texts, Bibliotheca Aegyptiaca VIII: ➤ 349, ᴱ*Groll* S., Papers 1 (1982) 278-302.

7551 **Izre'el** Shlomo, ❶ *Ha-Dialekt ha-'Akkadi* ... The Akkadian dialect of the scribes of Amurru in the 14th-13th centuries BC; linguistic analysis: diss. Tel Aviv 1985. 488 + 72 p. – KirSef 60 (1985) 706.

7552 *Janssen* C., Het gebruik van het herhaald meewerkend voorwerp [repeated indirect object] in Oud-Babylonische brieven: Akkadica 46 (1986) 50-58; Eng. 59.

7553 **Kinnier Wilson** J. V., The legend of Etana, a new edition 1985 ➤ 1,9103: RBO 43 (1986) 436-9 (M. *Vogelzang*); ZAss 76 (1986) 134-7 (D. O. *Edzard*).

7554 *Klein* Jacob, On writing monumental inscriptions in Ur III scribal curriculum: RAss 80 (1986) 1-7.

7555 **Kraus** F. R., Nominalsätze in altbabylonischen Briefen und der Stativ: Med Ned. Ak. lett. 47/2. Amst 1984, Nord-Hollands. 51 p. 0-4448-5606-4.

7556 *a)* *Krecher* Joachim, Understanding and translating Sumerian texts; – *b)* *Picchioni* Sergio A., Die Keilschriftrichtung und ihre archäologischen Implikationen; – *c)* *Hassa* Zuhair M., Speculations on Mesopotamian (decimal-sexagesimal) numerical system; – *d)* *Hunger* Hermann, The spread of Mesopotamian exact science into the Hellenistic world: Sumer 42 (1986) 44-47 / 48-54 / 55-60 ❹ 26-28 / 64-67.

7557 **Limet** Henri, Textes administratifs relatifs aux métaux: ARM 25. P 1986, RCiv. viii-291 p. 2-86538-155-2.

7557* **Livingstone** Alasdair, Mystical and mythological explanatory works of Assyrian and Babylonian scholars. Ox 1986, Clarendon. IX-270 p.; 7 pl. [JSS 37, 177, W. von *Soden*].

7558 *Monaco* Salvatore F., Parametri e qualificatori nei testi economici della Terza Dinastia di Ur II; Qualificatori non numerici: OrAnt 25 (1986) 1-20.

7559 **Rouault** Olivier, Éléments pour un logiciel [computer-program] assyriologique: CARNES 1/2. Malibu CA 1984, Undena. 82 p. $3.50. 0-89003-146-0. – RBO 43 (1986) 718-720 (P. *Talon*).

7560 **Sjöberg** Åke W., *al.*, Sumerian dictionary 2: B, 1984 ➤ 65,7989; 1,9115: RJSS 31 (1986) 81 (E. *Sollberger*: complete and reliable).

7561 **Soden** W. von, Einführung in die Altorientalistik 1985 ➤ 1,9116: RZAW 98 (1986) 475s (H.-C. *Schmitt*).

7562 *Soden* Wolfram von, The language of Ashur in the Mitanni empire (ca. 1450-1350 B.C.): Sumer 42 (1986) 106-9, ❹ 41-43.

7563 *Starr* Ivan, The place of the historical omens in the system of apodoses: BO 43 (1986) 628-642.

7564 *Vanstiphout* H. L. J., Un carré d'amour sumérien ou How once woman was won (résumé): Akkadica 50 (1986) 25s.

7565 *a)* *Vanstiphout* H., Some thoughts on genre in Mesopotamian literature; – *b)* *Steiner* Gerd, Die Inschrift der 'Geierstele' als literarischer Text; – *c)* *Finet* André, Allusions et reminiscences comme source d'information sur la diffusion de la littérature; – *d)* *Röllig* Wolfgang, Volksliteratur in mesopotamischer Überlieferung; – *e)* *Donbaz* Veysel, Publication of the Kültepe tablets housed in Ankara: ➤ 543, Rencontre 32, 1985/6, 1-11 / 33-44 / 13-17 / 81-87 / 149-153.

7566 *a) Veenhof* K. R., Two Akkadian auxiliaries, *ke'ûm* 'to be able' and *mu'ā'um* 'to want'; – *b) Vanstiphout* H. L. J., Some remarks on cuneiform *écritures*; – *c) Haayer* G., Languages in contact; the case of Akkadian and Sumerian: ➤ 47, ᶠHOSPERS J., Scripta 1986, 235-251 / 217-234 / 77-84.

7567 *Zadok* Ran, Some non-Semitic names in Akkadian sources: BeiNam 21 (1986) 244-8.

J2.7 Arabica.

7568 **Abu Nahleh** Lamis Y., A syntactic semantic analysis of object clitics and pronouns in Ramallah Palestinian Arabic: diss. Michigan, ᴰ*Hook* P. AA 1985. 214 p. 86-00394. – DissA 47 (1986s) 164-A.

7569 **Ahmed** Mokhtar, Lehrbuch des Ägyptisch-Arabischen. Wsb 1981, Harrassowitz. xiii-314 p. 3-447-02203-5: ᴿBO 43 (1985) 215-7 (A. J. *Gully*).

7570 **Beeston** A. F. L., Sabaic grammar: JSS Mon 6, 1984 ➤ 65,8004; £12: ᴿJSS 31 (1986) 270-5 (W. W. *Müller*, deutsch).

7571 **Beeston** A. F. L. *al.*, Sabaic dictionary 1982 ➤ 63,8166 ... 1,9131: ᴿOrientalia 55 (1986) 357-360 (R. *Weipert*: besser als *Biella*).

7572 **Behnstedt** Peter, *Woidich* Manfred, Die ägyptisch-arabischen Dialekte: TAVO B-50/1. Wsb 1985, Reichert. I. 129 p.; II. maps. 3-88226-227-3.

7573 **Biella** Joan C., Dictionary of Old South Arabic/Sabaean 1982 ➤ 63,8169 ... 1,9135: ᴿZDPV 102 (1986) 171-4 (E. A. *Knauf*).

7574 **Borg** Alexander, Cypriot Arabic; a historical and comparative investigation into the phonology and morphology of the Arabic vernacular spoken by the Maronites of Kormakiti village in the Kyrenia district of North-Western Cyprus: Abh. Kunde des Morgenlandes 47/4. Wsb 1985, Steiner für DMG. xii-203 p. – ᴿSalesianum 48 (1986) 765s (R. *Gottlieb*).

7575 **Brugman** J., *Schröder* F., Arabic studies in the Netherlands: Ned. Inst. Cairo, 1979 ➤ 61,a447: ᴿOLZ 81 (1986) 58-60 (W. *Reuschel*).

Garr W. Randall, Dialect geography of Syria-Palestine 1985 ➤ 7250.

7576 **Gaube** Heinz, [251] Arabische Inschriften aus Syrien: Beiruter Texte und Studien 17, 1978 ➤ 60,t782 ... 64,8155: ᴿJNES 45 (1986) 161-4 (P. E. *Chevedden*).

7576* **Hamilton** Alastair, William BEDWELL, the Arabist, 1563-1632: Browne Inst. Publ. 5. Leiden 1985, Brill./Univ. 163 p.; 13 pl. *f* 46. 90-04-07241-1. – ᴿBO 43 (1986) 808-810 (P. *Auchterlonie*); JSS 31 (1986) 114s (P. M. *Holt*).

7577 **Hopkins** Simon, Studies in the grammar of early Arabic based upon papyri datable to before 300 A.H./912 A.D.: London Univ. Or. Series 37, 1984 ➤ 1,9145; £28; 0-19-713603-6: ᴿJRAS (1986) 266-270 (J. *Blau*); JSS 31 (1986) 276-280 (J. D. *Latham*).

7577* *Knauf* Ernst A., Bemerkungen zur frühen Geschichte der arabischen Orthographie, II. Sprachen die vorklassischen Araber in Pausa **ʿAmrū?: Orientalia 55 (1986) 452s.

7578 **Nakano** Aki'o, Comparative vocabulary of Southern Arabic; Mahri, Gibbali and Soqotri: Studia Culturae Islamicae 29. Tokyo 1986, Institute for the Study of Languages and Cultures of Asia and Africa. ix-177 p.

7579 *Negev* Avraham, *al.*, Obodas the god: IsrEJ 36 (1986) 56-60; Nabatean inscr. facsimile.

7580 *O'Connor* M., The Arabic loanwords in Nabatean Aramaic [examining *Cantineau* J.: Nabatean emptied itself gradually of its Aramaic until it was decided to write nearly pure Arabic in Nabatean script]: JNES 45 (1986) 213-229.

7581 *O'Fahey* R. S., The writings by, attributed to, or on Aḥmad IBN IDRIS: BO 43 (1986) 660-7.

7582 **Pouzet** Louis, Une herméneutique de la tradition islamique; le commentaire des Arba'un al-Nawawīya de Muḥyī al-Dīn Yaḥyā AL-NAWAWĪ (m. 626/1277): Univ. S. Joseph A-13, Langue arabe et pensée islamique 13, 1982 ➤ 1,9160: ᴿJAOS 106 (1986) 595s (J. A. *Bellamy*: excellent; some alternatives); Orientalia 55 (1986) 199s (R. *Köbert*).

7583 **Prokosch** Erich, Osmanisches Wortgut im Ägyptisch-Arabischen. 1983: ᴿOLZ 81 (1986) 485-7 (Heidi *Stein*).

7584 **Roman** A., Étude de la phonologie et de la morphologie de la Koinè arabe [*Sībawayhi*, Kitab]. Aix-en-Provence 1983, Univ. [Marseilles: Lafitte]. 682 p.; p. 683-1190. – ᴿBSOAS 49 (1986) 390-2 (G. A. *Khan*).

7585 **Rosenhouse** Judith, The [North Israel] Bedouin Arabic dialects. Wsb 1984, Harrassowitz. xiii-348 p.; 5 maps. – ᴿZDMG 136 (1986) 645 (W. *Diem*).

7586 *Ryckmans* J., a) Une écriture minuscule sud-arabe antique récemment découverte: ➤ 47, ᶠHOSPERS J., Scripta 1986, 185-197; tables 198s; – b) Safaïtique [langue et religion autour du mont Ṣafā' SE Damas]: ➤ 595, SDB 11,60 (1986) 1-3.

7587 **Schregle** Götz, *al.*, Arabisch-Deutsches Wörterbuch [➤ 64,8173]. Lfg. 5-8. Wsb 1983s, Steiner. 383 p. DM 43. – ᴿDLZ 107 (1986) 281-3 (W. *Wiebke*).

7587* *Schub* Michael B., A normative syzygy, */kiddībᵘⁿ/ for 'inveterate liar' [should exist in Arabic because its opposite *ṣiddīqᵘⁿ* does], and a note on the origin of the elative: JQR 76 (1985s) 368-371.

7588 *Shahīd* Irfan, Arabic literature to the end of the Umayyad period [Cambridge History 1, 1984]: JAOS 106 (1986) 529-538.

7589 **Talmoudi** F., Texts in the Arabic dialect of Sūsa (Tunisia). Göteborg 1981, Univ. 166 p. – ᴿArOr 54 (1986) 203 (L. *Drozdík*).

7590 **Ullmann** Manfred, Arabisch 'asā 'vielleicht', Syntax und Wortart: Szb Bayer. P/H 1984/4, 1984 ➤ 1,9170: ᴿDer Islam 63 (1986) 153s (A. A. *Ambos*).

J3 Ægyptia.

7591 a) *Akiyama* Shinichi, ❶ The sḏm.f and sḏm.n.f forms in Middle Egyptian; – b) *Koyama* Masato, ❶ A list of ancient Egyptian literary works: Orient 28,1 (1985) 131-144 / 145-157.

7592 **Allen** James P., *al.*, Essays on Egyptian grammar: Yale Egyptological Studies I. Boston 1986, Museum of Fine Arts. vi-42 p. $8.50. 0-912532-90-0 [BO 43,829].

7592* *Allen* James P., The pyramid text of queens Jpwt and Wḏbt-n.(j): JAmEg 23 (1986) 1-26; 15 fig.

7593 **Barguet** Paul, Les textes des sarcophages égyptiens du Moyen Empire, introduction et traduction. P 1986, Cerf. 725 p. ill. F 270. 2-204-02332-9.

7593* *Barta* Winfried, Subjunktivische Konjunktionen als Einleitung von Umstandssätzen: GöMiszÄg 90 (1986) 7-10.

7594 **Beckerath** Jürgen von, Handbuch der ägyptischen Königsnamen: Mü-ÄgSt 20, 1984 ➤ 65,8046: ᴿJAmEg 22 (1985) 214s (D. *Lorton*).

7594* **Bradbury** Louis, Nefer's inscription on the death date of Queen Ahmose-Nefertary and the deed found pleasing to the King: JAmEg 22 (1985) 73-95; 3 fig.

7595 *a) Brashear* William, Holz- und Wachstafeln der Sammlung Kiseleff; – *b)*
Aguizy Ola el-, A palaeographical study of demotic papyri in the Cairo
Museum; – *c) Zauzich* Karl-T., 150 Jahre Erforschung demotischer
Ostraka: Enchoria 14 (1986) 1-19 ... / 67-70 / 129-134.

7596 **Bresciani** Edda, Le stele egiziane del museo civico archeologico di
Bologna. Bo 1985, Museo. 192 p. Lit. 30.000. – ᴿBO 43 (1986) 88-90 (A.
Leahy: critical).

7596* *Browne* Gerald M., *a)* Notes on Old Nubian [... texts]: Sudan Texts
Bulletin 7 (Ulster 1985) 6-13 [1-5; 14-29]; – *b)* Old Nubian colometry:
BeiSudan 1 (1986) 7-16.

7597 **Callender** J. B., Studies in the nominal sentence in Egyptian and Coptic:
Near Eastern Studies 24. Berkeley 1984, Univ. California. ix-221 p. –
ᴿCdÉ 61 (1986) 358-367 (L. *Depuydt*; specificity or emphasis; disturbing
typographical inaccuracy).

7598 **Černý** Jaroslav, Papyrus hiératiques de Deir el-Médineh Tome II (Nos
XVIII-XXXIV): Documents de Fouilles 22. Le Caire 1986, IFAO. 7 p.;
24 pl. 2-7247-0028-7.

7599 *Crevatin* Franco, Il mondo scritto e la formula efficace; due case-studies
egiziani antichi: ➤ 540*, Analisi 1985, AION-Clas 7 (1985) 117-129.

7600 *Cruz-Uribe* Eugene, *Šm' pn* 'this Upper Egypt': VAeg 2,1 (1986) 31-33.

7601 *Der Manuelian* Peter, An essay in document transmission; *Nj-k3-'nḫ*
[Keeper of the King's Property; his 'duty table'] and the earliest *ḥrjw rnpt*
['five epagomenal days']: JNES 45 (1986) 1-18; 8 fig.

7602 **Devauchelle** Didier, Ostraca démotiques du Musée du Louvre 1983
➤ 64,8198; 1,9190: ᴿCdÉ 61 (1986) 228-231 (C. J. *Martin*).

7603 **Doret** Eric, The narrative verbal system of Old and Middle Egyptian:
Cah. Orientalisme 12. Genève 1986, Cramer. 239 p. [JNES 46,242].

7604 **Edel** Elmar, Hieroglyphische Inschriften des Alten Reiches: Abh Rh/Wf
Ak 67,1981 ➤ 65,8054; 1,9192: ᴿOrientalia 55 (1986) 81s (J. *Osing*).

7605 **Faulkner** R. O., The ancient Egyptian Book of the Dead [➤ 1,9194]
²*Andrews* Carol. L 1985, British Museum. 192 p.; ill. £15. – ᴿJRAS
(1986) 263s (J. D. *Ray*: Faulkner's 1972 translation, but with new
illustrations from 24 of the Museum's finest manuscripts).

7606 **Fischer** Henry G., L'écriture et l'art de l'Égypte ancienne; quatre leçons
sur la paléographie et l'épigraphie pharaoniques: Collège de France. P
1986, PUF. 253 p.; ʈ08 pl. F 150 [JNES 46,76].

7607 **Franke** Detlef, Personendaten aus dem Mittleren Reich (20.-16.
Jahrhundert v.Chr.), Dossiers 1-796: ÄgAbh 41. Wsb 1984, Harrassowitz.
486 p. DM 66. – ᴿMundus 22 (1986) 14s (M. *Gutgesell*: male names).

7608 **Gaskins** Leanna, Notes on Middle Egyptian syntax. Berkeley 1978,
Univ. California. viii-217 p.

7609 *a) Goedicke* Hans, Gentlemen's salutations; – *b) Sun* Henry T. C., A
circumstantial sḏm.n.f of a verb of motion in BM 826: VAeg 2 (1986)
161-170 / 171-3.

7609* *Goedicke* Hans, *a)* Sinuhe's duel; – *b)* Abi-Sha(i)'s representation in Beni
Hasan: JAmEg 21 (1984) 197-201 / 203-210.

7610 *Goedicke* Hans, *a)* Inana as inventor: VAeg 2 (1986) 35-41; – *b)* Three
passages in the story of Sinuhe: JAmEg 23 (1986) 167-174.

7610* *a) Goelet* Ogden ᴶ, The term *štp-s3* in the Old Kingdom and its later
development; – *b) Friedman* Florence, *3ḫ* in the Amarna period: JAmEg
23 (1986) 85-98 / 99-106; 5 fig.

7611 *Green* Michael, m-k-m-r und w-r-k-t-r in der Wenamun-Geschichte:
ZägSpr 113 (1986) 115-9.

7612 *Greig* Gary,   The language of the hieratic ostracon O. Nash 1, from the 19th Dynasty; a grammatical analysis and translation: → 349*, ^E*Groll* S., Papers 1 (1982) 5-52.

7613 ^FGUTBUB A., Mélanges 1984 → 1,59; 2-905-39703-9:   ^RBO 43 (1986) 669-674 (P. *Germond*: pp. analyses sans titres).

7614 *a) Hallof* J., Die Erstellung eines Wörterbuches der ägyptischen Sprache mit Hilfe der Computertechnik; – *b) Callender* J. B., Problems of tense and aspect in Egyptian: ZägSpr 113 (1986) 20-24 / 8-18.

7615 **Johnson** Janet H.,   Thus wrote 'Onchshehonqy'; an introductory grammar of demotic: SAOC 45. Ch 1986, Univ. Oriental Institute. vii-106 p. $7 [JNES 46,242].

7616 *Junge* Friedrich,   Das sogenannte Narrativ/Kontinuative *jw=f ḥr (tm) sḏm*: JEA 78 (1986) 113-132.

7617 *Kanawati* Naguib,   New biographical inscriptions from the First Intermediate period [Macquarie Univ. Hawawish excavation]: GöMiszÄg 89 (1986) 43-51; 3 fig.

7617* ^E*Lüddeckens* Erich,   Ägyptische Handschriften 3., beschrieben von Ursula **Kaplony-Heckel**: Verzeichnis der Orientalischen Handschriften in Deutschland 19/3. Wsb 1986, Steiner. 142 p.

7618 **Lüscher** Barbara,   Totenbuch, Spruch 1, nach Quellen des Neuen Reiches: KlÄgTexte. Wsb 1986, Harrassowitz. ix-73 p. 3-447-02646-4.

7619 **Menu** Bernadette, [three articles on demotic texts in] Études sur l'Égypte et le Soudan anciens: CRIPEL 6. Lille 1981, Presses Univ. 264 p. – ^RJNES 45 (1986) 305 (R. *Jasnow*).

7620 *a) Osing* Jürgen, Vokalisation; – *b) Loprieno* Antonio, Zahlwort; – *c) Franke* Detlef, Verwandtschaftsbezeichnungen: → 591, LexÄg 6,47ss (1986) 1032-6 / 1054-7 / 1306-19.

7621 *Parlebas* J., Écriture idéographique, écriture cursive et iconographie dans l'Égypte pharaonique: → 356, ^E*Siebert* G., Méthodologie 1981, 107-114.

7622 *Patanè* Massimo,   *a)* Approche du système accentuel général du verbe égyptien: CdÉ 61 (1986) 211-7; – *b)* La geminazione nella lingua dell'Egitto antico: Aegyptus 66 (1986) 181-5.

7623 *Perdu* Olivier,   Prologue à un corpus des stèles royales de la XXVIe Dynastie: BSFrÉg 105 (1986) 23-38.

7624 *Quirke* Stephen,   The regular titles of the late Middle Kingdom: RÉgp 37 (1986) 107-130.

7625 *Roeder* H.,   Die Prädikation im nominalen Nominalsatz; ein logisch-semantischen Ansatz: GöMiszÄg 91 (1986) 77 p. (whole fasc.).

7626 *Schenkel* Wolfgang,   Das Wort für 'König (von Oberägypten)': GöMiszÄg 94 (1986) 57-73.

7627 **Silverman** David P.,   Interrogative constructions with JN and JN-JW in Old and Middle Egyptian [diss. Ch 1975]: BiblAeg 1. Malibu CA 1980, Undena. vi-144 p. $14; pa. $10.50. – ^RJNES 45 (1986) 76-79 (E. *Doret*); Orientalia 55 (1986) 82-85 (H. *Satzinger*).

7628 *Sturtewagen* Christian,   'A (piece of) wood fitting (for) a bolt' in Gardiner's Ramesside Administrative Documents 48,1 ? : Orientalia 55 (1986) 450s.

7629 *Thissen* Heinz-J., 'Tadel der Frauen' [in drei demotischen Belegen]: Enchoria 14 (1986) 159s.

7630 *a) Velde* H. te, Egyptian hieroglyphs as signs, symbols and gods; – *b) Heerma van Voss* M., Zwei ungewöhnliche Darstellungen des ägyptischen Sonnengottes: Visible Religion 4s (1985s) 63-72 / 73-76.

7631 *a*) *Velde* H. te, Scribes and literacy in ancient Egypt; – *b*) *Zaborski* A., The Cushitic article; – *c*) *Dijk* J. van, 'Anat, Seth and the seed of Prē': → 47, ^FHospers J., Scripta 1986, 253-263 / 317-331 / 31-51.

7632 **Vernus** Pascal, Le surnom au Moyen Empire; répertoire, procédés d'expression et structures de la double identité au début de la XIIe dynastie à la fin de la XVIIe dynastie: StPohl 13. R 1986, Biblical Institute. vii-146 p. Lit. 25.000. 88-7653-583-7.

7633 **Ward** William A., Essays on feminine titles of the Middle Kingdom and related subjects. Beirut 1986, American Univ. xviii-198 p. $30. [BO 43,831].

7634 **Ward** William A., Index of Egyptian administrative and religious titles in the Middle Kingdom with a glossary of words and phrases used 1982 → 64,8226; 85,8087: ^RJNES 45 (1986) 70-74 (W. K. *Simpson*: authoritative; many detailed comments).

7635 *Ward* William A., Reflections on methodology in Egypto-Semitic lexicography: → 115, Mem. Tufnell O., 1985, 231-248.

7636 *Westendorf* Wolfgang, [Ägypten] Einst-Jetzt-Einst; oder, Die Rückkehr zum Ursprung: WeltOr 17 (1986) 5-8.

7637 *Winand* Jean, Champ sémantique et structure en égyptien ancien; les verbes exprimant la vision: StAltÄgK 13 (1986) 293-314.

7638 *Wright* G. H. R., The book of the caverns (quererts) [sometimes found as ch. 168 of the Book of the Dead] and its imagery, '... bodies of things to be in the houses of death and of birth': WeltOr 17 (1986) 9s.

7639 *a*) *Youssef Ahmed* A., The modified participle; an Arabic approach to Egyptian grammar; – *b*) *Sayed* Ramadan el-, Formules de piété filiale; – *c*) *Goedicke* Hans, Zam3-t3wy ['union of the two lands' not 'unification' (by conquest)]: → 77, ^FMokhtar G., 1985, I, 1-3 / 271-292 / 307-324.

J3.4 **Coptica.**

7640 **Browne** Gerald M., *a*) Griffith's Old Nubian Lectionary 1982 → 63,8193; 65,8047; *b*) Chrysostomus Nubianus 1984 → 65,d578; PapyrCastroct 8.10: ^RBO 43 (1986) 104-8 (H. *Satzinger*).

7641 *Cruz-Uribe* Eugene, Notes on the Coptic Cambyses romance: Enchoria 14 (1986) 51-56.

7642 **Ernshtedt** P. V., ❸ *Issledovania* ... Coptic grammar researches. Moskva 1986, Nauka.

7643 **Giversen** Søren, The Manichaean Coptic papyri in the Chester Beatty library: Cahiers d'Orientalisme 14s. Genève 1986, Cramer. I. Kephalaia, xxvi-354 pl.; II. Homilies & varia, x-126 pl. ·

7644 **Goehring** James E., The letter of Ammon and Pachomian monasticism. B 1986, de Gruyter. 307 p. DM 178. 3-11-009513-0. – ^RExpTim 98 (1986s) 86 (J. D. *Ray*: proper names in the 'Theban dialect' p. 247s show it is Ahmimic, not Saidic).

7645 *Kasser* Rodolphe, *a*) Causes et procédés de la mutation de *n* en aleph ou *i* dans trois lexèmes coptes apparentés, B *ōnḫ* 'vie' et S *saanš* 'nourrir', S *pranš* 'archive'(?): Orientalia 55 (1986) 177-181; – *b*) L'identité linguistique du ms. Cambridge Univ. Lib. Or. 1700,1 à la périphérie de l'aire lycopolitaine: Muséon 99 (1986) 221-7.

7646 *Lambdin* Thomas O., Introduction to Sahidic Coptic 1982 → 64,8241 ... 1,9240: ^RJNES 45 (1986) 158-160 (Janet H. *Johnson*).

7647 **MacCoull** Leslie S. B., Coptic documentary papyri from the Beinecke Library (Yale University): Soc. Archéologie Copte, Textes et documents 17. Cairo 1986, Arab World. viii-63 p., 27 pl.

7648 *MacCoull* L. S. B., Further notes on the Greek-Coptic dictionary of DIOSCORUS of Aphrodito: Glotta 64 (1986) 253-7.

7649 **Messiḥa** Hishmat, Fragments of Coptic and Greek papyri from Kom Ichḳaw: ASAE Sup. 29. Cairo 1983. iii-36 p.; 43 pl. – ᴿOLZ 81 (1986) 550s (G. *Poethke*).

7650 *Mikhail* L. B., The second tenses in Coptic: ZägSpr 113 (1986) 137-141.

7651 **Orlandi** Tito, Omelie copte 1981 ➤ 62,8967 ... 65,8099: ᴿCdÉ 61 (1986) 180-2 (U. *Zanetti*).

7652 **Shisha-Halevy** Ariel, Coptic grammatical categories; structural studies in the syntax of Shenoutean Sahidic: AnOr 53. R 1986, Pont. Inst. Biblicum. ix-264 p. Lit. 90.000. 88-7653-255-2 [BO 43,830].

7653 *Thissen* Heinz-J., Koptische Kinderschenkungsurkunden; zur Hierodulie im christlichen Ägypten: Enchoria 14 (1986) 117-128.

7654 **Vycichl** W., Dictionnaire étymologique de la langue copte 1983 ➤ 64,8250; 1,9246: ᴿBO 43 (1986) 713s (R.-G. *Coquin*).

7655 **Zanetti** Ugo, Les lectionnaires coptes annuels, Basse-Égypte: Publ. Inst. Orientaliste 33. LvN 1986, Peeters. xxii-383 p. Fb 2350.

J3.8 Æthiopica.

7655* **Colin** Gérard, Synaxarius aethiopicus, Mois de maskaram: PatrOr 43/3, 195. Turnhout 1986, Brepols. p. 323-512.

7656 *Cowley* R. W., A Geʿez document reporting controversy concerning the Bible commentaries of IBN AṬ-ṬAIYIB: RasStEtiop 30 (1984ss) 5-13.

7657 **Haile** G., *Macomber* W. F., A catalogue of Ethiopian manuscripts ... microfilm, Collegeville I-VII, 1975-1983 ➤ 57,1009 ... 1,9249: ᴿOLZ 81 (1986) 261-3 (B. M. *Weischer*); OrChr 70 (1986) 212-5 (M. *Kropp*, 7s); OrChrPer 52 (1986) 220s (O. *Ranieri*, 8); RasStEtiop 30 (1984ss) 179-186 (L. *Ricci*, 7s).

7658 **Hammerschmidt** Ernst, Six Veronika, Äthiopische Handschriften 1. ... der Staatsbibliothek Preussischer Kulturbesitz: Verzeichnis der Orientalischen Handschriften in Deutschland 20/4, 1983 ➤ 64,8252; 65,8109: ᴿSalesianum 48 (1986) 390s (A. M. *Triacca*).

7659 **Uhlig** Siegbert, Hiob LUDOLFs 'Theologia aethiopica': ÄthFor 14. Wsb 1983, Steiner. 165 p.; p. 171-337. – ᴿSalesianum 48 (1986) 409s (A. M. *Triacca*).

7660 **Ullendorff** E., A Tigrinya chrestomathy 1985 ➤ 1,9253: ᴿJRAS (1986) 264s (R. W. *Cowley*).

7661 **Wagner** Ewald, Harari-Texte in arabischer Schrift: ÄthFor 13, 1983 ➤ 1,9254: ᴿJAOS 106 (1986) 368s (F. A. *Dombrowski*).

J4 Anatolica.

7662 *Barschel* Bernd, Der Modusbestand des Hethitischen – eine Altertümlichkeit?: MüStSprW 47 (1986) 5-21.

7663 **Friedrich** Johannes †, *Kammenhuber* Annelies, Hethitisches Wörterbuch² Lfg 3-7, 1978-82 ➤ 58,a343b ... 65,8118: ᴿOrientalia 55 (1986) 340-5 (A. *Archi*).

7664 **Güterbock** H. G., *Hoffner* H. A., Hittite Dictionary [3/1, 1980 ➤ 61,a557]; 3/2: Ch 1983, Univ. Or. Inst. 128 p. 0-918086-27-3. – ᴿBO 43 (1986) 157-165 (F. *Starke*).

7665 **Hoffmann** Inge, Der Erlass Telepinus 1984 ➤ 65,8120; 1,9264*: ᴿBO 43 (1986) 747-754 (T. R. *Bryce*); JAOS 106 (1986) 570-2 (G. *Beckman*).

7666 *a) Hoffner* Harry A.,J, Studies in Hittite grammar; – *b) Laroche* Emmanuel, Hittite *nakkuš–nakuššiš*; – *c) Hawkins* J. D., *Morpurgo Davies* A., Studies in hieroglyphic Luwian; – *d) Kammenhuber* Annelies, Die hethitischen Fragmente FHL 68 und 106: ↠ 42, ᶠGÜTERBOCK H., Kaniššuwar 1986, 83-94 / 137-140 / 69-81 / 111-3.

7667 *Kammenhuber* A., Hethitische Opfertexte mit *anaḫi, aḫrušḫi* und *ḫuprušḫi* und hurrischen Sprüchen: Orientalia 55 (1986) 105-130.390-423.

7668 **Melchert** H. Craig, Studies in Hittite historical phonology: ZvgSpr Egb 32, 1984 ↠ 1,9272: ᴿSalesianum 48 (1986) 1037s (R. *Gottlieb*).

7669 *a) Neu* Erich, Zum mittelhethitischen Alter der Tutḫalija-Annalen (CTH 142); – *b) Tischler* Johann, Bemerkungen zu den hethitischen Inventartexten; – *c) Gusmani* Roberto, Die Erforschung des Karischen: ↠ 81*, ᶠOBERHUBER K., Im Bannkreis 1986, 181-192 / 261-8 / 55-67.

7670 *Oshiro* Terumasa, Some aspects of hieroglyphic Luwian [< ◐ Oriento 28 (1985) 24-36]; Orient 22 (1986) 73-84.

7671 **Puhvel** Jaan, Hittite etymological dictionary, 1 (A); 2 (E-I): Trends in Linguistics, Documentation 1, 1984 ↠ 65,8133; 1,9275: ᴿJAOS 106 (1986) 568s (H. C. *Melchert*).

7672 **Tischler** Johann, Hethitisches-Deutsches Wörterverzeichnis 1982 ↠ 63, 8263 ... 1,9278: ᴿOLZ 81 (1986) 252s (R. *Sternemann*).

7673 **Tischler** Johann, Hethitisches etymologisches Glossar Lfg. 4, 1983 ↠ 1,9279: ᴿIndogF 91 (1986) 375s (E. *Neu*).

7674 **Wagner** Heinrich, Das Hethitische vom Standpunkte der typologischen Sprachgeographie: Testi linguistici 7. Pisa 1985, Giardini. 105 p. – ᴿSalesianum 48 (1986) 502s (R. *Gottlieb*).

7675 **Weitenberg** J. J. S., Die hethitischen u-Stämme [Diss. Amst. 1984]: Publ. Spr. Lit. 52, 1984 ↠ 65,8138; 1, 9281; *f* 120: ᴿBO 43 (1986) 165-8 (G. R. *Hart*).

7676 *Zinko* Christian, Kulturkontakte der Hethiter im Lichte des Wortschatzes: ↠ 542, Kulturkontakte 1986, 27-41.

7677 **Brixhe** Claude, *Lejeune* Michel, Corpus des inscriptions paléophrygiennes: Mém. 45, 1984 ↠ 1,9258: ᴿRÉG 99 (1986) 198 (J. *Raison*); RPLH 60 (1986) 275-8 (J.-L. *Perpillou*); VDI (1983,3) 202-210 (L. S. *Bayun*, V. E. *Orel*).

7678 *Carruba* Onofrio, Testi arcaici d'Anatolia: ↠ 540*, Analisi 1985, AION-Clas 7 (1985) 157-176.

7679 **Gusmani** Roberto, Lydisches Wörterbuch, Egb. [Lfg. 2, 1982 ↠ 64,8269]; Lfg. 3. Heid 1986, Winter. p. 117-193. – ᴿBeiNam 21 (1986) 377s (R. *Schmitt*).

7680 *a) Gusmani* Roberto, Zur Lesung der lydischen Inschrift aus Pergamon; – *b) Heubeck* Alfred, Bemerkungen zur altphrygischen Inschrift T-03; – *c) Neumann* Günter, Zur Syntax der neuphrygischen Inschrift Nr. 31: Kadmos 25 (1986) 155-161 / 75ss / 79ss.

7681 *Laroche* Emmanuel, Les laryngales de l'anatolien; état des questions: CRAI (1986) 134-140.

7682 *Lebrun* R., Observations sur la terminologie du 'temps' dans les langues anatoliennes anciennes: OrLovPer 17 (1986) 51-64.

7683 *Wallace* R. W., The Lydian word for 'lion'; WeltOr 17 (1986) 61-65.

Golden Peter B., Khazar studies [Khazar vocabulary in Turkish and related documents] 1980 → 9412.

J4.8 **Armena, georgica.**

7684 *Brock* Sebastian, Armenian in Syriac script: → 11, Mem. BERBÉRIAN H., 1986, 75-80.
7685 **Diakonoff** I. M., *Starostin* S. A., Hurro-Urartaian as an Eastern Caucasian language: Mü StSprW Bei 12 NF. Mü 1986, Kitzinger. x-103 p. 3-920645-38-1.
7686 *Minassian* Martiros, Formation du participe en *-eal* en Arménien ancien: → 11, Mém. BERBERIAN H. 1986, 557-589.

———

7687 **Aḫobadze** L., Beschreibung georgischer Handschriften, Athos-Sammlung Teil I. Tbilisi 1986, Mec'niereba. 153 p.
7688 **Gwaramia** R., Die altgeorgische Übersetzung der 'Vita des Johannes CHRYSOSTOMUS': Denkmäler der altgeorgischen Literatur 8. Tbilisi 1986, Mec'niereba. 192 p.
7689 **K'urc'ikidze** C'iala. Die georgische Version des apokryphen Nikodemus-Buches. Tbilisi 1985, Mec'niereba. 92 p.

J5 **Graeca** .1 *Grammatica, onomastica, inscriptiones*

7689* [*Adrados* F. dir.] **Gangutia** Elvira, *al.*, Diccionario griego-español 2, *allá - apokoinōnētos*. M 1986, Cons. Sup. Inv. p. 155-424 [WienerSt 100, 317-9, H, *Schwabl*].
7690 **Aura Jorro** Francisco, Diccionario griego-español, Anejo I. Diccionario micénico. M 1985, Cons. Sup. Inv. Ci. 480 p. [RÉG 100, 507, J.-L. *Perpillou*].
7691 **Bernand** André, Les portes du désert; recueil des inscriptions grecques ... 1984 → 1,9295: ᴿBO 43 (1986) 98-100 (R. S. *Bagnall*); Salesianum 48 (1986) 707 (R. *Della Casa*: ma non 'Bernard').
7692 **Betz** H. D., The Greek magical papyri in translation, including the demotic spells [< *Preisendanz* K., *Henrichs* A., amplified], I. Text. Ch 1986, Univ. lviii-339 p. £34. 0-226-00444-0 [BL 87,22, T. *Rajak*].
7693 *Bingen* Jean, Épigraphie grecque; les proscynèmes de Louqsor: CdÉ 61 (1986) 330-4.
7694 **Biondi** Alessandro, Gli accenti nei papiri greci biblici: Papyrol Castroct 9, 1983 → 63,8276 ... 1, 9296: ᴿJBL 105 (1986) 549s (F. T. *Gignac*: just plausible hypothesis; full of errors like 'roughts breathy'); VT 36 (1986) 371s (W. *Horbury*).
7695 **Blass** F., *Debrunner* A., ²*Rehkopf* F. ᵀᴱPisi Giordana, Grammatica del greco del NT: GLNT Sup 3, 1982 → 1,9298: ᴿEstE 61 (1986) 123s (A. *Vargas-Machuca*).
7696 **Blümel** Wolfgang, Die aiolischen Dialekte; Phonologie und Morphologie der inschriftlichen Texte aus generativer Sicht: ZvgSpr Egb. 30, 1982 → 1,9299: ᴿClasR 100 (1986) 147s (J. H. W. *Penney*); Mnemosyne 39 (1986) 145-152 (C. J. *Ruijgh*).
7697 *Bousquet* Jean, Une nouvelle inscription trilingue à Xanthos? [partie de la fameuse stèle du Létôon en araméen, lycien, grec]: R Archéol (1986) 101-6; 4 fig.

7698 ᴱBowman A. K., al., The Oxyrhynchus papyri: a) 45: Greco-Roman Memoirs 63, 1977 → 61, a591a: ᴿBO 43 (1986) 708-711 (Jean A. Straus); b): 50, 1983 → 64,8308; 65,8160: ᴿCdÉ 61 (1986) 156-163 (G. Nachtergael).

7699 Boyaval Bernard, Conclusion provisoires sur les étiquettes de momies en langue grecque: BIFAO 86 (1986) 37-89.

7700 Boyer James L., The classification of subjunctives; a statistical study: GraceTJ 7 (1986) 3-19.

7701 Brixhe Claude, Essai sur le grec anatolien au début de notre ère: TravMèm 2/1, 1984 → 65,8162: ᴿAntClas 55 (1986) 484s (M. Leroy); ArGlotIt 69 (1984) 163-5 (R. Gusmani).

7702 Bubeník Vít, The phonological interpretation of ancient Greek; a pandialectal analysis 1984 → 1,9302: ᴿRPLH 60 (1986) 407-9 (P. Monteil).

7703 Carrez M., Morel F., Dictionnaire grec-français du Nouveai Testament³, prèf. Margot J.-C. 1985 → 1,9304; 2-8309-0039-1 / 2-85300-712-X [NTAbs 30,216].

7704 ᴱCockle Helen M., The Oxyrhynchus papyri 52; Graeco-Roman memoirs 72, 1984 → 65, 8168: ᴿClasR 100 (1986) 121-5 (W. Luppe, deutsch).

7704* Corsten Thomas, Die Inschriften von Kios: Inschriften griechischer Städte aus Kleinasien 29. Bonn 1985, Habelt. xvi-223 p.; 5 pl. – ᴿGnomon 58 (1986) 629-633 (N. Ehrhardt).

7705 Cuvigny H., Wagner G., Les ostraca grecs de Douch (O. Douch) fasc. 1 (1-57): Doc. Fouilles 24. Le Caire 1986, IFAO. xi-47 p.; viii pl. 2-7247-0036-8.

7706 Cuvigny Hélène, Nouveaux ostraca grecs du Mons Claudianus: CdÉ 61 (1986) 271-286; 2 fig.

7707 Daniel Robert W. Griechische und demotische Papyri der Universitätsbibliothek Freiburg [Br]; Mitteilungen aus der Freiburger Papyrussammlung 4 / PapTAbh 38. Bonn 1986, Habelt. viii-115 p.; XVI pl. 3-7749-2275-6.

7708 Delaunois Marcel. Le système des modes en grec classique; concentrations sémantiques et nuances contextuelles: ÉtClas 54 (1986) 335-349.

7709 Dewailly Louis-Marie, Finns det många [Is there much] hendiadys i Nya Testamentet? SvEx 51s (1986s) 50-56.

7710 Diethart Johannes M., Corpus papyrorum Raineri, IX. Griechische Texte VI. W 1984, Hollinek. 116 p.; vol. of 42 pl. 3-85119-212-5. – ᴿBO 43 (1986) 93-97 (J. Gascou).

7711 Di Marco Angelico, Il 'perfetto' nei Vangeli; grammatica ed esegesi 1981, → 64,8346: ᴿOrpheus 7,1 (1986) 226s (S. Leanza).

7712 Di Segni Leah, Hirschfeld Yizhar, Four Greek inscriptions from Hammat Gader from the reign of Anastasius [c. 505 CE]: IsrEJ 36 (1986) 251-268; 1 fig.; pl. 23-25.

7713 Donnet D., Le traité de la Construction de la phrase de Michel le SYNCELLE de Jérusalem. Bru 1982, Inst. Belge de Rome. 576 p. – ᴿÉtClas 54 (1986) 104s (A. Allard).

7714 Dubois Laurent, Actualités dialectologiques; l'aoriste de títhēmi: RPLH 60 (1986) 99s.

7715 Dubuisson Michel, La place du grec dans la société romaine; à propos d'un ouvrage récent [Kaimio J., The Romans and the Greek language 1979 → 61,a629]: RBgPg 63 (1985) 108-115.

7716 Duhoux Yves, Introduction aux dialectes grecs anciens [→ 1,9311]; problèmes et méthodes; recueil de textes traduits: Lv Inst. Linguistique Pédagogique 12. LvN 1983, Cabay. 111 p. Fb 280. – ᴿSalesianum 48 (1986) 475s (R. Bracchi).

7716* *Figueras* Pau, Three dedicatory inscriptions from the Beersheva region: SBFLA 36 (1986) 265-276; pl. B.

7717 **Found** Jim, [E]*Olson* Bruce, Basic Greek in 30 minutes a day[2]. Minneapolis 1983, Bethany. 336 p. $10 [BAR-W 13/6,53].

7717* **Gallazzi** Claudio, *Pintaudi* Rosario, Ostraka greci del Museo Egizio del Cairo (O. Cair. GPW): Papyrologica Florentina 14. F 1986, Gonnelli. xvii-175 p.; ill.

7718 **Gatier** Pierre-Louis, Inscriptions de la Jordanie 2. Région centrale (Amman-Hasban-Madaba-Main-Dhiban): BAH 114 / Inscriptions Syrie 21. P 1986, Geuthner. 254 p.; XXXVI pl., 2 maps. – [R]SBFLA 36 (1986) 386-392 (M. *Piccirillo*).

7718* *Gignac* Francis T., *a*) Morphological phenomena in the Greek papyri significant for the text and language of the New Testament: → 32, [F]FITZMYER J., CBQ 48 (1986) 499-511; – *b*) The transformation of the second aorist in koine Greek: → 123, [F]WILLIS W., BASP 20 (1985) 49-54.

7719 **Greenlee** J. Harold, A concise exegetical grammar of New Testament Greek[5rev] [[1]1953, [4]1979]. GR 1986, Eerdmans. 79 p. 0-8028-0173-0.

7720 [E]**Grönewald** Michael, *al.*, Kölner Papyri 5: Rhein. Akad. Papyrologica Coloniensia 7. Opladen 1985, Westdeutscher-V. XV-352 p.; 48 pl. DM 68. 3-531-09920-5. – [R]BO 43 (1986) 711-3 (G. *Husson*).

7721 **Harlfinger** Dieter, *al.*, Specimina sinaitica ... gr. 1983 → 64,8334 ... 1,9319: [R]JBL 105 (1986) 361s (E. J. *Epp*); TrierTZ 95 (1986) 159s (E. *Sauser*).

7722 **Harrauer** Hermann, Griechisch Texte III [Lfg. 1, 1978]; Lfg. 2., Textband, Tafelheft: Corpus Rainer 6/2. W 1985, Hollinek. 63 p. + 103-159; pl. 25-38. – [R]CdÉ 61 (1986) 343s (J. *Bingen*).

7722* *Hull* Sanford D., Exceptions to APOLLONIUS' canon [two nouns in regimen are both articular or both anarthrous] in the NT: TrinJ 7 (1986) 3-16.

7723 *Krämer* Helmut, Zur explikativen Redeweise im neutestamentlichen Griechisch: → 39, [F]GREEVEN H., Text/Ethik 1986, 212-6.

7724 **Kramer** Bärbel, *Hagedorn* Dieter, Griechische Texte der Heidelberger Papyrus-Sammlung (P. Heid IV): Veröff NF 5. Heid 1986, Winter. 290 p.; XXVIII pl. 3-533-03822-X; pa. 1-1.

7725 **Létoublon** Françoise, Il allait, pareil à la nuit; les verbes de mouvement en grec; supplétisme et aspect verbal: ÉtComm 98. P 1985, Klincksieck. 308 p.; bibliog. p. 271-280. 2-86563-085-1.

7726 *Lillo* Antonio, The Arcadian datives type *"eti, pléthi*: MüStSprW 47 (1986) 121-5.

7727 [E]**Livrea** Enrico, Studi Cercidei (P. Oxy. 1082): PapyrTAbh 37. Bonn 1986, Habelt. xviii-189 p. 3-7749-2198-9.

7728 *López-Eire* Antonio, Jónico y ático: → 76, [F]MITXELENA L. 1985, 81-93.

7729 *Lovik* Gordon H., The future participle in the Greek New Testament: Calvary B 2,1 (1986) 29-32.

7730 *Mazzoleni* Danilo, Il lavoro nell'epigrafia cristiana: → 432, Spiritualità del lavoro 1985/6, 263-271; 13 fig.

7731 **Meimaris** Yiannis E., Sacred names, saints, martyrs and Church officials in the Greek inscriptions and papyri pertaining to the Christian Church of Palestine [diss. Hebr. Univ. J 1976]: Meletemata 2. Athenai 1985, National Hellenic Research Foundation; centre for Greek and Roman Antiquity. xix-292 p.; bibliog. p. 265-275.

7732 **Mills** Watson E., New Testament Greek, an introductory grammar. Lewiston NY 1985, Mellen. $50; pa. $13. – [R]Paradigms 2,1 (1986) 43s (S. *Sheely*).

7733 *O'Neil* J.L., The semantic usage of *tyrannos* and related words: Antichthon 20 (1986) 26-40.

7734 **Palmer** L.R., The Greek language: The Great Languages [replacing *Atkinson* F. 1931] 1980 → 61,a645 ... 64,8353: [R]JHS 106 (1986) 224s (Elizabeth *Tucker*).

7735 **Petzl** G., Die Inschriften von Smyrna 1982 → 63,8312; 65,8190: [R]Mnemosyne 39 (1986) 554-6 (H.W. *Pleket*).

7736 **Powers** Ward, Learn to read the Greek NT [3]1982 → 64,8357 ... 1,9340: [R]EvQ 58 (1986) 164-6 (Ruth B. *Edwards*).

7737 *Rainer* J.M., Über die atimie in den griechischen Inschriften: ZPapEp 64 (1986) 163-172.

7738 **Rea** J.R., The Oxyrhynchus papyri: *a*) **46**, 1978 → 61,a654; 62,9025*b*: [R]BO 43 (1986) 420-423 (Jean A. *Straus*); – *b*) **51**, 1984 → 65,8194: [R]CdÉ 61 (1986) 340-3 (G. *Nachtergael*).

7739 **Ringe** Donald A., The present tenses in Greek inscriptions: diss. Yale 1984. – 86-07563. – DissA 47 (1986s) 518-A.

7739* **Robertson** A.T., *Davis* W. Hersey, A new short grammar of the Greek New Testament[10] [[1]1908]: GR 1985 = 1933, Baker. 454 p. $13 pa. [BAR-W 13/6,53].

7740 **Romilly** Jacqueline de, A short history of Greek literature [Précis 1980], [T]*Doherty* Lillían. Ch 1985, Univ. xiv-293 p.; map. 0-226-14311-2; pa. 2-0.

7741 **Rupprecht** Hans-Albert, (*Hengstl* Joachim), Sammelbuch griechischer Urkunden aus Ägypten 16/1s (Nr 12220-12500-12719) [aus Zeitschriften 1979-82]. Wsb 1985, Harrassowitz. xii-xii-324 p. DM 126 + 110. – [R]CdÉ 61 (1986) 346 (A. *Martin*); Mundus 22 (1986) 120-2 (S. *Allam*).

7742 **Sacco** G., Iscrizioni greche d'Italia. Roma 1985, Porto. [AION 45 (1985) 721, F. *Vattioni*].

7743 **Savino** Ezio, Corso di lingua greca per il ginnasio, 1. Teoria; 2. Esercizi. F 1985, Le Monnier. iv-392 p.; iii-373 p. – [R]Salesianum 48 (1986) 497s (R. *Bracchi*: innovativo).

7744 **Shackelford** David G., Major sets of New Testament Greek synonyms not concertedly treated: diss. Mid-America Baptist Sem. 202 p. 86-13701. – DissA 47 (1986s) 1373-A.

7745 *Snyman* A.H., *Cronje* J.W., Toward a new classification of the figures (*schēmata*) in the Greek New Testament: NTS 32 (1986) 113-121.

7746 **Stephens** Susan A., Yale papyri in the Beinecke rare book and manuscript library [I. 1967]; II. : AmerStPapyrol 24. Chico 1985, Scholars. xxxvii-167 p.; XV (foldout) pl. $67. – [R]CdÉ 61 (1986) 335-9 (J. *Lenaerts*)..

7746* *Stylow* Armin U., Apuntes sobre epigrafía de época flavia en Hispania: Gerión 4 (1986) 285-311.

7747 **Threatte** L., The grammar of Attic inscriptions I, 1980 → 61,a663 ... 65,8208: [R]Mnemosyne 39 (1986) 448-452 (C.J. *Ruijgh*).

7748 *Wakker* G.C., Potential and contrary-to-fact conditionals in classical Greek: Glotta 64 (1986) 222-246.

7748* **Wenham** J.W., Initiation au grec du Nouveau Testament; grammaire — exercices — vocabulaire[2rev] [Elements 1965], [T]*Amphoux* C., al.: Beauchesne Religions 17. P 1986, Beauchesne. xix-270 p. 2-7010-1129-9.

7749 *Yarko* V. N., **☉** Is unified transliteration of Greek names possible?: VDI (1986,3) 221-3.

J5.2   Voces graecae (ordine alphabetico graeco)

7750 *agápē: Nikolaus* Wolfgang, Eros und agape; zum philosophischen Begriff der Liebe: ZEvEth 30 (1986) 399-420.

7751 *O'Callaghan* José, Agápē como título de trato [honorific address, 'Your Charity'] en el siglo Vᵖ?: Aegyptus 66 (1986) 169-173.

7752 *Manessy-Guitton* Jacqueline, Grec *Aigýptios*: ⇒ 38. ᶠGRANAROLO J. 1985, 139-148.

7753 *ainéō*: *Harding* Mark, The classical rhetoric of praise and the New Testament: RefTR 45 (1986) 73-82.

7754 **Dumitriu** Anton, *Alétheia,* incercarse asupra ideii de adevăr in Grecia antică. Bucuresti 1984, Eminescu. – ᴿSTBuc 37 (1985) 442-4 (I. I. *Ivan*); VerVid 44 (1986) 129-131 (J. *Uscatescu Barrón*).

7755 *Petersen* Hans, Wörter zusammengesezt mit *amphí*: Glotta 64 (1986) 193-213.

7756 *Holmberg* Bengt, Reciprocitetsnyanser i *allēlōn*: SvEx 51s (1986s) 90-99.

7757 *apóstolos: Agnew* Francis H., The origin of the NT apostle-concept; a review of research: JBL 105 (1986) 75-96 ['seafaring' in origin ... alleged Gnostic origin of religious sense...].

7758 **Mattioli** Umberto, *Asthéneia* e *andreía;* aspetti della femminilità nella letteratura classica, biblica e cristiana antica [ricerca in rapporto con La madre dei Maccabei, di prossima pubblicazione]: Univ. Parma, Ling. Lett. Latina 9, 1983 ⇒ 65,8227: ᴿLatomus 45 (1986) 443s (Simone *Deléani*); Salesianum 48 (1986) 145 (S. *Felici*).

7759 *didaktikós: Knecht* Ingebert, Zur Geschichte des Begriffs Didaktik: ArBegG 28 (1984) 100-122.

7760 *dikaiosýnē*: **Czarniak** Władysław, **☉** Sprawiedliwość ... La justice dans l'enseignement de saint Paul et dans l'Évangile de saint Matthieu: diss. ᴰ*Langkammer* H. Lublin 1986. xxiv-266 p. – RTLv 18,546.

7761 *heautoû*: **Woodard** Roger D., Generalization of the *heaut-* nonthird person reflexive pronoun in Greek; Xenophon to the NT: diss. North Carolina, ᴰ*Tsiapera* M. Chapel Hill 1986. 158 p. 86-18409. — DissA 47 (1986s) 1717-A.

7762 **Synodinou** Katerina, **☉** *Éoika-eikós kai syngeniká*: Univ. Publ. 17, Ioannina 1981 ⇒ 63,8357: ᴿMnemosyne 39 (1986) 153-8 (G. J. *Ruijgh*).

7763 *eikosi* = quite a few: *Hooker* James T., Helen and the duration of the Trojan War [Il 20,765]: ParPass 227 (1986) 111-3.

7764 *Slings* S. R., [*h*] *eilēpha:* Glotta 64 (1986) 9-14.

7765 *López Eire* Antonio, À propos de l'attique *ōn, oûsa, ón:* Glotta 64 (1986) 213-6.

7766 *ekklēsía: Rodríguez* Isidoro, Concepto filológico de 'ecclesia' y su supervivencia en el Nuevo Testamento: Carthaginensia 2 (1986) 3-22.

7767 **Menxel** François van, *Elpis* 1983 ⇒ 64,8392 ... 1,9380: ᴿSalesianum 48 (1986) 167 (M. *Cimosa*).

7768 **Nebe** Gottfried, Hoffnung bei Paulus ... elpis: SUNT 16, 1983 ⇒ 64,5647 ... 1,5645: ᴿTZBas 42 (1986) 269s (M. *Rese*).

7769 *Klauck* Hans-Josef, Dankbar leben, dankbar sterben; *eucharisteîn* bei EPIKTET: SNTU-A 11 (1986) 195-213.

7770 *eúchomai*: **Cimosa** Mario, Il vocabolario di preghiera nel Pentateuco greco dei LXX 1985 ⇒ 1,6595: ᴿClaretianum 26 (1986) 362s (B. *Proietti*);

JStJud 17 (1986) 244s (A. *Hilhorst*: useless preliminary to an announced more serious analysis).

7771 **Reynen** Hans, Eúchesthai und seine Derivate bei Homer [253-mal] 1983 ➤ 1,9385: ᴿSalesianum 48 (1986) 1042s (R. *Bracchi*).

7772 **Dombrowski** Bruno W. W., Der Name *Europa* [< '*ārab* / *ġrb*, sunset-land] auf seinem griechischen und altsyrischen Hintergrund; ein Beitrag zur ostmediterranen Kultur- und Religionsgeschichte in frühgriechischer Zeit. Amst 1984, Hakkert. xxiv-249 p. – ᴿSalesianum 48 (1986) 201s (R. *Della Casa*).

7773 *Brenk* Frederick E., *Hierosolyma;* splendid, perverted, and tragic name of Jerusalem: ➤ 377*b*, SBL Jerusalem summaries (1986) 12s.

7774 *Kudlien* Fridolf, *Katharós* 'erneuernd / neu (geboren)': Glotta 64 (1986) 15s.

7775 **Robson** Edward A., *Kai*-configurations in the Greek New Testament; diss. Syracuse NY 1980. – 345 p. (bibliog. p. 333-345); 460 p.

7776 **Rossi** C., *Kardía;* il lessico del cuore nella Bibbia: diss. ᴰ*Ceresa-Gastaldo* A. Genova 1985. [RivB 35,86].

7777 *Cheyns* André, Recherche sur l'emploi des synonymes *êtor, kêr* et *kradíē* dans l'Iliade et l'Odyssée: RBgPg 63 (1985) 15-73.

7778 *katanýssesthai:* **Harl** Marguerite, Les origines grecques du mot et de la notion de 'componction' dans la Septante et chez ses commentateurs: RÉAug 32 (1986) 3-21.

7779 *katapatéō:* Passoni dell'Acqua Anna, L'immagine del 'calpestare' dall'A.T. ai Padri della Chiesa: Anagénnēsis 4,1 (1986) 63-129.

7780 *Vellanickal* M., [*koinōnía...*] Ecclesial communio; a biblical perspective: Bible Bhashyam 12 (1986) 182-195.

7781 **Casevitz** M., Le vocabulaire de la colonisation ... *ktízō, oikízō* 1985 ➤ 1,9396: ᴿAnzAltW 39 (1986) (F. *Lochner von Hüttenbach*); RPLH 60 (1986) 109-111 (F. *Skoda*).

7782 *Hussen* G., À propos du mot *lóchion*, 'lieu de naissance', attesté dans un papyrus d'Égypte: RPLH 80 (1986) 89-94.

7783 *martyría:* Lash Nicholas, What might martyrdom mean? [< ᶠ*Styler* G. 1981, 183-198]: ExAud 1 (1985) 14-24.

'*ēd, mártys:* **Walton** Martin, Witness in biblical scholarship; a survey of recent studies 1956-1980: Research Pamphlet 15, 1986 ➤ 977.

7785 **Basset** Louis, Les emplois périphrastiques du verbe grec *méllein* 1979 ➤ 61,a779 ... 64,8417: ᴿAntClas 55 (1986) 481s (M. *Leroy*).

7786 *metánoia:* **Gaventa** Beverly R., From Darkness to Light; aspects of conversion in the NT: OvBT. Ph 1986, Fortress. 160 p. $9 pa. 0-8006-1545-8. – ᴿExpTim 98 (1986s) 85 (I. H. *Marshall*: ignores ecclesiastical dimension); JAAR 54 (1986) 776s (E. V. *Gallagher*); TTod 43 (1986s) 307 (Sharon H. *Ringe*).

7787 **Husson** Geneviève, *Oikía;* le vocabulaire de la maison privée en Égypte d'après les papyrus grecs [diss. 1978] 1983 ➤ 64,8408 ... 1,9401: ᴿCdÉ 61 (1986) 167s (J. *Bingen*).

7788 *Karavites* Peter, Homer; *horkia, horkos:* AncW 14 (1986) 115-128.

7789 *Mastrelli* C. A., Il problema etimologico del gr. *hósios:* ArGlotIt 70 (1985) 33-37.

7790 *Posch* Sebastian, Der 'Seelenbräu[tigam', *Zuckmayer* C. 1945] anders gedeutet (Zu den Begriffen 'Pfarrer' 'Pfarrei' / 'parochus' – 'parochia') [parochia < *paroikía*, aber parochus < *paréchō*, copiarius, bartender]: ➤ 81*, ᶠOBERHUBER K., Im Bannkreis 1986, 203-211.

7791 *parrhesía:* **Fabris** Rinaldo, La virtù del coraggio; la 'franchezza' nella

Bibbia 1985 ➤ **1**,9408: [R]CC 137 (1986,4) 611s (P. *Bovati*: conscio della problematica BARR-KITTEL sensa nominarla).

7792 **Maffeis** A. M., Il gruppo semantico di *peirázō* nei vangeli sinottici: diss. Univ. Cattolica, [D]*Ghiberti* G. Milano 1985. [RivB 35,86].

7793 *Frid* Bo, A brief note on *plēn* in Roman times: SvEx 51s (1986s) 65-71.

plērōma: **Fairman** Richard G., An exegesis of 'filling' texts which refer to the doctrine of filling: diss. Grace Theol. Sem. 1986 ➤ 7363.

7795 *Hadot* P., Sur divers sens du mot *pragma* dans la tradition philosophique grecque: Concepts et catégories dans la pensée antique [ed. *Aubenque* P. (P. 1980) 285-307]: ArBegG 28 (1984) 322.

7796 *Balaban* Oded, Aristotle's theory of *prâxis:* Hermes 114 (1986) 163-172.

7797 *Adams* Douglas Q., Two Greek words for 'beard', *hypēnē* and *pōgōn:* Glotta 64 (1986) 15-20.

7798 *rís:* **Skoda** Françoise, Les noms expressifs du nez en grec ancien: ➤ 38, [F]GRANAROLO J. 1985, 149-157.

7799 *Rikov* Georgi T., *rhōmē, rhōsis:* Linguistique Balkanique 25 (1982) 81s [*Hamp* E. P., Glotta 64 (1986) 246].

7800 *Lona* Horacio E., Der Sprachgebrauch von *sarx, sarkikos* bei IGNATIUS von Antiochien: ZkT 108 (1986) 383-408.

7801 **Lys** Daniel, L'arrière-plan et les connotations vétérotestamentaires de *sarx* et de *sōma* (étude préliminaire): VT 36 (1986) 163-204.

7802 *Pronay* Andreas, *hypókeisthai* – *hypokeímenon:* ArBegG 28 (1984) 7-48.

7803 *hypokritēs:* **Amory** Frederic, Whit[en]ed sepulchres; the semantic history of hypocrisy to the High Middle Ages: RTAM 53 (1986) 5-39.

7804 **Bia** S., *Hypomonē;* storia del termine e delle sue traduzioni latine nel NT: diss. Parma 1986, [R]*Scarpat* G. [RivB 35,86].

7805 *chará:* **Morrice** W., Joy in the NT, 1984 ➤ 65,8285; **1**,9421: [R]JPsy & T 14 (1986) 81s (H. W. *Holloman*).

7806 *Nolland* John, Grace as power [*Conzelmann* H., *cháris*]: NT 28 (1986) 26-31.

7807 *Sider* Robert D., *Cháris* and derivatives in the biblical scholarship of ERASMUS: ➤ 73, [F]*Meyer* R., Diakonia 1986, 242-260.

7808 *Jonge* M. de, The earliest Christian use of *christos;* some suggestions [begin with Paul, our oldest source; then Mark...; SNTS presidential address, Trondheim Aug. 20, 1985]: NTS 32 (1986) 321-343.

7809 *chrónos:* **Finazzi** Rosa B., I termini indicanti [il greco] 'tempo' in gotico: Rendiconti Ist. Lombardo 120 (1986) 63-68.

J5.5   Cypro-Minoa [➤ T9.1-4].

7810 *Best* J. G. P., *a*) The Zakro pithos inscription, again; – *b*) Two traditions in spiral inscriptions with Linear A texts: Talanta 14s (1982s) 9-15/17-25.

7811 **Bikaki** Aliki H., Ayia Irini; the potters' marks [? Linear B]: Keos Exc. 4. Mainz 1984, von Zabern. xv-64 p.; 28 pl. DM 65. – [R]AntClas 55 (1986) 566s (R. *Laffineur*); ClasR 100 (1986) 163s (R. L. N. *Barber*).

7812 **Brown** Raymond A., Evidence for pre-Greek speech on Crete from Greek alphabetic sources. Amst 1985, Hakkert. 408 p. – [R]Salesianum 48 (1986) 199s (R. *Gottlieb*).

7813 **Chadwick** J., Corpus of Mycenean inscriptions from Knossos I (1-

1063): Incunabula graeca 88. C 1986, Univ. xv-433 p.; 1063 fig. 0-521-32022-4.

7814 **Duhoux** Yves, L'étéocrétois 1982 ➤ 63,8410 ... 65,8292: ᴿArGlotIt 69 (1984) 162s (R. *Gusmani*).

7815 *a*) *Duhoux* Yves, The teaching of orthography in Mycenaean Pylos; – *b*) *Haecker* Hans-Joachim, Neue Überlegungen zu Schriftrichtung und Textstruktur des Diskos von Phaistos: Kadmos 25 (1986) 147-154/89-96.

7816 *Godart* Louis, L'interpretazione e la traduzione dei testi minoici e micenei: ➤ 540*, Analisi 1985, AION-Clas 7 (1985) 101-115.

7817 *a*) *Hallager* Erik, *Vlasakis* Maria, New evidence of Linear A archives from Khania; – *b*) *Janda* Michael, Zur Lesung des Zeichens *22 vom Linear B; – *c*) *Masson* Olivier, Un scarabée de Cambridge à inscription chypriote syllabique: Kadmos 25 (1986) 108-118/44ss/162s; 2 fig.

7818 *Heubeck* Alfred, Mykenisch *e-e-to/ke-re-si-jo we-ke*: MüStSprW 47 (1986) 79s/81-85.

7819 **Mitford** T., *Masson* O., The syllabic inscriptions of Rantidi-Paphos 1983 ➤ 65,8302: ᴿAJA 90 (1986) 134s (B. B. *Powell*); Mnemosyne 39 (1986) 550-4 (C. J. *Ruijgh*).

7820 *a*) *Woodard* Roger D., Dialectal differences at Knossos; – *b*) *Rutkowski* Bogdan, Some script signs on Aegean Bronze-Age vessels: Kadmos 26 (1986) 49-74/22-25.

J6 Indo-Iranica.

7821 *Back* M., Mitteliranische Forschungen: OLZ 81 (1986) 437-444 [*Skalmowski* W., *Tongerloo* A. van, Middle Iranian Studies, Lv 1982/4].

7822 **Collins** John F., A primer of ecclesiastical Latin. Wsh 1983, Catholic Univ. xviii-451 p. – ᴿSalesianum 48 (1986) 471s (B. *Amata*).

7823 **Ferrua** Antonio, Note al Thesaurus linguae latinae; addenda et corrigenda (A-D). Bari 1986, Edipuglia. 168 p. Lit. 25.000. – ᴿCC 137 (1986,4) 510 (G. *Caprile*).

7824 *a*) *Knobloch* Johann, Russ. *stakan* m. 'Trinkglas' und sein altiranischer Ursprung; – *b*) *Muth* Robert, Persicos odi, puer, adparatus; zu Horaz c. I 38: ➤ 81*, ᶠOBERHUBER K., Im Bannkreis 1986, 123s/171-180.

7825 *Rossi* Adriano-V., La competenza multipla nei testi arcaici; le iscrizioni di Bisotun [sic: 'senza colonne' in farsi (oggi)]: ➤ 540*, Analisi 1985, AION-Clas 7 (1985) 191-210; 1 fig.

7826 **Turner** R. L., A comparative dictionary of the Indo-Aryan languages [1966, supplements 1969, 1971], Addenda and corrigenda, ᴱ*Wright* J. C. L 1985, Univ. School of Oriental and African Studies. xi-168 p. £16. – ᴿBSOAS 49 (1986) 592 († T. *Burrow*).

J8.1 Philologia generalis.

7827 **Ax** Wolfram, Laut, Stimme und Sprache; Studien zu drei Grundbegriffen der antiken Sprachtheorie: Hypomnemata 84. Gö 1986, Vandenhoeck & R. 290 p.

7828 *Bagnall* Roger S., The computer and classical research: EchMClas 30 (1986) 53-62.

7829 **Kwok** Jack P., A historical appraisal of the principles employed in Greek lexicography: diss. Mid-America Baptist Theol. Sem. 1986. 214 p. 86-16550. – DissA 47 (1986) 1711-A.

7830 ᴱ*Zgusta* Ladislav, Theory and method in lexicography; Western and non-Western perspectives [Acta, Urbana IL meeting 1978]. Columbia SC 1980, Hornbeam. vii-189 p. Mostly on English dictionaries.

J8.2   Grammatica comparata.

7831 *Appleyard* D. L., Agaw Cushitic and Afroasiatic; the personal pronoun revisited: JSS 31 (1986) 195-236.

7832 **Blejer** Hatte A. R., Discourse markers in early Semitic, and their reanalyses in subsequent dialects, diss. Texas, ᴿ*Lehmann* W. Austin 1986. 644 p. 86-18423. – DissA 47 (1986s) 1712s-A.

7833 *Brown* John P., *Levin* Saul, The ethnic paradigm as a pattern for nominal forms in Greek and Hebrew: GenLing 26,2 (1986) 71-105; 31 tables with etymological parallels between Greek and Hebrew, classified by suffix morpheme.

7834 ᴱ**Bynon** James, Current progress in Afro-Asiatic linguistics 1978/84 ➔ 1,756: ᴿJAOS 106 (1986) 588s (R. *Aiello*).

7835 **De Francis** John, The Chinese language [mostly script], fact and fantasy. Honolulu 1984, Univ. 330 p.; 11 fig., map. $20. – ᴿAnthropos 81 (1986) 713-5 (R. *Malek*: sets a standard replacing all similar works); JAOS 106 (1986) 405-7 (W. G. *Boltz*: 'monosyllabic myth' and others blasted).

7836 *a) Diem* Werner, Alienable und inalienable Possession im Semitischen; – *b) Daiber* Hans, Semitische Sprachen als Kulturvermittler zwischen Antike und Mittelalter; Stand und Aufgaben der Forschung: ZDMG 136 (Festgabe XXXII International Congress of Asian and North African Studies, 1986) 227-291; Eng. 283s / 292-312; Eng. 313.

7837 *Dzhaukyan* G. B., ❿ About the so-called 'glottal theory' [*Gamkrelidze* T. V., *Ivanov* V. V.] in Indo-European phonetics: VDI (1986,3) 160-5; Eng. 166.

7838 **Gai** Amikam, The non-active participles in the ancient Semitic languages: ZDMG 136 (1986) 8-14.

7839 *Knauf* Ernst A., Bemerkungen zum ägyptisch-semitischen Sprach-vergleich 3. 4. [ḥṭ']: GöMiszÄg 94 (1986) 45-48.

7840 **Knobloch** Johann, Sprache und Religion III. Weihnachten und Ostern. Heid 1986, Winter. 77 p. [BeiNam 22,318, G. *Neumann*].

7841 *Lieberman* Stephen J., *a)* Word order in the Afro-Asiatic languages: ➔ 363, Congress IX-Dl, 1985/6, 1-8; – *b)* The Afro-Asiatic background of the Semitic N-stem; towards the origins of the stem-afformatives of the Semitic and Afro-Asiatic verb: BO 43 (1986) 577-628.

7842 **Loprieno** Antonio, Das Verbalsystem im Ägyptischen und im Semi-tischen; zur Grundlegung einer Aspekttheorie: GöOrFor 4/17. Wsb 1986, Harrassowitz. xv-213 p.; bibliog. p. 191-205. 3-447-02583-2.

7843 ᴱ**Martínez Díez** Alfonso, Actualización científica en filología griega: Orientaciones metodológicas 1. M 1984, Univ. Complutense. 723 p.

7844 *Muller* Jean-Claude, Early stages of language comparison from Sassetti to Sir William Jones (1786): Kratylos 31 (1986) 1-31.

7845 *Nespital* Helmut, Zum Verhältnis vom Genus verbi, Nominativ- und Ergativ-Konstruktionen im Indoarischen aus synchroner und diachroner Sicht: MüStSprW 47 (1986) 127-158.

7846 *Petráček* Karel, Quelques travaux en russe sur le chamito-sémitique dans un contexte archéologique: ArOr 54 (1986) 284-6.

7847 **Samadi** Mahlagha, Das chwaresmische Verbum [Diss. Mainz, ᴰ*Humbach* H.]. Wsb 1986, Harrassowitz. xvi-335 p. DM 78 [Kratylos 32,178, R. *Schmitt*].

7848 **Skoda** Françoise, Le redoublement expressif, un universal linguistique 1982 → 65,8343; 1,9482: ᴿMnemosyne 39 (1986) 459-463 (G. *Mussies*).
7849 **Steiner** Richard C., Affricated Ṣade in the Semitic languages 1982 → 64,8521; 65,8344: ᴿOLZ 81 (1986) 263-5 (F. *Rundgren*: beunruhigender Titel); Orientalia 55 (1986) 478 (E. *Lipiński*).

J8.3 **Linguistica generalis.**

7849* **Armengaud** François, La pragmatique [linguistique]: Que sais-je? 2230. P 1985, PUF. 127 p. F 29. 2-13-038973-2.
7850 **Baratin** M., *Desbordes* F., L'analyse linguistique dans l'Antiquité classique, I. Les théories 1981 → 65,8351: ᴿRTAM 53 (1986) 193 (P. *Swiggers*).
7851 **Brun** Jean, L'homme et le langage. P 1985, PUF. 120 p. – ᴿÉtudes 364 (1986) 685-7 (R. *Habachi*).
7852 ᴱ**Coulmas** Florian, Direct and indirect speech: Trends in Linguistics, StMon 31. B/NY 1986, Mouton de Gruyter. ix-370 p. 3-11-010599-3 / NY 0-89925-176-5.
7853 **Delfgaauw** Bernhard, Filosofie van de grammatica I. Weesp 1984, Wereldvenster. 201 p. ƒ 39,50. – ᴿNedTTs 40 (1986) 182s (G. *Nuchelmans*).
7854 **Dirven** René, *al.* [all Dutch/Flemish], The scene of linguistic action and its perspectivization by speak, talk, say and tell: Pragmatics & Beyond 3/6. Amst 1982, Benjamins. 186 p. ƒ 53. – ᴿRBgPg 62 (1984) 570s (J, *Buysschaert*).
7855 **Fowler** Roger, Linguistic criticism: Opus. Ox 1986, UP. 190 p. 0-19-219125-X; pa. 11-1.
7856 **Herbert** Robert K., Language universals, markedness theory, and natural phonetic processes: Trends in Linguistics StMon 25. B/NY 1986, Mouton de Gruyter. x-299 p. 3-11-010973-5 / NY 0-89925-123-4.
7857 **Hervey** Sándor, Semiotic perspectives. L 1982, Allen & U. 273 p. £16. – ᴿRelStR 12 (1986) 280 (D. *Jobling*).
7858 **Hock** Hans H., Principles of historical linguistics: Trends in Linguistics StMon 34. B/NY 1986, Mouton de Gruyter. xiii-722 p. – 3-11-010600-0/ NY 0-89925-220-6.
7859 *Jong* A. E. de, Revolutie in de taalfilosofie? De kritiek van AUSTIN en HEIDEGGER op de descriptieve taal: Bijdragen 47 (1986) 352-366; Eng. 367 [a word is not a sign; language is creative not representative...].
7860 **Kempson** Ruth, Teoría semántica, ᵀ*Cerdá* Ramón. Barc 1982, Teide. ix-227 p. – ᴿSalesianum 48 (1986) 1033 (R. *Della Casa*).
7861 **Matthews** P. H., Morfología; introducción a la teoría de la estructura de la palabra [Morphology 1974 → 61,a968 < Inflectional morphology], ᵀᴱ*Monroy Casas* Rafael. M 1980, Paraninfo. – ᴿSalesianum 48 (1986) 487s (R. *Della Casa*).
7862 *Murtonen* A., On structural growth in languages: AbrNahr 24 (1986) 139-154.
7863 *Newmeyer* Frederick J., Has there been a 'Chomskyan revolution' in linguistics? [Yes]: Language 62,1 (Baltimore 1986) 1-18.
7864 **Nöth** Winfried, Handbuch der Semiotik. Stu 1985, Metzler. xii-560 p. DM 78. 3-476-00580-1. [Bijdragen 47,467].
7865 ᴱ**Plank** Frans, Relational typology: Trends in Linguistics StMon 28. B/NY 1985, Mouton. xii-443 p. 3-11-009591-2 / NY 0-89925-086-6.
7866 **Pollock** John L., Language and thought. Princeton 1982, Univ. xii-297 p. £21.70. – ᴿHeythJ 27 (1986) 205-7 (E. *Nemeszeghy*).

7867 **Ramat** Paolo, Typologie linguistique: Linguistique nouvelle. P 1985, PUF. 139 p.; bibliog. p. 127-139.
7868 **Robins** R. H., Breve historia de la lingüística, [T]*Alcaraz Varo* E. M 1984, Paraninfo. 242 p. – [R]Salesianum 48 (1986) 793s (R. *Della Casa*).
7869 *Robins* R. H., The evolution of historical linguistics: JRAS (1986) 5-20.
7870 [E]**Sebeok** Thomas A., Encyclopedic dictionary of semiotics: Approaches to Semiotics 73. B/NY 1986, Mouton de Gruyter. [I. A-M; II. N-Z] III. Bibliog. 452 p. 3-11-010559-4 / NY 0-89925-137-4.
7871 **Slama Cazacu** Tatiana, Linguistique appliquée; une introduction: 'CLUC' 6. Brescia 1984, La Scuola. 340 p. – [R]Salesianum 48 (1986) 498 (R. *Della Casa*).
7872 **Szemerényi** Oswald, Richtungen der modernen Sprachwissenschaft [I. 1916-1950: 1971]; II. Die fünfziger Jahre (1950-1960): Sprachwissenschaftliche Studienbücher 1982 ⇒ 64,8555: [R]Emerita 57 (1986) 161s (F. R. *Adrados*); IndogF 91 (1986) 326-334 (P. *Kosta*).
7873 **Villar** Francisco, Ergatividad, acusatividad y género en la familia lingüística indoeuropea 1983 ⇒ 64,8558; 1,9509: [R]IndogF 91 (1986) 344-7 (K. H. *Schmidt*).

J8.4 *Origines artis scribendi* – The Origin of Writing.

7874 **Cardona** Giorgio R., Storia universale della Scrittura. Mi 1986, Mondadori. – [R]BbbOr 28 (1986) 185-196 (F. *Sardini*).
7875 **Escolar** Hipólito, [⇒ 752] Historia del Libro: Fundación G. Sánchez Ruipérez. M 1984, Pirámide. 524 p. – [R]CiuD 199 (1986) 183s (B. *Justel*).
7876 **Földes Papp** Károly, Dai graffiti all'alfabeto; la storia della scrittura. Mi 1985, Jaca. 222 p.: 216 fig. + color. pl. – [R]Salesianum 48 (1986) 480s (R. *Della Casa*).
7877 **Hamilton** Gordon J., The development of the early alphabet: diss. Harvard 1985. 361 p. 86-02286. – DissA 47 (1986s) 277-A.
7878 *Helck* Wolfgang, Gedanken zum Ursprung der ägyptischen Schrift: ⇒ 77, [F]MOKHTAR G. 1985, I, 395-408.
7879 *Helms* Svend, First words in Palestine [Um Hammad near Deir'alla straight west of Jawa; both have stamp-seal impressions 'on the way' to written speech, introduced from outside Palestine]: ILN Arch 3025 = 274, 7052 (1986) p. 66s.
7880 *Kaufman* Stephen A., The pitfalls of typology; on the early history of the alphabet: HUCA 57 (1986) 1-14; chart.
7881 **Kooy** G. van der, Early North-West Semitic script traditions, an archaeological study of the linear alphabetic scripts up to c. 500 B.C.; ink and argillary: diss. Leiden 1986, [D]*Hoftijzer* J. – Phoenix EOL 32,2 (1986) 11s.
7882 *Lodolini* Elio, L'origine degli archivi: Archeo 18 (1986) 18-23; ill.
7883 **Mallon** Jean, De l'écriture (publ. 1937-81) 1982 ⇒ 64,200: [R]Emerita 54 (1986) 167s (S. *Mariner Bigorra*).
7884 *Mazal* Otto, Paläographie und Paläotypie; zur Geschichte der Schrift im Zeitalter der Inkunabeln: Bibliothek des Buchwesens 8. Stu 1984, Hiersemann. viii-404 p. – [R]Salesianum 48 (1986) 979s (P. T. *Stella*).
7885 *O'Connor* M. P., Writing systems and native speaker analyses: ⇒ 392, SBL Seminars 1986, 536-543.
7886 *Puech* Émile, Origine de l'alphabet: RB 93 (1986) 161-213; 11 fig.; pl. II-III; à suivre (non pas 1986).
7886* **Sas** Benjamin, ⊕ *Rešît ha-alpabet* ... The genesis of the alphabet and its

development in the second millennium B.C. TA 1985, auct. xviii-346 p.; 29 fig.; 52 pl. [KirSef 61,77].

7887 *Schmandt-Besserat* Denise, a) An ancient [Sumerian] token system; the precursor to numerals and writing: Archaeology 39,6 (1986) 32-39; color. ill. - b) Clay symbols for data storage in the VIII Millennium B.C.: → 89, FPUGLESE S. 1985, 149-154.

7888 *Vacek* Jaroslav, Progress in the analysis of the Indus script: ArOr 54 (1986) 92-94.

7888* *Vycichl* Werner, L'écriture hiéroglyphique et son modèle sumérien; étude comparative: → 18, Mém. DAUMAS F., II (1986) 603-611.

J9.1   *Analysis linguistica loquelae de Deo* – **God-talk.**

7889 **Amen** Constancio C., Antony FLEW [Falsification 1951] and Christian theism; a critique: diss. DJordan M. Dallas 1986. 285 p. 86-11500. - DissA 47 (1986s) 931-A.

7890 *Armour* Leslie, Experience and the concept of God [*Flew* A., *Braithwaite* R.: what does religious language really say?]: ScEspr 38 (1986) 343-360.

7891 *Bader* Günter, 'Theologia poetica'; Begriff und Aufgabe: ZTK 83 (1986) 188-237.

7892 **Bagus** Lorenz, Religious language according to Ian Thomas RAMSEY in the light of St. Thomas AQUINAS: diss. Pont. Univ. Gregoriana, DHuber C. R 1986. 397 p. No 3371, xiv-274 p. - RTLv 18,571.

7893 **Bourg** Dominique, Transcendence et discours; essai sur la nomination paradoxale de Dieu: CogF 132, 1985 → 1,9534; F 85: RTS 47 (1986) 343s (G. H. *Tavard*).

7894 **Brown** Frank B., Transfiguration; poetic metaphor and the language of religious belief 1983 → 64,1169 ... 1,9535: RJRel 66 (1986) 105s (T. E. *Helm*).

7895 **Brun** Jean, L'homme et le language [... Jér Qoh Job]. P 1985, PUF. 254 p. - RRTPhil 118 (1986) 101s (M. *Cornu*).

7896 *Busch* Eberhard, God is God; the meaning of a controversial formula and the fundamental problem of speaking about God: PrincSemB 7 (1986) 101-113.

7896* *Cady* Linell E., Hermeneutics and tradition; the role of the past in jurisprudence and theology: HarvTR 79 (1986) 439-463.

7897 **Christ** Franz, Menschlich von Gott reden; das Problem des Anthropomorphismus bei SCHLEIERMACHER: ÖkT 10. Gütersloh 1982, Mohn. 299 p. DM 58. - RTLZ 111 (1986) 383-6 (T. *Jorgensen*).

7898 **Clendenin** Daniel B., Theological method in Jacques ELLUL: diss. Drew. Madison NJ 1985. - RelStR 13,187.

7899 *Di Marco* Angelico, Linguaggio tecnico e linguaggio su Dio: Laurentianum 27 (1986) 350-373.

7899* **Eliade** Mircea, Briser le toit de la maison; la créativité et ses symboles: Essais 229. P 1986, Gallimard. 258 p. F 110. 2-07-070600-1.

7900 **Geffré** C., Le christianisme au risque de l'interprétation: CogF 120, 1983 → 64,170 ...1,9557: RNRT 108 (1986) 914s (J. *Javaux*); Salesianum 48 (1986) 440s (C. *Bissoli*: equilibrato e arrischiato).

7901 **Geffré** C., El cristianismo ante el riesgo de la interpretación 1984 → 65,8413; 1,9558: RSalT 73 (1985) 334 (A. *Raffo*).

7902 **Gerhart** Mary, *Russell* Allan, Metaphoric process; the creation of scientific and religious understanding 1984 → 1,9560: RHorizons 13 (1986)

440s (J. V. *Apczynski*); JRel 66 (1986) 96s (F. B. *Brown*); RelSt 22 (1986) 282s (B. *Hebblethwaite*); TorJT 2 (1986) 297-9 (D. *Wiebe*).

7903 **Gervasoni** Maurizio, La 'poetica' nell'ermeneutica teologica di Paul RICŒUR, 1985 ➤ 1,9562: ᴿCC 137 (1986,1) 507s (P. *Cardoletti*); HumBr 41 (1986) 303 (B. *Belletti*).

7905 **Gómez Caffarena** José, Lenguaje sobre Dios: El problema de Dios hoy 9. M 1985, Fund. S. María. 77 p. – ᴿMiscCom 44 (1986) 228s (*ipse*).

7906 **Happel** Stephen, COLERIDGE's religious imagination [...religious language is a kind of poetic language]: Studies in Eng. Lit. Salzburg 1983, Inst. Anglistik. xii-943 p. – ᴿHeythJ 27 (1986) 97-99 (D. *Jasper*).

7907 **Heering** H. J., God ter sprake; reflecties over de taal van de religie. Meppel 1984, Boom. 192 p. *f* 29. – ᴿCollatV1 16 (1986) 244s (J. *Lammens*); GerefTTs 86 (1986) 53s (H. M. *Vroom*).

7908 *a)* **Heimbrock** Hans-Günter, Life without language? What religious education has to learn from the experiences of the hearing-impaired; – *b)* *Slee* Nicola, The development of religious thinking; some linguistic considerations: BrJRelEd 9 (1986s) 78-83 / 60-69.

7909 **Holland** Sherrill R. ᴵᴵᴵ, 'Fear not'; a study of Jacques ELLUL on the speaking and silent God: diss. Union [?NY] 1986. – RelStR 13,188.

7910 **Jeanrond** Werner G., Text und Interpretation als Kategorien theologischen Denkens [Diss. Ch 1984 ➤ 65,8422]: HermUnT 23. Tü 1986, Mohr. xi-163 p.; bibliog. p. 153-8. 3-16-145101-5.

7911 **Jennings** Theodore W.ᴶ, Beyond theism; a grammar of God-language. NY 1985, Oxford-UP. xiv-272 p. $30. – ᴿJTS 37 (1986) 685-7 (D. *Cupitt*); RelStR 12 (1986) 269 (W. *VanderMarck*: ALTIZER–influenced; his 'pre-meta-explicative logology' not yet fully at home in linguisticality).

7912 **Jones** Hugh O. † 1985, Die Logik theologischer Perspektiven; eine sprach-analytische Untersuchung [Hab.-Diss.]; ᴱ*Ritschl* D. Gö 1985, Vandenhoeck & R. 246 p. – ᴿRHPR 66 (1986) 474s (G. *Siegwalt*).

7913 **Knuth** Hans Christian, Verstehen und Erfahrung, hermeneutische Beiträge zur empirischen Theologie. Hannover 1986, Lutherhaus. 140 p. DM 19,80. [TLZ 112,456].

7914 **Kraml** Hans, Die Rede von Gott sprachkritisch rekonstruiert aus Sentenzenkommentaren: InnsbThSt 133, 1984 ➤ 1,9585: ᴿTR 82 (1986) 140-2 (L. *Hödl*).

7915 *a)* *Lane* Belden C., Language, metaphor, and pastoral theology; – *b)* *Bennett* Robert A., The power of language in worship: TTod 43 (1986s) 487-502 / 546-551 [472-486, *Edgerton* W.].

7916 **McFague** Sallie, Metaphorical theology; models of God in religious language 1982 ➤ 64,1219; 65,8432: ᴿHeythJ 27 (1986) 226s (Margaret M. *Yee*); RelStR 12 (1986) 204s (June *O'Connor*).

7917 **McQueen** Kenneth, Speech act theory and the roles of religious language: diss. McGill, ᴿ*McLelland* J. C. Montréal 1986. 296 p. – RTLv 18,574.

7918 **Malherbe** Jean-François, Le langage théologique à l'âge de la science; lecture de Jean LADRIÈRE: CogF 129, 1985 ➤ 1,9595; F 99; 2-204-02273-X: ᴿBrotéria 123 (1986) 230 (I. *Ribeiro da Silva*); ÉglT 17 (1986) 114-6 (B. *Garceau*); ÉTRel 61 (1986) 469s (J.-C. *Deroche*); RelStR 12 (1986) 270 (W. *VanderMarck*: the author was Ladrière's assistant); TS 47 (1986) 152s (R. *Schreiter*).

7919 *Martin* Terence J.ᴶ, The social rationality of theological discourse: Horizons 13 (1986) 23-42.

7920 *Melchiorre* Virgilio, Dire Dio, oggi: RasT 27 (1986) 410-430.

7921 *a)* *Meschonnic* H., Dieu absent, Dieu présent dans le langage; – *b)*

Gandillac M. de, Omninominabile Innominabile; – *c) Dragonetti* R., L'image et l'irreprésentable dans l'écriture de Saint AUGUSTIN: ➤ 16*, Mém. COPPIETERS D. 1985, 357-392 / 339-356 / 393-414.

7922 ᴱ**Michel** Marc, La théologie à l'épreuve de la vérité 1984 ➤ 65,347: ᴿGregorianum 67 (1986) 770s (J. *Dupuis*).

7923 *Molnár* Amedeo, Zur hermeneutischen Problematik des Glaubensdisputs in Hussitentum: ComViat 29 (1986) 1-14.

7924 **Monk** Robert C., *al.*, Exploring religious meaning³ʳᵉᵛ [¹1973, ²1980]. ENJ 1986, Prentice-Hall. xiii-253 p. $27 pa. [TDig 34,68].

7925 **Mtega** Norbert W., Analogy and theological language in the Summa contra gentiles; a textual survey of the concept of analogy and its theological application by St. Thomas AQUINAS [diss. Urbaniana, ᴰ*Mondin* B., R 1981]: EurHS 23/241. Fra 1984, Lang. 207 p. Fs 46. – ᴿRelStR 12 (1986) 270 (W. *VanderMarck*: unprintable).

7926 **Müller** Klaus, Thomas von AQUINS Theorie und Praxis der Analogie; der Streit um das rechte Vorurteil und die Analyse einer aufschlussreichen Diskrepanz in der 'Summa Theologiae' [diss. Gregoriana, R 1983, ᴰ*Huber* C.]: RgStTheol 29. Fra 1983, Lang. 368 p. Fs 74. – ᴿRelStR 12 (1986) 279 (W. *VanderMarck*: despite defects, rightly reduces analogy to just another aspect of linguistics).

7927 ᴱ**Noppen** J. P. Van, Theolinguistics: Studiereeks 8, 1981 ➤ 63,372 ... 65,8443: ᴿRTLv 17 (1986) 95s (E. *Brito*).

7928 *a) Pannenberg* Wolfhart, Wissenschaft und Existenz aus der Sicht des Theologen; – *b) Gadamer* Hans-Georg, Freundschaft und Selbsterkenntnis: ➤ 520, ᴱ*Bremer* D., Wissenschaft 1984/5, 87-94 / 25-33.

7929 **Pastor** Félix A., La lógica de lo inefable; una teoría teológica sobre el lenguaje del teismo cristiano [< EstE 1982-5]. R 1986, Pont Univ. Gregoriana. 329 p. Lit. 30.000. – ᴿSalesianum 48 (1986) 734 (L. A. *Gallo*).

7930 **Poque** Suzanne, Le langage symbolique dans la prédication d'AUGUSTIN d'Hippone; images héroïques [diss. Sorbonne 1982]. P 1984, Ét. Aug. xxx-410 p.; viii-310 p. – ᴿSalesianum 48 (1986) 402s (B. *Amata*).

7931 **Ramshaw-Schmidt** Gail, Christ in sacred speech. Ph 1986, Fortress. xi-130 p. $10. – ᴿCurrTM 13 (1986) 375s (J. C. *Rochelle*: lyric praise of a lyric hermeneutic; a tapestry of images; creative speech leaping into the abyss of meaning; breakage of the symbol as Yes-No-Yes movement in liturgy; if you still don't dig it, sign up for his course which will use her book as its text).

7932 *Raurell* Frederic, Risc d'insignificància i d'idolatria en el llenguatge religiós: ➤ 97, ᶠRUBÍ B. de = EstFranc 37 (1986) 1033-1062.

7933 **Rike** Jennifer L., Being and mystery; analogy and its linguistic implications in the thought of Karl RAHNER: diss. Chicago Divinity School, 1986. – RelStR 13,187.

Ruether Rosemary R., Sexism and God-talk 1984 ➤ 7104.

7934 *a) Ryden* Edmund, AQUINAS on the metaphorical expression of theological truth; – *b) Hill* William J., Rescuing theism; a bridge between Aquinas and HEIDEGGER: HeythJ 27 (1986) 409-419 / 377-393.

7935 *Santiago Guervós* Luis E. de, Contribución de la teología medieval a la concepción actual [GADAMER H.] del lenguaje en la hermenéutica: CiTom 113 (1986) 119-126.

7936 **Schüller** Bruno, Wholly human; essays on the theory and language of morality ['Man does not reflect on reality through the medium of language; instead, the language that a person has learned stipulates in advance .. what he will hold to be real and true'], ᵀ*Heinegg* Peter. Dublin/Wsh 1986,

Gill & M. / Georgetown Univ. 224 p. – ᴿRelStR 12 (1986) 275 (D. *Nelson*).

7937 *Schweizer* Harald, Anmerkungen zur Sprachverwendung in der Kirche: TüTQ 166 (1986) 209-223.

7938 **Scott** Nathan A.ᴶ, The poetics of belief; studies in COLERIDGE, ARNOLD, PATER, SANTAYANA, STEVENS, and HEIDEGGER. Chapel Hill 1985, NC Univ. 198 p. $24 [JAAR 55, 181-3, J. H. *Evans*].

7939 *Siegwart* Geo, Die Mehrdeutigkeit der Aussage 'Gott existiert': TPhil 61 (1986) 396-403.

7940 **Sonnet** Jean-Pierre, La parole consacrée; théorie des actes de langage; linguistique de l'énonciation et parole de la foi [→ 65,8457 ... 1,9625]; préf. *Chapelle* A., note exégétique *Radermakers* Jean: Parole consacrée et exégèse juive, BCILL 25. LvN 1984, Cabay. vi-197 p. Fb 520. – ᴿRelStR 12 (1986) 265 (W. *Vander Marck*).

7941 *Sonnet* Jean-Pierre, Les langages de la foi, à propos de [*Ladrière* J. 1984]: NRT 108 (1986) 404-419.

7942 **Soskice** Janet M., Metaphor and religious language 1985 → 1,9626: ᴿHeythJ 27 (1986) 225s (B. *Hebblethwaite*: astonishingly good, far ahead of the field); NBlackf 67 (1986) 545s (F. *Kerr*); TLond 39 (1986) 317-9 (K. *Surin*); TS 47 (1985) 523-6 (R. F. *Scuka*).

7943 *Staal* Frits, The sound of religion: Numen 33 (1986) 33-64. 185-224.

7944 *Talstra* Eep drs., Nieuwe namen voor de Naam ? Onze taal is het woord nog niet: GerefTTs 86 (1986) 65-79.

7945 a) *Toinet* Paul, Hermenéutica y teología; – b) *Elders* Leo J., El problema de la hermenéutica; – c) *Inciarte* Fernando, Hermenéutica y sistemas filosóficos; – d) *Ziegenaus* Antón, La superación de la 'diferencia hermenéutica', tarea de la teología: → 366, Biblia y hermenéutica 1985/6, 103-118 / 131-143 / 89-101 / 223-239.

7946 *Verlato* Micaela, Sprachinhalt und Interpretation; Bedeutung und Sinn in SCHLEIERMACHERS Auseinandersetzung mit der hermeneutischen Tradition: ZTK 83 (1986) 39-84.

7946* *Vogüé* A. de, Twenty-five years of Benedictine hermeneutics; an examination of conscience: AmBenR 36 (Atchison 1985) 402-452.

7947 **Wallace** Mark I., World of the text; theological hermeneutics in Karl BARTH and Paul RICOEUR: diss. ᴰ*Gilkey* L. Ch 1986. 295 p. – RTLv 18,540.

7948 **Weber** Hermann, An der Grenze der Sprache; religiöse Dimension der Sprache und biblisch-christliche Metaphorik im Werk Ingeborg BACHMANNS: kath. Diss. ᴰ*Hünermann* P. Tübingen 1986. 308 p. – RTLv 18,589.

J9.2 *Hermeneutica paratheologica* – **wider linguistic analysis.**

7949 *Åkerberg* Hans, Three components of interpretation; a psychological contribution to the question of hermeneutics: ST 40 (1986) 17-44.

7950 *Alonso Schökel* Luis, Una nota hermenéutica de QUEVEDO: Cuadernos de Poética 4,10 (Santo Domingo 1986) 7-11.

7951 **Auboyer** Jeannine, *al.*, Handbuch der Formen- und Stilkunde: Asien, ᵀ*Stoll* E., *Brandt* J. J. Stu 1980, Kohlhammer. 607 p., DM 69. – ᴿOLZ 81 (1986) 12-14 (Marlene *Njammasch*).

7952 **Ball** Milner S., Lying down together; law, metaphor, and theology. Madison 1986; Univ. Wisconsin. 198 p. $24 [JAAR 55, 131, M. C. *Taylor*].

7953 **Barthes** Roland, Essais critiques: I: Tel Quel, 1964 = 1984, 278 p.; 2-02005809-X. – [II? Points/Lit. 127] 1981; 280 p. – III. L'obvie et l'obtus: Tel Quel. 1982; 286 p.; 2-02-006248-8. – IV. Le bruissement de la langue, 1984; 417 p.; 2-02-006931-8. – [? V.] L'aventure sémiologique, 1985; 363 p. 2-02-008936-X. P, Seuil.

7954 *Bauw* Christine De, La réflexion ouverte et l'être religieux; lecture de Paul RICŒUR: RSPT 70 (1986) 197-215; Eng. 215.

7955 **Bellino** Francesco, La praticità della ragione ermeneutica; ragione e morale in GADAMER. Bari 1984, Levante. 188 p. Lit. 17.000. – ᴿCC 137 (1986,3) 538s (P. *Vanzan*).

7956 *Berger* Adriana, Cultural hermeneutics; the concept of imagination in the phenomenological approaches of Henry CORBIN and Mircea ELIADE: JRel 66 (1986) 141-156.

7957 **Bleicher** Josef, L'ermeneutica contemporanea [1980]. Bo 1986, Mulino. 344 p. Lit. 25.000. – ᴿHumBr 41 (1986) 960 (G. *Sansonnetti*).

7958 **Bouchard** Guy, Le procès de la métaphore: Brèches. Hurtubise HMH 1984. – ᴿLavalTP 42 (1986) 117-9 (A. *Carrier*).

7959 ᴱ**Branson** Mark L., *Padilla* C. René, Conflict and context; hermeneutics in the Americas; a report on the Context and Hermeneutics in the Americas conference [Tlaycapan Méx., Nov. 24-29, 1983]. GR 1986, Eerdmans. xii-323 p. 0-8028-0172-2.

7960 *Ciamarelli* F., Herméneutique et créativité; à propos de Paul RICŒUR: Revue Philosophique de Louvain 83 (1985) 410-412 [RSPT 70,168].

7961 **Cooper** J.C., Symbolism, the universal language. Wellingborough, Northamptonshire 1984 = 1982, Aquarian. 128 p. 0-85030-279-X.

7962 *Di Benedetto* Vincenzo, Nel laboratorio di Omero, I: Formularità e invenzione; II. Corrispondenze a distanza [*Perry* M. ...]: RivFgIC 114 (1986) 257-285 / 385-410.

7963 **Dillistone** F. W., The power of symbols. L 1986, SCM. viii-246 p. £7.50. 0-334-02261-4. – ᴿExpTim 98 (1986s) 217s (J. L. *Houlden*: also on Bible; author of Christianity and symbolism 1955).

7964 **Eco** Umberto, A theory of semiotics, ᵀwith *Osmond-Smith* David, 1979, xi-354 p. 0-253-35955-4. Semiotics and the philosophy of language [his ownᵀ] 1986, ix-242 p.; 0-253-35168-5; pa. 20398-8: Advances in Semiotics. Bloomington, Univ. Indiana.

7965 **Ellul** Jacques, The humiliation of the Word 1985 ⮕ 1, 9549: ᴿExpTim 98 (1986s) 148s (D. W. *Hardy*); TLond 39 (1986) 389s (P. *Avis*: disapproving).

7966 *Ellul* Jacques, *a)* La culture de l'oubli: FoiV 85, (1986) 13-22; – *b)* Sur la dialectique [< Interpretative essays 1981], ᵀ*Charcosset* Jean-Pierre: BCentProt 37,8 (1985) 3-26.

7967 *a) Ferrer Santos* Urbano, Algunas claves de la hermenéutica de GADAMER; – *b) Landazuri* Carlos O. de, Hermenéutica 'versus' semiótica en la pragmática transcendental de la acción de Karl-Otto APEL: ⮕ 366, Hermenéutica 1985/6, 173-191 / 193-221.

7968 **Gadamer** Hans Georg, Verità e metodo (1960; 1972), ᵀ*Vattimo* Gianni³ (¹1983). Mi 1986, Bompiani. xlvii-582 p.

7969 *Gadamer* Hans-Georg, L'homme et le langage / Qu'est-ce que la vérité? [< KlSchr 1976], ᵀ*Schouwey* Jacques: RTPhil 118 (1986) 11-20 / 21-34.

7970 **Greisch** Jean, L'âge herméneutique de la raison: CogF 133. P 1985, Cerf. 275 p. F 129. 2-204-02357-4 [ActuBbg 23,100]. – ᴿETL 62 (1986) 199 (E. *Brito*); NRT 108 (1986) 296 (J. *Javaux*).

7971 **Guirlanda** Paul, Faith, knowledge and community; a GADAMERIAN inquiry: diss. Graduate Theol. Union, Berkeley 1985. – RTLv 18,539.

7972 **Hagège** Claude, L'homme de paroles; contribution linguistique aux sciences humaines. P 1985, Fayard. 314 p. – ᴿRHPR 66 (1986) 468-470 (G. *Vahanian*).

7973 **Hekman** Susan J., Hermeneutics and the sociology of knowledge [*Gadamer* ...]. ND 1986, Univ. xii-224 p. $30 [RelStR 13,326, M. *Taylor*].

7974 **Howard** Roy J., Three faces of hermeneutics; an introduction to current theories of understanding. Berkeley, Univ. California. – ᴿHeythJ 27 (1986) 359 (Janet M. *Soskice*).

7975 **Ingbretsen** David A., Understanding and explanation; RICŒUR's critique of GADAMER: diss. notre Dame, 1986, ᴰ*Crosson* F. 300 p. 87-02206. – DissA 47 (1986s) 3773-A.

7975* *Ingendahl* Werner, Interpretation als Lebenspraxis; Modi der Erfahrung von und mit Literatur: ZSemiot 8 (1986) 331-344.

7976 **Jervolino** Domenico, Il Cogito e l'ermeneutica; la questione del soggetto in RICŒUR; préf. Ricœur & *Geraets* Théodore F., 1984 ➤ 1,9578: – ᴿRTPhil 118 (1986) 216 (P.-L. *Dubied*).

7977 **Kearney** R., Poétique du possible; phénoménologie herméneutique de la figuration: Bibl. Archives de Ph 44, 1984, ➤ 1,9581: ᴿNRT 108 (1986) 295 (P. *Gilbert*).

7978 *Keller* Joseph, The redemption of language: Encounter 47 (Indianapolis 1986) 159-168.

7979 **Klemm** David E., Hermeneutical inquiry; I. The interpretation of texts; II. The interpretation of existence: AAR StRel 43s. Atlanta 1986, Scholars. xiii-288 p.; viii-323 p.; bibliog. p. 273-323. 1-55540-032-9 [4-5]; pa. 5-3.

7980 **Klemm** David E., The hermeneutical theory of Paul RICŒUR; a constructive analysis. Cranbury NJ 1983, Bucknell Univ. 184 p. $22.50. – ᴿJRel 66 (1986) 95s (Mary *Gerhart*).

7981 **Knapp** Steven, *Michaels* Walter B., Against Theory 2; sentence meaning, hermeneutics. CHH. Berkeley 1986, Graduate Theological Union. 51 p.

7982 **Ladrière** Jean, L'articulation du sens 1984 ➤ 1,9587: ᴿSR 15 (1986) 106-8 (J.-P. *Rouleau*); TR 82 (1986) 142s (J. *Schmid*).

7983 *Ljung* Inger, Bildspräksanalys, språkfilosofi och litteraturvetenskap: DanTTs 49 (1986) 81-95 [< ZIT].

7984 *Loughlin* Gerard, Myths, signs and significations: TLond 39 (1986) 268-275.

7985 **Lundin** Roger, *al.*, The responsibility of hermeneutics 1985 ➤ 1,1325: ᴿTS 47 (1986) 741s (T. W. *Tilley*).

7986 *Meijers* S., Onze cultuurcrisis en onze hermeneutische opdracht: TRef 29 (Woerden 1986) 161-187 [< ZIT].

7987 **Nida** E. A., *al.*, Style and discourse 1983 ➤ 64,1892; 1,9603: ᴿJBL 105 (1986) 170s (M. *Silva*); JStNT 28 (1986) 121-3 (B. C. *Hewitt*: curiously regards 'red' and 'fast' as 'abstracts'); TLZ 112 (1987) 336s (W. *Schenk*).

7988 **Nkeramihigo** Théoneste, L'homme et la transcendance selon Paul RICŒUR. P 1984, Lethielleux. 299 p. – ᴿScEspr 38 (1986) 414-6 (J. *Naud*).

7989 **Ong** Walter J., Oralità e scrittura; le tecnologie della parola [1982 ➤ 64,1229], ᵀ*Calanchi* Alessandra, ᴱ*Loretelli* Rosamaria. Bo 1986, Mulino. 249 p. Lit. 18.000. – ᴿSMSR 52 (1986) 323s (G. Å. *Samoná*).

7990 **Penzo** Giorgio, Il comprendere in K. JASPERS e il problema dell'ermeneutica 1985 ➤ 1,9615: ᴿLetture 41 (1986) 667s (Annamaria *Pertoldi*); RasT 27 (1986) 94s (M. *Castellana*).

7991 **Rentsch** Thomas, HEIDEGGER und WITTGENSTEIN; Existenzial- und Sprachanalysen zu den Grundlagen philosophischer Anthropologie. Stu 1985, Klein-Cotta. xxi-243 p. [TPhil 62, 118-120, H. *Ollig*].

7992 **Ricœur** Paul, Il conflitto delle interpretazioni (Le conflit): Di fronte e attraverso 20. Mi 1986, Jaca. 518 p.

7993 RICŒUR Paul, La semantica dell'azione [1977],T; introd. *Pieretti* Antonio. Mi 1986, Jaca. 173 p. Lit. 19.000. – RCC 137 (1986,3) 307s (G. *Lorizio*).

7994 *Rioux* Bertrand, Philosophie du discours chez RICŒUR et le fondement du langage: LavalTP 42 (1986) 15-21.

7995 **Ross** J. F., Portraying analogy. C 1981, Univ. 244 p. – RJAAR 54 (1986) 360-2 (R. P. *Scharlemann*).

7996 *Scilironi* Carlo, L'ermeneutica dei simboli di P. RICŒUR: Sapienza 39 (1986) 315-329.

7997 **Scott** Edward A., On the way to ontology; the philosophy of language in the hermeneutic phenomenology of Paul RICŒUR: diss. Duquesne, DKeyes C. Pittsburgh 1985. 301 p. 86-14138. – DissA 47 (1986s) 1753-A.

7998 **Secretan** Philibert, L'analogie: Que sais-je? 2165. P 1984, PUF. 128 p. – RRThom 86 (1986) 690-3 (P.-C. *Courtes*).

7999 *Stahmer* Harold M., 'Sprachbriefe' und 'Sprachdenken'; Franz RO-SENZWEIG und Eugen ROSENSTOCK-HUESSY: BTZ 3 (1986) 307-329.

8000 **Wagner** Roy, Symbols that stand for themselves. Ch 1986, Univ. xiii-150 p. $36; pa. $11 [RelStR 13,52, J. *Holt*].

J9.3 *Critica reactionis lectoris* – **Reader-response criticism.**

8001 *a) Duranti* Alessandro, The audience as co-author; an introduction; – *b) Goodwin* Charles, Audience diversity, participation and interpretation: Text 6 (1986) 239-247 / 283-316.

8002 **Iser** Wolfgang, Der Akt des Lesens; Theorie ästhetischer Wirkung2rev (11976): Uni-Tb 636. Mü 1984, Fink. viii-358 p. 3-7705-1390-8.

J9.4 **Structuralism; deconstruction.**

8003 **Bolívar Botía** Antonio, El estructuralismo de Lévi-Strauss a Derrida: Historia de la filosofia 32. M 1985, Cincel. 216 p. 84-7046-401-9.

Greenwood David, Structuralism and the biblical text: Religion and Reason 32, 1985 → 929.

8005 **Harland** Richard, Superstructuralism: diss. New South Wales Univ. 1986. – DissA 47 (1986s) 3412-A.

8006 **Lategan** B. C., *Vorster* W. S., Text and reality; aspects of reference in biblical texts 1985 → 1,1323: RExpTim 97 (1985s) 280 (Margaret *Davies*: Vorster defends his structuralism from Mk 4 and 2 Sam 12; Lategan broadens and clarifies).

8007 **Berman** Arnold J., From the new criticism to deconstruction; the reception of structuralism and post-structuralism: diss. NYU 1986, DMeisel P. 561 p. 87-06719. – DissA 47 (1986s) 4387-A.

8008 **Flores** Ralph, The rhetoric of doubtful authority; deconstructive readings of self-questioning narratives, St. Augustine to Faulkner. Ithaca NY 1984, Cornell Univ. 175 p. $17.50. – RRelStR 12 (1986) 280 (D. *Jobling*: successful).

8009 **Merrell** Floyd, Deconstruction reframed. West Lafayette IN 1985, Purdue Univ. xi-261 p. $18.50. – ᴿRelStR 12 (1986) 280 (D. *Jobling*: it is fun to unthink all thinking, but the loss of faith in reason provokes fear).

J9.6 *Analysis narrationis* – Narrative-analysis.

8009* **Bar-Ephrat** Shimon, ❸ The art of narration in the Bible²ʳᵉᵛ (¹1979). J 1984.
8010 **Berlin** Adele, Poetics and interpretation of biblical narrative 1983 ➤ 64,1226 ... 1,1352: ᴿJBL 105 (1986) 125s (E. M. *Good*).
8011 ᴱ**Coats** George W., Saga ... narrative forms: JStOT Sup 35, 1985 ➤ 1,274: ᴿÉTRel 61 (1986) 280 (D. *Lys*).
8012 **Höffken** P., Elemente kommunikativer Didaktik in frühjüdischer und rabbinischer Literatur: Religionspädagogik 1. Essen 1986, Blaue Eule. 536 p. DM 56 [ZAW 99, 143, O. *Kaiser*].
8013 **Holzberg** Niklas, Der antike Roman; eine Einführung: Artemis Einführungen 25. Mü 1986, Artemis. 135 p.; bibliog. p. 125-135. 3-7608-1325-9.
8014 **Marchese** Angelo, L'officina del racconto; semiotica della narratività: Studio 105. Mi 1983, Mondadori. vi-246 p. 88-0022830-4. Lit. 16.000.
8015 **Ricœur** Paul, Time and narrative 1 [1983 ➤ 65,8451a], ᵀ*McLaughlin* Kathleen, *Pellauer* David, 1984 ➤ 65,8451b: ᴿRelStR 12 (1986) 247-251 (Morny *Joy*) & 251-4 (S. D. *Kepnes*).
8016 **Ricœur** Paul, Tempo e racconto I: Di fronte e attraverso 165. Mi 1986, Jaca. 340 p. Lit. 32.000 [RasT 28,536].
8016* **Rodríguez Adrados** Francisco, Historia de la fábula greco-latina [I] II. La fábula en época imperial romana y medieval. M 1979, Univ. Complutense. [p. 1-379; 381-727] 654 p. – ᴿGnomon 58 (1986) 193-8 (M. *Nøjgaard*).
8017 **Sternberg** Meir, The poetics of biblical narrative; ideological literature and the drama of reading. Bloomington 1985, Indiana Univ. xiv-580 p. – ᴿBiblica 67 (1986) 437-9 (L. *Alonso Schökel*); SBFLA 36 (1986) 409-411 (A. *Niccacci*).

J9.8 *Theologia narrativa* – Story-theology.

8018 **Bausch** William J., Storytelling; imagination and faith 1984 ➤ 65,1164; 1,1350: ᴿSpTod 38 (1986) 85s (V. P. *Branick* cannot accept 'Stories are always more important than facts').
8019 *Grimes* Ronald L., Of words the speaker, of deeds the doer [on narrative theology, in its infancy; most useful summary is *Goldberg* M., Theology and narrative, Nv 1982, Abingdon ➤ 65,8414]: JRel 66 (1986) 1-17.
8020 *Hardmeier* Christof, Old Testament exegesis and linguistic narrative: Poetics, International Review for the Theory of Literature 15 (Amst 1986) 89-109.
8021 **Hoffman** John C., Law, freedom, and story; the role of narrative in therapy, society, and faith. Waterloo ON 1986, W. Laurier Univ. x-163 p. 0-88920-185-4.
8022 **McCarthy** Carmel, *Riley* William, The Old Testament short story; explorations into narrative spirituality: Message of Biblical Spirituality 7. Wilmington 1986, Glazier. 229 p. $13; pa. $9. [JBL 105,753].
8023 **McKeating** Henry, The Bible – a story? L c. 1985, 'CEM'. 28 p. 0-905022-81-5. – ᴿExpTim 97 (1985s) 255 [C. S. *Rodd*: to introduce

children to the Bible; the author does not seem to have clarified his objectives].

8024 **Navone** John, Gospel love; a narrative theology: Good News Studies 12, 1984 ➤ 65,7670; **1**,8780: ᴿCBQ 48 (1986) 147s (J. M. *Reese*); RRel 45 (1986) 314s (T. J. *Tekippe*).

8025 **Navone** John, L'amore evangelico; una teologia narrativa. R 1986, Borla. 204 p. Lit. 12.000. – ᴿCC 137 (1986,3) 543s (Z. *Alszeghy*).

8026 **Navone** J., *Cooper* T., Narratori della Parola [1981 ➤ 63,1362]. Casale Monferrato 1986, Piemme. 327 p. [RivB 35,391].

Song Choan Seng, Tell us our names; story theology 1984 ➤ 6918.

8027 **Tilley** Terrence W., Story theology: Theology and Life 12, 1985 ➤ **1**,1369: ᴿHorizons 13 (1986) 181s (W. L. *Collinge*, also on AICHELE G., who will doubtless resent being thus 'framed'); TS 47 (1986) 186s (J. F. *Haught*).

(IV.) Apocrypha, Qumran, Judaismus

K1 **Pseudepigrapha** [= catholicis 'apocrypha'] .1 *VT, generalia.*

8027* ᴱ**Barnstone** Willis, The other Bible [... pseudepigrapha] 1984 ➤ 65,8464: ᴿChH 55 (1986) 251 (H. *Partrick*: nothing is included which ever had a real chance of being 'bible').

8028 **Bibeln**; tillägg till Gamla testamentet; de apokrypha oder deutero-kanoniska skrifterna: (Svenska) Bibelkommissionen. Sto 1986, Liber. 530 p.; 2 maps. Sk 170. 91-3809373-1. – [BL 87,43, G. W. *Anderson*].

8029 [**Caquot** A.] La littérature intertestamentaire: colloque 1983/5 ➤ **1**,458: ᴿRHE 81 (1986) 732s (A.-M. *Denis*); TüTQ 166 (1986) 232s (M. *Reiser*).

8030 ᴱ**Charlesworth** James H., The Old Testament pseudepigrapha, I. 1983 ➤ 64,253 ... **1**,9649; II. 1985 ➤ **1**,272: ᴿGregorianum 67 (1986) 537-542 (G. L. *Prato*, 1s); JSS 31 (1986) 87-89 (F. F. *Bruce*, 2); Month 248 (1986) 214s (J. A. *Crampsey*, 2).

8031 **Charlesworth** J. H., The OT Pseudepigrapha and the New Testament: SNTS Mon 54, 1985 ➤ **1**,9650: ᴿJStJud 17 (1986) 241s (M. de *Jonge*: far less meritorious than his 2-volume Pseudepigrapha).

8032 **Collins** John J., Between Athens and Jerusalem 1983 ➤ 64,8592 ... **1**,9652: ᴿJRel 66 (1986) 98s (S. *Cohen*).

8033 ᴱ**Díez Macho** Alejandro, Apócrifos del AT I-IV, 1982-4 ➤ 64,259 ... **1**,281.9653: ᴿBiblica 67 (1986) 133 (T. *Franxman*, 1-4); CiuD 199 (1986) 122s (J. L. del *Valle*, 1); Gerión 4 (1986) 370s (G. *Fernández*, 1-4); Judaica 41 (1985) 241s (M. *Petit*, 2-3); RechSR 74 (1986) 131-3 (A. *Paul*, 1); ScripTPamp 18 (1986) 267s (M. *Guerra*, 1); 268s (S. *Ausin*, 2s).

8034 *Grabar* Biserka, La prosa medievale croata, con speciale riferimento agli Apocrifi: Acme 39 (1986) 139-149.

8035 **McNamara** Martin, Intertestamental literature: OTMessage 23, 1983 ➤ 64,8597; **1**,9657: ᴿDivThom 88 (1985) 147s (G. *Testa*); EstE 61 (1986) 121s (A. *Vargas-Machuca*); LavalTP 42 (1986) 282s (P.-H. *Poirier*); TLZ 111 (1986) 19-21 (G. *Delling*).

8036 **Noll** S. F., The intertestamental period, a study guide: IBR Bibliographic Study Guides. Madison WI 1985, Theological Students Fellowship. vii-92 p. $3.50 [NTAbs 30,378].

8037 ᴱ**Sparks** H. F. D., The apocryphal Old Testament 1984 ➤ 65,8477; **1**,9569: ᴿCurrTM 13 (1986) 252 (E. *Krentz*: half as many items as

CHARLESWORTH, otherwise compares favorably); WestTJ 48 (1986) 373-5 (M. *Silva*).

8038 ᴱ**Stone** Michael E., Jewish writings of the Second Temple period: CompRNT 2/2, 1984 ➤ 65,311; **1**,9660: ᴿAntonianum 61 (1986) 183s (Z. I. *Herman*); Biblica 67 (1986) 135s (T. *Franxman*); CBQ 48 (1986) 160s (D. J. *Harrington*); Interpretation 40 (1986) 194s (J. C. *VanderKam*); JAAR 54 (1986) 362s (J. R. *Mueller*); JBL 105 (1986) 720-3 (A. J. *Saldarini*); JJS 37 (1986) 100s (S. *Brock*: more coherent than CompRer I); RevSR 60 (1986) 115s (B. *Renaud*); RQum 12,47 (1986) 441-6 (F. *García Martínez*); TS 47 (1986) 512-5 (J. A. *Fitzmyer*); TZBas 42 (1986) 433-5 (K. *Seybold*: three nagging problems in relation to canon).

8039 *Stone* Michael E., Categorization and classification of the Apocrypha and Pseudepigrapha: AbrNahr 24 (1986) 167-177.

8040 **Weidinger** E., Die Apokryphen; verborgene Bücher der Bibel. Aschaffenburg 1985, Pattloch. 572 p. DM 36. [SNTU-A 11,252].

κ1.2   Henoch.

8041 **Black** M., The book of Enoch 1985 ➤ **1**,9665: ᴿCrNSt 7 (1986) 603-6 (A.-M. *Denis*); JStJud 17 (1986) 86-92 (M. A. *Knibb*: not reliable); RelStR 12 (1986) 174 (J. H. *Charlesworth*).

8042 **Dean-Otting** Mary, Heavenly journeys; a study of the motif in Hellenistic Jewish literature: JudUm 8, 1984 ➤ 65,4666.8521; **1**,9666: ᴿNedTTs 40 (1986) 339s (P. W. van der *Horst*, also on *Himmelfarb* M., Tours of Hell 1985).

8043 ᴱ**Mosshammer** Alden A., Georgii Syncelli ecloga chronographica [using new manuscripts since *Dindorf* W. 1829]. Lp 1984, Teubner. xxxvii-507 p. DM 150. – ᴿJStJud 17 (1986) 262s (A. *Hilhorst*: the chronicle contains fragments of 1 Enoch and Jubilees, and references to PHILO and JOSEPHUS).

8044 [*Ödeberg* Hugo] **Hofmann** Helmut, Das sogenannte hebräische Henochbuch (3 Henoch): BoBB 58, 1984 ➤ 65,8486; **1**,9668: ᴿTR 82 (1986) 25s (Margarete *Schlüter*).

8045 **Rubinkiewicz** R., Die Eschatologie von Henoch 9-11 und das NT 1984 ➤ 65,8491, **1**,9673: ᴿBL (1986) 134s (M. A. *Knibb*); TLZ 111 (1986) 498-500 (F. *Dexinger*).

8046 *Sacchi* Paolo, Henochgestalt, Henochliteratur, ᵀ*Schäferdiek* K.: ➤ 597, TRE 15 (1986) 42-54.

8047 *a*) *Sacchi* Paolo, Testi palestinesi anteriori al 200 a.C. ['Vigilanti' e 'Astronomia' di Enoc]; – *b*) *Loprieno* Antonio, Il modello egiziano nei testi della letteratura intertestamentaria: ➤ 390, RivB 34 (1986) 183-203; Eng. 203s / 205-231; Eng. 232.

8048 **VanderKam** J. C., Enoch and the growth of an apocalyptic tradition: CBQ Mon 16, 1984 ➤ 65,8493; **1**,9576: ᴿRechSR 74 (1986) 135-8 (A. *Paul*); TLZ 111 (1986) 585s (F. *Dexinger*).

κ1.3   Testamenta.

8049 *Hilgert* Earle, 'By the sea of Jamnia', TNaph 6:1: ➤ 81, Mém. NIKIPROWETZKY V., Hellenica 1986, 245-255.

8050 **Hollander** H. W., *Jonge* M. de, The Testaments of the Twelve Patriarchs; a commentary: StVTPseud 6, 1985 ➤ **1**,9679: ᴿJStJud 17 (1986) 252-5 (A. *Hilhorst*).

8051 **Hultgård** A., L'eschatologie des Testaments des Douze Patriarches II, 1982 ➤ 63,8550 ... 1,9680: ᴿHenoch 8 (1986) 96s (A. *Moda*); RechSR 74 (1986) 134s (A. *Paul*).

8052 *Jonge* M. de, *a*) The future of Israel in the Testaments of the Twelve Patriarchs: JStJud 17 (1986) 196-211; – *b*) Two Messiahs in the Testaments of the Twelve Patriarchs?: ➤ 59, ᶠLEBRAM J., Tradition 1986, 150-162.

8053 *a*) *Kolenkow* Anitra B., The literary genre 'testament'; – *b*) *Collins* John J., The testamentary literature in recent scholarship: ➤ 255, Early Judaism 1986, 259-267 / 268-285.

8054 **Nordheim** E. von, Die Lehre der Alten II. Das Testament als Literaturgattung im AT und im alten Verderen Orient: ALHJ 18. Leiden 1985, Brill. vi-164 p. *f* 60. 90-04-07313-2 [BL 87,71s M.A. *Knibb*].

8055 **Schmidt** Francis, Le Testament grec d'Abraham; introduction, édition critique des deux recensions grecques, traduction [diss. ᴰ*Philonenko* M.]: TStAJ 11. Tü 1986, Mohr. ix-199 p. DM 98. 3-16-144949-5 [BL 87,117s C. *Hayward*].

8056 *Slingerland* Dixon, The nature of *Nomos* (law) within the Testament of the Twelve Patriarchs: JBL 105 (1986) 39-48.

K1.4 3-4 Esdras; 3-4 Maccabaei.

8058 *Gardner* Anne E., The purpose and date of 1 Esdras: JJS 37 (1986) 18-25; similarities to 2 Mcb, possibly circulating during the crisis itself.

8059 *Kraft* Robert, A., Towards assessing the Latin text of '5 Ezra' [prefixed to Vlg 4 Esdras]; the 'Christian' connection: ➤ 110, ᶠSTENDAHL K. = HarvTR 79 (1986) 158-169.

8060 **Muñoz León** Domingo, La Vorlage (¿griega?) de la Versión Armenia del 4⁰ de Esdras; un ejemplo de traducción targumizante: EstB 44 (1986) 25-100.

8061 **Talshir** Zipora, ⊕ First Esdras, origin and translation: diss. J 1984. 552 p. – KirSef 59 (1985) 309.

8062 *Zimmermann* Frank, The language, the date, and the portrayal of the Messiah in IV Ezra: HebSt 26 (1985) 203-218 [OTAbs 10,193].

8063 *Henten* Jan W. van, Datierung und Herkunft des Vierten Makkabäerbuches: ➤ 59, ᶠLEBRAM J., Tradition 1986, 136-149.

K1.5 Salomonis Psalmi (*et Odae epochae christianae*).

8064 *Caquot* André, Les Hasmonéens, les Romains et Hérode; observations sur Ps.Sal. 17: ➤ 81, Mém. NIKIPROWETZKY V., Hellenica 1986, 213-8.

8065 **Trafton** Joseph L., The Syriac version of the Psalms of Solomon 1985 ➤ 1,9694: ᴿScotJT 39 (1986) 566-8 (A. *Salvesen*).

8066 *Trafton* Joseph L., The Psalms of Solomon; new light from the Syriac version?: JBL 105 (1986) 227-237.

8067 *Drijvers* Han J.W., *a*) Die Oden Salomos und die Polemik mit den Markioniten im syrischen Christentum [< Symposium 1976, OrChrAn 205 (1978) 39-55]; – *b*) Kerygma und Logos in den Oden Salomos ... 23 [< ᶠ*Andresen* C. 1979, 153-172]; – *c*) The 19th Ode of Solomon; its interpretation and place in Syrian Christianity [< JTS 31 (1980) 337-355]: ➤ 153, East of Antioch 1984, VII / VIII / IX (original page-numbering).

8068 *Franzmann* Majella, 'Wipe the harlotry from your faces'; a brief note on Ode of Solomon 13,3: ZNW 77 (1986) 282s.

8069 **Lattke** Michael, Die Oden Salomos in ihrer Bedeutung für Neues Testament und Gnosis [I-II, 1979s ➤ 61,b125 ... 64,8648], III. Bibliographie 1799-1984; Beitrag *Franzmann* M.: OBO 25. FrS/Gö 1986, Univ./VR. xxxiii-478 p. Fs 125. 3-7278-0 [209-X (I-II)] 358-4 / 3-525-53 [330-6] 699-2.

8070 **Winterhalter** K., The odes of Solomon; original Christianity revealed: Spiritual Perspectives. St. Paul 1985, Llewellyn. xxx-275 p. $10 pa. 0-87542-875-4 [NTAbs 30,381].

K1.6 Jubilaea, Adam, Aḥiqar, Asenet.

8071 *a) Harrington* Daniel J., Palestinian adaptations of biblical narratives and prophecies 1. The Bible rewritten (narratives) [Jubilees, Temple Scroll, Pseudo-Philo, Josephus Antiquities]; – *b) Horgan* Maurya P., The Bible explained (prophecies) [18 Qumran pesharim]: ➤ 255, ^E*Kraft* R., Early Judaism 1986, 239-247-258.

8072 **Schwarz** Eberhard, [Jub 22,16 daté 175-164] Identität durch Abgrenzung; Abgrenzungsprozesse im Israël im 2. vorchristlichen Jahrhundert und ihre traditionsgeschichtlichen Voraussetzungen [Diss. 1980: EurHS 23/162 ➤ 62,9326; 64,8652]: Fra 1981, Lang. 231 p. 3-8204-5922-7: ^RÉTRel 61 (1986) 283s (T. *Römer*).

8073 **Lindenberger** James M., The Aramaic proverbs of Ahiqar [^D1974] 1983 ➤ 64,8662 ... 1,9703: ^RArOr 54 (1986) 193 (O. *Klima*); JBL 105 (1986) 114s (J. S. *Kselman*); JNES 45 (1986) 151 (S. A. *Kaufman*).

8075 **Chesnutt** Randall D., Conversion in Joseph and Aseneth; its nature, function, and relation to contemporaneous paradigms of conversion and initiation: diss. Duke, ^D*Charlesworth* J. Durham NC 1986. 412 p. 87-06829. – DissA 47 (1986s) 1418-A.

K1.7 Apocalypses, ascensiones.

8076 *Bauckham* Richard, The apocalypses in the new [*Charlesworth* 1983] Pseudepigrapha: JStNT 26 (1986) 97-117.

8077 **Acerbi** Antonio, Serra lignea; studi sulla fortuna della Ascensione di Isaia 1984 ➤ 65,8523: ^ROrpheus 7 (1986) 474-7 (Clementina *Mazzucco*); RB 93 (1986) 464 (M.-J. *Pierre*).

8078 *a) Himmelfarb* Martha, The experience of the visionary and genre in the Ascension of Isaiah 6-11 and the Apocalypse of Paul; – *b) Osiek* Carolyn, The genre and function of the Shepherd of Hermas: Semeia 36 (1986) 97-111 / 113-121.

8079 **Leemhuis** F., *al.*, The Arabic text of the Apocalypse of Baruch [with translation, also of Syriac in parallel]. Leiden 1986, Brill. viii-154. *f*76. 90-04-07608-5 [BL 87, 109, J. W. *Rogerson*].

8080 **Mueller** James R., The 'Apocryphon of Ezekiel', a critical study of pseudepigraphic fragments: diss. Duke, ^D*Charlesworth* J. Durham NC 1986, 292 p. 87-07332. – Diss A 47 (1986s) 4415-A.

8081 ^E**Pesce** M., Isaia, il Diletto e la Chiesa 1981/3 ➤ 64,412.8672 ... 1,9714*: ^RHenoch 8 (1986) 260s (P. G. *Borbone*); JBL 105 (1986) 545s (J. J. *Collins*); RivStoLR 22 (1986) 532-9 (L. *Cirillo*); TR 82 (1986) 280s (E. *Mühlenberg*).

8082 **Philonenko-Sayar** Belkis, *Philonenko* Marc, L'Apocalypse d'Abraham: Semitica 31. P 1981, Maisonneuve. 119 p. – ^RJStJud 17 (1986) 264-7 (H. E. *Gaylord*: survives only in Russian manuscripts, but with indications of earlier translation from Greek into Old Church Slavonic).

8082* *Murphy* Frederick J., Sapiential elements in the Syriac apocalypse of Baruch: JQR 76 (1985s) 311-327.

K2.1   Philo judaeus alexandrinus.

8083 *a*) *Alexandre* Manuel, Rhetorical argumentation as an exegetical technique in Philo of Alexandria; – *b*) *Lévy* Carlos, Le 'scepticisme' de Philon d'Alexandrie; une influence de la Nouvelle Académie?; – *c*) *Neusner* Jacob, Philo and the Mishnah; the matter of the soul after death; – *d*) *Runia* David T., Redrawing the map of early Middle Platonism; some comments on the Philonic evidence: ➤ 81, Mém. NIKIPROWETZKY V., Hellenica 1986, 13-27 / 29-41 / 53-59 / 85-104.

8084 *Alexandre* Manuel[J], A elaboração de uma Chreia no código hermenêutico de Fílon de Alexandria: Euphrosyne 14 (1986) 77-87.

8085 **Amir** Yehoshua [= *Neumark* Hermann; 11 Aufsätze], Die hellenistische Gestalt des Judentums bei Philon 1983 ➤ 64,8681...1,9722: [R]JBL 105 (1986) 178s (E. J. *Epp*: tit. pp.).

8086 *Belletti* Bruno, Alcune precisazioni sulla teologia di Filone Alessandrino: StPatav 33 (1986) 385-393.

8087 **Berchman** Robert M., From Philo to Origen; Middle Platonism in transition: BrownJudSt 69, 1984 ➤ 65,8534: [R]JTS 37 (1986) 557-9 (A. *Meredith*).

8088 *Boccaccini* G., Il concetto di memoria in Filone Alessandrino: Annali dell'Istituto di Filosofia 6 (F 1984) 1-19 [Judaica 41,64].

8089 *Carny* Pinhas, ❻ Rhetorical figures in Philo's allegory: Te'uda 3 (1983) 251-9; Eng. VIII.

8090 **Cazeaux** J., L'épée du Logos et le soleil du midi [Philon, De cherubim, De Abrahamo]: Coll. 13/2, 1983 ➤ 64,8688; 1,9729: 184 p. F 120. 2-903264-03-1. – [R]BL (1986) 114 (C. J. A. *Hickling*); RB 93 (1986) 465-7 (M.-J. *Pierre*).

8090* **Cazeaux** J., La trame... Philon 1983 ➤ 64,8689...1,9731: [R]RÉJ 145 (1986) 141-4 (Madeleine *Petit*).

8091 *Daubercies* Pierre, Reflexions sur la maturité humaine [... Philon]: EsprV 96 (1986) 120-8.

8092 *Davies* P. S., The meaning of Philo's text about the gilded shields [dedicated by Pilate to Tiberius in Jerusalem, Gai. 299s]: JTS 37 (1986) 109-114.

8092* *a*) *Goetschel* Roland, Philon et le judaïsme hellénistique au miroir de Nachman Krochmal [19ᵉ siècle]; – *b*) *Neher* André, Les références à Philon d'Alexandrie dans l'œuvre du Rav HANAZIR, disciple du Rav KOOK (Qol HaNevoua, 1970): ➤ 81, Mém. NIKIPROWETZKY V., Hellenica 1986, 371-383 / 385-390.

8093 *a*) *Laporte* John, The ages of life in Philo of Alexandria; – *b*) *Tobin* Thomas H., Tradition and interpretation in Philo's portrait of the patriarch Joseph; – *c*) *Hilgert* Earle, A survey of previous scholarship on Philo's De Josepho: ➤ 392, SBL Seminars 1986, 278-290 / 271-7 / 262-270.

8094 **Martín** Pablo J., Filón de Alejandría y la génesis de la cultura occidental: Oriente-Occidente. Buenos Aires 1986, Depalma. xii-168 p. [ZAW 99, 293, J. A. *Soggin*]. 950-14-0326-2.

8094* [T]*Mazzarelli* Claudio, Filone di Alessandria, Le origini del male [I cherubini... Caino... Immut. Dio], note *Radice* Roberto: Classici del Pensiero. Mi 1984, Rusconi. 540 p. [KirSef 61,27].

8095 **Méasson** Anita,   Du char ailé de Zeus à l'Arche d'Alliance; images et mythes platoniciens chez Philon d'Alexandrie [diss. Lyon 1982]. P 1986, Études Augustiniennes.   466 p.; bibliog. p. 415-424.   2-85121-072-6.

8096 *Ménard* J.-E., Philon d'Alexandrie: ➤ 578, Catholicisme XI, 49 (1986) 202-8.

8097 **Mendelson** Alan,   Secular education in Philo 1982 ➤ 63,8610 ... 1,9739: ᴿJTS 37 (1986) 208s (F. *Siegert*, deutsch); Mnemosyne 39 (1986) 493-5 (D. T. *Runia*).

8097* *Murphy* Frederick J.,   Divine plan, human plan; a structuring theme in Pseudo-Philo [Ant. Bib.]: JQR 77 (1986s) 5-14.

8098 **Radice** R.,   Filone, bibliografia 1983 ➤ 64,852 ... 1,9741:   ᴿRÉJ 145 (1986) 189s (Mireille *Hadas-Lebelle*: ✪ omis).

8099 *a) Reinhartz* Adele,   The meaning of *nomos* in Philo's Exposition of the Law; – *b) Westerholm* Stephen,   *Torah, nomos,* and law; a question of 'meaning':   SR 15 (1986) 337-345 / 327-336.

8100 *Rokéah* David, ✪ Philo of Alexandria, the Midrash and the primitive Halacha: Tarbiz 55 (1985s) 433-9; Eng. IIIs.

8101 *Runia* D. T.,   How to read Philo [a massive presence: 2632 pages of text; bibliographies, commentaries; Philo's aims, writings, audience; two examples, hebdomad and God-most-high]: NedTTs 40 (1986) 185-198.

8102 *Runia* David T.,   Mosaic and Platonist exegesis; Philo on 'finding' and 'refinding': VigChr 40 (1986) 209-217.

8103 *Wiefel* Wolfgang,   Das dritte Buch über 'Moses'; Anmerkungen zum Quaestionenwerk des Philo von Alexandrien: TLZ 111 (1986) 865-882.

8104 **Winston** David, *Dillon* John, Two treatises of Philo ... Gig., Deus immut.: BrownJudS 25, 1983 ➤ 64,8711; 65,8555:   ᴿJBL 105 (1986) 352-4 (T. H. *Tobin*: excellent); JQR 76 (1985s) 379-381 (D. M. *Hay*).

к2.4   *Evangelia apocrypha* – **Apocryphal Gospels.**

8105 ᴱ**Beylot** Robert,   Testamentum Domini éthiopien 1984 ➤ 1,9753:   ᴿJSS 31 (1986) 292-5 (R. W. *Cowley*); RHR 203 (1986) 438s (P. *Nautin*).

8106 *Bischoff* Bernhard,   Der Brief des Hohenpriesters Annas an den Philosophen Seneca — eine jüdisch-apologetische Missionsschrift (iv. Jht.?): ➤ 134, Anecdota 1984 ... [RHE 81,226].

8107 ᴱ**Bocciolini Palagi** L.,   Epistolario apocrifo di Seneca e San Paolo: Biblioteca Patristica 5.   F 1985, Nardini.   174 p. Lit. 20.000. – ᴿBenedictina 33 (1986) 576s (Clara *Burini*).

8109 **Cameron** Ron,   Sayings [of Jesus] traditions in the Apocryphon of James [diss. Harvard, ᴰ*Koester* H.]: HarvTheolSt 34, 1984 ➤ 64,8571: ᴿJBL 105 (1986) 741-3 (C. W. *Hedrick*: helps to 'legitimize the Church's favorite gospel, John').

8110 *Fiaccadori* Gianfranco,   Cristo sull'Eufrate [accettò l'invito di Abgar: amuleto ZPapEp 48 (1982) 149-170, *Maltomini* F.]: ParPass 226 (1986) 59-63.

8111 **Insoleza** A.,   Apocryphon Johannis; storia degli studi: diss. ᴰ*Sfameni-Gasparro* G. Messina 1985. [RivB 35,86].

8112 ᴱ**Klijn** A. F. J.,   Apokriefen van het Nieuwe Testament I, 1984 ➤ 65,8561: ᴿBijdragen 47 (1986) 70 (B. J. *Koet*); Streven 53 (1985s) 466 (P. *Beentjes*).

8113 *Lichtenberger* Hermann [*Hanhart* Robert], Apokryphen NT [AT]: ➤ 587, EvKL 1 (1986) 207-211 [203-7].

K2.6 Acta apocrypha apostolorum.

8114 **Bovon** F., *al.*, Les Actes apocryphes des Apôtres 1981 ➤ 62,311 ... **1,9764**: ᴿIstina 31 (1986) 331-3 (B. *Dupuy*).

8115 **D'Arenzio** L. A., Gli Atti apocrifi di Giovanni e le tradizioni gnostiche ed encratite: diss. ᴰ*Sfameni Gasparro* G. Messina 1985. [RivB 35,86].

8116 **Festugière** André-J., Les Actes apocryphes de Jean et de Thomas 1983 ➤ 64,8745 ... **1,9765**: ᴿLavalTP 42 (1986) 123s (P.-H. *Poirier*); OrChr 70 (1986) 196s (W. *Gessel*).

8117 ᴱ**Leloir** Louis, Écrits apocryphes sur les Apôtres; traduction de l'édition arménienne de Venise, I. Pierre, Paul, André, Jacques, Jean: CChrApocr 3. Turnhout 1986, Brepols. xxx-418 p. 2-503-41031-6; pa. 2-4. – ᴿÉTL 62 (1986) 432s (F. *Neirynck*).

8118 ᴱ**Junod** Eric, *Kaestli* Jean-D., Acta Iohannis 1983 ➤ 64,8746 ... **1,9766**: ᴿGregorianum 67 (1986) 175 (A. *Orbe*); LavalTP 42 (1986) 278-280 (P.-H. *Poirier*); RB 93 (1983) 627-630 (M.-J. *Pierre*); RÉByz 43 (1985) 267s (J. *Darrouzès*); RHR 203 (1986) 88 (P. *Nautin*); RivStoLR 22 (1986) 358-371 (W. *Schneemelcher*); TZBas 42 (1986) 440s (R. *Brändle*).

8119 **Junod** E., *Kaestli* J.-D., L'histoire des Actes apocryphes des apôtres ... Jean 1982 ➤ 63,8635 ... 65,8578: ᴿTR 82 (1986) 121s (N. *Brox*).

8120 **Poirier** Paul-H., La version copte de la Prédication et du Martyre de Thomas 1984 ➤ 65,8579: ᴿRHR 203 (1986) 319s (R.-G. *Coquin*); SR 15 (1986) 120 (J. K. *Coyle*).

8121 **Stoops** Robert F.ᴶ, Miracle stories and vision reports in the Acts of Peter: diss. Harvard ... – HarvTR 79 (1986) 482.

K2.7 Alia pseudepigrapha NT.

8122 *Horst* P. W. van der, *Kessels* A. H. M., Het visioen van Dorotheüs (Papyrus Bodmer XXIX): NedTTs 40 (1986) 97-111; Eng. 111: 343 lines from about 300 A.D. here translated into Dutch from Greek.

8123 *MacDonald* Dennis R. [also editor of this fascicle, The apocryphal acts of apostles], The forgotten novels of the early Church: Semeia 38 (1986) 1-6; 9-39, The Acts of Andrew / Andrew and Matthias (27-33, *Prieur* J.-M., response): 161-171, Conclusion, *Bovon* F., *Junod* E.; bibliography 173-181.

8124 **Robertson** Robert G., The dialogue of Timothy and Aquila; a critical text, introduction to the manuscript evidence, and an inquiry into the sources and literary relationships: diss. Harvard, ᴰ*Strugnell* J. CM 1986. 578 p. 86-19015. – DissA 47 (1986s) 2194-A; HarvTR 79 (1986) 478s.

8125 *a)* *Rordorf* Willy, Tradition and composition in the Acts of Thecla; the state of the question; – *b)* *Cartlidge* David R., Transfigurations of metamorphosis traditions in the Acts of John, Thomas, and Peter; – *c)* *Stoops* Robert F.ᴶ, Patronage in the Acts of Peter: Semeia 38 (1986 ➤ 8123) 43-52 / 53-66 / 91-100.

8126 *Rumianek* Ryszard, ❷ List do Laodycejczyków / Korintian do Pawła [Col 4,16; ed. HARNACK 1905], wprowadzenie, tłumaczenie i komentarz: STWsz 24,2 (1986) 227-9 / 231-6.

8127 **Suermann** Harald, Die geschichtstheologische Reaktion auf die einfallenden Muslime in der edessenischen Apokalyptik des 7. Jahrhunderts:

[Diss. Bonn 1985]: EurHS 23/256. Fra 1985, Lang. [NedTTs 41, 249, G. *Reinink*].

K3 **Qumran** .1 *generalia*.

8128 **Fujita** Neil S., A crack in the jar; what ancient [Qumran] Jewish documents tell us about the New Testament. Mahwah NJ 1986, Paulist. 308 p. $10. 0-8091-2745-8. – [R]ExpTim 98 (1986s) 54 (A. R. C. *Leaney*: useful and original).

8129 **Laperrousaz** E.-M., Les manuscrits de la mer Morte[6] [[1]1961]: Que sais-je? 953. P 1984, PUF. 120 p. 2-13-038030-1.

8130 *Laperrousaz* E.-M., Brèves remarques archéologiques concernant la chronologie des occupations esséniennes de Qoumran: RevQ 12,46 (1986) 199-212.

8131 *Lignée* Hubert, Qumran: → 582, DictSpir XII/2 (1986) 2858-2882.

8132 *a*) *Murphy-O'Connor* Jerome, The Judean desert; – *b*) *Brock* Sebastian P., Other manuscript discoveries: → 255, [E]*Kraft* R., Early Judaism 1986, 119-156 / 157-173.

8133 **Pollini** P., L'ebraistica italiana di fronte alle scoperte di Qumran: diss. Padova 1985, [D]*Prete* I. [RivB 35,86].

8134 *Wise* Michael, The Dead Sea Scrolls, I. Archaeology and biblical manuscripts: BA 49 (1986) 140-154; ill.

K3.4 *Qumran,* **Libri biblici** et pseudo-biblici; **commentarii**.

8135 **Brooke** G. F., Exegesis at Qumran; 4QFlorilegium in its Jewish context [diss. Claremont, [D]*Brownlee* W.]: JStOT Sup. 29, 1985 → 1,9789: [R]BL (1986) 113s (M. A. *Knibb*); CBQ 48 (1986) 554 (J. C. *VanderKam*); ETL 62 (1986) 422s (J. *Lust*); ÉTRel 61 (1986) 284s (F. *Smyth*); JTS 37 (1986) 492 (P. *Wernberg-Møller*); TLZ 111 (1986) 416s (S. *Holm-Nielsen*: says the dissertation is from Manchester); VT 36 (1986) 374s (H. G. M. *Williamson*).

8136 **Eisenman** R. H., James the Just in the Habakkuk Pesher [Paul is the Man of Lies]: StPostB 35. Leiden 1986, Brill. x-110 p. *f* 42. 90-04-07587-9 [BL 87,105s, P. S. *Alexander*: idosyncratic, follow up to his Maccabees, Zadokites].

8137 **Feltes** Heinz, Die Gattung des Habakukkommentars von Qumran (1QpHab); eine Studie zum frühen jüdischen Midrasch [Diss. Bochum]: ForBi 58. Wü 1986, Echter. 355 p. DM 48 [TR 83,338]. 3-429-01051-9.

8138 *Fröhlich* Ida, Le genre littéraire des Pesharim de Qumrân: RQum 12,47 (1986) 383-398.

8139 *García Martínez* F., Escatologización de los escritos proféticos en Qumrân: EstB 44 (1986) 101-116.

8140 *Lübbe* John, A reinterpretation of 4Q Testimonia: RQum 12,46 (1986) 187-197.

8141 *Lust* Johan, Ezekiel manuscripts in Qumran; preliminary edition of 4Q Ez a and b: → 384, Ezekiel 1985/6, 90-100.

8142 **Newsom** Carol, Songs of the sabbath sacrifice 1985 → 1,9793: [R]Harv-TR 79 (1986) 349-371 (E. *Qimron*: a great achievement, but many queries); IsrEJ 36 (1986) 282-4 (Esther G. *Chazon*); Syria 63 (1986) 450s (A. *Caquot*).

8143 **Nitzan** Bilha, Pesher Habakkuk. J 1986, Bialik Inst. 222 p. [ZAW 99, 295, Talia *Thorion-Vardi*].

8144 *Reeves* John C., What does Noah offer in 1QapGen X,15? [fat, not incense]: RQum 12,47 (1986) 415-9; franç. 419.
8145 **Schuller** Eileen M., Non-canonical psalms from Qumran; a pseudepigraphic collection: HarvSemSt 28. Atlanta 1986, Scholars [RQum 47,456]. xii-297 p. 0-891-30943-8.
8146 **Tanzer** Sarah J., The sages at Qumran; wisdom in the Hodayot: diss. Harvard. CM 1986. – RelStR 13,189.
8147 *Thorion-Vardi* Talia, a) Noch zu *k's* in 1 Q H IX,5; – b) *Mwr'* in Pešer Habaquq VI,5: RQum 12,46 (1986) 279-281 / 282 nur.

K3.5   *Milḥama, Serek...,* War, Temple scrolls.

8148 *Altshuler* David, On the classification of Judaic laws in the Antiquities of JOSEPHUS and the Temple Scroll of Qumran: AJS 7s (1982s) 1-14.
8149 *Callaway* Philip a) Source criticism of the Temple Scroll; the purity laws; – b) *Mî 'ad tūmām*, an abbreviated gloss?; – c) *'bryh* in the Temple Scroll XXIV,8: RQum 12,46 (1986) 213-222 / 263-8; franç. 268 / 269s.
8150 a) *Delcor* Mathias, Réflexions sur l'investiture sacerdotale sans onction à la fête du Nouvel An d'après le Rouleau du Temple de Qumrân (XIV,15-17); – b) *Dimant* Devorah, 4QFlorilegium and the idea of community as temple; – c) *Lemaire* André, L'enseignement essénien et l'école de Qumrân: → 81, Mém. NIKIPROWETZKY, Hellenica 1986, 155-164 / 165-189 / 191-203.
8151 *García Martínez* Florentino, El Rollo del Templo (11Q Temple), bibliografía sistemática: RQum 12,47 (1986) 425-440 [→ 669].
8152 *Hengel* M., *Charlesworth* J. H., *Mendels* D., The polemical character of 'On Kingship' in the Temple scroll; an attempt at dating 11QTemple: JJS 37 (1986) 28-38.
8153 **Maier** Johann, The Temple Scroll, an introduction, translation and commentary [1978], ᵀ*White* Richard: JStOT Sup 34, 1985 → 1,9801: ᴿJStJud 17 (1986) 108s (F. *García Martinez*).
8154 *Mink* Hans-Aage, The use of Scripture in the Temple scroll: ScandJOT 1,1 (1986) 20-50.
8155 *Schiffman* Lawrence H., Exclusion from the sanctuary and the city of the sanctuary in the Temple Scroll: → 36, Mem. GOITEIN S. = HebAnR 9 (1985) 301-320.
8155* *Tyloch* W., ℗ Le Rouleau du Temple; le plus important manuscrit de Qumran et l'époque de sa composition: Studia Religioznawcze 19 (1984) 27-38 [RHE 82,34*].
8156 **Wacholder**, Ben Zion, The dawn of Qumran 1983 → 64,8791 ... 1,9804: ᴿCuBi 39,283 (1984ss) 83-88 (F. *Sen*); Henoch 8 (1986) 97-99 (B. *Chiesa*); JStJud 17 (1986) 120-4 (A. S. van der *Woude*: irritating, not a gain to the study of the sect's origins); RechSR 74 (1986) 141-4 (A. *Paul*); SvTKv 62 (1986) 121-3 (T. *Kronholm*); Zion 51 (1986) 246-250 (Devorah *Dimant*).
8157 **Yadin** Y., The Temple Scroll 1983 → 65,8615; **1**,9805: ᴿBASOR 264 (1986) 91s (J. M. *Baumgarten*); BL (1986) 138s (M. A. *Knibb*); CBQ 48 (1986) 547-9 (J. A. *Fitzmyer*); PEQ 118 (1986) 76 (F. F. *Bruce*: 'a repromulgation of the Torah'); RÉJ 145 (1986) 400-4 (E.-M. *Laperrousaz*).
8158 **Yadin** Yigael, The Temple Scroll; the hidden law of the Dead Sea sect 1985 → 1,9806: ᴿJStJud 17 (1986) 124s (F. *García Martinez*: contains some

intuitions beyond the editio princeps, but no complete translation); TS 47 (1986) 515-8 (J. A. *Fitzmyer*).

8159 *Wise* Michael, The Dead Sea Scrolls 2. Nonbiblical manuscripts: BA 49 (1986) 228-243; ill.

8160 **Capper** Brian J., 'In der Hand des Ananias ...' Erwägungen zu 1 Q S VI,29 und der urchristlichen Gütergemeinschaft: RQum 12,46 (1986) 223-235; franç. 235s; Eng. 236.

8161 *Laubscher* F. D., The structural unity of the Manual of Discipline (1QS) 1:1-18a: ➤ 377a, IOSOT summaries (1986) 78.

8162 *Schiffman* L. H., The eschatological community of the Serekh-ha-'Edah: PAAR 51 (1984) 105-125 [< JStJud 17,144].

8163 **Charlesworth** James H., The discovery of a Dead Sea Scroll (4Q Therapeia); its importance in the history of medicine and Jesus research [Texas Tech conference] 1985 ➤ 1,e952: ᴿBL (1986) 115 (G. *Vermès*: virtually ALLEGRO's translation, without philological justification); IsrEJ 36 (1986) 118s (J. C. *Greenfield* debunks with NAVEH); JStJud 17 (1986) 242-4 (F. *García Martínez* favors rather Naveh: meaningless letters and words as writing-practice).

8164 *Naveh* Joseph, A medical document or a writing exercise?; the so-called 4Q Therapeia: IsrEJ 36 (1986) 52-55.

к3.6 Qumran et NT.

8165 **Allegro** John M., The Dead Sea Scrolls and the Christian myth [Westbridge 1979] 1984 ➤ 65,8616; 1,9808: ᴿBAR-W 12,4 (1986) 56s (J. J. *Collins*: the British publisher would not consent to include M. SMITH's Clement letter).

8166 **Carmody** Timothy R., The relationship of eschatology to the use of exclusion in Qumran and New Testament literature: diss. Catholic Univ., ᴰ*Fitzmyer* J. A. Wsh 1986. 310 p. 86-13468. – DissA 47 (1986s) 1359-A.

8167 **Eisenman** Robert, Maccabees, Zadokites, Christians and Qumran; a new hypothesis of Qumran origins: StPostB 34, 1983 ➤ 64,8798; 1,9812: ᴿHenoch 8 (1986) 99 (B. *Chiesa*: groundless); TLZ 111 (1986) 663-5 (G. *Baumbach*).

8168 **Thiede** C. P., Die älteste Evangelien-Handschrift? Das Markusfragment von Qumran und die Anfänge der schriftlichen Überlieferung des NTs. Wu 1986, Brockhaus. 80 p. – ᴿAegyptus 66 (1986) 297s (G. *Ghiberti*, favorevole); Streven 53 (1985s) 952s (P. *Beentjes*).

8169 **Thiering** Barbara E., The Gospels and Qumran 1981 ➤ 62,9433; 64,8800: ᴿRÉJ 145 (1986) 431s (C. Y. *Lambert*: négligeant tout bon sens).

8170 **Thiering** Barbara E., The Qumran origins of the Christian church 1983 ➤ 64,8799; 1,9818: ᴿRelStR 12 (1986) 68 (J. R. *Mueller*: 'ingenuity is not necessarily divination' — LIGHTFOOT); StPatav 33 (1986) 451s (G. *Segalla*).

к3.8 Historia et doctrinae Qumran.

8171 *Amussin* J. D., ᴱ*Gluskinya* L. M., ❸ A Qumran anti-Pharisaic pamphlet [*Allegro* J., Wiles 1964]: VDI (1986,3) 133-140; Eng. 140.

8172 *Baumgarten* Joseph M., 4 Q 503 (daily prayer) and the lunar calendar: RQum 12,47 (1986) 399-406; franç. 406s.

8173 **Burgmann** H., Zwei losbare Qumranprobleme; die Person des Lügenmannes, die Interkalation im Kalender [10 art. 1971-1981]. Fra 1986, Lang. 299 p. Fs 65. 3-8204-8368-3. – ᴿJStJud 17 (1986) 240s (F. *García Martínez*).

8174 **Callaway** Phillip R., The history of the Qumran community; an investigation of the problem: diss. Emory, ᴰ*Newsom* Carol. Atlanta 1986. 434 p. 86-26513. – DissA 47 (1986s) 3071-A; RelStR 13,190.

8175 *Carmignac* Jean, Roi, royauté et royaume dans la Liturgie Angélique: RQum 12,46 (1986) 177-186; deutsch 186.

8176 *Crotty* R. B., Qumran studies — challenge to consensus: RelTrad 7ss (Sydney 1984ss) 41-51 [< NTAbs 31,74].

8177 *Cryer* Frederick H., The 360-day calendar year and early Judaic sectarianism: ScandJOT 1,1 (1986) 116-122.

8178 *a) Davies* Philip R., Qumran beginnings; – *b) Nickelsburg* George W. E., 1 Enoch and Qumran origins; the state of the question and some prospects for answers; – *c) Trever* John C., The spiritual odyssey of the Qumran teacher; – *d) Murphy-O'Connor* Jerome, The Damascus Document revisited: ↠ 392, SBL Seminars 1986, 361-8 / 341-360 / 384-399 / 369-383.

8179 *García Martínez* Florentino, La 'nueva Jerusalén' y el templo futuro de ˹ los mss. de Qumran: ↠ 21, Mem. DíEZ MACHO A., Salvación 1986, 563-590.

8180 *Laperrousaz* E.-M., Notes sur l'évolution des conceptions de 'Guerre Sainte' dans les manuscrits de la mer Morte: RQum 12,46 (1986) 271-8.

8181 *Mędala* Stanisław, Recherches sur la problématique des documents de Qumran en Pologne: ↠ 377a, IOSOT summaries (1986) 90.

8182 *Milikowsky* Chaim, Law at Qumran; a critical reaction to Lawrence H. SCHIFFMAN, 'Sectarian law in the Dead Sea Scroll[s]; courts, testimony and the penal code': RQum 12,46 (1986) 237-248; Eng. 248s, franç. 249.

8183 *Nitzan* Bilha, ❾ Hymns from Qumran, *lipḥad wᵉlibhol*, evil ghosts, 4Q 510s: Tarbiz 55 (1985s) 18-46; Eng. Is. [further p. 440s. 603s; and 442-5 by J. *Baumgarten*, Eng. IV].

8184 **Schiffman** Lawrence H., Sectarian law in the Dead Sea Scrolls: BrownJudSt 33, 1983 ↠ 64,8809 ... 1,9834: ᴿJBL 105 (1986) 534-6 (Maurya P. *Horgan*: cemetery presumes normal childbearing).

8185 *Strickert* Frederick M., Damascus document VII,10-20 and Qumran messianic expectation [J. *Starcky* 1963]: RQum 12,47 (1968) 327-349; franç. 349.

8186 *Thiering* Barbara, The identification of the substitute sanctuary at Qumran: ↠ 377b, SBL Jerusalem summaries (1986) 10s.

8187 *Thorion* Yohanan, Beiträge zur Eforschung der Sprache der Kupfer-Rolle: RQum 12,46 (1986) 163-176; franç. 176.

8188 **Weinfeld** Moshe, The organizational pattern and the penal code of the Qumran sect; a comparison with guilds and religious associations of the Hellenistic-Roman period: NT & Orbis Antiquus 2. FrS/Gö 1986, Univ./VR. 100 p.

K4.1 Esseni, Zelotae.

8189 **Chiesa** B., *Lockwood* W., Ya'qūb al-QIRQISĀNĪ on Jewish Sects and Christianity, Kitāb al-anwārᵀ I, 1984 ↠ 65,8793: ᴿHenoch 8 (1986) 110s (P. G. *Borbone*); JQR 76 (1985s) 263s (L. *Nemoy*).

8190 *Horsley* Richard A., The zealots; their origin, relationships and importance in the Jewish revolt: NT 28 (1986) 159-192.

8191 *Kampen* John, A reconsideration of the name 'Essene' in Greco-Jewish literature in light of recent perceptions of the Qumran sect: HUCA 57 (1986) 61-81.
8191* **Violette** Jean Claude, Les Esséniens de Qoumrân: Les Portes de l'Étrange. P 1983, Laffont. 219 p.; maps. [KirSef 61,27].

K4.3 Samaritani.

8192 **Broadie** A., A Samaritan philosophy ... Memar Marqah 1981 ➔ 62,9460 ... 1,9841: ᴿHenoch 8 (1986) 109s (S. *Noja*).
8193 **Crown** Alan D., A bibliography of the Samaritans 1984 ➔ 65,806; 1,9843: ᴿRHR 203 (1986) 206s (J.-P. *Rothschild* disapproves alphabetizing von Gall under *v* and de Robert under *d*).
8194 *Crown* Alan D., The Samaritans in the Byzantine orbit: BJRyL 69 (1986s) 96-138.
8195 **Egger** Rita, Josephus Flavius und die Samaritaner; eine terminologische Untersuchung zur Identitätsklärung der Samaritaner: NT & Orbis Ant. 4. FrS/Gö 1986, Univ./VR. 412 p.; bibliog. p. 372-392. 3-7278-0373-8 / VR 3-525-53903-7.
8196 *Gaster* Moses, Les Samaritains (leur histoire, leurs doctrines, leur littérature [1923], ᵀ*Dubourg* Bernard. P 1984, OEIL. 220 p. – ᴿRÉJ 145 (1986) 186-8 (J.-P. *Rothschild*: Montgomery 1907 would have been better).
8197 *Lourenço* João, Os Samaritanos; un enigma na História Bíblica: Didaskalia 15,1 (1985) 49-72.
8198 **Montgomery** J. A., Les hommes du Garizim [1907]ᵀ: Les deux rives. P 1985, OEIL. 272 p. F 150. – ᴿVSp 140 (1986) 728s (H. *Troadec*: encore sous droit ottoman p. 26).
8199 *Purvis* James D., The Samaritans and Judaism: ➔ 255, ᴱ*Kraft* R., Early Judaism 1986, 81-98.
8200 **Rothschild** Jean-Pierre, Catalogue des manuscrits samaritains. P 1985, Bibl. Nationale. 188 p.; ill. – ᴿRÉJ 145 (1986) 404-6 (J. *Margain*).
8201 *Schur* Nathan, The Samaritans, as described in Christian itineraries (14th-18th centuries): PEQ 118 (1986) 144-155.
8202 *Stenhouse* Paul, The Kitab al-Tarikh of Abu l-Fath [... Samaritan history]: Studies in Judaica 1. Sydney 1985, Univ. Mandelbaum Trust. lxxvii-249 p. 0-949259-75-1.

K4.5 Ṣadoqitae, Qaraitae – Cairo Genizah; Zadokites, Karaites.

8203 *Bammel* Ernst, a) Sadduzäer und Sadokiden [< ETL 55 (1979) 107-115]; – b) Kirkisanis Sadduzäer [< ZAW 81 (1959) 265-270]; – c) Höhlenmenschen [< ZNW 49 (1958) 77-88]; – d) Zu 1QS 9,10f [< VT 7 (1957) 381-5]: ➔ 131, Judaica 1986, 117-126 / 107-111 / 95-106 / 112-6.
8204 **Davies** Philip R., The Damascus Covenant: JStOT Sup 25, 1983 ➔ 64,8831 ... 1,9847: ᴿCBQ 48 (1986) 301-3 (Maurya P. *Horgan*: opposition to Temple-Judaism did not begin with them, so when?); JQR 77 (1986s) 84-87 (E. *Qimron*).
8205 **Friedman** M. A., Jewish marriage in Palestine, a Cairo Geniza study I-II 1980s ➔ 62,9473 ... 65,8561: ᴿJQR 76 (1985s) 149-151 (M. *Gil*); Tarbiz 55 (1985s) 456-462; Eng. VI (Z. M. *Rabinovitz*).
8205* **Gil** Moshe, The Tustaris, family and sect 1981 ➔ 62,9474: ᴿJESHO 29 (1986) 104s (J. *Sadan*).

8206 **Goitein** S. D.,   A Mediterranean Society ... in the Genizah, 4. Daily Life
➤ 1,9850:   Berkeley 1983, Univ. California.   xxvi-492 p.; map. $ 38.50. –
ᴿSpeculum 61 (1986) 656-9 (A. L. *Udovitch*).

8207 **Golb** Norman, *Pritsak* Omeljian,   Khazarian Hebrew documents of the
tenth century.   Ithaca NY, Cornell Univ. $38.50.   0-8014-1221-8. – ᴿRÉJ
145 (1986) 193s (G. *Nahon*).

8208 *Gutwirth* Eleazar,   On the hispanicity of Sephardi Jewry [Geniza
fragments]:   RÉJ 145 (1986) 347-357; franç. 357.

8209 *Kahana* Menachem, ⊕ The critical edition of the Mekilta De-Rabbi
Ishmael in the light of the Genizah fragments: Tarbiz 55 (1985s)
489-524; Eng. Is.

8210 ꜰNemoy Leon: Studies in Judaica, Karaitica and Islamica, ᴱ*Brunswick*
S. R. 1982 ➤ 63,120; 64,84:   ᴿOLZ 81 (1986) 268-271 (H. *Simon*).

8211 *Prinz* Deborah R.,   A Geniza fragment attributed to Asher Ben Saul of
Lunel; text and study: HUCA 57 (1986) 121-212.

8212 *Qimron* Elisha, ⊕ The Halacha of Damascus Covenant — an
interpretation of 'Al Yitarev': ➤ 363, Congress IX-D1 1985/6, ⊕ 8-15.

8213 *Sadan* J.,   Genizah and Genizah-like practices in Islamic and Jewish
traditions: BO 43 (1986) 36-58.

κ5 Judaismus prior vel totus.

8214 **Abram** I. B. H.,   Joodse traditie als permanent leren.   Kampen 1986,
Kok. 336 p. ƒ45 [GerefTTs 86,192].

8215 **Alexander** Philip S.,   Textual sources for the study of Judaism 1984
➤ 65,8653; 1,9860:   ᴿJSS 31 (1986) 267-9 (A. P. *Hayman*).

8216 *Avril* A. C., *Lenhardt* P., La lettura ebraica della Scrittura con antologia di
testi rabbinici.   Bose 1984, Qiqayon.   126 p.   Lit. 7000. – ᴿSacDoc 31
(1986) 663-8 (R. *Barile*).

8217 *Cohen* Matty,   La maxime des hommes de la Grande Assemblée; une reconsidération: ➤ 81, Mém. Nikiprowetzky V., Hellenica 1986, 281-296.

   Faur José,   Golden doves with silver dots; semiotics and textuality in rabbinic
tradition: Jewish Literature and Culture 1986 ➤ 7289.

8219 **Fleischer** Ezra,   The Yozer [550-], its emergence and development.   J
1984, Magnes.   795 p.   965-223-520-2. – ᴿBO 43 (1986) 471-7 (W. J. van
Bekkum).

8220 **Fohrer** Georg,   Fede e vita nel giudaismo: StBPaid 69, 1984 ➤ 65,5981:
ᴿParVi 31 (1986) 151s (A. *Rolla*); Protestantesimo 41 (1986) 111s (D.
Garrone).

8221 **Gilat** Y. D.,   R. Eliezer Ben Hyrcanus; a scholar outcast 1984
➤ 1,9872:   ᴿJudaism 35 (1986) 495-7 (B. M. *Bokser*).

8222 *Goldenberg* Robert,   Hillel/Hillelschule (Schammaj/Schammajschule),
ᵀ*Wolter* Mariann: ➤ 597, TRE 15 (1986) 326-330.

8223 *Goldstain* Jacques,   To taste the Torah; a study of Jewish tradition
[< Christus 63 (P 1969) 389-395], ᵀ*Sebastian* G.: AmBenR 37 (1986)
197-207.

8224 *Goldstein* Israel,   Rabban Gamliel of Yavneh [Goldstein's first student
sermon, 1915; with four other Goldstein reprints]: Dor 15 (1986s)
273-280 (-304).

8225 **Hengel** Martin,   Rabbinische Legende ... S. b. Schetach und die achtzig
Hexen von Askalon 1984 ➤ 65,8666:   ᴿCBQ 48 (1986) 562s (B. T. *Viviano*:
an entertaining masterpiece); JStJud 17 (1986) 106s (A. S. van der *Woude*:

Meisterschaft); JTS 37 (1986) 506-8 (S. C. *Reif*); RB 93 (1986) 619s (É. *Nodet*); Zion 51 (1986) 363s (D. R. *Schwartz*).

8226 **Katunarich** Sergio M., L'ebraismo da allora a oggi; spunti di storia con cenni sui suoi rapporti col cristianesimo. Mi 1986, Univ. Cattolica. 325 p. Lit. 20.000.

8227 ^E**Kuntzmann** R., *Schlosser* J., Études sur le judaïsme hellénistique [Strasbourg 1983]: LDiv 119, 1984 ➤ 65,423: ^RBO 43 (1986) 477-9 (P. W. van der *Horst*); Compostellanum 31 (1986) 276-8 [E. *Romero Pose*]; ScEspr 38 (1986) 129-131 (P.-É. *Langevin*).

8228 **de Lange** Nicholas, Judaism: Opus. Ox 1986, UP. £10. 0-19-219198-5. – ^RExpTim 98 (1986s) 95 (W. W. *Simpson*).

8229 **Levinson** Pnina N., Einführung in die rabbinische Theologie 1982 ➤ 63,8270...1,9881: ^RRB 93 (1986) 620s (É *Nodet*).

Maier J., *Schäfer* P., Piccola enciclopedia dell'ebraismo 1985 ➤ 636.

8231 *Maier* Johann, Zum Problem der jüdischen Gemeinden Mesopotamiens im 2. und 3. Jh. n. Chr. im Blick auf dem CMC: ➤ 421, Codex Manichaicus 1984/6, 37-67.

8232 *Mayer* Günter, Rabbinica: TRu 51 (1986) 231-8.

8233 ^E**Mello** Alberto, Ritorna, Israele! La conversione nell'interpretazione rabbinica. R 1985, Città Nuova. 208 p. Lit. 11.000. – ^RCC 137 (1986,1) 92s (S. *Katunarich*).

8234 *Mendecki* Norbert, **❾** *a*) Diaspora babilońska – Amoraici i Saboryci: AnCracov 18 (1986) 245-250; 250 ...die Amoräer und die Saboräer; – *b*) Historia żydowskiej diaspory w III wieku po Chr. – centrum babilońskie: ColcT 56,1 (1986) 13-22; 23s; Die Geschichte der jüdischen Diaspora; – *c*) Palästina im 4. und 5. Jahrhundert n. Chr.: ColcT 56,4 (1986) 69-73; deutsch 73s.

8234* **Morgenstern** Benjamin, A companion to Pirke Avot. J 1983, Gefen. 221 p. $11. 965-229-008-4 [Bijdragen 48,82, F. De *Meyer*].

8235 *Moscovitz* Leib, **❾** On sounding the Shofar in the high court of Palestine on Shabat Rosh Hashanah: Tarbiz 55 (1985s) 608-10; rejoinder by *Fleischer* E. 611s; Eng. Vs.

8236 **Musaph-Andriesse** Rosetta C., Von der Tora bis zur Kabbala; eine kurze Einführung in die religiösen Schriften des Judentums: Kleine V.-Reihe 1509. Gö 1986, Vandenhoeck & R. 97 p. 0-525-33509-1.

8237 **Neusner** J., Ancient Judaism and modern category formation; 'Judaism', 'midrash', 'messianism', and canon in the past quarter-century: Studies in Judaism 1. Lanham MD 1986, UPA. xiv-123 p. $22.50; pa. $9.75. 0-8191-5395-8; 6-6 [BL 87, 111, A. P. *Hayman*].

8238 **Neusner** J., Formative Judaism 1982/4 ➤ 64,8886; 1,9885: ^RRB 93 (1986) 617s (É. *Nodet*).

8239 **Neusner** Jacob, Judaism in the matrix of Christianity. Ph 1986, Fortress. xix-148 p. $13; 0-8006-1897-1 [BL 87, 113, A. P. *Hayman*].

8240 **Neusner** Jacob, The Pharisees; rabbinic perspectives [abridgment of 1971 Rabbinic Traditions]: Studies in Ancient Judaism 1, 1985 ➤ 1,9886: ^RBL (1986) 131s (J. M. *Lieu*, 'since 1971 no discussion has been able to ignore Neusner's methodology or his conclusions').

8241 **Neusner** Jacob, Reading and behaving; ancient Judaism and contemporary gullibility: BrownJudSt 113. Atlanta 1986, Scholars. x-129 p. $25.50; sb./pa. $20.50 [JBL 105, 754].

8242 **Neusner** Jacob, The religious study of Judaism; description, analysis, interpretation; [II.] The centrality of context. Studies in Judaism. Lanham

MD 1986, UPA. xvi-172 p.; xiv-216 p. $23.50 / $24.50, pa. $11.75 [TR 83,338]. 0-8191-5393-1; 4-X / 50-4; 1-2.

8243 **Neusner** Jacob, Torah; from scroll to symbol in formative Judaism: Foundations of Judaism; method, teleology, doctrine, 3. Doctrine, 1985 → 1,9884: ᴿCBQ 48 (1986) 564s (E. J. *Fisher*: mission accomplished); Horizons 13 (1986) 420-2 (J. L. *Blau*: conclusion to Midrash/Messiah in Context).

8244 *a) Nickelsburg* George W. E., The modern study of early Judaism; – *b) Porton* Gary G., Diversity in postbiblical Judaism; *c) Charlesworth* James H., Jewish hymns, odes, and prayers (c. 167 B.C.E. - 135 C.E.); – *d) Saldarini* Anthony J., Reconstructions of rabbinic Judaism: → 255, ᴱ*Kraft* R., Early Judaism 1986, 1-30 / 57-80 / 411-436 / 437-477.

8245 **Niebuhr** Karl-Wilhelm, Katechismusartige Weisungsreihen in der frühjüdischen Literatur; Untersuchungen zum materialen Gehalt der Gesetzesforderung im Frühjudentum: Diss. Halle 1985. 195 + 156 p. – TLZ 112, 236-8.

8246 **Novak** David, Halakhah in a theological dimension. Chico CA 1985, Scholars. xi-174 p. $17. – ᴿRelStR 12 (1986) 276 (E. N. *Dorff*).

8247 **Ouaknin** Marc-Alain, **Smilevitch** Éric, Pirqê de Rabbi Eliézer: Les dix paroles. Lagrasse 1983, Verdier. 384 p. F 148. – ᴿEsprVie 96 (1986) 720 (A.-M. *Henry*).

8248 **Pérez Fernández** Miguel, Los capítulos de Rabbi Eliezer 1984 → 65,8679; 1,9888: ᴿEstE 61 (1986) 79s (R. *Aguirre*); JSS 31 (1986) 91s (G. *Brooke*); RB 93 (1986) 623s (É. *Nodet*); ScriptTPamp 18 (1986) 270-2 (S. *Ausin*).

8249 *Rash* Y., Rabbi Eliézer et son fourneau; les débats des Sages de Yabné: RechSR 74 (1986) 483-510; Eng. 558.

8250 ᴱ**Reeg** Gottfried, Die Geschichte von den zehn Märtyrern [ˈAqiba al.]: TStAJud 10, 1985 → 1,9892: ᴿJudaica 42 (1986) 255s (C. *Thoma*).

8251 **Rettberg** Daniel J., Paul BILLERBECK as student of rabbinic literature; a description and analysis of his interpretive methodology: diss. Dropsie, ᴰ*Goldenberg* D. Ph 1986. 210 p. 87-01938. – DissA 47 (1986s) 3783-A.

8252 **Roth** Joel, The halakhic process, a systemic analysis: Moreshet 13. NY 1986, Jewish Theol. Sem. vii-398 p. 0-87334-035-3.

8253 **Saldarini** A., Scholastic rabbinism, Fathers according to Rabbi Nathan 1982 → 63,8764 ... 1,9893: ᴿOLZ 81 (1986) 469s (P. *Schäfer*).

8254 **Schiffman** Lawrence H., Who was a Jew? Rabbinic and Halakhic perspectives on the Jewish-Christian schism 1985 → 1,9895: ᴿCurrTM 13 (1986) 53 (E. *Krentz*); Judaica 42 (1986) 101s (S. *Schreiner*).

8255 **Scholem** Gershom, Concetti fondamentali dell'ebraismo [Über einige Grundbegriffe 1970 ²1976], ᵀ*Bertaggia* Michele: Radici 7. Genova 1986, Marietti. vii-153 p. 88-211-8335-1.

8255* **Schwartz** Joshua, ❹ Ha-Yiššub ha-Yehûdî... Jewish settlement in Judaea after the Bar-Kochba War until the Arab Conquest. J 1986, Magnes [Immanuel 21, 138].

8256 **Sigal** Phillip, Judentum: Urban-Tb 359. Stu 1986, Kohlhammer. 276 p. DM 26 [TüTQ 167, 61].

8257 *a) Silberman* Lou H., Challenge and response; pesiqta Derab Kahana, chapter 26 as an oblique reply to Christian claims; – *b) Saperstein* Marc, Jews and Christians — some positive images: → 110, ᶠSTENDAHL K.: HarvTR 79 (1986) 247-253 / 236-246.

8258 **Smilévitch** Éric, Leçons des Pères du monde; Pirqé Avot et Avot de Rabbi Nathan version A et B; texte intégral traduit de l'hébreu: Les Dix Paroles. Lagrasse 1983, Verdier. 504 p. 2-86432-027-4.

8259 **Soloveitchik** Joseph B.,   Halakhic man.   Ph 1983, Jewish Publ. – [R]JRel 66 (1986) 194-8 (M. L. *Morgan*).

8260 *Standaert* Benoît,   Les trois colonnes du monde [Torah, culte, miséricorde: Pirqe Abot 1,2]; continuités et déplacements dans la tradition juive et chrétienne: CrNSt 7 (1986) 441-9.

8261 *Tabory* Joseph,   ⊕ When was the Scroll of Fasts abrogated? [shortly after (its compilation and) the destruction of the Second Temple; but Babylonian Jews retained it]: Tarbiz 55 (1985s) 261-5; Eng. IV.

8262 *Zlotnick* Dov,   Memory and the integrity of the oral tradition: → 11*, Mem. BICKERMAN E. = JANES 16s (1984s) 229-241.

K6   Mišna, *tosepta; Tannaim.*

8263 *Bar-Asher* Moshe,   La langue de la Mishna d'après les traditions des communautés juives d'Italie: RÉJ 145 (1986) 267-278.

8264 **Bokser** Baruch M.,   The origins of the Seder; the Passover rite and early rabbinic Judaism 1984 → 65,8686:   [R]BSOAS 49 (1986) 387s (J. R. *Segal*).

8265 **Brooks** Roger,   Support for the poor in the Mishnaic law of agriculture: BrownJudSt 43, 1983 → 64,8883 ... 1,9906:   [R]JBL 105 (1986) 162-4 (P. J. *Haas*); JStJud 17 (1986) 238-240 (H. E. *Gaylord*: also on four other NEUSNER Zeraim dissertations, praised).

8266 **Eilberg-Schwartz** Howard,   The human will in Judaism; the Mishnah's philosophy of intention: *a*) diss. Brown, [D]*Neusner* J.   Providence 1986, 392 p.   86-17553. – DissA 47 (1986s) 1756-A. – *b*) BrownJudSt 103. Atlanta 1986, Scholars.   xvi-250 p. $32; sb. $27.   0-89130-938-1 [BL 87, 104s, P. S. *Alexander*: DURKHEIMIAN].

8267 **Elman** Jack Y.,   Authority and tradition; Toseftan Baraitot in Talmudic Babylonia: diss. NYU 1986, [D]*Schiffman* L. 466 p. 87-06731. – DissA 47 (1986s) 4419-A.

8268 *Florsheim* Yoel,   ⊕ The relationship amongst second generation Babylonian Amoraim: Zion 51 (1986) 281-293; Eng. X.

8269 **Halivni** David W.,   Midrash, Mishnah, and Gemara; the Jewish pre-dilection for justified law.   CM 1986, Harvard.   ix-164 p. $22.50.   0-674-57370-6 [NTAbs 30,374]. – [R]JQR 77 (1986s) 59-64 (J. M. *Baumgarten*).

8269* *Kanarfogel* Ephraim,   The 'aliyah of 'three hundred rabbis' in 1211; Tosafist attitudes toward settling in the land of Israel: JQR 76 (1985s) 191-215.

8270 *Lightstone* Jack N.,   Scripture and Mishnah in earliest rabbinic Judaism: SR 15 (1986) 317-325.

8271 **Manns** Frédéric,   Pour lire la Mishna 1984 → 65,8690; 1,9910:   [R]Judaica 42 (1986) 58s (R. *Riesner*); TLZ 111 (1986) 267s (J. *Maier*).

8271* *Milikowsky* Chaim [follow-up to *Ta-Shema* Yisrael] ⊕ *Mahdorot* ... Recensions and text-types in rabbinic literature ... 11th-12th cent.: KirSef [60 (1985) 298-309] 61 (1986) 169s.

8272 **Nathan** Haya,   ⊕ The linguistic tradition of Codex Erfurt of the Tosefta: diss. Hebrew Univ.   J 1984. 100 p. – KirSef 60 (1985) 707.

8273 **Neusner** Jacob,   From Mishnah to Scripture; the problem of the unattributed saying ... Purities: BrownJudSt 67, 1984 → 65,8691:   [R]JBL 105 (1986) 546-8 (M. S. *Jaffee*: unclear how Neusner proves).

8274 **Neusner** J.,   A history of the Mishnaic law of Damages [→ 65,8694], *a*) IV. Shebuot, Eduyot, Abodah Zarah, Abot, Horayot; translation and explanation; – V. The Mishnaic system of damages: StJudLA 35.   Leiden 1985, Brill.   xxxi-275 p.; xxxi-228 p. ƒ156 + 104.   90-04-07269-1; 70-5

[NTAbs 31,125]. – *b*) 2. Baba Mesia: StJudLA 35/2, 1983 ➤ 64,8899: ᴿJBL 105 (1986) 354s (A. J. *Avery-Peck*).
8275 **Neusner** J., The Tosefta; its structure and its sources: BrownJudSt 112. Atlanta 1986, Scholars. xi-250 p. $40; sb. $30. 1-55540-049-3 [BL 87, 115, P. S. *Alexander*].
8276 **Neusner** Jacob, *Sarason* Richard S., The Tosefta translated from the Hebrew; first division, Zeraim (The order of agriculture). Hoboken 1986, KTAV. xxix-373 p. $59.50. 0-87068-693-3.
8277 **Peck** Alan J., The priestly gift in Mishnah, a study of the tractate Terumot: BrownJudSt 20, 1981 ➤ 62,9539...64,8904: ᴿOLZ 81 (1986) 259s (G. *Mayer*).
8278 **Rengstorf** K. H., Tosefta Zeraim 1983 ➤ 64,8905: 1,9917: ᴿJBL 105 (1986) 548s (R. S. *Sarason*).
8279 **Urbach** Ephraim E., The Halakhah; its sources and development, ᵀ*Posner* Raphael. J 1986, Massada. xvi-519 p.; bibliog. p. 513-8.
8280 **Wegner** Judith R., Woman in Mishnaic law; chattel or person?: diss. Brown. Providence 1986. – RelStR 13,190.

K6.5 **Talmud**, *midraš; Amoraim.*

8281 **Alon** Gedaliah, The Jews in their land in the Talmudic age, I, ᵀᴱ*Levi* Gershon, 1980 ➤ 61,9892...1,9920: ᴿBO 43 (1986) 775-7 (A. *Oppenheimer*).
8282 *Aminoah* Noah, L'attitude des 'Amora'im à l'égard des sources talmudiques antérieures: RÉJ 145 (1986) 5-19; on leur attribue des enseignements anonymes et des propos qui n'ont jamais existé.
8282* ᵀᴱ**Avery-Peck** Alan J., The Talmud of Babylonia, an American translation, VII. Tractate Besah: BrownJudSt 117. Atlanta 1986, Scholars. xix-378 p. 1-55540-054-X.
8283 *Ben Sasson* Menahem, ⊕ The Gaonate of r. Samuel b. Joseph ha-Cohen which was 'like a bath of boiling water' [newly noted Cairo Geniza letter about efforts in Ramla, Jerusalem, and Egypt to replace him]: Zion 51 (1986) 379-409; Eng. XIII.
8283* **Bokser** Baruch M., Post-mishnaic Judaism in transition; Samuel on Berakhot and the beginnings of Gemara: BrownJudSt 17, 1980 ➤ 61,b763...64,8912: ᴿJQR 76 (1985s) 269-271 (L. H. *Schiffman*).
8284 **Braude** W., *Kapstein* I., Tanna debe Eliyyahu 1981 ➤ 62,9554; 64,8913: ᴿBO 43 (1986) 186s (A. *Hultgård*); JQR 76 (1985s) 152-4 (L. S. *Kravitz*).
8285 **Freeman** Gordon M., The heavenly kingdom; aspects of political thought in the Talmud and Midrash. Lanham MD / J 1986, UPA / J Center for Public Affairs. viii-187 p. $25, pa. $12.50 [TR 83,338].
8286 *Glatt* Melvin J., Midrash, the defender of God: Judaism 35 (1986) 87-97.
8287 *Goldin* Judah, On the account of the banning of R. Eliezer ben Hyrqanus [bBabM 59b, pMo'ed Qatan 3:1,81cd]; an analysis and proposal: ➤ 11*, Mem. BICKERMAN E. = JANES 16s (1984s) 85-97.
8288 **Gradwohl** Roland, Wat is de Talmoed? 1985 ➤ 1,9927; ƒ14,50; 90-259-4294-6: ᴿCollatVl 16 (1986) 252 (J. *Lemmens*).
8289 **Jacobs** Louis, The Talmudic argument; a study of Talmudic reasoning and methodology 1984 ➤ 65,8709: ᴿRExp 83 (1986) 631s (D. E. *Garland*); Salesianum 48 (1986) 420 (R. *Vicent*).
8290 *Kirschner* Robert, Imitatio rabbini [T. Ber. 1:4...]: JStJud 17 (1986) 70-79.
8291 **Levinas** Emmanuel, Dal sacro al santo; cinque nuove letture talmudiche;

intr. *Cavalletti* Sofia. R 1985, Città Nuova. 164 p. Lit. 12.000. – ᴿCC 137 (1986,1) 198s (S. *Katunarich*).

8291* **Levine** Lee I., ❻ *Maᵗªmad ha-Ḥªkāmîm*... The rabbinic class in Palestine during the Talmudic period. J 1985, Ben-Zvi Foundation. 154 p.; 22 fig.; maps. 965-217-029-1 [KirSef 61,77].

8292 *Lightstone* Jack N., Talmudic rabbinism, midrash, and the fragmentation of Scripture: ➤ 392, SBL Seminars 1986, 614-630.

8293 *Morag* Šlomoh, ❻ On the Munaḥ of the Babylonian Masorah...: Lešonenu 48s (1984s) 297s.

8294 **Neusner** J., In the margins of the Yerushalmi; glosses on the English translation: BrownJudSt 55, 1983 ➤ 65,8717: ᴿRB 93 (1986) 622s (É. *Nodet*).

8295 **Neusner** Jacob, Judaism, the classical statement; the evidence of the Bavli: Chicago Studies in the History of Judaism. Ch 1986, Univ. xvii-270 p. $37 [JBL 105,754].

8296 **Neusner** Jacob, Midrash in context; essays in formative Judaism 1983 ➤ 64,8925; 1,9936: ᴿAbrNahr 24 (1986) 205s (R. *Hayward*); JBL 105 (1986) 160-2 (L. M. *Barth*: for history relies entirely on M. Avɪ-Yᴏɴᴀʜ 1946).

8297 **Neusner** Jacob, Das pharisäische und talmudische Judentum, ᴱ*Lichten-berger* Hermann: TStAJ 4, 1984 ➤ 65,8719; 1,9939: ᴿBijdragen 47 (1986) 327s (F. De *Meyer*); Gregorianum 67 (1986) 362s (G. L. *Prato*); Judaica 41 (1985) 117s (S. *Schreiner*); RÉJ 145 (1986) 131-4 (M. R. *Hayoun*); TLZ 111 (1986) 352-4 (L. *Wächter*).

8298 **Neusner** J., Talmud of Babylonia 17. Sotah 1984 ➤ 65,8720: ᴿRB 93 (1986) 623 (É. *Nodet*).

8299 **Neusner** Jacob, The Talmud of Babylonia, an American translation [1.6.23, 1984 ➤ 65,8721; 1,9940] 23. Arakhin: BrownJudSt 63. Chico CA 1984, Scholars. 258 p. 0-89130-739-7. – ᴿJTS 37 (1986) 493-504 (I. *Gamse*: not an advance on Sonsino).

8300 **Neusner** Jacob, The Talmud of the Land of Israel 34, 1982 ➤ 65,8723: ᴿJQR 77 (1986s) 74-81 (T. *Meacham*).

8301 *Neusner* Jacob, *a*) Toward a theory of comparison; the case of comparative midrash: Religion 16 (L 1986) 269... [< zɪᴛ]; *b*) When tales travel; the interpretation of multiple appearances of a single saying or story in Talmudic literature: JStNT 27 (1986) 69-88.

8302 **Ouaknin** Marc-Alain, Le livre brûlé; lire le Talmud. P 1986, Lieu Commun. 418 p.; bibliog. p. 403-9. F 125. 2-86705-066-9.

8303 *Porton* Gary G., Understanding rabbinic midrash: Library of Judaic Learning 5, 1985 ➤ 1,9943: ᴿJStJud 17 (1986) 270 (M. *Pérez Fernández*: ambivalent praise for unnecessary shortened repetitions of Porton's commentaries).

8303* **Rubin** M. David, ❻ *Kol ha-Miqra'ôt*... All biblical verses quoted in the Babylonian Talmud, with Rashi's comments. J 1985, Koren [Immanuel 21,139].

8304 **Salzer** Israel, Le Talmud, traité Pessahim, traduit de l'hébreu et de l'araméen: Les Dix Paroles (0243-0541). Lagrasse 1984-6, Verdier. 375 p.; 395 p. F 170 + 150. 2-86432-033-9; 51-7.

8305 **Stemberger** Günter, Der Talmud 1982 ➤ 63,8814... 1,9946: ᴿOLZ 81 (1986) 566-8 (J. *Conrad*).

8306 **Strack** H. L., ᴱ*Stemberger* G., Introduction au Talmud et au Midrash [Einleitung 1982 ➤ 63,8815]: Patrimoines, Judaïsme (0762-0829). P 1986, Cerf. 432 p. 2-204-02592-5.

8307 ᵀWewers Gerd A., Pea Ackerecke: Talmud Y 1/2. Tü 1986, Mohr. xix-231 p.; portr.; bibliog. p. xiv-xviii. 3-16-745068-1.

8308 Wewers Gerd A., Bavot Pforten; Talmud Y 4/1-3, 1982 → 63,8818: ᴿBO 43 (1986) 779s (D. *Goodblatt*).

8309 Wewers G. A., Horayot Entscheidungen: Übersetzung des Talmud Yeruschalmi 4/8, 1984 → 1,9949: ᴿNRT 108 (1986) 426 (X. *Jacques*).

8310 Wewers Gerd A., Probleme der Bavot-Traktate; ein redaktionskritischer und theologischer Beitrag zum Talmud Yerushalmi: TStAntJ 5, 1984 → 65,8730: ᴿGregorianum 67 (1986) 360 (G. L. *Prato*); Judaica 41 (1985) 242s (S. *Schreiner*).

к7.1 Judaismus mediaevalis, generalia.

8311 *David* Abraham, Bemerkungen zur Legende vom jüdischen Papst [< ❻ ᶠ*Habermann* A. 1983; Eng. Immanuel 15 (1982s) 58-96], ᵀ*Mach* Dafna: FreibRu 37s (1985s 'Immanuel-Supplement') 150-3.

8312 a) *Goetschel* R., Y a-t-il une philosophie juive?; – b) *Baudinet-Mondszain* M.-J., L'universel, l'image et la personne [... telle qu'elle apparaît dans la Bible]: Revue de Métaphysique et de Morale 90,3 ('Philosophies juives' 1985) 311-327 / 377-382.

8313 Kellner Menachem, Dogma in medieval Jewish thought from Maimonides to Abravanel: Littman Library of Jewish Civilization. NY 1986, Oxford-UP. xiv-310 p.; bibliog. p. 287-302. 0-19-710044-9.

8314 Lewis Bernard, The Jews of Islam 1984 → 65,8735; 0-691-07267-1: ᴿBO 43 (1986) 230s (J. M. *Landau*).

8315 *Meier* Beat, Zur Geschichte des spätmittelalterlichen Judentums; die Juden im Gebiet der heutigen Schweiz und der europäische Kontext: Judaica 42 (1986) 2-16.

8316 *Roth* Norman, 'Seis edades durará el mundo'; temas de polémica judía española: CiuD 199 (1986) 45-65.

8317 Simon Heinrich & Marie, Geschichte der jüdischen Philosophie 1984 → 65,8738; 1,9958: ᴿBO 43 (1986) 188-190 (H. J. *Heering*); RÉJ 145 (1986) 456s (M. R. *Hayoun*); TLZ 11 (1986) 21-23 (G. *Begrich*).

8318 Yassif Eli, Jewish folklore; an annotated bibliography. NY 1986, Garland. xxi-341 p. $65 [RelStR 13, 356, Carolyn *Lipson-Walker*].

к7.2 Maimonides.

8318* *Abramson* Shraga, ❻ Two identifications, (1) The 'western scholar' mentioned by Maimonides; (2) the Derisha on Even ha-ʿEzer §63: KirSef 61 (1986) 171-4.

8319 ᴱBleich J. David, With perfect faith; the [Maimonides] foundations of Jewish belief 1983 → 65,8743: ᴿRÉJ 145 (1986) 458-460 (C. *Sirat*).

8320 a) *Blumenthal* David R., Maimonides on angel names; – b) *Starobinski-Safran* Esther, La confrontation du judaïsme et de l'hellénisme dans Maïmonide, Guide des Égarés III,54: → 81, Mém. NIKIPROWETSKY V., Hellenica 1986, 357-369 / 391-400.

8321 Cohen Philip, ❻ Rambam al Hatorah; selected commentaries on verses of the Torah ²ʳᵉᵛ. J 1986, Mass. 284 p. 965-09-0043-8.

8322 ᴱDienstag Jacob I., Eschatology in Maimonidean thought 1983 → 64,258; 65,8745: ᴿHeythJ 27 (1986) 195s (L. *Jacobs*).

8322* *Dienstag* Jacob I., ❻ Maimonides' letter to the scholars of southern France on astrology; a bibliography: KirSef 61 (1986) 147-158.

8323 *Feinberg* Chaim, Maimonides and CORDOVERO; the rationalist and the mystic: Judaism 35 (1986) 325-339.

8324 *Fenton* Paul B., *a)* Le *taqwīm al-adyān* de Daniel IBN AL-MAŠIṬA [Leningrad Firkovič collection]; nouvelle pièce de la controverse maïmonidienne en Orient: RÉJ 145 (1986) 279-294; – *b)* ⊕ More light on the judge R. Hanan'el B. SAMUEL [A. Maimonides' father-in-law; Geniza data]: Tarbiz 55 (1985s) 77-107; Eng. III.

8325 **Goldfield** Lea N., Moses Maimonides' treatise on resurrection; an inquiry into its authenticity. NY 1986, KTAV. 167 p. $12. 0-88125-088-0. – RExpTim 98 (1986s) 221s (Julia *Neuberger*: exciting; she postulates other authors); FreibRu (1985s) 116s (C. *Thoma*).

8326 T**Hulster** J., Maimonide M., Épîtres: Les Dix Paroles. P 1984, Verdier. 200 p. F 75 [Judaica 41,59].

8327 *a) Ivry* Alfred L., Maimonides on creation; – *b) Staub* Jacob J., Gersonides and contemporary theories on the beginning of the universe: ➤ 387*, E*Novak* D., Creation 1984/6, 185-213 / 245-259.

8327* **Katchen** Aaron L., Christian Hebraists and Dutch Rabbis; seventeenth-century apologetics and the study of Maimonides' Mishneh Torah: Harvard Judaic Texts 3. CM 1984, Harvard Center for Jewish Studies. xvii-391 p. $28. – RJQR 76 (1985s) 377s (J. I. *Dienstag*).

8328 **Merced** Palacio de la, Maimónides y su época: Min. Cultura Andalucía. Córdoba 1986, Diputación Provincial. 183 p.; 59 fig. 84-505-3089-X.

8329 T**Nikiprowetzky** Valentin, *Zaoui* André, Moïse Maimonide, Le livre de la connaissance [= Mišne Tora I]; préf. *Pinès* Salomon: Quadrige. P 1985=1961, PUF. 428 p. 2-13-038669-5. – RÉTRel 61 (1986) 590s (J.-M. *Léonard*); RÉJ 145 (1986) 442s (M.-R. *Hayoun*).

8330 *a) Posen* Jacob, Die Einstellung des Maimonides zum Islam und zum Christentum: – *b) Levinger* Jakob, Die Prophetie als gesamt-menschliche Erscheinung nach der Lehre des Moses Maimonides; – *c) Giladi* Avner, Woher könnte der Titel 'Führer der Unschlüssigen' stammen?: Judaica 42 (1986) 66-73 (-79) / 80-88 / 89-98.

8331 E**Preisler** Zvi H., Moses Maimonides, The Mishneh Torah in the original Hebrew [but] with punctuation, biblical references and indices. J 1985, Ketuvim. 870 + viii p.

8332 *a) Romano* David, Mi-Mošě wᵉ-ʿad Moše lo qām kᵉ-Moše [Maimónides]; – *b) Bertola* Ermenegildo, Moshes Maimonide e il problema dell'esistenza di Dio: Sefarad 45 (1985) 179-184 / 185-206; Eng. 206.

8333 **Roth** N., Maimonides; essays and texts, 850th anniversary. Madison — 1985, Hispanic Seminary of Medieval Studies. 169 p. $10. 0-942260-59-7 [BL 87, 116s, S. C. *Reif*: holds Maimonides was never a rabbi].

8334 T**Russell** H. M., *Weinberg* J., The book of knowledge from the Mishneh Torah of Maimonides. NY 1983, Ktav. 144 p. – RRÉJ 145 (1986) 444s (M. R. *Hayoun*).

8335 *a) Stemberger* Günter, Maimonides als Mischna-Ausleger; *b) Simon* Heinrich, Leben und Tod in der Sicht des Maimonides: Kairos 28 (1986) 196-208 / 208-220.

K7.3 Alii magistri Judaismi mediaevalis.

8336 *Banitt* Menahem, RASHI, interpreter of the biblical letter 1985 ➤ 1,9979: RBO 43 (1986) 783-5 (A. van der *Heide*).

8337 **Kamin** Sara, ⊕ Rashi's exegetical categorization in respect to the

distinction between *peshat* and *derash*. J 1986, Hebr. Univ. 297 p. $20. 965-223-628-4 [ZAW 99, 291, Talia *Thorion-Vardi*].
8338 **Lehmann** Menasheh R., ⊕ Rashi's commentary according to a 1400 C.E. Yemenite manuscript. NY/J. – ᴿBethM 31,104 (1985s) 92s, 1 fig. (B. Z. *Luria*).

8338* **Ratzaby** Yehuda, ⊕ *Oṣar ha-lāšon* ... A dictionary of Judaeo-Arabic in R. SAADYA's Tafsīr. Ramat Gan 1986, Bar Ilan Univ. viii-151 p.; 3 facsimiles. – ᴿJQR 76 (1985s) 267s (L. *Nemoy*).
8339 *Bertola* Ermenegildo, Il 'Sefer chakmoni' (libro sapiente) di Shabbatai DONNOLO [morì 982]: Sefarad 44 (1984) 283-312; Eng. 312.
8340 *Blidstein* Gerald J., ⊕ ME'IRI's attitude towards Gentiles; between apologetics and internalization: ˙ Zion 51 (1986) 153-166; Eng. VI.
8341 **Cohen** Martin S., The Shi'ur Qomah; liturgy and theory in pre-Kabbalistic Jewish mysticism 1983 ➤ 64,8941 ... 1,9996: ᴿJAOS 106 (1986) 577s (D. J. *Halperin*: vitiated by assumption of a lost Urtext); JStJud 17 (1986) 96-98 (J. *Dan*: central treatise of two dozen Hekhalot; text good, comments not).
8342 *Dukan* Jacques, Un exégète de *piyyuṭim* en France au XIIIᵉ siècle [KARA Joseph; 16.XII.1985]: RÉJ 145 (1986) 250-6.
8343 *Fernández Tejero* Emilia, El tratado de Y. S. de NORZI sobre el *Ma'arik*: Henoch 8 (1986) 365-391; franç. 391s.
8344 **Gottfarstein** Joseph, Le Bahir, le livre de la clarté, traduit de l'hébreu et de l'araméen: Les Dix Paroles. Lagrasse 1986, Verdier. 171 p. 2-85432-021-5.
8344* **Groner** Tsvi, The legal methodology of HAI Gaon: BrownJudSt 66, 1985 ➤ 1,9991: ᴿJQR 76 (1985s) 237-245 (R. *Brody*).
8345 *Herring* Basil, Joseph IBN KASPI's Gevia' Kesef; a study in medieval Jewish philosophic Bible commentary 1982 ➤ 63,8823 ... 1,9992: ᴿRÉJ 145 (1986) 409-412 (Colette *Sirat*: rend orthodoxe un personnage qui ne s'y prête guère).
8345* *Maccoby* Hyam, NAHMANIDES and messianism, a reply: JQR [76s (1985s) 253-7, *Berger* D.] 77 (1986s) 55-57.
8346 ᵀᴱ**Perani** Mauro, Il Midrash Temurah; la dialettica degli opposti in un'interpretazione ebraica tardo-medievale: StBDehon 13. Bo 1986, Dehoniane. 104 p.; bibliog. p. 9-16. 88-10-40714-8.
8346* *Nemoy* Leon, Al-QIRQISĀNĪ on the occult sciences: JQR 76 (1985s) 329-367.
8347 **Rabinowitz** I., [Judah Messer LEON] The book of the honeycomb's flow 1983 ➤ 64,8975; 1,9994: ᴿJBL 105 (1986) 356s (J. L. *Kugel*).
8348 *Hayoun* Maurice R., MOÏSE de Narbonne [1300-1362] sur les *sefirot*, les sphères, et les intellects séparés ... d'IBN TUFAYL [m. 1185]: JQR 76 (1985s) 97-147.
8348* **Matt** Daniel C., Rabbi David BEN YEHUDAH he-Hasid, The Book of Mirrors 1982 ➤ 63,8848: ᴿJQR 76 (1985s) 155-7 (I. G. *Marcus*).

K7.4   *Qabbalâ, Zohar, Merkabâ* — **Jewish mysticism.**

8349 **Ashlag** Yehuda, Kabbalah, a gift of the Bible. J 1984, Research Centre of Kabbalah. 159 p. 0-943688-22-1.
8350 *Barnatán* M., Breve aproximación a la mística judía: El Olivo 23 (M 1986) 5-11.

8351 **Chernus** Ira, Mysticism in rabbinic Judaism 1982 ➤ 63,8837a...1,a1:
ᴿBijdragen 47 (1986) 72s (M. *Poorthuis*).

8352 **Dan** Joseph, The early Kabbalah: Classics of Western Spirituality.
NY/L 1986, Paulist/SPCK. 205 p. £12. 0-8091-2769-5. – ᴿExpTim 98
(1986s) 382 (G. S. *Wakefield*).

8353 **Dan** Joseph, Jewish mysticism and Jewish ethics. Seattle 1986, Univ.
Washington. 148 p. $20 [JAAR 55, 387-9, K. P. *Bland*].

8354 *García-Jalón* Santiago, El valor de la tradición en el Judaismo medieval
(estudio de la cuestión en el Sefer ha-Qabbalah de Abraham ʙᴇɴ Dᴀᴜᴅ):
ScripTPamp 18 (1986) 433-456; lat. 457; Eng. 457s.

8355 **Goetschel** Roland, La Kabbale: Que sais-je? N⁰ 1105, 1985 ➤ 1,a5:
ᴿRÉJ 145 (1986) 198s (M. R. *Hayoun*); RevSR 60 (1986) 268 (B. *Renaud*).

8356 **Gruenwald** I., Apocalyptic and Merkavah mysticism 1980 ➤ 61,4839...
65,8765: ᴿHenoch 8 (1986) 108s (Liliana *Rosso Ubigli*).

8357 **Matt** Daniel C., Zohar; the book of enlightenment, pref. *Green* Arthur.
NY/L 1984, Paulist/SPCK. 320 p. – ᴿExpTim 98 (1986s) 29 (R. *Howe*:
congenial to structuralists); Judaism 35 (1986) 251s (R. *Patai*).

8358 ᵀᴱMopsik Charles, Le Zohar... le Midrach ha Néélam: Les Dix Paroles.
Lagrasse 1984s, Verdier. 671 p.; 555 p. F 149 chaque. 2-86432-013-4;
33-9.

8359 ᴱSchäfer Peter, Geniza-Fragmente zur Hekhalot-Literatur: TStAntJ 6,
1984 ➤ 65,8770; 1,a12; DM 268: ᴿGregorianum 67 (1986) 360s (G. L.
Prato); JStJud 17 (1986) 270s (H. E. *Gaylord*: handsome); RTLv 17 (1986)
359-361 (P.-M. *Bogaert*).

8360 ᴱSchäfer Peter, al., Synopse zur Hekhalot-Literatur 1981 ➤ 62,9601...
1,a13: ᴿJSS 31 (1986) 266s (D. *Goodman*).

8361 **Schäfer** Peter, Konkordanz zur Hekhalot-Literatur, I, *a-k*: TStAntJ 12.
Tü 1986, Mohr. xii-364 p. 3-16-145030-2.

8362 **Scholem** Gershom, Le Nom et les symboles de Dieu dans la mystique juive 1983 ➤ 65,8785; 1,a15*: ᴿÉTRel 61 (1986) 128s (J.-M.
Léonard).

8362* *a) Scholem* G., Les derniers Kabbalistes d'Allemagne; – *b) Mosès* S.,
Langage et sécularisation chez G. Scholem; – *c) Mosse* G. L., La
sécularisation dans la théologie juive; – *d) Mayer* H., Mystique et
politique dans le 'Moïse et Aaron' d'Arnold Sᴄʜöɴʙᴇʀɢ: ArchivScSocRel
60s (1985) 9-25 / 85-96 / 27-41 / 97-107 [RHE 82,411].

8363 **Schweid** Eliezer, Judaism and mysticism according to Gershom Scholem;
a critical analysis and programmatic discussion [⊙], ᵀ*Weiner* David A.,
ᴱ*McCracken-Flesher* Caroline: Reprints & Translations. Atlanta 1985,
Scholars. 178 p. $23; pa. $17 [TDig 33,487].

8364 *Starobinski-Safran* Esther, Determinismus und Freiheit in der
mittelalterlichen Kabbala, ᵀ*Hruby* Kurt: Judaica 41 (1985) 66-78.

8365 **Uchelen** N. A. van, Joodse mystiek, Merkawa, tempel en troon; een
historische en literaire inleiding. Amst 1984, Amphora. 134 p. £27,50.
90-6446-061-2. – ᴿBijdragen 47 (1986) 73s (M. *Poorthuis*).

8366 *Uchelen* N. A. van, Ethical terminology in Heykhalot-texts: ➤ 59,
ꜰLᴇʙʀᴀᴍ J., Tradition 1986, 250-8.

8367 **Weiss** J. † 1969, Studies in Eastern European Jewish mysticism: Littman
Library. Oxford 1985, UP. viii-272 p. £18. 0-19-710034-1 [BL 87, 121s,
G. *Vermes*].

8368 *Wewers* Gerd A. †, Die Überlegenheit des Mystikers; zur Aussage der
Gedulla-Hymnen in Hekhalot Rabbati 1,2-2,3: JStJud 17 (1986) 3-22.

8369 **Zafrani** H., Kabbale, vie mystique et magie. P 1986, Maisonneuve & L. F 326 [Judaica 42,268].

K7.5 Judaismus saec. 14-18.

8370 *Abicht* Ludo, Het godsbeeld van de Chassidim: Streven 53 (1985s) 408-422.
8370* *Birnbaum* Eleazar, Mahzor Roma; the Cluj manuscript dated 5159 A.M. / 1399 C.E. and the public fast in Rome in 1321 C.E.: JQR 76 (1985s) 59-91; 4 phot.
8371 **Bowman** Steven B., The Jews of Byzantium 1204-1453. Univ. 1985, Alabama. 380 p. $42.50 [JAAR 55,134, S. D. *Benin*].
8372 *Elior* Rachel, Messianic expectations and spiritualization of religious life in the sixteenth century: RÉJ 145 (1986) 35-49; franç. 49.
8373 *Feiner* Shmuel, ⊙ The turning. point in the evaluation of Hasidism — Eliezer ZWEIFEL and the moderate Haskalah in Russia: Zion 51 (1986) 167-210; Eng. VIs.
8374 **Fishman** Talya, Kol SACHAL's critique of rabbinic tradition [anonymous treatise c. 1600]; a solution to the problem of *galut* [territorial or psychic exile, to be remedied by redemption]: diss. Harvard. CM 1986. 437 p. 86-20566. – DissA 47 (1986s) 2153-A.
8375 ᴱ**Gottlieb** Z., ⊙ Kitbê r. ʿObadyâh SFORNO [c. 1470-1550; exegesis of Prophets and Writings]. J 1983, Kook. ix-564 p. – ᴿHenoch 8 (1986) 111s (M. *Perani*).
8376 **Heschel** Abraham J., ᴱ*Dresner* Samuel H., The circle of the Baal Shem Tov; studies in Hasidism. Ch 1985, Univ. xlv-213 p. $25. – ᴿRelStT 6 (1986) 96s (Y. K. *Greenberg*).
8377 *Loewenthal* Tali, Early Hasidic teachings [Baal Shem Tov d. 1760] — esoteric mysticism or a medium of communal leadership?: JJS 37 (1986) 58-75.
8378 *Menjot* Denis, *González Castaño* Juan, Les Juifs de Mula [centre de Murcia] au XVᵉ siècle (notes socio-démographiques): RÉJ 145 (1986) 21-34.
8379 *Rothschild* Jean-Pierre, Deux bibliothèques juives comtadines vers 1630: RÉJ 145 (1986) 75-102.
8380 **Schoonhoven** E. Jansen, Jodendom, Christendom, Verlichting: J. G. HAMANN en M. MENDELSSOHN, een achttiende eeuws dispuut als bijdrage aan hedendaagse discussie: Toerusting. Nijkerk 1985, Callenbach. 183 p. *f*29,50 [TLZ 112,341, F. *Dexinger*].

K7.8 Judaismus contemporaneus.

8381 *Amon* Moshe, Marginal annotations on Rabbi [1865-1935, Isaac] KOOK's *Orot haKodesh* [ᴱ*Cohen* D. 1978]: SR 15 (1986) 55-64.
8382 **Bernstein** Saul, The renaissance of the Torah Jew. NY 1985, Ktav. 412 p. $20. 0-88125-066-X. – ᴿExpTim 98 (1986s) 153s (Julia *Neuberger*: narrow).
8383 **Breslauer** S. Daniel, Modern Jewish morality; a bibliographical survey. Westport CT 1986, Greenwood. 249 p. $40 [JAAR 55,419].
8384 *Cohen* Arthur A. *zal*, Life amid the paradigms or the absence of a Jewish critique of culture [1985 AAR plenary session]: JAAR 54 (1986) 499-520.
8385 **Della Pergola** Sergio, La trasformazione demografica della diaspora ebraica. T 1983, Loescher. 288 p. – ᴿRivStoLR 22 (1986) 169-172 (Elena *Loewenthal*).

8386 **Dobrinsky** Herbert C., A treasury of Sephardic laws and customs ... in North America. Hoboken/NY 1986, KTAV/Yeshiva Univ. xxii-520 p.; bibliog. p. 475-498. 0-88125-031-7; pa. 2-2.

8387 **Greenberg** Sidney, Light from Jewish lamps; a modern treasury of Jewish thoughts; intr. *Angoff* Charles. Northvale NJ 1986, J. Aronson. 465 p. 0-87668-938-7.

8388 *Grunberg* Bernard, Les premiers juifs mexicains (1521-1571): RÉJ 145 (1986) 359-382.

8389 *Haberman* Jacob, Some changing aspects of Jewish scholarship: Judaism 35 (1986) 183-197.

8390 **Hartman** David, A living covenant; the innovative spirit in traditional Judaism. NY 1985, Free Press. 340 p. $22.50 [JAAR 55, 152-4, M. S. *Jaffee*].

8391 **Helmreich** William R., The world of the Yeshiva; an intimate portrait of orthodox Jewry. NHv 1986, Yale Univ. 412 p. $15 pa. [JAAR 55,200].

8392 **Hoffman** Edward, The heavenly ladder; the Jewish guide to inner growth. NY 1985, Harper & R. xvi-140 p. $9 pa. [RelStR 13,49, R. *Bulka*].

8394 **Kolatch** Alfred J., The first/second Jewish book of why. Middle Village NY 1981/5, Jonathan David. ...; 423 p. 0-8246-0256-0; 305-2.

8395 **Kurzweil** Zvi, The modern impulse of traditional Judaism. NY 1985, Ktav. 156 p. $13 [JAAR 54,394].

8396 **Lutske** Harvey, The book of Jewish customs. Northvale NJ 1986, Aronson. 383 p.; ill. 0-87668-916-0.

8397 *Magonet* Jonathan, Jüdisches Selbstverständnis II. Das Werden des modernen Judentums: Diakonia 17 (Mainz 1986) 93-100.

8398 *Michelini Tocci* Franco, Note e documenti di letteratura religiosa e parareligiosa giuridica: AION 46 (1986) 101-8.

8399 **Nash** Stanley, In search of Hebraism, Shai HURWITZ [1861-1922] and his polemics in the Hebrew press: Studies in Judaism in Modern Times 3. Leiden 1980, Brill. xiv-410 p. *f*120. – ᴿOLZ 81 (1986) 255-8 (P. *Schäfer*).

8400 **Neusner** Jacob, Israel in America; a too-comfortable exile? Boston 1985, Beacon. xi-203 p. $15. – ᴿRelStT 6 (1986) 91s (A. *Rippin*: earlier essays unified).

8401 **Raphael** Marc L., Profiles in American Judaism; the Reform, Conservative, Orthodox and Reconstructionist traditions in historical perspective, 1985 → 1,a38: ᴿRelStT 6 (1986) 94s (D. *Cohn-Sherbok*).

8402 *Ribière* Germaine, Le peuple juif au présent: RencChrJ 19,79s (1985) 5-58 [78s, 5-8].

8403 **Rosenthal** Gilbert S., Contemporary Judaism, patterns of survival [= ²Four paths to one God; today's Jew and his religion 1973]. NY 1986, Human Sciences. xxii-401 p. $17 p. [TDig 34,90].

8404 **Rosenzweig** Franz, La Stella della Redenzione [1921], ᵀ*Bonola* G. Casale Monferrato 1985, Marietti. – ᴿAsprenas 33 (1986) 423-432 (O. *Di Grazia*).

8405 **Rosenzweig** Franz, Théologie athée (1914), ᵀᴱ*Schlegel* Jean-Louis [présent. *Petitdemange* Guy]: RechSR 74 (1986) 545-557 [537-544], Eng. 558 [559-574, *Bourel* D., Bulletin du judaïsme moderne].

8406 **Seguier** Marcel, Le Juif de l'Écriture [l'écrivain parallèle au croyant]; judaïsme et écriture nouvelle: Hatsour. Monaco 1985, Rocher. 365 p. 2-268-00329-9. – ᴿÉTRel 61 (1986) 129 (H. *Bost*: romancier; vol. 2 attendu, 'La phrase retrouvée').

8407 **Sonsino** Rifat, *Syme* Daniel B., Finding God; ten Jewish responses. NY 1986, Union Heb. Cong. 140 p. $8 pa. [TDig 34,92].

K8 *Philosemitismus* – **Judeo-Christian rapprochement.**

8408 *Adler* Joshua J., Know what to answer [to evangelical proselytizers ➤ 1,a43]: Dor 15 (1986s) 49-52.123s.

8408* **Angerstorfer** Ingeborg, MELITO und das Judentum: Diss. Rg 1986, D*Brox* N. – RHE 82,348.

8409 **Ankori** Zvi, ❶ Jews and Christian Greeks in their relation through the ages. TA 1984, Univ. 199 p. [Judaism 35,506].

8410 E**Bakker** L. A. R., *Goddijn* H. P. M., Joden en Christenen; een moeizaam gesprek door de eeuwen heen. Baarn 1985, Ambo. 181 p. f 28,50. – ROnsGLev 63 (1986) 111 (P. *Leenhouwers*); Streven 53 (1985s) 563s (P. *Beentjes*).

8411 E**Baumann** Arnulf H. *al.*, Luthers Erben und die Juden; das Verhältnis lutherischer Kirchen Europas zu den Juden. Hannover 1984, Luth.-VH. 144 p. DM 16,80. – RTLZ 111 (1986) 187s (H. *Kirchner*).

8412 *Baumbach* G., Das Neue Testament — ein judenfeindliches Buch? Zur Frage nach der Entstehung und Verbreitung antijüdischer Tendenzen im frühen Christentum: ZeichZt 40,6 (B 1986) 138-142 [< NTAbs 31,63].

8413 **Beck** Norman A., Mature Christianity; the recognition and repudiation of the anti-Jewish polemic of the New Testament 1985 ➤ 1,a48; 0-941664-03-1: RCurrTM 13 (1986) 374 (F. *Sherman*: interpretation, fine; new [inclusive] translation, no); TS 47 (1986) 700s (E. H. *Flannery*).

8414 *Ben Dasan* Isaia [= *Yamamoto* Shichihei], Gli ebrei e i giapponesi [❶ 1970 poi in 50 edizioni]. Mi 1986, Spirali. 220 p. Lit. 20.000. – RCC 137 (1986,4) 519 (G. *Pittau*).

8415 E**Biemer** Günter, *al.*, Was Juden und Judentum für Christen bedeuten; eine neue Verhältnisbestimmung zwischen Christen und Juden: Lehr- und Lerneinheiten für die Sekundarstufen; Lernprozess Christen Juden 3, 1984 ➤ 65,8796; DM 42,50: RTR 82 (1986) 316-8 (H. *Gahlen* empfiehlt).

8416 **Blackwell** Richard E.J, The use of Jewish narratives in Christian education to combat anti-Semitism in the Church: diss. Eastern Baptist Sem. 1986. 116 p. 87-02360. – DissA 47 (1986s) 3775-A.

8417 **Bremer** Natascha, Das Bild der Juden in den Passionsspielen und in der bildenden Kunst des deutschen Mittelalters. Fra 1986, P. Lang. 244 p.; 44 fig. $31 [RelStR 13,341, J. *Gutman*].

8418 *Breuer* Mordechai, ❶ MAHARAL of Prague's disputation with the Christians; a reappraisal of *be'er ha-gola*: Tarbiz 55 (1985s) 253-260; Eng. IIIs.

8419 **Brocke** Edna, *Bauer* Gerhard, Nicht im Himmel — nicht überm Meer; jüdisch-christliche Dialoge zur Bibel 1985 ➤ 1,a54: REvT 46 (1986) 190-5 (J. *Seim*).

8420 *Bruch* Richard, MENDELSSOHNs 'Jerusalem', ein jüdischer Beitrag zur religiösen Toleranz in der Aufklärungszeit: TGl 76 (1986) 252-263.

8421 *Bucci* Onorato, La genesi ellenistica dell'antigiudaismo romano; alle origini dell'antisemitismo cristiano [Convegno Greece and Rome in Eretz-Israel, Haifa/TA marzo 1985]: Lateranum 52 (1986) 51-82.

8422 **Busi** Frederick, The pope of antisemitism; the career and legacy of Édouard-Adolphe DRUMONT [1844-1917]. NY 1986, UPA. xiv-227 p. $26.50: pa. $12.50 [RelStR 13,270, H. *Schwartz*].

8423 *Campbell* Debra, David GOLDSTEIN and the rise of the Catholic Campaigners for Christ: CathHR 72 (1986) 33-50.

8424 *a) Campbell* W. S., Christianity and Judaism; continuity and discontinuity; – *b) Willebrands* J. C., Vatican II and the Jews; twenty years later; – *c) Hertzberg* A., Truth and tolerance; – *d) Fischer* E. J., The Pope and Israel; – *e) Sharry* L., Goodwill among Jews, Arabs and Christians: Christian Jewish Relations 1 (1985) 3-16 / 16-31 / 47-52 / 52-56 / 56-60 [< Judaica 41,254].

8425 **Caputo** G., *al.*, Il pregiudizio antisemitico in Italia; la coscienza democratica di fronte al razzismo strisciante. R 1984, Newton Compton. 242 [+ 14] p. – ᴿHenoch 8 (1986) 120s (G. *Busi*: tit. pp.).

8426 ᴱ**Cholvy** Gérard, Mouvements de jeunesse (Chrétiens et Juifs; sociabilité juvenile dans un cadre européen 1799-1968). P 1985, Cerf. 430 p. – ᴿÉTRel 61 (1986) 139-141 (J. *Pellegrin*: mouvements juifs et protestants mais surtout catholiques).

8427 **Cohen** Jeremy, The friars and the Jews 1982 → 63,8880 ... 1,a56: ᴿRHR 203 (1986) 325s (S. *Schwarzfuchs*); Zion 51 (1986) 113 (Ora *Limor*).

8428 *Cohn-Sherbok* Dan, Christianity and anti-Semitism: Month 248 (1986) 120-2.

8429 **Cutler** Allan H. & Helen E., The Jew as ally of the Muslim; medieval roots of anti-Semitism. ND 1986, Univ. x-577 p. $50 [JNES 46,76].

8430 **Delden** J. A. van (drs.), Israël is Gods volk! Amst 1985, Buijten & S. 79 p. ƒ 14,50. – ᴿPrakT 13 (1986) 401s (Marien van den *Boom*).

8431 **Delpech** François † 1982, [biographe du P. Théodore *Ratisbonne*], Sur les juifs; études d'histoire contemporaine, ᴱ*Comte* B. Lyon 1983, Presses Univ. 452 p. 19 art. [RHE 82,163].

8432 *De Rosa* Giuseppe, Ebrei e cristiani 'fratelli' nel 'fratello Gesù' [La visita di Giovanni Paolo II alla sinagoga di Roma 13.IV.1986 chiude definitivamente il lungo periodo di antisemitismo cristiano]: CC 137 (1986,2) 260-3 [264-273, *Caprile* G.].

8433 Il dono della Torah (un colloquio ebraico-cristiano): Quaderni di Vita Monastica 41. Camaldoli 1986. 149 p. → 373.

8434 **Druk** J. *al.*, De ander in beeld; Joden en Christenen over vooroordeel: OJEC 3. Kampen 1985, Kok. 94 p. – ᴿNedTTs 40 (1986) 247s (J. S. *Vos*).

8435 **Dubois** M.-J., *a)* Rencontres avec le Judaïsme en Israël; – *b)* L'exil et la demeure, journal de bord d'un chrétien en Israël (1962-1983). J 1983s, Olivier. 259 p., F 120 / 269 p., F 140. – ᴿMondeB 42 (1986) 55 (I. H. *Dalmais*).

8436 *Dupuy* Bernard, La juridiction du Pape sur les Juifs au Moyen Âge; une étude de l'Anonyme 1007 [*Stow* K. 1984]: Istina 31 (1936) 388-392; 392-5, sa traduction de l'Anonyme 1007.

8437 **Eckardt** A. Roy, Jews and Christians; the contemporary meeting. Bloomington 1986, Indiana Univ. xiv-178 p. $20 [RelStR 13,239, Denise L. *Carmody*].

8438 **Engelmann** H., Kirche am Abgrund; Adolf Sᴛᴏᴇᴄᴋᴇʀ [1838-1909] and seine antijüdische Bewegung [diss.]: SJVCG 5. B 1984, Kirche und Judentum. 185 p. – ᴿArLtgW 28 (1986) 170s (J. *Hennig*).

8439 *a) Etchegaray* Kard. Roger, Dankadresse [Laszt-Preis Univ. Beerscheba, 18.XII.1985]; – *b) Riegner* Gerhart M., Ansprache: FreibRu 37s (1985s) 25-28 / 28s.

8440 *Fabris* Renzo, L'antisemitismo; analisi di un fenomeno: HumBr 41 (1986) 5-22 (535-556, su Rᴏsᴇɴᴢᴡᴇɪɢ).

8441 *Ferrer-Chivite* Manuel, El factor judeo-converso en el proceso de consolidación del título 'Don': Sefarad 45 (1985) 131-173.

8442 **Flannery** Edward H., The anguish of the Jews; twenty-three centuries of antisemitism[2] *rev* [[1]1965]. NY 1985, Paulist. 369 p. $13 [JAAR 54,398].

8443 *Flint* Velrie I. J., Anti-Jewish literature and attitudes in the twelfth century: JJS 37 (1986) 39-57.

8444 *a) Fournier* M. H., L'évolution des relations entre Juifs et Chrétiens; – *b) Lesieur* R., L'évolution des Églises de la Réforme; – *c) Jouanin* Y., La place du Judaïsme dans le mouvement œcuménique; – *d) Landau* L., Prospectives pour le dialogue Judéo-Chrétien: Sens 38,7s (1986) 211-219 / 219-227 / 227-235 / 235-242 [< Judaica 42,272].

8445 *Fumagalli* Pier Francesco, I trattati medievali 'Adversus Judaeos', II. Il 'Pugio Fidei' ed il suo influsso sulla concezione cristiana dell'ebraismo: ScuolC 113 (1985) 522-545.

8446 **Gager** John G., The origins of anti-semitism... in antiquity 1983 → 64,9022 ... 1,a72: [R]JRel 66 (1986) 99-101 (A. J. *Droge*).

8447 [E]**Gerger** David A., Anti-semitism in American history. Urbana 1986, Univ. Illinois. 428 p. $30. 13 inedita + 1 reprint [TDig 33,456]. – [R]America 155 (1986) 428. 430 (L. *Smolar*).

8448 **Gilman** Sander L., Jewish self-hatred; anti-semitism and the hidden language of the Jews. Baltimore 1985, Johns Hopkins. xi-461 p. $28.50 [Judaism 35,505].

8449 **Gradwohl** R., Bibelauslegungen aus jüdischer Quellen, I. Die alttestamentlichen Predigttexte des [Ev.-kirch.] 3. Jahrgangs. Stu 1986, Calver. 253 p. DM 34. 3-7668-0800-1 [BL 87,64, A. *Gelston*].

8450 **Greive** Hermann, Geschichte des modernen Antisemitismus in Deutschland: Grundzüge 53, 1983 → 64,9027; 65,8821: [R]RÉJ 145 (1986) 475s (M. R. *Hayoun*).

8451 *Grossman* Avraham, ⊕ The Jewish-Christian polemic and Jewish biblical exegesis in twelfth century France (on the attitude of r. Joseph Qara to polemic): Zion 51 (1986) 29-60; Eng. II.

8452 **Häsler** A. A., Die älteren Brüder. Z 1986, Jordan. 266 p. [Judaica 42,269].

8453 **Harder** G., Kirche und Israel; Arbeiten zum christlich-jüdischen Verhältnis. B 1986, Inst. Kirche und Judentum. 280 p. [Judaica 42,206].

8454 *a) Hernando* Josep, Un tractat anònim 'adversus iudaeos' en català; – *b) Cortès* Enric, A propòsit de dos manuscrits fragmentaris hebreus apareguts de nou: → 97, [F]Rubí B. de = EstFranc 37 (1986) 1013-1024 / 1025-1030; 1 pl.

8455 **Herszlikowicz** Michel, Philosophie de l'antisémitisme. P 1985, PUF. 176 p. – [R]RThom 86 (1986) 659-665 (J.-M. *Joubert*).

8456 Hinweise für eine richtige Darstellung von Juden und Judentum in der Predigt und in der Katechese der Katholischen Kirche [Vatikan. Komm. Beziehungen zum Judentum, 24.VI.1985]: FreibRu 37s (1985s) 9-14; 14-16, Kommentar, *Ehrlich* E. L., *Thoma* Clemens; 15-16, *Johannes Paul* II, 28.X.1985, Mit dem Stamm Abrahams geistlich verbunden.

8457 [E]**Hostens** Michiel, Theognosia [anon., saec. IX/X], dissertatio contra Iudaeos: CCGr 14. Turnhout 1986, Brepols. lxxx-313 p. 2-503-40141-4; pa. 2-2.

8458 *Hruby* Kurt, Zum Besuch des Papstes in der römischen Hauptsynagoge: Judaica 42 (1986) 99s.

8459 *a) Hüssler* Georg, *Saier* Oskar, Festakademie für Dr. Gertrud Luckner 22.IX.1985; – *b) Thoma* Clemens, Freiburger Rundbrief — Dokument christlich-jüdischer Begegnung nach 1945: FreibR 37s (1985s) 34-36 / 37-41 (-48 al.).

8460 *Jacob* Edmond, Le dialogue judéo-chrétien d'après quelques études récentes II: RHPR [63 (1983) 311-322] 66 (1986) 329-337.

8461 *Janssen* Henk, Zijn Christendom en Jodendom in feite één geloof?: OnsGLev 63 (1986) 226-237.

8462 *Jean-Paul II*, Visite à la synagogue de Rome (13 avril 1986) [discours, aussi du président *Saban* Giacomo et du Grand-Rabbi *Toaff* Elio]: Istina 31 (1986) 416-429.

8463 *a*) Papst *Johannes Paul* II. in der Synagoge in Rom, Sonntag, 13. April 1986; – *b*) *Toaff* Elio, Israels Rolle im Heilsplan Gottes; – *c*) Oss. Rom 18.IV.86; – *d*) *Ehrlich* E. L., Kommentar: FreibRu 37s (1985s) 3-5 / 5s / 6s / 7.

8464 *Jeffery* Peter, Lateinische liturgische Zitate im 'Nizahon Yasan'; eine jüdische Kritik aus dem Mittelalter an der katholischen Liturgie, ᵀ*Sobiela* G.: Judaica 41 (1985) 108-114.

8465 **Katz** David S., Philo-Semitism and the readmission of the Jews to England 1603-1655: 1982 ➤ 63,8903; 64,9048: ᴿRÉJ 145 (1986) 452-4 (M. R. *Hayoun*).

8466 **Klappert** Bertold, Israel und die Kirche; Erwägungen zur Israellehre Karl BARTHs: TExH 207, 1980 ➤ 61,y332; 62,9669: ᴿTsTKi 57 (1986) 235s (M. *Saebø*).

8467 ᴱ**Klenicki** Leon, *Wigoder* Geoffrey, A dictionary of the Jewish-Christian dialogue. NY 1984, Stimulus ➤ 65,8831: ᴿCC 137 (1986,3) 537s (S. M. *Katunarich*).

8468 *Kniewasser* Manfred, Die Wirkungsgeschichte des Pariser Talmud-prozesses 1242/48 auf das Herzogtum Österreich: Kairos 28 (1986) 221-7.

8469 *a*) *Knoch-Mund* Gaby & Christoph, Kulturelle und religiöse Begegnung von Juden, Christen und Muslimen — Lehren der Vergangenheit; – *b*) *Schreiner* Stefan, Von den theologischen Zwangsdisputationen des Mittelalters zum christlich-jüdischen Dialog heute: Judaica 42 (1986) 137-140 / 141-157.

8470 *Kocher* Hermann, Schweizerischer Protestantismus und jüdische Flücht-lingsnot nach 1933; Tradition und Neuaufbrüche: Judaica 42 (1986) 28-40.

8471 **Kohn** Johanna, Haschoah; christlich-jüdische Verständigung nach Auschwitz; Vorw. *Ginzel* G. B.: FundTheolSt 13. Mü/Mainz 1986, Kaiser/Grünewald. 107 p. DM 19,80 [TLZ 112,101].

8472 **Kohn** Rachael, Hebrew Christianity and Messianic Judaism on the Church-Sect continuum: diss. McMaster 1985. – RelStR 13,187.

8473 ᴱ**Kremers** Heinz, Die Juden und M. LUTHER 1985 ➤ 1,602*: ᴿÖkRu 35 (1986) 222s (H. *Krüger*).

8474 *a*) *Kremers* Heinz, Der Beitrag des Neuen Testaments zu einer nicht-antijüdischen Christologie; – *b*) *Klappert* Bertold, Dass Jesus ein geborener Jude ist: ➤ 65*, ᶠMAYER R., Wie Gut 1986, 196-207 / 221-250.

8475 *Landucci* Pier Carlo, Ebrei e Cristiani: Renovatio 20 (1985) 219-227 [PalCl 15.I.1985, *Caprile* Giovanni 'da non confondersi con l'omonimo scrittore gesuita']; 461-8, *Boldorini* Alberto; 469s, risposta del Landucci.

8476 **Lapide** Pinchas E., Hebrew in the Church 1984 ➤ 65,8834; **1**,a86: ᴿCalvinT 21 (1986) 265-9 (P. *Sigal*: transliterations like *acadec* without accompanying *yitkadesh* are derisive rather than helpful); ChH 55 (1986) 84 (F. *Czerwinski*); RelStR 6 (1986) 84-86 (A. *Rippin*).

8477 **Lapide** P., *Luz* U., Jesus in two perspectives; ; a Jewish-Christian dialogue 1985 ➤ 1,a87: ᴿTS 47 (1986) 744 (D. J. *Harrington*).

8478 ᴱ**Lauer** Simon, Kritik und Gegenkritik in Christentum und Judentum:

JudChr 3, 1981 ➤ 63,8912: 65,8836: ᴿRÉJ 145 (1986) 420-3 (J.-P. *Rothschild*).
8479 *Levenson* J.D., Is there a counterpart in the Hebrew Bible to New Testament Antisemitism?: JEcuSt 22 (1985) 242-260.
8479* *Levine* R., Why praise Jews? Satire and history in the Middle Ages: Journal of Medieval History 12 (1986) 291-6.
8480 **Liebeschütz** Hans, Synagoge und Ecclesia 1983 ➤ 64,9058 ... 1,a91: ᴿRÉJ 145 (1986) 195s (M. R. *Hayoun*); ZRGg 38 (1986) 384s (H.-J. *Loth*).
8481 **Lindeskog** Gösta [1904-1984], Das jüdisch-christliche Problem; Randglossen zu einer Forschungsepoche: Ac U, Hist. Rel. 9. U 1986, Almqvist & W. 241 p.; bibliog. p. 219-241. 91-554-1915-1.
8482 **Lonsbach** Richard M., Friedrich NIETZSCHE und die Juden (1939), ²*Schlette* Heinz R. Bonn 1985, Bouvier. 102 p. – ᴿJudaica 42 (1986) 263s (P. *Maser*: dankbar zu begrüssen).
8483 **Lubarsky** Sandra B., Interreligious dialogue; four Jewish responses to religious pluralism: diss. Claremont 1986. – RelStR 13,187.
8484 **Maccoby** Hyam, Judaism on trial; Jewish-Christian disputations in the Middle Ages 1982 ➤ 64,9054; 65,8839: ᴿJQR 76 (1985s) 253-7 (D. *Berger*); RHR 203 (1986) 449s (S. *Schwarzfuchs*).
8485 *Macina* Robert, Le 'judéo-christianisme' de Franz ROSENZWEIG; compromis d'un Juif assimilé, esprit de système ou choix existentiel? Recherche d'une voie moyenne: RHPR 66 (1986) 429-450; Eng. 491.
8486 *McLain* Charles E., Israel's relation to the Church/Israel during the Church Age: CalvaryB 2,1 (1986) 51-66; 2,2 (1986) 39-55.
8487 **Maier** Johann, Jüdische Auseinandersetzung mit dem Christentum in der Antike: ErtFor 177, 1982 ➤ 63,8915 ... 65,8840: ᴿFranzSt 67 (1985) 362s (T. *Baumeister*); RÉJ 145 (1986) 188s (M. R. *Hayoun*); SvTKv 62 (1986) 77-79 (T. *Kronholm*).
8488 **Markish** Shimon, ERASMUS and the Jews ➒, ᵀ*Olcutt* Anthony. Ch 1985, Univ. viii-203 p. $25 [TS 48,401, M. R. *O'Connell*].
8489 **Michalski** Gabrielle, Der Antisemitismus im deutschen akademischen Leben in der Zeit nach dem I. Weltkrieg [diss. Paris VIII. 1975]: EurHS 3/128. Fra 1982, Lang. 244 p. – ᴿRÉJ 145 (1986) 480s (M. R. *Hayoun*).
8490 *a) Miller* Elizabeth M., The social context of the Jewish-Christian encounter; – *b) Wigoder* Geoffrey, The reaction of the Jews to LUTHER: Immanuel 20 (J 1986) 84-95 / 101-3.
8491 **Monti** J.E., Who do you say that I am? The Christian understanding of Christ and Antisemitism 1984 ➤ 65,8847; 1,a102 [Christian half of 1982 Vanderbilt forum; P. *Haas* was the Jewish representative]. NY 1984, Paulist. vii-98 p. $4. 0-8091-2598-6. – TsTNijm 26 (1986) 95.
8492 *Morris* Kevin L., The Vatican against Israel: Month 248 (1986) 302-5.
8493 **Mutius** Hans-Georg von, Die christlich-jüdische Zwangsdisputation zu Barcelona nach dem hebräischen Protokoll des Moses NACHMA-NIDES: JudUmw 5, 1982 ➤ 63,8920 ... 1,a103: ᴿRÉJ 145 (1986) 445s (G. *Dahan*).
8494 *Neher-Bernheim* Renée, L'assimilation linguistique des Juifs d'Alexandrie; une des sources de l'antijudaïsme antique: ➤ 81, Mém. NIKI-PROWETZKY V., Hellenica 1986, 313-9.
8495 ᴱ**Neusner** J., *Frerichs* J., 'To see ourserves as others see us' 1984/5 ➤ 1,300: ᴿTS 47 (1986) 316s (D. J. *Harrington*).
8496 *Neusner* Jacob, *a)* The Jewish-Christian argument in the first century; different people talking about different things to different people: RelStR 6 (1986) 8-19; – *b)* Den jødisk-kristne diskusjon i første århundre; hvordan to

grupper snakker forbi hverandre, ᵀ*Moxnes* Halvor: NorTTs 87 (1986) 205-217.

8497 **Oberman** Heiko A., The roots of anti-Semitism 1984 ⇥ 65,8850c; 1,a107: ᴿAndrUnS 24 (1986) 69s (K. A. *Strand*: the original scope of the work was LUTHER and the Jews).

8498 **Oesterreicher** J. M., The new encounter between Christians and Jews. NY 1986, Philosophical. 439 p. $25 [Judaica 42,269].

8498* *Olivari* M., Note sui rapporti tra ebrei e cattolici nei Cinquecento: Quaderni storici 21 (1986) 951-970 [RHE 82,318*].

8499 **Osier** J. P., L'évangile du Ghetto, ou comment les Juifs se racontaient Jésus. P 1984, Berg. 174 p. – ᴿIslamochristiana 12 (1986) 265s (J. M. *Gaudeul*).

8500 *a*) *Osten-Sacken* Peter von der, Christlich-jüdischer Dialog; – *b*) *Awerbuch* Marianne, Antijudaismus, antisemitismus: ⇥ 587, EvKL 1 (1986) 685-692 / 174-181.

8501 *Pacelli* Diana, La radice e i rami; intorno ai Sussidi per una corretta presentazione degli Ebrei e dell'ebraismo nella predicazione e nella catechesi della Chiesa cattolica: RasT 27 (1986) 352-364.

8502 *Pfister* Rudolf, Verantwortung, informative Texte; Jüdisch-christlicher Dialog. Stu-Neuhausen 1985, Hänssler. 302 p. – ᴿRHPR 66 (1986) 334 (E. *Jacob*).

8503 *Poirier* Paul-Hubert, Éléments de polémique anti-juive dans l'Ad Diognetum: VigChr 40 (1986) 218-225.

8504 **Poliakov** Léon, Geschichte des Antisemitismus 5. Die Aufklärung und ihre judenfeindliche Tendenz 1983 ⇥ 1,a114; DM 38: ᴿZkT 108 (1986) 92 (R. *Oberforcher*: Toledot Jeschu Jh. 9.-10. nicht 1.).

8505 **Poliakov** Leon, The history of anti-semitism; suicidal Europe, 1870-1933. NY 1986, Vanguard. xi-422 p. $22.50 [Judaism 35,505].

8506 **Praag** H. Van, Damit die Erde blüht; das Phänomen Israel [Het verschijnsel Israel]: Judentum Heute. Köln 1986, Scriba. 128 p. DM 16,80 3-921232-37-6 [BL 87,115s, R. B. *Salters*].

8507 *Raddatz* Alfred, Zur Vorgeschichte der 'Epistula seu liber contra Judaeos' AMULOS von Lyon: ⇥ 60, ᶠLENZENWEGER J., Ecclesia peregrinans 1986, 53-58.

8508 **Remaud** Michel, Chrétiens devant Israël serviteur de Dieu 1983 ⇥ 65,8863; 1,a118: ᴿBLitEc 87 (1986) 143s (L. *Monloubou*: on peut critiquer la critique de BENOIT P. sur MUSSNER F.); RencChrJ 19,78 (1985) 34s (G. *Passelecq*).

8509 **Remaud** Michel, Cristiani di fronte a Israele [cioè all'antisemitismo]; pref. *Lovsky* F.: Shalom. Brescia 1986, Morcelliana. 308 p. Lit. 16.000. – ᴿLetture 41 (1986) 885 (E. *Rivolta*).

8510 *Ribière* G. A., Réflexion à propos du Carmel d'Auschwitz [... offense et injure à nos frères juifs... une impossible fondation]: RencChrJ 20,82 (1986) 5-18.

8511 *Riegner* Gerhart M., Nostra aetate — 20 Jahre danach; – *b*) *Johannes Paul II* an Teilnehmer des Symposiums 19.IV.1985: FreibR 37s (1985s) 18-24 / 24s.

8512 *a*) *Riegner* G., 'Nostra aetate' veinte años después; – *b*) *Cabanellas* M., Sobre la recepción del D. C. 'Nostra aetate' en España; –) *Toledano* S., La nueva declaración del Vaticano y su repercusión entre los judíos: El Olivo 23 (1986) 73-95 / 95-107 / 107-121 [< Judaica 42,272].

8513 **Rosenberg** Stuart E., The Christian problem; a Jewish view. NY 1986, Hippocrene. xii-241 p. $16 [RelStR 13,325, J. *Carlson*].

8514 **Rosenberg** Stuart E. (rabbi), Christians and Jews: the eternal bond[2]; pref. *Hesburgh* T. NY 1985, Ungar. 200 p. $14. 0-8044-5800-6. – RSpTod 38 (1986) 190 (R. *Weber*: good on Jews).

8515 **Roynesdal** Olaf, Martin LUTHER and the Jews: diss. Marquette. Milwaukee 1986. 418 p. 87-08746. – DissA 47 (1986s) 4420-A.

8516 *Ruiz* Gregorio, España y los Judíos; una larga historia de rencor y tolerancia: RazF 213 (1986) 351-363.

8517 *Schmid* Augustin, Antijudaismus im NT ? : TGegw 23 (1985) 48-54.

8518 ESchoeps Julius H., Im Streit um Kafka und Judentum; Max BROD, Hans-Joachim SCHOEPS, Briefwechsel. Königstein 1985, Athenäum [NedTTs 41,241-3, R. *Hensen*].

8519 **Schoeps** Hans-Joachim, Jüdisch-christliches Religionsgespräch in neunzehn Jahrhunderten [1937] 1984 ➤ 1,a27: RJudaica 41 (1985) 120s (S. *Schreiner*); ZkT 108 (1986) 83 (G. *Fischer*).

8520 **Schreckenberg** Heinz, Die christlichen Adversus-Judaeos-Texte und ihr literarisches und historisches Umfeld (1.-11. Jh.): EurHS 23/172, 1982 ➤ 63,8936... 1,a129: RJudaica 41 (1985) 118-120 (P. *Maser*).

8521 **See** Wolfgang, Der Apostel Paulus und die Nürnberger Gesetze; Traktat über den abendlandlangen (sic) Antisemitismus der Christen anlässlich eines fünfzigsten Jahrestages [15.IX.1935]. B 1985, Wichern. 128 p. DM 14. – RZKG 97 (1986) 423-5 (K. *Haacker*).

8522 **Sgherri** Giuseppe, Chiesa e sinagoga nelle opere di ORIGENE 1982 ➤ 63, 8938... 1,a132: RAthenaeum 64 (1986) 285-9 (C. *Scaglioni*); Salesianum 48 (1986) 447s (B. *Amata*); TLZ 111 (1986) 455-7 (W. *Ullmann*).

8523 **Sherman** Shlomoh, Escape from Jesus; one man's search for a meaningful Judaism; pref. *Riskin* Shlomoh. Mount Vernon NY 1983, Decalogue. 222 p. [KirSef 59,442].

8524 **Simon** Marcel, Verus Israel; a study of the relations between Christians and Jews in the Roman Empire (A.D. 135-425) [c. 1948], TMcKeating H. NY 1985, Oxford-UP. 592 p. £30. – RTablet 240 (1986) 908s (Ulrich *Simon*).

8525 *Simpson* John W.J, The Jews of today according to twentieth-century German Protestant dogmatics: StudiaBT 13 (1983) 195-224.

8526 **Stefani** Piero, Tradimento fedele; la tradizione ebraica, provocazione per il cristiano, pref. *De Benedetti* P. 1983 ➤ 64,9087; 65,8874: RHumBr 41 (1986) 453 (F. *Montagnini*).

8527 *a)* *Stendahl* Krister bp., Die nächste Generation in den jüdisch-christlichen Beziehungen [< Boston 1983]; – *b)* *Rendtorff* Rolf, 'Das Land hatte vierzig Jahre Ruhe': KIsr 1 (1986) 11-15 / 9s.

8528 **Stow** Kenneth R., The '1007 anonymous' and Papal sovereignty; Jewish perceptions of papacy and papal policy in the high Middle Ages: HUC Sup 4, 1984➤ 1,a141: RJudaica 42 (1986) 260s (S. *Schreiner*); ScripB 17 (1986s) 21s (C. *Harper-Bill*).

8529 **Stroh** Hans, Juden und Christen — schwierige Partner..... Quell – RRHPR 66 (1986) 333s (E. *Jacob*; coquille p. 329).

8530 *Tamás* Bertalan, Ⓜ Antisemitism from Christian point of view: Theologiai Szemle 29 (1986) 147-153.

8531 *Torrance* David, *Lamont* Alastair, Anti-Semitism and Christian responsibility. E 1986, Handsel. 16 p. [TLZ 111,817].

8532 *Vasholz* R.I., Is the New Testament anti-Semitic?: Presbyterion 11,2 (1985) 118-123.

8533 EVogel Rolf, Ernst Ludwig EHRLICH und der christlich-jüdische Dialog

1984 ⇥ 1,a144: ᴿFreibRu 37s (1985s) 125 (P. *Fiedler*); TR 82 (1986) 244s (K.-H. *Minz*).

8534 *Waegeman* Maryse, Les traités Adversus Judaeos; aspects des relations judéo-chrétiennes dans le monde grec: Byzantion 56 (1986) 295-313.

8535 *Wallmann* Johannes, LUTHERs Stellung zu Judentum und Islam: Luther 57 (Wu 1986) 49-60.

8536 ᴱ**Walter** Rudolf, Das Judentum lebt — ich bin ihm begegnet [Erfahrung von D. *Sölle*, H. *Küng*, und noch 19 Christen]. FrB 1985, Herder. 167 p. – ᴿFreibRu 37s (1985s) 132s (E. L. *Ehrlich*).

8537 *Wilken* Robert L., Christianity and Judaism: ⇥ 585, EncRel 2 (1986) 431-8.

8538 *a*) *Willebrands* J. C., Is Christianity antisemitic?; – *b*) *Cracknell* K., Christianity and religious pluralism; the ethics of interfaith relations: Christian-Jewish Relations 2 (1985) 8-21 / 40-59.

8539 *a*) *Willebrands* Johannes. Notes pour une correcte présentation des juifs et du judaïsme dans la prédication et la catéchèse de l'Église Catholique (24.VI.1985); – *b*) *Siegman* Henry, La signification religieuse de la 'Terre d'Israël' dans les Notes catéchétiques; – *c*) *Fisher* Eugene J., L'évolution d'une tradition; de 'Nostra aetate' aux 'Notes', ᵀ*Delmotte* Marguerite; – *d*) *Waxman* Mordecai, Réflexions sur le dialogue à venir, ᵀ*Delmotte* M.: Istina 31 (1986) 207-219 / 184-7 / 163-180 / 148-162.

8540 *Willebrands* J. C., *a*) Vatican II and the Jews; twenty years later; – *b*) Is Christianity antisemitic?: Christian Jewish Relations (1985,1) 16-31 / (1985,2) 8-21 [Judaica 41,254s].

8541 *Winogradsky* Alexandre A., Présences hébraïques dans l'histoire de l'Église: RechSR 74 (1986) 511-536; Eng. 558.

8542 *Wytzes* J., AMBROSIUS en de Joden: KerkT 37 (1986) 2-20.

8543 **Yaseen** Leonard C., The Jesus connection; to triumph over anti-Semitism; pref. *Hesburgh* T. NY 1985, Crossroad. xvi-154 p. $10 pa. [TDig 33,495]. – ᴿSpTod 38 (1986) 190s (R. *Weber*: thin, gushy).

8544 **Zuidema** W., Gottes Partner; Begegnung mit dem Judentum [mehr Ethik als Dogmatik], ᵀ*Bunte* W.: Information Judentum 4, 1983 ⇥ 65,8883: ᴿArLtgW 28 (1986) 166s (J. *Hennig*).

XVII,3 Gnosis et religiones parabiblicae

M1.1   **Gnosticismus classicus.**

8545 **Buckley** Jorunn J., Female fault and fulfilment in Gnosticism: Studies in Religion. Chapel Hill 1986, Univ. North Carolina. xv-180 p.

8546 **Culianu** Ioan P., Gnosticismo e pensiero moderno; Hans JONAS. R 1985, Bretschneider. 155 p. – ᴿVigChr 40 (1986) 414 (G. *Quispel*: restrained).

8547 *Jaeschke* Walter, Gnostizismus — ein Schlagwort zwischen geschichtlicher Aufklärung und Häreseomachie: ArBegG 28 (1984) 269-280.

8548 *Ménard* J.-E., Le *pneuma (ruaḥ)* dans l'hellénisme et les gnoses: ⇥ 595, SDB 11,60 (1986) 165-172.

8549 ᴱ**Moraldi** Luigi, [⇥ 8616] Testi gnostici 1982 ⇥ 64,4116: ᴿRivStoLR 22 (1986) 152-160 (C. *Gianotto*).

8550 *a*) *Pearson* Birger A., Jewish sources in Gnostic literature; – *b*) *Smith* Morton, The Jewish elements in the magical papyri: ⇥ 392, SBL Seminars 1986, 422-454 / 455-462.

8551 a) *Pearson* Birger A.,   The problem of 'Jewish Gnostic' literature; – b) *Turner* John D.,   Sethian Gnosticism, a literary history: ➤ 374, ᴱ*Hedrick* C., Nag Hammadi 1983/6, 15-35 / 55-86.

8552 **Pétrement** Simone,   Le Dieu séparé; les origines du gnosticisme 1984 ➤ 65,8901; 1,a170:   ᴿGregorianum 67 (1986) 784s (A. *Orbe*); RHPR 66 (1986) 349s (P. *Maraval*); RTPhil 118 (1986) 81s (Françoise *Morard*).

8553 ᶠQUISPEL Gilles,   Studies in Gnosticism... ᴱ**Broek** B. van den, *al.*: ÉPR 91, 1981 ➤ 62,139... 64,100:   ᴿOLZ 81 (1986) 357-361 (H.-F. *Weiss*).

8554 **Quispel** G. [The birth of the child; some Gnostic and Jewish aspects < EranosJb 40 (1971) 285-209], *Scholem* G. [Three types of Jewish piety, < EranosJb 38 (1969) 331-348]; Jewish and Gnostic man: Eranos Lectures 3. Dallas 1985, Spring. 46 p. 0-88214-403-0 [NTAbs 30,378].

8555 *Quispel* G.,   Gnosis en katholicisme: Streven 53 (1985s) 710-714.

8556 **Rudolph** Kurt, Gnosis; the nature and history of an ancient religion 1983 ➤ 64,9119... 1,a173:   ᴿJTS 37 (1986) 202-6 (R. *Williams*); StPatav 33 (1986) 705s (G. *Segalla*).

8557 a) *Rudolph* Kurt,   Gnosis — eine spätantike Weltanschauung; ihre Denkstrukturen und Wurzeln; – b) *Lona* Horacio E.,   Die Auseinandetzung der Kirchenväter mit der Gnosis; – c) *Hofrichter* Peter, 'Gnosis und Johannesevangelium'; – d) Frankemolle Hubert,   Die Welt als Gefängnis; die gnostische Deutung des Menschen in der Welt — eine nicht nur historische Frage: BiKi 41,1 (1986) 2-7 / 8-14 / 15-21 / 22-33.

8558 **Schmithals** Walter,   Neues Testament und Gnosis: ErtFor 208, 1984 ➤ 65,8904; 1,a174:   ᴿBLitEc 87 (1986) 150 (S. *Légasse*); FreibRu 37s (1985s) 107 (C. *Thoma*); Gregorianum 67 (1986) 546s (G. L. *Prato*); Numen 33 (1986) 170s (G. G. *Stroumsa*).

8559 **Segal** Robert A.,   The Poimandres as myth; scholarly theory and Gnostic meaning: Religion and Reason 33.   B 1986, Mouton de Gruyter. viii-214 p.; bibliog. p. 171-209. 3-11-010791-0.

8560 **Stroumsa** Gedaliahu A. G.,   Another seed; studies in Gnostic mythology: NHS 24, 1984 ➤ 65,8995; 1,a176:   ᴿBO 43 (1986) 423-5 (J. *Helderman*); JTS 37 (1986) 206-8 (R. M. *Wilson*); VigChr 40 (1986) 96-101 (G. *Quispel*: ground-breaking).

8561 **Tardieu** Michel,   Écrits gnostiques; Codex de Berlin 1984 ➤ 65,8907; 1,a177:   ᴿGregorianum 67 (1986) 379 (A. *Orbe*).

8562 **Tardieu** Michel,   *Dubois* Jean-Daniel,   Introduction à la littérature gnostique, I. Collections retrouvées avant 1945: Initiations au christianisme ancien. P 1986, Cerf/CNRS. 152 p. F 130. – ᴿRivStoLR 22 (1986) 539-542 (C. *Gianotto*); RThom 86 (1986) 517 [J.-M. *Fabre*]; STBuc 38,3 (1986) 112-120 (T. *Baconsky*, rum.).

8563 *Tröger* Karl-Wolfgang, ⓜ Gnosis, New Testament, Church [Raday lecture Oct. 1984): Theologiai Szemle 28 (1985) 82-85.

8564 **Williams** Michael A.,   The immovable race [diss. ᴰ*MacRae* G. ➤ 1, a181!]; a Gnostic designation and the theme of stability in late antiquity: NHS 29, 1985:   ᴿJTS 37 (1986) 570-2 (R. M. *Wilson*); RHPR 66 (1986) 354 (D. A. *Bertrand*); VigChr 40 (1986) 411s (G. *Quispel*: good but some flaws).

8565 *Wilson* Robert M.,   Ethics and the Gnostics: ➤ 39, ᶠGREEVEN H., Text/Ethik 1986, 440-9.

M1.2   *Valentinus – Pistis sophia – ***Elchasai.**

8566 *Bammel* Caroline,   Herakleon: ➤ 597, TRE 15 (1986) 54-57.

8567 *Baumgarten* Joseph M., The book of Elkesai and Merkabah mysticism: JStJud 17 (1986) 212-223.

8568 *Buckley* Jorunn J., Tools and tasks; Elchasaite and Manichaean purification rituals: JRel 66 (1986) 399-411.

8569 **Cirillo** L., Elchasai e gli Elchasaiti 1984 → 65,4630; 1,a184a: ᴿProtestantesimo 41 (1986) 50s (G. *Gonnet*).

8570 *a*) *Cirillo* Luigi, Elchasaiti e Battisti di Mani; i limiti di un confronto delle fonti; – *b*) *Klijn* A. F. J., Alchasaios et CMC; – *c*) *Ries* J., La doctrine de l'âme du monde et des trois sceaux dans la controverse de Mani avec les Elchasaïtes: → 421, Codex Manichaicus 1984/6, 97-139 / 141-152 / 169-181.

8571 *Desjardins* Michel, The sources for Valentinian gnosticism; a question of methodology: VigChr 40 (1986) 342-7.

8572 **Luttikhuizen** Gerard P., The revelation of Elchasai [ᴰ1984 → 65,8562; 1,a184b]: TStAntJud 8. Tü 1985, Mohr. xii-252 p. DM 98. 3-16-144935-5. – ᴿAugR 26 (1986) 580s (E. *Peretto*); BL (1986) 126 (P. S. *Alexander*); JJS 37 (1986) 102 (S. *Brock*); JStJud 17 (1986) 257-9 (J. M. *Baumgarten*); Salesianum 48 (1986) 423 (R. *Vicent*); SNTU-A 11 (1986) 255-7 (H. *Giesen*).

8573 **Ménard** Jacques-Étienne, L'exposé valentinien; les fragments sur le baptême et sur l'eucharistie (NH XI,2): BCNH-T 14. Québec 1985, Univ. Laval. viii-109 p. Fb 1000. 2-7637-7057-6. – ᴿETL 62 (1986) 436s (A. de *Halleux*); ÉTRel 61 (1986) 266 (J.-D. *Dubois*: texte ingrat mais passionnant; aussi sur Résurrection et Silvanos); NRT 108 (1986) 763 (X. *Jacques*); TR 82 (1986) 463s (H.-J. *Klauck*); JTS 37 (1986) 566s (R. M. *Wilson*); Muséon 99 (1986) 213 (Yvonne *Janssens*).

M1.3 **Corpus hermeticum; Orphismus.**

8574 ᴱ**Hurst** André, *al.*, Papyrus Bodmer XXIX — vision de Dorothéos; avec *Kasser* R. *al.*, Description et datation du Codex des Visions. Genève-Coligny 1984, Fond. Bodmer. 129 p.; 9 pl. – ᴿRTPhil 118 (1986) 82s (É. *Junod*).

8575 **Iversen** Erik, Egyptian and Hermetic doctrine: Opuscula gr.-lat. 27, 1984 → 65,8924; 1,a189: ᴿBO 43 (1986) 406-8 (E. *Hornung*); ClasR 100 (1986) 323s (J. G. *Griffiths*).

8576 **Mahé** Jean-Pierre, Hermès en Haute-Égypte II. Le fragment du Discours Parfait et les Définitions herméneutiques arméniennes (NH VI,8.8a): BCNH Textes 7, 1982 → 63,8974*b*... 1,a191: ᴿÉTRel 61 (1986) 261s (J.-D. *Dubois*); JTS 37 (1986) 560-6 (F. *Siegert*, deutsch); TR 82 (1986) 377-380 (T. *Baumeister*, auch über vol. 1 und Ähnliches).

8577 **Whitehouse** David J. M., The hymns of the *Corpus Hermeticum*; forms with a diverse functional history: diss. Harvard... – HarvTR 79 (1986) 483s.

8578 *Casadio* Giovanni, Adversus orphica et orientalia: SMSR 52 (1986) 291-322.

8579 *Finkelberg* Aryeh, On the unity of Orphic and Milesian thought: HarvTR 79 (1986) 321-336.

8580 **Halleux** R., *Schamp* J., Les lapidaires grecs... orphique... d'Orphée 1985 → 1,a195: ᴿSalesianum 48 (1986) 978 (R. *Della Casa*).

8581 *Pérez Gago* Santiago, Proceso de identidad estética; *a*) Semblante órfico, selección *Ortega Jaldo* José L.; *b*) Órficos; selección *Espinosa Rubio* Luciano. Salamanca 1985, San Esteban. 179 p.; 127 p. [MélSR 43,227].

8582 **West** M. L., The Orphic poems 1983 ➤ 1,a197: [R]AntClas 55 (1986) 415-7
(Annie *Bonnafé*: passionant).

M1.5 **Mani,** *dualismus;* **Mandaei.**

8583 *Bammel* Ernst, Zur Frühgeschichte der Mandäer [< Orientalia 32 (1963)
220-5]: ➤ 131, Judaica 1986, 86-92.
8584 **Bianchi** Ugo, Il dualismo religioso ²1983 ➤ 64,9140: [R]AntClas 55
(1986) 502s (M. *Graulich*: rien sur Mexique).
8585 *a) Bianchi* Ugo, Osservazioni storico-religiose sul Codice Manicheo
di Colonia; – *b) Rudolph* Kurt, Jüdische und christliche Täufertraditio
nen im Spiegel des CMC; – *c) Strecker* Georg, Das Judenchristentum und
der Manikodex; – *d) Henrichs* Albert, The timing of supernatural events
in the CMC; – *e) Sundermann* Werner, Mani's revelations in the CMC
and in other sources; – *f) Römer* Cornelia, Mani, der neue Urmensch;
eine neue Interpretation der p. 36 des Kölner Mani-Kodex: ➤ 421, Codex Manichaicus 1984/6, 17-35 / 69-80 / 81-96 / 183-204 / 205-214 /
333-344.
8586 **Böhlig** A., Die Gnosis 3. Der Manichäismus 1980 ➤ 61,k315; 62,9787:
[R]VigChr 40 (1986) 406-8 (C. *Colpe*, auch über FELDMANN E. 1975).
8587 *Delcor* Mathias, *Aggoula* Basile. Une coupe mandéenne inédite du musée
du Louvre: CRAI (1986) 262-289.
8588 *Drijvers* Han J. W., *a)* Mani und Bardaisan; ein Beitrag zur
Vorgeschichte des Manichäismus [< [F]PUECH H. 1974, 459-469]; – *b)* Odes
of Solomon and Psalms of Mani; Christians and Manichaeans in
Third-Century Syria [< [F]QUISPEL G. 1981, 117-130]: ➤ 153, East of
Antioch 1984, XIII / X (original page-numbering).
8588* **Duvernoy** J., Le Catharisme, 1. La religion des cathares; 2. L'histoire
des cathares. Toulouse 1986, Privat. 404 p., 4 pl.; 398 p., 8 pl. F 135
chaque [RHE 82,267*].
8589 *Filoramo* Giovanni, Dal mito gnostico al mito manicheo; metamorfosi di
modelli culturali: ➤ 537, Trasformazioni 1982/5, 491-507.
8590 **Fontaine** P. F. M., The light and the dark; a cultural history of dualism,
I. Dualism in the archaic and early classical periods of Greek history.
Amst 1986, Gieben. xvi-293 p.; bibliog. p. 265-279. 90-70265-40-0.
8591 *a) Giversen* Søren, The inedited Chester Beatty Mani texts; – *b) Stroumsa*
G. G., Esotericism in Mani's thought and background; – *c) Poirier* P.-H.,
L'Hymne de la Perle et le manichéisme à la lumière du CMC; – *d) Sfameni
Gasparro* Giulia, Tradizione e nuova creazione religiosa nel manicheismo;
il *syzygos* e la missione profetica di Mani: ➤ 421, Codex Manichaicus
Coloniensis 1984/6, 371-380 / 153-168 / 235-248.
8592 **Klimkeit** Hans J., Manichaean art and calligraphy: IconRel 20, 1982
➤ 63,8986... 65,8934: [R]OLZ 81 (1986) 470-2 (J. P. *Asmussen*).
8593 *Klimkeit* Hans-J., *a)* Ausbreitung und Untergang einer Weltreligion; die
Geschichte des Manichäismus [*Lieu* S. 1985]: ZRGg 38 (1986) 370-2; – *b)*
Jesus' entry into Parinirvāna; Manichaean identity in Buddhist central
Asia: Numen 33 (1986) 225-240.
8594 **Koenen** L., *Römer* C., Neue Lesungen im Kölner-Codex: ZPapEp 66
(1986) 265-8.
8595 **Lieu** S., Manichaeism 1985 ➤ 1,a207: [R]JEH 37 (1986) 622s (W. H. C.
Frend).
8595* *Lieu* Samuel N. C., Some themes in later Roman anti-Manichaean
polemics II: BJRyL 69 (1986s) 235-275.

8596 **Ménard** J., De la Gnose au Manichéisme: Gnostica. P 1986, Cariscript. 105 p. F 89 [NRT 109,445, X. *Jacques*].

8597 *Merkelbach* R., *a*) Manichaica (7); ein Fragment aus der Epistula fundamenti; – *b*) Die Zahl 9999 in der Magie und der computus digitorum: ZPapEp 63 (1986) 303s [64 (1986) 53-55] / 305-8; fig. p. 307.

8598 *Quispel* Gilles, Alle origini del catarismo: SMSR 52 (1986) 101-112.

8599 Effacement du catharisme? (XIIIe-XIVe siècles): Cahiers de Fanjeaux 20. Toulouse 1985, Privat. 384 p. F 119. – [R]MélSR 43 (1986) 171 (H. *Platelle*).

8600 *Ries* Julien, *a*) Sacré, sainteté et salut gnostique dans la liturgie manichéenne copte; – *b*) Retour ou permanence du sacré?; – *c*) Homo religiosus, sacré, sainteté: → 493, Expression du Sacré 3 (1978/86) 257-288 / 1-13 / 331-384 (-397, bibliog.).

8601 **Rudolph** Kurt, Der mandäische 'Diwan der Flüsse', AbhLp 70/1, 1982 → 65,8936: [R]OLZ 81 (1986) 260s (B. *Brentjes*).

8602 *Stein-Schneider* Herbert, La 'confessio evangelica' du Catharisme occitan; nouveaux aspects du Catharisme; le Catharisme vu par lui-même: ÉTRel 61 (1986) 353-370.

8603 *Sundermann* Werner, Studien zur kirchengeschichtlichen Literatur der iranischen Manichäer: AltOrF 13 (1986) 40-92. 239-317.

8604 **Villey** André, ALEXANDRE de Lycopolis, Contre la doctrine de Mani: SourcesGn 2, 1985 → 1,a218: [R]ScripTPamp 18 (1986) 292-4 (M. *Merino*); Teresianum 37 (1986) 513 (M. *Diego Sánchez*); TLZ 111 (1986) 439 (T. *Holtz*); VigChr 40 (1986) 198-201 (G. *Quispel*).

M2.1 Nag'-Ḥammadi, generalia.

8605 [E]**Robinson** J., NHC Facsimile edition, Codex I, 1977 [→ 61,k355], Cartonnage [1980 → 62,9811; 63,9008]: [R]OLZ 81 (1986) 241-4. 551-4 (W.-P. *Funk*).

8606 **Arthur** Rose H., The wisdom goddess; feminine motifs in eight Nag Hammadi documents 1984 → 1,a220: [R]CBQ 48 (1986) 733s (S. L. *Davies*).

Hedrick Charles W., Nag Hammadi, Gnosticism and early Christianity 1986 → 374.

8608 *Poirier* Paul-Hubert, La bibliothèque copte de Nag Hammadi; sa nature et son importance: SR 15 (1986) 303-316.

8609 **Tuckett** C. M., Nag Hammadi and the Gospel tradition: Studies of the NT and its world. E 1986, Clark. XII-194 p. £12. – [R]CiTom 113 (1986) 629s (J. L. *Espinel*).

M2.2 *Evangelium etc. Thomae* – **The Gospel** (etc.) **of Thomas.**

8610 **Amersfoort** Jacobus van, Het Evangelie van Thomas en de Pseudo-Clementinen: diss. Utrecht, [D]*Quispel* G. 1984 → 65,8958: [R]NedTTs 40 (1986) 344 (B. *Dehandschutter*).

8611 *Crossan* J. D., Four other Gospels 1985 → 1,a228: [R]Interpretation 40 (1986) 316 (Pheme *Perkins*: raises questions but makes to real effort to explain); Themelios 12 (1986s) 56-60 (D. F. *Wright*); TLond 39 (1986) 402-4 (W. R. *Telford*: 'It find it difficult').

8612 **Davies** Stevan L., The Gospel of Thomas and Christian wisdom 1983 → 64,9186; 1,a229: [R]BibTB 16 (1986) 29 (P. J. *Kobelski*).

8613 [T]**Iyer** P., The Gospel according to Thomas, with complementary texts [and essays]. Santa Barbara 1983, Concord Grove. viii-130 p. $8.50 pa. 0-88695-005-8 [NTAbs 30,373].

8614 **Kuntzmann** Raymond, Le livre de Thomas [l'Athlète] (NH II,7): BCNH Textes 16. Québec 1986, Univ. Laval. xvi-201 p.

8615 **LaFargue** Michael, Language and gnosis; the opening scenes of the Acts of Thomas [diss. ^D*Georgi* D.]: Harvard Diss. Rel. 18, 1985 → 1,a231: ^RRelStR 12 (1986) 296 (B. A. *Pearson*).

8616 **Moraldi** Luigi [→ 8542], I Vangeli Gnostici 1984 → 1,a234: ^RVigChr 40 (1986) 101s (G. *Quispel*).

Poirier Paul-Hubert, La version copte de la Prédication et du Martyre de Thomas 1984 → 8120.

M2.3 *Singula scripta* – **Nag' Hammadi, various titles.**

8618 *Broek* Roelof van den, The theology of the Teachings of Silvanus: VigChr 40 (1986) 1-23.

8619 ^E**Janssens** Yvonne, Les leçons de Silvanos (NH VII,4) 1983 → 64,2905 ... 1,a243: 2-7637-7026-6: ^RGregorianum 67 (1986) 569 (A. *Orbe*); Muséon 99 (1986) 183-6 (P.-H. *Poirier*); RHR 203 (1986) 439s (P. *Nautin*: not a Gnostic text; in fact anti-Gnostic).

8620 **Cameron** Ron, Sayings traditions in the Apocryphon of James [NH; Diss. Harvard 1983] 1984 → 65,8970; 1,a240: ^RJAAR 54 (1986) 371s (S. E. *Robinson*).

8621 *Camplani* Alberto, Alcune note sul testo del VI codice di Nag Hammadi; la predizione di Hermes ad Asclepius: AugR 26 (1986) 349-368.

8622 **Chérix** Pierre, Le Concept de notre Grande Puissance (CG IV,4 [diss. Rome, ^D*Quecke* H.]; texte, remarques philologiques, traduction et notes: OBO 47, 1982 → 63,9045; 64,9213: ^RCdÉ 61 (1986) 177-180 (C. *Cannuyer*); ÉTRel 61 (1986) 266s (J.-D. *Dubois*); LavalTP 42 (1986) 274 (A. *Veilleux*); RelStR 12 (1986) 70 (B. A. *Pearson*).

8623 **Claude** Paul, Les trois stèles de Seth; hymne gnostique à la Triade (NH VII, 5): BCNH Textes 8, 1983 → 64,9204; 65,8978: ^RCBQ 48 (1986) 555-7 (Pheme *Perkins*, also on four other 1983 volumes of the series); ÉTRel 61 (1986) 262s (J.-D. *Dubois*).

8624 **Painchaud** L., Le deuxième traité du grand Seth (NH VII,2) 1982 → 63,9042 ... 1,a251: ^RCdÉ 61 (1986) 175-7 (E. *Lucchesi*).

8625 **Sevrin** Jean-Marie, Le dossier baptismal séthien; études 1985 → 1,a256: BCNH Études 2. Québec 1986, Univ. Laval. xx-306 p. 2-7637-7062-2. – ^RRTLv 17 (1986) 345s (P.-M. *Bogaert*).

8626 **Emmel** S., *Koester* H., *Pagels* Elaine, Nag Hammadi Codex III,5, The dialogue of the savior: NHS 26, 1984 → 65,8981: ^RCBQ 48 (1986) 335s (A. J. *Droge*); Enchoria 14 (1986) 175-187 (H.-M. *Schenke*); RHPR 66 (1986) 341 (D. A. *Bertrand*).

8627 *Gianotto* Claudio, Esegesi e interpretazione della Scrittura nel Testimonium Veritatis (NHC IX,3): → 365*, AnStoEseg 3 (1985/6) 149-162.

8628 **Helderman** Jan, Die Anapausis im Ev.-Ver.: NHS 18, ^D1984 → 65,8972...

1,a244:   RCBQ 48 (1986) 749s (H. W. *Attridge*); NedTTs 40 (1986) 343s (B. *Dehandschutter*); NT 28 (1986) 93s (A. F. J. *Klijn*).

8629 EKasser R., *al.*, Tractatus tripartitus, I. De supernis [editio princeps]. 1973 → 55,1560; 56,1454:   RRHPR 66 (1986) 339s (J.-D. *Dubois*).

8630 *Myszor* Wincenty, ℗ Chrzest jako milczenie; z gnostyckiej teologii chrztu w 'Tractatus tripartitus': ColcT 56,1 (1986) 25-28; 28s, Die Taufe als Schweigen.

8631 **Layton** Bentley, The Gnostic treatise on resurrection from Nag Hammadi 1979 → 61,k476; 63,9040:   ROLZ 81 (1986) 361-3 (H.-F. *Weiss*).

8632 *a) Layton* Bentley, The riddle of the thunder (NHC VI,2); the function of paradox in a Gnostic text from Nag Hammadi; – *b) Attridge* Harold W., The Gospel of Truth as an exoteric text: → 374, EHedrick C., Nag Hammadi 1983/6, 37-54 / 239-255.

8633 *McGuire* Anne, Conversion and Gnosis in the Gospel of Truth: NT 28 (1986) 338-355.

8634 *Ménard* J. E., Philippe (L'Évangile selon): → 578, Catholicisme XI,49 (1986) 165-7.

8635 **Meyer** Marvin, The letter of Peter to Philip: SBL diss. 53, 1981 → 62,9843... 1,a248:   RÉTRel 61 (1986) 267s (J.-D. *Dubois*).

8636 **Rouleau** Donald, L'Épître apocryphe de Jacques (NH 1,2): diss. Laval. 1986. 234 p. – RTLv 18,567.

8637 **Pasquier** Anne, L'Évangile selon Marie (BG 1) [de Berlin, non NH, mais]: BCNH 10, 1983 → 64,9209; 1,a253;   2-7637-6994-2:   RÉTRel 61 (1986) 264 (J.-D. *Dubois*).

8638 **Schenke** Gesine, Die dreigestaltige Protennoia (NHC XIII): TU 132, 1984 → 65,8982:   RBO 43 (1986) 715-7 (J.-E. *Ménard*); BZ 30 (1986) 263s (R. *Schnackenburg*); JTS 37 (1986) 568-570 (R. M. *Wilson* admires but does not agree).

8639 **Scopello** Maddalena, L'Exégèse de l'Âme, Nag Hammadi Codex ii,6: NHS 25, 1985 → 1,a255:   RETL 62 (1986) 435s (B. *Dehandschutter*).

8640 **Sevrin** Jean-Marie, L'exégèse de l'âme (NH II,6): BCNH-T 9, 1983 → 64,9183:   RÉTRel 61 (1986) 263s (J.-D. *Dubois*).

M3   **Religiones comparatae** – *Historia religionum.*

8641 **Abraham** William J., An introduction to the philosophy of religion 1985 → 1,a258:   RScotJT 39 (1986) 244s (P. *Byrne*).

8642 **Ackermann** Robert J., Religion as critique 1985 → 1,a259:   RJScStR25 (1986) 526s (R. A. *Segal*).

8643 **Adams** James L., EBeach George K., The prophethood of all believers. Boston 1986, Beacon. 350 p. $25 [JAAR 55,193].

8644 **Allen** Douglas, Mircea ELIADE y el fenómeno religioso [1982 → 64,9222], THernández Zulaica J.: Academia Christiana 25, 304 p. 1985 → 1,a260: RSalmanticensis 33 (1986) 266s (D. *Salado*).

8645 *a) Antes* Peter, Systematische Religionswissenschaft — eine Neuorientierung; – *b) Dhavamony* Mariasusai, Klassische Religionsphänomenologie und Missiologie; – *c) Kramm* Thomas, Vergleichende Theologie statt Missionswissenschaft?: ZMissRW 70 (1986) 214-221 / 222-231 / 101-111.

8646 **Ariarajah** Wesley, The Bible and people of other faiths: Risk Book 26, 1985 ➤ 1,a264; Fs 7,90. 2-8254-0840-9: ᴿÉTRel 61 (1986) 619 (J. *Pons*).

8647 **Arthur** –, In the hall of mirrors; problems of commitment in a religiously plural world [New/Junior Gifford Lectures 1985]. L 1986, Mowbray. 172 p. £7. 0-264-67090-6. – ᴿExpTim 98 (1986s) 162-4 (C. S. *Rodd*: frustrating, metaphorical; but makes him want more).

8648 **Bachofen** Johann J., Mutterrecht und Urreligion [1861] ᴱ*Kippenberg* Hans. Stu 1984, Kröner. 366 p. DM 25. – ᴿAnthropos 81 (1986) 703s (H. *Witte*).

8649 *Baudy* Dorothea, Heischegang und Segenszweig; antike und neuzeitliche Riten des sozialen Ausgleichs; eine Studie über die Sakralisierung von Symbolen: Saeculum 37 (1986) 212-227.

8650 *Baum* Hermann, Zum funktionalen Interesse philosophischer Reflexionen über das Phänomen Religion bei DESCARTES, KANT und SCHLEIERMACHER: NSys 28 (1986) 14-28; Eng. 28.

8651 **Bergeron** Richard, Le cortège des fous de Dieu; un chrétien scrute les nouvelles religions. Montréal 1982, Paulines. 511 p. [SR 15,29].

8652 **Bianchi** U., Saggi di metodologia della storia delle religioni 1970 ➤ 61,k527: ᴿAnzAltW 39 (1986) 74-76 (G. *Lorenz*).

8653 *a) Braaten* Carl E., The problem of the absoluteness of Christianity; – *b) Blenkinsopp* Joseph, Yahweh and other deities; conflict and accommodation in the religion of Israel; – *c) Perkins* Pheme, Christianity and world religions; NT questions; – *d) Wilken* Robert L., Religious pluralism and early Christian theology: Interpretation 40 (1986) 341-353 / 354-366 / 367-378 / 379-391.

8654 **Brakenhielm** Carl R., Problems of religious experience. U 1985, Univ. 158 p. Sk 105 [JAAR 54,397].

8655 ᴱ**Burkhardt** Frederick, *Bowers* Fredson, Works of William JAMES: The varieties of religious experience; intr. *Smith* John E.; notes *Skrupselis* Ignas. CM 1985, Harvard. li-669 p. $35. – ᴿRelStR 12 (1986) 265 (H. S. *Levinson*: superb critical edition of a classic).

8656 *Burkhart* Ernst, Heilsbedeutung der nichtchristlichen Religionen; die Aussagen des kirchlichen Lehramtes in kritischer Konfrontation mit einer neueren These: ForumKT 2 (1986) 1-23.

8657 ᴱ**Carrasco** David, *Swanberg* Jane M., Waiting for the dawn; Mircea ELIADE in perspective [1982 Univ. Colorado interdisciplinary seminar, with eleven excerpts from Eliade]. Boulder 1985, Westview. xix-139 p. [RelStR 13,46, Ilinca Z. *Johnston*].

8658 *Chidester* David, Michael FOUCAULT [1926-1984] and the study of religion: RelStR 12 (1986) 1-19.

8659 *Chirpaz* François, La experiencia de lo sagrado según Mircea ELIADE [< Études 360 (1984) 789-801], ᵀᴱ*Muñoz* Máxim: SelT 25 (1986) 217-224.

8660 **Ciattini** Alessandra, Sulla religione primitiva: Quad. Glottoantropologici 1. R 1986, Bagatto. 97 p. Lit. 10.000. 88-7755-581-5.

8661 **Clark** Stephen R. L., The mysteries of religion; an introduction to philosophy through religion. Ox 1986, Blackwell. x-277 p. £8 pa. 0-631-13419-0; pa. 4395-9. – ᴿExpTim 98 (1986s) 218 (D. A. *Pailin*: uses feminine always for God and for common-gender pronoun).

8662 **Corbin** Henry, Temple and contemplation [Eranos conferences on Islam], T*Sherrard* Philip (& Liadain): Islamic texts and context. L 1986, KPI. xii-413 p. $18 [TDig 34,64].

8663 *Coward* Harold [!] C., Pluralism, challenge to world religions 1985 ➤ 1,a285. 0-88344-710-X. – RAmerica 154 (1986) 102s (E. *Gorski*); Encounter 47 (1986) 178 (H. *Hatt*); ScotR 7 (1986) 88-90 (G. *Richards*); ScripTPamp 18 (1986) 995s (C. *Izquierdo*); TsTNijm 26 (1986) 84 (J.H. *Kamstra*).

8665 **Cragg** Kenneth, The Christ and the faiths; theology in cross reference. L 1986, SPCK. 360 p. £13.50. 0-281-04240-3. – RExpTim 98 (1986s) 284s (G. *D'Costa*); Themelios 12 (1986s) 101s (M. *Goldsmith*).

8666 *Dawson* Lorne, Neither [failure of] nerve nor ecstasy [in the academic study of religion]; comment on the Wiebe-Davis exchange: SR [13 (1984) 393-422] 15 (1986) 145-151 [153-164, *Alton* B.; 165-175, *Penner* Hans H.; 191-6, *Davis C.*; 197-203, *Wiebe* D.].

8667 **D'Costa** Gavin, Theology and religious pluralism. Ox 1986, Blackwell. 155 p. £19.50; pa. £7. 0-631-14517-6; 8-4. – RExpTim 98 (1986s) 2s (C.S. *Rodd*: 'Basil Blackwood'); Month 248 (1986) 277s (P. *Endean*); NBlackf 67 (1986) 549s (H.P. *Owen*); VerbumSVD 27 (1986) 305-8 (E. *Zeitler*).

8668 *D'Costa* Gavin, The pluralist paradigm in the Christian theology of religions: ScotJT 39 (1986) 211-224.

Denny Frederick M., The Holy Book in comparative perspective 1985 ➤ 1,561.

8669 **Despland** Michel, La religion en occident; évolution des idées et du vécu. Montréal 1979, Fides. xiii-579 p. – RRelStR 12 (1986) 112-115 (J.S. *Preus*: a landmark, though unnoticed for six years in the U.S.).

8670 **Desroche** Henri, O homem e suas religiões. São Paulo 1985, Paulinas. 196 p. [REB 46,229].

8671 a) *Donovan* Peter J., Do different religions share moral common ground?; – b) *Cohn-Sherbok* Dan, Ranking religions; – c) *Vink* A.G., The literary and dramatic character of HUME's Dialogues concerning natural religion: RelSt 22 (1986) 367-375 / 377-386 / 387-396.

8672 **Dupré** Wilhelm, Einführung in die Religionsphilosophie 1985 ➤ 1,a288: RTPhil 61 (1986) 441 (J. *Schmidt*).

8673 **Eliade** Mircea, Histoire des croyances et des idées religieuses [I. 1976 ➤ 58,c695; II. 1978 ➤ 61,m837] III. De Mahomet à l'âge des Réformes: BiblHist. P 1984, Payot. F 96; 2-228-13160-1. – RÉTRel 61 (1986) 575s (D. *Lys*).

8674 **Eliade** Mircea, A history of religious ideas [Is, 1979/82 ➤ 64,9258] III. Ch 1985, Univ. 360 p. $27.50. – RTTod 43 (1986s) 597s (R.E. *McLaughlin*).

8674* **Eliade** Mircea, Occultisme, sorcellerie et modes culturelles: Essais 206. P 1986, Gallimard. 183 p. 2-07-028257-0.

8675 **Ellwood** Robert S., Many peoples, many faiths; an introduction to the religious life of human kind³ rev [¹1976; ²1983]. ENJ 1986, Prentice-Hall. xii-356 p. $27 [TDig 34,67].

8676 **Evans** C. Stephen, Philosophy of religion; thinking about faith: Contours of classic philosophy 1985 ➤ 1,a292: RThemelios 12 (1986s) 66 (K. *Vanhoozer*).

8677 **Figl** Johann, Dialektik der Gewalt; NIETZSCHEs hermeneutische Religionsphilosophie, mit Berücksichtigung unveröffentlichter Manuskripte: Beiträge zur Theologie und Religionswissenschaft. Dü 1984, Patmos. 412 p. DM 54 [TR 83,421-3, P. *Köster*].

8678 *Figl* Johann, Phänomenologie der Religionen: ZkT 108 (1986) 409-421.

8679 *Gerlitz* Peter, Konvergenz und Divergenz im interreligiösen Dialog; zur religionsgeschichtlichen Problematik des Verstehens: SMSR 52 (1986) 129-157; 159s, 10 Thesen.

8680 *Ghedini* Francesco, Sull'indagine genealogica delle diverse religioni storiche in Friedrich NIETZSCHE, II: StPatav 33 (1986) 623-656; Eng. 657.

8681 **Godin** André, The psychological dynamics of religious experience [1981], ᵀ*Turton* Mary. Birmingham AL 1985, Religious Ed. 279 p. $14 pa. – ᴿHorizons 13 (1986) 192s (R. J. *Wicks*: in 'top five'); RelStR 12 (1986) 262s (C. M. *Bache*: more a pastoral and Christian apologia than the title suggests).

8682 [*Bertholet* Alfred], ⁴*Goldammer* Kurt, Wörterbuch der Religionen: Kröners Tb 125. Stu 1985, Kröner. xi-679 p. – ᴿSalesianum 48 (1986) 708 (R. *Sabini*: rifatto dal Bertholet dopo distruzione del manoscritto 1941; ritocchi significativi).

8683 **Grant** Robert M., Gods and the one God; Christian theology in the Graeco-Roman world: Library of Early Christianity 1. Ph/L 1986, Westminster/SPCK. 207 p. $19. – ᴿBAR-W 12,4 (1986) 54s (R. A. *Wild*); CCurr 36 (1986s) 231s (Pheme *Perkins*); RExp 83 (1986) 648 (E. G. *Hinson*); Themelios 12 (1986s) 103s (G. *Bray*).

8684 ᴱ**Hammond** Phillip E., The sacred in a secular age; toward revision in the scientific study of religion 1985 → 1,354: ᴿJScStR 25 (1986) 374-376 (M. E. *Marty*: focuses Bryan WILSON); RelStR 12 (1986) 136 (W. R. *Garrett*: authors a veritable Who's Who of the field, but more about what is than 'toward revision').

8685 ᴱ**Haubst** Rudolf, Der Friede unter den Religionen nach Nikolaus von KUES, Akten des Symposions in Trier 13.-15. Okt. 1982/4 → 65,506: ᴿTGegw 23 (1985) 129 (C. *Schedl*); TrierTZ 95 (1986) 148s (K. *Reinhardt*).

8686 **Heiler** F., Le religioni dell'umanità; volume di introduzione generale: Storia delle Religioni. Mi 1985, Jaca. xi-594 p. – ᴿAntonianum 61 (1986) 173-5 (M. *Nobile*).

8687 **Heller** David, The [Jewish, Catholic, Protestant, Hindu] children's God [imagery; transcripts]. Ch 1986, Univ. 165 p. $16 [RelStR 13,230, Elizabeth *Liebert*].

8688 **Hick** John, Problems of religious pluralism. NY 1985, St. Martin's. 148 p. $20. – ᴿCCurr 36 (1986s) 262-4 (M. *Brannigan*); ModT 3 (1986s) 375s & TLond 39 (1986) 497-9 (G. *Loughlin*).

8689 *Höhn* Hans-Joachim, Religion und funktionale Systemtheorie; zur theologischen Auseinandersetzung mit der Religionstheorie Niklas LUHMANNs: TGl 76 (1986) 38-69.

8690 *Holzmüller* Thilo, Projektion — ein fragwürdiger Begriff in der FEUERBACHrezeption? Die Projektionstheorie Hans-Martin BARTHs als Erklärungsmodell für Ludwig Feuerbachs Religionskritik: NSys 28 (1986) 77-99; Eng. 100.

8691 **Hospital** Clifford G., Breakthrough; insights of the great religious discoverers [Gautama, Krishna, Confucius, Lao-Tzu, Moses, Jesus, Muḥammad]. Maryknoll NY 1985, Orbis. xii-196 p. – ᴿGregorianum 67 (1987) 792 (J. *Dupuis*); RelStT 6 (1986) 55-57 (R. *Neufeldt*); SR 15 (1986) 250s (H. *Coward*).

8692 **Hughes** Edward J., Wilfred Cantwell SMITH, A theology for the world. L 1986, SCM. 242 p. £9. 0-334-02333-5. – ᴿExpTim 98 (1986s) 124 (Ursula *King*).

8693 **Hunter** Alastair G., Christianity and other faiths in Britain. L 1985, SCM. xvi-176 p. £7. – ᴿTLond 39 (1986) 328s (A. *Race*).

8694 **Jaeschke** Walter, Die Religionsphilosophie HEGELs: ErtFor 201, 1983 ➤ 64,9276 ... 1,a308: ᴿFreibRu 37s (1985s) 102s (G. *Klostermann*).

8695 **Hegel** G. W. F., Vorlesungen über die Philosophie der Religion, ᴱ*Jaeschke* Walter: Ausgewählte Nachschriften und Manuskripte 3-5, 1983/5/4 ➤ 1,a307: ᴿRTLv 17 (1986) 353-8 (E. *Brito*).

8696 **Hegel** Georg W. F., Die bestimmte Religion: ᴱ*Jaeschke* Walter: Vorlesungen über die Philosophie der Religion 2. Ha 1985, Meiner. xiii-1024 p. (2 vol.). – ᴿTPhil 61 (1986) 421s (J. *Splett*).

8697 **James** William, [➤ 8655] Las variedades de la experiencia religiosa; estudio de la naturaleza humana, ᵀ*Yvars* J. F.; pról. *Aranguren* José L.: Historia, Ciencia, Sociedad 199. Barc 1986, Península. 397 p. 84-297-2456-7. – ᴿActuBbg 23 (1986) 225s (J. *Boada*).

8698 *Kaiser* Otto, HEGELs Religionsphilosophie; ein Versuch, sie aus dem Ganzen seines Systems zu verstehen: NSys 28 (1986) 198-222.

8699 ᴱ**Kitagawa** Joseph M., The history of religions, retrospect and prospect 1983/5 ➤ 1,369: ᴿJRel 66 (1986) 226s (H. H. *Penner*).

8700 **Klimkeit** Hans-Joachim, Götterbilder in Kunst und Schrift: Studium Universale 2. Bonn 1984, Bouvier. 180 p. [Mundus 22,52].

8701 **Knitter** Paul F., No other name? A critical survey of Christian attitudes toward the world religions 1985 ➤ 1,a319; 0-88344-347-3: ᴿCCurr 36 (1986s) 474-7 (W. R. *Burrows*); EAsJT 4,2 (1986) 200-2 (M. G. *Fonner*); ÉTRel 61 (1986) 275s (A. *Gounelle*: demande une suite); Horizons 13 (1986) 116-8 (W. *Collinge*) & 118-121 (D. *Sheridan*) & 122s (Denise L. *Carmody*) & 123-6 (W. P. *Loewe*) & 127-130 (W. *Cenkner*); 130-5, response by Knitter; REB 46 (1986) 886-890 (Waldemar *Boff*); TLond 39 (1986) 147-9 (K. *Cracknell*); Vidyajyoti 49 (1985) 466-9 (G. *Gispert-Sauch*).

8702 **König** Franz, Der Glaube der Menschen; Christus und die Religionen der Erde 1985 ➤ 1,a320: ᴿTGl 76 (1986) 354s (W. *Beinert*).

8703 **Kolbe** Christoph, Heilung oder Hindernis; Religion bei FREUD, ADLER, FROMM, JUNG und FRANKL. Stu 1986, Kreuz. 315 p. 3-7831-0829-2 [ActuBbg 24,231, J. *Boada*].

8704 **Kramer** Kenneth, World Scriptures, an introduction to comparative religions. NY 1986, Paulist. 298 p. $13. 0-8091-2781-4 [ExpTim 98,351].

8705 *Kramer* Kenneth P., Autobiographical world theology [i.e. any theology must be self-oriented yet exclude no one]: Horizons 13 (1986) 104-115.

8706 **Kraus** H. J., Theologische Religionskritik 1982 ➤ 64,9283: ᴿProtestantesimo 41 (1986) 124-6 (V. *Subilia*).

8707 **Krüger** J. S., Studying religion; a methodological introduction to science of religion 1982 ➤ 63,9093: ᴿRelSAfr 7,1 (1986) 59-62 (I. A. *Ben-Yosef*).

8708 *Kühn* R., Aperçu sur la situation de la 'philosophie de la religion': Revue de Métaphysique et de Morale 90 (1985) 483-504 [RSPT 70 (1986) 308].

8709 **Küng** H., *al.*, Christentum und Weltreligionen 1984 ➤ 1,604: ᴿNZMissW 42 (1986) 69-74 (H. *Waldenfels*).

8710 **Küng** H., *al.*, Cristianesimo e religioni universali [1984]ᵀ: Saggi. Mi 1986, Mondadori. 527 p. – ᴿIslamochristiana 12 (1986) 252-6 (A. *Garon*).

8711 **Küng** Hans. *a)* Der Streit um den Religionsbegriff; – *b)* Zu einer ökumenischen Theologie der Religion: IZT (Concilium) 22 (1986) 1-4 / 76-80 (éd. franç. ᵀ*Givord* R., 9-13 / 151-9).

8712 **Kusar** Stjepan, Dem göttlichen Gott entgegen denken; der Weg von der metaphysischen zu einer nachmetaphysischen Sicht Gottes in der Religionsphilosophie Bernhard WELTES: FreibThSt 133. FrB 1986, Herder. x-419 p. DM 58. 3-451-20587-4. – RActuBbg 23 (1986) 228 (J. *Boada*: merece toda la atención de la teología fundamental).

8713 **Lähnemann** Johannes, Weltreligionen im Unterricht; eine theologische Didaktik für Schule, Hochschule und Gemeinde, 1. Fernostliche Religionen; 2. Islam. Gö 1986, Vandenhoeck & R. 297 p.; 299 p., ill. DM 34 + 36 [TLZ 112,629-631, U. *Tworuschka*].

8714 **Larson** Martin A., New thought; a modern religious approach. NY 1985, Philosophical. 458 p. $20 [JAAR 54,205].

8715 **Lewis** Ian M., Religion in context — cults [...anthropology] and charisma. C 1986, Univ. 139 p. £20; pa. £7. 0-521-30616-7; 1596-4. – RExpTim 98 (1986s) 157s (G. *Parrinder*: LÉVI-STRAUSS is mechanical and opaque; Mary DOUGLAS tends to incomprehensible whimsy).

8716 **Magnani** Giovanni, La crisi della metapsicologia freudiana. R 1981. – RBbbOr 28 (1986) 125s (I. *Testa Bappenheim*).

8717 **Makhlouf** Georgia, Les grandes religions: L'histoire des hommes. P 1986, Casterman. 78 p. 2-203-15706-2. – RÉTRel 61 (1986) 577s (D. *Lys* laisse mystérieux le rôle de Michaël WELPLY).

8718 *Manaranche* André, [Les immigrés:] La rencontre des religions: Communio 11,2 [non in IkaZ] (P 1986) 64-76.

8719 **Mathis** Terry R., Against John HICK; an examination of his philosophy of religion. Lanham MD 1985, UPA. ix-137 p. £10.25. – RJRel 66 (1986) 230s (C. *Gillis*); NBlackf 67 (1986) 50s (G. *D'Costa*); TLond 39 (1986) 306 (G. *Loughlin*: written while at Claremont where Hick is professor; unsuccessful).

8720 El mundo de las religiones, TSantidrián Pedro R.: Nueva imagen 2. Estella/M 1985, VDivino/Paulinas. 453 p.; pt 3325. 84-7151-399-4 /.

8721 **Munson** Thomas M., The challenge of religion; a philosophical appraisal. Pittsburgh 1985, Duquesne Univ. [distr. Humanities]. ix-228 p. $21; pa. $10 [RelStR 13,328, W. *Proudfoot*].

8722 [Natale] **Terrin** Aldo, Spiegare e comprendere la religione?: Caro salutis cardo, 1983 ➤ 64,9334: RNRT 108 (1986) 314s (J. M.).

8722* *Natale Terrin* Aldo, Sulla 'religione' nello studio delle religioni [*Eliade* M., van der *Leeuw* G.: ital. 1985]: St Patav 33 (1986) 373-383.

8723 **Neill** Stephen †, Crises of belief; the Christian dialogue with faith [¹other faiths] and no faith². L 1985, Hodder & S. 304 p. – RTLond 39 (1986) 65s (J. *Lipner*: stridently Christian, despite effort to be sensitive).

8724 *Netland* Harold A., Professor HICK on religious pluralism: RelSt 22 (1986) 249-262.

8725 *Neusner* Jacob, Why study religion?: BR 2,4 (1986) 4 only.

8726 **Pailin** David A., Attitude to other religions; comparative religion in seventeenth- and eighteenth-century Britain 1984 ➤ 65,9057: RJSS 31 (1986) 115-7 (N. *Daniel*); ScotJT 39 (1986) 142s (E. *Leach*).

8727 **Pailin** David A., Groundwork of philosophy of religion. 1986, Epworth. 258 p. £8.50. 0-7162-0418-5. – RExpTim 98 (1986s) 34s (C. S. *Rodd*: almost too clear).

8728 *Pals* Daniel, Reductionism and belief; an appraisal of recent attacks on the doctrine of irreducible religion [... *Segal* R.]: JRel 66 (1986) 18-36.

8729 **Panikkar** R., Le dialogue intrareligieux. P 1985, Aubier. F 98. 2-7007-0361-8. – RÉTRel 61 (1986) 458s (Jacky *Argaud*).

8730 **Parrinder** G., Le sexe dans les religions du monde. P 1986, Centurion. 274 p. F 99 [RHE 82,93*].

8731 **Pfüller** Wolfgang, Die Frage nach dem Wesen der Religion und das

Problem der Begründung ethischer Normen: NSys 28 (1986) 245-260; Eng. 260.

8732 **Picht** Georg, KANTs Religionsphilosophie [2 Vorlesungen 1965s]; Einf. *Rudolf* E. Stu 1985, Klett-Cotta. xxi-638 p. DM 68 [TLZ 112, 136-8, H. *Schleiff*].

8733 **Pollack** Detlef, Die Religiontheorie Niklas LUHMANNs und ihre systemtheoretischen Voraussetzung: Diss. Leipzig 1984. iii-170 p.; 20 p. – TLZ 112,425-7.

8734 **Proudfoot** Wayne, Religious experience. Berkeley 1985, Univ. California. xix-263 p. $25. – RTS 48 (1986) 352-4 (C. D. *Hardwick*).

8735 **Prozesky** Martin, Religion and ultimate well-being; an explanatory theory 1984 → 1,a349; also L, Macmillan; £20: RTLond 39 (1986) 50s (A. *Rudolph*: old-style HEGEL/FEUERBACH).

8736 **Puthenkalam** Xavier, Religious experience and faith; a critical evaluation of William JAMES' and William Ernest HOCKING's theories on religious experience in relation to faith: diss. DVergote A. Leuven 1986. – RTLv 18,572; TsTNijm 27,101.

8737 **Race** Alan, Christians and religious pluralism; patterns in the Christian theology of religions 1983 → 64,9309 ... 1,a351: RHeythJ 27 (1986) 452-4 (Ursula *King*); Vidyajyoti 49 (1985) 465s (G. *Gispert-Sauch*).

8738 *Race* Alan, Christianity and other religions; is inclusivism enough?: TLond 39 (1986) 178-186.

8739 *Raschke* Carl A., Religious studies and the default of critical intelligence [... *Ray* Richard, Is ELIADE's metapsychoanalysis an end run around BULTMANN's demythologization?: EGibbs L., Myth and the Crisis (Missoula 1975) 57-74]: JAAR 54 (1986) 131-8.

8740 **Ratnasekara** Leopold, Christianity and the world religions; a contribution to the theology of religions [diss. P Inst. Cath.]. Kandy 1982, National Seminary. xx-247 p. $8. – RVidyajyoti 49 (1985) 469s (G. *Gisbert-Sauch*: in note Ratnasekera).

8741 *Ratzinger* Joseph Kard., Pluralismus als Frage an Kirche und Theologie: ForumKT 2 (1986) 81-96.

8742 *Reati* Fiorenzo E., La 'Fenomenologia della Religione' di Geo WIDENGREN [Religionsvärld 1945 ²1953; ital. 1985]; una introduzione storico-critica alla lettura: HumBr 41 (1986) 234-241.

8743 *Ricœur* Paul, Le statut de la Vorstellung dans la philosophie Hégélienne de la religion: → 16*, Mém. COPPIETERS D. 1985, 185-206.

8744 *Ries* Julien, Les chemins du sacré dans l'histoire: Presence et pensée, 1985 → 1,a354: RGregorianum 67 (1986) 789s (J. *Dupuis*).

8745 ERies Julien, L'expression du sacré [III → 493] I-II, 1978/83 → 64,526; 1,a355: RÉglT 17 (1986) 407-411 (L. *Laberge*).

8746 ERies Julien, Le symbolisme dans le culte des grandes religions 1983/5 → 1,633: RTeresianum 37 (1986) 499 (L. *Borriello*).

8747 *Rise* Svein, Moderne religionskritikk, med særlig henblikk på religionskritikken hos FEUERBACH, FREUD, MARX og NIETZSCHE: TsTKi 57 (1986) 161-171.

8748 **Rolston** Holmes III, Religious inquiry — participation and detachment [AUGUSTINE, GHAZALI ...] 1985 → 1,a357: RScotJT 39 (1986) 284s (D. *Davies*: gives great satisfaction).

8749 **Ruland** Vernon, Eight sacred horizons; the religious imagination east and west 1985 → 1,a361: RRelStR 12 (1986) 262 (J. *Strong*: traditions we stand judged by rather than stand in judgment over).

8750 **Saldanha** Chrys, Divine pedagogy; a patristic view of non-Christian religions: BiblScR 57, 1984 ➤ 65,9073; 1,a363; 88-213-0079-X: ᴿActuBbg 23 (1986) 263; Gregorianum 67 (1986) 167s (J. *Dupuis*); Salmanticensis 33 (1986) 132s (R. *Trevijano*); StPatav 33 (1986) 667-670 (P. F. *Beatrice*).

8751 *Samartha* Stanley J., De Jordaan oversteken; naar een christelijke theologie der religies: Wereld en Zending 15 (Amst 1986) 126-130 [< ZIT].

8752 ᴱ**Sartori** L., Le scienze della religione oggi 1981/3 ➤ 64,532; 65,9074: ᴿDivThom 88 (1985) 171-3 (G. *Sanguineti*, sic).

8753 **Schaeffler** R., Religionsphilosophie 1983 ➤ 65,9075: ᴿExpTim 97 (1985s) 267s (G. *Wainwright*: 'creatively analytical'; takes first place amid 15 works of recent continental theology).

8754 **Schoen** Ulrich, Das Ereignis und die Antworten; auf der Suche nach einer Theologie der Religionen heute 1984 ➤ 1,a366: ᴿRHPR 66 (1986) 246s (J.-F. *Collange*).

8755 *Seckler* Max, Theologie der Religionen mit Fragezeichen: TüTQ 166 (1986) 164-184.

8756 **Sharpe** Eric J., Comparative religion; a history² [= ¹1975 + updating chapter]. La Salle IL 1986, Open Court. xvi-341 p. $32; pa. $15 [RelStR 13,326, Kathryn A. *Rabuzzi*].

8757 *Sheridan* Daniel P., a) Discerning difference; a taxonomy of culture, spirituality, and religion: JRel 66 (1986) 37-45; – b) Grounded in the Trinity; suggestions for a theology of relationship to other religions: Thomist 50 (1986) 260-278.

8758 **Siebert** Rudolf J., The critical theory of religion; the Frankfort school: Religion and Reason 29, 1985 ➤ 1,a370: ᴿTorJT 2 (1986) 291-5 (D. *Wiebe*: more on HABERMAS, and on theology).

8759 *Siegwalt* Gérard, La recherche chrétienne de Dieu dans la rencontre avec les religions non-chrétiennes: PosLuth 34 (1986) 210-224.

8760 ᴱ**Sievernich** M., *Seif* K., Schuld und Umkehr in den Weltreligionen 1983 ➤ 64,354; 65,9082: ᴿTGegw 23 (1985) 128s (B. *Häring*).

8761 **Skalicky** Carlo, Alle prese con il sacro; la religione nella ricerca scientifica moderna. R 1982, Herder / Univ. Lateranense. 352 p. – ᴿSapienza 39 (1986) 127s (R. M. *Pizzorni*).

8762 **Smart** Ninian, Worldviews; crosscultural explorations of human beliefs 1983 ➤ 65,9084: ᴿTsTKi 57 (1986) 156s (A. *Romarheim*).

8763 **Stackhouse** Max L., Creeds, society, and human rights; a study in three cultures [Greco-Roman as now transmuted; East German; India]. GR 1984, Eerdmans. 315 p. $20. – ᴿJAAR 54 (1986) 150s (R. L. *Shinn*).

8764 *Steege* Gerhard, Kindlichkeit und Glaubensreifung; theologische und psychologische Bemerkungen im Anschluss an ein Kapitel Religionskritik bei Sigmund FREUD: TVers 16 (1986) 131-159.

8765 **Thiel** Josef F., Religionsethnologie [Mundus 22,55 'religious theology']; Grundbegriffe der Religionen schriftloser Völker: Anthropos Coll. 33. B 1984, Reimer. 250 p.

8766 *Thorbjørnsen* Svein O., Nyere religions- og kristendomskritikk i Norge; presentasjon av noen utvalgte kritikere: TsTKi 57 (1986) 241-255.

8767 *Thorsen* Donald A. D., Michael POLANYI; a post-critical understanding of religious belief: AsburyTJ 41 (1986) 79-90.

8768 *Tiryakian* Edward A., Modernity as an eschatological setting; a new vista for the study of religions: HistRel 25 (1985s) 378-386 [< ZIT].

8769 *Tracy* David, The analogical imagination 1981 ➤ 62,4334... 1,a385: ᴿVidyajyoti 49 (1985) 206s (G. *Gispert-Sauch*).

8770 **Vergote** Antoine, Religion, foi, incroyance: Psychologie et sciences humaines 126. P 1983, Mardaga. 328 p. – RRTLv 17 (1986) 77-83 É. *Bocquet*).

8771 *Vernette* Jean,   Sectes et Gnoses; I. Où va la religion en Occident?; II. La nouvelle religiosité; III. Prolifération des sectes: EsprV 96 (1986) 129-133.145-150.161-170.

8772 **Waardenburg** Jacques,   Religionen und Religion; systematische Einführung in die Religionswissenschaft: Göschen 2228.   B 1986, de Gruyter. 227 p. DM 24,80 pa. – RZkT 108 (1986) 345 (W. *Kern*).

8773 *Wagner* Falk,   Was ist Religion? Studien zu ihrem Begriff und Thema in Geschichte und Gegenwart.   Gü 1986, Mohn.   596 p.   DM 98 [TLZ 112,582-6, H. *Moritz*].

8774 **Welte** B.,   Qu'est ce que croire? [Was ist Glauben 1982] 1984 → 65,8096; 1,a392: RScripTPamp 18 (1986) 337s (J. M. *Odero*).

8775 EWhaling Frank,   Contemporary approaches to the study of religion; I. The humanities; II. The social sciences 1984s → 1,411:   RScotJT 39 (1986) 276-9 (D. A. *Pailin*).

8776 **Whitehead** Alfred N.,   Wie ensteht Religion? [Religion in the making 1936].   Fra 1985, Suhrkamp.   128 p.   DM 24. – REvKomm 19 (1986) 432s (M. *Welker*).

8777 **Widengren** Geo,   Fenomenologia della religione T, pref. *Filoramo* Giovanni: Collana di Studi Religiosi.   Bo 1984, Dehoniane.   958 p. – RSalesianum 48 (1986) 746 (Ad. A.).

8778 **Williamson** Raymond K.,   Introduction to Hegel's philosophy of religion. Albany 1984, SUNY.   xii-388 p. $44.50; pa. $15. – RScotJT 39 (1986) 404-8 (T. L. S. *Sprigge*).

8779 *Yamdell* Keith,   Can there *be* a science of religion?: ChrSchR 15 (1985) 28-41.

8780 *Zimoń* Henryk,   Wilhelm SCHMIDT's theory of primitive monotheism and its critique within the Vienna school of ethnology: Anthropos 81 (1986) 243-260.

8781 **Zirker** Hans,   Crítica de la religión [*Comte ... Freud*] 1985 → 1,a401: REstE 61 (1986) 462 (J. *García Pérez*); PerspT 18 (1986) 412 (X. H.); RazF 213 (1986) 555 (también J. *García Pérez*).

M3.5   **Mythologia.** [→ 1464-1487].

8781* *Assmann* Jan, al.,   Funktionen und Leistungen des Mythos; drei altorientalische Beispiele: OBO 48, 1982 → 63,2079; 1,2047: RCdÉ 61 (1986) 79-81 (J. G. *Griffiths*); OLZ 81 (1986) 328s (C. *Onasch*).

8782 *Biallas* Leonard J.,   Myths, gods, heroes, and saviors. Mystic CT 1986, Twenty-Third.   301 p. $10 [RelStR 13,231, Ruth L. *Smith*].

8783 **Bloch** Raymond, al.,   D'Héraklès à Poseidon; mythologie et protohistoire: Hautes Études du Monde Gréco-Romain 14, 1985 → 1,a403: RRHR 203 (1986) 209s (D. *Bouvier*).

8784 **Bolen** Jean S.,   Goddesses in everywoman; a new psychology of woman [Artemis ... Hera ... Aphrodite]. SF 1984, Harper & R.   xiv-334 p. [RelStR 13,48, Kathryn A. *Rabuzzi*].

8785 **Bonnafé** Annie,   Eros et eris; mariages divins et mythe de succession chez Hésiode. Lyon 1985, Univ.   168 p.   F 90. – RRHR 203 (A. *Ballabriga*).

8786 *Cigognini* Mariadele,   Per una tipologia del motivo mitico della metamorfosi; il caso di Adonis e Mirra: SMSR 52 (1986) 5-32.

Cotterell Arthur,   A dictionary of world mythology 1986 → 608.

8788 **Detienne** M., L'invenzione della mitologia [1981 ➤ 63,9130], ᵀ*Cuniberto* F. T 1983, Boringhieri. 197 p. Lit. 20.000. – ᴿMaia 38 (1986) 261s (Silvana *Fasce*).

8789 **Doty** W. G., Mythography; the study of myths and rituals. University AL 1986. xix-326 p. $28.50. 0-8173-0269-7 [NTAbs 31,91].

8790 **Dumézil** Georges, Mythe et épopée [indo-européens]⁴: Bibliothèque des Sciences Humaines. P 1981 [I, ¹1968] – 1986 [II, ¹1971], Gallimard. 659 p.; 412 p. 2-07-027797-6.

8791 *Durand* Gilbert de, *al.*, Le mythe et le mythique. A. Michel. 224 p. [JAAR 55,644].

8792 *Grosse* Ernst U., Mythische und poetische Zeichen bei Gottfried BENN: LingBib [56 (1985) 53-74] 58 (1986) 80-85; franç. 86.

Haussig Hans W., *al.*, Wörterbuch der Mythologie I/4, 1986 ➤ 625*; 608.

8793 *Horsfell* Nicholas, Myth and mythography: ÉchMClas 29 (1985) 393-410.

8794 **Hübner** Kurt, Die Wahrheit des Mythos 1985 ➤ 1,a412: ᴿTüTQ 166 (1986) 231s (K. H. *Schelkle*).

8795 ᴱ**Izard** Michel, *Smith* Pierre, Between belief and transgression; structuralist essays in religion, history and myth [La fonction symbolique], ᵀ*Leavitt* John; intr. *Boon* James A. Ch 1982, Univ. xx-276 p.; p. 24-42, *Herrenschmidt* O., Sacrifice — symbolic or effective [KirSef 59,297].

8796 **Krolik** Sanford W., In the twilight of myth; a study in the phenomenology of religion: diss. Virginia 1985. 292 p. 86-08564. – DissA 47 (1986s) 560s-A.

8797 ᴱ**Limet** H., *Ries* J., Le mythe 1981/3 ➤ 64,513... 1,a416: ᴿAnthropos 81 (1986) 737 (K.-H. *Golzio*); SMSR 52 (1986) 167-9 (Ida *Paladino*).

8798 **Luft** U., Beiträge zur Historisierung der Götterwelt und der Mythenschreibung: StAeg 4, 1978 ➤ 61,k737: 63,9139: ᴿOLZ 81 (1986) 133-5 (J. *Zandee*).

8799 *a) Mennekes* Friedhelm, Zur Aktualität des Mythos; – *b) Lorenzer* Alfred, Symbol, Desymbolisierung und Zerstörung der Sinnlichkeit; – *c) Wedewer* Rolf, Kunst als symbolische Form: Kunst und Kirche 49,1 (Linz 1986) 26-30 / 21s / 23-25 [< zɪᴛ].

8800 *Müller* Hans-Peter, Mythos und Kerygma; anthropologische und theologische Aspekte: ZTK 83 (1986) 405-435.

8801 *Nethöfel* Wolfgang, Ethnotheologie; zur Struktur unserer Mythen: TZBas 42 (1986) 66-82; 8 fig.

8802 **Pandimakil** Peter G., The analysis of myth in the works of Claude LÉVI-STRAUSS; a study in structural anthropology of religion: diss. Pont. Univ. Gregoriana, ᴰ*Dhavamony* M. R 1986. 449 p. Extr. Nᵒ 3311, vi-130 p.; bibliog. p. 87-130. – RTLv 18,566.

8803 **Perera** Sylvia B., The scapegoat complex; toward a mythology of shadow and guilt. 1986, Inner City. 128 p. $12. [JAAR 55,409s, L. W. *Bailey*].

8804 *Power* William L., Myth, truth, and justification in religion: RelSt 22 (1986) 447-458.

8805 **Rahner** Hugo † 1968, ᴱ*Rosenberg* A., Griechische Mythen in christlicher Deutung 1984 = 1945 ➤ 1,a418: ᴿTLZ 111 (1986) 130s (U. *Mann*); TrierTZ 95 (1986) 242 (E. *Sauser*).

8806 **Ranke-Graves** Robert von, *a)* Griechische Mythologie; Quellen und Deutung. – *b)* Die Weise Göttin; Sprache des Mythos; – *c)* Hebräische Mythologie [➤ 1484]. 1985s, Reinbeck [GeistL 59 (1969) 308].

8807 *Timm* H., Remythologisierung? Der akkumulative Symbolismus im Christentum: E*Bohrer* K. H., Mythos und Moderne; Begriff und Bild einer Rekonstruktion im 19. und 20. Jahrhundert (Fra 1982) 432-456 [< JbBT 1,234].

8808 **Wind** Edgar, Pagan mysteries in the Renaissance. Ox 1980, Univ. xiii-345 p.

M4 Religio romana.

8809 *Belloni* G. G., Casi di identità, analogie e divergenze tra la testimonianza monetale romana imperiale e quella di altre fonti sulla religione e sui culti: → 574, ANRW 2/16/3 (1986) 1844-1867.

8810 *a) Brenk* Frederick E., In the light of the moon; demonology in the early imperial period; – *b) Szemler* G.J., Priesthoods and priestly careers in ancient Rome: → 574, ANRW 2/16/3 (1986) 2068-2145 / 2314-2331.

8811 **Champeaux** Jacqueline, Fortuna; recherches sur le culte de la Fortne à Rome et dans le monde romain des origines à la mort de César, I. Fortuna dans la religion archaïque: Coll. Éc. Fr. 64, 1982 → 65,9131: ᴿRHR 203 (1986) 67-71 (J. *Scheid*).

8811* *Clauss* Manfred, Heerwesen (Heeresreligion): → 594, RAC 13 (1986) 1073-1113.

8812 **Cox** Patricia, Biography in late antiquity, a quest for the holy man [diss. Ch] 1983 → 64,9850: ᴿÉtClas 54 (1986) 321s (B. *Coulie*).

8813 *a) Dassmann* Ernst, *al.*, Hausgemeinschaft; – *b) Ohly* Friedrich, Haus (Metapher): → 594, RAC 13,102 (1986) 801-905 / 906-1063.

8814 *Feeney* D. C., History and revelation in Vergil's underworld: PrCPgS 212 (1986) 1-24.

8815 *a) Forschner* Maximilian, Das Gute und die Güter; zur Aktualität der stoischen Ethik; – *b) Kidd* I. G., Posidonian methodology and the self-sufficiency of virtue; – *c) Bringmann* Klaus, Geschichte und Psychologie bei Poseidonios: → 527, Hardt 32 (1985) 325-350 (-9 discussion) / 1-21 (-28) / 29-59 (-66).

8816 *Foucault* Michel, Histoire de la sexualité, I. ...; 2. L'usage des plaisirs; 3. Le souci de soi: Bibliothèque des histoires. P 1984, Gallimard. ... 287 p.; 286 p. – ᴿJRS 76 (1986) 266-271 (A. *Cameron*).

8817 **Freyburger** Gérard, Fides; étude sémantique et religieuse depuis les origines jusqu'à l'époque augustéenne: Coll. ÉtAnc (0184-7112). P 1986, BLettres. 361 p. 2-251-32861-0.

8818 *a) Gagé* Jean, Les pratiques magiques d'épiphanie royale — *basiléia* — et la mystique impériale aux IIᵉ et IIIᵉ siècles; – *b) Tupet* Anne-Marie †, Rites magiques dans l'Antiquité romaine: → 574, ANRW 2/16/3 (1986) 2382-2403 / 2591-2675.

8820 **Grisé** Yolande, Le suicide dans la Rome antique 1982 → 65,9136... 1,a435: ᴿRBgPg 63 (1985) 149-151 (L. *Jerphagnon*); RÉLat 63 (1985) 366s (J.-L. *Voisin*).

8821 **Guillaumont** François, Philosophe et augure; recherches sur la théorie cicéronienne de la divination: Coll. Latomus 184. Bru 1984. 212 p. Fb 950. – ᴿAntClas 55 (1986) 441-3 (M. van den *Bruwaene*); RHR 203 (1986) 83-85 (R. *Turcan*).

8822 *a) Harris* J. R., Iconography and context; ab oriente ad occidentem; – *b) Colledge* Malcolm A. R., Interpretatio romana; the Semitic populations of Syria and Mesopotamia; – *c) Bailey* D. M., The procession-house of the great Hermaion at Hermopolis Magna; – *d) Soffe* Grahame, Christians,

Jews and pagans in the Acts of the Apostles: → infra 8823, ᴱ*Henig* M., Pagan gods 1986, 171-7 / 221-230; 13 fig. / 231-7; 6 fig. / 239-256; map.

8823 ᴱ**Henig** Martin, *King* Anthony, Pagan gods and shrines of the Roman Empire [Oxford meeting 1984] Mon 8. Ox 1986, Univ. Committee for Archaeology. 265 p.; ill. 0-947816-08-9: mostly Roman Britain, except Henig, Ita intellexit numine inductus tuo; some personal interpretations of deity in Roman religion, p. 159-169 + 9 infra.

8824 **Hickson** Frances V., Voces precationum; the language of prayer in the History of LIVY and the Aeneid of VERGIL: diss. North Carolina, ᴰ*Linderski* J. Chapel Hill 1986. 153 p. 86-18353. – DissA 47 (1986s) 2141-A.

8825 **Ide** A. F., Loving women; a study of lesbianism to 500 CE: Woman in History 3. Arlington TX 1985, Liberal Arts. 108 p. $6. 0-935175-00-8 [NTAbs 30,249].

8826 *Kierdorf* Wilhelm, 'Funus' und 'consecratio'; zu Terminologie und Ablauf der römischen Kaiserapotheose: Chiron 16 (1986) 43-69.

8827 *Lührmann* Dieter, SUPERSTITIO — die Beurteilung des frühen Christentums durch die Römer [Antrittsvorlesung Marburg 1983]: TZBas 42 (1986) 193-213.

8828 *a) Mayer* Marc, *Rodà* Isabel, Les divinités féminines de la fertilité et de la fécondité en Hispania pendant l'époque romaine; – *b) Le Glay* M., Archéologie et cultes de fertilité dans la religion romaine; – *c) Vella* H. C. R., Juno and fertility at the sanctuary of Tas-Silġ, Malta: → 550, ᴱ*Bonanno* A., Fertility cults 1985/6, 293-304 / 273-292 / 315-322.

8829 *Momigliano* A., *a)* How Roman emperors became gods: American Scholar 55,2 (Wsh 1986) 181-193 [NTAbs 30,338]; – *b)* Ancient biography and the study of religion in the Roman Empire: AnPisa 16 (1986) 25-44.

8830 *Montanari* Enrico, Problemi della demitizzazione romana: SMSR 52 (1986) 73-99.

8831 *a) Neverov* Oleg, Nero-Helios; – *b) Godfrey* Paul, *Hemsoll* David, The Pantheon; temple or rotunda?: – *c) Lloyd-Morgan* G., Roman Venus; public worship and private rites; – *d) Blagg* T. F. C., The cult and sanctuary of Diana Nemorensis; – *e) Wardman* Alan, Pagan priesthoods in the later Roman Empire: → 8823 supra, ᴱ*Henig* M., Pagan gods 1986, 17-7; 2 fig. / 195-209; 5 fig. / 179-188; 21 fig. / 211-9; 2 fig. / 257-262.

8832 *North* J. A., Religion and politics, from Republic to Principate [*Moreau* P. 1982; *Scullard* H. 1981; *MacBain* B. 1981; *Scheid* J. 1983/5]: JRS 76 (1986) 251-8.

8833 *Pöhlmann* Wolfgang, *al.*, Herrscherkult: → 597, TRE 15 (1986) 248-253 (244-8; 253-5).

8834 **Porte** Danielle, L'étiologie dans les Fastes d'OVIDE. P 1985, BLettres. 598 p. F 450. – ᴿ*RPLH* 60 (1986) 150-3 (J.-C. *Richard*).

8835 **Pouthier** Pierre, Ops et la conception divine de l'abondance dans la religion romaine jusqu'à la mort d'Auguste 1981 → 62,a27; 64,9394: ᴿAugM 31 (1986) 461 (J. *Oroz*).

8836 **Price** S. R. F., Rituals and power; the Roman imperial cult in Asia Minor 1984 → 65,9144; 1,a447: ᴿAmJPg 107 (1986) 296s (R. *Mellor*); Gnomon 58 (1986) 38-43 (P. *Herz*).

8836* **Richlin** Amy, The garden of Priapus; sexuality and aggression in Roman humor 1983 → 65,9146; 1,a449: ᴿLatomus 45 (1986) 194-6 (N. J. H. *Sturt*).

8837 **Schubert** Werner, Jupiter in den Epen der Flavierzeit [Diss. Heid 1982]: StKlPg 8. Fra 1984, Lang. 352 p. Fs 68. – ᴿClasR 199 (1986) 134s (D. C. *Feeney*); RÉLat 63 (1985) 535 (M. *Royo*).

8838 **Scullard** Howard H., Römische Feste, Kalender und Kult [Festivals and ceremonies of the Roman republic 1981 ➤ 62,a35], ᵀ*Buchholz* Maria: Kulturgeschichte der antiken Welt 25. Mainz 1985, von Zabern. 513 p.; 55 fig.

8839 **Sfameni Gasparro** Giulia, Misteri e culti mistici di Demetra: Storia delle Religioni 3. R 1986, Bretschneider. 371 p.; bibliog. p. 353-371. 88-7062-592-3.

8840 **Terpening** Ronnie H., Charon and the crossing; ancient, medieval and renaissance transformations of a myth: Bucknell Univ. L 1985, Assoc. Univ. Presses. 293 p. £30. – ᴿClasR 100 (1986) 355s (Helen *King*).

8841 *Veyne* Paul, Une évolution du paganisme gréco-romain; injustice et piété des dieux, leurs ordres ou 'oracles'; Latomus 45 (1986) 259-283.

8842 *Wieacker* Franz, Altrömische Priesterjurisprudenz: ➤ 51, ꜰKaser M., Iuris professio 1986, 347-370.

8843 *Zannini Quirini* Bruno, Religioni romane [survey of recent publications]: Studi Romani 34 (1986) 128-137.

M4.5 Mithraismus.

8844 *Clauss* Manfred, Mithras und Christus: HZ 243 (1986) 265-285.

8845 *Gaidon* Marie-Agnès, Sous un couvent des Carmes [Bordeaux]... un Mithraeum ! : Archéologia 219 (1986) 44-51; ill.

8846 **Lissi-Caronna** Elisa, Il mitreo dei [sic] Castra Peregrinorum (S. Stefano Rotondo): ÉPR 104. Leiden 1986, Brill. viii-52 p.; 9 fig.; 43 pl. 90-04-07493-7.

8847 **Merkelbach** Reinhold, Mithras 1984 ➤ 65,9155; 1,a458: ᴿGGA 238 (1986) 37-40 (H.-J. *Klimkeit*); Gnomon 58 (1986) 394 (R. *Turcan*); HistRel 26 (1986s) 87-89 (H. D. *Betz*); ZkT 108 (1986) 89-91 (E. *Ruschitzka*).

8848 *a)* *Merkelbach* Reinhold, Über einige Denkmäler der Mithrasreligion in österreichischen Sammlungen; – *b)* *Vermaseren* Maarten J., Töpfer und orientalische Religionen im Römerreich; ➤ 119, ꜰVetters H. 1985, 174s, / 170-3.

8849 *Sijpesteijn* P. J., Eine neue mithrische Gemme?: ZPapEp 64 (1986) 123s.

8850 *Turcan* Robert, Feu et sang; à propos d'un relief mithriaque: CRAI (1986) 217-229: 2 fig.

M5 Religio graeca.

8851 *Alexeyeva* E. M., ⊕ [Greek] Religious cults in Gorgippia [now Anapa]: SovArch (1986,4) 34-52; Eng. 52.

8852 *a)* *Alles* Gregory D., Verbal craft and religious act in the Iliad; – *b)* *Martin* Luther H., Greek goddesses and grain; the Sicilian connection; – *c)* *MacDonald* Dennis R., Odysseus's oar and Andrew's cross; the transformation of a Homeric theme in the Acts of Andrew: ➤ 392, SBL Seminars 1986, 99-103 / 104-9 / 309-313.

8853 ᴱ**Armstrong** A. H., Plotinus Enneads IV, 1-9; V, 1-9: Loeb 443s. CM/L 1984, Harvard/Heinemann. x-441 p.; x-319 p. £6.50 each [JTS 38,205, G. *O'Daly*].

8854 *Armstrong* A. Hilary, The hidden and the open in Hellenic thought: Eranos-Jb 54 ('The hidden course of events' 1985) 81-118.

8855 ᴱ**Barié** Paul, Antike Religion: Der altsprachliche Unterricht 28/2. Velber 1985, Friedrick & K. 92 p.

8856 *Benedum* C., Asklepios und Demeter; zur Bedeutung weiblicher Gottheiten für den frühen Asklepioskult: JbDAI 101 (1986) 137-157.

8857 **Berthiaume** Guy, Les rôles du mágeiros; étude sur la boucherie, la cuisine et le sacrifice dans la Grèce ancienne 1982 ➤ 63, 9192: ᴿSR 15 (1986) 399-401 (G. *Leroux*).

8858 *Bett* Richard, Immortality and the nature of the soul in the Phaedrus: Phronesis 31 (1986) 1-26.

8859 ᴱ**Betz** Hans D., The Greek magical papyri in translation, including the demotic spells, I. Texts [i.e. translation; vol. 2 will be indices also of Greek text editions]. Ch 1986, Univ. lviii-339 p. $40 [TDig 33,364]. 0-226-04444-0.

8860 *a) Bianchi* Ugo, PLUTARCO e il dualismo; – *b) Barthelmess* James, Recent work on the Moralia: ➤ 521, ᴱ*Brenk* F., Miscellanea 1985/6, 111-120 / 83-96.

8861 *Bonnet* Corinne, Le culte de Leucothéa et de Mélicerte, en Grèce, au Proche-Orient et en Italie: SMSR 52 (1986) 53-71.

8862 **Bortolotti** Arrigo, La religione nel pensiero di PLATONE dai primi dialoghi al Fedro: AcF Studi 86. F 1986, Olschki. 237 p. 88-222-3664-2.

8863 *Brunner* Fernand, Le dernier argument du Phédon de PLATON en faveur de l'immortalité de l'âme: RSPT 70 (1986) 497-520; Eng. 520.

8864 **Burkert** Walter, Die orientalisierende Epoche in der griechischen Religion und Literatur: Szb Heid 1984/1, 1984; DM 68. 3-353-03528-X. – ᴿAntClas 55 (1986) 511-3 (D. *Donnet*); ClasR 100 (1986) 151 (P. *Walcot*).

8865 **Burkert** Walter, Greek Religion, ᵀ*Raffan* John, 1985 ➤ 1,a464: ᴿHistRel 26 (1986s) 92-95 (G. D. *Alles*); RRelRes 28 (1986s) 95s (W. M. A. *Grimaldi*); ScripTPamp 18 (1986) 351 (J. *Morales*).

8866 *Calame* Claude, Facing otherness; the tragic mask in ancient Greece: HistRel 26 (1986s) 125-142.

8867 **Cassidy** William J.ᴵᴵᴵ, Intermediary divinities and personal piety in Greece and Mesopotamia; the rise of personal religion: diss. Graduate Theological Union. Berkeley 1985. – RelStR 13,189.

8868 *Cors i Meya* Jord, Homer i l'influx de la mitologia oriental: Faventia 7,1 (1985) 7-19.

8868* *Croon* Johan H., Heilgötter, ᵀ*Kehl* Alois: ➤ 594, RAC 13 (1986) 1190-1232.

8869 *Czerwińska* Jadwiga, ℗ Sophistarum doctrina de virtute apud THUCYDIDEM obvia: Meander 41 (1986) 211-223; lat. 223.

8870 **Daszewski** W. A., Dionysos der Erlöser; griechische Mythen im spätantiken Cypern: Trierer [Univ.] Beiträge zur Altertumskunde 2. Mainz 1985, von Zabern. 52 p.; 3 fig.; 19 color. pl. – ᴿBMosAnt 11 (1987) 378-380 (J. P. *Darmon*).

8871 **Despland** Michel, The education of desire; PLATO and the philosophy of religion. Toronto 1985, Univ. 395 p. [JAAR 55,389-391, C. *Raschke*].

8872 **Dietrich** Bernard C., Tradition in Greek religion. B 1986, de Gruyter. xvi-213 p. bibliog. p. 187-196. 3-11-010695-7.

8873 ᴱ**Easterling** P. E., *Muir* J. V., Greek religion and society 1985 ➤ 1,425: ᴿAncSRes 16 (1986) 61-63 (G. R. *Horsley*); ClasR 100 (1986) 258s (Emily *Kearns*).

8874 *Edson* C., Cults of Thessalonica [< HarvTR 41 (1948) 153-204]: ➤ 360, Thessaloniken 1985, 886-937; 7 fig.

8875 **Erbse** Hartmut, Untersuchungen zur Funktion der Götter im homerischen Epos: Untersuchungen zur Antiken Literatur und Geschichte 24. B 1986, de Gruyter. xiv-316 p.; bibliog. p. xi-xiv. 3-11-010777-5.

8876 a) *Frede* Michael,   The Stoic doctrine of the affections of the soul; – b) *Engberg-Pedersen* Troels,   Discovering the good; *oikeiōsis* and *kathēkonta* in Stoic ethics; – c) *Irwin* T. H., Stoic and Aristotelian conceptions of happiness: ➤ 540, Norms of Nature 1983/6, 93-110 / 185-184 / 205-244.

8877 **Freyburger-Galland** Marie-Laurie, *Freyburger* Gérard, *Tautil* Jean-Christian.   Sectes religieuses en Grèce et à Rome dans l'antiquité païenne: Realia (0245-8829).   P 1986, BLettres.   338 p. + 23 p.; map.   2-251-33809-8.

8878 **Gadamer** Hans-Georg,   The idea of the good in Platonic-Aristotelian philosophy, ᵀ*Smith* P. Christopher.   NHv 1986, Yale Univ.   182 p. $20 [JAAR 55,601s, M. *Despland*].

8879 *Garbrah* K.,   On the *theophaneia* in Chios and the epiphany of gods in war: ZPapEp 65 (1986) 207-210.

8880 **Garland** Robert,   The Greek way of death.   Ithaca NY 1985, Cornell Univ.   xvi-192 p. $22.50 [RelStR 13,68, P. *Sellew*].

8881 a) *Gladigow* B.,   Präsenz der Bilder — Präsenz der Götter; Kultbilder und Bilder der Götter in griechischer Religion; – b) *Metzler* D.,   Anikonische Darstellungen: Visible Religion 4s (Leiden (1986s) 114-133 / 96-113 [< ZIT]

8882 *Goodman* M. D., *Holladay* A. J.,   Religious scruples in ancient warfare: ClasJ 80 (1986) 151-171 [165-171, Jewish sabbatical year].

8883 **Gosling** J., *Taylor* C.,   The Greeks on pleasure 1982 ➤ 1,a486:   ᴿHeythJ 27 (1986) 206 (J. *Ferguson*).

8884 **Graf** Fritz,   Griechische Mythologie, eine Einführung: Einführungen 16.   Z 1985, Artemis.   198 p.; 10 fig. DM 19,80 [DLZ 107,361, F. *Jürss*].

8885 **Graf** F.,   Nordionische Kulte; religionsgeschichtliche und epigraphische Untersuchungen zu den Kulten von Chios, Erythrai, Klazomenai und Phokaia: Bibl. Helv. Rom. 21.   R 1985, Schweiz. Inst.   XX-490 p.; 3 pl.; 2 maps. Fs 143 [JHS 107,219, J. M. *Cook*].

8886 *Gregory* Timothy,   The survival of paganism in ancient Greece: AmJPg 107 (1986) 229 ...

8887 *Hägg* Robin,   Die göttliche Epiphanie im minoischen Ritual: MiDAI-A 101 (1986) 41-62.

8888 **Hamdorf** Friedrich W.,   Dionysos/Bacchus; Kult und Wandlungen des Weingottes.   Mü 1986, Callwey.   174 p.; 128 fig.

8889 a) *Harris* Bruce F.,   The idea of mercy and its Graeco-Roman context; – b) *Judge* Edwin A.,   The quest for mercy in late antiquity [papyri]: ➤ 54, ᶠKNOX D., God rich 1986, 89-105 / 107-121.

8890 *Hermary* A.,   Divinités chypriotes II: RepCyp (1986) 164-172; 1 fig.; pl. xxxiv-xxxv.

8891 **Hughes** Dennis,   Human sacrifice in ancient Greece; the literary and archaeological evidence: diss. Ohio State 1986, ᴰ*Tracy* S. 457 p. 86-12375. – DissA 47 (1986s) 943-A.

8892 *Inciarte* Fernando,   Skepsis und Glaube; zur Aktualität der hellenistischen Philosophie [*Hossenfelder* Malte 1985]:   TR 83 (1987) 177-186.

8893 *Kleve* Knut,   The daimonion of Socrates [impish unrolling of the evidence that he was mad, or something]: StIFgC 4 (1986) 5-18.

8894 *Koehl* Robert B.,   The Chieftain Cup and a Minoan rite of passage: JHS 106 (1986) 99-110.

8895 *La Genière* Juliette de,   Le culte de la Mère des dieux dans le Péloponnèse: CRAI (1986) 29-46; 10 fig.

8896 ᴱ**Lanternari** Vittorio, *Massenzio* Marcello,   I Greci e gli dei: Anthropos 11.   N 1985, Liguori.   141 p.; 24 fig.

8897 *Le Roy* Christian, Un règlement religieux au Létôon de Xanthos: RArchéol (1986) 281-300; 8 fig.

8898 *Lévêque* P., Les cultes de la fécondité/fertilité dans la Grèce des cités: ➤ 550, ᴱ*Bonanno* A., Fertility cults 1985/6, 242-256.

8899 **Loraux** Nicole, The invention of Athens; the funeral oration in the classical city [L'invention d'Athènes; histoire de l'oraison funèbre dans la 'cité classique' 1981], ᵀ*Sheridan* Alan. CM 1986, Harvard. xii-479 p. 0-674-46362-5.

8900 *Loucas* Éveline & Ioannis, Un autel de Rhéa-Cybèle et la Grande Déesse de Phlya: Latomus 45 (1986) 392-404; V pl.

8901 **Luck** Georg, Arcana mundi; magic and the occult in the Greek and Roman worlds. Baltimore 1985, Johns Hopkins Univ. xv-395 p. 0-8018-2523-7; pa. 48-2.

8902 **Malherbe** Abraham J., Moral exhortation; a Greco-Roman sourcebook: Library of Early Christianity 4. Ph 1986, Westminster. 178 p. $19 [RelStR 13,166, Pheme *Perkins*].

8903 *Mantzoulinou-Richards* Ersie, Demeter Malophoros, the divine sheep-bringer: AncW 13 (1986) 15-22.

8904 **Marglin** Frédérique A., Wives of the god-king [... hierodules; exponents of arts, music]; the rituals of the Devadasis of Puri. NY 1985, Oxford-UP. 388 p. $30 [JAAR 55,405-7, W. *Harman*].

8905 *May* Louise A., Above her sex; the enigma of the Athena Parthenos: VisRel 3 (1984)... [ÉTRel 61,437].

8906 **Mikalson** Jon D., Athenian popular religion 1983 ➤ 65,9192; 1,a501: ᴿMnemosyne 39 (1986) 543-5 (J. N. *Bremmer*).

8907 **Mora** F., Religione e religioni nelle Storie di ERODOTO. Mi 1986, Jaca [SMSR 52,181].

8908 *Motte* André, L'expression du sacré dans la religion grecque: ➤ 493, ᴱ*Ries* J., Expression du sacré 3 (1978/86) 109-256.

8909 **Moustaka** Aliki, Kulte und Mythen auf thessalischen Münzen [< Diss. Heid.]: Beiträge zur Archäologie 15, 1983 ➤ 65,9196; 1,a506: ᴿRNum 28 (1986) 216 (D. *Gerin*).

8910 *Neumer-Pfau* W., Die nackte Liebesgöttin; Aphroditestatuen als Verkörperung des Weiblichkeitsideals in der griechisch-hellenistischen Welt: Visible Religion 4s (1985s) 205-234.

8911 **Nilsson** Martin P., Cults, myths, oracles and politics in ancient Greece: SIMA pocket 43. Göteborg 1986 [= 1951 + notice of 16 reviews], Åström. 180 p. [Antiquity 61,439]. 91-86098-43-8.

8912 **Nussbaum** Martha C., The fragility of goodness; luck and ethics in Greek tragedy and philosophy. L 1986, Univ. xvii-544 p. bibliog. p. 512-525 $59.50; pa. $20 [RelStR 13,348, R. A. *Swanson*]. 0-521-25768-9; pa. 7702-7.

8913 **Parker** Robert, Miasma; pollution and purification in early Greek religion 1983 ➤ 64,9444 ... 1,a508: ᴿJHS 106 (1986) 234s (R. *Garland*); Mnemosyne 39 (1986) 538-543 (H. *Horstmanshoff*); RHR 203 (1986) 295-9 (C. *Jacob*).

8915 *Parry* Hugh, The Homeric hymn to Aphrodite; erotic *anankē*: Phoenix 40 (Toronto 1986) 253-264.

8916 **Pesce** D., La tavola di Cebete 1982 ➤ 65,9002: ᴿMnemosyne 39 (1986) 484-6 (J. Mansfeld, also on FITZGERALD-WHITE).

8917 *Piérart* Marcel, Michel FOUCAULT et la morale sexuelle des anciens: FreibZ 33 (1986) 23-43.

8918 *Places* Édouard des, Chronique de la philosophie religieuse des Grecs (1984-1986); BBudé (1986) 408-423.

8919 *Poliseno* Antonio,   L'etica nel mondo greco; dall'approvazione alla responsabilità: CivClasCr 7 (1986) 261-7.

8920 ᴱ**Pontrandolfo** Angela,   La città delle immagini; religione e società nella Grecia antica.   Modena 1986, Panini.   159 p.; 231 fig.

8921 *Rainer* Johannes M.,   Zum Problem der Atimie als Verlust der bürgerlichen Rechte insbesondere bei männlichen homosexuellen Prostituten: RIDA 33 (1986) 89-114.

8922 **Rankin** H. D.,   Sophists, Socratics and Cynics.   L/Totowa 1983, Croom Helm / Barnes & N.   263 p.   £18. – ᴿHeythJ 27 (1986) 469s (J. *Ferguson*).

8923 **Rutkowski** Bogdan,   The cult places of the [pre-Bronze Age] Aegean [= ²Cult places of the Aegean world 1972], ᵀ*Kozlowska* C.   NHv 1986, Yale Univ.   xix-267 p.; 315 fig. $35.   0-300-02962-4. – ᴿRelStR 12 (1986) 288 (W. A. *McDonald*).

8924 ᴱ**Schofield** M., *Striker* G.,   The norms of nature; studies in Hellenistic ethics.   C/P 1986, Univ. / Maison Sciences Homme.   vii-287 p. $50.   0-521-26623-8 / 2-7351-0147-9 [NTAbs 31,128].

8925 *Schröder* Richard,   Die Linie Dᴇᴍᴏᴋʀɪᴛs [... Lenin]: BTZ 3 (1986) 77-91.

8926 **Sergent** Bernard,   L'homosexualité dans la mythologie grecque 1984 ➤ 65,9209:   ᴿAmJPg 107 (1986) 426s (T. J. *Figueira*).

8927 **Settegast** Mary,   Plato prehistorian; 10,000 to 5,000 in myth and archaeology.   CM 1986, Rotenberg.   xvi-334; 151 fig. $36 [JNES 46,244].

8928 *Shapiro* H. A.,   The Attic deity Basile: ZPapEp 63 (1986) 134-6.

8929 **Simms** Ronda Rae,   Foreign religious cults in Athens in the fifth and fourth centuries B.C.: diss. Virginia 1985. 332 p. 86-15569. – DissA 47 (1986s) 3532-A.

8930 *Sippel* Donald V.,   Minoan religion and the sign of the double axe: AncW 14 (1986) 87-94.

8931 **Souza Brandão** Juanito de,   Mitologia grega I.   Petrópolis 1986, Vozes. 404 p. [REB 46,469].

8932 *Thummer* Erich,   Griechische 'Erlösungsdramen': ➤ 80*, ᶠOʙᴇʀʜᴜʙᴇʀ K., Im Bannkreis 1986, 237-259.

8933 **Tracy** Stephen V.,   I. G. II² 2336, contributors of first fruits for the Pythaïs: BeiKlPg 139.   Meisenheim 1982, Hain.   DM 64 [RelStR 13,68, Susan G. *Cole*].

8934 **Tsouvara-Souli** C., ☉ *Hē latreia...* Cult of female divinities in ancient Epirus: diss. Ioannina 1979 ➤ 65,9215:   ᴿJHS 106 (1986) 235 (Christiane *Sourvinou-Inwood*).

8935 **Vermaseren** M. J.,   Corpus cultus Cybelae Attidisque V. Aegyptus, Africa, Hispania, Gallia et Britannia: ÉPR 50/5.   Leiden 1986, Brill. xxiv-227 p.; 169 pl.; bibliog. p. xi-xxiv.   90-04-07679-4.

8936 **Vernant** Jean-Pierre, *Vidal-Naquet* Pierre,   Mythe et tragédie en Grèce ancienne: Textes à l'appui.   P 1986, Découverte.   301 p. 2-7071-1590-8.

M5.5   **Religiones anatolicae.**

8937 **Archi** A.,   Hethitische Orakeltexte etc.: KUB 52, 1983 ➤ 64,3361... 1,3408:   ᴿOLZ 81 (1986) 39s (V. *Haas*; ibid. Jᴀᴋᴏʙ-Rᴏsᴛ L., Oᴛᴛᴇɴ H.).

8938 **Beckman** Gary M.,   Hittite birth rituals² [diss. Yale 1977] 1983 ➤ 64,9469; 1,a538:   ᴿOLZ 81 (1986) 559-561 (M. *Popko*); ZAss 76 (1986) 143-6 (M. *Poetto*).

8939 *Ebach* Jürgen,   Hethitische Religion: ➤ 597, TRE 15 (1986) 290-7.

8940 **Freydank** Helmut,   Hethitische Rituale und Festbeschreibungen: KUB

51, 1981 → 63,9243; 65,9226: ᴿOrientalia 55 (1986) 475s (M. *Popko*); ZAss 76 (1986) 130-3 (S. *Košak*).

8941 **Haas** Volkert, *Thiel* Hans J., Die Beschwörungsrituale der Allaiturah(h)i und verwandte Texte: AOAT 31, 1978 → 58,c845a... 65,9230: ᴿOrientalia 55 (1986) 346-8 (A. *Archi*).

8942 **Jakob-Rost** Liane, Festritual für Telipinu von Kašha und andere hethitische Rituale: KUB 53, 1983 → 64,9478; 65,9232: ᴿOrientalia 55 (1986) 476s (M. *Popko*).

8943 *Kammenhuber* Annelies, Die luwischen Rituale KUB XXXV 45 + KBo XXIX 3 (II), XXXV 43 + KBo XXIX 55 (III) und KUB XXXII 9 + XXXV 21 (+) XXXII 11 nebst Parallelen (= Anlässlich der neuen luwischen Fragmente aus KBo XXIX [1983], I §§ 1-3): → 80*, ᶠOBERHUBER K., Im Bannkreis 1986, 83-104.

8944 **Klengel** Horst, Hethitische Gelübde[-] und Traumtexte sowie Rituale und Festbeschreibungen: KaB 56. B 1986, Akademie. xi-50 pl. 3-05-00142-9.

8945 *Kühne* Cord, Hethitisch *auli-* und einige Aspekte altanatolischer Opferpraxis: ZAss 76 (1986) 85-117; 5 fig.

8946 **Neu** Erich, Glossar zu den althethitischen Ritualtexten 1983 → 64,9484; 65,9239: ᴿOLZ 81 (1986) 250-2 (L. *Jakob-Rost*).

8947 **Otten** Heinrich, *Rüster* Christel, Festbeschreibungen und Rituale: KaB 30, 1984 → 65,9240; DM 43: ᴿMundus 22 (1986) 34s (K. *Hecker*).

8948 *a*) *Otten* Heinrich, Ein Ritual von Ašdu, der Hurriterin; – *b*) *Kellerman* Galina, The Telepinu myth reconsidered; – *c*) *Houwink ten Cate* P., The outline of the AN.TAH.ŠUM festival: → 42, ᶠGÜTERBOCK H., Kaniššuwar 1986, 165-171 / 115-123 / 95-110.

8949 **Salvini** Mirjo, *Wegner* Ilse, Die Rituale des AZU-Priesters: Corpus der Hurritischen Sprachdenkmäler 1 (Boğazköy), 2. R 1986, Multigrafica. 483 p.; 171 p.

8950 **Singer** Itamar, The Hittite KI.LAM festival I-II 1983s → 64,9490... 1,a552: ᴿBO 43 (1986) 168-171 (G. *Beckman*); IndogF 91 (1986) 377-380 (G. *Neumann*).

8951 *Taracha* Piotr, Zum Festritual des Gottes Telipinu in Hanhana und in Kašha: AltOrF 13 (1986) 180-3.

8952 *Wouters* W., La dées[s]e au bonnet 'pointu' [Fraktın, Ugarit, Alaca]: OrLovPer 17 (1986) 65-70.

M6 Religio canaanaea, syra.

8953 **Amir** David, ⊕ Gods and heroes; Canaanite epics from Ugarit (including some epics never before published in Hebrew), notes, glossary; concordance KTU/CTA/UT. Dan 1986, Beth Ussishkin. 42 p.

8954 *Bendala Galán* Manuel, Die orientalischen Religionen Hispaniens in vorrömischer und römischer Zeit, ᵀ*Koch* Michael: → 574, ANRW 2,18,1 (1986) 345-408; 8 fig.; 12 pl.

ᴱ**Bonnet** C., *Lipinski* E., *Marchetti* P., Religio Phoenicia: Studia Phoenicia 4, 1986 → 551.

8956 *Cooper* Alan M. [*Coogan* Michael D.] Canaanite religion, an overview [the literature]: → 585, EncRel 3 (1986) 35-45 [-58].

8957 **Daum** Werner, Ursemitische Religion 1985 → 1,a566: ᴿBL (1986) 101s (J. F. *Healey*); ÉTRel 61 (1986) 272s (K. *Smyth*); WeltOr 17 (1986) 155-8 (W. *Röllig*); ZAW 98 (1986) 462s (O. *Kaiser*).

8958 *a*) *Falsone* Gioacchino, Anath or Astarte? A Phoenician bronze statuette of the 'Smiting Goddess'; – b) Bisi Anna Maria, Le 'Smiting God' dans les milieux phéniciens d'Occident; un réexamen de la question: ⇒ 551, Religio phoenicia 1984/6, 53-76 / 169-187.

8959 Ferron Jean, La déesse TNT de Carthage; à propos d'un livre récent [Hvidberg-Hansen F. 1979]: Muséon 99 (1986) 15-37.

8960 Fredouille Jean-Claude, Heiden, AT-Judentum-NT, ᵀHoheisel Karl: ⇒ 594, RAC 13 (1986) 1113-1149 [-1190, -verfolgung, Noethlichs Karl L.].

8961 Freilich Donna, Is there an Ugaritic deity Bbt?: JSS 31 (1986) 119-130.

8962 Giveon Raphael, Remarks on the Tel Qarnayim goddess [female standing on horse (pottery relief) found also on Lachish gold leaf...]: BibNot 33 (1986) 7-9.

8963 a) Gordon C. H., Ḥby, possessor of horns and tail [UT Sup. 552; Ebla ...]; – b) Gruber Mayer I., Hebrew Qedēšāh and her Canaanite and Akkadian cognates: UF 18 (1986s) 129-132 / 133-148.

8964 Gubel E., 'Astarté à cheval?'; nota's omtrent een nieuwe Fenicische schaal [bowl from the sea near Byblos] (résumé): Akkadica 49 (1986) 31.

8965 Heider George C., The cult of Molek, a reassessment [< diss. Yale]: JStOT Sup 43, 1985 ⇒ 1,a572: ᴿExpTim 97 (1985s) 375s (J. Day); VT 36 (1986) 511s (J. A. Emerton); ZAW 98 (1986) 467 (G. Wanke).

8966 Holter Knut, Jahve og Dagon; et eksempel på en misjonsteologisk tilnær-ming til et gammeltestamentlig religionsmøte: TsTKi 57 (1986) 271-280.

8967 Hoskisson Paul Y., The deities and cult terms in Mari; an analysis of the textual evidence: diss. Brandeis. Boston 1986. 560 p. 86-06424. – DissA 47 (1986s) 211-A.

8968 Hvidberg–Hansen F. O., La déesse TNT; une étude sur la religion canaanéo-punique 1980 ⇒ 61,m177... 64,9499: ᴿJNES 45 (1986) 311-4 (G. W. Ahlström: too many errors).

8969 Kloos Carola, Yhwh's combat with the sea; a Canaanite tradition in the religion of ancient Israel. Amst/Leiden 1986, Van Oorschot / Brill. 245 p. ƒ84 pa. 90-0408096-1 [JBL 105,752]. ⇒ 2333, Ps. 29.

8970 Kuemmerlin-McLean Joanne K., Divination and magic in the religion of ancient Israel; a study in perspectives and methodology: diss. Vanderbilt, ᴰKnight D. Nv 1986. 287 p. 86-26559. – DissA 47 (1986s) 3073s-A.

8971 Lewis Theodore J., Cults of the dead in ancient Israel and Ugarit: diss. Harvard. CM 1986. 342 p. 86-20571. – DissA 47 (1986s) 2189-A.

8972 a) Lipiński Édouard, Zeus Ammon et Baal-Ḥammon; – b) Bordreuil P., Attestations inédites de Melqart, Baal Ḥamon et Baal Ṣaphon à Tyr (Nouveaux documents religieux phéniciens II); – c) Roobaert Arlette, Ṣid, Sardus Pater ou Baal Ḥammon? À propos d'un bronze de Genoni (Sardaigne); – d) Tokay Madeleine, Le bas-relief au sphinx de Damas: ⇒ 551, Religio phoenicia 1984/6, 307-332; 15 fig. / 77-86; 4 fig. / 333-345; 9 fig. / 99-118; 18 fig.

8973 McMurray Carl W. †, Stone and pillar cult among the western Semites, with special reference to Hebrews: diss. E 1934! 86-18607. – DissA 47 (1986s) 1770-A.

8974 Maier Walter A., ʿAšerah; extrabiblical evidence: HarvSemMon 37. Atlanta 1986, Scholars. 260 p. $22.

8975 Mazzoni Stefania, La dea alata con veste paleosiriana: EgVO 9 (1986) 83-96; 8 fig.

8976 Moor J. C. de, The crisis of polytheism in Late Bronze Ugarit: ⇒ 399, OTS 24, 1985/6, 1-20.

8977 Mullen E. Theodore, [cover-title] The Assembly of the Gods; [title-page] The divine council in Canaanite and early Hebrew literature: HarvSemMon

24,1980 ➤ 61,m199 ... 1,a578: ᴿJNES 45 (1986) 64-67 (D. *Pardee*, also on two other Harvard theses, HALPERN B. and FRIEDMAN R. 1981); Orientalia 55 (1986) 92-95 (O. *Loretz*); Syria 63 (1986) 442-4 (R. *Caquot*). *North* Robert, Ebla names and gods at Rome conference 1986/6 ➤ e274.

8978 *a*) *Noy* T., Seated clay figurines from the Neolithic period, Israel; – *b*) *Hvidberg-Hansen* F. O., Uni-Ashtarte and Tanit-Iuno Caelestis; two Phoenician goddesses of fertility reconsidered from recent archaeological discoveries; – *c*) *Meshel* Z., The Israelite religious centre of Kuntillet ʿAjrud, Sinai; – *d*) *Lipiński* E. [*Segert* S.], Fertility cult in ancient Ugarit; – *e*) *Hölbl* G., Egyptian fertility magic within Phoenician and Punic culture; – *f*) *Rooy* H. F. van, Fertility as blessing and infertility as curse in the ancient Near East and the OT: ➤ 550, ᴱ*Bonanno* A., Fertility cult 1985/6, 63-67 / 170-195 / 237-9 / 207-216 [217-221] / 197-205 / 225-235; ill.

8979 **Olmo Lete** Gregorio del, Interpretación de la mitología cananea; estudios de semántica ugarítica 1984 ➤ 65,236; 1,a579: ᴿBO 43 (1986) 758-760 (M. *Dijkstra*); JBL 105 (1986) 705s (R. H. *McGrath*).

8980 **Olmo Lete** G. del, Mitos y leyendas de Canaán según la tradición de Ugarit 1981 ➤ 62,a144 ... 65,9267: ᴿOrientalia 55 (1986) 194-7 (W. G. E. *Watson*: an achievement; numerous proposals).

8981 *Olmo Lete* G. del., *a*) The cultic literature of Ugaritic; hermeneutical issues and their application to KTU 1.112: ➤ 543, Rencontre 32, 1985/6, 155-164; 1 pl.; – *b*) La estructura del panteón ugarítico: ➤ 21, Mem. DÍEZ MACHO A., Salvación 1986, 267-304.

8982 *a*) *Olmo Lete* G. del, The 'divine' names of the Ugaritic kings; – *b*) *Hess* Richard S., Divine names in the Amarna texts: UF 18 (1986s) 83 / 149-168.

8983 **Pettey** Richard A., Asherah, goddess of Israel?: diss. Marquette, ᴰ*Pace* Sharon. Milwaukee 1985. 285 p. – DissA 47 (1986s) 212-A.

8984 *a*) *Quinzio* S., Il sacro nel pensiero ebraico; – *b*) *García Bazán* F., Il sacro e le religioni dell'Oriente: Fondamenti 4 (Brescia 1986) 125-139 / 141-172 [ZAW 99,118]; Eng. 217s.

8985 **Ribichini** S., Poenus advena; gli dèi fenici e l'interpretazione classica: StFen 19,1985➤ 1,a581: ᴿÉtClas 54 (1986) 175s (Corinne *Bonnet*); RStFen 14 (1986) 251-5 (L. *Troiani*).

8987 *Teixidor* J., Aramean religion: ➤ 585, EncRel 1 (1986) 367-372.

8988 *Thompson* J. A., Foreign religious influence on Israel: BurH 21,4 (1985) 89-97 [OTAbs 9,270].

8989 **Tubach** J., Im Schatten des Sonnengottes; der Sonnenkult in Edessa, Harran und Hatra am Vorabend der christlichen Mission. Wsb 1986, Harrassowitz. xviii-546 p.; 12 pl. DM 198. 3-447-02435-6 [BL 87,120, M. *Richardson*].

8990 *Will* Ernest, Du môtab de Dusarès au trône d'Astarté: Syria 63 (1986) 343-351; 7 fig.

8991 *a*) *Xella* Paolo, Le polythéisme phénicien; – *b*) *Ribichini* Sergio, Questions de mythologie phénicienne d'après PHILON de Byblos; – *c*) *Heltzer* M., Phoenician theophorous names with the root ʿMS; – *d*) *Elayi* J., Le roi et la religion dans les cités phéniciennes à l'époque perse (*Gubel* E., scène); – *e*) *Servais-Soyez* Brigitte, La 'triade' phénicienne aux époques hellénistique et romaine: ➤ 551, Religio phoenicia 1984/6, 29-39 / 41-52 / 239-247 / 249-261 (263-276) / 347-360.

M6.5 **Religio aegyptia.**

8992 **Armour** Robert A., Gods and myths of ancient Egypt. Cairo

1986, American Univ. [NY Columbia Univ.]. 206 p.; 53 pl. $15. [JNES 46,74].

8993 **Assmann** J., Ägypten — Theologie und Frömmigkeit einer frühen Hochkultur: Urban-Tb 366, 1984 → 1,a589: ᴿBL (1986) 99s (K. A. *Kitchen*).

8994 **Assmann** J., Re und Amun...: OBO 51, 1983 → 64,9524 ... 1,a590: ᴿOLZ 81 (1986) 333-6 (W. *Barta*).

8994* **Assmann** Jan, Sonnenhymnen in thebanischen Gräbern 1983 → 65, 9289; 1,a591: ᴿJAmEg 22 (1985) 223s (C. C. *Van Siclen*).

8995 *a*) *Assmann* Jan, Verklärung; – *b*) *Schoske* Sylvia, Vernichtigungsrituale; – *c*) *Goedicke* Hans, Vergöttlichung: → 591, LexÄg 6,47 (1986) 998-1006 / 1009-1012 / 989-992.

8996 *a*) *Avi-Yonah* Eva, 'To see the god ...'; reflections on the iconography of the decorated chamber in ancient Hierakonpolis; – *b*) *Tobin* Vincent A., The myth of Osiris: → 349*, ᴱ*Groll* S., Papers 2 (1985) 7-44; p. 45-82 = 56 fig. / 328-348.

8997 **Banna** Essam El-, À propos de la désignation 'Père des dieux' (*'it nṯrw*): BIFAO 86 (1986) 151-170.

8998 **Barguet** Paul, Les textes des sarcophages égyptiens du Moyen-Empire: LAPO 12. P 1986, Cerf. 725 p. F 270. 2-204-02332-9. – ᴿÉTRel 61 (1986) 439s (D. *Lys*).

8999 *Barta* Winfried, *a*) Osiris als Mutterleib des unterweltlichen Sonnengottes in den Jenseitsbüchern des Neuen Reiches: JbEOL 29 (1985s) 98-105; – *b*) Bemerkungen zur 'grossen Litanei' im Buch der Anbetung des Re im Westen: ZägSpr 113 (1986) 83-88.

9000 *Battaglia* Emanuela, Due liste di sacerdoti [in greco]: Aegyptus 66 (1986) 85-99.

9001 **Beinlich** H., Die 'Osirisreliquien'; zum Motiv der Körperzergliederung in der altägyptischen Religion: ÄgAbh 42, 1984 → 65,9295; 1,a597*; DM 148. 3-447-02498-4: ᴿBL (1986) 100s (K. A. *Kitchen*).

9002 *Bilolo* M., A l'enjeu politique de la théologie négative du Grand Hymne à Jati: GöMiszÄg 93 (1986) 29-35.

9003 *Borghouts* J. F., Nieuwjaar in het Oude Egypte [Inaug. Leiden 1986]. Leiden 1986, Ned. Inst. 36 p. [PhoenixEOL 32/2,7].

9004 **Brier** R., Zauber und Magie im alten Ägypten 1984 → 65,9302: ᴿAnz-AltW 39 (1986) 123 (P. *Haider*).

9005 **Brunner** Hellmut, Grundzüge der altägyptischen Religion: Grundzüge 50, 1983 → 64,9535 [3-534-08424-1!]... 1,a600: ᴿBO 43 (1986) 401-6 (U. *Luft*).

9006 *Brunner* Hellmut, Votivgaben: → 591, LexÄg 6,47 (1986) 1977-81.

9007 *Buchberger* Hannes, Wiedergeburt [... Wiederholung der Geburt]: → 591, LexÄg 6,48 (1986) 1246-6 [1261-4, *Gundlach* Rolf].

9007* **Cauville** Sylvie, La théologie d'Osiris à Edfou 1983 → 64,9539... 1,a603: ᴿJAmEg 22 (1985) 216s (R. J. *Leprohon*).

9008 *Cenival* François de, Comptes d'une association religieuse datant des années 29 à 33 du roi Amasis [541-537] (P. Démot. Louvre E 7840 bis): RÉgp 37 (1986) 13-29; pl. 3s.

9009 *Chauveau* Michel, Les cultes d'Edfa [6 k NW Sohag] à l'époque romaine: RÉgp 37 (1986) 31-43; pl. 5-8.

9010 *Chiodi* Silvia M., Demiurgia e ierogamia nel De Iside plutarcheo; un'esegesi platonica del mito egiziano: SMSR 52 (1986) 33-51.

9011 *a*) *Clère* Jacques J., Deux groupes inédits de génies-gardiens du quatrième prophète d'Amon Mentemḥat; – *b*) *Cuvigny* Hélène, Une prétendue taxe sur les autels, le *phoros bōmōn*; – *c*) *Meulenaere* Herman De, Une famille

sacerdotale thébaine: BIFAO 86 (1986) 99-106; 10 fig.; pl. III / 107-133 /
135-142; pl. IV-VII.

9012 *a) Colpe* Carsten, Ägypten; – *b) Assmann* Jan, Ägyptische Religion:
➤ 587, EvKL 1 (1986) 64-88 / 68-72.

9013 **Del Corno** Dario, *Cavalli* Marina, PLUTARCO, Iside e Osiride: Picc.
Bibliot. 179. Mi 1985, Adelphi. 225 p. Lit. 13.000. – ᴿClasR 100 (1986)
314 (J. G. *Griffiths*).

9014 **Derchain-Urteil** Maria-Theresia, Thot à travers ses épithètes dans les
scènes d'offrandes des temples d'époque greco-romaine: Rites égyptiens 3,
1981 ➤ 63,9325; 64,9544: ᴿOLZ 81 (1986) 139-141 (J. G. *Griffiths*).

9015 *Dijk* Jacobus van, Zerbrechen der roten Töpfe [breaking the *dšrt*-vessels,
in English]: ➤ 591, LexÄg 6,49 (1986) 1389-96.

9016 *a) Dijk* Jacobus van, The symbolism of the Memphite Djed-pillar; – *b)
Raven* Maarten J., A rare type of Osiris Canopus: OMRO 66 (1986)
7-17; 3 pl. / 21-27; 3 pl.

9017 *Donadoni* Sergio F., La preghiera egiziana [< La Preghiera I (1967)
219-232]: ➤ 152, Cultura 1986, 109-122.

9018 *Dunand* F., Religion populaire et iconographie en Égypte hellénistique et
romaine: VisRel 3 (1984)... [EŤRel 61,437].

9019 *Finnestad* Ragnhild B., On transposing 'soul' and 'body' into a monistic
conception of 'being'; an example from ancient Egypt: Religion 16 (L
1986) 359... [< ZIT].

9020 **Germond** Philippe, Sekhmet et la protection du monde: AegHelv 9,
ᴰ1981 ➤ 65,9314; 1,a610: ᴿOrientalia 55 (1986) 78-81 (P. *Vernus*).

9021 **Goedicke** Hans, Die Darstellung des Horus; ein Mysterienspiel in Philae
unter Ptolemäus VIII, 1982 ➤ 63,9332; 65,9317: CdÉ 61 (1986) 82-86
(J.-C. *Goyon*); OLZ 81 (1986) 450-2 (H. *Beinlich*).

9022 *Hafemann* Ingelore, Zur Religion der alten Ägypter [*Morenz* S. ²1984]:
Klio 68 (1986) 279...

9023 **Hari** R., New Kingdom, Amarna period: Iconography of Religions 16/6,
1985 ➤ 1,a619: ᴿVT 36 (1986) 509s (J. D. *Ray* at length).

9024 **Hart** George, A dictionary of Egyptian gods and goddesses. L 1986,
Routledge-KP. xv-229 p. £6. – ᴿSalesianum 48 (1986) 975s (R. *Sabin*).

9025 *Heerma van Voss* Matthieu, Le Livre des Morts au Nouvel Empire au
Musée de Leyde: BSFr.Eg 105 (1986) 10-22; 8 pl.

9026 **Hoffmeier** James K., Sacred in the vocabulary of ancient Egypt, ... dsr
1985 ➤ 1,a623: ᴿBO 43 (1986) 74-76 (W. *Barta*); Henoch 8 (1986) 90s (A.
Roccati); JAmEg 22 (1985) 235s (H. *Goedicke*); Salesianum 48 (1986) 1032
(R. *Sabin*).

9027 **Hornung** Erik, *al.*, Der ägyptische Mythos von der Himmelskuh; eine
Ätiologie des Unvollkommenen: OBO 46, 1982 ➤ 63,9342; 64,9566:
ᴿOLZ 81 (1986) 135-9 (U. *Verhoeven*).

9028 **Horst** Pieter W. van der, Chaeremon, Egyptian priest and Stoic
philosopher: ÉPR 101, 1984 ➤ 65,9333; 1,a627: ᴿRB 93 (1986) 468s
(M.-J. *Pierre*).

9029 *Hummel* Siegert, Notizen zu [ithyphallischem] Min: ActOrK 47 (1986)
7-12.

9030 *Jackson* Howard, *Kórē kósmou*; Isis, pupil of the eye of the world: CdÉ
61 (1986) 116-135.

9031 *Jacq* C., Egyptian magic [➤ 1,a628*b*], intr. *David* A. R. Wmr/Ch 1985,
Aris & P / Bolchazy-Carducci. xiv-162 p.; 46 fig.; front. £6. 0-85668-
299-3 / Ch 0-86516-118-6 [BL 87,98, K. A. *Kitchen*: as if he believed
in it].

9032 **Kruchten** Jean-Marie, Le grand texte oraculaire de Djéhoutymose. Bru 1986, Fond. Reine Élisabeth. 397 p.; 5 pl. [JNES 46,77].

9033 **Lalouette** Claire, La littérature égyptienne: Que sais-je? Nᵒ 1934: 1981 ➤ 62,a199: ᴿCdÉ 61 (1986) 231s (C. De *Wit*).

9034 **Lapp** Günther, Die Opferformel des Alten Reiches, unter Berücksichtigung einiger späterer Formen: DAI-K Sonderschrift 21. Mainz 1986, von Zabern. xxxvii-268 p.

9035 *Lemaire* André, Divinités égyptiennes dans l'onomastique phénicienne: ➤ 551, Religio phoenicia 1984/6, 87-98.

9036 ᴱ**Lüscher** B., Totenbuch Spruch I, nach Quellen des Neuen Reiches: KlÄgTexte. Wsb 1986, Harrassowitz. ix-73 p. DM 32. 3-447-02646-4 [BL 87,98s, K. A. *Kitchen*].

9037 *a) Malaise* Michel, L'expression du sacré dans les cultes isiaques; – *b*) *Duchesne-Guillemin* J., Le sacré dans le mazdéisme: ➤ 493, ᴱ*Ries* J., Expression du sacré 3 (1978/86) 25-107 / 15-24.

9038 **Morenz** Siegfried [1964], ²*Blumenthal* Elke, Gott und Mensch im alten Ägypten 1984 ➤ 65,9348; **1**,a634: ᴿMundus 22 (1986) 30 (Ingrid *Gamer-Wallert*).

9039 **Mostafa** Maha M. F., Untersuchungen zu Opfertafeln im Alten Reich 1982 ➤ 63,9351; **1**,a635*: ᴿCdÉ 61 (1986) 264-7 (Marie-Paule *Vanlathem*).

9040 **Myśliwiec** Karol, Studien zum Gott Atum, I., Die heiligen Tiere des Atum; II. Name — Epitheta — Ikonographie 1978s ➤ 61,m347 ... 63,9353: ᴿOLZ 81 (1986) 239-241 (H. A. *Schlögl*).

9041 *a) O'Connell* Robert H., An exposition of Coffin Text Spell 148 — the emergence of Horus; – *b*) *Schmidt* Brian, A grammatical analysis of a Coffin Text entitled Sailing from death to life: ➤ 349*, ᴱ*Groll* S., Papers 1 (1982) 102-137 [53ss *Hollander* Frances] / 138-155.

9042 **Ogdon** Jorge R., *a*) Some notes on the name and the iconography of the god *3kr*; VAeg 2 (1986) 127-135; – *b*) An exceptional family of priests of the early fifth dynasty at Gîza: GöMiszÄg 90 (1986) 61-65.

9043 **Oswalt** John N., The concept of Amon-Re as reflected in the hymns and prayers of the Ramesside period: diss. Brandeis. Boston 1968. xiii-294 p.; bibliog. p. 285-293.

9044 **Plas** Dirk van der, L'hymne à la crue du Nil: Egyptologische uitgaven 4. Leiden 1986, Ned. Instituut Nabije Oosten. 217 p.; 213 p. + LV pl. 90-6258-204-4.

9045 *Podvin* Jean-Louis, Quelques aspects de l'identification entre Pharaon et Amon-Re au début de la XVIIIᵉ Dynastie: GöMiszÄg 93 (1986) 49-60.

9046 *Posener-Kriéger* Paule, Wag-Fest [fête funéraire, en français]: ➤ 591, LexÄg 6,48 (1986) 1135-9.

9047 *Quaegebeur* Jan, *a*) Amenophis, nom royal et nom divin; questions méthodologiques: REgp 37 (1986) 97-106; – *b*) Thot-Hermès, le dieu le plus grand?: ➤ 18, Mém. DAUMAS F., II (1986) 525-544.

9048 *a) Schulman* Alan R., Some observations on the *3ḫ iḳr n R'* stelae; – *b*) *Demarée* R. J., More *3ḫ iḳr n R'*-stelae: BO 43 (1986) 302-349 / 348-351.

9049 *Séguenny* Edwige, *Desanges* Jehan, Sarapis dans le royaume de Kouch: CdÉ 61 (1986) 324-329.

9050 **Thomas** Angela P., Egyptian gods and myths: Shire Egyptology. Aylesbury 1986, Shire. 64 p.; 48 fig. £2.50. 0-85263-788-8 [BO 43,706]. – ᴿJAmEg 23 (1986) 224s (R. D. *Bianchi*).

9051 **Totti** Maria, Ausgewählte Texte der Isis- und Sarapis-Religion: Subsidia epigraphica 12. Hildesheim 1985, Olms. viii-231 p.

9052 **Van Siclen** Charles C.[III], The alabaster shrine of King Amenhotep III: Brooklyn Museum Archaeological Expedition to the precinct of the Goddess Mut at South Karnak. San Antonio 1986, auct. xv-59 p.; 13 fig.; 60 pl. 0-933175-05-1. [OIAc F86].

9053 **Van Siclen** Charles C.[III], The chapel of Sesostris III at Uronarti. San Antonio 1982, auct. 58 p.

9054 **Verhoeven** Ursula, *Derchain* Philippe, Le voyage de la déesse libyque; ein Text aus dem 'Mutritual' des Pap. Berlin 3053: Rites Égyptiens 5. Bru 1985, Fond. Reine Élisabeth. viii-87 p.; 9 pl.

9055 *Vittmann* G., Quellenindex zu J. F. BORGHOUTS, Ancient Egyptian magical texts: GöMiszÄg 94 (1986) 89-92.

9056 **Ward** William A., Index of Egyptian administrative and religious titles of the Middle Kingdom 1982 → 63,9378; 65,9371: [R]CdÉ 61 (1986) 238s (O. *Berlev*).

9057 **Werner** Edward K., The god Montu, from the earliest attestations to the end of the New Kingdom: diss. Yale. NHv 1985. 410 p. 86-13638. – DissA 47 (1986s) 1448-A.

9058 **Wild** Robert J., Water in the cultic worship of Isis and Sarapis: ÉPR 87, 1981 → 62,a222... 1,a670: [R]JEA 78 (1986) 209 (J. G. *Griffiths*).

9059 **Wirz** Gretel, Tod und Vergänglichkeit 1982 → 63,9381... 1,a671: [R]OLZ 81 (1986) 546s (E. *Hornung*).

9060 [F]ZANDEE J., Studies in Egyptian religion, [E]*Heerma Van Voss* M. al. 1982 → 63,171; 1,a672: [R]CdÉ 61,121 (1986) 76-78 (Gertie *Englund*).

M7 Religio mesopotamica.

9061 **Charpin** Dominique, Le clergé d'Ur au siècle d'Hammurabi (XIXe-XVIIIe siècles av. J.-C.: ÉPHÉH 4/2/22. Genève 1986, Droz. 519 p. [RelStR 13, 255, J. M. *Sasson*].

9062 *Cohen* Mark E., Sumerian hymnology; the Eršemma 1981 → 62,3108*; 63,9391: [R]ArOr 54 (1986) 302s (B. *Hruška*).

9063 **DiVito** Robert A., Studies in third millennium Sumerian and Akkadian onomastics; the designation and conception of the personal God: diss. Harvard. CM 1986. 451 p. 87-04476. – DissA 47 (1986s) 4075-A.

9064 *Farber* Walter, Associative magic; some rituals, word plays, and philosophy [to add to *Weiher* E. von, *bīt rimki* 1983]: JAOS 106 (1986) 447-9.

9065 *Foxvog* Daniel A., A third Arua [Temple ex-voto] summary from Ur III Lagash: RAss 80 (1986) 19-29.

9066 **Geller** Markham J., Forerunners to Udug-hul; Sumerian exorcistic incantations: FreibAltorSt 12, 1985 → 1,a682; 20 pl.; DM 56: [R]BSOAS 49 (1986) 566s (B. *Alster*); JRAS (1986) 260-3 (A. R. *George*; some errata).

9067 **Golzio** Karl-Heinz, Der Tempel im alten Mesopotamien und seine Parallele in Indien 1983 → 64,b87; 1,a685: [R]ArOr 54 (1986) 304 (B. *Hruška*).

9068 *Groneberg* Brigitte, Die sumerisch-akkadische Inanna/Ištar; Hermaphroditos?: WeltOr 17 (1986) 25-46.

9069 **Haas** Volkert, Magie und Mythen in Babylonien; von Dämonen, Hexen und Beschwörungspriestern: Bibliothek der Geheimen Wissenschaften 8. Lüneburg/Vastorf 1986, Merlin. 256 p.; ill. 3-87536-133-4.

9070 *Hall* Mark C., A hymn to the moon-god, Nanna: JCS 28 (1986) 152-163; 5 phot.; 1 facsim.

9071 *Heimpel* Wolfgang, The sun at night and the doors of heaven in Babylonian texts: JCS 28 (1986) 127-151.

9072 *Krebernik* Manfred, Die Götterlisten aus Fāra: ZAss 76 (1986) 161-204.
9073 *Lambert* W. G., The reading of the divine name Šakkan: Orientalia 55 (1986) 152-8.
9074 **McEwan** G. J. P., Priest and temple in Hellenistic Babylonia 1981 ➤ 62,a248 ... 1,a700: ᴿRAss 80 (1986) 77s (F. *Joannès*).
9075 *Panitschek* Peter, Mesopotamische Religion bei HERODOT; die Frau auf dem Turm in Herodot I.181.5-181.2: ➤ 542, Kulturkontakte 1986, 43-50.
9076 **Reiner** Erica, Your thwarts in pieces, your mooring rope out; poetry from Babylonia and Assyria: Michigan Studies in the Humanities 5. AA 1985, Michigan Univ. xiv-129 p. 9 documents. – ᴿRelStR 12 (1986) 282s (J. M. *Sasson*: elegies, underworld, Hymn to Sun, Righteous Sufferer ...).
9077 *Renger* Johannes, Babylonische und assyrische Religion: ➤ 587, EvKL 1 (1986) 349-352.
9078 **Starr** Ivan. The rituals of the diviner [Yale diss. 1974] BiblMesop 12, 1983 ➤ 65,9405: ᴿArOr 54 (1986) 304s (B. *Hruška*).
9079 **Wiggermann** Franciscus A. M., Babylonian prophylactic figures; the ritual texts: Proefschrift. Amst 1986, Free Univ. 356 p. 20 pl. 90-6256-080-6.
9079* *Wiggermann* F. A. M., The staff of Ninšubura; studies in Babylonian demonology II: JbEOL 29 (1985) 3-29; 5 fig.; bibliog. 29-34. 133.
9080 *Zawadzki* Stefan, New data concerning *qīpu* and *šangu* of Ebabbar Temple in Sippar in the Neo-Babylonian and early Persian periods: Eos 74,1 (1986) 85-89.

M7.4   Religio persiana, *Iran*.

9081 **Boyce** Mary, ⸱A Persian stronghold of Zoroastrianism 1977 ➤ 58,d238*b*; 61,m515; ᴿIndIraJ 29 (1986) 128s (N. *Sims-Williams*).
9082 *Carter* Martha L., Trifunctional Pharro [Kushan deity]: StIran 15 (1986) 90-98; 9 fig.
9083 **Colledge** M. A. R., The Parthian period: Iconographie des Religions 14/3. Leiden 1986, Brill. xiv-47 p.; XLVIII pl. *f*84 [NRT 109, 145]. 90-04-07115-6.
9084 **Lankarany** F.-T., Daēnā im Avesta, eine semantische Untersuchung: StIndIranMon 10. Reinbek 1985. vii-190 p. – ᴿEWest 35 (1985) 294-6 (G. *Gnoli*).
9085 **Mosig-Walburg** Karin, Die frühen sasanidischen Könige als Vertreter und Förderer der zarathustrischen Religion; eine Untersuchung der zeitgenössischen Quellen: EurHS 3/166, 1982 ➤ 64,9674; 65,9423: ᴿOLZ 81 (1986) 277-9 (O. *Klíma*).

M8   Religio islamica *et proto-arabica*.

9086 *Aasi* Ghulam H., The Qur'an and other religious traditions: Hamdard 9,2 (1198) 65-91.
9087 *Adelowo* E. Dada, The Bible and the Qur'an as sources of theology, ethics, politics, history and culture: NigJT 1,2 (1986) 28-45 [< TKontext 8/2, 20].
9087* **Argyriou** Astérios, MACAIRE Makrès et la polémique contre l'Islam: ST 314. Vaticano 1986, Biblioteca. x-346 p.
9088 *Barbulesco* Luc, Rencontres à la Dernière Heure; quelques récits eschatologiques en Islam égyptien: Istina 31 (1986) 301-6.
9089 **Basetti-Sani** Giulio, Louis MASSIGNON (1883-1962) [ordained a Greek Catholic priest in 1950]. F 1985, Alinea. 287 p. – ᴿHumBr 41 (1986)

249-251 (F. *Peirone*); OrChrPer 52 (1986) 469s (V. *Poggi*); StPatav 33 (1986) 399-402 (Jeannette *Najem Sfair*).

9090 *Beck* Herman, Sultan Ismaël en de nakomelingen van de Profeet Mohammed; religio en realpolitik in Marokko rond het jaar 1700: NedTTs 40 (1986) 1-13; Eng. 13.

9091 *Bergman* Jan, Allah oder Gud; reflexioner kring namn, gudsföreställningar, uppenbarelse, översättning och kommunikationssituationer: ➤ 46*, ᶠHARTMAN S. 1983, 11-20.

9092 *Bouamama* Ali, L'imaginaire dans le Coran: RevSR 60 (1986) 90-99.

9093 **Bouamrane** Chikh, *Gardet* Louis, Panorama de la pensée islamique 1984 ➤ 1,a753: ᴿRHR 203 (1986) 198-200 (J. *Jolivet*).

9094 *Boudiba* Abdelwahab, Sexuality in Islam, ᵀ*Sheridan* Alan. L 1985, Routledge-KP. 288 p. – ᴿRelStR 12 (1986) 310 (Margot *Badran* compares with SABAH ➤ 9137).

9095 *Bowersock* G. W., An Arabian Trinity [Dusares, on Nazareth gem. ...]: ➤ 110, ᶠSTENDAHL K. = HarvTR 79 (1986) 17-21; 465s on *nouaemith*.

9096 *a) Caspar* Robert, Quelques types de sainteté en Islam; – *b) Cragg* Kenneth, Sainthood and spirituality in Islam: StMiss 35 (1986) 123-159 / 179-198.

9097 **Charnay** Jean-Paul, L'Islam et la guerre; de la guerre juste à la révolution sainte: Géopolitique et stratégies. P 1986, Fayard. 358 p. F 92. – ᴿÉtudes 365 (1986) 704s (R. *Leveau*).

9898 ᴱ**Cortés** Julio, El Corán. Barc 1986, Herder. 784 p. pt 1000. 84-254-1570-5 [ActuBbg 24,281, R. de *Sivatte*].

9099 **Cragg** Kenneth, The call of the minaret ²ʳᵉᵛ [¹1956]. Maryknoll NY / Ibadan 1985, Orbis / Daystar. x-358 p. $14 [RelStR 13,230, J. *Renard*]. – Also L 1986, Collins: ᴿRefTR 45 (1986) 83s (B. J. *Hall*).

9100 **Crone** Patricia, Slaves on horses; the evolution of the Islamic polity 1980 ➤ 63,9452; 64,9695: ᴿJNES 45 (1986) 165-7 (D. *Pipes*: wild cards that will probably have little influence).

9102 **Denny** Frederick M., An introduction to Islam 1985 ➤ 1,a762; $17.50: ᴿParadigms 2,1 (1986) 49s (J. D. *Cave*).

9103 **Eaton** Charles L., Islam and the destiny of man. Albany 1985, SUNY. 242 p. $36.50; pa. $12. – ᴿParabola 11,2 (1986) 100.102-4 (Jane I. *Smith*: beautiful).

9104 **Endress** Gerhard, Einführung in die islamische Geschichte: Elementarbücher, 1982 ➤ 1,a764: ᴿOLZ 81 (1986) 52-55 (H. *Preissler*: Bibliographie p. 247-316).

9105 *Frank* Richard M., Ambiguities of understanding [Islam: *Smith* W. C. 1981]: JAOS 106 (1986) 313-321.

9106 **Gardet** Louis, Regards chrétiens sur l'Islam. P 1986, Desclée-B. 219 p. F 96 [NRT 109,938]. – ᴿIslamochristiana 12 (1986) 243-6 (M. *Borrmans*).

9107 *Gilliot* Claude, Bulletin d'islamologie et d'études arabes: RSPT 70 (1986) 439-464.

9108 ᵀᴱ**Gramlich** R., [Aḥmad al-ĠAZĀLĪ, *Tajrīd*...] Der reine Gottesglaube; das Wort des Einheitsbekenntnisses. Wsb 1983, Steiner. 51 p. – ᴿAION 46 (1986) 296-308 (Carmela *Baffioni*).

9109 **Hajjar** Joseph, Bible et témoignage chrétien en pays d'Islam 1983 ➤ 64,9709; 65,9456: ᴿSMSR 52 (1986) 172s (Ida *Paladino*).

9110 **Halm** Heinz, Die islamische Gnosis; die extreme Schia und die Alawiten. Z 1982, Artemis. 406 p. – ᴿSTWsz 24,1 (1986) 292-7 (W. *Dembski*).

9111 **Harpigny** Guy, al., Aspects de la foi de l'Islam [conférences 1984]. Bru 1985, Fac. univ. Saint-Louis. 248 p. – ᴿRThom 86 (1986) 333s (J. *Jomier*:

conférenciers bien choisis; l'abbé Harpigny [positions catholiques] 'a mené a bien cette entreprise').

9112 **Hock** Klaus, Der Islam im Spiegel westlicher Theologie; Aspekte christlich-theologischer Beurteilung des Islams im 20. Jahrhundert: Kölner Veröff. RelGesch. 6. Köln 1986, Böhlau. 403 p. DM 64 [TR 83, 156, L. *Hagemann*].

9113 **Irving** T. B., The Qur'an; the first American version. Brattleboro VT 1985, Amana. xliii-401. $17.50. – [R]TS 47 (1986) 734-6 (C. *De Celles*: five English translations are available, especially N. DAWOOD).

9114 [E]**Jargy** Simon, Les Arabes et l'Occident: Arabiyya 4. Genève 1982, Labor et Fides. 131 p. [TR 83,247, A. *Khoury*].

9115 **Jomier** J., Un cristiano lee el Corán 1985 → 1,a778: [R]BibFe 12 (1986) 135s (C. *Barcía*).

9116 **Juynboll** G. H. A., Muslim tradition; studies in chronology, provenance and authorship of early hadīth 1983 → 65,9461; 1,a781: [R]JAOS 106 (1986) 374-6 (J. A. *Bellamy*).

9117 **Kedar** Benjamin Z., Crusade and mission; European approaches toward the Muslims 1984 → 65,9464; 1,a783; [R]EngHR 101 (1986) 168s (P. W. *Edbury*); RHist 276 (1986) 430-2 (C. *Cahen*); Speculum 61 (1986) 431-3 (J. *Waltz*).

9118 *Khan* Abrahim H., Metatheological reflections on recent Christian acknowledgment of Muḥammad as prophet; inter-faith dialogue and the academic study of religion: TorJT 2 (1986) 188-203.

9119 **Khoury** Adel T., Gottes ist der Orient — Gottes ist der Okzident; Lebensweisheit des Islams 1983 → 65,9466: [R]OLZ 81 (1986) 164-6 (K.-W. *Tröger*).

9120 *Köbert* Raimund, Frühe und spätere Koranexegese; eine Ergänzung: Orientalia [35 (1966) 28-32] 55 (1986) 174-6.

9120* *Leiser* Gary, The *Madrasa* and the Islamization of the Middle East; the case of Egypt: JAmEg 22 (1985) 29-47.

9121 **Lewis** Bernard, Le retour de l'Islam, [T]*Jolas* Tina, *Paulme* Denis. P 1985, Gallimard. 428 p. F 180. – [R]Études 365 (1986) 704 (H. *Loucel*).

9122 **Lüling** Günter, Die Wiederentdeckung des Propheten Muhammad ... 1981 → 62,a312 ... 65,9475: [R]Der Islam 63 (1986) 335-7 (W. *Raven*); OLZ 81 (1986) 479-483 (T. *Lohmann*).

9123 **Masson** Denise, Monothéisme coranique et monothéisme biblique; doctrines comparées [= [2]Le Coran et la révélation judéo-chrétienne 1958]. 1976, reprint. P 1984, Maisonneuve. 823 p. F 212. – [R]RSPT 70 (1986) 444 (C. *Gilliot*).

9124 *Mazaf* Otto, Die Bedeutung des Islam für die abendländische Wissenschaft: Biblos 34 (1985) 284-302.

9125 [TE]**Michel** Thomas F., IBN TAYMIYYA; a Muslim theologian's response to Christianity (Al-Jawâh al-Sahîh): Studies in Islamic philosophy and science. Delmar NY 1984, Caravan. x-470 p. – [R]Hamdard 9,3 (1986) 95-98 (A.-H. *Sehmi*); Islamochristiana 12 (1986) 248-250 (M. *Borrmans*); RThom 86 (1986) 335s (J. *Jomier*).

9126 *Michel* Thomas, Pope John Paul II's teaching about Islam [*Borrmans* Maurice, ... aux jeunes de Casablanca (text Eng./Arab.)]: Seminarium 37 (1986) 73-82 / [44-72 (13-32)].

9127 *Mooren* Thomas, Die Provokation des Gesetzes und der eine Gott bei dem islamischen Mystiker Ḥusayn b. Manṣûr AL-ḤALLÂJ und bei Jesus von Nazareth: TPhil 61 (1986) 481-506.

9128 *a) Nakamura* Kōjirō, Early Japanese pilgrims to Mecca; – *b) Oda*

Yoshiko, Muḥammad as the judge; an examination of the specific quality of Muḥammad's charismatic authority: Orient 22 (1986) 47-57 / 58-72.

9129 **Niewöhner-Eberhard** Elke, Sa'da [Yemen]; Bauten und Bewohner in einer traditionellen islamischen Stadt: TAVO B-64, 1985 → 1,a796; DM 148: ᴿMundus 22 (1986) 331s (E. *Ehlers*).

9130 **Ormsby** Eric L., Theodicy in Islamic thought; the dispute over al-GHAZĀLī's 'Best of all possible worlds'. Princeton 1984, Univ. xvi-312 p. – ᴿAION 46 (1986) 116s (A. *Ventura*).

9131 **O'Shaughnessy** Thomas J., Word of God in the Qur'an [= ² Koranic Concept 1948]: BibOrPont 11a, 1984 → 65,9484; 1,e798: ᴿActOrK 47 (1986) 173 (E. K. *Keck*); Anthropos 81 (1986) 357s (J. *Henninger:* ²gemildert); Der Islam 63 (1986) 334s (H. *Schützinger*); RHR 203 (1986) 433-5 (G. *Monnot*).

9132 **Piamenta** M., [Islam in everyday Arabic speech 1979 → 1,9158] The Muslim conception of God and human welfare as reflected in everyday Arabic speech 1983 → 1,9159: ᴿJAOS 106 (1986) 378 (J. B. *Broderick:* falls short).

9133 *Räisänen* Heikki, Islamsk Koranutläggning och kristlig bibelexeges: SvEx 51s (1986s) 203-213.

9134 ᴱ**Renard** John, IBN ABBAD of Ronda, letters on the Sufi path: Classics of Western Spirituality. NY/L 1986, Paulist/SPCK. 238 p. £11.50. 0-8091-2730-X.– ᴿExpTim 98 (1986s) 190 (G. S. *Wakefield*).

9135 *Rizzardi* Giuseppe, *a)* La controversia cristiano-islamica latina nei secoli XI-XIV: Renovatio 20 (1985) 569-576; 21 (1986) 139-152; – *b)* I teologi del secolo XII si interrogano sull'Islam: TItSett 11 (1986) 79-104; Eng. 104.

9136 ᴱ**Rousseau** Richard W., Christianity and Islam; the struggling dialogue 1985 → 1,a808; 0-940866-03-X: ᴿÉTRel 61 (1986) 274s (A. *Gounelle*).

9137 **Sabah** Fatna A., Woman in the Muslim unconscious, ᵀ*Lakeland* Mary Jo. Elmsford NY 1984, Pergamon. 132 p. $22.50; pa. $10. – ᴿRelStR 12 (1986) 310 (Margod *Badran*, firmly spells 'Fatna').

9138 **Schimmel** Annemarie, *a)* Islam in the Indian subcontinent: HbOr 2/4/3, 1980 → 62,a339; 65,9494; – *b)* Der Islam im indischen Subkontinent: Grundzüge 48. Da 1983, Wiss. v-163 p. DM 44. – ᴿOLZ 81 (1986) 582-4 (E. *Serauky*).

9139 **Schirrmacher** Christine, 'Prophet' aus der Wüste; Mohammed: Telos 2803. Berneck 1984, Schwengeler. 121 p. [Mundus 22,54].

9140 *Schumann* Olaf, Einige Bemerkungen zur Frage der Allgemeinen Menschenrechte im Islam: ZEvEthik 30 (1980) 155-174.

9141 **Schuon** Frithjof, Christianity/Islam; essays in esoteric ecumenism, ᵀ*Polit* Gustavo, 1985 → 1,a814: ᴿHamdard 9,4 (1986) 89-106.

9142 *Seidensticker* Tilman, Zur Frage eines Astralkultes im vorislamischen Arabien: ZDMG 136,3 (1986) 493-511.

9143 **Siauve** Marie-Louise, L'amour de Dieu chez GHAZALI; une philosophie de l'amour à Baghdad au début du XIIᵉ siècle: Études musulmanes 28. P 1986, Vrin. xii-324 p. – ᴿRThom 86 (1986) 694 (J. *Jomier*, aussi sur sa traduction du 'Livre de l'amour' 1986).

9144 *Siddiqi* Mazheruddin, Greek civilization and Islam: Hamdard 9,3 (1986) 77-88.

9145 *Tröger* Karl-W., Tolerance and intolerance in Islam [< Kairos 26 (1984) 89-101], ᵀᴱ*Asen* B.: TDig 33 (1986) 119-125.

9146 *Troll* Christian W., Christian/Muslim dialog [< StiZt 110 (1985) 723-734], ᵀᴱ*Asen* B.: TDig 33 (1986) 129-133.

9147 *a*) **Tworuschka** Monika, Analyse der Geschichtsbücher zum Thema Islam; – *b*) **Tworuschka** Udo, Analyse der evangelischen Religionsbücher zum Thema Islam: Studien zur internationalen Schulbuchforschung 46s, Deutschland 1s. Braunschweig 1986, Eckert. xxi-343 p., DM 29; xix-300 p., DM 27. [180 Bücher analysiert: TLZ 112, 463-6, J. *Lähnemann*].

9148 **Watt** W. Montgomery, *Murmura* Michael, Der Islam [I. 1980 → 61,m797]; II. Politische Entwicklungen und theologische Konzepte: Religionen der Menschheit 25/2. Stu 1985, Kohlhammer. xxi-502 p. DM 110. 3-17-005707-3. – ᴿBO [40 (1983)] 43 (1986) 810s (G. H. A. *Juynboll*); TLZ 111 (1986) 578-581 (T. *Lohmann*).

9149 **Watt** W. Montgomery, Islam and Christianity today 1983 → 65,9503; 1,a828: ᴿHeythJ 27 (1986) 201 (H. *Beck*); Vidyajyoti 49 (1985) 36-41 (C. M. *Troll*).

M8.5 Religiones Indiae *et variae*.

9150 **Abe** Masao, Zen and western thought, ᴱ*La Fleur* William R. Honolulu 1985, Univ. Hawaii. 308 p. $25 [JAAR 54,391]. – ᴿParabola 11,1 (1986) 108-110.114 (J. J. *Buckley*).

9151 **Acharuparambil** Daniel, Espiritualidad hinduista [cf. → 1,a832]: BAC 437. M 1982, Católica. xxviii-292 p. – ᴿCiTom 113 (1986) 149 (D. S.).

9152 **Arokiasamy** S., Dharma, Hindu and Christian, according to Roberto DE NOBILI; analysis of its meaning and its use in Hinduism and Christianity: Documenta Missionalia 19. R 1986, Pont. Univ. Gregoriana. 376 p. Lit. 45.000 [NRT 109,767, J. *Masson*].

9153 *Bishop* Peter, Keeping up with recent studies, XIII. Hinduism: ExpTim 97 (1985s) 227-231s, list of 60 books considered.

9154 *Brown* C. Mackenzie, Purāna as Scripture; from sound to image of the holy word in the Hindu tradition: HistRel 26 (1986s) 68-86.

9155 ᴱ**Bsteh** Andreas, Sein als Offenbarung in Christentum und Hinduismus 1983/4 → 65,480: ᴿGregorianum 67 (1986) 159s (J. *Wicki*).

9156 **Channa** V. C., Hinduism. New Delhi 1984, National. x-202 p. rs. 90. – ᴿVidyajyoti 49 (1985) 532s (G. *Gispert-Sauch*).

9157 **Chatterjee** Margaret, GANDHI's religious thought: Library of Philosophy and Religion. L 1983, Macmillan. xiv-194 p. – ᴿVidyajyoti 49 (1985) 248-250 (J. *Neuner*).

9158 **Coward** Harold, *al.*, JUNG and Eastern thought. Albany 1985, SUNY. xvi-218 p. – ᴿSR 15 (1986) 251-3 (J. P. *Dourley*).

9159 **Dammann** Ernst, L'Africa: Storia delle Religioni 10. Mi 1982, Jaca. xvi-328 p. Lit. 38.000. – ᴿAntonianum 61 (1986) 780s (M. *Nobile*).

9160 **Dumoulin** Heinrich, Encuentro con el Budismo. Barc 1982, Herder. 226 p. – ᴿTVida 27 (1986) 328 (A. *Bentué*).

9161 ᶠDUMOULIN Heinrich, Fernöstliche Weisheit und christlicher Glaube, ᴱ**Waldenfels** Hans 1985 → 1,45: ᴿMüTZ 37 (1986) 136-8 (P. *Schmidt-Leukel*).

9162 **Fernando** Antony, *Swidler* L., Buddhism made plain 1985 → 1,948: ᴿCurrTM 13 (1986) (J. C. *Rochelle*); Horizons 13 (1986) 463-5 (D. *Swearer*).

9163 **Girardot** Norman J., Myth and meaning in early Taoism. Berkeley 1983, Univ. California. 422 p. – ᴿJAAR 54 (1986) 173s (Judith A. *Berling*).

9164 **Griffiths** Bede, Expérience chrétienne; mystique hindoue [The marriage of East and West 1982 → 63,9529]: Rencontres 40. P 1985, Cerf. 205 p. F 120. [SR 16,383, A. *Couture*]. – ᴿVSp 140 (1986) 751-3 (B. *Durel*).

9165 **Hardy** Friedhelm,   Viraha-Bhakti; the early history of Kṛṣṇa devotion in South India 1983 ➤ **1**,a856: [R]HeythJ 27 (1986) 366s (M. *Barnes*).

9166 *Hinüber* Oskar von, Buddhismus ➤ 587, EvKL 1 (1986) 554-9 (-560).

9167 **Hultkrantz** Ake, The study of American Indian religions, [E]*Vecsey* Christopher: AAR Studies in Religion 29. Atlanta 1983, Scholars. viii-134 p. $13. – [R]RHR 203 (1986) 221s (J.-P. *Roux*).

9168 **Kendall** Laurel, Shamans, housewives, and other restless spirits; women in Korean ritual life. Honolulu 1985, Univ. 234 p. $20. – [R]HistRel 26 (1986s) 216-9 (J. M. *Kitagawa*).

9169 **Khoury** Adel T., Buddha für Christen, eine Herausforderung; intr. *Meier* Erhard: Herderbücherei 1303. FrB 1986, Herder. 192 p. DM 10 [TR 83,159, K. *Meisig*].

9170 **Kinsley** David R., Hindu goddesses; visions of the divine feminine in the Hindu religious tradition. Berkeley 1986, Univ. California. viii-281 p. $35 [TDig 34,79]. – [R]RelStR 12 (1986) 185 (G. *Yocum*).

9171 *Kirkland* J. Russell, The roots of altruism in the Taoist tradition: JAAR 54 (1986) 59-77.

9172 [E]**LaFleur** William R., Dōgen [1200-1253 Zen] studies: Juroda East Asian Buddhism 2. Honolulu 1985, Univ. Hawaii. 168 p. $19 pa. – [R]CurrTM 13 (1985) 380 (J. C. *Rochelle*: high quality, not easy).

9173 *Lederle* Matthäus †, Dialog mit dem Hinduismus: GeistL 59 (1980) 380-8.

9174 **Lipner** Julius J., The face of truth; a study of meaning and metaphysics in the Vedāntic theology of Rāmānuja. Albany 1986, SUNY. xiii-183 p. $44.50; pa. $19. – [R]TS 47 (1986) 736-8 (F. X. *Clooney*).

9175 **Mehta** J. L., India and the west; the problem of understanding: Studies in World Religions 4. Chico CA 1985, Scholars. xvii-268 p. $13.75. – [R]RelStR 12 (1986) 264 (C. *Chapple*: minimal and secondary on India; really on Sartre, Heidegger, Gadamer ...).

9176 **Meier** Erhard, Kleine Einführung in den Buddhismus: Herderbücherei 1158, 1984 ➤ 65,9522: [R]TLZ 111 (1986) 94s (K.-W. *Tröger*: empfohlen).

9177 **Niwano** Nikkyó, El Budismo para el hombre de hoy. Barc ———, ADEBE. 412 p. – [R]Studium 26 (M 1986) 158 (J. G. *Valles*: sin fecha).

9178 [E]**Nosco** Peter, Confucianism and Tokugawa culture. Princeton 1984, Univ. 290 p. $32.50. 9 art. – [R]JAOS 106 (1986) 386-8 (R. L. *Backus*).

9179 **O'Flaherty** Wendy D., Dreams, illusions and other realities 1984 ➤ **1**,a877: [R]CurrTM 13 (1986) 381s (R. *Roschke*: breathless); RelStR 12 (1986) 216-220 (Gananath *Obeyesekere*); SMSR 52 (1986) 328-330 (I. P. *Culianu*).

9179* **O'Flaherty** Wendy D., Tales of sex and violence; folklore, sacrifice and danger in the Jaiminīya Brāmaṇa. Ch 1985, Univ. 145 p. $17 [JAAR 55,1718, L. *Rocher*].

9180 **Oort** H. A. Van, The Iconography of Chinese Buddhism in traditional China: IconRel 12/5/1s. Leiden 1986, Brill. xii-30 p., XLVIII pl.; viii-27 p., XLVI pl. 90-04-07822-3; 3-1.

9181 *Oswald* Julius, Meditation – Buddhismus – Bewusstseinswandel; ein Literaturbericht: ZkT 108 (1986) 62-67.

9182 **Panikkar** Raimundo, Der unbekannte Christus im Hinduismus: Dialog der Religionen. Mainz 1986, Grünewald. 166 p. DM 39 [TR 83,157-9, K. *Meisig*].

9183 *Reynolds* Frank E., *Hallisey* Charles, Buddhism, an overview: ➤ 585, EncRel 2 (1986) 334-351 (-560 *al.*, places; schools; texts...).
9184 **Rizvi** Saiyid A. A., A history of Sufism in India. New Delhi 1978/83, Munshiram Manoharlal. xii-467 p.; xii-535 p. – ᴿSevartham 11 (1986) 144-9 (P. *Jackson*).
9185 *Rutledge* Paul, Southeast Asian religions; a perspective on historical Buddhism within the developing states of Southeast Asia: EAsJT 4,2 (1986) 138-152; bibliog. 152-6.
9186 *Seemann* Rainer, Versuch zu einer Theorie des Avatāra; Mensch gewordener Gott oder Gott gewordener Mensch?: Numen 33 (1986) 90-140.
9187 **Sheth** Noel, The divinity of Krishna (diss. 1980) 1984 ➤ 1,a889: ᴿHist-Rel 26 (1986s) 333-5 (W. K. *Mahony*).
9188 **Smet** Robert, Le problème d'une théologie hindoue-chrétienne selon Raymond PANIKKAR 1983 ➤ 64,9783; 1,a890: ᴿSMSR 52 (171s (Paola *Pisi*).
9189 *Starkloff* Carl F., New tribal religious movements in North America; a contemporary theological horizon: TorJT 2 (1986) 215-225.
9190 *Stietencron* Heinrich von, Hinduism: ➤ 597, TRE 15 (1986) 346-355.
9191 **Stoltzman** William, The pipe and the Christ [Lakota religion compared with Christianity]. 1986, Tipi. 222 p. $8. [ExpTim 98,383].
9192 **Straelen** Henry van, Ivresse ou abandon de soi; le Zen démystifié. P 1985, Beauchesne. 235 p. – ᴿSR 16 (1987) 384 (R. *Cagnon*: il a enseigné en japonais pendant trente ans, mais il est fermé au dialogue interreligieux, même haineux).
9193 **Strolz** Walter, Heilswege der Weltreligionen 2. Christliche Begegnung mit Hinduismus, Buddhismus und Taoismus. FrB 1986, Herder. 255 p. DM 38. 3-451-20112-2. – ᴿActuBbg 23 (1986) 269s (J. *Boada*).
9194 **Strong** John S., The legend of King Aśoka. Princeton 1983, Univ. xii-336 p. $37.50. – ᴿIndIranJ 29 (1986) 70-73 (J. W. de *Jong*); JAAR 54 (1986) 151-3 (P. J. *Griffiths*).
9195 **Teasdale** Wayne, Towards a Christian Vedanta; the encounter of Hinduism and Christianity according to Bede GRIFFITHS: diss. Fordham. NY 1985. – RelStR 13,186.
9196 *Vroom* H. M., Aan het nihilisme voorbij; de godsdienstfilosofie van NISHITANI [Keiji b. 1900: Was ist Religion? (1961) 1982]: NedTTs 40 (1986) 143-158; Eng. 158s 'whether Christianity can be viewed as a genuine alternative for nihilism and Zen'.
9197 ᴱ**Waghorne** Joanne P. *al.*, Gods of flesh, gods of stone; the embodiment of divinity in India [Religion in South India conference]. Chambersburg PA 1985, Anima. 208 p. $13 pa. [TDig 33,364].
9198 **Waldenfels** Hans, Faszination des Buddhismus; zum christlich-buddhistischen Dialog 1982 ➤ 63,9547... 65,9532: ᴿTPhil 61 (1986) 283s (R. *Sebott*).
9199 *Walf* Knut, Tao = God? Peilingen in zijn en van Yao: TsTNijm 26 (1986) 145-155; Eng. 155s [a person? nothingness? can be reached only by silence or intuitive knowledge].
9200 **Yu** David C., Guide to Chinese religion. 1985, G. K. Hall. 200 p. $45 [JAAR 54,207].
9201 **Zago** Marcello, Buddhismo e cristianesimo in dialogo; situazione – rapporti – convergenze. R 1985, Città Nuova. 429 p. Lit. 40.000. 88-311-3531-7. – ᴿEAPast 23 (1986) 94s (C. *Arévalo*); ÉglT 17 (1986) 418s

(A. *Couture*); Gregorianum 67 (1986) 588 (J. *López-Gay*); Teresianum 37 (1986) 221s (D. *Acharuparambil*).

XVII,1. Historia Medii Orientis Biblici

G1 *Syria, Canaan,* Israel Veteris Testamenti.

9202 **Ahlström** Gösta, Who were the Israelites? Winona Lake IN 1986, Eisenbrauns. x-134 p. $12.50. 0-931464-24-2.

9203 ᴱ**Baras** Z., *al.*, Eretz Israel from the destruction of the Second Temple to the Muslim conquest, I. Political, social and cultural history [II. **Tsafrir** Y., Archaeology and art] 1982/4 ➤ 1,265: ᴿBO 43 (1986) 771-6 (D. *Adan-Bayewitz*, D. *Sperber*).

9204 *Bruzzone* G. Battista, Storia biblica e calendario: BbbOr 28 (1986) 33-40.

9205 **Castel** François, Historia de Israel y de Judá 1984 ➤ 65,9541; 1,a903: ᴿEstE 61 (1986) 91s (J. *Iturriaga*); Teresianum 37 (1986) 237 (J. *Martín de Lucas*).

9206 **Castel** F., Storia d'Israele e di Giuda dalle origini al II secolo d.C. Mi 1986, Paoline. Lit. 14.000. – ᴿParVi 31 (1986) 462s (A. *Bonora*).

9207 **Cazelles** Henri, Histoire politique d'Israel 1982 ➤ 63,9564... 1,a906: ᴿBZ 30 (1986) 119s (J. *Scharbert*).

9208 **Cazelles** H., Historia política de Israel 1984 ➤ 65,9543; 1,a907: ᴿComSev 19 (1986) 81s (V. J. *Ansede Alonso*); Compostellanum 31 (1986) 275s (J. *Precedo Lafuente*).

9209 **Cazelles** H., Storia politica di Israele; dalle origini ad Alessandro Magno: Picc. Enc. Biblica 1. R 1985, Borla. – ᴿRClerIt 67 (1986) 876s (G. *Borgonovo*).

9209* **Clair-Hellon** O., La fresque biblique; au commencement. P 1986, Lombard France. 152 p.; dessins de Torton J., Lambert C. F 90. – ᴿMondeB 46 (1986) 56 (F. I. *Fransen*: réserves).

9210 **Clauss** Manfred, Geschichte Israels (von der Frühzeit bis zur Zerstörung Jerusalems, 587 v.Chr.). Mü 1986, Beck. 238 p.; 26 fig.; bibliog. p. 213-223. DM 32. 3-406-31175-X. – ᴿBbbOr 28 (1986) 232 (D. *Sardini*); FreibRu 37s (1985s) 112s (Y. *Ilsar*).

9211 **Donner** Herbert, Geschichte des Volkes Israel und seiner Nachbarn in Grundzügen [I. 1984 ➤ 65,9546; 1,a910] II. Von der Königszeit bis zu Alexander dem Grossen, mit einem Ausblick auf die Geschichte des Judentums bis Bar Kochba: Grundrisse ATD 4. Gö 1986, Vandenhoeck & R. vii-511 p. DM [29,80 +]36,80.– ᴿZAW 98 (1986) 464s (H.-C. *Schmitt*). – I: CBQ 48 (1986) 111s (W. R. *Wifall*); BO 43 (1986) 455s (H. *Jagersma*); FreibRu 37s (1985s) 114 (D. *Kinet*); JBL 105 (1986) 306s (J. A. *Dearman*).

9212 **Elazar** Daniel V., *Cohen* Stuart A., The Jewish polity; Jewish political organization from biblical times to the present. Bloomington 1985, Indiana Univ. x-303 p. $27.50. 0-253-33156-0. – ᴿRRelRes 28 (1986s) 92-94 (W. P. *Baumgarth*).

9213 ᴱ**Eph'al** I., The history of Eretz-Israel I. Introduction; the early period. 1982. – ᴿZDPV 102 (1986) 179s (R. *Zadok*).

9214 **Goldschmidt** Arthur E.ᴶ, A concise history of the Middle East². Boulder 1983, Westview. xvi-416 p.; maps; bibliog. p. 377-395 [KirSef 60,617].

9215 **Grant** Michael, The history of ancient Israel 1984 ➤ 65,9550; 1,a915: ᴿJBL 105 (1986) 515s (J. *Bright* tries to be fair); JJS 37 (1986) 109s (J.

Hughes: many factual errors); Mid-Stream 25 (1986) 244s (R. *Lowery*: footnotes 'sparce').

9216 **Hecke** Karl-Heinz, Juda und Israel... in vor- und frühstaatlicher Zeit [1982 Diss.] 1985 ➤ 1,a919: ᴿColcT 56,3 (1986) 190-3 (J. W. *Roslon*).

9217 *Henige* David, Comparative chronology and the Ancient Near East; a case for symbiosis: BASOR 261 (1986) 57-68.

9218 *Herion* Gary A., The impact of modern and social science assumptions on the reconstruction of biblical history: JStOT 34 (1986) 3-33.

9219 **Jablonski** Edward, A pictorial history of the Middle East; war and peace from antiquity to the present. GCNY 1984, Doubleday. xxv-294 p.; ill.; maps (Palacios R.) [KirSef 60,617].

9220 ᴱ**Jonge** M. De, Outside the Old Testament: CamCW 4. C 1986, Univ. 263 p. £32.50; pa. £12. 0-521-24249-5; 8554-2. – ᴿExpTim 97 (1985s) 381 (C. S. *Rodd*: high quality).

9221 **Knauf** Ernst A., Ismael 1985 ➤ 64,9814a ... 1,a924: ᴿMundus 22 (1986) 287s (W. *Röllig*); TLZ 112 (1987) 256s (S. *Holm-Nielsen*).

9222 *Koizumi* Tatsuhito, Toward the establishment of a scientific history of Israel — from the nomadic period to the organization of the four leading tribes: AnJapB 12 (1986) 29-76.

9223 *Lemaire* A. Qui est Bar Ga'yah roi de KTK? JAs 272 (1984) 473s.

9224 **Lemaître** Alain J., The cultural history of the Holy Land. L 1984, Aurum. 95 p.; ill.; map [KirSef 60,617].

9225 **Malamat** A., ❺ *Yiśra'el* ... Israel in biblical times; historical essays 1983 ➤ 64,199; 65,210: ᴿBASOR 262 (1986) 94s (B. *Halpern*).

Mayes A. D. H., The story of Israel between settlement and exile 1983 ➤ Nᵒ 1956 supra.

9227 **Mayeur** Marc, Histoire du peuple d'Israël. P 1983, Pensée Universelle. 189 p. [KirSef 60,623].

Mazar Benjamin, The early biblical period 1986 ➤ 191.

9229 *Mendecki* Norbert, ❺ Filistyni. Aramejczycy i Kananejczycy [1500-1000 a.C.]: ColcT 56,3 (1986) 43-45; deutsch 45s.

9230 *Merrillees* Robert S., Political conditions in the Eastern Mediterranean during the Late Bronze Age: BA 49 (1986) 42-50; ill.; p. 50 The Mitanni by Marie-Henriette *Gates*.

9231 **Metzger** M., Breve storia di Israele [1963, ⁶1983], ᵀ*Stagi* P. Brescia 1985, Queriniana. 271 p. [RivB 35,91, O.*Carena*]. – ᴿAsprenas 33 (1986) 331s (A. *Rolla*); CC 137 (1986,1) 95 (S. *Katunarich*); ParVi 31 (1986) 156s (M. *Milani*) & 463-5 (A. *Rolla*).

9232 **Miller** J. Maxwell, **Hayes** John H., A history of ancient Israel and Judah. Ph/L 1986, Westminster/SCM. 523 p.; 29 maps. $28/£17.50. 0-664-21262-X / 0-334-02042-5. – ᴿBAR-W 12,6 (1986) 4.6.8 (P. *Machinist*: unwisely dispenses with footnotes); ExpTim 98 (1986s) (C. S. *Rodd*: superb; but 'Jordan River' is an Americanism).

North Robert, Symposium on the mythic in Israel's origins 1986 ➤ e186.

9233 **Schiffmann** Ilya, Phönizisch-punische Mythologie und geschichtliche Überlieferung in der Widerspiegelung der antiken Geschichtsschreibung: Coll. StFen 17. R 1986, Cons. Naz. Ric. [OIAc Aug. 87].

9234 *Segalla* Giuseppe, [➤ 3010] Panorama storico del NT: LoB 3/5, 1984 ➤ 1,b343; ᴿParVi 30 (1985) 157s (F. *Mosetto*).

9235 *Simpson* William K., Personnel accounts of the early twelfth dynasty; Papyrus Reisner IV with translation and commentary, with Indices to Papyri Reisner I-IV and palaeography IV (*Der Manuelian* Peter). Boston 1986, Museum of Fine Arts. 47 p.; 33 pl. $80 [JNES 46,78].

9236 **Soggin** J. A., Storia d'Israele 1984 ➤ 65,9574: 1,a943: ᴿComSev 19 (1986) 241-3 (M. de *Burgos*: imprescindible para las siguientes generaciones); EstE 61 (1986) 244s (J. R. *Busto Saiz*); Gregorianum 67 (1986) 143-7 (G. L. *Prato*: valido tentativo); ParVi 30 (1985) 436-441 (P. *Sacchi*); RechSR 74 (1986) 626 (J. *Briend*: déconcerte: prend position sans donner ses arguments); RivStoLR 22 (1986) 147-151 (G. L. *Boschi*); STEv 8,16 (1985) 280-4 (W. *Nelson*: scettico);TZBas 42 (1986) 433 (O. *Bächli*).

9237 **Soggin** J. Alberto, A history of Israel [ital. ᵀ*Bowden* John] 1984 ➤ 65,9573; 1,a944: ᴿBS 143 (1986) 277s (E. H. *Merrill*: post-ALBRIGHT; fails); CurrTM 13 (1986) 178s (R. *Nysse*: not good; a scholar's scholar); JJS 37 (1986) 106-8 (J. *Hughes*: careless, not only in printing); JTS 37 (1986) 450s (E. W. *Nicholson*); RHPR 66 (1986) 215s (P. de *Robert*); RB 93 (1986) 144-6 (J.-M. de *Tarragon*); TLond 39 (1986) 56-58 (A. *Phillips*; brisk, never dull, encourages the right questions); Vidyajyoti 49 (1985) 528-530 (P. M. *Meagher*); ZAW 98 (1986) 476s (H.-C. *Schmitt*).

9238 *Soggin* J. Alberto, *a*) La storiografia israelitica più antica: ➤ 391, Storiografia 1984/6, 21-27; – *b*) Le origini d'Israele; problemi, proposte e prospettive [< Lincei Roma 10.II.1986]: Henoch 8 (1986) 129-145; franç. 145-7.

9239 **Stubblefield** David B., The consistency of George Ernest WRIGHT in his affirmation of the historicity of the biblical events of the premonarchial period: diss. SW Baptist Sem. 271 p. 86-12699. – DissA 47 (1986s) 1381-A.

9240 *Thiel* Winfried, Verfehlte Geschichte im Alten Testament: TBei 17 (Wu 1986) 248-266 [< ZIT].

9241 *a*) *Villard* P., Un roi de Mari à Ugarit; – *b*) *Wyatt* N., The hollow crown; ambivalent elements in West Semitic royal ideology: UF 18 (1986s) 387-412 / 421-436.

9242 *Whitelam* Keith W., Recreating the history of Israel: JStOT 35 (1986) 45-70.

9243 *Wolf* Kirsten, An Old Norse record of Jewish history: JQR 77 (1986s) 45-54.

9244 ᴱ**Wollman-Tsamir** Pinchas, The graphic history of the Jewish heritage, I. The Biblical period,² ᵀ*Hoenig* Sidney B. al. NY 1982, MP. 224 p.; ill. [KirSef 59,308].

Q2 **Historiographia** – *theologia historiae.*

9245 *Alessandri* Giovanni, Storiografia-narrazione o storiografia-problema?: CC 137 (1986,1) 58-63.

9246 **Altizer** T. J. J., History as apocalypse 1985 ➤ 1,a949: ᴿTorJT 2 (1986) 295-7 (Joanne *McWilliam*).

9247 *a*) *Bartnik* Czesław, ❷ Historiologia; – *b*) *Górski* Karol, ❷ La vérité dans l'histoire; – *c*) *Gogacz* Mieczysław, ❷ L'homme c'est un sujet ou l'objet de l'histoire?: AtKap 106 (1986) 214-231 / 232-241 / 242-253.

9248 **Butterfield** Herbert, † 20.VII.1979, The origins of history, ᴱ*Watson* Adam [manuscript unchanged] 1981 ➤ 63,9612; also L 1981, Methuen. 252 p. £12.50. – ᴿRBgPg 62 (1984) 858s (J. *Paquet*).

9249 *Celada* Gregorio, Cristianismo e historia; drama de una ruptura: CiTom 113 (1986) 417-445.

9249* ᴱ**Crawford** M., Sources for ancient history 1983 ➤ 65,380[.9583]; 1,a959: ᴿGymnasium 93 (1986) 293s (Kai *Brodersen*).

9250 *Ebach* J., 'Ein Sturm vom Paradiese her'; Walter BENJAMINS Geschichtsphilosophie und die hebräische Bibel: ➤ 155, Ursprung 1986, 48-74.

9251 *Ferguson* Duncan S., AUGUSTINE on history; a perspective for our time: EvQ 58 (1986) 39-52.

9252 **Finley** M. I., Ancient history, evidence and models. NY 1986, Viking. x-131 p. $18 [RelStR 13,258, A. T. *Kraabel*].

9253 *Freyne* S., Our preoccupation with history; problems and prospects: PrIrB 9 (1985) 1-18.

9254 EFriedman R., [6 essays] The poet and the historian 1983 ➤ 62,264: RBO 43 (1986) 764-6 (R. *Polzin*); JTS 37 (1986) 465-7 (E. W. *Nicholson*).

9255 **Furet** F., In the workshop of history, T. Ch 1984, Univ. vi-259 p. £29 [RHE 82,183*].

9256 **Garbini** Giovanni, Storia e ideologia nell'Israele antico: Biblioteca di storia e storiografia dei tempi biblici 3. Brescia 1986, Paideia. 254 p. Lit. 30.000.

9257 *Gilman* James E., R. G. COLLINGWOOD and the religious sources of Nazism: JAAR 54 (1986) 111-128.

9258 **Glover** Willis B., Biblical origins of modern secular culture; an essay in the interpretation of Western history 1984 ➤ 1,e973; $24; RJAAR 54 (1986) 375s (J. H. *Moorhead*); RExp 83 (1986) 646s (E. G. *Hinson*).

9259 **Goetz** H. W., Die Geschichtstheologie des OROSIUS: ImpulsFor 32, 1980 ➤ 61,q75 ... 65, 9589: RWienerSt 99 (1986) 304s (Dorothea *Weber*).

9260 *a) Grossi* Vittorino, [XII Congresso Nazionale ATI] 'Verità e storia'; nota previa dalla tradizione cristiana [*La Potterie* I. de ...]; – *b) Molari* Carlo, Spunti sul tema: RasT 27 (1986) 180s / 181-3 [260-8-270, *Bof* G., *Giannoni* P.].

9261 **Häringer** Thomas, Geschichtsphilosophie bei Raymond ARON; wissenschaftstheoretische Untersuchung der Begriffe Verstehen, Erklären und Kausalität in Arons Werk: diss. Innsbruck 1986. 119 p. – RTLv 18,539.

9262 **Hall** Robert G., Revealed history; a Jewish and Christian technique of interpreting the past: diss. Duke 1986, DSmith D. M. 359 p. 87-07326. – DissA 47 (1986s) 4419-A.

9263 **Hengel** Martin, La storiografia protocristiana [1978 ➤ 60,6613], TESoffritti Omero: StBPaid 73, 1985 ➤ 1,a978: RÉTRel 61 (1986) 592s (Letizia *Tomassone*); Orpheus 7 (1986) 468s (Maria Laura *Astarita*).

9264 **Herrmann** Siegfried, Geschichtsbild und Gotteserkenntnis; zum Problem altorientalischen und alttestamentlichen Geschichtsdenkens [< FSeeligman 3 (1983) 15-38]: ➤ 171, Ges. St. 1986, 9-31.

9265 **Jarausch** Konrad H., *Arminger* Gerhard, *Thaller* Manfred, Quantitative Methoden in der Geschichtswissenschaft; eine Einführung in die Forschung, Datenverarbeitung und Statistik: Die Geschichtswissenschaft. Da 1985, Wiss. x-211 p. DM 66 [ÉtClas 55,227, Corinne *Bonnet*].

9266 **Kevane** Eugene, The Lord of history; Christocentrism and the philosophy of history 1980 ➤ 61,q89 ... 64,9865: RScripTPamp 18 (1986) 939-945 (J. M. de *Torre*).

9267 EKirby John, [➤ 65,367 puts first:] *Thompson* William M., VOEGELIN and the theologian; Toronto Studies in Theology 10. Toronto 1983, Mellen. vii-377 p. – RTorJT 2 (1986) 147s (D. *Wiebe*).

9268 *Knebel* Sven K., 'Geschichtlichkeit' oder, Der Buchstabe des Grafen Yorck [= Hermeneutisches Colloquium, Berlin 1985]: ZRGg 38 (1986) 359-369.

9269 *Leadbetter* W. L., The wood versus the trees; Chester G. STARR [³1983] and the generalist approach to ancient history: ➤ 45*, ᶠHARRIS B., Anc-SRes 16 (1986) 169-173.

9270 ᴱLeGoff Jacques, *Nore* Pierre, Constructing the past; essays in historical methodology [< 1974 Faire l'histoire]. C/P 1985, Univ./Sciences de l'Homme. $39.50. – ᴿNBlackf 67 (1986) 342s (M. *Bentley*).

9271 **Logister** Wiel M. E., Heilsgeschiedenis en jodendom; de Israëls-geschiedenis van PANNENBERG in discussie [... *Rendtorff* R.]. Nijmegen 1984, Gottmer. 109 p. – ᴿETL 62 (1986) 410 (J. *Lust*).

9272 **Lohfink** Gerhard, Gottes Taten gehen weiter; Geschichtstheologie als Grundvollzug neutestamentlicher Gemeinden [6 Predigten] 1985 ➤ 1,197: ᴿTR 82 (1986) 30 (H. *Merklein*).

9273 **McCullagh** C. B., Justifying historical descriptions. C 1984, Univ. x-252 p. £25; pa. £8. 0-521-26722-6; 31830-6. – ᴿExpTim 98 (1986s) 91 (J. *Barton*).

9274 ᴱMcIntire C. T., *Wells* Ronald A., History and historical understanding [Calvin College papers] 1984 ➤ 1,377: ᴿTorJT 2 (1986) 139-142 (Joanne M. *Dewart*).

9275 *a) Meissner* Burkhard, Pragmatikē historía; POLYBIOS über den Zweck pragmatischer Geschichtsschreibung; – *b) Zemlin* Michael-J., Die historische Theorie im Geschichtsdenken RANKES: Saeculum 37 (1986) 313-351 / 352-365.

9276 *Mellor* D. H., History without the flow of time: NSys 28 (1986) 68-76; deutsch 75.

9277 *Mistrorigo* Luigi, Eric VOEGELIN; ordine e politica: Studium 82 (R 1986) 623-635.

9278 **Müller** D., Parole et histoire; dialogue avec W. PANNENBERG 1983 ➤ 65,9600; 1,a990: ᴿProtestantesimo 41 (1986) 184s (V. *Subilia*: conferma alcuni suoi giudizi negativi).

9279 **Nicolai** Walter, Versuch über HERODOTS Geschichtsphilosophie: Bibliothek. Klas. Alt-W. 2/77. Heid 1986, Winter. 54 p.

9280 **Niño** Rodríguez A., La historia de la historiografía, una disciplina en construcción: Hispania 46 (1986) 395-417 [RHE 82,184*].

9281 **Oakeshott** Michael, On history and [two shorter] other essays. Ox 1983, Blackwell. 198 p. £12. – ᴿHeythJ 27 (1986) 360-3 (J. *Bradley*).

9282 *Partner* Nancy F., Making up lost time; writing on the writing of history [*Butterfield* H., *Ladurie* E. ...]: Speculum 61 (1986) 90-117.

9283 *Prato* Gian Luigi, La storiografia nella Bibbia e la sua collocazione tra la storiografia greca e la storiografia nell'antico oriente: ➤ 391, Storiografia 1984/6, 9-19.

9284 *Rajak* Tessa, The sense of history in Jewish intertestamental writing: ➤ 399, OTS 24, 1985/6, 124-145.

9285 **Russell** Anthony F., Logic, philosophy of history based on the work of R. G. COLLINGWOOD [< diss. Ottawa], foreword *Williams* Brooke: Studies in Semiotics 1. Lanham MD 1984, UPA. xx-527 p. – ᴿHistTheory 25 (1986) 215-9 (E. O. *Golob*).

9285* **Sacks** Kenneth, POLYBIUS on the writing of history 1981 ➤ 64,9882: ᴿGnomon 58 (1986) 139-145 (K.-E. *Petzold*).

9286 **Schulte** Hannelis, L'origine della storiografia nell'Israele antico, ᵀ*Gatti* V. 1982 ➤ 64,9886 ... 1,b4: ᴿParVi 30 (1985) 73-77 (G. *Marocco*).

9287 ᴱ**Tadmor** H., *Weinfeld* M., History, historiography and interpretation 1978/83 ➤ 64,429 ... 1,b10: ᴿBZ 30 (1986) 299-301 (J. *Scharbert*); CBQ 48 (1986) 772-4 (D. W. *Baker*); OLZ 81 (1986) 457s (G. *Wallis*); SMSR 52 (1986) 161-5 (F. *Mazza*).

9288 *Tomassone* Letizia, La critica di KIERKEGAARD alle filosofie della storia: Protestantesimo 41 (1986) 129-141.

9289 **Tresmontant** Claude, L'histoire de l'Univers et le sens de la création 1988 ➤ 1,b13: ᴿNRT 108 (1986) 309 (A. *Toubeau*).

9290 **Van Seters** John, In search of history 1983 ➤ 64,9896...1,b14: ᴿBiblica 67 (1986) 109-117 (K. *Koch*: die Gattungen haben nicht nur soziologische, sondern auch semantische Funktion); BZ 30 (1986) 122s J. *Scharbert*); JbAC 29 (1986) 189-191 (Friedhelm *Winkelmann*); JTS 37 (1986) 451-4 (J. W. *Rogerson*: to make his point, the author must define history as 'articulating the people's identity').

9291 **Vischer** E., Geschichte der Geschichtsschreibung; eine Nachlese. Bern 1985, Francke. 310 p. Fs 70 [HZ 244,364, E. *Schulin*].

9292 *Vischer* Wilhelm, ᵀᴱ*Gossman* Lionel, The boundaries of the city [1877]; on the limits of historical knolewdge: HistTheory 25 (1986) 33-51.

9293 **Weber** Wolfgang, Priester der Klio; historisch-sozialwissenschaftliche Studien zur Herkunft und Karriere deutscher Historiker und zur Geschichte der Geschichtwissenschaft 1800-1970: EurHS 3/216. Fra 1984, Lang. 613 p. [RHE 82,94, J.M. *Hannick*].

Q3   *Historia Ægypti* – **Egypt.**

9294 *Amer* Amin A. M. A., A further note on Maya: Orientalia [43 (1974) 153-161, *Hari* R.] 55 (1986) 171-3.

9295 *a) Angonoa Gilardi* Franca, I condizionamenti del potere 'assoluto' del Faraone; – *b) Criscuolo* Lucia, Le istituzioni pubbliche nell'Egitto tolemaico; – *c) Geraci* Giovanni, La formazione della provincia romana d'Egitto; – *d) Bastianini* Guido, Le istituzioni pubbliche 'dell'Egitto romano: ➤ 546, Egitto 1984/5, 47-59 / 133-145 / 163-180 / 197-209.

9296 *Bagnall* Roger S., *Worp* K. A.,A., Dating by the moon in Nubian inscriptions: CdÉ 61 (1986) 347-357.

9297 *Barta* Winfried, *a)* Zur Berechnung der Zyklusjahre 1 des 25jährigen Mondzyklus: GöMiszÄg 94 (1986) 7-12; – *b)* Zur Bezeichnung des Jahres in Datumsangaben: ZägSpr 113 (1986) 89-92.

9298 *Beckerath* Jürgen von, Neue Überlegungen zum ägyptischen Kalender: Saeculum 37 (1986) 1-7.

9299 **Berman** Lawrence M., Amenemhet I: diss. Yale, ᴰ*Simpson* W. NHv 1985. 249 p. 86-12942. – DissA 47 (1986s) 1303s-A.

9300 *Bibé* Celia, La rédécouverte d'expressions mathématiques modernes dans les anciens textes égyptiens: GöMiszÄg 94 (1986) 13-15.

9301 **Blumenthal** Elke, Altägyptische Reiseerzählungen; die Lebensgeschichte des Sinuhe, der Reisebericht des Wen-Amun: Univ.-Bibl. 928, 1982 ➤ 64,9999; M 1,50: ᴿOLZ 81 (1986) 23s (W. *Barta*).

9302 **Bowman** Alan K., Egypt after the Pharaohs, 332 B.C.-A.D. 642; from Alexander to the Arab Conquest. Berkeley 1986, Univ. California. 264 p.; 4 fig.; 144 pl.; bibliog. p. 248-258. $25 [AJA 91,623, R. S. *Bagnall*]. 0-7141-0942-8.

9303 *Bresciani* Edda, Il possibile nome del figlio maggiore di Nectanebo II [= nome del padre]: ➤ 11*, Mem. BICKERMAN E. = JANES 16s (1984s) 19-21.

9304 **Bryan** Betsy M., The reign of Tuthmosis IV: diss. Yale. NHv 1980. viii-493 p.; bibliog. p. 454-477.

9305 *Bryan* Betsy M., The career and family of Minmose, high priest of Onuris: CdÉ 61,121 (1986) 5-30.

9306 ᴱ**Burkhardt** Adelheid, *al.*, Urkunden der 18. Dynastie [Lp 1906-9; B 1955-8] Übersetzung zu den Heften 5-16. B 1984, Akademie. 509 p. – ᴿArOr 54 (1986) 202s (B. *Vachala*).

9307 *Burstein* S. M., The Ethiopian war of Ptolemy V; an historical myth?: BeiSudan 1 (1986) 17-23.

9308 *Casperson* Lee W., The lunar dates of Thutmose III: JNES 45 (1986) 139-150; 1 fig.

9309 *Chappaz* Jean-Luc, Le sarcophage de Houner, épouse [et non frère] du vizir [de Ramsès II] Ra-Hotep, et deux fragments inédits du Musée d'Art et d'Histoire de Genève: CdÉ 61,121 (1986) 31-42.

9310 *Clarysse* Willy, Le mariage et le testament de Dryton en 150 avant J.-C.: CdÉ [57 (1982) 317, *Lewis* N.] 61 (1986) 99-103.

9311 [*Helck* W.], ᵀ**Cumming** Barbara, Egyptian historical records of the later eighteenth dynasty 1982 ➤ 65,9635: ᴿJEA 78 (1986) 221s (C. C. *Van Siclen*); JNES 45 (1986) 244s (E. *Cruz-Uribe*).

9311* **Curto** Silvio, L'antico Egitto 1981 ➤ 64,a6; Società e costume 9; 88-02-03650-0. – ᴿBO 43 (1986) 69-74 (H. *Satzinger*).

9312 *Dautzenberg* N., *a*) Zu den Regierungszeiten in Manethos 1. Dynastie: GöMiszÄg 92 (1986) 23-28; – *b*) Zu den Königen Chaires und Cheneres bei Manetho: GöMiszÄg 94 (1986) 25-29.

9313 **Demicheli** Anna Maria, Rapporti di pace e di guerra dell'Egitto Romano con le popolazioni dei deserti africani: Univ. Genova Fond. Poggi 12, 1976 ➤ 61,9189; Lit. 5000: ᴿGnomon 58 (1986) 182-4 (J. *Schwartz*).

9314 **Dormion** Gilles, *Goidin* Jean-Patrice, Khéops; nouvelle enquête; propositions préliminaires. P 1986. RCiv. 110 p.; map. 2-86538-158-7.

9315 **Fischer-Elfert** H. W., Literarische Ostraka der Ramessidenzeit in Übersetzung: KlÄgTexte. Wsb 1986, Harrassowitz. x-93 p. DM 36. 3-447-02611-1 [BL 87,96, K. A. *Kitchen*].

9316 **Franke** Detlef [➤ 65,8058] Personendaten aus dem Mittleren Reich (20.-16. Jahrhundert v. Chr. Dossiers 1-796): AegAbh 41. Wsb 1984, Harrassowitz. 486 p. DM 66. 3-447-02484-4. – ᴿBO 43 (1986) 76-79 (H. De *Meulenaere*).

9317 **Geraci** G., Genesi della Provincia Romana d'Egitto 1983 ➤ 64,a10... 1,b38: ᴿCdÉ 61 (1986) 165s (A. *Martin*); ClasR 100 (1986) 274s (Jane *Rowlandson*).

9318 *Goedicke* Hans, Inana as inventor [advisor and treasurer up to Hatshepsut]: VAeg 2 (1986) 35-41.

9319 *Götte* Karin, Eine Individualcharakteristik ptolemäischer Herrscher anhand der Epitheta-Sequenzen beim Weinopfer: RÉgp 37 (1986) 63-80.

9320 **Gomaà** Farouk, Die Besiedlung Ägyptens während des Mittleren Reiches: TAVO Bei B-66. Wsb 1986s, Reichert. I. Oberägypten 453 p.; II. Unterägypten 398 p. 3-88226-279-6; 80-X.

9321 **Gottschalk** Gisela, Die grossen Pharaonen; die bedeutendsten Gottkönige Ägyptens in Bildern, Berichten und Dokumenten; ihr Leben, Zeit, ihre Kunstwerke. Herrsching 1984, Pawlak. 272 p.; ill. [Mundus 22,51].

9322 *Grandet* Pierre, Les songes d'Atia et d'Octavius; note sur les rapports d'Auguste et de l'Égypte: RHR 203 (1986) 365-379.

9323 *Grenier* Jean-Claude, Le prophète [Pakhôm, stèle] et l'Autokratôr [(? empereur romain) mentionné là-dessus]: RÉgp 37 (1986) 81-89.

9324 **Grimal** Nicolas-Christophe, Les termes de la propagande royale égyptienne de la XIXᵉ dynastie à la conquête d'Alexandre: AIBL Mém 6. P 1986, Imp. Nationale. vi-764 p.; bibliog. p. 13-41.

9325 **Grist** Jehon M., The identity of the Ramesside queen Tyti: diss. California. Berkeley 1966. 469 p. 86-24775. – DissA 47 (1986s) 2630-A.

9326 **Gutgesell** Manfred, Der Friedensvertrag; Ramses und die Hethiter, Geheimdiplomatie im Alten Orient. Hildesheim 1984, Bernard. 50 p.; ill.

9327 *Habachi* Labib, Devotion of Tuthmosis III to his predecessors; à propos of a meeting of Sesostris I with his courtiers ...

9328 **Helck** Wolfgang, Politische Gegensätze im alten Ägypten; ein Versuch: Hild. ÄgBei 23. Hildesheim 1986, Gerstenberg. 98 p. 3-8067-8099-4.

9329 *Helck* Wolfgang, Wenamun: → 591, LexÄg 6,48 (1986) 1215-7.

9330 EIsraelit-Groll Sarah, Pharaonic Egypt, the Bible and Christianity 1985 → 1,476: RBO 43 (1986) 679-686 (M. *Green*).

9331 EKambitsis Sophie, Le Papyrus Thmouis 1 colonnes 68-160: Papyrologie 3. P 1985, Sorbonne. x-196 p; XVI pl.

9332 **Kitchen** K. A., The third intermediate period in Egypt (1100-650 B.C.)[2] [= [1]1972 with supplement, p. 527-599 + index p. 600-8]. Wmr 1986, Aris & P. xvii-608 p. 0-85668-298-5.

9333 **Kitchen** K. A., Ramesside inscriptions [→ 1,b51s] V, 11-14; VI, 15-20, 1983; ROLZ 81 (1986) 338-40 (J. v. *Beckerath*).

9334 **Koenig** Viviane, Pyramides et pharaons. Poitiers 1983, F. Nathan. 80 p.; 10 pl. – RJAmEg 23 (1986) 223s (R. S. *Bianchi*).

9335 **Kruchten** Jean-Marie, Le decret d'Horemheb 1981 → 64,a34; 1,b57: RCdÉ 61 (1986) 225-8 (S. *Allam*).

9336 **Lalouette** C., Textes sacrés et textes profanes de l'ancienne Égypte I. Des Pharaons et des hommes; traductions et commentaires: UNESCO Connaissance de l'Orient 1984 → 65,9655; 2-07-070142-5: RBL (1986) 105s (K. A. *Kitchen*).

9337 **Lichtheim** Miriam, Ancient Egyptian literature, a book of readings 3. The late period 1980 → 61,q262c; 65,9658: RJNES 45 (1986) 243s (R. K. *Ritner*).

9338 *Lorton* David, Terms of coregency in the Middle Kingdom: VAeg 2 (1986) 113-120.

9339 *Luft* Ulrich, Noch einmal zum Ebers-Kalender [Medizinischer Papyrus, Rückseite; *Krauss* R.]: GöMiszÄg 92 (1986) 69.

9340 **Malek** Jaromir, In the shadows of the pyramids; Egypt during the Old Kingdom. Norman 1986, Univ. Oklahoma. 128 p.; ill. $22.50 [JNES 46,243].

9341 *Martin* Alain, La dédicace impériale de Coptos I. Portes 84: CdÉ 61 (1986) 318-323.

9342 *Martin-Pardey* Eva [erste], *Beckerath* Jürgen von [zweite], *Graefe* Erhart [dritte] Zwischenzeit: → 591, LexÄg 6,49 (1986) 1437-42-48-51.

9343 *Martin-Pardey* Eva, Wesir (vizir, *t3tj*): → 591, LexÄg 6,48 (1986) 1227-35.

9344 *Meulenaere* Herman De, Un général du Delta, gouverneur de la Haute Égypte: CdÉ 61 (1986) 203-210.

9345 **Miller** William K., The genealogy and chronology of the Ramesside period: diss. Minnesota, DRapp G. Minneapolis 1986. 204 p. 86-15122. – DissA 47 (1986s) 1448-A.

9346 **Moftah** Ramses, Studien zum ägyptischen Königsdogma im Neuen Reich: DAI-K Sond. 20. Mainz 1985, von Zabern. xiv-370 p. DM 88. – RJAmEg 22 (1985) 234s (H. *Goedicke*).

9347 *a)* *Onasch* Angela, Der Aufbau der ägyptischen Beamtenschaft des Neuen Reichs I; – *b)* *Schaefer* Alisa, Zur Entstehung der Mitre-

gentenschaft als Legitimationsprinzip von Herrschaft: ZägSpr 113 (1986) 24-44 / 44-55.
9348 **Pomeroy** Sarah S., Women in Hellenistic Egypt 1984 ➤ 65,9664; 1,b73: ᴿGnomon 58 (1986) 417-421 (R. *Scholl*).
9349 *Ray* J.D., Psammuthis and Hakoris [Dynasty 29, 440-380]: JEA 78 (1986) 149-158.
9350 **Redford** Donald B., a) Sais and the Kushite invasions of the eighth century B.C.; – b) Egypt and Western Asia in the Old Kingdom: JAmEg 22 (1985) 5-15; 3 fig. / 23 (1986) 125-143.
9351 **Rice** E.E., The grand procession of Ptolemy Philadelphus: Ox. Clas. Mon. 1983 ➤ 65,9666; 1,b76: ᴿRelStR 12 (1986) 67 (J.H. *Sieber*); RivFgIC 113 (1985) 464-9 (Maria Letizia *Lazzarini*).
9352 **Roccati** Alessandro, La littérature historique sous l'Ancien Empire égyptien: LAPO 11, 1982 ➤ 63,9699...1,b77: ᴿCdÉ 61 (1986) 232-4 (N. *Kanawati*); NRT 108 (1986) 451s (J.-L. *Ska*).
9353 **Salmon** Pierre, Introduction à l'histoire de l'Afrique. Bru 1986, Hayez. 200 p., 22 fig.; map. Fb 595. – ᴿCdÉ 61 (1986) 269s (A. *Mekhitarian*).
9354 *Schulman* Alan R., The royal butler Ramessessamiron [AA 1983, AmResEg]: CdÉ 61 (1986) 187-202; 199-202, 54 known royal butlers.
9355 *Stadelmann* Rainer, Vierhundertjahrstele: ➤ 591, LexÄg 6,47 (1986) 1039-1044.
9356 **Swelim** Nabil M.A., Some problems on the history of the Third Dynasty: Archaeological and Historical Studies 7, 1983 ➤ 64,a64: ᴿBO 43 (1986) 408s (B. van de *Walle*).
9357 **Thomas** J. David, The epistrategos in Ptolemaic and Roman Egypt 2. The Roman Epistrategos: Abh. Rh/Wf Akad 6, 1982 ➤ 64,a65: ᴿDLZ 107 (1986) 48s (G. *Poethke*).
9358 *Treu* Kurt, Antike Literatur im byzantinischen Ägypten im Lichte der Papyri: BySlav 47,1 (1986) 1-7.
9358* **Trigger** B.G., *al*., Ancient Egypt, a social history 1983 ➤ 64,a66; 1,b85: ᴿAncSRes 16 (1986) 110-7 (B.G. *Ockinga*); CdÉ 61 (1986) 234-7 (M. *Malaise*).
9359 **Trigger** B.G., *al*., Historia del Egipto antiguo, ᵀ*Faci* Juan. Barc 1985. 548 p.; 59 fig.; 5 pl. – ᴿGerión 4 (1986) 345-7 (J.J. *Urruela*).
9360 **Troy** Lana, Patterns of queenship in ancient Egyptian myth and history: Boreas 14. U 1986, Univ. xiv-236 p.; 104 fig. Sk 147   91-554-1919-4 [AntiqJ 67,144].
9361 *Vandorpe* Katelijn, The chronology of the reigns of Hurganophor and Chaonnophris [207-186, Edfu dedication]: CdÉ 61 (1986) 294-302.
9362 **Way** Thomas von der, Die Textüberlieferung Ramses' II. zur Qadeš-Schlacht; Analyse und Struktur: Hildesheimer ÄgBei 22, 1984 ➤ 65,9677; DM 59: ᴿMundus 22 (1986) 47s (Ingrid *Gamer-Wallert*).
9363 a) *Whitehorne* J.E.G., Strategus and Protostatae; – b) *Wipszycka* Ewa, La valeur de l'onomastique pour l'histoire de la christianisation de l'Égypte; à propos d'une étude de R.S. BAGNALL: ZPapEp 62 (1986) 159-172 / 173-181.

Q4 Historia Mesopotamiae.

9364 *Astour* Michael C., The name of the ninth Kassite ruler [Agum (II Kakrime) as WEIDNER after all, but his epithet rather than name Agum]: JAOS 106 (1986) 327-331; 1 fig.
9365 **Beaulieu** Paul-Alain, The reign of Nabonidus, king of Babylon (556-539

B.C.): diss. Yale, DHallo W. NHv 1985. 390 p. 86-12940. – DissA 47 (1986s) 1447s-A.

9366 **Capomacchia** Anna Maria G., Semiramis, una femminilità ribaltata: Storia delle Religioni 4. R 1986, Bretschneider. 76 p. 88-7062-590-7.

9367 **Chadefaud** Catherine, *Coblence* Jean-Michel, Les premiers empires: L'histoire des hommes. P 1986, Casterman. 2-203-15704-6. – RÉTRel 61 (1986) 577s (D. *Lys*).

9368 **Cooper** Jerrold S., The curse of Agade 1983 ➤ 64,a83; 65,9686: ROrientalia 55 (1986) 459-464 (W. H. P. *Römer*: zahlreiche Vorschläge).

9369 **Cooper** Jerrold S., Sumerian and Akkadian royal inscriptions, I. Presargonic inscriptions: AOS Translations. NHv 1986, American Oriental Soc. 118 p. [RelStR 13,255, J. M. *Sasson*].

9370 *Ellis* Maria D., The chronological placement of King Rim-Anum [1749, some 50 years later than hitherto]: RAss 80 (1986) 65-72; 1 fig.

9371 **Forbes** C., Documents of the Assyrian Empire (1115-612 B.C.); a collection of Assyrian sources on the imperialism of the Neo-Assyrian period from Tiglath-pileser I to the Babylonian conquest: Documents of the Ancient Near East for Secondary School Studies 2. Melbourne 1986, Australian Institute of Archaeology. 0-909923-15-9 [OIAc Ag. 87].

9372 **Gaster** Theodor H., Die ältesten Geschichten der Welt [1952], TBengs W.; Nachwort *Pfeiffer* M. wB 1983, Wagenbach. 223 p. – ROLZ 81 (1986) 233-5 (H. *Klengel*).

9373 **Glassner** Jean-Jacques, La chute d'Akkadé; l'événement et sa mémoire: Berliner Beiträge zum Vorderen Orient 5. B 1986, Reimer. vii-125 p.; bibliog. p. 99-117. 3-496-00878-4.

9374 *Glombiowski* Krzysztof, ❷ De Babylonis expugnatione a Cyro, Persarum rege, facta quid scriptores antiqui tradiderint: Meander 41 (1986) 375-387; lat. 387 [includitur liber Danielis].

9375 **Graziani** Simonetta, I testi mesopotamici datati al regno di Serse (485-465 a.C.): AION 46,2 Sup. R 1986, Herder. xxi-143 p.

9376 **Heinsohn** Gunnar, Altmesopotamische Historiographie; von Geisterreichen zur Rekonstruktion; Probleme und Verwunderungen in der Geschichtsschreibung zur 'Zivilisationswiege' Südmesopotamien — Darstellung und Lösungsvorschläge in einem chronologischen Überblick. Bremen 1986, Univ. ii-58 p. [BO 43,831].

9377 EKuziščina M., ❸ Istočnikovedenije... Near East history, textbook for university students of history faculties. Viš.Šk. 1984. 392 p. – RVDI (1986,3) 186-191 (K. *Avetisyan*, V. V. *Simonov*).

9378 *Mendecki* Norbert, ❷ Narody i państwa starożytnego Wschodu...: ColcT 56,2 (1986) 35-40; 41s, Völker und Staaten des Alten Orients in der 2. Hälfte des 2. Jahrtausends v. Chr.

9379 *Menzel-Wortmann* Brigitte, Der Lúgal danibata in neuassyrischer Zeit: 20, FDELLER K., MesopT 21 (F 1986) 213-227.

9380 *Oelsner* Joachim, Materialien zur babylonischen Gesellschaft und Kultur in hellenistischer Zeit: Assyriologia 7. Budapest 1986, Univ. 693-462-058-2 [OIAc Ag. 87].

9381 **Pettinato** Giovanni, Semiramide 1965 ➤ 1,b114: RLetture 41 (1986) 422-4 (G. *Ravasi*).

9382 *Postgate* J. N., *a*) Administrative archives from the city of Ashur in the Middle Assyrian period: ➤ 563*, Sumer 42 (1986) 100-5, ❹ 36-40; – *b*) Middle Assyrian tablets; the instruments of bureaucracy: AltOrF 13 (1986) 10-39.

9383 *a*) *Renger* Johannes, Neuassyrische Königsinschriften als Genre der

Keilschriftliteratur — zum Stil und zur Kompositionstechnik der Inschriften Sargons II. von Assyrien; – *b*) *Pedersén* Olof, The libraries in the city of Assur; – *c*) *Lipiński* E., The king's arbitration in ancient Near Eastern folk-tale: ➤ 543, Rencontre 32, 1985/6, 109-128 / 143-7 / 137-142.

9384 **Roux** Georges, La Mésopotamie; essai d'histoire politique, économique et culturelle, préf. *Bottéro* Jean: L'Univers Historique. P 1985, Seuil. 476 p. [AulaOr 5,340].

9385 *Spieckermann* Hermann, Aramäer: ➤ 587, EvKL 1 (1986) 235-7.

9386 *a*) *Steiner* G., Structural patterns in the history of ancient Mesopotamia; – *b*) *Biggs* Robert, Ancient Mesopotamia and the scholarly traditions of the third millennium; – *c*) *Steible* Horst, Remarks on the written tradition of the conflict between Lagaš and Umma: Sumer 42 (1986) 61-63 / 32s / 29-31.

9387 **Tovar** Antonio, *Röllig* W., *Gamer-Wallert* I., Historia del Antiguo Oriente [= Tovar ¹1956 rev.]. Barc 1984, Hora. xi-326 p.; 4 maps. 84-85950-01-1. – ᴿBO 43 (1986) 395s (Marisa *Ramos Sainz*).

9388 **Walker** Marcie F., The Tigris frontier from Sargon to Hammurabi; a philologic and historical synthesis: diss. Yale. ᴰ*Hallo* W. NHv 1985. 280 p. 86-13633. – DissA 47 (1986s) 1304-A.

9389 **Wilkinson** Richard H., Mesopotamian coronation and accession rites in the Neo-Sumerian and early Old-Babylonian periods, c. 2100-1800 B.C.: diss. Minnesota, ᴰ*Reisman* D. Minneapolis 1986. – 340 p. 87-00599. – DissA 47 (1986s) 3532-A.

Q4.5 *Historia Persiae, Iran.*

9390 **Amiet** Pierre, L'âge des échanges inter-iraniens 3500-1700 avant J.-C.: Notes et documents des Musées de France 11. P 1986, Réunion Musées. 332 p.; 207 fig. 2-7118-0290-6.

9391 *Brodersen* Kai, The date of the secession of Parthia from the Seleucid kingdom: Historia 35 (1986) 378-381.

9392 *Brown* Stuart C., Media and secondary state formation in the Neo-Asyrian Zagros; an anthropological approach to an Assyriological problem: JCS 38 (1986) 107-118; 2 fig.

9393 **Burn** A. R., Persia and the Greek defence of the West, c. 546-478. L 1984 [AION 45,711].

9394 *Dijk* Jan van, Die dynastischen Heiraten zwischen Kassiten und Elamern: eine verhängnisvolle Politik [23. Orientalistentag Wü 1985]: Orientalia 55 (1986) 159-170.

9395 **Frei** Peter, *Koch* Klaus, Reichsidee und Reichsorganisation im Perserreich: OBO 55, 1984 ➤ 65,9730; **1**,b133: ᴿCBQ 48 (1986) 530s (J. W. *Betlyon*).

9396 **Frye** Richard N., The history of ancient Iran 1984 ➤ 65,9731; **1**,b134: ᴿGnomon 58 (1986) 133-6 (J. *Duchesne-Guillemin*).

9397 *Gnoli* Gherardo, The quadripartition of the Sassanian Empire: EWest 35 (1985) 265-270.

9398 *Grayson* A. Kirk, Assyria's foreign policy in relation to Elam in the eighth and seventh centuries: ➤ 563*, Sumer 42 (1986) 146-8, ❹ 79-81.

9399 ᴱ**Harmatta** J., From Hecateus to Al-Ḥuwārizmi..., Pre-Islamic Central Asia 1984 ➤ **1**,b136: ᴿArOr 54 (1986) 193s (O. *Klíma*).

9400 *Hegyi* D., Athen und die Achämeniden in der zweiten Hälfte des 5. Jahrhunderts v.u.Z.: Oikoumene 4 (1983) 53-59 [AION 45,711].

9401 **Lewis** David M., Sparta and Persia [Cincinnati Bradeen lectures 1986]:

CinciClasSt 1, 1977 ➤ 61,q593; 62,a599: ᴿAnzAltW 39 (1986) 168-171 (G. *Kipp*: high quality).
9402 *Lewis* David M., Persians in Herodotus: ➤ 92, ᶠRAUBITSCHEK A., Greek historians 1985, 101-117.
9403 *McEwan* G. J. P., A Parthian campaign against Elymais in 77 B.C.: Iran 24 (1986) 91-94.
9404 **Savory** Roger, Iran under the Sefavids. C 1980, Univ. x-277 p.; 35 fig.; map. – ᴿWeltOr 17 (1986) 198-200 (H. *Gaube*).
9405 *Stève* M.-J., La fin de l'Élam; à propos d'une empreinte de sceau-cylindre: StIran 15 (1986) 7-21; Eng. 21.
9406 **Walser** Gerold, Hellas und Iran: ErtFor 209, 1984 ➤ 65,9741; 1,b141: ᴿArOr 54 (1986) 191s (J. *Klíma*).
9407 **Wolski** Jósef, Iran, siedziba imperiów w starożytności, I. Achemenidzi: Nauka dla Wszystkich 403. Wrocław 1986, Polska Akad. 83-04-02447-0 [OIAc Ag. 87].

Q5 *Historia Anatoliae*: **Asia Minor, the Hittites, Armenia.**

9408 **Allen** R. E. E., The Attalid Kingdom 1983 ➤ 64,a117... 1,b144: ᴿMnemosyne 39 (1986) 529-531 (A. van *Hooff*).
9409 *Beal* Richard H., The history of Kizzuwatna and the date of the Šunaššura treaty: Orientalia 55 (1986) 424-445.
9410 *Bryce* Trevor R. [➤ b839], Madduwatta and Hittite policy in western Anatolia: Historia 35 (1986) 1-12.
9411 *Gindin* L. A., *Tsymbursky* V. L., ❹ The ancient Greek version [Cypria] of the historical event reflected in a Hittite text [KUB XXIII]: VDI 176 (1986,1) 81-87; Eng. 87.
9412 **Golden** Peter B., Khazar Studies [Khazar vocabulary in Turkish and related documents]; an historical-philosophical inquiry into the origins of the Khazars: BibOrHung 25/1, 1980 ➤ 1,b148: ᴿRÉJ 145 (1986) 437s (G. *Nahon*).
9413 *Heinhold-Kramer* Susanne, Untersuchungen zu Piyamaradu: Orientalia [52 (1983) 81-97] 55 (1986) 47-62.
9414 **Ludwig** Dieter, Struktur und Gesellschaft des Chazaren-Reiches im Licht der schriftlichen Quellen [Inaug. Diss. Münster]. B 1982, Papyrus. 364 p.; 238 p. – ᴿDer Islam 63 (1986) 168-170 (D. M. *Dunlop*).
9415 *Moiseyeva* T. A., ❹ The Phrygian state in the eighth and early seventh centuries B.C.: VDI (1986,3) 9-31; Eng. 32.
9416 **Siegelová** Jana, Hethitische Verwaltungspraxis im Lichte der Wirtschafts- und Inventardokumente. Praha 1986, Narodni Muzeum. 3 vol. [OIAc Ag. 87].

Q6 **Historia graeca** *et hellenistica incluso Alexandro.*

9417 *Aalders* G. J. D., CASSIUS Dio and the Greek world: Mnemosyne 39 (1986) 282-304.
9418 *Bekkum* W. J. van, Alexander the Great in medieval Hebrew literature; stemma of relations between Hebrew sources of the Alexander traditions: JWarb 49 (1986) 218-226.
9419 *Betz* Hans D., Hellenismus: ➤ 597, TRE 15 (1986) 19-35.
9420 *Bichler* Reinhold, Die 'Reichsträume' bei HERODOT; eine Studie zu Herodot's schöpferischer Leistung und ihre quellenkritische Konsequenz: Chiron 15 (1985) 125-147.

9421 **Blundell** Sue, The origins of civilization in Greek and Roman thought. Wolfeboro NH 1986, Croom Helm. v-234 p. $32.50 [RelStR 13,258, M. E. *Clark*].

9422 **Bosworth** A. B., A historical commentary on ARRIAN's history of Alexander I, books I-III, 1980 ➤ 61,q684... 1,b162: ᴿGnomon 58 (1986) 145-154 (G. *Wirth*).

9423 *Bosworth* A. B., Alexander the Great and the decline of Macedon: JHS 106 (1986) 1-12.

9424 ᴱ**Calame** C., L'amore in Grecia: Storia e società 1983 (³1984 ➤ 1,b164): ᴿMaia 37 (1985) 285-7 (Elisabetta *Nano*).

9425 **Callender** Gae, Aspects of ancient Greece I-II and Teachers Handbook. Sydney 1985, Shakespeare Head. A$10; 9; 20. 0-7302-0210-0; 1-9; 2-? – ᴿAncSRes 16 (1986) 176-180 (R. *Muffet*).

9426 **Carlier** P., La royauté en Grèce avant Alexandre: ÉtTr Histoire Romaine 6, 1984 ➤ 1,b167: xiv-562 p.; 6 fig.; 4 maps: ᴿJHS 106 (1986) 236s (N. R. E. *Fisher*, comparing DREWS R.).

9427 **Connor** W. Robert, THUCYDIDES 1984 ➤ 85,9768; 1,b168: ᴿHistTheory 25 (1986) 95-106 (D. B. *Tompkins*); HZ 243 (1986) 397s (W. *Schuller*).

9428 *a*) *Connor* W. Robert, Narrative discourse in Thucydides [comment, *Robinson* Paul]; – *b*) *Dewald* Carolyn, Practical knowledge and the historian's role in Herodotus and Thucydides: ➤ 92, ꟘRAUBITSCHEK A., Greek historians 1985, 1-17 [19-23] / 47-63.

9429 **Corcella** Aldo, ERODOTO e l'analogia [i.e. pre-inductive thinking]. Palermo 1984, Sellerio. 311 p. Lit. 18.000. – ᴿClasR 100 (1986) 310s (D. *Fehling*); RPLH 60 (1986) 117s (C. *Coulet-Caquot*).

9430 *Croke* Brian, J. B. BURY and his History of Greece: ➤ 45*, ꟘHARRIS B., AncSRes 16 (1986) 79-94; portr.

9431 *Devine* A. M., *a*) The battle of Gaugamela; a tactical and source-critical study: AncW 13 (1986) 87-115; 2 fig.; – *b*) Demythologizing the battle of the Granicus: Phoenix 40 (Toronto 1986) 265-278.

9432 **Fine** John V. A., The ancient Greeks; a critical history 1983 ➤ 65,9774; 1,b173: ᴿGnomon 58 (1986) 744-6 (W. *Schuller*).

9433 **Finley** M. I., Politics in the ancient world (Wiles lectures, Belfast 1980) 1983 ➤ 65,9775; 0-521-27570-9: ᴿÉchMClas 30 (1986) 66-68 (J. F. *Drinkwater*); Gnomon 58 (1986) 496-509 (C. *Meier*).

9434 **Finley** Moses I., L'invention de la politique; démocratie et politique en Grèce et dans la Rome républicaine. P 1985, Flammarion 217 p. – ᴿRÉLat 63 (1985) 348 (J.-C. *Richard*).

9435 ᴱ**Finley** M. I., El legado de Grecia, una nueva valorización [1981 ➤ 1,b174],ᵀ: Estudios y Ensayos 117. Barc 1983, Grijalbo. 483 p. 16 pl. – ᴿFaventia 7,2 (1985) 127-9 (J. *Martínez Gázquez*).

9436 **Fornara** Charles W., Translated documents of Greece and Rome, I., Archaic times to the end of the Peloponnesian War². Cambridge 1983, Univ. $15. 0-521-29946-2. – ᴿAncSRes 16 (1986) 57-61 (M. J. *Osborne*).

9437 *French* Valerie, *Dixon* Patricia, The Pixodaros affair; another view [Alexander's role in the assassination of Philip]: AncW 13 (1986) 73-82 (83-85, appendix, The reliability of PLUTARCH).

9438 **Gafurov** Bobojan G., *Tsibukides* Dimitris I., ❸ Alexander the Great and the Orient. Moskva 1980, Nauka. 456 p.; 4 color pl. – ᴿAncW 13 (1986) 71s (I. *Prilutskaya*).

9439 *Gammie* John G., HERODOTUS on kings and tyrants; objective historiography or conventional portraiture?: JNES 45 (1986) 171-195.

9440 **Gehrke** Hans-Joachim, Jenseits von Athen und Sparta; das dritte Griechenland und seine Staatenwelt. Mü 1986, Beck. 216 p.

9441 [E]**Grant** Michael, Greece and Rome; the birth of western civilization. L 1986, Thames & H. 240 p.; 281 fig. + 95 colour. £20 [Antiquity 60, 178].

9442 *Greenwalt* William, HERODOTUS and the foundation of Argead Macedonia: AncW 13 (1986) 117-122.

9443 **Gruen** Erich S., The Hellenistic world and the coming of Rome 1984
➤ 1,b178: [R]ClasR 100 (1986) 91-96 (J. *Briscoe*); RÉLat 63 (1985) 349 (J.-L. *Ferrary*).

9444 **Hammond** N. G. L., Three historians of Alexander 1983 ➤ 64,a159...
1,b179: [R]AmJPg 107 (1986) 123-5 (A. M. *Devine*); ÉchMClas 29 (1985) 454-468 (E. *Badian*).

9445 **Hammond** N. G. L., A history of Greece to 322 B.C.[3] [[1]1959]. Ox 1986, Clarendon. xxiv-691 p.; ill. 0-19-873096-9; pa. 5-0.

9446 *Hammond* N. G. L., The kingdom of Asia and the Persian throne: Antichthon 20 (1986) 73-85.

9447 **Hart** John, HERODOTUS and Greek history 1982 ➤ 64,a171, 1,b181:
[R]Gnomon 58 (1986) 444s (J. *Cobet*).

9448 **Hemmerdinger** B., Les manuscrits d'HERODOTE et la critique verbale [< ms 1887. *Desrousseaux* A. M.] 1981 ➤ 65,9785; 1,b183: [R]Maia 38 (1986) 259-261 (G. B. *Alberti*).

9449 *Hershbell* Jackson P., PLUTARCH and the Milesian philosophers: Hermes 114 (1986) 172-185.

9450 **Högemann** Peter, Alexander der Grosse und Arabien: Zetemata 82. Mü 1985, Beck. ix-236 p.

9451 **Hooker** J. T., Sparta, Geschichte und Kultur [The ancient Spartans 1980], [T]*Bayer* E. Stu 1982, Reclam. 320 p.; 22 fig.; 35 phot.; 2 maps. –
[R]AnzAltW 39 (1986) 171-5 (G. *Kipp*).

9452 *Hornblower* Simon, El mundo griego 479-323 a.C. [The Greek world 1983 ➤ 65,9786]: Historia de las civilizaciones clásicas. Barc 1985, Crítica. 415 p. – [R]Gerión 4 (1986) 348s (D. *Plácido*).

9453 **Hude** Charles, HERODOTI Historiae I-IV / V-IX: Scriptorum classicorum bibliotheca oxoniensis. Ox 1979 = 1908 / 1984([1]1908) = [3]1927, Clarendon. I. xvii [no page-numbers]; II. iii-424 p. 0-19-814526-8; 7-6.

9454 **Keuls** Eva C., The reign of the phallus; sexual politics in ancient Athens 1985 ➤ 1,b189: [R]AJA 90 (1986) 361-3 (H. A. *Shapiro*); AmJPg 107 (1986) 599s (Jane M. *Snyder*).

9455 **Kreissig** H., Geschichte des Hellenismus 1982 ➤ 65,9790: [R]AnzAltW 39 (1986) 76-78 (R. *Urban*).

9456 **Kunstler** Barton L., Women and the development of the Spartan polis; a study of sex roles in classical antiquity: diss. Boston Univ. 1983.

9457 **Lacey** W. K., Die Familie im antiken Griechenland [The family in classical Greece 1968], [T]*Winter* U.: KGantW 14. Mainz 1983, von Zabern. 332 p. DM 45 [Gymnasium 94,85, K. *Brodersen*].

9458 **Lang** Mabel L., Herodotean narrative and discourse: Oberlin Martin Classical lectures 28, 1984 ➤ 1,b191: [R]JHS 106 (1986) 208s (J.H. *Westlake*).

9459 *Leimbach* Rüdiger, Militärische Musterrhetorik; eine Untersuchung zu den Feldherrnreden des THUKYDIDES. Stu 1985, Steiner. 136 p. DM 48.
– [R]ClasR 100 (1986) 311s (H. D. *Westlake*).

9460 *Liviabella Furiani* Patrizia, Il fenomeno donna nella Grecia antica: GitFg 38 (1986) 275-282.

9461 *McNeal* Richard A., PROTAGORAS the historian: HistTheory 25 (1986) 299-318.

9462 *Marcucci* Marcello, Necessità politica e realtà in TUCIDIDE (rileggendo W. JAEGER): Maia 38 (1986) 13-25.

9463 **Mastrocinque** Attilio, Manipolazione della storia in età ellenistica; i Seleucidi e Roma 1983 → 65,9795; 1,b199: ᴿGnomon 58 (1986) 136-9 (W. *Orth*).

9464 **Osborne** Robin, Demos; the discovery of classical Attica. C 1985, Univ. xiv-284 p. $49.50 [RelStR 13,68, A. T. *Kraabel*].

9465 **Ostwald** Martin, From popular sovereignty to the sovereignty of law; law, society, and politics in fifth-century Athens. Berkeley 1986, Univ. California. xxii-663 p. 0-520-05426-1.

9466 *Piejko* Francis, Antiochus Epiphanes saviour of Asia [OGI 253]: RivFgIC 114 (1986) 425-436.

9467 *Plácido* Domingo, De Heródoto a Tucídides: Gerión 4 (1986) 17-45.

9468 **Préaux** C., El mundo helenístico; Grecia y Oriente (323-146 a.C.) I-II, ᵀ*Lagasta* Faci. Barc 1984, Labor. 633 p. – ᴿCiuD 199 (1986) 175 (F. *Díez*).

9469 *Pritchett* W. Kendrick, THUCYDIDES' statement on his chronology: ZPapEp 62 (1986) 205-211.

9470 ᴱ**Prontera** Francesco, STRABONE, contributi allo studio della personalità e dell'opera I 1984; II. ᴱ**Maddoli** Gianfranco 1986. Perugia, Univ.

9471 **Ramírez Trejo** A., HERÓDOTO, padre y creador de la historia cientifica: Cuadernos del Centro de Estudios Clásicos 12. México 1984, U.N.A.M. Inst. Investig. Fg. 192 p. – ᴿJHS 106 (1986) 209 (J. M. *Alonso-Núñez*).

9472 **Rengakos** Antonios, Form und Wandel des Machtdenkens der Athener bei THUKYDIDES [Diss. Fr 1982]: Hermes Einz. 48. Wsb 1984, Steiner. 149 p. – ᴿRPLH 60 (1986) 118s M. *Nouhaud*).

9473 *Roberts* Jennifer T., Aristocratic democracy; the perseverance of timocratic principles in Athenian government: Athenaeum 64 (1986) 355-369.

9474 **Roebuck** Carl, The world of ancient times [reprint]. NY 1966, Scribner's. xxv-758 p. 0-684-13726-7. $24. – ᴿAncSRes 16 (1986) 54-56 (Louise *McInerney* defends its continuing use as textbook, not indicating whether 1966 or a recent year was the date of the reprint).

9475 *Sacks* Kenneth, Rhetoric and speeches in Hellenistic historiography: Athenaeum 64 (1986) 383-395.

9476 *a) Scardigli* Barbara, Scritti recenti sulle Vite di PLUTARCO (1974-1986) [bibliografia in ordine alfabetico dei personaggi greci poi romani]; – *b) Pelling* Christopher B. R., Synkrisis in Plutarch's Lives: → 521, ᴱ*Brenk* F., Miscellanea 1985/6, 7-22 [23-59] / 83-96.

9477 **Schachermeyr** Fritz, Griechische Frühgeschichte 1984 → 65,9808; 1,b209: ᴿGGA 238 (1986) 1-13 (A. *Heubeck*); Phoenix 40 (Toronto 1086) 341-3 (D.*Brown*).

9478 **Schuller** Wolfgang, Frauen in der griechischen Geschichte. Konstanz 1985, Univ. 142 p.; 34 fig. – ᴿKlio 68 (1986) 638s (Isolde *Stark*).

9479 *Serra* José P., Pedagogia e exemplo na Historiografia Grega: Euphrosyne 14 (Lisboa 1986) 53-76.

9480 **Šofman** A. S. ⊕ The decline and fall of the empire of Alexander of Macedon. Kazan 1984, Univ. 224 p. – ᴿAncW 13 (1986) 68-70 (D. *Tsibukides*).

9481 *Spahn* Peter, Das Aufkommen eines politischen Utilitarismus bei den Griechen [Antrittsvorlesung Bielefeld]: Saeculum 37 (1986) 8-21.

9482 **Steinbrecher** Michael,   Der delisch-attische Seebund und die athe-
nisch-spartanischen Beziehungen in der kimonischen Ära (ca. 478/7-
462/1): Palingenesia 21.   Stu 1985, Steiner.   173 p.   DM 48. – ᴿHZ 243
(1986) 395s (A. *Giovannini*).
9483 **Syriopoulos** C. T., ❻ *Eisagogē* ... Introduction to ancient Greek history [from the data of a century of archeology]; the transitional times from
the Mycenean to the Archaic 1200-700 B.C.: Ath. Archeol. Soc. 99. Athenai 1983, auct. lv-1201 p.; 19 pl. + 2 color.; 6 maps [JHS 107,241s, A. R.
Burn].
9484 *Thompson* Wesley E.,   The stasis at Corinth: StFgIC 4 (1986) 155-171.
9485 *Tripodi* Bruno,   L'ambasceria di Alessandro I di Macedonia ad Atene
nella tradizione erodotea (HDT. 8,136-144):   AnPisa 16 (1986) 621-635.
9486 **Tsibukides** D., ❼ Ancient Greece and the Orient [Hellenistic period].
Moskva 1981, Nauka.   254 p.; Eng. 243-7. – ᴿAncW 13 (1986) 70s (V.
Sergeyev).
9487 **Vatai** Frank L.,   Intellectuals in politics in the Greek world 1984
➤ 1,b215; $47.50;   0-7099-2613-8:   ᴿAncSRes 16 (1986) 119-121 (P.
Bicknell: disappointing); Gnomon 58 (1986) 1-3 (Ingomar *Weiler*).
9489 *a*) *Verkinderen* F.,   Les cités phéniciennes dans l'empire d'Alexandre le
Grand; – *b*) *Hauben* H.,   Philocles, king of the Sidonians and general of the
Ptolemies: ➤ 553, Cinquième = Akkadica 47 (1986) 82 / 80.
9490 **Waters** K. H.,   HERODOTOS the historian; his problems, methods and
originality 1984 ➤ 1,b218:   0-805-11928-4:   ᴿClasR 100 (1986s) 305s
(Stephanie *West*); ÉchMClas 30 (1986s) 305s (K. H. *Kinzl*); Gnomon 58
(1986) 545s (J. *Cobet*); JHS 106 (1986) 207s (H. D. *Westlake*).
9491 *Whitehead* David, Women and naturalisation in fourth-century Athens;
the case of Archippe: ClasJ 80 (1986) 109-114.
9492 **Will** W.,   Athen und Alexander; Untersuchungen zur Geschichte der
Stadt von 338 bis 322 v. Chr. [diss. 1980]: MüBeiPapF 77, 1983 ➤ 65,9916;
1,b219:   ᴿGymnasium 93 (1986) 299-301 (P. *Guyot*).
9493 ᴱWirth Gerhard, *Hinüber* Oskar von,   ARRIANS Alexanderzug und
Indische Geschichte, griechisch und deutsch: Tusculum. Mü 1985,
Artemis.   1153 p.   DM 98. – ᴿGymnasium 93 (1986) 297-9 (R. *Schmitt*);
Mundus 22 (1986) 126-9 (K.-H. *Golzio*).
9494 *Young-Bruehl* Elisabeth, What THUCYDIDES saw: HistTheor 25 (1986)
1-16.
9495 **Ziółkowski** John E., THUCYDIDES and the tradition of funeral speeches at
Athens: Monographs in Classical Studies. NY 1981, Arno.   219 p. $25. –
ᴿEos 74 (1986) 129-131 (R. *Turasiewicz* ❷); Gnomon 58 (1986) 482-9 (A.
Kleinlogel).

Q7   **Josephus Flavius.**

9496 *Bammel* Ernst,   *a*) Zum Testimonium Flavianum [< ᶠ*Michel* O. 1974,
9-22]; – *b*) A new variant form of the Testimonium Flavianum [< ExpTim
85 (1973s) 145-7]; – *c*) Jesus as a political agent in a version of the Josippon
[< Jesus and the politics of his day 1984, 197-209]; – *d*) Joasar [Ant 17,164;
18,26 ...; < ZDPV 90 (1974) 61-68]: ➤ 131, Judaica 1986, 177-189 / 190-3 /
289-301 / 28-34.
9497 **Bartlett** John R.,   Jews in the Hellenistic world; Josephus, Aristeas, the
Sibylline Oracles, Eupolemus: CamCW 1/1, 1985, ➤ 1,b222:   ᴿJStJud 17
(1986) 92s (F. *Garcia Martinez*); ZAW 98 (1986) 459 (H.-C. *Schmitt*).
9498 *Brisset* A.,   Les suppressions dans les 'Antiquités judaïques' [livres 17-20,

2-5 siècle] de Flavius Josèphe: CahRenan 32,137 (1984) 215-8 [NTAbs 30,332].

9499 *Cancik* Hubert, Geschichtsschreibung und Priestertum — Zum Vergleich von orientalischer und hellenischer Historiographie bei Flavius Josephus, contra Apionem, Buch I: ➤ 68*, ᶠMAYER R, Wie gut 1986, 41-62.

9500 *Cohen* Shaye J. D., Alexander the Great and Jaddus the High-Priest according to Josephus [A 11, 302-347]: AJS 7s (1982s) 41-68.

9501 *Crawford* L., Quelques mots sur Yosippos, fils de Matthias, dit Flavius Josèphe: CahRenan 33,140 (1985) 27-36 [NTAbs 30,332].

9502 **Deutsch** Guy N., Iconographie de l'illustration de Flavius Josèphe au temps de Jean Fouquet: ALGH 12. Leiden 1986, Brill. xi-225 p.; bibliog. p. 193-201; 148 fig. 90-04-07121-0.

Egger Rita, Josephus Flavius und die Samaritaner: OBO 1986 ➤ 8195 [< Diss. 1985 ➤ 1,b229].

9503 **Feldman** Louis H., Josephus and modern scholarship (1937-1980) 1984 ➤ 65,810; 1,b230: ᴿAmJPg 107 (1986) 298 (S. W. *Hirsch*); JStJud 17 (1986) 100s (F. *García Martínez*); Orpheus 7,1 (1986) 181-4 (Maria Laura *Astarita*); RÉJ 145 (1986) 134-7 (Mireille *Hadas-Lebel*); TPhil 61 (1986) 569s (J. *Beutler*).

9504 **Feldman** Louis H., Josephus, a supplementary bibliography [adds 1800 items to H. *Schreckenberg* 1968/1979, plus 1976-83]: Reference Library of the Humanities. NY 1986, Garland. xvii-696 p. $90 [TDig 33,361]. 0-8240-8792-5.

9505 ᴱFeldman L. H., *Hata* G., ❶ Josephan studies II. Tokyo 1985, Yamamoto Shoten. 552 p. 4 pl. 17 art. mostlyᵀ.

9506 *a) Franchet d'Espèrey* Sylvie, Vespasien, Titus et la littérature; – *b) Coleman* K. M., [Flavius Josèphe ...]; The emperor Domitiàn and literature: ➤ 574, ANRW 2/32/5 (1986) 3048-3086 / 3087-3115.

9507 *Gafni* L., *a)* Josephus' Gebrauch des Ersten Makkabäerbuchs; – *b)* Die babylonische Yeschiwa: HBeiWJ 1 (1985)... [< ZAW].

9508 *Gibbs* John G., *Feldman* Louis H., Josephus' vocabulary for slavery: JQR 76 (1985s) 281-310.

9509 **Hahn** István, Josephus Flavius, Apión ellen, avagy a zsidó nep ősi voltáról: Prométheusz 5. Budapest 1984, Helikon. 135 p. 16 pl. [KirSef 60,385].

9510 *Horsley* Richard A., High priests and the politics of Roman Palestine; a contextual analysis of the evidence in Josephus [*Smallwood* E. Mary, 1962]: JStJud 17 (1986) 23-55.

9511 *Ilan* Tal, ❶ A pattern of historical errors in the writings of Josephus: Zion 51 (1986) 357-360; Eng. XII.

9512 *Kokkinos* Nikos, Which Salome did Aristobulus marry? [Jos. Ant. 18,137; coin]: PEQ 118 (1986) 33-50; 4 fig.

9513 **Marichalar** Salvador pról., Flavio Josefo, La guerra de los judíos: 'Sepan cuantos' 374. M 1982, Porrúa. xlii-300 p. [KirSef 60,385].

9514 *Martin* Thomas R., Quintus Curtius' presentation of Philip Archidaeus and Josephus' accounts of the accession of Claudius: AmJAncH 8 (1983) 161-190.

9515 **Mason** Steven N., Josephus on the Pharisees; a redaction-critical study: diss. St. Michael, ᴰ*Longenecker* R. Toronto 1986. 694 p. – RTLv 18,548.

9516 *Parente* Fausto, Flavius Josephus' account of the anti-Roman riots preceding the 66-70 war, and its relevance for the reconstruction of Jewish eschatology during the first century A.D.: ➤ 11*, Mem. BICKERMAN E. = JANES 16s (1984s) 183-205.

9517 **Pelletier** André,   Flavius Josèphe, Guerre des Juifs III (livres IV-V) 1982 ➤ 63,9843 ... 65,9832: ᴿRBgPg 63 (1985) 123s (J. *Schamp*).
9518 **Poortman** Wilco C.,   Bijbel en Prent II: *a*) Boekzaal van de Nederlandse Prentbijbels; *b*) Boekzaal van de werken van Flavius Josephus in de Nederlandse taal. Haag 1986, Boekencentrum. 305 p. ƒ185. – ᴿStreven 53 (1985s) 950s (P. *Beentjes*).
9519 *Prato* Gian Luigi, [pre-Giuseppe] Cosmopolitismo culturale e auto-identificazione etnica nella prima storiografia giudaica: ➤ 391, RivB 34 (1986) 143-182; Eng. 182.
9520 **Rajak** Tessa, Josephus 1983 ➤ 64,a211 ... 1,b240: ᴿJBL 105 (1986) 350-2 (S. J. D. *Cohen*); JRS 76 (1986) 324-6 (M. *Stern*); Mnemosyne 39 (1986) 497-9 (P. W. van der *Horst*); NT 28 (1986) 286s (G. D. *Kilpatrick*).
9521 **Rengstorf** Karl H.,   A complete concordance to Flavius Josephus II-IV, 1975-83, ƒ1900; Supplement/Gesamtregister, *Schreckenberg* H. 1979, ƒ80 ➤ 64,a214 ... 1,b242: ᴿEvQ 58 (1986) 262-5 (J. N. *Birdsall*).
9522 **Schwartz** Seth,   Josephus and Judaism from 70 to 100 of the common era: diss. Columbia. NY 1985. 432 p. 86-04673. – DissA 47 (1986s) 277-A.
9523 *Schwartz* Seth,   The composition and publication of Josephus's *Bellum Iudaicum* Book 7:   HarvTR 79 (1986) 373-386.
9524 *Thérond* Bernard,   Discours au style indirect et discours au style direct dans La guerre des Juifs de Flavius Josèphe: ➤ 81,   Mém. NIKI-PROWETZKY V., Hellenica 1986, 139-152 [115-137, *Feldman* L., *Paul* A. 1986 ➤ supra Nᵒ 1440*].

Q8   *Historia epochae NT*   –   Seleucids to Bar-Kochba.

9525 **Aalders** G. J. D.,   Synagoge, kerk en staat in de eerste vijf eeuwen. Kampen 1985, Kok. 105 p. 90-22425-70-1. – ᴿNedTTs 40 (1986) 180 (K. A. D. *Smelik*).
9526 *Amir* Yehoshua,   *a*) Der Begriff Iudaïsmos — zum Selbstverständnis des hellenistischen Judentums [< Fifth World Congress Jewish St. 3 (1969) 263-8]; – *b*) Das jüdische Paradox auf dem Hintergrund der hellenistischen Judenfeindschaft [< ᴱ*Stern* M., Nation and History 1 (1983) 27-34]; – *c*) Homer und Bibel als Ausdrucksmittel im 3. Sibyllenbuch [< Scripta Classica Israelica 1 (1974) 73-89]: ➤ 127, Studien 1985, 101-113 / 114-123 / 83-100.
9527 **Anderson** Gordon L.,   The legal basis for the treatment of Christianity, 30-312 C.E.: diss. Minnesota, ᴰ*Spencer* R.   Minneapolis 1986. 543 p. 87-03396. – DissA 47 (1986s) 3848-A.
9528 *Avi-Yonah* Michael,   The Jews under Roman and Byzantine rule [1946]ᵀ. J 1984 = 1976, Magnes. 965-223-530-X.
9529 *Baldwin* Barry, SUETONIUS. Amst 1983, Hakkert. 579 p. – ᴿFaventia 8,1 (1986) 158-162 (A. *Valls*).
9530 *Bammel* Ernst,   *a*) Die Rechtsstellung des Herodes [< ZDPV 84 (1968) 73-79]; – *b*) Die Neuordnung des Pompeius und das römisch-jüdische Bündnis [< ZDPV 75 (1959) 76-82]; – *c*) The organization of Palestine by Gabinius [< JJS 12 (1961) 159-162]; – *d*) Pilate and Syrian coinage [< JJS 2 (1951) 108-110]; – *e*) Pilatus' und Kaiphas' Absetzung [inedi-tum]; – *f*) Die Schatzung des Archelaos [Kilikien 36 n.Chr.; < Historia 7 (1958) 497-500] ➤ 131, Judaica 1986, 3-9 / 10-16 / 17-20 / 47-50 / 51-58 / 35-38.
9531 **Barker** E.,   From Alexander to Constantine; passages and documents illustrating the history of social and political ideas 336 B.C.-A.D. 337 [=

Oxford 1956]. Lanham MD 1985, UPA. xxv-505 p. $19.75. 0-8191-4757-4 [NTAbs 31,118].

9531* *Baumbach* Günther, Herodes, Herodeshaus: ➤ 597, TRE 15 (1986) 159-162.

9532 **Beard** Mary, *Crawford* Michael, Rome in the late Republic; problems and interpretations. L 1985, Duckworth. ix-106 p. £15; pa. £6. – RClasR 100 (1986) 270-3 (Miriam *Griffin*).

9533 **Bengtson** H., Marcus Antonius 1977 ➤ 58,c489: RAnzArchW 39 (1986) 78-80 (H. *Aigner*).

9534 **Benko** Stephen, Pagan Rome and the early Christians 1984 ➤ 1,b254; £15; also Bloomington, Indiana Univ.: RAmerica 154 (1986) 251s (R. M. *Grant*); AugM 31 (1986) 438 (J. *Oroz*); ClasR 100 (1986) 333s (R. P. C. *Hanson*); JBL 105 (1986) 743-5 (L. M. *White*: nearly every Greek citation contains a mistake).

9535 **Birken** G., Augustus; Leben und Taten des Caesar Augustus. Essen 1984, Magnus. 496 p. DM 19,80. – RGymnasium 93 (1986) 312s (Ines *Stahlman*).

9536 E**Boardman** John, *al.*, The Oxford history of the classical world. Ox 1986, Univ. x-882 p.; figs. (listed p. 862-872); 20 colour. pl.; 10 maps. 0-19-872112-9.

9537 **Bombelli** Luciano, I frammenti degli storici giudaico-ellenistici: DARFICLET 103. Genova 1986, Univ. 193 p.

9538 **Braund** David C., Augustus to Nero; a sourcebook on Roman history 31 BC-AD 68. L 1985, Croom Helm. 334 p. $23. 0-7099-3206-5. – RAnc-SRes 16 (1986) 122-5 (B. *Jones*).

9539 *Brooten* Bernadette J., Jewish women's history in the Roman period; a task for Christian theology: ➤ 110, FSTENDAHL K. = HarvTR 79 (1986) 22-30.

9540 **Bruce** F. F., Zeitgeschichte des Neuen Testaments: WissTb 6. Wu 1986, Brockhaus. 222 + 271 p. DM 29,80. – RStreven 53 (1985s) 949s P. *Beentjes*).

9541 *Bruun* Christer, Some comments on early Claudian consulships: Arctos 19 (1985) 5-18.

9542 *Callatay* François de, Les derniers rois de Bithynie; problèmes de chronologie: RBgNum 132 (1986) 5-30; pl. I-V.

9543 *Chamoux* François, Vues nouvelles sur Marc Antoine: ÉchMClas 30 (1986s) 231-243.

9544 **Cimma** Maria Rosa, Ricerche sulle società di Publicani: Ist. Diritto Rom.-Med. 59, 1981 ➤ 65,9861; Lit. 14.000: RAntClas 55 (1986) 547s (Huguette *Jones*).

9545 **Cizek** E., Neron. P 1982, Fayard. 475 p. F 95 [Gymnasium 94,86, Bohumila *Mouchová*].

9546 *a) Cohen* Shaye J. D., The political and social history of the Jews in Greco-Roman antiquity; the state of the question; – *b) Gager* John G., Judaism as seen by outsiders: ➤ 225, EKraft R., Early Judaism 1986, 33-56 / 99-116.

9547 **Dix** Thomas K., Private and public libraries at Rome in the first century B.C.; a preliminary study in the history of Roman libraries: diss. Michigan, DFrier B. AA 1986. 294 p. 86-21274. – DissA 47 (1986s) 2149-A.

9548 **Downing** F. Gerald, Strangely familiar; an introduction reader to the first century. Manchester 1985, auct. iii-210 p. [RQum 47,456].

9549 **Dzielska** Maria, ⊕ APOLLONIUSZ z Tiany; legenda i rzeczywistość:

Rozprawa habilitacyjne 78. Kraków 1983, Univ. 148 p. – ^REos 74 (1986)
144-6 (M. *Salamon*, Eng.).

9550 *Edgeworth* Robert J., Nero the bastard: Eos 74,1 (1986) 103-111.

9551 *Feldman* Louis H., How much Hellenism in Jewish Palestine? HUCA 57
(1986) 83-111.

9552 *Février* Paul-Albert, L'histoire Auguste et le Maghreb: AntAfr 22
(1986) 115-128.

9553 *a) Finkel* Asher, The departures of the Essenes, Christians and R.
Yohanan Ben Zakkai from Jerusalem; – *b) Klingenberg* Eberhard, Urteil,
Schiedsspruch und Vergleich im römischen, griechischen und jüdischen
Recht; – *c) Ehrlich* Ernst L., Der Reformprozess in der jüdischen
Geschichte: ➤ 68*, ^FMAYER R., Wie gut 1986, 29-40 / 63-75 / 76-89.

9554 *Fischer* Thomas, Zur Struktur der römischen Herrschaft über Judäa und
seine Nebengebiete von Pompejus bis Hadrian (63 v. bis 135 n. Chr.):
Jahrbuch der Ruhr-Universität (Bochum 1986) 37-46.

9555 **Gascou** Jacques, SUÉTONE historien [diss. 1979]: BibliothÉcFrAR 255,
1984 ➤ 1,b279: ^RClasR 100 (1986) 243-5 (A. *Wallace-Hadrill*); Gnomon
58 (1986) 321-6 (D. *Flach*).

9556 *Gichon* Mordechai, New insight into the Bar Kokhba war and a
reappraisal of Dio CASSIUS 69.12-13: JQR 77 (1986s) 15-43.

9557 **Giebel** M., Augustus: Bildmonographien 327. Ha-Reinbek 1984,
Rowohlt. 156 p. DM 8,80. – ^RGymnasium 93 (1986) 561s (F. X. *Herrmann*).

9558 *a) Gilboa* A., The intervention of Sextus Julius Caesar, governor of
Syria, in the affair of Herod's trial; – *b) Geiger* Joseph, The last Jewish
revolt against Rome; a reconsideration: ➤ 34, ^FFUKS A., ScrClasIsr 5
(1979s) 185-194 / 250-7.

9559 **Goodman** Martin, State and society in Roman Galilee 1983 ➤ 1,b281:
^RClasR 100 (1986) 108-111 (A. *Wasserstein*); IsrEJ 36 (1986) 115-7 (L. I.
Levine).

9560 **Griffin** Jasper, Latin poets and Roman life. L 1985, Duckworth.
xiv-226 p. – ^RAncSRes 16 (1986) 100-109 (N. *Horsfall*: mostly sex-life;
titillating).

9561 **Griffin** Miriam, Nero, the end of a dynasty 1985 ➤ 1,b284; also NHv
1985, Yale Univ. 320 p. $25. – ^RClasR 100 (1986) 98-100 (R. *Seager*);
RelStR 12 (1986) 290 (J. S. *Ruebel*; now our most reliable biography).

9562 *Griffin* Miriam, Philosophy, Cato and Roman suicide: GreeceR 33
(1986) 64-75. 192-202.

9563 *Grünhagen* Wilhelm, Ein Porträt des Domitian aus Munigua: MadMit
27 (1986) 309-323; pl. 51-54.

9564 **Guevara Castillo** Hernando, Ambiente político del pueblo judío en
tiempos de Jesús: Academia Christiana 13. M 1985, Cristiandad. 285 p.
[RQum 47,456].

9565 **Harari** Ruth, Hérode-le-Grand ou le refus d'un peuple. P 1986, Cerf.
192 p. F 91. – ^REsprV 96 (1986) 554 (S. *Légasse*: sans recherche); MondeB
45 (1986) 54 (P. I. *Fransen*).

9566 *Hengel* Martin, Hadrians Politik gegenüber Juden und Christen: ➤ 11*.
Mem. BICKERMAN E. = JANES 16s (1984s) 153-182.

9567 **Hengst** Daniël den, The prefaces in the Historia Augusta 1981
➤ 65,9881: ^RAnzAltW 39 (1986) 146s (W. *Lackner*).

9568 *Holladay* C. R., Fragments from Hellenistic Jewish authors, I. Historians:
SBL TTr 20 / Pseud 10, 1983 ➤ 64,8594.a266; 1,b290: ^RGnomon 58 (1986)
268-270 (N. *Walter*); JJS 37 (1986) 118s (M. *Goodman*: good on

individuals; general introduction unsatisfactory); JSS 31 (1986) 262-4 (Tessa *Rajak*); ScripB 16 (1985s) 42s (M. *Prior*).

9569 **Horsley** G. H. R., New documents illustrating early Christianity 3, 1983 ➤ 63,8297; 65,8176: ᴿGnomon 58 (1986) 458s (P. *Stockmeier*, 1-3); RB 93 (1986) 309s (J. *Murphy-O'Connor*).

9570 **Horsley** R. A., *Hanson* J. S., Bandits, prophets, and Messiahs 1985 ➤ 1,b291; $20: ᴿCalvaryB 2,1 (1986) 68 (G. H. *Lovik*); CCurr 36 (1986s) (N. *Fujita*: 'the common people in the time of Jesus'); ChH 55 (1986) 508-510 (R. M. *Grant*); TTod 43 (1986s) 440-2 (R. *Lim*).

9572 *Horst* P. W. van der, Schriftgebruik bij drie vroege Joods-Hellenistische historici; Demetrius, Artapanus, Eupolemus: AmstCah 6 (1985) 144-161.

9573 *Hosaka* Takaya, Die Christenpolitik des jüngeren PLINIUS: AnJapB 12 (1986) 87-125.

9574 **Ide** A. F., Martyrdom of women; a study of death psychology in the early Christian church to 301 C.E. Garland TX 1985, Tanglewüld. ix-97 p. $7 pa. 0-923667-00-4 [NTAbs 31,122].

9575 **Jagersma** H., Geschiedenis van Israël 2. Von Alexander de Grote tot Bar Kochba 1985 ➤ 1,b294: ᴿStreven 53 (1985s) 467s (P. *Beentjes*).

9576 **Jagersma** H., A history of Israel from Alexander the Great to Bar Kochba. Ph 1986, Fortress. – ᴿAustralBR 34 (1986) 72 (B. R. *Doyle*).

9577 **Jones** Brian W., The emperor Titus 1984 ➤ 65,9887; 1,b295: L/NY 1984, Croom Helm / St. Martin's. 227 p. $32. 0-7099-1430-X. – ᴿAncSRes 16 (1986) 63-67 (A. R. *Birley*).

9578 ᴱ**Kaegi** Walter E., *White* Peter, Rome, late Republic and Principate: Readings in Western Civilization 2. Ch 1986, Univ. viii-308 p. 0-226-06936-2; pa. 7-0.

9579 **Kahn** Arthur D., The education of Julius Caesar. NY 1986, Schocken. x-514 p. $28.50 [RelStR 13,349, R. P. *Sonkowsky*].

9580 **Kasher** Aryeh, The Jews in Hellenistic and Roman Egypt; the struggle for equal rights: TSAntJ 7,1985 ➤ 1,b298: ᴿGregorianum 67 (1986) 361s (G. L. *Prato*); JStJud 17 (1986) 255-7 (H. G. *Kippenberg*: gegen TCHERIKOVER A.); Judaica 42 (1986) 104 (R. *Riesner*); Salmanticensis 33 (1986) 114-7 (R. *Trevijano*).

9581 *Kasher* Aryeh, ❶ The connection between the Hellenistic cities in Eretz-Israel and Gaius Caligula's rescript to install an idol in the temple: Zion 51 (1986) 135-151; Eng. V.

9582 **Kortekaas** G. A. A., Historia Apolloni regis Tyrii; prolegomena, text edition of the two principal Latin recensions: Mediaevalia Groningana 3. Groningen 1984, Bouma. XXXII-470 p. ƒ120. – ᴿGnomon 58 (1986) 368-370 (H. E. *Stiene*).

9583 *Kowalska* Elżbieta, ❷ The triumph, a sacral and political institution in republican Rome: Meander 41 (1986) 33-48. 71-84.

9584 **Lambrecht** Ulrich, Herrscherbild und Principatsidee in SUETONs Kaiserbiographien; Untersuchungen zur Caesar- und zur Augustus-Vita: Diss. Alte Gesch. H 19. Bonn 1984, Habelt. 176 p. – ᴿRivFgIC 113 (1985) 89-93 (G. *Traina*).

9585 **Langevin** G., Les premiers chrétiens 1-3, 1983 ➤ 64,281: ᴿRBgPg 64 (1986) 160-2 (B. *Coulie*).

9586 **Leaney** A. R. C., The Jewish and Christian world 200 BC to AD 220: CamCW 7, 1984 ➤ 65,9890; 1,b304: ᴿChH 55 (1986) 355s (F. *Czerwinski*); JStJud 17 (1986) 92-94 (F. *García Martínez*: a brief history plus a résumé of the other volumes); RHR 203 (1986) 431s (A. *Caquot*: not 'Learney', also in Index); ScripTPamp 18 (1986) 965s (G. *Aranda*).

9587 **Levi** Mario A., Augusto e il suo tempo: La Storia. Mi 1986, Rusconi. 578 p.; ill.

9588 **Levick** Barbara, The government of the Roman Empire; a sourcebook. Totowa NJ 1985, Barnes and Noble. xxvi-260 p.; 8 maps. $28.50. 0-389-20572-9 [NTAbs 31,124].

9589 **Linder** Amnon, ❶ *Ha-Yehudim we-ha-Yahᵃdut ba-huqqê*... Roman imperial legislation on the Jews 1983 ➤ 64,a276; 65,9893: ᴿKirSef 61 (1986) 77s (Rivkah *Fishman-Duker*).

9590 ᵀᴱ**Lo Cascio** Ferdinando, APOLLONIO Tianeo, epistole e frammenti: Ist. Sic. Biz. 12, 1984 ➤ 1,b307: ᴿMaia 38 (1986) 87s (E. *Valgiglio*); RivFgIC 114 (1986) 379 (G. *Ballaira*).

9591 **Lucrezi** F., Leges super principem; la 'monarchia costituzionale' di Vespasiano: Univ. N Pubb. Fac. Giuridica 195. N 1982, Jovene. viii-282 p. Lit. 17.500 [NTAbs 31,124].

9592 **McCulloch** Harold Y.ᴶ, Narrative cause in the annals of TACITUS [diss. Michigan 1977]: BeiKlasPg 160. Königstein 1984, Hain. xii-232 p. DM 48. 3-445-02327-1. – ᴿAntClas 55 (1986) 461s (A. *Martin*).

9593 *McGing* B. C., The governorship of Pontius Pilate; Messiahs and sources: PrIrB 10 (1986) 655-71.

9594 *MacMullen* Ramsey, Women's power in the Principate: Klio 68 (1986) 434-443.

9595 *Mor* Menachem, *Rappaport* Uriel, A survey of 25 years (1960-1985) of Israeli scholarship on Jewish history in the Second Temple period (539 B.C.E. – 135 C.E.): BibTB 16 (1986) 56-72.

9596 **Murmelstein** Wolf, Gli ebrei nell'Impero Romano; dalla distruzione del Secondo Tempio alla divisione dell'Impero Romano. R 1984, Collegio Rabbinico Italiano. 31 p.

9597 **Nash** Ronald H., Christianity and the Hellenistic world 1985 ➤ 1,b137: ᴿÉTRel 61 (1986) 445 (F. *Vouga*: apologétique); ScotJT 39 (1986) 135-7 (Judith H. *Lieu*, compares to LEANEY).

9598 **Nicolet** Claude, Strutture dell'Italia romana (sec. III-I a.C.), ᵀ*Razzano* Maria: Storia 15. R 1984 = 1977, Jouvence. 449 p.; bibliog. p. 405-444. Lit. 50.000. – Cf. ➤ 61,r199.

9599 **Novara** Antoinette, Les idées romaines sur le progrès d'après les écrivains de la République; essai sur le sens latin du progrès [often linked with decline: diss. Sorbonne]: HistAncMéd 9. P 1982, BLettres. 884 p. (2 vol.) – ᴿClasR 100 (1986) 254-6 (J.-M. *Alonso-Núñez*).

9600 **Orrieux** Claude, Les papyrus de Zénon [vulgarisation de sa thèse (attendue), Les archives de Zénon 1980]; l'horizon d'un grec en Égypte au IIIᵉ siècle avant J.-C.: 1983 ➤ 64,8351... 1,9336: ᴿClasR 100 (1986) 172s (Jane *Rowlandson*).

9601 **Otzen** Benedikt, Den antike jødedom; politisk udvikling og religiøse strømninger fra Aleksander den Store til Kejser Hadrian 1984 ➤ 65,9902; 1,b320: ᴿJStJud 17 (1986) 112s (A. S. van der *Woude*).

9602 **Paul** A., Il mondo ebraico al tempo di Gesù; storia politica 1983 ➤ 64,a288b; 65,9904: ᴿStPatav 33 (1986) 434s (G. *Segalla*).

9603 **Pearson** Birger A., *Goehring* James E., The roots of Egyptian Christianity: Studies in Antiquity and Christianity. Ph 1986, Fortress. xxix-319 p.

9604 **Roddaz** Jean-Michel, Marcus Agrippa 1984 ➤ 1,b331: ᴿAmJPg 107 (1986) 130-2 (M. *Reinhold*); ClasR 100 (1986) 96-98 (R. *Seager*); Gymnasium 93 (1986) 314s (P. *Herz*); RÉLat 63 (1985) 353-6 (J.-M. *André*).

9605 ^ESafrai Shmuel, ☉ At the end of the Second Temple and in the period of the Mishnah [updated original of The Jewish People in the First Century 1974-6 ➤ 58,b272]. J 1983, Ministry of Education. 207 p.; ill. [RelStR 13,172, D. *Kraemer*].

9606 ^ESanders E. P., Jewish and Christian self-definition I-III, 1980-2 ➤ 62,561*ab*...1,b334: ^RTsTKi 57 (1986) 218-220 (O. *Skarsaune*: 'jø-disk-kristen dialog').

9607 Saulnier Christiane, (*Perrot* Charles), Histoire d'Israël III. De la conquête d'Alexandre à la destruction du temple 1985 ➤ 1,a940: ^RAngelicum 63 (1986) 639s (P. *Zerafa*); EsprV 96 (1986) 138s (L. *Monloubou*); ETL 62 (1986) 172 (J. *Lust*); Études 364 (1986) 713 (P. *Gibert*); JStJud 17 (1986) 118 (A. S. van der *Woude*: Temple destroyed in 70, not 135 as title implies; less adequate on Geistesgeschichte than OTZEN); MondeB 42,1 (1986) 54 (P. I. *Fransen*); RTPhil 118 (1986) 419s (T. *Römer*); VSp 140 (1986) 725s (H. *Troadec*).

9608 Schäfer Peter, Der Bar Kokhba-Aufstand 1981 ➤ 62,a790... 1,b337: ^ROLZ 81 (1986) 40-42 (W. *Wiefel*).

9609 Schäfer Peter, Geschichte der Juden... von Alexander 1983 ➤ 64,a304... 1,b338: ^RHZ 243 (1986) 404-6 (K. *Bringmann*).

9610 *Schneewein* Gerhart, Gegenstand und Absicht in den Biographien PLUTARCHS: ➤ 25, ^FEGERMANN F. 1985, 147-162.

9611 [*Schürer* Emil] ^EVermes Geza *al.*, The history of the Jewish people in the age of Jesus Christ [I. 1973 ➤ 55,6676; II. 1979 ➤ 61,r5] III, 1-2. E 1986, Clark. xxi-704 p.; 705-890 and Index. £25; £35. 0-567-02244-7; 72-5. ^RExpTim 98 (1986s) 22s (P. R. *Ackroyd*).

9612 Schürer-Vermes, ^T*Soffritti* G. & O., Storia del popolo giudaico al tempo di Gesù Cristo [I] 1985 ➤ 1,b342: ^RAntonianum 61 (1986) 777-9 (M. *Nobile*); ParVi 31 (1986) 373s (A. *Rolla*); StPatav 33 (1986) 435s (G. *Leonardi*).

9613 Segal Alan F., Rebecca's children; Judaism and Christianity in the Roman world. CM 1986, Harvard. $20 [Judaica 42,206]. – ^RAmerica 155 (1986) 407-9 (Margaret R. *Miles*); TS 48 (1986) 347s (R. F. *O'Toole*).

9614 Segalla G., Panorama storico del NT 1984 ➤ 1,b343: ^RStPatav 33 (1986) 454s (A. *Moda*).

9615 ^{TE} Sherk Robert K., Translated documents of Greece and Rome, 4. Rome and the Greek East to the death of Augustus 1984 ➤ 65,9918; 1,b344: ^RAncSRes 16 (1986) 180-3 (B. *Marshall*).

9616 Sherwin-White A. N., Roman foreign policy in the east, 168 B.C. to A.D. 1: 1984 ➤ 65,9919; 1,b345: ^RAntClas 55 (1986) 524s (A. *Martin*); RPLH 60 (1986) 346-8 (Marianne *Bonnefond*).

9617 Simon Marcel, Verus Israel, a study of the relations between Christians and Jews in the Roman Empire (135-425) [1964], ^T*McKeating* H.: Littman Library. Ox 1986, Univ. xviii-533 p. 0-19-710035-X.

9618 Smolak Kurt, Christentum und römische Welt [Textsammlung für höheren Unterricht]. W 1984, Hölder-PT. 176 p.; 192 p.; ill. – ^RRHE 81 (1986) 652 (Renate *Pillinger*).

9619 Sonnabend Holger, Fremdenbild und Politik; Vorstellungen der Römer von Ägypten und dem Partherreich in der späten Republik und frühen Kaiserzeit: EurHS 3/286. Fra 1986, Lang. 324 p.

9620 ^ESørensen Villy, Seneca, ein Humanist auf Neros Hof, ^T*Wesemann* M. Mü 1984, Beck. 320 p. [AnzAltW 40, 242, H. *Strohm*].

9621 Sordi Marta, The Christians and the Roman Empire [1983 ➤ 65,9921], ^T*Bedini* Annabel. L/Norman OK 1983, Croom Helm/Univ. 215 p. 0-709-4421-7? / 0-4061-2011-8.

9622 *a) Speyer* Wolfgang, Das Verhältnis des Augustus zur Religion: – *b) Hall* John F.[III],   The Saeculum Novum of Augustus and its Etruscan antecedents: → 574, ARNW 2/16/3 (1986) 1777-1805 / 2564-2589.

9623 **Spinosa** Antonio,   Tiberio, l'imperatore che non amava Roma: Le scie. Mi 1985, Mondadori. 228 p. – [R]Salesianum 48 (1986) 407s (S. *Maggio*).

9624 **Stemberger** G.,   Die römische Herrschaft im Urteil der Juden: ErtFor 195, 1983 → 64,a312 ... 1,b349: [R]NorTTs 87 (1986) 49s (H. *Moxnes*).

9625 [E]**Stern** Menahem,   Greek and Latin authors on Jews and Judaism [I. 1976 → 61,k159; II. From Tacitus to Simplicius 1980 → 61,r118]; III. Appendices and Indices 1984 → 65,9934; 1,b351: [R]AntClas 55 (1986) 428-430 (Thérèse *Liebmann-Frankfort*); Athenaeum 64 (1986) 265-7 (L. *Troiani*); JSS 31 (1986) 92-96 (G. *Brooke*); RÉLat 63 (1985) 303s (J. *Fontaine*).

9626 **Stern** M.,   Die Vertreibung der Juden aus dem antiken Rom: HBeiWJ 1 (1985) 1 ... [< ZAW].

9627 **Sullivan** J. P.,   Literature and politics in the age of Nero. Ithaca NY 1985, Cornell. 218 p. $22.50. 0-8014-1740-6 [NTAbs 31,129]. – [R]ClasR 100 (1986) 256-8 (G. B. *Townsend*); ÉchMClas 30 (1986s) 312-5 (J. G. *Fitch*).

9628 **Sysling** H.,   De Bar-Kochba-opstand, historie en legende: Ter Herkenning 14,3 [or 47,3, < GerefTTs 86,256] (1986) 165-176.

9629 **Talbert** Richard J. A.,   The Senate of imperial Rome 1984 → 1,b355: [R]ClasR 100 (1986) 100-102 (G. P. *Burton*).

9630 **Tassin** Claude,   Le judaïsme de l'exil au temps de Jésus: CahÉv 55. P 1986, Cerf. 76 p. F 22. 0222-9714.

9631 *Tsafrir* Yoram,   The transfer of the Negev, Sinai and southern Transjordan from *Arabia* to *Palaestina*: IsrEJ 36 (1986) 77-86.

9632 **Virlouvet** Catherine,   Famines et émeutes à Rome des origines de la république à la mort de Néron: CollÉcFrR 87. R 1985, École Française. 133 p.

9633 **Wallace-Hadrill** A., Suetonius 1983 → 65,9931; 1,b357: [R]ClasJ 82 (1986s) 159-162 (R. C. *Lounsbury*); ÉchMClas 29 (1985) 469-477 (E. *Champlin*: better than Baldwin B.); Mnemosyne 39 (1986) 187-190 (A. B. *Breebaart*).

9634 [E]**Wellesley** Kenneth, Tacitus, Annales: 1/2. BSGR. Lp 1986, Teubner. xxi-201 p. 3-322-00270-5.

9635 **Wendland** Paul,   La cultura ellenistico-romana nei suoi rapporti con giudaismo e cristianesimo: Biblioteca di storia e storiografia dei tempi biblici. Brescia 1986, Paideia. 421 p. Lit. 40.000.

9636 **Whittaker** Molly,   Jews and Christians, Graeco-Roman views: CamCW 6, 1984 → 65,9932; 1,b358: [R]AncSRes 16 (1986) 67-69 (C. *Ehrhardt*); JJS 37 (1986) 120 (M *Goodman*); JTS 37 (1986) 491s (C. C. *Rowland*: more significant than Leaney).

9637 **Wilken** Robert L.,   The Christians as the Romans saw them 1984 → 65,9933; 1,b359: [R]Interpretation 40 (1986) 219s (P. J. *Achtemeier*); Month 248 (1986) 213 (A. *Meredith*); RB 93 (1986) 310s (J. *Murphy-O'Connor*); WWorld 6 (1986) 229s (W. *Sundberg*).

9638 **Wilken** R. L.,   Die frühen Christen, wie die Römer sie sahen. Graz 1986, Styria. 231 p. Sch. 298 [RHE 82,66*].

9639 **Will** Édouard, *Orrieux* Claude, Ioudaïsmos — Hellènismos; essai sur le judaïsme judéen à l'époque hellénistique. Nancy 1986, Presses Univ. 228 p. [JBL 105,757].

9640 ^E**Wiseman** T. P.,   Roman political life 90 B.C. - A.D. 69 [Competition and cooperation p. 3-19; *Patterson* Jeremy, Politics in the Late Republic, 21-43; *Levick* Barbara, Politics in the Early Principate, 45-68]: Studies in History 7. Exeter 1985, Univ.   vi-82 p. £1.25. – ^RRelStR 12 (1986) 291 (C. R. *Philips*).

9641 **Woodman** A. J.,   Velleius PATERCULUS, the Caesarian and Augustan narrative (2,41-93): ClasTCom 25. C 1983, Univ. xx-294 p. £32.50. – ^RClasR 100 (1986) 53-55 (B. M. *Levick*).

9642 **Yavetz** Zwi,   Julius Caesar and his public image [1979]: Aspects of Greek and Roman Life. L/Ithaca NY 1983, Thames & H./Cornell Univ. $45. 0-500-40043-1/. – ^RAncSRes 16 (1986) 125-8 (R. *Develin*); ÉchMClas 30 (1986) 80-83 (S. *Treggiari*).

Q9   *Historia imperii romani*   –   **Roman-Byzantine Empire.**

9643 **Alonso-Núñez** J. M.,   The ages of Rome. Amst 1982, Gieben. 28 p. ƒ12. – ^RRBgPg 64 (1986) 148 (P. *Salmon*).

9644 **Arce** Javier,   Estudios sobre el emperador Fl. Cl. Juliano (Fuentes literarias, epigrafía, numismática) 1984 → 1,b361: ^RFaventia 8,1 (1986) 171-3 (G. *Carrasco Serrano*).

9645 *Baldwin* Barry,   Historiography in the second century [A.D.: happiest and prosperous, but without writers (GIBBON)]; precursors of Dio CASSIUS: Klio 68 (1986) 479-486.

9646 **Barnes** Timothy D.,   Constantine and Eusebius 1984 → 65,9943; 1,b363: ^RMnemosyne 39 (1986) 218-221 (R. van den *Broek*); RHR 203 (1986) 207-9 (R. *Turcan*).

9647 *Barnes* T. D.,   The conversion of Constantine: EchMClas 29 (1985) 371-392.

9648 [**Blackmore** James H.] Second Acts; a continuation of Luke's account of the early Church, A.D. 64-313. Raleigh NC, Edwards & B. 136 p. – ^RRExp 83 (1986) 302s (Penrose St. *Amant*: a popular history by an anonymous author).

9649 a) *Brauch* Thomas L.,   The emperor Julian's theocratic vocation; – b) *Hendrix* Holland, Beyond 'imperial cult' and 'cults of magistrates': → 392, SBL Seminars 1986, 291-300 / 301-8.

9650 **Brind'Amour** Pierre,   Le calendrier romain, recherches chronologiques 1983 → 1,b366; 2-7603-4702-8: ^RJRS 76 (1986) 289s (J. *Briscoe*); Latomus 45 (1986) 431s (E. *Liénard* †); Salesianum 48 (1986) 375s (R. *Della Casa*).

9651 **Cameron** Averil (f.),   Procopius [of Caesarea] and the sixth century: Classical Life and Letters. L 1985, Duckworth. xiii-297 p. £29.50. – ^RClasR 100 (1986) 219s (R. *McCail*).

9652 **Christ** K.,   Römische Geschichte und Wissenschaftsgeschichte I 1982 → 64,a342* ...1,b371: ^RMaia 38 (1986) 274s (L. S. *Amantini*).

9653 *Criscuolo* Ugo,   Giuliano e l'ellenismo; conservazione e riforma: Orpheus 7 (1986) 272-292.

9654 a) *Daiber* Hans,   OROSIUS' Historiae adversus paganos in arabischer Überlieferung; – b) *Schäfer* Peter, Der Aufstand gegen Gallus Caesar [351 n. Chr.]: → 59, ^FLEBRAM J., Tradition 1986, 202-249 / 184-201.

9655 **Décarreaux** Jean,   Byzance ou l'autre Rome. P 1982, Cerf. 274 p. – ^RScEspr 38 (1986) 142 (G. *Pelland*: louanges in recto; réserves in obliquo).

9656 **Demandt** Alexander,   Der Fall Roms; die Auflösung des römischen Reiches im Urteil der Nachwelt 1984 → 65,9953; 1,b372: ^RRÉByz 43 (1985) 285 (A. *Failler*).

9657 **Dyson** Stephen L., The creation of the Roman frontier. Princeton 1985, Univ. xii-324 p.; 4 fig. 0-691-03577-6. – RClasR 100 (1986) 273s (L. *Keppie*: not about mid-east Limes, but 'How the West was Won' 400 - 50 B.C.); HZ 243 (1986) 152s (H. E. *Herzig*); JRS 76 (1986) 288s (S. *Mitchell*).

9658 *Eisenstein* Herbert, Die Erhebung des Mubarqa' in Palästina [841 A.D.]: Orientalia 55 (1986) 454-8.

9659 **Elliott** Thomas G., Ammianus Marcellinus and fourth century history 1983 → 1,b373; $35: RGnomon 58 (1986) 656s (G. *Sabbah*).

9660 **Flach** Dieter, Einführung in die römische Geschichtsschreibung: Die Altertumswissenschaft. Da 1985, Wiss. ix-337 p.

9661 **Fouquet** Claude, *Grimal* Pierre, Julien; la mort du monde antique: Confluents. P 1985, BLettres. 364 p. F 99. 2-252-33425-4. – RAugM 31 (1986) 452s (J. *Ortall*).

9662 *González* Julián, *Fernández* Fernando, Tabula Siarensis, Fortunales Siarenses et Municipia Ciuium Romanorum: Ivra 32 (dated 1981) 1-36 [= ZPapEp 55 (1984) 55-100; Ivra adds photos, and says the find (La Cañada near Seville) was in Spring 1982; Ivra 31 (dated 1980) 135-7 had said the find was Spring 1981].

9663 **Grabar** A., L'iconoclasme byzantin [1957 remanié]: Idées et Recherches. P 1984, Flammarion. 400 p. F 290. – RRSPT 70 (1986) 178s (J.-P. *Jossua*).

9664 **Grant** M., The Roman Emperors; a biographical guide to the [92] rulers of imperial Rome, 31 BC - AD 476. NY 1985, Scribner's. xv-367 p.; ill.; 11 maps. $25. 0-684-18388-9 [NTAbs 30,373].

9665 *a) Harris* William V., The Roman father's power of life and death; – *b) Pomeroy* Sarah B., Copronyms and the exposure of infants in Egypt: → 102, Mem. SCHILLER A., 1986, 81-95 / 147-162.

9666 **Holum** Kenneth G., Theodosian empresses 1982 → 64,a347 ... 1,b380: RLatomus 45 (1986) 466s (A. *Chastagnol*: de valeur); Mnemosyne 39 (1986) 533-8 (H. C. *Teitler*).

9667 *Holum* Kenneth G., a) Flavius Stephanus, proconsul of Byzantine Palestine [536]: ZPapEp 63 (1986) 231-9; – b) Proconsul Andreas *philoktistes*, of Byzantine Palestine: IsrEJ 36 (1986) 61-64.

9668 **Hussey** Joan M., The Orthodox Church in the Byzantine Empire: Oxford History of the Christian Church. Ox 1986, Clarendon. 408 p. £35. 0-19-826901-3. – RExpTim 98 (1986s) 185 (A. K. *McHardy*).

9669 **Jerphagnon** Lucien, Julien dit l'Apostat, histoire naturelle d'une famille sous le Bas-Empire. P 1986, Seuil. 308 p. F 99. – RRHPR 66 (1986) 355 (F. *Chalaye*).

Jerphagnon Lucien, Vivre et philosopher sous l'Empire chrétien 1983 → d331*.

9671 *Klein* Richard, Julian Apostata: Gymnasium 93 (1986) 273-292.

9672 **Lassère** Jean-Marie, Ubique populus ... Afrique romaine (146-235) 1977 → 61,r164; 62,k279: RRÉAug 31 (1985) 169-171 (C. *Lepelley*).

9673 ELieu S. N. C., The emperor Julian, panegyric and polemic; Claudius MAMERTINUS, John CHRYSOSTOM, EPHREM the Syrian: Translated texts for historians, Gr. 1. Liverpool 1986, Univ. viii-146 p., map. [RHE 82,37*].

9674 **MacMullen** R., Christianizing the Roman Empire 1984 → 65,9961; 1,b386: RÉchMClas 29 (1985) 495s (T. D. *Barnes*); JAAR 54 (1986) 596-8 (D. E. *Groh*).

9675 *MacMullen* Ramsay, 'What difference did Christianity make?': Historia 35 (1986) 322-343.

9676 *Markus* R. A., The end of the Roman empire; a note on Eugippius, Vita

S. Severini 20 [first Western writer to consider Roman domination finished]: Nottingham Medieval Studies 26,1-7 [RHE 81,741].

9677 **Martin** Paul M., L'idée de royauté à Rome; 1. De la Rome royale au consensus républicain. Clermont-Ferrand 1982, Adosa. xxvi-412 p.; 2 maps: F 300. – ᴿRBgPg 64 (1986) 149s (H. *Bardon*).

9678 ᴱ**Mendelssohn** Ludwig, APPIANI [Alexandrini] historia romana II. Lp 1986 = 1905, Teubner. xvi-645 p.

9679 ᴱ**Morrison** Karl F., The Church in the Roman Empire: Readings in Western Civilization 3. Ch 1986, Univ. viii-248 p. $20; pa. $8. [RelStR 13,263, E. *Ferguson*].

9680 **Munier** Charles, L'Église dans l'empire romain (IIᵉ-IIIᵉsiècles), II. Église et cité 1979 → 61,r194: ᴿAugR 26 (1986) 586-8 (B. *Studer*).

9681 *Nathanson* Barbara G., Jews, Christians, and the Gallus revolt in fourth-century Palestine: BA 49 (1986) 26-36; ill.

9682 **Neri** Valerio, Ammiano e il cristianesimo; religione e politica nelle 'Res gestae' di Ammiano Marcellino: Studi di Storia Antica 11. Bo 1985, Coop. univ. 244 p. Lit. 24.000 – ᴿGnomon 58 (1986) 644-7 (J. *Szidat*).

9683 **Neri** Valerio, Costanzo, Giuliano e l'ideale del civilis princeps nelle storie di Ammiano Marcellino: Quad. 1. R 1984, Studi Bizantini e Slavi. 78 p. ᴿGnomon 58 (1986) 753-6 (R. *Klein*).

9684 *a) Nobbs* Alanna E., A revolt in the time of Diocletian; the evidence of the Paniskos papyri; – *b) Brennan* Brian, Sources for Constantius II: → 45*, ᶠHARRIS B., AncSRes 16 (1986) 132-6 / 137-145.

9685 **Pack** Edgar, Städte und Steuern in der Politik Julians; Untersuchungen zu den Quellen eines Kaiserbildes: Coll. Latomus 194. Bru 1986. 420 p.

9686 **Patlagean** Evelyne, Povertà ed emarginazione a Bisanzio [1977, parte centrale]. ᵀᴱ*Barone* Giulia. Bari 1986, Laterza. 331 p. Lit. 35.000. – ᴿSileno 12 (1986) 171s (Anna *Quartarone Salanitro*).

9687 *Patzer* Harald, SALLUST und THUKYDIDES [< Neue Jahrbücher für Antike 4 (1941) 124-136]: → 203, Ges. Schr. 1985, 20-32.

9688 *Poucet* Jacques, Les origines de Rome; tradition et histoire 1985 → 1,b390: ᴿGerión 4 (1986) 329-340 (J. *Martínez-Pinna*).

9689 **Quacquarelli** Antonio, Reazione pagana e trasformazione della cultura (fine IV secolo d.C.): VetChr Quad. 19. Bari 1986, Edipuglia. 248 p. Lit. 32.000. – ᴿÉTRel 61 (1986) 593s (Letizia *Tomassone*; recueil d'essais qu'il avoue pas assez approfondis).

9690 *Rathbone* D.W., The dates of the recognition in Egypt of the emperors from Caracalla to Diocletianus: ZPapEp 62 (1986) 101-131.

9691 **Rawson** E. ms., Intellectual life in the late Roman republic. Baltimore 1985, Johns Hopkins Univ. ix-355 p. $29.50 0-8018-2899-6 [NTAbs 30,378].

9692 **Sahas** Daniel J., Icon and Logos; sources in eighth century iconoclasm. Toronto 1986, Univ. 215 p. $37.50 [RelStR 13,77, R. L. *Wilken*].

9693 **Shahîd** Irfan, Rome / Byzantium and the Arabs 1984 → 65,9974*ab*; 1,b393: ᴿClasR 100 (1986) 111-7 (G. W. *Bowersock*); HZ 243 (1986) 403s (E. *Kettenhofen*); RÉByz 43 (1985) 301s (J.-C. *Cheynet*); SBFLA 36 (1986) 381-4 (M. *Piccirillo*).

9694 **Siniscalco** Paolo, Il cammino di Cristo nell'impero romano 1983 → 64,a366 ... 1,b394: ᴿRÉAug 31 (1985) 172 (R. *Braun*); Salesianum 48 (1986) 155s (R. *Farina*).

9695 **Thelamon** Françoise, Païens et chrétiens au IVᵉ siècle; l'apport de l' 'Histoire Ecclésiastique' de RUFIN d'Aquilée, 1981 → 62,m114; 64,a368: ᴿRÉAug 31 (1985) 181-3 (C. *Lepelley*).

9696 **Wells** C., The Roman Empire: History of the Ancient World 6, 1984
➤ 65,9981; 1,b399: ᴿZRGg 38 (1986) 373s (J. M. *Alonso-Núñez*, auch kurz
über 1-5: Deutscher Taschenbuch-V. Geschichte der Antike).

9697 *Williams* Wynne, Epigraphic texts of imperial subscripts; a survey:
ZPapEp 66 (1986) 181-207.

9698 *a) Zecchini* Giuseppe, La tabula siarensis [near Seville 1982 ➤ 9662;
'most important epigraphic discovery of the eighties'] e la 'dissimvlatio' di
Tiberio; – *b) Lebek* Wolfgang D., Schwierige Stellen der Tabula siarensis:
ZPapEp [55 (1984) 55-100] 66 (1986) 23-29 [citing Ivra as 1983 and with *u*
despite his own *v* above] / 31-48.

XVIII. Archaeologia terrae biblicae

T1 **General biblical-area archeologies.**

9699 **Albright** W. F., ❺ The archaeology of Palestine⁴, ᵀ*Totoki* E., *Tomura* M.,
Tokyo 1986, Kirisuto Kyōdan. 291 p. + × (index); 63 fig.; 32 phot.
Y 4200 [BL 87,22].

9700 **Algulin** Ingemar, Nyklassicism som litterär tradition: SIMA pocket 39.
Partille 1986, Åström. 24 p.

9701 **Andrén** Arvid, Deeds and misdeeds in classical art and antiquities: SIMA
pocket 36. Göteborg 1986, Åström. 176 p.; 21 fig.

9702 **Baez-Camargo** Gonzalo, Archaeological commentary on the Bible 1984
[1979 ²1982 ➤ 64,a376: ... 1,b402]: ᴿBible Bhashyam 11 (1985) 189s (G.
Mangatt); Gregorianum 67 (1986) 591 (G. L. *Prato*); RExp 83 (1986) 458s
(J. E. *Drinkard*: not fully recommended).

9703 *Bahn* Paul G., *Paterson* R. W. K., The last rights [sic]; more on
archaeology and the dead: OxJArch 5 (1986) 255-271.

9704 *Bashilov* V. A., *Loone* E. N., ❻ On the levels of knowledge and cognitive
aims of archaeology: SovArch (1986,3) 192-208; Eng. 208.

9705 *Bastet* Frederik L., Hinter den Kulissen der Antike [Wandelingen door
de antieke wereld]. ᵀ*Dörner* Eleonore: Kulturgeschichte der antiken Welt
32. Mainz 1985, von Zabern. 337 p.; ill.

9706 ᴱBiran A., Biblical archaeology today 1984/5 ➤ 1,455: ᴿJStJud 17
(1986) 235-8 (A. S. van der *Woude*); PhoenixEOL 32,2 (1986) 58 (K. R.
Veenhof).

9707 ᴱBlaiklock E. M., *Harrison* R. K., The new international dictionary of
biblical archaeology 1983 ➤ 64,a380 ... 1,921: ᴿVT 36 (1986) 372s (Judith
M. *Hadley*: on Baalbek only a reference to Heliopolis, where only the
Egyptian site is treated; under Philadelphia nothing on 'Amman).

9708 **Brown** Raymond E., Recent discoveries and the biblical world 1983
➤ 64,a384 ... 1,b407: ᴿBAR-W 12,1 (1986) 17s (K. N. *Schoville*: bias
against fundamentalists).

9709 *Deichmann* Friedrich W., Einführung in die christliche Archäologie 1983
➤ 64,a388 ... 1,b415: ᴿTrierTZ 95 (1986) 67 (E. *Sauser*).

9710 *Demarest* Arthur A., Archaeology and religion: ➤ 585, EncRel 1 (1986)
372-9.

9711 **Dowley** Tim, Dicovering the Bible; archaeologists look at Scripture.
Glasgow c. 1985, Marshall Pickering. ... color ill. £9.

9712 *Eydoux* Henri-Paul, L'archéologie; histoire des découvertes. P 1985, La-
rousse. 296 p.; 300 fig. F 295. – ᴿÉtudes 364 (1986) 416 (P. du *Bourguet*).

9713 **Fagan** Brian M., The adventure of archaeology. Wsh 1985, National Geographic. 388 p.; (color.) ill. – [R]Antiquity 60 (1986) 153s (G. *Daniel*: high praise).

9714 *Fritz* Volkmar, [*Wischmeyer* Wolfgang], Archäologie, biblisch [NT]: → 587, EvKL 1 (1986) 254-7 [-8].

9715 **Gallay** Alain, L'archéologie demain. P 1986, Belfond. 320 p. 2-7144-1883-X [Fornvännen 82,235, C.-A. *Moberg* †].

9716 *Gening* Vladimir F., ⊕ The object and subject-matter of archaeology. – [R]SovArch (1986,3) 209-219; Eng. 219 (L. S. *Klein*: 'object' redundant).

9717 **Gibbon** Guy, Anthropological archaeology 1984 → 65,a2; 1,b422: [R]AJA 90 (1986) 102s (R. *Whallon*).

9718 *Ginouvès* René, 'Images de l'archéologie'; un premier vidéodisque pour l'archéologie classique: RArchéol (1986) 227-244.

9719 [E]**Green** Ernestine L., Ethics and values in [NS America] archaeology 1984 → 65,383; 1,429: [R]BAR-W 12,3 (1986) 14.16.18 (J. F. *Strange*).

9720 **Hackwell** W. John, Digging to the past; excavations in ancient lands. NY 1986, Scribner's. 50 p. 0-684-18692-1. [BAR-W 13/4, 8, O. *Borowski*; adv. 13/5,67 'ages 8-12'].

9721 [E]**Hankey** Henry, Archaeology; artifacts and artifiction: SIMA pocket 37. Göteborg 1985, Åström. 32 p.; ill. [Antiquity 60,148].

9722 **Hodder** Ian, Reading the past, current approaches to interpretation in archaeology. C 1986, Univ. xi-194 p.; bibliog. p. 179-190. 0-521-32743-1; pa. 3960-X. [Antiquity 61, 322s, J. *Gardin* & 458-473, J.C. *Barrett*].

9723 *Hodder* Ian, Digging for symbols in science and history; a reply: PrPrehS [51 (1985) 329-334, *Yengoyan* Y.] 52 (1986) 352-6.

9724 *Holt* Frank L., Egyptomania; have we cursed the Pharaohs?: Archaeology 39,2 (1986) 60-63.

9725 **Hoppe** Leslie J., What are they saying about biblical archaeology? 1984 → 65,a8; 1,b425: [R]CBQ 48 (1986) 309 (Patricia M. *Bikai*: severe); Interpretation 40 (1986) 196.198 (J. A. *Callaway*: mostly on the buzz about Ebla).

9726 **Lowenthal** David, The past is a foreign country. C 1985, Univ. 489 p. £10 pa. – [R]Antiquity 60 (1986) 152s (S. *Piggott*: boring pedantry).

9727 **McIntosh** Jane, The practical archaeologist; how we know what we know about the past. NY 1986, Facts on File. 192 p.; ill. $19 [JNES 46,77].

9728 **Magall** Mirian [Mundus 22,53], Archäologie und Bibel; wissenschaftliche Wege zur Welt des Alten Testaments. Köln 1985, DuMont. 250 p.; 120 fig. + 12 color.

9729 **Matthiae** Paolo, Scoperte di archeologia orientale: Universale 686. Bari 1986, Laterza. xv-240 p.; bibliog. p. 225-233.

9730 **Meyers** E., *Strange* J., Archaeology, the Rabbis and early Christianity 1981 → 62,k678 ... 1,b431: [R]SvTKv 62 (1986) 79-81 (Thérèse L. *Robertz*).

9731 **Meyers** E.M., *Strange* J. E., Les rabbins et les premiers chrétiens 1983 → 65,a17b; 1,b432: [R]Judaica 42 (1986) 102s (M. *Petit*, [T]*Hruby* K.); RencChrJ 19,79s (1985) 88s (A. *Perchenet*); TLZ 111 (1986) 139s (W. *Wiefel*).

9732 **Moscati** Sabatino, Le nuove frontiere dell'archeologia: *a*) Archeo Dossier 18. Novara 1986, De Agostini. 66 p.; (color.) ill. – *b*) [discorso inaugurale]: AntRArch 11,1 (1986) 2-8.

9733 **Müller-Karpe** Hermann, Frauen des 13. Jahrhunderts v. Chr. Mainz c. 1986, von Zabern. 201 p.; 112 fig.; 18 color. pl. DM 40 [one chapter: Ein Frauengrab in Assur, is in AntWelt 17,3 (1986) 40-49; p. 49 'Jahrtausends' in the title].

9734 **Muszyński** H., *Mędala* S., ✆ Archeologia Palestyny w zarysie [outline] 1984 ➤ 65,a21: ᴿCBQ 48 (1986) 726s (R. *North*).
9735 **Odden** Teresa, Heritage of the Pharaohs, 50 minute color video film. Palo Alto CA 1984, 400 Webster 94301. $30. – ᴿArchaeology 39,1 (1986) 71s (E. *Cruz-Uribe*); fasc. 3, p. 75, several statements of the review retracted by the Editor.
9736 **Sekiya** S., ❿ An illustrated OT archaeology²ʳᵉᵛ. Tokyo 1986, Yoru-dan-sha. 139 p.; ill. (13 color). Y 4500 [BL 87,28].
9738 *Shanks* H., Archeology as Politics: Commentary 82,2 (NY 1986) 50-52 [< NTAbs 31,73: refutes G. W. *Bowersock* (Grand Street, Autumn 1981) charges against M. *Avi-Yonah, A. Negev, Y. Yadin*].
9739 *Snodgrass* Anthony, A salon science? [archaeology uncertain of fundamentals? *Boardman* J. 1985 *al*.]: Antiquity 60 (1986) 193-8.
9740 **Snyder** Graydon F., Ante pacem; archaeological evidence of Church life before Constantine. Macon GA 1985, Mercer. xiv-174 p.; 47 fig.; 50 pl. $20. – ᴿBA 49 (1986) 249-251 (J. F. *Strange*); CurrTM 13 (1986) 181-3 (E. *Krentz*); TZBas 42 (1986) 437 (B. *Reicke*).
Soden Wolfram von, Einführung in die Altorientalistik 1985 ➤ 7561.
9742 ᴱ**Spriggs** Matthew, Marxist perspectives in archaeology 1984 ➤ 65,398; 1,445*: ᴿArchaeology 39,5 (1986) 66 (P. *Wells*, also on same series: ERICSON P., Prehistoric quarries; HIETALA H., intrasite spatial analysis; and the best, MILLER D., Ideology, power and prehistory); PrPrehS 52 (1986) 336-8 (S. *Shennan*).
9743 **Testini** Pasquale, Archeologia cristiana; nozioni generali dalle origini alla fine del secolo VI; propedeutica, topografia cimiteriale, epigrafia, edifici di culto². Bari 1980, Edipuglia. xviii-840 p.; 435 fig.; 3 pl. – ᴿSalesianum 48 (1986) 408s (R. *Della Casa*).
9744 *Trebolle Barrera* Julio, Arqueología y Biblia en los últimos veinte años [< IglViva]: RBibArg 48 (1986) 175-9.
9745 a) *Trigger* Bruce T., Prospects for a world archaeology; – b) *Doran* Jim, Formal methods and archaeological theory; a perspective: WoArch 18 (1986) 1-20 / 21-37.
9746 *Yamauchi* E. M., The proofs, problems and promises of biblical archaeology: EvRT 9 (1985) 117-138 [OTAbs 10,120].

T1.2 **Musea, organismi, expositiones.**

9747 *Amiet* Pierre, Jordanie, la voie royale; 9000 ans d'art [musée du Sénat, Paris]: Archéologia 219 (1986) 14-27; (color.) ill.
9748 L'archéologie allemande au Proche- et Moyen-Orient [Instituts: B Gö Mü Tü Köln Mainz Saarbrücken; Iraq, Israël, Jordanie, Syrie, Turquie; fouilles]: LIAO 8 (1986) 15-69, mostly in English.
9749 **Ashworth** William B., Jesuit science in the age of Galileo: an exhibition of rare books from the history of science collection March 24 - July 31, 1986. Kansas City 1986, Linda Hall Science Library. 31 p. 43 items (ill.).
9749* *Bator* Andrzej, ✆ Egyptian exposition in Warsaw Univ. [1-15. IV. 1985]: PrzOr (1986) 261s.
9750 **Bienkowski** Piotr, *Southworth* Edmund, Egyptian antiquities in the Liverpool museum I. A list of the provenanced objects. Wmr 1986, Ares & P. xxv-107 p., 7 pl. £30 [JNES 46,75]. 0-85668-376-0.
9751 *Bongard-Levin* G. M., *Dandamayev* M. A., ❽ Soviet research on the ancient Orient, 1981-1985: VDI 176 (1986,1) 3-16.

9752 *Boorn* G. Vanden, Treasures from Turkey [exposition Leiden 22.VI-22.IX. 1986]: Akkadica 48 (1986) 40.

9753 **Bothmer** Dietrich von, The Amasis painter and his world; vase-painting in sixth-century B.C. Athens, intr. *Boegehold* Alan L.: Exposition NY Metropolitan Museum 1985, al. Malibu/L 1985, Getty Museum / Thames & H. 246 p.; ill.

9754 **Brunner-Traut** Emma, *Brunner* Helmut, Die ägyptische Sammlung der Universität Tübingen 1981 → 62,a936 ... 1,b467: ᴿJNES 45 (1986) 160s (W. H. *Peck*: admirable).

9755 **Buroh** Knut, *al.*, Hieroglyphenschrift und Totenbuch; die Papyri der ägyptischen Sammlung der Universität Tübingen; Ausstellung und Katalog 18. Tü 1985, Attempto. 103 p. DM 20. – ᴿMundus 22 (1986) 187 (Ingrid *Gamer-Wallert*: really annotated editions of a dozen large papyri, out of Tübingen's 2000 Egyptological pieces already catalogued in 1981).

9756 *Caquot* André, Rapport sur l'activité de l'École Biblique et Archéologique française de Jérusalem pendant l'année 1985-1986: CRAI 519-523. [Athènes 608-621, *Will* E.; Rome 572-588, *Favier* J.].

9757 *Carazzali* Giulia, La terra tra i due fiumi [mostra T 1985, F 1986] – venti anni di archeologia italiana; la Mesopotamia dei tesori: HumBr 41 (1986) 264-7.

9758 *Catling* Hector, The Hellenist school ... 100 years of British contributions to the archaeology of Greece: ILN Arch. 3027 = 274,7054 (1986) p. 82s.

9759 *Caubet* Annie, Exposition, Les Phéniciens et le monde méditerranéen Bru / Luxembourg 1986: LIAO 8 (1986) 103.

9760 **Corteggiani** Jean-Pierre, L'Égypte des Pharaons au Musée du Caire²ʳᵉᵛ [¹1979]. P 1986, Hachette. 192 p.; 120 phot. 2-0101-2297-6.

9761 a) *Curto* Silvio, La storia del Museo Egizio di Torino, da privato a universitario a pubblico; – b) *Montevecchi* Orsolina, La papirologia nella cultura italiana; – c) *Donadoni* Sergio, Egittologia e papirologia: → 546, Egitto 1984/5, 1-8 / 105-122 / 123-132.

9762 a) Da Ebla a Damasco; diecimila anni di archeologia in Siria. Mi 1985, Electa. 369 p. Lit. 30.000. – ᴿCC 137 (1986,1) 504s (G. L. *Prato*). – b) *Gates* Marie-Henriette, From Ebla to Damascus; the archaeology of ancient Syria [exposition LA etc.]: BAR-W 12,3 (1986) 62-67; (color.) ill.; → 1,b516, *Weiss* H.

9763 ᴱ*Desse-Berset* Nathalie, L'archéologie allemande (fédérale) au Proche et Moyen-Orient: LIAO 8 (1986) 13-62.

9764 **Dewachter** Michel, *al.*, La collection égyptienne du Musée Champollion. Figeac 1986, Musée C. 2-906398-00-4 [OIAc Oc87].

9764* *Dewachter* Michel, La première liste connue des antiquités égyptiennes de la Bibliothèque du Roy (1684) [Bibl. nat.]: RÉgp 37 (1986) 164-6.

9765 **Drenkhahn** Rosemarie, Elfenbein im Alten Ägypten; Sonderausstellung zum 20-jährigen Bestehen des Deutschen Elfenbeinmuseums Erbach 6.IX-30.XIII. Erbach 1986, Elfenbeinmseum. 87 p. DM 10 [Mundus 23,94].

9765* *Eitan* Avi [interview with *Shanks* H.], [Israel] Antiquities director confronts problems and controversies [... 'failure to permit scholars access to the Dead Sea Scrolls', p. 2; 'I have now demanded from Père BENOIT, as chief editor ... a detailed report on the progress', p. 37]: BAR-W 12,4 (1986) 30-38.

9766 Excavation opportunities 1986 [for volunteers paying travel cost and $20-$30 per day board]: BAR-W 12,1 (1986) 54-65 [+ 12,2 p. 10, Yarmouth].

9767 **Ferrazzini** Pierre-Alain, photos, Treasures of the Israel Museum, Jerusalem. J 1985, Museum. xii-205 p.; 100 pl. [BAR-W 13/4, 9, H. O. *Thompson*].

9768 **Gordon** Cyrus H., The Philadelphia tradition of Semitics; a century of Near Eastern and Biblical studies at the University of Pennsylvania: SBL BSNAm 13. Atlanta 1986, Scholars. 80 p. $14; sb./pa. $12 [JAAR 55,431]. 1-55540-023-X.

9769 *a*) **Grafman** Rafi, Israel museum guide. J 1983. – *b*) Highlights of archaeology from the Israel museum I. J 1984. 159 p.; 51 photos + 26 color., mostly by N. *Slapak*. – ᴿBAR-W 12,1 (1986) 16s (O. *Borowski*).

9770 **Haarlem** W. M. van, *Lunsingh Scheurleer* R. A., Gids voor de afdeling Egypte, Allard Pierson Museum Amsterdam = PhoenixEOL 32,1 (1986). 121 p.; 72 fig. 90-71347-02-8.

9771 *Hägg* Robin, The Swedish Institute in Athens; report for the academic years 1982-83 and 1983-84: OpAth 16 (1986) 131-5.

9772 **Hodjash** Svetlana, *Berlev* Oleg, The Egyptian reliefs and stelae in the Pushkin Museum of Fine Arts, Moscow. Leningrad 1982, Aurora. 311 p.; 213 phot.

9773 **Homès-Fredericq** Denyse, *Franken* H. J., Pottery and potters, past and present; 7000 years of ceramic art in Jordan: Tübingen Ausstellungskatalog 20. Tü 1986, Attempto. iii-263 p.; ill.

9774 *Jaeger* Bertrand, Pour une meilleure information sur les expositions égyptiennes: GöMiszÄg 89 (1986) 89-94.

9775 Jahresbericht 1985 des Deutschen Archäologischen Instituts [B, R, Athen, Kairo, Istanbul, M...]: ArchAnz (1986) 765-830.

9776 **Jantzen** Ulf, Einhundert Jahre Athener Institut, 1874-1974: DAI Geschichte und Dokumente 10. Mainz 1986, von Zabern. viii-111 p.; 9 pl.

9777 ᴱ**Kákosy** László, *Roccati* Alessandro, La magia in Egitto ai tempi dei faraoni [mostra Milano 1985]. Modena 1985, Panini. 147 p. Lit. 25.000. – ᴿHumBr 41 (1986) 474s (G. *Carazzali*).

9778 **King** Philip J., American archaeology in the Mideast ... ASOR 1983 ⇢ 64,a468 ... 1,b491: ᴿBA 19 (1986) 62s (T. W. *Davis*: reserves); JAmEg 22 (1985) 204s (B. *Brier*: ALBRIGHT and WRIGHT were fundamentalists).

9779 *Lafaurie* Jean, La Revue Numismatique à 150 ans: RNum 28 (1986) 7-50; 11 portr. + pl. 1-2; 2 facsím.

9781 **McDonald** John K., Treasures of the Holy Land; ancient art from the Israel museum: BA 49 (1986) 155-165; ill.

9782 **[Marfoe** Leon] A guide to the Oriental Institute museum. Ch 1982, Univ. xiii-137 p.; 68 fig. $3.75. – ᴿJNES 45 (1986) 59s (P.R.S. *Moorey*).

9783 **Muscarella** O. W., Ladders to heaven [1979 Toronto exhibition] 1981 ⇢ 62,a969* ... 65,a59: ᴿJNES 45 (1986) 60-62 (W. *Farber*).

9784 *a*) **Ornan** Tallay, A man and his land; highlights from the Moshe Dayan collection [exhibition catalogue]. J 1986, Israel Museum. 136 p.; ill. 065-278-047-2. – *b*) [*Shanks* H.], Dayan collection [1986 Israel Museum exposition, Jerusalem] opens amidst controversy: BAR-W 12,4 (1986) 6.8.

9785 **Pietrangeli** Carlo, I musei vaticani; cinque secoli di storia. R 1985, Quasar. 286 p.; 213 fig. Lit. 90.000. – ᴿCC (1986,3) 206s (A. *Ferrua*).

9786 **Pietrangeli** Carlo, La Pontificia Accademia Romana di Archeologia; note storiche: Atti 3/4. R 1983, Bretschneider. 95 p.; 37 fig. 88-7062-536-2.

9786* ᴱ**Quarantelli** Ezio, ᵀ*Haydock* Juliet, *Binns* Míchael [cf. *Invernizzi* A. ⇢ 1,b486] The land between two rivers; twenty years of Italian archaeology in the Middle East; the treasures of Mesopotamia. Torino 1986, Quadrante. xxx-443 p.; color pl. p. 143-200; 295-300. Exhibition catalog + 27 signed articles.

9787 **Sabbahy** Lisa K., Ramses II, the Pharaoh and his time; exhibition catalog, Brigham Young Univ. 25 Oct. 1985 – 5 Apr. 1986. Provo UT 1985. 109 p.; 76 color. phot.

9788 **Saleh** Mohamed, *Sourouzian* Hourig, Die Hauptwerke im Ägyptischen Museum Kairo; offizieller Katalog, Antikendienst Arabische Republik Ägypten. Mainz 1986, von Zabern. 268 p.; 270 color. phot. 3-8053-0640-7 (904-X, Museum ed.).

9788* *Seybold* Irmtraut, Kurze Geschichte der Orientalistik in Graz: → 542, Kulturkontakte 1986, 1-4.

9789 *Sichelen* Laurence Van, La femme au temps des pharaons [exposition Bru, 'nonante-six œuvres du Caire']: Archéologia 210 (1986) 16-25; (color.) ill.

9790 *a*) Treasures of the Holy Land: Ancient Art from the Israel Museum; NY Met 1986, Los Angeles and Houston 1987: ArchNews 14 (Tallahassee 1985) 49-51. – *b*) *Shanks* H., Ancient Israelite art sparse in impressive show at Met [NY, 'Treasures of the Holy Land'; pieces from Israel cannot be attributed to biblical Israelites]: BAR-W 12,6 (1986) 64-68; ill.; – *c*) *Tadmor* Miriam, Treasures of the Holy Land; ancient art from the Israel museum, [exhibition NY Met 1986, then LA; Houston]: Archaeology 39,5 (1986) 60-63.

9791 **Thompson** David L., Mummy portraits in the J. Paul Getty museum [= ²The Artists of the Mummy Portraits ¹1976 → 65,a444 + catalog]. Malibu CA 1982. 70 p.; ill. – ᴿJNES 45 (1986) 301-4 (Lorelei H. *Corcoran*).

9792 **Tyloch** Witold, *a*) Oriental studies in... Poland 1983 → 65,e80; **1**,b513: ᴿOLZ 81 (1986) 444s (Heidi *Stein*). – *b*) ❷ Research and popularization of Ancient Near East culture in Poland: PrzAr (1986) 95-98.

9793 ᴱVercoutter J., Livre du centenaire 1880-1980. Le Caire 1980, IFAO → 61,104: ᴿJAmEg 22 (1987) 211-4 (A. R. *Schulman*).

9794 *Wenning* Robert, Eine römische Grabbüste aus Palästina in Münster: Boreas 9 (1986) 221-5; pl. 37,1s.

9795 *Zahle* Jan, Dansk arkæologi i Middelhavslandene 1973-1984: MusTusc 56 (1984ss) 11-46.

T1.3 *Methodi,* **Science in archeology.**

9796 *Arndt* Allen A., *Coulson* William D. E., The development of a field computer for archaeological use at Naukratis in Egypt: JAmEg 22 (1985) 105-115; 11 fig.

9797 **Barisano** Emilio, Télédétection et archéologie: Rech. Arch. Techniques 14. P 1986, CNRS. 52 p.; 11 phot.; 4 (foldout) maps. F 130. 2-222-03264-4.

9798 *a*) *Beauchesne* F., *Barrandon* J. N., Analyse globale et non destructive des objets archéologiques cuivreux par activation avec des neutrons rapides de cyclotron; – *b*) *Frost* Dominique C., *Chatellier* Jean-Yves, Contribution méthodologique à l'analyse quantitative des propriétés mécaniques des roches fragiles élastiques: RArchéom 10 (1986) 75-85 / 69-74.

9799 *a*) *Bintliff* J. L., Archaeology at the Interface; an historical perspective; – *b*) *Aspinall* A., Hard science; too hard for archaeology? – *c*) *Gaffney* C. F., Explanation at the method and theory interface; – *d*) *Lewthwaite* J. C.,

Archaeologists in academe; an institutional confinement?; – *e) Arnold*
C.J., Archaeology and history; the shades of confrontation and cooperation; – *f) Lloyd* J.A., Why should historians take archaeology
seriously?: → 548*, Archaeology at the Interface 1986, 4-31; 2 fig. /
130-132 / 88-93 / 52-87 / 32-39 / 40-51.

9800 *Bresson* A., Épigraphie grecque et ordinateur; le cas des timbres
amphoriques rhodiens: Épigraphie hispanique, problèmes de méthode et
d'histoire (1984) 241-259 [< RÉG 100,60].

9801 *a) Chapman* Rupert L. III, Excavation techniques and recording systems;
a theoretical study: PEQ 118 (1986) 5-26 [defense of the KENYON system,
called 'scientific', against the objections of the AHARONI system, called
'proto-scientific']. – *b) Rainey* Anson E., Broad lateral exposure is a must
in archaeology [the 'Kenyon approach' is a vestigial appendage of a
misguided era]: BAR-W 11,5 (1985) 22, supporting R. *Boraas* cited 11,1
(1985) 66-68.

9802 ᴱ**Cruwys** E., *Foley* R.A., Teeth and anthropology [Durham conference
1985]: BAR-Int 291. Oxford 1986. 231 p.; 99 fig. [AJA 91,616, D.K.
Charles].

9803 *Deriu* A., *al.*, Provenance and firing techniques of geometric pottery
from Pithekoussai; a Mössbauer investigation: ArchStorAnt 8 (1986)
99-116.

9804 *Dorner* Josef, Einige Bemerkungen über eine neue Methode für die
Bestimmung des Neigungswinkels von Pyramiden: GöMiszÄg 94 (1986)
31-37.

9805 *Dupont* Pierre, Naturwissenschaftliche Bestimmung der archaischen
Keramik Milets: → 569, ᴱ*Müller-Wiener* W., Milet 1980/6, 57-71 [73-80,
Walter-Karydi Elena], pl. 3-5.

9806 *Elliott* Carolyn, *al.*, Petrographic and mineral analyses used in tracing
the provenance of Late Bronze Age and Roman basalt artefacts from
Cyprus: RepCyp (1986) 80-93; 4 fig.; pl. XX-XXIII.

9807 *Fischer* Peter M., The Cyclopean-built wall of the Mycenaean citadel of
Midea; a survey using electronic distance measuring equipment: JField 13
(1986) 499-503; 2 fig.

9808 *Goedicke* Christian, *Slusallek* Klaus, *Kubelik* Martin, Thermolu-
mineszenzdatierungen in der Architekturgeschichte dargestellt an Hand
von Villen im Veneto: Berliner Beiträge zur Archäometrie 6. B 1983,
Staatliche Museen. 185 p. incl. 82 fig.

9809 *Gowlett* J.A.J., *al.*, Radiocarbon dates from the Oxford AMS system;
archaeometry datelist 2-4: Archaeometry 27 (1985) 237-246; 28 (1986)
116-125. 206-221.

9810 *a) Grimanis* A.P., Instrumental neutron activation analysis of ancient
limestone sculptures; – *b) Russodimos* G., The annual rings of forest trees;
structure and uses: → 559, Science 1985/6, 17-20 / 7-10.

9811 *Hancock* R.G.V., A rapid INAA [instrumental neutron activation
analysis] method to characterize Egyptian ceramics: JArchSc 13 (1986)
107-117; 4 fig. (map) [161-170, *Vitali* Vanda, *Franklin* Ursula M.].

9812 *Hedges* Robert E.M., *Gowlett* John A.J., Radiocarbon dating by
accelerator mass spectometry: ScAm 254,1 (1986) 100-107.

9813 ᴱ**Hietala** Harold, Intrasite spatial analysis in archaeology [cf. → 1,b451].
C 1984, Univ. 284 p. £30 – ᴿAnthropos 81 (1986) 330 (R.J. *Lawrence*).

9814 ᴱ**Ingersoll** Daniel, Experimental archeology. NY 1977, Columbia Univ.
xviii-423 p.; ill. 0-231-03658-2. 18 technical articles.

9815 *Kampffmeyer* Ulrich, *al.*, Arcos; ein Computer zeichnet römische

Keramik; die Ergebnisse der Testuntersuchung mit dem ARCOS 1 im Landesamt für Denkmalpflege: Mainzer Zeitschrift 81 (1986) 191-200; 9 fig.

9816 *King* R. H., *al.*, A multivariate analysis of pottery from southwestern Cyprus using neutron activation analysis data: JArchSc 13 (1986) 361-374; 3 fig.

9817 *Levin* Aaron M., Excavation photography; a day on a dig: Archaeology 39,1 (1986) 34-39; color. ill.

9818 *a) Liritzis* Y., Reappraisal of Minoan kilns by thermoluminescence and neutron-activation/XRF analyses; – *b) Laloy* J., *Massard* P., Nouvelle méthode thermique d'étude des foyers préhistoriques: RArchéom 8 (1984) 7-20 / 33-40.

9819 *Maréchal* Joëlle, Microdosages de la matière organique des os [... élimination des polluants pour datation C 14]: LIAO 8 (1986) 71-74.

9820 *a) Ottaway* Barbara S., Is radiocarbon dating obsolescent for archaeologists? – *b) Gabasio* Martine, *al.*, Origins of carbon in potsherds: ➤ 573, 12th Radiocarbon Conference 1985/6, 732-8 / 711-8.

9821 **Parkes** P. A., Current scientific techniques in archaeology. NY 1986, St. Martin's. xi-271 p. $35 [JNES 46,243].

9822 **Poulsgaard Markussen** Erik, Calculus; computers in classical archaeology. Odense 1986, Univ. 15 p.

9823 ᴱ**Rapp** Georgeᴶ, *Gifford* John A., Archaeological geology. NHv 1983, Yale. 435 p.; 136 fig. – ᴿAJA 90 (1986) 348s (K. W. *Butzer*).

9824 **Richards** J. D., *Ryan* N. S., Data processing in archaeology 1985 ➤ 1,b550: ᴿAJA 90 (1986) 476s (Susan *Lukesh*); JArchSc 13 (1986) 201 (C. *Orton*).

9825 **Rottländer** Rolf C. A., Einführung in die naturwissenschaftlichen Methoden in der Archäologie: Arch. Venatoria 6. Tü 1983, Archaeologia Venatoria. vii-604 p.; 93 fig.

9826 *Schvoerer* M., *al.*, Datation des céramiques par thermoluminescence...: ➤ 558, ᶠ*Hackens* T., Datations 1981/4, 125-139 (–201); 13 fig.

9827 *Witte* Reinhard, Einige Fragen zur Zusammenarbeit von Altertums- und Naturwissenschaften: Klio 68 (1986) 285s [on *Maier* Franz G., Altertumswissenschaft und Computer: Xenia 3. Konstanz 1982. Univ. 21 p.].

9828 *Wolff* S. R., *al.*, Classical and Hellenistic black glaze ware in the Mediterranean; a study by epithermal neutron activation analysis: JArchSc 13 (1986) 245-259.

9829 *Yellin* J., *Dothan* Trude, *Gould* Bonnie, The provenience of beerbottles from Deir el-Balah; a study by neutron activation analysis: IsrEJ 36 (1986) 68-76.

T1.4 *Exploratores* – **Excavators, pioneers.**

9830 *a)* **Blinderman** Charles, The Piltdown inquest. Buffalo 1982, Prometheus. 261 p.; ill. $23. [Antiquity 61, 423]; – *b) Costello* Peter, The Piltdown hoax: beyond the [John T.] HEWITT connection [he in 1952 confessed the responsibility]: Antiquity 60 (1986) 145-7 [cf. 59s, *Daniel* G., from readers' letters].

9831 *Clark* J. Desmond, [African prehistory] Archaeological retrospect 10: Antiquity 60 (1986) 175-192; pl. XXX-XXXI.

9832 **Daniel** Glyn, [† 1. III. 1987]. memoirs, Some small harvest. L 1986, Thames & H. 448 p.; 53 fig. £13. 0-500-01387-X. [AntiqJ 67, 217. J. *Hopkins*].

9833 *Daxelmüller* Christoph, GASTER, Moses, 17.IX.1856-5.III. 1939: ⇒ 586, EnzMär 5 (1986) 735-9.

9834 **Drower** Margaret S., Flinders PETRIE – a life in archaeology 1985 ⇒ 1,b564: ᴿAntiquity 60 (1986) 66s (D. *Jeffreys*) & 2s (G. *Daniel*); PEQ 118 (1986) 73s (P. R. *Ackroyd*).

9834* **Eccles** Robert S., E. R. GOODENOUGH, a personal pilgrimage: BSch-NAm, 1985 ⇒ 1,b565: ᴿTLZ 111 (1986) 740s (G. *Delling* †).

9835 [cover: The Rabbi was a spy] *Fierman* Floyd S., Rabbi Nelson GLUECK – an archaeologist's secret life in the service of the OSS [... helped US map contingency plans against Nazi Rommel...]: BAR-W 12,5 (1986) 18-22 [22, 'the archaeological community can be glad ... that Glueck was a partisan and not an impartial archaeologist']; – BAR-W 13/1,17; 13/3,64.66 (B. *Rothenberg*). protests, 13/5,69, reply.

9836 *Gordon* T. Crouther, Digging in Galilee [1925; *Garstang* J., *Turville-Petre* F.]: PEQ 118 (1986) 81-90; 4 fig.

9837 *Gran-Aymerich* E. & J., *a*) Charles-J. TISSOT [1828-1884]; – *b*) Pierre PARIS [1897-1931] – *c*) L'abbé Henri BREUIL [1877-1961]; – *d*) Léon HEUZEY [1831-1922]: Archéologia (1986) 209,67-72 / 211, 71-74 / 212,69-73 / 213,71-75.

9838 *Gran-Aymerich* Evelyne & J., Les grands archéologues: Georges PERROT 1832-1914, Asie Mineure; Edmond POTTIER 1855-1934, Myrina-Smyrne; Gustave JÉQUIER 1868-c. 1940 Mésopotamie-Egypte; Auguste MARIETTE créateur de l'árchéologie égyptienne: 1821-1881. Archéologia 216 (1986) 73-79 / 217 (1986) 55-59 / 218 (1986) 75-79 / 219 (1986) 71-79; ill.

9838* **Henze** Dietmar, Enzyklopädie der Entdecker und Erforscher der Erde [I. c. 1975] II. K – Lar. Graz 1985, Akademisch. xiv-150 p. DM 66. [Mundus 23,66, H. *Wilhelmy*].

9839 **Kramer** Samuel N., In the world of Sumer; an autobiography. Detroit 1986, Wayne State Univ. 255 p. $37.50. – ᴿAntiquity 60 (1986) 239s (S. *Lloyd*); RelStR 12 (1986) 282 (J. M. *Sasson*: superb).

9840 **Leakey** Mary D., Disclosing the past; an autobiography 1984 ⇒ 1,b574: ᴿArchaeology 39,6 (1986) 68s (Diana C. *Crader*).

9841 *Leighton* Robert, Paolo ORSI (1859-1935) and the prehistory of Sicily: Antiquity 60 (1986) 15-20; pl. VIII.

9842 *Liventhal* Viveca, Christian T. FALBE, naval officer and archaeologist (Carthage): MusTusc 56 (1984s) 360s; dansk 337-360; 3 fig.

9843 **Lloyd** Seton, The interval; a life in Near Eastern archaeology. Faringdon OX 1986, Lloyd Collon. xvi-186 p.; 29 fig. 0-9511828-0-3.

9844 *McGovern* Francis H. & John N., Paul Émile BOTTA [6.XII.1802-29.III.1870]: BA 49 (1986) 109-113.

9845 **Millard** Alan, [discoveries of] Treasures from Bible times 1985 ⇒ 1,b433; 0-85648-587-X: ᴿEvQ 58 (1986) 356-8 (D. *Schibler*).

9846 **Millard** Alan, [Découverte moderne des] Trésors des temps bibliques, ᵀ*Doriath* A., *Rat* S. P 1986, Sator/Cerf. 189 p. F 158. 2-7350-0088-5 / 2-204-02414-7. – ᴿÉTRel 61 (1986) 440s (D. *Lys*: magnifiquement illustré); NRT 108 (1986) 744s (X. *Jacques*: photocomposé à Dole, imprimé à Hong Kong).

9847 *Mulvaney* D. J., [autiobiog.] Archaeological retrospect 9: Antiquity 60 (1986) 96-107; pl. XVII-XVIII.

9848 *Oerter* Wolf B., František LEXA [b. 1876; Begründer der tschechischen Ägyptologie]: Enchoria 14 (1986) 71-78.

9849 *Ryan* Donald P., Giovanni Battista BELZONI [5.XI.1778 – 3.XII.1823; first excavator of Thebes Vallery of the Kings]: BA 49 (1986) 133-144; ill.

9850 SCHLIEMANN: *a*) **Llewelyn-Davis** Melissa, The man behind the mask: BBC 50 minute color video. Ch 1982, Films Inc. $198; rental $90. – ᴿArchaeology 39,6 (1986) 71.74 (J. B. *Rutter*: tasteless character assassination its only goal). – *b*) **Calder** William M.ᴵᴵᴵ, *Traill* David A., Myth, scandal, and history; the Heinrich Schliemann controversy and a first edition of the Mycenaean diary. Detroit 1986, Wayne State. 273 p. [RelStR 13,259, W. A. *McDonald*: mean-spirited and a failure]. – *c*) **Cottrell** Leonard, The Bull of Minos; the discoveries of Schliemann and Evans [1953, ²1971] ᴱ*Levi* Peter. NY 1984, Facts on File. 224 p.; 16 color pl. $20. [BAR-W 13/5, 6-8, F. *Stubbings*]. – *d*) *Traill* David A., Schliemann's mendacity; a question of methodology: AnSt 36 (1986) 91-98. – *e*) **Döhl** Hartmut, Heinrich Schliemann, Mythos und Ärgernis: Bucher Report. Mü 1981, Bucher. 144 p.; 112 fig. [AJA 91,492, C. G. *Thomas*]. – *f*) *Schliemann* Sophia [his wife, 1852-1932], Schliemann's excavations: AncW 14 (1986) 81-85 [86, bibliography added].

9851 *Schmitt* Rüdiger, Dänische Forscher bei der Erschliessung der Achaimeniden-Inschriften: ActOrK 47 (1986) 13-26.
ᴱ**Shanks** Hershel, Who's who in biblical studies and archaeology 1986 ⇒ 650.

9852 *Werber* Gertrud, FRAZER, James George 1.I.1854 - 7.V.1941: ⇒ 586, EnzMär 5 (1986) 220-227.

9853 *Whitteridge* Gordon, Charles MASSON of Afghanistan; explorer, archaeologist, numismatist and intelligence agent. Wmr 1986, Aris & P. ix-181 p.; 14 fig. $35.

9854 *Wickremeratne* L. Ananda, The genesis of an Orientalist; Thomas W. RHYS DAVIDS in Sri Lanka. 1985, South Asia. 246 p. rs 90 (JAAR 54, 207].

9855 *Winstone* H. V. F., Uncovering the ancient world [MARIETTE, SCHLIEMANN; mostly British excavators]. L 1985, Constable. 394 p.; 101 fig. + 16 colour. £15. – ᴿAntiquity 60 (1986) 153 (J. N. *Postgate*).

ᴛ1.5   *Materiae primae* – **metals, glass.**

9856 *Argentum,* SILVER-GOLD: *Kessler* Rainer, Silber und Gold, Gold und Silber; zur Wertschätzung der Edelmetalle im Alten Israel: BibNot 31 (1986) 57-69.

9857 **Clark** Grahame, Symbols of excellence; precious materials as expressions of status. C 1986, Univ. ix-426 p.; 43 fig.

9858 *Yener* K. Aslihan, The archaeometry of silver in Anatolia; the Bolkardağ mining district (Toros near Cilician Gates): AJA 90 (1986) 469-472.

9859 *Cuprum,* COPPER: **Knapp** A. Bernhard, Copper production and divine protection; archaeology, ideology and social complexity on Bronze Age Cyprus: SIMA pocket 42. Göteborg 1986, Åström. vi-161 p.; 4 fig.; 11 pl.; 2 maps.

9859* **Hauptmann** Andreas, 5000 Jahre Kupfer in Oman, I., Die Entwicklung der Kupfermetallurgie vom 3. Jahrtausend bis zur Neuzeit: Museum Veröff. 33. Bochum 1985, Deutsches Bergbau-Museum. 137 p. DM 20. [Mundus 23,235-7, K. *Schippmann*].

9860 **Gale** N. H., *Stos-Gale* Z. A., Oxhide copper ingots in Crete and Cyprus and the Bronze Age metals trade: AnBritAth 81 (1986) 81-100; 9 fig. (maps).

9861 *Kunç* Şeref, Analyses of İkiztepe metal [copper] artifacts: AnSt 36 (1986) 99-101.

9862 *Ferrum,* IRON: *Košak* Silvin, 'The gospel of iron': → 42, FGÜTERBOCK H., Kaniššuwar 1986, 125-135.

9863 **Košak** Silvin, Hittite inventories [basically metals, expanded to gems, textiles ... showing wide range of Hittite trade] 1982 → 63,8253; 65,a161: RJAOS 106 (1986) 569s (C. *Carter:* useful despite blemishes).

9864 *Plumbum,* LEAD: **Nriagu** Jerome O., Lead and lead poisoning in antiquity: Environmental Science and Technology. NY 1983, Wiley. xi-437 p.

9865 *Stannum,* TIN: *Fuchs* Robert, Zinn / Zink: → 591, LexÄg 6,49 (1986) 1409-14 / 1404-9.

9866 *Vitrum,* GLASS: **Barag** D., Catalogue of Western Asiatic glass in the British Museum, I. 1985 → 1,b607: RAntiqJ 66 (1986) 419-421 (A. von *Saldern*).

9867 *Gorelick* L., *Gwinnett* A. J., Further investigation of the method of manufacture of an Ancient Near Eastern cast glass vessel: Iraq 48 (1986) 15-18; pl. I-IV.

9868 **Harden** Donald B., Catalogue of Greek and Roman Glass in the British Museum I, 1981 → 64,a584; 1,b612: RGnomon 58 (1986) 77-79 (Clasina *Isings*).

9869 *a) Harden* Donald B., Study and research on ancient glass; past and future; – *b) Grose* David F., Glass forming methods in classical antiquity; some considerations: JGlass 26 (1984) 9-24 / 25-34; 13 fig.

9870 **Hayes** John W., Greek and Italian black-glass wares and related wares in the Royal Ontario Museum. Toronto 1984, Museum. XI-205 p.; 295 fig. $45. 0-88854-302-6. REchMClas 30 (1986) 198-201 (Helena *Fracchia*).

9871 **Herrmann** C., Formen für ägyptische Fayencen: OBO 60, 1985 → 1,b615: RRStFen 14 (1986) 109s (Lorenza-Ilia *Manfredi*): VT 36 (1986) 512 (J. D. *Ray*).

9872 *Kaczmarczyk* A., *Hedges* R., Ancient Egyptien faience 1983 → 64,a586; 1,b616: RZDPV 102 (1986) 183s (H. G. *Bachmann*).

9873 **Ščapova** Yu. L., Ⓖ Essays on the early history of glassmaking. Moskva 1983, MGU. 199 p. – RSovArch (1986,1) 293-9 (T. I. *Makarova*).

9874 *Seefried* Monique, Glass in Cyprus from the Late Bronze Age to Roman times: RepCyp (1986) 145-9 [187-191, *Grose* D. F., Kourion].

9875 *Taniichi* Takashi, Roman and post-Roman glass vessels depicted in Asian wall paintings: Orient 22 (Tokyo 1986) 128-139; 10 fig.

9876 *Tite* M. S., *Bimson* M., Faience; an investigation of the microstructures associated with the different methods of glazing: Archacometry 28 (1986) 69-78; 9 fig.

T1.6   *Silex,* flints, stone tools.

9877 *Adam* E., Investigating the function of stone artefacts; methods and problems: → 559, Science 1985/6, 3-6.

9878 ECauvin M. C., Traces d'utilisation sur les outils néolithiques du Proche-Orient 1982/4 → 64,709; 1,b624: RJAOS 106 (1986) 362s (Ingolf *Thuesen*).

9879 **Champion** Timothy, *al.,* Prehistoric Europe. L 1984, Academic. 359 p., 197 fig. £14.50. – RPrPrehS 52 (1986) 357s (G. *Renfrew*).

9880 EEricson J. E., *Purdy* B. A., Prehistoric quarries and lithic production: New Directions in Archaeology 1984 → 65,a178: RAJA 90 (1986) 99 (J. *Clark*).

9881 *Fuchs* Robert, Wetzstein [whetstone]: → 591, LexÄg 6,48 (1986) 1240-3.

9882 **Gamble** Clive, The palaeolithic settlement of Europe. C 1986, Univ. xix-471 p.; 80 fig. [AJA 91, 617, L. G. *Straus*].

9883 *Hübner* Ulrich, *Knauf* Ernst E., Ein safaitischer Schlägel vom Ğebel Qurma [3 k E Azraq]: ZDPV 102 (1986) 110-112; pl. 9-11.

9884 *Kaiser* Werner, Vor- und Frühgeschichte: → 591, LexÄg 6,47 (1986) 1069-1076; map.

9885 *Montenat* Christian, Un aperçu des industries préhistoriques du Golfe de Suez et du littoral égyptien de la Mer Rouge: BIFAO 86 (1986) 239-255; pl. XXX-XXXVI.

9886 *Ohel* Milla Y., Milking the stones, or An Acheulean aggregation locality on the Yiron plateau in Upper Galilee: PrPrehS 52 (1986) 247-280; 14 fig.

9887 *Rollefson* Gary O., Chipped stone artifacts from two prehistoric sites from the Moab survey (Worschech): ZDPV 102 (1986) 53-64; 3 fig.

9888 **Roodenberg** J. J., Le mobilier en pierre de Bouqras; utilisation de la pierre dans un site néolithique sur le Moyen Euphrate (Syrie): Ned. Hist. – Arch. 61. Leiden 1986, Nederlands Instituut voor het Nabije Oosten. vii-207 p.; bibliog. 188-201; Eng. p. 202-5; 87 fig. 90-6258-061-0.

9889 **Torrence** Robin, Production and exchange of stone tools; prehistoric obsidian in the Aegean: New Studies in Archaeology. C 1986, Univ. xiv-256 p.; 56 fig. £27.50. 0-521-25266-0 [AntiqJ 67, 138, D. *Roe*].

9890 *Yalçınkaya* Işın, *Minzoni-Déroche* Angela, ❶ Un essai de lexique [turc-français] pour les descriptions techniques des outils en pierre: Belleten 50,196 (1986) 1-8; 13 fig.

T1.7 **Technologia antiqua.**

9891 *a) Argoud* Gilbert, Le lavage du minerai en Grèce; – *b) Vergnieux* Robert, L'eau et les mines d'or dans le désert arabique [i.e. Égyptien]: → 562, Eau/techniques 1981/6, 85-92 / 101-8; 4 fig.

9892 **Balthazar** Judith W., Copper and bronze working in early through middle Bronze Age Cyprus: diss. Pennsylvania, ᴰ*Muhly* J. Ph 1986. 734 p. 87-03177. – DissA 47 (1986s) 3793-A.

9893 **Bogoslovskij** E. S. ❹ Drevne-egipeckie mastera, po materialam iz Der el-Medina. Moskva 1983. 366 p. – ᴿOrAnt 25 (1986) 134-6 (A. *Roccati*).

9893* **Craddock** P. T., *Hughes* M. J., Furnaces and smelting technology in antiquity: OccP 48. L 1985, British Museum. 0-85159-048-1 [OIAc Oc87].

9894 **Fintsi** Yehuda, Woodcraft in the biblical period in the light of comparative material from the Ancient Near East and rabbinic literature: diss. Bar-Ilan, ᴰ*Feliks* Y. TA 1986. – RTLv 18,541.

9895 *a) Fuchs* Robert, Vergolden, versilbern; – *b) Rothenberg* Beno, Verhüttung: → 591, LexÄg 6,47 (1986) 992-5 / 995-8.

9896 **Hill** Donald, A history of engineering in classical and medieval times 1984 → 1,b645: ᴿBSOAS 49 (1986) 627 (K. N. *Chaudhuri*); ClasR 100 (1986) 175s (K. D. *White*).

9897 *Kaptan* Ergun, Early mining in the Tokat province, Anatolia; new finds: Anatolica 13 (1986) 19-30; 9 fig.

9898 ᴱ**Kingery** W. D., Ancient technology to modern science: Ceramics and Civilization 1. Columbus 1985, American Ceramic Soc. 342 p.; ill.; 6 color. pl. [Antiquity 60, 148].

9899 *a) Louis* Pierre, L'eau dans les techniques en Grèce au temps d'Aristote; – *b) Casevitz* Michel, Les utilisations de l'eau dans les techniques en lisant DIODORE de Sicile, STRABON et PAUSANIAS: → 562, Eau/techniques 1981/6, 7-14 / 15-19.

9900 *Lüling* G., Archaische Metallgewinnung und die Idee der Wiedergeburt ['Metall'-Etymologie]: ➤ 188, Sprache 1985 ...

9901 **Oleson** J.P., Greek and Roman mechanical water-lifting devices; the history of a technology 1984 ➤ 64,a196; **1**,b653: ᴿClasR 100 (1986) 176s (K. D. *White*) ParPass 226 (1986) 77-80 (V. *Marone,* E. *Pugliese Carratelli*).

9902 *Provera* Mario, Il lavoro al tempo di Gesù [... arti e mestieri (acquedotti, lavorazione del metallo, ceramica, legno); pastori]: ParVi 31 (1986) 365-9.

9903 *a) Rostoker* William, Ancient techniques for making holes in sheet metal; – *b) Jüngst* Hans, Supposed references to reaction soldering in Alcman, Sophocles and Antiphanes: AJA 90 (1986) 93s; pl. 7/95-98.

9904 *Scheel* Bernd, Studien zum Metallhandwerk im alten Ägypten II. Handlungen und Beischriften in den Bildprogrammen der Gräber des Mittleren Reiches: StAltÄgK 13 (1986) 181-205.

9905 *Strommenger* Eva, Early metal figures from Assur and the technology of metal casting: ➤ 563*, Sumer 42 (1986) 114s, ❹ 51s.

9906 *a) Tite* M.S., Egyptian blue, faience and related materials; technological investigations; – *b) Photos* E., *al.,* Extractive iron metallurgy on Thasos and the East Macedonian mainland: ➤ 559, Science 1985/6 39-41/43-47.

9907 **Van de Mieroop** Marc G., The Early Isin craft archive [875 cuneiform documents]: diss. Yale. NHv 1983. 268 p. 86-22023. – DissA 47 (1986s) 2142-A.

9908 *Verlinden* Colette, La métallurgie minoenne et la fonte à la cire perdue; expérimentations sur un procédé antique: BCH 110 (1986) 44-52.

9908* **Wikander** Orian, Exploitation of water-power or technological stagnation? A reappraisal of the productive forces in the Roman Empire 1984 ➤ **1**,b661: ᴿClasR 100 (1986) 177s (G. E. *Rickman*: a joy to read).

T1.8 Architectura.

9909 **Adam** Jean-Pierre, L'architecture militaire grecque 1982 ➤ 63,a248; 65,a201: P 1982, Picard. 264 p.; 285 phot.; 144 fig. F 500. – ᴿRBg Pg 63 (1985) 225s (P. *Fontaine*).

9910 **Adam** Jean-Pierre, La construction romaine; matériaux et techniques 1984 ➤ 65,a200; **1**,b664: ᴿRÉLat 63 (1985) 388-391 (M. *Royo*).

9911 *Aurenche* Olivier, Mesopotamian architecture from the 7th to the 4th millenia, ᵀ*Anderson-Gerfaud* P.: Sumer 42 (1986) 71-80; 23 fig.; franç. p. 80.

9912 **Braemer** Frank, L'architecture domestique du Levant à l'âge du fer 1982 ➤ 63,a253; 64,a626: ᴿBASOR 264 (1986) 92-94; 1 fig. (Y. *Shiloh*); RBgPg 63 (1985) 224s (M. *Otte*).

9913 ᴱ**Callebat** Louis, *Fleury* Philippe, VITRUVE, De l'architecture X: Coll. Budé. P 1986, BLettres. xlii-304, (double 2-56). 2-251-01309-1.

9914 *Franken* H.J., De puinhopen van het verleden [debris-heaps ➤ **1**,b418; but title continues 'dwellings']: onderzoek naar het wonen in de oudheid met behulp van stratigrafische analyse van ruïneheuvels: Palaestina Antiqua 4. Kampen 1984, Kok. 104 p. *f.* 17,90. – ᴿGerefTTs 86 (1986) 43s (C. *Houtman*).

9915 **Ginouvès** René, *Martin* Roland, Dictionnaire méthodique de l'architecture grecque et romaine, I. Matériaux, techniques de construction et formes du décor: Coll. Éc. Fr. Rome 84. P/R 1985, Boccard/Bretschneider. viii-307 p.; 65 pl. [BMosAnt 11, 374s, P. *Bruneau*].

9916 **Glaser** F., Antike Brunnenbauten in Griechenland 1983 ➤ 65,a219; **1**,b683: ᴿAcArchH 38,1s (1986) 319s (M. *Szabó*).

9917 *Görg* Manfred, Ein weiterer Tonnagel des Ur-Nammu von Ur III [Louvre, provenance unknown, but from a wall; 'he built and named a canal...']: BibNot 34 (1986) 22-24; 3 fig.

9918 *Golvin* Jean-Claude, *Vergnieux* Robert, Étude des techniques de construction dans l'Égypte ancienne, *a*) (III). La décoration des parois (son principe et les équivoques qu'elle peut entraîner en ce qui concerne la datation des édifices): ➤ 97, ᶠMOKHTAR G. 1985, I, 325-338; 4 pl.; – *b*) IV. Le ravalement des parois, la taille des volumes et des moulures: ➤ 18, Mem. DAUMAS F., I (1986) 299-321; 5 pl.

9919 *Green* Yosef, Tiles and bricks in biblical poetry: Dor 15 (1986s) 160-2.

9920 *Gregori* Barbara, 'Three-entrance' city-gates of the Middle Bronze Age in Syria and Palestine: Levant 18 (1986) 83-102; 16 fig.

9921 **Heinrich** Ernst, Die Paläste im alten Mesopotamien 1984 ➤ 65,a222: ᴿGnomon 58 (1986) 167-172 (G. R. H. *Wright*).

9922 **Heinrich** Gerhard F., Palast, Moschee und Wüstenschloss; das Werden der arabischen Kunst 7.-9. Jahrhundert. Graz 1984, Akad. DV. 166 p.; 72 fig.; 64 pl. – ᴿKairos 28 (1986) 120-2 (K.-W. *Tröger*).

9923 **Herzog** Ze'ev, Das Stadtor in Israel und in den Nachbarländern, ᵀ*Fischer* Moshe. Mainz 1986, von Zabern. x-178 p.; 116 fig. DM 148. 3-8053-0572-9. [AntiqJ 67, 195, A. J. *Frendo*].

9924 *Hirschfeld* Yizhar, The rural dwelling house in the Hebron hills and building tradition in Palestine: BAngIsr 6 (1986s) 13-28; 8 fig. (map).

9925 *a*) *Hrouda* Barthel, Bemerkungen zur Architektur des 4. und 3. Jahrtausends v. Chr. in Mesopotamien; – *b*) *Jakob-Rost* Liane, Zur Zikkurrat von Borsippa: ➤ 80*, ᶠOBERHUBER K., Im Bannkreis 1986, 69-78 / 79-82; 2 fig.

9926 **Hult** Gunnel, Bronze Age ashlar masonry in the Eastern Mediterranean; Cyprus, Ugarit, and neighboring regions: SIMA 66, 1983 ➤ 64,a640; 1,b686: ᴿJAOS 106 (1986) 581-4 (B. *Knapp*: material fine, interpretation less).

9927 *Jacobson* David M., Hadrianic architecture and geometry: AJA 90 (1986) 69-85; 14 fig.

9928 **Lackenbacher** Sylvie, Le roi bâtisseur; les récits de construction assyriens 1982 ➤ 63,a270 ... 65,a226: ᴿJAOS 106 (1986) 572s (Cheryl T. *Meltzer*); OLZ 81 (1986) 145s (O. *Tunca*).

9929 **MacDonald** William L., The architecture of the Roman Empire, I. an introductory study² [➤ 64,a646]; II. an urban appraisal: Yale Publications in the History of Art 17/35. NHv 1982/6, Yale Univ. xxi-225 p., 135 fig.; x-316 p., 213 fig., 5 maps, $35 each. [RelStR 13, 349, W. *Coulson*].

9930 **Mango** Cyril, Byzantine architecture. L 1986, Faber & F. 215 p. £13 [ÉtClas 55, 237, A. *Ghéquière*].

9931 *Margueron* Jean, Stratigraphie et architecture de terre: Syria 63 (1986) 257-303; 15 fig.

9932 *Meyers* C., sap 'Türschwelle': ➤ 599, TWAT 5,7s (1986) 898-901.

9933 **Preziosi** Donald, Minoan architectural design; formation and significance [➤ 65,b629]: Approaches to Semiotics 63 [but it is about buildings, not sentences]. Amst 1983, Mouton. xxxi-522 p.; ill. – ᴿAntClas 55 (1986) 558-560 (R. *Laffineur*).

9934 *Reeves* C. N., Two architectural drawings from the Valley of the Kings [ostraca known since 1906 but not recognized as such]: CdÉ 61,121 (1986) 43-49; 4 fig.

9935 *Richardson* Peter, *a*) Law and piety in Herod's architecture: SR 15 (1986) 347-360; – *b*) Religion and architecture; a study in Herod's piety,

power, pomp and pleasure: BCanadB 45 (Ottawa 1985) 3-29 [< NTAbs 31,73].
9936 *Thornton* M. K., Julio-Claudian building programs; eat, drink, and be merry: Historia 35 (1986) 28-44.
9937 **Tunca** Önhan, L'architecture religieuse protodynastique en Mésopotamie: Akkadica Sup 2, 1984 ➤ 1,b705: I. xxii-278 p., 278 fig.; II. 156 p., 200 fig.; RBO 43 (1986) 500-3 (P. R. S. *Moorey*); ZAss 76 (1986) 310-314 (G. R. H. *Wright*).
9938 *Van Beek* Gus W., Arches and vaults in the Ancient Near East: ScAm 257,1 (1987) 96-103.
9939 **Wagner** Peter, Der ägyptische Einfluss auf die phönizische Architektur: Diss. Klas. Arch. 12, 1980 ➤ 61,s291 ... 1,b706: ROLZ 81 (1986) 17-19 (G. *Rühlmann*).
9940 *Walsh* Vicky A., *McDonald* William A., Greek Late Bronze Age domestic architecture; toward a typology of stone masonry: JField 13 (1986) 493-9; 7 fig.
9941 **Wright** G. H. R., Ancient building in South Syria and Palestine 1985 ➤ 1,b709: RHenoch 8 (1986) 399s (J. A. *Soggin*); ZAW 98 (1986) 482 (O. *Kaiser*: Pionierarbeit).

T1.9   *Supellex*; **furniture, objects of daily life.**

9942 **Bresciani** Edda, Vivere nell'Antico Egitto: Archeo Dossier 22. Novara 1986, De Agostini. 66 p.; (color.) ill.
9943 **Cimmino** Franco, Vita quotidiana degli Egizi²ʳᵉᵛ [¹1974]. Mi 1985, Rusconi. 368 p.; ill. Lit. 25.000. 88-18-12019-0. – RLetture 41 (1986) 415-7 (F. *D'Adamo*).
9944 **Coleman** William L., Today's handbook of Bible times and customs 1984 ➤ 1,b714: RBS 143 (1986) 277 (F. D. *Lindsey*).
9945 **Fayer** Carla, Aspetti di vita quotidiana nella Roma arcaica, dalle origini all'età monarchica: Arch 22, 1982 ➤ 63,a185; 64,a559: RRÉLat 63 (1985) 382s (A. *Grandazzi*).
9946 **Hamman** A., Die ersten Christen [La vie quotidienne 1979 ➤ 60,y677], TSchmidt Katharina. Stu 1985, Reclam. 281 p. DM 29,80. – RBiblos 35 (1986) 407 (W. G. *Wieser*).
9947 **Metzger** Martin, Königsthron und Gottesthron; Thronformen und Throndarstellungen in Ägypten und im Vorderen Orient im dritten und zweiten Jahrtausend vor Christus und deren Bedeutung für das Verständnis von Aussagen über den Thron im AT [Hab. Diss. Hamburg 1968]: AOAT 15, 1985 ➤ 1,b720: RSvTKv 62 (1986) 174-7 (T. N. D. *Mettinger*); ZAW 98 (1986) 318 (O. *Kaiser*: seit 1971 im Druck).
9948 a) *Roccati* Alessandro, Il quotidiano degli Egizi attraverso i papiri di Torino; – b) *Curto* Silvio. L'umanesimo nella civiltà egizia; – c) *Pestman* P. W., L'ambiente indigeno nell'età tolemaica visto attraverso i papiri del Museo Egizio di Torino: ➤ 546, Egitto 1984/5, 41-46/61-73/146-161.
9949 **Romant** Bernard, Life in Egypt in ancient times [1978-81], TSmith J. Geneva 1986, Minerva. 143 p.; (color) ill.
9950 **Romer** John, Vita quotidiana nella Valle dei Re, TErnesti Gabriella: Palme. Mi 1986, A. Mondadori. 302 p.; 39 color. fig.; 4 maps.
9951 *Simpson* Elizabeth, *Payton* Robert, Royal wooden furniture from Gordion [west-central Turkey]: Archaeology 39,6 (1986) 40-47; color. ill.
9952 *Songer* Harold S., Anointing with oil; what does it mean?: BibIll 12 (Nv 1986) 32-34 [OTAbs 10,13].

9953 **Stead** Miriam, Egyptian life. L 1986, British Museum. 72 p.; 93 (colour.) fig. + covers. 0-7141-2040-5.
9954 **Thompson** J. A., Handbook of life in Bible times: Master Reference Collection. DG/Leicester 1986, Inter-Varsity. 384 p. $35. 0-87784-949-8 / 0-85110-633-1 [NTAbs 31,129]. – ᴿExpTim 98 (1986s) 196 (C. S. *Rodd*); Furrow 57 (1986) 805 (M. *Neary*).

T2.1   *Res militaris*;   **weapons.**

9955 *Bietak* Manfred, Zu den nubischen Bogenschützen aus Assiut; ein Beitrag zur Geschichte der Ersten Zwischenzeit: ➤ 77, ᶠMOKHTAR G. 1985, I, 87-97; 3 fig.; 4 pl.
9956 *a) Bishop* M. C., The military *fabrica* and the production of arms in the early Principate; – *b) van Driel-Murray* C., The production and supply of military leatherwork in the first and second centuries A.D.; a review of the evidence; – *c) Oldenstein* J., Manufacture and supply of the Roman army with bronze fittings: ➤ 549, Military equipment II (1985) 1-42 / 43-81 / 82-94.
9957 **Bittner** Stefan, Tracht und Bewaffnung des persischen Heeres zur Zeit der Achaimeniden: Interdisziplinäre Wissenschaft 1. Mü 1985, Friedrich. 379 p.; 45 pl.
9958 ᴱ**Chiaramonte** Treré C., Nuovi contributi sulle fortificazioni pompeiane: Acme Quad. Mi 1986, Cisalpino. 113 p., LV pl. – ᴿParPass 227 (1986) 158-160 (S. *De Caro*).
9959 **Dintsis** Petros, Hellenistische Helme: Archaeologica 43. R 1986, Bretschneider. xxi-394 p.; vol. of 83 pl., 14 foldouts, 22 maps.
9960 **Ducrey** Pierre, Warfare in ancient Greece, ᵀ*Lloyd* Janet. NY 1986, Schocken. 315 p.; 170 fig. + 32 color.; 4 maps. $55 [RelStR 13, 348, W. M. *Calder*].
9961 *Garner* Gordon, Siege warfare in Bible times: BurHist 22,1 (1986) 4-13 [OTAbs 10,21].
9962 **Gilliam** J. F., Roman army papers: Mavors Roman Army Researches 2. Amst 1986, Gieben. 471 p.
9963 *Golvin* Jean-Claude, *Reddé* Michel, Quelques recherches récentes sur l'archéologie militaire romaine en Égypte: CRAI (1986) 172-198; 12 fig.
9964 *James* Simon, Part of a Roman helmet from Jerusalem [*Warren* 1870, PEF collection]: PEQ 118 (1986) 109-112; 2 fig.
9965 **Junkelmann** Marcus, Die Legionen des Augustus; der römische Soldat im archäologischen Experiment: KuGAtW 35. Mainz 1986, von Zabern. 313 p.; 80 pl.
9966 **Lazenby** J. F., The Spartan army. Wmr 1985, Aris & P. xiii-210 p.; 13 pl.; 14 maps. £16. – ᴿClasR 100 (1986) 327s (S. *Hodkinson*).
9967 **Lendle** Otto, Texte und Untersuchungen zum technischen Bereich der antiken Poliorketik: Palingenesia 19. Wsb 1983, Steiner. xxii-218 p.; 67 fig. DM 96. – ᴿRBgPg 64 (1986) 167s (L. *DeLannoy*).
9968 **Malbran-Labat** Florence, L'armée et l'organisation militaire de l'Assyrie d'après les lettres des Sargonides trouvées à Ninive: 1982 ➤ 63,a299 ... 1,745: ᴿOrientalia 55 (1986) 89s (G. B. *Lanfranchi*).
9969 *a) Miller* R. *al.*, Experimental approaches to ancient Near Eastern archery; – *b) Raymond* Anan, Experiments in the function and performance of the weighted atlatl [spearthrower]: WoArch 18 (1986) 178-195 / 153-177.
9970 **Ober** Josiah, Fortress Attica; defense of the Athenian land frontier

404-322 B.C.: Mnemosyne Sup. 84. Leiden 1985. xii-243 p.; 8 pl.; 11 maps. *f* 76. – ᴿAJA 90 (1986) 363-5 (M. H. *Munn*).

9971 *a) Paddock* John, Some changes in the manufacture and supply of Roman helmets under the late Republic and early Empire; – *b) Scott* Ian R., First century military daggers and the manufacture and supply of weapons for the Roman army; – *c) Coulston* J. C., Roman archery equipment: ➤ 549, Military equipment II (1985) 142-159/160-213; 2 pl. / 220-366; 47 fig.

9972 *a) Rink* Bernhard, Exercitus romanus, die schlagkräftigste Armee ihrer Zeit; – *b) Brentjes* Burchard, Kriegswesen im Alten Orient: Altertum 32 (1986) 143-151; 8 fig. / 133-142; 9 fig. [177-181 Byzantiner, *Irmscher* Johannes].

9973 **Saddington** D. B., The development of the Roman auxiliary forces from Caesar to Vespasian (49 B.C. – A.D. 79). Harare 1982, Univ. Zimbabwe. 287 p. $40. – ᴿAnt Clas 55 (1986) 528s (Marie-Thérèse *Raepsaet-Charlier*).

9974 **Secunda** Nick, The army of Alexander the Great: Men-at-Arms 1984 ➤ 1,b750: ᴿArchaeology 39,4 (1986) 68s (R. A. *Bauslaugh*: useful on uniforms and equipment, otherwise jargon; there are already 80 volumes in this Men-at-Arms series).

9975 *Shatzman* Israel, The beginning of the Roman defensive system in Judaea: AmJAncH 8 (1983) 130-160; map.

9976 **Spalinger** Anthony J., Aspects of the military documents of the ancient Egyptians: Yale NERes 9, 1983 ➤ 63,a302...1,b751: ᴿJNES 45 (1986) 304s (E. *Cruz-Uribe*).

9977 **Speidel** M. P., Centurions and horesemen of Legio II Traiana: Aegyptus 66 (1986) 163-8.

9978 *a) Tubb* Jonathan N., Some observations on spearheads in Palestine in the Middle and Late Bronze Ages; – *b) Mitchell* T. C., Another Palestinian inscribed arrowhead: ➤ 115, Mem. TUFNELL O., 1985, 189-196; 2 fig. / 136-150; 2 fig.; 3 pl.

9979 **Vidal-Naquet** Pierre, The black hunter [opposite of 'cultivated hoplite']; forms of thought and forms of society in the Greek world, ᵀ*Szegedy-Maszak* Andrew. Baltimore 1986, Johns Hopkins Univ. xv-367 p. $28.50 [RelStR 13, 348, Mary C. *McBay*].

T2.2 **Vehicula.**

9980 *Bagnall* Roger S., The camel, the wagon and the donkey in later Roman Egypt: ➤ 123, ꟳWILLIS W., BASP 20 (1985) 1-6.

9981 *Decker* Wolfgang, Wagen: ➤ 591, LexÄg 6,48 (1986) 1130-5.

9982 **Green** Miranda J., The wheel as a cult-symbol in the Romano-Celtic world with special reference to Gaul and Britain: Coll. Latomus 183. Bru 1984. 408 p.; 85 pl. Fb 2250. – ᴿAntClas 55 (1986) 506-8 (C. *Sterckx*: irritations mineures).

9983 *Hofmann* Ulrich, Zaumzeug: ➤ 591, LexÄg 6,49 (1986) 1355-7; 1 fig.

9984 *Kellermann* D., ᵃ*gālāh* 'Wagen': ➤ 599, TWAT 5,9s (1986) 1062-6.

9985 *Littauer* M. A., *Crouwel* J. H., *a)* The earliest-known three-dimensional evidence for spoked wheels: AJA 90 (1986) 395-8; 1 fig.; pl. 23; – *b)* A near Eastern bridle bit of the second millennium B.C. in New York: Levant 18 (1986) 163-7; 4 fig.; pl. XLII.

9986 *Moorey* P. R. S., The emergence of the light horse-drawn chariot in the Near East c. 2000-1500 B.C: WoArch 18 (1986) 196-215.

9987 *Özgen* Engin, A group of terracotta wagon models from [Sürüç, c. 2000 B.C.; Gaziantep and Adana museums] southeastern Anatolia: AnSt 36 (1986) 165-171; 3 fig.; pl. XV-XVI.

9988 *Schauensee* Maude de, *Dyson* Robert H.[J], Hasanlu horse trappings and Assyrian reliefs: → 122, [F]WILKINSON C., NEArt 1983, 59-77; 25 fig.

9989 *Sherratt* A.G., Two new finds of wooden wheels from later neolithic and Early Bronze Age Europe: OxJArch 5 (1986) 243-8; 2 fig.

9990 *Tappeiner* Margret, Ein Beitrag zu den Wagenzügen auf den Stelen aus Daskyleion: EpAnat 7 (1986) 81-95; 4 fig.; pl. 13-14; ◐ 95.

9990* [E]**Treue** Wilhelm, Achse, Ras und Wagen; fünftausend Jahre Kultur- und Technikgeschichte² [¹1965 plus contributions by 12 other experts]. Gö 1986, Vandenhoeck & R. 412 p., ill. DM 88 [Mundus 23, 123, K. *Kaufhold*].

T2.3 Nautica.

9991 *Amadasi Guzzo* M.G., *Guzzo* P.G., Di Nora, di Eracle gaditano e della più antica navigazione fenicia: [E]*Olmo Lete* G. del, Fenicios 1986, II. 59-68; 69-71, tavole comparative di alfabeti fenici.

9992 *a)* *Amadasi Guzzo* M.G., *Guzzo* P.G., Di Nora di Eracle gaditano e della più antica navigazione fenicia; – *b)* *Gasull* P., Problemática en torno a la ubicación de los asentamientos fenicios en el sur de la Península: AulaOr 4 (1986) 59-71 / 193-202; 3 fig. (mapa, barcos).

9993 *Bass* George F., A Bronze Age shipwreck at Ulu Burun (Kaş) [W Antalya]; 1984 campaign: AJA 90 (1986) 269-296; 34 fig.; pl. 17. [p. 177 → 548].

9994 *Casson* Lionel, Greek and Roman shipbuilding: American Neptune 45 (1985) 10-19 [ClasR 100,171].

9995 *Catling* H.W., The date of the Cape Gelidonya ship and Cypriot bronzework: RepCyp (1986) 68-71.

9996 *Clarke* R.W., The Punic ship – the condition of the conserved timbers, Spring 1984: Mariner's Mirror 71 (1985) 153-6 [AION 45, 710].

9997 *Cohen* Orna, The lifting operaton of the [2000-year-old] Kinneret boat, and some aspects of the conservation: BAnglsr 6 (1986s) 34s; 2 fig. [50-52, summary of Shelley *Wachsmann* lecture].

9998 [E]**Crumlin-Pedersen** Ole, *Vinner* Max, Sailing into the past – the International Ship Replica seminar. Roskilde, Denmark 1986, Viking Ship Museum. 237 p.; ill [IntJNaut 16, 357, P. *Adam*].

9999 *Elayi* J. & A.G., The Aradian pataecus [war-galley figurehead, on coins of Arados on Syrian coast, not Arad in S. Israel]: AmNumM 31 (1986) 1-5.

a1 **Ericsson** C.H., Navis oneraria 1984 → 65,a297; 1,b777: [R]ClasR 100 (1986) 170s (G.E. *Rickman*: muffed); Gnomon 58 (1986) 376s (A. *Göttlicher*).

a2 *Frame* Grant, Some Neo-Babylonian and Persian documents involving boats: OrAnt 25 (1986) 29-42; 43-50 facsim.

a3 *Gabbert* Janice J., Piracy in the early Hellenistic period; a career open to talents: GreeceR 33 (1986) 156-163.

a4 *Galili* E., *Shmueli* E., *Artzy* Michael, Bronze Age ship's cargo of copper and tin: IntJNaut 15 (1986) 25-37; 11 fig.

a5 **Gianfrotta** Piero A., Archeologia subacquea / Il passato sommerso; scoperte di tutti i tempi dal Mediterraneo agli oceani: Archeo Dossier 5/17. Novara 1985s, De Agostini. 66 p. ognuno; (color.) ill.

a6 *Gibbons* D.J.L., *Parker* A.J., The Roman wreck of c. AD 200 at

Plemmirio, near Siracusa (Sicily); interim report: IntJNaut 15 (1986) 267-304; 30 fig.

a7 *a) Hauben* Hans, Another [grain-transport] boat of Kleopatra II?; – *b) Minnen* P. van, A woman *naúklēros* [owner of ship transporting grain]: ZPapEp 66 (1986) 148 / 91s.

a8 **Höckmann** O., Antike Seefahrt: ArchäolBiblioth, 1985 ➤ 1,b795: [R]ClasR 100 (1986) 354 (G. E. *Rickman*: high praise); MünstHand 5,1 (1986) 74-79 (P. *Kracht*).

a9 *Kadry* Ahmed, The solar boat of Cheops: IntJNaut 15 (1986) 123-131; 6 fig.

a10 **Kola** Andrzej, *Wilke* Gerard, ☉ Archeologia podwodna I. Torun 1985, Univ. Kopernika. 284 p.; 122 fig. zł 143. – [R]IntJNaut 15 (1986) 349 (J. *Kirkman*).

a11 *Langa* Pedro, La teología náutica en la catequesis de los Padres: TEspir 30 (1986) 107-117.

a12 *Liberati* Anna Maria, Le naumachie: ArchViva 5/9 (1986) 74-78; ll.

a13 *Linder* Elisha, The Khorsabad wall relief; a Mediterranean seascape [*Albenda* P., Assur 3 (1983)] or river transport of timbers?: JAOS 106 (1986) 273-281.

a14 **Lipke** P., The royal ship of Cheops: BAR-Int. 225, 1984 ➤ 1,b799; £12: [R]Fornvännen 81 (1986) 60s (A. *Fischer*).

a15 **McCaslin** Dan E., Stone anchors in antiquity: SIMA 61, 1980 ➤ 61,s325 ... 64,a720: [R]AnzAltW 39 (1986) 229-231 (S. *Hiller*).

a16 *Manfredini* Arrigo D., Les naviculaires et le naufrage: RIDA 33 (1986) 135-148.

a17 **Meijer** F., History of seafaring in the classical world, [T]*Giles* Norman, *Mulder* Hotze. Beckenham, Kent/NY 1986, Croom Helm/St. Martins. 248 p.; ill. £25 [IntJNaut 16, 184, A. J. *Parker*].

a18 **Morrison** J.S., *Coates* J.F., The Athenian trireme; the history and reconstruction of an ancient Greek warship. C 1986, Univ. xxii-266 p.; 75 fig.; 15 maps. £22.50. 0-521-32202-2 [AntiqJ 67, 159, S. *McGrail*].

a19 *Murray* William R., The symbols on the Athlit ram: ➤ 548, AJA 90 (1986) 192.

a20 *Nardi* Enzo, De urinatoribus; ovvero dei 'sub' [sommozzatori] nell'antichità: AtAcBo mor 73 (1984s) 51-63.

a21 *a) Raban* Avner, The ancient harbours of Israel in biblical times (from the Neolithic period to the end of the Iron Age); – *b) Hohlfelder* Robert L., The building of the Roman harbour at Kenchreai; old technology in a new era; ➤ 571, [E]*Raban* A., Harbours 1983/5, 11-44 / 81-86.

a22 **Reddé** Michel, Mare nostrum; les infrastructures, le dispositif et l'histoire de la marine militaire sous l'Empire Romain: BiblÉcFrAR 260. R 1986, École Française. 737 p.; bibliog. p. 691-704; 73 fig. 2-7283-0114-X.

a23 *Rickman* Geoffrey E., The archaeology and history of Roman ports: ➤ 548, AJA 90 (1986) 200.

a24 *a) Riesner* Rainer, Das Boot vom See Gennesaret: BiKi 41 (1986) 135s; – *b) Mendecki* Norbert, ☉ De navi piscatoria in Genesareth recenter reperta: RuBi 39 (1986) 490-2.

a25 *Rosen* Baruch, An incorrect representation of a sailing boat in the Madaba mosaic: IsrEJ 36 (1986) 97s.

a26 *a) Rougé* Jean, La navigation intérieure dans le Proche Orient antique; – *b) Goyon* Jean-Claude, Transports par voie d'eau et organisation étatique de la vallée du Nil à l'époque pharaonique: ➤ 562, Eau/techniques 1981/6, 39-49 / 51-64; 5 fig.

a27 *Toby* A. Steven, World's first warships [Thera frescoes]; tubs or ocean greyhounds: IntJNaut 15 (1986) 339-346.

a28 *Tooley* A.M.J., An unusual type of model boat: JEA 78 (1986) 189-192.

a29 *Tsalas* H., The construction of a replica of an ancient ship: ➤ 559, Science 1985/6, 53-56.

a30 *Vallespín Gómez* Olga, The [Roma-era] copper wreck (Peco del Cobre): IntJNaut 15 (1986) 305-322; 12 fig.

a31 *Veligianni* Chrissoula, Hypostoloi und Trierarchos auf einer neuen Inschrift aus Amphipolis: ZPapEp 62 (1986) 241-6.

a32 *Werner* Edward K., Montu and the 'Falcon Ships' of the Eighteenth Dynasty: JAmEg 23 (1986) 107-13; 19 fig.

a33 *Wessetzky* V., Über eine besondere Art der Schiff-Fahrt auf dem Nil im Alten Ägypten: Ann. Budapest. class. 9s (1985) 105-110; 4 fig.

a34 **Westerberg** Karin, Cypriote ships: SIMA pocket 22, 1983 ➤ 64,a740 ... 1,b818: ᴿClasR 100 (1986) 162s (Veronica *Tratton-Brown*); RArchéol (1986) 154-6 (A. *Hermary*).

a35 *Worthington* I., I.G. II² 1631, 1632 and Harpalus' ships: ZPapEp 65 (1986) 222-4.

т2.4 *Athletica,* **sport, games.**

a36 *Baldwin* Barry, The sports fans of Rome and Byzantium [< Liverpool Classical Monthly 9 (1984) 28-30]; ➤ 129, Studies 1985, 493-5.

a37 *Bérard* Claude, L'impossible femme athlète: ArchStorAnt 8 (1986) 195-202; pl. 60-62.

a38 **Cavallaro** M. Adele, Spese e spettacoli; aspetti economici-strutturali degli spettacoli nella Roma giulia-claudia: Antiquitas 1/34. Bonn 1984, Habelt. x-286 p.

a39 *Clavel-Lévêque* Monique, L'espace des jeux dans le monde romain; hégémonie, symbolique et pratique sociale: ➤ 574, ANRW 2/16/3 (1986) 2405-2563.

a40 *Dewey* Arthur J., The hymn in the Acts of John; dance as hermeneutic: Semeia 38 (1986 ➤ 8123) 67-80.

a41 *a) Evjen* Harold D., Competitive athletics in ancient Greece; the search for origins and influences; – *b) Rystedt* Eva, The foot-race and other athletic contests in the Mycenaean world; the evidence of the pictorial vases: OpAth 16 (1986) 51-56 / 103-116; 25 fig.

a42 **Gehrke** Hans J., Die Olympischen Spiele im Rahmen des antiken Sports: A U 28,5 (1985) 14-31 [AnzAltW-Did. 12 (1986)1].

a43 **Gryse** Bob De, De spelen van Zeus; mythe en werkelijkheid van de antieke Olympische Spelen. Bru 1982, Elsevier. 168 p.; ill. – ᴿRBgPg 63 (1985) 194s (P. *Salmon*).

a44 **Humphrey** John H., Roman circuses, arenas for chariot racing. L 1986, Batsford. xiv-703 p.; 323 fig. £45. – ᴿGreeceR 33 (1986) 219 (B.A. *Sparkes*).

a45 **Johnston** Robert K., The Christian at play 1983 ➤ 64,a746; 1,b832: ᴿEvQ 58 (1986) 284s (P. *Helm*).

a46 *Katzoff* Ranon, Where did the Greeks of the Roman period practice wrestling?: AJA 90 (1986) 437-440; 1 fig.

a47 *Kyle* Donald G., Non-competition in Homeric sport; spectatorship and status: Stadion 10 (1984) 1-19; franç. 274.

a48 *Lee* Hugh M., The order of the footraces in the ancient Olympic Games: ➤ 548, AJA 90 (1986) 193.

a49 *Millard* Alan, [Terracotta gaming board, pl.1, from Gezer; not 'degenerated Ashtoreth plaque']: BAngIsr 6 (1986s) 46-8 [from lecture-summary; also on *pym*-weight and incense-burners].

a50 **Miller** James, Measures of wisdom; the cosmic dance in classical and Christian antiquity: Visio 1. Toronto 1986, Univ. xiii-652 p., ill. 0-8020-2553-6.

a51 **Olivová** Vera, Sport and games in the ancient world 1984 ➤ 1,b836: ^RStadion 10 (1984) 247-9 (M.B. *Poliakoff*).

a52 *Perpillou-Thomas* Françoise, La panégyrie au gymnase d'Oxyrhynchos (IIe-IVe s. après J.-C.): CdÉ 61 (1986) 303-313.

a53 *Poliakoff* Michael, Deaths in the pan-Hellenic games; addenda et corrigenda: AmJPg [106 (1985) 171-198, *Brophy* R. & M. inadequately clinical in comparison with another known report] 107 (1986) 400-2.

a54 *Pusch* Edgar B., Zwanzig-Felder-Spiel: ➤ 591, LexÄg 6,49 (1986) 1427-9.

a55 **Rieche** Anita, Römische Kinder- und Gesellschaftsspiele. Stu 1984, Ges. für Vor./Frühgesch. 80 p.; 46 fig.

a56 **Scanlon** Thomas F., *a)* Greek and Roman athletics, a bibliography 1984 ➤ 1,b839: ^RClasJ 82 (1986s) 268-271 (H. D. *Evjen*). – *b)* Boxing gloves and the games of Gallienus: AmJPg 107 (1986) 110-4.

a57 *a) Schmidt* Sabine, Mark Aurel und Spectacula; – *b)* Lee Hugh M., Athletics and the bikini girls from Piazza Armerina [Sicily]: Stadion 10 (1984) 21-43 / 45-76; franç. 275s.

a58 *Thompson* James G., The bull-jumping exhibition at Mallia: ArchNews 14 (1985) 1-8; 6 fig.

a59 **Thuillier** Jean-Paul, Les jeux athlétiques dans la civilisation étrusque: B.Ec.Fr.A-Rome 256. R 1985, École Française. 755 p.; 67 fig. [AJA 91, 628, Ingrid *Edlund-Berry*].

a60 **Weiler** I., Der Sport bei den Völkern der alten Welt 1981 ➤ 62,b194 ... 1,b844: ^RAnzAltW 39 (1986) 89-93 (M. *Lämmer*); Stadion 10 (1984) 249-253 (M. B. *Poliakoff*).

a61 **Young** David C., The Olympic myth of Greek amateur athletics. Ch 1985, Ares. xii-202 p. – ^RClasJ 82 (1986s) 268-271 (H. D. *Evjen*).

T2.5 Musica.

a62 *Badalì* Enrico, La musica presso gli Ittiti; un aspetto particolare del culto in onore di divinità: BbbOr 28 (1986) 55-64.

a63 *Baines* John, The stela of Emhab [drum competition]; innovation, tradition, hierarchy: JEA 78 (1986) 41-53; pl. VIII.

a64 **Barker** Andrew, Greek musical writings, I. The musician and his art 1984 ➤ 65,a333; 1,b847: ^RRPLH 60 (1986) 288s (Annie *Bélis*).

a65 **Bélis** Annie, L'aulos phrygien: RArchéol (1986) 21-40; 11 fig.

a66 *Demsky* Aaron, When the priests trumpeted the onset of the Sabbath [Jerusalem Temple-mount inscription 'to the place of trumpeting']: BAR-W 12,6 (1986) 50-52. 72.

a67 **Grözinger** Karl E., Musik und Gesang in der Theologie der frühen jüdischen Literatur 1982 ➤ 63,3079 ... 1,b856: ^ROLZ 81 (1986) 468s (G. *Pfeifer*).

a68 **Haïk-Vantoura** Suzanne, Les 150 psaumes dans leurs mélodies antiques; la musique de la Bible révélée; une notation millénaire décryptée. P 1985, Fond. Roi David. I (ps. 1-75) xlix-407 p.; II (ps. 76-150) p. 408-852. – ^RRÉJ 145 (1986) 127-131 (Denise *Jourdan-Hemmerdinger*).

a69 *Jones* Ivor H., Musical instruments in the Bible I: BTrans 37 (1986) 101-116; 5 fig.

a70 *Kilmer* A. D., *Civil* M., Old Babylonian musical instructions relating to hymnody: JCS 38 (1986) 94-97; facsimiles 98.

a71 *Koitabashi* Matahisa, ❶ Singers in the cuneiform texts from Ugarit: Orient 28,1 (1985) 56-64; Eng. 55s.

a72 *Krapf* Gerhard, Bach's use of the chorale as an agent of exegesis: RelStT 6 (1986) 20-26.

a73 **Kuen** A., Oui à la musique; la musique dans la Bible et dans l'Église. St. Légier 1986, Emmaüs. 110 p. Fs. 11. 2-8287-0031-3 [NTAbs 31, 131].

a74 **Luck** George, Arcana mundi; music and the occult in the Greek and Roman worlds. Baltimore 1985, Johns Hopkins Univ. 395 p. $30; pa. $13 [JAAR 54,400].

a75 **Mizuno** N., ❶ *a*) A history of the music of the Jewish people. Tokyo 1980, Rocco Shuppan. – *b*) The hymns of the Jews: Jerusalem Library. Tokyo 1986, Jerusalem Shūkyō-Bunka Kenkyū-jo. 197 p. Y 1200. 4-900454-08 [? OTAbs 10,96].

a75* *Music* David W., [sic in OTAbs 10 (1986) 9] Musical instruments of the seventh century B.C.: BibIll 12 (Nv 1986) 51-55.

a76 **Paquette** Daniel, L'instrument de musique dans la céramique de la Grèce antique; études d'organologie: Biblioth. S. Reinach 4, 1984 ➤ 65,a345; **1**,b860; 2-7018-0008-0: ᴿAJA 90 (1986) 111 (Jane M. *Snyder*); AntClas 55 (1986) 585-7 (F. *Duysinx*); RArchéol (1986) 170-2 (Annie *Bélis*: accumule les erreurs, les analyses fausses, et les naïvetés ... pourtant utile; *aulós* justement n'est pas 'flûte'); RPLH 60 (1986) 289-291 (Annie *Bélis*).

a77 **Rashid** Subhi A., Musikgeschichte in Bildern 2/2, Mesopotamien. Lp 1984, VEB Deutscher Verlag für Musik. 183 p.; 202 fig.; map. – ᴿBO 43 (1986) 503-7 (Marcelle *Duchesne-Guillemin*); MesopT 21 (1986) 281-4 (A. *Invernizzi*); ZAss 76 (1986) 138-140 (D. O. *Edzard*).

a78 **Rouget** Gilbert, Music and trance; a theory of the relations between music and possession [1980], ᵀwith *Biebuyck* Brunnhilde. Ch 1985, Univ. xix-395 p.; 8 fig. $60; pa. $20 [RelStR 13,46, G. *Yocum*].

a79 *Tutundjian* Christian, A wooden sistrum handle: VAeg 2 (1986) 73-78; 6 fig.

a80 *Weintraub* David, Music and prophecy: Dor 14 (1985s) 94-100.

a81 **Werner** Eric, The sacred bridge, II. The interdependence of liturgy and music in Synagogue and Church during the first millenium 1985 ➤ **1**,6628: ᴿRB 93 (1986) 313 (R. J. *Tournay*).

a82 *West* M. L., The singing of hexameters; evidence from Epidaurus: ZPapEp 63 (1986) 39-46.

a83 *Zav'jalov* V. A., *Meškeris* V. A., Zur Darstellung eines baktrischen Musikanten mit Panflöte: Altertum 32 (1986) 174-6; 1 fig.

a84 **Ziegler** C., Catalogue des instruments de musique égyptiens, Musée du Louvre 1979 ➤ 60,s608; **1**,b871: ᴿJAmEg 22 (1985) 228s (C. C. *Van Siclen*).

T2.6 **Textilia.**

a85 **Biga** M. G., *Milano* L., Testi amministrativi; assegnazioni di tessili (Archivio L 2769): ARET 4, 1984 ➤ 65,a354: ᴿBO 43 (1986) 428-436 (H. *Waetzoldt*).

a86 *Brenner* Athalya, 'White' textiles in biblical Hebrew and mishnaic Hebrew: HebAnR 4 (1980) 39-44 [OTAbs 10,125].

a87 *Daniel* R.W., Two rare words [1. *gynaikyphē* 'woman-woven' rather than 'Frauen-Weiberei']: ZPapEp 66 (1986) 59s.

a88 *Deblauwe* Francis, Female figurines with head-shawl from Tell Halaf: OrLovPer 17 (1986) 275-9.

a89 *a) del Francia* Loretta, Tissus coptes d'Antinoé à Florence; – *b) Rutschowscaya* M.H., Le matériel du tisserand égyptien d'après les collections du Musée du Louvre; – *c) Nauerth* Claudia, Bemerkungen zum koptischen Josef: RSO 58 (1984) 55-83 / 153-178 / 135-9.

a90 *Egger* Gerhart, Ein spätantikes Bildnis auf einem koptischen Textil: ➤ 52, ᶠKENNER H. 1982, 112-6.

a91 *Gauthier* Philippe, Les chlamydes et l'entretien des éphèbes athéniens; remarques sur le décret de 204/3: Chiron 15 (1985) 149-163.

a92 **Gourlay** Yvon J.-L., Les sparteries [basket-weaving] de Deir el-Médineh, XVIIIᵉ-XXᵉ dynasties, 1. Techniques; 2. Objets: Documents de Fouilles 17,1s. Le Caire 1981, IFAO. viii-94 p., 152 fig., 40 pl.; vi-170 p., 22 pl. – ᴿJAmEg 22 (1985) 215s (D.P. *Ryan*); OLZ 81 (1986) 19s (N. *Driskell, M. Stafford*).

a93 *Hagemann* Sabine, Webstuhl: ➤ 591, LexÄg 6,48 (1986) 1160s; 3 fig.

a94 **Hall** Rosalind, Egyptian textiles: Shire Egyptology. Aylesbury 1986, Shire. 72 p. £2.50. 0-85263-800-0 [BO 43,707]. – ᴿJAmEg 23 (1986) 224 (R.D. *Bianchi*).

a95 *Kakovkin* A., ❻ Two Coptic textiles with patriarch Joseph: SGErm 50 (1985) 43s; 4 fig.

a96 *Knauer* Elfriede R., Ex oriente vestimenta; trachtgeschichtliche Beobachtungen zu Ärmelmantel und Ärmeljacke: ➤ 574, ANRW 2,12,3 (1985) 578-741; 22 fig.; XXXIV pl.

a97 *Malul* Meir, 'Sissiktu' and 'sikku' [garment] – their meaning and function: BO 43 (1986) 20-36.

a98 *a) Milla* H., Greek clothing regulations; sacred and profane ? – *b) Culham* Phyllis, 'Again, what meaning lies in colour ! ' : ZPapEp 55 (1984) 255-265 / 64 (1986) 235-245.

a99 **Nelson** Cherilyn N.S., A methodology for examining ancient textiles and its application to VI-XIX century textiles from Akhmim, Egypt: diss. Minnesota. Minneapolis 1986. 332 p. 86-27032. – DissA 47 (1986s) 3089-A.

a100 *Petruso* Karl M., Wool-evaluation at Knossos and Nuzi: Kadmos 25 (1986) 26-37.

a101 *Renner* Dorothee, Die koptischen Textilien in den vatikanischen Museen 1982 ➤ 64,a793; 1,b894: ᴿDLZ 107 (1986) 226-8 (B. *Brentjes*); OLZ 81 (1986) 20-23 (A. *Effenberger*); RivArCr 62 (1986) 409-411 (Rossana *Martorelli*).

a102 *Roesch* Paul, L'eau et les textiles; Chorsial de Béotie: ➤ 562, Eau/techniques 1981/6, 93-99; 4 fig.

a103 **Sollberger** Edmond, Administrative texts chiefly concerning textiles (L. 2752): ARET 8. R 1986, Univ. xii-228 p. XXVI pl. Lit. 75.000.

a104 **Tata** Giovanni, The development of the Egyptian textile industry [Neolithic to Greek]: diss. Utah 1986, ᴰ*Hammond* P. 286 p. 87-03485. – DissA 47 (1986s) 3797-A.

a105 *Thompson* Deborah, *a)* 'Miniaturization' as a design principle in Late Coptic textiles of the Islamic period; observations on the classification of Coptic textiles: JAmEg 22 (1985) 55-71; 15 fig.; – *b)* The evolution of two traditional Coptic tape patterns; further observations on the classification of Coptic textiles: JAmEg 23 (1986) 145-156; 11 fig.

a106 **Tölle-Kastenbein** Renate,   Frühklassische Peplosfiguren; Typen und Repliken: Antike Plastik 20. B 1986, Mann. 88 p.; 72 pl.

a107 *Vogelzang* M.E., *Bekkum* W.J. van,   Meaning and symbolism of clothing in Ancient Near Eastern texts: ➤ 47, ᶠHOSPERS J., Scripta 1986, 265-284.

a108 *Wietheger* Cäcilia,   Ein koptischer 'Josephsstoff' im Gustav-Lübcke-Museum zu Hamm: GöMiszÄg 94 (1986) 75-78; 2 fig.

T2.7   *Ornamenta corporis,* jewelry, mirrors.

a109 *Bell* Martha R.,   A Hittite pendant from Amarna: AJA 90 (1986) 145-151; 3 fig.; pl. 8.

a110 *Börker-Klähn* Jutta, *Krafzik* Ute,   Zur Bedeutung der Aufsätze aus Alaca Höyük: WeltOr 17 (1986) 47-60; 10 fig.

a111 *Buchholz* Hans-Günter,   Spätbronzezeitliche Ohrringe Zyperns in Gestalt von Rinderköpfen und ihr Auftreten in Griechenland: AcPraeh 18 (1986) 117-155; 27 fig.

a112 **Caner** Ertuğrul,   Fibeln in Anatolien I: Praeh. Bronzefunde 14/8, 1983 ➤ 64,a796; 1,b904:   ᴿBO 43 (1986) 194-201 (O. W. *Muscarella*); PraehZ 61 (1986) 218-220 (R. M. *Boehmer*).

a113 *Curtis* John,   Late Assyrian jewellery from Ur: ➤ 563*, Sumer 42 (1986) 149-154.

a114 **Deppert-Lippitz** Barbara,   Griechischer Goldschmuck: Kulturgeschichte der antiken Welt 27.   Mainz 1985, von Zabern. 322 p.; 225 fig.

a115 **Fellmann** Berthold,   Frühe olympische Gürtelschmuckscheiben aus Bronze: Olympische Forschungen 16. B 1984, de Gruyter. xi-128 p.; 32 fig.; 49 pl. 3-11-009729-X. - ᴿBabesch 61 (1986) 230s (M. *Stoop*).

a116 **McGovern** Patrick E.,   Late Bronze Palestinian pendants; innovation in a cosmopolitan age: JStOT/ASOR Mon. 1. Sheffield 1985, JStOT. xx-184 p.; 79 fig.; 25 pl. [JNES 46,77].

a117 *Madl* H.,   *ādāh* 'schmücken': ➤ 599, TWAT 5,9s (1986) 1074-9.

a118 *Mayer-Opificius* Ruth,   Schmuck als Schutz [it means amulets, though some of the pins look rather lethal]: AntWelt 17,3 (1986) 27-30; 6 fig.

a119 *Myśliwiec* Karol,   Quelques remarques sur les couronnes à plumes de Thoutmosis III: ➤ 77, ᶠMOKHTAR G. 1985, II, 149-159; 5 fig.; VI pl.

a120 **Zazoff** P.,   Die antiken Gemmen 1983 ➤ 65,a379; 1,b920:   ᴿGGA 238 (1986) 165-190 (Marie-Louise *Vollenweider*).

T2.8   **Utensilia.**

a121 *Altenmüller* Hartwig,   Ein Zaubermesser des Mittleren Reiches: StA-HÄgK 13 (1986) 1-27; 8 fig.; pl. 1-4.

a122 **Cain** H.-U.,   Römische Marmorkandelaber [Diss. Mü]: Hell.-kais. Skulptur 7, 1985 ➤ 1,b926:   ᴿClasR 100 (1986) 349s (R. *Ling*).

a123 *Clamer* Christa,   The Dayan collection; the [NK Egypt] stone vessels: IsrMusJ 5 (1986) 19-36; ill.

a124 *Cotterell* B., *al.,*   Ancient Egyptian water-clocks; a reappraisal: JArchSc 13 (1986) 31-50; 14 fig.

a125 *Diethart* Johannes M.,   Neue Papyri zur Realienkunde [Haushaltsgeräte, Behälter, Kleidung]: ZPapEp 64 (1986) 75-81.

a126 *Doyen* J.-M.,   L'outillage en os des sites de Tell Abou Danné et d'Oumm el-Marra (campagnes 1975-1983); quelques aspects de l'artisanat en Syrie du nord du IIIᵉᵐᵉ au Iᵉʳ millénaire: Akkadica 47 (1986) 30-75; ill.

a127 *Fullerton* Mark D., The archaistic perirrhanteria [ritual basins] of Attica: Hesperia 55 (1986) 207-217; pl. 41-44.

a128 *Gauthier* Marie-Madeleine, Objets d'art du métal en Terre Sainte [coupe de Resafa]: Bull. Antiquaires (1984) 177-184.

a129 **Gershuny** Lilly, Bronze vessels from Israel and Jordan: Prähistorische Bronzefunde 2/6, 1985 ⇒ 1,b933: ᴿAnthropos 81 (1988) 719 (Alexandra *Aredeleanu-Jansen*).

a130 *Gevaryahu* Haim M.I., *Luaḥ seper*; [Ezek 37,16...]; wood tablets as writing material in the Bible: ⇒ 377*a*, IOSOT summaries (1986) 43.

a131 **Hengel** M., Achilleus in Jerusalem [Messingkanne] 1982 ⇒ 63,a467; 65,a774: ᴿZDPV 102 (1986) 180-2 (Anneliese *Kossatz-Deissmann*).

a132 *Hoddinott* Ralph, The Rogozen treasure [500 B.C. Achemenid-style Thracian glass *phialai* and jugs found in Bulgaria 1985]: ILN 274, 7061 (1986) 'Archaeology 3032', 56s; ill.

a132* *Howes Smith* P.H.G., A study of the 9th-7th century metal bowls from Western Asia: IrAnt 21 (1986) 1-88; 5 fig.; 4 pl.

a133 *Kaplony* Peter, Zepter: ⇒ 591, LexÄg 6,49 (1986) 1373-89.

a133* *Lang* J.R.S., al, Bronze bowls with handles from Nimrud – a note [atomic absorption spectometry]: OxJArch 5 (1986) 109-117.

a134 *Khalil* Lutfi A., A bronze caryatid censer from Amman: Levant 18 (1986) 103-110; 2 fig.; pl. XVI-XVII.

a135 *Malamat* Avraham, 'Doorbells' at Mari; a textual-archaeological correlation: ⇒ 545*, Rencontre 30ᵉ 1983/6, 160-7.

a136 *Ritner* Robert K., Unrecognized decorated linch pins from the tombs of Tutankhamon and Amenhotep II: GöMiszÄg 94 (1986) 53-55; 5 fig.

T2.9 *Pondera;* **Weights and Measures**

a137 *Altenmüller* Hartwig, Zum Abwiegen von Metall im Alten Reich und zur Redewendung '*jw.s m jnr*': GöMiszÄg 89 (1986) 7-14: 'It is on the stone', i.e. the scale shows that the weighed metal does not amount to the weight-standard used.

a138 **Basnizki** L. (1885-1957), ᴱ*Glaser* Werner, Der jüdische Kalender; Entstehung und Aufbau. Fra 1986 = 1938, Athenäum. 69 p. DM 19,80. 3-7610-0387-0 [BL 87, 101, S. C. *Reif:* 'charming'].

a139 *Galaz* M. Teresa, Algunos problemas de métrica griega; ritmo, pies, metros: Faventia 7,1 (1985) 21-32.

a140 *Gatier* Pierre-Louis, Deux poids syriens de la fondation Piéridès: Syria 63 (1986) 375-8; 4 fig.

a141 *a) Holland* Lionel, Islamic bronze weights from Caesarea Maritima; – *b) Kolbas* J., Mamlūk bronze weights; an extinct species?: AmNumM 31 (1986) 171-201; pl. 33-36 / 203-6; 2 fig.

a142 *Hori* Akira, A consideration of the Ancient Near Eastern systems of weight: Orient 22 (1986) 16-32; 4 fig.; photos p. 3-36.

a144 **Manns** Frédéric, Some weights of the Hellenistic, Roman and Byzantine periods, ᵀ*Kloetzli* Godfrey: SBF Museum 7. J 1984, SBF. 48 p.; 13 pl.

a145 *Martin-Pardey* Eva, Waage [balance-scale]: ⇒ 591, LexÄg 6,47 (1986) 1081-6.

a147 *Naegele* J., Translation of *talanton* 'talent': BTrans [1978, 237, *Fry* E.] 37 (1986) 441-3.

a148 *Parise* Nicola F., *a)* Unità ponderali egee: ⇒ 564, Traffici micenei 1984/6, 303-314; – *b)* Pesi egei per la lana: ParPass 227 (1986) 81-88.

a149 **Richardson** William F., Numbering and measuring in the classical

world. Auckland 1985, St. Leonards. 62 p. $11 pa. – ᴿÉchMClas 30 (1986) 211s (Patricia A. *Clark*).
a150 *Stronk* J.P. Linear A liquid measure; a contribution: Talanta 14s (1982s) 27 only.
a151 *Zaccagnini* Carlo, The Dilmun standard and its relationship with Indus and Near Eastern weight systems: Iraq [44 (1982) 137, *Roaf* M.] 48 (1986) 19-23.

T3.1 **Ars,** *motiva, pictura.*

a152 *Badawy* Alexandre, L'art copte; les influences orientales (Perse et Syrie): RSO 58 (1984) 13-48; 32 fig.
a153 **Barbet** Alix, La peinture murale romaine; → 1,b971; les styles décoratifs pompéiens. P 1985, Picard. 285 p.; 200 fig.; 8 color. pl. F 480. – ᴿBMosAnt 11 (1986) 367-370 (Nicole *Blanc*); ClasR 100 (1986) 346s (R. *Ling*); RBgPg 64 (1986) 86-91 (C. *Delplace*).
a154 *Barnett* R.D. †, Six fingers in art and archaeology: BAngIsr 6 (1986s) 5-12; 3 fig.
a155 **Bernard** B., De Bijbel in de schilderkunst 1984 → 1,b975; also Kampen 1985, Kok: ᴿCollatVl 16 (1986) 118s (Agnes *Pas*).
a156 **Bernard** Bruce, The Bible and its painters; intr. *Gowing* Laurence, 1983 → 1,b976: ᴿBR 2,2 (1986) 14-17; 2 color fig. (Jane *Dillenberger*).
a157 **Boardman** John [ᵀ*Koenigs* Wolf], *Dörig* José, *al.*, Die griechische Kunst. Mü 1984 [= 1966], Hirmer. 240 p.; 215 fig.; 304 phot. + LII color. 3-7774-3690-9.
a158 **Boespflug** François, Le Credo de Sienne [Nicée-Constantinople en collage de bois XVᵉ siècle]. P 1985, Cerf. 52 p.; color. pl. (Loose H.) F 97. 2-204-02406-6. – ᴿÉTRel 61 (1986) 134 (D. *Lys*).
a159 *Bourguet* Pierre du, L'origine du geste de protection divine du groupe peint copte du Christ et d'Apa Mena: → 77, ᶠMOKHTAR G. 1985, I, 105-8; 2 fig.; 2 pl.
a160 **Bouyet** Louis, Vérité des icônes; la tradition iconographique chrétienne et sa signification. Limoges 1984, Droguet & A. 144 p. – ᴿRThom 86 (1986) 166s (J.-P. *Rey*: courageux; 'nous conseillons aux [non-initiés] de commencer par «lire» [les titres? ou les livres mêmes? de] la très bonne bibliographie').
a161 *Brunner-Traut* Emma, Vorderansicht [humans and animals are almost always shown in profile in Egyptian art, except for (sometimes) the head (and chest); exceptions mostly 'pre-canonical']: → 591, LexÄg 6,47 (1986) 1062-7.
a162 **Bruno** Vincent J., Hellenistic painting techniques; the evidence of the Delos fragments: Columbia Studies in the Classical Tradition 11. Leiden 1986, Brill. viii-66 p.; 2 fig.; 16 colour. pl. [AJA 91, 626, Ann O. *Koloski-Ostrow*].
a163 **Burckhardt** Titus, L'art de l'Islam, langage et signification: La Bibliothèque de l'Islam, Essais. P 1985, Sindbad. 312 p.; 106 color phot. (Michaud R.) - ᴿRThom 86 (1986) 700s (J. *Jomier*).
a164 **Canby** Jeanny V., The child in Hittite iconography: → 71, ᶠMELLINK M., Anatolia 1986, 54-69; 15 fig.
a165 *a)* *Carrière* Paul, Art sacré et mission de l'Église; – *b)* *Schönborn* Christophe, Le Temple comme lieu maternel de l'Église; – *c)* *Berthoud* Émile, L'Art Sacré et son évolution au cours des siècles: EsprV 96 (1986) 609-613 / 613-7 / 618-623.

a166 **Cormack** Robin,   Writing in gold; Byzantine society and its icons.   L
1985, Philip.   270 p.; 100 fig. £15.   0-540-01085-5. – ᴿAntiqJ 66 (1986)
443-5 (Lucy-Anne *Hunt*).

a167 *a)* *D'Amicone* Elvira,   Arte minore nel Museo Egizio di Torino; – *b)*
Leospo Enrichetta,   Un cantiere torinese; la tomba dipinta di Gebelein: ➤
546, Egitto 1984/5, 27-40 / 9-17; 8 piante.

a168 *Davis* Ellen N.,   Youth and age in the Thera frescoes: AJA 90 (1986)
399-406; 1 fig.

a169 *Dijk* Jacobus van,   Wepset [one of the names of the fire-spitting uraeus; in
English]: ➤ 591: LexÄg 6,48 (1986) 1218-20.

a170 **Dillenberger** Jane,   Style and content in Christian art.   L 1986, SCM.
240 p. £10.50.   0-334-02344-0. – ᴿExpTim 98 (1986s) 382s (J. *Bates*).

a171 *Dunbabin* Katherine M.D.,   Sic erimus cuncti ... the skeleton in
Graeco-Roman art [a. at the banquet; b. Trimalchio; c. skull allegory; d.
animated skeleton; e. funerary art; f. conclusion]: JbDAI 101 (1986)
185-255; 59 fig.

a172 ᴱ**Ettinghausen** R.,   *Yarshater* E.,   Highlights of Persian art: Persian Art
Series 1.   Boulder/Leiden 1979, Westview/Brill. xviii-392 p. ƒ156. 0-89158-
295-9. – ᴿBO 43 (1986) 209-211 (K. *Rührdanz*); JRAS (1986) 116s (Fateme
Keshavarz).

a173 *Fehlig* A.,   Königskrone und Horusauge: GöMiszÄg 90 (1986) 11-25.

a174 *Giunchedi* Francesco,   Erotismo [a differenza di pornografia, può essere
inerente all'espressione artistica]: RasT 27 (1986) 401-9.

a175 **Goldman** B.,   The sacred portal, a primary symbol in ancient Judaic art
(1966): Brown Classics in Judaica. Lanham MD 1986, UPA. 215 p.; 30 pl.
$15.75.   0-8191-5269-2 [BL 87,107, N. de *Lange*: not worth reprinting].

a176 **Grabar** André,   Las vías de creación en la iconografía cristiana [Les voies
1979], ᵀ*Díes del Corral* Francisco. M 1985, Alianza.   342 p. –
ᴿScripTPamp 18 (1986) 922-8 (J.A. *Iñiguez*).

a177 **Grinten** F. van der,   *Mennekes* F., Mythos und Bibel ... Gegenwartskunst
1985 ➤ 1,b996: ᴿGeistL 59 (1986) 471 (J. *Sudbrack*).

a178 **Gross** Karl,   Menschenhand und Gotteshand in Antike und Christentum,
ᴱ*Speyer* W. 1985 ➤ 1,b997: ᴿTüTQ 166 (1986) 233s (H.J. *Vogt*).

a179 **Hall** Emma S.,   The Pharaoh smites his enemies; a comparative study:
MüÄgSt 44. Mü 1986, Deutscher Kunstv. xxvi-49 p.; bibliog. p. ix-xxiv;
92 fig. 3-422-00838-1.

a180 **Hannestad** Niels,   Roman art and imperial policy: Jutland Arch.Soc. 19.
Aarhus 1986, Univ. 485 p.; 203 fig., II plans.   87-7288-043-0.

a181 *Hatzopoulos* M.B.,   A reconsideration of the Pixodarus affair: Studies in
the history of art 10 (1982) 59-66 [AION 45,712].

a182 **Hebron** Miriam E.,   Statistical studies of the iconography of the dragon
in biblical texts of the 13th and 14th centuries 1985 ➤ 1,d2; iv-60 p.; ill.
£4: ᴿRB 93 (1986) 137 (F. *Langlamet*).

a183 **Hellemo** Geir,   Kristus på keisertronen; en undersøkelse av apsi-
deutsmykning og katekeser fra det 4. århundre med særligt vekt på
eschatologiproblemet: diss. Oslo, 1985. – NorTTs 87 (1986) 40.

a184 **Himmelmann** N.,   Alexandria und der Realismus in der griechischen
Kunst 1983 ➤ 65,a417; 1,d5: ᴿGymnasium 93 (1986) 330-2 (E. *Pochmarski*).

a185 *Holmes* Y.L.,   Syncretism in Christian Coptic art [< Symposium
Jerusalem 1982]: ➤ 349*, ᴱ*Groll* S., Papers 2 (1985) 83-96.

a186 **Hurwit** Jeffrey M.,   The art and culture of early Greece, 1100-480 B.C.
Ithaca NY 1985, Cornell Univ. 367 p.; 154 fig. $49.50. – ᴿAJA 90 (1986)

485-7 (R.R. *Holloway*); RelStR 12 (1986) 289 (W.D.E. *Coulson*: not for teachers or students).

a187 **James** T.G.H., Egyptian painting and drawing in the British Museum. L 1985, Museum. 71 p.; 84 fig.

a188 *Kilström* B.I., Bibel och liturgi i medeltida kyrkokonst: Kyrkohistoriskårsskrift (U 1985) 53-60 [RHE 82,485].

a189 *Kühnel* Bianca, Likeness and vision; loca sancta tradition and apocalyptic inspiration in Christian medieval imagery: IsrMusJ 5 (1986) 57-66; 12 fig.

a190 **Lalouette** Claire, L'art égyptien: Que sais-je, Nº 1909, 1981 ➤ 62,a199 [Nº 1934?]: ᴿCdÉ 61 (1986) 247s (Constant De *Wit*).

a191 **Leroy** Jules, Les peintures des couvents du Ouadi Natroun: IFAO Peinture murale chez les Coptes 2 / Publ. 581, 1982 ➤ 63,a471; 149 pl.: ᴿBO 43 (1986) 426-8 (P. van *Moorsel*); Orientalia 55 (1986) 197-9 (H. *Quecke*).

a192 *Lipiński* Edward, The Syro-Palestinian iconography of woman and goddess [*Winter* U. 1983]: IsrEJ 36 (1986) 87-96.

a193 **Magall** M., Kleine Geschichte der jüdischen Kunst: Du Mont TB 144, 1984 ➤ 1,d19; 129 fig.; DM 18,80: ᴿHenoch 8 (1986) 112s (G. *Tamani*).

a194 *Maser* Peter, Christliche Kunst: ➤ 587, EvKL 1 (1986) 696-708.

a195 **Meer** Fritz van der, Die Ursprünge christlicher Kunst, ᵀStoks Franz. FrB 1982, Herder. 224 p.; 49 pl. + 47 color. – ᴿRHE 81 (1986) 135-7 (Renate *Pillinger*).

a196 **Miles** Margaret, Image as insight; visual understanding in Western Christianity [centrality of pictures, sculpture, architecture in its development]. Boston 1985, Beacon. xiii-200 p.; 22 fig. $25. – ᴿTS 47 (1986) 732-4 [Diane *Apostolos-Cappadona*: her visual samples annoying].

a197 *Monloubou* L., La Bible et l'image: EsprVie 96 (1986) 715-9.

a198 *Müller* Maya, Zum Werkverfahren an thebanischen Grabwänden des Neuen Reiches: StAltÄgK 13 (1986) 149-164; 4 fig.; pl. 13-18.

a199 *Onasch* Konrad, Recht und Grenzen einer Ikonensemiotik: TLZ 111 (1986) 241-258.

a200 *Ovadiah* Asher, Art of ancient synagogues in Israel: Gerión 4 (1986) 111-127.

a201 **Pfeiffer** Heinrich, Gottes Wort im Bild; Christusdarstellungen in der Kunst. Mü/Wu 1986, Neue Stadt / Brockhaus. 104 p.; 83 (color.) fig. DM 68. 3-87996-149-2 / Wu 3-417-24308-4. – ᴿGeistL 59 (1986) 469s (J. *Sudbrack*).

a202 *Pietrzykowski* Michał, The origins of the frontal convention in the arts of the Near East: Berytus 33 (1985) 55-59; fig. 1-11 in 34 (1986) 135-8.

a203 *Plazaola* Juan, Influjo de la iconología del Seudo-Dionisio en la iconografia medieval: EstE 61 (1986) 151-171.

a204 **Pollitt** J.J., Art in the Hellenistic age. C 1986, Univ. xiii-329 p.; bibliog. p. 293-301; 300 fig. £15. 0-521-27672-1. [ÉtClas 55, 115, A. *Wankenne*].

a205 *Quacquarelli* Antonio, La lettera cristologica (gammadia), I. Nell'iconografia dei primi secoli: VetChr 23 (1986) 5-19; 11 fig.

a206 *Rassart-Debergh* Marguerite, Les grands thèmes de la peinture kelliote, ses sources d'inspiration, sa place dans la peinture copte antérieure au Xᵉ siècle: ➤ 551*, Kellia 1984/6, 183-196.

a207 **Reinach** A., Textes grecs et latins relatifs à l'histoire de la peinture ancienne ('Recueil Milliet') [1921] ²*Rouveret* A.: Deucalion. P 1985, Macula. xxiii-461 p. – ᴿRÉLat 63 (1985) 390s (M. *Royo*).

Revel-Neher Élisabeth, L'arche d'alliance dans l'art juif et chrétien du second au dixième siècles; le signe de la rencontre 1984 ➤ 1873.

a209 **Robins** Gay, Egyptian painting and relief: Shire Egyptology. Aylesbury 1986, Shire. 64 p.; 56 fig.; map. £2.50. 0-85263-789-6 [BO 43, 706].

a210 **Schiller** Gertrud, Ikonographie der christlichen Kunst, Gü 1981-6, Mohn. I. Leben Jesu 1966 ³1981; 484 p.; 585 fig. – II. Passion 1966 ²1983; 671 p.; 816 fig. – III. Resurrection 1971 ²1986; 604 p.; 721 fig. [IV.1 ...] – IV. 2 Maria 1980; 472 p.; 839 fig. – Register 120 p. 3-579-04135-5; 6-3; 7-1; 9-8.

a211 **Schönborn** Christoph, Die Christus-Ikone²ʳᵉᵛ [¹L'icône du Christ 1976] 1984 ➤ 1,d41: ᴿTLZ 111 (1986) 134-6 (K. *Onasch*); Orpheus 7 (1986) 482-4 (C. *Crimi*); TrierTZ 95 (1986) 247 (E. *Sauser*).

a212 *Schulman* Alan R., The iconographic theme 'Opening of the mouth' on stelae: JAnEg 21 (1984) 169-196; 27 fig.

a213 **Sed-Rajna** Gabrielle, L'art juif: Que sais-je? 1985 ➤ 1,d44: ᴿRÉJ 145 (1986) 181-3 (Sonia *Fellous*).

a214 *Shapiro* Alan, The origins of allegory in Greek art: Boreas 9 (Münster 1986) 4-23; pl. 1-3.

a215 *Singer* Suzanne F., Paper-cuts; an ancient art form glorifies biblical texts: BR 2,2 (1986) 28-35; ill.

a216 *Smulders* A., L'arbre sacré et les animaux fantastiques dans les reliefs d'ivoire phéniciens du premier millénaire: ➤ 553, Cinquième = Akkadica 47 (1986) 81.

a217 **Steinberg** Leo, The sexuality of Christ in Renaissance art and in modern oblivion 1984 ➤ 1,d48: ᴿBbbOr 28 (1986) 222-4 (T. M. Carlo *Dinis*); CurrTM 13 (1986) 314.316 (T. *Peters*).

a218 *Stock* Alex, 'Wenn du es mit Andacht anschaust'; zum Status des Christusbildes: ZkT 108 (1986) 301-310.

a219 *Stouphi-Poulemenou* Ioanna, ❻ Early Christian portrayals of Christ and the Byzantine Pantocrator: TAth 57 (1986) 793-826; 35 pl.

a220 **Stylianou** A.J., The painted churches of Cyprus; treasures of Byzantine art: Trigraph. Athenai 1985, Leventis. 517 p.; 301 fig. + 10 color. pl. – ᴿCahArch 34 (1986) 195-7 (T. *Velmans*).

a221 **Thiel** Josef F., Christliche Kunst in Afrika. B 1984, Reimer. 355 p. DM 88. – ᴿTR 82 (1986) 325 (K. J. *Tossou*).

a222 *Tomandl* Herbert, Die Thronuntersätze vom Amuntempel in Merce und Jebel Barkal; ein ikonographischer Vergleich [... captives]: VAeg 2 (1986) 63-72; 5 fig. [101-111, 8 fig., mit *Hofmann* Inge, Bemerkungen zu einem meroitischen Gefangenentypus].

a223 **Wichelhaus** Manfred, *Stock* Alex, Bildtheologie und Bilddidaktik; Studien zur religösen Bildwelt, 1981 ➤ 63,a502; 3-491-78376-3: ᴿBijdragen 47 (1986) 341s (W. *Tillmans*).

a224 **Wilson** Eva, Ancient Egyptian designs: Pattern Books. L 1986, British Museum. 100 p.; 100 fig. £1.95. 0-7141-8061-0.

a225 *Winter* U., Der 'Lebensbaum' in der altorientalischen Bildsymbolik: ➤ 338*, ᴱ*Schweizer* H., Bäume 1986, 57-88.

T3.2 Sculptura.

a226 **Alexander** Robert L., The sculpture and sculptors of Yazilikaya. Newark DE 1986, Univ. Delaware. 167 p. $29.50 [RelStR 13,256, J. M. *Sasson*).

a227 **Bober** Phyllis P., *Rubinstein* Ruth, (*Woodford* Susan), Renaissance artists and antique sculpture; a handbook of sources. Ox/L 1986 Univ. Press/H. Miller. 522 p.; 203 pl. £45 [ÉtClas 55,238, A. *Ghéquière*].

a228 **Börker-Klähn** Jutta, Altvorderasiatische Bildstelen und vergleichbare Felsreliefs 1982 ⮕ 63,a512 ... 1,d77: ᴿOrientalia 55 (1986) 320-327; 1 fig. (Ursula *Seidl*: zahlreiche Vorschläge).

a229 **Bol** Peter C., Antike Bronzetechnik; Kunst und Handwerk antiker Erzbilder [⮕ 1,d78]: Archäologische Bibliothek. Mü 1985, Beck. 212 p.; 136 fig. – ᴿClasR 100 (1986) 284-6 (M. *Vickers*).

e230 *Callieri* Pierfrancesco, Rilievi funerari palmireni nella collezione Zeri: ArchStorAnt 8 (1986) 223-244; pl. 63-69 [*Vattioni* F., Le iscrizioni, 245-8, pl. 67-69].

a231 **Chadefaud** Catherine, Le statues porte-enseignes de l'Egypte ancienne (1580-1085 av. J.-C.); signification et insertion dans le culte du Ka royal. P 1982, auct. xiii-231 p. £30. 2-903986-00-2. – ᴿJAmEg 22 (1985) 224-6 (C. C. *Van Siclen*); JEA 78 (1986) 216-221 (R. A. *Caminos*: hopeless botch-work).

a232 *Charikov* A. A., ⓖ Specific features of [238 pieces of] stone sculpture of Kazakhstan: SovArch (1986,1) 87-102; 4 fig.; Eng. 102.

a233 **Croissant** Francis, Les protomés féminines archaïques; recherches sur les représentations du visage dans la plastique grecque de 550 à 480 av. J.-C. 1983 ⮕ 1,d79: ᴿAntClas 55 (1986) 576-8 (R. *Laffineur*); RArchéol (1986) 81-88 (B. *Holtzmann*).

a234 *Dolce* Rita, Due testine policrome del Museo del Louvre; in margine alla problematica delle 'maschere' femminili dell'età del Bronzo nell'Asia Anteriore antica: Orientalia 55 (1986) 63-69; p. IV-VII.

a235 **Fehr** Burkhard, Bewegungswesen und Verhaltensideale; physiognomische Deutungsmöglichkeiten der Bewegungsdarstellung an griechischen Statuen des 5. und des 4. Jhs. v. Chr. Bad Bramstedt 1979, Moreland. viii-143 p.; 23 fig. DM 68. 3-7749-2138-5. – ᴿBabesch 61 (1986) 219s (E. M. *Moormann*); Gnomon 58 (1986) 723-9 (A. H. *Borbein*).

a236 **Fittschen** Klaus, *Zanker* Paul, Katalog der römischen Porträts in [Rom], III. Kaiserinnen- und Prinzessinnenbildnisse; Frauenporträts 1983 ⮕ 1, d84: ᴿAJA 90 (1986) 370s (Diana E. E. *Kleiner*); AntClas 55 (1986) 619-624 (J. C. *Balty*); ClasR 100 (1986) 345s (M. A. R. *Colledge*).

a237 *Flourentzos* P., Two Late Bronze faience rhyta from a private collection in Nicosia: Levant 18 (1986) 169; pl. XLIV.

a238 **Fridh-Haneson** Britt Marie, Le manteau symbolique; étude sur les couples votifs en terre cuite assis sous un même manteau 1983 ⮕ 64,a899: ᴿAntClas 55 (1986) 598s (R. *Laffineur*); ClasR 100 (1986) 340s (C. E. *Vafopoulou-Richardson*).

a239 *Gophna* R. al., ⓖ A forgotten stone mask from er-Ram in the land of Benjamin: Qadmoniot 19 (1986) 82s; ill.

a240 *Hallett* C. H., The origins of the classic style in sculpture: JHS 106 (1986) 71-84.

a241 **James** T.G.H., *Davies* W. V., Egyptian sculpture (1983) ⮕ 1,d91: ᴿAncSRes 16 (1986) 56s (E. *Thompson*).

a242 **Kiss** Zsolt, Études sur le portrait impérial romain en Égypte: Travaux d'arch. médit. 23. Wsz 1984, Acad. 204 p.; 270 fig. 83-01-03621-4. – ᴿAntClas 55 (1986) 624-6 (F. *Baratte*); BO 43 (1986) 101-4 (C. *Vermeule*: a heroic book).

a243 **Kleiner** G., ²*Parlasca* K. (*Linfert* A.), Tanagrafiguren; Untersuchungen zur hellenistischen Kunst und Geschichte. B 1984, de Gruyter. xiv-368 p.; 63 pl. DM 198. – ᴿGymnasium 93 (1986) 332-4 (E. *Pochmarski*).

a243* **Kröger** Jens,   Sasanidischer Stuckdekor 1982 ↠ 63,a523; 64,a909: ᴿJNES 45 (1986) 62-64 (Prudence R. *Harper*).

a244 **Leprohon** Ronald J.,   Stelae 1/1, The Early Dynastic period to the Late Middle Kingdom: Corpus Antiquitatum Aegyptiacarum, Boston 2. Mainz 1985, von Zabern.

a246 **Maystre** Charles,   Tabo I, statue en bronze d'un roi méroïtique; Musée National de Khartoum, Inv. 24705: Univ. Genève, Centre Ét. Or. 2. Genève 1986, Georg. 78 p.; 45 fig.; 4 pl. 2-8257-0134-0.

a247 *Menzel* Heinz,   Römische Bronzestatuetten und verwandte Geräte; ein Beitrag zum Stand der Forschung: ↠ 574, ANRW 2,12,3 (1985) 127-169; XXV pl.

a248 **Niemeier** Jörg-Peter,   Kopien und Nachahmungen im Hellenismus; ein Beitrag zum Klassizismus des 2. und frühen 1. Jhs. v. Chr: DissKlasArch 20. Bonn 1985, Habelt. 246 p.; 38 fig. [AJA 91, 624-6, Brunilde S. *Ridgway*].

a249 **Orphanides** Andreas G.,   Bronze Age anthropomorphic figurines in the Cesnola collection at the Metropolitan museum of art: SIMA pocket 20, 1983 ↠ 64,a488.a916: ᴿRArchéol (1986) 156s (A. *Hermary*).

a250 **Orthmann** Winfried,   Iranische Bronzen aus der Sammlung Beitz: Saarbrücker Bei. Alt. K. 37, 1982 ↠ 65,a481: ᴿBO 43 (1986) 798s (Barbara *Malecka-Kaim*).

a251 *Palagia* Olga,   Imitation of Herakles in ruler portraiture; a survey, from Alexander to Maximinus Daza: Boreas 9 (Münster 1986) 137-151; pl. 23.

a252 **Pfrommer** Michael,   Studien zu alexandrinischer und grossgriechischer Toreutik frühhellenistischer Zeit: ArchäolFor 16. B 1986, Mann. 288 p.; 2 fig.; 63 pl. [Mundus 22,313].

a253 *Schäfer* Thomas,   Römische Schlachtenbilder: MadMit 27 (1986) 345-363; pl. 61-66.

a254 **Stewart** H. M.,   Egyptian stelae, reliefs and paintings, 3. The late period 1983 ↠ 1,d118: ᴿJEA 78 (1986) 225-9 (A. *Leahy*).

a255 **Tindel** Raymond,   Gilded figure of Baal: Or. Inst. Featured Object 4. Ch 1986, Univ.

a256 *Tore* Giovanni,   Di un bronzo figurato da Beirut nel Museo Archeologico Nazionale di Cagliari: ↠ 61, ᶠLILLIU G. 1985, 63-69 [one of the little pointed-cap figures of which there are still many in Beirut].

a257 *Touloupa* Evi,   Das bronzene Reiterstandbild des Augustus aus dem nordägäischen Meer: MiDAI-A 101 (1986) 185-205; 9 fig.; pl. 36-45.

a258 **Walker** Susan, *Burnett* Andrew,   *a*) The image of Augustus; Exhibition, L 1981, British Museum. 47 p.; 49 fig.; maps ↠ 62,b339; – *b*) Augustus; Handlist of the Exhibition: Occ. Papers 16. L 1981, British Museum. 64 p. – ᴿJbNumG 34 (1984) 185s (W. *Kuhoff*).

a259 **Walter** Hans,   Die Gestalt der Frau; Bildwerke von 30.000 – 20 v. Chr.; anthropologische Betrachtungen. Stu 1985, Urach. 88 p.; 80 fig.

a260 *Winter* Irene J.,   Eannatum and the 'King of Kiš'?: another look at the Stele of the Vultures and 'cartouches' in early Sumerian art: ZAss 76 (1986) 205-212; 6 fig.

a261 **Wood** Susan,   Roman portrait sculpture 217-260 A.D.: the transformation of an artistic tradition: Columbia Studies in the Classical Tradition 12. Leiden 1986, Brill. 150 p.; 87 fig.; LXIV pl. [AJA 91, 498, Elaine K. *Gazda*]. 90-04-07282-9.

a262 **Wrede** Henning, Die antike Herme: Trierer Beiträge zur Altertumskunde 1. Mainz 1986, von Zabern. ix-96 p. 3-8053-0866-3.

т3.3   *Glyptica*: **stamp and cylinder seals,** scarabs, amulets.

a263 **Aruz** Joan, The Aegean and the Orient in the Neolithic and Bronze Ages; the evidence of stamp and cylinder seals: diss. NYU 1986, ᴰ*Kopcke* G. 1355 p. (5 vol.) 86-26849. – DissA 47 (1986s) 3088-A.

a264 **Avigad** Nahman, [225] Hebrew bullae from the time of Jeremiah; remnants of a burnt archive. J 1986, Israel Expl. Soc.   139 p.; ill. $20 965-221-006-4. – ᴿPhoenixEOL 32,2 (1986) 59s (K. R. *Veenhof*).

a265 *a) Avigad* Nahman, Three ancient seals [Neriyahu the king's son; Tan'el; Shamash'azar]; – *b) Bordreuil* Pierre, A note on the seal of Peqah the armor-bearer, future king of Israel: BA 49 (1986) 51-53 / 54s; ill.

a266 *a) Boardman* John, *Moorey* Roger, The Yunus cemetery group; haematite scarabs; – *b) Amiran* Ruth, Some cult-and-art objects of the EB I period; – *c) Beck* Pirhiya, A new type of female figurine [Aphek]: ➤ 87, ᶠPORADA E., Insight 1986, 35-48; pl. 13-19 / 7-9; 5 fig.; pl. 2-5 / 29-34; pl. 12.

a267 *a) Boehmer* Rainer M., Drei Siegel mit Spiralstabmuster aus Hattusa; – *b) Özgüç* Nimet, Two seal impressions from Kültepe and the Kırık Bayır relief; – *c) Özgüç* Tahsin, Glazed faience objects from Kanish: ➤ 87, ᶠPORADA E., Insight 1986, 49; pl. 20-21 / 197-200; pl. 39-40 / 201-8; 1 fig.; pl. 41-46.

a268 *Bordreuil* Pierre, Charges et fonctions en Syrie-Palestine d'après quelques sceaux ouest-sémitiques du second et du premier millénaire: CRAI (1986) 290-308; 9 fig.

a269 *a) Bordreuil* P., Un cachet moabite du musée biblique de Palma de Mallorca; – *b) Acquaro* E., Motivi iconografici negli scarabei ibicenchi: ➤ 353, ᴱ*Olmo Lete* G. del, Fenicios 1986, II. 119s; 1 fig. / 105-110 [111-8, *Gubel* E.].

a270 *a) Bordreuil* P., Un cachet moabite du musée biblique de Palma de Mallorca; – *b) Acquaro* E., Motivi iconografici negli scarabei ibicenchi; – *c) Gubel* E., The iconography of the Ibiza gem MAI 3650 ['Smiting Baal'] reconsidered: Aula Or 4 (1986) 119s; phot. / 105-110 / 111-118; 4 fig.

a271 **Boysan** Nilüfer, *Marazzi* Massimiliano, *Nowicki* Helmut, Sammlung (hethitisch-)hieroglyphischer Siegel I. Vorarbeiten 1983 ➤ 64,a948; **1**,d133: ᴿOLZ 81 (1986) 147-9 (R. *Lebrun*).

a272 **Brentjes** Burchard, Alte Siegelkunst des Vorderen Orients 1983 ➤ 64,a951: ᴿZDMG 136,3 (1986) 631s (P. *Yule*).

a273 **Buchanan** Briggs †, ᴱ*Moorey* P.R.S., Catalogue of ancient Near Eastern seals in the Ashmolean museum, II. ➤ 65,a503: The prehistoric stamp seals 1984: ᴿBSOAS 49 (1986) 567s (W. G. *Lambert*: prehistoric? includes all third millennium); RArchéol (1986) 153s (J.-L. *Huot*).

a274 *Chanteloup* Jacqueline de, Amulettes représentant la main dans l'Égypte ancienne: VAeg 2,1 (1986) 7-22; 42 fig. p. 9.

a275 **Collon** Dominique, Catalogue of the Western Asiatic seals in the British Museum, Cylinder Seals II, 1982 ➤ 63,a559; 65,a507: ᴿOrientalia 55 (1986) 91s (S. *Mazzoni*).

a276 **Collon** Dominique, Catalogue of the Western Asiatic seals in the British Museum; Cylinder Seals III, Isin-Larsa and Old Babylonian periods. L 1986, British Museum. 243 p.; 48 pl. 0-7141-1120-1.

a277 *a*) *Collon* Dominique, The green jasper cylinder seal workshop [? Byblos]; – *b*) *Kelly-Buccellati* Marilyn, Sealing practices at Terqa; – *c*) *Margueron* Jean-Claude, Une corne sculptée à Émar; – *d*) *Homès-Fredericq* Denyse, Coquillages et glyptique araméenne: ➤ 87, ᶠPORADA E., Insight 1986, 57-63; 24 fig.; map p. 70; pl. 22-23 / 133-142; pl. 27a / 153-8; fig. p. 159; pl. 29 / 111-8; pl. 25.

a278 *a*) *Collon* Dominique, A North Syrian cylinder seal style; evidence of North-South links with 'Ajjul; – *b*) *Tushingham* A. D., A selection of scarabs and scaraboids: ➤ 115, Mem. TUFNELL O., 1985, 57-65; 23 fig. / 197-213; 17 fig.

a279 *Culican* William, *a*) The iconography of some Phoenician seals and seal impressions; – *b*) Melqart representations on Phoenician seals: ➤ 146, Opera 1986, 211-264 [281-311] / 195-210.

a280 **Devauchelle** Didier, Ostraca démotiques du Musée du Louvre, I. Reçus: BiblÉt 92. Le Caire 1983, IFAO. vii-261 p.; 49 p. + 72 pl. ➤ 64,8198; 1,9190: ᴿJAmEg 22 (1985) 208-210 (E. *Cruz-Uribe*).

a281 *Dewachter* Michel, Le scarabée funéraire de Néchao II et deux amulettes inédites du Musée Jacquemart-André: RÉgp 37 (1986) 53-62; 2 fig.; pl. 11-13.

a282 *a*) *Dolce* Rita, Some remarks about a distinctive group of Kassite glyptic art; – *b*) *Amiet* Pierre, Kassites ou Élamites?; – *c*) *Dyson* Robert H.ᴶ, *Harris* Mary V., The archaeological context of cylinder seals excavated on the Iranian plateau: ➤ 87, ᶠPORADA E., Insight 1986, 71-78; pl. 24 / 1-6; 1 fig.; pl. 1 / 79-110; map.

a283 *Elayi* Josette, Le sceau du prêtre Ḥilqiyahu: Semitica 36 (1986) 43-46; pl. XI.

a284 **Gignoux** Philippe, *Gyselen* Rika, Sceaux sasanides 1982 ➤ 65,a510: ᴿIndIraJ 29 (1986) 129-133 (D. N. *Mackenzie*).

a285 **Giveon** R., Egyptian scarabs from Western Asia from the collections of the British Museum: OBO arch. 3, 1985 ➤ 1,d140: ᴿBbbOr 28 (1986) 123s (Maria Pia *Cesaretti*); BO 43 (1986) 702-5 (W. A. *Ward* corrects 23 of the 420 objects); WeltOr 17 (1986) 150 (Ingrid *Gamer-Wallert*).

a286 **Giveon** Raphael, *Kertesz* Trude, Egyptian scarabs and seals from Acco from the collection of the Israel department of antiquities and museums. FrS 1986, Univ. 48 p.; 20 pl. – (176 drawings; 176 phot.) 3-7278-0371-1. ᴿSBFLA 36 (1986) 393 (A. *Niccacci*).

a287 **Gorelick** L., *Williams-Forte* E., Ancient seals and the Bible 1983 ➤ 64,a962 ... 1,d143: ᴿJAOS 106 (1986) 307-311 (O. *Keel,* ᵀ*Keel-Leu* Hildi); MesopT 21 (1986) 280s (A. *Invernizzi*).

a288 *Gubel* E., Syro-Cypriote cubical stamps; the Phoenician connection: ➤ 553, Cinquième = Akkadica 47 (1986) 79.

a289 **Hallager** Erik, The master impression; a clay sealing from the Greek-Swedish excavations at Kastelli, Khania: SIMA 69. Göteborg 1985, Åström. 75 p.; bibliog. p. 34-38; 31 fig. 91-86098-28-4.

a290 *Homès-Fredericq* Denyse, La glyptique des archives inédites d'un centre provincial de l'empire assyrien aux Musées Royaux d'art et d'histoire, Bruxelles: ➤ 545*, Rencontre 30ᵉ 1983/6, 247-259; 4 fig.

a291 *Homès-Fredericq* Denyse, *al.,* Glyptica V [résumés d'articles 1983]: Akkadica 48 (1987) 10-34.

a292 *Israel* Felice, Observations on Northwest Semitic seals [*Herr* L. 1978]: Orientalia 55 (1986) 70-77.

a293 **Karg** Norbert, Untersuchungen zur älteren frühdynastischen Glyptik Babyloniens; Aspekte regionaler Entwicklungen in der ersten Hälfte des

3. Jahrtausends: DAI BaghFor 8, 1984 ➤ 65,a521: ᴿMundus 22 (1986) 105-7 (W. *Röllig*): RAss 80 (1986) 95 (P. *Amiet*).

a294 **Keel** Othmar, *Schroer* Silvia, Studien zu den Stempelsiegeln aus Palästina/Israel I: OBO 67,1985 ➤ 1,d152: ᴿActOrK 47 (1986) 179-185 (Tine *Bagh*).

a295 *a) Keel* Othmar, A stamp seal research project and a group of scarabs with raised relief; – *b) Asher-Greve* J. M., *Stern* W. B., Practical advice[s] for collecting data on cylinder seals: Akkadica 49 (1986) 1-16 / 17-19.

a296 **Kjaerim** Poul, The stanp and cylinder seals: Falaka Dilmun 1/1, Jutland Pub. 17/1, 1983 ➤ 64,a973 [Kjærum]: ᴿMesopT 21 (1986) 279s (A. *Invernizzi*).

a297 *Kunath* Siegward, Ein Skarabäus von Qarn Ḥaṭṭīn: BibNot 32 (1986) 22-24.

a298 *Lemaire* André, Nouveaux sceaux nord-ouest sémitiques: Syria 63 (1986) 305-325; ill.

a299 **Martin** Geoffrey T., Scarabs, cylinders and other ancient Egyptian seals; a checklist of publications 1985 ➤ 1,d158: ᴿVAeg 2 (1986) 156s (C. *Van Siclen*).

a300 *a) Mayer-Opificius* R., Betrachtungen zum Verwendungszeitraum altorientalischer Rollsiegel; – *b) Becking* Bob, A remark on a post-exilic seal: UF 18 (1986s) 237-240; 4 fig. / 445s.

a301 *a) Meerten* Reinier van, Zwei Hauptformeln der altkretischen Siegel; – *b) Younger* John G., Aegean seals of the Late Bronze Age; stylistic groups V. Minoan groups contemporary with LM III A 1: Kadmos 25 (1986) 102-7 / 118-140.

a302 *Møller* Eva, Cylinder seals from the [1835-1906 tea trader, John] Horniman museum, London: Iraq 48 (1986) 65-72; pl. XI-XII.

a303 *Moore* Michael S., The Judean 'lmlk' stamps; some unresolved issues: RestQ 28 (1985s) 17-26.

a304 *Morrisson* C., Sceaux byzantins inédits de la collection Henri Seyrig: CRAI (1986) 420-435; 3 pl.

a305 *a) Özgüç* Nimet, Seals of the Old Assyrian Colony period and some observations on the seal impressions; – *b) Porada* Edith, A subject for continuing conversation [cylinder seal]: ➤ 71, ᶠMELLINK M., Anatolia 1986, 48-53; 11 fig. / 84-92; 17 fig.

a306 **Platon** Nikolaos, *Pini* Ingo, Die Siegel der Nachpalastzeit /ᶦUndatierbare spätminoische Siegel: Corpus der minoischen und mykenischen Siegel 2/4. B 1985, Mann. lxxvi-304 p.; ill.

a307 **Schaeffer-Forrer** Claude F.-A., Corpus des cylindres-sceaux de Ras Shamra-Ugarit et d'Enkomi-Alasia I, 1983 ➤ 64,a992 ... 1, d166: ᴿOLZ 81 (1986) 149-151 (Evelyn *Klengel-Brandt*); RAss 80 (1986) 81-88 (D. *Collon*); ZDMG 136 (1986) 111-3 (W. *Röllig*).

a308 *Shaked* S., *Naveh* J., Three Aramaic seals of the Achaemenid period: JRAS (1986) 21-26; 4 pl.

a309 *Shiloh* Yigal, ❺ A hoard of Israelite seal-impressions on bullae from the City of David: Qàdmoniot 19 (1986) 2-11; ill.

a310 *Sijpesteijn* P. J., Ostracon copticum amstelodamense 1: CdÉ 61 (1986) 173s.

a311 **Śliwa** J., Egyptian scarabs, scaraboids and plaques from the Cracow collections 1985 ➤ 1,d168: ᴿBO 43 (1986) 701s (G. *Hölbl*).

a312 *Stern* Ephraim, Two Phoenician glass seals from Tel Dor: ➤ 11*, Mem. BICKERMAN E. = JANES 16s (1984s) 213-216; 2 fig.

a313 *Sürenhagen* Dietrich,   Ein Königssiegel aus Kargamis [in Lidar/Urfa gefunden]:   MDOG 118 (1986) 183-190; 3 fig.
a314 **Teissier** Béatrice, Ancient NE cylinder seals ... Marcopoli 1984 ➤ 1,d170: ᴿSyria 63 (1986) 438-441 (P. *Amiet*).
a315 *Trokay* M., Art cassite; kudurru et sceaux-cylindres; art officiel et art vivant (résumé): Akkadica 49 (1986) 33s.
a316 **Tufnell** Olga, (*Martin* G. T., *Ward* William A.), Studies on Scarab Seals [I. 1978 ➤ 60,s266], II. Scarab seals and their contribution to history in the early second millennium B.C. 1984 ➤ 65,a534; also p. 203-397 and £17.50: ᴿRB 93 (1986) 138-140 (B. *Couroyer*).
a317 *Venit* M. S., Toward a definition of Middle Assyrian style [sealings]: Akkadica 50 (1986) 1-14; 15-21 = 23 fig.
a318 *Verga* S., Scarabei in pietra dura nel museo archeologico regionale di Palermo: RStFen 14 (1986) 153-178; 2 fig.; pl. XXV-XXVII.
a319 **Vollenweider** M., Musée d'art et d'histoire de Genève, Catalogue raisonné des sceaux cylindres et camées 3. Mainz 1983, von Zabern. xx-242 p.; 245 fig. – ᴿJAOS 106 (1986) 372s (D. *Collon*).
a320 *Ward* William A., Scarab typology and archaeological context: AJA 91 (1987) 507-532; 8 fig.
a321 **Weingarten** Judith, The Zakro master [220 Cretan seals] and his place in prehistory: SIMA pocket 26, 1983 ➤ 64,a998: ᴿAJA 90 (1986) 105 (E. L. *Bennett*); AntClas 55 (1986) 563-5 (R. *Laffineur*: homogeneous glyptic group from Kato Zakro House A); RBgPg 64 (1986) 200s (J. *Vanschoonwinkel*).
a322 *Werr* Lamia A., The Sippar workshop of seal engraving: AJA 90 (1986) 461-3.
a323 *a) Winter* Irene J., The king and the cup; iconography of the royal presentation scene on Ur III seals; – *b) Klengel-Brandt* Evelyn, Siegelabrollungen auf der altbabylonischen Tafel VAT 712; – *c) Mayer-Opificius* Ruth, Bemerkungen zur mittelassyrischen Glyptik des 13. und 12. Jhdts. v. Chr.; – *d) Paley* Samuel M., Inscribed Neo-Assyrian and Neo-Babylonian cylinder seals and impressions: ➤ 87, ᶠPORADA E., Insight 1986, 253-268; pl. 62-64 / 143-7; 15 fig.; pl. 27 b / 161-7; 14 fig.; pl. 30 / 209-220; pl. 47-50.

T3.4   Mosaica.

a324 **Alexander** M. A., *al.*, Corpus des mosaïques de Tunisie, II. Thuburbo Majus, 2. Les mosaïques de la région des Grands-Thermes. Tunis 1985. xvii-121 p.; LIX pl.; 22 foldout plans. – ᴿBMosAnt 11 (1986) 381-3 (J.-P. *Darmon*).
a325 **Balmelle** C., *al.*, Le décor géometrique de la mosaïque romaine; répertoire graphique et descriptif des compositions linéaires et isotropes. P 1985, Picard. 431 p.; 254 pl. F 650. – ᴿClasR 100 (1986) 346 (R. *Ling*: revised < BMosAnt 1973).
a326 **Blázquez** J. M., *Mezquiriz* M. A., *al.*, Mosaicos romanos de Navarra: Corpus de mosaicos de España 7. M 1985, Cons. Sup. Inv. 111 p.; 31 fig.; 62 pl. [AJA 91,500, D. *Parrish*].
a327 **Boeselager** Dela von, Antike Mosaiken in Sizilien; Hellenismus und römische Kaiserzeit [Diss. Basel 1977]: Archaeologica 40, 1983 ➤ 1,d177; Lit. 270.000: ᴿAntClas 55 (1987) 630s (Janine *Balty*).
a328 *Michaelides* D., A season mosaic from Nea Paphos: RepCyp (1986) 212-221; 4 fig.; pl. XLV.

a329 **Parrish** David,   Season mosaics of Roman North Africa [diss. Columbia]: Archaeologica 46, 1984 ➤ 65,a547; **1**,d192:   ᴿAJA 90 (1986) 122-4 (D. W. *Rupp*); AntClas 55 (1986) 633-5 (Janine *Balty*: sévère); Athenaeum 64 (1986) 511s (S. *Maggi*).

a330 **Piccirillo** Michele,   *a*) I mosaici di Giordania, catalogo [esposizione Italia-Austria-Germania 1986s], + 8 essays, *al.* R 1986, Quasar. 236 p.; 109 fig., 56 color. pl.   88-85020-73-9. – *b*) Byzantinische Mosaiken aus Jordanien, ᵀ*Buschhausen* H.   W 1986, NÖ-Landesregierung.   251 p. – ᴿSBFLA 36 (1986) 375s (P. *Kaswalder*).

a331 *Stähli* Hans-Peter,   '... was die Welt im Innersten zusammenhält'; die Mosaike von Beth-Alpha — bildliche Darstellungen zentraler Aussagen jïdischen Glaubens: Judaica 41 (1985) 79-98; 6 fig.

a332 **Van Elderen** Bastiaan,   The mosaics of Jordan.   84 slides and text. $114. – ᴿArchaeology 39,5 (1986) 69 (Christine *Kondoleon*).

a333 **Wilson** R.J.A.,   Piazza Armerina.   Austin 1983, Univ. Texas.   124 p.; 58 fig. $12.50   0-292-76472-3. – ᴿÉchMClas 30 (1986) 206s (P. D. *Emanuele*).

т3.5 *Ceramica*, **pottery**   [➤ *singuli situs*].

a334 **Arnold** Dean E.,   Ceramic theory and cultural process: New Studies in Archaeology.   C 1985, Univ.   xi-268 p. £19.50.   0-521-25262-8. – ᴿAntiqJ 66 (1986) 406 (R. *Hodges*).

a335 ᴱ**Barrelet** M.-T.,   *Gardin* J.-C.,   À propos des interprétations archéologiques de la poterie; questions ouvertes: Mémoire 64.   P 1986, RCiv.   165 p.; 21 fig. [RelStR 13, 343, J. *Frane*]. F 176.   2-86538-149-8.

a336 **Beazley** J. D.,   The development of Attic black-figure [Sather Classical Lectures 24].   Berkeley 1986, Univ. California.   xxvii-117 p.; 104 pl. 0-520-05593-4.

a337 **Bernardini** Paola,   La ceramica a vernice nera dal Tevere: Museo Nazionale Romano, Ceramiche 5/1.   R 1986, De Luca.   286 p.; 19 fig.; LXIII pl.

a338 **Betancourt** Philip P.,   The history of Minoan pottery.   Princeton 1985, Univ. ➤ **1**,d202:   xxi-226 p.; 134 fig.; 32 pl. – ᴿAJA 90 (1986) 484s (G. *Walberg*).

a339 *Blakely* Jeffrey A., *Horton* Fred L.ᴶ,   South Palestinian Bes vessels of the Persian period: Levant 18 (1986) 111-119; 1 fig.; pl. XVIII-XXV.

a340 **Böhr** E.,   Der Schaukelmaler [ᴰ1976] 1982 ➤ 64,b25 ... **1**,b979:   ᴿAcArchH 38,1s (1986) 322s (J. Gy. *Szilágyi*).

a341 **Bothmer** Dietrich von,   The Amasis painter and his world; vase-painting in sixth-century ʙ.ᴄ. Athens; intr. *Boegehold* Alan L.   Malibu/L 1985, Getty Museum/Thames & H.   248 p.; 365 fig.; 8 color. pl. $60; pa. $22.50. – ᴿAJA 90 (1986) 360s (Sarah P. *Morris*).

a342 *a*) *Clamer* Christa,   A middle Bronze Age pottery boot from Tell Lachish; – *b*) *Hankey* Vronwy & Henry,   A Mycenaean pictorial krater from Lachish, level VI; – *c*) *Hennessy* J. B.,   Chocolate-on-White ware at Pella; – *d*) *Prag* Kay,   The imitation of Cypriote wares in Late Bronze Age Palestine: ➤ 115, Mem. Tᴜꜰɴᴇʟʟ O., 1985, 50-56; 8 fig. / 88-99; 4 fig. / 100-113; 3 fig. / 154-166; 1 fig.

a343 **Coulson** William D. E.,   The Dark Age pottery of Messenia: SIMA pocket 43.   Göteborg 1986, Åström.   146 p.; 15 fig.   91-86098-46-2.

a344 **Díez Fernández** Florentino,   Cerámica común romana de la Galilea ➤ 64,b27: [diss. Inst. Cath., Paris 1980]. M 1983, Biblia y Fe.   247 p., ill. – ᴿJAOS 106 (1986) 369s (E. M. *Meyers*).

a345 *Edwards* Charles M.,   Corinthian moldmade bowls; the 1926 reservoir: Hesperia 55 (1986) 389-409.

a346 *Edwards* Michael,   'Urmia ware' and its contribution in north-western Iran in the second millenium B.C.; a review of the results of excavations and surveys: Iran 24 (1986) 57-77; 4 fig.

a347 *Efe* Turan,   Patterned reserved-slip decoration in the Early Bronze Age of western Anatolia: Anatolica 13 (1986) 1-16; chart 17.

a348 *Ferrari* Gloria,   Eye-cup: RArchéol (1986) 5-20; 15 fig.

a349 **Haerinck** E.,   La céramique en Iran pendant la période parthe...: Iran-Ant Sup. 2, 1983 ➤ 64,b37 ... 1,d215:   ᴿBO 43 (1986) 507-9 (W. *Vogelsang*); MesopT 21 (1986) 288-291 (E. *Valtz*); OLZ 81 (1986) 385 (B. *Brentjes*).

a350 **Hemelrijk** Jaap M.,   Caeretan hydriae: Kerameus 2/5, 1984 ➤ 1,d218; 3-8053-0740-3:   ᴿBabesch 61 (1986) 221s (L. B. van der *Meer*: 'humourous' and 'relativating').

a351 *Hershkovitz* Malka,   Miniature ointment vases from the Second Temple period: IsrEJ 36 (1986) 45-51; 3 fig.

a352 *Hoffman* Bettina, *Juranek* Heinz,   The reconstruction of production techniques for relief-decorated Terra Sigillata: ➤ 561, The many dimensions of pottery 1982/4, 167; 1 fig.

a353 **Jones** R. E.,   Greek and Cypriote pottery; a review of scientific studies: Fitch Laboratory 1. Athens 1986, British School.   938 p.; 188 fig. [Antiquity 60, 178].

a354 **Kemp** B. J., *Merrillees* R. S.,   Minoan pottery in second millenium Egypt: DAI-K, 1980 ➤ 62,b420 ... 1,d221:   ᴿBO 43 (1986) 85-87 (Emily *Vermeule* regrets her delay); WeltOr 17 (1986) 152-4 (Vronwy *Hankey*).

a355 *Killebrew* Ann,   The pottery workshop in ancient Egyptian reliefs and paintings: ➤ 349*, ᴱ*Groll* S., Papers 1 (1982) 60-101.

a356 *Koehler* Carolyn G., *Matheson* Philippa M. W.,   Amphoras on computers: ➤ 548, AJA 90 (1986) 224.

a357 **Kurtz** Donna C.,   The Berlin painter 1983 ➤ 65,a420:   ᴿBabesch 61 (1986) 222s (L. *Byvanck-Quarles van Ufford*).

a358 *Medvedskaya* I. N.,   A study of the chronological parallels between the Greek geometric style and Sialk B painted pottery: IrAnt 21 (1986) 89-120; VIII pl.

a359 *Mershen* Birgit,   Recent hand-made pottery from northern Jordan; Berytus 33 (1985) 75-80; 17 fig.

a360 **Mountjoy** P. A.,   Mycenaean decorated pottery, a guide to identification: SIMA 73. Göteborg 1986, Åström. 238 p.; 283 fig. 91-86098-32-2. – ᴿAJA 91 (1987) 493s (Gisela *Walberg*: a guide to the use of A. FURUMARK, The Mycenaean pottery).

a361 **Philon** Helen, *al.,*   Early Islamic ceramics: Benaki Museum Athens, Catalogue of Islamic Art I. L 1980, Sotheby-PB. – ᴿJAmEg 22 (1985) 197-201 (G. T. *Scanlon*: sumptuous).

a362 *Popham* Mervyn,   A late Minoan III C pyxis in the Andreades collection: OxJArch 5 (1986) 157-164 [perhaps for cremation].

a363 *Schaus* Gerald P.,   Two Fikellura vase painters: AnBritAth 81 (1986) 251-295; 12 fig. [+ A-B]; pl. 13-16.

a364 *Scheibler* Ingeborg,   Formen der Zusammenarbeit in attischen Töpfereien des 6. und 5. Jahrhunderts v. Chr: ➤ 58, ᶠLAUFFER S., III (1986) 785-804; 2 fig.; 6 phot.

a365 *Spencer* John R.,   Samaria ware; the study of a pottery type and its implications for the eighth century B.C.E.: ➤ 377b, SBL Jerusalem summaries (1986) 7.

a366 **Stucki** Willi, Unterlagen zur Keramik des Alten Vorderen Orients: von ihren Anfängen bis zum Ende der Vordynastischen Zeit [I 1980 ➤ 62,b43]; II. Z 1984, EA. ➤ 65,a587; 262 p. DM 174. 3-85657-00[1-2]; 2-0. – ᴿBO 43 (1986) 193s (D. *Meijer*); Mundus 22 (1986) 304s (W. *Röllig*: unhelpful organization, countless errors).

a367 *Tadmor* Miriam, Naturalistic depictions in the Gilat sculptured vessels [nude woman with churn, ram with jars]: IsrMusJ 5 (1986) 7-12; ill.

a368 *Trinkaus* Kathryn M., Pottery from the Damghan Plain, Iran; chronology and variability from the Parthian to the early Islamic periods: StIran 15 (1986) 23-88; 23 fig.; franç. 88.

a369 *Tutundzic* Sava P., The group of narrowing necked jars and one-loop-handled vessels at Maadi in relation to the Palestinian ceramic ware: Recueil de Travaux de la Faculté de Philosophie 15 (Beograd 1985) 11-32.

a370 *Venit* Marjorie S., Early Attic black figure vases in Egypt: JAmEg 21 (1984) 141-154; 22 fig.

a371 *Vitali* V. *al.*, La stabilité des céramiques par rapport à l'environnement: RArchéom 8 (1984) 41-44.

a372 *Whitbread* I. K., The characterisation of argillaceous inclusions in ceramic thin sections: Archaeometry 28 (1986) 79-88; 1 fig.

a373 *Wickede* Alwo von, Die Ornamentik der Tell Halaf-Keramik; ein Beitrag zu ihrer Typologie: AcPraeh 18 (1986) 7-33; 54 fig.

T3.6   Lampas.

a374 **Beaune** Sophie A. de, Lampes et godets au paléolithique: Gallia Préhistoire Sup. 23. P 1986, CNRS. 286 p.; 93 fig.; 16 pl. F 320 [Antiquity 61,423].

a375 *Deneauve* Jean, Note sur quelques lampes africaines du IIIe siècle [apr. J.-C. ... Carthage]: AntAfr 22 (1986) 141-161; 21 fig.

a376 *Geus* C.H.J. de, Signum ignis signum vitae; lamps in ancient Israelite tombs: ➤ 47, ᶠHOSPERS J., Scripta 1986, 65-75.

a377 **Goethert-Polaschek** Karin, Römische Lampen; Katalog der [779] römischen Lampen des Rheinischen Landesmuseums Trier: Trierer Grabungen und Forschungen 15. Mainz 1985, von Zabern 338 p.; 77 pl.; map. [AJA 91, 630, Norma *Goldman*].

a378 *a*) *Khairy* Nabil I., *'Amr* Abdel-Jalil A., Early Islamic incribed pottery lamps from Jordan; – *b*) *Amr*, Some unusual glazed Mamluke saucer lamps: Levant 18 (1986) 143-153; 12 fig.; pl. XXXVIII-XLI / 155-161; 4 fig.

a379 *Radt* Wolfgang, Lampen und Beleuchtung in der Antike: AntWelt 17,1 (1986) 40-58; 42 fig., some with 10 to 30 clear informative portrayals.

T3.7   Cultica   [➤ 8809-9085].

a380 **Alp** Sedat, Beiträge zur Erforschung des hethitischen Tempels 1983 ➤ 64,b72; 65,a597: ᴿOrientalia 55 (1986) 345s (M. *Popko*).

a381 *Amiran* Ruth, A suggestion to see the copper 'crowns' of the Judean Desert treasure as drums of stand-like altars: ➤ 115, Mem. TUFNELL G. 1985, 10s; 7 fig.

a382 *Brown* John P., The *Templum* and the *saeculum*; sacred space and time in Israel and Etruria: ZAW 98 (1986) 415-433.

a383 *Chen* Doron, The design of the ancient synagogues of Galilee: SBFLA 36 (1986) 235-240; 3 fig.

a384 *Christensen* J., Tempel – bjerg – paradis; en forestillingskreds og dens konstans [Mari, Ugarit; Ps, Dt-Jes, Ezek; 1 Hen 17-36; 4 Ezra]: DanskTTs 49 (1986) 51-61 [< ZAW].

a385 *a) Corboud* Pierre, L'oratoire et les niches-oratoires; les lieux de la prière; – *b) Quecke* Hans, Gebet und Gottesdienst der Mönche nach den Texten: ➤ 551*, Kellia 1984/6, 85-92 / 93-103 (-6).

a386 *Davies* J.G., *a)* Altar, ᵀ*Roehl* W.: ➤ 587, EvKL 1 (1986) 100-102; – *b)* Basilica, cathedral, and church: ➤ 585, EncRel 2 (1986) 71-77; 7 fig.

a387 **Gandolfo** Francesco, Le basiliche armene, IV-VII secolo: CNRS/Univ. Roma, Studi di architettura medioevale Armena 5. R 1982, De Luca. 141 p.; 76 pl. – ᴿBO 43 (1986) 791s (J. *Wilkinson*).

a388 **Golzio** Karl-Heinz, Der Tempel im alten Mesopotamien ... Indien 1983 ➤ 64,b87 ... 1,a681; *f*80: ᴿBO 43 (1986) 795-8 (J.M.C. *Pragt*, R. *Leenders*).

a389 **Heinrich** Ernst, Die Tempel und Heiligtümer im alten Mesopotamien; Typologie, Morphologie und Geschichte: DAI Denkmäler der antiken Architektur 14, 1982 ➤ 63,a661 ... 65,a609: ᴿJNES 45 (1986) 322-6 (Sally *Dunham*); ZDMG 136 (1986) 113s (W. *Röllig*).

a390 *Ilan* Z., Galilee, survey of synagogues [1982-6]: ➤ a507, ExcSIsr 5 (1986) 35-37; map.

a391 *Jaritz* Horst, Die Kirche des Heiligen Psōti vor der Stadtmauer von Assuan: ➤ 77, ᶠMOKHTAR G. 1985, II, 1-19; 3 fig.; 3 pl.

a392 *Lanciers* Eddy, Die ägyptischen Tempelbauten zur Zeit des Ptolemaios V. Epiphanes (204-180 v.Chr.) Teil 1: MiDAI-K 42 (1986) 81-98.

a393 **Negev** A., Tempel, Kirchen und Zisternen 1983 ➤ 64,b101 ... 1,d267: ᴿBA 49 (1986) 253 (D.F. *Graf*); TRu 51 (1986) 229 (L. *Perlitt*).

a394 *Perlman* Isadore, *Gunneweg* Jan, *Yellin* Joseph, Pseudo-Nabataean ware and the pottery of Jerusalem [*Avigad* N. 1980]: BASOR 262 (1986) 77-82; 1 fig.

a395 **Rutkowki** Bogdan, The cult places of the Aegean [supersedes Cult Places in the Aegean world 1972]. NHv 1986, Yale Univ. xix-267 p.; 315 pl. $40 [AJA 91,491, J. *Rexine*].

a396 ᴱ**Safrai** Zeev, ⊕ *Bêt ha-Kᵉnesset* ... The ancient synagogue; selected studies. J 1986, Shazar Center. 210 p.; 25 fig. 965-227-033-4 [KirSef 61,77].

a397 *Van Siclen* Charles C.ᴵᴵᴵ, Ostracon DM 41228; a sketch plan of a shrine reconsidered: GöMiszÄg 90 (1986) 71-77; 4 fig.

T3.8 **Funeraria;** *Sindon,* **the Shroud.**

a398 **Andrews** Carol, Egyptian Mummies 1984 ➤ 65,a627; 1,d273; 0-7141-2027-8: ᴿAncSRes 16 (1986) 174-6 (Joan *Beck*: beautiful).

a399 **Balma Bollone** P.B., L'impronta di Dio; alla ricerca delle reliquie di Cristo 1985 ➤ 1,d274: ᴿSindon 27,34 (1985) 84s (G. *Ghiberti*).

a400 **Bianchi** Luca, Le stele funerarie della Dacia. R 1985, Bretschneider. vii-315 p.; 137 fig. [AJA 91, 631, W.E. *Mierse*].

a401 *Bolshakov* A.O., System analysis of tomb complexes in Old Kingdom Egypt: VDI 177 (1986,2) 98-137; Eng. 137.

a402 *Borghini* Alberto, A proposito di gambe o piedi incrociati nelle rappresentazioni funerarie antiche: Athenaeum 64 (1986) 439-452.

a403 *Bulst* Werner, Turiner Grabtuch und Exegese heute – II. Neues zur Geschichte des Tuches: BZ 30 (1986) 70-91; 6 phot.

a404 *Chapman* Rupert, Executions or atrocities?: a note on Tomb P19 at Jericho: BAngIsr 6 (1986s) 29-33; 1 fig.

a405 **Chappaz** Jean-Luc, Les figurines funéraires égyptiennes ... 1984 ➤ 65,a632: ᴿBO 43 (1986) 699s (K. *Martin*); JAOS 106 (1986) 576s (Joyce L. *Haynes*); OrAnt 25 (1986) 131-4 (S. *Pernigotti*).

a406 **Dentzer** Jean-Marie, Le motif du banquet couché 1982 ➤ 63,a515 ... 1,d284: ᴿSyria 63 (1986) 169-172 (J. *Teixidor*).

a407 **De Puma** Richard D., Etruscan tomb-groups; ancient pottery and bronzes in Chicago's Field Museum of Natural History. Mainz 1986, von Zabern. xiv-131 p.; 37 fig.; 48 pl. 3-8053-0870-1.

a408 **Drews** Robert. In search of the shroud of Turin 1984 ➤ 65,a639; 1,d285: ᴿBibTB 16 (1986) 31 (Pheme *Perkins*).

a409 **Dubarle** A. M., Histoire ancienne du linceul de Turin 1985 ➤ 1,d286: ᴿAevum 60 (1986) 308s (G. *Ghiberti*); AnBoll 104 (1986) 460-4 (P. *Devos*); EsprV 96 (1986) 544 (R. *Desvoyes*); Études 365 (1986) 38s (P. du *Bourguet*); RevSR 60 (1986) 271 (C. *Munier*).

a410 *Dubarle* A. M., Le linceul de Turin dans les publications récentes [*Heller* J., *Gilly* R. ...]: EsprV 96 (1986) 59-64.

a411 **Edel** E., Die Inschriften der Grabfronten der Siut-Gräber in Mittel-Ägypten aus der Herakleopolitenzeit; eine Wiederherstellung nach den Zeichnungen der Description de l'Égypte: Abh Rh/Wf Ak 71. Opladen 1984, Westdeutscher-V. 210 p. – ᴿOrAnt 25 (1986) 137s (A. *Roccati*).

a412 *Flusser* David, 'The house of David' on an ossuary: IsrMusJ 5 (1986) 37-40; 3 fig.

a413 *Fossati* Luigi, Sindonologia; è utile l'analisi radiocarbonica?: StCattMi 30 (1986) 130-2.

a414 *Germer* Renate, Die Verwendung von Flechten [plaiting] bei der Mumifizierung: StAltÄgK 13 (1986) 95-98.

a415 *Goško* T. Yu., *Otroščenko* V. V., ⓑ Cimmerian burials in catacomb and shaft-and-chamber tombs: SovArch (1986,1) 168-183; 8 fig.; Eng. 183.

a416 *Healey* John F., The Ugaritic dead; some live issues [not 'life issues' as Contents]: ➤ 368, Münster 18 (1986s) 27-32.

a417 *Holt* Frank L., The missing mummy of Alexander the Great [*Schwartz* Stephan A., The Alexandria project, an extraordinary true adventure in psychic archaeology (Dell 1983) outrageous]: Archaeology 39,1 (1986) 80.

a418 *Jenni* Hanna, Das Dekorationsprogramm des Sarkophages Nektanebo's II = AegHelv 12 (1986). v-67 p.; 3 pl.

a419 **Koch** Guntram, *Sichtermann* Hellmut, Römische Sarkophage 1982 ➤ 65,a651; 1,d299: ᴿGGA 238 (1986) 201-220 (Heide *Froning*).

a420 *Kohlbeck* Joseph A., *Nitowski* Eugenia L. (now Carmelite Sr. Damian) New evidence may explain image on shroud of Turin; chemical tests link shroud to Jerusalem: BAR-W 12,4 (1986) 18-29; (color.) ill. [History of the Shroud and of the 'STRUP' investigation team by Walter *McCrone*, pp. 26s and 22]; letters 12,6 p. 18s. 69-73.

a421 **Konikoff** Adia, Sarcophagi from the Jewish catacombs of ancient Rome; a catalogue raisonné. Stu 1986, Steiner. 65 p.; 16 pl.

a422 *Kuyper* J. de, Jusqu'à ce que la mort nous sépare; responsabilités funéraires d'une reine hittite (résumé): Akkadica 50 (1986) 24.

a423 **Lapp** Günther, *al.*, Särge des Mittleren Reiches aus der ehemaligen Sammlung Khashaba [quondam owner]: ÄgAbh 43, 1985 ➤ 1,d300: ᴿBO 43 (1986) 696-8 (Diana *Magee*).

a424 **McLauchlin** Barbara K., Lydian graves and burial customs [Sardis ...]: diss. California. Berkeley 1985. 443 p. 86-10138. – DissA 47 (1986s) 954-A.

a425 *Meacham* William, O the archaeological evidence for a coin-on-eye Jewish burial custom in the first century A.D.: BA 49 (1986) 56-58; 59s, rejoinder by Rachel *Hachlili* and Ann *Killebrew*.

a426 *Merrillees* R.S., A late Cypriote Bronze Age tomb and its Asiatic connections: → 115, Mem. TUFNELL O. 1985, 114-135; 22 fig.

a427 **Mollina Paquez** Marino, ¿Un reto a la ciencia? El lienzo de Turin. Novelda 1985, Aguado. – ᴿSindon 27,34 (1985) 86 (L.d.V.).

a428 *Mourlon Beernaert* Pierre, L'énigme du linceul de Turin; un signe, non une preuve: LVitae 41 (1986) 277-290.

a429 **O'Rahilly** A. [1884-1969], The Crucified [1950, on the Shroud], ᴱ*Gaughan* J.A.. Dublin 1985, Kingdom. xxxv-488 p. 0-9506015-5-1 [NTAbs 31, 103].

a430 **Parlasca** Klaus, Syrische Grabreliefs 1982 → 65,a659; 1,d308: ᴿAJA 90 (1986) 138s (Elaine K. *Gazda*); ClasR 100 (1986) 166s (M.A.R. *Colledge*); Latomus 45 (1986) 477s (R. *Chevallier*).

a431 *Podella* Thomas, Ein mediterraner Trauerritus: UF 18 (1986s) 163-9; 5 fig. (figurines with hands on head).

a432 *Polz* Daniel, Die Särge des (Pa-)Ramessu [Vezir unter Haremhab]: MiDAI-K 42 (1986) 145-166; 6 fig.; pl. 20-23.

a433 **Prieur** Jean, La mort dans l'Antiquité romaine. Rennes 1986, Ouest-France. 224 p. F 88. – ᴿÉtudes 364 (1986) 849s (P. *Vallin*).

a434 *Rahmani* L.Y., *a*) Some remarks on R. HACHLILI's and A. KILLEBREW's 'Jewish funerary customs': PEQ [115 (1983) 109-132] 118 (1986) 96-100; – *b*) On some [three] recently discovered lead coffins from Israel: IsrEJ 36 (1986) 234-250; 2 fig.; pl. 27-33.

a435 **Ricci** Giulio, L'Uomo della Sindone è Gesù[3]. Mi/R 1985, Cammino/Centro Sindonologia. 148 p. Lit. 50.000. – ᴿCC 137 (1986.2) 298s (V. *Marcozzi*).

a436 *Rössler-Köhler* Ursula, Einige Beobachtungen an Dekorationsteilen der Königsgräber des N[euen] R[eiches]: BO 43 (1986) 277-302.

a437 **Rolle** Renate, Totenkult der Skythen, I. Das Steppengebiet: Vorgeschichtliche Forschungen 18, 1979 → 62,a128: – ᴿZfArch 20 (1986) 139-142 (A. *Häusler*).

a438 **Siliato** Maria Grazia, L'uomo della Sindone; indagine su un antico delitto.[2] Casale Monferrato 1985, Piemme. 205 p. Lit. 20.000. – ᴿCC 137 (1986,3) 314s (D. *Chianella*).

a439 **Skupinska-Løvset** Ilona, Funerary portraiture of Roman Palestine: SIMA pocket 21, 1983 → 64,b158; 65,a667: ᴿAJA 90 (1986) 139s (Elaine K. *Gazda*).

a440 **Solé** Manuel, La Sábana Santa de Turín. Bilbao 1985, Mensajero. 483 p. – ᴿCiuD 199 (1986) 152s (F. *Díez*); Sindon 27,34 (1985) 86s (P. *Coero Borga*).

a441 **Steck** Wolfgang, Begräbnis AT-NT: → 587, EvKL 1 (1986) 387-9.

a442 **Stewart** H.M., Mummy-cases and inscribed funerary cones in the Petrie collection. Wmr/Ch1986, Aris & P. / Bolchazy-Carducci ix-84 p.; 25 pl. 0-85668-312-4 / Ch 0-86516-075-9.

a443 *Tribbe* Frank C., The shroud of Turin, mystical visions ['expressions of ascetics compared with the Shroud'] and retrocognition: Sindon 27,34 (1985) 43-51.

a444 *Trummer* Regina, West-östliche Grabbautraditionen: → 542, Kulturkontakte 1986, 67-77; 2 fig.

a445 **Ventura** Raphael, Living in a city of the dead; a selection of topographical and administrative terms in the documents of the Theban necropolis: OBO 69.   FrS/Gö 1986, Univ./VR.   xiv-227 p.; 3 fig. [JNES 46,78].

a446 *Vriezen* Karel J. H.,   Ein Basaltsarkophag aus Umm Qēs (Gadara) in Jordanien: ZDPV 102 (1986) 113-133; 1 fig.; pl. 12-15.

a447 *Westergård-Nielsen* Nanna,   Macedonian tombs; the construction and origin of the vaulted chamber tomb: MusTusc 56 (1984ss) 173s; dansk 149-173; 11 fig.

a448 *Wiebach* Silvia,   Die Begegnung von Lebenden und Verstorbenen im Rahmen des Thebanischen Taifestes: StAltÄgKu 13 (1986) 263-291.

a449 **Wilson** Ian [chairman of British Society for the Turin Shroud], The evidence of the shroud. ... O'Mara.   158 p.; ill.   £10.50. – RTablet 240 (1986) 1111s (D. *Sox,* resigned secretary of same British society: rehash of Wilson's 1978 volume; Edessa equation, FILAS' coin over eyes, and A. WHANGER's 145 points of congruity on a 9 mm coin A.D. 695 — only cloud the issue; WILD's BAR-W ignored).

a450 **Wilson** I.,   The mysterious Shroud.   GCNY 1986, Doubleday.   xviii-158 p.; 90 phot. $20.   0-385-19074-3 [NTAbs 30,359].

T3.9   *Numismatica,* **coins.**

a451 **Acquaro** E., present,   Studi di numismática púnica: RStFen Sup 11.   R 1983, Cons. Naz. Ric.   81 p.; XVLII pl. [AulaOr 5,332, M. *Campo*].

a452 *Akhunbabaev* Kh. G., Ⓞ Concerning a group of Sogdian coins: SovArch (1986,4) 254-261; 2 fig.

a453 *a) Alfaro Asins* C.,   Sistematización del antiguo numerario [coinage] gaditano; – *b) Villalonga* L.,   Economía monetaria en la Península Ibérica ante la presencia cartaginesa durante la segunda guerra púnica: → 353, EOlmo Lete G. del, Fenicios 1986, II. 121-134; IV pl. + 5 color. / 157-162.

a454 *Arnold-Biucchi* Carmen, *Metcalf* William E.,   New light on the mint of Caesarea Cappadociae [largest such find ever recorded, 900 to 2500 silver coins]: → 548, AJA 90 (1986) 212.

a455 *Bakhoum* Soheir,   Programme monétaraire et tendance romanisante de l'atelier d'Alexandrie sous Marc-Aurèle: BIFAO 86 (1986) 33-36; 1 pl.

a456 *a) Barrandon* J. N.,   Détermination du titre des monnaies d'argent par analyse par activation au moyen des neutrons rapides; – *b) Mancini* C., Silver evaluation in Roman Republican Victoriatus: RArchéom 8 (1984) 61-69 / 30-32.

a457 **Bassoli** Ferdinando,   Monete e medaglie nel libro antico dal XV al XIX secolo [ristampe < Esopo]: Biblioteconomia 21.   F 1985, Olschki. 95 p. – RRNum 28 (1986) 213 (J.-B. *Giard*).

a458 **Betlyon** J. W.,   The coinage and mints of Phoenicia; the pre-Alexandrine period: HarvSemMon 26.   Chico CA 1982, Scholars.   171 p. – RAulaOr 4 (1986) 343 (M. *Campo*).

a459 *Betlyon* John W.,   Coins excavated between 1970 and 1983 at Tell el-Ḥesi: PEQ 118 (1986) 66-69.

a460 *a) Burnett* Andrew,   The iconography of Roman coin types in the third century BC; – *b) Foss* Clive,   The coinage of Tigranes the Great; problems, suggestions and a new find; – *c) Dilmaghani* J.,   Parthian coins from Mithradates II to Orodes II; – *d) Barclay* Craig,   A countermarked as of Vespasian from South Italy: NumC 146 (1986) 67-75; pl. 8-9 / 19-66; pl. 5-7 / 216-224 / 226-230.

a461 *Buttrey* T. V., *Johnston* Ann, *al.,* Greek, Roman and Islamic coins from Sardis 1981 → 62,b496; 1,d332;   RAJA 90 (1986) 117s (J. H. *Kroll*).

a462 *a) Carbè* Anna, Note sulla monetazione di Selinunte; – *b) Lazzarini* Lorenzo, Note sulle monete bronzee di Kebren nella Troade; – *c) Martini* Rodolfo, Cronologia delle emissioni orientali di Marcus Antonius (II): RitNum 88 (1986) 3-20; 3 pl. / 27-35; 5 fig. / 37-75; fig. 89-175.

a463 *Classen* Carl J., Virtutes Romanorum nach dem Zeugnis der Münzen republikanischer Zeit: MiDAI-R 93 (1986) 257-279; pl. 118-131.

a464 **Deppert-Lippitz** Barbara, Die Münzprägung Milets vom vierten bis ersten Jahrhundert v. Chr.: Typos 5,1984 ➤ 1,d339: RJbNumG 34 (1984) 180s (D. O. A. *Klose*); NumC 146 (1986) 233-260 (P. *Kinns*); RBgNum 132 (1986) 187s (T. *Hackens*).

a465 *Devauchelle* Didier, *ḥ ḏ*: deben (20 drachmes) ou kite (2 drachmes); Enchoria 14 (1986) 157s.

a466 *Düfel* Hans, Die Reformation auf Münzen und Medaillen [*Schnell* H. 1983; *Whiting* R. 1983 ...]: Luther 57 (Wu 1986) 81-85; 13 fig.

a467 *Ehrhardt* Christopher T. H. R., Roman coin types and the Roman public [*Crawford* M. 1983]: JbNumG 34 (1984) 41-54; deutsch 163s.

a468 *Fischer* Thomas, Literaturüberblicke der griechischen Numismatik; Seleukiden: Chiron 15 (1985) 283-389.

a469 *Geissen* Angelo, Zu Beamtennamen auf Münzen von Hypaipa: EpAnat 7 (1986) 113-122; pl. 18; ❶ 123.

a470 ᴱ**Heckel** Waldemar, *Sullivan* Richard, Ancient coins of the Graeco-Roman World; the Nickle [Arts Museum, Univ. Calgary 1981] Numismatic Papers. Waterloo ON 1984, W. Laurier Univ. xii-310 p.; 7 pl. – RPhoenix 40 (Toronto 1986) 374-6 (R. T. *Williams*).

a471 **Howgego** C. J., Greek imperial countermarks; studies in the provincial coinage of the Roman Empire: Spec. Publ. 17. L 1985, Royal Numismatic Soc. 317 p.; 33 pl.; 36 maps. £35. – RNumC 146 (1986) 265-7 (D. R. *Walker*).

a472 *a) Jacobson* David M., A new interpretation of the reverse of Herod's largest coin; – *b) Houghton* Arthur, The elephants of Nisibis; – *c) Moore* Wayne, The divine couple of Demetrius II, Nicator, and his coinage at Nisibis; – *d) Weigel* Richard D., An Augean Stables coin type from Nicaea: AmNumM 31 (1986) 145-165; pl. 32 / 107-124; pl. 27-29 / 125-143; pl. 30-31 / 167-9; 2 fig.

a473 **Kindler** A., The coinage of Bostra 1983 ➤ 65,a702; 1,d350; £24: RPEQ 118 (1986) 74s (R. *Reece*: the real records only pp. 105-128; the rest comment).

a474 *a) King* C. E., A small hoard of fourth century [A.D.] bronze coins from Egypt; – *b) Weiser* Wolfram, Ein Fund von rhodischem Kleingeld aus hellenistischer Zeit: ZPapEp 66 (1986) 285-291; pl. XIII / 209-215; pl. VII.

a475 *Kokkinos* Nikos, A retouched new date on a coin of Valerius Gratus: SBFLA 36 (1986) 241-6; pl. I-II.

a476 *Krupp* Michael, Die Münzen Jonatan Hyrkanos II: ➤ 68*, ꟳMAYER R., Wie gut 1986, 12-28.

a477 *Le Rider* Georges, Les Alexandres d'argent en Asie Mineure et dans l'Orient séleucide au IIIᵉ siècle av. J.-C. (c. 275 - c. 225); remarques sur le système monétaire des Séleucides et des Ptolémées: JSav (1986) 3-51; 4 pl.

a478 **Levy** Brooks E., *Bastien* Pierre, Roman coins in the Princeton University Library, I. Republic to Commodus. Wetteren 1985. 191 p.; XXVIII pl. – RRitNum 88 (1986) 262-4 (V. *Picozzi*).

a479 **Martin** Thomas R., Sovereignty and coinage in classical Greece. Princeton 1986, Univ. xiv-332 p.; 2 fig. $32 [AJA 91,622s, R. A. *Billows*].

a480 **Meshorer** Ya'akov, City-coins of Eretz-Israel and the Decapolis in the
Roman period [☉ 1984 → 1,d357]. J 1985, Israel Museum. 123 p.; 283
coin phot., etc. 965-278-036-7.

a481 **Meshorer** Y., Ancient Jewish coinage 1982 [< 1966]. – ᴿQadmoniot 19
(1986) 120 (M. *Broshi*).

a482 a) *Meshorer* Yaakov, Jewish Numismatics; – b) *Meyers* Eric M., *Kraabel*
A. Thomas, Archeology, iconography, and nonliterary written remains:
255, ᴱ*Kraft* R., Early Judaism 1986, 211-220; 22 fig. / 175-210.

a483 *Michaux - van der Mersch* Françoise, Un trésor de monnaies archaïques
de l'époque achéménide (Turquie ouest): RBgNum 132 (1986) 168-173; pl.
XV.

a484 **Mildenberg** Leo, ᴱ*Mottahedeh* Patricia E., The Kochba war: Typos 6,
1984 → 1,d36; 3-7941-2634-3: ᴿBO 43 (1986) 205s (A.N. *Zadoks*, J.
Jitta); CBQ 48 (1986) 563s (L.J. *Hoppe*); Gnomon 58 (1986) 326-331 (M.
Hengel); IsrEJ 36 (1986) 117s (Y. *Meshorer*); JStJud 17 (1986) 109-112 (M.
Piccirillo); TLZ 111 (1986) 185-7 (K. *Matthiae*); WeltOr 17 (1986) 179-184
(T. *Fischer*).

a485 *Miller* M.C.J., The Macedonian pretender Pausanias and his coinage:
AncW 13 (1986) 23-27.

a486 **Morrisson** C., al., L'or monnayé, I. Purification et altérations de Rome à
Byzance; préf. *Grierson* P.: Cah Ernest-Babelon 2. P c. 1985, C.N.R.S.
282 p. – ᴿRNum 28 (1986) 218-220 (D. *Nony*).

a487 *Moysey* Robert A., The silver stater issues of Pharnabazos and Datames
from the mint of Tarsus in Cilicia: AmNumM 31 (1986) 7-61; pl. 1-5.

a488 *Naster* Paul, Ambrosiai petrai dans les textes et sur les monnaies de Tyr:
→ 551, Religio phoenicia 1984/6, 361-370; 18 fig.

a489 *Reade* Julian, A hoard of silver currency from Achaemenid Babylonia:
Iran 24 (1986) 79-89; 4 fig; 4 pl.

a490 *Rebuffat* F., Alexandre le Grand et Apollonia de Pisidie: RNum 28
(1986) 65-71; 4 fig.

a491 *Sfameni Gasparro* Giulia, Iside-Dikaiosyne in una serie monetale
bronzea di Catania; un aspetto nuovo dell'iconografia isiaca: SMSR 52
(1986) 189-211.

a492 *Talamo* Clara, Nota sui rapporti tra la Lidia e le città greche d'Asia da
Gige a Creso: AnItNum 30 (1983) 9-37.

a493 **Tall** Safwan K. al-, Development of coinage in Jordan throughout
history. Amman 1986, Central Bank. 116 p. – ᴿSBFLA 36 (1986) 370 (P.
Kaswalder).

a494 *Tamburelli* Giovanni, L'impronta sindonica della monetina rilevata dal
computer: Sindon 27,34 (1985) 15-20.

a495 **Troxell** Hyla A., The coinage of the Lycian league: Numismatic Notes
and Monographs 162, 1982 → 64,b227 ... 1,d379: ᴿBelleten 50,198 (1986)
929-932 (Oğuz *Tekin*); RBgPg 64 (1986) 205 (J.P. *Callu*).

a496 **Vacano** Otfried von, Typenkatalog der antiken Münzen Kleinasiens. B
1986, Reimer. 530 p. [Mundus 22,312].

a497 *Vardanyan* H. Ye., Elymaean coins; a chronological systematization of
bronze emissions in the second century A.D.: VDI 176 (1986,1) 99-116; 4
fig.; 2 pl.; Eng. 116s.

a498 *Vickers* Michaël, Persépolis, Athènes et Sybaris; questions de monnayage
et de chronologie: RÉG 99 (1986) 239-270.

a499 a) *Villaronga* L., Economía monetaria en la Península Ibérica ante la
presencia cartaginesa durante la segunda guerra púnica; – b) *Camp* M.,
Algunas cuestiones sobre las monedas de Malaca; – c) *Alfaro Asins* C.,

Sistematización del antiguo numerario gaditano [3052 coins in seven series, six Punic]: AulaOr 4 (1986) 157-162 / 139-152; 2 fig.; 3 pl. / 121-134; 4 pl.
a500 **Waggoner** Nancy M., Early Greek coins from the collection of Jonathan P. Rosen 1983 → 1,d383: ᴿRBgPg 64 (1986) 202 (R. *Weiller*).
a501 *Zehnacker* Hubert, Où en est le 'Roman Imperial Coinage'? [*Kent* J. 1981; *Sutherland* C. 1984]: BBudé (1986) 202-5.
a502 *a) Zehnacker* Hubert, La solde de l'armée romaine, de Polybe à Domitien; – *b) Preston* Hugh S., Roman Republican coin hoards; an age correction and some other comments: AnItNum 30 (1983) 95-121 / 83-93; 1 fig.

T4 *Situs,* **excavation-sites** .1 *Chronica,* **bulletins.**

a503 *a) Aurenche* Olivier, Chronique archéologique [rapports signés dans leur langue d'origine]: Syria 63 (1986) 386-415; ill. – *b)* ᴱ*Bordreuil* P., *Gubel* E., Bulletin d'antiquités archéologiques du Levant inédits ou méconnues III: Syria 63 (1986) 417-435; 17 fig.
a504 Chronique archéologique, fin: RB [92 (1985) 389-430] 93 (1986) 236-284; 27 fig.; maps. Communications attribuées, en français.
a505 Excavations: IsrEJ 36 (1986) 99-115; map; 273-9; map; most signed, infra.
a506 ᴱ*Piccirillo* Michele, Ricerca storico-archeologica in Giordania VI (1986): SBFLA 36 (1986) 335-367, pl. 65-80, 41 signed articles, many infra; + 368-392, book-reviews.
a507 ᴱ*Pommerantz* Inna, Excavations and surveys in Israel 5 (1986) [< Hadashot Arkheologiyot]. vii-127 p.; 62 fig.; 9 phot.; 2 maps. 0334-1607. Signed articles on some 100 sites, some infra.
a508 Recherches archéologiques en Israël, Lv 1984, Peeters (Amis Belges). 255 p. Fb 1200. 90-6831-017-8. – ᴿBO 43 (1986) 491-3 (Hanna *Blok*).
ᴱ**Rast** Walter E., Preliminary reports of ASOR-sponsored excavations, 1980-4: BASOR Sup. 24, 1986 → 354.
a509 *Segal* Arthur, Archaeological research in Israel 1960-1985: BibTB 16 (1986) 73-77.
a510 ᴱ**Shanks** H., *Mazar* B., Recent archeology in the land of Israel, ᵀ*Finkelstein* Aryeh. Wsh 1984, BAR (soc.). 194 p. $20. – ᴿBA 49 (1986) 127s (W. E. *Rast*).
a511 **Vogel** E. K., *Holtzclaw* B., Bibliography of [archeology research at] Holy Land sites, II. (1970-1981) [< HUCA]. Cincinnati 1982, HUC. 92 p. $5. 0-87820-625-6 [NTAbs 30,381].

T4.2 *Situs effossi,* **syntheses.**

a513 *Arata Mantovani* Piera, L'archeologia siro-palestinese e la storia di Israele; rassegna di studi archeologici 3 [14 scritti]: Henoch 8 (1986) 223-242.
a514 **Bagatti** Bellarmino, Antichi villaggi cristiani di Giudea e Neghev: SBF min 24, 1983 → 64,b241... 1,d397: ᴿBO 43 (1986) 791 (J. *Wilkinson*); RHE 81 (1986) 756 (Jacqueline *Lafontaine-Dosogne*).
a515 **Brug** John F., A literary and archaeological study of the Philistines: BAR-Int 265. Ox 1985. vi-312 p.; 30 fig.
a516 *Chute* Richard, An examination of T. L. THOMPSON's analysis of Early Bronze Age IV/Middle Bronze Age I Syro-Canaan [climate shift], undergraduate prize essay (summary): BAR-W 12,3 (1986) 10.
a517 **Dothan** Trude, The Philistines 1982 → 64,a824... 1,d401: ᴿOLZ 81 (1986) 14-17 (H. *Klengel*); ZDPV 102 (1986) 177-9 (Karin M. v. *Filseck*).

a518 *a) Gregori* Barbara, *Palumbo* Gaetano,   Presenze micenee in Siria-Palestina [111 siti elencati]; – *b) Lepore* Ettore,   Modo di produzione egeo in relazione al Mediterraneo occidentale: ➤ 564, Traffici micenei 1984/6, 365-383; 11 maps / 315-322.

a519 *Levy* Thomas E.,   The chalcolithic period; archaeological sources for the history of Palestine: BA 49 (1986) 82-108; ill.

a520 **Negev** Avraham,   Nabatean archaeology today: Kevorkian NE Art. NY 1986, NY Univ. xiv-155 p.; 66 fig.; bibliog. p. 143-8. 0-8147-8760-X.

a521 *Piccirillo* Michele, Archeologia e vangelo; la Terra Santa: ArchViv 5/10 (1986) 13-30; ill.

a522 *Rolla* Armando,   La Palestina postesilica alla luce dell'archeologia: ➤ 391, RivB 34 (1986) 111-124; Eng. 125.

a523 *Ron* Zvi Y. D.,   '... and built a tower ... a booth in a vineyard ... a lodge ...' [15,000 stone field towers, (earliest) few Hellenistic, (visible) in Israel]: ➤ 377*a*, IOSOT summaries (1986) 115.

a524 **Stern** Ephraim,   Material culture of the land of the Bible in the Persian period 538-332 B.C. [D1973] 1982 ➤ 63,a838; 65,a751: RBerytus 33 (1985) 169s (J. *Wilson*); Gnomon 58 (1986) 339-342 (R. *Wenning*).

a524* *Strange* John,   The transition from the Bronze Age to the Iron Age: ScandJOT 1,1 (1986) 1-19.

a525 **Tsafrir** Y., ❿ The archaeology of Roman and Byzantine Palestine. J 1985, Ben-Zvi. 462 p. – RQadmoniot 19 (1986) 120s (M. *Broshi*).

T4.3 **Jerusalem,** *archaeologia et historia.*

a526 **Avigad** N.,   Discovering Jerusalem 1983 ➤ 64,b265 ... **1**,d416: RBA 49 (1986) 248s (V. *Fritz*); Henoch 8 (1986) 233-6 (Piera *Arata Montanari*).

a527 *Bagatti* Bellarmino, *Alliata* Eugenio,   Nuovi elementi per la storia della Chiesa di S. Giovanni ad 'Ain Karem: SBFLA 36 (1986) 277-296; pl. 9-28.

a528 *Bahat* Dan,   Does the Holy Sepulchre Church mark burial of Jesus? [*Corbo* V. 1981s important but unsatisfactory; no more specific answer to the question is given]: BAR-W 12,3 (1986) 26-45; (color.) ill.

a529 *Bahat* Dan, *Reich* Ronny,   Une église médiévale dans le quartier juif de Jérusalem: RB 93 (1986) 111-4; 1 fig.; pl. I.

a530 *Bahat* Dan,   Les portes de Jérusalem selon MUKADDASI [*Le Strange* G. 1896, reprinted Beirut 1965]; nouvelle identification: RB 93 (1986) 429-435; 1 fig.

a531 *Bailey* Lloyd R.,   Gehenna, the topography of hell: BA 49 (1986) 187-191; ill.

a532 *Bammel* Ernst,   *a)* Nicanor and his gate [< JJS 7 (1956) 77s]; – *b)* Jesus and 'setting up a brick' [from the Temple to worship: < ZRGg 20 (1968) 364-7]: ➤ 131, Judaica 1986, 39-41 / 205-8.

a533 *Barkay* Gabriel,   The garden tomb; was Jesus buried here? [... two different sites vie]: BAR-W 12,2 (1986) 40-53: impossible because tomb dug before 700 was not afterward used before 300 [p. 54s, epitaph of one Eusebius 'near where the body of the Lord lay', *Murphy-O'Connor* J.]; p. 26 corrected in BAR-W 12/4 (1986) 64: 1885 Garden Tomb publisher was Ludovic de Vaux, not Roland prenatally; BAR-W 12,4 (1986) 14-17.58: Garden tomb authenticity defended [but not in informative letter by sponsors].

a534 *Barkay* Gabriel, *Kloner* Amos,   Jerusalem tombs from the days of the First Temple [under École Biblique]: BAR-W 12,2 (1986) 22-39; (color.) ill.

a535 *Bedouelle* Guy, Le désir de voir Jérusalem; histoire du thème des deux cités: Communio 11,3 (1986) 38-52 [non in IkaZ].

a536 **Ben-Arieh** Y., Jerusalem in the 19th century, I. The Old City 1984 → 1,d418: ᴿPEQ 118 (1986) 156s (M. *Hannam*).

a537 **Ben-Dov** M., In the shadow of the Temple; the discovery of ancient Jerusalem [*Hepîrût hār ha-bayit* 1982], ᵀ*Friedman* Ina → 1,d419; also SF 1985, Harper & R. 381 p. $25. 0-06-015362-8 [NTAbs 31,119].

a538 *a*) *Ben-Dov* Meir, Herod's mighty Temple mount; – *b*) *Shanks* Hershel, Excavating in the shadow of the Temple mount [not as effective as it should have been]: BAR-W 12,6 (1986) 40-49 / 20-38; (color.) ill.

a539 *Brlek* Metodio, Il Monte Sion a cinquanta anni dal ritorno dei Frati Minori: TerraS 62,5 Sup. (1986). 28 p.

a540 *Cannuyer* C., Les Géorgiens dans l' 'Historia hierosolimitana' de Jacques de Vɪᴛʀʏ [< Thèse de licence, LvN 1982]: Revue de Kartvélologie 40 (1983) 175-187 [RHE 81 (1986) 719].

a541 *Cohn* Erich W., The history of Jerusalem's Benjamin Gate; a case of interrupted continuity [Jer 20,2; Zech 14,10; Theodosius, Daniel, Burchard]: PEQ 118 (1986) 138-143.

a542 **Corbo** Virgilio C., Il Santo Sepolcro di Gerusalemme 1982 → 63,a863 ... 1,d428: ᴿJbAC 29 (1986) 213-8 (Renate *Rosenthal-Heginbottom*: unge-stützte Feststellungen).

a543 *Dequeker* Luc, David's Tomb in the City of David; a biblical tradition reconsidered: → 377a, IOSOT summaries (1986) 33.

a544 *Edelstein* G., 'En Ya'el [1668.1277 S Jerusalem]: → a507, ExSIsr 5 (1986) 30-33; 3 phot. (floor mosaics).

a545 *Ehrlich* E. L., La lettre 'Redemptionis anno' de Jean-Paul II sur Jérusalem [< Jüdische Rundschau (Basel 11.V.1984)]: Istina 31 (1986) 181-3 [texte (< OssRom 20.IV.1984) p. 196-200].

a546 *Fumagalli* Pier Francesco, Gerusalemme nel dialogo ebraico-cristiano: StCattMi 30 (1986) 113-7.

a547 [*Garner* Gordon] Jerusalem City of David excavations 1978-1984: BurH 21,4 (1985) 75-88.

a548 **Gilbert** Martin, Jerusalem, rebirth of a city → 1,d441; also L 1985, Chatto & W. xvi-238 p.; ill.; 11 maps. £15. – ᴿPEQ 118 (1986) 74 (Gillian *Webster*: vintage photos; aspects of Zionism).

a549 *Golan* David, Hadrian's decision to supplant 'Jerusalem' by 'Aelia Capitolina': Historia 35 (1986) 226-239.

a550 *Gros* Marie-Dominique (N. D.-Sion), Jérusalem, du nouveau à l'Ecce Homo: MondeB 45 (1986) 49s; 3 fig.

a551 *Hammer* Karl, Die christliche Jerusalemsehnsucht im 19. Jahrhundert; der geistige und geschichtliche Hintergrund der Gründung Johann Ludwig Sᴄʜɴᴇʟʟᴇʀs [1860 Waisenhaus]: TZBas 42 (1986) 255-266.

a552 *Heutger* Nicolaus, Königliche Gräber in Jerusalem: BiKi 41 (1986) 85s [177s *Riesner* R., Herodes].

a553 Jérusalem dans les traditions juives et chrétiennes; colloque des 11 et 12 novembre 1982, Bru.: Publ. Institutum Iudaicum. Lv, Peeters. 127 p. 9 art. [109-127, *Schoors* A., en Is 40-55; 15-23, 2Esd, 2Baruch; 81-96, *Guigui* A., talmud et midrach; 33-53, 4 fig., *Dequeker* L., L'iconographie du Temple dans les synagogues].

a554 *Kaswalder* P., Tombeau des Rois: TerreS (mai 1986) [EsprV 97,127, J. *Daoust*].

a555 *a*) *Klauck* Hans-Joseph, Die heilige Stadt; Jerusalem bei PHILO und Lukas; – *b*) *Brox* Norbert, Das 'irdische Jerusalem' in der altchristlichen Theologie; Kairos 28 (1986) 129-151 / 152-173.

a556 **Kloner** Amos, The 'third wall' in Jerusalem and the 'cave of the kings' (Josephus War 5,147) [south of École Biblique]: Levant 18 (1986) 121-9; 3 fig.; pl. XXVI-XXIX.

a557 **Kollek** Teddy, *Pearlman* Moshe, Jerusalem, sacred city of mankind; a history of forty centuries.[5] TA 1985, Steimatzky. 288 p.; (color.) ill. $29. – [R]GeistL 59 (1986) 477s (P. *Imhof*).

a558 **Konzelmann** Gerhard, Jerusalem; 4000 Jahre Kampf um eine heilige Stadt[3]. Ha 1984, Hoffmann & C. 495 p.; maps [KirSef 60,617].

a559 *Laperoussaz* E.-M., La discontinuité visible près de l'extrémité sud du mur oriental du Ḥaram esh-Shérif marque-t-elle l'angle sud-est du 'Temple de Salomon'?: → 377*a*, IOSOT summaries (1986) 77.

a560 **Martin** I., Six New Testament walks in Jerusalem. SF 1986, Harper & R. 240 p. $13 [BAR-W 13/5, 14, J. *Murphy-O'Connor*, negative].

a561 *Mazar* A., Jerusalem, the Ophel — 1986: → a507, ExcSIsr 5 (1986) 56-58; fig. 25.

a562 *Meshorer* Yaakov, Ancient gold ring [found in Jerusalem 1974] depicts the Holy Sepulchre: BAR-W 12,3 (1986) 46-48; (color.) ill.

a563 **Peters** F.E., Jerusalem [an anthology]. Princeton 1985, UP. 650 p. – [R]Dor 15 (1968s) 53 (S. *Liptzin*).

a564 **Peters** F.E., Jerusalem and Mecca; the typology of the holy city in the Near East: StudNECiv 11. NY 1986, NY Univ. xi-269 p.; bibliog. p. 243-258. 0-8147-6598-X.

a565 *Pringle* D., Magna Mahumeria (al-Bira); the archaeology of a Frankish new town in Palestine: → 1,801, [F]SMAIL R., Crusade and Settlement 1985 ...

a566 *Provera* Mario, Gerusalemme nel pensiero e negli scritti di san GEROLAMO: TerraS 62 (1986) 42-46; foto.

a567 **Rapcsányi** László, Jeruzsálem. Budapest 1984. – [R]Theologiai Szemle 28 (1985) 64.

a568 *Riesner* Rainer, Das Prätorium des Pilatus; zwei moderne Lokalisierungsvorschläge: BiKi 41 (1986) 34-37; plan.

a569 *Routtenberg* Hyman, Jerusalem in rabbinic literature: Dor 14 (1985s) 119-123.179-182; 15 (1986s) 45-48. 118-122.

a570 **Shiloh** Yigal, Excavations at the City of David I (1978-1982): Qedem 19, 1984 → 65,a979; **1**,d467: [R]ETL 62 (1986) 173s (E. *Eynikel*: Shiloh dates MACALISTER's 'Jebusite' and KENYON's 'Maccabean' ramp to 10th cent. B.C.); Henoch 8 (1986) 229-233 (Piera *Arata Mantovani*); RB 93 (1986) 142-4 (P. *Benoit*).

a571 *Shiloh* Yigal, *Tarler* David, Bullae from the city of David: BA 49 (1986) 196-209; ill.

a572 **Smeenk** R.D., Jeruzalem, lofzang of roestige pot. Franeker 1984, Wever. 186 p.; ill. *f* 24,50. – [R]GerefTTs 86 (1986) 186s (H. *Mulder*).

a573 *Steiner* Margreet L., A note on the Iron Age defence wall on the Ophel hill of Jerusalem: PEQ 118 (1986) 27-32; 4 fig.

a574 **Storme** Albert, Il Monte degli Olivi [Le Mont des Oliviers c. 1964], [T]*Baratto* Claudio: Luoghi Santi di Palestina. J 1985, Franciscan. 186 p. [KirSef 60,627].

a575 *Tolotti* Francesco, Il S. Sepolcro di Gerusalemme e le coeve basiliche di Roma: MiDAI-R 93 (1986) 471-512; 16 fig.

a576 **Ussishkin** David, ⊕ The village of Silwan; the necropolis from the period of the Judean kingdom. J 1986, Yad Ben-Tzvi. 965-217-034-8 [OIAc Ag. 87].

T4.4 *Situs alphabetice*: **Judaea, Negeb.**

a577 *'Ajrûd: Meshel* Zeev, The inscriptions of Kuntillet 'Ajrud [*one* only 'Amaryau said to my lord ... may you be blessed by Yahweh of Teiman and his Asherah']: ➤ 377*a*, IOSOT summaries (1986) 92.

a578 *Arad*: *Mazar* Amihai, *Netzer* Ehud, On the Israelite fortress at Arad: BASOR 263 (1986) 87-91.

a579 *Hospers* J. H., Enkele oudhebreeuwse Brieven uit Tell 'Arād, Israel (c. 600 v.Chr.): JbEOL 24 (1983) 100-6 [AION 45,719].

a580 *Kaswalder* Pietro, Tell Arad: TerraS 62 (1986) 62-64; 3 fig.

a581 *Ashkelon* 1985-6: ➤ a507, ExcSIsr 5 (1986) 2-6; fig. 3 (map)-4 (L. *Stager*, D. *Esse*).

a582 *Ašdod: Canivet* Maria T., Ashdod II-III, excavations 1963-5 [p. 186-190]: ➤ 139, Scritti 1986, 101-151 [-167].

a583 *Batash* (Timna) 1984-6: ➤ a507, ExcSIsr 5 (1986) 6-9 (A. *Mazar*, G. L. *Kelm*).

a584 *Kelm* G. L., *Mazar* A., Tel Batash (Timnah) 8th 1985: IsrEJ 36 (1986) 107-9.

a585 *Beersheba*: **Herzog** Z., Beer Sheba II. The early Iron Age settlements: TA Inst. Arch. Publ. 7, 1984 ➤ 65,a812; 1,d480: ^RSyria 63 (1986) 163-9 (F. *Braemer*).

a586 *Mayerson* Philip, *a*) The Beersheba edict [ed. *Alt* A.]; – *b*) Nea Arabia (P. Oxy. 3574; an addendum to ZPE 53 [chiefly a justification of his claim there that also others more expert than himself equate Idumeans with Arabs]; ZPapEp 64 (1986) 141-8 / 139s.

a587 *Bet-Ter*: *Ussishkin* David, Betar, the last stronghold of Bar-Kochba: BAngIsr 6 (1968s) 49s [lecture summary].

a588 *Bethlehem*: *Compagnoni* Pia, Betlemme, città messianica: TerraS 62 (1986) 196-204.

a589 *Sered* Susan S., Rachel's Tomb and the Milk Grotto of the Virgin Mary; two women's shrines in Bethlehem: JFemStRel 2,2 (1986) 7-22 [< ZIT].

a590 **Netzer** Ehud, Greater Herodium: Qedem 13,1981 ➤ 62,b613 ... 1,d496: ^ROLZ 81 (1986) 157-9 (K.-H. *Bernhardt*); RB 93 (1986) 461 (É. *Nodet*).

a591 *Netzer* Ehud, Herodium — Herod's summer palace and burial place [lecture summary]: BAngIsr 6 (1986s) 57-60; 2 fig.

a592 *Zias* Joseph, Was Byzantine Herodium a leprosarium?: BA 49 (1986) 182-6; ill.

a593 *Deir*, ḥirbat, 1981-4: *a*) ➤ a504, RB 93 (1986) 276-284; fig. 20-27; pl. XIV-XV (Y. *Hirschfeld*, R. *Birger*); – *b*) monastère byzantin: MondeB 43 (1986) 51-53; 6 fig. (Y. *Hirschfeld*, R. *Birger*; ^T*Comte* Francine).

a594 *Eilat*: *Flinder* Alexander, The search for Ezion-geber, King Solomon's Red Sea port [1 K 9,26; lecture summary]: BAngIsr 6 (1986s) 43-45; map.

a595 *Pratico* Gary D., Where is Ezion-Geber? a reappraisal of the site archaeologist Nelson GLUECK identified as King Solomon's Red Sea port: BAR-W 12,5 (1986) 24-35; (color.) ill.

a596 *En Gedi* 1985-6: ➤ a507, ExcSIsr 5 (1986) 27-29 (A. *Ofer*, Y. *Porath*).

a597 *Far'a S: Tubb* Jonathan N., The pottery from a Byzantine well near Tell Fara [south]: PEQ 118 (1986) 51-65; 6 fig.

a598 *Gezer*: **Dever** William G., *al.*, Gezer IV; the 1969-71 seasons in Field VI, the Acropolis. J 1986, Annual of the Nelson Glueck School of Biblical Archaeology. viii-275 p.; ill.; vol. of 120 pl. + loose plans.

a599 *Dever* William G., Late Bronze Age and Solomonic defenses at Gezer; new evidence: BASOR 262 (1986) 9-34; 18 fig.

a600 *Rosenbaum* Jonathan, *Seger* Joe D., Three unpublished ostraca from Gezer: BASOR 264 (1986) 51-60; 6 fig.

a601 *Finkelstein* Israel, ❶ The date of Gezer's outer wall: BarIlAn 293 (1983) 7-18; Eng. VII.

a602 *Singer* Itamar, Merneptah's campaign to Canaan and the fate of the kingdom of Gezer [MACALISTER's trench 14-16 north = Egyptian governor's residency contemporary to American stratum XIV]: ➤ 377*a*, IOSOT summaries (1986) 126.

a603 *Hebron*: Rumeideh ('biblical Hebron') 1985: ➤ a507, ExcSIsr 5 (1986) 92s (A. *Ofer*).

a604 *Heymar*; *Bar Yosef* Ofer, *Alon* David, ❶ Excavations in the Nahal Heymar cave [W Sedom]: Qadmoniot 19 (1986) 62-71; ill.

a605 *Izbet Ṣartah*: *a*) *Kochavi* M., Ein richterzeitliches Ostrakon aus 'Izbet Ṣartah; – *b*) *Dotan* A., Das Alphabet von 'Izbet Ṣartah: HBeiWJ 1 (1985) [< ZAW].

a606 *Jamma*: *Van Beek* Gus W., Are there beehive granaries at Tell Jemmeh? A rejoinder: BA 49 (1986) [p. 20, *Currid* J.] 245-7.

a607 *Jericho*: *Kenyon* K., *Holland* T., Excavations of Jericho IVs, 1982s ➤ 63,a927a/65,a832: ᴿSyria 63 (1986) 161-3 (H. de *Contenson*).

a608 *Bienkowski* Piotr, Jericho in the Late Bronze Age. Wmr 1986, Aris & P. 240 p.; 62 fig.; bibliog. p. 175-190. £22 [Antiquity 60,174]. 0-85668-320-5.

a609 *Prag* Kay, The intermediate Early Bronze – Middle Bronze Age sequences at Jericho and Tell Iktanu [E. Jordan] reviewed: BASOR 264 (1986) 61-72; 8 fig.

a610 *Compagnoni* Pia, Il deserto di Giuda 1985 ➤ **1**,d400: ᴿPrOrChr 36 (1986) 183 (P. *Ternant*).

a611 *Karkom* 1986: ➤ a507, ExcSIsr 5 (1986) 47s (E. *Anati*); ➤ 1810-1812.

a612 *Lachish*: *a*) *Ussishkin* David, Levels VII and VI at Tel Lachish and the end of the Late Bronze Age in Canaan; – *b*) *Callaway* Joseph A., A new perspective on the hill county settlement of Canaan in Iron Age I; – *c*) *Dever* William G., Relations between Syria-Palestine and Egypt in the 'Hyksos' period: ➤ 115, Mem. TUFNELL O. 1985, 213-228; 1 fig.; 4 pl. / 31-49 / 69-87.

a613 *Rosen* Arlene M., Environmental change and settlement at Tel Lachish, Israel: BASOR 263 (1986) 55-60; 3 fig.

a614 *Maresha* 1985, Byz. church mosaic: IsrEJ 36 (1986) 277-9, 1 fig. (A. *Klemer*, H. *Stark*).

a615 *Miqne* (Ekron) 1985-6: ➤ a507, ExcSIsr 5 (1986) 72-77; fig. 36-38 (D. *Eitam, al.*).

a616 *Lipiński* E., Guadalhorce; une inscription du roi d'Éqron [... serviteur d'Esarhaddon, if chemical fingerprints match Muqanna' pottery]: AulaOr 4 (1986) 85; phot.

a617 *Dothan* Trude, *Gitin* Seymour, Tell Miqne 1985: IsrEJ 36 (1986) 104-7.

a618 *Gunneweg* Jan *al.*, On the origin of pottery from Tel Miqne – Ekron: BASOR 264 (1986) 3-16; 3 fig.

a619 *Mišmar*: *Amiran* Ruth, A new type of chalcolithic ritual vessel and some implications for the Naḥal Mishmar hoard: BASOR 262 (1986) 83-87; 2 fig.

a620 *Oboda*: **Negev** A.,   The Late Hellenistic and Early Roman pottery of Nabatean Oboda: final report: Qedem 22 [0333-5844]. J 1986, Hebrew Univ. xxii-144 p.; 1200 + fig. [NRT 109,753, X. *Jacques*].

a621 *Qitmit*: *Beit-Arieh* Yitshak, *a*) ❶ An Edomite temple at Horvat Qitmit [30k E Bersheba]: Qadmoniot 19 (1986) 72-79; ill. [79-81, *Beck* Pirhiya, goddess]. – *b*) Qitmit, an Edomite shrine in the Judean Negev: ➤ 377a, IOSOT summaries (1986) 16.

a622 *Negeb*: *a*) *Cohen* Rudolph,   Solomon's Negev defense line contained three fewer fortresses [than the over-40 he had maintained]: BAR-W [11,3 (1985)] 12,4 (1986) 40-45: Ritma, Mesora, and Haroʻa were of Persian era. – *b*) *Finkelstein* Israel, [unsatisfied with COHEN] The Iron Age sites in the Negev highlands — military fortresses or nomads settling down?: BAR-W 12,4 (1986) 46-53.

a623 *Cohen* R., *Schmitt* J., Drei Studien [Negeb fortresses, Bet-Awen, Gat]: TAVO B 44, 1980 ➤ 61,s781: RZDPV 102 (1986) 175s (E. A. *Knauf*).

a624 *Seled*: *Kloner* Amos, ❶ A burial cave of the Second Temple period at Givʻat Seled in the Judean Shephelah: Qadmoniot 19 (1986) 102-5; ill.

a625 *Subayta*: Shivta 1985: IsrEJ 36 (1986) 11 (A. *Negev*, S. *Margalit*). – Église, 1985: RB 93 (1986) 267-9; fig. 15; pl. XIb (A. *Negev*, S. *Margalit*).

a626 **Rosenthal-Heginbottom** Renate, Die Kirchen von Sobota und die Dreiapsidenkirchen des Nahen Ostens; Beitr. *Chen* Doron: GöOrFor 2/7. Wsb 1982, Harrassowitz. xi-281 p.; 77 pl. [KirSef 59,454].

a627 *Uzza*: Beit-Arieh Y., ❶ Horvat ʻUzza [49k E Beersheba] — a border fortress in the eastern Negev: Qadmoniot 19 (1986) 31-40; ill.; 49s, bulla, *Beck* P.

T4.5 Samaria, Sharon.

a628 *Burj Aḥmar*: **Pringle** Denys, (*Cartledge* Judith, *al.*) The red tower (al-Burj al-Ahmar); settlement in the Plain of Sharon at the time of the Crusaders and Mamluks, A.D. 1099-1516: Brit. Sch. J Mon 1. L 1986, British School of Archaeology in Jerusalem. vii-206 p.; 70 fig.; 48 pl.; bibliog. p. 195-200. 0-9500542-6-7.

a629 *Caesarea M.*: **Levine** L. I., *Netzer* E., Excavations at Caesarea Maritima 1975, 1976, 1979; final report: Qedem 21. J 1986, Hebrew Univ. xi-206 p.; ill. [NRT 109,443, X. *Jacques*].

a630 *Betz* Artur, Zur Pontius Pilatus-Inschrift von Caesarea Maritima: ➤ 52, FKENNER H. 1982, 33-36.

a631 *a*) *Oleson* J.P., Herod and VITRUVIUS; preliminary thoughts about harbour engineering at Sebastos, the harbour of Caesarea Maritima; – *b*) *Breitstein* Stephen, Some logistic aspects of the excavations of Caesarea harbour: ➤ 571, ERaban A., Harbours 1983/5, 165-172 / 195-204.

a632 *Finkielsztejn* Gérald, *Asklepios leontoukhos* et le mythe de la coupe de Césarée Maritime [*Will* E. 1983]: RB 93 (1986) 419-428; 4 fig.

a633 *Mayerson* Philip, CHORICIUS of Gaza on the watersupply system of Caesarea: IsrEJ 36 (1986) 269-272.

a634 *Wenning* Robert, Die Stadtgöttin von Caesarea Maritima: Boreas 9 (Münster 1986) 113-129; pl. 15-16.

a635 *Artzy* Michal, *Schiøler* Thorkild, The dam at the kibbutz Maʻagan Michael [Caesarea]: MusTusc 56 (1984ss) 336; dansk 331-6; 6 fig.

a636 *Dor*: Stern Ephraim. *Sharon* Ilan, Tel Dor 1985; Roman-Hellenistic; some Iron Age; Persian: IsrEJ 36 (1986) 101-4.

a637 *Dauphin* Claudine, Temple grec, église byzantine et cimetière musulman; la basilique de Dor en Israël: PrOrChr 36 (1986) 14-22; 5 phot.; plan.

a638 Dor, église byzantine, 1983: RB 93 (1986) 269; pl. XII (C. *Dauphin*).

a639 Dor 1985: ➤ a507, ExcSIsr 5 (1986) 24-27 (E. *Stern*, I. *Sharon*).

a640 *Stern* Ephraim, Two favissae from Tel Dor, Israel: ➤ 551, Religio phoenicia 1984/6, 277-287.

a641 *Dothan*: *Wenning* Robert, *Zenger* Erich, Ein bäuerliches Baal-Heiligtum im samarischen Gebirge aus der Zeit der Anfänge Israels; Erwägungen zu dem von A. MAZAR zwischen Dotan und Tirza entdeckten 'Bull Site': ZDPV 102 (1986) 75-86; 3 fig.

a642 *Emmaus/Amwas*: *Gichon* Mordechai, The bath-house at Emmaus [Lecture summary]: BAngIsr 6 (1986s) 54-57; plan.

a643 *Gerizim*: *Magen* Yitshak, Ⓒ A fortified town of the Hellenistic period on Mount Gerizim: Qadmoniot 19 (1986) 91-101.

a644 *Jaffa-Tel Aviv*: *Burdajewicz* Mariusz, À propos des temples philistins de Qasileh [temples 'philistins', *Mazar* A., Qedem 12, 1980]: RB 93 (1986) 222-235; 5 fig.

a645 *Mazar* Amihai, Excavations at Tell Qasile, 1982-1984; preliminary report: IsrEJ 36 (1986) 1-15; 6 fig.; pl. 1-3.

a646 *Miḥmas*: *Patrich* Y. al., Ⓒ Jewish caves of refuge in the cliffs of Nahal Mikhmas: Qadmoniot 19 (1986) 45-50.

a647 *Ramat ha-Nadiv* (Zikhron Ya'aqov) 1984-5: IsrEJ 36 (1986) 275-7; 1 fig.; (Y. *Hirschfeld*, Rivka *Berger*).

a648 *Šiloh*: *Finkelstein* Israel, Shiloh yields some, but not all, of its secrets; location of tabernacle still uncertain: BAR-W 12,1 (1986) 22-41; (color.) ill.

a649 *Kaswalder* Pietro, Tel Seilun. la biblica Shilo: TerraS 62 (1986) 143-5.

a650 *Tirṣa*: *Garner* Gordon, Tirzah, an early capital of Israel: BurHist 22,1 (1986) 14-24 [OTAbs 10,21].

a651 *Yafit*: *Magen* Y., Ⓒ Two tumuli at Moshav Yafit in the Jordan valley: Qadmoniot 19 (1986) 42-45; ill.

a652 *Zikhrin* 1466.1634 [? same on map p. 237]: RB 93 (1986) 269-276; fig. 16-19; pl. XIII (M. *Fischer*).

T4.6   **Galilaea; pro tempore** *Golan*.

a653 *Akko*: *De Palma* Claudio, Tell Akko: ArchViva 5/9 (1986) 16-34; ill.

a654 (Fortuna) *Canivet* Maria T., Akko nelle sue vicende storiche dalle origini all'occupazione romana [< Rendiconti Ist. Lombardo 88 (1989) 171-182]: ➤ 139, Scritti 1986 69-82 [-100].

a655 *Beth Alpha*: *Dequeker* L., Le zodiaque de la synagogue de Beth Alpha et le Midrash: Bijdragen 47 (1986) 2-29; Eng. 30; 1 fig.

a656 *Ammûdîm*: *Chen* Doron, The ancient synagogue at Ḥorvat 'Ammudim [Umm el-'Ammed, *Kohl-Watzinger* 1916, 71]; design and chronology: PEQ 118 (1986) 135-7: 1 fig.

a657 *Anafa*: *Fuks* Gideon, Tel Anafa [= Akhadar 2105.2869 near Šamîr; = ? Arsinoe] — a proposed identification: ➤ 34, IsrClas St 5 (1979s) 178-184.

a658 *Beth-Shan*: **Yadin** Yigael, *Geva* Shulamit, Investigations at Beth-Shean; the early Iron Age strata: Qedem 23. J 1986, Hebr. Univ. xv-95 p.; ill. – ᴿBAngIsr 6 (1986s) 37-42; 1 fig. (R. *Chapman*).

a659 [*Beth-Yeraḥ*] *Currid* John D., The beehive building of ancient Palestine: BA 49 (1986) 20-24 [storehouses].

a660 *Capharnaum*: *Corbo* Vergilio C., Cafarnao dopo la XIX campagna di scavo: SBFLA 36 (1986) 297-308; 2 foldout plans; pl. 29-38.

a661 *Fischer* Moshe, The Corinthian capitals of the Capernaum synagogue; a revision: Levant 18 (1986) 131-142; 2 fig.; pl. XXX-XXXVII.

a662 Cafarnao 18° 'Virglio Corbo e Stanislao Loffreda. 1885': TerraS 62,1 (1986) 15-17.

a663 *Chen* Doron, On the chronology of the ancient synagogue at Capernaum: ZDPV 102 (1986) 134-143; 4 fig.

a664 *Preuss* Margarete / *Hofmann* Friedhelm, Die Brotvermehrungskirche in Tabgha erhielt Bronzeportale: HLand 118/2s (1986) 19s / 21s.

a665 *Dan*: *Biran* A., **O** An incense altar and other discoveries at Dan: Qadmoniot 19 (1986) 27-31; ill.

a666 *Biran* Avraham, The dancer from Dan [LB clay-mould plaque], the empty tomb and the altar room: IsrEJ 36 (1986) 168-187; 15 fig.; pl. 19-21.

a667 *Gamla* [217.248, E Bethsaida-Julias] 1984-6, synagogue: ➤ a507, ExcSIsr 5 (1986) 38-41, fig. 15-18 (S. *Gutmann*, D. *Wagner*).

a668 *Golan* survey 1985: IsrEJ 36 (1986) 273-5 (Claudine M. *Dauphin*).

a669 *Goren-Inbar* N., *Perlman* I., Chemical mapping of basalt flows at [Golan Heights] paleolithic sites: Archaeometry 28 (1986) 89-99; 3 fig. (map).

a670 *Haifa*: *Herrera* M.D., *Balensi* J., More about the Greek geometric pottery at Tell Abu Hawam: Levant [17 (1985) 131-8] 18 (1986) 169-171.

a671 *Kearsley* Rosalinde A., The redating of Tell Abu Hawam III and the Greek pendant semicircle skyphos: BASOR 263 (1986) 85s.

a672 *Hermon* 1985-6: ➤ a507, ExcSIsr 5 (1986) 78-81; fig. 39-41 (S. *Dar*).

a673 *Dar* Shimon, Mount Hermon 1985: IsrEJ 36 (1986) 99s.

a674 *Jotapata*: *Meshel* Z., *Roll* Y., **O** A fortress and an inscription of Diocletian at Yotvata: Qadmoniot 19 (1986) 106-112; ill.

a675 *Keisan*: **Briend** J., *Humbert* J., *al.*, Tell Keisan ➤ 63,d10... 65,a909: ᴿOrAnt 23 (1984) 314-6 ['OA', AION 45 (1985) 720, not on p. 673].

a676 *Kinneret/Urayma*: *Fritz* F., *Rösel* N., **O** Four seasons of excavation at Tel Kinnarot: Qadmoniot 19 (1986) 23-27; ill.

a677 *Fritz* Volkmar, Kinneret; Vorbericht über die Ausgrabungen auf dem Tell el-'Orēme am See Genezaret in den Jahren 1982-1985: ZDPV 102 (1986) 1-39; 20 fig.; pl. 1-8.

a678 *Fritz* Volkmar, Kinneret, Ergebnisse der Ausgrabungen auf dem Tell el-'Orēme am See Gennesaret: AntWelt 17,1 (1986) 13-36; 13 (color.) fig.

a679 *Hübner* Ulrich, *a)* Aegyptiaca vom Tell el-'Orēme: SBFLA 36 (1986) 253-264; 3 fig.; pl. 5-7; – *b)* Die 4. Grabungskampagne 1985 auf dem Tell el-'Orēme am See Gennesaret: HLand 118,4 (1986) 6-12; 8 fig.

a680 *Megiddo*: **Davies** Graham I., Megiddo: Cities of the biblical world. C/GR 1986, Lutterworth/Eerdmans. xii-116 p.; 22 fig.; 21 pl. /GR 0-8028-0247-8.

a681 *Davies* G.I., Megiddo in the period of the Judges: ➤ 399, OTS 24, 1985/6, 34-53.

a682 **Yadin** Yigael, ᴱ*Lindsay* Shira, Megiddo — city of destruction: 29-minute color film. Bloomington IN 1982, Univ. Audio-Visual Center. $400; rental $25. – ᴿArchaeology 39,1 (1986) 67.72 (W.G. *Dever*).

a683 *Milson* David, The design of the royal gates at Megiddo, Hazor, and Gezer: ZDPV 102 (1986) 87-92.

a684 *Meroth* (Kh. Marus, N. Safed) — 1986: ➤ a507, ExcSIsr 5 (1986) 64-68; fig. 31-33; photos 5-6 (synagogue and 'academy').

a685 *Montfort*: *Frenkel* R., *Gatzov* N., **O** The history and plan of Monfort [sic] Castle: Qadmoniot 19 (1986) 52-57 [51, Nahal Khezib human relief].

a686 *Nazareth*: **Bagatti** Bellarmino. Scavi di Nazaret 2, 1984 ➤ 65,a914; 1,d610: ᴿBO 43 (1986) 791s (J. *Wilkinson*).

a687 *Piccirillo* Michele, *a*) Il museo di Nazaret presso l'Annunziata: TerraS
62 (1986) 69-71; – *b*) Un nouveau musée à Nazareth, ᵀ*Comte* Francine:
MondeB 44 (1986) 49-51; 4 fig.

a688 *Loffreda* Stanislao, La casa della Vergine a Nazaret: SBFLA 36 (1986)
211-234.

a689 **Folda** Jaroslav, The Nazareth capital and the Crusader shrine of the
Annunciation: Mon Fine Arts 42. Univ. Park PA 1986, Univ./College Art
Ass. of America. xvii-101 p.; 77 pl. – ᴿSBFLA 36 (1986) 442-6 (E.
Alliata).

a690 *Sepphoris* 1985: ➤ a507, ExcSIsr 5 (1986) 101-4; fig. 53 (E. *M[e]yers, al.*).

a691 Sepphoris 3d, 1985: RB 93 (1986) 252-4 (J. *Strange*, T. *Longstaff*).

a692 *Meyers* Eric & Carol L., *Netzer* Ehud, Sepphoris 'ornament of all
Galilee' [mostly on Michigan excavation 1931 though subtitled 'new
excavations' and showing some unusual finds]: BA 49 (1986) 4-19; ill.

a693 **Miller** Stuart S., Studies in the history and traditions of Sepphoris [diss.
NYU 1980]: StJudLA 37, 1984 ➤ 65,a920; **1**,d622: ᴿJBL 105 (1986)
550-2 (E. M. *Meyers*); JQR 76 (1985s) 260-2 (D. *Goodblatt*).

a694 *Te'o* [2035.2819 W. Hula; chalcolithic]: ➤ a507, ExcSIsr 5 (1986) 107-9;
fig. 54-55 (E. *Eisenberg*).

T4.8 *Transjordania*: **East-Jordan.**

a695 *Banning* E. B., Peasants, pastoralists and pax romana; mutualism in the
southern highlands of Jordan: BASOR 261 (1986) 25-50; 11 fig.

a696 ᴱ**Dexinger** F., *al.*, Jordanien 1985 ➤ **1**,d632: ᴿAnzAltW 39 (1986) 108s
(W. *Muth*).

a697 **Dornemann** R. H., The archaeology of the Transjordan in the Bronze
and Iron ages [< London Univ. diss. 1970 updated to 1978] 1983
➤ 64,b452; 65,a928: ᴿPEQ 118 (1986) 72s (M. F. *Oakeshott*).

a698 **Gatier** Pierre-Louis, Inscriptions de la Jordanie, 2. Région centrale
(Amman - Hesban - Madaba - Main - Dhiban): Inscriptions grecques et
latines de la Syrie 21 / BAH 114. P 1986, Geuthner. 255 p.; xxxvi pl.
2-7053-0267-0.

a699 ᴱ**Hadidi** Adnan, Studies in the history and archaeology of Jordan I
1980/2➤ 64,b453; 65,a930: ᴿBO 43 (1986) 206s (Margaret *Steiner*).

a700 *Hart* Stephen, Some preliminary thoughts [i.e. 1984 survey conclusions]
on settlement in southern Edom: Levant 18 (1986) 51-58; 4 fig.

a701 *Kennedy* David, *MacAdam* Henry I., Latin inscriptions from Jordan,
1985: ZPapEp 65 (1986) 231-6; 2 fig.; pl. XI.

a702 *K[h]ouri* Rami, The decapolis of Jordan: Aramco World Magazine
[Nov. 1985) 28-35 [< BS 143 (1986) 271].

a703 *Mayerson* Philip, The Saracens and the limes: BASOR 262 (1986) 35-47.

a704 **Parker** S. Thomas, Romans and Saracens; a history of the Arabian
frontier: ASOR diss. 6. Winona Lake 1986, Eisenbrauns. $25 [BASOR
263,54].

a705 *a*) *Piccirillo* Michele, I mosaici di Giordania; – *b*) *Vannini* Guido, La
terra di Giordania: ArchViva 5,7 (1986) 14-39; ill. / 40-44; ill.

a706 *Sauer* James A., Transjordan in the Bronze and Iron ages; a critique of
GLUECK's synthesis: BASOR 263 (1986) 1-26; 18 fig.

a707 *Zayadine* Fawzi, Ammon, Moab et Edom; une longue histoire commune
avec Israël: MondeB 46 (1986) 10-16.17-20(22s) [25ss, Moab, *Worschech*
U., *Puech* É.].

a708 *Abu Ḥamid* [16k N DeirʿAlla], First season of joint excavations [Yarmouk Univ.-CNRS]: SBFLA 36 (1986) 341 (G. *Dollfus*, Z. *Kafafi*).

a709 *Amman:* **Almagro Gorbea** Antonio, El palacio omeya de Amman, I. La arquitectura 1983 ⇥ 1,d646; 84-7472-055-9: ᴿBO 43 (1986) 815s (J. *Wilkinson*).

a710 *Kafafi* Zeidan A., White objects from ʿAin Ghazāl, near Amman: BASOR 261 (1986) 51-56; 4 fig.

a711 *Azraq:* *Garrard* Andrew, *al.*, Prehistoric environment and settlement in the Azraq basin; an interim report on the 1984 excavation season: Levant 18 (1984) 5-24; 9 fig.; IV pl.

a712 *Dariḥ*, ḫirba [220.040, 30 k S Kerak] 1985: RB 93 (1986) 247-252; fig. 7s; pl. V-VI (F. *Villeneuve*); MondeB 46 (1986) 49s.

a713 *Dibon:* **Horn** Siegfried H., Why the Moabite Stone was blown to pieces: BAR-W 12,3 (1986) 50-61; (color.) ill. [12,5 p. 75, reader's correction: Ahab had 2000 chariots, not 1000].

a714 *Worschech* Udo, **Knauf** Ernst A., Dimon [Jes 15,9] und Horonaim [Jer 48,3; ed-Der]: BibNot 31 (1986) 75-96; 6 fig.; 2 pl.

a715 *Feinan* 1984: RB 93 (1986) 236-8, pl. IVa (A. *Hauptmann*).

a716 *Ghassul:* **Dillfus** Geneviève, Il y a 6000 ans dans la vallée du Jourdain: MondeB 46 (1986) 5s (-9, *Thalmann* J., *Balensi* Jacqueline).

a717 *Hanbury-Tenison* Jack, Hegel in prehistory [Ghassulian archeology between KENYON-HENNESSY positivism and New Anti-Empiricism]: Antiquity 60 (1986) 108-114.

a718 *Ghrareh* Edomite fortress 600 B.C.: SBFLA 36 (1986) 348s, pl. 86 (S. *Hart*).

a719 *Hallabat* qaṣr 1984s: SBFLA 36 (1986) 363-7 (G. *Bisheh*).

a720 *Hesbân:* **Storfjell** J. Bjørnar, The stratigraphy of Tell Hesbân, in the Byzantine peiod: diss. Andrews Univ., ᴰ*Geraty* L. Berrien Springs MI 1983. – AndrUnS 24 (1986) 49.

a721 *Irbid*/Beit Ras 1983-6: SBFLA 36 (1986) 361-3 (C. *Lenzen*, E. *Knauf*).

a722 *Jawa:* **Helms** S.W., Jawa – lost city of the black desert 1981 ⇥ 63,d70 ... 65,a974: ᴿIsrEJ 36 (1986) 280s (A. *Kempinski*: archeology, science fiction, psychoanalysis).

a723 *Jerash*, sanctuaire de Zeus: RB 93 (1986) 238-247; fig. 2-6 (J. *Seigne*).

a724 ᴱ**Zayadine** Fawzi, Jerash archaeological project 1981-3, I. Amman 1986, Dept. Antiquities. 492 p.; 142 pl. – ᴿSBFLA 36 (1986) 372-4 (P. *Kaswalder*).

a725 *Segal* Arthur, ❶ Gerasa — an archaeological-historical review: Qadmoniot 19 (1986) 12-22;

a726 *Karak:* **Worschech** U. F. C., Northwest Ard el-Kerak 1983 and 1984, a preliminary report: BibNot Beih. 2. Mü 1985. 88 p.; 29 fig.; XXIV pl. DM 8. – ᴿZAW 98 (1986) 481s (H.-C. *Schmitt*).

a727 *Worschech* Udo, Die sozio-ökologische Bedeutung frühbronzezeitlicher Ortslagen in der nordwestlichen Arḍ el-Kerak; ein Vorbericht: ZDPV 102 (1986) 40-52; 3 fig. [ledge-handles...].

a728 *Lejjun* (E Kerak), limes arabicus: RB 93 (1986) 256-261; fig. 10-11 (S. T. *Parker*).

a729 *a)* *Leonard* Albert ᴶ, The 1985 season of excavation at Kataret es-Samra, Jordan; – *b*) *Wimmer* Donald H., Late Iron Age architecture at Tell Safut, Jordan; – *c*) *Haeckl* Ann E., The principia of the Roman legionary fortress at El-Lejjun [Limes Arabicus, not Megiddo], Jordan (1980, 1982, 1985): ⇥ 548, AJA 90 (1986) all p. 232.

a730 Limes arabicus 1985: Syria 63 (1986) 401-5 (S. T. *Parker*).

a731 *Madaba:* RB 93 (1986) 261-7: fig. 12-14; pl. VII-XI (M. *Piccirillo*).

a732 *Piccirillo* Michele, Il palazzo bruciato di Madaba: SBFLA 36 (1986) 317-327; 328-334, fig. 7-10, Ceramica, *Alliata* E.

a733 *Piccirillo* Michele, Découverte d'une maison patricienne au centre de Madaba: MondeB 42 (1986) 49s; 5 fig.

a734 *Ma'in:* *Piccirillo* Michele, Ma'in in Giordania, un eremitaggio e un cimitero bizantino: TerraS 62 (1986) 109-111.

a735 *Mazar:* **Yassine** Khair, Tell el Mazar I, Cemetery A. Amman 1984, Univ. Jordan. xxv-195 p.; 69 fig.; bibliog. p. v-xxi. $32 [BL 87,29].

a736 *Mudeibi'a:* *Negueruela* I., La fortaleza moabita de Mudeibi'a, en Jordania: Trabajos da Prehistoria 40 (1983) 357-365 [AION 45 (1985) 721].

a737 **Nebo:** *a)* 1986: SBFLA 36 (1986) 349-351; pl. 67-70 (M. *Piccirillo*); – *b)* fouilles / cité: MondeB 44 (1986) 4-19.30-39 (M. *Piccirillo*).

a738 **Piccirillo** Michele, La Montagna del Nebo: SBF Guide 2. Assisi 1986, Porziuncola. 109 p. – ᴿSBFLA 36 (1986) 369s (P. *Kaswalder*).

a739 *Pella:* *Potts* Timothy, An ivory-decorated box from Pella (Jordan): Antiquity 60 (1986) 217-9; pl. XXVI.

a740 *Petra:* American expedition 1986: SBFLA 36 (1986) 346-8 (P. *Hammond*).

a741 Petra, installations de banquet: RB 93 (1986) 254-6; fig. 9; pl. IV b (D. *Tarrier*).

a742 *Hammond* Philip C., Petra, the timeless: Archaeology 39,1 (1986) 18-25; color. ill.

a743 *Hammond* Philip C., *Jordan* David J., *Jones* Richard N., A religio-legal Nabataean inscription from the Atargatis / Al-'Uzza temple at Petra: BASOR 263 (1986) 77-80; 2 fig.

a744 *Khairy* Nabil I., Three unique objects from Petra [Katuteh 1981; winged Eros...]: PEQ 118 (1986) 101-8; 6 fig.

a745 **Khouri** Rami G., Petra, a guide to the capital of the Nabataeans. L 1986, Longman. 160 p.; ill.; maps. £6.75 [Antiquity 61,423].

a746 ᴱ**Lindner** Manfred, Petra, neue Ausgrabungen und Entdeckungen. Bad Windsheim 1986, Delp. 328 p.; 340 fig. DM 39.80 [TR 83,107-9, R. *Wenning*].

a747 *Banning* Edward B., *Köhler-Rollefson* Ilse, Ethnoarchaeological survey in the Bēdā area, Southern Jordan: ZDPV 102 (1986) 152-170; 3 fig.; pl. 15-18.

a748 *Eadie* John W., *Oleson* John P., The water-supply systems of Nabataean and Roman Ḥumayma [S Petra]: BASOR 262 (1986) 49-76; 27 fig.

a749 *Sa'idiyeh:* → 595, SDB 11,60 (1986) 119-126; fig. 944-9 (J. B. *Pritchard*).

a750 (Mafraq, Fedein) *Samra:* SBFLA 36 (1986) 354-361, pl. 75-77 (J.-B. *Humbert*); → a729a.

a751 *Sela':* *Haag* E., Sæla': → 599, TWAT 5,7s (1986) 872-880.

a752 *Udruh:* *Homès-Fredericq* Denyse, Udhruh, een antieke karavaanstad en oase in de Jordaanse woestijn [exposition Bru *al.* 1987]: Akkadica 50 (1986) 42s.

a753 *Killick* Alistair, [Udruh], Nabataean pottery legacy: ILN Arch 3030 = 274,7059 (1986) 66 [p. 72s, *Lyall* Gavin, travel from Petra to Dubai].

a754 *Umm Ḥammâd:* *Helms* S. W., Excavations at Tell Um Hammad, 1984: Levant 18 (1986) 25-50; 19 fig.

a755 *Umm Rasās* (30 k SE Madaba) 1st 1986: SBFLA 36 (1986) 351-4; pl. 70-74 (M. *Piccirillo*).

a756 *Piccirillo* Michele, Um er-Rasas Kastron Mefaa in Giordania: TerraS 62,6 Sup. (1986). 32 p.; ill.

τ5.1   **Phoenicia** – *Libanus*, **Lebanon.**

a757 *a*) *Baurain* Claude, Portées chronologique et géographique du terme 'phénicien'; – *b*) *Bunnens* Guy, Aspects religieux de l'expansion phénicienne: ➤ 551, Religio phoenicia 1984/6, 7-28 / 119-125.

a758 **Elayi** Josette, The Phoenician cities and the Assyrian Empire in the time of Sargon II: ➤ 563*, Sumer 42 (1986) 129-132, ❹ 71-73.

a759 *Garbini* G., 'Paisà' [Herodotus 7,89 puts origin of Phoenicians near 'Eritrean Sea', Persian Gulf not Red Sea; but really they were installed before 2000]: ParPass 214 (1984) 39-41.

a760 ᴱ*Gubel* E., *al*. [*Homès-Fredericq* D., introd.] Studia Phoenicia [Namur] III 1985 ➤ **1**,556: ᴿSalesianum 48 (1986) 984s (R. *Gottlieb*).

a761 **Spanuth** Jürgen, Die Phönizier, ein Nordmeervolk im Libanon. Osnabrück 1985, Zeller. 234 p. [ÉtClas 55,231, Corinne *Bonnet*].

a762 *Baʿalbek:* **Habachi** René, Le moment de l'homme [= réédition de] Commencement de la créature [1965, et de] La colonne brisée de Baalbeck [1968, philosophie de Vie et mort; rien de l'archéologie]: Connivence. P 1984, Desclée-B. 272 p. – ᴿRThom 86 (1986) 171 (J.-M. *Fabre*).

a763 *Strobel* Karl, *a*) Zur Rekonstruktion der Laufbahn des C. Velius Rufus [70-89 n.Chr.; Statuenbasis Baalbek]; – *b*) [Derselbe c. 84] Zu den Vexillationsziegelstempeln von Mirebeau bei Dijon: ZPapEp 64 (1986) 265-286 / 257-264.

a764 *Byblos:* *Peña* Ignacio, Un estilita a Biblos: SBFLA 36 (1986) 247-252; pl. 3-4.

a765 *Prag* Kay, Byblos and Egypt in the fourth millennium B.C.: Levant 18 (1986) 59-74; 1 fig.; pl. V-XII.

a766 **Salles** J. F., La nécropole 'K' de Byblos: RCiv Mém. 2, 1980 ➤ 61,s999: ᴿAulaO 4 (1986) 352s (C. *Gómez Bellard*).

a767 *Thissen* Heinz J., Die Königin von Byblos; zu Plut. Is. 15: GöMiszÄg 90 (1986) 79-84.

a768 **Nibbi** Alessandra, *a*) Ancient Byblos reconsidered 1985 ➤ **1**,d729: ᴿBO 43 (1986) 689-692 (W. A. *Ward*: her guesswork has not changed the textbook-view). – *b*) Wenamun and Alashiya reconsidered 1985 ➤ **1**,e388: ᴿMuséon 99 (1986) 358s (C. *Vandersleyen*: on parlera de la géographie avant/après Nibbi).

a769 ʿAqura (-Byblos): *Elayi* J.,   Un isolat de culture phénicienne [headers-stretchers wall corner]: RStFen 14 (1986) 113s; 1 fig.

a770 *Kāmid al-Lōz:* **Hachmann** R., *al*., Bericht über... Kāmid el-Loz 1971-4, 1982 ➤ **1**,d732: ᴿZAss 16 (1986) 306-9 (M. *Görg*).

a771 **Frisch** Bertram, *al.*, Kamid el-Loz 6. Die Werkstätten der spätbronzezeitlichen Paläste: Saarbrücker Bei 33, 1985 ➤ **1**,d735: ᴿSyria 63 (1986) 441s (H. de *Contenson*).

a772 **Sidon:** *Ben-Dov* Meir, ❹ The sea and the land fort at Sidon: Qadmoniot 19 (1986) 113-9; ill.

a773 **Engle** Anita, The Proto-Sidonians; glassmakers and potters: Readings in Glass History 17. J 1983, Phoenix. 102 p.; 60 fig.

a774 **Schmidt-Dounas** Barbara, Der lykische Sarkophag aus Sidon 1985 ➤ **1**,d742*b*; ᴿAJA 90 (1986) 488 (Susan *Kane*); DLZ 107 (1986) 317-9 (M. *Oppermann*).

a775 **Stucky** Rolf A., Tribune d'Echmoun; ein griechischer Reliefzyklus des

4. Jahrhunderts v.Chr. in Sidon, 1984 → 65,b13; **1**,d743: ᴿBO 43 (1986) 482-4 (J. W. *Betlyon*); JHS 106 (1986) 249 (G. B. *Waywell*).

a776 **Tyrus:** *Rey-Coquais* Jean-Paul, Tyr après les Phéniciens: Archéologia 211 (1986) 22-29; (color.) ill.

т5.2   *Situs mediterranei* **phoenicei et punici.**

a777 **Blázquez** J. M., Fenicios y Cartagineses en la Península Ibérica 1980 → 61,m936 ... 64,b527: ᴿJESHO 29 (1986) 214-6 (G. *Bunnens*).

a778 *Culican* William, a) Aspects of Phoenician settlement in the West Mediterranean; – b) Quelques aperçus sur les ateliers phéniciens: → 146, Opera 1986, 629-648 [673-684] / 649-671.

a779 *Du Buit* F. M., Phéniciens: → 578, Catholicisme XI,49 (1986) 141-3.

a780 *Garbini* Giovanni, 1979; un bilancio per gli studi fenici: RStFen 14 (1986) 117-128.

a781 a) *Hoz* J. De, Las lenguas e la epigrafia prerromanas de la península ibérica; – b) *Gonzalbes Gravioto* E., La administración local en la Hispania cartaguesa [AION 45,707]: Actas del VI congreso español de estudios clásicos (M 1983) I, 351-396 / II, 7-17.

a782 *Lebrun* R., Observations sur les relations entre la Phénicie et l'Anatolie au premier millénaire avant J.-C.: → 553, Cinquième = Akkadica 47 (1986) 80.

a783 ᴱNiemeyer H. G., Phönizier im Westen 1979/83 → 64,727; 65,b17: ᴿAulaO 4 (1986) 353s (G. del *Olmo Lete*); IsrEJ 36 (1986) 281s (E. *Stern*); VDI (1986,3) 192-202 (V. I. *Kozlovskaya*, A. Yu. *Sogomonov*: 'Phoenician expansion in the Mediterranean', international symposium in Köln 24-27.IV.1979).

Olmo Lete Gregorio del, *Aubet Semmler* Maria Eugenia, Los Fenicios en la Península Ibérica, I. Arqueología, cerámica y plástica; II. Epigrafía y lengua; glíptica y numismática; expansión e interacción cultural 1986 → 353.

a785 *Parzinger* Hermann, *Sanz* Rosa, Zum ostmediterranen Ursprung einer Gürtelhakenform der Iberischen Halbinsel: MadMit 27 (1986) 169-194; 7 (foldout) fig.

a786 *Pérez* C. J., Bibliografía sobre los Fenicios en la península ibérica: AulaO 4 (1986) 315-338; → 7473ss.

a787 ᴱSpaltenstein François, Commentaire des Punica di SILIUS Italicus (livres 1 à 8): Univ. Lausanne lett. 28. Genève 1986, Droz. xx-563 p.

a788 **Tejera Gaspar** A., Las tumbas fenicias y púnicas del mediterráneo occidental (estudio tipológico); Anales fil./letras. Sevilla 1979, Univ. 202 p.; 14 maps. – ᴿAulaO 4 (1986) 341-3 (G. del *Olmo Lete*).

---

a789 *Almuñécar:* **Molina Fajardo** F., Almuñécar en la antigüedad; la necrópolis fenicio-púnica de Noy. Granada 1982 [AION 45, 708:] ᴿRArchéolog (1984) 368 (G. *Clerc*).

a790 *Cagliari:* **Manfredi** Lorenza-Ilia, Amuleti punici di Cagliari: AION 46 (1986) 161-6; 14 fig.

a791 **Bartoloni** Piero, Studi sulla ceramica fenicia e punica di Sardegna: StFen 15, 1983 → 65,b31: ᴿRBgPg 64 (1986) 197 (J. *Debergh*).

a792 a) *Bernardini* Paolo, Precolonizzazione e colonizzazione fenicia in Sardegna; – b) *Botto* Massimo, I commerci fenici nella Sardegna e la fase precoloniale: EgVO 9 (1986) 101-116 / 125-149.

a793 **Hölbl** Günther, Ägyptisches Kulturgut im phönikischen und punischen Sardinien: ÉPR 102. Leiden 1986, Brill. I. Text, xxi-430 p., 76 fig.; bibliog. p. xv-xxi; II. Anmerkungen, Indices; 244 p., 183 pl + V color. 90-04-07183-0; 4-9.

a794 **Moscati** Sabatino, Italia Punica. Mi 1986, Rusconi. lxiv-416 p. [Aula-Or 5,327, M. *Fernández-Miranda*].

a795 *Rowland* R.J., Beyond the frontier in Punic Sardinia: AmJAncH 7 (1982) 20-39.

a796 *a*) *Maass-Lindemann* Gerta, Vasos fenicios de los siglos VIII-VI; su procedencia y posición dentro del mundo fenicio occidental; – *b*) *Bisi* A.M., La coroplastica fenicia d'Occidente (con particolare riguardo a quella ibicenca); – *c*) *Perea Caveda* A., La orfebrería púnica de Cádiz: ⇥ 353, ᴱ*Olmo Lete* G. del, Fenicios 1986, I. 227-230; 2 fig.; 8 color. pl. [al. 241-283] / 285-294 / 295-312; 10 pl. + 4 color.

a797 *Mozia:* *Acquaro* E., Mozia, la campagna di 1985 [*Moscati* S., stele]: RStFen 14 (1986) 82-89; pl. V-XII [91s; 1 fig.; pl. XIII].

a798 *Tusa* V., Il giovane di Mozia: RStFen 14 (1986) 143-152; pl. XX-XXIV.

a799 *Sirai:* *Santoni* V., Ceramica fenicia dal nuraghe Sirai di Carbonia: RStFen 14 (1986) 181-4; 1 fig.; pl. XXVIII.

a800 *Sulcis:* **Moscati** Sabatino, Le stele di Sulcis; caratteri e confronti: Coll. Studi Fenici 23. R 1986, Cons. Naz. Ric. 106 p.; 6 fig.; XXIII pl.

a801 **Bartoloni** Piero, Le stele di Sulcis; catalogo: Coll. Studi Fenici 24. R 1986, Cons. Naz. Ric. 248 p.; CLI pl.

a802 *Taršiš:* *Wagner* C.G., Tartessos y las tradiciones literarias: RStFen 14 (1986) 201-228.

a803 **Koch** M., [1 Kg 10,22 ...] Tarschisch und Hispanien ... 1984 ⇥ 65,b35; 1,d774: ᴿAulaO 4 (1986) 348s (G. del *Olmo Lete*).

a804 *Tharros:* *Acquaro* E., Tharros XII, la campagna del 1985: RStFen 14 (1986) 95-97; pl. XIV-XVI [99, *Garbini* G., iscrizione punica pl. XVII].

a805 *Toscanos:* *a*) *Niemeyer* H.G., El yacimiento fenicio de Toscanos; balance de la investigación 1964.1979; – *b*) *Schubart* H., Asentimientos fenicios en la costa meridional de la península ibérica; – *c*) *Bendala Galan* M., La perduración púnica en los tiempos romanos; el caso de Carmo: Huelva arqueológica 6 (1982) 101-130 [AION 45,707s] / 71-99 / 193-203.

a806 *a*) *Aubet Semmler* M.E., Los fenicios en España, estado de la cuestión y perspectivas; – *b*) *Escacena* J.L., Gadir; – *c*) *Schubart* H., El asentamiento fenicio del s. VIII a.C. en el Morro de Mezquitilla (Algarrobo, Málaga); – *d*) *Pellicer* Catalán, Sexi fenicia y púnica; – *e*) *Niemeyer* H.G., El yacimiento fenicio de Toscanos, urbanística y función; – *f*) *Gómez Bellard* C., Asentamientos rurales en la Ibiza púnica: ⇥ 353, ᴱ*Olmo Lete* G. del, Fenicios 1986, I, 9-30; 9 fig.; IX pl. + 5 color. / 39-52; 4 fig. XIV pl. / 59-79; 11 fig.; VI pl. / 85-107; 10 fig. / 109-126; 8 fig. / 177-192; 6 fig.

a807 *Blázquez* J.M., La colonización fenicia en la Alta Andalucía (Oretania) S. VIII-VI A.C.: RStFen 14 (1986) 53-80; pl. I-IV; foldout map.

T5.3 **Carthago.**

a808 **Benichou-Safar** Hélène, Les tombes puniques de Carthage 1982 ⇥ 65,b38; 1,d780: ᴿCBQ 48 (1986) 101s (W.G.E. *Watson*); RBgPg 64 (1986) 173-5 (J. *Debergh*); RStFen 14 (1986) 111s (Daniela *Ferrari*).

a809 *Fantar* Mhamed, Les tombes puniques de Carthage [*Bénichou-Safar* H. 1982]: AntAfr 20 (1984) 95-103.

a810 *Ribichini* Sergio, Morte e oltretomba a Cartagine [*Benichou-Safar* H. 1982]: SMSR 51 (1985) 353-364.

a811 *a) Bonnet* Corinne, Le culte de Melqart à Carthage; un cas de conservatisme religieux; – *b) Huss* Werner, Hannibal und die Religion; – *c) Amadasi Guzzo* Maria Giulia, La documentazione epigrafica del *Tofet* di Mozia e il problema del sacrificio *molk*: ➤ 551, Religio phoenicia 1984/6, 209-222; 4 fig. / 223-238 / 189-207.

a812 **Brown** Susanna S., Late Carthaginian child sacrifice and sacrificial monuments in their Mediterranean context [tophet 750-146 B.C.]: diss. Indiana 1986, ᴰ*Jacobsen* T. 410 p. 87-07776. – DissA 47 (1986s) 4425s-A.

a812* *Clover* Frank M., Felix Karthago: DumbO 40 (1986) 1-16; 17 fig.

a813 **Hans** Linda-Marie, Karthago und Sizilien; die Entstehung und Gestaltung der Epikratie auf dem Hintergrund der Beziehungen der Karthager zu den Griechen und den nichtgriechischen Völkern Siziliens 1983 ➤ **1**,d786: ᴿGerión 4 (1986) 350-2 (P. A. *Barceló*).

a814 *a) Huret* H. R., *Roskams* S. P., [➤ 65,b42] Salammbo I, The site and finds other than pottery; – *b)* **Fulford** M. G., *Peacock* D. P. S., 2. The pottery and other ceramic objects: Excavations at Carthage. Sheffield 1984, Univ., for British Academy. xiv-271 p., 78 fig., 30 pl.; xi-284 p., 96 fig., 6 pl. £55 [AntiqJ 67,175, J. *Hayes*]. 0-906090-15-6 [6-4 vol. 1; 7-2 vol. 2].

a815 **Huss** Werner, Die Geschichte der Karthager: HbAltW 3/8, 1985 ➤ **1**,d789: ᴿMundus 22 (1986) 191s (K. *Christ*).

a816 **Lancel** S. *al.*, Byrsa, rapports préliminaires I. des fouilles 1974-6; II. [➤ 64,b588] sur les fouilles 1977s, niveaux et vestiges puniques: ÉcFR 41. R 1982, École française de Rome. 351 p., 5 foldout maps; 417 p., 10 foldout maps. – ᴿAulaO 4 (1986) 350s (G. del *Olmo Lete*).

a817 *Leroy* Frédéric, Les citernes de Carthage et Dougga: Archéologia 218 (1986) 16-21; (color.) ill.

a818 *Lund* John, Punic Carthage in the light of recent excavations: MusTusc 56 (1984ss) 380s; dansk 363-380; 11 fig.

a818* *Ridley* R. T., To be taken with a pinch of salt; the destruction of Carthage: ClasPg 81 (1986) 140-6.

a819 *Tsirkin* Ju. B., Carthage and the problem of *polis*, ᵀ*Chistonogova* L.: RStFen 14 (1986) 129-141.

a820 *Tusa* V., I Cartaginesi nella Sicilia occidentale: Kokalos 28s (1982s) 131-149 [*al.*: AION 45 (1985) 709].

a821 *Yorke* R. A., *Davidson* D. P., Survey of building techniques at the Roman harbours of Carthage and some other North African ports: ➤ 571, ᴱ*Raban* A., Harbours 1983/5, 157-164.

T5.4 **Ugarit** – *Ras Šamra.*

a822 **Callot** Olivier, Une maison à Ougarit 1983 ➤ 64,b601; 65,b58: ᴿOLZ 81 (1986) 462-4 (C. *Tietze*).

a823 *Callot* Olivier, La région nord du Palais Royal d'Ugarit: CRAI (1986) 735-755; 8 fig.

a824 **Craigie** P. C., Ugarit and the OT 1983 ➤ 64,b603 ... **1**,d808: ᴿHenoch 8 (1986) 244s (P. G. *Borbone*).

a825 **Del Monte** G. F., Il trattato fra Muršili II di Ḫattuša e Niqmepaʿ di Ugarit: OrAntColl 18. R 1986, Istituto per l'Oriente. xiv-204 p. [ZAW 99,139, J. A. *Soggin*].

a826 **Hendel** Ronald S., Parallel themes in the Ugaritic epic poem and the Hebrew Bible [< diss. Harvard], 1985 Dahood Memorial prize essay,

Anaheim SBL meeting. – BAR-W 12,2 (1986) 11; subject assigned for the 1986 $1000 prize is 'The impact of Ugaritic on Old Testament studies'.

a827 **Kinet** Dirk, Ugarit... AT: SBS 104, 1981 ➤ 63,d173... 65,b61: ᴿBZ 30 (1986) 127s (A. *Schmitt*).

a828 *Lagarce* Jacques, Herstellung von Kupferrohbarren in Ras Ibn Hani (Syrien): AcPraeh 18 (1986) 85-90; 4 fig.

a829 *a) Lipiński* E., Scribes d'Ugarit et de Jérusalem; – *b) Aartun* R., Herkunft und Sinn des Namens Aqht im Ugaritischen Material: ➤ 47, ᶠHOSPERS J., Scripta 1986, 143-154 / 9-14.

a830 *a) Soldt* W. H. van, The palace archives at Ugarit; – *b) Wansbrough* John, Ugarit in chancery practice: ➤ 545*, Rencontre 30ᵉ 1983/6, 196-204 / 205-9.

a831 *Soldt* W. H. van, The queens of Ugarit: JbEOL 29 (1985s) 68-73.

a832 **Stucky** Rolf A., Ras Shamra, Leukos Limen; die nachugaritische Besiedlung von Ras Shamra: IFAPO Mission Archéologique de Ras Shamra 1, 1983 ➤ 64,b620; 65,b67: ᴿBO 43 (1986) 485-8 (J. *Lund*); DLZ 107 (1986) 901s (B. *Brentjes*: 'Shambra').

a833 **Tyloch** Witold, ✪ Odkrycia w Ugarit a Stary Testament 1980 ➤ 62,b834; 63,d181: ᴿOLZ 81 (1986) 35s (Z. J. *Kapera*).

a834 *a) Zwicker* Ulrich, Untersuchungen an Silber aus den Grabungen von Ugarit (Ras Shamra, Syrien) und Vergleich mit Silber von antiken Münzen; – *b) Herbrodt* Suzanne, Die Goldschale aus Ras Šamra im Museum Aleppo; ein Beitrag zu den Beziehungen zwischen Ägypten, der Ägäis und Vorderasien: AcPraeh 18 (1986) 157-176; 25 fig. / 91-116; 23 fig.

T5.5   **Ebla.**

a835 *Archi* Alfonso, *a)* Berechnungen von Zuwendungen an Personengruppen in Ebla: AltOrF 13 (1986) 191-205; – *b)* Die ersten Zehn Könige von Ebla: ZAss 76 (1986) 213-7.

a836 *Chiera* Giovanna, Il messaggero di Ibuba [Ebla]: OrAnt 25 (1986) 81-86.

a837 **Edzard** Dietz O., Verwaltungstexte verschiedenen Inhalts (aus dem Archiv L. 2769): ARET 2, 1981 ➤ 62,b841: ᴿJNES 45 (1986) 79-81 (P. *Michalowski*); OLZ 81 (1986) 556-9 (W. *Sommerfeld*).

a838 **Matthiae** Paolo, I tesori di Ebla 1984 ➤ 65,b87; 1,d835: ᴿHenoch 8 (1986) 397s (Piera *Arata Mantovani*).

a839 *a) Matthiae* Paolo, The archives of the Royal Palace G of Ebla; distribution and arrangement of the tablets according to the archaeological evidence; – *b) Archi* Alfonso, The archives of Ebla: ➤ 545*, Rencontre 30ᵉ, 1983/6, 53-71 / 72-86; ill.

a840 *Negoiţă* Athanasie, Les nouvelles découvertes d'Ebla (roum.): STBuc 37 (1985) 666-673.

a841 **Pettinato** Giovanni, Ebla; nuovi orizzonti della storia, Mi 1986, Rusconi. 451 p.; 38 fig.; 25 pl.; bibliog. p. 415-433. 88-18-12036-0.

a842 *a) Pinnock* Frances, The lapis lazuli trade in the third millennium B.C. and the evidence from the royal palace G of Ebla; – *b) Shaath* Shawqi, Three new steatite pyxides from northern Syria in the Aleppo museum: ➤ 87, ᶠPORADA E., Insight 1986, 221-8; pl. 51-52 / 237-243; pl. 56-58.

a843 *Postgate* J. N., Abu Essalabikh Tell Mardikh; Sumer and Ebla: Sumer 42 (1986) 68-70 [27s, *Moon* J. A., ceramic sequence].

a844 *Stieglitz* Robert R., Notes on riverine-maritime trade at Ebla: ➤ 571, ᴱRaban A., Harbours 1983/5, 7-10.

a845 *Waetzoldt* Hartmut, Ohne Parallelstellen geht es nicht, oder: Lesung

eblaitischer Wörter und Namen — eine Glücksache [*Pettinato* G. inedita; *Krebernik* M. ...]: JAOS 106 (1986) 553-5.
a846 *Xella* Paolo, 'Le grand froid', le dieu *Baradu madu* à Ebla: UF 18 (1986s) 437-444.

T5.8 **Situs effossi Syriae** *in ordine alphabetico.*

a847 *Kohlmeyer* Kay, Euphrat-Survey 1984, zweiter Vorbericht: MDOG 118 (1986) 51-65; 8 fig.
a848 **Meijer** Diederik J. W., A survey in northeastern Syria: Uitgaven Ned. Inst. Istanbul 58. Leiden 1986, Nederlands Instituut voor het Nabije Oosten. 59 p.; 34 fig.; bibliog. p. 56-58. 90-6258-058-0.
a849 **Peña** L., *al.*, Les cénobites syriens 1983 ↠ 64,d931*b*; 65,b113: ᴿBO 43 (1986) 489s (J. *Wilkinson*); Syria 63 (1986) 172-4 (J.-L. *Biscop*).
a850 *Peña* Ignacio, La desconcertante vida de los monjes sirios, siglos IV-VI [síntesis de Les stylites syriens 1975, Les reclus syriens 1980, Les cénobites syriens 1983]: El peso de los días 22. Salamanca 1985, Sígueme. 159 p.; ill. pt 1000. 84-201-0983-8 [ActuBbg 24,127, J. *Vives*]. – ᴿLumenV 35 (1986) 547s (F. *Ortiz de Urtaran*); RazF 213 (1986) 662 (M. *Alcalá*).
a851 *Aleppo:* ᴱ**Gaube** Heinz, **Wirth** Eugen, Aleppo; historische und geographische Beiträge zur baulichen Gestaltung, zur sozialen Organisation und zur wirtschaftlichen Dynamik einer vorderasiatischen Fernhandelsmetropole: TAVO B-58, 1984 ↠ 65,b110; DM 267: ᴿMundus 22 (1986) 61s (H. *Müller*).
a852 *Amrit: Puech* Émile. Les inscriptions phéniciennes d'Amrit et les dieux guérisseurs du sanctuaire: Syria 63 (1986) 327-342; 4 fig.
a853 *Apamée* 1984/5: Syria 63 (1986) 391-7 (J.-C. *Balty*).
a854 *Canivet* Maria T., Ricerche archeologiche nell'Apamene (Siria) [< Rendiconti Ist. Lombardo 103 (1969) 799-812]: ↠ 139, Scritti 1986, 173-186 (-206; 207-296 Huarte).
a855 *Bassit:* a) *Courbin* Paul, Bassit; - b) *Braemer* Frank, La céramique à engobe rouge de l'âge du Fer à Bassit; - c) *Gagnier* Pierre-Yves, Les restes fauniques: Syria 63 (1986) 175-220; 59 fig. [+ 387-391] / 221-246; 11 fig. / 247-255.
a856 *Bīʿa: Strommenger* Eva, *al.*, Ausgrabungen in Tall Biʿa 1984; MDOG 118 (1986) 7-44; 27 fig.
a857 *Boṣra:* **Dentzer** J.-M., Hauran I., Recherches archéologiques sur la Syrie du sud à l'époque hellénistique et romaine 1-2: BAH 124. P 1986, Geuthner. xiv-217 p.; p. xii + 219-426. 2-7053-0262-X. – ᴿBerytus 33 (1985) 167s (G. W. *Bowersock*); SBFLA 36 (1986) 371s (P. *Kaswalder*).
a858 *Dentzer* Jean-Marie, Les sondages de l'arc nabatéen et l'urbanisme de Boṣra: CRAI (1986) 62-86; 12 fig.
a859 *Farioli Campanati* Raffaella, a) Die italienischen Ausgrabungen in Bosra (Syrien); der spätantike Zentralbau der Kirche der Hll. Sergius, Bacchus und Leontius: Boreas 9 (Münster 1986) 173-185; pl. 24-25; - b) Gli scavi della chiesa dei SS. Sergio, Bacco e Leonzio a Bostra: Berytus 33 (1985) 61-74; 10 fig.
a860 **Sartre** Maurice, a) Bostra, des origines à l'Islam; – b) Inscriptions grecques et latines de la Syrie 13/1 Bostra Nos. 9001-9472 [↠ 64,8365]: BAH 117/113. P 1985/2, Geuthner. 278 p.; 60 fig. / 441 p.; LXXX pl. – ᴿSBFLA 36 (1986) 385s (M. *Piccirillo*).
a861 a) *Berthier* Sophie, Sondage dans le secteur des Thermes Sud à Buṣrā 1985; – b) *Bresenham* Mary, Descriptive and experimental study of

contemporary and ancient pottery techniques at Buṣrā: Berytus 33 (1985) 5-45; 140 fig. / 89-101; 15 fig. [47-50, 103-142 *al.*].

a862 *Danné:*   **Lebeau** Marc,   La céramique de l'âge du Fer II-III à Tel Abou Danné et ses rapports avec la céramique contemporaine en Syrie 1983 ➤ 64,b610; **1,d865**:   ᴿBASOR 262 (1986) 95s (Patricia M. *Bikai*); OLZ 81 (1986) 50-52 (B. *Brentjes*).

a863 *Dumayr* [45 k NE Damàscus]: *Ehrhardt* Norbert,   Die ala Vocontiorum und die Datierung des Tempels von Dmeir: ZPapEp 65 (1986) 225-230.

a864 *Dura-Europos:*   **MacDonald** David,   Dating the fall of Dura-Europos [could be 257]: Historia 35 (1986) 45-68; 3 fig.

a865 *Goldstein* Jonathan,   The central composition of the west wall of the synagogue of Dura-Europos: ➤ 11*, Mem. BICKERMAN E. = JANES 16s (1984s) 99-142; 13 fig.

a866 *Harmatta* J.,   Dura-Europos and its connection with Iranian Mesopotamia: Ann. Budapest class. 9s (1985) 45-48.

a867 *James* Simon,   Dura-Europos and the chronology of Syria in the 250s AD: Chiron 15 (1985) 111-124.

a868 *a)* *Leriche* Pierre, *al.*,   Le site de Doura-Europos; état actuel et perspectives d'action [reprise après 50 ans]; – *b)* *Downey* Susan B.,   The citadel palace at Dura-Europos; – *c)* *Allara* Anny,   Les maisons de Doura-Europos; questions de typologie; – *d)* *Leriche* P.,   Chronologie du rempart de brique crue de Doura-Europos; – *e)* *Augé* Christian,   Note sur les monnaies de Doura-Europos 1984; – *f)* *Rebuffat* René,   Le bouclier de Doura; – *g)* *James* Simon,   Evidence from Dura Europos for the origins of late Roman helmets; – *h)* *Arnaud* Pascal,   Doura-Europos, microcosme grec ou rouage de l'administration arsacide? Modes de maîtrise du territoire et intégration des notables locaux dans la pratique administrative des rois arsacides: Syria 63 (1986) 5-25; 11 fig. / 27-37; 9 fig. / 39-60; 14 fig. / 61-82; 14 fig. / 83s; 3 fig. / 85-105; 4 fig. / 107-134; 21 fig. / 135-155.

a869 *St. Clair* Archer,   The Torah shrine at Dura-Europos; a re-evaluation: JbAC 29 (1986) 109-117; pl. 14-15.

a870 *Emar:* **Arnaud** Daniel,   Recherches au pays d'Aštata, Emar VI: Synthèse 18. P 1985s, RCiv. I. Textes sum. acc. 382 p.; II. Planches 383-756; ensemble F 364; 2-86538-138-2. – III. Textes sum-acc. 494 p. F 325. 2-86538-137-4.

a871 *Ḥalaf:* *Moscati* Sabatino,   Due statue di Tell Halaf e i troni fenici: LinceiR 41,3 (1986) 53-56; pl. I-III.

a872 *Halawa:* **Orthmann** W.,   Halawa 1977-9:   1981 ➤ 65,b131:   ᴿBO 43 (1986) 201-4 (D. J. W. *Meijer*).

a873 *Ḥamidiyya* (30 k S Qamišli): **Eichler** Seyyare, *al.*,   Tall al-Hamidiya I. Vorbericht 1984: OBO arch 4, 1985 ➤ **1,d883**:   ᴿZAss 76 (1986) 158s (W. von *Soden*).

a874 *Ḥammām:* *Meyer* D. J. W.,   Tell Hammām in Noord-Syrië; een vluchtig overzicht van de architectuur uit vier campagnes: PhoenixEOL 32,2 (1986) 31-47; fig. 16-27.

a875 *Kôm:* **Dornemann** Rudolph H.,   A neolithic village at Tell el Kowm in the Syrian desert: SAOC 43. Ch 1986, Univ. Oriental Institute.   xii-89 p.; 46 pl. 0-918986-15-1.

a876 *Laḍiqiyya:* *Saadé* Gabriel,   Découvertes archéologiques à Lattaquié [1978-1985]: Syria 63 (1986) 157-9.

a877 *Mari* 4, Actes du colloque international CNRS 620, À propos d'un cinquantenaire 1983/5 ➤ **1,565**:   ᴿRHist 276 (1986) 191-3 (S. *Dupré*).

a878 *Margueron* Jean, Mari; principaux résultats des fouilles conduites depuis 1979: CRAI (1986) 763-785; 10 fig.

a879 *a) Margueron* Jean, Quelques remarques concernant les archives retrouvées dans le palais de Mari; – *b) Finet* André, Typologie des lettres des archives 'royales' de Mari: → 545*, Rencontre 30e, 1983/6, 141-152 / 153-9; ill.

a880 **Dossin** Georges, *Finet* André, Correspondance féminine, transcrite et traduite: ARM 10. P 1978, Geuthner. iv-300 p. F 250. – ᴿOLZ 81 (1986) 247-250 (J. *Benger*).

a881 **Talon** P., Textes administratifs des salles 'Y et Z' du Palais de Mari: ARM 24, 1985 → 1,d896: BL (1986) 105 (A. R. *Millard*: Nᵒ 75 may mention Hazor; vol. 22s also presented). BO 43 (1986) [113-]142-8 (J. M. *Sasson*).

a882 [Équipe dirigée par] **Durand** J.-M., [*Bardot* G., *al.*], Archives administratives de Mari 1: ARM 23, 1984 → 65,b142: ᴿJAOS 106 (1986) 356s (M. *Stol*).

a883 **Kupper** Jean-Robert, Documents administratifs de la Salle 135 du Palais de Mari, transcrits et traduits: ARM 22, 1983 → 65,b145: ᴿJAOS 106 (1986) 355s (M. *Stol*: with this volume, publication of ARM is transferred from Geuthner to ADPF); Syria 63 (1986) 445-8 (A. *Lemaire* aussi sur *Talon* ARM 24).

a884 *Charpin* Dominique, *Durand* Jean-Marie, 'Fils de Sim'al'; les origines tribales des rois de Mari: RAss 80 (1986) 141-183; 5 phot.; 2 facsim.

a885 **Sasson** Jack M., Dated texts from Mari, a tabulation: ARTANES 4, 1980 → 63,d297; 65,b148: ᴿJNES 45 (1986) 245s (B. J. *Beitzel*).

Anbar Moshe, ⊕ *Ha-šᵉbaṭîm ha-ᵃmoriyîm* ... The Amorite tribes in Mari and the installation of the benê Israel in Canaan, 1985 → 1950.

a887 **Dalley** Stephanie, Mari and Karana 1984 → 1,d893: BSOAS 386s (F. *Joannès*, français); WeltOr 17 (1986) 158s (J. R. *Kupper*: 30 corrections).

a888 *Melebiya:* printemps 1985: Akkadica 46 (1986) 1-28; 28-49 pl. (*Lebeau* M., *al.*).

a889 *Munbāqa: Machule* Dittmar, *al.*, Ausgrabungen in Tall Munbāqa 1984: MDOG 118 (1986) 67-145; 41 fig. [161-3, Metall].

a890 *Palmyra: Fiema* Zbigniew T., An inscription from the temple of Bel in Palmyra reconsidered: BASOR 263 (1986) 81-83; 1 fig.

a891 *Gawlikowski* Michel, Les comptes d'un homme d'affaires dans une tour funéraire à Palmyre: Semitica 36 (1986) 87-99; pl. XIV-XVI.

a893 ᴱ**Tanabe** Katsumi, Sculptures of Palmyra I: Memoirs I. Tokyo 1986, Ancient Orient Museum. 499 p.; 475 fig.; 2 maps. – ᴿMesopT 21 (1986) 292s (A. *Invernizzi*).

a894 *Will* Ernest, La déesse au chien de Palmyre; note additionnelle: Syria 63 (1986) 383s.

a895 *Zahrnt* M., Zum Fiskalgesetz von Palmyra und zur Geschichte der Stadt in hadrianischer Zeit: ZPapEp 62 (1986) 279-293.

a896 *Qitar: McClellan* Thomas L., El-Qitar; third season of excavation, 1984-5: AbrNahr 24 (1986) 83-106; 12 fig. [107-119, tomb, *Sagona* A. G.].

a897 *Resafa:* **Mackensen** Michael, Resafa I.; eine befestigte spätantike Anlage vor den Stadtmauern von Resafa... Sergiupolis: DAI, 1984 → 65,b159; 1,d927: ᴿMundus 22 (1986) 113s (K. *Schippmann*).

a898 **Ulbert** Thilo, Die Basilika des Heiligen Kreuzes in Resafa-Sergiupolis: DAI. Mainz 1986, von Zabern. xi-230 p.; 96 fig.; 87 pl.; 12 Beilagen. 3-8053-0815-9.

a899 *Tawi:* **Kampschulte** I., *Orthmann* W.,   Gräber des 3. Jahrtausends v.Chr. im syrischen Euphrattal I. Ausgrabungen bei Tawi 1975 und 1978: SaarbrückerBei-AltK 38, 1984 ➤ 1,b166; DM 70:   ᴿZAss 76 (1986) 146-151 (Kay *Kohlmeyer*).

T6.1 **Mesopotamia:** *generalia.*

a900 **Asher-Greve** Julia M.,   Frauen in altsumerischer Zeit: BibMesop 18, 1985 ➤ 1,1502.b87 [ᴰ1979]: ᴿMesopT 21 (1986) 273-7 (A. *Invernizzi*).

a901 ᴱ**Barrelet** Marie-Thérèse,   L'archéologie de l'Iraq 1978/80 ➤ 61,924... 1,d933: ᴿGnomon 58 (1986) 46-50 (Kay *Kohlmeyer*).

a902 ᶠDɪᴀᴋᴏɴᴏꜰꜰ I. M.,   Societies and languages of the ancient Near East 1982 ➤ 64,27: ᴿOLZ 81 (1986) 23-28 (C. *Zaccagnini*, Eng.).

a903 **Klengel-Brandt** Evelyn,   Assyrien, die archäologischen Denkmäler: Kleine Schriften 3.   B 1982, Vorderasiatisches Museum.   32 p.; ill.

a904 ᴱ**Nissen** H.-J., *Renger* J.,   Mesopotamien und seine Nachbarn, Renc. 25, 1978/82 ➤ 63,701; 1,d943:   ᴿJAOS 106 (1986) 365-7 (N. *Yoffee*: Mesopotamian studies were born and nurtured in the concern with Mesopotamia's impact... most significantly on ancient Israel).

a905 **Parrot** A.,   Sumer und Akkad[4], 1983 ➤ 64,b718; 65,b175; 3-406-08999-2 [!]:   ᴿBO 43 (1986) 793s (J. *Börker-Klähn*).

a906 Register Assyriologie 1968-72, Realien und Wörter: [ᴱ*Hirsch* H.] AfO Beih 21.   Horn, Österreich 1986, Berger.   iv-110 p.

a907 *Röllig* Wolfgang,   Assur - Geissel der Völker; zur Typologie aggressiver Gesellschaften: Saeculum 37 (1986) 116-128.

a908 *a*) *Scholz* Bernhard,   Mesopotamien und das Ausland; Gastarbeiter im alten Vorderasien; – *b*) *Galter* Hannes D.,   Das Šamši-Adad-Syndrom; Assyrien und die Folgen kultureller Innovationen: ➤ 542, Kulturkontakte 1986, 5-12 / 13-26.

a909 *Sarianidi* V. I., ❸ Mesopotamia and Bactria in the 2nd Millennium B.C.: SovArch (1986,2) 34-45; 8 fig.; Eng. 46.

a910 **Stein** Aurel,   Limes report [1938s], ᴱ*Gregory* Shelah, *Kennedy* David: BAR-Int 272. Ox 1985. – ᴿMesopT 21 (1986) 284-8 (A. *Invernizzi*).

a911 *Trenkwalder-Piesl* Helga,   Die österreichischen Ausgrabungen in Iraq; 1978 bis 1984: ➤ 81*, ᶠOʙᴇʀʜᴜʙᴇʀ K., Im Bannkreis 1986, 269-281; 5 fig.

a912 **Zadok** Ran,   Assyrians in Chaldean and Achemenian Babylonia: Assur 4/3, 1984 ➤ 65,9718: ᴿMesopT 21 (1986) 272s (P. *Negri Scafa*).

T6.3 *Mesopotamia,* **inscriptiones.**

a913 **Alberti** Amedeo, *Pomponio* Francesco,   Pre-Sargonic and Sargonic texts from Ur edited in UET 2 Supp: StPohl 13.   R 1986, Biblical Press. xv-134 p.; IV pl. 88-7653-585-3. – ᴿZAss 76 (1986) 118-120 (J. *Bauer*).

a914 *Cooper* Jerrold S.,   Sumerian and Akkadian royal inscriptions, I. Presargonic inscriptions: AOS Tr 1.   NHv 1986, American Oriental Soc. x-118 p.   0-940490-82-X.

a915 **Dalley** S., *Postgate* J. N.,   The tablets from Fort Shalmaneser 1984 ➤ 65,b181:   ᴿArOr 54 (1986) 198s (J. *Pečírková*).

a916 *Doherty* Timothy J. G.,   Die Keilschrifturkunden der Sammlung H. Grimme: ZAss 76 (1986) 76-84.

a917 **Donbaz** V., *Grayson* A. K.,   Royal inscriptions on clay cones from Ashur now in Istanbul 1984 ➤ 65,b183; 1,d952:   ᴿZAss 76 (1986) 301s (R. *Borger*).

a918 **Donbaz** Veysel, *Yoffee* Norman, Old Babylonian texts from Kish conserved in the Istanbul archaeological museums: BiblMesop 17. Malibu CA 1986, Undena. viii-94 p.; 23 fig.; VI pl. 0-89003-087-1; pa. 6-3.

a919 *Donbaz* V., More Old Assyrian tablets from Assur: Akkadica 42 (1985) 1-14; 15-23 = pl.

a920 *Driel* G. van, Neo-Babylonian texts from the Louvre [*Durand* J.-M., *Joannès* F., 1981s]: BO 43 (1986) 5-20.

a921 **Durand** Jean-Marie, Documents cunéiformes de ... l'ÉPHÉ 1, 1982 ➤ 63,d273: ᴿJNES 45 (1986) 328s (R. D. *Biggs*: tablets acquired by V. *Scheil*; the interesting ones were published long ago; many entrusted to scholars have disappeared, but some turned up at the Collège de France and will be published in vol. 2).

a922 **Durand** Jean-Marie, Textes babyloniens d'époque récente: RCiv Cah 6, 1981 ➤ 63,d273; 64,b721: ᴿOrientalia 55 (1986) 85-88 (G. J. P. *McEwan*). *Durand* J.-M., [Mésopotamie], *Masson* E. [Hittites]: ➤ 346*, [*Barucq* A.] Écrits de l'Orient ancien et sources bibliques 1986.

a923 *Ellis* Maria D., The archive of the Old Babylonian Kititum Temple and other texts from Ishchali [*Greengus* S. 1979]: JAOS 106 (1986) 757-786.

a924 *Fales* Frederick M., Cento lettere neo-assire 1983 ➤ 65,b186: ᴿBO 43 (1986) 439-445 (K. *Watanabe*).

a925 *a*) *Foster* B. R., Archives and empire in Sargonic Mesopotamia; – *b*) *Postgate* J. N., Administrative archives from the city of Assur in the Middle Assyrian period: ➤ 545*, Rencontre 30ᵉ 1983/6, 46-52 / 168-183.

a926 **Frankena** R., Kommentar zu den altbabylonischen Briefen aus Lagaba und anderen Orten: StCunBöhl 4, 1978 ➤ 61,q413: ᴿOrientalia 55 (1986) 190-2 (N. *Yoffee*).

a927 **Freydank** Helmut, Mittelassyrische Rechtsurkunden und Verwaltungs-texte II [32 Tafeln]: Vorderasiatische Schriftdenkmäler 21, 1982 ➤ 63, 2511: ᴿOLZ 81 (1986) 455-7 (G. *Wilhelm*).

a928 **Greengus** Samuel, Old Babylonian tablets from Ishchali and vicinity 1979 ➤ 65,b192: ᴿOrientalia 55 (1986) 336-9 (N. *Yoffee*).

a929 **Gurney** O. R., The Middle Babylonian legal and economic texts from Ur 1983 ➤ 1,d959: ᴿBSOAS 49 (1986) 565s (W. H. *Van Soldt*).

a930 **Gwaltney** W. C., The Pennsylvania Old Assyrian texts: HUC sup 3, 1983 ➤ 64,b722... 1,d960: ᴿJAOS 106 (1986) 567s (H. D. *Galter*).

a931 **Jacob-Rost** Liane, *Marzahn* Joachim, Assyrische Königsinschriften auf Ziegeln aus Assur 1985 ➤ 1,d962; DM 48: ᴿMundus 22 (1986) 104s (W. *Farber*); ZAss 76 (1986) 302-305 (W. *Richter*).

a932 **Joannès** Francis, Textes économiques de la Babylonie récente: ÉtAssyr 5, 1982 ➤ 63,d281; 64,b724: ᴿJNES 45 (1986) 81s (R. H. *Sack*: needed; index frustrating).

a933 *Joannès* Francis, Les archives d'une famille babylonienne sur des tablettes d'argile trouvées à Borsippa: Archéologia 219 (1986) 56-61; ill.

a934 **Klengel** Horst, Altbabylonische Texte aus Babylon 1983 ➤ 64,b726; 65,b196: ᴿOLZ 81 (1986) 245-7 (W. von *Soden*).

a935 *Koshurnikov* S. G., *Yoffee* N., Old Babylonian tablets from Dilbat in the Ashmolean museum: Iraq 48 (1986) 117-130.

a936 **Kraus** F. R., Altbabylonische Briefe in Umschrift und Übersetzung, X [208] Briefe aus kleineren westeuropäischen Sammlungen. Leiden 1985, Brill. xix-189 p. 90-04-07075-3. – ᴿBO 43 (1986) 732-6 (W. von *Soden*); JSS 31 (1986) 238-240 (D. J. *Wiseman*).

a937 *Lafont* Bertrand, Tablettes cunéiformes [12] de l'abbaye de Solesmes: RAss 80 (1986) 9-18.

a938 **Leichty** Erle, intr. *Reade* J. E., Catalogue of the Babylonian tablets in the British Museum, 6: Tablets from Sippar 1. L 1986, British Museum. xliv-308 p.; 2 maps. 0-7141-1115-5.

a939 **Livingstone** Alasdair, Mystical and mythological explanatory works of Assyrian and Babylonian scholars [diss. Birmingham 1980, DLambert W.]. Ox 1986, Clarendon. ix-270 p.; 7 pl. £30. 0-1908-5462-3. – RAntiqJ 66 (1986) 421s (S. *Dalley*).

a940 **McEwan** G. J. P., The Late Babylonian tablets in the Royal Ontario Museum 1982 → 63,d286; 65,b198: RJNES 45 (1986) 329-331 (R. D. *Biggs*); RAss 80 (1986) 79-81 (F. *Joannès*).

a941 **McEwan** Gilbert J. P., Late Babylonian texts in the Ashmolean museum: Ox Cuneiform Texts 10. Ox 1984, Clarendon. ix-126 p.; 88 facsimiles. £20. – RJRAS (1986) 97 (W. G. *Lambert*); ZAss 76 (1986) 154-8 (W. von *Soden*).

a942 **McEwan** Gilbert J. P., Texts from Hellenistic Babylonia in the Ashmolean Museum 1982 → 63,d285 ... 1,d966: ROrientalia 55 (1986) 468-472 (W. *Farber*: kritisch).

a943 *Maidman* M. P., The Nuzi texts of the British Museum: ZAss 76 (1986) 254-288.

a944 **Matouš** Lubor, *Matoušová-Rejmová* Marie, Kappadokische Keilschrifttafeln mit Siegeln aus den Sammlungen der Karlsuniversität in Prag 1984 → 65,b201; Kčs 45; RArOr 54 (1986) 305s (B. *Hruška*).

a945 *Michel* Cécile, Réédition des trente tablettes 'cappadociennes' de G. CONTENAU [1919]: RAss 80 (1986) 105-136; 137-140 facsimiles.

a946 *Negri Scafa* Paola, Gli scribi di Nuzi in funzioni diverse da redattori di testi; osservazioni preliminari: → 20, FDELLER K. MesopT 21 (F 1986) 249-259.

a947 **Neugebauer** O., Astronomical cuneiform texts; Babylonian ephemerides of the Seleucid period for the motion of the sun, the moon, and the planets I-III: Sources in the History of Mathematics 5. NY 1983, Springer. xxxvii-789 p.; 225 fig. – ROLZ 81 (1986) 229-232 (H. *Hunger*).

a948 **Owen** David I., [988 hand-copied Ur-III] Neo-Sumerian archival texts primarily from Nippur ... 1982 → 63,d291 ... 1,d971: RJNES 45 (1986) 326-8 (P. *Michalowski*).

a949 *Parpola* S., The Neo-Assyrian text corpus project of the University of Helsinki: Akkadica 49 (1986) 20-24.

a950 *Römer* W. H. P., Keilschrifttexte im Leidener Staatlichen Altertumsmuseum II. einige Urkunden aus dem Ur III-Zeit: OMRO 66 (1986) 31-58; 18 pl.

a951 **Sigrist** Marcel, Ur-III-Texte: Verstreute Publikationen aus Zeitschriften. B 1986. I.199 p. II.251 p. III.223 p. IV.275 p. V.249 p. Almost wholly facsimiles.

a952 **Stol** M., Letters from collections in Philadelphia, Chicago and Berkeley, transliterated and translated: Altbabylonische Briefe in Umschrift und Übersetzung 11. Leiden 1986, Brill. viii-129 p.; 5 facsimiles. 90-04-07705-7.

a953 *a) Veenhof* Klaas R., Cuneiform archives; an introduction; – *b) Tunca* Ö., Le problème des archives dans l'architecture religieuse protodynastique; – *c) Garelli* Paul, Les archives inédites [de provenance incertaine] centre provincial de l'empire assyrien; – *d) Greenfield* Jonas C., Aspects of archives in the Achaemenid period: → 545*, Rencontre 30e 1983/6, 1-36 / 37-45 / 241-6 / 289-295.

a954 **Weiher** Egbert von, Spätbabylonische Texte aus Uruk II. B 1983, Mann. ix-289 p.; ill. – EOLZ 81 (1986) 346-351 (J. *Oelsner*).

a955 **Westenholz** Aage, Literary and lexical texts and the earliest administrative documents from Nippur: BiblMesop 1, 1975 ➤ 57,7689b; 58,a017: ᴿOrientalia 55 (1986) 184s (D. O. *Edzard*).

т6.5 **Situs effossi Iraq** *in ordine alphabetico.*

a956 *Ajājā:* **Mahmoud** Asad, Neo-Assyrian sculptures from Saddikanni (Tell Ajaja): Assur 4/2. Malibu CA 1983, Undena. 0-89003-147-9. – ᴿBO 43 (1986) 794s (M. van *Loon*).

a957 *Arbān:* **Moortgat-Correns** Ursula, Die Eingangsfassade vom Palast des Mušēzib-Ninurta in ʿArbān-Šadikanni; ein Rekonstruktionsversuch: ZAss 76 (1986) 295-300; foldout fig.

a958 *Aššur:* **Pedersen** Olof, Archives and Libraries in the city of Assur 1985 ➤ 1,d981: ᴿWeltOr 17 (1986) 160s (W. *Röllig*).

a959 *Miglus* Peter A., Ein mittelassyrischer Anbau am Alten Palast in Assur: MDOG 118 (1986) 191-216; 14 fig.

a960 *Babylon:* **Oates** Joan, Babylon: Ancient Peoples and Places. L 1986, Thames & H. 216 p.; 137 fig. £6 pa. [Antiquity 60,178].

a961 *a) Hrouda* B., Zur Thronraumfassade der Südburg in Babylon; – *b) Nissen* Hans J., 'Sumerian' vs. 'Akkadian' art; art and politics in Babylonia of the mid-third millennium B.C.; – *c) Baffi Guardata* Francesca, Iconographic contributions of Palestinian glyptic to the Mitannian 'common style'; – *d) Moortgat-Correns* Ursula, Einige Bemerkungen zur [Mari] 'Statue Cabane'; – *e) Brandes* Mark A., Commemorative seals ? [Uruk]: ➤ 87, ᶠPORADA E., Insight 1986, 119-122; 7 fig. / 189-196 / 15-19 / 183-7; 2 fig.; pl. 36-38 / 51-55; 2 fig.

a962 *Borsippa:* *Reade* J.E., RASSAM's excavations at Borsippa and Kutha, 1879-82; Iraq 48 (1986) 105-116; 3 fig.; pl. XIII-XIX.

a963 *Der:* *Meyer* L. de, *Gasche* H., *al.*, Mission archéologique belge en Iraq; aperçu des travaux de la campagne de 1985: Akkadica 47 (1986) 1-29; ill.; giant foldout plan of Tell Der.

a964 *Habūba:* *Algaze* Guillermo, Habuba on the Tigris; archaic Nineveh reconsidered: JNES 45 (1986) 125-135; 3 fig.

a965 *Hamrin*-Sabra: *Tunca* Ö., La stèle de Baradan Bawi: Akkadica 43 (1985) 1-4; 2 fig.

a966 *Ḥatra:* *Invernizzi* Antonio, Traiano a Hatra? [no; testa più tardiva]; MesopT 21 (F 1986) 21-50; Eng. 51.

a967 *Imliḥîya:* **Boehmer** Rainer M., *Dämmer* Heinz W., Tell Imlihiye, Tell Zubeidi, Tell Abbas 1985 ➤ 1,e1: ᴿMundus 22 (1986) 267-9 (K. *Schippmann*).

a968 *Jarmo:* **Braidwood** L. & R., *al.*, Prehistoric archeology along the Zagros flanks 1983 ➤ 64,b751; 1,e5: ᴿOrient 28,1 (1985) 184-194 (A. *Tsuneki* ◑).

a969 *Khorsabad:* **Albenda** Pauline, The palace of Sargon, king of Assyria; monumental wall-reliefs at Dur-Sharrukin, from the original drawings made at the time of their discovery in 1843-1844 by Botta and Flandin. P 1986, RCiv. 188 p.; 197-280, French ᵀᴱ*Caubet* Annie; 97 fig.; 153 pl. F 352 [JNES 46,241]. 2-86538-152-8.

a970 *Albenda* Pauline, *Guralnick* Eleanor, Some fragments of stone reliefs from Khorsabad: JNES 45 (1986) 231-242; 10 fig. [fragments indeed].

a971 *Kifrin:* *Invernizzi* Antonio, Kifrin – *bech(ch)ouphrein* [Euphrates S Ana]: MesopT 21 (F 1986) 53-83; Eng. 84.

a972 *Nimrud:* *a) Winter* Irene J., The program of the throneroom of

Assurnasirpal II; – *b*) *Mallowan* Barbara P.,   Magic and ritual in the
Northwest Palace reliefs; – *c*) *Paley* Samuel M.,   Assyrian Palace reliefs;
finished and unfinished business: ➤ 122, ᶠWILKINSON C., NE Art 1983,
16-31; 16 fig. / 32-39; 12 fig. / 48-58; 5 fig.

a973 **Herrmann** Georgina, [1500!] Ivories from Room SW 37 Fort
Shalmaneser; 1s. Commentary and Catalogue: Ivories from Nimrud
(1949-1963) 4/1s. L 1986, British School of Archaeology in Iraq. 288 p.,
fig., 1 colour. pl.; vol. of 422 pl. £100. 0-903472-10-4.

a974 *Ninive:* a) *Parpola* Simo, The royal archives of Nineveh; – *b*) *Reade*
Julian, Archaeology and the Kuyunjik archives; – *c*) *Kwasman* T., Neo-
Assyrian legal archives in the Kouyunjik collection: ➤ 545*, Rencontre 30*
1983/6, 223-236 / 213-222, fig. 1-3 / 237-240.

a974* **Brackman** Arnold C., The luck of Nineveh. L 1980, Eyre Methuen.
viii-349 p.; 4 pl. 0-413-40170-7.

a975 *Qadissiya:* *Shukri* Sabah J. al-, *al.*, The salvage of the antiquities of the
Qadissiya Dam basin: Sumer 42 (1986) 9-12 (-25), ❹ 9-12 (-25).

a976 *Salābīḫ:* **Postgate** J. N., The west mound surface clearance: Abu
Salabikh Excavations 1, 1983 ➤ 64,b767 ... 1,e16: ᴿJAOS 106 (1986) 373s
(Elizabeth *Carter*).

a977 **Martin** Harriet P., *al.*, Graves 1 to 99: Abu Salabikh Excav. 2. L 1985,
Brit. Sch. Iraq. vi-224 p; 147 fig.; 32 pl. 0-903472-09-0. – ᴿMesopT 21
(1986) 277-9 (P. *Fiorina*).

a978 *Seleucia* (-Ctesiphon): *Valtz* Elisabetta, Trench on the east side of the
Archive Square (Seleucia, 12th season): MesopT 21 (F 1986) 11-20.

a979 *Shanidar:* **Solecki** Rose L., [An early village site at Zawi Chemi Shanidar
1981 ➤ 61,t940 ... 64,b769], answer to F. G. *Fedele*, MesopT [17 (1982)
178] 21 (1986) 261-4.

a980 *Uch:* ᴱGibson M., Uch Tepe I, 1981 ➤ 65,b249 (Ugh): ᴿZAss 76
(1986) 314-8 (D. *Sürenhagen*).

a981 *Umma:* **Foster** Benjamin R., Umma in the Sargonic period 1982
➤ 63,d338 ... 1,121: ᴿOrientalia 55 (1986) 186-190 (A. *Alberti*).

a982 *Ur:* **Gockel** Wolfgang, Die Stratigraphie und Chronologie der
Ausgrabungen des Diyala-Gebietes und der Stadt Ur ... 1982 ➤ 64,b708;
65,b252: ᴿOLZ 81 (1986) 459-462 (D. *Sürenhagen*).

T6.7   **Arabia.**

a983 **Bowersock** G. W., Roman Arabia 1983 ➤ 64,b788 ... 1,e30: ᴿClasPg 81
(1986) 262s (M. P. *Speidel*).

a983* *Bowersock* G. W., The Arabian Area; Scritti A. MOMIGLIANO (Como
1983) 43-47 [AION 45 (1985) 718].

a984 *Donner* Fred M., XENOPHON's Arabia: Iraq 48 (1986) 1-14.

a985 **Högemann** Peter, Alexander der Grosse und Arabien [< Diss. Wü
1982]: Zetemata 82. Mü 1985, Beck. ix-236 p. 3-406-30493-1. – ᴿZDPV
102 (1986) 182 (E. A. *Knauf*: only then did our 'Arabia' become part of
Greek 'Arabia').

a986 **MacAdam** Henry I., Studies in the history of the Roman province of
Arabia; the northern sector [< diss, Manchester]: BAR-Int 295. Ox 1986.
xv-420 p.; 12 fig.; 24 pl. £25 [AJA 91, 635, J. W. *Betlyon*].

a987 **Parker** S. Thomas, Romans and Saracens; a history of the Arabian
frontier: ASOR diss. 6. Winona Lake IN 1986, Eisenbrauns. xiv-247 p.;
74 fig. 7 pl. 0-89757-106-1: ᴿSBFLA 36 (1986) 378-381 (E. *Alliata*).

a988 **Sartre** M., Trois études sur l'Arabie romaine et byzantine: Coll. Latomus

178, 1982 → 65,a933: ᴿPEQ 118 (1986) 158 (J. *Bowsher*, also on BOWER-
SOCK).
Shahid Irfan,   Rome/Byzantium and the Arabs 1984 → 9693.
a990 *Stiegner* Roswitha G.,   Altsüdarabien — Teil des Alten und des Neuen
Orients?: → 542, Kulturkontakte 1986, 79-91; 3 fig.

---

a991 **Bahrain:** *Lowe* Anthony,   Bronze age burial mounds on Bahrain: Iraq
48 (1986) 73-84.
a992 **Mārib:** **Brunner** Ueli,   Die Erforschung der antiken Oase von Mārib...:
DAI-San'a, Archäologische Berichte aus dem Yemen 2, 1983 → 1,e41:
ᴿJNES 45 (1986) 315-7 (R. D. *Tindel*).
a993 **Ṣa'da:** **Gingrich** Andre,   Beiträge zur Ethnographie der Provinz Ṣa'da
(Nordjemen): Szb W ph/h 462. W 1986, Öster. Akad. 186+❹17 p.; 27
fig.; 18 pl.; bibliog. p. 172-6. 3-7001-0741-2.

T6.9 **Iran, Persia;** Asia centralis.

a994 ꟳBOYCE Mary, Papers = Acta Iranica 2/24s, 1985 → 1,26: ᴿStIran 15
(1986) 275-280 (P. *Gignoux*).
a995 *Brentjes* Burchard,   Archäologisches zu den Wanderungen der
Indoiraner: AltOrF 13 (1986) 224-238.
a996 **Carter** Elizabeth, *Stolger* Matthew W.,   Elam; surveys of political history
and archaeology: Near Eastern Studies 25.   Berkeley 1986, Univ.
California. xiv-328 p. (3 p. errata insert). – ᴿAJA 90 (1986) 350s (B. R.
Foster); WeltOr 17 (1986) 162s (H. *Koch*); ZAss 76 (1986) 151-4 (D. O.
Edzard).
a997 ꟳFISCHER K., ᴱOzols Jacob, *Thewalt* Volker,   Aus dem Osten des
Alexanderreiches; Völker und Kulturen zwischen Orient und Okzident:
Iran, Afghanistan, Pakistan und Indien 1983 → 65,50: ᴿGnomon 58
(1986) 372-4 (J. *Seibert*).
a998 **Smith** Philip E. L.,   Palaeolithic archaeology in Iran: Amer. Inst. Iranian
St. 1. Ph 1986, Univ. Museum. 111 p.; 15 fig. [JNES 46,244].
a999 *Tosi* M.,   The archaeology of early states in Middle Asia: OrAnt 25
(1986) 153-187.

b1 **Bisitun:** *Vogelsang* W.,   Four short notes on the Bisutun text and
monument: IrAnt 21 (1986) 121-140.
b2 *Schmitt* Rüdiger,   Bisitun — Babylon — Elephantine; Dareios' Thema mit
Variationen: → 80*, ꟳOBERHUBER K., Im Bannkreis 1986, 223-230.
b3 **Dahan-i Ghulaman:** *Genito* B.,   Dahan-i Ghulaman; una città achemenide
tra centro e periferia dell'impero: OrAnt 25 (1986) 287-317.
b4 **Hissar:** *Yule* Paul,   Tepe Hissar — neolithische und kupferzeitliche
Siedlung in Nordostiran: Materialien zur Allgemeinen und Vergleichenden
Archäologie 14, 1982 → 64,b814; 25 fig.; DM 11: ᴿPraehZ 61 (1986)
99-109 (R. *Dittmann*).
b5 **Laristan:** **Pohanka** Reinhard,   Burgen und Heiligtümer in Laristan,
Südiran; ein Surveybericht: Szb W 466, IranKom 19. W 1986, Österr.
Akad. 47 p., 19 fig. 3-7001-0760-9.
b6 **Naqš-i Rustam:** *Tanabe* Katsumi,   A study of the investiture of Narseh at
Naqsh-i Rustam — anahitah or queen of queens?:   Orient 22 (1986)
105-119; 17 fig.
b7 **Natanz:** **Blair** Sheila S.,   The Ilkhanid shrine complex at Natanz, Iran:

Harvard Middle East papers, classical 1. CM 1986, Univ. Center for ME studies. 102 p.; 7 fig.; 136 pl. [JNES 46,75].

b8 *Nuš-i Jan:* **Curtis** John, Nush-i Jan III. The small finds 1984 ⇸ 65,b284; 1,e63: ᴿBO 43 (1986) 800-3 (P. R. S. *Moorey*); OLZ 81 (1986) 387s (W. *Kleiss*).

b9 *Persepolis:* **Roaf** Michael, Sculptures and sculptors at Persepolis 1983 ⇸ 64,b826: ᴿAJA 90 (1986) 113s (Margaret C. *Root*).

b10 ᴱ**Shahbazi** A. Shapur, Corpus Inscriptionum Iranicarum I/1/1, Old Persian Inscriptions of the Persepolis Platforms. L 1985, Lund Humphries. 24 p.; XLVIII pl. – ᴿActOrK 47 (1986) 165-7 (B. *Utas*).

b11 **Walser** Gerald, Persepolis; *a*) die Königspfalz des Darius, 1980 ⇸ 61,t290; 63,d364; – *b*) la cité royale de Darius, ᵀ*Scheidegger* J. FrS 1981, Office du Livre. – ᴿBO 43 (1986) 803-8 (Michael *Roaf*).

b12 **Sumner** W. M., Achaemenid settlement in the Persepolis plain: AJA 90 (1986) 3-31.

b13 *Calmeyer* P., Dareios in Bagestana und Xerxes in Persepolis; zur parataktischen Komposition achaimenidischer Herrscherdarstellungen: Visible Religion 4s (1985s) 77-95 [< ᴢɪᴛ].

b14 *Sogdiana:* **Grenet** Frantz, L'art zoroastrien en Sogdiane; études d'iconographie funéraire: MesopT 21 (F 1986) 97-131.

b15 *Sokhta:* **Piperno** M., Aspects of ethnical multiplicity across the Shahr-i Sokhta graveyard: OrAnt 25 (1986) 257-270.

b16 *Susa:* **Lafont** Bertrand, À propos de la ville de Suse et d'un fragment d'enveloppe: RAss 80 (1986) 75s.

b17 *Schmandt-Besserat* Denise, Tokens at Susa: OrAnt 25 (1986) 93-125; pl. IV-X.

b18 *Toprak-kala:* **Grenet** Frantz, Palais ou palais-temple? Remarques sur la publication du monument de Toprak-kala [*Rapoport* J., *al.* 1984]: StIran 15 (1986) 123-135.

b19 *Tureng:* **Cleuziou** S., Tureng Tepe and burnished grey ware; a question of frontier?: OrAnt 25 (1986) 221-256.

b20 *Yahya:* **Amiet** Pierre, Antiquités trans-élamites [... Yahya, Iblis]: RAss 80 (1986) 97-104; 5 fig.

b21 **Lemberg-Karlovsky** C. C., Excavations at Tepe Yahya, Iran 1967-1975; the early periods: American School of Prehistoric Research Bulletin 38. CM 1986, Peabody Museum. xvii-346 p.; ill. 0-87365-541-9.

---

b22 **Briant** Pierre, L'Asie centrale ['Bactria'] et les royaumes proche-orientaux du premier millénaire (c. VIIIᵉ-IVᵉ siècles avant notre ère): Mémoire 42. P 1984, RCiv. 118 p.; 4 maps. F 70. 2-86538-092-0. – ᴿBO 43 (1986) 755s (J. M. *Balcer*).

b23 *a*) **Callieri** Pierfrancesco, I sigilli e le cretule del nord-ovest del sub-continente indiano e dell'Afghanistan dai Seleucidi ai Sasanidi; – *b*) *Vidale* Massimo, Lo studio dell'organizzazione industriale di Moenjodaro (Sind, Pakistan); elementi analitici per un sistema informativo 'a crescere': AION 46 (1986) 157-9.311-4 / 315-348; 12 fig.

b23* **Francfort** Henri-Paul, Fouilles d'Aï Khanoum [Afghanistan], III. Le sanctuaire du temple à niches indentées 2. Les trouvailles: Mémoires 27. P 1984, de Boccard. 145 p.; 32 fig.; XLI pl. – ᴿGnomon 58 (1986) 768-770 (Berthild *Gossel-Raeck*).

b24 **Bernard** Paul, Fouilles d'Aï Khanoum, IV. Les monnaies hors trésors; questions d'histoire gréco-bactrienne: Mémoires DAF Afghanistan 28. P

1985, de Boccard.   xix-181 p.; 3 fig.; 13 pl. F 460 [JHS 107,238, Susan *Sherwin-White*].

b25 *Debroy* B.,   Natural catastrophes and the Indus Valley civilization; Annals Bhandarkar 66 (1985) 1-12.

b26 ᴱ**Possehl** Gregory L.,   Harappan civilization; a contemporary perspective 1982 ⇥ 64,383; **1**,e81; 0-85668-211-X. – ᴿBO 43 (1986) 518-528 (E. C. L. *During-Caspers*).

          т7.1 **Aegyptus,** *generalia.*

b27 **Brugsch** Heinrich K.,   Recueil de monuments égyptiens dessinés sur lieux et publiés sous les auspices de son Altesse le vice-roi [1862-1885], 7. Teile in einem Band. Hildesheim 1981, Olms. 3-487-06979-2.

b28 *Condon* Virginia, [Seven royal hymns 1978, 58,d831... 65,9305] 'Two variant accounts?' by JANSSEN: VAeg [1/3,109] 2 (1986) 23-29.

b29 **Erman** A., *Ranke* H.,   La civilisation égyptienne: BiblHist. P 1985 = 1963, Payot. 751 p.; 285 fig.

b30 **Gomaà** Farouk,   Die Besiedlung Ägyptens während des Mittleren Reiches, 1. Oberägypten und das Fayyum: TAVO-B 66. Wsb 1986, Reichert. 463 p.

b31 ᴱ**Geus** Francis,   Archéologie du Nil moyen [... revue], Lille 1986, auct. 159 p. F 80 [JNES 46, 76].

b32 ᴱ**Grimal** N.-C.,   Prospection et sauvegarde des antiquités d'Égypte 1981 ⇥ 63,734; 65,b306: ᴿCdÉ 61 (1986) 248-251 (P. *Lacovara*).

b33 ᴱ**Israelit-Groll** Sarah,   Pharaonic Egypt; the Bible and Christianity [Hebrew Univ. symposium 'The Bible and Ancient Egypt', 4-6 Apr. 1984; 23 lectures] 1985 ⇥ **1**, 476; $30: ᴿIsrEJ 36 (1986) 285s (S. *Ahituv*: a single paper on the 'Christianity' of the title).

b34 ᴱ**James** T. G. H.,   Excavating in Egypt ...[1882-]1982 ⇥ 63,56; 64,a466: ᴿCdÉ 61 (1986) 251-3 (J. L. *Chappaz*).

b35 **King** Joan W.,   Historical dictionary of Egypt: African historical dictionaries 36.   Metuchen NJ 1984, Scarecrow. xiii-719 p.; bibliog. p. 633-719.

b36 *Leclant* Jean, *Clerc* Gisèle,   Fouilles et travaux en Égypte et au Soudan, 1984-1985, I. Égypte: Orientalia 55 (1986) 236-297; pl. VIII-LIV. 95 sites.

b37 *Leclant* Jean, *Asurmendi* Jesús, *al.*,   La Bible et l'Égypte: MondeB 45 (1986) 3-17 (-46).

b38 **Liebling** Roslyn,   Time line of culture in the Nile Valley and its relationship to other world cultures. NY 1986, Metropolitan Museum of Art. Unnumbered long vertical pages opening out into one continuous sheet.

b39 *Pernigotti* Sergio,   L'Egitto dei Faraoni: Archeo Dossier 11 (1986), 66 p., (color.) ill.

b40 ᶠSÄVE-SÖDERBERGH T.,   Sundries 1984 ⇥ 65,126: ᴿBO 43 (1986) 674-9 (E. S. *Bogoslovsky*: tit. pp. analyses).

          т7.2 **Luxor,** *Karnak;* **Thebae.**

b41 **Abd el-Raziq** Mahmud,   Die Darstellungen und Texte des Sanktuars Alexanders des Grossen im Tempel von Luxor: DAI-K 16. Mainz 1984, von Zabern. 62 p.; 16 pl. DM 88. – ᴿJAmEg 22 (1985) 252 (H. *Goedicke*).

b42 [*Golvin* J.-C., *al.*] Cahiers de Karnak 7, 1978-1981. P 1982, RCiv. 399 p. + ◐35 p. – ᴿJAmEg 22 (1985) 226-8 (C. C. *Van Siclen*, ample summaries).

b43 *Goyon* Jean-Claude, Thèbes, an 1000: MondeB 45 (1986) 18-22.

b44 **Jacquet** Jean,   Karnak-Nord V, le trésor de Thoutmosis Iᵉʳ, étude
architecturale 1983 ➤ 64,b901; 1,e102:   ᴿOLZ 81 (1986) 547-550 (Mag-
dalena *Stoof*).

b45 **Lalouette** Claire, Thèbes ou la naissance d'un Empire: Pharaons 2.   P
1986, A. Fayard. 650 p.; 4 maps; bibliog. p. 615-621. F 140. 2-213-
01734-4. – ᴿRHist 276 (1986) 427s (B. *Mathieu*).

b46 *Leclant* Jean, *Clerc* Gisèle, Karnak, (-Nord), [... p. 276 mission féminine
AWARE = American Women's Archaeological Research in Egypt, Pylon
10,1985], Luxor, Thebes left bank [... Budapest Univ. L. *Kákosy* 1984,
tomb of a Ramesses II official; Polish mission at Hatshepsut and
Thutmoses III funerary temples]: Orientalia 55 (1986) 272-285.

b48 *Masson* E., Nouvelles données sur la dégradation des grès de Karnak
(Égypte): RArchéom 9 (1985) 31-43.

b49 *Murnane* William J.,   False-doors and cult practices inside Luxor Temple:
➤ 77, ᶠMOKHTAR G. 1985, II, 135-148; 3 fig.; 2 pl.

b50 **Nelson** Harold H.,   The great hypostyle hall at Karnak I/1, The wall
reliefs, ᴱ*Murnane* William J.: OIP 106, 1981 ➤ 65,b318: ᴿCdÉ 61 (1986)
89-91 (R. van de *Walle*); JNES 45 (1986) 74s (D.P. *Silverman*).

b51 **Redford** Donald B.,   *a)* New light on Temple J at Karnak: Orientalia 55
(1986) 1-15; pl. I-III; – *b)* The Ashkelon relief at Karnak [hypostyle hall
outer wall near list not mentioned on Fig. 1] and the Israel stela: IsrEJ 36
(1986) 188-200; 1 fig.; pl. 22-26.

b52 **Saghir** Mohammed El-, *al.*, Le camp romain de Louqsor (avec une étude
des graffites gréco-romains du temple d'Amon): Mémoire 83. Le Caire
1986, IFAO. viii-127 p.; 71 fig.; XXII (foldout) pl. 2-7247-0033-3.

b53 *Schuller-Götzburg* Thomas,   Der Kultweg in den südlichen Räumen des
Tempels von Luxor: VAeg 2 (1986) 145-9; plan.

b54 **Traunecker** Claude, *al.*, La chapelle d'Achôris à Karnak 1981
➤ 64,b909 ... 1,e107: ᴿJAmEg 22 (1985) 217-9 (R.J. *Leprohon*); OLZ 82
(1986) 331-3 (R.S. *Bianchi*).

b55 **Traunecker** Claude, *Golvin* Jean-C., Karnak, Résurrection d'un site. FrS
1984, Office du Livre. 238 p; 153 fig. + 44 color. 2-228-00040-X. – ᴿBO
43 (1986) 79-81 (P.A. *Clayton*).

b56 **Van Siclen** Charles C.ᴵᴵᴵ,   The alabaster shrine of King Amenhotep II.
San Antonio 1986, auct. xv-59 p. 0-933175-05-1.

b57 *Van Siclen* Charles C.,   Amenhotep II's bark chapel for Amun at North
Karnak: BIFAO 86 (1986) 353-9; 4 fig.; pl. XLIII-LXI.

b58 [ᴱ*Wenta* E.] The Temple of Khonsu 1s, 1979/81 ➤ 62,k10: 1,e108: ᴿOLZ
81 (1986) 129-132 (S. *Wenig*).

---

b59 **Abitz** Friedrich,   Ramses III. in den Gräbern seiner Söhne: OBO 72.
FrS/Gö 1986, Univ./VR. 148 p.; 31 fig. (Anhang). 3-7278-0369-X / Gö
3-525-53701-X.

b60 **Arnold** Dieter,   Der Tempel des Königs Mentuhotep von Deir el-Bahari
3. Die königlichen Beigaben: DAI-K 23, 1981 ➤ 61,t373*b* ... 65,b324:
ᴿJNES 45 (1986) 307s (W.J. *Murnane*).

b61 **Bietak** Manfred, *Reiser-Haslauer* Elfriede, Das Grab des Ankh-Hor
1978/82 ➤ 65,b326: 1,e110: ᴿJEA 78 (1986) 214s (A. *Leary*).

b62 *Desroches-Noblecourt* Christiane, La Vallée des Reines retrouvera-t-elle sa
splendeur passée?: Archéologia 209 (1986) 22-37, (color.) ill.

b63 *Dodson* Aidan, Was the sarcophagus of Ramesses III begun for Sethos II?: JEA 78 (1986) 196-8.

b64 a) *Duc* Michel, La tombe aux vignes [=] b) *Nelson* Monique, La tombe de Sennefer maire de Thèbes: Archéologia 212 (1986) 30-35 / 36-41; (color.) phot.

b64* **Godlewski** Włodzimierz, Le monastère de St. Phoibammon: Deir El-Bahari 5, Wsz 1984, Państwowe. 83-01-05648-7 [OIAc Oc87].

b65 **Hegazy** E., *Tosi* M., A Theban private tomb, 295: Äg. Veröff. 45. Mainz 1983, von Zabern. 33 p.; 12 pl. – ᴿCdÉ 61 (1986) 91s (A. *Mekhitarian*).

b66 *Krauss* Rolf, Zum archäologischen Befund im thebanischen Königsgrab Nr. 62: MDOG 118 (1986) 165-181; 8 fig.

b67 **Laskowska-Kusztal** Ewa, Deir el-Bahari III. Le sanctuaire ptolemaïque. Wsz 1984, PWN. 140 p.; 81 pl.; 17 foldouts. 83-01-04512-4. – ᴿAntiqJ 66 (1986) 429s (P. A. *Clayton*).

b68 a) *Leblanc* Christian, DɪODORE, le tombeau d'Osymandyas et la statuaire du Ramesseum; – b) *Wysocki* Zygmunt, The discovery and reintegration of two niches in the East Chamber of Queen Hatshepsut's main sanctuary at Deir el-Bahri: ➤ 77, ᶠMOKHTAR G., 1985, ii,69-82; 6 pl. / 361-370; 6 fig.; 4 pl.

b69 *Nelson* Monique, Les récentes découvertes au Ramesseum: BSocFrÉg 106 (1986) 7-26; 5 fig.; IV pl.

b70 *Schaden* Otto J., Clearance of the tomb of king Ay (WV 23): JAmEg 21 (1984) 39-64; 39 fig.

b71 *Smith* Scot E., An assessment of structural deterioration of ancient Egyptian monuments and tombs in Thebes: JField 13 (1986) 503-510; 8 fig.

b72 *Wysocki* Zygmunt, The temple of Queen Hatshepsut at Deir el Bahari; its original form: MiDAI-K 42 (1986) 213-228; 5 fig.; pl. 30-31.

b73 **Morimoto** Iwataro, *al.*, Ancient human remains from Qurna, Egypt: Studies in Egyptian Culture 4. Tokyo 1986, Waseda Univ. [OIAc Ag87].

b74 *Qurna:* Osing J., Der Tempel Sethos' I in Gurna 1977 ➤ 60,t891; 62,k23: ᴿJAmEg 23 (1986) 225s (A. *Spalinger*).

---

b75 *Deir el-Medineh:* Bierbrier Morris, The tomb-builders of the Pharaohs 1984 ➤ 1,2378: ᴿArchaeology 39,3 (1986) 73.76 (Lisa *Sabbahy*).

b76 **Gasse** Annie, Catalogue des Ostraca figurés de Deir El-Médineh Nos 3100-3372 [fasc. 5]: Documents de Fouilles 23. Le Caire 1986, IFAO. vi-57 p.; 7 color. fig.; 40 pl. 2-7247-0032-5.

b77 *Keller* C. A., How many draughtsmen named Amenhotep? A study of some Deir el-Medina painters: JAmEg 21 (1984) 119-129.

b78 **Romer** John, [Deir el-Medineh] Ancient lives; the story of the Pharaohs' tombmakers 1984 ➤ 1,d311; 0-297-78646-6: ᴿBO 43 (1986) 419.

т7.3 **Amarna.**

b79 *Artzi* Pinchas, Observations on the 'library' of the Amarna archives: ➤ 545*, Rencontre 30ᵉ 1983/6, 219-2.

b80 *Bell* Martha R., A Hittite pendant from Amarna ['crock of gold' hoard found 1933; 18th dynasty]: AJA 90 (1986) 145-151.

b81 *Bongioanni* Alessandro, Giubileo di Akhenaten; realtà storica o finzione letteraria: Atti T mor/fg 120 (1986) 161-171.

b81* **Brink** Ulrich, Echnaton in der altägyptischen Kunst — wie der Monotheismus propagiert wurde; eine Analyse aus religionsgeschichtlicher und medizinischer Sicht. Gö 1986, Verein für Wiss. Schrifttum. 26 p. [Mundus 23,222].

b82 *Donadoni* Sergio F., Ekhnaton e il suo dio [< StClasOr 1 (1951) 19-34]: ➤ 152, Cultura 1986, 33-48.

b83 *Freu* Jacques, La correspondance d'Abimilki, prince de Tyr, et la fin de l'ère amarnienne: ➤ 38, FGRANAROLO J. 1985, 23-60.

b84 **Heitz** J.-G., *al.*, Index documentaire d'El-Amarna, I.D.E.A., I, 1982 ➤ 63,9665... 65,b346: RBO 43 (1986) 488s (A. F. *Rainey*: the idea was good).

b85 *Hulin* Christopher, *a)* The history of the Amarna period in Egypt; – *b)* The archaeology of the Amarna plain; – *c)* The worshippers of Asiatic gods in Egypt: ➤ 349*, EGroll S., Papers 1 (1982) 191-207 / 208-268 / 269-278.

b86 **Kemp** Barry J., *al.*, Amarna reports 1s, 1984s ➤ 65,b349; 1,e143: RAJA 90 (1986) 103-5 (K. *Grzymski*); BO 43 (1986) 81-84 (M. *Eaton-Krauss*).

b87 **Kemp** Barry J., Amarna reports III. L 1986, Egypt Exploration Soc. 212 p.; 104 fig. [Antiquity 60, 178]. 0-85698-101-X.

b88 [*Kemp* B.J., Amarna 21.I.-28.III.1985]: ➤ b36, Orientalia 55 (1986) 267-9.

b89 *Kessler* Dieter, Zu den Jagdszenen auf dem kleinen goldenen Tutanchamunschrein: GöMiszÄg 90 (1986) 35-43.

b90 **Krauss** Rolf, Das Ende der Amarnazeit: ÄgBei 7, 1978 ➤ 61,q251... 1,e146: RJAmEg 23 (1986) 226-8 (A. *Spalinger*).

b91 *a)* *Leprohon* Ronald J., The reign of Akhenaten seen through the later royal decrees; – *b)* *Bell* Lanny, Aspects of the cult of the deified Tutankhamun: ➤ 77, FMOKHTAR G. 1985, II, 93-105 / 31-59; 2 pl.

b92 *a)* *Loeben* Christian E., Eine Bestattung der grossen königlichen Gemahlin Nofretete in Amarna? Die Totenfigur der Nofretete; – *b)* *Dijk* J. van, *Eaton-Krauss* M., Tutankhamun at Memphis; – *c)* *Martin* Geoffrey T., Shabtis of private persons in the Amarna period: MiDAI-K 42 (1986) 99-107; 2 fig.; pl. 6-7 / 35-41; 3 fig.; pl. 4 / 109-129; pl. 8-19.

b93 *Munro* Irmtraut, Zusammenstellung von Datierungskriterien für Inschriften der Amarna-Zeit nach J.J. PEREPELKIN 'Die Revolution Amenophis' IV', Teil I ⊕ 1967: GöMiszÄg 94 (1986) 81-87.

b94 **Perepelkin** Yu. Ya., ⊕ Amenhotp IV's revolution [1, 1967] 2. Moskva 1984, Nauka. 288 p. – RGöMiszÄg [I. 61, 53-63] 93 (1986) 85-93 (E. S. *Bogoslovsky*: his unfinished vol. 3 will be partly published in VDI).

b94* Ratié Suzanne, Quelques problèmes soulevés par la persécution de Toutankhamon: ➤ 18, Mém. DAUMAS F., II (1986) 545-550.

b95 **Redford** Donald B., Akhenaten, the heretic king 1984 ➤ 65,b351... 1, e151: RBA 49 (1986) 253s (A. *Spalinger*); BSCAS 49 (1986) 245s (J. D. *Ray*); JBL 105 (1986) 500s (J. *Van Seters*).

b96 *Ritner* Robert K., Unrecognized decorated linch pins from the tombs of Tutankhamon and Amenhotep II: Gö MiszÄg 94 (1986) 53-56.

b97 **Schlögl** Hermann A., Echnaton – Tutanchamun; Fakten und Texte 1983 ➤ 64,b862... 1,e153: ROLZ 81 (1986) 336s (W. *Helck*).

b98 *Tefnin* Roland, Réflexions sur l'esthétique amarnienne, à propos d'une nouvelle tête de princesse: StAltÄgKu 13 (1986) 255-261; pl. 23-24.

b99 *Tietze* Christian, Amarna (Teil II), Analyse der ökonomischen Beziehungen der Stadtbewohner: ZägSpr 113 (1986) 55-78.

b100 *Traunecker* Claude, Aménophis IV et Néfertiti; le couple royal d'après les talatates du IXe pylône de Karnak: BSocFrÉg 107 (1986) 17-44;

11 fig. 'Talatate': bloc de grès de petit module du temple d'Aménophis IV
à Thèbes.

T7.4 **Memphis,** *Saqqara; Giza.*

b101 *Berlandini* J., Petite statuaire memphite au musée du Louvre; la dyade de
Sementaouy et la statuette de Tchay: REgp 37 (1986) 3-11; pl. 1s.
b102 **Crawford** Dorothy J., *al.*, Studies on Ptolemaic Memphis 1980 ➤ 62,k31:
ᴿOLZ 81 (1986) 452-4 (L. *Kákosy*).
b103 **Davies** W. V., *al.*, The mastabas of Mereri and Wernu: Saqqara Tomb 1 /
Archaeological Survey Memor 36, 1984 ➤ 65,b359; 1,e156: ᴿBO 43 (1986)
409-411 (N. *Kanawati*).
b104 *Devauchelle* Didier, *al.*, Présentation des stèles nouvellement découvertes
au Sérapéum: BSocFrEg 106 (1986) 31-44; 6 fig.
b105 *Jeffreys* D. G., *al.*, Memphis 1984: JEA 72 (1986) 1-14; 8 fig.
b106 *Jones* Michael & Angela M., Apis expedition at Mit Rahinah; preliminary report of the fourth season, 1984: JAmEg 22 (1985) 17-28; 12 fig.
b107 *Malek* Jaromir, The monuments recorded by Alice LIEDER in the
'Temple of Vulcan' at Memphis in May, 1953: JEA 78 (1986) 101-112;
3 fig.
b108 *Martin* Geoffrey T., *al.*, The tomb chambers of Iurudef; preliminary
report on the Saqqara excavations, 1985: JEA 72 (1986) 15-22; pl. II-V.
b109 *a) Rassart-Debergh* M., Décoration picturale du monastère de Saqqara;
essai de reconstitution / À propos de trois peintures / La peinture copte
avant le XIIe s.; – *b) Van Moorsel* P., *Huybers* M., Repertory of the
preserved wall-paintings from the monastery of Apa Jeremiah at Saqqara;
– *c) Torp* H., Le monastère copte de Banouit: Miscellanea coptica,
AcArchN 9 (1981) 9-124.207-220.221-285 / 125-186 / 1-8 [RBgPg 63 (1985)
205-7, J. *Lafontaine-Dosogne*; RHE 82,189].
b110 *Raven* Maarten J., De herontdekking van het graf van Maya:
PhoenixEOL 32,2 (1986) 47-54; fig. 28-29.
b111 *Schulman* Alan R., A birth scene (?) from Memphis: JAmEg 22 (1985)
97-103; 8 fig.
b112 *Smith* H. S., *Jeffreys* D. G., A survey of Memphis, Egypt: Antiquity 60
(1986) 88-95; 4 fig.; pl. XIX.
b113 *Stadelmann* Rainer, Die Oberbauten der Königsgräber der 2. Dynastie in
Sakkara: ➤ 77, ᶠMOKHTAR G, II, 295-307; 3 fig.

―――――――――

b114 *Cannuyer* Christian, Les pyramides d'Égypte dans la littérature
médio-latine: RBgPg 62 (1984) 673-681.
b115 **David** A. R., The pyramid builders of ancient Egypt; a modern
investigation of Pharaoh's workforce. L 1986, Routledge-KP. x-269 p.;
32 pl. 0-7100-9909-6. – ᴿVAeg 2 (1986) 219s (C. C. *Van Siclen*: really on
W. PETRIE's Fayum Kahun).
b116 *Dorner* Josef, *a)* Einige Bemerkungen über eine neue Methode für die
Bestimmung des Neigungswinkels von Pyramiden : GöMiszÄg [57 (1982)
49-54] 94 (1986) 31-37; – *b)* Form und Ausmasse der Knickpyramide; neue
Beobachtungen und Messungen: MiDAI-K 42 (1986) 45-58; 5 fig.; pl. 5.
b117 **Edwards** I. E. S., The pyramids of Egypt; the classic text, revised and
fully illustrated. NY ²1986, Viking = Hmw ²1985, Penguin. xxii p.; 60
fig.; 63 pl. + XXI color.; bibliog. p. 307-322. NY 0-670-80153-4.

b118 *Isler* Martin, On pyramid building: JAmEg 22 (1985) 129-142; 28 fig.

b119 *Krivsky* Ladislav, Stepped and true pyramids — symbolization of the rising sun: GöMiszÄg 90 (1986) 45-49.

b120 **Lehner** Mark, The pyramid tomb of Hetep-heres and the satellite pyramid of Khufu: DAI-K, Sonderschrift 19. Mainz 1985, von Zabern. 90 p., 27 fig. DM 88. 3-8053-0814-0. − ᴿBO 43 (1986) 692-6 (J. *Brinks*).

b121 **Mendelssohn** Kurt, The riddle of the pyramids. L 1986, Thames & H. 224 p.; 112 fig. + 15 colour. £8. 0-500-27388-8. − ᴿExpTim [91 (1979s) 137-140] 98 (1986s) 86 (A. *Wainwright*).

b122 **Stadelmann** Rainer, Die ägyptischen Pyramiden 1985 → 1,e169; DM 68: ᴿMundus 22 (1986) 210s (J. *Brinks*).

b123 *Wegner* Josef W. & Gary, Reexamining the Bent Pyramid: VAeg 2 (1986) 209-215; 5 fig.; II pl.: contains a still-undiscovered gallery.

---

b124 *a) Verner* Miroslav, Excavations at Abusir 1984/5: ZägSpr 113 (1986) 154-160; − *b*) Abusir, Saqqâra: → b36, Orientalia 55 (1986) 252-4-261.

T7.5 Delta Nili.

b125 *Abû Billû:* **Abd el-Al** A., *al.*, Stèles funéraires de Kom Abu Bellou. P 1985, RCiv. 143 p.; 47 pl. − ᴿAegyptus 66 (1986) 286-8 (G. *Casanova*).

b126 *Vitali* Isabella, Un contributo per l'interpretazione delle stele di Kom Abou Billou [Terenouthis]: RSO 58 (1984) 245-265.

b127 *Alexandria: a) Balconi* Carla, Alessandria nell'età augustea; aspetti di vita; − *b*) *Daris* Sergio, I villaggi dell'Egitto nei papiri greci: → 546, Egitto 1984/5, 181-196 / 211-231.

b128 *Fiema* Zbigniew T., A Hebrew inscription from Kom el-Dikka, Alexandria, Egypt [*brkm/h*]: JAmEg 22 (1985) 117.

b129 ᴱ**Grimm** G., *al.*, Alexandrien 1981 [→ 62,k435, *Hinske* N.]: ᴿAnzAltW 39 (1986) 198-200 (A. *Jahne*).

b130 *Rejmer* Jerzy, ☻ Alexandria of ORIGEN's times: Meander 41 (1986) 443-458; lat. 458.

b131 *Wickert* Ulrich, Alexandrien: → 587, EvKL 1 (1986) 81-83 (-85, Theologie).

b132 Les *Kellia:* → b36, Orientalia 55 (1986) 239-241.

b133 ᴱ**Kasser** R., Survey archéologique des Kellia (1981) 1983 → 65,b379; 1,e188: ᴿRÉAug 32 (1986) 184-7 (N. *Duval*); RÉByz 44 (1986) 328-330 (Suzy *Dufrenne*).

b134 *Marsa Matruḥ: White* Donald, Excavations on Bates's Island, Marsa Matruh, 1985: JAmEg 23 (1986) 51-84; 43 fig.

b135 *Maṭarîya:* **Saleh** A.A., The site of Tell el-Hisn-Matarîyah 1981/3: Excavations at Heliopolis, ancient Egyptian Ounu I-II. Cairo 1981-3, Univ.

b136 *Mendes: Holz* Robert K., *al.*, Mendes I, 1980 → 62,k32 ... 65,b382: ᴿJEA 78 (1986) 207-9 (Helen *Jacquet-Gordon*).

b137 *Naucratis: Coulson* W., *Leonard* A., Naucratis: Cities of the Delta I, 1981 → 62,k35 ... 65,b386 (Naukratis): ᴿJEA 78 (1986) 210-3 (M. *Jones*).

b138 *Coulson* William D.E., *Wilkie* Nancy C., Ptolemaic and Roman kilns [three, near Naukratis] in the Western Nile Delta: BASOR 263 (1986) 61-75; 20 fig.

b139 *Qanṭîr-Dabʿa: Bietak* Manfred, Stratigraphie und Seriation; Arbeiten zur Erschliessung der relativen Chronologie in Ägypten: → 119, ᶠVETTERS H. 1985, 5-9.

b139* **Snape** S. R.,   Six archaeological sites in Sharqiyeh province.   Liverpool 1986, Univ. x-93 p.
b140 *Tanis* 31st, 24 Sept. - 26 Nov. 1984: ➤ b36, Orientalia 55 (1986) 246-8.
b141 **Uphill** E. P.,   The temples of Per-Ramesses 1984 ➤ 65,b392; 1,e199: ᴿBO 43 (1986) 687-9 (E. S. *Bogoslovsky*).
b142 Pi-Ramsès perdue, Tanis retrouvée: MondeB 45 (1986) 23-30, ill. (J. *Yoyotte*).
b143 *Yahudîya:* **Kaplan** Maureen F.,   The origin and distribution of Tell el Yahudiyeh ware: SIMA 62, 1980 ➤ 61,s546 ... 65,a571:   ᴿAnzAltW 39 (1986) 231s (S. *Hiller*).

т7.6 *Alii situs Aegypti alphabetice.*

b144 *Abydos:* O'Connor David,   The 'cenotaphs' of the Middle Kingdom at Abydos: ➤ 77, ᶠMOKHTAR G. 1985, II, 161-177; 6 fig.; 1 pl.
b145 *Aḥmim: Brovarski* Edward,   Akhmim in the Old Kingdom and First Intermediate period: ➤ 77, ᶠMOKHTAR G. 1985, I, 117-153; 8 pl.
b146 **Kuhlmann** Klaus P.,   Materialien zur Archäologie und Geschichte des Raumes von Achmim 1983 ➤ 64,b840; 1,e204:   ᴿOLZ 81 (1986) 447s (R. S. *Bianchi*).
b147 *Asasif:* **Burkard** Günter,   Grabung im Asasif 1963-1970, III. Die Papyrusfunde: ArchVeröff 22. Mainz 1986, von Zabern. 88 p.; 86 pl. 3-8053-0037-9.
b148 *Aswan:* **Dreyer** Günter,   Elephantine VIII; der Tempel des Satet; die Funde der Frühzeit und des Alten Reiches: DAI-K, arch. Veröff. 39. Mainz 1986. 155 p.; 63 fig.; also 63 pl. 3-8053-0501-X [OIAc F86].
b149 Éléphantine: MondeB 45 (1986) 32-39, ill. (G. *Posener*).
b150 *Dahla:* [**Fakhry** A., Nachlass] ᴱ*Osing* J. *al.*, Denkmäler der Oase Dachla 1982 ➤ **1**,e214: ᴿCdÉ 61 (1986) 94s (H. De *Meulenaere*); JAmEg 22 (1985) 219-22 (R. J. *Leprohon*).
b151 **Valloggia** Michel,   Balat I, Le mastaba de Medou-Nefer: Fouilles 31/1. Le Caire 1986, IFAO. xv-239 p.; 24 fig. [vol. II, 96 pl.]. 2-7247-0037-6.
b151* *Dendera: Colin* Marie-Ève,   Le Saint des Saints (ou le sanctuaire des barques) du temple de Dendera à travers ses inscriptions dédicatoires: ➤ 18, Mém. F. DAUMAS I (1986) 109-131.
b152 *Fayûm: Bresciani* Edda,   L'attività archeologica dell'università di Pisa in Egitto (1985); Medinet Madi nel Fayum: EgVO 9 (1986) 7s; 6 pl.
b153 *Idfu: Kurth* Dieter,   Information über ein von der Deutschen Forschungsgemeinschaft gefördertes Projekt zur philologischer Gesamtbearbeitung der Inschriften des Tempels von Edfu: GöMiszÄg 92 (1986) 93s.
b154 **Kurth** Dieter,   Die Dekoration der Säulen im Pronaos des Tempels von Edfu 1983 ➤ 64,b893; 65,b419:   ᴿCdÉ 61 (1986) 256-264 (Sylvie *Cauville*).
b155 **Germond** Philippe,   Les invocations à la Bonne Année au temple d'Edfou = AegHelv 12 (1986). 108 p.
b156 *Hammamât: Gundlach* Rolf,   Wadi Hammamat: ➤ 391, LexÄg 6,47 (1986) 1099-1114 [1095-1124, wadi Natrûn, *al.*; ➤ 751*].
b157 *Hawâwîš:* **Kanawati** Naguib,   The rock tombs of El-Hawawish, Cemetery of Akhmim [➤ 62,b971] ... III-IV. Sydney 1982s, Macquarie Anc. Hist. Asn. 48 p.; 35 fig.; 11 pl. / 48 p.; 34 fig.; 14 pl. £17.75 each. 0-908299-95-2; 06-0. – ᴿJEA 78 (1986) 223-5 (N. *Strudwick*).

b159 **Kharga:** Cruz-Uribe Eugene, [Khargha 650 k SSW Cairo] The Hibis temple project: JAmEg 23 (1986) 157-166; 7 fig.

b160 **Devauchelle** Didier [➤ 65,8052], Wagner Guy, Les graffites du Gebel Teir (6 k N Kharga): Recherches d'Archéologie PgHist 22. Le Caire 1984. x-60 p.; 34 pl. – ^EEnchoria 14 (1986) 171-3 (R. Jasnow).

b161 **al-Kōm al-Aḥmar** / Šārūna 3d 1986: GöMiszÄg 93 (1986) 65-80; 5 fig. (J. Brinks ... W. Schenkel).

b162 **Kôm Ombo:** Kemp Barry J.,   Kom Ombo; evidence for an early town: ➤ 77, ^FMOKHTAR G. 1985, II. 39-53; 13 fig.; 3 pl.

b163 **Philae:** Grossman Peter,   Die Kirche des Bischofs Theodoros im Isistempel von Philae; Versuch einer Rekonstruktion: RSO 58 (1984) 107-117.

b164 **Selwît:** Zivie Christiane M.,   Le temple de Deir Chelouit [II 56-89, inscriptions du Naos, 1983 ➤ 64,b879], Le Caire 1986,IFAO.   III 90-157, ix-211 p.; 20 pl.   2-7247-0026-0 [5-2 complet]: ^RCdÉ 61 (1986) 92s (P. Derchain).

b165 **Siut:** **Edel** Elmar,   Die Inschriften der Grabfronten der Siut-Gräber in Mittelägypten aus Herakleopolitenzeit: Abh.Rh/W.Akad. 71, 1984 ➤ 65,b427: DM 96: ^RMundus 22 (1986) 13s (Ingrid Gamer-Wallert).

T7.7 Situs Nubiae et alibi.

b166 a) **Batta** Ernst,   Obelisken; Ägyptische Obelisken und ihre Geschichte in Rom: Taschenbuch 765.   Fra 1986, Insel.   205 p.; 93 fig.   3-458-32465-8. – b) Bedon Robert,   Les obélisques de Rome antique: Archéologia 216 (1986) 55-65; ill. – c) Demougeot Émilienne,   Obélisques égyptiens transférés à Rome en 357 et à Constantinople en 390: ➤ 18, Mém. F. DAUMAS I (1986) 153-172.

b167 **Červíček** Pavel,   Rock pictures of Upper Egypt and Nubia: AION 46,1 Sup.   R 1986, Herder.   viii-117 p.; 6 maps; 50 phot.

b168 **Fattovich** Rodolfo,   Remarks on the peopling of the northern Ethiopian-Sudanese borderland in ancient historical times: RSO 58 (1984) 85-106.

b169 **Hinkel** Friedrich W.,   Exodus from Nubia [Auszug aus Nubien 1978 ➤ 62,k73; 63,d477]. B 1978, Akademie.   90 p.; 51 fig.; 131 pl. + 21 color. – ^RJAmEg 22 (1985) 208s (R. S. Bianchi).

b170 **Kirwan** L. P.,   The birth of Christian Nubia; some archaeological problems: RSO 58 (1984) 119-134.

b171 **Leclant** Jean, Clerc Gisèle,   Fouilles et travaux ... au Soudan 1984-1985: Orientalia 55 (1986) 298-313: pl. LV-LXVII: 32 sites; p. 313-9, Découvertes d'objects égyptiens et égyptisants hors d'Égypte.

b172 **Marks** Anthony E., al.,   The archeology of the eastern Sudan; a first look: Archaeology 39,5 (1986) 44-50; color. ill.

b173 **Moorsel** Paul van,   New discoveries in Nubia; proceedings of the colloquium on Nubian studies, The Hague 1979: Eg. Uitgaven 11, 1982 ➤ 65,713; ƒ95: ^RCdÉ 61 (1986) 95-98 (E. Strouhal).

b174 **Oltre l'Egitto,** Nubia; l'avventura dell'archeologia dalle rive del Nilo ai deserti del Sudan (Milano Galleria del Sagrato 15 gen.-15 mar. 1985). Mi 1985, Electa.   143 p.; 146 fig.

b175 **Steinmeyer-Schareika** A.,   Das Nilmosaik 1978 ➤ 60,t931 ... 63,d467: ^RAnzAltW 39 (1986) 94-96 (E. Walde).

b176 **Vos** Mariette de,   L'egittomania in pitture e mosaici romano-campani della prima età imperiale: ÉPR 84, 1980 ➤ 61,q345 ... 63,a111:   ᴿAegyptus 66 (1986) 288-290 (Orsolina *Montevecchi*).

---

b177 *Abu Simbel: Leclant* Jean,   Abou Simbel et la Nubie, 25 ans après: CRAI (1986) 686-700.

b178 *Cyrene:* **White** Donald,   The extramural sanctuary of Demeter and Persephone at Cyrene, Libya; background and introduction to the excavations.   Ph 1984, Univ. Museum.   xviii-143 p.; 121 fig.; 2 pl. – ᴿAJA 90 (1986) 358-360 (S. *Brown*).

b179 *Dongola:* ➤ b171, Orientalia 55 (1986) 301-3; pl. lvii.

b180 *Faras:* **Karkowski** Janusz,   The pharaonic inscriptions from Faras: Faras 5, 1981 ➤ 64,b884:   ᴿJEA 78 (1986) 213s (E. F. *Wente*).

b181 *Ferghana:*   **Bulygina** T. N.,   ⓔ New finds of Egyptian artifacts in Ferghana: SovArch (1986,2) 247-253; 1 fig.

b182 *Kassala:* **Sadr** K.,   Preliminary report on the archaeological settlement pattern of the [Sudan] Kassala area: AION 46 (1986) 1-34; 10 fig.; 2 pl.

b183 *Kerma:* ➤ b171, Orientalia 55 (1986) 300s; pl. LVIII-LXI.

b183* **Bonnet** Charles,   Kerma, territoire et métropole; quatre leçons au Collège de France: Bibl. Générale 9.   Le Caire 1986, IFAO. vii-51 p.; 9 fig.; XVI pl.   2-7247-0041-4.

b184 *O'Connor* David,   Kerma and Egypt; the significance of the monumental buildings, Kerma I, II, and XI: JAmEg 21 (1984) 65-108; 12 fig.

b185 *Lambesa: Janon* Michel,   Recherches à Lambèse, III. Essais sur le temple d'Esculape: AntAfr 21 (1985) 35-102; 57 fig. Eng. 265.

b186 *Meroë:*   **Török** L.,   Economic offices and officials in Meroitic Nubia (a study in territorial administration of the Late Meroitic kingdom): StAegyptiaca 5, 1979 ➤ 61,t441; 64,b981:   ᴿJNES 45 (1986) 84 (E. *Cruz-Uribe*).

b187 *Török* L.,   A contribution to post-Meroitic chronology; the Blemmyes: RSO 58 (1984) 201-243.

b188 ᴱ*Wenig* S.,   Meroitische Forschungen 1980/4 ➤ 65,708 ᴱ*Hintze* F.: ᴿJAmEg 22 (1985) 206-8 (R. S. *Bianchi*).

b189 *Williams* Bruce,   A chronology of Meroitic occupation below the Fourth Cataract: JAmEg 22 (1985) 149-195; 19 fig.

b190 *Naqʿa:* **Gamer-Wallert** Ingrid,   Der Löwentempel von Naqʿa in der Butana (Sudan) III. Der Reliefschmuck: TAVO B-48/3.   Wsb 1984, Reichert.   373 p.; 105 fig. DM 320. – ᴿMundus 22 (1986) 99-101 (ipsa).

b191 **Zibelius** Karola,   Der Löwentempel von Naqʾa in der Butana (Sudan), IV. Die Inschriften.   Wsb 1984, Reichert.   100 p.; 27 fig. DM 98. – ᴿMundus 22 (1986) 215-220 ('from the summary').

b192 **Ahmed** Khidir Abdelkarim,   Meroitic settlement in the Central Sudan; an analysis of sites in the Nile Valley and western Butana: Cambridge Monographs in African Archaeology 8 / BAR-Int 197.   Ox 1984. xii-308 p.; ill.; bibliog. p. 289-308.   0-86054-252-1.

b193 *Qastul:* **Williams** Bruce B.,   Excavations between Abu Simbel and the Sudan frontier, 1. The A-group royal cemetery at Qastul: cemetery L: OINE 3.   Ch 1986, Univ. Oriental Inst.   xxxviii-388 p.; 110 pl. $85 [JNES 46,244].

b194 *Qitna:* **Strouhal** Eugen,   Wadi Qitna and Kalabsha-South: Late Roman – Early Byzantine tumuli cemeteries in Egyptian Nubia 1, 1984 ➤ 65,b440: ᴿBO 43 (1986) 411-6 (B. G. *Trigger*).

b195 **Mallows** Wilfrid, The mystery of the Great *Zimbabwe* — the key to a major archeological enigma. L 1985, R. Hale. 217 p.; 29 fig.; 29 pl. £14. – RAntiquity 60 (1986) 154s (D. W. *Philippson*: no mystery at all since G. C. THOMPSON 1931).

T7.9 **Sinai.**

b196 *Beit-Arieh* Itzhaq, Two cultures in southern Sinai in the third millennium B.C.: BASOR 263 (1986) 27-54; 23 fig.

b197 *Dijkstra* Meindert, The statue Sinai 346 and the tribe of the Kenites [*bn qn* clan of smiths at Serâbîṭ el-Kâdim]: ➤ 377*a*, IOSOT summaries (1986) 34.

b198 EGaley John, (*Weitzmann* K., *Forsyth* G.), Sinai and the monastery of St. Catherine [German 1979; cf. Eng. 1976➤ 60,t6]. Cairo 1985, American Univ. [NY, Columbia]. 189 p.; ill. [Galey]. $45. – RTDig 33 (1986) 479s (W. C. *Heiser*).

b199 **Meïmaris** Yiannis, Catalogue of Arabic manuscripts in St. Catherine's monastery, Mount Sinai. Athenai 1985, National Hellenic research foundation. 156 + 70 p.; 142 fig. + 20 color. – ROrChrPer 52 (1986) 441-4 (*Khalil Samir*).

b200 *Bar-Yosef* O. al., Nawamis [sg. (& pl.)] and habitation sites near Gebel Gunna, southern Sinai: IsrEJ 36 (1986) 121-167; 14 fig.; pl. 17-18.

b200* **Wilson** Charles W., Sinai and the south, including a short description of the Negev [appendix to Picturesque Palestine 1880], pref. *Vilnay* Z. J c. 1980, Ariel. 154 p.; ill., map.

T8.1 **Anatolia,** *generalia.*

b201 E*French* D. H., Recent archaeological research in Turkey [from reports duly attributed, many infra]: AnSt 36 (1986) 174-218.

b202 Land of civilizations, Turkey (❶ ❶ Eng.: exposition 2.IV-2.VI.1985, Tokyo Idemitsu Museum). Tokyo 1985, Middle Eastern Culture Center. 397 p.; 404 fig.

b203 *Laminger-Pascher* Gertrud, Das lykaonische Koinon und die Lage der Städte Barata, Dalisandos und Hyde: AnzW 128 (1986) 238-259.

b204 *MacMullen* Ramsay, Frequency of inscriptions in Roman Lydia [... *Jalabert* L. 1908]: ZPapEp 65 (1986) 237s.

b205 *a*) *Marazzi* M., Gli 'Achei' in Anatolia; un problema di metodologia; – *b*) *Re* L., Presenze micenee in Anatolia; – *c*) *Kilian* Klaus, Il confine settentrionale della civiltà micenea nella tarda età del bronzo: ➤ 564, Traffici micenei 1984/6, 391-403 / 343-358; 12 fig. / 283-293; 11 fig.

b206 **Todd** Ian A., The prehistory of Central Anatolia, I. The neolithic period: SIMA 60, 1980 ➤ 61,t553 ... 65,b460: RAnzAltW 39 (1986) 227-9 (S. *Hiller*).

b207 *Waelkens* Marc, Die kleinasiatischen Türsteine; typologische und epigraphische Untersuchungen der kleinasiatischen Grabreliefs mit Scheintür. Mainz 1986, von Zabern. xxiii-334 p.; 90 fig.; 109 pl. DM 198. [Mundus 23,301, P. *Calmeyer*].

T8.2 **Boğazköy,** *Hethaei* – **The Hittites.**

b208 *Bittel* Kurt, Hartapus and Kızıldağ: ➤ 71, FMELLINK M., Anatolia 1986, 103-111; 11 fig.

b209 a) *Bittel* Kurt, Bildliche Darstellungen Hattušili's III. in Ägypten; –
b) *Berman* Howard, New Boghazköy joins and duplicates: ➤ 42,
ᶠGÜTERBOCK H., Kaniššuwar 1986, 39-44; 5 fig. / 33-37.

b210 **Bittel** Kurt, Hattuscha, Hauptstadt der Hethiter; Geschichte und Kultur
einer altorientalischen Grossmacht. Köln 1986, DuMont. 226 p.; bibliog.
p. 213-221.

b211 *Marazzi* Massimiliano, Die Hieroglypheninschrift am Löwentor von
Boğazköy; Diskussionsbeitrag: OrAnt 25 (1986) 51-57.

b212 *Neve* P., Die Ausgrabungen in Boğazköy-Hattuša 1985: ArchAnz
(1986) 365...; 37 fig.

b213 *Otten* Heinrich, Das hethitische Königshaus im 15. Jahrhundert v.Chr.:
AnzW 128 (1986) 21-34, 8 fig.

b214 a) *Otten* Heinrich, Archive und Bibliotheken in Hattuša; – b) *Mauer* G.,
Die Karriere des Schreibers Tattamaru, Sohn des Šaḫurunuwa: ➤ 545*,
Rencontre 30ᵉ 1983/6, 184-190 / 191-5

т8.3 **Ephesus.**

b215 *Bammer* Anton, Das Heiligtum der Artemis von Ephesos 1984
➤ 65,b466: ᴿAntClas 55 (1986) 574s (C. *Delvoye*).

b216 a) *Büsing* Hermann, Zweierlei Mass am Artemision von Ephesos?: – b)
Ganschow Thomas, Überlegungen zum Parthermonument von Ephesos:
ArchAnz (1986) 205-8; 1 fig. / 209-221; 3 fig.

b217 **Elliger** Winfried, Ephesos; Geschichte einer antiken Weltstadt:
Urban-Tb 375. Stu 1985, Kohlhammer. 200 p. [Mundus 22,131].

b218 a) *Jobst* Werner, Zur Bau- und Bildkunst der Spätantike in Ephesos; –
b) *Karwiese* Stefan, Koressos – ein fast vergessener Stadtteil in Ephesos; –
c) *Mitsopoulos-Leon* Veronika, Töpferateliers in Ephesos: ➤ 52, ᶠKEN-
NER H. 1985, 195-206 / 214-225 / 247-251.

b219 *Masson* Olivier, Remarques sur l'onomastique d'Éphèse (à propos de
l'Index Ephesos VIII.2): ZPapEp 64 (1986) 173-183.

b220 **Rogers** Guy M., Founding an identity; C. Vibius Salutaris and Ephesos
in A.D. 104: diss. Princeton 1986. 280 p. 86-27943. – DissA 47 (1986s)
3157-A.

b221 *Rogers* G. M., Demetrios of Ephesos; silversmith and *neopoios*?:
Belleten 50,198 (1986) 877-882; ❶ 883.

b222 a) *Sauer* Georg, Ephesos und Petra; Beobachtungen zur Stadtplanung in
hellenistischer Zeit; – b) *Merić* Recep, Zur Lage des ephesischen
Aussenhafens Panormos; – c) *Engelmann* Helmut, Die Bauinschriften des
Prytaneions von Ephesos: ➤ 119, ᶠVETTERS H., 1985, 95-97 / 30-32 /
155-7; auch viele andere kleinste Artikel über Ephesos.

b223 *Vetters* Hermann, Ephesos; Vorläufiger Grabungsbericht für die Jahre
1984 und 1985: AnzW 128 (1986) 75-110; 110-161 Fundmünzen, *Karwiese*
Stefan. 41 (foldout) fig.; XXXVI (color.) pl.

b224 *Vetters* Hermann, Ephesus 1985: AnSt 36 (1986) 193-5.

т8.4 **Pergamum.**

b225 **Filgis** Meinard N., *Radt* W., Die Stadtgrabung 1/1. Das Heroon:
Altertümer von Pergamon 15. B 1986, De Gruyter.

b226 *Radt* W., Pergamon 1985; Trajaneum restoration; city excavation: AnSt
36 (1986) 208-210.

b227 *Radt* W., Pergamon; Vorbericht über die Kampagne 1985: ArchAnz (1986) 415...; 13 fig.

T8.6 *Situs Turchiae,* **Turkey sites** in alphabetical order.

b228 *Aizanoi:* *Hoffmann* Adolf, Aizanoi; erster Vorbericht über die Arbeiten im Stadion, 1982-1984: ArchAnz (1986) 683-698; 16 fig.

b229 *Alahan:* **Gough** Mary, Alahan, an early Christian monastery in southern Turkey [excavated by † Michael Gough, 1955-1973]. Toronto 1985, Pontifical Institute of Medieval Studies. 235 p. $22.50 [RelStR 13,76s, R. *Ousterhout*].

b230 *Alanya:* castle, 1985: AnSt 36 (1986) 174s (M. O. *Arık*).

b231 *Anemurium* 1985 (Univ. British Columbia): AnSt 36 (1986) 174-6 (J. *Russell*).

b232 *Russell* James, Excavations at Anemurium (Eski Anamur) [İcel], 1985: ÉchMClas 30 (1986) 173-183.

b233 *Ancyra:* a) *Mitchell* Stephen, Galatia under Tiberius; – b) *Halfmann* Helmut, Zur Datierung und Deutung der Priesterliste am Augustus-Roma-Tempel in Ankara: Chiron 16 (1986) 17-33 / 35-42.

b234 *Antiochia:* *Wickert* Ulrich, Antiochien: → 587, EvKL 1 (1986) 185-7 (185s, Theologie).

b235 *Aphrodisias* 1985: a) AnSt 36 (1986) 176-181 (K. *Erim*); – b) [his awaited] Aphrodisias, city of Venus Aphrodite. L 1986, Muller-Blond-White.

b236 **Reynolds** J., *Tannenbaum* R., Jews and Godfearers at Aphrodisias: Cambridge PgSup 12. C 1986 (Trinity Hall). 160 p. £15. 0-96014-08-5 [ClasR 100,v adv].

b236* **Budde** Ludwig, St. Pantaleon von Aphrodisias in Kilikien, Türkei: Beiträge zur Kunst des christlichen Ostens 9. Recklinghausen 1986, Bongers. 298 p. [Mundus 23,222].

b237 *Beşik:* 1985, AnSt 36 (1986) 181s (M. *Korfmann*).

b238 *Korfmann* M., al., Beşik-Tepe 1984: ArchAnz (1986) 303...; 28 fig.; 8 pl.

b239 *Cafer* Höyük 1985: AnSt 36 (1986) 182-5 (J. *Cauvin*, O. *Aurenche*).

b240 ᴱ*Cauvin* J., *Aurenche* O., Cahiers de l'Euphrate 4 [mostly Cafer Hüyük in Malatya; also el-Kown etc.] 1985 → 1,e320; F 210: ᴿIsrEJ 36 (1986) 286s (O. *Bar-Yosef*).

b241 *Çavustepe* 1985: AnSt 36 (1986) 185-7 (A. *Erzen*).

b242 *Dereağzı:* **Morganstern** James, The Byzantine church at Dereağzı and its decoration: IstMittBeih 29. Tü 1983, Wasmuth. 205 p. DM 112 [RelStR 13,77, R. *Ousterhout*].

b243 *Didyma* 1985: AnSt 36 (1986) 189 (K. *Tuchelt*).

b244 *Tuchelt* Klaus, Fragen zum Naiskos von Didyma: ArchAnz (1986) 33-50; 13 (foldout) fig.

b245 *Gödecken* Karin B., Beobachtungen und Funde an der Heiligen Strasse zwischen Milet und Didyma, 1984: ZPapEp 66 (1986) 217-253; 7 fig.; pl. VIII-XI.

b246 *Ferzant:* *Özgüç* Tahsin, ⦿ Nouvelles observations sur les objets trouvés dans le cimitière hittite de Ferzant: Belleten 50,197 (1986) 383-92, Eng. 393-402; 44 fig. map.

b247 *Fındık:* *Berndt* Dietrich, Findik, eine antike Stätte im phrygischen Bergland: AntWelt 17,1 (1986) 2-12; 15 (color.) fig.

b248 *Göreme:* **Rodley** Lyn, Cave monasteries of Byzantine Cappadocia. C 1986, Univ. xviii-266 p.; 59 fig.; 188 pl. $79.50. – ᴿBelleten 50,197 (1986) 607-610 (Yıldız *Ötüken*).

b249 **Thierry** Nicole, Haut Moyen Âge en Cappadoce; les églises de la région de Çavuşin [entre Ürgüp et Avanos], I: IFAP-BAH 102. P 1983, Geuthner. xvii-200 p.; 60 fig.; 200 pl. – ᴿRÉByz 44 (1986) 330s (J. *Darrouzès*.

b250 *Hierapolis* 1985: AnSt 36 (1986) 195s (Daria D. *Ferrero*).

b251 *Lane* Eugene N., A Men-stele from Phrygian Hierapolis [*Robert* L., BCH 107 (1983) 511-5], further considerations: EpAnat 7 (1986) 107-9; pl. 17; ❶ 110.

b252 **Ritti** Tullia, Hierapolis scavi e ricerche I. Fonti letterarie ed epigrafiche; II. **d'Andria** Francesco e ~, Le sculture del Teatro; i rilievi con i cicli di Apollo e Artemide. R 1985. ...; 205 p.; 53 pl. – ᴿAJA 90 (1986) 499s (S. *Mitchell*).

b253 *Iasos:* **Pecorella** Paolo E., La cultura preistorica di Iasos in Caria; pref. *Levi* Doro: Archeologia 51. R 1984, Bretschneider. 139 p.; 19 fig.; 59 pl. Lit. 200.000. – ᴿGnomon 58 (1986) 784-6 (M. *Korfmann*).

b254 *Kültepe:* a) *Özgüç* Tahsin, Some rare objects from the Karum of Kanish; – b) *Matouš* Lubor, Ein aA Vertrag über gemeinsame Haushaltungsführung aus der Zeit der Kültepe-Schicht Iᵇ: → 42, ᶠGÜTERBOCK H., Kaniššuwar 1986, 173-8; 7 fig. / 141-146; 4 facsimiles.

b255 *Özgüç* Tahsin, New observations on the relationship of Kültepe with Southeast Anatolia and North Syria during the Third Millennium B.C.: → 71, ᶠMELLINK M., Anatolia 1986, 31-47; 43 fig.

b256 *Lidar*, Gritille (Samsat 50 k NW Urfa): *Redford* Scott, Excavations at Gritille (1982-1984); the medieval period, a preliminary report: AnSt 36 (1986) 104-123; 15 fig. (maps); pl. IX-XI.

b257 *Limyra:* **Ganzert** Joachim, Das Kenotaph für Gaius Caesar [nepos Augusti] in Limyra [SW Türkei] (Diss. 1981): IstFor 35, 1984 → 1,e338: ᴿAJA 90 (1986) 134-6 (J. *Pollini*); OLZ 81 (1986) 385-7 (Erika *Simon*).

b258 *Miletus* 1985: AnSt 36 (1986) 206 (W. *Müller-Wiener*).

b259 *Müller-Wiener* Wolfgang, al., Milet 1983-1984, Vorbericht: IstMitt 35 (1985) 13-138; 3 + 56 + 16 fig.; pl. 5-30; foldouts 1-2.

b260 a) *Heilmeyer* Wolf-Dieter, Die Einordnung Milets in die Siedlungszonen der griechischen Frühzeit; – b) *Schiering* Wolfgang, Zu den Beziehungen zwischen der ältesten Siedlung von Milet und Kreta; – c) *Müller-Wiener* Wolfgang, Zur Erforschung der hellenistischen Monumente Milets: → 569, Milet 1980/6, 105-112 / 11-15; pl. 1 / 121-8; fig. 27s.

b261 *Kleine* Jürgen †, Pergamenische Stiftungen in Milet: → 569, ᴱ*Müller-Wiener* W., Milet 1980/6, 129-140; pl. 13.

b262 *Rusyayeva* A.S., ❶ Miletus – Didyma – Borysthenes – Olbia; the colonization of the lower Bug region: VDI 177 (1986,2) 25-64; Eng. 64.

b263 *Nicaea* (İznik) theatre, 6th 1958 [presumably for 1985]: AnSt 36 (1986) 199s (B. *Yalman*).

b264 *Oenoanda:* Coulton J.J., Oenoanda; a) The Agora; – b) with *Stenton* E.C., The water supply and aqueduct: AnSt 36 (1986) 61-90; 10 fig. / 15-19; 9 fig.; VII pl.

b265 *Perga:* **Galanis** Evangelos, ❻ *Pérgē tēs Pamphylías*... political and ecclesiastical history of the ancient city: Analecta Vlatadon 40. Thessalonica 1983, Inst. patriarcal d'études patristiques. 236 p. – ᴿRHE 81 (1986) 352 (V.T. *Istavridis*: matériel archéologique p. 60-62, 121-3).

b266 *Sardis* 1985: AnSt 36 (1986) 210-212 (C.H. *Greenewalt* ᴶ).

b267 **Hanfmann** G.M.A., Sardis from prehistoric to Roman times 1983 → 64,d74 ... 1,e347: ᴿVDI 176 (1986,1) 165-170 (T.A. *Moiseeva*).

b268 *Gschnitzer* Fritz, Eine persische Kultstiftung in Sardeis und die

'Sippengötter' Vorderasiens: → 80, FOBERHUBER K., Im Bannkreis 1986, 45-54.

b269 *Ramage* Nancy H., Two new Attic cups and the siege of Sardis: AJA 90 (1986) 419-424; 4 fig.; pl. 27.

b270 *Ratté* Christopher, *Howe* Thomas N., *Foss* Clive, An early imperial pseudodipteral temple at Sardis: AJA 90 (1986) 45-68; 7 fig.; pl. 3-4.

b271 **Yegül** F. K., The Bath-Gymnasium complex at Sardis: Report 3. CM 1986, Harvard. xx-180 p.; 457 fig. $45. 0-674-06345-7 [NTAbs 31, 130].

b271* *Termessos* [SW Asia Minor]: **Pekridou** Anastasia, Das Alketas-Grab in Termessos: IstMit Beih. 32. Tü 1986, Wasmuth. 133 p.; 13 fig.; 36 pl.; map. DM 68 [Mundus 23,39s, F. *Eckstein*].

b272 *Troja: Schachermeyr* Fritz, Troia in hethitischen Texten?: → 119, FVETTERS H. 1985, 13-15.

b273 *a*) *Korfmann* Manfred, Troy, topography and navigation / Beşik Tepe; new evidence for the period of the Trojan sixth and seventh settlements; – *b*) *Güterbock* Hans G., Troy in Hittite texts ? Wilusa, Ahhiyawa, and Hittite history; – *c*) *Watkins* Calvert, The language of the Trojans: → 566*, Troy 1984/6, 1-16, fig. 1-13. 17-28, fig. 14-23 / 33-44 / 45-62.

b274 **Wood** Michael, In search of the Trojan War, six BBC films [including 'The singer of tales' and 'Empire of the Hittites'], 55 minutes each. LA 1985, KCET. – RArchaeology 39,6 (1986) 70s (S. S. *Brown*).

b275 *Tur Abdîn:* **Bell** Gertrude, The churches and monasteries of the Tur ʿAbdin, EMango M. M. 1982 → 65,b351; 1,e364: ROrChr 70 (1986) 202-4 (A. *Palmer*).

b276 *Urfa*, Edessa: *Marfoe* Leon, *al.*, The Chicago [Urfa province] Euphrates archaeological project 1980-1984; an interim report: Anatolia 13 (1986) 37-122; 42 fig. (-169 skeletal, *Alpagut* B.).

b277 *Huxley* G., Baanes the notary on ʿold Edessa': GrRByz 24 (1983) 253-7.

b278 *Xanthos:* **Asheri** David, Fra Ellenismo e Iranismo. Bo 1983, Patron. 192 p. – RRArchéol (1986) 408s (P. *Demargne*); RHistDFrançÉ (1984) 613-6 (C. *Le Roy*).

b279 **Balland** André, Fouilles de Xanthos, 7. Inscriptions d'époque impériale du Létôon 1981 → 63,d578; 64,d85: RGnomon 58 (1986) 43-46 (H. *Halfmann*).

b280 *Demargne* P., Le décor sculpté des monuments funéraires de Xanthos; principes explicatifs d'un art grec au service d'une idéologie orientale: → 356, ESiebert G., Méthodologie 1981, 85-89.

b281 *Yortan:* **Kamil** Turhan, Yortan cemetery in the Early Bronze Age of western Anatolia: BAR-Int 145, 1982 → 63,a707; 1,e365: RRB 93 (1986) 460s (É. *Nodet*).

T8.9 **Armenia, Urarṭu.**

b282 *Cengiz* Işık, ❶ Tische und Tischdarstellungen in der urartäischer Kunst: Belleten 50,197 (1986) 413-446; 45 fig.

b283 **Der Nersessian** Sirarpie, *Mekhitarian* Arpag, Miniatures arméniennes d'Ispahan. Bru 1986, Éditeurs d'Art. 218 p.; 124 fig. 2-87103-022-0.

b284 **Eichler** Seyyare, Götter, Genien und Mischwesen in der urartäischen Kunst: ArchMIran Egb 12, 1984 → 65,b536; DM 75: RMundus 22 (1986) 98s (K. *Hecker*).

b285 **Kaspar** Elke & Hans-Dieter, Urartu, ein Weltreich der Antike; ein Reisehandbuch. Nordlingen 1986, Korient. 3-925696-01-6 [OIAc Ag87].

b286 *Salvini* Mirjo, Assyrian and Urartaean written sources for Urartaean history: Sumer 42 (1986) 155-9.

b287 **Zakrzewska-Dubasowa** M., ⊘ Ormianie w dawnej Polsce. Lublin 1982, Lubelskie. – ᴿRoczOr 45,1 (1986) 127-137 (J. P. *Datkevič*).

b288 **Zimansky** Paul, Ecology and empire; the structure of the Urartian state 1985 → 1,e371: ᴿAJA 90 (1986) 482s (O. W. *Muscarella*).

т9.1 Cyprus.

b289 *Christol* Michel, Proconsuls de Chypre: Chiron 16 (1986) 1-14.

b290 *Cordano* Federica, L'isola di Cipro in STRABONE II 5,21 e X 5,14: ParPass 223 (1985) 280-3.

b291 **Hadjioannou** Kyriakos, ⊚ *Hē archaîa Kýpros*... Ancient Cyprus in Greek sources, 5. supplements and indices. Nicosia 1983. x-441 p.; 2 pl.; 10 maps. C£15. – ᴿClasR 100 (1986) 337 (F. G. *Maier*).

b292 *Helck* Wolfgang, Zypern und Ägypten: → 591, LexÄg 6,49 (1986) 1452-5.

b293 *Karageorghis* Vassos, *a)* Chronique des fouilles et découvertes archéologiques à Chypre en 1985. BCH 110 (1986) 823-880; 130 fig.; *b)* L'archeologia a Cipro: Archeo 15 (1986) 22-29; (color.) ill. 17, p. 18-23.

b294 **Kyrris** Costas P., History [+ geography] of Cyprus. Nicosia 1985, Nicocles. 450 p.; XVI pl. – ᴿDLZ 107 (1986) 539-542 (R. *Koerner*).

b295 *a) Mazzoni* Stefania, Continuity and development in the Syrian and the Cypriote common glyptic styles; – *b) Karageorghis* V., Tiarae of gold from Cyprus: → 87, ᶠPORADA E., Insight 1986, 171-182; pl. 31-35 / 129-132; pl. 26.

b296 **Morris** Desmond, The art of ancient Cyprus 1985 → 1,e377; £60: ᴿAntiquity 60 (1986) 157s (H. W. *Catling*); Archaeology 39,5 (1986) 66s.76 (D. *Soren*).

b297 **Orphanides** Andreas G., Towards a theory for the interpretation of material remains in archaeology; the Bronze Age anthropomorphic figurines from Cyprus: diss. SUNY. Albany 1985. 247 p. 86-14606. – DissA 47 (1986s) 1380-A.

b298 **Peltenburg** E. J., Recent developments in the later prehistory of Cyprus: SIMA pocket 16, 1982 → 63,d600 ... 1,e378: ᴿRB 93 (1986) 459s (É. *Nodet*).

b299 *Rosser* John, Crusader castles of Cyprus: Archaeology 39,4 (1986) 40-47; color. ill.

b300 **Schürmann** Wolfgang, Katalog der kyprischen Antiken im Badischen Landesmuseum Karlsuhe: SIMA 20/9, 1984 → 65,b552*b*: ᴿGnomon 58 (1986) 766-8 (A. *Hermary*).

b301 *Wachsmann* Shelley, Is Cyprus ancient Alashiya? new evidence from an Egyptian tablet [Amarna 114]: BA 49 (1986) 37-40; ill.

b302 **Webb** Jennifer M., Cypriote Antiquities in the Abbey Museum, Queensland, Australia: SIMA 20/12. Göteborg 1986, Åström. 88 p., ill.

b303 *a) Yon* Marguerite, Cultes phéniciens à Chypre; l'interprétation chypriote; – *b) Caubet* Annie, Les sanctuaires de Kition à l'époque de la dynastie phénicienne; – *c) Baslez* M.-F., Cultes et dévotions des Phéniciens en Grèce; les divinités marines: → 551, Religio phoenicia 1984/6, 127-152 / 153-168 / 289-305.

b304 *Amathous: Empereur* Jean-Yves, *Verlinden* Colette, Le port antique d'Amathonte: Archéologia 215 (1986) 32-37; (color.) ill.

b305 *Hermary* Antoine, *al.*,   Rapport sur les travaux de la missions de l'École française à Amathonte en 1985: BCH 110 (1986) 881-907; 44 fig.

b306 **Aupert** P., *al.*, Amathonte I, Auteurs anciens, – monnayage – voyageurs – fouilles – origines – géographie: ÉtChyp 4/Mémoire 33, 1984 → **1**,e381: ᴿRivArCr 62 (1986) 412-4 (Rossanna *Martorelli*).

b307 *Athienou:* **Dothan** Trude, *Ben-Tor* Amnon, Excavations at Athienou, Cyprus 1971-72: Qedem 16, 1983 → 64,d117; **1**,e384: ᴿPEQ 118 (1986) 157 (E. *Peltenburg*).

b308 *Enkomi:* **Courtois** Jean-Claude, Alasia III. Les objets des niveaux stratifiés d'Enkomi (fouilles C. F.-A. SCHAEFFER 1947-1970): Mission archéologique d'Alasia 6. P 1984, RCiv. 244 p.; 49 fig.; XXV pl. [RÉG 100,488s, O. *Masson*].

b309 **Lagarce** Jacques & Élisabeth, Alasia IV; deux tombes du Chypriote Récent d'Enkomi (Chypre) tombes 1951 et 1907: Mémoire 51. P 1985, RCiv. 162 p.; 42 fig. 2-86538-119-8.

b310 *Episkopi:* **Swiny** Stuart, The Kent State University expedition to Episkopi Phaneromeni 2: SIMA 74/2. Nicosia 1986, Åström. xv-171 p.; 73 fig. 91-86098-40-3.

b311 *Hala Sultan Tekke:* *Åström* Paul, *a*) Hala Sultan Tekke — an international harbour town of the Late Cypriote Bronze Age; – *b*) (*al.*) Iron artifacts from Swedish excavations in Cyprus: OpAth 16 (1986) 7-17; 24 fig. / 27-41; 19 fig.

b312 *Idalion:* Lipiński Édouard, Le Baʿana' d'Idalion: Syria 63 (1986) 379-382.

b313 *Kalavasos:* **Todd** Ian A., Vasilikos valley project, 1. The Bronze Age cemetery in Kalavasos village: SIMA 71/1. Göteborg 1986, Åström. 306 p.; 46 fig.; bibliog. p. 219-226. 91-86098-38-1.

b314 *Khirokitia:* Le Brun A. & O., L'extension vers l'est de l'occupation pré-céramique de Khirokitia; la tranchée 6: RepCyp (1986) 1-11; 3 fig.; pl. 1.

b315 *Kissonerga: Peltenburg* E. J., *al.*, Excavations at Kissonerga – Mosphilia 1985: RepCyp (1986) 28-39; 2 fig.; pl. V-VI.

b316 *Kition:* **Yon** Marguerite, *Caubet* Annie, *al.*, Kition-Bamboula III: Le sondage L-N 13 (Bronze récent et géométrique I): Mém. 56. P 1986, RCiv. 203 p.; 363 fig. F 180. [Mém. Nᵒ wrongly given as 53, also 2-86538-125-2, both of which are *Pardee*].

b317 *Paphos:* *Maier* F.-G., *Wartburg* Marie-Louise von, *a*) Excavations at Kouklia-Palaepaphos; fourteenth preliminary report, season 1985: Rep-Cyp (1986) 55-61; 3 fig.; pl. XII-XV; – *b*) Ausgrabungen in Alt-Paphos: ArchAnz (1986) 145-193; 78 fig.

b318 **Karageorghis** Vassos, Palaepaphos-Skales, an iron age cemetery in Cyprus: DAI-Ausg. Alt-Paphos 3, 1983 → **1**,e405: ᴿAntClas 55 (1986) 570-2 (R. *Laffineur*).

b319 **Maier** F., *Karageorghis* V., *al.*, Paphos, history and archaeology 1984 → **1**,e400: ᴿAntiquity 60 (1986) 166s (H. W. *Catling*).

т9.3   *Graecia,* **Greece** – mainland sites in alphabetical order.

b320 *Catling* H. W., Archaeology in Greece, 1985-86: [Brit. Sch. Athens] ArchRep 32 (1985s) 3-101; 152 fig.

b321 ❺ Excavations 1983 (Abdera, Philippi, Amphipolis, Vergina, Epidaurus and 23 others): PrakArch 139 (for 1983, in 1986) 1-270; 182 pl.

b322 *Touchais* Gilles, Chronique des fouilles et découvertes archéologiques en Grèce en 1985: BCH 110 (1986) 671-761; 152 fig.

b323 **Amphipolis:** *Voutiras* Emmanuel, Victa Macedonia; remarques sur une dédicace d'Amphipolis: BCH 110 (1986) 347-355; 4 fig.

b324 **Athenae: Camp** John M., The Athenian Agora; excavations in the heart of classical Athens: New Aspects of Antiquity. L 1986, Thames & H. 231 p.; 189 fig.; 10 colour. pl. $30 [AJA 91,495, R. R. *Holloway*].

b325 *Jeppesen* Kristian, [Danish] Some critical remarks on the traditional Erechtheion theory: MusTusc 56 (1984ss) 105-122 [Eng. AJA 83 (1979) 381-394; 87 (1983) 325-333].

b326 *La Follette* Laetitia, The chalkotheke on the Athenian Acropolis: Hesperia 55 (1986) 75-87; 4 fig.; pl. 20-24.

b327 *Meyer* Laure, L'acropole d'Athènes, travaux de restauration: Archéologia 212 (1985) 62-66; ill.

b328 *Roberts* Sally B., The Stoa gutter well, a Late Archaic deposit in the Athenian agora: Hesperia 55 (1986) 1-74; 44 fig.; pl. 1-19.

b329 **Mountjoy** P. A., Four early Mycenaean wells from the south slope of the Acropolis at Athens: Misc. Graeca 4, 1981 → 63,a637 [index!]: [R]Anz-AltW 39 (1986) 232-4 (S. *Hiller*).

b330 *Townsend* Rhys F., The fourth-century skene of the theater of Dionysus at Athens: Hesperia 55 (1986) 421-438; 7 fig.; pl. 91, 92.

b331 **Wickens** Jere M., The archaeology and history of cave use in Attica, Greece, from prehistoric through late Roman times (67 as habitation): diss. Indiana, [D]*Jacobsen* T., 1986. 712 p. 87-04046. – DissA 47 (1986s) 4121s-A.

b332 **Buthrotum:** *Prifti* Peter R., Hellenic colonies in ancient Albania: Archaeology 39,4 (1986) 26-31; color. ill.

b333 **Corinthus:** *Williams* Charles K [II], Corinth 1985; east of the theater: Hesperia 55 (1986) 129-173; 4 fig.; pl. 25-37 [163-175. 183-205, Coins, also 1978-80, *Zervos* Orestes H.].

b334 *Benson* J. I., An early protocorinthan workshop and the sources of its motifs: Babesch 61 (1986) 1-20; 46 fig.

b335 **Salmon** J. B., Wealthy Corinth 1984 → 1,5184: [R]Athenaeum 64 (1986) 250s (L. *Moretti*); Gymnasium 93 (1986) 558s (K. H. *Kinzl*).

b336 *Slane* Kathleen W., Two deposits from the early Roman cellar building, Corinth: Hesperia 55 (1986) 271-318; 20 fig.; pl. 61-70 [→ 1,431].

b337 **Biers** Jane C., Corinth XVII; the great bath on the Lechaion Road. Princeton 1985, Amer. Sch. Athens. xiv-112 p.; 8 fig.; 56 pl. – [R]AJA 90 (1986) 496-9 (F. K. *Yegül*); Gnomon 58 (1986) 670-2 (W. *Martini*).

b338 **Adamsheck** Beverley, Kenchreai IV, 1979 → 61,t615: [R]Gnomon 58 (1986) 172-5 (P. *Hellström*).

b339 **Delphi:** *Walsh* John, The date of the Athenian stoa at Delphi: AJA 90 (1986) 319-336.

b340 **Epidaurus: Tomlinson** R. A., Epidauros 1983 → 64,d155: [R]ÉchMClas 30 (1986) 204-6 (H. *Williams*).

b341 **Mycenae: Xenakē-Sakellariou** Agnē, *Hoi thalamotoi taphoi...* Les tombes à chambre de Mycènes; fouilles de Chr. TSOUNTAS (1887-1898). P 1985, de Boccard. ☺ 333 p.; franç. 334-357; 144 + XIV pl.

b342 *Bader* Tiberiu, Neue Beiträge zu den mykenischen Schwertern von Typ A aus Rumänien: ZfArch 20 (1986) 1-15.

b343 *Bell* Martha R., [Fayûm] Gurob tomb 605 and Mycenaean chronology: → 77, [F]MOKHTAR G. 1985, I, 61-86; 6 pl.

b344 *a) Dayton* J. E., The Mycenaeans and the discovery of glass / Geology, archaeology and trade; – *b) Sherratt* E. S., Patterns of contact; manufacture and distribution of Mycenaean pottery, 1400-1100: → 65,697, [E]*Best* J., Interaction and acculturation in the Mediterranean II 1980/2

[90-6032-195-2] 169-177.153-168 / 179-192; 3 maps [N.B. p. 223-238, plates for *Møller* E., Crete seals, vol. I p. 85].

b345 **Lehmann** Gustav A., Die mykenisch-frühgriechische Welt and der östliche Mittelmeerraum in der Zeit der 'Seevölker'-Invasion um 1200 v. Chr.: Rh/Wf Akad Vortrag G 276. Opladen 1985, Westdeutscher-V. 74 p.

b346 *a) Lo Porto* F. G., Le importazioni micenee in Puglia; bilancio di un decennio di studi; – *b) Valente* I., Indizi di presenza micenea nella Sicilia occidentale durante la media età del bronzo; – *c) Guzzardi* L., Elementi di tradizione micenea nell'architettura funeraria calabrese; – *d) Tomasello* F., L'architettura funeraria in Sicilia tra la media e tarda età del Bronzo; le tombe a camera del tipo a tholos: ➤ 564, Traffici micenei 1984/6, 13-17; 11 fig. / 123-6; 8 fig. / 71-73; 7 fig. / 93-100; 10 fig.

b347 **Schachermeyr** Fritz, Mykene und das Hethiterreich: Szb W 472 / Mykenische Forschung 11. W 1986, Österr. Akad. 367 p.; 36 fig. 3-7001-0777-3.

b348 **Harding** Anthony F., The Mycenaeans and Europe 1984 ➤ 65,b606; 1,e440: RAJA 90 (1986) 357s (R. R. *Holloway*).

b349 *Nichoria:* **McDonald** William A., *al.*, Excavatons at Nichoria in southwest Greece, III. Dark Age and Byzantine occupation. Minneapolis 1983, Univ. Minnesota. xxxii-527 p. (80 pl.) $49.50. – RÉchMClas 30 (1986) 193-7 (J. W. *Hayes*).

b350 *Olympia:* **Bol** Renate, Das Statuenprogramm des Herodes-Atticus-Nymphäums: DAI-Olympische For. 15, 1984 ➤ 1,e445: RClasR 100 (1986) 342s (M. A. R. *Colledge*); Orpheus 7,1 (1986) 227-9 (Maria Laura *Astarita*).

b351 *Orchomenus:* **Mountjoy** Penelope A., Orchomenos V. Mycenaean pottery from Orchomenos, Eutresis and other Boeotian sites: BayrAk ph/h 89, 1983 ➤ 64,b47: RClasR 100 (1986) 36s (E. *Schofield*).

b352 *Paradimi:* **Bakalakis** Georgios, *Sakellariou* Agni, Paradimi [in Thrakien: nur Gefässe 1930 ohne Grabungsnotizen]: Heid Akad, Balkan-Mon 2. Mainz 1981, von Zabern. viii-88 p.; 73 fig.; XLV pl.; 16 Beilagen. – RAnzAltW 39 (1986) 224-7 (S. *Hiller*).

b353 *Philippes* [École française 1985]: BCH 110 (1986) 789s (M. *Sève*).

b354 **Abrahamsen** Valerie Ann, The rock reliefs and the cult of Diana at Philippi: diss. Harvard, DMiles Margaret R. CM 1986. 241 p. 86-19009. – DissA 47 (1986s) 1764s-A; HarvTR 79 (1986) 467.

b355 *Phocis:* **Fossey** John M., The ancient topography of eastern Phokis. Amst 1986, Gieben. xiii-234 p.; 29 fig.; 68 pl.

b356 *Pylus:* **Sergent** Bernard, Pylos et les enfers: RHR 203 (1986) 5-39; Eng. 5.

b357 *Soli:* **Tran Tam Tinh,** Soloi, la basilique: fouilles 1964-1974, 1. Sainte-Foy QU 1985, Univ. Laval. xliii-160 p.; 257 fig.; 23 maps. – RPhoenix 40 (Toronto 1986) 372-4 (C. *Delvoye*).

b358 *Tegea:* **Østby** Erik, The archaic temple of Athena Alea at Tegea [generally explained as a Byzantine church]: OpAth 16 (1986) 75-102; 30 (foldout) fig.

b359 *Thebae:* **Braun** Karin. *Haevernick* Thea E., Das Kabirenheiligtum IV. Bemalte Keramik und Glas 1981 ➤ 1,e454: RRArchéol (1986) 169s (G. *Siebert*).

b360 **Demand** Nancy H., Thebes in the fifth century; Heracles resurgent: States and Cities of Ancient Greece. L 1982, Routledge-KP. x-196 p.; 10 pl.; 4 fig. (2 maps) £10. – RClasR 100 (1986) 89-91 (G. *Huxley*).

b361 *Thessalonica: a) Vickers* Michael, Hellenistic Thessaloniki [< JHS 92

(1972) 156-170]; – *b*) *Bakalakis* G., Vorlage und Interpretation von römischen Kunstdenkmälern in Thessaloniki [< ArchAnz 88 (1973) 671-684]: ➤ 360, *Thessalonikēn Philippou Vasilissan* 1985, 486-499; 4 fig. / 500-513; 14 fig.

b362 **Tiryns:** *Moser von Filseck* Karin, Der Alabasterfries von Tiryns: ArchAnz (1986) 1-32; 13 fig.

T9.4 Creta.

b363 **Blome** P., Die figürliche Bildwelt Kretas 1982 ➤ 64,d173: ᴿDLZ 107 (1986) 778-781 (K. *Zimmermann*).

b364 ᴱ**Darcque** Pascal, *Poursat* Jean-C., L'iconographie minoenne: BCH Sup. 11, 1985 ➤ 1,868: ᴿAJA 90 (1986) 353 (Karen P. *Foster*).

b365 *Gómez Fuentes* Alejandro, El estado minoico y el modo de producción asiático: Zephyrus 37s (Salamanca 1984s) 249-254.

b366 **Higgins** Reynold, Minoan and Mycenaean art²ʳᵉᵛ: World of Art Library. L 1981, Thames & H. 216 p. 187 fig. + 54 color. £3. – ᴿGnomon 58 (1986) 563s (W. *Schiering*).

b367 *a*) *Niemeier* Wolf-Dietrich, Creta, Egeo e Mediterraneo agli inizi del Bronzo Tardo; – *b*) *Dickinson* O., Early Mycenaean Greece and the Mediterranean; – *c*) *French* Elizabeth, Mycenaean Greece and the Mediterranean world in the LH III: ➤ 564, Traffici micenei 1984/6, 245-260; 25 maps / 271-6 / 277-282.

b368 **Snyder** Geerto A. S., Minoische und Mykenische Kunst 1980 ➤ 61,t643 ... 63,d671: ᴿAnzAltW 31 (1986) 237-242 (S. *Hiller*).

b369 **Haghia Triada:** **Halbherr** F., *Stefani* E., *Banti* L., Haghia Triada nel periodo tardo palaziale: Annuario Atene 55 (1977). R 1980, Bretschneider. 365 p.; 260 fig.; 8 pl. – ᴿAnzAltW 39 (1986) 234-7 (S. *Hiller*).

b370 **Walberg** Gisela, Provincial Middle Minoan pottery 1983 ➤ 1,e473: ᴿJHS 106 (1986) 249s (J. A. *MacGillivray*); RBgPg 64 (1986) 195s (J. *Vanschoonwinkel*).

b371 *Kavousi: Day* Leslie P., *al.*, Kavousi, 1983-4; the settlement at Vronda: Hesperia 55 (1985) 355-387; 14 fig.; pl. 77-84.

b372 *Knossos: Koehl* Robert B., A marinescape floor from the palace at Knossos: AJA 90 (1986) 407-417; 4 fig.; pl. 24s (26 color.).

b373 *Marinatos* Nanno, *Hägg* Robin, On the ceremonial function of the Minoan polythyron: OpAth 16 (1986) 57-73; 16 fig.

b374 *Niemeier* Wolf-Dietrich, Zur Deutung des Thronraumes im Palast von Knossos: MiDAI-A 101 (1986) 63-65; 19 fig.; pl. 11-13.

b375 **Popham** M. R., *al.*, The Minoan unexplored mansion at Knossos: BritSchAth Sup. 17, 1984 ➤ 65,b636: ᴿAntiqJ 66 (1986) 154s (P. *Warren*); Antiquity 60 (1986) 242s (G. *Cadogan*); ClasR 100 (1986) 117-9 (S. *Hood*).

b376 **Gesell** Geraldine C., Town, palace, and house cult in Minoan Crete: SIMA 67, 1985 ➤ 1,e466: ᴿGnomon 58 (1986) 468-470 (G. *Walberg*).

b377 *Sippel* Donald V., The supposed site of the Cretan labyrinth: AncW 14 (1986) 67-79.

b378 *Wall* S. M. *al.*, Human bones from a Late Minoan IB house at Knossos: AnBritAth 81 (1986) 333-388; 11 fig.; pl. 21-37.

b379 *Kommos: Shaw* Joseph W., Excavations at Kommos (Crete) during 1984-5: Hesperia 55 (1986) 219-269; 11 fig.; pl. 45-60 [➤ 1,e480].

b380 *Malia: Darcque* Pascal, *Baurain* Claude, Les coquillages dans l'art crétois: Archéologia 211 (1986) 30-44; (color.) ill.

b381 *Pelon* Olivier, Un dépôt de fondation au palais de Malia: BCH 110 (1986) 3-19; 15 fig.

b382 **Phaistos:** *Weingarten* Judith, The sealing structures of Minoan Crete; MM II Phaistos to the destruction of the palace of Knossos: OxJArch 5 (1986) 279-298; 4 fig.

T9.5 Insulae graecae.

b383 **Åström** P., *al.*, Studies in Aegean chronology: SIMA pocket 25, 1984 ➤ 65,b643; 1,e484: ᴿPEQ 118 (1986) 156 (Vrowny *Hankey* admires and uses vigor).

b384 ᴱ**Holloway** R. Ross, Italy and the Aegean, 3000-700 B.C.: Archaeologia Transatlantica 1. LvN 1981, Univ. 158 p.; 155 fig.– ᴿAntiquity 60 (1986) 73s (J. F. *Cherry*).

b385 McDONALD William A.: Contributions to Aegean archaeology; studies in honor of ~, ᴱ**Wilkie** Nancy C., *Coulson* William D. E.: Univ. Minn. Center for Ancient Studies, 1, 1985 ➤ 1,90: ᴿAJA 90 (1986) 357 (J. L. *Davis*).

b386 **Cyclades:** Le nouveau Musée d'Art des Cyclades à Athènes: Archéologia 210 (1986) 39-41.

b387 **Ekschmitt** Werner, Kunst und Kultur der Kykladen, I. Neolithikum und Bronzezeit; II. Geometrische und archaische Zeit: KuGAntW 28. Mainz 1986, von Zabern. 244 p., 110 fig.; 276 p., 127 fig., 64 pl.

b388 *Frost* Frank J., Here and there in the Cyclades; an historian and archaeologist looks around and remembers his wanderings: AncW 14 (1986) 97-114.

b389 ᴱ**MacGillivray** J. A., *Barker* R. L. N., The prehistoric Cyclades 1983/4 ➤ 1,859: ᴿAJA 90 (1986) 481s (J. E. *Coleman*, also on KNAPP-STECK 1981/5).

b390 **Preziosi** Pat G., Early Cycladic sculpture; an introduction. Malibu CA 1985, Getty Museum. 92 p.; 82 fig. 0-89236-101-8 [AJA 90,505].

b391 *Søren* Dietz, The Aegean area in the age of the Trojan war — a sketch (in Danish): MusTusc 56 (1984ss) 47-64; Eng. 64s.

b392 **Delos:** *Will* E., Delos 35: Le sanctuaire de la déesse syrienne. P 1985, de Boccard. 167 p.; 66 fig.; 40 pl.; 4 foldouts. F 550 [JHS 107,249, R. A. *Tomlinson*].

b393 **Ialysos:** *Macdonald* Colin, Problems of the twelfth century BC in the Dodecanese [< diss.]: AnBritAth 81 (1986) 125-151; 10 fig.

b394 **Melas** E. M., The [east Dodecanese] islands of Karpathos, Saros and Kasos in the Neolithic and Bronze Age: SIMA 68. Göteborg 1985, Åström. 337 p.; ill.; bibliog. p. 182-191. 91-86098-23-3 [AntiqJ 67,141].

b395 **Keos:** **Georgiou** Hara S., Keos 6; Ayia Irini specialized domestic and industrial pottery. Mainz 1986, von Zabern. xiv-63 p.; 22 pl. DM 65. 3-8053-0849-3 [AntiqJ 67,142, P. *Warren*].

b396 **Davis** Jack L., Ayia Irini, period V: Keos 5. Mainz 1986, von Zabern. xxi-125 p.; 68 pl.

b397 [**Kouveli** south of Boeotia] *Gregory* Timothy E., A desert island survey in the gulf of Corinth: Archaeology 39,3 (1986) 16-21; color. ill.

b398 **Lesbos:** *Williams* Caroline & Hector, Excavations at the acropolis of Mytilene, 1985: ÉchMClas 30 (1986) 141-154.

b399 **Melos:** **Renfrew** Colin, *al.*, The archaeology of cult; the sanctuary at Phylakopi [Melos]: Brit.Sch.Athens Sup. 18. L 1985, Thomas & H. 526 p.; 130 fig.; 70 pl. £35. – ᴿAntiquity 60 (1986) 155s (P. *Warren*).

b400 **Rhodus: Berthold** Richard M., Rhodes in the Hellenistic age 1984
→ 65,b657; 1,e499: ᴿGnomon 58 (1986) 412-7 (J. *Deininger*).

b401 **Samothrace: Lehmann** Phyllis W., *Spittle* Denys, Samothrace V. The
temenos: Bollingen Series 60, 1982 → 64,d196... 1,e506: ᴿRArchéol
(1986) 174-6 (R. *Ginouvès*).

b402 **Thera:** *Vanschoonwinkel* Jacques, *a)* Théra et la jeune civilisation
mycénienne: AntClas 55 (1986) 5-41; – *b)* Les fouilles de Théra et la
protohistoire égéenne: ÉtClas 54 (1986) 223-247; 11 fig. (map); bibliog.
p. 248-252.

b403 **Marinatos** Nanno, Art and religion in Thera; reconstructing a Bronze
Age society. Athenai 1984, Mathioulakis [→ 65,b663]: 128 p.; 83 fig. (4
foldout). – ᴿAJA 90 (1986) 353s (Karen P. *Foster* compares Egyptian
heb-sed).

b404 *Palivou* Clairy, Notes on the town plan of Late Cycladic Akrotiri, Thera;
AnBritAth 81 (1986) 179-194; 10 fig. [297-312 pottery, *Sotirakopoulou*
Panayiota].

---

b405 *a) Biaggi* Cristina, The significance of the nudity, obesity and sexuality
of the Maltese goddess figures; – *b) Battiti Sorlini* Giulia, The megalithic
temples of Malta, an anthropological perspective; – *c) Renfrew* Colin, The
prehistoric Maltese achievement and its interpretation: → 550, ᴱ*Bonanno*
A., Fertility cult 1985/6, 131-9, franç. 139 / 141-150 / 118-130.

т9.6 Urbs Roma.

b406 **Anderson** James C.ᴶ, The historical topography of the imperial fora:
Coll. Latomus 182, 1984 → 65,b665: ᴿRBgPg 63 (1985) 164-7 (P. *Gros*).

b407 ᴱ**Bietti Sestieri** Anna Maria, Preistoria e protostoria nel territorio di
Roma: Lavori e studi di archeologia 3. R 1984, De Luca. 204 p.

b408 **Boersma** Johannes D., Amoenissima civitas; Block V.ii at Ostia;
description and analysis of its visible remains: Scrinium 1. Assen 1985,
Van Gorcum. xxiii-484 p.; 608 fig. 90-232-2049-8. – ᴿAntiqJ 66 (1986)
434s (M. *Todd*).

b409 *Boersma* Johannes, *al.*, Excavations in the House of the Porch (V.ii. 4-5)
at Ostia: Babesch 61 (1986) 77-137; 71 fig. [138-143, *Heres* T. L., house of
Columns].

b410 *Capizzi* C., A proposito del VIII° volume dell'‵Inscriptiones christianae
urbis Romae saeculo septimo antiquiores′: OrChrPer 52 (1986) 408-420.

b411 **Cizek** E., La Roma di Nerone [Néron 1982], ᵀ*Bonini* Mario: Storia della
Civiltà. Mi 1984, Garzanti. 419 p.; 14 fig. – ᴿSalesianum 48 (1986) 129
(S. *Maggio*).

b412 **Coarelli** Filippo, Il foro romano, II. periodo repubblicano e augusteo:
Lectiones planetariae 1985 → 1,e516: ᴿGnomon 58 (1986) 58-64 (P. *Gros*).

b413 **Coarelli** F., Roma sepolta. R 1984 [23-26 Pyrgi, Astarte: AION 45
(1985) 656].

b414 **Conticello de' Spagnolis** Marisa, Il tempio dei Dioscuri nel Circo
Flaminio: Lavori e studi di archeologia 4. R 1984, De Luca. 67 p.; 23
fig.; 2 foldout plans.

b415 ᴱ**Cozza** Lucos, Tempio di Adriano: Lavori e studi di archeologia 1. R
1982, De Luca. 58 p.; 70 fig.

b416 **Eisner** Michael, Zur Typologie der Grabbauten im Suburbium Roms:
MDAI-R Ergh. 26. Mainz 1986, von Zabern. 255 p.; 60 pl. 3-8053-
0756-X.

b417 *Freibergs* G., *Littleton* C. S., *Strutynski* U., Indo-European tripartition and the Ara Pacis Augustae; an excursus in ideological archeology: Numen 33 (1986) 3-25; 3 fig.

b418 *Grenier* Jean-Claude, *Coarelli* Filippo, La tombe d'Antinoüs à Rome: MélEcFrR-A '98 (1986) 217-253.

b419 **Guidobaldi** F. & A., Pavimenti marmorati di Roma dal IV al IX secolo 1983 → 64,d206: ᴿRivArCr 62 (1986) 398-405 (X. *Barral i Altet*).

b420 *Heitz* Carol, Les monuments de Rome à l'époque de Grégoire le Grand: → 433*, Grégoire 1982/6, 31-39.

b421 **Kleiner** Fred S., The Arch of Nero 1985 → 1,e521*: ᴿAJA 90 (1986) 492s (Mary T. *Boatwright*); RÉLat 63 (1985) 385s (G.-C. *Picard*).

b422 *Koeppel* Gertrud M., Maximus videtur rex; the collegium pontificum on the ara pacis Augustae: ArchNews 14 (1985) 17-22; 2 fig.

b423 **Pace** Pietrantonio, Gli acquedotti di Roma. R c. 1984, Art Studio. 330 p.; ill. Lit. 50.000. – ᴿAntRArch 10,5 (1985) 63.

b424 **Panimolle** Giuseppe, Gli acquedotti di Roma antica. R 1984, Abete. 322 p.; 262 p.; (color.) ill. – ᴿAntRArch 10,3 (1985) 86 (R. A. *Staccioli*).

b425 *Pavoncello* Nello, Ancora un'epigrafe ebraica nel chiostro di S. Giovanni in Laterano di Roma [1588 d.C.]: Henoch 8 (1986) 393-5.

b426 **Pfanner** Michael, Der Titusbogen 1983 → 64,d215... 1,e524*: ᴿArchNews 14 (1985) 69s (Diana & F. *Kleiner*); Arctos 19 (1985) 312s (Heikke *Solin*); RArchéol (1986) 185-8 (P. *Gros*: important).

b427 **Rasch** Jürgen J., Das Maxentius-Mausoleum an der Via Appia in Rom: Univ. Karlsruhe / DAI, Spätantike Zentralbauten in Rom und Latium 1, 1984 → 65,b674; DM 160: ᴿClasR 100 (1986) 344s (M. A. S. *Colledge*: project begun in 1939).

b428 **Smith** Gary E., A guide to the Roman amphitheatres → 1,e526*: LA 1984, Westland. vi-90 p.; 144 phot. $15; pa. $10. – ᴿArchaeology 39,1 (1986) 71 (J. H. *Humphrey*).

b429 **Sugano** Karin, Das Rombild des HIERONYMUS 1983 → 65,d552; 1,e527*: ᴿAnBoll 104 (1986) 248s (P. *Devos*); REAug 31 (1985) 200-2 (Y.-M. *Duval*).

b430 **Torelli** Mario, Lavinio e Roma; riti iniziatici e matrimonio tra archeologia e storia. R 1984, Quasar. 264 p. [AJA 91,497, W. V. *Harris*].

b431 *Tracey* Robyn, The forum of Augustus; where were the statues? [in the exedrae, then in front of them]: → 45*, ᶠHARRIS B., AncSRes 16 (1986) 146-168; 7 fig.

T9.7 *Roma,* **Catacumbae.**

b432 **Brettman** E. S., Vaults of memory; Jewish and Christian imagery in the catacombs of Rome [catalogue of 199-item exhibit]. Boston 1985, International Catacomb Society. 40 p. $15 pa. [NTAbs 31,120].

b433 *Drzymała* Kazimierz, ❷ Grób św. Piotra Apostoła w Rzymie: RuBi 39 (1986) 353-362.

b434 *Eck* Werner, Inschriften aus der Vatikanischen Nekropole unter St. Peter [1983-4]: ZPapEp 65 (1986) 245-293; pl. XIV-XXVI.

b435 *Fasala* Umberto M., Lavori nella catacomba 'ad duas lauros': RivArCr 62 (1986) 7-37; 11 fig.

b436 **Ferrua** Antonio, Sigilli su calce nelle catacombe: Sussidi allo studio delle antichità cristiane 8. Vaticano 1986, Pont. Ist. Archeologia Cristiana. 127 p.; 7 fig.

b437 **Konikoff** Adia, Sarcophagi from the Jewish catacombs of Ancient Rome, a catalogue raisonné. Stu 1986, Steiner. 67 p.; 16 pl. 3-515-04464-7.

b438 *Martimort* Aimé G., À propos des reliques de saint Pierre [*Guarducci* M. 1983, *Walsh* J. 1982]: BLitEc 87 (1986) 92-111; Eng. 82: insensitivity to objections.

b439 *Mazzoleni* Danilo, Tre iscrizioni della catacomba di Priscilla: RivArCr 62 (1986) 265-273; 4 fig

b440 *a) Mazzoleni* Danilo, Papa Damaso e l'archeologia cristiana; – *b) Reekmans* Louis, L'œuvre du pape Damase dans le complexe de Gaius à la catacombe de saint Callixte; – *c) Guyon* Jean, L'œuvre de Damase dans le cimetière 'aux deux lauriers' sur la via Labicana; – *d) Umberto* M., Santuari sotterranei di Damaso nelle catacombe romane — i contributi di una recente scoperta; – *e) Pergola* Philippe, Nereus et Achilleus martyres; 'l'intervention de Damase à Domitille: → 566, Saecularia Damasiana 1984/6, 5-13 / 259-281 / 225-258 / 173-201 / 203-224.

b441 **Mielsch** Harald, *Hesberg* Henner von, Die heidnische Nekropole unter St. Peter in Rom; die Mausoleen A-D: Pont. Acc. Romana di Archeologia, Atti III, Memorie 16,1. R 1986, Bretschneider. 79 p.; 62 fig.; 9 (foldout) pl. 88-7062-604-0.

b442 *Paschia* Gheorghe, L'importance religieuse-morale et historique-littéraire des épitaphes des cimetières romains (en roumain): STBuc 38,1 (1986) 23-42.

b443 **Stevenson** James [† 1983], The catacombs; life and death in early Christianity. Nv 1985 = 1978, Nelson. 179 p., 144 pl. $9 pa. [RelStR 13,264, J. H. *Elliott*).

T9.8 *Roma,* **Ars palaeochristiana.**

b444 ᴱ**Carletti** Carlo, Iscrizioni cristiane di Roma, testimonianze di vita cristiana (secoli III-VII): Biblioteca patristica 7. F 1986, Nardini. 181 p.; bibliog. p. 155-161.

b445 **Carletti** Carlo, Regio VII — Volsinii; – **Mazzoleni** Danilo, Regio VII — Centumcellae: Inscriptiones christianae Italiae septimo saeculo antiquiores. Bari 1985, Edipuglia. xvi-84 p.; xii-35 p. Lit.35.000; 20.000. – ᴿ137 (1986),1) 311 (A. *Ferrua*).

b446 *Ferrua* Antonio, Ultime osservazioni alle iscrizioni cristiane di Roma incertae originis [*Silvagni* A., *Ferrua* 1979]: RivArCr 62 (1986) 41-60.

b447 *Passigli* Susanna, Una questione di topografia cristiana; l'ubicazione della Basilica dei SS. Primo e Feliciano sulla Via Nomentana: RivArCr 62 (1986) 311-332.

b448 *Pillinger* Renate, Monumenti paleoscristiani in in Bulgaria: RivArCr 62 (1986) 275-310; 30 pl.

b449 **Ritz** Sándor, Cielo [esterno-interno della basilica di S. Stefano Rotondo, fotocopie (color.)]. R 1986, La Roccia. Senza paginazione.

b450 **Sörries** Reiner, Die Bilder der Orthodoxen im Kampf gegen den Arianismus... Ravenna 1983 → 64,d250: ᴿJbAC 21 (1986) 22-8 (E. Johanna *Claus-Thomassen*); TR 82 (1986) 204-6 (W. *Gessel*).

T9.9 *(Roma) Imperium occidentale,* **Europa.**

b451 ᴱ**Chiaramonte Treré** Cristina, Nuovi contributi sulle fortificazioni pompeiane: Acme Quad. 6. Mi 1986, Cisalpino. 115 p.; LV pl. Lit. 28.000. 85-205-0533-9.

b452 **d'Andria** Francesco, I Greci in Italia: Archeo Dossier 20. Novara 1986, De Agostini. 66 p.; (color.) ill.

b453 *Duval* Noël, Une hypothèse sur la basilique de Rutilius à Mactar et le temple qui l'a précédée; Études d'archéologie chrétienne nord-africaine XI: RÉAug 31 (1985) 20-45.

b454 **Ennabli** Liliane, Les inscriptions funéraires chrétiennes de Carthage II 1982 → 64,b583; 1,e544: ᴿRÉAug 31 (1985) 168s (J.M. *Lassère*).

b455 *Février* Paul-Albert, Baptistères, martyres et réliques: RivArCr 62 (1986) 109-138.

b456 *Fischer* Hagen, Zur Entwicklung Ostias und Puteolis vom 1. Jh. v.u. Z. bis zum 3. Jahrhundert: MünstHand 5,1 (1986) 3-15; Eng. 15; franç. 16.

b457 [*Formigli* E. and others on the mode and place of origin] Due Bronzi da Riace; rinvenimento, restauro, analisi ed ipotesi di interpretazione 1985 [→ 1,e547]; R 1985, Ministero Beni Cult. 231 p.; 35 pl.; vol. of 106 (color.) pl. – ᴿClasR 100 (1986) 282-4 (J. *Boardman*).

b458 *Marcadé* Jean, Rapports techniques et publications archéologiques: à propos des bronzes de Riace: RArchéol (1986) 89-101.

b459 **Greco** Emanuele, *Theodorescu* Dinu, Poseidonia – Paestum, II. L'agora Éc. Française de Rome 42, 1983 → 1,e550: ᴿGnomon 58 (1986) 51-58 (H. *Riemann*).

b460 **Gros** Pierre, Byrsa III: rapport sur les campagnes de fouilles de 1977 à 1980; la basilique orientale et ses abords: Mission Archéologique Française à Carthage, Coll. Éc. Fr. 41. R 1986, École Française. 220 p.; 188 fig. 2-7283-0082-8.

b461 *Irmscher* Johannes, Spätantike und Christentum; Forschung und Forschungsstätten in der DDR: Sileno 12 (1986) 5-9.

b462 **Kockel** Valentin, Die Grabbauten vor dem Herkulaner Tor in Pompeji: Bei. Erschliessung hellenist/ kais. Skulptur und Architektur. Mainz 1983, von Zabern. xiii-212 p.; 41 fig.; 70 pl. – ᴿRArchéol (1986) 183-5 (P. *Gros*).

b463 **Maggi** Giuseppe, Ercolano; fine di una città. N 1985, Loffredo. 182 p. Lit. 23.000. – ᴿCC 137 (1986,4) 631 (G. *Caprile*).

b464 *Mazzotti* Mario †, S.Apollinare in Classe; indagini e studi degli ultimi trent'anni: RivArCr 62 (1986) 199-219; III foldout plans.

b465 **Prévot** Françoise, Recherches archéologiques franco-tunisiennes à Mactar V. Les inscriptions chrétiennes: CollÉcFrR 34, 1984 → 65,b708; 1,e557; 2-7283-0080-1: ᴿGregorianum 67 (1986) 591-4 (J. *Janssens*).

b466 **Strocka** Volker M., Casa del Principe di Napoli (VI 15, 7-8): DAI-Häuser in Pompeji 1, 1984s→ 1,e558; 3-8030-1032-2: ᴿAntiqJ 66 (1986) 433s (A. *Wallace-Hadrill*).

b467 **Van der Poel** Halsted B., *al.*, Corpus Topographicum Pompeianum 3A, The insulae of Regions I-V. Austin 1986, Univ. Texas. xxv-86 p.; maps 3-9; VII phot. 0-930084-06-3.

b468 **Wilkes** J.J., Diocletian's palace, Split [Spalato, Yugoslavia], residence of a retired emperor [1982 Sanders Lecture]. Sheffield 1986, Univ. 103 p. £6. [AJA 91,635, J.H. *Humphrey*].

b469 **Wojcik** Maria Rita, La villa dei papiri ad Ercolano; contributo alla ricostruzione dell'ideologia della nobilitas tardo-repubblicana: Soprintendenza Pompei Mon. 1. R 1986, Bretschneider. 333 p.; 129 pl.

XIX. Geographia biblica

U.1 **Geographies.**

b470 **Andulsalam** Adel, The rural geographic environment of the Syrian coastal region and the Shizuoka region; a comparative study of Syria and

Japan: Studia Culturae Islamicae 24. Tokyo 1985, Inst. Asia Africa. vii-174 p. [JNES 46,241].

b471 **Aharoni** Y., Das Land der Bibel 1984 ➤ 65,b711; 1,e561: ᴿÉTRel 61 (1986) 110 (J. *Pons*).

b472 **Barthold** W., An historical geography of Iran [Ⓖ 1903, ²1971 ᴱ*Livshits* V., ᵀ*Soucek* Svat], ᵀ*Bosworth* C.: Modern Classics in Near Eastern Studies 1984 ➤ 1,e563: ᴿBSOAS 49 (1986) 225s (D. O. *Morgan*); JRAS (1986) 115s (A. D. H. *Bivar*); Der Islam 63 (1986) 159s (B. *Spuler*).

b473 **Ehlers** Eckart, Iran; Grundzüge einer geographischen Landeskunde 1980 ➤ 62,k293; 64,d267: ᴿArOr 54 (1986) 397s (Adéla *Křivavová*).

b474 **Eybers** Ian H., A geography of biblical Israel and its surroundings. Pretoria 1984 = 1978, Kerkboekhandel Transvaal. 156 p.; maps [KirSef 61,79].

b475 ᴱ**Grothusen** Klaus-Detlef, Türkei: Südosteuropa-Handbuch 4. Gö 1985, Vandenhoeck & R. 844 p.; 165 fig. DM 264. – ᴿMundus 22 (1986) 325-7 (M. *Ursinus*; vol. 1. Yugoslavia, 2, Romania, 3. Greece; cites 'Pogrom' but not 'Türkologischer Anzeiger').

b476 Israel von A-Z; Daten, Fakten, Hintergründe. Neuhausen 1986, Hänssler. 136 p.; 120 fig.; 21 maps [Mundus 22,223].

b477 **Karmon** Yehuda, ᴱ*Storkebaum* Werner, Israel, eine geographische Landeskunde: Wissenschaftliche Länderkunde 22. Da 1983, Wiss. xx-269 p.; 34 fig.; 43 phot.; maps. – ᴿFreibRu 37s (1985s) 134s (Y. *Ilsar*).

b478 **Salibi** Kemal, Die Bibel kam aus dem Lande Asir; eine neue These über die Ursprünge Israels [The Bible came from Arabia 1985 ➤ 1,e574]ᵀ. Ha 1985, Rowohlt. 220 p. DM 36. – ᴿEvKomm 19 (1986) 549s (P. *Maiberger*).

b479 *Salamé-Sarkis* Ḥassān, Et si la Bible venait d'Arabie? A propos du livre de Kamal SALIBI [1985 ➤ 1,e574]: Berytus 33 (1985) 143-165.

b480 **Schliephake** Konrad, Wirtschafts- und stadtgeographische Strukturen in der Türkei, in Syrien und Jordanien; Berichte und Protokolle zur Exkursion Vorderer Orient des Geographischen Instituts der Universität Würzburg 26.IX-31.X.1983: Wü geog. Manuskripte 15. Wü 1985, Geog. Inst. 233 p.; maps. DM 19 [Mundus 22,158].

b481 **Sitwell** N. H. H., The world the Romans knew. L c. 1985, Hamish Hamilton, 222 p.; 43 fig.; 14 maps. £13 [Antiquity 60,178].

b481* **Wolf** Klaus, *Jurczek* Peter, Geographie der Freizeit und des Tourismus. Stu 1986, Ulmer. 167 p.; 11 fig. [Mundus 23,261].

U1.2 Historia geographiae.

b482 *a)* **André** J., *Filliozat* J., Pline l'ancien, Histoire naturelle VI/2 [Asie centrale], 1980 ➤ 61,r210: ᴿRBgPg 64 (1986) 135s (G. *Bunnens*); – *b)* **Desanges** Jehan, Pline l'ancien, Histoire naturelle V,1-46 (Iᵉʳᵉ Partie, L'Afrique du Nord): CollBudé, 1980 ➤ 61,r210: ᴿPBgPg 64 (1986) 134s (G. *Bunnens*: commentaire hors proportion).

b483 *Bühlmann* Walter, Die Mosaikkarte von Madaba in Jordanien: HLand 118,1 (1986) 5-9; 5 fig.

b484 *Casson* Lionel, The location of Tabai (Periplus maris erythraei 12-13) [north of Ras Hafun at southern ledge of Somali Horn of Africa]: JHS 106 (1986) 179-182.

b485 *a)* *Clausi* Benedetto, Scuola e geografia nella tarda antichità; il 'Versus de Asia et de universi mundi rota' [< ISIDOR. Hisp.]; – *b)* *Musti* Domenico,

L'itinerario di PAUSANIA; dal viaggio alla storia: → 537, Trasformazioni 1982/5, 737-780 / 679-690.

b486 *Debergh* Minako,   La carte du monde du P. Matteo RICCI (1602) et sa version coréenne (1708) conservée à Osaka: JAs 274 (1986) 417-453; 5 fig.; Eng. 453s.

b487 **Dilke** O. A. W.,   Greek and Roman maps: Aspects of Greek and Roman life [→ 1,e587]: L/ Ithaca NY 1985, Thames & H. / Cornell Univ. 224 p.; 62 fig. $25. 0-8014-1801-1. – ᴿÉchMClas 30 (1986) 208-210 (Mary E. H. *Walbank*).

b488 *Duchesne-Guillemin* Jacques,   Origines iraniennes et babyloniennes de la nomenclature astrale: CRAI (1986) 234-250; 7 fig.

b489 **Enan** Mohamed A.,   Section of the manuscripts of history and travel books: Catalogues of the [Moroccan] Royal Library, 1. Rabat 1980. 480 p. – ᴿJAOS 106 (1986) 376s (Maya *Shatzmiller*).

b489* *Fezer* F.,   Kartographie mit Hilfe der 'Spacelab'-Aufnahmen: Spektrum der Wissenschaft (Heid 1986) 28-38 [Mundus 23,250].

b490 *Frézouls* Edmond,   Quelques enseignements du Périple de la Mer Érythrée: Ktema 9 (1984) 305-325.

b491 **Gerricke** Helmuth,   Mathematik in Antike und Orient. B 1984, Springer. 3-540-11647-8 [OIAc Oc87].

b492 *Gingerich* Owen, [Greek-] Islamic astronomy: ScAm 254,4 (1986) 74-83; ill.

b493 **Habicht** Christian,   PAUSANIAS' Guide to Ancient Greece: Sather Classical Lectures, 50. Berkeley 1985, Univ. California. xv-207 p.; bibliog. 181-6; 34 fig. 0-520-05398-2.

b494 ᴱ**Hamann** Günther,   Aufsätze zur Geschichte der Naturwissenschaften und Geographie: Szb W ph/h 475. W 1986, Österr. Akad. 220 p. 3-7001-0797-8.

b495 *Horváth* János †,   L'univers d'HÉRODOTE: Ann. Budapest, class. 7 (1979) 37-44.

b496 *Högemann* Peter,   Die Bedeutung des Indischen Ozeans für die Weltmächte von Altertum und Neuzeit; geophysikalische und geopolitische Konstanten in der Geschichte: Saeculum 37 (1986) 34-44.

b497 **Janni** P.,   La mappa e il periplo; cartografia antica e spazio odologico: Univ. Macerata, lett./fil. 19, 1984 → 65,b738; 1,e595: ᴿMaia 38 (1986) 88 (F. *Della Corte*).

b498 **Laor** Eran, (*Klein* Shoshana), Maps of the Holy Land; cartobibliography of printed maps, 1475-1900. NY/Amst 1986, Liss/Meridian. xx-201 p.; ill. 0-8451-1705-X [JNES 46,243].

b499 **Miller** Konrad, Mappae arabicae (1926) ᴱ*Gaube* Heinz: TAVO B-65. Wsb 1986, Reichert. I. xiii-207 p. (biog. ix-xiii, *Husslein* Gertrud); II. 111 pl. 3-88226-293-1.

b500 ᴱ**Musti** Domenico, *Beschi* Luigi, PAUSANIA, Guida della Grecia I. L'Attica 1982 → 1,e606: ᴿRÉG 99 (1986) 393 (F. *Chamoux*).

b501 *Nicolet* Claude, *Gaultier* Dalcher Patrick, Les 'quatre sages' de Jules César et la 'mesure du monde' selon Julius Honorius; réalité antique et tradition médiévale: JSavants (1986,4) 157-209; 9 fig.

b502 ᴱ**Parroni** Piergiorgio, POMPONIUS Mela, De chorographia libri tres: Storia e Letteratura 1984 → 1,e608: ᴿRPLH 60 (1986) 142-5 (A. *Silberman*).

b503 **Peters** Arno, Die neue Kartographie / The new cartography. Klagenfurt / NY 1983, Univ. Carinthia / Friendship. 163 p.; 135 maps [challenges Europe-centered maps: RelStR 13,64, J. H. *Elliott*].

b504 ᵀᴱRackham H., al., PLINY [The Elder], Natural history, with an English translation: Loeb Classical Library. CM/L 1969-1986, Harvard/ Heinemann. 10 vol.

b504* Sack Robert D., Human territoriality, its theory and history: Studies in historical geography 7. C 1986, Univ.

b505 Şahin Sencer, a) STRABON XII 3,7 p. 543, Der Fluss Gallos, die Stadt Modr < en > e in Phrygia; Epiktetos und die Schiffbarkeit des Sangarios; – b) Malagina/Melagina am Sangarios: EpAnat 7 (1986) 125-181; 8 fig.; map; pl. 19; ❶ 182 / 153-166; 5 maps; phot.; ❶ 167.

b506 Seibert Jakob, Die Eroberung des Perserreiches durch Alexander den Grossen auf kartographischer Grundlage: TAVO B-68. Wsb 1985, Reichert. 233 p.; 29 loose maps. DM 88. [Mundus 23,42s, K. Schippmann: details on Persian road system].

b507 a) Serbat Guy, Pline l'Ancien; État présent des études sur sa vie, son œuvre et son influence; – b) Kádár Zoltán, (Berényi-Révész Maria), Die Anthropologie des Plinius Minor: ➤ 574, ANRW 2,32,4 (1986) 2069-2183; bibliog. 2183-2195; index 2195-2200 / 2201-2224.

b508 Sommerlatte Herbert W. A., Der Papyrus von Turin; seine Geschichte und seine Bedeutung als eine sehr frühe geographische und geologische Darstellung [Des mines d'or et le Wadi Hammamat]: AntWelt 17,3 (1986) 31-39; 8 fig.

b509 Tsafir Yoram, The maps used by Theodosius; on the pilgrim maps of the Holy Land and Jerusalem in the sixth century C.E.: DumbO 40 (1986) 129-145; 9 fig.; 4 maps.

U1.4 Atlas – maps.

b510 Baines John, Málek Jaromir, Atlante dell'antico Egitto [Atlas 1980 ➤ 62,k335], ᵀBona Gaspare, ᴱRoccati Alessandro: Civiltà del passato. Novara 1985, De Agostini. 240 p.; 130 color. fig.; 150 fot. + 250 color.; 16 maps. – ᴿSalesianum 48 (1986) 706 (R. Sabin).

b511 Beitzel Barry J., The Moody atlas of Bible lands 1985 ➤ 1,e612: $30: ᴿAndrUnS 24 (1986) 265-7 (W. H. Shea).

b512 Cohen Rudolph, Map of Sede-Boqer West (167) 12-03. J 1985, Archaeological Survey of Israel. [OIAc Oc87].

b513 Cornu Georgette, Atlas du monde arabo-islamique à l'époque classique, I ➤ 64,d328; II ➤ 1,e615. Leiden 1983/5, Brill. xii-92, maps 1-6; x-87, maps 7-15. ƒ52 + 56. – ᴿJRAS (1986) 270s (C. F. Beckingham: to accompany projected MUQADDASI edition; third instalment awaited).

b514 ᴱFlon Christine, The world atlas of archaeology [Le grand atlas de l'archéologie, P 1985, Encyclopaedia Universalis], ᵀᴱWood Michael. L 1985, Beazley. 424 p. £30. – ᴿAntiquity 60 (1986) 153s (G. Daniel: superb).

b515 Friesel Evyatar, Carta's Atlas on the Jewish people in modern times. J 1983, Carta. 160 p. – ᴿRÉJ 145 (1986) 464-6 (J. Shatzmiller).

b516 Levi Peter, Atlante del mondo greco [1980 ➤ 62,k348], ᵀMenghi Martino. Novara 1986, de Agostini. 239 p.; 211 fig.

b517 May H., ³Day John, Oxford Bible Atlas 1984 ➤ 65,b762; 1,e619: ᴿBA 49 (1986) 128 (D. C. Hopkins); VT 36 (1986) 379s (J. L. Peterson).

b518 a) ᴱNagy B. T., [Jerusalem Arbeitsteam] Studienatlas zur Bibel — Handbuch zur historischen Geographie der biblischen Länder. Stu, Hänssler. 172 p.; 106 maps. DM 49,80. – ᴿLuthTKi 10 (1986) 76-78 (H. P. Mahlke). – b) Das Land der Bibel in Bildern; 8 Farbbild Poster: Pictorial

Archive, Wide Screen Project. Deutsche Ausgabe: Stu-Neuhausen 1984, Hänssler. – RFreibRu 37s (1985s) 133 (P. *Fiedler*).

b519 **Pacomio** L., *Vanetti* P., Piccolo atlante biblico; storia, geografia, archeologia della Bibbia 1985 ➤ 1,e620: RStPatav 33 (1986) 431 (G. *Leonardi*).

b520 E**Patterson** J. H., *Wiseman* D. J., *al.*, New Bible atlas. Wheaton 1985, Tyndale. 128 p. $15 [RelStR 13,342, J. H. *Elliott*].

b521 Reader's Digest [E*Frank* H.], TE*Rossi* Fantonetti, Il grande atlante della Bibbia; la storia, i luoghi, i costumi della Terra Santa. Mi 1986, Selezione. 304 p. 88-7045-062-7.

b522 **Rhymer** Joseph, Atlante del mondo biblico [Atlas of the biblical world 1983], T*Gonella* Anna M. T 1986, Soc. Ed. Internazionale. 223 p. 88-05-03891-1.

b523 **Robinson** Francis, Atlas of the Islamic world 1982 ➤ 64,d334... 1,e621: RRBgPg 64 (1986) 781s (Annette *Destrée*: some good maps, but not really an atlas).

b524 **Rogerson** John, Atlas of the Bible 1985 ➤ 1,e622; also NY 1986, Facts on File: RBAR-W 12,5 (1986) 6 (J. *Fleming*, also on BEITZEL).

b525 **Rogerson** J., Nouvel atlas de la Bible, T*Trope* Simon & Gisèle, 1985 ➤ 1,e623: REsprV 96 (1986) 134s (L. *Monloubou*: splendide); ÉTRel 61 (1986) 278 (J. *Pons*); Études 365 (1986) 714s (J. *Trublet*); NRT 108 (1986) 743s (X. *Jacques*).

b526 **Rogerson** John, Atlas van de Bijbel. Amst 1985, Elsevier. 236 p. – RStreven 53 (1985s) 468s (P. *Beentjes*).

b527 **Scagnetti** Francesco, *Grande* Giuseppe, Roma Urbs Imperatorum aetate [in cinque colori; cartina ridotta a 70 × 85 cm, dalle due versioni 100 × 120 in nove e cinque colori]. R 1981, Maggiore Cristina. – RSalesianum 48 (1986) 404 (B. *Amata*).

b528 E**Talbert** Richard J. A., Atlas of classical history 1985 ➤ 1,e626; 0-7099-2421-6: RAncSRes 16 (1986) 117-9 (Rosalyn *Bird*); ClasR 100 (1986) 153s (S. *Mitchell*); ÉtClas 54 (1986) 208s (H. *Leclercq*); Gnomon 58 (1986) 733-5 (P. *Janni*).

u1.5 **Photographiae.**

b529 E**Brunner-Traut** Emma, Ägypten; Geschichte – Kunst – Menschen. Stu 1984, Klett-Cotta. Fotos Michelle Parra-Alédo. – RWeltOr 17 (1986) 151s (Ingrid *Gamer-Wallert*).

b530 **Cole** Dan, *Bahat* Dan, *Shanks* Hershel, Jerusalem archaeology slide set, 6 maps, 133 views; – Biblical archaeology slide set, 134 views; – New Testament archaeology slide set, 2 maps 178 views [selected out of several thousand submitted]. Wsh 1986, BAR. $120; $100; $160. – BAR-W 12,3 (1986) 3-6: 'the only slide set ever reviewed by IsrEJ'. RJBL 105 (1986) 171s (H. D. *Lance*: errors in manual); PEQ 118 (1986) 71s (J. R. *Bartlett*: more background-information needed).

b531 **Dowley** T., High above the Holy Land [28 air-photos with text by *Bruce* F. F.]. L 1986, Hodder & S. 64 p. £10. 0-340-39088-3 [BL 87,31].

b532 **Germesin** Elena, Türkei. Luzern 1985, Reich. 208 p.; 110 color. ill. [Mundus 22,168].

b533 **Hartmann-von Monakow** Lore, Fahrten im Hula-Tal. Z 1983, Freunde Kirjath-Jearim. 68 p.; (color.) ill. (Hartmann T.); maps [KirSef 60,617].

b534 *Malek* Jaromir, *Miles* Elizabeth, Nineteenth-century 'studio photographs' of Egypt in the collection of the Griffith Institute, Oxford: VAeg 2 (1986) 121-6; some fifty sites.

b535 **Wünsche** Erica, *Schwerberger* Michael, Ägypten 1985 → 1,e663: [R]Mundus 22 (1986) 214 (Emma *Brunner-Traut*: 'little archaeology, lots of life and landscape').

U1.6　**Guide books,** *Führer.*

b536 **Baedeker** Karl, [< Palestine and Syria[5] 1912] Baedeker's historical Palestine; handbook for travellers [facsimiles of the Palestine excursions]. NY 1985, Hippocrene. ix-174 p.; maps [KirSef 60,617].

b537 **Charvit** Yossi, 'Lève-toi et promène-toi sur cette terre de long en large' [Gn 13]. Kiryat-Arba' 1983, Midrešet Hebron. vi-105 p.; ill.; maps [KirSef 60,617].

b538 **Devir** Ori, Off the beaten track in Israel; a guide to beautiful places. NY 1985, Adama. 199 p.; 66 fig. + 100 color.; 92 maps. $15 [BAR-W 13/3,10].

b539 **Doyle** Stephen, The pilgrim's new guide to the Holy Land 1985 → 1,e643: [R]BibTB 16 (1986) 151 (L. J. *Hoppe*: prayer services).

b540 [E]**Göttler** Gerhard, Die Sahara; Mensch und Natur in der grössten Wüste der Erde: Kulturreiseführer. Köln 1984, DuMont. 386 p. DM 35. – [R]Mundus 22 (1986) 63 (J. H. *Hohnholz*).

b541 **Gorys** Erhard, Das heilige Land; historische und religiöse Stätten von Judentum, Christentum und Islam in dem 10000 Jahre alten Kulturland zwischen Mittelmeer, Roten Meer und Jordan 1984 → 65,b773; DM 38: [R]Der Islam 62 (1985) 181s (B. *Spuler*).

b542 **Higgins** Paul L., Pilgrimages to Rome and beyond; a guide to the holy places of southern Europe [Greece; Delos ...; Pergamum]. ENJ 1985, Prentice-Hall. 130 p. $9. – [R]BAR-W 12,3 (1986) 14 (J. *Murphy- O'Connor*).

b543 [E]**Huhn** Martin, *Wende* Wolfgang, Wege nach Jerusalem [Förderung der Jugendbegegnung]; zum Verständnis des Judentums. Dü 1985, dkv [Der kleine Verlag]. 77 p. – [R]FreibRu 37s (1985s) 118 (P. *Fiedler*).

b544 **Kamil** Jill, Upper Egypt; historical outline and descriptive guide to the ancient sites. L 1986, Longman. [xii-] 227 p.; ill. 0-582-78314-3.

b545 **Keel** Othmar, *al.*, Orte und Landschaften der Bibel I. 1984 → 65,b775; 1,e648 [II. 1982 → 63,d816]: [R]Reformatio 35 (1986) 72-76 (M. *Rohner*); Theologiai Szemle 29 (1986) 60s (I. *Karasszon*); TR 82 (1986) 107-9 (R. *Wenning*).

b546 **Murphy-O'Connor** Jerome, The Holy Land. an archaeological guide from earliest times to 1700[2rev] [[1]1980 → 61,t825]. Ox 1986, UP. xviii-382 p.; 124 fig.; 2 maps. $10 pa. 0-19-285158-6 [NTAbs 31,125].

b547 **Parker** Richard B., *Sabin* Robin, Islamic monuments in Cairo; a practical guide, [3]*Williams* Caroline. Cairo 1985 [[1]1981], American Univ. $12.50. – [R]JAmEg 23 (1986) 217s (J. M. *Bloom*).

b548 **Ravasi** Gianfranco, La città del Dio vivente; viaggio all'interno di sette Chiese del Nuovo Testamento. Mi 1985, Àncora. 153 p. Lit. 8.000. – [R]CC 137 (1986,4) 197s (J. *Janssens*).

b549 **Richards** H. J., Pilgrim to the Holy Land — a practical guide[2rev]. 1985, Mayhew McCrimmon. 256 p. £5. – [R]CleR 71 (1986) 193 (A. F. *Richards*, no kin).

b550 **Scheck** Frank R., Jordanien; Völker und Kulturen zwischen Jordan und Rotem Meer: Kunst-Reiseführer. Köln 1985, DuMont. 495 p.; 181 fig.; 92 phot. + 41 color. DM 38. – [R]Mundus 22 (1986) 254s (H. *Mergner*).

b551 **Strelocke** Hans, Ägypten und Sinai; Geschichte, Kunst und Kultur im Niltal, von Pharaonen bis zur Gegenwart[9rev]. Köln 1984, DuMont. 472 p. DM 34. – [R]Der Islam 62 (1985) 163s (B. *Spuler*).

b552 **Wagner** Jörg & Heike,   Die türkische Südküste; das neue Reiseland mit seinen alten Kulturstätten[2rev]. Stu 1986, Kohlhammer.   264 p.; 224 fig. DM 98. [Mundus 23,303, J. *Hohnholz*].

U.1.7   Onomastica.

b553 *Beschaouch* Azedine,   De l'Africa latino-chrétienne à l'Ifriqiya arabo-musulmane; questions de toponymie tunisienne: CRAI (1986) 530-546, 5 fig.

b554 *Calderini* Aristide,   E*Daris* Sergio, Dizionario dei nomi geografici e topografici dell'Egitto greco-romano 4/3.   Mi 1986, Cisalpina.

b555 *Darnell* John C.,   Irem and the ghost of Kerma [*i.e. irm* cannot be Kerma as PRIESE claimed, though *i3m* can]: GöMiszÄg 94 (1986) 17-23.

b556 *Görg* Manfred,   Zu einigen mesopotamischen Toponymen in der Liste Amenophis' III. im Tempel von Soleb: GöMiszÄg 94 (1986) 39s.

b557 **Groom** Nigel,   A dictionary of Arabic topography and placenames; transliterated Arabic-English with an Arabic glossary of topographical words and placenames.   Beirut/L 1983, Liban/Longman.   369 p. – RBSOAS 49 (1986) 215s (R. B. *Serjeant*).

b558 *Herrmann* Peter,   Zwei Ortsnamen in Lydien; Agatheira und Tibbai: EpAnat 7 (1986) 17.19.

b559 *Hobson* Deborah,   The village of Heraklia in the Arsinoite nome [evidenced in 144 papyri]:   → 123, FWILLIS W., BASP 20 (1985) 101-115.

b559* *Hrouda* B.,   Zum Itinerar YBC 4499: ZAss 76 (1986) 289-294; 2 maps, 2 phot.

b560 **Marazzi** Massimiliano,   L'Anatolia hittita, repertori archeologici ed epigrafici: Quaderni di Geografia Storica 3.   R 1986, Univ.   xv-201 p.; 19 fig.

b561 *Masson* O.,   La liste des villes de Chypre chez PLINE l'Ancien (V,130): RepCyp (1986) 183-6.

b562 *Mayer* Walter,   Taide oder Waššukanni? Name und Lage der Hauptstadt Mitannis: UF 18 (1986s) 231-6.

b563 *Michałowski* Piotr,   The earliest Hurrian toponymy; a new Sargonic inscription: ZAss 76 (1986) 4-11; 6 fig.

b564 *Muscarella* Oscar W.,   The location of Ulhu and Uiše in Sargon II's Eighth Campaign, 714 B.C.: JField 13 (1986) 465-475.

b565 **Na'aman** Nadav,   Borders and districts in biblical historiography; seven studies in biblical geographical lists: Jerusalem Biblical Studies 4.   J 1986, Simor.   275 p.

b566 *O'Connor* David O.,   The locations of Yam and Kush and their historical implications;   JAmEg 23 (1986) 27-50; 3 fig.

b567 **Oppenheimer** A., (*Isaac* B., *Lecker* M.), Babylonia Judaica in the Talmudic period: TAVO-B 47, 1983 → 1,e679:   RBO 43 (1986) 781-3 (D. *Sperber*: identifies Babylonian sites mentioned in Talmudic literature).

b568 *Osing* Jürgen,   Die ägyptischen Namen für Charga und Dachla [both are *t3 n wḫ3t*, 'Oasis-land'; with *rsjt* 'south' = Kharga]:   → 77, FMOKHTAR G. 1985, II, 179-193.

b569 *Pitard* Wayne T.,   Is the area of Apum–Damascus mentioned in the Mari archives?:   BASOR 264 (1986) 73-77.

b570 *Röllig* W.,   Aims and organization of the Répertoire géographique des textes cunéiformes and historical geography: Sumer 42 (1986) 40-43.

b571 **Zgusta** Ladislav,   Kleinasiatische Ortsnamen 1984 → 1,e688:   RGGA 238

(1986) 191-200 (W. *Blümel*); JNES 45 (1986) 317-322 (H. G. *Güterbock*: classical names, but not for localizing Hittite toponyms).

U2.1 *Geologia;* **soils, mountains, earthquakes.**

b572 ᴱ**Arad** V., *Ehrlich* A., The geology of Lebanon; bibliography 1772-1984. J 1985, Geological Survey of Israel. [OIAc Oc87].

b573 *Ashton* R. H. J., Rhodian bronze coinage and the earthquake of 229-226 B.C.: NumC 146 (1986) 1-18: pl. 1-4.

b574 **Baz** Farouk el-, The geology of Egypt; an annotated bibliography 1984 ➤ 1,e691: ᴿBO 43 (1986) 397s (E. *Paulissen*).

b575 *Boye* P., *Holzapfel* C., *Wittenberg* J., Biogeographische Betrachtung einer Gebirgsregion in Südjordanien: Natur und Museum 116 (Fra 1986) 385-402 [Mundus 23,248].

b576 *Elliott* Carolyn, Whole-rock and mineral chemistry used in tracing the sources of certain stone artefacts from Cyprus: PEQ 118 (1986) 77.

b577 **Hosney** Hassan M., Geophysical investigations in the Gulf of Suez; consequence for the tectonic evolution of the northern Red Sea: diss. Kiel 1985. viii-188 p. – Mundus 23,81.

b578 **Jarrab** Ghaleb H., Late proterozoic crustal evolution of the Arabian Nubian shield in the wadi 'Araba area, SW-Jordan: Geologisch-paläontologische Dissertationen 2. Braunschweig 1984, Techn. Univ. 107 p. – Mundus 23,81.

b579 **Kronberg** Peter, Fernerkundung der Erde; Grundlagen und Methoden des Remote Sensing in der Geologie. Stu 1985, Enke. ix-394 p.; 246 fig. DM 148. [Mundus 23,318-320, H. *Leser*].

b580 *Provera* Mario, *a)* Il monte della Transfigurazione o Tabor; – *b)* Il monte Hermon; – *c)* Nebo / Ulivi: ParVi 30 (1985) 153 / 223s / 52-55.

b581 ᴱ**Rapp** G.ᴶ, *Gifford* J. A., Archaeological geology 1985 ➤ 1,442: ᴿIsrEJ 36 (1986) 284s (M. *Inbar*).

b582 *Soren* D., *al.*, Archaeological excavations and analyses of earthquake-affected strata at Roman Kourion, Cyprus: RepCyp (1986) 202-206; 2 fig.; pl. XLIV.

b583 **Wittig** Michael A., Athos, der Heilige Berg von Byzanz. Wü 1985, Augustinus. 135 p.; ill. DM 12,80. –ᴿIkiZ 76 (1986) 63 (B. *Spuler*).

U2.2 *Hydrographia:* **rivers, seas, salt.**

b584 **Ammendola** A., Il mare nella Bibbia. N 1985, Apostolato del mare. 242 p. Lit. 10.000 [RasT 27,279].

b585 **Arad** Varda, *al.*, The Dead Sea and its surroundings, bibliography of geological research. J 1984, Geological Survey of Israel. 111 p. [KirSef 59,286].

b586 *a) Bonneau* Danielle, Le nilomètre; aspect technique; – *b) Sambin* Chantal, Les horloges hydrauliques dans l'Égypte ancienne: ➤ 562, Eau/techniques 1981/6, 65-73 / 75-83; 3 fig.

b587 *Crouzel* Henri, Puits et sources [Écriture... ORIGÈNE]: ➤ 582, DictSpir XII/2 (1986) 2614-7.

b588 *Desanges* Jehan, Rome et les riverains de la mer Rouge au IIIᵉ siècle de notre ère; aperçus récents et nouveaux problèmes: Ktema 9 (1984) 249-259; map.

b589 **Grewe** Klaus, Planung und Trassierung römischer Wasserleitungen: Frontinus-Ges. Sup 1. Wsb 1985, Chmielorz. 108 p.; ill.

b590 **Kelletat** Dieter, Deltaforschung; Verbreitung, Morphologie, Entstehung und Ökologie von Deltas [Mississippi etc.; since *Credner* G. 1878]: ErtFor 214. Da 1984, Wiss. 158 p.; 48 fig. DM 43. – RMundus 22 (1986) 66 (H. *Wilhelmy*).

b591 *Kleinschroth* Adolf, Die Verwendung des Hafirs [künstlichen Wasserspeichers] im meroitischen Reich: BeiSudan 1 (1986) 79-95; 9 fig.

b592 *Kunin* Robert, Water in Bible times: Dor 15 (1986s) 195-8.(267-9, Nm 19).

b593 *Leemans* W. F., Les grands fleuves du Proche-Orient comme sources de prosperité; pourvoyeurs d'eau et voies de commerce [*McAdams* R.; *Margueron* J.]: JESHO 29 (1986) 89-99.

Pace G., **Panimolle** G. Roma, acquedotti 1984 ⇢ b423s.

b594 **Piacenti** Franco, Perfluoropolyethers as water repellents for the protection of stone: Sumer 42 (1986) 90s.

b595 *Schenkel* Wolfgang, Wasserwirtschaft: ⇢ 591, LexÄg 6,48 (1986) 1157s [1156s, Wasseruhr; an article on 'Water' is announced as a Nachtrag].

b596 *Simon* Erika, Aígyptos-Neilos; archaische Darstellungen des Nil: ⇢ 520, EBremer D., Wissenschaft 1984/5, 95-102; 8 phot.

b597 *Werner* Dietrich, Rom, die wasserreichste Stadt des Altertums; Bemerkungen aus bautechnischer Sicht: Altertum 32 (1986) 36-42; 3 fig.

U2.3 **Clima, pluvia.**

b598 *Ben-Yoseph* Jacob, The climate in Eretz Israel during biblical times: HebSt 26 (Madison 1985) 225-239 [OTAbs 10,131].

b599 **Boedeker** Deborah, Descent from heaven; images of dew in Greek poetry and religion: AmerClasSt 13, 1984 ⇢ 1,e728; 0-89130-807-5: EAntClas 55 (1986) 386s (D. *Donnet*).

b599* *Fabry* H.-J., *sā'ar, śā'ār* 'Sturmwind': ⇢ 599, TWAT 5,7s (1986) 893-8.

b600 *Ginter* Boleslaw, *Kozlowski* Janusz K., Kulturelle und paläoklimatische Sequenz in der Fayum-Depression — eine zusammenfassende Darstellung der Forschungsarbeiten in den Jahren 1979-1981: MiDAI-K 42 (1986) 9-23.

b601 *Hassan* Fekri A., Holocene lakes and prehistoric settlements of the Western Faiyum, Egypt: JArchSc 13 (1986) 483-501; 6 fig.

b602 *Holmberg* B., *'āb* 'Wolke': ⇢ 599, TWAT 5,7s (1986) 978-982.

b603 **Jacobeit** Jucundus, Die Analyse grossräumiger Strömungsverhältnisse als Grundlage von Niederschlagsdifferenzierung im Mittelmeerraum: Würzburger geog. Arb. 63. Wü 1985, Univ. Geog. Inst. iv-284 p.; 35 fig. DM 30. – RMundus 22 (1986) 65 (H. *Blume*: Strömung = 'pressure').

b604 *Kurth* Dieter, Wind: ⇢ 591, LexÄg 6,48 (1986) 1266-72.

b605 **Neuser** Kora, Anemoi 1982 ⇢ 63,d900... 65,b840: RRBgPg 63 (1985) 158-162 (R. *Turcan*).

b606 *Vercoutter* Jean, Les 'affamés' d'Ounas et le changement climatique de la fin de l'Ancien Empire: ⇢ 77, FMOKHTAR G. 1985, II, 327-337 [Gn 41,1-8].

U2.5 *Fauna;* **Animals.**

b607 *Barasch* M., Animal metaphors of the messianic age; some ancient Jewish imagery: Visible Religion 4s (1985s) 235-249 [< ZIT].

b608 *Barnett* R. D., Lachish, Ashkelon and the camel; a discussion of its use in southern Palestine: ⇢ 115, Mem. TUFNELL O., 1985, 15-30; 4 fig.

b609 *Bartosiewicz* L., Multivariate methods in archaeozoology: AcArchH 38,1s (1986) 279-294; 7 fig.

b610 *Behrens* Peter, Widder [ram]: → 591, LexÄg 6,48 (1986) 1243-5.

b611 *Benecke* Norbert, *Reymann* Wolfgang, 'Bonesort-Ziaga' – ein System zur computergestützten Datenanalyse von Tierresten aus archäologischen Ausgrabungen: ZfArch 20 (1986) 81-90.

b612 **Bevan** Elinor, Representations of animals in sanctuaries of Artemis and other Olympian deities: BAR-Int 315. Ox 1986, BAR. 337 p.; p. 338-559, 49 fig. £25. 0-86054-403-6.

b613 *Beyse* K.-M., *ēdær*, Herde: → 599, TWAT 5,9s (1986) 1103-7.

b614 *a) Boehmer* Rainer M., Ein früher neusumerischer Wisent [bison] aus Uruk; – *b) Palmer* Leonard R. †, The virgin she-goat; an Aegeanist approach to Near-Eastern iconography: → 80*, ᶠOBERHUBER K., Im Bannkreis 1986, 25-30; 2 fig., 2 pl. / 193-201.

b615 **Boessneck** Joachim, *Driesch* Angela von den, Knochenfunde aus Zisternen in Pergamon: DAI-Istanbul. Mü 1985, Univ. 90 p.

b616 *Boessneck* Joachim, *Driesch* Angela von den, Eine Equidenbestattung in spätfrühdynastischer Zeit [Biʿa]: MDOG 118 (1986) 45-50; 1 fig. [147-160, Munbāqa].

b617 *Boessneck* J., *Schaffer* J., Tierknochenfunde aus Didyma II: ArchAnz (1986) 251-301; 12 fig.; 32 pl.

b618 **Brinkhuizen** D.C., *Clason* A.T., Fish and archaeology; studies in osteometry, taphonomy, seasonality and fishing methods: BAR-Int. 294. Ox 1986, BAR. 139 p.; 7 fig. 0-86054-378-1.

b619 *Butzer* Karl W., Wüste, Wüstentiere [in English: desert(-fauna)]: → 591, LexÄg 6,49 (1986) 1292-7.

b620 *Byl* Simon, Notule relative au glissement de sens de *stelio* (gecko, petit reptile): Latomus 45 (1986) 143-6.

b621 *Červiček* P., Anser sacer [goose]: BeiSudan 1 (1986) 121-6; 1 fig.

b622 **Clutton-Brock** J., *Grigson* C., Animals and archaeology, 3. Early herds and their flocks: BAR-Int. 203. Ox 1984, BAR. 410 p.; ill.

b623 **Cohen** C., *Sivan* D., The Ugaritic hippiatric texts 1983 → 64,d448; 1,e760: ᴿBO 43 (1986) 172-4 (M. *Stol*); OLZ 81 (1986) 551s (W. *Herrmann*).

b624 *Collins* A.O., Locust: BibIll 12 (Nv 1986) 18-21 [OTAbs 10,42].

b625 *Drexhage* Hans-Joachim, Eselpreise im römischen Ägypten; ein Beitrag zum Binnenhandel: MünstHand 5,1 (1986) 34-47; Eng. franç. 48.

b626 *Driesch* Angela von den, Tierknochenfunde aus Qasr el-Sagha / Fayum (Neolithikum und Mittleres Reich): MiDAI-K 42 (1986) 1-8 [25-34, Mollusken, *Alexandrowicz* S.].

b627 *a) Driesch* Angela von den, Fischknochen aus Abu Salabikh/Iraq; – *b) Green* Anthony, A note on the Assyrian 'goat-fish', 'fish-man' and 'fish-woman': Iraq 48 (1986) 31-38 / 25-30. pl. V-X.

b628 **Elgayoum** Salah E.A., Study on the mechanisms of resistance to camel diseases: GöBeitr. Land- und Forstwirtschaft in den Tropen und Subtropen 22. Gaimersheim 1986, Margraf. 152 p. [Mundus 23, 249].

b629 *Finkenstaedt* Elizabeth, Cognitive vs. ecological niches in prehistoric Egypt [... animals]: JAmEg 22 (1985) 143-7.

b630 **Frayn** Joan M., Sheep-rearing and the wool trade in Italy during the Roman period 1984 → 65,b866; 0-905205-22-7: ᴿÉchMClas 30 (1986) 184-192 (A. M.*Small*); JRS 76 (1986) 333 (M. S. *Spurr*); RÉLat 63 (1985) 346s (J. *Rougé*).

b631 *Fuchs* Robert, Wachs (Bienenwachs): ➤ 591, LexÄg 6,47 (1986) 1088-94; 1 fig.

b632 *Giveon* Raphael, Cattle-administration in Middle Kingdom Egypt and Canaan: ➤ 18, Mem. DAUMAS F. I (1986) 279-284.

b633 a) *Handoussa* T., Le chien d'agrément en ancienne Égypte; – b) *Derchain* Philippe, Djédi et le boeuf (pWestcar VIII,24 - IX,1): GöMiszÄg 89 (1986) 23-41 / 15-17 (-21).

b634 *Helck* Wolfgang, Viehwirtschaft, Viehzählung: ➤ 591, LexÄg 6,47 (1986) 1036-8-9.

b635 *Hesbert* René-Jean †, Le bestiaire de GRÉGOIRE: 433*, Grégoire 1982/6, 455-466.

b636 a) *Hesse* Brian, Animal use at Tell Miqne-Ekron in the Bronze Age and Iron Age; – b) *Miller* Robert, Elephants, ivory, and charcoal; an ecological perspective: BASOR 264 (1986) 17-27 / 29-43.

b637 **Hofmann** Inge, *Tomandl* Herbert, Die Bedeutung des Tieres in der meroitischen Kultur: BeiSudan Beih. Wien 1986, Univ. 208 p. Sch 350 [BeiSudan 1,213-5, Inhalt].

b638 *Hofmann* Inge, Der Pferdekopf am Löwenthron [Merce] Beg.N.ii: VAeg 2 (1986) 47-50; 2 fig.

b639 *Hofmann* Inge, *Tomandl* Herbert, Die Widderplastiken in der Meroitischen Kunst: BeiSudan 1 (1986) 58-78; 18 fig.

b640 **Houlihan** Patrick F., The birds of ancient Egypt; Natural History of Egypt 1. Wmr 1986, Aris & P. xxx-191 p.; 199 fig.; map. 0-85668-283-7.

b641 **Hübner** Wolfgang, Zodiacus christianus: BeiKlPg 144, 1983 ➤ 64,d458; 65,b875: RGnomon 58 (1986) 67-69 (G. *Stemberger*).

b642 *Kawami* Trudy S., Greek art and Persian taste; some animal sculptures from Persepolis: AJA 90 (1986) 259-267; pl. 15-16.

b643 **Klein** Richard G., *Cruz-Uribe* Kathryn, The analysis of animal bones from archaeological sites 1984 ➤ 65,b877; 1,e784: RAntiqJ 66 (1986) 137s (Annie *Grant*); Archeology 39,4 (1986) 66 (Pamela *Crabtree*; for describing collections; better for the excavator is *Coy* Jennie, First Aid for animal bones); JArchSc 13 (1986) 600s (P. *Halstead*).

b644 **Koch-Harnack** Gundel, Knabenliebe und Tiergeschenke 1983 ➤ 65,b878; 1,e785: RAmJPg 107 (1986) 430-2 (T. J. *Figueira*).

b645 **Kozloff** Arielle P., *al.*, More animals in ancient art from the Leo Mildenberg collection. Mainz 1986, von Zabern. 3-8053-0927-9 [OIAc Ag 87].

b646 *Kronholm* T., *næšær* 'Adler': ➤ 599, TWAT 5,5s (1986) 680-9.

b647 **Lamberton** Robert D., *Rotroff* Susan I., Birds of the Athenian Agora: Excavation Picture Book 22, 1985 ➤ 1,e790: RClasR 100 (1986) 179 (W. G. *Arnott*).

b648 **Lapucci** Carlo, Animali e caccia nei proverbi. F 1983, Olimpia. 212 p. – RSalesianum 48 (1986) 504s (R. *Della Casa*).

b649 **Mainoldi** Carla, L'image du loup et du chien dans la Grèce ancienne d'Homère à Platon 1984 ➤ 1,e795: RRivFgIC 113 (1985) 446-451 (Maria Serena *Mirto*); RPLH 60 (1986) 119s (A. *Bonnafé*).

b650 a) *Mallowan* Barbara, Three Middle-Assyrian bronze/copper dogs from Tell al Rimah; – b) *Seidl* Ursula, Ein Pferde-Pektorale; – c) *Barnett* Richard D., The [bankrupt 1841 British merchant] Burgon lebes and the Iranian winged horned lion: ➤ 87, FPORADA E., Insight 1986, 149-152; pl. 28 (one with very fetching smile) / 229-233; 4 fig.; pl. 54-55 / 21-27; 1 fig.; pl. 6-11.

b651 **Martin** Geoffrey T., *al.*, The sacred animal necropolis at North Saqqâra;

the southern dependencies of the main Temple complex 1981 ➤ 63,d435; 1,e797: ᴿCdÉ 61 (1986) 253-6 (Helen *Jacquet-Gordon*).

b652 *Martin* Karl, Vogel(fang)[-aussendung; semiotisch, *al.*]: ➤ 591, LexÄg 6,47 (1986) [1044-] 1051-4. ➤ 1808*b*.

b653 ᴱ*Meadow* R.H., *Uerpmann* H.-P., Equids in the ancient world [Uerpmann: N. Syria Shams ed-Din Tannira]: TAVO Beih. A-19/1,1. Wsb 1986, Reichert. [246-265]. [Mundus 23,85].

b654 *Mertens-Horn* Madeleine, Studien zu griechischen Löwenbildern: MiDAI-R 93 (1986) 1-61; 5 fig.; pl. 1-19.

b655 *Mielsch* Harald, Hellenistische Tieranekdoten in der römischen Kunst: ArchAnz (1986) 747-763; 17 fig.

b656 *Müller* Ulrike, Vervex aethiopicus oder ovis steatopygia? Eine Fallstudie zur antiquarischen Gelehrsamkeit [Vat. Mus. Sala degli Animali]: Mi-DAI-R 93 (1986) 183-8; pl. 60-61.

b657 **Nessia** [Backman] Lematé L., ❿ Man and animals in the Bible [franç.],ᵀ. TA 1984, Am ha-Sefer. 80 p. – KirSef 59 (1985) 296.

b658 *Neu* Erich, Zur Datierung der hethitischen Pferdetexte: ➤ 42, ᶠGÜ-TERBOCK H., Kaniššuwar 1096, 151-163.

b659 *Newall* Venetia, [*al.*], Frosch: ➤ 586, EnzMär 5 (1986) 393-401 [-430].

b660 **Olsen** Stanley J., Origins of the domestic dog; the fossil record. Tucson 1985, Univ. Arizona. xiv-118 p.; 4 fig.; 34 phot. $20. 0-8165-0909-3 [pa. $12, Norman, Univ. Oklahoma]. – ᴿArchaeologia 39,4 (1986) 66 (Pamela *Crabtree*: palaeontology); JArchSc 13 (1986) 389s (S. *Payne*).

b661 **Pardee** Dennis, Les textes hippiatriques: Ras Shamra II / Mém. 53. P 1985, RCiv. 77 p.; ill. F 82. 2-86538-125-2. – ᴿZAss 76 (1986) 305s (W. *Richter*).

b662 *Pierce* Linda J., Report on the mule remains, 1984 excavations at Kourion: RepCyp (1986) 207-211; 1 fig.

b663 **Pilali-Papasterio** Angeliki, Die bronzenen Tierfiguren aus Kreta: Prä-historische Bronzefunde 1/3. Mü 1985, Beck. xi-182 p.; 44 fig.; 26 pl.

b664 *Pitsch* Helmut, Zoologischer Garten: ➤ 591, LexÄg 6,49 (1986) 1420-3.

b665 *a*) *Prummel* Wietske, *Frisch* Hans-Jörg, A guide for the distinction of species, sex and body size in bones of sheep and goat; – *b*) *Grine* Frederick E., *al.*, Analysis of enamel ultrastructure in archaeology; the identification of Ovis aries and Capra hircus dental remains: JArchSc 13 (1986) 567-577; 15 fig. / 579-595.

b666 *Reese* David S., *al.*, On the trade of shells and fish from the Nile River: BASOR 264 (1986) 79-84; 3 fig.

b667 *Ringgren* Helmer, ʾ*egœl* 'Kalb': ➤ 599, TWAT 5,9s (1986) 1056-1061.

b668 *Schenda* Rudolf [*al.*], Fisch: ➤ 586, EnzMär 4 (1984) 1196-1211 [-1240].

b669 **Schochet** Elijah J., Animal life in Jewish tradition; attitudes and relationships 1984 ➤ 65,b892 (Shochet): ᴿRelStR 12 (1986) 79.

b670 **Scholfield** A.F., AELIAN, On the characteristics of animals, with an English translation: Loeb Classical Library 446.448. CM/L, Harvard/Heinemann. I. 1971 = 1958; 359 p. – II. 1971 = 1959; 413 p. – III. 1972 = 1959; 445 p. 0-674-99491-4; 3-0; 4-9.

b671 **Sergent** Frédéric, Le bœuf et le Nil; l'élevage bovin dè l'Égypte ancienne à l'Égypte moderne; diss. vétérinaire, Paris XIII 1986. – BSocFrÉg104 (1985) 56.

b672 *Stein* G.J., Village level pastoral production; faunal remains from Gritille Höyük, southeast Turkey: Masca 4,1 (1986s) 2-11; 5 pl.

b673 *Stendeback* F.J., *sûs* 'Pferd': ➤ 599. TWAT 5,7s (1986) 782-791.

b674 *Stetkevych* Jaroslav, Name and epithet; the philology and semiotics of animal nomenclature in early Arabic poetry: JNES 45 (1986) 89-124.

b675 *Tammisto* Antero, Representations of the kingfisher (Alcedo atthis) in Graeco-Roman art: Arctos 19 (1985) 217-242; 6 fig.

b676 a) *Toperoff* S. P., Canines / dove, turtle and pigeon / eagle | in Bible and midrash; – b) *Cohen* Noah J, Prevention of cruelty: Dor 15 (1986 114-7.181-5.260-3 / 97-13 [in the Bible God has a concern for animals greater than for vegetation].

b677 *Uther* Hans-Jörg, [al.], Fuchs: ➤ 586, EnzMär 5 (1986) 447-478 [-537].

b678 *Van Siclen* Charles C.[III], A new document for Senenmut ['overseer of fowl-houses', Tchay Thebes tomb 349]: VAeg 2 (1986) 151-4; 2 fig.

b679 *Zivie* Alain-Pierre, Cavaliers et cavalerie au Nouvel Empire; à propos d'un vieux problème: ➤ 77, [F]MOKHTAR G. 1985, II, 379-388.

b680 a) *Zobel* H.-J., '*Ez*, 'Ziege': ➤ 599, TWAT 5,9s (1986) 1193-9; – b) *Störk* Lothar, Ziege: ➤ 591, LexÄg 6,49 (1986) 1400s.

U2.7 Flora; *plantae biblicae et antiquae.*

b681 **André** Jacques, Les noms des plantes dans la Rome antique 1985 ➤ 1,e833: [R]RPLH 60 (1986) 133s (P. *Flobert* says this is not a revised edition of Lexique des termes de botanique en latin 1956, but shows that it really is); Salesianum 48 (1986) 197s (R. *Bracchi*).

b682 *Aufrère* Sydney, Remarques au sujet des végétaux interdits dans le temple d'Isis à Philae: BIFAO 86 (1986) 1-32.

b683 **Bierkamp** M., *Frey W., Kürschner* H., Bibliography of the geobotanical literature on southwest Asia: TAVO A-25. Wsb 1986, Reichert. 104 p. [Mundus 23,248].

b684 **Bietak** Manfred, Ein altägyptischer Weingarten in einem Tempelbezirk, Tell el Dab'a: AnzW 122/2. Wien 1986, Österr. Akad. p. 268-278 [Mundus 23,131].

b685 **Bleibtreu** Erika, Die Flora der neuassyrischen Reliefs ➤ 64,d489; 1980: [R]Orientalia 55 (1986) 193s (J. E. *Reade*).

b686 **Blunt** Wilfrid, The compleat naturalist; a life of Linnaeus. L 1984, Collins. 256 p.; (colour.) ill. £7 pa. – [R]Antiquity 60 (1986) 161 (S. *Piggott*).

b687 **Cirillo** Domenico, Il papiro [1796]; pref. *Gigante* M. 1983 ➤ 65,b904: [R]CdÉ 61 (1986) 169s (J. *Lenaerts*).

b688 *Compagnoni* Pia, Alcuni alberi della Bibbia [mandorlo, fico, sicomoro, palma]: TerraS 62 (1986) 175-181.

b689 **Dimbleby** Geoffrey W., The palynology [pollen analysis] of archaeological sites: Studies in Archaeological Science. L 1985, Academic. 190 p.; 36 fig.; £34.50. – [R]Antiquity 60 (1986) 149 (R. A. *Housley*).

b690 **Dittmar** Johanna, Blumen und Blumensträusse als Opfergabe im alten Ägypten: MüÄgSt 43. Mü 1986, Deutscher Kunstv. 178 p.; 187 fig. [Mundus 23, 188, Ingrid *Gamer-Wallert*].

b691 **Frey** W. H., *al.*, Südkaspisches Tiefland und Elburzgebirge (Iran) Vegetation 1:500,000: TAVO Karte A VI 5. Wsb 1985, Reichert [Mundus 22,258].

b692 *Friiss* I., *al.*, The botanical identity of the Mimusops in ancient Egyptian tombs: JEA 78 (1986) 201-4; 2 fig.

b693 **Germer** Renate, Flora des pharaonischen Ägyptens: DAI-K Sonderschrift 14, 1985 ➤ 1,e843: DM 128: ᴿMundus 22 (1986) 240s (Ingrid *Gamer-Wallert*).

b694 *Germer* Renate, *a*) Weihrauch: – *b*) Weizen; – *c*) Weide [willow, salix]: ➤ 591, LexÄg 6,48 (1986) 1167-9 / 1209s / 1164 [-6, —Aufrichten].

b695 *Germer* Renate, Zeder, Zypresse: ➤ 591, LexÄg 6,49 (1986) 1357s/1455s.

b696 ᵀᴱ**Goujard** Raoul, COLUMELLE, Les arbres: Coll. Budé. P 1986, BLettres. 149 p. [34-88 doubles]. 2-251-01330-X.

b697 *Kaplony* Peter, Wappenpflanze: ➤ 591, LexÄg 6,48 (1986) 1146-52.

b698 ᴱ**Kürschner** H., Contributions to the vegetation of southwest Asia: TAVO A-24. Wsb 1986, Reichert. 221 p. [Mundus 23,253; 250:] *Frey W.*, *Probst W.*, A synopsis of the vegetation of Iran, p. 9-43; – *Kürschner*, A physiognonomical-ecological classification of the vegetation of southern Jordan, p. 45-79.

b699 *Kürschner* H., Die syntaxonomische Stellung der subalpinen Dornpolsterformationen am Westrand SW-Asiens: Phytocoenologia 14 (Stu 1986) 381-397 [Mundus 23,254].

b700 **Löschert** Wilhelm, Palmen. Stu 1985, Ulmer. 151 p.; 30 fig.; 18 phot. + 80 color. DM 78. – ᴿMundus 22 (1986) 251 (J. H. *Hohnholz*).

b701 *Loon* Maurits van, The [Byblos sarcophagus; Megiddo ...] drooping lotus flower: ➤ 87, ꟳPORADA E., Insight 1986, 245-252; pl. 59-61.

b702 *Mallowan* Barbara, The Assyrian tree [wrongly called 'palmette']: ➤ 563*, Sumer 42 (1986) 141-5; 22 fig.

b703 *Mayer Modena* Maria Luisa, A proposito di alcune denominazioni della 'canna' e della 'radice' in ambito indomediterraneo: AION-Clas 8 (1986) 271-282.

b704 **Meiggs** Russell, Trees and timber in the ancient Mediterranean world 1982 ➤ 64,d499 ... 1,e858: ᴿGnomon 58 (1986) 761-4 (Wilhelmina F. *Jashemski*).

b705 *Mendoza* Ruben, Plant and animal domestication; direct versus indirect evidence: Antiquity 60 (1986) 7-14; 1 fig.

b706 **Ottosson** M., *sûp* 'Schilf[-meer]': ➤ 599, TWAT 1,7s (1986) 794-6 (H. *Lamberty-Zielinski*) [-800].

b707 **Razzag** Ayed A., Einfluss des Standorts auf den Aufforstungserfolg in Jordanien; Untersuchungen zur Entwicklung einer forstlichen Standortsgliederung für die jordanischen Erosionsschutz-Aufforstungen: Göttinger Beiträge zur Land- und Forstwirtschaft in den Tropen und Subtropen 13. Gaimersheim 1986, Margraf. 173 p. [Mundus 23,84].

b708 *Reinhard* K. J., *al.*, Privies, pollen, parasites and seeds; a biological nexus in historic archaeology: Masca 4,1 (1986s) 31-36; 3 fig.

b709 *Runnels* Curtis N., *Hansen* Julie, The olive in the prehistoric Aegean; the evidence for domestication in the Early Bronze Age: OxJArch 5 (1986) 299-308.

b709* **Sigrist** René M., Les šattukku dans l'Ešumeša durant la période d'Isin et Larsa 1984 ➤ 65,b924; 1,e863: ᴿJSS 31 (1986) 237s (J. N. *Postgate*: spelled *šattukku* throughout but *šatukku* in Contents).

b710 **Sjöquist** Karl-Erik, *Åström* Paul, Pylos, palmprints and palmleaves: SIMA pocket 31. Göteborg 1985, Åström. 107 p. 37 fig. [Antiquity 60,66].

b711 *Talon* Philippe, Le coton et la soie en Mésopotamie?: Akkadica 47 (1986) 75-78.

b712 *Sourvinou-Inwood* Christiane, Altars with palm-trees, palm-trees and parthenoi: BInstClas 32 (1985) 125-146; pl. 7-8.

b713 *Vernus* Pascal, Wald: ➤ 591, LexÄg 6,48 (1986) 1143-5, en français.

b714 *Winter* Urs, Der stilisierte Baum; zu einem auffalligen Aspekt altorientalischer Baumsymbolik und seiner Rezeption im Alten Testament: BiKi 41 (1986) 171-7.

U2.8 Agricultura, alimentatio.

b715 *Arnaldi* Girolamo, L'approvvigionamento di Roma e l'amministrazione dei 'patrimoni di S. Pietro' al tempo di GREGORIO Magno: Studi Romani 34 (1986) 25-39.

b716 *Bondì* Sandro F., Pranzo a Cartagine: Archeo 16 (1986) 36-39; ill.

b717 *a) Bonnet* Françoise, Aspects de l'organisation alimentaire aux Kellia; – *b) Devos* Paul, Règles et pratiques alimentaires selon les textes; le salut par l'ascèse?: → 551*, Kellia 1984/6, 55-71 / 73-83(-84).

b718 *Broshi* Magen, The diet of Palestine in the Roman period — introductory notes: IsrMusJ 5 (1986) 41-56; ill.

b719 **Bruins** Hendrik J., Desert environment and agriculture in the Central Negev and Kadesh-Barnea during historical times. Nijkerk 1986, Midbar. 90-71666-01-8 [OIAc Oc87].

b720 *Bryer* Anthony, Byzantine agricultural implements; the evidence of medieval illustrations of Hesiod's Works and Days: AnBritAth 81 (1986) 45-80; 19 fig.

b720* **Cutler** Daniel S., The Bible cookbook. NY 1985, Morrow. 416 p. $20 [BR 3/1,10, Joan *Nathan*].

b721 **Detienne** Marcel, *Vernant* Jean-Pierre, *al.*, La cucina del sacrificio in terra greca: Società antiche 3, 1982 → 65,9169: **1**,e890: ᴿSalesianum 48 (1986) 713s (R. *Della Casa*).

b722 **Edwards** John, The Roman cookery of APICIUS; a treasury of gourmet recipes and herbal cookery translated and adapted for the modern kitchen. Vancouver 1984, Hartley & M. xxix-322 p. 0-88179-008-7. – ᴿÉchMClas 30 (1986) 93s (Mary Ella *Milham*).

b723 *Endesfelder* Erika, Die Nährungsmittel der alten Ägypter und ihre Zubereitung: Altertum 32 (1986) 18-26; 7 fig.

b724 **Frankel** Rafael, ❶ *Tôlᵉdôt 'ibbûd*... The history of the processing of wine and oil in Galilee in the period of the Bible, the Mishna and the Talmud: diss. TA 1984. 2 vol.; maps. – KirSef 60 (1985) 620.

b725 *Frankel* R., Khirbet el-Quṣeir [1734.2603 east of 'Akko; elaborate oil-press reconstructions]: → a507, ExcSIsr 5 (1986) 88-91; fig. 46-49.

b726 *a) Garnsey* P.D.A., Grain for Athens; – *b) Rowlandson* Jane, Freedom and subordination in ancient agriculture; the case of the *basilikoì geōrgoi* of Ptolemaic Egypt: → 98, ᶠSTE CROIX G., Crux 1985, 62-75/ 327-347.

b727 *Gichon* M., The upright screw-operated pillar press in Israel [for oil]: ScrClasIsr 5 (1979s) 206-244; 13 fig.

b727* **Goodman** Naomi, *al.*, The Good Book cookbook. NY 1986, Dodd Mead. 225 p. $17 [BR 3/1,11, Joan *Nathan*].

b728 *Gottwald* Norman K., The participation of free agrarians in the introduction of monarchy to ancient Israel; an application of H.A. LANDSBERGER's framework for the analysis of peasant movements: Semeia 37 (1986 → b873) 77-102; bibliog. 102-6.

b729 *Greppin* John A.C., Some etymological notes on Gk. *staphylinos* 'carrot': Glotta 64 (1986) 248-252.

b730 *Grottanelli* Cristiano, Agriculture: → 585, EncRel 1 (1986) 139-149.

b731 **Hanson** Victor D., Warfare and agriculture in classical Greece: BiblStAntichi 40, 1983 → 64,d531; **1**,e900: ᴿAthenaeum 64 (1986) 205-218 (P. *Harvey*).

b732 *Harvey* Paul,   New harvests reappear; the impact of war on agriculture [*Hanson* V. 1983]:   Athenaeum 64 (Pavia 1986) 205-218.

b733 **Hopkins** D. C.,   The highlands of Canaan; agricultural life in the early Iron Age: Social World of Biblical Antiquity 3.   Sheffield 1985, Almond/JStOT (with ASOR). 326 p.; 3 maps. £20; pa. £10.50.   0-907459-38-2; 9-0 [BL 87,32, J. R. *Bartlett*].

b734 *Janssen* Jac. J.,   Agrarian administration in Egypt during the Twentieth Dynasty: BO 43 (1986) 351-366.

b735 *Jones* Glynis, *al.*,   Crop storage at Assiros [Mycenean Bronze Age Macedonia]:   ScAm 254,3 (1986) 96-103; ill.

b736 *Kemp* Barry J.,   Large Middle Kingdom granary buildings (and the archaeology of administration]: ZägSpr 113 (1986) 120-136; 8 fig.

b737 *Kingsley* Bonnie M.,   Harpalos in the Megarid (333-331 B.C.) and the grain shipments from Cyrene (SEG IX 2 + = Tod, Greek Hist. Inscr. II no. 196):   ZPapEp 66 (1986) 165-177; map.   ➤ a7 *Hauben*.

b738 *Krasnov* Yu. A.,   ☉ An early history of the wooden plough: SovArch (1986,1) 103-120; 10 fig.; Eng. 120.

b739 *Le Bonniec* Henri,   Un témoignage d'ARNOBE sur la cuisine du sacrifice romain: RÉLat 63 (1985) 183-193.

b740 *Love* J.,   The character of the Roman agricultural estate in the light of Max WEBER's economic sociology: Chiron 16 (1986) 99-146.

b741 *Manniche* Lise,   The tomb of Nakht, the gardener, at Thebes (No. 161) as copied by Robert HAY [1826/32]:   JEA 78 (1986) 55-72; 13 fig. (65 facsimiles) [79-90, *Quirke* Stephen, hieratic texts].

b742 *Meyer* Christine,   Wein [-krug, -opfer, -trauben; *al*]:   ➤ 591, LexÄg 6,48 (1986) 1169-82 [1190-2; 1182-90].

b743 **Neeve** P. W., De,   Colonus; private farm-tenancy in Roman Italy 1984 ➤ 65,8950:   RÉchMClas 29 (1985) 494s (K. R. *Bradley*).

b744 **Reed** Stephen A.,   Food in the Psalms: diss. Claremont 1986, DKnierim R. 562 p. 87-05185. – DissA 47 (1986s) 4116-A; RelStR 13,189.

b744* *Reekmans* Tony,   The motives of the Roman farmer's economic options: ➤ 18, FVEREMANS J. 1986, 259-273.

b745 **Rindos** David,   The origins of agriculture 1984 ➤ 65,b953; 1,e924: RAnthropos 81 (1986) 365s (W. G. *Smith*: 'cultural selectionism as a viable alternative to genetic-based sociobiology and equilibrium-based cultural ecology'); JArchSc 13 (1986) 95s (D. R. *Harris*).

b746 **Robert** Jean Noël,   La vie à la campagne dans l'antiquité romaine: Realia. P 1985, BLettres. 320 p.; ill.

b747 *Rosenthal* Uwe,   Eine Weinpresse im biblischen Moab [Dēr plateau south of Arnon 1985]: BibNot 34 (1986) 25-27; 2 pl.

b748 **Ruyt** Claire de,   Macellum, marché alimentaire des Romains 1983 ➤ 65,b955; 1,e925:   RRÉLat 63 (1985) 383-5 (R. *Adam*).

b749 *Scholl* Reinhold,   Ein Koch namens Spinthēr in [Zenon] PSI VI 615?: ZPapEp 63 (1986) 279s.

b750 *Sijpesteijn* P. J.,   'Christians for Christians' inscription No. 15 [*pykri* hardly 'barley and wheat sown together', but maybe *sitokrithos* = *pyrokrithos*, mixed together; *krithopyros* is a ? hybrid of barley and wheat]: ZPapEp 62 (1986) 150.

b751 *Spalinger* Anthony,   *a*) Baking during the reign of Seti I: BIFAO 86 (1986) 307-352; – *b*) Foods in P. Bulaq 18: StAltÄgK 13 (1986) 207-247.

b752 *Spurr* M. S.,   Agriculture and the Georgics: GreeceR 33 (1986) 164-187.

b753 *Stager* Lawrence E.,   The firstfruits of civilization [agriculture in Canaan ...]:   ➤ 115, Mem. TUFNELL O., 1985, 172-187.

b754 **Tchernia** A., Le vin de l'Italie romaine; essai d'histoire économique d'après les amphores: BiblÉcFrAR 261. R 1986, École française. xii-410 p.; 5 pl. etc.; 9 (foldout) maps. F 360. 2-7283-0106-9 [JRS 77,279].

b755 *Turcan* Marie, L'eau dans l'alimentation et la cuisine romaine: → 562, Eau/techniques 1981/6, 21-28.

b756 *Van Andel* Tjeerd H., *al.*, Five thousand years of land use and abuse in the southern Argolid: Hesperia 55 (1986) 103-128; 15 fig.

b757 **Vandier** J., Manuel d'archéologie égyptienne, VI. Bas-reliefs et peintures; scènes de la vie agricole à l'Ancien et au Moyen empire 1978 → 60,s424 ... 64,d559: ᴿOLZ 81 (1986) 235-9 (J. F. *Romano*).

b758 *Venzke* Margaret L., Aleppo's mālikāne-dīvānī system [... land-tenure and taxation]: JAOS 106 (1986) 451-469.

b759 *Verner* Miroslav, A slaughterhouse from the Old Kingdom [Abusir. Raneferef pyramid complex; *Fischer* H., Or 29 (1969) 168 ...]: MiDAI-K 42 (1986) 181-9; 8 fig.; pl. 27.

b760 *Vesel* Živa, Les traités d'agriculture en Iran [... d'époque médiévale]: StIran 15 (1986) 99-108; Eng. 108.

b761 **Watson** Andrew M., Agricultural innovation in the early Islamic world 1983 → 1,e936: ᴿJESHO 29 (1986) 217s (C. *Cahen*).

U2.9 **Medicina** *biblica et antiqua*.

b762 *Angel* J. L., *Bisel* S. C., Health and stress in an Early Bronze Age population [two, Karataş and Kalınkaya]: → 71, ᶠMELLINCK M., Anatolia 1986, 12-30; 27 fig.

b763 **Başer** K. H. C., Herb drugs and herbalists in Turkey: Studia culturae islamicae 27. Tokyo 1986, Inst.Lang.Cult.Asia & Africa. vii-296 p.

Charlesworth J. H., Discovery ... 4Q Therapeia 1985 → 8163.

b764 ᴱ**Debru** A., HIPPOCRATE, La consultation, ᵀ*Littré* F.; préf. *Jouanna* J. P 1986, Harmann. xviii-278 p. – ᴿRÉG 99 (1986) 384s (P. *Demont*).

b765 *Dow* Sterling, The cult of the hero doctor [*hērōs iatrós*]: → 123, ᶠWILLIS W., BASP 20 (1985) 33-47.

b766 **Duminil** Marie-Paule, Le sang, les vaisseaux, le cœur dans la Collection hippocratique; anatomie et physiologie 1983 → 1,e957: ᴿRBgPg 64 (1986) 166s (A. *Lejeune*).

b767 *Dzierżykray-Rogalski* T., *Promińska* É., Sur la paléopathologie dans l'Alexandrie musulmane: → 77, ᵀMOKHTAR G. 1985, II. 243-7.

b768 **Feldman** David M., Health and medicine in the Jewish tradition. NY 1986, Crossroad. $18 [Judaica 42,204].

b769 ᵀᴱ**Festugière** A.-J., Aelius ARISTIDE, Discours sacrés; rêve, religion, médicine au IIᵉ siècle après J.-C.; préf. *LeGoff* J. Propylées. P 1986, Macula. 188 p.; map. 2-86589-016-3.

b770 *Fischer* Peter M., *al.*, Prehistoric Cypriot skulls; a medico-anthropological, archaeological and micro-analytical investigation: SIMA 75. Göteborg 1986, Åström. 93 p.; 112 fig. 91-86098-34-9.

b771 **Furley** David J., *Wilkie* J. S., GALEN on Respiration and the Arteries. Princeton 1984, Univ. vii-289 p. $39. 0-691-08286-3. – ᴿAntClas 55 (1986) 426 (R. *Joly*); ClasR 100 (1986) 31s (J. T. *Vallance*).

b772 *Galeazzi* O., Gli ex-voto di Bithia; una interpretazione storico-medica: RStFen 14 (1986) 185-199.

b773 **Ghalioungui** Paul, The physicians of pharaonic Egypt 1983 → 1,e960: ᴿCdÉ 61 (1986) 239-242 (H. De *Meulenaere* ne condamne pas absolument).

b774 *a)* *Ghalioungui* Paul, Quelques contributions récentes de la médecine à l'égyptologie; – *b)* *Godron* Gérard, Notes sur l'histoire de la médecine et l'occupation perse en Égypte; – *c)* *Lang* Bernard, Le 'tb' et le 'ḫ3ty' dans les textes médicaux de l'Égypte ancienne: ➤ 18, Mem. DAUMAS F., I (1986) 273-8; 1 fig. / 285-297 / [II] 483-494.

b775 **Gourevitch** Danielle, Le triangle hippocratique dans le monde gréco-romain; le malade, sa maladie et son médecin 1984 ➤ 1,e964: ᴿLatomus 45 (1986) 444-7 (J.-M. *André*).

b776 **Grmek** Mrko D., Le malattie all'alba della società occidentale; ricerche sulla realtà patologica del mondo greco preistorico, arcaico e classico [1983 ➤ 65,b983], ᵀ*Albertini* R. Bo 1985, Mulino. 600 p. – ᴿOrpheus 7 (1986) 406-8 (V. *Citti*).

b777 *Harer* W. Bensonᴶ, Pharmacological and biological properties of the Egyptian lotus: JAmEg 22 (1985) 49-54.

b778 **Herrero** Pablo † 1976, La thérapeutique mésopotamienne, ᴱ*Sigrist* Marcel, préf. *Vallat* François: Mémoire 48, 1984 1,e972: ᴿBO 43 (1986) 738-744 (M. J. *Geller*).

b779 **Khattabi** Mohamed A., Section of the manuscripts of medicine, pharmacy and allied sciences: Catalogues of the [Moroccan] Royal Library, 2. Rabat 1982. 256 p. – ᴿJAOS 106 (1986) 377 (Maya *Shatzmiller*).

b780 *King* Helen, Agnodike and the profession of medicine: PrCPgS 212 (1986) 53-75; 2 phot.

b781 **Kudlien** Fridolf, Die Stellung des Arztes in der römischen Gesellschaft; freigeborene Römer, Eingebürgerte, Peregrine, Sklaven, Freigelassene als Ärzte: ForschAntSklav 18. Stu 1986, Steiner. vi-228 p.

b782 *Kudlien* Fridolf, Überlegungen zu einer Sozialgeschichte des frühgriechischen Arztes und seines Berufs: Hermes 114 (1986) 129-146.

b783 **Kühn** Josef-Hans, *Fleischer* Ulrich, Index hippocraticus, I. A-D. Gö 1986, Vandenhoeck & R. xxxiv-200 p.

b784 *Lateiner* Donald, The empirical element in the methods of early Greek medical writers and HERODOTUS; a shared epistemological response: Antichthon 20 (1986) 1-20.

b785 *a)* *Lausdei* Claudio, Osservazioni testuali su PLINIO ed altri autori medici; – *b)* *Vázquez* Buján, Codicologie et histoire des textes médicaux [P BN lat 11.219]: ➤ 538, Testi di Medicina 1984/5, 101-111 / 75-88.

b786 *Löfstedt* Bengt, Zu einigen lateinischen HIPPOKRATES-Übersetzungen; Arctos 19 (1985) 75-79.

b787 *Manchester* K., Tuberculosis and leprosy in antiquity; an interpretation [< Medical History]: Masca 4,1 (1986s) 22-30; 7 pl.

b788 *Manuli* Paola, Lo stile del commento; GALENO e la tradizione ippocratica: ➤ 530, ᴱ*Giannantoni* G., La scienza ellenistica 1982/5, 375-394.

b789 *a)* *Martini* Carlo M., Arte medica e saggezza umana; – *b)* *Grmek* Mrko D., Il medico dell'antichità greco-romana di fronte alla morte: Fondamenti 5 (De medicina, 1986) 11-23 / 67-82.

b790 *Mirković* Miroslava, Zwei neue Stempel von Augenärzten aus Obermösien: ZPapEp 64 (1986) 217s.

b791 ᴱ**Mudry** Philippe, La préface du 'De medicina' de CELSE (texte tr. comm.): BiblHelv 19. Lausanne 1982, Inst. Suisse de Rome. 228 p. – ᴿEmerita 54 (1986) 153s (D. *Ollero*).

b792 **Müri** Walter, Der Arzt im Altertum; griechische und lateinische Quellenstücke von Hippokrates bis Galen⁵, intr. *Grensemann* Hermann: Tusculum. Mü 1986, Artemis. 530 p.

b793 *Norman* Naomi J., Asklepios and Hygieia and the cult statue at Tegea: AJA 90 (1986) 425-430; 2 fig.; pl. 28.

b794 *Philips* Allan K., Observation on the alleged New Kingdom sanatorium at Deir el-Bahari [*Marciniak* M. 1981, hieratic ink-graffito, priest Nebwau came 'to be healed completely' [or? just 'to have a good time']: GöMiszÄg 89 (1986) 77-83.

b795 *Pleket* H. W., Arts en maatschappij in het oude Griekenland; de sociale status van de arts; Tijdschrift voor Geschiedenis 96 (1983) 325-347.

b796 **Preuss** Julius, Biblical and talmudic medicine [1923], TE *Rosner* Fred. NY 1983, Hebrew. xxix-652 p. 0-88482-861-1.

b797 *Pugliese Carratelli* Giovanni, Nuove note sulla scuola medica di PARMENIDE a Velia: ParPass 227 (1986) 108-111.

b799 **Riddle** John M., DIOSCORIDES on pharmacy and medicine, pref. *Scarborough* John. Austin 1985, Univ. Texas. xxviii-298 p. 0-292-71514-7.

b800 *a) Robert* C. A., Palaeopathology; cottage industry or interesting discipline?: – *b) Chapman* J., Human sociobiology and archaeology: ➤ 548*, Archaeology/Interface 1986, 110-7; 11 pl. / 94-109; 2 fig.

b801 **Sezgin** Fuat, Geschichte des arabischen Schrifttums [➤ 63,8189; 65,8038] 3. Medizin, Pharmazie, Zoologie, Tierheilkunde; 4. Alchimie, Chemie, Botanik, Agrikultur [5. Mathematik; 6. Astronomie]. Leiden 1970s, Brill. xi-498 p.; xi-399 p. – ᴿOLZ 81 (1986) 55-58 (M. *Fleischhammer*).

b802 *Skoda* Françoise, Une métaphore agricole en dermatologie: RPLH 60 (1986) 215-222.

b803 **Stückelberger** Alfred, Vestigia DEMOCRITEA; die Rezeption der Lehre von den Atomen in der antiken Naturwissenschaft und Medizin: Schweizerische Beiträge AltW. 17. Ba 1984, Reinhardt. 215 p. Fs 58. – ᴿAntClas 55 (1986) 492s (R. *Joly*).

b804 **Thite** Ganesh Umakant, Medicine, its magico-religious aspects according to the Vedic and later literature. Poona 1982, Continental Prakashan. 12 + 254 p. rs 60. – ᴿOLZ 81 (1986) 193-5 (K. *Mylius*).

b805 *Touwaide* Alain, Un recueil grec de pharmacologie du Xᵉ siècle illustré au xivᵉ siècle, le Vaticanus gr. 284: Scriptorium 39 (Bru 1985) 13-56.

b806 *Vásquez Buján* Enrique, Diez años de estudios sobre las antiguas traducciones latinas de HIPOCRATES: Euphrosyne 14 (Lisboa 1986) 147-152.

b807 *Veenhof* K. R., Spijkers met koppen I [press-errors about trepaning in Isin]: PhoenixEOL 32,2 (1986) 54-57.

b808 *a) Wiseman* Donald J., Medicine in the OT world; – *b) Hemer* Colin J., Medicine in the NT world: ➤ 261, ᴱ*Palmer* B., Medicine 1986, 13-42. 242-9 / 43-83. 250-257.

b809 *a) Youtie* L. C., The Michigan medical codex P. Mich. Inv. 21; – *b) Marganne* Marie-Hélène, Compléments à l"Inventaire analytique des papyrus grecs de médecine'; - *c) Künzl* Ernst, Zum Verbreitungsgebiet der Okulistenstempel [296 signacula medicorum oculariorum]: ZPapEp 65 (1986) 123-149; pl. VI-VII; 66 (1986) 149-156 / 65 (1986) 175-186 / 200-202; 2 maps.

b810 *Zias* Joseph, *Numeroff* Karen, Ancient dentistry in the Eastern Mediterranean, a brief review: IsrEJ 36 (1986) 65-67.

U3 *Duodecim Tribus:* **Israel Tribes;** *Land-Ideology.*

b811 **Ahlström** Gösta W., Who were the Israelites? Winona Lake IN 1986, Eisenbruns. x-134 p. $13 [RelStR 13,257, W. L. *Humphreys*].

b812 *a*) *Ben-Chorin* Schalom, Israel; Land der Väter, Land der Söhne; – *b*) *Schubert* Kurt, Das 'heilige' Land — Ursache aller Konflikte: Kunst und Kirche 4 (Linz 1986) 225-9 / 230-6.

b813 **Blanchard** William M.[J], Changing hermeneutical perspectives on 'The Land' in biblical theology: diss. Southern Baptist Sem. 1986, [D]*Ward* W. 192 p. 86-09084. – DissA 47 (1986s) 553-A.

b814 **Brueggemann** Walter, A Terra na Bíblia [The Land 1977 → 58,7876],[T]. São Paulo 1986, Paulinas. 274 p. [REB 46,228].

b815 **Davies** William D., The territorial dimension of Judaism: Quantum 1982 → 63,e55... 65,d15: [R]Kairos 28 (1986) 252s (G. *Stemberger*).

b816 *Goldschmidt* Joseph, Der Staat Israel im jüdisch-religiösen Bewusstsein [Ⓞ 1960; Eng. often], [T]*Mach* Dafna: FreibRu 37s (1985s, 'Imma-nuel-Supp.') 157-165.

b817 **Gruber** Franz, Impressionen aus Israel als dem Land der Verheissung: Kath. Akad. Gesch. 3/1. W 1984, Kath. Akad. 27 p. [Mundus 22,51].

b818 [E]**Hoffman** Lawrence A., The land of Israel; Jewish perspectives. ND 1986, Univ. 348 p. $30 [JAAR 55,422].

b819 **Kallai** Zecharia, Historical geography of the Bible; the tribal territories of Israel, [T]*Abrahams* I., *Perla-Puder* Shoshana. Leiden 1986, Brill. xii-543 p.; 4 maps. *f* 125 [TR 83,338]. 965-233-631-4.

b820 *Kallai* Zechariah, The settlement traditions of Ephraim; a his-toriographical study: ZDPV 102 (1986) 68-74.

b821 **Kickel** W., Das gelobte Land; die religiöse Bedeutung des Staates Israel in jüdischer und christlicher Sicht; Vorw. *Gollwitzer* H., 1984 → 1,f8: [R]ArLtgW 28 (1986) 167s (J. *Hennig*).

b822 *Kickel* Walter, 'Sammlung des Volkes Gottes in Jerusalem'; die Theologie der württembergischen Templer im Vergleich zur heutigen Israeltheologie: Judaica 42 (1986) 171-187.

b823 *Luz* U., Israel und sein Land — aus der Sicht des Neuen Testaments: ZeichZt 39 (1985) 266-9.

b824 **Na'aman** N., Borders and districts in biblical historiography: JBiblicalStudies 4. J 1986, Simor. 275 p. $24. 965-242-005-0 [BL 87,34, J. R. *Bartlett*].

b825 *Na'aman* Nadav, The Canaanite city-states in the Late Bronze Age and the inheritance of the Israelite tribes: Tarbiz 55 (1985s) 463-488; Eng. I.

b826 **Niemann** Hermann M., Die Daniten: FRLANT 135, 1985 → 1,f11: [R]Biblica 67 (1986) 292-5 (H. *Engel*); TLZ 111 (1986) 496-8 (E. *Gerstenberger*).

b827 **Ohler** Annemarie, Israel, Volk und Land 1979 → 60,u884... 1,f12: [R]FreibRu 37s (1985s) 122s (Veronika *Kubina*).

b828 *Olson* Dennis T., Biblical perspectives on the land: WWorld 6 (St. Paul 1986) 18-27.

b829 **Pragai** Michael J., Faith and fulfilment; Christians and the return [of Jews] to the Promised Land. L 1985, Valentine & M. 308 p. – [R]FreibRu 37s (1985s) 126 (P. *Fiedler*).

b830 La tierra prometida. M 1983, S.M. 123 p. – [R]RelCu 31 (1985) 102 (V. D. *Canet*).

b831 **Walker** James B., Israel — covenant and land. E 1986, Handsel. ii-13 p. [TLZ 111,504].

b832 *Wilken* Robert L., Early Christian chiliasm, Jewish messianism, and the idea of the Holy Land: → 110, [F]STENDAHL K. = HarvTR 79 (1986) 298-307.

b833 **Yakobovitch** Yiśrael (Emanuel), ❿ Ereș Yiśrael ba-Torah.   J 1983, Dept. Education.   48 p. [KirSef 59,289].

U4   *Limitrophi*, adjacent lands.

Anbar Moshe,   The Amorite tribes in Mari 1985 ➤ 1950.

b835 **Banerjee** Gauranga N.,   Hellenism in Ancient India[2rev].   New Delhi 1981, Munshiram Manoharlal.   viii-276 p.

b836 **Bouzek** Jan,   The Aegean, Anatolia and Europe; cultural interrelations in the second millennium B.C.: SIMA 29, 1985 ➤ 1,f23; Sk 275:   [R]Fornvännen 81 (1986) 143s (S. Hood, *Eng.*); PrPrehS 52 (1986) 368s (A. F. *Harding*).

b837 *Box* Bobby D.,   Edom; who can bring me down?: BibIll 12 (Nv 1986) 41-50 [OTAbs 10,41].

b838 *a) Bresciani* Edda,   I Semiti nell'Egitto di età saitica e persiana; – *b) Montevecchi* Orsolina,   Egiziani e Greci; la coesistenza delle due culture nell'Egitto romano; – *c) Tibiletti* Giuseppe,   Tra paganesimo e cristianesimo; l'Egitto nel III secolo; – *d) Manfredi* Manfredo,   Cultura letteraria nell'Egitto greco e romano: ➤ 546, Egitto 1984/5, 93-104 / 233-245 / 247-269 / 271-285.

b839 **Bryce** Trevor R. [➤ 9410],   The Lycians in literary and epigraphic sources: a study of Lycian history and civilisation to the conquest of Alexander the Great, I.   K 1986, Museum Tusculanum.   xvi-273 p.   87-7289-023-1.

b840 *Buit* F. M. du,   Philistins: ➤ 578, Catholicisme XI,49 (1986) 194s.

b843 *Crocker* P. T.,   Cush [Sudan, not Ethiopia] and the Bible: BurHist 22,2 (1986) 27-38 [OTAbs 10,43].

b846 *Donadoni* Sergio F.,   I testi egiziani sui Popoli del Mare [< RivStoIt 77 (1965) 300-314]: ➤ 152, Cultura 1986, 89-103.

b847 *Edel* Elmar,   Der Seevölkerbericht aus dem 8. Jahre Ramses' III (MH II. pl. 46,15-18); Übersetzung und Struktur: ➤ 77, [F]MOKHTAR G. 1985, I,223-237.

b848 *Karavites* Peter,   *Philotes*, Homer and the Near East: Athenaeum 64 (1986) 474-481.

b849 *Lamberg-Karlovsky* C. C.,   Third millennium structure and process; from the Euphrates to the Indus and the Oxus to the Indian Ocean: OrAnt 25 (1986) 189-219.

b850 **Lehmann** Gustav A.,   Die mykenisch-frühgriechische Welt und der östliche Mittelmeerraum in der Zeit der 'Seevölker'-Invasionen um 1200 v.Chr.: Rhein/Wf Ak g 276.   Opladen 1985, Westdeutscher-V.   74 p. – [R]Gnomon 58 (1986) 626-9 (W. *Helck*); HZ 243 (1986) 146s (G. *Neumann*).

b851 [E]Nagel Peter,   Graeco-Coptica; Griechen und Kopten im byzantinischen Ägypten: Wiss. Bei 48/1/29. = Halle 1984, Luther-Univ.   273 p.; ill.

b852 *Nibbi* Alessandra,   The Sea Peoples; some problems concerning historical method; Annuaire de l'Université de Sofia, Fac. Hist. 77/2 (1985) 310-317.

b853 **Sedlar** Jean W.,   India and the Greek world; a study in the transmission of culture 1980 ➤ 62,k793: [R]Gnomon 58 (1986) 510-5 (F. F. *Schwarz*).

b854 **Sitarz** Eugen,   Kulturen am Rand der Bibel; Sachbuch über Völker und Götter im Geschichtsfeld Israels 1983 ➤ 64,a414; 65,d48:   [R]FreibRu 37s (1985s) 105 (Martina *Schlatterer*).

b855 **Strange** John, Caphtor/Keftiu 1980 ➤ 61,3591 ... 65,d50:   [R]ZDPV 102 (1986) 191-3 (H. M. *Niemann*).

b856 *Tardieu* Michel, Ṣābiens coraniques et 'Ṣābiens' de Ḥarran: JAs 274 (1986) 1-44; Eng. 44.

u4.5 *Viae* – **Routes, roads.**

b857 **Bittel** Kurt, Beobachtungen an und bei einer römischen Strasse im östlichen Galatien. Heidenheim 1985. 55 p.; 35 fig.

b858 *Roll* Israel, *Ayalon* Etan, Roman roads in western Samaria: PEQ 118 (1986) 113-134; 13 fig. (maps).

u5 *Ethnographia,* **Sociologia** [servitus ➤ 4873-4889].

b859 **Alföldy** Géza, Römische Socialgeschichte[2rev] [[1]1975, reprinted 1979]: Wiss. Paperbacks 8. Wsb 1984, Steiner. 212 p.; 1 fig. DM 24. [Eng. ➤ 1,f54]. – [R]ClasR 100 (1986) 331s (M. S. *Spurr*: no real updating).

b860 **Anderson** Ray S., *Guernsey* Dennis B., On being family; a social theology of the family. GR 1985, Eerdmans. vii-168 p. $12 pa. – [R]RelStR 12 (1986) 276 (L. G. *Jones*: useful; 'unfortunately the sociological chapters rarely add to the overall position').

b861 *Arbuckle* Gerald A., Theology and anthropology; time for dialogue; TS 47 (1986) 428-447.

b862 *Baldwin* Barry, Strikes in the Roman Empire [< ClasJ 59 (1963) 275s]: ➤ 129, Studies 1985, 513s.

b863 *Bergman* Jerry, A brief history of the failure of American corrections [i.e. crime-prevention]: JAmScAf 38 (1986) 27-37.

Bouwman G., De weg van het woord ... [social-psychological interpretation of Acts church] 1985 ➤ 4046.

b864 [E]**Buss** Andreas E., Max WEBER in Asian studies: International Studies in Sociology and Social Anthropology 42. Leiden 1985, Brill. 130 p. *f*42 [RelStR 13,51, G. *Yocum*].

b865 *Cartaxo Rolim* Francisco, Max WEBER e sua proposta de comunidade fraternal: REB 46 (1986) 795-813.

b866 *Cipriani* Roberto, Dalla sociologia 'religiosa' alla sociologia della religione: RasT 27 (1986) 559-565.

b867 *Conrad* Robert, A book worth discussing, [*Bellah* Robert N., *al.*, 1985] Habits of the heart; individualism and commitment in American life [social scientists' effort to counter current individualism with an 'older biblical and republican tradition']: CurrTM 13 (1986) 171-3.

b868 *Cowling* G., The biblical househould [*bayit*]: ➤ 377a, IOSOT summaries (1986) 29.

b869 *Culianu* Ioan P., Civilization as a product of wilderness; Hans Peter DUERR [Traumzeit 1978, arguably influenced by Paul K. *Feyerabend* 1975 'anything goes'] and his theories of culture: NedTTs 40 (1986) 305-311.

b870 *Diakonoff* I. M., Women in Old Babylonia not under patriarchal authority: JESHO 29 (1986) 225-238.

b871 *Dosch* Gudrun, Gesellschaftsformen, die in Nuzi-Texten nachgewiesen werden können: ➤ 20, [F]DELLER K., MesopT 21 (F 1986) 191-207.

b872 **Downing** F. Gerald, Strangely familiar 1985 ➤ 1,f67; an introductory reader to the first century — to the life and loves, the hopes and fears, the doubts and certaities of pagans, Jews, and Christians: [R]JStNT 27 (1986) 119 (F. F. *Bruce*: sociological sourcebook).

b873 *a) Elliott* John H. [also editor of this fascicule on] Social-Scientific criticism of the New Testament and its social world; more on method and models; – b) *Malina* Bruce J., Normative dissonance and Christian origins: Semeia 35 (1986) 1-26; bibliog. 27-33 / 35-55; bibliog. 57-59.

b874 *Fenn* Richard K., Sources of social credit in first-century Palestine; immanence and authority in the Jesus movement: ExAud 2 (1986) 19-33.

b875 a) *Franke* Detler, Witwe; – b) *Feucht* Erika, Waise: ➤ 591, LexÄg 6,48 (1986) 1279-82 / 1142s.

b876 **Freedman** D., *Graf* D., Palestine in transition 1983 ➤ 64,262... 1,f74: ᴿBO 43 (1986) 175-8 (G. *Ahlström*).

b877 **Freeman** Derek, Liebe ohne Aggression; Margaret MEAD's Legende von der Friedfertigkeit der Naturvölker. Mu 1983, Kindler. 384 p. – ᴿZEthnol 111 (1986) 142-5 (G. *Hartmann*).

b878 *Flanagan* Kieran, To be a sociologist and a Catholic; a reflection: NBlackf 67 (1986) 256-270.

b879 *Fuks* Alexander, The sharing of property by the poor in Greek theory and practice: ScrClasIsr 5 (1979s) 46-63.

b880 a) *Gager* John G., The DODDS hypothesis; – b) *Bregman* Jay, *Logismós* and *pistis*: ➤ 395, ᴱ*Smith* R., Pagan and Christian anxiety 1979/84, 1-11 / 217-231.

b881 *García Recio* J., Los šībūtum [ancianos] en el reino de Mari: ➤ 21, Mem. DÍEZ MACHO A., Salvación 1986, 305-325.

b882 *Gill* Robin, New studies in the sociology of religion [*Pickering* J. on DURKHEIM 1984; *Turner* B. 1983]: HeythJ 27 (1986) 66-68.

b883 *Goriely* Georges, Athéisme, socialisme, sociologie: Athéisme, ProbHist-Chr 16 (1986) 89-98.

b884 *Gottwald* Norman K. ➤ b728 [editor of this fascicle], Social scientific criticism of the Hebrew Bible and its social world; the Israelite monarchy: Semeia 37 (1986) 1 (-8 introd.)-147.

b885 **Gottwald** Norman K., As tribos de Iahweh; uma sociologia da religião do Israel libertado 1250-1050 [1979➤ 60,g5a]. São Paulo 1986, Paulinas. – ᴿEstudosB 8 [REB 45,180 (1985!)] 50-52 (Ana F. *Anderson*, G. *Gorgulho*); RCuBíb 10,39s (1986) 154-160 (A. *Ferreira Martins*); REB 46 (1986) 722 (–: hipotética, conjetural).

b886 a) *Gugolz* Alfred, Un maestro della sociologia religiosa, Carl MAYER; – b) *Burgalassi* Silvano, Sui significati della ricerca socioreligiosa; – c) *Voyé* Liliane, Gli indicatori socioreligiosi; sviluppi attuali: Religioni e Società 1,1 (R 1986) 49-67 / 115-9 / 120-8.

b887 *Gutiérrez* Gustavo, Teología y ciencias sociales [< Páginas 9/63s (1984) 4-15], ᴱ*Casas* Josep: SelT 25 (1986) 169-182.

b888 **Hallett** Judith P., Fathers and daughters in Roman society 1984 ➤ 1,f82: ᴿAmJPg 107 (1986) 125-130 (Suzanne *Dixon*); ClasPg 81 (1986) 354-8 (R. P. *Saller*); ClasR 100 (1986) 102-5 (Susan *Treggiari*); ÉchMClas 30 (1986s) 76-78 (T. *Fleming*: flawed; filiafocality a silly coinage).

b889 **Hervieu-Léger** D., Vers un nouveau christianisme? Introduction à la sociologie du christianisme occidental. P 1986, Cerf. 398 p. F 135. – ᴿRSPT 70 (1986) 494s (J.-P. *Jossua*).

b890 **Hopkins** Keith, Death and renewal: Sociological Studies in Roman History 2, 1983 ➤ 65,d99: ᴿJRS 76 (1986) 258 (W. G. *Runciman*); Latomus 45 (1986) 219-221 (P. *Salmon*); RÉLat 63 (1985) 362-6 (P. *Moreau*).

b891 **Houtart** François, Religion et modes de production précapitalistes. Bru 1980, Univ. (vi-) 279 p. Fb 550. 2-8004-0710-7.

b892 **Hurst** Antony, Rendering unto Caesar. L 1986, Churchman. 133 p. £5. 1-85093-039-2. – ᴿExpTim first choice 97,12 (1985s) (C. S. *Rodd*: by a latecome Anglican priest on the sociology of organizations, highly praised).

b893 **Kee** Howard C.,   Christian origins in sociological perspective 1980
➤ 61,u242 ... 64,d696: ᴿDeltioVM 15,1 (1986) 54s (S. *Agouridis*).

b894 **Kippenberg** H.G., ❶ Kodai Yudaya Shakai-shi [Religion und
Klassenbildung² 1982 ➤ 63,e169], ᵀ*Okoizumi* Y., *Konno* K. Tokyo 1986,
Kyōbunkwan   283 + 19 p. Y 3800 [BL 87,85].

b895 ᴱ**Klengel** H., Gesellschaft und Kultur im alten Vorderasien 1979/82
➤ 64,663; 65,d110: ᴿBASOR 263 (1986) 93s (N. *Yoffee*).

b896 **Lane** Dermot A., Foundations for a social theology; praxis, process and
salvation. Ramsey NJ 1984, Paulist. 192 p. $7. – ᴿMid-Stream 25 (1986)
133-5 (J. *Gros*).

b897 ᴱ**Lang** B., Anthropological approaches to the OT 1985 ➤ **1**,295: ᴿBib-
TB 16 (1986) 156 (R. *Gnuse*); ÉTRel 61 (1986) 562s (D. *Lys*); Inter-
pretation 40 (1986) 305s (B.O. *Long*); TLond 39 (1986) 397s (A.C.J.
Phillips).

b898 *Laub* Franz, Sozialgeschichtlicher Hintergrund und ekklesiologische
Relevanz der neutestamentlich-frühchristlichen Haus- und Gemeinde-
Tafelparänese — ein Beitrag zur Soziologie des Frühchristentums: MüTZ
37 (1986) 249-271.

b899 *Mack* B.L., Gilgamesh and the Wizard of Oz: Forum 1,2 (Bonner MT
1985) 3-29: NT scholars, instead of trying to relate all the logia and
traditions (from Jesus to the Gospels) to a single mysterious moment,
should try to relate them to many human social moments [NTAbs 30,139].

b900 **Malherbe** Abraham J., Social aspects of early Christianity²ʳᵉᵛ [¹1977]
1983 ➤ 64,d710,**1**,f100: ᴿTLZ 111 (1986) 27s (G. *Theissen*).

b901 **Malina** Bruce, Christian origins and cultural anthropology; practical
models for biblical interpretation. Atlanta 1986, Knox. – ᴿBibTB 16
(1986) 107-110 (J.H. *Neyrey*) & 111-5 (L.J. *White*).

b902 **Malina** Bruce J., The New Testament world; insights from cultural
anthropology 1981 ➤ 62,k763 ... **1**,f101; also L 1983, SCM. £6. – ᴿHeythJ
27 (1986) 191s (M.F.C. *Bourdillon*: has not kept abreast of anthropologists' querying 'limited good' influence).

b903 *a)* *Malina* Bruce J., 'Religion' in the world of Paul; *b)* *Neyrey* Jerome
H., Review articles on two social scientific studies of the Bible; social
science modeling and the NT [*Malina* B., Christian origins (only!); *White* L.
also on Malina; *Kazmierski* C. on MAYER A., Der zensierte Jesus]: BibTB
16 (1986) 107-110 [111-5; 116s].

b904 **Mann** M., The sources of social power; 1. A history of power from the
beginning to A.D. 1769 [... Middle East, Greece, Rome]. C 1986, Univ.
ix-549 p. 0-521-30851-8; pa. 1349-X. [JRS 77, 193, G. *Woolf*].

b905 *Martel* Gilles, Une grille d'analyse des mouvements messianiques
appliqués au cas de Louis RIEL [... *Desroche* Henri, Dieux d'hommes;
dictionnnaire des messianismes et millénarismes de l'ère chrétienne (P 1969,
Mouton)]: SR 15 (1986) 205-220.

b906 *Martínez Cortés* Javier, Sociología de la increencia en España
[< Pastoral Misionera 21 (1985) 143-157], ᴱ*Gari* José A.: SelT 25 (1986)
205-213.

b907 **Mayer** Anton, Der zensierte Jesus; Sociologie des NTs 1983 ➤ 64,
d718 ... **1**,f103 [Mayer!]: ᴿActuBbg 23 (1986) 41-43 (J. *Boada*); BíbTB 16
(1986) 116-8 (C. *Kazmierski*); Salesianum 48 (1986) 424s C. *Bissoli*: l'autore
un pubblicista che conosce molte cose nell'ambiente della sociologia).

b908 **Meeks** Wayne A., The moral world of [i.e. surrounding] the first
Christians: Library of Early Christianity 6. Ph 1986, Westminster. 182 p.
$19 [RelStR 13,261, Pheme *Perkins*].

b909 *Meeks* Wayne A., A hermeneutics of social embodiment: → 110, ᶠSTENDAHL K. = HarvTR 79 (1986) 176-186.

b910 ᴱ**Moore** Robert L., *Reynolds* Frank E., Anthropology and the study of religion: Studies in Religion and Society 1984 → 1,384: ᴿSMSR 52 (1986) 336s (I. P. *Culianu*).

b911 *Mosala* Itumeleng J., Social scientific approaches to the Bible; one step forward, two steps backward: JTSAf 14,55 (1986) 15-30.

b912 *Na'man* Nadav, Ḥabiru and Hebrews; the transfer of a social term to the literary sphere: JNES 45 (1986) 251-269.

b913 **Novak** Michael, Freedom with justice; Catholic social thought and liberal institutions. SF 1984, Harper & R. xiv-253 p. $18. 0-06-066317-0. – ᴿCurrTM 13 (1986) 177s (H. T. *Mayer*).

b914 *Oppermann* Ralf, Die Rebellionsthese in GOTTWALDs 'The tribes of Yahweh': BibNot 33 (1986) 80-99.

b915 **Osiek** Carolyn, What are they saying about the social setting of the NT? 1984 → 65,d131; 1,f114: ᴿBibTB 16 (1986) 80 (D. *Rhoads*).

b916 *Phillips* Charles R.ᴵᴵᴵ, The sociology of religious knowledge in the Roman Empire to A.D, 284: → 574, ANRW 2/16/3 (1986) 2677-2773.

b917 **Pickering** W. S. F., DURKHEIM's sociology of religion; themes and theories 1984 → 65,d136; 1,f117: ᴿJScStR 25 (1986) 259-261 (R. *Robertson*).

b918 **Ponsetto** Antonio, Max WEBER, ascesa, crisi e trasformazione del capitalismo. Mi 1986, Angeli. 240 p. Lit. 20.000. – ᴿHumBr 41 (1986) 957 (B. *Belletti*).

b919 *Poole* FitzJohn P., Metaphors and maps; towards comparison in the anthropology of religion: JAAR 54 (1986) 411-441; bibliog. 441-457.

b920 *Quack* Anton, The ambivalent relationship between mission and anthropology; criticisms and suggestions: VerbumSVD 27 (1986) 221-234.

b921 *Raphael* Freddy, L'étranger et le paria dans l'œuvre de Max WEBER et de Georg SIMMEL: ArchivScSocRel 31,1 (Autour de Max Weber) 63-82 [*al.* 5-170].

b922 *Riesner* Rainer, Soziologie des Urchristentums; ein Literaturüberblick: TBei 17 (Wu 1986) 213 ... [< ZIT].

b923 **Rogerson** J. W., Anthropology and the OT 1984 → 60,8503 ... ᴿÉTRel 61 (1986) 561s (D. *Lys*).

b924 *Rogerson* John, Anthropology and the Old Testament: PrIrB 10 (1986) 90-102.

b925 *Salamone* Frank A., Missionaries and anthropologists; an inquiry into their ambivalent relationship: Missiology 14 (1986) 55-70.

b926 **Samuel** Alan E., From Athens to Alexandria; Hellenism and social goals in Ptolemaic Egypt: Studia Hellenistica 26, 1983 → 64,d734: ᴿCdÉ 61 (1986) 164s (J. *Bingen*).

b927 **Schöllgen** Georg, Ecclesia sordida? Zur Frage der sozialen Schichtung frühchristlicher Gemeinden am Beispiel Karthagos zur Zeit TERTULLIANS: JbAC Egb 12, 1985 → 65,d154; 1,f134: ᴿChH 55 (1986) 220s (R. M. *Grant*); JTS 37 (1986) 214-6 (W. H. C. *Frend*); MüTZ 37 (1986) 140s (H. *Frohnhofen*); NRT 108 (1986) 453s (N. *Plumat*); RÉLat 63 (1985) 412-6 (J. *Fontaine*); RömQ 81 (1986) 125-8 (R. *Klein*); TR 82 (1986) 289-292 (E. *Feldmann* erwartet Ähnliches über Hippo); VigChr 40 (1986) 83-86 (J. van *Winden*).

b928 *a*) *Scroggs* Robin, Sociology and the New Testament; – *b*) *Malina* Bruce J., Interpreting the Bible with anthropology; the case of the poor and the rich: Listening 21 (1986) 138-147 / 148-159.

b929 *Segal* Robert A., The 'de-sociologizing' of the sociology of religion: ScotR 7,1 (1986) 1-28.
b930 *Seyfried* Karl-Joachim, Zwerg [dwarf]: ➤ 591, LexÄg 6,49 (1986) 1432 [1436s, Zwilling, twin, *Baines* J. R].
b931 **Sharashenidze** Dzh. M., Ⓡ *Formi ekspluatatsii* ... Forms of labour utilization in Sumer state economy in the second half of the III millennium B.C. Tbilisi 1986, Metsniereba [OIAc Ag87].
b932 *Sherwin-White* A. N., The letters of PLINY; a historical and social commentary. Ox 1985, Clarendon. xv-808 p. £45 [ÉtClas 55,109].
b933 **Stambaugh** J. E., *Balch* D. L., The New Testament in its social environment: Library of Early Christianity 2. Ph 1986, Westminster. 210 p.; 16 maps. 0-664-21906-3 [NTAbs 30,380]. $19; pa. $13. – ᴿBR 2,3 (1986) 12.60 (Carolyn *Osiek*); ChH 55 (1986) 503 (E. G. *Hinson*); CurrTM 13 (1986) 371s (E. *Krentz*); TS 47 (1986) 518s (D. J. *Harrington*); TTod 43 (1986s) 601s (B. J. *Malina*: informative for us but would the persons described recognize themselves?).
b934 *Stevenson* Kenneth W., Van GENNEP and marriage — strange bedfellows? A fresh look at the rites of marriage [Rites de Passage 1908: the three pre-marriage phases (powerlessness, cultural inversion, temporary suspension of cultural mores) reflected in rituals: Syrian-Armenian, Coptic-Ethiopic, Byzantine, later]: EphLtg 100 (1986) 138-151.
b935 **Sutherland** Ray K., The political role of the assemblies in ancient Israel: diss. Vanderbilt, ᴰ*Knight* D. Nv 1985. 176 p. 86-16376. – DissA 47 (1986s) 1365s-A; RelStR 13,189.
b936 *Talmon* Shemaryahu, a) The Judaean ʿam haʾareṣ in historical perspective [< 4th world congress 1965/7, 71-76]; – b) The emergence of Jewish sectarianism in the early Second Temple period [< ᴱ*Schluchter* W., Max WEBERs Sicht 1985, 233-280]: ➤ 227, King, cult 1986, 68-78 / 165-201.
b936* **Taylor** Mark K., Beyond explanation; religious dimensions in cultural anthropology. Macon 1986, Mercer Univ. 262 p. $25 [TTod 44,119, P. C. *Hodgson*].
b937 **Theissen** Gerd, Studien zur Soziologie des Urchristentums²: WUNT 19, 1983 ➤ 64,d747 ... 1,f144: ᴿRechSR 74 (1986) 249s (J. *Guillet*).
b938 **Theissen** Gerd, Estudios de sociología del cristianismo primitivo, ᵀ*Ruiz* F., *Vidal* S. 1985 ➤ 1,f147: ᴿCiTom 113 (1986) 402s (J. L. *Espinel*); ComSev 19 (1986) 435-8 (V. J. *Ansede Alonso*); EstAg 21 (1986) 184 (A. *Rodríguez*); NatGrac 33 (1986) 178s (D. *Montero*); PerspT 13 (1986) 397-9 (A. *Casalegno*); RazF 213 (1986) 553 (V. *Ramallo*).
b939 **Thiel** W., Die soziale Entwicklung Israels in vorstaatlicher Zeit 1985 ➤ 1,f148: ᴿExpTim 97 (1985s) 344 (R. J. *Coggins*: MENDENHALL and GOTTWALD dismissed; ex-amphictyony elements valued).
b940 *Thompson* L. A., Observations on the perception of 'race' in imperial Rome: Proceedings of the African Classical Associations 17 (1983: final volume) 1-21.
b941 **Tidball** Derek, The social context of the NT 1984 ➤ 64,d751 ... 1,f150: ᴿJAAR 54 (1986) 617s (J. V. *Spickard*).
b942 **Towler** Robert, The need for certainty; a sociology study of conventional religion 1984 ➤ 1,f152: ᴿTLond 39 (1986) 71-73 (G. *James*: 4000 letters about Honest to God).
b943 **Vidich** Arthur J., *Lyman* Stanford M., American sociology; worldly rejections of religion and their directions 1985 ➤ 1,f158: ᴿJAAR 54 (1986) 364s (W. H. *Swatos*); TTod 43 (1986s) 273-5. 278s (R. K. *Fenn*:

American sociology largely formed by transmutations of the Protestant heritage).

Watson F. B., Paul... a sociological approach 1986 → 4634*.

b944 **Welskopf** E. C. †, Soziale Typenbegriffe im alten Griechenland und ihr Fortleben in den Sprachen der Welt, I-II [last of the series to appear; III-V are also on Greece, 1981; VI on German 1981, VII on 'world-languages' 1982; → 1,f143]; Belegstellenverzeichnis altgriechischer sozialer Typenbegriffe von Homer bis Aristoteles. B 1985, Akademie. xxxvii-1022 p.; 966 p. DM 150. – ᴿClasR 100 (1986) 330s (T. J. *Saunders*).

b945 **Wilson** Robert R., Sociological approaches to the Old Testament: GuidesBS, 1984 → 65,d170; 1,f169: ᴿBibTB 16 (1986) 42 (D. C. *Benjamin*); CBQ 48 (1986) 97-9 (J. *Ferrie*); Interpretation 40 (1986) 81 (B. O. *Long*); JBL 105 (1986) 303 (T. W. *Overholt*).

b946 **Zeitlin** Irving M., Ancient Judaism; biblical criticism from Max WEBER to the present 1984 → 65,d173; 1,f172: ᴿRelSt 22 (1986) 151-3 (R. *Carroll*: unscholarly defense of KAUFMANN against ALT - NOTH - von RAD); ScotJT 39 (1986) 255-7 (P. *Addinall*); TLond 39 (1986) 55s (R. *Clements*).

U5.3 Commercium, oeconomica.

b947 *Abulafia* David, The merchants of Messina; Levant trade and domestic economy: PBritSR 54 (1986) 196-212.

b948 *Andreyev* V. N., ⊕ The instability of wealth in fifth and fourth century Athens: VDI (1986,3) 68-93; Eng. 93.

b949 *a) Aravantinos* Vassilis L., Tebe e il ruolo dei centri elladici in età premicenea; – *b) Doumas* Christos G., Trade in the Aegean in the light of the Thera excavations: → 564, Traffici micenei 1984/6, 215-231 / 233-240; 19 fig.

b950 *Badalyants* Yu. S., ⊕ Trade and other economic ties between Rhodes and the North Black Sea area in the Hellenistic period: VDI 176 (1986,1) 87-99; Eng. 99.

b951 **Bagnall** Roger S., Currency and inflation in fourth century [A.D.] Egypt: BASP Sup 5. Atlanta 1985, Scholars. vii-81 p.; 2 pl. 0-89130-780-7.

b952 *Ben-Tor* Amnon, The trade relations of Palestine in the Early Bronze Age: JESHO 29 (1986) 1-27.

b953 **Blázquez** J. M., Economía de la Hispania romana [18 art., 1957-76], 1978 → 1,f179; 84-85432-002: ᴿBabesch 61 (1986) 226s (H. W. *Pleket*).

b954 *Bleiberg* Edward, The King's privy purse during the New Kingdom; an examination of *inw*: JAmEg 21 (1984) 155-169.

b955 **Boardman** John, I Greci sui mari; traffici e colonie [The Greeks overseas... trade, 1964 → 63,e246], ᵀGilotta Fernando, intr. *Cristofani* Mauro: Archeologia. F 1986, Giunti. xi-330 p.; 313 fig.

b956 *Bogaert* Raymond, Grundzüge des Bankwesens im alten Griechenland; Xenia 18. Konstanz 1986, Univ. 30 p. 3-87940-281-7.

b957 **Brun** Patrice, Eisphora, syntaxis, stratiotika; recherches sur les finances militaires d'Athènes au IVᵉ siècle avant J.-C.: AnnLittBesançon 50. P 1983, BLettres. iii-196 p. F 180. – ᴿRBgPg 64 (1986) 146s (P. *Salmon*).

b958 *Burelli Bergese* Laura, Sparta, il denaro e i depositi in Arcadia: AnPisa 16 (1986) 608-619.

b959 *Casson* Lionel B., Rome's trade in the Indian Ocean; the routes, the ships, the ports: → 548, AJA 90 (1986) 203.

b960 *Cataudella* Michele R., Aspetti e strumenti della politica monetaria ateniese fra V e IV secolo: Sileno 12 (1986) 111-135.

b961 *a) Charvát* Petr, The name Anzu-ᵈSùd in the texts from Fara [*Deimel* A. *al.*, apparently a human being useful for tracing economic and social life]; – *b) Vogelzang* [sic] Marianna E., Kill Anzu! on a point of literary evolution [divinity in a myth]: ➤ 543, Rencontre 32, 1985/6, 45-53 / 61-70.

b962 *Cotton* Hannah M., A note on the organization of tax-farming in Asia Minor (CICERO, Fam. XIII,65); Latomus 45 (1986) 367-373.

b963 *Crawford* Michael H., Coinage and money under the Roman republic; Italy and the Mediterranean economy 1985 ➤ 1,f185; £65: ᴿAthenaeum 64 (1986) 525-9 (Alessandra *Gara*); HZ 243 (1986) 661-3 (D. *Kienast*).

b964 *Daniel* R. W., *Sijpesteijn* Pieter J., Remarks on the camel-tax in Roman Egypt: CdÉ 61 (1986) 111-5.

b965 *Deller* Karlheinz, Ein Assyrer tilgt Schulden: OrAnt 25 (1986) 21-27.

b966 **De Martino** Francesco, Wirtschaftsgeschichte des alten Rom [Storia economica 1979s ➤ 63,e281], ᵀ*Galsterer* Brigitte 1985 ➤ 1,f190: ᴿHistJb 106 (1986) 439s (P. *Herz*).

b967 **Di Porto** Andrea, Impresa collettiva e schiavo; 'manager' in Roma antica (II sec. a.C. - II sec. d.C): Univ. Roma, Ist. Diritto Rom./Or. 64. Mi 1984, Giuffrè. 497 p. 88-14-00631-8 [JRS 77,205, J. *Percival*].

b968 ᴱ**Garnsey** P., *al.*, Trade in the ancient economy 1983 ➤ 64,375; 1,f203: ᴿEngHR 101 (1986) 207 (C. J. *Howgego*).

b969 *Gras* Michel, La coupe et l'échange dans la Méditerranée antique: ➤ 18, Mém. DAUMAS F., II (1986) 351-359.

b970 **Gras** Michel, Trafics tyrrhéniens archaïques: Bibl.Éc.FrAR 258. R 1985, École française. 774 p. 8 pl. F 490. – ᴿArchéologia 216 (1986) 82s (C. *Rolley*).

b971 **Green** Henry A., The economic and social origins of Gnosticism: SBL diss. [St. Andrew's 1982] 77, 1985 ➤1,f212: ᴿETL 62 (1986) 438s (A. de *Halleux*); IrBSt 8 (1986) 49s (R. M. *Wilson*).

b972 **Greene** Kevin, The archaeology of the Roman economy. L 1986, Batsford. 192 p.; 73 fig. £12.50 pa. 0-7134-4594-7 [AntiqJ 67,166, M. *Fulford*].

b973 **Grunert** Stefan, Thebanische Kaufverträge des 3. und 2. Jahrhunderts 1981 ➤ 65,d196: ᴿOLZ 81 (1986) 340-343 (B. *Menu*).

b974 *Gutgesell* Manfred, Wirtschaft: ➤ 591, LexÄg 6,48 (1986) 1275-8.

b975 *Hawkins* J. D., Royal statements of ideal prices; Assyrian, Babylonian, and Hittite: ➤ 71,ᶠMELLINK M., Anatolia 1986, 93-102.

b976 **Höhfeld** Volker, (*Doğan* Yaman), Persistenz und Wandel der tradi-tionellen Formen des Fremdenverkehrs in der Türkei: TAVO B-71 [zu Blatt A-X-19]. Wsb 1986, Reichert. 207 p.; 40 fig.; 18 maps. 3-88226-287-7.

b977 **Joannès** Francis, Textes économiques de la Babylonie récente 1982 ➤ 64,b724; 1,f222: ᴿOLZ 81 (1986) 31-35 (H. *Freydank*); Orientalia 55 (1986) 85-89 (G. J. P. *McEwan*).

b978 *Kennedy* D. A., Documentary evidence for the economic base of early Neo-Babylonian society II. A survey of Babylonian texts, 626-605 B.C.: JCS 28 (1986) 172-244.

b979 *Kleiman* Ephraim, ❶ Were fairs in Tannaitic and Amoraic Palestine artificial and redundant?: Zion 51 (1986) 471-484; Eng. XVI [rejoinder of Z. *Safrai* 485s].

b980 *Knapp* A. Bernard, Production, exchange, and socio-political complexity on Bronze Age Cyprus: OxJArch 5 (1986) 35-53; bibliog. 53-60.

b981 *Kozyreva* N. V., ❷ The use of silver as a means of payment in Old Babylonian Mesopotamia: VDI 176 (1986,1) 76-81; Eng. 81.

b982 *a) Kupiszewski* Henryk, Antichrese und Nutzpfand in den Papyri; – *b) Benöhr* Hans-P., Finanzielle Transaktionen zwischen CICERO und CAESAR in den Jahren 54 bis 50 v.Chr.: ➤ 51, FKASER M., Iuris professio 1986, 133-149 / 21-43.

b983 *Kuyper* J. de, Collectief of privé-landeigendom in Mari ? (résumé): Akkadica 49 (1986) 31.

b984 *Lage* F., La crítica del comercio en los profetas de Israel: Moralia 7 (1985) 3-28.

b985 **Lévy** Jean-Philippe, L'économie antique[3]. Que sais-je? N° 1155. P 1981, PUF. 128 p. 2-13-036870-0.

b986 *Lohfink* Norbert, Gottes Reich und die Wirtschaft in der Bibel: IkaZ 15 (1986) 110-123; = Les aspects économiques du Règne de Dieu [... jubilé, Lv 25; Christianisme primitif]: Communio 11,3 (P 1986) 53-70.

b987 *Love* John, Max WEBER and the theory of ancient capitalism: Hist-Theory 25 (1986) 152-172.

b988 *Macve* Richard H., Some glosses on Ste. Croix's 'Greek and Roman accounting': ➤ 98, FSTE. CROIX G., Crux 1985, 233-264.

b989 *a) Maluquer de Motes* J., La dualidad comercial fenicia y griega en Occidente; – *b) Belén* M., Importaciones fenicias en Andalucía Occidental; – *c) González-Prats* A., Las importaciones y la presencia fenicias en la Sierra de Crevillente (Alicante): ➤ 353, EOlmo Lete G. del, Fenicios 1986, II = AulaO 4 (1986) 202-210 / 263-275; 5 fig.; 3 pl. / 279-301; 12 fig.; 1 pl.

b990 *a) Marazzi* Massimiliano, Repertori archeologici sui traffici micenei nel Mediterraneo orientale: Egitto, Cipro, Vicino-Oriente; – *b) Vincentelli* I., *Tiradritti* F., La presenza egea in Egitto; – *c) Pacci* M., Presenze micenee a Cipro; – *d) Liverani* M., La ceramica e i testi; commercio miceneo e politica orientale; – *e) Zaccagnini* C., Aspects of copper trade in the Eastern Mediterranean during the Late Bronze Age: ➤ 564, Traffici 1984/6, 323-6 / 327-334 / 335-342 / 405-412 / 413-424.

b991 *Martin* Cary J., A demotic land lease from Philadelphia [Darb el-Gerza], P. BM 10560: JEA 78 (1986) 159-173.

b992 *Mian* Franca, Due componenti socio-economiche nella Bibbia; ricchezza e povertà: Renovatio 21 (1986) 497-524.

b993 *Van De Mieroop* Marc, *a)* Gold offerings of Šulgi: Orientalia 55 (1986) 131-151; – *b)* Tūram-Ilī, an Ur III merchant: JCS 38 (1986) 1-23; 25-80 facsimiles.

b994 **Migeotte** L., L'emprunt public dans les cités grecques; recueil des documents et analyse critique: ÉtAnc. Québec/P 1984, Sphinx/BLettres. iii-436 p.; 5 pl. [JHS 107, 225s, R. *Osborne*].

b995 **Morris** Holly Jane, An economic model of the Late Mycenaean kingdom of Pylos: diss. Minnesota, DRaup P. Minneapolis 1986. 229 p. 87-06945. – DissA 47 (1986s) 4426-A.

b996 *Montgomery* Hugo, 'Merchants fond of corn'; citizens and foreigners in the Athenian grain trade: Symbolae 61 (Oslo 1986) 43-61.

b997 **Oakman** Douglas E., The economic aspect in the words and ministry of Jesus: diss. Graduate Theological Union. Berkeley 1986. 309 p. 86-28717. DissA 47 (1986s) 3453-A. – RelStR 13,189.

b998 *Oren* E., al., ⊕ A Phoenician emporium on the border of Egypt: Qadmoniot 19 (1986) 83-90; ill.

b999 **Peacock** D. P. S., *Williams* D. F., Amphorae and the Roman economy; an introductory guide. L 1986, Longman. xix-239 p.; 139 fig. £28. 0-582-49304-8 [AntiqJ 67,164, A. *Fitzpatrick*].

d1 **Perepelkin** Jurij J., Privateigentum in der Vorstellung der Ägypter des Alten Reichs, ᵀ*Müller-Wollermann* Renate. Tü 1986. – ᴿGöMiszÄg 93 (1986) 95 (S. *Allam*); 94 (1986) 81-87 (Irmtraut *Munro,* Datierungskriterien vol. 1).

d2 *Perreault* Jacques, Céramique et échanges; les importations attiques au Proche-Orient du VIᵉ au milieu du Vᵉ siècle av. J.-C. – Les données archéologiques: BCH 110 (1986) 145-175.

d3 **Peruzzi** Emilio, Money in early Rome: Ac F Studi 73, 1981 → 1,f240: ᴿRÉLat 63 (1985) 345s (P. M. *Martin*); Salesianum 48 (1986) 401 (R. *Bracchi*).

d4 **Pinches** T. G. [copied 1892-4], ᴱ*Finkel* I. L., Neo-Babylonian and Achaemenid economic texts: CunTBab 55-57, 1982 → 63,d293; 64,b732 (65, d192): ᴿOrientalia 55 (1986) 464-8 (M. A. *Dandamayev*).

d5 *Provera* Mario, Il commercio al tempo di Gesù: ParVi 31 (1986) 303-6.

d6 **Raphaël** Freddy, Judaïsme et capitalisme; essai sur le controverse Max WEBER et Werner SOMBART: Sociologie d'aujourd'hui, 1982 → 64,d726; F 180: ᴿRB 93 (1986) 621 (É. *Nodet*).

d7 *Sauren* H., Le banquier prémonitaire [sic]: → 553, Cinquième = Akkadica 47 (1986) 83.

d8 **Sigrist** Marcel, Textes économiques néo-sumériens de l'Université de Syracuse 1983 → 64,b733: ᴿJAOS 106 (1986) 565 (W. *Heimpel*: 489 Ur-III tablets); JCS 38 (1986) 120-6 (M. *Cooper*).

d9 **Silver** Morris, Prophets and markets; the political economy of ancient Israel: Social Dimensions of Economics, 1983 → 65,d218; 1,f248: ᴿJESHO 29 (1986) 213s (C. de *Geus*); KirSef 59 (1985) 306.

d10 **Snell** Daniel C., Ledgers and prices; early Mesopotamian merchant accounts: Yale NERes 8, 1982 → 62,e398 ... 65,d220: ᴿJAOS 106 (1986) 367s (M. A. *Powell*); Orientalia 55 (1986) 327-336 (H. *Waetzoldt*: zahlreiche Vorschläge).

d11 *Soden* Wolfram von, Weinen und Freude über Geldgeschäfte in Kaniš: WeltOr 17 (1986) 17s.

d12 **Spek** Robartus J. van der, Grondbezit in het Seleucidische Rijk: diss. Amst Vrije Univ. 1986, ᴰ*Neeve* P. de. x-293 p.; bibliog. p. 257-278. 90-6256-2349-X. – PhoenixEOL 32,2 (1986) 10s.

d13 **Stech** Tamara, *Pigott* Vincent C., The metals trade in southwest Asia in the third millennium B.C.: Iraq 48 (1986) 39-59; bibliog. 59-64.

d14 *Stos-Gale* Z. A., *al.,* The copper trade in the south-east Mediterranean region; preliminary scientific evidence: RepCyp (1986) 122-141; bibliog. 142-4.

d15 **Teixidor** Javier, Un port romain du désert, Palmyre et son commerce: Semitica 34, 1984 → 1,f253: ᴿRÉLat 63 (1985) 359-361 (A. *Chastagnol*: sur le tarif de Léningrad en araméen et grec).

d17 **Ugas** G., *Zucca* R., Il commercio arcaico in Sardegna. Cagliari 1984. [AION 45, 708].

d18 *Whitehorne* John, The valuation of gold dowry objects in papyri of the Roman period: ArPapF 32 (1986).

d19 **Yankovskaya** N. B., ⊛ Wholesale trade in Kanish, nineteenth century B.C.; *uṭṭātu,* the smallest money unit: VDI 177 (1986,2) 17-23; Eng. 23s.

U5.7   **Nomadismus;** ecology.

d20 ᴱ**Aurenche** Olivier, Nomades et sédentaires; perspectives ethnoarchéologiques: RCiv Memoire 4, 1984 → 1,f264: 235 p., c. 150 fig.; 2-86538-

088-2: ᴿAJA 90 (1986) 477s (A. B. *Smith*); Antiquity 60 (1986) 150s (I. *Hodder*: merits attention).

d21 *Braidwood* Linda S. & Robert J., Prelude to the appearance of village-farming communities in southwestern Asia: → 71, ᶠMELLINK M., Anatolia 1986, 3-11.

d22 **Briant** Pierre, État et pasteurs au Moyen-Orient ancien: Production pastorale et société 1982 → 63,d918; 65,d229: ᴿBO 43 (1986) 59-68 (E. van der *Vliet*); Orientalia 55 (1986) 95-97 (C. *Zaccagnini*).

d23 **Eph'al** Israel, The ancient Arabs; nomads on the border of the Fertile Crescent, 8th-5th centuries B.C. 1982 → 63,e73 ... 65,d35: ᴿZAss 76 (1986) 128-130 (D. O. *Edzard*).

d24 *Frenkley* Helen, The search for roots; Israel's biblical landscape reserve [Neot Kedumim]: BAR-W 12,5 (1986) 36-43; color phot. (Nogah Hareuveni).

d25 *Talon* Ph., Les nomades et le royaume de Mari: Akkadica 48 (1986) 1-9.

U5.8 **Urbanismus.**

d26 ᴱAdkins Arthur W. H., *White* Peter, The Greek polis: Readings in Western Civilization 1. Ch 1986, Univ. viii-351 p. 0-226-06934-6; pa. 5-4.

d27 *Applebaum* Shim'on, Jewish urban communities and Greek influences: → 34, ᶠFUKS A., ScrClasIsr 5 (1979s) 158-177.

d28 *Arthur* Paul, Problems of the urbanization of Pompeii; excavations 1980-81; AntiqJ 66 (1986) 29-44; 5 fig.; 4 pl.

d29 **Bernhardt** Rainer, Polis und römische Herrschaft in der späten Republik (149-31 v. Chr.): Unters. Ant. Lit. Gesch. 21. B 1985, de Gruyter. viii-318 p. DM 138. – ᴿClasR 100 (1986) 267-270 (J. *Briscoe*); Gnomon 58 (1986) 515-8 (F. W. *Walbank*).

d30 *Bietak* Manfred, Ein Staatsakt als Beginn des Städtewesens im Alten Ägypten?: → 81*, ᶠOBERHUBER K., Im Bannkreis 1986, 17-23; 4 fig.

d31 **Borst** Otto, Babel oder Jerusalem? Sechs Kapitel Stadtgeschichte. Stu 1984, Theiss. 637 p. [Mundus 22,49].

d32 *Brink* C.M.E. van den, Nederzettingsonderzoek in de Noord-Oostelijke Nijldelta, Egypte [vakgroep 1984s]: PhoenixEOL 32,2 (1986) 13-30; 15 fig. (3 maps).

d33 *a*) *Cadell* Hélène, Pour une recherche sur *astu* et *polis* dans les papyrus grecs d'Égypte; – *b*) *Étienne* R., ... à Ténos; – *c*) *Fouchard* A., ... chez PLATON: Ktema 9 (1984) 235-246 / 205-211 / 185-204.

d34 **Classen** Carl J., Die Stadt im Spiegel der Descriptiones und laudes urbium in der antiken und mittelalterlichen Literatur bis zum Ende des zwölften Jahrhunderts²: Beiträge Alt-W 2. Hildesheim 1986, Olms. 128 p.

d35 *Conn* H. M., Lucan perspectives and the city: Missiology 13 (Scottdale PA 1985) 409-428.

d36 **Cuneo** Paolo, Storia dell'urbanistica nel mondo islamico. R 1986, Laterza. 457 p.; 601 fig. Lit. 70.000. – ᴿDLZ 107 (1986) 885-7 (B. *Brentjes*).

d38 **Dan** Y., ⊕ The city in Eretz Israel during the Late Roman and Byzantine periods 1984 → 65,d243; 1,f275: ᴿByzantion 56 (1986) 511s (Rivkah *Fishman-Duker*).

d39 **Dreher** M., Sophistik und Polisentwicklung: EurHS 3/191. Fra 1983, Lang. 183 p. Fs 44. – ᴿGymnasium 93 (1986) 296 (F. X. *Herrmann*).

d40 *Duthoy* Robert, Qu'est-ce qu'une *polis*? Esquisse d'une morphologie succincte: ÉtClas 54 (1986) 3-20 [< Didactica Classica Gandensia 23 (1983) 251-285 néerl.].

d41 **Effenterre** Henri van, La Cité grecque, des origines à la défaite de Marathon: La Force des Idées, 1985 → 1,f277; F 150: ᴿClasR 100 (1986) 261 (A. M. *Snodgrass*: puts origins a thousand years before *de Polignac*); Gnomon 58 (1986) 711-5 (N. *Ehrhardt*).

d42 **Ferretto** Carla, La città dissipatrice; studi sull'excursus del libro decimo dei Philippika di TEOPOMPO: Università hist. 2. Genova 1984, Melangolo. 149 p. Lit. 15.000. – ᴿAntClas 55 (1986) 420s (J. *Labarbe*).

d43 **García y Bellido** A., Urbanística de las grandes ciudades del mundo antiquo²ʳᵉᵛ [¹1966]: Bibliotheca archaeologica 5. M 1985, Cons. Sup./ Inst. Esp. Arq. xxvii-384 p.; 195 fig.; 22 pl.; 2 maps. pt 1500. 84-00-05908-5 [NTAbs 30,372]. ᴿSalesianum 48 (1986) 715 (R. *Vicent*).

d44 **Gauthier** Philippe, Les cités grecques et leurs bienfaiteurs (IVᵉ-Iᵉʳ siècle avant J.-C.); contribution à l'histoire des institutions: BCH Sup 12. P 1985, de Boccard. viii-236 p. – ᴿRivFgIC 114 (1986) 462-471 (I. *Savalli*).

d45 **Gawantka** Wilfried, Die sogenannte Polis 1985 → 1,f278: ᴿRPLH 60 (1986) 283s (H. van *Effenterre*).

d46 *Geus* Cornelis de, The profile of an Israelite city [vertical aspects not shown on plans]: BA 49 (1986) 224-7; 4 fig.

d47 **Greco** Emanuele, *Torelli* Mario, Storia dell'urbanistica; il mondo greco 1983 → 64,d825: ᴿRArchéol (1986) 163-5 (R. *Martin, G. Vallet*).

d48 **Gutwein** Kenneth C., Third Palestine; a regional study in Byzantine urbanization 1981 → 63,e318; 64,d827: ᴿBASOR 264 (1986) 86-88 (J. *Schaefer*).

d49 **Hakim** Beslim Selim, Arabic-Islamic cities; building and planning principles. L 1986, KPI. 192 p.; 43 fig.; 71 pl. $75 [JNES 46,76].

d50 **Harrison** R. K., [26] Major cities of the biblical world 1985 → 1,f279: ᴿRExp 83 (1986) 461s (J. E. *Drinkard*); SR 15 (1986) 405s (Eileen *Schuller*; by theologians, not archaeologists; why Thebes and not Qumran?).

d51 *Hoffman* Michael A., A model of urban development for the Hierakonpolis region from predynastic through Old Kingdom times: JAmEg 23 (1986) 175-187; 3 fig.

d52 **Kolb** Frank, Die Stadt im Altertum 1984 → 65,d248; 1,f282: ᴿAthenaeum 64 (1986) 515-7 (Laura *Boffo*); DLZ 107 (1986) 283-6 (P. *Musiolek*); Eos 74 (1986) 150-4 (L. *Mrozewicz* ❷); HZ 243 (1986) 654-6 (H.-J. *Gehrke*).

d53 **Kotter** Wade R., Spatial aspects of the urban development of Palestine during the Middle Bronze Age: diss Arizona 1986, ᴰ*Schiffer* M. 559 p. 86-15826. – DissA 47 (1986s) 1380-A.

d54 **Leschhorn** Wolfgang, 'Gründer der Stadt'; Studien zu einem politisch-religiösen Phänomen der griechischen Geschichte: Palingenesia 20. Stu 1984, Steiner. xi-436 p. DM 54. – ᴿHZ 243 (1986) 393s (J. *Seibert*).

d55 **Liverani** Mario, L'origine delle città: Libri di base 99. R 1986, Riuniti. 157 p.

d56 **Loraux** N., La cité, l'historien, les femmes: Pallas 32 ('La femme dans l'antiquité grecque' 1985) ... [RÉLat 63,455].

d57 **Majak** I. L., ❸ Rim pervych tsarej, genezis rimskogo polisa [Rome of the first emperors, genesis of the Roman polis]. Moskva 1983, Univ. 267 p.; 13 fig.

d58 *Müller-Wiener* Wolfgang, Von der Polis zum Kastron; Wandlungen der Stadt im ägäischen Raum: Gymnasium 93 (1986) 435-475; pl. I-IV.

d59 *Negbi* Ora, The climax of urban development in Bronze Age Cyprus: RepCyp (1986) 97-116; pl. XXIV-XXV; bibliog. p. 117-121.

d60 **Pelletier** André, L'urbanisme romain sous l'empire 1982 → 64,d831;

1,f289: ᴿAntClas 55 (1986) 615s (J. C. *Balty*); AugM 31 (1986) 464 (J. *Ortall*).

d61 *Pissavino* Paolo, Polis e democrazia in Atene; linee preliminari di ricerca [*Meier* C.]: Athenaeum 64 (Pavia 1986) 218-222.

d62 **Polignac** François de, La naissance de la cité grecque; culte, espace et société; VIIIᵉ-VIIᵉ siècles avant J.-C.: Textes à l'appui. P 1984, Découverte. 189 p. F 96. – ᴿClasR 100 (1986) 261-5 (A. M. *Snodgrass*).

d63 **Rhodes** P. J., The Greek city states; a source book. L 1986, Croom Helm. xx-266 p. 0-7099-2222-1; pa. 4223-0.

d64 *Scorie* Alex, Slums, sanitation, and morality in the Roman world [...almost every house in Pompeii had a latrine, but very unhygienic disposal; not so many at Ostia ... nothing really on morality]: Klio 68 (1986) 399-433.

d65 *Sealey* Raphael, How citizenship and the city began in Athens: AmJAncH 8 (1983) 97-129.

d66 **Serangeli** F., Insediamento e urbanizzazione nella Palestina del Bronzo Antico 1980 → 61,u416 ... 65,d255: ᴿBASOR 262 (1986) 93s (G. *Palumbo*: weak).

d67 **Starr** Chester G., Individual and community; the rise of the *polis*, 800-500 B.C. NY 1986, Oxford-UP. x-133 p. $17 [RelStR 13,348, J. C. *Hippen*]. 0-19-503971-8.

d68 **Trench** William, The social gospel and the city; implications for theological reconstruction in the work of Washington GLADDEN, Josiah STRONG, and Walter RAUSCHENBUSCH [... biblical images of the city]: diss. Boston Univ. 1986, ᴰDeats P. 447 p. 86-21433. – DissA 47 (1986s) 2625-A; RelStR 13,189.

d69 ᴱWeiss Harvey, The origins of cities in dry-farming Syria and Mesopotamia in the third millennium B.C. Guilford CT 1986, Four Quarters. 167 p.

d70 *Yoshinari* Kaoru, ❹ Towns in the ancient Egypt: Orient 28,1 (1985) 176-183.

U5.9 *Demographia,* **population-statistics.**

d71 *Broshi* Magen, *Gophna* Ram, Middle Bronze Age II Palestine; its settlements and population [106,000, then 138,000; 250 persons per hectare]: BASOR 261 (1986) 69-90.

d72 **Casarico** Loisa, Il controllo della popolazione nell'Egitto romano, 1. Le denunce di morte: Corpora Papyrorum Graecarum 2. Azzare VA(rese) 1985, Tibiletti. [OIAc Oc87]. xxv-263 p.; lxxxii pl. a parte. – ᴿSalesianum 48 (1986) 962s (R. *Della Casa*).

d73 **Domurad** Melodie R., The populations of ancient Cyprus: diss. Cincinnati 1986. 291 p. 86-27574. – DissA 47 (1986s) 3463s-A.

d74 **Gallo** Luigi, Alimentazione e demografia della Grecia antica 1984 → 1,f301; Lit. 8000: ᴿClasR 100 (1986) 328 (S. *Hornblower*).

d75 *Garner* Gordon, How many people? Archaeology and population numbers: BurHist 22,2 (1986) 39-48 [OTAbs 10,20].

d76 *Hansen* M. H., Demography and democracy; the number of citizens in fourth-century Athens; Proc. Clas. Assoc. 83 (L 1986) 16s (summary).

d77 **Osborne** Robin, Demos; the discovery of classical Attika [diss.]: ClasSt. C 1985, Univ. xiv-284 p.; 12 pl. £25. – ᴿClasR 100 (1986) 265-7 (G. *Shipley*: prosopography made dynamic).

d78 *Otto* E., Gibt es Zusammenhänge zwischen Bevölkerungswachstum,

Staatsbildung und Kulturentwicklung im eisenzeitlichen Israel? [... oppression resulted in urbanization etc.]: ➤ 351, ᴱKraus O., Regulation 1986, 73-87.

d79 Seibert Jakob, Demographische und wirtschaftliche Probleme Makedoniens in der frühen Diadochenzeit: ➤ 58, ᶠLAUFFER S. III (1986) 835-851.

d80 **Symonovich** F.A., ⊕ Population of the Late Scythian kingdom's capital (according to the material of the eastern burial ground of Scythian Naples). Kiev 1983, Nauk. Dumka. 172 p.; ill. – ᴿSovArch (1986,1) 281-5 (I.N. Khrapunov).

d81 Tomadl Herbert, Zur Demographie und sozialen Schichtung der Feinde Meroes: BeiSudan 1 (1986) 97-113; 8 fig.

U6 Narrationes peregrinorum et exploratorum; Loca sancta.

d82 **d'Abbadie** Arnould, Douze ans de séjour dans la Haute-Éthiopie: ST 304, 1983 ➤ 65,d269: ᴿRasStEtiop 30 (1984ss) 192-8 (L. Ricci).

d83 **Artola** A.M., La Tierra, el Libro, el Espíritu; experiencia bíblica en Tierra Santa. Bilbao 1986, Desclée-B. 569 p. – ᴿEstAg 21 (1986) 641 (C. Mielgo: sirve más para conocer al autor, que ... Palestina o la Biblia); NatGrac 33 (1986) 559 (D. Montero: transmitir su experiencia bíblica en Tierra Santa).

d84 Belle G. Van, Le voyage de Charlemagne à Jérusalem et a Constantinople; pour une approche narratologique: RBgPg 64 (1986) 465 ...

d85 **Ben-Arieh** Yehoshua, The rediscovery of the Holy Land in the nineteenth century². J 1983, Magnes. 266 p.; ill. $25. – ᴿTLZ 111 (1986) 137 (K.-D. Schunck).

d86 ᴱ**Büttner** Martin, al., Grundfragen der Religionsgeographie, mit Fallstudien zum Pilgertourismus: Geographia Religionum 1. B 1985, Reimer. 286 p.; ill. DM 48. – ᴿMundus 22 (1986) 141 (M. Domrös).

d87 **Buhl** Marie-Louise, al., The Danish naval officer Frederik Ludvig NORDEN; his travels in Egypt 1737-38 and his voyage I-II [1755; plates by Marcus Tuscher]. K 1986, Royal Danish Acad. 87-7304-168-8 [OIAc Aug. 87].

d88 **Clayton** Peter A., a) The rediscovery of ancient Egypt; artists and travellers in the 18th century. L 1982, Thames & H. 192 p. £16. – ᴿCdÉ 61 (1986) 218s (H. De Meulenaere: superbly published). – b) Das wiederentdeckte Ägypten in Reiseberichten und Gemälden des 19. Jahrhunderts. Bergisch Gladbach 1983, Lübbe. 192 p. DM 72. – ᴿDer Islam 62 (1985) 366s (U. Erker-Sonnabend, Eng.).

d89 Colbi Paolo S., La ripresa dei pellegrinaggi dopo la fine del regno crociato: TerraS 62 (1986) 149-151.

d90 ᴱ**Da Costa** M.G., The Itinerário of Jerónimo LOBO; ᵀLockhart Donald M., notes Beckingham C.F.: Hakluyt 2/162. L 1984, Hakluyt Soc. xxxvi-417 p.; 2 pl. £15. – ᴿBSOAS 49 (1986) 395 (D.L. Appleyard).

d91 ᴱ**Fischer** Rudolf, Babylon; Entdeckungsreisen in die Vergangenheit. Stu 1985, Thienemann/Erdmann. 352 p.; 50 fig. [Mundus 22,50].

d92 **Freier** Elke, Grunert Stefan, Eine Reise durch Ägypten ... LEPSIUS 1842-5: 1984 ➤ 65,d277: ᴿBO 43 (1986) 667-9 (B. Vachala).

d93 **Gauthier** Marie-M., Les routes de la foi 1983 ➤ 1,f325: ᴿSpeculum 61 (1986) 498s (Elizabeth A.R. Brown).

d94 **Gebhardt** Jürgen, Reisen und Erkenntnis; Ursprünge und Folgen des 'wissenschaftlichen' Reisens im 19. Jahrhundert: ZRGg 38 (1986) 97-113

(114-132, *Salewski* Michael; 133-166, *Löhneysen* W. von, Deutsche in Griechenland).

d95 *Gurney* J.D., Pietro DELLA VALLE; the limits of perception: ➤ 57, FLAMBTON A., BSOAS 49 (1986) 103-116.

d96 *Guth* Klaus, Die Wallfahrt — Ausdruck religiöser Kultur: LtgJb 36 (1986) 180-204.

d97 TEHoll Béla, Ⓜ PÉCSVÁRADI Gábor, Jeruzsálemi utazás [1520]. Budapest 1983, Szépirodalmi. 271 p.; 7 pl. [KirSef 60,625].

d98 Hunt E.D., Holy Land pilgrimage in the Later Roman Empire AD 312-460: 1982 ➤ 63,e359 ... 1,f332: RBySlav 47 (1986) 226-9 (W. *Ceran*).

d98* TEJaneras S., EGÈRIA, Pelegrinatge: Escriptors cristians 237s. Barc 1986, Fund. Metge. 140 p. [AnBoll 105,159-164, P. *Devos*].

d99 Labarge Margaret W., Medieval travellers; the rich and restless. L 1982, H. Hamilton. xvi-237 p.; ill., facsims.; bibliog. p. 213-224 [KirSef 60,623].

d100 EMaraval P., Égérie: SChr 296, 1982 ➤ 64,d870; 65,d287: RHenoch 8 (1986) 123 (B. *Chiesa*); Mnemosyne 39 (1986) 211-4 (A.P. *Orbán*); RPLH 60 (1986) 336-9 (M.J. *Rondeau*).

d101 Maraval Pierre, Lieux saints et pèlerinages d'Orient 1985 ➤ 1,f342: RBLitEc 87 (1986) 308s (Fernand *Crouzel*); CiuD 199 (1986) 127 (F. *Díez*); Gregorianum 67 (1986) 573s (J. *Janssens*); JEH 37 (1986) 481s (H.E. *Mayer*); JTS 37 (1986) 232-5 (G. *Fowden*); NRT 108 (1986) 918s (N. *Plumat*); RTPhil 118 (1986) 84s (É. *Junod*); RuBi 39 (1986) 80s (B. *Nadolski*: 'Mireval'); TPhil 61 (1986) 579-581 (H.J. *Sieben*); ZKG 97 (1986) 281s (G.G. *Blum*).

d102 *Maraval* Pierre, Une querelle sur les pèlerinages autour d'un texte patristique (GRÉGOIRE de Nysse, lettre 2): RHPR 66 (1986) 131-146; Eng. 257.

d103 Miller Max, Introducing the Holy Land. Macon GA 1982. x-189 p. $14. RBA 49 (1986) 62 (Z. *Garber*).

d104 *Pedrale* Giuseppina, Santa Brigida di Svezia, una eccezionale pellegrina di Terrasanta: TerraS 62 (1986) 82-85.

d105 *Pinault* David, Pénitence, pèlerinage et l'emploi d'images bibliques dans un ouvrage d'HONORÉ d'Autun: BLitEc 87 (1986) 273-280; Eng. 242.

d106 *Provera* Mario, Il pellegrinaggio al tempo di Gesù: ParVi 31 (1986) 230-3.

d107 Safrai Shmuel, Die Wallfahrt im Zeitalter des Zweiten Tempels [Ⓗ 1965], TKries-Mach Dafna von; ForJüdChrD 3, 1981 ➤ 62,k825 ... 64,d883: RFreibRu 37s (1985s) 124 (O. *Kaiser*).

d108 Salas Antonio, Tierra Santa, impresiones de un peregrino. M 1986, Biblia y Fe. 336 p. – RBibFe 12 (1986) 249s (M. *Sáenz Galache*).

d109 *Scheffer* Lia, [FABRI Felix, BREYDENBACH Bernhard von] A pilgrimage to the Holy Land and Mount Sinai in the 15th century: ZDPV 102 (1986) 144-151.

d110 Sicard Claude, EMartin M., I. Lettres...; II. Relations...; III. Parallèle géographique: IFAO BÉt 83ss, 1982 ➤ 63,264: RCdÉ 61 (1986) 219-224 (B. van de *Walle*).

d111 ESiniscalco P., Scarampi Lella, EGERIA, Pellegrinaggio in Terra Santa: Collana di testi patristici 48. R 1985, Città Nuova. 215 p. 88-311-3048-X. – RTeresianum 37 (1986) 509 (M. *Diego Sánchez*).

d112 Skyrms James F., The rituals of pilgrimage in the Middle Ages: diss. Iowa 1986, DGiesey R. 637 p. 87-08027. – DissA 47 (1986s) 4484-A.

d113 EStanford W.B., Finopoulos E.J., The travels of Lord CHARLEMONT in Greece and Turkey, 1749. L 1984, Trigraph. xii-244 p.; ill.

d114 *Stone* Michael E., Holy Land pilgrimage of Armenians before the Arab conquest: RB 93 (1986) 93-110; franç. 93.

d115 *Thier* Ludger, Christus peregrinus; Christus als Pilger in der Sicht von Theologen, Predigern und Mystikern des Mittelalters: ➤ 60, FLENZENWEGER J., Ecclesia peregrinans 1986, 29-42.

d116 **Tidrick** Kathryn, Heart-beguiling Araby. C 1981, Univ. xii-244; 13 fig.; 2 maps. £12.50. - RRBgPg 64 (1986) 782s (J. *Ryckmans*).

d117 *Väänänen* Veikko, Itinerarium EGERIAE 3,6; une méprise consacrée: Arctos 19 (1985) 251-3.

d118 *Veronese* Alessandria, Le comunità ebraiche del Vicino Oriente e di Egitto nelle relazioni di viaggio dei pellegrini ebrei italiani del XV secolo: EgVO 9 (1986) 157-163.

d119 EVolkoff Oleg V., Voyages en Égypte pendant les années 1678-1701 [... R. *Huntington*]: Voyageurs occidentaux en Égypte 23, 1981 ➤ 64,d890: RArPapF 32 (1986) 77 (U. *Luft*).

U7 *Crucigeri* - **The Crusades.**

d120 **Beltjens** A., Le soleil des Vivants [Gérard, héros de la non-violence au milieu de la première croisade]. Liège 1986, Dessain. 388 p.; 20 fig. [NRT 109,793, L.-J. *Renard*].

d120* *Brand* C. M., The fourth crusade; some recent interpretations: MedHum 12 (1984) 33-45 [47-60, *Laiou* A; RHE 82, 384*].

d121 **Bresc-Bautier** Geneviève, Le cartulaire du chapitre du Saint-Sépulcre de Jérusalem: AIBL Doc. Croisades 15. P 1984, Geuthner. 434 p. - RRHE 81 (1986) 169-172 (J. *Pycke*).

d121* **Burns** Robert J., Muslims, Christians and Jews in the Crusader kingdom of Valencia 1984 ➤ 65,d303: RDer Islam 63 (1986) 349s (H. *Möhring*); Islamochristiana 12 (1986) 235s (J. *Lacunza Balda*).

d122 **Cahen** Claude, Orient et Occident au temps des Croisades 1983 ➤ 64,d896; 65,d304: REngHR 101 (1986) 216s (C. J. *Tyerman*); RBgPg 64 (1986) 330s (J. *Richard*).

d123 *Daoust* J., Saint Louis croisé idéal? [*Le Goff* J.]: EsprVie 96 (1986) 713-5.

d124 **Demurger** Alain, Vie et mort de l'ordre du Temple, 1118-1314. P 1985, Seuil. 338 p., 26 fig. - RRHist 275 (1986) 484-6 (Geneviève *Bresc-Bautier*).

d125 *Dunkel* Franz, Das fünffache Jerusalem-Kreuz: HLand 118,1 (1986) 10s [= 1928].

d126 *Hillenbrand* Carole, The Islamic world and the Crusades: ScotR 7 (Stirling 1986) 150 ... [< ZIT].

d127 **Holt** P. M., The age of the Crusades; the Near East from the XIth century to 1517. L 1986, Longman. xiii-250 p. [RHE 82,384*].

d128 **Housley** Norman, The Avignon papacy and the Crusades, 1305-1378. Ox 1986, Clarendon. xii-348 p. £27.50 [RHE 82,433, F. *Hockey*].

d129 **Hutait** Aḥmad, 'Izz AD-DÎN, Geschichte des Sultans BAIBARS...: Bibliotheca Islamica 31. Wsb 1983, Steiner. 336 p. DM 64. - RBSOAS 49 (1986) 219 (P. M. *Holt*).

d130 EHuygens R. B. C., *Mayer* H. E., *Rösch* G., GUILLAUME de Tyr, Chronique (Chronicon, lat.), éd. critique: CCMed 63.63A. Turnhout 1986, Brepols. 627 p.; VI (color.) pl. - CETEDOC 24 microfiches, 149 p. 2-503-03631-7; pa. 2-5.

d131 *Impellizzeri* Salvatore, Aux racines de l'idée de croisade et sa survie dans les idéologies politiques: Nicolaus 12 (Bari 1985) 339-348.

d132 EJacobsen P. C., METELLUS von Tegernsee, Expeditio hierosolymitana

[1. Kreuzzug]: Quellen und Untersuchungen MA 6, 1982 → 63,e409; 65,d316: ᴿRBgPg 64 (1986) 331s (J. *Richard*).

d133 *Jacoby* David,   The Kingdom of Jerusalem and the collapse of Hohenstaufen power in the Levant: DumbO 40 (1986) 83-101.

d134 **Jacquin** Gérard,   Le style historique dans les écrits latins et français de la quatrième Croisade: diss. Sorbonne Nouvelle, Paris-III, 1985. – RÉLat 63 (1985) 31.

d135 [ᶠPRAWER J.,] **Kedar** B. Z. *al.*,   Outremer – studies in the history of the Crusading Kingdom of Jerusalem 1982 → 63,133 ... 65,112: ᴿQadmoniot 19 (1986) 58s (Y. *Friedman*).

d136 *Kedar* Benjamin Z.,   Ungarische Muslime in Jerusalem im Jahre 1217: AcOrH 40 (1986) 325-7.

d137 *Kenaan-Kedar* Nurith,   Symbolic meaning in Crusader architecture: CahArchéol 34 (1986) 109-117; 4 fig.

d138 *a*) *Köhler* Michael A.,   Al-Afḍal und Jerusalem – was versprach sich Ägypten vom ersten Kreuzzug?; – *b*) *Noth* Albrecht,   Heiliger Kampf (Ǧihād) gegen die 'Franken'; zur Position der Kreuzzüge im Rahmen der Islamgeschichte: Saeculum 37 (1986) 228-239 / 240-260.

d139 **Mayer** Hans-Eberhard,   Das Siegelwesen in dem Kreuzfahrerstaaten: Abh. Bayr. Akad. ph/h 83. Mü 1978. 101 p.; 4 pl. – ᴿRNum 28 (1986) 220-2 (J. *Richard*).

d140 **Partner** Peter,   The murdered magicians; the Templars and their myth 1982 → 63,e418 ... 1,f379: ᴿRBgPg 64 (1986) 332s (H. *Platelle*).

d141 **Riley-Smith** Jonathan,   The First Crusade and the idea of crusading. L/Ph 1986, Athlone/Univ. Pennsylvania.   227 p.; 2 maps. £22 / $30 [JAAR 55,426].   0-485-11291-4/.

d142 *Satō* Tsugitaka,   Iqṭā´ policy of Sultan Baybars I [1260-77]: Orient 22 (1986) 85-104.

d143 *Schein* Sylvia,   The image of the Crusader Kingdom of Jerusalem in the thirteenth century [< diss. C 1980]: RBgPg 64 (1986) 704-717.

d144 **Serper** Arye,   HUON de Saint-Quentin, poète satirique et lyrique; étude historique et édition de textes.   Potomac MD 1983, Studia Humanitatis. 142 p. [1-63 Croisés]; music [KirSef 60,626].

d145 **Setton** Kenneth M.,   [→ 362] The papacy and the Levant (1204-1571) [Is → 60,y321], III. The sixteenth century to the reign of Julius III; – IV. The sixteenth century from Julius III to Pius V: AmPhSoc Mem 161s. Ph 1984. 564 p.; p. 565-1180. $45 each. – ᴿOrChrPer 52 (1986) 229-231 (V. *Poggi*); RHE 81 (1986) 189-191 (J. *Richard*).

d146 ᴱ**Zacour** Norman P., *Hazard* Harry W.,   The impact of the Crusades on the Near East: [ᴱ*Setton* K.] History of the Crusades 5.   Madison 1985, Univ. Wisconsin.   599 p. $40 [JAAR 54,397]. – ᴿRHE 81 (1986) 573-5 (J. *Richard*); RHist 276 (1986) 195s (C. *Cahen*).

d147 **Siberry** Elizabeth,   Criticism of crusading, 1095-1274.   Ox 1985, Clarendon.   xii-257 p. [KirSef 60,626].

d148 **Slattery** Maureen,   Myth, man, and sovereign saint; King Louis IX in Jean de JOINVILLE's Sources: Amer Univ Stud 2/11.   NY 1985, Lang. x-212 p. $26.90. – ᴿÉglT 17 (1986) 399 (K. C. *Russell*).

U8   *Communitates Terrae Sanctae* – **The Status Quo.**

d149 **Anschütz** Helga, *Harb* Paul,   Christen im Vorderen Orient; Kirchen, Ursprünge, Verbreitung; eine Dokumentation.   Ha 1985, Deutsches Orient-Institut. 167 p. [Mundus 22,221].

d150 **Anschütz** Helga,   Die syrischen Christen vom Tur 'Abdin 1984
➤ 65,d333; 1,f384:   ᴿOrChr 70 (1986) 205-211 (H. *Kaufhold*); TLZ 111
(1986) 773s (F. *Winkelmann*); TR 82 (1986) 204 (W. *Cramer*).

d151 *Assad* Maurice,   Christian education in Egypt; past, present and future:
NESTR 7,1 (1986) 44-61.

d152 **Avineri** Shlomo,   *a*) The making of modern Zionism; the intellectual
origins of the Jewish state. NY 1981, Basic. – *b*) Histoire de la pensée
sioniste; les origines intellectuelles de l'État juif, ᵀ*Spatz* Erwin. P 1982,
Lattès. 336 p. – ᴿRÉJ 145 (1986) 483s (C. *Sirat*).

d153 **Baulig** Harald,   Das frühe Christentum in Hermopolis Magna; Beiträge
zur Geschichte des christlichen Ägypten: Diss. Trier 1984. – Chiron 15
(1985) 390.

d154 ᴱ**Braude** Benjamin, *Lewis* Bernard,   Christians and Jews in the Ottoman
Empire; I, The Central Lands; II. The Arab-speaking countries 1982
➤ 65,d336; 1,f385: ᴿRHR 203 (1986) 215s (S. *Schwarzfuchs*).

d155 *Carmel* Alex,   Über den christlichen Beitrag zum Wiederaufbau
Palästinas im 19. Jahrhundert: ➤ 68*, ᶠMAYER R., Wie gut 1986, 90-95.

d156 **Carter** B. L.,   The Copts in Egyptian politics. L 1986, Croom Helm.
(xii-)328 p.; bibliog. p. 305-320. 0-7099-3417-3.

d157 **Cobban** Helena,   The Palestinian Liberation Organisation; people, power,
and politics. C 1984, Univ. xii-305 p. £22.50; pa. £7. – ᴿDer Islam 63
(1986) 150 (W. *Ende*).

d158 **Coen** Fausto,   Israele, quarant'anni di storia. Casale Monferrato 1985,
Marietti. xii-204 p. Lit. 18.000. – ᴿCC 137 (1986,1) 405s (G. *Rulli*).

d159 **Cohen** Amnon,   Jewish life under Islam; Jerusalem in the sixteenth
century 1984 ➤ 65,d341: ᴿJAOS 106 (1986) 591s (M. R. *Cohen*); JSS 31
(1986) 285-7 (N. A. *Stillman*).

d160 *Colpe* Carsten,   Die Mhagrāyē – Hinweise auf ein arabisches
Judenchristentum?: ➤ 108, ᶠSPULER B., IkiZ 76 (1986) 203-217.

d161 **Desramaut** Francis,   L'orphelinat Jésus-Adolescent de Nazareth en
Galilée au temps des Turcs, puis des Anglais (1896-1948). R 1986,
LAS(alesianum). 318 p. – ᴿSalesianum 48 (1986) 1057s (*ipse*).

d162 **Donini** Pier Giovanni,   Le minoranze nel Vicino Oriente e nel Maghreb.
Salerno 1985, Laveglia. 188 p. – ᴿIslamochristiana 12 (1986) 241s (R.
Bellani).

d163 *a*) *Dubois* Marcel,   Un chrétien devant Israël; – *b*) *Rash* Yehoshua,
Nouveaux judaïsmes israéliens: Études 364 (1986) 225-237 / 239-251.

d164 **Ekins** Larry,   Enduring witness; the [mainline Protestant] Churches and
the Palestinans II. [I. 1981 by M. C. *King*]. Geneva 1985, WCC. 135 p.
$6.25. – ᴿCCurr 36 (1986s) 233s (Rosemary R. *Ruether*).

d165 **Epelbaum** Didier,   Le Troisième Temple; Israël, de l'utopie à l'histoire. P
1985, Hachette. 178 p. F 75. – ᴿÉtudes 364 (1986) 708 (D. *Bourel*).

d166 **Gerber** Haim,   Ottoman rule in Jerusalem 1800-1914: Islamkundliche
Unters. 101. B 1985, Schwarz. 343 p. – ᴿAcOrH 40 (1986) 356s (T.
Iványi); Der Islam 63 (1986) 353-5 (M. *Ursinus*).

d167 **Gerber** Haim, *Barnai* Jacob,   The Jews in Izmir in the 19th century
(Ottoman documents from the Shar'i Court). J 1984, Misgav (Sephardi
Heritage) 1. 114-vi p. – ᴿAcOrH 40 (1986) 355s (T. *Iványi*); Der Islam 63
(1986) 367s (J. M. *Landau*).

d168 **Gil** Moshe, Palestine during the first Muslim period I-III. TA 1983,
Ministry of Defence. 688 p.; 762 p.; 742 p. ᴿBSOAS 49 (1986) 572s
(M. R. *Cohen*).

d169 *Griffith* Sidney H.,   Greek into Arabic; life and letters in the monasteries of Palestine in the ninth century; the example of the Summa Theologiae Arabica: Byzantion 56 (1986) 117-138.

d170 **Guirguis** Fouad, The difficult years of survival; a short account of the history of the Coptic Church. NY 1985, Vantage. xi-89 p. $8 [TDig 33,364].

d171 **Heyer** Friedrich, Kirchengeschichte des Heiligen Landes: Urban-Tb 357, 1984 → 65,d353; 1,f402: RCrNSt 7 (1986) 141-165 (L. *Perrone*, comparando il manoscritto disponibile a Heidelberg).

d172 **Hussar** Bruno, Quand la nuée se levait...; Juif, prêtre, Israélien; un itinéraire 1983 → 65,d354; 1,f405: RPrOrChr 36 (1986) 180 (F. *Bouwen*).

d173 *Khalil Samir*, La spiritualità copta ieri e oggi: CC 137 (1986,2) 14-28.

d174 *Kley* Hans D., Athos – die bedrohte Stille; Erfahrungen aus der griechischen Mönchsrepublik: LuthMon 25 (1986) 303s [419, *Konstantinou* Grigorios].

d175 **Kolta** Kamil S., Christentum im Land der Pharaonen; Geschichte und Gegenwart der Kopten in Ägypten 1985 → 1,f411: ROstkSt 35 (1986) 207s (H. *Tretter*).

d176 **Krämer** Gudrun, Minderheit, Millet, Nation? Die Juden in Ägypten 1914-1952: Studien zum Minderheitsproblem im Islam 7/Bonner OrSt 27. Wsb 1982, Harrassowitz. viii-477 p. DM 72. – ROLZ 81 (1986) 273s (H. *Motzki*).

d177 **Lewis** B., The Jews of Islam 1984 → 65,8735; 1,f413: RSpeculum 61 (1986) 679-681 (A. *Levy*).

d178 **Männchen** Julia, Gustaf DALMANS Leben und Wirken in der Brüdergemeine [sic], für die Judenmission und an der Universität Leipzig, 1855-1902: Diss. Greifswald 1985. 260 p. – TLZ 112,77.

d179 **Mérigoux** Jean-Marie, Les chrétiens de Mossoul et leurs églises pendant la période ottomane de 1515 à 1815. Mossoul 1983. 154 p. – RIsla- mochristiana 12 (1986) 259s (P. *Bouwen*).

d180 **Moosa** Matti, The Maronites in history. Syracuse NY 1986, Univ. 391 p. $35 [JNES 46,78].

d181 **Muzikář** Josef, *al.*, Palestinska otázka... (The Palestinian question; its origins and development until the end of the first Arab-Israeli war in 1949). Praha 1983, Academia 260 p. Kčs 35. – RArOr 54 (1986) 196-8 (M. *Mendel*, Eng.).

d182 *Nusselein* Ernst W., Die Geschichte einer Schule – 100 Jahre Schmidt-Schule [Jerusalem]: HLand 118/2s (1986) 11-18 (1-10 Jubi- läumsfest).

d183 EReinharz Jehuda, Dokumente zur Geschichte des deutschen Zionismus 1882-1914: Baeck-Inst. 37, 1981 → 63,e445; 64,d932: RRÉJ 145 (1986) 476 (Dominique *Bourel*).

d184 **Roldanus** J. (*Hofstra* J., *Post* P.), De Syrisch Orthodoxen in Istanbul; een volk, uit een ver verleden overgebleven. Kampen 1984, Kok. – RNedTTs 40 (1986) 249s (L. van *Rompay*).

d185 **Rotter** Ekkehart, Abendland und Sarazenen; das okzidentale Araberbild und seine Entstehung im Frühmittelalter: Studien zur Sprache, Geschichte und Kultur des islamischen Orient 11. B 1986, de Gruyter. xii-290 p. DM 158. [Mundus 23, 293, H. *Müller*].

d186 **Schölch** Alexander, Palästina im Umbruch 1856-1882; Untersuchungen zur wirtschaftlichen und soziopolitischen Entwicklung: Berliner Islamst. 4. Stu 1986, Steiner. 272 p. [Mundus 23,305].

d187 **Shmuelevitz** Aryeh, The Jews of the Ottoman Empire in the late fifteenth and sixteenth centuries; administrative, legal and social relations as reflected in the responsa. Leiden 1984, Brill. xi-207 p. *f* 68. – ᴿBSOAS 49 (1986) 397s (C. *Imber*).

d188 *Szteinke* Anzelm, ❷ Polacy w Kustodii Ziemi Świętej: RuBi 39 (1986) 493-5.

d189 **Timm** Stefan, Das christlich-koptische Ägypten in arabischer Zeit: TAVO B-41/1, 1984 ➤ 65,d376; 1,f427: ᴿTLZ 111 (1986) 750-2 (H.-M. *Schenke*).

d190 **Tuchman** Barbara, Bibel und Schwert; Palästina und der Westen vom frühen Mittelalter bis zur Balfour-Deklaration 1917 [Bible and Sword NYU 1956 = Macmillan 1980; ned. 1983 ➤ 64,d937]. Fra 1983, Fischer. 383 p. – ᴿFreibRu 37s (1985s) 135s (Y. *Ilsar*).

d191 **Waltz** Viktoria, Die Erde habt ihr uns genommen; 100 Jahre zionistische Siedlungspolitik in Palästina. B 1986, Arab. Buch. 436 p. [Mundus 23,306].

d192 *Zafrani* Haïm, Judaïsme d'Occident musulman; les relations judéo-musulmanes dans la littérature juridique; le cas particulier du recours des tributaires juifs à la justice musulmane et aux autorités représentatives de l'État souverain: Studia Islamica 64 (1986) 125-149.

XX. Historia Scientiae Biblicae

Y1 **History of Exegesis** .1 **General.**

d193 **Aland** Kurt, A history of Christianity, I. From the beginnings to the Reformation [Geschichte der Christenheit], ᵀ*Schaaf* James L., 1985 ➤ 1,f432: ᴿChH 55 (1986) 82 (T. *Renna*); JEH 37 (1986) 349s (W. H. C. *Frend*); TTod 43 (1986s) 112-4 (R. E. *McLaughlin*).

d194 **Aland** Kurt. Kirchengeschichte in Zeittafeln und Überblicken: Siebenstern 1411. Gü 1984, Mohn. 125 p. DM 10. – ᴿTLZ 111 (1986) 36s (K. *Matthiae*).

d195 ᵀ**Bouquet** S., *al.*, Thèmes et figures bibliques: Les Pères dans la Foi. P 1984, Desclée-B. 336 p. – ᴿBLitEc 87 (1986) 155s (H. *Crouzel*: péricopes de plusieurs Pères, en rapport avec typologie/allégorie).

d196 *Brändle* Rudolf, Rechtgläubigkeit, Ketzerei, Streit unter Brüdern – drei Exempla aus der Alten Kirche [i. Rom und Korinth; ii. Sturz des CHRYSOSTOMOS; iii. AUGUSTIN und Pelagius]: TZBas 42 (1986) 375-385.

d197 **Comblin** José, A força da Palavra [... helenismo, reforma, modernidade ...]. Petrópolis 1986, Vozes. 408 p. [REB 46,895].

d198 **Dattrino** Lorenzo, Patrologia. R 1982, 'Ut unum sint'. 294 p. – ᴿSalesianum 48 (1986) 712 (S. *Felici*).

d199 ᴱ**Di Berardino** Angelo, *a)* Du concile de Nicée (325) au concile de Chalcédoine (451); les Pères latins; présent. *Quasten* Johannes: Initiation aux Pères de l'Église 4. P 1986, Cerf. 799 p. 2-204-02437-6. – *b)* Patrology IV. The golden age of Latin patristic literature from the Council of Nicaea to the Council of Chalcedon, intr. *Quasten* Johannes; ᵀ*Solari* Placid. Westminster MD 1986, Christian Classics. xxviii-667 p. $48; pa. $40. 0-87061-186-7; pa. 7-5. – ᴿTDig 33 (1986) 484 (W. C. *Heiser*: the 1978 Italian original was really the continuation of Quasten's Patrology I-III, 1950-60).

d200 **Dwyer** John C., Twenty centuries of Catholic Christianity [... judged against the original revelation of Jesus as received by the first Christians]. NY 1985, Paulist. x-406 p. $10 pa. [Horizons 14,375, L. *Biallas*].

d201 **Feri** Roberta, Prontuario patristico; sussidio per la consultazione della collana 'Testi patristici', I. Testi 1-55. R 1986, Città Nuova. 75 p. 88-311-3000-5.

d202 **Frank** Karl S., Grundzüge zur Geschichte der Alten Kirche: Grundzüge 55, 1984 ➤ **1**,f441: ᴿTPhil 61 (1986) 257s (H. J. *Sieben*).

d203 ᴱ**Frede** Hermann J., Kirchenschriftsteller; Verzeichnis und Sigel²: Vetus Latina 1/1, 1981 ➤ 62,2017; 65,d390: ᴿCBQ 48 (1986) 714s (A. *Cody*).

d204 **Frend** W. H. C., The rise of Christianity, 1984 ➤ 65,d391; **1**,f442: ᴿAntiqJ 66 (1986) 176-8 (R. P. C. *Hanson*); BAR-W 12,1 (1985) 14-16 (R. *Grant*: the author was originally an archeologist); CurrTM 13 (1986) 245s (K. K. *Hendel*); DowR 104 (1986) 44-46 (A. *Louth*); Interpretation 40 (1986) 104.106 (G. E. *Saint-Laurent*); JAAR 54 (1986) 337-342 (D. M. *Smith*: treatment of NT period will raise eyebrows); JEH 37 (1986) 351 (J. *Gaudemet*); JRel 66 (1986) 431-6 (S. H. *Griffith*); JRS 76 (1986) 301s (E. D. *Hunt*); RExp 83 (1986) 126s (E. G. *Hinson*).

d205 **Gelmi** Josef, Los Papas, retratos y semblanzas, 1986. ᴿRazF 213 (1986) 439 (M. *Alcalá*).

d206 **Gnilka** Christian, Chrêsis, die Methode der Kirchenväter im Umgang mit der antiken Kultur I., Der Begriff des 'rechten Gebrauchs' 1984 ➤ 65,d393; **1**,f445: ᴿAnthropos 81 (1986) 720-724 (K.-H. *Golzio*); HeythJ 27 (1986) 192s (A. *Meredith*); Muséon 99 (1986) 196s (J. *Mossay*); PerspT 18 (1986) 111-3 (F. *Taborda*); RÉAug 32 (1986) 176s (J. *Fontaine*); RHPR 66 (1986) 352 (J. *Doignon*); TGl 76 (1986) 133-7 (O. *Gigon*); VerbumSVD 27 (1986) 97s (A. *Kehl*).

d207 **Gonzales** Justo L., The story of Christianity, I. The early Church to the dawn of the Reformation; II. The Reformation to the present day. SF 1984s, Harper & R. xviii-429 p.; xiii-414 p. $13 each, pa. – ᴿHorizons 13 (1986) 162-4 (M. J. *Gallagher*).

d208 **Grant** R., ²*Tracy* D., A short history of the interpretation of the Bible 1984 ➤ 65,d394; **1**,f447: ᴿTR 82 (1986) 449-451 (P.-G. *Müller*).

d209 ᴱ**Greschat** Martin, Das Papsttum Is: Gestalten der Kirchengeschichte 1Is, 1984 ➤ **1**,351: ᴿRömQ 81 (1986) 135 (E. *Gatz*); TGl 76 (1986) 138s (M. *Gerwing*); TPQ 134 (1986) 290-5 (R. *Zinnhobler*); TR 82 (1986) 124s (R. *Bäumer*).

d210 ᴱ**Greschat** Martin, Gestalten der Kirchengeschichte 1-4, 1983s ➤ **1**,350. f448: ᴿTPQ 134 (1986) 89-91 (R. *Zinnhobler*).

d211 **Haendler** Gert, Zur Kirchenväterausgabe Corpus Christianorum: TLZ [107 (1982) 486-8] 111 (1986) 778-782.

d212 *Hünermann* Peter, Patristische Preziosen [ᴱ*Gessel* Wilhelm, Bibliothek der griechischen Literatur: Patristik 1-18, 1971-83]: TüTQ 166 (1986) 59-61.

d213 *Kannengiesser* C., L'essor actuel de la patristique: FoiTemps 16 (1986) 156-162.

d214 *La Potterie* Ignace de, Ⓖ Reading of the Holy Scriptures 'in the Spirit'; is the patristic way of reading the Bible still possible today? [< CC Ag. 1986], ᵀ*Kontogiannis* S., *Mavropheidis* S.: DeltioVM 15,2 (1986) 23-39.

d215 **Liébaert** J., Les Pères de l'Église, I. du Iᵉʳ au IVᵉ siècle: BiblHist-Christianisme 10. P 1986, Desclée. 190 p.; 2 maps. F 92 [NRT 109,791].

d216 **Lowry** Charles W., The first theologians. Ch 1986, Gateway. 443 p.

d217 **Margerie** Bertrand de, Introduction à l'histoire de l'exégèse I-III, 1980-3 ➤ 61,u595...**1**,f460: ᴿRÉAug 31 (1985) 173s (Y.-M. *Duval*, 1); RThom 86 (1986) 496-502 (M.-V. *Leroy*).

d218 **Margerie** B. de, Introduzione alla storia dell'esegesi [I-II, 1983 ➤ 64,d597; 1984 ➤ 65,d405] III. R 1986, Borla. – RSacDoc 31 (1986) 674-680 (R. *Barile*).

d219 *a) Mondésert* Claude, Comment publier aujourd'hui les Pères de l'Église?; – *b) Mandouze* André, Des pères de l'Église aux fils de Vatican II: ➤ d774, Migne 1975/85, 339-347 / 433-443.

d220 *Mühlenberg* Ekkehard, Alte Kirche: ➤ 587, EvKL 1 (1986) 102-8.

d221 **Murphy** Francis X., The Christian way of life: Message of the Fathers 18. Wilmington 1986, Glazier. 224 p. $16; pa. $10 pa. [TS 48,586 D. *Callam*].

d222 **Penna** Romano, L'ambiente storico-culturale delle origini cristiane; una documentazione ragionata: La Bibbia nella storia 7, 1984 ➤ **1**,f463; RParVi 30 (1985) 158s (F. *Mosetto*).

d223 EPennington M. Basil, *al.*, The living Testament; the essential writings of Christianity since the Bible. SF 1986, Harper & R. xxxiii-382 p.; $23; pa. $15 [TDig 34,81].

d224 **Peters** sr. Gabriel, I Padri della Chiesa, I. dalle origini al Concilio di Nicea [Lire les Pères], T*Vicario* L. 1984 ➤ **1**,f464: RAsprenas 32 (1985) 473s (L. *Longobardo*); ScuolC 113 (1985) 584-7 (C. *Pasini*).

d225 **Peters** sr. Gabriel, I Padri della Chiesa; II. ... a Gregorio Magno [Lire les Pères de l'Église], T*Vicario* Luigi: Cultura cristiana antica. R 1986, Borla. 374 p. Lit. 25.000 88-263-0427-0. – RBenedictina 33 (1986) 236s (Clara *Burini*); StPatav 33 (1986) 455s. 706s (C. *Corsato*).

d226 *Petitmangin* Pierre, Les patrologies avant MIGNE: ➤ d774, E*Mandouze* A., Migne 1985/85, 15-32; 33-38, La bibliothèque des Pères 1575-1788 [39-51, *Boisset* Jean, citations chez CALVIN].

d227 EPuech H.-C., Storia del cristianesimo, T*Pierini* Maria N. Bari 1983, Laterza. 767 p. – RRivStoLR 22 (1986) 356-8 (F. *Bolgiani*: severissimo, cominciando da 'Henry'–Ch. Puech, di cui l'unico contributo è stato eliminato).

d228 *Pierard* Richard V., The Christian quest for a usable past: JEvTS 29 (1986) 3-14 [< ZIT].

d229 **Ramsey** Boniface, Beginning to read the Fathers 1985 ➤ **1**,f467; also L 1986, Darton-LT: RChH 55 (1986) 507s (E. *TeSelle*); Furrow 57 (1986) 673s (sr. Aengus *O'Donovan*); TS 47 (1986) 319s (J. *Lienhard*).

d230 **Rudnick** Milton, Speaking the Gospel through the ages; a history of evangelism 1984 ➤ **1**,f469: RRExp 83 (1986) 317-9 (L. *Drummond*).

d231 *Savon* Hervé, L'athéisme jugé par les chrétiens des premiers siècles: ProbHistChr 16 (1986) 11-24.

d232 **Simonetti** Manlio, Lettera e/o allegoria; un contributo alla storia dell'esegesi: SEA 23. R 1985, Inst. Patristicum Augustinianum. 386 p. – [RasT 28,538s, S. *Spera*].

d233 *Smend* Rudolf [*Roloff* Jürgen], Bibelexegese AT [NT]: ➤ 587, EvKL 1 (1986) 450-5 [-461].

d234 **Spada** Domenico, La fede dei Padri: Subsidia Urbaniana 15. R 1985, Pont. Univ. Urbaniana. 659 p. Lit. 45.000. [ActuBbg 24,276, J. *Vives*].

d235 *Staats* Reinhart, Väter der Alten Kirche in der Evangelischen Kirche: Monatshefte für ev. Kirchengeschichte des Rheinlandes 34 (Dü 1985) 1-18 [< ZIT].

d236 *Torjesen* Karen Jo, The new florilegia; GLAZIER's Message of the Fathers: TS 47 (1986) 691-8.

d237 **Urban** Linwood, A short history of Christian thought. NY 1986, Oxford-UP. xvi-319 p. $28; pa. $11 [TS 48,585, J. *Heft*].

d238 **Vallin** P., Les chrétiens et leur histoire [plutôt 'la mémoire' que l'histoire classique de l'Église]: Le Christianisme et la foi chrétienne, manuel de théologie 1. P 1985, Desclée. 309 p. F 120. – [R]NRT 108 (1986) 449s (B. *Joassart*: série dirigée par J. DORÉ).

d239 **Verbraken** Pierre-Patrick, Les premiers siècles chrétiens[2] 1984 ➤ 1,f476: [R]EsprV 96 (1986) 557s (A.-M. *Henry*).

Y1.4   *Patres apostolici et saeculi II* – **First two centuries.**

d240 [E]**Burini** Clara, Gli apologeti greci; traduzione, introduzione e note: Collana di testi patristici 59. R 1986, Città Nuova. 498 p. 88-311-3059-5.

d241 *Grant* Robert M., Forms and occasions of the Greek Apologists: SMSR 52 (1986) 213-226.

d242 **Le Boulluec** Alain, La notion d'hérésie dans la littérature grecque, I. De Justin à Irénée; II. Clément d'Alexandrie et Origène [diss. Paris-IV, 1984] 1985 ➤ 1,f554: [R]Muséon 99 (1986) 363-6 (A. de *Halleux*); RSPT 70 (1986) 592-6 (G.-M. de *Durand*).

d243 **Osborn** E. F., Anfänge christlichen Denkens; Justin, Irenäus, Tertullian, Klemens [1981 ➤ 63,e473], [T]*Bernard* J. Lp 1986, St.-Benno. 387 p. M 26,50 [RHE 82,263*].

d244 *Padovese* Luigi, Lo 'scandalum incarnationis et crucis' nell'apologetica cristiana del secolo secondo e terzo: Laurentianum 27 (1986) 312-334.

d245 *a) Paulsen* Henning, Apostolische Väter; – *b) Mühlenberg* Ekkehard, Apologeten: ➤ 587, EvKL 1 (1986) 231-4 / 211-3.

d246 **Robinson** Thomas, Orthodoxy and heresy in western Asia Minor in the first Christian century; a dialogical response to Walter BAUER: diss. McMaster. Hamilton ONT 1985. – RelStR 13,190.

d247 **Schille** G., Frei zu neuen Aufgaben; Beiträge zum Verständnis der dritten urchristlichen Generation. B 1986, Ev.-V. 111 p. DM 10,50 [NTAbs 31,116].

---

d248 CLEMENS A.: **Blair** Harold A. †, The kaleidoscope of truth; types and archetypes in Clement of Alexandria [Stromateis not random, but arranging archetypes in their cosmic order]. L 1986, Churchman. 171 p. £9. 1-85093-020-1. – [R]ExpTim 98 (1986s) 186 (Frances M. *Young*: a priest with no scholarly pretensions).

d249 **Brackett** John K., A form critical study of the Protreptikos and the Paedagogos [ae/o sic] of Clement of Alexandria: diss. Emory. Atlanta 1986. – RelStR 13,190.

d250 **Nikolaou** Theodor, Ⓖ Die Willensfreiheit und die Affekte der Seele nach Klemens von Alexandrien. Thessaloniki 1981. 166 p. [TLZ 112,287, F. *Winkelmann*].

d251 [TE]**Pini** Giovanni, Clemente Alessandrino, Stromati; note di vera filosofia: Letture cristiane delle origini, Testi 20. T 1985, Paoline. 913 P. 88-215-0766-1.

d252 *Places* Édouard des, Les citations profanes de Clément d'Alexandrie dans le IIIe Stromate: RÉG 99 (1986) 54-62.

d253 *Rizzerio* L., Considerazioni sulla nozione di 'fede' in Clemente Alessandrino; un esempio di sintesi tra cultura classica e pensiero cristiano (Str. II 8,4-9,7): Sandalion 8s (Sassari 1985s) 147-179.

d254 *Senzasono* Luigi, Un passo di Clemente Alessandrino ed Eraclito: CivClasCr 7 (1986) 185-192.

d255 **Wyrwa** Dietmar, Die christliche Platonaneignung in den Stromateis des Clemens von Alexandrien 1983 ➤ 64,d986 ... **1**,f488: ᴿGregorianum 67 (1986) 173s (A. *Orbe*); TLZ 111 (1986) 530s (H. G. *Thümmel*).

d256 CLEMENS R.: **Bowe** Barbara E., A church in crisis; ecclesiology and paraenesis in Clement of Rome; diss. Harvard, ᴰ*Koester* H. CM 1986. 241 p. 86-19011. – DissA 47 (1986s) 1765-A.

d257 **Valdes de la Colina** Jesús, La enseñanza cristiana de San Clemente Romano: diss. ᴰ*Merino* M. Pamplona 1985. – RTLv 17,498.

d258 *Ziegler* Adolf W., Politische Aspekte im Ersten Klemensbrief: Forum KT 2 (1986) 67-74.

d259 **Strecker** Georg, Die Pseudoklementinen III/1, Konkordanz zu den Pseudoklementinen 1., Lateinisches Wortregister: Die Griechisch-Christlichen Schriftsteller der Ersten Jahrhunderte. B 1986, Akademie. xiv-581 p. 3-05-000115-1.

d260 *Cuenca Molina* Juan F., El judeo-cristianismo y la ley; a propósito del nomismo de las 'Homilías Clementinas': Carthaginensia 2 (1986) 35-54.

d261 DIDACHE etc.: *Schöllgen* Georg, Die Didache als Kirchenordnung; zur Frage des Abfassungszweckes und seinen Konsequenzen für die Interpretation: JbAC 29 (1986) 5-26.

d262 ᴱ**Wengst** Klaus, Schriften des Urchristentums; Didache (Apostellehre), Barnabasbrief, Zweiter Klemensbrief, Schrift an Diognet 1984 ➤ **1**,f495: ᴿZkT 108 (1986) 208-210 (L. *Lies*).

d263 ᴱ**Metzger** Marcel, Les Constitutions Apostoliques I, Livres I-II: SChr 320, 1985 ➤ **1**,f494: ᴿEsprV 96 (1986) 220 (Y.-M. *Duval*); RHPR 66 (1986) 347 (P. *Maraval*: le texte dit Paralipomènes, Navé, non Chroniques/Nun); ZKG 97 (1986) 272-5 (G. *Schöllgen*).

d264 **Metzger** Marcel, Les Constitutions Apostoliques II, Livres III-VI: SChr 329. P 1986, Cerf. 415 p. 2-204-02603-4.

d265 **Fiensy** David A., Prayers alleged to be Jewish; an examination of the Constitutiones Apostolorum: BrownJudSt 65, 1985 ➤ **1**,f493: ᴿJTS 37 (1986) 589-591 (T. A. *Kopeček*).

d266 *Stander* H. F., A stylistic analysis of chapter 4 of the Epistle to Diognetus: Acta Classica 27 (1984) 130-2 [*Hilhorst* A., Diogn. 4,6 refers only to Jewish, not partly Greek, worship: JStJud 17 (1986) 131].

d267 HERMAS: *Sanz Valdivieso* Rafael, Hermas y la transformación de la Apocalíptica: Carthaginensia 2 (1986) 145-160.

d268 *Staats* Reinhart, Hermas: ➤ 597, TRE 15 (1986) 100-8.

d269 IGNATIUS A.: [*Bauer* W.] ²**Paulsen** H., Die Briefe des Ignatius von Antiochia und der Brief des POLYKARP von Smyrna: HbNT 18, 1985 ➤ **1**,f500: ᴿAugR 26 (1986) 307 (P. *Grech*); TPhil 61 (1986) 257 (H. *Sieben*); TR 82 (1986) 461s (J. A. *Fischer*).

d270 *Bergamelli* Ferdinando, Nel Sangue di Cristo; la vita nuova del cristiano secondo il martire S. Ignazio di Antiochia: EphLtg 100 (1986) 152-170.

d271 *a*) *Grech* Prosper, El problema hermenéutico del siglo segundo; – *b*) *Alves de Sousa* Pío G., Jesucristo, centro de la Escritura y Tradición; un principio hermenéutico en Ignacio de Antioquía; – *c*) *Viciano* Alberto, Principios de hermenéutica bíblica en el Tratado 'Adversus Iudaeos' de TERTULIANO: ➤ 366; Hermenéutica 1985/6, 591-600 / 625-635 / 637-644.

d271* **Lowry** Charles W., The first theologians [John's Gospel; Ignatius letters ...]. Ch 1986, Gateway. 443 p. 0-89526-804-3.

d272 **Schoedel** William R., Ignatius of Antioch; a commentary on the Letters: Hermeneia, 1985 ➤ **1**,f502: ᴿBiblica 67 (1986) 592-595 (R. *Joly*: volume luxueux et du meilleur goût); Themelios 12 (1986s) 62s (C. *Hemer*); TR 82 (1986) 460s (J. A. *Fischer*); TS 47 (1986) 715s (G. H. *Ettlinger*).

d273 **Smith** James D., The Ignatian long recension and Christian communities in fourth century Syrian Antioch: diss. Harvard Div., ᴰ*Koester* H. CM 1986. 168 p. – RTLv 17 (1986) 498.

d274 IRENAEUS: *Doutreleau* Louis, S. Irénée: Missi (1986,6) [< EsprV 97,120, J. *Daoust*].

d275 *a) Grant* Robert M., Carpocratians and curriculum; Irenaeus's reply; – *b) Pearson* Birger A., Christians and Jews in first-century Alexandria; – *c) Trakatellis* Demetrios bp., JUSTIN Martyr's Trypho: → 110, ᶠSTENDAHL K. = HarvTR 79 (1986) 127-136 / 206-216 / 287-297.

d276 **Greer** Rowan A., Broken lights and mended lives; theology and common life in the early Church [... Irenaeus, Nyssenus, Augustine ...]. University Park 1986, Pennsylvania State Univ. xiv-237 p. $19.50 [TDig 34,72].

d277 **Lundström** Sven, Die Überlieferung der lateinischen Irenäusübersetzung: AcU, St. Lat. 18. U 1985, Almqvist & W. 166 p. Sk 99. – ᴿGnomon 58 (1986) 623-6 (F. *Weissengruber*).

d278 **Orbe** Antonio, Teología de San Ireneo, I, Comentario al Libro V del 'Adversus Haereses': BAC 25. M 1985, Católica. xlviii-704 p. – ᴿCompostellanum 31 (1986) 285s (E. *Romero-Pose*); ETL 62 (1986) 439s (A. de *Halleux*); OrChrPer 52 (1986) 479-481 (G. *Pelland*).

d279 *a) Perkins* Pheme, Ordering the cosmos; Irenaeus and the Gnostics; – *b) Parrott* Douglas M., Gnostic and orthodox disciples in the second and third centuries; – *c) Wisse* Frederik, The use of early Christian literature as evidence for inner diversity and conflict; – *d) Gero* Stephen, With Walter BAUER on the Tigris; encratite orthodoxy and libertine heresy in Syro-Mesopotamian Christianity: → 374, ᴱ*Hedrick* C., Nag Hammadi 1983/6, 221-238 / 193-219 / 177-190 / 287-307.

d280 **Rousseau** Adelin, *Doutreleau* Louis, Irénée de Lyon, Contre les hérésies II: SChr 293s, 1982 → 63,e512b; 64,e4: ᴿRBgPg 63 (1985) 125s (W. *Evenepoel*: this is the fifth and last 'book' to appear; a revision of IV, 1964 is contemplated).

d281 **Rousseau** Adelin, Irénée de Lyon, Contre les hérésies; dénonciation et réfutation de la Gnose au nom menteur [→ 65,d437;1,f505 < SChr en un volume]. P 1984, Cerf. 750 p. F 100. – ᴿRHR 203 (1986) 440s (A. *Le Boulluec*).

d282 JUSTINUS M.: *Denning-Bolle* Sara, Christian dialogue as apologetic; the case of Justin Martyr seen in historical context: BJRyL 69 (1986s) 492-510.

d283 *Joly* Robert, Parallèles païens pour Justin, Apologie I, XIX: → 81, Mém. NIKIPROWETZKY V., 1986, 473-481.

d284 *Keresztes* Paul, Justin, Roman law and the logos [pagans know only half, not the Incarnate]: Latomus 45 (1986) 339-346.

d285 *Marin* Marcello, Note introduttive sulla presenza di Paolo nel Dialogo con Trifone di Giustino: → 365*, AnStoEseg 3 (1985/6) 71-83.

d286 *Munier* Charles, La structure littéraire de l'Apologie de Justin: RevSR 60 (1986) 34-54.

d287 *Wartelle* André, Une bibliographie de saint Justin, philosophe et martyr [*Davids* Adelbert, Nijmegen 1983]: RÉAug 32 (1986) 138-141.

d288 MELITO S.: *Norris* Frederick W., Melito's motivation: AnglTR 68 (1986) 16-26.

d289 PAPIAS: **Körtner** Ulrich H. J., Papias von Hierapolis: FRLAnt 133, 1983

➤ 64,e25 ... 1,f512: – ᴿJbAC 29 (1986) 192-4 (P. *Lampe*); Salmanticensis
33 (1986) 129-131 (R. *Trevijano*).

d290 **Kürzinger** J., Papias von Hierapolis und die Evangelien des NT 1983
➤ 64,e26 ... 1,f513: ᴿCrNSt 7 (1986) 553-563 (L. *Cirillo*).

d291 PERPETUA: *Rossi* Mary Ann, The Passion of Perpetua, Everywoman of
late antiquity: ➤ 395, ᴱ*Smith* R., Pagan and Christian anxiety 1979/84,
53-86.

d292 POLYCARPUS: *Nielsen* Charles M., Polycarp and Marcion; a note: TS 47
(1986) 297-9.

Y1.6 **Origenes.**

d293 *Bammel* Ernst, *a*) Origen Contra Celsum i.41 and the Jewish tradition
[< JTS 19 (1968) 211-213]; – *b*) Christian origins in Jewish tradition [<
NTS 13 (1966s) 317-335]; – *c*) Der Jude des Celsus [ineditum]: ➤ 131,
Judaica 1986, 194s / 220-238 / 265-283.

d294 *Bernard* Jean, L'étymologie du nom d'Origène [not Horus but Hebr. *ôri*
'my light']: BLitEc 87 (1986) 83-92; Eng. 82.

d295 *Bunge* J.`G., Origenismus – Gnostizismus; zum geistesgeschichtlichen
Standort des Evagrios Pontikos: VigChr 40 (1986) 24-54.

d296 *Burke* Gary T., Celsus and the Old Testament: VT 36 (1986) 241-5.

d297 **Crouzel** H., Origène 1985 ➤ 1,f516; 2-249-61142-4: ᴿBLitEc 87 (1986)
139s (B. de *Guibert*, à la fin de la Chronique origénienne de Crouzel);
EsprV 96 (1986) 217 (Y.-M. *Duval*); ETL 62 (1986) 443-7 (A. de *Halleux*);
Gregorianum 67 (1986) 200 (*ipse*); RSPT 70 (1986) 606-9 (G.-M. de
Durand: sur l'Écriture, défense plutôt qu'explication); Salesianum 48 (1986)
437 (B. *Amata*); TR 82 (1986) 464s (Maria-Barbara von *Stritzky*); TS 47
(1986) 747ss (G. H. *Ettlinger*); ZKG 97 (1986) 276-9 (R.P.C. *Hanson*: very
anxious to vindicate Origen's orthodoxy; misses his total blindness to
poetry).

d298 **Crouzel** Henri, Origene; ᵀ*Fatica* Luigi: Cultura cristiana antica. R
1986, Borla. 376 p. 88-363-0635-4.

d299 **Crouzel** Henri, Origène: Chrétiens aujourd'hui 10, 1984 ➤ 1,f516: ᴿChH
55 (1986) 503s (J.W. *Trigg*); Teresianum 37 (1986) 154s (M. *Diego
Sánchez*).

d300 *Crouzel* Henri: Chronique origénienne; deux congrès pour le dix-hui-
tième centenaire de la naissance d'Origène [Rome 9-11.V.1985; Innsbruck ...]: BLitEc 87 (1986) 125-9 (-139).

d300* *Crouzel* Henri, L'édition DELARUE [Charles 1685-1739, son neveu
Charles-Vincent 1707-] d'Origène rééditée par J.-P. MIGNE: ➤ d774,
ᴱ*Mandouze* A., Migne 1975/85, 225-253.

d301 **Crouzel** H., *Simonetti* M., Origène, Traité des principes 5: SChr 312, 1984
➤ 65,d452; 1,f517: ᴿRB 93 (1986) 631 (M. J. *Pierre*).

d302 *Dillon* John M., Aisthêsis noêtê; a doctrine of spiritual senses in Origen
and in PLOTINUS: ➤ 81, Mém. NIKIPROWETZKY V., Hellenica 1986,
443-455.

d303 **Godin** A., ÉRASME lecteur d'Origène 1982 ➤ 64,e17; 65,d457: ᴿVigChr
40 (1986) 193-8 (H. J. de *Jonge*).

d304 **Hällström** Gunnar [af], Fides simpliciorum according to Origen of
Alexandria: Comm. Hum. Litt. 76, 1984 ➤ 1,f521: ᴿChH 55 (1986) 220
(J. W. *Trigg*); JTS 37 (1986) 574 (W. H. C. *Frend*); TLZ 111 (1986) 125s (H.
Kraft).

d305 ᴱ**Harl** Marguerite, Origène, Philocalie 1-20, Sur les Écritures...: SChr

302, 1983 → 64,e18 ... 1,f522: ᴿBijdragen 47 (1986) 215s (J. *Declerck*); RHR 203 (1986) 74-76 (A. *Le Boulluec*).

d306 *Hovland* C. Warren, The dialogue between Origen and Celsus: → 395, ᴱ*Smith* R., Pagan and Christian anxiety 1979/84, 191-216.

d307 *Laporte* Jean, Philonic models of Eucharistia in the Eucharist of Origen: LavalTP 42 (1986) 71-91.

d308 **Lies** Lothar, Wort und Eucharistie bei Origenes; zur Spiritualisierungstendenz des Eucharistieverständnisses[2] [Diss. Würzburg 1977]: InnsbTheolSt 1. Innsbruck 1982, Tyrolia. 363 p. Sch 480 pa. – ᴿTLZ 111 (1986) 374-6 (K.-H. *Kandler*).

d309 *McCartney* Dan G., Literal and allegorical interpretation in Origen's Contra Celsum: WestTJ 48 (1986) 281-301.

d310 *Nardi* Carlo, Attualità del senso psichico origeniano della Scrittura: Nicolaus 12 (Bari 1985) 349-356 [< ZIT].

d311 *Norderval* Øyvind, Origenes som teologisk utfordring?: NorTTs 87 (1986) 219-243.

d312 **Rius-Camps** Josep, El Peri Archon d'Origenes; radiografia del primer tractat de teología dogmàtico-sapiencial [inaug.]. Barc 1985, Fac. Teología. 90 p. – ᴿScripTPamp 18 (1986) 928-930 (J.-I. *Saranyana*).

d313 **Schütz** Werner, Der christliche Gottesdienst bei Origenes: Theol. Monographien, 1984→ 1,7810: BLitEc 87 (1986) 135s (H. *Crouzel*).

d314 *Simonetti* Manlio, Eusebio e Origene; per una storia dell'origenismo: AugR 26 (1986) 323-334.

d315 *a) Simonetti* Manlio, La controversia origeniana; caratteri e significato; – *b) Crouzel* Henri, Origene e l'Origenismo; le condanna di Origene; – *c) Bianchi* Ugo, L'anima in Origene e la questione della metensomatosi: → 476*, L'origenismo; AugR 26 (1986) 7-31 / 295-303 [51-61] / 33-50.

d316 **Torjesen** Karen Jo, Hermeneutical procedure and theological method in Origen's exegesis: PatrTSt 28 [0553-4003]. B 1986, de Gruyter. xi-183 p. 3-11-0102021-0.

d317 **Trigg** J. W., Origen; the Bible and philosophy in the third-century Church 1985 → 64,e24; 1,f529: ᴿBibTB 16 (1986) 159s (L. J. *White*); CleR 71 (1986) 37s (J. A. *McGuckin*); JEH 37 (1986) 141s (N. de *Lange*); JTS 37 (1986) 217-220 (Frances M. *Young* applauds imminent demise of supposed incompatibility of Hellenic and Hebraic); RSPT 70 (1986) 605s (G.-M. de *Durand*); TLond 39 (1986) 161-3 (C. *Stead*).

d318 **Tripolitis** Antonia, Origen: Amer. Univ. St 7/8. Fra 1985, Lang. xi-150 p. $21.60. – ᴿChH 55 (1986) 86s (P. J. *Gorday*).

Y1.8 **Tertullianus.**

d319 *Braun* René *al.*, Chronica Tertullianea 1984 / et Cyprianea 1985: RÉAug 31 (1985) 293-312 / 32 (1986) 255-283.

d320 ᴱ**Glover** T. R., Tertullian, De spectaculis, with an English translation: Loeb Classical Library 250. CM/L 1984, Harvard / Heinemann. xxvii-229 p. [P. 231-446 M. Felix].

d321 *Haendler* Gert, Tertullianforschung in Nordeuropa: TLZ 111 (1986) 1-10.

d322 **Hoffmann** R. Joseph, Marcion, on the restitution of Christianity... Paulinist theology: diss. Oxford 1982: 1984 → 65,d466; 1,f540: ᴿRB 93 (1986) 310s (J. *Murphy-O'Connor*); TRu 51 (1986) 404-413 (G. *May*: better just to overlook it).

d323 **Hoppe** Heinrich, Sintassi e stile di Tertulliano [1903], ᵀ*Allegri* G.,

Piccinato A.; AntClasCr 26, 1985 ➤ **1**,f540:   ᴿMaia 38 (1986) 277 (F. *Giovannini*).

d324 ᵀᴱ**Isetta** Sandra, Tertulliano, L'eleganza delle donne; de cultu feminarum: Bibl. Patristica 6. F 1986, Nardini. 223 p. Lit. 23.000.

d325 *Mattei* Paul, Tertullien De Monogamia, critique textuelle et contenu doctrinal [... préalable à une édition]: RivStoLR 22 (1986) 68-88.

d326 ᴱ**Turcan** M., Tertullien, Les spectacles: SChr 332. P 1986, Cerf. 367 p. F 207 [NRT 109, 449, A. *Harvengt*].

Y2   *Patres graeci* – The Greek Fathers.

d327 **Barrois** Georges A., The Fathers speak; St. BASIL the Great, St. GREGORY of Nazianzus, St. GREGORY of Nyssa; selected letters and life-records. Crestwood NY 1986, St. Vladimir. 224 p. $9 [TDig 34,68].

d328 **Bartolomei** Maria Cristina, Ellenizzazione del cristianesimo; linee di filosofia e teologia per una interpretazione del problema storico: Methodos 12, 1984 ➤ 1,f545: ᴿRSPT 70 (1986) 591s (G.-M. de *Durand*: 'di filosofica e teologica').

d329 **Buby** Bertrand, Research on the biblical approach and the method of exegesis appearing in the Greek homiletic texts of the late fourth and early fifth centuries [< diss. Dayton 1982]: Marian Library studies 13s (Dayton 1982) 224-394; bibliog. p. 233-251.

d330 *Dorival* Gilles, La postérité littéraire des chaînes exégétiques grecques [Oxford 1983]: RÉByz 43 (1985) 209-226.

d331 *Høeg* Kristan, De græske kirkefædres kristendom: DanTTs 49 (1986) 268-278 [< ZIT].

d331* **Jerphagnon** Lucien, Vivre et philosopher sous l'Empire chrétien 1983 ➤ 64,e34; 65,d478: ᴿRBgPg 63 (1985) 199s (Marie-Claire *Lambrechts*).

d332 **Le Boulluec** Alain, La notion d'hérésie dans la littérature grecque 1985 ➤ 1,f554: ᴿAustralBR 34 (1986) 84-86 (E. *Osborn*); ChH 55 (1986) 506s (R. M. *Grant*).

d333 *Leloir* Louis, Les Pères du désert et la Bible: VSp 140 (1986) 167-181.

d334 *Martin* Annik, La réconciliation des lapsi en Égypte; de Denys à Pierre d'Alexandrie, une querelle de clercs: RivStoLR 22 (1986) 256-269.

d335 *Madec* G., 'Platonisme' des Pères: ➤ 578, Catholicisme XI,50 (1986) 491-507.

d336 *Mangiagalli* Maurizio, Metafisica classica e rivelazione cristiana tra d[e]ellenizzazione e rigorizzazione: Sapienza 39 (1986) 145-182.

d337 **Meijering** E. P., Die Hellenisierung des Christentums im Urteil Adolf von HARNACKs: VerhNedAkad Lett. 128, 1985 ➤ 1,f557: ᴿJTS 37 (1986) 269-272 (A. H. *Armstrong*).

d338 ᴱ**Mondésert** Claude, Le monde grec ancien et la Bible: Bible de tous les temps 1, 1984 ➤ 1,299: ᴿCBQ 48 (1986) 581-4 (J. M. *Reese*, also on Moyen Âge); ChH 55 (1986) 85s (D. J. *Grimes*); ÉglT 17 (1986) 395s (L. *Laberge*); EsprV 96 (1986) 444s (L. *Monloubou*); Gregorianum 67 (1986) 150-2 (J. *Janssens*, anche su Le Moyen Âge); JEH 37 (1986) 448-450 (G. *Bonner*); RThom 86 (1986) 486-490 (M.-V. *Leroy*); SBFLA 36 (1986) 434-440 (F. *Manns*: donne aussi le contenu de vol. 2, 4, 8); SR 15 (1986) 117s (É. *Lamirande*); TS 47 (1986) 146s (J. T. *Lienhard*).

d339 **Mortley** Raoul, From word to silence; I. The rise and fall of logos; II. The way of negation: Theophaneia 30s. Bonn 1986, Hanstein. 168 p.; 292 p. 3-7756-1240-8; 1-6.

d340 *Puelma* Mario, Die Rezeption der Fachsprache griechischer Philosophie im Lateinischen: FreibZ 33 (1986) 45-69.

d341 *Riggi* Calogero, Impatto culturale tra paganesimo e cristianesimo; problematiche attuali sulla d[e]ellenizzazione: ➤ 518, [E]*Amata* B., Cultura 1985/6, 67-76.

d342 **Rist** John M., Platonism and its Christian heritage: Collected Studies 221; 16 art. 1962-1983: 1985 ➤ 1,234*: [R]RHE 81 (1986) 741 (F. *Hockey*); TPhil 61 (1986) 415 (F. *Ricken*).

d343 [F]*Roey* A. Van, After Chalcedon, [E]*Laga* C., *al.*, 1985 ➤ 1,117: [R]CrNSt 7 (1986) 614s (J. *Gribomont* †).

d344 **Simonetti** Manlio, Cristianesimo antico e cultura greca 1983 ➤ 65,d485: [R]Asprenas 32 (1985) 476s (L. *Longobardo*).

d345 *a*) *Simonetti* Manlio, Vecchio e nuovo nell'esegesi patristica greca del IV secolo; – *b*) *Romano* Francesco, Genesi e strutture del commentario neoplatonico: ➤ 537, Trasformazioni 1982/5, 385-411 / 219-237.

d346 *Stead* Christopher, Die Aufnahme des philosophischen Gottesbegriffes in der frühchristlichen Theologie; W. PANNENBERGs These [ZKG 70 (1959) 1-45] neu bedacht, [T]*Wildberg* Christian: [R]TRu 51 (1986) 346-371 [371, Beobachtung [E]*Ritter* A. M.].

d347 ATHANASIUS: [TE]**Cattaneo** Enrico, Atanasio, Lettere a Serapione; lo Spirito Santo. R 1986, Città Nuova. 192 p. Lit. 10.000. – [R]CC 137 (1986,4) 90s (G. *Ferraro*).

d348 *Kannengiesser* Charles, Bulletin de théologie patristique [Athanase et son siècle, 9 livres; commentaires (*Poffet* J., *Duval* Y.), christologies...]: RechSR 74 (1986) 575-614.

d349 [TE]**Meijering** E. P., Athanasius, Contra gentes: Philos. Patrum 7. 1984 ➤ 65,d494: [R]CrNSt 7 (1986) 183s (C. *Kannengiesser*).

d350 ARIUS: *Williams* R., Arius and the Melitian schism: JTS 37 (1986) 35-52.

d351 BASILIO di Cesarea, la sua età, la sua opera e il Basilianesimo in Sicilia 1979/83 ➤ 1,539: [R]GitFg 35 (1986) 155-9 (E. C.); Orpheus 7 (1986) 424-430 (C. *Crimi*); RHE 81 (1986) 535-9 (B. *Gain*).

d352 **Fecioru** Dumitru, [en roumain] St Basile le Grand, Écrits I: Homélies sur l'Hexaéméron; Homélies sur les Psaumes. Bucureşti 1986, Institut Biblique et de Mission. 650 p. – [R]STBuc 38,4 (1986) 114-6 (N. V. *Dură*).

d353 **Gain** Benoît, L'Église de Cappadoce au IVe siècle d'après la correspondance de Basile de Césarée (330-378): OrChrAn 225. R 1985, Pont. Inst. Stud. Orientalium. xxxi-464 p. – [R]EstE 61 (1986) 483-6 (G. M. *Colombás*: importante); OrChrPer 52 (1986) 477s (F. van de *Paverd*).

d354 *Halleux* André de, L'Économie dans le premier canon de Basile: ETL 62 (1986) 381-392.

d355 *Pouchet* Jean-Robert, Les rapports de Basile de Césarée avec DIODORE de Tarse: BLitEc 87 (1986) 243-272; Eng. 242.

d356 [TE]**Sesboüé** Bernard, Basile de Césarée Contre Eunome; suivi de EUNOME, Apologie: SChr 299.305, 1982s ➤ 63,e561 ... 65,714: [R]TR 82 (1986) 36-38 (W.-D. *Hauschild*).

d356* *Van Dam* Raymond, Emperor, bishops, and friends in late antique Cappadocia [Basil ...]: JTS 37 (1986) 53-76.

d357 **Tiraboschi** P., La dottrina esegetica di S. Basilio: diss. Univ. Cattolica, [D]*Pizzolato* P. L. Milano 1984 [RivB 35,86].

d358 CHRYSOSTOMUS: **Schatkin** Margaret A. [[T]On Babylas], *Harkins* Paul W. [[T]Demonstration that Christ is God], Saint John Chrysostom, apologist:

Fathers of the Church 73. Wsh 1985, Catholic Univ. 298 p. – [R]RelStR 12 (1986) 299 (D. G. *Hunter*: Schaktin introduction more adequate].

d359 CYRILLUS A.: **Burguière** Paul, *Evieux* Pierre, Cyrille d'Alexandrie, Contre Julien I-II: SChr 322. P 1985, Cerf. 324 p. F 139 [JTS 38,215, H. *Chadwick*]. 2-204-02466-X.

d360 **Carones** A., La dottrina esegetica di Cirillo d'Alessandria: diss. Univ. Cattolica, [D]*Pizzolato* P. Milano 1984 [RivB 35,86].

d361 CYRILLUS H.: *Grego* Igino, San Cirillo di Gerusalemme, il grande catecheta del sec. IV (387-1987): TerraS 62 (1986) 160-4.

d362 EUSEBIUS C.: **Chesnut** Glenn F., The first Christian histories; Eusebius, SOCRATES, SOZOMEN, THEODORET, and EVAGRIUS[2rev] [[1]1977 ➤ 61,q64]. Macon GA 1986, Mercer Univ. xiv-296 p.; bibliog. p. 259-287. 0-86554-164-7; pa. 203-1.

d363 *a*) *Curti* Carmelo, L'esegesi di Eusebio di Cesarea; caratteri e sviluppo; – *b*) *Calderone* Salvatore, Eusebio e l'ideologia imperiale: ➤ 537, Trasformazioni 1982/5, 459-478 / 1-26.

d364 [TE]**Forrat** Marguerite, [texte *Places* É. des], Eusèbe de Césarée, Contre Hiéroclès: SChr 333. P 1986, Cerf. 236 p. F 147. [RHE 82,360*]. 2-204-02690-5.

d365 **Mosshammer** Alden A., The 'Chronicle' of Eusebius and Greek chronographic tradition 1979 ➤ 61,q970... 64,a173: [R]Gnomon 58 (1986) 237-240 (R. Van *Compernolle*).

d366 **Places** Édouard des, Eusèbe de Césarée, La Préparation Évangélique XII-XIII: SChr 307, 1983 ➤ 64,e65... 1,f581: [R]Bijdragen 47 (1986) 333s (J. *Declerck*); RÉByz 44 (1986) 293 (J. *Wolinski*); RHR 203 (1986) 321s (A. *Le Boulluec*).

d367 **Places** Édouard des, Eusèbe de Césarée commentateur: THist 63, 1982 ➤ 63,a578... 1,f590: [R]CrNSt 7 (1986) 182s (C. *Moreschini*): EsprV 96 (1986) 218 (Y.-M. *Duval*, aussi sur PrépÉv XI et XIIs); RHR 203 (1986) 320s (P. *Nautin*).

d368 **Twomey** Vincent, Apostolikos thronos; the primacy of Rome... Eusebius, ATHANASIUS 1982 ➤ 63,u583... 1,f592: [R]JTS 37 (1986) 220-2 (H. *Chadwick*); TLZ 111 (1986) 679-681 (F. *Winkelmann*).

d369 GREGORIUS NAZIANZENUS: *Chaussy* Yves, Dom LOUVARD et l'édition de Saint Grégoire de Nazianze: RÉAug 31 (1985) 71-81.

d370 [TE]**Moreschini** Claudio, Gregorio Nazianzeno, I cinque discorsi teologici; lettere teologiche; il mistero cristiano; poesie (carmina arcana): Collana di Testi Patristici 58. R 1986, Città Nuova. 297 p. 88-311-3058-7.

d371 [E]**Mossay** J., II symposium nazianzenum 1981/3 ➤ 64,519*... 1,f596: [R]CrNSt 7 (1986) 390-3 (M. *Paparozzi*).

d372 GREGORIUS NYSSENUS: **Apostolopoulos** Charalambos, Phaedo Christianus; Studien zur Verbindung und Abwägung des Verhältnisses zwischen dem platonischen 'Phaidon' und dem Dialog Gregors von Nyssa 'Über die Seele und die Auferstehung': EurHS 20/188. Fra 1986, Lang. 416 p. Fs 75 [TR 83,111, W. *Gessel*].

d373 *Barrois* Georges, The alleged Origenism of St. Gregory of Nyssa: StVlad 30 (1986) 7-16.

d374 **Canévet** Mariette, Grégoire de Nysse et l'herméneutique biblique; études des rapports entre le langage et la connaissance de Dieu 1983 ➤ 64,e73... 1,f599: [R]TLZ 111 (1986) 839-841 (K. *Treu*).

d375 J. DAMASCENUS: *Déroche* Vincent, L'authenticité de l''Apologie contre les Juifs' de Léontios de Néapolis [citée par Jean Damascène]: BCH 110 (1986) 655-669.

d376 MARCELLUS A.: **Lienhard** Joseph T., Contra Marcellum; the influence of Marcellus of Ancyra on fourth-century Greek theology: Hab.-Diss. FrB 1986, DFrank. – RHE 82,347.

d377 METHODIUS O.: **Prinzivalli** Emanuela, L'esegesi biblica di Metodio di Olimpo D 1985 ➤ **1**,f603: ROrpheus 7 (1986) 420-4 (Clementina Mazzucco).

d378 PAULUS S.: Norris F. W., Paul of Samosata; 'procurator ducenarius'; JTS 35 (1984) 50-70 [RHE 81,741].

d379 SYNESIUS: Barnes T. D., a) Synesius in Constantinopole; – b) When did Synesius become bishop of Ptolemais?: GrRByz 27 (1986) 93-112 / 325-9.

d380 Liebeschuetz J. H. W. G., Why did Synesius become bishop of Ptolemais?: Byzantion 56 (1986) 180-195.

d381 **Vollenweider** Samuel, Neuplatonische und christliche Philosophie bei Synesios von Kyrene [Diss. Zürich 1983, DAltendorf H.]: ForKiDG 35, 1985 ➤ **1**,f608: RCrNSt 7 (1986) 181s (É. des Places); RHE 81 (1986) 227 (A. de Halleux: d'une remarquable maturité); ZKG 97 (1986) 279-281 (G. G. Blum).

d382 THEODORUS M.: **Bultmann** Rudolf, Die Exegese des Theodor von Mopsuestia, Hab.-Diss. Marburg 1912, EFeld H., Schelkle K. 1984 ➤ 65,d526: RTPhil 61 (1986) 578s (H. J. Sieben).

Y2.4 **Augustinus.**

d383 a) Amata Biagio, S. Agostino, 'De opere monachorum'; una concezione (antimanichea?) del lavoro; – b) Nazzaro Antonio V., Il lavoro nei motivi esegetici di Ambrogio; – c) Messana Vincenzo, Il lavoro nella prospettiva pelagiana: ➤ 432, EFelici S., Spiritualità del lavoro 1985/6, 59-78 / 79-93 / 185-203.

d384 Basevi Claudio, La conversión como criterio hermenéutico de las obras de San Agustin: ScripTPamp 18 (1986) 803-826 (-870 al.).

d385 Caserta Aldo, Sant'Agostino in Campania e a Napoli: Asprenas 33 (1986) 411-421.

d386 Ceresa-Gastaldo Aldo, Fede e sapere nella conversione di Agostino: Renovatio 21 (1986) 487-495.

d387 **Chadwick** Henry, Augustine: Past masters. Ox 1986, UP. 122 p. $15 pa. [TDig 34,62]. 0-19-287535-3; pa. 4-5. – RCleR 71 (1986) 460s (J. McGuckin); Month 248 (1986) 244s (B. R. Brinkman); NBlackf 67 (1986) 505s (Gillian R. Evans).

d388 Coyle Kevin, Augustine's use of Scripture: CanadCathR 4 (Dec. 1986)...

d389 **Cremona** Carlo, Agostino d'Ippona; la ragione e la fede. Mi 1986, Rusconi. 332 p. Lit. 28.000. – RCC 137 (1986,3) 48-52 (G. Mucci).

d390 **Ferrari** Leo C., The conversions of Saint Augustine. Villanova PA 1984, Univ. 88 p. – RRÉAug 31 (1985) 317 (D. Marianelli).

d391 ELa Bonnardière A.-M., Saint Augustin et la Bible: Monde de la Bible 3. P 1986, Beauchesne. F 270 [NRT 109, 908, V. Roisel].

d392 **Lange van Ravenswaay** J. Marius J., Augustinus totus noster; das Augustinusverständnis bei Johannes CALVIN: Diss. Tübingen 1986. 269 p. – TLZ 112,76.

d393 Larrabe José Luis, Naturaleza y gracia en la conversión de san Agustín (en el XVI centenario): NatGrac 33 (1986) 317-325.

d394 Marafioti Domenico, La conversione di sant'Agostino; l'ora della grazia: RasT 27 (1986) 136-152.

d395 *McEvoy* James, Anima una et cor unum; friendship and spiritual unity in Augustine: RTAM 53 (1986) 40-92.

d396 *McGuckin* John A., The enigma of Augustine's conversion: CleR 71 (1986) 315-325.

d397 *Madec* Goulven, *al.*, Bulletin Augustinien pour 1984 / 1985-6: RÉAug 31 (1985) 313-401 / 32 (1986) 284-392.

d398 *Madec* Goulven, Augustin et le néoplatonisme: RICathP 19 (1986) 41-52.

d399 *Markus* R. A., Pelagianism; Britain and the Continent: JEH 37 (1986) 191-204.

ᴱ**Mayer** Cornelius, Augustinus-Lexikon 1986 ➤ 637*.

d400 *Miccoli* Paolo, Storia e profezia nel pensiero di s. Agostino: Studium 82 (R 1986) 477-500.

d401 **O'Connell** Robert J., Imagination and metaphysics in St. Augustine [Aquinas Lecture]. Milwaukee 1986, Marquette Univ. iv-70 p. [TS 48,399, W. C. *Marceau*].

d402 *O'Daly* Gerard, Augustins Theologie: ➤ 587, EvKL 1 (1986) 326-332.

d403 **Oort** J. van, Jerusalem en Babylon, een onderzoek van Augustinus' De stad van God en de bronnen van zijn leer der twee steden (rijken): diss.Utrecht 1986, ᴰ*Quispel* G. Haag 1986, Boekencentrum. x-366 p. – [Bijdragen 48,344s, G. *Rouwhorst*].

d404 **Pelikan** Jaroslav, The mystery of continuity; memory and eternity in the thought of Saint Augustine. Charlottesville 1986, Virginia Univ. x-187. $15 pa. [TS 48,588, E. *TeSelle*].

d405 **Poque** Suzanne, Le langage symbolique dans la prédication d'Augustin d'Hippone; images héroïques: ÉtAug 1984 ➤ 1,f622: ᴿRÉAug 32 (1986) 301-3 (D. *Marianelli*).

d406 *Rivinius* Karl J., Reflections on the life and work of St. Augustine: Verbum 27 (1986) 3-19.

d407 ᴱ**Rodríguez** J.-M., Agostino d'Ippona, Le confessioni, libro 6; *Madec* G., 7; *Mara* M.-G., 8; *Siniscalco* P., 9. Palermo 1985, Augustinus. 112 p. Lit. 13.000. – ᴿCC 137 (1986,1) 88s (D. *Marafioti*).

d408 *Smith* Warren T., Augustine of Hippo: ➤ 585, ᴱ*Eliade* M., EncRel 1 (1986) 520-527.

d409 *Turrado* Argimiro, La utopía y la dialéctica vital de la Biblia como característica esencial de la mentalidad de san Agustín: EstAg 21 (1986) 451-473.

d410 *Wankenne* J., Une découverte importante; les lettres inédites de saint Augustin [*Divjak* J. 1981]: ➤ 118, ᶠVEREMANS J. 1986, 373-382.

Y2.5 *Hieronymus* – **Jerome.**

d411 *Banchich* Thomas M., EUNAPIUS and Jerome: GrRByz 27 (1986) 319-324.

d412 **Bartelink** G. J. M., Hieronymus, Liber de optimo genere interpretandi (Ep. 57): Mnemosyne Sup. 61, 1980 ➤ 62,1305: ᴿGnomon 58 (1986) 222-5 (P. *Serra Zanetti*).

d413 *Bartelink* Gerard, Hieronymus über die Schwäche der conditio humana: Kairos 28 (1986) 23-32.

d414 *Fodor* István, Le lieu d'origine de S. Jérôme; reconsidération d'une vieille controverse [avant OLAHUS, l'hongrois BRODARICS István mentionne Stridon, qui peut être le Stridon/Strigon de Pannonie]: RHE 81 (1986) 498-500.

d415 *Force* Paul, La deuxième partie du Saint Jérôme du P. CAVALLERA: BLitEc-Chr 2 (1986) 12-18.

d416 *Grego* Igino, *a*) San Girolamo e i suoi amici romani: Asprenas 32 (1985) 429-444; – *b*) San Girolamo maestro di spiritualità: Asprenas 33 (1986) 305-329.

d417 *a*) *Gribomont* Jean, Lavoro e Parola di Dio in S. Girolamo; – *b*) *Riggi* Calogero, Dimensione religiosa del lavoro nel mondo pagano in EPIFANIO (Haer. 80,1-3); – *c*) *Pasquato* Ottorino, Vita spirituale e lavoro in Giovanni CRISOSTOMO; 'modelli' di un rapporto: → 432, Spiritualità del lavoro 1985/6, 205-212 / 39-58 / 105-139.

d418 ᴱLardet Pierre, S. Jérôme, Apologie contre Rufin: SChr 303, 1983 → 64,e134... 1,ƒ629: ᴿJTS 37 (1986) 595s (H. *Chadwick*: expert on the unangelic doctor); Mnemosyne 39 (1986) 525-7 (G. *Bartelink*); RÉAug 31 (1985) 184-7 (P. *Jay*).

d419 Lardet P., *a*) S. Hieronymi Contra Rufinum, Opera 3/1: CCLat 79, 1982 → 64,e646; 65,d547: ᴿRÉAug 31 (1985) 183s (Y.-M. *Duval*). – *b*) digesserunt *Gouder* Eddy, *Tombeur* Paul: CETEDOC. Turnhout 1986, Brepols. 29 p.; 3 microfiches.

d420 *a*) *Moreschini* Claudio, Gerolamo tra Pelagio e ORIGENE; – *b*) *Opelt* Ilona, Origene visto da San Girolamo; – *c*) *Murphy* F.X., Magistros meos nec muto nec accuso; RUFINUS on Origen: → 476*, L'origenismo, AugR 26 (1986) 207-216 / 217-222 / 241-9.

d421 *Nautin* Pierre, Hieronymus, ᵀ*Wolter* Mariann: → 597, TRE 15 (1986) 304-315.

d422 Rice Eugene F.ᴶ, Saint Jerome in the Renaissance 1985 → 1,ƒ633: ᴿChH 55 (1986) 226s (A. *Rabil*); RelStR 12 (1986) 301 (R.L. *Harrison*).

d423 *Scourfield* J.H.D., Jerome, Antioch, and the desert; a note on chronology: JTS 37 (1986) 117-121.

d424 *Visotzky* Burton L., HILLEL, Hieronymus and PRAETEXTATUS: → 11*, Mem. BICKERMAN E. = JANES 16s (1984s) 217-224.

Y2.6 Patres Latini alphabetice.

d426 ᴱFontaine J., *Pietri* C., Le monde latin antique et la bible: Bible de tous les temps 2, 1985 → 1,ƒ638: ᴿBrotéria 123 (1986) 575s (F. de Sales *Baptista*); RThom 86 (1986) 490-6 (M.-V. *Leroy*); TsTNijm 26 (1986) 297 (F. van de *Paverd*).

d427 Gryson Roger, Le recueil arien de Vérone 1982 → 64,e85: ᴿRBgPg 64 (1986) 139s (J. *Schamp*).

d428 Hagendahl Harald, Von Tertullian zu Cassiodor; die profane literarische Tradition in dem lateinischen christlichen Schrifttum: Ac. Göteborg gr./lat. 44, 1983, 164 p. – ᴿRÉAug 31 (1985) 175-9 (J. *Fontaine*).

d429 AMBROSIUS: Lamirande E., PAULIN de Milan et la 'Vita Ambrosii'; aspects de la religion sous le Bas-Empire: Recherches théologie 30. P/Montréal 1983, Desclée/Bellarmin. 204 p. $15. – ᴿCrNSt 7 (1986) 396-8 (Elena *Giannarelli*).

d430 Nauroy Gérard, Exégèse et création littéraire chez Ambroise de Milan; étude sur les prédications du De Jacob et du De Joseph: diss. Paris IV, 1985. – RÉLat 63 (1985) 31.

d431 Paredi Angelo, Sant'Ambrogio; l'uomo, il politico, il vescovo. Mi 1985, Rizzoli. 444 p. Lit. 20.000. – ᴿCC 137 (1986,2) 300s (A. *Ferrua*); RivLtg 73 (1986) 435s (G.M. *Medica*); StCattMi 30 (1986) 151 (A. *Zaccuri*).

d432 Zelzer Michaela, [→ 65,d61] S. Ambrosii, Epistularum liber decimus... Opera 10 / CSEL 82, 1982: ᴿRÉAug 32 (1986) 249-254 (H. *Savon*).

d433 CAESARIUS A.: ᴱDelage M.-J., Césaire d'Arles, Sermons au peuple III

(Sermons 56-80): SChr 330. P 1986, Cerf. 318 p. F 208 [NRT 109,451, A. *Harvengt*].

d434 CHROMATIUS A.: **Truzzi** C., ZENO, GAUDENZIO e Cromazio; testi e contenuti della predicazione cristiana per le chiese di Verona, Brescia e Aquileia (360-410 ca.) [153 sermons]: TRicSRel 22. Brescia 1985, Paideia. 349 p. Lit. 40.000 [NRT 109,110, V. *Roisel*].

d435 CYPRIANUS: **Bouet** P., *al.,* Cyprien, traités; concordance, documentation lexicale et grammaticale: Alpha-Omega A-67. Hildesheim/NY 1986, Olms/Widmann. XLIV-1399 p. (2 vol) [TPhil 62, 593s, H. *Sieben*].

d436 ᵀᴱ**Clarke** G. W., The letters of St. Cyprian of Carthage 1s: Ancient Christian Writers 43s, 1984 ⇒ 65,d562; **1,**f649: ᴿTR 82 (1986) 34-36 (G. *Schöllgen*).

d437 *Stritzky* Maria-Barbara von, Erwägungen zum Decischen Opferbefehl und seinen Folgen unter besonderer Berücksichtigung der Beurteilung durch Cyprian: RömQ 81 (1986) 1-25.

d438 GREGORIUS M.: **Colgrave** Bertram, The earliest life of Gregory the Great, by an anonymous monk of Whitby; text, translation and notes. C 1985, Univ. ix-180 p.

d439 **Evans** Gillian R., The thought of Gregory the Great: Studies in Medieval Life and Thought 4/2. C 1986, Univ. xi-164 p. £25/$39.50 [TDig 34,48]. 0-521-30904-2. – ᴿExpTim 98 (1986s) 184s (S. N. C. *Lieu*).

d440 *Gillet* R., Grégoire Iᵉʳ le Grand: ⇒ 581, DHGE XXI,125 (1986) 1387-1420.

d441 **Paronetto** Vera, Gregorio Magno, un maestro delle origini cristiane d'Europa 1985 ⇒ **1,**f656*: 88-382-3522-8: ᴿAugR 26 (1986) 608s (L. *Navarra*); JEH 37 (1986) 486s (R. A. *Markus*); VetChr 23 (1986) 186-9 (A. *Quacquarelli*).

d442 *Petersen* Joan M., The Dialogues of Gregory the Great in their late antique cultural background [diss. London 1981]: Studies and Texts 69, 1984 ⇒ **1,**f657; $23: ᴿCrNSt 7 (1986) 393-6 (A. de *Vogüé*); JEH 37 (1986) 112-4 (P. *Meyvaert*).

d443 **Richards** Jeffrey, Gregor der Grosse 1983 ⇒ 64,e129*b;* **1,**f659: ᴿTrierTZ 95 (1986) 79s (E. *Sauser:* ein ausgesprochenes 'Lesebuch').

d444 **Richards** J., Il console di Dio; la vita e i tempi di Gregorio Magno. F 1984. – ᴿVetChr 23 (1986) 199-206 (Risa S. *Calì*).

d445 HILARIUS P.: **Brennecke** Hanns C., Hilarius von Poitiers: ⇒ 597, TRE 15 (1986) 315-322.

d446 HIPÓLITO de Roma, La tradición apostólica: Ichthys 1. Salamanca 1986, Sigueme. 123 p. [Teresianum 38,472, M. *Diego Sánchez*].

d447 ᴱ**Marcovich** Miroslav, Hippolytus, refutatio omnium haeresium [introd. Eng.]: PatrTSt 25. NY/B 1986, de Gruyter. xvi-541 p. DM 298. 0-89925-211-7. – ᴿExpTim 98 (1986s) 184 (S. G. *Hall*).

d448 *Marcovich* Miroslav, Hippolyt von Rom, ᵀ*Schröter* M.: ⇒ 597, TRE 15 (1986) 381-7.

d449 LACTANTIUS: ᴱ**Monat** Pierre, Lactance, Institutions divines I: SChr 326. P 1986, Cerf. 271 p. F 179. – ᴿBFaCLyon 79 (1986) 65s.

d450 LEO M.: **Saenz** Alfredo, San León Magno y los misterios de Cristo. Paraná 1984, Mikael. 334 p. – ᴿDivinitas 30 (1986) 201s (C. *Petino*).

Y2.8 **Documenta orientalia.**

d451 *Daucourt* Gérard, Les anciennes églises d'Orient: EsprV 96 (1986) 584-8.

d452 *Breydy* Michel, Vestiges méconnus des Pères cappadocéens en syriaque: ParOr 12 (Kaslik 1984s) 239-252 [< ZIT].

d453 *Brock* Sebastian, An early Syriac commentary on the liturgy: JTS 37 (1986) 387-403.

d454 *Drijvers* Han J.W., *a*) East of Antioch; forces and structures in the development of early Syriac theology [< Oxford Patristic Conference 1983]; – *b*) Rechtgläubigkeit und Ketzerei im ältesten syrischen Christentum [< Symposium 1972, OrChrAnal 197 (1979) 291-308]: ➤ 153, East of Antioch 1984, 1-27 / III (original numbering, 291-308).

d455 **Gwaramia** R., The Old-Georgian versions of the 'Life of John Chrysostom' and its peculiarities according to a 968 Manuscript [edition in Georgian]: Old-Georgian Literature 8. Tbilisi 1986, Mec'niereba. 192 p.

d456 **Kawerau** Peter, Die Chronik von Arbela: CSCOr 467s, Syri 199s, 1985 ➤ 1,f669: ᴿRHE 81 (1986) 543-8 (J. M. *Fiey*: ne cite pas Fiey).

d457 **Suermann** Harald, Die geschichtstheologische Reaktion auf die einfallenden Muslime in der edessenischen Apokalyptik des 7. Jahrhunderts [Diss. Bonn]: EurHS 23/256. Bern 1985, Lang. 254 p. Fs 54. 3-8204-5674-9 [Bijdragen 48,89, M. *Parmentier*].

d458 ABUQURRA Théodore, Traité du culte des icônes; introduction et texte critique, ᴱ**Dick** Ignace: Patrimoine arabe chrétien 10. Beirut 1986, St-Paul. xxviii-272 p.

d459 APHRATES: *Vööbus* Arthur, Aphrahat: ➤ 594, RAC Sup (1986) 497-506.

d460 ATHANASIUS: ᴱ**Lorenz** Rudolf, Der zehnte Osterfestbrief des Athanasius von Alexandrien [the one Syriac text in photocopy; German tr. and analysis]: BZNW 49. B 1986, De Gruyter. 96 p. DM 44. 3-11-010652-3. – ᴿExpTim (1986s) 184 (S. G. *Hall*).

d461 **Martin** Annik, Histoire 'acéphale' et index syriaque des lettres festales d'Athanase d'Alexandrie: SChr 317, 1985 ➤ 1,f679: ᴿJTS 37 (1986) 576-589 (T. D. *Barnes*).

d462 BARHEBRAEUS: *Poirier* Paul-Hubert, Bar Hebraeus sur le libre arbitre: OrChr 70 (1986) 23-36.

d463 DOROTHEUS: *Esbroeck* Michel van, Une lettre de Dorothée, comte de Palestine, à Marcel et Mâri en 452: AnBoll 104 (1986) 145-159 (avec texte arabe).

d464 EPHRAEM: **Brock** Sebastian, The luminous eye; the spiritual world vision of St. Ephrem [Placid Lectures]. R 1985, C.I.I.S. 166 p. $7. [Bijdragen 48,86, M. *Parmentier*].

d465 **Petersen** William L., The Diatessaron and Ephraem Syrus as sources of Romanos the Melodist: [diss. ᴰ*Quispel* G. ➤ 65,d585]: CSCOr 475, Subsidia 74. Lv 1986. xxxiv-216 p. 0070-0444. – ᴿRB 93 (1986) 634s (M.-J. *Pierre*); RÉByz 44 (1986) 317s (J.-P. *Mahé*).

d466 ᴱ**Ter-Pétrossian** Lévon, ᵀ*Outtier* Bernard, Textes arméniens relatifs à S. Éphrem: CSCOr 473, arm. 15s. Lv 1985, Peeters. xx-122 p. (Arm.); viii-85 p. 0070-041X.

d467 ĠAZZI Sulaiman Al- (Xᵉ-XIᵉ s.), Écrits théologiques en prose, texte établi par **Edelby** Néophytos: Patrimoine arabe chrétien 9. Beirut 1986, St. Paul. vii-313 p.

d468 GERONTICON latine reddidit **Arras** Victor: CSCOr 477, aethiopici 80. Lv 1986, Peeters. viii-254 p. 0070-0398.

d469 GREGORIOS: **Gerhards** Albert, Die griechische Gregoriosanaphora 1984 ➤ 65,d586; 1,f688: ᴿOstkSt 35 (1986) 197-9 (H. M. *Biedermann*); VigChr 40 (1986) 304s (H. *Wegman*).

d470 JOHANNES Apam.: ᴱLavenant René, Jean d'Apamée, Dialogues et traités: SChr 311, 1984 ➤ 65,d587; 1,f690: ᴿBLitEc 87 (1986) 79s (H. *Crouzel*); NRT 108 (1986) 276s (C. *Martin*); RÉByz 43 (1985) 270 (B. *Flusin*).

d471 MARCUS M.: *Durand* Georges-Matthieu de, Études sur Marc le Moine, III, Marc et les controverses occidentales: BLitEc 87 (1986) 163-188; Eng. 162.

d472 MAXIMUS CONF.: Maxime le Confesseur, Vie de la Vierge, ᴱEsbroeck Michel-Jean van: CSCOr 478s; iberici 21s. Lv 1986, Peeters. xviii-189 p.; xxxix-145 p. 0070-0436.

d473 NARSAÏ: ᴱSiman E. P., Narsaï, cinq homélies sur les paraboles évangéliques. P 1984, Cariscript. 210 p. – ᴿVetChr 23 (1986) 429-431 (G. A. *Desantis*).

d474 SERUG Yaʻaqob: Jacques de Seroug, Six homélies festales en prose, ᵀᴱRilliet François: PatrOr 43/4,196. Turnhout 1986, Brepols. P. 517-663.

d475 SIMEON: ᴱGoguadze Nargiza, Old [Simeon] Metaphrases Collection (September Lectures): Old-Georgian Literature 7. Tbilisi 1986, Mecʻniereba. 552 p.

Y3 Medium aevum [➤ κ7].

d476 ᴱAbbiati S., *Agnoletto* A., *Lazzati* M. R., La stregoneria; diavoli, streghe, inquisitori dal Trecento al Settecento: Studio 114. Mi 1984, Mondadori. vii-371 p. – ᴿRivStoLR 22 (1986) 379-384 (Marina *Romanello*).

d477 *Bataillon* Louis J., De la lectio à la praedicatio; commentaires bibliques et sermons au XIIIᵉ siècle: RSPT 70 (1986) 559-574; Eng. 575.

d478 *Baumgärtner* Ingrid, 'De privilegiis doctorum'; über Gelehrtenstand und Doktorwürde im späten Mittelalter: HistJb 106 (Fr 1986) 298-332.

d479 **Chenu** M.-D., La teologia come scienza nel XIII secolo [= it. ¹1971 < fr. 1927]. Mi 1985, Jaca. 180 p. [STEv 9/18,296].

d480 **Coletti** V., Chiesa ed eresia tra latino e volgare, sec. XII/XIII. Genova 1981, Bozzi. 108 p. – ᴿProtestantesimo 41 (1986) 52 (G. *Gonnet*: dispense universitarie).

d481 **Dinzelbacher** Peter, Visionen und Visionsliteratur im Mittelalter: Mon. Gesch. MA 23, 1981 ➤ 64,e177: ᴿRPhil 61 (1986) 585s (R. *Berndt*).

d482 **Dronke** P., Women writers of the Middle Ages 1984 ➤ 1,f703: ᴿMaia 38 (1986) 257-9 (L. *Robertini*).

d483 **Enright** Michael J., Jona, Tora and Soissons; the origin of the [Pippin 751] royal anointing ritual: Arbeiten zur Frühmittelalterforschung 17. B 1985, de Gruyter. ix-198 p. DM 114. 3-11-010628-0 [Bijdragen 48,89, M. *Schneiders*].

d484 ᴱElder E. Rozanne, The roots of the modern Christian tradition [Kalamazoo conference 1982]. Kalamazoo 1984, Cistercian. xxii-340 p. – ᴿTLond 39 (1986) 126s (G. M. *Jantzen*).

d485 **Erbstösser** Martin, Ketzer im Mittelalter. Lp Edition 1984. 235 p.; 106 (color.) fig. M 68. – ᴿTLZ 111 (1986) 114s (G. *Haendler*).

d486 **Evans** Gillian R., [➤ d588] The language and logic of the Bible; the earlier Middle Ages 1984 ➤ 65,d597; 1,f707; ᴿJRel 66 (1986) 437s (E. Ann *Matter*); JRS 76 (1986) 329s (Margaret *Gibson*); NBlackf 67 (1986) 96s (L. J. *Bataillon*).

d487 **Gold** Penny S., The lady and the virgin; image, attitude and experience in twelfth century France. Ch 1985, Univ. 182 p. $20. – ᴿJAAR 54 (1986) 582s (Rosemary R. *Ruether*).

d488 *Graus* František, Verfassungsgeschichte des Mittelalters: HZ 243 (1986) 529-589.

d489 **Haren** Michael, Medieval thought; the western intellectual tradition from antiquity to the thirteenth century 1985 ➤ 1,f710; also L, Macmillan: ᴿChH 55 (1986) 360s (D. V. *Monti*).

d490 **Kleineidam** E., Universitas studi Erffordensis; Überblick über die Geschichte der Universität Erfurt, I. Spätmittelalter 1392-1460 ²ʳᵉᵛ [¹1964]: ErfTSt 14. Lp 1985, St. Benno. xxix-480 p. [RHE 82,108, J. *Paquet*].

d491 *Kuster* K. J., *Cormier* R. J., Old views and new trends; observations on the problem of homosexuality in the Middle Ages: Studi Medievali (1984) 587-610 [RHE 81,783].

d492 **Lubac** H. de, Esegesi medievali; i quattro sensi della Scrittura 1/1: Opera omnia 17. Mi 1986, Jaca. 407 p. Lit. 54.000 [RasT 28,538s, S. *Spera*].

d493 **McNally** Robert E., The Bible in the early Middle Ages [reprints], Atlanta 1986 = 1959, Scholars. 121 p. $10. 0-89139-912-8 [ExpTim 98,119].

d494 **Oursel** Raymond, *al.*, The monastic realm, ᵀ*Mills* Donald. NY 1985, Rizzoli. 287 p.; 299 fig. $65 [BAR-W 13/5, 12.14, S. *Gardner*].

d495 *Patroni Griffi* Filena, L'amore nel secolo XII negli studi recenti del P. Lᴇᴄʟᴇʀᴄǫ: Benedictina 33 (1986) 145-7.

d496 **Radding** C. M., A world made by men; cognition and society, 400-1200. Chapel Hill 1985, Univ. NC. xi-286 p. $28 [RHE 82,68*]. – ᴿAmHR 91 (1986) 901s (K. F. *Drew*).

d497 **Riché** Pierre, Le scuole e l'insegnamento nell'Occidente Cristiano [Écoles 1979 ➤ 61,u949], ᵀ*Messina* Nicolò. R 1984, Jouvence. 496 p.; bibliog. p. 433-463. Lit. 55.000.

d498 ᴱ**Riché P.**, *Lobrichon* G., Le Moyen Âge et la Bible: Bible de tous les temps 4, 1984 ➤ 1,306.d605: ᴿAevum 60 (1986) 356s (G. L. *Potestà*); RHE 81 (1986) 306-310 (H. *Silvestre*: titres sans pp., ensuite observations approfondies); RivStoLR 22 (1986) 151s (J. *Gribomont*); Speculum 61 (1986) 744s (J. H. *Bentley*).

d499 *Roberts* Michael, Biblical epic and rhetorical paraphrase in Late Antiquity: ARCA 16, 1985 ➤ 1,f719: ᴿGnomon 58 (1986) 740-2 (M. *Wissemann*); RÉLat 63 (1985) 424s (J.-L. *Charlet*).

d500 *Ruello* Francis, Bulletin d'histoire des idées médiévales [éditions; études]: RechSR 74 (1986) 253-304.

d501 *Segura Graíño* C., Las mujeres en el medievo hispano. M 1984, Cuadernos de Investigación Medieval. 56 p. – ᴿHispania 45 (1985) 446-8 (A. *Muñoz Fernández*) [RHE 82,311*].

d502 **Shannon** Albert C., The medieval Inquisition. Wsh 1983, Augustinian. viii-153 p. $10. – ᴿHeythJ 27 (1986) 91s (B. *Hamilton*: the book finds nothing to blame).

d503 **Sieben** Herman J., Die Konzilsidee des lateinischen Mittelalters 1984 ➤ 1,f721: ᴿTS 47 (1986) 162 (J. M. *McDermott*).

d504 **Skinner** Andrew C., Veritas hebraica; Christian attitudes toward the Hebrew language in the high Middle Ages: diss. Denver 1986. 360 p. 86-17677. – DissA 47 (1986s) 1847-A.

d505 **Smalley** Beryl, The study of the Bible in the Middle Ages ³ [= ²1952 with few addenda; ¹1941] 1983 ➤ 1,f722; xxxviii-406 p. – ᴿRHE 81 (1986) 341 recommande BTAM 13 (1985) 760s (H. *Silvestre*).

d506 *a*) *Steinmetz* David C., The superiority of pre-critical exegesis [< TTod 37 (1980) 27-38]; – *b*) *Frye* Roland M., Metaphors, equations and the faith [< TTod 37 (1980) 59-67]: ExAud 1 (1985) 74-82 / 47-53.

d507 **Stock** Brian, The implications of literacy; written language and models of interpretation in the eleventh and twelfth centuries. Princeton 1983, Univ. x-604 p. £38.80. – RHeythJ 27 (1986) 320 (G. R. *Evans*: seminal).

d508 ANSELMUS: *Gilbert* Paul, Justice et miséricorde dans le 'Proslogion' de saint Anselme [... similitude de plan du 'Monologion']: NRT 108 (1986) 218-238.

d509 AQUINAS: *Lobato* Abelardo, MAIMÓNIDES, Averroes y Tomás de Aquino; diálogo de tres culturas: ComSev 19 (1986) 33-64.

d510 **Vos** Arvin, Aquinas, CALVIN, and contemporary Protestant thought 1985 ➤ 1,f726: RCalvinT 21 (1986) 237-9 (R. J. *Feenstra*); ChH 55 (1986) 517s (E. *TeSelle*); ExpTim 97 (1986s) 345 (N. *Tanner*); ModT 3 (1986s) 273s (F. *Kerr*); RefTR 45 (1986) 58 (R. *Doyle*); ScotBEvT (1986) 65s (P. *Helm*: ecumenical theology of the best kind); Themelios 12 (1986s) 63 (T. *Lane*); TS 47 (1986) 542-4 (J. H. *Wright*).

d511 *Grijs* Ferdinand de, La Summa Theologiae traduite en français [I-III, Cerf 1984s]: Bijdragen 47 (1986) 421-434; Eng. 435.

d512 *Wohlman* Avital, De la foi à la foi par la raison; MAÏMONIDE et Thomas d'Aquin: RSPT 70 (1986) 521-557; Eng. 558.

d513 BONAVENTURA: **Fleming** John V., From Bonaventure to Bellini; an essay in Franciscan exegesis 1982 ➤ 65,6964: RTTod 43 (1986s) 503-9 (J. W. *Dixon*).

d514 CASSIODORUS: *Scivoletto* Nino, Cassiodoro e la 'retorica della città': GitFg 35 (1986) 1-24.

d515 CUSANUS: EHaubst Rudolf, Der Friede under den Religionen nach Nikolaus von Kues, Symposion Trier 1982/4 ➤ 65,506: RTLZ 111 (1986) 112-4 (K.-H. *Kandler*).

d516 DIONYSIUS: *Rorem* Paul, Biblical and liturgical symbols within the Pseudo-Dionysian synthesis [diss. Princeton, DFroehlich K.]: Studies and Texts 71, 1984 ➤ 65,d617; 1,f732: RJTS 37 (1986) 228-230 (A. *Louth*); TLZ 111 (1986) 365-7 (E. *Mühlenberg*).

d517 TELilla Salvatore, Ps. Dionigi l'Areopagita, Gerarchia celeste, teologia mistica, lettere: Collana di Testi Patristici 56. R 1986, Città Nuova. 186 p. 88-311-3056-0.

d518 GEUFROI: **Perry** Anne J. A. † 21.III.1980 [auto], EBeck Jonathan, La Passion des jongleurs [texte de Geufroi, Bible des sept estaz du monde; diss. Emory, DBeck, Atlanta 1978]: Textes Dossiers Documents 4, 1981 ➤ 64,1815: RÉglT 17 (1986) 92-94 (L. *Laberge*).

d519 GULIELMUS S.T.: **Bell** David N., The image and likeness; the Augustinian [not Eastern as *Dechanet* J.] spirituality of William of St. Thierry [< diss. Oxford 1975]. Kalamazoo 1984, Cistercian. 282 p. $20. – RTLond 39 (1986) 150-2 (G. *Mursell*).

d520 HONORIUS A.: *a) Iñiguez* José Antonio, La simbología del templo cristiano en el comienzo del período gótico — Honorio de Autún y SICARDO de Cremona; – *b) Menchen* Bartolomé, Algunos puntos de interés en la hermenéutica de Fray Luis de LEÓN, y de su tiempo: ➤ 366, Hermenéutica 1985/6, 667-681 / 487-495.

d521 HRABANUS M.: *Böhne* Winfried, Hrabanus Maurus: ➤ 597, TRE 15 (1986) 606-610.

d522 HUGO S.V.: *Châtillon* Jean, Hugo von St. Viktor, TSchäferdiek K.: ➤ 597, TRE 15 (1986) 629-635.

d523 INNOCENTIUS IV: *Melloni* Alberto, Interpretari et addere Euangelio; aspetti dei fondamenti biblici della christianitas in Sinibaldo Fieschi/Innocenzo IV: CrNSt 7 (1986) 239-264; Eng. 436.

d524 JOACHIM F.: **Daniel** E. Randolph, Joachim of Fiore, Liber de concordia Novi ac Veteris Testamenti: TrAmPh 73/8, 1983 ➤ **1**,f737: ᴿSpeculum 61 (1986) 429-431 (Sandra L. *Zimdars-Swartz*).

d525 **Gigante** M., S. Tommaso e la storia della salvezza; la polemica con Gioacchino da Fiore: La Ripresa 3. Salerno 1986, Ist. Sup. Scienze Religiose. 382 p. – ᴿAsprenas 33 (1986) 230s.

d526 **Lubac** H. de, La posterità spirituale di G. da Fiore II, 1984 ➤ 65,d624: ᴿStPatav 33 (1986) 711s (G. *Segalla*: panorama troppo vasto).

d527 **McGinn** Bernard, The Calabrian abbot; Joachim of Fiore in the history of western thought 1985 ➤ **1**,f740: ᴿChH 55 (1986) 515s (K. F. *Morrison*); Speculum 61 (1986) 965-8 (R. E. *Lerner*); TS 47 (1986) 323-5 (D. F. *Duclow*).

d528 **West** D., *Zimdars-Swartz* S., Joachim of Fiore 1983 ➤ 65,d626; **1**,f741: ᴿChH 55 (1986) 365s (G. A. *Zinn*).

d529 **Workman** Deborah S., The Spirit clothed in flesh; the significance of the Sabbath Age in Joachim of Fiore's theology of history: diss. Kent State 1986, ᴰ*Baird* J. 268 p. 86-28952. – DissA 47 (1986s) 3423-A.

d530 JULIANA N.: ᴱ**Pezzini** Domenico, Giuliana di Norwich, Libro delle rivelazioni. Mi 1984, Ancora. 354 p. – ᴿSalesianum 48 (1986) 138 (G. *Groppo*).

d531 ᴱ**Llewelyn** Robert, Julian, woman of our day. L 1985, Darton-LT. xii-144 p. £5. – ᴿTLond 39 (1986) 492s (Grace M. *Jantzen*).

d532 RAMUS P.: *Risse* W., Petrus Ramus und sein Verhältnis zur Schultradition: RSPT 70 (1986) 49-66 [2-100, al. Pierre de la Ramée].

d533 RICARDUS S. V.: **Cunningham** Lawrence S., The [Paulist 1979-83; Richard of St. Victor etc.] classics of western spirituality; some recent volumes: RelStR 12 (Macon 1986) 104-110.

d534 ROLLE R.: *Clark* J. P. H., Richard Rolle [1300-49] as a biblical commentator [... Thren Apc Ps Magnificat]: DowR 104 (1986) 165-213.

d535 RUPERTUS T.: **Timmer** D. E., The religious significance of Judaism for XIIth-century monastic exegesis; a study in the thought of Rupert of Deutz, c. 1070-1129. 219 p. [diss., date and place not indicated in RHE 82,99*].

d536 SEDULIUS: *Small* Carolinne D., Rhetoric and exegesis in Sedulius' Carmen Paschale: ClasMedK 37 (1986) 223-244.

d537 TAUBER: *Dell'Omo* Mariano, La Bibbia nei sermoni di Tauber: RivAscM 11 (1986) 176-184.

d538 ZACHARIAE J.: **Zumkeller** Adolar, Leben ... des J. Zachariae († 1428): Cassiciacum 34, 1984 ➤ **1**,752: ᴿZKG 97 (1986) 108-110 (J. *Hödl*).

Y4.1 **Luther**, *post-centenarium*.

d539 *Aardweg* Gerard V. M. van den, Martin Lutero dallo psichiatra: StCattMi 28 (1984) 100-3.

d540 **Atkinson** James, Martin Luther, prophet to the Church Catholic 1983 ➤ 65,d633; **1**,f755: ᴿEvQ 58 (1986) 90s (D. F. *Wright*).

d541 **Atkinson** James, Lutero, la parola scatenata — l'uomo e il pensiero 1983 ➤ 65,d633: ᴿSTEv 15 (1985) 142-5 (G. *Corradini*).

d542 **Bach** H., Handbuch der Luthersprache; Laut- und Formenlehre in Luthers Wittenberger Drucken bis 1545; 2. Druckschwache Silben, Konsonantismus 1985 ➤ **1**,f757: ᴿDLZ 107 (1986) 510-512 (J. *Schildt*).

d543 **Beintker** Horst, Leben mit dem Wort; Handbuch zur Schriftauslegung Martin Luthers. Erlangen 1985, Luther. 533 p. DM 30. – ᴿBTZ 3 (1986) 336-9 (W. *Kritschell*).

d544 **Brecht** Martin, Martin Luther, his road to Reformation 1483-1521 [1981
➤ 63,e7331], ᵀ*Schaaf* James L. Ph 1985, Fortress. xvi-557 p.; 44 fig. $37.
– ᴿAndrUnS 24 (1986) 267-9 (K. A. *Strand*); JTS 37 (1986) 254-6 (G.
Yule); RelStR 12 (1986) 301 (S. H. *Hendrix*: will replace H. BOEHMER 1925
on the younger Luther, though follows extra-chorum BIZER, unduly credits
STAUPITZ, and holds Luther's mother née Ziegler not Lindemann).

d545 **Busquets** Joan, ¿Quién era Martin Lutero?, ᵀ*Periel* Maite: Salamanca
1986, Sígueme. 311 p. – ᴿNatGrac 33 (1986) 566s (G. *Rodríguez*).

d546 **Busquets** Joan, Martí Luter; valoració actual de la Reforma. Barc 1986,
Curial. 287 p. – ᴿRCatalT 11 (1986) 472s (J. M. *Marquès*).

d547 **Congar** Yves, Martin Lutero; la fede, la riforma [1983 ➤ 64,e226],
ᵀ*Mandalari* M. T. 1984 ➤ 65,d645; 1,f766: ᴿRivStoLR 22 (1986) 585s
(P. C. *Bori*).

d548 **Delius** H. U., Augustin als Quelle Luthers; eine Materialsammlung 1984
➤ 1,f767: ᴿCrNSt 7 (1986) 639 (G. *Pani*); RHE 81 (1986) 639 (P. *Denis*:
écarte les œuvres de jeunesse; Luther a lu Augustin dès 1509).

Ebeling Gerhard, Lutherstudien III 1985 ➤ 155*.

d549 *Elshtain* Jean B., Luther *sic* — Luther *non* [a freedom-fighter, but
paradoxical]: TTod 43 (1986s) 155-168.

d550 ᴱ**Furcha** E. J., Encounters with Luther; papers from the 1983 McGill
Luther symposium 1984 ➤ 65,575: ᴿSR 14 (1985) 390s (D. *Janz*).

d551 **García Villoslada** Ricardo, Martin Lutero I., Il frate assetato di Dio
[²1976], ᵀ*Cerutti* C. M. *al.*: Sestante. Mi 1985, Ist. Prop. Libraria. 790 p.
– ᴿSalesianum 48 (1986) 715s (A. M. *Triacca*).

d552 *Grane* Leif [æresdoktor Oslo 3.IX.1986], Hvor havde han det fra?
Bemærkninger til den nyere diskussion om Luthers vej til reformationen:
NorTTs 87 (1986) 193-203.

d553 *Gritsch* Eric W., Martin — God's court jester 1983 ➤ 64,e239; 65,d659:
ᴿChH 55 (1986) 98s (P. E. *Pederson*: more serious than its title).

d554 *Hagen* Kenneth, Luther in Norway [< Oslo address 1980]: LuthJb 53
(1986) 31-54.

d555 ᴱ**Hammer** Gerhard, *zur Mühlen* Karl-Heinz, Lutheriana; zum 500.
Geburtstag M. Luthers von den Mitarbeitern der Weimarer Ausgabe.
Köln 1984, Böhlau. 483 p. [5 art. de Comm. Ps]. – ᴿRHE 81 (1986) 638s
(P. *Denis*).

d556 **Harran** Marilyn J., Luther on conversion; the early years 1983
➤ 65,d660: ᴿCathHR 72 (1986) 102-4 (J. S. *Preus*: a daring book on a
burned-out subject); ChH 55 (1986) 229s (B. A. *Gerrish*).

ᴱ**Iserloh** Erwin, *Müller* Gerhard, Luther und die politische Welt 1983/4
➤ 445.

d557 **Janz** Denis R., Luther and late medieval Thomism; a study in theological anthropology. Waterloo ONT 1983, Laurier Univ. 186 p. – ᴿRHE
81 (1986) 676s (P. *Denis*).

d558 ᴱ**Jürgens** Heiko, *al.*, D. Martin Luthers Werke, kritische Gesamtausgabe
62: Ortsregister zur Abteilung Schriften Band 1-60 einschliesslich geo-
graphischer und ethnographischer Bezeichnungen. Weimar 1986, Böhlau.
408 p. M 11 [TLZ 112,17, S. *Bräuer*].

d559 **Junghans** Helmar, Der junge Luther und die Humanisten 1985 ➤ 1,f777;
3-525-55391-9; M 45; also Gö/VR. – ᴿGregorianum 67 (1986) 778s (J. E.
Vercruysse); RTLv 17 (1986) 367s (J. F. *Gilmont*); TLZ 111 (1986) 602-4
(B. *Moeller*: löst Erstarrungen).

d560 *Junghans* Helmar, Aus der Ernte des Lutherjubiläums 1983: LuthJb 53
(1986) 55-137; 138 Register (c. 100 items).

d561 **Lienhard** Marc, Martin Luther; un temps, une vie, un message 1983
➤ 64,e252; 65,d666: [R]RHR 203 (1986) 329-331 (G. *Audisio*); ScotJT 39
(1986) 138-140 (J. *Atkinson*).

d562 **McGrath** Alister E., Luther's theology of the Cross; Martin Luther's
theological breakthrough 1985 ➤ 1,f785: [R]TS 47 (1986) 328s (P. *Misner*).

d563 **Manns** Peter, Martin Luther, praef. *Lohse* E. 1982 ➤ 64,e255 [Eng.1983
➤ 64,e256]: [R]TLZ 111 (1986) 519-522 (S. *Bräuer*: now that the incense and
gunpowder-smoke of the centenary have drifted).

[E]**Mat** Michèle, *Marx* Jacques, [➤ 1,f788] Luther, mythe et réalité 1984
➤ 467.

d564 **Mülhaupt** E., Luther im 20. Jahrhundert; Aufsätze [39: 1936-80] 1982
➤ 64,207; DM 30: [R]Protestantesimo 41 (1986) 53-55 (V. *Subilia*).

d565 *Mülhaupt* Erwin, Sieben Kleine Kapitel über die Lebenswege Luthers
und Käthes [from notes of *Klepper* Jochen for continuation of 'Die Flucht
der Katharina von Bora' 1951 under title 'Das ewige Haus']: Luther 57
(1986) 1-18.

d566 **Olivier** Daniel, Luthers Glaube; die Sache des Evangeliums in der Kirche
1982 [1978 ➤ 60,y932; Eng. 1982 ➤ 64,e266]: [R]Luther 57 (1986) 149s
(R.-A. *Kliesch*).

d567 *a*) *Ottlyk* Ernö, Ⓜ Luther on preaching; – *b*) *Kocsis* Elemér, ... in
Calvinism; – *c*) *Szigeti* Jenö, ... in Free Churches: Theologiai Szemle 29
(1986) 268-274 / 275-8 / 278-281.

d568 [E]**Ruokanen** Miikka, Luther in Finland: Luther-Agricola-Gesellschaft
A-22. Helsinki 1984. 218 p. [RHE 82,392].

d569 [E]**Skowronek** Alfons, Martin Luther in ökumenischer Reflexion, Wsz
1982/4 ➤ 65,543: [R]DivThom 88 (1985) 166-9 (S. *Cavallotto*); ScripTPamp
18 (1986) 308-310 (K. *Limburg*).

d570 *Smolinsky* Heribert, Ⓟ 'Od kacerza do wspólnego nauczyciela' ... Vom
Ketzer zum gemeinsamen Lehrer; Martin Luther in der deutschen
katholischen Geschichtsschreibung des 20. Jahrhunderts: AnCracov 18
(1986) 535-546.

d571 *Steinmetz* David C., Luther in context. Bloomington 1986, Indiana
Univ. 146 p. $8 [TTod 44,394, F. *Posset*].

d572 **Süssmuth** Hans, Das Luther-Erbe in Deutschland; Vermittlung zwischen
Wissenschaft und Öffentlichkeit [23 Art. für 1983 meist von Journalisten].
Düsseldorf 1985, Droste. 374 p. [TPhil 62,284, W. *Löser*].

d573 **Thomas** Terry C., The Paul-Luther relationship in terms of their
interpretation of Scripture: diss. Marquette, [D]*Hagen* K. Milwaukee 1985.
282 p. 86-04963. – DissA 47 (1986s) 219s-A.

d574 *Weber* Wolfgang, Bemerkungen zu Luthers praktischem Beitrag bei de
Ausbreitung und Durchsetzung seiner Lehre: ZKG 97 (1986) 309-333 [*al.*,
189; 205].

d575 [E]**Yule** George, Luther, theologian for Catholics and Protestants 1985
➤ 1,413: [R]JEH 37 (1986) 632s (P. N. *Brooks*); RefTR 45 (1986) 61 (R.
Doyle; Yule and Ian SIGGINS are Australian); TLond 39 (1986) 239s
(Daphne *Hampson*: fails to show that Luther is anything of the sort).

Y4.3 Exegesis et controversia saeculi XVI.

d576 **Aland** Kurt, A history of Christianity, 2. From the Reformation to the
present [1980], [T]*Schaaf* James L. Ph 1986, Fortress. 644 p. [JAAR
55,419]. $30.

d577 **Bainton** Roland H., The Reformation of the sixteenth century (1952),

²*Pelikan* Jaroslav.   Boston 1985, Beacon.   xv-278 p. $10 pa. [TDig 33, 352].

d578 **Simpler** Steven J.,   Roland H. BAINTON, an examination of his Reformation historiography: Texts and Studies in Religion 24. Lewiston NY 1985, Mellen. 253 p. $50 [TDig 33,488].

d579 **Bentley** J.,   Humanists and Holy Writ 1983 ➤ 64,e290; 65,d693:   ᴿCath-HR 72 (1986) 79s (C. A. L. *Jarrott* †); JBL 105 (1986) 552-4 (E. J. *Epp*); JRel 66 (1986) 76s (J. *Wicks*).

d580 *Boughton* Lynne C.,   Supralapsarianism and the role of metaphysics in sixteenth-century Reformed theology: WestTJ 48 (1986) 63-96.

d581 **Bujanda** J. M. De,   Index des livres interdits [analyse critique de tous les Indices ᴱ*Reusch* H. 1886], 1. (Paris 1544-1556); 2. (Louvain 1546-1558); 5. (Espagne 1551-9): Centre d'Études de la Renaissance.   Sherbrooke 1986-5-4, Univ. 587 p.; ...; 799 p. [RHE 82,369s, J.-F. *Gilmont*].

d582 **Collett** Barry,   Italian Benedictine scholars and the Reformation; the congregation of Santa Giustina of Padua: Historical Monographs.   Ox 1985, Clarendon. x-287 p. $46 [TDig 33,357].

d583 ᴱ**De Molen** Richard L.,   Leaders of the Reformation 1984 ➤ 1,f811: ᴿAndrUnS 24 (1986) 270-2 (K. A. *Strand*).

d584 **Dent** C. M.,   Protestant Reformers in Elizabethan Oxford 1983 ➤ 65, d696: ᴿHeythJ 27 (1986) 464s (D. *Loades*); JTS 37 (1986) 645s (C. *Haigh*).

d585 **Dickens** A. G., *Tonkin* John M.,   The Reformation in historical thought.   Ox 1986, Blackwell. xii-443 p. – ᴿHistTheor 25 (1986) 336-342 (G. R. *Elton*).

d586 **Eire** Carlos M.,   War against the idols; the reformation of worship from Erasmus to Calvin.   NY 1986, Cambridge-UP. x-325 p. $37.50 [TDig 34,67].

d587 **Estep** William R.,   Renaissance and Reformation.   GR/Exeter 1986, Eerdmans/Paternoster. xxi-331 p. £19.50. / 0-8028-0050-5. – ᴿExpTim 98 (1986s) 249 (P. N. *Brooks*: not history repeats itself, but historians repeat one another; no advance on the very successful same title of Vivian GREEN 1960); SWJT 29,2 (1986s) 44 (A. *Outler*).

d588 **Evans** G. R., [➤ d486] The language and logic of the Bible [II.] The road to reformation 1985 ➤ 1,f811: ᴿNBlackf 67 (1986) 292s (O. *Lewry*).

d589 *a) Fatio* Oliver,   Quelle Réformation? Les commémorations genevoises de la Réformation à travers les siècles; – *b) Bedouelle* Guy, Les historiens catholiques et la Réforme protestante; – *c) Lienhard* Marc, Luther... *Ganoczy* Alexandre, Calvin avait-il conscience de réformer l'Église?: – *d) Duquoc* Christian,   Fonction contemporaine de la Réforme; – *e) Ricca* Paolo,   Réforme et œcuménisme: RTPhil 118 (1986) 111-130 / 131-144 / 145-159.161-177 / 179-186 / 187-195.

d590 *Honée* Eugène,   Hereniging door schikking; over de institutionele grondslag van de duitse godsdienstgesprekken vóór Trente: TsTNijm 26 (1986) 217-238; 239, Reunion through settlement; the German religious discussions before Trent.

d591 **Horst** Ulrich,   Zwischen Konziliarismus und Reformation; Studien zur Ekklesiologie im Dominikanerorden: Diss. hist. 22. R 1985, Ist. Storico S. Sabina. 189 p. – ᴿRSPT 70 (1986) 325 (Y. *Congar*).

d592 **Iserloh** Erwin,   Katholische Theologen der Reformationszeit [Is, 1984s ➤ 1,362] 3. Katholisches Leben und Kirchenreform im Zeitalter der Glaubensspaltung 46. Münster 1986, Aschendorff. 102 p.; 2 fig. DM 24. – ᴿJEH 37 (1986) 496s (A. D. *Wright*, 1-2); RHE 81 (1986) 637s (J.-F. *Gilmont*).

d593 **Jones** R. Tudur,   The great reformation; from Wyclif to Knox — two centuries that changed the course of history 1985 ► 1,f818:   0-85110-468-1:   RExpTim 97 (1985s) 346 (P. N. *Brooks*; good, unsubtle).

d594 **Lienhard** Marc, *Willer* Jakob,   Strassburg und die Reformation². Morstadt 1982, Kehl.   372 p. – RLuther 57 (1986) 48 (W. A. *Schulze*).

d595 **Merlo** Grado G.,   Valdesi e valdismi medievali [trasformatisi in chiesa riformata con Chanforan 1532]. T 1984, Claudiana.   158 p. Lit. 14.000. – RAevum 60 (1986) 363s (G. L. *Potestà*); Protestantesimo 41 (1986) 117-9 (O. *Coïsson*); cf. p. 175-7 (e 149-55) su *Audisio* G. 1984; RHR 203 (1986) 214s (G. *Audisio*).

d596 **Miller** J.,   Scripture and the English Reformation: diss. Fuller. Pasadena 1982 ► 64,e310 [ZAW 98 (1986) 116: allegorical and symbolical interpretations were rejected in theory but not altogether in practice].

d597 *Mitchell* Mary Jane, *al*.,   A catalog of Reformation tracts [Flugschriften] in the heritage room of the James White Library, Andrews University: AndrUnS 24 (1986) 81-98; facsimiles 99-112; p. 173-180, *Strand* Kenneth A.,   Two notes concerning pamphlet literature of the Reformation era.

d598 **Oberman** H. A.,   I maestri della Riforma; la formazione di un nuovo clima intellettuale in Europa [Werden und Wertung 1979 ► 60,y980, Eng. 1981 ► 65,d704]. Bo 1982, Mulino.   521 p. Lit. 30.000. – RProtestantesimo 41 (1986) 174s (G. *Gonnet*).

d599 **Ohly** Friedrich,   Gesetz und Evangelium; zur Typologie bei Luther und Lucas CRANACH; zum Blutstrahl der Gnade in der Kunst: Münster Univ. Schr. 1.   Münster 1985, Aschendorff.   v-125 p.; 32 fig.; 1 foldout. DM 16 [TLZ 112,211s, Helga *Neumann*].

d600 **Pauck** Wilhelm † 1981, EPauck Marion, his wife,   From Luther to Tillich; the Reformers and their heirs. SF 1985, Harper & R.   xxiii-223 p. $20. – RHorizons 13 (1986) 424s (A. B. *Crabtree*: brilliant).

d601 **Pelikan** Jaroslav,   Reformation of Church and dogma (1300-1700): A history of the development of doctrine 4, 1984 ► 65,d705; 1,f828:   RCurrTM 13 (1986) 380s (T. F. *Mayer*).

d602 *Russell* Elizabeth,   Marian Oxford and the counter-reformation: ► 22*, FDuBoulay P. 1985, 212-227.

d603 **Russell** Paul A.,   Lay theology in the Reformation; popular pamphleteers in southwest Germany 1521-1525.   C 1986, Univ.   xvi-287 p. £27.50 [ScotJT 40, 466-8, E. *Cameron*].

d604 **Schmidt** Peter,   Das Collegium Germanicum in Rom und die Germaniker; zur Funktion eines römischen Ausländerseminars, 1552-1914: Bibliothek des Deutschen Historischen Instituts in Rom 56.   Tü 1984, Niemeyer.   xvi-364 p. – RTüTQ 166 (1986) 67-70 (R. *Reinhardt*).

d605 **Seguenny** André, *al*.,   Bibliotheca dissidentium; répertoire des non-conformistes religieux des seizième et dix-septième siècles, 7 [*Franck* S., (compléments à *Kaczerowsky* K.) et deux autres]: Bibliotheca bibliographica aureliana 106.   Baden-Baden 1986, Koerner.   192 p. [RHE 82,341, J.-F. *Gilmont*].

d606 **Sell** Alan P. F.,   The great debate; Calvinism, Arminianism and salvation. Worthing 1982, Walter.   £3. – RScotJT 39 (1986) 140s (A. *Heron*).

d607 **Spitz** Lewis W.,   The Protestant Reformation, 1517-1559: Rise of Modern Europe 1985 ► 1,f832:   RJAAR 54 (1986) 613-5 (A. *Fix*).

d608 **Weir** David A.,   Foedus naturale; the origins of federal theology in sixteenth century Reformation thought: diss. St. Andrews 1984.   255 p. 86-09023. – DissA 47 (1986s) 559s-A.

d609 **Welti M.**, Breve storia della Riforma italiana [1985 ⇥ 1,f833], [T?] Casale Monferrato 1985, Marietti. xvi-172 p. Lit. 14.000. – [R]Protestantesimo 41 (1986) 22-27 (G. *Spini*).

d610 **Willis** John R., A history of Christian thought; 3. From Luther [mostly on his contemporaries] to Marx. Pompano Beach FL 1985, Exposition. ix-386 p. $20. – [R]TS 47 (1986) 718s (G. H. *Tavard*).

Y4.4   Periti aetatis reformatoriae.

d611 AGRICOLA: **Kjeldgaard-Pedersen** Steffen, Gesetz, Evangelium und Busse; theologiegeschichtliche Studien zum Verhältnis zwischen dem jungen Johann Agricola (Eisleben) und Martin Luther: Acta Theologica Danica 16, 1983 ⇥ 64,e248: [R]LuthJb 53 (1986) 144-6 (M. *Schloemann*).

d612 ARMINIUS: **Bangs** Carl, Arminius, a study in the Dutch reformation. GR 1985, Asbury. 388 p. $11. 0-310-29481-9. – [R]ÉTRel 61 (1986) 603s (A. *Gounelle*: père des 'Resmontrants').

d613 **Nicholas** James & William, The works of James Arminius [1560-1609; 1825-75 London edition reprint], introd. *Bangs* Carl. GR 1986, Baker. xliv-770 p.; viii-754 p.; vii-658 p. $75 [TDig 34,58].

d614 BELLARMINUS: **Sieben** Hermann J., Robert Bellarmin und die Zahl der Ökumenischen Konzilien: TPhil 61 (1986) 24-59.

d615 BEZA: *Raitt* Jill, Beza, guide for the faithful life: ScotJT 39 (1986) 83-107.

d616 BUCER: **Hammann** G., Entre la secte et la cité; le projet d'Église du Réformateur Martin Bucer, 1491-1551: Histoire et Société 3. Genève 1984, Labor et Fides. 483 p. – [R]CrNSt 7 (1986) 415-8 (L. *Donvito*).

d617 BUGENHAGEN: *Holfelder* Hans H., Bugenhagens Theologie — Anfänge, Entwicklungen und Ausbildungen bis zum Römerbriefkolleg 1525: Luther 57 (Wu 1986) 65-80.

d618 *a)* *Leder* Hans-Günter, Zum gegenwärtigen Stand der Bugenhagenforschung: De Kennung 8 (1985) 21-45 [*al.*, 5-100, 500.Gb.1985]; – *b)* *Gülzow* Henneke, D. Johannes Bugenhagen-Pommer und das Mare Balticum: Mare Balticum (1985) 85-90 [*al.* -97; TLZ 112,200].

d619 CAJETAN: *Lohse* Bernhard, Cajetan und Luther — zur Begegnung von Thomismus und Reformation: KerDo 32 (1986) 150-169; Eng. 169.

d620 **Wicks** Jared, Cajetan und die Anfänge der Reformation: KLK 43, 1983 ⇥ 64,e326... 1,f842: [R]JTS 37 (1986) 642s (G. *Rupp*); TLZ 111 (1986) 202-4 (W. *Rochler*).

d621 CALVIN: *Békési* Andor, Ⓜ Calvin's Hermeneutics: Theologiai Szemle 28 (1985) 21-26.

d622 *a)* *Bouwsma* William J., The quest for the historical Calvin; – *b)* *McGrath* Alister E., John Calvin and late medioeval thought; – *c)* *Fischer* Danielle, L'histoire de l'Église dans la pensée de Calvin: ArRefG 77 (1986) 47-57, deutsch 57 / 58-78. deutsch 78 / 79-125, Eng. 129.

d623 [E]**Chaunu** Pierre, L'aventure de la Réforme; le monde de Jean Calvin. P 1986, Hermé/Desclée-B. 295 p. F 420. 2-86665-036-0. – [R]ÉTRel 61 (1986) 596s A. *Gounelle*: ouvrage d'art; dernier chapitre faux et injuste).

d624 *Clifford* Alan C., John Calvin and the Confessio fidei gallicana: EvQ 58 (1986) 195-206.

d625 *Fuchs* E., La morale selon Calvin: Histoire de la morale. P 1986, Cerf. 186 p. 2-204-02502-X. – [R]ÉTRel 61 (1986) 600-2 (J. *Ansaldi*).

d626 **Ganoczy** A., *Scheld* S., Die Hermeneutik Calvins 1983 ⇥ 65,d719; 1,f843: [R]ZKG 97 (1986) 123-5 (W. H. *Neuser*).

d627 *a) Heron* Alasdair J. C., Calvinismus; – *b) Neuser* Wilhelm, Calvins Theologie: → 587, EvKL 1 (1986) 615-621-630.

d628 ᴱ**McKim** Donald K., Readings in Calvin's theology 1984 → 1,f846: ᴿCalvinT 21 (1986) 233-5 (J. A. *De Jong*).

d629 ᴱ**Potter** G. R. †, *Greengrass* M., John Calvin: Documents of Modern History. L 1983, Arnold. xvi-176 p. £5. – ᴿHeythJ 27 (1986) 92s (N. P. *Tanner*).

d630 **Selinger** Suzanne, Calvin against himself. Hamden CT 1984, Archon. 238 p. – ᴿChH 55 (1986) 523s (E. *Dean*); JEH 37 (1986) 501s (R. *Bauckham*).

d631 *Szabó* László, Ⓜ Calvin the exegete: Theologiai Szemle 29 (1986) 231-5 [216-231, in Romania-Transylvania, L. *Tőkés*].

d632 CHEMNITZ: *Müller* Gerhard, Martin Chemnitz (1522-1586); ein Reformator der zweiten Generation: Luther 57 (Wu 1986) 119-127.

d633 *Volk* Ernst, Der andere Martin; eine Erinnerung an den lutherischen Theologen Martin Chemnitz: LuthTKi 10 (1986) 81-95. 145-155...

d634 DIEGO V.: **Vázquez Janeiro** Isaac, Tratados castellanos sobre la predestinación y sobre la Trinidad y la Encarnación, del Maestro Fray Diego de Valencia OFM (siglo XV); identificación de su autoría y edición crítica: Bibliotheca Theologica Hispana, Textos 2. M 1984, Inst. F. Suárez. 184 p. – ᴿRTLv 17 (1986) 231s (E. *Brito*).

d635 DIEGO Z.: **Bolado Ochoa** G., Fray Diego de Zuñiga O.S.A. [Didacus a Stunica 1536-c.1599, not to be confused with his homonym † 1531, adversary of Erasmus and Lefèvre; but Zuñiga also is better known as an exegete]: una filosofia como enciclopedía de las ciencias o los artes en el siglo XVI [diss. Salamanca 1984]: RAg 26 (1985) 105-150 [RHE 82,147].

DIETENBERGER Johannes, Phimostomus scripturariorum ['A muzzle for biblists' on urgent questions of the day, such as Scripture and Tradition, Purgatory, veneration of saints] Köln 1532, ᴱ*Iserloh* Erwin, *Fabisch* Peter *al.*: Corpus Catholicorum 38, 1985 → 1037.

d637 ERASMUS: **Augustijn** Cornelis, Erasmus. Baarn 1986, Ambo. 200 p. *f*39,50 [GerefTTs 86,257].

d638 **Augustijn** Cornelis, Erasmus von Rotterdam; Leben – Work – Wirkung, ᵀ*Baumer* Marga E. Mü 1986, Beck. 201 p. DM 48 [WienerSt 100,343, Christine *Harrauer*].

d639 *Augustijn* Cornelis, Erasmus and Menno SIMONS: MennoniteQR 60 (Goshen IN 1986) 497-508 [< ZIT].

d640 **Boyle** Marjorie O., Rhetoric and reform; Erasmus' civil dispute with Luther: HarvHistMon 71, 1983 → 65,d726: ᴿJRel 66 (1986) 207 (B. A. *Gerrish*).

d641 **Carrington** Jane L., Erasmus and the problem of language [he liked it clear but also allusive]: diss. Cornell. Ithaca NY 1986. 311 p. 86-28449. – DissA 47 (1986s) 3161-A.

d642 *Halkin* Léon-E., Érasme et Luther; le choc de deux réformes: FoiTemps 16 (1986) 453-473.

d643 *Heine* Susanne, Glaubensentscheidung und Glaubenserziehung; zur pädagogischen Aktualität der Kontroverse zwischen Erasmus und Luther: EvT 46 (1986) 113-127.

d644 *Herding* O., Erasmus v. Rotterdam: → 592, LexMA 3 (1986) 2096-2100.

d645 *Hoffmann* M., Erasmus on Church and ministry: Erasmus of Rotterdam Society Yearbook 6 (Fort Washington MD 1986) 1-30 [RHE 82,267*].

d646 **Holeczek** Heinz, Erasmus deutsch 1. Die volkssprachliche Rezeption des Erasmus von Rotterdam in der reformatorischen Öffentlichkeit 1519-1536

[< Diss. Freiburg 1981] 1983 ➤ 1,f854:   RTLZ 111 (1986) 444-7 (S. *Bräuer*: schreibt 'frommann-holzboog').

d647 TEMarc'hadour Germain, *Galibois* Roland, Erasme de Rotterdam et Thomas More, correspondance: Centre Études Renaissance 10. Sherbrooke 1985, Univ. L-267 p. [RHE 82,310-2, F. *Bierlaire*].

d648 *Margolin* Jean-Claude, Quinze années de travaux érasmiens (1970-1985): BiblHumRen 48 (1986) 585-619.

d649 *Padberg* Rudolf, Erasmus von Rotterdam und die Einheit der Kirche; zur Erinnerung an den 450. Todestag des Rotterdamers am 11. Juli: Catholica 40 (1986) 97-109.

d650 **Rummel** Erika, Erasmus' Annotations on the New Testament; from philologist to theologian.. Toronto 1986, Univ. xii-234 p. $35 [RelStR 13,352, R. *Kolb*].

d651 *Rummel* Erika, Nameless critics in Erasmus' Annotations on the NT: BiblHumRen 48 (1986) 41-57.

d652 *a) Tracy* J.D., Humanists among the scholastics; Erasmus, MORE and LEFÈVRE d'Étaples on the humanity of Christ; – *b) Thompson* C.R., Three American Erasmians [*Hudson* H.; *Smith* P.; *Bainton* R.]: Erasmus of Rotterdam Yearbook 5 (1985) 30-51 / 4 (1984) 1-36 [RHE 82,389].

d653 FLACIUS: **Keller** Rudolf, Der Schlüssel zur Schrift; die Lehre vom Wort Gottes bei Matthias Flacius Illyricus [Diss. Erlangen 1982]: ArbGTL 5. Hannover 1984, Luth.V. 211 p. DM 25. – RTLZ 111 (1986) 44s (E. *Koch*).

d654 FRANCK Sebastian, [1499-1542; Catholic (priest) till 1525], 280 paradoxes or wondrous sayings, TEFurcha E.J.: Texts and Studies in Religion 5. Lewiston NY 1986, Mellen. 509 p. $60 [TDig 34,69].

d655 HUSS: *Machilek* Franz, Hus, Hussiten: ➤ 597, TRE 15 (1986) 710-735.

d656 *Molnár* Amedeo, La norma biblica nell'hussitismo, TConte Gino: Protestantesimo 41 (1986) 65-80.

d657 KNOX: *Kyle* Richard, John Knox's methods of biblical interpretation; an important source of his intellectual radicalness: JRelSt 12,1 (Cleveland 1984) 57-70 [< ZIT].

d658 LEFÈVRE: *Bedouelle* Guy, Une adaptation anglaise des Épistres et Évangiles de Lefèvre d'Étaples et ses disciples: BiblHumRen 48 (1986) 723-734.

d659 **Hughes** Philip E., Lefèvre [d'Étaples], pioneer of ecclesiastical renewal in France 1984 ➤ 1,f857: RAndrUnS 24 (1986) 189-191(D.A. *Augsburger*); CathHR 72 (1986) 93s (H. *Heller*); ChH 55 (1986) 227s (R.A. *Mentzer*); GraceTJ 7 (1986) 261s (J.E. *McGoldrick*).

d660 MALDONADO: **Schmitt** Paul, La Réforme catholique; le combat de Maldonat (1534-1583): THist 74, 1985 ➤ 1,f859; F 240. 2-7010-1117-5: RÉTRel 61 (1986) 295 (P. *Petit* n'aime pas 'La réforme catholique'; 'Maldonat en son temps' aurait suffi); RHE 81 (1986) 722 (P. *Denis*).

d661 MORE: **Marius** Richard, Thomas More. NY 1984, Knopf. 562 p. $23. – RRExp 83 (1986) 319 (B.J. *Leonard*: captivating); also L 1986, Collins Fount. xxiv-562 p. £7.95. 0-00-626998-2. – RExpTim 98 (1986s) 64 ('Paidagogos': lawyerly in his use of the truth; as coarse as Luther in polemics; mocked other executions as well as his own; but never spoke evil of Jews; educated women but not for priesthood; noble to the core).

d662 PROPST: **Rudloff** Ortwin, Bonae litterae et Lutherus; Texte und Untersuchungen zu den Anfängen der Theologie des Bremer Reformator Jakob Propst: Hospitium Ecclesiae 14. Bremen 1985. 274 p. – RAugLv 36 (1986) 155s (A. *Zumkeller*).

d663 QUENSTEDT: TEPoellot Luther, The nature and character of theology; an introduction to the thought of Johann A. Quenstedt from Theologia didactico-polemica sive systema theologicum. St. Louis 1986, Concordia. 207 p. $13 pa. [TDig 33,485].

d664 SCHWENCKFELD: McLaughlin R. Emmet, Caspar Schwenckfeld [1489-1561], reluctant radical; his life to 1540. NHv 1986, Yale Univ. xii-250 p. $25 [TDig 33,479].

d665 TURRETIN: *Muller* Richard A., Scholasticism Protestant and Catholic; Francis Turretin on the object and principles of theology: ChH 55 (1986) 193-205.

d666 Phillips Timothy R., Francis Turretin's idea of theology and its bearing upon his doctrine of Scripture: diss. Vanderbilt, DFarley E. Nv 1986. 837 p. 86-16370. – DissA 47 (1986s) 1372-A; RelStR 13,190.

d667 VIRET: Bavaud Georges, Le Réformateur Pierre Viret (1511-1571), sa théologie: Histoire et Société 10. Genève 1986, Labor et Fides. 361 p. – REsprV 96 (1986) 540s (J. *Pintard*).

d668 WYCLIF: Fountain David, John Wycliffe, the dawn of the Reformation. Southampton 1984, Mayflower. 133 p. $4.50 pa. – RGraceTJ 7 (1986) 153s (J. E. *McGoldrick*).

d669 Kenny Anthony, Wyclif 1985 → 1,f870: RRHR 203 (1986) 217s (J.-C. *Margolin*); Theologiai Szemle 29 (1986) 57s (T. *Gorilovics*, Csilla *Lévai*).

d670 ZWINGLI: Gäbler Ulrich, Huldrych Zwingli; eine Einführung in sein Leben und sein Werk. Mü 1983, Beck. – RNedTTs 40 (1986) 90 (K. M. *Witteveen*).

d671 Gäbler Ulrich, Huldrych Zwingli, his life and work, TGritsch Ruth C. L. Ph 1986, Fortress. xiii-196 p. $25 [TDig 34,70].

d672 Locher Gottfried W., Die reformatorische Katholizität Huldrych Zwinglis: TZBas 42 (1986) 1-13.

d673 Spijker W. van 't, Gereformeerde Scholastiek III. Zwingli en Bucer: TRef 29 (Woerden 1986) 136-160 [< ZIT].

d674 Stephens W. Peter, The theology of Huldrych Zwingli. Ox 1986, Clarendon. 348 p. $52 [TDig 33,490]/ £27.50. 0-19-826677-4. – RExpTim 98 (1986s) 60 (P. N. *Brooks*: excellent).

d675 Winzeler Peter, Zwingli als Theologe der Befreiung: Polis 12. Ba 1986, Reinhardt. 113 p. [TLZ 112,442-4, J. *Rogge*].

Y4.5   *Exegesis post-reformatoria* – **Historical criticism to 1800.**

d676 Apologia Bibliorum [1697] (A Biblia védelmezése). Budapest 1985, Református Sajtóosztály. – RTheologiai Szemle 28 (1985) 382s (J. *Szigeti*).

d677 Avis Paul, Foundations of modern historical thought, from Machiavelli to Vico. L 1986, Croom Helm. ix-179 p. £20. – RTLond 39 (1986) 406 (L. *Houlden*).

d678 Bauer Barbara, Jesuitische 'ars rhetorica' im Zeitalter der Glaubens-kämpfe: Mikrokosmos 18. Fra 1986, Lang. ix-651 p. [TPhil 62,285, N. *Brieskorn*].

d679 Betts C. J., Early Deism in France [< diss. DShackleton R.] 1984 → 65,d741: RChH 55 (1986) 237s (W. A. *Poe*).

d680 Cohen Charles L., God's caress; the psychology of Puritan religious experience. NY 1986, Oxford-UP. 310 p. $30 [JAAR 55,382-4, T. D. *Bozeman*].

d681 Dompnier Bernard, Le venin de l'hérésie; image du protestantisme et combat catholique du XVIIe siècle; préf. *Delumeau* Jean: Chrétiens dans l'histoire. P 1985, Centurion. 288 p. – ᴿRThom 86 (1986) 506s (B. *Montagnes*).

d682 **Greaves** Richard L., Saints and rebels; seven nonconformists in Stuart England. Macon GA 1985, Mercer Univ. 223 p. $19 [JAAR 55,151, E. *More*].

d683 *Howley* Robert J. P., The notion of deism in relation to 17th and 18th century thought: diss. ᴰ*Pailin*. Manchester 1986. 418 p. – RTLv 18,574.

d684 **Laplanche** F., L'écriture, le sacré et l'histoire; érudits et politiques protestants devant la Bible en France au XVIIᵉ siècle: Études de l'Institut de recherches des relations intellectuelles entre les pays de l'Europe occidentale au XVIIᵉ siècle (Nijmegen) 12. Amst 1986, APA-Holland. xxxvi-1017 p.; 12 fig. F 220 [RHE 82,270*].

d685 *Martin-Achard* Robert, Aperçus [historiques] sur l'enseignement de l'Ancien Testament à l'Académie et à l'Université de Genève: RTPhil 118 (1986) 373-388.

d686 **Marty** Martin E., Pilgrims in their own land; 500 years of religion in America. Boston 1984, Little Brown. 500 p. $25. – ᴿRExp 83 (1986) 320s (B. J. *Leonard*: flies in the face of right-wing effort to re-Protestan[t]ize America).

d687 **Michel** Karl-Heinz, Anfänge der Bibelkritik; Quellentexte aus Orthodoxie und Aufklärung. Wu 1985, Brockhaus. 125 p. DM 19,80. – ᴿStreven 53 (1985s) 83s (P. *Beentjes*).

d688 **Reedy** Gerard, The Bible and reason; Anglicans and Scripture in late seventeenth-century England 1985 → 1,f883: ᴿJEH 37 (1986) 633-5 (M. *Goldie*); ScotR 7 (1986) 78s (D. W. *Bennington*: the Jesuit author is associate professor of English at Fordham).

d689 **Reventlow** H., Bibelautorität ... England 1980 → 61,y108a ... 1,f885: ᴿTsTKi 57 (1986) 301-6 (M. *Sæbø*).

d690 **Reventlow** Henning, The authority of the Bible and the rise of the modern world 1985 → 65,d748 ... 1,f686: ᴿCurrTM 13 (1986) 51s (R. *Gnuse*); JJS 37 (1986) 113s (P. *Wernberg-Møller*: absorbing); JRel 66 (1986) 332s (S. C. *Pearson*); ModT 3 (1986s) 205s (D. *Nineham*); RExp 83 (1986) 122 (E. G. *Hinson*); Thomist 50 (1986) 485s (L. *Boadt*); TLZ 111 (1986) 655s (S. *Wagner*).

d691 **Shapiro** Barbara J., Probability and certainty in seventeenth-century England; a study of the relationships between natural science, religion, history, law, and literature. Princeton 1983, Univ. 347 p. – ᴿHeythJ 27 (1986) 327 (G. F. *Nuttall*: too ambitious).

d692 ᴱ**Spencer** S. I., French women and the age of Enlightenment. Bloomington 1985, Indiana Univ. xvii-242 p. $35. – ᴿJournal of Modern History 58 (1986) 935-7 (D. *Goodman*) [RHE 82,312*].

d693 **Zaret** David, The heavenly contract; ideology and organization in pre-revolutionary Puritanism. Ch 1985, Univ. x-214 p. $22.50. – ᴿWestTJ 48 (1986) 404-7 (D. A. *Weir*).

d694 ALBERTI: **Sandt** Hubertus W. M. van de, Joan Alberti, een Nederlandse theoloog en classicus in de achttiende eeuw → 65,d751: diss. Utrecht 1984: ᴿRB 93 (1986) 296-8 (P. B. *Decock*).

d695 BACH: ᴱ**Petzoldt** Martin, Bach als Ausleger der Bibel 1985 → 1,304: ᴿTLZ 111 (1986) 537s (Helene *Werthemann*).

d696 BINGHAM: *Barnard* L. W., Joseph Bingham [c. 1702], the French Reformed Church and the comprehension question: HeythJ 27 (1986) 249-261.

d697 CHALLE: *Moureau* François, Robert Challe [Difficultés sur la religion proposées au père Malebranche 1767s, [E]*Deloffre* F. 1983] et le roman de la religion; notes critiques: RHR 203 (1986) 185-194.

d698 CHERBURY: *Pailin* David A., Herbert von Cherbury, [T]*Schröter* M.: → 597, TRE 15 (1986) 62-66.

d699 EDWARDS: **Clark** Stephen M., Jonathan EDWARDS, The history of redemption [30-sermon Nachlass]: diss. Drew. Madison NJ 1986. 429 p. 87-02256. – DissA 47 (1986s) 3786-A.

d700 **Sairsingh** Krister, Jonathan Edwards and the idea of divine glory; the trinitarian foundation of Edwards' theology and its ecclesial import: diss. Harvard 1986. – RelStR 13,188.

d701 GENET: **Pollock** James R., François Genet [17th century moralist]; the man and his methodology: AnGreg 237. R 1984, Pont. Univ. Gregoriana. 298 p. – [R]RHE 81 (1986) 195-8 (B. *Neveu*).

d702 GOODWIN: *Dallison* Anthony, The latter-day glory in the thought of Thomas Goodwin [c. 1650; = 'The latter-day glory in English Puritan thought', Gospel Magazine (July 1969) 316-331, foreshadowing *Murray* I., The Puritan hope 1971; [E]*Toon* P., Puritans 1970]: EvQ 58 (1986) 53-68.

d703 **Burgess** John P., The problem of Scripture and philosophical affairs as reflected in the Puritan revolution: Samuel RUTHERFORD, Thomas & John Goodwin, and Gerrard WINSTANLEY: diss. Chicago Divinity School 1986. – RelStR 13,191.

d704 *a) Knox* R. Buick, The Presbyterianism of Samuel RUTHERFORD; – *b) Thompson* John, Christian doctrine, yesterday and today: → 44, Mem. HAIRE J., IrBSt 8 (1986) 143-153 / 122-134.

d705 HAHN: [E]**Brecht** M., (*Paulus* R.), Die Kornwestheimer Tagebücher 1772-1777 des Philipp Matthäus Hahn: Texte zur Geschichte des Pietismus 8/1. B 1979, de Gruyter. 520 p.; ind. citat. bibl. DM 175 [RHE 82,346].

d706 HAMANN: **Corbin** Henri, Hamann [J. G. 1530-88], philosophe du luthéranisme. P 1985, Berg. 152 p. 2-900269-38-5. – [R]ÉTRel 61 (1986) 455 (J.-D. *Kraege*).

d707 HERDER: **Bunge** Marcia J., The restless reader; Johann Gottfried Herder's interpretations of the New Testament: diss. Chicago Divinity School 1986. – RelStR 13,190.

d708 *Herms* Eilert, Herder J. G. von (1744-1803): → 597, TRE 15 (1986) 70-95 (661-9, Humanität).

d709 HUME: *Addinall* Peter, Hume's challenge [Treatise 1739s, Dialogues 1779] and [William] PALEY's response: ExpTim 97 (1985s) 232-6.

d710 *Kulenkampff* Jens, Hume, David (1711-1776): → 597, TRE 15 (1986) 688-691.

d711 INGHAM: [E]**Heitzenrater** Richard F., Diary of an Oxford Methodist, Benjamin Ingham, 1733-1734. Durham NC 1985, Duke Univ. 304 p. $37.50 [JAAR 55,399s, R. E. *Luker*].

d712 JANSENIUS: *Ceyssens* Lucien, Autour de la bulle *Unigenitus*; *a)* la bulle *Pastoralis officii* (1718); – *b)* Correspondance de Don Alexandre ALBANI, neveu du pape Clément XI: Antonianum 61 (1986) 340-380 / 707-725.

d713 *Ceyssens* L., Autour de la bulle Unigenitus; Louis XIV: → 45, [F]HALKIN L. = Bull. Belge Rome 55s (1985s) 123-166 (-206).

d714 *Ceyssens* Lucien, Autour de la bulle Unigenitus; Madame de MAINTENON (1635-1719): AugLv 36 (1986) 101-154.

d715 **Vasquez** Isaac, L'œuvre sur le jansénisme [*Ceyssens* L.] 1979 → 60,z29: [R]RBgPg 64 (1986) 352s (J.-P. *Massaut*).

d716 LEIBNIZ: *Sparn* Walter, Das Bekenntnis des Philosophen; G. W. Leibniz als Philosoph und Theologe: NSys 28 (1986) 139-177; Eng. 177s.

d717 LESSING: **Michalson** G., Lessing's 'ugly ditch'... 1985 → 1,f906: ᴿJRel 66 (1986) 449s (W. *Wyman*); JTS 37 (1986) 676-9 (D. A. *Pailin*).

d718 **Lüpke** Johannes von, Wege der Weisheit; Studien zu Lessings Theologiekritik: Diss. Tübingen 1985. iv-376 p. – TLZ 112,637.

d719 MOLNÁR: *Takács* Béla, Ⓜ Molnár János, a Jesuit polemicist in the 18th century; Theologiai Szemle 29 (1986) 39-44.

d720 MONTAIGNE: *Boudou* Bénédicte, Montaigne et l'interprétation des Écritures-Saintes: Bulletin de la Société de l'Histoire du Protestantisme Français 132,1 (P 1986) 5-22 [< ZIT].

d721 MÜHLENBERG: ᴱ**Aland** Kurt, Die Korrespondenz Heinrich Melchior Mühlenbergs aus der Anfangszeit des deutschen Luthertums in Nordamerika, I: 1740-1752: Texte zur Geschichte des Pietismus 3/2. B/NY 1986, de Gruyter. xx-573 p. DM 295 [BTZ 4,269, P. E. *Hoffman*].

d722 SCHMIDT: L'œuvre exégétique d'un théologien strasbourgeois du 17ᵉ siècle, Sébastien Schmidt [1617-1696]: → 83*, ᶠPETER R. = RHPR 66 (1986) 71-78; Eng. 129.

d723 SIMON R., Additions à BREREWOOD, ᴱ*Le Brun* J. 1983 → 64,e385... 1,f914: ᴿRÉJ 145 (1986) 415-7 (B. E. *Schwarzbach*).

d724 SOUTH: *Reedy* Gerard, The Bible and reason; Anglicans and Scripture in Late Seventeenth-Century England [South Robert, STILLINGFLEET Edward, TILLOTSON John]. Ph 1985, Univ. Pennsylvania [RTPhil 119,119 (sic), Maria Cristina *Pitassi*; maigre sur SIMON].

d725 SPINOZA: *Siebrand* Heine J., Is God an 'open place' in Spinoza's philosophy of religion?: NSys 28 (1986) 261-273; deutsch 274s; 275-283, answer of *Naess* Arne.

d726 TOLAND: *Romagnani* Gian Paolo, 'Ideologia NEWTONiana' e 'illuminismo radicale' [Toland J.] nel recente dibattito storiografico; RivStoLR 22 (1986) 102-146.

d727 VOLTAIRE: **Trapnell** H. William, Christ and his 'associates' in Voltairian polemic; an assault on the Trinity and the Two Natures ['Like other absurdities masquerading as divine mysteries, the dogma was vulnerable to Voltairian satire' p. 253]: Stanford French and Italian Studies 26. Saratoga CA 1982, Anma. 268 p. – ᴿSR 15 (1986) 128s (G. *Vallée*).

d728 WESLEY: *MacCormack* J. T., The forgotten notes of John Wesley: IrBSt 8 (1986) 22-42.

Y5 *Saeculum XIX – Exegesis* – 19th Century.

Berger Klaus, Exegese und Philosophie: SBS 123s 1986 → 1138.

d730 **Cook** Ramsay, The regenerators; social criticism in Late Victorian English Canada. Toronto 1985, Univ. 291 p. $32; pa. 16 [JAAR 55,386s, R. T. *Handy*].

d731 **Duke** James O., The rise of biblical criticism; a review [*Reventlow* H. 1985; *Rogerson* J. 1985]: JAAR 54 (1986) 561-5.

d732 **Farley** Edward [→ 5160], Theologia; the [post-Enlightenment North American Protestant seminary] fragmentation and unity of theological education 1983 → 65,5814: ᴿHeythJ 27 (1986) 83-85 (J. E. *Thiel*).

d733 **Groh** John E., Nineteenth century German Protestantism; the Church as a social model. Wsh 1982, UPA. xxii-614 p. – ᴿTLZ 111 (1986) 756-8 (K. *Nowak*: durchaus sekundär).

d734 ᴱ**Gunn** G., The Bible and American arts and letters 1983 → 64,271: ᴿBibTB 16 (1986) 33 (J. F. *Craghan*).

d735 **Hefetz** Menahem, ⊕ The use of the Holy Scriptures in the propaganda of the Hohenstaufens: diss. Univ. Bar-Ilan. Ramat-Gan 1982. – KirSef 59 (1985) 313.

d736 ᴱ**McConica** James M., The Collegiate University; ᴱ**Sutherland** Lucy S., **Mitchell** L. G., The eighteenth century: [ᴱ*Aston* T. H.] The history of the University of Oxford 3.5. Ox 1986, Clarendon. xxiv-775 p., ill. £60; xx-949 p., ill., £75 [RHE 82,309s, G. *Temple*: magnificent].

d737 **Hoffecker** W. Andrew, Piety and the Princeton theologians 1981 → 62,m346 ... 65,d787: ᴿThemelios 11 (1985s) 104 (B. *Demarest*).

d738 **Kselman** Thomas A., Miracles and prophecies in nineteenth-century France. New Brunswick 1983, Rutgers Univ. $27.50. – ᴿEngHR 101 (1986) 531s (M. *Larkin*: 'Mariology and the miraculous have been a major source of embarrassment to Catholic intellectuals').

d739 **Marty** Martin E., Modern American religion, I. The irony of it all, 1893-1919 [four types of modernizing, one of reaction]. Ch 1986, Univ. xi-386 p. $25 [TDig 34,85: first volume of four].

d740 **Reardon** Bernhard M. G., Religion in the age of romanticism 1985 → 1,f929: ᴿJTS 37 (1986) 649-652 (D. *Jasper*); TLond 39 (1986) 408s (A. *Mason*).

d741 *Reardon* Bernhard M. G., Keeping up with recent studies XIV. Nineteenth century religious thought; A. Continental and Roman Catholic [in English only]: ExpTim 98 (1986s) 35-39; B. British and American: ExpTim 98 (1986s) 100-104, mostly bibliography.

d742 **Robinson** David, The unitarian and the universalist. Westport 1985, Greenwood. 368 p. $35 [JAAR 55, 176-9, M. D. *Morrison-Read*].

d743 **Rogerson** J., OT criticism in the nineteenth century 1984 → 65,d784: ᴿChH 55 (1986) 241s (D. L. *Pals*); Horizons 13 (1986) 416s (W. *Brueggemann*: splendid but not easy); Interpretation 40 (1986) 418.420 (M. *Hillmer*); NBlackf 67 (1986) 144s (P.*Joyce*); TrinJ 7 (1986) 86-92 (M. *Wise*); TTod 43 (1986s) 605s.608 (B. C. *Ollenburger*).

d744 ᴱ**Smart** Ninian, *al.*, Nineteenth century religious thought in the West III. 1985 → 1,399.f934: ᴿJTS 37 (1986) 654-662 (N. *Lash*); Month 248 (1986) 140 (C. *Gunton*, 3); NBlackf 67 (1986) 196s (H. F. G. *Swanston*, 2); NRT 109 (1987) 473 (P. *Gilbert*); ScotJT 39 (1986) 413-8 (R. H. *Roberts*, 1); TLond 39 (1986) 320-3 (D. W. *Hardy*, 1-3); TS 47 (1986) 544-6 (J. E. *Thiel*).

d745 **Smith** Gary S., The seeds of secularization; Calvinism, culture, and pluralism in America 1870-1915. GR 1985, Eerdmans (Christian Univ.) viii-239 p. $15 pa. – ᴿRRelRes 28 (1986s) 189s (W. H. *Swatos*).

d746 **Valenze** Deborah M., Prophetic sons and daughters; [heterodox Methodist] female preaching and popular religion in industrial England. Princeton 1985, Univ. xvi-308 p. $38.50 [Horizons 14, 156s, Amanda *Porterfield*).

d748 **Vree** Jasper, De Groninger godgeleerden; de oorsprong en de eerste periode van hun optreden (1820-1843) [diss. Vrije Univ., ᴰ*Augustijn* C.]. Kampen 1984. 367 p. ƒ65. – ᴿNedTTs 40 (1986) 248s (A. de *Groot*).

d749 **Welch** Claude, Protestant thought in the nineteenth century [I. 1985 = 1972 → 54,a394]; II. 1870-1914. NHv 1985, Yale Univ. xii-315 p. $25 [TDig 33,493]. 0-300-0-[1535-6]; 3369-9. – ᴿExpTim 98 (1986s) 155s (B. M. G. *Reardon*); TS 47 (1986) 750s (J. E. *Thiel*: admirable).

d750 ᴱ**Wells** David F., Reformed theology; essays in its modern expression in America; **Princeton**, *Noll* Mark A.; HODGE C., *Wells* D.; WARFIELD B., *Hoffecker* W.; **Westminster**, *Godfrey* W.; MACHEN J., *Reid* W.; VAN TIL

C., *Roberts W.;* **Dutch Schools,** *Bratt* J.; BERKHOF L., *Zwaanstra* H.;
DOOYERWEERD H., *McIntire* C.; **Southern,** *Smith* Morton H.; DABNEY R.,
Kelly D.; THORNWELL J., *Whitlock* L.; **Neo-Orthodoxy,** *Voskuil* D.;
NIEBUHR Reinhold, *Fackre* G.; NIEBUHR H. Richard, *Reid* M.; ... the
future, *Boice* J. GR/Exeter 1986, Eerdmans/Paternoster. £20. 0-8028-
0096-3 [EvQ 58,38 adv].

d751 BAUR: *Gerrish* B. A., Baur F. C. (1792-1860): ➤ 585, EncRel 2 (1986)
    84s (84 also BAUER Bruno by *Harvey* Van A.).

d752 **Meijering** E. P.,   F. C. Baur als Patristiker; die Bedeutung seiner
    Geschichtsphilosophie und Quellenforschung.   Amst 1986, Gieben.
    ix-183 p.; portr.; bibliog. p. 171-5.   90-70275-68-0.

d753 BUSHNELL: ᴱCherry Conrad,   Horace Bushnell, sermons.   NY 1985,
    Paulist.   237 p. $13 [JAAR 55,381s, C. E. *Johnson*].

d754 **Peterson** Edward R.,   The Horace Bushnell controversy; a study of heresy
    in nineteenth century America, 1828-1854: diss. Iowa, ᴰ*Bozeman* T. Iowa
    City 1985. – 453 p. 86-11129. – DissA 47 (1986s) 944-A; RelStR 13,191.

d755 ᴱ**Smith** David L.,   Horace Bushnell, selected writings on language,
    religion, and American culture. Atlanta 1984, Scholars.   187 p. $9.75; sb.
    $8.25 [JAAR 55,381s, C. E. *Johnson*].

d756 DREY: **Harskamp** A. van,   Theologie, tekst in context [sic]; op zoek naar
    de methode van ideologiekritische analyse van de theologie, geillustreerd
    aan het werk van Drey, MÖHLER en STAUDENMEIER: Cath. diss.
    Nijmegen, ᴰ*Schillebeeckx* E.   viii-497 p.; 123 p. – TsTNijm 26 (1986) 289.

d757 *Thiel* John E., J. S. Drey on doctrinal development; the context of
    Theological Encyclopedia [Kurze Einleitung 1819]: HeythJ 27 (1986)
    290-305.

d757* FINNEY: **Weddle** David L.,   The Law as Gospel; revival and reform in
    the theology of Charles G. Finney.   Pittsburgh 1985, Scarecrow.   281 p.
    $23.50. [JAAR 55,189s, K. J. *Hardman*].

d758 GUÉRANGER: *Yon* Ephrem,   Autour de Dom [Prosper] Guéranger;
    questions du XIXᵉ siècle et actualité liturgique: NRT 108 (1986) 76-92.

d759 HEGEL G. W. F.,   Three essays [ᴱ*Nohl* H. 1907 omitted in ᵀ*Knox* T. 1948;
    'Life of Jesus'], ᵀ*Fuss* P., *Dobbins* J. 1984 ➤ 65,d805: ᴿJAAR 54 (1986)
    586s (P. C. *Hodgson*).

d760 **Asendorf** Ulrich, LUTHER und Hegel 1982 ➤ 65,d804; 1,f948: ᴿTRu 51
    (1986) 414-420 (J. *Ringleben*).

d761 **Davis** Richard A.,   Hegel's concept of property; diss. Marquette.
    Milwaukee 1985.   150 p. 86-04951. – DissA 47 (1986s) 200s-A.

d762 *Devos* Rob,   God, mens wordend; Hegels visie op het christendom:
    Streven 53 (1985) 3-13.

d763 **Franz** Albert,   Glauben und Denken; Franz Anton STAUDENMEIERS
    Hegelkritik als Anfrage an das Selbstverständnis heutiger Theologie:
    Eichstätter Studien NF 18, 1983 ➤ 1,f949:   ᴿTR 82 (1986) 155-9 (C.
    Kronabel).

d764 *Greco* Carlo,   La crisi della coscienza moderna nella filosofia della
    religione di Hegel [ᴱ*Jaeschke* W. 1983]: RasT 27 (1986) 97-119.

d765 **Huber** Herbert,   Idealismus und Trinität, Pantheon und Götter-
    dämmerung; Grundlagen und Grundzüge der Lehre von Gott nach dem
    Manuskript Hegels zur Religionsphilosophie [Diss. München 1983]:
    Weinheim 1984, Acta Humaniora.   207 p. – ᴿZRGg 38 (1986) 376-8 (E.
    Schadel).

d766 *Ravven* H. M.,   Unmasking the true Hegel; a critique of Emil
    FACKENHEIM's Hegelianism: JRelSt 13 (Cleveland 1985s) 25-40 [< ZIT].

d767 *Schlitt* Dale M., Hegel on religion and identity: ÉglT 17 (1986) 195-221.

d768 **Verene** Donald P., Hegel's recollection; a study of images in the Phenomenology of spirit. Albany 1985, SUNY. xiv-148 p. $39.50; pa. $24.50. – RRelStR 12 (1986) 265 (P. C. *Hodgson*: unique, valuable).

d769 HORT: *Glasswell* Mark E., Hort, Fenton John Anthony (1828-1892), T*Wildemann* B.: → 597, TRE 15 (1986) 584-6.

d770 JOWETT: *Hinchliff* Peter, Ethics, evolution and biblical criticism in the thought of Benjamin Jowett and John William COLENSO: JEH 37 (1986) 91-110.

d771 KANT: **d'Aviau de Ternay** H., Traces bibliques dans la loi morale de Kant: Bibliothèque des Archives de Philosophie NS 46. P 1986, Beauchesne. 296 p. 2-7010-1130-2. – RÉTRel 61 (1986) 615 (J. *Ansaldi*).

d772 *Godlove* Terry F.J, Recent work on Kant on religion: RelStR 12 (1986) 229-233.

d773 LAMAR: *Allen* C. Leonard, Baconianism and the Bible in the Disciples of Christ; James S. Lamar and 'The Organon of Scripture': ChH 55 (1986) 65-80.

d774 MIGNE: E**Mandouze** A., *Fouilheron* J., Migne et le renouveau des études patristiques; Actes du Colloque de Saint-Flour, 7-8 juillet 1975: THist 66, 1985 → 1,611: RNRT 108 (1986) 585s (V. *Roisel*); RThom 86 (1986) 508s (B. *Montagnes*); ScripTPamp 18 (1986) 692-5 (M. *Merino*).

d775 *Hamman* Adalbert, Les principaux collaborateurs des deux Patrologies de Migne [*Soltner* S., GUÉRANGER, PITRA; CATRICE P., DRACH P.]: → d774, E*Mandouze* A., Migne 1975/85, 179-191 [193-209; 211-224].

d776 *Savart* Claude, Un éditeur révolutionnaire au service de la tradition: → d774, E*Mandouze* A., Migne 1975/85, 145-158.

d777 NIETZSCHE: **Biser** Eugen, Gottsucher oder Antichrist? Nietzsches provokative Kritik des Christentums 1982 → 64,e416: RGregorianum 67 (1986) 184s (S. *Decloux*).

d778 **Ledure** Yves, Lectures 'chrétiennes' de Nietzsche: MAURRAS, PAPINI, SCHELER, DE LUBAC, MARCEL, MOUNIER. Maubourg 1984, Cerf. 166 p. F 66 [TR 83,152-4, J. *Figl*].

d779 ORR: **Scorgie** Glen G., A call for continuity; the theological contribution of James Orr: diss. D*Cameron* J. St Andrews 1986. – RTLv 18,558.

d780 *Hoefel* Robert J., B. B. WARFIELD and James Orr; a study in contrasting approaches to Scripture: ChrSchR 16 (GR 1986) 40-52 [< ZIT].

d781 PFLEIDERER: **Leigh** Bruce K., Otto Pfleiderer and Protestant theology in nineteenth-century Germany: diss. Chicago 1985. – RTLv 18,557.

d782 SCHLEIERMACHER Friedrich, Jugendschriften 1787-1796, E*Meckenstock* Günter: Kritische Gesamtausgabe 1/1, 1984 → 1,f967: RRelStR 12 (1986) 235-8 (A. L. *Blackwell*).

d783 *Fischer* Hermann, F. D. E. Schleiermacher (1768-1834) rappresentante del protestantesimo moderno: RasT 27 (1986) 324-337.

d784 **Gerrish** B., A prince of the Church, Schleiermacher 1984 → 65,d811; 1,f966: RJRel 66 (1986) 78s (R. *Crouter*).

d785 E**Peiter** Hermann, Friedrich Schleiermacher, Der christliche Glaube nach den Grundsätzen der evangelischen Kirche im Zusammenhange dargestellt (1821-22), 1-2 (3. Marginalien und Anhang, E*Barth* Ulrich): Kritische Gesamtausgabe 1/7. B 1980(-4), de Gruyter. lxvi-357 p.; viii-409 p.; DM 248 (xxv-672 p.; DM 242) → 63,e910: RRelStR 12 (1986) 238-240 (B. A. *Gerrish*: 1-2 paperback appeared 1984).

d786 **Proudfoot** Wayne, Religious experience [Schleiermacher (also JAMES,

OTTO, and even BARTH) by vindicating the subjective limit inquiry].
Berkeley 1985, Univ. California. xix-263 p. $25. – ᴿRelStR 12 (1986) 272
(P. C. *Hodgson*: important, controversial).

d787 *Turnwald* Erik, Ein bisher unbekannter Brief Friedrich Schleiermachers
vom 15. Dezember 1800 an F. H. C. SCHWARZ, Pfarrer in Münster bei
Butzbach [so richtig p. 391; aber im Inhalt p. II 'an F. H. C. Barth']: ZKG
97 (1986) 391-403.

d788 **Wyman** Walter E., The [Schleiermacher] concept of 'Glaubenslehre':
AAR 144, 1983 → 65,d814*a*; ᴿRechSR 74 (1986) 454-7 (J. *Doré*; ibid. sur
GERRISH B., KELLER-WENTORF C.; ᴱFRERICHS J.; ᴱSORRENTINO S.).

d789 SERWATOWSKI: *Bednarz* Michał, ℗ Ks. Walerian Serwatowski —
wybitny biblista polski XIX w.: → 367, Sympozjum 1985 = RuBi 39
(1986) 274-8.

d790 SMITH: **Riesen** R. A., Criticism and faith in ... A. B. DAVIDSON, W. R.
Smith, G. A. Smith 1985 → 1,f930: ᴿAustralBR 34 (1986) 83s (I.
Breward); ChH 55 (1986) 245s (L. G. *Taft*); RefTR 45 (1986) 23s (A. M.
Harman); WestTJ 48 (1986) 198-200 (W. S. *Reid*).

d791 SPURGEON: *Whitcomb* John C., C. H. Spurgeon, biblical inerrancy, and
premillennialism [*Skinner* C., Lamplighter and son, 1984]: GraceTJ 7
(1986) 229-234.

d792 STRAUSS: *Geisser* Hans-Friedrich, Glück und Unglück eines Theologen
mit seiner Kirche — am Beispiel der beiden Tübinger Johann Adam
MÖHLER und David Friedrich Strauss: ZTK 83 (1986) 85-110.

d793 **Graf** Friedrich W., Kritik und Pseudo-Spekulation; D. F. Strauss als
Dogmatiker im Kontext der positionellen Theologie seiner Zeit ᴰ 1982
→ 64,e421; 1,f972: ᴿJAAR 54 (1986) 175 (F. S. *Fiorenza*); TLZ 111 (1986)
54-57 (K. *Nowak*).

d794 **Gunton** Colin, Enlightenment and alienation [... Strauss D. F.]. L 1985,
Marshall-MS. 166 p. £8 [ScotJT 40,613-6, D. *Brown*].

d795 **Lawler** Edwina G., David F. Strauss and his critics; the Life of Jesus
debate in early nineteenth-century German journals: AmerUnivSt7/16.
NY 1986, Lang. 164 p. $20.55. 0-8204-0292-7 [JStNT 28,126].

d796 **Madges** William, The core of Christian faith; D. F. Strauss and his
Catholic critics: diss. Chicago Divinity School, 1986. – RelStR 13,188.

d797 TROELTSCH: ᴱ*Renz* H., *Graf* F. W., Troeltsch-Studien 3. Protestantismus
und Neuzeit. Gü 1984 → 1,393: ᴿZKG 97 (1986) 149-156 (M. *Wichelhaus*,
sehr detailliert).

d798 WELLHAUSEN: **Rudolph** Kurt, Wellhausen als Arabist: SzblLp 123/5,
1983 → 64,e425: ᴿOLZ 81 (1986) 478s (B. *Spuler*).

d799 *a*) *Smend* R., Julius WELLHAUSEN; – *b*) *Kaltenborn* C.-J., Adolf von
HARNACK; – *c*) *Goichot* E., Alfred LOISY; – *d*) *Altner* G., Albert
SCHWEITZER; – *e*) *Klein* G., Rudolf BULTMANN... [*al.*; ALBRECHT R.,
Mutter TERESA: RITSCHL D., M. L. KING jr.]: → 1,350.f926, ᴱ*Greschat*
M., Gestalten der Kirchengeschichte, Die Neueste Zeit 1985s...

d800 ZUNZ: *Rahe* Thomas, Leopold Zunz [1794-1886] und die Wissenschaft
des Judentums; zum hundertsten Todestag: Judaica 42 (1986) 188-199.

Y5.5 *Crisis modernistica* – **The Modernist era.**

d801 *d'Andigné* Amédée, Le Syllabus est-il toujours actuel?: PenséeC 221
(1986) 27-50.

d802 *Campanini* Giorgio, Pio X fra tradizione e rinnovamento: RasT 27
(1986) 153-173.

d803 *Colombo* Giuseppe, La teologia tra fede e cultura nella prima metà del secolo XX: TItSett 11 (1986) 3-23.

d804 **Giorgi** L., La questione modernista e il protestantesimo italiano: Centro storia modernismo, fonti e documenti 11s. Urbino 1984, Univ. p. 361-563. – RProtestantesimo 41 (1986) 58s (L. *Santini*).

d805 *Guelluy* R., Les antécédents de l'Encyclique 'Humani generis' dans les sanctions romaines de 1942; CHENU, CHARLIER, DRAGUET: RHE 81 (1986) 421-497.

d806 **Kurtz** Lester R., The politics of heresy; the modernist crisis in Roman Catholicism. Berkeley 1986, Univ. California. xii-267 p. $32.50 [TDig 34, 80].

d807 **Laboa** Juan M., El integrismo, un talente limitado y excluyente. M 1985, Narcea. 190 p. 84-277-0691-X. – REstE 61 (1986) 236s (R. *Sanz de Diego*).

d808 *McWilliam* Joanne, Patristic scholarship in the aftermath of the modernist crisis: AnglTR 68 (1986) 106-124.

d809 *Maguire* Daniel C., Catholicism and modernity: Horizons 13 (1986) 355-370. 383-8; responses by Lisa S. *Cahill* 371-5; Avery *Dulles* 375-8; William E. *May* 378-381; Bernard E. *Cooke*, 381-3.

d810 *Olivier* Paul, Les modernismes et les modernistes; travaux récents [*Weaver* M., *Poels* H., *Loome* T., *Poulat* E., *Schultenover* D., *Leonard* E. ...]: RechSR (1986) 399-440.

d811 *Toinet* Paul, Le modernisme sur ses vieux jours [... et l'ultra-modernisme (*Poulat*) ... Jeunesse de l'antique Église]: RThom 86 (1986) 211-256.

d812 ARINTERO: *Bandera* Armando, La obra eclesiológica del P. [Juan G.] Arintero; cronología con mística al fondo [... ¿Contagio de modernismo?]: CiTom 113 (1986) 497-626 [597-609, un prólogo inédito].

d813 BLONDEL: *Favraux* Paul, L'unité de l'œuvre blondélienne: NRT 108 (1986) 356-373.

d814 **Henrici** Peter, Blondel Maurice, Die Logik der Tat; aus der 'Action' von 1893 ausgewählt und übertragen[2] *rev* [[1]1957]: Christliche Meister 27. Einsiedeln 1986, Johannes/Benziger. 110 p. DM 15 [TR 83, 132, H. *Verweyen*].

d815 **Hooff** Anton E. van, Die Vollendung des Menschen; die Idee des Glaubensaktes und ihre philosophische Begründung im Frühwerk Maurice Blondels [Diss. FrB 1982] 1983 ➤ 1,f993: RHeythJ 27 (1986) 219s (Agneta *Sutton*].

d816 *Izquierdo* César, La crítica del historicismo bíblico en 'Histoire et dogme' de Maurice Blondel: ➤ 366, Hermenéutica 1985/6, 159-171.

d817 **König** Otto, Dogma als Praxis und Theorie; Studien zum Begriff des Dogmas in der Religionsphilosophie Maurice Blondels und während der modernistischen Krise (1888-1908) [Diss. 1978]: GrazerTSt 9. Graz 1983, Univ. Inst. Ök. Theol. 448 p. [RTLv, 249-251, E. *Brito*]. – RRechSR 74 (1986) 438s (P. *Olivier*).

d818 **Pacheco** Mario, A génese do problema da Acção em Blondel (1878-1882), sentido de um projecto filosófico. P 1982, Fund. Gulbenkian. – RRechSR 74 (1986) 435s (P. *Olivier*).

d819 *Verweyen* Hansjürgen, Die 'Logik der Tat'; ein Durchblick durch M. Blondels 'L'Action' (1893): ZkT 108 (1986) 311-320.

d820 CORNOLDI: **Malusa** Luciano, Neotomismo e intransigentismo cattolico; il contributo di Giovanni Maria Cornoldi per la rinascita del tomismo: RicFilStF 3. Mi 1986, Ist. Prop. Libraria. 512 p. Lit. 30.000. – RSapienza 39 (1986) 473-5 (A. G. *Manno*).

d821 CURCI: **Mucci** Giandomenico, Il primo direttore della 'Civiltà Cattolica'; Carlo Maria Curci tra la cultura dell'immobilismo e la cultura della storicità; pref. *Salvini* G.; *Spadolini* G.   R 1986, CC.   xxviii-232 p. Lit. 25.000. – ᴿCC 137 (1986,2) 508s (G. *Martina*); RasT 27 (1986) 574-6 (N. *Galantino*).

d822 DÖLLINGER: **Boudens** Robrecht, (*Kenis* Leo),   Alfred PLÜMMER, Conversations with Dr. Döllinger, 1870-1890: BiblETL 67, 1985 ➤ 1,f995; Fb 1800; 90-6186-178-0: ᴿDowR 104 (1986) 62-66 (unsigned); Gregorianum 67 (1986) 581-3 (J. *Wicki*); JEH 37 (1986) 662s (W. R. *Ward*); TR 82 (1986) 475s (W. *Brandmüller*); TS 47 (1986) 170s (J. T. *Ford*).

d823 GASSER: ᴱO'Connor James T,   The gift of infallibility; the official relatio on infallibility of Bishop Vincent Gasser at Vatican Council II.   Boston 1986, St. Paul.   126 p. $5; pa. $4.

d824 VON HÜGEL: **Kelly** James J.,   Baron Friedrich von Hügel's philosophy of religion 1983 ➤ 64,e469... 1,f966:   ᴿHeythJ 27 (1986) 358s (Ellen *Leonard*).

d825 *Weitlauff* Manfred,   Hügel, Friedrich von (1852-1925); ➤ TRE 15 (1986) 614-8.

d826 LABERTHONNIÈRE: **Perrin** Marie-T.,   Jeunesse 1980 ➤ 1,f998; Dossier 1983 ➤ 1,f997:   ᴿMélSR 43 (1986) 48-50 (L. *Debarge*).

d827 *Virgoulay* René,   Présence de Laberthonnière; sur quelques publications récentes: RevSR 60 (1986) 55-62.

d828 LAMENNAIS: **Le Guillou** M. & L.,   La condamnation de Lamennais 1982 ➤ 63,e952... 1,g1:   ᴿRHE 81 (1986) 586-593 (R. *Aubert*).

d829 *Plongeron* Bernard,   Entre Bossuet et Lamennais; quelques équivoques historiques de 'politique chrétienne':   SR 15 (1986) 277-301.

d830 *Chaussé* G.,   Un évêque [d'abord] mennaisien au Canada; Mgr. Jean-Jacques LARTIGUE: ➤ 112,   ꟳSYLVAIN P., Les ultramontains 1985, 105-120 . 313-8.

d831 LE ROY: **Mansini** Guy,   'What is a dogma?' The meaning and truth of dogma in Édouard Le Roy and his scholastic opponents [Diss. ᴰ*Wicks* J.: 1985 ➤ 1,g2:   ᴿTS 47 (1986) 719s (D. *Donovan*).

d832 LOISY: *Dietrich* Wendell S.,   Loisy and the liberal Protestants: SR 14 (1985) 303-311.

d833 **Poulat** Émile,   Critique et mystique; autour de Loisy ou la conscience catholique et l'esprit moderne 1984 ➤ 65,d864; 1,g4:   ᴿBLitEc 87 (1986) 230s (A. *Dartigues*); RHE 81 (1986) 211-6 (R. *Aubert*).

d834 MERRY DEL VAL: *Dick* John A.,   Cardinal Merry del Val and [i.e. (p. 355) 'a major conspirator against'] the Malines Conversations [(p. 332) important for 'the development of post-Modernist Roman Catholic theology'; 'a positive move toward the unfettering of Roman Catholic theology from the shackles of anti-Modernist rigidity and frenzy']: ETL 62 (1986) 333-355.

d835 NEWMAN, OXFORD MOVEMENT: *Connolly* G.,   The transubstantiation of myth; towards a new popular history of XIXth-cent. Catholicism in England [... Oxford movement, Irish immigration]: JEH 35 (1984) 78-104 [RHE 81,784].

d836 *Galeota* Gustavo,   I discorsi parrocchiali di John Henry Newman: Asprenas 33 (1986) 53-64.

d837 *Merrigan* Terrence,   Newman's Oriel experience; its significance for his life and thought: Bijdragen 47 (1986) 192-211.

d838 *a) Merrigan* Terrence,   Newman's progress towards Rome; a psychological consideration of his conversion to Catholicism; – *b) Eigelsbach*

Jo Ann. The intellectual dialogue of Friedrich von HÜGEL and Wilfrid WARD: DowR 104 (1986) 95-112 / 144-157.

d839 *Mobbs* Frank, The making of a *Roman* Catholic; Newman in Rome 1846-7: CleR 71 (1986) 248-253.

d840 *Morales* José, Semblanza religiosa y significado teológico del movimiento de Oxford: ScripTPamp 18 (1986) 459-516; lat. 517; Eng. 517s.

d841 **Otellini** Steven D., Newmann on the episcopacy: diss. Nº 3318, Pont. Univ. Gregoriana, D*Beyer* J., R 1986. 198 p. – RTLv 18,558.

d842 **Rowell** Geoffrey, The vision glorious; themes and personalities of the Catholic revival in Anglicanism 1983 ➤ 1,g32: RJTS 37 (1928s (D. M. *Thompson*).

d843 *Townsend* Ralph D., PUSEY (Edward Bouverie): ➤ 582, DictSpir XII/2 (1986) 2678-2680.

d844 E**Weaver** Mary Jo, [➤ 344*] Newman and the Modernists. Lanham MD 1985, UPA. viii-232 p. $25.75; pa. $12.25. – RTS 47 (1986) 749s (J. *Griffin*: TYRRELL believed that if the modernist premiss were condemned, so was Newman; but Newman was more obedient to authority, and did not deserve comparison with 'VOLTAIRE's enigmatic features').

d845 RENAN: **Fraisse** Simone, Renan au pied de l'Acropole; du nouveau sur la 'Prière'; Cahiers renaniens 8. P 1979, Nizet. 85 p. [RHE 82,167, H. *Silvestre*].

d846 *Mollier* Jean-Yves, [549] Lettres inédites d'Ernest Renan à ses éditeurs Michel et Calmann Lévy. P 1986, Calmann-Lévy. 342 p. [RHE 82,411-4, H. *Silvestre*].

d847 TYRRELL: *Goichot* Émile, Sur 'l'affaire Tyrrell'; documents inédits: RHE 81 (1986) 95-116.

d848 *Guasco* Maurilio, Autorità e popolo nella Chiesa; Tyrrell e la rivista 'Il rinnovamento': HumBr 41 (1986) 44-55.

d849 *Holmes* J. Derek, PETRE (Maude Dominica) 1863-1942: ➤ 578, Catholicisme XI,49 (1986) 92s.

d850 *Nichols* Aidan, George Tyrrell and the development of doctrine: NBlackf 67 (1986) 515-530.

d851 **Schultenover** David G., George Tyrrell, In search of Catholicism 1981 ➤ 62,m920 ... 1,g46: RRechSR 74 (1986) 430-4 (P. *Olivier*: important, remarquablement informé: trop chronologique, sans esprit synthétique).

d852 **Chenu** Marie-Dominique, Une école de théologie; La Saulchoir 1985 ➤ 1,g41: RÉglT 17 (1986) 112-4 (R. *Garceau*); FoiTemps 16 (1986) 186s (P. *Scolas*); MélSR 43 (1986) 172s (G. *Mathon*); ScEspr 38 (1986) 133-5 (T. R. *Potvin*); VSp 139 (1985) 698s (R.-L. *Oechslin*).

d853 WISEMAN: **Schiefen** Richard J., Nicholas Wiseman and the transformation of English Catholicism 1984 ➤ 1,g50: RSR 14 (1985) 391s (C. *Davis*).

Y6 *Saeculum XX* – 20th Century Exegesis.

d854 *Fogarty* Gerald P., American Catholic approaches to Sacred Scripture: ➤ 27, FELLIS J. T., Studies 1985 ...

d855 E**Johnson** James T., The Bible in American law / EPhy Allene S., The Bible and popular culture ...: Bible in American Culture 4.7, 1985 ➤ 1,305.1599: RTLZ 111 (1986) 173-7 (G. *Wendelborn*).

d856 E**Marsden** George, Evangelicalism and modern American. GR 1984, Eerdmans. 220 p. $9. – RRExp 83 (1986) 321s (B. J. *Leonard*).

d857 **Buber** M., La fede dei profeti [🌑 1942; deutsch 1964 ²1984], ᵀ*Poma* Andrea. Casale Monferrato 1985, Marietti. xliv-240 p. – ᴿHenoch 8 (1986) 267-9 (C. *Ciancio*).

d858 **Buber** Martin, Ecstatic confessions [German 1909], ᴱ*Mendes-Flohr* Paul. SF 1985, Harper & R. xxxv-160 p. $6.30. – ᴿCCurr 25 (1985s) 470-2 (M. *Verman*: 'Buber, mysticism and feminism'); RExp 83 (1986) 485s (B. J. *Leonard*).

d859 **Berry** Donald L., Mutuality; the vision of Martin Buber 1985 ➤ 1,g61: ᴿTTod 43 (1986s) 110-112 (J. F. *Moore*).

d860 ᴱ**Bloch** Jochanan, *Gordon* Haim, Martin Buber; Bilanz seines Denkens [Ben-Gurion Univ. Kongress 1978] 1983 [➤ 1,457 gives editors reversed, dates 1979/84, and title Eng.]: ᴿFreibRu 37s (1985s) 1102 (M. *Weinrich*).

d861 **Dreyfus** Théodor, Martin Buber: Témoins spirituels d'aujourd'hui, 1981 ➤ 63,c987; 1,g65: ᴿIstina 31 (1986) 230s (A. *Derczanski*); RÉJ 145 (1986) 213-5 (M. R. *Hayoun*, avec 7 autres Buberiana).

d862 **Oesterreicher** John, The unfinished dialogue; Martin Buber and the Christian way. NY 1985, Philosophical. $15 [Judaica 42,206].

d863 **Polo** Alex, The realm of the between in Martin Buber's writings and its implications to the history of religions: diss. Fordham, NY 1986, ᴰ*Moore* D. 235 p. 86-15689. – DissA 47 (1986s) 1372-A; RelStR 13,187.

d864 *Rebell* Walter, Mystik und personale Begegnung bei Martin Buber: ZRGg 38 (1986) 345-358.

d865 **Sánchez Meca** Diego, Martin Buber; fundamento existencial de la intercomunicación 1984 ➤ 1,g71: ᴿAugM 31 (1986) 425s (E. *Rivera de Ventosa*).

d866 **Bultmann** Rudolf, Theologische Enzyklopädie, ᴱ*Jüngel* E., *Müller* K. W. 1984 = 1936 ➤ 65,d909; 1,g74: ᴿTGl 76 (1986) 474s (B. *Dieckmann*).

d867 **Bultmann** R., NT and Mythology ᵀᴱ*Ogden* S., 1984 ➤ 1,g75: ᴿHorizons 13 (1986) 419 (T. B. *Ommen*); TLond 39 (1986) 163s (R. *Morgan*).

d868 *Cahill* P. Joseph, Bultmann; reminiscence and legacy [he and Charlesworth both found at Marburg a preoccupying indifference to B.'s memory and manuscripts]: TS 47 (1986) 473-496.

d869 **Evang** Martin, Der junge Bultmann (bis ca. 1920): Diss. Bonn, ᴰ*Grässer* E., 1986s. – RTLv 18,556.

d870 **Herrmann** Eberhard, Vad har Bultmanns teologi med kunskapsteoretiska frågor att göra?: SvTKv 62 (1986) 103-8.

d871 ᴱ**Hobbs** Edward C., Bultmann... centenary 1984/5 ➤ 1,475: ᴿRExp 83 (1986) 469s (W. *Ward*: high praise).

d872 ᴱ**Jaspert** Bernd, Rudolf Bultmanns Werk und Wirkung 1984 ➤ 65,28*; 1,g82: ᴿCBQ 48 (1986) 157s (B. F. *Meyer*); Protestantesimo 41 (1986) 112-4 (B. *Corsani*).

d872* *Lindemann* Walter, Der Briefwechsel zwischen Barth und Bultmann: LuthMon 25 (1986) 207-9 [*al.* 197-220].

d873 *Schmithals* Walter, Zu Rudolf Bultmanns 100. Geburtstag [8 Editionen, 6 andere Schriften]: TRu 51 (1986) 79-91.

d874 **Cullmann:** **Dorman** Theodore M., The hermeneutics of Oscar Cullmann: diss. Fuller Theol. Sem. – StudiaBT 13 (1983) 272s.

d875 **Schlaudraff** Karl-Heinz, 'Heil als Geschichte'? Zur Cullmann-Rezeption und Cullmann-Kritik in der neutestamentlichen Wissenschaft des deutschsprachigen Protestantismus seit 1946: Diss. Tübingen 1986. 313 p. – TLZ 112,638.

d876 **Farrer:** **Curtis** Philip, A hawk among sparrows; a biography of Austin

Farrer 1985 → **1**,g96: ᴿTLond 39 (1986) 67s (J. L. *Houlden*: the telephone ensures that such witty data will no longer be preserved).

d877 HESCHEL: **Merkle** John C., The genesis of faith; the depth theology of A.J. Heschel [→ **1**,g105]. NY 1985, Macmillan. 292 p. $20. – ᴿTTod 43 (1986s) 109s (J. F. *Moore*); Worship 60 (1986) 180s (P. *Johnson*).

d878 HOLTZMANN: *Merk* Otto, Holtzmann, Heinrich Julius (1832-1910): → 597, TRE 15 (1986) 519-522.

d879 HOSKYNS: **Parsons** Richard E., Sir Edwyn Hoskyns as a biblical theologian 1985 → **1**,g107: ᴿCleR 71 (1986) 387 (W. G. *Morrice*); NBlackf 67 (1986) 551s (K *Grayston*).

d880 KÄSEMANN: *Ferrario* Fulvio, L'obbedienza della fede nella riflessione di E. Käsemann: Servitium 44 (1986) 87-96.

d881 KNOX: *Dayras* Solange, A Gallic view of Ronald Knox: CleR 71 (1986) 277-283.

d882 LAGRANGE M.-J., Personal reflections and memoirs, ᵀ*Wansbrough* Henry, 1985 → **1**,g112: ᴿHorizons 13 (1986) 171s (Ellen *Leonard*); RB 93 (1986) 315 (P. *Benoit*: name of Christopher WILDING as associate translator overlooked in the book).

d883 *Paretsky* Albert, M.-J. Lagrange's contribution to Catholic biblical studies: Angelicum 63 (1986) 509-531.

d884 MACHOVEC: **Augustin** M., Marxistischer Philosoph und Humanist; Milan Machovec und die Bedeutung alttestamentlicher Traditionen in seinem philosophischen Denken; ein Beitrag zum Dialog zwischen Christen und Marxisten; mit einem Essay von Machovec: Diss. Osnabrück. Essen 1985, Blaue Eule. 226 p. DM 28. – ZAW 99,132.

d885 MARTINI: **Garzonio** Marco, Cardinale a Milano in un mondo che cambia nella testimonianza di Carlo Maria Martini 1985 → **1**,g115: ᴿHumBr 41 (1986) 478 (T. *Goffi*).

d886 MESTERS: [P.] **Cavalcanti** Tereza M., A lógica do amor; pensamento teológico de Carlos Mesters [diss. Rio de Janeiro 1984]. São Paulo 1986, Paulinas. 126 p. – ᴿEstudos Bíblicos 12 [REB 46,4] (1986) 53s (L. *Garmus*).

d887 MOWINCKEL: *Sæbø* Magne, Sigmund Mowinckel and his relation to the literary critical school: ST 40 (1986) 81-93.

d888 NINEHAM: a) *Baker* Tom, Nineham as churchman: – b) *Downing* F. Gerald, Towards a fully systematic scepticism — in the service of faith; – c) *Cupitt* Don, A sense of history; TLond 39 (1986) 341-9 / 355-361; bibliog. 367 / 362-6.

d889 PEAKE: *Hooker* M.D., Ministerial training; the contribution of A.S. Peake: EpworthR 12,3 (1985) 64-76 [NTAbs 30,129].

d890 PERRIN: *Mercer* C.R., Norman Perrin's pilgrimage; releasing the Bible to the public: ChrCent 103,17 (1986) 483-6 [NTAbs 30,260].

d891 PIROT: *Ribaut* J.-P., Pirot, Louis, 10.VIII.1881-5.XII.1939: → 578, Catholicisme XI,50 (1986) 455s.

d892 POELS: *Fogarty* Gerald P., The case of Henry Poels [only Catholic U. professor before Charles CURRAN to have been dismissed for disagreeing with the ordinary magisterium]: America 155 (1986) 180-184.

d893 VON RAD: *Childs* Brevard S., Gerhard von Rad in American dress: → 69, ᶠMAYS J., 1986, 77-86.

d894 ROSENZWEIG Franz, a) Die Schrift; Aufsätze, Übertragungen und Briefe, ᴱ*Thieme* Karl; – b) Das Büchlein vom gesunden und kranken Menschenverstand, ᴱ*Glatzer* Nahum N. Königstein 1984, Athenäum. 259 p.; 128 p. – ᴿTZBas 42 (1986) 84s (K. *Seybold*).

d895 SCHLIER: **Schneider** Alfred, Wort Gottes und Kirche im theologischen Denken von Heinrich Schlier [Diss.]: EurHS 23/150. Bern 1981, Lang. 347 p. – RTR 82 (1986) 31-34 (P. *Kuhn*).

Y6.4 **Theologi influentes** *in exegesim saeculi XX*.

d896 **Avis** Paul, The methods of modern theology. L 1986, Marshall Pickering. xiii-240 p. £13. 0-551-01347-8. – RExpTim 98 (1986s) 154 (Ruth *Page*: 8 theologians; SCHLEIERMACHER criticized, RAHNER and LONERGAN not; PANNENBERG on BARTH on SCHLEIERMACHER; RITSCHL, TENNANT, TILLICH).

d897 **Bauer** Johannes B., Entwürfe der Theologie 1985 ➤ 1,323: RTLZ 111 (1986) 910-3 (R. *Marschner*).

d898 Bonn Agreement 1831: Old Catholics and Anglicans 1931-1981, EHuelin Gordon. Oxford 1983, UP. xi-177 p. £12.50. – RHeythJ 27 (1986) 335s (R. L. *Stewart*).

d899 **Ericksen** Robert P., Theologians under Hitler — G. KITTEL, P. ALTHAUS, E. HIRSCH. NHv 1985, Yale. 245 p. $20. 0-300-02926-8. – RÉTRel 61 (1986) 458 (B. *Reymond*: après le long ostracisme, les plus intéressants à étudier); JRel 66 (1986) 441-3 (R. W. *Lovin*); TLond 39 (1986) 235s (E. *Robertson*); TS 47 (1986) 720-3 (B. J. *Verkamp* is upset by the claim that their theologizing could have integrity while they opted for a political system now discredited); TTod 43 (1986s) 142.144 (W. *Harrelson*).

d900 EHodgson Peter, *King* Robert, Readings in Christian theology [= 2Christian theology, 11982]. L 1985, SPCK. xi-418 p. £15. 0-281-04169-5. – RExpTim 98 (1986s) 89 (G. *Slater*: 'sacramental theology' no longer missing; also new 'alternative visions', CONE, GUTIÉRREZ, RUETHER).

d901 *Jaki* S. L., Un siècle de Gifford Lectures: Archives de Philosophie 49 (1986) 3-49 [RSPT 70 (1986) 290].

d902 **Kent** John H. S., The end of the line? The development of Christian theology in the last two centuries 1982 = 1978 ➤ 64,e523...1,g126: RRExp 83 (1986) 327s (D. R. *Stiver*).

d903 **Poór** József, Ⓜ Protestant theology in Hungary 1945-1985. Budapest 1986, Kossuth. 185 p. – RTheologiai Szemle 29 (1986) 185-7 (J. *Szigeti*).

d904 BALTHASAR Hans Urs von, Le persone del dramma; l'uomo in Dio / l'uomo in Cristo: TeoDrammatica 2s, 1982s ➤ 65,d954; 1,g132: RRivStoLR 22 (1986) 592s (A. *Bodrato*).

d905 **Balthasar** Hans Urs von, Teodrammatica, 4. L'azione; 5. L'ultimo atto; TSommavilla Guido: Già e non ancora 129. 138. Mi 1986, Jaca. 474 p.; 448 p. Lit. 49.000; 46.000. 88-16-30129-5; 38-4. – RTItSett 11 (1986) 265-273 (E. *Babini*, 4).

d906 **Balthasar** H. Urs von. The glory of the Lord I. 1982 ➤ 64,e529 ... 1,g130: RHeythJ 27 (1986) 231-3 (J. *O'Donnell*: a classic, a superior translation).

d907 **Balthasar** Hans Urs von, The glory of the Lord 2. Studies in theological style. 1. Clerical styles 1985 ➤ 1,g131: RAmerica 154 (1986) 194s (E. T. *Oakes*); Horizons 13 (1986) 430s (D. P. *Sheridan*); TLond 39 (1986) 135-7 (B. *Horne*).

d908 **Balthasar** Hans Urs von, The glory of the Lord, a theological aesthetics, III. Studies in theological style; lay styles; TLouth Andrew, al., ERiches John. SF/E 1986, Ignatius/Clark. 524 p. $35/£15. [TDig 33,457]. / 0-567-09325-5. – RDoctLife 36 (1986) 557s (G. *Daly*); ExpTim 98 (1986s) 154s

(M. J. *Townsend*: profound book, good translation); Month 248 (1986) 245 (J. *McDade*).

d909 **Balthasar** Hans Urs von, Theologik [3d title of trilogy after Ästhetik (Glory) and Dramatik] I. Wahrheit der Welt; II. Wahrheit Gottes [III. erwartet: Geist der Wahrheit]. Einsiedeln 1985, Johannes. xxii-312 p.; 336 p. 3-265-10297-1; 8-6.

d910 **Balthasar** Hans Urs von, Puntos centrales de la fe [Zentren], T*Albizu* J. L.: BAC. M 1985, Católica. 395 p. – RCiudD 199 (1986) 128 (S. *Folgado Flórez*); NatGrac 37 (1986) 179s (A. *Villalmonte*).

d911 **Godenir** Joseph, ˙Jésus l'unique; introduction à la théologie de H. U. von Balthasar 1984 ➤ 65,d955; F 90: RÉtudes 364 (1986) 139 (R. *Marlé*).

d912 *a) Lacoste* Jean-Yves, [Minima Balthasariana; fragments d'un séminaire (*Chantraine* G. *al.*, Bru 1984s)] Du phénomène à la figure; pour réintroduire à 'La gloire et la croix'; – *b) Gilbert* Paul, L'articulation des transcendantaux selon H. U. von Balthasar; – *c) Moscow* Miriam, Passion et action de Dieu au Samedi Saint; – *d) Lafontaine* René, 'Arrivés à Jésus, ils le trouvèrent mort' (Jo XIX,39); H. U. von Balthasar, théologien du samedi Saint: RThom 86 (1986) 606-616 - 629 - 635 - 643.

d913 **Schrijver** Georges De, Le merveilleux accord de l'homme et de Dieu... Balthasar (D1976) 1983 ➤ 65,d963; 1,g137: RHeythJ 27 (1986) 230s (J. *O'Donnell*: rich).

d914 **BARTH** Karl, Esquisse d'une dogmatique [cours Bonn 1946], T*Ryser* Fernand, *Mauris* Édouard; préf. *Gisel* Pierre: Traditions chrétiennes 17. P/Genève 1984, Cerf/Labor et Fides. 254 p. F 59. – RÉglT 17 (1986) 106s (J. *Pambrun*).

d915 **Barth** Karl, Al servicio de la palabra. Salamanca 1985, Sígueme. 267 p. – RBibFe 12 (1986) 132s (M. *Saenz Galache*).

d916 **Alemany** José J., Karl Barth: ¿una teología socialista? [*Marquardt* W. 1972]: IglV 122s (1986) 215-223.

d917 *a) Amberg* Ernst-Heinz, [Karl Barth und] Barmen 1934-1984, ein Literaturbericht: TLZ 111 (1986) 161-174; – *b) Hauschild* Wolf-Dieter, Zur Erforschung der Barmer Theologischen Erklärung von 1934: TRu 51 (1986) 130-165; – *c) Manenschijn* Gerrit, Strijd om [Barth, 'de vader van'] Barmen: GerefTTs 86 (1986) 1-27.

d918 **Balthasar** H. U. von, La teologia di Karl Barth [K. B., Darstellung 1951 ²1961], T*Moretto* Giovanni: Già e non ancora 117. Mi 1985, Jaca. 418 p. Lit. 30.000. 88-16-30117-1. – RSTEv 9,18 (1986) 282-4 (P. *Bolognesi*).

d919 **Becker** Dieter, Karl Barth und Martin BUBER — Denker in dialogischer Nachbarschaft? Gö 1986, Vandenhoeck & R. 279 p. – RRHPR 66 (1986) 487s (sr. *Marie-Jeanne* K.).

d920 **Bohrer** Rudolf, Prophetie und Seelsorge... E. THURNEYSEN 1982 ➤ 64,e544... 1,g142: RTheologiai Szemle (1986) 120-2 (I. *Karasszon*).

d921 *a) Bornkamm* Karin, Die reformatorische Lehre vom Amt Christi und ihre Umformung durch Karl Barth; – *b) Ebeling* Gerhard, Über die Reformation hinaus? Zur Luther-Kritik Karl Barths; – *c) Gestrich* Christof, Die hermeneutische Differenz zwischen Barth und Luther angesichts der neuzeitlichen Situation: ➤9, Barth 100. Gb. = ZTK Bei 6 (1986) 1-32 / 33-75 / 136-157.

d922 *Brinkman* M. E., Karl Barth — 10 mei 1886 — 10 mei 1986: GerefTTs 86 (1986) 233-8.

d923 *Casalis* Georges, Karl Barth und unsere theologische Existenz heute?: ÖkRu 35 (1986) 281-295.

d924 *a) Bromiley* Geoffrey W., Introduzione alla teologia di Karl Barth

[< Certezze 59s (1959); Introduction 1979]; – b) *Runia* Klaas, La dottrina della Scrittura secondo K. Barth [< Certezze (1967)]; – c) *Bolognesi* Pietro, ... della predestinazione; – d) *Klooster* Fred H., ... della riconciliazione [< WestTJ]: STEv 9,18 (1986) 145-209 / 210-232 / 233-255 / 256-279 [280s, opere di Barth tradotte in italiano].

d925 **Davaney** Sheila G., Divine power; a study of Karl Barth and Charles HARTSHORNE. Ph 1986, Fortress. xi-224 p. $17 [RelStR 13,334, Anna *Case-Winters*].

d926 **Fraser** David A., Foundation for Christian ethics; Karl Barth's Christological anthropology and the social sciences: diss. Vanderbilt. Nv 1986. – RelStR 13,188.

d927 a) *Frederikse* T.C., Waarom en hoe HAITJEMA Barth in Nederland bijviel; – b) *Hasselaar* J.M., VAN RULER treedt Barth in de weg; – c) *Vos* A., De onderzoeksproblematiek van Barths dogmatiek; – d) *Neven* G.W., Katholisering van Karl Barths theologie?: KerkT 37 (1986) 90-105 / 106-9 / 110-127 / 291-302.

d928 *Gollwitzer* Helmut, Das Ereignis Karl Barth: ZeichZt 40 (1986) 110-3 [< ZIT].

d929 a) *Groó* Gyula, Ⓜ What have I learned from Karl Barth?; – b) *Jánossy* Imre, Ⓜ My encounters with Karl Barth: Theologiai Szemle 29 (1986) 133-7 / 138-141.

d930 a) *Gunton* Colin, Barth, the Trinity, and human freedom (response, *Campbell* Cynthia M.); – b) *Werpehowski* William, Narrative and ethics in Barth (*Hunsinger* George); – c) *Lindbeck* George, Barth and textuality (*Thiemann* Ronald F.); – d) *Welker* Michael, Barth's theology and process theology (*Suchocki* Marjorie): TTod 43 (1986s) 316-330 (331-3) / 334-353 (354-360) / 361-376 (377-382) / 383-397 (398-402) [403-418; Mozart and excerpts].

d931 **Hafstad** Kjetil, Wort und Geschichte; das Geschichtsverständnis Karl Barths: BeiEvT. Mü 1985, Kaiser. 432 p. DM 98 [ScotJT 40, 451, A.E. *McGrath*].

d932 *Harrison* Peter, Correlation and theology; Barth and TILLICH re-examined: SR 15 (1986) 65-76.

d933 *Hunsinger* George, Beyond literalism and expressivism; Karl Barth's hermeneutical realism: ModT 3 (1986s) 209-223.

d934 **Jüngel** Eberhard, Karl Barth, a theological legacy [3 reprints + 2 inedita 1982], ᵀ*Paul* Garrett E. Ph 1986, Westminster. 168 p. $14 [RelStR 13,334, P. *Hodgson*].

d935 **Kooi** C. van der, De denkweg van de jonge Karl Barth [➤ 1,g154]; een analyse van de ontwikkeling van zijn theologie in de jaren 1909-1927 in het licht van de vraag naar de geloofsverantwoording: diss. Amst Vrije Univ. 1985. 293 p. ƒ32,50. 90-6256-186-1. – ᴿBijdragen 47 (1986) 78s (J. *Wissink*).

d936 a) *Kraege* Jean-Denis, Rupture et continuité; à l'occasion du centième anniversaire de la naissance de Karl Barth; – b) *Gounelle* André, Foi et religion; esquisse d'une confrontation entre Barth, BONHOEFFER et TILLICH: ÉTRel 61 (1986) 487-521 / 523-532.

d937 a) *Krötke* Wolf, Gott und Mensch als 'Partner'; zur Bedeutung einer zentralen Kategorie in K. Barths Kirchlicher Dogmatik; – b) *Grözinger* Albrecht, Offenbarung und Praxis; zum schwierigen praktisch-theo-logischen Erbe der dialektischen Theologie; – c) *Jüngel* Eberhard, Zum Verhältnis von Kirche und Staat nach K. Barth; – d) *Trowitzsch* Michael, K. Barth; Erinnerung in angefochtener Zeit: ➤ 9, Barth 100.Gb. (1986) 158-175 / 176-193 / 76-135 / 194-239.

d938 **Lapide** Pinchas, Ieder komt tot de Vader; Karl Barth, Barmen en een poging tot een nieuwe christologie. Kampen 1985, Kok. 89 p. ƒ13,90. – ᴿKerkT 37 (1986) 77 (J. A. B. *Jongeneel*).

d939 *a) Link* Christian, Fides quaerens intellectum; die Bewegung der Theologie Karl Barths; – *b) Eicher* Peter, 'Doch was geht uns die Kirche an?' Eine katholische Besinnung nach Karl Barth; – *c) Lochman* Jan M., Karl Barths ökumenische Solidarität; am Beispiel Osteuropa; – *d) Bonjour* Edgar, Karl Barth und die Schweiz: → 478*, Symposium = TZBas 42,4 (1986) 279-302 / 313-331 / 332-351 / 303-312.

d940 *Merkel* Friedemann, Karl Barth und der kirchliche Gottesdienst: JbLtgHymn 30 (1986) 30-42; Eng. 42.

d941 *Neuer* Werner, Der Briefwechsel zwischen Karl Barth und Adolf SCHLATTER: TBei 17 (1986) 86-96…

d942 *Peters* Albrecht, Karl Barth und Martin LUTHER: Luther 57 (Wu 1986) 113-9.

d943 **Phillips** Donald E., Karl Barth's philosophy of communication. Hildesheim 1981, Olms. xvi-404 p. DM 48. – ᴿHeythJ 27 (1986) 227-230 (R. *Brecher*: sloppiness verging on illiteracy).

d944 *Pizzuti* Giuseppe M., Karl Barth e la teologia cattolica: Asprenas 33 (1986) 37-52.

d945 *a) Rendtorff* Trutz, Karl Barth und die Neuzeit; Fragen zur Barth-Forschung; – *b) Nossol* Alfons, Die Rezeption der Barthschen Christologie in der katholischen Theologie der Gegenwart; – *c) Roberts* Richard H., Die Aufnahme der Theologie Karl Barths im angelsächsischen Bereich; Geschichte – Typologie – Ausblick: EvT 46 (1986) 298-314 / 351-369 / 369-393 (… *al.*).

d946 *Reuss* András, Ⓜ Karl Barth at the Amsterdam assembly of the World Council of Churches: Theologiai Szemle 29 (1986) 286-293.

d947 **Reymond** Bernard, *a)* Théologien ou prophète? Les francophones et Karl Barth avant 1945. Lausanne 1985, L'Âge d'Homme. 250 p. – *b)* Karl Barth – Pierre MAURY, 'Nous qui pouvons encore parler…', correspondance 1928-1956. Lausanne 1985, L'Âge d'Homme. 299 p. – ᴿÉTRel 61 (1986) 474s (*ipse*); RHPR 66 (1986) 486s (G. *Siegwalt*).

d948 *Sequeri* Pierangelo, 'La teologia reclama uomini liberi'; l'istanza critica nella Dogmatica di Karl Barth: TItSett 11 (1986) 285-296; Eng. 297 [135-151].

d949 ᴱ*Smend* Rudolf, Karl Barth und Walter BAUMGARTNER; ein Briefwechsel über das Alte Testament: → 9, Barth 100. Gb. (1986) 240-271.

d950 **Spieckermann** Ingrid, Gotteserkenntnis; ein Beitrag zur Grundfrage der neuen Theologie Karl Barths [Diss. Gö 1982, ᴰ*Geyer* H.]: BeiEvT 97. Mü 1985, Kaiser. 236 p. DM 78 [ScotJT 40,451, A. E. *McGrath*].

d951 *a) Sykes* Stephen W., Karl Barth on the heart of the matter; – *b) Rosato* Philip J., The influence of Karl Barth on Catholic theology [Symposium, Gregorian, Rome May 10, 1986]: Gregorianum 67 (1986) 679-690 / 659-678; franç. 691.678.

d952 *Thiemann* Ronald, The significance of Karl Barth for contemporary theology: Thomist 50 (1986) 512-539 (-689, *al.*).

d953 *Thomsen* Henning, Praedestinationen — et centralt element i Karl Barths teologi: DanTTs 49 (1986) 117… [< ZIT].

d954 **Torjesen** Leif P., Resurrection and ideology; the theological origins and political setting of Karl Barth's attack on natural theology: diss. Claremont 1985. 544 p. 86-07841. – DissA 47 (1986s) 1374-A.

d955 *Torrance* T. F., *a)* Karl Barth and the Latin heresy; – *b)* The legacy of Karl Barth (1886-1986): ScotJT 39 (1986) 461-482 / 289-308.

d956 *Vanzan* Piersandro, Riscoprire SCHLEIERMACHER per fare luce anche su Barth [*Sorrentino* S. 1981-5]: CC 137 (1986,3) 500-8.

d957 *a) Wenz* Gunther, Zwischen den Zeiten; einige Bemerkungen zum geschichtlichen Verständnis der theologischen Anfänge Karl Barths: – *b) Meckenstock* Günter, Karl Barths Prolegomena zur Dogmatik; Entwicklungslinien vom 'Unterricht in der christlichen Religion' bis zur 'Kirchlichen Dogmatik': NSys 28 (1986) 284-295 / 296-310; Eng. 295/310.

d958 **Winzeler** Peter, Widerstehende Theologie, Karl Barth 1920-35 [Diss.]: Im Lehrhaus 1, 1984 → 65,d976; DM 31: ᴿTZBas 42 (1986) 89 (O. *Bächli*).

d959 **Zellweger-Barth** Max, My father-in-law; memories of Karl Barth, ᵀ*Rumscheidt* H. M. Pittsburgh c. 1986, Pickwick. 51 p. $6 [JAAR 55,648].

d960 BINGHAM: **McKenzie** Brian A., Fundamentalism, Christian unity, and pre-millennialism in the thought of Rowland Victor Bingham (1872-1942); a study of anti-modernism in Canada: diss. St. Michael, ᴰ*Moir* J. Toronto 1986. – RTLv 18,557.

d961 **BONHOEFFER** Dietrich, Spiritual care, ᵀᴱ*Rochelle* Jay C. Ph 1985, Fortress. 93 p. $5. – ᴿRelStR 12 (1986) 263 (G. *Meilaender*: goal not to build character but to uncover sin).

d962 Beiträge zur Theologie und Wirkungsgeschichte Dietrich Bonhoeffers. B 1985, Ev.-V. 211 p. 18 art. – ᴿTheologiai Szemle 29 (1986) 124s (I. *Szebik*).

d963 **Bethge** Eberhard & Renate, *Gremmels* Christian, Dietrich Bonhoeffer — a life in pictures. L 1986, SCM. 240 p. [RTPhil 119,529].

d964 *a) Clements* Keith, Bonhoeffer; theist or moralist?; – *b) Holyer* Robert, Toward an eschatology of the past [Bonhoeffer interpreted against MacINTYRE: hope beyond life possible only for those who find life itself meaningful]: TLond 39 (1986) 203-9 / 209-218.

d965 **Feil** Ernst, The theology of Dietrich Bonhoeffer, ᵀ*Rumscheidt* Martin 1985 → 1,g170; $20: ᴿHorizons 13 (1986) 184s (G. B. *Kelly*: superb translation of a ponderous Feil).

d966 *Huber* Wolfgang, 'Was das Christentum oder auch wer Christus für uns heute eigentlich ist' — Dietrich Bonhoeffers Bedeutung für die Zukunft der Christenheit: ZeichZt 40 (1986) 106-110 [< ZIT].

d967 *Jánossy* Imre, Ⓜ What does the memory of Dietrich Bonhoeffer oblige us to?: Theologiai Szemle 29 (1986) 141-6.

d968 **Kelly** Geffrey B., Liberating faith; Bonhoeffer's message for today 1984 → 1,g172: ᴿScotJT 39 (1986) 400-2 (M. *Keeling*); SpTod 38 (1986) 82s (Geraldine *Wodarczyk*).

d969 **Lange** F. de, Grond onder de voeten; burgerlijkheid bij Dietrich Bonhoeffer — een theologische studie [diss.]. Kampen 1985, Van den Berg. xiv-474 p. *f*42,50. 90-6651-040-4. – ᴿTsTNijm 26 (1986) 92 (H. D. van *Hoogstraten*: een origenele bijdrage).

d970 *Mohaupt* Lutz, Zwischen Pazifismus und Verschwörung; Gerechtigkeit und Schuld im Denken Dietrich Bonhoeffers: Luther 57 (Mu 1986) 127-143.

d971 **Morris** Kenneth E., Bonhoeffer's ethic of discipleship; a study in social psychology, political thought and religion. Univ. Park 1986, Pennsylvania State Univ. 192 p. $18. 0-271-00428-2. – ᴿExpTim 98 (1986s) 149s (R. *Preston*).

d972 *Oakley-Smith* T., *Summers* H., Theos or thanatos; who did Bonhoeffer worship? NduitseGT 27 (1986) 61-71 [< GerefTTs 86,191].

d973 *Peters* Tiemo R., Kirche – Wagnis für andere; Impulse für die Ekklesiologie im Werk Dietrich Bonhoeffers: StiZt 204 (1986) 485-496.

d974 *Tödt* Heinz E., Zur Neuausgabe von Dietrich Bonhoeffers Werken: EvT 46 (1986) 181-9.

d975 BREMOND: *Blanchet* Charles, À la recherche de la source divine; Henri Bremond 1865-1933 [*Goichot* É. 1982; *Blanchet* A. 1975...]: NRT 108 (1986) 321-341.

d976 EBELING: *Moda* Aldo, Per una lettura dell'ultimo Ebeling: StPatav 33 (1986) 361-372.

d977 EBNER: **Wucherer-Huldenfeld** Augustinus K., Personales Sein und Wert; Einführung in den Grundgedanken Ferdinand Ebners. W 1985, Böhlau. 309 p. DM 60 [TR 83,312s, B. *Casper*].

d978 FOSDICK: *Ferguson* Duncan S., The Bible in Protestant liberalism; the hermeneutics of Harry Emerson Fosdick: JRelSt 12,2 (Cleveland 1984) 14-26 [< ZIT].

d979 GAEBELEIN: **Rausch** David A., Arno C. Gaebelein, 1861-1945; irenic fundamentalist and scholar. NY 1983, Mellen. 297 p. $40. – RGraceTJ 7 (1986) 154s (D. S. *Dockery*).

d980 GUARDINI: **Gerl** Hanna-Barbara, Romano Guardini 1885-1968; Leben und Werk 1985 ➤ 1,g189; 3-7867-1146-1: RGregorianum 67 (1986) 583-5 (J. *Wicki*); ZKG 97 (1986) 428s (G. *Schwaiger*).

d981 *Hofmann* Peter, Der fragende Guardini; philosophische Anmerkungen zu den 'Theologischen Briefen an einen Freund': ZkT 108 (1986) 45-54.

d982 *Sommavilla* Guido, Romano Guardini (1885-1968), ritorno di un grande [*Gerl* H....]: Letture 41 (1986) 691-710.

d983 HEIDEGGER: **Avens** Robert, The new gnosis; Heidegger, HILLMAN, and angels. NY 1984, Spring. 154 p. $12 [JAAR 55,129s, R. A. *Underwood*].

d984 *Santiago Guervós* Luis E. de, Fenomenología y hermenéutica en el pensamiento de Martín Heidegger: CiuD 199 (1986) 93-103 [197-209... en GADAMER].

d985 HENRY Carl P. H., Confessions of a theologian; an autobiography. Waco 1986, Word. 416 p. $15 [CalvinT 22,329-331, J. H. *Kromminga*].

d986 **Patterson** Bob E., C. F. H. Henry 1984 ➤ 65,e5; 1,g196: RScripB 17 (1986s) 20s (R. C. *Fuller*).

d987 HERRMANN: *Mahlmann* Theodor, Herrmann, Wilhelm (1846-1922): ➤ 597, TRE 15 (1986) 165-172.

d988 HIRSCH: *Birkner* Hans-J., Hirsch, Emanuel (1888-1972): ➤ 597, TRE 15 (1986) 390-4.

d989 EMüller Hans M., Die Umformung des christlichen Denkens in der Neuzeit; ein Lesebuch von Emanuel Hirsch. Tü/Goslar 1985, Katzmann/Thuhoff. 349 p. [NedTTs 41,260, R. *Hensen*].

d990 IWAND: *Seim* Jürgen, Die Lehre von Evangelium und Gesetz bei Hans J. Iwand: EvT 46 (1986) 231-246.

d991 JENKINS: **Harrison** Ted, The Durham phenomenon [Anglican bishop David Jenkins, whose comments on the Resurrection aroused a furore ➤ 1,4731.g299R]. L 1985, Darton-LT. 184 p. £2. 0-232-51671-5. – RExpTim 98 (1986s) 58 (R. *Lunt*: a man for whom concern and exploration matter more than an obscurantist 'credo quia impossibile').

d992 JOHANNES XXIII: EAlberigo G., Fede, tradizione, profezia; studi su Giovanni XXIII et sul Vaticano II: TRicScRel 21. Brescia 1984, Paideia. 290 p. – RRHE 81 (1986) 776-8 [R. *Aubert*].

d993 **Hebblethwaite** Peter, John XXIII, pope of the council. L 1984, Chapman. viii-550 p. £15. 0-225-66419-4. – RBrotéria 123 (1986) 577-9 (M. de *Almeida*); Gregorianum 67 (1986) 517-531 (M. *Chappin*).

d994 *Melloni* Alberto, Concordanza degli scritti di A. G. Roncalli / Giovanni XXIII: CrNSt 7 (1986) 353-360 [515-552, carteggio con C. COSTANTINI (*Simonato* Ruggero)].

d995 JOHANNES PAULUS II: **Wojtyła** Karol, Faith according to Saint John of the Cross [diss. 1948], ᵀ*Aumann* Jordan. SF 1985, Ignatius. 276 p. [RelStR 13,57, L. J. *Biallas*].

d996 **Wojtyła** Karol (Pope John Paul II), The Word made flesh; the meaning of the Christmas season. SF 1985, Harper. 129 p. $12.95 [JAAR 54,397].

d997 **Wojtyła** Karol, Ejercicios espirituales para jóvenes. M 1982, BAC. 154 p. – ᴿTVida 27 (1986) 331 (E. *Reyes*).

d998 **Arias** Juan, El enigma Wojtyła. M 1985, El País. 413 p. – ᴿRazF 213 (1986) 329 (M. *Alcalá*).

d999 **Buttiglione** Rocco, Il pensiero di Karol Wojtyła 1982 ➤ 65,e11; franç. ➤ 1,g198: ᴿRivStoLR 22 (1986) 594s (A. *Olivieri*).

e1 *Kalinowski* G., La réforme du thomisme et de la phénoménologie chez Karol Wojtyła selon Rocco Buttiglione: Archives de Philosophie 49 (1986) 127-146 [RSPT 70 (1986) 290].

e2 *Corpas de Posada* Isabel, La verdad sobre el hombre en los escritos de Juan Pablo II: TXav 36 (1986) 225-246.

e3 *Dec* Ignacy, Person als Subjekt; zum Personbegriff bei Karol Wojtyła: TG1 76 (1986) 294-307.

e4 *Hebblethwaite* Peter, HUSSERL, SCHELER and Wojtyła; a tale of three philosophers: HeythJ 27 (1986) 441-5.

e5 **Hogan** Richard M., *Le Voir* John M., Covenant of love; Pope John Paul II on sexuality, marriage, and family in the modern world. GCNY 1985, Doubleday. 246 p. $16. – ᴿTTod 43 (1986s) 116.118s (Mary P. *McGinty*).

e6 *Kowalczyck* Stanisław, Le personnalisme polonais contemporain [Wojtyła K. ...]: DivThom 88 (1985) 58-76.

e7 **Zizola** Giancarlo, La restaurazione di papa Wojtyła. Bari 1985, Laterza. 264 p. Lit. 15.000. – ᴿHumBr 41 (1986) 314s (T. *Goffi*).

e8 **Zizola** Giancarlo, La restauración del Papa Wojtyła. M 1986, Cristiandad. – ᴿRazF 213 (1986) 440s (M. *Alcalá*).

e9 JÜNGEL: **Webster** John B., Eberhard Jüngel, an introduction to his theology. C 1986, Univ. viii-182 p. £20 [TR 82,435]. 0-521-30708-2. – ᴿExpTim 98 (1986s) 150 (I. R. *Torrance*).

e10 KASPER: *Nichols* Aidan, Walter Kasper and his theological programme: NBlackfr 67 (1986) 16-23.

e11 KING: **Hanigan** James P., Martin Luther King, Jr. and the foundations of nonviolence (< diss.). Lanham MD 1984, UPA. iii-328 p. $24.75; pa. $14.50. – ᴿHorizons 13 (1986) 203s (P. G. *Coy*).

e12 ᴱ**Washington** James M., A testament of hope; the essential writings of Martin Luther King, Jr. SF 1986, Harper & R. 676 p. $22.50 [JAAR 54,633].

e13 KÜNG H., Does God exist? 1980 ➤ 61,y358c; 65,e18: ᴿRelStT 6 (1986) 27.34 (L. *Sabourin*).

e15 **Pozzo** Guido, Magistero e teologia in H. Küng e P. SCHOONENBERG [diss. Gregoriana 1982] 1983 ➤ 65,e23: ᴿScripTPamp 18 (1986) 375 (J. L. *Illanes*).

e16 *Kerr* Fergus, Küng's case for God: Vidyajyoti 49 (1985) 118-123.

e17 *Kiwiet* John, Hans Küng 1985 ➤ 1,g201: ᴿRefTR 45 (1986) 21s (G. A. *Cole*).

e18 LONERGAN: *a*) *Crowe* Frederick E., Bernard Lonergan as pastoral theologian; – *b*) *Sala* Giovanni B., KANTs antithetisches Problem und

Lonergans rationale Auffassung von der Wirklichkeit: Gregorianum 67 (1986) 451-470; franç. 470 / 471-515; Eng. 516.

e19 *Drilling* Peter J., Lonergan's method and Christian ministry: ScEspr 38 (1986) 181-202.

e20 **Dunne** Tad, Lonergan and spirituality; towards a spiritual integration. Ch 1985, Loyola Univ. ix-230 p. $12.95 [TDig 33,360].

e21 *Helminiak* Daniel A., Lonergan and systematic spiritual theology: NBlackf 67 (1986) 78-92.

e22 *Keefe* Donald J., A methodological critique of Lonergan's theological method: Thomist 50 (1986) 28-65.

e23 ᴱ**Lawrence** Fred, Lonergan workshop V/VI. Atlanta 1985/6, Scholars. 342 p./260 p. $13.50/. – ᴿExpTim 98 (1986s) 92 [99,124] (G. *Slater*).

e24 **Meynell** Hugo A., The theology of Bernard Lonergan: AAR 42. xii-139 p. Atlanta 1986, Scholars. xii-139 p. [ExpTim 99,124, G. *Slater*]. 1-55540-015-9; pa. 6-7.

e25 **O'Callaghan** Michael C., Unity in theology; Lonergan's framework for theology in its new context [diss. Tübingen, ᴰ*Kasper* W.] 1980 ➤ 62, m562...65,e26: ᴿHeythJ 27 (1986) 83s (G. *Walmsley*).

e26 *Robert* Pierre, Théologie et vie spirituelle; rencontre avec Bernard Lonergan [un an et demi avant sa mort 26.XI.1984]: ScEspr 38 (1986) 331-341.

.e27 *Roy* Louis, La contribution de Bernard Lonergan à la théologie contemporaine [*Tracy, O'Callaghan, Crowe*]: SR 14 (1985) 475-485.

e28 *Sala* J. B., Bernardo Lonergan; um teólogo examina a própria mente: Brotéria 122 (1986) 182-192.

e29 **Lubac** Henri de, The Christian faith; an essay on the structure of the Apostles' Creed, ᵀ*Arnandez* Richard. SF 1986, Ignatius. 353 p. $13 pa. [TDig 34,83].

e30 **Lubac** Henri de, *a)* Entretien autour de Vatican II: 1985 ➤ 1,g217: ᴿCC 137 (1986,4) 308 (G. *Mucci*); EfMex 4,10 (1986) 124-9 (F. *Guillén Preckler*); – *b)* Diálogo sobre el Vaticano II 1985 ➤ 1,g218: ᴿRazF 213 (1986) 329s (M. A. *López-Barajas*).

e31 **Lubac** Henri de, Lettres de M. Étienne GILSON commentées. P 1986, Cerf. 204 p. F 78. 2-204-02489-9. – ᴿActuBbg 23 (1986) 240s (J. *Pegueroles*).

e32 **Maier** Eugen, Einigung der Welt in Gott; das Katholische bei Henri de Lubac [Diss. FrB] 1983 ➤ 64,e602...1,g223: ᴿTrierTZ 95 (1986) 155s (E. *Sauser*).

e33 *Neufeld* Karl H., Henri de Lubac S.J. als Konzilstheologe; zur Vollendung seines 90. Lebensjahres: TPQ 134 (1986) 149-159.

e34 **LUHMANN** Niklas, Religious dogmatics and the evolution of societies [Funktion der Religion 1977 ch. 2], ᵀ*Beyer* Peter: Studies in Religion and Society 9. Lewiston NY 1984, Mellen. liii-137 p. $50. – ᴿTDig 33 (1986) 370 (W. C. *Heiser*: first access in English to this 15-year-controverted scholar).

e35 **NEWBIGIN** Lesslie, Unfinished agenda; an autobiography. GR 1985, Eerdmans. 263 p. $12. – ᴿEAsJT 4,2 (1986) 203s (M. G. *Fonner*); RExp 83 (1986) 637s (E. G. *Hinson*).

e36 *Williams* Stephen, Theologians in pursuit of the enlightenment [GUNTON C., Newbigin L., LOUTH A.]: TLond 39 (1986) 368-374.

e37 NIEBUHR: **Brown** Robert M., The essential Reinhold Niebuhr; selected essays and addresses. NHv 1986, Yale Univ. 264 p. $20. 0-300-03464-4. – ᴿExpTim 98 (1986s) 155 (T. *Baird*); TTod 43 (1986s) 267-270 (H. T. *Kerr*, also on Fox R.).

e38 **Cooper** John W., The theology of freedom; the legacy of Jacques
MARITAIN and Reinhold Niebuhr. Macon GA 1985, Mercer Univ. 185 p.
[JAAR 55,597, D. *Brackley*].

e39 **Fox** Richard W., Reinhold Niebuhr, a bibliography. NY 1985, Pantheon.
X-340 p.; 16 pl. [TDig 33,362]. $20. – ᴿEcuR 38 (1986) 237-240 (P.
Abrecht).

e40 ᴱ*Harries* Richard, Reinhold Niebuhr and the issues of our time. L 1986,
Mowbray. x-205 p. £7 pa. – ᴿMonth 248 (1986) (P. *Logan*); TLond 39
(1986) 490-2 (S. *Platten*).

e41 NIEBUHR H. R.: **Fowler** James W., To see the Kingdom; the theological
vision of H. Richard Niebuhr. Lanham MD 1985, UPA. 292 p. $13.75
[JAAR 54,399].

e42 **Grant** C. David, God the center of value; value theory in the theology of
H. Richard Niebuhr. Fort Worth 1984, Texas Christian Univ. X-185 p.
$17. – ᴿHorizons 13 (1986) 200s (T. A. *Byrnes*).

e43 ᴱ**Wells** David F., Reformed theology in America; a history of its modern
development [from Princeton Theology (*Hodge* C., *Warfield* B.) by Mark
Noll to the Niebuhrs]. GR/Exeter 1985, Eerdmans/Paternoster. 317 p.
£20. 0-8028-0096-3. – ᴿExpTim 98 (1986s) 248 (P. *Toon*).

e44 *Clutter* Ronald T., The reorganization of Princeton Theological Seminary
reconsidered: GraceTJ 7 (1986) 179-201.

e45 OTTO: **Almond** Philip C., Rudolf Otto; an introduction to his
philosophical theology 1984 ➤ 65,e38; 1,g235: ᴿJScStR 25 (1986) 263s
(P. C. *Appleby*).

e46 PANNENBERG: **Fraijó** Manuel, El sentido de la historia; introducción al
pensamiento de W. Pannenberg. M 1986, Cristiandad. 328 p. – ᴿRazF
214 (1986) 360 (J. *Gómez Caffarena*); SalT 74 (1986) 832s (J. *Conill
Sancho*).

e47 *Martínez Camino* Juan A., La teología de W. Pannenberg interpretada por
M. FRAIJÓ; crítica de una crítica: EstE 61 (1986) 425-433.

e48 **Müller** Denis, Parole et histoire; dialogue avec W. Pannenberg 1983
➤ 65,e41: ᴿEstE 61 (1986) 471s (J. J. *Alemany*: claro, conscienzudo).

e49 **Pedrazzoli** Mauro, Intellectus quaerens fidem; fede-ragione in W.
Pannenberg ... RAHNER, BLONDEL e PASCAL: StAnselm 80, 1981
➤ 62,m576: ᴿActuBbg 23 (1986) 230 (J. *Boada*).

e50 PAULUS VI: *a) Danneels* G. card., *al.*, Le rôle de G. B. Montini — Paul VI
dans la réforme liturgique: colloque (Ist. Paolo VI —) LvN, 17.X.1984. —
b) Silvestrini A., *al.*, Paul VI et les réformes institutionnelles dans l'église:
colloque (Ist. Paolo VI —) FrS, 9.XI.1985: RHE 81 (1986) 671s [R.
Aubert].

e51 PIUS X, XI, XII: *Aubert* R., *a)* Pie X; *b)* Pie XI; *c)* Pie XII: ➤ 578,
Catholicisme XI,50 (1986) 279-287-300-311.

e52 **POHIER** Jacques, Dieu fractures 1985 ➤ 1,g241: ᴿEsprV 96 (1986) 344-6
(P. *Jay*); LumièreV 35,176 (1986) 89-91 (C. *Duquoc*); RevSR 60 (1986) 125s
(C. *Wackenheim*); Theologiai Szemle 29 (1986) 123s (I. *Karasszon*).

e53 **Pohier** Jacques, God — in fragments, ᵀ*Bowden* John. L 1985, SCM. –
ᴿNorTTs (1986) 62-64 (R. *Leivestad*); Tablet 240 (1986) 93s (A. *Nichols*;
delphic conclusions not inspiring hope); TLond 39 (1986) 291-6 (E.
Robertson: his When I say God 1977 had an effect comparable to
ROBINSON's Honest to God).

e54 **Pohier** J., God in fragmenten. Hilversum 1986, Gooi & S. 366 p. Fb 1100
[CollatVl 16,507].

e55 *Butterworth* Robert, Pohier's liberation of God [God in fragments 1985:

'Job like Pohier at least was honest enough to refuse the dead theological comfort of "friends" ']:   Month 248 (1986) 191-7.

e56 **RAHNER** K., Aimer Jésus [3 art.], [E]*Doré* Joseph: JJC 24.   P 1885, Desclée. F 68. – [R]VSp 140 (1986) 742s (P.-T. *Camelot*).

e57 **Rahner** Karl,   Le courage du théologien [< Karl Rahner im Gespräch (1964-1982) 1982s], [E]*Imhof* P., *Biallowons* H., [T]*Bagot* J. 1985 ➤ 1,g247; F 110:   [R]ÉglT 17 (1986) 116-8 (A. *Peelman*); ÉTRel 61 (1986) 464-6 (A. *Dupleix*).

e58 **Imhof** Paul, *Biallowons* Hubert,   Glaube in winterlicher Zeit; Gespräche mit Karl Rahner aus den letzten Lebensjahren.   Dü 1986, Patmos. 3-491-77631-7. – [R]EstE 61 (1986) 482s [J. *García Pérez*].

e59 *Rahner* Karl,   Le culte du Cœur de Jésus aujourd'hui [< SchriftenTh 16, 305-320]:   VieCons 58 (1986) 259-272.

e60 **Rahner** Karl,   Expériences d'un théologien catholique, [TE]*Mengus* Raymond.   P 1986, Cariscript.   50 p.

e61 *Rahner* Karl, [E]*Krauss* Meinold,   La fatica di credere.   Cinisello Balsamo 1986, Paoline.   125 p. Lit. 9000. – [R]CC 137 (1986,2) 103 (P. *Vanzan*).

e62 **Rahner** Karl,   Mój problem; K. Rahner odpowiada na pytania młodzieży [1982 ➤ 64,e612], [T]. Wsz 1985, Pax.   100 p. – [R]AtKap 107 (1986) 181s (S. *Knap*).

e63 **Callahan** Annice,   Karl Rahner's spirituality of the pierced heart [< Boston College diss.]. Lanham MD 1985, UPA.   xix-177 p. $11.50 pa. – [R]Horizons 13 (1986) 191s (J. J. *Buckley*: ch. 1-4 before Vat. II; 5-6 after); RelStR 12 (1986) 271 (M. *Downey*: masterful; unusually delivers what it promises on relation between systematic theology and spirituality).

e64 *Maas-Ewerd* Theodor,   Odo CASEL OSB und Karl Rahner SJ; Disput über das Wiener Memorandum 'Theologische und philosophische Zeitfragen im katholischen deutschen Raum' [< Hab.-Diss. 1981]: ArLtgW 28 (1986) 193-234.

e65 *Neufeld* K. H.,   Karl Rahner zu Busse und Beichte: ZkT 108 (1986) 55-61.

e66 *Peters* Albrecht,   Zwischen Gottesmystik und Christuszeugnis; zur Theologie Karl Rahners (5.3.1904 - 30.3.1984): TRu 51 (1986) 269-314.

e67 **Taylor** Mark L.,   God is love; a study in the theology of Karl Rahner [critique and alternative]: [J]AAR 50.   xv-416 p. $25; pa. $19 [TDig 34,93].

e68 **Vass** George,   Understanding Karl Rahner I-II, 1985 ➤ 1,g256 [Westminster MD Christian Classics edition 1985 puts before this title 'A theologian in search of a philosophy']: [R]America 154 (1986) 102 (V. *Guagliardo*); HeythJ 27 (1986) 84-86 (J. *Macquarrie*); TS 47 (1986) 726-8 (R. *Kress*: unfavorable, not only because of dubious English; cavalier treatment of God's universal salvific will is 'most dismaying').

e69 *Verweyen* H.,   Wie wird ein Existential übernatürlich? ... Rahner: TrierTZ 95 (1986) 115-131.

e70 **Vorgrimler** Herbert,   Understanding Karl Rahner; an introduction to his life and thought [K. R. verstehen, eine Einführung 1985 ➤ 1,g257], [T]*Bowden* John.   L 1986, SCM.   x-198 p. 0-334-01723-8. – [R]ExpTim 98 (1986s) 62s (R. *Butterworth*: the present Pontiff refused to be photographed with Rahner wearing a tie).

e71 **RATZINGER** Joseph,   Les principes de la théologie catholique, esquisse et matériaux, [T]*Maltier* J.: Croire et savoir.   P 1985, Téqui.   445 p. – [R]ScEspr 38 (1986) 273-5 (B. *de Margerie*).

e72 *Ratzinger* J. (*Messori* V.),   Informe sobre la fe: BAC pop. 66, 1985 ➤ 1,g259: [R]Burgense 27 (1986) 319s (N. *López Martínez*); CiTom 113 (1986) 159 (A. *Bandera*); RazF 212 (1985) 216-8 [M. *Alcalá*].

e73 **Ratzinger** Joseph [Gespräch mit *Messori* Vittorio], Zur Lage des Glaubens 1985 ⇥ 1,g260; 215 p.; DM 28: ᴿTPhil 61 (1986) 609 (M. *Kehl*); TR 82 (1986) 50s (H. U. von *Balthasar*).

e74 **Ratzinger** Joseph, interview with *Messori* Vittorio, The state of the Church 1985 ⇥ 1,g258: ᴿTS 47 (1986) 311-4 (J. J. *Hughes*).

e75 **Ratzinger** Joseph, (*Messori* V.), Entretiens sur la foi. P 1985, Fayard. 252 p. F 75. − ᴿNRT 108 (1986) 442s (A. *Toubeau*).

e76 **Ratzinger** J., *Messori* V., A fé em crise? O Cardeal se intérroga. São Paulo 1985, Ed. Pedagógica e Universitária. 154 p. − ᴿRCuBíb 10,37s (1986) 159s (A. *Charbel*).

e77 *Cipriani* Settimio, Il 'rapporto sulla fede' del Cardinale Ratzinger [*Messori* V. 1985; 'tra lucidità e pessimismo' ... certe riserve]: Asprenas 32 (1985) 445-452.

e78 **Biot** François, *Bernard* Stéphan, Lève-toi et marche; réponse à Ratzinger. P 1985, Témoignage Chrétien. − ᴿQVidCr 131s (1986) 225 (E. *Vilanova*).

e79 **Thils** Gustave, En dialogue avec l'"Entretien sur la foi' [*Ratzinger* J. 1984]. Lv 1986, Peeters. 96 p. [EsprV 97,64].

e80 **Velasco** Rufino, Réplica a Ratzinger, a propósito de su libro 'Informe sobre la fe'. Bilbao 1986, Desclée-B. 94 p. − ᴿNatGrac 33 (1986) 590 (A. *Villalmonte*: 'Recomendamos ... como una pertinente crítica a la poco oportunada exposición de [aquel] difficilis, querulus, iners, pavidusque futuri').

e81 **RAUSCHENBUSCH** Walter, Selected writings, ᴱ*Hudson* Winthrop S.: Sources of American Spirituality 1, 1984 ⇥ 1,233*; $15; 0-8091-0356-7. − ᴿGregorianum 67 (1986) 190-2 (C. *O'Neill*).

e82 **ROSENZWEIG**: *Friedmann* Friedrich G., Franz Rosenzweigs neues Denken: Orientierung 50 (1986) 255-260.

e83 **SCHILDER**: *Minnen* J. M. van, Licht in den rook; de theologie van Prof. Dr. K. Schilder: GerefTTs 86 (1986) 80-100.

e84 **SCHILLEBEECKX** E., Gott ist jeden Tag neu 1984 ⇥ 65,e56: ᴿTGegw 29 (1986) 187s (A. *Schmied*).

e85 *Borgman* Erik, Theologie tussen universiteit en emancipatie; de weg van Edward Schillebeeckx: TsTNijm 26 (1986) 240-258; Eng. 258.

e86 **Schoof** T., The Schillebeeckx case 1984 ⇥ 65,e63: ᴿSpTod 38 (1986) 271-3 (P. *Philibert*).

e87 **SMITH**: **Clemens** Keith W., The theology of Ronald Gregor Smith. Leiden 1986, Brill. 328 p. *f*120. 90-04-07298-5. − ᴿExpTim 98 (1986s) (A. D. *Galloway*).

e88 **TEILHARD DE CHARDIN** Pierre, Lettres à Jeanne Mortier. P 1984, Seuil. 187 p. − ᴿScEspr 38 (1986) 143-6 (J. *Langlois*: et les réponses?).

e89 **TILLICH** Paul, Dogmatik; Marburger Vorlesung von 1925, ᴱ*Schüssler* W. Dü 1986, Patmos. 397 p. DM 49,80 [TLZ 112,838-41, H. *Fischer*].

e90 **Tillich** Paul, Teología sistemática, I. La razón y la revelación; el Ser de Dios [1951]; II. La existencia de Cristo [c. 1951]. Salamanca 1981, Sígueme. 382 p.; 246 p. [III. 1984 ⇥ 1,g273]. − ᴿEstJos 40,79 (1986) 137 (S. *Ros García*).

e91 **Tillich** Paul, Perspectivas da Teología Protestante nos séculos dezenove e vinte, intr. *Braaten* Carl E. São Bernardo do Campo SP 1986, Imprensa Metodista. 232 p. [REB 46,723].

e92 ᴱ**Adams** James L. *al.*, The thought of Paul Tillich. SF 1985, Harper & R. xi-404 p. $25. − ᴿCurrTM 13 (1986) 320 (C. W. *Filer*: GILKEY L., TRACY D. noteworthy).

e93 **Albrecht** R., *Schüssler* W., Paul Tillich, sein Werk [= P. Tillich, sein

Leben (I. 1978 < Eng. 1976) II]. Dü 1986, Patmos.   224 p. DM 39,80 [TGl 77,498, A. *Seigfried*].

e94 **Carreras** P., Religió i cultura en Paul Tillich; el diàleg entre la religió i la cultura: Horitzons. Barc 1985, Claret. 80 p. 84-7263-363-2. – ᴿEstE 61 (1986) 468 (J. J. *Sánchez*).

e95 **Newport** John P., Paul Tillich 1984 → 65,e69; 1,g277: ᴿWestTJ 48 (1986) 207-212 (R. W. *Vunderink*).

e96 *Pastor* Félix-A., Itinerario espiritual de Paul Tillich; consideraciones ante un centenario: Gregorianum 67 (1986) 47-85; Eng. 86.

e97 *Richard* Jean, Les religions non chrétiennes et le christianisme dans la première dissertation de Tillich sur SCHELLING [Cinquième Colloque Tillich, Montpellier 5-6.I.1985]: SR 14 (1985) 415-434.

e98 *Rössler* Andreas, Paul Tillichs Programm einer evangelischer Katholizität: ÖkRu 35 (1986) 415-427.

e99 *Schnübbe* Otto, Die Botschaft der Rechtfertigung als Überwindung der Sinnkrise bei Paul Tillich: Luther 57 (Wu 1986) 99-113.

e100 *Schwöbel* Christoph, Tendenzen der Tillich-Forschung (1967-1983): TRu 51 (1986) 166-223.

e101 WITTGENSTEIN: *Diamond* Malcolm L., Wittgenstein and religion [*Edwards* J.; *Nielsen* K. 1982]: RelStR 12 (1986) 17-22.

e102 **Kerr** Fergus, Theology after Wittgenstein. Ox 1986, Blackwell. xii-202 p.; bibliog. p. 191-8. £22.50. 0-631-14688-8. – ᴿExpTim 98 (1986s) 86s W. D. *Hudson*; raises the question of whether even God can be 'bodiless').

Y6.8   *Tendentiae exeuntis saeculi XX* – **Late 20th Century Movements.**

e103 ᴱ**Alberigo** G., *Jossua* J. P., La réception de Vatican II: CogF 134, 1985 → 1,g279a: ᴿComSev 19 (1986) 444s (M. *Sánchez*); EsprV 96 (1986) 10-12 (P. *Jay*); MélSR 43 (1986) 113 (M. *Hu[f]tier*); TS 47 (1986) 533s (C. J. *Peter*: awaited in English); VSp 140 (1986) 738-742 (P.-T. *Camelot*).

e104 ᴱ**Alberigo** Giuseppe, *Jossua* Jean-Pierre, Il Vaticano II e la Chiesa 1985 → 1,g279b: ᴿRivStoLR 22 (1986) 572-5 (A. *Bodrato*: intenzione esplicita di controbilanciare l'immagine negativa proposta dal card. RATZINGER).

e105 ᴱ**Alberigo** G., *al.*, Kirche im Wandel... nach II. Vat. 1982 → 64,468b: ᴿTsTKi 57 (1986) 313s (Ola *Tjørhom*).

e106 **Balasuriya** Tissa (m.), Planetary theology 1984 → 1,8032.8218: ᴿÉglT 17 (1986) 403s (R. P. *Hardy*: enthusiastic).

e107 **Beeck** Frans J. van, Catholic identity after Vatican II; three types of faith in the one Church. Ch 1985, Loyola Univ. xi-133 p. $9 [Horizons 14,385-7, Margaret Mary *Reher*].

e108 *Bernardin* card., The Church in the third millennium: CanadCathR 4 (Apr. 1986).

e109 *Biser* Eugen, Religiöse Spurensuche; Christentum in postsäkularisierter Zeit: StiZt 204 (1986) 609-624.

e110 **Blasig** W., Christ im Jahr 2000: 1984 → 1,g281: ᴿClaretianum 26 (1986) 353s (B. *Proietti*).

e111 ᴱ**Bryant** M. Darrol, The future of Anglican theology 1984 → 1,551: ᴿSR 15 (1986) 110-2 (Joanne M. *Dewart*).

e112 **Bühlmann** Walbert, The church of the future; a model for the year 2001 [1984 → 1,g284], ᵀ*Groves* Mary. Maryknoll NY/Melbourne/Slough 1986, Orbis/Dove/St. Paul. xiii-207 p. $11 pa. [TDig 33,461]. – ᴿAmerica 155 (1986) 430s (J. J.*Hughes*); CleR 71 (1986) 155s (S. E. *Hall*); Spiritus 27 (1986) 330 (F. *Richard*).

e113 **Bühlmann** Walbert, ❷ Gdzie żyją wiarą; kościół u progu XXI wieku. Wsz 1985, Verbinum. [AtKap 108,524, J. *Salamon*].

e114 *Chmiel* Jerzy, ❷ De scientia biblica post Vaticanum II; XX anni Const. dogm. 'Dei Verbum' (1965-1985): RuBi 39 (1986) 1-4 (21-23).

e115 **Cox** Harvey, Religion in the secular city; toward a postmodern theology 1984 → 65,e73; 1,g287: ᴿJScStR 24 (1985) 222s (C. J. *Bourg*).

e116 **Cox** Harvey, La religión en la ciudad secular; hacia una teología postmoderna. Santander 1985, SalTerrae. 255 p. – ᴿSalT 73 (1985) 855s (J. A. *García*).

e117 **Davis** Charles, What is living, what is dead, in Christianity today? Breaking the liberal-conservative deadlock. SF 1986, Harper & R. 131 p. $17 [JAAR 55,420].

e118 [ᶠSᴀʀᴛᴏʀɪ Luigi → 1,119 (bibliog. 215-30)] ᴱ*Dianich* S., *Tura* E. R., Venti anni dopo il Concilio Vaticano II; contributi sulla sua recezione in Italia 1985: ᴿStPatav 33 (1986) 406-410 (C. *Scilironi*).

e119 **Dreyfus** François-Georges, Des Évêques contre le Pape; essai sur la crise du catholicisme français. P 1985, Grasset. 238 p. – ᴿRHPR 66 (1986) 380s (R. *Mehl*: si l'on ne le savait pas luthérien, on penserait certainement que c'est un intégriste catholique, côté RATZINGER non LEFEBVRE).

e120 **Drummond** Richard H., Toward a new age in Christian theology [... interreligious dialogue]: American Society of Missiology 8, 1985 → 1,g291; 0-88344-514-X. – ᴿGregorianum 67 (1986) 791s (J. *Dupuis*); PhilipSac 21 (1986) 315-7 (E. M. *Domingo*); RHPR 66 (1986) 470s (G. *Vahanian*); ScotJT 39 (1986) 562s (B. *Russell*).

e121 **Gill** Jerry H., On knowing God; new directions for the future of theology. Ph 1981, Westminster. 174 p. $10. 0-664-24380-0. – ᴿRelStR 12 (1986) 264s (P. *Mullins*).

e122 **Fichter** Joseph, The Holy Family of Father Moon. KC 1985, Leaven. 155 p. $8 pa. – ᴿBToday 24 (1986) 60 (C. *Stuhlmueller*: this Jesuit sociologist defends the Unification Church's right to exist, and compares its origins with those of Christianity).

e123 *Firet* J., De bediening van het geheimnis; over het beroep van predikant op de grens van het derde millennium: GerefTTs 86 (1986) 193-206.

e124 ᴱ**Floristán** Casiano, *al.*, El Vaticano II, veinte años después 1985 → 1,345: ᴿScripTPamp 18 (1986) 323-7 (J. M. *Odero*).

e126 *Haas* Johannes, Kirche in der Jahrtausendwende; eine Literaturauslese zur Kirchenzukunft: TPQ 134 (1986) 182-189.

e127 **Häring** Bernard, **McBrien** Richard, **La Verdiere** Eugene, A Christian agenda for A.D. 2001. Canfield 1984, Alba. 3 cassettes. $30. – ᴿRRel 45 (1986) 948s (Mary Catherine *Barron*).

e128 **Hebblethwaite** Peter, Synod extraordinary; the inside story of the Roman Synod, Nov./Dec. 1985. L 1986, Darton-LT. 146 p. £4. 0-232-516650. – ᴿExpTim 97 (1985s) 382 (J. *Kent*: gallant attempt to interest us in a non-event; he still hopes for more collegial power for the episcopate, 'a very unlikely body on which to base a satisfactory form of open Catholicism').

e129 **Hourdin** Georges, Au Pape Jean-Paul II et aux évêques du Synode; sur la nécessité d'achever le Concile. P 1985, Desclée. 176 p. F 72. – ᴿCC 137 (1986,4) 202s (G. *Caprile*: superficiale).

e129* **Kasper** W., Il futuro dalla forza del Concilio; sinodo straordinario dei vescovi 1985, documenti e commento: GdT 164. Brescia 1986, Queriniana. 106 p. Lit. 9000. – ᴿNRT 108 (1986) 931s (A. *Toubeau*).

e130 **Kaufman** Gordon, Theology for a nuclear age. Manchester/Ph 1985, Univ./Westminster. 66 p. $13; pa. $9. – ᴿCommonweal 113 (1986) 156-8

(Joan D. *Chittister*); RHPR 66 (1986) 471s (G. *Vahanian*); TorJT 2 (1986) 395-7 (D. B. *Stoesz*).

e131 **Koenig** Franz card., Chiesa dove vai? Gianni *Licheri* interroga. R 1985, Borla. 122 p. Lit. 10.000. – ᴿCC 137 (1986,3) 431-3 (G. *Caprile*: testimonianza fra le più autorevoli).

e132 **Koenig** Franz, Iglesia, ¿adónde vas? Gianni *Licheri* entrevista al Cardenal, ᵀ*García Abril* Jesús: Servidores y Testigos 26. Santander 1986, Sal Terrae. 111 p. 84-293-0737-0. – ᴿActuBbg 23 (1986) 235s (I. *Riudor*: optimista y esperanzador); RazF 213 (1986) 554s (M. *Alcalá*).

e133 **Koenig** Franz, [interviews with *Licheri* Gianni], Where the Church is heading. L 1986, St. Paul. 122 p. £5. 0-85439-251-3. – ᴿExpTim 98 (1986s) [C. S. *Rodd* recommends highly].

e134 ᴱ**Küng** H., *Tracy* D., Theologie — wohin? 1984 → 65,513: ᴿÖkRu 35 (1986) 218s (B. *Jaspert*).

e135 *Latourelle* René, Du Concile au Synode extraordinaire [1985]; à propos de deux ouvrages récents [Réception/Célébration de Vatican II, 1984s]: ScEspr 38 (1986) 380-391.

e136 **Lindbeck** George A., The nature of doctrine; religion and theology in a postliberal age 1984 → 1,g303: ᴿJTS 37 (1986) 277-282 (D. F. *Ford*: important); ModT 3 (1986s) 110-3 (M. *Corner*); TLond 39 (1986) 51-53 (M. *Kitchener*).

e137 *Loza* José, La exégesis bíblica 20 años después de la Dei Verbum II: EfMex... 4,11 (1986) 11-39.

e138 **Martin** Malachi, Vatican. Secker & W. £11. – ᴿTablet 240 (1986) 863s (A. *Greeley*: 'Martin speaks for the "hard" right of contemporary Catholicism', grossly unfair to his patron BEA).

e139 **Martini** C. M., Parole sulla Chiesa; meditazioni sul Vaticano II per i laici dei Consigli pastorali. Mi/Casale Monferrato 1986, Centro Ambrosiano/Piemme. 144 p. Lit. 10.500 [NRT 109,136, A. *Toubeau*].

e140 *Martini* Carlo M., La Chiesa italiana a un anno da Loreto [raduno 1985; relazione Napoli 1986]: Asprenas 3 (1986) 163-178.

e141 *Mera* Ramón, Vaticano II; balance de un balance: MiscCom 44 (1986) 201-224.

e142 **Mondello** Vittorio, Quale vescovo per il futuro? La dottrina dell'episcopato nella Chiesa 1984 → 65,6893: ᴿCC 137 (1986,3) 540s (G. *Mucci*: sembra far RAHNER limitare il Papa).

e143 *Muck* Terry present., Into the next century; trends facing the Church: ChrTod (Jan. 17 insert, 1986) 1-32 [< BS 143 (1986) 268].

e144 **Newbigin** Lesslie, The other side of 1984; questions for the churches. Geneva 1983, WCC. 75 p. – ᴿScotJT 39 (1986) 402-4 (D. M. *Murray*).

e145 ᴱ*O'Connell* Timothy E., Vatican II and its documents; an American appraisal: Theology and Life 15. Wilmington 1986, Glazier. 260 p. $11 pa. [Horizons 14,383, Anita M. *Hyslop*].

e146 *Ollig* Hans L., Schwierigkeiten mit der neuzeitlichen Rationalität; Anmerkungen zur jüngsten Vernunftkritik [*Sloterdijk* P., Kritik der zynischen Vernunft (Fra 1983; 60.000 Exemplare in kurzer Zeit verkauft); *Bergfleth* G., Zur Kritik der palavernden Vernunft 1984; *Böhme* H. & G., Das Andere der Vernunft 1983]: TPhil 61 (1986) 86-109.

e147 *Ottlyk* Ernő, Ⓜ The Second Vatican Council was convened 20 years ago: Theologiai Szemle 29 (1986) 44-49.

e148 **Parente** Pietro, A venti anni dal Concilio Vaticano II; esperienze e prospettive. R 1985, Città Nuova. 85 p. Lit. 6000. – ᴿCC 137 (1986,4) 308 (G. *Mucci*).

e149 **Perini** Giuseppe, Il Concilio e il post-concilio negli scritti del Card. G. SIRI [... fantascienza negli studi biblici p. 115]: DivThom 88 (1985) 100-144.

e150 **Ramm** B., After fundamentalism 1983 ➤ 64,e643 ... 1,g314: ᴿRExp 83 (1986) 113s (W. L. *Hendricks*: pun; he is also *going after* it).

e151 **Ratzinger** Joseph, Fede e futuro [conferenze e conversazioni]. Brescia 1984, Queriniana. 118 p. Lit. 9000. – ᴿCiVit 41 (1986) 485 (Susanna *Bellizzi*).

e152 *Ruether* R. R., Waarom blijf ik in die kerk? [= Crises and challenges of Catholicism today, lecture 1985]: Streven 53 (1985s) 483-495.

e153 **Rynne** Xavier, John Paul's extraordinary synod; a collegial achievement. Wilmington 1986, Glazier. xi-132 p. $8 [RelStR 13,335, J. *Ford*: his Vatican-II flair has mellowed].

e154 ᴱ**Savart** C., *Aletti* J.-N., Le monde contemporain et la Bible; Bible de tous les temps 8, 1985 ➤ 1,311: ᴿRHPR 66 (1986) 379s (E. *Goichot*).

e155 **Stark** Rodney, *Bainbridge* William S., The future of religion; secularization, revival, and cult formation. Berkeley 1985, Univ. California. 571 p. $29.50. –ᴿJAAR 54 (1986) 615-7 (S. C. *Porter*).

e156 ᴱ**Strecker** Georg [NT p. 61-145] Theologie im 20. Jahrhundert; Stand und Aufgaben [AT, *Schmidt* Werner H., p. 1-60]: Uni-TB 1238, 1983 ➤ 64,358; 1,g321: ᴿHeythJ 27 (1986) 340s (M. *Lattke*: merits translation).

e157 **Taylor** Mark C., Erring, a postmodern a/theology 1984 ➤ 1,g323: ᴿJAAR 54 (1986) 153-6 (C. A. *Raschke*: duly bewildered); also JAAR 54 (1986) 523s.543-7 (Edith *Wyschogrod*), 525-9 (T. J. J. *Altizer*), 529-534 (A. *Lingis*), 534-543 (J. *Prabhu*); reply by *Taylor*, 547-555; JRel 66 (1986) 324 ... (W. *Lowe*); RelStR 12 (1986) 256-9 (P. C. *Hodgson*: first full-scale deconstructive theology, anticipated by himself 1982 and ALTIZER T. 1982) & 259-261 (E. *Holzwarth*: what literary theory would be if literature did not exist).

e158 **Taylor** Mark C., Errance, lecture de Jacques DERRIDA [Erring, a postmodern A/Theology 1984],ᵀ. P 1985, Cerf. 286 p. [SR 16,382, Anne *Fortin*].

e159 **Thils** Gustave, Pour une théologie de structure planétaire: RTLv Cah 6, 1983 ➤ 64,e647; 1,g325: ᴿActuBbg 23 (1986) 104 (J. *Boada*).

e160 **Tillard** J. M. R., Haben wir das Zweite Vatikanum 'rezipiert'? [< OneInC 21 (1985) 276-283]: TGegw 29 (1986) 65-72.

e161 *Vályi-Nagy* Ervin, Zur Lage der heutigen deutschsprachigen Theologie; Bemerkungen eines ungarischen Theologen: EvT 46 (1986) 4-11.

e162 *Vanzan* Piersandro, Sinodo straordinario dei vescovi a vent'anni dal Concilio; un bilancio [prolusione del card. G. *Danneels* basata su 99 risposte preliminari 'e dialogo/diatriba a distanza tra pretoriani del Papa e teologi affetti dal complesso antiromano' (p. 124) fa chiaro che abbiamo compreso e applicato male lo spirito e la lettera di Vat. II]: RasT 27 (1986) 120-135.

e163 **Vattimo** G., La fine della modernità; nichilismo ed ermeneutica nella cultura post-moderna. Mi 1985, Garzanti. 189 p. Lit. 16.000. – ᴿProtestantesimo 41 (1986) 142-8 (Elena *Bein Ricco*).

e165 **Wildiers** Max, Theologie op nieuwe wegen. Antwerpen/Kampen 1985, Ned.-B./Kok. 121 p. *f*17,50 [NedTTs 41,162, R. *Reeling Brouwer*].

e166 *Williams* John, The shape of the church to come?: TLond 39 (1986) 194-202.

e166* **Winling** Raymond, La théologie contemporaine (1945-1980) 1983 ➤ 64,e649; 65,e82: ᴿRTLv 17 (1986) 228 (E. *Brito*: comme il l'admet, pratiquement sur France-Allemagne-Belgique, 'la théologie catholique qui vise le renouveau et même la théologie officielle est un fait européen').

e167 **Wogaman** J. Philip, Faith and fragmentation; Christianity for a new age [a broken vessel, which can yet convey living water]. Ph 1985, Fortress. xi-196 p. $11. – ᴿRelStR 12 (1986) 269 (S. *Crocco*); TS 47 (1986) 705s (R. L. *Maddox*: liberal Protestant concern that Christianity can measure up to the modern, rarely whether correct it).

Y7 (*Acta*) **Congressuum** .2 biblica: **nuntii,** *rapports, Berichte.*

e168 *Calloud* Jean, Rencontre nationale des groupes 'Sémiotique et Bible', La Tourette (Couvent Le Corbusier) 28 Août - 2 Septembre 1986: SémiotB 43 (1986) 32-35 [*al.* 30-32].

e169 *Catchpole* David R., Studiorum Novi Testamenti Societas, the fortieth general meeting, 19-23 August 1985 [Trondheim]: NTS 32 (1986) 293-6; Membership list, 297-320.

e170 *a) Chmiel* Jerzy, ❷ Prawo (das Gesetz) w Nowym Testamencie; Sympozjum biblijne w Brixen 1985; – *b) Woźniak* Jerzy, ❷ Konferencja syriologiczna w Lejdzie [Leiden 30-31.VIII] (1985); – *c) Wodecki* Bernard, ❷ Dni Judaistyczne w Pieniężnie [Judaism; Verbite seminary, Pieniężno 16-17.IV.1986]: RuBi 39 (1986) 495s / 497s / 498-500.

e171 *Delorme* J., [*Panier* L.], Parole, figure et parabole; résumés des communications, Colloque 10ᵉᵐᵉ anniv. [Le Corbusier 13-15.VI.1986]: SémiotB 43 (1986) 1-7.

e172 *Díez Merino* Luis, *a)* Los estudios arameo-targúmicos en el IX Congreso de Estudios Judíos (Jerusalén) [4-12.VIII.1985]; – *b)* Los estudios arameo-targúmicos en el Segundo Simposio Bíblico Español (15-18 sept. 1985, Córdoba): EstB 44 (1986) 195-219 / 221-6: resumen detallado de cada estudio.

e173 [*Evers* Georg], Erste Asiatische Arbeitstagung zum Bibelapostolat, Hong Kong 27.-31.X.1985: TKontext 7,2 (1986) 115s.

e174 *Fenton* Paul, Deuxième conférence internationale de la Société d'Études Judéo-Arabes [Jérusalem 13-15.VIII.1985]: RÉJ 145 (1986) 389-392.

e175 *Focant* Camille, La réception des écrits néotestamentaires dans le christianisme primitif; Colloquium biblicum lovaniense XXXVI [26-28.VIII.1986]: RTLv 17 (1986) 466-9.

e176 *Fusco* Vittorio, VIII colloquio sull'interpretazione [Lc 15,11 ...; Macerata 17-19 marzo 1986]: RivB 34 (1986) 400.

e177 *Gratsěas* G., ❻ From the 36th Congress of Journées Bibliques de Louvain [26-28.VIII.1986; Reception of NT texts in the early Church]: DeltioVM 16,1 (1987) 58-65.

e178 *Haim* Abraham, Deuxième Congrès international pour l'étude du patrimoine juif sépharade et oriental (Jérusalem Mount Scopus 23-28.XII.1984): RÉJ 145 (1986) 103-115.

e179 *Leonardi* Giovanni, Settimana Biblica Nazionale dell'A[ssociazione]BI, Roma 15/19 settembre 1986: StPatav 33 (1986) 725-736.

e180 *Liebster* Wolfram, Christlicher Glaube als 'unüberbrückbarer religiöser Gegensatz zum Judentum'? Neutestamentliche Wissenschaft im Dritten Reich; ein Tagungsbericht, Arnoldshain 17.-19. Januar 1986: Judaica 42 (1986) 240-254.

e181 *Lust* J., The IOSOT-Congress in Jerusalem 1986: ETL 62 (1986) 448-450.

e182 *Macuch* Rudolf, Internationales Samaritanistenkolloquium (7.-9.X.-1985); ZDMG 136,3 (1986) *37*s.

e183 *Maggiani* Silvano, La Bibbia nella liturgia; interpretazione e prassi; XV

Settimana di Studio dell'Associazione di Professori e Cultori di Liturgia: RivLtg 73 (1986) 694-8.

e184 *Mędala* Stanisław, ● Biblia i informatyka [LvN 2-4.IX.1985]: ColcT 56,3 (1986) 173-180.

e185 *Mesters* Carlos, 'Como a água do rio que carrega o barquinho das comunidades' — sobre o uso da Bíblia no VI Encontro Intereclesial das Comunidades de Base: → 459, REB 46 (1986) 569-577.

e186 *North* Robert, Symposium on the mythic in Israel's origins [Rome Feb. 10-11, 1986, Accademia dei Lincei]: Biblica 67 (1986) 440-8.

e187 *Passoni dell'Acqua* Anna, *a)* XXVIII settimana biblica nazionale per professori [10-14.IX.1984, Storiografia nella Bibbia]; – *b)* Convegno di Studi Veterotestamentari, Bocca di Magra 1-4.IX.1985: ParVi 30 (1985) 61-64 / 457-460.

e188 *Petzold* Lothar, Biblisches Erzählen; Werkstattbericht vom 2. Bibel-kongress in Görlitz: CLehre 39 (B 1986) 68-75 [< ZIT].

e189 Primer encuentro latinoamericano de pastoral bíblica, Bogotá 22-26. VII.1985: Medellín 12,45 (1986) 141s [TKontext 8/1,71]; – declaración final: RBibArg 48 (1986) 60-64.

e190 *Saenz Galache* M., II Simposio Bíblico español [Córdoba, 15-18. IX.1985]: BibFe 12 (1986) 139s.

e191 *Shanks* Hershel, *a)* Israel's turn at the Annual Meeting [ASOR, SBL, AAR, Anaheim Nov. 23-26, 1985]: BAR-W 12,2 (1986) 4.6-8; 12 portraits; – *b)* Summer's star — the [1986 Jerusalem] meetings of the International Organization for the Study of the OT: BAR-W 12,6 (1986) 14.16.

e192 *a)* *Söding* Thomas, Tagung der deutschsprachigen kath. Neutestamentler in Brixen vom 18. bis 23. März 1985; – *b)* *Schnackenburg* R., 40. Generalversammlung der Studiorum Novi Testamenti Societas 19.-23. August 1985 in Trondheim/Norwegen: BZ 30 (1986) 147-9 / 150-2.

e193 *Walsh* Jerome T., Report of the Forty-Ninth General Meeting of the Catholic Biblical Association [Washington D.C. 6-9.VIII.1986]: CBQ 48 (1986) 700-7.

e194 *Weren* Wim, Studiebijeenkomst over de relatie tussen het joodse volk en de christelijke kerk [annual international seminar founded 1982 by Paul *Van Buren* of Boston and David *Hartman* of Jerusalem; 1 (1984) Christology; 2 (Dec. 28, 1985 - Jan. 29, 1986) Jewish and Christian interpretation of the Hebrew Bible]: TsTNijm 26 (1986) 282s.

Y7.4 (*Acta*) *theologica:* **nuntii.**

e195 ABC (Asiatic Bishops Conferences), 4th Meeting, Tokyo 16-25.IX.1986, Call and mission of the laity in Asia, church and world: EAPast 23,4 (1986) 462-481 [< TKontext 8/2,125-7, G. *Evers*].

e196 AECAWA (Association of the Episcopal Conferences of Anglophone West Africa), Christianity and Islam in dialogue: Lagos, Nigeria 20-27.X.1986: Weltkirche 9 (1986) 283-6 [< TKontext 8/2,121, N. B. *Abeng*].

e197 *Alturo i Perucho* Jesús, El setè col·loqui internacional de paleografia [Londres 18-21.IX.1985]: Faventia 8,1 (1986) 145-8.

e198 *Anzulewicz* Piotr, ● Ku teologii pokoju [of peace]; sympozjum sekcji dogmatycznej teologów polskich (Łódź-Łagiewniki, 16-18.IX.1985): ColcT 56,4 (1986) 161-5.

e199 *Aubert* Roger, L'image de JANSÉNIUS jusqu'à la fin du XVIIIᵉ s.; colloque Lv 7-9.XI.1985, dir *Eijl* E. Van: RHE 81 (1986) 275-7.

e200 *Bérubé* Camille, Importancia y actualidad de Juan Duns ESCOTO; sobre el VI Congreso Escotista Internacional (Cracovia 1986): NatGrac 32 (1985) 291-8.

e201 BIRA (Bishops' Institute for Religious Affairs [Angelegenheiten]) IV/3, 'Unterscheidung des Geistes, der in und jenseits der Kirche in Asien tätig ist', Hong Kong 2-7.XI.1986: UCA News (12.XII.1986) 21-26 [< TKontext 8/2,123s, G. *Evers*].

e202 *Caprile* Giovanni, Il colloquio di Brescia su 'PAOLO VI e i problemi ecclesiologici del Concilio' [19-21.IX.1986]: CC 137 (1986,4) 480-490.

e203 *Chossonery* Charles, Première rencontre de théologiens africains et européens; Colloque de Yaoundé, 4-11 avril 1984: Spiritus 25 (P 1984) 421-431.

e204 *Collet* Giancarlo, 'Theologien der Dritten Welt', ein Tagungsbericht [SEDOS 6.-10.V.1986]: NZMissW 42 (1986) 287-290.

e205 a) *Connor* Bernard F., Studiedagen katholieke theologen van zuidelijk Afrika [Lesotho 9-11.X.1985]; – b) *Hoogen* T. van den, Studiedag over de betrokkenheid van feministische theologen bij vrouwengroepen [WKTN 18.I.1986]: TsTNijm 26 (1986) 77s / 78s.

e206 Episcopalian Pastoral (COPA) meeting in Limón, Costa Rica, 4-8.I.1985, Racism and marginality of Indian and Black in Latin America: Pastoralia 7,14 (1985) 9-73 [< TKontext 8/2,130s, M. von *Lay*].

e207 *Espeja* Jesús, a) Buena nueva para los pobres; Coloquio teológico Dominicano [Bogotá sept. 1986]: CiTom 113 (1986) 611-6; – b) Teología y magisterio [II. Jornadas teológicas 'Juan XXIII', 3-5.IV.1986]: CiTom 113 (1986) 373-381.

e208 *Evers* Georg, Christen und Muslime; Zeugnis und gegenseitige Achtung zwischen Einzelpersonen und Gemeinschaften; 15. Journées Romaines, Frascati 1.-7. Sept. 1985 [< HerdKor 39 (1985) 11]: TKontext 7,1 (1986) 118-120.

e209 *Evers* Georg, Gott, der Schöpfer und Erlöser in asiatischen Kontexten, Siebte Theologische Konsultation der Asiatischen Theologischen Vereinigung (ATA), Manila, 21.-26. Jan. 1985: TKontext 7,1 (1986) 112s.

e210 *Evers* Georg, Jesus macht frei zum Dienst; Achte Vollversammlung der Asiatischen Christlichen Konferenz, Seoul, 26. Juni - 2. Juli 1985: TKontext 7,1 (1986) 113-5.

e211 *Evers* Georg, Konsultation zum Afrikanischen Konzil, Yaoundé 11.-22. April 1984: TKontext 7 (1986) 108.

e212 *Evers* Georg, Viertes Afrikanisches Kontinentaltreffen der Afrikanischen Sektion von EATWOT (Ecumenical Association of Third World Theologians), Kairo 24.-28. Aug. 1985: TKontext 7,1 (1986) 110-2.

e213 [*Evers* G.] Theologisches Arbeiten mit Volksliteratur; zweite theologische Seminar-Arbeitung, Hong Kong 29.10.-15.11.1984: TKontext 7,2 (1986) 114s.

e214 *Fernández* Niceto, Symposium cristiano-marxista en Budapest: Studium 26 (M 1986) 511-532.

e215 *Fernández* Pedro, Inculturación y liturgia; jornadas de estudio de la Asociación Española de Profesores de Liturgia (Madrid, 2-3.IX.1986): Phase 26 (1986) 527-530.

e216 *Fornet-Betancourt* Raúl, Evangelisierung der Kultur und Inkulturation des Evangeliums, Internationale Theologietagung, San Miguel, Buenos Aires, 2.-6.IX.1985: TKontext 7,1 (1986) 116-8.

e217 *Forte* Bruno [*Valentini* Donato], Forum ATI [Associazione Teologica Italiana, XI Congresso Trento 9-13.IX.1985: semplice rendiconto, non

Acta come sembrerebbe dalla copertina; similmente nei fascicoli successivi, art. sciolti], Conclusioni del gruppo di studio 'Trinità-Carità-Chiesa'; rassegna della stampa [una lettura ...]: RasT 27 (1986) 80-82 [-86].

e218 *Görman* Ulf, First European conference on science and religion [Loccum 13-16.III.1986]: SvTKv 62 (1986) 142-4.

e219 *Goñi Gaztambide* José, El erasmismo en España: ScripTPamp 18 (1986) 117-145; Lat. 153s; Eng. 154s; bibliog. 145-152.

e220 *a) Hernández Martínez* José M., El anuncio de María a los jóvenes (6.º congreso para agentes de pastoral) [Roma 28-30.XII]; – *b) Billet* Bernard, Les 41ᵉˢ journées de la Société française d'études mariales 'Marie et la fin des temps; études patristiques' [Francheville 5-7.IX.1985]: EphMar 36 (1986) 159-166 / 157-9.

e221 *Ildefonso de la Inmaculada*, XLI Semana de estudios marianos, organizada por la Sociedad Mariológica Española (Zaragoza, 10-13 de septiembre de 1986): EphMar 36 (1986) 363-8.

e222 In Christ, women's strength: fourth ecumenical women's conference, Madras Oct. 1986: CCA News (15.XI.1986) 11 [< TKontext 8/2,124s, G. *Evers*].

e223 International congress of Calvin-researchers in Debrecen [25-28.VIII. 1986]: Theologiai Szemle 29 (1986) 321-6.

e224 *a) Ioniță* Alexandru M., La 46ᵉᵐᵉ conférence théologique inter-confessionnelle, Cluj-Napoca, les 12-13 nov. 1985; – *b) Șebu* Sebastian, Le rôle de l'Église ...; – *c) Gross* Michael, L'unité et l'intégrité du monde crée; – *d) Cornițescu* Emilian, La responsabilité chrétienne devant les nouveaux dangers qui menacent la vie sur notre planète: [tout en roumain]: STBuc 38,1 (1986) 91-96 / 102-9 / 96-102 / 110-116.

e225 *Juan Bosco de Jesús*, El IV simposio internacional josefino, Kalisz (Polonia), 22-29 de septiembre de 1985: EstJos 40,79 (1986) 101-120.

e226 Die Kirche und die menschliche Entwicklung in Afrika heute; siebte Vollversammlung von SECAM [Symposium of the Episcopal Conferences of Africa and Madagascar] Kinshasa 15.-22.VII.1984: TKontext 7,2 (1986) 113s.

e227 *Klimkeit* Hans-J., Religionsgeschichtliche Kongresse in Australien; 1. 15. Kongress der IAHR [International Association for History of Religions] Sydney 18.-23.VIII.1985; – 2. Studienkonferenz Brisbane 25.-27.VIII.1985: ZRGg 38 (1986) 69.

e228 *Kocher* H., Zum Blockseminar, 'Aspekte jüdisch-christlicher Beziehung im 19. und 20. Jahrhundert' (Ev. Fak. Bern 25.II-1.III.1985): Judaica 41 (1985) 175-7.

e229 *Lemieux* Raymond, Le congrès annuel de la Société canadienne de Théologie [Montréal 18-20.X.1985]: LavalTP 42 (1986) 115s.

e230 *Lewek* Antoni, *a)* Cours pastoral national sur le thème 'L'Eucharistie, sacrement de l'Église' [9-11.IX.1985]: BInfWsz (1986,3) 3-17; – *b)* Symposium de la section des homilètes polonais sur le thème 'Théorie et pratique homilétiques des Églises non catholiques' [11-12.IV.1985]: BInfWsz (1986,1) 14-21; – *c)* [G. K.], Symposium national sur 'Le renouveau postconciliaire de l'Église en Pologne' [7-8.IV.1986]: BInfWsz (1986,6) 8-15.

e231 *Lotti* Paola, Corso residenziale di storia religiosa (sec. XIII-XIV), Assisi, 30 giugno-18 luglio 1986: StPatav 33 (1986) 719-724.

e232 *Maggiani* Silvano, XXVIII convegno liturgico-pastorale, Roma 5-7 febb. 1986: RivLtg 73 (1986) 423-7.

e233 *Marra* Bruno, XII Congresso Nazionale ATISM [Associazione

Teologica Italiana per lo Studio della Morale, 1-4.IV.1986]; Eutanasia; diritto alla morte: RasT 27 (1986) 365-374.

e234 *Martínez Cortes* Javier,   V Congreso de Teología, 'Dios de vida, ídolos de muerte': SalT 73 (1985) 673-9.

e235 *Mattai* Giuseppe,   La carità forma della Chiesa e del mondo; riflessioni sull'XI Congresso dell'A(ssociazione) T(eologica) I(taliana) 9-13.IX.): Asprenas 32 (1985) 391-408.

e236 *Mund* Gaby, *al.*,   'Versöhnung in jüdisch-christlichen Beziehungen; gegenseitige Toleranz oder geteilte Verantwortung?'; Bericht vom internationalen Kolloquium des ICCJ [Internationalen Rat(es) von Juden und Christen (sic)] in Dublin 21.-25. Juli 1985:   Judaica 41 (1985) 238-240.

e237 *Nebel* Richard,   Internationale Konferenz über Befreiungstheologie in Vancouver [6.-8.II.1986]: ZMissRW 70 (1986) 310-2.

e238 *a*) *Nickel* Edgar,   Bericht über die 25. Internationale Altkatholische Theologenkonferenz vom 2.-7. September 1985, in Warschau; Verkündigung des Evangeliums in einer gewandelten Welt; – *b*) *Parmentier* Martien F.G.,   Katholisch und ökumenisch – Grundbestimmungen unserer Verkündigung; – *c*) *Balakier* Edward,   Polish sources of the ideology of the National Church organised by Bishop Franciszek HODUR: IkiZ 76 (1986) 66-78 / 79-95 / 96-108.

e239 *Pasini* Cesare,   AGOSTINO a Rus Cassiciacum; Colloquio internazionale, Gazzada [Varese], 2-4 ottobre 1986:   ScuolC 114 (1986) 729-737.

e240 *Peyrot* Lucilla,   Laboratorio di teologia sistematica; I incontro, Roma, 'La Facoltà di Teologia' [senz'altra qualifica anche sotto], 12-13 marzo 1986:   Protestantesimo 41 (1986) 224-7.

e241 *Pazzini* Domenico,   Il quarto colloquio origeniano internazionale di Innsbruck, 2-7 settembre 1985: StPatav 33 (1986) 491-502.

e242 *Piegsa* Joachim,   'Die Relevanz des Glaubens für das sittliche Handeln'; Bericht über den Internationalen Fachkongress der Moraltheologen und Sozialethiker in Brixen 1985: ForumKT 2 (1986) 58-66.

e243 Polskie Towarzystwo Teologiczne w Krakowie: *a*) III sesja syndonologiczna 12.II.1985 [*Waliszewski* S., Całunowe echo w pierwszym tysiącleciu (*Savio* P.); *Chmiel* J., Świadectwo IV. Evangelii]; – *b*) 'Bóg, który wyzwał', 24.IV.1985 [*Jelonek* T., Biblijna koncepcja wolności; *Chmiel* J., Wyzwalająca moc Boga ST: *Jankowski* A., Idea wyzwolenia w soteriologii św. Pawła]; – *c*) Dei verbum, 20.XI.1985 [... *Hałas* S., Żywe Słowo Boga 1 Pt]: RuBi 39 (1986) 51.

e244 *Robert* Pierre,   Le LONERGAN Workshop 1986 ['Meaning and mystery']: ScEspr 38 (1986) 241-3.

e245 *Robertson* Edwin [invited Baptist, Aachen 10-14.IX.1986] At the Katholikentag: Tablet 240 (1986) 1028s.

e246 *Rostagno* S.,   In margine all'XI congresso ATI [Trento 8-13.IX.1985]: Protestantesimo 41 (1986) 36-41.

e247 [*Ruh* Ulrich],   'Nicht bei Fehldeutungen und Mängeln stehen bleiben'; Botschaft an die Christen in der Welt / Schlussbericht [römische Bischofssynode]: HerdKor 40 (1986) 38-40-48.

e248 *a*) *Rus* Remus,   La 47ᵉ conférence théologique interconfessionnelle — Bucarest, les 22-23 mai 1986; – *b*) *Dura* Nicolae V.,   L'intégrité de la création [roumain]: STBuc 38,4 (1986) 79-96 / 96-106.

e249 *Rusecki* Marian, ❷ XVIIᵉ rencontre des 'théologiens fondamentalistes' polonais: ColcT 56,1 (1986) 161-6.

e250 *Salzano* Teresa,   'Il dialogo ebraico-cristiano, oggi'; VI colloquio ebraico-cristiano, Camaldoli 31 ott.- 3 nov. 1985:   St Patav 33 (1986) 503-513.

e251 **Sartori** Luigi,   Verso il Congresso [ATI XII 1985]; 'Verità Chiesa e Missione':   RasT 27 (1986) 442-9 [566-9, O. *Di Grazia*].

e252 *Scheffczyk* Leo,   Bilanz des Konzils; zur Bischofs-Sondersynode [Rom 24.XI-8.XII.1985]: ForumKT 2 (1986) 134-144.

e253 *Schilson* Arno,   Im Streit um Aufklärung und Offenbarungsglauben; zu einem Arbeitsgespräch in Wolfenbüttel über Johann Melchior GOEZE [1717-1786]: Orientierung 50 (1986) 234-6.

e254 *a) Schreiter* Robert,   Theologie, academisch en kerkelijk [Catholic Theological Society, SF 5-8.VI.1985]; – *b)* CTS Ch 12.-15. Juni, 'Theologie in de kontekst van Noord-Am.' – *c) Haes* R. de,   Beleving en viering van het heilige in Afrika [CERA (Centre d'Études des Religions Africaines) Kinshasa 16-22.II.1986]; – *d) Hoogen* T. van den,   Theologen tussen het gezag van de hiërarchie en van het volk van God [WKTN 19.IV.1986]: TsTNijm 26 (1986) 172s / 284s / 173s / 174s.

e255 Unterwegs zu einer indischen Befreiungstheologie; Neunte Jahrestagung der Indischen Theologischen Association; Madras, 28-31.XII.1985: TKontext 7,2 (1986) 117-9.

e256 *Vandekerkhove* Juliaan,   De buitengewone bischoppensynode 24 nov. - 8 dec. 1985 — een kroniek: CollatVl 16 (1986) 216-235.

e257 *Vanneste* A.,   Les semaines théologiques de Kinshasa [(1964-1982) XV. 14-20.IV.1985, Le charisme de la vie consacrée]: ETL 62 (1986) 450-3.

e258 *Yanguas* José M.,   Un congreso de teología moral, Roma, 7-12 abril, 1986:   ScripTPamp 18 (1986) 905-915.

       Y7.6   *Acta congressuum philologica:* **nuntii.**

e259 *Bélis* Annie,   La musica greca antica; convegno internazionale di studi, Urbino (18-20 octobre 1985): RArchéol (1986) 401-3.

e260 *Čekalova* A. A.,   ❾ International conference 'The crisis of the [Roman Empire] third century; its consequences, reflections in ideology and cultures (6-9 Nov. 1984, Halle):   VDI (1986,3) 219-221.

e261 *Gras* Michel,   Aspects de la recherche sur la colonisation grecque; à propos du Congrès d'Athènes [Scuola Italiana 15-20 oct. 1979]: RBgPg 64 (1986) 5-21.

e262 *Macuch* Rudolf,   Second international congress on Greek and Arabic studies in Delphi (1.-6.VII.1985): ZDMG 136,3 (1986) *36s*.

e263 *Meier* Johannes,   16. internationaler Kongress der Geschichtswissenschaften [Stu Aug. 1985]:   ZMissRW 70 (1986) 64-66.

e264 *Pąkcińska* Maria,   ❾ LXXX sprawozdanie z działalności Polskiego Towarzystwa Filologicznego 22.X.1983 - 21.IX.1984:   Eos 74 (1986) 171-180.

e265 *Rolley* Claude,   Naples antique [25° Convegno della Magna Grecia, Taranto 1985]:   Archéologia 212 (1986) 44-47; ill.

       Y7.8   *Acta congressuum orientalistica et archaeologica;* **nuntii.**

e266 *a) Brice* William C.,   The Manchester conference on Aegean prehistory (Apr. 1986); – *b) Coldstream* J. Nicholas,   The international archaeological colloquium in Nicosia on Cyprus between the Orient and the Occident (Sept. 1985); – *c) Karageorghis* Vassos,   The Erlangen-Nürnberg colloquium on copper artifacts from the SE Mediterranean; – *d) Rupp* David W.,   The Brock University symposium on 'Western Cyprus:

connections' (St. Catherines, Ont., March 21s, 1986): Kadmos 25 (1986) 170s / 168ss / 87s / 171s.

e267 *Brown* Stuart E., [*al.*], La IVᵉ rencontre islamo-chrétienne de Tunis (21-26 avril 1986) 'La spiritualité, exigence de notre temps': Islamochristiana 12 (1986) 169-176, topheavy with Tunisians, French, Catholics [163-179, ❷ 9-13].

e268 *a) Englund* Gertie, Egyptology and informatics [Round Table, Leiden July 1-4]; – *b) Strudwick* Nigel, Announcement of a newsletter on the use of computers in Egyptology and related subjects: GöMiszÄg 93 (1986) 99s.

e269 *Forest* J. D., Préhistoire de la Mésopotamie et exploration récente du Djebel Hamrin [colloque international Paris 17-19.XII.1984]: LIAO 8 (1986) 80s.

e271 *Homès-Fredericq* Denyse, (en français) Third international conference on the history and archaeology of Jordan, Tübingen 6-12/4/1986: Akkadica 48 (1987) 35-39; titles of all communications and summary of Belgians (her own).

e272 *Moraru* Alexandru, L'Église anglicane et l'œcuménisme; ses relations avec l'Église Orthodoxe Roumaine [diss.] I: OrtBuc 37 (1985) 549-634.

e273 *Muranyi* Miklos, Third international colloquium, From Jāhiliyya to Islam; aspects of social, cultural, and religious history in the period of transition, 30.VI-6.VII.1985, Jerusalem: ZDMG 136 (1986) *1*s.

e274 *North* Robert, Ebla names and gods at Rome conference [Univ. Rome, July 15-17, 1985]: Biblica 67 (1986) 137-143.

e275 *Pergola* Philippe, Seminario di Archeologia cristiana (Archeologia e cultura della tarda antichità e dell'alto medioevo), resoconto delle sedute 1984-5: RivArCr 62 (1986) 333-387.

e276 Rencontre assyriologique internationale 33 (Paris 7-10.VII. 1986): Akkadica 50 (1986) 22-26: tous les titres; résumés des Belges; 26-41 'La coopération' (ongoing research).

e277 *Stevens* André, Symposium international sur l'architecture de terre, Pekin 1-12.XI.1985: LIAO 8 (1986) 92s.

e278 *Sturtewagen* Christian, The fourth international congress of Egyptology (Munich, August 26 - September 1, 1985): Orientalia 55 (1986) 182s.

e279 *Switsur* Roy, The 12th international radiocarbon conference [Trondheim 1985]: Antiquity 60 (1986) 139-142.

e280 Twelfth archaeological conference in Israel, 18-19 Feb. 1986, Ramat Aviv, TA Univ.: IsrEJ 36 (1986) 279s.

e281 *Urbaniak* Katarzyna, ❷ Third international Coptological congress [Aug. 20-25, 1984, Warszawa]: PrzOr (1985) 132-4.

e282 *Vladyko* N. N., ❸ An all-union [vsyesoyuzniy] scientific seminar 'New methods of research, conservation and restoration of archaeological finds' (Kiev, 1984]: SovArch (1986,3) 296-300.

e283 *Yanusherich* Z. V., *Pashkevich* G. A., ❸ The 6th Symposium of the International Working Group on Palaeobotany (The Netherlands, 1983): SovArch (1986,3) 286-290.

Y8 *Periti*, Scholars, Personalia, organizations.

e284 *Bodrato* Aldo, Dalla ragion dialettica alla ragion simbolica; Jean-Pierre JOSSUA, itinerario di un teologo: HumBr 41 (1986) 585-596.

e285 *a) Bottoni* Giovanni C., Studio Biblico Francescano, inaugurazione dei nuovi locali ed attività didattica e scientifica: TerraS 62 (1986) 17-21; –

b) Buscemi A. M., Studium Biblicum Franciscanum cronaca 1985-6: SBFLA 36 (1986) 455-469.

e286 ᴱ**Briggs** Ward W., *Benario* Hubert W., Basil Lanneau GILDERSLEEVE [1831-1924], an American classicist: AJP Monographs [but it is a collection of essays]. Baltimore 1985, Johns Hopkins. xii-115 p.; portr. $13. – ᴿClasR 100 (1986) 357s (H. *Lloyd-Jones*).

e287 ᴱ**Calder** William M., *al.*, WILAMOWITZ nach 50 Jahren [24 Vorträge 25.IX.1981]. Da 1985, Wiss. xviii-802 p.; portr. DM 159: ᴿClasR 100 (1986) 295-300 (H. *Lloyd-Jones*).

e288 **Canfield** Joseph M., The incredible SCOFIELD and his book [... his 'conversion'; his dispensationalist Bible 1909. reedited 1917, 1920...]. Asheville NC 1984. 289 p. $10. – ᴿSTEv 8,16 (1986) 301s (P. *Bolognesi*).

e289 *Caquot* André, Rapport sur l'activité de l'École Biblique [Jérusalem] 1985-6: CRAI (1986) 519-523.

e290 [*Crocker* John R., secr., *Valentino* Carlo, assistente] Acta Pontificii Instituti Biblici 9,3 (1986s) 155-227; 222-6, summaria dissertationum.

e291 *Davies* W. D., Reflections on thirty years of biblical study: ScotJT 39 (1986) 43-64.

e293 **Getz** Gene A., MBI, the story of Moody Bible Institute ²ʳᵉᵛ. Ch 1986, Moody. 250 p.; bibliog. p. 211-224. 0-8024-8375-5.

e294 ᴱ**Gozzo** S. M., Memorie autobiografiche del P. Gabriele M. ALLEGRA OFM, missionario in Cina [essenzialmente una storia illustrativa della versione cinese della Bibbia]. R 1986. 264 p. – ᴿAntonianum 61 (1986) 193-6 (B. *Bonansea*).

e295 *Karavidopoulos* Johannes, Das Studium des Neuen Testaments in der griechisch-orthodoxen Kirche in Vergangenheit und Gegenwart: BTZ 3 (1986) 2-10.

e296 **Kneppe** Alfred, *Höfer* Josef W., Friedrich MÜNZER, ein Althistoriker zwischen Kaiserreich und Nationalsozialismus. Bonn 1983, Habelt. viii-310 p. DM 48. – ᴿClasR 100 (1986) 358s (F. *Millar*).

e297 *Lewis* Bernard, *Goldenberg* David M., [In September 1986 Dropsie College became the] Annenberg research institute for Judaic and Near Eastern studies; statement of purpose: JQR 77 (1986s) 1-4.

e298 *Lindner* Wulf-Volker, *al.*, Bibliographie Marie-Louise HENRY, 75. Gb.: TLZ 111 (1986) 925s.

e299 *Neumann* Edith, Frederick NEUMANN [10.I.1899-13.V.1967]: ExAud 1 (1985) iii-xiv (-xvi).

e300 *Nilson* John, La teologia cattolica contemporanea negli Stati Uniti, ᵀ*Rosati* Maria: CrNSt 7 (1986) 361-377.

e301 **Prenter** Regin, Erindringer. Århus 1985, Aros. 198 p. Dk 185. – ᴿNorTTs 87 (1986) 61s (Karstein M. *Hansen*).

e301* ❸ Report of activities, Historical Society of Israel and Zalman Shazar center — 1985-1986: Zion 51 (1986) 505-517.

e302 *Rikhof* Herwi, 'Auf Gott hin denken'; Piet SCHOONENBERG SJ 75 Jahre alt, ᵀ*Unger* Elisabeth: Orientierung 50 (1986) 217-220.

e303 **Rivinius** Karl J., Die Anfänge des 'Anthropos'; Briefe von P. Wilhelm SCHMIDT an G. F. von HERTLING 1904-8 und andere Dokumente: Missionspriesterseminar 32. Bonn/St. Augustin 1981, Steyler. 230 p.; 17 fig. DM 32,50. – ᴿTLZ 111 (1986) 133s (K. *Nowak*).

e303* *Sabugal* Santos, El Colegio Internacional y el Instituto Patristico (historia e importancia): AnAug 48 (1985) 393-401.

e304 *Semaan* Wanis A., The first Protestant theological seminary in Lebanon: NESTR 7,1 (1986) 8-22.

e305 *Stercal* Claudio,   I laici nelle facoltà di teologia: TItSett 11 (1986) 274-281 [Olanda; Penisola Iberica].

e306 *Stuhlmacher* Peter,   Ernst KÄSEMANN zum 80. Geburtstag: TLZ 111 (1986) 860-2.

e307 *Vilar* Vicente,   Los estudios de Antiguo Testamento en España en nuestro tiempo [Simposio 1982/4]: AnVal 11 (1985) 313-325.

e308 *Will* Ernest,   Rapport sur l'École Française d'Athènes 1985s: CRAI (1986) 608-621.

Y8.5   *Periti,* **in memoriam.**

e309 Obituaries: AntiqJ 66 (1986) 499-511; ETL 62 (1986) 84*-86*; KirSef 61 (1986) 88-90; REB 46 (1986) 208-221. 451-460. 706-717. 880-5; RHE 81 (1986) 140*.336* (A. van *Belle*).

e310 Almagro Basch, Martin [➤ 65,e102; 1,g351] 17.IV.1911 - 28.VIII.1984, archéologie africaine: AntAfr 22 (1986) 7-10, phot. (G. *Souville*; bibliog.).

e311 Ambroz, Anatoly Konstantinovič, 25.VI.1929-12.VIII.1985: SovArch (1986,2) 284-7 portr.; bibliog. (V. P. *Darkevič*, S. A. *Pletneva*).

e312 Amy, Robert, 1904 -18.III.1986; archéologie de Palmyre: RArchéol (1986) 395s, phot. (P. *Gros*).

e313 Anthes, Rudolf, 1.III.1896-5.I.1985; JAmEg 22 (1985) 1-3 (H. G. *Fischer*); Expedition 22 (1985) 34-36; ZägSpr 113,1 (1986) I-III (S. *Wenig*).

e314 Bacht, Heinrich, S.J., † 25.I.1986: Catholica 40 (1986) 246 (W. *Löser*).

e315 Balog, Paul, 15.VIII.1900-6.XI.1982, numismatica araba: AnItNum 30 (1983) 261-271 (G. *Oman*; bibliog.).

e316 Baltensweiler, Heinrich, 10.XII.1926-24.X.1984: Neutestamentler, Pfarrer: TZBas 42 (1986) 364s; phot. (E. *Stegemann*, R. *Brändle*).

e317 Bar-Adon, Pessah [➤ 65,114; 1,g363] 1907-10.I.1985: BASOR 261 (1986) 3 (B. *Mazar*).

e318 Barnett, Richard David, 23.I.1909-29.VII.1986; British Museum: BAngIsr 4 (1985s) 4-6 (D. *Barag*); PEQ 118 (1986) 159 [The Times 6.VIII].

e319 Barreca, Ferruccio, 1923 -29.XII.1986, soprintendente archeologo Cagliari-Oristano: RStFen 14,2 (1986) I-IV (S. *Moscati*).

e320 Basham, Arthur Llewellyn, 24.V.1914-27.I.1986; Indologist: JAOS 106 (1986) 411s (K. G. *Zysk*); BSOAS 49 (561s (K. *Ballhatchet*: 24.VI.1914).

e321 Bauch, Andreas, 28.II.1908-24.X.1985: hist. et ars ant. Eccl.: RHE 81 (1986) 239s (K. *Hausberger*).

e322 Beauvoir, Simone de, 1908-1986: Orientierung 50 (1986) 131s (Adelheid *Müller-Lissner*).

e323 Benton, Sylvia, 18.VIII.1887-12.IX.1985; Greek archeology: AnBritAth 81 (1986) vii-x.

e324 Bernareggi, Ernesto [➤ 65,e103; 1,g365], 28.VIII.1917-1.VIII.1984; redattore: AnItNum 30 (1983) 273.

e325 Björquist, Manfred, bp., aet. 101: TsTKi 57 (1986) 76s (S. O. *Thorbjørnsen*).

e326 Blake, Eugene Carson [➤ 1,g366], 7.IX.1906-31.VII.1985: ÖkRu 35 (1986) 4-6 (H. *Krüger*); PrincSemB 7 (1986) 79s.

e327 Blankenburg, Walter, 31.VII.1903-10.III.1986; Mitarbeiter: JblLtgHymn 30 (1986) vii.

e328 Brassloff, Fritz L., 30.VIII.1907-3.III.1985; Mitarbeiter: Judaica 41 (1985) 49s (M. *Cunz*).

e329 Braudel, Fernand, aet. 83, 28.XI.1985; RHist 275 (1986) 435-443 (J.-F. *Bergier*).

e330 Brongers, Hendrik Antonie, aet. 81, 5.II.1986; Near East and OT: NedTTs 40 (1986) 238s (C. van *Leeuwen*).

e331 Büchler, Curt F., 11.VII.1905-2.VIII.1985; Bible ms. and printed texts: Speculum 61 (1986) 759s (P.O. *Kristeller*, *al*.).

e332 Butin, Jacques-Dominique, 30.IV.1933-24.I.1986; NT: RevSR 60 (1986) 132-4 (J. *Schlosser*; bibliog.).

e333 Butler, Christopher, Abbot O.S.B., † 20.IX.1986: ScripB 17 (1986s) 12s (B. *Hume*).

e334 Caird, George Bradford, 1917-1984: Proc. British Academy 71 (1985) 494-521 (J. *Barr*); also separate, L £1.50.

e335 Carli, Luigi Maria, arcivescovo, 1914 -14.IV.1986: PenséeC 223 (1986) 56-66 (P. E.).

e336 Carmignac, Jean, 1914 -2.X.1986; rédacteur: RQum 12,47 (1986) 323s, portr. (E. *Puech*: 'venu tardivement aux études sémitiques', diss. 'Notre Père' Inst. Cath. 1960).

e337 Carrière, Gaston, O.M.I., 21.III.1913-29.VI.1985; histoire de sa congrégation: RHE 81 (1986) R. *Boucher*).

e338 Cataudella, Quintino, 4.XII.1900-6.VII.1984: Gnomon 58 (1986) 286s (G. *Salanitro*); ed. Sileno; Orpheus 7 (1986) 247-253 (Giuseppina *Basta Donzelli*).

e339 Caton-Thompson, Gertrude [➤ 1,g371], aet. 97, 18.IV.1985; excavated with PETRIE at Abydos: AntiqJ 66 (1986) 501s.

e340 Cattaneo, Enrico, mons., 7.I.1912-24.X.1986: liturgista: ScuolC 114 (1986) 658 (M. *Navoni*).

e341 Cavalleri, Giuseppe, mons., prof., 1902 -5.VIII.1986: RivLtg 73 (1986) 699-703 (R. Dalla *Mutta*).

e342 Chagall, Marc [➤ 1,g372] 7.VII.1887-1.IV.1985: TLond 39 (1986) 116-121 (Andrew *Bowden*, 'Homage to Chagall the theologian').

e343 Christern, Jürgen, 1928 -29.IX.1983; Nordafrika Frühkirchenbau: Gnomon 58 (1986) 189s (P. *Grossmann*); AntAfr 21 (1985) 7-11, phot. (N. *Duval*); bibliog. 11s (R. *Christern-Briesenick*).

e344 Corcoran, Cassian F., O.F.M., 15.VIII.1922-14.VII.1986; VT-NT: CBQ 48 (1986) 699s (A. A. *Di Lella*).

e345 Craigie, Peter Campbell [➤ 1,g378], 18.VIII.1938-26.IX.1985; Ezekiel-exegesis, Ugarit: UF 18 (1986s) i (C. M. *Foley*).

e346 Danielski, Wojciech, 10.IV.1935-24.XII.1985, hist. liturg.: RuBi 39 (1986) 373-467; portr. (a parte) (Z. *Wit*, al.; 420-430 bibliog., E. *Lenart*).

e347 David, Martin, 3.VII.1898-9.IV.1986: PhoenixEOL 32,2 (1986) 4-6; portr. (F. R. *Kraus*).

e348 Deichgräber, Karl, 10.II.1903-16.XII.1984; Klas. Pg.: Gnomon 58 (1986) 475-480 (H. *Gärtner*).

e349 Delaney, John D., aet. 74, 10.IV.1986; Catholic publishing [ETL 62,227].

e350 De Marco, Alberto, S.J., 6.XII.1911-21.IV.1986; ex-collaboratore: CC 137 (1986,4) 575s.

e351 Dockx, Stany-Isnard, O.P., 1901 -9.XI.1985; chronologies néotestamentaires [ETL 62,434].

e352 Dujčev, Yvan, 18.IV.1907-26.IV.1986, archiviste et historien: RHE 81 (1986) 279s (Enrica *Follieri*).

e353 Dumézil, Georges, aet. 89, 11.X.1986; mythologie: CRAI (1986) 524s (A. *Caquot*).

e354 Dumoulin, Alexis, 1898 -16.XII.1985: RBgNum 132 (1986) 215s (T. *Hackens*).

e355 Dupont-Sommer, André [➤ 64,e729 ... 1,g390] 23.XII.1900-14.V.1983; secrétaire perpétuel: CRAI (1986) 9-23; portr. (A. *Caquot*).

e356 Eliade, Mircea, 9.III.1907-22.IV.1986; religion comparée: RHE 81 (1986) 708s (J. *Ries*); RTLv 17 (1986) 329-340 (aussi J. *Ries*); HistRel 26 (1986).

e357 Emmen, Egbert, 18.III.1902-9.XI.1985: KerkT 37 (1986) 48-50.

e358 Falus, Robert, 2.X.1925-1.VIII.1983; litt. grecque: Ann. Budapest. class. 9s (1985) 7-9 (J. *Harmatta*).

e359 Farid, Shafik, 1911-V.1983; Nubian and Coptic antiquities: VAeg 2 (1986) 3-5; bibliog.

e360 Filas, Francis L., S.J. [➤ 1,g395] 1916-15.II.1985: EstJos 40,79 (1986) 98s; Sindon 27,34 (1985) 108s; portr. (P. *Coero Borga*).

e361 Fina, Kurt, aet. 59, 3.V.1983: HistJb 106 (1986) 236-9 (H. *Glaser*).

e362 Firkovič, Semei Adolfovič, 28.XI.1897-16.IV.1982: RoczOr 45,1 (1986) 123-6.

e363 Flanagan, Neal M., O.S.M., aet. 65, 22.XI.1985; NT exegete, Chicago, Ireland, Africa, Berkeley: CBQ 48 (1986) 290s (M.D. *Guinan*); AcPIB 9,3 (1986s) 221 [gives aet. 66, † 1986].

e364 Fletcher, Joseph F.J, 1934-1984, central Asiatic history: AcOrH 40 (1986) 329.

e365 Floridi, Ulisse Alessio, S.J., 18.III.1920-7.XI.1986; Russia, America Latina; ex-collaboratore: CC 137 (1986,4) 577-9.

e366 Foster, Kenelm, O.P., 1910 -6.II.1986: NBlackf 67 (1986) 138-140 (B. *Bailey*) & 401-418, appreciations.

e367 Fournier, Pierre, † 4.X.1986: CRAI (1986) 500s (A. *Caquot*).

e368 Friedrich, Gerhard, † 18.I.1986; Neutestamentler: KerDo 32 (1986) 69 (R. *Slenczka*).

e369 Fritz, Kurt von, 25.VIII.1900-16.VII.1985, Klas. Pg.: Gnomon 58 (1986) 283-6, phot. (W. *Ludwig*).

e370 Gardet, Louis, 1904 -17.VII.1985: Islamochristiana 12 (1986) 1-26; Hamdard 9,4 (1986) 113s phot. (H.M. *Said*: † 1986).

e370* Gelb, Ignaz J., 1907-1985: Orientalia 56,55*.

e371 Gispen, Willem Hendrik, 7.VIII.1900-24.IX.1986; Pentateuch Prov. Reg. comm.: GerefTTs 86 (1986) 230-2 (M.J. *Mulder*); PhoenixEOL 32,2 (1986) 7.

e372 Godwin, Harry, sir, 1901-12.VIII.1985; pollen analysis; JArchSc 13 (1986) 299-301, phot. (G. *Clarke*).

e373 Goell, Theresa, aet. 84, 18.XII.1985; excavator of Nemrud Dagh: Bar-W 12,3 (1986) 8.

e374 Goitein, Shelomo Dov [➤ 1,g407], 3.IV.1900-6.II.1985: Der Islam 63 (1986) 189-191; phot. (F. *Rosenthal*); Speculum 61 (1986) 760s (R.S. *Lopez, al.*).

e375 Gribomont, Jean, O.S.B., 17 -IX.1920-22.III-1986; dir. Vulgate AT: RHE 81 (1986) 279 (L. *Leloir*); CrNSt 7 (1986) 615s; TAth 57 (1986) 897s (E.D. *Moutsoulas*); VetChr 23 (1986) 213.

e376 Groslier, Bernard-Philippe, 1926 -29.V.1986, directeur de recherche au CNRS: CRAI (1986) 355s (A. *Caquot*).

e377 Gross, Walter Hatto, 30.III.1913-24.XII.1984; klas. Archäologe: Gnomon 58 (1986) 83s (R. *Winkes*).

e378 Habelt, Rudolf, 30.IX.1916-19.X.1984, Verleger: Gnomon 58 (1986) 573s (K. *Böhner*).

e379 Hales, Edward E.Y., aet. 77, 7.VII.1986; converti au catholicisme; histoire des Papes [RHE 82,445].

e380 Hanfmann, George Maxim A., 1911 -13.III.1986, Sardis excavator: BAR-W 12,4 (1986) 8s; CRAI (1986) 215s (A. *Caquot*); JGlass 28 (1986) 124.

e381 Hansen, Susanna H., 1914-11.VII.1986, secretary: Annual Newsletter of the Scandinavian Institute of Asian Studies 20 (K 1986s) 61 (P. *Mohr*).

e382 Hill, Dorothy Kent, 3.II.1907-9.III.1986: AJA 90 (1986) 473s (J.W. *Poultney*).

e383 Hiltner, Seward, † 19.XI.1984; pastoral counseling: PrincSemB 7 (1986) 76-78.

e384 Horváth, János [→ 64,e750], 7.X.1911-3.II.1977; Philologie Latine: Ann. Budapest. class. 7 (1977) 3-6 (aussi J. *Harmatta*).

e385 Hubatsch, Walther, 17.V.1915-29.XII.1984; deutsche Geschichte: ZRGg 38 (1986) 186-9 (M. *Salewski*).

e386 Hubbeling, Hubertus Gezinus, † 8.X.1986; Mitherausgeber: NSys 28 (1986) vor 245.

e387 Hutt, Anthony, aet. 53, 13.X.1985: Iran 24 (1986) IV (D. *Stronach*).

e388 Ingholt, Harald, 1896 -28.X.1985; archéologie syrienne: CRAI (1986) 353s (A. *Caquot*).

e389 Isaac, Glynn Llewelyn, 1937 -6.X.1985, paleontologist: Antiquity 60 (1986) 55 (J.D. *Clark*).

e390 Isaye, Gaston, S.J., † 15.XII.1984; 'métaphysique et sciences de la nature': NRT 108 (1986) 715-738 (M. *Leclerc*).

e391 Jaeschke, Gotthard, 1894 -29.XII.1983: Der Islam 62 (1986) 1-4, phot. (J. *Benzing*; bibliog.).

e392 Jeffreys, M.V.C.: BritJREd 8 (1986) 128s.

e393 Joffroy René, 1915-1986; directeur adjoint: RArchéol (1986) 393 (G.C. *Picard*).

e394 John, Uwe, 22.IX.1942-6.IV.1985; jus romanum: ZSav–R 103 (1986) 656-8 (J.G. *Wolf*).

e395 Jongeling, Bastiaan, 13.III.1913-12.I.1986; Qumran-Texte: JStJud 17 (1986) 2 (A.S. van der *Woude*).

e396 Kay, Hugh, 1923 -14.VI.1986; executive editor: Month 248 (1986) 220s (P. *Hackett*).

e397 Kearns, Conleth J., 1902-   : PrIrB 9 (1985) 137s (W.J. *Harrington*).

e398 Kenyon, Kathleen Mary, dame, [→ 60,1193; 62,m732] 1906-1978: Proc. British Academy 71 (1985) 555-582 (A.D. *Tushingham*); also separately, L £1.50.

e399 Kessel, Eberhard, 1.IV.1907-17.I.1986; neuere Geschichte: HZ 243 (1986) 211-5 (W. *Baumgart*).

e400 Korngut, Adolf, 14.I.1907-3.II.1973; filolog.: Meander 41 (1986) 459s (W. *Tyszkowski*).

e401 Krivochéine, Basile [→ 1,g428] 30.VI.1900-23.IX.1985, archevêque russe de Bruxelles: RHE 81 (1981) 278s (E. *Voordeckers*; † 22.IX); Byzantion 56 (1986) 5-15; portr. (also E. *Voordeckers*, here † 21.IX; bibliog.).

e402 Landucci, Pier Carlo, mons., 1.XIII.1900-28.V.1986; contro l'evolu- zionismo di TEILHARD, MARCOZZI, LYONNET, CARLO COLOMBO 'il cosiddetto "teologo" di Paolo VI'): Renovatio 21 (1986) 537-542 (F. *Spadafora*).

e403 Lammens, Gerrit Nicolaas, 17.VIII.1923-3.XII.1985; liturgie: GerefTTs 86 (1986) 28s (J.J. van *Nijen*).

e404 Laoust, Henri, 1905-1983: CRAI (1986) 502-548; portr. (C. *Pellat*).

e405 Larcade, Geneviève, 1918-1985: secrétaire: RICathP 18 (1986) 97-99 (A. *Lanavère*).

e406 Lazzati, Giuseppe, 22.VI.1909-18.V.1986; patrologo; Rettore dell'Univ. S. Cuore, Milano: RHE 81 (1986) 792s [R. *Aubert*]; VetChr 23 (1986) 214.

e407 Leek, Franz Filce, 5.II.1903-26.I.1985; paleo-odontologist: ZägSpr 113,2 (1986) VII (E. *Strouhal*); JEA 78 (1986) 175-8; portr. (D.M. *Dixon*: b. 6.II; bibliog.).

e408 Leroi-Gourhan, André, 25.VIII.1911-19.II.1986; préhistorien: Archéologia 212 (1986) 6-10 (B. & G. *Delluc*); Antiquity 60 (1986) 136 (P. *Bahn*); AntiqJ 66 (1986) 499; CRAI (1986) 143-5 (A. *Caquot*).

e409 Leser, Paul, 23.II.1899-19.XII.1984; Entstehung des Pfluges: Anthropos 81 (1986) 261-3, phot. (J. *Henninger*).

e410 Lindt, Andreas, 2.VII.1920-9.X.1985; hist. eccl. moderne: RHE 81 (1986) 396s (M. *Weitlauff*).

e411 Loos, Milan, 22.V.1923-10.VI.1985; hist. eccl.: BySlav 46 (1985) 4 p. avec portr. entre p. 152 et 153.

e412 Lotar, Peter, 12.II.1910-12.VII.1986; Schriftsteller: Orientierung 50 (1986) 183-5 (Beatrice *Eichmann-Leutenegger*).

e413 Lukonin, Vladimir Grigoryevič [➤ 65,e204; 1,g439], 21.I.1932-10.IX.1984: SovArch (1986,1) 319 (E. V. *Zeimal*).

e414 Lutz, Cora E., aet. 78, 28.III.1985; Cebes...: Speculum 61 (1986) 763s (F. C. *Robinson, al.*).

e415 Lutz, Heinrich. 1922 -18.V.1986; Wiener Historiker: Orientierung 50 (1986) 134-6 (H. R. *Schlette*).

e416 Luyten, Norbert, O.P., 1909 -10.IX.1986 [ETL 62 (1986) 457].

e417 Lyonnet, Stanislas, S.J., 23.VIII.1902-8.VI.1986; prof. NT, Pont. Ist. Biblico: AcPIB 9,2 (1986) 144s (A. *Vanhoye*); Butlettí de l'Associació Bíblica de Catalunya 30 (1986) 2s (J. *O'Callaghan*); Trenta Giorni 4 (1986s) 70s (I. de *la Potterie*).

e418 MacRae, George W. [➤ 1,g443], 27.VII.1928-6.IX.1985: CBQ 48 (1986) 95 (D. J. *Harrington*).

e419 Maggi, Cirillo, 31.I.1913-1.VII.1986: RitNum 88 (1986) 241 (L. *Colombetti*).

e420 Mallwitz, Alfred, 2.X.1919- 1986; Bauforschung, Olympia: MiDAI-A 101 (1986) VI-XIV, portr., bibliog. (K. *Herrmann*).

e421 Merle, Jean-Baptiste, 1907 -25.IV.1986: RICathP 18 (1986) 105 (J. *Vieillard*).

e422 Miller, Josef, S.J., 22.IV.1890-24.XI.1985; Moraltheologe: ZkT 108 (1986) 1-4 (E. *Coreth*; bibliog.).

e423 Moeller, Charles, † 3.IV.1986; secr. Unité des Chrétiens: RTLv 17 (1986) 253-7 [ETL 62 (1986) 457].

e424 Moereels, Lodewijk, S.J., 27.I.1899-21.VII.1986; collaborator: OnsGErf 60 (1986) 293-6; portr. (J. *Andriessen*; bibliog. 297-301).

e425 Moloney, Robert, S.J., aet. 74, 17.III.1986: HeythJ 27 (1986) 349s (J. A. *Munitiz*).

e426 Mosca, Bruno, 27.I.1902-22.IX.1985: AteneR 31 (1986) 182s (A. *Santoro*).

e427 Neill, Stephen Charles [➤ 65,e223], 1900-1984: ProcBrAc 71 (1985) 603-614, portr. (K. *Cragg*, O. *Chadwick*).

e428 Nissiotis, Nikos A., 1925 -18.VIII.1986: 'Philosophie der Theologie': TüTQ 166 (1986) 242 (M. *Seckler*); ÖkRu 35 (1986) 369-372 (L. *Vischer*).

e429 Oeing-Hanhoff, Ludger, 22.XII.1923-6.V.1986; philosophische Grundlagen der Theologie: TüTQ 166 (1986) 161-3 (W. *Kasper*).

e430 Oppenheimer, K. E. H., 21.XII.1905 - c. 1985: KerkT 37 (1986) 353-7.

e431 Paciórkowski, Ryszard, 9.II.1908-15.VIII.1981, apologetica: STWsz 24,1 (1986) 5-18 (W. *Tabaczyński*; bibliog.).

e432 Paret, Rudi [➤ 65,e229], 3.IV.1901-31.I.1983; Arabist: ZDMG 136 (1986) 1-7; portr. (W. W. *Müller*).

e433 Pearlman, Moshe, aet. 75, 5.IV.1986, Bible popularizer: BAR-W 12,4 (1986) 9.

e434 Pellegrino, Michele, card., 25.IV.1903-10.X.1986; patrologo: RÉAug 32 (1986) 205s; fondatore: RivStoLR 22 (1986) i.

e435 Phillips, Charles W., 1901-1985: Sutton Hoo excavator: Antiquity 60 (1986) 53s; pl. VIII (G. *Daniel*).

e436 Podipara, Placid J., C.M.I. [➤ 1,g472], 3.X.1899-27.IV.1985: Syriac, Oriental churches: OrChrP 52 (1986) 249-256.

e437 Poucha, Pavel, XII.1905-15.I.1986; inner-Asian philology: ArOr 54 (1986) 362-8 (J. *Šíma*; bibliog. since ArOr 1976).

e438 Puech, Henri-Charles, 20.VII.1902-11.I.1986: religions hellénistiques: CRAI (1986) 26-28 (A. *Caquot*); manichéisme, gnose: RHE 80 (1985!) 943 (R. *Aubert*); directeur: RHR 203 (1986) 3s; phot. (A. *Guillaumont*).

e439 Rambaud, Michel H., 1921 -22.IX.1985; César, Ciceron: ÉtClas 54 (1986) 1s (Madeleine *Bonjour*).

e440 Raskolnikoff, Mouza, 1940-1986: Ktema 9 (1984!) 1.

e441 Reuss, Joseph, Prälat, 23.V.1904-4.II.1986; NT, Komm., Hilfswissenschaften: BiKi 41 (1986) 38s (B. *Mayer*); BZ 30 (1986) 312s (auch B. *Mayer*).

e442 Robert, Louis [➤ 1,g476], 15.II.1904-31.V.1985, epigrafista: Aegyptus 66 (1986) 203 (Lucia *Criscuolo*); AJA 90 (1986) 171s (G.W. *Bowersock*); CRAI (1986) 356-366, portr. (J. *Pouilloux*); Gnomon 58 (1986) 81-83; portr. (P. *Herrmann*); RArchéol (1986) 143-9; phot. (P. *Gauthier*).

e443 Ruiz González, Gregorio, S.J., aet. 49, 29.VIII.1986 (auto accident): Islamochristiana 12 (1986) 199s (M. de *Epalza*); AcPIB 9,3 (1986s) 220 († 29.VII).

e444 Rumiński, Estanislao A., 15.I.1929-10.III.1984: EstJos 40,79 (1986) 95-98 (*Juan Bosco de Jesús*).

e445 Rupp, Gordon, † 19.XII.1986: historien de LUTHER, observateur à Vatican II [RHE 82,445].

e446 Russu, Ion I., 4.XII.1911-12.IX.1985: philologia comparativa: IstVArh 37 (1986) 110s (Emilia *Dorufiu-Boilă*).

e447 Ryan, Dermot, abp.; Ugaritologist: PrIrB 9 (1985) 136 (S. *McPolin*).

e448 Scattolon, Gioacchino, mons., 18.VIII.1901-30.VIII.1986; primo direttore: ParVi 31 (1986) 435-7; fot. (G. *Canfora*).

e449 Scharper, Philip J., aet. 65, 5.V.1986; Catholic publishing [ETL 62,227].

e450 Schedl, Claus, 3.VIII.1914-19.VI.1986: TGegw 29 (1986) 204(-212, aus seiner Abschiedsvorlesung).

e451 Schuster, Heinz, † 17.IX.1986: Diakonia 17 (1986) 361s (H. *Erharter*).

e452 Seston, William [➤ 1,g489], † 2.X.1983; antiquités Maroc-Libye: AntAfr 20 (1984) 7-9, phot. (M. *Euzennat*).

e453 Sevenster, Gerhard, 13.XI.1895-10.VIII.1985; NT ethics and Christology: NedTTs 40 (1986) 172s (J. *Smit Sibinga*); NT: KerkT 37 (1986) 47s.

e454 Simon, Marcel, 1907 -26.X.1986; histoire des religions: CRAI (1986) 592-4 (A. *Caquot*); Ktema 9 (1984!) 1.

e455 Skilliter, Susan, aet. 54, 16.IX.1985; secr., V.-Pres.: JRAS (1986) 93s (G. *Goodwin*).

e456 Sohrweide, Hanna (f.), 1919-6.XII.1984: Der Islam 63 (1986) 1-4 (Barbara *Flemming*).

e457 Spannaus, Günther, 25.VIII.1901-4.VII.1984; Völkerkunde: ZEthnol 111 (1986) 11-13; phot. (P. *Fuchs*).

e458 Stanford, William Bedell, 6.I.1910-30.XII.1984: Odyssey editor: Gnomon 58 (1986) 79-81 (J. V. *Luce*).

e459 Stauffer, Richard [➤ 65,e267; 1,g494], 17.V.1921-9.XI.1984: Bulletin de la Société d'Histoire Protestante française 132 (1986) 459s (M. *Reulos*).

e460 Stiernon, Lucien, 27.III.1921-11.I.1985: RÉByz 44 (1986) 336.

e461 Stolz, Benedikt, O.S.B., 6.I.1895-28.IV. (im Alter von 92 Jahren) Altprior und unersetzbare Säule der Abtei Dormitio: HLand 118/2s (1986) 24s (N. *Egender*).

e462 Strasburger, Hermann, aet. 75, 4.IV.1985: röm. Hist.: Gnomon 58 (1986) 187-9, portr. (W. *Schmitthenner*).

e463 Strigl, Richard A., 1.I.1926-27.III.1985, Kirchenrecht: MüTZ 37 (1986) 59s (W. *Aymans*).

e464 Thielicke, H.: LuthMon 25 (1986) 149-151 (H.-O. *Wölber*).

e465 Thom, Alexander, aet. 91, XI.1985; British megalithic: Antiquity 60 (1986) 136s (A. *Burl*).

e466 Tovar, Antonio [➤ 1,g500], 14.V.1911-7.XII.1985: CRAI (1986) 1s (P. *Grimal*).

e467 Toynbee, Jocelyn Mary Catherine, aet. 88, 31.XII.1985; commentator on Vatican excavation: AntiqJ 66 (1986) 509.

e468 Travlos, John, 1908 -28.X.1985; Athens archeology: AJA 90 (1986) 343-5 (H. A. *Thompson*).

e469 Trottier, Aimé, C.S.C., 1923 -21.II.1986: EstJos 40 (1986) 259s.

e470 Tüchle, Hermann, mgr., 7.XI.1905-22.VIII.1986; Église médiévale et moderne; Festschrift/Bibliog. 1975 ᴱ*Schwaiger* G.: RHE 81 (1986) 651 (K. *Hausberger*).

e471 Tufnell, Olga [➤ 1,g502], 26.I.1905-11.IV.1985: PEQ 118 (1986) 1-4 (Margaret S. *Drower*; bibliog.); Levant 18 (1986) 1s (R. *Henry*, Vronwy *Hankey*).

e472 Urbański, (Zenoń) Alberto, O.Carm., 20-XII.1911-1.III.1985; Auschwitz, Dachau: EstJos 40,79 (1986) 91-94 (*Juan Bosco de Jesús*).

e473 Uricchio, Nicola, S.J., aet. 71, 1986: AcPIB 9,3 (1986s) 221.

e474 Vawter, Bruce, C.M., 11.VIII.1921-1.XII.1986; OT exegete; ed. OTAbs [9 (1986) before 233].

e475 Verdonk, W. E., 17.VI.1928-10.II.1986: KerkT 37 (1986) 193s (A. J. *Bronkhorst*).

e476 Verkhovskoy, Serge S., 1907 -4.VIII.1986; dogma: StVlad 30 (1986) 283-7; phot. (J. *Meyendorff*), 288ss (V. *Kesich*).

e477 Vermaseren Maarten J. [➤ 1,g507], 7.IV.1918-9.IX.1985; Eastern religions in the Roman Empire: NedTTs 40 (1986) 82s (R. van den *Broek*).

e478 Visser 't Hooft, Willem A. [➤ 1,g509], 20.IX.1900-4.VII.1985: ÖkRu 35 (1986) 1-4 (H. *Krüger*).

e479 Voeltzel, René, 1912 -15.VIII.1986: RHPR [ᶠ61,4 (1981)] 66 (1986) 387-9 (R. *Mehl*).

e480 Vogeleisen, Gérard, 29.VI.1929-25.X.1985; pédagogie religieuse: RevSR 60 (1986) 129-131 (G. *Adler*; bibliog.).

e481 Vogt, Joseph, 1895-1986: RivStorAnt 15 (1985) 302.

e482 Volckaert, Julius, S.J., aet. 83, 20.VII.1986: AcPIB 9,3 (1986s) 221.

e483 Volk, Ludwig, S.J., † 4.XII.1984, Kirchenhistoriker: FreibRu 37s (1985s) 54s.

e484 Volterra, Edoardo [➤ 65,e284; 1,g512] 7.I.1904-19.VII.1984: Atti Torino mor/fg 120 (1986) 206-7 (G. *Provera*).

e485 Wallace-Hadrill, John Michael, 1916 -3.XI.1985; 1965-74, ed.: EngHR 101 (1986) 561-3 (K. *Leyser*); RHE 81 (1986) 351s (F. *Hockey*); Speculum 61 (1986) 767-9 (G. *Constable, al.*).

e486 Walsh, James, S.J., † 1986, co-founder: Way 26 (1986) 179.

e487 Wambacq, Benjamin, O.Praem., aet. 80, 12.XII.1986; secr. Pont. Commissionis Biblicae; AcPIB 9,3 (1986s) 221.

e488 Wångstedt Sten, 13.XII.1904-23.IV.1986: ägypt. Demotisch: Enchoria 14 (1986) VIIs, portr. (R. *Holthoer*).
e489 Weider, Bjarne O., bp., aet. 72, 17.VIII.1985: TsTKi 57 (1986) 48 (O. *Skjevesland*).
e490 Westphal-Hellbusch, Sigrid, 10.VI.1915-1.II.1984; Iraq-Iran Archäologie: ZEthnol 111 (1986) 1-5; phot. (Gisela *Dombrowski*; 6-10 bibliog.).
e491 Wewers, Gerd A., 18.II.1944-18.XII.1985, Talmud: BTZ 3 (1986) 330-5 (C. *Colpe*); JStJud 17 (1986) 1 (H. G. *Kippenberg*).
e492 Wolff, Hans Julius, 27.VIII.1903-23.VIII.1983: juristische Gräzistik: Aegyptus 66 (1986) 200-2 (J. *Hengstl*).
e493 Yadin, Yigael [→ 65,293; 1,g516], 21.III.1917-28.VI.1984: Theologiai Szemle 28 (1985) 52 (I. *Karasszon*).
e494 Zepos, Panayotis, 1.XII.1908-18.V.1985; hist. legis: ZSav-R 103 (1986) 659-662 (P. *Dimakis*).
e495 Zsindely, Endre, 4.V.1929-25.IV.1986: Theologiai Szemle 29 (1986) 250-2 (K. *Benda*).

Index Alphabeticus: Auctores – *Situs (omisso al-, tell, abu etc.)*
ᴰdiss./dir. ᴱeditor ꟳFestschrift ᴹmentio, de eo ᴿrecensio ᵀtranslator † in mem.

Aageson J 4611
Aalders G 9417 9525
Aarde A van 3582
Aardweg G d539
Aartun R a829*b*
Aasi G 9086
Aatsma H ᵀ1159
Abad J 6268
Abaitua C 6155
Abbà G 6455 ᴿ540 5236 5769
Abbadi S 7500
Abbadie J ᴿ3204
d'Abbadie A d82
Abbas a967
Abbiati S ᴱd476
Abd el-Al A b125
Abd el-Raziq M b41
Abdera b321
Abdul-Razaq M ᴱ563*
Abe G 2162 6797 **M** 9150
Abecassis A 405 2818*b*
Abeele B Van den ᴿ522
Abel O 3983
Abela A ᴰ1640
Abeng N ᴿ6225 6865 e196
Aberbach D ᴿ1110 **M** 2820 ᴱ1200

Abercrombie J 1133 1226 ᴿ2003 N ᴿ904
Aberdam P ᵀ400
Abesamis C 400
Abicht L 8370
Abir S 1416
Abitz F b59
Abogunrin S 6797*b*
Abou Assaf A 7501
Abrabanel I ᴹ2895
Abraham W 8641
Abrahams I ᵀb819
Abrahamsen V ᴰb354
Abram I 8214
Abramowitz C 2861*a* ᵀ2161
Abramowski L ᴰ5549
Abrams M 600 **R** ᴱ3346
Abramsky S 2011
Abramson S 8318*
Abrecht P ᴿe39
Ábrego J ᴰ2763 ᴿ2575 ᵀ2586
Abruden D 2294*
Abu Billu b125 b126
Abu Hamid a708
Abulafia b947
Abu l-Faṭḥ ᴹ8202
Abu Nahleh L ᴰ7568

Abuqurra T d458
Abusch T 1620
Abu Simbel b177
Abusir b124*ab* b759
Abydos 1763 b144 e339
Accatoli L 6107*d*
Acerbi A 8077
Achard P ᴱ515
Achtemeier E 1320 2936 5098* ᴹ996 ᴿ2679 **P** 3730 4043 4382 4548 ᴱ600* ᴿ3779 4436 5722 5799 9637
Achuparambil D 9151 ᴿ9201
Ackermann R 8642
Ackroyd P 1070* ᴿ892 2251 2786 2928 9611 9834
Acquaro E a269*b* a270*b* a797 a804 ᴱa451
Adam A ᴿ6012 **E** 9877 **G** ᴿ857*ab* 997* 6419 **J** 9909 9910 **K** ᴹ5622 **P** ᴿ9998 **R** ᴿb748
Adams A ᴱ4320 **D** 7797 ᴰ7012 **H** 6347 **J** 6456 8643 ᴱ274 e92 **K** 844
Adamsheck B b338

Ddiss./dir. Eeditor FFestschrift Mmentio, de eo Rrecensio Ttranslator † in mem.
Sub **de, van** etc.: cognomina *americana* (post 1979) et *italiana* (post 1984); **non** reliqua.

Ddiss./dir. Eeditor FFestschrift Mmentio, de eo Rrecensio Ttranslator † in mem.
Sub **de, van** etc.: cognomina *americana* (post 1979) et *italiana* (post 1984); **non** reliqua.

Ddiss./dir. Eeditor FFestschrift Mmentio, de eo Rrecensio Ttranslator † in mem.
Sub de, van etc.: cognomina americana (post 1979) et italiana (post 1984); non reliqua.

[D]diss./dir. [E]editor [F]Festschrift [M]mentio, de eo [R]recensio [T]translator † in mem.
Sub **de**, **van** etc.: cognomina *americana* (post 1979) et *italiana* (post 1984); **non** reliqua.

Ddiss./dir. Eeditor FFestschrift Mmentio, de eo Rrecensio Ttranslator † in mem.
Sub de, van etc.: cognomina *americana* (post 1979) et *italiana* (post 1984); non reliqua.

Ddiss./dir. Eeditor FFestschrift Mmentio, de eo Rrecensio Ttranslator † in mem.
Sub de, van etc.: cognomina americana (post 1979) et italiana (post 1984); non reliqua.

Ddiss./dir. Eeditor FFestschrift Mmentio, de eo Rrecensio Ttranslator † in mem.
Sub **de, van** etc.: cognomina *americana* (post 1979) et *italiana* (post 1984); **non** reliqua.

Ddiss./dir. Eeditor FFestschrift Mmentio, de eo Rrecensio Ttranslator † in mem.
Sub **de, van** etc.: cognomina *americana* (post 1979) et *italiana* (post 1984); **non** reliqua.

ᴰdiss./dir. ᴱeditor ᶠFestschrift ᴹmentio, de eo ᴿrecensio ᵀtranslator † in mem.
Sub **de, van** etc.: cognomina *americana* (post 1979) et *italiana* (post 1984); **non** reliqua.

ᴰdiss./dir. ᴱeditor ᶠFestschrift ᴹmentio, de eo ᴿrecensio ᵀtranslator † in mem.
Sub **de, van** etc.: cognomina *americana* (post 1979) et *italiana* (post 1984); **non** reliqua.

Ddiss./dir. Eeditor FFestschrift Mmentio, de eo Rrecensio Ttranslator † in mem. Sub de, van etc.: cognomina americana (post 1979) et italiana (post 1984); non reliqua.

Ddiss./dir. Eeditor FFestschrift Mmentio, de eo Rrecensio Ttranslator † in mem.
Sub de, van etc.: cognomina *americana* (post 1979) et *italiana* (post 1984); non reliqua.

Ddiss./dir. Eeditor FFestschrift Mmentio, de eo Rrecensio Ttranslator † in mem.
Sub **de, van** etc.: cognomina *americana* (post 1979) et *italiana* (post 1984); **non** reliqua.

Ddiss./dir. Eeditor FFestschrift Mmentio, de eo Rrecensio Ttranslator † in mem.
Sub de, van etc.: cognomina americana (post 1979) et italiana (post 1984); non reliqua.

Rordorf W 1463*b* 6431
8125*a* R597
Rorem P 1000 Dd516
Rosa J 5954*
Rosario J R6852
Rosati M Te300
Rosato P 5712 d951*b*
Roscam Abbing P 5482*
Roschinski H 7531
Roschke R R3636 R9179
Rose M 1372 E495
Roselli A E421
Rosemont J 1484*
Rosen A a613 B a25 H
7312
Rosenau H 5652
Rosenbaum J a600
Rosenberg A 1701 2739
E8805 F R5241 R 3101
R3136 S 8513 8514
Rosenbloom N 1548
Rosenhouse J 7585
Rosenkranz R D5919
Rosenstiehl J 4409*b*
Rosenstock-Huessy E
213 M7999
Rosenthal G 8403 U
b747
–Heginbottom R a626
Ra542
Rosenthaler F e374
Rosenzweig F 8404 8405
d894 M1594* 7999
8440 8485 e82
Ros García S 3351*b*
R3165 e90
Roshwald M 2127*
Roskams S a814*a*
Rosłon J 2290 R4108
9216
Rosner F Tb796
Ross J 4017 7995 S
R3110
Rossano P E394 1288
R3047
Rossé G 3492* 3855
4287* 4866*
Rossel W 3521
Rosser J b299
Rossi A 2170*c* 7825
C D7776 G E84
Md291
–Fantonetti C Eb521
Rosso Ubigli L 6995*e*
R1650 8356
Rossow F 3522

Rostagno B 1001 e246
R5188 7144 T6655*b*
Rostoker W 9903*a*
Rotenberg M 1152*
Roth J 5391 8252 N
8316 8333 R 4863 W
R2083
Róth E 7313
Rothenberg 9835 B
9895*b* M 2506
Rothermundt J 1002
Rothschild J 8200 8379
R235* 1158 7339 8193
8196 8478
Rotroff S b647
Rotter E d185 H R6481
Rottländer P E6766 R
9825
Roty M 647
Rotzetter A 6632
Rouault O 7559
Rouet A 3007*
Rougé J a26*a* Rb630
Rouget G a78
Rougier L 3008*a*
Rouillard H 1613 D1916
Rouiller G 3249* 3934
R1224
Rouleau D D8636 J
E496 R7982
Rouner L E497
Rousseau A d280 d281
F 3948* 5430 J M3192
R E335 9136
Routtenberg H a569
Rouveret A Ea207
Rouwhorst G Rd403
Roux A 6243 G 9384 J
3637* R9167 P 1529
1530
Rowatt G D2748*a*
Rowell G d842 R7191
Rowland C 3148 R2808
9636 R a795
Rowlandson J b726
R9317 9600
Rowold H 2425* R6049
Roy L e27
Roynesdal O D8515
Royo J R221 5615 6384
6666 M R8837 9910
a207
Ru G de R2520 3005
T4413
Rubeaux F 4288*a*
Rubí B de F97

Rubianes 3638*a*
Rubin M 8303*
Rubinkiewicz R 2181
5709*b* 8045 E266
Rubinstein E 7344 a227
Ruckstuhl E 3677 4305
Rudavsky T E336
Rudloff O d662
Rudnick M d230
Rudolph A R8735 E
8732 K 8556 8557*a*
8585*b* 8601 d798
Ruebel J R9561
Rücker H 6911
Ruedi-Weber H 3360
Rüger H E1325
Rühlmann G R9939
Rührdanz K Ra172
Ruello F Rd500
Rüster C 8947
Rueter A R993
Rüterswörden U D7462
Ruether R 6827*b*
7104-7107 e158 M5662
d900R R5106 7110
7133 d164 d487
Ruffin M D2958
Rufinus A 4556 M9695
Ruh U 1701*b* 5209*b*
e247 E648 R3697
Ruhbach G 6327
Ruijgh G 7762 R7696
7747 7819
Ruiz G 2895 3957*
6651*c* 8516 T2272 T
Tb938
–Arenas O 5211
–de la Peña J 5285 5820
R5132
–Díaz A 6032
–Garrido C 648* T5967
–González G †e443
Ruland V 8749
Ruler A van M6645
d927*b*
Rulla L 5286
Rulli G Rd158
Rumeideh a603
Rumianek R 8126
Rumiński E †e444
Rummel E d650 d651
Rumscheidt H Td959 M
R6608 6710 Td965
Runciman W Rb891

ᴰdiss./dir. ᴱeditor ᶠFestschrift ᴹmentio, de eo ᴿrecensio ᵀtranslator † in mem.
Sub de, van etc.: cognomina americana (post 1979) et italiana (post 1984); non reliqua.

ᴰdiss./dir. ᴱeditor ᶠFestschrift ᴹmentio, de eo ᴿrecensio ᵀtranslator † in mem.
Sub **de**, **van** etc.: cognomina *americana* (post 1979) et *italiana* (post 1984); **non** reliqua.

ᴰdiss./dir. ᴱeditor ᶠFestschrift ᴹmentio, de eo ᴿrecensio ᵀtranslator † in mem.
Sub **de**, **van** etc.: cognomina *americana* (post 1979) et *italiana* (post 1984); **non** reliqua.

ᴰdiss./dir. ᴱeditor ᶠFestschrift ᴹmentio, de eo ᴿrecensio ᵀtranslator † in mem.
Sub **de, van** etc.: cognomina *americana* (post 1979) et *italiana* (post 1984); **non** reliqua.

kórē kósmou 9030
kósmos 4209*
kradíē 7777
krithópyros b750
ktízō 7781

Leontoûchos a632
logismós b880b
lógos 4214 4220
lóchion 7782
lýtron 5930

Mathētēs 3341
martyría 7783
mártys 977 4108
méllō 7785
metá 4708
metánoia 7786
moicheúein 3568
mystērion 3568

Naúklēros a7b
neópoios b221
nēpios 4900a
nómos 4628c 8099ab

Hoi dé 3728
oikeiōsis 8876b
oikía 7787
oikízō 7781
oikodomē, -eîn 4524
oikos 4654
hórkos 7188
hósios 7789
hóti 4970

Paideía 4943
parabolē 3764
paréchō, párochos 7790
paroikía 7790
parrhēsía 3764 4090 7791
peirázō 7792
péplos a106
perirhantērion a127
pímplēmi 7363
pístis b880b
plēn 7793
plērōma 4870 7793
pneûma 8548
pneumatikós 4772
polis a819 d26-d67
ponērós 3434
prâgma 7795
prâxis 7796
protomē a233
procheirotonéō 4108

pykri b750
pōgōn 7797

Rís 7798
rhōmē, rhôsis 7799

Sárx, sarkikós 7800 7801
sképsis 8892
skýphos a671
staphylinós b729
stoicheîa 4957
sýnkrisis 9476
sýzygos 8591
sykophantéō 3998
syneídēsis 4515 4699R
schēma 7745
sôma 7801
sotēría 5914

Tálanton a147
tapeinós 4769*c
télos 4639
títhēmi 7714
tópos 4282
triērarchos a31
týrannos 7733

Hypēnē 7797
hypókeisthai, -keímenon
  7802
hypokritēs 7803
hypomonē 7804
hypóstoloi a31

Phanerós 3444
phiálē a132
philótēs b848
phoròs bōmōn 9011b
phroneîn 4846

Chará 7806 7807
cháris 3963 7807 7808
chlamýs a92
chreía 2986 2991 3279
christòs 7808
chrónos 7809

Pseudómenos 3425

Hōs 3964* mē 4695

ordine hebraico
† aram. ‡ ug./ph. ʾarab. * akk.

aleph
mu'ā'um *7566a

abba † 3499 5122 6354a
ebyon 6586
eben 1787
'gwz 7476
ᵃgālāh 9984
āhab 7328
ôr d294
Urim 1875 7329
eḥad 7330 7552
elohim 2340
'yt † 7300
amēn 7331
āmar 348
('nš, iššâ) našim 1703*
ārak 7331*
ārar 7332
Asasel 1892
Ašerâ 1872* 7333 8964
  8974 8983 8990 a577
  Astart 7514
'šbnw 2901

beth
bā'-šaḥaq 2359
bayit 2376 b868 bêt
  Yiśrā'ēl 7334 bit rimki
  *9064
ba'al 2502 -puš † 7523*
  -Ṣapon 1797
Iblis b20
Baradu madu *a846
brk(m/h) b128 bᵉrākâ
  1900 3616
bᵉrît 1925 1991 6797
bāśār 1416 7335

ghimel
gābāh 7336
gabbatha † 7511
geber zakî 1633
ghṭ ‡ 7490b
ganna mašāru *2182
gardali 7337

daleth
dābār 2720*
David 2046
dôr 2537
dal 6586
dam 7338
derek 1703*
dᵉraqon 7339
deraš 3225 madrasa° 9121*
dešeh 1449

he

hebel 2536
hāyāh 1782 7297a YHWH
  1783
hāzāh 7340
hēn 396b *hinneh* 7341

waw

we 7253
waw 7243
wqht † 705

zayin

zebaḥ 7287
zākar 7342
zaʿaq 7343

ḥeth

ḥubbal 2665
ḥāzaq 7344
ḥṭ' 7839
ḥokmâ 2634
ḥasqbōl ‡ 7541
ḥ'ršm ‡ 7487
ḥuppudum *7346
ḥafir º b591
ḥerem 5428d 7347
Ḥerem 7347
ḥesed 2277 2867 7345
ḥāsēr 2564

ṭeth

ṭôb 2277 7348

yod

yabin º 1678
yad 7349*
yādāh: tôdâ 3616
yadaʿ: daʿat Elohim 2867
yōm 7350
yônâ 7351
yasar 7352
y'r † 7523*
yārā 7354
yārah: tora 5334 8099b
  mwr' 8147b
yāṣā 7353
yt ‡ 7524
ytb: môtab º 8990

kaph

ke ‡ 7356
k's 8147a
kābas 1461

---

kiddîb º 7587*
kî 7357
kanwarta *7358
kapporet 2094
ketmān º 4698

lamed

le 2058 ‡ 7524
lō' 1787
le'ûm *7566a
lā'ak 7362 *me lā'kâ* 7362
Leviathan 2425*
Lilit 7457 7514
lāmad 7359 *lāmēd* 7361
  malmad 7360

mêm

m't 7455
ambaru *7545
mdl ‡ 7361
(ʿal-) mawet 7457
mṭ 7490b
mî yôdēaʿ 2071
mālē' 7363
melek 2038b 2158 a303
  -śārîm 2875
mun-du *7364
maśśa' 2875
māšiaḥ 5443-5452
nimšal 3505
mšr ‡ 7490

nûn

n- 7251
nābî' 7365
mabbûl 7287
ngš ‡ 7475
nedîriyyâ' † 7366
nēr 7382
nāzîr 7367
naḥa lat 7368
naḥat 7369
nawamis º b200
nouaemith º 9095
nēs 7370
nāpaḥ 7371
nāpal 7372
nepeš 7373
niṣṣeb 7374
neṣaḥ 7375
nāṣal 7376
nāṣar 7377
nāqab 7378
nāqāh nāqî 7379
nāqam 7380
nāqap 7381

---

nāśā' 7383 *nāsî'* 7385
nāśag 7384
nāśā' 7386
nāšak 7387
ne šāmâ 7388
nešep 7389
nāšaq 7390
nešer b646
nātak 7391
nātan 7392 *Ne tînîm* 2178
nātaq 7394
nātar 7395
nātaṣ 7393
nātaš 7396

samech

sābab 7397 *me sibbâ*
  2098
sābal 7398
se gullâ 7399
sāgar 7400
se dom 7401
sûg 7402
sôd 7403
sûs b673
sôp 7404 *sûpāh* 7405
sûr 7406
swt 7407
sāhar 7408
sākak, sukkâ 7409 *siktu*
  *a97
sākal 7410
Sākal 7467
sākan 2527
sālaḥ 7411
sālal, mesillâ 7412
sāmak, se mîkâ 7412*
sanwērîm 7346
sinnurbum *7441
sā'ad 7413
sa'ar b599*
sap 9932
sāpad 7413*
sāpah 7414
sāpaq 7415
sāpar 7416
sāqal 7417
sārar 7420
seren 7419
sārîs 7418
sātam 7421
sātar 7422

ʿayin

'ab b602
ʿābar 7424

ʾbryḥ 8149c ʿibrî 4435*
7424 7425
ʿᵃbôṭ 7423
ʿēgel b667
ʿad 1845 7426
ʿādāh a117
ʿēder b613
ʿēd 977 7438 ʿēdâ 7436
7437
ʿôz 7427 ʿēz b680a
ʿûl 7428 ʿawel 7429
ʿāwôn 7431
ʿûp 7432
ʿēṣ 1789 -perî 1449
ʿûr 7433 ʿēr 2970 ʿiwwer
7434 ʿîr 2376
ʿālaz 7439
ʿal 7475
ʿôlām 7430
ʿam 7440 -hā-āreṣ b936a
ʿammatu *1472
ʾms ‡8991
ʿemeq 7336
ʿôneh 2970 ʿāni 6586
ʿanāwîm 6616
ʿasā ⁰7590
ʿṣb 2527* ʿēṣeb 1449
ʿārab 7441 grb ⁰7772
ʿrgz ‡7476d

pê

pagrâ †7335
pî šᵉnayim 1937
pym a49
pāqad 7443
pirigalu *7490b
ephphatha 3811

ṣade

ṣôʾn 2802ᴿ
ṣᵉbāʾot 1774
ṣedeq 7446-7448 ṣᵉdāqâ
7445 saddîq 2939
ṣiddîq ⁰7587*
ṣelem 7449
ṣql ‡7476d
ṣrk ‡7476

qoph

qābāh 7451
qôdes 7452-7454 Qᵉdēšâ
8963b
qōl 926*
qîpu *9080
qḥt 7455
qillešôn 7456

qms †7523*
qāṣar 7336

rêš

rôʾš 2805
rabboni ‡7511
rādâh 1461
ruaḥ 8548
tᵉrûmâ 1889
rûš 6586
raz 7457
rāḥep 7457
rîb 7287 7458
rᵉpāʾîm 7459
ryqny †7523*

śin

śadādum *7460
śadeh 7297b 7460*
Śāṭān 2421 2422
śmḥ 7461
śar 7462

šin

saʿy ⁰1678
Šᵉʾol 7463
šᵉʾîrît 7464
šābaʿ 7465
šîbūtum *b881
šadday 5099
šāhaz 7466
šîr ʿagābîm 2801
škm 7468
miškan 7457
ṣālôm 5400 5401 5428a
7469
šem 7470
šangu *9080
šāpaṭ 7471 mišpaṭ 7446
šeqel 7472
šryr †7523*
šattukku b709*

tau

Tʾummîm 1875 7329
tūmām 8149b
tôʿēbâ 7349
tofet a811c a812
tšby(t) †7523*

Genesis

–: 1362-1722
1-3: 1095 1526 1566
1: 1416-1562 7523*
1,1-2,4: 1425b

1,2: 7457
1,11s: 1449
1,14-19: 1450
1,21: 1451
1,25-27: 1452a
1,26: 1454-1458
1,28: 1459 1596 2319
2-6: 4924
2s: 176 1058 1452b 1453
1563-1612 2039
2: 1425d 7061
2,3: 1463a
2,4-25: 1605
2,5-3,24: 1596
2,7: 1452a
2,8: 1606
2,9: 1606*
2,15: 1581*a 1606 1607
2,23: 1607*
2,24: 1608
2,25-3,7: 1608*
3: 1425f 1609
3,7.21: 1452a
3,14: 1774-1785
3,15: 1611
3,16: 1610
3,25: 1612
4: 1613ss
4,1.17: 1614
4,8: 3500*
4,26: 1618
5: 1619
6ss: 1452b 1620-1632
6,3: 1632
6,13: 2910
7,1: 1633
8,20-9,17: 1634
8,20s: 1635
9,6: 1204d
9,20-27: 1636
10: 1636 1637
11: 1452b 1638 1639
11,27-25,18: 1640
12-39: 6072
12-25: 1648
12s: 1640-1649
14: 1650-1654 1688
14,18-20: 1652
15: 1655-1664
15,1: 1688b
15,6: 1665 7263
16: 1666
16,1-16: 1994
16,6: 1667

12-20: 1935*
12,2-6: 1936
15: 1899*
15,12: 1840*
21,17: 1937
21,18-21: 6473
21,22s: 4298
21,33: 4459f
24,1-4: 1939 1940
25,5-10: 1940*
25,12: 1941
26,3: 1941*
28,28: 7346
30,6: 2760
32: 1942
32,1-43: 1943a
32,8-13: 7310
33: 1944
33,2: 1945
34,5: 1943b

Josue, Joshua

-: 1957-1964*
2: 1965 1966
3,1: 1966*
7,1-8,29: 1968
8,30-35: 1969a
8,30: 1992
9: 1969*
10,12-15: 1970
11: 1971
13-22: 1972
13,3: 1973
15,10: 1974
18,1-10: 1975
20: 1976
24: 1977

Judicum, Judges

-: 1960 1978-1981
2,10-3,6: 1982
3,31: 7360
4s: 1983 1986
5: 1984 1985
5,13-17: 1988
6,11-24: 1989
6,13: 1990
9: 1991
10,6-12,7: 1995
11,29-40: 1993 1994
13-16: 1996
14s: 1998*
14: 1105
16,21: 1999
18-21: 2038b
19: 6482

19,1-30: 1994

Ruth

-: 1960 2000-2010

1 Samuel

-: 2727
1-2 K 10: 2012
1-12: 176
2,1-10: 396
2,4-8: 2025
2,10.15: 5451
2,11-26: 2026a
3: 2026
3,4: 2027
8,4-22: 2038c
9-31: 2039
10,27-11,15: 2040a
12,3-5: 2040b
13-2 Sam 8: 2041
13-2 Sam 1: 2042
13-31: 176
13,21: 7456
15: 2043 2044
16-2 Sm 5: 2055
16-18: 2056-2062
28,3-25: 2064

2 Samuel

-: 2463
1,19-27: 2065
2,4: 2066
5,3: 2066
5,5: 2066*
6,3: 2067
6,9: 2067b
7: 2066
9-20: 2068*a
11s: 2069
11: 2069*
12: 8006R
12,1-4: 2070
12,17: 2070*
12,22: 2071
13,1-22: 1994
14,5-17: 2070
14,26: 7472
18,19-19,5: 2075
18,33: 2075
22,26s: 2077
24: 47*R

3 Regum, 1 Kings

-: 2078-2088
1s: 2068*a

3-10: 2089
3: 2069
3,1: 2086*
3,4-15: 2088
6: 2090
7: 2091-2097
7,21: 2093*
7,27-39: 2091
9-11: 2121
9,26: a594
10: 2097
11s: 2098
11,19: 2098*
16,29-2 K 13,25: 2110
17s: 176
17,1: 2107
17,7-24: 3969
17,17-24: 2112
17-19: 2111
18,1-16: 2113
21: 2114
22,1-38: 2114*

4 Regum, 2 Kings

-: 2115-2142
3,26: 2117
4,42: 7476d
5: 4102
5,1-19: 2118
6,25: 2119
8: 2120
11: 2122
12,5-17: 2123
14,7: 2124
15,30: 2125
17: 2125*
17,4-6: 2126
18,13-19,37: 2129
18,23: 7441
20,2: 2127*
20,12-19: 2128
20,13: 2138
21H,9: 2664
25,27-30: 2141 2142

Paralipomenon 1 Chron.

-: 2143-2152
6,33: 2153
16,8-36: 4389
21,1-22,1: 2421
23: 2154
24: 2155
25,8: 2156
28,9: 2157

1,2: 1685
2,4: 2462*

Proverbia

–: 2496-2508
1-9: 2509
1,4: 1451
1,20-33: 2510 2511
3,9: 2512
6,30: 2512
7,18: 1670
8,1-35: 2510
8,22-31: 1095
9,1-6: 2230 2510
9,13: 2510
12,28: 2513 7457
18,8: 2514
19,5: 2515
20-29: 2509
24; 26: 1058
25-29: 2516
25,4: 7353
25,27: 2517a
30,19: 2518
30,21-33: 2517
31,1-31: 2518*

Ecclesiastes, Qohelet

–: 2434 2519-2535 2633
5280d 7895
1,2: 2536
1,4: 2537
1,12-3,15: 2538
2,10.24: 2539
10,9: 2527*
12,5: 2539*

Sapientia Salomonis

–: 2540-2549 5280e
2: 2550
4,7-19: 2551
7,2: 1670
11-19: 2552
11,2-19,22: 2553
13,1-9: 2554

Ecclesiasticus, Sirach

–: 2173 2546 2555-2563
14,2: 2564
30,39: 2564
35,12: 2564
44-50: 2565-2567
44,16-45,26: 2568
44,19-21: 2569
47,12-22: 2570
51,1-12: 2571

1 Isaias

–: 2619-2645 2886
1: 2647
1,1: 2645
1,13: 2648
1,18-20: 2649
1,21ss: 2650
2-4: 2651
2,1-5: 2652
5,1-7: 2653 2655
6,1-9,6: 2656
6,1-8,18: 2657
6: 2658
6,9-13: 2658*
6,9: 2659
6,13: 2635
7,3: 2660
7,14: 2661-2664
9,2: 7461
9,5: 2661
10,27: 2665
10,32s: 2666
11,1-9: 5428c
11,6: 2668
13-23: 2900
13s: 2668*
14,12-15: 2669
15,9: a714
19,16-25: 2670
19,25: 2671
21,1-10: 2672
23: 2673
23,10: 2674
24,16: 7457
28,15.18: 7340
32,17: 2668
33: 1239
33,14-16: 2321
34,14: 7457
35: 2675
35,10: 2676
36s: 2677

2(-3) Isaias

–: 2717
40,4: 2689
40,6: 5292
40,12-31: 2689* 2690
40,20: 2691
43,1-7: 2692
44,1-5: 2693
45,20-25: 2694
49,22: 2695
50,1-9: 2706
50,1: 4603*
52,13-53,12: 2701

53: 4752 4850
56-66: 2707s
56-59: 2709
56,9-57,13: 2710
58,8: 7461
60: 2711 2712a
60,4: 2695
61,2: 2712b
62: 2713
63,16: 2714
66: 2715

Jeremias

–: 214 2716-2747 2905
3587 7895 a264
1: 2748
1,1-10: 2748*a
2,4: 2748*b
2,31: 396
4-6: 2749
5: 2750
7: 2751a
7,22: 1787b
9,22s: 2752
12: 2753
12,8: 2754
14,13: 2755
15: 2753
20,2: a541
20,7: 2756
25,10s: 2757
25,38: 7351
26: 2651a
31: 2759
31,7-9: 2757*
31,31-34: 2797b
31,31: 2758 2762
31,33: 2760
32,10-14: 2762
36-45: 2763
36: 2764
46-51: 2900
46,16: 7351
47,1-7: 2752
48,3: a714
50,2-51,58: 2764*
50,16: 7351
51: 2380
51,59-64: 2765

Lamentationes

–: 2722 2766-2772
1,3: 2771
5: 2276

14,41: 3847
14,47: 3848
14,62: 3849
14,72: 3850
15: 3851
15,28: 3853
15,34: 3854 3855
16: 3856
16,4: 3850
16,7: 3857* 7008
16,8: 3858
16,9-20: 3859

Lucas

–: 1264 3861-3958
1,1-38: 3940*
1,2: 5214
1,11.26: 3941
1,26-38: 3944
1,46-55: 2297 3942-3947
1,48: 3948
1,68-79: 3948*
2,3-5: 3351
2,7: 3950 3951 4282
2,11: 3952
2,12: 3955
2,25-32: 3955*
2,29-32: 3956
2,49: 3957
2,50s: 3957*
3,21: 3958
3,33: 3958*
4: 2183
4,9-12: 3383
4,16-30: 3960 3961
4,17: 3962
4,22-30: 3968a
4,22: 3963
4,23: 3964
4,25: 3964*
4,29s: 3965
5,1-11: 3966
5,29-35: 3968b
6,4: 3967
6,17-26: 3968
6,30-49: 3402
7,11-17: 3969
7,20: 3970
7,35: 3971a
7,36-50: 3971
7,36: 7021
8,2: 7021
8,12: 7002
8,26-39: 3973

9,28-36: 3974
10,11-32: 372
10,16s: 4000
10,20: 3975
10,25-37: 1254
10,29: 3976
10,38-42: 3977 3978
10,42: 3979
11,3: 3979*
11,5-8: 3980
11,17: 3501
11,37-54: 3585
12,13s: 3980*
12,15-21: 3970
12,49: 3981*
12,54-56: 3981*
13,10-17: 3982
13,11: 3982*
13,31-34: 4000
14,1-6: 3982
14,16-23: 3983
15,1-11: 3984*a
15,1-17,10: 3984
15,3-22: 3986
15,3-6: 3985
15,8-10: 7077
15,11-32: 3986*-3989
16,1-8: 3990
16,19-31: 6614
17: 4001
17,6: 3564
17,7-10: 3991 3992
17,21: 3993
18: 2463
18,9-14: 3994
19,1-10: 3970 3995
19,8: 3998
19,41-44: 4000
20,27-40: 3999
21: 4001
21,20-24: 4000
21,34-36: 4903
22s: 4002-4007
22,20: 4708
22,24-30: 4008
22,35-53: 4008*
22,39-46: 4009
22,61: 4010a
23,8: 4010b
23,26-32: 4000
23,45: 4011
23,47: 4012
24: 4013-4016
24,3-35: 4017*
24,12: 4017
24,34: 4017*a

24,42s: 4018
24,50-53: 4019

Johannes

–: 4129-4210
1-5: 4154
1: 4211-4225
1,1-18: 4215
1,8: 4226
1,17: 4227
1,19-42: 4228
1,19s: 3374
1,45-51: 4229
2-11: 4230
2,1-12: 4232-4235
2,1-11: 4191
2,1: 4235*
2,7-9: 4236
3: 4237 4238
3,29: 4239
4,1-42: 4240-4244
4,7-38: 4243
4,46-54: 4245
5,1-18: 4246
5,1-9: 4247
5,19-30: 4248
5,35: 4249
6: 3805a 4250-4253
6,14s: 4253
6,60: 4254
6,67-69: 4253
7,37-39: 4255 4256
7,53-8,11: 4257b
8s: 4259a
8,1-11: 4257 4258
8,12-59: 4260
8,25: 4261a
8,56: 4249
9: 4262a 4263
10,1-30: 4264
10,1-21: 4265 4266
11,1-46: 4267-4270
11,9s: 4271
11,14s: 4271*
11,25: 4272
12,1-11: 4272*a
12,20-26: 4272*
12,31-34: 4273a
12,34: 4273*
12,44: 4274
13-21: 4275-4306
13-17: 4276 4278
13,1-38: 4279
13,1-18: 4280
13,34: 3583
14: 4281

14,2s: 4282
14,6: 4282*
14,15: ᴰ4283
16,8-11: 4286a
16,21: 4191
17: 4287 4288
17,1-26: 4215
18-21: 4292
18s: 4289-4291
18,28-19,22: 4292*
18,28-19,16: 4293-4296*
18,37: 3374
19,19s: 4296a
19,25: 4234 4235*
19,29: 4300b
19,32-35: 4298*
19,37: 4299
19,39-42: 4298
19,39: d912d
20,1-18: 4299*a 4303
20,6s: 4300a 4301
20,16s: 3445 4297*
20,17: 4302
20,22b: 4304
20,31: 3470
21: 4230 4305 4306b
21,11: 4387

Actus Apostolorum

−: 4020-4074
1: 4075-4078
1,8: 4079 4105
1,15-26: 3687
2: 1239 4080 4081
2,16-21: 4082
2,30-37: 4083
2,38: 4104
2,41-47: 4084
2,46-3,2: 4083
3,1-10: 4085
3,19-21: 4086
3,21: 4087
3,22-26: 4082
4,23-31: 4089
4,24-31: 4090
4,32-35: 4091-4093
6,1-7: 4094
7,2-53: 4078
7,41-48: 4096
7,42: 4097
7,58: 4098
8: 4099
8,5-25: 4100 4101
8,9-40: 4102
8,14-17: 4103
8,16: 4104

8,26-40: 4105
9,1-19: 4106
9,1-7: 4124*
9,1: 4098
9,3: 4106*
10,41: 4108
10,44-48: 4104
12: 4109
12,17: 4989*
12,20-23: 4110
13,16-41: 4115
15s: 4116
15: 4117a 6206
15,21: 4118
16,1-3: 4119
16,6-15: 4119*
16,10: 4120
16,11-34: 866
17,16-34: 4121
17,18: 4122
17,22-31: 4123
18,12: 4435ᴿ
18,23: 4124
19,1-7: 4104
19,37: 4125
20,18-35: 4125*
27,9: 4126*
28,28: 4127

Ad Romanos

−: 4145 4548-4575
1-6: 4575*
1: 4576
1,3s: 5523
1,18-3,20: 4585
1,18-2,29: 4577
1,18-32: 4578a 4579
1,18-25: 4580
1,18-23: 4581
1,18: 499*
1,26: 6511
2: 4582
2,2-16: 4582*
2,12-27: 4583
3,21-31: 4585
3,21-26: 4785
3,21: 4586
3,27: 4587
3,29s: 4588
4: 1058
4,25: 5523
5: 4589 4590
5,1-11: 4591
5,12-19: 4592
5,18: 4675
5,20-7,6: 4593

Ad Romanos − 967

6,1-8,30: 4596
6: 4595
6,1-11: 4597
6,4-5: 4597
7: 4598
7,7-13: 4599
7,7-12: 4600 4601a
7,7s: 4602
7,14-25: 4603
7,14: 4603*
7,22-25: 4604
8: 4225
8,4: 4605
8,9-23: 4547
8,14-39: 4606
8,18-30: 4607-4609
8,26f: 4610
8.26: 4605
9: 4638a
9-11: 4611-4637 4901
9,1-5: 4614b
9,4: 4316
10,4: 4639
10,14-17: 4814
11: 4626b
11,17-21: 4640
11,25-32: 4641
11,25-27: 4642
12-15: 4643
12,1s: 4644 4645
12.6-8: 4646
13: 4647
13,1-10: 4649
13,1-9: 4648
13,1-7: 866 4650 4651
13,1: 4651*
15,16: 4626c
16: 4653
16,3.5: 4654
16,7: 4655

1 Ad Corinthios

−: 3020 4145 4656-4673
   5428f
1-4: 4674
1-3: 4677
1: 6023ᴿ
1,18-3,20: 4676
1,18: 4675
2,9: 4678
2,12: 4679
4,9: 4680
4,14-17: 4681a
5,1-7: 4681*

1 Ad Timotheum

−: 4113 4119 4893 4907-4923
1,10: 4686
2,8-15: 4924
2,9-5: 4925
2,11-14: 7061
2,11: 7006
3,15: 4926
3,16: 5523
6,20: 4927

2 Ad Timotheum

1,5: 4928
4,8s: 4454*

Ad Hebraeos

−: 398* 4914 4929-4953
1,1-4: 4954
1,8s: 4955
2,9s: 4955*
3,7-4,13: 4956
4,14: 4955*
5,1-10: 4955*
5,10: 4957
5,14: ᴰ4958
6,20: 4957
7,1-10: 4960
8-10: 4961
9s: 4961*
9,1-14: 4952
9,3s: 4963
9,4: 1874*b
9,11: 4962b
9,27s: 4955*

10,5: 4963*
11: 4964
12,22: 4380

1 Petri

−: 1246 3020 4914 4965-4982 5280g e243c
1,11: 4983
2,4-10: 4984
2,9s: 4985
2,17: 4986
2,18ss: 4976a
3,13-4,6: 4987
3,18-20: 4988
3,19s: 4988 7214
3,19: 4988b
4,12-19: 4988*
5,3: 4989a
5,13: 4989*

2 Petri

−: 4990 4991 5009 5010
3: 4992
3,13: 7199
3,16: 4993

Jacobi, James

−: 1246 4586 4805 4994-5003
1: 5003*
2: 14-26: 5004
4,4: 5004*
5,17s: 5005

1-3 Johannis

−: 1246 4307-4315 4914

1 Johannis − 969

2,18: 4315*
3,1-3: 4316
5,6-8: 4298*
2-3 Jn: 4317-4319

Judae

−: 5006-5010

Apocalypsis, Revelation

−: 4139 4320-4377
2s: 4378 4379
3,12: 4380 4384
4-22: 4381
5,1-14: 4382a
5,1-6: 4381*
6,2: 4383
7,9-17: 4382b
9,13: 4384
12,1: 4385
13: 2835 4385*
13,16-18: 4386
13,18: 4387 4388
16,14s: 4389*
17: 4385*
18: 4390a 4391
18,17: 47*ᴿ
20,1-15: 4402*a
21s: 4403
21,1-8: 4382c
21,1: 7199
21,2: 4380
22,6-21: 4404
22,17: 4405

FINIS − Elenchus of Biblica 2, 1986 − END OF INDEX

TIPOGRAFIA POLIGLOTTA DELLA PONTIFICIA UNIVERSITÀ GREGORIANA
PIAZZA DELLA PILOTTA, 4 - ROMA

Luis ALONSO SCHÖKEL

A Manual of Hebrew Poetics

Subsidia Biblica 11

xii-228 p.; Lit. 24.500 **1988** 88-7653-567-5

Theodore KWASMAN

Neo-Assyrian Legal Documents

in the Kouyunjik Collection of the British Museum

Studia Pohl, Series Maior 14

lviii-526 p.; Lit. 57.000 **1988** 88-7653-587-X

Stephen F. MILETIC

"One Flesh": Eph. 5,22-24; 5,31.

Marriage and the New Creation

Analecta Biblica 115

138 p.; Lit. 30.000 **1988** 88-7653-115-7

Biblical Institute Press – Piazza della Pilotta 35 – 00187 Roma

Carol STOCKHAUSEN

Moses' Veil
and the Glory of the New Covenant.
The exegetical substructure of 2 Cor 3,1-4,6

Analecta Biblica 116

x-202 p.; Lit. 40.500   **1989**   88-7653-116-5

Aurora LEONE

Gli animali da trasporto
nell'Egitto greco, romano e bizantino

Papyrologica Castroctaviana 12

102 p.; Lit. 19.500   **1988**   88-7653-579-9

John Paul HEIL

Romans
Paul's Letter of Hope

Analecta Biblica 112

x-126 p.; Lit. 30.000   **1987**   88-7653-112-2

Biblical Institute Press – Piazza della Pilotta 35 – 00187 Roma

Bruna COSTACURTA

La vita minacciata:

il tema della paura nella Bibbia Ebraica

Analecta Biblica 119

360 p.; Lit. 48.000   **1988**   88-7653-119-X

Santiago BRETÓN

Vocación y misión;
formulario profético

Analecta Biblica 111

xii-267 p.; Lit. 42.000   **1987**   88-7653-111-4

Pietro BOVATI

Ristabilire la giustizia

Analecta Biblica 110

446 p.; Lit. 45.000   **1986**   88-7653-110-6

Biblical Institute Press – Piazza della Pilotta 35 – 00187 Roma

ISBN 88-7653-569-1

RECEIVED
AUG 1 4 1989
KENRICK
SEMINARY LIBRARY

7793ß